Film Reviews
1907-1980

A SIXTEEN-VOLUME SET,

Including an Index to Titles

Garland Publishing, Inc.
New York and London
1983

Contents

OF THE SIXTEEN-VOLUME SET

VARIETY

Film Reviews
1964-1967

VOLUME ELEVEN

Garland Publishing, Inc.
New York and London
1983

Library of Congress Cataloging in Publication Data
Main entry under title:

Variety film reviews.
  Includes index.

  1. Moving-pictures—Reviews.   I. Daily variety.
PN1995.V34   1982   791.43'75   82-15691
ISBN 0-8240-5200-5 (v. 1)
ISBN 0-8240-5210-2 (v. 11)

Manufactured in the United States of America

Printed on acid-free,
250-year-life paper

User's Guide

The reviews in this collection are published in chronological order, by the date on which the review appeared. The date of each issue appears at the top of the column where the reviews for that issue begin. The reviews continue through that column and all following columns until a new date appears at the top of the page. Where blank spaces occur at the end of a column, this indicates the end of that particular week's reviews. An index to film titles, giving date of review, is published as the last volume in this set.

1964

Pie In The Sky

Allen Baron & Merrill Brody (Dorothy B. Reed) production. Directed and written by Baron. No release set. Stars Lee Grant, Richard Bray. Camera, Donald Malkames; editor, Ralph Rosenblum; 2d unit camera, Brody; music composed, conducted by Robert Mersey; asst. director, Richard Wolf. Reviewed at Lytton Center, Los Angeles, Dec. 23, '63. Running time, **86 MINS.**

Suzy .... Lee Grant
Brill .... Richard Bray
Carl .... Michael Higgins
Paco .... Roberto Marsach
Brill's father .... Robert Allen
Rose .... Sylvia Miles
Rick .... Jaime Charlamagne
Farmer's Wife .... Ruth Attaway
Farmer .... Robert Earl Jones
Artificial Inseminator.... Cnarles Jordon
Preacher .... Roscoe Browne
Pickpocket .... Rick Colitti
Brill's older sister....... Muriel Franklin
Pitchman .... Monroe Arnold
Haberdasher .... Boris Marshalov
Doorman .... Spencer Davis
Gas station attendant........ Fred Feldt
Hot-dog vendor .... Bill DaPrato
Delicatessen man.......Joseph Leberman
Bartender .... Milton Luchan
Truckdriver .... Mel Brown
Brill's brother .... Danny Dresser
Brill's sisters . Debby Bliss, Susie Dresser
Rick's gang .... Edward Greenberg, Willie Tomlin, Carmelo de la Cruz, Orlando Rosa, John Evans, Johnny Paczynski

With his second attempt at directing and writing, N.Y. filmmaker Allen Baron has created an extremely realistic, sometimes harsh, but heartwarming film of a few important and formative days in the life of a nine-year-old boy. A previous effort, "Blast of Silence," after creating a stir at the 1961 Locarno Film Fest, was picked up by Universal but never got off the ground in the U.S.

A better film is "Pie In the Sky." With the expert handling and advertising by a major distrib, it could realize on gentle appeal. Despite the obvious emphasis on children, this pic is for grownups.

Readily admitting his debt to the European directors, particularly Truffaut, Bergman and De Sica, Baron shot his film in 26 days on a $180,000 budget, of which $80,000 has been deferred pending release. Filmed entirely in N.Y. and farm country outside N.Y., the sporadically engrossing story's greatest flaw is lack of some needed bridging sequences to connect the small hero's adventures. Whether this hit-and-miss narration is due to a limited budget (and insufficient cover shots) or a possible addiction to "new wave" fast cutting, it is a shortcoming and, if still possible, should be remedied.

Brill (Richard Bray) runs away from his farm home when his father (Robert Allen) speaks harshly to him after he has accidentally damaged the roof. The lad, knowing that his widowed father finds it tough going to provide for his large brood, believes that he can make his fortune in New York City.

Arriving in Manhattan, Brill meets a gang of shoe-shine boys and paper carriers who work under the "protection" of Rick, a teenage punk (Jaime Charlamagne), who takes half their earnings. Paco, a Puerto Rican boy (Roberto Marsach), about Brill's age, befriends him, helps him get a job selling papers and takes him home for the night. Next day Brill wins most of Rick's money in a crap game and he and Paco take off for a night in Manhattan, which includes everything from 42nd Street pizza parlors to a Central Park hansom cab.

When Rick's gang beats him up for winning their money, Brill is rescued by Suzy, a prostitute (Lee Grant), who takes him home to patch him up. He remains with her that night and next day she treats him to new clothes, then the unlikely pair explore New York's daytime attractions.

Returning from an errand, Brill sees Suzy and another call girl, Rose (Sylvia Miles), being taken away by the police. Deciding to return home, he buys a bicycle for the journey. On his way out of the city, he is spotted by Rick's gang who give chase, but he gets away when Paco intercepts his pursuers. On the highway a truck wrecks the bike and Brill takes refuge for the night with an elderly Negro couple (Ruth Attaway and Robert Earl Jones). Next day he arrives home, a tired but wiser prodigal son, to turn over what is left of his "fortune" to his father.

Most of the action has to be carried by the non-professional Bray, an attractive towheaded type who tends to be self-conscious when a scene is contained or requires much emotion but for the most part he is delightfully natural, particularly during the action sequences, in exchanges with Paco, or roaming Central Park with Suzy. Miss Grant's "philanthoropic prostitute" role is an actress's holiday, tender with the boy, abrupt with her customers, flippant with merchants who know her trade, and moving in a scene with an abandoned lover (Michael Higgins). The latter scene is the weakest in the film, saved only by Miss Grant's convincing reading.

The gang sequences, while reminiscent of Luis Bunuel's "Los Olvidados," are free of that film's brutality, and are well-handled. Baron occasionally skirts the edge of vulgarity by writing provocative opening phrases for some key speeches but succeeds in avoiding actual suggestiveness. Paco's explanation to Brill of Suzy's "love for sale" profession is the typically exaggerated fabrication of a precocious child.

The incident between Brill and the Negro couple begins awkwardly, in an almost patronizing vein, but is saved by the dramatically humorous realism of his departure. The boy can't find his money and thinks they've stolen it. Finding that he has only dropped it, he's too ashamed to apologize and runs out. However, upbringing wins over embarrassment and he comes back and drops some money in the farmer's lap. The latter's "This ain't no hotel," shouted at the fleeing lad, is both a declaration of self respect and chastisement of the boy.

Besides the outstanding acting of Miss Grant, Bray and Marsach (the latter is really a find and steals every scene he's in), excellent performances in a smaller scale are provided by Charlamagne, Miss Miles, Miss Attaway, Higgins and Allen. All kids in pic are non-pros. In some colorful but brief vignettes, Charles Jordan is an "artificial inseminator" of cows who gives Brill a ride and finds it hard to explain where his bull is; Rick Collette is a pickpocket who, observed at work by the boys on a Fifth Avenue bus, gets hijacked by the cool Paco; Roscoe Browne is a fire-and-brimstone sidewalk preacher in Times Square.

Donald Malkames' clear, crisp photography is one of the film's greatest assets, considering the entirely-on-location shooting. The night scenes on 42nd Street were done from a hand-trundled cart bearing a concealed cameraman who kept contact with Baron via a two-radio intercom. Some of these long tracking shots along one of the world's busiest streets are amazing as is the bicycle chase through upper Manhattan. Ralph Rosenblum's editing, too imitative of the Europeans, uses fast cuts recklessly, even when the plot does not require them. Whether this choppiness is his own interpretation of pace or the influence of Baron, it hurts the film.

The sound recording by James Shields and Charles Federmack has the feeling of post-synchronization, frequently too strident and putting a shrillness on some voices, but Baron insists that post-sync work was kept to a minimum, most of film being recorded on the spot. Robert Mersey's delightful score has a definite Caribbean flavor (pic was originally planned with a Puerto Rican setting) but the jauntiness is perfect for the N.Y. setting and the antics of the boys, many of whom are Puerto Rican.

"Pie In the Sky" (which may get a title change) is a good film that could have been better with those much-needed bridging shots and a clearer, better-plotted script. A possible "sleeper," even in its present form, it's one of those too-rare motion pictures that send you out of the theatre the better for having seen it. *Robe.*

Willy
(GERMAN)

Exploitation angle: Negro G.I. sires son of fraulein; faces German race prejudice.

Hollywood, Dec. 17.

Allan A. Buckhantz production. No star billing. Directed by Buckhantz. Screenplay, Guenter Rudorf, as adapted from his play by Marcus Scholz; camera, Ludwig Berger; editor, Klaus Dudenhoefer; music, Nicholas Carras; assistant director, Frank Guthke. Reviewed at MGM Studios, Dec. 17, '63. Running time, **73 MINS.**

Willy .... Hubert Persicke
Klara .... Hannelore Schroth
Grandmother.... Edith Schultze-Westrum
Herbst .... Joseph Offenbach
Scott .... Peter Kuiper
Teacher .... Klaus Behrendt
Brother .... Reinhard Kolldehoff
Agent .... Kurt A. Jung
Secretary .... Viktoria Von Campe
Herbert .... Wilhelm Fricke
Wolfgang .... Arnfried Lerche

A timely and provocative subject—the struggle of a 15-year-old "illegitimate colored occupation child of German nationality" to find a place for himself in the hostile environment of modern West Germany—is given only skin-deep treatment in this post-dubbed import. At its core, "Willy" is a film of social significance. Had it been approached and developed with greater sensitivity and penetration, the ABA production might have generated considerable commercial impact in any country. But what emerges is a two-dimensional, black-and-white dramatization, haphazardly directed, transparently acted and crudely dubbed. Although it explores a pertinent problem of our time, and has merit as such, the cinematic imagination and/or trenchant social statement necessary for acceptance in the domestic art house sphere is lacking.

Produced and erratically directed by Allan A. Buckhantz from a shallow, glancing scenario by Guenter Rudorf, "Willy" tells of the plight of an "Afro-Aryan" boy who is the offspring out of wedlock of a German fraulein and a Negro G.I. who met during the post-war occupation of Germany. The film depicts the struggle of the boy, who was raised by his mother after his father returned permanently to the U.S., to locate and succeed in a job following graduation. Small town prejudicial pressures persuade his mother to allow him to seek a better life in Hamburg, on the assumption that perhaps the more impersonal environment of a larger city will enable him to get along better. The picture thus concludes on a note of hope, not solution.

All of the performances are severely handicapped by the dubbing. Hubert Persicke plays the title role, with Hannelore Schroth in the key role of his troubled, mistreated mother and Edith Schultze-Westrum, Joseph Offenbach and Peter Kuiper in other major characterizations.

Production contributions are rather haphazard. A title song by Nicholas Carras and Ric Marlow adds a somewhat jarringly commercial note over the titles, which come at the tag-end of the film.

Tube.

Entrega Inmediata
(Special Delivery)
(MEXICAN)

Columbia Pictures release of a Posa Films International S. A. production. Stars Cantinflas (Mario Moreno). Features Gina Romand, Claudio Brook, Guillermo Zetina, Fanny Cano, Maria Amelia, Alberto Catala. Directed by Miguel M. Delgado; screenplay, Jaime Salvador; camera, Gabriel Figueroa; music, Gustavo Cesar Carrion. Nitery sequence by Rafael de Cordoba y Ballet Espanol. Reviewed at Million Dollar Theatre, Los Angeles, Dec. 23, '63. Running time, **112 MINS.**

Himself .... Cantinflas
Carlota .... Gina Romand
Spy .... Claudio Brook
Female agent .... Fanny Cano
Baby .... Maria Amelia
Professor .... Alberto Catala

With the proven international appeal of Cantinflas and the excellent production values his films now contain, it is puzzling why Posa Films or Columbia, who distributes in the U.S., make no greater effort to sell his pix in the non-Spanish-speaking market. The "little man" has the universality of Chaplin and the commercial appeal of Jerry Lewis and it requires no knowledge of languages to derive pleasure from his peccadilloes. To realize, however, how many more laughs lie in "what" he says, one should view his films in a theatre filled with "understanding" Latins.

This time around, Cantinflas is a "special delivery messenger" who becomes the victim of every comedy cliche in the book—from the beautiful spy to the beautiful "baby" palmed off on him.

As the innocent involved in intrigue, the comedian gets away fast with an establishing shot that identifies him immediately as funny and ineffectual — an encounter with a bakeryman so contrived and so hilarious that you're sure it will be used again. Naturally, it gives the pic an equally funny close.

For northern audiences, much of the evident plot could be edited out. Indeed when Cantinflas is absent from the screen, the flimsiness of the script is embarrassingly evident. An exception is a well-staged nitery sequence featuring dancer Rafael de Cordoba. Here the imaginative camerawork of Gabriel Figueroa gets a real workout with a series of closeups that show off the machine-gun rapidity of de Cordoba's footwork.

The comedian, after h a v i n g established the unkempt, swivel-hipped figure the world knows best, works in several disguises including an elegant, ancient boulevardier and a slicked-down, be-spectacled undertaker. He also uses planted opportunities to show his dancing and singing prowess.

Gina Romand as a gorgeous, Gabor-ish spy, Maria Amelia as the orphan "baby" who turns out to be a pulchritudinous senorita who gets her Cantinflas, and Fanny Cano as a pretty government agent, provide beaucoup cheesecake for the pic, and turn in fairly good jobs of acting. Claudio Brook's chief spy and Alberto Catala's professor-accomplice, like most of the supporting cast, are stamped from worn, familiar moulds.

Director Miguel M. Delgado plays it safe, giving Cantinflas his head while keeping the plot moving, albeit slowly, when the star is off-screen. G a b r i e l Figueroa's photography is excellent throughout but particularly so in the nitery sequence. Gustavo Cesar Carnion's music, with the exception of the nitery and a closing musical sequence, is used merely to underscore humorous or would-be suspenseful key scenes.

Robe.

L'Appartement Des Filles
(Girls' Apartment)
(FRENCH)

Paris, Dec. 23.

UGC-Sirius release of Paul Graetz-Transcontinental Film production. Stars Mylene Demongeot, Sylva Koscina, Renata Ewert, Sami Frey. Directed by Michel Deville. Screenplay, Nina Companez, Deville from novel by Jacques Robert; camera, Claude Lecomte; editor, Nina Companez. At Marignan, Paris. Running time, **88 MINS.**
Melanie .... Mylene Demongeot
Elena .... Sylva Koscina
Lolotte .... Renata Ewert
Tibere .... Sami Frey
Christophe .... Jean-Francois Calve
Francois .... Daniel Ceccaldi

Slight comedy, about a gangster playboy trying to seduce any of three air hostesses to smuggle gold for him, is breezy enough to gloss over a certain repetitiveness in treatment. Familiar affair does not appear to have the uniqueness or tang for arty use abroad, but could be an okay dualer or playoff item on its general entertainment qualities. Local chances are fine.

The would-be smuggler is naturally transformed by love for one of the hostesses, who include a blase snob, an adventurous one and a sentimental femme. The last named naturally gets him. Director Michel Deville can not energize the slim material into much even if he does give it a glossy finish.

There are a bunch of promising people in this but without enough

of personal flair and zest to give this the right drive that comedies of this ilk need.

Sami Frey tries hard but does not have the dash for the small-time smuggler, who mends his ways. Mylene Demongeot has a graceful pouting dottiness as the lovestruck blonde if inclined to play things on one note. The girls at play appear quaint rather than giving this a pithy romp.

Film has a neat production gloss. And director Michel Deville still shows promise as a new, sophisticated comedy director even if he needs to get down to business instead of embroidering needlessly.

Mosk.

Le Mepris
(Contempt)
(FRENCH-ITALIAN)
(COLOR)

Paris, Dec. 30.

Cocinor release of Rome Paris Film-Concordia-Champion Films production. Stars Brigitte Bardot, Jack Palance; features Michel Piccoli, Fritz Lang, Georgia Moll. Written and directed by Jean-Luc Godard from novel by Alberto Moravia. Camera (Technicolor), Raoul Coutard; editor, Agnes Guillemot. At Lord Byron, Paris. Running time, **100 MINS.**
Camille .... Brigitte Bardot
Jeremie .... Jack Palance
Fritz Lang .... Fritz Lang
Paul .... Michel Piccoli
Francesca .... Georgia Moll

Crossing Brigitte Bardot with an arty, personal director, ex-New Waver Jean-Luc Godard, was not a bad idea. Miss Bardot appears, at last, as an actress in her own right with her trademark nude scenes not forced but aptly stemming from the plot. However, thus appears less accessible for depth use with best bet as an arty booking in the U.S.

Slim tale has Miss Bardot married to a hack scriptwriter called in by an egotistical American producer to rewrite scenes on an epic he is making in Italy with Fritz Lang himself directing. Film details her sudden intimations of contempt for her husband because of a series of incidents. It ends in her beginning to give into the assiduous courting of the producer and with both killed in an auto accident when she leaves her husband and goes off to Rome with the producer.

Main appeal is in the filmic manner as far as this pic is concerned. Based on an Alberto Moravia novel, Jean-Luc Godard still makes this a personally told tale. Though full of inside film talk, grandiloquent phrasings, sudden sharp elipses or quick repeat montage scenes of early incidents to make a point, this does have a decisive visual flair that lays bare these figures and discourses on that popular modern theme re the dissolution of a couple.

Miss Bardot, who oldtimers like H. G. Clouzot, Claude Autant-Lara, Julien Duvivier and Christian Jaque tried to force to act in the more general mold, here is given her head as a young married woman who is physically amorous but begins to doubt her respect for her husband.

She handles her lines well and displays a feel for a scene, and a timing and presence scarcely seen in her more undraped pix. There is a pre-title love scene that unveils her familiar chassis, as well as others, but none of this is out of

character with her sensual, free wheeling character.

Jack Palance has fire and frenzy as an officious film producer while Fritz plays himself with a gentle air of wisdom. His filming of "Ulysces" does have some symbolic ties with the tale but none of this is overdone.

One brilliant scene has Miss Bardot and her husband, sharply etched by Michel Piccoli, lolling about in their half finished Rome apartment that is full of shrewd observation, delineation of character and witty aspects. Here her growing distaste for her husband, because of his seeming lack of manlihood, is brought forth clearly yet subtly. But then the film just jogs on and repeats its points and builds to an arbitrary ending of the accidental death.

It will not be an easy film for circuit spotting. But by spreading in arty houses, this could be given more legs especially well sold. And then there is the Bardot name and exposure. It will also call for smart arty theatre handling, with perhaps the revelation of Miss Bardot as an actress, as well as a sex symbol, its main handle. Color is good if sometimes overindulged for mood effects. Godard has soft pedaled his penchant for jump cuts but still uses intellectual editing techniques that sometimes jar if they do not mar the general mood and development of the story.

This marks a step forward for both Miss Bardot and Godard if it still is not exactly an outright exploitation offering. Its hybird aspects call for careful placement but it may be worth it on its unorthodox aspects for arties.

Joe Levine's Embassy Pictures has this for the world but has sold it for France and Italy. There is no attempt to find short cuts for languages and all of Palance's dialog is translated by his secretary. This makes it both easier to handle for depth with subtitles and, respectively, harder to dub. English title is "Ghost at Noon."

Mosk.

The Pink Panther
(TECHNIRAMA-COLOR)

High-gloss n o n s e n s e with standout comic highlights and brilliant playing by Peter Sellers. His clowning and a star roster add up to topgrade fodder for escapists.

London, Jan. 7.

United Artists release of a Mirisch-G.-E. production. Stars David Niven, Peter Sellers, Robert Wagner, Capucine, Claudia Cardinale. Directed by Blake Edwards. Screenplay, Edwards and Maurice Richlin; music, Henry Mancini; camera, Philip Lathrop; editor, Ralph E. Winters. Reviewed at Odeon, Leicester Square, London. Running time, **115 MINS.**
Sir Charles .... David Niven
Insp. Jacques Clouseau ... Peter Sellers
George .... Robert Wagner
Simone Clouseau .... Capucine
Princess Dala .... Claudia Cardinale
Angela Dunning ..... Brenda De Banzie
Greek "Cousin" .... Fran Jeffries
Tucker .... Colin Gordon
Defense Attorney ...... John Le Mesurier
Saloud .... James Lanphier
Artoff .... Guy Thomajan
Novelist .... Michael Trubshawe
Greek shipowner .... Riccardo Billi
Hollywood starlet .... Meri Wells
Photographer .... Martin Miller

This is film making as a branch of the candy trade, and the pack is so enticing that few will worry about the jerky machinations of the plot. The production crams in so many appealing plusses that the whole luscious affair defies mental probing. And it is delivered with such an impudent, tongue-in-cheek elegance by Blake Edwards, as director and partwriter, that there is no inclination to brood over the occasional lapses. Quite apart from the general air of bubbling elegance, the pic is intensely funny. The yocks are almost entirely the responsibility of Peter Sellers, who is perfectly suited as a clumsy cop who can hardly move a foot without smashing a vase or open a door without hitting himself on the head. When memory of the o t h e r s subsides, "Panther" will be a vintage record of the farcical Sellers at his peak.

Mood of jaunty distraction is splendidly launched by the witty and diverting titles from DePatie-Freleng Enterprises, who use the cartoon figure of an insolent pink panther with fine ingenuity. Action starts rolling in fairly-tale style. These are few cumbersome moments in the film, for scripters Edwards and Richlin have a complicated plot to outline and it takes some alertness to pick up the threads and join them together. The "Panther" is a priceless jewel owned by the Indian Princess Dala (Claudia Cardinale), vacationing in the Swiss ski resort of Cortina. The other principals are introduced in their various habitats, before they converge on the Princess and her jewel.

In Rome, a dashing and elusive thief pulls off another coup, and later turns out to be Sir Charles Lytton (David Niven). In Los Angeles, his nephew George (Robert Wagner) has himself photographed in student cap-and-gown, so that the uncle who supports him will not know his true profession, which is similar to his own. In Paris, Simone Clouseau (Capucine) is almost caught in the act of passing a stolen jewel to a "fence," and makes a quick getaway. And Simone turns out to be the wife of Inspector Jacques Clouseau (Peter Sellers) who has been chasing the phantom thief for 15 years to no avail.

After this, the stage is set for a saucy and improbable imbroglio in Cortina. There is little point in tracking the twists of the plot, which only serves the useful purpose of putting all the characters in unlikely juxtaposition. Sir Charles manipulates an introduction to the Princess, whose jewel he is after, and then, via champagne, tries a little gentle seduction.

The other ingredients come straight from the Keystone Kops, and the highspot is a bedroom scene. The Inspector and his wife prepare for bed, but the cop does not know that there are two men, Sir Charles and George, concealed in the room, unable to escape. This classic situation of trousers-down comedy comes to a satisfying climax when the Inspector climbs thankfully into bed with his spouse, and is doused in champagne that she was trying to hide. The whole scene fizzes riotously, and it says much for the expertise of Blake Edwards' direction that the pace and interest do not languish after it.

Final comic setpiece at a costume ball does not quite reach these heights, but its satisfactory. With both Sir Charles and nephew George after the jewel, the fireworks unexpectedly explode in profusion. There's even a car chase, ending in a pileup in the village square.

The end is neat. Sir Charles and George seem to be caught at last. At the trial, they call the Inspector as their witness. He has to confess that every time a big jewel theft has been accomplished over the last 15 years, not only has Sir Charles. been present, but also the Inspector himself. Absentmindedly he pulls a handkerchief from his pocket. Attached to it is the missing "pink panther," which has been planted on him. So the Inspector goes to jail and the crooks go free.

It is Peter Sellers who swipes the stellar honors. His razor-sharp timing is superlative, and he makes the most of his ample opportunities. His doting concern for criminal wife, his blundering ineptitude with material objects, and his dogged pursuit of the crook all coalesce to a sharp performance, with satirical overtones.

David Niven produces his familiar brand of debonair ease. Robert Wagner has a somewhat undernourished role. Capucine, sometimes awkward and over-intense as if she were straining for yocks, is nevertheless a good Simone. The sultry Claudia Cardinale also does well as the Princess, and carries off her main scene, amorously tipsy with Sir Charles.

The Swiss locales are agreeably captured by Philip Lathrop's camera, and the lensing is firstrate throughout, making tasteful use of Technicolor and the Technirama process. Svelte music comes from Henry Mancini, also responsi-

ble for the cabaret number, "Meglio Stasera" (It Had Better Be Tonight), delivered with verve by newcomer Fran Jeffries. The tune is good enough to catch on.

Editor Ralph E. Winters includes no unnecessary footage. Result should be an international winner. *Otta.*

The Man From Galveston

Originally pilot for WB's "Temple Houston" vidseries. Undernourished as theatrical fare.

Hollywood, Jan. 7.
Warner Bros. release of Michael Meshekoff production. Stars Jeffrey Hunter, Preston Foster, James Coburn, Joanna Moore, Edward Andrews. Others in cast: Kevin Hagen, Martin West, Ed Nelson, Karl Swenson, Grace Lee Whitney, Claude Stroud. (No character names). Directed by William Conrad. Screenplay, Dean Riesner, Michael Zagor; camera, Bert Glennon; music, David Buttolph. Reviewed at World Theatre, Jan. 7, '64. Running time, **57 MINS.**

This is the pilot film that spawned Warner Bros.' "Temple Houston" television series. The studio has converted it into a theatrical feature. And it was accompanying feature with "Four for Texas" last week in several L.A. theatres. As a pilot, it was obviously successful, having paved the way for the series. As a theatre feature, however, it is mighty skimpy fare—barely acceptable as a running mate.

Jack Webb, until recently tv production chief at Warners, was exec producer of the Michael Meshekoff production. William Conrad directed from a screenplay by Dean Riesner and Michael Zagor. Yarn is concerned with the adventures of a brash young attorney (Jeffrey Hunter) attached to an early Texas circuit court, or a kind of roving frontier judiciary who stormed into small towns with all the fanfare and razz-ma-tazz of Ringling Bros. Plot describes Hunter's implication in a case involving an old flame who has been accused of murder. Hunter fingers the real killer in some absurdly contrived courtroom melodramatics.

Hunter is colorful as the cocky lawyer, Preston Foster correctly irritable as a circuit judge, James Coburn reliable as a rather hapless marshal, Joanna Moore pretty and sincere as the accused woman. Competent in key support are Edward Andrews, Kevin Hagen, Martin West and Ed Nelson. Dexterous photography by Bert Glennon is a plus factor. *Tube.*

Strait-Jacket

Shocker about an axe murderess drawn along lines of "Psycho." Although rather crude and imitative, b.o. future seems favorable.

Hollywood, Dec. 5
Columbia Pictures release of William Castle production. Stars Joan Crawford; features Diane Baker, Leif Erickson, Howard St. John, John Anthony Hayes. Directed by Castle. Screenplay, Robert Bloch; camera, Arthur Arling; editor, Edwin Bryant; music, Van Alexander; assistant director, Herbert Greene. Reviewed at Academy Awards Theatre, Dec. 5, '63. Running time, **93 MINS.**

Lucy Harbin	Joan Crawford
Carol	Diane Baker
Bill Cutler	Leif Erickson
Raymond Fields	Howard St. John
Michael Fields	John Anthony Hayes
Emily Cutler	Rochelle Hudson
Leo Krause	George Kennedy
Mrs. Fields	Edith Atwater
Dr. Anderson	Mitchell Cox
Frank Harbin	Lee Yeary
Stella Fulton	Patricia Krest
Carol (3 yrs.)	Vickie Cos
1st Little Girl	Patty Lee
2nd Little Girl	Laura Hess
Shoe Clerk	Robert Ward
Beauty Operator	Lyn Lundgren

"Strait-Jacket" could be summed up as a chip off the old Bloch. Writer Robert Bloch's "Psycho," that is. In crossing the basic plot design of that 1960 Bloch-buster with the instrument of murder (the axe) and at least one of the ramifications of the celebrated Lizzie Borden case, Bloch has provided the grisly ingredients for producer-director William Castle to concoct some marketable "chop" sey. Although it lacks the slickness, marquee stature and, obviously, the originality to generate anything approaching the response to "Psycho," it should be a moneymaker for Columbia.

Heads really roll in this yarn, which commences with a dual hatchet job on a cheating husband and his lady friend who are discovered bedroominating by the wife (Joan Crawford), whose three-year-old daughter witnesses in horror, the 40 some odd whacks per victim administered by her mother. Mom goes to the insane asylum and daughter grows up into Diane Baker. They are reunited 20 years later when mom is released. Whenever the film begins to bog down from this point on, which it tends to do, Bloch just gives 'em the axe, the axe, the axe. Three more victims fall by the wayside before the mystery — which to the more alert customers shouldn't prove very mysterious—is solved. The story is purposely manipulated to lead the audience astray, with the result that at least several of the characters and situations are awfully hokey and contrived. But whenever it's time to go chop-chop, "Strait-Jacket" is scary enough for anyone, and that saves the show.

Miss Crawford does well by her role, delivering an animated performance. Miss Baker is pretty and histrionically satisfactory as her daughter. Some of the supporting work is quite inept, but competent characterizations are fashioned by Leif Erickson, Howard St. John, John Anthony Hayes and Rochelle Hudson. Some of Castle's direction is stiff and mechanical, but most of the murders are suspensefully and chillingly constructed, along the order of the bloodbath blueprints for "Psycho."

Capable assists have been contributed to the production by cameraman Arthur Arling, editor Edwin Bryant (especially good on the homicidal knitting), production designer Boris Leven, composer Van Alexander and soundman Lambert Day. *Tube.*

Das Grosse Liebesspiel
(The Big Love Game)
(GERMAN)

Berlin, Jan. 7.
Nora release of Team-Film and Stadthallen production. Stars Lilli Palmer, Hildegard Knef, Nadja Tiller. Directed by Alfred Weidenmann. Screenplay, Herbert Reinecker; camera, Georg Bruck-

bauer; music, Charly Niessen. At Gloria Palast, Berlin. Running time, **133 MINS.**

The actress	Lilli Palmer
The call-girl	Hildegard Knef
The divorced woman	Nadja Tiller
The secretary	Daliah Lavi
The elderly lady Elisabeth Flickenschildt	
The French girl	Daniele Gaubert
The wife of the director	Alexandra Stewart
The diplomat	Paul Hubschmid
The school director	Martin Held
The chief	Peter van Eyck
The pupil	Thomas Fritsch
The student	Peter Parten
The policeman	Walter Giller

The Germans have a way with overdoing things, even with films. This pic, dramaturgically reminiscent of Max Ophuls' "La Ronde," gives evidence of it. There's a bit too much of just everything in this vehicle. The dialog sequences are much too wideopen. There's too much philosophical talk. The women in this are too fond of getting a man. The boys get the girls too easily. Much is too heavily played out. As a result, the film doesn't have what it should have had in the first place: Charm. And the pic is much too long.

Alfred Weidenmann undoubtedly is one of Germany's better directors. He knows his trade but why didn't he know when to stop? The late Lubitsch set a good example years ago. Also Ophuls did. What makes a delicate film really delicate? When much is left to the viewer's imagination. For this film, the viewer doesn't need much if any imagination. Commercially, the film has the potentials for a big local success. Artistically this doesn't amount to much. Foreign prospects are on the slim side.

Entire film centers more or less on the bed and what the film calls love. It starts out with a call girl (Hildegard Knef) who teaches the ways of love. The boy utilizes his newly acquired knowledge on the young wife of his school professor (Alexandra Stewart), while, in turn, the professor (Martin Held) has an erotical escapade with a sultry secretary (Daliah Lavi). And so it goes on.

There are some plus points with regard to the acting but they're not enough to make this an internationally attention-getting film. For the record, the best polished performances are turned in by Held and Miss Knef. Many if not most of the other name stars in this lean too heavily on the mere routine.

The film may please those who like to hear such phrases as "you want to sleep with me" over and over again. But otherwise this 133-minute film has a tendency to bore the average patron. *Hans.*

Il Maestro Di Vigevano
(The Teacher from Vigevano)
(ITALIAN)

Rome, Jan. 14.
Dino DeLaurentiis production and release. Stars Alberto Sordi, Claire Bloom; features Vito de Taranto, Ya Doucheskaya, Guido Spadea, Tullio Scovazzi, Lilla Ferrante, Piero Mazzarella, Eva Magni, Ignazio Gibilisco, Bruno de Cerce, Egidio Casolari Directed by Elio Petri. Screenplay, Petri, Age, Scarpelli, from story by Lucio Mastronardi. Camera, Otello Martelli. Sets, Gastome Corsetti. Music, Nino Rota. Editor, Ruggero Mastroianni. At Cinema Corso, Rome. Running time, **112 MINS.**

Mombelli	Alberto Sordi
Ada	Claire Bloom
Dean	Vito de Taranto
Eva	Ya Doucheskaya
Nanini	Guido Spadea
Rino	Tullio Scovazzi
Cuore	Lilla Ferrante
Bugatti	Piero Mazzarella

Widow Nanini	Eva Magni
Varaldi	Ignazio Gibilisco
Cippolone	Bruno de Cerce
Filippi	Egidio Casolari

First major disappointment from the usually reliable Alberto Sordi, this film uncertainly wavers between the pathetic and comic, ultimately disappointing in both sectors. It has a built-in b.o. base at home thanks to the Sordi rep, but will need hard sell to overcome inevitably downbeat word-of-mouth. Export chances are iffy.

Based on a much-talked-of novel by the same title, "Vigevano" deals with a tradition-bound and colorless elementary school prof (Sordi) who only slowly and reluctantly bows to his wife (Claire Bloom) and her dreams of riches in other fields. She gets him to invest in a shoe factory of their own, but both it and the family—thanks to her extra-curricular dalliances—soon go to pieces and, after his wife's sudden death in a car crash, he is forced to return to the grey and dismal professorship for which he was trained.

The glaring error of the picture, and one which Sordi committed once before, but less violently, in "The Boom," is to feed laugh-expectant audiences an almost steady diet of pathos and gloom. The few laughs that come up once in a while only distract and clash with tone of the remainder of the pic. Sordi's portrayal of the mixed-up professor is never clearly patterned, and the jumps from pathos to bathos to satire to comedy upset each mood as it is created. Nor does Claire Bloom's diligent, but basically wasted effort, raise tone of pic, while a large supporting cast ranges from anonymity to gross caricature (as in the overdone portrayal of the school headmaster by Vito De-Taranto).

Not aided by a meandering pace which all too frequently lags, Elio Petri's direction lacks force and insight of his earlier efforts. Technical kudos are in the top Italo tradition. *Hawk.*

Mail Order Bride
(PANAVISION—COLOR)

Partially successful western that misfires in the stretch. Solid production and acting values -could pave way for profitable b.o.

Hollywood, Jan. 8.

Metro release of Richard E. Lyons production. Stars Buddy Ebsen, Keir Dullea, Lois Nettleton. Directed and screenplay by Burt Kennedy, based on short story by Van Cort; camera (Metrocolor), Paul C. Vogel; editor, Frank Santillo; music, George Bassman; assistant director, Eli Dunn. Reviewed at the studio, Jan. 8, '64. Running time, **83 MINS.**

Will Lane	Buddy Ebsen
Lee Carey	Keir Dullea
Annie Boley	Lois Nettleton
Jace	Warren Oates
Marietta	Barbara Luna
Lank	Bill Smith
Matt	Jimmy Mathers
Hanna	Marie Windsor
Sheriff Linley	Paul Fix
Charlie Mary	Doodles Weaver
Preacher Pope	Denver Pyle
Sister Sue	Kathleen Freeman
Young Old Maid	Abagail Shelton
Lily	Diane Sayer
Bartender	Ted Ryan

Metro's "Mail Order Bride" is two-thirds of a satisfying western with special appeal for the family trade. Until that critical juncture, the Richard E. Lyons production exudes an air of unpretentious charm and an outdoor vigor that, coupled with some breathtaking location photography and a few frisky performances, makes it a pretty palatable ear of frontier corn.

Had scenarist-director Burt Kennedy and story writer Van Cort chosen not to resolve their yarn by resorting to the tired, primitive device of separating the good guys from the bad guys and letting them go at it, they might have come up with a dark horse boxoffice contender for the studio. But as it is, Metro may have to rely more on personality rather than story values to cash in. All things considered, "Mail Order Bride" could and should emerge a profitable venture but less successful than it might have been.

The film is concerned basically with the emotional growth to maturity of a young hellion (Keir Dullea) whose deceased father has legally stipulated that his Montana ranch be run by an old buddy and erstwhile lawman (Buddy Ebsen) until such time as the latter deems his son fit to take over. As the major move in his campaign to tame and gentle the young colt in his charge, Ebsen scans the Montgomery Ward catalog, sashays to Kansas City in search of a bride for Dullea and brings back Lois Nettleton for instant wedlock, frontier style. She just happens to have a six-year-old son with her.

The wedded couple comes to a temporary understanding and just when it begins to appear that the story may be developed naturally and eventually resolve itself into a reasonably believable happy ending, writers Kennedy and Cort veer off on their foolish tangent. They proceed to turn an until then merely colorfully ornery critter (Warren Oates) into a first class, full fledged, and totally absurd heavy, and the picture never recovers from this mortal blow. The happy ending develops anyway, but it just isn't the same after all the contrived chaos and confusion. The simple charm and glow of the film is all but destroyed.

Dullea, who attracted favorable attention with his work in "Hoodlum Priest" and "David And Lisa," continues to impress and takes another stride in what should develop into a bright career. Without question one of the most gifted young actors to hit the screen in some time, he shold be utilized more frequently and to greater advantage by Hollywood filmmakers. He scores in this outing with a histrionic vitality that gives more to the character than he gets from the script. Equally impressive is Lois Nettleton, another outstanding talent on the rise.

Ebsen, whose "Beverly Hillbillies" popularity won't hurt the boxoffice any, gives a firm and reserved portrayal of the perceptive guardian. Oates, another accomplished young player, delivers a virile performance. Sound support is contributed by Barbara Luna, Paul Fix, Marie Windsor, Denver Pyle, Bill Smith, Kathleen Freeman, Abagail Shelton and moppet Jimmy Mathers.

Shot on location in Northern California's High Sierras, the picture benefits from some stunning panoramic views, appreciatively captured and conveyed through Paul Vogel's picture postcard color photography. Another major assist is George Bassman's alternately plaintive and whimsical score, heavy on the country style harmonica, banjo and fiddle.

On the whole, editor Frank Santillo has done a taut job, and additionally knowing craftsmanship is displayed by art directors George W. Davis and Stan Jolley and soundman Franklin Milton. *Tube.*

Misadventures of Merlin Jones
(COLOR)

Disney with more miss than hit comedy.

Buena Vista release of Walt Disney production. Stars Tommy Kirk, Annette; features Leon Ames, Stuart Erwin, Alan Hewlitt, Connie Gilchrist, Dal McKennon, Norman Grabowski. Directed by Robert Stevenson. Screenplay, Tom and Helen August, from story by Bill Walsh; camera (Technicolor), Edward Colman; editor, Cotton Warburton; music, Bob Brunner for orchestration, Richard M. Sherman and Robert B. Sherman for title sing. Previewed in New York Jan. 3, '64. Running time, **88 MINS.**

Merlin Jones	Tommy Kirk
Jennifer	Annette
Judge Holmby	Leon Ames
Police Captain Loomis	Stuart Erwin
Professor Shattuck	Alan Hewitt
Mrs. Gossett	Connie Gilchrist
Detective Hutchins	Dal McKennon
Norman	Norman Grabowski

Fun and boxoffice conquests footnote Walt Disney's experimentations with a boy who could turn into a shaggy dog, and then an absent-minded professor who starteled the world, including himself, with the high-flying flubber. "Shaggy Dog" and "Absent Minded Professor" were funny pictures built around a gimmick and proved smash successes.

This new one, "The Misadventures of Merlin Jones," is another try at a gimmick and had at the outset, it would seem, the potential for another amusing absurdity. Sad to say, it just doesn't come off.

Amiable characters are sketched in the tale of a college student who sockets himself into being an electrofied brain with the ability to receive other people's thoughts. And from this base, the pic goes into the field of hypnosis with his subjects including a chimpanzee at the college lab, and a judge who moonlights as the anonymous writer of crime fiction.

As it plays out, there's little high voltage in the misadventures of the title character, Tommy Kirk. His girl, Annette, is a pretty co-ed, and nothing more. Leon Ames is the sometimes exasperated judge-writer and Stuart Erwin is a cop. Alan Hewitt is a smart-aleck prof at the college's psychology department, and Norman Grabowski is a brawny and dumb student with a reputation for football agility and disagreeableness to the chimp.

They all play it well enough, or at least as well as they can under the unsnappy direction by Robert Stevenson and a screenplay by Tom and Helen Auguest which lacks the necessary comedic shock.

Music is fair, and the technical work is all top-drawer.

The Disney name will help the sale, of course. But it's an innocuous comedy that, after the first couple of reels, hopefully would, but doesn't, jell. *Gene.*

La Ragazza Di Bube
(Bebo's Girl)
(ITALIAN)

Rome, Jan. 14.

Lux-Paramount release of a Lux-Ultra-Vides production by Franco Cristaldi. Stars Claudia Cardinale, George Chakiris. Features Marc Michel, Dany Paris, Emilio Esposito, Monique Vita, Mario Lupi, Pier Luigi Catocci, Carla Calo, Bruno Scipioni, Ugo Chitti. Directed by Luigi Comencini. Screenplay, Comencini, Marcello Fondato, from novel by Carlo Cassola. Camera, Gianni di Venanzo. Music, Carlo Rustichelli. Previewed in Rome. Running time, **110 MINS.**

Mara	Claudia Cardinale
Bube	George Chakiris
Stefano	Marc Michel
Liliana	Dany Paris
Mara's father	Emilio Esposito
Ines	Monique Vita
Lidori	Mario Lupi
Ciolfi	Pier Luigi Catocci
Mara's mother	Carla Calo
Mauro	Bruio Scipioni
Arnaldo	Ugo Chitti

Claudia Cardinale's career comes full circle—from striking beauty to undisputed talent—with her title performance in "Bebo's Girl." It's the female acting stint of the year in these parts, and it should win her solid recognition everywhere. Role and name will also, with an assist from George Chakiris', help chances for pic itself, which would otherwise be much more limited because of subject matter.

Based on a Carlo Cassola best-seller, to which it is reputedly very faithful, "Bebo's Girl" tells of the strange muted love of a country girl for a man she scarcely knows, a partisan who has killed a man during the war and who is eventually caught and jailed for the crime. Though offered chances of a new life and love with a solid, steady writer, she prefers to remain faithful to her briefly-known wartime hero and await his release from jail.

Slowly developed, pic grows on one just as consistently as the character of Mara (Claudia Cardinale) grows in stature as she pursues her seemingly impossible romance with an ever-distant and elusive target. It is a credit to Miss Cardinale and to director Luigi Comencini as the odds pay off in the end in the characterization of the strong, silent, woman who almost blindly follows her instinct to the end against all odds and reason.

Pic is underplayed in every sector, with George Chakiris ably following the pattern in a self-effacing, but nevertheless effective role, as the partisan who befriends Mara. Marc Michel is also good as the man who offers the girl security but is turned down. Others in the large cast provide colorful wartime backdrop of types. By Yank standards, the build-up is undeniably slow, and though this pays off later, some scissoring would help the pace.

Gianni di Venanzo's camerawork deserves the extra bow this Italo craftsman usually gets; his chiaroscuro work on settings, as well as his fine closeups of Miss Cardinale especially, are of the highest standard. Carlo Rustichelli's music is neatly reminiscent in atmosphere, while other credits measure up in a painstaking production effort. *Hawk.*

The Man Who Couldn't Walk

Adequate supporting item about a band of British jewel thieves. Shop-worn, but with scattered compensations.

Hollywood, Jan. 8.

Butcher's Film-Distributors Ltd. release of Jock MacGregor-Umesh Mallik production. No star credits. Directed by Henry Cass. Screenplay and story, Mallik; camera, James Harvey; editor, Robert Hill; music, Wilfred Burns. Reviewed at Joe Shore's projection room, Jan. 8, '64. Running time, **63 MINS.**

The Boss	Eric Pohlmann
Keefe	Peter Reynolds
Carol	Pat Clavin
Luigi	Reed de Rouen
Cora	Bernadette Miles
Enrico	Richard Shaw
Beppo	Martin Cass
Maria	Margot van der Burgh
Lou	Martin Cordon
Joey	Maurice Bannister

"The Man Who Couldn't Walk" is a routine but acceptable supporting melodrama about a band of jewel thieves. This low budget indie has going for it some efficient direction, several skillful performances and a script that once or twice emerges from its shell of contrivance and formula and comes through with a fairly lively scene or some lifelike dialog. The Jock MacGregor-Umesh Mallik production, a presentation of a new American-Canadian company, Falcon Pictures, will make a serviceable companion feature.

Evidently the Falcon campaigners have some hard exploitation sell in mind. judging from their ad layout which stresses the notion that the film tells "the story behind the scandal that shocked London . . . baring untold secrets of vice, intrigue and international party girls." This come-on, however, is a fraud, as those who see the picture will discover. What happens on the screen isn't even remotely related to recent scandalous developments in England.

Mallik's yarn, however, does have a London background, and concerns the problems of a brash safecracker who is recruited into a gang of thieves headed by a wheelchair-confined consul general of a Central American republic. In the process of an ultimately unsuccessful diamond heist, the safecracker discovers that his boss is the man who, years before, had killed his father. This coincidence, which would have benefitted the story had it been bypassed in favor of a more natural conclusive device, leads to an overly involved climax.

The most noteworthy character in Mallik's yarn, the one that gives the film a necessary shot in the arm, is that of the likably cocky safecracker, played with amiable self-assurance by Peter Reynolds. Eric Pohlmann is a strong plus factor as the invalid mastermind and Pat Clavin has a sultry quality as the heavy's stepdaughter. Skillful direction by Henry Cass aides throughout. James Harvey's camerawork shows occasional flair, but Wilfred Burns' music tends to be too bouncy and frivolous for the serious events that are transpiring.
Tube.

Man In The Middle
(C'SCOPE)

Engrossing military courtroom drama. U.S. officer goes beserk on racial issue. Good cast. So-so b.o. prospect.

Hollywood, Jan. 6.

Twentieth-Fox release of Walter Seltzer production. Stars Robert Mitchum, France Nuyen, Barry Sullivan, Trevor Howard, Keenan Wynn; features Sam Wanamaker. Alexander Knox. Directed by Guy Hamilton. Screenplay, Keith Waterhouse, Willis Hall from Howard Fast's novel, "The Winston Affair"; camera, Wilkie Cooper; editor, John Bloom; music, Lionel Bart; assistant director, Kip Gowans. Reviewed at the studio, Jan. 6, '64. Running time, **94 MINS.**

Lt. Col. Barney Adams	Robert Mitchum
Kate Davray	France Nuyen
General Kempton	Barry Sullivan
Major Kensington	Trevor Howard
Lt. Winston	Keenan Wynn
Major Kaufman	Sam Wanamaker
Colonel Burton	Alexander Knox
Lt. Morse	Gary Cockrell
Lt. Bender	Robert Nichols
Colonel Shaw	Michael Goodliffe
Sgt. Jackson	Errol John
Major Smith	Paul Maxwell
Capt. Gunther	Lionel Murton
Colonel Thompson	Russell Napier
Capt. Dwyer	Jared Allen
Colonel Mayburt	David Bauer
Major Wyclif	Edward Underdown
Major Poole	Howard Marion Crawford
Staff Sgt. Quinn	William Mitchel
Cpl. Zimmerman	Al Waxman
Cpl. Burke	Glenn Beck
Cpl. Baxter	Frank Killibrew
Lt. at Sikri	Edward Bishop
Major Clement	Terence Cooper
Major Hennessy	Graham Skidmore
Col. Burnside	Terry Skelton
Col. Winovich	Paul Blomley
Col. Kelly	Alistair Barr
Major McCabe	Brian Vaughan
Major Cummings	Julian Burton

The Howard Fast novel, "The Winston Affair," has been retitled "Man in the Middle" and cinematically fashioned into a property that starts off with promise and concludes on a note of disappointment. This Walter Seltzer production has something going for it in the basic nature of the story, which is provocative, and the cast names headed by Robert Mitchum and including France Nuyen, Barry Sullivan, Trevor Howard, Keenan Wynn, Sam Wanamaker and Alexander Knox. Snappy exploitation could mean talkability and saleability, in some measure.

Film itself, concerning a court martial involving both American and British interests in India at the end of World War II, has as its drawback a certain amount of vagueness as to character delineation and story motivation. All things revolve around Keenan Wynn, as an American lieutenant who has killed a British sergeant and consequently goes to trial. The onlooker is set to wondering just what makes him tick.

At the very end it's unfolded that Wynn is a psycopath and not responsible for his crime. And meanwhile, words are spoken copiously a b o u t British-American political conflict and the need to resolve the issue through Wynn's getting the rope.

At the outset the stage is set for what might have been strong dramatic conflict. Good part of the potential is permitted to go unrealized. Why not more intensity, and wallop, in the screenplay by Keith Waterhouse and Willis Hall? Why not more pinpointing of the story's key angle's in Guy Hamilton's direction? These were called for but undelivered. A shortage of clarity and organization in the story-telling renders "Man in the Middle" unqualified for any special recognition. It's a pro job, of sorts, but a letdown.

Mitchum's portrayal of the defense attorney is a fair job of emoting, though actor is looking pudgy in this outing. France Nuyen's Eurasian nurse part has little bearing on the story. Trevor Howard stands out as the British medical officer who makes it clear that Wynn was out of his mind when he murdered, having mentally constructed a cause of hate in a man he loathed because of his attachment to a Negro girl and, also, a man who threatened his authority.

Barry Sullivan, Sam Wanamaker, and Alexander Knox work out well enough in other featured parts.

Film, which originated as an enterprise of Entertainment Corp. of America, credits Max E. Youngstein as exec producer. Youngstein had headed the short-lived ECA and when the latter folded, 20th-Fox took it over. It was studio-filmed in England and on location in India. Wilkie Cooper's camera work is on the right track all the way and John Bloom's editing is particularly close, adding to the sense of movement. Music · by Lionel Bart is a modest contribution.
Gene.

Dr. Strangelove: Or How I Learned to Stop Worrying and Love The Bomb

Despite grim theme a funny comedy. Good b.o. prospect if properly exploited.

Hollywood, Jan. 13.

Columbia Pictures release of Stanley Kubrick production. Stars Peter Sellers, George C. Scott; costars Sterling Hayden, Keenan Wynn, Slim Pickens; features Peter Bull, James Earl Jones, Tracy Reed. Directed by Kubrick. Screenplay, Kubrick, Terry Southern, Peter George, based on book, "Red Alert," by George; camera, Gilbert Taylor; editor, Anthony Harvey; music, Laurie Johnson. Reviewed at Directors Guild Theatre, Jan. 12, '64. Running time, **102 MINS.**

Group Capt. Lionel Mandrake	
President Muffley	Peter Sellers
Dr. Strangelove	
General "Buck" Turgidson	
	George C. Scott
General Jack D. Ripper	Sterling Hayden
Colonel "Bat" Guano	Keenan Wynn
Major T. J. "King" Kong	Slim Pickens
Ambassador de Sadesky	Peter Bull
Miss "Foreign Affairs"	Tracy Reed
Lt. Lothar Zogg (Bombardier)	
	James Earl Jones
Mr. Staines	Jack Creley
Lt. H. R. Dietrich	Frank Berry
Lt. W. D. Kivel	Glenn Beck
Capt. G. A. "Ace" Owens	Shane Rimmer
Lt. B. Goldberg	Paul Tamarin
General Faceman	Gordon Tanner
Admiral Randolph	Robert O'Neil
Frank	Roy Stephens
On Defense Team	Laurence Herder
On Defense Team	John McCarthy
On Defense Team	Hal Galili

Producer - director S t a n l e y Kubrick has with skill and daring fashioned a sharply satirical comedy on a subject as sensitive as Top Security—a nuclear holocaust—in the Columbia Pictures release, "Dr. Strangelove: Or How I Learned to Stop Worrying and Love the Bomb." This is an ideal vehicle for exploitation, and should do very well at the b.o.

Nothing would · seem to be farther apart than nuclear war and comedy, yet Kubrick's caper eloquently tackles a "Fail-Safe" subject with a light touch. While there are times when it hurts to laugh because somehow there is a feeling that the mad events in "Strangelove" could happen, it emerges as a most unusual combination of comedy and suspense.

Screenplay by Kubrick, Peter George and Terry Southern, based on the book, "Red Alert," by George, is imaginative and contains many an offbeat touch. Some of the characters have a broad brush in their depiction, but this is the very nature of satire. Kubrick also directed the film by his own production company, and successfully captured the incongruous elements of "Strangelove" with a deft, professional touch.

It all begins when a Strategic Air Command general, a right-winger whose similarity to persons still living is more than passing, who on his own initiative orders bomb-carrying planes under his command to attack Russia. He immediately seals in the base, so that there is no way for the President or anyone else to contact him, nor to countermand his orders, since he has given them in a top-secret code only he knows. From here on it's a hectic, exciting series of events, alternating between the General who has started it all, the planes enroute to the USSR, and the Pentagon's war room, where the Chief Executive is trying his best to head off the nuclear war.

Again it would seem no setting for comedy or satire, but the writers have accomplished this with biting, piercing dialogue and through characterizations. The climax is one with a grim post-script, as the Pentagon begins worrying about the mineshaft-gap in the post-nuclear era, while the Red envoy sneaks some pictures of the War Room. The moral is obvious.

Peter Sellers is excellent, essaying a trio of roles — a British R.A.F. captain assigned to the U.S. base where it all begins, the President and the title character, Dr. Strangelove, a German scientist aiding the U.S. whose Nazi mannerisms overcome him

George C. Scott as the fiery Pentagon General who seizes on the crisis as a means to argue for total annhilation of the Russia offers a top performance, one of the best in the film. Odd as it may seem in this backdrop, he displays a fine comedy touch. Sterling Hayden is grimly realistic as the General who takes it on his own to send our nuclear bomb-carrying planes to attack Russia. He is a man who blames the Communists for flouridation of water, and just about everything else. As the cigar-chomping General, Hayden emerges a tragi-comic figure.

There are uniformly fine supporting performances from Slim Pickens, Keenan Wynn, Peter Bull, James Earl Jones, Shane Rimmer, Paul Tamarin and Tracy Reed, latter the only femme in the cast, very good in a bit role, as the Pentagon General's mistress.

Production is handsomely mounted, with fine work by art director Peter Murton; Wally Veevers, special effects; Laurie Johnson's music, and excellent photography by Gilbert Taylor.

Daku.

The Incredible Mr. Limpet
(COLOR)

Fantasy of a man with a successful yen to be a fish. Outlook okay.

Weeki Wachi, Fla., Jan. 19.

Warner Bros. release of John Rose production. Stars Don Knotts, Carole Cook, Jack Weston, Andrew Duggan, Larry Keating. Directed by Arthur Lubin. Screenplay, Jameson Brewer and Rose, from novel by Theodore Pratt; camera (Technicolor), Harold Stine; editor, Donald Tait; music, Frank Perkins; songs, Sammy Fain and Harold Adamson. At Weeki Wachee, Fla., Jan. 18, '64. Running time, **102 MINS.**

Henry Limpet .... Don Knotts
Bessie Limpet .... Carole Cook
George Stickle .... Jack Weston
Admiral Harlock .... Andrew Duggan
Admiral Spencer .... Larry Keating

The seemingly unlikely area of Weeki Wachee, Florida, came to be the locale of a worldwide press premiere of Warners' "The Incredible Mr. Limpet." But actually it was not so unlikely at all.

Film itself if far out in nuttiness, theme-wise. You might even say insane. It has to do with a man who wishes so hard to become a fish that he indeed turns into one. And then, after the piscatorial metamorphosis, he guides the U.S. Navy into the best ways of destroying Nazi submarines during World War II. Henry Limpet, as the man, is Don Knotts and Henry Limpet, as the fish, is man-made animation. It was presented via an underwater screening in Weeki Wache Springs, with a glass-enclosed audience 20 feet under the surface of the water looking on to a specially-engineered, submerged screen. So it was fitting.

This kind of presentation obviously was gimmick. The important factor is that the picture is fun, and the WB junket surely should help a bit in the saleability—what with about 250 reporters from the press and radio—television presumably, at least, spelling the title right.

Producer John Rose is a former longtime production associate of Walt Disney, and his work is mightily suggestive of Disney. It's one of those basic fantasy items which could emerge as a powerhouse at the boxoffice. This reviewer pegs it as an imaginative cinemative outing that has got to be at least agreeable, and then there's the possibility it might register so soundly as to be particularly meaningful commercially.

The important thing is that the audience adjusted to accept the fantastic notion about a milquetoast citizen, with an envy for the apparently tranquilized life of a fish, who just transforms. And Arthur Lubin, as the director, working from a screenplay by Jameson Brewer and producer Rose, which in turn was from the original by Theodore Pratt has worked it in amusingly.

Music backgrounding by Frank Perkins is on the beam and several songs by Sammy Fain and Harold Adamson make for a positive asset.

Harold Styne's photography, in Technicolor, is sharp and the animation effects are fair enough, being a little short of the Disney standards.

Don Knotts is married to Carole Cook and he has more of an eye for the denizens of a fishbowl than he had for her. An interloper is Jack Weston, as a sailor with an eye for Miss Cook. Andrew Duggan and Larry Keating are admiralty brass who become parties to the situation involving the incredible man who has turned into fish and helps knock the windpipes out of those Nazi U-boats.

The screenplay by Brewer and Rose provides a good number of clever and lively lines, including one by Lady Fish who invited Henry Limpet, in fish form, off to the spawning grounds.

Particularly captivating in the yock role is Weston, who for some reason, just has difficulty in believing that his friend, Knotts, has spouted gills. Knotts measures in ideally. Others all fine. *Gene.*

Man's Favorite Sport
(COLOR)

Hot and cold running fish story about an incomplete angler. With Rock Hudson could do fairly well at b.o.

Hollywood, Jan. 14.

Universal release of Howard Hawks production. Stars Rock Hudson, Paula Prentiss; features Maria Perschy, Charlene Holt. Directed by Hawks. Screenplay, John Fenton Murray, Steve McNeil, from Pat Frank's story, "The Girl Who Almost Got Away"; camera (Technicolor), Russell Harlan; editor, Stuart Gilmore; music, Henry Mancini; assistant director, Tom Connors Jr. Reviewed at Grauman's Chinese, Jan. 14, '64. Running time, **120 MINS.**

Roger Willoughby .... Rock Hudson
Abigail .... Paula Prentiss
Easy - .... Maria Perschy
Cadwalader .... John McGiver
Tex .... Charlene Holt
Major Phipps .... Roscoe Karns
Policeman .... James Westerfield
Screaming Eagle .... Norman Alden
Fisherman Skaggs .... Forrest Lewis
Program Chairman ...... Regis Toomey
Customer Bush .... Tyler McVey
Marcia .... Kathie Browne

At its best, "Man's Favorite Sport?" generates some uncommonly adroit visual comedy, principally of the slapstick variety. But the picture is only spasmodically scintillating, for producer-director Howard Hawks apparently has forgotten that brevity is the soul of wit and that two hours is too long a stretch for one witty but limited gag premise. The Universal release doesn't look like a boxoffice world-beater but, if cleverly and appealingly marketed, could turn into a moderate moneymaker. Rock Hudson's name will be a main value.

The comically ripe premise of the John Fenton Murray-Steve McNeil scenario from a story by Pat Frank, is what happens when a celebrated but fraudulent piscatorial authority and fishing equipment salesman for Abercrombie & Fitch who doesn't know how to fish is suddenly ordered by his unaware boss to compete in a fishing tournament? For a while, the adventures of this angler (Hudson) romps along with a kind of breezy Field & Stream charm, bolstered by some inventive slapstick ideas, cleverly devised characters and occasionally sharp dialog. But then, poof, the fish story begins to sag under the weight of its bulky romantic midsection and lumbers along tediously and repetitiously to a long overdue conclusion.

Matters are helped along somewhat by an attractive and spirited cast, but not enough to keep the film consistently amusing. Hudson gives what must undoubtedly be the most watered-down performance of modern times. Not since Esther Williams hung up her bathing suit has a screen thespian been so thoroughly drenched. It's a game performance, and an ingratiating one.

Paula Prentiss, looking more attractive than in any of her previous pictures, continues to blossom as a film actress and gives evidence that she may be able to successfully incorporate her comedic skills into the romantic image necessary for premium leading lady assignments. At the moment she's about halfway between Carol Burnett and the Rosalind Russell of about two decades ago. A few more outings and PP could conceivably join the celebrated alliterate sorority of the screen, whose charter members include the late MM, BB, CC and DD.

In Maria Perschy and Charlene Holt, Hawks has come up with a couple of very decorative new dolls, especially the former, brought over from Austria. Hawks also benefits from some first-class comedy support chipped in by John McGiver as Hudson's toupee-domed employer, Roscoe Karns as a dedicated angler who worships Hudson, James Westerfield as a sympathetic but duty-bound policeman and Norman Alden, who is particularly outstanding and memorable as a quasi-Indian con man with an unmanageable yen for wampum. There's additionally support from Forrest Lewis, Regis Toomey and Tyler McVey.

Hawks purportedly utilized unorthodox directorial techniques, such as filming in sequence a day at a time in order to capture an air of comic spontaneity. Since some of the sight gag passages are uproarious, there is a lot to be said for this technique. But it appears that the main trouble with Hawks' day-at-a-time approach to comedy is that there were too many days or not enough comedy or a combination of both. Editor Stuart Gilmore could still do a lot of good for this film with a snip here and there.

Handsomely photographed by Russell Harlan, the picture boasts some colorful rustic settings by art directors Alexander Golitzen and Tambi Larsen and a characteristically novel, infectiously effervescent musical score by Henry Mancini, along with a sprightly title tune he wrote in partnership with lyricist Johnny Mercer. *Tube.*

This is My Street
(BRITISH)

Seamy tale of the back streets, with novelettish ingredients in a modishly realistic setting; favorable b.o. prospects.

London, Jan. 15.

Warner-Pathe release of a Peter Rogers production. Stars Ian Hendry, June Ritchie. Directed by Sidney Hayers. Screenplay by Bill McIlwraith from Nan Maynard's novel; music, Eric Rogers; camera, Alan Hume; editor, Roger Cherrill. Reviewed at Warner-Pathe Private Theatre, London. Running time, **94 MINS.**

Harry .... Ian Hendry
Margery .... June Ritchie
Lily .... Avice Landon
Steve .... Meredith Edwards
Kitty .... Madge Ryan
Charlie .... John Hurt
Jinny .... Annette Andre
Maureen .... Philippa Gail
Sid .... Mike Pratt
Paul .... Tom Adams
Doris .... Hilda Fenemore
Phyllis .... Susan Burnet
Mark .... Robert Bruce
Joe .... John Bluthal
Granny .... Margaret Boyd
Fred .... Carl Bernard
Ransome .... Patrick Cargill
Isabel .... Margo Johns
Fingus .... Derek Francis
Molly .... Ursula Hirst
Gindy .... Sheraton Blount

"Live Now, Pay Later" in 1962 was the film that registered Ian Hendry as a highly watchable personality. And now "This is My Street" gives him a similar role as a fast-talking and feckless womanizer and hitches him again to his partner in the earlier film, June Ritchie. If comparisons have to be made, this successor lacks the cunning and the veracity of the earlier pic, but much of the crudity in the plotting is disguised by the crisp direction of Sidney Hayers and by the excellent performances of both Hendry and Miss Ritchie. Only those with vivid memories of the past will be disappointed in this one.

Ian Hendry is the flashy Harry, lodger in a mean London street close to the railroad tracks. His eyes rove constantly over the worthy contours of Margery (June Ritchie), who lives next door with her chunky and dreary husband. Not daunted by her marital status, Harry makes an insolent play for her, and she haughtily rebuffs him. Togetherness is achieved when her little girl gets lost, and Harry does a Galahad routine in finding her.

Margery is ripe for romance, being churned up with her sordid surroundings, her unimaginative and clumsy spouse, and the general lack of purpose. So they torridly bed down in the backroom of a drinking club in which Harry has an interest. He's also a peddler of fake jewellery.

So far, so illicitly sexy — until Margery's educated sister returns for a visit. She has an upper-crust suitor in tow but this again does not frighten Harry. He is tiring of Margery's jealousy and possessive grip, and chases her sister with added zest. Margery is brusquely discarded, and doesn't like it. When Harry succeeds to the extent of planning marriage with sister Jinny, Margery settles for suicide. She doesn't succeed, but the notes she leaves behind enlightens everyone about Harry's lack of scruples, and it ends in boy-leaves-girls bit.

Not content with this meaty, but more or less adequate, storyline, scripter Bill McIlwraith indulges in a sub-plot that topples into unconvincing melodrama. It also connects little with the main proceedings, and it is couched in such corny and contrived terms that it rouses unwanted yocks. The flighty Maureen (Phillipa Gail) picks up a rich dentist and milks him for money without much finesse.

But while Hendry and Miss Ritchie are around, the film keeps up interest. Hendry, in particular, is exactly right, filling out the conventional character of the guy who won't settle for as much as the material allows. He also scores with some glib dialog allotted him.

Miss Ritchie is also fine as the embittered Margery, and gives her best pic portrayal to date. She effectively translates Margery's frustration, and makes her credible and moving. Avice Landon is also quietly correct as her mother. Newcomer Annette Andree registers as Jinny, with a capacity for fun.

Phillipa Gail overplays the grasping Maureen, turning her to caricature, but admittedly she has little chance in the part. Other performances are often stiff and exaggerated, though John Hurt makes an impression as a highly irrelevant barman who privately dotes on Maureen. Mike Pratt is well suited as the coarse Sid, Margery's husband.

Sidney Hayer's direction never loiters, and makes fine use of the seedy London settings. Editor Roger Cherrill also knows when to stop. Alan Hume's photography is sharp. An appropriately jazzy musical soundtrack come from Eric Rogers, and it tends to sum up the whole hectic affair. It looks like a promising contender at local firstruns, and marks a further step in the progress of Hendry, who has international potential outside of this type pic.
Otta.

Children of The Damned
(BRITISH-PANAVISION)

Unsatisfactory followup to 1960 British sci-fi shocker. Approached too pretentiously.

Hollywood, Jan. 9.
Metro release of Lawrence P. Bachmann production. No star credits. Directed by Anton Leader. Screenplay, Jack Briley; camera, David Boulton; editor, Ernie Walter; assistant director, Ted Sturgis. Reviewed at the studio, Jan. 9, '64. Running time, **90 MINS.**
Col. Tom Lewellin .... Ian Hendry
Dr. David Neville .... Alan Badel
Susan Eliot .... Barbara Ferris
Colin Webster .... Alfred Burke
Diana Looran .... Sheila Allen
Paul .... Clive Powell
Mark .... Frank Summerscales
Rashid .... Mahdu Mathen
Aga Nagalo .... Gerald Delsol
Nina .... Roberta Rex
Mi-Ling .... Francnesca Lee
Harib .... Harold Goldblatt
Mr. Davidson .... Patrick Whyte
General Miller .... Tom Bowman
Professor Gruber .... Martin Miller
Russian Official ...... Andre Mikhelson

Like most sequels, "Children Of The Damned" isn't nearly as good as its predecessor — Metro's 1960 release, "Village Of The Damned," nor is it likely to be as successful at the boxoffice. What weakens this sequel is the fact that, unlike the original, it is burdened with a "message." The attempt at endowing it with moral significance is heavyhanded, unnecessary and too pretentious an aim for so relatively modest a production venture.

The Lawrence P. Bachmann production, filmed in England by Englishmen, is apt to rely commercially on the same exploitation angles that helped sell the earlier production. The same customers, recalling the above average quality of the original, figure to be attracted back, but they will be disappointed. The new but unsatisfactory approach to the same basic situation will confuse and irritate them. As for those who weren't there the first time around, they should be completely mystified by the events of this film.

Jack Briley's screenplay broadens the scope to an international scale of what was originally a taut little sci-fi shocker. This time those strange, handsome, parthenogenetic children with the genius IQ's, destructive dispositions and raygun eyes are not mere invaders from the outer limits bent on occupying earth, but are actually premature samplings of man as he will be in, say, a million years. And they have arrived for a curious purpose—to be destroyed, presumably to enable the silly, warlike contemporary man to learn some sort of lesson. The only lesson to emerge clearly from all of this, however, is—if you're going to get eyeball to eyeball with modern man, you'd better blink because if you don't he'll just blow you to bits.

There are one or two genuinely funny lines in Briley's scenario and they are inherited by the character of a geneticist played engagingly by Alan Badel. A few of Badel's scenes with Ian Hendry, who plays an idealistic psychologist, are the best in the picture. Otherwise it's tedious going, and Anton Leader's lethargic direction doesn't help any. Barbara Ferris has a key role, as do Alfred Burke, Sheila Allen and moppet Clive Powell. Memorable they aren't.

Technical credits are generally capable, but not especially distinguished. *Tube.*

491
(SWEDISH)
Stockholm, Jan. 14.
Svensk Filmindustri production and release. Stars Lars Lind, Leif Nymark, Stig Tornblom, Lars Hansson. Sven Algotsson, Torleif Cederstrand, Bo Andersson, Lena Nyman; features Frank Sundstrom, Ake Gronberg, Mona Andersson. Directed by Vilgot Sjoman. Screenplay by Lars Goerlin after his best selling novel; camera, Gunnar Fischer; music, Georg Riedel. Reviewed at Svensk Filmindustri, Stockholm. Running time, 105 MINS.
Krister .... Lars Lind
Nisse .... Leif Nymark
Egon .... Stig Tornblom
"Pyret" .... Lars Hansson
"Jingis" .... Sven Algotsson
"The Butcher" ..... Torleif Cederstrand
"The Fish" .... Bo Andersson
Sieva .... Lena Nyman
The Inspector .... Frank Sundstrom
The Preacher .... Ake Gronberg
Kajsa .... Mona Andersson
The Examiner .... Jan Blomberg
German sailor ...... Siegfried Wald
German sailor .... Wilhelm Fricks
Policeman .... Erik Hell
Policeman .... Leif Liljeroth

This is the most-discussed film in Sweden at the present time. The State Censorship Board voted to ban it, giving as a reason for the action that the pic was against the law of pornography. The producer has appealed to the government, and chances are that it will allow the film to be shown eventually, after certain cuts.

The title, "491," was taken from the Bible, where one of the disciples asked Jesus: "How many times shall I forgive my enemies, will seven times be enough" and Jesus answered: "Not seven times, but 70 times seven times . . .," the preacher in the film saying this means that we have promised the forgiveness for '490 sins, but the Lord has said nothing about the 491st sin.

This is a so-called social drama about six criminal teenagers, who are chosen by the authorities for an experiment. Together with a teenage social worker and student, they live in a house where they are free to do almost anything they like. But every morning they must report to the authorities and describe how they have spent their day.

However, not everything is as it should be. The Inspector to whom they report every day shows homosexual tendencies and gets involved with two of the teenagers. When they ask him for payment, he refuses saying: "People, in my position are accused so often that the authorities pay no attention to it any longer; you are welcome to go to the police with your complaints."

One night the teenagers sneak aboard a German ship in the harbor, looking for alcohol. There they meet the teenage girl Steva (Lena Nyman) who has been raped by one of the sailors. They take her along back to where they live. And later on, they use her as a prostitute when they need money.

The film ends tragically. In their desire to hurt everybody around them, the teenagers force Steva to have unnatural sexual contact, a scene well described in the novel. This is not actually shown in the film except that certain noises together with the dialog give a very good idea of what's happening.

The film is said to have been made as a social drama in order to describe that not everything is as wonderful as it could be in a welfare country. If the idea has been to shock, the producer has been very successful.

Nudity does not exist in the picture except for a few, and compared with other films, innocent scenes. The girl, Steva, is seen nude backside a couple of times, and that is about all. In other cases, as when she is raped, the camera shows the faces of the people around and just about how they feel.

This film presents no happy ending, and there is no "crime does not pay" angle.

Most of the actors are non-pros. Lars Lind, as Krister, a social worker who lives with the boys, is a widely known actor here. Same applies to Frank Sundstrom as the homo Inspector. The six teenagers are all new faces, who have never appeared in films before, but all contribute fine performances. Lena Nyman, as Steva, has been seen in pix and tele, playing minor roles. She does very well in an unsympathetic role. Direction and screenplay is tops.

However, this still is a dark, cruel film. The teenagers speak an obscene language. The most surprising thing is that the censors banned this under the law against pornography. Since Swedish censors are very careful about films showing violence, this film could have been banned for this alone.

This is the second pic made by director Vilgot Sjoman, a disciple of Ingmar Bergman. His first film, "Alskarinnan," has been picked as a foreign production for the next Oscar race.

"491" seems very dubious for export, except in countries where "Swedish sin" has a market. Since the Swedish censors are known as one of the most liberal regarding sex, the question is what censorship in other countries will say.

Overlooking the dark, brutal story this tells, the film is artistically a masterpiece as far as acting, direction, camerawork and music are concerned. *Winq.*

Mondo Cane No. 2
(ITALIAN—COLOR)
Rome, Jan. 15.
Cineriz production and release. A film by Gualtiero Jacopetti and Franco Prosperi. Directed by Mario Maffei and Giorgio Cecchini. Camera (Technicolor), Benito Frattari; music, Nino Oliviero; editor, Mario Morra; commentary, Gualtiero Jacopetti. At Modernissimo, Rome. Running time, **97 MINS.**

Followup film to the much-discussed and successful "Mondo Cane" may have the same bite and controversiality as its prototype. But it in no way measures up to the No. 1 pic. Its returns, though very promising, are likely to pay the consequences of this.

Subject is naturally exploitable, It's once again a discussion piece, has many unusual facets to it. But somehow, this lacks the sweep, the feeling for humanity (sick and controversial though it may have been) which contributed to the wide success of the first one.

Once again, here we have the juxtaposition by contrast of beast and man, and their treatment in distant corners of the earth. Once again, one is made to ponder on the follies of civilization and the sanity of the native. Once again, the sacred is closely matched to the profane, allowing the audience to draw its own conclusions. But here more than before, there is a feeling of construction, of following a pre-set pattern rather than happening on to the unusual by chance.

The sequence showing cranes dying out because of a lake polluted by a man-made factory, for one obvious example, closely resembles the one in "M.C. No. 1" showing the extermination of tortoises on a Bikini atoll, both in montage and theme. Other sequences border on the revolting, though it's unfortunately known that there's an audience for such footage somewhere.

In every way, the picture is faithful to its predecessor (lush lensing and music score, etc.), but only rarely measures up to it—though, often topping other similar local efforts of the recent past. Gualtiero Jacopetti's commentary is incisive and outspokenly characteristic. But one again has the feeling that pic is less his personal effort than that of a team attempting to get the "feel" of his previous hits ("Women of the World" was the other) into material which he himself did not shot. *Hawk.*

Batmanova, Singing Slave
(RUSSIAN-COLOR-SONGS)
(Kinopanorama)
Paris, Jan. 12.

Mosfilm production and release. With Tamara Semina, Dimitri Smirnov, Evgueni Leonov, Sergue Filippov. Directed by Roman Tikhomirov. Screenplay, L. Zakharov, E. Guerken, S. Vogelsohn; music, Nicolai Strelnikov; camera (Sovcolor), E. Chapiri; editor, M. Pen. At Kinopanorama, Paris. Running time, 92 MINS.
Batmanova .... Tamara Semina
Andrei .... Dimitri Smirnov
Nikita .... Evgueni Leonov
Prince .... Sergue Filippov

Russia now comes up with a one-projector Kinpanorama (akin to the Yank one-camera Cinerama) process and uses it for an operetta pic. It is set in an old style sort of Graustarkian Russia of old, with a wicked Prince and two lovers. Not the sort of pic for arty houses abroad but with enough general entertainment aspects for lingo spots.

Batmanova is an ex-Russian serf who comes back to the Court of a ruthless selfish 19th Century Prince as his lead singer after conquering Paris. The Prince wants her but she loves a young nobleman who is technically still a serf to the Prince since his papers have been lost.

All the obvious plotting finally leads to the happy ending. There is the comic sidekick and his girl, ballroom scenes, some nice terp bits, and rhythmic songs and pleasant voices. Playing and song dubbing is good. This also makes its social points about classes if it is disguised in the usual operetta shenanigans.

Players have the right larger than life stances, and, if pic sometimes repeats itself, this has movement and lightness not usually seen in Russo musical pic. Sovcolor seems less washed out than usual. *Mosk.*

La Pupa
(The Doll)
(ITALIAN)
Rome, Jan. 15.

Cineriz release of a Guido Glambartolomei production for Royal Films. Stars Michele Mercier; features Ettore Manni, Riccardo Garrone, Lia Zoppelli, Francesco Mule, Rossella Como. Directed by Giuseppe Orlandini. Screenplay, Ugo Guerra, Luciano Martino, Roberto Gianviti, from story by Martino and Guerra; camera, Raffaele Masciocchi; music, Nino Oliviero. At Mazzini, Rome. Running time, 107 MINS.
Pupa .... Michele Mercier
Barone .... Riccardo Garrone
Gianni .... Ettore Manni
Elena .... Lia Zoppelli

Exploitable item which could overcome basically local story approach via adroit selling for foreign market possibilities.

Rather confused story line has several people in a small north Italian town trying to buy what formerly was the local call house from its onetime madam, who refuses to sell out. When she eventually dies, a series of intrigues finally winds place in hands of a onetime employee, the "Pupa" of the title.

Humor is frequently gross and lowdown, and the situations overelaborated and obvious. But here and there, between leers, there's a genuine laugh, or two. Most of acting honors go to Michele Mercier, as the enterprising filledejole. A colorful cast with Francesco Mule, Riccardo Garrone, and Ettore Manni gives okay backstopping. Other credits are consistent. *Hawk.*

Belgium Fest

Guns of the Trees

Anguish in the "beat" milieu of Manhattan. Life is harrowing. Suicide is heroine's answer. Limited playoff probable.

Knokke, Jan. 14.

NACG release and production. With Adolfas Mekas, Frances Stillman, Ben Carruthers, Argus Carruthers. Written, directed, edited and photographed by Jonas Mekas with additional photography by Sheldon Rochlin; poetry read by Allan Ginsberg and Stuart Perkoff. At Belgian Experimental Film Fest. Running time, 85 MINS.
Gregory .... Adolfas Mekas
Barbara .... Francis Stillman
Ben .... Ben Carruthers
Argus .... Argus Carruthers

Greenwich Village's Jonas Mekas has made a film in the modern vein with a series of scenes rather than a narrative style, plus inserted poetry read on the sound track. It takes a look at a certain American anxiety which is stated more in a surface style than with any depth. It is thus mainly an arty entry and limited, at best, to specialized showings.

Item reflects the so-called beatnik philosophy of hatred of, and anguish over, convention, American materialism and the ugliness of life there, at least from view of such characters. Some rant. Some join protest marches. Some accept things. Others opt for suicide.

Basically film concerns a girl who feels that everything is worthless and horrible. She finally kills herself when nobody can help her, including a priest, a tormented intellectual and two life-esteeming friends. The film poses the problem about who is guilty but remains somewhat too romantic and sentimental in its accusations and intimations.

Everybody may be guilty it seems to say, or that life is just harrowing and one must live it aware of its failings. Failings of the pic itself are to show these characters in a convincing perspective within their society or environment. It is true many have no direct contact with it and evolve in their own clicks and groups.

Film sometimes waxes grandiloquent. Characters seem sterile and self-pitying rather than tragic. But, at moments some insight and feeling of plight comes through. Frances Stillman is properly intense and lost as the girl while Adolfas Mekas has a tormented gauntness as the intellectual who can not help her.

It is Ben and Argus Carruthers who give a poetic fillup to the pic in their dignified, quiet attachment and genuine care for each other. They are a married couple. She works. He tries but usually fails. She is a pert Negro actress with refreshing looks and presence while he has sharp projection and the ability to create a mood.

Footage is technically good with some fine imagery on New York's lower East Side life. Mekas displays filmic knowhow, though a tendency to obvious symbols and overindulges in breast beating. *Mosk.*

Die Parallelstrasse
(Parallel Streets)
(GERMAN-COLOR)
Knokke, Jan. 7.

Gesellschaft Film production and release. Directed by Ferdinand Khittl. Screenplay, Bodo Bluthner, Khittl; camera (Eastmancolor), Ronald Martini; editor, Irmgard Henrici. At Belgian Experimental Film Fest. Running time, 95 MINS.

Pic is a canny gimmick rather than a regular film in its own right. It works some good diverse color documentary scenes, in various parts of world, into a sort of suspense, search film in which a group of men are trying to resolve the meaning of these apparently unrelated scenes. It makes for a strangely absorbing pic if somewhat too arch in treatment. This has arty and playoff possibilities if well handled.

A group of men sit alongside another who instructs them that they must find out who the man is hinted about in a series of scenes. They are lensed in black and white and the documents in color. They see, as does the audience, the scenes and comment on them.

Also rung in are the facts that they can not leave till they solve the riddle. They discuss and analyze to seemingly no avail as the scenes are shown to them. There is a man in South America of Germanic origin who has built a life for himself but must move on, another man who died in some exotic South Sea Isle, lost cities and useless new ones.

The documentary scenes are good in their own right and do get some edge from the discussions. If nothing is really proved, the far-out approach makes this a clever new wrinkle on travel documentaries. It won the top prize at this recent Belgian Experimental Film Fest where the jury felt it added a new dimension to travel aspects and created its own form and outlook.

Anyway, it has enough color and entertainment, in spite of its tricky and talky cementing aspects, to have this something that could pay off with regular audiences as well as more selective ones. It is a gimmick that has worked. Color is good and editing sharp with a solid counterpointed musical score. *Mosk.*

Futari
(Couple)
(JAPANESE)
Knokke, Jan. 7.

Richie production and release. Written and directed and edited by Donald Richie. Camera, Clifford Harrington. With Smila Stefanovitch, Kiyoshi Hosoya. At Belgian Experimental Film Fest. Running time, 60 MINS.
Woman .... Smila Stefanovitch
Man .... Kiyoshi Hosoya

Donald Richie, an American, has written a definitive book on the Japanese cinema. And now he has made a film there which shows a feeling for the architecture, mood and atmosphere of that country where he has lived for many years. However, it is somewhat too mannered and literary and, along with its length, looks like primarily only for specialized and arty situations abroad, preferably supported by another medium length film.

This deals with the affair between a pretty thirtyish American woman and a handsome 26-year-old Japanese boy. The film rocks back and forth in time, makes its points in slow, posed scenes with commentary by both the man and woman on the incidents. She speaks in English and he in Japanese, so it would need no subtitles in the U.S.

Neither can speak to the other but theirs is a more than physical love and Richie manages to catch this in well-observed scenes. The woman is waiting for the boy and relives their affair in a series of scenes that have no chronological order but convey their first love, the boy's anger when he feels just a sort of object and humiliation and their finally deciding to try again in spite of the many things that separate them.

Obviously influenced by "Hiroshima Mon Amour," this has the same intermingling of time and events. Richie also uses sound adroitly if sometimes he forces up the sound level to give a feeling of anger rather than letting it emulate from the characters.

Playing is graceful and easy. This is more a muted series of incidents than a richly narrative pic. It sometimes overdoes symbols and effects. Film's slowness and repetitions often get in the way of its theme and characterizations. But both players respond nicely. Richie shows some definite filmic flair and can be promising when he assimilates his obvious influences and learns how to integrate his characters more fully into life rather than posing them.

It has a good technical polish and is a promising, if somewhat arty start. *Mosk.*

Zulu
(BRITISH-COLOR)

Joseph E. Levine's first adventure into British production, with stirring yarn of factually-based epic military exploit; loaded with exploitation angles, it looms as sturdy b.o. prospect.

London, Jan. 23.

Paramount release (Embassy in U.S.) of Joseph E. Levine presentation of Diamond Films Ltd. production. Stars Stanley Baker, Jack Hawkins, Ulla Jacobsson, James Booth, Michael Caine. Narration, Richard Burton. Directed by Cy Endfield. Screenplay, John Prebble and Endfield, from original story by Prebble; music, John Barry; camera, Stephen Dade; editor, John Jympson. Reviewed at the Plaza, London. Running time, **135 MINS.**
Lieut. John Chard ....Stanley Baker
Rev. Otto Witt ....Jack Hawkins
Margareta Witt ....Ulla Jacobsson
Private Henry Hook ......James Booth
Lieut. Gonville Bromhead .Michael Caine
Colour-Sergeant Bourne ....Nigel Green
Private Owen ....Ivor Emmanuel
Sergeant Maxfield ....Paul Daneman
Corporal Allen ....Glynn Edwards
Private Thomas ....Neil McCarthy
Private Hitch ....David Kernan
Private Cole ....Gary Bond
Private 612 Williams ......Peter Gill
Lance-Corporal ....Tom Gerrard
Surgeon Reynolds ....Patrick Magee
Private 593 Jones ....Richard Davies
Gunner Howarth ....Dafydd Havard
Private 716 Jones ....Denys Graham
Corporal Schiess ....Dickie Owen
Hughes ....Larry Taylor
Sergeant Windridge ....Joe Powell
Stephenson ....John Sullivan
Sick Man ....Harvey Hall
Adendorf ....Gert Van Den Bergh
Commissary D'lton ......Dennis Folbigge
Company Cook ....Kerry Jordan
Bugler ....Ronald Hill
Cetewayo ....Chief Buthelezi
Jacob ....Daniel Tshabalala
Red Garters ....Ephraim Mbhele
Dance Leader ....Simon Sabela

Joseph E. Levine makes an impressive debut in British film production with "Zulu," a picture with potent b.o. potential, and one that also allows ample scope for his flamboyant approach to showmanship. This has all the proven ingredients for bigscale exploitation, which will clearly be reflected in the boxoffice returns.

Based on a famous heroic exploit, when a handful of British soldiers withstood an onslaught by 4,000 Zulu warriors, the Stanley Baker-Cy Endfield production is distinguished by its notable onscreen values, which are enhanced by top-quality Technicolor-Technirama lensing by Stephen Dade. It also has an intelligent screenplay by John Prebble and Endfield, which avoids most of the obvious cliches. It keeps the traditional British stiff upper-lip attitudes down to the barest minimum.

Authenticity is helped by the extensive use of Natal locations. The picture gets off to a memorable start with scenes of mass wedding celebrations, in which young barebreasted Zulu maidens, each carrying a small spear as proof of their chastity, perform a tribal dance with the warriors they are to marry. (Incidentally, this provides the basis for one of the promotional aids, already receiving exploitation locally via the introduction of the "Zulu Stomp" in dance halls and clubs.)

The defense of the garrison at Rorke's Drift took place on Jan. 22, 1879, and significantly the world preem of the filmic reconstruction of that episode took place on the 85th anni. At the time the garrison heard the news that the 4,000 Zulu braves were on the way, reports had just come in that a far larger garrison had been completely wiped out, and there was no prospect of help from any other source.

Senior officer at Rorke's Drift at the time was a lieutenant in the Royal Engineers, who had been sent to build a bridge over the River Buffalo, and he assumed command and rejected advice to evacuate the garrison. At this point in the yarn, the script focusses briefly on an inevitable conflict with another lieutenant, a professional who feels he has a hereditary right to command, but once the leadership is firmly established, private squabbles are set aside to prepare the maximum defense with the minimum resources.

There were just eight offices and 97 men, apart from the sick and wounded, to resist wave after wave of Zulu attackers, some armed with spears and others with rifles captured from the British. The perimeter defenses, consisting of a few upturned wagons and a wall hastily built of mealie bags, could not withstand the weight of the attack for long, and bitter and bloody hand-to-hand fighting ensued. Yet the defenders, their numbers seriously depleted, held their positions, and after an epic battle lasting through the night, the attackers withdrew with a salute to the bravery of their opponents. Eleven of the defenders received the Victoria Cross, the highest British military decoration.

Endfield's skillful and forceful direction adroitly builds up the suspense to the start of the campaign. And the ensuing battle scenes which continue through to the end of the film have a powerful sweep, yet are never repetitive. The mood and the tempo is occasionally changed by a variety of human touches, one of the best of which shows the defenders (all from a Welsh regiment and noted for their voices) singing "Men of Harlech" in answer to tribal war chants coming from the Zulu warriors.

One of the more obvious cliches in this type of yarn is apt to be the malingerer who displays great heroism in a moment of crisis. There is such a situation in "Zulu," but the cliche is avoided, largely because of the excellent performance by James Booth. Indeed, the high allround standard of acting is one of the notable plus features. Stanley Baker, a solid and reliable performer, turns in a thoroughly convincing portrayal as the resolute RE officer, with an effective contrasting study by Michael Caine as a supercilious lieutenant. Their admission, after the battle is over and won, that neither had had previous combat experience, is another of the warm human touches which are sprinkled through the film.

Jack Hawkins has an offbeat role as a missionary who pleads in vain with Baker to evacuate the garrison, and then urges the men to obey the biblical "Thou Shalt Not Kill" commandment and lay down their arms. As always, he plays it with consummate skill. Ulla Jacobsson has little to do as his daughter, though attractively provides a negative feminine interest. Both fade out of the picture around the halfway mark, when Baker sends them off in their wagon, rather than risk a demoralizing influence on the men.

Richard Burton contributes a brief and dignified narration. There are also a number of solid supporting contributions, especially from Nigel Green, Ivor Emmanuel, Paul Daneman, Glynn Edwards and many other members of the big cast. High grade technical qualities round off a classy production. *Myro.*

La Cuisine Au Beurre
(Cooking With Butter)
(FRENCH-FRANSCOPE)

Paris, Jan. 21.

Valoria release of Corona-Dear Film production. Stars Fernandel, Bourvil; features Claire Maurier, Henri Vilbert, Michel Galabru, Andrex. Directed by Gilles Grangier. Screenplay, Jean Levitte, Pierre Levy-Corti, Raymond Castans; camera, Roger Hubert; editor, Madeleine Gug. At Marignan, Paris. Running time, **90 MINS.**
Fernand ....Fernandel
Andre ....Bourvil
Christiane ....Claire Maurier
Maitre ....Henri Vilbert
Postman ....Michel Galabru
Barman ....Andrex

What should have been an almost bawdy comedy comes out a tidy, compact situation affair that appears primarily a local bet, on the pull of the starred one-name comics appearing in their first pic together, Bourvil and Fernandel. It's primarily a dualer or exploitation possibility on its theme in the foreign market.

Fernandel has spent 13 years holed up with a buxom Bavarian woman since the war. Her husband's impending return from Siberia has him going back to France at last. But he finds his wife remarried and his old bistro turned into a fancy restaurant by her new husband. Bourvil is the latter.

Then Fernandel feigns he has been in Siberia and is taken in by his ex-wife and her husband. And complications arise when it seems he has to give her a divorce since he is legally still the husband. Then come all sorts of dodges until Fernandel gives in and is also faced by his ex-Bavarian mistress whose husband has gone back to his Siberian girl friend.

Fernandel uses his heavy mugging and familiar gestures to etch an acceptable portrait of the feckless, slothful ex-husband while Bourvil is more subtle as the sensitive member of the triangle. But direction keeps the comedy in low gear and it too often depends on the earthy shenanigans of the duo. And these are not inventive enough to give this the depth it needs.

Film technically is good and appears good for boxoffice results here if it would need the hardsell overseas. *Mosk.*

Dark Purpose
(COLOR)

Silly, clumsily plotted suspense meller set against some lovely Italo scenery. Weak b.o. indicated.

Universal release of Galatea-Lyre-Brazzi-Barclay-Hayutin production. Stars Shirley Jones, Rossano Brazzi, George Sanders; features Georgia Moll, Micheline Presle. Directed by George Marshall. Screenplay, David P. Harmon, based on novel by Doris Hume Kilburn; camera (Technicolor), Gabor Pogany; music, Angelo F. Lavagnino; editor, Giancarlo Cappelli; assistant director, Frank Marchione.

Reviewed at Universal, N. Y., Jan. 13, '64. Running time, **97 MINS.**
Karen Williams .... Shirley Jones
Count Paolo Barbarelli .. Rossano Brazzi
Raymond Fontaine .... George Sanders
Cora Barbarelli .... Georgia Moll
Monique Bouvier .... Micheline Presle

How all the respectable talents involved could have succeeded in turning out such a silly melodrama is the only mystery contained in "Dark Purpose." Perhaps they were touched by the Mediterranean sun, which so brilliantly lights the Italian Riviera landscapes and provides the pic — periodically — with a certain amount of eye appeal. "Purpose," otherwise, has very little.

Shirley Jones, Rossano Brazzi and George Sanders are toplined in this obvious bit of film-flammery. Brazzi is seen as a double-dealing Italo count who seeks to pass off his mentally ill wife, Georgia Moll, as his daughter in order to wed a pretty young American art expert, Miss Jones. Sandres is along just for the ride in his role as Miss Jones' art appraiser boss, while Micheline Presle turns up from time to time as Brazzi's unhappy mistress.

David P. Harmon's screenplay, which opens with Sanders and Miss Jones arriving at Brazzi's villa on a commission to appraise his various art treasures, makes an unsuccessful attempt to combine mystery and romance, spiced with wit. In the latter connection, Sanders, the acid-tongued critic of the world-at-large, is called upon—in effect—to parody some of his best remembered roles. Brazzi seems equally ill-at-ease as the narrative lumbers along, requiring him first to appear as a rather world weary intellectual and then as a love-crazed killer, dropping clues and suggesting menace with all the subtlety of the cat in a Tom & Jerry cartoon. The mice of the piece don't fare much better, and there are times when the Technicolor camera, which does so handsomely by the scenery, does anything but flatter the Misses Jones, Moll and Presle.

Vet George Marshall has directed the tale with no apparent enthusiasm or sense of discipline. This is evident in lines or dialog which meet with unsolicited laughs, as when Brazzi, with murder in his heart, batters at Miss Jones' door and is told by her: "Please don't come in, I've just taken a tranquilizer!"

Steve Barclay produced, with Paul Baron and Harvey Hayutin as exec producers. *Anby.*

Dead Ringer

Double dose for Bette Davis buffs. Hokey suspense meller with star as twin killer.

Hollywood, Jan. 14.

Warner Bros. release of William H. Wright production. Stars Bette Davis, Karl Malden, Peter Lawford; features Philip Carey, Jean Hagen. Directed by Paul Henreid. Screenplay, Albert Beich, Oscar Millard, from story by Rian James; camera, Ernest Haller; editor, Folmar Blangsted; music, Andre Previn; assistant directors, Charles L. Hansen, Lee White. Reviewed at the studio, Jan. 14, '64. Running time, **115 MINS.**
Margaret and Edith .... Bette Davis
Sgt. Hobson .... Karl Malden
Tony Collins .... Peter Lawford
Sgt. Hoag .... Philip Carey
Dede .... Jean Hagen
Paul Harrison .... George Macready
Matriarch .... Estelle Winwood
George .... George Chandler
Garcia .... Mario Alcalde
Henry .... Cyril Delevanti
Janet .... Monika Henreid
Dan .... Bert Remsen
Apt. Manager .... Charles Watts
Capt. Johnson .... Ken Lynch

Aggressive salesmanship and the Bette Davis name will probably have to carry the boxoffice burden for this old-fashioned suspense melodrama about homicidal twin sisters. The story doesn't hold up very well under close scrutiny, so the William H. Wright production will have to rely on the wicket support of the less discerning, less selective picturegoer and the incurable Bette Davis buff. A big initial impact should be the target for the Warner Bros. release. Beyond that, it's apt to be tough commercial sledding.

Miss Davis, who, along with Joan Crawford, seems to have launched a new shocker-oriented career with the recent "Baby Jane," enacts the pivotal dual role in the Albert Beich-Oscar Millard screenplay from a story by Rian James. For some rather foggy and dubious reason inconsistent with the character itself, the relatively "nice" poor sister (Edith) murders the relatively unappealing rich one (Margaret) and assumes her identity. For some equally unconvincing reason, the boys down at homicide fail to deduce the pretty obvious crime, and the truth also eludes Edith's ardent beau, police sergeant Jim Hobson (Karl Malden). After three months of successful masquerade, Edith is confronted by Margaret's enterprising lover, Tony (Peter Lawford), who has been "vacationing" abroad ever since, it is disclosed, he and Margaret disposed of her mate. The question, then, is not which twin gets the Tony, but whether Tony gets the twin before she gets him. The ending, alas, is pure hokum.

The enactment of twins is nothing new to Miss Davis, who did it before 18 years ago in "A Stolen Life." She achieves good contrast in her dual portrayal and carries on gamely and with considerable histrionic relish in the combination assignment. It is not, however, a very rewarding role for her, although there is always a certain bonus challenge in the enactment of twins. If nothing else, twice as much lower case Bette Davis is better than none, though not nearly as good as one upper case Bette Davis.

Malden is his usual reliable self as the somewhat dense policeman. Lawford seems rather ill-at-ease as the mercenary lover boy. Others of passing import are Philip Carey, Jean Hagen, George Macready, Estelle Winwood, George Chandler, Mario Alcalde, Cyril Delevanti, Monika Henreid, Bert Remsen, Charles Watts and Ken Lynch. Paul Henreid's directorial tempo is somewhat cumbersome and lethargic in spots, particularly in the early going, but then he hasn't a very fresh or distinguished piece of material with which to work.

The most impressive thing about "Dead Ringer" is the rich and macabre musical score composed for the occasion by Andre Previn. It is the most virile aspect of the picture. Ernest Haller's photography is a plus factor. As noted, the film drags now and then, a negative characteristic that might have been—and still might be—smoothed over by editor Folmar Blangsted. Perry Ferguson's art direction is apt and impressive. *Tube.*

Madmen of Mandoras

Unsatisfactory supporting item.

Hollywood, Jan. 22.

Crown International release of Carl Edwards production. No star credits. Directed by David Bradley. Screenplay, Richard Miles, from story by Steve Bennett; camera, Stanley Cortez. Reviewed at World Theatre, Jan. 22, '64. Running time, **74 MINS.**
Phil Daly .... Walter Stocker
Kathy Day .... Audrey Caire
Camine .... Carlos Rivas
John Coleman .... John Holland
Suzanne .... Dani Lynn
Frank Dvorak .... Marshall Reed
Alaniz .... Nestor Paiva
David Garrick .... Scott Peters
Padua .... Pedro Regas
Tom Sharon .... Keith Dahle
Mr. H .... Bill Freed

The sting of this "B" will poison any double feature program unlucky enough to inherit it. Ineptly written and chaotically directed, the Carl Edwards production for Crown International is a melodramatic fiasco that is apt to cause even less discerning audiences to squirm.

Hitler rides again in the Richard Miles scenario from an original story by Steve Bennett. This time he turns up in the Caribbean isle of "Mandoras," to which he had been transported after an operation in which his head was decapitated and "perpetuated" by last-ditch Nazi fanatics in order to preserve that teeming brain. But der Fuehrer is foiled again in his plot to overthrow the world by means of a deadly nerve gas.

Prominently embroiled in this dramatically incoherent rumpus are Walter Stocker, Audrey Caire, Carlos Rivas, Dani Lynn and Bill Freed, latter as Hitler. The picture is currently paired with "Comedy Of Terrors" in a city-wide L.A. engagement. *Tube.*

Sekstet
(Sextet)
(DANISH)

Copenhagen, Jan. 21.

Flamingo Studio release of Johan Jacobsen production. Stars Ingrid Thulin, Ghita Norby. Directed by Annelise Hovmand. Original story by Paul Bach; screenplay, Paul Bach, Annelise Hovmand; camera, Kalle Andersson, Niels Carstens; music, Erik Fiehn, Sahib Shihab. At the Imperial Bio, Copenhagen. Running time, **94 MINS.**
Elaine .... Ingrid Thulin
Lena .... Ghita Norby
Peter .... John Kelland
Robert .... Axel Strobye
John .... Ole Wegener
Rachel .... Hanne Ulrich

Even before its release, this Danish New Wave film drew international attention. An English-speaking version was shot simultaneously with the Danish edition for a London preem. Its top femme star is Sweden's Ingrid Thulin, protege of Ingmar Bergmann. Its producer-director team, Johan Jacobsen and Annelise Hovmand, created a minor uproar in the U.S. with their film, "A Stranger Knocks." And "Sextet" represents yet another new twist in cinematic treatment of the subject of sex.

Twist is the word for it. "Sextet" involves six people, all emotionally and sexually twisted into terrifying knots. Miss Thulin plays a novelist whose creative powers are running dry while she gushes hysterical tears and guzzles raw whiskey in an attempt to hold on to her second husband, Axel Strobye. He has tired of her but feels pity for her teenage daughter, Hanne Ulrich. Not enough pity, however, to check his own prowling instincts when he suddenly finds himself confronted with a young innocent but animalistic woman, Ghita Norby, who is shocked by the discovery that her two suitors feel more for each other than ordinary male friendship.

The action takes place in and around a summer house somewhere in a coastal region that allows for some fine scenic shots. But interest is concentrated primarily on the six people who are forced by bad weather to spend a night together. Director Annelise Hovmand directs her camera crew better than her actors. The film contains a lot of superior footage having photographic beauty. Her weak point, however, is her direction of the players. Actually, only Miss Thulin speaks her lines convincingly. And it is unfortunate that so many of the lines are rather programmatic. The lonely are damned, she yells in case anybody should have missed this all too obvious point. And it is the only point made by this film.

All in all, the film certainly will stir interest. The scenes where the two young men fight in a way that seems a concealed way of making love is strong stuff but discreetly handled. The traditional boy-meets-girl-in-bed sequence is surprisingly boring, but Miss Norby is a doll with rather fine porcelain features. Besides her film work, she is an established dramatic actress of the stage. *Kell.*

The Comedy of Terrors
(PANAVISION-COLOR)

Horror comedy about a mortician who "creates" his own clients. Okay b.o. prospect.

Hollywood, Jan. 20.

American International release of James H. Nicholson-Samuel Z. Arkoff production. Stars Vincent Price, Peter Lorre, Boris Karloff; features Basil Rathbone, Joyce Jameson, Joe E. Brown. Directed by Jacques Tourneur. Screenplay, Richard Matheson; camera (Pathecolor), Floyd Crosby; editor, Anthony Carras; music, Les Baxter; assistant director, Robert Agnew. Reviewed at Joe Shore's screening room, Jan. 20, '64. Running time, **88 MINS.**
W. Trumbull .... Vincent Price
Felix Gillie .... Peter Lorre
Amos Hinchley .... Boris Karloff
John F. Black .... Basil Rathbone
Cemetery Keeper .... Joe E. Brown
Amaryllis Trumbull ..... Joyce Jameson
Mrs. Phipps .... Beverly Hills
Riggs .... Paul Barsolow
Phipp's Maid .... Linda Rogers
Black's Servant .... Lurce Nicholson
Mr. Phipps .... Buddy Mason

The tongue-in-check approach to the horror film has become a speciality of American International Pictures over the past few years, but this latest effort in that category leaves much to be desired. The raw material for a jovial spoof of chillers was there, but the comic restraint and perception necessary to capitalize on those natural resources is conspicuously missing. Still AIP is apt to get some pretty fair boxoffice mileage over the short haul out of "The Comedy of Terrors" thanks largely to moppet support and its innate exploitability, but beyond its irresistible attraction for younger children the film is limited in audience range and appeal.

Too many producers have been known to spoil the froth. This picture boasts no fewer than four who fall roughly into that exalted category: "producers" James H. Nicholson and Samuel Z. Arkoff, "co-producer" Anthony Carras and "associate producer" R i c h a r d Matheson, who is also credited with the screenplay. Matheson's scenario is rich in satiric promise, but realizes its potential only momentarily and fitfully.

Story has to do with a tippling mortician (Vincent Price) who, in arrears on his rent, takes it upon himself to "create" his own customers. He gets his comeuppance thanks to a combination of three unlikely factors: the virtual indestructibility of his Shakespeare-obsessed landlord - victim (Basil Rathbone), the bizarre romance that erupts between his mistreated, would-be coloratura spouse (Joyce Jameson) and his unwilling, tone-deaf henchman (Peter Lorre), and the unexpectedly effectual intervention of his senile father-in-law (Boris Karloff).

In order for a film of this nature to be effective and fully satisfying to more than the most childish audience faction, it must be developed and executed with a deft touch so that the comic-satiric approach does not crush the horror-suspense aspects of the story. No such deftness is displayed here. Under Jacques Tourneur's heavy-handed direction, "The Comedy of Terrors" is neither sufficiently comical nor terrifying.

As deliciously grotesque a gallery of histrionic rogues as could conceivably be assembled on one Hollywood sound stage has been herded together for this project, making the result all the more disappointing. Evidently they have all been instructed to ham it up with all the uninhibited thespic flourish they can muster, and they have followed their orders extremely well. Alas, too well. Comedy such as this should be allowed to ooze out of a subtly wry approach. Outrageous overacting only serves to smother the satiric essence. Poof, goes the spoof. In addition to the aforementioned players, others who cavort briefly across the screen are Joe E. Brown, Beverly Hills, Paul Barsolow, Linda Rogers, Luree Nicholson, Buddy Mason and a cooperative cat named "Rhubarb."

Workmanlike assists to the production have been fashioned by such craftsmen as cameraman Floyd Crosby, editor Anthony Carras, art director Daniel Haller and composer Les Baxter. *Tube.*

Les Parapluies De Cherbourg
(The Umbrellas of Cherbourg)
(FRENCH-COLOR-SONGS)

Paris. Jan. 28.
20th-Fox release of Madeleine-Parc-Beta Films production. With Catherine Deneuve, Anne Vernon, Nino Castelnuovo, Marc Michel, Ellen Farmer, Mireille Perrey. Written and directed by Jacques Demy, with music by Michel Legrand. Camera (Eastmancolor), Jean Rabier; editor, A. M. Cotret. Previewed in Paris. Running time, 95 MINS.
Genevieve .... Catherine Deneuve
Guy .... Nino Castelnuovo
Mother .... Anne Vernon
Cassard .... Marc Michel
Aunt .... Mireille Perrey
Madeleine .... Ellen Farmer

It takes nerve to make a pic in which all dialog is sung when tuners rate low at the b.o. in France. "West Side Story" was the exception here. Also, there is no dancing and this is not a filmed operetta or opera. Picture is an original, eye-filling, fetching affair that appears to have the legs for both arty house and even more general situations abroad provided its way is eased with tact and taste.

Jacques Demy went to the port town of Cherbourg to make this simple tale of a boy and girl in love. He is depicted leaving for the army, with said girl pregnant, and she giving in to her mother's blandishments and marrying a well-heeled suitor. He comes back and finally marries a childhood friend and they see each other briefly one Christmas night as both go back to their regular lives.

Seemingly banal and sentimental on the surface, director-writer Demy has avoided these aspects by tasteful handling and the right balance in emotion, compassion and narrative. The feeling develops from the pic as the singing allows the tale to be taken on its own terms.

Thus, once everybody singing their lines is accepted, this takes on a sort of fabled feel. Pic becomes touching without being mawkish, simple sans being trite, and lovely to look at. So the lovers seemingly floating down a street is quite acceptable as are the gorgeous colors that can make tawdry interiors attractive and real streets almost surreal.

Michel Legrand has supplied a richly tuneful score that still is not ostentatious and also serves as a sharp counterpart to help story points and enhance the moods. The bright sets and the excellent color work are also assets.

Catherine Neneuve, a winsome looking type, that other directors have forced to act, here is allowed to be herself. She etches a fine portrait of a 16-year-old in love. Nino Castelnuovo has presence and poise as the boy. Others are all fine in their supporting roles. The dubbed voices, done in playback and recorded before shooting started, are all fitting for the various characters. They have the folksy, natural air that make them vibrant.

The fragile story has the slice of life, romantic look of the pre-war Hollywood comedies, but possessing a feeling and beguiling flair all its own. It looms a film that could make its way everywhere on its intrinsic rightness in atmosphere and tone. But it will need a helping hand via proper selling. Critics and word-of-mouth should help, too.

It is something old, in a disarming story, which has been done up in a bright, new package. It has fine production dress.

20th-Fox is distributing this pic in France, Belgium and Switzerland. Film has already won the top critical award of the year, the Prix Louis Delluc, even before release. It will probably break the jinx on musical pix on its home grounds. The title stems from an umbrella store owned by the girl's mother. *Mosk.*

Seven Days in May

Novel about military plot to overthrow the American Government makes absorbing cinema, with Burt Lancaster, Kirk Douglas, Fredric March and Ava Gardner among the names. Major production. Global boxoffice.

Paramount release of joint production by Seven Arts, Kirk Douglas's Joe Productions and John Frankenheimer's Company, with Edward Lewis as individual producer. Stars Burt Lancaster, Kirk Douglas, Fredric March, Ava Gardner; features Edmond O'Brien, Martin Balsam, George Macready. Directed by John Frankenheimer. Screenplay, Rod Serling, from novel of same title by Fletcher Knebel and Charles W. Bailey II; camera, Ellsworth Fredricks; editor, Ferris Webster; music, Jerry Goldsmith. At Paramount homeoffice Jan. 23, '64. Running time, 120 MINS.
Gen. James M. Scott .... Burt Lancaster
Col. Martin Casey ...... Kirk Douglas
Pres. Jordan Lyman .... Fredric March
E'eanor Holbrook ..... Ava Gardner
Sen. Raymond Clark ... Edmond O'Brien
Paul Girard .... Martin Balsam
Christopher Todd .... George Macready
Sen. Prentice .... Whit Bissell
Harold McPherson .... Hugh Marlowe
Arthur Corwin .... Bart Burns
Col. Murdock .... Richard Anderson
Lt. Hough .... Jack Mullaney
Col. "Mutt" Henderson Andrew Duggan
Col. Broderick .... John Larkin
White House Physician
                      Malcolm Atterbury
Esther Townsend .... Helen Kleeb
Admiral Barnswell ..... John Houseman
Bar Girl .... Colette Jackson

A combination of competents has drawn from the novel of the same title a strikingly dramatic, realistic and provocatively topical film in "Seven Days in May." Fletcher Knebel-Charles W. Bailey II's book detailed a military plot to overthrow the Government of the United States "in the not-too-distant future." It is fascinating in its reflections of present-day political attitudes and its exploration of what could conceivably happen momentarily.

The Capitol Hill and Pentagon and White House maneuverings, as taken from the popular book and deftly transcribed in screen form by Rod Serling, appear more genuinely for-real today than anybody's version of a twilight zone. It is done with such absence of false melodrama—that there's not a suggestion of far-fetchedness in the basic premise.

What "Seven Days in May" undertakes is the proposition that extremists could reach the point where they'd try to uproot the present form of government. Perhaps self-deluded as God's appointees, that would wrest control and thus become the nation's "deliverers."

Such a man, in the fiction at hand, is Gen. James M. Scott, played with authority by Burt Lancaster. He's a member of the Joint Chiefs of Staff, burning with patriotic fervor and seeking to "save" the country from the perils of a just-signed nuclear pact with Russia. He enlists the support of fellow chiefs, their codified correspondence being in the form of betting of a Preakness horse race. Their plan of seizure is to be consummated in seven days in May.

Edward Lewis's production is neither over-elaborate in mounting and trappings nor in running time. It's compact and a trim two hours. An abundance of exciting story is gotten across.

Preachiness is avoided except for the reflective comment by the

President near the finis, when Scott and his cohorts are ingeniously proved to be the conspirators and are put to rest. The President, portrayed by Fredric March as an idealistic rather than forceful man, states: "The enemy is an age, a nuclear age. Out of this comes a sickness. And every now and then we look for a man in red, white and blue. For some of us it was a Senator McCarthy. For others a General Walker. And now a General Scott."

The performances are excellent down the line, under the taut and penetrating directorial guidance of John Frankenheimer. Both Serling and Frankenheimer have outstanding credits in television, as writer and director, respectively, and their experience somewhat shows through with this theatrical production. It achieves some of its wallop at times via the quiet underplay (it has its explosive moments, too) that has been witnessed in the top-quality drama that tv has sporadically yielded.

Kirk Douglas is masterfully cool and matter of fact as Gen. Scott's aide, utterly devoted until he comes to be suspicious. He goes to the President with information that has got to be checked out in those fateful seven days.

(Incidentally, the final of the seven days is a Sunday and this is to mesh with the Preakness race; but, to be captious, or at least observant, there's no such thing as a horserace on Sunday in the States.)

Edmond O'Brien is standout as a southern senator with an addiction to bourbon and an unfailing loyalty to the President. He is among the trusted few assigned to investigate the evidence of the dastardly plot.

Ava Gardner is not so much the ingenue any more, but works out well enough as the Washington matron who has had an affair with Lancaster and is amenable to a go with Douglas. Martin Balsam is truly vivid as a Presidential aide, as is George Macready as Secretary of the Interior, both at the side of the President in tracking down the origin of the conspiracy.

In lesser but nonetheless significant parts, all handled meaningfully, are Whit Bissell, Hugh Marlowe, Bart Burns, Richard Anderson, Jack Mullaney, Andrew Duggan and others. Duggan particularly is on view only a short time but comes through with remarkable effect.

The conclusion is logically written out; there's no letdown as the President works out his subtle resolution of the vast problem at hand.

Ellsworth Frederick's photography is pertinently graphic and editor Ferris Webster has scored sharply with the editing. Music by Jerry Goldsmith is so unobtrusive as to be barely heard, and yet it's a definite complement to the action.

This is a truly moving picture play, with dramatic power that is certain to be felt in foreign lands. There's obviously a keen awareness of the U.S. Presidency by peoples abroad, this awareness having been enhanced by the assassination of President John F. Kennedy, and should add to the global interest in "Seven Days in May."

Paramount has a worldwide hit.

Gene.

Mort, Ou Est Ta Victoire?

(Death, Where Is Your Victory)
(FRENCH—TOTALSCOPE)

Paris, Jan. 28.

Gaumont release of Filmel production. Stars Pascale Audret, Laurent Terzieff, Michel Auclair; features, Olivier Despax, Elisabeth Ercy, Jacques Monod. Directed by Herve Bromberger. Screenplay, Daniel-Rops, Frederic Grendel, Bromberger from novel by Daniel-Rops; camera, Pierre Petit; editor, Pierre Ginette. At Colisee, Paris. Running time, **135 MINS.**

Laure	Pascale Audret
Thierry	Laurent Terzieff
Jean	Michel Auclair
Rene	Olivier Despax
Alix	Elisabeth Ercy
Doctor	Jacques Monod

Sudsy pic, obviously aimed at the distaff trade, rates as a grand soap opera. The heroine does not age in 20 years but goes through a melodramatic calvary that is lacking in depth or characterization. Based on a runaway bestseller, it could emerge an okay home item but it seems a slim export possibility.

The troubles she has before she becomes a nun entitle her to a private wailing wall. An orphan, she is accused of lesbian tactics with the daughter of a family bringing her up because the son turns over letters to his father that have passed between the two girls. The story pussyfoots on this, and it might have been girlish elan, but not giving in to the boy brings this revenge.

Then she goes to work in a parochial school where an old priest tries to help her find herself. A man with an invalid wife falls for her. She sacrifices her virginity to a shady doctor. And so it goes, till she decides to become a nun, not seemingly from faith, but because of her harrowing life.

Attempted modern direction, via overlapping sound, half the screen fading in on another image and sharp ellipses in time and place, does not help give this forced drama any weight or true emotional feeling.

Pascale Audret deserves plaudits for her attempt to breathe life into this synthetic creature but she can not overcome the pompous tale. Others walk through their roles and just serve to fill out Miss Audret's mortal troubles. Pic has already received a Catholic Film Office Prize. Pic is technically ordinary.

Mosk.

One Man's Way

Rev. Norman Vincent Peale biopic, capably dramatized for most part but bogged down in spots by story's inherent wordiness. Limited appeal, needs special-angle selling.

Hollywood, Jan. 24.

United Artists release of Frank Ross production. Stars Don Murray; features William Windom, Virginia Christine, Carol Ohmart; introduces Diana Hyland. Directed by Denis Sanders. Screenplay, Eleanore Griffin, John W. Bloch, based on Arthur Gordon's book, "Minister To Millions"; camera, Ernest Laszlo; editor, Philip W. Anderson; music, Richard Markowitz; assistant director, Herbert Greene. Reviewed at 20th, Jan. 24, '64. Running time, **100 MINS.**

Norman Peale	Don Murray
Ruth Peale	Diana Hyland
Rev. Clifford Peale	William Windom
Anna Peale	Virginia Christine
Evelyn	Carol Ohmart
Mary	Veronica Cartwright
Dr. Gordon	Liam Sullivan
Mrs. Gordon	June Dayton
Bishop Hardwick	Ian Wolfe
Lafe	Charles Lampkin
Instructor	Arthur Peterson, Jr.
Mrs. Thompson	Hope Sommers
Miss Collingswood	Virginia Sale
Leonard Peale (as a child)	Rory O'Brien
Robert Peale (as a child)	David Bailey
Norman Peale (as a child)	Mickey Sholdar
Feldman	Paul Marin
Jack Wilson	Hank Stanton
Organist	Bryon Byrne
Gas Station Attendant	Eddie Ryder
Harry (Reporter)	Edward Peck
Elder Marcus	John Harmon
Elder Thompson	Joseph Hamilton
Prof. Aiken	Tom Palmer
Alma	Sandra Gale Bettin
Margaret Peale	Wendy Ferdin
Elizabeth Peale	Sharyl Locke
John Peale	Butch Patrick
Robert Peale (grown)	Gerald Gordon
Leonard Peale (grown)	Tom Skerritt
Mr. Melton	Vernon Rich
Tom Rayburn	Bing Russell
Receptionist	Ann Morgan Guilbert
Mr. Boardman	Edward Prentiss
Rod Allenberry	Arthur Marshall
Mae Michaels	Geraldine Wall
John Hellman	Jon Lormer
Woman	Jean Carson

The story of the Fifth Avenue metaphysical clergyman, Norman Vincent Peale, is told with considerable dramatic efficiency in "One Man's Way." Unfortunately, the milestones of Peale's life, being principally of a "spiritual" and therefore physically uneventful nature, are of the type not easily convertible into motion picture image drama. This challenge has been met with a good deal of dramatic resourcefulness by the creative team of the Frank Ross production, but there are stretches where artistic ingenuity appears to bog down and give way either to apparent "contrivance" for the sake of visual impact or else to the inevitable in a religiously-oriented film—the long, wordy preachment from the pulpit.

The United Artists release is fortunate to have some highly engaging players in its leading roles, notably Don Murray as Peale and a newcomer, Diana Hyland, as the girl who becomes his wife. But "One Man's Way" is a film decidedly limited in range of audience appeal, and it will take more than a few attractive personalities or the power of positive thinking, with which Peale is identified in real life, to make it a boxoffice success.

The screenplay by Eleanore Griffin and John W. Bloch, based on Arthur Gordon's book, "Minister To Millions," traces Peale's life from a childhood incident through his triumph in the relatively recent disapproval within the Protestant fold over his self and religion-promoting methods. Along the way, screenplay pauses to examine some of the more eventful phases of his life such as his awakening to his destiny, his three years at the seminary, his first sermon, his wholesome courtship and his happy marriage.

Murray delivers a firm, earnest and intense delineation of the celebrated and enormously glib minister, coming through with special force and conviction where his histrionic talent is needed the most—in those lengthy and verbose pulpit passages. Miss Hyland, a fresh and interesting new personality, makes an auspicious screen bow, playing her part radiantly and vivaciously. Effective in key characterizations are William Windom as Peale's minister father and Virginia Christine as his devoted mother. Balance of support is generally efficient.

Director Denis Sanders has extracted the maximum degree of dramatic voltage out of the script, but in searching for moments of levity or whimsy he has, in several instances, settled for devices that emerge a trifle too "cute" and shopworn. On the whole, though, he's done a commendable job, as have cameraman Ernest Lazzlo, editor Philip W. Anderson, art director Edward Jewell and composer Richard Markowitz.

Tube.

A Global Affair

Infant abandoned in UN building creates international snarl. Lacklustre romanticomedy and lean b.o. candidate.

Hollywood, Jan. 22.

Metro release of Hall Bartlett production. Stars Bob Hope; features Lilo Pulver, Michele Mercier, Elga Andersen, Yvonne DeCarlo, Robert Sterling, Miiko Taka, John McGiver, Nehemiah Persoff, Mickey Shaughnessy, Jacques Bergerac. Directed by Jack Arnold. Screenplay, Arthur Marx, Bob Fisher, Charles Lederer, from story by Eugene Vale; camera, Joseph Ruttenberg; editor, Bud Molin; music, Dominic Frontiere; assistant directors, Tom Shaw, Lee Lukather. Reviewed at Stanley Warner BevHills Theatre, Jan. 22, '64. Running time: **84 MINS.**

Frank Larrimore	Bob Hope
Sonya	Lilo Pulver
Randy	Robert Sterling
Lisette	Michele Mercier
Duval	Jacques Bergerac
Dolores	Yvonne DeCarlo
Yvette	Elga Andersen
Fumiko	Miiko Taka
Segura	Nehemiah Persoff
Panja	Tanya Lemant
Snifter	John McGiver
Jean	Georgia Hayes
Gavin	Edmund Ryan

Even Bob Hope is unable to enliven this drab romantic comedy about an abandoned waif who becomes the center of a United Nations controversy. Boxoffice prospects are anything but encouraging for the Seven Arts-Hall Bartlett production and Metro release.

According to the screenplay by Arthur Marx, Bob Fisher and Charles Lederer from a story by Eugene Vale, the forsaken infant, after being discovered in the internationally owned territory of the UN building, is placed in the temporary custory of a department head (Hope) and quickly becomes the object of a politically-motivated international competition to officially adopt it. After being wooed by beauteous representatives of various nations, Hope decides to adopt the child himself, and proclaims it "the world's first truly international citizen" before the General Assembly. As the film concludes on this note of pretentious preachment, one almost expects to see, superimposed on the screen, an announcement that the picture is a public affairs presentation of MGM.

Public service, maybe, but as entertainment it fails. The script is flat and childish and littered with superficial gag dialog at the expense of reality. The outcome is never in doubt and the characters are stereotypical. Jack Arnold's direction is lethargic and fails to clarify many of the points the screenplay is apparently trying to make.

Hope has little with which to work, and doesn't get much comedy mileage out of this vehicle. Lilo Pulver and Michele Mercier make good impressions, former as a Russian agent, latter as the Belgian doll who ultimately lands Hope. Elga Andersen and Yvonne De-

Carlo etch key distaff roles with oomph, and Robert Sterling, John McGiver and Mickey Shaughnessy chip in comic support that isn't very comical. Nehemiah Persoff and Jacques Bergerac are among those wasted. Denise & Danielle Monroe share the role of the baby and just about steel the show—about par for the course for infant thespians.

A level of competence is attained by such craftsmen as lensman Joseph Ruttenberg, editor Bud Molin, art directors George W. Davis and Preston Ames and composer Dominic Frontiere. "So Wide The World," a marketable ballad by Frontiere and Dorcas Cochran, is sung tenderly behind the main titles by Vic Dana. *Tube.*

A Yank In Viet-Nam

Timely exploitation meller filmed in troubled land. Promising.

Hollywood, Jan. 24.

Allied Artists release of Wray Davis production. Stars Marshall Thompson, Enrique Magalona, Mario Barri, Kieu Chinh. Directed by Thompson. Screenplay, Jane Wardell, Jack Lewis, from latter's story; camera, Emmanuel I. Rojas; editors, Basil Wrangell, Orven Schanzer; music, Richard LaSalle; assistant director, Nguyen Van Duc. Reviewed at the studio, Jan. 24, '64. Running time, **80 MINS.**

Maj. Benson .... Marshall Thompson
Andre .... Enrique Magalona
Houng .... Mario Barri
Kieu Chinh .... Herself
Col. Haggerty .... Urban Drew
Kastens .... Donald Seely
Chau .... Hoang Vinh Loc
Quon .... My Tin
Father Francois .... Rene Laporte
Col. Thai .... Doan Chau Mau
Kim .... Pham Phuoc Chi
Dr. The .... Nam Chau
Madame The .... Kieu Nanh
Viet Cong Leader .... Le Van
Cung .... Nam Luong

Allied Artists has a marketable piece of merchandise in "A Yank in Viet-Nam," an action melodrama filmed entirely on location in that strife-torn nation. Although undistinguished as screen literature and devoid of revealing insight into the nature of that conflict, the Wray Davis production, thanks to its newsy title and timely, topical subject matter, should fulfill profitably the commercial destiny for which it has been consciously designed—the top half of an exploitation doubleheader.

The Jane Wardell-Jack Lewis scenario from the latter's original yarn describes the perils encountered in South Viet-Nam by a Yank Marine major (Marshall Thompson) after his helicopter is shot down by Viet Cong forces. The balance of the picture is concerned with the efforts of Thompson and a guerrilla band of Viet-Namese to rescue a doctor who has been captured by the enemy, during which mission Thompson falls madly in love with the doc's daughter (Kieu Chinh).

Thompson does a workmanlike job in a dual capacity as actor-director, although several scenes could have been sped up a bit. Miss Chinh, who makes her screen bow, is a pretty and appealing heroine. Enrique Magalona has strength as the mute guerrilla leader and Mario Barri warmth as one of the fighters. Balance of support is adequate, and the level of production performance is satisfactory for a budget picture. *Tube.*

The Leather Boys
(BRITISH)

Salty mean-street melodrama, delivered with vigor that helps to disguise a flabby story-line. Delayed release may affect its b.o. chances because it's a tardy ripple in the realistic wave.

London, Jan. 28.

British Lion-Garrick release, through BLC, of a Raymond Stross production. Stars Rita Tushingham; features Dudley Sutton, Gladys Henson, Colin Campbell. Directed by Sidney J. Furie. Screenplay, Gilliam Freeman, based on novel by Eliot George; music, Bill McGuffie; camera, Gerry Gibbs; editor, Reginald Beck. Reviewed at the Empire, London. Running time, **108 MINS.**

Dot .... Rita Tushingham
Reggie .... Colin Campbell
Pete .... Dudley Sutton
Gran .... Gladys Henson
Reggie's Mother .... Avice Landon
Reggie's Father .... Lockwood West
Dot's Mother .... Betty Marsden
Uncle Arthur .... Martin Mathews
Boy Friend .... Johnny Briggs
Les .... James Chase
Mr. Lunnis .... Geoffrey Dunn
Mrs. Stanley .... Dandy Nicholls
Woman Receptionist ... Elizabeth Begley
Brenda .... Valerie V[illegible]n
[illegible] .... Jill Mai Meredith
Man-in-Jeans .... Brian Phelan
Merchant Seaman .... Oliver Mac. Greevy
School Teacher .... Sylvia Kaye
School Girl (1) .... Sandra Caron
School Girl (2) .... Tracy Rogers
Bus Conductress ..... Carmel McSharry
Publican's Wife .... Joyce Hemson

This film has become a talking-point, sight unseen, in the current hassle about independent producers claiming a raw deal from the two major circuits. Completed nine months ago, it has now been slotted into a March date on the A.B.C. circuit and gets a West End preem. In this instance, the lapse of time has probably damaged its commercial possibilities, for familiarity has bred some indifference to mention of "queers" and "bleeders" while the sight of dirty dishes has lost much of its novel charm, if it ever had any.

Unluckily, too, the film hasn't the potency of situation or depth of insight shown by its predecessors. Main theme is the doomed marriage of a couple of immature kids. Reggie (Colin Campbell), who spends a riotous leisure as a motor-cyclist, hitches up with Dot (Rita Tushingham), who sees the union as a release from parental control. They honeymoon at a holiday camp, out of season and rainswept, and dissension sets in immediately.

Dot is a sociable twister, but Reggie moodily sits on the sidelines, for no good reason. The crackup comes when Dot turns out an incompetent wife, chary of making beds and relying on a daily diet of canned beans. This dampens Reggie's sex urge and he departs to live with grandma and takes up with a "buddy" called Peter (Dudley Sutton).

Despite Pete's insistent affection, his reluctance to associate with girls, and his housekeeping ability, Reggie does wise up to the fact that he's a homosexual. As the audience gets the drift early, this somewhat punctures the plot. The couple gag around on their bikes, with Dot making a few resentful appearances. She claims to be pregnant in order to get her husband back, but the trick does not work. And their final reconciliation is prevented when Reggie returns home to find Dot has invited another guy around to share the bed.

So Reggie decides to go to sea with Pete. But he sees the light just in time, when Pete meets up with a bunch of sailors, who are blatantly man-crazy. After this highly improbable revelation—exaggerated in conception and execution—Reggie retreats into the middle distance, looking shattered.

Virtues of the pic lie in Sidney Furie's direction and in the two male performances. Furie has a sharp eye for sleazy detail, and he uses the underprivileged backgrounds to telling visual effect. There are occasions when the treatment falls into caricature, but not enough to destroy authenticity. Gilliam Freeman's screenplay, culled from a novel by Eliot George, is also capable in its ear for verbal mannerisms, but it doesn't give coherence to the characters. Little sympathy can be stirred up for any of them, with the possible exception of Pete. Both Dot and Reggie behave with childish petulance, and their immaturity doesn't appeal.

Dudley Sutton, however, registers strongly as the spry, loyal Pete. He subtly indicates the forced gaiety, the need for popularity, that disguise his sexual inclinations and the loneliness they bring him. Newcomer Colin Campbell, too, makes a promising debut as the uncomprehending Reggie, displaying a sturdy sincerity that is often effective. Rita Tushingham is also good as Dot, but she is allowed to overplay the girl's perversity and incompetence in the early stages, making it all the harder to believe that any husband would return after once having escaped.

Other working-class types are competently filled out by Gladys Henson, Avice Landon, and Betty Marsden, with a superb half-minute from Geoffrey Dunn as a whispering undertaker. Bill McGuffie comes up with background music in the expected jazzy vein. Gerry Gibbs' lensing of seaside, cafe, and grim streets is appropriately grainy. Editing, by Reginald Beck, is taut.

"The Leather Boys" is, in fact, a crisp and capable film in last season's package. Even if it had been given to the public as soon as it was completed, it wouldn't have jostled in the top drawer with "Saturday Night, Sunday Morning" or "A Kind of Loving." Indeed, even nine months ago, it would have begun to show its age. *Otta.*

Pressure Of Guilt
(JAPANESE-TOHOSCOPE)

Hollywood, Jan. 28.

Toho Co. Ltd. release of Ichiro Sato-Hideyuki Shiino production. Stars Keiju Kobayashi, Tatsuya Nakadai. Directed by Hiromichi Horikawa. Screenplay, Shinobu Hashimoto; camera, Hiroshi Murai; music, Toru Takemitsu. Reviewed at Toho La Brea Theatre, Jan. 28, '64. Running time, **113 MINS.**

Ochiai .... Keiju Kobayashi
Hamano .... Tatsuya Nakadai
Wakida .... Hisashi Ikawa
Munekata .... Koreya Senda
Hirao .... Akira Nishimura
Muramatsu .... Mayumi Ohzora
Munekata's wife .... Chikage Awashima
Ochiai's wife .... Nobuko Otoba

The prolific Toho Co. of Japan has arrestingly contrived murder melodrama in "Pressure Of Guilt." The Ichiro Sato-Hideyuki Shiino production leads its audience through a maze of psychological blind alleys before untangling itself into a surprise conclusion. Although the story seems somewhat hokey and overly involved, it has been portrayed with force and conviction by a talented cast and directed with considerable cinematic flair by Hiromichi Horikawa, erstwhile young assistant to the renowned Akira Kurosawa. All in all, it is a competent display of filmmaking, and should be a popular entry with Japanese audience.

Shinobu Hashimoto's scenario depicts the unexpected and ironic twists and turns that evolve in the course of an investigation by a public prosecutor (Keiju Kobayashi) into the case of a young woman who has been found strangled. The woman happens to have been the cheating wife of an elderly attorney who is an outspoken foe of capital punishment and in whose employ toils the apparent murderer (Tatsuya Nakadai). However, a young burglar has been charged with the crime, has confessed to the investigator, and has been condemned to death. Pangs of conscience, coupled with Kobayashi's extra-curricular sleuthing, lead Nakadai to reveal himself as the killer. At this point, scenarist Hashimoto switches from psychological fast balls and begins throwing curves. When the dust clears, the burglar turns out to have been the actual murderer, Nakadai has committed suicide and Kobayashi is in the hospital having—of all things—an operation for piles.

Kobayashi gives an outstanding delineation of the conscientious prosecutor whose search for the truth hampers the progress of his career up the politically-involved law enforcement ladder. Hisahi Ikawa makes a vivid impression as the embittered, tubercular young burglar. Nakadai performs with intensity as the ill-fated man in the middle. Lovely Mayumi Chzora plays capably as his fiancee, and others who score in prominent roles are Akira Nishimura, Koreya Senda and Chikage Awashima. Solid production performance is attained by cameraman Hiroshi Murai, art director Hiroshi Mizutani and composer Toru Takemitsu. *Tube.*

Ladies Who Do
(BRITISH)

Mild, stereotyped farce, which largely squanders the talents of its promising team of stars; moderate prospects in undemanding locations.

London, Jan. 28.

British Lion-Bryanston release, through BLC, of a George H. Brown production. Stars Peggy Mount, Robert Morley, Harry H. Corbett, features Miriam Karlin, Dandy Nichols, Avril Elgar. Directed by C. M. Pennington-Richards. Screenplay, Michael Pertwee, from an idea by John Bignell; music, Ron Goodwin; camera Geoffrey Faithfull; editor, Oswald Hafenrichter. Reviewed at the Odeon, Marble Arch, London. Running time, **85 MINS.**

Mrs. Cragg .... Peggy Mount
Colonel Whitforth ..... Robert Morley
James Ryder .... Harry H. Corbett
Mrs. Higgins .... Miriam Karlin
Emily Parish .... Avril Elgar
Mrs. Merryweather ...... Dandy Nichols
Mr. Tait .... Jon Pertwee
Mr. Stang .... Nigel Davenport
Foreman .... Graham Stark
Inspector .... Ron Moody
Police Driver .... Cardew Robinson
Dr. MacGregor .... John Laurie
Ryder's Chauffeur .... Arthur Howard
Mrs. Parish .... Margaret Boyd
Miss Pinsent .... Joan Benham
Compressor Driver ..... Brian Rawlinson
Driller .... Harry Fowler

The only man who comes out of this one with much credit is John Bignell. It was his original idea, and it should have fared better. A troop of women, who daily clean the offices of highpowered financial tycoons, band together in a stockbuying syndicate—getting their tips about the future movements of shares from the waste baskets and blotting pads of their employers. This basis plot is neat and promising, but most of the bloom has faded in its translation to the screen.

Heading the team of charwomen is Mrs. Cragg (Peggy Mount), who has Colonel Whitforth (Robert Morley) as a lodger. He is the man with the speculative outlook who forms a company with Mrs. Cragg and her cleaning cronies. He holds meetings to sift the scraps of paper they bring to him.

The company booms for a while but it looks like foundering when the colonel invests the lot in a pig-farm on dubious information. The rambling plot also takes in the maneuvers of James Ryder (Harry H. Corbett), a selfmade property dealer who has bought the street in which Mr. Cragg lives and intends to rip the houses down and replace them with offices.

It is Mrs. Cragg's fight to save the street which occupies the last half of the film, and which sets it sagging. Climax is a revolt of dames who prevent the demolition men from working their machinery by pratfalling around with their groceries, letting the air out of auto tires, etc. Director C. M. Pennington-Richards lacks the light touch for this kind of frolic, and the capers lack zest. In fact, the direction throughout is as lissom as a bulldozer and heavily deflationary.

Michael Pertwee's script is replete with ponderous gags, and is also short on gaiety. It is the playing that sustains mild interest, and induces the odd yock every ten minutes or so.

Peggy Mount, in less than her usual stentorian form, gives some body to the thin material, but Robert Morley, his ebullience subdued, is almost entirely wasted in these unlikely proceedings. Harry H. Corbett is agreeable as the fastbuckmaking tycoon who gets his comeuppance, but the character is not extravagant enough for his comic gifts. Miriam Karlin, in an impersonation lifted intact from her "Rag Trade" tv skein, deserves more prominence while Avril Elgar dithers nicely as a charwoman with slowmoving greymatter.

Minor comic cameos from Graham Stark, as an officious foreman, and Ron Moody, as a harassed cop, give a slight boost to the closing minutes. The film has a musical theme, from Ron Goodwin, that is quite fetching and might improve out of its context. Editing, by Oswald Hafenrichter, can do little to give point and pace to the plodding direction.

The pity is that the idea might have been lifted into higher realms if it had developed with the flair of the postwar Ealing comedies. *Otta.*

Montevideo
(The House In Montevideo)
(GERMAN)
(Color)

Berlin, Jan. 28.
Constantin release of Hans Domnick production. Stars Heinz Ruehmann and Ruth Leuwerik; features Paul Dahlke, Ilse Page, Michael Verhoeven. Hanne Wieder. Directed by Helmut Kaeutner. Screenplay, Kaeutner and Curt Goetz; camera (Eastmancolor), Guenther Anders; music, Franz Grothe; editor, Klaus Dudenhoefer. At Zoo Palast, Berlin. Running time, **122 MINS.**

Professor Traugott Naegler	Heinz Ruehmann
Marianne, his wife	Ruth Leuwerik
Atlanta	Ilse Page
Pastor Riesling	Paul Dahlke
Herbert	Michael Verhoeven
Mayor	Fritz Tillmann
Druggist	Herbert Kroll
Martha	Doris Kiesow
Carmen del la Rocco	Hanne Wieder
Attorney	Viktor de Kowa

There seems little doubt that Hans Domnick's "House In Montevideo" will shape as one of the big German boxoffice hits of current season. The names of Heinz Ruehman and Ruth Leuwerik, both on top of the German popularity list, will lure the masses in this country. As will Curt Goetz. The late author-director-actor has still a powerful name. Incidentally, this Domnick production is a remake of the 1951 Goetz film. Foreign chances seem best in German-lingo countries. Chances elsewhere are dubious because the humor in this is perhaps too Germanic.

As contrasted with the old "Montevideo," which drew millions of German cinemagoers 12 years ago, the new one is double in many ways, both on cost and length. It is in color and Panavision. Artistically, it seems as though the color as well as the widescreen and the length (122 minutes) are superfluous. The producers' argument is of course, that color and widescreen are things that tele can't offer.

The best about this new film are still the Goetz' dialog sequences. Even if they are often silly, they contain wit and fun. Wisely enough, Kaeutner saved much of the original. Unfortunately, he occasionally lets Goetz go too far. "Montevideo" then becomes a rather banal film.

Plot concerns a smalltown school professor and father of 12 offsprings (Ruehmann) who suddenly has the chance to inherit a fortune from a sister in Montevideo whom he once chased out of the house because of her "immoral standards of living." The late sister placed a complicated clause in her will: The money goes only to a member of the professor's family if this member gets an illegitimate child. The only member in question is a 17-year-old daughter Atlanta (Ilse Page) because the professor's next daughter is only 12. But morality of course, wins out. The professor puts up with the fact that the money is "lost" although he would have loved to have had it. But film has it that he gets the money anyway. According to the contrived story, it suddenly becomes known that for a far-fetched reason his own marriage has not been valid and he's the father of 12 (and a 13th even due to come) illegitimate kids.

The acting is mainly very good. Ruehmann is right at home with his part, a grudging but likeable school professor. One feels that he "studied" Goetz and, in fact, he is at least as good as the late Goetz who created the role himself. Miss Leuwerik is better than in her previous pix. She isn't so much of a stereo Leuwerik anymore, but a bit "different" and often really funny personality. Fine performances are turned in by such dependable actors as Paul Dahlke as a down-to-earth pastor and Fritz Tillmann as the smalltown's mayor.

An especially strong performance is contributed by Miss Page in the role of the professor's eldest daughter, Atlanta. A Berlin stage actress, she should find more utilization in native films. Good support is given by Michael Verhoeven, Miss Page's young lover, and Viktor de Kowa, the attorney who takes care of the late sister's strange will.

Technically, film just reaches a fair standard. The color isn't exactly an advantage. Film occasionally has the flavor of operatic corn. But the average patron will hardly feel this amiss. *Hans.*

Nurse On Wheels
(BRITISH)

Lacklustre offspring of the "Carry On" cycle. Comic adventures of a British country nurse likeably played by Juliet Mills. Apt to be less successful than some of its forerunners.

Hollywood, Jan. 30.
Janus Films release of Peter Rogers (Anglo Amalgamated) production. Stars Juliet Mills, Ronald Lewis. Directed by Gerald Thomas. Screenplay, Norman Hudis, from Joanna Jones' novel, "Nurse Is A Neighbour"; camera, Alan Hume; editor, Archie Ludski; music, Eric Rogers. Reviewed at Beverly Canon Theatre, Jan. 30, '64. Running time, **86 MINS.**

Joanna	Juliet Mills
Henry Edwards	Ronald Lewis
Deborah	Joan Sims
Abel Worthy	Noel Purcell
Jones	Esma Cannon
Vicar	Raymond Hutley
Miss Farthington	Athene Seyler
George Judd	Norman Rossington
Doctor Harold	Ronald Howard
Mrs. Wood	Joan Hickson
Mrs. Beacon	Renee Houston
Tim Taylor	Jim Dale
Mr. Beacon	George Woodbridge
Dr. Golfrey	David Horne
Examiner	Deryck Guyler
Nurse Merrick	Barbara Everest
Policeman	Brian Rawlinson
Ann Taylor	Amanda Reiss
Miss Maitland	Virginia Vernon

They just don't "carry on" the way they used to be in these British comedies, and the diminishing comic inspiration is apt to be reflected by diminishing returns at the Yankee boxoffice. "Nurse on Wheels" is the latest effort of producer Peter Rogers and director Gerald Thomas, the team that, together with many of the actors who aappear in this rather lacklustre romantic farce, ground out no less than six "Carry On" films.

There are some fine comedy performance in this featherweight exercise, but only in widely scattered instances are the players helped along much by the Norman Hudis screenplay from Joanna Jones' novel, "Nurse Is a Neighbour." Yarn has to do with the experiences encountered by a newly-assigned young district nurse (Juliet Mills) in a rural community populated by the most accident-prone individuals ever to hit the screen-outside of a Tom & Jerry cartoon.

Miss Mills delivers a winning performance as the sweet and wholesome nurse who goes haywire only when she's behind the wheel of an automobile. Ronald Lewis scores as the wealthy farmer who wins her hand after one major romantic misunderstanding and a few narrow escapes as her passenger in a razzle-dazzle driving sequence, best sustained comic passage in the picture. Colorful performances are turned in by Joan Sims, Noel Purcell, Raymond Hutley, Athene Seyler, Norman Rossington, Ronald Howard, George Woodbridge, David Horne and Virginia Vernon, most of them as zany townspeople who become patients of Miss Mills. Deryck Guyler chips in a solid partrayl of a harassed driving examiner, and Esma Cannon manages an effective characterization of the nurse's daffy mother.

Director Thomas has made the most of the generally uninspired material, with the aid of such British craftsmen as cameraman Alan Hume, editor Archie Ludski and composer, Eric Rogers. *Tube.*

The Brass Bottle
(COLOR)

Diverting and skillfully executed modern dress variation of A l a d d i n e s q u e Arabian Nights opera. Joke wears thin in spots, but on whole an amusing item with b.o. potential.

Hollywood, Feb. 7.

Universal release of Robert Arthur production. Stars Tony Randall, Burl Ives; features Barbara Eden, Kamala Devi, Edward Andrews. Directed by Harry Keller. Screenplay, Oscar Brodney, based on novel by F. Anstey; camera (Eastman), Clifford Stine; editor, Ted J. Kent; music, Bernard Green; assistant director, Joseph Kenny. Reviewed at Hollywood Paramount Theatre, Feb. 7, '64. Running time, **89 MINS.**

Harold Ventimore .... Tony Randall
Fakrash .... Burl Ives
Sylvia .... Barbara Eden
Tezra .... Kamala Devi
Professor Kenton ..... Edward Andrews
Seymour Jenks .... Richard Erdman
Hazel Jenks .... Kathie Browne
Martha Kenton .... Ann Doran
William Beevor .... Philip Ober
Samuel Wackerbath ...... Parley Baer
Senator Grindle .... Howard Smith
Belly Dancer .... Luiu Porter
Dr. Travisley .... Alex Gerry
Eddie .... Herb Vigran
Joe .... Alan Dexter
Lawyer Jennings .... Robert Lieb
Seneschal .... Jan Arvan
Mrs. McGruder .... Nora Marlowe
Miss Gidden .... Aline Towne

Universal has an engaging item for easygoing audiences in "The Brass Bottle," a kind of contemporary takeoff on the traditional lamp-and-genie opera. Although the Robert Arthur production has occasional flaws that are apt to be detected by the more discerning, thus limiting to some extent its enticement of choosier filmgoers, there are enough entertainment rewards in it to insure a satisfactory boxoffice future. The appealing performance of its stars, generally resourceful direction of Harry Keller and slick display of cinemagic savvy by Arthur's technical staff combine to keep the story sufficiently diverting and the production desirably glossy.

Oscar B r o d n e y ' s screenplay, based on a novel by F. Anstey, is on the whole serviceable and on occasion downright hilarious. Beneath the surface of this simple story of a young architect whose life is complicated by the sudden advent of a benevolent but disoriented genie lurks an almost imperceptible spoof of the foibles of modern society. Some of this takes the form of sight gags, such as a truly choice one in which the genie is seen descending out of thin air and into his master's automobile via the Let-Hertz-Put-You-In-The-Driver's-Seat technique. But alongside these delectable passages are others of a rather heavyhanded nature, such as a sultanesque dinner party sequence of distinctly excessive proportions that eventually smothers the comic quotient of the simple, original idea. The joke wears thin.

Tony Randall, as skillful and engaging a light comic actor as there is around today, is perfect as the befuddled architect. It's a good character, a man without greed and with whom an audience will be only too happy to relate. The character also provides the moral of the story "what we attain too easily we esteem too lightly—and it has little value." Burl Ives makes an excellent genie. The film's best running gag is his anachronistic impulse to destroy all of Randall's enemies, with the latter continually having to persuade him that such methods are obsolete in the 20th century.

Barbara Eden is decorative and sincere as Randall's romantic interest. Edward A n d r e w s is a comedy stickout as her unimpressed father, whose dislike of Randall backfires when genie Ives transforms him into a mule. The mule does some fine acting, too. There are also Kamala Devi and Lulu Porter who chip in sexy efforts. Richard Erdman and Ann Doran score in prominent characterizations, and useful support is contributed by Philip Ober, Parley Baer, Howard Smith, Alex Gerry, Herb Vigran and Kathie Browne, among others.

It's a field day for art directors Alexander Golitzen and Henry Bumstead, set decorator Oliver Emert and special photographic effects man Roswell Hoffman and, save for one or two slight irregularities in the latter department, they all come through with flying colors. Ted J. Kent's editing is a valuable assist in bringing off the visual trickery, and there are additional s t a l w a r t contributions from cameraman Clifford Stine, composer Bernard Green, choreographer Hal Belfer and soundmen Waldon O. Watson and Frank H. Wilkinson. *Tube.*

Father Came Too
(BRTISH-COLOR)

Indefatigable assembly of every "do-it-yourself" home building gag in the book; fun for slapstick addicts.

London, Feb. 11.

Rank release of a Julian Wintle-Leslie Parkyn production. Stars James Robertson Justice, Sally Smith, Leslie Phillips, Stanley Baxter; features Ronnie Barker, James Villiers, Timothy Bateson, Raymond Huntley, Vanda Hudson, Cardew Robinson, Barbara Roscoe, Sydney Bromley, Geoffrey Dunn; guest stars, Fred Emney, Eric Barker, Peter Jones, Hugh Lloyd, Terry Scott, Kenneth Cope. Directed by Peter Graham Scott. Screenplay, Jack Davies, Henry Blight; camera, Reg Wyer; music, Norie Paramor; editor, Tom Priestley. Reviewed at New Victoria, London. Running time, **93 MINS.**

Sir Beverley Grant
James Robertson Justice
Roddy Chipfield .... Leslie Phillips
Dexter Munro .... Stanley Baxter
Juliet Munro .... Sally Smith
Josh .... Ronnie Barker
Benzil Bulstrode .... James Villiers
Mr. Wedgewood ...... Raymond Huntley
Mr. Trumper .... Geoffrey Dunn
Mrs. Trumper....... Anita Sharp Bolster
Lana .... Barbara Roscoe
Fire Officer .... Cardew Robinson
Nell Gwynne .... Vanda Hudson
Mr. Gallagher .... Eric Barker
Sir Francis Drake......... Fred Emney
Ron .... Kenneth Cope
Charles II .... Peter Jones
Executioner .... Terry Scott
Mary, Queen of Scots....... Hugh Lloyd

This is the type of frenetic comedy where the actors are less in need of talent than of stamina. The constant aim is a string of belly laughs aimed at the less mature filmgoer. Director Peter Graham Scott plus Jack Davies and Henry Blyth, the scriptwriters, have jettisoned wit in favor of broader appeal. The result is exhausting, but will amuse the easygoing. Useful programmer of a familiar type.

Flimsy storyline spotlights a couple of newlyweds, anxious to break away from her domineering pappy, by getting their own house. The gullible groom is slicktalked by an estate agent into buying "a desirable property," which turns out to need so much conversion that it would need half the loot from Fort Knox to finance it. So the gullible pair, with the interference of father and the dubious aid of the local builder and handiwork firm, set out on a disastrous "Do It Yourself" jig which provides a compendium of every known gag about paperhanging, whitewash, blown fuses, crashing rooftops, woodworm, moving in the bath, lazy workmen, stupid yokels, arguments about decoration, and so on. It culminates in the house catching fire and the one-horse local fire brigade disastrously ruining a local pageant.

For audiences with an insatiable appetite for this type of frolic, the scriptwriters and director have done a breezy job, assisted by a competent cast which provide some good telegraphed laughs and dutifully gloss over the frail passages. James Robertson Justice, as the irascible actor - manager, bumbles through his role in his usual formidable fashion. Stanley Baxter and Sally Smith are a likeable pair as the "babes in the domestic wood." Playing the glib estate agent who has a yen to become a famous actor-playwright is Leslie Phillips. He has played this type of part often; hence, he's excellent.

Useful spots in lesser roles come from guest star Eric Barker, as a fussy bankmanager; James Villiers playing a suave upperstrata interior decorator; Barbara Roscoe, Raymond Huntley, Geoffrey Dunn, Sidney Bromley, Timothy Bateson and Cardew Robinson. As the character in charge of the local fire brigade who plays havoc with the local pageant Robinson is excellent.

A jaunty score by Norrie Paramor, sound color lensing by Reg Wyer and a creditable job by Tom Priestley, whose task as editor is not so much to edit as to decide which gags are expendable, all contribute to this film. *Rich.*

Syd For Tana River
(South of Tana River)
(DANISH—COLOR)

Copenhagen, Feb. 4.

Asa release of Henning Karmark production. Directed by Bent Christensen, Sven Methling. Original story and screenplay by Finn Holten Hansen; camera, Erik Jensen, Henrik Fog-Moller; music, Bent Fabricius-Bjerre. At Kino-Palaeet, Copenhagen. Running time, **95 MINS.**

Axelson .... Paul Reichhardt
Schmidt ....William Rosenberg
Derek .... Axel Strobyby
Dupont ....Bent Christensen
Eva ....Charlotte Ernst
Hitching ....Terry Mathews
The game warden ....Ronald Burgess
Native boy ....Toto

This may reach the foreign market so eagerly sought by Danish film producers but only as a rather flat A production. The film, in other words, can boast no national identity except for the semi-Danish names of the leading characters. Is the Axelson, instead of the Danish Axelsen, supposed to make things easier on the international ear?

For the international eye, there is a lot of nicely photographed African landscape and some rather obviously faked animal lensing. For the very tolerant international mind, there is the story about a young Danish girl's father who has in many ways gone astray in the bush. The hero is a big game warden (Axel Stroyby) who catches his own very frail game (Charlotte Ernst). The father (Paul Reichhardt) winds up a sort of a hero, but for justice's sake, a dead one.

Bent Christensen, who has acknowledged cinematic talent, was brought along as director for no reason that meets the eye. But he plays and directs himself in a marvelously funny role as a villain who likes drink and meets his fate by whisky in a chillingly funny way. Music is by Bent Fabricius-Bjerre alias the Bent Fabric of "Alley Cat" record fame. That and Christensen's drunkard are truly international. *Kell.*

La Visita
(The Visit)
(ITALIAN)

Rome, Feb. 4.

Dear-20th-Fox release of a Zebra Film (Moris Ergas) production. Features Sandra Milo, Francois Perier, Mario Adorf, Angela Minervini, Gastone Moschin, Didi Perego. Directed by Antonio Pietrangeli. Story and screenplay, Pietrangeli, Scola, Maccari; camera, Armando Nannuzzi; editor, Eraldo da Roma; music, Armando Trovajoli. At Corso Cinema, Rome. Running time, **115 MINS.**

Pina .... Sandra Milo
Adolfo ....Francois Perier
Cucaracha ....Mario Adorf
Chiaretta ....Angela Minervini
Renato ....Gastone Moschin
Nella ....Didi Perego

One of the best entries in a busy local season, "The Visit" (not to be confused with the recent Anthony Quinn - Ingrid B e r g m a n starrer, which originally held the same title) is a well-made, often penetrating study of two people sizing up one another with a view to eventual marriage. Ironically, it might do better abroad than in its home territory, though basically an arty entry.

Story concerns meeting, in a small Po Valley town, of man who answered a lonely hearts column plea and the woman who placed item. Over a brief weekend away from work, they have ample time to catch one another's defects, flash back to previous life and loves, and make up their minds as to whether the negative elements can be outweighed by the downbeat prospects of the alternative a future on their lonesome.

The mutual scrutiny is often bitter and almost cruel, and characters unfold to display their respectively least attractive foibles. Solution is left open, but there's considerable doubt at the fadeout that the man ever will be back, despite his repeated assurances. Antonio Pietrangeli has directed ably, holding down what could have been out-and-out farce and caricature to human limits.

Sandra Milo's limning of the woman in question is one of the best Italo performances of the year, neatly following up her role in Federico Fellini's "8½." She gets a strong assist from makeup and costuming—close to grotesque but not overdoing it—(devised by Piero Gherardi) who did the same stint on "8½".

Francois Perier plays his role well, though at times his Gallic origin and training show through too patently in his playing of the p o t e n t i a l suitor. Mario Adorf makes the most of his part as the village idiot while Gastone Moschin is competent as usual as the woman's onetime lover. Didi Perego has a good bit. Angela Minervini is properly pert and a tempting distraction for the village visitor.

Technical credits are excellent, from Armando Nannuzzi's expert lensing to Armando Trovajoli's topical and apt scoring. *Hawk.*

Francoise ou La Vie Conjugale
(Francoise Or Conjugal Life)
and
Jean-Marc ou La Vie Conjugale
(Jean-Marc Or Conjugal Life)
(FRENCH-FRANSCOPE)
Paris, Feb. 11.

Prodis release of Films Borderie-Terra Films-Joly Film production. Stars Marie-Jose Nat, Jacques Charrier; features Georges Riviere, Gianni Esposito, Macha Meryl, Michele Girardon. Directed by Andre Cayatte. Screenplay, Cayatte, Louis Sapin, Maurice Auberge; camera, Roger Fellous; editor, Paul Cayatte. At Ambassade-Gaumont and Mercury, Paris. Running time, **115 MINS.** each.

Francoise .... Marie-Jose Nat
Jean-Marc .... Jacques Charrier
Roger .... Michel Subor
Olivier .... Gianni Esposito
Lawyer .... Michele Girardon
Boss .... Georges Riviere
Mother .... Jacqueline Porel

Two films have been made for somewhat more than the price of one on the same subject, the breakup of a young married couple. In the first, the viewpoint of wife is given while in the second the husband's view is outlined. Fairly surface exposition in both labels it's more a gimmick production than any unique film advance.

Both pix deal with the same two young students, Jean-Marc and Francoise, who have an affair, marry when she is pregnant and finally break up when both want different things with petty suspicions hastening the dissolution. In "Jean-Marc" (told by the husband), the wife is a headstrong, climbing, selfish type while the husband is more noble and trusting. In "Francoise" she sacrifices herself quietly for her husband but is finally driven to extramarital affairs by his failure to comprehend.

Problems of adjustment, female freedom and conflicting outlooks are sifted through in these two pix but mainly in a rather cursory manner. In trying to line up pros and cons on both sides for the couple, the film remains somewhat cold in observation and unfoldment. Events are sometimes dragged in to create some point or allow for a needed misunderstanding rather than springing from the characters or more naturally from the narrative.

"Jean-Marc" is the flimsier of the two since the husband is the more dull character. "Francoise" has a bit more form but also skirts melodrama rather than drama. Some points about the behavior of the wife in the husband's pic are naturally unclear as are the vice-versa aspects in the wife's version.

If seeing both versions straightens out why each did what at a certain time, it is only on fairly superficial points. So both pix emerge fairly okay little situation dramas with neither offering much for the foreign market.

And it does not seem very likely that seeing one would necessarily bring on the desire to see the other. Since they are not sequels, making one package of both fairly long (115 minutes each) pix would

only emphasize the fairly lack-lustre characters and synthetic treatment.

Films are both glossy. Marie-Jose Nat has a genuine charm and presence as the either two-faced or self-effacing wife. Jacques Charrier is somewhat stolid in both pix and is hard put to engender the noble aspirations of working with delinquents in one or the feeble, mediocre aspects of his character in the other.

Director Andre Cayatte, an ex-lawyer, really has drawn up two briefs rather than penetrating looks at the difficulties of human communications and the problems of a couple. As briefs they are somewhat cold and didactic. And he has also compounded a filmic felony by producing a largescale soap opera.

If the two pix could not stand on their own for foreign spots, the local gimmick of opening both at nearby houses could help give them some interest. But it is doubtful that they would display the draw and interest to have same audiences wanting both. If the aim was to draw men to the man's version and women to the woman's, or vice-versa, both pix have more than a distaff sheen. *Mosk.*

La Bonne Soupe
(The Good Soup)
(FRENCH—FRANSCOPE)

Paris, Feb. 11.

20th-Fox release of Belstar-Dear Film-Andre Hakim production. Stars Marie Bell, Annie Girardot; features Claude Dauphin, Jean-Claude Brialy, Raymond Pellegrin, Sacha Distel, Christian Marquand, Felix Marten, Franchot Tone. Written and directed by Robert Thomas from play by Felicien Marceau. Camera, Roger Hubert; editor, Henri Taverna. At Marignan, Paris. Running time, **100 MINS.**

Old Marie-Paule .... Marie Bell
Young Marie-Bell .... Annie Girardot
Croupier .... Claude Dauphin
Jacquot .... Jean-Claude Brialy
Armand .... Raymond Pellegrin
Odilon .... Felix Marten
Millionaire .... Franchot Tone
Lucien .... Christian Marquand
Boss .... Bernard Blier
Brother .... Daniel Gelin

Insouciant pic is reminiscent of pre-war French pix via an aging person telling a tale of the trials and tribulations in his climb through society to the top or slide to the bottom. It tries for irony, charm and wit to gloss over the essential slim theme. This one is intermittently clever but without the drive needed.

However, an engaging group of actors give it more style than the flat direction can manage. Hence, this has a certain footloose, gentle immorality. It deals with a girl who goes from being seduced by a clothing salesman, to becoming a joy girl. Then she really falls in love with him, only to lose him. She becomes a kept woman and then finally marries for money to lose all when she is caught making love to her son-in-law.

All this is told to a croupier one night by an aging woman (Marie Bell). She plays it with theatrical flourish that is acceptable while Annie Girardot gives an edge and glitter to her guileful but still sympathetic character of the young one.

Men are played by adroit actors with Claude Dauphin standout as the infatuated listener as is Bernard Blier as her bumptious lover who

keeps her in style. It is technically acceptable. Adapted from a play that was a hit here and flopped in the U.S., this looks in for okay returns at home with some foreign chances on its theme and fairly entertaining progression. It skirts vulgarity but manages to avoid it via the spirited playing. Scenes of her days as a prostie are reminiscent of "Irma La Douce" with the ability to keep it fairly risible rather than scabrous. *Mosk.*

Sedotta E Abbandonata
(Seduced and Abandoned)
(ITALO-FRENCH)

Rome, Feb. 4.

Paramount release of Lux-Ultra-Video (Rome)-Lux-C.C.F. (Paris) coproduction by Franco Cristaldi. Features Stefania Sandrelli, Saro Urzi, Lando Buzzanca, Leopoldo Trieste, Aldo Puglisi, Umberto Spadaro, Rocco D'Assunta, Lola Braccini, and with Paola Biggio, Lina La Galla, Gustavo D'Arpe, Vicenzo Licata. Directed by Pietro Germi. Screenplay, Pietro Germi, Luciano Vincenzoni, Age, Scarpelli, from story by Germi and Vincenzoni; camera, Ajace Parolin; music, Carlo Rustichelli; editor, Roberto Cinquini. At Fiamma, Rome. Running time, **118 MINS.**

Agnese .... Stefania Sandrelli
Vincenzo .... Saro Urzi
Antonio .... Lando Buzzanca
Rizieri .... Leopoldo Trieste
Peppino .... Aldo Puglisi
Ascalone .... Umberto Spadaro
Orlando .... Rocco D'Assunta
Amalia .... Lola Braccini
Matilde .... Paola Biggio
Potenza .... Oreste Palella
Francesca .... Lina La Galla
Ciarpetta .... Gustavo D'Arpe
Profumo .... Vincenzo Licata

Pietro Germi has followed up his successful "Divorce, Italian Style" with another grotesque comedy in a similar vein. It is to his credit that he brings this off. Mainly because it lacks the once-in-a-lifetime performance by Marcello Mastroianni which gave "Divorce" its clincher, "Seduced" doesn't look headed for exactly the same top figures. But an adroit sell could put it in the big leagues nevertheless.

Germi once again zeroes in on Sicilian manners and mores and, more specifically on a vintage Italo law which, as a line in film says, is known to every Sicilian schoolboy. Said law automatically frees a man guilty of forcible seduction and abduction just as long as he marries the girl in question. Once again, too, the director's principal barbs in a pointed picture are against the Southern Italians' exasperated concept of honor, to attain which any solution, cruel or primitive though it may be, is valid.

Here too, Germi and his fellow writers have couched their message in a rousingly risible script which, though it at times over-elaborates a point, and is ultimately not as hilarious as "Divorce" makes its strong points while amusing the patron. Briefly, Agnese is seduced by Peppino, her sister's fiance. When the matter is finally revealed, it precipitates a series of involved maneuvers by her father, Vincenzo, to save the family honor by having Peppino forcibly marry the girl.

Tale loses in the telling, for Germi has paced his pic on various levels. It can be taken as a mystery item, whose outcome maintains suspense, or as straight comedy, or as gay grotesque, whose subsurface implications are grim indeed. Much of the time, the story is played fortissimo, literally to the town square and its assemblage of onlookers, all of whom know the true facts, but

(who) hypocritically play along for tradition's sake.

In one final brutal jab, Germi even makes the father die while the rest of the family—and populace—remains uninformed at his behest, so as not to ruin the face-saving triumph of the wedding and feast. The ultimate implication, tag-line as it were, is that "they lived unhappily ever after."

The picture is filled with brilliant directorial touches, the characters are always upper case on the screen, both literally via Germi's predilection for closeups, and dramatically, via full-blooded portrayals. Saro Urzi is standout as the father. Aldo Puglisi, a previously little-known Sicilian actor, is a find as the seducer, while Stefania Sandrelli strikingly fits the part of the victimized girl, a symbol of sorts for such woman. Leopoldo Trieste and Lando Buzzanca are excellent, too (both were in "Divorce") in other roles, as are Umberto Spadaro, as a lawyer and Paola Biggio, as a sister. Supporting cast is colorful.

Pic has very notable assists, in rendering its memorable Sicilian setting, from lenser Ajace Parolin's black and white camera, and from Carlo Rustichelli's aptly lilting musical score. *Hawk.*

Psychomania

Low-budgeter for the sexploita tion market; good b.o. poten tial in that area.

Victoria Films release of a Del Tenney production. Stars Lee Philips, Shepperd Strudwick; features Jean Hale, Lorraine Rogers, Margot Hartman, Sylvia Miles, Kay Elhardt. Directed by Richard L. Hilliard. Screenplay, Robin Miller; camera, Louis McMahon; music, W. L. Holcombe. Reviewed at World Theatre, N.Y., Feb. 14, '64. Running time, 90 MINS.
Elliot Freeman .... Lee Philips
Adrian Benedict ....Shepperd Strudwick
Carol Bishop .... Jean Hale
Alice St. Clair ....Lorraine Rogers
Lynn Freeman ....Margot Hartman
Dolores Martello .... Kaye Elhardt
Charlie Perone ....James Farentino
Palmer .... Richard Van Patten
Janet (Lolita) Terhune ....Sheila Forbes
Silvia .... Sylvia Miles
Mr. Melbourne .... Day Tuttle
Inspector Grey .... Mike Keene
Max .... Mike O'Dowd

Sex and horror are a reliable formula for b.o. success in exploitation houses and "Psychomania" takes full advantage of it. But, unfortunately, this low-budgeter's approach is so crude that it frequently borders on the pornographic.

In light of the film's theme and its tasteless handling, this Victoria Films release may encounter censorship problems in some states. While there are no artistic values in the Del Tenney production, it unquestionably adds up to sock fare for the sexploitation market.

Robin Miller's screenplay depicts the murder of a couple of shapely femmes. A wealthy Korean War vet for whom one of the victims posed in his art studio is a prime suspect. So are a lot of other sordid characters.

A good part of the action takes place at a girls' college which appears to be an excuse for the inmates to display their charms from multitudinous angles. Murders, incidentally, are delicately alternated between assignation scenes that leave little to the imagination.

Lee Philips fails to put much color into his role of the war vet with a yen for painting nude models. Shepperd Strudwick is realistic as Philips' attorney despite some awkward lines.

Lorraine Rogers and Kaye Elhardt are pretty victims while Jean Hale is an attractive near-victim. Their talent, as well as that of the rest of the cast, is largely obscured by Richard L. Hilliard's inept direction and the debauchery of the script.

Louis McMahon's camerawork is fairish as is the W. L. Holcombe score. The title credits acknowledge cooperation of the Stamford (Conn.) Police Dept. The picture hardly improves Stamford's civic image or that of the surrounding area. *Gilb.*

Die Oese
(The Loop)
(GERMAN)
Oberhausen, Feb. 11.
Atlas production and release. With Branka Pepric, Bekim Fehmiu, Plaka Kostic, Slobodan Dimitriuvic, Bata Stoikovic. Directed by Jakov Lind. Screenplay, Jakov Lind; camera, Milan. Babic; music, Pim Jacobs; editor, Ytsen Brusse. Previewed at Oberhausen Film Fest. Running time, 50 MINS.

For the international critic, most of the German pix are either mere routine, superficial escapist fare or, if they try to achieve something different, morbidly intellectual.

This little pic, "The Loop," is neither fish nor fowl. It is technically primitive, but of some interest for several reasons. It was financed by Atlas-Film, West Germany's most ambitious distributing outfit, and authored and directed by Jakov Lind, an Austrian-born poet living in London, and is an original. It's his first directorial effort. Atlas took interest in his "Loop" idea and let him go ahead. Film was lensed in Yugoslavia with a cast mostly composed of Yugoslavs whose voices later were dubbed into German. So the pic is a strange German one.

Plot is simple. A pretty girl goes to a Yugoslav spa for the holidays. Four local boys take an immediate interest in the curvacious blonde. She flirts with everyone and there's a substantial exchange of kisses, yet no one reaches his goal. She would rather tell strange stories than go to bed with one of the boys. The theory is that a sexy-looking gal needn't be sexy at all. The boys find out that she is actually boring. Title, incidentally, stems from the girl's job. She works in a factory that produces such things as buttons, hooks, loops, etc.

Film has some original dialog sequences of which some are truly and others involuntarily funny. Acting by Branka Pepric is so convincing one thinks she portrays herself. But she's a member of the Belgrade Theatre. The boys in this are nothing but sparring partners. For a beginner, Lind didn't do too bad a job. Film is partly rather amusing. Technically, however, there's nothing impressive about it.

Where to place such a 50-minute vehicle? Atlas will release it together with another featurette, "The Weekend," to be directed by Detten Schleiermacher this coming September. This may be okay for some native offbeat houses but hardly anything for export. *Hans.*

Ratai
(The Body)
(JAPANESE — COLOR — GRANDSCOPE)
Shochiku release of a Shochiku (Masao Shirai-Shigeru Wakatsuki) production. Directed by Masashige Narusawa. Screenplay by Narusawa, based on novel by Kafu Nagai; camera (Eastman Color-Grandscope), Ko Kawamata; art director, Koji Uno; music, directed by Toru Takemitsu, Joji Iwata. Features Michiko Saga, Minoru Chiaki, Kazuko Matsuo, Mitsuko Takara, Yusuke Kawazu, Hiroyuki Nagato, Eitaro Shindo. Reviewed at Kabuki Theatre, Los Angeles, Feb. 11, '64. Running time: 85 MINS.
Sakiko Okamura..........Michiko Saga
Her father .... Ichiro Sugai
Her mother ....Kumeko Urabe
Sasaki .... Minoru Chiaki
Kimiko ....Kazuko Matsuo
Marie Angel ....Mitsuko Takara
Sota ....Yusuke Kawazu
Takasugi ....Hiroyuki Nagato
Hyodo ....Eitaro Shindo
Proprietress of sex club .. Isuzu Yamada
Naka ....Chieko Naniwa
The handsome boy ....Isao Sasaki

"The Body," had it been made by an American company with the same theme and intent, would have gone straight to the sexploitation outlets. Its naive approach to a controversial subject—the debasement of woman—and a professional slickness to its technical aspects, particularly fine color camerawork, makes this Japanese effort a flexible film that can either be used as bottom-half of an art house bill or, dubbed, dumped on the thrill market.

Mashashige Narusawa uses his proven know-how as a director to polish up the rough edges of his own script. As a screenwriter, he couldn't lick the problem of giving coherence and meaning to a story that had to be kept suggestive and sexually enticing; as the film's director, his big problem was to keep the story from getting in the way. As a result, "The Body" is willing but the flash is weak.

Michiko Saga stands out as the poor little girl who finds that luxury demands high prices. Her combination of childish mannerisms and guileless immorality forecast her sordid future. Outstanding in support are Minoru Chiaki and Eitaro Shindo as two of her "teachers" and Mitsuko Takara and Kazuko Matnu as Nipponese ecdysiasts. The pair, plus the heroine, provide considerable nudity. *Robe.*

Ensign Pulver
(PANAVISION-COLOR)

Mildly amusing sequel to "Mister Roberts."

Hollywood, Feb. 20.
Warner Bros. release of Joshua Logan production. Stars Robert Walker, Burl Ives, Walter Matthau, Tommy Sands, Millie Perkins; features Kay Medford. Directed by Logan. Screenplay, Logan, Peter S. Feibleman, based on play by Thomas Heggen and Logan from novel by Heggen; camera (Technicolor), Charles Lawion; editor, William Reynolds; music, George Duning; assistant director, Daniel McCauley. Reviewed at the studio, Feb. 20, '64. Running time, 104 MINS.
Ensign Pulver .... Robert Walker
Captain .... Burl Ives
Doc .... Walter Matthau
Bruno .... Tommy Sands
Scotty .... Millie Perkins
Head Nurse .... Kay Medford
Billings .... Larry Hagman
LaSueur .... Gerald O'Loughlin
Gabrowski .... Sal Papa
Taru .... Al Freeman Jr.
Insigna .... James Farentino
Skouras .... James Coco
Payne .... Don Dorrell
Carney .... Peter L. Marshall
Stretch .... Robert Matek
Mila .... Diana Sands
Dowdy .... Joseph Marr

Except for widely scattered flashes of mild amusement, "Ensign Pulver" doesn't have much going for it, and only audiences with the most easygoing dispositions are likely to cotton to the comic and sentimental overstatement with which the Warner Bros. release is afflicted. Almost everything has been exaggerated by Joshua Logan, who produced, directed and co-scripted with Peter S. Feibleman. It is difficult to reconcile this watered-down progeny of "Mister Roberts," a tremendous Warner success in 1955, with the fact that the same Logan directed the original Broadway production of "Roberts," which he co-authored with the late Thomas Heggen.

The sequel finds the still immature "Pulver," (Robert Walker) with the aid of "Doc," (Walter Matthau) still attempting to follow in Roberts' footsteps in harassing the enemy (the obnoxious Capt. Morton) to keep morale as high as possible among the men of the delapidated cargo ship ingloriously servicing some obscure South Pacific bases at the tail-end of World War II. The Logan-Feibleman plot contrives to cast Pulver and the captain (Burl Ives) adrift in a life raft, where the former obtains background information that enables him, after they are rescued, to persuade Ives to have himself transferred.

There is more than a twist of Lemmon (Jack) to Walker's delineation of "Pulver." In fact, recollections of the former cast invite regrettable comparisons all around. Young Walker is simply not being himself, and it shows through. Ives does what little he can with the distasteful role of the ambitious captain. There has been an attempt to provide psychological motivations for the inexplicably monstrous behavior of this character. The explanations are unconvincing and unnecessary. Better a villain than a Freudian screwball. Matthau employs several expressions as "Doc," and repeats them alternately, mostly in reaction takes.

Tommy Sands does some earnest emoting as an emotionally disturbed seaman, but it's in a lost cause. Millie Perkins is adequate in a romantic role, and Kay Medford gets in a few comic licks as a nurse. Supporting work is generally satisfactory, although Logan's awkward, heavyhanded direction puts a strain on everyone from principals to ensemble players.

Charles Lawton's Technicolor photography conjures up some extremely attractive seascapes and beachscapes. There are one or two spots where William Reynold's editing seems a bit slow on the draw, leaving the actors dangling with silly, superfluous expressions on their faces. Leo K. Kuter's art direction is convincing and George Duning's music provides the proper punctuation, comic and dramatic. *Tube.*

Constance Aux Enfers
(Constance in Hell)
(FRENCH-SPANISH)
Paris, Feb. 15.

CCFC release of Capitole-Louxor-Balcazar production. Stars Michele Morgan, Dany Saval; features Simon Andreu, Claude Rich, Maria Pacome. Directed by Francois Villiers. Screenplay, Jacques Sigurd from novel by Jean-Pierre Ferriere; camera, Manuel Berenger; editor, Christian Gaudin. At Colisee, Paris. Running time, **95 MINS.**

Constance	Michele Morgan
Starlet	Dany Saval
Young Man	Simon Andreu
Student	Claude Rich
Marie	Maria Pacome

Melodrama about a middleaged woman caught up in the machinations of a conniving young couple emerges more melodrama than drama on its telegraphed proceedings, sleek rather than penetrating direction and obvious playing. It appears more a playoff than arty item for abroad.

Michele Morgan is a forlorn piano-teaching widow who watches the lascivious carryings-on of a lewd starlet and her young lover from her window. If appalled, she is drawn to the affair, and when she sees him murder her in a jealous rage, she takes him in and hides him.

Love develops, at least on her part, but then it appears the girl is alive and she has been used for blackmail purposes. Plot is somewhat far-fetched on this point but it picks up a bit when the widow gets her vengeance and finally has the boy really killing the starlet out of jealousy.

Miss Morgan tries hard and does give her character a bit of edge and even some depth. But the crude acrid playing of Dany Saval, as the starlet, seems misguided. Simon Andreu is effective as the feckless young man.

Direction lacks the nervous edge to give this item the mounting progression and solid movement it needs to overcome the script shortcomings. This is given an okay production dress with interior shooting in Spain and exteriors in Paris well matched. *Mosk.*

Carry On Jack
(BRITISH-COLOR)

Ribald romp on the ocean wave suggests another potential grosser in the rich "Carry On" vein.

London, Feb. 18.

Warner-Pathe release of a Peter Rogers production for Anglo Amalgamated. Stars Bernard Cribbins, Juliet Mills, Charles Hawtrey, Kenneth Williams, Donald Houston; features Percy Herbert, Ed Devereaux, George Woodbridge, Jimmy Thomason, Anton Rodgers, Patrick Cargill. Directed by Gerald Thomas. Original screenplay by Talbot Rothwell; camera, Alan Hume; editor, Archie Ludski; music, Eric Rogers. Previewed at Studio One, London. Running time; **91 MINS.**

Albert	Bernard Cribbins
Sally	Juliet Mills
Walter	Charles Hawtrey
Captain Fearless	Kenneth Williams
Howett	Donald Houston
Angel	Percy Herbert
Patch	Peter Gilmore
Hook	Ed Devereaux
Carrier	Jim Dale
Ancient Carrier	Ian Wilson
Coachdriver	Barry Gosney
Ned	George Woodbridge
First Sea Lord	Cecil Parker
Second Sea Lord	Frank Forsyth
Nelson	Jimmy Thompson
Hardy	Anton Rodgers
Spanish Governor	Patrick Cargill
Captain of Guard	Jan Muzurus

Latest of the "Carry On" gang's shenanigans is an energetic skit on "Mutiny of the Bounty," even bringing in joshing of certain characters and scenes from the nautical opus. In a more modest way "Carry On, Jack" should prove equally bountiful at the boxoffice. Previous supporters of the "Carry Ons" will know just what to expect, even though only two of the "resident" c o m p a n y — Charles Hawtrey and Kenneth Williams—are on parade. This one, however, has an added credit in its very okay costuming and art work. Producers of more ambitious pix than this have often been more sparing in their attention to detail.

Talbot Rothwell has concocted a plot that gives ample scope for fast action. The dialog, without being particularly witty, has a lively tang. Mood is set by an opening cameo showing the epic, "Kiss Me, Hardy" incident, played with brief, witty aplomb by Jimmy T h o m p s o n and Anton Rodgers. From then on director Gerald Thomas, a shrewd hand with such rambunctious staff, steers his cast through a maze of mixups and misadventure. Rothwell's invention rarely flags and the director offers little chance for the filmgoer to analyze critically the proceedings between yocks.

The screenplay involves a serving wench taking the place aboard H.M.S. Venus of a green midshipman who, with the local nitwit, is press-ganged on to the same ship, a flogging that misfires, an operation at sea, an hilarious walking the plank sequence, a phony mutiny and the finale, when the Venus, now commanded by the middy, the girl and the birdbrain, puts the Spanish Armada out of action. All these, and other familiar incidents, are on hand to milk provide plenty of laughter.

William and Hawtrey have one or two scenes together which might be even funnier but for the fact that the style of both gifted comedians is similar. But Williams, playing the precious Captain Fearless, who hates the sea and violence, is in excellent form while Hawtrey plays his familiar nincompoop with the ease of long experience. Bernard Cribbins, as the sorely tried middy, Donald Houston, as the bullying second in command, and Percy Herbert, as his aide, bring some virile body to the proceedings and Jim Dale, George Woodbridge, Patrick Cargill, Ian Wilson, Ed Devereaux and Cecil Parker (gueststarring as First Lord of the Admiralty) add some amusing touches. Only sizeable femme role is played by Juliet Mills. Daintily attractive though she is, Miss Mills doesn't seem very comfortable in the robust male surroundings.

Art director Jack Shampan has done a creditable job both aboard the Venus and on shore at the harbor. Alan Hume's color lensing and Eric Rogers' light score fit the mood. Archie Ludski's unfussy editing helps a comedy that stands up against any of its predecessors. This should mean good news for most exhibitors. *Rich.*

Alta Infedelta
(High Infidelity)
(Italian)
Rome, Feb. 18.

Dino DeLaurentiis release of a Gianni Hecht Lucari (Documento Film) production.

(SCANDALOSO)
With Nino Manfredi, Fulvia Franco, John Law. Directed by Franco Rossi. Camera, Ennio Guarnieri.

Francesco	Nino Manfredi
Raffaella	Fulvia Franco
Stranger	John Law

(LA SOSPIROSA)
With Monica Vitti, Jean Pierre Cassel, Sergio Fantoni. Directed by Luciano Salce. Camera, Ennio Guarnieri.

Gloria	Monica Vitti
Tonino	Jean Pierre Cassel
Paolo	Sergio Fantoni

(PECCATO NEL POMMERIGGIO)
With Claire Bloom, Charles Aznavour. Directed by Elio Petri. Camera, Ennio Guarnieri.

Giulio	Charles Aznavour
Laura	Claire Bloom

GENTE MODERNA
With Ugo Tognazzi, Michele Mercier, Bernard Blier. Directed by Mario Monicelli. Camera, Gianni di Venanzo.

Cesare	Ugo Tognazzi
Zoraide	Michele Mercier
Reguzzoni	Bernard Blier

At Metropolitan, Rome. Running time, **130 MINS.**

Four-part pic combines fast-paced, m o d e r n, unprejudiced stories on topical subjects with adroit direction and popular performances for a strong b.o. parlay on the local market. Film is a promising export entry as well, thanks both to names (for some area) and pure content and handling.

Taken in segments, each has its plus points from an audience-appeal viewpoint. "Scandaloso," perhaps the most carefully made of the lot, has an apathetic husband on a seaside vacation suddenly become jealous of his wife until he realizes that her handsome and seemingly virile suitor is really courting him. It's a surprise ending, but with more than a bit of human insight and psychology, ably acted out by Fulvia Franco, Nino Manfredi, and Yank thesp John Law.

"La Sospirosa" allows Monica Vitti one of her rare comic escapades. And she makes the most of the situation as the over-jealous wife so engaged in checking on her husband that she fails to realize her own betrayal. Most intellectual segment of the bunch, and perhaps the least successful, is "Peccato nel Pommeriggio," in which Claire Bloom and Charles Aznavour, wife and husband, have an "illicit" afternoon affair away from the usual marital routine, with a deep bow to Harold Pinter's "The Lover," which treats a similar theme.

Mario Monicelli's saucy, racy "Gente Moderna" winds the foursome on an earthy, Boccaccio-like note, about a man who gambles his wife's honor at cards and loses, only to fool the winner into believing he's really won. Michele Mercier and Ugo Tognazzi ably play the couple, but Bernard Blier steals the show as the third man.

Technical credits are good, pic unspools smoothly and entertainingly, and everyone has a good time. *Hawk.*

Shock Treatment
(C'SCOPE)

Shallow but flashy exploitation shocker for less discerning customers. Flamboyant salesmanship and marquee names will help at b.o., but lacks story stature for staying power.

Hollywood, Feb. 19.

20th-Fox release of Aaron Rosenberg production. Stars Stuart Whitman, Carol Lynley, Roddy McDowall, Lauren Bacall. No character names. Balance of cast: Olive Deering, Ossie Davis, Donald Buka, Pauline Myers, Evadne Baker, Robert Wilke, Bert Freed, Judith DeHart, Judson Laire, Lili Clark, Douglas Dumbrille. Directed by Denis Sanders. Screenplay, Sidney Boehm, based on novel by Winfred Van Atta; camera, Sam Leavitt; editor, Louis Loeffler; music, Jerry Goldsmith; asst. director, Joseph E. Rickards. Reviewed at World Theatre, Feb. 19, '64. Running time, **93 MINS.**

Exploitation allure and a respectable array of marquee name-bait will have to tote the boxoffice burden for this flashy but hokey melodramatic trifle. This Aaron Rosenberg production for 20th-Fox is undistinguished fare. Escape, shock and superficial sensation are offered—and although there are always takers for this kind of entertainment, the bulk of modern filmgoers require a more convincing story framework than "Shock Treatment" has to offer.

Sidney Boehm's s c r e e n p l a y, based on a novel by Winfred Van Atta, relates the woes of a professional actor (Stuart Whitman) hired to pose as a psycho to obtain entry into the state mental hospital where he is to investigate the intentions of a psychotic patient (Roddy McDowall) who has just been sent up for murdering an elderly philanthropist and supposedly burning $1,000,000 of her cash. The question is whether McDowall has actually hidden the loot in cahoots with the assistant medical director of the hospital (Lauren Bacall). The answer, as Whitman discovers after going through hell, is no. But in the process Miss Bacall goes mad and Whitman finds love with a luscious manic-depressive (Carol Lynley).

Whitman is on "the mark" on this one, but he gives it a good college try. Miss Lynley is stuck in an undernourished role—a kind of Lustre Creme lunatic. McDowall cops acting honors with the spirited portrayal of a deranged gardener who would just as soon snip off a head as a deteriorated branch. Miss Bacall has seen better parts. Her role is absurd. Supporting work is passable and Denis Sanders' direction is fairly lively, considering the material provided.

Sam Leavitt has chipped in some frisky photography and Jerry Goldsmith a creepy score. The rest of the credits are satisfactory, but the picture isn't. *Tube.*

Twice A Man

New York-made experimental pic shot narrow-gauge and blown up to 35m with good color rendition. Limited to buffs primarily.

Gregory J. Markopolous release and production. Written, directed, lensed (Eastman Color), edited by Gregory J. Markopolous. Commentary spoken by Olympia Dukakis; music, Tchaikovski. With Olympia Dukakis, Paul Klib, Violet Roditi, Albert Torgesen. Previewed in Paris. Running time, **55 MINS.**
Youth .... Paul Klib
Friend .... Albert Torgessen
Young Woman .... Olympia Dukakis
Old Woman .... Violet Roditi

Film won a $2,000 prize at the recent Belgian Experiment Film Festival. The word "experimental" is central. There is a tendency to exploit technique for its own sake, and to go arty as the thing. Meanwhile it tells of a youth whose love objects include his stepmother and another man. Shot in Manhattan in 16 millimeter and expanded to 35m, this is a Greek tragedy done in modern dress and with avant garde editing and cutting.

A la Alain Resnais and Michelangelo Antonioni modes, short quick scenes within the context of another build up the past or comment on the action and psychology. Commentary is intended as counter-point. Characters sometimes ambulate through deserted modern vistas of NY or are suddenly transplanted to beaches.

Supposedly telling of a young man loved by his step-mother, but also having had some · relations with a man, it also scoots about in time via showing the step-mother young and then old. Not acted but posed slowly and calculatingly. Filmmaker Gregory J. Markopolous is enamoured of composition, color and plastic beauty.

But there is a tendency to wallow in it. Theme and mood and atmosphere suffer accordingly. So this is a difficult arty pic mainly for buffs or more hardy art house clientele. It will need hard, persistent and personal sell. However Markopolous does seem to have visual flair if presently too abusive of privilege as a director.

Color is exemplary and blows up from 16m to 35m very well. Less wispy personal attempts at transposing Greek heredity to Gotham today, and more starch in narration and theme, possibly would better have self-served. As is he is foo esoteric. *Mosk.*

He Rides Tall

Conventional l o w e r berth western.

Hollywood, Feb. 19.
Universal release of Gordon Kay production. Stars Tony Young, Dan Duryea, Jo Morrow; features Madlyn Rhue. Directed by R. G. Springsteen. Screenplay, Charles W. Irwin, Robert Creighton Williams, from story by Irwin; camera, Ellis W. Carter; editor, Russell Schoengarth; music, Irving Getz; assistant director, Raoul Pagel. Reviewed at the studio, Feb. 19, '64. Running time, **84 MINS.**
Marshal Morg Rocklin ..... Tony Young
Bart Thorne .... Dan Duryea
Kate McCloud .... Jo Morrow
Ellie Daniels .... Madlyn Rhue
Josh McCloud .... R. G. Armstrong
Dr. Sam .... Joel Fluellen
Gil .... Carl Reindel
Onie .... Mickey Simpson
Burt .... George Murdock
Lefty .... Michael Carr
Crowley .... George Petrie

"He Rides Tall" is a "B" western, barely distinguishable from dozens of others that have gone. before it over the years. Black-and-white in characterization, mechanical in style and modest in production value, it will suffice as a supporting item only where westerns are most ardently and indiscriminately appreciated. Care should be taken not to burden a sophisticated major attraction with it.

The Gordon Kay production for Universal benefits from a typically uninhibited, overplayed performince by Dan Duryea as a villain with a merry disposition. Duryea's characterization, although outrageously exaggerated, gives the picture a necessary dose of levity and color. Otherwise it's dreary going.

Young plays with intensity, but is rather wooden as the somewhat inept hero who is rarely there when his presence is most urgently required. Jo Morrow portrays the bad girl, Madlyn Rhue the good girl, neither of them very convincingly. Capable character support is dispatched by R. G. Armstrong, Joel Fluellen, Carl Reindel and several others. R. G. Springsteen's direction is mechanical and production efforts are conventional but efficient. *Tube.*

Becket
(TECHICOLOR-PANAVISION)

Richard Burton-Peter O'Toole in a dramatic tour de force. Richly mounted, vividly realized costume drama with exceptional dialog. An exciting film and a bit of a history lesson.

Paramount Pictures release of Hal Wallis production. Stars Richard Burton and Peter O'Toole. Directed by Peter Glenville. Screenplay by Edward Anhalt, based on play by Jean Anouilh; editor, Anne Coates; production designer, John Bryan; manager, Denis Holt; art director, Maurice Carter; costume designer, Margaret Furse; camera (Technicolor), Geoffrey Unsworth; score, Laurence Rosenthal, conducted by Muir Mathieson. Previewed at DeMille Theatre, N. Y., Feb. 28, 1964. Running time, **148 MINS.**
Thomas Becket .... Richard Burton
King Henry II .... Peter O'Toole
Louis of France .... John Gielgud
Bishop of London ..... Donald Wolfit
Queen Matilda .... Martita Hunt
Queen Eleanor .... Pamela Brown
Pope Alexander III .... Paola Stoppa
Cardinal Zambello .... Gino Cervi
Brother John .... David Weston
Archbishop of Canterbury. Felix Aylmer
Duke of Leicester ...... Inigo Jackson
Gwendolen .... Sian Phillips
French Girl ...... Veronique Vendell
English peaasnt .... Gerald Lawson
His Daughter .... Jeniffer Hilary
Prince Henry .... Riggs O'Hara
Bishop of Winchester... John Phillips
Bishop of York ..... Frank Pettingell
Bishop of Chichester .... Hamilton Dyce
Farmer's Daughter .... Linda Marlow
William of Corbeil .... Patrick Newall
Brother Philip ...... Geoffrey Bayldon
Pope's Secretary .... Graham Stark
French Tailor .... Victor Spinetti
Girl on Balcony .... Magda Knopke
Henry II's Barons .... Niall MacGinnis,
Percy Herbert, Christopher Rhodes,
Peter Jeffrey

Leave aside the chance that this one, made in the Shepperton Studio of Britain, may go into the record as Hal Wallis' finest film ever. The buffs of cinema will argue that. Enough to declare that this is a very fine, perhaps great, motion picture, a credit to the industry as well as Wallis. It is costume drama but not routine, invigorated by story substance, personality clash, bright dialog and religious interest. Not least among its virtues is the pace of the narrative in the astute handling of Peter Glenville, with his advantage of having also mounted the stage play from which the film is derived.

Patrons, and perhaps many reviewers, will tend to heap all of the credit on the actors. They deserve what they get but a judicious weighing of values, putting first things first, cannot slight Glenville, the tight screenplay of Edward Anhalt, the art direction of Maurice Carter, the costume design of Margaret Furse, the production design of John Bryan and, very much, the swift-flow of Anne Coates' cutting. In brief, "Becket" proves again that a great film is the harmoniously combined amalgam of many professional talents assembled by a canny showman.

The screenplay owes much to Jean Anouilh's original stage script. He created the basic conflict which ties the whole panorama together. The quality of "intellectualism" in the French dramatist has been nicely dispersed by Anhalt and Glenville for the mass market and most fans will barely know they are having an intellectual as well as an emotional experience. True, there are some remaining incongruities in the dialogue. The ear is occasionally jolted back into the 20th Century when hearing terms such as "perennial adolescent" and "gate crasher."

Which is not to quibble since the modern psychology of Anouilh lends fascination to these 12th Century shenanigans by investing them with special motivational insights rare in costume drama. The basic story is, of course, historic, the murder on Dec. 29, 1170 in the Cathedral of Canterbury of its archbishop, Becket, by barons from the entourage of Henry II, great-grandson of William the Conquerer. For fictional purposes, Becket and the King had been old roustabouts together, much as, later in English history, Henry IV and Falstaff were. Liberties apart, the killing of the primate in the sanctuary was one of the great scandals of the Middle Ages. The incident yields Hal Wallis and Paramount an angle with history classes and parochial schools.

The relationship of King and Archbishop is the taut string on which many emotional notes reverberate. Beginning as easy familiars of hunt, tavern and council, the pair come to head-on clash as exponents of royal and ecclesiastical privilege. The irony of the plot lies in Henry making Becket archbishop as a political trick only to have his chum turn serious Christian on him.

In the title role, Richard Burton gives a generally convincing and resourceful performance. It is strangely theatrical when he intones Latin phrases at the altar during his consecration as archbishop, and later. The transition from the cold, calculating Saxon courtier of a Norman king into a duty-obsessed sincere churchman is not easily managed. Burton does manage, though there may be wisecracks that religious conversion is far off his personal publicity and as an archbishop he is playing against type, thespically and journalistically.

It would not be warranted to assert that, as Henry II, Peter O'Toole steals the picture from Burton. Still it emerges as the fatter role, the more colorful, and the more likely to get a "best actor" nomination a year from now. The King is an unhappy monarch who has known little affection in life. His mother (Martita Hunt) and his wife (Pamela Brown) are mere figures in the dynastic game. He despises them. His four sons, including the stupid boy, Henry III, bore him. His only satisfying companionship has been provided by the Saxon Becket. Hating-loving, miserably lonely when deserted by his friend, O'Toole makes of the King a tormented, many-sided, baffled, believable human being. More believable than the aloof Becket can seem.

The latency of homosexuality in the relationship is more than hinted. A line of dialog describes the King's reaction to rejection "as if Becket were a woman." There is a scene, earlier, of comparable significance. Becket has given up his mistress, heartbreakingly played by Sian Phillips, to the king because he owes him a return of favor for another wench. The mistress takes the first opportunity to kill herself rather than sleep with the king. Revolted by the blood, the monarch wishes not to be alone that night. There is an implication that the two men share the one bed, the king in torment of conscience, Becket as the comforting presence.

In the large cast, there are a variety of sharply etched vignettes. The brutalized barons are well primed ahead as capable of assassination most foul. The Bishop of London, when passed up for the

Canterbury see, becomes, as delineated by Sir Donald Wolfit, a man of strong personality and dubious morality. Anything to get the job in the end and get back at a Saxon pig. Strangely assorted sly faces appear around Pope Alexander III to whom Becket appeals when threatened with a royal frame for embezzlement. This tide of Italian olive oil reaches the very feet of the white-robed reigning Pontiff (Paola Stoppa) who, however, mixes some compassion with banishment to a monastery.

Incidentally, all of the opening titles and credits are represented as hand-lettered on parchment, a nice touch in itself, to suggest the age and the cultural level. Fans should be edified, too, by the introduction into Henry's court of a great novelty—forks. As for the French king (Sir John Gielgud) and his retinue, they are a curiously effete bunch. But it all makes good theatre.

Imagination in casting stumbled in the choice of Felix Aylmer, as the earlier Archbishop of Canterbury who helps the plot along by dying. The trouble is that Aylmer has done so many such elderly roles that quavery voice is now his trademark. He was too predictable. Martita Hunt was also rather stereotype as the Queen-Mother, though in this instance she had few lines.

If there is no central boy-girl romance in "Becket," there are plenty of trollops, including Veronique Vendell, as a French lass under the royal sheets, and Jenifer Hilary, a peasant girl whose one line is, "Shall I undress, my Lord?" Anyone for tennis?

David Weston, as a youthful monk, symbolizes religious sincerity and dies alongside Becket on the altar.

"Becket" comes alive and stays alive as an entertainment. It has a wealth of values running for it's boxoffice success. There is more than plot and counter-plot, broadsword and local color. Plainly great care went into the production in Technicolor and Panavision. (Of the musical score by Laurence Rosenthal it may be said, as an intended compliment, that it serves without obtruding. It appears that the liturgical detail was carefully researched to its period. The cathedral set was necessarily constructed mostly for Geoffrey Unsworth's camera angles rather than for facsimile's sake.

But judgment reverts to the essential merits. The power of this feature film is rooted in characterization. It is endowed with depth and dialog, two elements often skimped in costume epics.
Land.

Kissin' Cousins
(PANAVISION-COLOR)

Lesser Presley tunefilm. He plays double role and sings eight songs. Weak story.

Hollywood, Feb. 21.
Metro release of Sam Katzman production. Stars Elvis Presley; features Arthur O'Connell, Glenda Farrell, Jack Albertson, Pam Austin, Cynthia Pepper, Yvonne Craig. Directed by Gene Nelson. Screenplay, Gerald Drayson Adams, Nelson, from story by Adams; camera (Metrocolor), Ellis W. Carter; editor, Ben Lewis; assistant director, Eli Dunn. Reviewed at Crest Theatre, North Long Beach, Feb. 21, '64. Running time, **96 MINS.**
Josh Morgan .... Elvis Presley
Jodie Tatum .... Elvis Presley
Pappy Tatum .... Arthur O'Connell
Ma Tatum .... Glenda Farrell

Captain Robert Salbo....Jack Albertson
Selena Tatum .... Pam Austin
Midge .... Cynthia Pepper
Azalea Tatum .... Yvonne Craig
General Alvin Donford .. Donald Woods
Master Sgt. William George Bailey
.... Tommy Farrell
Trudy .... Beverly Powers
Dixie .... Hortense Petra
General's Aide .... Robert Stone

This new Elvis Presley concoction is a pretty dreary effort, one that certainly won't replenish the popularity of Sir Swivel. Presley needs — and merits — more substantial material than this if his career is to continue to flourish as in the past. A few more like this and Cuhnel Parker may have to press the panic button.

Presumably, Metro is counting heavily on the support of ruralites to bring home the boxoffice bacon. The ammunition is Elvis in a dual role, a bunch of songs, a backwoods setting and a bevy of decorative young females in a minimum of wardrobe. But producer Sam Katzman and staff have forgotten several "little" things like a well-devolped storyline and characterizations that are at least remotely related to life. Without these vital ingredients, "Kissin' Cousins" is a commercial long shot, city or country.

Gerald Drayson Adams came up with a ripe story premise, but he and director-co-scenarist Gene Nelson appear to have run dry of creative inspiration in trying to develop it. Yarn is concerned with the problem faced by the U.S. government in attempting to establish an ICBM base on land owned by an obstinate hillbilly clan. To solve the problem, the Air Force sends in a lieutenant (Presley) who is kin to the stubborn critters, among whom is his lookalike cousin (Elvis in a blond wig, no less).

At the root of the failure of "Kissin' Cousins" are two principal factors. One is the business of bursting into song out of context in the middle of a scene. This used to be reasonably acceptable to audiences, but now it is beginning to evolve into an anachronism. Smoother, slicker, more convincing techniques for lapsing into song are necessary in the modern musical. The other prime negative factor in this film is the synthetic, two-dimensional pivotal character, the one portrayed by Presley. The star's character must be appealing. It must have depth and substance to enable his young fans to relate to him.

Histrionically, Presley does as well as possible under the circumstances. He also sings eight songs. Arthur O'Connell is excellent as the patriarch of the mountain clan, but what a mountainous waste of talent. Glenda Farrell is good as his hick wife, and delivers one musical number effectively. Jack Albertson handles a comedy role capably, and Donald Woods a straighter assignment with pro finesse.

The film features three luscious females — Pam Austin, Cynthia Pepper and Yvonne Craig. Miss Craig gets the biggest play and, with a racy, cuddly performance, makes the strongest impression. Miss Austin sort of vanishes inexplicably about halfway through the story. Evidently she is the femme lead on the cutting room floor. Beverly Powers chips in some fancy cleavage to the cause.

Some of Ellis W. Carter's photography is striking. Capable credits are also attained by editor Ben Lewis, art directors George W. Davis and Eddie Imazu and musical director Fred Karger. *Tube.*

Gunfight At Comanche Creek
(PANAVISION-COLOR)

Serviceable program western with Audie Murphy.
Hollywood, Feb. 24.

Allied Artists release of Ben Schwalb production. Stars Audie Murphy, Ben Cooper, Colleen Miller, DeForest Kelley, Jan Merlin. Directed by Frank McDonald. Screenplay, Edward Bernds; camera (De Luxe), Joseph F. Biroc; editor, William Austin; music, Marlin Skiles; assistant director, Don Torpin. Reviewed at the studio, Feb. 24, '64. Running time, **90 MINS.**
Gifford .... Audie Murphy
Carter .... Ben Cooper
Abbie .... Colleen Miller
Troop .... DeForest Kelley
Nielson .... Jan Merlin
Marshal Shearer .... John Hubbard
Winton .... Damian O'Flynn
Janie .... Susan Seaforth

Devised and executed with journeyman efficiency, "Gunfight at Comanche Creek" is tailor-made to satisfy the tastes of the Audie Murphy branch of the International Society of Western Film Addicts. Its palatability diminishes somewhat as one ascends the audience selectivity scale, but as a program western, the role for which it has been designed, it is right on target. Allied Artists should get ample boxoffice mileage out of the Ben Schwalb production.

Serviceably written by Edward Bernds and tautly directed by Frank McDonald, "Gunfight at Comanche Creek" describes, with a minimum of outrageous contrivance, the risky adventures of a member of the National Detective Agency, circa 1875, in ferreting out and bringing to justice a gang of badmen whose technique it is to spring prisoners from jail, fatten their bounties by implicating them in further hoist, and then shooting them for purposes of collecting the sizeable bounty stipend.

Murphy plays the detective who risks his neck in guinea pig fashion to uproot the gang from within. His low-pressure, easygoing histrionic style may not be great acting, but it's ideally suited to the western hero mold. Useful performances are also delivered by Ben Cooper, Colleen Miller, DeForest Kelley, Jan Merlin, John Hubbard, Damian O'Flynn and Susan Seaforth.

The film is handsomely decked out in Panavision and De Luxe Color and contains knowing production efforts in the western vein by cameraman Joseph F. Biroc, editor William Austin, art director Edward Jewell and composer Marlin Skiles. However, the use of a narrator's voice tends, in spots, to be superfluous and condescending. *Tube.*

L'Annee Du Bac
(Graduation Year)
(FRENCH)

Paris, Feb. 25.
Prodis release of CICC-Bertho Films-Carlton Film Export production. With Jean Desailly, Simone Valere, Paul Amiot, Jacques Rispal, Elisabeth Wiener. Written and directed by Jose Andre Lacour; camera, Andreas Winding; music, Claude Carrere. At Avenue, Paris. Running time, **90 MINS.**
Father .... Jean Desailly
Mother .... Simone Valere
Mic .... Paul Amiot
Nicky .... Catherine Lafond
Evelyne .... Elisabeth Wiener

Adapted from a hit play of a few years ago, this loses nearly everything in transfer to the screen. Its theme about the misunderstandings of the young generation with the older folks is somewhat old hat and sans the insights, thesping or revealing direction to keep it from falling into familiarity. It is mainly a local item.

A group of young boys are disillusioned with their fathers when the truth comes out about them. One kills himself, one runs off and another forgives. A few girls help them in their decisions or aid them. But no feeling for the characters comes through.

Jose Andre Lacour, who scripted and directed, also is hamstrung by uninspired thesps. He seems unable to give this movement or snap. Technical credits are only par and even the renown of the play, which spawned many present name thesps, will not help this one.
Mosk.

D'Ou Viens-Tu Johnny?
(Where Are You From Johnny?)
(FRENCH-COLOR)

Paris, March 3.
Imperia release of Hoche Films-SNC-Gueville production. Stars Johnny Hallyday; features Sylvia Vartan, Evelyne Dandry, Henri Vilbert, Pierre Barrouh. Directed by Noel Howard. Screenplay, Yvan Audouard, Christian Plume; camera (Eastmancolor), Walter Wottitz; editor, R. Lichtig. At Marignan, Paris. Running time, **100 MINS.**
Johnny .... Johnny Hallyday
Gigi .... Sylvie Vartan
Magali .... Evelyne Dandry
Christophe .... Henri Vilbert
Django .... Pierre Barrouh

Trying to cash in on the pull of rock and twist singer Johnny Hallyday is the mainstay of this would-be action film. Otherwise it is ineptly directed, haltingly played and mainly for local chances on the Hallyday tag.

The handsome blonde youth here gets a chance to sing one song before the titles. But after that he hardly has any more to parade his vocal talents as he goes back to his home in the plains section of France. He is chased by gangsters whose cache of dope he has destroyed.

There are some riding scenes, and also a vague love affair. Sylvie Vartan, also a rock fave, is forlornly unable to show any acting possibilities while Hallyday at least does have a fairly magnetic presence.

This feeble film, with its halting story values and flat direction, will not help Hallyday's rep much with youngsters. Regular filmgoers will not stand much of it since they get a staple of fine actioners and westerns from the U.S. Pic is a miss. However, it looks like it did not have too big a nut and could possibly make its way on playoff via Hallyday's popularity with the younger population It is technically fair.
Mosk.

7 Faces of Dr. Lao
(COLOR)

Western morality play in fantasy framework. Striking multi-portrayal by Tony Randall and lots of production flair. But, overall, doesn't quite hit the mark.

Hollywood, Feb. 28.

Metro release of George Pal production. Stars Tony Randall; features Barbara Eden, Arthur O'Connell, John Ericson. Directed by Pal. Screenplay, Charles Beaumont, based on novel by Charles G. Finney; camera (Metrocolor), Robert Bronner; editor, George Tomasini; music, Leigh Harline; assistant director, Al Shenberg. Reviewed at Warner Beverly Theatre, Feb. 28, '64. Running time, 100 MINS.

Dr. Lao	Tony Randall
Clint Stark	Arthur O'Connell
Angela Benedict	Barbara Eden
Ed Cunningham	John Ericson
Mike Benedict	Kevin Tate
Sarah Benedict	Argentina Brunetti
Tim Mitchell	Noah Beery
Carey	Royal Dano
Lucas	John Douchette
James Sargent	Frank Cady
Mrs. Howard Cassin	Lee Patrick
Luther Rogers	John Qualen
Kate Rogers	Minerva Urecal
George E. George	Eddlie Little Sky
Mrs. Peter Ramsey	Peggy Rae
Mr. Peter Ramsey	Frank Kreig
Lean Cowboy	Dale McKennon
Fat Cowbooy	Chubby Johnson
Toothless Cowboy	Douglas Fowley

Cinematic ingenuity and a noteworthy performance by Tony Randall are the outstanding attributes of this sometimes fascinating but not altogether successful fantasy. Some of the parts are decidedly better than the whole, which does not quite come off. The George Pal production for Metro should be a fairly popular novelty number with family audiences, but its commercial horizons are somewhat limited.

There are several captivating passages in Charles Beaumont's scenario from Charles G. Finney's novel, "The Circus Of Dr. Lao." But there are also superfluities, inconsistencies and a lack of proper character focus in the approach taken by Beaumont and producer-director Pal. Plot describes the repercussions in a small frontier desert town visited by a curious Oriental whose magical powers enable the townspeople to obtain a clearer perspective of themselves in the course of their adventures in his oddity of a circus—a bizarre tent occupied by such mythical creatures as Merlin, Appolonius of Tyana, Pan, Medusa and the Abominable Snowman, all of them portrayed by Randall.

Several sequences featuring these characters, notably one involving a town gossip whose fortune is told—truthfully—by the blind Appolonius, and another illustrating the plight of the exhausted, aged Merlin, are especially forceful. But the film bogs down in its failure to shed true light on the principal characters. They simply lack substance. And a climatic passage involving a seven-headed sea serpent seems calculated primarily for purposes of spectable, and adds little other than production value to the picture.

It's a histrionic tour de force for Randall, a flashy demonstration of his characterizational versatility. Another fine character actor, Arthur O'Connell, registers as a heavy who sees the error of his ways. Barbara Eden, a dependable and highly decorative actress, plays a somewhat shallow romantic role with sincerity, as does John Ericson as her heartthrob, a courageous newspaper editor. Others of value and prominence include Kevin Tate, Argentina Brunetti, Noah Berry, Royal Dano, John Douchette, Frank Cady, Lee Patrick, John Qualen and Minerva Urecal.

Pal has mounted quite an impressive fantasy production spectacle, and to this end has received stalwart aid from a gifted staff of artists and technicians. Robert Bronner's nimble, dexterous cinematography is a big asset, so is George Tomasini's acutely sharp and perceptive editing. The work of these two is particularly telling on a dance sequence in Pan's lair. Especially substantial art direction by George W. Davis and Gabriel Scognamillo, reinforced by the savvy set decoration of Henry Grace and Hugh Hunt, further enhances the quality appearance of the production. An unorthodox score with international variety and character has been put together for the occasion by Leigh Harline.

William Tuttle's makeup work on Randall is—in a word—superb. And last, but not least, a veritable fun zone has been created by the special visual effect team of Paul B. Byrd, Wah Chang, Jim Danforth, Ralph Rodine and Robert R. Hoag. *Tube.*

Hot Enough For June
(BRITISH-COLOR)

Likeable spoof of espionage racket which ambles along pleasantly but lacks the surprises and thrills which would have notched this comedy-thriller several points higher; good booking proposition.

London, March 10.

Rank release of a Betty E. Box-Ralph Thomas production. Stars Dirk Bogarde, Sylva Koscina, Robert Morley, Leo McKern; features Roger Delgado, John Le Mesurier, Noel Harrison, John Standing, George Pravda, Richard Pasco, Eric Pohlmann, Richard Vernon, Alan Tilvern, Norman Bird, William Mervyn. Directed by Ralph Thomas. Screenplay by Luke Heller, from Lloyd Davidson's novel, "Night of Wenceslas"; camera, Ernest Steward; editor, Alfred Roome; music, Angelo Lavagnino. At Odeon, Haymarket, London. Running time, 98 MINS.

Nicholas Whistler	Dirk Bogarde
Vlasta Simenova	Sylva Koscina
Colonel Cunliffe	Robert Morley
Simenova	Leo McKern
Josef	Roger Delgado
Allsop	John Le Mesurier
Roddinghead	Richard Vernon
Cunliffe's Secretary	Amanda Grinling
Johnnie	Noel Harrison
Fred	Derek Nimmo
Lorna	Jill Melford
Leon	Brook Williams
Pavelka	George Pravda
Plakov	Richard Pasco
Glaushka	Eric Pohlmann
German Research Man	Gertan Klauber
Simenova's Aide	Alan Tilvern
Embassy Janitor	Frank Finlay
Washroom Attendant	John Standing
Labor Exchange Clerk	Norman Bird
Business Man	William Mervyn
Russian Dancers	Igor Meggido and Partner

A faster pace from director Ralph Thomas and a few more red herrings and surprise situations from screenwriter Luke Heller could have worked wonders in lifting this amiable enough spoof of espionage into a top league comedy-thriller. As is, "Hot Enough For June" (title hinges on a code phrase) is a pleasant entertainment, enhanced by some amusing acting, and is a safe booking for most audiences.

With the James Bond spy thrillers much in the news, advent of "June" is timely, but it is by no means a skit on the Bond adventures. It is simply a genial leg-pull of some of the situations which, in tougher circumstances, Bond might easily be facing. Dick Bogarde, who plays the hero with ingratiating efficiency, is an unsuccessful writer content to live on national assistance. When the Labor Exchange unexpectedly sends him to take up a post as a trainee junior-executive in a glassworks, Bogarde at first tries to duck the job, but finds the combination of a good salary and useful expenses irresistible. He is assigned to visit a Czech factory and bring back a written message which he guilessly believes to be a simple commercial job. He does not know that he is now attached to the Espionage Department of the Foreign Office. Keig, gullible Bogarde is, in fact, an innocent dupe.

He arrives behind the Iron Curtain unaware that he is a spy, falls for the pretty girl who drives his car and still does not know that she is a spy, too, and also the daughter of the local Red Secret Police chief. When the truth about his phoney business connection dawns on him and he finds that his local contact has been liquidated he slowly gathers that he is on the spot.

Soon Bogarde is on the run from the Secret Police and needs the help of the girl, several disguises and a heap of luck as, bewildered, he blunders to eventual safety. But the local secret cops are themselves so hamstrung that the reluctant agent's dilemma never seems overly risky. And audiences will have little sense of participation in a dangerous exploit. Rather will they sit back, benevolently, and watch the escape and the romance wander along to an inevitable happy conclusion.

Bogarde proceeds gently from innocence to bewilderment, and then to resourcefulness. But a few nail-biting incidents would have helped to make this more exciting. He is partnered by the attractive Sylva Koscina, a Continental miss who projects sex quietly and not through abnormal vital statistics. She proves herself to be a shrewd aid to Bogarde. And they have a couple of minor affairs which are mainly left discreetly to the imagination. But there's no imagination about Miss Koscina looking delectable in deshabille.

Most of the humor comes from witty prods at the expense of the Foreign Office and the Iron Curtain Party system. Instead of the highly skilled and dangerous business that it is, international espionage is made to look very much of a hit-and-miss lark. Robert Morley is superb as the boss of the department, with his Old Etonian tie, benign plottings and general appearance of a well-poised walrus. His aide, John Le Mesurier, is also an amusing civil servant. He and Morley share a couple of bright scenes. Leo McKern, chief of the local Secret Police, is Morley's oldtime adversary, and they have one outstanding short sequence when they discuss their respective tricks of the trade.

Other actors who fit engagingly into the scene are Roger Delgado, Richard Vernon, Alan Tilvern, Eric Pohlmann, George Pravada and Richard Pasco. Apart from the studio work (location was in Padua) which is effective in simulating Prague. Syd Cain's artwork is okay. Ernest Steward's camera brings some good color backgrounds while Alfred Roome has edited smoothly. A nightclub sequence is unfortunately overly-abbreviated. "Hot Enough For June" is a sound enough production just lacking in the brisk tempo and element of outrageous surprise which it needs for a lift. *Rich.*

L'Homme De Rio
(The Man From Rio)
(FRENCH-COLOR)

Paris, March 3.

UA release of Ariane-UA production. Stars Jean-Paul Belmondo; features Francoise Dorleac, Jean Servais, Milton Ribeira, Adolfo Cellis, Simone Renant. Directed by Philippe De Broca. Screenplay, Jean-Paul Rappeneau, Ariane Mnouchkine, De Broca; camera (Technicolor), Edmond Sechan; editor, Laurence Mery. At Mercury, Paris. Running time, 110 MINS.

Adrien	Jean-Paul Belmondo
Agnes	Francoise Dorleac
Catalan	Jean Servais
Lola	Simone Renant
Tupac	Milton Ribeira
Di Valdes	Adolfo Celli

Smartly paced adventure opus has its tongue in cheek but plays it without creating on the action. Story is an acceptable excuse for a witty pic that moves along briskly and emerges almost on a par with the Yank-made situation comedy and adventure pix.

And this is a compliment since American pictures have a special brand and tone that has made them an international commodity.

This film, too, plays seriously, yet has a slightly offbeat flavor in adding a skeptical French touch to it. The hero is a nice French soldier who is only interested in having a good time with his girl on a week furlough. But he gets caught up in 2 series of wild adventure when she is kidnapped.

Director Philippe De Broca has kept this darting along while Jean-Paul Belmondo is an ingratiating actor who also takes chances on his derringdo if he lacks a grace and dash in doing it. But he more than makes up for it by his vitality, gusto and frank, simple common sense.

Belmondo finds his girl whisked off by two strange men, they turn out to be Brazilian Indians of an old historic tribe, and he follows them onto a plane and winds up in Rio de Janeiro. Plotting always stays coherent in overcoming all the needs like finding a way to the plane, his retrieving the girl and finally stumbling upon the mystery. It seems three statutes contained a key to a fabulous treasure. It ends with the villain's comeuppance. The hero manages to get back to Paris in time not to be AWOL.

Belmondo sways on the ledges of high buildings, has fights on scaffoldings, is almost eaten by an alligator, has to jump out of a plane and has many fights. It is all done with invention, speed and knowhow. Others play alongside Belmondo well and some savory gags liven up things between action segs.

The color is bright, Rio and Paris are nicely used for their photogenic qualities. And the film is generally entertaining and bright. It has been backed by United Artists which has it for worldwide distribution. It has the movement and snap for playoff chances and an all-out action treatment may also have this as an arty house possibility, too. *Mosk.*

The Long Ships
(BRITISH-YUGOSLAVIAN-COLOR)

Boisterous adventure. Despite hefty faults, should find a good market with those just looking for an eyeful.

London, March 3.

Columbia release (through BLC) of a Warwick-Avala (Irving Allen) production. Stars Richard Widmark, Sidney Poitier, Russ Tamblyn, Rosanna Schiaffino, Oscar Homolka; features Edward Judd, Lionel Jeffries, Bebe Loncar, Clifford Evans, Gordon Jackson, Paul Stafino, David Lodge, Colin Blakely, Jeanne Moody. Directed by Jack Cardiff. Screenplay by Berkely Mather, Beverley Cross from Franz Bengtsson's novel; camera, Christopher Challis; editor, Geoff Foot; music, Dusan Radic. At Odeon, Marble Arch, London. Running time, 124 MINS.
Rolfe .... Richard Widmark
El Mansuh .... Sidney Poitier
Orm .... Russ Tamblyn
Aminah .... Rosanna Schiaffino
Gerda .... Beba Looncar
Krok .... Oscar Homolka
Sven .... Edward Judd
King Harald .... Clifford Evans
Ylva .... Jeanne Moody
Rhykka .... Colin Blakely
Vahlin .... Gordon Jackson
Olla .... David Lodge
Raschid .... Paul Stassino
Aziz .... Lionel Jeffries

Any attempt to put this into the epic class falls down because of a hodge-podge of a storyline, a mixture of styles and insufficient development of characterization. Result is nothing more than a boisterous adventure yarn. Still, this British-Yugoslav meller is often quite an eyeful and should attract those who like straightforward adventure without the trimmings of subtlety. Where the pic scores particularly is in the way director Jack Cardiff has used seascapes and color for fine, poetic effect. His sea scenes are topnotch and concession to artwork is skilfully disguised. His directorial eye, based largely on his long experience as a top lenser, is enhanced by the work of Christopher Challis, himself no mean camera juggler.

The plot, which has obviously suffered in both editing and in censorial slaps, is a conglomeration of battles, double-crossing, seastorms, floggings, unarmed combat with occasional halfhearted peeks at sex. Throughout there's a great deal of noise and the entire experience is a very long drag. Film concerns the rivalry of the Vikings and the Moors in search of a legendary Golden Bell, the size of three men and containing "half the gold in the world." Leaders of the rival factors are Richard Widmark, an adventurous Viking con man, who plays strictly tongue in cheek, and Sidney Poitier, dignified, ruthless top man of the Moors. In contrast to Widmark, he seeks to take the film seriously. The clash in styles between these two is a minor disaster.

Curiously, Widmark's performance is the more impressive, even allowing for his accent, which smacks more of the Bowery than the Barbary Coast. He does emerge as a real, vital being. Poitier's less robust, more subtle performance is often lost in the surrounding babel. A tavern orgy, the progress of the Vikings' ship through dangerous waters, the discovery of the bell and a scene where Widmark nearly comes to a sticky end on a particularly unpleasant torture gadget called the Mare of Steel are all well done. And there is one fantastic sequence, funnier than was probably intended, in which the sex-starved Viking prisoners raid Poitier's harem, and which

might well have been trotted direct from the old Crazy Gang shows.

Apart from Widmark and Poitier, the remainder of the male cast mainly gets lost in the physical adventures and under their hirsute beards. However, Oscar Homolka as an ale-swigging, lusty shipbuilder; Clifford Evans, as King Harald; and Lionel Jeffries, as a blacked-up eunuch, have their moments. Colin Blakly, Edward Judd and Russ Tamblyn are among those also ran. On the femme side Rosanna Schiaffino brings beauty to the role of Poitier's No. 1 wife but Beba Loncar, taken on the perilous journey by Widmark as a hostage, is colorless though, again, easy on the eye.

Beverley Cross and Berkely Mason have hewn a script out of Franz Bengtsson's novel, rather than written it. Director Cardiff, seemingly acknowledging defeat, has, as indicated, concentrated largely on the visual aspects. Disappointment "The Long Ships" undoubtedly is, but it still has enough rough-and-ready action to amuse a great number of cinemagoers. At the end of the film's run, the Odeon, Marble Arch will be pulled down and converted into a modern cinema. It is a pity that it could not have wound up with a more satisfying film.   Rich.

Les Dames du Bois du Boulogne
(Women of the Bois du Boulogne)
(FRENCH-ENGLISH TITLES)

Los Angeles, March 3.

Brandon Films release of a Les Films Raoul Ploquin (Robert La Vallee) production. Directed by Robert Bresson. Stars Paul Bernard, Maria Casares, Elina Labourdette; features Lucienne Bogaert, Jean Marchat. Screenplay by Bresson, based on episode in Diderot's novel, "Jacques le Fataliste"; dialogue by Jean Cocteau; camera, Phillippe Agostini, Maurice Pecqueux, Marcel Weiss; editor, Jean Feyte; art directors, Max Douy, James Allan, Robert Clavel; music, Jean-Jacques Grunewald. Reviewed at Royce Hall, UCLA, L.A. Running time, 90 MINS.
Jean .... Paul Bernard
Helene .... Maria Casares
Agnes .... Elina Labourdette
Agnes' mother .... Lucienne Bogaert
Jacques .... Jean Marchat

Reviewed for the record. This, the second feature by French director Robert Bresson, was made in 1944 during the German occupation and has, until now, had comparatively little exposure even in France and none here. Its appeal today lies in its cinematic value as an example of Bresson's formative period. Film's potential audiences likely will be in the more serious arty houses, university film courses and film societies.

In contrast to the later and better-known Bresson films, such as "Pickpocket," "A Man Escapes" and "Trial of Joan of Arc," notable for their stark realism and documentary style. "Les Dames" seems startlingly sophisticated. Even more surprising, considering the time and conditions of filming, it is entirely Gallic with no trace of Germanic influence.

Bresson's tale of revenge, based on an incident in Diderot's 18th-Century novel, "Jacques le Fataliste," tells of a spurned woman's vengeance on her lover, the girl who replaces her in his affections, and the girl's mother. Updating the story to contemporary Paris, Bresson creates and maintains suspense by confining the plot almost entirely to the four principal characters, continously understating the action. This gives the film a formalized, deliberate pace that

might have become tiring without the exceptionally talented cast. They're right at home with the late Jean Cocteau's intelligent, sophisticated dialogue — as brittle and scintillating as the society in which the characters move.

Maria Casares, as the woman scorned, dominates the films with a chilling, electric performance. Her beautiful mask of a face remains outwardly impassive, conveying expression solely through her eyes, her superbly controlled voice and an uncanny ability to suggest evil. Despite the excellent, almost naive, performance by Paul Bernard as her principal victim he's too weak, too guileless to be truly sympathetic. Elina Labourdette, given a greater range of expression in which to create the good girl, temporarily bad, who becomes the object of Bernard's affections, at times, seems to be pushing but is generally effective. Lucienne Bogaert is superb as the girl's mother — a weak, impoverished gentlewoman who reluctantly but unfalteringly sells her daughter's innocence. Jean Marchat is on screen only in a tiny but important incident at the beginning as a suitor of Miss Casares.

Philippe Agostini's topnotch camerawork brings visual life as well as the proper feeling of claustrophobia to the film's settings—for the most part, the apartments of Miss Casares and her female victims. Outside locations are used simply to set a mood or establish an important plot incident such as the first meeting of Bernard with the daughter and mother in the Bois du Boulogne— hence the title.

Jean Feyte's editing remains outstanding despite the almost certain alterations in the film which must have occurred since its completion. The delicate score by Jean-Jacques Grunewald is in the proper Bresson mood of understatement.   Robe.

The World Of Henry Orient
(COLOR)

Amusing comedy. Two newcomer-ingenes harrass amorous life of Peter Sellers. Pan Arts off to good debut.

United Artists release of Pan Arts production, produced by Jerome Hellman. Stars Peter Sellers, Paula Prentiss, Angela Lansbury; features Tom Bosley, Phyllis Thaxter, Bibi Osterwald; introduces Tippy Walker, Merrie Spaeth. Directed by George Roy Hill. Screenplay, Nora & Nunnally Johnson based on novel by Nora Johnson; camera De Luxe (color), Boris Kaufman, Arthur J. Ornitz; editor, Stuart Gilmore; music, Elmer Bernstein; assistant directors. Michael Hertzberg, Roger Rothstein. Reviewed at RKO 86th St. Theatre, March 5, '64. Running time, 115 MINS.
Harry Orient .... Peter Sellers
Stella .... Paula Prentiss
Isabel Boyd .... Angela Lansbury
Frank Boyd .... Tom Bosley
Mrs. Gilbert .... Phyllis Thaxter
Boothy .... Bibi Osterwald
Valeri Boyd .... Tippy Walker
Marian Gilbert .... Merrie Spaeth
Joe Byrd .... Peter Duchin
Sidney .... John Fiedler
The Store Owner ...... Al Lewis
The Doctor .... Fred Stewart
Emma .... Philippa Bevans
Kafritz .... Jane Buchanan

In "The World of Henry Orient," the first feature to be made by the indie Pan Arts Co., United Artists has a picture with across the board appeal, strong for both family trade and hipper film comedy audiences. The Peter Sellers starrer also serves to introduce two promising young femme performers, Tippy Walker and Merrie Spaeth, both of whom make impressive debuts, especially Miss Walker. Additional fine performances and some bright direction by George Roy Hill mark the pic for hefty boxoffice contention all around.

Producer Jerome Hellman guided this production through many harrowing days as an all-New York try. Despite the problems, which included craft union hassles incident to being the first film ever lensed in its entirety at Michael Myerberg's Long Island Studios, as well as scheduling problems involving Seller's other commitments. "Orient" has come off an often-funny and always fetching production.

Nora and Nunnally Johnson's screenplay, based on Mrs. Johnson's novel, deals with the adventures of two young schoolgirls in Manhattan and their infatuation with a nutty avant garde pianist named Henry Orient (Sellers). One of the girls, played by Miss Walker, is the daughter of wealthy parents who spend most of their time galavanting around the world while leaving their offspring to live with another family. She is given to wild flights of fancy and her imagination is what first drums up the crush on Orient. At a ritzy eastside private school she befriends a more stable youngster, Miss Spaeth, who is captivated by her pal's vicarious and actual adventures and the two become best friends.

Pic traces the duo in their often-relentless pursuit of Orient whose talent at the piano is less than distinctive but whose ardor for ladies, especially married ones, is unbounded. The young femmes soon develop the knack of showing up constantly at just the wrong time for Orient, providing the springboard for several very funny bits of broad comic playing by Sellers. He turns in a skillful performance as the vain yet cowardly "lover," coming up with a nifty display of virtuosity.

Miss Walker makes quite an impressive debut, creating a wild yet sympathetic character. She demonstrates a flair for both comedy and drama and evokes considerable warmth and vivacious personality on the screen. As her chum, Miss Spaeth also contributes admirably in a less flashy role as the more down to earth of the two. She too displays intuitive feeling and spirit, which makes her pic debut likewise strong.

Although it is primarily the girls' picture (probably the first time anyone has "stolen" a pic from Sellers, several others contribute fine performances. As Miss Walker's selfish mother, Angela Lansbury delivers skillfully. She is the epitome of the dominating wealthy wife, who suddenly discovers her daughter after years of ignoring her. Misinterpreting the youngster's crush on Orient, Mommy ends up having an affair with the pianist while trying to clear the matter up, all of which ultimately leads to her losing both daughter and husband. Latter is played by Tom Bosley who lends warmth and sincerity to his newfound relationship with the neglected daughter.

Paula Prentiss overplays as an object of Orient's amorous intentions. She mugs and mutters excessively and in the process defeats much of the comic impact she is building to in many of the scenes. Nonetheless she does deliver some disarming bits from time to time. Phyllis Thaxter provides a fine and simple performance as Miss Spaeth's divorced mother and cafe sock singer Bibi Osterwald has some delightful moments as Miss Thaxter's pal.

Hill has directed the film with a smooth, even flow, nicely balancing the moments of crisis in the girls' lives with the high comedy of the Sellers character. He has come up with some clever directorial ideas which he skillfully employed to give the picture a successful style and warm spirit.

Photography by Boris Kaufman and Arthur J. Ornitz is firstrate. They have photographed some excellent Gotham color scenery and contributed substantially to the film's atmosphere and polish. There are some rough spots in Stuart Gilmore's editing, the cutting in a couple of the more complicated scenes not matching too well. But, overall, he has created a well-cut print. Elmer Bernstein's score is pleasant and effective.

"Orient" is the Easter attraction at Radio City Music Hall, N. Y., and is a fitting presentation for the holiday season there. It stands to come up with a substantial b.o. showing and should duplicate this performance when it goes into regular release nationally in June. The only requirement will be a carefully-designed ad campaign which can capitalize on both its family and more sophisticated audience appeal.   *Kali.*

Schloss Gripsholm
(The Gripsholm Castle)
(GERMAN-COLOR-C'SCOPE)

Berlin, March 10.
Gloria release of Independent (Georg Richter and Kurt Hoffmann) production. Stars Jana Brechowa, Walter Giller, Hanns Lothar and Nadja Tiller. Directed by Kurt Hoffman. Screenplay, Herbert Reinecker, based on novel by Kurt Tucholsky; camera (Eastmancolor), Richard Angst; music, Hans-Martin Majewski; sets, Otto Pischinger. At Gloria Palast, West Berlin. Running time, **99 MINS.**
Lydia .... Jana Brechova
Kurt .... Walter Giller
Karlchen .... Hanns Lothar
Billie .... Nadja Tiller
Frau Kremser .... Agnes Windeck

"Gripsholm," taken from a popular holiday tale of the late (1935) Kurt Tucholsky, one of the most prominent raconteurs of Germany's pre-Hitler era, may disappoint those who read and fell in love with the original. But leaving Tucholsky out of the game, this pic proves a good piece of entertainment for the average German film patron. Taking into account that "Gripsholm" has some special assets, for example a charming leading lady (new to German film, Czech Jana Brechowa), this may qualify itself for some export deals. However, much will depend on a good dubbing job.

This is the second film which Kurt Hoffmann, of "Aren't We Wonderful" prominence, directed and produced via his (and Georg Richter's) Independent-Film. It cost about $325,000. While in the original it was a young Berlin couple in love back in '20's who spend their holidays in the famous Swedish castle of Gripsholm, it's now a Hamburg twosome of 1963. The two, Walter Giller and Jana Brechowa, flirt, quarrel and poke fun at each other. Eventually Giller's friend, Hanns Lothar, shows up in the north and flirts with the girl and vice versa. Eventually the girl's friend, Nadja Tiller, joins the trio and flirts (and vice versa) with Giller.

Many of Tucholsky's phrases and dialog sequences have been saved. Oddly enough, this is both the film's drawback and advantage. Much that is said sounds strange and often even has a false ring. But at the same time it's cute and amusing dialog. Tucholsky was a master of the word and wordplay. The big question persists as to whether such can be adequately translated.

The acting is both pro and con. Jana Brechowa's works is the best of the film. She's a unique personality and easy to watch. Walter Giller is sympathetic and has many nice moments. Hanns Lothar is excellent while Nadja Tiller seems a miscast. A special word of praise goes to Richard Angst for his fine lensing. In fact, the pic is a beautiful bit of publicity for tourism in Sweden.   *Hans.*

A Tiger Walks
(COLOR)

Synthetic Disney concoction that should please the kiddies but hardly the adults.

Hollywood, March 13.
Buena Vista release of Walt Disney production. Stars Brian Keith, Vera Miles, Pamela Franklin; features Sabu, Edward Andrews, Una Merkel, Peter Brown, Kevin Corcoran. Others in cast: Frank McHugh, Arthur Hunnicutt, Merry Anders, Jack Albertson, Connie Gilchrist, Theodore Marcuse, Frank Aletter, Donald May. (No character names.) Directed by Norman Tokar. Screenplay, Lowell S. Hawley, based on book by Ian Niall; camera (Technicolor), William Snyder; editor, Grant K. Smith; music, Buddy Baker; assistant director, John C. Chulay. Reviewed at the studio, March 13, '64. Running time, **91 MINS.**

Where else but in a Walt Disney picture could a fierce Bengal tiger at large be the object of sympathy and affection and the terrorized community it prowls represent the antagonistic element? So it is in "A Tiger Walks," a suspense drama with overtones of morality and political satire. The Buena Vista release, co-produced by Bill Anderson, does not succeed in its bid for adult enjoyment, principally because the film's center of comic and dramatic gravity is synthetic and childish. But most kids will probably get a boot out of it, and that should see it through at the boxoffice, although it's apt to be a proportionately modest entry by Disney standards.

The varying reaction of people to the threat of a tiger on the loose serves as the nucleus of Lowell S. Hawley's screenplay, based on the book by Ian Niall. It boils down to a choice between rooting out the tiger and destroying it before it chews someone up (an unspeakably malicious view, as scanned by Hawley) or taking great pains to bring the big cat back alive and healthy. Since "Rajah" happens to be a Disney tiger—a lovable species that only chews up bad guys and would never even harm a dog, provided that it was a good dog—there's never any question as to the outcome.

Principal character, a sheriff torn between his duty to protect the community and his daughter's concern that the tiger be spared—a cause that (absurdly) sweeps the country—is essayed in persuasive style by Brian Keith. Pamela Franklin is capable as the daughter, as is Vera Miles as her mother. Edward Andrews carries the satirical ball as a pompous, double-talking boob of a governor. The ball gets fumbled, but it's hardly Andrews' fault. Others of more than minor value are Sabu, Una Merkel, Peter Brown, Kevin Corcoran, Frank McHugh, Arthur Hunnicutt, Merry Anders, Jack Albertson, Connie Gilchrist, Theodore Marcuse, Frank Aletter and Donald May. Doodles Weaver is very good as a country journalist.

Resourceful direction by Norman Tokay and editing by Grant K. Smith, along with alert photography by William Snyder, make the most of big cat footage in maintaining an element of suspense and menace for the moppets. They are not as successful with people footage.   *Tube.*

Paris When It Sizzles
(COLOR)

Glamorously mounted and cast but otherwise undistinguished romantic romp around Paree.

Hollywood, March 9.
Paramount release of Richard Quine-George Axelrod production. Stars William Holden, Audrey Hepburn; with Gregoire Aslan, Ramond Bussiere, Christian Duvallex, Thomas Michel. (No character names.) Directed by Quine. Screenplay, Axelrod; camera (Technicolor), Charles Lang Jr.; editor, Archie Marshek; music, Nelson Riddle; ass't director, Paul Feyder. Reviewed at studio, March 9, '64. Running time, **108 MINS.**

"Paris When It Sizzles" fizzles. The Richard Quine-George Axelrod production, written by the latter and directed by the former, will have to rely on the popularity of its stars and the glamor and richness of its production values to make a respectable commercial showing. But the boxoffice battle won't easily be won by the Paramount release. For at the foundation of all this technical sheen is a romantic comedy that, as scenarist Axelrod himself describes the story-within-a-story that weaves through the film, is "contrived, utterly preposterous and totally unmotivated."

Axelrod's 108-minutes of marshmallow-weight hokum is concerned with the evolution of a romantic relationship between a somewhat broken down, middleaged screenwriter (William Holden) and his Tessie the Typist, an adorable Givenchy wenchy also known as Audrey Hepburn. Their affair is more or less paralleled in the creative ramblings of Holden's mind as he dreams up an artificial cloak-and-dagger screenplay. Suddenly, having finished his yarn, he realizes he loves Miss Hepburn, concludes his career as a Hollywood hack and sets off with her apparently in pursuit of That Great Honest Movie Script In The Sky—the one, evidently, that Axelrod couldn't attain this time out.

The basic error in this film seems to be the artificiality of the shell in which the takeoffs are encased. In other words, the supposedly "realistic" situation is synthetic, so that the audience is never enabled to anchor itself between the imaginative flights of fancy scattered throughout the picture. Pretty soon one ceases to be concerned with the story and settles for watching the pretty images darting and dancing across the screen.

Prettiest image by far is Miss Hepburn, a refreshingly individual creature in this era of the exaggerated curve. Holden handles his assignment commendably. Both give a lot more than they have gotten. Satisfactory performances of a minor nature are dispatched by Gregoire Aslan, Ramond Bussieres, Christian Duvallex and Thomas Michel. Chipping in extended, uncredited cameos are Tony Curtis and Noel Coward, with smaller bits in the same vein by Mel Ferrer and Marlene Dietrich. The singing voices of Fred Astaire and Frank Sinatra are heard, former in a chorus of "That Face," latter singing one line of a tune in a parody of main titles that is one of the more amusing passages of the film.

Quine's slick, breezy direction is backed up by Charles Lang Jr.'s agile, colorful photography (some nifty views of poor, over-exploited Paree). Jean D'Eaubonne's elegant sets, Archie Marshek's expressive editing and Nelson Riddle's flavorful score. Miss Hepburn's "wardrobe and perfume" are credited to Hubert de Givenchy. The wardrobe is neat and functional, but unexciting from a fashion standpoint. This reviewer couldn't smell the perfume, only the picture.

Tube.

Night Must Fall

Flashy but somewhat spotty remake of thriller from the thirties. B.o. possibilities may hinge on selling ingenuity.

Hollywood, March 12.

Metro release of Karel Reisz-Albert Finney production, directed by Reisz. Stars Finney; features Mona Washbourne, Susan Hampshire, Sheila Hancock. Others: Michael Medwin, Joe Gladwin, Martin Wyldeck, John Gill. (No character names.) Screenplay, Clive Exton, adapted from Emlyn Williams' play; camera, Freddie Francis: editor, Philip Barnikel; music, Ron Grainer. Reviewed at studio, March 12, '64. Running time, **99 MINS.**

Artfully composed and strikingly photographed, this British-manufactured reproduction of Metro's 1937 shock-suspense thriller could, if perceptively marketed, generate a respectable boxoffice showing. Although the new Metro version lacks the restraint, clarity and subtlety of its 27-year-old forerunner, it makes up, to some degree, in cinematic flamboyance what it lacks in dramatic tidiness and conviction.

The key to the commercial strongbox, at least in this country, is Albert Finney, current fair-haired boy of international filmdom via "Tom Jones." His performance as the cunning madman is vivid and explosive, and it might not be too far from wrong to suppose that the entire project may have germinated out of his desire to tackle the character. He did. It should be noted, co-produce the venture with Karel Reisz, who also directed.

Vagueness in key dramatic junctures hampers the new version, constructed by scenarist Clive Exton around the skeleton of Emlyn Williams' original stage play. There's also a jarring tendency to bully the imagination rather than just tease it. For example, some doubt formerly existed as to the contents of the little bag carried around by the principal character. No such mystery pervades this version. Finney wields his axe in the very first scene, and much is made thereafter of his relationship with the resultantly independent head. When the bizarre tale arrives at its critical phases, scenarist Exton doesn't pause to explain the odd deductions and behavior of some of the central characters. For example, the young heroine all too abruptly and seemingly unaccountably senses there's something amiss in the house (as if Suddenly Last Summer, Olivia knew there was something evil, etc. etc.). Not only that, but when she returns to find heads have rolled again she has the audacity (and downright lack of good sense, it seemed to this reviewer) to confront and tame the murderer.

That these story lapses and irregularities seem less than drastic is a tribute to the dazzling execution and a batch of tangy performances. Finney, in the role played so well by Robert Montgomery 27 years ago, is fascinating to watch as his dispositions shift with maniacal rootlessness. It's an inventive, stimulating portrayal by a gifted actor. Yet Finney's thespic thunder is often stolen by Mona Washbourne's masterful delineation of the lonely "invalid" who becomes his victim. In one brief, flickering passage, in which she hesitantly suggests he can refer to her as "mother," Miss Washbourne creates an indelible image. Susan Hampshire is fragile and charming as the astonishingly intrepid maiden and Sheila Hancock spirited as a rather pathetic maid who has been compromised by Finney.

Reisz's perceptive, razzle-dazzle direction features dramatically abrupt cuts and transitions, often with images of one scene overlapping into the audio of the next — with telling effect. The picture has been strikingly photographed by Freddie Francis, arrestingly knit by editor Philip Barnikel and reinforced with a deliciously sinister score by Ron Grainer.

Tube.

Saturday Night Out
(BRITISH)

Poorly constructed pic with some reasonable thesping and directorial talent socked by tawdry predictable situations and weak dialog; okay as dualer for undiscerning audiences.

London, March 10.

Compton Cameo release of a (Robert Hartford-Davis) Michael Klinger, Tony Tenser Tekli production. Features Heather Sears, Bernard Lee, Erica Romberg, John Bonney, David Lodge, Nigel Greene, Francesca Annis, Colin Campbell, Inigo Jackson, Derek Bond, Patsy Rowlands, Searchers. Directed by Robert Hartford-Davis. Screenplay, Donald and Derek Ford; camera, Peter Newbrook; music, Robert Richards; editor, Alastair McIntyre. At Rialto, London. Running time, **96 MINS.**

Penny	Heather Sears
Hudson	Bernard Lee
Wanda	Erica Romberg
Lee	John Bonney
Jamie	Colin Campbell
Harry	Inigo Jackson
Paddy	Nigel Green
Marlene	Carolline Mortimer
Arlene	Vera Day
Club Manager	David Burke
Joe	Freddie Mills
Arthur	David Lodge
Cathy	Wendy Newton
Barman	Barry Langdon
Paul	Derek Bond

Robert Hartford-Davis is a sound director, but "Saturday Night Out" has fallen apart mainly because of poor, undistinguished dialog and predictable situations. There are some good glimpses of thesping, and locales are satisfactorily presented. But the four or five situations are only thinly interlocked, and the result adds up to a fair omnibus, dualer for not too demanding audiences.

Several sailors in the Merchant Navy descend on London with 15 hours' shore leave and the film depicts their brief adventures. Since most of the folks involved are concerned mainly with the delights of dames and drink, the results are predictable and the gals-and-guzzle routine palls. The incidents barely touch each other except in the most superficial way.

Astute business man George Hunter (Bernard Lee) turns the tables on a blackmailing dame (Erica Romberg) and her cameraman "business partner"; seaman David Lodge makes a beeline for his regular London dockside popsy and spends the 15 hours with her; another (Inigo Jackson) gets crocked and clipped in a sleazy Soho drinking club while his naive young pal gets involved with a young girl for whom he jumps ship to marry. John Bonney is picked up by an incredible beatnik girl (Heather Sears) and also falls in love somewhat incredibly. None of these incidents provides ultra bite or excitement, though the Bernard Lee-Erica Romberg blackmailing affair has a mildly neat twist. Campbell and Miss Annis provide a few moments of genuine and likeable wistfulness and the lark between Miss Sears and Bonney has a satirical air which unfortunately becomes over pretentious.

Lodge and Lee are as solidly dependable as ever. Remainder of the cast does workmanlike jobs against heavy odds. Worst anecdote is also, regrettably, the longest, that in which Jackson makes a fool of himself in the drinking club. The scriptwriters throw no new light on a situation in which many suckers have found themselves, and in the tavern and club scenes the dialog rarely rises higher than this sample: "I didn't get your name." "No, I didn't throw it." The Brothers Ford screenplay writers are also woolly and adrift when their dialog enters the realms of second-hand philosophy.

Among the lesser roles, Carole Mortimer and Vera Day stand out as cheap nightclub come-on girls. Nigel Green, as an whiskey-swigging tar, is effective, though hardly necessary to the action. The various London locales are conscientiously adequate and Peter Newbrook's camerawork is okay. A selling point among younger patrons is the appearance as pub entertainers of the popular and locally pop vocal group, The Searchers.

Hartford-Davis has done a routine but uninspired job as director and producer. Perhaps the greatest disappointment in the film is the appearance of Miss Sears, after a longish layoff, in a role which gives poor scope for her talent.

Rich.

Nothing But The Best
(BRITISH-COLOR)

Sharp, satirical comedy about a ruthless young man who stops at nothing to climb the social and business ladder. Stylishly directed and acted and should provide entertainment for most audiences.

London, March 10.

Warner-Pathe release of a Domino (David Deutsch) production for Anglo Amalgamated. Stars Alan Bates, Denholm Elliott, Millicent Martin; features Harry Andrews, Pauline Delany, Alison Leggatt, Lucinda Curtis, James Villiers, Avice Landon, Ernest Clark, Paul Curran, Godfrey Quigley. Directed by Clive Donner. Screenplay by Frederic Raphael from Stanley Ellin's short story; camera, Nicholas Roeg; editor, Fergus McDonell; music, Ron Grainer; title song, lyrics by Raphael, music by Grainer. At Warner Theatre, London. Running time, **99 MINS.**

Jimmy Brewster	Alan Bates
Charlie Prince	Denholm Elliott
Mr. Horton	Harry Andrews
Ann Horton	Millicent Martin
Coates	Godfrey Quigley
Mrs. March	Pauline Delany
Nadine	Lucinda Curtis
Ferris	Nigel Stock
Hugh	James Villiers
Denis	Drewe Henley
Mrs. Horton	Avice Landon
Roberts	Ernest Clark
Gerry	William Rushton
Ex-Politician	Peter Madden
Clergyman	Angus Mackay
Jutson	Howard Lang
Mr. Brewster	Paul Curran
Mrs. Brewster	Alison Laggalt

Clive Donner has done a standout job as director of this stylish British comedy which takes a sly, penetrating peek at the social climbing upper classes that use the Old School tie, social connections, well padded bank balances and the Smart Set background to further their material ambitions. Some of the situations and dialog (it was screenplayed by Frederic Raphael from a satirical short story by Stan Ellins) may be a shade too pretentious and smart aleck to suit every taste. But "Nothing But The Best," with its impeccable acting, sharp exchanges and colorful London scene should attract prosperous patrons and advantageous word-of-mouth.

It is ruthless in its unpeeling of the dubious foibles and mannerisms of its characters, none of whom fails to have an axe to grind. It lightheartedly but shrewdly exposes the weaknesses of this bunch of opportunists. In its way, this is a fable of the times, the story of an ambitious young man of humble background who, excited by the glitter of money, business power and an entry into the fascinating world of Hunt Balls, Ascot, smart restaurants, shooting, hunting, fishin' and the rest of the trappings, lies, bluffs, smiles, cheats, loves, and smoothtalks his way to marrying the boss' daughter, and doesn't stop at murder en route.

"The Best," which is a blackish comedy of the type of "Kind Hearts and Coronets," lightheartedly but deftly pinpoints an empty world in which a bank balance and social facade is of all importance. The pic is something of a rich man's "Room At The Top," and goes for knowing smiles rather than belly laughs, though these are not ignored.

Alan Bates, showing a previously unexplored vein of comedy, is first-class as the dubious hero. This is a measured, confident performance that appeals even when he is behaving at his worst. Many of the top scenes are those with Denholm Elliott who, in fact, turns in the best acting of the lot. It is a loss to the film when Bates decides that he is becoming an encumbrance and must be bumped off. Elliott plays a shabby, unscrupulous young remittance-man, whose blueblooded past has been blotted by his attraction for forgery. The two scrape up an acquaintance in a shabby bar and Elliott becomes Bates's guide in the ways of the upper classes. He shows him how to crash the best society, dress, and hide his uneducated background in a sea of insignificant small talk. In fact, he shows him the complete ropes in exchange for a temporary lodging in the hero's bedsitter. Elliott's playing is flawless in its observation and underplaying.

Two femme performances also hit the target. Heroine is Millicent Martin, the girl who became internationally known as the songstress on the tele program, "That Was The Week That Was." Playing a straight role, her first big opportunity in pix, Miss Martin, with her red hair and pale skin, looks lovely. Though, at the moment, she fails to project much warmth or heart, she does well as a blase young debutante with a nice line in smart backchat. She is particularly good with cool comedy.

Pauline Delany also scores as a very sexy, young landlady with an eye for Bates and the main chance. Supporting roles are given full weight by such dependables as Harry Andrews, Godfrey Quigly, Alison Leggatt, Ernest Clark and Avice Landon, with Lucinda Curtis showing promise as a telephonist. James Villiers goes through his paces with his usual aplomb as a debonair young aristocrat.

The film has several punchy situations and an ironic twist which leaves the audience in doubt as to whether the young murderer will get his deserved comeuppance. Nicholas Roeg's photography of several scenes such as London river by night, a depressingly hearty Hunt Ball and a near-seamy suburb is nifty. Fergus McDonnell's astute cutting is a large aid to Donner's intelligent interpretation of the script. The murder routine has a hilarious aftermath but is perhaps an unnecessary and unbelievable intrusion in the hero's spry adventures in a glossy jungle.

Rich.

The Empty Canvas

Italian-made melodrama has marquee names but slim prospect.

Hollywood, March 3.

Embassy Pictures release of Joseph E. Levine-Carlo Ponti production. Stars Bette Davis, Horst Buchholz, Catherine Spaak. Directed by Damiano Damiani. Screenplay, Torino Guerra, Ugo Liberatore, Damiani, based on novel by Alberto Moravia; camera, Roberto Gerardi; editor, Renzo Lucidi; music, Luis Enriquez Bacalov. Reviewed at Lido Theatre, L.A., March 3, '64. Running time, **118 MINS.**

Dino's Mother	Bette Davis
Dino	Horst Buchholz
Cecilia	Catherine Spaak
The Princess	Daniela Rocca
Balestrieri's Wife	Lea Padovani
Cecilia's Mother	Isa Miranda
Balestrieri	Leonida Rapaci
Cecilia's Father	George Wilson
Tenant	Marcella Rovena
Emma	Daniela Calvino
Waiters	Renato Moretti, Edoardo Nevola
Cashier	Jole Mauro
Detective	Mario Lanfranchi

Perhaps there's a niche for this one in the epidermis circuit, that shadowy offshoot of the art house sphere where voyeurs and related oglers gather to contemplate maidens in the altogether. For "The Empty Canvas" is nothing more than a celluloidal peepshow pretending to be art. Despite Bette Davis and Horst Buchholz on the marquee, the Embassy release, a Joseph E. Levine package from Italy, is devoid of lure.

Hero of the yarn is a wealthy lad (Buchholz) who, just after having discovered he has no talent as a painter and is about to exchange the squalor of his artist's environment for the luxury of his mother's (Miss Davis) estate, meets and falls immediately in love with a shallow, self-centered prostitute (Catherine Spaak). And when Buchholz falls, he really falls. Soon he's proposing marriage and, evidently to impress his point, he covers the nude Miss Spaak head to toe under a blanket of banknotes on his mother's bed and showers the rest of a roll of moolah around the room. This cues two of the funniest lines — when Miss Davis bursts unexpectedly into her room and considers the scene, she merely advises her son to "please put the money you don't want to keep back in the safe." Just after Miss Davis leaves, Miss Spaak observes, "You know, you're mother is quite nice." The rest of the film describes, somewhat anticlimactically, the crackup and recovery of Buchholz.

For gifted thespians the likes of Buchholz and Miss Davis, the Carlo Ponti production is a sorry vehicle. Miss Spaak, however, is another matter. She's the best towel-filler since BB, and has the looks to be a big star. She even looks good as a money sandwich. The film has been directed at a haphazard, staccato tempo by Damiano Damiani.

Tube.

Le Journal D'Une Femme De Chambre
(Diary of a Chambermaid)
(FRENCH-FRANSCOPE)

Paris, March 6.

Cocinor release of Speva-Filmsonor-Dear Film production. Stars Jeanne Moreau; features Georges Geret, Michel Piccoli, Francoise Lugagne, Jean Ozenne, Daniel Ivernel, Gilberte Geniat, Dominique Sauvare. Directed by Luis Bunuel. Screenplay, Bunuel, Jean-Claude Carriere from book by Octave Mirbeau; camera, Roger Fellous; editor, Louisette Hautecoeur. At Colisee, Paris. Running time, **100 MINS.**

Celestine	Jeanne Moreau
Joseph	Georges Geret
Husband	Michel Piccol
Wife	Francoise Lugagne
Father	Jean Ozenne
Claire	Dominique Sauvage

The noted Mexican director of Hispano origin, Luis Bunuel, who started his career here in 1930 with the famed surrealistic pic, "The Age of Gold," returned to make another pic here. A look at rustic insularity in the 1920s, it lays bare human pettiness but does it with a flair and objectivity. This makes the film funny, revealing and, overall, quite engrossing.

A bouncy, zesty ripe 32-year-old maid, Jeanne Moreau, is on her way to a job with a landed family in the country. And a rugged lot they are. There is the father who is a foot fetishist, his sickly daughter who dreads marital duties with her rakish, skirtchasing husband, an ominous racist handyman and an eccentric old military man next door who insists on throwing rubbish on their land because of an old feud.

The maid is soon chased by the husband and also is asked to try on old-fashioned high-button boots by the father. The latter is found dead one morning, with the boots clutched in his hands. Follows the rape of an eight-year-old girl. Sure it is the fascistic handyman, the maid frames him even if drawn to him sexually. But he gets off because of lack of evidence to become a pillar in the French fascist movement while she marries the rich, zany military man.

Bunuel has embroidered all this richly with revealing characterization, a fee for the period and a refusal to become moralistic or to take sides. He seems to point up that everybody, and everything, is not the best of all possible worlds. There are no heroes or heroines, and the only innocent is the child. Via this treatment the characters become clear while human comportment reveals its weaknesses and foibles via suggestion.

The old man would rather miss while trying to shoot animals, whom he prefers alive. The bigot professes a love for country and religion and wants to get along with his masters and yet can be a racist of the worst sort. The chambermaid is sly, shrewd and also not above using these fading rich folks to get ahead even if she is somewhat scathingly derogatory towards them.

Miss Moreau has the acid self protection and mixture of engaging forthrightness to make her role brim with a bright force that probes the antics and outlooks of the other characters. If they are all abject, there is no moralizing which makes this an adult, multifaceted production.

Georges Geret has menace and weight as the violent fascist. Michel Piccoli is rightly contemptible as the marauding husband while Jean Ozenne's old, perverse landowner is a gem of taste and tact in delineation. Francoise Lugagne has the correct vapidity as the frigid, sickly wife. Dominique Sauvage is an emerging fresh moppet thesp.

Lensing has the sharp gradations to give a photographic feel of the times. Director Bunuel again shows he is one of the more personable film creators at work today. But, the pic calls for careful handling and looms mainly an arty bet abroad. 20th-Fox has it for all markets except France, Belgium and Switzerland. Its robust storytelling also tags this for playoff possibilities, too.

Mosk.

La Tulipe Noire
(The Black Tulip)
(FRENCH-COLOR)

Paris, March 10.

Dicifrance release of Mediterranee-Mizar-Agatha Films productions. Stars Alain Delon; features Virna Lisi, Dawn Addams, Akim Tamiroff, Francis Blanche. Directed by Christian-Jaque. Screenplay, Henri Jeanson, Paul Andreota, Christian-Jaque from book by Alexandre Dumas; camera (Eastmancolor), Henri Decae; editor, Jacques Desagneaux. At Ambassade-Gaumont, Paris. Running time, **115 MINS.**

Julien	Alain Delon
Guillaume	Alain Delon
Caroline	Virna Lisi
Marquis	Akim Tamiroff
Marquise	Dawn Addams
Father	Francis Blanche

Producer Georges Cheyko has a costume swashbuckler. Nice production dress, the Alain Delon name and generally good action stuff, with a touch of the French Revolutionary period recreation, if satirical, make this loom a neat local item. It also appears a playoff possibility abroad with a little tightening up of some court intrigue.

Delon plays two brothers, one a bandit who is also a nobleman and his twin who has been away. Though he robs from the rich he does not give to the poor; he's really in it for himself. But the people, on the verge of revolution, think he is their leader and savior.

Marked on the face he calls in his look-alike brother to take his place. Latter turns out to be a real revolutionary and becomes a truly heroic Black Tulip, the name for the bandit. Film has its share of swordplay, decadent noble court intrigues, fights and horseplay, plus a leavening of romance, to make it par for this type of historical production.

Delon has dash in his dual role and he is well supported by Virna Lisi, as the peasant sweetheart, Dawn Addams, as a haughty noblewoman; and Akim Tamiroff, as a Marquis. Director Christian-Jaque has mounted this well but lacked the zest and dynamics to keep it moving all the time. But it has enough drive in the last half to bring it off.

Color is fine and production dress rich. Its best bet is for the action markets and for playoff on its fairly literate if familiar scripting.

Mosk.

The Son Of Captain Blood
(COLOR)

Sean Flynn, son of Errol, following in his father's swashbuckling footsteps. Hackneyed vehicle.

Paramount release of Harry Joe Brown production. Stars Sean Flynn; features Alessandra Panaro, Jose Nieto, Ann Todd. Directed by Tulio Demicheli. Screenplay, Casey Robinson, adapted from characters created by Rafael Sabatini; camera (Technicolor), Alejandro Ulloa; music, Gregoria Garcia Segura; assistant director, Yakima Cannut. Reviewed at the studio, March 11, '64. Running time, **88 MINS.**

Robert Blood	Sean Flynn
Abbigail	Alessandro Panaro
De Malagon	Jose Nieto
Arabella	Ann Todd

Nearly 30 years have passed since Errol Flynn sailed across the screen as "Captain Blood." Now, following in the "Blood" line of his late sire, young Sean Flynn fittingly limns the title role in this sequel. This unusual second generation duplication of actor and character provides the otherwise outmoded Paramount release with a promising exploitation of word-of-mouth gimmick.

The only really noteworthy aspect of the filmed-in-Spain Harry Joe Brown production is the emergence of young Flynn in the same swashbuckling image as that projected by his famous father, much as Doug Fairbanks Jr. once carried on in the tradition of Fairbanks Sr. The resemblance is striking. Flynn fils, when he learns to act, could become a popular screen personality in romantic adventurer roles. He's handsome, dashing and appears to have inherited his father's athletic prowess, judging by his agile swordplay and generally graceful moves. As a thespian, however, there's an enormous amount of room for improvement. Less artificial dialog than he has been afforded as "Robert Blood" might help in this regard, of course. When he bellows, "you swine," it just doesn't have that Errol Flynn ring to it, and that's because it's counterfeit —an imitation, an echo.

As for the picture, it's little more than a pack of sea adventure cliches. Written by Casey Robinson, the yarn describes young Blood's adventures at sea with the same gang of corsairs who served his pop, as lovable a band of buccaneers as ever yo-ho-ho'd across the Caribbean.

Alessandra Panaro is a pretty adornment as Flynn's romantic interest, and Ann Todd is durably attractive and about the best performer around as the lad's courageous mother—the same Arabella played by Olivia de Havilland back in 1935.

The production, directed by Tulio Demicheli, is fairly rich in physical values. Skillfl contributions have been made by cameraman Alejandro Ulloa and composer Gregoria Garcia Segura, among others.

Tube.

Comment Trouvez-Vous Ma Soeur?
(How Do You Like My Sister?)
(FRENCH)
Paris, March 17.

UGC-Sirius release of Mannic production. With France Anglade, Jacqueline Maillan, Michel Serrault, Claude Rich, Dany Robin, Jacques Charon. Directed by Michel Boisrond. Screenplay, Annette Wademant; camera, Jean-Louis Picavet; editor, Julien Coutellier. At Balzac, Paris. Running time, **80 MINS.**

Cecile	France Anglade
Mother	Jacqueline Maillan
Father	Michel Serrault
Francois	Claude Rich
Leopold	Jacques Charon
Martine	Dany Robin
Daniel	Daniel Haudepin

Director Michel Boisrond now has two pix in firstruns here and this looks likely to win same dating. He shows himself one of the abler commercial directors for this type of film. This vehicle lacks the comic drive or inventiveness for much export chances but should be an okay playoff item on its home grounds.

A pretty girl falls in love with her kid brother's teacher, and this details how she finally gets him. There are plenty of complications and some bright cameo bits via Jacqueline Maillan, as the bird-brained m o t h e r, and Jacques Charon, as a would-be Lothario who is used to get the teacher jealous.

Boisrond gives this familiar affair a nice pacing if the plotting, characterization a n d situations lack the fillip to make the comedy more lively and the effect more risible. As is, it might also serve for programmer fare in other Continental spots if it lacks the weight for much of a chance in the U.S. It is technically sharp.
Mosk.

The Fall of the Roman Empire
(TECHNICOLOR, ULTRA-PANAVISION)

Mighty theme, mighty pictorial sweep. A highpowered spectacle from Samuel Bronston.

Paramount release of Samuel Bronston production (associate producers, Michael Waszynksi and Jaimes Prades). Stars Sophia Loren, Alec Guinness, Stephen Boyd, Christopher Plummer, James Mason; features John Ireland, Mel Ferrer, Omar Sharif, Anthony Quayle. Directed by Anthony Mann. Original screenplay, Ben Barzman, Basilio Franchina, Philip Yordan; camera (Technicolor), Robert Krasker; set and production design, Veniero Colasanti-John Moore; score, Dimitri Tiomkin; second unit director, Yakima Canutt; editor, Robert Lawrence; consultant, Will Durant. Previewed March 12, 1964 at DeMille Theatre, N.Y. Running time, **185 MINS.**

Marcus Aurelius	Alec Guinness
Lucilla	Sophia Loren
Livius	Stephen Boyd
Timonides	James Mason
Commodus	Christofer Plummer
Verulus	Anthony Quayle
Ballomar	John Ireland
Cleander	Mel Ferrer
King of Armenians	Omar Sharif
Julianus	Eric Porter
Niger	Douglas Wilmer
Claudius	Peter Damon
Polybius	Andrew Keir
Victorius	George Murcell
Helva	Lena Von Martens
Tauna	Gabriella Licudi
Lentulus	Rafael Luis Calvo
Virgilianus	Norman Wooland
Marcellus	Virgil Texera
Cornelius	Michael Gwynn
Marius	Guy Rolfe
Caecina	Finlay Currie

This made-in-Spain Samuel Bronston production is a giant-size, three-hour, sweepingly pictorial entertainment carrying (1) a natural boxoffice title (2) an appeal to universal interest, and (3) a strong cast. It probably tells all that most film fans will want to know about the glory, grandeur and greed of Rome. Others may be inspired to read Gibbon, Lecky, Spengler, Edith Hamilton or the production's own consultant, Will Durant. Suffice that this is a film with incessant action, cleverly directed by Anthony Mann and handsomely photographed in Technicolor and Ultra-Panavision by Robert Krasker. It looms as a moneymaker for Bronston and Paramount.

Economic calculations naturally relate to the actual negative cost, the break-even figure, whether roadshowing, generally the most expensive form of going to market, slows or builds the harvest. But overall, and around the globe, the prognosis on "The Fall of The Roman Empire" spells out big.

The production reeks of expense —harness and hay for all those horses, arroz con pollo for all those Spanish extras, annuities for all those stars. Attention will focus upon the marblesque replica of downtown Rome in pagan days with temples, squares, forums, statuary, mosaic floors, columned chambers, luxury suites and a plunge for Caesar. If these Veniero Colasanti-John Moore sets cost a fortune they pay off in stunning camera angles and give the show special word-of-mouth.

Director Mann and many of his colleagues on "El Cid" traderated until now as Bronston's best grosser, repeated on "Fall." There are some points of technical resemblance but the two features are quite different. This one is bigger and, candidly, better. The humanities are especially well served in the first half, dominated by Alec Guinness as the dying emperor, Marcus Aurelius.

As with "El Cid," the associate producers under Bronston are again Michael Waszynski from Poland and Jaimes Prades from Spain. Robert Lawrence is also repeating as film editor, and a mighty task it must have been to bring this immense panorama together. Finally there is the old horse-fall expert, Yakima Canutt, on encore. The cavalry and chariot elements are wonderfully well handled throughout. There is a madcap mountain road drag race between two chariots driven by Stephen Boyd and Christopher Plummer, and/or stand-ins. They career on precipice's edge, knock over fences, saplings and assorted obstacles. It makes an exciting sequence.

The monumental challenge of telescoping one of history's great erosions of power into a few short years of time and with focus upon a few central characters has been accomplished with much professional competence by authors Ben Barzman, Basilio Franchina and Philip Yordan. The off-screen narration fore and aft helps maintain perspective and avoidance of the over-simplification of inter-personal relationships. The astute use of wall maps, the motif backgrounds for the credits and Dimitri Tiomkin's doom-hinting score are all distinct aids worthy of remark.

The story gets underway speedily. Marcus Aurelius has been campaigning for years in the bleak northern frontiers of Rome. He is dying and knows it, intends to disinherit his undependable son and neglects to do so. Stephen Boyd, a true-blue Tribune, will not claim the succession but instead supports the son, his old wrestling club chum. The entire subsequent plot swings on the failure of intention of the noble and just emperor to assure the continued peace and prosperity of Rome. In all of which the daughter, played attractively by Sophia Loren, the film's top name, is a desperately unhappy witness and victim.

There is much dialog about the factors which favor, and which oppose, good relations among peoples. The arrogance and cynicism in the Senate is part and parcel of the decline, as much as the vain and cruel Commodus, a man quick with the torch to homes, merciless in the ordering of wholesale crucifixions. An anti-intellectual as well as a sadist, this personage is played with smiling malice by Christopher Plummer. He, Guinness and James Mason as a cultivated and honorable Roman minister to Marcus Aurelius pretty much wrap up the acting honors for another empire, Great Britain. Anthony Quayle is also an arresting figure as an aging gladiator who is slain on the spot when ill-advised enough, late in the picture, to reveal that he, not Marcus Aurelius, was the true sire of Commodus.

Omar Sharif, a star in Egypt, a bit player here, probably because his English remains imperfect, has barely enough footage to attract notice. Mel Ferrer has a curious cameo, that of a blind politician who cold-bloodedly poisons Aurelius, perhaps a sufficient symbol of the prevailing viciousness which plots for and is attracted to power. The very end of the film has Commodus (Plummer) dead at last but Boyd refusing the throne. Whereupon all the wheelers and dealers of the day start a veritable auction to knock down the allegiance of the Roman legions to the highest bidder. The off-screen narrator points the obvious moral—venal troops in a corrupt society implies susceptibility to invasion by barbarians.

There are some artfully cast types as commanders, governors and senators of antiquity, among them Eric Porter, Finlay Currie, George Murcell, Douglas Wilmer, Peter Damond. Miss Loren is the only woman role rating closeup. John Ireland has little to do as the conquered chief of the northern tribes.

On several previous occasions Stephen Boyd has acted in the armor of Rome. He is pictorially ideal. Add that in the present instance he may have given his best performance in pagan uniform, thanks to Mann's direction.

Some tedium tends to develop toward the end of the film, a sense of climax on climax on climax until a too-muchness threatens. Partly this is a result of going from the personal closeups of the forepart to the mob scenes necessary to tie the tale up. However, the pace is always firm and the film is steadily cinematic in the sense of "motion" in the pictures. The action takes place about 150 years after Christ but before Christianity has infiltrated the Roman Empire. The theme rests, therefore, wholly on historic and not religious interest in appealing to scholastic tieups, which, at a guess, ought to be a valuable factor in the ticket-selling tactics. The film is already contracted for 38 roadshows engagements in the U.S.-Canada market between now and June.

This is a crowded film. There are a wealth of pictorial details and characterization touches which recur in memory. The iron discipline of the Roman army, the brutalities of pagan punishments, the milling hell of shoulder-to-shoulder battle, the superficial civilization which cracks under stress, all come through. Mann saves until toward the finish the great duel between the good guy and the bad guy, a scene comparable to the broadsword exercise involving Charlton Heston in "El Cid." It has been staged for suspense and menace values and rates high as derring-do.

Large in theme and concept, colorful in treatment, "The Fall of The Roman Empire" is Sam Bronston's greatest coup de cinema. It has large earning potential.
Land.

Law of the Lawless
(TECHNISCOPE-COLOR)

Wordy western with a salable cast of familiar vets and youngsters. Fair programmer.

Hollywood, March 13.

Paramount release of A. C. Lyles production. Stars Dale Robertson, Yvonne

De Carlo. Directed by William F. Claxton. Screenplay, Steve Fisher; camera (Technicolor), Lester Shorr; editor, Otho Lovering; asst. director, Harry Hogan. Reviewed at the studio, March 13, '64. Running time, **87 MINS.**

Judge Clem Rogers	Dale Robertson
Ellie Irish	Yvonne De Carlo
Sheriff Ed Tanner	William Bendix
Joe Rile	I r ce Cabot
Big Tom Stone	Barton MacLane
Pete Stone	John Agar
Bartender	Richard Arlen
George Stapleton	Jody McCrea
R nd McDonald	Kent Taylor
Silas Miller	Bill Williams
Deputy Tim Ludlow	Rod Lauren
Hotel Clerk	George Chandler
Tiny	Lon Chaney
Tuffy	Donald Barry
Johnson Brothers	Roy Jenson, Jerry Summers, Reg Parton
Drifter	Alex Sharp

A fundamental advantage enjoyed by the western over most other film forms is the intrinsic opportunity it affords to tell a simple story with a maximum of action and visual, outdoor values. And yet the trend in recent years seems to be away from these very aspects that built the great appeal of the sagebrush idiom. "Law Of The Lawless" suffers from this recently-developed affliction of pretension and stuffiness. It is a verbose, inner-directed western, one that by and large settles for words where action, though costlier, might be a more profitable dramatic method. The modestly-designed A.C. Lyles production for Paramount is fortified with a cast loaded with seasoned veterans, most of them reassuringly familiar faces to the oater buff. As such, it should rack up some boxoffice mileage in the program western category in spite of its flaws.

The original screenplay, written by Steve Fisher, is concerned with the frontier struggle in the 1880's between forces of law and order and advocates of the expiring anarchy of the gun. It boils down to the firm stand of a judge (Dale Robertson) who prevails over all manner of threat, challenge and attempt to influence during the trial of a gunman over which he has been summoned to preside. The story is riddled with motivational holes and mysteries, and the execution under director William F. Claxton is rather lethargic, but there are scattered moments of impact and one sequence of explosive combat to perk up the customer.

Few actors fit so snugly into the western mold as Robertson. Yvonne De Carlo is decorative in a dubiously-conceived role. Other seasoned players who do about as well as possible under the circumstances include William Bendix, Bruce Cabot, Barton MacLane, John Agar, Richard Arlen, Kent Taylor, Bill Williams, George Chandler, Lon Chaney and Donald Barry. Younger members of the cast include Rod Lauren and Jody McCrea.

Capable production efforts are contributed to the cause by cameraman Lester Shorr, editor Otho Lovering and art directors Hal Pereira and Al Roelofs. *Tube.*

Volles Herz Und Leere Taschen

(A Full Heart and Empty Pockets)
(GERMAN-ITALIAN)

Berlin, March 17.

Columbia-Bavaria release of Loewant (Franz Antel) production made in collaboration with Geos Film, Rome. Stars Thomas Fritsch, Alexandra Stewart; Gino Cervi. Directed by Camillo Mastrocinque. Screenplay, Franz Antel, Kurt Nachmann, Eduard Anton; camera, Ricardo Pallottini; settings, Hertha Hareiter; editor, Adolph Schlyssleder. At Marmorhaus, West Berlin. Running time, **98 MINS.**

Rik	Thomas Fritsch
Laura	Alexandra Stewart
Botta	Gino Cervi
Jane	Senta Berger
Minelli	Linda Christian
Elga	Dominique Boschero
Borgia	Francoise Rosay
Sabine	Helga Lehner
Editor-in-chief	Massimo Serato
Luigi	Manfred Spichs

There is an abundance of about everything in this German-Italian coproduction which had its world preem in Berlin—sex, honest love, dolce vita, comedy, corruption, blackmailing, politics. But it's all very much on the naive side. There are pix which border on the ridiculous. This is the case with "Empty Pockets." Film stars young Thomas Fritsch, a new idol with the German teenage set, whose name may guarantee some good results in this country. But is is doubtful whether such a banal pic will contribute to his prestige.

The plot itself is not so bad and could have furnished the basis for an interesting film had the writers done a competent job. The script is confusing and lacks polishing all through. And sex, in such quantities, requires delicacy which the films lacks, too. They simply went overboard on everything.

Curly-haired Fritsch, a boyish German dreamer, strolls about Rome's Via Veneto. He is as poor as a church mouse. But not long. A weighing machine suddenly spells countless coins. The money enables the lucky fellow to enter a restaurant. He is the 10,000th customer and gets 10,000 Lira for that reason. He wins also, all by pure luck, an auto. He gets the position of a managing director. And he jumps from bed to bed. Meets the most exciting girls. After a while even the most naive viewer must get the impression that so much sex in bed would be physically too much for such a small boy with such thin arms.

In the end, Fritsch is as poor as at the start. But he has the satisfaction of having found a decent newspaper gal whom they chase off the staff because she wrote an article against a corrupt industrialist.

The cast is international. In addition to German Fritsch, there are Canadian-born Alexandra Stewart, Italians Gino Cervi and Massimo Serato; Austrian Senta Berger, Rome-based, former Hollywoodite Linda Christian, French Francoise Rosay and others. There are some scenes which reveal director Mastrocinque's light hand and some beautiful shots of Rome's streets, but that's not enough to make a worthwhile film. *Hans.*

The Devil-Ship Pirates

(BRITISH-MEGASCOPE—COLOR)

Impressively mounted adventure meller for action-exploitation mart.

Hollywood, March 17.

Columbia Pictures release of Anthony Nelson Keys production. Stars Christopher Lee, Andrew Keir, John Cairney, Duncan Lamont. Directed by Don Sharp. Screenplay, Jimmy Sangster; camera (Eastman), Michael Reed; editor, James Needs; music, Gary Hughes; assistant director, Bert Batt. Reviewed at the studio, March 17, '64. Running time, **84 MINS.**

Captain Robeles	Christopher Lee
Tom	Andrew Keir
Harry	John Cairney
The Bosun	Duncan Lamont
Pepe	Michael Ripper
Sir Basil	Ernest Clark
Manuel	Barry Warren
Angela	Suzan Farmer
Jane	Natasha Pyne
Meg	Annette Whiteley
Antonio	Charles Houston
Miller	Philip Latham
Bragg	Harry Locke
Quintana	Leonard Fenton
Mandrake	Jack Rodney
Gustavo	Barry Linehan
Pedro	Bruce Beeby
Grande	Michael Peake
Pablo	Johnny Briggs
Smiler	Michael Newport
The Vicar	Peter Howell
Mrs. Blake	June Ellis

The production skills of Britain's Hammer Film artisans convert this otherwise routine adventure melodrama into a slightly better than average entry of its genre. The solidity of these physical values, coupled with a dramatic concept that stresses action elements, should override to some extent certain story deficiencies and the obscurity of the players to Yank audiences and make the Columbia release a serviceable partner in an exploitation dualer for the male-oriented adventure market. The kids will like it, too.

The Anthony Nelson Keys production, resourcefully written by Jimmy Sangster and directed with an action flourish by Don Sharp, tells the tale of a remote English village taken over in 1588 by a band of buccaneer cutthroats who, after briefly serving the ill-fated cause of the Spanish Armada against the British fleet, have dropped anchor on the English coast to repair damage to their vessel, then opportunistically seized control of the town on the pretense of having won a naval victory. Film describes the method by which the townspeople, despite treachery in the ranks, manage to outwit their captors.

Production designer Bernard Robinson merits credit for the richness of the sets, and Michael Reed's Eastman Color photography appreciatively captures the beauty of the period backgrounds and costumes. There is skill, too, in the efforts of such craftsmen as editor James Needs, soundman Ken Rawkins and composer Gary Hughes. *Tube.*

Muscle Beach Party

(PANAVISION—COLOR)

Sequel to "Beach Party" iffy prospect, but could take off.

American International Pictures release of James H. Nicholson-Robert Dillon production. Stars Frankie Avalon, Annette Funicello, Luciana Paluzzi, John Ashley; features Don Rickles, Jody McCrea, Dick Dale and the Del Tones, Candy Johnson, Morey Amsterdam, Buddy Hackett; introduces Little Stevie Wonder. Directed by William Asher. Screenplay, Robert Dillon, from story by Dillon, Asher; camera (Pathecolor), Harold Wellman; editor, Eve Newman; music, Les Baxter; asst. director, Clark Paylow. Reviewed at Directors Guild of America, March 20, '64. Running time, **94 MINS.**

Frankie	Frankie Avalon
Dee Dee	Annette Funicello
Julie	Luciana Paluzzi
Johnny	John Ashley
Jack Fanny	Don Rickles
Theodore	Peter Turgeon
Deadhead	Jody McCrea
Dick	Dick Dale
Candy	Candy Johnson
Cappy	Morey Amsterdam
S. Z. Matta	Buddy Hackett
Flex Martian	Rock Stevens
Sniffles	Deloses Wells
Donna	Donna Loren
Animal	Valora Noland
Lisa	Alberta Nelson
Floe	Amedee Chabot
Biff	Larry Scott
Rock	Bob Seven
Tug	Steve Merjanian
Riff	Dan Haggerty
Sulk	Chester Yorton
Mush	Gene Shuey
Clod	Gordon Cohn

This is American International's followup to "Beach Party," its click of a year ago.

Perhaps the momentum generated by the forerunner, accompanied by more of the same vigorous salesmanship, can pave the way for another moneymaker. But there are reasons to suspect that the sequel may fall short of its flashy predecessor in the boxoffice department.

For one thing, the novelty of surfing has worn off, leaving in its wake little more than a conventional teenage-geared romantic farce with songs. For another, sequels rarely match the drawing power of an original, especially when the cycle is linked to a passing fad. For "Muscle Beach Party" to make the grade, it will take all the allure of its glossy, sexy, razzle-dazzle production image, the relentlessly swinging beat of its music, and the appeal of its youthful stars to the fan mag set.

The James H. Nicholson-Robert Dillon production was scripted by Dillon from a yarn he concocted with the director of the enterprise, William Asher. The clash of three factions at a beach site sets off the romantic, comedic and musical fireworks. At one end is a group of youthful surfers. At another is a band of Atlasian musclemen. Catalyst is a wealthy, fickle contessa. Whenever the story bogs down, which it does quite often, someone runs into camera range and yells, "surf's up!" This is followed by a series of cuts of surfers in action. It's all very mechanical.

Best novelty aspect of the film, and one that should be exploited, is the gallery of extraordinary musclemen—as spectacularly repulsive an array of beefcake as probably has ever crossed the screen. There's plenty of cheesecake, too. In fact, skin keeps crowding in front of the camera, relegating the story action to the background in some cases. You can safely term "Muscle Beach Party" a torso opera. And the torsos are generally wiggling—in whole or in part. There's enough anatomical energy expended in this picture to propel a man to the moon.

Frankie Avalon and Annette Funicello top the cast and do most of the singing. There are eight tunes, six by the team of Roger Christian, Gary Usher and Brian Wilson, two by Guy Hemric and Jerry Styner. The songs aren't very good, but the two by the latter team sound the most commercial. Key roles are essayed by pretty Luciana Paluzzi as the contessa, Don Rickles as a junior grade Vic Tanny, and Buddy Hackett as the contessa's business manager. Others of prominence are John Ashley, Peter Turgeon, Jody McCrea, Dick Dale and the Del Tones, Morey Amsterdam, and a prodigious hunk of man named Rock Stevens. None of the acting is particularly noteworthy. Candy Johnson, a gyrating sexpot, contributes some high-voltage bumps and grinds. The film introduces Little Stevie Wonder, a lad who can really wail. Peter Lorre puts in an unbilled appearance.

The physique of the production is in pretty good shape, thanks to the efforts of such craftsmen as photographer Harold Wellman,

editor Eve Newman and art director Lucius Croxton. Les Baxter's score is serviceably frenetic. The main titles by Butler-Glouner Inc. set the stage with flair and humor.
Tube.

What A Way To Go
(CINEMASCOPE-COLOR)

Big, gaudy comedy. Telegraphs too many of its yoks and lacks consistent style, but has a powerhouse cast and enough laughs to indicate good boxoffice response.

20th-Fox release of Arthur P. Jacobs production. Stars Shirley MacLaine, Paul Newman, Robert Mitchum, Dean Martin, Gene Kelly, Bob Cummings, Dick Van Dyke. Directed by J. Lee Thompson. Screenplay. Betty Comden, Adolph Green, based on story by Gwen Davis; camera (De Luxe color), Leon Shamroy; music, Nelson Riddle; special songs, Julie Styne; editor, Marjorie Fowler; assistant director, Fred R. Simpson. Reviewed at Criterion Theatre, N. Y., March 23, '64. Running time, 111 MINS.
Louisa .... Shirley MacLaine
Larry Flint .... Paul Newman
Rod Anderson .... Robert Mitchum
Leonard Crawley .... Dean Martin
Jerry Benson .... Gene Kelly
Dr. Steffanson .... Bob Cummings
Edgar Hopper .... Dick Van Dyke
Painter .... Reginald Gardiner
Mrs. Foster .... Margaret Dumont
Trentino .... Lou Nova
Baroness .... Fifi D'Orsay
Rene .... Maurice Marsac
Agent .... Wally Vernon
Polly .... Jane Wald
Hollywood Lawyer .... Larry Kent

"What A Way To Go" is a big, gaudy, gimmicky comedy which continually promises more than it delivers by way of wit and/or belly-laffs. Still, with the many yoks and unsubtle clowning it does have, and with a cast headed by Shirley MacLaine and four of Hollywood's top male stars, it looks to establish a fine grossing record at the b.o. The disappointment is that—had it been played and directed with more original wit and sense of cinema style—it might have been a swinging classic.

The screenplay by Betty Comden and Adolph Green, based on a story by Gwen Davis, is, at its very promising basis, the sad, sad story of a little poor girl from Ohio who, though she wants only true love, is married and widowed in succession by four diverse types who eventually make her the richest woman in the world. It's a sort of ironic True Story, related in flashbacks from a psychiatrist's couch after the troubled, multi-widowed heroine has tried unsuccessfully to sign all her dough over to the Internal Revenue Service.

Essentially, the film is a series of blackout sketches, enlivened from time to time as Miss MacLaine tells of her marriages in styles of various types of films. Thus, in recalling her life with a Thoreau-reading idealist, Dick Van Dyke, she sees it in the jerky, exaggerated terms of a silent movie romance; her life with a beatnik, abstract-impressionist painter, Paul Newman, in Paris, is viewed as sexy French film (including a series of takeoffs on the bathtub scene from "The Lovers"), complete with English subtitles; and her life with tycoon Robert Mitchum is remembered as one of those overdressed Ross Hunter productions.

Some of these parodies are very funny but, with the exception of the silent film and "The Lovers" sequences, there often isn't much difference between the style of the parody and that of the encasing flashback. For all the laughs based on Miss MacLaine's too many costume changes in the Ross Hunter parody, it seemed (to at least one, not especially clothes conscious reviewer) that the star was just as overburdened with not particularly becoming clothes in most of the rest of the film. There is also

the added problem that director J. Lee Thompson too often allows his punch lines to be telegraphed, and there's no surer way to kill a blackout.

Yet, there is much that hits the correctly wild and wacky tone that Comden and Green intended. Many individual lines stick in the memory. There's the blunt advice of that fine old vet of so many Marx films, Margaret Dumont, to daughter Shirley MacLaine, who prefers to marry a poor-but-honest type instead of the rich boy: "You have something to sell. Take a mother's advice—sell it now!" Or Dean Martin's genial comment about the squalor in which Miss MacLaine and first husband Van Dyke live: "Why shouldn't you be happy? You have a good roof under your feet and (looking into a soup pot) you certainly have all the grass you can eat!"

The Parisian episode with Paul Newman also has a dizzy kind of eccentricity which is fun. Though abstract impressionism may well have had it, both as an art form and a source of humor, there still are a lot of laughs to be had from a painting chimpanzee named Frieda and a machine which paints in response to sonic impulses. Perhaps the most consistently amusing flashback is the final one featuring Gene Kelly. When the richer-and-richer heroine marries him, he is a happy-go-lucky roadhouse entertainer who suddenly hits it big in Hollywood and quickly gets a head to match. One of his final triumphs is producing, directing and starring in a comedy 5-1/2 hours long ("They said it couldn't be done! My next picture will run 8 hours!) before he is literally loved to death by his fans.

Kelly, in fact, gives the most consistently stylish performance in the film, closely followed by Newman. Mitchum, Bob Cummings (as the psychiatrist) and Martin (as the guy who finally wins her) do what they have always been doing quite naturally. Being on so much of the time, Miss MacLaine obviously has the toughest assignment, and while she is always appealing, there are indications that she needs the supervision of a director with a dominating talent for comedy.

Picture has been gaudily, expensively mounted in CinemaScope and brilliant DeLuxe color. Producer Arthur L. Jacobs, whose debut production this is, certainly didn't stint. A couple of songs by Julie Styne, including an hilarious production number (choreographed by Kelly) which might have come out of "Follow The Fleet", may well serve to hypo promotion on the film. All other technical credits are okay.   *Anby.*

Tamahine
(C'SCOPE—COLOR)

Romanticomedy with Nancy Kwan. An uninspired effort.

Hollywood, March 25.
Metro (in association with Seven Arts) release of John Bryan production. Stars Nancy Kwan, John Fraser, Dennis Price. Directed by Philip Leacock. Screenplay, Denis Cannan, based on novel by Thelma Nicklaus; camera (Eastman), Geoffrey Unsworth; editor, Peter Tanner; music, Malcolm Arnold. Reviewed at the studio, March 25, '64. Running time, 85 MINS.
Tamahine .... Nancy Kwan
Richard .... John Fraser
Poole .... Dennis Price
Madame Becque .... Coral Browne
Storekeeper .... Dick Bentley

Clove .... Derek Nimmo
Diana .... Justine Lord
Cartwright .... Michael Gough
Oliver .... James Fox
Housemaster .... Allan Cuthbertson
Mrs. MacFarlane .... Noel Hood
Bash .... Derek Fowlds
Fiend .... Robin Stewart
Mrs. Spruce .... Viola Keats
Major Spruce Howard Marion Crawford
Mrs. Cartwright .... Lally Bowers
Mr. O'Shaughnessy .... Max Kirby
Mrs. O'Shaughnessy ..... Joan Benham
Lord Birchester .... William Mervyn
Manservant .... Ian Fleming
Nun .... Barbara Cavan
Nun .... Bee Duffell

"Tamahine" is the British equivalent of a "Tammy" picture. It stars Nancy Kwan, a kind of Eurasian Sandra Dee, as the title character, a kind of cross between "Tammy" and "Tondelayo" who comes across the sea to a staid English boys' school and, before you can spell Gauguin, just upsets the institution with her naughty but nice Tahitian ways. The future looks rather bleak for this contrived, stale and predictable effort, a product of Associated British Picture Corp. and joint presentation of Metro and Seven Arts.

The John Bryan production, filmed in England and on location in Paris and Bora-Bora (a South Seas isle), was written by Denis Cannan from the novel by Thelma Nicklaus. In describing the impact of this Polynesian girl on the flabbergasted scholastic community, the script focuses on her more intimate relationship with an uncle (Dennis Price), a lonely widower-headmaster, and a cousin-once-removed (John Fraser), a spirited student. Utilizing her instinctive insight and athletic prowess (she out-hurdles, out-shimmies, out-foots and out-swims every male on campus—she's a regular superwoman), "Tamahine" sets everything in order at the school.

As actress, Miss Kwan leaves a lot to be desired, but she's a decorative heroine. Any dramatic contrivance seems to suffice in order to get her soaking wet or down to her panties. Fraser, an up-and-coming young British actor, works at maximum percentage of efficiency, as does that old pro, Dennis Price. Derek Nimmo and Justine Lord are effective in a romantic sub-plot.

Geoffrey Unsworth's photography capitalizes on scenic values. Peter Tanner's editing seems sluggish in spots. Polynesian airs and conventional screen melodies of the western world alternate in Malcolm Arnold's rather uninspired score. Philip Leacock's direction injects occasional moments of amusement, but the prevailing tone is forced and artificial.
Tube.

The Best Man

Skillful conversion to screen of Gore Vidal's play. Election year accent on national politics should boost b.o. chances.

Hollywood, March 18.
United Artists release of Stuart Millar-Lawrence Turman production. Stars Henry Fonda, Cliff Robertson, Edie Adams, Margaret Leighton, Shelly Berman, Lee Tracy, Ann Sothern; features Gene Raymond, Kevin McCarthy. Directed by Franklin Schaffner. Screenplay, Gore Vidal, from his play; camera, Haskell Wexler; editor, Robert E. Swink; music, Mort Lindsey; assistant director, Richard Moder. Reviewed at Directors

Guild of America, March 18, '64. Running time, 102 MINS.
William Russell .... Henry Fonda
Joe Cantwell .... Cliff Robertson
Mabel Cantwell .... Edie Adams
Alice Russell ...... Margaret Leighton
Sheldon Bascomb ...... Shelley Berman
Art Hockstader .... Lee Tracy
Mrs. Gamadge .... Ann Sothern
Don Cantwell .... Gene Raymond
Dick Jensen .... Kevin McCarthy
Mahalia Jackson .... Herself
Howard K. Smith .... Himself
T. T. Claypoole ..... John Henry Faulk
Oscar Anderson .... Richard Arlen
Mrs. Claypoole .... Penny Singleton
Speechwriter .... George Kirgo
Tom .... George Furth
Janet .... Anne Newman
Mrs. Merwin .... Mary Lawrence
Sen. Lazarus .... H. E. West
Zealot .... Michael MacDonald
Gov. Merwin ...... William R. Eberson
Mrs. Anderson .... Natalie Masters
Cleaning Woman .... Blossom Rock
Bill Stout .... Himself
Chairman .... Tyler McVey
Doctor .... Sherwood Keith

Gore Vidal's substantial and provocative drama of political in-fighting on the national level has been skillfully converted to film in this Stuart Millar - Lawrence Turman production. Although not an especially fresh or profound piece of work, it is certainly a worthwhile, lucid and engaging dramatization of a behind-the-scenes party power struggle that accompanies a contest for presidential nomination. The fact that this is a presidential election year should improve the boxoffice destiny of the United Artists relase.

Sly references and character similarities to certain controversial politicians will help, too. But for all of its merit, "The Best Man" does not shape up as a surefire big moneymaker because there will be those who will be offended by some of its points-of-view (although, opportunistically exploited, this could be reversed into a positive commercial factor as a word-of-mouth germinator). In short, a clever, robust ad-promo campaign will be required to bring out the full audience potential.

Vidal's straightforward, sharply-drawn scenario describes the bitter struggle for a party's presidential nomination between an ambitious, self-righteous character assassin (many will see him as a Nixon-McCarthy composite) and a scrupulous intellectual (of Stevensonian essence) who, ultimately faced with a choice of resorting to his opponent's smear tactics or bowing out of the race gracefully, decides he'd rather be right than president —leading to a somewhat pat and convenient conclusive development.

Between these two antagonists, portrayed with conviction and sensitivity by Cliff Robertson and Henry Fonda, respectively, stands the imposing figure of the mortally ill but still politically virile ex-president, a character likely to be associated with Harry S. Truman. Lee Tracy repeats his Broadway characterization in the role and just about steals the show with his expressive, colorful portrayal. Another flashy performance—perhaps a trifle too flashy—is Shelley Berman's as a jittery informer.

Of the three females involved, Ann Sothern has the meatiest part (an influential lady delegate) and makes the most of it. Edie Adams, as Robertson's wife, and Margaret Leighton, as Fonda's spouse, make do with roles of rather secondary

import. Kevin McCarthy registers solidly as Fonda's campaign manager (he's a fine southpaw dart-thrower), and Gene Raymond is excellent, too, as the rival manager. John Henry Faulk scores in a key portrayal. Balance of support is satisfactory, with prominent work from Howard K. Smith and, melodically, Mahalia Jackson. Vidal himself has a brief walk-on as a Senator.

Director Franklin Schaffner has done a fine job, especially in his execution of scenes to match the razzle-dazzle of a political convention. Schaffner came up through the live television ranks ("Playhouse 90," etc.) and his staging of these sequences reflects the air of spontaneity that is a hallmark of that medium.

Dexterous lenswork by Haskell Wexler and trim editing by Robert E. Swink are sizable assists, as are the authentic-looking artwork of Lyle R. Wheeler and unobtrusive score by Mort Lindsey. But what gives "The Best Man" its distinction and flavor is Vidal's writing—his bold, tangy dialog, her perceptive, intelligent point-of-view and his admirable hero. *Tube*

Ring of Spies
(British)

Painstaking but unexciting reconstruction of Britain's Portland Spy case. Neatly acted and directed.

London, March 24.
British Lion release of Leslie Gilliat production. Stars Bernard Lee, William Sylvester, Margaret Tyzack. Features David Kossoff, Nancy Nevinson, Thorey Walters, Patrick Barr, Hector Ross, Newton Blick. Directed by Robert Tronson. Screenplay, Frank Launder and Peter Barnes; camera, Arthur Lavis; editor, Thelma Connell. At Rialto, London. Running time, 90 MINS.
Henry Houghton ...... Bernard Lee
Gordon Lonsdale ...... William Sylvester
Elizabeth Gee .... Margaret Tyzack
Peter Kroger .... David Kossoff
Helen Kroger .... Nancy Nevinson
Commander Winters....Thorley Walters
Marjorie Shaw .... Gillian Lewis
Lt. Downes .... Brian Nissen
P. O. Meadows .... Newton Blick
Capt. Ray .... Philip Latham
Anderson .... Cyril Chamberlain
Christina .... Justine Lord
Capt. Warner .... Patrick Barr
Chief Supt. Croft .... Derek Francis
Supt. Woods .... Hector Ross

Three years ago five British spies were sentenced to long spells of forced reflection for their part in the Portland Spy Case. This film purports to give "the inside story" of the case. Instead, it merely presents a realistic documentary of the surface events leading up to the uncovering of the spies. It is not a highly exciting operation, but there is interest in watching the thorough, painstaking way in which the authorities seize on the blunders of the spies and eventually land them in the Old Bailey. There's precious little cloak-and-dagger stuff of the James Bond vintage and merely emphasizes that truth is not always stranger or more exciting than fiction.

Use of authentic backgrounds in London and on the South Coast and the fact that the five actors playing the leads use the spies actual names are a reminder that what the tab-buyer is watching is authentic stuff. Else it would seem

fairly flat entertainment and seems unlikely to create standout prospects at the boxoffice.

Henry Houghton (Bernard Lee) is sacked from the British Embassy at Warsaw as a bad security risk. He is transferred to records at the Portland Underwater Weapons Establishment. With a chip on his shoulder and a desire for easy money he is readily blackmailed into borrowing secret documents from Portland. He inveigles Elizabeth Fry, a respectable spinster who is in charge of the safe keys, to help him. The Russian contact passes the info on to a middle aged couple in the suburbs who are ostensibly bookdealers. They ingeniously transmit it by short wave to Russia.

Like most crooks who come into money Houghton becomes a boastful spendthrift. Soon the spy ring is under observation. The whole paraphenalia of hidden microphones, "tails" and undercover security men swings into action. Unwittingly Houghton and Fry lead the police to Lonsdale, the contact, and he in turn to the little house in suburbia. Then the police move in and cash-in on the gang's over-assurance.

Bernard Lee and Margaret Tyzack play the dupes with conviction, William Sylvester is a suave, formidable Lonsdale and David Kossoff and Nancy Nevison successfully complete the quintet as the fake bookdealers. Dialog is straightforward and there are one or two lighter touches such as when two-spy-catchers decline to leave Lord's cricket ground in the middle of an over, and when two police-women disguised as nuns, following the suspects in a car, resort to such dialog as: "Hurry up, Amy, or some bastard will cut in on us."

Robert Tronson has directed with a documentary touch, editing is okay and Norman Arnold's artwork satisfactory. But, somehow, "Ring of Spies" seemed a much more fascinating project as read in the newspaper headlines three years ago. *Rich.*

Cherchez L'Idole
(Find the Idol)
(FRENCH—FRANSCOPE)
Paris, March 24.
UGC-Sirius release of France Cinema-Adelphia production. Stars Dany Saval, Franck Fernandel, Berthe Grandval, Dominique Boschero; features Nancy Holloway, Johnny Hallyday, Charles Aznavour, Frank Alamo. Directed by Michel Boisrond. Screenplay, Richard Balducci, Annette Wademant; camera, R. Lemoigne; editor, Genevieve Vaury. At Normandie, Paris. Running time, 90 MINS.
Corinne .... Dany Saval
Robert .... Franck Fernandel
Gisele .... Berthe Grandval
Vanni .... Dominique Boschero

Modest budgeted, snappy little programmer cashes in on the big interest in rock and pop singers via ringing many known ones in through a simple chase story. No characterization or depth here, but a brisk pic that should pay off on its home marts if export is limited.

A young worker is talked into robbing a jewel which he hides in a guitar when chased. But he has remorse, breaks with a climbing, ruthless girl who egged him into the theft, and tries to find the

guitar and return the jewel. But naturally one of five noted singers may have it. The film is concerned with the chase for it.

So Sylvie Vartan and Johnny Hallyday, two of the lead rockers here, get to do a number as well as singer-cleffer Charles Aznavour, French twist singer Frank Alamo and U.S. belter Nancy Holloway, now a local fixture on the song scene.

Miss Vartan and Hallyday, being themselves, show they register better than when trying to act. Aznavour's bonhomie and intense song thrust come through as well as Miss Holloway's musky appeal and song knowhow.

Comic Fernandel's son, Franck Fernandel, is a pleasantly homely, young actor who shows presence and individuality while Berthe Grandval has charm. Dany Saval is rightly odious as the climbing crime-provoking mistress. Director Michel Boisrond just keeps this moving, and story does not get in the way, which gives it natural charm for monied youngsters if oldsters may abstain. It is technically okay. *Mosk.*

Advance To the Rear
(PANAVISION)

Glenn Ford, Melvyn Douglas starred in wacky comedy about raw recruits in Civil War period; shapes as moneymaker for Metro.

Metro release of Ted Richmond production. Stars Glenn Ford, Melvyn Douglas, Stella Stevens; features Jim Backus, Joan Blondell, Andrew Prine, Jesse Pearson. Directed by George Marshall. Screenplay, Samuel A. Peeples, William Bowers, based on novel by Jack Schaefer; camera, Milton Krasner; editor, Archie Marshek; music, Randy Sparks. Previewed in N. Y., March 27, '64. Running time, 97 MINS.
Capt. Jared Heath .... Glenn Ford
Martha Lou .... Stella Stevens
Col. Claude Brackenby...Melvyn Douglas
Gen. Willoughby .... Jim Backus
Jenny .... Joan Blondell
Pvt. Owen Selous .... Andrew Prine
Corp. Silas Geary .... Jesse Pearson
Sgt. Beauregard Davis..... Alan Hale
Hugo Zattig .... James Griffith
Capt. Queeg .... Whit Bissell
Thin Elk .... Michael Pate

"Advance to the Rear," an Army comedy with a Civil War background, is the wacky sort of laughmaker that promises to be a boxoffice "sleeper." Pic stars Glenn Ford, Melvyn Douglas, and Stella Stevens, and includes such featured players as Joan Blondell, Alan Hale and Jim Backus. There is much to be savored in this Ted Richmond production, and it is a vehicle which should make a trim profit for Metro. Maybe some will find some of the antics ridiculous, as often they are, but the pic holds audience interest, which is all to the good.

"To the Rear" is filled with amusing verbal exchanges, several clever visual comedy sequences and some pert performances by the highly capable cast.

Film is from Jack Schaefer's novel, "The Company of Cowards," but Metro has changed the tag to this probably more saleable one. It concerns the exploits of a Union Army company of misfits, headed by vet career officer, Douglas, who follows the strict rule that he must be absolute commander of his outfit, right or wrong. In this case, most of the time he is wrong even if a West Point grad. Some of the misfits in the outfit include a bone-crushing muscle man, a punch-drunk former fighter, an arsonist and a klepto.

Yarn's complications take in a Confederate femme spy, a group of ladies of ill-repute, a band of renegades and an Indian chief. Aside from the scene where the infantry company is ordered to take over the usual cavalry mounts and learn how to drill on horseback, which is sheer slapstick, the sequence where the company, sans uniforms and guns, attacks the southern troops and a "battle episode" in which a hurriedly-built rock catapult and other missiles are used prove to be highlights.

Ford follows his usual low-pressure, authoritative portrayal of the Union captain, who is constantly held back by his superior, Col. Douglas. Miss Stevens makes an excellent femme spy, displaying real thespian ability in her role as a southern miss. Douglas comes close to thefting this pic with his rather jovial interpretation of the peace-loving inept commander.

Veteran Alan Hale does a yeoman job as the company sergeant while Miss Blondell, relegated to the part of the lady in charge of the prosties, makes something of a minor role. Backus is superb as the pompous general. James Griffith, Jesse Pearson, Andrew Prine, Whit Bissell and Michael Pate are best of a large supporting cast.

Direction by George Marshall is one of his better efforts, being especially topflight on visual comedy episodes. Milton Krasner's lensing is unusually fine. Archie Marshek has edited with smartness, making for a fast flow of action. Randy Sparks' western-type score provides a commendable assist to the action. New Christy Minstrels are credited with playing and singing the music. *Wear.*

Yesterday, Today And Tomorrow
(ITALIAN-COLOR)

Engaging contrivance of three episodes given big lift by Sophia Loren and Marcello Mastroianni. Good moneymaking potential.

Hollywood, March 24.

Embassy Pictures release of Carlo Ponti production. Stars Sophia Loren, Marcello Mastroianni. Directed by Vittorio De Sica. Screenplay, ("Adelina"), Eduardo De Filippo, Isabella Quarantotti; ("Anna"), Cesare Zavattini, Billa Billa, from short story by Alberto Moravia; ("Mara"), Zavattini; camera, Giuseppe Rotunno; editor, Adriana Novelli; music, Armando Trovajoil; assistant director Luisa Alessandri. Reviewed at Warner BevHills Theatre, March 24, '64. Running time, **120 MINS.**

(1) "ADELINA" (NAPLES)

Adelina ... Sophia Loren
Carmine ... Marcello Mastroianni
Pasquale Nardella ... Aldo Giuffre
Lawyer Verace ... Agostino Salvietti
Amedeo Scapece ... Lino Mattera
Bianchina Verace ... Tecla Scarano
Elvira Nardella ... Silvia Monelli
Auctioneer ... Carlo Croccolo
Police Captain ... Pasquale Cennamo

(2) "ANNA" (MILAN)

Anna ... Sophia Loren
Her Lover ... Marcello Mastroianni
The Other Man ... Armando Trovajoli

(3) "MARA" (ROME)

Mara ... Sophia Loren
Rusconi ... Marcello Mastroianni
Grandmother ... Tina Pica
Umberto ... Giovanni Ridolfi
Grandfather ... Gennaro Di Gregorio

The wonders of Italy and Sophia Loren are the objects of intimate attention in this breezy, non-cerebral, three-episoder. Glamorously mounted and sensually inclined, Joseph E. Levine's Embassy release is an engaging trifle and has what it takes to make lots of money in any market. A minor drawback to its popularity and appeal in the mass exhibition circuit in which it has been unleashed is the use of sub-titles, a bothersome distraction to which the average easygoing customer, unlike his culture-conscious cousin who inhabits the art house, is not accustomed.

All three parts, separate entities save for the fact that they are set in Italy and co-star Miss Loren and Marcello Mastroianni, have been directed for Carlo Ponti with cinematic flair and invested with sensual gusto by Vittorio De Sica.

The first episode, "Adelina," illustrates the method by which a Neopolitan black-marketeer evades imprisonment over a seven-year span. The law says pregnant women may not be arrested, so she sees to it. This creates an exhausted, mercy-begging husband, a la "Conjugal Bed."

Episode number two, "Anna," is a brief interlude describing the abrupt dissolution of an affair between a Milanese Rolls-Royceterer and her lover. Third item, "Mara," is the flashiest but hokiest of the three. It explores the adventures in Rome of a lovable prostitute, a fanciful client and a confused young student priest. It amounts to an elaborately contrived excuse to get Miss Loren into a bikini.

Mastroianni and Miss Loren both are excellent in all three of their characterizations. Of the supporting players, the most vivid and lasting impressions are made by Giovanni Ridolfi and Tina Pica in the "Mara" episode and Aldo Giuffre in the "Adelina" installment. Ridolfi has all the earmarks of a teenage heartthrob.

Rich production values dress up "Yesterday, Today And Tomorrow" (a meaningless title), a reflection of the astute contributions of such men as photographer Giuseppe Rotunno, composer Armando Trovajoli, editor Adriana Novelli and art director Ezio Frigerio. *Tube.*

Une Ravissante Idiote
(A Ravishing Idiot)
(FRENCH)

Paris, March 24.

SNC release of Belles Rives production. Stars Brigitte Bardot, Anthony Perkins; features Gregoire Aslan, Andre Luguet, J. M. Tennberg, Charles Millot. Directed by Edouard Molinaro. Screenplay, Molinaro, Andre Tabet, Georges Tabet from book by Charles Exbrayat; camera, Andreas Winding; editor, Robert Isnardon. At Marignan, Paris. Running time, **110 MINS.**

Penny ... Brigitte Bardot
Harry ... Anthony Perkins
Bagda ... Gregoire Aslan
Dumfrey ... Andre Luguet
Cartwright ... J. M. Tennberg

Main handles for this uneven situation comedy-actioner are the names of Brigitte Bardot and Anthony Perkins. But Miss Bardot is only caught with her scanties twice, for quick flashes, and this does not quite have the inventive spark, balanced mock seriousness and comedic aspects for anything but playoff possibilities abroad.

Miss Bardot is made to play a dimwitted girl with a horselaugh who turns out to be a British secret agent. She takes up with Perkins, who is a disgruntled Britain of Russo origin, who gets mixed up with Russian spies. Naturally all turns out for the best after some killings, romantic byplay and usual complications.

Miss Bardot is shapely, pouting and nimbly silly, but without the right comic touch and timing as yet. Perkins is forced to play his timid, smiling stereotype which also does not get much help from the uneven scripting and direction.

It just lacks the free wheeling creativeness to give this the pace and zest it calls for to achieve that suspension of disbelief that this type of film demands. The supporting players are properly heavy-handed and menacing. This does get a good production dress and the proper lush lensing. B.B. will have to be the main selling point and it looks more promising at home than for foreign cinematic climes. *Mosk.*

Flight From Ashiya
(PANAVISION—COLOR)

Poorly engineered action melodrama about Air Rescue Service exploits. Handsome mounting and decorative players will have to carry b.o. ball.

Hollywood, March 16.

United Artists release of Harold Hecht production. Stars Yul Brynner, Richard Widmark, George Chakiris; features Suzy Parker, Shirley Knight, Daniele Gaubert. Directed by Michael Anderson. Screenplay, Elliott Arnold, Waldo Salt, based on Arnold's novel; camera (Eastman), Joseph MacDonald, Burnett Guffey; editor, Gordon Pilkington; music, Frank Cordell; assistant director, Milton Feldman. Reviewed at Goldwyn Studios, March 16, '64. Running time, **102 MINS.**

Sgt. Mike Takashima ... Yul Brynner
Col. Glenn Stevenson ... Richard Widmark
Lt. John Gregg ... George Chakiris
Lucille Carroll ... Suzy Parker
Caroline Gordon ... Shirley Knight
Leila ... Daniele Gaubert
Tomiko ... Eiko Taki
Sgt. Randy Smith ... Joe de Reda
Japanese Boy Charlie ... Mitsuhiro Sugiyama
Capt. Walter Mound ... E. S. Ince
Doctor Horton ... Andrew Hughes

Save for some physical production flair and a respectable array of marquee names, there's very little in this Japanese-American coproduction to whet a picture-goer's appetite or reward his curiosity. A joint enterprise of Japan's Daiei Motion Picture Co. Ltd. and America's Harold Hecht Films, with the latter individual as producer, the United Artists release is a hodge podge of aerial, nautical and romantic melodrama, unstable and overly-involved in dramatic design and fuzzy in thematic destination or resolution. "Flight From Ashiya" never really gets off the ground.

The three-pronged scenario by Elliott Arnold and Waldo Salt, based on the former's novel, traces the pasts of three members of the Air Rescue Service as they participate in a daring air-sea operation to save a small group of survivors shipwrecked in a typhoon. Lengthy flashbacks illustrate the personal problems of :(1) Yul Brynner, a Japanese-Polish pararescueman who has a tragic affair with an Algerian girl, (2) Richard Widmark, an Air Force officer who has a tragic affair with an American magazine shutterbug, and, (3) George Chakiris, who has a tragic affair with his own conscience as he absurdly blames himself for a disaster. None of the three characters is sharply or substantially drawn and none of the three stories is clearly resolved.

The dramatic architecture of the film is rickety and erratic, with at least one redundancy and so many flashbacks that a spectator is unable to get his bearings. At one point there is even a flashback-within-a-flashback. What rewards there are, are strictly physical or pictorial. Some spectacular and convincing special effects by the Daiei craftsmen enrich the production, and these efforts are backed up by those of cinematographers Joseph MacDonald and Burnett Guffey (there's at least one strikingly-composed and colored interior sequence), and art director Tom Shimogawara. Frank Cordell's music is melodic and atmospheric. Editor Gordon Pilkington could still do a lot for this film with his shears, especially in the lethargic romantic passages.

Michael Anderson's direction is more successful in bringing flavor and impact to action sequences than it is in the more introspective love scenes or static cockpit exchanges. There's nothing very impressive in the histrionic department. Brynner is rather wooden. There's at least one spot where he fails to convey a required nuance of expression. Widmark is the most effective, but even he gets a little sticky around the edges. Chakiris' range of expression is narrow. Of the three leading ladies, lovely Daniele Gaubert makes the most vivid impression as Brynner's ill-fated Algerian lady love. Suzy Parker has surprisingly little to do, considering that she's top billed of the three females. Shirley Knight labors with the part of Widmark's sweetheart, a role that requires her to say and do some very odd things. *Tube.*

Faites Sauter La Banque
(Rob the Bank)
(FRENCH)

Paris, March 24.

Comacico release of Copernic production. Stars Louis De Funes; features Anne Doat, Georges Wilson, Yvonne Clech, Jean-Pierre Marielle, Jean Valmont. Directed by Jean Girault. Screenplay, Jacques Vilfrid, Girault, Louis Sapin; camera, Andre Germain; editor, J. M. Gautier. At Marignan, Paris. Running time, **90 MINS.**

Garnier ... Louis De Funes
Durand ... Jean-Pierre Marielle
Daughter ... Anne Doat
Policeman ... Georges Wilson
Philippe ... Jean Valmont

Louis De Funes, a middleaged little man, has proved himself an adept comedian on stage and on screen. But the limpid, low budgeted lack-lustre film vehicles he's been in so far may kill him off at the boxoffice. And this pic will not help. And is not much for export.

Direction is flaccid and a good idea rarely brought off. De Funes is a storekeeper who is fleeced of his money by a shady banker. He decides to rob the bank by burrowing under the street, from his store to the bank vault. And thus to retrieve his money.

But the obvious plotting, quickie look of the production and the ordinary thesping around De Funes soon make the laughter forced and the idea overworked. He can vacillate from determined sadism to winning archness and has a flawless sense of timing.

He seems to need a writer and director that could channel this high comic presence into the right vehicles. This may do alright here. Below par lensing also detracts.
Mosk.

Voir Venise Et Crever
(See Venice and Die)
(FRENCH-DYALISCOPE)

Paris, March 24.
Cocinor release of Metzger & Woog. Marceau - Cocinor, Fichberg, Adelphia Films production. With Sean Flynn, Karin Baal, Pierra Mondy, Ettore Manni, Hans Messemer. Directed by Andre Versini. Screenplay, Jacques Robert, Versini from book by James Hadley Chase; camera, Andre Germain; editor, Henri Taverna. At Lord Byron, Paris. Running time, 85 MINS.
Michel .... Sean Flynn
Maria .... Karin Baal
Paul .... Pierre Mondy
Giuseppe .... Ettore Manni
Karel .... Hans Messemer

Actor - scripter Andre Versini shows himself sans much in handling his first directorial stint on a familiar spy actioner. Mainly home playoff chances are in store for this.

The son of a deceased famous secret service man gets embroiled with saving an old friend of his father's who has been deemed a traitor. But the youth finds him being tortured by Reds in Venice and rescues him after the usual fights, suspense and love interest.

Sean Flynn, son of the late Errol, is a good looking youth but, as yet, lacks much of the charm and projection of his father. Others fill in adequately in stereotype roles of friends, valet, heavies and bystanders. Fights lack the snap and precision that these films need. The story does not get the avid treatment and interest it requires.

Result is that this lags despite some good scripting and the Venice background. Technically okay, this coproduction (has minority German and Italo investments) emerges hybrid rather than a solid action opus. Too many nationalities seemingly have spoiled the filmic broth. *Mosk.*

The Crimson Blade
(BRITISH-MEGASCOPE-
COLOR)

Presentable partner in a dual exploitation package from Britain. Adventure meller with historical roots.

Hollywood, March 19.
Columbia Pictures release of Anthony Nelson Keys production. Stars Lionel Jeffries, Oliver Reed, Jack Hedley, June Thorburn. Directed and screenplay by John Gilling; camera (Eastman), Jack Asher; editor, John Dunsford; music, Gary Hughes; assistant director, Douglas Hermes. Reviewed at the studio, March 19, '64. Running time, 83 MINS.
Colonel Judd .... Lionel Jeffries
Sylvester .... Oliver Reed
Edward .... Jack Hedley
Clare .... June Thorburn
Pablo .... Michael Ripper
Jacob .... Harold Goldblatt
Major Bell .... Duncan Lamont
Philip .... Clifford Elkin
Constance .... Suzan Farmer
Sergeant Grey .... John Harvey
Drury .... Charles Houston
Lieut. Hawke .... Michael Byrne
Beverley .... John Stewart
Cobb .... Harry Towb

King Charles I .... Robert Rietty
Fitzroy .... John H. Watson
Blake .... Douglas Blackwell
Gonzales .... Leslie Glazer
Lieut. Wyatt .... John Woodnutt
Duncannon .... Eric Corrie
Chaplain .... Denis Holmes

Columbia has marketable exploitation merchandise in its British-spawned coupling of "The Crimson Blade" and "Devil-Ship Pirates," two historically-motivated adventure melodramas endowed with the coat of production polish that is a specialty of Hammer Films. Lack of cast names recognizable to Yank audiences will probably limit the draw, but it's an attractive twin-bill for youngsters in that the events are not only liberally invested with action but convey a rough idea of two periods of English history. "Blade" is concerned with 17th century Royalist underground resistance to the forces of Oliver Cromwell.

Anthony Nelson Keys produced the Associated British-Hammer entry, which was written and directed by John Gilling. Gilling, on the whole, has done a highly commendable job. His original screenplay has its holes and contrivances (some of the poorest marksmen in history seem to pull Cromwell triggers), but it is fairly strong on characterization, and that's the heart of any script. As for the execution, Gilling is especially fortunate in having enlisted the services of some highly skillful players.

Lionel Jeffries creates an interesting, shaded portrait of a "Roundhead" colonel torn between concern for his daughter, who's serving the Royalist cause, and his duty to Cromwell, which he dispatches in ruthless fashion. Oliver Reed limns with intensity a treacherous officer in love with Jeffries' daughter, attractively played by June Thorburn. Jack Hedley is capable as the title character, except that there's no such thing as the title character since the "Crimson Blade" is referred to as the "Scarlet Blade" in the picture itself. Apparently, crimson blades are out this year.

Balance of support is effective, and so are the efforts of the production team. Particularly valuable are Bernard Robinson's handsome production designs and Jack Asher's valuable easy-to-follow photography. Also commendable are John Dunsford's editing and Gary Hughes' musical score.
Tube.

The Chalk Garden
(BRITISH—COLOR)

Over theatrical, but smoothly performed drama with obvious femme appeal; has old fashioned wordiness, but the central situation is sound. A classy film which calls for discriminating promotion for maximum results.

London, April 3.
Rank-Universal release of a Ross Hunter production for Quota Rentals Ltd. Stars Deborah Kerr, Hayley Mills, John Mills; features Edith Evans, Felix Aylmer, Elizabeth Sellars, Lally Bowers, Toke Townley, Tonie Macdonald. Directed by Ronald Neame. Screenplay, John Michael Hayes from Enid Bagnold's play; camera (Technicolor), Arthur Ibbetson; editor, Jack Harris; music, Malcolm Arnold. Previewed at Leicester-Square Theatre, London. Running time, 106 MINS.
Miss Madrigal .... Deborah Kerr
Laurel .... Hayley Mills
Maitland .... John Mills
Mrs. St. Maughan ...... Edith Evans
Olivia .... Elizabeth Sellars
Judge McWhirrey .... Felix Aylmer
Anna .... Lally Bowers
Shopkeeper .... Toke Townley
Mrs. Williams .... Tonie Macmillan

"The Chalk Garden" makes no bones about its legit background. Enid Bagnold's drama had a healthy 17 months' run at the Haymarket in 1956 and producer Ross Hunter and director Ronald Neame have not done much to disguise the original. Maybe they've treated it over - reverently, and impatient audiences may yearn for a shade more physical action and clash between the characters. As it is, the drama is rooted in delving into the minds, motives and reactions of the five standout characters.

Its strong, if old-fashioned, theatrical situation has been given an overwordy script by John Michael Hayes, but at least it is literate prose despite a number of cliches. Three generations of skilled actresses make the film sound bait for femme patrons, and, overall, it is a reasonable bet for better class houses.

But one thing "Garden" is not, despite all advance ballyhoo. It is not the much-heralded adult role for Hayley Mills that was promised. Miss Mills vigorously plays a 16-year-old girl, in some ways perceptive beyond her years. But audiences will feel that a well applied hairbrush on her derriere could have swiftly ironed out some of the problems that beset her and the surrounding adults.

The child suffers from the feeling that she is not loved. Her mother has remarried and her grandmother is more obsessed with her arid garden. So the confused, unhappy girl grows up in a world of fantasy and lying. On to the scene comes a mystery woman as governess. Deborah Kerr's background turns out to be that of a woman straight from prison after a suspended sentence for bumping off her stepsister.

She sees in her charge exactly the same problems that led her to the dock and quietly but firmly starts to straighten out the child. When her guilty secret comes out in a predictable, but powerful and oddly moving scene, the child is restored to her mother and Miss Kerr stays on to assist grandmother Edith Evans with turning her chalk garden into something worthwhile.

On paper, this sounds like a ripe old piece of Victoriana, but curiously it works, largely because of confident, smooth performances by all concerned. Highly colored it may be, but this is the sort of situation that does produce a plot, something which is too often missing from modern pictures. The gloss which Hunter has successfully employed in previous films is here again and he finds a ready disciple in director Neame. The house on the South Coast of Britain is redolent of elegance and better class living ("two glasses for each wine") and the characters are all obstinately wellbred, despite their early upbringing. And the production design, wardrobe and set dressing departments have not put a foot wrong.

Edith Evans, who played the eccentric grandmother on the stage, is a figure of forbidding dignity though hardly sinister enough to suggest the selfishness and mistaken pride which motivates the plot. Anyway, Miss Evans' technique is always a joy to watch. Miss Kerr looks an unlikely jailbird but gives an aloof and understanding performance while John Mills is fine as a manservant of sound philosophy.

Skillfully blending tomboyishness with some sensitive scenes requiring rather more subtle talent, Miss Mills again registers as one of the most promising newcomers in the business. Elizabeth Sellars, a sorely neglected British thesp, has a brief, showy scene as the estranged mother with which Miss Sellars copes adequately. Felix Aylmer repeats his stage role, that of the judge who sentenced Miss Kerr to death and brings her past to a head. He does it with the now effortless skill that he has employed in a long string of portrayals of judges, archbishops, parliamentarians, surgeons and similar eminent pillars of society. *Rich.*

FBI Code 98

Routine suspense meller examining FBI heroics. Modestly produced. Okay companion entry.

Hollywood, April 2.
Warner Bros. release of Stanley Niss production. Stars Jack Kelly, Ray Danton, Andrew Duggan, Philip Carey, William Reynolds, Peggy McCay, Kathleen Crowley, Merry Anders, Jack Cassidy. Directed by Leslie H. Martinson. Screenplay, Niss; camera, Robert Hoffman; editor, Leo H. Shreve; music, Max Steiner; assistant director, James T. Vaughn. Reviewed at the studio, April 2, '64. Running time, 94 MINS.
Robert P. Cannon .... Jack Kelly
Fred Vitale .... Ray Danton
Alan W. Nichols .... Andrew Duggan
Insp. Leroy Gifford ..... Philip Carey
SA Edward P. Fox .... William Reynolds
Deborah Cannon. ...... Peggy McCay
Marian Nichols ...,.... Kathleen Crowley
Grace McLean .... Merry Anders
Walter Macklin .... Jack Cassidy
Joseph Petersen ...... Vaughn Taylor
Lloyd Kinsel .... Eddie Ryder
SAC Gibson White ..... Ken Lynch
SA Bernard Lyons ..... Charles Cooper
SA Philip Vaccaro ...... Paul Comi
Timothy Farrell .... Bob Hogan
Anita Davidson .... Laura Shelton
Carl Rush .... Robert Ridgely
Assistant Director ... Francis De Sales
SA Alan Woodward ..... William Quinn
SA Vernon Lockhart .... Ross Elliott
Narrator .... William Woodson

"FBI Code 98" was originally intended by Warner Bros. as a tv special, but now is being channeled into theatres. It's a routine melodramatization of crime detection methods employed by the FBI. The Stanley Niss production is shy the commercial stature or dramatic impact to carry a program but, despite its overextended length, is engrossing enough to serve as a companion item.

Written by the producer, the picture is burdened with rather pompous and often irrelevant narration about the superb technique of the FBI. All right, already. It is also marred by dubious story developments and some questionable character motivations. The strongest asset is its dramatic illustration of the way the FBI zeroes in on a culprit, in this case a deranged and embittered employee of a large electronics company who is out to dispose of the firm's three top executives. Since his method is to blow up an aircraft in which all three are passengers, the FBI enters the picture.

The trio of execs are played competently by Jack Kelly, Ray Danton and Andrew Duggan. Equally satisfactory as their respective romantic or matrimonial partners are Peggy McCay, Merry Anders and Kathleen Crowley. Philip Carey and William Reynolds are the chief FBI participants, Jack Cassidy a key figure in a romantic triangle and Vaughn Taylor the mad bomber who gets nailed. They and others in support perform ably, if mechanically.

Leslie H. Martinson's direction is efficient, an appraisal that applies to the production of such men as photographer Robert Hoffman, editor Leo H. Shreve, art director William Campbell and composer Max Steiner. *Tube.*

The Great Armored Car Swindle

Adequate "B" crime meller. Brevity its greatest asset.

Hollywood, March 30.
Falcon Pictures release of Peter Lambert production. Stars Peter Reynolds, Dermot Walsh, Joanna Dunham. Directed by Lance Comfort. Screenplay, Lambert, from novel by Laurence Meynell; camera, Basil Emmott; editor, Peter Pitt; music, Albert Elms; assistant director, Peter Medak. Reviewed at Joe Shire's screening room, March 30, '64. Running time, 58 MINS.
Eric .... Peter Reynolds
Robert .... Dermot Walsh
Cherry .... Joanna Dunham
Eva .... Lisa Gastoni
Peter de Savory .... Brian Cobby
Ernest Winlatter .... Jack Allen
Debt Collector .... Geoffrey Denton
Telling .... Arnold Diamond
Mintos .... Richard Golding
Mel .... John Heller
Ernest's Secrettary ...... Mercia Mansfield
Alex .... Peter Walker
Wilson .... Eric Corrie
Evans .... Desmond Cullon-Jones
Cappel .... Charles Russell
Boxer .... Joe Wadham
Lofty .... Gertan Klauber
Security Officer .... John Lawrence

Any second feature that runs only 58½ minutes has a distinct programming advantage in this age of the inflated epic and too often overgrown "B." This attribute of brevity is the most beneficial commercial characteristic of "The Great Armored Car Swindle," an otherwise routine crime melodrama with vague political and contrived romantic overtones. The Falcon Pictures release, produced by Peter Lambert, will be a serviceable companion item.

Lambert's screenplay, from a novel by Laurence Meynell, relates the ill-fated extra-curricula activities of a young English businessman who becomes a pawn in some international intrigue involving a shipment of currency to a Middle Eastern government threatened by Communist infiltration. The scheme is aborted when the poor fellow's neglected wife becomes suspicious and does some snooping around.

Peter Reynolds plays the mixed-up fortune hunter and does a fair job of it considering the fuzziness and inconsistency of the character he's portraying. Joanna Dunham is adequate as the wife, and so are Dermot Walsh, Lisa Gastoni, Brian Cobby and Jack Allen in the major roles.

Workmanlike if undistinguished craftsmanship is contributed by cameraman Basil Emmott, editor Peter Pitt, art director John Earl and composer Albert Elms. Lance Comfort's direction is competent, in a mechanical sort of way. *Tube.*

Selvmorderskolen
(School for Suicide)
(DANISH)

Copenhagen, March 31.
Palladium production and release. Features Jorgen Ryg, Axel Strobye, Hans W. Petersen, Lone Hertz. Written and directed by Knud Leif Thomsen; camera (Eastmancolor), Henning Kristiansen; music, H. C. Lumbye, Bent Fabricius Bjorre. Reviewed at Palladium Theatre, Copenhagen. Running time, 95 MINS.
S .... Jorgen Ryg
Dr. X .... Axel Strobye
Funeral agent .... Hans W. Petersen
Public Health nurse ...... Bodil Udsen
Fashion model .... Tina Norley
Secretary 1 .... Judy Gringer
Secretary 2 .... Helle Hertz
Girl in Park .... Lone Hertz

Knud Leif Thomsen speaks a very simple language in this film which, in spite of its title, is more of a farce than a tragedy. Intent is clearly satirical. Without allowing his characters too many lines to speak (and thus clutter up foreign screens with subtitles), the director tries hard to sustain his visual gags with a lot of meaningful decor.

"School for Suicide" is in color, and the tint job shines brightly in the modern apartment where the anonymous Mr. S (Jorgen Ryg) tries in vain to commit suicide, fed up as he is with being relieved of all personal problems by the Welfare State.

So he goes to the richly furnished and sexily secretaried (Helle Hertz) School for Suicide, state-run naturally, but he is a poor pupil who only gives the Public Health nurse a lot of trouble, standing on his head till he can walk again.

Next visit is to Survival Consultant, supplied by the State with lavish furniture and a curvacious secretary (Judy Gringer) who by exposing her curves for the patient's myopic inspection proves him perfectly normal.

Suicide and survival consultant alike are played by Axel Strobye with fittingly square-jawed determination. Strobye also portrays several other characters, all designed to symbolize the Big Brother of the Welfare State. In between, private initiative is represented by a funeral agent, very busy, and a sexdoll lolling on a park bench.

The point soon sinks in and it begins to put on a little heavily for and imagination and that is given little chance of its own. Still,

this film has a lot of funny and satirical points. The leading role, as played by Jorgen Rye, shows him to be a real comedian in his portrayal of quitely desperate citizen. *Kell.*

The Strangler

Psychological murder meller reminiscent of Boston. Strong exploitation angles that should override story weaknesses.

Hollywood, March 31.
Allied Artists release of Samuel Bischoff-David Diamond production. Stars Victor Buono, David McLean, Diane Sayer, Davey Davison, Ellen Corby. Directed by Burt Topper. Screenplay, Bill S. Ballinger; camera, Jacques Marquette; editor, Robert Eisen; music, Marlin Skiles; assistant director, Clark Paylow. Reviewed at the studio, March 31, '64. Running time, 89 MINS.
Leo Kroll .... Victor Buono
Lt. Benson .... David McLean
Barbara .... Diane Sayer
Tally .... Davey Davison
Mrs. Kroll .... Ellen Corby
Posner .... Michael M. Ryan
Sgt. Clyde .... Baynes Barron
Dr. Sanford .... Russ Bender
Clara .... Jeanne Bates
Eggerton .... Wally Campo
Thelma .... Mimi Dillard
Dr. Morton .... Byron Morrow
Intern .... John Yates
Artist .... James Sikking
Helen .... Selette Cole
Jack Rosten .... Robert Cranford
Attendant .... Victor Masi

Similarities between "The Strangler" and the recent string of still-unsolved murders in Boston should, if emphasized in molding the picture's public "image," make the Samuel Birchoff-David Diamond production a profitable exploitation entry for Allied Artists.

Another connection that might prove useful in selling the film to the public is its fundamental relationship to a popular enterprise of 20 years ago, "The Lodger," which it resembles in genre (psychological murder melodrama), story (a madman who slays the ladies) and anatomical construction of star (Laird Cregar-Victor Buono).

Bill S. Ballinger's scenario describes the latter phases of the homicidal career of a paranoid schizophrenic (Buono) whose hatred of women has been motivated by a possessive mother who has completely warped his personality. His fetish for dolls ultimately betrays him to the police just as he is in the act of applying the coup de grace to distaff victim No. 11.

Dramatically skillful, direction by Burt Topper and a firm level of histrionic performance help "The Strangler" over some rough spots and keep the picture from succumbing to inconsistencies of character and contrivances of story scattered through the picture. An especially harmful note might very well turn out to be the somewhat shopworn psychological nature of the story, which pins everything on mama in an era when mamas have sunk to new lows in prestige.

Bueno for Buono, a convincing menace all the way. There's always a place on the screen for a fat man who can act, and Buono has the avoirdupois field virtually to himself in these calorie-counting times. Among those who give satisfactory accounts of themselves as law enforcers are David McLean, Michael M. Ryan, Baynes Barron and Russ Bender. Buono's victims, an array of ladies who set what surely must be a new speed record for undressing, are Diane Sayer, Jeanne Bates and Selette Cole, all of whom per-

form creditably. The one that got away is played capably by newcomer Davey Davison, an actress with a boy's name but a woman's body. Mean old mama is portrayed with finesse by Ellen Corby.

Observant photography by Jacques Marquette, sharply etched editing by Robert Eisen, careful art direction by Hal Pereira and Eugene Lourie and a creepy musical score by Marlin Skiles dress up the production in very presentable style. *Tube.*

The Carpetbaggers
(70m SUPER PANAVISION—COLOR)

From Harold Robbins' best-seller, a lusty but erratic, sometimes distasteful film. Could be hot moneymaker.

Hollywood, April 6.
Paramount release of Joseph E. Levine production. Stars George Peppard, Alan Ladd, Bob Cummings, Martha Hyer, Elizabeth Ashley, Lew Ayres, Martin Balsam, Ralph Taeger, Archie Moore, Leif Erickson, Carroll Baker. Directed by Edward Dmytryk. Screenplay, John Michael Hayes, from Harold Robbins' novel; camera (Technicolor), Joseph MacDonald; editor, Frank Bracht; music, Elmer Bernstein; asst. director, D. Michael Moore. Reviewed at studio, April 6, '64. Running time, **150 MINS.**
Jonas Cord Jr. .... George Peppard
Nevada Smith .... Alan Ladd
Dan Pierce .... Bob Cummings
Jennie Denton .... Martha Hyer
Monica Winthrop ..... Elizabeth Ashley
McAllister .... Lew Ayres
Bernard B. Norman .... Martin Balsam
Buzz Dalton .... Ralph Taeger
Jedediah .... Archie Moore
Jonas Cord Sr. .... Leif Erickson
Rina .... Carroll Baker
Morrissey .... Arthur Franz
Amos Winthrop .... Tom Tully
The Prostitute .... Audrey Totter
Moroni .... Anthony Warde
Denby .... Charles Lane
David Woolf .... Tom Lowell
Ellis .... John Conte
The Doctor .... Vaughn Taylor
Cynthia Randall ...... Francesca Bellini
Jo-Ann .... Victoria Jean

Joseph E. Levine's screen version of "The Carpetbaggers" is lusty, vulgar and gusty and, on one notable occasion, painfully brutal. It projects with harsh, driving force—often erratically—the same two basic elements that propelled the novel into the bestseller lists. One is the underlying connection of its principal characters to several real and glamorous people around whom there has always circulated a certain aura of mystery. The other is a notorious reputation —a hint of sexual wickedness. Add to these alluring features an array of fairly salable marquee names and a physical production of considerable opulence and Paramount, by accompanying it into the marketplace with an explosive ad-promo campaign, would seem to have an attraction of great money-making potential.

That's the sunny side of the picture, but there's a negative side, too. For despite its gaudy and glamorous sugarcoating, "The Carpetbaggers" is hardly to be recommended for youngsters and there will be adults who will find this a rather distasteful melodrama that wears awfully thin long before its kingsized running time of 150 minutes is expended.

The story of a ruthless, emotionally unstable chemical-aircraft-film tycoon is told in a vague, often lurching manner in John Michael Hayes' scenario out of Harold Robbins' tome. The career of the "hero"—a heel in fact—is traced sketchily from the point at which he succeeds his just-deceased father (whom he detests) in business to the phase in which he manages to pull himself together emotionally after an unbroken string of brutally cold-blooded dealings, business and personal.

Psychological facets of the story are fuzzy, and vital motivational information about the focal character is withheld to the point where it no longer really seems to matter why he is the miserable critter he is. His sudden reform is little more than an unconvincing afterthought.

There's nobody to root for in "The Carpetbaggers." And Hayes' screenplay never seems to miss an opportunity to slip in connotations of sex, whether or not they are necessary. The dialog is frequently clever, but thoroughly artificial. And there is an accompanying narration that seems quite superfluous and too pretentious.

There are several competent performances. George Peppard growls and glowers his way through the pivotal role, wearing one basic expression—a surly, like-it-or-lump-it look—but there is an underlying animal magnetism to this performance that demonstrates Peppard just needs the right film to make a big explosion. The late Alan Ladd limns with conviction one of the few appealing characters—the cowboy star who ultimately restores Peppard to his senses. The climactic fistfight between these two will make the audience wince.

Carroll Baker has the flashy role of a Harlowesque sexpot, and makes the most of it. Elizabeth Ashley, currently a toast of Broadway, is considerably less auspicious in this screen assignment as the hero's long-suffering wife.

Other major roles are played capably by Bob Cummings, Martha Hyer, Lew Ayres, Martin Balsam, Ralph Taeger, Archie Moore and Leif Erickson, with satisfactory support from Arthur Franz, Tom Tully, Audrey Totter, Anthony Warde, Charles Lane, Tom Lowell, John Conte, Vaughn Taylor, Francesca Bellini and Victoria Jean.

Director Edward Dmytryk has fashioned some high-voltage individual scenes out of Hayes' melodrama, but overall has not been able to avoid a rollercoaster effect in the flow of the story. The going gets pretty tedious and erratic after the first few vicious clashes of personality. Energetic cinematography by Joseph MacDonald is an asset, but more editing by Frank Bracht wouldn't hurt this picture a bit. Lavish, colorful sets have been designed by art directors Hal Pereira and Walter Tyler. Edith Head's costumes are sleek and revealing. A lot of skin to go along with skin-deep characterizations. Elmer Bernstein's pulsating score sounds a great deal like the one he composed for "Walk on the Wild Side." *Tube.*

Rhino
(COLOR)

Engaging African adventure, filmed on-the-spot. Humorous approach compensates for occasional story lapses. Favorable b.o. prospects.

Hollywood, April 10.
Metro release of Ben Chapman production. Stars Harry Guardino, Shirley Eaton, Robert Culp. Directed by Ivan Tors. Screenplay, Art Arthur, Arthur Weiss, from Arthur's story; camera (Metrocolor), Sven Persson, Lamar Boren; editor, Warren Adams; music, Lalo Schifrin. Reviewed at Wiltern Theatre, April 10, '64. Running time, **92 MINS.**
Alec Burnett .... Harry Guardino
Dr. Jim Hanlon .... Robert Culp
Edith Arleigh .... Shirley Eaton
Jo-Po .... Harry Mekela
Haragay .... George Lane

Production ingenuity and a sense of humor combine to distinguish "Rhino" from most of the stark, stock African adventure melodramas of recent years. Pound for pound, dollar for dollar, it's one of the best films of its type since Metro's "King Solomon's Mines." There are flaws aplenty, to be sure, especially in its haphazard story construction, but the favorable elements prevail and should pave the way to commercial success for the Ivan Tors enterprise, produced by Ben Chapman.

The Metro release was filmed at the Umfolozi Game Reserve in Zululand, South Africa, and the on-the-spot photography gives the picture that fresh, authentic flavor that cannot be duplicated by mere educated splicing of stock wild animal footage, the method employed in so many Dark Continent dramas of the past several years. The screenplay provided for this ambitious enterprise was penned by Art Arthur and Arthur Weiss, and they have come up with a servicable and, in several instances, highly amusing script for the occasion. It concerns the idealistic and sometimes physical tangle between a white hunter (Harry Guardino) and a zoologist (Robert Culp) as they beat around the African bush in search of nearly extinct white rhino—the object being to tranquilize a male and female specimen via hypodermic needle gun so that they may be captured and transported to a game reserve for purposes of preserving the vanishing species. Guardino's greed causes complications until he reforms after his life is saved by Culp.

Although scattered story artificialities and irrelevancies mar the flow and blunt the impact of "Rhino," it is on the whole an engaging film. Director Tors rates major credit for the success of the enterprise, but he also is responsible for such superfluities as a brushfire sequence, evidently inserted for pictorial value, and a pulsating animal stampede that is clumsily incorporated into the story.

The better-than-average humor quotient that reinforces "Rhino" is, for the most part, a credit to the creative perception of Tors, the finesse of the cast principals, and the resourcefulness of the production staff. For example, there is a tongue-in-cheek fistfight sequence between Guardino and Culp in which "reaction" shots of the friendly neighborhood wild beasts have been inserted as if to comment ironically, "who's civilized and who's really the animal around here, anyway?" Warren Adams' editing has a lot to do with the humorous impact of this passage, as does the intimate animal photography by Sven Persson and Lamar Boren. The camerawork is an especially telling plus factor in this film, notably during the climactic rhino charges.

In Guardino and Culp, the picture is endowed with two solid actors, neither a particularly big name but both intelligent and spirited performers. The girl in the story is Shirley Eaton. Miss Eaton hails from England but will soon belong to the world. She's a knockout, and knows a thing or two about acting which, in her case, is enough.

Fred Turtle's soundwork is alert and vivid, and Lalo Schifrin has contrbiuted an unorthodox musical score with a bright personality. It's got that Mancini-like sparkle. Even the main titles come up with a few surprises like "animal immobilization" by Ian Player (golfer Gary's brother) and "psychopharmacology" by Keith S. Ditman. *Tube.*

The Quick Gun
(TECHNISCOPE—COLOR)

Routine lower-berth western with Audie Murphy.

Hollywood, April 7.
Columbia Pictures release of Grant Whytock production. Stars Audie Murphy. Directed by Sidney Salkow. Screenplay, Robert E. Kent, based on story by Steve Fisher; camera (Technicolor), Lester Shorr; editor, Whytock; music, Richard LaSalle; asst. director, Herbert S. Greene. Reviewed at the studio, April 7, '64. Running time, **89 MINS.**
Clint Cooper .... Audie Murphy
Helen Reed .... Merry Anders
Scotty Grant .... James Best
Spangler .... Ted de Corsia
Tom Morrison .... Walter Sande
Rick Morrison .... Rex Holman
Reverend Staley .... Charles Meredith
Dan Evans .... Frank Ferguson
Cagle .... Mort Mills
Donovan .... Gregg Palmer
George Keely .... Frank Gerstle
Dr. Stevens .... Stephen Roberts
Mitchell .... Paul Bryar
Elderly Man .... Raymond Hatton
Mike .... William Fawcett

Current king of the budget western field appears to be Audie Murphy, who rides again in this conventional sagebrusher from Admiral Pictures. The Columbia release is a little long for the companion slot in a program, but the added pictorial values of Techniscope and Technicolor compensate somewhat for its tendency to drag in the latter half. Although there are no surprises in the Grant Whytock production, there's enough action to appease the diehard western buff.

Murphy is cast as a gunslinger in the process of reforming in Robert E. Kent's screenplay from a story by Steve Fisher. Riding back to his home town, he comes in contact with a band of desperadoes who want to enlist his aid in their plan to raid the town, in which he is not thought of too highly. Instead he alerts the townspeople to the threat and supports them in the defense.

Murphy is an appealing western hero, still boyish in appearance but all man when it comes to scruples fists or six-shooters. Reliable, hard-working Merry Anders is his romantic partner. Third member of the triangle is sheriff James Best, and it doesn't take long to see that he's going to bite the dust. Bite he does. Best performs ably, and so does "heavy" Ted de Corsia, who has a great laugh for a villain. Adequate in key roles are Walter Sande, Rex Holman, Charles Meredith, Frank Ferguson and Mort Mills. Sidney Salkow's direction is undistinguished, but creditable.

Satisfactory, if stock, production contributions are made by cameramen Lester Shorr, are director Robert Purcell and composer Richard LaSalle. Producer Whytock did the editing. He should have done more of it. *Tube.*

Panic Button
(SONGS)

Banal as in 'B.' Chevalier, Parker, Mansfield names make the appeal for marquees. Filler.

Gorton Associates release of Yankee (Ron Gorton) production. Stars Maurice

Chevalier, Jayne Mansfield, Michael Connors, Eleanor Parker; features Akim Tamiroff, Carlo Croccolo. Directed by George Sherman. Screenplay, Hal Biller from original story by Gorton (dramatized by Mort Friedman, Gorton). Tradeshown in N.Y., April 3, '64. Running time, **90 MINS.**

Phillipe Fontaine	Maurice Chevalier
Angela	Jayne Mansfield
Frank	Michael Connors
Louise	Eleanor Parker
Pandowski	Akim Tamiroff
Guido	Carlo Croccolo

This indie production was started back in 1961, being filmed in Rome and Venice, Italy. It has been a long time in getting to market. Despite a cast headed by Maurice Chevalier, Eleanor Parker and Jayne Mansfield, this is skimpy fare for lower half of dualers.

"Panic Button" starts out like a meller, turns to sexy, romantic comedy and winds up as a wild, slapstick farce which strains credulity. When it is catching glimpse of Rome and the canals of Venice, this manages to hold interest. But in between are sandwiched some banal comedy, stilted acting and absurd story development.

Yarn is concerned with a syndicate (Pagano Enterprises) which finds it must pay heavy income taxes unless it can lose $500,000 in a month's time. Idea has been used, in various forms, previously on the screen. But here it's manhandled on scripting and thespian efforts. Syndicate decides the production of a tele pilot film in Rome is the best and fastest way to drop that kind of coin.

Even the charm of Chevalier's singing two standards fails to save this tale as it is unfolded with one after another stilted performance, and indifferent direction. Plot has the dramatic pilot short winning the prize at the Venice Film Fest as the most original comedy shown at this show.

Chevalier, cast as a washed-up actor, does well enough when given half a chance. But in this production he is not the Chevalier of "Fanny," for instance. Statuesque Jayne Mansfield is the amateur thespian enlisted to co-star with Chevalier in the tele short. In her few love scenes with Michael Connors she does surprisingly well, and, of course, looks her usual self in a bikini.

The camera is flattering to neither Miss Mansfield nor Chevalier. Connors makes an okay production chief working on the tv pilot. Akim Tamiroff is an eccentric drama instructor, recruited as the pilot's director, but not up to his usual standard. Often rated one of medium's neglected talents Eleanor Parker walks through her role of Chevalier's ex-wife. Italo comic Carlo Croccolo makes something of a minor role.

George Sherman has directed much better pix, but perhaps he should not be faulted in view of the material given him. It looks as if several cameramen worked on this but none is listed nor is the film's editor. Where the title was dug up is anybody's guess. *Wear.*

Parliamo Di Donne

(Let's Talk About Women)

(ITALO-FRENCH)

Rome, April 7.

Cineriz release of Fairfilm (Marlo Cecchi Gori)-Concordia Film (Paris) coproduction. Stars Vittorio Gassmann; features Sylva Koscina, Antonella Lualdi, Walter Chiari, Eleonora Rossi Drago, Giovanna Ralli, Jeanine Valerie. Directed by Ettore Scola. Screenplay, Scola and Ruggero Maccari; camera, Sandro D'Eva; editor, Marcello Malvestiti; music, Armando Trovajoli. At Metropolitan, Rome. Running time, **110 MINS.**

Fairfilm producer Mario Cecchi Gori continues to ring the bell with slick, fast-paced comedies, and his latest is no exception. "Parliamo," apart from apt direction and writing, has Vittorio ("Easy Life") Gassmann for an additional b.o. boost. This should give it notable projection both in this country and abroad. Theme being the female of the species, and man's involvement therewith, thus also has fewer limitingly local aspects to brake foreign audience interest.

As patterned in Gassmann's previous "I Mostri," film is series of vignettes, all featuring Gassmann but in various roles. And all wind with O. Henry-styled blackouts. Some are lightweight, a few telegraph their solutions, but most are frankly outspoken in terms of language and situation, though never vulgar.

Most statements are risible throughout while the fadeout one is given an ironic dimension not known to protagonist. Variously involved with Gassmann are such attractive and able partners as Sylva Koscina, as the girl who waits too long to be seduced by him; Antonella Lualdi, who has a last fling with him before rushing off to get married to another man; Eleonora Rossi Drago, Giovanna Ralli and others.

The star here truly deserves his rank. Gassmann is on screen throughout, in various guises, and does an outstanding job in the several characterizations, obviously relishing every bit of it. The audience is with him all the time. Walter Chiari is also good in a segmentary role, while Umberto D'Orsi and others provide okay backdrop action.

Lensing by Sandro D'Eva is classy, and the settings also raise this notches above the usual routine Italo comedy. Ettore Scola's direction (his first feature pic chore after longtime writing stints) is spirited and fast-paced.

Added to the production's gloss is an apt musical backdrop by Armanda Trovajoli, replete with current hit tunes and one future one, the title song sung by Michele. *Hawk.*

Frenesia D'Estate

(Summer Frenzy)

(ITALO-FRENCH)

Rome, April 7.

Cineriz release of a Gesi-Cisa- Federiz-Les Films Agiman co-production. Features Vittorio Gassman, Philipe Leroy, Michele Mercier, Sandra Milo, Umberto D'Orsi, Graziella Granata, Gabriella Giorgielli, Amedeo Narrari, Leo Padovanni. Directed by Luigi Zampa. Screenplay, Age, Scarpelli, Benvenuti, DeBernardi, Mario Monicelli; camera, Marcello Gatti; editor, Eraldo da Roma; music, Gianni Ferrio. At Arlecchino, Rome. Running time, **110 MINS.**

Lightweight comedy of summer doings at an Italian Riviera resort. This is uneven, alternating okay moments being thrust by tedious ones. Chances are offy, both in Italy and abroad, though names will help carry it here.

Several plot lines are intertwined, not always too clearly, in contributions by five scripters assembled for this item. Strangely, for a director of Luigi Zampa's stature, few of characters come off with any depth. The exception, and it's the episode which takes up the most footage, involves Michele Mercier and Vittorio Gassmann. He's an army officer, she's appearing in a visiting French transvestite show which he sees on a weekend furlough.

Though 100% woman, she can't convince him she's only subbing as a female impersonator for a defecting colleague. Gassmann is good, and Miss Mercier is easy on eyes, and the sequence brings forth the pic's main laughs. Others appear in minor capacity. Sandra Milo is wasted as a pastry vendor. Philipe Leroy, as a vocal operator, and others are relegated to minor appearances. In another good segment, Amedeo Nazzari almost steals picture as an elderly male model posing as a rich nobleman and trying hard to act athletically young in order to impress Gabriella Giorgielli, a local femme, and thus make his longtime mate, Lea Padovani, jealous.

Zampa's direction, as noted, is haphazard and obviously burdened by too many plot skeins. Technical credits good. Breezy musical track by Gianni Ferrio helps this. *Hawk.*

Amore in 4 Dimensioni

(Love in 4 Dimensions)

(ITALO-FRENCH)

Titanus release of an Adelphia Comp. Cinematografica (Rome)-France Cinema Productions (Paris) coproduction. Features Cylva Koscina, Franca Rame, Gastone Moschin, Franca Polesello, Carlo Bagno, Isa Crescenzi, Carlo Giuffre, Philipe LeRoy, Lena von Martens, Fabrizio Capucci, Michele Mercier, Alberto Lionello. Directed by Massimo Mida, Jacques Romain, Gianni Puccini, Mino Guerrini. Camera, Dario Di Palma, Carlo di Palma, Tonino delli Colli; editor, Franco Fraticelli; music, Franco Mannino. At Corso Cinema, Rome. Running time, **105 MINS.**

Four-episoder in the currently popular comedy vein, with polish and piquant aspects to indicate a lively "fifth" dimension, namely b.o. prowess in most situations both here and in the foreign market. Format and exploitable aspects naturally assist in making film saleable.

First bit, "Love and the Alphabet" shows the primary urge overcoming lingual obstacles in tale of Sicilian country yokel being won over by old-maidenish northern gal. It's ably acted out by Franca Rame, as the woman, and by Carlo Giuffre, as the illiterate country boy.

Second segment is "Love and Life," in which Sylva Koscina sets up another woman to seduce her husband so she can be free for her own lover, only to have latter falling for the very gal she's hired to do the job. Sylva Koscina is the wife, Gastone Moschin the husband, and Franca Polsello, the saucy third element.

Number three is "Love and Art," perhaps the subtlest of quartet. Here, a noted but lazy scripter weekly closes an eye when an assistant scripter (whose contributions, he realizes, are very vital to his fading career) falls for his wife. Philipe Leroy is the writer, Lena Von Martens is a looker as his wife, and Fabrizio Capucci sketches a neat cameo as the assistant.

Fourth item outlines a new highscaled pickup gimmick devised by a call girl, Michele Mercier. She poses as a recent widow prone to fainting spells in the city cemetery, where well-to-do widowers pick her up, later to be conned via the usual racket. Miss Mercier performs ably and is most easy to look at, but it's Alberto Lionello who displays a fresh comic personality (and a startling resemblance — physical and artistic) to Peter Sellers. He should go places in local pix.

Direction by four different people is on even, pro level. They milk situation for whatever they are worth. All segments have slick patina and savvy pace and mountings, assisted by lensing by three cameramen and single musical scorer, Franco Mannino. The pic is skillfully put together technically. *Hawk.*

Tomorrow's Yesterday

(ISRAEL)

Tel Aviv, April 14.

Geva Films release of the Baruch Agadati Itzhak Agadati production. Written, directed and photographed by Baruch Agadati, edited by Nellie Bogor, commentary written by Gavriel Zifroni and Aharon Amir, narrated by Zalman Levyoush, Ya'acov Ben Hertzel and Rivka Michaeli. Music written, arranged and conducted by Noam Sherif. Black and white. Reviewed at the Yaron cinema, Tel Aviv. Running time, **90 MINS.**

Members of young Collective settlement: Meir Teomi, Avraham Ne'eman, Rephael Klatchkin, Moshe Churgel.

Combining actual documentary material shot in Israel during the last 53 years and excerpts from his 1932 first Hebrew-speaking feature-film shot in the then-called Palestine, Baruch Agadati, dancer-painter-artist-film showman assembeled a variety of scenes, historic occasions and everyday scenes depicting the life of the Pioneers, grandparents and fathers of what became 16 years ago the State of Israel.

Being himself one of the youngsters sent by his parents in Tzarist Russia to study in the first Hebrew Highschool, Hertzliya, in the then just founded city of Tel Aviv, back in 1909, Agadati proves in this semi-documentary feature, his love of the subject, his poetic skill and his searching eye. The result is a sometimes moving, sometimes entertaining panorama of people and ways of living, of historic vignettes and ancient newsreels.

The narration (and the excerpts from the 1932 "This is the Land") aims at projecting the naive, idealistic past, with a grain of contemporary "salt." "They looked funny, our elders — but they meant it," kind of benignantly approving. It works, most of the time and evokes the mood that adds a sentimental thrill to the healthy curiosity. Apart from the many informative scenes, there is a rhythm to this film, and a synthesis of folklore and popular music, extremely fascinating most of the time, by Noam Sherif.

To audiences abroad, Jewish and non-Jewish, there should be enough appeal in this fare, in spite of the local nature of many scenes. Adequate English narration would suffice. Apart from the beauty of many shots, there are candid shots of such international figures as Albert Einstein (in the 1930s visiting Weitzmann), Winston Churchill (in the 1920s present at the wedding of Lord Samuel, among exotic Shieks and the late King Abdalla of Jordan), Lord Balfour and General Allenby.

Framing the picture are shots of Baruch Agadati, among his water-color-on-silk-with-oil-effect paintings (an original device of his), In his forty-five year old wooden hut, a living contrast to the now-building 33-stories Shalom skyscraper, just two blocks away. The picture does well bridging the 50 years between these two. *Port.*

Argentina Fest

Los Tarantos
(The Tarantos)
(SPANISH-COLOR)
Buenos Aires, April 14.
Tecisa production. Stars Carmen Amaya, with Sarita Lezana, Daniel Martin, Margarita Lozano, Carlos Villafranca, Antonio Singla, Aurelio Galan, Antonio Gades. Directed by F. Rovira Beleta. Screenplay, Beleta; camera, Rafael Perez de Rozas; music, Emilio Pujol, Fernando G. Morcillo, Jose Sola, Andres Batistax. At Buenos Aires Film Fest, April 8, '64. Running time, 92 MINS.

To a reviewer who had previously felt that the "Romeo and Juliet" theme had just about had its final reworking for this generation, anyway in "West Side Story"), "Los Tarantos" comes as a stunning surprise. The pic (Spain's entry in this year's foreign language Oscar derby) is a wild, pulsating drama, exotic in its passions and its color. Film is a fine bet for artie release in the U.S. The film immediately recalls "Black Orpheus" in its remarkably successful fusion of music, dance and drama, a romantic folktale set in a grimly realistic setting with no apparent clash between cinema styles. Director F. Rovira Beleta has, in fact, succeeded in blending his extremely stylized tale with a completely real physical background to an extent seldom matched by most American musicals.

"Tarantos" comes close to being a "dance opera," as it unfolds the tragic story of a pair of young lovers whose marriage is opposed by their feuding gypsy families. The setting is Barcelona and the gypsy camps high on the outskirts of the city. The gypsies don't live so much by their dancing as in their dancing and it's in the flamenco and the constant kinesthetic beat that the story rolls on at a furious, relentless pace. Rovira's accomplishment is that the dancing never seems quaint, nor are there any "set pieces." The vigor and the strength of the dancing make the tale.

Setting the pace for the entire film is the performance of the late Carmen Amaya who, as the gutsy mother of the gypsy "Romeo," comes across as a sort of musically exalted Katina Paxinou. The remainder of the dancing actors come close to matching her, which is indeed praise.

Most importantly, however, the film succeeds as a film. Color and camerawork are extraordinary. The individual images are rough and alive and seldom artily self-conscious. Director Rovira has seen to it that next to "Los Tarantos," "Carmen" would probably look like a Romberg operetta. *Anby.*

Oldas Es Kotes
(Cantata)
(HUNGARIAN)
Buenos Aires, April 14.
Hungarofilm presentation of an Estudios Hunnia production. Stars Zoltan Latinovits, with Miklos Szakats, Andor Ajtay, Bela Barsi, Edit Domjan, Gyula Bodrogi, Maria Medgyai. Directed by Miklos Jancso. Screenplay, Jancso, based on story by József Lengyel; camera, Tamas Somlo; music, Balint Sarosi. At Buenos Aires Film Fest, April 6, '64. Running time, 101 MINS.

If this film can be taken as an indication, the arts in Hungary are now swinging to the kind of personal statements which, common in the West, are seldom made in Red Bloc countries. "Cantata" is an extremely subjective tale, the search by a young doctor to find some meaning in his life as he pushes towards material success. Unfortunately, like so many first novels which tackle the same dilemma, the central character, rather fuzzy and vague though undoubtedly sincere, is overshadowed by a number of much more interesting subsidiary characters.

Story covers several days in the life of this doctor, beginning with his routine in the hospital, taking him back to his old bohemian haunts and, finally, to a visit to the farm where he grew up and where his father is now dying. Although director Miklos Jancso has not been fully successful in dramatizing in cinematic terms the hero's interior emotions, the film does contain a number of vivid, poignant scenes, including a closeup view of a heart operation which, though disturbingly clinical, is quite appropriate.

There is also an amusing sequence set in an artist's studio where the doctor's old friends raptly watch a crazily avant garde picture totally concerned with geese. (Says the artist angrily: "I have just shown you the film and you ask me what I am trying to say!").

Less interesting are the doctor's encounters with a couple of former amours, as well as his final resolution that life, after all, is meant to be lived in full commitment to one's family and friends. Film's view of a rather hip, intellectually active Hungarian society is something of an eye-opener, but is hardly enough to indicate any commercial b.o. success Stateside. Film is well-acted and all technical credits are firstrate. *Anby.*

Tudor
(RUMANIAN)
Buenos Aires, April 14.
Bucaresti Film Studio production. Features Emanoil Petrut, George Vraca, Lica Georghiu, Alex Giugaru, Geo Barton, Olga Tudorache, Ion Besoiu, Amza Pelea, Toma Dimitriu. Directed by Lucian Bratu; camera, Constantia Ciubotaru; screenplay, Mihnea Georghiu. At Buenos Aires Film Fest. Running time, 139 MINS.

"Tudor" is an "epic" that might best be described as anemic Eisenstein. It would tend to suggest that the Rumanian film industry is not yet prepared to undertake large scale productions of this type.

Film goes back to Rumanian history during the first half of the last century, showing the struggle of the people for liberty, with the Boyards and Turks as oppressors.

Tudor, the hero, is murdered at the very moment his revolution is approaching success, and there is a great deal of intrigue in the upper echelons of society.

Dialogue is at times appalling, and the whole pic has a naive air, too simple characterization, a general lack of subtlety and poor handling of mass scenes. Lensing, in black and white scope, is unimaginative. It all adds up to a Western in which the peasants are the good guys and the nobles, the heavies. Social content is on a rudimentary scale.

This pic unlikely to earn exposure in the West. *Chile.*

The Man in the Photograph
(YUGOSLAV)
Buenos Aires, April 14.
A Jadran Film (Zagreb) production. Features Nicola Milic, Olavera Markovic, Milan Pusic, Tomanija Duricko, Janez Vrhovec, Severin Bjelic. Directed by Vladimir Pogacic. Screenplay, Dragoslav Ilic; camera, Milorad Markovic. At Buenos Aires Film Fest, April 2, '64. Running time, 88 MINS.

An interesting script is wasted by director Vladimir Pogacic. The story, set in wartime occupied Yugoslavia, concerns Zhiko, a little man who tries to avoid involvement in the issues of his time specifically expressed in the struggle between the Germans and the Partisans. A series of circumstances, which are strange but at the same time credible, puts him right in the middle of things, forcing him to make a choice.

Zhiko finally dies a hero's death, but his dilemma is hardly convincing because the pic does not penetrate deeply enough and the action fails to build up suspense and excitement. Technical credits are barely adequate and the acting is not impressive. Strictly for the Yugoslav market. *Chile.*

Placeres Conyugales
(Conjugal Pleasures)
(ARGENTINA)
Buenos Aires, April 14.
Argentina Sono Film presentation of a Nicolas Carreras-Guido Parisier production. Stars Luis Sandrini, Ana Maria Campoy, Diana Maggi, Ambar La Fox. Directed by Luis Saslavsky. Screenplay, Abel Santa Cruz and Saslavsky, based on a play by Carlos Llopis; camera, Alberto Etchebehere; music, Lucio Milena. At Buenos Aires Film Fest, April 6, '64. Running time, 93 MINS.

Take "La Ronde" and cross it with "Kind Hearts and Coronets," and you might come up with something resembling "Placeres Conyugales" (Conjugal Pleasures). This broad, stylish farce looks to clean up in its home market, though it's hardly weighty enough to buck the competition outside Spanish speaking territories. Pic, based on a well-known play here, shows its legit origins, both in the exaggerated acting manner and in its formalistic progression of scenes. In this case, however, that only adds to the charm

Story, set in Buenos Aires circa 1900, concerns the woefully inept attempts of a wife and her would-be lover to murder her appealing, nitwit of a spouse. The wife, played with amusingly bland sweetness by Ana Maria Campoy, reasons that since she cannot bear the idea of committing adultry, there is nothing to do but dispatch her husband,

which she forthwith attempts to do via arsenic and homemade bombs. A large portion of the B.A. population is eradicated, but her husband lives on and, in a twist finish, he survives to marry a girl he'd had his eye on all the time.

In the key role of the husband, Luis Sandrini is wonderfully foolish and total sincere. Subsidiary performances are in the same vein. Luis Saslavsky's direction has an appropriately airy bounce, nicely complemented by the handsome period sets and costumes. In this case, color photography would have been a definitely plus, but the black-and-white lensing is quite okay, as are all technical credits. *Anby.*

Young Sanchez
(SPANISH)
Buenos Aires, April 14.
I. F. I. Espana, S.A. production. Stars Julian Mateos, with Carlos Otero, Ermanno Bonetti, Luis Ciges, Consuelo de Nieva, Luis Del Pueblo, Juan Torres, Manuel Bronchud, Miguel Graneri, Luis Romero, Manuel Ruiz, Sanchez Merayo. Directed by Mario Camus. Story and screenplay, Ignacio Aldecoa and Camus; camera, Victor Monreal; music, Enrique Escobar; editor, Juan Luis Oliver. At Buenos Aires Film Fest, April 5, '64. Running time, 106 MINS.

Exposes of some of the evils which surround professional boxing unfortunately are rather old cinema hat. Otherwise, "Young Sanchez" might be expected to cause a much greater stir in the international market than now seems indicated. This official Spanish entry at the Buenos Aires festival is nicely acted, directed and photographed, but none of these virtues can disguise the fact that it's basically a cliche. John Garfield, Robert Taylor, Tyrone Power, et. al., did the same story back in the 1930s and 1940s.

For overseas audiences the picture has a certain uniqueness in its contemporary Spanish locale. But the same things happen in these gyms and arenas as used to happen in those just off Broadway. In the title role, Julian Mateos gives an excellent performance as a young boxer who, disillusioned by early doublecrosses, sets out to make as much dough as he can, either clean or dirty. In appearance Mateos looks something like a husky Alain Delon and overall the film recalls the Delon-Visconti "Rocco and His Brothers." But "Young Sanchez" has none of that earlier film's social and psychological complexities. *Anby.*

Les Tontons Flingueurs
(FRENCH)
Buenos Aires, April 14.
Gaumont (Paris), Corona Filmproduktion (Munich), Ultra Film (Rome) coproduction. Features Lino Ventura, Bernard Blier, Francis Blanche, Claude Rich, Sabine, Sinjen, Horst Frank, Charles Regnier. Directed by Georges Lautner. Adapted by Albert Simonin from his novel "Grisbi or Not Grisbi"; dialogue, Michel Audiard; music, George Delerue. At Buenos Aires Film Fest, April 5, '64. Running time, 97 MINS.

An uneven film, marred by a far too slow beginning, turns into a slapstick farce once it gets into stride. Though not consistently good, this has amusing situations and some first-rate gags.

Fernand (Lino Ventura), owner of a small tractor factory, gets himself involved with gamblers and gangsters when asked to take care of a dying friend's daughter. The friend headed the syndicate, whose members are far from enthusiastic at the idea of a takeover by an outsider. And trouble soon brews, to the tune of mayhem with all kinds of weapons. Fernand, after a great deal of ammunition has been spent, proves himself the boss and everyone who hasn't been killed in the process feels quite happy.

Ventura plays his usual tough, but in a light vein while Bernard Blier turns out to be an amusing heavy.

"Les Tontons" may become successful in specialized situations particularly in Latin America, but from an artistic point of view, it's only real asset is Michel Audiard's sophisticated and ingenious dialogue. Should be good in the home market. Stateside chances are slim. *Chile.*

Nadeje
(The Hope)
(CZECHOSLOVAK)
Buenos Aires, April 14.
A Barrandov Film Studio production. Stars Hana Hegorova, Rudolf Hrusinsky; features, Frantisek Peterka. Otta Simanok, Vaclav Neuzil, Frantisek Vicena, Jaroslav Nikolny, Josef Barta. Directed by Wael Kachyna. Screenplay, Jan Prochaszka, Karel Kachyna; camera, Josef Vanis; music, Jan Novak; editor, Jan Chaloupek. At Buenos Aires Film Fest, April 8, '64. Running time, 92 MINS.

A slow, heavy pace prevents this pic from being attractive from the point of view of conventional entertainment, limiting its possibilities even in selected arty situations. But this does not prevent it from being a piece of serious and honest filmmaking.

Story concerns Lucin, a laborer on a construction job, who has swapped his self-respect for alcohol. When the pic begins, he is well on his way to becoming a Bowery-type character. His fellow workers despise and dislike him, except Magdalena. She has an uncertain reputation of her own and gives him her help and love, desperately trying to return him to the straight and narrow.

The relationship between these two characters is beautifully developed, without at any moment indulging in romantic overtones. In fact, the honesty of their presentation leads to the film's limitations as entertainment. Director Kachyna does not idealize his characters or try to make them personally attractive. Instead, he views them with sympathy and understanding for their plight, suggesting a great deal more about their lives and problems than is actually said. He is greatly helped by two good performances, of which Hana Hegorova's is outstanding.

Story is told in a straightforward manner, without unnecessary embroidery. Lensing and other technical credits are good. The film's ending only implies hope of regeneration, instead of forcing a definitive happy end. In toto, it is an interesting and positive approach to the theme of an individual unable to adopt to society. *Chile.*

Zerwany Most
(The Lost Bridge
(POLISH)
Buenos Aires, April 14.
Film Polski release of a Iluzjon Studio production (Warsaw). Features Tadeusz Lomnicki, Elzbieta Kepinska, Lidia Korsakowna. Wojciech Siemian. Mieczyslaw Voit. Directed by Jerzy Passendorfer. Screenplay, Roman Bratny; camera, Antoni Nurzynski; music, Tadeusz Baird. At Buenos Aires Film Fest, April 3, '64. Running time, 85 MINS.

The postwar struggle between Ukranian fascists and the Polish army is a somewhat local matter. And it evokes no emotional echo with foreign patrons. Hence the film, however competently and honestly made, does not succeed in bringing out universal issues.

Photography and acting are good but the historical background is taken too much for granted. If the pic had been more explicit regarding this, its foreign chances would have been much improved. As it stands, they are very limited. The story concerns a Polish officer who, disguised as a Ukrainian infiltrates the enemy, killing their leader and afterwards finds it a hard job to prove that he is actually Polish. *Chile.*

The Thin Red Line
(C'SCOPE)
War meller crammed with action but fuzzy in characterization. Strong fare for action market.

Hollywood, April 17.
Allied Artists release of Sidney Harmon production. Stars Keir Dullea, Jack Warden; features James Philbrook, Ray Daley, Robert Kanter, Merlyn Yordan, Kieron Moore. Directed by Andrew Marton. Screenplay, Bernard Gordon, from James Jones' novel; camera, Manuel Berenguer; editor, Derek Parsons; music, Malcolm Arnold; assistant director, Jose Maria Ochoa. Reviewed at the studio, April 17, '64. Running time, 90 MINS.
Pvt. Doll .... Keir Dullea
1st Sgt. Welsh .... Jack Warden
Col. Tall .... James Philbrook
Capt. Stone .... Ray Daley
Fife .... Robert Kanter
Judy (Doll's wife)........ Merlyn Yordan
Lieut. Band.............. Kieron Moore
Capt. Gaff.............. James Gillen
Pvt. Mazzi .... Steve Rowland
S Sgt. Stack.......... Stephen Levy
Medic .... Mark Johnson

Aficionados of the action-packed war film will savor the crackling, combat-centered approach of "The Thin Red Line," an explosive melodramatization of the Yank assault on Guadalcanal in World War II. It's a man's picture, a solid entry for the action market. But it is limited by shortcomings in the area of characterization. In its attempt at deeper insight into the mental and emotional stresses that govern men's behavior at the front, the Philip Yordan production and Allied Artists release lacks the necessary motivational clarity and dramatic eloquence to attract the attention of the more discerning picturegoer.

Bernard Gordon's scenario, turbulently gleaned from James Jones' novel, focuses its characterization gaze at two figures prominently implicated in the taking of that small but significant piece of Pacific real estate. One is a resourceful private (Keir Dullea), the other a war-wise, sadistic sergeant (Jack Warden). The two quickly become enemies but it is no surprise when, ultimately, one dies in the other's arms after saving the other's life. In addition to this pivotal intramural conflict, there are other hostilities including the one between Japan and the United States.

The movements, chaos and bloody brutality of front-line conflict are vividly and vigorously depicted, a credit to the willing cast, talented production staff, and especially to director Andrew Marton, who again demonstrates his flair for the crowd scene, his keen sense of detail yet perspective of overall patern in designing and executing mass movements of men. He is backed up stalwartly in this regard by Manuel Berenguer's alert, often striking photography and Derek Parsons' perceptive editing. Another major asset to Sidney Harmon's production is Malcolm Arnold's surging, expressive musical score. As a physical production, it's an outstanding effort.

Dullea and Warden are colorful antagonists, former's intensity contrasting sharply with the latter's easygoing air. Firm histrionic support is chipped in by James Philbrook, Ray Daley, Robert Kanter and Kieron Moore, with smaller but equally capable assists from James Gillen, Steve Rowland, Stephen Levy and Mark Johnson. Merlyn Yordan participates in a

flashback sequence that is rather artificial and irrelevant and could be deleted. She's the only female in the picture. *Tube.*

Never Put It In Writing

Sporadically amusing trifle about Pat Boone in pursuit of a letter he's mailed. Mild b.o. prospect.

Hollywood, April 14.
Allied Artists release of Andrew Stone production. Stars Pat Boone. Written and directed by Stone; camera, Martin Curtis; editor, Noreen Ackland; music, Frank Cordell; assistant director, Ted Wallis. Reviewed at the studio, April 14, '64. Running time, 93 MINS.
Stephen Cole .... Pat Boone
Danny O'Toole .... Milo O'Shea
Katie O'Connell ...... Fidelma Murphy
Lombardi .... Reginald Beckwith
Mr. Breeden .... Harry Brogan
Miss Bull .... Nuala Moiselle
Adams .... John Le Mesurier
Adams' Secretary...... Sarah Ballantine
Security Officer .... John Gardiner
Oscar .... Colin Blakeley
Taxi Driver .... Derry Power
Tower Man .... Bill Foley
Receptionist .... Polly Adams
Maid .... Julia Nelson
Pringle .... Ed Deveraux
Foreman, Sorting Office .. Seamus Healy
Young Woman .... Karal Gardner
Judge .... John Dunbar
Judge's Wife .... Susan Richards
Basil's Girl Friend......Liz Lanchbury

Filmed in Ireland and England by Andrew and Virginia Stone, "Never Put It In Writing" is a diverting, frivolous novelty constructed around an unusual "chase" in which the pursuer is simply trying to intercept a letter he himself had mailed, much to his later regret.

Pat Boone plays the desperate young man in pursuit and, although his presence may help push a few extra wickets, the Seven Arts production for Allied Artists release appears to lack sufficient allure for a solo boxoffice flight. It would, however, make a suitable featured companion on an unpretentious program package—or secondary running mate to a major attraction of less than epic proportions.

The picture was written, produced and directed by Andrew Stone, in capable enough fashion on all three counts. Many of the players of Ireland's Abbey Theatre cavort in the film, and their participation gives it a lift in atmospheric values.

The lightweight plot, stretched pretty thin, describes Boone's feverish efforts to catch up with a letter he has mailed to the boss of the London insurance firm for which he works, accusing him of nepotism in having selected his nephew, not Boone, for a general manager-junior partner post the latter feels he deserves. The chase begins when Boone discovers that it is indeed he, not the nephew, who had been promoted. The upshot is a merry romp from Belfast to London, during which he picks up two allies and tangles with, among others, an officious secretary, a tipsy pilot and several gendarmes.

Boone turns in a creditable performance as the hotshot insurance agent. The girl with whom he plays post office is Fidelma Murphy of the Abbey, a pretty colleen who tends to overemote. The outstanding participant is Milo O'Shea, who's a delight as a devious, opportunistic "friend" of Boone's. Others of more than passing import are Reginald Beckwith as the pilot, Sarah Ballantine as the secretary, John Le Mesurier as the boss and Colin Blakely as the nephew.

Skillful contributions to the production include those of cameraman Martin Curtis, editor Noreen Ackland (under Mrs. Stone's supervision), composer Frank Cordell and stunt flying expert Charlie O'Hara. A frisky and salable title song has been written by Boone, and he sings it enthusiastically over the main titles. *Tube.*

The Third Secret

Absorbing if uneven psychological mystery meller. B.O. prospect depends on smart salesmanship.

Hollywood, April 16.

Twentieth-Fox release of Robert L. Joseph production. Stars Stephen Boyd, Jack Hawkins, Richard Attenborough, Diane Cilento, Pamela Franklin. Directed by Charles Crichton. Screenplay, Joseph; camera, Douglas Slocombe; editor, Frederick Wilson; music, Richard Arnell; assistant director, Peter Bolton. Reviewed at the studio, April 16, '64. Running time, **103 MINS.**

Alex Stedman .... Stephen Boyd
Frederick Belline .... Jack Hawkins
Alfred Prince-Gorham .... Richard Attenborough
Anne Tanner .... Diane Cilento
Catherine Whitset ...... Pamela Franklin
Dr. Milton Gillen .... Paul Rogers
Alden Hoving .... Alan Webb
Mildred Hoving .... Rachel Kempson
Lawrence Jacks .... Peter Sallis
Mrs. Peltce .... Patience Collier
Mrs. Bales .... Freda Jackson
Miss Humphries .... Judi Dench
Dr. Leo Whitset .... Peter Copley
Lew Harding .... Nigel Davenport
Dermot McHenry ... Charles. Lloyd Pack
Police Secretary .... Barbara Hicks
Police officer ...... Ronald Leigh Hunt
Floor manager .... Geoffrey Adams
Mark .... James Maxwell
Mr. Bickes .... Gerald Case
Nurse .... Sarah Brackett
Mr. Morgan .... Neil Arden

When a renowned psychoanalyst is deemed a suicide, the emotional repercussions on the patients he was treating are bound to be severe. The puzzle surrounding his sudden and unaccountable death, as it is put together piece by piece by one of his agitated patients, is the plot pursued by "The Third Secret," an engrossing, if not altogether convincing, mystery melodrama of the weighty psychological school. The British-made Robert L. Joseph production, a 20th-Fox release, should be a welcome attraction for the diehard mystery buff, but it is better equipped to absorb an audience than to allure one. **Word of mouth will be a helpful boxoffice factor and with smart admanship this picture can intrigue customers generally. The trick is to build advance curiosity.**

Producer Joseph's original scenario has strengths and weaknesses. It is literately written, with a liberal sprinkling of sharp dialog and interesting observations. On the other hand, it is hampered by occasional vaguenesses, a tendency toward pretentiousness, motivational question marks, and an early tipoff that doesn't figure to elude the discerning mystery enthusiast.

Stephen Boyd, as the inquisitive patient of the deceased analyst, conducts a private investigation to determine whether the death was actually a suicide (contradicting everything the noted doctor stood for) or a murder committed by one of his patients, of whom there were only four, according to the analyst's daughter (Pamela Franklin). The investigation leads Boyd —an American telenewscaster living in England—from patient to patient, a fruitless path until he unearths "The Third Secret," which stands for the truth.

A lack of animation in spots is evident in Boyd's performance, but there are moments when he catches the spark of the character. Young Miss Franklin does a highly professional job as the daughter. She's a young actress of great potential. The three ex-patients visited by Boyd are Jack Hawkins as a judge, Diane Cilento as a secretary and Richard Attenborough as an art gallery owner. All three are effective, with Attenborough especially distinguished and memorable in his characterization. Chief support, competently etched, is contributed by Paul Rogers, Alan Webb, Rachel Kempson and Peter Sallis.

"The Third Secret" is a rather talky film, but Charles Crichton has done a commendable job of keeping it taut and as visually stimulating as possible. To this end, he benefits from the aid of such craftsmen as photographer Douglas Slocombe, editor Frederick Wilson and art director Tom Morahan. Richard Arnell's score is richly endowed with an aura of eerie imminence. *Tube.*

The Golden Arrow
(ITALIAN—TECHNIRAMA—COLOR)

Erratically written and executed adventure fantasy. Special effects trickery its only b.o. bait.

Hollywood, April 15.

Metro release of Titanus production. Stars Tab Hunter, Rossana Podesta. Directed by Antonio Margheriti. Screenplay, Bruno Vailati, Augusto Frassineti, Filippo Sanjust, Giorgio Prosperi, Giorgio Arlorio; camera (Technicolor), Mario Capriotti; editor, Giorgio Serandrei; music, Mario Nascimbene; assistant director, Ettore Fizzarotti, Giovanni Fago. Reviewed at the studio, April 15, '64. Running time, **91 MINS.**

Hassan .... Tab Hunter
Jamila .... Rossana Podesta
Thin Genie .... Umberto Melnati
Absent-Minded Genie ... Giustino Durano
Baktiar .... Mario Feliciani
Sabrath .... Jose Jaspe
Mokbar .... Giampaolo Rosmino
Prince of Bassora .... Renato Baldini
Prince of Aleppo ...... Rosario Borelli
Prince of Samarkand . Ceco Zamurovich
Prince of Bassora's General .... Calisto Calisti
Queen of Rocky Valley .... Dominique Boschero
Capt. Hamit ..... Abdel Moneim Ibrihim
Bandit .... Claudio Scarchilli
Magician of Rocky Valley .... Omar Zoulfikar

An adventure fantasy from Italy's Titanus picturemakers, "The Golden Arrow" is fashioned in roughly the same vein as "Captain Sindbad," a boxoffice winner for Metro last year. However, this import, owing to its lack of dramatic cohesion and rather unimaginative creative approach to the wide-open **possibilities of special effects spectacle, isn't apt to duplicate the success of its forerunner. Vivid, hard-sell exploitation of fantasy angles might stimulate attendance of the moppets and adults with childlike appetites for screen adventure.**

It took all of five scribblers to grind it out. Tab Hunter plays the lead, a dashing bandit who discovers he's the rightful heir to the sultanship of Damascus but must come by a magic golden arrow to properly stake his claim and assert his authority. With the aid of three whimsical genies, he accomplishes this goal.

Hunter is okay, but he does a lot of grinning and gaping, as if puzzled by the language cross-currents of the post-dubbed production. Rossana Podesta is that inevitable Damascus prop, the beautiful princess waiting for her Prince Charming. The balance of the cast performs in mechanical fashion under Antonio Margheriti's haphazard direction.

Fernando Mazza's special effects are generally satisfactory, best being his illusory construction of flaming monsters in human silhouette. Mario Capriotti's lenswork is adequate, but the editing by Giorgio Serandrei is choppy and gets the film off to a false start from which it takes a long time to recover. Flavio Mogherini's art direction is impressive but Mario Nascimbene's musical score is often somewhat incompatible with the dramatic events it accompanies. *Tube.*

Nightmare
(BRITISH)

Chilly melo, loosely concocted, but with some tense moments. Fair dualler.

London, April 17.

Rank release of a Hammer Film for Universal. Stars David Knight, Brenda Bruce, Moira Redmond, Jennie Linden. Features George A. Cooper, John Welsh, Irene Richmond, Timothy Bateson, Hytie Jessop. Written & produced by Jimmy Sangster. Directed by Freddie Francis; music, Don Banks; camera, John Wilcox; editor, James Needs. Previewed April 15, '64 at Rank Private Theatre, London. Running time: **83 MINS.**

Henry Baxter .... David Knight
Grace .... Moira Redmond
Mary .... Brenda Bruce
Janet .... Jennie Linden
John .... George A. Cooper
Mrs. Gibbs .... Irene Richmond
Doctor .... John Welsh
Barman .... Timothy Bateson
Woman in White .... Clytie Jessop
Sir Dudley .... Hedger Wallace
Maid .... Julie Samuel
Janet (as child) .... Elizabeth Dear
Mother .... Isla Cameron

Best feature of this highly contrived chiller is the direction and lensing (by Freddie Francis and John Wilcox respectively) of the atmosphere of a house where eerie things happen in the way of shadows, significant noises and the fleeting appearances of a phantom-like woman in white. A fair atmosphere is worked up by Francis and Wilcox, and it is aided by a useful musical score by Don Banks and sound editing by James Needs. But Jimmy Sangster's screenplay and dialog do not match these plusses. Dialog, in particular, often lapses into bathos. With minor stellar appeal, "Nightmare" can be functional only as a second feature in support of a strong bring-em-in top pic.

Jennie Linden's mother was committed to an asylum when the child was 14, after stabbing her husband. This preys on the child's mind and she is convinced that she may have inherited a streak of madness. She certainly is the victim of bad dreams. She is taken from school to her home where she is apparently safely guarded by the attention of an adoring housekeeper (Irene Richmond), her school mistress (Brenda Bruce), her young guardian (David Knight) and a nurse, (Moira Redmond), posing as a companion. But Knight and Miss Richmond are clandestine lovers. Their object is attained when the adolescent is goaded into murdering Knight's wife in a fit of panic, and is taken to a mental institution. But with both safely out of the way Miss Redmond becomes suspicious that her newly acquired husband wants to murder her. She takes the initiative but is trapped by the vigilance of the school mistress and family chauffeur (George A. Cooper).

The attempts by Knight and Miss Redmond to prey on the mind of the girl are elaborately worked out and, though highly **incredible, serve as a workmanlike plot for such a modest** thriller.

"Nightmare" has several of the ingredients of a successful thriller cocktail but these have not been shaken with enough guile to click satisfactorily. *Rich.*

Where Has Poor Mickey Gone?
(BRITISH)

Naive attempt by unknowns to produce a low budget chiller on cooperative basis.

London, April 17.

Compton-Cameo release of a Ledeck-Indigo Production. No star credits. Produced and directed by Gerry Levy. Original story & screenplay by Peter Marcus; camera, Alan Pusney; editor, Howard Lanning; music, Graham Whettam; title song written & sung by Ottilie Patterson. Previewed April 14, '64 at Hammer Theatre, London. Running time, **58 MINS.**

Emilio Dinelli .... Warren Mitchell
Mick .... John Malcolm
Ginger .... Raymond Armstrong
Tim .... John Challis
Kip .... Christopher Robbie
Girl .... Karol Hagar
Boy .... Joseph Cook
Detective .... Philip Newman

Attempts by unknowns to produce modest films on a co-operative basis supposedly are to be encouraged. But this one is too naive and lacking in expertise to stand much chance except that, at 58 minutes, it is a welcome length for a filler. Filmed on location with direct sound, it lacks punch as an essay in the macabre. Its straggling script has some down-to-earth saltiness, Warren Mitchell, the best known name, gives a professional performance and John Malcolm, as Mick, chief of the layabouts, is a podgy offbeat character who may do well as a character actor. But these are about all the bouquets that can be tossed to this misfire.

Malcolm leads a little gang of streetcorner roughs and they set out in search of mischief. Tossed out of a sleazy club, they assault a couple of streetcorner lovers and then decide to rob a basement workshop run by an Italian. All this is padding. The film really starts when they break into the premises to find that it is the workshop of a stage magician who makes novelty sideshows for carnivals.

Only Mitchell as the magician provides a performance that creates the intended atmosphere. The rest appear to have been given undue head by the producer-director Gerry Levy and the result is flat. *Rich.*

The Evil of Frankenstein
(BRITISH-EASTMANCOLOR)

Baron Frankenstein in trouble again in another of the horror pix. Okay for its natural audience.

London, April 16.

Rank release of a Hammer Film for Universal. Stars Peter Cushing. Features Peter Woodthorpe, Duncant Lamont, Sandor Eles, Katy Wild, David Hutcheson. Producer, Anthony Hinds. Directed by Freddie Francis. Story & screenplay by John Elder; camera, John Wilcox; music, Don Banks; editor, James Needs. Previewed at Rank Private Theatre, London. Running time; **84 MINS.**

Baron Frankenstein ...... Peter Cushing
Zoltan .... Peter Woodthorpe
Hans .... Sander Eles
The Creature .... Kiwi Kingston
Beggar Girl .... Katy Wild
Burgomaster .... David Hutcheson
Chief of Police .... Duncant Lamont
Priest .... James Maxwell
Burgomaster's Wife ..... Caron Gardner
Drunk .... Howard Goorney
Hypnotised Man .... Timothy Bateson
Landlord .... Alister Williamson
Bodysnatcher .... Tony Arpino

The horrific adventures of Baron Frankenstein are still providing Hammer Films with rich boxoffice loot. In this one the finale shows Frankenstein's castle going up in flames. But it is a safe bet that the sinister scientist will have got away to scare another day. Peter Cushing plays the Baron with his usual seriousness, avoiding tongue-in-the-cheek, and he is the main prop in the proceedings. Some of his fellow thesps tend to ham it up to the make-believe's detriment.

Director Freddie Francis, an upcoming horror specialist, must hereafter rap down severely on such actor fancies. Only by playing the films deadpan can audiences be indulgent enough to accept them for the harmless nonsense that they are. Direction here is deft enough over the more preposterous stretches. Special effects help, viz the Baron's crazy apparatus. Result, there is always something going on.

This time Cushing returns to the Castle which is his scientific playground and is bent on reviving and co-ordinating the brain of one of his homemade monsters. Earlier this character had escaped, but is found, conveniently preserved in a glacier. The Baron has sundry other problems on his plate, notably a drunken, blackmailing hypnotist, a deaf and dumb beggar girl, the local Burgomaster and the police, but keeps a fairly stiff upper lip throughout.

John Elder's dialog occasionally raises unintented laughter and John Wilcox's lensing is adequate. A great deal of the artwork smacks of backcloth and models. Peter Woodthorpe, Sandor Eles, Katy Wild, David Hutcheson, Caron Gardner and Duncant Lamont form the main support for Cushing, while Kiwi Kingston is the Creature, an uncomfortable role through which he shuffles with macabre aplomb. *Rich.*

La Mort D 'Un Tueur
(Death of a Killer)
(FRENCH)

Paris, April 14.

Comacico release of Copernic-Ciledial production. Stars Robert Hossein: features Marie-France Pisier, Simon Andreu, Robert Dalban. Directed by Robert Hossein. Screenplay, Hossein, Louis Martin, Claude Desailly, Georges and Andre Tabet; camera, Jean Boffety; editor, Marie-Sophie Dubus. At Triomphe, Paris. Running time, **75 MINS.**

Massa .... Robert Hossein
Maria .... Marie-France Pisier
Luciano .... Simon Andreu
Albert .... Robert Dalban
Tony .... Jean Lefebre

Actor Robert Hossein sometimes turns to writing and directing. This one has him combining all. It's still his penchant for trying to make arty gangster pix. Too much posing, farout psycho plotting with incestuous angles and slow pacing make result pretentious rather than probing. What might have been an okay actioner becomes a plodding affair. Mainly for playoff in France.

Hossein comes back from the jug convinced that a friend turned him in. He also has had an unhealthy interest in his pert sister which is shown in a series of flashbacks as he stalks the old friend who is now living with the sister.

So it appears he mainly hates this man for having won over his sister. Comes the showdown with a Russian roulette contest between him and his ex-friend via each trying a shot at the other with one bullet in a revolver. He wins but is turned in by his sister and shot down by the police.

There is even a symbolical girl, played by the actress who does the sister, who has a wordless affair with Hossein while some rich people ogle strippers and exotic dancers in another room. Hossein is stolidly acceptable as a thesp but too predictable as scripter-director. He alternates long shots and close shots for each scene with long pauses that make little dramatic effect.

Trying for tragedy there is not the requisite depth of characterization or relentless situation which is necessary. *Mosk.*

Mishpahat Simchon
(The Simchon Family)
(ISRAELI)

Noy Productions Ltd. presentation of Shlomo Nouman and Yair Pecker. Starring Meir Margalith. Directed by Yoel Zilberg. Script by Leo Filler and Yoel Zilberg; camera, Marco Yocovlevitz; editor, Helga Cranston; music, Dov Seltzer. Reviewed at the Allenby, April 12. Running time, **88 MINS.**

Noah Simchon .... Meir Margalith
Zira .... Shoshana Kotler
Gabi .... Oded Katler
Na'ava .... Rina Ganor
Orna .... Tikva More
Zwirn .... Zalman Levinah
Eddie Calvert & band

This story, scripted from a popular radio series that was broadcast for almost two years, trice weekly, has local coloring, familiar scenes and faces. It used to react to actual and topical problem and reflected everyday life in each installment. As a film it retains the local quality but fails notwithstanding the bright personality and warm humor of its star, Meir Margalith, to make the satirical points that might have added general interest in the story. It is shallow when criticising the artificial high standard of living. The only scene in which director Yoel Zilberg managed to convey this is the nightmarish reception held at the vague African State, upon installation in a diplomatic career. It brilliantly spoofs local cocktail parties and other ostentatious affairs.

Technically the picture is of varying quality. Standard shots and crude prints achieve neorealistic nature in a comedy that is anything but neorealistic. Zilberg's direction and Helga Cranston's editing (she used to edit Laurence Olivier's pictures) help make the series of scenes into a quick-lough-getting film. The director also managed to supervise cleverly Meir Margalith's first film assignment. This legit actor, long an outstanding comedy star of Moliere, Schweik and other standard works, comes across naturally in this film. Zilberg should also be credited for good supporting performances by Shraga Friedman and Elisheva Michaeli, as accomplices of Simchon in furnishing the penthouse.

Some of the other actors, young and old, give credible and natural performances, and only crude scenes (like the photo studio and the nightclub set) expose the film's weaknesses. These are not made up for by Dov Seltzer's score, into which he incorporated his local hit, "Speak to Me With Flowers," and two twist tunes.

Because of its professional shortcomings, the film deserves a lesser success than is evident at the boxoffice. It is the younger set, who have been listening to the radio series, who crowd the cinemas in all three major cities joined by the people who are going to watch Meir Margalith, who had been awarded, on Independence Day, the highly respected Israel Prize for his lifework in the Israeli theatre.

For audiences abroad this "B" picture holds limited interest, mainly as a way of seeing the changed scene of Israel, still associted by many as a land of pioneers, idealistic and romantic human beings. Watching "Mishpahat Simchon" might give them a view of other Israeli scenes, not necessarily the most important or telling ones. *Port.*

Paradis Retur
(Paradise and Back)
(DANISH)

Copenhagen, April 7.

Nordisk Film production and release. Stars Poul Reichhardt, Lise Ringheim, Elsebeth Reingaard, Christoffer Bro. Directed by Gabriel Axel. Story, screenplay by Peter Ronild; camera, Jorgen Skov; music, Bent Fabricius-Bjerre. Reviewed at Palads Theatre, Copenhagen. Running time, **90 MINS.**

Tonnemann .... Poul Reichhardt
The Lady .... Lise Ringheim
Mona at 11 .... Nina Larsen
Mona at 16 .... Elsebeth Reingaard
Mona at 36 .... Winnie Sorensen
Tom at 11 .... Henning Olsen
Tom at 16 .... Christoffer Bro
Tom at 36 .... Poul Clemmensen
Borge .... Kjeld Jacobsen
The Actor .... Preben Lerdorff Rye

Peter Ronild is bogged down by his social selfconsciousness but lifted by this true poetic spirit in this loose-jointed story about offbeat people who have either chosen or been fated to live in shacks near a vast Copenhagen city dump. It is in a marshy region next to an army shooting range. Ronild's screenplay has practically no outer drama, but Gabriel Axel has directed with a firm eye for whatever dramatic scraps he finds among the spoils.

"Paradise" is an earnest attempt to make a film that remains true to its intentions. Unfortunately, the intentions are more often naive than rawboned. Several sequences are handled in an experimental style that by now must be considered rather oldhat, newsreel shots frozen in the middle of the action and attempted take-offs on the syle of the silents.

But no audience can help but feel sympathy towards this collection of misfits. There's Poul Reichhardt, the man with the dreams of travels on the high seas; Kjeld Jacobsen, who during the war had found security in a Nazi uniform; the children are just children, still innocent of the predicament of their surroundings; the youngsters, groping toward their various guiding lights and desires. Latter two are played with exceptional restraint by Elsebeth Reingaard and Christoffer Bro.

There is no direct action, but a certain pattern gradually is formed. War is always a threat, but peacetime society threatens even more with its inertia and ignorance. Reichhardt had joined the resistance movement during the last World War but hates the dirty gun work. The children, even in the city dump of a welfare state, pursue their schooling towards various careers.

The film cannot make up its mind how and when to end, and so it has five different endings, all of them seemingly pessimistic. Even though this is in black and white, the film is not without its touches of color. It looks like respectable business looms at some art theatres for this pic. *Kell.*

The Silent Playground
(BRITISH)

Above-average low budget second feature, featuring new blood. Merits enthusiastic reception.

London, April 16.

British Lion release through BLC of a Focus Film Production. Stars Jean Anderson, Bernard Archerd, Roland Curram. Produced by George Mills. Written & directed by Stanley Giulder; camera, Martin Curtis; editor, Peter Musgrave; music, Tristram Carey. Previewed April 15, '64 at British Lion Private Theatre. Running time, **75 MINS.**

Lacey .... Roland Curram
Duffy .... Bernard Archerd
Mrs. Lacey .... Jean Anderson
Mavis .... Ellen McIntosh
Alan .... John Ronane
Dr. Green .... Desmond Llewellyn
Jane Wilson .... Rowena Gregory
Sgt. Clark .... Basil Beale

Brought in in 24 days at a modest $75,000, with entire location shooting and a little known cast, this is one of British Lion's frequent recent attempts to prove that the dualler can be top level product in entertainment and technical content. This exciting little drama amply proves the distributors' point. It is a quality production which scores heavily against some of its loftier rivals. Writer-director Stanley Boulder has had documentary experience but this is his first essay in feature work. His screenplay is taut, economic and natural in dialog and his direction is unfussy and alert. Technically he has smart aid, with crisp cutting, an evocative unobtrusive score by Tristram Carey and fine lensing by Martin Curtis which not only captures the atmosphere of the London suburb in which the pic was shot but produces some really attractive, bleak photography in river and snow sequences.

The story, which has a useful reminder to parents and moppets, "never take sweets from a stranger," concerns a mentally retarded youth who loves kids. Returning from the hospital where he is an out-patient he hands out highly colored barbituate tablets to youngsters in a cinema matinee queue. End of show finds a number of unconscious children slumped in their seats. All are dangerously ill. Then begins the patient fight for their lives at the local hospital, while the police hunt for the donor of the tablets. The two themes are neatly married, with the tracking down of the hapless youth having mounting tension.

Jean Anderson, who plays the half-wit's worried mother with dignity, is the best konwn name in the cast, though Bernard Archard, a brisk, credible police officer, is a w.k. tv thesp. Newcomer Roland Curram is a pitiable creature as the quarry and looks full of promise. Ellen McIntosh and John Ronane provide a slight, but likeable romantic interlude, Miss McIntosh being the widowed mother of three key children being hunted by the cops before they take the tablets. Desmond Llewellyn, Rowena Gregory and a bunch of others, including several talented moppets, form a solid supporting cast.

The film never seeks sensationalism or the mawkishness that could have arisen through the time of action, which is immediately pre-Christmas. Despite a lack of marquee bait, "The Silent Playground" booked with another carefully chosen film demands keen attention from exhibs. *Rich.*

Il Pelo Nel Mondo
(Go, Go, Go, World)
(ITALIAN)
(Color)

Rome, April 7.
Atlantica release of a Marco Vicario production. Directed by Renato Marzi, Anthony Dawson. Camera (Eastmancolor), Giovanni Raffaldi, Giancarlo Lari, Marcello Gallinelli; editor, Mario Morra; music, Nino Oliviero. At Capranica, Rome. Running time, **95 MINS.**

Latest in Italian documentary-feature skein of the "Mondo Cane" genre is one of the better ones, rising head and shoulders over the mass of exploitation items which have drugged the market in recent months. Elegant lensing, rather than some of the cheap pickup stuff used in many other similar pix, gives it the flash of class. And a witty, ironic commentary (in the Italian version seen, at least; an English language and French version are also ready) add to film's plus points. It should find a suitable market in many areas.

But it must be added that the rash of previous pix along these lines has severely limited possibilities of originality for this one. There are, to be sure, several in-

---

teresting, colorful, and sensational bits. But there are also many not so entertaining.

Blood, gore and folklore are musts here, too, and there are the now-familiar bits showing strange Eastern eating habits, Southern Italian religious ceremonies, tribal customs and the oft-seen shots of aged Yank tourists cavorting in Hawaii, lensed with ridiculous intent and here definitely over-indulged and in bad taste.

Other musts are the Spanish bulls running through a town, exploitable strip numbers, the U.S. Bowery, the Cannes bikini bit, Hong Kong sampan poverty row, etc. Effective windup with a moral is montage of the Italian auto mania, followed by clean, free zooming of a brace of jet planes into and beyond the Italian Alps.

Mario Morra's editing plays part in making this latter bit, and its adroit in most other transitions from sequence to sequence.

Nino Oliviero's musical score provides a major assist in general tone of lushly outfitted production. Incom Studios have fashioned some very effective animated titles. *Hawk.*

La Calda Vita
(The Warm Life)
(ITALO-FRENCH)

Rome, April 5.
Unidis release of a Jolly Film-Les Films Agiman co-production. Features Catherine Spaak, Gabriele Ferzetti, Jacque Perrin, Fabrizio Capucci. Directed by Florestano Vancini. Screenplay, Vancini. Fondato, Bartolini. Camera (Eastmancolor), Roberto Guardi. Music, Carlo Rustichelli. At Modernissimo, Rome. Running time, **97 MINS.**

Uneven pic. Some good human and physical values. But basic lack of warmth, hence low believability prevents ultimate satisfaction. Cast names will help in Italy, but elsewhere, release is on its own, with iffy chances.

Two youngsters on the make take a young girl along on an island vacation. She's basically game, but can't decide between the introverted Jacques Perrin and extroverted (but slightly neurotic) Fabrizio Capucci. Eventually she falls for older third man who happens by, Gabriele Ferzetti. At windup, however, and after introvert has committed suicide, gal decides not to get involved with anyone and goes off alone.

Catherine Spaak is once more easy to look at, acts with professional aplomb despite so-so material, and also provides exploitable footage along the way. Vancini's direction is technically fine, but he fails in bringing his characters to life, at least in case of two youngsters, resolving sequences involving them with almost endless staring and brooding (on the part of Perrin), and cavorting or pouting (by Capucci). Closing part of pic, mostly between Miss Spaak and Ferzetti, are on different plane and ring true, thanks also to a solid performance by thesps. There is a definite feeling of stylistic influence, conscious or not, by Michelangelo Antonioni and his "Avventura"—also because of island setting.

Camerawork in splendid Sardinian settings is a technical plus. So is Carlo Rustichelli's musical

---

scoring. Miss Spaak also sings song (Non e M'eute), over titles in her now-characteristic effective style. *Hawk.*

Argentina Fest

El Demonio En La Sangre
(Demon in the Blood)
(ARGENTINE)

Buenos Aires, April 14.
Columbia Pictures presentation of a Sergio Kogan production. Features Rosita Quintana, Arturo Garcia Buhr, Ubaldo Martinez, Wolf Ruvinski, Pinky, Ernesto Bianco, Lidia Lamaison. Directed by Rene Mugica. Screenplay, Augusto Roax Bastos, Tomas Eloy Martinez; camera, Ricardo Younis, Oscar Melli; music, Rodolfo Arizago. At Buenos Aires Film Festia, April 10, '64. Running time, **75 MINS.**

Director Rene Mugica's technical but not story virtuosity is evident throughout this three-part Argentine episodic pic detailing various ways in which evil takes hold of rather ordinary people. Unfortunately for the viewer, evil (and/or the devil) doesn't seem to be too inventive. The first episode is made up of the hallucination of a near-mortally wounded Negro boxer, who has a vision of his manager hypnotizing him into destroying all the people who have been good to him. The second is a sort of watered-down "Tell-Tale Heart," in which a murdered wife comes back to haunt her husband and his mistress. The third is an ironic tale of a puritan husband, his bored wife and a stranger, who may or may not be the devil and who sets out to seduce the wife. *Anby.*

His Own Blood
(RUSSIAN)

Buenos Aires, April 14.
Lenfilm presentation. Stars Evgueni Matvie, Via Artmane, with Anatoli Papanov, Vladimir Ratomski, Igor Seliuzhonok, Yura Fisenkov, Tania Doronina, Vera Povetnika, Andrei Danilov, Kola Morozov. Directed by Mijail Ershov. Screenplay, Fiodor Knorre; camera, Oleg Kujovarenco; music, V. Basner. At Buenos Aires Film Festival, April 10, '64. Running time, **92 MINS.**

Honesty of emotion and simplicity of treatment are the virtues of "His Own Blood," an appealing love story set in the closing days of World War II. Pic, however, does not seem to possess the kind of dramatic distinction which might create boxoffice interest in the international market.

Story concerns a returned soldier and his "courtship" of a sweet young woman who, with her three small children, has been abandoned by her husband. The soldier eventually persuades the woman to bring her children and set up housekeeping with him. Title derives from the contest over custody of the children between the step-father and the real father which ensues when the woman dies suddenly during an emergency operation (for reasons never specified, at least in the Spanish subtitles seen by this reviewer).

Central roles are nicely played by Evgueni Matvie and Via Artmane. *Anby.*

Mount Venus
(GERMAN)

Buenos Aires, April 9.
A Gala Selection release, produced by Franz Seitz and featuring Marissa Mell, Nicole Radal, Monica Flodquist, Ina Duscha, Claudia Marus, Christine Granberg and Jane Axell. Directed and written by Rolf Thiele. Director of Photography, Wolf Wirth. Camera, Rudolf Schloemp. At Buenos Aires Film Festival. Running time, **92 MINS.**

Though this "Mount Venus" may look like an art film at first sight, it is in reality arty. Photography is beautiful, even exciting and certainly difficult, from a technical point of view. Each frame is carefully balanced; a great many shots are made against the light of large windows and there are also some near-high key effects. Wolf Wirth and Rudolf Schloem certainly deserve credit for their excellent work.

The same can not be said for director Thiele, who handles his actresses as if they were models and even, in some cases, fails to individualize them properly. Stylistically the film is beautiful to look at; in content it is empty and, worse, pretentious. A sort of femenine "Waiting for Godot," that is not only heavyhanded but lacks humor. Godot in this case is not a mysterious entity, but a gynecologist named Alphonse. It would appear that all the vapid symbolism of this pic adds up to the simple fact that woman needs man and that lesbianism is not an easy way out. It certainly seems a roundabout way four estabishing such a truism.

"Mount Venus," might stand a chance at art-houses delving in the seudo-erotic and arty. *Chile.*

Psyche 59

Dim, dense psychological meller. Oscarwinner Patricia Neal name will have to carry.

Hollywood, April 21.

Columbia Pictures release of Phillip Hazelton production. Stars Curt Jurgens, Patricia Neal, Samantha Eggar, Ian Bannen. Directed by Alexander Singer. Screenplay, Julian Halevy, from the novel by Francoise des Ligneris; camera, Walter Lassally; editor, Max Benedict; music, Kenneth V. Jones; assistant director, David Bracknell. Reviewed at the studio, April 21, '64. Running time, 94 MINS.

Eric Crawfird .... Curt Jurgens
Alison .... Patricia Neal
Robin .... Samantha Eggar
Paul .... Ian Bannen
Mrs. Crawford .... Beatrix Lehmann
Madame Valadier .... Elspeth March
Susan .... Sandra Lee
Jean .... Shelley Crowhurst

Presence of Academy Awardwinner Patricia Neal should help boxoffice prospects of "Psyche 59," and it's going to need all the help it can get. As a matter of fact, a synopsis should be provided each customer, to clarify what's going on in this Columbia release. The psychological melodrama that occurs on the screen is muddled, monotonous and opaque.

Four weirdos cavort mysteriously in Julian Halevy's contrived screenplay from the novel by Francoise des Ligneris. It's not always clear which character is to be despised, but there are times when all four seem to fall into that category. Pivotal figure in the bizarre tale is the psychosomatically blind wife (Miss Neal) of an industrialist (Curt Jurgens) who is trying to plug the gap in her memory that is responsible for her non-vision. She's the only one in the theatre who doesn't know. The audience easily deduces that she went "blind" when she caught hubby Jurgens in the sack with her baby sister (Samantha Eggar). It's also no surprise when she regains her sight upon finding them in the hay again, after which she feigns blindness long enough to convince herself they're sick, sick, sick.

Further compounding the deficiencies of Halevy's scenario are Alexander Singer's deliberately-paced, artsy-craftsy direction (too much technical razzle-dazzle at the expense of clarifying dramatic matters) and Max Benedict's careless editing, which evidently eliminates scenes even if they render subsequent events mighty peculiar. Walter Lassally has contributed some flashy photographic strokes. Sensitive sound by George Stephenson and Red Law, expressive art direction by John Stoll and a creepy score by Kenneth V. Jones are assets to the Troy-Schenck production, produced in England by Phillip Hazelton.

Miss Neal manages a persuasive portrayal of the blind woman. Jurgens is pretty sour and unpleasant as her roving mate. Samatha Eggar plays the vixen with spirit and oomph. Any excuse to get her into something flimsy and revealing seems to suffice, even when it's irrelevant—such as when she admires and narcissistically paws herself in front of a full-length mirror in scanty panties. at, whatever the epidermis-to-clothing ratio. Ian Bannen plays Fortunately, she's pleasant to look a "friend of the famliy" in love with Miss Eggar. Most of the time he just sulks and sulks around in the background. Beatrix Lehmann plays a fifth screwball—Miss Neal's astrologically-oriented grandmother.

The title apparently has something to do with the date at which the heroine went blind, although that's a guess. All it really accomplishes is to make the picture sound five years old. *Tube*

Pyro

Weak horror meller barely adequate for companion status on a shock program.

Hollywood, April 17.

American-International release of Sidney-W. Pink-Harry E. Eller production. Stars Barry Sullivan and Martha Hyer. Directed by Julio Coll. Screenplay by Louis De Los Arcos and Sidney W. Pink from a story by Pink. Produced by Pink and Richard C. Meyer; camera, Manuel Berenguer; editor, Margaret Ochoa; music, Jose Sola. Reviewed in Joe Shore's projection room, April 17, '64. Running time, 99 MINS.

There are several saleable elements in this Spanish-lensed Pink-Eller production for American International release. Among them the familiar names of Barry Sullivan and Martha Hyer, some attractive Panacolor photography and fire sequences which offer a good exploitation peg. Film, however, is so weighted with stilted dialog and plot absurdities that it emerges barely servicable for even the lesser half of a double bill, a position which it has been assigned to occupy with AIP's "Goliath and the Vampires."

Nearly half the picture is spent on Sullivan's extra-marital dabblings with Miss Hyer. He is an American engineer in Spain at work on a dam and she apparently just a resident Bad Apple. When Sullivan returns to the family fold Miss Hyer sets fire to his house. His wife and child die and he is horribly disfigured. Mummy-swathed in bandages, Sullivan flees the hospital swearing vengeance on his ex-mistress which he ultimately achieves, along the way having adopted a new identity and a slightly altered face (revealed a mask in denouement) though exhibiting none of the madness with which searching police insist he is afflicted until finale.

It is the sort of picture which with a less awkward script might have found a profitable niche on the horror circuit, but burdened as it is with inadvertently laugh-provoking dialog and only a modicum of the necessary horror-suspense, it falls far short of the mark. Julio Coll directed from a script by Louis De Los Arcos and Sidney W. Pink from a story by Pink.

Sullivan and Miss Hyer play it straight all the way, something which, particularly in the case of Sullivan, must have demanded all of their professional discipline. Sherry Moreland as Sullivan's wife is wooden and of the Spanish cast only Fernando Hilbeckas a friend of Sullivan's makes a positive impression. Make-up man Carmen Martin did a first rate job on Sullivan's chared face. Manuel Berenguer's camerawork is good. *Fess.*

Bande A Part
(Gang of Outsiders) (FRENCH)

Paris, April 28.

Columbia Films release of Anouchka Films, Orsay production. Stars Anna Karina, Sami Frey, Claude Brasseur; features Louisa Colpeyn. Written and directed by Jean-Luc Godard from novel, "Fool's Gold," by D. and B. Hitchens. Camera, Raoul Coutard; editor, Agnes Guillemot. Previewed in Paris. Running time, 95 MINS.

Odile .... Anna Karina
Franz .... Sami Frey
Artur .... Claude Brasseur
Aunt .... Louisa Colpeyn

Ex-Waver Jean-Luc Godard still looms one of the most inventive and personal among the younger filmmakers in France today. So his pix are filled with personal gags, homages to past and present masters, and his own angles. If it sometimes makes them restricted to art and buff releases, they always have a sweep, and humor that have them also capable of more direct adhesion by art and selective, and even regular audiences.

This one seems his most accessible pic since his first one "Breathless" and his recent Brigitte Bardot starrer, "Contempt." Careful handling could have this a solid specialized item abroad on its general gusto. If unorthodox, Godard here avoids his usual jump cuts, free ellipses and prowling camera. It is made completely in exterior and real interiors. And the pic benefits from this in giving its rambling tale a cogency and realistic basis to its breezy carryings-on.

Two friends, Franz and Artur, meet a waif-like girl, Odile, in an English course they are taking. She lives with a relative in a house outside of Paris and there is a pile of money kept loosely in a wardrobe. It seems the money has never been declared. At any rate, she mentions it to the youths and they decide to steal it with her help.

The youths have a sketchy background if they manage to be able to own a car. Artur belongs to an underworld-type family of thieves while Franz's family is unclear. The girl, Odile, goes along with the holdup against her will. It ends in catastrophe when Artur's uncle, who wanted in on it, kills him when they try to do it without him. Artur manages to get him before dying.

Franz and Odile go off with some of the money to some distant land and new adventures with a sequel promised by the voice of Godard himself on the soundtrack. In fact, he makes several little speeches during the film on the comportment and outlooks of his characters.

There is neat observation about the antics of this strange trio. If seemingly outside of life, they do give an impression of yearning and wanting something that is unattainable. The holdup is one way to it. They play at cowboys in mock games, do a dance in a cafe together. They tell little tales and finally get down to the partly successful holdup.

Anna Karina has a fragile, wide-eyed appearance as the girl which fit the part. Besides this, she brings a dramatic intensity that keeps her from slipping into sentimentality. She can even sing a song on a subway, comment on the sadness around her and her deep compassion, without having it seem wrong.

Sami Frey is intense and brooding as Franz while Claude Brasseur has an animal aggressiveness as the little hoodlum who has sparks of decency and warmth and finally dies in the heroic manner of many of his film gangster, heroes. Godard obviously admires the silent and 1930's Yank action pix and comedies. Hence, he manages to capture the freewheeling human simplicity of those days and still seem modern and fresh.

Excellent lensing also is an asset. Godard shows he is a complete filmic creator in being able to mark each scene with visual authority, movement and interest. However, this penchant also sometimes makes his films too private and repetitious for general public acceptance. Thus, it calls for tactful handling. Made for $100,000, Columbia should have an okay value out of it with the right placement.

Its telling points are its inventive pace and observation and its refusal to make concessions. Accepted on its own terms by more discerning audiences, this has comedic and dramatic potency. It could also conceivably pay off if patrons are primed for it. *Mosk.*

The Bargee
(BRITISH—TECHNICOLOR)

Patchy comedy with sound local marquee bait; enlivened by Hugh Griffith, but fails to fulfill its promise.

London, April 28.

Warner-Pathe release of an Associated British presentation of a (W. A. Whittaker) Galton-Simpson production. Stars Harry H. Corbett, Hugh Griffith, Eric Sykes; features Julia Foster, Miriam Karlin, Ronnie Barker, Derek Nimmo, Eric Barker, Norman Bird. Directed by Duncan Wood. Original story and screenplay, Ray Galton & Alan Simpson; camera, Harry Waxman; editor, Richard Best; music, Frank Cordell. At Empire Theatre, London. Running time, 106 MINS.

Hemel .... Harry H. Corbett
Joe .... Hugh Griffith
The Mariner .... Eric Sykes
Ronnie .... Ronnie Barker
Christine .... Julia Foster
Nellie .... Miriam Karlin
Foreman .... Eric Barker
Doctor Scott .... Derek Nimmo
Waterways Supervisor .... Norman Bird
Tomkins .... Richard Briers
Policeman .... Brian Wilde
Office Official .... George A. Cooper
Girl in Office .... Grazina Frame
Cynthia .... Jo Rowbottom
Barman .... Edwin Apps
Announcer .... Godfrey Winn

Maybe this scrappy comedy suffers from an overdose of interbreeding. It is the first production of Ray Galton and Alan Simpson, tv script creators of BBC's prominent "Steptoe and Son" series. It is the first feature film directed by Duncan Wood, responsible for staging the "Steptoe and Son" episodes. And it stars Harry C. Corbett (Steptoe Jr.). Anyway, the Steptoe influence looms large and has thrown this yarn of a bargee off balance. With a refreshing new background of the British waterways, a capable cast and an acceptable enough yarn, it still fails to click, though it will provide spasmodic amusement for the easy-going.

Corbett plays a dyed-in-the-wool marriage-shy bargee who loves the life and particularly the freedom it gives him with the dames. He builds up a reputation as the

"Casanova of the Canals." But on the screen evidence, this is merely the result of a few skirmishes with two or three riverside femmes. There is no motivation in his character and it is fair to assume that either the censor or the distributors have clipped out much of the incident that would have given weight to his amorous exploits. Woven into a string of motley situations is the fact that he is eventually lured out of bachelordum through getting the daughter of an irascible lock-keeper into the family way. It's a slim incident on which to hang a comedy which never makes up its mind whether to be farce or not.

There are a few intriguing glimpses into the way of life of the fast lying bargee clan. Harry Waxman's color photography adds greatly to the refreshing charm of the British countryside. Though, of course, the weather always seems to be good and the life of a bargee is thus shown to be rather more delectable than it probably is. Although some of the dialog is richly perky and a few of the situations prompt laughs in somewhat haphazard fashion the storyline is not strong enough and Wood's direction is too meandering.

It rests with the cast to give the screenplay of Galton and Simpson a much needed lift. And here the production team is well served. The pic mainly comes to life when Hugh Griffith dominates the screen with a rictously overplayed and gloriously hammed-up performance as the heroine's irascible dad. Eyes bulging, his dialog pumped to life by Griffith's own turn of phrase he gives a joyful performance of ire, cunning and boisterous boozy comedy. This performance does most to keep "The Bargee" afloat. Miriam Karlin also makes a brief, larger-than-life appearance as an irate barmaid who has been two-timed by Corbett. But, inexcusably, the character is allowed to disappear early in the proceedings.

With Steptoe-ish intonations, gestures and philosophy, Corbett can do little to shake off his tv image but fulfills the part of the "anti-hero" with vigor. His buddy, Ronnie Barker, is a tubby little character comedian, highly likable but not likely to become a star but should have a profitable future as a feature player.

On the distaff side, apart from Miss Karlin, there's nothing outstanding. Julia Foster is no more than adequate as a colorless heroine, though Jo Rowbottom and Grazina Frame contribute a brace of lively bits. Derek Nimmo makes sharp impact as a nervous young doctor. Nimmo has one fine scene with Griffith when he breaks the news to the father that his daughter is pregnant and Griffith vainly tries to make the young medico marry her. This is a choice piece of comedy.

Biggest calamity is the casting of Eric Sykes, a witty, eccentric comedian, as a nincompoop of a landlubber who is a river menace with his little cruiser. Sykes is, inevitably, the fall guy who lands in the river. Throughout the pic, he has to cope with a role which is badly written.

A brisker pace, a little less (or a little more) genuine slapstick and considerably more gaiety could have made "The Bargee" a far more tempting vehicle than it is.

Rich.

Parias De La Gloire
(Pariahs of Glory)
(FRENCH-DYALISCOPE)

Paris, April 20.

Gaumont release of Paris-France Films, Films Marly, Oceeans Films, Sagittario Film production. Stars Curt Jurgens, Maurice Ronet, Folco Lulli; features Roland Lesaffre, Tiny Yong. Directed by Henri Decoin. Screenplay, Roger Delpay; camera, Frederic Larraya; editor, Juan Soler. At Ambassade, Paris. Running time, **95 MINS.**

Lud .... Curt Jurgens
Ferrier .... Maurice Ronet
Borsky .... Folco Lulli
Cook .... Roland Lesaffre
Girl .... Tiny Yong

French filmmakers do not make many pix on the Indo-Chinese and Algerian wars, but when they do, they do so gingerly. But this one is full of cliches, grandiloquence and pretentiousness, without even a helping leavening of well-done action sequences, to make this primarily a local bet.

A French outpost company awaits reinforcement in the jungle during the Indo-Chinese troubles. A plane with a German planter in it makes a forced landing nearby. It seems he was a German officer during the last World War and a Frenchman hates him immediately since his brother had been killed by a German officer.

Of course, it turns out to be him but under fire they help each other and die in each others' arms as the French officer gives the German back his war decoration that he had confiscated. A worthwhile theme about allaying war hatreds is smothered in conventional, forced histrionics and heroics.

Lacklustre direction does not help nor do ordinary production aspects. Curt Jurgens uses too many false mannerisms and overplays his role of the German. Maurice Ronet is listless as the French German-hater. Others are adequate. The few fighting scenes are only passable in their execution.

Mosk.

Goliath and The Vampires
(ITALIAN-COLOR)

Musclebound action fantasy. All brawn, no brain.

Hollywood, April 22.

American International release of Paolo Moffa production. Stars Gordon Scott. Directed by Giacomo Gentilomo. Screenplay, Sergio Corbucci, Ducci Tezzari; camera (Colorscope), Alvaro Mancori; editor, Eraldo Da Roma. Reviewed at Iris Theatre, April 22, '64. Running time, **91 MINS.**

Goliath .... Gordon Scott
Astra .... Gianna Maria Canale
Buono .... Jacques Sernas
Julia .... Leonora Ruffo
Magda .... Annabella Incontrera

Even the most ardent devotees of these overstuffed, simpleminded muscle spasms from Italy figure to be disenchanted with this latest entry in that league. Ludicrously written and crudely executed, the American International release may, through hefty exploitation campaigning, rack up some rupees in early dates before word-of-mouth catches up with it.

Erstwhile "Tarzan" Gordon Scott is the new "Goliath." In this one, his brawny biceps are pitted against a superhuman, sanguinary fiend who is enslaving the populace of an ancient region by turning them into bloodless robots subjected to his will. Just when it looks as if the home team hasn't got a chance, the monster unaccountably makes the mistake of assuming Goliath's identity, providing the audience with the odd climactic spectacle of Gordon Scott fighting himself to the death.

Scott's historionics are about as subtle as a statement by Cassius Clay. Also prominently implicated in the dubbed Paolo Moffa production and Dino De Laurentiis presentation are Gianna Maria Canale as a villainess and Jacques Sernas as a kindly chemist.

Tube.

A Place To Go
(BRITISH)

Well worn theme of London's East End family life. One or two handy performances, but minor appeal.

London, April 21.

British Lion-Bryanston release through BLC of a Bryanston presentation of a Michael Relph-Basil Dearden production. Stars Mike Sarne, Rita Tushingham, Bernard Lee. Features Doris Hare, Jerry Verno, David Andrews, William Marlowe, Roy Kinnear, Barbara Ferris, Norman Shelley. Produced by Michael Relph. Directed by Basil Dearden. Screenplay by Relph from Michael Fisher's novel; camera, Reginald Wyer; editor, John D. Guthridge; music, Charles Blackwell. Previewed April 15, '64 at Columbia Theatre, London. Running time, **86 MINS.**

Matt .... Bernard Lee
Catherine .... Rita Tushingham
Ricky .... Michael Sarne
Lil .... Doris Hare
Betsy .... Barbara Ferris
Jack Ellerman .... John Slater
Jim .... David Andrews
Charle Batey .... William Marlowe
Pug .... Michael Wynne
Sally .... Marjorie Lawrence
Bunting .... Roy Kinnear
Magistrate .... Norman Shelley
Nobby Knowles .... Jerry Verno

The experienced team of Michael Relph and Basil Dearden might well have been expected to come across with a more lively, incisive treatment of even such a tired old theme as "A Place To Go." But it has defeated them, and despite one or two brisk directorial touches and a few dependable performances, they are left wallowing in cliches. "A Place To Go" has an apt title, for it is the sort of film that may pass away an hour and a half, providing a person has no place to go but the cinema.

Usually with a keen feeling for comment on social problems, this time Relph and Dearden have settled for treading unadventurously along a familiar route. The scene is Bethnal Green in London's East End, and here Dearden has captured some vivid atmosphere, ably supported by Reginald Wyer's crisp photography. But the plot is a ragbag of incidents that seem to have been used in so many similar films too often. A flick knife fight, young hero involved in crime with a petty local gang, sentimental mum not wanting to leave her surroundings, boozeups in the local taverns, tippling, independent dad, young married daughter and husband living at home with baby and desperately yearning for a place of their own, but not doing much about it, boys wrangling over birds, furtive under-the-canal love making. It's all there, but no imagination has been brought to bear to give the job a lift.

Dialog ranges from the corny to the breezy, via brusque sentimentality. Situations occur but do little to jog the plot along. The makers of this film have unsuccessfully tried to disguise the fact that they have no pertinent views or comment to make on their subject. They have relied on a workmanlike cast, and two or three engaging performances crop up. It introduces pop singer Mike Sarne, who as well as warbling a couple of numbers, has the leading juve role. His is a new face and fresh personality and, in time, experience may well provide the screen with a useful young thesp. Rita Tushingham brings her usual, perky, gamine-like quality to the role of his self-possessed girl friend. Lacking conventional good looks, Miss Tushingham has a sparkling offbeat personality and livens the screen whenever she appears. She will have to guard against getting typed in this kind of role, however, if her real potentiality is to be developed. Doris Hare and Bernard Lee, with the experience of seasoned troupers, ring every laugh and possible sob out of their chores, John Slater is a credible minor crook and William Marlowe occasionally shows a glimpse of subtle viciousness as a young hood. David Andrews and Barbara Ferris cope with thankless tasks as the newlyweds, and Jerry Verno, Norman Shelly and Roy Kinnear weigh in with dependable cameos.

The Relph-Dearden record is good enough to ride a complete flop in films, but it can be even more precarious to turn out a piece of comparative nothingness. Location shots, artwork and editing are all satisfactory and Charles Blackwell's theme song may prove a hit parade challenger. Lack of marque bait may not matter overmuch in Britain, where Miss Tushingham has a pull and Sarne a ready made adolescent pop following, but abroad its chances are edgy.

Rich.

Gladiators 7
(SPANISH-ITALIAN—C'SCOPE—COLOR)

Heavyhanded period action meller for male-oriented, hit-and-run exploitation mill.

Hollywood, April 20.

Metro release of Cleto Fontini-Italo Zingarelli production. Directed by Pedro Lazaga. Screenplay, Sandro Continenza, Bruno Corbucci, Alberto De Martino, Giovanni Grimaldi; camera (Eastman), Adalberto Albertini, Eloy Mella; editor, Otello Colangeli; music, Marcello Giobini. Reviewed at the studio, April 20, '64. Running time, **92 MINS.**

Darius .... Richard Harrison
Aglaia .... Loredana Nusciak
Panurgus .... Livio Lorenzon
Hiarba .... Gerard Tichy
Milon .... Edoardo Toniolo
Xeno .... Joseph Marco
Flaccus .... Barta Barry
Vargas .... Tony Zamperla
Lucia .... Franca Badeschi
Livius .... Enrique Avila
Macrobius .... Antonio Molino
Mados .... Antonio Rubio
Ismere .... Emila Wolkowics

Hard-sell exploitation of action and sex elements, together with saturation bookings, should help to get the mostest for Metro out of this import, which is handicapped by lack of cast names recognizable to Yank audiences.

For even in these overstuffed, quasi-historical, post-dubbed extravaganzas in which the Italians specialize, there is a limit to heroic indestructibility beyond which audience concern evaporates and the necessary element of suspense dwindles to zero. This saturation point is reached in "Gladiators 7," a Spanish-Italian coproduction filmed in Rome and Madrid.

Four writers toiled on the cliche-riddled screenplay of the Cleto Fontini-Italo Zingarelli production, a mutual enterprise of Rome's Film Columbus SPA and Madrid's Atenea Films. Setting of the story is Sparta of first century A.D., a so-called "democracy," but actually under the yoke of Rome and governed by native tyrants. Film describes the successful effort of a patriot Spartan (Richard Harrison) to overthrow one of these tyrants, a chore in which he is aided by a handful of gladiators. Even Clark Kent wouldn't have a chance against these seven gladiators. It would be safe to estimate that 100 assorted Romans and Spartans are slain in hand-to-hand combat by this tiny band. Yet there they are at the ending——a happy, intact septet. Not even a bloody nose.

The acting is stiff and mechanical, and the dubbing doesn't help histrionic matters any. Chief roles are essayed without distinction by Harrison, Gerard Tichy and Loredana Nusciak. Director Pedro Lazaga has engineered several vigorous action sequences (a bullring bout between a bull and a bare-handed gladiator, though shopworn, is the best action passage), but otherwise his guidance is erratic in tempo and dramatically heavyhanded. Camerawork is energetic but the editing is crude and abrupt. Other production contributions are adequate. *Tube.*

The New Interns

Flashy sequel to "The Interns." Same highly marketable formula. Should be equally as popular, especially with younger, less demanding audiences.

Hollywood· May 5.
Columbia Pictures release of Robert Cohn production. Stars Michael Callan, Telly Savalas, Stefanie Powers, Barbara Eden, Kay Stevens. Inger Stevens; introduces George Segal. Directed by John Rich. Screenplay, Wilton Schiller, based on characters from Richard Frede's novel, "The Interns"; camera, Lucien Ballard; editors, Gene Milford, Eda Warren; music, Earle Hagen; asst. director, Michael Moder. Reviewed at Beverly Theatre, April 20, '64. Running time, **122 MINS.**
Dr. Alec Considine...... Michael Callan
Dr. Lew Worship .... Dean Jones
Gloria Worship .... Stefanie Powers
Laura Rogers .... Barbara Eden
Dr. Riccio .... Telly Savalas
Dr. Tony Parelli .... George Segal
Didi Loomis .... Kay Stevens
Nancy .... Inger Stevens
Freddie .... Jimmy Mathers
Beep .... Michael Vandever
Dr. Phil Osterman .... George Furth
Madeline .... Ellie Wood
Mrs. Hitchcock .... Lee Patrick
Clarke .... Greg Morris
Welanski .... Adam Williams
Chaum .... Gordon Kee
Stella .... Sue Ann Langdon
Bobbie .... Dawn Wells
Dr. Cranchard .... Gregory Morton
Dr. Hellman .... Michael Fox

Utilizing the same formula that proved commercially successful on "The Interns" two years ago, producer Robert Cohn has fashioned a followup that is superior in some respects to the original. Unless there has been a radical shift in the disposition of young audiences toward medical characters and hospital hi-jinks—a thoroughly exploited theatre of operations in recent entertainment annals—the new Columbia release should at least duplicate the success of its predecessor.

With attractive young players as marquee bait and a cool, hip, hot-rod-tempoed style to back it up, the film is shrewdly geared for youthful cinematic appetites. It is a kind of Hippocratic "Beach Party," with stethoscopes instead of surfboards. Also detectable in its combined comic-dramatic approach are elements of "West Side Story" and "Carry On, Nurse."

Actually, there are many things wrong with "The New Interns," insofar as more discerning audiences would be concerned. Principal flaw is the transparency of the central dramatic situations created by writer Wilton Schiller. The alert filmgoer could easily remain a step ahead of Schiller's plot machinations. And no doubt eight out of 10 doctors would agree that any resemblance between the lovable, one-big-happy-family bunch of interns and the real McCoy is purely coincidental. But such reservations aren't apt to modify the enjoyment of the less finicky, less selective mass audience.

Three principal romantic vignettes are interwoven in Schiller's dramatic fabric. One is light, two are heavy. The lighthearted facet, played for laughs, pairs Michael Callan as a girl-crazy dorm screwball and Barbara Eden as his unpredictable prey. "Obstetrician" Dean Jones and "nurse" Stefanie Powers team up in the most predictable of the three yarns as a couple whose matrimonial security is threatened by his sterility. Third story, the most melodramatic and contrived, involves hopeful surgeon George Segal, who has a

Dead-End-Kid past, and social worker Inger Stevens, whose life is wrecked by the vicious intrusion of a trio of delinquents. Overall thematic shell into which these three episodes are inserted is the depiction of the process by which candidate medics manage to mature into resident doctors.

Four principal members of the cast—Callan, Miss Powers, Telly Savalas, and Kay Stevens—are holdovers from the original. The others are new. Histrionic honors are won by the three male leads; Callan (the comedy standout), Jones (with a persuasive delineation) and Segal (a young man with modified Brando-like mannerisms who is officially "introduced" in this film). Savalas reels off another sound, reliable performance as the thrift-conscious administrative head of the hospital. Miss Powers wins the honors in the distaff department. An up-and-coming actress with a kind of Doris Day "wholesomeness" of style (at least in this vehicle), she's never looked better. Miss Eden hasn't much of a role, but does what she can with it. Inger Stevens has a tendency to overemote. Kay Stevens clowns it up in her customary fashion. Others of import in a film crammed with sub-plots are Ellie Wood, George Furth, Greg Morris, Lee Patrick, Adam Williams, Sue Ann Langdon, Dawn Wells, Gregory Morton, Michael Fox and young Jimmy Mathers. All perform creditably.

The kaleidoscopic style of the picture posed a challenge to director John Rich in maintaining dramatic momentum and coherence, and he has risen to the occasion. It's a commendable piece of directorial work. Astute, sometimes flashy, photography by Lucien Ballard and crisp, taut editing by Gene Milford and Eda Warren are major assists. Don Ament's art direction is convincing, Earle Hagen's musical score unobtrusively useful. *Tube.*

Wild And Wonderful
(COLOR)

Slight but often diverting trifle about a boozing, possessive canine. The dog should give it some b.o. bark.

Hollywood, April 21.
Universal release of Harold Hecht production. Stars Tony Curtis, Christine Kaufmann. Directed by Michael Anderson. Screenplay, Larry Markes, Michael Morris, Waldo Salt, from screen story by Richard M. Powell and Phillip Rapp, based on story by Dorothy Crider; camera (Eastman), Joseph LaShelle; editor, Gene Milford; music, Morton Stevens; asst. director, L. V. McCardle Jr. Reviewed at Grauman's Chinese, April 21, '64. Running time, **88 MINS.**
Terry Williams ...... Tony Curtis
Giselle .... Christine Kaufmann
Rufus .... Larry Storch
Doc .... Marty Ingels
Papa .... Jacques Aubuchon
Rousseleau .... Jules Munshin
Inspector Duvivier .... Marcel Hillaire
Pamela .... Sarah Marshall
Hercule .... Cliff Osmond
Dr. Reynard .... Marcel Dalio
Simone .... Fifi D'Orsay
Andre .... Vito Scotti
bartender .... Steven Geray
Mayor .... Stanley Adams
Musician .... Shelly Manne
Announcer .... Maurice Marsac
LeBeque .... Louis Mercier
Puffer .... Dante Cesari
Monique .... Danica d'Hondt
Gustav .... Guy De Vestel
Jacquot .... Pierre Olaf

Universal has what appears to be a profitable commodity in "Wild and Wonderful," a romantic comedy built around the antics of a

sheltered French movie star poodle whose jealousy is aroused when its mistress marries an American jazz musician. The joke is stretched thin, but easygoing audiences are apt to be amused by the feats performed by the talented pooch, and ardent dog lovers should find it irresistible. Tony Curtis and Christine Kaufman costar in the Harold Hecht production, but it's the dog, "Monsieur Cognac," that steals the picture.

The complicated writing credit goes as follows: screenplay by Larry Markes and Michael Morris and Waldo Salt from a screen story by Richard M. Powell and Phillip Rapp based on a story by Dorothy Crider. That's a lot of writers to filter a one-joke premise through. The going gets cumbersome in the middle stages, when the gag begins to drag and deteriorates to variations on a theme, but the film gets a fortunate life in a climactic television takeoff sequence that may not be an entirely fresh idea (it's a parody of a "Person to Person" type of program) but is executed well and comes off quite funny. The solution to the male canine's possessive passion for its mistress, apparent all along, is a female canine.

Curtis breezes through his role amiably and professionally, and Miss Kaufmann is a most decorative romantic partner. The attractiveness of Mrs. Curtis is emphasized by an array of glamorous gowns by Valentino of Rome. But histrionic honors are snared by the guzzling poodle, a virtual shoo-in for this year's PATSY. Behind every PATSY contender there's a trainer, in this case Frank Weatherwax, who's done an adroit job with "Cognac" and several other poodles. Jules Munshin is outstanding as the harassed director of the fractured tv show. Additional strong support is provided by Larry Storch, Marty Ingels, Jacques Aubuchon, Pierre Olaf, Marcel Hillaire and Sarah Marshall in key roles. Lesser support is equally gregarious, right down the line.

On the whole director Michael Anderson has extracted the maximum comedy mileage out of his material. The film is glamorously lensed by Joseph LaShelle and trimmed to a mercifully taut 88 minutes by editor Gene Milford. An excellent replica of the Montmartre district of Paris as well as some striking interiors have been designed by art directors Alexander Golitzen and Edward S. Haworth and constructed, on an elaborate scale, at Universal Studios. Morton Stevens' first motion picture score is effervescent and pleasing to the ear. *Tube.*

The Finest Hours
(BRITISH—TECHNICOLOR)

Engrossing documentary tribute to Sir Winston Churchill. Subject a colorful and classy boxoffice draw for all audiences.

London, May 1.
Columbia release through BLC of Jack Le Vien's production. Narrator, Orson Welles. Voices of Patrick Wymark, Faith Brook, George Baker, George Westbury, David Healy. Directed by Peter Baylis; screenplay by Victor Wolfson, based on Sir Winston Churchill's memoirs of "The Second World War"; camera, Hone Glendinning; research chief, Mary Baylis;

music, Ron Grainer. Opened April 30, '64 at Columbia Theatre, London. Running Time: **116 MINS.**

With infinite patience and enthusiasm Jack Le Vien has produced a fascinating tribute to Sir Winston Churchill which, while not kowtowing to the man, amply reveals Le Vien's admiration and respect for Britain's great war leader. It should prove a big, classy booking for all discriminate audiences, the man and the subject alone being enough to spark the interest of ducat buyers. Without the interest and co-operation of Churchill Le Vien's task would have been impossible. As it is, he and his team of researchers and technicians have done a sound job in compressing such a large canvas into the workmanlike span of 116 minutes.

As a tribute to Churchill, his career and, particularly his spectacular war effort, "The Finest Hours" amply fulfils its design. But as a permanent contribution to history it can be but a footnote. There is no critical appraisal in the film. The audience will get fascinating glimpses of the many faces of this man as warrior, statesman, orator and family man but there is no attempt to analyse any errors of judgment or consider the causes for the many setbacks in his mercurial 60-year career. But it does reveal clearly the tenacity, loyalty, world patriotism, courage and energy of one of the great men of this or any age. With all its omissions and facile scamper over many years it clearly reveals why both Britishers and the world had such confidence in the outcome of the Second World War, even in the darkest days. The fuel was there. Churchill was the flame that lit the fire which helped the Allies to defeat the Nazi and Italian tyranny.

He rallied a nation and, promising nothing but blood, sweat and tears, urged it to victory. The film begins symbolically. A small boy on the sands is building a fortress which starts to crumble and the Union Jack begins to sag. Across the screen is the silhouette of cigar-smoking Churchill. But from then on Le Vien tosses aside symbolism and shows facts. Many of them are familiar, culled from old newsreels, but there is also a lot of special shooting which gives new life to the picture. Even the newsreels are given fresh vitality and seem updated by color tinting which blends dramatically into the framework of the film.

The pic shows Churchill's birthplace at Bleinheim. Then him as a lad, a Sandhurst cadet, and a young officer in action in Cuba and South Africa. It portrays his entry into Parliament his rise to Minister status, his rejection into the wilderness, his comeback, the passionate devotion he put into his work as First Lord of the Admiralty, his taking over the Prime Ministership at time of crisis, his constant unflagging waging of war, then his post-war rejection and his final comeback as Prime Minister.

This is the pattern of his lifetime, showing events fitting him for what he must have sensed was his ultimate destiny. Many of the famous speeches are represented with the telling phrases, cajoling, rallying, warning, impish, witty and, above all, scornfully galling to the enemy. These when not actually spoken by Churchill in newsreels are put over by Patrick Wymark excellently. The thesp does not attempt an imitation of Churchill, but uncannily catches his intonation and the spirit of the typical Churchil phrases. Orson Welles delivers a commentary which is unobtrusive and remarkably subdued for Welles. It effectively binds the whole thing together. Other voices are those of Faith Brook as his mother, George Baker as his father and George Westbury as Churchill as a boy. "George Westbury," incidentally, is actually Marjorie Westbury, a longtime radio actress.

But Churchill is revealed not only as a man of vivid words, but also one of action. Nothing was too much trouble to satisfy his unquenchable curiosity and his desire to be in the thick of things. He and his cigar were familiar figures in every battle zone, either waddling across the desert in an outrageous garb, with pitch helmet, flying linen jacket and huge sand umbrella, inspecting troops and the tanks which were always a prime factor in war in his opinion, or attending high power conferences among warleaders and statesmen, on land, on sea and in the air. The film reveals that he was never far behind the men he was steeling to bigger and greater efforts. Yet it also shows how he had time to attend to the more human side of war, ticking off pompous officials for their handling of such matters as rationing which effected every housewife and watching the welfare of Gibraltar's famous apes.

"The Finest Hours" shows his rare moments of relaxation, writing and painting, and though never obtrusive there are several glimpses of his wife as a reminder that family life has always been important and close to him. Clearly, there are many big moments that have been omitted in favor of what some which seem trivial but, overall, Le Vien has done a notable job, a labor of love which will also turn out to have rich rewards for him.

Peter Baylis as director and Harry Booth as editorial co-ordinator have had their work cut out to compress a big subject into a wieldly whole. Mary Baylis and her team of researchers and Hone Glendinning's lensing are also worthy attributes, plus an imaginative score by Ron Grainer.

Victor Wolfson's screenplay, which avoids banality, over effusivess and pomposity maintains a dignity and occasional humor which are a plus to this very sound reminder of a man of stature. Perhaps Le Vien has merely laid the groundwork for a more exhaustive study of a complex personality but meanwhile the old wardog and those who admit his stature can be satisfied that Le Vien's team have, in no way, done him wrong.

Rich.

Voice of the Hurricane

Latest Moral ReArmament film has African setting but otherwise, is repeat of previous efforts. Potential limited.

Selected Picture Corp. release of a RAM (Scoville Wishard) production. Features Murial Smith, Phyllis Konstam, Reginald Owen. Directed by George Fraser; screenplay, Alan Thornhill, based on play by Peter Howard and Thornhill; camera (Technicolor), Rickard Tegstrom; editor, Harry Marker; sound, Fred Hendriksz; music composed and conducted by Ian Freebairn-Smith; additional musical arrangements, Paul Dunlap; art director, W. Cameron Johnson; costumes, Athena; lighting, Don Carstensen; special effects, Thol O. Simonson. Reviewed in N.Y., April 29, '64. Running time, **80 MINS.**

Mary .... Muriel Smith
Janet Lord .... Phyllis Konstam
Nigel Charter .... Reginald Owen
Mark Pearce .... William Close
Dolly Charter .... Jane Wax
Richard Lord .... David Cole
Humphrey Lord ..... William Pawley Jr.

This latest brave new whirl by the Moral ReArmament movement at selling their philosophy through the film medium should repeat the success and/or lack of it, that has befallen previous efforts. "Voice of the Hurricane," while booked into the Trans-Lux 52nd Street following present run, appears to have little appeal for the commercial market. What MRA could use is a member who heads a large chain of theatres.

As with previous efforts, Peter Howard provided the original material, adapted for the screen by Alan Thornhill from a play written by the pair. This time a nationalist uprising in Africa is used as the catalyst for the "big trouble" which, as always, is resolved by the message.

Average filmgoers, not seeking panacea but entertainment, will consider the technical excellence in most departments a waste of effort. Richard Tegstrom's lovely Technicolor photography is the film's greatest asset. If, as stated, some location shots were made in East Africa, Tegstrom has blended them beautifully with footage shot in the U.S., probably at MRA headquarters at Mackinac Island, Michigan. Attempts to make American foliage resemble that of Africa more often than not succeed.

Director George Fraser, hampered by the uninspiring stilted dialog given his cast and by the script's poorly-planned plot structure, has little luck with his actors. Only Muriel Smith fails to succumb to the hopeless task of breathing life into some very unlively characters. She also headed MRA's first film effort, the 1961 "Crowning Experience," and in this effort, as the servant who also is the rebellion leader, is impressive, particularly when given an opportunity to sing. Far too young, as the plot states, to have brought up the young rebel of the household (a part overplayed consistently with wild-eyed fanaticism by David Cole), it is her dignity and dedication that come closest to bringing off the intended message.

William Pawley Jr. as the youth's father works hard to create a pukka sahib but the part, as written, is a caricature of a bigoted, class-obsessed Britisher with no redeeming qualities. Reginald Owen's District Officer, intended to be an arrogant arm of the government, only succeeds in becoming a silly boor. Phyllis Konstam and Jane Wax are alternately reserved and hysterical as their wives.

Sanest member, and the natural spokesman for MRA, is William Close as an open-minded member of Parliament who illogically finds himself the house guest of Cole's family through a chance meeting. The native types, other than Miss Smith, are given little opportunity to create an impression which leaves the arguments rather one-sided.

Ian Freebairn-Smith's music is pleasant and two uncredited songs, sung by Miss Smith, are both refreshing and provocative. One, a child's number, has clever double-meaning lyrics that are a comment on the British. However, the title tune, a protest song, could be misused by ethnic groups or unthinking ballad singers.

Harry Marker's editing is crisp with only one slip, a series of short takes which are out of logical sequence. Other technical work is first rate.

Robe.

Blood Feast
(COLOR)

Totally inept horror shocker.

Hollywood, May 5.

Box Office Spectaculars Inc. release of David F. Friedman production. No star credits. Directed by Herschell G. Lewis. Screenplay, A. Louise Downe; camera (Eastman), Lewis; editors, Robert Sinise, Frank Romol; music, Lewis. Reviewed at Pix Theatre, April 29, '64. Running time, **58 MINS.**

Pete Thornton .... Thomas Wood
Ramses .... Mal Arnold
Suzette .... Connie Mason
Police Captain .... Scott H. Hall
Mrs. Fremont .... Lyn Bolton
Trudy .... Toni Calvert
Tony .... Gene Courtier
Girl On Beach .... Ashlyn Marton
Girl In Apartment ...... Sandra Sinclair
High Priest .... Al Golden
Truck Driver .... Craig Maudslay Jr.

Incredibly crude and unprofessional from start to finish, "Blood Feast" in an insult even to the most puerile and salacious of audiences. The very fact that it is taking itself seriously makes the David F. Friedman production all the more ludicrous. It is a fiasco in all departments.

A. Louise Downe's senseless screenplay is concerned with a ubiquitous madman's gory campaign to restore life to an Egyptian love goddess, evidently by synthesizing the organs and entrails of his many young female victims.

Herschell G. Lewis served in the three-ply capacity of director-cameraman-composer, and has failed dismally on all three counts. The acting is amateurish, top to bottom.

Tube.

Woman of Straw
(BRITISH—EASTMANCOLOR)

Contrived plot and plodding direction. But lush background and hot marquee bait could tempt ducat buyers.

London, April 29.

United Artists release of a Michael Relph & Basil Dearden production. Stars Gina Lollobrigida, Sean Connery, Ralph Richardson. Features Johnny Sekka, Laurence Hardy, Alexander Knox, Peter Madden, Edward Underdown, George Curzon, Andre Morell. Produced by Relph. Directed by Dearden. Screenplay by Robert Muller and Stanley Mann from Catherine Arley's novel: camera, Otto Heller; editor, John D. Gutheridge; music arranged by Muir Mathieson. Reviewed April 28, '64 at Odeon, Leicester Square, London. Running Time: **117 MINS.**

Maria .... Gina Lollobrigida
Anthony Richmond .... Sean Connery
Charles Richmond .... Ralph Richardson
Thomas .... Johnny Sekka
Baines .... Laurence Hardy
Fenton .... Danny Daniels
1st Executive ...... Edward Underdown
2nd Executive .... George Curzon
3rd Executive .... A. J. Brown
Yacht Captain .... Peter Madden
Lomer .... Alexander Knox
Judge .... Andre Morell

John ....:...... Robert Bruce
Wardress .... Peggy Marshall

Gina Lollobrigida, Sean Connery and Sir Ralph Richardson add up to a trio of marquee names sufficiently intriguing to give exhibs valuable lures for the crowds. But it is unlikely that customers will work up much enthusiasm (some femmes excepted) for this plodding meller-murder which rolls to a preposterous c l i m a x. Women should fancy lush gowns and the general air of magazine luxury. It starts off more promisingly than it turns out in the latter segment. That usually perceptive writer Robert Muller and the experienced Stanley Mann have collaborated to produce a screenplay from Catharine Arley's novel which fails to spark much animation.

Director Basil Dearden seems, here, to have temporarily misplaced the vigorous insight that has earned him some top credits. Best that can be said of "Straw" is that it looks handsome, what with Lollo, some scenes of Majorca and the English countryside and some ornate artwork. It also sounds good, which is in the way of a nosegay to Muir Mathison, conductor and arranger of the Sinfonia orchestra. He plus sound editor Roy Baker and sound recordist Stevens give full play to some of the more familiar passages of Beethoven, Merlioz, Mozart and Rimsky-Korsakov. These highclass tunesmiths get big play because, in the film, Richardson is just nuts about listening to endless tape recordings of such maestros.

But the film gets bogged down by stilted dialog and by the situations, which are as high as the Empire State Building. Richardson is a multimillionaire, an illmannered, sour tycoon condemned to spend his life in a wheelchair. He takes it out of anybody handy. These include his nephew-secretary, his major-domo, colored houseboy, his yacht skipper and his dogs. He even tosses some well considered snarls in the direction of Miss Lollobrigida who is hired by the nephew as the old man's nurse. As a result of all this humiliation there are several people who are not unhappy when he is found dead in the bunk of his yacht.

Interplay in the relationship and emotions of the characters involved make fair picturegoing in the early stages. But when the plot gets down to the mystery of whether he died from natural causes or whether he was the victim of mayhem then it descends into under average mishmash.

It transpires that Miss Lollobrigida has been hired by the nephew (Sean Connery) to lure the tycoon into marriage and so get her mitts on his bulky estate when he dies. Connery is due for 3,000,000 bucks as his share of the plot. Unfortunately after the nuptials Lollo gets quite fond of her peppery husband and is sad when he comes to a sudden end. Nevertheless, she is pulled in for murder and it turns out that Connery had doublecrossed her in several ways. He, of course, is the culprit but gets his desserts in a finale so phoney and contrived that it will provoke yocks in the audience if they are not stunned.

Richardson manages to extract what fun there is out of the desultory proceedings and even manages to dominate the screen when he is a corpse. Miss Lollobrigida, when not changing her highclass duds, is out of her depth in what must be a serious role if it is to jell, while the welldressed Connery wanders around with the air of a man who can't wait to get back to being James Bond again. Alexander Knox handles the role of the top cop with unobtrusive politeness and Johnny Sekka, Laurence Hardy and Peter Madden are other conscientiously on hand. But it is one of those films in which everybody stands around meaningful g l a n c e s registering menace, cynicism, disbelief, suspicion or plain dumbness. It is also one of those pix that needs a more ruthless editor than John Gutheridge is allowed to be. When a car has to traverse the winding roadway up to the mansion it isn't necessary to show the whole journey. It also slows up matters when a closed elevator constantly is shown travelling the full length of the shaft.

Otto Heller has done some bright lensing on both scenery and people and it isn't his fault that the mansion owned by the irascible tycoon is built like a cross between the UNO Building, Versailles and the British Museum. Chief knuckle rapping, however, must go to director Dearden for allowing the entire setup to limp along without thrill or surprises.

Rich.

The Playgirls and The Vampire
(ITALIAN)

Fang, bat and tomb opera. Mediocre.

Hollywood, April 29.
Gordon Films Inc. release of Tiziano Longo production. With Lyla Rocco, Walter Brandi, Maria Giovanni. Written and directed by Piero Regnoli; camera, Aldo Greci; editor, Mario Arditti; music, Aldo Piga. Reviewed at Pix Theatre, April 29, '64. Running time, 70 MINS.

This post-dubbed shocker from Italy (currently second-billed to "Blood Feast" in L.A. theatres and drive-ins) is a strictly second-rate horror melodrama, a totally shopworn, sex-propelled fang-bat-and-tomb opera.

Written and directed without imagination by Piero Regnoli, the film follows the adventures of an itinerant company of showgirls stranded in a castle haunted by a rather inept and confused vampire.

The actors are limited to two expressions—leer or fear—depending upon which side of the grave they occupy. The bulk of production contributions to the Gordon Films Inc. presentation are lacking in style or finesse, *Tube.*

Suna No Onna
(The Woman in the Dunes) (JAPANESE)

Cannes, April 30.
World Film release of Teshigahara production. Stars Eiji Okada, Kyoko Kishida. Directed by Hiroshi Teshigahara. Screenplay, Kobo Abe; camera, Hiroshi Segawa; music, Tohru Takemitsu; editor, F. Suisui. At Cannes Film Fest (in competition). Running time, 127 MINS.
Man .... Eiji Okada
Woman .... Kyoko Kishida

Trust the Japanese to come up with the film to beat with their first competing pic at the Cannes Film Fest. A basically simple tale takes on two profound and symbolic sides as to the very meaning of life and mankind yet it can be accepted on its own grounds as an offbeat adventure that befalls an entomologist while hunting insects in a barren sand dune part of the country. Thus this primarily is for arty situations abroad and will also call for knowing placement and handling because of its unusual treatment and theme.

The young man falls asleep during his expedition and is found by some townspeople who tell him they know where he can spend the night. They let him down to a house set in the side of a dune cliff. Here he finds a woman living alone. But next morning things suddenly take a strange turn. The ladder he came down on has been pulled up and he is told he cannot go up but must help this woman to fill lowered buckets with sand every night.

Then the film shows the man's attempts to escape, his rage at the woman and his finally giving in and even becoming her lover. When she is taken away, due to some problem in an approaching birth, he decides to stay even though he has a chance to escape. The discovery of a way of getting water in this barren land presumably is one of the things leading to his decision.

All this is done with a firm feel for atmosphere, human comportment and a knowing balance between the far-fetched aspects of the situation and a peek at man's general mores, outlooks and behavior. It seems they are kept there by a mysterious syndicate that sells the sand at cut-rate prices. So it seems like a look at man's exploitation of man, the way people can accept their fate, revolt and final acquiesce. Or it may be a parable about how everybody at some time accepts his lot if there are attempts to change it. But one is left with the feeling that some things, man or his environment, must be changed before true choice is available.

But no matter what the meanings may be, director Hiroshi Teshigahara displays a flawless feel for texture and observation. Perhaps one drawback may be that the characters are almost as mercilessly delineated as the insects the man collects. But underneath is a pulsating, if sometimes gritty, compassion for man's general fate and the state of his so-called liberty.

Eiji Okada is examplary as the civilized man caught in a trap he eventually adapts while Kyoko Kishida is touching, annoying, beguiling or irritating in turn as the simple woman who accepts her lot and can only give of herself. And the first erotic scene between the two shapes one of the most tasteful and yet intense moments to be seen on the screen for many a moon. No leering or patronizing here, but a true feel for the very life force sans any embellishments of romance or reason.

The sharp, contrasting black and white photography is perfect for the tale while the editing is solid. The strange pound or sighing music effectively counterpoints this tall tale. This is unique film but visually direct. It is a pic that should excite critical appraisal and word-of-mouth which could be an aid in foreign climes.

In all departments this is a veritable tour-de-force since practially only two personages are involved for more than two hours. There is sometimes a mixture of naturalism mysticism and straight narration that do not quite give this the final boost to achieve greatness. But it emerges a most unorthodox pic which is the stuff for festivals. Care and planning are called for if bought for the U. S., but it could well be worth it.
Mosk.

Cannes Festival

One Potato, Two Potato

Yank indie treats miscegenation with tact, not exploiting the theme. It looms a good specialized bet if well placed with its unknown but excellent thesps.

Sam Weston-Bowalco production and release. With Barbara Barrie, Bernie Hamilton, Richard Mulligan. Directed by Larry Peerce. Screenplay, Raphael Hayes; camera, Andrew Laszlo; editor, Robert Fritch; music, Gerald Fried. At Cannes Film Fest (In Competition). Running time, 122 MINS.
Julie .... Barbara Barrie
Frank .... Bernie Hamilton
Joe .... Richard Mulligan
Ellen Mary .... Marti Merika
Judge .... Harry Bellaver
William .... Robert Earl Jones
Johnny .... Sam Weston
Ann .... Faith Burwell

Cannes, May 4.
Made in Ohio on a subscription basis for a reported $250,000, this is a tender, tactful look at miscegenation that speaks in human rather than polemic terms. If some Southern markets may be difficult, this pic could well emerge an indie with solid arty and some general possibilities in most parts of the U.S., with foreign chances also potent.

Set in a midwest U.S. location (northern tier), it deals with a seemingly well-adjusted y o u n g Negro office worker who meets a young white divorcee who has a little girl. Their idyll grows slowly and gently as both react on normal planes with the color no apparent problem. But it sometimes intrudes when a policeman brands her a streetwalker because she is out late at night with him. The point is made that if he had been white this would not have happened. But after a kiss and professions of love, his parents object strongly and try to make him conscious of the problems marriage would bring.

But the woman's simple, sage declaration of love's lack of boundaries and color lines leads to marriage. He suddenly withdraws from all his friends and they live with his parents in a farm outside the town. Tastefully done is the father-in-law's final acceptance of the wife after a child is born.

Then along comes the woman's first husband who has made his fortune after leaving her and demands the custody of the little girl. His unconscious jealousy of the Negro husband, and insistence that the girl's life would be made difficult if brought up in these surroundings backs this up.

A sympathetic judge locates the girl in a good home, since he feels that as long as prejudice exists the little girl's life could be touched by it. All this is helped by fine delineations of character and added help from some new faces and the on-the-spot lensing.

Barbara Barrie has a striking presence and manages to mix intensity with need to etch a firm, moving character as the woman who finally finds the right man only to have her child taken away on racist principles. Bernie Hamilton is taking as the Negro husband who suddenly finds his manhood and very human liberty threatened by something that prevents him being a complete man.

Others are fine, especially the sober playing of Robert Earl Jones as the father; Richard Mulligan, as the ex-husband and Marti Merika, as the little girl. Rarely has a Yank moppet performance been so natural.

Director Larry Peerce, for his first pic, has wisely told his story without many heavy symbolical and overdramatic embellishments. This sometimes leads to faltering in some spots that repeat already made points rather than enhancing them. One scene, when the distraught husband revisits scenes of their early courting, is gratutitous. But otherwise there is a fine feeling for the characters, story and theme.

Film is poignant. And its simple, precise direction, script and thesping make the big scenes effective. For example, the grandfather's slowly being won over to life and out of his dogged, if not stated, opposal to his daughter-in-law, the woman's breakdown after the verdict and the little girl's hitting her mother because she doesn't understand why she is sent off to a home.

This is an independent production on a touchy theme that is faultlessly handled. Pic should get plenty of attention on this alone if tastefully placed and sold. Music is also an asset in its counterpointing and underlining of the characters and theme. Technical credits are fine and the lensing excellent. At a time when civil rights battles are almost daily affairs, this has an additional selling point.

This is an excellent beginning for all concerned in this first production. It also showed its class by being one of the first non-Hollywood pix to be invited directly in competition for some time at Cannes. It is true that another indie, "Long Day's Journey Into Night," was picked by the Hollywood Fest Selection Committee two years ago, but it did have known stars in it. Film was reportedly turned down by the Committee for showing at any fest and its direct fest invite on its own marits is commendable. *Mosk.*

100,000 Dollars Au Soleil

(100 000 Dollars In the Sun)
(FRENCH-FRANSCOPE)

Cannes, May 5.

Gaumont release of Gaumont-Trianon-Ultra Films production. Stars Jean-Paul Belmondo, Lino Ventura, Reginald Kernan; features Andrea Parisy, Gert Froebe, Bernard Blier. Directed by Henri Verneuil.; screenplay, Marcel Julian, Michel Audiard, Verneuil from novel by Claude Veillot; camera, Marcel Grignon; editor, Claude Durand. At Cannes Film Fest (In Competition). Running time, **120 MINS.**

Rocco .... Jean-Paul Belmondo
Ploue .... Lino Ventura
Steiner .... Reginald Kernan
Girl .... Andrea Parisys
Boss .... Gert Froebe
Driver .... Bernard Blier

Henri Verneuil made the international hit, "Any Number Can Win" which landed him a contract with Metro for three U.S. pix. This one belongs to Metro for all countries except France, Switzerland and Belgium. It is also an adventure opus in true Yank style. Film may lack the suspense and dramatic aspects of the earlier vehicle, on a holdup that goes awry, but has some solid action segs and shapes an oft-told, but still evergreen affair.

This has two adventurous buddies, who drive trucks in Africa, at each others' throats when one tries to abscond with some contraband loot and a girl. Film details the chase by the friend with an ironic ending as the girl runs off with the loot and leaves the two men behind, pals again after a big-scale brawl. Also involved is a mysterious adventurer who was supposed to drive the contraband truck.

This had been cooked up by the trucking owner unknown to the drivers until it was revealed unwittingly by someone. There are neatly done truck-driving scenes as the two try to stop each other on a hazardous winding mountain road, some solid drunk and fight scenes, and a comic relief in a talkative driver who always shows up to help when they get into trouble.

Jean-Paul Belmondo is the breezy would-be escapee with the loot and girl. He is in good form in essaying a familiar character. He has the sympathetic qualities that make his escapade picturesque rather than shady. After all, he is only beating some crooks at their own game. Lino Ventura has the beef and brawn as his angry friend. Yank actor Reginald Kernan is effective as the other man who cleans up Afro towns as revolutions change the various governments.

Director Verneuil has utilized on-the-spot Afro sites well. If the tale is too classic, it almost has the zest and brashness to stand up to its Yank models. Dialog has a tendency to stop the action cold to bring off some salty slang.

Pic is technically good if the music is too insistent. *Mosk.*

La Donna Scimmia

(The Ape Woman)
(ITALIAN)

Interfilm release of a C. C. Champion (Carlo Ponti) production. Stars Ugo Tognazzi, Annie Girardot; features Achille Majeroni, Filippo Pompa Marcelli, Linda de Felice, Elvira Paoloni. Directed by Marco Ferreri. Story and screenplay, Ferreri and Rafael Azcona; camera, Aldo Tonti; editor, Mario Serandrei; music, Teo Usuelli. At Cannes Film Fest (In Competition). Running time, **000 MINS.**

Antonio Focaccia ..... Ugo Tognazzi
Maria .... Annie Girardot

Marco Ferreri, who recently did well with his offbeater, "Ape Regina" (Conjugal Bed), has another attention-getter in this unusual tale. It again is concocted with the assistance of his favorite author, Rafael Azcona. While it lacks the audience identification aspects which made "Bed" an international conversation piece, it has other exploitable story aspects to attract attention with savvy bally. Ugo Tognazzi, of course, is a repeater from "Bed," and should help draw those who appreciated the previous Ferreri pic.

Bitter and ironic as they come, this story sounds wilder than it really is in the telling, though certainly downbeat. Antonio (Ugo Tognazzi) has for years lived by expedients, disliking the routine of steady occupation. One day he meets Maria, a fully normal woman, except for fact that her skin is covered with a thick coat of hair. He decides to exploit her and assure himself a steady living, setting her up as a sideshow in a garage. Later, both out of pity and interest, he marries the freak, and can thus also accept a French nitery's offer to have his wife star in a novel strip number. Back from Paris, wife learns she is to have a baby, and eventually dies in childbirth, together with the infant. To meet expenses, Antonio first accepts, then regrets an offer from a museum to have bodies enbalmed and shown in public. Broke once more but wanting the bodies back in order to give them a decent burial, he has to sign a set of IOU's. And to pay these, he is forced once more to set up a freak show and exhibit the wife and child's mummies to the public.

Admittedly, the windup is especially bitter in its comment on Roman society and could cause some adverse average audience comment. An alternate ending has been lensed, in which ironic aspects are maintained but the impact softened. Director shot this himself, but is known not to be too happy with it. In Italy, the first few days saw the pic circulating with truncated windup (ending at wife's death), but original footage was restored at Ferreri's immediate complaint.

It is to Ferreri's credit, and to his actors' prowess, that such an offbeat theme comes off at all, though each viewer will have and make his own mental reservations and comments. Tognazzi is good as the exploiter. Annie Giradot is appealing and often strangely moving as the object of attention. Technically, the pic could have used some smoother continuity, but otherwise is outfitted in okay fashion. *Hawk.*

Goldstein

Far out fable or satire this is still a Yank indie pic with an inventive drive; it has the dramatic force and comedy which could make it an arty or specialized entry at home or abroad.

Cannes, May 5.

Montrose production and release. With Lou Gilbert, Ellen Madison, Thomas Erhart, Benito Carruthers, Jack Burns, Charles Fischer, Nelson Algren. Written and directed by Benjamin Manaster, Philip Kaufman. Camera, Jean-Phillippe Carson; editor, Adolfas Mekas; music, Meyer Kupferman. At Cannes Film Fest (Critics Section). Running time, **85 MINS.**

Old Man .... Lou Gilbert
Sally .... Ellen Madison
Sculptor .... Thomas Erhart
Jay .... Benito Carruthers
Mr. Nice .... Charles Fischer
Doctor .... Severn Darden
Aid .... Anthony Holland
Nelson Algren .... Himself
(Critics Section). Running time, **115 MINS.**

A couple of Chicago filmmakers have created visual fireworks in this fable of city life. No matter what anyone chooses to label it—satire or legend, the pic is far out, riotously funny, in a macabre sort of way. It also is touching at times. This calls for special handling in the arty house manner and could well be worth it for this type of audience.

The non-Hollywood indie rarely has obtained the specialized attention that foreign arty pix get in the U.S. Though "David and Lisa" broke through, most still have to go the foreign film fest route, with most of them doing better abroad than at home. "Goldstein" made a dent on viewers at Cannes and should get plenty of foreign interest and possible sales. And it could create plenty of attention on its home grounds.

Chicago has already displayed its biting satirical aspects in legit and boites via the "Second City," Mike Nichols and others. Now it shows this can be placed on film. On the surface, this vehicle uses the old Hebrew legend of the Prophet Elijah who would disappear when recognized. Here, a giddy old tramp comes out of the lake near Chicago and gets mixed up in a lot of adventure before disappearing into the late again marked only by a floating hat.

Also embroiled are a dedicated artist, who refuses his rich father's money, and is a sculptor of scrap metal, a girl he has dropped (she gets an abortion) a gentle parisitic character who dreams of some-day working as a building wrecker, and assorted types and characters, including a guest shot by Chicago writer Nelson Algren.

And who is "Goldstein"? Actually, his name only appears on the side of a delivery truck seemingly guided by an invisible driver. The old tramp gets into the truck and throws out all sorts of electrical and household appliances since this Goldstein seems to deal in furnishings of all kinds. Is he Godot, God?, hope? a Father figure? or what? It really does not matter for the intrinsic insight, sharp comedics and bright visual inventiveness keep this rolling along no matter what the deeper aspects of it all may be.

Two sanctimonious, artsy-craftsy abortionists fly in to help the girl out of her troubles. There is a jolting scene during the operation but it is handled with tact and no false, horrific closeups. It is rugged but in a sane sort of way.

The old tramp wheels about a fiddling beggar who feigns infirmity and even drags him upstairs to the man's home. There a widow is enamored of him and gives him a bath and her dead husband's orthodox Jewish hat and gabardine. The old man is chased into a meat packing house by a sadistic fat guard who does not like his eating manners. Here the sculptor, seeing the chase, intervenes and throws the fat man into a vat and saves the tramp from being smoked. And then ever is chasing after him through the pic.

The sculptor goes to see Algren who spins a tale of conscience that has something to do with the man's chase and the artist's dilemma in chosing between art and love, easy money and dedication. Even the funny set-pieces, like a group playing at horror films in a bar, fall into place in this look at unsettled, city types.

The shots in a scrap metal center of the crushing of cars and burning piles of autos and metal, give this scene a look of a post-Atomic Bomb explosive landscape. The city of Chicago is a photogenic, dramatic and comic background to this fast moving unorthodox but absorbing offbeat pic. Its new buildings, in which a car can drive to the top via circling ramps, the old and new sectors and the packinghouse sections all combine to make a point about the excitement or coldness of a big city.

It ends with the sculptor's last mad dash, in his search for the tramp-prophet, out into the country for an idyllic last scene of the simple and restful aspects of nature. This is the type of different pic that might enrage some, beguile and titillate others, and entertain still others. Thus this film has to be sold with finesse, but the talents, originality and knowhow of this production denote that the socalled U.S. "film underground" belongs on the surface and in the film picture.

Gotham filmmaker Adolfas Mekas, who made the pic "Hallelujah, the Hills," that scored at Cannes last year, did a brilliant job of editing. He has meshed the rambling tale together with firmness and clarity.

And, for a first film co-directors Benjamin Manaster and Phillip Kaufman display a sure feel for telling imagery, neat shaping of both pro and non-pro thesps, and a wry wit and pro aplomb that belie this is an initial effort. No matter who did what, they should go on working together since they seem to mesh their work perfectly. Expert lensing and a creative musical score, that both underlines or revs up the scenes, are also great assets to this difficult but engaging vehicle.

Benito Carruthers, as the would-be housewrecker, has dash and projection. It is a wonder he has not been snapped up by Hollywood. He has appeared in several Gotham-made indies. Ellen Madison adds a bit of depth to her sporadic role as the left-behind girl while Lou Gilbert is rankish as the tramp. Thomas Erhart has the proper intensity for the sculptor. The others are fine including Algren, playing himself. *Mosk.*

Postava K Podpiraní
(Order and Discipline)
(CZECHOSLOVAKIAN)
Cannes, May 5.

Czech State Film production and release. With Karel Vasicek, Consuela Moravkov, Pavel Bertl. Written and directed by Pavel Juracek. Camera, Jan Curik; editor, Zdenek Stenlik. At Cannes Film Fest (Critics Section). Running time, 40 MINS.
Herold .... Karel Vasicek
Cat Seller .... Consuela Moravkov
Joseph Killian .... Pavel Bertl

Czech short feature pic has enough originality, candor and offbeat comedics to rate a good possibility for arty chances abroad with another short feature or as supporting fare. The chances are also inherent in this bureaucratic spoof that shows the influences of the noted Czech writer Franz Kafka, who wrote in German, and was only translated into Czech for the first time last year.

Like Kafka's universe, this too deals with a little man caught up in bureaucracy or drifting in a world that does not seem to have a place for him, whether he overdoes his obedience to its tenets or not. This chap hires a cat in a statecat rental store which then mysteriously disappears. And he goes around to various state agencies trying to find out what happened to it.

The endless corridors, with people bicycling through them, the waiting crowds for one Joseph Killian, who can solve most things, and the sharp delineation of typed characters, feeling for solitude (with a right comic flair to balance anguish) make this an unusual, fetching 40-minute pic. It is doubly unusual coming from the country considered the most subservient, hidebound Eastern block.

Killian (Pavel Bertl) is never found and the hero, neatly played in a gentle, self-effacing way by Karel Vasicek, tries to pin down a man in a cafe. Point is mae that order and discipline only keep society in line, but it is stated with an ironic touch.

So here is a decidedly experimental pic that succeeds in being penetrating and direct. Mixing of hidden camera techniques, when the hero asks for the cat store, also jells as a neat counterpart to the serio-comedic fable. It is well lensed and also works in an anti-Stalinist nod, too. A definitely promising new director is unveiled in Pavel Juracek. French and English title of "Joseph Killian" seems more fitting for this. *Mosk.*

La Herencia
(The Inheritance)
(ARGENTINIAN)
Cannes, May 5.

America Films production and release. Written and directed by Ricardo Aleventosa from a story by Guy De Maupassant. With Juan Vardagier, Natan Pinzol, Marisa Griebel, Alba Mujica. Camera, America Hoss; editor, J. Rimaldi. At Cannes Film Fest (Critics Section). Running time, 75 MINS.
Leopoldo .... Natan Pinzol
Friend .... Juan Vardagier
Corelia .... Marisa Girebel
Aunt .... Alba Mujica

Film is a successful broadside at some aspects of human selfishness and pettiness that is ferocious in its stigmatizing of these faults. But it also has a knowing observation that make this a comedy of manners rather than a class attack or political pic.

Its clever flair, inventive visual aspects and homogenious acting combine to make this a spry comedy. This could well be an arty or specialized entry abroad if well placed. Critics and word-of-mouth could help.

A tale of the French writer Guy De Maupassant is perfectly adapted to the Argentina of today. An office worker marries a fellow workers's daughter. An aunt leaves a will donating a fortune when her niece has a daughter. But the husband is seemingly sterile. All sorts of things are tried to build him up and finally the office Don Juan is invited. He is left alone with the wife and promptly seduces her.

With the birth of the child comes riches. The real father is dropped, and the family leads a high life. A telling last shot has everybody going to eat at a big party while the child is forgotten outside in its baby carriage. Writer-director Ricardo Alventosa shows the right balance of black humor and revealing characterization.

These people never seem to read the front pages of the papers where revolutions and upheavals are reported. They are sometimes fetchingly human if their lack of emotion and feeling seems to be a part of the times as well as of them.

Natan Pinzol looks like Buster Keaton and has the same deadpan reactions and intimations of an interior sensitivity and hurt. Possessing the sharp satire of such Italo pix as "Conjugal Bed" and "Divorce, Italian Style," it is still a personal and original work, and denotes an already mature and knowing filmmaker in director Alventosa for his first film. It is technically fine with production dress good. *Mosk.*

La Vie a L'Envers
(Other Side of Life)
(FRENCH)
Cannes, May 5.

SETEC release of A.J. Films production. With Charles Denner, Anna Gaylor, Nane Germon, Yvonne Clech. Jean Yanne. Written and directed by Alain Jessua. Camera, Jacques Robin; editor, Micole Marko. At Cannes Film Fest (Critics Section). Running time, 92 MINS.
Jacques .... Charles Denner
Viviane .... Anna Gaylor
Mother .... Nane Germon
Madame .... Yvonne Clech
Boss .... Jean Yanne

Film is a controlled, canny look at a case of alienation, the lapsing into insanity of a seemingly personable young office worker. If specialized and downbeat, it has rightness, without being clinical. Looks likely as an arty house bet abroad.

Living with a pretty, if futile little actress who does ad films, a young man works in a rental agency. He has lapses, though seems fairly lucid. He may make up little tales, suddenly decide to get married and walk out on the wedding party and then disappear for days at a time.

Each step is well logged out and photographically handled. His visions of being alone in Paris, his mixing of day and night and a new feeling for the textures of objects all adroitly show his advancing withdrawal from life. His hapless little wife's attempted suicide almost jolts him but then he gets worse and finally ends up in an asylum where he thinks the nurse who brings him food is his wife.

Charles Denner has an expressive face and bearing and gives the role and the film a pathetic and almost emotional pitch that is not too much a part of the general mood. Anna Gaylor is fetchingly banal to add an additional emotional twinge to this look at a breakdown.

There is a technical firmness and finesse that belies his is a first film for director Alain Jessua. More compassion, or a closer link between life and the denial of it, should have made this film even more successful. As is, it is a fine beginning. Film needs firm, personal handling. Jessua looks like a coming talent to be reckoned with here. *Mosk.*

Prima Della Rivoluzione
(Before the Revolution)
(ITALIAN)
Cannes, May 5.

Cineriz release of IRIDE Cinematografica production. With Francesco Barilli, Adriana Asti. Alain Midgette, Morando Morandini. Written and directed by Bernardo Bertolucci. Camera, Aldo Scavarda; music. Gino Paoli. At Cannes Film Fest (Critics Section). Running time, 115 MINS.
Gina .... Adriana Asti
Boy .... Francesco Barilli
Agostino .... Alain Midgette
Teacher .... Morando Morandini

Twenty - three - year - o'd director Bernardo Bertolucci shows a firm hand in putting a personal tale on the screen and keeping it revealing in spite of length and a fragmentary technique. This is a tender, probing look at a coming of age of a well-to-do boy that may have certain private ties with Italo customs and outlooks but builds up the universality to make it of interest for offshore markets too.

It is thus a film that needs careful handling but could do for arty and specialized bookings abroad on its insight and fervid and obvious'y sensitive feeling. The upper-class boy has a tortured poorer friend who is abnormally sensitive to things about him that never bother the former. Then the friend commits suicide.

So he begins to question his own life and outlook. It leads to meeting the leftist mentor of the dead boy, talks with militant leftists or fading landowners, etc. Intertwined is his initiation to love by a beauteous if unstable young aunt. He finally realizes he cannot escape and marries the girl he is supposed to and takes his place in his own class.

Film does not take sides or pontificate. To the contrary, it shows one case and its various aspects. There is a tendency to talk things out too much at times but Bertolucci has a firm feel for the visual points of his scenes and counterpoints the talk and sight values expertly.

Adriana Asti has weight and dimension as the aunt while Francesco Barilli has the right mixture of stuffiness and yearning as the mixed-up youth. There is able support from Alain Midgette, as his anguished friend and film critic Morando Morandini, as the helpful teacher, doing an okay segue into acting.

Film is technically excellent with sharp lensing that sometimes goes into color to underline a romantic or pertinent scene. Bertolucci appears an impressive newcomer to Italo pictures if he can broaden his scope in future films. *Mosk.*

Shabe Quzi
(The Hunchback's Night)
(IRANIAN)
Cannes, May 5.

Iran Nema production and release. With P. Saberi, P. Hakemi, M. A. Keshavarz, K. H. Sahami, S. Venus. Directed by Farrokh Gaffary. Screenplay, J. Moqadam, Gaffary from a tale in "The Arabian Nights"; camera, G. Hayarpetian; editor, M. Ragnar. At Cannes Film Fest (Critics Section). Running time, 95 MINS.

Arzi .... P. Saberi
Girl .... P. Hakemi
Boss .... M. A. Keshavarz
Hunchback .... K. H. Sahami
Old Man .... S. Venus
Hairdresser .... F. Gaffary

Iran, ex-Persia, is known to make about 30 pix per year but has hardly ever been heard of at festivals or in the west. This one is a fine start and should focus interest on the future turnout of that country or director Farrokh Gaffary. He shows neat narrative skill, a flair for atmosphere and a sophisticated way of putting a pic together that keeps its national feel, but likely will have appeal anywhere.

Since it is mainly a well-told tale, that mixes macabre comedy, folklore and moralism, the pic appears more likely for only specialized chances abroad, with some arty aspects. Perhaps this still is somewhat special for depth playoff. But its generally fetching look also could have this of use in keys.

A sickly hunchback, of a traveling troupe of players, dies during a practical joke. His terrified comrades leave his body in a hallway. But it seems he has the list of a smuggling gang on him and he has been left near the shop of a man, who is sending an assistant out of the country with some drugs.

So the body gets passed about considerably and creates a lot of complications. All this leads to the unmasking of several con-men and crooks, and in breaking up an unwanted wedding by a young girl to an elderly man. All this is handled with wit, smartly etched characterizations, and still has the ability to keep it interesting.

Picture also gives a fresh look at life, especially in Iran. It manages to tweak foibles, fads and attitudes. Acting is rightly clear and direct. It is technically fine, with Gaffary looming as a promising, new talent with a definite pro touch visible in this first pic. Good handling could make this pay off.   *Mosk.*

Island Of The Blue Dolphins
(COLOR)

Wholesome family fare. Idyllic tale of abandoned Indian girl. Weak in some story areas. Will need and is getting sell.

Universal release of Robert B. Radnitz production. No star credits. Directed by James B. Clark. Screenplay, Ted Sherdeman, Jane Klove, based on Scott O'Dell's novel; camera (Eastman), Leo Tover; editor, Ted J. Kent; music, Paul Sawtell; asst. director, Phil Bowles. Reviewed at the studio, May 4, '64. Running time, 93 MINS.
Karana .... Celia Kaye
Ramo .... Larry Domasin
Tutok .... Ann Daniel
Aleut Captain .... George Kennedy
Chowig .... Carlos Romero
Kimki .... Hal Jon Norman
The Priest .... Martin Garralaga
Spanish Captain .... Alex Montoya
Lurai .... Julie Payne

The bittersweet true-life tale of an Indian maiden who persevered alone for 18 years on a small island in the Santa Barbara chain during the first half of the 19th century is idyllically but rather superficially dramatized in Robert B. Radnitz's production of "Island of the Blue Dolphins." The Universal release, based on Scott O'Dell's novel, is a commendable undertaking in that it certainly fills a programming need in the area of wholesome, uplifting fare for children.

Yet, although it is a highly respectable artistic effort in several departments, the film falls somewhat short of the mark at its dramatic core, failing to convey with full emotional impact or chronological clarity the spiritual and physical dimension of the Indian girl's prolonged adventure in solitude. A kind of narrative poetry seems to be missing in the scenario by Ted Sherdeman and Jane Klove (the sort of quality so much more easily conveyed in a novel than in a film), and the vital element of character change or personality erosion is absent in the performance of Celia Kaye, who makes her screen debut in the demanding role of the maiden.

Still, souped up with imaginative selling, the picture might make its mark at the boxoffice as a choice item for the moppet brigade—especially for little girls. It's the kind of attraction that, were it endowed with, say, the Disney banner, would be a shoo-in. But, lacking that adornment or significant marquee name bait, the Universal entry is unusually dependent upon salesmanship to make the grade.

The part of the isolated girl would be an extremely difficult one for any actress, requiring long stretches where the only spoken word is of the soliloquy variety. For a newcomer like Miss Kaye, it is an even more challenging assignment. There are expressive flashes in her performance, but the spark and soul required to capture the essence of this strange true-life character is by and large a missing ingredient in her depiction.

The story relates the girl's long ordeal on the island after her father is murdered by a wicked white trapper, the balance of her tribe migrates to the mainland and her little brother is killed by wild dogs. Supposedly, the story spans an 18-year stretch although one would have to read that fact to know it. Neither the script nor Miss Kaye's portrayal clarifies that aspect. Although her canine companion dies, presumably of old age, nothing about Miss Kaye's appearance or disposition suggests nearly two decades of erosion.

Just about the most expressive performance in the film is that of the dog, "Rontu," for which much of the credit is due trainer Frank Weatherwax. Principal roles are essayed capably by young Larry Domasin, Ann Daniel, George Kennedy and Carlos Romero. Wherever the script was afforded him the opportunity, director James B. Clark has engineered the events of the story with vigor and skill. But inspiration tends to run out when the written source runs dry.

The picture is beautifully photographed in Eastman Color by Leo Tover. Except for some listlessness in the latter half, it is adeptly edited by Ted J. Kent. Shooting took place near Anchor Bay, about 150 miles north of San Francisco. In selection of site and design of set, art directors Alexander Golitzen and George Webb have performed their services perceptively. Paul Sawtell's plaintive Indianesque score is a vital asset to a production so dominated by nature and solitude.   *Tube.*

Acosada
(Harassed)
(ARGENTINE)
Santiago, May 5.

Gloria Films production and release. Stars Libertad Leblanc, Nestor Zavarce; features Eva Moreno. Directed by Albert Dubois. Screenplay, Alberto Diego; camera, Ignacio Scuto; music, Amadeo Monges. At Teatro Santiago (Santiago, Chile). Running time, 80 MINS.

On the surface, this film has the ingredients to make it a hit on the garterbelt circuit. Libertad Leblanc appears in the nude during a beach scene and in her undies plus laboriously putting on her stockings. She even gets beaten up for the benefit of those with more sadistic inclinations. Yet the film is remarkably non-erotic because of a poor plot, hopelessly deficient acting and equally bad direction and editing.

The story takes a singer from Buenos Aires to Caracas (where most of the pic was lensed). But her contract was faked by a gentleman who deals in dope and she is soon in all sorts of trouble. Pic does not have the courage of its convictions, being neither an out-and-out meller nor a sexy musical. Plenty of songs are dragged in to satisfy those who prefer music to sex.

Miss Leblanc shapes up well physically, but not so well in her acting. The film obviously is aimed at the more illiterate segments of the Spanish language market and should go good big with this group.   *Chile.*

A Jolly Bad Fellow
(BRITISH)

Bright comedy that never quite comes to full boil; witty moments fight more arid patches, but the fun makes this a useful b.o. contender.

London, May 5.

British Lion-Pax release (through BLC) of a Pax presentation of a Michael Balcon (Donald Taylor) production. Stars Leo McKern, Janet Munro; features Maxine Audley, George Benson, Patricia Jessel. Directed by Don Chaffey. Screenplay, by Robert Hamer and Taylor from C. E. Vulliamy's novel, "Don Among the Dead Men"; camera, George Gibbs; editor, Peter Tanner; music, John Barry. Previewed at Columbia Theatre, London. Running time, 96 MINS.
Bowles-Ottery .... Leo McKern
Delia .... Janet Munro
Clarinda .... Maxine Audley
Dr. Brass .... Duncan Macrae
Hughes .... Dennis Price
Dr. Wooley .... Miles Malleson
Dr. Fisher .... Leonard Rossiter
Epicen .... Alan Wheatley
Mrs. Pugh-Smith .... Patricia Jessel
Fred .... Dinsdale Landen
Inspector Butts .... George Benson
The Master .... Mark Dignam
Armstrong .... Jerome Willis
Superintendent .... Ralph Michael
Willie Pugh-Smith .... Mervyn Johns
The Waiter .... Raymond Ray

This is the type of witty, offbeat comedy that used to be a favorite of the old Ealing Films setup. And significantly, it is a Michael Balcon production, and part was written by the late Robert Hamer, one of the brightest in the Ealing stable. It has roots in "Kind Hearts and Coronets," with the same urbane flavor and mocking eyelifting at the humorous side of murder. "A Jolly Bad Fellow," which is a fairly frail title (but probably preferable to "Don Among the Dead Men," title of the original novel), is a lighthearted entry entertaining while it lasts. But this is unlikely to stick in patrons' memories.

Leo McKern plays a science professor in a stuffy little University town. He is a firm believer that gossipers, hypocrites and stuffed-shirts are more menace to the world than many major criminals and should be given the heaveho. When, by accident, he hits on a formula that makes a mouse first hysterically gay before it turns up its toes and dies, and which shows no trace of poison, he sees his chance. He first humiliates a pompous colleague and then bumps off a nosey woman, a rival professor for a lectureship and his girl assistant who is trying to trap him into marriage, before the cops get suspicious. In a final showdown, he gets his comeuppance by an ironic twist.

The screenplay by Hamer and producer Donald Taylor moves slowly but smoothly. It sparks some witty lines and situations. Although Don Chaffey's direction is polished and spry, the fun rarely fully boils to its rich potentiality, since satire is forced too often to rub shoulders with slapstick. However, McKern gives a well-rounded, amusing performance as the professor with liberal ideas and a roving eye for a pretty face. Every gesture, and every throwaway line by McKern shrewdly helps to build up a character who carries the film and in whose activities patrons will never lose interest.

Fitting into the authentic University background of stuffy ritual are a number of lesser lights who surround McKern with distinction. Maxine Audley, as his farseeing, tolerant wife plays with attractive poise. Janet Munro, as his young assistant, is a nubile lass rather more convincing in the boudoir than the laboratory. Patricia Jessel handles the unconvincing character of the local gossip with plenty of bounce. Duncan Macrae, Dennis Price, Miles Malleson, Alan Wheatley, Mervyn Johns and others fit snugly into the roles of dons and professors. The climaxes of the murders are less effective on screen than they may have seemed on paper, but help to carry the yarn along with zest.

George Gibbs has essayed some smooth photography. Peter Tanner's editing is unobtrusive and the art department has done sound work with the various interior settings. An illicit weekend, shared by McKern and Miss Munro, is helped a lot by its location and amusing shrewd observation of the kind of dispirited British seaside hotel at which such extra-matrimonial jaunts are liable to take place. A quiet but lively musical score by John Barry suits the mood of the playful comedy well.

Rich.

Wartezimmer zum Jenseits
(GERMAN)
Berlin May 5.

Constantin-Film release of Rialto Film Preben Philipsen (Berlin) production. Stars Hildegard Knef, Goetz George and Richard Muench. Directed by Alfred Vohrer. Screenplay, Eberhard Keindorff and Johanna Sibelius, based on a book by James Hadley Chase; camera, Bruno Mondi; music, Martin Boettcher. Preemed in 50 West German cities. Running time, **88 MINS.**

Lorelli	Hildegard Knef
Don Micklem	Goetz George
Alsconi	Richard Muench
Crantor	Carl Lange
Dickes	Heinz Reincke
Lady Helen	Adelheid Seeck
Carlos	Pinkas Braun

Crime pictures, or what the domestic trade calls "Krimis," currently have a big following in Germany. The greater part of them comes from the Berlin-based Rialto-Film Preben Philipsen. Under the supervision of Horst Wendlandt, the Berlin Rialto topper, the company has turned out 16 such "Krimis" in the last four years. And nearly all of them made money.

Rialto's latest crime pic, "Waiting-Room For the Other Side," based on the book "Pay Or Die" by British James Hadley Chase, looks like another native b.o. click. It offers that right mixture of thrill, horror and humor which large segments of this country's film patrons obviously go for. It's a technically well-made, swiftly paced and expertly directed production. Also, it has a good cast. These plus factors compensate for the somewhat superficial script. Wendlandt sees to it that his crime pix are never too long. This one runs 88 minutes and qualifies for some foreign situations.

Story is a simple one. A British millionaire has been murdered because he wouldn't pay 100,000 pounds demanded by an international gangster syndicate. His nephew and only heir to his fortune sets out to track down the evildoers by himself. He is one of the few survivors when the film ends. Due to internal quarrels, one gangster kills the other in the fadeout. Also the chieftain becomes the victim of his own men.

Cast includes a number of familiar stars. Best known internationally is Hildegard Knef (Neff), as an elegant gangster moll who turns against her boss. Goetz George is the young revenger while Richard Muench contributes an effectual study of a gangster boss sitting in

a wheelchair. Carl Lange, whose marked face is a menace in itself, plays one of his sinister men.

Alfred Vohrer's direction reveals knowhow. He already has several similar pix to his credit. The lensing by vet cameraman Bruno Mondi, with exteriors shot on actual locations in London and Trieste, is a plus. As is Martin Boettcher's fine score. Pic was made for about $375,000.

Hans.

Du Grabuge Chez Les Veuves
(Trouble Among Widows)
(FRENCH)

Paris, May 5.

Cocinor release of Marceau-Cocinor, Laetitia production. Stars Danielle Darrieux, Dany Carrel; features Jean Rochefort, Enzo Doria, Jacques Castelot, Pascale De Boysson. Directed by Jacques Poitrenaud. Screenplay, Denys De La Patelliere, Albert Simonin from book by Jean-Pierre Ferriere; camera, Armand Thirard; editor, Gilbert Natot. At Balzac, Paris. Running time, **95 MINS.**

Judith	Danielle Darrieux
Isabell	Dany Carrel
Laforet	Jean Rochefort
Angelo	Enzo Doria
Cyril	Jacques Castelot
Gilberte	Pascale De Boysson

Film has a good idea that is not completely brought off. It tries to play for broad, black humor and drama at the same time, with both suffering as a result. Abroad, its best chances are for dualer use or specialized situations on its stylish performances by Danielle Darrieux and Dany Carrel.

A young widow sees a more matronly woman, dressed in black, turn up at the funeral of her husband and lament about him. Since her husband was a fairly dreary, selfish type she wonders about this. But it seems that the husband had helped this woman by turning a cache of cocaine into heroin. Now this woman is trying to find out where it is since the man died before delivering it.

The young woman catches on and finds the stuff, and suddenly is courted by the other woman's gigolo and a police inspector. It turns out the young woman had murdered her husband and everybody gets their comeuppance. Director Jacques Poitrenaud has not been able to fuse the serious and comic elements. Result is that the film vacillates and has only intermittently successful scenes.

Miss Darrieux is elegant and even pitiable as an aging woman who tries everything to hold a young gigolo while Dany Carrel is properly conniving and selfish as the other woman. Male roles are adequate. Probably the best impact is made by Pasquale De Boysson as the spinster sister-in-law who gets a whiff of the cocaine by mistake.

This is technically good with a fine production look. *Mosk.*

Cannes Festival

The Visit
(GERMAN-FRENCH-ITALO-U.S.)
(CINEMASCOPE)

Cannes, May 5.

20th-Fox release of Deutschefox-Cinecitta-Dear Film-Siecle-PECF production. Stars Ingrid Bergman, Anthony Quinn; features Irina Demick, Claude Dauphin, Valentina Cortese, Romolo Valli, Paolo Stoppa, Eduardo Ciannelli, Jacques Dufilho. Directed by Bernhard Wicki. Screenplay, Ben Barzman from play by Friedrich Durrenmatt; camera, Armando Nannuzzi; editor, Samuel Beetley. At Cannes Film Fest. Running time, **100 MINS.**

Karla	Ingrid Bergman
Serge	Anthony Quinn
Anya	Irina Demich
Badrick	Claude Dauphin
Doctor	Paolo Stoppa
Painter	Romolo Valli
Mathilde	Valentina Cortese
Innkeeper	Eduardo Ciannelli
Frisch	Jacques Dufilho

(In English)

An example of international film mixing, pic is based on a Swiss-German's play English adaptation, with a Swiss-German director, Yank scripter and U.S., French, German and Italo thesps. All this does not quite jell and film's main selling points remain the Ingrid Bergman and Anthony Quinn names.

Offbeat theme about a woman's vengeance on a man and a township that wronged her as a girl, slants this mainly for an arty approach, with playoff leaning on the star names. Its parable on the corruptive power of money, and the hatred engendered by betrayed love, seems somewhat stilted. However, there is a strange old European atmosphere. So 20th-Fox will probably have to handle this carefully in most markets for best results. There may also be an asset in the offbeat casting of Miss Bergman and Quinn for curio values even if both are monumentally miscast.

Miss Bergman is a fabulously rich woman who comes back to a mythical independent European township that smacks of mittel-Europa. The town is rundown with its industries all but gone. As an ex-resident, she is counted on as a savior and a big dance is put on in her honor. But here she drops a bombshell in demanding the death of Quinn, a man who had wronged her, before she would give $2,000,000 to the township and its people.

At first, greeted with rage, the people back Quinn, and then begin to hate him and finally try to kill him outright and then in the guise of a new law that can execute him for past actions. It seems he had been Miss Bergman's lover when she was a 17-year-old slavey. When she was pregnant, he trumped up court proceedings against her on her alleged immorality and had her run out of town to marry a woman with a business.

Miss Bergman landed in a house of ill-repute, saw her child die and then ended up marrying a millionaire. She had bought up the industries and mines of the town and closed them while preparing her colossal revenge. She finally

relents at the end when they condemn Quinn to death, and decides it is a better and more fitting punishment to keep him alive among people who wanted his blood. This is a switch from the play in the Alfred Lunt-Lynn Fontanne N. Y. production.

Miss Bergman first appears with harsh makeup and then intermittently looks baroque, beautiful or drawn. If again proving her projective presence she is hard put to be able to repress her natural fresh, good natured character and replace it by a grim, determined woman full of spite and hatred.

Quinn's rugged stature and virility are also repressed with difficulty to betray a little man, while the fact that both still look capable of love also somewhat waters down the theme. There is thus a break with the original play in which the characters were very old.

Film also brushes broadside satires on human cupidity. On stage, the outright baroque qualities were able to make the symbolical aspects sharper while on film the changeover seems more general and too sudden for top impact.

Besides Miss Bergman and Quinn many solid international actors enact small roles well. But they are mere stereotypes. Irina Demich is supposed to mirror the maid that Miss Bergman once was and is thus a reflection of a part which is carried off no more than adequately.

Sets look tacky and theatrical rather than really run down and poverty stricken while lensing has the right gray tones and the technical dress is fine. Director Bernhard Wicki has obtained some fire in isolated scenes to underline the theme of the corruption of power and riches.

Miss Bergman hovering over the town on a balcony in far out dresses, flanked by a leopard, is effective as is the crowd's hunting of her escaped leopard which is an excuse to track Quinn. *Mosk.*

La Peau Douce
(The Soft Skin)
(FRENCH)

Cannes, May 12.

Athos films release of SEDIF-Films Du Carrosse production. Stars Jean Desailly, Francoise Dorleac, Nelly Benedetti; features Daniel Ceccaldi, Jean Lanier. Directed by Francois Truffaut. Screenplay, Truffaut, J. L. Richard; camera, Raoul Coutard; editor, Claudine Bouche. At Cannes Film Fest. Running time, **115 MINS.**

Pierre	Jean Desailly
Nicole	Francoise Dorleac
Franca	Nelly Benedetti
Clement	Daniel Ceccaldi
Michel	Jean Lanier
Odile	Paule Emanuele

Francois Truffaut, whose inventive charm got him an international name via his personal pix on childhood, timidity and personal freedom and love, now comes up with an austere, well-made look at a case of adultery. It appears primarily an arty house bet on its discretion, adroit observation and theme, with depth distrib calling for hardsell.

Heretofore full of free-wheeling inventivessness in his scenes, Truffaut now goes in for a clean, uncluttered study of a man's first extra-marital affair in 12 years that leads to tragedy.

Film details the matter-of-fact homelife of a semi-successful high-brow magazine editor and lecturer who one day becomes enamored of an airline hostess. It seems that her freshness brings on desire or some obscure need for adventure. He manages to get a date with her and love comes quickly, and is carried on when they get back to Paris. The wife senses something wrong and catches him in a lie. It leads to a decision to divorce. But when she finds out it is a young girl she calmly takes down a rifle and shoots him dead.

One of the flaws in the pic is that the three rather colorless people suddenly do unusual things without any sort of preparation for this side of them. People may suddenly do strange things but the film's almost classic treatment makes them jolting rather than dramatically right.

But Truffaut does show that he can make a solidly carpentered film like anybody else. There are some irrepressibly witty scenes.

Direction is sharp and lensing has the clear gradations and compositions to fit this prosaic pic. Thesps are all fairly ordinary characters, and also have a lack of positive drive that almost makes them drab at times. But they are ordinary people. Life may be ambiguous and unsorted in these things but the film exploits this rather than making it dramatically satisfying. Francoise Dorleac has the feckless quality for the girl while Jean Desailly the reserve and phlegmatic qualities of a supposedly set man who succumbs to the flesh. Nelly Benedetti is more unclear as the seemingly settled housewife who is capable of murder when her home is threatened.

This marks a more mature turn for director Truffaut and a seeming decision to treat more reserved and settled aspects rather than the lowlife, groping youth, gangster and bohemian milieus he has dealt with before. It is more adult if the spontaneous spark of his previous pix is not there.

But this finely made pic could hit with more selective audiences who will accept its muted style and subdued acting. Truffaut adequately displays his filmic talents if he has somewhat overblown a fairly banal situation. It seems that adultery is no longer a laughing matter among ex-Wave filmmakers.
Mosk.

Die Tote Von Beverly.. Hills
(The Dead One of Beverly Hills)
(GERMAN—COLOR)
Cannes, May 5.
<small>Constantin release of Modern Art Film (Hans-Juergen Pohland) production. Stars Heidelinde Weis. Klausjuergen Wussow; features Horst Frank, Wolfgang Neuss, E. F. Fuerbringer. Directed by Michael Pfleghar. Screenplay, Peter Laregh, Hans-Juergen Pohland and Michael Pfleghar, after same-titled novel by Curt Goetz; camera (Eastmancolor), Ernst Wild; music, Heinz Kiessling. At Cannes Film Fest. Running time, 110 MINS.
Lu .... Heidelinde Weis
C.G. .... Klausjuergen Wussow
Dr. Maning .... Horst Frank
Ben .... Wolfgang Neuss
Sostlov .... E. F. Fuerbringer
Swendka .... Peter Schuette
Peter Dehne .... Bruno Dietrich
Priest .... Herbert Weissbach</small>

This film commanded attention long before its completion in Germany since the first German postwar feature pic that was shot (80%) in Hollywood. Young producer Hans-Juergen Pohland put all his money into the production (budgeted at $300,000) and employed young Michael Pfleghar, prominent creator of many German musical tele programs, as director. "Beverly Hills" meant Pfleghar's debut as a feature film director.

In Germany, film can cash in on the same-titled satirical bestseller by the late Curt Goetz. Also the fact that a young German producer took the risk to make a picture in Hollywood is an exploitation factor in Germany. Despite all ambition and devotion, the film's artistic outcome doesn't quite come up to expectations. Although it has been sold to a number of countries, the film's foreign chances appear mild.

That the production didn't make the grade is primarily the fault of an inadequate script. As a satire, the film is not funny enough. Much is involuntarily funny because of the German—or even Berlinese—spoken in Hollywood. Much is banal in flavor. Quite obviously, the German film team had no leisure in Hollywood. All had to go fast. Of course, this doesn't excuse the improperly prepared script.

The story is simple: The body of a dead, young girl has been found in BevHills. The detective who sets out to solve the case discovers a daybook of the murdered girl and —in flashbacks—the girl's erotical life story is retold. The girl, a mixture of Lulu and Lolita, had countless romances and one of them broke her neck: Two dancing sisters murdered her because of jealousy.

Pfleghar tried to achieve something that he thought different. He let the flashbacks run in color and the detective story in black and white photography. His flair for imagination is felt now and then, but he couldn't overcome the deficiencies in the script. Also, one feels that the satirical essence of the novel, which made amusing reading, doesn't qualify itself too well for filmization.

The film's biggest plus point is Heidelinde Weis in first big screen role. This Viennese actress is undoubtedly a promising talent. Her portrayal of the Lulu-Lolita type of Goetz' Lu is a complete delight. And her face is a pleasant departure from so many a conventional screen puss. There is nothing exciting about the acting by the others. The musical score is fine and the lensing in parts interesting. Other technical credits come up to average.
Hans.

Kvarteret Korpen
(Raven Street)
(SWEDISH)
Cannes, May 5.
<small>Europa Film production and release. With Thommy Berggren, Keve Hjelm, Emy Strom, Ingvar Hirdwall. Written and directed by Bo Widerberg. Camera, Jan Lindestrom; editor, Wic Kjellin. At Cannes Film Fest. Running time, 100 MINS.
Anders .... Thommy Berggren
Father .... Keve Hjelm
Mother .... Emy Strom
Sixten .... Ingvar Hirdwall
Elsie .... Christina Framback</small>

Swedish films lately have been filled with anguish about the absence of God, the dark doings of alienated delinquents or the lack of communication and faith among people. This one sparks a difference by being a look at the Sweden of the '30's which combines a universal outlook. With foreign fare seemingly limited to the more titilating and dynamic this tender, well-observed pic about the coming of age of a young man may find it difficult going in the U.S.

With the right personal handling and placement, it could be worth a try on its intrinsically fine characterization; and faultless emotions. However, film is slow and relies on a muted series of scenes to build to its moments of truth.

The well-contrasted lensing brings out the 30's look adequately. The bare, little street of the action is also well notated with its characters, and children. A young writer tries to break out and finally does. That is the essence of it. But in the process, the first rays of worker determination and the need to raise the level of the poverty-stricken sections of the popula'n are well limned.

Thommy Berggren has the right elan, divided loyalties and final strength to break with this gray life even if it means leaving a pregnant girl in the lurch. Keve Hjelm is fine as the pathetic father while Emy Strom gives strength and depth to the mother. The allusions to politics and feel of the times are applicable to most countries in depression days.

Film is thus an estimable effort that will still find it hard to make its way outside of Sweden. A bit more dramatic edge would have made it even more effective. As is, director Bo Widerberg shows himself one of the more gifted among the Swedish newcomers. This is his second film and denotes a deep pro flair.
Mosk.

Aimez-Vous Les Femmes?
(Do You Like Women?)
(FRENCH)
Cannes, May 5.
<small>Comacico release of Pierre Kalfon-Film Number One production. Stars Edwige Feuillere, Sophie Daumier, Guy Bedos; features Gerard Sety, Roger Blin, Guido Alberti. Directed by Jean Leon. Screenplay, Roman Polanski, Gerard Brach from book by Georges Bardawil; camera, Sacha Vierny; music, Ward Swingle. At Cannes Film Fest. Running time, 100 MINS.
Aunt .... Edwige Feuillere
Violette .... Sophie Daumier
Nephew .... Guy Bedos
Leader .... Guido Alberti
Inspector .... Gregoire Aslan
Reporter .... Gerard Sety</small>

Fairly sprightly spoof on involved suspense pix also has the offbeat premise about an innocent mixed up with a sect that likes to eat comely girls, literally. All turns out well after some far-fetched adventures. Playoff on its theme and general inventiveness seems the lot for this film offshore, with arty chances more limited.

Eating in a vegetarian restaurant, a young writer finds a dead man in the wash room. It disappears when he gets the police but holding the hat gets him involved with

a pretty girl. From there on it entails murders by both the secret sect and a bunch of gangsters who want a statue filled with opium that was shipped to the sect. Bouncing between is the bewildered young man.

After weird poison dart murders, love, gang fights and the twin sister of the heroine being served in a big dish and saved in the nick of time, it has the usual happy ending. Director Jean Leon, for his first production, shows a feeling for maintaining the right mock seriousness but sometimes lacks the inventiveness, pace and visual byplay to sustain it throughout.

Players are acceptable if they mainly lack the weight and presence to add a sheen and mock plausibility to their shenanigans. Bedos is gently perplexed if he still lacks the necessary timing. He hints promise. Sophie Daumier is appealing physically while tragedienne Edwige Feuillere has a romp as a zany aunt. Chalk this up as a madcap offbeater that manages to sustain interest though sometimes it repeats itself.

Perhaps canny spotting and hypoing could make this a playoff item with legs. It has good technical credits and okay production dress with a plus in the zesty music of Ward Swingle which already is out on Mercury records stateside.
Mosk.

Primero Yo
(Me First)
(ARGENTINIAN)
Cannes, May 12.
<small>AAA release of Hector Olivera production. With Alberto De Mendoza, Susana Freyre, Marilina Ross, Ricardo Areco, Hector Gance, Mercedes Sombra. Directed by Fernando Ayala. Screenplay, Luis Pico Estrada; camera, Ricardo Younis; editor, Atilio Rinaldi. At Cannes Film Fest. Running time, 90 MINS.
Juanjo .... Alberto De Mendoza
Ines .... Susana Freyre
Laura .... Marilini Ross
Jacie .... Ricardo Areco
Horacio .... Hector Gance</small>

A feckless, rich playboy's comeuppance is handled without the necessary depth in characterization or the ability to make its theme more than surface. It thus emerges mainly a Latino language possibility on its acceptable pacing and smooth, if predictable unfoldment.

The man in question is a noted auto racer and also a most successful Don Juan if he no longer seems to take too much pleasure in these things. A son of 20 years, comes to stay with him. The youth is sensitive, reserved, and the opposite of his selfish but charming father.

So comes the boy's initiation to love by his father's mistress and his finding real love with a young girl. But this love is destroyed when his father seduces her on a bet. He feels his son is not ready for marriage and this should be only fun for his son. But the boy commits suicide, and the father is left alone.

Director Fernando Ayala has given this a fairly proper feeling for the milieu but has lacked the edge to make these people more than cardboard characters. However, the love scenes are well done. Technical and production aspects are only fair.
Mosk.

Krik
(First Cry)
(CZECHOSLAVAKIAN)

Cannes, May 5.

Czech State Film release and production. No Star credits. Directed by Jaromil Jires. Screenplay, Ludvik Askenazy, Jires; camera, Jaroslav Kucera; music, Jan Klusak. At Cannes Film Fest. Running time, **80 MINS.**
Slavek .... Joself Abrham
Ivana .... Eva Limanova
Teacher .... Eva Kopecka

Film displays frozen shots to emphasize a point, simultaneous unfolding of past, present and even future time, with a leavening of a simple love story. There's also comment on that most banal and yet most moving and important human event, namely the birth of a baby. This has tenderness and insight but is somewhat diffuse in impact and limited in character probing. It is thus mainly specialized entry for abroad.

It is time for the young husband to get his wife to the hospital for her baby. As he goes about his work as a tv repairman he thinks back on their meeting and courtship, shown as he feels them, as well as his growing awareness of the world around him into which his child will be born. This allows for allusions to the A-Bomb, his taking sides in a racial rumpus as well as contrasting his wife's outlooks during her delivery and just before it.

Propaganda is held in check through adroit imagery, pacing and editing. But it is there, if muted. Acting is uncluttered and simple as is fitting to this unpretentious but taking little pic. Screenplay is meritorious and Jaromil Jires emerges a director of promise for his first pic.

It just lacks the poetic and lyrical breadth to make the spontaneous and worked out scenes fuse into a moving as well as interesting look at the emotions at play. But it makes it points on man's general unawareness and also does not paint a rosy picture of young life in that country today. *Mosk.*

La Douceur Du Village
(Village Sweetness)
(FRENCH—COLOR—SCOPE)
Cannes, May 7.

Films de La Pleiade release of Pierre Braunberger production. Conception by Francois Reichenbach. Camera (Eastmancolor), Reichenbach. J. M. Ripert; editor, J. Rboy. At Cann e Film Fest. Running time, **47 MINS.**

Documentary on village life is a gently chiding look at the seasons and existance changes entailed. It has a clever envelope in linking sequences via a teacher's series of lessons to young students. It is full of inventive juxtapositions of images, cannily but not woundingly satiric, and a pic that could well be good fodder for supporting art fare abroad or for video usage.

Livestock and its place in the village outlook is the beginning, followed by morals, lectures on work and laws, war peace etc. Each gets a neat blending of scenes taken around the village during a better part of a year by filmmaker Francois Reichenbach and an assistant. Lensing is excellent, notations clever and this is a stimulating essay-type pic with foreign chances positive.

La Nina De Luto
(The Girl in Mourning)
(SPANISH—COLOR)
Cannes, May 7.

Eco Films, Impala release and production. No Star credits. Written and directed by Manuel Summers. Camera (Eastmancolor), Francisco Fraile; editor, Pedro Del Rey. At Cannes Film Fest. Running time, **84 MINS.**
Rocio .... Maria Jose Alfonso
Raphael .... Alfredo Landa

Though death is the mainspring in the workings of this pic, it packs many comic moments and manages to make its point about the stifling of the life force and life itself by outmoded, anachronistic mores and habits. Only drawback is a predictability in the progression and happenings with not enough bite to be irony. As is, it is a solid Latin language circuit bet with some more general and even art chances if well sold.

A young couple in a small Southern Hispano town have been kept apart by the period of mourning, six months, she has had to face due to the death of a near relative. The townspeople are provincial and old fashioned and frown on any sort of joy or contentment during the period.

They are reunited and marriage is looming when her grandfather dies. Comes the mourning period and this time he revolts only to be subdued by the girl's fears of being compromised, what people will think, and her stern family. But love seems to be winning and she is ready to go off to another town with him when her father dies. He goes off sadly alone.

Main plus aspects are the easy characterizations, if familiar, and the inventive little sidelight happenings that enhance the scenes. And director-writer Manuel Summers also contrives to keep this tasteful and in line if it does suffer in not having enough depth in its parody that eventually lets it get repetitive. *Mosk.*

Pacsirta
(The Lark)
(HUNGARIAN)
Cannes, May 5.

Hungarofilm release of Hunnia Film production. With Antal Pager, Klari Tolnay, Anna Naby, Zoltan Litinovits, Mari Torocsik. Directed by Laszlo Ranody. Screenplay, Tamas Huszty from book by Dezso Kosztolani; camera, Gyorgy Illes; music, Ferenc Farkas. At Cannes Film Fest. Running time, **100 MINS.**
Akos .... Antal Pager
Wife .... Klari Tolnay
Pacsirta .... Anna Nagy
Miklos .... Zoltan Litinovits
Margit .... Mari Torocsik

A noted Hungarian novel about smalltown stuffiness at the turn-of-the-century is translated to the screen with delicacy and taste. But its literary tang and academic treatment limit this to lingo and special situations abroad.

A homely daughter has made a couple almost recluses. Mirrors are covered, the girl does all the cooking and the man's retirement makes them even more remote from the general social life of their town. The daughter's visit to an uncle, to try for a possible match with a peasant widower, brings realization and an understanding of their outlooks to the parents.

The man feels old before his time but the wife, still fetching, dreams of once more being seen about. He goes back to an old drinking club and is struck by the pompous, petty and rather fetid

---

lives led and realizes that he and his wife have really hated their homely daughter and selfishly hidden this feeling.

Anna Nagy, seen here as a pretty girl in real life, deserves a nod for letting herself be made so ugly. She also fills the role with a sad understanding of the irritating and pitiable character of this shunned girl. Antal Pager is excellent as the father. Others in smaller parts also register well.

Director Laszlo Ranody has a flair for recreating the times and sometimes gets a true feeling of sadness, satire and poignance into this tale without making the characters one-dimensional. It is elegantly lensed and a smooth period piece just lacking a deeper and more encompassing look at the times. *Mosk.*

Black Like Me

Quick playoff could mean quick payoff for tale of man who pigmented his skin to see the whites as a Negro does. Exploitable title and saturation selling indicate potential moneymaker. Film technically bad.

Continental Distribution Co. release of a Julius Tannenbaum production. Stars James Whitmore; features Sorrel Booke, Robert Gerringer, Al Freeman Jr., Lenka Peterson, Roscoe Lee Browne, Clifton James, Will Geer, Thelma Oliver. P. J. Sidney. Directed by Carl Lerner. Screenplay by Carl and Gerda Lerner, based on John Howard Griffin's book, "Black Like Me." Camera, Victor Lukens, Henry Mueller II; editor, Lora Hayes; sound, Stanley Kasper; music, composed and conducted by Meyer Kupferman asst. director, Edward Wells; make-up, Herman Buchman. Reviewed in N.Y., May 14, '64. Running time, **107 MINS.**
John Finley Horton .... James Whitmore
Dr. Jackson .... Sorrel Booke
Ed Saunders .... Robert Gerringer
Tom Newcomb .... Al Freeman Jr.
Christophe .... Roscoe Lee Browne
Eli Carr .... Clifton James
Farmer .... Will Geer
Georgie .... Thelma Oliver
Frank Newcomb .... P. J. Sidney
Bus Driver .... Don Priest
Mason .... Walter Mason
Hodges .... John Marriott
Lucy Horton .... Lenka Peterson
Burt Wilson .... Richard Ward
Salesman .... Stanley Brock
Nice Young Man ...... David Huddleston
Vertell .... Billy Allen
Stretch .... Llewellyn B. Skinner
Hoodlum .... Matt Clark
Mary Saunders ...... Sarah Cunningham
Mrs. Townsend .... Eva Jessye
Charles Maynard .... Alan Bergmann
The Priest .... Ralph Dunn

Early bookings and promotion indicate Continental intends purely commercial selloff for this what's-it-like-to-be-a-Negro film. It's skeded to open in 60 N.Y. area houses on May 20. Even so, film will require careful handling in many situations.

Planned heavy promotion (early ads are highlighting more lurid aspects) should attract wider audiences than those reached by John Howard Griffin's book and original magazine series. Title and theme, exploitedly shrewdly, could easily recover medium-sized production cost and rack up profit. Best playoff appears to be, after first general saturation attempts, via sexploitation houses and drive-ins.

Film is first directorial effort of Carl Lerner, a N.Y. film editor. He also did the screenplay in collaboration with wife Gerda. Although some of his ideas are effective, such as the recurring use, as a symbol of the color-bar, of a white-line-divided highway, and some of the dialogue, particularly that spoken by the lesser Negro characters, natural and interesting, the technical obstacles were frequently too much for him. What may have started out as a seriously conceived cinematic version of Griffin's book wound up as a wishy-washy effort that will do the cause of integration little good.

The script, although credited as being based on Griffin's book, diary and articles, makes such changes as fictionalizing Griffin's, and other characters', names, indicating that other facts may have also been altered. The original outlet for the story was serialization in Sepia, a national Negro-market magazine. In the film the articles are printed in a Negro-market magazine called Black and Tan, published, of all things, by a white Texas millionaire.

This is only one of many illogical and poorly-conceived incidents. Whitmore, also supposedly Texan, speaks with northern accent. His hitchhiking through the south results in rides with only white motorists; he never appears to be in danger of losing his obviously good clothing, luggage and money; he carries his white driver's license on his person. His articles, printed while he's still making the experiment, have pictures showing him as both white and Negro but no one recognizes him although he has persistently used his own name. All of which apparently violates the cautions which surrounded the real journalistic venture.

Another major detraction from plausible acceptance of the film is James Whitmore's obvious makeup. If the original Griffin made the change, as claimed, with injections, Whitmore would have been well advised to have tried the same method. Instead, he looks like a high-school Othello. Although he works hard to be convincing, his reactions are frequently illogical because of script demands and occasionally, as in his furious rebuttals to white men who question him about his sex life (as a Negro), completely unconvincing.

Stress on sex (done through these conversations rather than any actual involvement between members of the two races—this, indeed, is pointedly avoided) is undoubtedly meant to titillate, as are the occasional recourses to strong language. Latter is acceptable because it is natural to the situation but the sex discussions are repetitive and poorly handled.

Acting, generally, mixes exaggeration, self consciousness and naturalness. Sometimes colorful, it too often lacks credence. Supporting players, also victims of the script, have little time to create lasting characterizations. Two are successful. Richard Ward's bootblack who teaches Whitmore how to "pass" as colored and David Huddleston as the one white driver who doesn't bug him about his sex life are very good. Impressive also are Roscoe Lee Browne, Llewellyn B. Skinner, Billie Allen, Thelma Oliver, Alan Bergmann, Robert Gerringer, P. J. Sidney and Al Freeman Jr.

Victor Lukens and Henry Mueller's black and white camerawork suggests they may have operated as separate units, shooting concurrently to save time and money, then joining sequences. One tracking shot through a Negro neighborhood, despite the jerky effect of a concealed or hand-held camera, makes up in realism for some steadier but unimaginative interior sequences. Sound, only fair throughout, has a hollow, echo-chamber effect in some intimate scenes that is most annoying.

Although Lerner is a film editor by profession, film's cutting was handled by Lora Hayes, apparently with little supervision. Too frequent cuts tend to makes episodes jumpy and continuity sporadic. Apparently no dissolves were used, making the flashbacks hard to adjust to. Film, while not overlong, could benefit by excision of some meaningless bits. Shorter running time would also help in the fast turnover market for which it is headed.

Meyer Kupferman's music is neither help nor hindrance although one bit of Whitmore playing classical music on an upright is very bad. *Robe.*

For Those Who Think Young
(TECHNICOLOR-TECHNISCOPE)

Another beach party aimed at those who attend young. Summer fare has several new faces. Heavy commercial tie-ins indicate beaucoup cross-plugs.

United Artists release of Aubrey Schenck-Howard W. Koch production. Produced by Hugh Benson. Directed by Leslie H. Martinson. Stars James Darren, Pamela Tiffen, Paul Lynde; features Tina Louise, Nancy Sinatra, Claudia Martin, Woody Woodbury. Screenplay by James O'Hanlon, George O'Hanlon, Dan Beaumont, from story by Beaumont; camera (Technicolor, Techniscope), Harold E. Stine; editor, Frank P. Keller; sound, Hugo Grenzbach, John Wilkinson; music, composed-conducted by Jerry Fielding song, "For Those Who Think Young," Jerry Livingston, Mack David; art direction, Hal Pereira, Arthur Lonergan; set decoration, Sam Comer, James Payne. Reviewed in N.Y., May 6, '64. Running time, **96 MINS.**

Gardner "Ding" Pruitt III	James Darren
Sandy Palmer	Pamela Tiffin
Woody Woodbury	Himself
Sid Hoyt	Paul Lynde
Topaz McQueen	Tina Louise
Karen Cross	Nancy Sinatra
Kelp	Bob Denver
Sue Lewis	Claudia Martin
Edgar J. Cronin	Robert Middleton
Dr. Pauline Thayer	Ellen McRae
Beach Girl	Amedee Chabot
Gus Kestler	Louis Quinn
Sessue	Sammee Tong
Dean Watkins	Addison Richards
Mousie	Mousie Garner
Lou	Benny Baker
Laura Pruitt	Anna Lee
Mrs. Harkness	Sheila Bromley
Cronin Associates	Jack LaRue, Allen Jenkins, Robert Armstrong
Detectives	George Raft, Roger Smith
Butler	Alberto Morin
Reporter	Byron Kane

This slanted pitch to the young in tastes should be very successful as it contains every status symbol by which young America apparently measures itself. Its principal contribution to the future of films, however, is the introduction of many new and pretty faces and several new talents.

With such surefire exploitable angles as youth, fun, music and unconcern, "For Those Who Think Young" should slice itself a nice piece of summer business, hitting the market in early June. Pepsi-cola, from whence came the title as any addict knows, is only the most prominent of the film's many plugs for consumer products from ice cream to tv sets, suggesting plugs in return.

Director Leslie Martinson probably found this frothy foolishness a breeze after "PT 109" and wisely made no effort to corral his skittish colts. The result is much fast action and surface charm.

That slight feeling of familiarity in James and George O'Hanlan and Dan Beaumont's script which will bug more attentive viewers is due to the presence, therein, of heavy helpings from some more than twice-told tales. The prime ingredients are all there—college setting, ageless students, surfing, b.m.o.c., wild oats sowing and reaping, wolf into lamb. The heavy helpings of cheese cake, beefcake and well-buttered corn make for a hi-caloric screen diet!

Rich boy James Darren and poor girl Pamela Tiffin tie the most romantic knots in the plot's flimsy thread, with several second-teams providing comedy relief. Paul Lynde is film's biggest talent waste, being relegated to stooging for nitery comedian Woody Woodbury. Making his screen debut, Woodbury's heavily - scrubbed version of his nitery routine comes off as dullsville but he shows considerable personality and, in his straight scenes, some acting promise.

Nancy Sinatra and Bob Denver, second-banana romantics, get little screen time but make it count. Denver, as Darren's bearded beatnik buddy, overplays for the most part but provides film's top moment — a reverse switch on Senor Wences. It can't be described in words but is hideously hilarious. Miss Sinatra, pretty without being beautiful, has something better going for her—a delightful personality and the suggestion of a latent acting ability which needs a greater challenge than provided here.

Cast members who come on strong if briefly include Ellen McRae, a delightful sociology prof; Amedee Chabot, a stunning blonde beauty with one scene, who creates a heat wave by letting her seat wave; Claudia Martin, a sorority type who spends more time on the phone than did the late A. G. Bell.

Familiar faces, including some long-absent ones, include Tina Louise as an ex-stripper who tutors math students, Robert Middleton, Benny Baker, Anna Lee, Jack La Rue, Allen Jenkins, Robert Armstrong, George Raft and Roger Smith. Their roles, other than Middleton's villainous grandfather, are inconsequential.

Harold Stine's Technicolor photography makes the most of the beautiful scenery, whether created by Mother Nature or Wally Westmore. Latter, incidentally, loaded down his principal femmes with such heavy eye makeup, particularly Miss Tiffin, it makes them look half-asleep most of the time. Frank Keller's crisp editing only slips a few times, although he failed to catch one glaring booboo. Miss McRae is bedded down on a sofa with lots of pillows in Woodbury's apartment when she passes out, but awakens on his bed, which has been moved to a terrace for his own use.

Jerry Fielding's music is, appropriately, as flavorsome and substantial as cotton candy. Darren sings Jerry Livingston and Mack David's title tune, the cast joining in on a couple of others. One, "Surf's Up," is the outlet for Kelp's wild bit. *Robe.*

Gorath
(TOHOSCOPE—COLOR)

Japanese scifi film with exploitation possibilities for general market.

Hollywood, May 15.

Brenco presentation of Toho production. Features Ryo Ikebe, Akihiko Hirata, Jun Tazaki, Yumi Shirakawa, Takashi Shimura. Directed by Inoshiro Honda. Screenplay, Takeshi Kimura; camera (Eastman-Color), Hajime Koizumil; special effects, Eiji Tsuburaya; music, Kan Ishii. Previewed at Egyptian Theatre, May 15, '64. Running time, **83 MINS.**

Exploitation potential of this Japanese-made scifi is considerable, pegged on pic's subject of a giant celestial body hurtling toward Earth and certain destruction of our own planet. Japanese producers in the past have displayed great ingenuity along this line of scientific speculation, and "Gorath," name of the onrushing flaming object, lends certain credence. Special effects are particularly interesting, but the story itself is possibly too scientific for popular reception and onlooker is left in constant state of wonderment except for the overall premise. A hard-driving campaign, however, should help attract certain trade.

Eastman-color film, produced by Toho, has been acquired for world distribution (except the Far East, retained by Toho) by Edward L. Alperson and Stanley Meyer's Brenco Pictures, with Allied Artists to handle Southern California release. Pic is dubbed in English, generally a first-class endeavor, so it's aimed for general release instead of strictly the foreign and art-house exposure.

Its short length of 83 minutes makes it a handy entry in most theatres, but there is need of sharp editing, particularly in its opening, which for seven minutes concentrates on shots of the various constellations and a lecture, no less, on astronomy and movement of the heavens. Plot picks up in Tokyo, where scientists have discovered a monstrous red-hot orb racing toward Earth, and efforts are launched to see what can be done about avoiding disaster when they collide.

A space ship, venturing too near the titanic body with 6,000 times the gravitational pull of Earth, is able to send back valuable information before it crashes, and the Japanese begin to plot their desperate plan with the other nations of the world. The world is saved at the last minute by rockets installed in bases at the South Pole exploding and moving the earth out of orbit sufficiently for Gorath to pass by.

Names of Japanese thesps are unknown in this country, but turn in very creditable performances, particularly Ryo Ikebe, the scientist most responsible for saving the earth. Particular credit goes to Eiji Tsuburaya for his spectacular special effects, and Inoshiro Honda's direction catches the spirit of the Takeshi Kimura screenplay. Color photography by Hajime Koizumi is another strong asset, as is Kan Ishii's mood music. *Whit.*

Trouble-Fete
(CANADIAN)

Montreal, May 6.

France Film release of Cooperatio Production. Producer, Jean-Claude Lord, director, Pierre Patry; screenplay, Lord & Patry; camera, Jean Roy; editing, Lucien Marleau; music, Claude Leveilles. With Lucien Hamelin, Louise Remy, Percy Rodriguez, Henri Tremblay, Yves Corbeil. Premiere at St. Denis, Montreal. Running time, **95 MINS.**

(In French)

This interesting, low-budget, cooperative film venture follows the familiar paths of a young student in revolt against conformity, but who is misunderstood and causes himself more trouble than would seem worthwhile. Although melodramatic in places it takes on a contemporary validity being set against Quebec's present day social unrest.

Vigorously directed, played with naturalism and intense conviction, and brilliantly photographed with touches of avant-garde techniques, this is a welcome addition to the growing number of Canadian feature films now being planned and produced. It's Canada's official entry at his year's Cannes film festival, and is a good commercial proposition for any country.

Prat.

Girl With Green Eyes
(BRITISH)

Thoughtfully directed, tenderly written and acted with immense vitality, this romance should provide a ready b.o. dividend, with careful selling.

London, May 15.

United Artists release of Woodfall Film (Oscar Lewenstein) production. Stars Peter Finch, Rita Tushingham; features Lynn Redgrave, T. P. McKenna, Arthur O'Sullivan, Eileen Crowe, Joe Lynch, Yolande Turner, Marie Kean. Directed by Desmond Davis. Screenplay by Edna O'Brien; camera, Manny Wynn; editor, Brian Smedley-Aston; music, John Addison. Previewed May 14, '64, at Leicester Square Theatre, London. Running time, **91 MINS.**

Eugene Gaillard .... Peter Finch
Kate Brady .... Rita Tushingham
Baba Brennan .... Lynn Redgrave
Josie Hannigan .... Marie Kean
Mr. Brady .... Arthur O'Sullivan
Malachi Sullivan .... Julian Glover
Priest .... T. P. McKenna
Joanna .... Lislott Goettinger
Bertie Counihan .... Patrick Laffan
Mrs. Byrne .... Eileen Crowe
Aunt .... May Craig
Andy Devlin .... Joe Lynch
Mary McIntosh .... Yolande Turner
Jack Holland .... Harry Brogan
Davey .... Michael Hennessy
Patrick Devlin .... Joe O'Donnell
Lodger .... Michael O'Brien
Ticket Collector .... Dave Kelly

This first film directed by Desmond Davis, who was a cameraman with Tony Richardson on "Loneliness of Long Distance Runner" and "Saturday Night, Sunday Morning," has the smell of success, though it may need careful nursing till word-of-mouth gets around. Certainly, in Davis, a bright new talent emerges. He is imaginative, prepared to take chances and has the sympathy to draw perceptive performances from his cast. "Girl With Green Eyes" is the sort of deceptively, simple love story that offers the unwary director scores of chances for stumbling, but Davis does not noticeably waver.

Producer Oscar Lewenstein (theatre man), lenser Manny Wynn and scenarist Edna O'Brien, who has adapted her own novel, are all first-timers. This enthusiasm, with the knowhow of Richardson behind it, has given the film its keen vitality, despite the leisurely theme.

Story is set in Dublin where two shopgirls share a room. One (Rita Tushingham) is a quiet, withdrawn girl in the painful throes of awakening. The other (Lynn Redgrave) is a vivacious, gabby, good-natured colleen with a roving eye for the boys. But when the two girls casually meet a quiet, middle-aged writer (Peter Finch), the friendship that starts up is, naturally, between Miss Tushingham and Finch. At first, she is to him just an amusing child whose eagerness and intensity give him a kick. Gradually, he finds that she is taking a far bigger place in his life, fulfilling a need and a hunger.

Sexually, their romance is slow to unfold and not very satisfactory. Her background, shyness and religion are barriers. He is a divorced man which brings down on them the fury of her peasant family. But somehow the association flowers until she realizes that it holds no future for either of them. And with a newly developed wisdom, she leaves and starts a new life in London. The ending is abrupt, a piece of unfinished business very true to life and just right.

The story is told by Miss O'Brien with a skillful sense of mood. Particularly she etches beautifully the uncertainty, gaucherie and tenderness of the girl and the patient restrained need of the man. Sometimes the dialog is a shade too artificial, but rarely strays too far into arty-craftiness. The humor and pathos are pleasantly interwoven.

Finch does a standout job as the tolerant writer who, despite occasional lapses into impatience, develops a fine understanding of the problems of the girl. Miss Tushingham is often moving, sometimes spritely and always interesting to watch in her puzzled shyness. Miss Redgrave, latest of the famous Redgrave family to make her mark, makes an ebullient wench. The trio are surrounded by such tornotch Irish character actors as Eileen Crowe, T. P. McKenna, May Craig, Arthur O'Sullivan, Marie Kean, Joe Lynch and Patrick Laffan. There is a neat, bitchy cameo by Finch's real life wife, Yolande Turner.

Technically, Davis pulls one or two tricks that come off very well, with the aid of brisk cutting. Notably a long duolog between Finch and Miss Tushingham which is uninterrupted but which, by change of scene and clothes, clearly indicates a passage of time spent wrestling over a perpetual problem. Some of the sound is inclined to be thick but this may well be due to the not always comprehensible Irish lingo.

The bustle of Dublin is nicely contrasted with the bleakness of the Irish countryside from which the heroine has fled. Manny Wynn's camerawork, the artwork and choice of locations all contribute usefully. John Addison has come up with a melodius but unobtrusive score.

With lashings of femme appeal and a warm emotional quality, this is a very worthy adult British pic which will repay attention by exhibs. It certainly adds laurels to the careers of Finch and Miss Tushingham. Pic introduces Miss Redgrave as a lively newcomer to the scene. It makes the next chore of director Davis, which is to be "The Uncle," something worth awaiting.

Rich.

Viva Las Vegas
(PANAVISION—COLOR)

Potent pairing of Presley and Ann-Margret insures bright b.o. future for this sleek but skimpy concoction of romance and songs.

Hollywood, May 15.

Metro release of Jack Cummings production. Stars Elvis Presley, Ann-Margret; features Cesare Danova, William Demarest, Nicky Blair. Directed by George Sidney. Screenplay, Sally Benson; camera (Metrocolor), Joseph Birok; editor, John McSweeney Jr.; music, George Stoll; asst. director, Milton Feldman. Reviewed at Hollywood Paramount Theatre, May 15, '64. Running time, **85 MINS.**

Lucky Jackson .... Elvis Presley
Rusty Martin .... Ann-Margret
Count Elmo Mancini ... Cesare Danova
Mr. Martin .... William Demarest
Shorty Farnsworth .... Nicky Blair

The sizzling co-star combination of Elvis Presley and Ann-Margret will be enough to carry "Viva Las Vegas" over the top for Metro. The picture is fortunate in having two such hot commodities for bait, because beyond several flashy musical numbers, a glamorous locale and one electrifying auto race sequence, the Jack Cummings production is a pretty trite and heavy-handed affair, puny in story development and distortedly preocupied with anatomical oomph. For all its shortcomings, however, it shapes up as a robust boxoffice entry.

The film is designed to dazzle the eye, assault the ear and ignore the brain. Vegas, of course, is the setting of Sally Benson's superficial contrivance about an auto racing buff (Presley) trying to raise funds to purchase an engine for the racer with which he hopes to win the Grand Prix. His main obstacle is a swimming instructress (A-M) who doesn't approve of his goal, but ultimately softens.

Hackneyed yarn provides the skeletal excuse for about 10 musical interludes, a quick tour of the U.S. gambling capital and that one slam-bang climactic sequence that lifts the film up by its bootstraps just when it is sorely in need of a lift. This depiction of an auto race is one of the most exciting passages of its type ever put on film. The driver's eye-view position in which the audience is placed as the cars whoosh over the swoops and dips of the desert highway engenders a genuine sensation of giddiness in the spectator—much like that generated by a roller coaster ride in Cinerama.

The pickings are lean outside of this show-stopping kicker. A few of the musical specialties have some merit and sparkle. The title tune gives Presley his meatiest and most commercial sounding material. His co-star's best number, although not her most sensually torrid, is the "My Rival" routine in which she laments the competition of his would-be profession. They pair up most successfully on "The Lady Loves Me," which has the earmarks of a fairly popular wax entry.

Neither EP nor A-M fares too well histrionically, but then this isn't the kind of vehicle that demands high-powered emoting. Their fans will probably be pleased enough with their showing. Cesare Danova provides the romanticompetition for Elvis in the thankless role of an Italian racing champion. This character gets a pretty big play throughout the film, but when the chips are down and he dies in a horrifying crash near the climax nobody seems to give a hoot. The only visible reaction is a kind of fleeting scowl and tch-tch-what-a-shame head wag by Presley as he zips to victory. William Demarest and Nicky Blair contribute likeable characterizations.

Any excuse to stare at a derriere in motion seems good enough for director George Sidney and cameraman Joseph Biroc. The provocative pulchritude of Ann-Margret and assorted other chicks and chorines makes the sexy scrutiny downright pleasurable to the male eye, but there is a certain lack of tastefulness or subtlety about the film's obsession with peeping at anatomical contours and epidermis simply for the sake of peeping.

There is a lot of visual flair to the Sidney-Biroc approach, and this is fortified with the razzle-dazzle editorial style of John McSweeney Jr. that keeps the production hopping even when it veers off on superfluous or irrevelevant tangents, which it does more than once. Other plus values are the showy art direction by George W. Davis and Edward Carfagno and a fairly expressive score by George Stoll.

Tube.

Cannes Festival

The Pumpkin Eater
(BRITISH)

Sensitively-made quality production. Strong cast. Perceptive screenplay.

Cannes, May 10.

Columbia release of a Romulus-Jack Clayton production. Stars Anne Bancroft, Peter Finch, James Mason. Features Cedric Hardwicke, Richard Johnson. Produced by James Woolf; director, Jack Clayton. Screenplay by Harold Pinter from a novel by Penelope Mortimer. Camera Oswald Morris; editor, James Clark; settings, Edward Marshall; music, George Delerue. At Cannes Film Festival, May 9, '64. Running time, **118 MINS.**

Jo Armitage .... Anne Bancroft
Jake Armitage .... Peter Finch
Bob Conway .... James Mason
Mr. James .... Cedric Hardwicke
Giles .... Richard Johnson
Psychiatrist .... Eric Porter
Mrs. James .... Rosalind Atkinson
Dinah .... Frances White
Mr. Armitage .... Alan Webb
Doctor .... Cyril Luckham
Beth Conway .... Janine Gray
Woman in Hairdressers .. Yootha Joyce
"King of Israel" .... Frank Singuineau

A wealth of talent has been harnessed to make "The Pumpkin Eater" a notable British film, and a worthy selection to represent the U.K. at the Cannes film festival. This Romulus production for Columbia release should command healthy support at the boxoffice from a public which appreciates literate writing and fine acting.

Harold Pinter's screenplay is based on a witty novel by Penelope Mortimer, and his script vividly brings to life the principal characters in this story of a shattered marriage, though Pinter's resort to flashback technique is confusing in the early stages.

Jack Clayton's direction gets off to a slow, almost casual start, but the pace quickens as the drama becomes more intense. He has used the considerable acting talents at his command for the maximum results.

Anne Bancroft is exceptionally good. She plays the mother of several young children who leaves her second husband to marry Peter Finch, a scriptwriter with a promising career ahead. And as he succeeds in his work, so she becomes aware of his increasing infidelites, and she becomes a case for psychiatric treatment. The role may sound conventional enough, but not as played by Miss Bancorft; she adds a depth and understanding which puts it on a higher plane. The contrasts in her moods and her appearance from radiant happiness to morbid depressions have a chilling and realistic quality.

Peter Finch's performance as the husband is among the best in his career. It is a mature interpretation, and always impressive. To him, casual infidelities are the natural prerequisites of a successful writer. The marital conflicts that come in their wake, as well as the reconciliations that follow, are presented with powerful dramatic force.

Notwithstanding the scope offered by these two roles, James Mason stands out in a much smaller part. He plays a deceived husband with a sinister, malevolent bitterness, to provide one of the acting highlights of the picture. And, typically of this grade of British film, there are the noteworthy supporting cameos, particularly from Cedric Hardwicke as Anne Bancroft's father, Richard Johnson as her second husband, Yootha Joyce in one telling scene in a hairdresser's, and from Eric Porter, Alan Webb, Janine Gray and others.

Technically, the production is first rate, and a credit to Romulus and producer James Woolf. Fine camera work by Oswald Morris, superb editing by James Clark, effective sets by Edward Marshall, and a sensitive score by George Delerue are among the standout features. *Myro.*

White Caravan
(RUSSIAN)
Cannes, May 12.

Mosfilm release of Grouzia production. With Ariadna Chenguelaia, Imet Kokihani, Spartak Bagachvili, Marat Eliozivili. Directed by Elder Chenguelaia, Tomaz Meliava. Screenplay, Marat Eliazichvili; camera, Tito Kalatozichvili; music, I. Guedjaze. At Cannes Film Fest. Running time, **100 MINS.**

Maria	Ariadna Chenguelaia
Guela	Imet Kokihani
Martia	Spartak Bagachvili
Balta	Marat Eliozivili

Made in the Georgian section of Russia, in its own dialect, this pic about sheepherders sometimes intimates that man can not live by bread and work alone. But the man who wants to try to lead another life is brought into line by tragedy. If quaintly old fashioned, this has a nice feel for landscapes, faces and the general lot of the almost archaic sheepmen on their yearly primitive treks.

But the deeper treatment to keep this from making the characters stereotypes and symbols, rather than individuals, is only intermittently present. Result is a visually fine but predictable and quaint Russo pic. It thus looks limited abroad.

Film is about the trek of the sheepmen from their rocky mountain homes to the winter pastures. On the way one meets and falls in love with a girl working in a fishery. There are also gamey contrasts between their way of life and city methods. But these are stacked in many cases and this has a sad feeling rather than a dynamic flair.

Lensing is starkly contrasting and eye filling. Playing agreeable, especially by the fetching, pretty Ariadna Chenguelaia who gives breadth and scope to the role of the girl. *Mosk.*

Kokkina Fanaria
(Red Lights)
(GREEK)
Cannes, May 12.

DM release of Damskinos-V. G. Michaelides production. With Jenny Karezi, Georges Foundas, Despo Dimantidou, Marie Chronopoulou, Katerina Helmi Dimitris Papamichael. Directed by Vassili Georgiades. Screenplay, Alekos Galanos based on his own play; camera, Nicos

Gardelis; music, St. Xarchos. At Cannes Film Fest. Running time, **120 MINS.**

Princess	Jenny Karezi
Mike	Georges Foundas
Peter	Dimitris Papamichael
Mary	Marie Chronopoulou

Playoff possibilities, on its story about the last days in a Greek bagnio before the laws closed them, are the main foreign chances for this academically-made pic. Characters are too stereotyped for any arty house possibilities, but some shearing could bring it down for more general release.

Pic deals with a few of the girls and their affairs with men. Two manage to find comprehensive men to take them away from it all while others continue privately in their most ancient of professions.

Film plays it all out for sentiment though much of it is telegraphed. But this does have some neatly done atmospheric scenes in the sporting house if it eschews any objectionable bits or practically any nudity. Main selling point is obvious.

This is technically fair if the street set is somewhat stagey. But its wholehearted attempt to treat prosties as people, and soft pedaling their sad story backgrounds, takes some of the familiar stigma away. The age-old theme might serve for putting this pic in foreign orbit for regular distrib. Beauteous femmes is an added asset. *Mosk.*

Deus E O Diabo Na Terr Do Sol
(God and the Devil in Land of Sun)
(BRAZILIAN)
Cannes, May 12.

Luiz Augusto Mendes-Copacabana production and release. With Yona Magalhaes, Geraldo Del Rey, Othon Bastos. Written and directed by Glauber Rocha. Camera, Wlademar Lima; editor, L. Ririra; music, Villa-Lobos. At Cannes Film Fest. Running time, **120 MINS.**

Rosa	Yona Magalhaes
Manuel	Geraldo Del Rey
Sebastien	Othon Bastos
Antonio	Mauricio de Valle
Congaceiro	Lidlo Silva

Brazil walked off with the top award at the Cannes Fest two years ago, and has since shown a vital film outlook at other festivals. Twenty-five year old Glauber Rocha's lyric fable looks at the mixture of good and evil in man and has a driving force that keep it from falling into melodrama. As effective as it is, the film needs careful handling abroad where its best bet is for arty spots.

Besides its comments and reflections on religious and bandit inspired revolts in the backwoods sections of Brazil in 1940, it has the outward look of a western but played in a tragic manner. Use of folk-type songs sets up a fine background or this saga of a cowman who kills his boss when the latter tries to rob him of his just dues for his work. He runs off with his wife and joins a self-styled Negro Saint who preaches child sacrifice and bloodshed.

His wife ends up killing the so-called Saint and they flee to join with a bandit chief who is being relentlessly stalked by a paid gunman. The man finishes by fleeing and and leaving everything behind as he runs towards freedom and the sea.

Rocha shows he is not afraid to

use the full visual panoply of the screen to spin his romancero. If he sometimes rises to almost delirious heights of drama and effect, he always keep his theme in hand. Expert lensing, stalwart acting and a fine musical score have this coherent.

This does not flag panaceas, propaganda or dogma. Its point seems to be that man must find his way on earth before being fogged down with any obscure aspects such as his social, personal and religious life.

There is the right blend of symbolical and human sides in its characters but this could throw off audiences in the playoff. Rocha emerges a director to be watched, having a dynamic visual flair and ability. Pic should do well on its own native markets. Its international career will depend partly on whether the hard outlooks will be accepted on their fable qualities. *Mosk.*

Lotna
(POLISH—COLOR)
Cannes, May 13.

Polski Film release of Kadr production. With Bozena Kurowska, Jerzy Pichelski, M. Loza, Jerzy Moes, Adam Pawlikowski. Directed by Andrzej Wajda. Screenplay, Wojciech Zukrowski, Wajda from book by W. Zukrowski; camera (Sovcolor), Jerzy Lipman; music, Tadeusz Baird. At Cannes Film Fest. Running time, **85 MINS.**

Ewa	Bozena Kurowska
Choda	Jerzy Pichelski
Laton	M. Loza
Grabokswi	Jerzy Moes
Wodnicki	Adam Pawlikowski

Polski director Andrzej Wajda, whose "Kanal" and "Ashes and Diamonds" made somewhat of a dent in Yank marts two years ago (if limited biz) now has a baroque tale of a cavalry horse that appears mainly for possible playoff chances abroad.

Film does mix color and sepia effectively to underline but sometimes romanticizes and makes a plea for futile heroism. Set in the the era at the start of the Second World War, it shows the Poles still fighting with lances and cavalry against the first German foot troops. But soon the tanks foreshadow the German superiority in equipment that soon is to crush the daring horsemen. It is summed up in the appearance of the first tank that runs over a fallen horse.. Tale is about a white thoroughbred horse that passes to various people in a military outfit till he breaks a leg, and is shot.

This might symbolize the end of an old type of Polish life. War is mainly a backdrop to this tale and director Wajda embroiders well. But this remains a small if absorbing pic that is more an offbeat curiosity than having enough weight to do well abroad at arty houses. *Mosk.*

Siberska Ledi Magbet
(Siberian Lady Macbeth)
(YUGOSLAVIAN)
Cannes, May 12.

Avala Films production and release. With Olivera Markovic, Ljuba Tadic, Bojan Stupica, Miodrag Lazovic. Directed by Andrzej Wajda. Screenplay, Sveta Likic from novel by Nicolai Leskov; camera, Alexandre Sekulouic; music, Dimitri Shostakovitch. At Cannes Film Fest Running time, **90 MINS.**

Sergei	Olivera Markovic
Wife	Ljuba Tadic
Kulak	Bojan Stupica
Husband	Miodrag Lazovic

A Polish director made this Russo tale of Czarist days in Yugoslavia. But it still has a deep Slavic ring in its fine settings, correct larger-than-life acting and its adroit visual stylization. Pic. could rate arty and special playoff possibilities abroad with tie-ins also apparent on the Dimitri Shostokovitch music used for the background.

Based on both the book, and the opera which Shostokovitch wrote, pic also has an operatic ring via its characters bound by fate and also the stifling social climate of the times. A husky, sensual woman lives on a big farm with her brutish father-in-law while her husband is long absent in town.

One day she takes a rakish peasant laborer to bed with her but is discovered by the father. She then poisons him and has the peasant move in. The husband's return has him liquidated as well as a young heir, only to be caught and sent to Siberia.

Director Andrzej Wajda is not afraid to try for broad symbolic strokes. Result achieves the right classis mold, and too, gives a measure of tragic implacacility to these two people trying to escape their fates. Thesps have the right heavyweight bearing. Technical credits and production dress are firstrate. *Mosk.*

El Leila El Akhira
(The Last Night)
(EGYPTIAN)
Cannes, May 12.

Gamal El-Leissi production and release. Stars Faten Hamama; features Ahmed Mazhar, Mahmoud Moursi. Directed by Kamal El-Cheikh. Screenplay, Youssef El-Sebai; camera, Abdel-Halim Nasr; editor, Said El-Cheikh. At Cannes Film Fest. Running time, **120 MINS.**

Wife	Faten Hamama
Doctor	Ahmed Mazhar
Husband	Mahmoud Moursi

If there is any wonder about what happened to Yank B films, this shows they are now being made in Egypt. Suspense item does have some script ideas but relies on far-fetched plotting and stereotyped characters. It is fairly slickly done but primarily a lingo entry. Pic is reminiscent of such prewar Yank pix as "Gaslight" and "Spellbound."

A woman awakens one day to find she is married to her brother-in-law, has usurped her sister's role, and 15 years have gone by. It does maintain some fairly interesting, provoking early scenes, but then bogs down and runs too long. The husband had substituted her for her sister killed in a bombing raid in which she had lost her memory.

A sympathetic doctor thwarts the attempts of the husband to kill her to keep the inheritance. Leading Egyptian actress Faten Hamama shows pro bearing and projection as the maltreated heroine. Others are only adequate. Direction is workmanlike if uninspired.

Lensing is flat and musical score seems to be a pot-pourri of known Western tunes of various kinds from pop through folk to the classics. *Mosk.*

Mujhe Jeene Do
(Let Me Live)
(INDIAN)

Cannes, May 12.
Ajanta Arts-Moni Battacharjee production and release With Sunil Dutt, Waheeda Rehman. Nirupa Roy. Directed by Moni Battacharjee Screenplay, Aga Joni Kashmiri; camera, A. Bhattacharya; music Jaidev, Sahir. At Cannes Film Fest. Running time, 95 MINS.
Jernail .... Sunil Dutt
Chameli .... Waheeda Rehman

Naive tale of the saga of a bandit has the format of an oater but without the right segueing from actioner to myth. Hence, this mainly is a home item except for possible lower slotting in dualers abroad.

A snarling bandit is finally tamed by a pretty courtesan singer he abducts. But their short time together ends in tradgedy when the police finally get him. However, it is intimated he is one of the last of the outlaws and that his son will go straight.

Direction gives this a measure of old fashioned posturing but does have an obviously sincere, if limited, talent. Acting is in the broad style, with technical credits about par. *Mosk.*

The Unsinkable Molly Brown
(PANAVISION—COLOR)

Flaws Don't Matter, This Is Big Boxoffice Tunepic.

Hollywood, May 22.
Metro release of Lawrence Weingarten (Roger Edens) production. Stars Debbie Reynolds, Harve Presnell; features Ed Begley, Jack Kruschen, Hermione Baddeley. Directed by Charles Walters. Screenplay, Helen Deutsch, based on the Meredith Willson musical (book by Richard Morris); camera (Metrocolor), Daniel L. Fapp; dances, Peter Gennaro; editor, Fredric Steinkamp; special effects, A. Arnold Gillespie, Robert R. Hoag, J. McMillan Johnson; asst. director, Hank Moonjean; orchestrations, Calvin Jackson, Lee Arnaud, Jack Elliott, Alexander Courage; conductor-musical supervisor, Robert Armbruster. Tradeshown May 22, 1964 at Egyptian Theatre. Running time, 128 MINS.
Molly Brown .... Debbie Reynolds
Johnny Brown .... Harve Presnell
Shamus Tobin .... Ed Begley
Christmas Morgan ...... Jack Kruschen
Mrs. Grogan ..... Hermione Baddeley
Prince Louis de Laniere
.... Vassili Lambrinos
Baron Karl Ludwig von Ettenburg
.... Fred Essler
Polak .... Harvey Lembeck
Mr. Fitzgerald .... Lauren Gilbert
Mrs. Wadlington .... Kathryn Card
Broderick .... Hayden Rorke
Mr. Wadlington .... Harry Holcombe
Mrs. Fitzgerald .... Amy Douglass
Monsignor Ryan .... George Mitchell
Grand Duchess Elise Lupovinova
.... Martita Hunt
Mr. Cartwright .... Vaughn Taylor
Roberts .... Anthony Eustrel
Mrs. McGraw .... Audrey Christie
Jam .... Grover Dale
Murphy .... Brendan Dillon
Daphne .... Maria Karnilova
Joe .... Gus Trikonis

The market is overdue for a major musical. And Metro has one in Lawrence Weingarten's production of "The Unsinkable Molly Brown." It looms as one of the top moneymakers of the year. A rowdy and sometimes rousing blend of song and sentiment, the converted stage tuner should prove an almost totally pleasurable experience for most audiences.

The Helen Deutsch scenario stems, of course, from the book by Richard Morris for the stage production. The film is adorned with the music and lyrics of Meredith Willson, although a number of his songs for the legiter have been excised and one new production number ("He's My Friend") has been added. The dramatic story remains virtually intact in Miss Deutsch's translation. It relates the adventures of Molly Brown, a hillbilly heroine who rises from poverty to become one of the richest and most celebrated women of her time. Shortly after her marriage to Leadville Johnny Brown he strikes it rich, and the rest of the picture depicts her feverish efforts to cut the mustard with snooty Denver society.

In essence, it's a pretty shallow story since the title character, when you get right down to it, is obsessed with a very superficial, egotistical problem beneath her generous, razzmatazz facade. On top of that, Willson's score is rather undistinguished. Still, the picture overpowers these fundamental weaknesses by dint of a lavish, striking physical production, several vivacious musical numbers and a skilled and spirited cast.

Debbie Reynolds gives what is probably the outstanding performance of her career as the title character. She has thrust herself into the role with an enormous amount of verve and vigor. At times her approach to the character seems more athletic than artful. But overall it's a successful delineation that's neither provocative nor substantial enough to carry the story on her shoulders.

Harve Presnell, who created the role on Broadway in 1960, makes a generally auspicious screen debut as the patient Johnny. His fine, booming voice and physical stature make him a valuable commodity for Hollywood. He seems to be a fairly expressive actor, despite a tendency to posture or gesture artificially from time to time, especially in musical numbers. This ought to have been corrected by director Charles Walters.

Such stagey movements are inconsistent with the element of realism that must prevail on the screen. Natural outdoor settings require reasonably natural behavior and believable story developments, unlike the stage, where an artificial and less intimate framework allows greater histrionic license. On the whole, director Walters has maintained the balance, but one or twice he has slipped up.

The supporting cast is very good. Ed Begley will surprise a lot of people with his peppery song-and-dance characterization of Molly's father, a man who loves a jug and a jig. But a sequence in which, wild-eyed, he heaves a cream pie at the camera to conclude a brawl doesn't come off. Hermione Baddeley is outstanding as the whimsical mother of the snobbish, nouveau-riche Mrs. McGraw, a role played with a keen sense of timing and reaction by Audrey Christie. Others who do well in featured support are Jack Kruschen and Martita Hunt, and there is capable work in lesser parts by virtually the entire remainder of the cast.

Photographically, the film reflects an astute piece of work by Daniel Fapp, indoors and out. There are many majestic views of the Colorado Rockies to dazzle the eye. Although the echo bit is overdone on Presnell's songs. Fredric Steinkamp's editing is generally observant and efficient. George W. Davis and Preston Ames have fashioned some memorable sets, particularly the ostentatiously vulgar Pennsylvania Avenue, Denver, residence of the Browns.

Robert Armbruster rates praise for the lively manner in which he has supervised and conducted the music for the production. Peter Gennaro's choreography is an outstanding contribution, especially on the film's two best numbers, the "Belly Up To The Bar" saloon strut in the first half and the "He's My Friend" shindig in the latter part. Morton Haack's costumes are appropriately resplendent.

Other noteworthy efforts are those of set decorators Henry Grace and Hugh Hunt, recording supervisor Franklin Milton, orchestrators Calvin Jackson, Leo Arnaud, Jack Elliott and Alexander Courage, associate producer-musical arranger Roger Edens, and the special visual effects team of A. Arnold Gillespie, Robert R. Hoag and J. McMillan Johnson. *Tube.*

French Dressing
(BRITISH)

Promising comedy idea fizzles rather than fizzes; engaging acting by James Booth and newcomer Alita Naughton in uneven pic with minor marquee appeal.

London, May 19.
Warner-Pathe release of Associated British presentation of Kenneth Harper production. Stars James Booth, Marisa Mell, Roy Kinnear, Alita Naughton; features Bryan Pringle, Robert Robinson. Directed by Ken Russell. Screenplay by Peter Myers, Ronald Cass, Peter Brett, from original story by Myers & Cass; added dialog by Johnny Speight; camera, Ken Higgins; editor, Jack Slade; music, Georges Delrue. Previewed May 19, '64 at 20th-Fox Private Theatre. Running time, 86 MINS.
Jim .... James Booth
Henry .... Roy Kinnear
Francoise Fayol .... Marisa Mell
Judy .... Alita Naughton
The Mayor .... Bryan Pringle
Robert Robinson .... Himself
Westebourne Mayor........ Norman Pitt
Bridgmouth Mayor .... Henry McCarthy
Vladek .... Sandor Eles

It's a pity to see a promising comedy idea go busted through sheer lack of bright wit and irony. "French Dressing" is a light comedy which needed the satirical touch, but instead suffers from a flat, heavy treatment. This squelches many of the lighter, more promising moments. This clings to the hoary idea that anything French is automatically, in British eyes, saucy, provocative and full of sexy connotations. Earnest attempts by new director Ken Russell to get out of the groove only occasionally click. Overall, the pic fizzles.

Peter Myers and Ronald Cass (abetted by Peter Brett and Johnny Speight) have conjured up the neat idea of boosting a typical British seaside resort, the British weather, local authority pomposity, starlet sexpots and a film festival. But they haven't produced the style or imagination to give their jokes a real kick.

Gormleigh-on-Sea is one of those British holiday resorts that suffer from acute dull-itis. A bright young deckchair attendant (James Booth) cons the local entertainments manager and the mayor into running a film festival. They persuade an ambitious young French actress to be the star of the proceedings which lead to some inevitable disasters and coy jokes such as a total washout at the opening of a new Nudist Beach and a riot at a premiere. Only quick thinking by the young American journalist girl friend of James Booth saves the situation.

Too much stodgy joking does not aid predictable slapstick situations. Quick cutting and speeding up of camerawork are not enough to disguise the fact that this is not a souffle but mainly an indigestible pancake.

Pic was shot in the genuine surroundings of Herne Bay, a South coast resort, and briefly at Le Touquet, so the atmosphere's okay. There are also one or two pleasant shots of the deserted beach in the early morning and at sundown. But there are lost opportunities. A breezy dance by Booth and the entertainments boss (Roy Kinnear) on Le Touquet promenade would have enhanced the mood if the screen had been bursting with prancing holidaymakers.

Booth, as the ambitious boy,

brings the same effervescence to his role as he provided as the corporal in "Zulu" but he gets little help. Roly-poly Roy Kinnear is a funny man within limits, but his range is not varied enough to carry a full starring role. Bryan Pringle suffers agonies as the banal mayor with a roving eye and an I.Q. of unsurpassed stupidity.

Viennese Marisa Mell as Francoise Fayol, or "F.F.", has her moments in an obvious parody of Brigitte Bardot but the most refreshing item is cover model Alita Naughton, a tomboyish American girl, making her screen debut. She has not yet learned any tricks and gives a natural and pleasant performance as Booth's jealous girl friend. There is also a telling bit by tv personality Robert Robinson, playing himself. He is covering the festival and in a role presumably written by himself he provides the tongue-in-cheek touch of sophisticated wit that the entire film badly lacks.

Director Russell certainly has a go at bringing freshness to old-hat happenings though they don't often come off. He is a new man who promises better things. Ken Higgins' lensing is sound and Georges Delerue, who scribed the music for the French hit, "Jules and Jim," has provided a lively score, but with several cliches. For instance, a one day trip to France by Booth and Kinnear (inevitable lingo difficulties) brings out a Gallic influence, the sinking of a waterlogged float draws out an expected snatch of "Rule Britannia," etc.

"French Dressing" will provide mild fun for the undemanding, but the idea deserved a far more audacious approach. As it is, what should have been champagne remains, obstinately, ginger beer.

Rich.

The Human Vapor
(JAPANESE—COLOR)

Handy Japanese entry for sci-fi exploitation market, sparked by clever special effects.

Hollywood, May 20.

Brenco presentation of Toho production. Features Yoshio Tsuchiya, Kaoru Yachigusa, Tatsuya Mihashi, Keiko Sata. Directed by Inoshiro Honda; special effects, Eiji Tsuburaya. Reviewed at World Theatre, May 20, '64. Running time, **79 MINS.**

Mizuno, The Vapor Man	Yoshio Tsuchiya
Fujichiyo	Kaoru Yachigusa
Okamoto	Tatsuya Mihashi
Kyoko	Keiko Sata

"The Human Vapor," packaged with "Gorath" (reviewed in VARIETY May 20 issue) for general release in U. S., projects imaginative sci-fi qualities and with its companion picture shapes as an okay entry for the exploitation market. Japanese-made (like its teammate), film is the stronger of the two insofar as story development is concerned and leans heavily on expert special effects for its story premise. This deals with a man who finds, as a result of a scientific experiment, that he is capable of transforming himself at will from human to Vapor.

Brenco Pictures has acquired "Vapor," like "Gorath" produced by Toho, for world distribution outside the Far East. Like the other, too, "Vapor" has been dubbed in English but the result is far from gratifying—unlike "Gorath" — and spectator is always aware that lips and words never match, thus decreasing realism. Narrative is sufficiently interesting, however, to hold the audience as plot follows efforts of the Tokyo police to destroy the Vapor Man as he uses his superhuman powers to commit a series of crimes for the sake of his love, a beautiful dancer.

Special effects by Eiji Tsuburaya —responsible also for "Gorath"— create a dynamic effect as the man, portrayed by Yoshio Tsuchiya, turns into vapor, which permits him to be indestructible. Interesting vistas are afforded of various parts of Tokyo, and there's a classic Japanese dance for followers of this art. Eastman-color lensing is artistic.

Inoshiro Honda's direction fits the occasion, and competent performances are handled also by Kaoru Yachigusa, as the dancer; Tatsuya Mihashi, a detective; and Keiko Sata, a femme reporter.

Whit.

I Walk In Moscow
(RUSSIAN)

Cannes, May 13.

Mosfilm production and release. With Nikita Mikhalkov, Alexei Loktev, Evgueni Steblov, Galina Polskikh. Directed by Gheorghi Daniela. Screenplay, Guennadi Chpalikov; camera, Vadim Youssov; editor, D. Dara. At Cannes Film Fest. Running time, **76 MINS.**

Alena	Galina Polskikh
Volodia	Alexei Loktev
Kolia	Nikita Mikhalkov
Sacha	Evgueni Steblov

Russo situation comedy has some light moments and inventiveness. It displays a neat comedic look at youthful insouciance. But it's mainly a nice little film sans the drive to make it more than a dualer possibility abroad.

Two young men meet on the subway one summer day in Moscow. The pic details a series of adventures that has one falling in love, a friend's marriage almost ruined and various little incidents around Moscow.

Film sometimes takes potshots at human pettiness or bureaucracy but this is mainly sentimental. Young players have charm and freshness, and it is technically good.

Mosk.

A Distant Trumpet
(PANAVISION—COLOR)

Physically handsome but plodding and predictable cavalry adventure. Plugs a summer programming gap with Troy Donahue - Suzanne Pleshette - Diane McBain.

Hollywood, May 21.

Warner Bros. release of William H. Wright production. Stars Troy Donahue, Suzanne Pleshette, Diane McBain; features James Gregory, William Reynolds, Claude Akins, Kent Smith. Directed by Raoul Walsh. Screenplay, John Twist, from adaptation by Richard Fielder and Albert Beich of novel by Paul Horgan; camera (Technicolor), William Clothier; editor, David Wages; music, Max Steiner; asst. directors, Russell Saunders, William Kissel. Reviewed at the studio, May 21, '64. Running time, **117 MINS.**

Lt. Hazard	Troy Donahue
Kitty	Suzanne Pleshette
Laura	Diane McBain
General Quoit	James Gregory
Lt. Mainwaring	William Reynolds
Seely Jones	Claude Akins
Secretary of War	Kent Smith
Capt. Gray	Judson Pratt
Major Prescott	Bartlett Robinson
Cranshaw	Bobby Bare
Sgt. Kroger	Larry Ward
Slattery	Richard X. Slattery
Jessica Prescott	Mary Patton
Capt. Brinker	Russell Johnson
Maj. Miller	Lane Bradford

The summer market is always ripe for at least one cavalry 'n' injun' opera, and this year's candidate for that function is Warner's "A Distant Trumpet." The William H. Wright production should adequately fill that program hole. Youngsters are likely to respond to its adventurous image, and a fair turnout of the fan mag set might be generated by the dangling of such glamour bait as Troy Donahue, Suzanne Pleshette and Diane McBain.

The last gasp of the Southwestern tribe of Chiricahua Indians in opposing the encroaching white man is covered by John Twist's screenplay from an adaptation by Richard Fiedler and Albert Beich of a novel by Paul Horgan. Donahue enacts the role of an idealistic second lieutenant from West Point who arrives at a remote outpost in the middle of the Arizona desert and is thrust into two sizzling circumstances—the battle against War Eagle and the romantic squeeze play between Misses Pleshette and McBain.

The film just seems to mark-time-march in the "middle act" of its 117-minute running (walking) time, but things perk up for the big battle sequence, and the momentum is sustained to the end. Eventually, War Eagle gives in quietly. As for Miss McBain, she makes the idiotic mistake of scolding Donahue for demanding better treatment of the Indian. Miss Pleshette, lucky girl, winds up the army wife.

The stunning location terrain of the Red Rocks area of New Mexico and Arizona's Painted Desert gives the production a tremendous pictorial lift. The scenery is appreciatively regarded through William Clothier's Technicolored lens. Art director William Campbell has designed a believable fort. Max Steiner's score is a driving dramatic force and hard to erase from the mind, but the use of the main theme seems a trifle excessive. The picture would benefit from a lot more pruning by editor David Wages. One of the film's best features is Howard Shoup's costume design—authentic in conveying the period and very becoming to the ladies.

Raoul Walsh's direction is generally competent, but the climactic battle strategy is a bit fuzzy and the Indians seem incredibly inept in combat, as depicted. Hardly a white man bites the dust, yet the Redmen consistently get picked off like ducks at a shooting gallery. How one-sided can you get?

Donahue's range of expression is very slim. There isn't a great deal of difference between the way he gazes into a girl's eyes or faces up to a hundred armed Chiricahuas. Obviously he ought to be conveying more fear when he stares at the girl.

Miss Pleshette and Miss McBain would make any picture look good. Their roles hardly tap what histrionic resources may lurk beneath those beautiful facades. James Gregory gives one of his gritty, prudent-veteran performances as good General Quait. William Reynolds has the looks to go places one of these days—when he gets the right part, perhaps. A colorful characterization is pitched in by Claude Akins, with competent support from the balance of the cast.

Tube.

The Killers
(COLOR)

Uninspired remake of the old yarn. Barely a trace of the original Hemingway. Exploitation entry for crime buffs.

Hollywood, May 19.

Universal release of Donald Siegel production. Stars Lee Marvin, Angie Dickinson, John Cassavetes; features Ronald Reagan, Clu Gulager, Claude Akins, Norman Fell. Directed by Siegel. Screenplay, Gene L. Coon, from story by Ernest Hemingway; camera (Pathe Color), Richard L. Rawlings; editor, Richard Belding; music, Johnny Williams; asst. director, Milton Feldman. Reviewed at the studio, May 19, '64. Running time, **95 MINS.**

Charlie	Lee Marvin
Sheila Farr	Angie Dickinson
Johnny North	John Cassavetes
Browning	Ronald Reagan
Lee	Clu Gulager
Earl Sylvester	Claude Akins
Mickey	Norman Fell
Miss Watson	Virginia Christine
Mail Truck Driver	Don Haggerty
George	Robert Phillips
Receptionist	Kathleen O'Malley
Gym Assistant	Ted Jacques
Mail Truck Guard	Iivin Mosley
Salesman	Jimmy Joyce

Spawned as the pilot ("Johnny North") of Revue's projected series of two-hour films for television, but scratched when NBC balked at what was deemed an overdose of sex and brutality, this rehash of "The Killers" has been redirected to theatrical exhibition, where it emerges a throwback to the period of crime and violence that monopolized the screen in the late '30s and early '40s. In spite of the slick, modern cinematic techniques with which it has been invested by producer-director Donald Siegel and staff, the film is essentially an anachronism, in parts bordering on parody of an outmoded style.

Only the most devoted buffs of the crime melodrama will get much of a charge out of this exercise in hate, double-cross and sadism. The Universal release will have to make its mark as an exploitation entry in the male-dominated crime-and-action market. Any attempt to lure a discerning audience with the Hemingway credentials is apt to be abortive and ineffectual.

Gene L. Coon's scenario is similar in basic structural respects, but different in character and plot specifics, to Mark Hellinger's 1946 vintage elaboration on Hemingway's concise short story. In this version, the "hero" (John Cassavetes) is a racing car driver, which provides the background for some flashy track scenes. But Coon's screenplay is burdened with affected dialog and contrived plotwork. Virtually nothing of the original Hemingway remains. And the dramatic style engineered by director Siegel is mostly on the artificial side, too.

Of the actors, Cassavetes and Clu Gulager come off best, the former arousing interest with his customary histrionic drive and intensity, the latter fashioning a colorful study in evil, a portrait of playful sadism. Lee Marvin has some impact as another distorted menace, approaching his role with the cold-blooded demeanor for which he is celebrated. Angie Dickinson lacks depth or variety as the female in the middle of it all. Claude Akins and Norman Fell have some strong moments, but Ronald Reagan fails to crash convincingly through his good-guy image in his portrayal of a ruthless crook.

The picture is notable for photographic flair and d e x t e r i t y. Richard L. Rawlings' c a m e r a maneuvers keep the screen alive with interesting views of the action, witnessed from elevated positions, titled angles, sudden zooms and such. Other assets to the production are contributed by editor Richard Belding, art directors Frank Arrigo and George Chan, and composer Johnny Williams.

A song, "Too Little Time" by Henry Mancini and Don Raye, is sung by Nancy Wilson. On first hearing, it doesn't make a very strong impression. *Tube.*

Hey There, It's Yogi Bear
(CARTOON—COLOR)

Marketable hot weather cartoon feature for the moppet mart. Will have to buck its own freevee competition.

Hollywood, May 19.
Columbia Pictures release of William Hanna-Joseph Barbera production. Voices of Daws Butler, Don Messick, Julie Bennett, Mel Blanc, Jean Vander Pyl, Hal Smith, J. Pat O'Malley. Directed by Hanna, Barbera. Screenplay, Barbera, Warren Foster, Hanna; camera (Eastman), Frank Paiker, Norman Steinback, Roy Wade, Charles Flekal, Frank Parrish, Ted Bemiller, Bill Koller; editors, Greg Watson, Warner Leighton, Tony Milch, Donald A. Douglas, Larry Cowan, Ken Spears; art directors, Richard Bickenbach, Iwao Takamoto, William Perez, Jacques W. Rupp, Willie Ito, Tony Sgroi, Ernest Nordli, Jerry Eisenberg, Zigmond Jablecki, Bruce Bushman; music, Marty Paich; sound, Bud Myers; animators, Don Lusk, Irv Spence, George Kreisl, Ray Petterson, Jerry Hathcock, Grant Simmons, Fred Wolf, Gerry Chiniquy, Don Peterson, Ken Harris, George Goepper, Edwin Aardal, Ed Parks, Kenneth Muse, Harry Holt background designers, F. Montealegre, Robert Gentle, Art Lozzi, Richard H. Thomas, Ron Dias, Fernanda Arce, Dick Kelsey, Bob Abrams, Don Peters, Tom O'Loughlin, Dick Ung, Curtiss D. Perkins; animation director, Charles A. Nichols; story sketches, Dan Gordon; production supervisor, Howard Hanson. Reviewed at the studio, May 19, '64. Running time, **89 MINS.**

The small output of full-length theatrical cartoons in recent years leaves the field pretty wide open for this Hanna-Barbera concoction. Thanks to that element of scarcity plus the lingering popularity of the "Yogi Bear" character as an animated television "personality," the Columbia release shapes up as a marketable vacation season entry for the popsicle brigade.

However, it's never easy for a commodity that's popular on television to make a profitable transition to the theatrical screen, where it must then buck the competition of its freely-observed home counterpart. Few are the attractions or performers successful in bridging this historically hazardous gap. Something special must be emphasized in the selling to lure the stay-at-homers. In the case of "Hey There, It's Yogi Bear," fresh secondary characters and five new songs might serve as commercial reinforcements f o r the main bait, which is the appealing title figure.

The expanded feature version, written by Joseph Barbera, Warren Foster and William Hanna, is artistically accomplished in all departments, although the 89-minute route puts something of a strain on characters attuned to much shorter hauls. The script gets a bit redundant along the way and resembles, in basic plot structure, the storylines of some full-length c a r t o o n s that have gone before it.

Yarn is concerned with two issues. One is Yogi's running battle of wits with Ranger Smith of Jellystone Park. The other has to do with his romance with Cindy Bear, whose love for Yogi lands her in grave difficulty as a high-wire performer in a circus operated by a wicked impresario whose sadistic dog, "Mugger," emits a wheezing laugh that is pure black evil. Yogi, with the aid of Boo Boo, rescues Cindy and the threesome is returned to Jellystone by Ranger Smith for a happy ending.

The pleasant, if not especially distinguished, refrains are incorporated smoothly into the story. One of them, "Ven-e, Ven-o, Ven-a," is sung by James Darren. The songs were written by Ray Gilbert and Doug Goodwin, with the exception of the title tune, composed by David Gates. Marty Paich penned the e x p r e s s i v e musical score. The infectious voice of "Yogi" belongs to Daws Butler. Other prominent voices are those of Don Messick and Julie Bennett.

The artisans who toiled for producers-directors Hanna and Barbera are too numerous to single out for specific comment here. The names of those who contributed their artistic savvy to the impressive cartoon production are noted in the above credits.

Tube.

Flipper's New Adventure
(COLOR)

Salable sequel to last year's click. Healthy moppet prospect.

Hollywood, May 20.
Metro release of Ivan Tors production. Stars Luke Halpin, Pamela Franklin; features Helen Cherry, Tom Helmore, Francesca Annis, Brian Kelly. Directed by Leon Benson. Screenplay, Art Arthur, from story by Tors based on character created by Ricou Browning, Jack Cowden; camera (Metrocolor), Lamar Boren; editors, Warren Adams, Charles Craft; music, Henry Vars; assistant director, Edward Haldeman. Reviewed at the studio, May 20, '64. Running time, **92 MINS.**

Sandy	Luke Halpin
Penny	Pamela Franklin
Julia	Helen Cherry
Sir Ralsey Hopewell	Tom Helmore
Gwen	Francesca Annis
Porter Ricks	Brian Kelly
L. C. Porett	Joe Higgins
Gill	Lloyd Battista
Sea Captain	Gordon Dilworth
Convict	Courtney Brown
Second Convict	William Cooley
Coast Guard Commander	Dan Chandler
Dr. Clark Burton	Ricou Browning
Veterinarian	Ric O'Feldman
Veterinarian	Robert Baldwin

Following roughly the same formula that clicked so profitably a year ago with "Flipper," producer Ivan Tors has fashioned a sequel that is equal to the original in virtually every respect. There is no reason to suspect, therefore, that the Metro release won't attract the same mass audience that responded to its predecessor. Since there have been no similar boy-dolphin

seascapades in the interim, the novelty of this curious amphibian-esque camaraderie should still be fresh enough to coax another look-see out of vacationing aquabrats.

Art Arthur's fish opera, from a story by Tors, transports the audience with Flipper the dolphin and his young pal (Luke Halpin), who take off for the open sea when their togetherness is threatened. Setting up a home-away-from-home on an uninhabited isle in the Bahamas, they become implicated in a situation involving a wealthy British family being held captive by three thugs. The hapless thugs are no match for junior and his pet, who communicate much better than most people do.

The charm of the picture, as with its forerunner, is in the antics of the talented, remarkably responsive dolphin — whether going it alone or romping with its young master. Outside of this novel and appealing nucleus, it's strictly an ordinary film. The song intrusions are just that—musical tangents that serve no story purpose save to exhibit the dolphin's talents. The three tunes ("Flipper," "Imagine" and "It's a Cotton Candy World") were written by By Dunham and Henry Vars, who also penned the background score. Chris Crosby and Jerry Wallace do the warbling.

For Master Halpin, it's a repeat characterization, and he seems at home in the role, wet or dry. The young English actress, Pamela Franklin, capably portrays his girlish playmate. Francesca Annis enacts her older sister, a role that has no payoff. Helen Cherry (Mrs. Trevor Howard) and Tom Helmore are competent as parents of the girls, and Brian Kelly, who will star in the same role in the forthcoming "Flipper" vidseries, is attractive as Halpin's worried father. Joe Higgins and Gordon Dilworth are good in brief character parts, and Lloyd Battista brings menace to the role of the chief convict.

Leon Benson's resourceful direction is backed up by Lamar Boren's photographic skill and ingenuity (there's a fine underwater fight sequence at the climax), the trim editing of Warren Adams and Charles Craft (although one song sequence could be deleted at no detriment to the picture) and the all-important training of "Flipper" by a s s o c i a t e producer Ricou Browning. The Metrocolored film was shot in Florida and the Bahamas, a very attractive setting.

Tube.

Honeymoon Hotel
(PANAVISION—COLOR)

Drab sex-propelled farce. Fresh cast faces—Goulet and Morse —may stir mild response at outset, but long-range b.o. chances appear slim.

Hollywood, May 27.
Metro release of Pandro S. Berman production. Stars Robert Goulet, Nancy Kwan, Robert Morse, Jill St. John; features Keenan Wynn, Anne Helm, Elsa Lanchester. Directed by Henry Levin. Screenplay, R. S. Allen, Harvey Bullock; camera (Metrocolor), Harold Lipstein; editor, Rita Roland; music, Walter Scharf; asst. director, Al Jennings. Reviewed at the studio, May 27, '64. Running time, **89 MINS.**

Ross Kingsley	Robert Goulet
Lynn Hope	Nancy Kwan
Jay Menlow	Robert Morse
Sherry	Jill St. John
Mr. Sampson	Keenan Wynn
Cynthia	Anne Helm
Chambermaid	Elsa Lanchester
Room Clerk	Bernard Fox
Mrs. Sampson	Elvia Allman
Mabel	Sandra Gould
Mr. Hampton	David Lewis
Nancy Penrose	Chris Noel
Fatso	Dale Malone
Hogan	Pauline Myers

Metro's "Honeymoon Hotel" is one of the bolder sex farces to come along in some time. Sex has been known to sell, of course, so the picture will find a certain receptive audience, but whether or not it will be large enough to make for good boxoffice in all situations is another matter. Much will depend upon how effective the exploitation will be in generating initial curiosity and selling Robert Goulet and Robert Morse. They are fresh screen personalities from legit, which could become plus factors, but due to the picture's flimsy and familiar content Goulet and Morse are being introed under somewhat of a handicap.

The Pandro S. Berman production, written lasciviously by R. S. Allen and Harvey Bullock, has to do with a couple of oversexed bachelors sharing a room in a Caribbean resort hotel which caters exclusively to honeymooners. The plot implicates them in a series of mixups, mostly of the quick-hide-in-the-closet variety.

The Goulet-Morse pairing is roughly reminiscent of the Dennis Morgan-Jack Carson "Two Guys From..." arrangement of years back. Of the two, Morse makes the better impression. Having succeeded in "Business Without Really Trying" on Broadway, he's forced to try very hard in this vehicle, left as he is to his own comedic resources. However, Morse, who resembles a young Tom Ewell, could prove a valuable comedy commodity to have around Hollywood. Goulet is adequate. He gets to sing only one song, the title ditty by Sammy Cahn and James Van Heusen, and that offscreen. It sounds likes a highly commercial.

Nancy Kwan and Jill St. John are the principal femmes involved. Miss Kwan's flashiest contribution is a sudden outburst of terpsichore, for no apparent reason, which she executes racily to Miriam Nelson's choreographic blueprint. Miss St. John, looking more voluptuous than ever, plays one of those stacked and accommodating nitwits—a role with which she is now firmly associated. Her best moment is an unscheduled nose-first crash into a glass door. Keenan Wynn and Elsa Lanchester gamely cope with inane parts, and Anne Helm plays a prominent role in the bedroom-hopping proceedings.

Henry Levin's frivolous direction is backed up by Harold Lipstein's glamorous photography, a fairly trim editing job by Rita Roland and an unobtrusive score by Walter Scharf. The plush setmanship of art directors George W. Davis and Paul Groesse is an asset, with one exception—the twin beds in the "My Blue Heaven Suite" of the Boca Roca (honeymooners only) Hotel occupied illegally by the two male stars. How thoughtful of the hotel management to anticipate their predicament. *Tube.*

Monsieur
(FRENCH-FRANSCOPE)

Paris, May 26.

Comacico release of Copernic, Corona, Sancro Film production. Stars Jean Gabin; features Liselotte Pulver, Philippe Noiret, Mireille Darc, Gaby Morlay. Directed by Jean-Paul Le Chanois. Screenplay, Claude Sautet, Pascal Jardin from play by Claude Gevel; camera, Louis Page; editor, Emma Le Chanois. At Marignan, Paris. Running time, **90 MINS.**

Monsieur .... Jean Gabin
Elizabeth .... Liselotte Pulver
Husband .... Philippe Noiret
Suzanne .... Mireille Darc
Natalie .... Berthe Grandval
Grandmother .... Gaby Morley

Sleek, familiar comedy is tailored for the phlegmatic but powerful pic presence of vet star Jean Gabin. It is all telegraphed and in the pre-war groove: to wit, a rich man is masquerading as a gentleman's gentleman and straightening out a mixed up well-to-do family. It should get good results in the home marts though foreign chances are somewhat limited.

Saved from suicide by a streetwalker (his ex-maid), after the death of his young wife, a banker finds out that his wife had been cuckolding him. He decides to start a new life as a valet, passing off the girl as his daughter.

Said family has the young man falling in love with the maid and the wife on the verge of cheating due to her husband's neglect via his business. But all is straightened out and the ex-banker takes over his own fortune again to wrest it from greedy in-laws. He adopts the ex-prostie.

Film is suavely directed if it lacks the bite to remove its cliche ring and patronizing air of class relations and goody-goody aspects of its characters. But this may provide needed family fare here but may not do so well in arty houses in the foreign markets. It is technically good.

Gabin is his usual self-indulgent self if he soft pedals his anger scenes. Others do all right in their stereotyped roles. Adapted from a pre-war play, this still seems too theatrical. *Mosk.*

Cyrano Et D'Artagnan
(Cyrano and D'Artagnan)
(FRENCH-ITALO-SPANISH)
(COLOR)

Paris, May 26.

Cocinor release of Circe Prod., GESI, Agata Film production. Stars Jose Ferrer, Jean-Pierre Kessel, Sylva Koscina, Dahlia Lavi. Written and directed by Abel Gance with assistance of Nelly Kaplan. Camera (Eastmancolor), Otello Martelli; editor, Gance, Miss Kaplan, Eraldo Daroma. At Colisee, Paris. Running time, **160 MINS.**

Cyrano .... Jose Ferrer
D'Artagnan .... Jean-Pierre Cassel
Ninon .... Sylvia Koscina
Marion .... Dahlia Lavi

French film pioneer Abel Gance has turned out a disarming swashbuckler, with a good leavening of zesty 17th Century French period fantasy and a looksee at the love affairs of the times. Pic needs some shearing but could be a neat foreign playoff item on its entertainment qualities, straightforward adventure and pulsating feel for the pre-war adventure epics.

It is naturally not realistic but Gance plays it sans tongue-in-cheek and with a gusto which belies his age. Color has fine tones to catch the period sets and costuming. The casting is right. Jose Ferrer again dons the long nose of the poet, inventor, writer, roisterer Cyrano, which won him an Academy Award in the Yank version of the Edmond Rostand play.

This is no lovesick Cyrano but his known aspects and story are neatly played on by writer-director Gance. If D'Artagnan and his Musketeers are made to play second fiddle to Cyrano, Jean-Pierre Cassel gives him a youthful exuberance and drive. Pic shows them both leaving home for Paris, meeting and then joining forces in Paris to help the country from going into revolution. Cardinal Richilieu for once is not a complete heavy.

First part of this pic can be tightened up, but it does have some smart swordplay ending with an excellently done version of Cyrano taking on 100 men and winning. Second part, on a criss-cross love affair involving them and two courtesans, has the right mixture of lustful innocence and charm to make a most comedic look at courtship.

It seems one girl wants Cyrano and the other seeks D'Artagnan but they feel the opposite. They frame the idea of wearing masks on their nightly visits which the women find charming and love frays, in spite of each thinking she has the other man, is successful. But then comes the unmasking and the troubles to be wound up when the country is saved from revolution. The women realize that love is more than skin deep.

Gance manages to avoid a feeling of the old and passe by his obvious relish for the charade. If it may be mistaken for an average actioner, it does have the breadth and dash for specialized situations. Production of dress is good. Dahlia Lavi and Sylva Koscina are beauteous and correctly bright and innocent in their gay carryings-on to remove any leering qualities. *Mosk.*

Bedtime Story
(COLOR)

Sporadically funny romantic farce about a couple of con men in competition. Names of Brando and Niven will help wicket activity.

Hollywood, May 12.

Universal release of Stanley Shapiro production. Stars Marlon Brando, David Niven, Shirley Jones. Directed by Ralph Levy. Screenplay, Shapiro, Paul Henning; camera (Eastman), Clifford Stine; editor, Milton Garruth; music, Hans J. Salter; asst. director, Joseph E. Kenny. Reviewed at Grauman's Chinese, May 12, '64. Running time, **99 MINS.**

Freddy .... Marlon Brando
Lawrence .... David Niven
Janet .... Shirley Jones
Fanny Eubank .... Dody Goodman
Andre .... Aram Stephan
Col. Williams .... Parley Baer
Mrs. Sutton .... Marie Windsor
Miss Trumble .... Rebecca Sand
Miss Harrington .... Frances Robinson
Sattler .... Henry Slate
Dubin .... Norman Alden
Anna .... Susanne Cramer
Frieda .... Cynthia Lynn
Hilda .... Ilse Taurins
Gina .... Francine York

Universal's latest comedy entry, "Bedtime Story," has some widely scattered zany interludes that should appeal more to the mass than the class audience, and, with the aid of such respectable marquee cargo as Marlon Brando and David Niven, could get off to a fast start at the boxoffice. As a summer entry it will divert the less discriminating, although there are times when even such major league performers as Brando and Niven have to strain to sustain the overall meager romantic comedy material provided by such comedy craftsmen as Stanley Shapiro (also the producer) and Paul Henning.

Some of the lines snap and crackle, and several of the situations (done with slapstick overtones) in which Brando and Niven find themselves involved as con men in competition on the French Riviera are broadly funny if not in the best of taste. A burlesque bit with Brando posing as a mentally deficient scion of royalty doesn't do any credit to the talents of the actor or the writers or the director.

The credits introduction designed by Pacific Title effectively sets the mood for the spoofing to come. And the production department has not spared in providing glamorous background as well as exterior and interior sets for the screenplay that has Niven as a bigtime operator and Brando a relatively petty practitioner of the confidence art who comes to challenge the "king of the mountain" in his own background. The mercenary contest centers around "American soap queen" Shirley Jones, who turns out to be merely the penniless winner of a soap queen contest.

Brando wins the girl, but he loses the histrionic contest to Niven, whose effortless flair for sophisticated comedy is not matched by his co-star. Actually, Brando has some expressive takes, but the very qualities that make him a dramatic star of the first magnitude seemingly limit him as a comic actor. There is a heaviness about his performance. Of course, the script frequently puts a strain on both men, who are portraying characters utterly devoid of substance or soul. An attempt is made at the climax of the picture to endow the character played by Brando with a heart, but this abrupt switch to sentimentality is incongruous.

Ralph Levy's direction of the proceedings is sporadically effective, yet on the whole rather mechanical. Miss Jones is attractive but doesn't generate the required light touch for full comedy effect. Aram Stephan is amusing as a gendarme who aids Niven in his sexploits. Others of note include Dody Goodman, Parley Baer, Marie Windsor, Rebecca Sand, Frances Robinson, Henry Slate, Norman Alden, Susanne Cramer, Cynthia Lynn, Ilse Taurins and Francine York.

There is dexterity and lustre to much of Clifford Stine's Eastman Color photography, and the handsome, sometimes gaudy sets by Alexander Golitzen and Robert Clatworthy make for good viewing. Milton Carruth's editing is efficient, and Hans J. Salter's score lends occasional atmospheric value to the film, on which Robert Arthur served as exec producer. *Tube.*

633 Squadron
(PANAVISION—COLOR)

Technically slick depiction of a costly RAF mission in World War II. Story weaknesses limit audience range, but it's a solid entry for action markets.

Hollywood, May 19.

United Artists release of Cecil F. Ford production. Stars Cliff Robertson, George Chakiris; features Maria Perschy, Harry Andrews, Donald Houston. Directed by Walter E. Grauman. Screenplay, James Clavell, Howard Koch, from Frederick E. Smith's novel; camera (De Luxe), Edward Scaife, John Wilcox; editor, Bert Bates; music, Ron Goodwin; asst. director, Ted Sturgis. Reviewed at Goldwyn Studios, May 19, '64. Running time, **94 MINS.**

Wing Com. Roy Grant.... Cliff Robertson
Lt. Erik Bergman........George Chakiris
Hilde Bergman .... Maria Perschy
Air Marshal Davis ....Harry Andrews
Wing Com. Tom Barrett Donald Houston
Squadron Leader Bill Adams
Michael Goodliffe
F/Lt. Gillibrand .... John Meillon
F/Lt. Scott .... John Bonney
F/Lt. Hoppy Hopkinson ... Angus Lennie
F/Lt. Bissel .... Scot Finch
Barmaid .... Barbara Archer
F/Lt. Singh .... Julian Sherrier
Sergeant Mary .... Suzan Farmer
F/Lt. Evans .... John Church
F/Lt. Nigel .... Sean Kelly
F/Lt. Frank .... Geoffrey Frederick
F/Lt. Jones .... Johnny Briggs
F/Lt. Reynolds .... Jeremy Wagg
F/Lt. Grenier .... Edward Brayshaw
Innkeeper .... Arnold Locke
F/Lt. Miner .... Peter Kriss
Thor .... Drewe Henley
Johanson .... Richard Shaw
Ericson .... Cavan Malone
Goth .... Chris Williams
S.S. Woman .... Anne Ridley

Cinematically, "633 Squadron" is a spectacular achievement, a technically explosive depiction of an RAF unit's successful but costly mission to demolish an almost impregnable Nazi rocket fuel installation in Norway. The Cecil F. Ford production, filmed in its entirety in England, contains some of the most rip-roaring aerial action photography ever recorded on celluloid. Unfortunately, this technical prowess is not matched by the drama it adorns.

The characters of the James Clavell-Howard Koch scenario from the novel by Frederick E. Smith are somewhat shallowly drawn and fall into rather familiar war story molds and behavior patterns. Viewer feels no deeply personal sense of loss at their deaths—a major shortcoming in a picture where virtually everyone of import dies. This lack of deep character penetration and definition, added to the short supply of surefire marquee names, could reduce the impact of the United Artists release in any exclusive first-run situations. However, this is the type of entertainment that will have tremendous appeal for fanciers of war action. It should pick up healthy boxoffice momentum in the nabes and drive-ins, and all situations in which less finicky filmgoers are most apt to get at it.

Cliff Robertson skillfully rattles off the leading assignment, that of a Yank wing commander whose squadron is chosen for the dangerous mission. George Chakiris is adequate though miscast and rather colorless as a Norwegian resistance leader who is to pave the way for the vital bombing raid. Maria Perschy supplies decorative romantic interest as Chakiris' sister and eventually Robertson's girl. Harry Andrews and Donald Houston deliver businesslike delineations of English officers. Support is generally spirited.

Under Walter Grauman's vigorous direction, producer Ford's talented staff and crew have fashioned an impressive physical production, distinguished particularly by the dazzling photography, aerial and otherwise, of Edward Scaife and John Wilcox. The climactic sequence—the big raid—is a noteworthy cinematic effort, one that will jar an audience right out of its seats.

Also worthy of high praise for the stimulating physique of this production are such artisans as special effects expert Tom Howard, editor Bert Bates, production designer Michael Stringer, sound recordists John Bramall and J. B. Smith, and second unit director Roy Stevens. Ron Goodwin's musical score tends to be a bit laborious in spots, but serves its atmospheric purpose in others. Lewis J. Rachnil served as exec producer of the Mirisch Corp. presentation.

Tube.

Les Amoureux Du France

(The Lovers of the France)
(FRENCH-COLOR-FRANSCOPE)

Paris, May 2.

CFDC release of Boreal, Stella Films production. With Marie-France Pisier, Olivier Despax, Catherine Rouvel, Henri Garcin, Bernard Meusnier. Written and directed by Pierre Grimblat after Pierre Marivaux and an idea by Francois Reichenbach. Camera (Eastmancolor), Jean-Marc Ripert: editor, Albert Jurgenson; scenes covering the voyage photographed by Francois Reichenbach. Previewed in Paris. Running time, **95 MINS.**

Olivier .... Olivier Despax
Heiress .... Marie-France Pisier
Lisa .... Catherine Rouvel
Brother .... Bernard Meusnier
Gamekeeper .... Henri Garcin

This seems more of a floating ad for the S.S. France than a feature film in its own right. Pic tries to mix fantasy, situation comedy and romantic byplay during a trip of this ship from France to Brazil. But it lacks characterization, zest and sustained comedics to make this more than a local bet. Foreign art chances are slim and playoff strictly for the lower half of dualers.

A ruined, rich young nobleman is sent off by his father to try to marry the daughter of a rich businessman friend. The boy changes places with his valet and the girl with her secretary. So both pairs fall in love with a final happy ending getting the ruined noble family the needed money. Director Pierre Grimblat has used New Wave tactics of mixing past and present via flashbacks, breaking with time and place at will and erratic cutting.

There are witty scenes, such as two duellists from the gymnasium carrying on all over the ship. But this is somewhat too intermittent and fragile to keep this entertaining for its feature footage. It bogs down halfway through and its callow personages, played by wooden thesps, do not help.

Documentarist Francois Reichenbach has shot side footage on regular passengers and the ship's functioning. But he tries for wit to force the tone and make it patronizing rather than revealing. Color is good and technical credits fine. The ship itself emerges well from this overloaded but fragile pic.

Mosk.

Robinson Crusoe On Mars

(TECHNISCOPE—COLOR)

Highly promising b.o. prospect —a stimulating and skillful sci-fi takeoff on the adventure classic. Class effort in its field, rates vigorous salesmanship.

Hollywood, May 28.

Paramount release of Aubrey Schenck production. With Paul Mantee, Vic Lundin, Adam West. Directed by Byron Haskin. Screenplay, Ib Melchior, John C. Higgins, based on Daniel Defoe's "Robinson Crusoe"; camera, Winton C. Hoch; editor, Terry Morse; music, Van Cleaye; asst. director, Arthur Jacobson. Reviewed at the studio, May 28, '64. Running time, **109 MINS.**

Commander Chris Draper.... Paul Mantee
Friday .... Vic Lundin
Colonel Dan McReady .... Adam West

Paramount has a dark horse boxoffice prospect in "Robinson Crusoe On Mars," a fascinating futuristic takeoff on Daniel DeFoe's two-and-a-half-century-old adventure classic. It's an enthralling screen experience for people of all ages, and an especially enticing number for lovers of adventure and for children on the prowl for exciting vacation entertainment. The Aubrey Schenck-Edwin F. Zabel production is an outstanding achievement of its genre, a class science fiction film that is a tribute to the creative and cinematic ingenuity of all who toiled on it. Boxoffice response may not be astronomical but, given the proper sendoff and word-of-mouth stimulus, should prove highly profitable.

Man, you think we've got turmoil here on earth? Compared to the Mars that materializes in this screenplay by Ib Melchoir and John C. Higgins, nothing-but-nothing ever happens in our celestial neighborhood. The adventure begins when the modern (astronaut) counterpart of Crusoe (Paul Mantee) has to eject himself from his spacecraft after narrowly avoiding collision with a meteor. On the surface of an extremely inhospitable Mars, he and his monkey companion manage to survive through discovery of fresh means by which they are able to breathe (a yellow rock that exhales oxygen fumes), drink (watery underground caverns beneath the planet's arid and fiery crust) and eat (a pod that resembles a hot dog).

The problem of loneliness is solved when "Crusoe" finds his "Friday" (Vic Lundin), a runaway slave of an interplanetary mining team from another galaxy. Friday's masters have to go down in sci-fi history as the most hostile and persistent critters in the universe. The way they bombard Mars just to polish off this one little slave defies reason. Eventually, Crusoe and Friday, having become comrades and learned to communicate, make their way through great earthquake-spawned fissures (the Martian canals) to the polar ice cap, where they survive a devastating meteor explosion and resultant thaw, and are rescued by a spacecraft from earth.

Astronomers may scoff, or at least have reservations, about many of these dramatic simplifications, but ordinary folk aren't apt to be troubled by any scientific data discrepancies. What may bother some of the more finicky customers is a vagueness in topographical and meteorological explanation. The title is another debatable facet. Although it's a highly exploitable handle, it serves to kill some of the suspense inherent in the screenplay, since those familiar with the Defoe work will not only be aware of the happy outcome but also will be a step ahead of certain plot developments.

Mantee and Lundin, relative unknowns to film audiences, are well cast, appealing and more than competent in their delineations. Adam West is very capable in his abbreviated portrayal, at the outset, of Mantee's ill-fated astronaut colleague.

Aubrey Schenck's production is vigorously and resourcefully directed by Byron Haskin and expertly photographed in Technicolor by Winton C. Hoch. The picture was shot against the almost otherworldly landscape of Death Valley. Art directors Hal Pereira and Arthur Lonergan rate praise for their selection of appropriate sites.

Van Cleave's musical score is eerily indigenous to the hostile environment. Highly commendable work has been obtained from editor Terry Morse and soundmen Harold Lewis and John Wilkinson. Last, but not least, a low bow to special photographic effects man Lawrence Butler, whose optical illusions make a big contribution to "Robinson Crusoe on Mars."

Tube.

Samurai From Nowhere

(JAPANESE—GRANDSCOPE)

Beautifully made Japanese study of unemployed Samurai. One for the Cineaddicts.

Hollywood, May 21.

Shochiku Films of America release of Gin-ichi Kishimoto production. Stars Isamu Nagato; features Tetsuro Tamba, Shima Iwashita; Chieko Baisho, Seiji Miyaguchi. Directed by Seiichiro Uchikawa. Screenplay, Hideo Ogumi, from story by Shugoro Yasmamoto; camera, Yoshiharu Ohta; music, Masaru Sato. Reviewed at Kabuki Theatre, May 21, '64. Running time, **93 MINS.**

Ihei Misawa .... Isamu Nagato
Gunjuro Ohba .... Tetsuro Tamba
Otae .... Shima Iwashita
Chigusa .... Chieko Baisho
Tatewaki Komuro .... Seiji Miyaguchi

Students of the cinema and motion picture industry would do well to expose themselves to this intriguing import from Japan. In several respects, it is an exceptional artistic achievement. It affords the inquisitive filmgoer a fascinating glimpse of feudal Japan, but more than that it is the manner in which the film is constructed that is apt to excite the technique-conscious observer. The picture has flaws, but they are relatively insignificant compared to its merits.

"Samurai From Nowhere" tells the story of a "ronin," or unemployed samurai who, having lost his master, has taken to hustling as a means of livelihood. This particular ronin happens to be a marvelous person, a character so appealing as to be irresistible to an audience. One might describe him as a composite of Robin Hood, Don Quoxite and the Cisco Kid, although his disheveled appearance and deceptively ordinary physique is more akin to the comic sidekicks of those three heroic figures.

At any rate, all he seeks is 10 gold pieces by which he and his wife (whom he has rescued from a fate of concubine to a deranged feudal Lord—a maneuver for which he is being pursued) can cross a checkpoint to sanctuary in a neighboring domain. His exceptional strength of character almost wins him a cherished position as master of martial arts, but his hustling ways deprive him of this honor. Ultimately, in his desperate attempt to cross the border, he is assaulted by a swarm of guards and officials but, with the unexpected aid of his former rival (another masterful warrior), he manages to subdue his opponents in as vicious and gory a skirmish as one might ever witness on the screen.

The film's outstanding components are the endearing nature of the central character and the striking cinematic technique of depicting the swordplay. The trigger-quick fashion in which these scenes of intimate and deadly combat are cut and knit brings to them an extraordinary visual and emotional impact. The cinematographic image is quicker than the eye, and never has it been so graphically illustrated. The illusion of battle is conveyed with a terrifying ferocity.

Isamu Nagato is memorable as the focal figure. Tetsuro Tamba is excellent as his frightening foe who becomes his ally in the clutch. The rest of the players are more than competent under Seiichiro Uchikawa's skillful direction. The film may be far too gory for the more squeamish spectator, and its delayed exposition proves troublesome over the first half, but its cinematic rewards more than make up for these shortcomings. *Tube.*

Kapo

(ITALIAN—FRENCH)

Lionex Films release of a Vides-Zebra-Cineriz-Francinex (Morris Ergas) production. Directed by Gillo Pontecorvo. Features Susan Strasberg, Laurent Terzieff, Emmanuelle Riva, Didi Perego. Story and screenplay, Pontecorvo and Franco Solinas; camera, Alexander Sekulovic, Goffredo Bellisario; editor, Roberto Cinquini; music, Carlo Rustichelli. Reviewed at N.Y., May 23, 1964. Running time, **116 MINS.**

Edith (Nicole) .... Susan Strasberg
Sascia .... Laurent Terzieff
Teresa .... Emmanuelle Riva
Sofia .... Didi Perego
And Gianni Garko, Annabella Besi, Graziella Galvani.

This Italian-French coproduction was important enough to have been the Italian nominee for the 1960 "best foreign language" Academy Award and it won Susan Strasberg a "best actress" trophy at the 1961 Mar del Plata Film Festival. It is just now, however, getting a U.S. release.

The delay, undoubtedly due to its subject matter (fight for survival in a Nazi concentration camp) and its length, won't help any. The only conceivable market are art situations where heavier fare is the policy. While many imports are cut severely to make them acceptable in U.S., this one escaped. Careful and considerable cutting would improve both the film and its chances.

Basically Italian, nothing in "Kapo" identifies it as an Italian film. Assorted nationalities make up the featured part of the cast. Inserted newsreel shots of concentration camps, blended with staged footage, bear undertones of propaganda.

Partially dubbed, but bearing no

credits, the voices for the principals are sometimes good but generally poor. They more or less match the actors but not always their expressions or emotions.

Miss Strasberg plays Edith, a young French Jewess, confined in a German concentration camp. After her parents are killed, she is helped by another prisoner, Sofia (Didi Perego) to change her identity to that of Nicole, a prisoner who had died.

To survive, Nicole begins to collaborate with the Nazis and eventually becomes a "kapo," a trustee. Film concentrates on actions of the prisoners. Only one German, a young S.S. officer (played sympathetically), is given much footage.

Teresa, a French partisan (Emmannelle Riva) who has befriended Nicole, finally gives up and commits suicide. Some male Russian prisoners are brought into the camp and Nicole falls for one, Sascia (Laurent Terzieff). Under his influence she reforms and finally sacrifices her life to help the others escape.

Director Pontecorvo's examination of the degradation of human beings under the Nazis dwells too long on depicting of camp facilities and prisoner behavior. Effective in her early Anne Frank-ish scenes. Miss Strasberg is less so as a harsh-voiced female guard. She's frequently overshadowed by Miss Riva whose expressive face says more than do others with pages of dialog.

Laurent Terzieff, as Sascha, acts Russian, sounds English and looks German, quite a trick for a Frenchman. Miss Perego is most effective as a tough survivalist.

Alexander Sekulovic and Goffredo Bellisario's black and white photography captures the cold, miserable hopelessness of the camp and the tragic futility in the faces of the prisoners. Robert Cinquin's editing is efficient but insufficient. Carlo Bustichelli's score makes repeated use of a harpsichord theme identified with Miss Strasberg, indicating the more dramatic moments by increasing the volume. *Robe.*

Lady In a Cage

Unappealing shock melodrama. Dim b.o. prospect.

Hollywood, May 25.

Paramount release of Luther Davis production. Stars Olivia de Havilland; features Ann Sothern. Directed by Walter Grauman. Screenplay, Davis; camera, Lee Garmes; editor, Leon Barsha; music, Paul Glass; asst. director, Howard Alston. Reviewed at the studio, May 25, '64. Running time, **94 MINS.**

Mrs. Hilyard .... Olivia de Havilland
Sade .... Ann Sothern
The Wino .... Jeff Corey
Randall .... James Caan
Elaine .... Jennifer Billingsley
Essie .... Rafael Campos
Malcolm Hilvard .... William Swan
Junkyard Proprietor ...... Charles Seel

As pessimistic an appraisal of human nature as has come along in some time is advanced by "Lady In a Cage." Evidently the Luther Davis production was designed to shock an audience, but its distorted, distastefully sordid view of life makes it a noxious, repulsive film. A campaign to condition prospective customers to the gruelling experience that awaits them is being launched by Paramount in advance of the picture. This might engender

some brief initial curiosity and attendance, but once the customers begin to "condition" each other the boxoffice bubble will quickly burst.

There's not a single redeeming character or characteristic to producer Davis' sensationalistically vulgar screenplay. It is haphazardly constructed, full of holes sometimes pretentious and in bad taste. Had the basic premise—of an invalid woman trapped in her private home elevator when the power is cut off—been developed simply, neatly and realistically, gripping dramatic entertainment might have ensued. But Davis has chosen to employ his premise as a means to expose all the negative aspects of the human animal. He has infested the caged woman's house with as scummy an assortment of characters as literary imagination might conceive. Among those who greedily invade her abode are a delirious wino (Jeff Corey), a plump prostitute (Ann Southern) and three vicious young hoodlums (James Caan, Jennifer Billingsley and Rafael Campos). The crowning disillusionment, perhaps intended as some stroke of irony, is the revelation of the woman's own base nature. There's just nobody to root for in this picture.

Olivia de Havilland plays the unfortunate woman in the elevator, and gives one of those ranting, raving, wild-eyed performances often thought of as Academy Award oriented. Actually, the role appears to require more emotional stamina than histrionic deftness. Miss de Havilland does about as well as possible under the dire circumstances. So does Miss Sothern as the prostie. When the picture ends, she's locked up in a closet but nobody seems to care. Corey is sufficiently pitiful as the wino. Caan, as the sadistic leader of the little ratpack, appears to have been watching too many early Marlon Brando movies. Miss Billingsley and Campos are unpleasantly gregarious. The cast is rounded out adequately by William Swan, Charles Seel and Scat Man Cruthers.

Directorial guide of this hysterical orgy is Walter Grauman. With the assistance of cameraman Lee Garmes and editor Leon Barsha, he has spared the audience none of the lurid details. Art directors Hal Pereira and Rudy Sternad have designed, evidently according to the specifications of the script, an incongruously luxurious residence in an impoverished, dilapidated neighborhood. A largely atonal score by Paul Glass accompanies the action. *Tube.*

Marnie
(COLOR)

Latest Hitchcock melodramatics holds sturdy b.o. prospects. Exploitable and well-acted.

Hollywood, June 2.

Universal release of Alfred Hitchcock production. Stars Tippi Hedren, Sean Connery; features Diane Baker, Martin Gabel. Directed by Hitchcock. Screenplay, Jay Presson Allen, from novel by Winston Graham; camera (Technicolor), Robert Berks; editor, George Tomasini; music, Bernard Herrmann; assistant director, James H. Brown. Reviewed at Directors Guild Theatre, June 1, '64. Running time, 130 MINS.

Marnie .... Tippi Hedren
Mark Rutland .... Sean Connery
Lil Mainwaring .... Diane Baker
Sidney Strutt .... Martin Gabel
Bernice Edgar .... Louise Latham
Cousin Bob .... Bob Sweeney
Man at the Track .... Milton Selzer
Susan Clabon .... Mariette Hartley
Mr. Rutland .... Alan Napier
Sailor .... Bruce Dern
First Detective ...... Henry Beckman
Sam Ward .... S. John Launer
Rita .... Edith Evanson
Mrs. Turpin .... Meg Wyllie

Alfred Hitchcock's first production since "The Birds" early last year emerges with sufficient suspense and melodramatics to be sturdy box-office for Universal. Pic carries the familiar Hitchcock brand of audience-teasing dramaturgy which may be exploited profitably for all situations and comes near to returning director, after his off-format "Birds," to the type of filmantics which originally established him as b o. lure. Opening sequences, however, are so slow that it sometimes appears as if director is more interested in wooing his own particular talents than pleasing his audience.

"Marnie" is the character study of a thief and a liar, but what makes her tick remains clouded even after a climax reckoned to be shocking but somewhat missing its point. Hitchcock builds on this premise of character-development in sometimes over-lackadaisical fashion, but once in his story generally keeps the action fairly fast-paced—provided audience can overlook certain puzzling aspects, such as why the lady became a thief—and gets strong performances from his two stars and other cast members. An anti-climatic note is hit in closing scene which leaves spectators wondering if the heroine will get her come-uppance.

Tippi Hedren, whom Hitchcock intro'd in "Birds," returns in a particularly demanding role and Sean Connery makes his American film bow, as the two principal protagonists in this adaptation of Winston Graham's bestseller. Complicated story line, as scripted by Jay Presson Allen, offers Miss Hedren as a sexy femme who takes office jobs, then absconds with as much cash as she can find in the safe, changing color of her tresses and obtaining new employment for similar purposes. Plot becomes objective when she is recognized by her new employer, book publisher Connery, as the girl who stole $10,000 from a business associate, and rather than turn her in marries her.

That's merely the beginning, and balance of unfoldment dwells on husband's efforts to ferret mystery of why she recoils from the touch of any man—himself included—and why other terrors seem to overcome her. The secret is partially cleared after a session with girl's mother, who reveals a series of shocking events which took place when femme was a

small child. Still militating against full understanding of plot is unexplained reason for her constant thieving.

Miss Hedren, undertaking role originally offered Princess Grace Kelly of Monaco for a resumption of her screen career, lends credence to a part never sympathetic. It's a difficult assignment which she fulfills satisfactorily, although Hitchcock seldom permits her a change of pace which would have made her character more interesting. Connery handles himself convincingly, but here, again, greater interest would have resulted from greater facets of character as he attempts to explore femme's unexplained past. Diane Baker, as his dead wife's sister out to marry him, registers interestingly, and Louise Latham as Miss Hedren's mother socks over a strangely dramatic role. Martin Gabel is in briefly as Miss Hedren's first victim in pic.

As usual, with Hitchcock's product, technical credits are highly placed. Robert Burk's color photography is fluid and deft, production design by Robert Boyle interesting as narrative swings from offices to luxurious country manor, and George Tomasini's editing sharp, the trio having worked previously on director's "Birds." George Milo's set decorations are properly artistic, Bernard Herrmann's music score blends appropriately with the action and Edith Head designed several beautiful outfits for both Miss Hedren and Miss Baker. *Whit.*

Stage to Thunder Rock
(TECHNISCOPE-COLOR)

Western with underlying psychological motivations that should be a solid programmer in most situations. Cast of familiar faces and longtime pros adds to its appeal.

Hollywood, June 5.

Paramount release of A. C. Lyles production. Stars Barry Sullivan, Marilyn Maxwell, Keenan Wynn; features Scott Brady, Lon Chaney, John Agar, Wandrix. Directed by William F. Claxton. Screenplay, Charles Wallace; camera, W. Wallace Kelley; editor, Jodie Copelan; music, Paul Dunlap; assistant director, Russ Haverick. Reviewed at studio, June 1, '64. Running time, **84 MINS.**

Sheriff Horne .... Barry Sullivan
Leah Parker .... Marilyn Maxwell
Ross Sawyer .... Keenan Wynn
Sam Swope .... Scott Brady
Henry Parker .... Lon Chaney
Dan Carrouthers ...... John Agar
Mrs. Swope .... Wanda Handeix
Myra Parker .... Anne Seymour
Mayor Ted Dollar .... Allan Jones
Reese Sawyer .... Ralph Taeger
Julie Parker .... Laurel Goodwin
Judge Bates .... Robert Strauss
Seth Harrington ..... Robert Strauss
Sarita .... Argentina Brunetti
"Shotgun" .... Rex Bell Jr.
Sandy Swope .... Suzanne Cupito
Toby Sawyer .... Wayne Peters

Within the rapidly diminishing sphere of the program western, A. C. Lyles has developed what appears to be a successful pattern of mixing action and outdoor drama within a framework of simple psychology to provide acceptable screenfare in the low budget field.

Action has generally been the keynote of the oaters, although changes in theatre attendance, added cost of color and wider screens have forced westerns into an added dimension. There is a lot of talk and even some underlying Freudian motivation involved in Lyles' production of what formerly might have been just a simple guns and girls story.

"Stage," ignoring the underlying elements, is still basically the story of a couple of gunslingers after the same guys for different reasons. The issue of mortality involved is one that stirs up some thought. However, Charles Wallace's screenplay and William F. Claxton's direction keep the plot moving sufficiently to center on suspense and action rather than on more scrutable areas. The plot telegraphs its ending as well as many of the relationships in between, but for those less demanding filmgoers it offers enough material to be generally satisfying. Tale tells of a lawman forced to capture or kill the father and his two sons with whom he was raised. Town businessmen, distrusting him for his personal feelings, have hired a paid gunman in their interests and the fight becomes one of morality between the two men. Interspersed, but unclear in its basic motivation, is the story of a hard-luck rancher and his family, whose own drives for betterment nearly cause them to aid the wrong side.

Lyles continues casting with familiar faces and longtime pros, many of whom have become identified with his pix. Barry Sullivan is staunch, hard and strongwilled as the lawman in a performance well suited to the role. And Marilyn Maxwell and Scott Brady are fine in equally undemanding but plausible performances. Keenan Wynn has a strikingly evil character delivery and the character work of Lon Chaney, Anne Seymour and, particularly, Ralph Taeger, stands out throughout. Laurel Goodwin and John Agar add a healthy, youthful romantic look, while Wanda Hendrix, Allan Jones, Robert Strauss, Robert Lowery and Argentina Brunetti are well cast.   *Dale.*

Seance on a Wet Afternoon
(BRITISH)

Downbeat subject skilfully handled by Bryan Forbes and sound cast; astute selling needed to put over a chilly pic that compels admiration but lacks sympathy.

London, June 2.
Rank release of an Allied Film Makers presentation of a Richard Attenborough-Bryan Forbes production. Stars Kim Stanley, Richard Attenborough; features Nanette Newman, Marian Spencer, Judith Donner, Patrick Magee, Arnold Bell, Mark Eden, Gerald Sim. Written and directed by Forbes, from Mark McShane's novel; camera, Gerry Turpin; music, John Barry; editor, Derek York. At Odeon, Haymarket, London. Running time, **116 MINS.**
Myra .... Kim Stanley
Bill .... Richard Attenborough
Women at First Seance . Margaret Lacey
                              Maria Kazan
Man at Seances .... Lionel Gamlin
Mrs. Wintry .... Marian Spencer
Amanda .... Judith Donner
Mr. Clayton .... Mark Eden
Mrs. Clayton .... Nanette Newman
Beadle .... Gerald Sim
Weaver .... Arnold Bell
Woman at Second Seance
                         Margaret McGrath
Bus Conductor ...... Frank Singuineau
Walsh .... Patrick Magee

Selected as Britain's official entry at the San Sebastian Film Fest, this is a skillful picture, and on many counts, admirable picture. Bryan Forbes' writing and direc-

tion have created an aptly clammy atmosphere and he's backed by some shrewd thesping. But the theme is downbeat and unlikely to whip up much sympathetic reaction among patrons. Astute selling may be necessary to put over a film that lacks warmth and heart and which deals with a subject that is alien to many.

Onus of the acting falls heavily on Kim Stanley and Richard Attenborough. Capture of Miss Stanley for one of her rare screen appearances is a major triumph for Allied. Yet though she is an exciting actress to watch, she is much Method and technicalities occasionally get in the way of her rendering of a role that provides a leading actress with plenty of scope.

Even her rendering of lines often slows down the pace of proceedings and director Forbes appears to have let Miss Stanley dictate that pace a shade too often. It throws extra responsibility on Richard Attenborough as her weak, loving and downtrodden husband. Here is a splendid piece of trouping which rings true throughout. It's another smart move by Attenborough in becoming accepted as a character actor after longish years in younger parts. The two make a fascinating team in this film, though the audience always will feel outside their activities rather than with them.

The star is a medium of dubious authenticity, who inveigles her spouse into a nutty plan which she confidently believes will give her the recognition due to her. Idea is to "borrow" a child, make out it has been kidnapped, collect the ransom loot and wait for the story to pump up to front page sensation. Then she aims to hold a seance and reveal clues which will enable the cops to find the child unharmed. She believes the deception is justified to put over her claim for spiritualism.

Attenborough realizes that the scheme is booked for disaster but goes through with it for love and pity for his wife. Safety demands that he kill the child in the end but he'll not go along with this. At the inevitable showdown he realizes that his wife is not a gifted spiritualist but merely crazy.

The film throughout is pitched on sombre key with much macabre reference to a son that the couple never had but in whom Miss Stanley implicitly believes. The dankness of the house in which her shabby machinations evolve is well caught, thanks to deft artwork and Gerry Turpin's searching camera.

Forbes well-written, imaginative script is a study in grey, abetted by the fine lensing of Turpin, a newish arrival on the lensing scene. An exciting, ingenious highspot involves complicated production when Attenborough is due to collect the ransom money. It has been shot with hidden cameras in Leicester-square and Piccadilly at London's busiest hour. Result is an air of intense, exciting realism. So realistic, in fact, that parts of it had to be reshot. Without realizing that a film was being shot, the negative revealed several w.k. characters such as Sir John Gielgud captured while strolling in London about their daily business.

John Barry has provided an evocative musical score and Ray Simms' artwork is impeccable. Though the acting relies mainly on the intelligent performances of Miss Stanley and Attenborough it is boosted by telling bits from such as Nanette Newman, as the distraught mother of the kidnapped child, Judith Donner, as the moppet, Patrick Magee, Arnold Bell and Mark Eden. Scenes between the guilty couple and the police are particularly tactfully handled. A standout opening holds the interest from the start and this rarely falters even though the wheels are seen to be going round a shade too patently.

The seances have a fascinating, forbidding eeriness and may prove uncomfortable for the many who find spiritualism hard to take. "Seance" is, in many ways, a remarkable picture. It offers food for thought, conjecture and debate and has a sure grip on its theme. Yet, though compelling, it is in many ways too mechanically clinical and lacks many of the qualities needed to endear it to a wide audience.   *Rich.*

The Living and the Dead
(RUSSIAN—SCOPE)

Paris, June 9.
Mosfilm production and release. Stars Kirill Larov, Anatoly Papanov, Aleksei Glazurin. Written and directed by Alexandre Stolper from book by Constantin Simonov. Camera, Nikolai Olonovsky; editor, I. Orionovskaya. At Kinopanorama, Paris. Running time, **130 MINS.**
Correspondent .... Anatoly Papanov
Serpiline .... Aleksei Glazurin
Friend .... Kirill Larov

News has been coming out of Russia lately about tugs-of-war between artists and the state reps, and the gains and losses in freer expression in all the arts and especially films. This trend shows up in a cut version here. It does seem more outspoken on certain subjects like Siberia, war losses and anti-stalinism.

This film has some forthright (for Russia) talk and soft pedals the usual legendary, exemplary and sturdy Russo military man, be he officer or recruit. Other pix have shown some soldiers expressing fear or common sense when outnumbered by the enemy, but they have usually redeemed themselves. It is only partially so in this pic.

There also have been a few evidences of some thaw in Russo films before via the anti-Stalinistic aspects of Gregori Chonkrai's "Clear Skies." Then the heroic war tales started up again. Now here is a big scale war vehicle that questions Russo heroism and also pokes at Stalin's pre-war purges. If it still balances with some bravery, this has a feel for the waste of war and Russo unpreparedness that is something new. This alone could give this curio value perhaps for some Yank specialized chances. If sheared to 130 minutes from its reported 210 minute original length this depicts man within the context of war.

A war correspondent is followed as he finds himself drafted into fighting, losing his party card, and hounded as a deserter and renegade till one kind move gets him reinstated with a lower rank. Also involved is a high-ranking officer who had been sent to Siberia dur-

ing the Stalin pre-war purges. Let out to command, he brings this up to other officers who only show shame for not speaking up earlier.

It is unusual to see anything like this cropping up in a Soviet war pic. Rugged is a scene of the slaughter of a group of badly-equipped Russki soldiers by German tanks and soldiers as well as the shooting down of three unescorted bombers by German Messerschmitts. Aside from the political aspects, this resembles other war pix from that country in its ability to humanize the many characters and also do action scenes with fervor and yet, for once, show the dirt, dreariness and horror of war.

Scope screen is well utilized. Alexandre Stolper, unknown in the West, has directed with a feel for the epic as well as the repetitiveness and sordidness of war.

Lensing is well contrasted. This looms as one Russo pic with some chances abroad. It still needs careful handling and release.
                                        Mosk.

Good Neighbor Sam
(COLOR)

Latest Jack Lemmon opus. Clever situation comedy with hot b.o. prospects.

Hollywood, June 4.

Columbia Pictures release of David Swift production. Stars Jack Lemmon, Romy Schneider, Dorothy Provine, Edward G. Robinson, Michael Connors. Directed by Swift. Screenplay, James Fritzell, Everett Greenbaum, David Swift, from novel by Jack Finney; camera (Eastman-color), Burnett Guffey; editor, Charles Nelson; music, DeVol; assistant director, R. Robert Rosenbaum. Reviewed at Beverly Theatre, June 3, '64. Running time, **130 MINS.**

Sam Bissel .... Jack Lemmon
Janet Lagerlof .... Romy Schneider
Minerva Bissel .... Dorothy Provine
Howard F..bets .... Michael Connors
Mr. Burke .... Edward Andrews
Reinhold Shiffner .... Louis Nye
Earl .... Robert Q. Lewis
Girl .... Joyce Jameson
Irene .... Anne Seymoer
Jack Bailey .... Charles Lane
Edna .... Linda Watkins
Phil Reisner .... Peter Hobbs
Sonny Blatchford .... Tris Coffin
Larry Boling .... Neil Hamilton
Miss Halverson .... Riza Royce
Millard Mellner .... William Forrest
The Hi-Lo's .... The Hi-Lo's
Simon Nurdlinger . Edward G. Robinson

Jack Lemmon's farcical flair finds further amusing exposure in this situation comedy which provides Columbia with one of its stronger entries of the season. Development of the Jack Finney tale gets slapstick screen treatment and despite, scriptwise, the solution of every situation being utterly forgotten and left dangling at pic's windup the David Swift production looks like whammo boxoffice.

Lemmon topbills star lineup in his usual competent and zany fashion but it is the Viennese Romy Schneider, making her first Hollywood-lensed feature, who shines the brightest. She displays talent as a comedienne—not apparent in "The Cardinal" and "The Victors"—and as the sexpot neighbor whom Lemmon attempts to help she's a fascinating newcomer to the Hollywood scene. Dorothy Provine, as Lemmon's understanding wife who reluctantly agrees to her spouse assisting her neighbor—and best friend—by posing as her husband so she may come into a $15,000,000 inheritance, has her best feature role to date and adds spice to the comedics of the basic situation.

Swift, who directed as well as produced and co-scripted with James Fritzell and Everett Greenbaum, sets an early breezy tempo for the nonsensical yarn which nevertheless would benefit by some judicial pruning. He makes broad use of comedy routines which pay off in several belly laughs. Gagging a filming of the familiar Hertz auto rental tv commercial of the "man in the driver's seat" is a particular standout, as the mechanics always go wrong. Certain straining is felt, however, toward the end which might be obliviated through sharp editing.

Narrative jumps with crazy, mixed-up situations, Lemmon playing low man on the totem pole of a San Francisco advertising agency until he suggests a new approach built around the average man in a campaign for a dissatisfied client about to ankle agency. Suddenly, he is important business-wise. He also finds himself called upon to play the "husband" to his next-door neighbor, who is divorced and must come up with a spouse if she is to meet the provisions of her grandfather's will in bequeathing her his $15,000,000 estate.

Unfoldment sometimes takes on the aspects of an oldtime bedroom farce as Lemmon is forced to introduce his neighbor as his wife to his boss and the client, a strait-laced bigot who believes in the sanctity of the home. There is further complication when the agency, unknown to Lemmon, has 20-foot-high faces of Lemmon and the neighbor emblazoned on ads all over town, advertising them as a couple who recommends the client's product. When the two of them frantically set out to change the faces and names on every billboard with a paint brush, they finally land in a bawdy house. All this creates plenty of humor, but the finale leaves their problems unsolved, viz., the neighbor getting her fortune and Lemmon putting himself right at the office.

Edward G. Robinson gets chuckles as the client, who demands a wholesome campaign and a wholesome man to conduct it, and Michael Connors as Miss Schneider's ex-spouse conducts himself in properly goofball style. Edward Andrews gets his share of laughs, too, as Lemmon's boss, and Robert Q. Lewis as Lemmon's neighbor who wants to know what's going on has his moments. Joyce Jameson scores briefly as a hooker who thinks Lemmon in his painter's clothes is out to brush her, and Anne Seymour and Charles Lane faithfully portray Romy's cousins also named in will.

Color camera work by Burnett Guffey is interesting, and Dale Hennesy's production design an asset. DeVol's music is particularly atmospheric, and Charles Nelson is credited as film editor.

Whit.

Des Pissenlits Par La Racine
(The Salad By the Roots) (FRENCH)

Paris, June 9.

Cocinor release of Ardennes Films-Transinter - Cocinor - Marceau - Columbua production. Stars Louis De Funes, Michel Serrault, Maurice Biraud; features Mireille Darc, Francis Blanche, Darry Cowl, Malka Ribowska. Directed by Georges Lautner. Screenplay, Calrence Weff, Albert Kantof, Michel Audiard, Lautner from novel by Weff; camera, Maurice Fellows; editor, Michele David. At Balzac, Paris. Running time, **100 MINS.**

Jockey .... Louis De Funes
Jerome .... Michel Serrault
Jo .... Maurice Biraud
Rockie .... Mireille Darc
Absalom .... Francis Blanche
Countess .... Malka Ribowska

Burlesque comedy about small-time lowlife has some funny bits. Pic veers between outright zany comedics and satire. It evokes enough yocks to have this a probable good local entry with offshore chances good for playoff spotting but arty aspects are more difficult.

Coming out of prison, an angry hoodlum tries to kill a man who had been with his girl. He is killed instead by mistake and his body put in a bass fiddle case. Most of the pic is about the doings with the cadaver as well as the winning of the moll.

Acting has the right, zesty flash for these happenings. Louis De Funes uses his neatly-timed mugging to advantage as the mistaken killer. Francis Blanche, as a madcap anthropologist, Maurice Biraud, as the Don Juan swindler, and Mireille Darc, as the girl, give ample support.

Director Georges Lautner has a way with parody pix though he has yet to find a more lightweight form of satire. But he keeps a fairly even keel in this. Swiss-based producer Arthur Cohn, who has this for the world outside of France, has an okay programmer. Already dubbed into English and called "Have Another Bier," this could do for lowercase slotting on Yank and British marts. It is technically good.

Mosk.

Gold For The Caesars
(CINEMASCOPE—COLOR)

Enough action and spectacle to please the sword-and-sandal crowd in this latest Italian import from Joseph Fryd.

Hollywood, June 8.

Metro-Goldwyn-Mayer release of an Adelphia Campagnia Cinematografica S.F.A. (Rome) production. Produced by Joseph Fryd. Directed by Andre De Toth. Features Jeffrey Hunter, Mylene Demongeot, Ron Randell, Massimo Girotti, Giulio Bosetti, Ettore Manni, Georges Lycan, Furio Meniconi. Screenplay by Arnold Perl, adapted from a novel, "Gold For the Caesars," by Florence A. Seward; camera (Technicolor), Raffaele Masciocchi; editor, Franco Fraticelli; music, Franco Mannino; sound, Giovanni Rossi; art director, Ottavio Scotti; set decorator, Arrigo Breschi; special effects, Erasmo Bacciucchi; costumes, Mario Giorsi; 2nd unit director, Riccardo Freda; asst. director, Jerzy Macc; Reviewed at the studio, June 8, 1964. Running time, **85 MINS.**

Lacer .... Jeffrey Hunter
Pennelope .... Mylene Demongeot
Rufus .... Ron Randell
Maximus .... Massimo Girotti
Scipio .... Giulio Bosetti
Luna .... Ettore Manni
Malendi .... Georges Lycan
Dax .... Furio Meniconi

Italian import is designed for spectacle and is as suitable as any of its kind for playing the exploitation-pix situations.

Jeffrey Hunter and Ron Randell are top-billed American names familiar to U.S. audiences, which may give the film a slight edge over some of its forerunners. Of course, the market has been flooded with Italian splurge product for years, so it remains a little harder to sell 'em today. But for the saturation bookings or as a second bill feature, "Gold" is at least an acceptable piece of product that may satisfy the more undemanding filmgers.

Hunter plays a Roman slave whose ability as an architect wins him respect, admiration but also envy from his rulers. It also wins him wine, women and revelry, but this is almost his downfall when he selects beautiful Mylene Demongeot, slave mistress of the Pro Consul, Massimo Girotti. Charged with a project of finding gold in a nearby valley ruled by the opposing Celts, Hunter runs the usual gamut of oppressive resistance, bloody battles and frantic activity in an easily telegraphed plot but one that moves nicely and fills the screen well.

Hunter is window-dressing in the film, looks good in his role but needs a little more guts in his acting of role. Randell is fine in a stereotyped part of an overbearing centurion. Miss Demongeot is there just for romantic interest. Most striking of performers is Giulio Bosetti, an evil conniver, while Massimo Girotti and Furio Meniconi are fine support throughout. Andre de Toth directed.

Dale.

Jack and Jenny
(GERMAN, COLOR)

Berlin, June 9.

Nora release of Arca-Winston (Berlin) production. With Brett Halsey, Senta Berger, Michael Hinz, Marion Michael, Eckart Dux. Directed by Victor Vicas. Screenplay, Kurt Nachmann, based on novel, "Early to Bed," by Anne Piper; camera (Agfacolor), Werner M. Lenz; music, Paul Misraki. At Marmorhaus, Berlin. Running time, **87 MINS.**

Jack .... Brett Halsey
Jenny .... Senta Berger
Josef .... Michael Hinz
Betsy .... Marion Michael
Eduard .... Eckart Dux
Mrs. Johannsen ...... Olga Tschechowa
Timothy .... Michael Verhoeven
Victor .... Friedrich Joloff
Barbara .... Claude Farell

Victor Vicas, Russian-born American living in Paris, already has directed several German pix. "Two Among Millions," one of these, was one of the better German pix of 1961. But his last German-lingo effort, "Jack and Jenny" misses the boat completely. Indeed, there is little to laud in this film.

What the creators of "Jack and Jenny" had in mind was a "frivolous comedy." Bed sequences galore, a substantial exhibition of femme nudity, daring dialog plus a lineup of "interesting" sex-conscious characters including a girl who lets herself be seduced as if it were nothing, a seven-times divorced playboy and even some homosexuals.

This so-called comedy is admittedly frank but seldom funny. It lacks charm, with and any sort of delicacy. Vicas has not only become the victim of a morbidly superficial script but also a victim of his German producer who wanted to bring, if in comedy form, some sex and perversion.

Jenny (Senta Berger) is a salesgirl and Jack (Brett Halsey) a painter. Both fall in love. All through the pic they have their affairs and then their quarrels. In the meantime, Jenny has a short-lived marriage with a rich ship owner which ends because both have soon their own adventures. A second marriage with an often-time divorced playboy also ends swiftly. She's already on the verge of a third marriage when she realizes the painter is actually the man she needs.

There is nothing noteworthy about the acting.

Hans.

Three Nuts in Search of a Bolt
(EASTMANCOLOR)

Nudie exploitation picture suitable only for specialty art houses that play nudie flims. Poorly written, but suitably cast. Has some comedy moments.

Hollywood, June 6.

Harlequin International Pictures release of a Tommy Noonan-Ian McGlashan production. Stars Mamie Van Doren, Noonan, Ziva Rodann, Paul Gilbert, John Cronin; features Peter Howard, T. C. Jones. Others: Charles Irving, Alvy Moore, Robert Kenneally, Marjorie Bennett, Arthur Gould-Porter, Pat O'Moore, Jennie Lee, Jimmy Cross, Curt Mercer, Richard Normoyle, Frank Kreig, Pat Noone, Kathy Waniata, Phil Arnold. Directed by Noonan. Screenplay, Noonan and McGlashan; camera, Fouad Said; editor, Bill Martin; art director, Carol Ballard; Music, Phil Moody; production manager, William J. Maginetti. Reviewed June 6, 1964. Monica Theatre, L. A. Running time: **80 MINS.**

Tommy Noonan made money on "Promises. Promises," first of his nudie-designed films, and it is conceivable he will again get some coin into the cash register with "Three Nuts" which, as bad a picture as it is, is still better than Noonan's first effort.

There are apparently enough specialty houses catering to the customers who like to see a pretty girl take her clothes off—and this is really what basically happens in "Nuts." In this case it's Mamie Van Doren who shows almost every inch of her delectable physiognomy in scenes from a nude beer bath to a torrid strip that bumps and grinds as far as the screen could possibly allow.

"Nuts" is supposed to be a comedy and there are some genuinely funny moments in it. The idea is fresh and could have been expanded into a pretty clever plot. Story concerns three "nuts" in search of a schnook to impersonate them all simultaneously with an expensive lady psychiatrist so they can get her advice by paying only one bill. Noonan, of course, is the schnook and a better one couldn't be found. He's wacky, ridiculous and slapstick throughout. The three patients are Miss Van Doren, who plays a stripper who is afraid of men; Paul Gilbert, excellent as a hard sell car salesman who loves to dupe the public, and John Cronin, a narcissistic model who hates girls.

Where "Nuts" is completely lost is in the dull, unbelievable and careless dialog in which the story is couched. There is too much activity and little tieing in so it comes out as just a mishmash of trite, cheap comedy. And could have been better.

But there are some momentary flashes of delightful comedy, as in the character bits of Marjorie Bennett and Phil Arnold and in the campy, satirical performance of T. C. Jones, who just about steals the show with an outlandish characterization of the psychiatrist's secretary. Ziva Rodann is fine as the doctor, also displays a few Playboy type shots herself, to add to the French post card effect. These, for some reason, are all in technicolor, as are the other stripper and nudie sequences, while the basic film is in black and white.

Other performances of note are by Charles Irving, Alvy Moore, Arthur Gould-Porter, Pat O'Moore, Jimmy Cross and Frank Kreig, all comedy bits. *Dale.*

Les Pas Perdus
(The Last Steps)
(FRENCH—TOTALVISION)
Paris, June 9.
SETEC release of Cinerora Productions production. Stars Michele Morgan; features Jean-Louis Trintignant, Catherine Rouvel, Jean Carmet. Directed by Jacques Robin. Screenplay, Rene Fallet, Robin from book by Fallet; camera, Guy Chichignoux; editor, Nadine Marquand. Previewed in Paris. Running time, **87 MINS.**
Yolande .... Michele Morgan
Georges .... Jean-Louis Trintignant
Lemartin .... Jean Carmet
Sonia .... Catherine Rouvel
Husband .... Michel Vitold

Laborious tale of a short-lived love affair between a middleaged upper class woman and a young worker is sans the insight into the feel for characters to have it come off. It also shows that filmmakers here find it hard to unearth any good vehicles for their young vet femme star Michele Morgan.

Turgidly told, but with playing that cannot cope with the stereotyped personages and telegraphed proceedings, this appears mainly a home bet with foreign chances not so good. Quickie production may have this an okay home playoff item, however.

Miss Morgan is encountered by worker Jean-Louis Trintignant in a station which she visits daily on her way home to the suburbs. Brief encounter leads to quick love and then her sudden decision to cut it off and stay with her husband since it is getting dangerous. May-December romance is told lacklustrely.

All of this makes the pic preachy instead of probing or incisive in its theme and telling. Miss Morgan is her usual gentle self but Trintignant, usually expressing charm in his pix, appears gauche. Technical credits and supporting playing are average. *Mosk.*

A Shot In The Dark
(PANAVISION—COLOR)

Peter Sellers and Blake Edwards in another romp of the bumbling Inspector Jacques Clouseau, brimful of slapstick and clicky prospects indicated.

Hollywood, June 19.
United Artists release of Mirisch (Blake Edwards) production, directed by Edwards. Stars Peter Sellers, Elke Sommer; features George Sanders, Herbert Lom. Screenplay, Blake Edwards, William Peter Blatty, based on plays by Harry Kurnitz, Marcel Achard; camera (DeLuxe Color), Chris Challis; music, Henry Mancini; editors, Ralph E. Winters, Bert Bates; asst. director, Derek Cracknell. Reviewed at Academy Awards Theatre, June 18, '64. Running time, **103 MINS.**
Inspector Jacques Clouseau .. Peter Sellers
Maria Gambrelli .... Elke Sommer
Chief Insp. Charles Dreyfus..Herbert Lom
Dominique Ballon .... Tracy Reed
Hercule Lajoy .... Graham Stark
Francois .... Andre Maranne
Henri Lafarge .... Douglas Wilmer
Madame Lafarge .... Vanda Godsell
Pierre .... Maurice Kaufman
Dudu .... Ann Lynn
Georges .... David Lodge
Simone .... Moira Redmond
Maurice .... Martin Benson
Kato .... Burt Kwouk
Receptionist .... Reginald Beckwith
Charlie .... Turk Thrust
Doctor .... John Herrington
Psychoanalyst .... Jack Melford

The late Al Christie once said, "The best comedy director is the one with the longest memory." Blake Edwards is a very good comedy director, as he has proved in numerous past excursions, more recently with "Pink Panther" and now "A Shot in the Dark," an audience picture indeed with a yock a minute and the look of boxoffice success.

Edwards again makes use of the talents (?) of Inspector Jacques Clouseau, the bumbling French sleuth of "Panther," for his star character in "Dark," a historic repeat for Peter Sellers whose timing and drollness hits classic lines. Edwards, too, draws extravagantly upon slapstick, uncorking comedy gags and routines almost forgotten in modern times but grist for early comedy kings, draining individual scenes of farcical potential and generally aiming his material for huge audience appreciation. Wisdom remains to be seen of projecting a second appearance of the hilariously inept detective so soon after the still-current firstrun showing of "Panther," since some of the spontaneous novelty may have worn off, but the laughs are still there abundantly through imaginative bits of business and a few strike belly proportions.

Sometimes the narrative is subordinated to these individual bits of business and running gags which evoke merriment. Spectators apparently care not, for each, though sometimes telegraphed ahead, provides the stuff that makes for handsome entertainment, though there may be those who object to such trivialities. Sellers becomes such a stylized individual in his handling of a murder case—which immediately becomes multiple when he takes over—that the audience almost works out in its own mind situations in which he might have plunged, and he can do no wrong. Even in the most nonsensical scene, and there are plenty, he's a powerhouse.

Based upon the French farce authored by Marcel Achard and adapted to the American stage by Harry Kurnitz, Blake transforms Seller's role from a magistrate, whose activities were limited to judicial chambers, into Inspector Clouseau, where more movement and greater area are possible. "Give me 10 men like Clouseau, and I could destroy the world!" his superior exclaims in despair, in summing up the character played by Sellers, sent to investigate a murder in the chateau of a millionaire outside Paris. When this chief inspector, portrayed by Herbert Lom, attempts to take him off the case, powers above return him to his investigations which revolve about chief suspect Elke Sommer, a French maid, whom the dick is convinced is innocent.

These chores take him to a nudist camp, a tour of Parisian nightclubs, where dead bodies are left in his wake, and to his apartment, where one of the funniest seduction scenes ever filmed unfolds to the tune of three in a bed and an exploding time bomb. It's never completely clear whether the detective solves his case in a windup that doesn't quite come off.

Sellers' skill as a comedian again is demonstrated, and Miss Sommer, in role of the chambermaid who moves all men to amorous thoughts and sometimes murder, is pert and expert. Lom gives punch and humor to star's often-distraught superior, George Sanders lends polish as the millionaire and Graham Stark excels as Sellers' dead-pan assistant. Burt Kwouk gets laughs as Sellers' Nipponese houseboy under constant orders to attack his employer at unexpected moments to keep detective on the qui vive.

Color photography by Chris Challis in turn makes expansive use of Paris streets, contributes tellingly and Henry Mancini's music score is a particular standout. Another potent asset, to launch a fast opening, is the witty titles from DePatie-Frelend Enterprises and amusing animation production by George Dunning, Ltd. Michael Stringer's production design also rates highly as does editing by Ralph E. Winters and Bert Bates. *Whit.*

The Moon-Spinners
(COLOR)

Disney plants a variety of film types in a colorful Cretan setting. Result is fast suspense-comedy with something for everyone.

New York, June 18.
A Buena Vista release of a Walt Disney production. Co-producer, Bill Anderson; associate producer, Hugh Attwooll. Features Hayley Mills, Eli Wallach, Peter McEnery, Joan Greenwood, Irene Papas, Pola Negri. Directed by James Neilson. Screenplay by Michael Dyne, based on a novel by Mary Stewart; camera (Technicolor), Paul Beeson, additional photography, John Wilcox, Michael Reed; editor, Gordon Stone; sound, Jonathan Bates; art director, Tony Masters; music, composed and conducted by Ron Grainer; title song by Terry Gilkyson; costumes, Anthony Mendleson; second unit director, Arthur J. Vitarelli; asst. director, John Peverall. Reviewed in N.Y., June 18, 1964. Running time: **118 MINS.**
Nikky Ferris .... Hayley Mills
Stratos .... Eli Wallach
Mark Camford.......... Peter McEnery
Aunt Frances .... Joan Greenwood
Sophia .... Irene Papas
Madame Hab'b .... Pola Negri
Anthony Gamble ..... John Le Mesurier
Lambis .... Paul Stassino
Mrs. Gamble........... Sheila Hancock
Alexis .... Michael Davis

Disney's race against time to find adequate vehicles for the popular but fast-growing Hayley Mills is nearing its end as she turns woman but he'll get plenty of mileage and good returns from this Grecian gambol.

With a mixture of American, English and Greek talents, engaged in a silly but zestful tale of villainy undone, told against some of the most photogenic landscapes in the world, Disney has provided exhibitors with a package that should provide fast and favorable returns in almost any situation. It is scheduled nationally, for a July 4 release.

Admittedly not for serious-minded filmgoers unless they're willing to forego logic for a chance to relax amid gorgeous surroundings, "Moon-Spinners" naturally concentrates on Miss Mills. With action the keyword in Michael Dyne's loosely-knit script, this keeps the young lady perpetually on the move. Her adventures into first-puppy-love and feats of derring-do are accomplished with equal amounts of energy. She's never still long enough for her virtue or her life to be in danger.

Director James Neilson puts almost all of his people through much the same paces, resulting in an overall impression of effusiveness. More irritating than the hectic movement is his habit of dropping really interesting bits of business into the plot with no explanation and no resolution, or not following through on obviously-planted story threads. In this he's aided and abetted by editor Gordon Stine's pinking shears.

Tale chiefly concerns two English females (Miss Mills and Joan Greenwood) becoming involved in a jewel-theft adventure that concerns the Moon-Spinners, the Cretan inn where they're staying. The intrigue includes an odd but colorful assortment of local types headed by Eli Walach, a most hissable villain, his sister (Irene Papas) and a young, mysterious Englishman (Peter McEnery).

Pola Negri makes a late entrance as a wierd, wealthy widow type who gets her kicks from jewels. It's rather obvious novelty casting, and the part isn't likely to tee-off a new screen career for the silent-screen siren. She looks appropriately exotic and sounds (naturally or dubbed?) like a road company Maria Ouspenskaya.

Wallach comes off best by playing his villainy straight—vicious, unfeeling and rotten to the core. He'd willingly shoot his nephew to keep the boy's mother from ratting on him. Irene Papas, a superb Greek actress with a wonderfully expressive face, gives more dignity and feeling to her tiny role than it deserves.

Only in a Disney film would Joan Greenwood be cast as a doting aunt. No one really believes that she's there to collect folksongs and provide niece Hayley with a holiday. That voice and slink are just as libidinous in Crete as they ever were in merry old England and the viewer is certain there's a rendezvous planned for later.

Outstanding in featured roles are Sheila Hancock as the lonely, alcoholic wife of Wallach's accomplice, played well by John Le Mesurier. McEnery makes a valiant, handsome and indestructible young hero. Forced to go through half the film with a wounded arm, he still works in a few fights, chases, acrobatics and even a little romance—anything but medical attention. Michael Davis and Paul Stassino are very good in roles calling more for energy than thespic promise.

Even the scenery, caught by the Technicolor camera of Paul Beeson, isn't the usually restful expanse of sea and sky. It presents contrasting moods of sunbaked villages, flapping windmills and tumbling temples, intermingled with brilliantly colored and unusually-designed interiors. Tony Masters' art direction competes on even terms with the multicolored exteriors.

Jonathan Bates' sound is sometimes uncomfortably highpitched. With Neilsen having most of his cast playing at the top of their voices, the result creates bedlam in a few frenetic sequences. Ron Grainer's music, a westerner's idea of Hellenic melodies, is pleasant and, in the temple scene, adds much to the feeling of suspense. Native dances and festive music are also used freely. Terry Gilkyson's title tune may recall, to some ears, the title tune of another Greek film. *Robe.*

The Seventh Dawn
(COLOR)

William Holden holds this one in hand, plus exotic background and action. Asia of Communist harassment. Prospects okay.

United Artists release of Charles K. Feldman presentation, coproduced by Karl Tunberg. Stars William Holden, Susannah York, Capucine; features Tetsuro Tamba, Michael Goodliffe, Allan Cuthbertson, Maurice Denham. Directed by Lewis Gilbert. Screenplay, Tunberg based on novel, "The Durian Tree," by Michael Keon; camera (Technicolor), Frederick Young; editor, John Shirley; music, Riz Ortolani; asst. director, Jack Causey. Reviewed at United Artists homeoffice, **June 18, '64.** Running time, **123 MINS.**

Ferris .... William Holden
Candace .... Susannah York
Dhana .... Capucine
Ng .... Tetsuro Tamba
Trumpey .... Michael Goodliffe
Cavendish .... Allan Cuthbertson
Tarlton .... Maurice Denham
C.P.O. .... Sidney Tafler
Ah Ming .... Buelah Quo
Judge .... Hugh Robinson
Morley .... Tony Price
Sedgwick .... Griffiths Alun
C.I.D. .... Christopher Allen
Lim .... Yap Mook Fui
Aide .... David Keith
Malay Engineer .... James Massang
General Osaki .... R. William Koh
Colonel Hsia .... Allan Wong
Captain Chey .... Ibrahim Bin
Captain Kiat .... Noel Chow
Lt. Nelson .... Hew Thian Choy
Tamil Cyclist .... David Weinman
Indian Unionist .... George Zakhariah
Chinese Unionist .... Seow
Walter .... Tomy Chang
Japanese Prisoner .... Kip Bahadun

Despite script deficiencies and some static direction, Charles K. Feldman's presentation for United Artists release, "The Seventh Dawn," has sufficient action-adventure elements to make it a reasonable boxoffice contender, with William Holden's name as lure.

Set in the Malayan jungle, circa 1945, the pic uses as its background a three-way struggle between Communist-inspired Malayan terrorists, British governors and the people of Malaya along with outsiders who have vested interests in the country. All are interested in freedom for the place but their motives vary considerably. These conflicts lead to bloody confrontations between the factions, a situation very much like the present-day situation in Southeast Asia.

Pivotal characters in the film each represent a faction, a fact which leads to some rather predictable problems and solutions as time passes. Personal relationships aren't helped much either by coproducer Karl Tunberg's screenplay, based on Michael Keon's novel "The Durian Tree." Although the script moves fairly fluently through the action passages, harmful slowdowns develop during personal moments between the characters. In general throughout the pic there are just too many words.

Lewis Gilbert's direction is not too successful in overcoming the more "private" scenes. His constant reliance on closeups and camera movement which "discovers" people in a shot becomes "trademarky" and hinders a faster clip. His handling of action sequences, on the other hand, is often sharply-timed and gives the pic its best moments.

Holden handles himself in credible fashion as a Yank co-leader of local guerilla forces during World War II who stays on after the war's end to become a major local land owner and who gets involved in the new politics because of his old-time friendship for the leader of the Red terrorists, played by Tetsuro Tamva. Holden is further involved because of his mistress, a Malayan loyalist portrayed by Capucine. These three had worked together on the same side during the previous combat. For further plot there's the blonde and attractive daughter of the British governor, a role essayed by Susannah York.

Inevitably and predictably Holden and Tamva eventually come to a showdown which the Yank wins. Capucine gets herself hanged by the British for refusing to give info against her old pal Tamva and Miss York, who has come to Malaya in youthful albeit alluring innocence, is politely rebuffed by Holden who doesn't want to spoil her by turning her into another mistress he'll never marry. Through it all Tamva aptly conveys the dedicated, Commie-indoctrinated Asian attitude with sometimes menacing effectiveness. Capucine goes to her death in plausible martrydom and Miss York provides the viewer with an eyeful along with some suitable thesping.

Effective support is also provided by Michael Goodliffe as the British governor, Allen Cuthbertson as a rigid English officer, Maurice Denham, a long cast of British and Asiatic players. The film was lensed entirely on location, in Malaya by Frederick Young whose camerawork in Technicolor has made fine use of the natural terrain. Editor John Shirley's cutting is somewhat choppy in spots and the film could easily have run under its present 123 minutes but he has assembled the package in oke fashion. Riz Ortolani has penned a good background score with some airplay potential and Maurice Binder's main title sets the pic off to a nice pictoral start.

Although it falters as a yarn with much impact when it comes to the people involved, "Seventh Dawn" gives Holden a chance to again play the rugged, independent hero and to do so with accustomed dash and surliness. This, plus the overall action pattern of the pic may be enough to overcome its problems and make it a sound b.o. prospect. *Kali*

Hide and Seek
(BRITISH)

Ineffectual thriller with untidy construction and muddled climax; good thesping dissipated in a so-so job.

London, June 16.

British Lion-Albion release, through BLC, of Albion Film Distributors presentation of a Hal E. Chester production. Stars Ian Carmichael, Janet Munro, Hugh Griffith, Curt Jurgens; features Keiron Moore, George Pravda, Edward Chapman, Kynaston Reeves, Una Venning, Cardew Robinson. Directed by Cy Endfield. Screen play by David Stone; screen adaptation by Robert Foshko from a story by Harold Greene; camera, Gilbert Taylor; editor, Thelma Connell; music, Muir Mathieson, Gary Hughes. Previewed June 15, '64 at Columbia Theatre, London. Running time, **90 MINS.**

David Garrett .... Ian Carmichael
Maggie .... Janet Munro
Hubert Marek .... Curt Jurgens
Frank Melnicker .... George Pravda
Wilkins .... Hugh Griffith
Paul .... Keiron Moore
Chambers .... Derek Tansley
Chauffeur .... Judy Parfitt
Tea Lady .... Esma Cannon
Secretary .... John Boxer
Constable .... Cardew Robinson
Bride .... Barbara Roscoe
Drunken Songwriter .... Tommy Godfrey
Idiot .... Lance Percival
Pompous Man .... Julian Orchard
McPherson .... Edward Chapman
Hunter .... Kynaston Reeves
Cottrell .... Frederick Peisley
Porter .... Charles Lamb
Mrs. Cromer .... Una Venning

Ineptness of the title pinpoints the fact that what might have been a crisp thriller has misfired. Looseness in script and editing is clearly obvious, so that there is padding in some stages and, at others, important points are glossed over or left absurdly unanswered. Rarely has a thriller petered out in such a scrappy manner. Only very undiscriminating audiences will be satisfied with this pic's lack of sustained suspense and its too obvious red herrings. Characters are introduced with the minimum of subtlety and key points are tossed away without explanation.

Story is hinged loosely on a chess game, but this is an artificial device which will irritate equally those who understand chess and those to whom it is a closed book. Shorn of such clumsy symbolism the yarn concerns a young professor of astronomy, working on a missile project, who meets the world chess champion, an old friend from behind the Iron Curtain. From then on the professor (Ian Carmichael) is enmeshed in a plot which involves his capture in a manner that will suggest that he has purposely defected to the foreigners.

Every key character that Carmichael encounters subsequently proves to be a member of a team run by a master businessman (Curt Jurgens) who is prepared to sell anything at a profit, even top brains to foreign powers. Unfortunately, the people Carmichael runs up against are all so obviously sinister or so suspiciously innocent that the conspiracy provides no surprise.

Carmichael is lured to a fortress in the North of England and manages to escape just before he is due to be shipped abroad. Just how he accomplishes this is only hinted at and in such a hazy, improbable way that the getaway has all the excitement of a wet fish. The journey northwards involves such cliches as an escape from a train and a cross-country chase, a scrap with a villain on a cliff edge and one or two abortive attempts to escape from "prison."

Main assets of this thriller, which lacks crispness, is in the art and location work, effective photography by Gilbert Taylor, and one or two pieces of determined acting which do their best to overcome the limp script. Carmichael is a likable hero who meanders through some unlikely adventures with simple faith. But the role of the girl who first tricks him is never developed sufficiently for Janet Munro's talents. But she has charm and assurance.

Hugh Griffith, as usual, extracts the most amusement from his role of the seemingly nutty, largehearted bargee, while Curt Jurgens is a suave, civilized villian, who accepts victory and defeat with an apparent boredom which seems to communicate itself to the audience. Keiron Moore plays a conventional thickear man and George Pravda, Cardew Robinson, Una Venning, Edward Chapman and Kynaston Reeves chip in with small but useful support.

Cy Endfield's direction is effective in isolated sequences, but it not authoritative enough to rescue the whole from its flabby lack of purpose and drive.   *Rich.*

Robin And The Seven Hoods
(PANAVISION—COLOR)

Wacky gangster comedy with powerhouse names of Sinatra, Martin and Crosby to assure heavy grosses.

Hollywood, June 18.
Warner Bros. release of Frank Sinatra production. Stars Frank Sinatra, Dean Martin, Sammy Davis Jr., Bing Crosby, Peter Falk. Features Edward G. Robinson, Barbara Rush, Victor Buono. Directed by Gordon Douglas. Screenplay, David R. Schwartz; camera (Technicolor), William H. Daniels; editor, Sam O'Steen; music, Nelson Riddle; songs, Sammy Cahn, James Van Heusen; asst. director, David Salven. Reviewed at Academy Awards Theatre, June 19, '64. Running time, **123 MINS.**
Robbo .... Frank Sinatra
John .... Dean Martin
Will .... Sammy Davis Jr.
Guy Gisborne .... Peter Falk
Allen A. Dale .... Bing Crosby
Marian .... Barbara Rush
Sheriff Potts .... Victor Buono
Six Seconds .... Hank Henry
Vermin .... Allen Jenkins
Tomatoes .... Jack LaRue
Sheriff Glock .... Robert Foulk
Hood .... Phil Crosby
Blue Jaw .... Robert Carricart
Hatrock .... Phil Arnold
Hood .... Sonny King

Warner Bros. has a solid money entry in "Robin and the Seven Hoods," a spoof on gangster pix of bygone days sparked by the names of Frank Sinatra, Dean Martin and Bing Crosby to give marquee power. The daffy doings of Chicago's hoodlums during the Prohibition era in a battle for leadership of the rackets backdrops action which usually is on the slightly wacky side, and film is loaded with appropriate production values. A threadbare story frequently tangents and some sharp editing should cut its present overlength footage, but the spirit of a hit is apparent and pic stacks up nicely as mass entertainment.

Eight song numbers by Sammy Cahn and James Van Heusen brighten the unreeling, and the three stars, as well as Sammy Davis, Jr., and Peter Falk, also starred, take advantage of these for standout sequences. Deftly directed by Gordon Douglas, who knows how to color his characters, Technicolor film is a joint effort by WB and indie companies headed by Sinatra and Martin, with Sinatra also acting as producer. Ending is weak, what was probably calculated to be a classic merely a letdown without any particular merit.

Scripter David R. Schwartz takes the legend of Robin Hood and his merrie men and retailors it loosely to the frolickings of Sinatra and his pack. In some measure the parallel is successful, at least as basis for a premise which gives the plot a gimmick springboard as Sinatra, as Robbo, the good-hearted hood, takes from the rich to give to the poor. Yarn opens in 1928 with the gangster kingpin of the day—Edward G. Robinson doing a cameo bit here —guest of honor at a lavish birthday party. After a sentimental rendition of "For He's a Jolly Good Fellow" by the assembled company of hoods, they shoot Robinson dead.

Thereafter it's for grabs as Peter Falk has himself elected as the new Number One, and Sinatra arrives to warn him to keep out of his territory. When Barbara Rush, daughter of the deceased Robinson and a delectable dish, tells Sinatra she'll pay him $50,000 if he'll avenge her father's murder, but she sends him the 50 grand anyway after the sheriff, who put the finger on Robinson, is buried in the cornerstone of the new Police Bldg. Sinatra orders Sammy Davis, one of his henchmen, to "dump" the money somewhere and Davis presents it to the Blessed Shelter Orphans Home in Sinatra's name, which immediately brings him public attention and adulation.

Hefty laugh situations are afforded as pic unreels, one of tops here the new gambling casino which Sinatra is opening being converted into a Skid Row mission when Falk and his crooked sheriff ally arrive for a raid. Setting allows Crosby, who plays a dignified secretary of the orphanage, and chorus of other stars to sock over "Mr. Booze" number. Top song number is "Style," sung by Sinatra, Crosby and Martin. Another biggie is "Bang, Bang," song-and-dancer done by Davis as his gang is wrecking Falk's expensive casino.

Falk scores with the comedic "All for One" song number as he elects himself tophand, and Martin, beating Sinatra in a $50,000 pool game, warbles "Any Man Who Loves His Mother" to good effect. Sinatra's big number is "My Kind of Town," after he's been acquitted of the sheriff's murder, and Crosby does well by **"Don't Be a Do-Badder" in the orphanage.**

Performance-wise, Falk comes out best. His comic gangster is a pure gem and he should get plenty of offers after this. Sinatra, of course, is smooth and Crosby in a "different" type of role rates a big hand. Martin, seems lost in the shuffle. Davis is slick and Miss Rush, going heavy, is beautiful to look at. Victor Buono offers able support as the sheriff supplanting Robert Foulk as a cop on the take. A lovely assortment of hood types back them effectively.

Technical credits are well handled, particularly William H. Daniels on color cameras and LeRoy Deane's art direction. Sam O'Steen generally lends good editing technique, and music score by Nelson Riddle is attuned to the action.   *Whit.*

The Insect
(JAPANESE)

Potent adult film fare by any nation's standards, but probably limited to art houses. However, graphic sexual scenes may make exploitation feasible for more general adult market. Life story of a prostitute and madame in post-war Tokyo.

San Francisco, June 12.
Shochiku release of Nikkatsu Corp. production. With Sachiko Hidari, Jitsuko Yoshimura, Seizaburo Kawazu, Kazuo Kitamura. Directed by Shohei Imamura. Screenplay by Imamura and Keiji Hasebe; camera, Masahisa Himeda; editor, Matsuo Tanji; musical score, Toshio Mayuzumi. Reviewed at Toho Rio Theatre, June 11, '64. Running time, **123 MINS.**
Tome Matsuki .... Sachiko Hidari
Nobuko .... Jitsuko Yoshimura
Matsunami .... Hiroyuki Nagato
Karasawa .... Seizaburo Kawazu
Chuji .... Kazuo Kitamura
Kamibayashi .... Daizaburo Hirata
Foreman .... Taiji Tonoyama
Honda .... Shoichi Tsuyuguchi
Rin .... Teruko Kishi
En .... Sumie Sasaki
En's lover .... Shoichi Kuwayama
Sawakichi .... Asao Koike
Rui .... Emiko Aizawa
Midori .... Masumi Harukawa
Madam .... Tanie Kitabayashi

Japanese filmmakers, who can be all blood- and thunder for a Samurai yarn, often turn demure when it comes to sex. Not so Shohei Imamura, director and co-writer of "The Insect." Taking his cue from the directors of Paris and Rome, Imamura has laced his film liberally with graphic portrayals of sex, including some incestuous incidents between the heroine and her stepfather.

The feature has startled Japan, reaped 14 awards there, and has been entered in the Berlin Film Fest. It looks like surefire material for art houses and may attract attention elsewhere because of frank handling of adult theme.

Despite the misleading title, Japanese translation was originally "The Insect Woman" which ought to be changed, this is not a monster picture, but a horror story of a much different sort. It chronicles the course of a peasant girl from a natural, instinctive (insect-like) childhood in Japan's northern mountains to postwar prostitution in Tokyo.

Imamura covers a period of 45 years by using a wide-gapped, episodic technique, consciously causing viewer alienation, never allowing the audience to become engrossed with the human aspects of the characters.

Story centers on survival efforts of Tome (Sachiko Hidari) and her constant reversals of romance and fortune, leading to life as prostitute and later as a madame. Even in her most squalid circumstances, she plods on with a touch of hope—or at least a refusal of despair. But Imamura's rather dour view of human behavior indicates— through various subplots which repeat patterns from one generation to the next—that man is an ugly bug.

Fortunately he avoids the whore with a heart of gold routine. Tome is appealing in the beginning, but as she ages, hardened by experience and rejections, she grows fiercer in her methods of self-preservation, even to the point of acting as a procuress scheming against her own daughter.

All of this is played against a panorama of the social upheavals of modern Japan. Imamura is an accurate sniper as he levels in on modern Japanese politics, religious confusion, commercialism, Westernization, the American Occupation and just about every other environmental influence.

If he seems impatient with human nature, almost naive in his expectations, Imamura must still be reckoned with for his right-on-target perceptions of individual and social weaknesses.

He enhances the authenticity of his observations by insisting on location filming (with expert camera work in black and white by Masahisa Himeda) and natural lighting (sometimes too dim and murky). The rambling film needs a bit of judicious trimming. It takes two hours to unfold its many elements and is difficult to sit through. However its cumulative effect is an overwhelming experience.

Performances are on the highest level, including Miss Hidari as the central figure, Kazuo Kitamura as her simpleton stepfather (and first lover), and Jitsuko Yoshimura as her illegitimate daughter. Lesser roles are handled splendidly by Teruko Kishi as a garrulous matriarch; Tanie Kitabayshi, usually a Japanese stage actress, in a florid performance as the madam who finds Tome at a religious meeting and introduces her to the red light district; and Seizaburo Kawazu as an aging businessman who seeks the favors first of Tome and later of her daughter.

Toshio Mayuzumi has provided a spare, effective score to underline major scenes. Subtitles at first seem laughable, but by film's end prove carefully planned and cogent. To convey the strong peasant accent of the mountain people, subtitles read like Beverly Hillbillies dialog, later switch to basic English for Tokyo scenes; and in a present day return to the mountains, the dialect has become softened because of educational advances.   *Mich.*

Masque of The Red Death
(PANAVISION-COLOR)

Latest Edgar Allan Poe entry portends good b.o.

Hollywood, June 16.
American International Pictures release of Roger Corman production. Stars Vincent Price. Features Hazel Court, Jane Asher. Directed by Corman. Screenplay, Charles Beaumont, R. Wright Campbell, from story by Edgar Allan Poe; camera (Pathecolor), Nicholas Roeg;

editor, Ann Chegwidden; music, David Lee; assistant director, Peter Price. Reviewed at Lytton Center, June 15, '64. Running time, **86 MINS.**

Prince Prospero .... Vincent Price
Juliana .... Hazel Court
Francesca .... Jane Asher
Gino .... David Weston
Alfredo .... Patrick Magee
Ludovico .... Nigel Green
Hop Toad .... Skip Martin
Man in Red .... John Westbrook
Senora Escobar .... Gay Brown
Senor Veronese .... Julian Burton
Anna-Marie .... Doreen Dawn
Scarlatti .... Paul Whitsun-Jones
Scarlatti's Wife .... Jean Lodge
Esmeralda .... Verina Greenlaw
Lampredi .... Brian Hewlett
Clistor .... Harvey Hall

Popularity of Edgar Allan Poe derived material at boxoffice has cued American International Pictures to make its seventh from that source, "Masque of the Red Death." Latest catches the flavor of past offerings in this field of horror and exploitation and should carry the same lure, particularly with the name of Vincent Price, star of most of AIP's Poe program, to build on.

Roger Corman, responsible for majority of former entries here, again produces and directs. He has garmented his film, lensed in England, with production values. His color camera work, his sets, music and plot unfoldment itself—if the latter is vague and a bit involved it still fits into the pattern intended—establish an appropriate mood for pic's tale of terror and in addition it's evident Corman doesn't take his subject too seriously.

Chief protagonist is a disciple of Satan himself in "Masque" screenplay by Charles Beaumont and R. Wright Campbell. Price is the very essence of evil, albeit charming when need be, and as film progresses the dark workings of his mind are stressed, tortuously intent on evil as a follower of the Devil. He plays Prince Prospero, a tyrannical power in Spain in the Middle Ages, who seizes a young girl and tries to make her choose between his saving the life of her beloved or her father, even as the Red Death is killing off most of his impoverished serfs. A strange and uninvited guest to the Bacchanalian orgy he is staging for his noble guests stalks through the festivities to transform the Masque Ball into a Dance of Death in a climactic sequence which sees the Prince a victim of his own evil.

Corman in his direction sets a pace calculated to divert the teenage taste particularly, and past experience with Poe makes him a worthy delineator of this master of the macabre. In Price is the perfect interpreter, too, of the Poe character, and he succeeds in creating an aura of terror. Hazel Court as his mistress, who calls on evil spirits to give her strength and understanding she desires as his court companion, is a beautiful woman who persuasively portrays her strange character, and Jane Asher lends interest as the girl. David Weston is competent as the boy she loves and Skip Martin impresses as a dwarf, the court jester who enlivens the party by burning alive a noble who slapped his sweetheart. Patrick Magee in this latter role handles part well.

Art direction by Robert Jones and lensing by Nicholas Roeg are particular standouts, giving class to pic, and David Lee's music score suitably backdrops the action. Editing by Ann Chegwidden is leisurely at times, sharp, too, where needed, and Jack Carter's choreography permits fast movement. *Whit.*

Les Animaux
(The Animals)
(FRENCH)

Paris, June 16.

Athos Films release of Tele Hachette, Ancinex production. Written and directed by Frederic Rossif. Adaptation and commentary by Madeleine Chapsal, spoken by Maurice Escande, Marcelle Ranson, Martine Sarcey, Jean-Marc Bory, Jean-Pierre Marielle; camera, Georges Barsky; editor, Rossif; music, Maurice Jarre. At Mercury, Paris. Running time, **80 MINS.**

Neatly compiled montage pic shifts from a thumbnail sketch about the formation of the world and life, via okay illustrations, to a look at the animal kingdom in its offbeat and simple moments. If it has some new and unusual scenes, this shapes a fair compendium of animal aspects.

But the scattered sources for all this footage sometimes make it more a curio album of miscellany than a complete, absorbing documentary or even an incisive look at animals. Film thus appears more for supporting or specialized fare abroad or for tele. It does not have the stature for arty possibilities unless extremely well hypoed and placed.

Director Frederic Rossif has found scenes on the cruelty of wild life, via a series of kills, the disarming and witty side (many times obviously staged). But added and specially shot scenes, like a dream look at jumping horses, if photographically stunning, do not have much to do with the general more naturalistic approach.

This is technically well put together and has an unobtrusive, lucid commentary plus a knowing underlining musical score by Maurice Jarre. *Mosk.*

Les Longues Annees
(THE LONG YEARS)
(FRENCH)

Paris, June 16.

Comacico release of Copernic production. Directed and compiled by Andre Tranche. Commentary written and spoken by Pierre Desgraupes, Pierre Demayet, Maurice Seveno. At Marignan, Paris. Running time, **85 MINS.**

Objective compilation pic gives a concise, if simplified, look at World War II via well-selected newsreel footage and some clips from other films. It ranges from the attack on Poland, the French defeat, Pearl Harbor, D-Day to the A-Bomb and beginning of the Atomic Era. If nothing new is added to all this, it still packs interest and emerges a fine tv bet for abroad and for dualer or specialized use with not enough original material for arty usage.

Commentary is also clear and concise. The mixture of French, German, Yank, British, Russian and Japanese footage again attests to the amazing ubiquity of cameramen during the last war. If not straining for it, this film does make clear the horror of war but sometimes even taps its gory glory.

Now, 20 years after the war, films of this type are growing and seem to be popular. It seems that it is now the time to look at the event dispassionately. At any rate it still shows the absorbing look of old film and their revocative powers if neatly and intelligently edited and mounted as in the case of this pic. Quality of images is also good. *Mosk.*

Devil Doll

British-made thriller based on the dummy's revenge against the ventriloquist. First U.S. release for new distributor could make it with fast playoff.

New York, June 19, 1964.

Associated Film Dist. Corp. release of Galaworldfilm-Gordon Films production (Kenneth Rive-Richard Gordon-Lindsay Shonteff), directed by Shonteff. Features William Sylvester, Bryant Haliday, Yvonne Romain, Sandra Dorne, Karel Stepanek, Francis de Wolff. Screenplay by George Barclay and Lance Z. Hargreaves, from original story by Frederick E. Smith; camera, Gerald Gibbs; editor, Ernest Bullingham; sound, Derek McColm; art director, Stan Shields. No other credits. Reviewed at N.Y., June 19, '64. Running time, **80 MINS.**

The Great Vorelli .... Bryant Haliday
Mark Engilsh .... William Sylvester
Marianne .... Yvonne Romain
Dr. Heller .... Karel Stepanek
Dr. Keisling .... Francis de Wolff
Aunt Eva .... Nora Nicholson
Uncle Walter .... Philip Ray
Bob Garrett .... Alan Gifford
Garrett's girlfriend ..... Pamela Law
Grace .... Heidi Erich
Soldier .... Antony Baird
Miss Penton .... Trixie Dallas
The Countess .... Margaret Durnell
Twist Dancer .... Ray Landor
Louisa .... Ella Tracey
Hans .... Guy Deghy
Hugo Novik .... David Charlesworth
Mercedes .... Lorenza Coalville
The Nurse .... Jackie Ramsden

As its initial release, the just-formed Associated Film Dist. Corp.'s "Devil Doll" is expected to be launched with an extensive ad-pub campaign and saturation bookings. If so, it could provide a fast return for the distributors.

The slow-paced import, however, never comes up to its title in the way of shocks, thrills, scares, sex or other dividends for the "meller" regulars, making it an uncertain bet once the saturation cream has beek skimmed. Filmed in England as a coproduction by Kenneth Rive and Richard Gordon, its gimmick—a ventriloquial dummy's revenge on his manipulator—has been done before and better by Cavalcanti and Michael Redgrave in a real "horror" classic—"Dead of Night" and "The Great Gabbo" of 1929.

"Devil Doll" was apparently also filmed with an eye to tv, depending heavily on closeups, not just of the principals but almost everyone and everything in the film. This is also an economical trick, allowing the use of a partial set only.

Lindsay Shonteff, who directed as well as co-produced, has permitted cameraman Gerald Gibbs to slow the dramatic pace down to a walk, sometimes grinding to a halt, while the camera lingers on a face or an object.

American newspaperman William Sylvester, assigned to do a story on a hypnotist-ventriloquist suspected of being a fake, takes his girlfriend, Yvonne Romain, along but both are impressed by the act. The hypnotist (Bryant Haliday), invited to perform at a charity affair at the home of Miss Romain's aunt, hypnotizes the girl and, without the others knowing it, leaves her in a trance. When she later becomes ill, Sylvester brings in a hypnotism specialist (Karel Stepanek) but without success.

Haliday plans to repeat, with the girl, an experiment he had done years previously in Berlin, transferring a human soul to the body of a dummy, which he will keep subservient and force it to carry out his demands.

While Sylvester is tracking down the truth, Haliday's dummy, Hugo, takes matters into his own hands.

Sylvester gives an honest, realistic touch to the role of the newspaperman. Haliday, however, burdened with a messy beard and one expression, the hypnotic stare, depends on his resonant voice to make the role credible. Miss Romaine and Sandra Dorne, as Haliday's assistant who is killed, have the proper physical charms for their roles, if little else. A few teasing shots of Miss Dorne almost becoming unclothed are about all the film has to offer the flesh-buyers.

Support, generally, is sufficient unto the purpose if somewhat uninspired. A cut above the others are Philip Ray as Miss Romain's uncle and Lorenza Coalville as the Berliner who provides Sylvester with the hypnotist's background.

George Barclay and Lance Z. Hargreaves' wobbly script might have made better material for a short subject than stretched into a feature. The film's 80 minutes makes it a short one by today's standards but editor Ernest Bullingham could well sacrifice another 10 or 12. At best, the future of "Devil Doll" is as a programmer. *Robe.*

Salach Shabati
(ISRAEL)

Tel Aviv, June 16.

Noah Films Ltd. release of Menahem Golan's production. Stars Haim Topol. Written and directed by Ephraim Kishon. Camera, Floyd Crosby; music, Yohanan Zarai; editors, Dani Shik, Jacko Erlich. Reviewed at Hod Cinema, Tel Aviv, June 15, '64. Running time, **110 MINS.**

Salach Shabati .... Haim Topol
Sosialit .... Gila Almagor
Siggi .... Arik Einstein
Habbubah .... Geualah Noni
Noymann .... Shraga Friedman
Frida .... Zaharira Harifai
Mrs. Shabati .... Esther Grinberg
Goldstein .... Nathan Meisler
Shimon .... Sheike Levi

Israel's leading satirist, Ephraim Kishon, has proven himself previously to be a prolific and successful writer in the dailies, of sketches and plays. His "Look Back, Mrs. Lot" or such Israeli comedies as "His Name Precedes Him" or "The Ketoubah," have been boxoffice hits in Israel and in other countries. In his first venture into films, he proves himself as a potential leader of the cinema. This comedy, depicting scenes and characters of the present day, has a touch of satire, a sensitive approach and a few pointed arrowheads which are sure to reach home.

Salach Shabati, a newcomer who arrives to Israel with a large family, is lazy, touching and funny at the same time. He is quick to size up his situation and appraise the possibilities in the transitory dwellings alloted his family. A few episodes mark his process of naturalization. At the end he manages to make the police force him to move into a modern apartment house, having mated his beautiful daughter with a member of the nearby kibbutz and one of his sons with a kibbutz girl.

In the process he has exposed vote-buying and other maladies of a young democracy among some of the problems facing both vets and newcomers in this melting-pot of a country.

Photographed professionally by Hollywood's Floyd Crosby, (whose first encounter with this country had been back in 1946, shooting "My Father's House") this is a picture that could very well hold the interest of foreign audiences. The brand of humor, though of local significance, has definite universal appeal while the unfailing charm of the star, Haim Topol, shows in a remarkable performance as Salach. Kishon's direction is smooth. When the pic is tightened here and there (as planned for showing at the Venice Festival), it would help in the world market.

The moody and gay music by Yohanan Zarai, with a title-song that is catching, adds luster to this first effort of Kishon.

Under Kishon's direction, the remainder of the cast, headed by Zaharira Harifai, Esther Grinberg, Gila Almagor and Shraga Friedman, contribute to the neat impression. One feels this is the first Israeli film which could fare well, both artistically and at the general boxoffice, despite minor shortcomings and lack of a dramatic story. *Rapp.*

Les Felins
(The Felines)
(FRENCH—FRANSCOPE)
Paris, June 23.
MGM release of Cipra-Jacques Bar production. Stars Alain Delon, Jane Fonda, Lola Albright; features Robert Oumansky, Carl Studer, Sorrel Booke, Del Negro. Directed by Rene Clement. Screenplay, Pascal Jardin, Charles Williams, Clement from book by Day Keene; camera, Henri Decae; editor, Fedora Zincone; music, Lalo Schiffrin. At Ambassade-Gaumont, Paris. Running time, 95 MINS.
Marc .... Alain Delon
Melinda .... Jane Fonda
Barbara .... Lola Albright
Vincent .... Robert Oumansky
Loftus .... Sorrel Booke
Nick .... Del Negro

Slickly turned out pic deals with the ironic come-uppance of a French Don Juanesque, a young, good-looking opportunist who comes up against some rugged U.S. gangsters and offbeat Yank femme personages to beat him at his own game. If the playing is skillful, direction neat and story unusual, all this still does not quite have the character and insight for outstanding arty chances abroad. Also it doesn't have enough clear progression and action for easy playoff. Home possibilities, however, appear excellent.

It thus needs careful handling and placement offshore. The Jane Fonda name, plus that of Alain Delon, a local thesp building a foreign following, could help as well as its sleek envelope and pacing. Film was actually shot in English primarily, and this version is called "Joy House" while the well-dubbed French version is the one under review.

It must be said Miss Fonda's French is very good. Also she has a charming accent, just right for the role of a lovesick but yet unpredictable waif-like girl. She turns in a bright performance as a perverse innocent neatly contrasted by Lola Albright's brittle presence as her ruthless aunt. Delon shows he has the projection and catching

appeal that mean imminent stardom.

Delon has seduced an American gangster's girl and is now in Monte Carlo spending money. But the thug does not like this and sends his men to literally get Delon's head. He escapes once and ends up chauffering for Miss Albright. But she is hiding a lover who killed her rich husband and plot is to exchange Delon's identity for his when they knock him off.

But Delon latches on, besides becoming Miss Albright's lover, when all is mixed up by Miss Fonda, who's in love with Delon. Climax has the thugs killing the lover by mistake. All would be well until Miss Fonda manages to get the killings blamed on Delon.

Director Rene Clement has given this a fastidious mounting full of action scenes, symbolical intentions and a generally fine pace that keep this from lagging even when things get telegraphed. Main problem is that all characters are primarily ruthless or slightly eccentric, or downright neurotic, without a balance of true feeling.

If a film with difficult chances, the right handling and hypoing could conceivably turn this into a neat playoff item on its general offbeat theme and story. Art chances are chancier. If reminiscent of Clement's other thriller, "Purple Noon," this one lacks the deeper social backgrounding of the thesps. So chalk this up as a mighty smooth item somewhat overdirected. Technical credits are tops. *Mosk.*

Les Durs A Cuire
(Hard Boiled Ones)
(FRENCH)
Paris, June 23.
Pathe release of Cimatel-Pathe production. Stars Roger Pittre, Jean Poiret, Michel Serrault; features Stephane Audran, Mireille Darc. Directed by Jack Pinoteau. Screenplay, Roger Pierre, Jacques Emmanuel, Pinoteau from the book by Michel Lebrun; camera, Claude Lecomte; editor, Georges Arnstam. At Balzac, Paris. Running time, 85 MINS.
Germain .... Roger Pierre
Louis .... Jean Poiret
Detective .... Michel Serrault
Ricka .... Stephane Audran
Josette .... Mireille Darc
Friend .... Hubert Deschamps
Doctor .... Claude Chabrol

This type of sly satire has not been seen in a French pic since Sacha Guitry's days. So it is rather dated if it does have some okay deadpan situations and fairly risible mordant humor. Dates as playoff or supporting fare are most likely for this abroad, with arty house chances slimmer. Home probabilities are okay.

A priggish, self-indulgent successful playwright, whose work is really done by an assistant, one day finds that somebody in his household is trying to kill him. Since he is noted for crime plays, he decides to get to the bottom of it. Suspects are his old military friend (who feels his talents have been warped by the charity he gets), the ghost writer, a perky secretary making passes at him and his feckless wife.

He gets to seduce the secretary, hires a private eye (who turns out a blackmailer) and then finds his attempts to wipe out his entourage lead to people being killed inadvertently.

Director Jack Pinoteau has tried to take potshots at New Wave tech-

niques of frozen shots, handheld cameras and on-the-spot lensing. But they do not help this essentially classic-type comedy. But it is well served by a group of young actors, and does wring some laughs if the outright madcap lucidity are missing. *Mosk.*

Circus World
(CINERAMA-TECHNIRAMA-70—COLOR)

Samuel Bronston - Cinerama-John Wayne parlay sure box-office. Action-full and color-full with warm family trade appeal. An American circus in Europe, circa 1910.

Paramount release of Samuel Bronston Production (Michael Waszynski, associate producer). Stars John Wayne, Claudia Cardinale, Rita Hayworth; features Lloyd Nolan, John Smith, Richard Conte. Directed by Henry Hathaway. Cameraman (Technicolor), Jock Hildyard. Second unit director, Richard Talmadge; second unit cameraman, Claude Renoir. Screenplay by Ben Hecht, Julian Halevy and James Edward Grant based on story by Philip Yordan and Nicholas Ray. Score by Dimitri Tiomkin. Production designed by John De Cuir; costumes by Renie; titles by Dong Kingman; film editor, Dorothy Spencer; special effects, Alex Weldon. Reviewed at Loew's Cinerama, N.Y., June 24, 1964. Running time, 135 MINS. Reserved seat scale top $3.50.
Matt Masters .... John Wayne
Toni Alfredo .... Claudia Cardinale
Lili Alfredo .... Rita Hayworth
Cap Carson .... Lloyd Nolan
Aldo Alfredo .... Richard Conte
Steve McCabe .... John Smith
Emile Schuman .... Henri Dantes
Mrs. Schuman .... Wanda Rotha
Giovana .... Katharyna
Flo Hunt .... Kay Walsh
Anna .... Margaret MacGrath
Molly .... Kathrine Ellison
Billy Rogers .... Miles Malleson
Hilda .... Katharine Kath
Bartender .... Moustache

Samuel Bronston's made-in-Spain-and-in-Cinerama "Circus World," which had its premiere last Thursday (25) at Loew's Cinerama Theatre on Broadway, is a bigscreen, big boxoffice wedding of spectacle and romance. It should please the masses everywhere, and especially women and children. The pace, as directed by Henry Hathaway, is unslackening. The plot combines action, color, European scenery, melodrama, disaster by fire and catastrophe by water. Underlying all is family-type sex, oldfashioned morality and ample schmaltz. Add for marquee appeal John Wayne as foster father to Italian sexkitten Claudia Cardinale and as the mooning, forever loyal, forever seeking sweetheart of Rita Rayworth.

While "Circus World" is the fourth Cinerama release to tell a story it is markedly different in narrative approach from the fantasy of "Brothers Grimm," the episode panoramics of "How the West Was Won," and the slapstick of "Mad World." No invidious comparison is intended by the observation that Cinerama adapts to "Circus" rather than the other way round. Though benefited by the curved screen in the optical sweep department, the story conveys the impression of not having been written or directed for camera stunts, as such. Certainly this is a far cry from rollercoasters and Lowell Thomas in a silk hat calling on a Himalayan king. The payoff formula of "Circus World" is straight story, people-within-pageant. At a negative cost of around $8,500,000 the economic prospects seem excellent.

A major value throughout is the photography of Jack Hildyard, whose credits include Sam Spiegel's "Bridge on the River Kwai" and Bronston's earlier "55 Days In Peking." Working harmoniously with Hathaway (after Frank Capra Sr. departed), a series of well-composed scenes in Super-Technirama-70 and Technicolor alternate with the private aspects of the circus yarn. A second unit directed by Richard Talmadge had Claude Renoir on camera.

Special effects are numerous, perhaps the most memorable being Alex Weldon's engineering coup, the capsizing on cue of a 4,000-ton freighter, loaded with the American circus folk, gear and animals, at Barcelona dockside. An implicit message of the whole story is that running a circus is hell, compounded by death plunges, the inflammability of canvas, and the superstitions of backstagers.

It is easy to imagine the logistics and technical burdens which were carried by production manager C. O. Erickson, circus coordinator Frank Capra Jr. (who stayed) and associate producer Michael Waszynski under Bronston. The hand of experience is manifest in the artful uses of different public buildings and localities of Spain. Barcelona's opera house was planked over to simulate the Hansa Circus Theatre of Hamburg, Circa 1910. The plaza at Chinchon, used for the bullfight scene in "Around the World in 80 Days," may also be recognized.

The circus atmosphere is believably real, except for the over-applauding audiences, a cliche practically no Hollywood director can resist. Producer Bronston went to pains in contracting on a run-of-picture basis the Franz Althoff Circus of Europe while also calling upon the consultation of Bob Dover and Umberto Bedini of Ringlings. Not the least amusing bit in the film is oldtimer Miles Malleson, of Britain, wearing a pearl-gray derby and sharp matching attire and sliding up to John Wayne, about to sail for Europe from Brooklyn, to remind him of the missing aerialist (Miss Hayworth). Guess who Malleson is? The circus reporter of Billboard. No doubt that little touch is out of the memory of co-scripter Ben Hecht.

The basic story is by Philip Yordan and Nicholas Ray, according to the souvenir program, with Ray dropped from the Cinerama mimeographed credit sheet. Julian Halvey worked with Hecht and James Edward Grant on the screenplay. The runaway aerialist returns to watch her daughter rehearsing on the lot, like Madame X of long ago, but this time (after the women in the audience have their little cry) there is a happy reunion of all, the final scene being the performance given hours after a terrible fire in which mother and daughter costar in a two-act. Miss Hayworth does 100 over-shoulder, one-arm somersaults on high, while the audience and the attendant nobility count them out. This is obviously a fond recall of Lillian Leitzel, who often hit and exceeded 100.

Something like a month of preparation and rehearsal was necessary so that the Misses Cardinale and Hayworth could carry out the illusion of climbing the rope and doing the wrist work. In these details, as in so much else, meticulous direction overcomes improbability. Her first role in three years, Rita Hayworth might come back in demand as result of this appearance. She looks very good indeed and acts with warmth and authority.

Miss Cardinale, in her fifth English-language film, is ideal for the girl - bursting - into - womanhood. There is one quick, sly touch when she innocently exposes bosom to her sweetheart, he being half-teased and half-embarrassed. The relationship to Wayne is developed with a steady sense of the interplay of the stern he-man and the passionate-natured ward.

Of Wayne it may be said that he is the center-pole, the muscle, the virility and the incarnate courage of this often down but never out circus. The role has been tailored to his talents and personality, since this globetrotting show carries, as did circuses of that day, an afterpiece Wild West performance, in which Wayne is the rooting-tooting-shooting central figure. One scene has him staging a stagecoach runaway on the Champs-Elysees to the delight of the Parisians of that day, who never heard of ballyhoo.

In one scene Wayne is getting back in shape for an old act of his and apparently throws himself off a stand to catch the saddle of a galloping white steed, but usually landing on the ground. It seems not to have been faked and, if so, is further evidence of the stamina of this hardy star who is also part of the myth of American manhood, western style.

John Smith from television is the horsemen who becomes the husband of the girl and partner of Wayne at the happy-happy finale. This appearance will boost his career. A small role allows little chance to Richard Conte who apparently didn't start that fire after all, and who thrills with the rest of the circusfolk when his ex sister-in-law makes her 100th somersault and comeback. Lloyd Nolan is the completely sincere and necessary reactive old friend to Wayne, a role he could play with half his brain and a quarter of his talent. Wanda Rotha as the manager-wife of a liontamer who rebels at working tigers, but works them, adds an interesting character cameo. Hathaway has injected a variety of humanizing little touches, though none for hokum's sake. There are smiles along the way but essentially this is strictly serious romantic melodrama with spectacularity thrown in.

The clowns are like circus clowns, funny enough but not Chaplin. The circus itself is big enough but not Barnum & Bailey. There is a sense of realism to the film, but nothing of today's denigration of human character. In "Circus World" human character is well thought of and well spoken of and even the Hamburg hustler, played effectively by Katharine Kath, is a decent sort whom your Aunt Nellie from Keokuk would like.

Realism derives in part from the able costume design of Renie and the production design of John De Cuir. The action is heightened on occasion by Dimitri Tiomkin's musical score. At other times the music is wisely muted. At least one melody recurs pleasantly and has some chance of standing by itself. The film has been edited with unobtrusive skill by Dorothy Spencer.

Sophisticates may pass "Circus World" by, feeling that they have had circus films. They may chafe at the heroics, rescues and the mother - and - lost - daughter bit. There is perhaps one line of dialog which narrowly misses drawing a titter, when Wayne says to Hayworth, "Lili, you've got guts!" Against such quibbles, circus films have often done big business and the prediction on Bronston's entry is just that. *Land.*

Night Of The Iguana

Powerful drama based on Tennessee Williams play; hefty profits anticipated with names of Richard Burton, Ava Gardner and Deborah Kerr to pull.

Hollywood, June 26.

Metro release of Seven Arts (Ray Stark) production. Stars Richard Burton, Ava Gardner, Deborah Kerr, Sue Lyon. Directed by John Huston. Screenplay, Anthony Veiller, Huston, from play by Tennessee Williams, adapted from Charles Bowden-Two Rivers Enterprises Inc., stage production; camera, Gabriel Figueroa; editor, Ralph Kemplen; music, Benjamin Frankel; assistant director, Tom Shaw. Reviewed at Metro studio, June 26, 1964. Running time: 117 MINS.

Rev. T. Lawrence Shannon .... Richard Burton
Maxine Faulk .... Ava Gardner
Hannah Jelkes .... Deborah Kerr
Charlotte Goodall .... Sue Lyon
Hank Prosner .... James Ward
Judith Fellowes .... Grayson Hall
Nonno .... Cyril Delevanti
Miss Peebles .... Mary Boylan
Miss Dexter .... Gladys Hill
Miss Throxton .... Billie Matticks
Teacher .... Eloise Hardt
Teacher .... Thelda Victor
Teacher .... Betty Proctor
Teacher .... Dorothy Vance
Teacher .... Liz Rubey
Teacher .... Bernice Starr
Teacher .... Barbara Joyce
Pepe .... Fidelmar Duran
Pedro .... Roberto Leyva
Chang .... C. G. Kim

The success that has marked past adaptations of Tennessee Williams plays to the screen gains momentum with "Night of the Iguana," a compelling drama unquestionably headed for solid boxoffice returns. Property is one of playwright's more impressive and finer undertakings, and its filmic translation is in kind.

This Ray Stark production, carrying the Seven Arts trademark, is rich in talents. Performances by Richard Burton, Ava Gardner and Deborah Kerr are superlative in demanding roles. Direction by John Huston is resourceful and dynamic as he sympathetically weaves together the often-vague and philosophical threads that mark Williams' writing. And the script by Huston and Anthony Veiller is a skillful transference to motion picture terms of the legiter, which won the N.Y. Drama Critics Award as best play of the 1961-62 season. A tale of loneliness and frustrations, all elements have been smoothly insinuated in what, with smart exploitation, should be one of Metro's better grossers of the year.

Unfoldment takes place mainly in a ramshackle Mexican seacoast hotel where Burton, an unfrocked minister and now guide of a cheap bus tour, takes refuge from his latest flock, a group of complaining American schoolteachers who refuse to believe he actually is a preacher who lost his church. Frankness in dealing with his emotional problems as first he is pursued by a young sexpot in the party, then his involvement with the aggressive, man-hungry hotel owner and a sensitive, itinerant artist travelling with her 97-year-old grandfather, produces compassionate undertones finely realized in situations evoking particular interest. Only occasional reference is made to a perversion theme, entire overall subject delicately handled. This is one of the best Tennessee Williams efforts to emerge on the screen.

Burton rises to a new stature in the difficult portrayal of the Reverend T. Lawrence Shannon, a part without glamour yet touched with magical significant force as he progresses to the point of a near-mental crackup. Miss Gardner, in the earthy role of Maxine Faulk, the proprietress, is a gusty figure as she makes her play for the depraved ex-minister, turning in a colorful delineation. Miss Kerr lends warm conviction as the spinster who lives by idealism and her selling of quick sketches, a helpless creature yet endowed with certain innate strength.

As the girl on the make for Burton—or any other male—Sue Lyon is enticing in her rather brief role and evinces acting ability. Grayson Hall, a particularly competent actress, delivers strongly as leader of the schoolteachers, bent on making Burton suffer for the girl's interest in him. Cyril Delevanti, too, is persuasive as Miss Kerr's grandfather, claiming to be the world's oldest poet and living only for the moment he finishes his latest work, 20 years in composition.

Black-and-white photography by top Mexican lenser Gabriel Figueroa is outstanding in catching the atmosphere of the various Mexican locations for picture, and Ralph Kemplen's editing is another definite asset. Art direction by Stephen Grimes likewise contributes strongly to overall excellence of film. *Whit.*

Seelenwanderung
(Transmigration of Souls)
(GERMAN)

Berlin, June 23.

Matthias Filmverleih release of Bavaria Atelier production. Stars Hanns Lothar, Wolfgang Reichmann, features Karin Schlemmer, Robert Meyn. Directed by Rainer Erler. Screenplay, Karl Wittlinger; Camera, Guenther Senftleben; editor, Johannes Nikel. At Bali Filmkunst, West Berlin. Running time, 78 MINS.

Bum .... Wolfgang Reichmann
Axel .... Hanns Lothar
Woman .... Karin Schlemmer
Another man .... Robert Meyn

The acquisition of this film for theatrical release is somewhat unusual. Originally a vidpic (and awarded as such with the prix Italia in 1962), it was purchased by a regular domestic pix distrib (Matthias-Film) which found that "Seelenwanderung" so good that it should be made available for the cinema, too. It remains to be seen how the German exhibs will react. Often they have shown open dislike for any film that has run on tv.

However, "Seelenwanderung" is a film worthy of cinema showing. Artistically, it's one of the best German productions in many months. It also hints that the artistic quality of many German tv feature films is above that of native theatrical pix.

Based on a script by Karl Wittlinger, successful German playwright, this is a satirical type of modern fairy tale. Two poor, good-natured fellow-tipplers, Bum and Axel, sit together and brood over the misery of their life. Already rather intoxicated, they get the fancy idea that the misfortune of Bum, who's the more intelligent of the twosome, lies with his soul. How to get rid of his soul? Axel talks Bum into putting his soul (symbolically) in a box which the two men take to a pawnbroker.

Without a soul, Bum soon strikes it rich. As an industrialist, he climbs up the ladder of success higher and higher, becomes unscrupulous, ignores his former good pal, and eventually dies of a heart attack. Axel, who has remained good-natured, is put in jail because caught stealing a bronze statue of his former friend.

The simple yarn has been brought to the screen with fine satirical sharpness by 30-year-old Rainer Erler who had been assistant director (of Kurt Hoffmann) for several years. It's at least a German feature film which shows accuracy, taste and imagination. Acting by Hanns Lothar and Wolfgang Reichmann, the two principal players, is excellent. Also the lensing is very good.

Production dress reveals the modest budget of just $75,000. Occasionally one feels that pic was originally made for video. Yet this is hardly a drawback. It's a sympathetic picture which could sled also into foreign arties. Also, it's a fine directorial debut for young Rainer Erler who now sets out to make a big theatrical pic. *Hans.*

Of Human Bondage
(BRITISH)

Stilted, downbeat remake of Somerset Maughan novel; Laurence Harvey, Kim Novak and title should stimulate business, but this meller will need shrewd selling.

Berlin, June 30.

Metro release and presentation in association with Seven Arts (James Woolf) production. Stars Laurence Harvey, Kim Novak; features Siobhan McKenna, Roger Livesey, Jack Hedley, Robert Morley, Nanette Newman. Directed by Ken Hughes (with additional scenes by Henry Hathaway). Screenplay by Bryan Forbes, from Somerset Maugham's novel; camera, Oswald Morris; editor, Russell Lloyd; music, Ron Goodwin. Previewed at Berlin Film Fest. Running time, **98 MINS.**

Mildred Rogers .... Kim Novak
Philip Carey .... Laurence Harvey
Dr. Jacobs .... Robert Morley
Norah Nesbitt .... Siobhan McKenna
Thorpe Athelny .... Roger Livesey
Griffiths .... Jack Hedley
Sally Athelny .... Nanette Newman
Mathews .... Ronald Lacey

Earlier filmgoers will recall the Leslie Howard/Bette Davis 1934 version of this story and, maybe, the 1946 entry starring Paul Henried and Eleanor Parker. The newest stab, with Laurence Harvey and Kim Novak, will not erase the memories. For those who come fresh to "Of Human Bondage," this perceptive but highly introspective yarn by Somerset Maugham may seem a hard-to-take slab of period meller.

It could cop plaudits at the Berlin Film Fest, where it's Britain's official flag waver, for Bryan Forbes' screenplay and Ken Hughes direction both extract the maximum from the rather dated material on hand. And Miss Novak comes up with a performance which, though uneven, reveals some unexpected flashes of depth. But Film Row's hucksters will need all the marquee-bait of title and star names to sell this.

The pic had a ruffled nascency, due primarily to clashes of opinion among top brass. Henry Hathaway quit to let in Ken Hughes as director and it's bruited that the star duo did not always see eye-to-eye on the chore in hand. Still, among the stolid patches there are some worthwhile moments which soften the overall disappointment of the film.

Story concerns a withdrawn, young medical student very conscious of his clubfoot who manages to become a doctor in London's East End despite being totally besotted with the tawdry charms of a promiscuous waitress. She plays Old Harry with his infatuated devotion and his dignity, walks out on him from his bed in order to marry another guy, returns when she is left broke and pregnant by her "husband" who turns out to be already married. Then she walks out again and finishes up first on the streets and then on her deathbed. He nearly gets off the hook when a pleasant, intelligent young writer woman falls for him and eventually after the good-time gal's death settles for the love of a good, homely, forgiving young woman who knows all.

Allowing for the fact that Forbes' screenplay is light on humor, Laurence Harvey nevertheless plays the role in such a stiff, martyred manner as to forfeit any sympathy or liking in the audience. He jumps through all the emotional hoops, infatuation, affection, shyness, outraged dignity, anger and compassion but so pompously that audiences may well feel that having made his uncomfortable bed he can darned well lie in it. The wreckage of his life and career could have had some of the tragic undertones of the "Blue Angel" professor, but Harvey's glum portrayal gives no hint of this.

The role that "made" Bette Davis doesn't serve the same purpose for Miss Novak. Yet she gamely tackles a wide range of emotions and seems to be far more aware of the demands of her role than is her co-star. Her gradual degradation from goodtime floozie to the dregs of the gutter is an exacting task and she manages to hold onlookers' interest in her fate.

Roger Livesy, and Nanette Newman, as his daughter, bring some needed life into the downbeat proceedings in the closing stages. Siobhan McKenna gives a short, but interesting performance as the writer who understands Harvey's moods while Jack Hedley is stalwart as his student buddy.

There is also Robert Morley to provide a characteristic, all-too-brief interlude as a bouncy, medical professor. Collectors of cinema trivia will notice, with interest, the fleeting appearances by highly-paid scriptwriter Forbes as a student-extra without any lines, an inexplicable throwback to his earlier business of being an actor.

Direction by Hughes (with, as credited, additional scenes by Henry Hathaway) is workmanlike considering the inflexible playing by his male star. Filmed at Ardmore Studios, near Dublin, the early-century London atmosphere is okay though there is over-much interior work. Oswald Morris' lensing excellently underscores the stuffiness and essential gloom of the settings. Ron Goodwin's music settles for a fairly heavy melodramatic touch which seems to call for the services of one of the oldtime silent cinema 88'ers and certainly fits the mood. *Rich*

McHale's Navy
(COLOR)

Wacky film version of tv series with big laugh and b.o. prospects.

Hollywood, June 25.

Universal release of Edward J. Montagne production, directed by Montagne. Stars Ernest Borgnine; features Joe Flynn, Tim Conway. Screenplay, Frank Gill Jr., G. Garleton Brown, from story by Si Rose; camera (Pathe Color), William Margulies; editor, Sam E. Waxman; asst. director, Phil Bowles; music, Jerry Fielding. Reviewed at Academy Awards Theatre. June 23, '64. Running time, **93 MINS.**

Lt. Comdr. Quinton McHale ... Ernest Borgnine
Capt. Wallace Binghamton .... Joe Flynn
Ensign Charles Parker ..... Tim Conway
Lester Gruber ...... Carl Ballantine
George Christopher ... Gary Vinson
Harrison "Tinker" Bell .... Billy Sands
Virgil Edwards .... Edson Stroll
Joseph Hanes .... Gavin MacLeod
Willy Moss .... John Wright
Takeo Fugiwara .... Yoshio Yoda
LeRoy Carpenter .... Bob Hastings
Andrea Bouchard ...... Claudine Longet
Margot Monet .... Jean Willes
Henri Le Clerc ...... George Kennedy
Chief de Gendarmes .... Marcel Hillaire
Japanese Captain .... Dale Ishimoto
Japanese J.G. .... John Mamo
French Girl .... Sandy Slavik

One wonders how America won the war in the Pacific, if the exploits of Lt. Comdr. Quinton McHale and his PT-boat crew were typical of that dark period in U.S. history. But then, "McHale's Navy," which Universal now presents as a full-length feature version of Revue's successful telepix series, doesn't attempt to prove any point. In this expansion of the vidshow studio comes up with one of the year's zaniest comedies. With its already-built-in audience, film is a sure firecracker at the wickets.

Edward J. Montagne, producer and sometimes-director of the vidpix, handles both chores in this longer color rendition and pulls out all the stops. Every corny gag ever devised for a pic finds welcome reception here, fitting in patly with action as loony as the goony bird and a magnified repeat of series, whose principal characters take over their same roles. Players, too, sock over their characters in proper screwball fashion and affair is one mad Navy romp, hearkening back to the days of Abbott & Costello, Martin & Lewis and other top comedy teams who used to spell magic at the boxoffice.

Like its original tv counterpart, action here depends upon outlandish situations in which McHale and his crew, who do things the "McHale" way first and the Navy's way second, get involved. In the present case, it's getting out of debt, first for getting themselves deeply in the red by restaging Australian horse race results for excitement-hungry Marines from week-old-but-track-fresh news sheets flown in, and again for dock damages inflicted by their runaway PT-boat. The wily sailors take advantage of a chance to recoup their losses with hard cash to pay off when they find the horse they've lost mysteriously quartered on an isolated South Pacific isle, and transport the nag aboard their boat to New Caledonia for entry as a ringer in the $7,000 Bastille Day sweepstakes.

One of the biggest laughs in the fun-laden unreeling is a Japanese submarine exec officer's reaction when through the periscope he sees the horse standing on the bow of the racing PT-boat but refuses to believe his eyes. Situation of disguising the horse, which otherwise would have been recognized, for the big race again provides boff response. Where pic is longest on yocks, however, is the clowning of Joe Flynn, as Capt. Wallace Binghamton and McHale's immediate superior, and Tim Conway's hamming—there's no other word—as McHale's own exec and as naive a gent as ever fell down a ship's ladder. Juve audiences particularly will find they've stolen the show, while taking nothing from Ernest Borgnine's credit as star of the proceedings.

Borgnine approaches his assignment with the same gusto as in tv and Flynn, whose goal in life first is to whip McHale's men into shape and send McHale to the brig permanently, second to whip the Japs, is immense, his longer exposure permitting added howls. Conway, too, makes every wall-eyed move count, and balance of crew who appear in teleseries shine anew. On distaff side, Claudine Longet appears as a cute lass of Noumea, and Jean Willes, owner of a gambling casino out to marry McHale, goes the limit.

Script by Frank Gill Jr., and G. Carleton Brown, from story by Si Rose, is aimed strictly for yocks. Trio of technicians who swing over from tv series handle assignments effectively, including William Margulies' clever color photography, Sam E. Waxman's fast editing and Russell Kimball's suitable art direction, credit for which Alexander Golitzen also shares. *Whit.*

The Troublemaker

Farfetched fable that attempts to kid the modern scene but winds up kidding itself has some moments of genuine comedy.

Janus Films release of Ozymandias-Seneca production (Robert Gaffney). Directed by Theodore J. Flicker. Features Tom Aldredge, Joan Darling, Flicker, James Frawley, Buck Henry. Original story and screenplay by Flicker and Henry; camera, Gayne Rescher; editor, John McManus; music composed, arranged, conducted by Cy Coleman; asst. director, Ben Berk. Reviewed in New York, June 22, '64. Running time, **80 MINS.**

Jack Armstrong .... Tom Aldredge
Denver James .... Joan Darling
Crime Commissioner Theodore J. Flicker
Sol, Sal & Judge Kelly .... James Frawley
T. R. Kingston .... Buck Henry
Building Inspector ...... Charles White
Fire Inspector ...... Godfrey Cambridge
Sanitation Inspector ..... Bernard Reed
Electrical Inspector .... Michael Currie
Dirty Old Man .... Leo Lerman
Interne .... Al Freeman Jr.
Psychiatrist .... Adelaide Klein
Miss Simmons .... Joy Claussen
Hooker .... China Lee
Girl on the Couch .... Betty Stanton
Kid .... Robbie Reed
Nazi Leader .... Francis Dux
Mr. Cohen .... Calvin Ander
Sal's Secretary ..... Graziella Narducci

"The Troublemaker" is self-defined as a combination of two theatrical traditions: the wild, free-winging, strongly visual early American film comedy and the sharply satiric, highly contemporary cabaret-theatre.

The resulting film can make some claims to the former definition but generally misses the boat on the latter. Indeed, during those moments when it is most enjoyable, the film is very oldfashioned and not a bit contemporary. The plot is a little eclectic but apparently they didn't want to suppress anything.

Many of the performers are alumni of "The Premise," an off-Broadway improvisational theatre with a well-deserved reputation for talent. That talent, however, has it rough trying to make the journey from Bleecker Street's stream-of-consciousness to Hollywood Blvd.'s (or its N.Y. counterpart) script-confinement.

At its best, and there are some hilarious sequences, "Troublemaker" depends on extended sight gags. There are lovely ones, when the so-called plot doesn't interfere: an old lady being absent-mindedly sealed behind a wall; a fight in an apartment; a picnic for two on an island in the middle of what looks like Seventh Ave., and others.

The theatrical fate of the film must be decided by how it is advertised and exploited. There's too little in it for the masses, yet the simple virtues of its comedy may prove a bit subtle for art-house buffs. There'll be trouble with the title which indicates nothing of the film's humor.

Attempts to be satirical get a bit heavyhanded, much depending on the familiarity of the viewer with psychoanalytic jargon. They evidently couldn't go all the way with it as they have this problem of releasing.

What plot there is concerns one of those catastrophe-prone, simple souls. Tom Aldredge plays Jack Armstrong, the All-American schnook, invading the big city to win fame and fortune. He encounters all the evils of the great metropolis, introduced to most of them by an old college chum, T. R. Kingston (Buck Henry).

Attempts to open a coffeeshop meet with disaster . . . several disasters, in fact, embodied in the crooked carcasses of civic officials. Thanks to T. R., Armstrong is unaware that results are accomplished by putting the right amount of money into the right pockets. His buddy is an expert putter.

When the dawn breaks, he rebels and starts a one-man clean-up campaign, turning a well-programmed catastrophe into utter chaos. How he finally resolves his problem provides three different endings to give the discriminating viewer a choice.

Theodore J. Flicker divides his talents between directing, collaborating with Buck Henry on the story and screenplay, and playing one of the key roles. Henry also doubles from writer to his role as T. R. It's the longest sustained imitation of Jack Lemmon, whom he strongly resembles in theatrical history. Joan Darling is correctly kooky as girlfriend.

Major menaces are essayed by James Frawley (as three of them), Charles White, Godfrey Cambridge, Bernard Reed and Michael Currie. They meet a fate worse than debt. Also outstanding is Adelaide Klein as a nervous psychiatrist. Funny bit is Carbridge's Irish brogue.

Technical credits are generally good. Gayne Rescher's camerawork shows considerable variance in definition and lighting but street shots are excellent and show imaginative thinking. Cy Coleman's music is appropriate to the zany atmosphere.

Whatever the advantages of improvised theatre may be, creating and depicting a completely-scripted film needs more training than improvisation provides. *Robe.*

The Patsy
(COLOR)

Jerry Lewis starrer headed as usual for potent ticket sales.

Hollywood, June 24.

Paramount release of Ernest D. Glucksman production. Stars Jerry Lewis; features Ina Balin. Everett Sloane, Phil Harris, Keenan Wynn, Peter Lorre, John Carradine, Hans Conreid. Directed by Lewis. Screenplay, Lewis, Bill Richmond; camera (Technicolor), Wallace Kelley; music, David Raksin; editor, John Woodcock; assistant directors, Ralph Axness, Howard Roessell. Reviewed at Picwood Theatre, June 24, '64. Running time, **100 MINS.**

Stanley Belt .... Jerry Lewis
Ellen Betz .... Ina Balin
Caryl Fergusson .... Everett Sloane
Chic Wymore .... Phil Harris
Harry Silver .... Keenan Wynn
Morgan Heywood .... Peter Lorre
Bruce Alden .... John Carradine
Professor Mule-rr .... Hans Conreid
Mayo Sloan .... Phil Foster
Sy Devore .... Richard Deacon
Barber .... Neil Hamilton
TV Newscaster .... Jerry Dumphy
Radio Newscaster .... Jerry Dexter
Shoe-shine Boy .... Scatman Crothers
Policeman .... Del Moore
Theatre-goer .... Nancy Kulp
Maitre d' .... Fritz Feld
Waiter .... Benny Rubin
Executive .... Jerome Cowan
Page .... Ned Wynn
Paul .... Henry Slate

Madcap adventures, which usually are misadventures, of Jerry Lewis usually assure stout b.o. response. His latest for Paramount release is no exception. If anything, his madcapping is a little bit more mad than usual, but he knows the pulse of his particular public and "The Patsy" is right. Scripted by Lewis in association with Bill Richmond, a slim story line has it ups and downs, sometimes being hilarious, frequently unfunny. It could have been built up through stronger plotting and tighter editing.

Premise of a group of film professionals—a producer, director, writer-gagman, press agent and secretary—who have lost their star in a plane disaster and find another meal ticket by grabbing a hotel bellboy and building him to stardom, is an okay device for situations but lacks development—which might have made a better comedy.

Lewis also directs in the part, and as the patsy of this pack of hangers-on, he indulges in his usual mugging and clowning, good for guffaws and enough nonsensical anticking to appeal to juve audiences especially. Top sequence, which clobbers the spectators, is his session with voice teacher Hans Conreid, where the high pitch of their voices not only cracks vases but breaks up the whole set. Another, in which he's appearing on Ed Sullivan's tv program, has him converting a sloppy sports outfit to formal attire, via use of black paint and judicious ripping, so he may attend a Hollywood black-tie event at Grauman's Chinese.

Lewis as the simple-minded Stanley, "discovered" as he is delivering ice to the forlorn group wondering how to salvage their own positions, socks over his customary brand of broad and nutty humor and gets good backing right down the line. Everett Sloane as the producer, Peter Lorre the director, Phil Harris the gagman, Keenan Wynn the p.a., and Ina Balin the secretary, deliver soundly, Miss Balin also in for romancing with Lewis. Conreid also is up to his usual zany comicking and John Carradine plays a valet, who has him outfitted at Sy Devore's (free plug for Hollywood haberdasher, with Richard Deacon undertaking this part).

Hedda Hopper plays herself in a nice scene, and others playing themselves in cameo roles are Ed Wynn, Rhonda Fleming, George Raft, Mel Torme. The Step Brothers do a quick terping routine, appearing, too, as dance instructors for Lewis, and Ed Sullivan does a gag guest-stint.

As usual, Lewis mounts his production handsomely and Ernest D. Glucksman as producer rates a hand for physical values. Wallace Kelley's color photography of Hal Pereira-Gary Odell's lush sets is firstclass and David Raksin's music score helps with the comic mood intended. *Whit.*

Bullet For a Badman
(EASTMAN COLOR)

Oater with a slightly new twist that should prove sufficient for the bread-and-butter bookings. Well cast.

Hollywood, June 25.

Universal release. Produced by Gordon Kay. Directed by R. G. Springsteen. Stars Audie Murphy, Darren McGavin. Features Ruta Lee, Beverley Owen. Screenplay by Mary and Willard Willingham, based on novel by Marvin H. Albert. Camera, Joseph Biroc; music, Frank Skinner, supervised by Joseph Gershenson; editor, Russell Schoengarth; asst director, Phil Bowles. Reviewed at Studio, June 25, 1964. Running time: **80 MINS.**

Logan Keliher .... Audie Murphy
Sam Ward .... Darren McGavin
Lottie .... Ruta Lee
Susan .... Beverley Owen
Pink .... Skip Homeier
Diggs .... George Tobias
Leach .... Alan Hale
Jeff .... Berkeley Harris
Tucker .... Edward C. Platt
Sammy .... Kevin Tate
Goldie .... Cece Whitney

As long as Audie Murphy keeps in the saddle, there's bound to be a steady stream of bread and butter oaters. And this time, in some respect, there's even a little jam to make this smallscale western a bit more palatable than usual. "Bullet" has everything—in fact it has a little too much. There is plenty of action, lots of good colorful scenery, the usual good man vs. badman and even a bloody violent Apache Indian fight.

But what makes the Gordon Kay production, directed by R. G. Springsteen, hold its interest is a slight plot twist. It isn't new to find the good guy fighting a bad guy who used to be his best friend until the law separated them. It is slightly different however, to find the major problem between them is that law abiding Murphy has married lawbreaker Darren McGavin's former wife, Beverley Owen, and raised their child, Kevin Tate, as his own. McGavin wants them back, even though she divorced him when he turned into a gunman and was sent to jail for life—from which he broke out, of course.

Most of the picture involves a hunt for McGavin, his eventual capture and then Murphy's efforts to get him and the stolen bank money back to town. To add to the problem, the rest of the posse gets greedy eyes, pitting Murphy against a passel of supposedly honest men who turn out to be as bad as McGavin.

"Bullet" starts out slowly; the Mary and Willard Willingham screenplay is unclear until well into the story. But it gets better as the action increases. The plot is telegraphed, the title itself indicating McGavin isn't going to come through this alive. And interspersed between it all are a few sermons on honesty, ethics and a man's attitude about his fellow man that are just a little preachy and unnecessary for this kind of mild, undemanding filmfare.

The cast is good. Murphy plays it a little softer than most of his previous roles and gives it a good sensitive flavor. McGavin is stylized but appealing. Top work comes from Skip Homeier, George Tobias, Alan Hale and newcomer Berkeley Harris, in general western heavy roles. And there's a lot to look at in Ruta Lee and Miss Owen, who both play honestly in undemanding roles that merely give it femme dressing. Cece Whitney has a good bit and Edward C. Platt is staunch.

Joseph Biroc's photography gives the picture a good look, particularly in rich night scenes, although some of the color in other spots has a rusty pastel quality that could have been toned down. *Dale.*

For Att Inte Tala Om Alla Dessa Kvinnor
(As For All These Women)
(SWEDISH—COLOR)

Stockholm, June 23.

Svensk Filmindustri production and release. Stars Jarl Kulle; features Bibi Andersson, Harriet Andersson, Eva Dahlbeck, Karin Kavli, Gertrude Fridh, Mona Malm, Barbro Hiort af Ornas, Allan Edwall, Georg Funkquist, Carll Billquist. Directed by Ingmar Bergman. Screenplay by Erland Josephson, Bergman; camera (Eastmancolor), Sven Nykvist. At Roda Kvarn, Stockholm. Running time, **80 MINS.**

Cornelius .... Jarl Kulle
"Bumble-Bee" .... Bibi Andersson
Isolde .... Harriet Andersson
Adelaide .... Eva Dahlbeck
Madame Tussaud .... Karin Kavli
Traviata .... Gertrud Fridh
Cecilia .... Mona Malm
Beatrice .... Barbro Hiort af Ornas
Jillker .... Allan Edwall
Tristan .... Georg Funkquist
A young man .... Carl Billquist
British radio announcer .. Jan Blomberg
French radio announcer .. Goran Graffman
Swedish radio announcer Gosta Pruzelius
German radio announcer Jan-Olof Strandberg
Men in black suits .... Ulf Johansson, Axel Duberg, Lars-Erik Liedholm
The driver .... L. O. Carlberg
Waitresses ... Doris Funcke, Yvonne Igell

This is a much awaited production since it's the color debut by Ingmar Bergman and a comedy after all dark, dramatic stories this Swedish director has done in recent years. The result is confusing. After each new Bergman picture the question always appears: What does he mean? The same question appears here, too, but maybe with a little change: What does he mean, and why?

This film is the story about a genius named Felix, a cellist. The great Felix is never seen in the film, but the whole story deals with the last four days of his life. Another great genius, the famous music critic Cornelius (Jarl Kulle) is to write his biography. He arrives at the chateau owned by Madame Tussaud, where the genius lives. He wants to see Felix, to ask him questions and try to get something personal for the biography. But a great genius can't be disturbed.

Everybody must do everything to satisfy the genius so he is in good condition if and when he desires to give one of his famous concerts. If he is not satisfied with his wife, let him have a mistress and if that isn't enough, get him one mistress for each night during the week. Of course, conventional names for people is not enough for the genius, he gives each person in his neighborhood a special name, like "Bumble-Bee," Isolde, Traviata, Tristan, etc.

Cornelius never get his chance to see the genius, but he meets all the women, and he speaks to the butler, the driver and the manager. Each one adds a new chapter about the genius.

The film starts at the funeral parlor with the genius in his casket, and all the women coming in, one by one, to say goodbye. From there, the audience is taken back and can follow the final four days in the life of the genius.

Cornelius, the music critic, as depicted here is not particularly sympathetic. He considers himself a genius who feels he understands what the maestro is doing better than the maestro himself. Some Swedish crix have translated this to mean that Felix, the cellist, is Ingmar Bergman himself. And all Swedish critics have been more or less harsh in reviewing this film.

The film is slow-moving most of the time. The fact that Bergman can get every actor or actress to do his best in any role can't save the audience from the tedious pace.

There might be a world market for this film thanks to the name of Ingmar Bergman, but it is doubtful of any great success. *Winq.*

Looking For Love
(SONGS—COLOR)

Comedy with music specifically designed for youth appeal and filled with promotional assists which could make it a successful boxoffice entry. Plenty of good songs sung by Connie Francis.

Hollywood, July 1.

Metro release of Euterpe-Franmet production. Stars Connie Francis, Jim Hutton, Susan Oliver; features Joby Baker, Barbara Nichols, Jay C. Flippen, Jesse White, Charles Lane, Joan Marshall. Cameo bits by George Hamilton, Yvette Mimieux, Paula Prentiss, Danny Thomas, Johnny Carson. Produced by Joe Pasternak. Directed by Don Weis. Screenplay, Ruth Brooks Flippen; camera (Metrocolor), Milton Krasner; editor, Adrienne Fazan; music, George Stoll; asst. director, William McGarry. Reviewed at Village Theatre, Westwood, June 29, '64. Running time, 84 MINS.

Libby Caruso .... Connie Francis
Paul Davis .... Jim Hutton
Jan McNair .... Susan Oliver
Cuz Rickover .... Joby Baker
Gaye Swinger .... Barbara Nichols
Mr. Ralph Front .... Jay C. Flippen
Tiger Shay .... Jesse White
Director .... Charles Lane
Miss Devine .... Joan Marshall
Themselves .... George Hamilton,
Yvette Mimieux, Paula Prentiss,
Danny Thomas, Johnny Carson

Bells ring when Connie Francis finds her true love in Joe Pasternak's frothy, pure entertainment romanceful comedy with music. More than likely, there will also be a fairly generous tinkle at the cash register for "Looking for Love," a typically lightweight concoction of youth appeal that is particularly marketable in the summer vacation period.

Ruth Brooks Flippen's screenplay, designed chiefly for rapid pace, punch and upbeat liveliness is full of holes. But Don Weis' direction, maintaining the invigorating, youthful energy the piece exudes, fills them up so easily they just don't seem to matter. There are plenty of laughs within the hokey framework and an overall feeling of relaxation and fun that should prove its most delectable virtue.

Moreover, it is refreshing to find a completely clean story on the screen. There is sex enough—a constant bevy of bosomy beauties streaming through—but it is wholesome, natural and simple. Just a girl-sees-boy, who doesn't have eyes for her, and goes after him until he's frothing at the mouth for her—only to find he isn't Mr. Right, after all. The audience, of course, knew this all along from the telegraphed plotline that early indicates Connie and her roommate, Susan Oliver, are really going to end up switching boyfriends.

Film is a real showcase for Miss Francis, among the nation's more popular singers to teen fans. She gets seven songs, including "Be My Love," a selection that can't help but remind, mirthfully in this case, of Mario Lanza, particularly since Miss Francis' name in the film is Libby Caruso and Lanza was well known for his portrayal of "The Great Caruso." She does the tune in one of the wackiest scenes in the picture, a bit of pure bedlam that features a guest cameo from Danny Thomas that also might add some fan appeal. Title song, by Hank Hunter and Stan Vincent, looks like a potential pop hit and a good piece of promotion for the film.

Singer reteams with several of the young performers who starred in her first picture, "Where the Boys Are." Jim Hutton is her erstwhile romantic attraction and plays the roll to the hilt in an easy and appealing performance. George Hamilton and Yvette Mimieux also have cameos along with one by Paula Prentiss which is the choicest moment in the picture. And tv star Johnny Carson also plays himself in one scene.

But the most significant major performance is that of Susan Oliver, who gives it a mixture of sarcastic comedy and wholesome reality that is strikingly attractive. Similarly, Jesse White and Jay C. Flippen are superb in comedy character portrayals of a typically loudmouth Hollywood agent and a wry, softly gruff businessman, respectively. Barbara Nichols is her usual dumb blonde and Charles Lane and Joan Marshall are fine in bits. Joby Baker has a fresh, young appeal as Miss Francis' final beau.

Picture's look is aided by costumes designed by Don Loper that should have extra femme appeal, as well as colorful sets by Henry Grace and Charles S. Thompson. There may develop an extra promotional asset in a lady valet, a wardrobe assist for working girls which figures highly in the story and is now being marketed by Miss Francis. *Dale.*

Bikini Beach
(PANAVISION—COLOR)

Same mixture as before indicates same success. Combination of young talent and old formula, accentuated by surfing, racing, beaucoup epidermis.

American International Pictures release of James H. Nicholson-Samuel Z. Arkoff production. Directed by William Asher. Features Frankie Avalon, Annette Funicello, Martha Hyer, Harvey Lembeck, Don Rickles, John Ashley, Jody McCrea, Keenan Wynn. Coproducer, Anthony Carras. Screenplay by Asher, Leo Townsend, Robert Dillon; camera (Pathecolor), Floyd Crosby; editor, Fred Feitshans; sound, Kathleen Rose; art director, Daniel Haller; set decorator Harry Reif; music score, Les Baxter; music coordinator, Al Simms; songs, Guy Hemric, Jerry Styner, Gary Usher, Roger Christian. Jack Merrill, Red Gilson; second unit director, Anthony Carras; asst. director, Clark Paylow. Reviewed at N. Y. World's Fair, July 4, 1964. Running time, 100 MINS.

Frankie & Potato Bug.. Frankie Avalon
Dee Dee .... Annette Funicello
Vivien Clements .... Martha Hyer
Harvey Huntington Honeywagon ...
.... Keenan Wynn
Eric Von Zipper .... Harvey Lembeck
Big Drag .... Don Rickles
Johnny .... John Ashley
Deadhead .... Jody McCrea
Candy .... Candy Johnson
Lady Bug .... Danielle Aubry
Animal .... Meredith MacRae
Sniffles .... Delores Wells
1st Officer.............. Paul Smith
2d Officer.......... James Westerfield
Donna .... Donna Loren
Clyde .... Janos Prohaska
So. Dakota Slim .... Timothy Carey
Teenage Werewolf Monster .. Val Warren
Also—Little Stevie Wonder, The Pyramids and The Exciters Band.

Success, they say, depends on three things—who says it, what he says and how he says it, with "what" being the least important. American International's variation on the three things would be, obviously, "Beach Party," "Muscle Beach Party" and, now, "Bikini Beach." What any of them say is of no importance at all because AIP has the secret of "how to say it."

There's no reason to believe that version number three shouldn't have a boxoffice success comparable to, if not greater than, its predecessors. Little of anything is introduced and the cast, other than Keenan Wynn and Martha Hyer, has the familiarity which youthful audiences find reassuring.

Introduction of some first-rate satire is so overloaded with coatings of slapstick that the satire will be lost on the great mass of youngsters who will provide the film's major support but it does make "Bikini Beach" more palatable for parents or pseudo-sophisticates among the teenagers who find themselves viewing it.

Frankie Avalon doubles as himself and as a horrendously-wigged and bespectacled English singer, The Potato Bug, who temporarily endangers his standing with his steady, Annette Funicello. Other types of opposition are Keenan Wynn, as a publisher who wants the surfers evicted in order to build a senior citizens community. He's straightened out fast by Martha Hyer, a teacher who spends so much time chasing him that she doesn't get much teaching done.

Funniest bit is Harvey Lembeck's travesty on the "wild one" type, complete with rat pack, souped-up cycles and neanderthalic mentality. There's some excellent writing in the part, which even spoofs the cyclists' adoration of the Hitler myth, and Lembeck uses every bit of it.

Most of the "Beach" gang are present with no sign of change. Candy Johnson, still wiggling, Jody McCrea, John Ashley, Meredith MacRae and Delores Wells tag along. Danielle Aubry provides some diversion as the Potato Bug's femme bodyguard who uses savatte (foot-biting) the way the Japanese use judo. Janos Prohaska, kept under covers as Clyde, Wynn's multi-talented chimpanzee, gets in quite a few laughs with his surfing, racing, twisting, fighting bits.

Don Rickles repeats as Big Drag, the friend of man (if the man is Big Drag), with Boris Karloff doing a walkon and gag exit. Outstanding but uncredited are character actress Renee Riano who upstages the kids every time she walks on and almost out-twists Miss Johnson in the end-of-pic credits runoff, and an unnamed but callipygian beauty who plays the "bikini" part of the pic's title. She walks like Amedee Chabot. There's a lovely fight that even parents will enjoy.

Technical credits are excellent throughout, with particular emphasis on Floyd Crosby's Pathecolor camerawork. Only negative reaction is caused by too-frequent use of superimposition. Always obvious, it is the greatest technical flaw still unsolved by film technicians, closely followed by the easily-detected treadmill used for this type shot.

William Asher's nimble direction never lets anything slow the pace he knows is necessary to this type of film. His script, with collaboration of Leo Townsend and Robert Dillon, is mostly a series of gags tied together with the frayed string of logic. The music is what one expects, ten tunes sprinkled generously throughout, and backfielded by Les Baxter's bouncy score. Soloists spotlighted are Little Stevie Wonder and two combos, The Pyramids and The Exciters. *Robe.*

La Bataille De France
(The Battle of France)
(FRENCH)

Paris, June 30.

Cocinor release of Zodiac production. Directed, compiled and conceived by Jean Aurel. Commentary written and spoken by Cecil Saint Laurent; editor, Claudine Bouche. At Lord Byron, Paris. Running time, **90 MINS.**

Sharply done compilation pic goes over the final happenings before the start of the last World War and the early, brief conquest of France. Images are new or rarely seen for the most part as is the theme. Film has interest for specialized showings abroad, and for tv, if it may not have the impact for arty theatre chances.

Commentary is delivered by author Cecil Saint Laurent along with a man who was a foreign minister at the time. They are seen in some shots but it is mainly footage from newsreels and archives that neatly sets up the last days of peace undermined by Hitler's demands and the other nations' giving until war was inevitable.

There is a good tempo and rugged scenes as the war devastates Poland and then bogs down until the Nazi onslaught through Belgium and Holland. The scenes of Nazi bombings and air might are spectacular as is the onward Blitzkreig rush. The big French mistakes are clearly outlined as the major part of the armies of both France and Britain are shipped to Belgium as the Nazis break through into France from the east.

Then the ending sums up Dunkirk where the British were evacuated to fight again at a great cost in men and material, with the French left defeated and Hitler entering Paris. The commentary is mainly effective.

It again shows that well-mounted historical footage still carries dramatic weight. Film makes the strange early aspects of the war clear and shows real leg work by director Aurel in amassing all this telling film from all over Europe. Pic is photographically good for the most part. *Mosk.*

Wonderful Life
(BRITISH-COLOR)

Shaky, unwitty script but pleasant enough vehicle for Cliff Richard.

London, July 3.

Warner-Pathe release of Elstree Distributors presentation of an Ivy (Kenneth Harper) Production. Stars Cliff Richard; features Susan Hampshire, The Shadows, Walter Slezak. Directed by Sidney J. Furie. Screenplay and original story by Peter Myers and Ronald Cass; camera (Technicolor), Kenneth Higgins; editor, Jack Slade; music & lyrics, Myers & Cass, additional songs & music, Richard and The Shadows, background score, Stanley Black; choreography, Gilliam Lynne. At Empire Theatre, London. Running time, **113 MINS.**

Johnnie	Cliff Richard
Lloyd Davis	Walter Slezak
Jenny	Susan Hampshire
Mood Musicians	Hank B. Marvin, Bruce Welch, Brian Bennett, John Rostill
Jerry	Melvyn Hayes
Barbara	Una Stubbs
Douglas Leslie	Derek Bond
Miguel	Joseph Cuby

Cliff Richard has already proved himself a likeable young guy with plenty of savvy as a performer on tv, stage, disks and pix. But more experienced talent than his still needs the aid of a brisk script, which "Wonderful Life" is not. It's his third musical film on the trot and though it will breezily satisfy his big British following and pay good dividends at the native boxoffice, it doesn't advance Richard's career as well as it might.

True, film musicals often get by on shaky storylines but these are usually decked out with lively jokes and badinage and Messrs. Peter Myers and Ronald Cass once again proved themselves somewhat sparing in this department. It's putting an unfair onus on Richard, at this stage of his career, to expect his still developing personality to buck several slack passages and remarkably unwitty wordage. Same thing happened to Elvis Presley at one stage and Richard's sponsors must take warning. However, the film is a light, engaging way of passing an hour or so and it has a youthful cast that spares no effort to please.

The film is set in the Canary Islands, and amid more sand than was used even in "Lawrence of Arabia," Richard and his colleagues cavort with ebullience and zeal. There are several songs that should challenge in the Top Twenty and some lively terping production scenes pep up the action when it is danger of capsizing.

Richard, the Shadows group and comedians Melvyn Hayes and Richard O'Sullivan are merchant sailors stranded in the Canaries where they come across Walter Slezak directing a diabolical "Beau Geste" epic. Caught up in this mish mash, leading lady Susan Hampshire is having a rough time. For love of the young lady the lads decide to boost her confidence by making an off-the-cuff musical version of the director's film. They use his equipment and his script without him knowing and, for plot purposes, Miss Hampshire is kept in the dark about the enterprise and is filmed surreptitiously. Richard is, of course, the young hero and they shoot his scenes when he is acting as stand in for the real star. Both pix turn out to be dogs, but Slezak's stuff is okay and Richard draws out a good performance from Miss Hampshire. So the two eventually "marry" the best parts of both films and turn out a winner. Alas, it is not as simple in the real thing!

Some spasmodic fun is created from this farfetched situation but, as has been hinted, the film relies overmuch on the songs and dances, the likeable young players and some good lensing by Kenneth Higgins for its credit side.

Sidney J. Furie is an on-the-ball young director but he has a tough struggle with some of the material at his disposal. The happiest flight of fancy is a sequence which sends up films down the ages. Richard, Miss Hampshire, and the rest show a pleasing sense of mimicry and satire as they josh such favorites as Valentino, the Marx Brothers, the Mack Sennett Cops, Shirley Temple, Garbo, Grable, Boyer, Fairbanks Senior, Bogart, Dick Powell, Tarzan and others right up to James Bond. It's a moot point whether Richard's public will be able to identify many of the parodied figures, but the middle aged will have a chortling time.

Richard gives a pleasing performance and chirps admirably while Miss Hampshire registers okay, though faced with the downbeat problem of having to portray a not-so-hot young thesp who has little confidence in her own ability. The Shadows and Hayes and O'-Sullivan also give with some useful support while Slezak and Derek Bond have some amusing byplay as a director and leading man who have gone slightly to seed. A standout is Una Stubbs, a lissome, peppy young woman who is an effervescent bundle of energy and talent and who looks set for a bright future.

Furie keeps his cast on the move considerably but tends to dwell overlong on desert sequences which provide lenser Higgins with plenty of scope, while Gillian Lynne earns plaudits for her choreography. Tighter editing would have kept the tempo at highest pitch. Altogether "Wonderful Life" is clean, pleasant family entertainment, a friendly show in which the determination to please by all concerned will communicate profitably to all but the most stony faced audiences. *Rich.*

Berlin Festival

The Pawnbroker

Portrait of concentration camp victim who runs a pawnshop in Harlem, with Rod Steiger effectively portraying title role; needs careful selling for best results.

Berlin, July 7.

Ely Landau and Herbert R. Steinmann presentation of an Ely Landau production, coproduced by Roger H. Lewis and Philip Langner. Stars Rod Steiger; features Brock Peters, Geraldine Fitzgerald, Jaime Sanchez. Directed by Sidney Lumet. Screenplay, Morton Fine, David Friedkin, from a novel by Edward Lewis Wallant; editor, Ralph Rosenblum; camera, Boris Kaufman; music, Quincy Jones. At Berlin Film Fest. Running time, **112 MINS.**

Sol Nazerman	Rod Steiger
Marilyn Birchfield	Geraldine Fitzgerald
Rodriguez	Brock Peters
Jesus Ortiz	Jaime Sanchez
Ortiz' Girl	Thelma Oliver
Tessie	Marketta Kimbrell
Mendel	Baruch Lumet
Mr. Smith	Juano Hernandez
Ruth	Linda Geiser
Bertha	Nancy R. Pollock
Tangee	Raymond St. Jacques
Buck	John McCurry
Robinson	Ed Morehouse
Mrs. Ortiz	Eusebia Cosme
Savarese	Warren Finnerty
Morton	Jack Ader
Papa	E. M. Margolese
Joan	Marianne Kanter

"The Pawnbroker," filmed in New York under the Ely Landau banner as the first production enterprise of Roger Lewis and Philip Langner, is a painstakingly etched portrait of a man who survived the living hell of a Nazi concentration camp and encounters further prejudice when he runs a pawnshop in Harlem. The picture will need individual handling and careful attention to obtain best results to compensate for the lack of the more conventional boxoffice ingredients.

Rod Steiger plays the embittered pawnbroker, and his personal credo is a reflection of his past experiences. He has lost his faith in God, the arts and sciences, he has no discriminatory feelings against white or colored man, but regards them all as human scum. Such is the character of the man whose pawnshop is actually a front for a Negro racketeer, whose main income comes from the slums and brothels.

There is little plot in the regular sense, but a series of episodes spanning just a few days of the present, which recall many harrowing experiences of the past. Some are absorbing, but others seem to lack the dramatic punch for which the director must have strived.

Sidney Lumet, who renews his association with Landau in this production (he also directed the Cannes award winner, "Long Day's Journey Into Night") has made novel use of the flashback technique which is employed from time to time to underscore a particular incident. Occasionally, they are prolonged in a familiar way. Others are quick flashes interspliced into a sequence to give something approaching a subliminal effect. Easily the most telling flashback follows a visit to the pawnshop by a Negro prostie (she's actually the girl friend of his Puerto Rican assistant) to hock a gold locket, and in a bid to better his offer, she tries to tempt him by bearing her breasts. Inevitably, that brings back an incident in the concentration camp when he was forced to watch his wife being stripped and raped.

One of the failings of the screenplay, which is based on the novel by the late Edward Lewis Wallant, is that some characters are too loosely sketched. Also some incidents are not adequately clarified at the time, though they are explained away later. Thoughtful re-editing could probably correct this, and would at the same time take up some of the slack and give the picture a tighter finish.

By the very nature of the subject, the pic is dominated by Steiger, and indeed virtually must stand or fall by his performance. He's an intelligent, experienced actor who knows most of the tricks of the trade, and puts them to good use. It is a faithful study of a man with a load of grief on his shoulders, though it is always in monochrome without any relief. Only once is there an expression of tenderness, and that is when his young assistant dies in arms, having stopped a bullet which young thugs intended for him.

Although appearing only in three scenes, Geraldine Fitzgerald makes a deep impression as a welfare worker who almost succeeds in getting through to him, but at the last moment he refuses to weaken. Brock Peters makes a striking character as the slum landlord, Jaime Sanchez gives a vital study as Steiger's young assistant, and Thelma Oliver reveals a forceful personality (and a lovely body, too) as the Negro prostie. Lesser roles are suitably filled by Marketa Kimbrell, who lost her husband in a camp, and with whom the pawnbroker is having a loveless affair; Baruch Lumet, as her dying father, who disapproves of the relationship; and Linda Geiser, as his wife, who is only seen in the concentration camp flashback.

As much of the action takes place in the dimly lit pawnshop, Boris Kaufman has little scope to maneuver his camera. But he has adroitly avoided a static effect and achieves a considerable amount of movement. Richard Sylbert's settings look authentic while the Quincy Jones score provides a good background effect. *Myro.*

Susuz Yaz
(Waterless Summer)
(TURKEY)
Berlin, June 30.
Hitit Film Ulvi Dogan (Istanbul) presentation. Stars Ulvi Dogan, Erol Tas, Hulya Kocyigit. Directed by Ismail Metin. Screenplay, Necati Cumali; camera, Ali Ugur; music, Yamaci. At Berlin Film Fest. Running time, 70 MINS.
Hassan .... Ulvi Dogan
Osman .... Erol Tas
Bahar .... Hulya Kocyigit

Using a style and technique that has been outdated in the West for at least a couple of decades, this Turkish production entered at the Berlin Film Fest, must be regarded for local consumption only, and cannot conceivably have any export chances in Europe.

Characters are crudely overdrawn, even to the point of the villain carefully twirling the ends of his mustache before planning an assault on his sister-in-law while her husband languishes in jail. The plot, such as it is, describes how the said villain tries to ruin other tobacco planters in the community by diverting the water supply to his land.

Meller develops predictably and seems overlong at 70 minutes. The three principals give unrestrained performances, but Hulya Kocyigit, as the young bride, is quite a beauty, and with proper guidance could go places. *Myro.*

Zeit Der Schuldlosen
(Time of the Innocent)
(GERMAN)
Berlin, June 30.
Columbia-Bavaria release of Peter Carsten production. With Erik Schumann, Peter Pasetti, Wolfgang Kieling. Directed by Thomas Fantl. Screenplay, Fantl and Siegfried Lenz; camera, Georg Krause; music, Hans Posegga; editor, Elisabeth Imholte. At Berlin Film Fest. Running time, 95 MINS.
Sason .... Erik Schumann
Baron .... Peter Pasetti
Engineer .... Wolfgang Kieling
Medico .... Hans Reiser
Hotel owner .... Heinz Leo Fischer
Banker .... Otto Brueggemann
Student .... Walter Wilz
Peasant .... Gustl Datz

This German pic, independently produced by actor Peter Carsten, offers an interesting plot, shows some good acting and looks technically allright. But it, somehow just misses the boat. The property was first a radio play and then a stage work. It looks as though it should have been limited to these two media. While it still may be good enough for tele, plot in this form hardly qualifies itself for a theatre feature pic. As seen by current German standards, Carsten's effort may be called interesting, even courageous, yet the outcome isn't convincing. Commercial prospects seem mild even in this country. Some foreign arty house chances seem likely.

Story is laid in an imaginary dictator's state. Three men try to kill the governor but fail and one is caught. The governor puts him in jail along with nine hostages who are allowed to use any means to make him reveal the names of the two men who were with him. Only if he speaks up, will the hostages be set free.

After some unsuccessful attempts at brute force to force him to speak the revolutionary is killed—but no one knows who did the killing. Four years later the political scene has changed in this country. One of the former hostages who's now on the side of the new regime brings his then inmates together and forces them to confess who killed the revolutionary four years ago. Film tries to explain that actually all were guilty.

A basic flaw with this film is that there's simply too much talk. It's the kind of philosophical talk that gets dull after a while.

Acting is generally good, especially on the part of Erik Schumann (the revolutionary). Direction by newcomer, 35-year old Thomas Fantl, could have been more imaginative and less deliberate in parts. Same goes for the lensing.

Pic cost only $112,500 and has virtually only two sets. Film doesn't make a big impression, but doesn't hurt the German prestige either. Also, it tries to say something. In this respect "Innocent" deserves praise because both are rare factors in current German filmmaking. *Hans.*

Os Fuzis
(The Guns)
(BRAZIL)
Berlin, July 7.
Copacabana Filmes (Rio de Janeiro) presentation of a Jarbas Barbosa production. Stars Atila Iorio, Nelson Xavier. Direction and screenplay, Ruy Guerra; camera, Ricardo Aronovich; music, Moacyr Santos. At Berlin Film Fest. Running time, 110 MINS.
Gaucho .... Atila Iorio
Mario .... Nelson Xavier
Luisa .... Maria Gladys
Sergeant .... Leonides Bayer

Susceptible peasants, who are too easily encouraged to believe in miracles, is the dominant theme of this Brazilian film, which takes an in-depth look at the problems and poverty of farmers living in an arid region in the northwestern part of the country. The subject has only restricted audience appeal, however, and cannot hope for more than limited arty house dates.

Ruy Guerra's screenplay and direction emphasize the simplemindedness of these gullible people who fall for a preacher's claim that he can bring water to the region through a scraggy and half-starved ox. The tale is too leisurely unfolded, however, and some scenes are held for unnecessarily long periods. Some lengthy sequences evoked a noisy audience reaction when screened at this festival.

When the ignorant peasants follow the preacher to the next village, there is a call to the government for protection. The arrival of a handful of soldiers leads to an uneasy and dangerous situation which results in two killings.

Production qualities are adequate, and the location lensing

gives a detailed picture of the arid, but not very attractive region Performances are up to standard. *Myro.*

Kanojox To Kare
(She and He)
(JAPANESE)
Berlin, June 30.
Iwanami Productions and Eizo-Sha Co. (Tokyo) presentation. Stars Aachiko Hidari, Eiji Okada, Kikuji Yamashita; features Mariko Igarashi. Directed by Susumu Hani. Screenplay, Hani and Kunio Shimizu; camera, Juichi Nagano; music, Toku Takemitsu. At Berlin Film Fest. Running time, 114 MINS.

With a delicate touch and a highly sensitive approach, director Susumu Hani has lifted a simple yarn about a lonely middleclass wife who is attracted to a junk peddler on to a high, artistic plane. The film, distinguished also by fine performances, may have limited commercial appeal in western countries, but could succeed in artie situations which cater to the buffs.

The "she" of the title is a young married woman, living in a comfortable apartment house which is adjacent to a slum area in which the inhabitants live in broken-down shacks. She and her husband are not even aware of the slums until the whole compound is destroyed by fire. It is then that she discovers that a junk merchant was a former college mate of her husband.

From then on, she appears to be irresistibly attracted to him, not in the physical sense, but as an escape from her loneliness. It is a strange and uneasy relationship, but it obviously fills a gap in her life. As she is childless, too, she welcomes the opportunity of showing her maternal instinct when she takes care of a sick blind girl who lives with the junk man.

An interesting feature of the story is the wife's attitude to her husband. When he returns from work, she is always at hand to help him on with his robe; not out of servility, but in conformity with convention. Yet when he protests her relationship, she openly defies him and walks out of the house. It is a state of mind which she cannot control, and its effect is heightened by the director's low-key dramatic style.

The portrait of the wife is tenderly etched by Sachiko Hildari; it is a superb performance, rich in contrasting qualities, and notable for its consistent sincerity. The junk man is played by a screen newcomer, Kikuji Yamashita, with considerable authority. He displays more screen expertise than many experienced actors. Eiji Okada has less scope as the husband, but fills a difficult role with understanding. Mariko Igarashi, an amateur from a blind Institute, makes the blind girl an appealing character. Neighbors at the apartment house and on the compound are played by non-pros, too, but they all respond to the director's guidance. Excellent camerawork and a subtle score set the high technical standard, though tauter editing would help. *Myro.*

Kesalla Kello Viisi
(This Summer at Five)
(FINLAND)
Berlin, June 30.
Elokuva Oy (Helsinki) presentation. Stars Martti Koski, Tuula Elomaa, Carita Gren. Direction and screenplay, Erkko Kivikoski; camera, Virke Lehtinen, music, Pentti Lasanen. At Berlin Film Fest, June 29, '64. Running time, 76 MINS.

Finland is one of the minor European film producing nations, and its stature internationally will not be helped by this entry at the Berlin Film Festival. It is a lowercase novelettish subject, and its export chances must be limited to the Scandinavian territory.

Although running only 76 minutes, the pic's slender story line is padded with interminable flashbacks and a number of totally irrelevant sequences. It is directed at a snail's pace, though the camera occasionally catches some of Finland's scenic attractions.

The screenplay puts the focus on a pair of young lovers on a camping holiday by the sea, but the young man feels that it is not working out the way it ought, and brings the affair to an end. They return to the city. While he spends the night with a pickup, the girl patiently waits outside his apartment.

Going home after her lonely vigil, she is knocked down by a car, and it is then that he realizes that he really is in love with her. Martti Koski and Tuula Elomaa play the young lovers in downbeat style, but Carita Gren shows a little more spirit as the pickup. *Myro.*

Olympische Winterspiele In Innsbruck
(Olympic Winter Games At Innsbruck)
(AUSTRIAN-COLOR)
Berlin, June 30.
Theo Hoermann production. Directed by Hoermann. Commentary, Dr. Kurt Jeschko and Hans Hoemberg; camera (Agfacolor), Alfons Benesch, Jan Boon and 12 other cameramen; music, Bert Breit; editors, Lilo Primavesi, E. Proell, H. Bernetti; narrators, Ernst Grissemann, Heinz Engelmann. At Berlin Film Fest. Running time, 92 MINS.

This full-length color documentary on the last Olympic Winter Games, Austria's official entry at the 1964 Berlin Film Fest, emerges as a good-natured contribution to winter sports. There is nothing demanding about the film to give it better than average chances. It will be chiefly an item for sports-minded patrons. Commercial prospects look best for this fall when the Olympic Games are held in Tokyo. Hans Schubert's Sportfilm (Munich) has acquired its world rights.

Starting out with the ignition of the Olympic Flame, film shows excerpts from what are supposedly the highlights of the Winter Games. There are bits of beautiful skating, footage of the more important ice hockey games, scenes of the various alpine disciplines, etc. Woven in are folklore, yodling, etc. In addition, the pic makes a plea for friendship and understanding between foreign nations for which sports are especially qualified.

One of this documentary's flaws lies with a rather provincial commentary which, however, can be improved if dubbed into foreign lingo. What can't be improved is film's look as a whole. Director-producer Theo Hoermann must be told that he tailored his documentary more for Austrian mentality t h a n for international appeal. Also a film of this type could be more imaginative, could stand sophisticated touches and a more demanding narration. Also, the variety of sports sequences lacks some smooth order while there is too little inside stuff.

However, there is some good color photography. Footage of the Tirolese mountains and that of the town of Innsbruck is often beautiful. But this is only a small compensation for an otherwise rather mediocre documentary on a major sports event. *Hans.*

Los Evadidos
(The Escaped)
(ARGENTINE)
Berlin, June 30.
Selecciones Huincul (SRL), Buenos Aires, presentation. Stars Jorge Salcedo, Tital Merello. Directed by Enrique Carreras. Screenplay, Sixto Pondal Rios; camera, Antonio Merayo; music, Tito Tibero. At Berlin Film Fest, June 29, '64. Running time, **98 MINS.**

There have been a number of distinguished films out of the Argentine in recent years, which makes it hard to understand how such an indifferent pic came to be selected as the country's official entry at this festival. At best, it can be rated a moderate "B" programmer.

Neither in its production nor in its story does the pic have much to commend it. Apart from a prolog prior to the credit titles (which shows a young thug brutally robbing a cab driver and later committing a cold-blooded murder) the entire action takes place inside a prison, where the inmates are plotting a mass escape. The breakout attempt, almost a classic of confusion, ends in mass killing of prison officials as the trigger-happy convicts meet resistance; and the officers, in turn, getting their revenge on the prisoners.

Only intriguing aspect of the pic are the glimpses of prison life in the Argentine. The prisoners wear their own clothes, apparently have no work to do and spend their days lounging around on their bunks, have their food and laundry sent in by friends or relatives. And they have a fairly free time when they have visits from wives or girl friends.

Technically, the pic matches the production's modest status. Direction is pedestrian, camerawork just adequate, and the acting is only so-so though always up to the demands of the subject. *Myro.*

Mahanagar
(The Great City)
(INDIA)
Berlin, July 7.
R. D. Bansal (Calcutta) presentation and production. Stars Anil Chatterji and Madhabi Mukherjee. Direction, screenplay and music, Satyajit Ray; camera, Subrata Mitra; editor, Dulal Dutta. At Berlin Film Fest. Running time, **122 MINS.**
Bookkeeper ....Anil Chatterji
His wife ....Madhabi Mukherjee

"Mahanagar" already has received a number of distinguished awards in India, and will undoubtedly collect further accolades as it travels the international route. Its style is typical of the director: leisurely probing a problem, with subtle character studies and a penetrating look at the subject. Inevitably, this is for the arty trade, though it may widen the director's already substantial following.

Satyajit Ray this time has taken a modern problem for his subject, and gives it the stylish look for which he is noted. The characters are as genuine as their economic difficulties: making ends on a limited income and increasing responsibilities is his theme. And it is played with utmost sincerity and understanding.

Principal characters are a bookkeeper and his wife. His salary at a local bank does not stretch to meet the day-to-day needs of a family, which includes aging parents and a couple of youngsters. So the wife takes a job as a door-to-door salesgirl, peddling knitting machines to rich housewives. It is a situation which hardly appeals to the husband, and he reacts even more strongly as he realizes that his wife enjoys her new life and the opportunity of meeting new people and visiting elegant homes. He is on the point of forcing her to quit when the bank pulls down the shutters and she is left as the breadwinner for the entire family.

Not much of a plot, admittedly, but as scripted by Ray it has depth, warmth and sincerity — qualities which are shrewdly exploited in his sensitive direction. It is an elegant, unhurried piece of filmmaking which will give considerable pleasure to selective audience, for it takes a perceptive look at a universal problem in an interesting setting. Incidentally, apart from direction and script, Ray also takes credit for the score, and the background music. a d m i r a b l y catches the mood of the pic.

The sensitive qualities of the production are enhanced by the principal performances, though Anil Chatterjee is inclined to be relentlessly sombre as the husband. A little more shading to his interpretation of the character would have helped. But Madhabi Mukherjee radiates charm as the wife, and plays her role with considerable sympathy and tenderness. There is a pleasant cameo by Vicky Redwood as an Anglo-Indian girl, and excellent support from Haradhan Banerjee and Haren Chatterjee. *Myro.*

A Hard Day's Night
(BRITISH)

The Beatles' film debut. Big b.o. and also stands up as a lively, offbeat and funny film.

London, July 8.
United Artists release of Walter Shenson production. Stars The Beatles (John Lennon, Paul McCartney, George Harrison, Ringo Starr); features Wilfrid Brambell, Norman Rossington, Victor Spinetti, Kenneth Haigh, Deryck Guyler, John Junkin, Anna Quayle. Directed by Richard Lester. Screenplay by Alun Owen; camera, Gilbert Taylor; editor, John Jympson; songs, Lennon & McCartney. Opened July 6, '64 at Pavilion, London. Running time, **83 MINS.**
John .... John Lennon
Paul .... Paul McCartney
George .... George Harrison
Ringo .... Ringo Starr
Grandfather.......... Wilfrid Brambell
Norm ....Norman Rossington
TV director ....Victor Spinetti
Shake .... John Junkin
Millie .... Anna Quayle
Man on train.......... Richard Vernon
Police Sgt. .... Deryck Guyler

From conception, the entry of the Beatles into feature film circles had to be a presold success. Curiosity, alone, will steer even non-fanatical admirers of this screwball showbiz phenomena to the wickets. Pertinent point, however, is whether the film itself clicks and whether the Liverpool lads have any future and the answer to both questions is a resounding "Yeah, yeah, yeah!"

"A Hard Day's Night" is a wacky, offbeat piece of filming, charged with vitality and inventiveness by Director Dick Lester, slickly lensed and put over at a fair lick. No attempt has been paid to build the Beatles up as Oliviers, they are at their best when the pic has a misleading air of off-the-cuff spontaneity. But they emerge as individual characters, not as a four-headed monster, and carefully handled, they may well develop the kind of cinematic zaniness that has not been seen since the Marx Brothers in their prime.

Running at 83 minutes, in black and white, it keeps Beatles within their ability. Alun Owen's screenplay is a slim vehicle with spiky, funny, offbeat dialog well turned to the Beatles' respective characteristics. It merely attempts to portray an exaggerated 36 hours in the lives of the Beatles. But, though exaggerated, the thin story line gives a shrewd idea of the pressure and difficulties under which they work and live.

Four set off by train to keep a live television date and, before taking off by helicopter for their next stint, they have some rum adventures. A skirmish with the police, mobbing by hysterical fans, then a press conference, riotous moments in a tavern, a jazz cellar, a gambling club and at tv rehearsals all work into the crazy tapestry and offer the Beatles a chance to display their sense of humor and approach to life.

It's all done with breeziness. Each of the boys has his individual moments, too. John Lennon in a bubble bath playing with a midget submarine, and also in surrealistic conversation with an intense young women (Anna Quayle). George Harrison being quizzed by a precious dress designer on the clothes trend for modern youth ("that's a very grotty shirt you're wearing!"), Paul McCartney concerned with his mythical grandfather. Ringo Harrison playing truant from the Group and finding the outside world a cold, unfriendly place. Each is an opportunity, nicely taken. The group activities include the sending up of the press at a conference, the deflating of a pompous character on a train, a smack at their own image in the tv rehearsals and, splendidly, a scene where the four briefly escape from routine and have an uninhibited frolic in mime in a field, which pinpoints the fact that success has virtually made them prisoners.

In fact, social significance could well be dug out—"A Hard Day's Night". But to do so would be to dig greater importance to the film than it warrants. It's wiser to accept the Beatles as potentially fine entertainers in a new field and with a new career that will need careful handling. To give the almost documentary storyline a boost scriptwriter Owen has introduced Paul's grand father, a mischief making mixer with an eye on the main chance. Played by Wilfrid Brambell with sharp perception his presence is a great buffer for the boys' throwaway sense of comedy. Norman Rossington as their harrassed road manager, John Junkin as their baggage man, Victor Spinetti, great as a neurotic tv producer, Deryck Guyler, a sympathetic police chief, Kenneth Haigh as the fashion conscious quizzer of Harrison, and Richard Vernon, briefly, as the pompous train traveller, are all rewardingly on hand to ensure that the Beatles are not left entirely to their own resources.

John Jympson's editing is brisk, though there are signs of whole chunks being cut out of the pic, and Gilbert Taylor's lensing matches the swift, darting mood of Lester's shrewd direction. Musically, there are a dozen or so numbers written by Lennon and McCartney many of which will be prominent in the Hit Parade. There is no musical score, as such but just as the new numbers are fitted logically into the action some of the Beatles old songs are adroitly used as background to miming sequences, thus adding to the fans' earful of Beatles' ditties, but without slowing down the pace of the film.

Most members of the audience will come away with memories of favorite gags or brief interudes in the film but overall impression will be of a fresh piece of filming that has the excitement of welcome new personalities breaking fresh ground. "Hard Day's Night" (their own zany choice of title) will not go down as the greatest film of the decade. But it is one that is going to be subject of much discussion. It will satisfy the legion of Beatles' followers and should make the Group a lot of new friends who have sensed that there must be more behind them than the vocal twanging which has brought them such swift fame (notoriety?) and fortune. *Rich.*

Berlin Festival

Faust
Berlin, July 8.
Kalmar Inc. (Calvin Floyd) production. Stars Robert Towner, Judy Peters, Roban Cody. Direction and screenplay, Michael Suman; camera, Tony Forsberg; music, Gordon Zahler. At Berlin Film Fest. Running time, **100 MINS.**
Faust ....Robert Towner
Margaret ....Judy Peters
Bolus ....Roban Cody

Calvin Floyd's Kalmar Inc. is the production company behind

this version of "Faust," which was directed and scripted by Michael Suman and filmed in Hollywood on a shoestring budget of around $100,000. It showed up at the Berlin festival as an invited entry, but it is difficult to understand how it achieved the dignity of presentation at an international event. Not surprisingly, its presentation on the final day of the fest was greeted with prolonged boos.

Although Floyd and Suman were undoubtedly motivated by sincerity their combined effort misfires sadly, and can virtually be regarded as a commercial write-off. It is amateurishly made, appallingly acted, and has almost nothing to commend it.

What the producers were aiming at is anybody's guess, and the official description that it is a "contemporary satirical fantasy and a playfully distorted counterpart of Goethe's 'Faust'" does not help overmuch. The involved storyline presents Faust as a young magician endeavoring to perform a feat of real magic something more ambitious than just illusion. The character of Mephistopheles comes in the guise of a psychiatrist called Bolus, who defies Faust to perform a trick which he cannot explain. All this is decorated with a lot of mumbo-jumbo about Halloween, including a masquerade, but none of the characters is clearly delineated, and it adds up to a depressing and distressing experience. The acting by the three principals, Robert Towner, Judy Peters and Roban Cody is, to put it generously, lamentable. That, too, goes for most of the other credits.   *Myro.*

Circe
(ARGENTINE)

Berlin, July 7.
Chase Films (Buenos Aires) presentation of a Manuel Antin production. Stars Graciela Borges, Alberto Argibay. Directed by Antin. Screenplay, Antin, Julio Cortazar, H. Grossi; camera, Americo Hoss; music, Adolfo Morpugo. At Berlin Film Fest. Running time, **83 MINS.**
Delia .... Graciela Borges
Mario .... Alberto Argibay
Hektor .... Walter Vidarte
Rolo .... Sergio Renan

Based on a legend, this Argentinian film (which was an invited entry to the Berlin festival), display her talent. Albert Argibay gives a sensitive study as the would-be lover. Walter Vidarte and Serge Renan give okay performances as the two other men. Technically, the film is up to par.   *Myro.*

Polnische Passion
(Polish Passion)
(STATELESS)

Berlin, July 7
Janusz Piekalkiewicz production. Directed and written by Piekalkiewicz. Camera, Mathias Chromecki; music, Oskar Sala. Commentary in German. At Berlin Film Fest. Running time, **80 MINS.**

Janusz Piekalkiewicz, a 39-year-old Pole living in Paris, dedicated his first full-length documentary film to the sufferings of his countrymen through the years of 1939 to 1945. He is an authority on this subject—he was a participant in the bloody Warsaw uprising and

an inmate of a Nazi concentration camp. In 1957, he fled his native country and became a stateless person. His documentary, therefore, seems to have no nationality.

There have been many films depicting Nazi brutality in Poland. Piekalkiewicz tried to give his documentary a different slant, showing the Stalinistic terror on Poland, a chapter which the producer-director-writer thought had been neglected in documentary films. He stresses his aim that "Polish Passion" isn't an anti-Russian film. It's anti-Stalin. The picture's release in East Bloc countries seems to be out of the question. Commercial prospects in western countries aren't easy to gauge. Nevertheless, it's a very interesting film.

This first concentrates on the Hitler-Stalin pact in 1939 and shows a lineup of excerpts from newsreel footage. Faces that history will never forget are shown, such as Hitler, Ribbentrop, Goering, etc. on one side, Stalin, Molotov, etc. on the other one. Molotov's visit in Berlin and Ribbentrop's visit to Moscow to sign the pact and Soviets and Germans meeting at the demarcation line are intensely interesting. Then the cruelty of the Gestapo and German concentration camps are shown as well as the annihilation camps in Siberia. Also corpses of Polish officers found in Katyn.

It reportedly took Piekalkiewicz three years to make this documentary. The long time may be explained by the fact that Piekalkiewicz' producing company is a two-man outfit. He has only a cameraman with him. Technically, it's a very good production. Footage has been put together with remarkable smoothness. The narration is refreshingly matter-of-fact and avoids sentimentality. But it draws emotional impact and brings heavy sympathies for the Poles. Poland belongs to those countries that suffered most in those grim years. The commentary says that there were more victims on Polish side than on the western allied side combined.   *Hans.*

Llanto Por Un Bandido
(Weeping for a Bandit)
(SPAIN-COLOR-SCOPE)
Berlin, July 7.
Agata Films (Madrid) presentation of a Jose Luis Dibildos production. Stars Francisco Rabal. Directed by Carlos Saura. Screenplay, Saura and Mario Camus; camera, Juan Jose Baena; music, Carlo Rustichelli. Pedro del Valle. At Berlin Film Fest. Running time, **95 MINS.**
El Tempranillo ....Francisco Rabal
Maria Jerouima.......... Lea Massari
Pedro Sanchez.......... Phillipe Leroy
El Lutos .... Lino Ventura

This outdoor Spanish pic, filmed on location in the rugged Sierra Morena in lush Eastmancolor and in C'Scope, is based on the character of a soldier who turned bandit after the Napoleonic wars, and who became a legend in his own lifetime. Film is virtually a period Western and could have moderate playoff chances.

The principal character is known as El Tempranillo (the early bird) and he takes to the mountains and brigandry after getting the taste for fighting during the war. He prefers the spoils of banditry to the poverty and

hunger of the country. He is joined in the hills by Pedro Sanchez, a liberal leader who escaped from a convict chain gang, but the two split when the bandit accepts the king's pardon and the gift of an estate.

Carlos Saura's direction puts emphasis on action and adventure while Juan Julio Baena's camera sweeps the countryside to achieve a colorful pictorial effect. Film has pace and atmosphere and is helped by an able cast.

Francisco Rabal makes a tough and uncompromising bandit, though capable of tenderness as evidenced in the scenes of his wedding night. Lea Massari is the bride who tries in vain to persuade him to change his mode of life, but her betrayal and death make him even more determined to seek vengeance. Phillipe Leroy and Lino Ventura head the strong supporting cast. A number of tough bandit-types have been recruited for lesser roles, adding conviction to the plot.   *Myro.*

Alleman
(The Human Dutch)
(HOLLAND)

Berlin, July 7.
Bert Haanstra presentation and production. Direction and screenplay, Haanstra; camera, Anton van Munster; music, Otto Ketting. At Berlin Film Fest. Running time, **90 MINS.**

Bert Haanstra, one of Europe's brightest documentary filmmakers, has taken a perceptive look at his 12,000,000 fellow Dutchmen in this highly entertaining, though somewhat gimmicky documentary pic. Film sustains high allround qualities, and could make useful supporting feature for most programs.

Holland is a country which has more water than land, and as viewed through Haanstra's camera is a fascinating country with its attractive architecture and its hundreds of canals. But this is no conventional travelog; the producer-director has set out to observe the habits and manners of the people, and hits the bullseye most of the time.

Haanstra is an expert at juggling his material to achieve a lively effect. There is one fine example of such sharp editing in a sequence in which various sporting teams are preparing for the "off," and another in which people react to a bust of Hitler in a junk store. In these, and other sequences, Haanstra's visual flair is heightened by his sense of comedy and timing.

The film has been smoothly photographed by Anton van Munster. His camera has unobtrusively caught the Dutch at work and play. Musical backgrounding is adequate.   *Myro.*

Herrenpartie
(Stag Party)
(GERMAN-YUGOSLAV)
Berlin, July 7.
Schorcht release of Neue Emelka (Munich) and Avala-Film (Belgrade) production. Stars Hans Nielsen, Goetz George, Rudolf Platte, features Mira Stupica. Milana Dravic, Oliviera Markovic. Directed by Wolfgang Staudte. Screenplay, Werner Joerg Lueddecke, Arsen Diclic; camera, Nenad Jovicic; music, Zoran Hristic. At Berlin Film Fest. Running time, **95 MINS.**
Friedrich Hacklaender ..... Hans Nielsen
Herbert Hacklaender .... Goetz George
Otmar Wengel .... Gerlach Fiedler
Karl Asmuth .... Friedrich Maurer
Willi Wirth .... Reinhold Bernt
Miroslava .... Mira Stupica
Seja .... Milana Dravic
Nada .... Ljubica Janicijevic
Lia .... Oliviera Markovic

Wolfgang Staudte, creator of some of Germany's most memorable postwar pix, has the reputation for preferring a risky pic which flops than a conventional film. His attitude is again evidenced by his latest, "Herrenpartie" which tackles a highly interesting and (for German standards) daring subject. It's intended to be a sincere film.

Unfortunately, the outcome doesn't ring true in several instances. But despite its deficiencies this still rates as one of the more important West German productions. Domestically, it won't be easy to sell it because it isn't exactly a pleasant theme for the Germans. But plot is exploitable for export. Perhaps this Schorcht release is going to spell more money abroad than at home. It is neither artistically nor technically an essential film, but its theme certainly stirs interest.

A group of German tourists, all men of a German lieder choir, makes a bus trip to Yugoslavia. The men reach a lonely Montenegrin village whose inhabitants are only women. Here their bus runs out of gas and they must look for help. But the village women refuse to aid them, and show a hostile attitude.

They are neither willing to forget nor to forgive what happened here during the war. The Germans took all their men as hostages and shot them. The women push the bus down the valley and even attempt to kill the German tourists. The viewer's sympathy remains on side of the women. Their attitude is humanly understood. The film's fadeout, however, makes reconciliation evident.

Staudte calls his effort a satirical attack on forgetfulness, ignorance and lack of tact on one side, and hate trauma on the other. The characters of the Germans are exaggerated on purpose. There is a nice German who's overly nice, a stupid one is overly stupid while some dialog is too witty.

The other (Yugoslav) side is grim tragedy, also officially; the women are all clad in black. This strange mixture of satire and tragedy doesn't quite come off. Staudte picked the extremes to make a provocative film. But the outcome is a film of only harmless calibre. It's indeed a pity for a highly interesting and important theme has been nearly wasted.

The acting by the Yugoslav players is convincing, but hardly anything special on part of the Germans. It's mostly cliche, often bordering on cabaret-type performances. Technically, the pic is not better than average. It's the interesting plot which gives it its importance.   *Hans.*

Soft Hands
(Original title not given)
(EGYPT-COLOR)

Berlin, July 7.
General Company release of Arab Film Production (Cairo) film. With Sabah, Ahmad Mazhar, Mariam Fakhreldin, Laila Taher and Salah Zoulfikar. Directed by Mahmoud Zoulfikar. Camera (Eastmancolor), Wadid Sirry, Aly Khrei-

rallah; music, Aly Ismail. At Berlin Film Fest. Running time, 75 MINS.

Egypt belongs to those nations that are most faithful to the Berlin festival. One thing all Arab entries always have had in common: they are, voluntarily or involuntarily, funny. And this goes for tragedies, dramas as well as comedies. Audience laughter stems mostly from the amateurish acting. This one is no exception either. "Soft Hands" a peculiar mixture of comedy, musical and social satire, can be described only as an item for some film buffs.

Naive plot centers around a prince who has been living so much beyond his means that he faces financial ruin. But only gradually he realizes that his good days of doing nothing are over, and that he has to change his life. The change means work and the title indicates that he has to use his "soft hands."

Acting and direction only can be called dilettantish. Also technically Arab film-making is still way behind normal picture standards. The Eastman color is quite good and in a way there are some interesting shots of Arab life. But it's hard to take this seriously.

Hans.

Sodrasban
(In The Current)
(HUNGARIAN)

Budapest, July 14.

Hungarofilm release of Hunnia production. With Andrea Drahota, Marianne Moor, Sandor Csikos, Janos Harkanyi, Andras Kozak, Tibor Orban, Gyula Szersen. Written and directed by Istvan Gaal. Camera, Sandor Sara; music, Andrad Szollosy. Reviewed in Budapest. Running time, 90 MINS.

Vadoc ... Andrea Drahota
Bobe ... Marianne Moor
Laci ... Sandor Csikos
Gabi ... Janos Harkanyi
Lujza ... Andras Kozak
Zoli ... Tibor Orban
Karesz ... Gyula Szersen

A needed new talent for Magyar films is unveiled in Istvan Gaal with his first feature pic. This has a definite visual flair as it looks at the effects of an accidental death on a group of young people. Observation and execution are sharp if the needed fillip of deeper probing of character is uneven at times. It is thus mainly for special situations in foreign climes while film fest airings also may help.

A group of school friends, five boys and two girls, are on holiday. Early scenes are fast and full of right character notations, bright and airy progression and an almost lyrical snap. They go for a swim and vie with each other as to how deep they can dive. Then a campfire is built and they dance about to suddenly discover one boy is missing.

Comes anguish, searching and then the calling of the police. Finally he is given up for lost. Then each one's reaction to the event is shown with more uneven results. One girl learns she is not really in love with her superficial suitor, a girl who felt something for the lost boy realizes her loss and his best friend the awe and understanding of mortality.

The dead boy's grandmother in austere mourning marks one of the most poignant parts of this as well as the finding, identification and burial of the boy. All have been marked by it as they go their ways.

Director-writer Gaal displays a true filmic feel in marking the drama and its effects. There may sometimes be a tendency to simplify a passion or mood.

But these are only youthful transgressions and Gaal should emerge a director to be heard from on local and international grounds in the future. Film is well done technically with the right sharpness in direction and editing. And there is fresh playing by a group of advanced students at the local acting school. Pic is the Magyar entry at the presently unspooling Karlovy Vary Film Fest in Czechoslavakia.

Mosk.

Uj Gilgames
(New Gilgames)
(HUNGARIAN)

Budapest, July 14.

Hungarofilm release of Hunnia production. With Ivan Darvas, Edit Domjan, Sandor Pecsi, Szilvia Dallos. Directed by Mihaly Szemes. Screenplay, Ida Andras, Joszef Solymar; camera, Barnabas Hegyi; music, Emil Petrovics. Reviewed in Budapest. Running time, 105 MINS.

David ... Ivan Darvas
Lilla ... Edit Domjan
Aradi ... Sandor Pecsi
Margo ... Szilvia Dallos

Though the theme is grim (a love affair between two cancer patients) this has the delicacy to keep it tasteful throughout. If the pic remains somewhat melodramatic, there is still a poignant note bolstered by sensitive direction and fine emoting. It is a specialized film for abroad but has the emotional content that could slant it for certain situations.

A young man with chest cancer has become fatalistic about it and stopped his work and dropped a longtime mistress. He meets a woman whose husband has left her because of her sickness. Love comes simply. She is cured and leaves the hospital to wait for him while he goes on working, the possible outcome being obscure. Perhaps the character background is sketchy, but the pic falters rarely in its main theme of human communication.

Director Mikhaly Szemes has refrained from any shock tactics and used a simple approach. Production makes its statement gently but forcefully in this way. Ivan Darvas has restraint as the man while Edit Domjan possesses the right tenderness. The others, too, are fine.

Fine technical aspects also help this fragile pic overcome its surface approach. Careful handling is called for but it might be worth it. Title refers to a Mesopotamian book of verses on the meaning of life and death.

Mosk.

Igen
(Yes)
(HUNGARIAN)

Budapest, July 14.

Hungarofilm release of Studio III production. With Ivan Darvas, Ilona Beres. Directed by Gyorgy Revesz. Screenplay, Ivan Boldiszar; camera, Ferenc Skecsenyi; music, Andras Mihaly. Reviewed in Budapest. Running time, 75 MINS.

Teres ... Ilona Beres
Janos ... Ivan Darvas

Ambitious theme of wartime psychic scars leading to a case of fear of life is not quite balanced by the script, direction and scope of this film. Result is a stylish if overblown love story that would qualify mainly for specialized or language situations abroad.

There seems an influence of New Wave methods since the film unrolls in memory and in the present. It also shows clever use of frozen images, sharp cutting and even a dash of expressionism. A man, whose pregnant wife was killed during the war, manages to fall in love again but does not want a child in a world which he feels menaced by the Atomic Bomb.

A strong love grows with his new wife but does not lessen the fear of responsibility for a child. When she becomes pregnant she promises to get an abortion.

Ivan Darvas and Ilona Beres are deft thesps who manage to give this couple life and freshness. Director Gyorgy Revesz has handled the love scenes with taste. But there is too much visual stylization for its own sake with an imperfect blending of the man's problems and needs, and their effects on his life.

Film is technically expert and this can be chalked up as an ambitious production that wants to comment on the past and present through a current love affair. Unfortunately it is too schematic on both planes to have them jive effectively and give the film that extra dimension to have it jell.

Mosk.

Karambol
(Collision)
(HUNGARIAN)

Budapest, July 14.

Hungarofilm release of Hunnia production. With Istvan Bujtor, Zsuzsa Balogh, Zoltan Latinovits, Tamas Vegvari, Eva Szabo. Directed by Felix Mariassy. Screenplay, Judith Mariassy; camera, Gyorgy Illes; music, Imre Vincze. Reviewed in Budapest. Running time, 90 MINS.

Terpinko ... Istvan Bujtor
Eva ... Zsuzsa Balogh
Weber ... Zoltan Latinovits
Csebli ... Tamas Vegvari
Eszter ... Eva Szabo

Tale of a loutish but fairly charming worker who gets his comeuppance through unrequited love is slickly turned out. It seems more Western than Eastern Bloc in motivations, execution and emphasis. But its surface look limits this more for playoff than arty theatre chances abroad.

An incredibly strong, uneducated young man runs off from the farm to stay with his sister in the big town. After bumming around, he finally gets a job in a factory and also becomes a champion weightlifter. Paralleled to his story is that of a young provincial, femme student who also goes to work in the city.

The boy has many women and marries one, only to possess her and then annul the marriage. The girl marries a dedicated scientist and becomes one herself. She crosses paths with the strong man when he becomes her helper. His assiduous attempts to seduce her, half by challenge and then by love, almost lead to tragedy when he causes an accident chasing her.

Director Felix Mariassy neatly blocks out characters and shows people who may be consciously or unconsciously unsatisfied with their lot. But the husband's character is left a bit sketchy and the needed power in building emotion and drama sometimes bogs down. So its tale of self realization does not have the dimension to suspend a certain familiar and even telegraphed progression.

Film is somewhat reminiscent of the British film, "This Sporting Life," without its tragic insights. Istvan Bujtor has an ease and drive in his playing of the brutish type while Zsuzsa Balogh is effective as the harassed girl. Others are adequate. Technically it is good. Script is crisp if not quite deep enough.

Mosk.

Foto Haber
(Haber's Photo Shop)
(HUNGARIAN)

Budapest, July 14.

Hungarofilm release of Hunnia production. With Zoltan Latinovits, Eva Ruttkai, Miklos Szakats, Antal Pager. Directed by Zoltan Varkonyi. Screenplay, Janos Erdodi, Deszo Radvanyi, Marianne Szemes; camera, Istvan Hildebrand; music, Frigyes Hidas. Reviewed in Budapest. Running time, 100 MINS.

Gabor ... Zoltan Latinovits
Annie ... Eva Ruttkai
Haber ... Miklos Szakats
Inspector ... Antal Pager

Hungarians want their own commercial-type films and this one fills the bill for the home market. This espionage tale has some suspense, a love story, a few twists (despite its familiar aspects) and action, to have it moderately entertaining. Export chances remain mainly for Eastern Bloc countries.

Film has a clever concoction of shady characters and a secret service man getting into a gang to find love and break it up. Front is a photo shop and they are after some atomic secrets for some unknown foreign power.

There are muggings, murders, love affairs and even a twist party before the gang is gunned down. Another twist is the secretive spy ring head turning out to be an old woman who has masqueraded as a shopkeeper. Zoltan Latinovits, one of the more popular leading men, has the dash and cool headedness for the undercover man while Eva Ruttkai is decorative in an ill-defined role used mainly for femme interest.

Direction is perky. This pic has already proved itself a hit with general audiences here, showing a local desire for more escapist fare and action films besides the more serious ones. It is technically good though the fights are only passably staged.

Mosk.

Elveszett Paradicsom
(Lost Paradise)
(HUNGARIAN)

Budapest, July 14.

Hungarofilm release of Hunnia production. With Mari Torocsik, Gyorgy Palos, Antal Pager. Directed by Karoly Makk. Screenplay, Imre Sarkadi, Makk; camera, Ferenc Szechenyi. Reviewed in Budapest. Running time, 98 MINS.

Zoltan ... Gyorgy Palos
Girl ... Mari Torocsik
Father ... Antal Pager

This tale about redemption through love sometimes forces things towards outright melodrama and tear jerking but has a force in characterization that keeps it coherent and intermittently moving. Thus, this pic mainly has playoff chances abroad on its lachrymose theme with arty chances slimmer.

A young doctor has been responsible for the accidental death of a woman in an abortion. He goes to see his old father to ponder what he will do and meets a young girl who brings love and a new determination to face his actions. The death of his elderly father also brings on his self-realization and a newfound strength.

Scenes of growing love are done with tact and skill. Mari Torocsik's simplicity and insight bolster the role of the girl while Gyorgy Palos has the mixture of weakness and intelligence to make his part also acceptable. Antal Pager's timing as the stalwart father keep this from being a stereotyped figure.

Lensing is rightly sombre while the visual symbols are not overdone in this uneven but generally well-done tale of love and responsibility. It just lacks that deeper forcefulness to make its ending acceptable. *Mosk.*

Eva A 5116
(HUNGARIAN)
Budapest, July 14.

Hungarofilm release of Hunnia production. Directed by Laszlo Nadasy. Screen play, Laszlo Rozsa, Nadasy; camera, Sandor Sara; editor, M. Kovacs. Reviewed in Budapest. Running time, 65 MINS.

Documentary is one of the first Hungarian cinema truth pix. It depicts the search for the parents of a Hungarian girl who had been brought up by a Polish family after being saved from a concentration camp during the last war. It is a forthright, well observed documentary good primarily as supporting arty house fare abroad, if pruned sagaciously.

Filmmakers first contacted a flock of people who thought the girl might possibly have been a lost child when her attempt to locate her parents after 19 years was written up in local papers. Then they had scenes of her setting out, her meeting with the various people and her return when all the attempts to make positive identifications proved futile.

Film makes an unhysterical comment on the horror of the camps as well as catching true, deep human emotions through the hopes of possibly finding a long lost loved one. The contrast of true feelings with the inhumanity of this not-so-long-ago brutal past gives the film its main force and power. Discreet lensing and editing are helpful. But the pic sometimes repeats itself so that some scenes are more padding than revealing.

But this is an engrossing document and is also well tied together. It is the type of cinema truth film that catches something vital while it is happening without losing its grip and turning into a peeping tom show. Shooting has a direct, sharp quality that helps in keeping the mood. The editing manages to keep the many people involved and the girl's reactions mostly clear and progressive. *Mosk.*

Parbeszed
(Dialog)
(HUNGARIAN)
Budapest, July 14.

Hungarofilm release of Hunnia production. With Imre Sinkovits, Anita Semjen. Istvan Sztankai. Written and directed by Janos Hersko. Camera, Gyorgy Illes; music, Imre Vince, Gyorgy

Gara. Reviewed in Budapest. Running time, 135 MINS.
Laszlo .... Imre Sinkovits
Judit .... Anita Semjen
Writer .... Istvan Sztankai

This film has as its basis a love affair that spans the troubled years of Hungarian history from 1945 to 1956. It sets out to be an epic look at this era if it is sometimes too local for international audiences. But there is curio value and interest in its handling of the touchy 1956 uprising as well as a flair for linking a couple's personal problems with those of the times. However, this is still a limited export vehicle and mainly for restricted arty and special situations more on its politico aspects than its human insight.

A militant Communist gets a good position after the war and marries a young girl who has been freed from a concentration camp. Life seems good till Stalinist types have him arrested during a purge of oldtime party men. He returns after four years to find himself estranged from his wife. She has had an affair with a progressive young writer. They try to take up again but find it difficult. Then comes the uprising and they are on opposite sides.

First it is shown as being done by those who do not want to overthrow Communism but want to go it their own way. The Russian tanks are shown coming in, and he goes over to that side. An ambiguous note is the girl remembering that Russo tanks freed her from the camp long ago. So this portion is sluffed over, and they manage to get together again.

Director Janos Hersko displays a feeling for period and skillfully uses techniques like frozen images, time ellipses and side commentary, if it all does not quite boil down to a balanced political drama. Pic probably means more on home grounds. It is acted adequately and is technically above average. *Mosk.*

Carry On Spying
(BRITISH)

Latest in profitable skein is well up to standard in ingenious yock raising; many of Old Gang to boost a slightly stronger storyline than usual; safe booking.

Warner-Pathe release of a Peter Rogers production from Anglo Amalgamated. Stars Kenneth Williams, Bernard Cribbins, Charles Hawtrey, Barbara Windsor; features Eric Pohlmann, Eric Barker, Victor Maddern, Judith Furse, Jim Dale. Directed by Gerald Thomas. Screenplay, Talbot Rothwell, Sid Colin; camera, Alan Hume; editor, Archie Ludski; music, Eric Rogers. Previewed at Anglo Private Cinema, London. Running time, 87 MINS.
Desmond Simkins ...Kenneth Williams
Harold Crump ....Bernard Cribbins
Charlie Bind .... Charles Hawtrey
Daphne Honeybutt....Barbara Windsor
Fat Man............... Eric Pohlmann
Chief .... Eric Barker
Lila .... Dilys Laye
Carstairs .... Jim Dale
Cobley .... Richard Wattis
Dr. Crow.............. Judith Furse
Milchmann .... Victor Maddern
Headwaiter .... John Bluthal

Current vogue for spy films is the latest target in the hit "Carry On" series and Talbot Rothwell and Sid Colin have dreamed up a useful enough storyline, laced with gags and situations sufficiently outrageous to provide the old Carry On hands with plenty of ammo for audience laughter. The team knows its job and does it unerringly, with Gerald Thomas helming the proceedings with his usual knowhow, which is to keep events moving so that the ultra-critical have little chance of standing back and pinpointing.

The Society for Total Extinction of Non-Conforming Humans (STENCH for short) has grabbed a secret formula and the British Operational Security Headquarters (B.O.S.H. in brief) tackles the job of getting back Formula "X" and outwitting its arch enemy, Doctor Crow. Through shortage of personnel, the assignment is handed to Simkins (Kenneth Williams), an agent in charge of training new spies, and three of his pupils.

The hapless, bungling quartet sets off for Vienna and their frenetic tracking down of the sinister Dr. Crow. The Fat Man and his accomplices lead them to the Algiers Casbah, an agent of the Society for the Neutralization of Germs and an Automatum Plant.

This thin if adequate storyline enables considerable dressing up in fantastic disguises, gunplay, double crossing and general horseplay. The film bristles with irrelevant gags, situations and zany dialog yet manages to keep a slight story form which sometimes has been abandoned in previous Carry On pix.

Best knockabout sequences take place on the Orient Express, in a Viennese restaurant, a murky quarter of the Casbah and in the Automatum Plant where the inept foursome nearly comes to a sticky end, but are rescued by good luck and the intervention of a beautiful spy. After the opening sequence, the cheerful nonsense rarely lets up. The cast supports the proceedings vigorously and with tongue firmly in check.

There are times when dialog could be sharper, but all technical departments exercise as much care

on their jobs as if they were handling a far more ambitious production. Thus, Eric Rogers' score is chirpy and Archie Budski's editing is as smooth as possible considering that episodes often crop up with seeming irrelevance. Alan Hume's photography is crisp, and special effects can take a bow for the explosions and the scenes in the Automatum plant.

Kenneth Williams' brand of "camp" comedy, while very funny in smallish doses, can pall when he has a lengthy chore as here. But Bernard Cribbins brings some useful virility to his fatuous role, Charles Hawtrey contributes his now familiar performance as the guileless one and Barbara Windsor proves a well-upholstered and perky heroine as the girl spy with a photogenic memory. Other parts are played characteristically and well by seasoned troupers, notably Eric Barker as the fussy British spy boss; Eric Pohlmann, as the heavy with dead seriousness except for a frolic in the Casbah, with Miss Windsor and Cribbins, disguised as Algerian charmers; Victor Maddern, Jim Dale, Judith Furse.

There are no signs that this series of wicket-clicking comedies is showing strain. And this adventure will stir up plenty amusement among noneggheads. *Rich.*

Miert Rosszak a Magyar Filmek
(Why Hungarian Films Are Bad)
(HUNGARIAN)
Budapest, July 14.

Hungarofilm release of Studio IV production. With Miklos Gabor, Ferenc Kallai, Zsuzsa Gordon, Tamas Major, Agi Margittai. Directed by Tamas Fejer. Screenplay, Istvan Csurka; camera, Barnabas Hegyi; music, Tihamer Vujicsics. Reviewed in Budapest. Running time, 92 MINS.
Fodor .... Miklos Gabor
Gergely .... Ferenc Kallai
Eva .... Zsuzsa Gordon
Poczik .... Tamas Major
Wife .... Agi Margittai
Alice .... Margit Bara

Attempt at satirizing general Hungarian film themes and methods lacks the snap or pace to have this jell. Also, its behind-the-scenes at a film studio would make this a difficult export item. But it has some curio value on the attempts to chide themselves through their films which is not too often seen in Eastern Bloc pix.

A down-and-out writer gets up an idea for a strong drama about the sad life of an ex-convict. It is accepted by a producer who wants to do an arty film. But the script goes through many changes as it is put before a production committee, various bureaucrats and higher ups. Would-be scenes in the proposed pic are shown in different ways and also contrasted to the varying beliefs, enthusiasms and final giving in by the writer and producer.

But all this is somewhat heavy-handed without the light touch needed to underscore the difficulties of Magyar film life. Thesps are also handicapped by the sluggish writing and direction. Brief color scene is good as are the general technical values and production dress. *Mosk.*

Old Shatterhand
(Superpanorama-Color)
(GERMAN-YUGOSLAV-FRENCH-ITALIAN)

Berlin, July 14.

Constantin release of CCC (Artur Brauner) production, made in collab with Avala-Film (Belgrade), Cri'er'on (France) and Serena (Italy). Stars Lex Barker, Pierre Brice, Guy Madison, Daliah Lavi. Directed by Hugo Fregonese. Screenplay, Ladislas Fodor, R A. Stemmle; camera (Eastmancolor), Siegfried Hold; music, Riz Ortolani; editor Alfred Srp. At Zoo Palast, Berlin. Running time 122 MINS.
Old Shatterhand...........Lex Barker
Winnetou ....Pierre Brice
Paloma ....Daliah Lavi
Bradley ....Guy Madison
Sam Hawkens.............Ralf Wolter
Bush ....Gustavo Rojo
Dixon ....Rik Battaglia
Rosemary ....Kitti Mattern
Tunjunga ....Alain Tissier

For the record, this is Artur Brauner's first big-scale western. The Berlin CCC topper thus cashes in on the amazing domestic Karl May ("the German Zane Grey") trend launched by another Berlin producer, Horst Wendlandt, two years ago.

"Old Shatterhand" may be called a Karl May western although it isn't a Karl May filmization. The exclusive filmization rights of the late author's western novels have been acquired by Wendlandt. But the popular Karl May characters (public domain) such as Old Shatterhand, Winnetou and Sam Hawkens are there. Ladislao Fodor, Hungarian-born American living in Switzerland, and Robert A. Stemmle, a German writer, dreamed up a new plot which follows about what Karl May had to say in his novels.

Supervised by Brauner, this is truly an international vehicle. Headed by Americans Lex Barker and Guy Madison, French Pierre Brice and Israeli beauty Daliah Lavi, the cast is composed of American, French, Italian, Yugoslav and German players. Similar variety of nationalities applies to the staff of this venture. And an American, Hugo Fregonese, directed.

Although one can find many faults with "Old Shatterhand," there is no denying that this "German western" will spell much coin in this country. And taking into account that action pix of this type find adherents everywhere, it should do well elsewhere, the more so because director Hugo Fregonese has given this the typical American action slant.

There is sure to be an inclination to draw comparisons between "Old Shatterhand" and its native predecessors, "Treasure of Silver Lake" and "Winnetou, Part I" two Rialto productions which have become mammoth moneymakers in Germany. And there is a difference. Brauner's horse opera concentrates more on violence and also has sex in the form of Daliah Lavi to offer. There is even an attempted rape in this film.

The screenplay is the weakest thing about "Old Shatterhand." It looks as though the various action scenes were the main thing. Typical of the rather thin script is the comedy relief which has a real corny quality. But actions fans won't find it amiss, because there is plenty of gunfire and bloodshed along this line.

Unscrupulous settlers, supported by vicious Union soldiers and officers, supply the Commanches with whisky for which these Redskins do everything. The white villains stir the feud between the Commanches and Apaches for their own benefit. There are the familiar complications and situations until justice is meted out. Old Shatterhand, the good white hero, and his friend Winnetou, chief of the Apaches, are naturally mainly responsible for the good party's victory.

Hugo Fregonese's direction of the battle sequences reveals much knowhow. Lex Barker is once more the grim but friendly hero, Old Shatterhand, while Pierre Brice is the handsome Apache chieftain. Guy Madison portrays Captain Bradley, one of the top villains. It's his Teutonic screen debut.

His performance is perhaps the most polished. The sex interest is supplied by Miss Lavi, the beautiful daughter of a white man and an Indian woman.

It's the first time that the 70m Superpanorama was used in a Karl May vehicle. There are impressive shots of the beautiful Yugoslav country which provided the "American background" for this European western. *Hans.*

London In The Raw
(BRITISH-COLOR)

Exploitation documentary which will depend mainly on its title to draw its audience.

London, July 15.

Compton-Cameo (Tony Tenser & Michael Klinger) Films presentation of a Troubadour (Arnold Louis Miller & Stanley A. Long) Films production. Written and directed by Miller; camera, (Eastman Color) Long; editor, Stephen Cross; narrator, David Gell; music, Synchro & Brull; research, Robert Gaddes. At Jacey Theatre, Piccadilly, London. Running time: 73 MINS.

The title "London In The Raw" suggests a startling expose of sin and vice in the home city of Christine Keeler, et al, and undoubtedly there's a gripping documentary to be made on such a topic. But this isn't it. The title is catchpenny but should attract some business from people expecting to get a vicarious kick out of the naughty goings on in the Metropolis. But there is little spark or inventiveness in the plodding script and lacklustre delivery by David Gell. Result is a series of tired, "on-the-surface" glimpses of the seamy side which never probe below the surface. On the plus side is some pleasantly unglaring Eastmancolor lensing by Stephen Cross.

A major snag is that though Arnold Louis Miller's script (he also directs and is co-producer) attempts to stick to a theme i.e. the loneliness and need for human contact that drives people to clip joints, hookers, night spots and so on, it constantly wanders and the theme seems to be dragged in merely to fit the pix's content. There is a rather dim feeling of "tut-tuttery" about the proceedings but with little suggestion that the makers care very deeply about the sleazy parish that they are featuring.

Co-operation has been given to the film by some known and reputable West End joints and so a somewhat whitewashed version of much' of London's jungle is the result. Among the many episodes loosely joined together with straightforward editing are visits to a body building centre, a gaming room at the 21, one or two other dance spots, a clip drinking joint, belly dancers at a City eaterie and so on. Two aspects touched on but not developed with any interest are down-and-outs drinking methylated spirits in a queasy cellar and registered drug addicts waiting the chimes of Big Ben at midnight, when they can go legitimately to an allnight chain drugstore and claim a limited, prescribed amount of dope to keep them going for another day. There is also a very unpleasant sequence showing a close up of an operation whereby men with thinning hair can have healthy hair transplanted to the bald patches. Among the brighter moments is a spirited jazz singing act by Joy Marsden at the popular Blue Angel Room.

Robert Gaddes' research has not turned up much that's new, informative or revealing and though a great deal of the location stuff has an air of authenticity some of the spots used (notably a clip drink salon) come out with an air of false respectability that is not true to most of the facts of life about such dens.

Camera has caught a few interesting faces and expressions among background human beings but too many of the characters look as if they are well aware that they are being lensed. The film will disappoint those who hope to find it a penny peepshow and, as a piece of film journalism, it lacks purpose, and a sharpness of eye and ear for the stories behind the story. Above all, it lacks courage in that its moralising is rather like a slap on the wrist with a damp lettuce leaf. *Rich.*

Banco A Bangkok
(FRENCH-COLOR-FRAN-SCOPE)

Paris, July 14.

Prodis release of PAC-CICC production. Stars Kerwin Mathews, Robert Hossin, Pier Angeli; features Dominique Wilms. Directed by Andre Hunebelle. Screenplay, Pierre Foucaud, Raymond Borel, Michel Lebrun, Richard aron, Patrice Rondard, Hunebelle from book by Jean Bruce; camera (Eastmancolor), Raymond Lemoigne; Editor, Jean Feyte. At Normandie, Paris. Running time, 115 MINS
O.S.S. 117..............Kerwin Mathews
Dr. Sinn.................Robert Hossein
Lila ....Pier Angeli
Eva ....Dominique Wilms

It looks as though the French filmmakers want their own James Bond pix, here in the form of an intrepid Yank Secret Service Man. Although color, scope and a bigger budget than usual was poured into this, it still lacks the lean perfection in mayhem, the controlled playing and outrageously piled on erotic, politico and bland seriousness of the Bond films. This may show well here and in some other foreign spots but looms as a lower-case dual feature, at best, for the U.S.

A rugged undercover man is called to an exotic Far Eastern locale to look into some strange goings-on in this case a bubonic plague seemingly brought on by anti-cholera vaccine. The man is attacked, followed, finds a lovely Eurasian and finally sees there is a secret organization dedicated to wiping out the weaklings of the world, and taking over.

Tired of East and West bumbling their fascist way of improving things is shown as not commendable. So the agent single-handedly finds the culprit, a Dr. Sinn, and manages to wipe out the whole group with the aid of two natives.

Kerwin Mathews lacks the needed stern projection to make his sexy, hardbitten superman the character needed for this pic. Pier Angeli is drawn and ill at ease as an Eurasian who falls for him while Robert Hossein is the standard menace. Even if there are some well done fights, this lags in building up complications after the inital spot angle is unfolded. On-the-spot Asian lensing is a plus.

This got the French Film Exhib Syndicate Golden Ticket Award at the recent Cannes Film Fest as a pic that would succeed at wickets and c'd not need festival or kudos. It looks to be an okay commercial entry here if it is not the sort to do much at the U. S. boxoffice where this type of pic is a staple. *Mosk.*

Ride The Wild Surf
(COLOR)

Exciting surf-riding aimed particularly at youthful trade.

Hollywood, July 24.

Columbia Pictures release of Jo and Art Napoleon production. Stars Fabian, Tab Hunter, Peter Brown, Susan Hart, Shelly Fabares, Barbara Eden, Anthony Hayes, James Mitchum. Directed by Don Taylor. Screenplay, Jo & Art Napoleon; camera (PatheColor), Joseph Biroc; music, Stu Phillips: editors, Eda Warren, Howard A. Smith: asst. director, R. Robert Rosenbaum. Reviewed at Columbia Studios, Hollywood, July 24, '64. Running time **101 MINS.**

Jody Wallis .... Fabian
Brie Matthews .... Shelly Fabares
Steamer Lane .... Tab Hunter
Augie Poole .... Barbara Eden
Chase Colton .... Peter Brown
Frank Decker .... Anthony Hayes
Lily .... Susan Hart
Eskimo .... James Mitchum
Mrs. Kilua .... Catherine McLeod
Swag .... Murray Rose
Charlie .... Roger Davis
Russ .... Robert Kenneally
Vic .... Paul Tremaine
Phil .... Alan LeBuse
TV Commentator .... John Kennell
Ally .... David Cadiente
Mr. Chin .... Yanqui Chang

A new background is provided for this latest youth market entry, the high waves of Hawaii and the wild surf riders. Ballyhoo possibilities are pegged on this spectacular sport—with all its spills and dangers—and a talented cast of young players whose appeal should spell satisfactory grosses for the Columbia release.

In a sense, the Jo and Art Napoleon production, lushly and sometimes sensationally filmed in the Islands, is a sports subject with a thin story line woven around its core. Young romance between various principals strikes a refreshing note, but interest lies mainly in the thrilling sport of riding the waves as they rise high and roar toward the beach. Exciting as many of these scenes are, too much emphasis is placed upon them without relief and such footage should be trimmed. Pic would benefit measurably by a good 15 to 20 minutes' shearing to make it more acceptable to exhibs' running time.

Narrative—by the producers—concerns a group of young surfers who travel to surfdom's Mecca, the north shore of Oahu, during their winter vacations. These include Fabian, Tab Hunter and Peter Brown, pals from California, who immediately become romantically involved with three charmers, Shelley Fabares, Susan Hart and Barbara Eden. Climax is aimed at who, among all the surfers gathered for yearly event, can outlast all others in riding in the mountainous waves on what is called "the last ride" and be acclaimed champion of the year.

Surfing scenes are adroitly handled and furnish a new slant on a sport which will be new to most inland audiences. Joseph Biroc's color photography is masterly, and direction by Don Taylor is brisk. The principals without exception are excellent, and good support is afforded by James Mitchum, Anthony Hayes, Catherine McLeod. Stu Phillips' music is a definite asset, as is Edward S. Haworth's art direction, and Eda Warren and Howard A. Smith are credited with film editing. *Whit.*

I'd Rather Be Rich
(COLOR)

Amusing romantic comedy with Sandra Dee in middle of a finance mixup. Good returns probable.

Hollywood, July 22.

Universal release of Ross Hunter production. Stars Sandra Dee, Robert Goulet, Andy Williams; features Maurice Chevalier, Hermione Gingold, Charlie Ruggles, Gene Raymond. Directed by Jack Smight. Screenplay, Oscar Brodney, Norman Krasna, Leo Townsend; camera (EastmanColor), Russell Metty; editor, Milton Carruth; music, Percy Faith; assistant director, Phil Bowles. Reviewed at Academy Award Theatre, July 21, '64. Running time, **96 MINS.**

Cynthia .... Sandra Dee
Paul .... Robert Goulet
Warren .... Andy Williams
Philip Dulaine .... Maurice Chevalier
Dr. Crandall .... Charlie Ruggles
Martin Wood .... Gene Raymond
Miss Grimshaw .... Hermione Gingold
Fred .... Allen Jenkins
Airlines Clerk .... Rip Taylor
Harrison .... Laurie Main
Albert .... Dort Clark
Cartwright .... Alex Gerry
MacDougall .... Hayden Rorke
Mrs. MacDougall .... Jill Jackson
Max .... Milton Frome

Ross Hunter has established himself as a slick light comedy producer. "I'd Rather Be Rich," is his latest effusion for Universal. It follows in the same romantic vein, and while lacking some of the schmaltz and sock of his past blockbusters, pic generally shapes as a money entry with mass appeal.

Names of Sandra Dee, Andy Williams, Robert Goulet and Maurice Chevalier provide the marquee lure for this situation affair which Hunter has embellished with his customary production values, making handsome use of extravagant settings and atmosphere. Despite film's exterior high polish, comedy is frequently forced and old-hat aspects of the plot interfere with spontaneity of movement. Enough skill is evinced, however, in handling the overall subject to keep pace at fairly quick tempo, there is a goodly sprinkling of laugh-lines and gags, and the basic situation coupled with glamor and youth-doings are refined to audience proportions.

Williams, one of the top singers in his field, makes his film bow as Sandra Dee's fiance and solos three numbers. In addition, he and Goulet, latter appearing in his second film after vaulting to fame in "Camelot" on Broadway, sing title song over the main title, effectively setting the mood. Screenplay by Oscar Brodney, Norman Krasna and Leo Townsend twirls around Miss Dee, granddaughter of fabulously wealthy Chevalier, trying to palm off Goulet as her absent finance, grounded by fog, to her supposedly dying—but doting — grandparent. Williams' arrival cues the expected mixup in trying to keep Chevalier from learning the true identities of the men.

Honors go principally to Chevalier as the conniving grandfather, who suddenly recovers from death's grip and schemes to have Goulet win his granddaughter. He's immense in this character as he periodically relapses to a supposedly dying state whenever the young ones appear.

Miss Dee hasn't much to do except look harassed but she acquits herself with her usual pert aplomb and attractively parades Jean Louis' lovely creations. Williams delivers nicely, particularly in the signing department—"Almost There," "Where Are You?" "It Had To Be You"—but Goulet suffers from unnatural stiffness. He scores mainly in his opening song number. Charlie Ruggles as the doctor, Hermione Gingold the nurse—appearing in a few amusing bits of business with Chevalier —and Gene Raymond as Chevalier's secretary, lend prominent support. Laurie Main is good as a family retainer.

Jack Smight's direction is generally bright and he benefits from expert technical assistance. Russell Metty's color photography, Alexander Golitzen and George Webb's artistic sets and decorations by Howard Bristol, Milton Carruth's tight editing and Percy Faith's music score furnish class mounting. *Whit.*

Intramuros
(The Walls of Hell)
(FILIPINO—ENGLISH SOUNDTRACK)

War film gains much of being shot on actual location; slight plot and lack of names limits to action market.

Hemisphere Pictures release of an Hemisphere-Eddie Romero production. Directed by Romero and Gerardo De Leon. Stars Jock Mahoney. Script by Romero, Ferde Grofe Jr., Cesar Amigo; photography, Felipe Sacdalan; music, Tito Areualo (no other credits provided). Reviewed at N.Y. July 23, 1964. Running time: **87 MINS.**

Lt. Sorenson .... Jock Mahoney
Nardo .... Fernando Poe Jr.
Papa .... Mike Parsons
Joker .... Oscar Roncal
Murray .... Paul Edwards Jr.
Tina .... Cecila Lopez
The Captain .... Vance Skarstead
Claude Wilson
The Guerrillas Ely Ramos Jr., Angel Buenaventura, Carpi Asturias, Arsenio Alonso, Pedro Navarro, Tommy Romulo, Fred Galang, Alex Swanbeck, Jess Montalban, Ben Sanchez, Reynaldo Sibal.

This made-in-the-Phillippines war film, which Hemisphere will release on Aug. 10 under title, "Walls of Hell," will find its proper outlet via the action market where it should do very well as this is the one aspect in which it is most outstanding.

The authenticity of its selling is the film's greatest asset (and its greatest economy)—the fortress of Fort Santiago, or as some call it —"Intramuros, the walled city of Manila." Use of newsreel footage and pre-credits narration set the scene. A huge, artillery-riddled carcass of a fortress, it has seen plenty of action since it was first built in 1574 and provides a setting that would have been close to impossible to duplicate.

"Walls of Hell" deals with last days of Intramuros — February, 1945 — when defeated Japanese troops holding Manila retreated into the walled city in a last-ditch defense, holding prisoner 10,000 Filipinos. Before the fortress was taken every Jap had been killed.

The slight script conceived by producer and co-director Eddie Romero with the help of Ferde Grofe Jr. and Cesar Amigo provides Romero and his co-director, Gerardo De Leon, with a frame of action in which they keep their few principals and many extras moving, like pawns in a chessgame of war. Although dialogue is fortunately kept to a minumum, even the little that sneaks through smacks of war-film cliches, the topper being the closing line—spoken to the battle-fatigued wounded and dying defenders—"Get the lead out. Don't you know there's a war on?"

There's no stinting on the action or the gunpowder, however. Most of the film's budget must certainly have gone to purchase of the latter. In the film's favor, besides the scene-stealing old fort, are the always present background sound of artillery barrage; suspenseful shots of parole and guerrilla tactics in the tunnels and passageways of the fort; the eloquent, silent suffering of the Filipino prisoners; and the use of English dialogue only when necessary, which isn't often.

Negative aspects are the later dubbed dialogue which allows little vocal expression; a stolidity of facial expression among most of the cast—even spreading to Jock Mahoney and the other professionals. There are occasional illogical incidents but not distracting enough to slow down the action.

Mahoney, as the American leader of the Filipino guerrillas, and Fernando Pope Jr., as an Intramuros escapee who triggers the escape of the prisoners, get most of the screen time. They're both efficient without being particularly impressive. Topping them, in smaller parts, are Mike Parsons, a younger Richard Todd type, as a seminarian-turned-soldier and Cecila Lopez, who rates little dialogue but is visually impressive as Mahoney's Filipino wife, a prisoner of the Japs. Paul Edwards gets star billing for some reason but his war correspondent part is not only unnecessary, he's sure to irritate bona fide correspondents by carrying weapons and participating in guerrilla actions.

Most of the technical credits are well handled and rate screen credits but many of them are unmentioned in the distributor's press book. Likewise, cast billings in the press book and ads vary greatly with the order they're given on the screen. *Robe.*

Karlovy Fest

Hamlet
(RUSSIAN—SCOPE)

Karlovy Vary, July 14.

Sovexport release of Lenfilm production. With Innokenti Smoktunovsky, Anastasia Vertinskaya, Mikhail Nazvanov, Elsa Radzin, Yuri Tolubeyev, Stepan Olexenko. Written and directed by Grigori Kozintzev from play by Shakespeare. Camera, Jonas Gritzius; music, Dmitri Shostakovitch. At Karlovy Film Fest. Running time, **140 MINS.**

Hamlet .... Innokenti Smoktunovsky
Ophelia .... Anastasia Vertinskaya
King .... Mikhail Nazvanov
Queen .... Elsa Radzin
Polonius .... Yuri Tolubeyev
Horatio .... Vladimir Erenberg
Laertes .... Stepan Olexenko

Russians have shown they can ably transpose Shakespeare to the screen, even without the language of the Bard, via a good "Othello" some years ago. Now comes a thoughtful "Hamlet" that has some cogent ideas, mounting and inspired acting. But if it has a knowing classic clarification about the character of the melancholy Dane, it perhaps simplifies a bit too much. And this pic adds some social touches that ultimately make him more a victim of his times than a truly tragic figure.

Thus director-adapter Grigori Kozintzev adds more depth in depicting the court of the times and even some looks at the countryside, court revels and a few outside scenes. This does not distract from Hamlet's basic torments at his father's death and the early remarriage of his mother to his uncle. The intimations that his father was murdered by his uncle comes from the ghost of his father whom he sees in full battle dress on the ramparts of Elsinore.

The mixture of real, social aspects and a scrupulous attention to rationality in Hamlet's actions, even if he does see a ghost, also are different from the usually deeper psychological interpretations handed to Hamlet more and more these days on stage and screen. This pic does have impressive settings, expert contrasting lens work and fine costuming and production values.

Innokenti Smoktunovsky has the young, smoldering blonde looks for Hamlet. However, all his acting is exteriorized, as are the soliloquies, and this sometimes clouds his unpredictable actions.

Anastasia Vertinskaya is a fragile exquisite Ophelia whose being strapped into iron underpinning for her mourning gown is an inspired touch. Her mad scene has the proper poignance. Other thesps are all fine. During this 400th Shakespeare Anni, the film might be worth arty house use abroad on its fine visuals, acting and mood even though it is mainly stripped of its intense human probing. Some cuts and changes of sequences are quite acceptable.

To dub or not to dub may be the question, but it would be hard to reconstitute the original language, and, since it is mainly its new outlooks that count, it would probably be better to slant it for arties in its original version and accept depth usage as limited. An English track might also be a needless added cost. Anyway, it is a pictorialy brilliant affair and does not force its outside scenes.
Mosk.

El Espontaneo
(The Rash One)
(SPANISH)
Karlovy Vary, July 14.
Ocean Films production and release. With Luis Ferrin, Anabel Jorda, Ana Maria Noe, Fernando Rey, Angel De Andres. Felix Ferandez. Written and directed by Jorge Grau. Camera, Federico G. Larraya; editor, Emilio Rodriguez. At Karlovy Vary Film Fest. Running time, 92 FINS.
Paco .... Luis Ferrin
Girl .... Anabel Jorda
Mother .... Ana Maria Noe
Painter .... Ferando Rey
Joaquin .... Angel De Andres
Old Man .... Felix Fernandez

Film adroitly blocks out the life of an adolescent youth who is destroyed by ambitions and desires that seem almost unattainable because of his education and background. If this is sometimes facile and contrived, often it mainly has a fine insight into character that should make this a neat language Hispano entry for the U.S. as well as possibly for some specialized spots on its general filmic know-how.

The boy is self reliant, proud

and of some obvious intelligence and personality if his training is meager. Fired from a hotel job, film details his hunt for a job and his realization that there seems no place for him at home or among his friends.

He finally learns that the glitter of bullfighting may be his only way to get needed money for his family. Without any training, he jumps into a bullring to gain attention, but is killed by the bull as a young girl he has befriended waits for him at a rendezvous.

The use of color to depict the mirage and draw of the bullring as a way out for poverty is successful. Young director Jorge Grau displays a fine feel for visual narration and handling of actors.

It is technically fine and also gives a picture of today's Spain, with its class and economic differences, without preachiness. Luis Ferrin displays a fine filmic presence and imbues the character of Paco, the youth, with charm.
Mosk.

Onna No Rekishi
(A Woman's Life)
(JAPANESE-SCOPE)

Karlovy Vary, July 14.
Toho production and release. Stars Hideko Takamine, Tatsuya Nakadai; features Tsutomu Yamazaki, Yuriko Hoshi, Akira Takarada. Directed by Mikio Naruse. Screenplay, Ryozo Kasahara; camera, Asaichi Nakai. At Karlovy Vary Film Fest. Running time. 120 MINS.
Nobuko .... Hideko Takamine
Akimoto .... Tatsuya Nakadai
.... Tsutomu Yamazaki
Koichi .... Akira Takarada
Hostess .... Yuriko Hoshi

A sentimental yarn about the trials of a woman over a period of years is given depth by the right taste, thesping and handling. This avoids soapy aspects and becomes a tender but forthright look at female problems without makewishness. This is still a subtle and simple pic on the surface, which may thus make it difficult for arty theatre chances, with playoff potentialities more probable.

A gentle, delicate woman marries a man she loves and bears him a son. He is unfaithful and later dies during the war. She manages to bring up her son only to have him killed in an auto crash after he weds a bar girl against his mother's will. She finally accepts the girl when she hears she is having a baby.

Director Mikio Naruse uses a simple but intelligent mounting that never overdoes the pathos. Each point is made with a minimum of dramatic effects which gives the film a poignance and insight. This could appeal to both regular and more distaff audiences.

Hideko Takamine has poise and dramatic flair that keep her development of character realistic. The scenes of the period are well recreated. Other acting roles are okay. Director Naruse is revealed as a most perceptive filmmaker with a dep understanding of femme with a deep understanding of femme psychology. *Mosk.*

Licem U Lice
(Face to Face)
(YUGOSLAVIAN)
Karlovy Vary, July 21.
Jadran Film production and release. With Ilija Dzuvalekovski, Hussein Cokie, Vladimir Popovic. Directed by Branko Bauer. Screenplay, Bogdan Jovanovic; camera, Branko Blazina; music, Branimir Sakac. At Karlovy Vary Film Fest. Running time, 80 MINS.
Milun .... Ilija Dzuvalekovski
Cumie .... Hussein Cokic
Ilya .... Vladimir Popovic

Crucible film appears more of interest to Eastern countries than the West on its theme of worker-director relationships within the Communist party. It fails to make the characters broad or revealing enough to give this much hope outside of the Iron Curtain countries.

A fervent Communist worker is brought up, at a meeting of the director and the worker-managers, on a charge of having written an anonymous letter to headquarters. He did not do it but the general lack of interest by most of the workers has him railroaded out of the party until others wake up and go against the director, finally voting him out rather than the worker.

Actors have presence but can not overcome the essential static qualities of this vehicle. It may be important in denouncing bureaucracy and clarifying workers' rights and more individual action in socialized countries. But its good intentions are not backed up either by depth in writing or directorial execution. *Mosk.*

Nugel Bujan
(Vice and Virtue)
(MONGOLIAN)
Karlovy Vary, July 14.
Mongolfilm production and release. With D. Icinchorloova, B. Dulamsurenova, L. Terbis. Written and directed by D. Cimit-Oser; camera, C. Senzav. At Karlovy Vary Film Fest. Running time, 70 MINS.
Mother .... D. Icinchorloova
Daughter .... B. Dulamsurenova
Monk .... L. Terbis

Mongolian film deals with pre-revolutionary corruption in the Buddhist temples of that era. It has two young people, a girl and a monk trying to find their way out of this life. Made for obvious propaganda reasons, this still has a charm in its naive techniques and unforced simplicity. Film is mainly of interest for the record since its homey look stamps it for home consumption primarily.

A young monk is attracted by a girl living with a sinful mother trying to sell her to rich men. But she manages to fight the men off and a pure friendship grows between her and the monk. When the latter finds his teacher is a liar, he leaves as does the girl.

Though made by somebody with little film training, this still makes its points adroitly, playing is direct in keeping with the general tenure of the pic. This is technically sparse but all this denotes some visual flair. *Mosk.*

Prawo I Piese
(The Law and the Fist)
(POLISH)
Karlovy Vary, July 21.
Polski State Film release of Kamera production. With Gustaw Holoubek, Jerzy Przybylski, Zbigniew Dobrzynski, Wieslaw Golas, Zofia Mrozowska. Directed by Jerzy Hoffman, Edward

Skorzewski. Screenplay, Josef Hen; camera, Jerzy Lipman; music, Krzystof Komeda. At Karlovy Vary Film Fest. Running time, 90 MINS.
Andrew .... Gustaw Holoubek
Milecki .... Jerzy Przybylski
Rudlowski .... Zbigniew Dobrzynski
Smolka .... Wieslaw Golas
Ann .... Zofia Mrozowska

This pic seems to be an attempt to make sort of a Polski Western with schematic characters and lots of action. But the lagging pace, lacklustre direction and less than robust acting relegate it mainly for the native market.

At the end of the war, Polish people move into the land vacated by the Germans. But some ruthless profiteers pose as representatives and intend to make off with loot from a deserted town they take over. One man stands up to them and foils it because he has a feeling these goods belong to the people. Situations and characters emulate oats operas but without their snap or precision. It is technically only passable. *Mosk.*

Obzalovany
(The Defendant)
(CZECHOSLOVAKIAN)
Karlovy Vary, July 21.
Czech State Film production and release. With Vlado Muller, Jaroslav Blazek, Miroslav Machacek, Milan Jedlicka, Pavel Bartl, Zora Jirakova. Directed by Jan Kadar, Elmar Klos. Screenplay, Vladimir Valenta, Kadar, Klos from story by Lenka Haskova; camera, Rudolf Milic; music, Zdenek Liska. At Karlovy Vary Film Fest. Running time, 90 MINS.
Kudrna .... Vlado Muller
Judge .... Jaroslav Blazek
Prosecutor .... Miroslav Machacek
Kudrnova .... Zora Jirakova

Taut courtroom drama has a nice wedding of talk, imagery and pacing. But it is much more than a mere suspense item. Film delves rather daringly into the economic ideological and ethical concepts of a socialist state. This may make it more difficult for wider release aboard, but it does have a theme and execution that could have it an arty theatre bet.

Practically all the action takes place during the trial with some useful flashbacks to underline a point. A man who built a needed state power plant on time is arrested for misuse of funds via premium payments to his workers which were not authorized. He felt they were needed but it seems some workers and bureaucrats abused it.

The man's plea is that some incentive was called for and he had the successful work to show for it. Nice editing, smooth direction and pacing by Jan Kadar and Elmar Klos keep this engrossing. The point is made that the judges may be passing a judgment on themselves, that one communist feels leniency towards the noted communist defendant may be misconstrued and that workers may not always be dedicated people.

Vlado Muller has a strong moral force and drive as the defendant. All other parts are well limned. The point is made that the token sentence given the head engineer, Muller, is unacceptable to him for he feels it glosses over the major issues of finding a way to make the system work.

This is an outspoken, forthright film with perhaps too much dialog for general audiences offshore. But the right selling of its theme could also help this in foreign climes. It is technically fine with excellent ensemble acting. *Mosk.*

Strainul
(The Stranger)
(RUMANIAN—C'SCOPE)
Karlovy Vary, July 21.
Bucaresti Film production and release. With Irina Petresco, Stefan Iordache, Serban Cantacuzino. Directed by Mihai Iacob. Screenplay, Titus Popovici; camera, Octavian Basti, Viorel Todan; music, Mircea Istrate. At Karlovy Vary Film Fest. Running time, **120 MINS.**
Sonia .... Irina Petresco
Andrei .... Stefan Iordache
Lucian .... Serban Cantacuzino
Romulus .... George Calboreanu
Father .... Fory Etterle

Against the background of wartime Rumania is spun an overlong tale of the friendship of two young boys from different groups. If the film does have a sincere note in the disarray of the youth from the worker class, the different events, allusions and incidents are sometimes confusing for anyone not in on Rumanian history of the time. Thus this pic mainly a language feature for abroad without the dramatic insight to give it a more universal feeling.

The poorer boy is a good student but just not able to find anything or anyone to believe in. It is the oncoming Communists who give him something to believe in. However, the propaganda is not blatant.

Film does have some nice aspects via knowing emoting by the younger players if the older ones tend to overplay their roles. It is technically good. This does show a budding individuality in Rumanian films and neater production dress plus interesting contemporary themes. It should be an okay item on its home grounds. *Mosk.*

Starci Na Chmelu
(The Hop Pickers)
(CZECH) •
(Color—Songs)
Karlovy Vary, July 21.
Czech State Film production and release. With Vladimir Pucholt, Milos Zavadil, Ivana Pavlova, Irena Kacirkova, Josef Kemr. Directed by Ladislav Rychman. Screenplay, Vratislav Blazek; camera (Agfacolor), Jan Stallich; music, Jiri Bazant, Vlastimil Hala, Jiri Malasek; choreography, Josef Konicek. At Karlovy Vary Film Fest. Running time, **90 MINS.**
Philipp .... Vladimir Pucholt
John .... Milos Zavadil
Joan .... Ivana Pavlova
Teacher .... Irena Kacirkova
Chairman .... Josef Kemr

The Czechs have probably come up with the first Eastern Bloc film musical that has charm and bounce (if a bit thin) that could hold some interest for Western playoff. It lacks the stature for big specialized handling but displays that U.S. tuner attitudes have been assimilated, rather than just copied. And it is a step forward in Eastern entertainment pix. This should do well at home and in like-minded countries if it does not run into censor troubles.

Pic is quite outspoken on adolescent morality problems, individualism and collectivism and twits slogans and bureaucracy. However, this keeps it light and gay with an ending that does not compromise. Color is rightly garish, but might have used more subtlety

in the love scenes. Pacing is lively and playing generally bright.

A group of adolescent boys and girls are picking hops one summer under school supervision. One boy wants privacy and has more personal outlooks and even manages to make an attic hideaway with filched objects. A girl discovers it and simple, innocent love develops. But a jealous more delinquent type spills all and they are suspected of immorality. To fight ostracism they really become lovers and accept school suspension and go off together while the informer has everybody turn their backs on him.

Dance numbers have the stylized, sharp movements developed from ordinary adolescent posturing and physical mannerisms as do the musical numbers. But the director's frequent cuts to show only feet or heads in the terps bits tends somewhat destroy the dance patterns. Still the dancers are disciplined. Dances and songs are catchy, if not distinguished. And for once, they move the action.

This pic, as other Czech films by newcomers, shows a new interest in style and content as well as a freshness and individual approach which are making the Czech pix the most refreshing among the Eastern countries. Film has a nice production dress and if it may still be uneven by Western standards, is a big step forward. *Mosk.*

A House Is Not A Home
Late Polly Adler's memoirs as a madam brought to screen. Spells trouble and grosses.

Hollywood, July 31.
Embassy release of Clarence Greene production. Stars Shelley Winters; features Robert Taylor, Broderick Crawford, Cesar Romero, Mickey Shaughnessy, Kaye Ballard, Ralph Taeger, Lisa Seagram, Meri Welles, Jesse White. Directed by Russell Rouse. Screenplay, Rouse & Greene, based on book by Polly Adler; camera, Harold Stine; editor, Chester Schaeffer; asst. director, William Mull; music, Joseph Weiss. Reviewed at Lytton Center Theatre, July 31, '64. Running time, **98 MINS.**
Polly Adler .... Shelley Winters
Frank Costigan .... Robert Taylor
Lucky Luciano .... Cesar Romero
Casey Booth .... Ralph Taeger
Sidonia .... Kaye Ballard
Harrigan .... Broderick Crawford
Sergt. John Riordan .. Mickey Shaughnessy
Madge .... Lisa Seagram
Lorraine .... Meri Welles
Rafferty .... Jesse White
Hattie Miller .... Connie Gilchrist
Laura .... Constance Dane
Gwen .... Allyson Ames
Angelo .... Lewis Charles
Vince .... Steven Peck
Bernie Watson .... Michael Forest
Harry .... Stanley Adams
Pete Snyder .... Dick Reeves
Dixie Keeler .... Roger Carmel
Muldoon .... J. Pat O'Malley
Sarah Ludwig .... Alice Reinheart
Max Ludwig .... Ben Astar
Bill Cameron .... Hayden Rorke
Happy Charlie .... Benny Rubin
Gabe .... Tom D'Andrea
Dorothy .... Gee Gee Galligan
Doctor .... Alex Gerry
Sam .... Edmon Ryan
Dr. Saunders .... George Casir
Bert .... Charles E. Fredericks
Matt .... Bayness Barron
Tim .... Jerry James
Dance Hall Manager .... Michael Ross
The Bald Headed Man .. Larry Barton
Oggle-eyed Man .... Steve Carruthers
Goggle-Eyed Man .... Billy Back
The Irate Wife .... June Gleason
Secretary .... Wynne Brown
A Man .... John Indrisano
Second Man .... Max Power
The Scarred Girl .... Sandra Scott
Girls: Amedee Chabot, Danica D'Hondt, Leona Gage, Sandra Grant, Diane Libby, Patricia Manning, Inga Nielson, Francine Pyne, Astri Schultz, Patricia Thomas, Raquel Welch, Edy Williams.

Picturization of late Polly Adler's autobiog of her New York bordello days when she operated the best-known tolerated spot emerges as a frank approach to subject of paid sex and will come under considerable fire from censorship and religious groups. From the opening blast made by Shelley Winters—in the Adler role—"I'm the madam of a brothel"—to the finale, illicit sex motivates the action, which also includes police payoffs and the character of Lucky Luciano. Release, a Joseph E. Levine presentation, unquestionably will benefit at the b.o. by his hard-sell campaign and film's content will evoke mass curiosity.

Film was not submitted for a Production Code seal and probably won't be. Legion of Decency has rated it as "B" (morally objectionable in part for all).

Russel Rouse and Clarence Greene—who respectively directed and produced—have gone in for sensational overtones in their screenplay, which embraces all the parlance and terms—including constant use of the words "whore" and "prostitute" — of a fancy house. They have successfully concocted a disputatious melodrama which some will deem in bad taste, while others will look at it as a true account of the seamier side of night-life. Whatever the contention of the viewer, seldom has the subject been covered with such candor. Film has been accorded rugged production and direction and likewise benefits by excellent acting, particularly by Miss Winters, whose delineation of the madam role is lively.

Narrative limns Polly Adler from her early sweatshop days in Brooklyn and her rape by its foreman to her becoming a foreman herself, backed by a bigshot bootlegger and racketeer. Her career is launched when she's asked to recruit some of her most attractive acquaintances for one of his parties and discovers easy money. She successively progresses from a simple apartment to the plushiest establishment in New York, where the topshots in town are her customers. Interwoven in plot is her romance with a young musician, who wants to marry her despite her profession but whom she refuses for this very reason. Penalty of this profession and how girls can never expect to lead a normal life is constantly pointed up, possibly as a sop to censors.

Miss Winters is a standout as she believably traces the character and a good cast backs her. Robert Taylor is the bootlegger; Cesar Romero portrays Luciano in an almost whitewashed part; Ralph Taeger appears as the musician. Kaye Ballard gets laughs as an early friend and Lisa Seagram and Meri Welles score nicely as two of Polly's "girls," whose lives end tragically. Broderick Crawford appears briefly as a politician, Mickey Shaughnessy a corrupt cop and Jesse White a conniving politician. Balance play their roles well.

Capable technical credits include Alexander Roelofs' very suitable art direction; Harold Stine's camera work; Edith Head's beautiful costumes; Chester Schaeffer's editing. Joseph Weiss' music score is especially atmospheric. *Whit.*

Station Six-Sahara
(BRITISH-MADE)

Sex melodrama with name of Carroll Baker to spark good chances in general market.

Allied Artists release of Victor Lyndon production. Stars Carroll Baker; features Peter Van Eyck, Ian Bannen, Denholm Elliott, Jorg Felmy, Biff McGuire. Directed by Seth Holt. Screenplay, Bryan Forbes, Brian Clemens; camera, Ray Sturgess; music, Ron Grainer; editor, Alastair McIntyre; asst. director, David Stacknell. Reviewed at Allied Artists Studios, July 30, '64. Running time, **97 MINS.**
Catherine .... Carroll Baker
Kramer .... Peter Van Eyck
Fletcher .... Ian Bannen
Macey .... Denholm Elliott
Martin .... George Felmy
Santos .... Mario Adorf
Jimmy .... Biff McGuire
Sailor .... Harry Baird

"Station Six-Sahara" is a sex melodrama, filmed in the Libyan Desert with the star name of Carroll Baker to give it importance in the American market, particularly in light of her sex-symbol role in the currently-released "Carpetbaggers." Story premise of a sexpot arriving at an isolated desert oil pipeline station where five lonely men have only thing in common—the nagging need for a woman—has been generally well developed and provides strong exploitation potential.

British-produced by Victor Lyndon and Seth Holt's direction deftly narrating the Bryan Forbes-Brian Clemens screenplay, good interest is early sustained despite fact that Miss Baker does not appear for first 42 minutes. Limited confines of the rude station settings puts emphasis strictly upon yarn unfoldment and permits Holt, to display his helming mettle while audience awaits entrance of femme star, only woman in cast. With her entry into plot, when a car roars out of the night and eager hands, after it crashes, lift her seductive figure out of the wreckage, attention picks up perceptibly as the men react in varying degrees and kind to her presence.

In tenor, story actually is an incident in the lives of the men as their strained and bitter existence is interrupted by a golden-tressed goddess who briefly upsets their thoughts and actions. With her sudden death — murdered by her divorced husband who was in the accident with her and cannot bear the thought of her leaving him for one of the others as he lies in his sick-bed—the men return to their former life of mutual contempt. Lack of an exciting climax reduces dramatic impact, but first-rate performances right down the line help overcome this fault.

Miss Baker, in what amounts actually to a smaller role, feelingly delineates this key character and makes her work count. Peter Van Eyck, in charge of the station which he operates with typical cold Teutonic efficiency, is smooth and convincing. Jorg Felmy, another German with icy self-control, underplays his role for excellent effect. Ian Bannen, a Scotsman with a sour sense of humor, and Denholm Elliott, a paper-spined Englishman who lives on memories of the desert war in World War II, persuasively portray their respective parts, and Mario Adorf, as a French-Spaniard, and Biff McGuire, the jealous ex-husband, offer good support. One of the best sequences in film, tensely enacted, is a poker session interrupted by femme's arrival.

Technical credits u n i f o r m l y furnish strong assists. Ray Sturgess' photography, Jack Stephens' art direction, Alastair McIntyre's editing and Ron Grainer's music score are definite assets. *Whit.*

Sing and Swing
(BRITISH—MUSICAL)

Quiet for a rock 'n' roller, this British import could make good filler due to short running time and harmless theme.

Universal release of a Three Kings Film (Lance Comfort) production. Directed by Comfort. Features David Hemmings, Joan Newell, Veronica Hurst, Ed Devereaux, Heinz Burt, Jennifer Moss, John Pike, Steven Marriott. Musical specialties by Kenny Ball and his Jazzmen, Gene Vincent, The Outlaws, Patsy Ann Noble, James Cavell. Original story, screenplay, Lyn Fairhurst; camera, Basil Emmott; film editor, John Trumper; sound, R. T. Macphee. C. Le Messurier; songs, Joe Meek, Norrie Paramor, Bob Barratt; asst. director, John Stoneman. Reviewed at Universal, N.Y., Aug. 3, '64. Running time, 78 MINS.

Dave Martin .... David Hemmings
Jill .... Jennifer Moss
Phil .... John Pike
Ron .... Heinz Burt
Ricky .... Steven Marriott
Margaret Martin .... Joan Newell
Herbert Martin .... Ed Devereaux
Kay Miller .... Veronica Hurst
Barbara .... Penny Lambirth
Mike Moss .... Peter Glaze
Mark Watson .... David Brner
Bob .... Anthony Ashdown
Bingo .... Douglas Ives
Columnist .... Nancy Spain

Made in England last year as "Live It Up," this tuner has been imported by Universal, evidently as a filler. They've skedded it as a December release.

Best thing about "Sing and Swing" is that, for a rock 'n' roller, it's comparatively quiet. Must be that famous British undertatement. Producer-director Lance Comfort has pulled quite a feat, finding space for 11 musical numbers in a 78-minute feature, although none of them are likely to push the Beatles off the charts. What space is left is taken up by Lyn Fairhurst's loosely-knit script about aspiring young talent and that "first big chance."

In this magic, make-believe world, rock 'n' roll combos are booked only into the smartest supper clubs. Like Dave Clark at the Persian Room, so to speak. And everyone quits work to grab their electric guitar whenever the mood comes, which is often.

Bit of originality is introduced with possibly rock 'n' roll's first bleached-blonde singer. A male singer. Well, it didn't hurt wrestling, did it? Heinz Burt, the peroxide practitioner, is something of a mystery. He has about two words of dialog but does all the singing of the former ("Live It Up") title number. Could be, the singing is dubbed.

Technical aspects are generally good. The musical numbers, once the numbness takes effect, sound alike.

David Baucr, as an American film producer, tells his publicity gal (Veronica Hurst) that all successful films have "Don't" in the title. This one doesn't. *Robe.*

First Men In The Moon
(BRITISH-COLOR)

Highly exploitable science-fiction comedy-drama.

London, Aug. 4.

BLC-Columbia release of a Charles H. Schneer production. Stars Edward Judd, Martha Hyer, Lionel Jeffries. Features Eric Chitty, Betty McDowall, Miles Malleson, Gladys Henson, Marne Maitland, Hugh McDermott. Directed by Nathan Juran. Special effects director, Ray Harryhausen. Screenplay, Nigel y Kneale, Jan Read, from H. G. Wells' novel; camera (Technicolor), Wilkie Cooper; editor, Maurice Rootes; music, Laurie Johnson. Reviewed at Columbia Theatre, London. Running time, 102 MINS.

Arnold Bedford .... Edward Judd
Cavor .... Lionel Jeffries
Kate Callender .... Martha Hyer
Gibbs .... Eric Chitty
Maggie .... Betty McDowall
Registrar .... Miles Malleson
Glushkov .... Lawrence Herder
Matron .... Gladys Henson
Dr. Tok .... Marne Maitland
Challis .... Hugh McDermott
U.N. Astronauts...... Gordon Robinson, Sean Kelly, John Murray Scott

Ray Harryhausen and his special effects men have had another high old time in Charles H. Schneer's Panavision, Technicolor piece of science-fiction hokum filmed in Dynamation. "First Man In The Moon," following Schneer's other all-action pix, is an exploiteer's dream. Family audiences should flock to the wickets. It is an astute blend of comedy, occasional thrills and special effects work. Film is a good example of the kind of fare that television cannot hope to match in the forseeable future.

Picture is based on H. G. Wells' novel and has been neatly undated. The novelist's fertile and prophetic imagination, crazy though some of

it may have seemed when his works were scribed, is a gift to screenplay writers. And Schneer hired two of the best in the sci-fi business in Nigel Kneale and Jan Read. They have turned out a good, solid job, though the film's ending tends to fall apart a bit. Apart from the intended comedy both the director (Nathan Juran) and the cast have treated it with essential seriousness.

Yarn starts with the arrival on the moon of three United Nations astronauts (Yank, Russian and British) amid world excitement. Pride of the astros receives a jolt when they find a small, faded Union Jack on the moon, together with a yellowed manuscript (a bailiff's receipt) with a scrawl which claims the discovery of the moon on behalf of Queen Victoria—date, 1899.

In a home, an aged man (Edward Judd) is tracked down by UNO investigators. He tells them the incredible story of how he, his fiancee and an eccentric professor actually did land on the moon. He and the girl escaped. The prof remained to continue his scientific investigations.

Judd, an aspiring playwright, partnered the professor on the crazy expedition which took off almost by accident, and his story told of adventures with the Selenites, dwarfs who live under the moon's surface, and of danger from the giant moon-cow and other unknown terrors. All this adds up to acceptable adventure stuff but sidetracked somewhat are the equally fascinating attempts of the professor and the moon's inhabitants to communicate. Allowing for dramatic license, the fact that the unknown journey to the moon may well be cracked within the lifetime of modern babes, gives an added point to the meeting of representatives of the earth and outer space.

But it's the physical adventures that will give the biggest kick to audiences.

The three principals play second fiddle to the special effects and art work, which are impressive in color, construction and animation. But Edward Judd gives a stalwart performance and in the earlier scenes shows a nice sense of comedy. Martha Hyer provides decoration and a hint of romance charmingly while Lionel Jeffries as the dedicated, whacky professor is immensely good fun in his eccentricity. At the same time, he's extremely credible when he seeks to make contact with the minds of the Moon Men. There is an unobtrusive score by Laurie Johnson and some first rate photography by Wilkie Cooper, not only on the moon, but in his delightful lensing of the attractive Victorian village of Dymchurch.

Take it as you like—as an out-and-out schoolboy adventure, or as a springboard for another, more serious probe of potential Earth-Moon relationship—Schneer's production still stands up as a healthy prospect. *Rich.*

Locarno Fest

Demanty Noel
(Diamonds of the Night)
(CZECHOSLAVAKIAN)

Locarno, July 28.

Czech State Film production and release. With Antonin Kumbera, Ladislav Jansky. Directed and edited by Jan Nemec. Screenplay, Arnost Lustig, Nemec from book by Lustig; camera, Jaroslav Kucera. At Locarno Film Fest. Running time, 64 MINS.

First Boy .... Antonin Kumbera
Second Boy .... Ladislav Jansky

This film is more a study of mood and atmosphere (an expressionistic rendering of a time when man gave vent to beastly tactics) than a forthright story production. It deals with the escape of two young boys from a concentration camp convoy during the last World War. It is grave, taut and jolting. Thus this is mainly an art item for abroad.

Picture also shows Western influences in mixing two levels of time during the boys' attempt to dash to freedom. They are reduced to primitivism and pic does not spare their bruises, fears and hurts in sharp scenes that display their inner feelings. Thus when one boy goes to a peasant hut to ask for bread he thinks of killing the women.

Then a group of doddering old men give chase and catch them and keep them in an inn while they feast and dance. They let them go and they run on as the pic ends. Director Jan N e m e c shows an ability to put man's instinct into visual terms.

It is starkly lensed for added bite with acute and cogent performances by the two boys on the run. The mixture of styles and forcefully. A definite talent, pictorial flair and narrative power are unveiled with this first pic by Nemec. He should be heard from at future festivals. *Mosk.*

Vysoka Zed
(The High Wall)
(CZECHOSLAVAKIAN)

Locarno, July 28.

Czech State Film production and release. With Radka Dulikova, Vit Olmen, Helena Kruzikova, Vaclav Lohnisky. Directed by Kare Kachnya. Screenplay, Jan Prochazka, Kashnya; camera, Josef Vanis; music, Jan Novak. At Locarno Film Fest. Running time, 70 MINS.

Jitka .... Radka Dulikova
Sick Ore .... Vit Olmer
Mother .... Helena Kruzikova
Janitor .... Vaclav Lohnisky

Film is a tender moppet film that also sustains some adult interest. About a 12-year-old girl's first stirring of love, it has telling insight, good pacing and a disarming sentimentality that never falls into bathos or forced pathos. It could be a nice playoff or specialized item for some foreign spots. Also it looks a natural for children's programs in theatres or on tv.

The girl has discovered a paralyzed young man in a hospital. She goes to see him every day. He is learning how to walk again after an accident and she helps, infuriates and generally sustains him. But she never is conscious that there is some deeper feeling in it for her.

The girl's poise, lack of self-consciousness and self reliance build a nice character. It's helped by Radka Dulikova's fine presence. A budding actress is definitely unveiled while Vit Omer is acceptable as the young man who does not realize the little girl's feelings.

But when she sees him with his fiancee and has a tantrum, this is quickly dispelled by a new interest, as children are prone to do. Director Karel Kachnya displays an expert flair in this fragile tale.

The other children and adults are all good. Well textured lensing is also an asset. The highlighted whites of the hospital grounds and the harsher grays of her outside life make a fine balance to this simple, but taking pic. *Mosk.*

Os Verdes Anos
(The Green Years)
(PORTUGUESE)

Locarno, July 28.
Antonio Cunha Telles production and release. With Rui Gomes, Isabel Ruth, Paulo Renato. Written and directed by Paulo Rocha with dialog by Nuno Braganca. Camera, Luc Mirot; editor, Margareta Manys; music, Carlos Parades. At Locarno Film Fest. Running time, 85 MINS.
Julio .... Rui Gomes
Ilda ....,........ Isabel Ruth
Alfonson .... Paulo Renato

Portugal, with little feature pic production, is little known at most film fests. But here is one film that unveils a new director with fine narrative skill and something to say. If its allusions may be somewhat too private for good art of theatre possibilities abroad, this has definite language chances and also may do for specialized spots. Film has sensitive feeling for young love and the attempts by youths to find themselves, as well as a feel for the country and its atmosphere.

An 18-year-old peasant youth comes to Lisbon to work for a shoemaker. He lives with his uncle who has found an okay niche for himself by concessions and self-effacement but has developed cynicism. The boy meets a young gal of 19, and love blooms. But she refuses marriage, because of his position. In a fit of inarticulate moral and physical suffocation, he kills her and runs amok.

The relations between the two young people are done with understanding and revelation. The city is also lovingly shown as is a sort of despair that attacks young people with little chance for achieving anything.

Perhaps this is a bit too muted and an exceptional case, but writer-director Paulo Rocha has managed to give this a more universal intensity by his knowing probing of character and a fine filmic flair. It is technically good and offers some promise for Portuguese pix. Acting is good and the music a fine counterpoint. *Mosk.*

Midareru
(Yearning)
(JAPAN)

Locarno, July 28.
Toho production and release. Stars Hideko Takamine, Yuzo Kayama. Directed by Mikio Naruse. Screenplay, Zenzo Hatsuyama; camera, Jun Yasumoto; music, Ichiro Saito. At Locarno Film Fest. Running time, 95 MINS.
Reiko .... Hideko Takamine
Koji .... Yuzo Kayama

After an involved start, about supermarket competition against small shop owners, this develops into a tender, knowing look at a love affair between a 37-year-old widow and her 25-year-old brother-in-law. But the effect is cumulative, and this will stand little chance in the Yank marts. This remains mainly a home item.

Whether a shop owner will commit suicide when he sees his business slipping may be true, but the early part of pic wastes too much time on this. Then it centers on the widow who has created a fairly successful store for the family. Now the young brother-in-law confesses his love but the remainder of the family wants to get rid of her, and turn the shop into a supermarket.

She remains true to her husband's memory and repulses the boy, even if she is attracted. The boy follows her and she admits she feels something for him but can not give in.

Last part of the film has a touching insight into reactions and feelings. Hideko Takamime displays a perfect balance between emotion and action that keeps her from being mawkish. Yuzo Kayama has the right intensity as the young man.

This is technically excellent and director Mikio Naruse displays top talent. He promises to emerge as one of the more interesting Japanese filmmakers. *Mosk.*

Den Stchastia
(A Day of Happiness)
(RUSSIAN SCOPE)

Locarno, July 28.
Sovexport release of Lenfilm production. Stars Tamara Semina, Alexei Batalov, Valentin Zoubkov. Directed by Jossif Heifitz. Screenplay, Youri Guerman, Heifitz; camera, Guenrikh Marandjian. At Locarno Film Fest. Running time, 100 MINS.
Choura .... Tamara Semina
Alexandre .... Alexei Batalov
Husband .... Valentin Zoubkov

Film is a perceptive look at the eternal triangle between a wife, husband and a man she has met in the street. But being Russian, it also brings in issues of professions, work and careers. Somewhat slow, it is primarily for specialized situations abroad with art or playoff possibilities very dobutful.

A young doctor "picks up" a married woman in the street. It is a harmless flirtation. Then she goes home to her husband just back from a geological tour. He decides to miss another trip to be with her but this leads to a tragdy in his crew, and he loses his job.

Then the doctor comes back into her life and love develops as the husband sinks lower. She finally decides to leave both and go back to teaching. The film ends on that note.

Direction builds a nice observation of the people and their everyday lives with a good serio-comic flair. But too many side issues make this uneven though it does maintain interest. Players are personable. It shows some easing in personal pic content from Russia with fine technical qualities. *Mosk.*

Nappali Sotetseg
(Darkness At Daytime)
(HUNGARIAN)

Locarno, July 28.
Hungarofilm release of Hunnia production. With Lajos Basti, Erika Szegedi, Ilona Beres, Ferenc Ladanyi, Margit Makay. Written and directed by Zoltan Fabri from book by Boris Palotai. Camera, Janos Toth; music, Peter Eotvos, Janos Gonda. At Locarno Film Fest. Running time, 100 MINS.
Naday .... Lajos Basti
Agnes .... Erika Szegedi
Potyi .... Ilona Beres
Janics .... Ferenc Ladanyi
Mother .... Margit Makay

Highly mannered study of a May-December romance during the last World War remains too contrived and cold to make it come off. Sleek direction keeps it lifeless. This appears primarily a home item with foreign possibilities dubious.

A middleaged writer falls in love with a young Jewish girl and gives her his daughter's identity papers to keep her. But the daughter is wanted for underground activities and the Jewish girl allows herself to be jailed for it in spite of his protestations.

The writer tells the story 20 years later and still wonders if he was a coward. Irony falls short as the direction academically plays for feeling and deeper characterization.

Also crimping the film is Lajos Basti's unfeeling, posturing performance as the writer. Erika Sezegedi and Ilona Beres are more telling and true as the mistress and daughter respectively. It has technical assurance but director Zoltan Fabri shows he is wasting fine filmic knowhow on a story and theme that he does not feel. Chalk it up as a gifted director searching for a story. *Mosk.*

Comizi D'Amore
(Study of Love)
(ITALIAN)

Locarno, July 28.
Arco Film release of Alfredo Bini production. Directed by Pier Paolo Pasolini. Commentary, Alberto Moravia, Cesare Musatti; camera, Mario Bernardo, Tonio Delli Colli; editor, Nino Baragli. At Locarno Film Fest. Running time, 90 MINS.

Cinema Truth pix have come late to Italy and seem a bit old hat generally, if new there. Here, offbeat filmmaker Pier Paolo Pasolini takes a tape recorder and camera around Italy to ask people about love. Result is talky, only intermittently revealing picture. It might have some pull for hardtops on its home grounds but not much for abroad.

All walks of people talk of love, prostitution, homosexuality, married and non-marital love, etc. Writer Alberto Moravia and psychologist Cesare Musatti are also worked in to comment on the idea. But it does not add up to much.

Maybe the drawback is that mostly exhibitionists accept the appearance of the camera. Pasolini does the questioning adequately but does not really get something new or drastically revealing. Lensing is flat and grainy. *Mosk.*

Gade Uden Ende
(Street Without End)
(DANISH)

Locarno, July 28.
Rialto Film production and release. With Sunny Nielsen, Zellita Torki, Connie Ohlsen, Poul Jacobsen. Written and directed by Moegens Vemmer. Camera, Bent Paulsen; editor, Bodil Andersen. At Locarno Film Fest. Running time, 80 MINS.
Sunny .... Sunny Nielsen
Lis .... Zellita Torki
Connie .... Connie Ohlsen
Jorgen .... Poul Jacobsen

This is a cross between a cinema truth and an expose treating that oldest of professions, prostitution. Film has a tendency of repeating itself, giving unnecessary aspects of a prostie's life. It thus appears more an exploitation item than an arty possibility abroad.

Pic does refrain from being over-explicit about actual carryings-on but appears slogging in its insistence on the degradation of it all without any true insights, even if the commentary is from real interviews with people living off vice.

The point of its unsavory, almost degenerate, aspects is also heavily drawn but appears more sanctimonious and heavyhanded in revealing this seamy world.

But there is obviously a sincerity about it. Solid, grimy lensing makes it clear there is nothing romantic or savory about this world.

But the mixture of styles, over-indulged reiterations and one-note feeling film has bogs down and loses true probing sifnificance. However, it has some value as a documentary. *Mosk.*

Le Schiave Esistano Ancora
(Slaves Still Exist)
(ITALIAN-COLOR)

Locarno, July 28.
GE-SI Cinematografical-Films Agiman production and release. Directed and written by Folco Quilici, Mario Malenotti. Camera (Eastmancolor), Aldo Nascimbene, Nanni Sacrpellini, Aldo Tonti, Adalberto Albertini, Giuseppi Pinori; editor, Eralda Da Roma. At Locarno Film Fest. Running time, 90 MINS.

Film tries to be a more reserved "Monde Cane" in parading its cameras around central Africa, India and the Near East to show that actual slavery and sales of humans still exist today. It uses UN articles and talks by noted journalists and writers to make its points. So it has some exploitation and human documentary interest for playoff and specialized chances abroad if some contrived and jolting footage also slant this for exploitation aspects.

The sale of children, harems (including some footage sold to the makers of an English woman who was in one), clandestine footage via hidden cameras and long focal length lenses to show actual sales of people are the more telling episodes of this meandering affair.

Then there are some questionable sequences like giant land crabs fondling human skeletons, supposedly of escaped slaves, and a re-enactment of slave tests to prove their bravery.

This masquerades as an expose affair with too many bits obviously thrown in for effect. It lacks the out and out vulgarity and slick lensing of "Monde Cane." This wants it both ways, as a human plea against this existence of barbarism and shock footage for its own sake.

It is well lensed in color, and black and white, for some night scenes. Film may pack the curio values to draw audiences on the heels of its predecessors. It will need savvy handling and hardsell but might be worth it. *Mosk.*

New York Sur-Mer
(New York On The Sea)
(FRENCH-U.S.)

Locarno, July 28.
SICA-Embassy production and release. Conceived and shot by Pierre-Dominique Gaisseau with assistance of Yan Yorrors, Jean Hamon. Commentary written and spoken by Philippe Labro; editor, Georges Arnstam. At Locarno Film Fest. Running time, **72 MINS.**

Ethnologist and anthropologist Pierre-Dominique Gaisseau made the Oscar-winning documentary on a trip through stone age New Guinea, "The Sky Above." Here he applies these outlooks to New York and insists mainly on ethnic remnants in this great cosmopolitan city. Result is somewhat tedious and one-sided, and is more exotic than a true or new look at Gotham.

So there is Chinatown, and then Jewish communities, Lithuanian, Ukrainian, Italian, Puerto Rican, Negro, etc. with all touched on and the insistence that they are clinging to old habits before finally giving in and becoming simple Americans like everybody else. Commentary has a tendency to be grandiloquent at times.

There is some fine lensing and exoticism in this approach but it could almost be done in any big international city. The immensity of Manhattan buildings is the film's keynote.

This does have a foreign-eye view of New York but gives very little of what it is actually like. It might be a little like only filming ancient Roman ruins in the Rome of today and saying it is an essay on modern Rome.

Pic was partly financed by Embassy Pictures in the U.S., which will distribute it there. It appears mainly a good supporting item, with some shearing called for. It also needs a more discreet commentary in English. The one shown here is the French version. English version is called "Only One New York." *Mosk.*

Goodbye In The Mirror
(ITALIAN)

Locarno, July 28.
Bobina production and release. With Rosa Pradell, Franco Volpino, Diane Stainton, Barbara Apostal, Charlotte Bradley. Written and directed by Storm De Hirsch. Camera, Giorgio Turi; editors, Miss De Hirsch. Louis Brigante; music, Norman Blagman Jeffey Menkes. At Locarno Film Fest. Running time, **80 MINS.**
Maria .... Rosa Pradell
Marco .... Franco Volpino
Berenice .... Diane Stainton
Sarah .... Charlotte Bradley

Constantly moving hand-held camera and too fragmented cutting and scenes mar this look at an almost thirtyish American girl living in Rome and looking for love and adventure. This pic therefore appears a difficult commercial item

with only some specialized arty or school showing its main bet.

Yet out of all these slivers of film, femme writer-director Storm DeHirsch manages to etch a handful of portraits that ring true if rarely thoroughly explored or allowed to come to life in teeming Rome. Camera literally roams non-stop over feet, features, objects, streets, etc. to allow only general impressions.

The girl permits two others to live in her apartment, a loose British girl and an intense Swede. But she is singularly ungenerous and slightly hysterical. And she soon throws them out. She has an affair with a good looking Italian boy, ruined when he finds she has been out all night with another. She is thus left alone and probably ready to go home.

Film points up the girl's lack of roots and disdain of foreigners whom she only uses. It also depicts as dabbling in arts without talent. It is a worthy theme as Yanks emerge the great travelers. However, this is a bit bogged down in too specialized and personalized outlooks.

Blown up from 16m film, this vehicle is still technically good with music sly, inquisitive, witty and a solid asset in underlining and counterpointing the erratic action. Acting is uneven. But Miss Storm has some visual ideas that might be more explicit when there is a better combining of style and content. As is, this is just too uneven for feature pic length. It might have been a sharp, incisive short. *Mosk.*

Limonodavy Joe
(Lemonade Joe)
(CZECH—COLOR)

Locarno, July 28.
Czech State Film production and release. With Karel Fiala, Olga Schoberova, Xveta Fialova, Rudolf Deyl, Milos Kopecky. Directed by Oldrich Lipsky. Screenplay, Jiri Brdecka; camera (Agfacolor), Vladimir Novotny; music, Jan Rychlik, Vlastimil Hala. At Locarno Film Fest. Running time, **95 MINS.**
Lemonade Joe .... Karel Fiala
Winnifred .... Olga Schoberova
Tornado Lou .... Xveta Fialova
Doug Badman .... Rudolf Deyl
Hogofogo .... Milos Kopecky

The people who made this spoof of American westerns obviously understand and love this type of pic. But if it is well imitated, with the right exaggerations, this eventually gets repetitious. Hence, judicious pruning is called for and its chances abroad seem mainly for specialized or playoff spots, hardsell needed for best results.

So it begins with a bangup saloon fight replete with timid pianist, brutes and the sexy singer. Into this scene comes a preacher with a comely daughter and Lemonade Joe, a white-clad avenger of wrongs who mops up the place. He takes only a soft drink and faints if he touches alcohol.

A new saloon serving only soft drinks is begun and gets all the play. Meanwhile, the singer has also fallen for Joe. But a new underworld tough is brought in for further complications till the happy ending. Color seems like a different tint for each scene which is effective.

The characters have the right concept of good and evil, but the killings always lead to the people getting up again. After a rapid beginning in western sets, pic begins to repeat. *Mosk.*

The System
(BRITISH)

Slight but amusing and often perceptive glimpse of youth at the seaside. Minor star draw, but both the pic and Oliver Reed are worth noting.

London, Aug. 4.
BLC release of a Bryanston presentation of a Kenneth Shipman — Michael Winner production. Stars Oliver Reed, Jane Merrow, Barbara Ferris, Harry Andrews, Julia Foster; features Ann Lynn, Guy Doleman, Andrew Ray, John Porter Davison, Clive Colin Bowler, John Alderton, Derek Nimmo, Jennifer Tafler. Directed by Winner. Screenplay, Peter Draper; camera, Nicolas Roeg; editor, Fred Burnley; music, Stanley Black. Reviewed at Columbia Theatre London. Running time, **90 MINS.**
Tinker .... Oliver Reed
Nicola .... Jane Merrow
Suzy .... Barbara Ferris
Lorna .... Julia Foster
Ella .... Ann Lynn
Philip .... Guy Doleman
Willy .... Andrew Ray
Grib .... John Porter Davison
Sneakers .... Clive Colin Bowler
Sammy .... Iain Gregory
David .... David Hemmings
Michael .... Mark Burns
James .... Derek Nimmo
Sylvie .... Pauline Munro
Larsey .... Harry Andrews
Jasmin .... Susan Burnet
Stan Atty .... Victor Winding
Sonia .... Jennifer Tafler

"The System" is the kind of modest British picture that might so easily have turned up as a 60-minute program on television. It is a slight anecdote, not explored as fully as it might have been, but made worthwhile by some bright direction, lensing and acting from young, eager talent. It would be leading with the chin to go all out and recommend it strongly for exhibs. But those who do book it, preferably with a strong, contrasted action film, will have a program that they'll not regret. The snag for Overseas is that it has no marquee appeal. However, the male lead, Oliver Reed, seems likely to rectify that situation if he gets the breaks.

Screenplay by Peter Draper concerns the activities of a bunch of local lads at a seaside resort who every summer work a system by which they 'take' the holidaying femmes for a lighthearted emotional ride. There's nothing vicious about it. It's simply young men in search of goodtime romances that will have to make do in their memories during the dreary offseason winter months. The youths work in the best spots for contacting the gals—the holiday photography shop, the cafes, the dance hall, the bowling alleys, and so on. Sometimes the visiting girls fall too heavily, but nobody gets hurt very much.

Tinker (Oliver Reed), a young beach photographer, is leader of the "come up and see my pad" gang. The film tells how, one summer, he himself gets taken. He falls heavily in love with a well-loaded, well-stacked fashion model, and that's against the "rules," even when the girl reciprocates. But the seven day romance enables him to see himself straight for once and realize that he's leading an aimless life. He is hurt, but there's a hint that he's passed an emotional crisis.

This thin yarn is an adroitly spun concoction of comedy, sentiment and pathos which, however, needs a strong sub-plot to sustain interest. Draper has decked out his situations with some neat dialog. mostly of the flip-talk variety, but there are one or two moments of genuine emotional depth between the young lovers. Some of the other characters, too, give body to the wispy story. Michael Winner has directed with a keen ear and eye for the behavior of modern youth. He and the screenplay also offer some obvious but realy ironic comment on life at a typical seaside resort. A wedding reception, a local dance, a beach party, the clash between the young roughneck hero and the uppity friends of the rich chick, and beach and bathing scenes are all displayed observantly and amusingly though there's some padding.

Reed, the brash but likeable young cut-rate Romeo, could be a considerable find. Behind his dark and rather glowering good looks, there's a wide mixture of smart alecky, genuine humor and animalism.

Most of the fresh young talent around him seems, at the moment, fairly undeveloped, but they take what opportunities are available. Jane Merrow is a promising, cool young thesp while Ann Lynn is expert in another of her studies of suffering, frustrated young womanhood. Barbara Ferris, John Alderton, David Hemmings, Andrew Ray and Jennifer Tafler also have their moments. Julia Foster, as a fluffy naive pickup, has only one short scene in which she is adequate.

A big plus is the lensing of Nicolas Roeg, whose inquisitive camera brings the seaside scene to graphic life and also gets some fine eventide effects across the sea. Stanley Black's score is workmanlike but the three songs, played by various groups, don't have overmuch pop chemistry. *Rich.*

East of Sudan
(BRITISH-COLOR)

Action-packed dualler making sound booking for easygoing audiences.

London, Aug. 5.
BLC release of a Charles H. Schneer production for Columbia Pictures. Stars Anthony Quayle, Sylvia Syms. Features rest of cast. Directed by Nathan Juran. Screenplay, Jud Kinberg; camera (Technicolor), Wilkie Cooper; editor. Ernest Hosler; music, Laurie Johnson. Reviewed at Columbia Private Theatre, London, Aug. 4. '64. Running time. 85 MINS.
Richard Baker ..... Anthony Quayle
Margaret Woodville ...... Sylvia Syms
Murchison .... Derek Fowlds
Asua .... Jenny Agutter
Kimrasi .... Johnny Sekka
Major Harris .... Harold Coyne
Gondoki .... Joseph Layode
Witch Doctor .... Ellario Pedro
Aide .... Desmond Davies
Second Major .... Derek Bloomfield
Arab .... Edward Ellis

Plenty of action in this workmanlike dualler, but not much overseas star appeal and much of the effect of the pic is lost because of its obvious studio setting. There is none of the stench and steam of the jungle and though special effects man Ted Samuels has contributed some useful tricks the whole affair is artificial. There is a lot of obvious processing, back projection and stock animal shots. The easygoing cinema patron will not worry unduly, however, and

be satisfied with the vicarious kick of sharing the actors' adventurous trek from Batash down the river to Khartoum.

The period is the 1880s, with the Sudanese Moslems fiercely resisting General Gordon in his attempts to stamp out slave trading. With Batash sacked, four refugees start a perilous journey to Khartoum. They are Anthony Quayle, an Army trooper, resourceful and rough and ready, a greenhorn of a lieutenant (Derek Fowlds) and Sylvia Syms, a prim, slightly priggish governess with her native charge (Jenny Agutter).

Quayle, Fowlds and Miss Syms are soon at each other's throats but find a common link in saving their skins in the tricky problems ahead. Quayle is the natural leader and he copes with a sinking boat and the other perils, though hampered by the inefficiency of Fowlds and difficulties arising from the petulant behavior of the governess. Said perils include skirmishes with various wild animals, the near-death of the young native girl when she hurtles into some falls, plus the unwelcome dangers of Moslems, slave traders and unfriendly natives. Eventually, with admirable aplomb, Quayle and Fowlds blow up an arsenal, rescue beleaguered British troops and run up the Union Jack. In between, Quayle and Miss Syms predictably find their mutual irritation turning into romance.

The stiff upper-lip dialog and somewhat coy joking supplied by screenwriter Jud Kinberg is probably admirably in period, but it makes for some heavy going and not a few unintentional yoks. However, Kinberg keeps the action jogging along satisfactorily and the actors cope, though somewhat with tongue in cheek. Minor productions highlights include an elephant stampede, the rescue by Quayle of the young girl from death by crocodile, a native dance and some sweeping desert warfare.

Quayle is a stalwart, dependable hero and Miss Syms does what she can with the material supplied to her, but her acting consists mainly of being on the receiving end of some unchivalrous treatment by Quayle and physical discomfort as she scrambles through the mock-scenery. Little Jenny Agutter is pleasantly charming as the young native girl and Fowlds is cast as the conventional fatuous officer figure who rises to the occasion at the finale. Among the natives Joseph Layode is a lively wicked chieftain and Johnny Sekka the pukka, educated prince who was once a slave and can't ever forget it. *Rich.*

The Square Root of Zero

Yank indie Gotham-based pic will not do much for the cause. It lacks the bite and filmic knowhow for impact.

Locarno, Aug. 4.
Mark-L Enterprises production and release. With Michael Egan, James Gavin, Leslie Davis, Don Woodbury, Mary Bower. Written and directed by William Cannon. Camera and editing, Sheldon Rochlin. At Locarno Film Fest. Running time, 80 MINS.
Zero .... Michael Egan
Allen .... James Gavin
Jane .... Leslie Davis
Arch .... Don Woodbury
May .... Mary Bower

Attempted spoof of rich girl meets poor (beatnik artist) boy in the Hollywood tradition, and of current mores and outlooks, with a love story interpolated, does not come off. It lacks the true filmic pace and zest of the very thing it is chiding. There are some good segs, but, overall, this does not have playoff legs and calls for specialized spotting and selling for best results.

A bearded beatnik writes seemingly penny-dreadful, true confession type stories in his head but never gets them down on his typewriter. Pic alternates between the imagined stories and the writer's room.

He and his pal, an abstract painter, go off to an island near N.Y. to camp out. The painter meets and falls for a rich girl whom both insult for her swag. When she thinks she has become pregnant, things pop but it seems it was not so as the painter and his pal escape after a mock drowning and funeral dirge.

Potshots at rich men who sneak off for rendezvous with a vacationing tart, a pixilated mother who writes tobacco road-type plays, the love affair and assorted types all lack the right comedic delineation, drive and blend of situation and parody to bring this off.

Result is the film lags and is not helped by self-conscious acting and weak delivery of ordinary dialog. It is technically okay. Director-writer William Cannon at times displays a flair for tenderness without sentimentality and parody without pettiness. But there is not enough of it.

It is not up to such other far-out U.S. pix as "Hallelujah the Hills" and "Goldstein." This is acceptable but uneven. It will not be one of those to help the non-Hollywood indie cause too much. *Mosk.*

Cerny Petr
(Black Peter)
(CZECHOSLOVAKIAN)
Locarno, July 28.
Czech State Film production and release. With Ladislav Jakim, Pavla Martinkova, Pavel Sedlacek, Jan Ostrcil, Bozena Matuskova, Vladimir Pucholt. Directed by Milos Forman. Screenplay, Jaroslav Papousek, Forman; camera, Jan Nemecek; editor, Miroslav Hajek. At Locarno Film Fest. Running time, 82 MINS.
Peter .... Ladislav Jakim
Pauline .... Pavla Martinkova
Lada .... Pavel Sedlacek
Father .... Jan Ostrcil
Mother .... Bozena Matuskova
Cenda .... Vladimir Pucholt

Film considers teenage life with understanding and wit that makes this good entertainment. It also has deeper shafts of parental and youthful coping. This could have playoff or specialized booking handles for offshore theatres, with word-of-mouth a probable added asset.

With only one young pro thesp involved, film has a freshness in playing coupled with breezy and pointed direction. A young boy gets his first job watching out for shoplifters in a small supermarket. His attempted courtship of a girl and his homelife fill out the film. If there is no real storyline, it has a series of nice vignettes.

The boy follows a suspicious looking man, who he thinks stole something, to no avail. His pomp-

ous father lectures him about this and his work. He tries to spy on his girl undressing in a bath house, then goes dancing and has a run-in with a drunken young worker. And so the pic goes on to end on a muted note regarding the older generation's incomprehension of the young one.

Ladislav Jakim has the right puzzled and touseled look as the semi-articulate youth trying to make his way in work and early love. He manages to express an inner sensitivity alongside his exterior charm. Others also score as does pro thesp Vladimir Pucholt, as the drunk.

Director Milos Forman displays a sharp, pictorial pace and the right lightness of touch to make these adventures risible as well as taking some pointed potshots at bureaucracy. But coming from an Eastern country, this is even more pertinent and telling.

Film is technically expert and maintains a feeling of spontaniety that comes from fine handling of non-pro actors and blending their reactions into an episodic framework. This reveals facets of the characters, life in that country today and parental and youthful relations that appear timeless and sans borders. *Mosk.*

Les Apprentis
(The Apprentices)
(SWISS)

Locarno, July 29.
Rialto Films release and production. Written and directed by Alain Tanner. Camera and editing by Ernest Artaria; music, Victor Fenigstein. At Locarno Film Fest. Running time, 80 MINS.

Patronal film, backed by various industries, is a surface look at apprentices. It has a nice visual flair and aligning of talk, work and the various types with okay associative patterns of cutting. But this remains primarily of local interest or for commercial usage only abroad.

Various young people talk about why they do what they do and pic shows them at home or at work. It refrains from much comment except in some spots where it denotes a certain lack of much outside interest by these people. Strictly a rote, comfortable, but not too demanding, life seem in store for most.

Pic has a good background score and is well lensed and edited. It treats its subject fairly but refrains from going into more depth or emerging with some more cogent commentary among this group of apprentices. Little personality shows throughly among them. *Mosk.*

El Shaytan El Saheir
(The Hostage)
(EGYPTIAN)

Karlovy Vary, Aug. 4.
Dollar Film production and release. With Samira Ahmed, Kamal El Chennaqui, Hassan Youssef. Written and directed by Kamal El Cheikh; camera, Mahmoud Nasr. At Karlovy Vary Film Fest. Running time, 85 MINS.
Mother .... Samira Ahmed
Father .... Kamal El Chennaqui
Son .... Hassan Youssef

It seems Egypt is intent on making films that are reminiscent of Yank "B" films without their snap or pace. These pix do not help festival interest or Egyptian films for that matter. Said commercial items would be better kept at home.

This is somewhat like a successful Yank pic, "The Window." But it has none of its attributes. A boy stows away in a moving van that turns out to be used by a murderer in which to transport a body. Most of the pic is taken up with the killers tracking the kid while his father tries to find him. Acting is bad and direction obvious. It is technically good.

Mosk.

En Dias Come Estos
(In Such Times As These)
(CUBAN)

Karlovy Vary, Aug. 4.

CAIC production and release. With Mequi Herrera, Rebecca Morales, Carmen Delgado, Jorge Fraga. Screenplay, Daura Olema; camera, Jose Tabic; music, Juan Blanco. At Karlovy Vary Film Fest. Running time, **82 MINS.**
Ellen .... Mequi Herrera
Friend .... Rebecca Morales
Mother .... Carmen Delgado
Fiance .... Jose Graga

Cuban film shows influences of modern European techniques in couching a tale of a rich girl's near conversion to the Cuban Revolution on two levels of time. It is naturally mainly a product for Eastern Bloc countries.

A rich girl has a fiance who is thinking of leaving Cuba. She tries to do something for her country by trying to teach illiterates in the mountains. Here she meets dedicated Communists and revolutionaries who spout dogma. Through it all, she thinks back to her lover and former life.

These are adroitly dovetailed but little life is given the characters or plot. Main story impetus is the possible invasion of the island to come from the U.S.

Acting is somewhat mannered and rarely gives substance to the ideas stressed throughout the pic. This is well lensed. The director evidently has some style but the production doesn't even adequately give an idea of the country today.

Mosk.

Tiempo D'Amore
(Time of Love)
(SPANISH)

Locarno, Aug. 4.

MGM release of Epoca Films production. With Julia Gutierrez. Enriqueta Carballeira, Augustin Gonzales, Julian Mateos, Lina Canalejas, Carlos Estrada. Directed by Julio Diamante. Screenplay, Elena Saez, Diamante; camera. J. Baldani editor, Pedro Del Ano. At Locarno Film Fest. Running time, 75 MINS.
Fiancee .... Julia Gutierrez
Alfonso .... Augustin Gonzales
Girl .... Lina Canale
Doctor .... Carlos Estrada

Sketch film may have some repercussions on its home ground where it shows up outmoded courting techniques and gives a grim picture of chances for a career. But for foreign spots, it looms only for language situations since it is somewhat sentimental, sketchy and only fair in the thesp and directorial departments.

First, a couple engaged for 12 years finally has the woman giving in to solace the man who has flunked a hard law test for the fourth time. By then, he seems to be losing interest in her. Follows an innocent working girl almost

seduced by a shrewd and smooth monied youth only to fight him off and go off alone. Then there is a young doctor's wife who is angered by their lack of money but relents when she sees him treating some poor people sans demanding payment.

Lead seg has some bite if it remains loose in character delineation while the second is telegraphed. The third is lachrymose and sudsy. Acting is only fair. While this does try to reflect a sort of static society, there is no depth, filmic flair or sharp outlook to sustain it.

Mosk.

Trois Femmes
(Three Women)
(CANADIAN)

Locarno, July 28.

Canadian National Film Board production and release. With Carol-Lynne Traynor, Ginette Letondal, Patricia Nolin. Directed by Georges Dufaux, Clement Perron for sketch on "Caroline," Pierre Patry for "Francoise" and Gilles Carle for "Solange." Lensing and editing by directors. At Locarno Film Fest. Running time. **85 MINS.**
Caroline .... Carol-Lynne Traynor
Francoise .... Ginette Letondal
Solange .... Patricia Nolin

Three sketches on three women make up this rather pretentious pic. Simple stories are overblown by heavy and portentous techniques, stream-of-consciousness commentary and arty camerawork. So this appears mainly a home product without much chance in foreign situations.

In one a young married woman feels her life is somewhat listless, in spite of a loving husband and child, because of his seeming forgetfulness about their anniversary. But his surprise recognition resolves everything. All this is done with her at work and thinking of her courtship and walking about aimlessly to a voice commenting on it. This rarely gives any true inkling of character.

Then a divorcee and career woman has her walks and comments on a hard period in her life, with some superfluous office intrigues while a tele show woman has a run-in with a rustic lass who stars on one of her programs. The last one is the only seg with some fairly witty scenes and less badly assimilated imitations of the New Wave techniques.

Film is technically okay while any thematic or subject matter is sacrificed for effect and gratuitously slick camerawork. Thesps are comely but can not do much with these surface essays on working women today. Film is in French.

Mosk.

Kennwort: Reiher
(Password: Heron)
(GERMAN)

Berlin, Aug. 4.

Nora release of Franz Seitz production (Munich) (produced in collab with Filmaufbau (Goettingen) and Independent-Produktion, Berlin. Stars Peter van Eyck, Marie Versini. Walter Rilla; features Fritz Wepper, Chez Hickmann, Elfriede Kuzmany. Directed by Rudolf Jugert. Screenplay. Herbert Reinecker. after novel "The River Line" by Charles Morgan; camera. Wolf Wirth, Hans Jura; music. Rolf Wilhelm; editor. Heidi Rente. Preemed in several West German cities. Running time. **97 MINS.**
William C. Barton ...... Peter van Eyck
Marie .... Marie Versini
Pierre, Marie's Father .... Walter Rilla
Philip .... Fritz Wepper
Frewers .... Chez Hickmann
Madame Claire .... Elfriede Kuzmany
Julian .... Geoffrey Toone

This is the German pic that captured most (four) of this country's 1964 Federal Film Prizes. Also, it repped West Germany at the recent Locarno Film Fest. If this is to be "the crown of German productions," the domestic filmmaking has truly reached a pitiful status. Admittedly, this Franz Seitz production employs a basically interesting plot and also attempts an ambitious for German film standards slant. But the outcome is rather mild. Internationally, there's simply nothing special about it. While it may do okay within its home-grounds, the film's foreign chances appear very slim.

This deals with Allied airmen shot down over German-occupied Belgium and France, and other Allied soldiers who escaped prison camps in that territory. An underground organization is smuggling them out into neutral Spain.

Film shows the odyssey of such a group. Central figure is William C. Barton, called "the Heron" because of his slender build. The group is nearly to its destination when a tragic incident occurs. Barton is watched while writing a letter to Germany. He is thought a spy for Germany and immediately killed by demand of the organization. Soon thereafter it's found out that the suspicion was unfounded, and that he was liquidated by mistake.

There are too many drawbacks to make this a convincing film. The script merely offers paper talk. Many sequences ring untrue. What also militates against genuineness is the language used in this film: The Allied escapees speak a beautiful German while the French come along with broken German. Conviction was sacrificed for conventional audience concession. Rudolf Jugert's direction is on the dull side.

Peter van Eyck, German-born American actor, one of Germany's most popular screenstars. enacts the central role in the manner German cinema patrons have seen him over and over again. Fritz Wepper adequately portrays a shot-down U.S. pilot. A good performance is contributed by French Marie Versini who's in the service of the underground organization. In a way, all are "interesting types," yet all have a tough time trying to overcome the deficiencies of the script.

On the positive side, there is good lensing by Wolf Wirth and Hans Jura. Incidentally, both walked off with the West German Federal Award for best camerawork. Award also went to young Fritz Wepper (best newcomer). In addition, "Password: Heron" got an award as the best German feature pic of the year. One would think that all these awards suggest an important film. Unfortunately, this isn't so.

Hans.

Naganiacz
(Manhunters)
(POLISH-DYALISCOPE)

Locarno. Aug. 4.

Polski State Film release of Kamera production. With Maria Wachowiak, Bronislaw Pawlik, Waclaw Kowalski, Ryszard Pietruski. Directed by Ewa and Czeslaw Petelski. Screenplay, Roman Bratny; camera. Stefan Matyjaszkiewicz; music. Tadeusz Baird. At Locarno Film Fest. Running time. **82 MINS.**
Michal .... Bronislaw Pawlik
Girl .... Maria Wachowiak

A harsh anecdote about wartime inhumanity and a doomed love affair unfortunately does not get the right direction, playing or dramatic strength it needs. Film appears mainly a specialized one on its central harrowing look at a German-Polish hunting party during the last war that turns into a massacre of some Jews, escaped from a concentration camp convoy.

Situated in a snowy country landscape, a young Pole helps a young Jewish girl, hiding her and her people in haystacks. A Nazi hunting group happens to go by and dogs flush out the Jews who are cold bloodedly slaughtered alongside the scampering game.

Here the situation is treated with tact and a lament for the times that could easily allow this beastliness. Film's main worth depends on this alone. Otherwise, the pic meanders about a group of dimly etched characters marking time as the war goes on around them. But direction and playing do little to build a probing feeling for the times and the people, with the side love affair of a Jewish girl and a Pole also somewhat lukewarm.

It is academically planned and deployed but sans the revelation and dramatic pitch to give it its full needed measure of irony and outrage. So this would need very careful handling and hardsell abroad for best chances on its anecdotal rather than filmic qualities. It is technically proficient.

Mosk.

Bandini
(INDIAN)

Karlovy Vary, Aug. 4.

Bimal Roy production and release. With Ashok Kumar, Nutan. Directed by Bimal Roy. Screenplay, M. Ghosh; camera, Kammal Bose; editor, M. Prabhalavkar. At Karlovy Vary Film Fest. Running time, **120 MINS.**
Kalyani .... Ashok Kumar
Bikash .... Nutan

This Indian film has technical proficiency but is too melodramatic and thematically simplified for much chance abroad. Its best bet is on Asian grounds where the mixture of sentiment, bravado and adventure would be more appreciated.

A young girl ends in prison when she poisons the wife of a man she was supposed to wed. The wife had been dangerous to his welfare as an underground worker during the pre-independence days of India. The girl's tribulations in prison, the love of a young doctor for her and her freedom are limed as well as flashbacks tying all together.

Acting is reserved and direction pictorially expert. But the limpid style and slow progression as well as the surface treatment keep this from having much chance in the Western market.

Mosk.

Retez
(The Chain)
(BULGARIAN—SCOPE)

Karlovy Vary, Aug. 4.

Film Bulgaria production and release. With Vassil Popiliev, Kina Dacheva, Ivan Bratanov. Directed by Lubomir Charlandjiev. Screenplay, Angel Waguenstein; camera, Emile Waguenstein; music, Kiril Zibulka. At Karlovy Vary Film Fest. Running time, **85 MINS.**
Man .... Vassil Popiliev
Woman .... Kina Dacheva
Peasant .... Ivan Bratanov

The evergreen theme of a man on the run is treated simply and honestly to have this an engaging if perhaps too thin film. Thus this primarily is a home item but denotes growing filmic skills in Bulgaria.

During the last war, a young communist is sentenced to death and heavily chained and sent off to be hanged. He escapes from the train and treks across the country dragging his chains. He at first fears to see people, fearing betrayal, but then realizes he must have faith in them.

After hallucinations he is finally picked up by a peasant who gets some partisans to help him. But he leaves the hut to spare them reprisals and is then saved from prison by a soldier who dies in the attempt. This does not dwell on heroics or action but on the man's gradual reactions to society again. It perhaps does not quite succeed in giving this a more profound transcending of the actual tale and theme. Direction does not have the needed intensity.

But the subject is handled with discretion and well played by Vassil Popiliev as the hunted man whose faith is restored. It is starkly lensed if editing is a bit too flaccid. *Mosk.*

Go-Daan
(The Cow Gift)
(INDIAN)

Locarno, Aug. 4.
Jetly Films production and release. With Raaj Kumar, Kamini Kaushal, Shubha Khote, Mehmood, Shashikala. Written and directed by Trilok Jetly from book by Premchand. Camera, Sudhin Mazumdar; editor, Shyam Das; Music, Ravi Shankar. At Locarno Film Fest. Running time, 110 MINS.
Hori .... Raaj Kumar
Dhania .... Kamini Kaushal
Jhunia .... Shubha Khote
Gobar .... Mehmood
Malti .... Shashikala
Rai .... Bepin Gupta

Posey pic is a long, uninspired account of a poor peasant's hardships as his own brother kills his coveted cow in jealousy. He falls into great poverty, and finally dies. There is no direct feeling for the times, drama and characters. And the obvious studio interiors of exteriors also do not help. It remains mainly a local item.

There was an attempt to give a picture of the pious, self deprecating peasant, but it is all done with such lack of earthiness or dynamism. It is technically passable, with the acting too stagey and obvious to rob the roles of their needed depth. *Mosk.*

Shehar Aur Sapna
(The City and the Dream)
(INDIAN)

Karlovy Vary, Aug. 4.
Sansar production and release. With Surekha Parkar, M. Krishna, Anwar Husain, David, Nana Palsikar. Written and directed by K. A. Abbas. Camera, Ramachandra. At Karlovy Vary Film Fest. Running time, 120 MINS.
Radha .... Surekha Parkar
Diwanna .... M. Krishna
Anwar .... Anwar Husain
Pandoo .... David
Johnny .... Nana Palsikar

This starts well in showing an overpopulated almost dehumanized city and its extremes in wealth and poverty. Then the story seems un-

real and melodramatic to make this mostly a home market release.

A young peasant ends up sleeping in the street and meets a girl whom he marries. Then their problems are gone into. If pic tries to deal with poverty with an optimistic, humanistic flair, it does not have the insight or feeling to make it come off. Result is stagey playing, forced sentiments and a generally inept film. If okay on its home grounds, it hasn't the quality for any untoward chances abroad. This technically reeks of inferior sets with ordinary acting and direction. *Mosk.*

Der Geteilte Himmel
(The Divided Sky)
(EAST GERMAN)

Karlovy Vary, Aug. 4.
Defa production and release. With Renate Blume, Eberhard Esche, Hans Hardt-Hardtloff, Erika Pelikowski. Directed by Konrad Wolf. Screenplay, Christa, Gerhard and Konrad Wolf. Will Bruckner, Kurt Barthel; camera, Werner Bergmann; music, Alfred Hirschmeier. At Karlovy Vary Film Fest. Running time, 110 MINS.
Rita .... Renate Blume
Manfred .... Eberhard Esche

Touchy theme of East and West Germany and their worker difficulties with bureaucracy are melded into a love story in this one. But this is somewhat too lifeless to make anything much come off. Result is a pic with primarily home chances in view, with even other Eastern Bloc export possibilities uncertain.

Director Konrad Wolf has tried to be impartial but has not been able to give life to his two lovers. The man is a scientist who can not get a new process for dyeing fabrics accepted in East Germany, and goes over to the West. The girl goes to see him there but realizes her place is in the East and leaves him to go back.

Intercutting of various levels of time, repeated symbols, places and imagery show some influence by the New Wave and others, but it is not too well assimilated in this overblown and essentially humorless, unfeeling pic. It becomes too portentous and the players are also somewhat formalistic rather than people in their own right. Lensing is too gray and editing slow. *Mosk.*

Behold A Pale Horse

Sensitive, artistic picture tracing the sociological attitudes of a Spanish guerrilla fighter who remains a one-man army 20 years after the Spanish Civil War. Film may prove provocative to thoughtful audiences, but looms essentially as art fare.

Columbia release of Fred Zinnemann production, directed by Zinnemann. Stars Gregory Peck, Anthony Quinn, Omar Sharif; features Raymond Pellegrin, Paola Stoppa, Mildred Dunnock, Daniela Rocca, Christian Marquand, Marietto Angeletti. Screenplay, J. P. Miller based on novel, "Killing a Mouse on Sunday," by Emeric Pressburger; camera, Jean Badal; editor, Walter Thompson; music, Maurice Jarre; asst. director, Paul Feyder. Reviewed Aug. 6, 1964, at Academy Theatre, L.A. Running time, 119 MINS.
Manuel Artiguez .... Gregory Peck
Capt. Vinolas .... Anthony Quinn
Father Francisco ...... Omar Sharif
Carlos .... Raymond Pellegrin
Pedro .... Paola Stoppa
Pilar .... Mildred Dunnock
Rosanna .... Daniela Rocca
Lieut. Zaganar ...... Christian Marquand
Paco Dages .... Marietto Angeletti
Maria .... Perette Pradier
Luis .... Zia Mohyeddin
Teresa .... Rosalie Crutchley

Hollywood, Aug. 7.
After a lengthy absence, director Fred Zinnemann returns to the screen with a film sensitive to intellect and to visual communication. "Behold a Pale Horse" is a provocative cinematic achievement but a substantial audience segment may label the picture tedious. This is a director's picture that compels the viewer to involve himself within subtle psychological emotions of a handful of people who represent a moral sociological attitude.

"Pale Horse" is rooted in the 1939 Spanish Civil War, using introductory newsreel footage of the fighting to set the background for a story that happens 20 years later and essentially concerns a Spanish guerrilla (Gregory Peck) who continues to live the war alone. He is thrown again into the fray in a personal attack against a vain and arrogant police captain (Anthony Quinn) who has vowed his death. The one-man fight against a corrupt and powerful adversary is an obvious losing battle, but the guerrilla's last stand, he knows, can be his most effective. It is a subtle story of political vendetta and sacrifice, but one which carries a great deal of strength and seems destined to respark controversy about the Loyalist-Falangist blood bath. ["Pale Horse" and all Columbia films have been banned from Spain by the Franco government.]

Peck is a worn-out, untidy, broken man who once again surges with force and energy in a characterization that ranks among the better in his long and respected career. Unflattering as a romantic image, this is a performance that is prestigious as an actor and one to which Peck brings both his own characteristic qualities of introspective underplaying as well as a slightly new dimension of hulking guts.

There also is an excellent performance from Quinn, who is coarse, crude and worldly as the arrogant police chief but shows his own insecurity beneath a physically courageous false front. Omar Sharif shows a warm, sensitive side in this film, playing the role

of a young priest born between obligations of personal morality and the official laws of government. It is a human performance of quality.

Marietto Angeletti has charm and a bright, empathetic flair as a youngster sent to enlist Peck for the assignment, while Mildred Dunnock, Daniella Rocca, Paola Stoppa, Raymond Pellegrin and Rosalie Crutchley show superb moments in lesser roles.

"Pale Horse" aimed as a major exposure picture, is actually an art picture, handsomely photographed by Jean Badal, scored by Maurice Jarre and edited by Walter Thompson.

Brot und Spiele
(Bread and Games)
(GERMAN - COLOR)

A Manfred Durnick production directed by Durnick. Camera (Agfacolor) Gunther Hahn, Juergen Stahf and Erich Grohmann; commentary Hans-Juergen Hsko; narrator, Richard Muench; music, Peter Thomas and Oskar Sala; editing Eva-Marie Crohmann. Previewed at Transocean, West Berlin. Running time, 90 MINS.

Manfred Durniok, young (30) German documentary film producer-director of shorts herewith presents his first full-length documentary. It's a slickly made film which, taking into account that documentaries are now much in vogue here, should be able to collect play dates in this country. If well handled, it might also reach some foreign markets.

Deals with peculiar characters and creatures ranging from head hunters in Borneo to chicken eaters in the Philippines, to a five-legged cow in India. Includes a bordello in Mexico, a joint in Boston, offbeat dining places in the Far East. Also photographed is beach life on Costa Brava, Spain, people in love in London's Hyde Park, Paris in the early morning hours, night life in Berlin, and so forth. *Hans.*

The Lively Set
(DRAMA WITH MUSIC-COLOR)

Young crowd stuff. Hero mad for speed. Rock 'n' roll diversions. Okay for intended market.

Hollywood, Aug. 12.
U release of Wm. Alland production. Stars James Darren, Pamela Tiffin, Doug McClure, Joanie Sommers. Directed by Jack Arnold. Screenplay, Mel Goldberg and William Wood; story, Goldberg and William Alland; camera, Carl Guthrie; editor Archie Marshek; art directors, Aexander Colitzen, Walter Simonds; sound, Waldon O. Watson and Josh Westmoreland; asst. director, James Welch; music, Bobby Darin; music supervision, Joseph Gershenson. Reviewed at Universal studio Aug. 11, '64. Running time, 95 MINS.
Casey .... James Darren
Eadie .... Pamela Tiffin
Chuck .... Doug McClure
Doreen .... Joanie Sommers
Marge .... Marilyn Maxwell
Paul Manning .... Charles Drake
Stanford Rogers ..... Peter Mann
Mona .... Carole Wells
Celeste .... Frances Robinson
Policeman .... Greg Morris
Ernie .... Ross Elliott
Moody .... Russ Conway
Prof. Collins ...... Martin Blaine
Himself .... Captain Max Schumacher
Himself .... Dick Whittinghill
Himself .... Mickey Thompson
Himself .... James Nelson
Himself .... Ron Miller
Himself .... Duane Carter
Himself .... Billy Krause

"The Lively Set" is quite a lively formula film full of bright, shiny teeth, well-groomed hair and wholesome, exuberant youth. Add racing cars, plus rock 'n' roll music. Result should be a pleasant boxoffice dish for the young crowd in particular.

Screenplay by Mel Goldberg and William Wood, based on story by producer William Alland and Goldberg, serves sufficiently to show off some exciting racing scenes and beautiful color photography which should appease appetites of racing buffs. Thin plot revolves around 22-year old ex-GI college student, James Darren, who'd rather devote time to building his dream car—a gas turbine job—than pursue academic studies. He even appears to love cars more than girls, until Pamela Tifflin, sister of hot-rod buff friend Doug McClure, tears him away long enough to fall in love and get engaged Darren then quits school and goes to San Francisco to build a turbine car for racing hero Peter Mann, who fires him after he almost cracks up car.

Undaunted, everybody chips in so Darren can build his own turbine car, which he does, and enters the Tri-State race against his nemesis Rogers. Highlight of film are the excellent sequences of speeding cars on snaking roads against the striking ruggedness of the Sierra Mountains. Credit goes to director Jack Arnold, cameraman Carl Guthrie and editor Archie Marshek for some of the most exciting race shots seen in a long time.

Darren and Miss Tifflin, who starred in "For Those Who Think Young," make a wholesome American-type couple and do adequately by their roles. Darren has it a shade better as there are moments when Miss Tifflin's performance seems weak, but the direction is more at fault here. Fine support is given by Marilyn Maxwell, Charles Drake, Russ Conway and Ross Elliott. Appearing as themselves in roles of race drivers are professionals Mickey Thompson, James Nelson, Duane Carter, Billy Krause and Ron Miller.

Joanie Sommers, already a successful singer, makes her film debut as McClure's girlfriend. She has a good scene on top of too much champagne and also sings two tunes, one of them—"If You Love Him"—a potential hit. Bobby Darin composed five tunes plus 'Most memorable, oc-sides "If You Love Him," are the song sung by James Darren, and a novelty tune, "Boss Barracuda," sung by the Surfaris.

Special credit goes to art director, Walter Simonds and Alexander Golitzen for their realistic 'ca of the Bonneville Salt Flats. *Bobb.*

Nobody Waved Goodbye
(CANADIAN)

Production touches and techniques notable and could make this a "David and Lisa" type sleeper. Story of juvenile problems deteriorating into crime has heart-tug quality necessary for good b.o.

Montreal, Aug. 14.
National Film Board release. Stars Peter Kastner and Julie Biggs. With Claude Rae, Toby Tarnow, Charmion King, Ron Taylor. Direction and screenplay by Don Owen. Camera, John Spotton; music, Eldon Rathburn. Reviewed

at Fifth Montreal International Film Festival at Place des Arts. Running time, 80 MINS.

This is one of the few features produced by the National Film Board of Canada and may well turn out to be a good box office bet, if properly handled promotionwise. In fact, with a good distribution setup, it could become a sleeper in the "David and Lisa" pattern, since there are similar qualities.

It's a simple story, simply told, about a couple of juves, the boy typically smartalecky, the girl attractive, decent and naive. From truancy and petty offenses, the road is downhill until by fadeout the young couple is split, the girl pregnant, and the boy having to decide whether to go back and face the music for theft, while there's still time to rehabilitate himself.

"Nobody Waved Goodbye" turned up in the next-to-closing spot of the Montreal film festival, and maybe it's a good thing, since it obviously left an impression that the Film Board, which until now has concentrated largely on documentaries, has the necessary talent, like Don Owen, who's sensitive to things around him, and can turn out a solid piece of film work relating to everyday people.

It's not a flawless film by any means. Some of the dialogue is dull. The acting in instances is bordering on bush league. The camera work veers to the pretentious. By and large, however, even if the story line becomes hokey and a little soap-operash in content, the film could be a winner.

Total production cost was approximately $75,000, which means that whoever undertakes North American and even world distribution, can make a good deal.

Film also has a good bit of light humor to take the edge off the sombre subject, and if the family characters sometimes ring corny because of the cliches used by the average middle class citizen, then the impact will be that much greater on the average film goer.

Peter Kastner and Julie Biggs have high and low points in the leads, but they're naturally charming enough to get away with momentary lapses in their performance.

Claude Rae and Charmion King, both experienced Canadian actors, are excellent in providing the right professional balance.

Others making appreciative contributions are Toby Tarnow, Charmion King, Ron Taylor, Robert Hill, Jack Beer, John Sullivan, Lynn Gorman, Yvor Barrie, Sharon Bonin, Norman Ettinger and John Vernon.

Pic was shot almost entirely in Toronto. *Laza.*

Kisses for My President

Comedy spoof of a lady President and the problems of her husband as "First Lady of the Land." Exploitation of the novelty idea, popularity of Fred MacMurray and saturation bookings may give it a boxoffice push, but picture telegraphs plot and jokes.

Hollywood, Aug. 12.
Warner Bros. release of Pearlayne (Curtis Bernhardt) Production, directed by Bernhardt. Stars Fred MacMurray, Polly Bergen; features Arlene Dahl, Edward Andrews, Eli Wallach. Screenplay, Claude Binyon and Robert G. Kane based on story by Kane; camera, Robert Surtees; editor, Sam O'Steen; music, Bronislau Kaper asst. director, Arthur Lueker. Reviewed, Aug. 11, '64, at Academy Theatre, Hollywood. Running time, 113 MINS.

Thad McCloud	Fred MacMurray
Leslie McCloud	Polly Bergen
Doris Reid	Arlene Dahl
Sen. Walsh	Edward Andrews
Valdez	Eli Wallach
John O'Connor	Donald May
Bill Richards	Harry Holcombe
Gloria McCloud	Anna Capri
Peter McCloud	Ronnie Dapo
Jackson	Richard St. John
Joseph	Bill Walker
Miss Higgins	Adrienne Marden

Saturation bookings, exploitation centered around the current political interest, family popularity of Fred MacMurray and the novelty idea of a lady President are all plus factors to give Curtis Bernhardt's produced and directed comedy spoof a push at the boxoffice. "Kisses For My President" is not, however, an electrifying comedy exercise, but essentially a one joke idea that telegraphs plotline, gags and obvious sightlines most of the way. Yet it is easy to take so the picture should have good general acceptance.

While there have been instances of women making a name for themselves in politics, (Margaret Chase Smith, of course, this year was the first woman to actually seek nomination to office of U. S. President) they have rarely been as (1) youthful, (2) glamorous or (3) unbelievable as Polly Bergen is in this role.

Perhaps it isn't Miss Bergen's fault. Actress has charm and a certain amount of strength, but the comic situations she is given in Claude Binyon and Robert G. Kane's screenplay and the complementary tongue-in-cheek characterizations surrounding her aren't always as right for her. The authors might complain too.

The picture's approach to problems confronting a married lady president, with family obligations, is strictly from fictionsville. It might have had benefit of more natural comedic situations if the unique premise had a more serious examination in terms of human relations.

However, the attention is placed on MacMurray, the "First Lady of the land" as the new President's husband. Obvious jokes like waiting in line to see his wife, femme decor of his bedroom as opposed to accented masculine appointments of the President's bedroom and a takeoff with MacMurray on the Jacqueline Kennedy tv tour of the White House lack sustained comedy impact. There are laughs, but they will be most strongly forthcoming from the undemanding filmgoer, for after a couple of scenes of the awkwardness of the male member of the family being lost in what is traditionally the wife's role in the White House, the attempts at fun become labored.

MacMurray is likeable and warm as the confused husband, a role typical of the pleasant characters he plays well. And Eli Wallach is excellent as a caricature of a South American dictator, although the role heaps too much satire upon satire. Arlene Dahl, who flames beautifully in color, looks blank in black and white with a role that leaves her looking and acting like an everyday Zsa Zsa Gabor. Edward

Andrews, playing it straight, has some good moments as an unscrupulous senator, while Donald May, moppet Ronnie Dapo, Bill Walker and Adrienne Marden are fine in lesser spots.

Bronislau Kaper's score is lilting and frequently spicy. Film uses process shots of Washington and some newsreel footage of crowd scenes in various areas. *Dale.*

Echo
(The Echo)
(POLISH)

Karlovy Vary, Aug. 11.
Polski State Film production and release. With Wienczyslaw Glinski, Barbara Horawianka, Jacek Blawut. Directed by Stanislaw Rozewicz. Screenplay, Tadeusz and Stanislaw Rozewicz; camera, Jerzy Wojcik; music, Wojciech Kilar. At Karlovy Vary Film Fest. Running time, 90 MINS.

Henry	Wienczyslaw Glinski
Wife	Barbara Horawianka
Son	Jacek Blawut

Muted melodrama is rich in this psychological film but does not have the depth and emotional power to make this look at a wartime collaborator's conscience penetrating enough to come off. It is thus chancey export fare for arty spots but is sans the action or pace for playoff.

A happily married man with a son is suddenly confronted with evidence that he had collaborated with the Gestapo during the last war. His defense is that he signed to do it to save his life and used his position to save a man. But the man has died. Pic delineates his reliving of what he did and his insistence it was not criminal even if it estranges his wife and son.

It ends with the man even being unable to kill himself. Direction is somewhat too measured and, if the theme of the collaborationist mind is interesting, this does not quite have the visual strength to make it a definitive study. Acting is good and direction observant. *Mosk.*

Murder Most Foul
(BRITISH)

Margaret Rutherford in another of her Miss Marple whodunits. Good for its natural strata.

Hollywood, Aug. 18.
Metro-Goldwyn-Mayer release of a Lawrence P. Buchmann production. Features Margaret Rutherford, Ron Moody, Charles Tingwell, Andrew Cruickshank, Dennis Price, Megs Jenkins. Produced by Ben Arbeid. Directed by George Pollock. Screenplay by David Pursall, Jack Seddon, based on Agatha Christie's "Mrs. McGinty's Dead"; camera, Desmond Dickinson; editor, Ernest Walter; sound, Allan Sones; art director, Frank White; music, composed and conducted by Ron Goodwin; asst. director, David Tomblin. Reviewed at studio, Aug. 17, 1964. Running time, 90 MINS.

Miss Marple	Margaret Rutherford
Driffold Cosgood	Ron Moody
Inspector Craddock	Charles Tingwell
Justice Crosby	Andrew Cruickshank
Mrs. Thomas	Megs Jenkins
Theatrical Agent	Dennis Price
Ralph Summers	Ralph Michael
Bill Hanson	James Bolam
Mr. Stringer	Stringer Davis
Sheila Upward	Francesca Annis
Eva McGonigall	Allison Seebohm
Police Constable Wells	Terry Scott

Margaret Rutherford has an audience all her own that gives considerable assurance of success to the newest Agatha Christie thriller to cast the doughty oldtimer in the role of Miss Marple, the eccentric amateur sleuth. For director George Pollock and screenwriters David Pursall and Jack Seddon, it continues an association that was highly successful earlier with "Murder At The Gallop" and "Murder She Said."

Miss Rutherford, in this instance, is the lone member of a murder jury who holds out for acquittal. Armed only with her experience in amateur mystery theatricals, she proceeds to unsnarl the case and prove herself far more professional than the investigating police. There is a mixture of satiric comedy and daredevil melodrama in the screenplay, which also includes a wealth of amusing and unusual characters who all turn up suspect at one time or another.

The picture, however, for all its comedy delight and charm, does not quite hold up to its predecessors. Miss Marple is beginning to wear a little thin as she retraces many of the same comedy situations and even some similar dialog. Audiences who have seen the other pix can pretty well guess the tale, leaving only the immediate visual amusement that comes from the typical Rutherford look — puffed out lower jaw, tweedy attire, staunch, rugged walk and beautiful timing.

Stringer Davis again plays the confused partner with a charming personality performance and Charles Tingwell completes the trio as the young inspector who ends up with the credit for solving the crime even though he flails Miss Marple all the way.

Also helpful, in richly flavorful roles are Ron Moody, an affected theatre director; Terry Scott, prototype of the dense police constable; Andrew Cruikshank, the judge, and Allison Seebohm, a wispy, introspective actress. Megs Jenkins, Ralph Michael, James Bolam, Francesca Annis are fine in other roles.

Ben Arbeid takes the producer credit earlier held by George H. Brown in the other pix. Production values are highlighted by Ron Goodwin's music with its tingling, clavichord sound.

Desmond Dickinson's photography, with acute angles and interesting lighting, gives it a sensitive, mysterious look. *Dale.*

The Big Parade of Comedy

Fourth—and most ambitious— in Robert Youngson's series of nostalgic excursions into films of yesteryear; good for secondary market.

Hollywood, Aug. 21.
Metro release of Robert Youngson production. Stars 51 Metro players. Screenplay, Youngson; music, Bernie Green; narrated by Les Tremayne. Reviewed at Metro studios, Aug. 20, '64. Running time, **90 MINS.**
Clark Gable, Cary Grant, Stan Laurel, Lucille Ball, Marie Dressler, Carole Lombard, Lionel Barrymore, Marion Davies, Lewis Stone, Lupe Velez, George K. Arthur, Jimmy Finlayson, Greta Garbo, Spencer Tracy, Oliver Hardy, Red Skelton, Wallace Beery, Jimmy Durante, Franchot Tone, Lee Tracy, Bert Lahr, Freddie Bartholomew, Leo Carrillo, Norma Shearer, The Marx Brothers, Katharine Hepburn, William Powell, Robert Taylor, Bud Abbott, Buster Keaton, Melvyn Douglas, Polly Moran, Nat Pendleton, Zasu Pitts, Asta, the dog, Jean Harlow, W. C. Fields, Myrna Loy, Joan Crawford, Lou Costello, Ted Healy and the Three Stooges, Robert Benchley, Gail Patrick, Chester Morris, Karl Dane, Dave O'Brien.

Robert Youngson's continuing series of nostalgic film memories drawn from motion pictures of the past digs deeply into Metro's backlog of greats and not-so-greats for this fourth effusion which should meet with the same response as its predecessors. Feature is slickly handled with know-how technique and may be easily exploited for the program market.

Preceded by "The Golden Age of Comedy" (DCA release, 1958), "When Comedy Was King" (20th-Fox, '60) and "Days of Thrills and Laughter" (20th, '61), this 90-minute entry composed of clips and sequences which many of the older generation will recall fondly and should tickle more youthful spectators, follows the same style of presentation. A running narration, this time by Les Tremayne, amusingly accompanies the broad slapstick and more refined comedy and a musical score helps point up the comic tenor of the action.

A total of 48 names, all on the star or top featured side, make this feature the most ambitious of Youngson's entire program. In the past, producer dealt only with silent footage; here, he makes extensive use of talking pix. Included in lineup of talent, which is virtually a grand parade of Metro's stellarites down through the years, are some of the same performers who appeared previously, such as Laurel & Hardy, Jean Harlow, Carole Lombard, Buster Keaton. On the grimmer side, 19 of those projected in comedy turns are now deceased.

Biggest laughs come from a couple of Laurel & Hardy comedies, embodying more footage than is devoted to most of the others. These depict the zany humor of the pair, one of the sequences showing them in kilts with Jimmy Finlayson, the other a bar scene with Lupe Velez in which slapstick at its funniest is the order. Clips from several Pete Smith Specialties featuring Dave O'Brien in a treatise on "sight" gags likewise panics, and wide exposure to further slapstick is provided via such comics as Abbott & Costello, the Marx Bros., Red Skelton, W. C. Fields, Jimmy Durante, Ted Healy and the Three Stooges.

Clips of varying lengths but all carrying interest also feature Clark Gable, Joan Crawford, Lucille Ball, Greta Garbo, William Powell and Myrna Loy, Marie Dressler and Wallace Beery, Robert Benchley, Karl Dane, Cary Grant, Lionel Barrymore, Keaton, Jean Harlow, Marion Davies, George K. Arthur, Melvyn Douglas, Gail Patrick, Robert Taylor, Katharine Hepburn. Flashes likewise are caught of Norma Shearer, Polly Moran, Bert Lahr, Freddie Bartholomew, Lewis Stone, Leo Carrillo, Spencer Tracy, Franchot Tone, Lee Tracy, Nat Pendleton, ZaSu Pitts, Chester Morris. Asta, the pooch, of "The Thin Man" fame, has his own time.

Youngson also wrote the narration and lyrics of the title song, composed by Bernie Green, who did the appropriate score. Jeanne Keyes is credited as research supervisor, a mammoth undertaking well executed. *Whit.*

Hilfe, Mein Frau Klaut
(Help, My Bride Steals)
(AUSTRIAN)

Vienna, Aug. 11.
Sascha Film production. Stars Peter Alexander, Connie Froboess; features Gunther Philipp. Directed by Werner Jacobs. Screenplay by Janne Furch, Stephan Gommermann; camera, Sepp Ketterer; musical direction, Johannes Fehring. At Kosmos Kino, Vienna. Running time, **95 MINS.**

There seems little need for this production, and there appears to be small need for an Austrian pic anyway. All preems are held here in third-class houses apparently so as to avoid the crix.

Story is good if old. A millionaire's daughter (Connie Froboess) is a kleptomaniac. Her lover (Peter Alexander) gets himself into loads of trouble. It's entertaining and well directed by Werner Jacobs, who at least deserves credit for good gags. And cameraman Sepp Ketterer is expert.

But on the negative side is the music of this would-be musical. As there are "no composers" in Austria, all were imported from West Germany. Three songs with the silly titles will be plugged. They are "Oh, Oh, Oh, Gloria," "Little-Bittle Moonshine" and "Wodka Beatle Boy." And for all this, the producers want a "state guarantee." *Maas.*

Master Spy
(BRITISH)

Routine spy meller has a few pilot gimmicks to make it satisfactory second-bill fare.

Allied Artists release of Eternal Film (Maurice J. Wilson) production. Directed by Montgomery Tully. Features Stephen Murray, June Thorburn, John Carson, Alan Wheatley, Marne Maitland. Screenplay by Wilson and Tully, based on "They Also Serve," by Gerald Anstruther, Paul White; camera, Geoffrey Faithfull; editor, Eric Boyd Perkins; music, Ken Thorne. Reviewed at Embassy, N.Y., Aug. 22, '64. Running time, **71 MINS.**
Boris Turganev ...... Stephen Murray
Leila .... June Thorburn
Paul Skelton .... Alan Wheatley
Richard Colman ...... John Carson
John Baxter .... John Brown
Captain Foster ...... Jack Watson
Dr. Pembury .... Peter Gilmore
Tom Masters .... Ernest Clark
Dr. Asafu .... Marne Maitland
Dr. Morrell .... Ellen Pollock
Sir Gilbert Saunders .. Hugh Morton
Richard Horton ...... Basil Dignam

Overall result of this British import is disappointing, especially as it contains a few story angles that warranted better work. A generally efficient, if uninspired, cast performance helps keep it fairly interesting.

Basically a tale of a Russian scientist who turns out to be a British counterspy, producer Maurice J. Wilson and director Montgomery Tully's collaborated screenplay contains a few provocative thought-stimulators. Their work in production and direction, unfortunately, doesn't indicate the same promise. Stephen Murray, as a Russian nuclear research scientist of some renown, defects to the British, who install him in a lab, connected with a hush-hush project, to continue his work. He's actually a Russian spy but is tripped up by an accidental incident involving his pretty assistant, June Thorburn. For a twist ending, Murray turns out to be a British spy who has gone through this elaborate routine to get him back into the good graces of the Russians. Why he couldn't have stayed there, in the responsible post he holds when the picture opens, goes unexplained.

Most interesting item in the plot is his disclosure, during a conversation with Miss Thorburn, that he learned all he knows about nuclear research "while a student at Cambridge." As this is certainly within the realm of possibility, the question posed is—"How many other Russians or Iron Curtain-natives have studied science at universities outside Russia, where are they today, and what are they doing?" A survey of graduate lists of some British and U.S. science schools might be in order.

Poorly lit black-and-white photography results in bad definition and many scenes seem out of focus. Other technical credits are equally routine. *Robe.*

The Gorgon
(BRITISH-COLOR)

Leisurely paced, nicely-made yarn, with sound cast and direction; useful booking preferably with a lively comedy.

London, Aug. 21.
Columbia release (through BLC) of a Hammer (Anthony Nelson Keys) production. Stars Peter Cushing, Christopher Lee; features Richard Pasco, Barbara Shelley, Michael Goodliffe, Patrick Troughton, Jack Watson. Directed by Terence Fisher. Screenplay by John Gilling, from story by J. Llewellyn Devine; camera (Technicolor). Michael Reed; editor, James Needs; music, James Bernard. Reviewed at Columbia Theatre, London. Running time, **83 MINS.**
Namaroff .... Peter Cushing
Meister .... Christopher Lee
Paul .... Richard Pasco
Carla .... Barbara Shelley
Heitz .... Michael Goodliffe
Kanof .... Patrick Troughton
Eatoff .... Jack Watson
Bruno .... Jeremy Longhurst
Sascha .... Toni Gilpin
Hans .... Redmond Phillips
Coroner .... Joseph O'Conor
Cass .... Alister Williamson
Policeman .... Michael Peake
Nurse .... Sally Nesbitt
Chatelaine .... Prudence Hyman

Though written and directed on a leisurely note, "The Gorgon" is a well-made, direct yarn that mainly gets its thrills through atmosphere rather than contrived horror. The period storyline is simple and predictable but John Gilling has turned out a well-rounded piece and Terence Fisher's direction is restrained enough to avoid any unintentional yocks. With a well contrasted film, could be a very useful dualler.

Set in the German village of Vandorf, this concerns a series of murders in which all the victims are turned to stone. Things come to a head- when a scientist comes to investigate the death by hanging of his son. The professor is also a victim of the unknown assassin and his other son turns up to pursue the inquiries further. He finds a village of fear, distrust and unknown evil, with local authorities too scared to allow investigation. •

There is evidence but, at first, no proof that the terror springs from an old legend of a supernatural Gorgon whose gaze kills and petrifies. But into which human being does her spirit and power penetrate, and why and when?

Old students will not be deterred by the fact that the identity of the villainess is early obvious, but will instead be beguiled by the commendable seriousness with which a sound cast carry off the eerie proceedings. Peter Cushing and Christopher Lee are old hands at this sort of lark and the only snag is that it is difficult to divorce them from past Frankenstein dramas. Barbara Shelley, as Professor Cushing's assistant, is a redheaded beauty with considerable thesping intelligence and charm who by now seems to rate bigger opportunities. There is a sound, straightforward hero in Richard Pasco. Michael Goodliffe, Jack Watson, Patricia Hyman, Patrick Troughton and Jeremy Longhurst add to the acting strength.

Highlights are the occasional glimpses of the mysterious Gorgon, a tough fight between Cushing and Pasco and the dank, mysterious atmosphere controved by lenser Michael Reed, art director Don Mingaye and special effects man Syd Pearson. Music by James Bernard and smooth editing by Eric Boyd Perkins are a distinct aid. *Rich.*

Zimmer 13
(Room 13)
(GERMAN)

Berlin, Aug. 11.
Constantin release of Rialto Film Preben Philipsen production. Stars Joachim Fuchsberger. Karin Dor, Richard Haeussler. Directed by Dr. Harald Reinl. Screenplay, Quentin Philips, adapted from Edgar Wallace's novel of same title; camera, Ernst W. Kalinke; music, Peter Thomas; editor, Jutta Hering. At Hili. West Berlin. Running time, **90 MINS.**

Jonny Gray .... Joachim Fuchsberger
Denise .... Karin Dor
Joe Legge .... Richard Haeussler
Pia Pasani .... Kai Fischer
Sir Marney ..... Walter Rilla
Sir John .... Siegfried Schuerenberg
Mr. Igle .... Hans Clarin
Dr. Higgins .... Eddie Arent
Blackstone-Edwards ... Benno Hoffmann

There is something about Rialto's Edgar Wallace filmizations which deserves praise. They are, unlike most other similar domestic thrillers, based on properly prepared scripts and technically well made. This also applies to "Room 13." Since the native crime thriller trend shows no letup as yet, this one will spell enough money to satisfy its producers. It looks okay also for some foreign situations.

As usual with such pix turned out by the Berlin-based Rialto, this offers the familiar mixture of thrill, horror and humor.- Suspense is well maintained, and there are plenty of victims along the 90 minutes. To balance with the bloody stuff, there is enough comedy relief coming from such characters as a scurrilous police medico, a stupid Scotland Yard inspector, some narrow-minded gangsters and the like.

A bunch of underworld characters has taken shelter in "Room 13" of a shady Soho nightspot. They plan to rob a train and hide the loot in the mansion of a respected English parliamentarian whom they force to keep quiet because of his association with the gangleader some 20 years ago.

Independently, a series of razor blade killings of women occur which have nothing to do with the train robbery. A private detective solves both cases. The end sees most of the robbers killed. A real surprise is the revelation who's to blame for the femme slayings.

Austrian-born Dr. Harald Reinl keeps the action rolling at full speed. Having already quite a number of Wallace pix to his credit, he knows how to handle this kind of production. His actress-wife, Karin Dor, plays the femme lead. Joachim Fuchsberger, one of Germany's better known film detectives, is the hero. Fine comerawork, a catchy score and tight editing round out the good technical setup. *Hans.*

Crooks In Cloisters
(BRITISH—COLOR)

Amusing joke that needed tighter, punchier screenplay. Star value overseas dubious, but useful light booking.

London, Aug. 18.
Warner-Pathe release of an Associated British Picture. Stars Ronald Fraser, Barbara Windsor, Gregoire Aslan, Bernard Cribbins. Produced by Gordon L. T. Scott. Directed by Jeremy Summers. Screenplay, T. J. Morrison and Mike Watts, from Watts' original story; camera (Technicolor), Harry Waxman; editor, Ann Chegwidden; music, Don Banks. Reviewed at A.B.C. Theatre, Harrow Road, London, Aug. 11, '64. Running time, **97 MINS.**.

Walt .... Ronald Fraser
Bikini .... Barbara Windsor
Lorenzo .... Gregoire Aslan
Squirts .... Bernard Cribbins
Specs .... Davy Kaye
Willy .... Melvyn Hayes
Phineas .... Wilfrid Brambell
Father Septimus ...... Joseph O'Conor
Brother Lucius .... Corin Redgrave
June .... Francesca Annis
Lady Florence ..... Patricia Laffan
Mungo .... Alister Williamson
Ship's Chandler ...... Russell Waters
Publican .... Howard Douglas
Newsagent .... Arnold Ridley
Bookmaker .... Max Bacon
Kate .... Barbara Riscoe
Strip Girl .... Karen Kaufman

Mike Watts hit on a neat enough idea for a comedy in "Crooks In Cloisters," but he and T. J. Morrison have not developed the script with enough punch or twists to make the affair very funny. However, with some popular British comedy favorites, a few surefire comedy situations and the pleasant scenery of Cornwall, attractively lensed by Harry Waxman, this should be an okay booking.

Ronald Fraser plays the boss of a small band of successful, amiable villains who are on the lam from the cops. They take over a deserted monastery in a remote island off the coast of Cornwall and pose as monks. While living the simple life they carry on the respective branches of their nefarious trade. Much of the simple fun comes from the settling down of the "monks" in their unaccustomed, abstemious life and how they gradually get to enjoy it. The script relies over-much on a string of episodes involving the problems of milking cows, tending pigs, cooking, a visit from inquisitive tourists and from a couple of real monks and similar going on, with considerable emphasis on the drawbacks of celibacy.

While these rumbustious frolics draw easy giggles the overall effect is too scrappy. The visit of the "kosher" monks, for instance, is a situation not fully explored. When one of the crooks cannot resist putting on hefty bets on his greyhound the police become suspicious and eventually the gang is caught.

Jeremy Summers extracts plenty of laughter from his directing but cannot provide the necessary punch and inventiveness that's lacking in the script. Artwork by Robert Jones, music by Don Banks and the editing of Ann Chegwidden are competent and the comedy lines and situations are evenly spread around the cast. Snag is that none of the characters is a real thug so there is no major internal conflict in the gang. Ronald Fraser cuts a smugly amusing figure as the boss turned "Father Superior" and Bernard Cribbins, Davy Kaye, Gregoire Aslan and Melvyn Hayes support him amusingly as fellow gangsters. The well padded, freshly scrubbed, pert Barbara Windsor, playing Fraser's moll, gives another of her now familiar portrayals as the goodhearted, vulgar, little tart and extracts a lot of fun out of her sudden passion for learning to cook.

Wilfrid Brambell as a layabout boatman who is hired to collect and deliver stolen goods, counterfeit money and jewelry for the gang is quite a character and Francesca Annis, Joseph O'Conor, Arnold Ridley and Howard Douglas contribute smaller but useful background bits of support. *Rich.*

Mary Poppins
(COLOR-SONGS)

Musical fantasy as only Walt Disney can do it, one of Disney's finest; boff returns indicated and suitable for all audiences.

Hollywood, Aug. 24.
Buena Vista release of Walt Disney production. Stars Julie Andrews, Dick Van Dyke. David Tomlinson, Glynis Johns; features Karen Dotrice, Matthew Garber, Ed Wynn, Hermione Baddeley, Elsa Lanchester. Arthur Treacher. Reginald Owen. Directed by Robert Stevenson. Co-producer, Bill Walsh. Screenplay, Walsh, Don DaGradi, based on "Mary Poppins" books by P. L. Travers; camera (Technicolor), Edward Colman; music and lyrics. Richard M. and Robert B. Sherman; editor. Cotton Warburton; assistant directors, Joseph L. McEveety, Paul Feiner; animation director, Hamilton S. Luske. Reviewed at Academy Award Theatre, Aug. 21, '64. Running time, **140 MINS.**

Mary Poppins .... Julie Andrews
Bert .... Dick Van Dyke
Mr. Banks .... David Tomlinson
Mrs. Banks .... Glynis Johns
Uncle Albert .... Ed Wynn
Ellen .... Hermione Baddeley
Jane Banks .... Karen Dotrice
Michael Banks .... Matthew Garber
Katie Nanna .... Elsa Lanchester
Constable Jones ...... Arthur Treacher
Admiral Boom .... Reginald Owen
Mrs. Brill .... Rita Shaw
Mr. Dawes Jr. .... Arthur Malet
Bird Woman .... Jane Darwell
Mr. Grubbs .... Cyril Delevanti
Mr. Tomes .... Lester Matthews
Mr. Mousley .... Clive L. Halliday
Mr. Binnacle .... Don Barclay
Miss Lark .... Marjorie Bennett
Mrs. Corry .... Alma Lawton
Miss Persimmon .... Marjorie Eaton

All the magic that audiences have come to associate with Walt Disney films down through the years comes to life with eloquent and delicious lustre in this musical fantasy based on the "Mary Poppins" books. It is the novelty picture of the year, the closest suggestion to "Peter Pan" ever glimpsed on the screen, and a shining new film star, Julie Andrews. For moppets and grownups alike it is a stimulating cinematic experience, a must-see, for it is an imaginative event seldom seen and when the count is in might very well be an Academy contender.

Disney has gone all-out in his dream-world rendition of a magical English nanny who one day arrives on the East Wind and takes over the household of a very proper London banker. Besides changing the lives of everyone therein, she introduces his two young children to wonders imagined and possible only in fantasy.

Producer has captured a mood so charming, so whimsical and delightful, that he fairly outdoes himself in his own realm of the high fanciful. Picture, despite its slight over-length, is a topflight accomplishment for all its many departments and its spirit communicates to the spectator, whatever the age.

Musically, the Technicolor film carries some of the most original songs of the season, to which Miss Andrews—of Broadway's "My Fair Lady"—responds with bright vivacity and fine voice. Cleffed by Richard M. and Robert B. Sherman, who also wrote the score, more than a dozen numbers further the action, with Miss Andrews' costars, Dick Van Dyke, David Tomlinson and Glynis Johns, also sharing honors. Among a spread of outstanding songs perhaps the most unusual is "Chim-Chim-Cheree," sung by

Van Dyke, which carries a haunting quality.

Dancing also plays an important part in unfolding the story and one number, the Chimney-Sweep Ballet, performed on the roofs of London and with Van Dyke starring here, is a particular standout. For sheer entertainment, a sequence mingling live-action and animation in which Van Dyke dances with four little penguin-waiters is immense.

Extensive use is made of animation. Disney's technique of combining live-action photography with animated cartoons never better limned. Many will be of the opinion that the long sequence in which he combines the two mediums, the "Jolly Holiday" number, in which merry-go-round horses ridden by the nanny, the two children and Van Dyke, break away from their carousel and gallop off across the countryside—is the most ingenious ever seen in a Disney film. Special effects play a vital part here, as in other sequences, such magical tricks as the nursemaid riding up a bannister, the airborne travels of the flying nanny, a teaparty on the ceiling, being effectively executed by Peter Ellenshaw, Eustace Lycett and Robert A. Mattey.

Miss Andrews' first appearance on the screen is a signal triumph and she performs as easily as she sings, displaying a fresh type of beauty nicely adaptable to the color cameras. Van Dyke, as the happy-go-lucky jack-of-all-trades, scores heavily, the part permitting him to showcase his wide range of talents.

The two children, Karen Dotrice and Matthew Garber, who want their father to pick a new nanny who will be fun and tell them stories when their former nanny, adroitly enacted by Elsa Lanchester, abruptly departs and leaves the household in an uproar, are particularly appealing. Tomlinson, as their harassed father, and Miss Johns, their nutty suffragette mother always on the go, perform uniquely. Ed Wynn, as Uncle Albert, who believes that anybody can fly if he laughs enough and is always laughing, amuses as he hosts his teaparty on the ceiling; Reginald Owen, as the eccentric Admiral Boom, who shoots his cannon from his rooftop ship promptly at 6 p.m., each evening, adds a humorous note, as do Arthur Treacher, a constable, and Hermione Baddeley, the Cockney maid.

Robert Stevenson's direction is sensitive and understanding as he catches all the nuances of the Mary Poppins character and the spell she casts, admirably scripted by Bill Walsh and Don DaGradi from the P.L. Travers' childhood books. Walsh also is credited as coproducer.

Particular credit also goes to Marc Breaux and Dee Dee Wood for their extraordinary choreography; Edward Colman's smooth photography; Carroll Clark and William H. Tuntke's distinguished art direction; Cotton Warburton's know-how editing; Tony Walton as costume and design consultant; Hamilton S. Luske's animation direction. Irwin Kostal supervised and arranged the music and conducted. *Whit.*

Send Me No Flowers
(COLOR)

Lightweight Doris Day-Rock Hudson marital comedy; good grosses indicated due to names.

Hollywood, Aug. 26.

Universal release of Martin Melcher (Harry Keller) production. Stars Doris Day, Rock Hudson, Tony Randall; features Hal March, Paul Lynde, Edward Andrews, Patricia Barry, Clint Walker. Directed by Norman Jewison. Screenplay, Julius Epstein, based on play by Norman Barasch, Carroll Moore; camera (Technicolor), Daniel Fapp; editor, J. Terry Williams; music, Frank De Vol; asst. director, Douglas Green. Reviewed at Academy Award Theatre, Aug. 25, '64. Running time, 100 MINS.

George	Rock Hudson
Judy	Doris Day
Arnold	Tony Randall
Mr. Akins	Paul Lynde
Winston Burr	Hal March
Dr. Morrissey	Edward Andrews
Linda	Patricia Barry
Vito	Clive Clerk
Milkman	Dave Willock
Cora	Aline Towne
Woman Commuter	Helen Winston
Nurse	Christine Nelson
Bert	Clint Walker

Perhaps it's because the possibilities inherent in a marital comedy with the same stars aren't endless, or because the basic premise here is too old-hat and not sufficient ingenuity is displayed in garmenting the familiar plot with necessary fresh habiliments, but whatever the cause, "Send Me No Flowers" doesn't carry the same voltage, either in laughs or originality, as Doris Day and Rock Hudson's two previous entries, "Pillow Talk" (1959) and "Lover Come Back" ('61). Film is amusing, however, and names of the two stars should spell satisfactory returns at b.o.

Adapted by Julius Epstein from the Broadway play by Norman Barasch and Carroll Moore, the thin story line romps around Hudson, a hypochondriac, overhearing his doctor discussing the fatal symptoms of another patient and believing them to be his own. In the belief he has only a few weeks to live, he sets about trying to find a suitable man to take his place as Miss Day's husband. Femme, at first rightfully distressed, learns her husband's true condition from the doctor, thinks he claimed to be dying to hide an affair with another woman, and throws him out of the house.

Norman Jewison in his direction weaves his characters in and out of this situation as skillfully as the script will permit, having the benefit, of course, of seasoned thesps in such roles. Miss Day is quite up to the demands of her part, indulging in a bit of slapstick in the opening sequence as she's locked out of the house in her nightgown, arms loaded with eggs and milk bottles. Hudson plays his character nobly. Tony Randall, costarred with the pair in the other two films, again plays Hudson's pal, this time his next door neighbor, who takes his friend's expected fate even harder than the soon-to-be-deceased and goes on a threeday drunk.

Some excellent trouping by Paul Lynde, as a cemetery salesman who loves his work, and Edward Andrews as the doctor, provide guffaws and high points in individual scenes. Clint Walker, in swing over from years in tv westerns, plays a millionaire Arizona sportsman once in love with Miss Day, whom Hudson considers for his wife after his "demise."

Harry Keller, making his bow as a producer after years as a director, is responsible for good physical values. Technical credits are uniformly expert, including Daniel Fapp's color photography, Frank De Vol's score, Jean Louis' gowns for femme star (who also warbles title song by Burt Bacharach and Hal David); J. Terry Williams' editing. *Whit.*

The Curse of The Mummy's Tomb
(BRITISH-COLOR)

Contrived horror thriller; thickly sliced ham that will get by as a dualer.

London, Aug. 25.

Columbia release (through BLC) of a Hammer (Michael Carreras) production. Stars Terence Morgan, Fred Clark, Ronald Howard; features Jeanne Roland, George Pastell, Jack Gwillim. Directed by Carreras. Screenplay, Henry Younger; camera (Technicolor), Otto Heller; music, Carlo Martelli; editor, Eric Boyd Perkins. Reviewed at Columbia Theatre, London. Running time, 80 MINS.

Adam Beauchamp	Terence Morgan
Alexander King	Fred Clark
John Bray	Ronald Howard
Annette Dubois	Jeanne Roland
Hashmi Bey	George Pastell
Inspector Mackenzie	John Paul
Sir Giles Dalrymple	Jack Gwillim
Professor Dubois	Bernard Rebel
The Mummy	Dickie Owen
Ra	Michael McStay
Jenny	Jill Mai Meredith
Jessop	Vernon Smythe

It needs a crystal ball to sort out the reasons for some of the contrived goings on in this modest and rather slapdash horror pic. But it doesn't need a soothsayer to guess, early, the identity of the heavy. After that it's merely a question of some fairly listless pondering as to when and how he'll get his comeuppance. With plenty of heads and severed hands rolling, liberally splashed with ketchup, there are probably enough kicks to satisfy indiscriminating audiences. But mediocre thesping and direction, obvious backcloths, ponderous dialog and occasional bewildering flashbacks make this a below-average entry from the Hammer horror stable.

Plot hinges around the discovery of an ancient tomb in the Egyptian desert, with a curse on anybody who opens it. Leader of the expedition intends giving the archaeological discoveries to the Egyptian government for its National Museum. But the expedition's smooth backer, a slick talking American showman, sees it as a coast-to-coast peepshow.

Murder and mayhem begins its gory trail and the motivation comes from a plausible stranger (Terence Morgan) who turns out to be a murderous descendant of the ancient Egyptian dynasty. That's a rough outline of Henry Younger's involved screenplay.

Though handsomely mounted, with the art department deserving a bow, even Otto Heller's camera cannot do much with some obviously phony backgrounds. Michael Carreras has directed the piece flatly, though there is a brisk finale.

Terence Morgan performs smoothly enough as the villain but is too patently up to no good from the start. Ronald Howard, Jack Gwillim and George Pastell are among those who provide sound support but the liveliest performance comes from Fred Clark. The pic introduces Jeanne Roland as the heroine. She hasn't much to do except look appropriately romantic. "Mummy's Tomb" falls well below the standard set by Hammer with its usually successful and competently-made horror fiction. *Rich.*

The Beauty Jungle
(BRITISH-COLOR)

Bright, fairly penetrating look of beauty contest jungle; exploitable title and brisk performances with plenty of femme appeal; good booking.

London, Aug. 25.

Rank release of a Val Guest production. Stars Ian Hendry, Janette Scott, Ronald Fraser, Edmund Purdom; features Kay Walsh, Jean Claudio, David Weston, Janina Faye, Norman Bird, Tommy Trinder, Jerry Matthews, Peter Ashmore. Directed by Guest. Screenplay, Robert Muller, Guest; camera (Eastmancolor), Arthur Grant; editor, Bill Lenny; music, Laurie Johnson. Reviewed at RFD Private Theatre. Running time, 114 MINS.

Don Mackenzie	Ian Hendry
Shirley	Janette Scott
Walter	Ronald Fraser
Carrick	Edmund Purdom
Armand	Jean Claudio
Mrs. Freeman	Kay Walsh
Freeman	Norman Bird
Elaine	Janina Faye
Charlie Dorton	Tommy Trinder
Harry	David Weston
Taylor	Francis Matthews
Organizer	Jerry Desmonde
Lucius	Peter Ashmore
Jean Watson	Jacqueline Jones
Miss Peru	Alizia Gur
Barbara	Jackie White
2nd Chaperone	Leila Williams
American Tourists	Paul Carpenter, Henry McCarthy
Globe Organizer	Raymond Young
Typist	Marianne Stone
Janet	Sylvia Steel
Angela	Eve Arden
Julie	Jacqueline Wallis
Caroline	Margaret Nolan
Cora	Nicki Peters

The Beauty Queen contest has become a highly exploitable affair the world over and this pic, which takes a knowing if not over-searching eye at the topic, has equally exploitable qualities. There's plenty of pulchritude in the beauty queens which director-writer Val Guest has assembled in his cast, and some lively, if not over subtle, comedy in this yarn of a girl who gains quick rewards, but finds the going full of disillusionment and pitfalls. It is a sound booking for some audiences.

Screenplay tends to soft pedal the problems involved and the writers (Guest and an observant journalist-author Robert Muller, who has studied the Beauty Queen scene) seem reluctant to come out with their views on whether such contests are degrading or even dangerous to comely damsels who take them too seriously, or whether they are just a harmless giggle. They "tut-tut" politely when a more ruthless scalpel would have helped. However, Guest's direction has provided an amusing film about an interesting if shallow phase of contemporary life.

Story concerns a pretty stenographer who is joshed by a local newspaper columnist into entering a seaside pier contest. She wins and he takes over and builds her up into a regular contestant at such junkets who progresses steadily around the familiar circuit and gets into the big time league of big money, overblown publicity, commercialism and spurious glitter that's the magnet

On the way, both she and the columnist get their share of disappointments before she comes to her senses and goes home in time to save some of her self-respect, and also prevent her kid sister from jumping on the same giddy carousel. Old students will recognize the validity of some of the backstage rivalry and chicanery that goes on in even the most reputable of such shenanigans, but these are not explored in depth.

Janette Scott, as the beauty queen, cops a role that proves finally that the British kid star is now a fully fledged, talented young woman with style. Ian Hendry, as the poor man's Svengali, is brisk and credible while Ronald Fraser, as his lenser buddy, also turns in a ripe performance.

The inevitable fading egotistic film star, who regularly judges such contests for the publicity and possible boudoir perks, is played with style and self-deprecating good humor by Edmund Purdom. Tommy Trinder, Kay Walsh, David Weston, Jean Claudio and Janina Faye also contribute rewardingly.

Pic displays an eyeworthy lineup of shapely young femmes as the leading contestants. Guest also had good judgment with some of the misfit types that are pulled into such contests with about as much chance of success as the Dodgers have of winning the English F.A. Cup Final.

Sharp editing, a light Laurie Johnson score and shrewd camerawork by Arthur Lenny give a lift to both the seaside resort sequences and the more ritzy surroundings of the Riviera. *Rich.*

Topkapi
(COLOR)

"Rififi" for laughs. Jules Dassin mixes suspense and humor with excellent results. Delightful cast makes most of firstrate script.

United Artists release of Filmways production, produced and directed by Jules Dassin. Stars Melina Mercouri, Peter Ustinov, Maximilian Schell; features Robert Morley, Akim Tamiroff, Gilles Segal, Jess Hahn. Screenplay, Monja Danischewsky, based on Eric Ambler's "The Light of Day"; camera (Color), Henri Alekan; music, Manos Hadjidakis; asst. directors, Tom Pevsner, Joseph Dassin. Tradeshown at Astor, N.Y., Aug. 26, 1964. Running time, 120 MINS.
Elizabeth Lipp .... Melina Mercouri
Arthur Simpson .... Peter Ustinov
William Walter ....Maximilian Schell
Cedric Page .... Robert Morley
Geven .... Akim Tamiroff
Giulio .... Gilles Segal
Fischer .... Jess Hahn
Harback .... Titos Wandis
Major Tufan .... Ege Ernart
First Shadow .... Senih Orkan
Second Shadow . Ahmet Danyal Topatan
Josef .... Joseph Dassin
Nanny .... Amy Dalby
Voula .... Despo Diamantidou

Still fascinated, evidently, by the intriguing world of high-level crime, Jules Dassin has taken a minor novel by Eric Ambler and turned it into a delightful and suspenseful comedy spoof of his own "Rififi."

The double elements of humor and suspense are about equally balanced throughout the film but, though close at times, laughs are never permitted to intrude when the master crime gets under way.

Monja Danischewsky's script has given Dassin a well-paced plot, liberally sprinkled with wit and incidents of both broad and satirical comedy. He has gathered as leading players a small, choice selection of talent that gives the final polish to the smooth yarn.

Although the sexual allure of Melina Mercouri is ever present (indeed she gives a remarkably frank interpretation of a nymphomaniac but suggests it, for the most part, with facial expressions and dialog rather than the embarrassingly detailed variations seen on the screen too often, of late), her greed is not restricted to males; she also has big eyes for fine jewelry—so fine that it is usually found in a museum.

The band of thieves whose adventures make "Topkapi" are a motley crew, indeed. Besides Miss Mercouri, it includes Maximilian Schell, master thief; Robert Morley, Gilles Segal and Jess Hahn. Added later, although it takes him some time and a bit of adventure to realize it, Peter Ustinov is an unwitting accomplice.

The basically simple plot, which is rich in detail and background, has the gang attempting to steal a fabulous jeweled dagger from the Topkapi Palace museum in Istanbul. The actual theft is depicted in a long sequence reminiscent of the one in "Rififi" but with a bit more levity.

Miss Mercouri has a holiday in a role that asks her to be equally enamored of gems and males. Her facial reaction to a large group of wrestlers is a delightful travesty on sex. She plays what could be a distasteful part with such abandon that no one could be offended. Schell, surprisingly, plays

his role somewhat tongue-in-cheek, never evidencing more than a surface interest in anything (including Miss Mercouri), other than his work.

Ustinov has probably the meatiest part in the film and one that allows him to use many of the unsubtleties in dominating scenes he has at his command. Morley is delightfully kooky as an expert in transistors, electronics and kindred subjects. Gilles Segal's silent but athletic role provides some of the film's top suspense moments. They're all excellently supported by Tamiroff, Joseph Dassin, Titos Wandis, Ege Ernart, Senih Orkan and Ahmet Danyal Topatan.

Henri Alekan's color camerawork makes the most of a film having been filmed almost entirely on location in Istanbul. The audience is given a crooks' tour of the colorful city. Actual events are worked into the continuity, such as the mass wrestling meet. There are no listed editor credits, indicating that Dassin more or less supervised this part of the post-filming work.

Manos Hadjikdakis' music, while interesting, too often comes over as a Grecian version of how Turkish music should sound.
Robe.

Samson And The Slave Queen
(Zorro Contre Maciste)
(ITALIAN-COLOR)

American International Pictures release of Roman Film. (Fortunato Misiano) production. Directed by Umberto Lenzi. Stars Pierre Brice, Alan Steel; features Moira Orfei, Maria Grazia Spina, Andrea Aureli, Massimo Serato. Screenplay, Lenzi and Guido Malatesta; camera (Colorscope), Augusto Tiezzi; music composed and conducted by Frances Colavagnino; Reviewed at RKO 86th St., N.Y., Sept. 2, 1964. Running time, 86 MINS.
Zorro .... Pierre Brice
Samson (Maciste) .... Alan Steel
Malva .... Moira Orfei
Isabella .... Maria Grazia Spina
Rabek .... Andrea Aureli
Garcia .... Massimo Serato

AIP's import from Italy, where it was filmed as "Zorro Contre Maciste," has enough vim and vigor, thanks to a spirited performance by Pierre Brice as Zorro, to please the less-demanding beefcake-and-biceps aficianados. Current double-billing for New York first run with Embassy's "A House Is Not A Home" provides an interesting program contrast of flesh display, male and female.

Teaming agility with brute strength is evidently an effort to maintain audience interest in the sinewy cinema field. Eventually, as it does here, interest will follow the adroit actor rather than the muscular male. Brice, one of the more promising young European thespians (best known for the German-made Karl May westerns, he has recently finished Columbia's "Major Dundee"), plays a dashing swordsman-bandit in a style that's both Doug Fairbanks and Gerard Philippe. His natural flair for heroics and a better-written part enable him to act circles around his costar, strong man Alan Steel, cast as the usual muscle-bound do-gooder.

Produced in Italy, the film's setting is Spain. (AIP's ads show Steel pulling down columns and a

female beating slaves—neither of which have anything to do with the story). The flimsy plot has Steel conned into helping Moira Orfei, evil aspirant to the throne, while Brice sides up with Maria Grazia Spina, another claimant to the crown. Eventually Brice and Steel join forces (blade and biceps) to rout Miss Orfei's baddies, led by villain Massimo Serato. Director Umberto Lenzi keeps his cast moving, with emphasis on fighting.

With exception of Brice, excellent throughout, acting is only adequate although Andrea Aureli, as a rascally bandit chief, breaks out of the mould occasionally. Film has one major drawback—an exceptionally poor color process, something called Colorscope, and highly unflattering to actors, especially Miss Spina (a blonde) who appears to have yellow jaundice. Photography, otherwise, is adequate as are other technical aspects. Frances Colavagnino's score is properly swashbuckling if not memorable. *Robe.*

The Secret Invasion
(DE LUXE COLOR— PANAVISION)

War drama's excellent technical work and frequent plot twists, plus beaucoup action, should give it needed boost at b.o.

United Artists release of Corman Co. (Gene Corman) production. Directed by Roger Corman. Stars Stewart Granger, Raf Vallone, Mickey Rooney, Edd Byrnes, Henry Silva. Story and screenplay, R. Wright Campbell; camera (Deluxe), Arthur E. Arling; editor, Ronald Sinclair; special effects, George Blackwell; music, Hugo Friedhofer; asst. director, Charles Griffith. Tradeshown at UA, home office, N.Y., Aug. 28, 1964. Running time, 95 MINS.
Major Richard Mace...Stewart Granger
Roberto Rocca .... Raf Vallone
Terrence Scanlon ...... Mickey Rooney
Simon Fell .... Edd Byrnes
John Durrell .... Henry Silva
Mila .... Mia Massini
Jean Saval .... William Campbell
German Commandant
                  Helmo Kindermann
General Quadri .... Enzo Fiermonte
Marko .... Peter Coe
Stephana .... Nan Morris
German Captain....Helmut Schneider
Italian Officer .... Giulio Marchetti
Fishing Capt. .... Nicholas Rend
Petar .... Craig March
Partisan Leader .... Todd Williams
First Monk .... Charles Brent
Wireless Operator.......Richard Johns
German Naval Lt. .... Kurt Bricker
Peasant Woman .... Katrina Rozan

"Secret Invasion," a war drama, has action — almost unceasingly. It was filmed entirely in Yugoslavia, under working title of "Dubious Patriots," with cooperation of the Yugoslavian government. Although the film's familiar-to-the-U.S.-market cast and its heavy emphasis on action are necessary for general audiences, its photographic plug for the country's scenic beauty should provide an effective form of repayment for the Tito government's assistance.

Although it should have little effect on the general appeal of the film, its technical excellence, especially in photography, art and set direction, spotlights its weaker departments, particularly the writing and acting.

Director Roger Corman and scripter R. Wright Campbell have evidently made an excellent study of previous films that dealt with war, prison, heroism and patriotism, as there are some familiar scenes in their bloody tale. Luckily, they all seem quite at home.

British officer Stewart Granger takes a team of specialists (in various forms of crime) into Yugoslavia in 1943 on an Allied mission. Criminals all, they're to be pardoned if successful, but it's apparent from the start that most of them won't make it. The experts — Raf Vallone, Mickey Rooney, Henry Silva, Edd Byrnes and William Campbell—provide expected resistance to the idea but realize, finally, they must succeed to survive.

Vallone, who gets top billing in Europe, carries most of the acting responsibility as the master criminal who takes charge once the operation begins. He gives one of his usual excellent performances and easily outdistances the efforts of the others. Granger's officer is all heroics, and little histrionics, except for his final scenes. Silva is excellent in last half of the film when he drops his cold-blooded, emotionless characteristics. This change stems from his accidentally killing the baby of one of the partisan women, well played by newcomer Mia Wassini.

Byrnes, Rooney and Campbell are hampered by poorly-written roles and, on the part of Rooney, frequent overacting. Byrnes' forger shows little depth of character, Campbell, supposedly a moster of disguise and dialect, is rarely convincing. Besides Miss Massini, good support is provided by Helmo Kindermann, as the fortress commandant, and Peter Coe, as the partisan leader. The use of a basically English soundtrack, but with non-English supporting players speaking in their own tongues, should facilitate foreign dubbing. Vallone's adeptness at both Italian and English enables him to do all his own speeches but Campbell's German is obviously dubbed.

Arthur E. Arling's color camerawork is the film's top asset. He has beautifully photographed the unfamiliar but photogenic Yugoslavian port of Dubrovnik, using the idyllic scenery as a background and, by contrast, a commentary on the fighting and killing which takes place against it. Other technical work complements Arling's artistry. A bit old-fashioned but frequently majestic, Hugo Friedhofer's score is the fullbodied type that makes a good soundtrack album. *Robe.*

The Comedy Man
(BRITISH)

Slight but well made anecdote about unsuccessful stock player. Maybe the joke's a bit too "in" for non-legit customers, but an engaging lightweight performance by Kenneth More is a distinct pull.

London, Sept. 4.

BLC release of British Lion presentation. Stars Kenneth More. Features Cecil Parker, Dennis Price, Billie Whitelaw, Angela Douglas, Norman Rossington, Edmund Purdom. Producer, Jon Penington. Director, Alvin Rakoff. Screenplay, Peter Yeldham, from Douglas Hayes' novel; camera, Ken Hodges; music, Bill McGuffie. Reviewed at Columbia Theatre, London, Sept. 3, '64. Running time, **92 MINS.**

Chick ... Kenneth More
Rutherford ... Cecil Parker
Tommy Morris ... Dennis Price
Judy ... Billie Whitelaw
Theodore ... Norman Rossington
Fay ... Angela Douglas
Prout ... Frank Finlay
Julian ... Edmond Purdom
Sloppit ... J. C. Devlin
Twins ... Valerie & Leila Croft
Indian Chief ... Freddie Mills,
Jan Kennedy ... Jill Adams

Douglas Hayes' lightweight novel about the struggle of a stock actor who has just passed the dangerous 40s, without making the grade, hardly scratches new ground. But its authenticity and atmosphere are complete and this well made little film recreates that atmosphere splendidly on the screen. It will provide wry chuckles and some pangs for most stock actors, but the joke may be rather too "in" for non-legits. Still, a well drawn performance by Kenneth More in a role which, he admits, might well have been the story of his life if the breaks hadn't come for him, adds greatly to the entertainment value of the film. "The Comedy Man's" slick, superficial blend of yocks and tears will make a sound dualer if booked with a more weighty pic.

Fired from a stock company in the sticks for being found with the leading lady, who happens to be the producer's wife, More comes to London for one more crack at making good in the big time. In the seedy atmosphere of theatrical digs, promiscuous affairs, doing the agents' rounds he suffers all the humiliations and disappointments. Eventually pride breaks down, he takes a job doing tv commercials as "Mr. Honeybreath," which brings him dough and recognition. But the desire for stage success still eats him and he walks out of one of his own dizzy parties to go back to legit work in the provinces and retain some shreds of professional pride.

This slight plot is neatly embellished with all the trimmings that help to build up a not too exaggerated peek at the feckless, heartbreaking hand-to-mouth lives led by these struggling thesps who live on hope. The shooting of the tv commercials, the rounds of the agents, life in digs, the flip talk at parties and in showbiz pubs, the local gags are all put over with pleasant enough gaiety. But More and some of the other actors have also opportunities, well taken, of showing the disillusionment and the desperate nagging anxieties that are part of the lot of the theatrical profession — especially in the lower echelon.

Peter Yeldham has, in fact, turned out a neat script and it is perceptively directed by Alvin Rakoff. More tackles both the frivolous and the more serious with deft artistry and Cecil Parker as the veteran actor failure, Edmund Purdom who gets a break as a film star, Dennis Price as a smoothie agent and Norman Rossington as an amorous salesmen living in the theatrical digs provide amiable support. On the distaff side there's a particuarly well rounded showing by Billie Whitelaw as an ex-flame of More's, who knows and loves him well enough to be able to accuse him of being a spectacular failure and a not spectacular success on tv, while Angela Douglas shapes up well as a naive young actress who is his current romance. Jacqueline Hill has a few moving moments as the wife of a flop actor who commits suicide.

In fact, "The Comedy Man" scores with several small, successful bits, notably by Frank Finlay, Alan Dobie, Jacqueline Hill, J. C. Devlin, Jill Adams and Derek Francis. Cutting and lensing are brisk and competent and the locale of the Shaftesbury Avenue world of agents offices, parties and taverns have a bitter authenticity that comes of the painfully sure knowledge by most of the folk connected with the film of the uneasy world that they are portraying. *Rich.*

The Last Man on Earth
(ITALIAN-U.S.)

American International Pictures release of Associated Producers (Robert L. Lippert) and Produzioni La Regina coproduction. Directed by Sidney Salkow. Stars Vincent Price; features Franca Bettoia, Emma Danieli, Giacomo Rossi-Stuart. Screenplay, Logan Swanson and William P. Leicester from Richard Mathesen's novel, "I Am Legend"; camera, Franco Delli Colli; editor, Gene Ruggiero; music, Paul Sawtell, Bert Shefter; asst. director, Carlo Grandone. Reviewed at RKO Palace, N.Y., Sept. 2, 1964. Running time, **86 MINS.**

Robert Morgan ... Vincent Price
Ruth ... Franca Bettoia
Virginia ... Emma Danieli
Ben Cortman ... Giacomo Rossi-Stuart
Umberto Rau, Christi Courtland, Tony Corevi, Hector Ribotta.

Although weak ammunition for even the bottom half of a double bill, AIP should have little trouble finding bookings for this programmer, thanks to the sales value of Vincent Price's name, an interesting title and proper promotion. In New York, film is playing first-run on bill with U's "I'd Rather Be Rich."

Credited as joint effort of Associated Producers (Robert L. Lippert) and Produzioni La Regina, general impression left by the film is that it is a quickly-made, extremely low budgeter, possibly a combination of Italian location and studio filming, polished in the U.S. Despite an English soundtrack and use of signs printed in English, there's a European look to the scenery, furnishings and most of the cast. Dubbing is poor for the most part, with exception of Price whose voice is well recorded.

Producer Lippert's budget evidently carried a high Price, judging by the cheaply built interiors and props, lack of names (even for Italians) and inadequate lighting for Franco Delli Colli's black and white photography. Logan Swanson and William Leicester's script, despite a basically interesting idea, has nothing really suspenseful in it to hold attention. Such plot loopholes as Price, for instance, leaving his house wearing a coat, walking into his garage in a sweater, then walking around his car in the coat, abound.

Thinking himself the only person alive after a plague that has also killed his wife (Emma Danieli) and child, Price, a scientist, fights a nightly battle with what appear to be vampires, trying to break into his house. Price's fellow scientist (Giacomo Rossi-Stuart) becomes a "creature" himself, although the script never explains how.

Director Sidney Salkow begins his film at a plodding pace, evidently to create suspense, and the plot remains immobile with the exception of a short chase sequence near the end. Technical work, including Paul Sawtell and Bert Shefter's score, is generally poor. *Robe.*

Guns At Batasi
(CinemaScope)
(BRITISH)

British drama mixing a professional soldier with politics in a story of morality. An artistic film that will depend on bookings and word-of-mouth.

Hollywood, Sept. 8.

20th Century-Fox release of George H. Brown production. Stars Richard Attenborough, Flora Robson, John Lefton, Jack Hawkins, Mia Farrow. Directed by John Guillermin. Screenplay, Robert Holles from his novel; original adaptation, Leo Marks, Marshall Pugh; additional material, C. M. Pennington-Richards; camera (CinemaScope), Douglas Slocombe; editor, Max Benedict; music, composed and conducted, John Addison; played by Sinfonia of London; asst. director Jan Darnley Smith. Reviewed at studio, Aug. 26, 1964. Running time, **102 MINS.**

Reg. Sgt. Major Lauderdale ... Richard Aattenborough
Colonel Deal ... Jack Hawkins
Miss Barker-Wise ... Flora Robson
Pvt. Wilkes ... John Leyton
Karen Ericksson ... Mia Farrow
Fletcher ... Cecil Parker
Lt. Boniface ... Errol John
Sgt. "Dodger" Brown ... Graram Stark
Capt. Abraham ... Earl Cameron
Sgt. Ben Parkin ... Percy Herbert
Sgt. "Muscles" Dunn ... David Lodge
Sgt. "Schoolie" Prideaux ... Bernard Horsfall
Sgt. "Aussie" Drake ... John Meillon
Corp. Abou ... Horace James
Captain ... Patricak Holt
Adjutant ... Alan Browning
Lieutenant ... Richard Bidlake
Archibong Shaw ... Joseph Layode
Russell ... Ric Hutton

Soldiering and politics don't mix, according to a well developed screenplay and story by Robert Holles which dissects with a piercing personal touch the strict disciplinary attitudes that govern a true British soldier and makes him retain his own individual pride in the face of political forces unappreciative of his principles.

Were "Guns" an American picture, with a more generally known cast and Americanized character identification, it might prove to be a highly commercial picture. However, the completely British elements involved turn the film into a specialty offering on the edge between art and general run. Its success will be dependent on selection of bookings and possible resultant word of mouth.

Producer George Brown and director John Guillermin, who have been successful in earlier British imports, come up with a strong and frequently exciting piece of work in this picture, the story of a British battalion caught in the midst of the African struggle for independence.

A small group of men, headed by a book regimental sergeant, are pitted in resistance to the new government prior to official word of the change. The valor of the sergeant, who risks his life to protect his station when an African lieutenant seizes command under a new regime, becomes the focal point of the story, mixing war drama with morality in a manner that makes a succinct point.

Sympathies may be with the British band and, particularly, with the sergeant, who acts strictly within his responsibilities, but his dismissal from post at the request of the new government is understandable from a political standpoint, even if unjust in his unfortunate position as a political victim.

Performances throughout are excellent. Richard Attenborough is tough, crisp and staunch as the sergeant, playing with as much starch as the character implies. Errol John has intense qualities of fanaticism as the lieutenant who siezes the government, and Jack Hawkins, in essentially a cameo spot, plays like the resigned war-horse he is meant to be. Flora Robson brings guts and an earthy quality to the role of a hardened Member of Parliament impressed with her own importance. Only romantic interest is provided with charm by John Leyton and Mia Farrow, latter the daughter of the late John Farrow and Maureen O'Sullivan and introduced in the film. Miss Farrow has a pensive, soft quality that indicates future potential.

Earl Cameron, Percy Herbert, David Lodge, Graham Stark, John Meillon, Bernard Horsfall, Alan Browning, Horace James and Bloke Modisane are all excellent in lesser roles. *Dale.*

Slottet
(The Castle)
(DANISH-COLOR)
Copenhagen, Sept. 1.

Palladium Studio production and release. Stars Malene Schwartz, Lone Hertz, Poul Reichardt. Directed by Anker. Based on novel by Ib Henrik Cavling; screenplay, Morten Schyberg; camera (Technicolor), Henning Bendtsen. Running time, **80 MINS.**

Bente Falk .... Malene Schwartz
Marianne Falk .... Lone Hertz
Regitze Falk .... Mimi Heinrich
Henrik Stenfelt ...... Poul Reichhardt
Family lawyer .... Karl Stegger
Cousin Hans .... Preben Marth
The butler .... Ole Monty
Metron .... Bodil Steen

This kind of film just isn't done any more, and probably will not be either by Palladium. For the umpteenth time, Anker has taken the corniest kind of dream story about girls of yesterday who rescue the family castle from its debts, first by hard work and then by trying to sell their lily-white bodies to some rich if nasty man. Finally, of course they find a knight with sufficient gold in both heart and coffer.

This film dream may still appeal to some people but perhaps not too many. Color photography by Henning Bendtsen is vivid. The well-established Danish actors all seem to be enjoying a private joke on the director. *Kell.*

Venice Films

Nothing But a Man
An American indie with insight into Negro life in the south as exemplified by a couple in crisis; well made, this needs special handling but could well be worth it.

Venice, Sept. 1.

Nothing But A Man Co. — Du Art Film Labs production and release. Stars Ivan Dixon, Abbey Lincoln; features Gloria Foster, Julius Harris, Leonard Parker, Yaphet Kotto, Stanley Greene. Directed by Michael Roemer. Screenplay, Robert Young, Roemer; camera, Robert Young; editor, Luke Bennet. At Venice Film Fest. Running time, **95 MINS.**

Duff .... Ivan Dixon
Josie .... Abbey Lincoln
Lee .... Gloria Foster

Will .... Julius Harris
Driver .... Martin Priest
Frankie .... Leonard Parker
Jocko .... Yaphet Kotto
Dawson .... Stanley Greene
Effie .... Helen Lounck
Doris .... Helene Arrindell
Pop .... Milton Williams
Raddick .... Melvin Stewart

Film deals meaningfully with the crisis in the life of a Negro couple in the South (U.S.). It is more about the need for dignity and human commitment than a didactic pic. Its intensity, fine acting and knowing mounting could make this a film with good chances for specialized bookings. Word-of-mouth and crix appraisal are likely plus factors.

It is fitting in these times for films to handle this theme. Right placement and selling could have it in for general as well as arty theatre interest. Southern chances are problematical. However, this could very well have the legs for arty and even playoff possibilities.

Somewhere in Alabama a railroad lineman falls in love with a local girl. He is also from Alabama but had been up North and overseas in the army. Ivan Dixon is in his mid-twenties as is she. If he has more instinct, she more intellectual, making for a good balance. If not unusually violent, Dixon does want to be accepted as a human being—a man. This gets him into trouble when he takes a town job after his marriage. Working in a local factory, Dixon is soon judged a troublemaker. He's fired and put on a blacklist. Shunning menial labor, he becomes frustrated and bitter. He tells off an Uncle Tomish father-in-law, has bouts of violence with his wife and inanimate objects. He finally runs off.

But the death of his father, a violent man, sees him going back to take his stand with his wife even if it means trouble. Though he will try to cope, this is not resignation but a step forward in his manhood. The film does not try for preaching but is effective in its modest way and in its awareness of character and place.

Perhaps there is a tendency to let this meander and bring out its growth in character and outlooks in talk rather than a more full-bodied integration with the social elements and human relations. But it rings true and appears one of those rare films delivering an insight into Southern life and the place of the Negro without patronizing or using false histrionics.

Abbey Lincoln has a striking presence and manages to give a feeling of strength and wisdom that is the bolster for her more direct but emotionally immature husband, played with intensity and intelligence by Dixon.

Michael Roemer has directed firmly with a feel for character delineation and progression. He has obtained a fine response from his mixed pro and non-pro cast. Lensing is sharp and direct and avoids pictorial quality for its own sake. The use of folk, jazz and spiritual music is excellent.

There is no exploiting of a timely theme here, but a searching attempt to look at the human side of the Negro's needs. This independent production is a credit to all involved and a plus for the non-Hollywood indies who can find a way of making the films they want on their own.

Picture has a good documentary flavor even if the whites involved are usually just external features.

This might have used a script with more dramatic scope and a direct tie-in with Southern life. But on its own level, the pic succeeds in making a strong plea about the human side of the Negro today. *Mosk.*

Hakujitsumu
(Day Dream)
(JAPANESE-SCOPE)

Venice, Sept. 1.

Shochiku release and production. Stars Kanako Michi, Akira Ishihama, Chojuro Hanakawa. Written and directed by Tetsuji Takechi from novel by Junichiro Tanizaki. Camera, Masayoshi Kayanuma. At Venice Film Festival. Running time, **93 MINS.**

Chieko .... Kanako Michi
Kurabashi .... Akira Ishihama
Dentist .... Chojuro Hanakawa

Though this pic is sprinkled throughout with female nudity, and with perverse and erotic love scenes, it is not offensive or in bad taste. Naturally it will have some censorships problems.

It is mainly a black comedy about desire and human behavior with specialized foreign booking chances for the more advanced film buffs plus the handlers of sex-ploitation pix.

Based on a 1926 book, it embodies some of the attitudes of the surrealist and expressionist pix of the times. That is, it gains its freedom in treatment and story by making it all a dream, and one that takes place under an anesthetic in a dentist's chair.

The feeling is set by excessive pointing up of the nosey, harrowing and eerie look of people getting their teeth fixed. Closeups give it a risible air by making it so grotesque that pain and latent fears of the dentist can be smiled, or laughed, at.

A young man and a pretty young girl have adjoining dentist chairs since the doctor seems to work on two at a time, aided by a nurse. He has been smitten by the girl and half under drugs seems to see her faint and the doctor suddenly strips off part of her clothes and bites deeply into her chest with the teeth marks quite clearly shown. Then she is singing in an empty night club, except for the dentist now turned into a menacing heavy.

The boy follows them and sees the dentist putting her to all sorts of tortures, helpless behind a strong window. She is strung up by the arms with her clothes cut off, subjected to shock treatments that make her writhe in agony with a scene in color showing her bleeding from knife wounds but still attracted to, and making love to, the heavy.

All this manages to have a risible yet serious air. It is both satirical and inventive in its own right.

Comes the awakening and the couple leaves the office while the

dentist gives a wicked look at the audience when another lovely girl takes a seat. Meanwhile the girl offers the boy a lift in her car and the teeth marks on her chest are shown as she covers them up as they drive off.

Of course this film could be accused of bad taste or pornography, and the many scenes of simulated love climaxes may add to this theory. But it also parodies and pokes fun at prudishness, sex overemphasis and the more lascivious love and adventure pix. It is neatly lensed and edited with a gory color scene imbedded in this primarily black and white pic.

Kanako Michi suffers admirably as the girl and is also good to look at while Akira Ishihama is a properly stalwart hero trying to save his girl by love, but not above killing her when he feels she does not deserve him. Chojuro Hanakawa is a creepy menace.

Pic was refused by the Venice fest, but might have been a worthy special entry. It would probably have raised howls both for and against it.

Director Tetsuji Takechi shows he knows his oldtime films and can give them a more personal and up to date look via the proper balance of over-statement and mock seriousness. It is a big hit in Japan but would need careful handling anywhere else with censor troubles all the way. *Mosk.*

Att Alska
(To Love)
(SWEDEN)

Venice, Sept. 1.

Sandrews production and release. Features Harriet Andersson, Zbigniev Czybulski, Isa Quenel, Tomas Svanfledt, Jane Friedman, Nils Eklund, Jan Erik Lindkvist. Written and directed by Jorn Donner. Camera, Sven Nikvist; music, Bo Nilsson; editor, Lennart Warren. At Venice Film Fest. Running time, **90 MINS.**

Louise .... Harriet Andersson
Fredrik .... Zbigniev Czybulski
Marta .... Isa Quenel
Jakob .... Tomas Svenfeldt
Nora .... Jane Friedman
Priest .... Nils Eklund
Speaker .... Jan-Erik Lindkvist

Second feature effort by young Swedish-Finnish director Jorn Donner is a quality entry about a widow who becomes merry. It has exploitable angles that should send it off to okay possibilities in many areas. Combo of arty story and development and tastefully handled but nevertheless exploitable love scenes set it up for this parlay. But it needs adroit handling to get the most from both sales points.

Among many other things, the pic is basically the story of the developing love affair of a still-young widow and a zany sort of travel agent. After her husband's death, the widow slowly comes out of her conformity shell in which she's lived for 10 years, and begins to enjoy life—and love-making—for the first time, thanks to the agent's assiduous attentions. At the same time, he begins slowly to mature and take a more serious attitude towards life. Neither attempts to dominate, both in a way resist a more binding link, and the end is left open as to whether or not the affair will continue.

But meanwhile, the fun has been had. It's documented in a completely honest, unleering manner though in great detail, taking up something about 80% of the pic. Unhypocritical handling brings off that rarity, the exploitation film with taste. Donner's direction skips over distracting bits, and concentrates on showing the awakening of the woman's sensuality and abandonment of her former conformity. Some may find the frequent bedroom scenes repetitious or even boring, but each is nevertheless there for a purpose.

Harriet Andersson is excellent as the widow with a beautifully modulated performance. Less successful is Zbigniev Czybulski's as her maturing lover. Often he appears to handle over-heavily a role which is to be treated lightly and with more charm. Isa Quensel has some good moments as the girl's condescending mother while Tomas Svenfeldt is okay as the boy.

Camerawork by Sven Nikvist rates a nod, as does the musical backdrop, often tongue-in-cheek, by Bo Nilsson. Other credits measure up, but it's Miss Andersson's and Donner's picture all the way.

Hawk.

The Case of The 44's
(BRITISH-DANISH)

Lightweight spoof of James Bond pix with okay playoff possibilities in general situations with exploitation fillip helping.

Venice, Sept. 3.

D. & A. Productions Ltd. release of Jon Penington-Bent Christensen Production for Passo Verde Films. Stars Ian Carmichael; features Bent Christensen, William Rosenberg, Lotte Tarp, Jessie Rindom, Carl Stegger, Gunnar Lauring, Peter Maalberg. Narration by Tony Hawes for Voice of Monty Landis. Written and directed by Tom McCowan. Camera, Henning Christiansen. Music, Bent Fabricius-Bjerre. Tradeshown in Venice. Running time, **73 MINS.**

Jim Pond .... Ian Carmichael
Miss 44 .... Lotte Tarp
Sinister Man .... Bent Christensen
English Photographer
William Rosenberg
Charlady .... Jessie Rindom
Carl S. Berg .... Carl Stegger
Laboratory Man .... Gunnar Lauring
Old Mon .... Peter Maalberg

Reportedly produced on a microscopic budget in Denmark, but boasting an English-language soundtrack, this pic should parlay into a moneymaker on its spoof humor take off of the James Bond and other spy-crime mellers, as well as some equally spoofed, but nevertheless present, sexploitation angles. It is often flimsy fluff, but could provide good filler fare for most situations.

After a not-too mysterious murder in Copenhagen, agent Jim Pond is called in from Scotland Yard. In Denmark, he rapidly gets enmeshed in intrigue and a chase for a blonde with a 44 bust, prime suspect for the crime. All thriller angles are given the once-over-lightly with tongue in cheek, and there's a particularly funny bit in which, a la "Doctor No," gal is subjected to "dangerous" experiment in radiation—this time from a man-catching perfume, complete with de-contamination, etc.

Often, humor falls flat and the goings get pretty silly and predictable, but there's enough to keep it going, including the intermittent appearance of a cast of pretty girls. Ian Carmichael is at ease in his tailor made role as the would-be investigator, playing it in the traditional tut-tut British key. Lotte Tarp is the statuesque beauty he is chasing, while Bent Christensen, William Rosenberg, Jessie Rindom, and a large cast fill out the roster ably.

Technically, pic has an added advantage, for export to all non-English marts, of having almost no pertinent dialog; most of the talk is handled by the speaker, making for easy dubbing jobs. Technically, it's a neat job, and other credits, including Henning Christiansen's lensing, Bent Fabricius-Bjerre's music, and editing by Christian Hartkop, are in keeping. *Hawk.*

Across the River

Venice, Sept. 1.

Sharff production and release. Stars Lou Gilbert, Kay Doubleday. Written and directed by Stefan Sharff. Camera, Tom Mangravili; music, Charles Gorss. At Venice Film Fest. Running Time, **85 MINS.**

Obadiah .... Lou Gilbert
Monica .... Kay Doubleday

Stefan Sharff, who heads the film department of Columbia University (N.Y.), has made a tender film fable that is both reminiscent of 1930 Hollywood comedies and still is a modern parable in its own right. Yet its pacing, feeling and outlook slant this more for arty chances. Playoff possibilities call for hardsell.

He has taken a bearded, old junk man and dealt with his apparently happy life on the outskirts of a big city. When the outer world intrudes, it leads him to stealing, the first feelings of femme need and to eventual tragedy. If there are echos of Harry Langdon and other like comedians, film still has a personal ring and today's sound of the big city turmoil.

Sharff has woven a series of incidents rather than tried to tell a story. The junkman lives in a cluttered shack across the river from Manhattan. He has a goat who lives with him and gives him milk which he exchanges for food and he makes enough for his undemanding existence by collecting and selling junk.

Then one day he meets a girl along the river and helps her when a man in a car tries to molest her. He takes her home and she lives there idyllically by his side though she is young. She needs a coat and he tries to get one for her but a policeman takes his money, gotten from junk sales, when he looks suspicious. This leads him to steal a coat.

Lou Gilbert has the right frisky, childish quality with an impish dash that makes him a touching, anachronistic but beguiling figure as the junkman. If almost inarticulate, his few words always deal with how he lives, but his actions denote a deep human contentment in his dissociation from life.

Kay Doubleday is a comely miss who has a fetching quality. Director Sharff, however, does not push his symbols. But he has achieved a truly fable-like quality in his mixture of seething city life and almost pastoral, poverty existence.

While there is no try for comedy in situation, it is there via the reactions and actions of this' unworldly old man. There also is a touch of drama and even poignance, sans mawkishness, when the outside world and its problems intrude.

This has fine photographic quality and its rambling style fits the theme of man's coping with, or abstaining from society. Here is an offbeat pic that needs personal handling and placement, but could be worthwhile.

Film got good response to a special showing at the Venice festival. *Mosk.*

Les Amities Particulieres
(Particular Friendships)
(FRENCH)

Venice, Sept. 1.

Lux release of Progefi-CCF-Lux production. Features Francis Lacombrade, Didier Haudepin, Louis Seigner, Michel Bouquet, Lucien Nat. Directed by Jean Delannoy. Screenplay, Jean Aurenche, Pierre Bost from book by Roger Peyrefitte; camera, Christian Matras; music, Jean Prodromides. At Venice Film Fest. Running time, **105 MINS.**

Georges .... Francis Lacombrade
Alexandre .... Didier Haudepin
Lauzon .... Louis Seigner
Priest .... Michel Bouquet
Superior .... Lucien Nat

This solidly hewn film details a sort of spiritual love affair between young boys, that might have hovered on homosexuality, in a Jesuit school. But pic skirts any more daring probing of the situation and forces an ending that is dramatically unsatisfying. However it has good, if plodding, observation of the school and its residents and might be art-house fodder, if well placed.

A priggish 16 year-old from a noble family comes to a Jesuit religious school. He quickly wins scholastic honors, but not many friends. He is religious and turns in an acquaintance's letter from a friend that is a harmless, if love, missive. The boy who signed it is expelled. Then he himself is enamored of a 12-year-old boy and a relationship starts.

They are soon exchanging love poems and meeting secretly. The older boy is completely taken by this nymphet-like youth and they even sign a blood pact. One day they playfully roll about in the hay and are caught by a priest-teacher. It leads to the older boy giving in and promising not to see the younger boy again. But the young one feels betrayed and commits suicide.

Didier Haudepin, as the sylph-like kid, is obviously intended as the victim of both the school and his supposedly true-blue friend when he is first seen with a sacrificial lamb in his arms during a service. If he is gracious, boyish and beguiling he can not manage the show of inner intensity, sensitivity and strength to accept his suicide.

Francis Lacombrade has the elegant, selfish archness as the intellectual young boy searching for beauty and not above lying to gain his ends. The various priests and the school system are made to seem somewhat impervious to youthful needs in the over-insistence on selflessness and dedication to higher principles rather than to ordinary friendships.

The direction is solid but too often stolid, and not able to imbue the film with the force and intensity of feelings and dramatic tensions it needs. But it has a fine production dress and it is technically firstrate. Adult players are acceptable. *Mosk.*

La Fleur De L'Age ou Les Adolescentes
(That Tender Age or The Adolescents)
(CANADIAN-FRENCH-ITALO-JAPANESE)

Venice, Aug. 31.

Canadian National Film Board release of a CNFB-Films Pleiade-Nanjin Club-Idi Cinematografica production. With Genevieve Bujold, Veronique Duval, Micaela Esdra, Miki Orie. Directed by Michel Brault, Jean Rouch, Gian Vittorio Baldi, Hiroshi Teshigahara. Screenplay, Alex Pelletier, Jean Rouch, Baldi, Kobo Abe; editor, Werner Nold, Claudine Bouche, Dominico Gorgolini, Kiyoshi Awazu. At Venice Film Fest. Running time, **110 MINS.**

GENEVIEVE
Genevieve .... Genevieve Bujold
Louise .... Louise Marleau
Bernard .... Bernard Arcand
MARIE-FRANCE ET VERONIQUE
Veronique .... Veronique Duval
Marie-France
Marie-France de Chabaneix
Daniele .... Nadine Ballot
Marc .... Marc Kalinoski
Michel .... Michel Aracheguesne
Mother .... Eliane Bonneau
Father .... Olivier Perrin
Friend .... Gilles Queant
Singer .... Didier Leon
Photographer .... Maurice Pialla
FIAMMETTA
Fiammetta .... Micaela Esdra
Livia .... Esmeralda Ruspoli
Ottavio .... Giancarlo Sbragia
Mino .... Muni Castel
Franco .... Franco Marino
Teacher .... Hilde Reiner
AKO
Ako .... Miki Irie

Sketch films, both national or international still seem popular. They sometimes do all right in Europe, but rarely in the U. S., and this may follow the example.

The film has four nations each providing a seg about female adolescents, with the ages ranging from 14 to 17. The girls are pretty and fresh, but no real outlook or feeling for this skittish age emerges.

Plots include a small infidelity among girl friends, a drifting girl and a more determined one, a poor little rich girl and a decent poor girl. But most are precious rather than incisive or revealing and the few good bits are mainly cancelled out by a lack of unity.

Canada's Michel Brault features two teenagers with crushes on the same boy. It meanders, is cute, but remains a fragile interlude as one flirts with the other's boyfriend on an outing.

Jean Rouch of France maintains that girls of 15 and 16 act like grown women and has one girl falling into a life of easy love without true pleasure while the other tries to find more feeling way in life. It is somewhat too didactic, but does have some fetching femme protraits and a few reveling scenes.

Japan's Hiroshi Teshigahara shows a 16 year-old girl's monotonous job and her fairly dank life with boys only after her body. She remains optimistic after near rape and other escapades. It has some forceful scenes, but not enough time to develop character or make a more dramatic point.

Last item is a lachrymose one about a rich girl with a widowed mother who finds herself isolated due to her mother's need for men and their life in a big moldering house. It's somewhat too sentimental and slow to add up to anything.

Pic might have some specialized chances abroad, with school showings indicated due to its theme plus some tv opportunities. It is technically good. *Mosk.*

The Brig

Venice, Sept. 2.
White Line Productions-David Stone release and production. Features Warren Finnerty, Jim Anderson, Henry Howard, Tom Lillard. James Tiroff. Directed and filmed by Jonas Mekas based on stage direction of Judith Malina, production design of Julian Beck of play by Kenneth Brown; editor, Adolfas Mekas. At Venice Film Fest.

Guards .... Warren Finnerty,
Jim Anderson, Henry Howard,
Tom Lillard
Prisoners .... James Tiroff,
Steven Ben Israel, Rufus Collins,
Gene Lipton

Jonas Mekas, pic critic of the Village Voice, filmmaker, ardent fighter against censorship and nominal head of the so-called U.S. "film underground" movement, shot this at the off-Broadway production of the now defunct Living Theatre repertory group. It emerges as a film in its own right besides a good document on the play's production.

An intensely roving camera tracks about the stage catching the harrowing routine in a U.S. Marine brig. There is no attempt to cut this into balanced scenes. Instead, the camera just records the play. There were probably repeats of sections for proper mounting, but it is essentially a record of the play from within rather than from an audience vantage point.

It is a day in a small prison with the men haplessly blasted into a routine that is supposed to regiment them. Since all military and prison life for that matter, depend on discipline and rules this leaves them time to spare.

There is a wild touch of violence as the men are beaten, insulted and degraded continually, also as a part of breaking down men's individuality for the group. The essential fact is that it transcends any reality or social protest, and becomes a study of a kind of excessive cruelty, totalitarianism or man's inhumanity to man.

Mekas has managed to keep his hand held camera fluid while catching the constant movement with usually telling force. It's repetitious, it is always in crescendo and has a dramatic edge as victims and victimizers seem to blend into a ballet like form. Sometimes a man cracks or one almost fights back at the beatings. But it is mainly a pattern that goes on and on and it does not seem to be one that will change the inmates and has already corrupted the keepers.

It also shows Judith Malina's controlled if feverish staging and is helped by Julian Beck's dark wired set that makes this brig a sort of rat's trap. Film won a documentary award at Venice and could be gauged a sort of study of a play's direction.

Blown up from 16m, it has the right, stark pictorial look and Adolfas Mekas has contributed fluid editing with fine balanced playing by a little known group of actors. *Mosk.*

Kradezat Na Praskovi
(The Man Who Stole Peaches)
(BULGARIAN)

Venice, Sept. 1.
Sophia Studios production and release. Features Nevena Nokanova, Rade Markovich, Michail Mickailov, Vassil Vatchev. Written and directed by Veulo Radev. Camera, Todar Stoyanov: music, Simeon Pironkov. At Venice Film Fest. Running time, 83 MINS.

Lisa .... Nevena Nokanova
Ivo .... Rade Markovich
Colonel .... Michail Mickailov
Ordonant .... Vassil Vatchev

Bulgarian entry at Venice is a first pic effort for onetime lenser Valo Redev, and it's a promising one. Film blends old-fashioned and modern techniques in telling its romantic tale. Its charm comes across, thanks also to able lensing. fine feeling for setting and neat performances. Nevertheless, as a commerciable entry in for A'n situations, this is a dubious risk. Its deliberately slow pace, and some of the very qualities which give it a certain stature, will mitigate against it in normal situations.

Story is set during the first World War around a Bulgarian concentration camp. While raiding a peach orchard, a young Serb officer and prisoner, Rade Markovic, meets Nevena Nokanova, young wife of the town's elderly commandant whose orchard contains the coveted peaches. After resisting for long, she finally confesses her love for Markovic and the couple spend many hours together in the loosely administered camp fringes. When the prisoners are sent elsewhere, one day, Markovic escapes to rejoin and flee with Nokanova but is shot by a guard.

Film's strength lies in its feeling for the transition period covered, the concentration camp, the delicacy in which it hints at the crumbling of the old and the coming of the new order in that country. Also, in how it tenderly tells an unabashedly romantic tale in the classic tradition. Principals score with able stints, especially beauteous Miss Nokanova and Rade Markovic. Strong contributions also from lenser Tadar Stoyanov and especially from Simeon Pironkov's lush and haunting musical score. *Hawk.*

Fail Safe

Suspenseful adaptation of the bestseller, but will "Dr. Strangelove," with identical plot, affect its b.o. chances?

Hollywood, Sept. 4.
Columbia Pictures release of Max E. Youngstein production. Stars Dan O'Herlihy, Walter Matthau, Frank Overton, Edward Binns, Larry Hagman, Henry Fonda; features Fritz Weaver, William Hansen, Russell Hardie, Russell Collins, Sorrell Booke. Directed by Sidney Lumet. Screenpay, Walter Bernstein, based on novel by Eugene Burdick, Harvey Wheeler; camera, Gerald Hirschfeld; editor, Ralph Rosenblum; asst. director, Harry Falk Jr. Reviewed at Columbia Studios, Sept. 2, '64. Running time, 112 MINS.

Gen. Black .... Dan O'Herlihy
Groeteschele .... Walter Matthau
Gen. Bogan .... Frank Overton
Col. Grady .... Edward Binns
Col. Cascio .... Fritz Weaver
The President .... Henry Fonda
Buck .... Larry Hagman
Secretary Swenson .... William Hansen
Gen. Stark .... Russell Hardie
Knapp .... Russell Collins
Cong. Raskob .... Sorrell Booke
Ilsa Wolfe .... Nancy Berg
Thomas .... John Connell
Sullivan .... Frank Simpson
Betty Black .... Hildy Parks
Mrs. Grady .... Janet Ward
Sgt. Collins .... Dom DeLouise
Foster .... Dana Elcar
Mr. Cascio .... Stuart Germain
Mrs. Cascio .... Louise Larabee
Jennie .... Frieda Altman

Standing on its own merits, "Fail Safe" (hyphen has been dropped for pic) is a tense and suspenseful piece of filmmaking dealing with the frightening implications of accidental nuclear warfare. It faithfully translates on the screen the power and seething drama of the Eugene Burdick-Harvey Wheeler book, capturing the full menace of the Strategic Air Command's fail-safe device in respect to its possible malfunction, and paints a vivid canvas of an imaginary situation which conceivably could arise in our relations with the Soviet Union. That it will create much word-of-mouth comment, perhaps even attract certain possible Governmental attention, there can be no doubt.

Simultaneously, however, the picture poses a rare problem of showmanship ethics and faith with the public. An earlier Columbia Pictures release (February-May, this year), "Dr. Strangelove: Or How I Learned to Stop Worrying and Love the Bomb," dealt with precisely the same situation: a U.S. plane loaded with hydrogen bombs is flying toward Moscow and because of technical difficulties barring any communication it is impossible to recall the bomber before it can drop its deadly cargo which unquestionably will launch a world holocaust.

Identical basic premise and attendant situations between the two story properties led to Columbia and others attached to the production of "Strangelove" to file a Federal Court suit early last year against the authors of "Fail Safe," the book's publishers and the production company — ECA — which had announced it would film the tome. Charge was made that "Safe" was plagiarized from book on which "Strangelove" was based. Controversy was finally resolved when Columbia took over the financing-distribution of "Safe" and Max E. Youngstein, whose ECA unit had planned its indie production before dissolving, swung over as producer.

What remains is how Columbia will exploit and present "Fail Safe," which is straight drama as compared with "Strangelove" being handled in serio-comic fashion.

There is the question of whether or not audiences will feel they are looking at the same property, despite its change in treatment—and having paid good money to do so —or whether they will overlook this fact and accept the new release on its own worth.

This is where the question of ethics and studio's faith with its public enters, never before encountered by a studio with two of its own releases within a single year. "Strangelove" was so long in profitable release that the majority of regular picturegoers who might catch "Safe" very likely saw its predecessor.

In any event, "Fail Safe" deserves to be seen. It is a gripping narrative realistically and almost frighteningly told as the U.S. goes all-out to halt the plane carrying the bombs, even to the extent of trying to shoot it down and advising the Russians of their peril and urging them to destroy the plane. Particularly dramatic are the sequences in which the President—tellingly portrayed by Henry Fonda—talks with the Russian Premier over the "hot wire."

As the moments dwindle toward the time the American plane gets through the Russian defense and unleashes its megaton load on Moscow, tension mounts to a degree seldom attained on the screen. The true art of picture-making— with its underplayed tenor in writing, acting, direction and editing—is graphically revealed here. Emotional heights are reached in the President's efforts to persuade the Russian chairman that this is not a sneak attack, and, failing in this, to finally agree, to avert certain war, for the U.S. to immediately bomb and totally destroy the city of N. Y.

First few reels, however, unlike the action when the full story line takes hold, are slow and pic's opening is awkward as producers reach back to well-forgotten techniques of other years. Producers seem unsure of themselves, unable to get into their plot which is too long formulating, and three lengthy sequences could be telescoped into one for a much-needed quick entry into the subject.

Fonda is the only big name in the cast, which uniformly is top-flight and socks over respective roles. Frank Overton, as the general in charge of the S.A.C. base in Omaha, home of the fail-safe mechanism which fails to act properly, is a particular standout; Dan O'Herlihy, Edward Binns and Fritz Weaver score as Army officers; Walter Matthau as a professor who urges that the U.S. attack the Soviets and Larry Hagman as the President's interpreter. Balance of smaller roles are also well played.

Youngstein's helming is generally firstclass and direction by Sidney Lumet, discounting the ragged beginning, is forceful and effective, draining all the possibilities of the Walter Bernstein screenplay. Art direction by Albert Brenner is outstanding as he atmospherically registers with the Omaha War Room, the Pentagon, the White House and other sets, and Gerald Hirschfeld's photography is properly stark and realistic. Ralph Rosenblum's sharp editing also contributes to the high level of dramatic intensity. *Whit.*

Fate Is The Hunter

Suspenseful melodrama with Glenn Ford and Rod Taylor to spark chances in general market.

Hollywood, Sept. 10.

Twentieth-Fox release of Aaron Rosenberg production. Stars Glenn Ford, Rod Taylor, Nancy Kwan, Suzanne Pleshette; features Jane Russell, Wally Cox, Nehemiah Persoff, Mark Stevens. Directed by Ralph Nelson. Screenplay, Harold Medford, based on book by Ernest K. Gann; camera, Milton Krasner; editor, Robert Simpson; assistant director, Ad Schaumer; music, Jerry Goldsmith. Reviewed at Academy Award Theatre, Sept. 9, '64. Running time, **106 MINS.**

McBane .... Glenn Ford
Sally Fraser .... Nancy Kwan
Capt. Jack Savage .... Rod Taylor
Martha Webster .... Suzanne Pleshette
Guest Star .... Jane Russell
Bundy .... Wally Cox
Ben Sawyer .... Nehemiah Persoff
Mickey Doolan .... Mark Stevens
Crawford .... Max Showalter
Peg Burke .... Constance Towers
Hutchins .... Howard St. John
Stillman .... Robert Wilke
Dillon .... Bert Freed
Wilson .... Dort Clark
Mrs. Hewelyn .... Mary Wickes
Proctor .... Robert F. Simon

"Fate Is the Hunter," based upon the Ernest K. Gann book, is a realistically-produced picture, sparked by good acting right down the line. Its greatest asset is a stirring climax which brings the story line to a satisfactory conclusion, but the buildup, while meeting expository requirements, frequently plods due to lack of significant lines and situations. On the whole, however, the film rates as a suspenseful melodrama and should do well in the general and action market, particularly with the names of Glenn Ford and Rod Taylor heading the cast.

The Aaron Rosenberg production deals with the cause of a spectacular plane crash in which 53 people are killed. As the various elements are considered, then discarded, the investigation finally centers on the dead pilot, reported to have been drinking a few hours before the tragedy. With the Civil Aeronautics Board and the F.B.I. already on the case, the airline's director of flight operations and old friend of the pilot pursues his own line of inquiry. In a final attempt to exonerate his friend and learn what really was responsible for the crash, he tries to reproduce the fatal flight exactly, aided by the stewardess, lone survivor, and tumbles upon the cause.

Ford as the operations director who was a war flyer with the dead pilot, Taylor, underplays his character for good effect. Part isn't as outgoing as Ford generally undertakes, but is dramatically forceful. Taylor's role is more flamboyant and colorful, most of it in flashback sequences as the Harold Medford screenplay limns the character of the man and what made him tick. In the crash sequence, teeing off narrative's chain of events, he, too, underplays to point up drama.

Ralph Nelson's taut direction gets the most out of his script, the crash emerging as a thrilling experience and with suspense mounting in Ford's reenactment of the fatality. Under his helming, too, Nancy Kwan, as Taylor's fiancee, and Suzanne Pleshette, the stewardess, register nicely, and Jane Russell makes an appearance as herself playing a World War II Army camp. Wally Cox, Nehemiah Persoff, Mark Stevens and Constance Towers competently handle important key roles.

Technical credits generally are firstclass, including Milton Krasner's photography, Robert Simpson's editing, art direction by Jack Martin Smith and Hilyard Brown, music by Jerry Goldsmith.

Whit.

Witchcraft

Okay eerie fare for horror market, packaged by 20th-Fox with "The Horror of It All" as special double bill.

Hollywood, Sept. 9.

Twentieth-Fox release of Robert L. Lippert-Jack Parsons production. Stars Lon Chaney, Jack Hedley, Jill Dixon, Viola Keats, Marie Ney, David Weston, Yvette Rees. Directed by Don Sharp. Screenplay, Harry Spalding; camera, Arthur Lavis; editor, Robert Winter; music, Carlo Martelli. Reviewed at Pix Theatre, Sept. 9, '64. Running time, **80 MINS.**

Morgan Whitlock .... Lon Chaney
Bill Lanier .... Jack Hedley
Tracy Lanier .... Jill Dixon
Helen Lanier .... Viola Keats
Malvina Lanier .... Marie Ney
Todd Lanier .... David Weston
Vanessa Whitlock .... Yvette Rees

Eerie music, low-key photography, competent acting and a gimmick-filled plot combine to make the horror-feature "Witchcraft" a good example of its kind.

The Robert Lippert-Jack Parsons production has the added feature of a plastic "witch deflector" for each viewer. This, along with heavy sell promotion should attract audiences addicted to horror films.

Lon Chaney, a veteran of two decades of screamers, tops the cast in a story about a coven of modern witches, led by a 300-year-old witch (Yvette Rees), who comes to life when housing developers level an ancient graveyard in rural England.

One partner in the building firm is Bill Lanier (Jack Hedley) whose family has been feuding with Whitlock family for centuries. Morgan Whitlock (Chaney), who also is the leader of the local coven, protests uprooting of the cemetery.

Lanier's partner dies mysteriously, then his Aunt Helen (Viola Keats). Lanier himself and his grandmother (Marie Ney) both survive attempted killings, but then his wife Tracy (Jill Dixon) is kidnapped to await a witches' sabbath.

Chaney tended to overact, but others in cast handled chores in workmanlike fashion, with Diane Clare particularly appealing as the ingenue.

Arthur Lavis' photography was competent for a horror story, with murky shots of church steeples and graveyards through ever-present fog.

Picture was filmed at Shepperton Studios, England.

Hogg.

Dalia And The Sailors
(ISRAEL)

Tel Aviv, Sept. 8.

Geva Films release of Mordechai Navon production. Directed by Menahem Golan, screenplay by Menahem Golan, Mania & Josh Halevi, based on the Halevi's play with additional dialog by Shai K Ophir. Camert, Harry Waxman; Music, Itzhak Graziani; editor, Nelly Bogor; songs, Na'omi Shemer. Reviewed at the Ben Yehuda Cinema, Tel Aviv. Running time, **100 MINS.**

Dalia .... Veronique Vandell
Jacko .... Shai K. Ophir

This is an Israeli musicomedy, fashioned, so to speak, on the prolific "Carry On . . ." series of English comedies. An Israeli girl, having been taken to Canada at an early age, by her migrating parents, comes of age (at least physically) and tries to make it back to Israel by stealing her way onto an Israeli freighter loading in Montreal.

The curvacious stowaway, Veronique Vandell, causes a lot of excitement aboard the boat. The crew (including almost a complete Who's Who of Israel's light entertainment stages), enjoys the hidden addition to their problems. The girl enjoys the general attention of the male crew, including the never-too-serious tension created by the "fear" that the captain might find her out.

The picture is a compilation of all the standing gags and standard, stock-situations prevalent in such stories. The mis-directed cable, the disappearing food and bedding, the mutual "cheating," on the part of captain and crew alike, as to what should be done and what is known about the bikini-clad stowaway.

Some scenes are lively in tempo and some of the performers, notably Shai K. Ophir, Joseph Bomba Tzur and Arik Einstein, use perfect timing in delivering lines and punchlines. The language-barrier and cross-section of the Israeli population evident in the crew makes for more local fun and a number of good laughs.

The camera work is excellent and the moods of ocean and engine-room are captured in sight and sound. Some of the songs are good and most of them are melodic enough to catch the ear. The whole thing comes to a mixed-up end after a "Captain's Ball," where the whole crew dresses like girls, to help cover-up for Dalia.

Menahem Golan's direction is restricted to good coordination of the many entertainment elements and talents, each of which is allowered to perform his usual (locally popular) routine. These seem to expose the best values of this film, in spite of the mild competition by Veronique Vandell exposing her features in the shower.

Rap.

Rattle of a Simple Man
(BRITISH)

Vulgarized, but exploitable version of successful play with a sex emphasis that should draw. British performance by Diane Cilento, the best thing in a disappointing pic.

London, Sept. 7.

Warner-Pathe release of a Sydney Box Production for Associated British. Stars Harry H. Corbett, Diane Cilento. Features Thora Hird, Michael Medwin, Charles Dyer, Barbara Archer. Produced by William Gell. Directed by Muriel Box. Screenplay by Charles Dyer from his original play; camera, Reg Wyer; editor, Frederick Wilson; music, Stanley Black. Reviewed at Warner Theatre, London, Sept. 7, '64. Running time, **96 MINS.**

Percy .... Harry H. Corbett
Cyrenne .... Diana Cilento
Mrs. Winterham .... Thora Hird
Ginger .... Michael Medwin
Chalky .... Charles Dyer
Ozzie .... Hugh Futcher
Fred .... Brian Wilde
Ricardo .... Alexander Davion
Marlo .... David Saire
Iris .... Barbara Archer
Organizer .... Michael Robbins
Papa .... George Roderick
Mama .... Marie Burke
District Nurse .... Carole Gray
Willie .... John Ronane
1st Stripper .... Ingrid Anthofer
2nd Stripper .... Karen Kaufman

Most of the charm and tenderness that occasionally illuminated Charles Dyer's successful play has been lost in this coarsened, fatuous film. There's plenty of exploitable sex which could drag in the customers, but the outcome is a sniggering item which effectively smothers the play's pivot, that of two lonely, unhappy people striving for brief contact.

Only a lively, vivid performance by the exciting Diane Cilento in a contrived role holds much interest, though a sound cast does spartan work in juggling the sparse material. The author, Charles Dyer, has broadened his intimate little play for the benefit of the screen and has heaved most of its values into the trash can.

A bunch of football fans from the North of England, characteristically drawn as noisy, boozing, lecherous nitwits, comes to London for the Cup Final and a night out among the sleazy bright lights. One of them (Harry H. Corbett), a particularly formless, repressed, mother-ridden oaf, is conned into a bet with his pals. He wagers his motorbike that he'll have an affair with a goodlooking, blonde tart that he picks up in a Soho drinking club. The girl lives in an air of fantasy and he is gulled into believing her yarns of rich parents, smart background and so on. The bedroom rendezvous is a pitiable farce in which he fails to take the opportunities cheerfully flung at him by the goodtime girl. Instead he weaves dreams of real love about the goldenhearted little prostie.

It is difficult to conceive that the girl would have wasted her time or that any man with red blood at all would have failed, however fumblingly, to accept her uninhibited invitations to the mattress. Instead, the two spin yarns in inept fashion. The girl's sympathy registers more as teasing. The man's shyness becomes boorish stupidity and so the whole coneption of the author's original idea falls flat on its face.

Diane Cilento, one of Britian's most exciting young actresses, has little scope for her intelligence, though she certainly looks a desirable dish and gives out refreshingly with the flip talk. Harry H. Corbett, a good actor sadly saddled with the "Steptoe and Son" image which he cannot yet fling off in films, does not get within shouting distance of the sympathy that his character should arouse. George Roderick and Marie Burke have good moments in a scene which reveals Miss Cilento's real background, and the author, Michael Medwin, Brian Wilde and Hugh Futcher parade stock types as northerners on a spree. Thora Hird cops a guestar billing in a one minute spot before the credit titles, as Corbett's clucking mum.

Artwork and locales project the usual sleazy drinking club, taverns and neon-lit West End streets inseparable from this type of film and Reg Wyer's photography is adequate throughout. Dyer has sacrificed his own play in rewriting for the screen and Muriel Box, a most competent director, has, in this instance, lost her way, failing to bring out the essence of a slim anecdote that had some charm and significance on the stage but, in this film, becomes a breezy but farfetched and tasteless romp.

Rich.

The Horror Of It All
(BRITISH)

Horror weakie; slim appeal even on lower half of exploitation bill.

Hollywood, Sept. 9.

Twentieth-Fox release of Robert L. Lippert production. Stars Pat Boone, Erica Rogers, Dennis Price, Andree Melly, Valentine Duvall, Jack Bligh; Erik Chitty, Archie Duncan, Oswald Laurence. Directed by Terence Fisher. Screenplay, Ray Russell; camera, Arthur Lavis; editor, Robert Winter; assistant director, Frank Nesbitt. Reviewed at Pix Theatre, Sept. 9, '64. Running time, 75 MINS.

Jack Robinson .... Pat Boone
Cynthia .... Erica Rogers
Cornwallis .... Dennis Price
Natalia .:................. Andree Melly
Reginal ....Valentine Duvall
Percival .... Jack Bligh
Grandpapa .... Erik Chitty
Muldoon .... Archie Duncan
Young Doctor .... Oswald Laurence

Director Terence Fisher and cast of "The Horror of It All" tried to play this Robert L. Lippert production for laughs, but they didn't pull it off. The filmed-in-England feature is a weak mixture of unfunny gags and standard horror situations that get laughs, when they aren't supposed to.

Lightweight fare for even the bottom half of a twin bill, the 20th Century-Fox release has only Pat Boone's name to attract viewers. But Boone's thesping is on a high school level and the one song he warbles, the title tune, is unlikely to go far on the charts.

The nonsensical story has Boone as an American who pursues his English fiancee, Erica Rogers, to her family mansion, where he finds a houseful of people who are eccentric, to say the least.

There's Valentine Dyall who is creepy and speaks in Lugosi-like tones; Andree Melly has long fingernails and likes blood; Archie Duncan is kept locked in a padded cell; Jack Bligh is an inventor 50 years too late, having just discovered the electric light and put together a horseless carriage. The only normal member of the clan other than Miss Rogers is the Grandpapa, played by Erik Chitty, who reads Playboy in his sickbed.

All this probably seemed amusing on paper, but it doesn't jell as, one by one, the family members get killed off, until an improbable climax is reached. Perhaps a team of top comedy writers could have made something here, but it didn't happen.

All production values are strictly routine. *Hogg.*

Venice Films

Il Deserto Rosso
(Red Desert)
(ITALO-FRENCH-COLOR)

Venice, Sept. 8.

Cineriz release of Film Duemila-Francoriz coproduction. Stars Monica Vitti, Richard Harris; features Carlo Chionetti, Xenia Valderi, Lili Rheims, Valerio Bartoleschi, Emanuela Carboni, Bruno Borghi, Peppe Conti, Giulio Cotignoli, Giovanni Lolli, Hiram Madonia, Giuliano Missirini, Arturo Parmisani, Carla Ravasi, Ivo Scherpani, Rita Renoir, Aldo Grotti. Directed by Michelangelo Antonioni. Screenplay, Antonioni, Tonino Guerra. Camera, (color) Carlo di Palma. Music, Giovanni Fusco. Editor, Eraldo da Roma. At Venice Film Festival. Running time, 120 MINS.

Giuliana .... Monica Vitti
Corrado .... Richard Harris
Ugo ....'............ Carlo Chionetti
Linda .... Xenia Valderi
Emilia .... Rita Renoir
Max .... Aldro Grotti
Son .... Valerio Bartoleschi.

A film of high quality and artistry in the now-traditional style of Michelangelo Antonioni, "Red Desert" should provoke infinite discussions about meanings, and entertainment values, but remains a film to see and see again for its intrinsic contribution to cinematography. The fact that film is also a milestone in color lensing approach provides an added fillip for the curioseeker and student. From a more practical standpoint, the pic has certain name values in Monica Vitti and Richard Harris, as well as that of Antonioni, but must basically be pegged for specialized outlets or general release conditioned by territory and preceded by an adroit preparatory campaign.

"Red Desert" is many things, and symbol-chasers should have a field day for interpretation. Basically, it is on one level an un-traditional study of a neurosis, on another a frightening fresco of the destructive dangers and crises implicit in present-day life, with its intensive pace, mechanization, disintegration of established values and traditions.

Antonioni's latest tells of a woman (Monica Vitti) who has tried suicide and emerged from the car crash with increased mental injuries. She nevertheless still desperately seeks an escape from the neurotic state of which she is conscious. Her quest for an "oasis" in the desert makes her seek the company of a colleague of her husband (Richard Harris) who is almost as unprepared and unwilling to sufficiently assist her as is her husband. Her crisis has its ups and downs, reaching a head after her son fakes a serious illness. She again seeks an escape, first by seducing the friend, later by thinking of sailing away in a ship docked nearby. Windup however finds her returned to her relative normality, having realized that there's no escape from her situation. There remains an implied hint that her problem may be resolved, but it remains only a hint.

Stylistically, the film is unmistakably Antonioni's—though he treats problems, situations, and moods which have in other guises been touched on by the films of Ingmar Bergman, for one. The pace is slow, objects play as important a role as humans, etc. The novelty here is color, and the director's contribution is masterful—perhaps the first time tint has been used creatively with such effect and power. It should prove a textbook for further efforts. But other elements, notably sound and music, also contribute strongly to the obsessive mood of anguish which Antonioni manages to instill, the anguish which the director suggests is in all of us and which in the Vitti character symbolizes modern civilization and the dangerous rhythm it is acquiring. A way out? Physical escape, a journey to a distant land where the relatively pure, calm, idyllic conditions of youth still exist (and which Antonioni depicts in a beautifully lensed insert illustrating a fairy tale told by the mother to her son during his fake illness) is becoming more and more difficult.

Conversely, the director suggests that all too often we are unwilling or unprepared to help our fellow man, provide the proper escape for him, due to an ultimate lack of communication. These and many more thoughts are provoked by a picture which stimulates from every angle. The color also hints a mood, vivid colors indicating normality, their absence a need for contact with the world, a loneliness, non-participation in life, pastels show relative tranquility. Greys dominate exteriors as well, and fog is also used symbolically as a sort of mobile screen between normality and the neurotic state. Factory noises, brief snatches of electronic music all help to add to the obsessive mood of the settings, as does the contrast between the monstrous cold and sterile modern structures (home, hotel, or factory) and the few crumbling remnants of the old way of life.

The acting spotlight is clearly on Miss Vitti, in keeping with the pic's theme, and she gives another of her moving incarnations of a desparate woman in quest of a solution to her inner struggle. Other roles are played against her. Richard Harris is effective as the friend (though at times his makeup proves disconcerting for those who've seen him in other pix), as is Carlo Chionetti, an improvised thesp, as her husband. Xenia Valderi, Aldo Grotti, and others have relatively little to do. Carlo di Palma deserves praise for the way he has carried out the director's intentions in color (Eastmancolor stock, Technicolor prints), which very often achieve the stature of a masterful moving abstract. Other credits measure up, not the least those for producers Antonio Cervi and Angelo Rizzoli, who made such an offbeat film financially possible. *Hawk.*

Tonio Kroeger
(GERMAN-FRENCH)

Venice, Sept. 2.

Schorcht release of Franz Seitz-Filmaufbau production, in collaboration with Mondex-Procinex. Stars Jean Claude Brialy, Najda Tiller; features Werner Hinz, Theo Lingen, Walter Giller, Gert Froebe. Directed by Rolf Thiele. Screenplay, Erika Mann, Ennio Flaiano, adapted from novelette by Thomas Mann; camera, Wolf Wirth; music, Rolf Wilhelm. At Venice film festival. Running time, 90 MINS.

Tonio Kroeger .... Jean Claude Brialy
Lisaweta Iwanowna .... Najda Tiller
Consul Kroeger .... Warner Hinz
Monsieur Knaak .... Theo Lingen
Merchant .... Walter Giller
Tonio's Mother .... Anaid Iplicjian
Gendarme .... Gert Froebe

This pic follows "Royal Highness", "Confessions of Felix Krull" and "The Buddenbrooks" and is the fourth Thomas Mann filmization. There is no doubt that this screen version of "Tonio Kroeger" is an ambitious enterprise, but the outcome is very much on the dubious side. It's neither a good nor a bad film in the conventional sense. It's the kind of film that is too demanding for the average patron, but not good enough for the more fastidious customer. Thanks to the powerful Thomas Mann name and a prominent cast, satisfactory returns should be achieved in Germany, but foreign chances seem to be limited strictly to the art house circuit.

The big question was: Could Thomas Mann's novelette which reflects the moods and daydreams of a sensitive young author be transferred to the screen? After seeing this film one is inclined to say no. The story is—at least in this form—of little interest, and just too little happens in this pic. The budget of $400,000, is rather high by domestic standards, and it remains a puzzle why so much money was used on such an un-filmable subject.

The characters never come to life. This particularly applies to Jean Claude Brialy who just walks through the scenes. He portrays Tonio Kroeger, the only son of a stiff Luebeck aristocrat and a music-loving Italian mother, who leaves his home town to become an author, a profession of which he's always dreamed. Wherever he is, be it Florence or Munich, the film tells in brief flashback episodes of his childhood. Brialy is a handsome lad, but he's an utterly inconvincing Tonio Kroeger.

Despite these drawbacks, "Tonio Kroeger" is not a bad film. It even has dignity. The latter results from Wolf Wirth's beautiful camerawork which gives this production a very pretty picture-book atmosphere. Unfortunately, it is one without much life.

Rolf Thiele, the director, tried hard to achieve a film of importance. It's possible that he underestimated the difficulties as Thomas Mann is hard to master.

The late German poet's daughter, Erika Mann, together with Ennio Flaiano, an Italian writer, wrote the script. "Tonio Kroeger" is a film which the Germans needn't be ashamed of. It has many flaws, it is dull, but it has dignity.

Hans.

King and Country
(BRITISH)

Courtmartial of World War I deserter, given emotional uplift via shrewd direction and sterling performances.

Venice, Sept. 6.

Warner-Pathe release of a BHE (Daniel M. Angel) production, coproduced by Joseph Losey, Norman Priggen. Stars Dirk Bogarde, Tom Courtenay and Leo McKern. Features Barry Foster. Directed by Losey; screenplay, Evan Jones; camera, Denys Coop; editor, Reginald Mills; settings, Peter Mullin; music, Larry Adler. Previewed at Venice Film Fest, Sept. 5, '64. Running time, 88 MINS.

Captain Hargreaves ... Dirk Bogarde
Hamp .... Tom Courtenay
Captain O'Sullivan .... Leo McKern
Lieutenant Webb .... Barry Foster
Captain Midgeley .... James Villiers
Colonel .... Peter Copley
Lieutenant Prescott ..... Barry Justice
Padre .... Vivian Matalon
Sparrow .... Jeremy Spencer
Sykes .... James Hunter
Wilson .... David Cook
Sergeant-Major .... Larry Taylor
Corporal M[illegible] .... Jonah Seymour
Corporal of the Guard ... Keith Buckley
Guard 'Charlie'........ Richard Arthur
Captain .... Derek Partridge
Lieutenant .... Brian Tipping
Soldiers ... Raymond Brody, Terry Palmer, Dan Cornwall

The story of Private Hamp, a deserter from the battle front in World War I, has already been told on radio, television and the stage, but undeterred by this exposure, director Joseph Losey has attacked the subject with confidence and vigor, and the result is a highly sensitive and emotional drama, enlivened by sterling performances and a sincere screenplay. "King and Country" may not have it easy at the wickets, but it is the sort of picture that could be helped by word of mouth, particularly if it follows a carefully selected route along the art house circuits.

The action takes place behind the lines at Passchendaele, where Hamp's battalion has been relieved for a few days rest. Not a single German soldier is seen or heard, and exploding shells are only heard as a background effect. The "enemy" which confronts the soldiers is the rain, the mud and the rats that invade the dugouts and the trenches.

Hamp, a volunteer at the outbreak of war, and the sole survivor of his company, decides one day to "go for a walk." In fact, he contemplates walking to his home in London, but after more than 24 hours on the road, and near the embarkation port of Calais, he's picked up by the Military Police and sent back to his unit to face court-martial for desertion.

The job of defending the private goes to Dirk Bogarde, a typically arrogant officer who accepts the assignment because it is his duty to do so. But during his preliminary investigation, he responds to Hamp's beguiling simplicity and honesty, coming to the inevitable conclusion that he was not responsible for his actions. That is the main line of defense at the court-martial, and is the subject of a magnificently powerful verbal duel between Bogarde and the medical officer, Leo McKern. It transpires that Hamp reported sick, complaining of nerves and insomnia, for which the doctor prescribed a potent laxative, convinced that he was nothing more than a coward suffering from cold feet.

Because war is a dirty business, and Hamp had let down his fellow soldiers, he is sentenced to death, with the execution to be carried out by firing squad at dawn before the battalion returns to the front line. When his fellow privates hear the verdict, they steal large quantities of rum from the officers rations, and have a glorious booze-up in the condemned cell, with the result they bungle the execution, and it is left to Bogarde to fire the deciding shot.

Though the main drama is played out in the improvised court room, director Losey has succeeded in giving fluency and movement to the subject, aided considerably by Denys Coop's stark camerawork, which brilliantly captures the scene and the mood of the story. However, the court-martial is the guts of the plot, and the dramatic tension is maintained without resort to the more conventional screen cliches.

Notwithstanding its technical excellence, the picture is carried by the outstanding performances of its three stars. Tom Courtenay, who has been collaring critical attention for the past couple of years or more, has never done anything better than this compelling study of a simple minded soldier, unable to accept the fact that he has committed a heinous crime, and unable to believe that he will suffer the maximum penalty. It is a performance that succeeds by its total sincerity. Bogarde's portrayal of the defending officer is also distinguished by its sincerity, and though his courtroom clash with the medico provides a dramatic highlight, it is achieved more through conviction than histrionic outburst. Completing the stellar trio, Leo McKern's study of the medical officer is faultless, and in his big scene he unerringly stands up to Bogarde's cross-examination, insisting that Hamp—like many other privates—was just a malingerer, and that the few moments he spent with him was enough to justify his diagnosis.

Solid support comes from the all male cast, notably from Barry Foster as a sympathetic officer, and Peter Copley as the presiding officer at the courtmartial.

Technical credits are above par, and are particularly noteworthy in a picture lensed in three and a half weeks. Reginald Mills has edited to a taut 88 minutes; Peter Mullins' mud soaked dugouts have a genuine look; and Larry Adler's score (which he plays himself) hypoes the dramatic situations.

"King and Country" reunites "The Servant" team of Losey and Bogarde. That could be a valuable exploitable angle, particularly among art-house devotees. *Myro.*

Il Vangelo Secondo Matteo
(The Gospel According to Matthew)
(ITALO-FRENCH)

Venice, Sept. 4.

Titanus release of Alfredo Bini production for Arco Films (Rome)-Lux Cie Cinematografique de France (Paris). With Enrique Irazoqui, Margherita Caruso, Susanna Pasolini, Marcello Morante, Mario Socrate, others. Written and directed by Pier Paolo Pasolini. Camera, Tonino delli Colli. Music, Luis Bacalov. Editor, Nino Baragli At Venice Film Festival. Running time, **142 MINS.**

Christ .... Enrique Irazoqui
Mary .... Margherita Caruso, Susanna Pasolini
Joseph .... Marcello Morante
John the Baptist .... Mario Socrate
Peter .... Settimio di Porto
Judas .... Otello Sestili
Matthew .... Ferruccio Nuzzo
John .... Giacomo Morante
Andreas .... Alfonso Gatto
Simon .... Enzo Siciliano
Philip .... Giorgio Agamben
Bartholomew .... Guido Cerretani
Jacob son of Alpheus .... Luigi Barbini
Jacob son of Zebedeus .... Marcello Galdini
Thaddeus .... Elio Spaziani
Thomas .... Rosario Migale
Caiphas .... Rodolfo Wilcock
Pontius Pilate .... Alessandro Tasca
Herod I .... Amerigo Bevilaqua
Herod II .... Francesco Leonetti
Herodiad .... Franca Cupane
Salome .... Paola Tedesco
Angel of Lord .... Rossana di Rocco
Joseph .... Eliseo Boschi
Mary of Bethunia .... Natalia Ginzburg

Offbeat, almost neo-realistic film version of the Saint Matthew Gospel, pic has many talking points and effective moments giving this latest scriptures transposition an interesting new dimension. It needs special handling, but religioso appeal should make it a worthwhile entry in many situations both here and abroad. Also looms as to eventual 16m. circuit fodder. Those "with it," will probably feel it a fascinating, even moving film; others may rate it a crashing bore; still others may fault its unconventional approach to (or illustration of) a tale which has remained essentially unchanged in concept over the centuries. In this sense, an ultimate Church and/or endorsement is vital to its commercial future.

Pier Paolo Pasolini has made a pic poles apart from the many which have told the story of Christ—though remaining faithful in its development and spoken text. To be premised also, is the fact that it's probably the first instance in which a Marxist (Pasolini) has tangled with this subject matter on film, and that the film is dedicated to the memory of the late Pope John, purportedly arguing that a dialog between the Church and the Left is possible.

Basically, Pasolini's approach has been to break with the long-traditional visual concepts of the Gospel and its people. Pic was filmed in Southern Italy, and the faces are deliberately those of Italians. Costumes are a simplification of tradition, and settings are also different from those "usually" seen or visualized. The effect is such that these factors become completely acceptable after an initial adjustment.

Thesps are all non-actors, and Enrique Irazoqui is a find as the man who plays Christ. (And Pasolini's Christ concept—as are other facets of the film—is revolutionary: The Saviour is here not the halo-topped Prince of fools but a battling leader, severe and unbending as he fights for his cause.) Faces have the craggy, unglamorous, rugged look of the working man or peasant. The music is similarly offbeat, containing Negro spirituals ("Motherless Child", sung in English for example), Russo folk songs, etc.

Yet as noted, the unconventional approach is rapidly accepted, and the pic aquires the look of a pageant—such as those enacted by citizens of many European villages every year—lensed in depth. Several times, the film soars to heights—as in the Calvary sequence, a masterful achievement which has the graphic immediacy of a newsreel document in a crescendo of tragedy and sorrow which is eminently moving and believable.

The picture is roughly hewn, and there are some jumpy parts which can be smoothed by editing. Lensing by Tonino delli Colli is a standout feature with its grey tone giving it a certain timelessness in keeping with Pasolini's choice of bleakly beautiful settings (as for example the setting for the Baptism). Musical blend of classics, spirituals, etc. was ably orchestrated by Luis Bacalov. *Hawk.*

La Femme Mariee
(The Married Woman)
(FRENCH)

Venice, Sept. 8.

Columbia Films release of Anouchka-Orsay Films production. Stars Macha Meril, Bernard Noel, Philippe Leroy. Written and directed by Jean-Luc Godard. Camera, Raoul Coutard; editor, J. Rozier. At Venice Film Fest. Running time, **98 MINS.**

Charlotte .... Macha Meril
Lover .... Bernard Noel
Husband .... Philippe Leroy

Jean-Luc Godard is a fast man with a film. Within five months he made two pix for Columbia Films worldwide release at a cost of about $100,000 each. The first was made in three weeks and this one in about four. It emerges as a witty, objective look at a day in the life of an adulterous married young woman.

Godard has taken that age old triangle of the wife, husband and lover and given it a fillip with the trappings of series of anecdotes, essay-like interludes and generally unorthodox treatment. In this case he uses negative, sharp ellipses, a fluid camera and almost all non-studio shooting.

But there is no moralizing and not much of a narrative quality here. The wife is seen with her lover at an afternoon tryst. A tasteful array of portions of the bodies and wisps of talk build a knowing, but non-suggestive beginning. He wants her to divorce her husband and marry him.

Then she is off to meet her husband, back from a business trip. He is a pilot on a private plane, and the film details the time with him and her child, and then another secret meeting with her lover whom she puts off by saying she has not seen her husband yet. She has also been told she is three months pregnant and does not know if it was her husband or lover, and has told neither.

That is about it, but interspersed are little comic segments. For instance, the woman's constant primping and reaction to things around her, subtle and even blatant pictorial parellel symbols, incidents and attitudes that mirror her seeming need for both the husband's security and the lover's excitement. There is nothing complex about her or does she see any problems of morality.

She is a basically an instinctive creature who is essentially decent, but is trying to keep both men distinct for she needs them both. Her belief is that life must be lived in the present and she is thus carried along by feeling alone.

The nude scenes all have a crystal-like lensing and an adroitness in composition and presentation that make them more ornamental than in any way pornographic.

However, a flaw lies in director Godard's subtitles which he does as a series of fragments. This sometimes leads to repetition, a lagging of interest and, at times, a preciosity.

Macha Meril has the proper innocent look that calls for forgiving anything she does, and make for an acceptance of her own moral outlock and comportment. She has a zesty offbeat quality and a vein of spontaniety that also help put over her role. She is well supported by Philippe Leroy as the direct husband and Bernard Noel as the more romantic lover.

Godard again shows in this pic that he has a natural flair for transposing ideas to pictorial terms, but has yet to blend this ability with a more sustained narrative manner. A series of discussions heighten character, but are mainly a sounding board for Godard's own ideas and sometimes are too pat and obvious.

The film is primarily an art possibility on its audacious, but deceptively simple, look at adultery with some distaff interest possible via word-of-mouth. It needs specialized handling but could pay off on its offbeat, outspoken attitudes and its refusal to compromise. It is technically tops. *Mosk.*

La Donna E Una Cosa Meravigliosa
(Woman Is a Wonderful Thing)
(ITALO-FRENCH)
(COLOR—BLACK & WHITE)

Venice, Sept. 9.

Cineriz release of Moris Ergas production for Zebra Films (Rome). Aera Films

(Paris). Features Sandra Milo, Vittorio Caprioli, Beba Loncar, Angela Minervini, Nani Colombo, others. Directed by Mauro Bolognini. Story and screenplay, Goffredo Parise, Giorgio Salvioni, Antonio Guerra, Leo Benvenuti, Piero de Bernardi. Camera, Gianni di Venanzo, Otello Martelli. Music, Carlo Rustichelli, Piero Piccioni. Tradeshown at Venice Film Festival. Running time, 90 MINS.

This two-episoder is a disappointing commercial entry short on the intended tongue-in-cheek humor though fairly big on production values. It might squeeze through on general situations if given a hard sell, but doubtful as an export entity unless drastically revamped.

First episode tells of a triangle tale between midget married to a circus fat lady, but secretly is love with another lilliputian. He tries by all means to dispose of spouse, but all attempts fail, the hefty lady apparently being unmurderable. Bit has its moments, but few of them, and rarely hits with barbed yocks previously put forth by a pic with similar themes. Though ably acted, the segment sometimes stoops to tasteless dialog, and ironic climax lacks sufficient punch.

Second bit records zany antics of a childless wife who turns her husband into an infant, eventually relegating him to a wheelchair, in which he ultimately dies. Sandra Milo has the talent and looks for her Judy Holliday-like role, but is poorly served by script which is more often silly than amusing, more frequently inept than inane. Director Mauro Bolognini's contribution is unrecognizable here, it's so far removed from his usual stylishness and the fault must be attributed to the scripting by a team of writers. It just does not come off, though it might have looked promising on paper.

Best point about the twin item is the music, by Piero Piccioni and Carlo Rustichelli, and the lensing, by Gianni di Venanzo and Otello Martelli. Title animation by humorist Zac is another standout contribution in an otherwise letdown item, in which much talent is wasted. *Hawk.*

La Suora Giovane
(The Novice)
(ITALIAN)

Venice, Sept. 7.
Italspettacolo production and release. Features Laura Efrikian, Jonathan Elliott, Maria Sardoch, Cesarino Miceli Picardi, Marcella Rovena, Aid Aste, Carlo Alighiero, Emilio Esposito. Written and directed by Bruno Paolinelli. Camera, Enrico Mencrer; music, Teo Usuelli. Tradeshown at Venice. Running time 97 MINS.
Serena .... Laura Efrikian
Antonino .... Jonathan Elliott
Anna .... Maria Sardoch
Mo .... C. M. Picardi
Iris .... Aid Aste
Serena's Father .... Emilio Esposito
Serena's Mother ...... Marcella Rovena

Based on the bestseller by Giovanni Arpino, "The Novice" emerges as a neat low-budgeter with arty possibilities on theme and treatment.

Lensed by a co-op group headed by director Bruno Paolinelli, the film is a faithful treatment of the novel. This dealt with a growing love story between a middle-aged man and a young novice nun. He at first follows her on her nightly trolley ride home. Fascinated by her glances, he speaks to her, and they begin nightly meetings, for prolonged chats, at the door of the

home in which she is serving as a night nurse to an invalid, and they confess their love. Just as he abandons his previous mistress and group of friends, however, a misunderstanding arises, and she leaves for another city. After trying to forget her, he visits her parents and discovers her whereabouts, learns that she wants to leave the convent and get married. Windup finds him still resisting further involvement, but weakening. (Alternate ending also lensed makes their reunion—not seen in book—more clear).

The film has stature thanks especially to sensitive acting by Laura Efrikian, a find as the domineering yet fragile novice. It's a striking performance. Jonathan Elliott is likewise effective as the man, though his role is necessarily a downbeat one. Emilio Esposito plays a neat portrayal as Serena's father, while others contribute apt performances to give the pic substance.

Dialog is another plus value. If at times literary, revealing its origin, it is intelligent and cut several notches above the norm. Bruno Paolinelli's direction is unobtrusive, concentrated on atmosphere, performances and respect for the original novel on which it is based. Only Teo Usuelli's music sometimes enters a discordant note by becoming noticeable per se, rather than backdropping action. Lensing and other technical credits are good. *Hawk.*

La Loutre
(The Otter)
(FRENCH)

Venice, Sept. 8.
Lisbon Films release and production. Stars Jean Richard, Dany Robin, Magali Noel; features Felix Marten, Claude Mann, Estella Blain, Paul Frankeur. Directed by Joseph Lisbona. Screenplay, Jean-Charles Pichon, Lisbona from the novel by Pichon; camera, Gricha Willy; editor, Jacques Mavel; music, Pier Piccione. At Venice Film Fest. Running time. 86 MINS.
Arthur .... Jean Richard
Isabelle .... Dany Robin
Clara .... Magali Noel
Robert .... Felix Marten
Marc .... Claude Mann
Helene .... Estella Blain
Bruneau .... Paul Frankeur
Judge .... Louis Seigner

This suspense item with a few last minute twists is simply mounted and is a possible playoff item for dualers outside its home grounds. If characterization is slight, it does not try to milk its motivations or cloud the progression with frills and directorial cleverness.

But this sometimes gives the film a pedestrian look that is intermittently overcome by sudden plot turns. A man of ordinary looks and means has a rather shrewish wife and a demanding, expensive mistress. He dreams of killing his wife and one day is finally goaded into it by his need for his mistress and the refusal of a divorce from the wife.

However he kills the mistress by mistake as she's in his wife's bed. It seems the wife had a visit from the mistress, struck her in anger and put her to bed. The couple hide the body, but it seems the mistress had been already poisoned before coming to see the wife.

All these turns are worked out simply, but lack a sharp edge of

observation and deep probing that would have it all come off.

Comic Jean Richard acquits himself acceptably in his first serious role while others are adequate. Director Lisbona needs some more roadwork and better material before he can be judged on his contribution to the current French film scene. *Mosk.*

Ca Ira-Il Fiume della Rivolta
(The River of Revolt)
(ITALIAN)
(Songs)

Venice, Sept. 7.
Moris Ergas production and release. Written and directed by Tinto Bras. Commentary, Giancarlo Fusco, spoken by Tino Buazzelli, E. M. Salerno. Music, Romolo Grano. Tradeshown at Venice. Running time, 110 MINS.

Well made, often fascinating, frequently a brutal montage, telling in pictures the essentials of the revolutions of this century. It uses film clips, stock footage, newsreel material, culled from what must be one of the largest pools of material on the subject extant. Its commercial values are spotty, indicating specialized handling in most areas. Impact could, however, be strong in certain key situations.

Beginning with the Russian Revolution, Tinto Bras' effort uses bits from w.k. pix (Eisenstein classics are frequently excerpted), rarely seen newsreel or library shots to illustrate the brutality of revolutionary movements that followed. There are frequent shots of violence, executions, mutilated bodies, etc., which are not for the queasy (and which preclude television exposure) but which graphically underline and justify the revolts which followed. Ideologically, the pic tries to be fair in giving both sides of situations, but the accent is nevertheless one in favor of the oppressed or underdogs. A greater balance could have resulted in a stronger film and would have removed all hints of bias. For example, the Spanish Revolution is seen solely from the side of the harassed and succumbing Reds, never showing (existing) footage of tortured priests and nuns and ravaged churches, indicating leftist brutality as well. In short, the director seems more intent in justifying the revolts than in keying the point that revolution is perhaps the bloodiest, cruelest of all types of war. Significant also is the brevity of footage dedicated to the Hungarian revolt, versus the lengthy rendering—albeit the most interesting because of rarity of material—of the Japanese invasion of China and others.

Film is brilliantly edited, material is vividly chosen, comment (with above reservations) is to the point, and the pic is technically okay. *Hawk.*

Lilith

Psycho drama downbeat all the way.

Hollywood, Sept. 11.
Columbia Pictures release of Robert Rossen production. Stars Warren Beatty, Jean Seberg; features Peter Fonda, Kim Hunter. Directed by Rossen. Screenplay, Rossen, based on novel by J. R. Salamanca; camera, Eugen Shuftan; editor, Aram Avakian; music, Kenyon Hopkins; assistant director, Larry Sturhahn. Reviewed at Beverly Theatre, Sept. 10, '64. Running time, 110 MINS.
Vincent Bruce .... Warren Beatty
Lilith Arthur .... Jean Seberg
Stephen Evshevsky .... Peter Fonda
Bea Brice .... Kim Hunter
Mrs. Yvonne Meaghan .... Anne Meacham
Dr. Lavrier .... James Patterson
Laura .... Jessica Walter
Norman .... Gene Hackman
Bob Clayfield .... Robert Reilly
Howie .... Rene Auberjenois
Vincent's Grandmother .. Lucy Smith
Mr. Gordon .... Maurice Brenner
Miss Glassman .... Jeanne Barr
Mr. Palakis .... Richard Higgs
Girl at the Bar .... Elizabeth Bader

"Lilith," originally selected to be the American official entry in this year's Venice Film Festival but withdrawn when it was reported to have been "pre-judged," is strictly for art house and selected audiences. Its subject of seduction in an insane asylum is neither pleasant nor conducive to mass entertainment. Columbia Pictures, which is releasing the Robert Rossen production, may well be confronted with a problem both in booking and exploiting the subject matter.

It's the story of a young man who becomes an occupational therapist in a private mental institution where patients share three conditions—schizophrenia, wealth and uncommon intelligence. Untrained in medicine, he nevertheless takes the job because he feels he can help suffering humanity.

Whatever clarity the narrative has in its early reels is shrouded in mist as his relations with a beautiful young patient begin to develop. Unfoldment is complex and often confusing. Rossen as producer-scripter-director frequently fails to communicate to the spectator. Audience is left in as much of a daze as the hero is throughout most of the film.

Warren Beatty undertakes lead role with a hesitation jarring to the watcher. His dialog generally is restricted to no more than a single, or at most two sentences, and often the audience waits uncomfortably for words which never come while Beatty merely hangs his head or stares into space. As he finds himself falling in love with Jean Seberg, a fragile girl who lives in her own dream-world and wants love, the change of character from one fairly definitive in the beginning to the gropings of a sexually-obsessed mind never carries conviction.

In adapting the J. R. Salamanca novel, Rossen approaches his task with obvious attempt to shock. Instead, he comes up with something distasteful and, by some standards, offensive. His story-line apparently is for the few who enjoy such offbeat subjects, and very often his sequences run into one another without interlinking explanation.

When Beatty starts work at the institution he meets all manner of people who seem sane but have their own quirks of behavior. He is assigned first to the elfin-like girl who responds to his honest desire to be of help, and realizes she is falling for him, which he reports to the doctor in charge. Gradually, he comes under her spell. There is a seduction scene in a forest; and later, repeated in her own room, to which he has easy access. The girl is strange, her love unbound by sex and he follows her to a building where she has gone with an older woman, one of the patients. On another occasion he's instrumental in the suicide of a patient who has begged Beatty to intercede for him in his love for the girl. Yarn ends with his own complete disintegration, and asking the doctors to help him.

Beatty cannot surmount the transformations of character to which he is constantly subjected. Miss Seberg is properly vague but is lovely in her role, and Peter Fonda as the youth who commits suicide is dramatically effective. Kim Hunter scores as head of the institution. Good support is offered by Anne Meacham, a patient; James Patterson, the doctor; Jessica Walter, the girl who didn't wait for Beatty to return from war; and Gene Hackman, her husband.

Rossen has accorded film excellent production mounting and Eugen Shuftan's camera work and Richard Sylbert's production design are first-class credits. Music score by Kenyon Hopkins, though fairly effective, sometimes overpowers the dialog so the lines are lost, and Aram Avakian's editing frequently is uneven. *Whit.*

The Luck Of Ginger Coffey

Well-produced drama of an Irish immigrant in Montreal but lacking general appeal; only spotty business indicated.

Hollywood, Sept. 18.

Continental Distributing release of Leon Roth production. Stars Robert Shaw, Mary Ure. Features Liam Redmond. Directed by Irvin Kershner. Screenplay, Brian Moore, based on his novel; camera, Manny Wynn; editor, Anthony Gibbs; music Bernardo Segall; assistant director, Martin Rich; sound, Stanley Kasper. Reviewed at Lytton Center Theatre, Sept. 17, '64. Running time, **100 MINS.**

Ginger .... Robert Shaw
Vera .... Mary Ure
MacGregor .... Liam Redmond
Joe McGlade .... Tom Harvey
Paulie .... Libby McClintock
Brott .... Leo Leyden
Fox .... Powys Thomas
Kenny .... Tom Kneebone
Stan Melton .... Leslie Yeo
Hawkins .... Vern Chapman
Marcel .... Paul Guevremont
Clarence .... Barry Stewart
O'Donnell .... Arch McDonell
Judge .... Oliva Legare
Policeman .... Jacques Godin
M. Beaulieu .... Maurice Beaupre
Old Billy .... Sydney Brown
Mme. Beaulieu .... Juliette Huot
Court Clerk .... Paul Hebert
Newspaper foreman .... Barney McManus
Hickey .... Clarence Goodhue

"The Luck of Ginger Coffey," filmed in Canada as a joint Hollywood-Dominion production, is a well-turned-out drama based on a Brian Moore novel. Its story of a flamboyant Irish immigrant in Montreal and his marital and job-holding troubles, however, while perhaps of certain interest to more mature audiences, lacks mass appeal so that its chances in the general market appear spotty.

Film was produced by Leon Roth and Irvin Kershner's Hollywood unit in association with Crawley Films Ltd., of Ottawa, in which Walter Reade-Sterling Inc., also was interested. Roth handled producer reins with an awareness of the drama in the author's screenplay, while Kershner directed, likewise capturing the mood of the script. The overall, despite its straightforward story-telling, is rather depressing and the youthful spectator who makes up the bulk of the b.o. attendance will find small interest in its two middle-aged characters, particularly since players are unknown to American filmgoers.

Robert Shaw and Mary Ure, two of Britain's more prominent thesps, delineate the lead roles as a married couple who have found the going in Montreal rough since they arrived from Dublin six months before to make their new home in Canada. The husband, who cannot keep a job, has spent the passage money on which the wife was depending to return them to Ireland should they not make the grade. A marital crisis therefore arises, since the wife believes that with her husband's superior attitude he will always be unable to hold a job in Canada. When he gets a $45-a-week newspaper proofreader's job, a salary she knows cannot keep them and their 14-year-old daughter, the wife moves out. In his efforts to re-win his wife's love the husband encounters further bad luck by being fired after the editor goes back on his word to promote him to a reporter, but film ends on a note indicating a happy future for couple.

Shaw plays his brash Irishman with sincerity and Miss Ure (his real wife in private life) lends credence to the wife, both scoring strongly. Liam Redmond as the hardboiled editor does a fine job with the part, and so does Tom Harvey as a friend of the couple. Libby McClintock is the daughter, and Powys Thomas does a standout job as a bitter proofreader. Film has been well cast in minor roles.

Manny Wynn's fluid camera catches interesting glimpses of Montreal in winter, and Bernardo Segall's music score is atmospherically effective. Harry Horner's production design and Anthony Gibbs' editing rate highly. *Whit.*

Goldfinger
(BRITISH—COLOR)

Another boxoffice bonanza for third James Bond film from the Broccoli-Saltzman stable; splendidly witty and zestful slice of fantastic hokum, with Sean Connery relishing every dame and fight.

London, Sept. 22.

United Artists release of an Eon (Harry Saltzman-Albert R. Broccoli) production. Stars Sean Connery, Honor Blackman, Gert Frobe. Directed by Guy Hamilton. Screenplay, Richard Maibaum and Paul Dehn, from Ian Fleming's novel; camera, (Technicolor), Ted Holmes; editor, Peter Hunt; music, John Barry. Reviewed at Odeon, Leicester-square, London. Running time, **112 MINS.**

James Bond .... Sean Connery
Pussy Galore .... Honor Blackman
Goldfinger .... Gert Frobe
Jill Masterson .... Shirley Eaton
Tilly Masterson .... Tania Mallet
Odd-job .... Harold Sakata
"M" .... Bernard Lee
Solo .... Martin Benson
Felix Leiter .... Cec Linder
Simmons .... Austin Willis
Miss Moneypenny .... Lois Maxwell
Midnight .... Bill Nagy
Capungo .... Alf Joint
Old Lady .... Varley Thomas
Bonita .... Nadja Regin
Sierra .... Raymond Young
Smithers .... Richard Vernon
Burnskill .... Denis Cowles
Kisch .... Michael Mellinger
Mr. Ling .... Bert Kwouk
Strap .... Hal Galili
Henchman .... Lenny Rabin

There's not the least sign of staleness in the Bond 007 formula, and this third sample looks like matching the mammoth grosses of "From Russia With Love" and may be exceeding them. In addition to its ample quota of action and girl-fancying, this film has extra piquancy from a script that's not afraid to laugh at its own conventions and from a production that uses a number of mechanical and electrical gimmicks to spice the mayhem. And the whole thing is given an affluent gloss that makes it ideal for escapists.

Some liberties have been taken with Ian Fleming's original novel by scripters Richard Maibaum and Paul Dehn, but without diluting its flavor. The mood is set before the credits show up, with Connery making an arrogant pass at a chick and spying a thug creeping up from behind; he's reflected in the femmes eyeballs. So he heaves the heavy into bathful of water and connects it deftly to a handy supply of electricity.

Thereafter the plot gets its teeth into the real business, which is the duel between Bond and Goldfinger. The latter plans to plant an atomic bomb in Fort Knox and thus contaminate the U. S. hoard of the yellow stuff so that it can't be touched, and thus increase tenfold the value of his own gold, earned by hard international smuggling. The first half-hour is gloriously sly 24-carat pleasure. Bond meets up with Goldfinger in Miami, where he's playing crooked poker. He's planted a blonde with a telescope in his hotel bedroom, and she can watch the other guy's fistful of cards in the patio below. And she tells Goldfinger what he's holding by transistor radio, which he listens to through a hearing aid.

But the blonde tries to run out on Goldfinger, so he snuffs her out. And this launches Bond on a chase, with plenty of fanciful trimmings. He's given an Aston-Martin that is equipped with radar, machine-guns, an ejector seat that hurtles unwanted passengers through the roof, and a smokescreen device. With this, he traces Goldfinger to a Swiss hideout, where he's captured after a car chase that wouldn't have been despised by the Keystone Kops. Hi-jacked back to the States where Goldfinger runs a stud farm, Bond meets up with Pussy Galore, with cleavage to match the monicker. And the entire preposterous affair comes to a dizzy climax with Bond foiling the Fort Knox coup, leaving himself three seconds before the bomb is timed to go off.

Sean Connery repeats his suave portrayal of the punch-packing Bond, who can find his way around the wine-list as easily as he can negotiate a dame. But, if backroom boys got star billing, it's deserved by Ken Adam, who has designed the production with a wealth of enticing invention. There's a ray-gun that cuts through any metal, and threatens to carve Bond down the middle. There's Goldfinger's automobile—cast in solid gold. And his farm is stocked with furniture that moves at the press of a button. Perhaps the most memorable visual incident is the crushing of a limousine, with a body inside, at a scrap yard. It's then put in the boot of another car and driven back to Goldfinger; he wants to rescue the gold it's made of.

Honor Blackman, with a large local rep for her tele success in "The Avengers" skein, makes a fine, sexy partner for Bond. As Pussy, Goldfinger's pilot for his private plane, she does not take things lying down—she's a judo expert who throws Bond until the final k.o. when she's tumbled herself. Gert Frobe, too, is near-perfect casting as the resourceful Goldfinger, an amoral tycoon who treats gold-cornering as a business like any other. And Harold Sakata scores as Odd-job, his chief henchman, who kills by throwing his bowlerhat at the jugular vein like a discus; it has a razor concealed in the brim. Shirley Eaton looks appropriately edible as the girl who gets bumped off. A neat cameo as Bond's Secret Service boss, "M," is supplied by Bernard Lee. Cec Linder, Tania Mallet and Nadja Regin are also okay in minor roles.

Guy Hamilton's direction is first-class, especially in the earlier scenes, but he tends to loiter a little in the middle stretches. The script, by Maibaum and Dehn, is a professional blend of excitement and offhand humor. After the battle of Fort Knox and Bond has been saved in the nick of time, his payoff is "And what kept you, then?" It's this tongue-in-cheek attitude that gives the script an extra kick.

Ted Moore's lensing does full justice to Adam's astute sets, which are great for Technicolor. The musical soundtrack is slickly furnished by John Barry, who also composed the title song (to lyrics by Anthony Newley and Leslie Bricusse) which is sung over the closing and opening credits by Shirley Bassey, with the expected intensity. *Otta.*

Godzilla Vs. The Thing
(JAPANESE-COLOR)

Latest Japanese sci-fi long on special effects but lacks appeal for general trade.

Hollywood, Sept. 17.

American International Pictures release of Toho production. Stars Akira Takarada, Yuriko Hoshi, Hiroshi Koisumi; features Yu Fujiki, Emi Ito, Yumi Ito. Directed by Inoshiro Honda. Screenplay, Shinichi Sekizawa; camera (Colorscope), Hajime Koizumi; music, Akira Ifukube; sound, Fumio Yanoguchi. Reviewed at Joe Shore Screening Room, Sept. 17, '64. Running time, **90 MINS.**

News reporter .... Akira Takarada
Girl photographer .... Yuriko Hoshi
Scientist .... Hiroshi Koisumi
2d reporter .... Yu Fujiki
Twin girls .... Emi Ito, Yumi Ito

"Godzilla Vs. The Thing" should be ultimate in monster pics, with four super-monsters plus an orgy of special effects that should satisfy devotees of this fare. But in spite of the slick production, the story and acting don't offer enough to attract large general audiences. Virtually all-Japanese cast, with unfamiliar faces and broad emoting typical of such Japanese pics, also detracts from general appeal.

Three leads, Akira Takarada,

Yuriko Hoshi and Hiroshi Koisumi, handle roles creditably as reporter, photographer and scientist who investigate giant egg washed ashore after typhoon. Pair of unscrupulous promoters, unnamed in credits, get control of egg and hope to make millions with it as tourist attraction.

Six-inch-tall twin girls, engagingly played by Emi and Yumi Ito, appeal to heroes to help return egg to their Pacific island. Egg is sacred to inhabitants of island, which was used in early atomic tests and as result is radioactive horror spot. The Thing, monstrous special effects creation like gigantic bee or hornet, returns twins to island when they get no help with egg.

Then Godzilla rises from sea as result of typhoon and goes on rampage. This dinosaur-like creature, several hundred feet tall, is indestructible as it plows through Japanese countryside, destroying and killing. Tanks, missiles and artificial lightning all fail to stop him.

It's apparent special effects men, headed by Eiji Tsuburaya, labored mightily to cook up monsters and their battles, the tiny twins and the military assaults against Godzilla. Direction by Inoshiro Honda and script by Shinichi Sekizawa keep story moving at lively pace, building up to tense, climactic scenes. Final result, however, is for viewer to wonder why any of them bothered. *Hogg.*

L'Age D'Or
(FRENCH)

First U.S. showing of Luis Bunuel's savage 1930 attack on morals, faith and society. Historic but hardly for general public.

Lincoln Center Film Festival presentation of Vicomte de Nolalles production. Produced, directed and edited by Luis Bunuel. Features Gaston Modot, Lya Lys. Screenplay, Bunuel and Salvador Dali; camera. Albert Dubergent; music, Wagner, Debussy, Beethoven, Mendelssohn and original music by Georges van Parys. Reviewed at Lincoln Center, N. Y., Sept. 21, 1964. Running time, 65 MINS.
Man .... Gaston Modot
Girl .... Lya Lys
Also Max Ernst. Pierre Prevert, Jose Artigas, Cardinal de Lamberdesque, Jacques Brunius.

Reviewed for the record. Luis Bunuel's second feature (1930) has never been shown commercially in the U.S. Its booking by the Lincoln Center Film Festival has some historical and novelty value but main interest is to film students and film buffs. There is a print at Eastman House but the expense of making prints for the few film societies that will ask for it may preclude any such venture.

Made two years after his surrealistic "Le Chien Andalou," this second effort created such a furor when first shown in Paris that, after a stormy run, it was finally banned by the French government. Bunuel's film was offensive to both society and church. Establishment teamed up to "eradicate" this impudent upstart. Bunuel has been having trouble with them ever since. The detestation is clearly mutual.

As shown at Lincoln Center, "L'Age D'Or" is an example of early sound in the French film. Not quite trusting in the new approach, lengthy printed (in French) intro prefaces each major sequence. At the Festival showing, the film was accompanied by an excellent live spoken translation in English.

A Bunuel film has been likened, perhaps with some exaggeration, to raw spirit poured onto an open wound, a stinging, cauterizing therapy of shock. In "L'Age D'Or," Bunuel early sets his pattern of condemnation of the "conventional morals, sentimentalism and the moral uncleanliness of society." He forecast his career-long obsession with sexuality and anti-religion. There's no denying that his talent for cinematic comment had power and persuasion in even this early work.

Although Salvador Dali is co-credited with the screenplay, there's little evidence of his contribution to the film beyond the occasional surrealistic treatment of an incident or a visual image indicative of his pictorial style.

Bunuel's anger at society, particularly its attitude on morality, seems not only dated today, but laugh provoking. The behavior of his libidinous hero and heroine, played by Gaston Modot and Lya Lys in a style straight out of "A Fool There Was," wouldn't cause raised eyebrows today at a Flatbush cocktail party.

As antique as his comments on morality now seem, those he makes against religion are still marked by violence, blasphemy and vilification, hence not for general audiences. This Jesuit-educated Spaniard uses for closing a sequence based on an excerpt from the writings of Marquis de Sade. It's a particularly brutal comment with a Jesus Christ-like figure staggering out of a sin castle.

There are some intentional moments of humor, some so broad that they were obviously influenced by the earlier American slapstick films. Others, while subtler, are also effective. One visual comment that still registers is in an early scene. Modot, having scandalized the crowd gathered at a ceremony to welcome some visiting bishops by publicly displaying his lust for Lya Lys, is forcibly separated from her and taken away. The crowd reviles him as he passes, for his gauche behavior and lack of respect for the occasion. He remains unmoved by their name-calling but, when a small dog begins to bark at him, it is too much. Breaking away from his guards, he boots the dog for a good ten yards. Though basically cruel, it is no more so than the impossible violence that makes up many screen cartoons. *Robe.*

The Outrage
(PANAVISION)

Star names should attract okay grosses but reaction to film may be lukewarm.

Hollywood, Sept. 17.
Metro release of A. Ronald Lubin production. Stars Paul Newman, Laurence Harvey, Claire Bloom; Edward G. Robinson; features rest of cast. Directed by Martin Ritt. Screenplay, Michael Kanin, from play, "Rashomon," by Fay and Michael Kanin, based on Japanese Daiei production, "Rashomon" and stories by Ryunosuka Akutagawa; camera, James Wong Howe; music, Alex North; editor, Frank Santillo; assistant director, Daniel J. McCauley; sound, Franklin Milton. Reviewed at Hollywood Paramount Theatre, Sept. 1 ,8'64. Running Time, 95 MINS.
Juan Carrasco .... Paul Newman
Husband .... Laurence Harvey
Wife .... Claire Bloom
Con Man .... Edward G. Robinson
Preacher .... William Shatner
Prospector .... Howard Da Silva
Sheriff .... Albert Salmi
Judge .... Thomas Chalmers
Indian .... Paul Fix

For the masses who keep theatres in operation a sense of wonderment undoubtedly will engulf them to the detriment of this film. "Outrage" is adapted from the Fay and Michael Kanin Broadway play, "Rashomon," which in turn was based on the Japanese Daiei film production of same tab which won considerable critical attention when released in 1951. It is the story of a killing of a Southern gentleman and the rape of his wife by a bloodthirsty bandit, told through the eyes of the three protagonists and then by a disinterested eye witness, each version differing.

What should attract at the box-office is lineup of star names, headed by Paul Newman as the Mexican outlaw, Laurence Harvey the victim, Claire Bloom the ravished spouse, and Edward G. Robinson as a con-man to whom the story is told by an old prospector. Newman as the violent and passionate killer plays his colorful character with a flourish and heavy accent, reminiscent of the late Holbrook Blinn's portrayal in "The Bad Man," which years ago set the model for demi-heroes (or badmen) of this type. He dominates the action mainly told in flashback sequences as the basic situation and consequent footage, is recounted four times.

Script by Michael Kanin unfolds in the American Southwest—probably the Arizona Territory—in the 1870's, a neat metamorphosis from the 12th Century Japan of the play and original Nipponese pic. Bandit character is retained, but the Samurai character becomes a Southern gentleman of fine family who is travelling through the West with his wife when set upon by a Mexican outlaw.

Plot takes its form, opening on platform of a deserted railroad station as the prospector and a preacher, who is leaving the town a disillusioned man, recite to Robinson the trial of the outlaw a few days previously, when three people testify to three totally different accounts of what "actually" happened. Outlaw confesses he tied up the husband, raped his wife before his eyes, then killed him with a dagger during a duel of honor. The widow claims bandit attacked her, and the husband regarded her with such contempt that she became enraged and plunged knife into his heart. An old Indian medicine-man, saying he

chanced along while husband was still alive, tells court that husband claimed he had stabbed himself because of his humiliation.

Narrative under realistic direction of Martin Ritt is developed along strictly dramatic lines through this point, then turns to broadest type of absurd slapstick and oldhat comedy situations as the prospector, who was the eye witness, describes the incident to con-man and preacher as he remembers it. Transition from drama to farce—and not in its most brilliant form—is so abrupt and the mood previously set so disrupted that's it's disturbing, almost an affront to the intelligence. There's the further business of an abandoned baby being discovered in the station, wholly without meaning and unbelievable, to further lessen any impact producers might hope for.

Harvey has little to do in first three accounts except remain tied to a tree, his turn coming in fourth when the prospector tells how he and bandit are shamed by the wife into fighting for her. He accidentally trips and falls upon the dagger, rising to state, dead-pan, "Ah tripped." Miss Bloom, who appeared in Broadway play, has her gamut during the four versions of her ravishment, running from pure innocence to her demand to the outlaw to kill her husband so she can go away with her new lover. In all, she delivers strongly, turning glibly from drama to comedy.

Robinson displays earthy humor as the cynical con-man and Howard Da Silva scores as the prospector, as does William Shatner in preacher role. Albert Salmi, Paul Fix and Thomas Chalmers also contribute in the A. Ronald Lubin production, which has benefit of several fine technical credits, particularly James Wong Howe's black-and-white photography. Additional plusses are Frank Santillo's editing; art direction by George W. Davis and Tambi Larsen; music by Alex North. *Whit.*

Murder Ahoy

Margaret Rutherford again as the spinster private-eye. Good b.o. anticipated.

Hollywood, Sept. 14.
Metro release of Lawrence P. Bachman production. Stars Margaret Rutherford; features rest of cast. Directed by George Pollock. Screenplay by David Pursall, Jack Seddon, based on Agatha Christie character; music, Ron Goodwin; camera, Desmond Dickinson; editor, Ernest Walter. Reviewed at Metro Studio, Sept. 11, 1964. Running time, 93 MINS.
Miss Marple .... Margaret Rutherford
Captain Rhumstone ..... Lionel Jeffries
Det. Insp. Craddock .... Charles Tingwell
Breeze-Connington .... William Mervyn
Matron Alice Fanbraid ... Joan Benham
Mr. Stringer .... Stringer Davis
Dr. Crump .... Nicholas Parsons
Bishop .... Miles Malleson
Lord Rudkin .... Henry Oscar
Humbert .... Derek Nimmo
Lt. Commander Dimchurch Gerald Cross
Shirley .... Norma Foster
Sgt. Bacon .... Terence Edmund
Millie .... Lucy Griffiths
Dusty Miller .... Bernard Adams
Kelly-Tramp .... Tony Quinn
Miss Pringle .... Edna Petrie

"Murder Ahoy" is another in the light-hearted series of Metro releases starring Margaret Rutherford as the indomitable spinster detective, Miss Marple. Although over-exposure is possible, this being fourth such pic, the Rutherford name and series itself had developed fans. Result should be ready-made 'audiences.

This latest escapade of England's best-known female Hawkshaw is up to slick, workmanlike standards of others in producer Lawrence P. Bachmann's series. Opening with a dead body and closing with unmasking of killer, script includes some hoary cliches, but, as directed by George Pollock, has saving grace of not taking itself too seriously.

Story begins with Miss Marple, a board member, at meet of trustees of Cape of Good Hope Reclamation Trust, a do-good foundation that saves wayward teenage boys by cooping them up on a cadet training ship under ex-Navy officers. One trustee is impatient to disclose important news about the cadet ship when he falls dead.

In typical bull-headed fashion, Miss Marple discovers victim died of poison in his snuff. Naturally the law, overplayed by Charles Tingwell as the Chief inspector, doesn't agree. So Miss Marple takes off for ship to do own investigating. There she finds a motley group of officers, headed by Lionel Jeffries as bearded, rather kookie captain, all with something to hide.

Despite brief stay in jail for her nosiness, Miss Marple is convinced she's right when body of a ship's officer is found hanging from yardarm and attractive ship's matron is killed by poisoned mousetrap. Spinster uncovers most of the ship's secrets, discovers the killer and winds up in an improbable sword duel with the culprit.

In spite of aforementioned cliches, including people creeping along dark corridors, sudden screams, and quick searches of empty rooms, the story sparkles with extras. These include brisk medical examiner (Nicholas Parsons) who has quip for every corpse, Stringer Davis as Miss Marple's bumbling aide, and Gerald Cross as Naval officer who has been hiding seasickness for a couple of decades.

Director Pollock and editor Ernest Walter, along with scripters David Pursall and Jack Seddon, share credit for smooth and well-organized story, sans loose ends too often found in film whodunits. Photography by Desmond Dickinson, while not over-obtrusive, catches spirit of production, and Ron Goodwin's musical score is bouncy and listenable.

Hogg.

Les Yeux Cernes
(Marked Eyes)
(FRENCH)

Paris, Sept. 29.

Cocinor release of Cocinor-Marceau production. Stars Michele Morgan, Robert Hossein; features Marie-France Pisier, Francois Patrice, Yvette Etievant. Directed by Robert Hossein. Screenplay, Hossein; Claude Desailly, Georges and Andre Tabet from an original by Hossein; camera, Jean Bossety; editor, Marie Sophie Dubois. At Ermitage, Paris. Running time, 80 MINS.
Widow .... Michele Morgan
Franz .... Robert Hossein
Clara .... Marie-France Pisier
Inspector .... Francoise Patrice
Mother .... Yvette Etievant

French, too, are giving their more veteran female stars suspense items to do. Here Michele Morgan suffers as a widow being blackmailed when she comes back, after a long separation, following the murder of her husband. But limp scripting and ordinary direction make this mainly a local item or, at best, a dualer in foreign marts.

Miss Morgan finds her husband was hated by everybody in a small Troylian town. She gets notes saying that something is known and she had better pay money. She is helped by a worker her husband fired, Robert Hossein. She begins to crack and suspect the man but a switch has it that she really murdered her husband and she tries to do in Hossein. The blackmailing was being done by a young girl who was Hossein's mistress.

Director Hossein tries to mix some forthright love scenes, suspense and Miss Morgan's well-known brooding face. They really jive and this plods rather than giving the banal tale the dynamic lift it needs.

Miss Morgan is made to walk all over muddy, wet and forest roads with high heels and is allowed only to look harassed, while Marie-France Pisier has the right surly qualities for the conniving blackmailer. Hossein directs himself woodenly. Otherwise, it is technically good. *Mosk.*

Diary of a Bachelor

Tame tale of modern Casanova. Gotham -- made film's lack of names and generally pallid comedy make it candidate for second billing.

American International Pictures release of Sandy Howard production. Directed by Howard Features William Traylor, Dagne Crane, Joe Silver, Denise Lor, Susan Dean, Jan Crockett, Eleni Kiamos, Arlene Golonka, Joan Holloway. Screenplay, Ken Barnett, camera, Julian Townsend; editor, Angelo Ross; music, composed and conducted, Jack Pleis. Reviewed in N. Y., Sept. 18, 1964. Running time, 90 MINS.
Skip O'Hara .... William Traylor
Joanne .... Dagne Crane
Charlie Barrett .... Joe Silver
Jana Woods .... Denoise Lor
Barbara .... Susan Dean
Angie Pisano .... Eleni Kiamos
Jennifer Watters .... Jan Crockett
Lois .... Arlene Golonka
Nancy Feather .... Joan Holloway
Barney Washburn ...... Mickey Deems
Marvin Rollins .... Dom De Luise
Bob Haney .... Jackie Kannon
Mother O'Hara .... Leora Thatcher
Bugsy .... Bradley Bolke
Harley Peterson .... Jim Alexander
Bartender .... Joey Faye
Thelma .... Beatrice Pons
Susan .... Joy Claussen
Carol .... Chris Noel
Belly Dancer .... Saliha Tekneci
Wanda Smith .... Bonnie Jones
Cynthia Brooks ...... Joanne Macormack
Victoria Ampolsk .... Ellen Nevdal

Although filmed in New York in 1963, Sandy Howard's comedy is just now being released by American International. As something of an experiment, the first date set was last week in Macon, Georgia. The ultimate future of this programmer, however, will be the bottom half of a double bill unless someone comes up with a miraculous promotion gimmick.

Not a cheaply-made film by any means, "Diary" has much going in its favor but not a good script or outstanding acting. Ken Barnett's screenplay tries to substitute a series of vignettes for a well-founded and credible plot. Living up to the title, most of the film

consists of a bachelor (William Traylor) confiding to his diary his prowess among the babes. When his fiancee (Dagne Crane) accidentally discovers and reads it, the plot becomes a series of flashbacks depicting his individual conquests. These range from dull to two really funny adventures.

William Traylor's hero is a major drawback as is Howard's indifferent and only occasionally imaginative directing. Traylor plays the fickle lover in such a smug manner that his easy and overdone conquest of a long list of really beautiful females is unbelievable and, usually, ridiculous.

Best acting is turned in by Eleni Kiamos as a screwball prostitute whose single scene with Traylor in a bar is film's highlight. Also outstanding is Arlene Golonka as a Greenwich Village artist whose unabashed propositioning of Traylor makes even that wolf type a bit apprehensive. Their tryst comes to naught because of an ill-timed visit by Miss Golonka's muscle-bound regular boyfriend. More photogenic than dramatically convincing, but a visual treat, nevertheless, are Denise Lor, Susan Dean, Joan Holloway and a long list of other beauties.

Joe Silver, as Traylor's best friend, is impressive in a rather thankless role. With the help of Mickey Deems, Jackie Kannon and, particularly, Dom De Luise, he makes the weekly poker party a laughgetting vignette.

Julian Townsend's photography is first rate but his mixture of studio shots and hand-held camera footage for street scenes creates an uneven visual pattern. Many Gotham locations are used, particularly Greenwich Village. Other technical credits are good. *Robe.*

The Train
(FRENCH-ITALIAN-U.S.)

John Frankenheimer save-the-art-of-France actioner with something for everybody. Should hightail to hefty international b.o. returns.

Paris, Sept. 25.

United Artists release of UA-Ariane-Dear Films production. Stars Burt Lancaster; features, Paul Scofield, Jeanne Moreau, Michel Simon, Suzanne Flon. Directed by John Frankenheimer. Screenplay, Franklin Coen, Frank Davis, Walter Bernstein from the book by Rose Valland; camera, Walter Wottitz, Jean Tournier; editor, Gabriel Rongier, David Brotherton; special effect, Lee Zavitz. Previewed in Paris. Running time, 140 MINS.
Labiche .... Burt Lancaster
Waldheim .... Paul Scofield
Christine .... Jeanne Moreau
Papa Boule .... Michel Simon
Villard .... Suzanne Flon
Pesquet .... Charles Millot

After a slow start, "The Train" picks up to become a colorful, actionful big-scale adventure opus that should prove a neat boxoffice item internationally. Burt Lancaster name will help while monickers for the more selective fans are Jeanne Moreau and Paul Scofield.

So it looks like UA has a fine showcase item for all audiences. Made in French and English in France, it was entirely lensed in real exteriors with unlimited access to old French rolling stock of the last war.

Stations and armored cars and

ordinary trains are blown sky high, they are strafed on the run or run wild to plow into each other. Steam driven trains have often been taken and photogenic film fodder ("La Roue" of Abel Gance and Buster Keaton's "The General" to name a couple) and it is again true here. Pic concerns an elaborate railroad resistance plot to keep a train full of French art treasures from being shipped to Germany near the end of the war.

At first there is impassioned talk of patrimony and France's duty to preserve these art treasures for the world. An earthy station master, Lancaster, if in the resistance, is reluctant to sacrifice men for paintings, especially with the war nearing its end. But he finally gives in when an old engineer, almost his foster father, is killed by the Germans for trying to hold up the art train.

An elaborate plot is put into action. Lancaster himself is made to drive the train by the fanatic German Colonel (Paul Scofield) to whom the art has become bigger than the war itself. But the resistance net has been alerted and they begin to change the names of stations and manage to make the Germans believe it is headed for Germany when it is making a round trip.

Director John Frankenheimer has a way with obsession and the visually plotted workings of a complicated movement. Here the resistance sides become an exciting human endeavor that transcend the war, time and even place. It boils down to two men, each fighting for something, if sometimes forced into it, or with reasons clouded, that are mainly exciting and catching on their execution rather than their deeper ideology.

Lancaster's rugged physique is serviceable as is his still active acrobatic elan. Scofield has the dandyish almost psychotic nature of a dilettante with unlimited power that gives his role a dark power.

French star Jeanne Moreau has a small but telling cameo bit as does Michel Simon as the dedicated old engineer who swings Lancaster into line to go all out for saving the train. But above all it is the railroad bustle, the trains themselves and some bangup special effects of bombing attacks and accidents that give the pic its main points.

Dialog is sometimes stilted and characterations are surface. Sharply contrasted lensing is also an asset as is knowing editing. Production dress is rightly unstinting.

Film opens here before the U.S. If the plot is the thing, it also makes a comment on courage and its ironic ending hits the right balanced note as executed hostages are intercut with the boxes of priceless paintings strewn alongside the train but intact as Lancaster limps off into the distance. *Mosk.*

Le Monocle Rit Jaune
(The Monocle's Sour Laugh)
(FRENCH)

Paris, Sept. 29.

Cocinor release of Marceau-Transinter Films production. Stars Paul Meurisse;

features Marcel Dalio, Olivier Despax, Robert Dalban, Barbara Steele, Renee Saint-Cyr. Directed by Georges Lautner. Screenplay, G. Remy, Jacques Robert, Albert Kantof; camera, Maurice Fellous; editor, Michelle David. At the Balzac, Paris. Running time, 95 MINS.

Le Monocle .... Paul Meurisse
Elie ....Marcel Dalio
Frederic .... Olivier Despax
Poussin .... Robert Dalban
Valerie .... Barbara Steele
Madame Hui .... Renee Saint-Cyr

Film is the third in a series devoted to the tongue-in-cheek adventures of a phlegmatic French secret service man. It has some good color in its Hong Kong lensing and some okay adventurous aspects and comedics. But this does not have the consistent imaginative tempo to keep it from lagging. It is thus a good home item with mainly dualer aspects for abroad on its general entertaining qualities. Paul Meurisse's clever limning of the main role also is a help.

The Monocle, Paul Meurisee, is a dandyish, flowery speaking man, who wears a monocle. But he is quick with his revolver which he carries like a bouquet of flowers with a dry reserve of French skepticism and wit. He is out to track down a group of terrorists who want to insure peace by killing off anybody connected with the A-Bomb.

Pic has some good chase and fight scenes but is far out balance of parody and action to bring it off entirely. However, it does pick up at the end for a bangup series of gags and twists.

Georges Lautner has directed briskly if he sometimes lacks the punch and mock seriousness to give the originality it strives for. Supporting players are good, camera work bright and editing solid. It just does not have the fillip to put it in the James Bond class which it strives for. *Mosk.*

La Repas Des Fauves
(Dinner for Savages)
(FRENCH-DYALISCOPE)

Paris, Sept. 22.

Prodis release of Terra Film-Films Borderie - FIF - Prod. - Vertice-Flora Film production. With France Anglade, Francis Blanche, Boy Gobert, Antonella Lualdi, Claude Nicot, Claude Rich. Directed by Christian Jaque. Screenplay, Claude Marcy, Henri Jeanson, Jaque from play by Vahe Katcha; camera, Pierre Petit; editor, Jacques Desagneaux. At Ambassade-Gaumont Paris. Running time, 105 MINS.

Sophie .... France Anglade
Francis .... Francis Blanche
Kaubach .... Boy Gobert
Francoise .... Antonella Lualdi
Victor .... Claude Nicot
Claude .... Claude Rich

This is a harrowing look at abject human nature during an incident under the Occupation of France in the last World War that plays it more for laughs than drama. This makes it somewhat theatrical, with heightened, if witty, dialog, taking precedence over motivation and drama. Pic looms a difficult arty subject if its outright romping in human pettiness gives it an unsavvory but biting look. This might give it some playoff or special situation legs abroad.

A group of friends gather for the birthday party of a dim-witted, comely girl and her fumbling, silly husband. Present is a collaborating and unsavory uncle, a blind veteran, a cocky teacher, a weak-willed doctor and an outspoken, patriotic girl.

Some Germans are killed outside the house and a sadistic Gestapo man tells them he will let them choose two hostages who will be shot if the terrorists are not caught. His knowing the husband, whose book store he patronizes, gives him this leeway with them if it's a sadistic game. If they do not choose he will take all seven.

So a lot of hair is let down and closet skeletons romp as most show the white feathers and are ready to cling to life at anybody's expense. It might have been valid but this is done with smirks and sacrifices insights to a queasy selfishness and clever talk.

However Christian Jaque has given this impeccable mounting and kept things moving in spite of an almost one-room locale, with acting all of a piece and well-balanced. This is mainly a slick unsavory jape at human baseness. *Mosk.*

Brollopsbesvar
(Wedding-Swedish Style)
(SWEDISH)

Stockholm, Sept. 22.

Minerva (Tore Sjoberg and Lorens Marmstedt) production and release. Stars Jarl Kulle, Christina Schollin, Edvin Adolphson, Lars Ekborg, Isa Quensel, Lena Hansson, Catrin Westerlund, Tor Isedal. Directed by Ake Falck. Screenplay, Lars Widding after idea by Stig Dagerman; camera, Rune Ericson; music, Georg Riedel; editor, Ingemar Ejve. At Roda Kvarn, Stockholm. Running time, 100 MINS.

Hilmer Westlund .... Jarl Kulle
Siri, his daughter........ Lena Hansson
Hildur Palm .... Christina Schollin
Victor Palm, her father Edvin Adolphson
Hilma Palm, her mother .. Isa Quensel
Irma Palm, her sister.Catrin Westerlund
Rudolph Palm, her brother .. Tor Isedal
Gunnar Palm, Irma's son .. Peter Thelin
Simon .... Lars Ekborg
Mary .... Margareta Krook
Svea .... Yvonne Lombard
Johan Borg .... Georg Arlin
Ivar .... Ove Tjernberg
Martin .... Lars Passgard
Soren .... Lars Lind
Philips .... Sigge Fischer
Bjuhr .... John Norrman
Loony-Anders .... Tommy Nilsson
Rullan .... Ulla Edin
Hagstrom .... Sten Mattsson
Karlsson .... Thor Zackrisson
Nisse Johansson .... Gosta Krantz
Wallinder .... Claes Esphagen
Mary Lou .... Jessie Flaws
The Beef Manager .... Fritiof Bjarne
The Pedlar .... Lasse Poysti

Late playwright Stig Dagerman left a number of unpublished works, one of them being this racy story from his own home-province during the '40s. There is to be a wedding in the village. Butcher Jarl Kulle, widower with a grown-up daughter, is going to be married to Christina Schollin, who has agreed to marry him because her former boyfriend sent back the engagement ring. Kulle isn't known among the women in village for a life in chastity.

After a number of complications, the two finally are married. At a dinner following, large quantities of liquor are consumed, and existing erotic and emotional conflicts between the people in the village are revealed.

Finally, the newlyweds return to their new home. Kulle is so drunk he falls asleep on the kitchen floor.

There are some erotic scenes that can be compared with those in "The Silence." However, for some reason these seem more natural in this story, perhaps, because the millieu is typically Swedish, and so are the characters.

Kulle again has a very good role as the butcher Westlund. However, he is in almost every Swedish film being made these days. Miss Schollin, as the girl he marries, is successful in portraying the girl of innocence among people where little innocence is left. Edvin Adolphson, grand old man of Swedish films, as her father, gives another of his great performances. A vivid portrayal is contributed by Georg Arlih, as the man from the almshouse. He thinks he is a great singer but when asked to sing at the wedding, he faints. When he wakes up, everybody tells him how much they enjoyed his singing.

Direction by Ake Falck is outstanding as are most of the other credits. This film looks likely to be a top money maker here. It should also do well abroad, provided it doesn't run into censorship difficulties. *Wing.*

Le Chat Dans le Sac
(The Cat in the Bag)
(CANADIAN)

Montreal, Sept. 29

National Film Board of Canada production (Jacques Bobet) written and directed by Gilles Groulx. Camera, Jean-Claude Labrecque; editing, Margot Payette and Sydney Perason; music, John Coltrane. Reviewed at Place des Arts, Montreal. Running time, 75 MINS.

Barbara .... Barbara Ulrich
Claude .... Claude Godbout
Manon J'sais-pas-qui ..... Manon Blain
Jean-Paul .... Jean-Paul Bernier
Veronique .... Veronique Vilbert
Toulouse .... Andre Leblanc
and Paul-Marie Lapointe, Jean-V. Dufresne, Pierre Maheu.

(In French)

This is the National Film Board of Canada's third feature film following "The Drylanders" and "Nobody Waved Goodbye" and the first by Gilles Groulx. Like so many first films by young directors these days it is described as "a personal statement," which is another way of saying that a story is purely incidental to the dialog and should not be expected.

Claude is a French-speaking Canadian living in Quebec who is worried about 'the cause' but whose grievances are expressed more in his mind than in bomb-throwing or protest marches. It is freedom of the spirit he seeks more than political freedom and after finding that his Jewish girl friend doesn't seem to worry about the situation as much as he does, he goes away in the middle of winter into the snowy countryside, there to conduct a dialog with himself and find immunity from outside influences. There is a reasonably satisfying conclusion.

This is all very tenuous and talkative and not likely to find a large audience to communicate with, even in Quebec. The young players are pleasant and natural enough, the camera work casual in the flexible hand-held manner, and the production relatively inexpensive. If the director succeeds in finding himself as a filmmaker as a result of it and goes on to more decisive things it may well have been worthwhile. *Prat.*

Hamlet
(ELECTRONOVISION)

Photographic record of recent Broadway stage play. Given two-day, reserved seat showing nationally, then withdrawn. A challenging experiment. Effective despite dark lighting.

Warner Bros. release of Wm. Sargeant Jr.-Alfred W. Crown Electronovision production (Alex Cohen, executive producer) of play by William Shakespeare as presented at Lunt-Fontanne Theatre on Broadway. Stars Richard Burton. Staged by John Geilgud. Director for Electronovision, Bill Colleran. Reviewed at Pantages, Hollywood, Sept. 23, 1964. Running time, 199 MINS.

Bernardo .... Robert Burr
Francisco .... Michael Ebert
Marcellus .... Barnard Hughes
Horatio .... Robert Milli
Claudius .... Alfred Drake
Voltimand .... Philip Coolidge
Cornelius .... Hugh Alexander
Laertes .... John Cullum
Polonius .... Hume Cronyn
Hamlet ....Richard Burton
Gertrude .... Eileen Herlie
Ophelia .... Linda Marsh
Ghost .... Voice of John Gielgud
Reynaldo .... Dillon Evans
Rosencrantz .... Clement Fowler
Guildenstern .... William Redfield
Player King .... George Voskovec
Player Prolog .... John Hetherington
Player Queen ...... Christopher Culkin
Lucianus .... Geoff Garland
Fortinbras .... Michael Ebert
Gentleman .... Richard Sterne
First Gravedigger .... George Rose
Second Gravedigger.....Hugh Alexander
Priest .... Barnard Hughes
Oaric .... Dillon Evans
English Ambassador.... Hugh Alexander
Others: Alex Giannini, Frederick Young, Claude Harz, Gerome Ragni, Linda Seff, Carol Teitel.

Filmic translation of Broadway stage production of "Hamlet" in new Electronovision process is impressive despite technical deficiencies of latest screening medium. It carries high drama, fine acting, catching many of forceful attributes of Richard Burton legiter as staged by Sir John Gielgud for Alex Cohen which made play important event and emerges as almost "living theatre" on screen. Innovating release via WB was for two days only, reserved seats.

Greatest cinematic fault is lack of light, sometimes verging on near-total darkness which detracts from full enjoyment but which duplicated stage conditions. Through use of 15 electronic camera setups there is fluidity about unfoldment which allows no static pauses; lens frequently carries spontaneity which even improves on stage production due to close-ups and more angles than allowed theatre spectator. Process itself, however, is detrimental to quality on screen which often is fuzzy and far below present-day standards.

Burton (starred on screen, not on Broadway) surmounts the technical hurdles in a superb performance, exploiting the inherent dramatic intensity and delivering one of finest Shakespearean performances ever viewed on screen. Being a record in photography of the play, sans costumes or settings, this may dull the Middle Ages realism for some. There are unexpected moments of humor which average production of bard's melancholy Dane does not contain, and these—perhaps because of suprise elements—sock over certain impact.

Vying with Burton in importance of performance is Hume Cronyn as Polonius, father of Ophelia and court adviser, who makes each scene count. Eileen Herlie is strongly cast as Queen, Hamlet' mother. Alfred Drake as Claudius, however, appears stiff, overplays sometimes for accepted screen idiom. George Rose is particularly a brief standout as gravedigger, and Robert Milli's Horatio also rates highly. Linda Marsh lacks force as Ophelia.

Film, produced by William Sargent Jr., and Alfred W. Crown from Gielgud legiter, and directed in Electronovision by Bill Colleran offers meritorious technical credits, headed by Bruce Pierce's editing.   *Whit.*

Cheyenne Autumn
(SUPER PANAVISION 70-COLOR)

Episodic, over - liesurely account of a historic Indian migration which misses as topgrade fare. Good grosses indicated, however, on star names and John Ford reputation for westerns.

Cheyenne, Wyo., Oct. 4.
Warner Bros. release of John Ford production, produced by Bernard Smith. Stars Richard Widmark, Carroll Baker, James Stewart, Edward G. Robinson, Karl Malden, Sal Mineo, Dolores Del Rio, Ricardo Montalban, Gilbert Roland, Arthur Kennedy; features Patrick Wayne, Elizabeth Allen, John Carradine, Victor Jory. Directed by Ford. Screenplay, James R. Webb, suggested by "Cheyenne Autumn," by Mari Sandoz; camera (Technicolor), William Clothier; editor, Otho Lovering; sound, Francis E. Stahl; music, Alex North; assistant directors, Wingate Smith, Russ Saunders. Reviewed at Lincoln Theatre, Cheyenne, Wyo., Oct. 3, '64. Running time, 00 MINS.
Capt. Thos. Archer ... Richard Widmark
Deborah Wright .... Carroll Baker
Wyatt Earp .... James Stewart
Sec. of Interior .. Edward G. Robinson
Capt. Wessels .... Karl Malden
Red Shirt .... Sal Mineo
Spanish Woman ..... Dolores Del Rio
Little Wolf .... Ricardo Montalban
Dull Knife .... Gilbert Roland
Doc Holliday .... Arthur Kennedy
2nd Lieut. Scott .... Patrick Wayne
Miss Plantagenet ...... Elizabeth Allen
Jeff Blair .... John Carradine
Tall Tree .... Victor Jory
Senior 1st Sergeant .... Mike Mazurki
Major Braden .... George O'Brien
Dr. O'Carberry ...... Sean McClory
Mayor Dog Kelly .. .. Judson Pratt
Pawnee Woman .... Carmen D'Antonio
Joe .... Ken Curtis

"Cheyenne Autumn" is a rambling, episodic account of a reputedly little-known historic Cheyenne Indian migration, 1,500 miles through almost unbelievable hardships and dangers to the tribe's home near the Yellowstone in Wyoming. Somewhere in the telling, the original premise of the Mari Sandoz' novel is lost sight of in a wholesale 'insertion of extraneous incidents whiich bear no little relation to the subject. As a result, picture lacks forceful qualities. While there is excitement in the various U.S. Cavalry - Indian skirmishes and the overall benefits by exquisite Technicolor photography in picturesque settings the film emerges an uneven piece of filmmaking.

John Ford directed and Bernard Smith produced. Physically, it is filled with excellent production values. These, however, are dissipated in effect by the script (or Ford) never cleaving to a direct line. Detracting considerably are several long comedy sequences which in striking slapstick proportions evoke laughs but project no valid reason for them other than to drag in James Stewart for marquee lure as a clownish— and totally unconvincing—Wyatt Earp. Feature, too, is sorely in need of trimming; its good passages do not compensate for an over-leisurely style of narration. Some of Ford's comic touches which in the past have carried sock entertainment are simply out of place here in what ostensibly is a serious indictment of the Government's shabby treatment of the Indians.

Action follows a small band of Cheyennes attempting to escape from their barren Oklahoma reservation to their own lush Wyoming lands, from which they were transported after having surrendered to the army in 1877. Originally more than 900, their number now has been decimated to 286 through starvation and lack of

medical attention. Wishing no violence, only escape to security, they manage to elude cavalry units sent after them until one segment decides to surrender. Episodic nature of story unfoldment reduces suspense and dramatic impact.

Richard Widmark in one of his hardboiled roles is persuasive as a cavalry captain sympathetic to the Indians, detailed to bring them back to the reservation and finally going to Washington to see the Secretary of the Interior in charge of Indian affairs. Gilbert Roland and Ricardo Montalban portray the historic Dull Knife and Little Wolf, respectively, leaders of the Cheyennes, and carry off their work with honors. Carroll Baker is somewhat lost as a Quaker schoolteacher who accompanied the Cheyennes because of her love for the children.

Stewart in the Earp character is in strictly for laughs, not for plot motivation, and Arthur Kennedy also is in briefly as Dic Holliday, neither having much to do. Karl Malden scores as a German captain of U.S. cavalry; Dolores Del Rio plays an Indian woman with conviction; Edward G. Robinson does well by the Interior Secretary part and Patrick Wayne plays a brash young lieutenant with feeling. Sal Mineo in an Indian role, Elizabeth Allen in role of a madam, John Carradine a gambler and Sean McClory an army doctor all are okay.

Color photography of William Clothier is topflight. Alex North composed the music score, which offers a rather heavy and pretentious overture, and James R. Webb scripted.   *Whit.*

Rio Conchos
(CINEMASCOPE-COLOR)

Slambang western. Lofty grosses indicated in general market.

Hollywood, Oct. 1.
Twentieth-Fox release of David Weisbart production. Stars Stuart Whitman, Richard Boone, Tony Franciosa, Edmond O'Brien; features Jim Brown, Warner Anderson, Wende Wagner. Directed by Gordon Douglas. Screenplay, Joseph Landon, Clair Huffaker, based on novel by Huffaker; camera (DeLuxe Color), Joe MacDonald; music, Jerry Goldsmith; editor, Joseph Silver; assistant director, Joseph R. Rickards; sound, Alfred Bruzlin, Elmer Morton. Reviewed at 20th-Fox Studios, Sept. 29, '64. Running time, 105 MINS.
Lassiter .... Richard Boone
Captain Haven .... Stuart Whitman
Rodriguez .... Tony Franciosa
Sally .... Wende Wagner
Colonel Wagner ...... Warner Anderson
Franklyn .... Jim Brown
Bloodshirt .... Rodolfo Acosta
Croupier .... Barry Kelley
Bandit .... Vito Scotti
Pardee Officer ...... House Peters. Jr.
Blondebeard .... Kevin Hagen
Pardee .... Edmond O'Brien

"Rio Conchos" is a big, tough, action-packed slam-bang western with as tough a set of characters as ever rode the sage. It is Old West adventure at its best, turned out with a punch and destined for lofty grosses in the general market, where femmes as well as males and moppets will find excitement in its Indian backdrop yarn.

Producer David Weisbart has woven the type of fanciful movement along with lush settings via on-the-spot color lensing in Arizona that pay off in hefty audience reaction. To this, Gordon Douglas has added his own version of what a lusty western should be in the

direction, getting the most from a batch of colorful characters. Music score by Jerry Goldsmith is a particularly valuable asset in striking a fast mood from the opening scene. Actors, headed by Stuart Whitman, Richard Boone, Tony Franciosa and Edmond O'Brien, disport themselves with a force seldom achieved in a film of this sort, each a standout and Boone and Franciosa in particular socking over superb performances.

Script by Joseph Landon and Clair Huffaker, adapted from latter's novel, limns the quest of four men for 2,000 stolen repeating rifles that a group of former Confederate soldiers have been running to the Apaches. Quartet is composed of Whitman, a Cavalry captain, who heads the party; Boone, an ex-Reb who hates Apaches; Franciosa, a Mexican gigolo-type killer whom the Army was about to hang; and Jim Brown, a cavalry corporal. Their destination is the camp of a demented Confederate gun-runner, O'Brien, who wants vengeance on the North for the South's defeat.

Plot pattern permits a gun fight with Mexican bulditos and further gunplay in a Border saloon seldom equalled for ferocity and thrills There is the Apache version of running-the-gauntlet, in which Whitman, Boone and Brown are dragged on the ground by horses and the Indians club them as they pass. Climax occurs with a wagonload of gunpowder being set off to destroy the camp.

Whitman acquits himself excellently in his tough role but interest principally lies in characters played by Boone and Franciosa, both killers and a director's dream. Brown, too, handles himself well, and Vito Scotti, as a laughing bandit, registers particularly in his brief menacing role before being killed. Wende Wagner, a newcomer, makes her screen bow as an Apache girl who helps the whitemen, speaking only in native tongue, and Rodolfo Acosta plays a florid Indian chief. O'Brien, as usual, qualifies as an impressive thesp but his role is minor.

Color photography by Joe MacDonald is interesting as he makes effective use of such backgrounds as Monument Valley and other Arizona locations, and Joseph Silver's editing is tight and dramatic. Other technical credits match the superiority of the picture as a whole.   *Whit.*

Echappement Libre
(Free Escape)
(FRENCH-FRANSCOPE)

Paris, Sept. 29.
CCFC release of Sud-Pacifique-Capitole Films - Perojo - Transmonde production. Stars Jean-Paul Belmondo, Jean Seberg; features Gert Froebe, Jean-Pierre Marielle, Renate Ewert, Enrico-Maria Salerno, Fernando Rey. Directed by Jean Becker. Screenplay, Didier Goulart, Maurice Fabre, Daniel Boulanger, Becker from a novel by Clet Coroner; camera, Edmond Sechan; editor, Monique Kirsanoff. At the Mercury, Paris. Running time, 95 MINS.
David .... Jean-Paul Belmondo
Olga .... Jean Seberg
Hode .... Jean-Pierre Marielle
Ferhman .... Gert Froebe
Mario .... Enrico-Maria Salerno
Countess .... Renate Ewert

Jean-Paul Belmondo seems to have developed into a permanent type for situation comedies here even if he has also proved histrionic versatility earlier in his career. His is either a likeable, petty gangster or a daring innocent caught up in far-fetched adventure. Here he combines both to have an uneven chase comedy with more chances at home than in the U.S. There it would mainly be a workable playoff item on his and Jean Seberg's names, with arty theatre chances misty.

A sort of picaresque spoof, without the far out parody of "That Man From Rio," this has smuggler Belmondo running off with a gold-plated car (he is to deliver) and his accomplice Miss Seberg. Chase goes through Lebanon, Greece and Italy to end in Germany where irony gets him off the hook and leaves him the girl.

Director Jean Becker has done an acceptable job, if lacking the snap and edge to give this the dash to ward off repetition and lagging. Belmondo is brash but too often just boorish with not enough help from the pace to help. Miss Seberg is a fetching German lass who brings love and a new leaf to the incorrigibly larcenous orphan Belmondo.

Lensing is somewhat too harsh for this situation comedy actioner. General supporting roles have the right mixture of menace and tongue-in-cheek seriousness. Chalk this up as an intermittently entertaining affair without the weight for untoward Yank chances.

Mosk.

Four Days in November
(DOCUMENTARY)

Assassination of President Kennedy treated as history and tribute of general interest.

Hollywood, Oct. 3.
United Artists release of David L. Wolper production. Producer-director, Mel Stuart. Script, Theodore Strauss; music, Elmer Bernstein; editor, William T. Cartwright; narrator, Richard Basehart. Reviewed at Screen Directors Guild, Oct. 2, 1964. Running time, **120 MINS.**

With "Four Days In November," David L. Wolper has produced a broad account of events of Nov. 22-25, 1963, that is solemn, sometimes majestic tribute to late President Kennedy.

Expertly pieced together from newsreel clips, footage by amateurs, some stock shots, and few scenes re-created for Wolper cameras, the documentary should hold great appeal for public, even though United Artists release tells little that's new.

Most striking plus value is suspense build-up, engendered by dramatic cutting back and forth between seemingly disparate scenes, which foreknowledge of events doesn't lessen. A minus rests in fact part of story could be depressing and painful for some, as when John Jr. salutes father's casket. More could be trimmed from 2-hour film, and occasionally script written by Theodore Strauss for narrator Richard Basehart—who described funeral as "some final act of purification" — gets sticky. Generally, it's restrained and factual.

Certain aspects of case highlighted in recent Warren Report aren't touched, particularly charges of poor coordination and rivalry of FBI and Secret Service. This data, made public long before report, logically could have been included, and spots existed for it in coverage of events leading up to fatal Nov. 22. No hint is given in this film that Dallas police were less than efficient, nor is mention made of Lee Harvey Oswald's trip to Mexico seeking Cuban visa or his earlier attempt to kill General Edward Walker. In view of Warren Report putting stamp of authenticity on these facts, they could be added before film is released.

Otherwise, producer - director Mel Stuart and film editor William T. Cartwright have created dramatic portrayal of recent history. Mood is set at opening as honor guard fires solemn 50-gun salute at state funeral. Then come words of John Kennedy, some hopeful, others prophetic ("this is not an easy job . . .").

Background of JFK's trip to Texas is told while film shuttles from politics to scenes of tranquil nation. Next comes step-by-step account of President's progress through Texas, along with contrasting scenes of Dallas newspaper maps of his route through city and close-up of Dallas Police Chief Curry, mindful of recent assaults on Adlai Stevenson, telling city "nothing must occur that is disrespectful to the President."

Effective device of camera panning through empty rooms of Oswald's boarding house and wife's home creates feeling of coming doom. Kennedy's happy speech in Fort Worth is shown, then pleasant ride past friendly crowds lining Dallas streets. Frequent shots of clocks ticking away toward 12:30 are interspersed with footage of procession.

Then in rapid succession come rifle shots, breakneck rush to hospital, pictures of growing crowds, and death announcement.

Remaining events of the four days are told in same fashion of suspense build-up and climax, including tracking down of Oswald, flight of body to Washington, succession of power to new President, Jack Ruby's slaying of Oswald and finally the fitting, impressive state funeral. Through it all are sensitive shots of public reaction, U.S. and abroad, including a few tearful quotes from man-in-street interviews.

Footage was so well assembled that transitions from pro to amateur camera work, from actual scenes to re-creations, were unnoticeable. Elmer Bernstein's score helped through rough spots.

Hogg.

Ubranie Prawie Nowe
(A Hand-Me-Down Suit)
(POLISH)

Cork, Sept. 29.
A Studio Film Unit Warsawa production. With Hanna Skarzanka, Kazimierz Borowiec, Magda Celowna, Lucyna Winnicka, Marian Rulka. Directed by Wlodzimierz Haupe. Screenplay by W. Haupe, based on a story by Jaroslaw Iwaszkiewicz; camera, Tadeusz Wiezan; music, Krzysztof T. Komeda. At Cork Film Fest. Running time, **95 MINS.**

This Polish film won the dubious honor of rating as the most unsympathetic entry shown at this festival. There is nothing pleasant about this production which looks as though director Haupe had only in mind to exaggerate everything.

The plot is overly morbid, the characters exceptionally ugly, the scenes dirty. In fact, nothing nice develops in this strange vehicle from Poland.

Pic centers on an elderly, ugly housemaid who has been saving money for years to provide herself with a dowry for a successful marriage. The title of the film is closely related to her problem. It is by no means easy for an aging maid to find a young, handsome bachelor. As a rural custom, the maid has to provide a prospective bridegroom with a suit. The maid here finds a husband who's more than twenty years younger than she is, but he soon dies of tuberculosis. Later, her money enables her to get an even younger man. Film plays in pre-war Poland when the country was still not Communistic. Perhaps its message is that then life was gloomy but that the new regime has changed the situation.

What militates against conviction here is definitely the fact that everyone is unlikable. Life isn't entirely like that. In any group there is at least some person who shows something that may be termed friendly. Haupe went overboard with regard to ugliness and unpleasantness and the outcome is a terribly unappetizing picture. That Haupe represents some talent is evidenced by the fact that he caught the atmosphere quite well. As per the nature of the film, dialog is rather dirty. Technically, the film has a good standard.

Hans.

Deutschland Gruesst Kennedy
(Germany Greets Kennedy)
(GERMAN—COLOR)

Cork, Sept. 29.
Deutsche Wochenschau Gmbil production. Directed by Manfred Purzer. Camera (Technicolor), Wilhelm Luppa, Georg Pahl, Kurt Rau; music, Franz Schubert, Robert Schumann, Gerhard Trede, Paul Lincke; commentator, Wolfgang Esterer. At Cork Film Fest. Running time, **58 MINS.**

This German documentary film covering the tour of Germany by the late John F. Kennedy, in June 1963, was generally called the most moving film shown at the Cork festival. JFK was loved and idolized by millions in many countries. And this was particularly so in Ireland where, after all, his forefathers came from. Film received the warmest applause and also fine crix acclaim in Cork. Although it is not an artistic masterpiece, it has many plus points. One concerns the beautiful color. And there seems little doubt but that this is an important historical document.

The documentary, one of West Germany's two major entries at the Cork Fest, shows Kennedy's Germany visit starting with his arrival in Cologne and ending with his departure from Berlin where he had received the biggest and most enthusiastic ovations in his life. Film tries to communicate an image of the winning personality of the American President and to capture, as well, the reaction of the German people to his youthful, yet potent personality. The character of Kennedy emerges in every shot of him in Cologne, Bonn, Frankfurt, Hanau, and, of course, Berlin. Film should deeply move anyone who had an affection for this leader.

The English title on the screen, incidentally, reads ". . . Go To Germany." It came from his words as he was leaving Germany: "I am leaving a note for my successor to read when he is discouraged. On it I have written 'Go To Germany'."

Hans.

Dokuritsu Kikanjutai Imada Shagekichu
(Outpost of Hell)
(JAPAN)

Cork, Sept. 29.
Toho production. With Tatsuya Mihashi, Makoto Sato, Yosuke Natsuki, Makoto Terada, Hiroshi Tachikawa. Directed by Senkichi Taniguchi. Screenplay, Masato Ide; camera, Kazuo Yamada. At Cork Film Fest. Running time, **98 MINS.**

This was more or less the most brutal film shown at the Cork festival. The brutality, however, is justified by the fact that this is an utterly realistic, compromiseless war feature. Its outcome is convincing. It's war as it is, with all its cruelty and senselessness. Film can be given export chances.

Action is set in 1945, when the Japanese front line of defense stretched along the desolate Manchurian border, an area exposed to imminent Soviet attacks. Film is a study of five Japanese soldiers with different backgrounds and attitudes. Their outpost of hell is a pillbox on the front line in which the entire action takes place. Their defense is actually senseless because all the neighboring pillboxes have been wiped out. The attacking Soviets ask them to surrender but they continue fighting until—one by one they are liquidated. And each one's death is intensively gruesome. One of the men, par example, is burned to a crisp by a Russian flame thrower.

Technically, film deserves highest praise. Acting is competent and direction displays cleverness. Film's message isn't quite clear, but it can be termed anti-war. But on the other hand, film cannot escape a certain glorification of heroism. The struggle of the soldiers who share a common central weapon, a heavy machine gun, reaches considerable heights. Nevertheless, this hard-hitting feature pic is of its kind a rather outstanding cinematic effort.

Hans.

Emil and the Detectives
(COLOR)

German childhood classic brought to life by Disney as amusing cops-and-robbers tale.

Hollywood, Oct. 10.

Buena Vista release of Walt Disney production. Stars Walter Slezak, Bryan Russell, Roger Mobley; features Heinz Schubert, Peter Ehrlich, Cindy Cassell. Directed by Peter Tewksbury. Screenplay A. J. Carothers, based on novel by Erich Kastner; camera (Technicolor), Erich Kastner; camera (Technicolor) Gunther Senftleben; editors, Thomas Stanford, Cotton Warburton; music, Heinz Schreiter; assistant director, Brigitte Liphardt. Reviewed at Academy Award Theatre, Oct. 9, '64. Running time, **99 MINS.**

Baron	Walter Slezak
Emil	Bryan Russell
Gustav	Roger Mobley
Grundeis	Heinz Schubert
Muller	Peter Ehrlich
Pony	Cindy Cassell
Nana	Elsa Wagner
Stucke	Wolfgang Volz
Frau Tischbein	Eva-Ingeborg Scholz
Desk Sgt.	Franz Nicklisch
Prof.	Brian Richardson
Dienstag	David Petrychka
Hermann	Robert Swann
Frieda	Ann Noland
Rudolf	Ron Johnson
Hans	Rick Johnson
Traffic Policeman	Paul Glawion
Officer Kiessling	Gerhard Retschy
Proprietor, Newsstand	Viktor Hospach
Waiter	Konrad Thoms
Dispatcher	Egon Vogel
Policeman	Gert Wiedenhofen
Bus driver	Georg Rebentisch
Butler	Rolf Rolphs
Parlor maid	Roswitha Habedank

Walt Disney has come up with an interesting project in this adaptation of the German childhood classic, "Emil and the Detectives," filmed entirely in West Berlin and making handsome use of its backgrounds. Bearing the customary distinguishable Disney mark to give it class and the producer's own brand of entertainment, film is particularly appropriate for specialized situations. Juve appeal is strong and there is also adult attraction—not, however, to the degree, say, of Disney's previous moppet classic, "Mary Poppins." Feature would benefit by some judicious shearing to eliminate certain repetition.

Produced five times before—twice in Germany, once each by British, Japanese and Brazilian producers — a German version, "Emil," was released in this country in 1938, adapted by Billy Wilder. Premise intrigues the imagination—it's tale of a youngster victimized by a pick-pocket and calling on a group of boy detectives to help him catch the thief, universal. Script by A. J. Corothers has caught the spirit of the Erich Kastner book and director Peter Tewksbury has helmed the adventures of the youthful pack in their determined goal with an eye to getting the most out of his subject.

The boy moppet leads—Bryan Russel in title role and Roger Mobley as leader of the detectives—are happy selections, and Disney found a superb pantomimic comedian in Germany for the pick-pocket role, Heinz Schubert, who displays a brand of sly humor all his own. Walter Slezak also is in as the comic Baron, leader of a three-man gang who forces Emil to help them rob a bank, and the antics of the "sleuths" in their trackdown of their quarry and later in capturing the bank robbers as they attempt to escape with their loot will find enthusiastic audience response.

One of the assets of the production is the Technicolor photography of Gunther Senftleben, who makes best use of his cameras in limning the Berlin locations. These add considerably to the effect of the narrative as the man-hunt continues through city streets and bombed-out buildings, and music score by Heinz Schreiter further contributes to the intended mood.

Bryan Russell, who like all the juve cast is American, displays a hardy understanding of his role and turns in a rousing performance, matched by Roger Mobley, who projects an authoritative presence. Brian Richardson is another juve standout and Ron and Rick Johnson are amusing as a pair of twins in the private-eye force.

Slezak is up to his sly comedy top as the grandiose robber-leader, but in the adult ranks it's Schubert who scores as the pick-pocket, his pantomime an achievement and joy. Peter Ehrlich also is good as the third hood, and Cindy Cassell as Emil's pestering cousin handles herself convincingly.

Art direction by Werner and Isabell Schlichting and editing by Thomas Stanford and Cotton Warburton, likewise add to film's general excellence. *Whit.*

Neprimirimite
(The Intransigents)
(BULGARIA)

Cork, Sept. 29.

A Bulgarian Cinematography (Sofia) production. With D. Zhegarats, S. Gestov, Y. Mastev, G. Vachkov, B. Banov. Directed by Yanko Yankov. Screenplay, Yankov; camera, T. Zakhariev; music, Al Raichev. At Cork Film Fest. Running time, **85 MINS.**

Both technically and artistically, Bulgarian pix have made obvious improvements in recent years. And this one gives evidence of the upward trend. Yanko Yankov, one of Bulgaria's more prominent directors, did much to create this one. If western releasing chances are slim, it's because the plot which makes it primarily an item for East Bloc countries. Also, the pic is too slow for western standards.

Action leads the viewer to Yugoslavia during the final phase of the last World War. A Bulgarian subdetachment of troops with lorries gets an urgent order to transport ammunition to an important strategical point. Film attempts to show the moral fibre of the men involved in this action. The dialog is mainly of a political nature, with it's Commie message blandly revealed.

Technically, the film reaches a satisfactory standard. The atmosphere is generally well captured. The acting is passable. But the average western patron cannot find much interest in what the conversation is about. Suspense is fair even if there are many dull moments along the line. Film should have been given more pace. They still have more leisure in the East. *Hans.*

Where Love Has Gone
(TECHNISCOPE—COLOR)

Girl-stabs-mom's-lover situation. Strong woman's film. Big grosses foreseen.

Hollywood, Oct. 11.

Paramount release of Joseph E. Levine production. Stars Susan Hayward, Bette Davis. Features Michael Connors, Joey Heatherton. Directed by Edward Dmytryk. Screenplay, John Michael Hayes, based on novel by Harold Robbins; camera (Technicolor), Joseph MacDonald; editor, Frank Bracht; music, Walter Scharf; assistant director, D. Michael Moore. Reviewed at Paramount Studios, Oct. 5, '64. Running time, **111 MINS.**

Valerie Hayden Miller	Susan Hayward
Mrs. Gerald Hayden	Bette Davis
Luke Miller	Michael Connors
Danielle Valerie Miller	Joey Heatherton
Marian Spicer	Jane Greer
Sam Corwin	DeForest Kelley
Gordon Harris	George Macready
Dr. Sally Jennings	Anne Seymour
Judge Murphy	Willis Bouchey
George Babson	Walter Reed
Mrs. Geraghty	Ann Doran
Mr. Coleman	Bartlett Robinson
Professor Bell	Whit Bissell
Rafael	Anthony Caruso

Sooner or later it was bound to happen—a film based on the celebrated onetime Hollywood scandal of the daughter of a film star stabbing to death her mother's paramour. Joseph E. Levine's latest contribution to screen art obviously take its cue in close detail from this incident which hit every headline in the nation and patently was inspiration for the Harold Robbins novel. Scene is changed from Hollywood to San Francisco, and the mother now is a society woman with a bent for sculpture.

"Where Love Has Gone" is a woman's problem picture, almost a soap-opera, carrying strong male as well as femme appeal and unquestionably slated for hefty reception at b.o. It excels in every department; well-produced and enacted, the subject is handled tastefully yet along near-sensational lines. Plot premise lends itself admirably to a hard-selling campaign; indeed, crackling dialog direct from picture is being used as catchlines in advertising—viz., *"you couldn't stand your daughter stealing your lover"* and *"I use sex like you use liquor"*—and exhibits will find plenty of meat for their promotion.

Sufficient ingenuity and shock value in character delineation have been interwoven into the John Michael Hayes screenplay to maintain high-tempoed interest as the yarn revolves around a bitter divorced couple come together again briefly to save their daughter after the 15-year-old girl kills her mother's lover. Flashback technique is utilized in expository footage to limn couple's romance and ultimate divorce after the husband has taken to drink and wife brings countless men into the home as both live under the ruthless domination of femme's aggressive mother. Production has been handsomely mounted, the rich tones of Technicolor and luxurious settings providing a particularly interesting pictorial backdrop.

Edward Dmytryk in his careful direction points up dramatic moments effectively as the daughter is taken into juvenile custody, later in an explosive climax at final custody hearing after girl has been cleared of a murder charge. Certain suspense is inserted in an attempt to blackmail the family for hot love letters written to the murdered man by both the mother and daughter. Film ends on a hopeful note after the mother commits suicide and the daughter is to live with her father after rehabilitation.

Susan Hayward and Bette Davis share top honors in impressive performances, former as the daughter whose life is a story of indiscretions. Miss Davis, smart in a white wig, plays the autocratic mother, who always sees that the family name is protected at any price, a scheming woman of unscrupulous methods and seemingless inexhaustible means. Picture is a brilliant showcase for both actresses and projects them in roles which will find much comment.

Michael Connors is deft and able as the husband, who now is a successful architect on his own after having previously been forced into his mother-in-law's employ. As the mixed-up teenager who never knew domestic happiness, Joey Heatherton is ideally cast and delivers a compelling portrayal. Jane Greer is both beautiful and excellent as a juvenile probation officer, DeForest Kelley impresses as an unscrupulous art critic who promotes Miss Hayward's sculpting career and Anne Seymour has a few good moments as a psychologist.

Technical credits are all highly-placed, including Joseph MacDonald's fluid camera work, art direction by Hal Pereira and Walter Tyler, Frank Bracht's fast editing and Walter Scharf's moving music score. Jack Jones sings title song by Sammy Cahn and James Van Heusen over credits. *Whit.*

Doeden Kommer Til Middag
(Death Comes At High Noon)
(DANISH)

Luebeck, Oct. 6.

Nordisk Films Kompagni (Copenhagen) production. Stars Poul Reichhardt and Helle Virkner. Directed by Erik Balling. Screenplay, Erik Balling; camera, Joergen Skov; music, Bent Fabricius-Bjerre. At Luebeck Film Fest. Running time, **100 MINS.**

Peter Sander	Poul Reichhardt
Eva Lindberg	Helle Virkner
Merete Lindberg	Brigitte Federspiel
John	Jan Priiskirn Schmidt
Bertil Lindberg	Morten Grunwald
Miss Joergensen	Kirsten Soeberg

Erik Balling, head of production of Copenhagen's Nordisk Films, has made a name for himself as a director. "Death," a crime pic with comedy ingredients, falls considerably short of two previous films. There's nothing about this which could give it special chances abroad.

Central figure is Peter Sander, author of many successful crime novels, who discovers a dead body in a deserted house. It's an elderly man who's been shot. Sanders sets out to solve the murder case. He has quarrels with the police who don't like the idea of an amateur interferring in such a matter. Lineup of characters includes some women and a moppet who is of particular value to Sander. There are several "logical suspects" until the case is cleared. The ending isn't too much of a surprise.

Some plus points about this average production are attractive Helle Virkner who supplies the romantic interest and a number of rather impressively photographed sequences. Otherwise it's a somewhat tedious film with quite a bit of routine acting which even includes the central figure (Sander). Plot has its weaknesses, too.

Hans.

Epilogue
'(DANISH)

Luebeck, Oct. 6.
Preben Philipsen release of Bent Christensen production. Stars Erno Mueller, Maud Berthelsen. Directed by Henning Carlsen. Screenplay, Leif Panduro; camera, Henning Kristiansen; music, Krzysztof Komeda. At Luebeck Film Fest. Running time, 93 MINS.
Martin .... Erno Mueller
Lis .... Maud Berthelsen
Gorm .... Buster Larsen
Officer .... Preben Neergaard
Fabian .... Joern Jeppesen
Photographer .... Paul Hagen
Ivan .... Morten Grunwald

"Epilogue" is neither fish nor fowl. It is an ambitious film, too pretentious. It is too confusing for the average patron. On the other hand, the more demanding viewer will find too many faults with it. This may qualify for some late-night tele utilization, but that's about all.

Henning Carlsen, 37-year-old Dane, who walked off with a top prize for his first feature film, "Dilemma," at the 1962 Mannheim festival, has directed "Epilogue" with too much devotion to what has become known as "nouvelle vague." But it's only a fair imitation.

Film is best photographically. In particular, this goes for the street sequences which benefit from fine documentary sharpness. It would seem that Carlsen's forte is the documentary field.

Plot concerns Erno Mueller, a former resistance fighter, who returns to his native Denmark after an absence of 17 years. He meets a girl about half his age and an intensively erotic affair ensues. However, soon both realize that there are too many differences between them. There's the man's constant trauma: He thinks back (repeatedly brief flashbacks) of the time when the Germans had occupied Denmark and the experiences he then had.

Acting often is not convincing. Erno Mueller's bitter looks border on the unpleasant. And it's somehow hard to believe how a young girl could fall for a man who is so utterly unromantic and unsympathic. What also militates against conviction is the twosome's philosophical chatter. The director's incompetent hand in handling the players often becomes evident. The score is interesting, having been done by Polish composer Krzysztof Komeda who wrote the music for several Polish hit pix.

Hans.

Ossa Krivi I Nichta
(All the Night Hides)
(GREEK)

Cork, Sept. 29.
Vaghelis Batarlas production. With Efi Economou, Petrous Fissoun. Andreas Douzos, Martha Vourtsi. Directed by Stelios Zografakis. Screenplay, Nicos Foscolos; camera, Vaghelis Caramanidis; music, Chr. Mourahas. At Cork Film Fest. Running time, 103 MINS.

The Greeks already have had so many interesting if not excellent films at festivals. But this one is a real disappointment. There is hardly anything noteworthy about this pic except the fact that it could not show everything at the Cork festival. For at request of the festival committee 350 feet of film had been cut. This happened to a substantial striptease sequence. The "art" of striptease is illegal in Eire.

Film concerns two young men of very different backgrounds and upbringing. One is the son of wealthy parents and the other one comes from poor surroundings. What both have in common is their predilection for a dangerous life which leads them into the hazards of the underworld. And they eventually become murderers. Along the line there is considerable sex tossed in.

Pic is overly melodramatic, with plot and situations oldhat. Moreover, there is unconvincing acting which eventually becomes involuntarily funny. A film like this seems out of place at a festival.

Hans.

The Young Lovers

Sensational story of young love and pregnancy, emphasizing problems of unwed father, may do well at b.o. despite script and acting deficiencies.

Hollywood, Oct. 9.
Metro release of Samuel Goldwyn Jr., production; no star credits. Directed by Goldwyn Jr. Script, George Garrett, from Julian Halevy novel; camera, Joe Biroc, Ellsworth Fredericks; editor, William A. Lyon; music, Sol Kaplan. Reviewed at Academy Awards Theatre, Hollywood, Oct. 7, '64. Running time 110 MINS.
Eddie Slocum .... Peter Fonda
Pam Burns .... Sharon Hugueny
Tarragoo .... Nick Adams
Debbie .... Deborah Walley
Mrs. Burns .... Beatrice Straight
Prof. Schwartz.......... Malachi Throne
Dr. Shoemaker........... Kent Smith
Prof. Reese .... Joseph Campanella
Karen .... Jennifer Billingsley
Mary Reese....... .... Nancy Rennick

Samuel Goldwyn Jr.'s "The Young Lovers" has a lot of things going for it that should translate into happy accounting for exhibs and Metro, even though it's an uneven production with awkward spots and slow build-up. While the story about young, unwed parents-to-be is no longer the shocker it would have been a generation ago, the talk is frank and switch on familiar theme to problems mainly those of unwed father, rather than of mother, will stir more than usual interest and controversy.

Most awkward parts come during opening scenes, as love affair between college students Peter Fonda and Sharon Hugueny is slowly built up. Lack of early conflict between characters causes story to drag and some of dialog between young lovers is too precious. But once the dramatic situation is set up, with the girl pregnant and wanting to marry, and the boy refusing, takes off at good pace.

Young Fonda has uncomfortable moments as an art student who intends to live free, bachelor life, and his voice doesn't carry conviction in several scenes. How much of this is attributable to direction, (film is producer Goldwyn's first as a director as well) rather than lack of acting experience by young Fonda, is difficult to assess. But his overall portrayal fits the character, and he delivers key bits of dialog well, as when he tells buddy, "Everything was just great until this (the pregnancy) happened." This, incidentally, sums up the dramatic conflict.

Lovely and appealing Miss Hugueny also suffers acting lapses, but scores by making apparent her three-step transition from shy teenager, to passionate lover, and on to wiser, more mature young adult. The director can share credit here.

With the focus on Fonda's role, the girl's search for an abortion is treated as a side issue in which he takes no part. Some viewers may feel the consequences of an abortion are not stressed enough. It is treated as a moral evil—and the girl finally rejects it on this point—but no mention is made of the fact that illegal surgery often is fatal, which could leave some young people with the feeling that if they have no moral objections, the only problem is finding enough money and right surgeon.

Lesser members of cast handle their roles in off-and-on fashion. Nick Adams is competent as Fonda's fast-talking college buddy, but looks ten years too old for the part. Deborah Walley as Adams' girl-friend is stereotyped as wise-cracking blonde. Mother of Miss Hugueny, Beatrice Straight, is a victim of ambiguities in the script which did not make clear until near the end whether or not she sympathized with her daughter. Malachi Throne is excellent as tough prof.

Responsibility for story-line and character lapses must be shared by producer-director Goldwyn and script George Garrett. But they deserve praise for film's credit side, which should count financially.

Photography, with credits shared by Joe Biroc and Ellsworth Fredericks, is uniformly excellent. Score by Sol Kaplan was unobtrusive and sets by Frank Wade catches college atmosphere accurately. Editor William A. Lyon must share some of criticism, along with Goldwyn, for unexplained time lapses and occasional choppy feeling. *Hogg.*

Italiani Brava Gente
(Italians Good People)
(ITALO-RUSSIAN)

Unheroic Italian soldiers, very heroic Soviets. Second thoughts about Mussolini. Needs editing for U.S.

Rome, Oct. 7.
Titanus release of Galatea- Coronet (Rome)-Mosfilm (Moscow) coproduction. Features entire cast. Directed by Giuseppe DeSantis. Screenplay, DeSantis, Ennio de Concini, Serghei Smirnov, Augusto Frassinetti, Giandomentico Giagni; from story by DeConcini and DeSantis. Camera, Antonio Secchi. Sets, Ermanno Manco. Editor, Mario Serandrei. Music, Armando Trovajoli. At Corso Cinema, Rome. Running time, 150 MINS.
Ferri .... Arthur Kennedy
Katia .... Gianna Prokhorenko
Gabrielli .... Raffaele Pisu
Sonja .... Tatiana Samoilova
Sermonti .... Andrea Checchi
Sanna .... Riccardo Cucciolla
Giuliani .... Valeri Somov
Medic Captain .... Peter Falk

An elaborately staged World War II pic showing adventures of an Italo regiment on the Soviet front, this is also one of first Soviet-Italian coproductions. It stands to fare quite well in Italy, but foreign chances are more spotty, unless a drastic shearing job is undertaken. For US, it has relative marquee names in Peter Falk and Arthur Kennedy.

Pic is one of those fresco items replete with characters chosen from all walks of life and places of birth, all thrown together into a war which few of them want. Basic attempt, to show Italian troops' unhappiness in fighting Mussolini's war, has been done before—and better—though not on Russo front, where more gruesome situations pertained. With few exceptions, acting roles are cameos; there's the fascist die-hard who fakes an injury when the chips are down; there's the cocky know-it-all who dies an ironic hero's death; there's the average G.I. who's doomed without knowing what it's really all about; above all, there are the stalwart Russians—whether partisans or soldiers—all of them idealized in sharp contrast to the more varied and not always heroic Italian types.

Too much has been thrown into the pot by director-scripter Giuseppe DeSantis and his collaborators. Isolated episodes stand out, others fail to convince through over-forcing. At all times when epic-sweeping scenes are on screen, DeSantis is in command: he is a master of the long-range boom shot, first displayed in his "Bitter Rice." But where the more intimate dynamics are to the fore, he often strives overly for the corny effect. Nor is he often served by good dialog, much of which is also in bad taste. And while in certain sequences which render the "war-is-hell" theme to good effect he is objective in his rationalization of what presumably went on during Italy's unhappy Russian campaign (see for example the rabbit "hunt" staged between opposing lines; or the episode in which Peter Falk, as a medic, crosses the lines to save a Soviet life but gets back too late to prevent shooting of a Russian hostage held pending his safe return), at others DeSantis and scripter-coproducer Ennio DeConcini show their cards too openly in composing rationalized hymns to (eventual) Russian-Italian friendships and in idealizing all the Soviet characters, even photographically. Except for some typical Italian touches, in fact, pic has distinct Russian film flavor about it, in way it was shot, in content, and in acting.

Midst dozens of characters, those limned by Arthur Kennedy and Peter Falk stand out, as do some of the Italians (Riccardo Cucciola as an ever-observing, rarely-speaking G.I., Andrea Checchi as a one-time Fascist colonel who "wises up"), and a few Soviet players (a very pretty Gianna Prokhorienko in a partisan role). Kennedy, wildly but effectively made up, registers despite a rhetorical part as the bald-pated do-not-die-officer with the phony arm injury, while Falk is excellent in his brief but winning role as the Italo medic sent behind Soviet lines.

And though he frames almost every shot in strategically placed sunflowers, cameraman Antonio

Secchi has done a topnotch job in lensing on Russian locations: there is no doubt about their authenticity. Where the pic rings false—or at least biased in its Monday a.m. quarterbacking—is in the juxtaposition of the humanly unheroic Italian G.I. with their at all times upwards-and-onwards Soviet counterparts who come off best, and not by little; they even have the best, heroically lit, camera angles. Pic might better have been titled "Soviets, Good People." *Hawk.*

Yksityisalue
(Private Territory)
(FINLAND)

Luebeck, Oct. 6.
Kurkvaara Filmi Oy (Helsinki) production. With Kalervo Nissilae, Kyllikki Forssell, Jarno Hiiloskorpi. Directed and written by Maunu Kurkvaara. Camera, Kurkvaara; music, Usko Merilaeinen. At Luebeck Film Fest. Running time, **82 MINS.**
Koski .... Kalervo Nissilae
His wife .... Kyllikki Forssell
Pena .... Jarno Hiiloskorpi
Secretary .... Sinikka Hannula
A friend .... Per-Olof Siren
Young Girl .... Sointu Angervo
Dr. Carlstedt .... Kaarlo Halttunen

In the Scandinavian filmmaking field, the Finns stand well in the shadow of what the Swedish and Danish producers are doing. The Finns have no Bergman and comparatively little money which may explain the film situation for that country. Yet every now and then, Finland comes along with a production that could stack up with the best product of the Scandinavian nations. This applies to "Private Territory." It's definitely an above-average Finnish production. Film has adequate acting and technically is well made. Foreign chances, of course, seem very limited.

Plot revolves around a prominent architect who has been found dead in his home. A young man, who just cannot believe that such a successful man would want to take his own life, tries to find out the reason for his so-called suicide. And he finds out there's a woman involved. But after a while he stops searching for the truth. He feels that every human being has the right to live his own life. "Private Territory" shouldn't be touched.

What militates against pic's foreign chances is the overly deliberate direction. Film moves along very slowly which results in many dull moments. But in its treatment of the subject matter, one senses the ambitions of the allround man Kurkvaara, who produced, directed, scripted and even lensed it. *Hans.*

Pigen og Pressefotografen
(Girl and Press Photographer)
(DANISH-COLOR)

Luebeck, Oct. 6.
Merry Film (Copenhagen) production. Stars Dirch Passer and Ghita Noerby. Directed by Swen Methling. Camera (Eastmancolor), Henning Christiansen; music, Ib Glindemann. At Luebeck Film Fest. Running time, **100 MINS.**
Bastian, a photographer... Dirch Passer
Lene, reporter .... Ghita Noerby
Soren, publisher .... Poul Hagen
Jarl Kulle .... Jarl Kulle (himself)

Danish filmites have previously shown that they can turn out a funny pic. This one is a wild

slapstick burlesque. It's nothing much for the crix, but it's likely that such crazy film may find a wide audience. Commercial chances look good even outside the homegrounds.

As the title indicates, this production figures in the newspaper field. Dirch Passer, a photographer on a large Danish daily, is constantly seeking real news scoops, and is quite successful even if it means disguising as a fireworker to get close to a top personality. Also, the comedy touches off a local problem—the housing shortage in the Danish capital. Married couples get priority on apartments in newly-built houses. Passer and his colleague, a cute femme reporter, exploit the opportunity in their own way. This is good for many funny situations.

These two players theft this film. Passer proves once more that he is a highly talented comedian while Ghita Noerby is the cute girl reporter. Director Sven Methling has made this in the wildest sort of way. But not without imagination. The sex, both with regard to dialog and situations, occasionally is carried quite far. But that's Denmark where they are very "progressive" in this particular field. Technically, this Eastmancolored comedy is okay. Sight gags add to the fun. *Hans.*

Il Goucho
(The Gaucho)
(ITALO-ARGENTINE)
(Songs)

Rome, Oct. 13.
Titanus release of a Mario Cecchi Gori (Fairfilm)—Clemente Lococo (Buenos Aires) coproduction. Stars Vittorio Gassmann; features Nino Manfredi, Silvana Pampanini, Amedeo Nazzari, Maria Grazia Buccella, Annie Gorassini, Nelli Panizza, Guido Gorgari, Sanchez Calleia, Nort Carpena, Aldo Vianello. Directed by Dino Risi. Screenplay, Ettore Scola, Tullio Pinelli, Ruggero Maccari, from story by Scola and Maccari; camera, Alfio Contini; music, Armando Trovajoli. At Adriano, Rome. Running time, **115 MINS.**
Marco Ravicchio ..... Vittorio Gassmann
Marucchelli .... Amedeo Nazzari
Luciana .... Silvana Pampanini
Stefano .... Nino Manfredi

The successful Vittorio Gassmann-Dino Risi actor-director team, which hit big money with "The Easy Life" (Il Sorpasso) has another winner in this one. It's lighter fare and not nearly as polished as the other, but it will do very well as a followup. The Gassman name is a big assist in those areas where "Sorpasso" scored, and the word that this is entertainment in the lightweight manner should get around. For the States, it has specialized chances.

Gassmann is now firmly set in his niche as the master of (charming) bluff and bluster. Here he leads a group of film stars to a South American Film Festival in Buenos Aires, returning after 10 days of animated experiences with the fest milieu and fringe characters. Principally, the group is hosted by a nostalgic Italian expatriate who has made his fortune in Gaucho-land, and who pours on the hospitality bit and empties his pocketbook to make the people from his homeland feel at home. He's made it, but another expatriate, a boyhood pal of Gassmann's, hasn't. Two characters are aptly contrasted, latter adding a poignant note as the failure who hates to admit it, and they are neatly portrayed by Amedeo Nazzari, excellent as the one who struck it rich, and Nino Manfredi as the Buster Keaton-faced failure.

Script is a bit too errant for proper continuity, but chances are audience won't worry unduly about jumps and discrepancies as long as leads are on screen—which is most of time. The South American scene is glimpsed with interest (all of the pic was lensed on location). And there are some solid contributions by such Italo players as Silvana Pampanini, in a parody of the glamor queen; Annie Gorassini and Maria Grazia Bucella, both as triumphs of body over brain, and also some thesps found on spot.

Risi and cameraman Alfio Contini have chosen some colorful location spots, scripters Scola, Maccari, and Pinelli have inserted some very funny dialog. But how much of this will register with foreign audiences (no matter how good the titles or dubbing) remains to be seen. Technical credits are tops. Armando Trovajoli has put together an aptly South-of-border score, to which Neil Sedaka chirps a couple of listenable tunes in the Latino idiom. *Hawk.*

Invitation to a Gunfighter

Offbeat but confusing western that must rely on Yul Brynner's drawing power at b.o. for any success. Too many crooks spoiled the plot.

Hollywood, Oct. 15.
United Artists release of Kramer Co. production. Stars Yul Brynner; features Janice Rule, Brad Dexter, Alfred Ryder, Milo Kellin, George Segal, Clifford David, Pat Hingle. Directed by Richard Wilson. Screenplay, Richard and Elizabeth Wilson, adapted by Alvin Sapinsley, based on story by Hal Goodman, Larry Klein; camera, Joe McDonald; music, David Raksin; editor, Bob Jones. Reviewed at Academy Award Theatre, Oct. 14, '64. Running time, **91 MINS.**
Jules Gaspard D'Estaing ... Yul Brynner
Ruth Adams .... Janice Rule
Kenarsie .... Brad Dexter
Doc Barker .... Alfred Ryder
Tom .... Mike Kellin
Matt Weaver .... George Segal
Crane Adams .... Clifford David
Sam Brewster .... Pat Hingle
Sheriff .... Bert Freed
McKeever .... Curt Conway
Tuttle .... Clifton James
Hickman .... Clarke Gordon
Schoop .... Arthur Peterson
Fiddler .... Strother Martin

"Invitation To A Gunfighter" has off-beat characters and plot but its box-office potential rests with die-hard Western fans and the marquee value of Yul Brynner's name. Much of the character development is illogical and the story has confusing aspects, adding up to a generally unsatisfactory film that will fail to benefit from word-of-mouth reports. Bottom of double bills may be the fate of this United Artists release, produced by the Kramer Company.

The story opens on a relatively routine situation, with George Segal as a mustered-out Confederate soldier returning to Pecos, New Mexico Territory, to find the town's boss has swindled him out of the family homestead. After an attempt to get the boss (Pat Hingle) fails, he kills a man and barricades himself in the house. To flush him out, the townspeople hire a dandyish but deadly gunfighter Jules Gaspard D'Estaing, played by Brynner.

Brynner handles the role as competently as the script permits. Initially, he's presented as a strong, silent Creole who is a deadly shot and a perfect poker player who also can play spinet and quote poetry—a real Paladin—with an arrogant but suave manner toward Janice Rule, wife of weakling Clifford David and one-time lover of Segal.

Perhaps too many cooks spoiled the script (screenplay by Elizabeth and Richard Wilson, adapted by Alvin Sapinsley, based on story by Hal Goodman and Larry Klein) because in mid-picture the gunman's character makes an abrupt, unforeshadowed change. Actually, he's part-Negro, son of a slave mother and Creole father. He has a grudge against the hypocritical, prosperous town leaders, and is out to harm them rather than kill Segal.

This interesting and unusual theme is marred, however, by the aforementioned character illogic and scenes such as one in which Brynner gets drunk and lurches down Main Street, smashing windows and stock of businesses while the local citizens follow in helpless dismay. This leads to Boss Hingle making peace with Segal and asking him to rid town of Brynner. Windup has gunfighter and boss dead, Segal with the girl.

Had the story focussed either on Brynner or on Segal alone it might have come through. As it was, it wasted an excellent performance by Segal (although he occasionally was over-intense) and by Hingle as pompous but ruthless stuffed-shirt. Brynner and Miss Rule were competent, even though the girl's chief function was as a foil for the men. Lesser roles were well-played by David Alfred Ryder, Brad Dexter, Curt Conway and Robert Freed once again as a sheriff.

Richard Wilson as director and co-scripter must accept much of the blame for failures. Color photography by Joe McDonald generally was excellent. Music by David Raksin was undistinguished and often obtrusive. The action was confined to Universal backlot (utilizing the Western town and the "Psycho" mansion for Hingle's home) but art director Robert Clatworthy made most of limited scope. Editing by Bob Jones may be responsible for omission of several characters' names and identification, but otherwise seemed adequate.

Hogg.

The Black Torment
(BRITISH-COLOR)

Period hokey-pokey, lushly mounted and suspense-holding, despite routine red herrings and farfetched yarn; good booking for double-bill houses.

London, Oct. 20.

Compton-Tekli release of a Michael Klinger and Robert Hartford-Davis) Tony Tenser production. Stars John Turner, Heather Sears; features Ann Lynn, Raymond Huntley, Joseph Tomelty, Peter Arne, Annette Whitely, Patrick Troughton, Norman Bird, Francis De Wolff. Directed by Robert Hartford-Davis. Screenplay, Donald and Derek Ford; camera (Eastmancolor), Peter Newbrook; editor, Alastair McIntyre; music, Robert Richards. Reviewed at Rialto, London. Running time, **85 MINS.**

Sir Richard Fordyce	John Turner
Lady Elizabeth	Heather Sears
Diane	Ann Lynn
Seymour	Peter Arne
Colonel Wentworth	Raymond Huntley
Mary	Annette Whiteley
Harris	Norman Bird
Apprentice	Roger Croucher
Sir Giles	Joseph Tomelty
Ostler	Patrick Troughton
Black John	Francis de Wolff
Jenkins	Charles Houston
Lucy Judd	Edina Ronay
Kate	Cathy McDonald

Set a British film in the 18th Century and stage it in some country mansion, and it's a fair bet that the characters will be involved in some pretty eerie hocus-pocus. "Black Torment" is such a period chiller, with a somewhat nonsensical story dominated by routine thrills. It is lushly lensed by Peter Newbrook in Eastmancolor, handsomely mounted and played with sufficient intensity to hold suspense. A trick ending is glibly explained away but until then customers will have had their fill of mild kicks. A useful dualler.

Donald and Derek Ford have concocted a story liberally laced with fear, rape, insanity, murderous intent and [illegible] of suspicious characters, any one of whom is liable to be up to no good.

Sir Richard Fordyce (John Turner) returns from honeymoon with his second wife (Heather Sears), the first having, four years previously, heaved herself to her death from a top window at Fordyce Manor. In the guvnor's absence, murky happenings have taken place. A girl has been raped, with his name on her lips, and the local yokels are full of suspicion of their lord and master. They swear they've seen him being chased on horseback by a white-gowned woman who shrieks "murderer" in the voice of the dead wife.

After the lord of the manor has gone nearly round the bend with anxiety, his paralyzed father has been found hanged and his new wife shoots him to ward off his murderous attempts, the situation is ironed out. But not until after much window banging, apparitions in the night and considerable leering by everybody at everybody else. Seems that the heavies are the dead woman's sister and the trusted steward, who was her cousin. They have been using the man's maniacal twin brother, who, understandably, is the skeleton in the family closet and has been kept in the background.

Robert Hartford-Davis, producer and director of the film, has given it the full treatment in the way of production values. And, despite some unintentional laughs, he has managed to keep the cast within the bounds that will retain audience speculation as to who's done what to whom, why and when.

Turner is the stalwart, perplexed victim of these murky proceedings. Miss Sears, despite a somewhat plummy vocal delivery, starts what is hoped will be a comeback following her early success in "Room At Top." But she will need stronger material than this film provides. Ann Lynn, as the conniving sister, gets little chance to sustain many recent fine impressions. There are dependable supporting stints by Joseph Tomelty, Annette Whiting, Francis de Wolff, Patrick Arne and Charles Houston. Edina Judd and Cathy McDonald have minor roles as murderous victims. It is Miss Judd who has the unfortunate task of setting the keynote of the film before the credits. She is chased panting through a wood but it is not her fault that her hysterical breathing rings through the theatre with the strength of Gale Force 9. Editing and music both okay.

Rich.

Le Voci Bianche
(I Castrati)
(ITALO-FRENCH—COLOR)

Rome, Oct. 13.

Cineriz release of a Franca Films-Federiz-Francoriz coproduction by Luciano Perugia and Nello Meniconi. Features Paolo Ferrari, Anouk Aimes, Vittorio Caprioli, Claudio Gora, Graziella Granata, Philippe Leroy, Jacqueline Sassard, Barbara Steele, Jean Tissier, Leopoldo Trieste, Jeanne Valerie, Sandra Milo, and with Alfredo Bianchini, Francesco Mule, Luigi Basagaluppi, Jacques Herlin, Gulio Battiferri, Guglielmo Spoletini, Anita Durante, Filippo Spoletini. Directed by Festa Campanile, Massimo Franciosa. Screenplay, Franciosa, Campanile, Luigi Magni; camert (Technicolor-Techniscope), Ennio Guarneri; music, Gino Marinuzzi Jr.; editor, Ruggero Mastroianni. At the Fiamma, Rome. Running time, **100 MINS.**

Meo	Paolo Ferrari
Carolina	Sandra Milo
Teresa	Graziella Granata
Lorenza	Abouk Aimee
Matteuccio	Vittorio Caprioli
Maria	Jeanne Valerie
Ascanio	Philippe Leroy
Guilia	Barbara Steele
Orcpreenobbi	Leopoldo Trieste
Eugenia	Jacqueline Sassard
Marchionne	Claudio Gora
Savello	Jean Tissier

Comedy-satire much in the manner of an Italian "Tom Jones," this has foreign possibilities on content and handling plus several exploitable pegs.

"White Voices" in the title are those of "castrates" which per historical fact were in 17th Century Rome to provide choir voices as well as the female thesping forbidden at the time for women. Often, poverty forced families to sell their sons into this profession. Pic deals with ne'er-do-well Roman, Meo, who first tries to sell his brother, who escapes. When he himself is trapped into being recruited, he pays off a surgeon not to perform the operation, and feigns the growing effeminecy it would have produced.

Though disgusted and frustrated, he plays along in fear of punishment, soon discovering that his "position" gives him a "safe" status with women at various courts and palaces he visits, femmes whom he resolutely proceeds to seduce, unsuspected by their husbands who feel him inoffensive. In this finale, however, he's caught, and rather than face beheading, he voluntarily agrees to the operation on theory that "it's better to lose one's virility than one's head."

This explosive subject is treated with tongue-in-cheek humor but is never openly tasteless or disgusting, as it easily might have been. Travesty aspects are all there, and very graphically rendered, too, in various exchanges between the "hero" and his colleagues, but they are rendered matter-of-factly as they presumably were in period covered. In fact, the plight of the group is exemplified in character well played by Vittorio Diprioli who eventually commits suicide when he realizes he is physically unable to consummate his love for a girl (Jeanne Valerie). And there is plenty of lusty good humor in hero's many affairs with a bunch of busty beauties, played by Graxiella Granata, Barbara Steele, Jacqueline Sassard, Anouk Aimee, and Sandra Milo, all of them striking looking femmes.

Script meanders a bit and a faster pace could have helped. Dialog, in tight Roman accent, is very good, though this facet may not register with foreign ears. An outstanding contribution to the pic is color lensing by Ennio Guarnieri (in Technicolor-Techniscope), among best efforts of the year in this sector, both for its interiors and the location shots which bring out the beauty of spectacular settings around Rome and Naples. Playing is suitable on all sides. Paolo Ferrari is fine as Meo. Vittorio Caprioli has a gem of a performance as a friend while Philippe Leroy solidly plays his aristocrat. Leopoldo Trieste again registers in a colorful bit. The women have little to do except look beautiful, and this they do.

In short, "Bianche" proves that even the most prohibitive subject matter (in fact, a principal problem has been to find a suitable title) can be made acceptable and even entertaining if handled with taste.

Hawk.

Ready For the People

Tv pilot which didn't sell reconverted to theatrical release; for lesser program market only.

Hollywood, Oct. 14.

Warner Bros. release of Anthony Spinner production. Stars Simon Oakland, Everett Sloane, Anne Helm, Richard Jordan, Karl Held. Directed by Buzz Kulik. Screenplay, E. M. Parsons, Sy Salkowitz, from magazine story by Eleazar Lipsky; camera, Carl Guthrie; music, Frank Perkins; editor, Robert B. Warwick; asst. director, Russell Llewellyn. Reviewed at WB studios, Oct. 13, '64. Running time, **54 MINS.**

Murray Brock	Simon Oakland
Paul Boyer	Everett Sloane
Connie Zelenko	Anne Helm
Eddie Dickinson	Richard Jordan
Dave Ryan	Karl Held
John T. McGrane	Bartlett Robinson
District Attorney	Simon Scott
Joe Damico	Louis Guss
Arnie Tomkins	Harold Gould
Dr. Michaels	Don Keefer
Karen Brock	Jo Helton
Nick Williams	William Bramley
Judge	Robert Lieb
Chaplain	King Calder

"Ready for the People" was made originally as an hour-long pilot for a prospective teleseries but didn't sell. To go out in theatrical release it is suitable only for program situations with less discriminating trade.

Plotline focuses on a prosecutor in the N.Y. District Attorney's office who, faced with trying a young man accused of murder, believes him innocent of the crime despite depositions of half a dozen eye-witnesses. His conscience is finally cleared after the baby-faced youth is executed, when he receives a letter from the boy confessing the crime which up to his last hour he had claimed he did not commit.

Simon Oakland acquits himself forcably as the prosecutor and Richard Jordan is the boy, inclined to overact with a heavy Southern accent. Everett Sloane is in briefly as Assistant D.A., Anne Helm is a blind pig hostess and Karl Held the attorney's aide, all okay.

Buzz Kulik's direction is routine and so is Anthony Spinner's producer helming. Technical credits are also average.

Whit.

L'Insoumis
(The Unvanquished)
(FRENCH)

Paris, Oct. 13.

MGM release of Delbeau-Cite Films-Cipra production. Stars Alain Delon; features Lea Massari, Georges Geret, Guy Laroche. Directed by Alain Cavalier. Screenplay, Cavalier, Jean Cau; camera, Claude Renoir; editor, Pierre Gillette. At Paris, Paris. Running time, **110 MINS.**

Thomas	Alain Delon
Dominique	Lea Massari
Lieutenant	Georges Geret
Husband	Guy Laroche

Familiar actioner about a man-on-the-run has an added fillip in situating it during the recent Algerian War. It thus may have some extra interest here but looms mainly a playoff item abroad on its good pacing and adroit if oft-told tale.

Director Alain Cavalier begins this tautly as a young man deserts the French Foreign Legion, gets tied up with the terrorist organization, the OAS, and then acquits himself by saving a woman hostage but finally paying for it with his death.

Film deftly showcases the rising talents, and thespic progress of new star Alain Delon. He shows that projection, ease and photogenic qualities that make his scenes usually telling. Perhaps some more variety and depth in future characterization will help, but the promise is there.

Pic has him getting wounded and killing a fellow guard when he tries to help a girl prisoner. He is given money by her and escapes, and then looks her up in France on his way home to Luxembourgh. Love comes as well as trailing by the French terrorists. He manages to get back to his home where he dies.

So the picture bogs down a bit after the initial dash as the characters are fairly conventional, and the action is often telegraphed. But it denotes an okay visual flair from director Cavalier, with fine production aspects and good supporting players. This should do well on its home grounds with playoff legs abroad on its neat action, tempo and theme.

Mosk.

San Francisco Fest

At Your Doorstep
(U Tvoyego Poroga)
(RUSSIAN)

Way - below - Soviet export average. Small prospects in States.

San Francisco, Oct. ?
Mosfilm studio production, directed by V. Ordynsky. Screenplay by S. Nagorny; I. Slabnevitch, photographer; V. Basner, composer. At San Francisco Film Fest. Running time, **79 MINS.**
The Mother .... N. Fedosova
The Father .... P. Liubeshkin
Liza .... L. Dziuba
Prokhorenko .... B. Yurtchenko
Perkalin .... I. Gorobetz

Russia has sent a number of distinguished films to the United States, where they have been well-received, but why "At Your Doorstep" was chosen as an export item is incomprehensible. A tired treatment of the war theme, pic is full of propaganda, p a t r i o t i s m and corny soldier jokes along with all the cliches about how stirring is the courage of those who rise to the occasion when threatened by overwhelming odds. Chances here look mighty slim.

Granted that the approach is a bit more intelligent than many similar pics from western nations, there are still loads of wornout situations, d e v e l o p m e n t s and chunks of dialog, making pic almost w h o l l y predictable. Its blatant emotionalism is heavily hammered home by V. Basner's weighty score.

Film deals with the German advance to the outskirts of Moscow during World War II, and the attempts of meager forces, supplemented by the citizenry, to defend the capital until the arrival of reinforcements.

Specifically, a small artillery unit sets up an anti-aircraft gun (to blast approaching tanks) in the kitchen garden of a p e a s a n t woman caring for her brood while her husband is off to war elsewhere. Having nowhere to go, she refuses to leave until it is too late and her home and family are eventually subjected to gunfire— a dramatic situation, certainly, but one that is left undeveloped.

What does create some interest is the interim proximity of military and civilian, and particularly the excellent performance of N. Fedosova as the peasant mother.

Not a stereotype of a slow and stolid, landbound woman, Miss Fedosova projects from beneath her massive reserve a great deal of warmth, intelligence, compassion and, most important, well-rounded humanity. She makes the film worth watching. *Sanf.*

The Naked Hours
(Le Ore Nude)
(ITALIAN)

Serious study of promiscuity. Well directed, good art booking bet.

San Francisco, Oct. 20.
Atlantica Cinematografica production, produced and directed by Marco Vicario. Featuring Keir Dullea, Rossana Podesta and Philippe Leroy. Screenplay by Alberto Moravia, T. Guerra and Vicario, based on a short story by Moravia. Carlo di Palma, camera; Riz Ortolani, music. At San Francisco Film Fest. Running time, **92 MINS.**
Aldo .... Keir Dullea
Carla .... Rossana Podesta
Massimo .... Philippe Leroy
Nonno .... Odardo Spadaro

Bare bottoms and adultery are becoming ho-hum cliches of art films, having by now, because of their abundance, lost the power to shock the audiences at which the pics are directed. It is time to move on to explore what is beneath the sensationalism. Which is exactly what producer - director Marco Vicario has done in "The Naked Hours," a work whose virtue is not innovation but refinement of style.

Seldom has the triangle situation been handled with the incisiveness and grace of this Italian film, and seldom has a picture dealing with sexual relationships for its entire running time seemed more tasteful in its graphic realism. This is because Vicario is not so worried about what happens in his characters' beds as what happens in their heads, and so probes the totality of the interacting relationships.

Simple story line deals with three days in the life of a woman, one day on a fling and two with her husband. From this framework there emerges, at a leisurely pace, the complex structure of personalities in a triangle.

Film marks the blossoming acting talents of Rossana Podesta, who walks away with the film by her portrayal of a borderline psychotic who acquiesces to her husband's taste for group sexplay, but never seeks outside affairs on her own until she meets a young student (Keir Dullea). Carla is one of those rare film femmes, a real and complete woman, and time and again Miss Podesta conveys her complexities with a tiny turn of the head, a slight change of expression in the eyes.

Less fully conceived is the part of the wooing student, but within the limits of the role, Dullea performs admirably. He retains all the sensitivity and cherubic quality of past roles while adding a new sense of freedom and a dash of maturity.

As the stoic husband who enjoys "group therapy," French actor Philippe Leroy manages to convey stolidly many of the fears besetting a man who substitutes uninhibited promiscuity for deeper commitments. But like Dullea's role, Leroy's is not fully conceived and left subservient to the study of Carla.

Odardo Spadaro contributes an effective bit as Dullea's grandfather, and smaller roles are handled competently.

Undoubtedly a nudie-dip scene involving Dullea and Miss Podesta during a night rainstorm will create some stir, but to single out the scene renders a disservice to the artistic unity of the film.

Riz Ortolani (composer of "Mondo Cane") has penned a spare and, at times, haunting score. Lamentably, cameraman Carlo di Palma has marred a generally well-photographed film by allowing too many sun flares, only one of which really contributes a visual effect that strengthens the mood of the scene.

Although it is too delicate and introspective for mass market, "The Naked Hours" should do excellent biz in art house situations.
Sanf.

Hvad med os?
(Epilogue)
(DANISH)
Strong Danish film with saucy new femme. Some promise for U. S.

San Francisco, Oct. 20.
Bent Christensen Filmproduktion, directed by Hennig Carlsen, produced by Bent Christensen. Featuring Erno Muller and Maud Berthelsen. Screenplay by Leif Panduro, Henning Kristiansen, photographer Krzystof Komeda, composer. At San Francisco Film Fest., Running time, **93 MINS.**
Martin .... Erno Muller
Lis .... Maud Berthelsen
Gorm .... Buster Larsen
Officer .... Preben Neegaard
Fabian .... John Jeppesen
Ivan .... Morten Grunwald

Bent Christensen, whose "Weekend" was successful in the United States, has come up with another winner though this one is a bit more obscure and less erotic, but making a far more telling statement. In addition, it introduces a fascinating and wonderful new actress in the person of Maud Berthelsen, a dark haired Danish dish, who spends most of her time as a cool Paris fashion model, but who comes through on screen as warm, sensual and thoroughly natural, despite a total lack of acting training.

Theme of "Epilogue" is that the times they are a-changing, and the similarity of the film's ideas to those contained in the Bob Dylan song is startling, though there is no evidence that the thoughts were not arrived at independently.

An expatriate returns to his native Copenhagen, obsessed with guilt about an incident in the past. He meets and begins an affair with a girl half his age who glows with a joie de vivre. A man of mental inflexibility and stunted development, he cannot comprehend the girl, who eventually leaves him when she efforts to communicate with him fail.

The man returns to look up several old partners in a wartime resistance murder of a Nazi collaborator. He is unable to get beyond guilt, beyond the past. The girl at first attributes his resultant somber dullness to age, eventually realizes that he is a "barely living corpse," obsessed with the evil of death, while she is busy revering and exploring the preciousness of life and trying to share her discoveries. After she leaves, the wartime accomplices, as chained to the past and as threatened by it as the expatriate, look him up and the ending incident of violence is a powerful, almost bitter comment on those who fail to grow.

As the older man, Erno Muller presents an image of fearful, sensitive sobriety; as the hip chick, Miss Berthelsen radiates youth, vitality, beauty, intuition and an extraordinary amount of cheerful good humor which saves the picture from ponderousness.

Henning Kristiansen's photography, evidently utilizing available light techniques, is occasionally murky, but for the most part exceptionally fine in producing vivid images. Krzystof Komeda's jazz score is undistinguished but adequate.

Film looks right for art house situations, especially those attracting youthful audiences; but many adults may resent pic's point.
Sanf.

My Fair Lady
(MUSICAL—TECHNICOLOR-SUPER PANAVISION 70)

Superlative amusement and entertainment. A b.o. gold mine.

Warner Bros. release of Jack L. Warner production. Stars Rex Harrison, Audrey Hepburn. Features Stanley Holloway, Gladys Cooper, Wilfred Hyde-White, Jeremy Brett. Directed by George Cukor. Based on "Pygmalion" by Bernard Shaw. Screenplay and Broadway musical by Lerner & Loewe and lyrics by Alan Jay Lerner. Music by Frederick Loewe, conductor, Andre Previn. Choreographer, Hermes Pan. Cameraman, Harry Stradling. Costumes and scenery, Cecil Beaton. Art direction, Gene Allen. Film editor, William Ziegler. Sound, Francis J. Scheid, Murray Spivack. World premiere Oct. 21, '64, at Criterion Theatre, N.Y. Running time, **170 MINS.**

Eliza	Audrey Hepburn
Prof. Higgins	Rex Harrison
Alfred Doolittle	Stanley Holloway
Col. Pickering	Wilfred Hyde-White
Mrs. Higgins	Galdys Cooper
Freddie	Jeremy Brett
Zoltan Karpathy	Theodore Bikel
Mrs. Pearce	Mona Washbourne
Mrs. Eynsford-Hill	Isobel Elson
Butler	John Holland

The great longrun stage musical made by Lerner & Loewe (and Herman Levin) out of the wit of Bernard Shaw's old play, "Pygmalion," has now been transformed into a stunningly effective screen entertainment. "My Fair Lady" in Technicolor and Super Panavision 70 must clean up for Warners. It has riches of story, humor, acting and production values far beyond the average big picture. It is Hollywood at its best, Jack L. Warner's career capstone and a film that will go on without now-forseeable limits of playoff in reserved seat policy and world rentals.

That Warner paid $5,500,000 for the rights alone is a staggering first fact. Add that after $20,000,000 the original stage production interest collects 47 ½% of the net. So a lot of people are going to again make it to the bank from this Midas musical.

Care and planning shine in every detail and thus cast a glow around the name of director George Cukor. Of course the original staging genius of Moss Hart cannot be overlooked as a blueprint for success. But like all great films "My Fair Lady" represents a team of talents. The delicate task of proper apportionment of credits will draw different answers but this reviewer would rate Rex Harrison's performance and Cecil Beaton's design of costumes, scenery and production as the two powerhouse contributions. Which, of course, in no way neglects appreciation of the master eye behind the camera, to wit, Harry Stradling.

Alan Jay Lerner's screenplay derived from his own stage libretto has not attempted to improve on a hit, although there is some re-arrangement, compression and telescoping for cinematic effects. Some of the action is "opened up." The color of London before World War I benefits through the camera creation of both working and upper class customs.

Gene Allen's art direction probably constitutes a major credit, even within the master-plan of Beaton. Francis J. Scheid and Murray Spivack handled the sound, a mighty undertaking. A plus value for the widescreen version is that anybody may sit anywhere and hear every lyric and see every facial nuance. An important aid to the over-all impression is the editing of the footage by William Zeigler, which is exceptionally smooth, although there are a number of sharp jumps of locale.

This is a man-bullies-girl plot with story novelty. An unorthodox musical without a kiss, the audience travels to total involvement with characters and situation on the rails of sharp dialog and business. The deft segues of dialog into lyric are superb, especially in the case of Harrison. One can only guess the preparation and takes necessary to get the effect. Technical maps and paraphernalia incident to Higgins scientific work in phonetics have been given much attention. It enchances the verbal obsessions of the Harrison role upon which all is based.

Main credit, following a prolonged garden of flowers, stars the title rather than Audrey Hepburn and Rex Harrison, who are billed below the show, and hence not strictly within the defined conditions of stardom. Some may wonder why Harrison is subordinate to the girl in the billing since he dominates "My Fair Lady" as he dominated "Cleopatra."

Only incurably disputions persons will consider it a defect of "Lady" on screen that Julie Andrews has been replaced by the better known Miss H. She is thoroughly beguiling as Eliza though her singing is dubbed by Marni Nixon.

Stanley Holloway repeats from the Broadway stage version. Again and again his theatrical authority clicks. How this great English trouper takes the basically "thin" and repetitious, "With A Little Bit O'Luck" and makes it stand up as gaiety incarnate.

Every one in the small cast is excellent. Mona Washbourne is especially fine as the prim but compassionate housekeeper. Wildred Hyde-White has the necessary proper gentleman quality as Pickering and makes a good foil for Harrison. Gladys Cooper brings aristocratic common sense to the mother of the phonetics wizard. The lovesick young man who sings outside the house, and is otherwise just a tenor from sub-plot has been assigned to Jeremy Brett. He photographs handsomely and sings with nice melody. The Hungarian charlatan speech expert who nearly upsets the masquerade at the high style ball is plausibly handled by Theodore Bikel.

The staging of the fashionable paddock scene at Ascot closely approximates the tableau used on the stage, though enlarged. Elsewhere in the picture there are a number of freeze-action bits but in general the story is told with strict realism, albeit dressed to the burst of Beaton's imagination. Women must dote on the gowns. All will be struck by the comfort and service for the well-to-do of the England that was. The house in which Higgins lives and where most of the action takes place is sheer recapture of a bygone era.

Hermes Pan cleverly handled the choreographic movement essential to some of the songs which travel all over the sets. The ballroom detail is of high style detailing.

A certain amount of new music by Frederick Loewe and added lyrics by Lerner are part of the adjustment to the cinematic medium. But it is the original stage score which stands out. Actually the numbers never went out of fashion so all that may reasonably be said is that a fresh peak of popularity may follow in the wake of the picture. Andre Previn handled the orchestra using arrangements of Alexander Courage, Robert Frankly and Al Woodbury.

Running some 10 minutes short of three hours "My Fair Lady" is a long film but only rheumatics will object to sitting that long. There is hardly a dull moment and, more to the point, there are many laughs, many humanly touching scenes, and song numbers that come smashing through. Audience applause must break out during the unspooling.

This is an occasion for general congratulations. Hollywood has seldom looked lovelier. *Land.*

The Soldier's Tale
(BRITISH-COLOR)

London, Oct. 14.

British Home Entertainment production. Stars Robert Helpmann, Brian Phelan, Svetlana Beriosova. Produced by Leonard Cassini and Dennis Miller. Directed by Michael Birkett; music by Igor Stravinsky; libretto by C. F. Ramuz; camera (Technicolor), Miller; editor, Richard Marden; score played by Melos Ensemble, conducted by Derek Hudson. Previewed at Film & Arts Private Theatre, London, Oct. 12, '64. Running time, **52 MINS.**

The Devil	Robert Helpmann
The Soldier	Brian Phelan
The Princess	Svetlana Beriosova

Designed initially for the upcoming pay-tv market, British Home Entertainment has put out this short film into release. Its appeal will be confined strictly to balletophiles. It is a morality fable in which Robert Helpmann, playing the Devil, has seven roles and enjoys a field day in acting, dancing and miming.

Simple and often attractive in its lensing it tells the tale of an Irish soldier who sells his violin (which represents his soul) to the devil. Helpmann as Lucifer, Brian Phelan as the soldier and the accomplished ballerina, Svetlana Beriosova, play the trio of roles with deft ability and it is always very attractive to the eye. Its appeal, however, must be regarded as strictly limited. *Rich.*

The Americanization Of Emily

Sometimes amusing comedy-drama with names of Julie Andrews and James Garner to attract. Unpleasant concept detracts.

Hollywood, Oct. 23.

Metro release of Martin Ransohoff production. Stars James Garner, Julie Andrews, Melvyn Douglas. Features James Coburn, Joyce Grenfell, Keenan Wynn. Directed by Arthur Hiller. Screenplay, Paddy Chayefsky, based on novel by William Bradford Huie; camera, Philip Lathrop; editor, Tom McAdoo; asst. director, Al Shenberg; music, Johnny Mandel. Reviewed at Academy Award Theatre, Oct. 21, '64. Running time, **115 MINS.**

Lt. Com. Charles E. Madison	James Garner
Emily Barham	Julie Andrews
Admiral William Jessup	Melvyn Douglas
Lt. Com. "Bus" Cummings	James Coburn
Mrs. Barham	Joyce Grenfell
Admiral Thomas Healy	Edward Binns
Sheila	Liz Fraser
Old Sailor	Keenan Wynn
Capt. Harry Spaulding	William Windom
Chief Petty Officer Paul Adams	John Crawford
Capt. Marvin Ellender	Douglas Henderson
Admiral Hoyle	Edmond Ryan
Young Sailor	Steve Franken
General William Hallerton	Paul Newlan
Lt. Victor Wade	Gary Cockrell
Enright	Alan Sues
Port Commander	Bill Frastr
Nurse Captain	Lou Byrne
Port Ensign	Alan Howard
Pat	Linda Marlowe
Nameless Broads	No. 1, Janine Gray; No. 2, Judy Carne; No. 3, Kathy Kersh

Designed as a romantic wartime comedy-drama, "The Americanization of Emily" has its glaring faults as well as its virtues. It carries a certain breeziness in some of its humorously ridiculous situations which evoke laughs, but on the other hand there are certain aspects which many audiences will find hard to stomach. Film's most potent selling point is the reappearance of Julie Andrews, after scoring so sensationally in Disney's "Mary Poppins," and James Garner in another of his light comedy roles.

"Emily," with Miss Andrews in title role as an English motor pool driver in World War II, takes place immediately before the Normandy invasion. Most of the action unspools in London where Garner, a lieutenant commander who makes avowed cowardice his career, is "dog robber" to Melvyn Douglas, an erratic Admiral and one of the heads of the oncoming onslaught on the French coast. Most of Garner's duties consist of rounding up delicacies and services, impossible to get, for his boss, until the admiral, a Navy traditionalist who believes his branch of the service is being overshadowed by the Army, orders him to make a film showing activities of Navy demolition on their landing at Omaha Beach.

Despite the motivating premise being approached via broad comedy strokes, its concept may be resented in many quarters and the impact of the intended humor consequently weakened. This basic idea builds around the admiral being beset with an obsession to have the first man killed on Omaha Beach a sailor, to show the Navy can have no peer in the service, and the script takes it from there. Idea is further distasteful in seeing one of the high chiefs of the Normandy invasion being delineated as some of an irresponsible lunatic.

Film, too, tends toward preachiness, when Garner in lengthy dialog spouts his philosophy of how war may be sidestepped.

While long on comedy and bits of business which pay off, film has its more realistic moments during the invasion but this footage is minimized. Pic is primarily interesting for the romance between Miss Andrews and Garner, the former struggling against being Americanized through her contact with the outgoing and freewheeling Garner.

Miss Andrews displays a charming presence. She makes the most of her character of a young Englishwoman widowed by the war, having lost, too, her father and brother; she describes herself aptly when she says, "I fall in love too easily, I shatter too easily." Part enables her both comedy and dramatic rendition.

Garner, usually okay, sometimes forces his comedy scenes but generally delivers a satisfactory performance. Douglas plays his admiral strictly for laughs.

James Coburn as a Navy officer is outstanding particularly for his comedy scenes. He participates in one of the most hilarious bits of biz in film, a running gag where Garner keeps breaking into his room and interrupting a pleasant little seance with what are billed as "The Three Nameless Broads," played respectively and with some attraction by Janine Gray, Kathy Kersh and Judy Carne. Joyce Grenfell as femme star's mother and Keenan Wynn a salty old salt likewise handle their roles well.

Martin Ransohoff as producer gives production satisfactory values and Arthur Hiller's direction of the Paddy Chayefsky screenplay maintains a swift pace. Philip Lathrop's camera work is effective, and added plus is afforded by Tom McAdoo editing, Johnny Mandel's music score and art direction by George W. Davis, Hans Peters and Elliot Scott.   *Whit.*

Der Damm
(The Dam)
(GERMAN)
Manheim, Oct. 20.

A Detten Schleiermacher production. With Petra Krause, Vlado Kristl, Felix Potisk, Erich Gloeckner. Directed by Vlado Kristl. Screenplay, Vlado Kristl; camera, Gerard Vandenberg; editor, Marlies Detjens. At Mannheim Film Fest. Running time, **90 MINS.**

Vlado Kristl, a Yugoslav living in Munich and remembered as a creator of several outstanding (Yugoslav) cartoons, presents his first full-length feature with this pic. The avantgardist Kristl aimed at making a film outside any producing routine and seemingly lost every control over himself. He went overboard in all directions. And "The Dam" looks like a waste of time.

This strange offering deals with love and all its ingredients and consequencies such as jealousy, loneliness, violence, confusion, complications and so forth. All are treated in a symbolical way with no apparent story line. Bits of situations, speeches, often abruptly interrupted, often repeated, often turned upside down leave the viewer no chance to make head or tail of what is going on.

A pic like this can't be taken seriously. Even if Kristl had in mind to make fun of the audience, he hasn't succeeded since this isn't even involuntarily funny. Author-director has had time, leisure and even money (his producer, Schleiermacher, let him do as he pleased) to direct his first full-length pic. But it turns out a minus effort.

Only a few players are in this one. The femme central figure is portrayed by Petra Krause, otherwise a tele announcer in Hamburg, as a paralyzed girl confined to a wheelchair. One of the male play-

ers is Felix Potisk, otherwise a Munich nightclub employee. Another male in the cast is Kristl himself.   *Hans.*

Wiano
(The Dowry)
(POLISH)

Film Polski release of Syrena (Warszawa) production. With Zofia Kucowna, Roman Wilhelmi, Marta Lipinska, Tadeusz Lomnicki, Zdislaw Karczewski. Directed by Jan Lomnicki. Screenplay, Jerzy Pomianowski; camera, Kurt Weber; music, Zbigniew Rudzinski. At Mannheim Film Fest. Running time, **95 MINS.**

The Poles seem to have taken a fancy to morbid peasant dramas. Their strange predilection for this type of screen fare borders, at least for Western viewers, on the unpleasant. "The Dowry" is another example. Of the films shown in the "first feature" section at the Mannheim festival, it was not well received. Foreign prospects look zero.

Central figures are a young man named Stasiek just released from prison and a girl by the name of Bronka who's a cripple. The limping maid is very much in love with the man and he's willing to marry her if she provides him with a dowry in form of her father's land on which they could settle and run a farm. It takes some time to talk her father into turning the land over to her. In the meantime, her lover finds back to his former fiancee. There's nothing left for the disillusioned cripple to do except to stab the ex-convict.

The whole pic teems with unpleasant faces and situations. Moreover, the treatment of subject matter is too conventional. It's the first feature film of Jan Lomnicki, a former shorts film producer who did well in this field. His directorial talents are obvious in several sequences but wasted on this pic. Acting may be called competent. A film like this can hardly contribute to prestige of the Polish film industry. Technically, "Dowry" is okay.   *Hans.*

Kitten With A Whip

Ann-Margret's name may draw. Unpleasant, violence - minded programmer.

Hollywood, Oct. 20.

Universal release of Harry Keller production. Stars Ann-Margret, John Forsythe; features Peter Brown, Patricia Barry, Richard Anderson. Directed by Douglas Hayes, Hayes, based on book by Wade Miller; camera, Joseph Biroc; editor, Russell F. Schoengarth; asst. director, Terence Nelson. Reviewed at Universal Studios, Oct. 20, '64. Running time, **82 MINS.**

Jody	Ann-Margret
David	John Forsythe
Ron	Peter Brown
Vera	Patricia Barry
Grant	Richard Anderson
Buck	James Ward
Midge	Diane Sayer
Mavis	Ann Doran
Varden	Patrick Whyte
Virginia	Audrey Dalton
Enders	Leo Gordon
Strip Tease Dancer	Patricia Tiara
Matron	Nora Marlowe
Martha	Frances Robinson
Peggy	Maxine Stuart
Saleslady	Mildred Von Hollen
Newscaster	Jerry Dunphy
Salty Sam	Doodles Weaver
Chauffeur	Hal Hopper

"Kitten With a Whip" is a return to the B's, suitable mainly for program situations. Its contrived plot carries an unpleasant theme

and film's only apparent reason is to offer a number of sadistic characters in the hope that the overall effect will be shocking. Sole box-office asset is name Ann-Margret —who should remain in musicals —likely to draw followers in the mistaken idea they are in for a round of entertainment.

Script by Douglas Hayes, who also directs, frames on a vicious femme juvenile hall escapee who breaks into the home of a politically-ambitious family man, whose wife is out of town, and refuses to leave. She threatens him with scandal should he call the police; then calls in a couple of strong-arm associates who take over the house and keep owner a virtual prisoner. Action is burdened with frequent uncalled-for violence of the type the MPAA Production Code assertedly is against.

Ann-Margret plays the unsympathetic lead with a display of over-acting and John Forsythe fares little better as her victim. Peter Brown and James Ward are the slap-happy goons. Richard Anderson, Patricia Barry and Diane Sayer head supporting cast.

Hayes' direction is on a par with his script and Harry Keller produced. Technical credits are okay.   *Whit.*

La Chasse A L'Homme
(Manhunt)
(FRENCH)
Paris, Oct. 20.

Gaumont release of Filmsonor-Procinex-Mondex-Euro International Films production. Stars Jean-Claude Brialy, Jean-Paul Belmondo, Claude Rich, Francoise Dorleac, Marie Dubois, Catherine Deneuve, Marie Laforet, Micheline Presle; features Mireille Darc, Bernadette Lafont. Directed by Edouard Molinaro. Screenplay, France Roche, Michel Audiard, Albert Simonin, Michel Duran; camera, Andre Winding; editor, Robert Isnardon. At the Ambassade-Gaumont, Paris. Running time, **90 MINS.**

Antoine	Jean-Claude Brialy
Fernand	Jean-Paul Belmondo
Julien	Claude Rich
Clotilde	Francoise Dorleac
Cashier	Marie Dubois
Secretary	Catherine Deneuve
Woman	Micheline Presle
Giselle	Marie Laforet
Flora	Bernadette Lafont

Lagging situation comedy about recalcitrant bachelors is too heavy-footed in story, execution and playing to give it the airy invention it strives for. Result makes for an okay local item, with slim specialized chances abroad and only fair exploitation possibilities on its theme.

On the way to get married, the prospective groom is talked out of it by hearing the tales of the marital woes of two pals. He runs off but gets bagged anyway by a con-girl as do his two pals who have left their respective spouses.

In spite of a good cast, this has too slight characterization and fairly lame mounting. However, there are speeded up and slowed down motion and some zany situations. Film just does not get off the ground even if Jean-Paul Belmondo does his usual lowdown character as a petty gangster caught in marital woes.

Others can not do much with their skimpy parts and also fail to rise above the unimaginative plot and stilted dialog. It is technically okay.   *Mosk.*

La Ronde
(The Round)
(FRENCH-COLOR-FRANSCOPE)
Paris, Oct. 27.

Pathe release of Paris-Film Production-Interopa-Robert and Raymond Hakim production. Stars Jean-Claude Brialy, Jane Fonda, Anna Karina, Catherine Spaak, Francine Berge, Marie Dubois, Claude Giraud, Jean Sorel, Maurice Ronet, Bernard Noel. Directed by Roger Vadim. Screenplay, Jean Anouilh from play by Arthur Schnitzler; camera (Eastmancolor), Henri Decae; editor, Victoria Mercanton. At Marignan, Paris. Running time, **110 MINS.**

Albert	Jean-Claude Brialy
Sophie	Jane Fonda
Rose	Anna Karina
Girl	Catherine Spaak
Actress	Francine Berge
Prostitute	Marie Dubois
Soldier	Claude Giraud
Husband	Maurice Ronet
Count	Jean Sorel
Author	Bernard Noel

Arthur Schnitzler's play on turn-of-the-century morals and sex and standing gets still another film time around by Robert and Raymond Hakim who produced the first one in 1950. But this is no remake, with a different outlook and time, the early 1900's Vienna is replaced by the Paris of 1914 on the eve of the First World War. It shapes an almost classic French film insouciant, elegant, witty and one track in its series of seductions as love is handed from one character to another until the round is completed when the last meets the first.

The first "La Ronde" had censorship trouble in some Yank states and naturally had low pressure group ratings. This may have the same, since the same subject matter, but there is no leering quality here. In fact, sex is treated so matter-of-factly that it is never offensive or rarely suggestive.

There is only one equivocal scene that has some tongue-in-cheek, below-the-belt connotations. This is the episode where Jane Fonda, as an erring young wife, is pictured with her lover. This could be sheared for better chances abroad. So this shapes an exploitable item offshore and at home, with arty theatre chances also inherent. But this calls for good placement. Controversy could provide a sales peg, too.

If the original was a harsher condemnation of the decadence of the times and the first pic version a more elegant, indulgent look at social decay, this one plays it more for a bittersweet attitude towards love's aspects, aided by the adroit scripting of playwright Jean Anouilh.

Roger Vadim's direction stresses the cluttered and cozy decors of the era. His treatment of love is almost modest to give this a sort of comedic air rather than an ironic undertone.

Sometimes this gets repetitious in its insistence on scene after scene of love trysts, but there is a good balance of types, and a wary, wry discretion that perks it up whenever it begins to lose interest. Film may not have the sexational aspects, in spite of its theme, for grind or circusing, but will create word-of-mouth which should help.

A prostie and a soldier have a brief fling with the soldier seducing a maid who is then taken over by the son of the house. He goes on to a young married woman, then to a girl he has picked up, etc. It all ends with the prostitute again as he has a drunken night out.

Nudity is only really present in some night club scenes. Otherwise director Vadim shrewdly keeps the love scenes, as torrid as some are, discreetly covered or shot from vantage points that are rarely unseemly.

Acting is of a high level as each does his or her little sequence with the backgrounds and decoration sometimes more important than characters.

Jane Fonda is especially beguiling and deceptively naive as the philandering wife, while Anna Karina is a right waif-like maid. Marie Dubois has the underlying good nature, under a vulgar exterior, as the sentimental prostie. Catherine Spaak depicts an adroit blending of innocence and guile as an emancipated young woman. Francine Berge displays a knowing mixture of sexual appetite and discreet longing as an actress.

The men are mainly foils but do well, too, with Claude Giraud a handsome, dashing but c r u e l soldier. Jean-Claude Brialy is a too eager young Don Juan. Maurice Ronet portrays a more fatuous but sympathetic husband. Jean Sorel is a rightly stuffy nobleman while Bernard Noel is cast as a seductive man of the world and author.

All this is done up in expert **color, unstinting production dress and a nice re-creation of the pre-World War I period.** Also worth mentioning is Maurice Binder's expertly conceived titles.

This turns out to be a bedroom oriented film that still sidesteps prurience. It will need good placement and selling for the U.S. where it may have difficult times in some spots and depth playoff.
Mosk.

It Happened Here
(BRITISH)

Mannheim, Oct. 18.
Rath Films Ltd. (London) production. With Pauline Murray, Sebastian Shaw, Nicolette Bernard, Bart Allison, Stella Kemball, Fiona Leland, Reginald Marsh, Bertha Russell, Ralph Wilson, John Harrington. Directed and written by Kevin Brownlow and Andrew Mollo. Camera, Peter Suschitzky; music, Jack Beaver; editor, Kevin Brownlow; commentators, Frank Philips, Alvar Lidell, John Snagg and Michael Mellinger. At Mannheim Film Festival. Running time, **99 MINS.**

Story-wise, "It Happened Here" may be classified as the most unusual European film seen in quite some time. It tells the story of what might have happened had England been occupied by the Germans. Critics can find some faults with this production, yet its outcome is certainly interesting and exciting. Many will even call it a "sensational" film. It may collect a lot of money if it finds a clever distributor who knows how to cash in on the unusual subject. It's indeed a highly exploitable subject. It will lead to heavy discussions everywhere.

The action takes place in England in 1943. The Germans have successfully invaded the country.

There's also a story line going through. It centers on the experience of an English nurse who, in order to help, joins the Fascist-controlled Immediate Organization. She soon finds out that her I.A. uniform alienates those around here. She eventually tries to help a wounded partisan. Her action is

discovered and she's punished for associating with "the other side." She's transferred to a country hospital and later arrested. She then falls into the hands of partisans. The ending sees an English SS unit surrendering to the partisans. The SS men are shot down by another group of partisans.

The film shows brutality on both sides. Its message is that Nazism leads to violence everywhere. Film poses the question: Can Nazism only be wiped out by Nazi methods? It's up to the viewer to decide this for himself.

As it lies in the nature of such a daring theme, film's ingredients will face controversy. There's naturally the question whether Hitler Germany would have found such kind of following in England as depicted in the film. But the creators of "It Happened Here" argue that Nazism is possible and, in fact, existing everywhere. (After all, there are still hundreds of Fascist groups in Europe, even in England.)

But despite all controversy, film reveals a tremendous task. Compliments galore should go to the two young men who created it: Kevin Brownlow (26) and Andrew Mollo (24), the former a professional film editor, the latter assistant director to Tony Richardson who, incidentally, contributed the money to complete the film. (Profits allegedly will be split 50-50.)

"It Happened Here" is a nonprofessional feature which began as an amateur project on 16m and remained so until financing was secured six years (!) after production had started. The early material was then "blown-up" and rest of the film was shot on standard 35m. Most of the cast is nonprofessional. One is hardly aware of this. Film cost a mere £7,000, which is just around $20,000. Taking all this and the spectacular outcome into account, this is indeed a sensational production. It may be added that film makes also technically a good impression. The lensing is particularly slick. The atmosphere is well caught. Also, the score utilizing a German march ("Volk ans Gewehr") and Bruckner's 9th Symphony is very effective. If the reviews should (and they will) be varied, they will be mainly because of the individual viewers' different political outlook and imagination. By all means "It Happened Here" rates as an unconventional enterprise in every field of the trade.
Hans.

San Francisco Fest

Zhivyot Takoy Paren
(There Is Such a Guy)
(RUSSIAN)

San Francisco, Oct. 24.
Gorky Film Studio production, written and directed by V. Shukshin. Features Leonid Kuravlev. Camera, V. Ginsburg; music, P. Tchekalov. At San Francisco Film Fest. Running time, **101 MINS.**
Pashka Kolokolnikov....Leonid Kuravlev
Nastya .... L. Alexandrova
Katya .... L. Budkova
The Journalist .... B. Akhmadullina
(English Subtitles)

This Russian feature is such a quiet work that the only notable thing about it—its extraordinary

gentleness and humanism—does not strike one until the final reel is unspooling.

The deceptively simple comedy follows a truck driver through a series of unsuccessful amorous pursuits, a moment as matchmaker and other minor misadventures. Nothing much happens, and even the climactic incident in which Pashka (Leonid Kuravlev) becomes a temporary hero is nearly insignificant.

But all the actions and events serve to reveal slowly the character of Pashka, a gentle and good young man who aspires to be a ladies' man and otherwise is content. Ever so subtly it becomes apparent that he is awakening from his peasant placidness to a more questioning awareness. Unfortunately, just as one is discovering this serious sub-theme, the pic changes course and hammers home its message in an unsuitable ending which negates the previous subtlety.

For the most part, however, this is a glowing little comedy which indicates a remarkable Russian willingness to indulge in a spoof of life in the interior, reaching a high point in a fashion show on a collective farm where the models display the latest chic outfits for egg-gathering.

Warmth and cheerful good humor suffuse the film, and its gentle satire marks the increasing maturity of Soviet pics. Writer-director V. Shukshin has fashioned a film of considerable merit, aided immeasurably by the faultlessly natural performance of Leonid Kuravlev as the bumbling hero. There may be some title confusion. Shown at the Frisco Film Fest as 'There Is Such a Guy," the subtitles on the film translate the Russian as "There's a Boy For You."
Sanf.

Between Tears And Smiles
(Sun Tai Sil Yen Yin)
(HONG KONG)

San Francisco, Oct. 23.
A Shaw Brothers, Ltd. production, directed by Lo Chen. Featuring Li Li Hua and Ivy Lee Po. Screenplay by Ching Wei; Liu Chi, photographer; Wang Fu-ling, composer. At San Francisco Film Fest. Running time, **135 MINS.**
Shen Fung Hsien,
Ho Li Ya .... Li Li Hua
Kwan Shiu-chu, acrobat....... Ivy Lee Po
Fan Chia Soo, student ..... Kwan Shan
Mrs. Shen .... Chen Yen-yen
General Chang .... Ching Niao
Uncle Shen .... Chiang Kwang-chao
Mrs. Tao .... Kao Pao-shu
(English Subtitles)

Like many Shaw Bros. pics, this one combines excellent production values with the most elaborate but naive sort of soap opera. Its sheer escapism and wholly unbelievable characters make it unsuitable for Occidental audiences, and its only chances here would seem to be for situations catering to Chinese-American communities.

Story, set in the early days of the Republic, concerns a well-to-do student's involvement in the lives of three girls and their families. One is rich and eligible, but not particularly interesting to the student. The second is a singer in dives. Both these roles are played with aplomb by the beautiful Li Li Hau. The third is an acrobat, who with her father, performs in the streets and passes the hat for sub-

sistence. She is played by Ivy Lee Po, ballyhooed as China's leading actress, but here she overdoes everything, particularly facial expressions.

Kwan Shan is colorless as the student, but his role is included only to move the plot along.

The plot is as torturous and circuitous as a Victorian novel's, but less credible than a Superman comic book. Impossible to detail here, suffice it to say that the student falls in love with the singer, is called away, and the girl is kidnapped by a lecherous general, whose villainy is portrayed so broadly (by Ching Niao) as to be ridiculous. The whole thing degenerates into a mishmash of bathos, derring-do, insanity and gore.

But the sets and costumes, for whom the credits are omitted in the English info, are handsome.
Sanf.

Samorastniki
(Wild Growth)
(YUGOSLAVIAN)

San Francisco, Oct. 24.
A Prolzvadnja Triglav film production, directed by Igor Pretnar. Screenplay by Vojko Duletic; camera, Mile de Gleria. At San Francisco Film Fest. Running time, **90MINS.**
Meta .... Majda Potokarjeva
Ozbej .... Rudi Kosmac
Karnicnik, his father Vladimir Skrbinsek
Karnicnika, his mother..Sava Severjeva
Meta's mother .... Vida Juvanova
Volbenk, Ozbej't brother.. Lojze Rozman
(English Subtitles)

Yugoslavia is still far behind cinematically, if one is to judge by "Samorastniki" ("Wild Growth" or "The Wildings"). It's a turgid melodrama about a pair of ill-fated medieval lovers.

Ozbej (Rudi Kosmac), son of a feudal landowner, has the misfortune not merely to seduce a peasant serf, Meta, attractively played by Majda Potokarjeva, but to fall in love with her. She returns the love, but such a match is not tolerated, and Ozbej's father, a despicable heavy etched in broad black strokes by Vladimor Skrbinsek, does everything he can think of to end the affair. Naturally, most of the actions are taken against Meta, and they include a lashing, torture by burning her hands, ostracism from the community, and ultimately eviction from her home and banishment from the district.

Through it all the lovers have continued to see each other. Then, ten years and five bastard children later, Meta is leaving under the banishment. Ozbej meets her on the road to tell her that he will remain at his paternal home because he will always have an income there. Meta understands. Ozbej ends, saying, "Well, goodnight."

Scene is one of about six false endings, and it is all pretty funny by the time pic is over. Film is strongly reminiscent of the Italian costumers and spectacles, and if it had been filmed in color and were dubbed, it might rate similar playoff. As it is, pic does not look right for the U.S.
Sanf.

Encounter in Salzburg
(WEST GERMAN)

San Francisco, Oct. 23.
Peter Bamberger production with Paris Inter Productions, directed by Max Friedman. Featuring Curt Jurgens, Nadia Gray, Daniele Gaubert. Screenplay by Thomas Muenster; Georg Kraus, photographer; Peter Thomas, composed. At San Francisco Film Fest. Running time, 100 MINS.
Hans Wilke, general director
.... Curt Jurgens
Felicitas, his wife .... Nadia Gray
Bernhard von Wangen .Victor de Kowa
Kroener, insurance agent Walter Giller
Manuela .... Daniele Gaubert
Insurance director .... Paul Dahlke
Fraulein Niederalt, secretary
.... Marte Harell

(English Subtitles)

Obviously a sincere attempt at significant cinema, "Encounter in Salzburg" is a noble failure, and the fault lies squarely with Thomas Muenster's leaden, superficial, screenplay.

Counterpointing the annual Salzburg production of the medieval morality play, "Everyman," with the 1964 life of a postwar German industrialist and millionaire (Curt Jurgens), Muenster laboriously tries to say something about life, death, society and boredom. The idea of contemporizing ancient and inadequate myths is as old as Euripides, but what Muenster has come up with contains less insight than the original "Everyman." Such cliches as "money isn't everything" or "work isn't everything" or "the patient will live only if he decides to" would not be very impressive in a freshman philosophy or drama course, let alone an adult film.

As the industrialist, Jurgens contributes an impressive performance, trying at every turn to override the inadequacies of the script and portray a man who on one level is suave and confident, and more deeply is troubled and unsure. But in the end, Jurgens cannot accomplish too much.

Film has him taking a sneak holiday in Salzburg to visit an old friend who portrays Death in the morality play. Their initial meeting, a long and philosophical discussion, while lacking dramatic punch, gives promise of an interesting pic as there are a few tentative thrusts at contrasting a modern Everyman with one from the Middle Ages; but from there everyhing goes downhill into a muddle of cliche.

He meets an art student (luscious Daniele Gaubert), makes her his mistress, has a heart attack at what is supposed to be a party rife with symbolism, which either hits the viewer over the head, or at other times never comes off, a shortcoming for which director Max Friedmann must bear the responsibility.

Pic's only high point occurs in a fantasy sequence in which the stricken Jurgens is battling for life.

In addition to Jurgens' performance, Victor de Kowa brings a great deal of intensity to his role as the actor-friend, Miss Gaubert is fine as the young mistress, and Nadia Gray does all she can with her small part as the neurotic, neglected wife.

Production values are excellent, particularly Georg Kraus's dramatic camera work and Peter Thomas's contemporary score, embodying pop, rock 'n' roll and jazz themes, as well as traditional strains, and bits of electronic sound in the fantasy sequence.
Sanf.

A Jester's Tale
(Dva Musketyri)
(CZECHOSLOVAKIA)

San Francisco, Oct. 24.
A Ceskoslovensky film production, directed by Karel Zeman. Screenplay by Zeman and Pavel Juracek; Vaclav Hanus, photographer; Jan Novak, composer. At San Francisco Film Fest. Running time, 83 MINS.
Petr .... Petr Kastka
Matej .... Miroslav Holub
Lenka .... Emilie Vasaryova
Veronica .... Valentina Thielova
Count Pinkles .... Eduard Kohout
Varga .... Karel Effa
Spanish Officer .... Jiri Holy

(English Subtitles)

Like "Lemonade Joe," another Czech satire currently making the festival rounds and reaping much praise, "A Jester's Tale" is a satiric and cinematic jewel but whose commercial possibilities do not seem readily apparent. Perhaps sharp promotion and word-of-mouth can spread the news of its superior quality, but this is the sort of feature likely to be dug up a decade or two hence by film societies and marveled over posthumously.

A sort of jester's eye view of the Thirty Years' War, film combines a comic romance with acid comments about the motivations of leaders in wars and the frequent lack of interest or conviction of the ordinary people called upon to participate in them.

Pic also combines animation and live photography in dazzling complexity, utilizing cartoon work, old engravings, straight scenes, sets, location shots, photomontage and special effects, sometimes just for the sheer pleasure of being clever. It is a film buff's delight.

The feature's wide-ranging humor includes broad slapstick, sharp satire and many subtly and simply funny bits. Plot revolves about an unlikely trio—Petr (Petr Kostka), a peasant impressed into service unwillingly, who escapes only to be captured by the other side but mistaken for a duke; Matej (Miroslav Holub), who impressed Petr, but is willing to change sides with a flick of his reversible cloak; and Lenka (Emilie Vasaryova), a lovely who joins them in their wanderings and adopts a jester's disguise. In their respective roles, Kostka, Holub and Miss Vasaryova give excellent comic performances, but this is director Karel Zeman's picture, a tour de force of imagination and technique, of humor without frivolousness.

On the minus side, there are a few moments of repetition and tedium, the film is not in color, and some of the contemporary graphics have an old-fashioned (eastern European) look about them. But these are minor drawbacks in view of the total work.
Sanf.

Youngblood Hawke

Big production of big novel has soap-operaish plot that should do well at b.o., particularly with women.

Hollywood, Oct. 29.
Warner Bros. release of Delmer Daves production, directed by Daves. Stars James Franciscus, Suzanne Pleshette, Genevieve Page; features Eva Gabor, Mary Astor, Lee Bowman, Edward Andrews, Don Porter, Mildred Dunnock, Kent Smith, John Dehner, John Emery. Screenplay by Daves, based on Herman Wouk novel; camera, Charles Lawton; music, Max Steiner; editor, Sam O'Steen. Reviewed at Warner Bros. Studio, Oct. 29, 1964. Running time, 137 MINS.
Youngblood Hawke... James Franciscus
Jeanne Green .... Suzanne Pleshette
Frieda Winter........... Genevieve Page
Fannie Prince.............. Eva Gabor
Irene Perry .... Mary Astor
Jason Prince.......... Lee Bowman
Quentin Judd..........Edward Andrews
Ferdie Lax .... Don Porter
Mrs. Sarah Hawke.....Mildred Dunnock
Paul Winter Sr............. Kent Smith
Scotty Hawke ....John Dehner
Georges Feydal.............John Emery
Ross Hodge.............. Mark Miller
Mr. Givney.............. Hayden Rorke
Mr. Leffer ...... Werner Klemperer
Jock Maas .... Barry Kroeger
Gus Adam................. Rusty Lane

Delmer Daves' "Youngblood Hawke" was made from Herman Wouk's big novel into a big picture, with more than a hint of soap opera, and should do spectacularly well at the boxoffice. Women particularly should go for episodic story about volcanic young author, his struggle for artistic integrity in materialistic world, his compulsive passion for a married woman, and his patient and good sweetheart who waits for him to come to his senses.

Could be argued that the Warner Bros. release could be shortened by 10% or more from its 2 hour, 17-minute length. It tends to show people and situations in black and white terms. An ever-present overtone of puritanism, which applies double standard to morals of male and female characters, also may annoy some.

But with the material at hand—only major change from book is that hero lives rather than dies at windup—cast and crew have come through with top performances. Producer-director-scripter Daves, who obviously must have lived the novel for many months, fashioned well the product he had, except for aforementioned lengthiness.

James Franciscus, as title character, Arthur Youngblood Hawke, comes through effectively even though he doesn't resemble Thomas Wolfe, late author said to be model for novel. Suzanne Pleshette hasn't much room to display talent in role of Hawke's editor who becomes his long-suffering sweetheart. Her portrayal is appealing, however.

Acting plaudits go to French thesp, Genevieve Page, as married society woman having affair with Hawke. She runs gamut of emotions from believable passion to complete degradation and despair. Less important parts are excellently played by Edward Andrews as that rare character, a sympathetic critic; Don Porter, as literary agent; Mildred Dunnock, Hawke's mother; Mary Astor as aging actress; Kent Smith, soon-undeceived husband of Miss Page; Werner Klemperer, repping Swiss financiers with whom Hawke becomes involved and who lead to his financial disaster.

Black and white camera work by Charles Lawton is outstanding in subtle capture of Hawke's rugged home country in Kentucky to excitement of New York. Art director Leo K. Kuter's sets, Hawke's attic lair especially, are well done. Score by Max Steiner is unobtrusive and editing by Sam O'Steen produces smoothly-integrated footage.
Hogg.

The Well
(El Pozo)
(MEXICAN)

San Francisco, Nov. 2.
Produced by Raul de Anda Jr.; directed by Raul de Anda Sr. Screenplay by Fernando Galiana and de Anda Sr.; camera, Ignacio Torres; composer, Raul Lavista. With Luis Aguilar and Sonia Furio. At San Francisco Film Fest. Running time, 105 MINS.
Jose Maria .... Luis Aguilar
Laura .... Sonia Furio
Manuel .... Dagoberto Rodriguez
Ana .... Sonia Infante
Dono Tencha ..... Hortensia Santoyena

(English Subtitles)

From Mexico comes this curiosity which shows what can happen when an element of one culture is taken over, undigested, by another.

Pic begins in the warm and folksy way with which Mexican filmmakers have scored so often. A widower and father of three is advised to seek a new wife, and the search has its appealing moments. The widower, Jose Maria (Luis Aguilar), finally chooses the prettiest prospect and is complimented for his good taste.

The girl, Laura (Sonia Furio), had always had her strange moments, but the marriage works in the beginning. Then comes the north-of-the-border element — the attempt to present a psychological thriller. Laura slips into insanity with a homicidal bent, and the film slips into overdone melodrama. It is more William Castle than Alfred Hitchcock, more Fannie Hurst than Tennessee Williams.

Pic is the sort which, if made in U.S. would play on a terror double bill aimed at the teen market. The Freudian implications of the attempted murder in the well, giving film its name, would intrigue the teeners a good half-hour after pic's end. *Sanf.*

The Calm
(RUSSIAN) (SCOPE)

Paris, Oct. 27.
Mosfilm production and release. With Vitali Koniaev, Gueorgui Martiniouk, Larissa Loujina, Vladimir Emelianov, Natalia Velitchko. Directed by Vadimir Bassov. Screenplay, Iouri Bondarev, Bassov from book by Bondarev; camera, Timofei Lebechev; music, V. Basner. At Palais De Chaillot, Paris, in Soviet Film Week. Running time, 150 MINS.
Serguei .... Vitali Koniaev
Constantin ....:.... Gueorgui Martiniouk
Nina .... Larissa Loujina
Assia .... Natalia Velitchko
Oouvarov .... Evgueni Lazarev
Sviridov............... Vsevolod Safonov

A stalwart young hero, a good Communist, is caught up in Stalinist machinations right after the last World War in this anti-Stalinist Russo pic that still shows care in allusions to the Party. Film points up the thaw in pix subject matter and treatment by the Russians in the last few years. Whether the disposing of Khrushchev will curtail more film outspokenness is yet to be seen.

This is technically solid with a nice feeling for the characters. It even treats a love affair with insight and modesty. Pic runs very long, and, perhaps, is too indigenous for much interest in the U.S. except for specialized showings on its theme. Sheared down a lot, it could fare better still.

As most Soviet heroes, this one is young, stalwart and pure if his morals do not deter him from becoming the lover of a separated married woman. He likes his spirited, innocent sister but holds a grudge against his father who took another woman during the war.

Then his father is arrested on some informer's charge and he is chucked out of the Party for not telling the ruling group about it. There are pros and cons during the voting for his ouster that take slams at the police tactics under Stalinism and its fanaticism. But this is countered by a final note claiming the Party is still omnipresent and the most important thing in a man's life even if it makes mistakes.

Perhaps this is a step forward in more personalized outlooks re human relations in a Russo pic as well as some self censure. But it lacks the needed robust handling and insight into character for more untoward Western chances. Acting is good but the heavies are painted too black.

One good, gray figure is a self taught worker in love with the hero's sister. Pic is another film dealing with more forthright Soviet problems during the recent arts thaw. *Mosk.*

Your Cheatin' Heart
(SONGS)

Musical bio of Hank Williams has great b.o. appeal for fans of late country singer-composer, but may be passed over by more sophisticated.

Hollywood, Oct. 26.
Metro release of Sam Katzman production. Stars George Hamilton, Susan Oliver, Red Buttons, Arthur O'Connell; features rest of cast. Directed by Gene Nelson. Screenplay, Stanford Whitmore; music, Fred Karger; editor, Ben Lewis. Reviewed at Academy Theatre, Oct. 23, '64. Running time, 100 MINS.
Hank Williams .... George Hamilton
Audrey Williams .... Susan Oliver
Shorty Younger .... Red Buttons
Fred Rose .... Arthur O'Connell
Ann Younger .... Shary Marshall
Teetot .... Rex Ingram
Sam Priddy .... Chris Crosby
Charley Bybee .... Rex Holman
Wilma, the Cashier .... Hortense Petra
Joe Rauch .... Roy Engel
Young Hank Williams .... Donald Losby
Boy Fishing .... Kevin Tate

The late "king" of country music, Hank Williams, still has enough fans to insure good boxoffice for "Your Cheatin' Heart." Four Leaf production based on his life. Producer Sam Katzman and director Gene Nelson have put together an entertaining, tuneful story that should attract other viewers, also.

George Hamilton resembles the singer-composer and the soundtrack voice of Hank Williams Jr. is close enough to his father's to add to audience satisfaction with the Metro release. Only highly sophisticated filmgoers, most of whom don't dig country music, are likely to bypass pic.

One of best scenes comes at opening, before titles, with Donald

Losby as 14-year-old Williams, orphan boy whose friend and protector, Rex Ingram, dies in poignant episode.

Story picks up on Hamilton and singer with medicine show and details his meeting with Susan Oliver (later to become his wife), Red Buttons and other members of itinerant band of struggling country musicians. Williams' singing and song-writing soon lead them to success in recordings, concerts and Grand Ole Opry.

After marriage of Williams and Miss Oliver, story takes off on important tangent that script—by Stanford Whitmore—fails to resolve satisfactorily. Williams obviously is unhappy with high-pressure life of rushing from concert halls to studios in rat race to cash in on popularity. At several points he accuses his wife of driving him beyond endurance, but nothing further is done to clear up problem. Each time Williams drinks to excess and misses engagements he is pictured as being in wrong. Of course, script was dealing with people still living and had to tread carefully.

Both Hamilton and Miss Oliver are appealing and as near life-sized in their portrayals as possible in this type story. Buttons and Arthur O'Connell are adequate in roles which have them as sympathetic co-workers and friends. Ingram and young Losby are particularly effective in opening scene, while small role of Kevin Tate as unnamed boy fishing on riverbank is excellent.

Score by Fred Karger keeps unobtrusive string arrangements of Williams' compositions constantly going in background. Nelson's direction seemed especially adept at tastefully portraying what could have been filmed too downbeat. But either Nelson or editor Ben Lewis is responsible for viewer confusion over passage of time. *Hogg.*

The Happy Sixties
(Los Felices 60)
(SPANISH—EASTMANCOLOR)

San Francisco, Oct. 30.
Tibidabo Films S.A. production, directed by Jaime Camino. Screenplay by Camino and Manuel Mira. Juan Gelpi, camera. At San Francisco Film Fest. Running time, 100 MINS.
Victor .... Jacques Doniol-Valcroze
Monica .... Yelena Samarina
Pep .... Daniel Martin
Pablo .... German Cobos
Virginia .... Eulalia Soldevila

(English Subtitles)

"The Happy Sixties" is a visually splendid film of the sort whose images will linger in the memory of the viewer long after he has left the theatre. Juan Gelpi's careful camera work stresses composition for strong visual impact, and director Jaime Camino's use of color then softens the images into exquisite works of art combining both strength and subtlety. First of all, Camino has chosen the picturesque resort area of Cadaques for location filming. He used Eastmancolor, and then insisted on laboratory color control to soften the effect. The result is less brilliant color than American films, but far richer (and for his film, more appropriate) than the pastels of which so many European filmmakers are so fond.

Dramatically the film is not so satisfying. Theme is a brief adul-

terous affair, born of boredom and highly superficial; but pic's observations are even more superficial. Obviously trying to avoid church condemnation, Camino avoids erotic scenes; but he also fails to indicate much motivation on any level, and shows very little of the thoughts or emotions involved as the affair is in progress. The build-up and the end are satisfactory, but the relationship itself is static and unexplored. Unfortunately, much of the middle of the film looks more like travelog than screen drama.

Still it is encouraging to see Camino, one of the young directors of the "new deal in Spanish cinema," taking the tentative steps toward adult filmmaking there.

As the bored young wife and mother, Yelena Samarina is a standout looker, slim and exceptionally photogenic. And she possesses a sort of natural elegance which conveys her well-to-do standing in the film. Married to Spanish painter Juan Manuel Lopez, she is a Russian-born emigrant now living in Spain; her voice is dubbed in the Spanish soundtrack.

Her lover is played by critic Jacques Doniol-Valcroze. He is pleasant, successful and temporarily drifting. These qualities he puts over well, and is given little else to do.

With proper ballyhoo, pic could do some art house biz, but will break no boxoffice records. *Sanf.*

There Was Once A Guy
(RUSSIAN)

Paris, Oct. 27.
Mosfilm release of Maxime Gorki Studio production. With Leonide Kouravlev, Lidia Alexandrova, Larissa Bourkova, Nina Sazonova. Written and directed by Vassili Choukchine. Camera, Valery Guinzbourg; music, Pavel Tchekalov. At Lord Byron, Paris, in Soviet Film Week. Running time, 99 MINS.
Pavel .... Leonide Kouravlev
Nastia .... Lidia Alexandrova
Katia .... Larissa Bourkova
Anissia .... Nina Sazonova
Marfa .... Anastasia Zouieva
Journalist .... Bella Akhmadoulina
Kondrat .... Boris Balakine

Simple comedy about a young truckdriver has a disarming feel for character and situation that keeps it from being banal. If not of the stature for arty chances abroad, it would rate specialized slotting on its entertaining values and unstinted look at class distinctions that seem to be springing up in Russia.

The hero is brash and forward with women and not interested in politics at all. He also harbors a resentment against the more involved people who seem to look down on his kind. They sometimes treat him as a sort of threat to their security and even a future revolutionary.

But all this is soft-peddled to a series of his adventures as he cannot score with a librarian, takes on airs he learns and manages to be matchmaker for an old friend.

Direction is easygoing, and gets the most from the comic interludes. It is sentimental without being too mawkish due to its spirited thesing and nice handling. If avoiding outright accusations, it also shows that the Party can be twitted and love looked at

with wit. But it is all in talk and not in the action. *Mosk.*

Apache Rifles
(DE LUXE COLOR)

Routine drama about U.S. Cavalry, Apaches and greedy whites. Acceptable for second spot.

Hollywood, Oct. 30.
20th-Fox release of Admiral Pictures Inc. production. Stars Audie Murphy. Features Michael Dante, Linda Lawson. Directed by William H. Witney. Screenplay, Charles B. Smith; camera, Arch R. Dalzell; editor, Grant Whytock. Reviewed at 20th-Fox Studio, Oct. 30, '64. Running time, 90 MINS.
Jeff Stanton .... Audie Murphy
Red Hawk .... Michael Dante
Dawn Gillis .... Linda Lawson
Mike Greer .... L. Q. Jones
Hodges .... Ken Lynch
Victorio .... Joseph A. Vitale
Sgt. Cobb .... Robert Brubaker

Grant Whytock's "Apache Rifles" is a low-budget U.S. Cavalry & Indians feature with a routine story, well enough made to bolster the bottom half of a twin bill. Audie Murphy as star might draw some fans and Arch R. Dalzell's scenic photography in De Luxe color will add to their enjoyment.

Otherwise, the 20th-Fox release differs from video Westerns only because it has slightly larger cast and some sub-plots.

Story concerns Murphy as commander of Arizona outpost and fierce fighter who at beginning hates Apaches. But through romance with Linda Lawson, part-Indian missionary, he comes to feel Apaches should be treated fairly and protected from greedy whites. His attempts to play fair are opposed by miners who seek gold on Apache territory and who manage to get him superseded by a more conventional officer, played by John Archer.

Climax sees Murphy at least partially vindicated and winning the girl, after a well-staged battle. One unusual scene, bordering on slapstick, has Murphy fighting white baddie in midst of hostile Indians. They cooperate in lying low every time warriors come near.

Murphy essentially portrays same tough, humorless but honorable character shown in his other pictures. Supporting cast is competent, with Robert Brubaker effective as Regular Army top sergeant.

Outside of camera work, production credits are not outstanding. No one is credited with score, but music seems typical for this type picture. Editing leaves no loose ends. *Hogg.*

Yesterday In Fact
(Naprawde Wczoraj)
(POLISH)

San Francisco, Oct. 30.
Film Polski production, directed by Jan Rybowski. Screenplay by Leopold Tyrmand; camera, Mieczyslaw Jahoda; composer, Gunther Schuller. At San Francisco Film Fest. Running time, 89 MINS.
Ewa .... Beata Tyszkiewicz
Editor .... Ewa Krzyzewska
Writer Nowak .... Andrzej Lapicki
Stolyp .... Gustaw Holoubek

(English Subtitles)

"Yesterday in Fact" looks like a dated film decked out in fancy modern dress, but it is actually a droll look both at human nature and at past and present film styles.

The impact of the work of Alain Resnais seems to be far-flung, and here Polish director Jan Rybkowski sees fit to use the complicated flashback technique and an ethereal place setting in the present, with sort of drifting semi-abstract people. But the flashbacks into the past remind one, not of Resnais, but of Francois Truffaut with his delight in twists on the films of earlier years.

Story concerns a successful writer on a promotion gambit at the height of his career, but he is in a state of crisis, unable to forget the girl he considers his ideal with whom he had a brief affair in the '40s. The flashbacks look exactly like a Bogart romance-suspense film of the era—up to a point.

Trenchcoat-clad, the writer (Andrzej Lapicki) is in a Polish coastal town, planning, partly for ideological reasons, to leave the country, but not without heading a smuggling plot to remove a priceless art treasure.

But he meets his nemesis, a beautiful blonde (Beata Tyszkiewicz) on a government mission to try to recover the same object, a triptych believed lost in the war. The whole thing reeks of the films of the late '40s. There is the seduction supper with the couple alone in an inn's dining room, geting high, turning out the lights, dancing to the radio, going upstairs, and the girl demurely saying goodnight and firmly shutting the door in the writer's face.

However, eventually he is invited into her room, and this is where the film departs from its antecedents. Instead of panning and out the window, the camera lingers to watch the proceedings. And what awkward encounters they are! Bodies and limbs getting in the way. Bothersome clothes and what to do about them. Both partners trying to take the initiative at once, or one or the other pouting or playing games.

The couple manages to have only one satisfying lovemaking experience, but it is enough to make our write-hero give up his plans of smuggling or departing. After taking the irreversible step of telling the local priest about the location of the triptych, he finds that the girl has gone.

Returning to the present, the writer meets the girl for the first time in many years at a banquet. The girl, matured and married, barely remembers the long ago incident, and the writer has recalled, re-examined and exorcised the affair which he had too ridiculously romanticized.

Done with a poker face, this is not outright comedy, yet it is not a "serious" film; rather, it is wry comment, remarkably well executed.

Pic contains a few anti-western digs, fairly well founded, and some astonishingly piercing self-critical thrusts.

As the blonde, Miss Tyszkiewicz is beguiling and always interesting, convincing in her portrayal of a woman both intelligent and sensuous, yet in the latter fickle and superficial. Lapicki, as the writer, could be a bit stronger, but turns in an at least adequate performance. Gustaw Holoubek plays a naval officer whose character is something of the other side of the coin of the writer's; his minor role is interesting and well handled. Other supporting players are less satisfactory.

Pic could play art houses here, but will require special handling, because its elements which seem most promotable can only lead to misinterpretation. *Sanf.*

Il Tempo S E Fermato
(Time Stood Still)
(ITALIAN-C'SCOPE)
Paris, Oct. 27.

J. Arthur Rank release of Prod. 22 Dicembre production. With Roberto Seveso, Natale Rossi, Paolo Quadrubbi. Written and directed by Ermanno Olmi. Camera, Carlo Belletto; editor, Giani Viola, Carla Colomba. At Studio De L'Etoile, Paris. Running time, **90 MINS.**
Natale .... Natale Rossi
Roberto .... Roberto Seveso
Salvetti .... Paolo Quadrubbi

Ermanno Olmi made two tender but unsentimental films that gained critical attention but did not do so well at the b.o. This pic promises to go the same route (after its belated release here), but still has the fine filmic qualities that could make for specialized handling for arty spots abroad.

Olmi made this for a big electric company in Milan and it wavers under documentary and patronal nomenclature. But the picture manages to be neither because of his unstinting interest in his two characters. Pic turns out to be an undidactic look at two generations of workmen starting to understand each other in the isolation of a dam site during winter.

There is an old man, who is set in his ways of winter watchman for a few months at the dam and until work starts up again. When his partner leaves, the regular replacement fails to arrive, a young student coming to the site.

Film then develops into a knowing if undramatic examination of the interest the two have in each other as well as their differences. The older man is set in his ways and the film watches his meticulous, ordered manner of doing chores, and somehow staves off monotony by Olmi's mature visual knowhow. He is interested in his people and that manages to keep them from being boring.

Film shows the student to be brash and fresh while the old man somewhat oldhat. But a storm brings them closer together as he takes care of the boy. That is all, but there is a poetic quality that keeps this film constantly engaging. It is also technically good with a plus in the colorful winter mountain scenery.

If not as finished or as incisive as the later "Sound of Trumpets" this pic has a sophisticated filmic aspect that denotes Olmi's definite talents. This lacks big dramatic effects, and this labels it a difficult commercial bet. *Mosk.*

Two in the Steppes
(RUSSIAN)
Paris, Oct. 27.

Mosfilm production and release. With Valery Babiatinski, Assou Nourekenov, Evguenia Presnikova. Directed by Anatoli Efros. Screenplay, Emmanuel Kararievitch based on his book; camera, Piotr Emelianov; music, Ter-Tatevossian. At Lord Byron, Paris, in Soviet Film Week. Running time, **81 MINS.**
Ogarkov .... Valery Babiatinski
Diourabaiev .... Assou Nourekenov
Maria .... Evguenia Presnikova

Another Russian war film with a more personal theme, and the fighting a backdrop, this film has enough brisk character insight and pace to make it a good cut above the ordinary. It still does not quite have the depth for top art possibilities abroad but could be an item of interest if well handled and sold.

Like "Ballad of a Solider," a 20-year-old solider gets caught up in a big military movement. He was supposed to deliver a message which he could not do. In the heat of reverses he is condemned to death when he comes back.

But German bombs kill the people who are supposed to execute him, and he is left with a guard. They go off together and get mixed up in many battles and skirmishes, with the guard finally killed. But the boy gives himself up only to be pardoned since all things have changed.

Film is directed with a good flair for incident and the confused, heroic backdrop of the war. The hero's devotion and refusal to escape is somehow not forced. He is just that way as is his silent but faithful guard.

Reminiscent of such Yank Westerns as "Last Train From Gun Hill" and "The Ride Back," about a gunman and law enforcer together on the way back to justice, this takes potshots at severe military law, and the sometimes too dogged Communist laws.

But the film does not try to delve too deeply into character and creates good, acceptable types, moves briskly and is engrossing if its denouement is too set. The director sometimes loses the thread at the beginning but does not falter once the two men are thrown together. Acting is excellent as are technical credits all down the line. *Mosk.*

Winnetou, Part II
(GERMAN-YUGO—C'SCOPE-COLOR)
Berlin, Oct. 27.

Constantin release of Rialto Film Pre-Ben Philipsen production, made in collab with Jadran Film and Atlantis-SCN. Stars Lex Barker, Pierre Brice and Anthony Steel. Directed by Dr. Harald Reinl. Screenplay, Harald G. Petersson, adapted from a novel by Karl May; camera, Ernst W. Kalinke; music, Martin Boettcher; settings, Vladimir Tadey; editing, Hermann Haller; general supervision, Horst Wendlandt. At Zoo Palast, Berlin. Running time, **104 MINS.**
Old Shatterhand .... Lex Barker
Winnetou .... Pierre Brice
Forrester .... Anthony Steel
Ribanna .... Karin Dor
Luke .... Klaus Kinski
Lieutenant Merril .... Mario Girotti
Colonel Merril .... Renato Baldini
Lord Castlepool .... Eddi Arent

Horst Wendlandt has done it again: Another big-scale Teutonic "western" made in Yugoslavia with an international cast headed by Lex Barker, Pierre Brice and (new to the German screen) Anthony Steel. It's the Berlin Rialto topper's third big filmization which he personally supervised. Since the "German Zane Grey" (Karl May) is still popular in German market, it looks as though this sequel to "Winnetou," budgeted at 4,000,000 D-Marks ($1,000,000) will collect a lot of coin in this country. Taking into account that "family type of features" are scarce everywhere, it can be granted certain foreign possibilities.

As often goes with pictures made in series, this is not as fresh as its predecessors. Also, characters, situations and complications have become a bit too familiar, a drawback for which the scriptor, Harald G. Petersson, must bear responsibility. Yet also "Winnetou, Part II" has its advantages.

Script employs the same central figures, Old Shatterhand, the heroic westerner of Teutonic origin, and Winnetou, the beautiful chieftain of the Apaches, portrayed by American Lex Barker and French Pierre Brice, respectively. Heavy (Anthony Steel) is trailed by his gang of sinister-looking evildoers. There is the conventional comic touch (Eddi Arent). Again there are the vicious pale faces who fuel up the Injun tribes for their own benefit. Again Old Shatterhand and Winnetou serve peace and justice.

If compared with "Treasure of Silver Lake" and "Winnetou, Part I," they counted more shooting and more dead bodies. But on the other hand, the love interest is more substantial in present release.

Barker and Brice turn in their usual performances. Anthony Steel comes along with the cliche study of a malicious adventurer, while Karin Dor, described (by May) as a girl as "beautiful as the dawn and as lovely as the rose in the mountains," enacts Ribanna. Miss Dor, wife of director Harald Reinl, is indubitably one of the prettiest women on the German screen. Remainder of cast includes Klaus Kinski, the insane type of hoodlum, Italians Mario Girotti, who takes Miss Dor to the altar, and Renato Baldini, an American colonel on the good guys' side.

Beautiful Yugoslav mountains substitute for the American western territory. Martin Boettcher has provided an appealing score. Quite good camerawork. Meanwhile, Horst Wendlandt is already shooting another ("Among Vultures") Karl May western, starring Stewart Grainger as Old Surehand, another May character. *Hans.*

Le Monde Sans Soleil
(World Without Sun)
(FRENCH-COLOR)
Paris, Oct. 27.

Columbia release of Requin Associes-Filmed-CEIAP-Arsay Films production. Directed by Jacques-Yves Cousteau. Camera (Eastmancolor), Pierre Goupil; editor, Georges Alepee; music, Serge Baudo. At the Publicis, Paris. Running time, **90 MINS.**

Underwater explorer and oceanographer Jacques-Yves Cousteau made a documentary about undersea explorations, "The World of Silence" that copped the grand prize at the Cannes Film Fest in 1956 and went on to fine art and playoff biz. This could easily repeat and maybe do better because it is a stronger pic than its predecessor.

Cousteau now seems to have unlimited means at his disposal and his work is concerned with charting oceans and perhaps showing a way that man can live in and exploit its resources. But all this is not didactic. The film actually is stunning visually and has an almost sci-fi aura, with the silvery frogmen uniforms, elaborate living conditions under the sea in bungalows. Then there is the flora and fauna of the Red Sea's continental undersea shelf where this absorbing documentary was made.

Commentary is succinct, lensing and color are topnotch. This is a constantly eye-filling spectacle. The men are shown living beneath the sea in prefabricated housing units. There are all the comforts. However, there is a change in personalities as the men get used to things and seem to lose contact with their earlier lives and do not talk much but seem at ease.

The forays to catch fish are always colorful as are the species involved. A descent to almost 1,000 feet in a two-man sub is also unique as the daily work of this unit. Sometimes the lurking shark is used for a dramatic flourish but, on the whole, this is fairly free from forced or hoked up fishy aspects.

Film looms as a good art bet, and possibly a playoff item abroad. There is also a knowing filmic feeling for mounting and editing that keeps it fluid and revealing without ever being pedantic.
Mosk.

Der Schut
(The Yellow Devil)
(GERMAN-YUGOSLAV-COLOR)
Berlin, Oct. 27.
Gloria release of CCC (Arthur Brauner) production, made in collaboration with Avala-Film, Belgrade. Stars Lex Barker, Marie Versini, Rik Battaglia. Directed by Robert Siodmak. Screenplay, Georg Marischka, after same-titled novel by Karl May; camera (Eastmancolor), Alexander Sekulovic; music, Martin Boettcher; editor, Ursula Kahlmaum. At Delphi Palast, West Berlin. Running time, 118 MINS.
Kara Ben Nemsi .... Lex Barker
Hadschi Halef Omar....... Ralf Wolter
Tschita .... Marie Versini
Annette .... Marianne Hold
Nirwan .... Rik Battaglia
Mubarek .... F. von Ledebur
Sir Lindsay .... Dieter Borsche
Archibald .... Chris Howland

Another large-scale German-Yugoslav Karl May filmization, again with Lex Barker as the Teutonic hero, this one has an Oriental background. There is no denying that Hollywood is doing such adventurous things much better. Yet there seems little doubt but that this one will collect a lot of coin in this country. Karl May, still much in vogue around here, is a powerful b.o. guarantee.

Robert Siodmak, the German American who returned from Hollywood several years ago, directed "Der Schut" with a twinkle in his eyes. Wisely enough, the adventurous plot is not taken too seriously. And there is a substantial

portion of comedy relief to balance with the suspense.

A dozen years ago, Siodmak made "The Crimson Pirate," an adventure yarn which combined suspense and comedy. This contains much the same ingredients, but the outcome is not too similar. Real flaw in this one is a rather superficial script. Although the experienced hand of the director is evident in many sequences, there is little imagination.

Nevertheless, the comedy is well taken care of. Ralf Wolter, as Hadschi Halef Omar, Lex Barker's faithful companion; Dieter Borsche, as Sir Lindsay, an Englishman, and Chris Howland, as the latter's stiff butler, provide many chuckles. The three are quite funny although their material doesn't exactly teem with fresh gags.

The simple yarn centers on Kara Ben Nemsi (Lex Barker), the tall and blond German adventurer, who's trying to track down "Der Schut," a villain in the disguise of a wealthy carpet dealer, who's been terrorizing the people of Monte Negro for quite some time. Of course, justice is meted out after the familiar complications, chases, fisticuffs and gunfights. Lineup of victims, unfortunately, includes the hero's wonder horse, Rih, who is to German Karl May fans nearly as popular as the author's star characters.

"Der Schut," incidentally, may be translated here into "Yellow Devil."

The beautiful Yugoslav rocky mountains supply the background for this adventure pic, certainly as asset. Martin Boettcher wrote the occasionally full-sounding score, another plus. *Hans.*

Roustabout
(SONGS-TECHNISCOPE-COLOR)

Elvis Presley name and co-billing of Barbara Stanwyck, plus musical production, should insure b.o. success. Script cliche-ridden.

Hollywood, Nov. 5.
Paramount release of Hal Wallis production. Stars Elvis Presley; features Barbara Stanwyck. Directed by John Rich. Screenplay, Anthony Lawrence, Allan Weiss; camera, (Technicolor), Lucien Ballard; editor, Warren Low; music, Joseph J. Lilley. Reviewed at Paramount Studio Nov. 4, '64. Running time, 101 MINS.
Charlie Rogers .... Elvis Presley
Maggie Morgan .... Barbara Stanwyck
Cathy Lean .... Joan Freeman
Joe Lean .... Leif Erickson
Mme. Mijanou .... Sue Ane Langdon
Harry Carver .... Pat Buttram
Marge .... Joan Staley
Arthur Nielsen............. Dabs Greer
Fred .... Steve Brodie
Sam .... Norman Grabowski
Lou .... Jack Albertson
Hazel .... Jane Dulo
Cody Marsh .... Joel Fluellen
Little Egypt .... Wilda Taylor

Elvis Presley-starrer, "Roustabout," is a gaudily-staged, tritely-scripted film looming as a box-office smash, based on lure of Presley name and co-billing of Barbara Stanwyck and expensive quality of the Technicolor. Techniscope frame provided for 11 Presley songs.

Composer-conductor Joseph J. Lilley's score and featured songs are best part of Hal Wallis pic, with Presley delivering latter in the pleasant, tuneful style he has developed. "I Never Had It So Good," "One Track Heart," and "Hard Knocks" all have hit possibilities. Production numbers staged by Earl Barton and vocal accompaniment by The Jordanaires, add to plus value of music.

Hoary script by Anthony Lawrence and Alan Weiss is loaded with cliches outdated in Tom Swift days. Presley, singer with tough exterior, becomes involved with carnival operated by Miss Stanwyck, who has Leif Erickson as grouchy, mean carny supervisor with lovely daughter, Joan Freeman. Erickson hates Presley when singer tries to woo daughter.

Cliches are too numerous to enumerate. Carny is failing financially because payments cannot be met on note held by bank. Presley's singing brings in customers and prosperity, but he deserts to another show after fight with Erickson and misunderstanding with Miss Freeman. Involved is lost wallet for which Presley is blamed, dark-haired vamp who pants after Presley, and ever-present phony spirit of carny camaraderie. Almost too inane to consider is showdown fight between Presley and Erickson, and musical finale with enemies and friends smiling happily.

Good cast tries its best to cope with nonsense, but it's losing battle. Miss Stanwyck's talents—she's had four Academy Award nominations in distinguished career—are totally wasted. Miss Freeman hasn't much to do except wring her hands when father and boyfriend get in fights, but does it prettily. Standouts in smaller roles are Pat Buttram as owner of rival carny and Steve Brodie, obnoxious customer in baseball-tossing game.

Direction by John Rich and editing of Warren Low both seem better than raw materials. Art directors Hal Pereira and Walter Tyler, set directors Sam Comer and Robert Benton, plus costumer Edith Head have provided colorful carnival settings. *Hogg.*

The Inheritance

Cinematic history of a union aims at commercial exhibition dates. Well-made documentary but major interest for members of garment industry and kindred spirits.

Amalgamated Clothing Workers of America and Harold Mayer Productions presentation. Produced and directed by Mayer. Narrated by Robert Ryan. Screenplay, Millard Lampell; editor, Lawrence Silk; camera, Edmund B. Gerard, Jesse Paley, Leonard Stark; sound, Al Gramaglia; music, composed and conducted by George Kleinsinger; song, "Pass It On," music, Kleinsinger, lyrics, Lampell. Background singers: Pete Seeger, Judy Collins, Tom Paxton, Page Gaynes, Barry Kornfeld, Millard Lampell, Carla Rotolo, John R. Winn. Reviewed in N.Y., Nov. 4, 1964. Running time, 60 MINS.

This documentary was planned originally as a cinematic history of the Amalgamated Clothing Workers of America but was broadened by producer-director Harold Mayer to depict the influx of workers into America since 1900, their problems and progress, and the resulting effects on both labor and management.

With this broader view, ACWA and Mayer have decided to try booking film into theatres on a commercial basis, first being local date at the Carnegie Hall Cinema which started Sunday (8). To date, no regular distribution deal has been made.

That it will have a limited appeal is assumed by ACWA but union figures it will interest most of labor groups in the U.S. particularly garment workers (whose activities dominate the film) and possibly naturalized and first-generation Americans. Beyond these groups "Inheritance" may attract documentary buffs as an excellent example in that field.

Mayer has combined old motion picture footage (some from newsreels, other from union's archives), old stills and photographs and some specially-filmed bridging shots. Narration by Robert Ryan is good but sporadic and actually has less importance than dubbed-in comments (with plenty of dialects) by types being depicted. Some soundtrack newsreel footage is also used when historical or political figures are shown. A group of folk singers add musical comment frequently throughout the film, with George Kleinsinger and Millard Lampell's "Pass It On" reprised several times. Gist of tune is that freedom has to be fought for by every new generation, it isn't to be taken for granted.

With ACWA's labor-political history, it is to be expected that Lampell's script is loaded, heavily, pro-unionism. Indeed, picture of management is never a pretty one (and no one speaks for its views). Only concessions are such begrudging capitulation remarks by such manufacturers as Hart, Schaffner & Marx. Film suggests that, after lengthy Chicago strike,

Shaffner only gave in to plea by Jane Addams.

Some of comments on society are considerably slanted, types being depicted as "blind" to mismanagement and exploitation of labor. The Vanderbilts are spotlighted as typical upper crust family. Time span ranges from 1901 influx of immigrants to the present with plenty of social and economic contrasts shown, as well as strikes and bloodshed, labor's perseverance and, particularly, selfmade benefits of the garment workers' union. It's a well-filmed and interesting glimpse of one side of the American labor struggle.

Short running time may relegate pic to second-half of bill even in art houses unless packaged with carefully selected short subject. All technical aspects of film are excellent. *Robe.*

Goodbye Charlie
(CINEMASCOPE-COLOR)

Novel idea but too far out for anything but mild reception. Must rely upon Curtis-Reynolds-Boone names.

Hollywood, Nov. 3.
Twentieth-Fox release of David Weisbart production. Stars Tony Curtis, Debbie Reynolds, Pat Boone. Features Joanna Barnes, Ellen McRae, Laura Devon. Directed by Vincente Minnelli. Screenplay, Harry Kurnitz, based on play by George Axelrod; camera (De'uxe Color), Milton Krasner; music, Andre Previn; editor, John W. Holmes; asst. director, David Hall. Reviewed at Academy Award Theatre, Nov. 2, '64. Running time, 117 MINS.
George .... Tony Curtis
Charlie .... Debbie Reynolds
Bruce .... Pat Boone
Janie .... Joanna Barnes
Franny .... Ellen McRae
Rusty ...., ... Laura Devon
Morton Craft .... Martin Gabel
Inspector .... Roger Carmel
Charlie Sorel .... Harry Madden
Starlet .... Myrna Hansen
Patron .... Michael Romanoff
Michael Jackson .... Himself
Butler .... Antony Eustrel
Guest on Yacht .... Donna Michelle
Sartori .... Walter Matthau

Even by delving into fantasy for its wildly implausible premise this picturization of George Axelrod's not-so-successful 1930 Broadway play doesn't come off as anything but the mildest type of entertainment. The basic idea—while novel and amusing as an idea—does not hold water in the development stage and what was calculated by producers as a kooky comedy reaches too far out for popular appreciation. Drawing voltage on its three stars, however—Tony Curtis, Debbie Reynolds and Pat Boone—may give film a good sendoff at boxoffice.

A joint effort of Curtis' indie Venice banner and 20th-Fox, story framework of the David Weisbart production takes form when a hotshot Hollywood-writer Lario named Charlie is thoroughly punctured by a gun-wielding Hungarian producer after catching him vis-a-vis with his wife, and writer is reincarnated as a luscious babe. The Harry Kurnitz screenplay carries a certain amount of laughs but the motivating idea apparently is beyond the scope of picture-making. Consequently every department, including cast, presses and humor is forced, to the detriment of audience reception.

Miss Reynolds takes on the task of creating an offbeat character as

the reincarnated late-departed who combines the lecherous mind and mores of her former male self with a sexy exterior and newfound femininity while announcing to the world she is the writer's widow. Curtis plays another writer, victim's best friend who arrives from his Paris home to deliver the eulogy and finds himself saddled not only with a debt-plagued estate, as executor, but his reborn pal as well, now a blonde who decides to cash in on former affairs with filmdon wives and plays cozy with the producer who shot Charlie.

Both make their work count as much as script will permit under Vincente Minnelli's direction, Debbie playing it wise and cool as she constantly shocks Curtis with her tactics. Biggest laughs come when femme seems oblivious of her charms as the late Charlie character shines through. Curtis lends the proper anxious note to the whole proceedings, while trying to work out the impossible aspects of the situation in which he finds both himself and his former friend. A surprise finale doesn't help matters much.

Boone is an over-rich boy with a mother complex who falls for Debbie and wants to marry her, while Walter Matthau puts goulash in the producer role. Joanna Barnes and Ellen McRae score nicely as two of Charlie's past girl friends, film wives, and Laura Devon is the producer's spouse responsible for bringing on the whole affair. Martin Gabel is in briefly as a Hollywood agent.

Minnelli's best touches are found in the yacht party where the shooting occurs, a form of prolog. Milton Krasner's color photography is excellent as are all the technical credits, including art direction by Jack Martin Smith and Richard Day, editing by John W. Holmes, music by Andre Previn. *Whit.*

An Evening With The Royal Ballet
(BRITISH-COLOR)

Terp addicts item. Four ballets danced by top interpreters. Probable market in selected art houses.

London, Nov. 3.
British Home Entertainment production. Produced and directed by Anthony Havelock-Allan. Stars Margot Fonteyn, Rudolf Nureyev, David Blair. Features Graham Usher, Antoinette Sibley, Merle Park. Codirector, Anthony Asquith; camera (Technicolor), Geoffrey Unsworth, Christopher Challis; editor, Richard Marden, James Clark. Previewed at Film & Arts Private Theatre, London, Oct. 12, '64. Running time, 85 MINS.

Ballet buffs will respond. Four ballets danced by Margot Fonteyn and Rudolf Nureyev. Released in advance of ultimate showing cinemas on tollvision in Britain. Directed with taste and affection by Anthony Havelock-Allan and Anthony Asquith, the film is well mounted and lensed and danced with great skill by Dame Margot, Nureyev, David Blair, Graham Usher, Antoinette Sibley and Merle Park.

The selected items, produced with the Royal Opera House's cooperation and photographed on

stage consist of Drigo's "Le Corsaire Ravel's "La Valse," Fokine's "Les Sylphides" by Chopin and Tschaikovsky's "Aurora's Wedding" from "The Sleeping Beauty." *Rich.*

Sweet Substitute
(CANADIAN)

Story of juvenile passions has an earthy quality that scores despite flaws in script and direction. Low budget independent production made in Vancouver.

Vancouver, Nov. 2.
Larry Kent production. Cast: Robert Howay, Carol Pastinsky, Angela Gann, Lannie Beckman, Robert Silverman, Bill Hartley, Mitzi Hurd and Virginia Dunsaith. Direction and screenplay by Larry Kent; camera, Richard Bellamy; editor, Sheila Reljac; music, Jack Dale; sound, Robin Spurgeon; graphics, Sonja Arentzson. Reviewed at University of B.C. Auditorium. Running time, 90 MINS.

"Sweet Substitute" is producerwriter-director Larry Kent's second feature film but is so superior to his first effort, "Bitter Ash," made a year ago, that it is hardly fair to draw comparisons. "Ash" gained a small measure of notoriety when shown to university audiences across Canada. It was actually a dull and tedious film, notable only for the fact that as a campus production brought in for a modest $5,000 outlay it was the first feature length film to be made in Vancouver and publicly exhibited.

Kent recouped his money on "Ash" and could have been excused for calling it quits at this point. But he went ahead with "Sweet Substitute" and has brought in what could be a distinct winner in its genre. Total production cost was about $10,000 and Kent will likely get this back from Canadian university showings he already has lined up. Film has been okayed by the B.C. film censor and if a distributor can be found to handle theatrical release in this country and the U.S. a healthy financial return should be realized.

Plot is simple, if cliched, and centres around a husky, teenage boy who can't concentrate on his studies because his mind is obsessed with sex. Although his frustrations get to the point of jeopardizing his college scholarship chances he is finally able to satisfy his driving adolescent biological urges with the nice but plain girl who has been helping him with his schoolwork. Pic ends on a sour note with the boy getting his scholarship but rejecting the helplessly pregnant girl in favor of engagement to a more sexy, socially-acceptable but less-accessible female. (Shades of "American Tragedy" by Dreiser!)

Character motivations as conceived by the author as not very convincing but script deficiencies are largely overcome by the enthusiastic way in which the non-professional cast has given life to the banal story line. Improvised dialogue, while sometimes lacking in wit, does have a natural quality to it.

Where the film scores heavily and comes off a winner is in the acting, editing and camera work.

Bob Howay gives his obsessed young male a sensitive reality that is completely believable. He gets wonderful support from Carol Pastinsky, a talented young actress as the plain Jane girl. Both these performances suggest them capable of handling better assignments.

Both photograph well and project. Angela Gann is excellent as the opportunist blonde sexpot and Lannie Beckman, Bob Silverman, Bill Hartley, Mitzi Hurd and Virginia Dunsaith handle their minor supporting roles creditably.

Film was shot entirely on location in Vancouver and Dick Bellamy's photography is professionally competent. His camera is artistically fluid and catches the mood of realism that the script often misses. Sheila Reljac, a seasoned film editor with Vancouver CBC-TV, has done a skillful job in integrating the visual and dramatic ingredients she was given to work with into a satisfying whole that is far greater than its individual parts. *Shaw.*

All Mixed Up
(Manji)
(JAPANESE-COLOR)

Unintended comic melodrama derived from lesbian relationship. Might be a gag success in special spots.

San Francisco, Oct. 26.
Daiei Motion Picture Co. Ltd. production, directed by Yasuzo Masumura, produced by Yonejiro Saito. Screenplay by Kanendo Shindo, based on a story by Jun'ichiro Tanizaki; camera, Setsuo Kobayashi; music, Tadashi Yamauchi. At San Francisco Film Fest. Running time, 90 MINS.
Mitsuko .... Ayako Wakao
Sonoko Kakiuchi .... Kyoko Kishida
Kotaro Kakiuchi .... Eiji Funakoshi
Eijiro Watanuki .... Yusuki Kawazu

From all the internal evidence of the film itself, it appears that "All Mixed Up" is an attempt at serious drama about several interrelationships affected by a lesbian affair. Too bad, because as a serious attempt, pic is to Western eyes, a failure—the crudest sort of soap opera. But if it is viewed as the slyest, most sophisticated sort of sex comedy, it is very funny indeed.

With all the intricacy of Moliere and more frankness than Henry Fielding, the pic not only follows relationship of a lawyer's dissatisfied wife with a beautiful girl in what are probably the most vivid screen presentations yet, it also deals with the girl's impotent lover, and the eventual involvement of the lawyer in the menage a quatre. There are also elements of blackmail, blood oaths, and numerous suicide pacts.

One of the reasons the film does not work as tragedy, or melodrama, is that even in their most miserable hours, all the characters are really enjoying themselves—and each other. Resultantly, an audience, even one with many Japanese-Americans, finds itself bursting into guffaws—not nervous giggles at bad filmmaking, but genuine laughs at funny situations which point up the absurd lengths to which people will let their emotions take them. That all this should be achieved by accident merely adds to the amusement.

As might be expected of a

Japanese film, the color photography by Setsuo Kobayashi is of the highest quality, including a few bits of the most exquisite, nonpornographic erotica.

Perhaps "All Mixed Up" should be released in this country as "an unintentional sex comedy," with emphasis on the lesbo angle. Art houses could clean up. It really is enjoyably funny. *Sanf.*

Gli Indifferenti
(A Time of Indifference)
(ITALO-FRENCH)

Rome, Nov. 3.
Interfilm release of a Lux-Ultra-Vide (Rome)-Lux Compagnie Cin. (Paris) coproduction. Stars Claudia Cardinale. Rod Steiger, Shelley Winters, Tomas Milian, Paulette Goddard. Directed by Francesco Maselli. Screenplay. Suso Cecchi D'Amico, based on novel by Alberto Moravia; camera, Gianni di Venanzo; music, Giovanni Fusco; editor, Ruggero Mastroianni. At Cinema Corso, Rome. Running time, 100 MINS.
Carla Ardengo........Claudia Cardinale
Lisa ....Shelley Winters
Mariagrazia Ardengo . Paulette Goddard
Leo Merumeci .... Rod Steiger
Michele Ardengo...........Tomas Milian

Director Francesco Maselli and scripter Suso Cecchi D'Amico have brought off a notable achievement in this film transcript of Alberto Moravia's first novel. It's not an easy morsel for the average patron, but a choice one for the discriminating who are willing to enter into its particular atmosphere and taste its refined subtleties and stylistic delights. Its name cast will help, of course. But there's a strictly downbeat, morbid and gloomy atmosphere to overcome, at least on a sales level. Hence, its chances appear spotty at best, despite its ranking as one of the noteworthy local achievements of the year.

Set in the late '20's, this tale of a family disintegrating in conformity, in taking the "easy" way out of things is topical now as well. Briefly, two youngsters in the family shown here try to break out of this web of indifference and rebel. But they are not conditioned, and eventually succumb to outside lures, as did their elders before them. Villain and only moving element in action is Leo Merumeci (Rod Steiger), once lover of Lisa (Shelley Winters), later of Mariagrazia (Paulette Goddard). And at film's end becomes the lover of the latter's daughter, Carla (Claudia Cardinale), while the son, Michele, becomes Lisa's lover after vainly trying to break out of the circle.

To top it all, Mariagrazia keeps running after a bored Leo even though he's successfully wrested ownership of house and home from her family. Everyone else, in the long run, hypocritically accepts the squalid situation out of personal convenience.

Not a pleasant tale, it's given a highly atmospheric reading by director Maselli, cameraman Gianni di Venanzo (mostly of the gloomy side), and by Giovanni Fusco's haunting score. D'Amico hews closely to Moravia's original in the feeling of her screenplay.

The playing is uniformly competent. Paulette Goddard probably walks off with honors as the aging mother still obsessed by her man and the maintenance of a status quo—at all costs. Her near-

finale scene, in which she suddenly and finally realizes part of the truth is shattering in its power. Rod Steiger is fine as the matter-of-fact heavy; Shelley Winters is good as the family stand-by; Tomas Milian is perfectly suited to the role of the once-idealistic youth whose ideals take a tumble. Claudia Cardinale, last but not least, gives a powerful subsurface portrayal of youth in torment.

All in all, this is strong stuff, handled adultly, drenched with atmosphere and abundant in closeups. It's a pic which grows on one, slowly but surely, and takes hold. But it takes patience.
Hawk.

John Goldfarb, Please Come Home
(CINEMASCOPE-COLOR)

Zany comedy that mostly doesn't come off. Shirley MacLaine name needed insurance.

Hollywood, Nov. 13.
Twentieth-Fox release of Steve Parker production. Stars Shirley MacLaine, Peter Ustinov, Richard Crenna. Features Wilfred-Hyde White, Jim Backus, Scott Brady, Fred Clark, Harry Morgan. Directed by J. Lee Thompson. Screenplay, William Peter Blatty; camera (DeLuxe Color), Leon Shamroy; editor, William B. Murphy; music, Johnny Williams; asst. director, John Flynn. Reviewed at Bruin Theatre, Westwood, Cal., Nov. 12, '64. Running time, 95 MINS.
Jenny ....Shirley MacLaine
Fawz ....l........ Peter Ustinov
John Goldfarb .... Richard Crenna
Whitepaper .... Jim Backus
Sakalakis .... Scott Brady
Overreach .... Fred Clark
Sarajevo .... Harry Morgan
Guz .... Wilfrid Hyde-White
Armud .... Patrick Adiarte
Maginot .... Richard Deacon
Brinkley .... Jerome Cowan
Samir .... Leon Askin
Cronkite .... David Lewis
Air Force General........Milton Frome
Editor .... Charles Lane
Pinkerton .... Jerry Orbach
Father Ryan .... Jackie Coogan
Specialty Dancers . Nai Bonet, Sultanna

The name of Shirley MacLaine is about the only ingredient to keep afloat this attempt at zany comedy that mostly doesn't come off. Designed as a fable lampooning U.S. international relations—in which a U-2 incident is dragged in and its hapless pilot landed in a mid-East kingdom where an oil-rich and sex-happy despot is grooming a football team to beat Notre Dame—the result doesn't live up to the potential offered by its premise. Film, though beautifully lensed in color and over-run with luscious harem babes, emerges pretty hit-and-miss fare. Final sequence of the nutty gridiron tussle in the middle of the desert, with oil wells suddenly spouting in the background, bundle laughs but these can't compensate for the long uninspired buildup.

Film, produced by Steve Parker and directed by J. Lee Thompson under their own banner for 20th release, takes its title from an ad placed by U.S. State Dept. in all Asian newspapers when the U-2 pilot, on a spying mission over Russia, is lost. The pilot, appropriately named "Wrong-Way" Goldfarb because of an uncanny proclivity (a former All-American halfback he ran 95 yards for a touchdown behind the wrong goal, and once took his team to Seattle when they were to play in Florida) has trouble with his automatic pilot, compasses go awry, and he's forced down in the kingdom of Fawzia, scene of all the goings-on.

Here he finds Miss MacLaine, an American mag photographer on an assignment to limn the sultan's harem and temporarily one of its most fetching inmates. Goldfarb, played by Richard Crenna, is given his choice of coaching King Fawz' team, comprised of dervishes, or being turned over to Russian as a spy. The William Peter Blatty script takes it from there as Shirley tries to elude the king's own amorous intentions for her and Crenna trying to save his neck.

Most amusing touches are the numerous sight gags as the king plays with his expensive toy train, continually barges about in a lux-

urious golf cart and a toy train carrying all sorts of small animals, etc. speeds through the various rooms. Constant switching back and forth from Fawzia and the Secretary of State in Washington slows down the action, but some of the thesping, always on a broad scale by such stalwarts as Harry Morgan, Fred Clark and Jim Backus, as State Dept. toppers, is good for occasional guffaws. The football game between the king's own and the Notre Dame squad, specially flown to Fawzia along with State Dept. officials, is a minor goofy classic.

Miss MacLaine, who earlier showed what little girls are made of in "What a Way to Go," nicely reprises via a flock of scanty harem garments and otherwise disports herself along comedic lines. Crenna makes the most of his wrong-way character. Reigning star of the picture, however, is Peter Ustinov as the sultan, who pulls out every plug in a more than broad performance. Wilfrid-Hyde White is smooth as the grand mufti and Scott Brady is the Notre Dame coach, who can't understand the State Dept's demand that his team lose the game.

Technical credits are well executed, including Leon Shamroy's fluid camera work, art direction by Jack Martin Smith and Dale Hennesy, Johnny Williams' music score. Jaye P. Morgan warbles title song cleffed by Don Wolf and Williams, over the credits.
Whit.

Father Goose
(COLOR)

Slick war comedy with names of Cary Grant and Leslie Caron to spark b.o. chances.

Hollywood, Nov. 12.
Universal release of Robert Arthur production. Stars Cary Grant, Leslie Caron; features Trevor Howard. Directed by Ralph Nelson. Screenplay, Peter Stone, Frank Tarloff, from novel by S. H. Barnett; camera (Technicolor), Charles Lang Jr.; editor, Ted J. Kent; music, Cy Coleman; asst. director, Tom Shaw. Reviewed at Academy Award Theatre, Nov. 10, '64. Running time 115 MINS.
Walter .... Cary Grant
Catherine................Leslie Caron
Houghton ....Trevor Howard
Stebbings .... Jack Good
Jenny .... Sharyl Locke
Anne .... Pip Sparke
Christine .... Verina Greenlaw
Elizabeth ....Stephanie Berrington
Harriet ....Jennifer Berrington
Angelique ....Laurelle Felsette
Dominique ....Nicole Felsette

Cary Grant comes up with an about-face change of character in this World War II comedy which at first may shock many of his more avid femme followers but provides the basis for some crackling good humor and a made-to-order plot unquestionably destined for handsome grosses at b.o. As a Japanese plane watcher on a deserted South Sea isle Grant plays an unshaven bum addicted to tippling and tattered attire, a long way from the suave figure he usually projects but affording him opportunity for nutty characterization. Leslie Caron and Trevor Howard are valuable assists to plottage which brings in a flock of refugee kids.

Under Ralph Nelson's shrewd helming the Peter Stone-Frank Tarloff screenplay takes amusing form as Grant, who plies the South Seas in his own cruiser at the beginning of the war, is pressed into service by Australian Navy Commander Howard to man a strategic watching station. Grant agrees only when an Aussie gunboat rams his launch, making it unusable. He is further disheartened when Howard secrets his liquid store on the island, with Howard revealing the whereabouts of the supply, bottle by bottle, only when the reluctant and complaining reports enemy planes, which then must be confirmed by watchers on other islands.

Into this harrassed existence, then, comes further harrassment when Grant crosses 40 miles of open sea in an eight-foot dinghy to rescue another watcher, but ends up with Miss Caron and seven young girls, marooned there when a pilot who was transporting them to safety from New Guinea was ordered to pick up survivors of a crashed bomber. Situation of Grant being unwillingly saddled with his femme flock cues the hilarity as Miss Caron, the height of primness until she becomes inebriated when she thinks she's dying of snake-bite, takes over.

Some of the gags are a bit shopworn but generally funny as Grant guns his character to the hilt. His romance with Miss Caron, too, ending in marriage by a chaplain over the radio, is a bit too sudden, after a single evening of her guzzling, but lends itself to the mood and spirit achieved in the overall unfoldment. Film has a fast climax as Grant puts out from the island in his repaired launch to draw the fire of a Japanese gunboat, and an American sub blasts the Nip craft out of the water.

Grant delivers with his customary aplomb, socking over his character in resounding fashion, and Miss Caron displays an aptitude for comedy. Howard, as the Aussie commander, spends most of his time at the radio talking with Grant, whose identifying code name is Mother Goose, a clever piece of acting in which patience to his civilian watcher's complaints is the dominating element. Jack Good gets a few laughs as his stuffy aide, and the seven young girls play their parts well.

Digby Wolfe's over-main-titles warbling of the song, "Pass Me By," cleffed by Coleman and Carolyn Leigh, is catchy, and technical credits are all on plus side. Deserving mentions are Charles Lang Jr.'s color photography, Ted J. Kent's editing, Alexander Golitzen-Henry Bumstead's art direction. Producer Robert Arthur coordinated his duties with sure showmanship. *Whit.*

Code 7, Victim 5
(BRITISH - TECHNISCOPE - TECHNICOLOR)

Poor man's James Bond has plenty of action but little wit and originality. Colorful South African background is asset. Should do well as second-biller.

A Columbia release of a Towers of London Films Ltd. (Harry Alan Towers) production. Directed by Robert Lynn. Stars Lex Barker, Ronald Fraser; features rest of cast. Screenplay, Peter Yeldham, based on orig story by Peter Welbeck: camera (Technicolor), Nicholas Roeg; editor, John Trumper; sound, Roy Taylor; music, composed and conducted, Johnny Douglas; asst. director, Roy Baird; second unit director, Egil S. Woxholt. Reviewed in N.Y., Nov. 5, 1964. Running time, **88 MINS.**

Steve Martin .... Lex Barker
Inspector Lean .... Ronald Fraser
Helga Swenson .... Ann Smyrner
Gina .... Veronique Vendell
Wexler .... Walter Rilla
Paul .... Dietmar Schoenherr
Anderson .... Percy Sieff
Kramer .... Gustel Gundelach

Still another "takeoff' on the successful James Bond films, this British-produced but South African-filmed variation has enough action and scenic beauty to enable it to do well in the thriller market. These assets aren't enough, however, to expect much more than routine success by today's more demanding standards.

Originally titled "Table Bay," a reference to its scenic Capetown background, producer Harry Alan Towers and director Robert Lynn have attempted to pad out a weak script with much emphasis on violence, sex and comedy. The photogenic backdrop, which includes sidetrips into a fantastic cavern, ostrich farms, big game country and beaucoup bathing beaches, is film's chief asset, helped by a good comedy performance by Ronald Fraser as a girl-happy police inspector.

Biggest drawback, besides Peter Yeldham's pulp mag script, is the casting of Lex Barker as an American private-eye, imported to trace a would-be assassin, intent on knocking off Walter Rilla, a South African millionaire. Barker may have been selected because of his European box-office pull (as result of his "Winnetou" westerns) but this won't mean anything in the U.S.

Females in the film, with exception of Ann Smyrner, who's excellent as Rilla's multi-talented secretary), are just scenery, even Veronique Vendell (one of the "bed girls" in "Becket"), featured as Rilla's oversexed step-daughter. Rilla, particularly, Dietmar Schoenharr and Gustel Gundelach are outstanding in major supporting roles.

As happens too often with acquired-films, credit sheets identify only characters who are to be publicized, making it impossible to point out lesser, but outstanding, work. A top South African actor, Gert Van Den Bergh, gets screen credit but is not identified in the printed credit sheet. Neither are Howard Davies and Sophia Spentzos.

There are only short glimpses of Negroes. All the villains are identified as German prisoners-of-war who didn't return home after WW II. There are no references to Afrikaans, apartheid or segregation. Except for the scenery, the story could be taking place anywhere.

Nicholas Roeg and Egil S. Woxholt's color camerawork is very complimentary to the country. Latter also supervised lengthen underwater sequence. Other technical credits are generally good. John Douglas' score is fast and jazzy and particularly appropriate to the stress on action. *Robe.*

Runaway
(NEW ZEALAND)

Auckland, Nov. 10.

Pacific Films (John O'Shea) production. Stars Colin Broadley, Deirdre McCarron, Nadja Regin, Tanya Binning; features Clyde Scott, Barry Crump, Selwyn Muru. Directed by John O'Shea. Screenplay by John Graham, O'Shea; camera, Anthony Williams. Reviewed at St. James Theatre Theatrette, Auckland. Running time, **102 MINS.**

Strength here is on the technical side, particularly the camerawork which is moody or sharp as the story requires. That is what distinguishes New Zealand's first locally-produced feature film in 12 years. What is lacking is a script. The story-line, an up-dated fable, is about a youth who leaves home in a huff and under a cloud. After a series of adventures on the road, he is last seen climbing to (presumably) his death on the rugged Southern Alps. As played by Colin Broadley the boy looks well in a sharp-boned, narrowed-eyed way and is not unsympathetic. But the script does not give him enough character depth to force audience involvement. The story is downbeat and, since nearly plotless as well, the final effect is vague.

Nadja Regin, an import from the Europe, registers in the role of a bad goodtime girl. Deirdre McCarron is composed as the girl who is picked up along the way. Small roles (some of which are inflated beyond their importance in the credit titles) are filled by Australian surf girl Tanya Binning, New Zealand author Barry Crump, who plays a character similar to himself, and Clyde Scott. A title song is sung with conviction by Rim D. Paul.

"Runaway" might have been better if producer-director John O'Shea, involved in this small-budgeter, had been able to resist some of the cliches that are associated with the arty film. There is the soaring camera bit, for instance, where the lovers go into their clinch and the screen fills with images of clouds and tree-tops. But on the plus side are the overall expert, camerawork by Anthony Williams, and the crisp editing most of the way. Film has generated considerable interest in this country, but it may require careful selling elsewhere where the fact that it's the first New Zealand feature pic in years will be less noteworthy *Dub.*

Rebels Against the Light

U.S. indie, made in Israel, tackles too many themes but blocks them out well. Its locale and okay treatment could slant this for specialized handling or some good playoff changes.

Paris, Nov. 10.

David Productions Ltd. release of Alexander Ramati production. Stars Diane Baker, David Opatoshu, Tom Bell, Paul Stassino, Didi Ramati; features Theodore Marcuse, Wolfe Barzell. Written and directed by Alexander Ramati from his own book; camera, Wolfgang Shushitsky; editor, Helga Cranston; music, Mel Keller with song by Naomi Shemer (sung by Soshana Damari). Previewed in Paris. Running time, **93 MINS.**

Susan .... Diane Baker
Daoud .... David Opatoshu
Dan .... Tom Bell
Salim .... Paul Stassino
Naima .... Didi Ramati
Nuri .... Theodore Marcuse
Ayub .... Wolfe Barzell

American writer, director and film scripter Alexander Ramati raised money by subscription to make this Yank indie entirely in Israel. It mixes a Biblical modern parable, a look at Jewish-Arab skirmishes in 1949, treating good and pacifistic Arabs as well as the terrorists and fighters, plus a tale of a Christian American girl on a pilgrimage to see the grave of her U.S. Jewish boyfriend who died during the Jewish-Arab skirmishes.

This is tightly plotted for what is essentially an action film, with some ideological handles. Result is that most of the story can not be handled in great depth. Pic moves along and has some colorful Israeli backgrounds and more insight into dealing with Arab actors than usually seen in either Israeli or foreign pix made there.

In 1949, a group of Arab terrorists still mine roads, harass Jewish outposts and also rob their own people, though they say it is their due, for needed guns, food and money. The terrorist leader of a small gang goes back to his own village for loot and kills the local policeman, thinking he's sold out to the Israelis. This then goes highly melodramatic, with the Jewish boy and American girl finally falling in love.

David Opatoshu has dignity as the old Arab, if he sometimes tends to theatrics because of the mixture of real and symbolical in his role. Diane Baker, as the girl and Tom Bell, as the boy, are fine in simplified parts. Didi Ramati is a touching Arab woman while Paul Stassino is acceptable as the fanatically, dedicated terrorist, the son.

This is technically good. Alexander Ramati has used colorful landscapes well and kept the mixture of stylization and reality clear and direct. Film has good specialized and some arty possibilities for the U.S., with playoff and dualer chances also inherent in its subject and treatment. *Mosk.*

Pajama Party
(PANAVISION-SONGS-COLOR)

Another American International musical aimed at youth market. Same profitable b.o. possibilities as past entries.

Hollywood, Nov. 5.

American International Pictures release of James H. Nicholson-Samuel Z. Arkoff production, coproduced by Anthony Carras. Stars Tommy Kirk, Annette Funicello, Elsa Lanchester, Harvey Lembeck, Jesse White, Jody McCrea, Ben Lessy, Donna Loren, Susan Hart, Bobbi Shaw, Candy Johnson. Features Buster Keaton, Dorothy Lamour. Directed by Don Weis. Screenplay, Louis M. Heyward; camera (Pathecolor), Floyd Crosby; music, Les Baxter; editors, Fred Feitshans, Eve Newman; asst. director, Clark Paylow. Reviewed at Directors' Guild Theatre, Nov. 4, '64. Running time, **82 MINS.**

Go-Go .... Tommy Kirk
Connie .... Annette Funicello
Aunt Wendy .... Elsa Lanchester
Eric Von Zipper .... Harvey Lembeck
J. Sinister Hulk .... Jesse White
Big Lunk .... Jody McCrea
Fleegle .... Ben Lessy
Vikki .... Donna Loren
Jilda .... Susan Hart
Helga .... Bobbi Shaw
Francine .... Cheryl Sweeten
Perfume Girl .... Luree Holmes
Candy .... Candy Johnson
Chief Rotten Eagle .... Buster Keaton
Head Saleslady ..... Dorothy Lamour
The Nooney Rickett 4 .... Themselves
Rat Pack . Andy Romano, Linda Rogers, Allen Fife, Alberta Nelson, Jerry Brutsche, Bob Harvey.
Maid .... Renie Riano
Toyless Model .... Joi Holmes
Little Boy .... Kerry Kollmar

Pajama Girls: Joan Neel, Patricia O'Reilly, Marion Kildany, Linda Opie, Mary Hughes, Patti Chandler, Laura Nicholson, Linda Benson, Carey Foster, Stacey Maxwell, Teri Hope, Margo Mehling, Diane Bond, Keva Page, Tom Basil, Kay Sutton, Connie Ducharme, Joyce Nizzari, Leslie Wenner.

Pajama Boys: Ray Atkinson, Frank

Alesia, Ned Wynn, Ronnie Rondell, Howard Curtis, Johnny Fain, Mike Nader, Rick Newton, Guy Hemric, Ed Garner, Frank Mortiforte, Ronnie David, Gus Trikonis, Bob Pane, Roger Bacon, Ronnie Dayton.

Past profitable showings of films turned out specifically for the youth market has cued American International to enter a fifth for this trade. Latest effusion evidences no wavering of expected returns and meets the demands of the specialized field, filled with names known to younger audiences and the type of goings-on that spells moola at the boxoffice. For adults, color feature can be passed up with no sense of loss (oldsters may become as confused as some of the characters). Young 'uns should turn in a gross comparable to film's predecessors—"Operation Bikini," "Beach Party," "Muscle Beach Party," "Bikini Beach."

As before there's strong accent on pulchritude and near-nudity via brief attire. Exuberance of youth guns the action which twirls around a personable young Martian—Tommy Kirk—arriving on earth to pave the way for an invasion. He lands during a swimming party tossed by an eccentric wealthy widow, Elsa Lanchester, and immediately falls for Annette Funicello, girl-friend of widow's lug nephew, Jody McCrea.

Action in the Louis M. Heyward script, which makes no effort to keep the narrative either taut or logical, includes two con men trying to rob widow of a large hoard of money hidden in the house, a leather- jacket gang set on causing trouble and finally the pajama party itself, certainly no relation to the kind Mother knew. Interspersed are seven songs mostly sung by Miss Funicello and Kirk, either dueting or solo, to lend musical flavor.

Miss Funicello, who appeared in last three of these pix, displays an engaging presence and registers solidly. Kirk likewise shows class and Miss Lanchester projects a rather zany character nicely. McCrea, a veteran in entire program, hams it up the way he should for such a part. Harvey Lembeck as the gang leader, Jesse White and Ben Lessy as the con men sock over their roles, as do Buster Keaton, playing an Indian, and Dorothy Lamour, dress store manager, in guestar renditions. Miss Lamour also warbles a single number effectively.

Bobbi Shaw as a non-English-speaking Swede but who knows all the holds is a standout as the sexy lure White uses to learn where the money is secreted, and Donna Loren, Susan Hart and Candy Johnson romp through for further distaff interest. Don Weis directs with a sure hand, Floyd Crosby's color photography is interesting and other technical credits likewise stack up. Guy Hemric and Jerry Styner are responsible for song numbers. Anthony Carras is listed as co-producer under James H. Nicholson and Samuel Z. Arkoff's top credit. *Whit.*

The T-A-M-I Show
(Electronovision)

Second Electronovision film can hardly miss with young rock 'n' roll addicts. Technically superior to "Hamlet," surefire teenage market appeal at lower ticket price.

An Electronovision production and presentation. Executive producer, William Sargent Jr. Producer, Lee Savin. Director, Steve Binder. With The Beach Boys, The Barbarians, Chuck Berry, James Brown and the Flames, Marvin Gaye, Gerry and the Pacemakers, Lesley Gore, Jan & Dean, Billy J. Kramer and The Dakotas, Smokey Robinson and The Miracles, The Supremes, The Rolling Stones. Choreography, David Winters; camera, Jim Kilgore; video engineer, Carl Hanseman; audio engineer, Lionel St. Peter; musical direction, Jack Nitsche. Reviewed at N.Y., Nov. 11, 1964. Running time, **113 MINS.**

This, the second Electronovision production, was filmed on Oct. 29 at Santa Monica Civic Auditorium before an invited audience of 5,000 teenagers. If national paid reception is even close to that the on-film cuffo audience gives the artists, this could be one of the biggest grossers of the year, despite its twelfth-month release.

Produced by Lee Savin and Electrovision president William Sargent Jr., the film, which is, en toto, a rock 'n' roll concert perpetuated by the camera, is almost certain to prove popular with the audience for which it was made the nation's biggest group of filmgoers, if we believe statistical reports.

Technically, "The T-A-M-I Show" (screen credits title as "Teenage Command Performance" but tie-in with Teenage Awards Music International will almost certainly keep the T-A-M-I tag on this first effort) is a better-filmed, better-paced production than was the Richard Burton "Hamlet." Sargent claims that this one even used less lighting than the Broadway theatre-filmed Shakespearean work but difference is in better placing and equalization of lighting power.

Director Steve Binder, who must also receive credit for the excellent editing as Electronovision is a cut-as-you-go process, has captured on film, possibly for the first time with authenticity, the teenage environment that fosters, maintains and passes judgement on the phenomenon that the young of the world call entertainment but which the adult world calls everything from mass hysteria to delayed maturity. Shooting the film before a live audience was inspired as the artists throw away all inhibitions at the slightest encouragement from their entranced viewers (who are brought on camera frequently). Indeed, psychiatrists might be wise to study this (and the considerable other footage which has been edited out) for a view of the teenagers making up the audience for some insight into what makes that generation tick.

Although presented as a concert, the program has been taken out of the static, confined feeling of most filmed stage presentations by the use of wide variety of camera angles, fast cutting, and visual effects that resemble dissolves and iris shots. Closeups are used frequently and usually to underscore the visual impact of a particular performer on the audience, whether it's flattering to the artist or not. Longer shots, used when the act consists of a larger group, are interspersed with closeups of particular members.

Show is emceed by Jan and Dean, young California males whose wild sense of comedy is perfect for this added chore. Besides the introductions, they also contribute several songs in their surfing style. All acts are backed by dance groups which vary in size according to the artists they're supporting. David Winters' choreography has added considerably to the show's solid punch. His wild and abandoned terpsichore, like most of the dances, of course, complement the musical styles of the singers.

For the adult ear, there's little or no variation in the song numbers presented. The beat never changes, whether it's old timer Chuck Berry or lovely Lesley Gore. After a while they all sound as though they're singing the same song. One major drawback of having a live audience is that the soundtrack is one continuous scream from beginning to end. The only variation is in decibels, going from very loud to just short of pandemonium.

Biggest impact is made by James Brown and the Flames. For a moment, something that sounds like a tortured "Prisoner of Love" comes through but winds with Brown, who makes Johnny Ray sound like the Good Humor Man, on the floor, writhing, moaning and making like the last stages of the d.t.'s. It's a bravura performance.

Also doing their bit are Gerry and the Pacemakers, The Miracles, Marvin Gaye, Lesley Gore, the Beach Boys (one of the best acts, particularly their delightful "Little Old Lady From Pasadena"), Billy J. Kramer and the Dakotas, the Supremes (three young sepia songstresses with real class), the Barbarians, the Rolling Stones and, for a finale, the entire group, sending the audience home in a state of shock. Although running time could be easily pared if faster runoff is needed, there's little need for it with present booking setup.

Exhibitors will be watching results of Saturday's Los Angeles saturation showing for possible forecast on regular engagement's business. *Robe.*

Allez France
(Go France)
(FRENCH-COLOR)

Paris, Nov. 10.

Prodis release of Film D'Art-Films Arthur Lesser-CICC production. Stars Robert Dhery, Colette Brosset; features Pierre Olaf, Robert Rollis, Diana Dors, Henri Genes, Catherine Sola. Directed by Dhery. Screenplay, Dhery, Pierre Tcherina; camera (Eastmancolor), Jean Tournier; editor, Albert Jurgenson. At Colisee, Paris. Running time, **92 MINS.**

Henri	Robert Dhery
Yvette	Colette Brosset
Sergeants	Robert Rollis
Diana Dors	Herself
Agent	Pierre Olaf
Sister	Catherine Sola
Friend	Henri Genes

Robert Dhery has concocted a neat comedy about the adventures of a group of French football fans in London for a game. Idea gags and execution are blocked out with precision, timing and finesse. If there are plenty of laughs, there is also a tendency to lack a more visual inventive turn which telegraphs many aspects.

It thus is sans that comedic fillip to give it a greater yock value. Yet, this has fine color lensing, snappy editing and good ensemble playing. It appears that Dhery, who got his start on the stage via such comedy revues as "La Plume De Ma Tante," which scored in the U. S., still thinks a little too much in these terms.

Film gets moving nicely at the soccer ball game. Dhery, to be married in two days, has sneaked over with some fellow fans for a last fling. A zealous fan knocks out his two front teeth and he has to go to a dentist. There he winds up trying on a policeman's coat and helmet.

A holdup of British pic star Diana Dors, next door, has him unwittingly disarming the man and then becoming a hero. He escapes and pic is then concerned with him on the lam, intermittently running into his drunken busload of pals, the pursuing police who want only to praise him and sundry mishaps and gags.

Repeated gags are all knowingly worked in but do not gain when they are repeated too much. On stage this has more overtones but not always as the desired point in a film.

And there is a tendency to use too much explaining and logic which sometimes kill a good gag.

If there is not much bite, there is a consistently gentle and amusing level in the pic that rarely lets down. Dhery, who hardly says a word, is always beguiling. Colette Brosset is fine as a brassy ex-hoofer, now a lady, who gets entangled in all sort of scraps trying to trap her brother-in-law-to-be. Others are all fine. Diana Dors plays the sexpot symbol well. Color is good and production dress excellent.

With dialog mostly in English, this is tailormade for British and Yank playoffs, with specialized spotting also indicated on its generally diverting aspects. It has a good mixture of French extended logic and English homey comic literalness that keep it refreshing throughout. Dhery now books like he is on the right film track for his brand of comedy.

This should go big on the Continent with Yank chances also good if well placed and sold. Its generally entertaining qualities should help it through most situations. *Mosk.*

Patate
(FRENCH-DYALISCOPE)

Paris, Nov. 10.

20th-Fox release of Belstar-Films Du Siecle-Ultra Films-Andre Hakim production. Stars Jean Marais, Danielle Darrieux, Pierre Dux, Anne Vernon, Sylvie Vertan; features Mike Marshall, Francois Charet. Directed and written by Robert Thomas from play by Marcel Achard; camera, Robert Le Febvre; editor, Henri Taverna. At Balzac, Paris. Running time, **90 MINS.**

Noel	Jean Marais
Patate	Pierre Dux
Wife	Danielle Darrieux
Mrs. Carradine	Anne Vernon
Alexa	Sylvie Vartan

The Marcel Achard play, "Patate," was a smash here (ran for six years), but a flop on Broadway. Pic version may repeat with local possibilities also not as great as its theatrical potential. A bitter, would-be inventor still has a beauteous wife with a good job, a sprightly daughter and hopes of finally making his inventions (toys of all kinds) pay off. He decides to ask a school chum, a man he hates and who labeled him Patate, meaning in Yank slang something like nitwit, to lend him some money.

This handsome successful man, married to a rich woman, is secretly having an affair with Patate's daughter. He decides to lend him money only to change his mind. Patate finds out about the liaison and decides to have his revenge. Then he relents. The daughter gets over her first love and looks headed for a rich marriage.

All this has been directed with a singular lack of visual knowhow or the right balance of comedy, irony and a skepticism to make this fairly petty rather than biting. However, the actors go their own way and manage to come off acceptably. Rock singer Sylvie Vartan is pert if gauche as the daughter. Pierre Dux is the abominable Patate with some inkling of charm. The others do okay in lesser roles if Jean Marais is miscast as the aging Don-Juanish friend.

It is technically par, with good production dress. Art chances in the U.S. appear chancey, with playoff there on its theme if not on the treatment. *Mosk.*

Akai Satsui
(Unholy Desire)
(JAPANESE)

Toho release of a Nikkatsu Corp. (Masayuki Takagi) production. Directed by Shohei Imamura. Features Masumi Harukawa, Akira Nishimura, Shigeru Tsuyuguchi, Ikuko Kusonoki, Haruo Itoga. Screenplay, Keiji Hasebe and Imamura from original story by Shinji Fujiwara; camera, Masahisa Himeda; music, Toshiro Mayuzumi. Reviewed at N.Y., Nov. 12, 1964. Running time, 150 MINS.

(English Subtitles)

Following up on boxoffice interest in his "Insect Woman," Nikkatsu Films has rushed along director Shohei Imamura's "Unholy Desire," which is the same mixture as before—cinematic erotica. Although U.S. title given the film, which opened Tuesday (17) at the Toho Cinema, is not a literal translation, or even close, it is apt and has exploitation value.

While technically excellent and evidencing great skill in such secondary aspects as depicting a slice of contemporary Japanese life, the emphasis on sex, natural and otherwise, is so great that repetition eventually dulls the viewer's ability to accept what he sees.

Major faults are Imamura's insistence on exaggerating the emotional experiences of his cast by holding scenes interminably, commenting at great length on the sensual natures of all concernec and bypassing chances to show more of contemporary life in Japan.

Principal characters are Sadako, a dull but attractive wife; Koichi, her condescending, ambitious husband; Hiraoka, an itinerant musician with a bad heart, who rapes the wife; and Yoshiko, the husband's mistress. After the original rape scene, when Hiraoka breaks into the house in search of money to buy medicine, he discovers that the wife is too afraid to tell the husband, returns and rapes her again but falls in love with her. He tries to get her to run away with him. The wife, having become pregnant, tries to buy off the rapist but finds herself becoming emotionally involved. Yoshio, her husband's mistress, trying to get evidence on the pair to show the husband, gets killed. The rapist dies of a heart attack, the wife returns home and, presumably, takes up a duller but more tranquil life.

Obsession with sex appears to be a growing effort on the part of **Japanese filmmakers to come up with something that will have commercial appeal in the U.S. market. More and more Japanese films contain extended sex sequences. Occasionally, these are necessary to the story. Usually, however, and this is such an instance, they're used purely for sexploitation.**

After repeated sessions of heavy breathing, struggles, rape, adultery, heart attacks and tubercular coughing spells, the viewer may begin to wonder if he will make it through the film himself. Mood-establishing shots are held to the point of boredom. Imamura and cameraman Masahisa Himeda try for frequent offbeat camera effects. Some are excellent, others only appear distorted.

Something new has been added to the Japanese sex film. Never a nation that cared for kissing, they've now taken it up with the passion of a child with a new toy, and make up with ferociousness what they lack in finesse. Imamura's fondness for symbolism has frequent outlets. The train is a recurring image, as a plot necessity and also to convey the sex act; caged white mice symbolize the limited world of the wife. Quickly established as a latent sensualist, she finds escape at first in laziness and gorging. She is slow-witted and self-indulgent, a woman who can never find, in her own mind, any explanation for the blow life has dealt her. Imamura conveys this to the viewer by flashbacks which are frequently confusing as she doesn't change appearance sufficiently in the time periods elapsed.

Entire cast is good within the limitations of their roles with Masumi Harkukawa particularly outstanding as the wife and an unidentified actress as her mother-in-law. Technical credits, other than an evident need for considerable editing, are first rate. Running time of film will also work against its exploitation in situations where the eroticism can be used as the principle selling point. *Robe.*

Das Hab' Ich Von Papa Gelernt
(I Learned It From Father)
(AUSTRIAN)

Vienna, Nov. 10.

Bavaria (Vienna) release of Vienna Stadthalle-Berolina production. Directed by Axel von Ambesser. Stars Willy Fritsch, Thomas Fritsch; features, Peter Vogel, Gertraud Jesserer, Paul Hoerbiger. Screenplay, Kurt Nachmann; camera, Hans Matula; music, Johannes Fehring. At Maria Theresia Kino, Vienna., Running time, 90 MINS.

Clemens Andermann	Willy Fritsch
Andreas, his son	Thomas Fritsch
Oskar Werner Vischer	Peter Vogel
Monika Holl	Gertraud Jesserer
Koewe, theatre director	Gustav Knuth
Knackert	Paul Hoerbiger
Christa Seebald	Marianne Chapula
Ebba Pedersen	Barbara Stanyk
Sebastian Delt	Franz Stoss
Neumann	Ljuba Welitsch
Joachim Lange	Peter Matic
Benno Sax	Fritz Muliar

The fact that this Austrian picture is a fraction better than the average 1964 film does not recommend it, however, for abroad. Kurt Nachmann, who scripted this, concocted a clever idea about father-son problems in our times. Director Axel von Ambesser responded by hiring father Willy Fritsch and son, Thomas.

The plot has a father as a Romeo and his son as a would-be-Romeo flop in business but successful in theatrical life, including motion pictures. It is a highly entertaining story. Gertrud Jesserer, a looker, is in the cast. Peter Vogel and Paul Hoerbiger stand out in the other leading roles.

Direction by Axel von Ambesser might have been better with fewer gags, these being strung too closely together. Cameraman Hans Matula also has done some original work. Johannes Fehring arranged the music, the theme melody being catchy. All technical credits are okay. *Maas.*

Svenska Bilder
(Swedish Portraits)
(SWEDISH)

Stockholm, Nov. 10.

Svensk Filmindustri production and release. Stars Monica Zetterlund, Birgitta Andersson, Hans Alfredson, Lars Ekborg, Georg Rydeberg, Siv Ericks; features Lissi Alandh, Sif Ruud, Ernst Hugo Jaregard, Gosta Ekman, Mille Schmidt, Margit Andelius, Julie Bernby, Stig Johansson, John Norrman, Julia Caesar, Sonya Hedenbratt, Tage Danielsson, Monica Nielsen, Martin Ljung. Directed by Tage Danielsson. Screenplay, Danielsson & Hans Alfredson; camera, Martin Bodin; music, Bengt-Arne Wallin. At the China, Stockholm. Running time, 106 MINS.

Mejram	Monica Zetterlund
Cikoria	Birgitta Andersson
Timjan	Hans Alfredsson
Bjorkman	Lars Ekborg
J. P. Hansson	Georg Rydeberg
Miss Larsson	Siv Ericks
Salvia	Lissi Alandh
Miss Fridlund	Sif Ruud
Karlman	Ernst Hugo Jargard
Bengtsson	Gosta Ekman
Detective	Mille Schmidt
Miss Pepping	Julie Bernby
Dad	Stig Johansson
Uncle	John Norrman
Great Grandfather	Julia Caesar
Mrs. Holm	Sonya Hedenbratt
A Cousin	Tage Danielsson
Sister Marta	Monica Nielsen
Drum-major	Martin Ljung

This is not the first Swedish attempt to make a satirical comedy about the human nature in general and Swedes in particular. But it is the first time that the result has been something of a masterpiece. One could say it is a Swedish "Hellzapoppin'" but at same time it might be wrong to compare it with that Universal production of 1941. The story is so different as is treatment of the material.

The whole thing involves the human fear of loneliness. Men hunt women, women hunt men, and it is during their hunting each other that they run sometimes into big dramatic situations or into somehing very funny, as in this picture. It is difficult to pick out any particular sequence, but there is a love scene that should have a chance of going into film history.

The cast is huge while the Direction by Tage Danielsson is tops.

Screenplay by Danielsson and Hans Alfredsson represents the new school in Swedish entertainment. These two formed their own company, called Svenska Ord (Swedish Words, Inc.). Later, they turned to the record business with a record label, Svenska Ljud (Swedish Sounds). Now they have entered motion pictures with Svenska Bilder (Swedish Pictures or Portraits). Their credits include a 90-minute show at the Berns Restaurant.

To mention one particular person in the cast above others is difficult. Many of them appears only in short sequences, others are seen throughout the film. Monica Zetterlund, jazz singer who has been touring the U. S., is seen here in a dramatic role. Birgitta Anderson, another widely known name from comedies, notches another victory in her career. In fact, there are many in this film in this category.

Film moves at top speed from the first to the last scene. When it is time to vote the best Swedish films of 1964, it will be difficult not to list "Svenska Bilder" among the top productions. *Winq.*

Those Calloways
(COLOR)

Latest Disney film, plotted around a Vermont backwoodsman trying to save wild geese from extinction, carries strong general appeal. Particularly interesting camera work limning wild life.

Hollywood, Nov. 10.

Buena Vista release of Walt Disney production, co-produced by Winston Hibler Stars Brian Keith, Vara Miles, Brandon de Wilde, Walter Brennan, Ed Wynn; features rest of cast. Directed by Norman Tokar. Screenplay, Louis Pelletier, based on book, "Swiftwater," by Paul Annixter; camera (Technicolor), Edward Colman; music, Max Steiner; editor, Grant K. Smith; asst. director, Tom Leetch. Reviewed at Academy Award Theatre, Nov. 9, '64. Running time, 132 MINS.

Cam Calloway	Brian Keith
Liddy Calloway	Vera Miles
Bucky Calloway	Brandon de Wilde
Alf Simes	Walter Brennan
Ed Parker	Ed Wynn
Bridie Mellot	Linda Evans
Dell Fraser	Philip Abbott
Jim Mellot	John Larkin
Doane Shattuck	Parley Baer
Nigosh	Frank de Kova
E. J. Fletcher	Roy Roberts
Ernie Evans	John Qualen
Whit Turner	Tom Skerritt
Charley Evans	Paul Hartman
Nat Perkins	Russell Collins
Ollie Gibbons	John Davis Chandler
Phil Petrie	Chet Stratton
Sarah Mellot	Renee Godfrey

Walt Disney has another winner in this warm tale of an idealistic Vermont backwoodsman and his family who put up everything they own to provide a sanctuary for the great flocks of wild geese that cross their sky every year. Film provides excitement, humor and drama of the sort producer specializes in, and he blends his forte of expertly-photographed wild life with a story which exerts strong general appeal.

Impressively lensed in color which catches the natural beauty of the actual Vermont wilderness both in the rich tones of Autumn and the mid-Winter snows, feature is realistically enacted by a cast headed by Brian Keith, Vera Miles and Brandon de Wilde, who compose the family. Disney and his co-producer, Winston Hibler, have peopled narrative with interesting smalltown New England characters, and Norman Tokar's deft direction points up the best features and possibilities of Louis Pelletier's nature book. Unfoldment, well-paced, is almost a saga of a man with a mission, fighting the odds of greed and indifference, but whose efforts finally pay off after he has nearly lost his life.

One of the most suspenseful sequences is the fight to the death with a wolverine after it has been wounded and takes refuge in a huge log jam, furnishing all the thrills of hand-to-hand combat as the vicious beast attacks de Wilde. A friendly hound trying to catch an otter in the deep snow is good for laughs, and interesting shots of wild geese in flight, both in formation and in solo closeup, lend certain enchantment, filmed by Dick Borden. Edward Colman's overall photography is a topflight achievement.

Keith makes a convincing forest man, raised among the Indians and now dedicated to saving the geese when city men move in and try to sell the nearby townspeople on disposing of their lands for shooting sites. Miss Miles is memorably effective as his sharp-tongued but loving wife and de Wilde is excellent both in his dramatic portrayal and shy romantic scenes with Linda Evans, likewise outstanding in her role. Walter Brennan, also co-starred as the town crier, is up to his usual standard in a warmhearted part.

Top support also comes from Ed Wynn, a hard-of-hearing villager; John Larkin, the shopkeeper, and the late Renee Godfrey, as his wife; Parley Baer, a penny-pinching businessman; Tom Skerritt, the town bully who gets his comeuppance from de Wilde in a street fight; Philip Abbott, a doubledealing salesman responsible for the fracas over the geese. Frank de Kova as an Indian also is effective.

Max Steiner's music score is a valuable assist and two songs by Richard M. and Robert B. Sherman, "The Cabin Raising Song" and "Rhyme-Around," add to general interest in the cabin-raising sequence. Grant K. Smith's editing is tight but moving and Carroll Clark and John B. Mansbridge's art direction fills the bill. Lloyd Beebe and William R. Koehler are credited for the animal unit.

Whit.

Per Un Pugno Di Dollari
(For a Fistful of Dollars)
(ITALO-GERMAN-SPANISH)
(COLOR)

Rome, Nov. 10.

UNIDIS release of a Jolly Film (Rome)-Constantin (Germany)-Ocean (Madrid) coproduction. Stars Clint Eastwood; features Marianne Koch, Josef Egger, Wolfgang Lukschy, John Wells, Daniel Martin, Pepe Calvo, Carol Brown, Benny Reeves. Directed by Bob Robertson. Screenplay, Robertson and Duccio Tessari from story by Toni Palombi. Camera (Technicolor-Techniscope), Jack Dalmas; title animation, Luigi Lardani; editor, Roberto Cinquini; music, Dan Savio. At Supercinema, Rome. Dunning time, 100 MINS.
Joe .... Clint Eastwood
Marisol .... Marianne Koch
Piripero .... Josef Egger
John Baxter .... Wolfgang Lukschy
Antonio Baxter .... Carol Brown
Ramon .... John Wells
Solvanito .... Pepe Calvo
Rubio .... Benny Reeves

Cracker-jack western made in Italy and Spain by group of Italians and an international cast, with a James Bondian vigor and tongue-in-cheek approach to capture both sophisticates and average cinema patrons. Early Italo figures indicate it's a major candidate to be sleeper of the year. Also that word-of-mouth, rather than cast strength or ad campaign, is a true selling point. As such, it should make okay program fare abroad as well.

Under local circumstances, it's very easy to overrate this. It's not one of those epics with sweep and grandeur nor was it intended as such. For worldwide release, it lacks the major male and female marquee names which have socked across some of the major Yank Westerns in past decade. Naturally, too, there's a curio point in seeing an oater made by an Italian named Sergio Leoni (who bills himself as Bob Robertson). But let there be no mistake. This is a hard-hitting item, ably directed, splendidly lensed, neatly acted, which has all the ingredients wanted by action fans and then some. In fact, it often overdoes the violent and sadistic angles, but in the acceptably exaggerated spirit of the Ian Fleming skein of things if such a transposition can be made.

Basically, it's about a loner, Joe (Clint Eastwood), who arrives in a small Southwestern settlement split by the rivalry of two families. For money, he plays both sides against the middle, eventually winning his longstanding battle with the heavy. Tale is well developed, and though there is plenty of cliche, such as "Her name is Marisol—but you'd best forget her," it's handled with an all-stops-out style, vigorous use of widescreen camera, effective juggling of closeups and long shots. Spanish landscapes pass well for Southwestern areas bordering on Mexico, as do costumes and types chosen, be they German, Italian, Spanish or "original" Yanks. The hurdle that prospective buyers would have to face are the proper dubbing jobs. Italo version is very well done, with Enrico Maria Salerno, one of best actors in country, lending his voice to Eastwood.

Eastwood handles himself very well as the stranger, shaping a character strong enough to beg a sequel for admirers of this pic. Others in the large cast, especially Pepe Calvo, as the town tavernkeeper, and John Wells (born Gian Maria Volonte) as the heavy, acquit themselves well and colorfully. Marianne Koch has little to do as a contented woman, Marisol, but is a handsome looker. As noted, script by Leoni and Duccio Tessari keeps the tongue well in cheek, and in that spirit, there are few who'll quibble over shooting of several men with a sixshooter.

Further plaudits go to title animation by Luigi Lardani, which sets the style of this film from the start. Also to Ennio Moricone's music, somewhat redundant but effective in the western vein.

Hawk.

Un Monsieur De Compagnie
(A Hail-Fellow Well-Met)
(FRENCH-COLOR)

Paris, Nov. 10.

20th-Fox release of PECF-Films Du Siecle-Dear Film production. Stars Jean-Pierre Cassel, Catherine Deneuve, Irina Demick, Jean-Claude Brialy, Sandra Milo; features Valerie Lagrange, Marcel Dalio. Directed by Philippe De Broca. Screenplay, Henri Lanoe, De Broca from book by Andre Couteaux; camera (Eastmancolor), Raoul Coutard; editor, Francois Javet. At Paris. Running time, 93 MINS.
Antoine .... Jean-Pierre Cassel
Nicole .... Irina Demick
Isabelle .... Catherine Deneuve
Maria .... Sandra Milo
Rich Boy ....Jean-Claude Brialy
Balthazar .... Jean-Pierre Marielle
Maid .... Valerie Lagrange
Millionaire .... Dalio

Philippe De Broca did the successful parody on adventure pix, "That Man From Rio," and now comes up with an inventive, droll takeoff on the marrying off of a good-natured, charming ne'er do well. It should show good international playoff and art returns on its general snap, and wit.

Since this tries to have an ironic, anarchic edge, as well as a happy ending, it sometimes loses out on a gag or repeats itself. But, on the whole, the eye-catching color, pounding pace, personable thesps and tongue-in-cheek speculating keep this engaging most of the way.

Antoine, played by Jean-Pierre Cassel, has been taught by a doting grandfather never to work and enjoy life's good things like women, food and drink. His tutor's death finds him penniless and out in the world.

First he takes over the girl of a friend but work soon stares him in the face. Follows a run-in with an eccentric rich boy who likes to play with trains. Then he ends up in Rome and is able to eat by becoming the lover of a voluptuous woman whose husband works at night. Later he moves in on a rich family. Threats of having to work have him fleeing this to end in London with a rich man. But he gives it all up for love and goes to work.

It is the avoidance of derision, or skepticism that keep this bowling along. Even a scene when he poses nude in an art studio is handled with cleverness to make it funny and insouciant.

Cassel has the right blend of charm, grace and quick wits to have him acceptable all through his fast, clever adventures. Catherine Deneuve is fluffily pretty as the woman who gets him to work. Sandra Milo is a sexy Italian, Irina Demick a free-loving model.

Switch on it all is that it is only a dream and almost a nightmare to the charming loafer. This is a clever, whipped-up romp. Gags are rarely over-worked and some are ingenious.

Production dress is fine and technical credits excellent. Pic marks De Broca as one of the leading comedy directors here. This is not in the more personal style, but in the situation comedy tradition.

Mosk.

Get Yourself A College Girl
(COLOR)

Comedy with music aimed at youth market and featuring top name rhythm musical group. Picture has an academic storyline and lacklustre appeal.

Hollywood, Nov. 19.

Metro release of Four Leaf production, produced by Sam Katzman. Stars Dave Clark Five, The Animals, Stan Getz & Astrud Gilberto, Jimmy Smith Trio, Freddie Bell, Roberta Linn & the Bell Boys; features rest of cast. Directed by Sidney Miller. Screenplay, Robert E. Kent; camera, Fred H. Jackman; editor, Ben Lewis; music, Fred Karger; asst. director, Eddie Saeta. Reviewed Nov. 11, 1964, Iris Theatre, Hollywood. Runnig Time, 87 MINS.
Terry .... Mary Ann Mobley
Marge .... Joan O'Brien
Lynne .... Nancy Sinatra
Sue .... Chris Noel
Gary .... Chad Everett
Senator .... Willard Waterman
Armand .... Fabrizio Mioni
Gordon .... James Milhollin
Ray .... Paul Todd
Donnie .... Donnie Brooks
Donna .... Hortense Petra
Dean .... Dorothy Neumann
Secretary .... Marti Barris
Bellboy .... Mario Costello

If there's a new trend, count on Sam Katzman to film it before the fad runs out and boxoffice fizzles. In "College Girl" the producer gives a lot of credit to Los Angeles' Whisky a GoGo nitery in patterning much of his Watusirhythm styled film around a club tagged the GoGo and pointing up the current interest in this frenetic, youthful music.

Major exploitable attraction in "College Girl" is the use of several of the musical groups now in vogue, including the newest smasheroos, the Dave Clark Five. But the academic Robert E. Kent screenplay and a bad dubbing job on the songs make little striking use of the groups, all of which are topbilled before the title and dramatic cast.

Clark quintet, for instance, do two dry, unimpressive numbers, and there is nothing more exciting about the Animals, Jimmy Smith Trio, Freddie Bell, Roberta Linn and the Bell Boys, the Standells or the Rhythm Masters. But what a wild—and costly—bill of fare if all these acts were really employed by one night club, as Katzman's picture seems to indicate.

There is, however, one classy musical number when Astrud Gilberto joins Stan Getz to recreate the disclick "The Girl From Ipanema." But, generally, music, supervised and conducted by Fred Karger, including title song written by Karger and director Sidney Miller and "The Swingin' Set," by Karger, Miller and Donnie Brooks, is listless and dull and doesn't have the energy even in performance by smash groups on screen that it does in clubs.

Picture is the stale tale of a pretty coed in a staid, exclusive girls' college who nearly flunks out when she is discovered as the composer of several hit pop tunes. She's saved from her fate during a Sun Valley vacation by a senator descendant of the school's founder who learns he can get winning votes in his campaign by getting in with the youngfolks.

Pretty Mary Ann Mobley plays the girl and looks nice even if her role is dull. Willard Waterman is the senator, one of several stereo-

typed roles played by James Milhollin, Fabrizio Mioni and Chris
Noel. Joan O'Brien, Nancy Sinatra and Chad Everett also head
the cast in roles of little proportion which they paly adequately
under the circumstances. Dorothy
Neumann is fine in a bit.

Dale.

The Time Travelers
(FANTASY—COLOR)

**Good idea, so-so acting and
other values. Okay for intended market.**

American International release of
William Redlin (Don Levy) production.
Directed and written by Ib Melchior from
story by Melchior and David Hewitt.
Asst. director, Clark Paylow; music, Rich-
ard Lasalle; camera (Pathecolor) William
Zsigmond; special effects, David Hewitt;
editor, Hal Dennis; art director, Ray
Storey; production manager, Tom Ram-
sey. Reviewed at Pix Theatre in Holly-
wood, Nov. 18, '64. Running Time, 82
MINS.
Dr. Erik von Steiner.....Preston Foster
Steve Connors .... Philip Carey
Carol White ... . Merry Anders
Varno .... John Hoyt
Councilman Willard.....Dennis Patrick
Gadra .... Joan Woodbury
Reena .... Dolores Wells
Danny McKee .... Steve Franken
Councilwoman ....,.... Gloria Leslie
The deviant .... Peter Strudwick
Technician .... Margaret Seldeen
Third technician... Forrest J. Ackerman

American International's "The
Time Travelers," because of its fascinating theme, should prove to be
good boxoffice draw, although the
film is weakened by some poor
acting performances, stilted writing and generally uneven direction.
The idea itself—that of a warp in
the space-time continuum—is one
that has been passed around for
many years and will probably continue to be as we enter the space
age.

Preston Foster and Philip Carey
are adequate as two scientists who
stumble upon a space warp while
playing around with a time portal
in their laboratory on a small college campus. No attempt is even
made to explain why or what they
are experimenting for. Merry
Anders, as the female lab assistant, and Steve Franken as the
comical little electrician, round
out the quartet who end up on
the other side of the "time portal"
in the year 2071, only to find the
earth desolate as a result of a dis-
asterous nuclear war (sound familiar?). Dennis Patrick and John
Hoyt do well by their roles as
councilmen of an underground society that is planning to leave earth
for a star, but other minor roles
are unconvincing. Some scenes
are so bad they aren't even funny,
like the so-called "love machine"
that looks like an old Wurlitzer,
and the robots, called "androids,"
who look like "The Thing" warmed
over.

All of this is in color, and
there's plenty of blood and guts at
the end to satisfy everyone.
David Hewitt's effects are stagey,
and William Zsigmond's camera
work and Hal Dennis' editing are
so-so.   *Bobb.*

Il Magnifico Cornuto
(The Magnificent Cuckold)
(ITALO-FRENCH)

Rome, Nov. 19.
Cineriz release of Alfonso Sansone-
Henryk Chroscicki coproduction for San-
cro Films—Les Films Copernic (Paris).
Stars Claudia Cardinale, Ugo Tognazzi;

features Bernard Blier, Michael Girar-
don, Salvo Randone, Jose Luis de Villa-
longa, Gian Maria Volonte, Paul Guers,
Philipe Nicaud, Suzy Andersen, Ettore
Mattia. Directed by Antonio Pietrangeli.
Screenplay, Pietrangeli, Diego Fabbri,
Stefano Strucchi, Maccari, Scola. Based
on play by Ferdinand Crommelynck. Cam-
era, Armando Nannuzzi. Editor, Eraldo
da Roma. Music, Armando Trovajoli. At
Cinema Corso, Rome. Running time,
123 MINS.
Mariagrazia ....Claudia Cardinale
Andrea .... Ugo Tognazzi
Corna D'Oro .... Bernard Blier
Christiana ....Michele Girardon
Belisario .... Salvo Randone
Presidente ......Jose Luis de Villalonga
Assessore ....Gian Maria Volonte
Gabriele .... Paul Guers
Doctor .... Philippe Nicaud
Wanda .... Suzy Andersen
Guest .... Alfonso Sansone
2nd guest.................. Ettore Mattia

Updated and freely adapted pic
version of Ferdinand Crommelynck's opus, "The Magnificent
Cuckold" shapes up a neatly commercial entry for home market,
while its export chances are enhanced by the Claudia Cardinale
name, its production stylishness,
and more than a dash of exploitable
angles.

Solidly constucted pic is more
sophisticated than most recent Italian satires on manners and morals.
Its main theme, however, is obsessive jealousy carried to extremes, with comic-ironic consequences. Andrea, a well-off hat
manufacturer, casually betrays his
wife, Mariagrazia, but circumstance shows him how relatively
easy it is to bring off: i.e. how
easy it would be for his wife to do
the same to him. Whole series of
coincidental events trigger doubt
in his mind about his (completely
innocent) spouse. At finale, of
course, she becomes disgusted by
his obsession and, just as Andrea
thinks he's licked his folly, she betrays him.

Pic is elegantly outfitted and
stylishly directed, though Antonio
Pietrangeli at times over-indulges
his points, especially at half way
mark, when mechanics of plot begin to show through a bit. Acting
is in keeping. Claudia Cardinale
makes a splendid and believable
wife. Ugo Tognazzi is in top form
as the husband. Michele Girardon
makes a statuesque smalltown
seductress, while Bernard Blier
and Salvo Randone outlines neat
bits as do Paul Guers and Philipe
Nicaud. Armando Nannuzzi is his
usual accomplished self behind the
camera. Armando Trovajoli's music also a plus.   *Hawk.*

The Crawling Hand

Mediocre shocker.

American International release of Jo-
seph F. Robertson production. Directed
by Herbert L. Strock. Stars Peter Breck,
Kent Taylor, Rod Lauren. Screenplay by
Strock and William Edelson; story by
Robert Young and Joseph Granston;
camera, Willard Van der Veer; editor,
Strock. Reviewed at Pix Theatre in Hol-
lywood, Nov. 18, '64. Running Time,
89 MINS.
Steve Curan.............Peter Breck
Doc Weitzberg.............Kent Taylor
Paul Lawrence............Rod Lauren
Marta Farnstrom...........Sirry Steffen
Mrs. Hotchkiss.............Arline Judge
Sheriff ....Alan Hale

The shocking thing about "The
Crawling Hand" is that it was
made at all. Film probably
wouldn't even make the television
late show except as the tail of a
double feature. Good promotion
might draw audiences into the
theatre, but nothing is going to
force them to sit through a study of
innocuous tedium that "The Crawling Hand" presents.

Peter Breck and Kent Taylor
seem embarrassed in the roles of
scientists who trace a missing astronaut to California after the
spaceman's craft explodes while re-
entering the atmosphere. The
catch is that the astronaut didn't
make it—but his hand did. Rod
Lauren is the medical student who
picks up the hand and takes it
home, not realizing he has a killer
in his closet.

The hand strangles his landlady
and tries to do the same to him but
doesn't succeed. Instead Lauren
himself becomes a Jekyll-Hyde
character whose hands have to
kill. You can tell when's in the
mood by the black make-up around
his eyes. Lauren's acting borders
on the pathetic, as does Swedish
import Sirry Steffen's, although the
latter at least has a nice body to
look at.

At the end the hand is destroyed and Lauren recovers. The
best scene is at the end when
Breck looks at the destroyed hand
with a look of complete disgust and
nausea.   *Bobb.*

La Mia Signora
(My Wife)
(ITALIAN)

Rome, Nov. 15.
Dino DeLaurentiis production and re-
lease. Stars Silvana Mangano, Alberto
Sordi; features Claudio Gora, Mariso
Fiorio, Laura Borel, Mario Conocchia.
Directed by Mauro Bolognini, Luigi
Comencini, Tinto Brass. Screenplay,
Rodolfo Sonego; camera, Otello Martelli,
Bruno Barcaroi; editor, Nino Baragli;
music, Armando Trovajoli. At Metro-
politan, Rome. Running Time, 115 MINS.
L'UCCELLINO
Directed by Tinto Bras
Husband .... Alberto Sordi
Wife .... Silvana Magano

ERITREA
Directed by Luigi Comencini
Eritrea ....Silvana Magano
Sartoletti .... Alberto Sordi
Onorevole ....Claudio Gora

I MIERI CARI
Directed by Mauro Bolognini
Marco .... Alberto Sordi
Clara ....Silvana Mangano

LUCIANA
Directed by Mauro Bolognini
Lucia ....Silvana Mangano
Giovanni .... Alberto Sordi
Roberta .... Marisa Fiorio
Commenda ....Mario Conocchia
Hostess ....Laura Borel

L'AUTOMOBILE
Directed by Tinto Brass
Husband .... Alberto Sordi
Wife ....Silvana Mangano

Dino DeLaurentiis has a seasonal hit in this five-parter. Italo success is assured and foreign earnings will be proportional, if much
lower. The Alberto Sordi—Silvana
Mangano tandem will guarantee
local grosses for some time to
come.

But principally, audiences will
pleasantly welcome back the Sordi
they love to laugh at—and with.
Lately, comedian's pix were becoming more and more "arty," and
audience response was in kind.
They'll be back in droves now to
see him mug, double-take, once
knit his eyebrows in inimitable
fashion in the five segments in
which he costars with Miss Mangano, who demonstrates her versatility in a series of sock cameos.

Some of the segments are rightly brief, like "L'Uccellino" or
"L'Automobile". Both are directed
by Tinto Brass with rapid strokes
satirizing a husband and a wife's
obsessions, respectively, for a bird
and for a Jaguar (car). They're
facile bits, but made effective by
brevity.

There are some sharp topical

barbs tossed in "Eritrea" as well,
in which Sordi hires a call girl to
help "soften" a government official into granting a building permit. Director Luigi Comencini's
episode also boasts a fine supporting bit by Claudio Gora.

Mauro Bolognini directed two
parts: "I Miei Cari" is a brutal bit
about the coldness of most hospital visits and the patient's helplessness. "Luciana" is a more developed item, perhaps the best of
the lot, about a brief airport interlude by two people who meet while
seeing wife and husband off on a
plane.

Just after takeoff, the plane is
forced back, but can't land until
fuel is used up to avoid complications of a potentially fatal crash.
Time is spent together by couple.
"Luciana" is variously amusing
and human in its development of
character and unfolding of personality.

Technically, the film rates highly, with lensing (Otello Martelli
and Bruno Barcaro), music (Armando Trovajoli) and editing (Nino Baragli) all of high calibre.
Piero Gherardi has designed some
trim dresses for Miss Mangano.
Hawk.

Dear Heart

Appealing mature romance yarn starring Glenn Ford and Geraldine Page. Good prospects in adult market.

Hollywood, Nov. 25.

Warner Bros. release of Martin Manulis production. Stars Glenn Ford, Gerald Page. Features Michael Anderson Jr., Barbara Nichols, Patricia Barry, Charles Drake. Directed by Delbert Mann. Screenplay, Ted Mosel, from his own story; camera, Russell Harlan; editor, Folmar Blangsted; music, Henry Mancini; asst. director, Carter DeHaven Jr. Reviewed at WB studios, Burbank, Cal., Nov. 24, '64. Running time 114 MINS.

Harry Mark .... Glenn Ford
Evie Jackson .... Geraldine Page
Patrick ....Michael Anderson Jr.
June .... Barbara Nichols
Mitchell .... Patricia Barry
Frank Taylor .... Charles Drake
Phyllis ....Angela Lansbury
Miss Tait................ Ruth McDevitt
Connie .... Neva Patterson
Miss Moore .... Alice Pearce
Mr. Cruikshank .... Richard Deacon
Zola ....Joanne Crawford
Miss Fox .... Mary Wickes
Peterson .... Peter Turgeon

"Dear Heart," a pleasant comedy-drama, is important for the screen return of Geraldine Page—who received Oscar nominations for each of her three previous film appearances—in a story which will hold meaning for femme audiences. It is the romance of two more mature persons, and as such its appeal will be stronger for adult rather than younger theatregoers, particularly since both are down-to-earth characters lacking entirely in glamor. Nonetheless with small promotion grosses should be satisfactory, if not spectacular, and there is the added plus of Glenn Ford's name for marquee voltage.

Produced by Martin Manulis and directed by Delbert Mann, film is well-turned-out in every department and writing by Tad Mosel, who adapted from his own story, is tops.

Due to its lacklustre qualities the picture would probably benefit by considerable shearing, from its current 114 minutes down to around 100 minutes or less, say, but even in this excess footage the directorial touches are always there to enliven character delineation and the two principals are ever alive to every possibility.

For Miss Page particularly, in the role of a small town postmistress who has missed the boat matrimonially through over-emphasis on good intentions which cause people to shy away from her, the feature is paved with opportunity. It is not a showy part, but one complete in acting technique as she arrives in New York to attend a postmasters' convention and here meets Ford, who is about to be married to an Altoona, Pa., widow with a 19-year-old son and is looking forward lustily to his finally becoming not only a husband but a father as well.

Miss Page registers impressively as she creates character, and Ford in a more conventional role but one which also permits certain characterization, provides an interesting foil for her, delivering one of his best performances. Both play their respective parts for a peculiar brand of comedy with serious undertones, and here is where the film especially excels.

Backing pair are several outstanding impersonations, including Angela Lansbury, the widow betrothed who doesn't care what Ford may do if only she is allowed an absence of "responsibilities"; Michael Anderson Jr., as her freesoul son; Barbara Nichols, the voluptuous and sexy hotel mag stand salesgirl whom Ford picks up for an evening of enchantment.

In smaller parts, Mary Wickes and Ruth McDevitt as a pair of postmistresses lend brief comedy rapture; Patricia Barry scores as Ford's previous vis-a-vis whenever he has been in town; and Charles Drake and Richard Deacon are a couple of conventioneers.

Mann's direction is particularly sure and able in his character development and Manulis has backed his production with good values. Title song, with lyrics by Jay Livingston and Ray Evans and music by Henry Mancini, shapes logically into one of the convention sequences, and Mancini's score also is appropriate. Russell Harlan's deft camera work, Folmar Blangsted's editing and Joseph Wright's art direction are definite assets.

Whit.

Moro Witch Doctor

Lower case in every department; for least discriminating situations only.

Hollywood, Nov. 23.

Twentieth-Fox release of Eddie Romero production. Stars Jock Mahoney, Margia Dean, Pancho Magalona; features Paraluman, Mike Parsons, Vic Diaz. Directed and written by Romero. Camera, Felipe Sacdalan; editor, Jovan Calub; music, Ariston Aveline. Reviewed at Iris Theatre, Hollywood, Calif., Nov. 17, '64. Running time, 61 MINS.

Jefferson Stark .... Jock Mahoney
Paula Cameron .... Margia Dean
Martin Gonzaga ...... Pancho Magalona
Felisa Noble .... Paraluman
Ackerman .... Mike Parsons
Salek .... Vic Diaz
Mulan .... Nemia Velasco
Datu Sumlang .... Bruno Punzalan
Mahmud ....Jay Ilagan

"Moro Witch Doctor," a lowbudgeter filmed in the Philippines with Jock Mahoney starred as an Interpol agent seeking to rub out an opium ring, is a confused piece of picture-making suitable only for the least discriminating trade. It's the type of minor B which went by the boards many years ago, and is further burdened with a narrator explaining much of the action instead of the participants handling dialog.

Written, produced and directed by Eddie Romero, its amateurish presentation attempts to follow Mahoney's assignment which takes him into the Moro country. Director was as mixed up as the spectator.

Mahoney has no chance at all with his role, Margia Dean walks through as a needless femme lead and Pancho Magalona helps star in his quest.

Technical credits are all far below par. *Whit.*

Le Tigre Aime La Chair Fraiche
(The Tiger Likes Fresh Flesh)
(FRENCH)

Paris, Dec. 1.

Gaumont release of Progefi production. Stars Roger Hanin, Maria Mauban, Daniela Bianchi; features Roger Dumas, Mario David. Directed by Claude Chabrol. Screenplay, Antoine Flachot, Jean Halain; camera, Jean Rabier; editor, Jacques Gaillard. At Elysees, Paris. Running time, 85 MINS.

Le Tigre .... Roger Hanin
Mother .... Maria Mauban
Mika .... Daniela Bianchi
Assistant .... Roger Dumas
Dubrowski .... Mario David

Mock serious action espionage undercovcr operator pic is obviously influenced by the James Bond success, but it lacks the ample means, right blend of tongue-in cheek heroics and brittle brightness. Its impact is not Bonded, looms mainly for dualer playoff abroad.

Claude Chabrol brings to bear his usual brash methods but it does not quite work with this theme. What should be surface cynicism somehow gets overemphasized and what should be unruffled mayhem becomes a bit overdone and distasteful, such as dwelling too long on a strangling or human infirmities.

Roger Hanin also lacks the necessary phlegm, composure and/or lightness for the two-fisted ladies' man secret service op. Others are okay and there is plenty of use of scientific methods, brutal battles, sex interludes and exotic locales.

But its indebtedness to Bond shows too much to have this suffer by comparison. A scene with a car masher, reminiscent of "Goldfinger," is used but pic overdoes it as it shows the heavy narrowly escaping rather than the bland sadism of the Bond episode where a body is allowed to go with it and then become a deft macabre pun. Here it is played for teasing easy sadism and does not work.

Even Daniela Bianchi, who was in "To Russia With Love," is here wasted as a pining daughter of the guarded Turkish diplomat who has a few nuzzling scenes with the hero and some bathing suit bits.

So chalk this up as an okay, sharply paced actioner for local use sans the legs needed for foreign mileage. *Mosk.*

Every Day's A Holiday
(BRITISH-COLOR)

Feeble story enlivened by energetic young pop performers. Several good pop songs and bright lensing of familiar holiday camp scene should attract younger filmgoers to this dualler.

London, Nov. 24.

Grand National release and presentation. Stars John Layton, Mike Sarne, Freddie & The Dreamers, Ron Moody, Liz Fraser; features Grazina Frame, The Baker Twins, The Mojos, Nicholas Parsons, Richard O'Sullivan. Produced by Maurice J. Wilson and Ronald J. Kahn. Directed by James Hill. Screenplay, Anthony Mariott, Jeri Matos and Hill, from Mariott's original story; camera (Technicolor), Nicholas Roeg; editor, Tristam Cones; music, Tony Osborne; choreography, Gilliam Lynne. Reviewed at Warner Theatre, London, Nov. 23, '64. Running time, 94 MINS.

Gerry .... John Leyton
Tim .... Mike Sarne
The Chefs......Freddie & The Dreamers
Professor .... Ron Moody
Miss Slightly .... Liz Fraser
Christine .... Grazina Frame
Jennifer .... Jennifer Baker
Susan .... Susan Baker
Themselves .... The Mojos
Julian Goddard .... Nicholas Parsons
Mrs. Barrington De Witt Hazel Hughes
Mr. Pullman .... Michael Ripper
Jimmy .... Richard O'Sullivan
Mike .... Tony Daines
Mr. Close .... Charles Lloyd Pack
Little Girl .... Nicola Riley
Vision Mixer .... Marion Grimaldi
Themselves .... The Leroys

It is possible to get away without a story in a musical if the performers, songs and dancing are top league. But even then a crisp, strong story line helps. "Every Day's A Holiday" has an abysmally thin and trite yarn; it is really carrying things too far to flatter scripter Anthony Mariot with a credit line for his original story.

But peppy, enthusiastic young pop performers give the framework zest and a likeable, ingenuous sense of fun. As a result, this lively song-and-dancalog should turn out a profitable dualler for houses that attract youthful cinemagoers. Nicholas Roeg's excellent color camerawork is a distince asset, too.

The romp is set in a holiday camp with several young people joining the staff as holiday workers. There is a touch of boy-meets-girl, a plot to foil the nosy, interfering aunt of one of the girls and the culmination of a tv talent show in which the film's leading young heroines emerge as stars.

None of the characters are developed overmuch. But Mike Sarne's rich, young would-be Romeo has some amusing aspects. Grazina Frame is a pleasant singing heroine and such talent as John Leyton, Freddie & the Dreamers (playing comedy chefs), The Mojos, The Baker Twins and the Leroys get to grips with the pop ditties, some of which seem likely hit material.

Liz Fraser, as the camp secretary, has little to do except to look sexy which presents her with no problem at all. Ron Moody, as a bogus operatic professor; Nicholas Parsons, playing a tempermental tv producer; Michael Ripper, Hazel Hughes and Patrick Newell are among the "non-popsters" who help to give a little body to their roles.

The mediocrity of the acting is obvious, but it is outweighed by the genuinely infectious enthusiasm put into their jobs by the cast and some useful contributions by choreographer Gillian Lynne and composer Tony Osborne.

The holiday camp setting provides familiar territory for many cinemagoers and is enhanced by the aforementioned slick work of lenser Roeg. Tristam Cones' editing is occasionally awry, but achieves its purpose of giving an air of speed in the lighthearted proceedings. *Rich.*

Fantomas
(FRENCH-COLOR-FRANSCOPE)

Paris, Nov. 24.

Gaumont release of PAC-Gaumont production. Stars Jean Marais, Louis De Funes, Mylene Demongeot; features Marie-Helene Arnaud, Jacques Dynam, Robert Dalban. Directed by Andre Hunebelle. Screenplay, Jean Halain, Pierre Foucaud from novel by Marcel Alain; camera (EastmanColor), Marcel Grignom, Jean Feyte. At Ambassador-Gaumont, Paris. Running time, 105 MINS.

Newsman .... Jean Marais
Juve .... Louis De Funes
Fiancee .... Mylene Demongeot
Countess .... Marie-Helen Arnaud

Inspector .... Jacques Dynam
Editor .... Robert Dalban

Far out super criminals, color, big screen and adventures are popping in French films as late on the heels of the successful James Bond pix. But local equivalents lack the tongue-in cheek arrogance, pace, and sheer entertainment gloss of the Bond films. This one is no exception and remains mainly a local bet.

A noted character of early silent film serials has been resurrected for it. A reporter fakes an interview with the mythical criminal Fantomas after a series of holdups. But it seems he exists and he kidnaps the scribe to transport him to his underground lair which is full of gadgets. Fantomas creates the face of the newsman to discredit him in many escapades. But he is finally tracked down only to escape once more.

There are some good chases in this if fights are only fair. The languid direction, absence of style and old fashioned action, sans the fillip of dynamic drive, loses this the acceptable entertainment qualities it might have had. Production values are good.

Jean Marais does some derring-do which belies his age and Louis De Funes is funny as the enraged, fumbling police inspector who is the usual butt of Fantomas. Marais also plays Fantomas since that fellow has taken his face. *Mosk.*

La Grande Frousse
(The Big Scare)
(FRENCH)
Paris, Nov. 24.
Pathe release of Attica-SNC production. Stars Bourvil; features Jean-Louis Barrault, Francis Blanche. Victor Francen, Raymond Rouleau, Veronique Nordey, Jean Poiret. Directed by Jean-Pierre Mocky. Screenplay, Gerard Klein. Mocky from book by Jean Ray; camera, Eugene Shuftan; editor, Marguerite Renoir; at Ermitage, Paris. Running time, 92 MINS.
Triquet .... Bourvil
Douve .... Jean-Louis Barrault
Mayor .... Raymond Rouleau
Calbert .... Victor Francen
Livina .... Veronique Nordey
Franquie .... Francis Blanche
Chabriant ....Raymond Rouleau
Loupiac .... Jean Poiret
Gosseran .... Jacques Dufilho

Combination satire on small-town human pettiness and suspense police comedy does not completely jell. But it never gets gritty. And this does have some atmosphere and far out characterization to slant this for special situations or playoff abroad. Arty house chances seem less promising.

A good-natured police inspector unwittingly captures a murderer who is sent to be beheaded. Guillotine does not work and he escapes from the executioner. Pic concerns the inspector's search for the man to keep him from doing anything wrong because technically he can no longer be put to death.

Searching for him in small town that has a myth about a monster he bungles on all sorts of hatreds and inhibitions among the people.

Director Jean-Pierre Mocky shows a mordant vein in all his pix and an almost queasy attack on human foibles. Here he soft pedals it a bit and shows practically compassion for these weird, inverted characters.

Bourvil has charm as the pleasant-natured policeman retired from the force for catching too many crooks outside the call of duty. Others are good and technical credits fine. Mocky definitely shows a personal flair and should emerge a pertinent filmmaker. Here he finds the right blend for his macabre humor and good narrative techniques. *Mosk.*

Verdammt zur Suende
(Condemned to Sin)
(GERMAN)
Berlin, Nov. 24.
Nora release of Eberhard Klagemann production. Stars Martin Held, Heidelinde Weis, Hildegard Knef, Tilla Durieux and Else Knott. Directed by Alfred Weidenmann. Screenplay, Eberhard Keindorff and Johanna Sibelius, based on novel "The Fortress" by Henry Jaeger; camera, Enzo Serafin; music, Herta Hareither. W-Berlin preem, Nov. 24, '64, at Marmorhaus. Running time, 104 MINS.
Hugo Starosta .... Martin Held
Eliese .... Else Knott
Mi-Mo Starosta .... Christa Linder
Albert Starosta .... Michael Ande
Bruno Starosta .... Rene Egiomue
Hermann Starosta ...... Sieghardt Rupp
Grand-Mother .... Tilla Durieux
Edeltraut .... Heidelinde Weis
Alwine .... Hildegard Knef

This Nora release reveals the dilemma of current German filmmaking: a qualified cast, a basically interesting plot, a name director, a fine cameraman—but the outcome is utterly disappointing. Film has—for Germany—"public appeal." But it's a cheap sort of appeal. A production like this can hardly make friends for this country's film industry abroad.

There is an overdose of what they call "sex," overly suggestive if not obscene situations and dialog sequences. Also repetition of gags, too muchness of corny slapstick ingredients. Note the title itself. What was originally titled "The Fortress" (based on a book written by a gangster in jail) emerges as "Condemned to (not for) Sin."

"The Fortress" is an old citadel which serves as the home for German refugee families after 1945. Action concentrates on Hugo Starosta and his breed. And what kind of breed! The father is beaten and constantly abused by his children. His wife has five children including one not by him—just a wartime episode. The daughter realizes that money is the thing and becomes a prostitute. Two sons dedicate themselves to sexual excesses. Another son, 15 of age, is taught the trade of sex by a girl. When she's expecting she avoids complications by turning to an elderly man whom she makes believe that he's the father of the coming child.

Lineup of characters includes Alwine, the disillusioned wife of a brutal man, who eventually strangles her. But the viewer doesn't learn what happens to the murderer. There are bed sequences galore throughout. Not one or two, rather 10 to 15.

Moreover, authorities (youth authorities, police, etc.) are abused and ridiculed. Indeed, how this film could—in this form—pass the censors is a puzzle. *Hans.*

Lucky Jo
(FRENCH)
Paris, Nov. 24.
UGC-Sirius release of Raitfeld-Belmont Films-EDE Films production. Stars Eddie Constantine; features Francoise Arnoul, Christiane Minazzoli, Pierre Brasseur, Claude Brasseur, Georges Wilson, Jean-Pierre Darras, Andre Cellier. Directed by Michel Dreville. Screenplay, Nina Companeez, Dreville from book by Pierre Lesou; camera, Claude Lecomte; editor, Nina Companeez. At Balzac, Paris. Running time, 85 MINS.
Jo .... Eddie Constantine
Mimi .... Francoise Arnoul
Inspector .... Pierre Brasseur
Fils .... Claude Brasseur
Simon .... Georges Wilson
Wife .... Christiane Minazzoll
Napo .... Jean-Pierre Darras
Gabriel .... Andre Cellier

American actor Eddie Constantine became a star here and on the Continent via roles in parody type gangster and G-Man style pix. He has been trying to change his image of late via working with younger directors and essaying slightly differing roles. But they have yet to jell and this one opens no new roads for his talents.

Instead of playing the usual self-assured, Scotch-drinking, two-fisted, skirt-chasing policeman in tongue-in-check plots, he is now a petty gangster down on his luck since he seems to bring bad luck to everybody on jobs. Fights abound and the action is crisply handled.

Constantine is forced to try to play for sympathy while it has always been his brashness that has somehow made him winning in spite of his arrogance. He doesn't quite bring it off and the serio-comic direction and plot also do not have this working-out for topflight results.

Director Michel Deville has a sharp way of going into a scene but doesn't seem to have the right balance of tenderness, irony and parody; hence, this lags. A group of good players surround Constantine to keep this going if it is only intermittently entertaining. *Mosk.*

The Guns of August
(Documentary)

Pulitzer Prize book converted into a fascinating documentary of World War I. For general audiences, and history classroom tieups.

Universal release of Nathan Kroll (Lawrence White) production. Edited by Miriam Arsham; scored and conducted by Sol Kaplan; narration text, Arthur B. Tourtellot, read by Fritz Weaver; stills and maps, Herbert Matter; animation, Dumont; special effects, D & G Studios; titles, Richard Erdoes, Wango Wen. Reviewed Nov. 23, '64, in N.Y. projection room. Running Time, 99 MINS.

Nathan Kroll, a refugee from radio where he functioned for years as arranger-conductor of mood music, has since made a number of attention-drawing shorts, notably the Martha Graham "Appalachian Spring" and the Pablo Casals "Master Class" vidpix series. He now appears as producer of a feature-length documentary derived from Barbara W. Tuchman's recall of that fateful August of 1914 when the lights of Europe went out, and the world that was was washed away in a bloody tidal wave.

The initial footage details at some length the royal and imperial nincompoops and their blundering ministers who between 1910 and 1914 were fully warned to the relentless drift to catastrophe and were totally incapable if the honesty and intelligence necessary to defuse the bombs. As in Miss Tuchman's book, the camera pans in on King Edward VII dead in London, George V beginning his reign. To the funeral came nearly all the crowned heads of the day. It is a concentrated panorama of the pomp and privilege so soon to fall ignominiously upon their collective, stupid, proud faces.

These foreshadowings may well be the most arresting of the footage assembled, more of it new, than in the battle sequences, and all of it educational to the modern generations who probably only dimly know about the 1914 vestiges of divine right. Especially revealing are the glimpses of old Franz Josef (in Vienna, not London) in his senility, a supposedly absolute emperor yet unable to control his own generals, who scarcely won a skirmish once hostilities broke out.

There remains much dispute concerning World War I, and these issues still generate some heat. Which is an element of useful promotion for Universal and Kroll. It is very likely that history classes and buffs will respond to the bait in a big way, though 1914 may not exercise quite the appeal to collectors as does the Civil War, which conflict suffers the defect of having no cinematic archives.

Universal financed the making of this documentary. At the very end there is a listing of the sources from which footage was obtained —many of them foreign and their aggregate providing further evidence of the great weight of interest in the struggle which may not have made the world safe for democracy but did make it unsafe for three-quarters of the monarchs.

Only a historian could perhaps adequately evaluate the various scenes. Enough to report for the commercial boxoffice interest that it is steadily engrossing. Seen in a smallish projection room the 99 minutes of old stock was a bit of an eye-strain, but it may be assumed that this factor will be minimal under modern exhibition conditions.

Kroll again used Miriam Arsham as editor, as on his shorts. Sandra E. Robertson was the assistant. It is plausible to assume they are very definite feature talent in these circumstances. The narration of Arthur B. Tourtellot is informative and nicely delivered by actor Fritz Weaver. No doubt there is a calculated neutrality at times in the commentary, since even now there are national sensitivities. Not, however, that the Germans do not emerge as the heavies.

The battlefield carnage avoids the arms and legs and skulls caught on barbed wire familiar to many a war film of the past 30 years. It is sufficiently grisly. Indeed there is a very strong lesson implicit. Not horror alone but unendurable indignity and boredom is the awful price of modern war.

Obvious pains were taken in all the technical aspects. Kroll had **Lawrence G. White as exec producer and Eugene Gelber as associate producer.** An important aspect was the score, handled effectively by Sol Kaplan. Special titles, maps, effects, animation help vary the narrative style and pace. It's a promising bet to pile up a good gross on a $40,000 investment, and the world is its boxoffice oyster. *Land.*

Ferry Across the Mersey
(BRITISH)

Another routine musical which will satisfy pop youngsters. Fair support to topliner pic with certain audiences.

London, Dec. 1.

United Artists release of a Brian Epstein presentation of a Suba Film. Stars Gerry & The Pacemakers. Features Cilla Black, Julie Samuel, The Fourmost, Jimmy Savile, Earl Royce & The Olympics, The Blackwells, The Black Knights, Eric Barker, T. P. McKenna, Deryck Guyler, George A. Cooper, Mona Washbourne, Patricia Lawrence, Mischa de la Motte. Produced by Michael Holden. Directed by Jeremy Summers. Screenplay uncredited, based on an idea by Tony Warren; camera, Gilbert Taylor; sound, Kevin Sutton; songs, Gerry Marsden; music, George Martin. Previewed at Mermaid Theatre, London, Nov. 30. Running time, **88 MINS.**

Gerry .... Gerry Marsden
Fred .... Fred Marsden
Chad .... Les Chadwick
Les .... Les Maguire
Dodie .... Julie Samuel
Colonel Dawson .... Eric Barker
Tresler .... Deryck Guiler
Mr. Lumsden .... George A. Cooper
Miss Kneave .... Patricia Lawrence
Aunt Lil .... Mona Washbourne
Dawson's Butler .... Mischa de la Motte
Hanson .... T. P. McKenna
Norah .... Margaret Nolan
Chinese Restaurant Manager.... Andy Ho

The Mersey Sound which put pop music on the map in this country gets a fair belting in this modest, routine picture designed to exploit Gerry and the Pacemakers, one of Britain's top pop groups. It will have useful support in U.K. but though the group is known in America for its disks and a fairly successful tour "Ferry Across The Mersey" is unlikely to have much export appeal. It is noisy, corny and full of cliches but Jeremy Summers has directed with zest and some vitality and the pic goes at a reasonable lick. The Liverpool scene shows up well with some adroitly picked location work and two or three unoriginal, but sprightly "Keystone Cop" sequences add considerably to its comedy content.

As so often, however, this kind of pic falls down because of laxness over the script, which is used mainly as a framework for putting over pop numbers. It is based on an idea by Tony Warren but the loose screenplay is uncredited, which is significant. Opening shows Gerry and the Pacemakers returning from a click U. S. trip. In flashback it shows how the group was formed, helped by a local chick who introduces the boys to a go-getting manager, and, despite a last minute mishap when they nearly lose their instruments and costumes, the lads win the European Beat Group Contest. Undoubtedly stronger material is needed if this type of film is ever to get out of a well-ploughed rut.

The thick local accent and idiom do not help for general consumption and there is a kind of noisy, frenetic, pumped up hysteria and lack of discipline about the proceedings which palls, even with its modest limits of 88 minutes. Gerry Marsden, as well as writing the songs, leads his group with ebulience but shows little sign of being an actor. As his rich girl friend Julie Samuel makes her debut. She is a pretty, young blonde, but her inexperience also shows up starkly. Jimmy Savile, a zany disk jockey, appears as himself, as does Cilla Black, a top British thrush, who sings one song and utters a few lines with a pallid personality and dubious success. T. P. McKenna scores as the manager and Mona Washbourne, Eric Barker, Deryck Guyler, Patricia Lawrence and George A. Cooper bring a little of their professional expertise to bear on unrewarding roles.

Most of the humor is naive in the extreme but director Summers gives the events as much pep as possible and has extracted some good fun from the frantic car chase sequences. Gilbert Taylor's lensing is vivid and effective and sound mixer Kevin Sutton has done a valiant, if not altogether successful, job in trying to discipline the sound when the Pacemakers and other groups are on a no-holds-barred beat wingding. *Rich.*

Casablan
(GREEK)

Greek-made study of problem of assimilation of various national strains of Jews into modern Israel. Low budget production indicates limited returns. English dialog.

Frisch-Natas Productions and Cinematographic Enterprises Anzervos Corp. (Alec Natas) presentation. Directed by Larry Frisch. Screenplay, Alex Maimon, based on Igal Mossinsohn's play "Casablan"; camera, Gregoris Danalis; editor, Gerassimos Papadatos; music, composed and conducted by Costa Capnissis. Reviewed in N.Y., Dec. 3, '64. Running time, **63 MINS.**

Casablan .... Nikos Kourkoulos
Rachel .... Maria Xenia
Abramov ....Lykourgos Kallergis
Yosh .... Demetris Ballas
Feldman .... Mitsos Lygizos
Mushiko .... Demos Starenios
Gina .... Aspa Nakopoulou
Neuberg ....Artemis Matsas

Although about Israel, this film was made entirely at the Anzervos Studios in Athens. Reason for this departure, according to director Larry Frisch, was that Igal Mossinsohn's play, when performed in Israel, caused so much upset that it was impossible to obtain backing or permission to make the film there. What has been put on the screen is so mild Israel's objection is incomprehensible. The very brief running time (63 minutes) could imply either considerable pruning or insufficient production funds to make a more complete film.

Despite some success in believable interpretation of various Israeli types by Greek actors, producer Alec Natas and director Frisch have created only another tale of a non-conformist, not too unlike the early John Garfield films. And as portrayed by Nikos Kourkoulos, there's very little to like about this antagonistic, surly ex-veteran who can't believe the war for independence (in which he was at home) is over and things aren't what they used to be.

The so-called controversy is the conflict between European-born Jews (with their better education, culture and living standards) and poorer ones from previously Arabian countries. Casablan, one of the latter, is a troublemaker, quick of temper and even quicker with a knife, who finds himself accused of a murder and with most of his neighbors against him. His former army commander, now a lawyer, defends him successfully but winds up with his girl. Story ends on a note of nothing solved. Film's makers might have been more successful by using a group of people instead of one member to get across the sociological differences that undoubtedly do exist. The viewer never really sympathizes with Casablan, as an individual or as a symbol.

Some of cast, particularly Maria Xenia as the girl, Lykourgos Kallergis as the police inspector, and Demetris Ballas as the lawyer, indicate more promise than their material permits. Others range from fair to poor. Generally, the film looks as though it had been made on a single set with a few location shots in actual buildings. **One short outdoor bit at a kibbutz appears out of place.** Photography is grainy and lighting is extremely poor. Costa Capnissis' score is only adequate.

The soundtrack, post-synchronized in English, according to Frisch, was done with all of the actors, except one, speaking their own lines. It is a good job, both lingually and mechanically. The film opens Dec. 12 at the Cameo. General prospects, however, are limited. *Robe.*

Kare John
(Dear John)
(SWEDISH)

Sandrew Film production and release. Stars Jarl Kulle, Christina Schollin. Features Morgan Andersson, Helen Nilsson, Synnove Liljeback, Eric Hell, Emy Storm, Hakan Serner, Hans Wigren, Erland Nordenfalk, Bo Wahlstrom, Stig Woxter. Directed by Lars Magnus Lindgren. Screenplay, Lindgren after a novel by Olle Lansberg. Camera, Rune Ericson. Music, Bengt-Arne Wallin. At Alcazar, Stockholm. Running time, **111 MINS.**

John Berndtsson .... Jarl Kulle
Anita .... Christina Schollin
Helent .... Helene Nilsson
Raymond .... Morgan Andersson
Dagny .... Synnove Liljeback
Lindgren .... Erik Hell
Mrs. Lindgren .... Emy Storm
Edwin .... Hakan Serner
Elon .... Hans Wigren
Kurt .... Erland Nordenfalk
Bosse .... Bo Wahlstrom
Taxi Driver .... Stig Woxter

Somehow a difficult film. Sexy without sex. It tells the story of John, captain on board a small vessel, who meets Anita, waitress at a small harbor village cafe. She has a daughter, a memory from a love affair at 18. An unmarried mother must be an easy conquest, he thinks, but learns that she isn't. The three, John, Anita and Helena, spend a day in Copenhagen, at the zoo. John is beginning to make plans, not for one night with Anita, but perhaps a whole life together. When he asks her to marry him, she does not dare to believe that a man can have any good intentions to an unmarried mother. All this leads to misunderstandings, and the next day John leaves the harbor disconsolate.

Novel by Olle Lansberg was something of a sensation here. Film follows text more closely than films usually do, but most of those "bad words" in the book have been deleted. Though largely located in bed, there is hardly any nudity. Certain censors may resist "message" of the film, that "physical love is sometimes the ground from which pure love will grow."

Film brings back the love couple from "Angels, Are There Any" of 1960, Jarl Kulle and Christina Schollin.

One confusing aspect is the many retrospections, a film technique of which too much is tiring.

Young Helene Nilsson as the five-six years old daughter of Miss Schollin is very convincing. Morgan Andersson is seen in a few scenes as Miss Schollin's brother, a young man very proud of his well-trained muscles. While the novel gave a good view of the crew on the vessel, the film gives very little about them.

Camera work by Rune Ericson is top grade. Ditto other technical credits. Director Lars Magnus Lindgren shows an ability that no doubt will make his name known as one of the best in the younger generation of Swedish film-makers.

Success within Sweden is sure, thanks to the novel. Abroad it should have good chances, as more of the famous Swedish sin.

Wing.

The Nasty Rabbit
(TECHNISCOPE-COLOR)

Company which has stressed sex and violence in previous efforts turns to comedy with tragic results.

Fairway-International release of Arch Hall (Nicholas Merriwether) production. Directed by James Landis. Features

Mischa Terr, Arch Hall Jr., Melissa Morgan, William Watters, Little Jack Little, Ray Vegas, John Akana, Harold Bizzy, Sharon Ryker. Screenplay, Arch Hall, Jim Critchfield; camera (Technicolor), William Zsigmond; editor, Anthony M. Lanza; asst. director, Daved Reed 3d. Reviewed in N.Y., Dec. 3, 1964. Running time, 85 MINS.

Mischa Lowzoff	Mischa Terr
Britt Hunter	Arch Hall Jr.
Cecelia	Melissa Morgan
Marshall Malouf and	
Malcolm McKinley	William Watters
Maxwell Stoppic	Little Jack Little
Gonzales	Ray Vegas
Col. Kobayaski	John Akana
Heinrich Krueger	Harold Bizzy
Jackie	Sharon Ryker
Gavin	Hal Bokar
Hubert Jackson	George Morgan
The Idiot	Leslie Kovacs
Pat & Lolly Vegas	Themselves
The Archers	Themselves

Fairway - International, which has had some past success with a series of exploitation-type features, with stress on sex and/or violence, as in "The Sadist," "Wild Guitars," and "The Choppers," has now made a stab at the comedy field. Their first such effort will need every bit of promotion it can get. Lacking the obviously exploitable title of past efforts, it may not fare as well.

Producer Nicholas Merriwether, director James Landis and the entire human cast share equally the guilt of creating an interminable 85 minutes of crashing boredom. Arch Hall and Jim Critchfield's script is a case of little work and no play. What was meant to be a funny takeoff on spy films does, indeed, take off on some past cinematic efforts but fails to borrow their wit along with their storylines.

The title-role rabbit not only gives the best performance, but also has the best lines. A series of pseudo-international types, played so offensively they are sure to alienate the countries they represent, are belabored by Mischa Terr, Melissa Morgan, William Watters, Little Jack Little, Ray Vegas, John Akana and Harold Bizzy, with possibly Terr and Miss Morgan the worst offenders. Arch Hall Jr. has added another trick —besides riding a motorcycle, he also plays a guitar. Sharon Ryker, a very pretty girl, needs at least two years with a voice coach.

The one professional touch to the film, and it is poor at the beginning, is William Zsigmond's Technicolor camerawork which gives the film a wasted surface gloss.

The sick story concerns a rabbit bearing a capsule of highly contagious bacteria (hence "nasty"), which the Russians hope to release in the U.S. After about a half-hour this epic, the release of the capsule is a consummation devoutly to be wished. *Robe.*

Taggart
(COLOR)

Western good for second spot in double bill is lifted from routine by good characterizations from Dan Duryea and Elsa Cardenas, plus spectacular photography.

Hollywood, Dec. 2.
Universal release of Gordon Kay & Associates production. Stars Tony Young, Dan Duryea; features rest of cast. Sarah Selby, George Murdock, Arthur Space, Bob Steele. Directed by R. G. Springsteen. Screenplay, Robert Creighton Williams, from Louis L'Amour novel; camera, William Margulies; editor, Tony Martinelli; music, Herman Stein. Reviewed at Universal Studios, Dec. 2, '64. Running time, 85 MINS.

Kent Taggart	Tony Young
Jason	Dan Duryea
Stark	Dick Foran
Consuela	Elsa Cardenas
Miriam	Jean Hale
Ben Blazer	Emile Meyer
Cal Dodge	David Carradine
Rusty Bob	Peter Duryea
Vince August	Tom Reese
Ralph Taggart	Ray Teal
Lola	Claudia Barrett
Sheriff	Stuart Randall
Lt. Hudson	Harry Carey
Army Sgt.	Bill Henry
Maude Taggart	Sarah Selby
Army Scout	George Murdock
Colonel	Arthur Space

Gordon Kay's "Taggart" is lifted above routine Western label by some deft characterizations—particularly by Dan Duryea and Elsa Cardenas—and spectacular color photography from William Margulies and crew. Universal release could add strength to double features, but its boxoffice potential atop the bill is dubious.

Tony Young in title role of man fleeing hired killers is tall, handsome and silent. His dead-pan acting is unimpressive, however, as is that of romantic interest Jean Hale.

Acting honors goes to Duryea as talkative, wise-cracking and cold-blooded hired killer following Young, and to Miss Cardenas, faithless wife and stepmother who double-crosses husband to flee with Duryea and gold. She adds a dash of sex not customary in modest budget Western.

Sex is only unusual facet of Robert Creighton Williams' script, which encompasses practically every device in Western corral, from cattle stampede straight through to lost gold mine, and Indian attack on wagon train and fort. Script is traditional in attitude toward Indians; only good ones are dead ones.

Director R. G. Springsteen has deftly molded this grab-bag of cliches into smooth-flowing narrative that does hold viewer interest. Tony Martinelli's editing is well-done and music by Herman Stein carries along action unobtrusively. *Hogg.*

Kiss Me Stupid

Lower grade Billy Wilder sex comedy with average to good b.o. prospects.

Lopert Pictures release of Mirisch presentation of a Phalanx (Billy Wilder) production. Stars Dean Martin, Kim Novak, Ray Walston. Felicia Farr, Cliff Osmond. Directed by Wilder. Screenplay by Wilder and I.A.L. Diamond from play, "L'Ora della Fantasia," by Anna Bonacci; camera, Joseph LaShelle; editor, Daniel Mandell; songs, George & Ira Gershwin; score, Andre Previn. Reviewed at Academy Awards Theatre, Hollywood, Dec. 11, 1964. Running Time, 126 MINS.

Dino	Dean Martin
Polly	Kim Novak
Orville J. Spooner	Ray Walston
Zelda Spooner	Felicia Farr
Barney Millsap	Cliff Osmond
Big Bertha	Barbara Pepper
Milkman	James Ward
Mrs. Pettibone	Doro Merande
Mr. Pettibone	Howard McNear
Waitress	Bobo Lewis
Johnny Mulligan	Tommy Nolan
Rev. Carruthers	John Fiedler
Bartender	Bern Hoffman
Truck driver	Henry Beckman

Coming into the market on a wave of notoriety generated by one of the sharpest condemnations the Roman Catholic Legion of Decency has issued in many years might conversely benefit "Kiss Me Stupid" in the beginning. However, once this curiosity factor is exhausted it is doubtful that this new Billy Wilder-I.A.L. Diamond sexploitation comedy will exhibit any exceptional boxoffice staying power. For, putting aside the LOD objection, Wilder is far from being in top form as a story teller and commentator in this instance, and he has got at best only plodding help from two of his principals, Dean Martin and Kim Novak.

A dirty sex exercise, "Kiss Me Stupid" ain't. However, it isn't for the kiddies. Yet it is not likely to corrupt any sensible audience. But there is a cheapness and more than a fair share of crudeness about the humor of a contrived double adultery situation that a husband-wife combo stumble into. In short, the Wilder - Diamond script—the credits say it was triggered by an Italian play, "L'Ora della Fantasia," by Anna Bonacci —calls for a generous seasoning of Noel Coward but, unfortunately, it provides a dash of same, only now and again.

Wilder, usually a director of considerable flair and inventiveness (if not always impeccable taste), has not been able this time out to rise above a basically vulgar, as well as creatively delinquent, screenplay. The version of the picture presented for review purposes was toned down from Wilder's original. Cuts were at the suggestion of both the distributor United Artists (which decided to remove its corporate label and use that of a subsidiary, Lopert Films, after the LOD "C" rating) and the Production Code Administration. Still the film seems overlong.

The thespic mainstays of "Kiss Me Stupid" are Ray Walston and Cliff Osmond, while Felicia Farr registers nicely as the former's attractive and sexually aggressive wife (within matrimonial limits until things get out of hand). Walston plays broadly and with suggestion of farce, never completely realized. If it had been this might

have provided a dimension of sophistication, to cover a multitude of original sins in this case. Walston's role of a suspicious, jealous husband, yet a character who has a certain validity, is permitted too early in the story development, however, to become stupid like the title says.

Moreover, Wilder has directed with frontal assault rather than suggestive finesse the means by which Walston and Osmond, a pair of amateur songwriters in a Nevada waystop—called Climax— on the route from Las Vegas to California, contrive to bag girl-crazy star Martin and sell him on their ditties. Idea is to make Martin stay overnight in Walston's house, to get latter's wife out of the way by creating a domestic crisis and substitute as wife for a night of accommodation with the celebrity a floozy from a tavern.

However, the jealous husband isn't up to carrying through the ruse after he gets a taste of Miss Novak, the tavern B maid. He winds up throwing Martin out of the house and spending the night with the accommodating gal while the wife he had abused into going back to mother ultimately winds up in bed, accidentally of course, with the completely confused, but nonetheless anxious, Martin.

Aside from the principals mentioned, members of the subordinate cast acquit themselves professionally in roles of little more than bit proportions. Doro Merande, as the mother of the character called Polly the Pistol (Miss Novak), has the meatiest secondary role and turns in a gem of a performance.

The score, which figures rather prominently as story motivation and is orchestrated appropriately under the baton of Andre Previn, carries the unusual credit of songs by Ira and George Gershwin. Introed are three unpublished melodies by the long deceased composer to which brother Ira has provided special lyrics. Numbers, pleasant but not exceptionally impressive, are "Sophia," "I'm A Poached Egg" and "All the Livelong Day." *Pry.*

Shmonah Be'ikvot Ekhad
(Eight Following One)
(ISRAEL)

Tel Aviv, Nov 21.
Noah Films release of Michael Kagan-Menahem Golan production. Stars Shai K. Ophir, also starring Bomba Tzur, Geula Gil and Elisheva Michaeli. Directed by Menahem Golan. Screenplay by Uriel Ofek, based on the Yemima Tshernovitz story. Camera. Izhak Herbet ("Mimish"). Music, Dov Seltzer. Editors, Dani Schik, Jacko Erlich. Reviewed at the Hod Cinema, Tel Aviv. Running time, 95 MINS.

Prof. Berger	Shai K. Ophir
Yankele	Bomba Tzur
Geulah	Geulah Gil
Bat Sheva	Elisheva Michaeli
Toppa	Eitan Priver
Tzvika	Ricko Nitai
Reznik	Shlomo Vishinsky
Wolf	Shmuel Wolf
Abu Ichya	Ya'akov Banai
Col. Rimon	Michael Kagan
Moshiko	Benny Cohen
Samelet	Lidia Ophir
Children: Tzion Ashkenozi, Gouri Segal, Tzvika Ram. Ruth Golan, Anat Baigon, Binyamin Goldslager. Alon Brown, Yoram Shwartz, Yoav Ammon.	

This new Israeli thriller-comedy is the kind of fare intended to please the family. Producer-director Menahem Golan mixed ingredients of espionage, cute children, humor, sentiment, patriotism dangers and music, into a combination "Emil and the De'ectives"-"James Bond" concoction, shot against the youthful backgrounds of a Kibbutz (collective settlement) and an Israeli Air Force Base.

A group of Kibbutz children, entertaining a cousin who came from Jerusalem and enjoyed their summer holiday, realize that an odd scholar has established his headquarters in the old ruins, which they consider their exclusive retreat. Upon closer examination and numerous visits with this "visitor," the kids suspect clandestine activities on the part of this ornithologist. He turns out to be bird-watching and Mirage III watching, seeking for details of this French supersonic fighter.

This adds up to adequate fare for Israel audiences but its appeal to foreign patrons seems to be limited. In spite of an Air Force fly-past, snatches of a local football match and a number of songs (written especially for film and pleasantly performed by Geula Gil and a children's choir) it is still rather simple, lacklustre entertainment. Yet some moments of sentiment and tension, some excellent photography by Itzhak Herbst and very decent performances by Shai K. Ophir and Bomba Tzur delight children and young patrons.

Among the relaxed performances directed by Menahem Golan, there are three second-generation performers (Segal and Ram are sons of parent-actors and radio-personalities, while Ruth Golan is daughter of the director), whose charm and ease are most promising.

Music and the editing are professional and the film should prove another step in the direction of badly needed run-of-the-mill film production. *Rapo.*

36 Hours
(PANAVISION)

Strong U.S.-German Military Intelligence melodrama; hefty grosses seen.

Hollywood, Dec. 8.

Metro release of a Perlberg-Seaton production, William Perlberg, producer. Stars James Garner, Eva Marie Saint, Rod Taylor; features Werner Peters. Directed by George Seaton. Screenplay, Seaton, based on Roald Dahl's "Beware of the Dog," and story by Carl K. Hittleman, Luis H. Vance; camera, Philip H. Lathrop; music, Dimitri Tiomkin; editor, Adrienne Fazan; asst. director, Donald Roberts. Reviewed at Metro studios, Dec. 7, '64. Running time, **115 MINS.**

Major Jefferson Pike	James Garner
Anna Hedler	Eva Marie Saint
Major Walter Gerber	Rod Taylor
Otto Schack	Werner Peters
Ernst	John Banner
General Allison	Russell Thorson
Colonel Peter MacLean	Alan Napier
Lt. Colonel Ostermann	Oscar Beregi
Captain Abbott	Ed Gilbert
German Guard	Sig Ruman
Elsa	Celia Lovsky
Corporal Kenter	Karl Held
Kraatz	Martin Kosleck
Charwoman	Marjorie Bennett
German Soldier	Henry Rowland
German Soldier	Otto Reichow
German Agent	Hilda Plowright
Denker	Walter Friedel
Lamke	Joseph Mell

"36 Hours" is a fanciful war melodrama limning an incident during that crucial number of hours immediately preceding D-Day which rates high in suspense and audience lure. The Perlberg-Seaton production takes its title from the span of time allotted a German psychiatrist to learn from a captured U.S. Intelligence officer fully briefed on the oncoming Allied invasion the exact point of landing. There are certain contrived aspects, but in the main an intriguing subject is nicely realized. James Garner, Rod Taylor and Eva Marie Saint embellish the top characters to herald a good sendoff.

Film's narrative projects a battle of wits between the two antagonists, and the interfering tactics of a high Gestapo agent insistent upon use of force rather than the more subtle means of prying vital information employed by the doctor. George Seaton's script—which he directs tellingly—is an imaginative approach to the situation of the German's desperate last-ditch attempt to pinpoint the Allies' strategy.

Based on Roald Dahl's "Beware of the Dog" and a story by Carl K. Hittleman and Luis H. Vance, it provides a behind-the-scenes glimpse of high Military Intelligence at work. Plot carries enough twists to hurdle a few more static periods and various parts are vibranly enacted.

Garner plays the American sent to Lisbon to confirm through a German contact that the Nazis expect the Allies to land in the Calais area rather than the secretly-planned Normandy beach. Drugged, he's flown under heavy sedation by the Germans to an isolated resort in Bavaria where upon regaining consciousness he's led to believe he has been an amnesia victim for six years.

Seaton builds his suspense through Garner accidentally discovering the German plan after he has mentioned Normandy as the Allies' landing site, then clouding the issue in the German minds. Conflict between the German doctor and Gestapo agent over Garner further motivates the action, which has Taylor helping Garner and Miss Saint, a German nurse, escape.

Taylor registers most effectively in the offbeat role of the German, playing it for sympathy and realistically. Garner in a derring-do part is okay and up to his usual sound brand of histrionics. Miss Saint also delivers strongly as the nurse drafted by the Nazis from a concentration camp and promised help by Taylor if she plays her part well—in the masquerade with Garner. As the Gestapo officer, Werner Peters is properly menacing, and John Banner is a brief standout as a German Home Guard soldier who shoots Peters so Garner and femme may escape into Switzerland.

William Perlberg's producer helming is expert and his technical backing perform in kind. Philip H. Lathrop's fluid camera work, Dimiri Tiomkin's atmospheric music score and Adrienne Fazan's tight editing add to general overall excellence of film. *Whit.*

Quick, Before It Melts
(PANAVISION-COLOR)

Goofball comedy about doings in Little America okay for general situations.

Hollywood, Dec. 3.

Metro release of Douglas Laurence-Delbert Mann production. Stars George Maharis, Robert Morse; features James Gregory, Anjanette Comer, Howard St. John, Michael Constantine, Norman Fell, Janine Gray, Yvonne Craig, Bernard Fox, Conlon Carter. Directed by Mann. Screenplay, Dale Wasserman, based on novel by Philip Benjamin; camera (Metro-Color), Russell Harlan; music, David Rose; editor, Fredric Steinkamp; asst. director, Erich von Stroheim Jr. Reviewed at Hollywood Paramount Theatre, Dec. 2, '64. Running time, **97 MINS.**

Peter Santelli	George Maharis
Oliver Cromwell Cannon	Robert Morse
Tiare Marshall	Anjanette Comer
Vice Admiral	James Gregory
Harvey T. Sweigert	Howard St. John
Mikhail Drozhensky	Michael Constantine
George Snell	Norman Fell
Diana Grenville-Wells	Janine Gray
Sharon Sweigert	Yvonne Craig
Leslie Folliott	Bernard Fox
Orville Bayleaf	Conlan Carter
Ben Livingston	Richard Lepore
Prison Guard	Hal Baylor
Ham Operator	Doodles Weaver
Shaggy Type	Frank London
Scientist	Nelson Olmsted
Military Men	Tom Vize, John Dennis, Hugh "Slim" Langtry, Fletcher Allen, Davis Roberts, Dale Malone
Bar Maids	Marjorie Bennett, Karen Scott
Milton Fox	Milton Fox

Do you know how to take the temperature of a seal? Do you believe a former Navy buddy can be reincarnated as a penguin? Do you think there are no femmes in Antarctica? "Quick, Before It Melts" out to explore such trivia and the doings at Little America when a team composed of a resourceful mag photographer and an introverted writer are assigned to cover a scientific mission there. It emerges as a light, slicky-pacer farce with plenty of laughs for the general market.

The Douglas Laurence-Delbert Mann production is headed by George Maharis, as the woman-crazy bulber, and Robert Morse, the shy scribbler who learns about women from a half-Maori airline hostess whom he meets in New Zealand. Film intro's a new looker, Anjanette Comer, in this role, swinging over from tv, and distaff end is further held up by Janine Gray and Yvonne Craig, both evincing promise. Backing such fresh talent are such hardies as James Gregory, the vice admiral commanding Little America; Bernard Fox, his public relations officer; Michael Constantine, a Russian exchange scientist; Conlon Carter, radio operator who uses a willing penguin to deliver messages; Norman Fell, a rival correspondent; and Howard St. John, bombastic publisher-boss of Maharis and Morse—and father of Morse' betrothed, played by Miss Craig.

Dale Wasserman screenplay, based on Philip Benjamin novel, is slotted in a light vein which seldom wavers and Mann's deft direction maintains a nonsensical note in keeping with the story line. Once ensconced at Little America, where the two magsters are continually in the bad graces of commanding officer when they try to get the Russian to defect to appease their publisher's demand for news, pair hit a zenith in complications when they sell the admiral, who hates women, on a publicity stunt to fly in a bevy of femmes from New Zealand to prove that Antarctica isn't as remote as it seems.

Both Maharis and Morse sock over their roles and Mann gets the most out of his supporting cast, all wrapping up the parts neatly. Film gets certain authentic polar background through Metro sending a camera unit to Alaska to lens ice and snow and photography of Russell Harlan is interesting. David Rose's music score accentuates comedic aspects of the unreeling, which Fredric Steinkamp tightly edited, and Laurence and Mann accorded film top production values. *Whit.*

Zorba The Greek

A paean to life, told in tragicomic terms, with a lusty performance by Anthony Quinn. Excessive length, deliberate pace dilutes the intended exuberance. For the arties.

International Classics release of Michael Cacoyannis production, directed by Cacoyannis. Stars Anthony Quinn, Alan Bates and Irene Papas. Screenplay, Cacoyannis, based on novel by Nikos Kazantzakis; camera, Walter Lassally; music, Mikis Theodorakis; asst. editor, Alex Archambault. Reviewed in N.Y., Dec. 8, 1964. Running time, **142 MINS.**

Alexis Zorba	Anthony Quinn
Basil	Alan Bates
The Widow	Irene Papas
Madame Hortense	Lila Kedrova
Mavrandoni	George Foundas
Lola	Eleni Anousaki
Mimithos	Sotiris Moustakas
Manolakas	Takis Emmanuel
Pavlo	George Voyadjis
Soul	Anna Kyriakou

To one who has not read the late Nikos Kazantzakis' widely praised novel, on which this International Classics (20th-Fox) film is based, it appears that producer-director-scenarist Michael Cacoyannis may have tried to be too faithful to the original. That would seem to be the most reasonable explanation for the picture's excessive length and overabundance of incident which, instead of contributing to the intended exuberance, only dilute it.

"Zorba The Greek" is a paean to life in all its diverse aspects, ranging from the farcical to the tragic, and as epitomized by the lusty title character. This Zorba, beautifully played by Anthony Quinn, is a wise and aging peasant, a free soul who is totally committed to life no matter what it holds. When his friend at one point asks him if—by pursuing a local widow—he is "looking for trouble," Zorba answers simply that "to be alive is to look for trouble—only death is not." And Zorba accepts the consequences of his own actions, as well as those over which he has had no control, with a kind of optimistic resignation which seems to say that, as love is life, so are hate and poverty and the impulse to survive.

To dramatize this theme, Cacoyannis has written a screenplay which is packed with incidents of varying moods, so packed, in fact, that some of the more important ones cannot be developed fully. The story takes place in a remote section of the island of Crete where Zorba has come as the self-appointed aide-de-camp to a young, inhibited Englishman of Greek parentage, played by Alan Bates. Latter, who describes himself as a writer who hasn't written anything in a long, long time, intends to reopen an old lignite mine he has inherited, both to earn his own keep and to help the struggling peasants.

Their subsequent adventures—rather loosely connected and wherein Bates finally learns to live a la Zorba—comprise the body of the film. At its best moments, "Zorba The Greek" is either tumultuously funny or brutally sad. Zorba's pursuit of an aging French courtesan, somehow mysteriously marooned in this bleak Cretan hamlet, is uproarious slapstick, eventually capped when, some months later, as she is dying of pneumonia in his arms, the ravenous peasants already are ransacking her house around her.

Also touching, though never quite clearly defined, is the sequence in which the introverted Bates finally decides to make love to the young widow, Irene Papas, who has chosen him over all the offers of the fiercely jealous townsmen. When the lady's number one suitor subsequently commits suicide in shame, the townsmen publicly execute the widow in a rite which erupts as a brief, appalling echo of the Greece of pre-history.

In such moments, Cacoyannis is brilliantly successful. There are other times, however, when he allows the film to be merely cute and picturesque, as when Zorba dupes the monks in a nearby monastery into thinking he has changed their water to wine, or when he goes on a spree in Athens. Also, perhaps because of the tight focus maintained on Quinn and Bates, one never quite believes that they really are living and working with the islanders around them. The islanders, photogenic as they are in their authentic way, thus emerge as looking like quaint extras (which, of course, they are) milling around two professional actors.

Quinn is excellent, and Bates, in a less flamboyant role, is equally good. Irene Papas is strikingly effective as the doomed widow, a role without dialog. Lila Kedrova plays the aging courtesan with all stops out, always halfway between laughter and tears and, grotesquely, reminding one of Shirley Temple as The Little Colonel. It's a busy but oddly interesting performance.

The physical production is excellent, especially the sharp black and white camerawork of the bleak Cretan locales, and the background score, which only becomes (or seems to become) intrusive when interest in the screen action lags.

"Zorba The Greek" is a natural for the arties, where audiences will appreciate its offbeat qualities and indulge its length. A careful buildup, plus good word of mouth, might permit it to successfully play general dates later. *Anby.*

The Last Woman Of Shang

(Ta Chi)

(CHINESE—EASTMAN COLOR—SHAWSCOPE)

Frank Lee presentation of a Shaw Bros. (Run Run Shaw) production. Directed by Yueh Feng. Stars Lin Dai, Pat Ting Hung; features Nam Koong-woon, Shin Yung-kyoon, Ching Miao, Chiang Kwong-t'sao; screenplay, Wang Yueh-ting; camera (Eastman Color), Ho Lan-shan; editor, Chiang Hsing-loong; musical score, Wang Foo-ling, lyrics, Chen Di-ye. Reviewed at New York, Dec. 10, 1964. Running time—**147 MINS.**

(English Subtitles)

Although Shaw Bros. have had some west coast exposure of their Hong-Kong-filmed product, particularly in the San Francisco area, they have not released any films in the eastern U.S. markets. As part of the plunge into the N.Y. art film situation, producer Run Run Shaw hopes his first will have a sufficient run to continue with a series for first-run showing at the Moss circuit's 55th Street Playhouse. If "Last Woman of Shang" which started Monday (14) does well, the series planned will include more of the same genre as "Woman," spectacle-filled and historically colorful.

Based on this first booking, however, an extremely limited market is indicated for more than a week or longer. Genuinely effective scenes of great magnitude are connected by lengthy, dull passages that have already been overdone by many earlier similar-themed Japanese films. Coast representative for Shaw, Frank Lee, will handle all distribution and bookings from his Frisco office for the time being, a smart move.

"Woman" was last film made by actress Lin Dai before her death earlier this year. Her fantastic popularity (likely one of reasons for U.S. move is to capitalize on already-made product starring her) was symbolized by mob scenes at her funeral in Hong Kong.

As Ta Chi, who becomes a queen in order to avenge her people and her father, slain by the king, Miss Dai, a lovely and talented actress, shows a wide range of expression that takes advantage of an admittedly colorful role. She pretty much carries the film and is at her best in the lengthy closing scene wherein she levels with her king-husband as to her true intentions and feelings. All the time the two of them barely avoid falling timbers in the palace which is burning and overrun with troops of the invading revolutionaries. As both are constantly on camera it is obvious they had to play the scene without doubles which is pretty risky handling of a valuable property.

Other than Miss Dai, only cast members who come up to western acting standards are Pat Ting Hung as her faithful handmaiden and, briefly, Ching Miao as the father of the hero. His wonderfully expressive face and natural acting remain in the viewer's memory long after his short scenes. Providing plenty of action but little acting, Nam Koong-woon as the prince-poet-soldier hero and Shin Yung-kyoon as King Chou head a large cast, with plenty of blood-letting and torture.

Although the 147-minute running time is of epic length, there are references in the synopsis to sequences not shown, indicating previous editing has been done but much more would help. One unusual facet of Chinese filmmaking, and one which quickly became annoying, is the attitude that laughter, in the minds of the Chinese, is associated with vulgarity, boorishness, drunkenness and never with honest enjoyment. Several characters, particularly King Chou and some of his ministers, go into endless fits of laughing whenever they wish to convey lechery, evil intent, etc. When "nice" characters want to convey happiness, they merely smile.

Filmed primarily at Shaw's Movie Town (Hong Kong prototype of the Italian Cinecitta), location work for the battle scenes was done in South Korea. The sameness about interpolated battle and spectacle scenes (building a tower, fleeing cities, etc.) suggests extensive footage having been shot and then cut into segments of varying length for use where needed. This is also true of court dance scenes, which have striking similarity to each other. Some interiors have obvious painted backdrops and little actual exterior work is shown, but costumes are opulent and on a par with the Japanese.

Besides the English subtitles, which tend to be too long and changed too quickly, the film also has Chinese subtitles. It seems that although the Chinese speak many dialects, they read only one version of Chinese. Hence, soundtrack uses Mandarin dialect but subtitles can be read in any area where Chinese are found. Screenplay supposedly stems from old Chinese legends but the plot contains large chunks of familiar Occidental tales including Shakespeare's "Othello" and "Coriolanus."

Music, only occasionally completely Chinese, does retain Oriental mood even when instruments are evidently western, such as lots of violins. As Shaw has always been able to profitably restrict his films to the Chinese-populated areas of the world, his move into U.S. market will probably be in nature of experiment. There would appear to be only limited appeal for even art houses in such films as this, however. *Robe.*

Strange Bedfellows

(COLOR)

Romantic comedy, with top-name cast and excellent support from comedians in small roles, should do well at b.o.

Hollywood, Nov. 24.

Universal release of Panama & Frank production. Stars Rock Hudson, Gina Lollobrigida, Gig Young; features Terry-Thomas, Edward Judd. Directed by Melvin Frank. Screenplay, Melvin Frank and Michael Pertwee, based on story by Norman Panama and Frank; camera (Technicolor), Leo Tover; editor, Gene Milford; music, Leigh Harline. Reviewed at Academy Theatre, Hollywood, Nov. 23, '64. Running time, **99 MINS.**

Carter	Rock Hudson
Toni	Gina Lollobrigida
Richard Bramwell	Gig Young
Harry Jones	Edward Judd
Assistant Mortician	Terry-Thomas
Taxi Driver	Arthur Haynes
J. L. Stevens	Howard St. John
Toni's Taxi Driver	David King
Mavis	Peggy Rea
Petracini	Joseph Sirola
Aggressive Woman	Nancy Kulp
Jolly Woman	Lucy Landau
Policeman	Bernard Fox
Mrs. Stevens	Edith Atwater
Old Man	James McCallion
Bagshott	Hedley Mattingly
Radio Dispatcher	John Orchard

"Strange Bedfellows" is another of those romantic marital comedies, based primarily on misunderstandings, which Universal issues with calendar-like regularity. Graced by the handsome virility of Rock Hudson, fiery beauty of Gina Lollobrigida, plus gowns by Jean Louis, beautiful photography by Leo Tover and comedy backing in the second rank, this Panama and Frank Production should mean happy days at the b.o.

Critics for the thinking man may scoff at the plot, which derives much of its drama from ancient device of each character not quite understanding what the others are up to. But story line differs enough so that it isn't simple carbon of all the Hudson-Tony Randall-Doris Day comedies that have come before.

Hudson is a trifle solemn as London-based U.S. oil executive who can rise to extreme top echelon if his corporate image is white-washed. This means he must patch up seven-year marriage to Miss Lollobrigida, who more than compensates for Hudson's stuffiness by her enthusiastic rapport with zany causes and kook advocates of ban-the-bomb marches and other suspect endeavors.

Gig Young is company p.r. man assigned to clear up Hudson's image, and he plays man-in-the-middle over-broadly. Edward Judd, Gina's British boyfriend who hopes to keep her and Hudson apart, is blandly competent in role.

But the unabashed comedians steal the show. Probably the funniest bit has Arthur Haynes and David King as taxidrivers with Hudson and Gina in their respective vehicles. The estranged lovers try to communicate with one another by way of two-way cab radio, with hilarity resulting from cabbies garbling of messages.

Terry-Thomas shines in cameo role as undertaker whose shop is in path of chase scene. Also amusing are Peggy Rea, who is bumped from Godiva role by Gina, Nancy Kulp as fanatic picket-line marcher and Lucy Landau as jolly advocate of freedom of expression.

Godiva role, incidentally, turns out to be dud from standpoint of those intrigued by "closed-set" publicity. Gina wear flesh-colored woolies that wouldn't create blushes in a Disney pic. Some bedroom scenes generate enough heat to compensate for disappointment, however.

Director Frank keeps story moving at lively clip, preventing viewers from dwelling on holes in plot, and editor Gene Milford's cutting has no apparent defects. Art directors Alexander Golitzen and Joseph Wright have done top job of recreating London, much of it on Universal's new "European" set. *Hogg.*

Psychomania

Well-produced shocker suitable for exploitation.

Hollywood, Dec. 10.

Emerson Pictures release of Del Penney production. Stars Lee Philips, with Sheppard Strudwick, James Farentino, Carol Bishop, Lorraine Rogers, Margot Hardtman. Directed by Richard Hilliard. Screenplay, Robin Miller; camera, Louis McMahon; editor, Robert Q. Lovett. Reviewed at Pix Theatre, Dec. 9, '64. Running time, **90 MINS.**

Elliott Freeman	Lee Philips
Lawyer	Sheppard Strudwick
Charlie Perone	James Farentino
Jean Hale	Carol Bishop
Alice S. Clair	Lorraine Rogers
Lynn Freeman	Margot Hardtman
Palmer	Richard Van Patten
Janet	Shiela Forbes
Inspector Gray	Mike Keene
Sylvia	Sylvia Miles

"Psychomania" is a low-budget, well-done shocker with a tightly-knit plot and a believable surprise ending which should have no trouble making up its low cost with good advance promotion.

Lee Philips does a fine acting job as the karate-expert artist from a family with a psychotic background, who gets involved in a pair of bizarre murders. Shepperd Strudwick and James Farentino are believable as the lawyer and a tough motorcycle hood respectively. Margot Hardtman seems forced as Philips' sister. Lorraine

Rogers is appropriately sexy as a young siren.

Richard Hilliard's realistic direction and Louis McMahon's excellent camera work help build the suspense of Robin Miller's screenplay to a satisfyingly real ending. Some of the dialog shows good imagination. Probably with a bigger budget, film could have been an excellent psychodrama.

Bobb.

The Disorderly Orderly
(COLOR)

Jerry Lewis in one of his funnier madcaps. Usual solid grosses indicated.

Hollywood, Dec. 11.

Paramount release of Paul Jones production. Stars Jerry Lewis; features rest of cast. Directed by Frank Tashlin. Screenplay, Tashlin, from story by Nora Liebmann, Ed Haas; camera (Technicolor), W. Wallace Kelley; music, Joseph Lilley; editor, John Woodcock asst. director, Ralph Axness. Reviewed at Bruin Theatre, Westwood, Cal., Dec. 10, '64. Running time, 80 MINS.
Jerome Littlefield .... Jerry Lewis
Dr. Jean Howard .... Glenda Farrell
Mr. Tuffington .... Everett Sloane
Julie Blair .... Karen Sharpe
Maggie Higgins ..... Kathleen Freeman
Susan Andrews .... Susan Oliver
Dr. Davenport .... Del Moore
    Others: Jack E. Leonard, Barbara Nichols, Alice Pearce, Danny Costello, Mike Ross, Benny Rubin, Frank Scannell, Milton Frome, John Macchia.

Jerry Lewis, wise in the ways of his audiences, comes up with the same formula that has meant money in the bank for past offerings. With producer Paul Jones at the helm to render his experience as a top comic filmaker and Frank Tashlin as combination scripter and director, "The Disorderly Orderly" is fast and madcappish, with Lewis again playing one of his malaprop characters that seem to suit his particular talents . . . and his public's taste.

Lewis dons hospital orderly attire for this quick-tempoed eTusion of happenings that naturally accrue from this character. Of story line there's only the slightest, of gags there are many, some not so funny but most on the hilarious **side that communicate to the comedian's particular public.** Lewis throughout plays everything broad, and as the orderly who always tries too hard usually leaves desolation in his wake. There's one of the fastest windups on record as two ambulances charge through the streets at breakneck pace, narrowly missing cars, trucks and public, and a stretcher on wheels bearing a panicked passenger rivals them in speed.

As the orderly, Lewis is himself almost a menial patient as he takes on all the symptoms of the individual patients in the plush sanitarium where he's employed. Ambitious to be a doctor, he flunked out in medical school because of this particular attribute. He's cured through some fancy script-figuring when Susan Oliver, one of the patients, offers him love and he discovers that he's really in love with Karen Sharpe, a nurse. Sandwiched within this premise is Lewis at work, at play, always in trouble.

Star is up to his usual comicking and Frank Tashlin's direction of his own screenplay is fast and vigorous in maintaining a nutty mood. Miss Sharpe is pert and cute, Miss Oliver ably transforms from a would-be suicide to a sexpot and Glenda Farrell, cast as head of

the sanitarium, displays the talent which once made her a star. Everett Sloane as board of directors chairman is heavy of the piece. Standouts also are contributed by Kathleen Freeman as a harrassed nurse and Alice Pearce as a talkative patient, Del Moore enacts a psychiatrist trying to oust Lewis from his negative thinking and Barbara Nichols and Jack E. Leonard are in for cameo roles. Sammy Lewis sings title song over the credits.

Jones as producer gives the Lewis picture the customary handsome mounting that always distinguishes comic's films and W. Wallace Kelley's color photography of Hal Pereira-Tambi Larsen's artistic sets lends class. Music score by Joseph Lilley and John Woodcock's editing also are on the plus side.

Whit.

Carry On Cleo
(BRITISH — COLOR)

Another slapstick entry from the "Carry On" stable; plenty of yocks from the familiar gang should pay off.

London, Dec. 8.

Warner-Pathe release of a Peter Rogers Production from Anglo Amalgamated. Stars Kenneth Williams, Kenneth Connor, Sidney James, Charles Hawtrey, Joan Sims, features Amanda Barrie, Jim Dale, Julie Stevens, Victor Maddern, Sheila Hancock. Directed by Gerald Thomas. Screenplay by Talbot Rothwell; camera (Eastmancolor), Alan Hume; editor, Archie Ludski; music, Eric Rogers. At Warner Theatre, London. Running time, 92 MINS.
Mark Antony .... Sidney James
Julius Caesar .... Kenneth Williams
Hengist .... Kenneth Connor
Seneca .... Charles Hawtrey
Calpurnia .... Joan Sims
Cleo .... Amanda Stevens
Gloria .... Julie Stevens
Sgt. Major .... Victor Maddern
Senna .... Sheila Hancock
Bilius .... David Davenport
Archimedes .... Michael Ward
Virginia .... Tanya Billing
Agrippa .... Francis de Wolff
Sosages .... Tom Clegg
Soothsayer .... Jon Pertwee
Galley Master .... Peter Gilmore
Brutus .... Brian Oulton
Spencius .... Warren Mitchell

Intended as a parody of the expensive original "Cleopatra," this latest entry from the "Carry On" stables relies on the bludgeon rather than the rapier, so isn't entirely successful in its purpose. But regarded as one of a successful string of knockabout pieces of slapstick it registers a full quota of yocks. Neither aficionado nor exhibitors will be disappointed. The title and cast should guarantee a boxoffice hit.

As usual, Peter Rogers' technical team is well up to scratch. Alan Hume's lensing, Eric Rogers' music and the editing by Archie Ludski all register satisfactorily. Gerald Thomas' formula for directing these groups is now cut-and-dried and any deviation would be a gamble. It is Talbot Rothwell's screenplay that is suspect. Though he has not allowed himself to be hampered overmuch by historical fact or William Shakespeare's "idea," from which the producer magnanimously admits this lark is derived, many characters and situations will not be familiar to all patrons and parodying the little known is a chancy business.

Accent in this frolic is less on situation than on dialog and so there is less action to hold the audience. Rothwell's dialog is unabashedly corny but this doesn't much matter. But it is also unusu-

ally bristling with plodding double entendres and tinged with a blueness which is less acceptable **than the all-out healthy vulgarity that has stamped pervious "Carry Ons."** Gags, both verbal and visual, suffer from repetition and few are as neat as Julius Caesar's woeful complaint, "Infamy! Infamy! Everybody's got it in for me!" Still, music hall flavor about the happenings to insure snickers, belly laffs and good humored chortles galore.

The practised cast of Old Regulars are also, mainly, up to form, with Sidney James as Mark Anthony and Kenneth Connor as Hengist, the Wheelmaker particularly prominent as they disport among the vestal virgins. Kenneth Williams has a few twittering moments as Caesar but again irritatingly overplays. Charles Hawtrey's main function is to look incongruous and carry the weight of some of the least subile sex patter. Jim Dale, Victor Maddern, Brian Oulton, Warren Mitchell and David Davenport are others who chip in with gusto.

On the femme side, Joan Sims is a hearty gal as Caesar's wife, Sheila Hancock is a shrill one as Hengist's spouse. Ianya Billing and Julie Stevens look stunning. But the best discovery is Amanda Barrie as the poor man's Cleopatra. Miss Barrie is a wide-eyed youngster who, as well as having femme appeal, shows distinct signs of a comic sense. Her takeoff of the Queen of the Nile gets nearer to the tongue-in-cheek sense of what Rogers and Thomas were aiming at than any of her more experienced colleagues. *Rich.*

Katu
(COLOR)

Brazilian nudie film. Not much.

Hollywood, Dec. 9.

Levinson release of Zygmunt Sulistrowski production. Directed & screenplay by Sulistrowski. Camera (color), Herbert C. Theisen. Reviewed at Hollywood Theatre, Dec. 8, '64. Running time, 84 MINS.

"Katu" is a nudie with a dash of Brazilian Indian travelog tossed in to springboard the story of a group of American nudists going to a deserted island off Brazil and living off the land for three months to win a wager. Produced and directed by Brazilian indie Zygmunt Sulistrowski, cast is completely unknown. Film, in color, is subtitled "The French Girl and the Nudists."

As an exploitation pic for limited booking it may draw some engagements but means nothing insofar as entertainment is concerned. Footage is mostly devoted to rear shots of the 13 naturists mostly in the raw disporting themselves on their island retreat, working, playing, swimming, et al, in static poses and movement. Sensation-seekers can do better than this. *Whit.*

Monstrosity

Agrees with its implication.

Hollywood, Dec. 10.

Emerson Pictures release of Cinema Venture production. Stars Frank Gerstle, with Erika Peters, Judy Bamber, Marjorie Eaton, Frank Fowler, Margie Fisco. Directed by Joseph Mascelli. Reviewed at Pix Theatre, Dec. 9, '64. Running time, 70 MINS.
Doctor .... Frank Gerstle
Nina .... Erika Peters
Bee .... Judy Bamber
Hazel .... Marjorie Eaton
Victor .... Frank Fowler
Zombie .... Margie Fisco

"Monstrosity" proves its name no misnomer. Film might go on second half of double bill, but by itself it stands as a poorly acted, poorly directed and poorly written attempt to shock.

Frank Gerstle walks through his role as a doctor making experiments to transplant human brain from one body to another for a rich old lady played by Marjorie Eaton. Experiments fail to produce anything but zombies, and it's difficult to distinguish the zombies from the other actors. Erika Peters, Judy Bamber and Margie Fisco are three bodies imported from Europe for the doctor's evil purpose, all three losing their foreign accents half-way through the film.

Joseph Mascelli's direction is sloppy, and even the sound is poor. Film ends with the entire evil house burning to the ground. Not a bad idea. *Bobb.*

Sinderella and The Golden Bra
(COLOR)

She didn't lose her slipper. Color nudie okay for its market.

Hollywood, Dec. 17.

Manson release of Paul Mart production. Features Suzanne Sybele, Bill Gaskin. Directed by Loel Minardi. Screenplay, Frank Squires, from story by Minardi, Squires, Les Szarvas, based on idea by Mart; camera (EastmanColor), Fou; music, Szarvas; editor, Karl Von; asst. director, Ronald Terry. Reviewed at Monica Theatre, Dec. 16, '64. Running time, 81 MINS.

Sinderella .... Suzanne Sybele
Prince David .... Bill Gaskin
King .... David Duffield
Godfather .... Sid Lassick
Stepmother .... Patricia Mayfield
Flossy .... June Faith
Fanny .... Joan Lemo
Adviser .... Gerald Strickland
First Page .... John Bradley
Matron .... Kay Hall
Village Maidens .... Althea Currier, Jackie De Witt, Justine Scott, Lisa Carole, Beverly Frankell, Donna Anderson

Once there was a prince in a fairytale kingdom who fell in love with a beautiful stranger who left her slipper behind her when she disappeared from the royal ball on the stroke of midnight. Only this cinematic version in color has her losing her golden bra, and her name is now Sinderella. For the nudie market the Paul Mart production should suffice.

Footage is pegged on the prince searching the kingdom for the maiden who will perfectly fit the bra, and there it is right there before the camera. But not one of the maids who strip down can mould themselves into the flimsy piece of gold, and the prince is disheartened, thinking he'll never find his love. But—you guessed it—there is a beauteous scullery maid, the stepdaughter of a living ogre with two daughters, who is the owner of the bra, whom the prince finally finds and they live happily ever after.

Suzanne Sybele, a Miss France in the Miss Universe contest, is Sinderella and Bill Gaskin the prince. Patricia Mayfield is the stepmother, June Faith and Joan Lemo the daughters, David Duffield the king and Sid Lassick the witless fairy godfather who sends Sinderella to the ball. They play for laughs under Loel Minardi's direction.

Exhibs also are offered a "dressed" version if they don't want the peeled product. *Whit.*

Controsesso
(COUNTERSEX)
(ITALO-FRENCH)

Rome, Dec. 15.

Interfilm release of Carlo Ponti production for Champion Films (Rome)—Les Films Concordia (Paris). Stars Nino Manfredi, Ugo Tognazzi; features Annamaria Ferrero, Dolores Wettach, Umberto D'Orsi, Renzo Marignano. Directed by Franco Rossi, Renato Castellani, Marco Ferreri. At the Quattrofontane, Rome. Running time, 118 MINS.

COCAINA DI DOMENICA
(Cocaine on Sunday)

With Manfredi, Miss Ferrero. Directed by Rossi. Screenplay, Cesare Zavattini, Benvenuti, DeBernardi; camera, Leonida Barboni; editor, Giorgio Serralonga.

Husband .... Nino Manfredi
Wife .... Annamaria Ferrero
Officer .... Renzo Marignano

IL PROFESSORE
(The Professor)

With Tognazzi. Directed by Ferreri. Screenplay, Ferreri, Rafael Azcona; camera, Roberto Gerardi; music, Teo Usuelli.

Professor .... Ugo Tognazzi

UNA DONNA D'AFFARI
(A Businesswoman)

With Manfredi, Miss Wettach, D'Orsi. Directed by Renato Castellani. Screenplay, Tonino Guerra, Giorgio Salvioni, Castellani; music, Roman Vlad; camera, Ennio Guerrieri; editor, Jolanda Benvenuti.

Maestro .... Nino Manfredi
Giovanna .... Dolores Wettach
Friend .... Umberto D'Orsi

Amusing episode entry, two-thirds of which have good grossing potential on the local market and special foreign situations, where exploitable angles will assist. Third item in trio by director Marco Ferreri, is more for the initiates via its subtlety, a must for Ferreri aficionados.

There's a certain vague link between three items exemplified by the title, but more clearly illustrated by their joint preoccupations with sexual frustrations of very different kinds. Initial episode, very skillfully directed by Franco Rossi, and neatly acted by Nino Manfredi and Annamaria Ferrero, may run into censorship trouble with production codes or censorial groups, as it's about narcotics, though treated for laughs. Man is safeguarding a bottle of cocaine as a guarantee for money loaned a friend. When the latter is arrested, the man's wife discovers the flask and, refusing to waste drug and fearful of otherwise disposing of it, takes some. Her subsequent agitation induces the reluctant husband to join her, but, after various incidents, the effect wears off and things return to normal. It's one to be seen rather than recounted, with prurient material nicely spoofed, a credit to the director and thespians.

Second seg is more "difficult," dealing with introverted, often "sick" life and the thoughts of village professor, Ugo Tognazzi, frustrated into woman-hating, coddled in a memory-ridden house by two vintage aunts, on his way to becoming a veritable male old maid, though suffering deeply inside. Bit has a shattering climax in which Tognazzi silently cries out his inner torment and frustrations. As noted, it's not for all palates, except for some surface humor which is not author's primary intent. Tognazzi is excellent. Lensing, in the copy seen, was a bit murky.

Final item, though point is a bit overextended, is the most generally risible of all. Musician meets a lovely girl on the street, follows her, and she unexpectedly agrees to meet him at his place. Scene is set, both are willing, but there, and on subsequent meetings one or another of woman's biz problems interrupts their affair at the crucial moments, as man's frustrations grow and grow.

Nino Manfredi is very amusing as the Maestro while a newcomer Dolores Wettach, is a very pretty find as the elusive target for his attentions. Bit is neatly staged by director Renato Castellani. Technical credits are tops, with Roman Vlad's classic musical backdropping, with modern interpolations, a major plus. *Hawk.*

House With An Attic
(Dom s Mezzaninom)
(RUSSIAN-COLOR)

Artkino presentation of Yalta Film Studios production. Directed by Y. Bazelian. Features Sergei Yakovlev, Nelly Myshkova, Ludmilla Gordeichuk, Olga Zhizneva, Yacov Leonidov, Sergei Kalinin; screenplay, P. Yerofeyev from story by Anton Chekhov; camera (Sovcolor), A. Rybuv; music, A. Muravlev. Reviewed at N.Y., Dec. 19, 1964. Running time, 85 MINS.

Though studied to the point of lethargy and photographed in some of the poorest color seen in years, much of the Chekhovian gift for conveying the influence of the times and social conditions on characters still comes through in this Russian import. Technical imperfections and stolid pace make it of little appeal, however.

There is excellent acting on the part of the cast, most of whom are members of the Moscow Art Players. Story details painter whose anti-social beliefs and failure to conform antagonize the sister of the girl he loves, causing the breakup of the affair. Title refers to the home of the sisters, the last view of which the artist carries in his memory for the rest of his life. Mostly an exercise in characterization, "House" is enjoyable if the viewer adjusts to the stately, sometimes stolid, pace of the film and the poor color process.

Director Y. Bazelian never hurries his actors, keeping dialog (and English subtitles) to a minimum. Not all talk is translated but the story is easy to follow. Sergei Yakovlev, blondly handsome, is sympathetic as the landscape artist who falls in love in vain with Ludmilla Gordeichuk, the younger sister of Nelly Myshkova. The latter, a do-gooder type immediately recognizable as such, is beautiful and coldly unresponsive and so completely dominates her sister that she ends the affair by merely disapproving. Yacov Leonidov as an "exemplary farmer," with whom Yakovlev lives (and is apparently supported by) and Sergei Kalinin as an overworked footman are also impressive. *Robe.*

Image of Love
(COLOR)

Slickly-made documentary is entertaining but is unlikely to go outside of art houses, and will need strong companion on double bill to succeed here.

Hollywood, Dec. 12.

Raab-Stoumen Productions, own release. Executive producer, Max L. Raab. Produced and directed by Lou Stoumen. Screenplay, Stoumen; camera, Arnold Engle; narrated by Anthony Newley. Reviewed at Cinema Theatre, Hollywood, Dec. 11, '64. Running time, 90 MINS.

Raab-Stoumen Productions has assembled a slick and intriguing documentary, "Image Of Love," search through ages for ideal image from numerous sources to trace by using bits and pieces of film of love. Boxoffice success outside of art houses is uncertain, however, and even on such specialized bookings it's not likely to be smash.

Slickness and well-edited pace is both weakness and strength of pic narrated by Anthony Newley. Viewers will not grow bored as scenes shift back and forth from nudes in ancient art to shots of modern beaches and Playboy's centerfold. But they are likely to leave with feeling only surface of enormous subject was skimmed.

Newley's narration is calm and intelligent as film uses clips from old features to show caveman love, then progresses through Greek, Roman, Medieval, Victorian and finally modern eras. Decision seems to be that tastes in love varied with needs of each specific age, but that underneath superficial differences, the attraction of the sexes has been much the same ever since Eve first saw an apple core.

This is hardly a new, startling revelation but Lou Stoument, who produced, directed and scripted, did his work with such finesse that the product adds up to 90 minutes of pleasant, un-momentous viewing. *Hogg.*

Clay
(AUSTRALIAN)

Melbourne, Dec. 14.

Giorgio Mangiamele production. Stars Janine Lebedew, George Dixon, Chris Tsalikis. Features rest of cast. Directed, scripted, photographed and edited by Giorgio Mangiamele. Previewed at St. Kilda Palais, Melbourne, Dec. 13, '64. Running time, 85 MINS.

Margot .... Janine Lebedew
Nick .... George Dixon
Chris .... Chris Tsalikis
Father .... Claude Thomas
Charles .... Robert Clarke
Deaf and Dumb Woman .... Sheila Florance
Mary .... Lola Russell
Businessman .... Cole Turnley

Main interest in this film is that it's the first all-Australian film to be made since 1955's "Jedda." It's the work of Italian-born Mangiamele who's been in Australia for some 12 years and has previously made three shorter films. It's been shot on a shoestring with understanding that unit will be paid at Equity rates if it eventually makes a profit. Shot in some seven weeks at a cost of about $22,250. The producer hopes it'll also be taken up by commercial cinema managements, or perhaps TV.

Photographer Mangiamele emerges streets ahead of scripter Mangiamele or director Mangiamele. Visually it's frequently a poem brought to life with some breathstakingly poignant and arty shots.

Story line is hackneyed, thin and downright muddled. It's whimsically told at beginning and end by the young Margot and concerns Nick, a refugee from the police who apparently is a killer, but it's never revealed who, how or when he did the deed—nor in fact any background on this character is given. Nick, with face downward in clay soil and drenching rain—after being haunted by police—is found by aged painter and his potter daughter Margot, and taken back to what apparently is potters' colony in wilds. Inevitably Nick and Margot fall in love — to chagrin of jealous neighbor Chris who's also enamoured with the girl. But love's young dream has Father's blessing. Chris of course goes to police, who seek out Nick, and there's a tearful scene with Margot driving car at full speed with Chris as passenger—who jumps out before the inevitable tree-crash—and finally there's Margot doing final recap on past events after car accident.

The film action is taken at too leisurely a pace, with little real dramatic conflict. Unfortunately too, some of the acting—and direction—never quite gets beyond the amateur status, sincere though it may be. This isn't helped by some rather obvious dubbing — particularly in the role of the girl—so that there's a slow hollow unnatural pace to a lot of it, reminiscent of early-type British films.

There're quite a few blind alleys in incident and character — which're quite gripping at the time — but seem to indicate that the scripter-director didn't quite know where he was going and changed in mid-stream. One such incident is of a deaf and dumb woman — beautifully portrayed by Sheila Florance — who accompanies a business man who presumably is her husband and watches him order expensive pottery, but isn't allowed the piece that catches her eye. It's only a cameo and would seem to have a lot of meaning behind it, but the incident isn't developed and therefore seemingly serves no useful purpose.

Because it's such a rarity—i.e. an Australian film, there could be a tendency here to praise it regardless. Fact is it shows much promise of what Mangiamele could do with better script and firmer direction. As it stands film might be okay for supporting feature.

Stan.

Lydia
(CANADIAN—COLOR)

Slight, but refreshing romance. Filmed in Greece, with pleasant locations. Good bet for discriminating audiences.

London, Dec. 15.

Libra Film (Julius Rascheff) Production. Features Gordon Pinsent, Anna Hagen, Benentino Costa, Malena Anousaki. Directed by Dedric d'Ailly. Screenplay by Rascheff, Binton Krancer; camera (Technicolor), Rascheff; editor, Krancer; music, A. Hajdu. Previewed at Films and Arts Theatre, London. Running Time, **83 MINS.**

Thomas .... Gordon Pinsent
Lydia .... Anna Hagen
Miki .... Benentino Costa
Marella .... Malena Anousaki

Unable to get backing in Canada, a new Toronto company, Libra, found its finance from Continental business men and shot this, its first pic, in and around the isles of Greece. It took only eight weeks and came in on a budget of $230,000, using mainly local technicians. Result, first shown in London in an attempt to interest distributors, is a modest, slight effort which has a naive charm, considerably enhanced by some refreshing location camerawork by producer Julius Rascheff of the Greek seascape. Discriminating houses could well take a chance with a film which, though not indigenous to Canada, shows plenty of enthusiastic knowhow by its makers.

The wispy story concerns an American, under sentence of death through an incurable illness, who visits the Greek islands to find peace and to come to terms with himself. At first, he cannot understand the great store which the Greeks put on local legends and myths, but gradually finds understanding.

He is brought into contact with an American girl through a small local lad who is steeped in mythology and regards the girl as his own personal siren. The man and girl fall in love but, knowing that he cannot be cured, he leaves the girl and the small boy to live out the legend.

Direction of the picture is over leisurely and, at times, the story and dialog are almost naive. But it has tenderness and puts over the timelessness and unimportance of material things which are a feature of Greece. Camerawork in Technicolor is largely in restful pastel shades and should do much to boost holiday trade in Greece. Editing also is a trifle lacking in tautness. There is also a long but tasteful nude lovemaking sequence on a lonely beach. Some of these padded inconsequential scenes might well have been trimmed to advantage.

There are only four main characters. The American man is played over glumly but with strong sincerity by Gordon Pinsent. Anna Hagen fills the title role passively, but pleasantly. Benentino Costa is an engaging imp while Malena Anousaki plays a local fortune teller strongly, though it's a role that never developes as significantly as might be expected. A. Hajdu's score is unobtrusive and well fitting to the generally gentle tenor of a piece that might have been jerked up boxofficewise, but only at the risk of vulgarization.

Rich.

Mediterranean Holiday
(COLOR—CINERAMA)

German-made 70m travelog gains much with added Burl Ives narration and projection in Cinerama. Natural for Cinerama houses though reminiscent of "Windjammer."

Walter Reade - Sterling (Continental) presentation of Bavaria Films (Georg M. Reuther) production. Directed by Hermann Leitner, Rudolph Nussgruber. Features Burl Ives, Captain Skoglund, officers and cadets of the "Flying Clipper." Screenplay, Gerd Nickstadt, Arthur Elliot, Hans Dieter Bowe, English narration by William Lovelock; camera (70m-Technicolor), Siegfried Hold, Heinz Hoelgher, Toni Braun, Klaus Konig, Bernard Stebich, aerial—Heinrich Schaefer, Heinz Holescher, prolog—Howard Dennis, Howard McKenzie, Edward Campbell; sound, Jean Neny; music, composed, conducted, Riz Ortoloni; songs, music, Ortoloni, lyrics George Weiss, sung by Katyna Ranieri; Burl Ives' songs from Decca Records album.
Reviewed at the Warner Cinerama Theatre, N. Y., Dec. 15, '64. Running time, **158 MINS.**

This 1962 travelog, filmed by producer Georg M. Reuther for Bavaria Studios in Munich, has been acquired by Walter Reade-Sterling, fitted up with a prolog to introduce narrator Burl Ives, given an English narration spoken by Ives and a score by "Mondo Cane" composer Riz Ortolani. The transition has been smooth and painless and with the decision to present it in the single-projector Cinerama process with the help of a special projector lens which compensates for the Cinerama screen (a bit deeper than standard 70m screen), another worthy feature has been added to the Cinerama library. Appeal should be general.

There's a considerable resemblance, in concept, to Louis de Rochemont's Cinemiracle "Windjammer," which also dealt with a sailing ship manned by cadets. This one, however, sails from Goteborg, Sweden to the countries bordering the Mediterranean. Their ship, oddly enough, is an American-designed, British-built three-master, with the English name "Flying Clipper," while the crew is Scandinavian, including 20 Swedish Merchant Marine cadets. Their cruise includes visits ashore in Egypt, Portugal, Yugoslavia, Turkey, Lebanon, Greece, Italy, Monaco and Spain and a lengthy sequence aboard the U.S. aircraft carrier "Shangri La" when one of the cadets needs an emergency appendectomy.

Ives, in a prolog shot by a Hollywood camera crew at Santa Monica pier, appears on screen to set the scene, but remains an off-screen singing and narrating voice through the remainder of the film. His occasional singing of sea chanties are lifted from one of his Decca albums. William Lovelock's narration, while erudite, also contains considerable whimsy.

There's little of the "familiar" Cinerama audience-encompassing feeling in the film (with exception of a wild busride down a mountain) but the projection is a natural for both land and marine shots. Best of the photography is the aerial filming by Heinrich Schaefer and Heinz Hoelscher. Color work throughout is tasteful and a great asset. Helicopter-made shots enable the viewer to see such stretches of little-visited country as the eerie Anatolian flatlands.

Portuguese fishing villages, Lisbon, Dubrovnik, Port Said, a trip up the Nile to Karnak, Luxor, Aswan (to say hello to the Begum Aga Khan at the late Aga Khan's mausoleum), Abu Simbel and the Valley of the Kings, Cairo, Gizeh (and a "race" to the top of the Great Pyramid), Beirut, Baalek, Les Cedres (the Cedars of Lebanon), Antalya, Goreme, Istanbul, the Shangri-La, Santurin, Mykenos, Kalymnos, Rhodes and Athens, Naples and Capri, Monaco and part of the Grand Prix de Monaco, Barcelona, Granada and Seville are stopping points for the ship. Bits of humor are introduced but the film's real appeal are the spectacular views of ship and ports and people.

"Mediterranean Holiday" was shown earlier in WR-S's "Wonderama" process but it was never completely satisfactory. Film will, of course, become available in standard 35 and 70m when necessary but the Cinerama projection adds much to its appeal as a cinematic treat.

The music, whether Ives' songs or Riz Ortolani's breezy score, ably underscores the screen imagery. Some songs, sung by Katyna Ranieri and written by husband Ortolani, are equally atmospheric. None stand out as commercial prospects.

Robe.

Hush . . . Hush, Sweet Charlotte

A shocker. Handsome follow-up to Robert Aldrich's "What Ever Happened to Baby Jane?" with same type of grosses indicated.

Hollywood, Dec. 17.

20th-Fox release of Robert Aldrich production, directed by Aldrich. Stars Bette Davis, Olivia de Havilland, Joseph Cotten; features Agnes Moorehead, Cecil Kellaway, Victor Buono, Mary Astor, Screenplay, Henry Farrell, Lukas Keller, from story by Farrell; camera, Joseph Biroc; editor, Michael Luciano; music, Frank De Vol; asst. directors, William McGarry, Sam Strangis, William F. Sheehan. Reviewed at Village Theatre, Westwood, Cal., Dec. 15, '64. Running time, **134 MINS.**

Charlotte .... Bette Davis
Miriam .... Olivia de Havilland
Drew .... Joseph Cotten
Velma .... Agnes Moorehead
Harry .... Cecil Kellaway
Big Sam .... Victor Buono
Jewel Mayhew .... Mary Astor
Sheriff .... Wesley Addy
Paul Marchand ...... William Campbell
John Mayhew .... Bruce Dern
Editor .... Frank Ferguson
Foreman .... George Kennedy
Taxi Driver .... David Willock
New Boy .... John Megna
Funeral Director .... Percy Helton
2nd Boy .... Kelly Flynn
Gang Leader .... Michael Petit
Young Girl .... Alida Aldrich
3rd Boy .... Kelly Aldrich
Boy Dancer .... William Aldrich
Town Gossips .... Ellen Corby,
Marianne Stewart, Helen Kleeb
Geraldine .... Carol De Lay
Cleaning Women ..... Mary Henderson,
Lillian Randolph, Geraldine West
Chauffeur .... William Walker
Ginny Mae .... Idell James
And .... Teddy Buckner All-Stars

Robert Aldrich's followup (but no relation) to "What Ever Happened to Baby Jane?" is a shocker, possibly the season's most hair-raising filmic event. It appears headed for the same type of audience reception that greeted the previous Bette Davis-Joan Crawford starrer. Miss Davis again stars, with Olivia de Havilland returning to the screen in the role which Miss Crawford started but due to continued illness had to abandon, much to Miss de Havilland's good fortune.

Many of the same elements of suspense and high drama, and oncoming insanity on the part of Miss Davis that characterized feature's predecessor are apparent here, in what is a brilliant production generally right down the line. There are moments when the going becomes complicated and overly contrived, when the happenings in the stately old Southern mansion about to be razed to make way for progress are too confusing to be readily understood. However, the spectator remains intent upon pic's unfoldment and "Hush . . . Hush" will be one of the talked-about films of the year.

Aldrich has established an atmosphere of foreboding, of mystery, of impending tragedy with tenacious regard to formative ingredient, and in a prolog provides a chilling opening sequence that sets the pattern for the main narrative. Both femme stars conform to this pattern with dramatic performances of considerable depth, evincing an intensity attuned to Aldrich's dynamic direction.

Miss Davis lives in the reflection of a dreadful past, the macabre murder and mutiliation of her married lover hanging over her as she frequently confuses the past with the present as her mental balance is threatened. Miss de Havilland, as her cousin, lives very much for the present—and future —as she attempts to soothe and rationalize with the deeply emotional mistress of the house.

Based upon a story by Henry Farrell, who also authored "Baby Jane," screenplay by Farrell and Lukas Heller (latter scripted "Jane") opens in 1927 in the Louisiana plantation house of Miss Davis' father, who warns a neighboring married man to break off all romantic relations with his daughter. That evening, during a grand ball in the mansion, the lover tells Miss Davis their romance is over. As he remains in the summer-house nearby, mulling over the scene that has taken place between them, he looks up in time to see a meat cleaver guillotining downward to chop off his hand at the wrist (closeup for the audience) and then the cleaver cuts off his head.

The main story swings to the present, again in the mansion where Miss Davis lives alone with her memories which threaten to destroy her. The house has been condemned by the Highway Commission and its occupant, whom the nearby towns-people regard as crazy, ordered to leave, but she refuses. Miss de Havilland arrives from the city, upon her cousin's invitation, but not with the intention of blocking the HC's condemnation as Miss Davis believes. She has her own idea of what she wants, and this includes Miss Davis' fortune, in which she's aided by Joseph Cotten as the family doctor. Narrative follows an incredible—sometimes too contrived—chain of events to a tragic finale.

Miss Davis' portrayal is reminiscent of "Jane" in its emotional overtones, in her style of characterization of the near-crazed former Southern belle, aided by haggard makeup and outlandish attire. It is an outgoing performance, and she plays it to the limit. Miss de Havilland, on the other hand, is far more restrained but none the less effective dramatically in her offbeat role. Cotten, in a briefer, less demanding part, persuasively enacts the physician once in love with Miss de Havilland and who grew up with the pair.

Support is particularly strong, outstanding here Agnes Moorehead as the slovenly but faithful housekeeper murdered when she returns to the house after being discharged. Victor Buono as Miss Davis' father in opening sequence is impressive, and Cecil Kellaway registers as a retired Lloyds of London insurance claims man who arrives to determine why no claim was made on the murdered man's policy years before. Bruce Dern as the victim, Mary Astor his widow, Wesley Addy the sheriff, Frank Ferguson a newspaper editor and William Campbell a smut mag reporter likewise are competent.

Music score by Frank De Vol is a valuable assist in building atmospheric mood and Michael Luciano's fast editing helps with suspense. Joseph Biroc's photography is interesting as is art direction by William Glasgow. Title song cleffed by Mack David and De Vol and sung by Al Martino carries a certain haunting quality.

Whit.

The Night Walker

Complicated chiller entry but okay for its particular market.

Hollywood, Dec. 2.

Universal release of William Castle production. Stars Robert Taylor, Barbara Stanwyck, Judith Meredith, Lloyd Bochner; features rest of cast. Directed by Castle. Screenplay, Robert Bloch; camera, Harold E. Stine; editor, Edwin H. Bryant; music, Vic Mizzy; asst. director, Terence Nelson. Reviewed at Wiltern Theatre, Dec. 1, '64. Running time, 86 MINS.

Barry Morland	Robert Taylor
Irene Trent	Barbara Stanwyck
Joyce	Judith Meredith
Howard	Hayden Rorke
Hilda	Rochelle Hudson
Manager	Marjorie Bennett
Malone	Jess Barker
Gardener	Tetsu Komai
Narrator	Ted Durant
The Dream	Lloyd Bochner

Latest in producer-director William Castle's parade of shockers, "The Night Walker," attains its goal as a chiller but the unfoldment is so complicated that audience frequently is lost. Film carries sufficient suspense and elements of shock, however, coupled with star names of Robert Taylor and Barbara Stanwyck, to reap satisfactory grosses in market for which it is aimed.

The Robert Block screenplay, slow in takeoff, twirls around the subject of dreams. It is personalized here in Miss Stanwyck, as widow of a blind electronics engineer who accuses her of unfaithfulness before he's killed in an explosion in his lab, having dreams so starkly real that she cannot determine whether they are illusionary or their events are actually happening. Involved is a handsome stranger who constantly appears, and who takes her to a chaptl where they are married by a wax minister. Climax carries a surprise twist.

Castle, who specializes in this type of product, is responsible for several sock moments that drew screams from preview audience and builds his suspense despite a confused story line. Miss Stanwyck scores as the weirdly perplexed widow who finds herself in horror situations, and Taylor is okay as her husband's attorney. Lloyd Bochner is the man in her dreams, also okay, Hayden Rorke makes the most of his jealous husband role, Judith Meredith registers nicely as a beauty shop attendant and Rochelle Hudson as the shop manager.

Music score by Vic Mizzy helps create suspense and technical credits are all plus side.

Whit.

Signpost To Murder
(PANAVISION)

Suspenseful melodrama that holds until final reel; moderate biz foreseen.

Hollywood, Dec. 9.

Metro release of Lawrence Weingarten production. Stars Joanne Woodward, Stuart Whitman; features Edward Mulhare. Directed by George Englund. Screenplay, Sally Benson, based on play by Monte Doyle; camera, Paul V. Vogel; music, Lyn Murray; editor, John McSweeney; asst. director, Wallace Worsley. Reviewed at Metro studios, Dec. 8, '64. Running time, 75 MINS.

Molly Thomas	Joanne Woodward
Alex Forrester	Stuart Whitman
Dr. Mark Fleming	Edward Mulhare
The Vicar	Alan Napier
Mrs. Barnes	Joyce Worsley
Supt. Bickley	Leslie Denison
Dr. Graham	Murray Matheson
Officer Rogers	Hedley Matingly
Auntie	Carol Veazie

"Signpost to Murder" shapes as a well-sustained piece of suspenseful melodrama—even if contrived in certain elements—until its final reel. Climax totally dismisses unexplained vital story points which make characters unbelievable in their reactions and what dramatic impact the picture had up to this point is lost. By today's standards, the Lawrence Weingarten production is overly short, only 75 minutes, but this may be a source of some comfort both to audiences and exhibs who are accustomed to several more reels in offerings undeserving of this overlength.

Joanne Woodward and Stuart Whitman star in this filmization of Monte Doyle's British play, scripted by Sally Benson, and George Englund directs. Situation of an escaped inmate of an English asylum for the criminally insane taking refuge in a nearby cottage where the wife's husband is out of town—but expected home momentarily—is built up strongly in Englund's direction.

He establishes mood, aided by a huge water wheel attached to house which provides a certain eerie audio effect, and draws realistic performances from his two principals. Either by design or through unfortunate circumstance the whole tenor of the film reverses in the closing minutes, when what is supposed to be a shock climax becomes hopelessly confusing.

Miss Woodward is up to her customary excellence as the femme who hides Whitman, the escapee, in her home, displaying warmth and acting depth. She is up against the somewhat incredible situation, however, that while being held prisoner by a presumed dangerous lunatic she willingly succumbs to his rather hesitant romantic advances within a matter of hours, and fails to inform the authorities when afforded the opportunity.

Whitman, underplaying his role, also registers strongly, coming through with the more consistent performance. He claims to have been an innocent victim when sent to the asylum after a plea of insanity following his wife having been found with her throat cut in her bathtub. He makes his escape after overpowering his doctor, banking on a point of British law that if a lunatic can maintain his freedom for 14 days he is eligible for a new trial.

Edward Mulhare as the doctor is impressive up to the finale, and Murray Matheson as the asylum head and Leslie Denison the police superintendent handle their characters competently. Alan Napier also is in briefly as a vicar who calls on Miss Woodward after her husband is found murdered, for which Whitman is accused.

Weingarten gives his production class mounting and has the benefit of top technical assistance. Paul C. Vogel's photography, art direction by George W. Davis and Edward Garfagno, editing by James McSweeney and music score by Lyn Murray are valuable assets.

Whit.

Marriage—Italian Style
(COLOR)

Clever Italian comedy with names of Sophia Loren and Marcello Mastroianni to spark biz in selected situations.

Hollywood, Dec. 17.

Embassy release of (Joseph E. Levine) Carlo Ponti production. Stars Sophia Loren, Marcello Mastroianni; features Aldo Puglisi, Tecla Scarano, Marilu Tolo, Pia Lindstrom, Giovanni Ridolfi, Vito Moriconi, Generoso Cortini. Directed by Vittorio De Sica. Screenplay, Eduardo de Filippo, Renato Castellani, Antonio Guerrea, Leo Benvenuto, Piero de Bernardi, based on play, "Filomena Marturano," by de Filippo; camera, (EastmanColor), Roberto Gerardi; editor, Adriana Novelli; music, Armando Trovaioli; asst. director, Luisa Alessandri, Franco Indovina. Reviewed Dec. 15, '64. Running time, 102 MINS.

Filomena Marturano	Sophia Loren
Domenico Soriano ..	Marcello Mastroianni
Alfredo	Aldo Puglisi
Rosalie	Tecla Scarano
Diane	Marilu Tolo
Cashier	Pia Lindstrom
Umberto	Giovanni Ridolfi
Riccardo	Vito Moriconi
Michele	Generoso Cortini
Lawyer	Raffaello Rossi Bussola
Mother	Vincenza Di Capua
Priest	Vincenzo Aita

(English Subtitles)

Previous boxoffice success of the Italo "Yesterday, Today, Tomorrow," pairing Sophia Loren and Marcello Mastroianni, and latter's "Divorce—Italian Style," no doubt sparked the filming of "Marriage—Italian Style," again with the same stars and as clever a piece of picture-making as has come from abroad in many a day. Production by Carlo Ponti, who did "Yesterday," compares favorably with top Hollywood features in point of quality, story and performances and should be an excellent grosser for its particular market.

Militating somewhat against general acceptance of film is the use of English subtitles—all well done—to cover Italian dialog, and the added possibility that the public may become confused by title similarity and figure it's a reissue of "Divorce—Italian Style." Here, though, is comedy done in the grand style, its amusing yarn of a Neapolitan prostitute becoming a playboy's mistress handled tongue-in-cheek with a fine flair which will be appreciated by more mature audiences.

Vittorio DeSica's adroit direction is the epitome of sophistication, never permitting bad taste to cloud the spicy brothel scenes, and he slips naturally from comedy to the drama that gives story strong buildup toward the end. Finale is a reprise of film's earlier light spirit. Director, too, makes the most of his Naples background and color photgrpahy is particularly interesting.

Both Miss Loren and Mastroianni register fine impressions. Equally adept at either comedy or drama, they respond tellingly to the situation which arises over femme, who was picked out of a brothel 22 years previously by playboy and his constant companion ever since, through a ruse forcing him to marry her in the belief she is on her deathbed. Miss Loren properly ages through the years but still is the tempting personality she always is, and Mastroianni continues to exhibit his masculine wiles.

A competent cast backs the pair, with Aldo Puglisi as the valet and Tecla Scarano the maid special standouts. Giovanni Ridolfi, Vito Moriconi and Generoso Cortini play the three sons of femme star, who tells Mastroianni that one of them is his, which brings on the hilarious climax. Pia Lindstrom (Ingrid Bergman's daughter) also appears briefly (very) as cashier in male star's pastry shop.

Technical credits, particularly camera work by Roberto Gerardi, rate highly and all provide valuable assets.

Whit.

Sex and the Single Girl
(TECHNICOLOR)

Fast-paced, sophisticated comedy with top cast and pre-built title add up to b.o.

Hollywood, Dec. 11.
Warner Bros. release of Richard Quine-Reynard Production. Stars Tony Curtis, Natalie Wood, Henry Fonda, Lauren Bacall, Mel Ferrer; features rest of cast. Directed by Richard Quine. Screenplay, Joseph Heller and David R. Schwartz, story by Joseph Hoffman, based on book by Helen Gurley Brown; camera, Charles Lang; editor, David Wages; music, Neal Hefti. Reviewed at Academy Theatre, Hollywood, Dec. 8, '64. Running time, **114 MINS.**

Bob Weston	Tony Curtis
Helen Brown	Natalie Wood
Frank	Henry Fonda
Sylvia	Lauren Bacall
Rudy	Mel Ferrer
Gretchen	Fran Jeffries
Susan	Leslie Parrish
The Chief	Edward Everett Horton
Motorcycle Cop	Larry Storch
Helen's Cabbie	Stubby Kaye
Randall	Howard St. John
Dr. Anderson	Otto Kruger
Holmes	Max Showalter
Sylvester	William Lanteau
Hilda	Helen Kleeb
Sylvia's Cabbie	Curley Klein
Themselves	Count Basie Orchestra

With pre-built title, modernized slapstick scenes and snappy lines that could feel censor's shears in Kansas City, "Sex And The Single Girl" has ingredients of boxoffice smash. True, plot has weak points but few viewers will care while following antics of top cast in which Tony Curtis, Natalie Wood, Henry Fonda, Lauren Bacall, Fran Jeffries, Leslie Parrish, Edward Everett Horton and Larry Storch are extremely funny.

Helen Gurley Brown's how-to-do-it book for single girls is takeoff point for story by Joseph Hoffman, scripted by Joseph Heller and David R. Schwartz. Miss Wood is Dr. Helen Brown of International Institute of Advanced Marital and Pre-Marital Studies, who is target of scandal mag editor Curtis. Curtis is bent on exposing her to be 23-year-old virgin without background for advising single girls about sex.

In plot convolution far too complex to detail here, Curtis poses as his neighbor, Henry Fonda, who has monumental wife trouble, and goes to Miss Wood for advice. Inevitably, they fall for one another, with Miss Wood ignorant of Curtis' identity as ogre out to ruin her career.

As usual in this type of farce, male and female leads have fewer comic lines than supporting players. But Curtis registers exceptionally well when detailing supposed marital problems to adviser. His timing in confessing to "inadequacies" shows great comic talent. And one of funniest bits in pic comes when poised, self-assured "Dr. Brown" finds she has romantic problem of own, crumples into tears and places long-distance call to "Mother."

Fonda and Miss Bacall as warring husband and wife also serve up effective scenes as they battle over Fonda's non-existent wild life as head of Sexy Sox Inc.

Edward Everett Horton shines as boss of Curtis' mag, who harangues aides to make publication "the most disgusting scandal sheet the human mind can recall." Fran Jeffries and Leslie Parrish are properly, or improperly, funny as

Curtis' amorous girlfriend and dumb blonde secretary, respectively. Mel Ferrer has little to do as Miss Wood's steady, but gets big laugh with confession he became psychiatrist because he "liked to hear dirty stories."

Standout scene for those who dig slapstick is wild freeway chase involving most of cast, plus Larry Storch as motorcycle cop who is driven to madness by zany drivers. Helen Kleeb's role as receptionist who changed her style while reading Dr. Brown's book is a miniature gem. Other small roles are well done, including Stubby Kaye and Curley Klein as cab drivers. Count Basie and Orchestra portrayed themselves with classy version of title tune (which won't make top 40) and "What Is This Thing Called Love?"

Production values of Richard Quine-Reynard Production, released by Warner Bros., are uniformly high. Director Quine keeps fast pace and probably is responsible for small, bright touches, such as showing without comment neurotic symptoms of members of scandal mag's staff. Charles Lang's Technicolor photography and art direction by Cary O'Dell provide suitably lavish settings. David Wages' editing results in smooth-running pictures. Neal Hefti's score is eminently tuneful. *Hogg.*

The Pleasure Seekers
(SONGS-CINEMASCOPE-COLOR)

Pleasant remake of "Three Coins in the Fountain" with new Madrid setting; equally pleasant grosses expected.

Hollywood, Dec. 23.
Twentieth-Fox release of David Weisbart production. Stars Ann-Margret, Tony Franciosa, Carol Lynley, Gardner McKay, Pamela Tiffin, Andre Lawrence; features Gene Tierney, Brian Keith, with Isobel Elsom. Directed by Jean Negulesco. Screenplay, Edith Sommer, based on novel by John H. Secondari; camera (DeLuxe Color), Daniel L. Fapp; music, Lionel Newman; editor, Louis Loeffler; asst. director, Joseph Lensi. Reviewed at 20th-Fox Studios, Dec. 22, '64. Running time, **106 MINS.**

Fran	Ann-Margret
Emilo	Tony Franciosa
Maggie	Carol Lynley
Pete	Gardner McKay
Susie	Pamela Tiffin
Andres	Andrew Lawrence
Jane Barton	Gene Tierney
Paul Barton	Brian Keith
Neighbor man	Vito Scotti
Dona Teresa	Isobel Elsom
Jose	Maurice Morsac
Marian	Shelby Grant
Martinez	Raoul De Leon
Flamenco Dancer	Antonio Gades
Guitarist	Emilio Diego

Twentieth-Fox' big 1954 grosser, "Three Coins in the Fountain," is back in new-dress as "The Pleasure Seekers." Background has been switched to Madrid from Rome, but the basic plot structure fashioned around the romantic adventures of three American girls residing there still provides a happy story line and a new generation of theatre-goers either won't know the difference or shouldn't mind the reprise. The David Weisbart production has been turned out with an eye both to pictorial and human values and under the direction of Jean Negulesco, who also helmed "Fountain," a light-toned picture emerges which should strike a popular note at the boxoffice. All that's lacking is the terrific title song that helped the original.

Studio is booking pic in some of the situations which previously had skedded its "John Goldfarb, Please Come Home," following latter's forced withdrawal from distribution on order of a N.Y. Supreme Court justice. With its story of youth and fresh treatment, "Pleasure Seekers" may prove a profitable substitute.

Trio of young femme charmers —Ann-Margret, Carol Lynley and Pamela Tiffin—spice the events that allow photographically the lush use of various Spanish locations, including Madrid and Toledo. Foiling for them romantically are Tony Franciosa, Gardner McKay and Andre Lawrence, and for complications Brian Keith. Good casting permits excellent acting right down the line in characters that carry spectator interest.

There is the added plus of Ann-Margret warbling four songs cleffed by Sammy Cahn and James Van Heusen, catchy and well suited to the action. One, "Everything Makes Music When You're in Love," with actress clad in a brief bikini on a Spanish beach, affords a lively dance number.

Script by Edith Sommer based on the John H. Secondari novel interweaves the lives of the three

girls who share the same Madrid apartment. Ann-Margret, ambitious to be a dancer and singer, is in love with Lawrence, a struggling Spanish doctor; Miss Lynley, secretary to Keith, head of a big American news agency and a married man, carries a torch for him and later turns to McKay; Miss Tiffin is all out for Franciosa, a wealthy Spanish playboy who offers everything but marriage. Romances progress in troubled waters and here the story takes form. Finale comes as a logical outgrowth of various situations.

Ann-Margret delivers what is perhaps her best performance to date and gets the most footage, occasioned by her four song numbers which she socks over gustily. Miss Lynley, no less effective, however, registers as the embittered secretary who had an affair previously with Franciosa, and Miss Tiffin is pert and appealing in her romancing McKay. The four men without exception ably carry out their respective assignments; McKay, making his first feature appearance after a long stand in "Adventures in Paradise" teleseries, is a cinch to continue in important casting. Gene Tierney acquits herself capably as Keith's jealous wife and Isobel Elsom stands out as Franciosa's patrician mother.

Daniel L. Fapp's color photography is handsome and art direction by Jack Martin Smith and Edward Carrere is quality straight through. Lionel Newman provides a tuneful musical backdrop for the fast unfoldment via Louis Loeffler's tight editing and Robert Sidney's choreography and Flamenco dances performed by Antonio Gades lend additional interest.
Whit.

Weekend a Zuydcoote
(FRENCH-COLOR)

Paris, Dec. 29.
Pathe release of Paris Film-Robert and Raymond Hakim-Interopa Film production. Stars Jean-Paul Belmondo, Francois Perier; features Jean-Paul Marielle, Pierre Mondy, Georges Geret, Albert Remy, Francois Guerin, Catherine Spaak. Directed by Henri Verneuil. Screen play, Francois Boyer from novel by Robert Merle; camera (Eastmancolor), Henri Decae; editor, Claude Durand. At Normandie, Paris. Running time, **120 MINS.**

Julien	Jean-Paul Belmondo
Alexandre	Francois Perier
Curate	Jean-Paul Marielle
Dhery	Pierre Mondy
Pinot	Georges Geret
Virret	Albert Remy
Lieutenant	Francois Guerin
Jeanne	Catherine Spaak

This solidly made and well-produced tale of the evacuation of Dunkirk, as seen from the French side during the last world war, looks to do fine biz here, with good playoff possibilities stateside and worth dubbing rather than playing it in arty houses. It is 1940, and the French and English have been routed by the Germans and are being driven into the sea around Dunkirk and the nearby Belgian sea resort of Zuydcotte. The British are intent on evacuating their men first and the French are a bit abrasive about this but not bitter.

The constant German strafings, bombings and shellings are the background for this tale as it picks out four French soldiers and a girl, who will not leave her seaside house. One man is decent and set on getting to England. Then there is the goldbricker, a personable, talky type only longing for his wife and a priest who thinks his calling does not rule out fighting.

They barge about the beach and also find their own beachhead in an abandoned ambulance. The goldbricker manages to get out but the others are picked off one by one to end on a potent image of war's futility as the girl comes looking for the decent lad as he expires on a now-abandoned beach.

If the girl's pigheadedness in staying on in her house is sometimes overdone, it allows for some digressions from war's grime and grimness as the good guy saves her from rape by killing two fellow Frenchmen.

The crowds on the beaches, the endless explosions, the panic and bravery are all well handled by director Henri Verneuil who has marshalled his pacing and epic values well. The characters tend to be stereotypes rather than just people caught up in war. But they are well depicted via robust, salty dialogue.

20th-Fox already has this for the U. S. and Canada and should have a fine playoff item. The name of Jean-Paul Belmondo, who scored in "That Man From Rio," is an added asset. Catherine Spaak is somewhat gauche as the hardheaded girl but is good to look at. But in this impressive production, the good overall acting makes it one of the four local pix with top export chances.   *Mosk.*

Les Aventures De Salavin
(The Adventures of Salavin)
(FRENCH)
Paris, Dec. 15.
United Artists release of Horizons production. Stars Maurice Biraud; features Christiane Minazzolli, Mona Dol, Genevieve Fontanel, Dominique Rozan, Max Montavon. Directed by Pierre Granier-Deferre. Screenplay, R. M. Arlaud, Granier-Deferre from novel by George Duhamel; camera, Rene Bucaille; editor, Jean Ravel. At Balzac, Paris. Running time, 100 MINS.
Salavin .... Maurice Biraud
Marguerite ...... Christiane Minazzolli
Mother .... Mona Dol
Marta .... Genevieve Fontanel
Friend .... Dominique Rozan

Pic is a pedestrian affair about a pedestrian type. The inane rebellion of a little man against his lot and life seem somewhat oldhat and without particular feeling and narrative to lift him into a more important figure or to give the film the comic relief needed.

The hero lives with his mother and has a petty clerical job with no women in his life. One day he pulls his boss' ear on a whim and is fired. Then come days of unemployment and his growing self-pity. But all this is done in drab tone and a literary manner.

Director Pierre Granier-Deferre has been content to tell his tale via a series of anecdotes that bodes a flair for pace at times but is so repetitive it finally leads to monotony.

Maurice Biraud shows a growing thespic maturity in giving the vacillating, petty figure of the hero a sort of aura that is not in the script. Usually cast in light roles he hints that he can bring off deeper characterizations. Supporting cast is okay and technical credits par. This looks like a chancey export item.   *Mosk.*

Polizeirevier Davidswache
(Police Station Davidswache)
(GERMAN)
Berlin, Dec. 15.
Atlas release of Ernst Liesenhoff production. Stars Wolfgang Kieling, Hannelore Schroth, Guenther Ungeheuer. Directed by Juergen Roland. Screenplay, Wolfgang Menge; camera, Guenter Haase, editor, Sussane Paschen. Preemed at Zoo Palast, West Berlin. Running time, 101 MINS.
Police Sgt. Glantz .. Wolfgang Kieling
Margot .... Hannelore Schroth
Schriever .... Guenther Neutze
Bruno .... Guenther Ungeheuer
Laepke .... Horst Neutze
Kohlhammer .... Helmut Oeser
Miss Schmelz .... Johanna Koenig
Manfred .... Juergen Draeger
Bruenjes .... Fred Berthold
Cherie .... Silvana Sansoni

At last, here is a German film that rates praise. It is well directed and acted, has suspense and competent dialog sequences and reaches its intended documentary sharpness. Pic is semi-documentary type of vehicle dealing with Hamburg's famous Reeperbahn, possibly the old world's biggest amusement district or, as sometimes claimed "the filthiest mile in the world." Taking into account that Reeperbahn is an international tourist attraction, this Atlas release may interest foreign buyers.

"Davidswache" is the name of Hamburg's most cited police station, located in this city's St. Pauli district in which is located the notorious Reeperbahn. Film depicts 48 hours of the tough job the cops have in that area.

All incidents are based on true happenings, only the names of the characters have been changed. There are the big and little gangsters, the racketeers, the juvenile hoodlums, the clip joints, the dubious striptease places, the prosties, the curio-seeking tourists, drunkards, the unfaithful husbands and also one of those female impersonators. To make the whole thing more genuine, real Reeperbahn characters have been utilized.

Plot concerns a criminal just released from four years in jail who seeks revenge on the cop who trapped him. The policeman is accidentally shot by the criminal's bride. Story, especially in the fadeout, has a rather melodramatic flavor, yet is supposedly authentic.

The 38-year old director Juergen Roland, a former reporter with 10 films to his credit, proves that he knows his story. Roland, the creator of the prominent German tv series, "Steel Net" (the German version of the stateside "Dragnet"), with "Davidswache" has created an important film. It points up how rough, difficult and even heroic the life of the policeman can be in that Hamburg area.

There are several outstanding performances, especially by Wolfgang Kieling, the police sergeant, and Guenther Ungeheuer, who turns in an impressive study of a notorious criminal. A promising characterization is turned in by newcomer Juergen Draeger as a juvenile good-for-nothing. Out of place, however, seems Hannelore Schroth, an accomplished actress, who enacts Ungeheuer's naive bride. Incidentally, also a large contingent of Americans gets into the picture—sailors of a U. S. warship who get involved with clip-joint operators.

Technically, the film also has high standard. Guenter Haase's camerawork deserves particular praise. Pic may put the Reeperbahn in a very unfavorable light. But the Hamburg police authorities granted this venture their full assistance.   *Hans.*

Geld und Geist
(Money and Spirit)
(SWISS—COLOR)
Zurich, Dec. 15.
Monopol-Films A. G. Zurich release of Neue Film A.G. Zurich (Franz Schnyder) production. Directed by Schnyder. Screenplay, Richard Schweizer and Schnyder, based on the Jeremias Gotthelf novel; camera (Eastmancolor), Konstantin Tschet; music, Robert Blum; features Peter Arens, Elisabeth Berger, Margrit Winter, Erwin Kohlund, Max Haufler, Margrit Rainer, Fritz Nydegger, Verena Hallau, Ruedi Walter, Mathias Wieman. At Corso Theatre, Zurich; Running time, 116 MINS.

(Swiss--German Dialog)

This color-and-widescreen filmization of a peasant novel by Jeremias Gotthelf, 19th century Swiss classical poet, is the only Swiss feature film produced this year. Because of its locally-slanted theme, the popularity of the novel and its (for Switzerland) steep budget of 1,000,000 Swiss francs ($233,000), it looks like a neat bet for the local market, especially for middle-age and older patrons whose tastes veer toward unsophisticated filmmaking. But for more demanding audiences, it has little to offer beside some handsome exteriors in color and a few above-par performances. Commercial chances outside of Switzerland are negligible.

Basically a Romeo and Juliet yarn with a happy ending, this concerns two peasant families in the Bernese Oberland whose son and daughter, respectively, find each other after many obstacles caused by one father's plans to "sell" his daughter to a rich old neighbor in return for the latter's heritage. The plan misfires when the father dies in an accident, with the son's mother reuniting the young lovers on her deathbed.

In the Gotthelf novel, this emerges as a richly characterized, sincere and poetic tale of Swiss peasant life in the last century, but it is reduced to an often maudlin tear-jerker in the film version, with flat characters and lack of atmosphere.

Direction by Franz Schnyder is clumsy and uninspired. Lensing by Konstantin Tschet, done mostly on location, offers some nice pictorial values. Performances are uneven, but include some convincing portrayals, notably by Max Haufler, as the greedy father; Ruedi Walter, as the rich neighbor, and Margrit Winter, as the dying mother.   *Mezo.*

Le Consequenze
(The Consequences)
(ITALIAN)
Rome, Dec. 22.
Supercinematografica release of a Gaia Cin. Production. Features Marisa Solinas, Venantino Venantini, Pierre Massimi, Marina Berti, Mario Valdemarin, Germano Giglioli, Massimo Tonna, Claudio Gora, Jole Fierro, Gala, Raffi. Written and directed by Sergio Capogna. Camera, Otello Spila; music, Franco Pisano. At Roxy Theatre, Rome. Running time, 100 MINS.
Marisa .... Marisa Solinas
Valerio .... Venantino Venantini
Simone .... Mario Valdemarin

Sergio Copogna disappoints with this second effort after an interesting debut with another indie effort made some years back. Though interestingly cast and dealing with a provocative subject, this lacks strong direction and is weakly scripted. Original censorship ban in Italy, presumably because of abortion topic, may help it to some exploitation coin, but pic lacks legs for depth.

Well-intentioned pic wants to show consequences facing a girl who too soon and too rapidly wants to break with conventions and patterns of life. She has several flings with men, most of them disappointing, before facing up to the hard realities. Final shaking factor is detailed operation, performed illegally, during which youngster flashes back over her adventures.

Acting is very uneven. Marisa Solinas is too static and blank in the lead. Venantino Venantini seems little interested in his role as a painter. Other men fare somewhat better, Pierre Massimi, Mario Valdemarin, and Massimo Tonna coming through with some sincere thesping efforts.

Continuity is shaky, dialogue frequently banal and unreal, thus upsetting the value of okay sequences in this film. Franco Pisano's music frequently drowns out the dialogue, and is at times played several notches too loud.   *Hawk.*

Yolanta
(RUSSIAN-COLOR)

Interesting operatic film based on Tchaikowsky's last work; hefty outlook for art houses and certain longhair regular sites.

Los Angeles, Dec. 22.
Artkino release of Riga Film Studio production. Stars Natalya Rudnaya, Fyodor Nikitin, Yuri Perov, Alexander Belyavsky; features Pyotr Glebov, Valentina Usakova, Valdis Sandberg. Directed by V. Gorikker. Screenplay, Gorikker, based on opera "Yolanta," by Peter Y .Tchaikowsky, text by M. I. Tchaikowsky, original play. "King Rene's Daughter," by H. Hertz; camera (Magicolor), V. Mass: Reviewed at Europa Theatre. Dec. 21, '64. Running time, 80 MINS.
Yolanta .... Natalya Rudnaya
(sung by Galina Oleinichenko)
King Rene .... Fyodor Nikitin
(sung by Ivan Petrov)
Vaudemont .... Yuri Perov
(sung by Z. Andjaparidze)
Duke Robert ...... Alexander Belyavsky
(sung by Pavel Lisitsian)
Eon-Hakkia .... Pyotr Glebov
(sung by V. Valaitis)
Martha .... Valentina Ushakova
(sung by Y. Verbitskaya)
Bertrand .... Valdis Sandberg
(sung by V. Yaroslavtsev)

Operatic film version of Tchaikovsky's last work features excellent performances and singing, poetic English subtitles and effective cinematic treatment. Well-mounted color production of Riga Film Studio is heart-warming and melodic, with broad appeal that should spell satisfactory grosses in artie bookings. With proper selling, Artkino (Russian) release looks good for selected longhair commercial situations as well.

Based on Danish play "King Rene's Daughter" by H. Hertz, opera preemed in Moscow in 1893, two years after completion. More familiar to European audiences, libretto by M. I. Tchaikovshy is uncomplicated fairy tale of a princess of feudal France blind since birth, her loving father whose paternalism hides this fact from her, and young knight who sparks her ultimate recovery.

In title role, Natalya Rudnaya is outstanding as the royal maid. Initially serene and innocent, performance develops believably through shock at learning of her blindness, desire for cure, clumsiness in her first steps in a world of depth perception and final coquetry as the now-complete virgin is joined to her lover.

Yuri Perov is topnotch as knight Vaudemont, projecting youth, nobility and virility. As the well-meaning but blundering father, Fyodor Nikitin excels, particularly in chapel scene clutching a crucifix in poignant prayer while a Moorish healer invokes Allah in his daughter's behalf. Pyotr Glebov as the healer projects proper mysticism.

Alexander Belyavsky comes across as Yolanta's betrothed who gives way to Vaudemont in final scenes. Valentina Ushakova and Valdis Sandberg score in lesser roles as wet-nurse and guard, respectively.

Performers are of necessity mimes, making character delineations all the more noteworthy. Singing voices of principals are clear and true, with lip sync perfect. Orchestra and chorus are Bolshoi Opera talent under B. Khaikin's direction.

English subtitles are poetic, blank verse used in sober passages while trimeters and tetrameters translate livelier moments, enhancing medieval atmosphere. Titles are trapped within confines of libretto whose basic flaw is too-quick plot resolution after measured buildup.

Director V. Gorikker has avoided pitfall of photographing a stage presentation, keeping V. Mass' camera fluid but unobtrusive. Smooth editing makes for brisk 80-minute unreeling. V. Zorin's sound and G. Likums' sets are plus values. Magicolor process reproduces exteriors faithfully, but interiors are too artificial at times. Color quality in first two reels caught was uneven. *Murf.*

3 Notti D'Amore
(Three Nights of Love)
(ITALIAN)
(Color-Songs)

Rome, Dec. 22.
Unidis release of Silvio Clementelli production for Jolly-Unidis. Stars Catherine Spaak; features Renato Salvatori. John P. Law, Enrico Maria Salerno, Diletta D'Andrea. Directed by Luigi Comencini, Renato Castellani, Franco Rossi. Camera (Technicolor), Mario Montuori, Roberto Gherardi. At Cinema Barberini, Rome. Running time, 122 MINS.

FATEBENEFRATELLI
Directed by Luigi Comencini. Screenplay, Castellano, Pipolo; music, Giuseppe Fusco; editor, Renato Cinquini.
Ghiga .... Catherine Spaak
Fra Felice .... John P. Law

LA VEDOVA (The Widow)
Directed by Renato Castellani. Story and screenplay, Marcello Fondato; Music, Carlo Rustichelli; editor, Yolanda Benvenuti.
Giselle .... Catherine Spaak
Nicola .... Renato Salvatori

LA MOGLIE BAMBINA
(Child Bride)
Directed by Franco Rossi. Screenplay, Franciosa, Luigi Magni; music, Piero Piccioni; editor, Giorgio Serralonga.
Cirilla .... Catherine Spaak
Giuliano .... Enrico Maria Salerno
Gabriella .... Diletta D'Andrea

———

Neatly assembled, stylishly produced episoder which rises head-and-shoulders above the mass of most others in the latest Italo trend for fragmented features. Tough exploitable, it's done with taste, and it boasts fine production values in color, sets, and costumes plus some topnotch performances. Should rouse audience interest in many world areas if lingual versions are given as much care as went into original.

Opener, directed by Luigi Comencini, has Catherine Spaak as an expensive call girl who wrecks her current keeper's car and winds up in a convent, and up to her neck in a cast. Slowly, a friendship with a male novice grows into love on his part, and he leaves the order before taking his final vows. Switch at finale finds gal becoming a nun, nursing him after accident. Catherine Spaak is excellent as the convert while John P. Law registers as the man she torments. There's some neat backing by others in the colorful cast. Episode is given the right touch and balance by director Comencini. The subject is naturally touchy, but it's handled with just the right discretion so as not to offend any except the most susceptible.

Second segment is an amusing spoof of Sicilian Mafia traditions. And how they affect the foreign widow of a local Mafia leader who brings his body back from their honeymoon trip to Paris. Not knowing what she's doing, she approaches local men, mostly with innocent intent, only to have them bumped off by the late boss' henchmen. Some of the material displays facets of Sicilian manners and mores already documented by such pix as "Divorce, Italian Style" yet it's still risible and effective as ably guided by Renato Castellani. Some colorful village types help. Renato Salvatori plays one of the victims in pro fashion.

Third is the modern bit by Franco Rossi, in which Miss Spaak is the youthful bride of Enrico Salerno. Latter resolves his many complexes by betraying her after first resisting a similar cure she deliberately if unwisely suggests herself. Ending here, as in other bits, is a switch, in keeping with episode pic tradition. Last fragment also has a topless bit as a fillip. Whole is neatly acted by Enrico Maria Salerno and Miss Spaak. This is the latter's best picture, nailing down her versatility and great potential.

Above-mentioned stylishness of the entire production is helped by the merit of cameramen Mario Montuori and Roberto Gherardi and Oscar-winning costume stylist Piero Gherardi, whose imprint is felt throughout. *Hawk.*

1965

The Yellow Rolls-Royce
(BRITISH-COLOR)

Lush triple-decker with starry marquee value, skillfully tailored to woo world markets; light comedy, romance and thesping spell big success.

London, Jan. 5.
Metro release of an Anatole De Grunwald production. Stars Rex Harrison, Jeanne Moreau, George C. Scott, Shirley MacLaine, Art Carney, Alain Delon, Ingrid Bergman, Omar Sharif; features Joyce Grenfell, Moira Lister, Edmund Purdom, Lance Purcival, Isa Miranda. Directed by Anthony Asquith. Screenplay by Terence Rattigan; camera (Metrocolor), Jack Hildyard; editor, Frank Clarke; music, Riz Ortolani. At the Emp.re, London. Running time, 122 MINS.
(1)
Marquess of Frinton .... Rex Harrison
Marchioness of Frinton . Jeanne Moreau
John Fane .... Edmund Purdom
Lady St. Simeon .... Moira Lister
Duchess d'Angouleme.... Isa Miranda
Norwood .... Roland Culver
Harnsworth .... Michael Hordern
His Assistant .... Lance Percival
Taylor .... Harold Scott
(2)
Mae Jenkins .... Shirley MacLaine
Paolo Maltese .... George C. Scott
Stefano .... Alain Delon
Joey .... Art Carney
Bomba .... Riccardo Garrone
(3)
Mrs. Gerda Millett ...Ingrid Bergman
Davich .... Omar Sharif
Miss Hortense Astor ..... Joyce Grenfell
Ferguson .... Wally Cox
Mrs. Millet's Chauffeur...Carlo Groccolo

With a sizzling international cast that shrewdly sets its bead on the full, potential world market, the team of Anatole De Grunwald, Anthony Asquith and Terence Rattigan have produced a sleek piece of entertainment in "The Yellow Rolls-Royce." It is handsomely tinted, lushly lensed and though leisurely in its approach, this has style, humor and some effective thesping. It's a triple-decker that should draw the crowds, first for its marquee value and second because Rattigan's screenplay, though slight, is literate and polished. Metro has a great start to the New Year with this glossy package.

Film consists of three separate anecdotes, linked only by ownership of the elegant Phantom 11 Rolls-Royce auto, which appears in each of the three playlets and handsomely dominates the scene. The film might have packed more punch if the characters involved had been interwoven, but there is still plenty to relish in the trio of yarns.

First one concerns Lord Frinton (Rex Harrison), a Foreign Office big shot who buys the car as an anni gift for his wife (Jeanne Moreau). It is the eve of his Ascot Week house party during which his nag wins the Royal Gold Cup. His Lordship's elation is cut short when he discovers his wife and a Foreign Office minion (Edmund Purdom) in a passionate embrace in the back seat of the Rolls, blinds drawn. Naturally piqued, he returns the motor car to the showroom.

Much mileage later, in the 30's, the car is bought in Italy by gangster George C. Scott as a present for his current moll, hatcheck gal Shirley MacLaine. He is showing Miss MacLaine the historical monuments of the land of his fathers, but she is bored. Until, that is, the hot business of flying to the States to bump off a competitor takes Scott back to America briefly. During this time the dame falls for a street photographer and

again the comfortable, accomodating back seat of the Rolls is pressed into service for l'amour.

Finally, in 1942, the Phantom 11 is acquired by Ingrid Bergman playing a hectoring American woman. Hitler is attacking Yugoslavia and she becomes involved when she finds that she has smuggled an archpatriot (Omar Sharif) across the border. She and the car do yeomen work in helping the guerillas wage war. She and Sharif also find time for a leap into the hay via the hospitable Rolls before she goes home, shipping the bus with her. What happens to it in the U.S. is anybody's guess.

Harrison is immaculate as the fastidious Lord and Miss Moreau, though having some difficulty with the English lingo, also copes admirably, with Purdom a suave young lover. There also are nice touches by Moira Lister and Isa Miranda. Roland Culver, as a typical butler of the period helps considerably. The opulent luxury of upperclass living in England in the 30's is beautifully captured both by the writer and the director. Background scenery of Italy is easy on the eye in the second section of the production. Miss MacLaine gives a cunningly blended performance of comedy and pathos as Scott's gal, her scenes with Delon being a subtle contrast from those with the tough gangster, played well, though sometimes inaudibly, by Scott. Art Carney tags along as Scott's buddy but hasn't much chance of making real impact.

Final instalment has an uneven performance by Ingrid Bergman, not at her best in character-comedy, but rather more effective during the war sequences. Sharif, as the partisan, and Joyce Grenfell, briefly, as Miss Bergman's companion, both aid and abet the star well in an episode that is of somewhat different mood from the other two.

All three filmlets have a number of choice, brief scenes. Jack Hildyard's lensing, Riz Ortolani's music and the colorful settings, artwork and costumes all add up to the type of cinema-filling escapist entertainment that should bring nothing but good news at the boxoffice. The film is superficial and untaxing but always gently amusing and full of warmth, with full kudos for the technical jobs.

With a British producer, who was born in Russia, the casting director must have felt free to experiment. Result, is that Britain is represented by Harrision and the impressive Rolls-Royce and Jeanne Moreau bats for France as a British peeress. A Frenchman (Alain Delon) plays an Italian, an American (Scott) pinchhits for a man of Italian extraction, a Swede (Miss Bergman) plays a Yank and an Egyptian (Sharif) represents Yugoslav. This sounds like an international boxoffice parlay that should pay off handsomely.
Rich.

Two On A Guillotine
(Panavision)

Well-developed chiller for the exploitation market; good grosses expected.

Hollywood, Jan. 8.
Warner Bros. release of William Conrad production. Stars Connie Stevens, Dean Jones, Cesar Romero; features Parley Baer, Virginia Gregg, Connie Gilchrist, John Hoyt, Russell Thorson. Directed by Conrad. Screenplay, Henry Slesar; camera, Sam Levitt; music, Max Steiner; editor, William Ziegler; asst. director, Phil Rawlins. Reviewed at Warner Bros. Studios, Jan. 7, '65. Running time, 107 MINS.
Melinda Duqueste,
Cassia Duquesne ....Connie Stevens
Val Henderson .... Dean Jones
"Dukee" Duquesne........Cesar Romero
"Buzz" Sheridan......... Parley Baer
Dolly Bast .... Virginia Gregg
Ramona Ryerdon........Connie Gilchrist
Carl Vickers.............. John Hoyt
Marmichael .... Russell Thorson

"Two On a Guillotine," faintly reminiscent of the type of terror pix Warner Bros. turned out a decade and more ago. stacks up as a firstrate entry for the exploitation market, where with smart bally hefty grosses may be anticipated. The William Conrad production packs enough chilling elements to sustain audience interest at a fairly high pitch, which, however, could be heightened through tighter editing and deletion of a long non-essential sequence.

Starring Connie Stevens, Dean Jones and Cesar Romero, plot is premised on the daughter of a departed former top magician having to spend seven consecutive nights in her father's Los Angeles home, where she undergoes some terrifying experiences. This is a stipulation of the will; otherwise, the estate valued at $300,000 is to be divided equally between magician's housekeeper and onetime press agent. Helping Miss Stevens, as the daughter, is a young newspaper reporter, Jones, who is instrumental in bringing events to a climax.

Conrad, who also directs the Henry Slesar - John Kneubuhl screenplay, succeeds early in developing a fast tempo that builds suspensefully and draws believable performances from his cast. Miss Stevens, who sheds her usual cute enactment, swings into a dramatic groove persuasively and acquits herself nicely. Jones does well in a straight leading part and Romero, as the magician whose greatest feat was to make use of a specially-built guillotine and who predicted he would return from the grave, is good in a shorter role. Virginia Gregg as the housekeeper and Parley Baer as the press agent are in for dramatic renderings.

If in the final reel the narrative attains to the incredible, this isn't fully realized until the film ends. Technical credits are all on the plus side. *Whit.*

Baby The Rain Must Fall

Downbeat drama about irresponsible rockabilly singer, his wife and child has effective spots, but is slow-moving and must rely on marquee value of stars for b.o. appeal.

Hollywood, Jan. 7.
Columbia release of Pakula-Mulligan Production. Stars Lee Remick, Steve McQueen, Don Murray; features rest of cast. Directed by Robert Mulligan. Screenplay, Horton Foote, based on Foote's play, "The Traveling Lady"; camera, Ernest Laszlo; editor, Aaron Stell;

music Elmer Bernstein. Reviewed at Columbia Studios Jan. 7, '65. Running time, 93 MINS.
Georgette Thomas....... Lee Remick
Henry Thomas......... Steve McQueen
Slim ....Don Murray
Judge Ewing .... Paul Fix
Mrs. Ewing........Josephine Hutchinson
Miss Clara .... Ruth White
Mr. Tillman.............Charles Watts
Mrs. Tillman .... Carol Veazie
Catherine .... Estelle Hemsley
Margaret Rose .... Kimberly Block
Mrs. T. V. Smith... Zamah Cunningham
Counterman ....George Dunn

Chief assets of Pakula-Mulligan's "Baby The Rain Must Fall" are outstanding performances by its stars and an emotional punch that lingers. Steve McQueen is exactly right as irresponsible rockabilly singer, Lee Remick portrays his wife sensitively, and newcomer Kimberly Block is charming and unaffected as their six-year-old daughter.

But boxoffice draw of this Columbia release depends on stars, because its somber, downbeat story meanders and has plot holes that leave viewers confused and depressed.

McQueen, raised by dictatorial spinster (Georgia Simmons) who disapproves his singing in roadhouses, is troublesome rebel. When story opens he is free on parole for a stabbing, and is joined by Miss Remick and Kimberly, wife and daughter he had kept secret. Opposite him in temperament, wife sets to work to keep him out of trouble and build family life while holding job so he can try to sell songs.

Miss Remick is vividly alive in spontaneous-appearing scenes with daughter. But director Robert Mulligan apparently was so determined to avoid soap-opera cliches that he did not permit actress to register negative emotion beyond look of distraught unhappiness even though sad events should have allowed room for tears. Underplaying of Miss Remick's role makes it impossible to interpret her feelings at finale, and viewers are in dark whether she is unhappy because husband is being returned to prison or simply because family is broken up.

Kimberly Block, making debut, is free of child-acting mannerisms, and an appealing moppet.

Other cast members are adequate, but roles suffer from editorial cuts (confirmed by director) that leave sub-plots dangling. Don Murray, as boyhood friend of McQueen, gets star billing but role lacks meaning because only scene of Josephine Hutchinson, mother of his dead wife, was cut to shorten film still over-long. Paul Fix, husband of Miss Hutchinson, is in similar position.

Some minor roles are effectively played, especially those of Miss Simmons as crusty foster mother, and Zamah Cunningham as nosy woman on bus.

Credit for picture's emotional power goes to Horton Foote who scripted from own play. Production values are excellent, particularly Ernest Laszlo's black-and-white camera work. Art director Roland Anderson and set decorator Frank Tuttle have provided realistic settings. Elmer Bernstein's score, in rockabilly style, is appropriate and Aaron Stell's editing shows no flaws. *Hogg.*

Gertrud
(DANISH)

Paris, Jan. 5.

Ursuline and AZ Distribution release of C. P. production. With Nina Pena Rode, Ebbe Rode, Axel Gebuhr, William Knoblauch. Written and directed by Carl Theodore Dreyer from a play by Hjalmar Soderberg. Camera, Henning Bendtsen; editor, Edith Schlussle; music, Jorgen Jersild. At Monte Carlo, Paris. Running time, **120 MINS.**

Gertrud	Nina Pena Rode
Lidman	Ebbe Rode
Kanning	Axel Gebuhr
Jansson	William Knoblauch

Film is an event for film buffs and specialists in the first film in nine years by the noted Danish veteran (at 75) Carl T. Dreyer since his Venice prizewinning "The Word." He was also responsible for such classics as "Passion of Joan of Arc," voted one of the greatest all-time films in Brussels in 1958, "Day of Wrath" and others.

Aside from its inside pull, this does not have any concessions for general audiences. Pic would need specialized, personalized handling in selected arty spots for best results. From a turn-of-the-century secondary Swedish play, Dreyer has woven what looks like a meditation on love.

This eschews trying to reconstruct the 1907 period in which it takes place but tries for a timelessness in presenting a theme that has been in most of Dreyer's work. It is, namely, that reconciling true love with ordinary life and religion has always been a problem for those who will not compromise. And if these more idyllic people do accept life, it is usually, as the heroine puts it, a belief in carnal pleasure and the irremediable solitude of the soul.

The heroine is a thirtyish woman who has been an opera singer. She had broken off a liaison with a poet who seemed more interested in his work than her and then married his friend. An affair with a young musician is also disappointing since it was deep physical love for her but an adventure for him. So she leaves all these men, including the poet, who comes back to be feted in his native land. He finds that he's ruined his life by breaking with her.

Follows a look at her as an old woman who had devoted herself to a fairly solitary life of learning but has felt it was all worth it since she had loved, even if incompatibly. Actually Dreyer handles themes that have been of much concern to others. That is, the problems of communication, the couple and the conflict between needs, ideals and ethics.

Yet this, with echos of Ibsen, in its social haranguing for female independence, and Strindberg, in its difficulty in male and female understanding, lends itself admirably to Dreyer's dry but penetrating style.

Perhaps Dreyer repeats things and has found no need to adapt the more fashionable pace and greater tie with the remainder of society and the times inherent in most films today treating these themes. But it still remains the work of a master craftsman and has the right timing and mixture of imagery and dialog that keep this absorbing if it may skirt banality, tedium and repetition for average audiences.

Hence, this is one of those uncompromising pix that will find it hard-going in today's markets. It was world preemed at two arty houses in Paris.

Nina Pena Rode has the right luminous quality for the romantic, uncompromising Gertrud while the men are acceptable if sometimes overindulgent in their roles as either hypocrites, staid and settled males. But the actors all take a second place to director Dreyer's mood, visual compositions and dry dialog that relegate the thesps to subordinated roles to the ideas and outlooks. *Mosk.*

The Outlaws Is Coming

Three Stooges in fast slapstick western, a natural for trio's particular market.

Hollywood, Jan. 5.

Columbia Pictures release of Norman Maurer production. Stars Three Stooges (Larry Fine, Moe Howard, Joe De Rita); features Adam West, Nancy Kovack, Mort Mills, Don Lamond, Rex Holman. Directed and story by Maurer. Screenplay, Elwood Ullman; camera, Irving Lippman; music, Paul Dunlap; editor, Aaron Nibley; asst. director, Donald Gold. Reviewed at studio, Jan. 4, '65. Running time, **88 MINS.**

Larry	THE
Moe	THREE
Curly (Joe)	STOOGES
Kenneth Cabot	Adam West
Annie Oakley	Nancy Kovack
Trigger Mortis	Mort Mills
Rance Roden	Don Lamond
Sunstroke Kid	Rex Holman
Mr. Abernathy	
Witch Doctor	Emil Sitka
Cavalry Colonel	
Charlie Horse	Henry Gibson
Chief Crazy Horse	Murray Alper
Bartender	Tiny Brauer
Bob Dalton	Joe Bolton
Wyatt Earp	Bill Camfield
Johnny Ringo	Hal Fryar
Billy the Kid	Johnny Ginger
Jesse James	Wayne Mack
Bat Mastereson	Ed. T. McDonnell
Cole Younger	Bruce Sedley
Wild Bill Hickok	Paul Shannon
Belle Starr	Sally Starr

Like all "Three Stooges" comedies, "The Outlaws IS Coming!" depends chiefly on the corny horseplay and situations in which the trio become involved. This time out, their antics are set down in one of the fastest slapstick westerns. Entry fits patly in the particular market for which it's aimed.

The Norman Maurer production (Maurer directed and wrote story from Elwood Ullman fashioned screeplay) projects trio in the roaring Wyoming of 1871, after a brief opening in Boston where as employees of the Society for the Preservation of Wildlife they're fired and accompany the editor west to halt the slaughter of buffalo. They become the target of every gunslinger west of the Mississippi when it's apparent the editor and the Stooges are interfering with a gangleader's plans to start the Indians on the warpath after all the buffalo have been killed. Easterners are aided by Annie Oakley, who falls for the handsome editor and does his shooting for him.

Action is broad and every time-honored routine of westerns down through the years is drawn upon to provide yocks, laced with references to the present (viz., a skunk named Elvis, and that certain razor blade tv commercial beep-beep to cover some dialog). It's a special effects holiday, too, adding to general amusement as unbelievable feats are performed. If there are several anticlimaxes, no matter, unless one is an editing purist—the laughs continue. One story gimmick has practically every celebrated badman of the West—Bob Dalton, Johnny Ringo, Billy the Kid, Jesse James, Cole Younger, Belle Starr — plus such lawmen as Wyatt Earp, Bat Masterson and Wild Bill Hickok, guns glued to their holsters, facing editor and the Stooges.

Stooges display their usual brand of comedics and get hefty backing right down the line. Adam West is gallant as the somewhat square young editor, and Nancy Kovack makes a fine impression as the beauteous Annie Oakley, engaging in a knock-down-drag-out street brawl with Belle Starr, played by Sally Starr. Mort Mills is properly trigger-happy as a gunman heavy and Don Lamond dastardly as the unscrupulous gang-boss of the West.

Maurer's work as producer-director is on the happy side and photography by Irving Lippman and music by Paul Dunlap lend quality. Richard Albain is responsible for clever special effects. *Whit.*

Angelique Marquise Des Anges
(FRENCH-ITALO-GERMAN)
(Color-Dyaliscope)

Paris, Jan. 5.

Prodis release of Francos Films-CICC-Gloria Films-Fonorama production. Stars Michele Mercier, Robert Hossein; features Claude Giraud, Jean Rochefort, Madeleine Lebeau, Philippe Lemaire, Giuliano Yemma. Directed by Bernard Bordérie. Screenplay, Claude Brule, Francis Cosne, Daniel Boulanger, Borderie from book by Serge and Anne Golon; camera (Eastmancolor), Henri Persin; editor, Christian Gaudin. At the Paris, Paris. Running time, **120 MINS.**

Angelique	Michele Mercier
Peyrac	Robert Hossein
Lawyer	Jean Rochefort
Nicolas	Giuliano Yemma
King	Jacques Toja
Cousin	Claude Giraud
Courtesan	Madeleine Lebeau
Father	Bernard Lajarraige

Costumer of 17th Century adventures is a sort of local "Forever Amber," with an innocent but sensual beauty caught up in court intrigues, love and history. It has some tactful nudity and love scenes plus okay action. Its attempts to recreate the times however, are off. This looms mainly a playoff item abroad on its color, scope, and possible value of the best-selling book on which it is based.

Angelique is the comely daughter of a broke nobleman who is married off to a terribly scared man. But love blooms until the imprisonment of her husband for witchcraft.

Tripartite coproduction is part of the European answer to big-scale U.S. pix and this may have good production value but not the bombastic action fillip or more spectacular pageantry and name values of the Yank counterparts. However, European chances seem fine.

Michele Mercier as Angelique, is lovely and not stingy in showing her fine chassis. It is only that she does not quite display a more complex character to make her fiery temperament more bouncy. She appears sweet rather than headstrong.

Director Bernard Borderie has done okay with the romantic settings. But trying to make for a more profound sense in the trial and execution of her husband is somewhat flat. Film needed a more robust out and out tongue-in-cheek flair or true seriousness.

However, the production values are good and the male roles acceptable. *Mosk.*

Unter Geiern
(Among Vultures)
(GERMAN-FRENCH-YUGO-COLOR)

Berlin, Jan. 5.

Constantin release of Rialto Film Preben Philipsen production, made in collab with Societe Nouvelle de Cinematographie (Paris) and Jadran-Film, Zagreb. Stars Stewart Granger, Pierre Brice, Elke Sommer; features Goetz George, Walter Barnes. Directed by Alfred Vohrer. Screenplay, Eberhard Keindorff, Johanna Sibelius, based on same-titled novel by Karl May; camera (Eastmancolor), Karl Loeb; music, Martin Boettcher; editor, Hermann Haller. UFA Pavillon, West Berlin. Running time, **102 MINS.**

Old Surehand	Stewart Granger
Winnetou	Pierre Brice
Annie	Elke Sommer
Martin Baumann	Goetz George
The Old Baumann	Walter Barnes
Preston	Sieghardt Rupp
Weller	Mila Baloh

The amazing German Karl May trend continues. "Among Vultures" is the fourth big-screen May filmization which the Berlin Rialto topper, Horst Wendlandt, the initiator of this trend, personally supervised. It is the first Karl May western to star Stewart Granger as Old Surehand, another popular May character. This Teutonic horse opera looks like a stout domestic b.o. contender. Also this type of film will sled into foreign markets, the more because it is a production of truly international calibre. Made by the Berlin-based Rialto in collab with French, Italian (Atlantis Film, Rome) and Yugoslav partners, it employs French Pierre Brice, American Walter Barnes, Italian Renato Baldini, Germans Elke Sommer, Goetz George and numerous Yugoslav players. The colorful cast is headed by a former Hollywood star of British descent, Granger.

The film's title refers to a gang of white villains ("The Vultures") who terrorize gold diggers and settlers in Arizona. Their string of crimes includes the killing of the family of Baumann, a bear hunter and good friend of Old Surehand, a westerner in the service of justice. These white badmen make their crime look like as though committed by the redskins. This makes good old Bauman an Indian hater, but Old Surehand and his pal, Winnetou, Apache chief, see to it that justice is meted out. The evildoers are liquidated one by one.

The number of killings is remarkably high in this one. But this doesn't make "Among Vultures" a faithful Karl May vehicle for the late German writer. Yet the many juvenile patrons won't think this amiss.

Wisely enough, Alfred Vohrer has directed this with a twinkle in his eye. He doesn't take the bloody action too seriously. Fun is always cropping up. Incidentally, this is Vohrer's first western. After a series of moneymaking crime thrillers (Edgar Wallace filmizations), he now shows that he's also quite at home in the western camp.

Granger contributes a colorful

portrayal of Old Surehand. It won't make the critics rave but one can imagine youngsters will take a fancy to this well - built crack shot, and his mannerisms. With his nonchalance eventually paired with tongueincheek, his impressive white hair and beautiful teeth, he makes a hero the femmes will go for. Pierre Brice is again cast as Winnetou, already a legendary figure with German filmgoers. Goetz George and American Walter Barnes have several good scenes while blond Elke Sommer supplies some sex interest.

Lineup of technical credits includes fine camera work by Karl Loeb. Once more the beautiful Yugoslav landscapes prove good substitute for the American territory. But Martin Boettcher, who has become a "specialist" on music for German Karl May films, ought to dream up new melodies. His western scores are getting monotonous. Otherwise, there is much knowhow and cleverness associated with this production.

Hans.

The Rounders
(PANAVISION—COLOR)

Humorous look at life of modern cowboys, with drawing power of two top stars, should do well at b.o.

Hollywood, Dec. 17.

Metro production and release. Stars Glenn Ford, Henry Fonda; features Sue Ann Langdon, Hope Holiday, Chill Wills. Directed by Burt Kennedy. Screenplay, Kennedy, from novel by Max Evans; camera (Metrocolor), Paul C. Vogel; editor, John McSweeny; music, Jeff Alexander. Reviewed at Vogue Theatre, Hollywood, Dec. 16, '64. Running time, **85** MINS.

Ben Jones .... Glenn Ford
Howdy Lewis .... Henry Fonda
Mary .... Sue Ann Langdon
Sister .... Hope Holiday
Jim Ed Love .... Chill Wills
Vince Moore .... Edgar Buchanan
Agatha Moore ...... Kathleen Freeman
Meg Moore .... Joan Freeman

Metro's "The Rounders" is a pleasant, sometimes funny story about two saddle bums of today's West, Glenn Ford and Henry Fonda. Star cowboys, plus striking color photography and story attributes should result in good audience word-of-mouth to make this entry a comfortable boxoffice hit.

The two are itinerant broncbusters who travel New Mexico-Arizona area, breaking horses for ranchers, then blowing all their money in town. Plan for quitting this hard life to run a bar in Tahiti is nothing more than dream to chronically-broke pair. Eventually, they create impression they would not leave their work no matter how much money they had.

Story of men who stick to tough jobs is not new. Neither is the basic conflict between Ford and proud, stubborn roan stallion he can't completely break. But director Burt Kennedy's mixture of two plot lines, told in low key, sans heroics, adds up to different film fare.

Fonda, as drawling, easy-going character he has often played, is right foil for more emotional Ford, whose explosiveness often leads to trouble. Latter's thesping is believable and effective. All other roles

are minor, but Chill Wills does excellent portrayal of stingy rancher who gets pair to do his roughest work at short prices. (For four days breaking 20 broncs, they earn $7 a head; for a winter rounding up and herding 100-plus stray cattle the price is still $7 a head.)

Femme roles are extremely minor. Kathleen Freeman and Joan Freeman do well as sisters who welcome pair with home cooking and friendly kisses whenever they stop at father's ranch. Father (Edgar Buchanan) is bearded old slob who makes best moonshine whisky in the county.

Most hilarious scene comes when Ford and Fonda meet pair of strippers from Las Vegas (Sue Ane Langdon and Hope Holiday) while blowing pay during festival and rodeo. Midnight nude swimming party in state fishing hatchery leads to girls leaving clothing on shore while group flees warden. Waitress' aprons cover girls barely in ensuing sequence, but this should not be objectionable to family trade.

A testy roan unnamed in script but called "Ol' Fooler" by studio, provides climax to story when Ford and Fonda bet all their money roan can throw any rider in rodeo. Moment of truth for Ford comes when horse is injured and vet says he must be killed.

Kennedy's direction and John McSweeny's editing are generally effective, although more cutting in early scenes would have created better pace. Realistic sets were provided by art directors George W. Davis and Urie McCleary and set decorators Henry Grace and Jack Mills. Director of photography Paul C. Vogel's color cameras caught sweep and beauty of Southwest. Many scenes were filmed in Coconino National Forest.

Pic is one of few in recent years credited as a studio (Metro) production. Richard E. Lyons was producer.

Hogg.

Act of Murder
(BRITISH)

Workmanlike dualer; thriller sex triangle with some imaginative touches and crisp action.

London, Jan 12.

Warner-Pathe release of an Anglo Amalgamated (Jack Greenwood) production. Stars John Carson, Anthony Bates, Justine Lord; features Duncan Lewis, Richard Burrell, Dandy Nichols, Robin Wentworth, Michael Brennan. Directed by Alan Bridges. Screenplay by Lewis Davidson; camera, James Wilson; editor, Derek Holding; music Bernard Ebbinghouse. Previewed at Corner Theatre, London. Running time. 62 MINS.

Tim Ford .... John Carson
Ralph Longman .... Anthony Bates
Anne Longman .... Justine Lord
Will Peterson .... Duncan Lewis
Maud Peterson .... Dandy Nichols
John Quick .... Richard Burrell
Pauline .... Sheena Marshe
Watson .... Norman Scace
Constable .... Robin Wentworth
Publican .... John Moore
Police Sergeant .... Michael Brennan
Charlie .... Kenneth Laird
Bobbie .... Marianne Stone

Brief running time of this workmanlike support feature—62 minutes—naturally militates against all but superficial character-drawing, motivation and plot development. Nevertheless, it's a commendable job and, within its modest limits, has production values that fully stand up to some more ambitious features. With the right top feature, it could be useful booking.

Suspenseful credit titles lead crisply into the yarn. This concerns a young married couple—business man and ex-thesp wife—who for their vacations, rather foolishly swap their house in the country with a couple who purport to run a swagger non-existent West End apartment. The interlopers start to move out the couple's valuable china and antiques but are interrupted. When the couple return posthaste to their home they find no theft, but signs of the place being disturbed, plus a poisoned dog and chickens. This creates a strained atmosphere between husband and wife and she stalks out to return to London, an offered job on the stage, and her ex-lover's bed.

Whodunit and why are tantalizingly dangled in front of the audience. It turns out to be the work of the heavy, an actor who is an ex-flame of the young wife and sees his opportunity to break up their married life by bringing her back to the bright lights. Climax, which results in the husband murdering the actor and then committing suicide, is farfetched and could probably have been resolved more logically with more running time.

Alan Bridges has directed with economic tautness and feeling for audience tingles. Lewis Davidson's screenplay keeps the action moving, though some dialog, especially his attempts at comedy, teeter on the verge of naivete. Bernard Ebbinghouse's music is atmospheric. James Wilson has done a sound lensing job.

Justine Lord, a blonde looker; Alan Bate, as the stuffy young husband; and John Carson, as the jealous lover, complement each other's work satisfactorily. Duncan Lewis, Richard Burrell, Dandy Nichols, Robin Wentworth and Michael Brennan provide useful support in lesser roles.

Rich.

Man in the Dark

Well-made, lightweight meller looks okay for dualers in American market; British little known to U.S. audiences biggest handicap.

Universal release of Mancunian Film Corp. (Tom Blakely) production. Stars William Sylvester, Barbara Shelley, Elizabeth Shepherd, Alex Davion, Mark Eden (guest, Rennie Carroll, Barry Aldis). Directed by Lance Comfort. Screenplay, James Kelly, Peter Miller, based on story by Vivian Kemble; camera, Basil Emmott; editor, John Trumper; musical direction, Brian Fahey, "Concerto," composed by Peter Hart; "Princess and Disc Jockey Bounce," composed by Fahey, songs, "Blind Corner" and "Where Ya Going," by Stan Butcher, Syd Cordell. Previewed in N.Y. Jan 15. '65 Running time. 80 MINS.

Paul .... William Sylvester
Anne .... Barbara Shelley
Joan .... Elizabeth Shepherd
Ricky .... Alex Davion
Mike .... Mark Eden
Ronnie .... Ronnie Carroll
Inspector .... Frank Forsyth
Dancers ... Joy Allen, Unity Grimwood, Wendy Martin

Yarns about a blind man or sightless girl are not exactly new to the films. And this one concerning a blind composer, isn't either. Despite its tried-and-true formula and telegraphed plot, film manages to be fairly entertaining, mainly because its deftly directed. Absence of names (it was produced in England) consigns this meller for U.S. to lower portion of some dual bills.

There's clipped British accent, which comes through very interestingly. Basically this is the fable of a man who lost his sight in an auto-racing accident. A composer, both for recording artists and tele, he's taken for a ride by his beautiful wife and her new lover, a portrait painter.

The murder plot of this pair, who decide to do away with the composer to inherit his considerable fortune, is cleverly contrived with the real culprit in the plot neatly concealed until the final moment. The sightless composer has obtained recordings of several incriminating conversations and is able to baffle the artist by following his movements by sounds alone. And he finally saves his own life by out-talking the artist on his own grounds. Surprise climax has his wife and her new sweetheart arriving to find him very much alive. This enables the blind composer to hop the same plane with his comely, blond secretary.

William Sylvester is quite competent as the blind composer while Barbara Shelley proves adequate as his faithless wife. Elizabeth Shepherd thefts many scenes as the composer's efficient if beautiful secretary, who secretly is in love with him. Alex Davion suffices as the portrait painter, being well cast as the he-man lover of the composer's wife. Mark Eden, as the composer's friend and agent, does splendidly in a contrasting role.

Direction by Lance Comfort goes far in making a routine story quite palatable. "Concerto," the main theme used so often in the pic, is a composition by Peter Hart. It's a nice effort, as is "Princess and Disc Jockey Bounce," by Brian Fahey, who also deserves a pat for his musical direction. This "Bounce" number provides the lone production bit of the film—a sort of song and dance routine. Basil Emmott's camera work is uniformly fine.

Wear.

Andy

Outstanding pic about grown-up mental retard and his problems in modern society. Good prospects for arties and some regular situations.

Hollywood, Jan. 18.

Universal release of Deran Productions Inc film Stars Norman Alden; features rest of cast Written, produced, and directed by Richard C Sarafan Camera, Ernesto Cappares, editor, Aram Avakian, asst directors, Larry Sturhahn, Paul Leaf Reviewed at Universal Studio, Jan 15, '65 Running Time, 86 MINS

Andy .... Norman Alden
Mrs. Chadakis .... Tamara Daykarhanova
Mr Chadakis .... Zvee Scooler
Margie .... Ann Wedgeworth
Bartender .... Murvyn Vye
Sommerville .... Al Nepor
Simovich .... Warren Finnerty
Thelma .... Sudie Bond

A touching, honest, and effective treatment of typical day and night in the life of the title character, a 40-year-old mental retard, "Andy" boasts excellent performances, sparse but hard-hitting dialog, topnotch production values, and fast pace. Free of sensationalism and vulgarity and never maudlin, pic has strong adult and adolescent appeal. Universal release shapes up as potential top-grosser in artie using eyes, face, grunts, hands and body stance to project variety of emotions while being in turn loved, jeered, pitied, and befriended by others.

Richard C. Sarafian produced and directed his own screenplay which uses slum setting, thus permitting fast character definition and minimum talk. It's an effective cinematic device, but the good and bad in human nature which he exposes so well is readily exterpolated to all levels of society, assuming that audiences have the guts to do so.

Sarafian involves Andy in many brief encounters, all coming across with three standouts. One features a saloon brawl, with bartender Murvyn Vye standing by feeling sympathy for Andy while low life beats up latter; after all, he is a businessman. Ann Wedgeworth's barmaid Margie likes Andy, but she breaks date when more attractive score enters. Both are very good in these bits, while Sudie Bond does smash job as worn-out hooker who grabs Andy as last resort, hustles him home where she makes usual hurried preparations for male company, repeats her search for temporary affection, then dismisses him casually come morning.

Sarafian's direction is consistent and excellent, particularly his emphasis on noise and stark visual contrasts which depicts within limitations of film the idiot's near-complete dependence on animal sense perception. Ernesto Cappares' camera is integral in successful capture of proper mood. Aram Avakian's editing is extremely sharp to very end, when tempo slows (but not uncomfortably so) as parents see how much son means to them and they move away where Andy may be kept under their watchful eyes.

All other technical credits on this New York locationer are big plusses. *Murf.*

Tomb of Ligeia
(BRITISH-COLOR® WIDESCREEN)

Disappointing pic form Edgar Allan Poe tale; light biz possible with heavy exploitation push.

Hollywood, Jan. 14.

American International release of Roger Corman production. Stars Vincent Price, Elizabeth Shepard; features rest of cast. Directed by Corman. Screenplay, Robert Towne, based on story by Edgar Allan Poe; camera (Fathecolor), Arthur Grant; editor, Alfred Cox; music, Kenneth V. Jones; asst. director, David Tringham. Reviewed at Joe Shore Screeening Room, L.A., Jan 14, '65. Running time, 80 MINS.

Verden Fell .... Vincent Price
Lady Ligeia-Lady Rewena .... Elizabeth Shepard
Christopher Gough .... John Westbrook
Kendrick .... Oliver Johnston
Lord Trevanion .... Derek Francis
Dr. Vivian .... Richard Vernon
Parson .... Ronald Adam
Peperel .... Frank Thornton
Livery Boy .... Denis Gilmore

More Poe but no go about sums up "The Tomb of Ligeia," a tedious and talky addition to American International's series of chill-pix based on tales by the 19th Century U.S. author. Roger Corman produced and directed a script that resists analysis and lacks credibility, with all performances blah monotones and color lensing of no help. Widescreen pic tries serious supernatural approach minimizing gore angles, but it doesn't jell so neither suspense addicts nor bloodhounds will dig it. Strictly lowercase material, but saturation-exploitation bookings might help.

Amid ruins of English abbey lives widower Vincent Price, near grave of first wife Ligeia buried under strange circumstances some years before. His odd behavior is unexplained until finale when it turns out he was mesmerized by wife on her death bed.

Price disappoints in attempt to project character's inner struggle to escape spell, since no one knows why he acts kooky. Elizabeth Shepherd vacillates between too-stiff patrician elegance and unconvincing terror in role of second wife who is subjected to endless repetitions of brief, ineffective horror bits involving black cat, saucer of milk, and dead fox. She also plays first wife, but latter's footage is brief and still life. Fiery climax puts Ligeia, hubby, and that darn cat to merciful ashen rest, with second wife rescued by lawyer-hero. Other roles include man-servant, squire, gravediggers and house wench, all as cliche as performances given them.

Camera work is routine, except for a few setups using abbey walls to frame scenes. Verdant exteriors are pleasant but are so intercut as to destroy repeatedly what little suspense has been built up on the inside. Music is too busy and totally ineffective, telegraphing every flop shock situation. Pic runs 80 minutes, but seems twice as long. Other technical credits of England's Shepperton Studios are acceptable.

Sole plus factor is opening title work by Francis Rodker who provides artistic and eerie suggestions of quality that doesn't follow. *Murf.*

L'Age Ingrat
(That Tender Age)
(FRENCH-DYALISCOPE)

Paris, Jan 12.

Valoria release of Gafer production Stars Jean Gabin, Fernandel; features Marie Dubois, Franck Fernandel, Noel Roquevert, Paulette Dubost Directed by Gilles Grangier Screenplay, Claude Sautet, Pascal Jardin, Grangier, camera, Robert Le Feberre; editor, J. Douarinou Sadeul At Marignan, Paris Running time, 100 MINS

Adelphe .... Fernandel
Emile .... Jean Gabin
Antoine .... Franck Fernandel
Marie .... Marie Dubois
Mother .... Paulette Dubost
Tourist .... Noel Roquevert

Veteran film stars Jean Gabin and Fernandel have formed their own company, Gafer, and tried to come up with a family pic with this, their first effort. But the cliches of this tale about two fathers trying to marry off their respective offsprings make it in no way better than the usual vehicle of this type.

Result is it may do alright here, where the stars have some draw, but it's sans any real foreign appeal. Abroad it is mainly the Gabin and Fernandel monickers that will have to attract patrons.

This plot is predictable and obvious as Gabin, a hardbitten Parisian, bundles his family into his car to go down South to meet the in-laws of his prospective son-in-law. There is the horse-faced, good natured Fernandel who tries to break them into easier going Southern ways.

The sleepless country night, the budding friendship of the fathers and their differences are tried for laughs till a jealous hassle between the would-be newlyweds leads to some complications ending in a fight between Gabin and Fernandel with the two making up.

Gabin is somewhat pudgy in this as he walks through his part except for his inevitable angry scene when Fernandel is his usual big talking, bland self. But director Gilles Grangier has given this pedestrian mounting which does not help overcome the flat script.

Franck Fernandel, Fernandel's real son, also plays the son in the pic and acquits himself well in an insipid role. Marie Dubois shows she can act but can't do much to bring the more intense Gabin daughter character to life. *Mosk.*

The Naked Kiss

Good Programmer showcasing Constance Towers as reforming prostie. Sexploitation promo may help in certain situations, but lowercase slotting in general prospect.

Hollywood, Jan. 13

Allied Artists release of Leon Fromkess-Sam Firks production, written, produced and directed by Samuel Fuller Stars Constance Towers, Anthony Risley, Michael Dante; features Virginia Grey, Patsy Kelly, Betty Bronson and rest of cast. Canera, Stanley Cortez; editor, Jerome Thoms; music, Paul Dunlap; asst. director, Nate Levinson. Reveiwed at Allied Artists studio, Jan 12, '65 Running time, 90 MINS.

Kelly .... Constance Towers
Griff .... Anthony Eisley
Grant .... Michael Dante
Candy .... Virginia Grey
Mac .... Patsy Kelly
Miss Josephine .... Betty Bronson
Bull .... Marie Devereux
Dusty .... Karen Conrad
Rembrandt .... Linda Francis
Edna .... Barbara Perry
Mike .... Walter Mathews
Bunny .... Betty Robinson
Kip .... Gerald Michenaud
Peanuts .... Christopher Barry
Tim .... George Spell
Angel Face .... Patty Robinson
Officer Sam .... Neyle Morrow
Farlunde .... Monte Mansfield
Barney .... Fletcher Fint
Zookie .... Gerald Milton
Redhead .... Breena Howard
Marshmallow .... Sally Mills
Hatrack .... Edy Williams
Young Delinquent .... Michael Barrere
Nurse .... Patricia Gayle
Receptionist .... Sheila Mintz
Jerry .... Bill Sampson

Good Samuel Fuller programmer about a prostie trying the straight route, "The Naked Kiss" is primarily a vehicle for Constance Towers. Hooker angles and sex perversion plot windup are handled with care, alternating with handicapped children "good works" theme. Some good performances and experienced direction raise this social meller above humdrum, but it seems destined for lowercase market in adult situations, but sexploitation buildup could pay off in appropriate houses.

Action starts fast with brawl between hardened prostie Kelly (Miss Towers) and cheating pimp who shaved her head, after which she takes to sticks, looking believably washed out on eventual arrival in burg where she promptly makes it with local cop Griff. Role is played routinely throughout by Anthony Eisley except for fine touch when (after sex) he consigns her to living-room couch for rest of night.

Pic bogs down at this point in cliches, as hooker rejects berth in nearby red-lighter run by an effective hard-bitten Virginia Grey, instead taking up rehabilitation of crippled children under wing of Patsy Kelly who makes the most of her few lines. Between helping kids, an unwed mother, and keeping another girl from going wrong, Kelly develops romance with Grant, scion of town's founding family who sponsors moppet clinic. Latter character is combination playboy-philanthropist, played okay by Michael Dante.

Switcheroo finds Kelly arrested for Grant's murder when she discovers his interest in children extends beyond hospital care, but molested child is found to cue downbeat ending. Miss Towers' overall effect is very good, director Fuller overcoming his routine script in displaying blonde looker's acting range. Betty Bronson of early film fame radiates in a landlady bit, while other thesps are adequate.

Stanley Cortez kept his camera mobile, sharing credit with Fuller and Miss Towers for rescuing pic from morbid and banal depths probable in less-experienced hands. Other technical credits are professional. Not a sleeper, but good. *Murf.*

How To Murder Your Wife

Far-fetched Lemmon Flavored farce will overcome any flaws. Good b.o. anticipated.

Hollywood, Jan 14.

United artists release of Murder Inc. (Jack Lemmon, George Axelrod, Richard Quine) production. Stars Lemmon, Virna Lisi. Features Claire Trevor, Eddie Mayehoff, Terry-Thomas. Directed by Quine. Screenplay by Axelrod; camera (Technicolor), Harry Stradling; editor, David Wagner; music, Neal Hefti; choreography, Robert Sydney; assistant director, Carter DeHaven. Reviewed at Cinema I, N.Y. Jan. 7 '65. Running time, 118 MINS.

Stanley Ford .... Jack Lemmon
Mrs. Ford .... Virna Lisi
Charles .... Terry-Thomas
Harold Lampson .... Eddie Mayehoff
Edna .... Claire Trevor
Judge Blackstone .... Sidney Blackmer
Tobey Rawlins .... Max Showalter
Dr. Bentley .... Jack Albertson
District Attorney .... Alan Hewitt
Harold's Secretary .... Mary Wickes

A variety of ingredients for box-office success have been blended into "How To Murder Your Wife" and, even though the finished product hasn't turned out to be the comic souffle that was intended, there is still probably enough going for it to bring the Jack Lemmon starrer (and coproduction) for United Artists a goodly hunk of action at the wickets.

George Axelrod's plot deals with the antics of a bachelor cartoonist, played by Lemmon, who has a policy of acting out the escapades of his newsprint sleuth hero to test their creaibility before actually committing them to paper. So it is that, awakening one morning to find himself married to an Italian dish who had popped out of a cake at a party the night before and after trying to make a go of this unwanted wedlock, he simulates the "murder" of said spouse one evening by dumping a dummy likeness of her into a building site construction form which workmen subsequently fill with concrete.

When Lemmon's wife, played by Italo newcomer to Yank pix, Virna Lisi, spots the cartoonist's sketches of his "crime" on his work table she panics and flees. The strip appears in the papers and, unable to explain his wife's whereabouts, Lemmon is arrested for murder and brought to trial in a silly courtroom scene in which he is freed by an all-male jury the members of which he convinces all secretly hanker after emancipation themselves. She returns later anyway.

All of this has moments of fine comic style but, overall, emerges as prefabricated as Lemmon's comic strip character. The comedian's efforts are considerable and consistent but finesse and desire (being part owner as well as topliner) aren't enough to overcome the fact that Axelrod's script doesn't make the most of its potentially antic situations.

Richard Quine, who is also partnered in the venture along with Axelrod and Lemmon via their Murder Inc. indie formed for the making of the pic, directed the film. Although he brings some bright spots into focus, the pace of the pic often falters. All the mugging and agility of Lemmon and his costars can't save these lagging moments.

Figuring prominently in this department are Terry-Thomas and Eddie Mayehoff. The British film comic plays Lemmon's valet and assistant on the acted out capers of the comic strip sleuth. As one more dedicated to the cartoonist's bachelorhood than even the animator himself, Terry-Thomas cavorts about doing his best to break up the marriage. His contributions are zesty in his splay-toothed tradition.

Mayehoff overdoes in the mugging department, a factor which tends to annoy because of the redundant, one-joke nature of his portrayal. He is Lemmon's attorney who has long felt that the cartoonist should marry and fights off Lemmon's attempt at annulling the marriage. As his domineering wife, Clair Trevor does a pat job of giving her spouse the rolling pin treatment.

Miss Lisi, who gets top starring billing with Lemmon, is a blonde looker who makes one wonder what the animator is so upset about when finding himself with her for a mate. She seems potentially more provocative than she actually comes across. Her acting covers the role effectively and she displays a flair for comedy but the promise she

displays isn't given sufficient development.

Technical credits are fine. Harry Stradling's Technicolor camera has captured the goings on nicely. Neal Hefti has penned some smoothly-swinging music and David Wages has edited the film soundly, although tightening of the 118 minutes could heighten some scenes. Supporting cast backs up ably.

That all of the potential of "How To Murder Your Wife" doesn't quite come off may be a disappointment to Lemmon and Terry-Thomas followers and believers in the tradition of UA comedy smashes but there is sufficient style, action and marquee bait here to keep ticket sellers busy and the UA-Murder Inc. treasurers happy. A hefty promo campaign is planned to help this aim along. *Kali.*

Girl Happy
(SONGS-PANAVISION-COLOR)

Plush Elvis Presley songfest with slick bo.o indicated.

Hollywood, Jan. 14.

Metro release of Joe Pasternak production. Stars Elvis Presley; features Shelley Fabares, Gary Crosby, Nita Talbot, Joby Baker, Mary Ann Mobley, Harold J. Stone, Chris Noel. Directed by Boris Sagal. Screenplay, Harvey Bullock, R. S. Allen; camera (Metrocolor), Philip H. Lathrop; music, George Stoll; editor, Rita Roland; asst. director, Jack Aldworth. Reviewed at Hollywood-Paramount Theatre, Jan. 13, '65. Running time, 96 MINS.
Rusty Wells .... Elvis Presley
Valerie .... Shelley Fabares
Big Frank .... Harold J. Stone
Andy .... Gary Crosby
Wilbur .... Joby Baker
Sunny Daze .... Nita Talbot
Deena .... Mary Ann Mobley
Romano .... Fabrizio Mioni
Doc .... Jimmy Hawkins
Sgt. Benson .... Jackie Coogan
Brentwood von Durgenfeld .Peter Brooks
Mr. Penchill .... John Fiedler
Betsy .... Chris Noel
Laurie .... Lyn Edgington
Nancy .... Gale Gilmore
Bobbie .... Pamela Curran
Linda .... Rusty Allen

Elvis Presley, who gets around more than most top stars (viz., "Viva Las Vegas," released last July, and "The Roustabout," late November), has another musical winner in this Joe Pasternak production. A story line unburdened by anything but lightness and a dozen song numbers belted out in singer's customary style provide the type of pleasant fare which Presley's fans have come to expect. Film, lavishly produced in a glamorous background, shapes as a money entry.

As usual, songs and production numbers highlight the action, which is liberally sprinkled with a score of Bikini-clad lovelies. Perhaps the two top numbers are "She's Evil," in which star is backed by his three-man combo and Shelley Fabares, femme lead, and "Wolf Call," which Presley reprises for a romantic climax. Nita Talbot lends an attractive presence, too, as a stripper chirping "Good News." Another production number which juve audiences can swing to is "The Clam," a slick-paced rock 'n' roller.

Locale of the Harvey Bullock-R. S. Allen screenplay is the resort city of Fort Lauderdale, Fla., where Easter Week is celebrated by thousands of sun-seeking collegians. Presley, as leader of a hot musical combo, has the extra-curricular assignment of keeping an eye—or else—on Miss Fabares, daughter of a tough Chicago nitery owner, to keep her out of trouble. Director Boris Sagal takes this somewhat-hackneyed story premise and endows it with quick-tempoed action in which song numbers fit patly.

Presley undertakes his role with growing naturalness and, of course, scores with his singing. Miss Fabares is cute and pretty in an undemanding role, and star gets strong support from Gary Crosby, Joby Baker and Jimmy Hawkins (as his combo) both musically and in the comedy field. Mary Ann Mobley as a charmer has her moments, Harold J. Stone gustily socks over the father role

and Fabrizio Mioni and Peter Brooks play students. Jackie Coogan amuses as a cop.

Philip H. Lathrop's color photography is a visual asset, as is the art direction by George W. Davis and Addison Hehr. George Stoll's musical score nicely captures the proper mood, which Rita Roland's editing maintains at a speedy clip. The Jordanaires melodically provide vocal backgrounds. *Whit.*

One Way Pendulum
(BRITISH)

Wayout comedy that, sparked by clever trade and consumer selling, could make it; otherwise, will have rough going.

Lopert Pictures Corp. presentation of a Woodfall Film production. Produced by Michael Deeley. Directd by Peter Yates. Features Eric Sykes, George Coe, Julia Foster, Jonathan Miller, Peggy Mount, Alison Leggatt, Mona Washbourne, Douglas Wilmer. Screenplay, N. F. Simpson, based on his play of same name; camera, Denys Coop; editor, Peter Taylor; sound, Steve Delby; music, composed by Richard Rodney Bennett, conducted by Marcus Dods. Reviewed in N.Y., Jan. 18, 1965. Running time 90 MINS.
Mr. Groomkirby .... Eric Sykes
Defense counsel, friend......George Cole
Sylvia ....Julia Foster
Kirby....................Jonathan Miller
Mrs. Gantry........t......Peggy Mount
Mrs. Groomkirby..........Alison Leggatt
Aunt Mildred......... Mona Washbourne
Judge, Maintenance man .Douglas Wilmer
Stan ....Kenneth Farringdon
Det. Insp. Barnes........ Glyn Houston
Counsel caretaker......Graham Crowden
Court Clerk cleaners' assistant ....
.... Walter Horsbruch
Usher office clerk .... Frederick Piper
Policeman, bus conductor........Vincent Harding
Voice of Gormless ....Tommy Bruce

While it is unlikely that anyone will come up with a lucid explanation of what "One Way Pendulum" is about, there are sufficient ingredients in the quasi-surrealistic comedy to provide a good ad copywriter with the germ of a clever promotion campaign.

A swinging film version of a British play that had some measure of success in London several years ago, the selling stumbling-block presented by the absence of any boxoffice names is somewhat compensated for by the zany style of the so-called story with acting to match. If Lopert strikes the right selling approach, "Pendulum" could create something of a stir in those art houses that dig British comedy. It is a natural to be taken up by collegiate types and borderline intellectuals.

Adapted from his own play by N. F. Simpson, what there is of a plot deals with an eccentric British family whose antics resemble normal behavior as Salvador Dali resembles Grandma Moses. The "story" is actually a series of character sketches that sometimes merge but more frequently stamp the individual concerned as an eccentric in his own right.

Although Simpson's people behave like the logical forebears of such recent British exports as the Beatles, they are portrayed by the able cast as dead serious types, which only accents the absurdity of their behavior.

Papa (Eric Sykes) seeks change from his humdrum existence as an insurance clerk by erecting a do-it-yourself replica of the Old Bailey in his living room only to find a trial underway when he gets it finished; the mother (Alison

Leggatt repeating her stage role), seemingly the sane one, goes along with her oddly-behaviored family until she adds her own bit by engaging a charwoman (Peggy Mound), not to clean, but to eat the family's leftovers. Son (Jonathan Miller—one of the original "Beyond The Fringe" quartet) segues between teaching a group of stolen weight scales, (kept in the attic) of a British type that "speaks" the weight, to sing the "Hallelujah Chorus" and serving, ex-officio, as the defendant in his father's trial scene (having committed 43 murders). Nearly rational is daughter (Julia Foster), whose only concern is for what she considers a physical deformity—her arms don't reach her knees. Another member of the family, Aunt Mildred (Mona Washbourne), spends her days in a wheelchair waiting to depart—for anywhere.

Several characters double from real life associates of the father to various participants in the trial. Particularly outstanding is Douglas Wilmer's dry, impeccable Judge whose acquittal of the son, despite his admitted guilt, is the only logical outcome as far as the father is concerned.

Peter Yates has directed with a technique that treats comedy as deadly serious and is responsible for much of the antic spirit that keeps the film animated during most of its chaotic run. Denys Coop's excellent camerawork and Reece Pemberton's art work ably catch the drabness of the British middle-class in which Simpson has set his story. Richard Rodney Bennett's music properly avoids the opportunity to match the extreme form of the plot.

Although the attempt to blend farce and fantasy is only intermittently successful, there are comparatively few dull passages in the film and should please the rather special audience it must find.
Robe.

Erzaehl Mir Nichts
(Don't Tell Me Any Stories)
GERMAN-COLOR)
Berlin, Jan. 19.
Columbia-Bavaria release of Parnass-Film (Theo Maria Werner) production. Stars Heidelinde Weis and Karl Michael; features Georg Thomalla, Alice Treff, Thomas Reiner, Ursula Borsodi. Directed by Diterich Haugk. Screenplay, Jo Hanns Roesler, Theo Maria Werner, and Dietrich Haugk, after a novel by Roesler; camera (Eastmancolor), Guenter Senftleben; music, Karl Bette; editor, Claus von Boro. At the Marmorhaus, West Berlin. Running time, 102 MINS.
Martine Doerner ... Heidelinde Weis
Dr. Nikolaus Feyl...Karl Michael Vogler
Hugo Bach ....Georg Thomalla
Rosalinde Bach ....Ursula Borsodi
Wastl Bach ....Lothar Roehrig
Dr. Waldemar Hecht......Thomas Reiner
vl's aunt .... Alice Treff
Emmerich Mehler ......Alfred Pongratz

This one marks the debut of a new German producer, Theo Maria Werner, Columbia's former press chief for Germany. He produced the pic, via his own Parnass-Film unit, for Columbia on whose payroll he had been for many years. Internationally, there is nothing special about this production. But for the German market several plus points are apparent. It is primarily an item for the local market where it looks like a good commercial bet.

This type of feature pic has become rather rare in Germany. It is a genuine love story, a film without those eternal bed sequences. There's only one intimate scene but handled with taste.

Plot is rather simple but benefits from a series of amiable situations. It centers on a young, handsome divorce attorney. He fools around with the girls and divorced women. Marriage is out of the question for him because he finds that all females are about the same and they begin to bore him after a while. Then he meets a girl who is "different." It's mutual affection. But when the girl finds out about his many previous affairs, she believes that she is just another victim, and deserts him. Girl pretends she's married which complicates the affair. Of course, the pair are reconciled and reunited ultimately.

Performances of the two principal players, Heidelinde Weis and Karl Michael Vogler, are refreshing enough to overcome the drawbacks contained in the script. Lineup of good supporting players includes Thomas Reiner, as Vogler's colleague, who shows promise.

Theo Maria Werner can be credited with producing one of the more enjoyable German pix. But it is not much of a film for the reviewers. But bulk of native film patrons will undoubtedly like it. All in all, this is a satisfactory beginning for Werner who intends to produce a second film soon. Technically, his initial production measures up. *Hans.*

Dr. med, Hiob Praetorius
(Praetorius)
(GERMAN-COLOR)
Berlin, Jan. 19.
Constantin release of Hans Domnick and Independent Film (Kurt Hoffmann) production. Stars Heinz Ruehmann, Liselotte Pulver; features Fritz Rasp, Fritz Tillmann, Werner Hinz. Directed by Kurt Hoffmann. Screenplay, Heinz Pauck and Istvan Bekefi, adapted from stageplay of same title by Curt Goetz; camera (Eastmancolor), Richard Angst; music, Franz Grothe. At Gloria Palast, West Berlin. Running time, 92 MINS.
Dr. med. Hiob
Praetorius...............Heinz Ruehmann
Violetta Hoellriegel......Liselotte Pulver
Shunderson .... Fritz Rasp
Dr. Klotz.................Fritz Tillmann
Hoellriel ....Werner Hinz
Prof. Speiter...............Peter Luehr
Dr. Watzmann........Claus Schwarzkopf

This is a remake of the 1949 German Curt Goetz filmization of the same title. While the old "Praetorius" pic cost $200,000, budget for this new one, this time in Eastmancolor and Panavision, was exactly twice as much or $400,000. Americans may remember the Goetz story: Joseph L. Mankiewicz filmed it, under the title of "People Will Talk," with Cary Grant and Jeanne Crain, for 20th-Fox back in 1951.

The new German production is nothing for the crix. Yet it is in the heavy money class in this country. Big draw here will be Heinz Ruehmann and Liselotte (Lilo) Pulver, currently top stars with German audiences. Also the name of the late Curt Goetz is still powerful around here.

Kurt Hoffman has directed a vehicle full of cliches. There is little imagination along the 92 minutes,

---

some performances are merely routine. Moreover, the whole thing has been transferred into ultra-modern (the hospital, etc.) surroundings. Only the dialog still reminds of the Goetz original. This is a great pity for "Praetorius" rates as one of the few truly witty pieces of German boulevard literature. Unfortunately, there is nothing very witty about this pic. Everything remains on the surface.

This concerns the story of a highly successful medico who's a big philantropist as well. He has his own outlook upon life and his own way of helping human beings. His attitude brings him many friends and admirers, but also enemies. Latter includes a jealous colleague who sets out to "track down" his background. There seems to be something fishy about the good medico's past. Remainder is familiar to those who have seen the play or the 1951 film.

Heinz Ruehmann enacts an amiable medico's who's, however, not faithful to the Goetz pattern. Ruehmann is once more Ruehmann and not the strange outsider, Dr. Praetorius, once so brilliantly and intelligently portrayed by the late Goetz himself on the screen. Quite obviously, director Hoffmann let safety play first fiddle by presenting Ruehmann to native audiences as they have known this actor for decades.

His partner is Swiss-born Lilo Pulver. She is lovely to look at and thoroughly sympathetic, but the scurrilous touch her role actually demands is completely missing. A polished performance is contributed by Fritz Rasp as Shunderson. It's a brilliant acting job by this German vet player.

There is fine color photography by oldtimer Richard Angst. The score was written by another vet, Franz Grothe, who contributed his 154th film score since 1929. A top German production that seems to fall short. *Hans.*

The Man From Button Willow
(COLOR CARTOON-SONGS)

First animated western feature is okay for kiddie market but much too naive for teenagers and their elders.

United Screen Arts presentation of a Phyllis Bounds Detiege production. Voices of Dale Robertson, Howard Keel, Edgar Buchanan, Barbara Jean Wong, Herschel Bernardi, Ross Martin, Verna Felton, Shep Menken, Pinto Colvig, Cliff Edwards, Thurl Ravenscroft, John Hiestand, Clarence Nash, Edward Platt, Buck Buchanan. Directed by David Detiege. Screenplay, David Detiege; production designer, Ernie Nordi; music, George Stoll, Robert Van Eps; songs, Phil Bounds, Dale Robertson, George Bruns, Mel Henke; editors, Ted Baker, Sam Horta; camera (color), Max Morgan. Reviewed at Preview Screening Room, N.Y., Jan. 21, '65. Running time, 87 MINS.

In "The Man from Button Willow," exhibs have a sweet, simple little picture ideally suited for the moppet trade. Being promoted as the first animated western feature ever made, the picture is, however, much too naive in story and artistic design to cause much stir among jaded, "Bonanza"-bred teenagers and their elders. Film's biz prospects thus will be limited by what it can pick up in what is generally known as the afternoon trade. Offsetting this handicap to some ex-

---

tent may be the fact that since there is such a dearth of suitable product for the very young fry, pic should be around for a long, long time.

Star Dale Robertson, whose new distribution firm, United Screen Arts, is getting underway with this pic, obviously was much in on the film's planning. Not only is he credited for penning some of pic's songs and does he supply the voice for its stalwart hero, he also was obviously the physical model for the hero. Latter is a well-to-do, jut-jawed rancher whom the government calls upon from time to time to protect its interests and those of innocent landholders whose property is coveted by speculators anticipating the building of the transcontinental railroad.

That plotline, however, only comes to the fore in the closing quarter of the film. Most of the running time is devoted to a more or less conventional cartoon view of life on the farm, wherein the rancher's little Chinese ward and her horse, dog, bird and other furred and feathered friends frisk about in a series of pleasant, if exceedingly mild, adventures. The windup, which finds the Robertson character (named "Justine Eagle") saving the life of a U.S. senator and immediately extolling the virtues of democracy, adds a dash of patriotism to the corn pudding.

Picture has been nicely animated in strictly conventional style. The occasional songs are bouncy, though hardly memorable, and the uncredited color is good.
Anby.

Sylvia

Story of a prostie who reforms. Strong femme appeal and bright b.o. through natural exploitation.

Hollywood, Jan. 27.

Paramount release of Martin H. Poll production. Stars Carroll Baker, George Maharis; features Joanne Dru, Peter Lawford, Viveca Lindfors, Edmond O'Brien, Aldo Ray, Ann Sothern, Lloyd Bochner. Directed by Gordon Douglas. Screenplay, Sydney Boehm, based on novel by E. V. Cunningham; camera, Joseph Ruttenberg; editor, Frank Bracht; asst. director, Dick Moder; music, David Raksin. Reviewed at Paramount Studios, Jan. 25, '65. Running time, **115 MINS.**

Sylvia West .... Carroll Baker
Alan Macklin .... George Maharis
Jane Phillips .... Joanne Dru
Frederick Summers ...... Peter Lawford
Irma Olanski .... Viveca Lindfors
Oscar Stewart .... Edmond O'Brien
Jonas Karoki .... Aldo Ray
Grace Argona ....Ann Sothern
Bruce Stamford III ...... Lloyd Bochner
Lola Diamond .... Paul Gilbert
Big Shirley .... Nancy Kovack
Father Gonzales .... Jay Novallo
Gavin Cullen .... Gene Lyons
Muscles .... Anthony Caruso
Pudgey .... Val Avery
Gus .... Alan Carney
Pancho .... Manuel Padilla
Anne .... Majel Barrett
Mrs. Karoki .... Shirley O'Hara

"Sylvia" is the story of a prostitute who turns to decency. The Martin H. Poll production is episodic until its closing reels, covering a period of 14 to 15 years as a private investigator digs into her obscure past to learn who she really is; consequently, considerable dramatic impact is lost due to film's rambling flashback treatment. However, by the very nature of the title character's rise to fiancee of a fabulously wealthy man there is unusually strong femme appeal. With its high exploitation potential, coupled with the sex buildup of Carroll Baker for her upcoming "Harlow" starrer, payoff should be profitable.

Miss Baker is joined in stellar spot by George Maharis as the private eye who ultimately falls in love with the woman he is tracing. Actually, although hers is the motivating character, top honors go to Maharis for a consistently restrained performance which builds, while actress suffers somewhat from the spotty nature of her haphazard part. They do not come together until late in the pic, after Maharis has completed his long and exhaustive search into femme's past—film then substitute romance for sordidness for a satisfactory finale.

Under Gordon Douglas' telling direction of Sydney Boehm's screenplay based on the E. V. Cunningham novel, sequences limning title character's past are generally individually strongly etched. Action follows Maharis as his assignment takes him around the country to the different scenes of his quarry's career. He learns through records and from people who once knew her history of Sylvia from the time she was raped at age of 14 by her drunken stepfather up through various stages of her trail of vice. Dick is hired by Peter Lawford as Miss Baker's fiance, suspicious of the stories femme, now cultured, modestly wealthy and author of a published book of modern poetry, tells him of her family background.

Miss Baker delivers in okay fashion although the part isn't particularly a powerhouse and her character isn't a sexpot. Maharis is more successful, scoring decisively. Pair is strongly backed by an exceptionally able cast.

Ann Sothern as a blowsy cashier in a penny arcade where Sylvia once worked is a definite standout. Viveca Lindfors likewise scores as a Pittsburgh librarian who once befriended the little 14-year-old before she was seduced and sent on her scarlet way. Edmond O'Brien also registers as a married salesman who took her from Mexico to N.Y. Particularly effective is Joanne Dru, once picked up with Sylvia on a charge of prostitution but now respectably wed to a banker, who fills in Maharis on the most tragic portions of Sylvia's past and how she was able finally to break away to live a decent life. Lawford is okay in his role although he hasn't much to do.

One of the most colorful characters is played by Nancy Kovack, as a voluptuous dancer once arrested with Sylvia, who belts over her part in slick fashion. Aldo Ray is the stepfather, and Jay Novello impresses in his brief appearance as a Mexican priest.

Joseph Ruttenberg turns in good photography and art direction by Hal Pereira and Roland Anderson captures story demands. Other technical credits also are okay. Paul Anka sings title song over credits, clefted by Paul Francis Webster and David Raksin.

Whit.

Le Bambole
(The Dolls)
(ITALIAN, SONGS)

Rome, Feb. 2.

Columbia-Celad release of Gianni Hecht Lucari production for Documento Films. Features Gina Lollobrigida, Elke Sommer, Monica Vitti, Virna Lisi, Nino Manfredi, Maurizio Arena, Akim Tamiroff, Jean Sorel, Gianni Rizzo, Piero Focaccia, Orazio Orlando. Music, Armando Trovajoli; editor, Roberto Cinquini, Giuliana Bettoja. At Fiamma, Rome. Running Time, **100 MINS.**

LA TELEFONATA
(THE PHONE CALL)

Directed by Dino Risi. Story and screenplay, Rodolfo Sonega. Camera, Ennio Guarnieri.

Wife .... Virna Lisi
Husband .... Nino Manfredi

TRATTATO DI EUGENETICA
(TREATISE IN EUGENICS)

Directed by Luigi Comencini. Screenplay, Tullio Pinelli, from story by Luciano Salce and Steno; Camera, Carlo Montuori.

Ulla .... Elke Sommer
Massimo .... Maurizio Arena
Valerio .... Piero Focaccia

LA MINESTRA
(THE COUP)

Directed by Fianco Rossi. Story and screenplay, Rodolfo Sonego, and Luigi Magni; camera, Roberto Gerardi.

Giovanna .... Monica Vitti
Husband .... John Carlsen
Richetto .... Orazio Orlando
Peppe .... DeSimone

MONSIGNOR CUPIDO
(MONSIGNOR CUPID)

Directed by Mauro Bolognini. Story and screenplay, Leo Benvenuti, Piero deBernardi; camera, Leonida Barboni.

Beatrice .... Gina Lollobrigida
Monsignor Arendi ...... Akim Tamiroff
Vincenzo .... Jean Sorel

Episode entry makes for okay lightweight fare, giving Columbia, which is handling most world areas, a good investment in the Gianni Hecht—Documento production. Lollobrigida - Sommer-Vitti-Lisi name parlay also will assist as marquee bait as well as provide some eye-popping exploitation ingredients. It's one of the better and more balanced of the many seg entries recently made in Italy.

"The Phone Call" is a brief and piquant item spoofing longwinded calls by mothers-in-law. It's neatly limned by Virna Lisi, and especially by Nino Manfredi, who plays the harried husband distracted by a sunbathing neighbor when his own amorous approaches to his wife are interrupted by a never-ending session on the Ameche.

An Elke Sommer in top form makes a delight out of "Treatise." Looker has never been better or displayed a more winning personality than she does here in playing a Nordic type who descends on Rome to find the perfect male with whom to make love, have a child, but not marry. Maurizio Arena and Piero Focaccia, latter a find in his first pic role (he's a pop singer), play two contrasting local suitors. Luigi Comencini directed with good pace.

"The Coup" is more biting, dealing with various attempts by a desperate wife to get her no-good husband killed by someone—anyone—for money. Director Franco Rossi, with strong assists from writers Rodolfo Sonego and Luigi Magni (the latter's dialogue is especially lively) makes the story believable. Monica Vitti gives a topnotch performance, vastly different from her stints in Antonioni films, as the scheming wife. John Carlsen, Orazio Orlando and others populate a colorful supporting cast.

"Monsignor Cupid," based by scripters DeBernardi and Benvenuti on a tale by Boccaccio, tells how a sex-starved hotel owner's wife tricks a Monsignor into favoring her seduction of his male secretary, unbeknownst to all but the couple. Somewhat mechanical and predictable in its construction, this nevertheless allows for plenty of tongue-in-cheek humor while never passing the borderline of bad taste. Gina Lollobrigida is fine as the beauty with designs, Jean Sorel makes an okay target for her attention, and Akim Tamiroff is the ebullient monsignor who falls for her scheming.

Technical credits are good throughout. Armando Trovajoli has put plenty of savvy into his musical blend, which includes a number of current pop hits.

Hawk.

Dear Brigitte
(C'SCOPE—COLOR)

Excellent family comedy pic starring James Stewart as egghead pop who finds out son is math genius. Solid supporting cast and actual appearance by Brigitte Bardot spell top money in general market.

Hollywood, Jan. 28.

20th-Fox release of Fred Kohlmar production produced by Henry Koster. Stars James Stewart; features Fabian, Glynis Johns, Cindy Carol, Billy Mumy, John Williams, Jack Kruschen, Ed Wynn. Directed by Koster. Screenplay, Hal Kanter, based on novel "Erasmus With Freckles" by John Haase; camera (DeLuxe Color), Lucien Ballard; editor, Marjorie Fowler; music, George Duning art direction, Jack Martin Smith, Malcolm Brown; sound, Alfred Bruzlin, Elmer Raguse; asst. director, Fred R. Simpson. Reviewed at 20th-Fox Studios, Jan. 26, '65. Running time, **100 MINS.**

Prof. Robert Leaf .... James Stewart
Kenneth .... Fabian
Vina Leaf .... Glynis Johns
Pandora Leaf .... Cindy Carol
Erasmus Leaf .... Billy Mumy
Peregrine Upjohn .... John Williams
Dr. Volker .... Jack Kruschen
George .... Charles Robinson
Dean Sawyer .... Howard Freeman
Terry .... Jane Wald
Unemployment Office Clerk . Alice Pearce
Argyle .... Jesse White
Lt. Rink .... Gene O'Donnell
The Captain .... Ed Wynn

An entertaining comedy with something for everyone, "Dear Brigitte" shapes up as an excellent family pic. Fine direction of a very competent cast of comic talents, backstopped by firstrate technical know-how, make this Fred Kohlmar-Henry Koster production a strong contender for top grosses in the general market.

Hal Kanter's screenplay, based on John Haase's novel "Erasmus With Freckles," focuses on poet-professor Robert Leaf who's not only pro-humanities but very much anti-science. James Stewart is perfect in characterization of the idealistic voice in academic wilderness, as nuclear labs and computer setups encroach upon his domain of arts and letters at mythical modern university.

Complications arise when 8-year-old son Erasmus turns up tone-deaf, then color-blind (hence unsuited for artistic career) but displays mathematical genius which indicates great scientific future. Kanter's yarn is lightweight, but a sufficiently strong fiber to support a string of varied and effective comedy situations, including Erasmus' puppy love for Brigitte Bardot to whom he secretly writes letters from Sausalito riverboat home.

In role of Stewart's wife, Glynis Johns is standout as steadying influence on hubby, son Billy Mumy, teen-age daughter Cindy Carol and latter's boy friend Fabian who puts kid's genius to work figuring out winning horses. Rambling throughout zany proceedings as one-man Greek Chorus is Ed Wynn, delivering strongly in role of retired ferryboat skipper.

When son's talents make headlines, Stewart refuses all attempts at exploitation, including projected tv show pitting moppet against top adult brains and called "Beat the Kid." Jack Kruschen excels as psychiatrist who uncovers Erasmus' yen for Miss Bardot. When pop ankles campus and files for unemployment loot, Alice Pearce does smash bit as bureaucratic clerk, a highlight segment.

Miss Johns brings hubby around to using son's gift at handicapping for non-profit arts foundation in partnership with an urbane academic fraud socked over by John Williams, and his bookie-pal Argyle played by appropriately toutish Jesse White. Campus dean Howard Freeman and Gene O'Donnell as cop succeed in bringing final order out of laff-getting chaos. Charles Robinson and looker Jane Wald decorate domestic settings as Bohemian neighbors.

Erasmus' yen for Miss Bardot is satisfied in final scenes with trip to Paris for meeting with Gallic symbol. Actual appearance by Miss Bardot in five-minute seg is her first family pic exposure, and overall impact of grace and charm could open up new career angles. Contract forbids use of her name in credits and paid advertising, but she's in the title, in the film, and good.

Pic is a Fred Kohlmar production, but Koster did two-hat chores as prod-director, getting the most out of talented cast framed by Lucien Ballard's color and widescreen camera which is a bit too static in overuse of medium shots. Marjorie Fowler's tight editing to 100 minutes prevented vignettes from wearing thin, and George Duning's non-obtrusive music is effective. Grade A art direction by Jack Martin Smith and Malcolm Brown gives pic an attractive backdrop. Opening titles are Computer-Contemporary, and Pacific Title gets the nod here. Sharper ears will catch unbilled voice bit by Richard (Dick) Lane as horse race broadcaster. All other technical credits are topnotch. *Murf.*

Young Fury
(COLOR-TECHNISCOPE)

Routine oater defeated by weak script despite some good new faces among vet names and topnotch production values.

Hollywood, Feb. 1.
Paramount release of A. C. Lyles production. Stars Rory Calhoun, Virginia Mayo, Lon Chaney, Richard Arlen, John Agar; features Preston Pierce, Linda Foster, Robert Biheller, William Bendix and rest of cast. Directed by Christian Nyby. Screenplay, Steve Fisher, from story idea by Lyles and Fisher; camera (Technicolor), Haskell Boggs; editor, Marvin Coil; music, Paul Dunlap; asst. directors, Mike Caffey, Howard Roessell. Reviewed at Paramount Studios, Jan. 25, '65. Running time, 79 MINS.

Clint McCoy	Rory Calhoun
Sara McCoy	Virginia Mayo
Bartender	Lon Chaney
Sheriff Jenkins	Richard Arlen
Dawson	John Agar
Tige	Preston Pierce
Sally	Linda Foster
Biff	Robert Biheller
Alice	Merry Anders
Kathy	Joan Huntington
Pancho	Marc Cavell
Stone	Jody McCrea
Farmer	Rex Bell, Jr.
Peters	Wm. Wellman, Jr.
Jeb	Reg Parton
Slim	Jay Ripley
Curly	Kevin O'Neal
Gabbo	Jerry Summers
Pony	Fred Alexander
Sam	Dal Jenkins
Blacksmith	William Bendix

Tale of post-Civil War juve gangs plus commendable slotting of young thesps in major roles amid rich Paramount production elements cannot overcome stereotyped plot mechanics to which Steve Fisher's screenplay ultimately succumbs. Routine performances by vet names alternate with scenes of excessive brawling and cruelty, none of which ever gets plot rolling or produces a major sympathetic character. A. C. Lyles production shapes up as strictly routine programer.

Groups of immature youths wandering bewildered in the backwash of political upheavals have formed basis for other films set in periods following wars and economic depressions. Particular group here is headed up by Preston Pierce, playing well the role of Tige, rootless adolescent of the 1870's who takes his gang to home town upon hearing that father Clint has headed there one jump

ahead of the Dawson crowd which is out to get Pop for alleged finking.

Tige and crew bust into town, succeeding to temporary power and indulging in many repetitious and wanton acts of destruction. Situation might be believable in today's climate of non-involvement, but total gutlessness of frontier townfolk, as typified by ineffective sheriff Richard Arlen, strains credulity. Nihilism of the hoods is exploited, not explored, in scenery-wrecking rumbles around and within saloon operated by Virginia Mayo, wife of Rory Calhoun's Clint who had (illogically) deserted because of her promiscuity but left an infant Tige in her care.

Calhoun is generally wooden except in underplayed confrontation with Tige, when he forces son and other despicable scum to realize shallowness of drifter-gunfighter existence. Miss Mayo is on briefly as remorseful mother, ditto John Agar as Dawson whose arrival in town is by final reel almost welcome relief. Richard Arlen's longtime facial and vocal masculinity is at odds with the vapid lawman he plays, and the late William Bendix has a cameo bit as village smithy. Lon Chaney walks through bartender role.

Pierce shows much promise as new film face, also Linda Foster as young girl forced into plot as romantic interest for Tige. Robert Biheller registers okay as another punk, but he relies too much on "West Side Story" rather than "Dead End" to develop character.

Techniscope and Technicolor camera of Haskell Boggs, art direction by Hal Pereira and Arthur Lonergan, editing of Marvin Coil, Paul Dunlap's music, and Harold Lewis' sound are firstrate, but director Christian Nyby is stymied by Steve Fisher's screenplay which lapses into cliche after 15 of pic's 79 minutes. Lyles' prominent casting of young thesps in major studio pix is laudable. *Murf.*

The Blue Beast
(Aoi Yaju)
(JAPANESE)

Toho presentation of a Toho (Sanezumi Fujimoto-Masakatsu Kaneko) production. Directed by Hiromichi Horikawa. Features Tatsuya Nakadai, Yoko Tsukasa, Koreya Senda, Keiko Awaji, Jun Tazaki, Ichiro Nakaya. Screenplay, Yoshio Shirasaka; camera, Asakazu Nakai; music, Sei Ikeno. Reviewed at Toho Cinema, N.Y., Jan. 28, 1965. Running time: 95 MINS.

(English Subtitles)

Although a bit late arriving in the U.S. (film is about four years old), this Japanese variation on "A Room At The Top" is an interesting and well-handled look at an aspect of life that Westerners may have thought existed only in the land of Miltown and the status symbol. Unlike the British film about the ruthlessness of ambition, this one winds with the climber getting cut down.

Director Hiromichi Horikawa, whose forte is a no-holds-barred look at modern Japanese mores, is able to give his slight tale more force by having an excellent cast headed by one of Japan's most promising young actors—Tatsuya Nakadai—as his anti-hero. Nakadai, whose versatility grows with

every role he undertakes, has much of the "naturalness" of Toshiro Mifune but is young enough to eventually acquire an even wider range than that estimable thespian. He also has that fortunate facility of responding to the ideas of widely varying directors, having worked with most of the top ones.

A smooth character, whose honest demeanor hides the ambition that devours him (symbolized by the title of the film), Nakadai doesn't hesitate to use friends, business acquaintances, and especially the women in his life, to get ahead. A minor executive in a publishing-house beset with labor troubles, he plays labor against management and eventually abandons both for a connection with a top political figure. The latter incident, also reminiscent of "Room At The Top," is to be by way of the bridal path—having made the politico's daughter pregnant. When success is finally at hand, however, Nakadai is killed by one of the union radicals he had betrayed earlier.

Besides Nakadai's completely believable portrayal, impressive performances are given by Yoko Tsukasa as the politico's daughter, Keiko Awaji as a former girl student amour and Koreya Senda as the politician, trapped by Nakadai's machinations. Technically, film is good but not particularly outstanding. However, Horikawa's use of symbolism is outstanding, particularly in the closing sequence where the dying Nakadai imagines a tile column in his hallway is the finally attainable building of the politician. *Robe.*

None But The Brave
(PANAVISION-COLOR)

Frank Sinatra's first directorial job (also produces, stars) emerges fastpaced World War II actioner; good b.o. indicated for general market.

Hollywood, Jan. 27
Warner Bros. release of Frank Sinatra production (coproduced by Sinatra's Artanis Productions and Toho Films' Tokyo Eiga Ltd.), directed by Sinatra. Stars Sinatra, Clint Walker, Tommy Sands, Brad Dexter, Tony Bill; features Tatsuya Mihashi, Takeshi Kato. Screenplay, John Twist, from story by Kikumaru Okuda; camera (Technicolor), Harold Lipstein; editor, Sam O'Steen; asst. director, David Selven; music, Johnny Williams. Reviewed at Hollywood Paramount Theatre, Jan. 26, '65. Running time, 105 MINS.

Maloney	Frank Sinatra
Capt. Bourke	Clint Walker
Lieut. Blair	Tommy Sands
Skt. Bleeker	Brad Dexter
Keller	Tony Bill
Lieut. Kuroki	Tatsuya Mihashi
Sgt. Tamura	Takeshi Kato
Cpl. Craddock	Sammy Jackson
Cpl. Ruffino	R. Bakalyan
Pvt. Johnson	Rafer Johnson
Pvt. Dexter	Jimmy Griffin
Pvt. Searcy	Chris. Dark
Pvt. Hoxie	Don Dorrell
Pvt. Magee	Phil Crosby
Pvt. Waller	John H. Young
Pvt. Swensholm	Roger Ewing
Hirano	H. Suguro
Col. Fufimoto	K. Sahara
Lt. Pvt. Ando	M. Tanimura
Pvt. Tokumaru	Hidao Dazai
Pvt. Goro	S. Kurabe
Pvt. Ishii	T. Inagaki
Pvt. Sato	K. Hato
Pvt. Arikawa	Toro Ibuki
Pvt. Okuda	R. Shunputei

Marking the first joint screen venture actually filmed by an American and Japanese company in the U. S., "None But The Brave" manages a high level of interest for World War II buffs via its unusual premise and action-adventure backdrop, with indications pointing to good reception in general market Reminiscent of the "Kataki" theme—almost an elaboration of the Shimon Wincelberg two-character drama—feature, beautifully mounted in Technicolor, was made by Frank Sinatra's Artanis Productions and Toho Films' Tokyo Eiga Co Ltd, and boasts both an American and Nipponese cast.

Sinatra, who also stars with Clint Walker and produces, makes his directorial bow in this story by Kikumaru Okuda and is responsible for some good effects in maintaining a suspenseful pace. The compact and mostly tenseful screenplay by John Twist — who spent considerable time in Japan on project—and Katsuya Susaki tells its story through the eyes of a Japanese lieutenant, commanding a small detachment of Imperial troops forgotten on an uncharted South Pacific island where an American plane carrying U.S. Marines crashlands.

A truce is arranged by the Japanese commander and Walker, the American pilot and senior officer, after Sinatra, as a pharmacist's mate, amputates the leg of one of the Japanese soldiers wounded in a skirmish with the Americans. Americans' radio is believed destroyed in the crash, and with no means of communication for the Japanese it seems that both sides are destined to sweat out the war on the island, where they lead an uneasy existence together. Truce carries a provision, stipulated by the Japanese, that should either side again become part of the war fighting will be immediately resumed. Shooting starts when the Americans' radio is repaired and a destroyer comes to their aid, resulting in Japanese being wiped out to a man and only five Americans left.

One of the most interesting aspects of film, which was lensed on island of Kanai, Hawaii, for about one-half the footage, with Japanese technicians assisting, is the style of acting adopted by Japanese cast, headed by Tatsuya Mihashi as the lieutenant. Total of 11 Japanese thesps were used, and their peculiar vocal style lends added realism since they speak only in their native tongue, with English subtitles. Sole exception is Mihashi, one of Japan's leading actors, who registers strongly in a different type of character than American audiences have come to expect.

Sinatra, although topbilled, plays second fiddle in footage to Walker, who with Mihashi are the dominating figures. Sinatra appears only intermittently; his character only important in the operation scene which he enacts dramatically. Walker gives a lusty performance as the flier, a professional soldier who knows war and how to approach it.

Starred with Sinatra and Walker are Tommy Sands, who gives an over-enthusiastic portrayal of a young lieutenant; Brad Dexter, cast as a sergeant; and Tony Bill, the radio operator, both okay. An interesting performance is delivered by Takeshi Kato, playing second in Japanese command, and other Japanese players likewise add to overall effect. American casters also competently handle their roles.

On the technical side, Harold Lipstein's Panavision-Technicolor photography is particularly impressive and Sam O'Steen's editing fast. LeRoy Deane's art direction fills the bill and Johnny Williams' music score provides excellent background. Special effects are credited to E. Tsuburaya, expertly contrived. *Whit.*

Il Disco Volante
(The Martians)
ITALIAN

Rome, Feb. 2.
Dino DeLaurentiis production and release. Features Alberto Sordi, Silvana Mangano, Monica Vitti, Eleonora Rossi Drago, Guido Celano, Alberto Fogliani, Liana del Balzo, Lars Bloch. Directed by Tinto Brass. Story and screenplay, Rodolfo Sonego; camera, Bruno Barcarol; music, Piero Piccioni; editor, Tatiana Casini. At Galleria, Rome. Running time, **93 MINS.**
Brigadiere .... Alberto Sordi
Marsicano .... Alberto Sordi
Don Giuseppe .... Alberto Sordi
The Count .... Alberto Sordi
Mercedes .... Monica Vitti
Clelia .... Eleonora Rossi Drago
Vittoria .... Silvana Mangano

Only occasionally amusing science fiction blend with realism in this film. It will have to ride on the Alberto Sordi name as well as those of Monica Vitti and Silvana Mangano for drawing power.

Film banks strongly on multiple roles by Sordi for its comedic impact, but while the comedian is up to form in one or two of his characters, others misfire, thus diminishing effect of the gimmick

in itself. Firstly, the types are physically too similar. Secondly, Sordi—at least here—is not on a par with a Guinness or Sellers.

Third, script is somewhat nuclear on the exact delineation of some of his characters.

Sonego's screenplay, in fact, might be charged with the major faults of this pic notably in its recurrent attempts to preach a thesis. This ranges from the standard exposure of corruption and decadence in today's society to the world's unwillingness to face up to new realities, "personified" by "invading" Martians. In fact, people (mostly impersonated by Sordi) don't want to believe the evidence of the invaders' presence.

Sordi alternately plays a libidinous accountant who seduces the mayor's wife; a drunkard curate; a somewhat puzzled gendarme; and an effeminate nobleman, but rarely seems fully at ease. Women are similarly wasted. Silvana Mangano comes off best as a peasant woman. Monica Vitti and Eleonora Rossi Drago have relatively little to do in minor roles. There's some able backing from sideline characters played by Guido Celano, Liana del Balzo and others.

Tinto Brass' direction is fairly smooth, and he milks his effects thanks also to lenser Bruno Barcarol and designer Gianni Polidori, who has designed some imaginative inhabitants. Piero Piccioni's music is a bit obsessive. *Hawk.*

The Guide
(INDIAN—COLOR)

Best for the art situations.

Stratton International presentation of Tad Danielewski production, directed by Danielewski. Features Dev Anand, Waheeda Rehman, Kishore Sahu, Leela Chitnis, Anwar Hussein, K. N. Singh, Levy Aaron, Rashid Khan, Dilip Dutt, Sheila Burghart. Screenplay by Pearl S. Buck and Danielewski, based on novel by R. K. Narayan; camera (Eastman Color), Fali Mistry; sound, Barot; art director, Ram Yedekar; music, S. D. Burman; choreography, Hiralal. Reviewed in N.Y., Feb. 5, '65. Running time, **120 MINS.**

This initial effort by Stratton International (made up of writer Pearl Buck and producer-director Tad Danielewski) is an outstanding example of what can be accomplished when a western film director and a western writer choose to make an otherwise completely-Oriental film.

Although Miss Buck has turned to the writings of another for her film material, she retains the Indian heart of R. K. Narayan's novel while telling it in a manner more suitable to western ways of thinking; adapting it so that the universality of the plot comes across without losing the particular Indian flavor of the style. The soundtrack is in English but most of the principals are easy to understand.

Even with their success, however, the potential market for "The Guide" is still the art theatre. Film opened Feb. 9 at the Lincoln Arts Theatre. Lacking exploitable angles usually necessary when a non-stellar film also spurns the usual sexploitation bit, "The Guide" is nevertheless a good film, with

much in its favor. But it will need sharp promotion unless Stratton will be satisfied with the long, slow payoff.

Danielewski isn't always able to keep the Indian tendency towards scenery chewing under control, particularly with leading man Dev Anand, but this is less of a problem than his failure, in the closing sequences, where the audience is expected to believe that the hero has changed, morally and spiritually, into the sainted creature the natives have created. As the emotional transformation was evidently beyond Anand, Danielewski should have used other means of conveying, cinematically, this necessary change.

The plot, a fairly universal one, centers about a brash, young guide whose gift of gab is second only to his taking advantage of the opportunities that come his way—whether it's conning a snobbish archeologist who hires him or seducing the customer's wife.

When the wife (Waheeda Rehman) turns out to be an extremely talented (but frustrated) dancer, the guide sees an opportunity to exploit her. When the situation becomes evident, the husband (Kishore Sahu) abandons his wife. With the help of the guide, she does become a famous dancer, and with success and wealth come boredom and dishonesty.

The guide, found guilty of forging her name to a check, is sent to prison. When released, he hits the skids and, shabby and penniless, wanders about the country. He finds succor with a group of innocent villagers who believe that his big words and slick manner are a mark of wisdom. When a drought strikes the country, however, they turn to him for advice and he finds himself being regarded as a saint. His too-rapid tongue finally tricks him into saying he'll fast until rain comes. The story would then have you believe that, at this point, a spiritual rebirth occurs and the guide sacrifices himself rather than shatter the villagers' belief in his sanctity.

Anand is at his best when he's flippant and brash and speaking the satirical lines provided early in the picture. He rarely, however, captures the asceticism the character requires as the film progresses. Miss Rehman, a lovely, petite type, has considerable range of emotion and is a superb dancer. The producers have managed to satisfy the Indian-public demand for musical sequences by having her dance often, in a variety of settings, but always in keeping with the storyline.

Also outstanding are Sahu as the husband, Leela Chitnia as Anand's mother and a wide assortment of Indian character actors, impressive but unfamiliar to American audiences. One poor performance (and a generally tasteless bit that could easily be edited out) is given by Sheila Burghart as a hardfaced, unfeeling American television reporter.

The settings, beautifully photographed by Fali Mistry in color (the screen says Pathe but Danielewski says that the color is Eastman Color, which was processed by Pathe in New York), vary from the tiny Indian village where the guide lives to Bombay and New

Delhi. One sequence even takes place in the Edward Durrell Stone-designed U.S. Embassy in New Delhi.

Art direction is topnotch, with as much detail given to the usual ugly Indian version of a Western room with art nouveau figurines, bad reproductions of French paintings and clashing colors as to the natural beauties of the countryside and cities.

Music, credited to S. D. Burman, is bits and pieces of Indian music, U.S. jazz and Latin rhythms. *Robe.*

Minnesota Clay
(ITALO-FRANCO-SPANISH)
(COLOR)

Rome, Feb. 2.
Titanus release of an Ultra-Jaguar-Francolondon coproduction. Features Cameron Mitchell, Ethel Rojo, Georges Riviere, Alberto Cevenini, Diana Martin, Fernando Sancho, Antonio Casas. Directed by Sergio Corbucci. Screenplay, Adriano Bolzoni, Corbucci, from story by Bolzoni; camera (Eastmancolor), Jose Fernandez Aguayo; music, Piero Piccioni; editor, Franco Fraticelli. At Corso Cinema, Rome. Running Time, **95 MINS.**
Minnesota Clay .... Cameron Mitchell
Estella .... Ethel Rojo
Fox .... Georges Riviere
Nancy .... Diana Martin
Andy .... Alberto Cevenini
Jonathan .... Antonio Casas
Ortiz .... Fernando Sancho
Lt. Evans .... Julio Pena
Tubbs .... Nando Poggi
Millicet .... Joe Kamel

Latest of Italo-made oaters, "Minnesota Clay," shapes as a good programmer, boasting okay playoff possibilities in Italy and some other areas where western are in major demand. With an open campaign to cash in on the runaway success of "Pugno di Dollari" (a more effective entry) by pushing its Italian origin, this has a chance at some extra money, though it should gross nowhere near total of the previous pic.

Brought in at moderate cost, this film has undeniable production values. And in the cost-vs.-net parlay lie its interesting aspects. It should bring in a neat return on its investment. Among the cliches and novelty plot gimmicks, of which the former abound, this leans heavily on the angle of making its star, Cameron Mitchell (Minnesota Clay), a vet gunfighter escaped from unjust imprisonment He's impaired by faulty eyesight.

Also melded in are rival gang incidents, betrayal and jealousy of a Mexican spitfire camp follower, meeting of hero with his long-lost daughter and familiar wrinkles. Paced somewhat reflectively and overly dialogued, the pic could do with some speeding up.

Mitchell is stolid not to say stiff and uncolorful as the hero, Georges Riviere plays his villain, Fox, in the accepted convention. Ethel Rojo and Diana Martin lend their very different good looks to the contrasting femme roles. Others are capable, with Antonio Casas playing the reliable friend of the family and Fernando Sancho portraying the Mexican bandit chief with all the stops out. Pic takes good advantage of scenery, mostly in Spain. Most of the technical aspects will satisfy all except the most expert westernophiles. *Hawk.*

Love Has Many Faces
(COLOR)

Lushly produced romantic yarn laid in Acapulco. Pedestrian story may be lifted to okay grosses via the Lana Turner name and strong exploitation.

Hollywood, Feb. 1.
Columbia Pictures release of Jerry Bresler production. Stars Lana Turner, Cliff Robertson, Hugh O'Brian; features Ruth Roman, Stefanie Powers, Virginia Grey, Ron Husmann. Directed by Alexander Singer. Screenplay, Marguerite Roberts; camera (PatheColor), Joseph Ruttenberg; music, David Raksin; editor, Alma Macrorie; asst. director, Richard Moder. Reviewed at Columbia Studios, Jan. 28, '65. Running time, **104 MINS.**
Kit Jordon .... Lana Turner
Pete Jordon .... Cliff Robertson
Hank Walker .... Hugh O'Brian
Margot Eliot .... Ruth Roman
Carol Lambert .... Stefanie Powers
Irene Talbot .... Virginia Grey
Chuck Austin .... Ron Husmann
Lieut. Riccardo Andrade Enrique Lucero
Don Julian .... Carlos Montalban
Manuel Perez .... Jamie Bravo
Maria .... Fannie Schiller
Ramos .... Rene Dupreyon

High life among American beach bums in Acapulco is lavishly dramatized in this Jerry Bresler production starring Lana Turner, Cliff Robertson and Hugh O'Brian. Effectively tintfilmed in the actual locale, story line carries little more than pedestrian interest but the Turner name and a sound promotional campaign playing up the romantic entanglements of plot very likely will lift feature to okay grosses in the mass market.

Miss Turner portrays a millionairess in the Marguerite Roberts script, surrounded by moochers—including her husband, Robertson—and desperately striving for unfound-happiness in her own particular brandy-swilling world. Narrative concerns the love affairs—the many faces of love—at the glamorous resort, giving opportunity for extravagant use of the exotic tropical background. Climax is lensed on a Mexican ranch which raises bulls for the Mexico City bullring, where femme star is gored but brought closer to her husband in a near-happiness windup.

Alexander Singer's direction gets the utmost in values from his story and cast, although none of latter is particularly sympathetic. Miss Turner has chance to wear some dazzling creations by Edith Head as she segues from her yacht to her beach cabana and luxurious home, the object of her husband's indifference and O'Brian's bold attention. O'Brian is an expert in the art of sharing his company for money and as a sideline indulges in friendly blackmail, in this case Ruth Roman, a wealthy divorcee.

Miss Turner lends conviction in a demanding part and Robertson is forceful as her husband who married her for her money but finds his life distasteful. O'Brian turns in a good job as a beach parasite who sells his wares to avid young touristas, Miss Powers inserts the proper note of freshness and Miss Roman hits just the right chord as the woman who knows she's being taken by O'Brian but plays it his way. Enrique Lucero gives a good account of himself as the Acapulco police officer investigating the suicide, as does Carlos Montalban as the ranch owner.

Technically, Joseph Ruttenberg's color photography is particularly outstanding and Alfred Sweeney's art direction catches the flavor of the story and setting. Alma Macrorie's fast editing is another potent assist, particularly her handling of the sequence in which Miss Turner is gored and Robertson and Jaime Bravo come to her aid to distract the bull's wild charges. David Raksin's music score also is effective. *Whit.*

Clarence, The Cross-Eyed Lion
(COLOR)

Young matinee crowd should go for story about African animals, which has enough comedy and suspense to hold interest.

Hollywood, Feb. 7.
Metro release of Ivan Tors production. Stars Marshall Thompson, Betsy Drake, Richard Haydn; features Cheryl Miller, Alan Caillou, Maurice Marsac. Directed by Andrew Marton. Screenplay, Alan Caillou, based on story by Art Arthur and Marshall Thompson; camera (Metrocolor), Lamar Boren; editor, Warren Adams; music, Al Mack. Reviewed at Picwood Theatre, Los Angeles, Feb. 6, 1965. Running time, **92 MINS.**
Dr. Marsh Tracy .... Marshall Thompson
Julie Harper .... Betsy Drake
Rupert Rowbotham ...... Richard Haydn
Paula .... Cheryl Miller
Carter .... Alan Caillou
Gregory .... Maurice Marsac

Ivan Tors' "Clarence, The Cross-Eyed Lion" is a natural for moppet trade, with some slapstick comedy, appealing animals and sufficient danger to provide suspense without fright. Parents will find the animals and superb color photography by Lamar Boren easy to take, but its doubtful many adults will buy tickets for themselves only.

Human performers generally take secondary roles to East African flora and fauna. Marshall Thompson is adequate as head of "Wameru Study Center for Animal Behavior," while Cheryl Miller is bright and natural as his teenage daughter with an affinity for beasts. Mild love interest develops between Thompson and Betsy Drake, anthropologist making study of gorilla life.

Central character is cross-eyed lion who has grown up gentle beast because faulty vision gives him no chance to develop hunting ability. This trait doesn't impress timid schoolmaster Richard Haydn, and some of most comic scenes result from Haydn's ludicrous fright.

All minor roles are filled effectively, but Maurice Marsac seems over-board as chief heavy. He is leader of band of mercenaries and rebels who plot to kidnap Miss Drake's gorillas and sell them at going price of $6,000 each.

But villains are foiled by native troops led by Alan Caillou, an extremely-British officer. Climax comes when Clarence traps Marsac in comic sequence reminiscent of a Three Stooges' chase.

Art directors George W. Davis and Edward Imazu and set decorators Henry Grace and Jack Mills re-creation of African setting had authentic touch, even though Metro release was filmed entirely at studio's animal center north of Los Angeles. Director Andrew Marton and editor Warren Adams share credit for smoothly-paced scenes. Al Mack's score is unobtrusive, and Shelly Manne plays some swinging jazz behind animated titles. *Hogg.*

Crack In The World
(COLOR)

Scientists nearly blow up the world when an experiment backfires. Okay for sci-fi trade.

Hollywood, Feb. 2.
Paramount release of Bernard Glasser-Lester A. Sansom production. Stars Dana Andrews, Janette Scott, Kieron Moore, Alexander Knox. Directed by Andrew Marton. Screenplay, Jon Manchip White, Julian Halevy, from story by White; camera (Technicolor), Manuel Berenguer; editor, Derek Parsons; music, John Douglas; asst. director, Jose-Maria Ochoa. Reviewed at Paramount Studios, Feb. 1, '65. Running time, **96 MINS.**
Dr. Stephen Sorenson .... Dana Andrews
Mrs. Maggie Sorensen.....Janette Scott
Ted Rampion .... Kieron Moore
Sir Charles Eggerston .Alexander Knox
Masefield .... Peter Damon
Markov .... Gary Lasdun
Steele .... Mike Steen
Simpson .... Todd Martin
Rand .... Jim Gillen

Outer space, thoroughly investigated during recent years through countless cinematic excursions, makes way for Project Inner Space in this latest pseudo-scientific effusion to hit the screen. "Crack in the World," distinguished principally by some startling special effects, imaginatively focuses on an ill-fated experiment to tap the unlimited energy residing within the earth's core which nearly blows up the world. Subject is adaptable to strong exploitation which should meet with acceptable reaction in its particular market.

Produced in Spain by Bernard Glasser and Lester A. Sansom for Philip Yordan's Security Pictures, the Paramount release carries a more legitimate premise than the regular science-fiction entry, strictly fictional in tone and context. Here is an entirely logical scientific operation, of drilling through the earth's crust to reach the molten mass called Magma, which brought to the surface under controlled conditions, could give the world all the energy it would ever want.

Slow in takeoff and inclined to over-clinical scientific exposition, action gradually hits its stride when the experiment backfires and results in giant earthquakes, tidal waves and general destruction in various parts of the world. Scientists conclude the only way to halt the great crack which is threatening the earth with extinction is to blow a hole ahead of its path with a nuclear bomb, but this only serves to divert the direction and double the pace. Windup sequences are confusing and means by which the destruction of the world is barely averted unclear.

The human story of the scientists involved is minimized somewhat to the catastrophic events resulting from their experiments, but there is one suspenseful sequence in which three of the men descend into a volcano to place the nuclear bomb and one falls to his death in the molten lava. Andrew Marton displays a lively understanding of his subject and his direction is vigorous.

Dana Andrews plays part of the scientist in charge of the operation, dying with fast cancer, and Kieron Moore his assistant who believes his superior's plan will end in the disaster which eventuates, both handling their roles okay. Janette Scott is Andrew's scientist-wife, actually in love with Moore, a rather thankless role which she sparks as much as possible, and Alexander Knox in brief appearance heads a commission which gives the go-signal for great experiment.

Eugene Lourie and Alex Weldon rate a big hand for special effects and Lourie's art direction also is unusual. Manuel Berenguer's color photography occasionally generates excitement, John Douglas' music score provides good backing to the action and Derek Parsons' editing is mostly on plus side. *Whit.*

Onibaba
(The Demon)
(JAPANESE)

Toho Co. Ltd. release of Hisao Itoya-Setsuo Noto-Tamotsu Minato production. Stars Nobuko Otowa, Jitsuko Yoshimura, Kei Sato. Directed by Kaneto Shindo. Original screenplay by Shindo; camera, Kiyomi Kuroda; music, Hikaru Hayashi. Tradeshown in N.Y., Feb. 4, '65. Running time, **103 MINS.**
The woman .... Nobuko Otowa
The young woman .... Jitsuko Yoshimura
Hachi .... Kei Sato
The warrior .... Jukichi Uno
Ushi, the merchant .... Taiji Tonomura

(English Subtitles)

This Japanese film may be the most nude, sexiest pic to be unveiled in New York so far. Raw fare is sometimes high adventure and exciting, at other times dull in its so-called symbolism. Too often, this turns out to be a potpourri of ravenous eating and blatant sex. Picture may give censors a field day. In big cities and drive-ins looks like strong meat.

Basic plot shows an elderly woman and her daughter-in-law, stranded without any means of support, during the civil wars of 16th Century Japan. They live among the reeds, many of them grown higher than their heads. When wounded, exhausted warriors wander in, women kill them. The victims are stripped of their weapons and clothing, which they sell in return for food. They live undisturbed until Kei Sato returns from the fighting with news that the older woman's son and husband of the younger woman is dead.

Sato immediately tries to lure the younger femme to his hut for nightly trysts. He succeeds, and for the next two reels (between the killings of wounded warriors) the director focuses attention on this affair. In case any sleepy member of the audience there is the symbolism of mating birds (with sound effects) as gal goes rushing through the reeds for her nightly seances. A few of the closeups covering these nightly trysts still remain in the film—and they are unlike American screen ways, to say the least. Both women are seen bare-breasted.

There is another shot in the farmer trader's hut showing nude woman (posterior view) which is only explained by earlier dialog passages in which the trader indicates he is not adverse to trading sex for food.

The older woman tries to halt the affair her daughter-in-law is having, finally uses a hideous mask to frighten her away from this funloving male.

Nobuko Otowa is superb as the older woman while Jitsuko Yoshimura contribs an excellent characterization as the daughter-in-law, especially in the "romantic" sequences. Sato is well cast as the former farmer youth who escapes from the fighting forces for more peaceful days back on the farm. Taiji Tonomura makes the tough-bargaining farmer merchant as odious as he is supposed to be.

Kaneto Shindo, who has turned out many successful Nipponese dramas, (particularly the highly acclaimed "The Island") directed with blunt strokes. He also did the original screenplay—hence he knew what he wanted. Lensing by Kiyomi Kuroda obviously needed a steady hand, with the result that few of the more intimate details are overlooked. Music accentuates the more horrendous sequences.

Wear.

Lausbubenges Chichten

(Tales of a Young Scamp)
(GERMAN-COLOR)

Berlin, Feb. 2.

Columbia-Bavaria release of Franz Seitz production. Stars Hansi Kraus, Kaethe Braun, Heidelinde Weis. Directed by Helmut Kaeutner. Screenplay, Kurt Heuser and Georg Laforet, based on a story by Ludwig Thoma; camera (Eastmancolor), Heinz Pehlke; music, Rolf Wilhelm; editor, Klaus Dudenhoefer. At Atelier am Zoo, West Berlin. Running time, **102 MINS.**

Ludwig	Hansi Kraus
Frau Thoma, his mother	Kaethe Braun
Aennchen, his sister	Renate Kasche
Filser	Michl Lang
Franzi	Friedrich von Thun
Aunt Frieda	Elisabeth Flickenschildt
Rafenauer	Beppo Brem
School director	E. F. Fuerbringer
Cora	Heidelinde Weis

The German market is overdue for a major juvenile picture. And there was some hope that there would be one in Helmut Kaeutner's filmization of Ludwig Thoma's "Tales of a Young Scamp," a smart piece of Bavarian literature which has remained (Thoma died in 1921) fresh and popular up to the present. But the filmic outcome is rather moderate. Not only that the film lacks the satirical wit of the original, it is also remarkably provincial. Even if young patrons won't be aware of the film's flaws, it's doubtful whether they will take a fancy to this modestly entertaining, old-fashioned offering. Commercial chances appear limited, even for Germany.

This relates 15 of the 18 episodes contained in the book. There are the lovable jokes and tricks with which Ludwig, the young scamp, annoys the adults. The little good-for-nothing makes toys explode, white mice run into an elderly couple's sleeping room, substitutes Aunt Frieda's darling (a parrot) with a black cat, lets a train go in the wrong direction, etc. The dialog and the lovable characters of the original are all there, but any other similiarity stops with them. What militates against the good overall impression is that the whole thing doesn't come off smoothly. Action is uneven, the flashbacks are confusing. And there are too many dull moments.

When producer Franz Seitz handed Kaeutner the directorial job, he thought of the director's cabaret background. A cabaret type of feature pic may not have been a bad idea. But what Kaeutner has brought to the screen is too slow.

On the plus side, there is a lineup of enjoyable characters. The most polished performance is turned in by vet actress Elisabeth Flickenschildt whose portrayal of a scurrilous old spinster aunt is a acting masterpiece. Also Kaethe Braun, as the young scamp's mother and Heidelinde Weis, as his pretty cousin, stand out. Moppet Hansi Kraus who enacts the title role is not as funny as one would have expected. Technically, this film is okay. The color photography displays romantic beauty. Although this is definitely a German yarn, one is inclined to feel that others might have made more of it.

Hans.

The High Bright Sun

(BRITISH-COLOR)

Conventional cloak-and-dagger stuff set against the Cypriot troubles of 1957; action is spasmodic, but acting is smooth and makes for sound wicket draw.

London, Feb. 2.

Rank release of a Betty E. Box-Ralph Thomas production. Stars Dirk Bogarde, George Chakaris, Susan Strasberg, Denholm Elliott, Gregoire Aslan; features Colin Campbell, Joseph Furst, Nigel Stock. Directed by Ralph Thomas. Screenplay, Ian Stuart Black; camera (Eastmancolor), Ernest Steward; music, Angelo Lavagnino; editor, Alfred Roome. Previewed at Leicester-square Theatre, London. Running time, **114 MINS.**

Major McGuire	Dirk Bogarde
Haghios	George Chakaris
Juno Kozani	Susan Strasberg
Baker	Denholm Elliott
Skyros	Gregoire Aslan
Emile	Colin Campbell
Dr. Andros	Joseph Furst
Mrs. Andros	Katharine Kath
Prinos	George Pastell
Alkis	Paul Stassino
Colonel Park	Nigel Stock

Betty E. Box and Ralph Thomas elected to make this film because they regarded it "as a suspenseful drama which could be played against any background." They certainly have played safe. Though set in Cyprus during the 1957 troubles, this sits firmly on a fence and makes virtually no attempt to analyze the troubles, the causes or the attitudes of the cardboard characters. However, the characters go through their paces smoothly and occasional bursts of action jerk placidity into a sound suspense drama that should do good business with audiences that don't want particularly to know why something is happening so long as it is.

Film comes out with the British looking at times rather silly and at others very dogged, the Cypriots clearly detesting the British occupation, the Turks shadowy almost to a point of non-existence and America, represented by Susan Strasberg, merely a bewildered intruder.

Miss Strasberg, a dewy-eyed young American archeaology student of Cypriot parentage, is visiting Cypriot friends who, unbeknown to her, are mixed up in the local terrorist racket. She gets to know more than is good for her and is torn between loyalty to the Cypriots and to the British, as represented by an Intelligence major (Dirk Bogarde) whose job it is to keep alive the unhelpful young dame for whom he has fallen. He tackles the job with unconventional methods and stiff upper lip.

There is some leisurely direction by Ralph Thomas which occasionally flares up to excitement with bomb-lobbing, gunplay and a final chase to the airport, but Thomas's helming must be tabbed as conscientious and efficent rather than inspiring. He is served with a more than useful cast. Miss Strasberg brings intelligence and charm to a sketchy role while Bogarde has no trouble with a part as the major which scarcely strains his thesping ability. George Chakaris, a hotheaded young terrorist, glooms through his part, and, surprisingly, for an actor of his skill, succeeds in making it both flat and dull. Compensation is provided by Denholm Elliott, who is becoming a notorious scene stealer. Elliott is a sardonic, seemingly drunken and shiftless buddy of Bogarde's who is very much on the ball. His introductory scene is a little gem but fortunately for the remainder of the cast, if not the picture, his part splutters out into fragmentary but always telling quick appearances. Nigel Stock provides some routine humor as a blimpish colonel. Gregoire Aslan, Joseph Furst, Katharine Kath, George Pastell and Paul Stassino have no difficulty in putting over the Cypriot patriots convincingly.

Ian Stuart Black's screenplay moves smoothly but with few surprises, though there is one choice joke of a running red herring which make a neat payoff gag, and Black's dialog has a fair quota of dry, throwaway wisecracks of which Bogarde and Elliott take full advantage. Mostly shot on location, with long shots in Cyprus and Greece (close action stuff is primary in Italy), the pic is colorful and helped by Alfred Roome's cutting and an atmospheric score by Angelo Lavagnino.

Rich.

The Greatest Story Ever Told

(ULTA PANAVISION 70—TECHNICOLOR-CINERAMA)

Lavish, well-produced telling of birth, ministry, death and resurrection of Jesus Christ. A big picture.

United Artists release. Produced, directed and coscripted (with James Lee Barrett) by George Stevens. Executive Producer, Frank I. Davis; associate producers, George Stevens Jr., Antonio Vellani. No stars. Max Von Sydow top-featured. Photography by William C. Mellor, Loyal Griggs. Sound, Franklin Milton, William Steinkamp, Charles Wallace. Film editors, Harold F. Kress, Argyle Nelson Jr., Frank O'Neill. Set design, David Hall. Art direction, Richard Day, William Creber. Costumes, Vittorio Nino Novarese, Marjorie Best. Second unit directors, Richard Talmadge, William Hale. Special visual effects, J. McMillan ohnson, clarence Slifer, A. Arnold Gillespie, Robert R. Hoag. Choral supervision, Ken Darby. Musical score composed and conducted by Alfred Newman. Previewed Feb. 8, 1965, at Warner Cinerama Theatre, N.Y. Running time, **225 MINS.**

Jesus	Max Von Sydow
Mary	Dorothy McGuire
Joseph	Robert Loggia
Herod The Great	Claude Rains
Herod Antipas	Jose Ferrer
Herodias	Marian Seldes
Aben	John Abbott
Captain of Lancers	Rodolfo Acosta
Chuza	Philip Coolidge
Herod's Commander	Michael Ansara
Philip	Dal Jenkins
Archelaus	Joe Perry
John the Baptist	Charlton Heston
The Dark Hermit	Donald Pleasence
Judas Iscariot	David McCallum
Matthew	Roddy McDowell
James the Younger	Michael Anderson Jr.
James the Elder	David Sheiner
Peter	Gary Raymond
Simon the Zealot	Robert Blake
Andrew	Burt Brinckerhoff
John	John Considine
Thaddaeus	Jamie Farr
Philip	David Hedison
Nathaniel	Peter Mann
Thomas	Tom Reese
Pontius Pilate	Telly Savalas
Claudia	Angela Lansbury
Pilate's Aide	Johnny Seven
Questor	Paul Stewart
General Varus	Harold J. Stone
Melchior	Cyril Delavanti
Bathazar	Mark Lenard
Caspar	Frank Silvera
Mary Magdalene	Joanna Dunham
Mary of Bethany	Janet Margolin
Martha of Bethany	Ina Balin
Lazarus	Michael Tolan
Veronica	Carroll Baker
Man at Tomb	Pat Boone
Uriah	Sal Mineo
Bar Armand	Van Heflin
Old Aram	Ed Wynn
Woman of No Name	Shelley Winters
Theophilius	Chet Stratton
Annas	Ron Whelan
Speaker of Capernaum	John Lupton
Scribe	Russell Johnson
Joseph of Arimathaea	Abraham Sofaer
Caiaphas	Martin Landau
Shemiah	Nehemiah Persoff
Nicodemus	Joseph Schildkraut
Sorak	Victor Buono
Emissary	Robert Busch
Alexander	John Crawford
Roman Captain	John Wayne
Simon of Cyrene	Sidney Poitier
Barabbas	Richard Conte
Tormentor	Frank De Kova
Dumah	Joseph Sirola

The prophets should speak with respect of this Biblical epic. It should attain global payoff with all deliberate slow speed, with particular expectations from Catholic countries. It is a big, powerful moving picture demonstrating vast cinematic resource. Minor reservations remain to be mentioned and there must be the worrying factor of the film's negative cost ($20,000,000) and the wearying factor (for some) of its four-hour length. But now that it is finally in reserved seat operation, "The Greatest Story Ever Told" is the word made manifest. Plainly United

Artists, the ones of great faith, will not recant on the hard-sell mission.

In such a spectacle there can be no story surprise or suspense in the ordinary sense. Only anticipation of the director's interpretation of individual scenes and prototypes. Producer-Director George Stevens has elected to stick to the straight, literal, orthodox, familiar facts of the Four Gospels. He has scorned plot gimmicks and scanted on characterization quirks. There are no neurotic kings, no chariot races, no tortures, no necrophilic foamings over a man's head served on a platter to a crazy, mixed-up, hot-country girl. There is a veil dance but it could be presented at a parish tea.

What Stevens puts on view, overall, is panoramic cinema, cannily created backgrounds, especially the stupendous buttes of Utah. He is infinitely skilled in staging street mobs or bringing horsemen into menacing silhouette against the horizon of parched terrain. The film is rich in production values of professional competence. Late David Hall's design, the art direction of Richard Day and William Creber are painstakingly detailed. So, too, as to the costumes of the era created by Vittorio Nino Novarese and Marjorie Best. All is photographed in Ultra Panavision 70 and Technicolor for the single lens Cinerama projection process. Co-equal on the cameras were Loyal Griggs, may his years be many, and the late William C. Mellor.

Stevens is not particularly original in his approach to the galaxy of talent, some 60 roles. Hollywood's recent years fad for cameo bits by featured players may suffer some discredit in the light of the triviality of footage and impact by such players as Carroll Baker, Pat Boone, Richard Conte, Ina Balin, Frank De Kova, Victor Buono, Marian Seldes, Paul Stewart. Angela Lansbury is a mere flash in the Panavision, literally a face glimpsed on the stairway beckoning Pontius Pilate (Telly Savalas) come hear her advice. She has no lines but seems to be saying, "Ponti, Sweets, don't get involved in this case!" Equally transitory is Shelley Winters, the Woman of No Name (but a couple of lines), who is cleansed of leprosy and whom Stevens didn't bother to establish. Sal Mineo's curing of crippled legs is more explicit, an okay cameo.

Roddy McDowell is recruited by Jesus to become one of the 12 Apostles but has almost nothing to do on camera thereafter except look thoughtful. John Wayne is ill-at-ease and a waste of name, many may feel, as the captain of the soldiers who escort the Redeemer to the cross. Van Heflin is luckier than others in that his bit (awe reaction) at the tomb of Lazarus leaves some actor identification with the beholder. Claude Rains is standout in the opening sequence as the dying ruler of Judea.

(All of the Apostles are pictured as hardly more than boys. Their pictorial immaturity may be historic but is disconcerting. Nor do they seem natives of a Jewish land.)

Quite properly Stevens has focussed on the birth, ministry, execution and resurrection of the Son of God. In the casting of Jesus there is occasion for compliment. The performance of the Swedish actor, Max Von Sydow, and his English diction, are ideal. Here indeed is a "blessing."

Though Stevens passes up nearly all chances to infuse flamboyance into the minor characters he has clearly pondered the nature of the Redeemer's personality in terms of camera drama. The key word for Jesus rightly is love. From the projection of compassion and kindness which the Swedish actor achieves with amazing artistry, and whatever help the director provided, presumably a total partnership, comes in the end as an undeniable Deposit of Faith, in the theological phrase.

There is a final moment on the cross just at the moment death intervenes which is a marvel of illusion, the very synthesis of the suffering Christ of 2,000 years of church art. It has got to profoundly move millions of people. And just in this potential multitude lies United Artists' hope of financial salvation.

The Jesus of this epic is, of course, gentle. But he is much more. He is also virile, a great cross-country walker, practically a mountain-climbing Saviour. The sheer precipice face of Utah rock up which he climbs might not unfairly be described as a miracle of athletic prowess. This sequence narrowly avoids seeming like scenery for scenery's sake.

Stevens and Von Sydow contrive many beguiling touches to exhibit the Redeemer's humanity. His courtesy is unfailing, and so his understanding. He is discouraged by human nature, yes, but never intolerant or fanatic. Von Sydow supports a great many long-held closeups in which the single element of acting is the exquisite utilization of his gaze. Seldom has a player had the talent (or the chance) to show so much. He is a tower of strength and sensitivity, both, and must be expected to win "Best Actor" in the Oscars a year hence.

One novelty in conception and casting centres on Donald Pleasence, an enigmatic symbol-figure curiously introduced by Stevens as "The Dark Hermit." He substitutes for the Devil who tempts Christ with a promise of human power and glory. On the whole this underplayed Tempter is more caption than content. However, he fuses into the mise en scene as do all the incidental figures. It is a compliment of no subtlety to acknowledge that while Stevens and his editors, Harold F. Kress, Argyle Nelson Jr. and Frank O'Neill, have fractured and fragmented many a small role, there are few visibly awkward bits. Some may not like the decision to have the one person who helps Christ bear the cross on the way to agony a Negro, played without dialog by Sidney Poitier. Against that, it may be argued that Stevens sought throughout to include Negro, Near East and Oriental types in the groupings. Christianity is, by emphasis, a universal religion.

Possibly the most unfortunate casting in the picture is that of Ed Wynn as Old Aram whose sight is restored by Jesus. Unfortunate because every time he speaks he is nobody but himself, Ed Wynn. Such casting was a lapse on Stevens' part, the Hollywood chichi sort of thing, against which the director is usually superior.

The delicacy of the Virgin Mary role had to be faced. Who may fairly pass on camera in this secular age as the Mother of God? Sufficient to remark that Dorothy McGuire is plausible. Her large, soft, womanly eyes and pensive expression are right. Few will quibble that, as the mother of the Holy Babe and the mother of the grown man of 33, she is unmarked by age. It was obviously a deliberate decision of the screenplay of James Lee Barrett and Stevens to withhold from the Virgin all speech. Risks were minimized and she was used essentially for necessary symbolism. A reviewer may only guess that the Marianists, always a potent bloc in the Catholic Church, should be satisfied with Miss McGuire.

Certain characters are probably obligatory, if somewhat stereotyped, namely John the Baptist, Herod Antipas and Judas Iscariot. They have 2,000 years of Passion Plays and sermon continuity. Stevens seems to have little to say about these men. He is content with pedestrian reference. The Baptist (Charlton Heston) is the only out-and-out fanatic in the picture but this takes the form of roaring demands that Herod "repent." Herod, in the remarkably curbed performance of Jose Ferrer, is no worse than a cynical administrative stooge for the Romans with hardly a hint of sexual hanky panky with the Inbal Dancers from Israel who are part of his provincial court. Judas Iscariot is, as usual, a question mark. How does a man who has followed the Master for three years prove so vile?

Stevens and his collaborator apparently foresaw that Judas stands in need, for modern psychology, of some explication. Not much is possible if the treatment is to maintain its franchise as a religious documentary based on Scripture. There are planted reaction shots as if on various occasions Judas is inwardly doubting or denying Jesus and there is ore scene to suggest his penury. The difficulty lies in Stevens' choice of actor. David McCallum has a wholesome, almost boyish, face. Perhaps the idea was that just this sort shaves basketball points. It is not particularly convincing to watch his doublecross, and it's downright confusing that he cares so little for the 30 pieces of silver, over whose counting Stevens is distinctly dilatory. Judas does not hang himself, as usually represented, but flings himself into the temple fire, rather Buddhist-like, many will think.

In the light of the Vatican Council's recent clearing of the Jews of the hoary accusation of deicide, this re-tell of Gospel tactfully sidesteps offense to Jesus' landsmen. The priests of the Temple are more fussy, time-serving and prideful than calcu-

lately evil though one of them, played by the late Joseph Schildkraut, chides them for politicking against a good man.

There is an abundance of symbolic scenes and groupings. The film opens and closes with a dolly-in upon the dome of a cathedral and a giant figure of Christ in mural. Inevitable, no doubt, is the crescendo of heavenly choirs at certain points, turning the picture into a liturgical service. In New York's Warner Cinerama Theatre at last week's preview the sound volume was ear-splitting on occasion and so distractive as to prevent a calm assessment of Alfred Newman's musical score which, without the assault upon the nervous system, is generally competent and attractive. Charles Wallace is credited for sound and the recording supervisors are Franklin Milton and William Steinkamp.

Special visual effects warrant mention, though it is easy to misstate such credits. The sense of antiquity and of a civilization hewn out of granite and field stone is well suggested. Jerusalem in the background, the palaces and courtyards in perspective is the presumed work of J. McMillan Johnson, Clarence Slifer, A. Arnold Gillespie, Robert R. Hoag. If the vision of the Jerusalem hints at a city as sprawling as Greater New York, that is a harmless eccentricity of the cinematic mind.

Full justice to such a production crew can hardly be recorded. Where draw the line of contribution of second unit directors Richard Talmadge and William Hale? One may only imagine the valiant labors of the set dressers, the hairdressers, the scriptcheckers, the production managers. In the hierarchy under Stevens there are the undefinable implications of exec producer (Frank I. Davis) and the associate producers (George Stevens Jr. and Antonio Vellani) and the "creative association" of Carl Sandburg. The script credits acknowledge Old and New Testaments, Fulton Oursler and Henry Denker as "sources."

In the end this is the timeless tale of the Saviour. It has been screened with marked artistry if conservative attitude. As an entertainment the appeal is preponderantly to the religiously bent. Heretofore Biblical spectacles have drawn from the masses not always available to ordinary film offerings. That is the presumed market for "The Greatest Story Ever Told." The sum of its merits is impressive. The residue of its defects is unimportant. The film looks like the money it cost, or at least most of it and though it may need some selling, there is a lot to sell. *Land.*

Mata-Hari
(FRENCH)

Paris, Feb. 9.
CCFC release of Filmel-Films Du Carrose-Simar production. Stars Jeanne Moreau; features Jean-Louis Trintignant, Frank Villard, Claude Rich, Marie Dubois, Georges Riguier. Directed by Jean-Louis Richard. Screenplay, Francois Truffaut, Richard; camera, Michel Kelber; editor, Kenout Peltier. At Paris, Paris. Running time, **95 MINS.**

Mata-Hari	Jeanne Moreau
Francois	Jean-Louis Trintignant
Pelletier	Frank Villard
Julien	Claude Rich

Fiancee	Marie Dubois
Ludovic	Georges Riguier

That familiar femme spy of World War I, Mata-Hari, rides again in this adventurous, good natured pic about her work, love and final demise before a firing squad one foggy morn. No outrageous romanticism or overdone suspense here, but mainly a look at a woman, both shrewd and vulnerable, hard and fragile. It's all carried off mainly because of knowing presence and work of actress Jeanne Moreau. Pic will have to be handled with care and well spotted for foreign market because of downbeat character of opus.

Why she is a spy for the Germans during the war is not explained. She just is, and does not seem to feel any remorse about it all even when she falls in love with a French army officer. She fakes Oriental dancing and likes to live well but tempers her excesses and concessions with gentleness and love.

Miss Moreau has a way of imbuing a scene with guile and freshness that still has the underlying feel of a knowing mood of lost hopes, chances and love. It perks up the pic which returns to those innocent pre-war days when things were direct, clear and told visually.

So meeting her German liaison she may be nice to a cat that is kicked by the man. So she is shown as basically good. Her spying is her need for money, she has a poor sponging father she is always providing with money and she has many servants. She can accept gifts from men and share her bed only to revolt when she finds a true emotion from another.

That seems to be the essence of this film. A look at a woman in her fragile complication, annoying paradoxes and final seductiveness. However, it just lacks the dash and poetic grasp to bring this off entirely. Too many times it appears flat and pedestrian if suddenly braced by an inventive touch, like her execution or her last day of love with a French lieutenant before he is killed.

Director Jean-Louis Richard does not cheat. He tells his tale clearly and can make the war episodes seem real and crowd scenes big and rousing though they are shot with a limited number of people. Supporting cast is excellent but it is the muted, spontaneous work of Miss Moreau that gives this a consistency not always present in its basic story.

Ex-New Wave filmmaker Francois Truffaut ("The 400 Blows") has contributed a generous script and dialog that always enhances rather than slows the imagery. All it lacks is the fillip of directorial observation that would have made it rewardingly dramatic as well as charming. *Mosk.*

Lord Jim
(BRITISH-COLOR)

Hefty production values in this Joseph Conrad drama and marquee names should spell sturdy boxoffice. But too much verbiage makes performance of Peter O'Toole a disappointment.

London, Feb. 17.
Columbia Pictures release of Columbia-Keep Films coproduction, produced, directed and written by Richard Brooks. Stars Peter O'Toole, James Mason, Curt Jurgens, Jack Hawkins, Eli Wallach, Paul Lukas, Akim Tamiroff, Dahlia Lavi; features Newton Blick, Noel Purcell, Marne Maitland, Jack MacGowaran, Christian Marquand, Icizo Itami, Tatsuo Sainto. Adapted from Joseph Conrad's novel; camera (Technicolor), Frederick A. Young; music, Bronislau Kaper; editor, Alan Osbiston. At Odeon, Leicester Square, London, Feb. 16 '65. Running Time: 154 MINS.

Lord Jim	Peter O'Toole
Gentleman Brown	James Mason
Cornelius	Curt Jurgens
Marlow	Jack Hawkins
The General	Eli Wallach
Stein	Paul Lukas
The Girl	Dahlia Lavi
Schomberg	Akim Tamiroff
Waris	Ichizo Itami
Du-Ramin	Tatsuo Saito
Brierly	Andrew Keir
Robinson	Jack MacGowran
Malay	Eric Young
Capt. Chester	Noel Purcell
Capt. of Patna	Walter Gotell
Moslem Leader	Rafik Anwar
Elder	Marne Maitland
Doctor	Newton Blick
Magistrate	A. J. Brown
French Officer	Christian Marquand

The marquee names and the hefty production values of "Lord Jim" should ensure sturdy wicket activity. Many may be disappointed with Richard Brooks' handling of the Joseph Conrad novel. The storyline is often confused, some of the more interesting characters emerge merely as shadowy sketches. Brooks, while capturing the spirit of adventure of the novel, only superficially catches the inner emotional and spiritual conflict of its hero. In this he is not overly helped by Peter O'Toole whose performance is self indulgent and lacking in real depth.

The film starts clumsily with a note of moralizing that is offputting. The scene is laid in the form of a commentary curiously unctuous from Jack Hawkins, who plays the skipper who commanded Lord Jim when he first went to sea. Mercifully, the commentary soon disappears.

The story, for those unfamiliar, concerns a young merchant seaman apparently endowed with all the qualities needed for a great career. In a moment of cowardice he deserts his ship during a storm and his life is dogged throughout by remorse and an urge to redeem himself. After many adventures he chooses to die when he could have saved his own life. His search for a second chance takes him to South Asia. There he becomes the conquering hero of natives oppressed by a fanatical war lord. It is there, though what Brooks offers is a feast for the eye, that the film parts company from Conrad, becoming the wildest, if lively melodrama. In lesser ways Brooks has failed to interpret Conrad but this was perhaps necessary if he was to bring to the cinema a visual sense of what Conrad wrote with masterly understatement.

There is nothing to cavil about in some of the spectacular scenes. The battle between the natives and war lords' armies, the storm at sea, the locale of the Oriental ports and island life are vigorously and atmospherically brought to life on the screen and clearly neither expense nor detail have been spared in a massive job of logistics.

Brooks has teetered between making it a fullblooded, no-holds-barred adventure yarn and the fascinating psychological study that Conrad wrote. O'Toole, though a fine, handsome figure of a man, goes through the film practically expressionless and the audience sees little of the character's introspection and soul searching. Nor does O'Toole age throughout his many adventures, so that all sense of the passage of time is lost. The star seems almost bored with his chore.

Of the rest of the cast the two who stand out, mainly because they are provided with the best opportunities, are Eli Wallach and Paul Lukas. Wallach gives an arresting show as the arrogant, ruthlessly and yet intelligent despot. Lukas, playing the trader who provides Lord Jim with his "second chance," is dignified and convincing. James Mason is dragged in as Gentleman Brown, the wily bowler-hatted buccaneer, and is most effective within the limits of the role. Curt Jurgens is a soft-bellied figure of a man as the treacherous conniver and Akim Tamiroff, Ichizo Itami, Tatsuo Saito, Jack MacGowran, Walter Gotell and Christian Marquand are among those who provide fitting chorus to O'Toole. Dahlia Lavi, referred to throughout as "The Girl," is an arresting, dark haired beauty and combines strength and feminine appeal admirably, but the romantic side of the film is virtually nil.

Shot in Technicolor, the camerawork by Frederick Young does full justice to the exotic backgrounds and the rest of the technical crew can take a bow, with the possible exception of Bronislau Kaper, whose florid score is stuffed with cliches.

The many plusses in "Lord Jim" will satisfy those to whom Conrad is unknown. Brooks' conception is one thing. His failure to jerk O'Toole into anything like the acting performance that his appearances in "Lawrence of Arabia" and "Becket" suggest is another matter. *Rich.*

Yoho
(FRENCH)
Paris, Feb. 23.
Warner Bros. release of CAPAC-Paul Claudon production. Stars Pierre Etaix; features Luce Klein, Philippe Dionnet, Claudine Auger. Directed by Pierre Etaix. Screenplay, Jean-Claude Carriere, Etaix; camera, Jean Boffety; editor Henri Lanoe. At Colisee, Paris. Running Time, 98 MINS.

Yoho	Pierre Etaix
Yoho, as a child	Philippe Dionnet
Isolina	Claudine Auger
Wife	Luce Klein

Pierre Etaix proved he had a personal comic filmic flair in his Oscar-winning short "Happy Anniversary," and his first feature pic, "The Suitor." He now cements it with his second full-length pic that should have a good international career in store if given careful selling and art exposure first before playoff attempts.

Only drawback is Etaix's penchant for carefully worked out gags that bring smiles and often laughs but not the big yocks. This makes the pic highly entertaining but needing harder sell in general situations, with film buffs and more knowing and selective audiences more certain.

Etaix also shows he has a poetic elan and can evoke mood wistfulness and good nature without ever being mawkish. He emerges as one of the leading film comic creators on the world scene.

In the meantime, this effort will do very well. It begins in 1925 with Etaix as a bored melancholy millionaire. The films of the time are brilliantly evoked as only sound effects and music are used with the jerky silent movements also well utilized.

Gags abound as his great mansion is shown plus the entertainments that try to cheer him up as well as his servants' peccadillos. Great doors creak, as do shoes, and all attempts can not remove his sadness over a girl who once left him.

A circus performing for him has her appear with a son. The stock market crash coincides with the sound film and his losing his money and going off to find his girl and son. Then it takes up with the son's restoration of the mansion and making a fortune only to go off also to the old circus life, and leaving behind all the modern fortune he has built up as a great clown.

The first half is actually brilliant as Etaix shows his surety of comic touch and inventiveness. It recreates the silent comedies with today's attitudes.

The second part, which pokes fun at tele, mundane types and rushing progress, is still sure but perhaps too good natured and not biting enough to equal the more successful initial segment.

Etaix also has excellent ideas for transition shots and depicting the passing of time and small fugitive emotions. As a boy his discovery of the mansion is done with persuasive, lyrical comedies. He handles his other actors well and is a consummate film creator.

There will be inevitable comparisons to such early film greats. But Etaix has his own developed comic talents that spring from situation, character and emotions, and are usually adroit and amusing.

Pic may be the French entry at the coming Cannes Film Fest. *Mosk.*

Pas Question Le Samedi
(Impossible on Saturday)
(FRENCH-ISRAELI)
Paris, Feb. 16.
Athos release of Athos Fims-Steiner Film production. Stars Robert Hirsch. Directed by Alex Joffe. Screenplay, Ferry and Joffe, from a story by S. Tevet, J. Steiner; camera, Jean Bourgoin; editor, Eric Plumet. At the Mercury, Paris. Running Time, 105 MINS.

Italian, American, Israeli, German, Scotsman, Frenchman	Robert Hirsch

Whimsical pic made in Israel by the French travels the familiar route of a man trying to redeem himself after death by watching, as an unseen character, whether his acts can be patched up on earth to earn him a berth in heaven. Humor is telegraphed and obvious, but this does have the saving grace of simplicity and a tour-de-force via the playing of seven roles by legit theatre actor Robert Hirsch.

Hirsch, with the Comedie-Francaise here, thus tries for the success that Alec Guinness and Peter Sellers have had before him in similar type pix in which they played multiple parts. He is somewhat too theatrical with makeup often too apparent. But he does have a way of getting to the core of a type of nationality. His impersonation of a German woman trying to pass herself off as a man is a gem.

It sometimes uses Jewish stereotype humor too patly. But on the whole, this manages to give it the essential folksy air that's never objectionable. Hirsch is shown as an 80-year-old conductor, with a fondness for women, who dies in Israel. His orthodox dead father, a tailor in life, comes down to get him but tells him he must redeem himself before he can ascend. The man, older than his father, finds he has had many illegitimate children and he can only get his passport to heaven if they come to Israel and marry.

The will states this, with money to go to the city of Jerusalem if not fulfilled. So Hirsch appears as an American son, an Italian, an Israeli, a German daughter, a Scottish son, a French son and as the old man. He watches invisibly with his father as the American tries to get the will fulfilled.

There are some comic moments as well as some longish segments. Its goodnatured, uncomplicated unwinding could make this a possible playoff item for the U.S. with the proper hypoing of the Hirsch bits an added handle. But it will need plenty of hardsell.

However, the modishness of Jewish humor could get it even more attention despite its heavy-handed ladling out of it. Alex Joffe has directed with lightness if not too much invention. The Israeli players lend authenticity for a good counterpoint to the fantasy of this unambitious but fairly amusing film.

Production is shaping up as a sleeper here. Right handling could possibly have it repeat abroad.
Mosk.

Dm-Killer
(GERMAN - AUSTRIAN)

Berlin, Feb. 16.

Nora release of Siener Stadthallen production. Stars Curd Jurgens, Walter Giller, Charles Regnier; features Daliah Lavi, Elga Andersen, Elisabeth Flickenschildt. Directed by Rolf Thiele. Screenplay, Peter Norden; camera, Wolf Wirth; music, Erwin Halletz. At the Marmorhaus, West Berlin. Running time, 110 MINS.

Kurt Lehnert	Curd Jurgens
Charly Bauer	Walter Giller
Ronald Bruck	Charles Regnier
Lolita	Daliah Lavi
Inge Moebius	Elga Andersen
Frau Bauer	Elisabeth Flickenschildt
District Attorney	Hubert von Meyerinck
Gerda Bruck	Erika Beer
American	Ivan Desny
Otto Krueger	Stanislav Ledinek
Priest	Balduin Baas
Schulz	Heinrich Trimbur

Helped by its plot and acting, this is truly an amusing and enjoyable German - language film.

The story is interesting enough to make this a worthwhile bet for foreign buyers. Domestically, it is good enough for satisfactory returns. Despite the films flaws, it may even appeal to the more demanding patrons. This has something which is rather rare in German-lingo productions, wit and originality.

Yarn centers around three lovable crooks just released from jail. They want to strike it rich and one of them whom they call "the professor" has an idea: The sale of Volkswagen to the U.S. Normally, a Stateside buyer has to wait 10 to 18 months to get such a German car. They manage to ship over large consignments of such cars in less than no time. And they manage to make a fortune but it would not be a comedy if they did not end up in jail again. There is some social-criticism mixed with satirical ingredients. It may be added that the plot is partly based on facts.

Rolf Thiele shows with this that he is still one of Germany's better film directors. There are many scenes which reveal directorial imagination, with the handling of the players particularly praiseworthy. True to his rep, he has inserted quite a bit of sex in this.

Unfortunately, some of this is needlessly exaggerated and some even borders on the tasteless. For example, this applies to some scenes in a brothel. Yet the fun plays the dominating factor.

It chiefly comes off on account of the three principal players each being truly a type of his own. Curd Jurgens is an elegant he-man who has his own way with women and particularly effective. Charles Regnier, "the professor," supplies a fine study of an intelligent crook while Walter Giller contributes an amusing study of a somewhat stupid knave. There is outstanding support all down the line. Wolf Wirth, one of Germany's finest cameramen, has contributed good, imaginative lensing. There are good technical credits in other departments. *Hans.*

Extraconjugale
(Extraconjugal)
(ITALIAN)

Rome, Feb. 16.

Cineriz release of a Dario Sabatello production for D. S. Prods. Features Renato Salvatori, Franca Rame, Gastone Moschin, Maria Perschy, Lando Buzzanca, Liana Orfei, Enzo LaTorre, Agata Flori, Lena von Martens. Previewed in Rome. Running time, 100 MINS.

LA ROCCIA (THE SHOWER)
Directed by Massimo Franciosa. With Moschin, Lena von Martens, Buzzanca, Orfei. Screenplay, Castellano and Pipolo; camera, Tonino delli Colli; music, Luis Enriquez Bacalov.

IL MONDO E' DEI RICCHI (WORLD BELONGS TO THE RICH)
Written and directed by Mino Guerrini. With LaTorre, Flori, Rame; camera, Enrico Menczer; music, A. F. Lavagnino.

LA MOGLIE SVEDESE (THE SWEDISH WIFE)
Directed by Guiliano Montaldo. With Salvatori, Maria Perschy. Screenplay, Massimo Franciosa, Luigi Magni, Guiliano Montaldo from idea by Castellano and Pipolo; camera, Alfio Contini; music, Piero Umiliani.

Episoder with okay sales points which will satisfy a market still unsated by the recent burst of segmented features. Exploitable and humorous, with plenty of easy-to-look-at femmes who will partly make up for a lack of marquee stature.

Though building slowly, the opening item, "La Doccia," is an imaginative and sometimes surrealistic tale of how a faithful husband happens into an extracurricular situation and begins to relish it. It's neatly acted by Gastone Moschin and Lena von Martens, a looker with a future. Lando Buzzanca overacts as an unwelcome brother-in-law while Liana Orfei plays the wife. Some cuts are needed at the start to help the pace.

"The World Belongs To the Rich" contains some good ideas, but develops them somewhat pretentiously and haphazardly. It's about a provincial milktoast who acquires strength of action when he thinks he's won millions in a football pool. It turns out that office pals played a trick on him, but reactions are ironically effective anyway and his moment of glory serves a purpose. Director Mino Guerrini introes some spoofs of cheap literature and stripteases (illustrated by a striking Agata Flori), but this segment is the weakest of the three.

Third fable, by Giuliano Montaldo, has Renato Salvatori bringing his new Swedish wife back to Rome and his Sicilian family. The shock effect on them and on the neighborhood of her nordic free-wheeling habits, and the stirring of long-forgotten jealous reactions on the part of the husband, make for risible sequences with an ironic twist at the finale. It's neatly packaged, well-scripted and rousingly acted and directed. Salvatori is fine as the man, Maria Perschy is comely and able as his import, with topnotch backing from a colorful supporting cast.

Production credits are uniformly slick, with various musical accompaniments (and a click title tune by Annamaria Izzo, "Come Tutti gli Altri") adding to the general values. *Hawk.*

I Tre Volti
(Three Faces of a Woman)
(ITALIAN-COLOR)

Rome, Feb. 17.

Dino DeLaurentiis production and release. Features Soraya, Richard Harris, Alberto Sordi, Esmeralda Ruspoli, Jose DeVillalonga, Goffredo Alessandrini, Renato Tagliani, Alberto Giubilo, Ivano Davoli. Directed by Michelangelo Antonioni, Mauro Bolognini, Franco Indovina. Camera (Technicolor) Carlo di Palma, Otello Martelli, music, Piero Piccioni; editors, Nino Baragli, Eraldo da Roma. At Supercinema, Rome. Running time, 120 MINS.

IL PROVINO (The Screen Test)
Preface and screenplay by Antonioni. Camera, Carlo di Palma; Editor, da Roma.

Princess Soraya	Soraya
Reporter	Ivano Davoli
Photographer	Giorgio Sartarelli
Designer	Piero Tosi
American producer	Ralph Serpe

GLI AMANTI CELEBRI (Famous Lovers)
Directed by Bolognini. Screenplay, Tullio, Pinelli, Clive Exton; camera, Martelli; editor, Baragli.

Linda	Soraya
Robert	Richar Harris
Hedda	Esmeralda Ruspoli
Rudolph	Jose de Villalonga

LATIN LOVER
Directed by Indovina. Screenplay, Indovina, Alberto Sordi, Rodolfo Sonego; camera, Martelli; editor Baragli.

Mrs. Melville	Soraya
Armando Tucci	Alberto Sordi
Agency manager	Goffredo Alessandrini
TV reporter	Renato Tagliani
TV reporter	Alberto Giubilo

Episoder ably confectioned to present onetime Empress Soraya to international audiences, pic can expect an interested following especially in areas where there's been an unflagging curiosity in the Princess. Italy, Germany, France and Britain are among these markets, but the slickness of the film and its other inlaid values give it an added potential in other areas as well. Name values of Richard Harris, Alberto Sordi, plus the Michelangelo Antonioni directorial credit on the initial seg, offer further assists.

Antonioni's start-off item, listed as a "preface," provides background to remainder of film as it details the sequence of true events leading up to Soraya's decision to embark on her screen career, with the accent on the night on which her secret screen test took place. Given an alternately realistic and surrealistic treatment by Antonioni, sequence has a weird fascination and a dose of suspense in its "inside" glimpse of studio goings-on.

Mauro Bolognini's ironic follow-up tale, about the chilling of a torrid and headline-making love affair between a married society girl and a writer on the skids, is fiction, though numerous semi-coincidences with real-life events can be read into it. Soraya appears more relaxed here as well as strikingly beautiful. No heavy acting burden is thrust upon her, but both alone and in her sparring with Richard Harris—fine as her lover—she performs ably and exudes an undeniable fascination.

Third segment winds pic on light note, sparked by an irresistible performance by Sordi, in his element as a fully licensed "Latin Lover" hired by a Rome travel agency to entertain a busy and dynamic female executive type played by Soraya—during a whirlwind biz visit to Rome.

He soon finds himself a superfluous and unappreciated item on her agenda, especially after she deserts him for another party during a visit to a nightclub, and the threatened loss of face among other Via Veneto gigolos is hard to take. Windup sees her saving the situation by faking an amorous airport embrace before a swarm of lenshounds. His reputation is safe. As in other bits, Soraya's role is perfectly constructed to project her qualities and beauty without overly taxing or stressing the dramatic angles. Sordi, as noted, is perfect in another well-served performance.

Physically, the film is lushly outfitted and the gloss of the Technicolor-Techniscope lens job is a further plus. Lush is also the word for Piero Piccioni's musical score. But since the principal attraction of this vehicle remains Soraya, it can be said in short that no better or more glorified screen test could have been constructed for her, that she passes with flying colors, and that pic should legitimately whet audience appetite for a more challenging follow-up film by this new screen personality.

Hawk.

The Sound of Music
(MUSICAL—TODD-AO—COLOR)

Superb screen adaptation of Rodgers & Hammerstein legit musical; boffo returns.

Hollywood, Feb. 27.

Twentieth-Fox release of Robert Wise production, directed by Wise. Stars Julie Andrews, Christopher Plummer; features Eleanor Parker, Richard Haydn, Peggy Wood; with Charmian Carr, Heather Menzies, Nicholas Hammond, Duane Chase, Angela Cartwright, Debbie Turner, Kym Karath, Anna Lee, Portia Nelson, Ben Wright, Daniel Truhitte, Norma Varden, Gil Stuart, Marni Nixon, Evadne Baker, Doris Lloyd. Screenplay, Ernest Lehman; from stage musical with music and lyrics by Richard Rodgers & Oscar Hammerstein 2d, book by Howard Lindsay & Russel Crouse; music, Rodgers; lyrics, Hammerstein, Rodgers; production design, Boris Leven; camera (DeLuxe Color), Ted McCord; editor, William Reynolds; asst. director, Ridgeway Callow; sound, Murray Spivack, Bernard Freericks. Reviewed at Carthay Circle Theatre, Feb. 26, '65. Running time (without intermission), **173 MINS.**

Maria	Julie Andrews
Capt. Von Trapp	Christopher Plummer
The Baroness	Eleanor Parker
Max Detweiler	Richard Haydn
Mother Abbess	Peggy Wood
Liesl	Charmian Carr
Louisa	Heather Menzies
Friedrich	Nicholas Hammond
Kurt	Duane Chase
Brigitta	Angela Cartwright
Marta	Debbie Turner
Gretl	Kym Karath
Sister Margaretta	Anna Lee
Sister Berthe	Portia Nelson
Herr Zeller	Ben Wright
Rolfe	Daniel Truhitte
Frau Schmidt	Norma Varden
Franz	Gil Stuart
Sister Sophia	Marni Nixon
Sister Bernice	Evadne Baker
Baroness Ebberfie'd	Doris Lloyd

The magic and charm of Rodgers — Hammerstein — Lindsay — Crouse 1959 stage hit are sharply blended in this filmic translation which emerges one of the top musicals to reach the screen. The Robert Wise production is a warmly-pulsating, captivating drama set to the most imaginative use of the lilting R-H tunes, magnificently mounted and with a brilliant cast headed by Julie Andrews and Christopher Plummer which must strike a respondent chord at the boxoffice. Slated for roadshowing, the Todd-AO film cloaked in the superb tints of DeLuxe Color bears the mark of assured lengthy runs and should be one of the season's most successful entries, particularly with Miss Andrews—fresh from her "Mary Poppins" triumph — to further spark attention.

Wise drew on the same team of creative talent associated with him on "West Side Story" to convert the stage property, with its natural physical limitations, to the more expansive possibilities of the camera. Ernest Lehman again wrote the screenplay after the Howard Lindsay—Buck Crouse stage version, a moving portraiture of persons and events; Saul Chaplin served in the exacting post of associate producer; and Boris Leven used all his artistry as production designer on sets strikingly beautiful.

For the story of the Von Trapp family singers, of the events leading up to their becoming a top concert attraction just prior to World War II and their fleeing Nazi Austria, Wise went to the actual locale, Salzburg, and spent 11 weeks limning his action amidst the pageantry of the Bavarian Alps. Ted McCord catches the beauty and fascination of the terrain with his facile cameras, combining the splendor of towering mountains and quiet lakes with the Old World grace of the historic City of Music, a stunning complement to interiors shot in Hollywood. Against such background the tale of the postulant at Nonnberg Abbey in Salzburg who becomes governess to widower Captain Von Trapp and his seven children, who brings music into a household that had, until then, been run on a strict naval office regimen, with no frivolity permitted, takes on fresh meaning.

Richard Rodgers composed two new songs for the picture, for which he also wrote the lyrics, as he did with added numbers to the remake of "State Fair." Pair, "I Have Confidence in Me," sung by Miss Andrews, and "Something Good," an Andrews-Plummer duet, replace three songs from the original stage show which didn't blend well into changes made by Lehman in the libretto. While neither is as catchy, perhaps, as certain of the other songs, both are made into interesting numbers.

Of particular interest is the sequence simulating part of the famous Salzburg Festival and actually shot in the spectacular Felsenreitschule, or Rocky Riding School. The stage of the vast amphitheatre is backgrounded by scores of arched tunnels carved out of the rocky mountain that surrounds the city and it forms an impressive backdrop for the climactic scenes of the film, which show the Von Trapp family making their escape after an appearance onstage while storm troopers are waiting for them in the audience.

Miss Andrews endows her role of the governess who aspires to be a nun but instead falls in love with Navy Captain Von Trapp and marries him, with fine feeling and a sense of balance which assures continued star stature.

Plummer also is particularly forceful as Von Trapp, former Austrian Navy officer who rather than be drafted into service under Hitler prefers to leave his homeland. He scores with several song numbers, outstanding here "Edelweiss," and is bound to be cast importantly in future films.

Playing the part of the baroness, whom the captain nearly married, Eleanor Parker acquits herself with style. Peggy Wood is especially outstanding as the Mother Abbess, sympathetic to the young postulant who cannot seem to conform to the abbey's disciplined regulations. One of the film's top moments is her singing "Climb Every Mountain," to encourage the girl after she returns from the Von Trapp estate. Richard Haydn as Max, the impresario who launches the Von Trapp family on their singing career, and in a character foreign to past roles also registers effectively.

The seven children are ably portrayed, topped by Charmian Carr as the eldest, who displays a nice voice with her singing of "Going On 17" in a folksy number with Daniel Truhitte. Nicholas Hammond and Duane Chase play the two boys, and Heather Menzies, Angela Cartwright, Debbie Turner and Kym Karath the younger girls.

Marni Nixon, whose voice was used for Audrey Hepburn's in "My Fair Lady," Natalie Wood's in 'West Side Story" and Deborah Kerr's in "King And I," makes a brief appearance here, her first film role, as Sister Sophia. She sings with Miss Wood and four other nuns in the number, "Maria." Ben Wright lends menace as a Nazi leader, Daniel Truhitte plays young Rolfe, who turns Nazi, and Anna Lee is among the sisters.

Various song numbers have been without exception expertly staged. "My Favorite Things," sung by Miss Andrews and the children, is perhaps the most warmly presented, while "Do-Re-Mi," showing femme and the moppets picnic-bound through the streets of Salzburg, the most spritely. Miss Andrews' opening title song atop mountain marks an effective start of the picture which is prologued by aerial views through the mountains, and "Lonely Goathered," a puppet number backed by hers and children's voices, provides a light note. Moppets' "So Long, Farewell" is charming, and various reprises throughout the film lend additional interest.

Every technical credit is topflight and impressive. William Reynolds' editing is bright, never permitting pause, and costumes designed by Dorothy Jeakins catch the flavor needed. Set decorations by Walter Scitt and Ruby Levitt are in keeping with the high excellence of the picture itself, choreography by Marc Breaux and Dee Dee Wood lends color and sound by Murray Spivack and Bernard Freericks a decided asset. Special photographic effects by L. B. Abbot and Emil Kosa, Jr., are a further plus. Irwin Kostal's arranging-conducting of the beautiful score is one of most potent assets.

Whit.

Escape By Night
(BRITISH)

Routine prison-break drama suitable for second billing thanks to some better than routine performances.

Allied Artists presentation of Maurice J. Wilson production. Directed by Montgomery Tully. Features Terence Longdon, Jennifer Jayne, Harry Fowler. Screenplay by Wilson and Tully, based on Rupert Croft-Cooke's novel, "Clash By Night"; camera, Geoffrey Faithful, Alan McKabe; editor, Maurice Rootes; music, John Veale. Reviewed at RKO Palace, N.Y., Feb. 25, '65. Running Time: **75 MINS.**

Martin Lord	Terence Longdon
Nita Lord	Jennifer Jayne
Doug Roberts	Harry Fowler
Victor Lush	Peter Sallis
Ronald Grey-Simmons	Alan Wheatley
Mrs. Grey-Simmons	Vanda Godsell
Ernie Peel	Arthur Lovegrove
Mrs. Peel	Hilda Fenemore
Sydney Selwyn	Mark Dignam
Inspector Croft	John Arnatt
Danny Watts	Richard Carpenter
George Brett	Stanley Meadows
Mawsley	Robert Brown
Bart Rennison	Tom Bowman
The Intruder	Ray Amsten

British import being used by Allied Artists as second-bill material is getting better than average N.Y. exposure due to current showing as supporting fare with "None But The Brave." Although too weak to stand on its own, the oft-told tale of human crosstypes found in an assortment of escaped convicts comes off fairly well thanks to several good performances.

Tight budget has meant tight production and it shows. Much of action takes place at night or in dimly-lit interiors to save lighting. Big chunk of financing was evidently spent in climactic barn burning where the convicts are taken after mobsters hijack a bus taking them from one jail to another. Outside cohorts of gangleader Tom Bowman, who pulled job to release him, pour paraffin over barn's thatched roof and tell police guards and rest of convicts to remain inside until following day or barn will be set afire. Picture then concentrates on reactions of group left behind to possibility of escape, with some flashbacks.

Director Montgomery Tully, unable to provide much room for his cast to swing, has chosen to stress characterizations rather than action. This, as expected, brings in such extremes as psychotic murderer Peter Sallis (currently playing Dr. Watson in "Baker Street" on B'way) and lay preacher Mark Dignam (in trouble because he likes boys). These types are kept in the background fortunately, until Sallis sets the barn afire.

Most impressive portrayals are top-billed Terence Longdon, jailed for killing an intruder who tried to rape his wife; Doug Roberts, crook reformed by Longdon and Alan Wheatley, an ex-Army officer jailed for fraud. Technical credits are only fair except barn-burning which is very ably presented and provides most of film's action.
Robe.

Ballad In Blue
(BRITISH)

Banal, hearts-and-flowers yarn about blind child. Presence of Ray Charles may boost the wicket take; otherwise this a chancey operation.

London, Feb. 23.
Warner-Pathe release of an Alsa Films (Herman Blaser) production. Stars Ray Charles, Mary Peach, Tom Bell, Dawn Addams; features Piers Bishop, Joe Adams, Betty McDowell. Directed by Paul Henreid. Screenplay, Burton Wohl, based on original story by Henreid and Wohl; camera, Bob Hike; editor, Ray Poulton; music, Stanley Black. Previewed at Rialto Theatre, London. Running time 88 MINS.
Himse'f .... Ray Charles
Steve Collins .... Tom Bell
Peggy Harrison .... Mary Peach
Gina Graham .... Dawn Addams
David .... Piers Bishop
Mrs. Babbidge .... Betty McDowell
Margaret .... Lucy Appleby
Fred .... Joe Adams
Antonia .... Monika Henreid
Antonia's Protector .... Brendan Agnew
Headmaster .... Vernon Hayden
Dr. Leger .... Leo McCabe
Themselves ...... Ray Charles orchestra
and The Raelets

"Ballad In Blue" is one of those worthy, sincere efforts which becomes a sloppy, banal bore through flattish writing and direction. Ray Charles' aficionados may welcome the chance of hearing and watching the blind entertainer, but there is little else to stir much interest at the boxoffice. Since Paul Henreid directed the pic and is partly responsible for the original story, he must take much of the blame for its lack of vigor and interest. The story is predictable and at times embarrassingly naive.

Charles plays himself on a European tour. He befriends a small blind boy and his widowed mother, a young ballet dancer who is coddling her handicapped child. Charles, the wife's young lover (Tom Bell) and Dawn Addams, one of Bell's previous flames, all try to show the young mother (Mary Peach) that she is sapping the lad's independence. Eventually they persuade her to let her son have an eye operation. At fadeout it looks as if the kid will regain his sight and that Miss Peach and Bell will be hearing the altar call.

This frail storyline is ploddingly directed by Henreid. Only Miss Addams brings much animation to her role. Miss Peach and Bell are adequate and the small boy (Piers Bishop) and his little friend (Lucy Appleby) are played in a matter of fact way by two moppets who at least avoid cuteness. In fact, the boy's philosophical approach to his affliction is so adult that it is unconvincing. There is a nice, sharp bit by Monika Henreid, director Henreid's daughter, at a cocktail party which stands out among the general levelness of the other thesping.

As an actor, Charles is clearly most uncomfortable and stilted. But he does some pleasant work at the piano, backed by his orchestra and the Raelets. Joe Adams as his manager, and Betty McDowell, as an understanding neighbor, provide smooth support. Filmed in Dublin (this was the pic which reopened the Ardmore Studios at Bray) and on location in London and Paris, the settings are okay, as are sound and camerawork. But without more convincing star performances plus sharper writing and helming, the limpness of the film is apparent throughout.
Rich.

Le Ciel Sur La Tete
(Heaven On One's Head)
(FRENCH-COLOR)
Paris, Feb. 23.

Gaumont release of Gaumont-Galatea production. With Andre Smogghe, Jacques Monod, Marcel Bozzufi, Yves Brainville, Guy, Trejan. Directed by Yves Ciampi. Screenplay, Alain Satou, Jean Chapot, Ciampi; camera (Eastmancolor), Edmond Sechan; aerial views by Guy Tabary; editor, Georges Alepee. At Ambassade-Gaumont, Paris. Running time, 107 MINS.
Gaillac .... Andre Smogghe
Commandant .... Jacques Monod
Captain .... Marcel Bozzufi
Commander .... Yves Brainville
Minister .... Guy Trejan

President De Gaulle's feeling for national grandeur seems to be the basis for this pic. It uses the French aircraft carrier Clemenceau to spin a weak sci-fi affair which is really a slightly fictionalized documentary on the running of this mighty ship. Mixing nonactors and pros is unwieldy and this shapes a non-pro film.

This appears limited for export because of its lack of characterization, flaccid story values and repetitious exploring of the carrier. There is some nice stuff on jet landings and takeoffs and an A-Bomb drill.

But here the airmen are limned with stereotype strokes, to wit, the knowing leader, the fighter sans feelings, the more humane one, the more free-wheeling type, etc. Story is about a flying saucer that appears around the ship and the

suspicions of it being either a Russo or American satellite.

Stock and recreated footage show anxious governments, a state of alert and the Russians destroying something let off by the saucer. Color is good as are the air shots. This can be chalked up as a fairly neatly-made documentary about an aircraft carrier in crisis even if the actual would-be fictional sides are weak and obvious.
Mosk.

A Swingin' Summer
(WIDESCREEN—COLOR)

Colorful and tuneful programmer with several promising young thesps amid Lake Arrowhead settings. Excellent prospects for top-slotting in teenage and young adult situations.

Hollywood, Feb. 26.
United Screen Arts release of Reno Carell-National Talent Consultants Production, produced by Carell; exec producers, Ken Raphael, Larry Goldblatt. No stars. Features entire cast Directed by Robert Sparr. Screenplay, Leigh Chapman, from original story by Carell; camera (Techniscope and Technicolor), Ray Fernstrom; editors, James T. Heckert, William E. Lee; music, Harry Betts; asst. director, Rusty Meek. Reviewed at Lytton Center of Visual Arts, L.A., Feb. 24, '65. Running time, 81 MINS.
Mickey .... James Stacy
Rick .... William A Wellman Jr.
Cindy .... Quinn O'Hara
Turk .... Martin West
Shirley .... Mary Mitchell
Tony .... Robert Blair
Jeri .... Raquel Welch
Mr. Johnson .... Allan Jones
Sandra .... Lili Kardell
The Gals .... Diane Bond, Diane Swanson, Irene Sale, Kathy Francis, Laurie Williams
Themselves Gary Lewis & The Playboys, The Righteous Bros., The Rip Chords, Donnie Brooks
Hoods .... Reno Carell, Buck Holland, Glen Stensil

A breezy bouncing bunch of boys, babes, bosoms, buttocks and bodies bob about in this bucolic beach-bash broth. There is action, some top wax names, and lush Lake Arrowhead settings. Reno Carell-National Talent Consultants production qualifies as a solid entry in the youth market. The story never intrudes.

Leigh Chapman's yarn spotlights two guys and a gal who operate an Arrowhead teen terpery, and the completely-solvable problems in romance and business which they encounter. Director Robert Sparr set a fast pace, aided by a talented group of thesps, notably top-featured James Stacy (all names are below the title), William A. Wellman Jr. and Quinn O'Hara.

Latter two are the love interest, Wellman playing the sober youth who wants to make good on his own, with Miss O'Hara his everlovin' gal. Wellman is somewhat wooden and mechanical, but has good potential. Miss O'Hara is a knockout who can go places.

Stacy breezes through role of pair's light-hearted biz partner, but shows terrif potential in comedy or dramatic roles from brief flashes of talent permitted by script. Out of such pix comes future names, and Stacy is worth the big push.

Martin West scores as the smiling louse who complicates romance, and bubble-gum-chewing Mary Mitchell registers solidly in comic support. Robert Blair turns good-guy after waterski "chicken" race with Stacy, an inventive updating of the old hot-rodder bit no longer "in." but in earlier scenes Blair's baddie is a little weak.

The egghead chick who becomes a swinger is socked over by Raquel Welch, and it's hard to look away when she's in view. Draped about in all scenes are dozens of beauties, a modern equivalent of the Goldwyn Girls, who enhance the Arrowhead scene, itself an eyecatcher throughout. Singer Allan Jones and Lili Kardell appear briefly in cameos.

Alternating with bits of story development are Gary Lewis & The Playboys, The Righteous Bros., The Rip Chords, and Donnie Brooks, all current wax faves who provide seven well-staged song and dance numbers which set toes to tapping. Mike Blodgett's choreography rates a well-done. Dramatic climax (the chase) is also imaginative, using speedboats instead of cars. Jody Miller warbles okay under titles.

Ray Fernstrom's Techniscope and Technicolor camera fluidity is outstanding, while editors James T. Heckert and William E. Lee have handled their Moviolas excellently (although a few awkward transitions might be trimmed from pic's tight 81 minutes). Harry Betts' music is sparse but helps action. Goldwyn Studio sound department maintains its excellence here, and other technical credits are firstrate. Exec producers Ken Raphael and Larry Goldblatt and producer Reno Carell can all take a bow, which latter does anyway in a hoodlum bit.
Murf.

Young Cassidy
(COLOR)

Interesting characterization by Rod Taylor of Irish playwright Sean O'Casey highlights episodic biopic; indications spotty.

Hollywood, Feb. 11.
Metro release of "John Ford film," produced by Robert D. Graff, Robert Emmett Ginna. Stars Rod Taylor; features Maggie Smith, Julie Christie, Edith Evans, Michael Redgrave, Flora Robson. Directed by Jack Cardiff, Ford. Screenplay, John Whiting, based on "Mirror in My House," autobiog by Sean O'Casey; camera (Metrocolor), Ted Scaife; music, Sean O'Riada; editor, Anne V. Coates; asst. director, John Questad. Reviewed at Warner Beverly Theatre, Feb. 10, '65. Running Time, 107 MINS.
John Cassidy .... Rod Taylor
Daisy Battles .... Julie Christie
Lady Gregory .... Edith Evans
W. B. Yeats .... Michael Redgrave
Mrs. Cassidy .... Flora Robson
Nora .... Maggie Smith
Archie .... Jack MacGowran
Bassie Ballynoy .... Pauline Delany
Mick Mullen .... Philip O'Flynn
Tom .... T. P. McKenna
Ella .... Sian Phillips

"Young Cassidy," biopic of Irish playwright Sean O'Casey in his sprouting years based on late author's autobiography, "Mirror in My House," is notable principally for the top-rating performance of Rod Taylor in title role. Story of a rebel who rises to literary greatness, like the majority of screen bio narratives, is episodic; in attempting to cover the many facets of career, film consequently lacks the cohesion necessary for a full dramatic enactment of a historic personality. Reception is foreseen as spotty, dependent upon whatever draw Taylor possesses and interest generated in promotion.

Originally started under John Ford's direction but taken over in mid-stream by Jack Cardiff when illness forced Ford to withdraw, pic opens in 1911 Dublin during the troubled times of opposition to the British. It is a period when Cassidy—name given himself by O'Casey in his third-person writing —was feeling the stirrings of a talent which was to elevate him ultimately to the position of one of Ireland's great playwrights. First half of film scans Cassidy's participation in the events of the times, loosely treated, although there are a few realistically-effective, bloody revolutionary sequences; the second half, and this is when the biographical aspects come alive, concerns the man.

Ford's handiwork in prepping the John Whiting screenplay seems discernible particularly in the rebellion scenes and in building the character of Cassidy. Film throughout gets rugged direction.

Taylor delivers a fine, strongly-etched characterization, believable both in his romantic scenes and the writer who comes up the hard way. Splendid support is afforded particularly by Maggie Smith, as his one love but who leaves him so he can progress better without her; by Flora Robson, as his understanding mother, Edith Evans as Lady Gregory, who played a potent force in helping him to the top. Julie Christie also scores colorfully as a tart with whom Cassidy has a torrid affair; Philip O'Flynn as his close friend; Michael Redgrave as the poet Yeats; Jack MacGowran, the brother; Sian Phillips, the sister.

Photographically the picture catches much of the poverty of Dublin and also limns the Abbey Theatre through Ted Scaife's deft focusing. Producer chores were in the hands of Robert D. Graff and Robert Emmett Ginna, who arranged good technical treatment right down the line. *Whit.*

Le Bonheur
(Happiness)
(FRENCH-COLOR)
Paris, March 2.

Columbia Films release of Parc Film-Mag Bodard production. With Jean-Claude Drouot, Claire Drouot, Sandrine Drouot, Olivier Drouot, Marie-France Boyer. Written and directed by Agnes Varda. Camera (Eastmancolor), Claude Beausoleil; editor, Janine Verneau. At Studio Publicis, Paris. Running time, 84 MINS.

Husband .... Jean-Claude Drouot
Wife .... Claire Drouot
Emilie .... Marie-France Boyer

Adultery seems to be a favorite theme with ex-New Wavers here. After Francois Truffaut's tragic and austere look with "The Soft Skin," and Jean-Luc Godard's insolent appraisal in "A Married Woman," femme director Agnes Varda takes a more humane and original attitude towards it.

But the theme here is also family life in a fresh tale of a worker and his family in everyday life. The drama comes slowly and

without undue plotting, or over-emphasis.

The father is a good looking, faithful carpenter and she is a completely dedicated wife, her whole life being her husband and two pretty children. She also does dressmaking at home to bolster the income.

He meets a girl in a post office, and love blossoms quickly. He is soon her lover and yet finds he also needs his wife and family. One day he tries to explain this to his wife who has noticed his happier outlook. She tries to accept it but on a picnic, she slips off and drowns herself.

After his heartbreak, he can still take up his life with the other girl who he soon marries and who then takes over the children. But there is no real amorality here, if it may seem so, in recounting this fragile but physically, lovely film.

Film does not stump for polygamy but tries to show a case where love blossoms for two people.

But the pic leads to tragedy in this case and the underlining aspect of life going on is never cruel or cynical. That is the quality of this offbeat pic. It's stunningly filmed love scenes and nudity are always in proper perspective and never leering.

All this may encounter censor troubles and it is naturally strictly an arty house bet. But there is a tendency on writer-director Varda's part to play this on more an intellectual than emotional level. This keeps it from having any moving impact and more a slice of life than a probing drama.

Jean-Claude Drouot is effectively charming as the father. Same goes for his wife, played by his real life wife, Claire. Marie-France Boyer is okay as the undemanding mistress.

Here is a film that may be construed differently by many and could be a controversial subjection, with censorship problems likely. But it may also arouse pros and cons for specialized arty playoff. It will probably rep France at the coming Cannes Film Fest. *Mosk.*

Die Abenteuer des Werner Holt
(Adventures of Werner Holt)
(EAST GERMAN)
Berlin, March 2.

Progress release of DEFA production. With Klaus-Peter Thiele, Manfred Karge, Arno Wyzniewski. Directed by Joachim Kunert. Screenplay, Claus Kuechenmeister and Joachim Kunert; camera, Rolf Sohre; music, Gerhard Wohlgemuth; editor, Christa Stritt. Previewed at Moewe, East Berlin. Running time, 165 MINS.
Werner Holt .... Klaus-Peter Thiele
Gilbert Wolzow .... Manfred Karge
Sepp Gomulka .... Arno Wyzniewski
Christian Vetter ...... Guenter Junghans
Peter Wiese .... Peter Reusse
Marie Krueger .... Dietlinde Greiff
Uta Barnim .... Angelica Domroese
Professor Holt ...... Wolfgang Langhoff
Gertie Ziesche .... Maria Alexander
Guendel Thiess ...... Monika Woytowicz
General Wolzow .... Wolf Kaiser

This one looms as one of the most ambitious productions turned out by the East German DEFA in quite some time. Film, which was two years in the making, centers around young German soldiers during the final phase of the last World War. It has considerable merit as to acting, direction and atmosphere. Pic also benefits from

technical brilliancy. Its long running time and absence of any star names make it a problematical export item. Yet it looks like a good bet for some special situations. At any rate, "Werner Holt" is powerful and interesting enough to classify it as a prestige item for DEFA, sole producing outfit in the other part of Germany.

Adapted from an East German bestseller (of same title) by Dieter Noll, film opens in spring in 1945. The Red Army is already deep in the heart of Germany and the war is hopelessly lost for the Germans. But there are still quite a few German soldiers who, faithful to their beloved "Fuehrer," continue the merciless fight. Central figures are two young Nazi soldiers who have been close friends for many years. One is an intellectual fanatic who wants to defend Hitler Germany to the last drop of his blood. The other one is the sensitive type. Although he, too, is addicted to the Nazi regime, he keeps brooding over justice and the meaning of this war and gradually realizes its senselessness. There are countless flashbacks which show how the two spent their school days together and how they became friends. Pic tells how these two young men gradually separate. Werner Holt does not want to die for Hitler. He turns against his former friend and becomes a deserter. Ironical twist for the fanatic is that he is hung by SS men who think him a deserter. The impressive fadeout shows how sensitive lad kills the SS unit by his machine gun from a cellar window.

Picture is overloaded with characters and situations which occasionally tend to confuse. Adding to the confusion are the many flashbacks but, nevertheless, they hold the viewer's interest. Atmosphere of the wartime era which has documentary sharpness throughout has been excellently caught by the director. The genuine atmosphere is indeed one of the major assets of the production.

Another asset is the acting. This particularly applies to the two young male stars. Klaus-Peter Thiele, who portrays the title role, the more sensitive lad, looks like a bet for any Western nation. Manfred Karge, the young intellectual fanatic, turns in a highly competent performance, too. The large lineup of competent players includes Wolfgang Langhoff, as Holt's divorced father, who gave up his highly paid job in the chemical industry because he didn't want to serve the Hitler regime, and Hans-Joachim Hanisch, who contributes a fine study of a typical German master-sergeant. Pic's strong anti-war message and anti-Nazi attitude is evident all through.

Joachim Kunert has done a strong directorial job. His handling of the mostly young and unknown players is excellent. There are a number of sentimental cliche scenes but those are actually only minor drawbacks. The fight sequences often are spectacular.

Technically, the film is firstrate. It's a costly production. But since the film industry is State-owned in East Germany, they have no financial worries. *Hans.*

Dead Birds
(Color)

Excellent documentary in the making of which Michael Rockefeller lost his life.

Directed and edited by Robert Gardner. Written by Peter Mathieson; camera, Eliot Elisofon; sound, Michael Rockefeller; editing, Jestrup Lincoln; ethnography, Karl Heider; titles, Peter and Joyce Chopro. At The Movie, San Francisco, Jan. 21, 1965. Running time, 85 MINS.

Death and mystery pervade "Dead Birds," an exquisite documentary financed by the Peabody Museum at Harvard and The Netherlands government. It was on the 1961 expedition to study tribal life in New Guinea that sound technician Michael Rockefeller mysteriously disappeared, and presumably died. While this tragic fact draws public attention to the film, once seen it stands on its own as an outstanding example of the possibilities of factual filmmaking.

Unlike "The Sky Above, the Mud Below," which detailed the perils of a New Guinea expedition, no white man intrudes in "Dead Birds," which concentrates on the daily life of a personable tribesman and his engaging family.

They are surrounded by, and ever aware of, death. There are almost weekly wars with a neighboring tribe, futile, perpetual conflicts necessary to dispel the bad luck which befalls a tribe with an unavenged death. And between the skirmishes, there is the daily preoccupation as the warriors climb watchtowers to guard against enemy invasion.

When a death occurs, even a great feast is instantly forgotten as the whole community goes into mourning and prepares the elaborate ritual funeral in which a chair, the tribe's only formal furniture, raises the spirit above the earth towards the heavens.

Ritual, mystery, magic abound. Girls' fingers are cut off in mourning. Warriors are forever weaving cloth strips and decorating them with shells as tokens for the dead. Blades of grass are magic when formed into bows and arrows. Children play games of war in ritualistic imitation of their elders. Everywhere, nature is full of omens, boding good or evil.

The battles themselves are often abortive shouting matches in which the warriors, so proud at home, reveal their very human fears and reluctance.

Between battles, life is farming drudgery borne mainly by the women and children, with the warriors doing only the heaviest work. But one of the strangest things is that there is little strife within the community. All the hostility seems directed at the enemy.

All of this is superbly filmed in color by Life magazine's Eliot Elisofon, who has pulled no punches and shows the bloody gore as well as the pastoral beauty of this simple existence. Peter Mathieson's poetic narration, spoken by director Robert Gardner, has the quality of some fable or ancient tale which contributes a seductive surface romanticism. The obscure New Guinea mountain valley is exotic, distant, harboring an existence predating history and, at first glance, totally foreign to contemporary life. Yet before it is over, the film subtly implies that the remote valley is really only a day away and this is the story of man in microcosm; the sophisticated modern world has not grown up, it has only covered up.

Gardner has fashioned a fascinating, beautiful and disturbing film which well deserves its several awards received at European film festivals.

Currently in its American preem engagement at Frisco's tiny arty, The Movie. "Dead Birds" is now available only in 16m, but negotiations are underway for commercial distribution with 35m prints. While the subject matter may sound unlikely, pic's superior quality in all areas makes it a strong contender for art house cc'n. *Sanf.*

Dr. Terror's House Of Horrors
(BRITISH—COLOR)

Five slightly macabre anecdotes, thinly linked, provide some ingenuity and occasional shudders. Useful entry as co-feature at most houses.

London, Feb. 23.
Regal Films International release (Paramount in U.S.) of an Amicus (Milton Subotsky-Max J. Rosenberg) production. Stars Peter Cushing, Christopher Lee, Max Adrian, Michael Gough, Neil McCallum, Ann Bell, Jennifer Jayne, Bernard Lee, Roy Castle; features Alan Freeman, Kenny Lynch, Ursula Howells, Peter Madden, Jeremy Kemp, Tubby Hayes' Quintet. Russ Henderson Steel Band. Directed by Freddie Francis. Screenplay by Subotsky; camera (Technicolor), Alan Hume; editor, Thelma Connell; music, Tubby Hayes. Reviewed at Studio One, London. Running time, 98 MINS.
Dr. Schreck .... Peter Cushing
Franklyn Marsh .... Christopher Lee
Biff Bailey .... Roy Castle
Bob Carroll .... Donald Sutherland
Jim Dawson .... Neil McCallum
Bill Rogers .... Alan Freeman
Dr. Blake .... Max Adrian
Tod .... Edward Underdown
Deirdre .... Ursula Howells
Caleb .... Peter Madden
Valda .... Katy Wild
Ann Rogers .... Ann Bell
Carol Rogers .... Sarah Nicholls
Drake .... Jeremy Kemp
Sammy Coin .... Kenny Lynch
Shine .... Harold Lang
Dambala .... Thomas Baptiste
Bailey's Band ...... Tubby Hayes Quintet
Eric Landor .... Michael Gough
Pretty Girl .... Isla Blair
Nicolle .... Jennifer Jayne
Detective .... Al Mulock

Five short horror episodes, thinly linked, provide a usefully chilly package deal which will offer audiences several mild shudders and quite a lot of amusement. It should be a useful dualer at most houses. Even though occasional giggles set in, the cast, headed by experienced horror practitioners such as Peter Cushing, Michael Gough, Christopher Lee and Max Adrian, sensibly play it straight. Unintentional laughter is mainly caused by odd lines and phrases in Milton Subotsky's screenplay. Helmed by Freddie Francis, who also is an old hand with macabre sprees, both as cameraman and director, the film has good production values and several imaginative directing touches.

Five young men traveling on a routine train journey, meet up with the sixth passenger. He's a mysterious, bearded stranger (Peter Cushing who reveals himself as Dr. Schreck. With the aid of a pack of Tarot Cards, he foretells the grisly deaths in store for the quintet.

The five stories involve a young architect who, while altering his old family home for a client, is savaged by a werewolf; a pop musician who is struck down by voodoo after hijacking a voodoo sacred melody and performing it in a nightclub; an American doctor who is kidded by his partner that his young French wife is a vampire, so he sticks a stake through her heart; an arrogant art critic who murders an artist and is then haunted by (shades of Edgar Allen Poe) the artist's creeping, dismembered hand and a suburban chap who find that he has been harboring in his garden a creeping vine which has a grudge against the human race. The film emerges as a kind of Cinemagers Digest of how to come to a sticky end.

These playlets are insufficiently developed to sustain prolonger interest, though one or two of them, notably the creeping vine and the voodoo disaster, merit deeper treatment, but they provide some useful thesping changes. Cushing has little to do, but Christopher Lee as the art critic and Michael Gough as his artist victim are vivid characters. Roy Castle makes his first screen appearance effectively as the pop musician. A long list of sound mummers who weigh in with approximately sinister or matter-of-fact performances. The Tubby Hayes Quintet and the Russ Henderson Steel Band hit the musical highnotes. Hayes also contributed the musical score.

Technicolor lensing by Alan Hume is good and, in fact, production values are modest but very sound. Regal International Films release in the United Kingdom, with Paramount taking over for the States. *Rich.*

The Love Goddesses

Clips and quips of old and new film sex symbols has great appeal for film buffs, but disappointment for sensation-seekers.

Walter Reade-Sterling presentation of a Saul J. Turell-Graeme Ferguson production. Written by Turell and Ferguson; narrated by Carl King. Music, Percy Faith; editors, Nat Greene, Howard Kuperman; consultants William K. Everson, Paul Killiam, James A. Lebenthal; research, Georges LaBrousse, Gideon Bachmann. Reviewed at N.Y., Feb. 15, '65. Running Time: 87 MINS.

The idea of a quasi-documentary on the trends in sex during the history of motion pictures was an excellent one. The influence of the motion picture medium on the social behavior and morals of the peoples of the world has, undoubtedly, been an important one. What dilutes any value that this cinematic analysis of the screen's "love goddesses" might have had is the incomplete picture it gives of the subject; the second-choice examples used of some admitted prototypes; and a tendency to interpolate too much of the company's own product. The commercial appeal, initially, must come from the provocative title.

Film buffs will enjoy the technically-excellent compilation for its older examples and well as those from the early sound era.

Although credit is given to Paramount Pictures, Columbia Pictures, RKO Radio Pictures, United Artists, The Rank Organization, Romulus Films and, for older material, the Killiam-Sterling Film Collection, George Eastman House, Museum of Modern Art and Editions Jean-Jacques Pauvert, the greater part of the footage is from Paramount. The most recent material used is from 1959 vintage and, then, from Walter Reeade-Sterling films "Room at The Top" and "Expresso Bongo."

Although self-styled the story of "sex in the movies," it is comparatively innocent as much of the sex appeal of early film "goddesses" was less literal than is common today. The attempt to convey eroticism in these earlier examples, today only provides laughter. However, a few really effective examples of sex appeal, particularly Marlene Dietrich, were as evident then as they are today.

Roles range from Lillian Gish in D. W. Griffith's "True Heart Susie" to Simone Signoret in "Room At The Top." Along the way, such varying types are studied as Theda Bara, Mae Marsh, Fannie Ward, Agnes Ayres, Nita Naldi, Pola Negri, Lya de Putti, Clara Bow, Gloria Swanson, Louise Brooks, Hedy Lamarr, Greta Garbo, Jean Harlow, Bette Davis, Ruby Keeler, Carole Lombard, Ginger Rogers, Jeanette MacDonald, Myrna Loy, Mae West, Barbara Stanwyck, Lana Turner, Betty Grable, Dorothy Lamour, Rita Hayworth, Elizabeth Taylor, Marilyn Monroe, Sophia Loren, Audrey Hepburn, Brigitte Bardot, and Claudette Colbert.

Intended, undoubtedly, as humorous comment on the channels which American affection can take, are inserts of Shirley Temple and Hayley Mills. Some of the older segments provide, surprisingly, considerable merit: a scene from "Professional Sweetheart" (1933) in which Norman Foster, to later become a director, acts circles around Ginger Rogers as an unbelievably innocent husband; astonishingly lovely Louise Brooks in "Diary of a Lost Girl"; Sessue Hayakawa "branding" Fannie Ward in "The Cheat"; Dietrich in both "Blonde Venus" and "Morocco," particularly the latter where, dressed in male evening clothes, she does a nightclub turn; Carole Lombard and Clark Gable in "No Man Of Her Own"; Lana Turner and that sweater in "They Won't Forget"; and Rita Hayworth in "Gilda."

Biggest disappointments are footage on Garbo, Bette Davis, Marilyn Monroe and Elizabeth Taylor. Generally unheralded but competing equally with and sometimes surpassing) the femmes are an equally long list of male names that range from Horst Buchholz to Rudolph Valentino. The black and white photography is firstrate and the comment on both films and players intelligent, adequate and sometimes witty. *Robe.*

Joy in the Morning
(COLOR)
Lightweight young marriage tale starring Richard Chamberlain and Yvette Mimieux. Okay for smaller situations.

Metro release of Henry T. Weinstein production. Stars Richard Chamberlain, Yvette Mimieux; features Arthur Kennedy, Oscar Homolka, Donald Davis, Joan Tetzel, Sidney Blackmer. Directed by Alex Segal. Screenplay, Sally Benson, Alfred Hayes, Norman Lessing; based on novel by Betty Smith; camera (Metrocolor), Ellsworth Fredricks; music, Bernard Herrmann; editor, Tom McCarthy; asst. director, Sheldon Schrager. Reviewed at Beverly Theatre, March 3, '65. Running time, 101 MINS.
Carl Brown ..... Richard Chamberlain
Annie McGairy .... Yvette Mimieux
Patrick Brown .... Arthur Kennedy
Stan Pulaski .... Oscar Homolka
Anthony Byrd .... Donald Davis
Beverly Karter .... Joan Tetzel
Dean James Darwent .. Sidney Blackmer

Undoubted appeal of the Betty Smith novel fails to come through in any appreciable measure in its filmic translation, at best a lightweight entry in today's demanding market. Richard Chamberlain and Yvette Mimieux topbill cast. While their names may exert certain attraction, particularly in light of actor's hold on tv audiences via his "Dr. Kildare" series and femme's draw with younger contingent, indications point only to lesser-situation booking.

Story is of a young couple's first year of marriage at a small midwestern college in late '20s where groom is working has way through law school. Weakness of picture lies in the treatment. There is an absence of anything unusual happening and nothing is accomplished to overcome this lack through strong buildup of characterization. There are laughs, but mostly in the wrong places when action apparently gets away from the director. Visually, the Henry T. Weinstein production carries appropriate values cloaked in Metrocolor, and the two stars are backed by a substantial cast headed by Donald Davis, Arthur Kennedy, Oscar Homolka, Joan Tetzel and Sidney Blackmer.

Chamberlain seldom appears at ease as the young husband-student who has difficulty in making ends meet as he takes a night watchman job to augment his day jobs, leaving only scarce time for family life and classes. Miss Mimieux fares a little better, as she babysits to help out, then leaves Chamberlain when she finds she's pregnant so he won't have additional worries. Kennedy as the husband's father brings them together again in a gruff role; Davis is the faithful friend of the bride who sees her through some rough times; and Miss Tetzel likewise scores as the mother for whom femme star babysits, kept by Homolka, who hires Chamberlain as watchman.

Alex Segal's direction of the Sally Benson-Alfred Hayes-Norman Lessing screenplay is uneven but he manages at times to establish a nice feeling of young marriage. Color photography by Ellsworth Fredricks, music score by Bernard Herrmann, editing by Tom McCarthy and art direction by George W. Davis and Carl Anderson are assets. Chamberlain sings title song, by Sammy Fain and Paul Francis Webster, in good voice. *Whit.*

Wild Seed

Cutting might qualify as lowerhalfer on dual bills. Script inept and performances. Dim prospects.

Hollywood, March 3.
Universal release of Pennebaker (Albert S. Ruddy) production. Directed by Brian G. Hutton. Features Michael Parks, Celia Kaye. Screenplay, Les Pine, based on story by Pine and Ike Jones; camera, Conrad Hall; editor, Hugh Fowler; music, Richard Markowitz. Reviewed in Hollywood, March 3, '65. Running Time: 99 MINS.

Fargo	Michael Parks
Daffy	Celia Kaye
Mr. Collinge	Ross Elliott
Mr. Simms	Woodrow Chambliss
Hobo	Rupert Crosse
Mrs. Simms	Eva Novak
Policeman	Norman Burton
Constable	Merritt Bohn
Bartender	Anthony Lettier

Contemporary social drama about runaway gal and guy who takes her across country, "Wild Seed" is defeated by static acting, weak script and faulty character motivation. Exec producers Marlon Brando Sr. and Walter Seltzer have sponsored some new talent in what emerges as a blah, downbeat debut. Universal release is overlong and tedious. But with cutting could be acceptable if lowercased in general market.

One of Universal's lower-budget "New Horizon" pix, it will be held up in release to follow "Bus Riley's Back In Town," also with Parks.

Les Pine's screenplay fails to generate either interest or sympathy in describing hitch-hike of Celia Kaye from foster parents in N.Y. to real pop in L.A. The role must carry forward the plot, but through uninspired dialog and actress' inability to project required inner strength misses the mark. And with this failure goes the pic.

Top-featured Michael Parks (all names are below the title) plays the con artist who latches onto the gal for what she can do for him, exploiting human nature in everyone he encounters. Throughout pic he's a guy who could not care less, and the feeling becomes infectious. Combining James Dean looks and mannerisms of a nitery imitation of Marlon Brando, Parks sticks with the gal to a saccharine, slightly-upbeat ending which suggests, he doesn't have anything better to do. His potential is hard to evaluate, he being as seen here less an actor than a reactor.

Director Brian G. Hutton makes little of script and principals, but occasionally interesting staging, aided by Conrad Hall's camera, captures the dreary mobility of riding the rods. Both are bowing in respective posts as is Albert S. Ruddy as producer.

Woodrow Chambliss and Eve Novak (she a onetime silent star) are on briefly as middle-aged foster parents who try to reclaim their teenager. Other supporting players are adequate in trite bits.

Pic's 99 minutes are too much and Hugh Fowler's editing could be tightened some 15-20 minutes to give much-needed pace. Music by Richard Markowitz doesn't help mood, except at end where its apparent fuzziness parallels the plot resolution. Remaining technical credits okay.

Film has undergone several title changes, and script is understood to have been kicking around for some years, which might explain the uneven results. In closing titles Elliott-Kastner is cited ("without whose help . . ."), but his specific contributions are unexplained in titles. At one time he was an agent at MCA. *Murf.*

La 317 Section
(Platoon 317)
(FRENCH)

Paris, March 9.
Rank release of Rome-Paris Film-Benito Perojo production. With Jacques Perrin, Bruno Cremer, Pierre Fabre, Manuel Zarzo. Written and directed by Pierre Schoendoerffer from his own book. Camera, Raoul Coutard; editor, Armand Psenny. Previewed in Paris. Running time, 94 MINS.

Torrens	Jacques Perrin
Willsdorf	Bruno Cremer
Roudier	Pierre Fabre
Perrin	Manuel Zarzo

Guerrilla war in Asia is the background for this tale of a French patrol trying to join its group during the last days of the French-Indochinese War in 1954. With developments in Vietnam today, this has some possible uptodate and exploitation value abroad on its theme. It shapes a possible good playoff item on subject and treatment if it does not rise above its framework for untoward arty theatre chances.

Four Frenchmen have 41 Laotians under their command as they strike out in the jungle after the fall of Dien Bien Phu which practically spells French defeat at Viet Minh Communist hands. Ambushes, attacks on villages and the slow destruction of the group make up the core of the film.

There is the young almost callow lieutenant who turns out alright, the hardbitten sergeant who had served with the Germans, and other fairly stock characters. But with the enemy hardly ever seen, and no ordinary dialog, this is a fairly taut, unvarnished look at aimless warfare. Heroics are held to a minimum.

A needed lift in direction is also apparent, pic sometimes being plodding without any needed insight into war's harrowing aspects.

Good, harsh lensing, location shooting in Cambodia and acceptable thesping are assets. This may have good local chances if foreign outlooks depend on promotional knowhow and the film's timeliness. *Mosk.*

The Satan Bug
(PANAVISION—COLOR)

Suspenseful melodrama of a threat to destroy the earth. Hefty returns indicated in general market, with strong exploitation.

Hollywood, March 2.
United Artists release of Mirisch-Kappa production, produced-directed by John Sturges. Stars George Maharis, Richard Basehart, Anne Francis, Dana Andrews; features John Larkin, Richard Bull, Martin Blaine, Edward Asner, Frank Sutton. Screenplay, James Clavell, Edward Anhalt, based on novel by Ian Stuart; camera (DeLuxe Color), Robert Surtees; music, Jerry Goldsmith; editor, Ferris Webster; asst. director, Jack Deddish. Reviewed at Directors Guild Theatre, March 1, '65. Running time, 114 MINS.

Lee Barrett	George Maharis
Dr. Hoffman	Richard Basehart
Ann	Anne Francis
The General	Dana Andrews
Veretti	Edward Asner
Donald	Frank Sutton
Michaelson	John Larkin
Cavanaugh	Richard Bull
Martin	Martin Blaine
Reagan	John Anderson
Mason	Russ Bender
Johnson	Hari Rhodes
Raskin	John Clarke
Tasserly	Simon Oakland
Dr. Baxter	Henry Backman
Dr. Ostrer	Harold Gould
Dr. Yang	James Hong

"The Satan Bug" is a superior suspense melodrama and should keep audiences on the edge of their seats despite certain unexplained, confusing elements which tend to make plot at times difficult to follow. Film's theme of a threat of almost instantaneous world extinction via an awesome destructive virus is packed with shock values suitable for strong exploitation and better than average b.o. returns are indicated.

Based on a novel by Ian Stuart (nom de plume for Britisher Alistair MacLean), producer-director John Sturges builds his action to a generally chilling pace after a needlessly-slow opening which establishes America's experiments in bacteriological warfare at a highly-secret top-security research installation in the desert. The scientist who develops the deadly virus known as the Satan Bug, so lethal it can cause instant death over great areas, is murdered and flasks containing the liquid mysteriously spirited out of the lab.

Script by James Clavell and Edward Anhalt projects George Maharis as a former Army Intelligence officer recalled to find the virus before it can be put to the use threatened by a millionaire paranoiac who master-minded the theft and claims to hate war. He wipes out a small Florida community to show what he intends doing if the research lab isn't immediately dismantled as first step in his goal toward halting war, then announces that a vial of the virus has been planted somewhere in Los Angeles and will next be set off to the entire destruction of the city. Unfoldment follows Maharis and other Government agents working against time to save the city, with exciting climax in a helicopter high over Los Angeles as Maharis struggles with the fanatic, who posed as one of the lab scientists, for possession of the final flask.

Maharis makes a good impression as the investigator, although his character isn't developed sufficiently—a fault also applying to other principals—due to overspeedy editing in an attempt to narrate story at fever pitch. Richard Basehart as the millionaire who somehow gets through Government screening to become one of the hush-hush installation's top scientists suffers through inept development, and Dana Andrews is in as a general in charge of the case. Anne Francis, playing latter's daughter, is dragged in apparently for whatever lure her name might exact on marquee, nice to look at. Competent support is afforded by John Larkin, Richard Bull and Martin Blaine, as Government men, and Edward Asner and Frank Sutton as Basehart's strong-arm henchmen.

Robert Surtees' Panavision camera work is interesting, DeLuxe Color further enhancing its overall excellence, and Jerry Goldsmith's music score provides exciting overtones. Ferris Webster's editing blows both hot and cold, but is good for much of the suspense. *Whit.*

De L'Amour
(About Love)
(FRENCH)

Paris, March 2.
Cocinor release of Films De La Pleiade-Cocinor-Marceau production. Stars Anna Karina, Elsa Martinelli, Michel Piccoli, Jean Sorel. Directed by Jean Aurel. Screenplay, Cecil Saint Laurent, Aurel, based on the book by Stendhal; camera, Edmond Richard; editor, Agnes Guillemont. At Lord Byron, Paris. Running Time, 90 MINS.

Helene	Anna Karina
Raoul	Michele Piccoli
Mathilde	Elsa Martinelli
Antoine	Jean Sorel
Wether	Bernard Garnier
Serge	Philippe Avron
Sophie	Joanna Schimkus

Here is one of those insouciant, arbitrarily but glib looks at love in the French manner. It is a bit sketchy and familiar, but the pic has neat mounting, adroit playing and remains within tasteful bounds. Hence, it is an exploitation or arty house item. Word-of-mouth could also help.

Vaguely based on Stendhal's aphoristic book on love, film is updated and proves a series of sketches bound together by the same character, a little in the manner of "La Ronde." Main ingredients are the first seduction during a pickup, a Don Juan-type's breaking with a girl not because she cheats on him but because she does not tell him about it, and a battle between him and a modern, predatory female.

Two sparring people, a fetching girl and a charming young man, have their bout counterpointed by boxing sounds and divided into rounds by a character who spies on the first few sketches.

A ladies' man dentist easily seduces a girl in his chair to have a shortlived affair. Then, one day he finds himself impotent with a girl who is too easy. When he finally gets her, by her making him jealous, he is ready for new conquests.

Diretcor Jean Aurel keeps this bubbly, even if the outlook is mainly cynical and detached, because of his flair for visual revelation of character. Writer Cecil Saint Laurent is also the commentator and eavesdropper on some of the couples.

Anna Karina is warm, beguiling and flirty without vulgarity, as the first girl seduced while Joanna Schimkus is saucy as the dentist's paramour. Michel Piccoli and Elsa Martinelli are shrewd and engaging as the hunter and hunted alternately.

Crisp lensing and fine technical polish also help. This is an amusing lightweight trifle that could have local and foreign exploitation legs. *Mosk.*

Le Voleur De Tibidabo
(The Thief of Tibidabo)
(FRENCH-SPANISH)

Paris, March 2.
CFDC release of NEF-Sirius-UGC-JET production. Stars Maurice Ronet, Anna Karina. Directed by Maurice Ronet. Screenplay, Jean-Charles Tacchella, Remo Foriani, Ronet; camera, Andre Leventi, editor, J. Ayar. At Biarritz, Paris. Running Time, 115 MINS.
Nicolas .... Maurice Ronet
Maria .... Anna Karina

Popular actor Maurice Ronet has turned director of this film. It has not worked out well. Attempted picaresque comedy lacks the swift pace, electric lift and visual inventiveness to make this familiar tale catching. It plods and is overlong. Mainly local chances for this.

Ronet is a carefree Frenchman selling ice cream in Barcelona. He helps a friend supposedly trying to escape from a girl but the fellow has robbed a shop. Ronet is suspected and pic is about his imbroglios with a lot of colorful underworld characters and his love affairs.

All is straightened out after a flock of chases. But this is laborious rather than free-wheeling and Ronet has directed without a clearcut progression. So he is followed by shady characters after his money but also liking him.

But if a musical number is suddenly brought on, it has no grace, chases are overlong and confused. Attempts at wit, satire and tenderness just lack the right pitch and flair. Ronet is somewhat stiff though Anna Karina is gracious and fetching though her part is too ill defined to make much impact.

Film also shows a slipshod dubbing job with too many voices off. So chalk this up as a would-be lightweight comedy that has no pretentions and some freshness in its lack of guile but not the necessary talents to bring it off. Perhaps using another actor or more careful work on the script could give Ronet another chance behind the camera. His acting status is still high but not helped by this one. *Mosk.*

Une Fille Et Des Fusils
(A Girl and Guns)
(FRENCH)

Paris, March 2.
Films De La Pleiade release of Films 13-Pierre Braunberger production. With Jannie Magnan, Amidou, Pierre Barouh, Jean-Pierre Kalfon, Jacques Portet. Written, directed and edited by Claude Lelouch. Camera, Jean Colon. Previewed in Paris. Running Time, 110 MINS.
Martine .... Janine Magnan
Amidou .... Amidou
Pierre .... Pierre Barouh
Jean .... Jean-Pierre Kalfon
Jacques .... Jacques Portet

Claude Lelouch is a young filmmaker who has shown some knowhow with two previous pix. This one has a more subdued, yet effective story, but also goes off the rails via overdone violence and mayhem. Mainly a specialized item for abroad on its brashness. Arty chances are slimmer but exploitation possibilities bright.

Lelouch uses a personable group of young players to depict four workers who decide to become professional gangsters. They are influenced by films and gangster books. They proceed to live a strenuous life to learn about the underworld.

This idea at first is intriguing and handled with snap. They quit jobs and devote themselves to their training. One boy's deafmute girl is the only femme allowed with them. When they are ready their first important job leads to involuntary killing and their killing each other since they differ on what to do.

Approach is too unsettled to make this pay off. Idea of it being boyish and playful at first soon gets out of hand as they go from petty shoplifting to more lethal jobs too abruptly. Lelouch overdoes zoom shots, fast cutting and fancy angles. But instead of just telling his tale, he overstresses morality. This makes the last half somewhat banal.

The players are all fresh and engaging but remain unformed, and the film is almost childish on some of its angles.

But Lelouch does display a notable flair for action sequences and the use of on-the-spot lensing. For a film made almost entirely with exteriors and with newcomers, it has a remarkably fine technical finish. *Mosk.*

Fanny Hill: Memoirs of a Woman of Pleasure

A disgrace to the film industry. Sexploitation film aimed at t e obvious exp... ; of the notorious John Cleland novel has little quality and a dull, smutty approach. A slipshod, guttersnipe production.

Hollywood, March 13.
Favorite Films release of Famous Players Corp. production. Produced by Albert Zugsmith. Stars Miriam Hopkins, Letitia Roman; features Walter Giller, Alex D'Arcy, Helmut Weiss, Chris Howland, Ulli Lommel, Cara Garnett. Directed by Russ Meyer. Screenplay, Robert Hill, based on the novel by John Cleland; camera, Heinz Hilscher; editor, Alfred Srp; music, Erwin Halletz; Assistant director, Elfie Tillack. Reviewed at Four Star Theatre, L.A., March 12, '64. Running Time: 104 MINS.
Mrs. Maude Brown ...... Miriam Hopkins
Fanny Hill .... Letitia Roman
Hemingway .... Walter Giller
The Admiral .... Alex D'Arcy
Mr. Dinklespieler .... Helmut Weiss
Mr. Norbert .... Chris Howland
Charles .... Ulli Lommel
Phoebe .... Cara Garnett
Martha .... Karin Evans
Hortense .... Syra Marty
Grand Duke .... Albert Zugsmith
Fiona .... Christiane Schmidtmer
Fenella .... Heide Hansen
Emily .... Erica Ericson
Amanda .... Patricia Houstoun
Johnny .... Marshall Raynor
Mrs. Snow .... Hilda Sessack
Percival .... Billy Frick
James .... Jurgen Nesbach
Mudge .... Herbert Knippenberg
Lotus Blossom .... Susanne Hsiao
Niece .... Renate Hutte
Girl .... Ellen Velero

Hollywood has frequently taken the rap for a good many scurrilous accusations and attacks it has not deserved. As a commercial industry involved in the presentation of an artistic, but mass appeal, communications product, there are those areas of production that sometimes fall victim to the so-called high-minded, purist reactions and end up with an unwarranted slap in the face. Not so with Albert Zugsmith's production of "Fanny Hill." This picture deserves every slap it may get—and more. It is an insult to the integrity and sensibility of the Hollywood motion picture industry, a setback for the business.

John Cleland's 18th century book, on which the title and obvious exploitation elements of the picture is based, was banned for 200 years, until recently. The book, while a vivid descriptive account of sexual pleasures, has a bawdy, lusty and lively point of view. Had Zugsmith filmed it with taste and with proper facilities, it might have made a special and probably successful film. What he has done instead is taken the first chapter, filled it with ridiculous, smutty, cheap bedroom activity in the manner of a low class nudie and then tried to save the day by cutting to the end. Fanny herself loses her virginity and marries her true love in the end, which apparently makes all the vulgar tomfoolery in between proper.

Ads for the picture call it "a female 'Tom Jones'." Would that it had the same bawdy style done with the same believable mood and artistic quality. There will probably be plenty of interest on the part of the public response to such ads, but in the end these insult the public. No self-respecting exhibitor of prominence should bow to such cheap exploitation and no respectable house should dupe its patrons into seeing the picture under this veil. It is doubtful if most major dailies will accept its advertising. Money might be made on the first round, but the loss of community respect multiplied over the nation must be detrimental to the film industry.

Aside from the slipshod manner in which the film is made, a chief fault is in Robert Hill's academic screenplay and Russ Meyer's dull direction. Dialog is as low as can be found and the storyline is just old fashioned, thin and uninteresting.

Production itself has a couple of clever laughs, like the shop sign for the piemaker, M. Sennett. And there are some deliciously motley character people throughout, like a silent bit by Ellen Velero and, in fact, a bit by Zugsmith himself as the Grand Duke.

Miriam Hopkins, so fine an actress in the past in many first class films, is woefully disgraced by inadequate material and ludicrous situations as the madame, who notes, "It isn't much, but we call it a house." Letitia Roman is pretty as Fanny and Ulli Lommel, who looks emaciated without his clothes, does have a few moments of interest as Fanny's suitor. Walter Giller has an evil sensitivity as one lusty patron and Karin Evans could be fine as a grumbling maid if the role were well written. Others are generally inadequate throughout.

To comment on the film's design, it was badly dubbed with no background or normal room sounds, leaving it with a dull aural thud. Editing is sloppy and there seems little attempt at matching the photography. Scenes look like day and night at the same time. Picture runs much like a documentary, with a good deal of narration throughout and a busy series of lithographs aimed at the plates of a book as the film takes it sway through the ordeals of Fanny, the country lass who never once found out about the house she thought was a home. *Dale.*

Atragon
(COLOR-WIDESCREEN)
(Japanese-English Dubbed)

Highly-exploitable sci-fi thriller with topical gimmicks, well-directed and mounted.

American-International release of Toho Company (Japan) production, executive producer Yuko Tanaka. No stars; features Tadao Takashima, Yoko Fujiyama, Yu Fujiki; with Kenji Sawara, Akemi Kita, Tetsuko Kobayashi, Akihiko Hirata, Hiroshi Koizumi, Jun Tazaki, Ken Uehara. Directed by Inoshiro Honda. Screenplay, Shinichi Sekizawa; camera (anamorphic, Pathecolor), Hajime Koizumi; special effects, Eiji Tsuburaya; music, Akira Ifukube. Reviewed at Joe Shore's Screening Room, L.A., March 11, '65. Running Time: 90 MINS.

Hollywood, March 12.
A threat to the world from underseas kingdom whose weapons can be repulsed only by amphibious battleship named "Atragon" makes for special effects holiday in this English-dubbed Japanese sci-fi pic, originally "Kaitei Gun-

kan" (Atoragon) from Toho. Good acting, fast-paced direction and editing and contemporary political theme result in sock exploitationer for American-International release in action situations. Excellent prospects for showmanly exhibs.

Director Inoshiro Honda competently handles good cast topfeaturing Tadao Takashima as photog who stumbles onto civil engineer kidnap plot. Shinichi Sekizawa's clever screenplay intros plans of undersea Mu Empire to control world via modern weapons and planned earthquakes, since submerged kingdom is threatened by earth crust movements. Mu agents come up via sub to snatch key people, including Yoko Fuijiyama, secretary to shipping magnate who was Imperial Navy admiral in World War II.

Yu Fujiki, sub skipper and father of gal, was never captured and set up shop on Pacific Island where he built air-surface-submerged battleship. Mu Empire demands earth's surrender, fearing only superweapon Atragon, sketches of which were recovered from father's rammed sub. Gal and admiral can't persuade him to have a now-united world (sic), but her later kidnapping by Mu-men and sabotage attempt change his mind.

Special effects by Eiji Tsuburaya are consistently excellent, including futuristic weapons, inevitable monster, underwater explosions and fine miniature work depicting Mu-caused earthquake which levels parts of Tokyo.

Honda (whose forte is as Japan's sci-fi expert) has effectively employed Western actors in scenes where United Nations defense efforts are shown, and mob scenes are believably staged. Editing interpolates jet aircraft, army, and navy footage as it cross-cuts in crescendo from Atragon base to Mu Empire to world capitals on earth. Climax finds Atragon boring into enemy kingdom, destroying power plant with weapon which freezes targets, and blowing up everything. The good guys are all saved, natch, and family reconciliation is achieved.

Hajime Koizumi's widescreen and color camera (processed here by Pathe Labs) is a solid asset throughout, while Akira Ifukube's music is unobtrusive. Yuko Tanaka was exec producer for Toho and coordinated things admirably to turn a lightweight programmer into a solid exploitation pic. Other uncredited technical chores are topnotch. *Murf.*

Nightmare In The Sun
(COLOR)

Mediocre programmer with murder theme. Poor script and performances mean lowercasein discriminatory situations.

Hollywood, March 7.

Zodiac Films release of Afilmco (Ricky Dupont) Production produced by Marc Lawrence and John Derek. No stars; features entire cast. Directed by Lawrence. Screenplay, Ted Thomas, Fanya Lawrence, from story by director and George Fass; camera (DeLuxe Color), Stanley Cortez; editors, Douglas Stewart, William Shenberg; music, Paul Glass; art direction, Paul Sylas; sound, Glen Glenn; asst. director, Frank Parmenter. Reviewed at Pix Theatre. L.A., March 6, '65. Running Time, 80 MINS.

Hitch-hiker	John Derek
Sheriff	Aldo Ray
Husband	Arthur O'Connell
Wife	Ursula Andress
Truckdriver	Sammy Davis Jr.
Scoutmaster	Allan Joslyn
Junk dealer	Keenan Wynn
Bartender	Chick Chandler
Motorcyclists	Richard Jaeckel, Robert Duvall
Married couple	Lurene Tuttle, George Tobias
Unidentified	Douglas Fowley, John Marley, Bill Challee, Michael Petit, James Waters, John Sebastian

Story about man hunted for murder by people who know he's innocent, "Nightmare In The Sun" features trite script and generally poor performances. Color lensing of modern cowtown melodrama reflects artistic barrenness of this Marc Lawrence - John Derek production. Zodiac Films release is currently (and properly) lowercased, although cast of familiar names might make possible exploitation push in hick situations.

The Ted Thomas - Fanya Lawrence script puts banalities into mouths of players who recite same unconvincingly, with stock situations introduced to no avail, ditto several cameo bits.

All names appear after title with current star-guestar sleights of pen, with Derek, Aldo Ray, Arthur O'Connell and Ursula Andress topfeatured in that order. Ad layouts have moved Miss Andress to top of list, although footage is relatively brief as bored wife of jealous Arthur O'Connell who has been cuckolded by many, including sheriff Aldo Ray. In psychotic rage, O'Connell kills her but confession is stifled by Ray who has other plans.

Idea is to place blame on Derek, hitch-hiker transient who has also made it with Miss Andress before moving on. Pic concerns itself with Derek's huntdown within few miles of town. Gimmick doesn't pan out, with O'Connell and Ray unbelievably bad, Miss Andress passable until early death, and Derek merely fair. Latter gives a more mature image than before, having escaped longtime slicked-down baby-face appearance. Stronger material might revive a dormant career.

Unconvincing motorcyclists Richard Jaeckel and a psycho Robert Duvall, bird-loving Lurene Tuttle-George Tobias married couple, junk dealer Keenan Wynn, truckdriver Sammy Davis, Jr., and bartender Chick Chandler, are encountered by Derek but lend nothing. Allan Joslyn is scoutmaster who finks after Derek has saved a kid from death, but by that time O'Connell has killed Ray in another rage so the fugitive goes free. Other players are equally flat.

Director Lawrence never gets film rolling, despite Stanley Cortez' camera which lends life and movement to a few scenes. Other technical credits are okay, including editing by Douglas Stewart (also associate producer) and William Shenberg which gives some pace. *Murf.*

Kungsleden
(The Royal Road)
(SWEDISH—COLOR)

Warner-Tonefilm release of Nordisk Tonefilm production. Stars Mathias Henrikson, Maude Adelson; features Lars Lind, Guy De La Berg, Johannes Blind. Directed by Gunnar Hoglund. Screenplay by Hoglund and Bosse Gustafson from novel by Gustafson; camera (Eastmancolor), Bertil Wiktorsson; music, Karl-Erik Welin. At the Grand, Stockholm. Running Time, 107 MINS.

"You"	Mathias Henrikson
Leni Wodak	Maude Adelson
"The other man"	Lars Lind
German tourist	Guy De La Berg
Andreas	Johannes Blind

Up in northern Sweden, north of the Arctic Circle, between the mountains is a trail popular among tourists walking there every summer. A Swedish King is known for having walked this trail more than once, hence the name of this pic. Bosse Gustafson's book about this trail has been filmed by Nordisk Tonefilm. But it is a confusing pic and not a very entertaining one.

Story deals with "You" (Mathias Henrikson) walking the trail at the present time. He recalls the last time he has done so, 10 years ago, then with the Jewish girl Maude Adelson. Their first night in the mountains turned into romance, but the third night he had raped her in a brutal scene. She told him after this raping that they couldn't continue.

But 10 years later, he's walking the trail again and discovers Maude is just about one day ahead of him. Later he finds her dead in a mountain stream. After having buried her he returns to a nearby cottage, the place of the drama of 10 years ago.

The next morning he discovers somebody else has been sleeping in one of the cottages. And he begins to suspect him of having killed Maude. After a chase in the high mountain passes, Mathias brings about the death of his suspect. Henrikson is very good as "You," both as the teenage youth of 10 years ago and as the grownup man. Maude Adelson, as Leni with memories from a concentration camp in Hitler's Germany, gives a standout performance. These two are the only important characters in the pic, as the "other man" is seen only briefly.

The audience likely will be confused because the film leaves it undecided if the girl was killed by accident or if she was murdered.

Picture has several nude scenes and the very crude rape scene. Technically, it is well-done and should have a chance abroad provided the censors are not too tough. *Wing.*

Par Un Beau Matin D'Ete
(On a Nice Summer Day)
(FRENCH-FRANSCOPE)
Paris, March 9.

Prodis release of Sud-Pacifique Films-Films Borderie-Benito Perejo-Jolly Films production. Stars Jean-Paul Belmondo; features Sophie Daumier, Analia Gade, Gabriele Ferzetti, Georges Geret, Akim Tamiroff, Geraldine Chaplin. Directed by Jacques Deray. Screenplay, Michel Audiard, Didier Goulard, Maurice Fabre, Georges Bardawill, Deray from a book by James Hadley Chase; camera, M. Charvein; editor, Monique Kirsanoff. At Ambassaed-Gaumont, Paris. Running Time, 105 MINS.

Francis	Jean-Paul Belmondo
Monique	Sophie Daumier
Zelda	Geraldine Chaplin
Paitler	Gabriele Ferzetti
Max	Georges Geret
Frank	Akim Tamiroff

Jean-Paul Belmondo is one of the busiest stars on the scene here. He again plays his usual breezy, but vulgar hoodlum with a way with women and holding his own toughness in the underworld. But this rather too solidly treated kidnaping tale is unbalanced by his character and its seriousness.

It is the familiar one about the kidnapped heiress falling for one of her imprisoners, and pulls the usual suspense and action strings. Belmondo and a yeasty, good-looking sister use the sucker stunt he bursts into a room where she supposedly is about to be defiled by a man she has picked up.

Then an aging racketeer talks them into a kidnaping job. They break into an isolated house where an artist, his wife and child live. The artist is sent out to contact the father, with his family as hostages.

Personal problems among all these assorted characters bring on complications. Belmondo fights it out with one of the gunmen, jealous when the hostage girl seems to be falling for him. It all ends in the usual irony.

Belmondo is his usual vigorous self and acquits himself although the situations, slanted for realism, take the edge off his good work.

Geraldine Chaplin, daughter of Charles Chaplin, has a fragile presence, with a hint of inner strength, which hints future promise. She photographs well and has an attention-arresting quality. Akim Tamiroff is fine as the ringleader with others also adequate. However, this lacks the needed dramatic edge to make it a more than routine gangster film. *Mosk.*

Bus Riley's Back In Town
(COLOR)

Ann-Margret and slick production should make this over-mellow drama an initial success but has little staying power.

Universal release of Elliott Kastner production. Features Ann-Margret, Michael Parks, Janet Margolin, Brad Dexter, Jocelyn Brando, Larry Storch. Directed by Harvey Hart. Screenplay, Walter Gage; camera (Eastmancolor), Russell Metty; editor, Folmar Blangsted; music, Richard Markowitz. Reviewed in N.Y., March 12, '65. Running Time: 93 MINS.

Laurel	Ann-Margret
Bus Riley	Michael Parks
Judy	Janet Margolin
Slocum	Brad Dexter
Mrs. Riley	Jocelyn Brando
Howie	Larry Storch
Spencer	Crahan Denton
Gussie	Kim Darby
Carlotta	Brett Somers
Paula	Mimsy Farmer
Mrs. Nichols	Nan Martin
Joy	Lisabeth Hush
Mrs. Spencer	Ethel Griffies
Woman Customer	Alice Pearce
Benji	Chet Stratton
Stretch	David Carradine
Egg Foo	Marc Cavell
Mr. Griswald	Parley Baer

Where to pinpoint the blame for this well-intended major feature's failure is difficult. Certainly some of it must be allotted to former tv-director Harvey Hart's inexperience with the bigger-screen medium, and his lack of control over several of the thespians involved (this is his feature debut), but the erratic, chopped-up screenplay is also a major fault. Originally announced as the work of William Inge, screen credit is now given to Walter Gage, evidently a pseudonym for the several studio writers who had a go at it. Bits of Inge remain.

That both producer Elliott Kastner and Universal thought big is evident in the assignment of top-drawer technicians in every other department. Cameraman Russell Metty (his use of Eastmancolor is lovely), editor Folmar Blangsted, art directors Alexander Golitzer and Frank Arrigo, set decorators John McCarthy and Oliver Emert, sound men Waldon O. Watson and Lyle Cain—between them, they share 17 Oscar nominations. Their efforts give "Bus Riley" a slickness and a surface polish that makes a most attractive package but boxoffice endurance must rest with the film's dramatic impact and that is where the trouble lies.

Although Ann-Margret is the marquee lure for "Bus Riley," the story centers on the title character, played by newcomer Michael Parks. Actually his second role (first, "Wild Seed," held up by Universal to take advantage of greater audience identification provided by "Riley"). Gives Parks more opportunity than is provided the average film-debuting actor. He has an evident potential but needs the tight supervision and inspiration of a screen-knowledgeable director. He tends to rely overmuch on "method" methods—the tightly-constricted gesture, the stammer, the withdrawn, hunched-shoulder, hooded-eye type of acting that, sometimes adequate on the stage, is rarely effective on the wide screen of a motion picture theatre. Fortunately, Parks responds to the interplay provided by a bona fide talent. His scenes with Janet Margolin are his best, those with Ann-Margret, his poorest.

A simple plot—young ex-serviceman seeking an identity and faced with the problem of succumbing to the wiles of bad girl (Ann-Margret) or meeting responsibility head on (with implied support of good girl) —there's insufficient background provided for some principal characters while an over importance is given to some minor parts.

Besides Parks' promise as a future screen talent and the too-brief but beautifully-played contribution of Miss Margolin as the girl to whom "Bus Riley" is drawn as the antithesis of the worldly Ann-Margret character, there are few outstanding performances. Crahan Denton, as a latently homosexual undertaker, does demonstrate, in three knee-pats and a single line, how to quickly establish a morally-sick type, but other roles are routinely written and played, several almost caricatures of early Inge types.

"Bus Riley" will get top treatment in promotion because of its production values and should provide good double-bill programming for an easy return of investment. Only the filmgoers who seek solid story material and better than good performances will feel gypped.
Robe.

The Lost World of Sinbad
(WIDESCREEN-COLOR)
(Japanese-English Dubbed)

Sinbad gone Samurai with average fantasy result. Toshiro Mifune only marquee name value. Okay prospects for lowercasing with stronger exploitation pic.

Hollywood, March 12.
American-International release of Toho (Japan) (Yuko Tanaka) production. Stars Toshiro Mifune; features Makoto Satoh, Jun Funado, Ichiro Arishima. Directed by Senkichi Taniguchi. Screenplay, Takeshi Kimura; camera (anamorphic, Pathecolor), Shinichi Sekizawa; special effects, Eiji Tsuburaya; music, Masaru Satoh. Reviewed March 11, '65. Running Time: 94 MINS.

Far East relocation and rework of Sinbad character emerges as somewhat heavyhanded Samurai meller, although relieved with broad comic bits which help restore mood of light fantasy. English-dubbed by AIP, pic, originally called "Daitozoku" (Samurai Pirate), a 1963 product of Toho Co., has good direction and production values despite moderate pace. Presence of toplined Toshiro Mifune lends marquee lure via thesp's international reputation. Interesting special effects help, but AIP release will be best lowercased on dual exploitation bill.

Mifune plays Sinbad in Takeshi Kimura's rambling screenplay which kicks off with Sinbad bribing way out of death sentence, only to lose jewel treasure to pirates who leave him to die at sea. Washed ashore, he's nursed by a fallen wizard who has lost his touch because of predilection for pretty girls, proof of which recurs throughout pic.

Sinbad becomes embroiled in palace politics as guard. Evil premier, radiant princess pining for overseas lover but coveted by premier who's poisoning her father, the King, wicked lady-in-waiting and a witch named Granny keep the pot boiling, while Mifune plays it straight. Latter has commanding presence, a bit too severe herein although thoroughly virile.

Premiere's takeover plot is foiled by Sinbad with bandit troupe led by lady rice-slinger from local teahouse. Arrival of prince and defeat of premier (and pirate chieftain who has been in cahoots) sees lovers fading in clinch and Sinbad returning to sea.

Subplot humor comes mainly from old wizard becoming Granny (after trapping real one in flash after she's become a flying insect), and finally shaking his mammary fixation. Granny's power is turning people to stone by hypnosis, and at climax (attempting to petrify princess) she becomes stoned herself from mirror reflection. Villain dies from being crushed by moat gate under hordes of released political prisoners.

Thesping averages out good, Mifune's stiffness offset by magicians' very good characterizations, while others are appropriately broad. Also, director Senkichi Taniguchi has partially succeeded in creating lightness, aided by Shinichi Sekizawa's wide and colorful camera which lends fluidity, but crowd scenes and spectacular derring-do are lacking. Sea battles and fire-arrow joust are noteworthy, however. Editing could be tightened some 10-15 minutes to enhance pace.

Special effects by Eiji Tsuburaya involve the two magicians, also Sinbad's kite flight into castle, all okay though far from sensational. Music by Masaru Satoh is adequate. Yuko Tanaka was exec producer for Toho. Other uncredited technical work (including Pathe Lab processing) is professional. *Murf.*

My Blood Runs Cold
(PANAVISION)

Suspense programmer from dullsville. Cliche script and so-so acting make exploitation prospects doubtful despite some marquee names.

Hollywood, March 8.
Warner Bros. release of William Conrad production, directed by Conrad. Features Troy Donahue, Joey Heatherton, Barry Sullivan, Nicolas Coster, Jeanette Nolan. Screenplay, John Mantley, from story by John Meredyth Lucas; camera, Sam Leavitt; editor, William Ziegler; music, George Duning; art direction, LeRoy Deane; sound, Stanley Jones; asst. director, Russell Llewellyn. Reviewed at Warner Bros. Studio, March 2, '65. Running Time, 103 MINS.

Ben Gunther	Troy Donahue
Julie Merriday	Joey Heatherton
Julian Merriday	Barry Sullivan
Harry Lindsay	Nicolas Coster
Aunt Sarah	Jeanette Nolan
Sheriff	Russell Thorson
Lansbury	Ben Wright
Mrs. Courtland	Shirley Mitchell
Henry	Howard McNear
Mayor	Howard Wendell
Mr. Courtland	John Holland
Owen	John McCook

A dull suspense programmer handicapped by cliche-ridden script and disappointing performers, "My Blood Runs Cold" emerges as weak sequel to prod.-director William Conrad's "Two On A Guillotine." Presence of some marquee names may help, but Warner Bros. release is overlong rehash of stereotyped melodrama and short on suspense. Occasionally interesting direction and photography of rugged northern Calif. coast helps, but overall it's a dim prospect for intended exploitation. With 20 minutes cut it could be acceptable as lowercase entry in general market.

Conrad again uses Sam Leavitt's b&w Panavision camera and William Ziegler's editing this time out in tepid tale by John Mantley, without the audience identification with principals, humor, or suspense that characterized "Guillotine." A spoiled brat daughter played unevenly by Joey Heatherton, wealthy and dictatorial father limned with near embarrassment by Barry Sullivan, and a psychotic fugitive from an asylum essayed unconvincingly by Troy Donahue are the principals in a reincarnation theme.

Add Nicolas Coster's weak-spirited country-club boyfriend of Miss Heatherton and Jeanette Nolan's plain-talking aunt (inevitable in potboilers to explain plot angles which major characters cannot project).

As a talent showcase, pic presents Miss Heatherton in inconsistent characterization of gal conned by Donahue into believing the pair are really 19th century lovers whose affair put a skeleton into the family closet. Sometimes she's trying to be cute, other times a pouter. Blond looker might well be developed along latter lines for roles once played by Susan Hayward, since other young film femmes seem to prefer nice-girl roles.

Donahue fails to project as the psycho who has found an old diary on which he bases his pitch. Despite role which permits vacant stares and mystical references, he is inadequate, feeling being all the stops are pulled out. Even when ordered by Barry Sullivan to lay off, there's little animation. Donahue is top-featured, all names coming after title.

Boyfriend Nicolas Coster gets most out of his minor part, displaying good potential. Jeanette Nolan, in bizarre costumes and with sharp dialog, creates some interest in artificial role. Supporting players are adequate in stock characterizations. Climactic battle in sand plant between Donahue and Coster is well-directed, but predictable.

George Duning's music is incidental, with a spinet piano leitmotif for Donahue's mysterioso scenes. Other Warner technical credits are professional. *Murf.*

Samurai Assassin
(JAPANESE)

Toho International release of Toho-Mifune (Tomoyuki Tanaka-Reiji Miwa) production. Directed by Kihachi Okamoto. Stars Toshiro Mifune; features Keiju Kobayashi, Yunosuke Ito, Koshiro Matsumoto, Michiyo Aratama, Nami Tamura, Kaoru Yachigusa. Screenplay, Shinobu Hashimoto, based on Jiromasa Gunji's "Samurai Nippon"; camera, Hiroshi Murai; music, Katsu Sato. Reviewed in N.Y., March 10, '65. Running Time: 122 MINS.

(English Subtitles)

Toshiro Mifune and a samurai plot go together like Lunt and Fontanne or Laurel and Hardy. Some of the resulting films are superb, some are only very good. "Samurai Assassin" belongs to the latter group. Confirmed samurai-film patrons will get their money's worth and the film should do well for Toho, who's bringing Mifune in from Japan to spark the N.Y. opening March 18.

Originally called simply "Samurai," the film, which Mifune coproduced as well as acted in, is also Japanese entry in forthcoming Mar del Plata Film Festival. Director Kihachi Okamoto has generally dealt in the past with film of a more contemporary nature but with heavy stress on action and violence (in most samurai films these two qualities are the same). Like the maker of westerns, he knows that the story must be kept simple and the byplay between good and bad full of colorful movement. Only in the resolution of plot does the Japanese director sometimes steer away from the western-like format. Boy rarely gets girl and is often killed.

Mifune, again a wandering samurai, Shane-like in his odd combination of controlled strength and personal sense of humor, seeks an opportunity to so demonstrate his ability that he'll be asked to join the ranks of a recognized feudal lord. This opportunity presents itself when he joins a group of revolutionaries intent on assassinating the Chief Minister who shares the spreading belief that Japan should open its doors to the western nations. Also illegitimate, Mifune hopes to find the solution to the identity of his father. The finally assassinated lord, of course, was his father.

Led by Mifune, the entire cast, particularly the men, give excellent portrayals. Keiju Kobayashi as an equally proficient at arms but intellectually superior comrade of Mifune (who Mifune is ordered to kill as a suspected spy) is particularly outstanding. Michiyo Aratama as a restaurant owner who falls in love with the uncouth, swaggering Mifune is lovely and convincing in an easily unbelievable role.

Hiroshi Murai's crisp black and white photography is most effective in the outdoor, dead-of-winter panoramas and fight scenes. Interiors are sometimes overlit - in contrast with heavily-shadowed exterior scenes.

There's much violent swordplay but who wants a samurai who leaves his sword sheathed all the time? Or a cowboy who never draws his gun.　　　*Robe.*

Major Dundee
(PANAVISION-COLOR)

Cavalry-Indians yarn starring Charlton Heston. Rugged action but continuity at times ragged and too many delaying sequences. But good chances in adventure-melodrama market.

Hollywood, March 1.
Columbia Pictures release of Jerry Bresler production. Stars Charlton Heston, Richard Harris, Jim Hutton, James Coburn, Michael Anderson Jr.; features Mario Adorf, Brock Peters, Warren Oates, Senta Berger. Directed by Sam Peckinpah. Screenplay, Harry Julian Fink, Oscar Saul, Peckinpah; story, Fink; camera (Pathe Color), Sam Leavitt; music, Daniel Amfitheatrof; editors, William A. Lyon, Don Starling, Howard Kunin; asst. directors, John Veitch, Floyd Joyer. Reviewed at Academy Award Theatre, Feb. 25, '65. Running Time, 134 MINS.

Major Amos Charles Dundee	Charlton Heston
Captain Benjamin Tyreen	Richard Harris
Lieutenant Graham	Jim Hutton
Samuel Potts	James Coburn
Tim Ryan	Michael Anderson Jr.
Teresa Santiago	Senta Berger
Sergeant Gomez	Mario Adorf
Aesop	Brock Peters
O. W. Hadley	Warren Oates
Sergeant Chillum	Ben Johnson
Reverend Dahlstrom	R. G. Armstrong
Arthur Hadley	L. Q. Jones
Wiley	Slim Pickens
Captain Waller	Karl Swenson
Sierra Charriba	Michael Pate
Jimmy Lee Benteen	John Davis Chandler
Priam	Dub Taylor
Captain Jacques Tremaine	Albert Carrier
Riago	Jose Carlos Ruiz
Melincha	Aurora Clavell
Linda	Begonia Palacios
Doctor Aguilar	Enrique Lucero
Old Apache	Francisco Reyguera

Somewhere in the development of this Jerry Bresler production the central premise was sidetracked and a maze of little-meaning action substituted. What started out as a straight story-line (or at least, idea)—a troop of U.S. Cavalry chasing a murderous Apache and his band into Mexico to rescue three kidnapped white children and avenge an Indian massacre—devolves into a series of sub-plots and tedious, poorly-edited footage in which much of

the continuity is lost. There are certain salable ingredients, however. To wit, type of violence inherent in its subject matter, and presence of Charlton Heston.

Interestingly lensed in Panavision and PatheColor against the actual Mexico terrain, film would benefit by a good 20 to 25-minute snap-up, especially of sequences having virtually no bearing on main plot and which serve to reduce pace to a crawl instead of adhering to rapid movement the topic requires. Sam Peckinpah's direction of individual scenes is mostly vigorous but he cannot overcome the weakness of screenplay of whose responsibility he bears a share with Harry Julian Fink and Oscar Saul. Use of off-screen narration, ostensibly from the diary of one of the troopers on the march, reduces impact and is a further deterrent to fast unfoldment.

Heston delivers one of his regulation hefty portrayals and gets solid backing from a cast headed by Richard Harris as the Rebel captain, who presents a dashing figure. Jim Hutton as an energetic young lieutenant and James Coburn an Indian scout likewise stand out. Michael Anderson Jr., is the bugler, sole survivor of the Indian massacre, who kills the Apache when a trap is laid for him, and Mario Adorf a sergeant, and Brock Peters a Negro trooper, all handling their roles well. For distaff interest, Senta Berger, as widow of a Mexican doctor, provides the slight romance in pic.

Photography by Sam Leavitt is one of the high marks of picture, which has a rousing music score by Daniel Amfitheatrof. Three editors are credited, including William A. Lyon, Don Starling and Howard Kunin, which may account in part for film's lack of continuity through too many cutters.

Mitch Miller's Sing Along Gang sing the "Major Dundee March," composed by Amfitheatrof and lyrics by Ned Washington, over opening credits.　　　*Whit.*

The Truth About Spring
(COLOR)

Strong family film starring Hayley Mills.

Hollywood, March 1.
Universal release of Alan Brown production. Stars Hayley Mills, John Mills, James MacArthur; features Lionel Jeffries, Harry Andrews, Niall MacGinnis, Lionel Murton, David Tomlinson. Directed by Richard Thorpe. Screenplay, James Lee Barrett, based on story by Henry de Vere Stacpoole; camera (Technicolor), Edward Scaife; music, Robert Farnon; editor, Thomas Stanford; asst. directors, Ted Sturgis, Pedro Vidal. Reviewed at Beverly Theatre, Feb. 23, '65. Running Time, 102 MINS.

Spring Tyler	Haley Mills
Tommy Tyler	John Mills
William Ashton	James MacArthur
Cark	Lionel Jeffries
Sellers	Harry Andrews
Ceary	Niall MacGinnis
Simmons	Lionel Murton
Skelton	David Tomlinson

"The Truth About Spring" carries enough young-love interest and the doings of a couple of engaging characters to qualify nicely for the family trade and for those situations where name of Hayley Mills may draw. Former moppet star plays a tomboyish 18-year-old (her actual age) whose life with her father aboard a tumbledown fishing smack in the Caribbean has scarcely prepared her to cope with the emotional problems of growing up. Film's light, escapist treatment would benefit by judicious trimming, particularly of some of the earlier overly-meandering footage, to accelerate pace but in the main its entertainment potential is realized.

Producer Alan Brown's initial pic under the banner of Quota Rentals Ltd., Technicolor feature was lensed entirely on location along Spain's Costa Brava, which accounts for a number of unusually interesting and picturesque scenic backdrops. Richard Thorpe has inserted plenty of comedy in his direction of the James Lee Barrett screenplay which limns John Mills (Hayley's actual father) as a good-natured, lazy past-master of getting something - for - nothing. His guile and ability to con others out of almost anything has left him with a couple of dangerous rivals.

When one of these, Lionel Jeffries, master of the dirtiest ship afloat and piratically-inclined, finally catches up to him, Mills sells him on sharing in a treasure map, which he knows Mills has and for which Mills extracts $1,000 advance. Complications arise when Jeffries' doublecrossing partner, Niall MacGinnis, accosts Mills for his part in the hoard, buried on an uncharted Caribbean isle, which turns out to be only the powdery skeletons of dozens of slaves. The romance unfolds in this plot structure between Hayley and James MacArthur, a wealthy and somewhat stuffy young Philadelphian just out of law school, who leaves his millionaire uncle's yacht upon Mills' invitation to spend the rest of his vacation with Mills and his daughter.

Miss Mills — her wardrobe consists of a couple of pairs of faded blue jeans and pair of ragged shirts until final two scenes in a dress — ably demonstrates she is bridging her adolescent years with true aplomb. She handles comedy with as much fine feeling as she does scenes in which she feels the springing of love. Mills, begrizzled with a mighty beard, goes in

heavily for facial contortions but with a twinkle which makes him a rather lovable character. MacArthur, perhaps because the role called for it, is stiff.

Jeffries socks over his comical character with lush delivery, and Harry Andrews, with a patch over one eye, is his leering mate. MacGinnis plays his menace for comic effect, and David Tomlinson has a few nice scenes as MacArthur's uncle, with a fondness for bikini-clad young ladies aboard his yacht.

Technical credits are headed by Edward Scaife's dexterous color camera work, and balance stack up well. Danny Street sings title song by Robert Farnon and David Heneker, over the credits. *Whit.*

Where Was Your Majesty Between 3 and 5?
(HUNGARIAN-COLOR)

Vienna, March 23.
Studio I Mafilm (Budapest) production. Stars Iren Psota and Ivan Darvas. Directed by Karoly Makk. Screenplay, Miklos Hubay, after a novel by Koloman Mikszath; camera (Eastmancolor), Gyorgy Illes; music, Emil Petrovics. At Kuenstlerhauskino, Viennese Fest of Gaiety. Running Time: 87 MINS.

As evidenced by their entries at film festivals, the Hungarian producers are getting better and better. This one is another example. It's an imaginative mixture of feature players plus cartoon pic. It is nothing much for the fastidious patron, but this type of production stands a solid chance with general audiences. "Your Majesty" was one of the most applauded entries at the recently terminated Fifth Viennese Festival of Gaiety. Audiences there took an obvious fancy to the films' beautiful colors, witty characters, amusing plot and unusual situations. It has foreign market possibilities.

Action occurs in 1485 when King Matthias Corvinus conquered Vienna. But the handsome king then conquered something else, women. Indeed, he had a way with the dames. This made the queen repeatedly inquire. "Where were you between 3 and 5 a.m.?" This rather lavish renaissance comedy answers this question in a charming way. There are quite a few delicate scenes along the line.

Ivan Darvas is the dashing king and the lineup of tempermental and beautiful women is headed by Iren Psota, a multi-sided actress, reputedly a big name in the Magyar country.

Karoly Makk, who has already a good number of Hungarian pix to his credit, shows directorial skill and brilliance in many sequences. At times, the film appears overly slow and a bit long. The different mentality may be admitted but it can't be overlooked that the pic is repetitious. However, this is another prestige item for Hungary. Technically, it's a fine effort, the color being a particular asset. *Hans.*

Le Coup De Grace
(FRENCH)

Paris, March 16.
Setec release of Sofracima-Roger Blais Films production. Stars Danielle Dar-

rieux, Emmanuelle Riva; features Michel Piccoli, Jean-Jacques Legarde. Directed and written by Jean Cayrol, Claude Durand. Camera, J. M. Bousaguet; editor, Odile Terzieff. Previewed in Paris. Running Time, **105 MINS.**

Helene	Danielle Darrieux
Sophie	Emmanuelle Riva
Bruno	Michele Piccolo
Jean	Jean-Jacques Legarde

A valid subject, the return of a man who denounced many people to the Germans during the last war. His face is changed and he has his imbroglios with families of those he had destroyed. But it is handled in a too talky, static a manner to make this anything but arty house fodder abroad, and limited at best even for this.

The returned informer falls in love with the sister of one of his victims. The family is a gray lot, full of self pity, whining and aimlessness that is suddenly jolted when word comes that the squealer may be back in town.

Finally unmasked, he hides in an old submarine pit only to be shot down like a dog. Michel Piccoli does imbue the denouncer part with a feeling of hopelessness and almost squalid lifelessness. But the slow direction, aimless dialog and plodding action rarely give this the needed drama.

Danielle Darrieux is adequate as the wife of a man sent up by the returnee. But Emmanuelle Riva is too full of overdone mannerisms as the old maidish girl who falls for the doomed man. Its theme may get it some specialized play here. But it does not shape up with the needed quality for better chances abroad.

Lensing is sombre and gray in keeping with the mood. Firsttime directors Jean Cayrol and Claude Durand rely too much on talk to give this a more visual flair.

Mosk.

The Ipcress File
(BRITISH-COLOR)

Spy thriller introducing Len Deighton's investigator Harry Palmer. Short on thrills, but neat characterizations plus able, arty direction; sound booking for all situations.

London, March 23.
Rank release of a Harry Saltzman production. Stars Michael Caine; features Nigel Green, Guy Doleman, Sue Lloyd, Gordon Jackson. Directed by Sidney J. Furie. Screenplay, Bill Canaway and James Doran from Len Deighton's novel; camera, (Technicolor); Otto Heller; editor, Peter Hunt; music, John Barry. At Leicester Square Theatre, London, March 18, '65. Running Time, **109 MINS.**

Harry Palmer	Michael Caine
Dalby	Nigel Green
Ross	Guy Doleman
Jean	Sue Lloyd
Carswell	Gordon Jackson
Radcliffe	Aubrey Richards
Bluejay	Frank Gatliff
Barney	Thomas Baptiste
Housemartin	Oliver MacGreevy
Alice	Freda Bamford
Charlady	Pauline Winter
Edwards	Anthony Blackshaw
Inspector Keighley	Stanley Meadows
Sir Robert	Peter Ashmore
Police Station Sgt.	Glynn Edwards
Prison Doctor	Szolt Vadaszffy

The James Bond films have a strong lead in the motion picture spy field in Britain, though plenty new runners are threatened. Harry Saltzman and A. R. Broccoli, who produce the Bond razamatazz, are diversifying by bringing to the screen a kind of "anti-Bond" spy in the character of Harry Palmer, based on Len Deighton's novel, "The Ipcress File." The result is probably rather more true to the facts of Intelligence life than the Bond world of fantasy but the present offering is at time so soft-pedalled that audiences will probably be screaming for more kicks and more of the glamorous, rollicking nonsense that puts the Bond pix into a class of their own.

However, despite the shortage of thrills and other defects, "Ipcress File" is a soundly made film which should prove a worthwhile booking at most situations. It has an intelligent director, Sidney J. Furie, excellent color lensing and a leading actor, Michael Caine, who has considerable star potential. Shrewdly used London locations as a background to the plot also give the film a useful ring of authenticity.

Intelligence man Harry Palmer (Michael Caine) is an undisciplined sergeant who is seconded to intelligence work and finds that it is more legwork and filling in forms then inspired hunches and glamorous adventure. Unlike, Bond, Palmer is a fairly undistinguished young man who wears spectacles, cooks his own meals and gets results despite his occasional blunders rather than by a flash technique. He has an eye for dames and a cool line of insolent chatter but is almost completely the opposite of Bond in appearance, outlook and behavior. The image is unlikely to topple that of Secret Agent 007, but may well find its own following.

Present adventure concerns the steps taken to retrieve a missing boffin and involves the agent being captured by the enemy and subjected to acute brainwashing. There is the odd murder or so, but these are done in a matter of fact way, totally unlike the bizarre cloak-and-dagger feats of the Ian Fleming yarns. The screenplay is an interesting one when its various episodes are considered, but Bill Canaway and James Doran have not invested it with any real high spots. Pic does not build up to the type of suspense usually demanded of such thrillers.

Furie's direction, allied with Otto Heller's camera, provides some striking effects. But sometimes he gets carried away into arty-crafty fields with low angle shots and symbolism adding to the confusion of the screenplay instead of tightening the slim storyline. There is a Hitchcockian atmosphere, in that much of the action takes place against unspectacular backgrounds, such as a science museum, a traffic jam in a London street, a supermarket, a huge underground carpark and the unglamorous offices in which the investigator and his superiors work.

Caine obviously is a very good actor and he skillfully resists any temptation he may have had to pep up the proceedings. In fact, his consistent underplaying adds considerably to the pull of the picture. Nigel Green and Guy Doleman, playing Caine's rival superiors, both give excellent performances. Green, in particular making much of the ex-Army major who doesn't quite ring true.

Sue Lloyd is an attractive leading femme as the colleague of Caine, but does not get many opportunities for showing her prowess. Gordon Jackson, Thomas Baptiste, Frank Gatliff, Oliver MacGreevy, Freda Bamford and Aubrey Richards are among a large cast who stand out. And it is one of the film's credits that so many not-too-familiar faces are used, thus adding a lot to the realism.

John Barry has given the film some twangy music. Peter Hunt's cutting is smoothly efficient. Overall, the film largely achieves the non-spectacular effects at which it has clearly aimed. But it would have helped if Furie's direction had been a little less stylised, particularly in the very long brainwashing torture sequence and a trifle more lively in the "documentary" aspect. *Rich.*

Zebra in the Kitchen
(COLOR)

Animal comedy has enough slapstick and animal scenes to appeal to grade schoolers, who also may be interested because Jay North, tv's Dennis the Menace, is starred.

Metro release of Ivan Tors Production. Features Jay North, Martin Milner, Andy Devine. Directed by Ivan Tors. Screenplay, Art Arthur, based on story by Elgin Ciampi; camera (Metrocolor), Lamar Boren; editor, Warren Adams; music, Warren Barket; assistant director, Eddie Saeta. Reviewed at Picwood Theatre, L.A., March 13, 1965. Running Time, **92 MINS.**

Chris Carlyle	Jay North
Dr. Del Hartwood	Martin Milner
Branch Hawksbill	Andy Devine
Isobel Moon	Joyce Meadows
Adam Carlyle	Jim Davis
Anne Carlyle	Dorothy Green
Wilma Carlyle	Karen Green
Councilman Pew	Vaughn Taylor
Sergeant Freebee	John Milford
Councilman Lawrence	Tris Coffin
Chief of Police	Merritt Bohn
Sheriff	Robert Clarke
Mr. Richardson	Percy Helton
Tim	Jimmy Stiles
Kookie	Dal Jenkins
Ribs	Gordon Wescourt
Greenie	Gary Judis
Preston Heston	Robert Lowery
Newscaster	Wayne Thomas
Nearsighted Man	Doodles Weaver
Judge	Jon Lormer
Man in Man-Hole	Vince Barnett
Man in Tub	Phil Arnold

"Zebra In The Kitchen" is another pleasant and interesting animal feature from Ivan Tors that should appeal chiefly to grade school set. Starring role for TV's Dennis, Jay North, should hold some marquee appeal. Adults probably will not be attracted to attend alone. Parents who take children will find story and characterizations over-simplified and in many instances, over-stereotyped. But Lamar Boren's color photography is attractive, and slapstick scenes of escaping zoo animals taking over town will amuse all in audience.

Despite title, animal star is tame wildcat Jay North has raised from cub on farm. When family moves to city, cat must be put in zoo, headed by Martin Milner, as animal expert, and Andy Devine, head keeper. Zoo is outmoded and woefully inadequate, but Milner's appeals to Council for new facilities go unheeded.

Milner portrays role with unsmiling grimness, while Devine plays frog-voiced, kind-hearted buffoon he has delineated during past 30 years and more. Jay North runs through his scenes with little

more effort than would be devoted to a vidseries. In fact, the human actors are virtual bit players manipulated to bring about film's big sequence, in which Jay unlocks animal cages and zoo beasts go frolicking off to town. This permits numerous brief scenes of character actors reacting to sudden appearance of zebra in kitchen, elephant in window, tigers in hall.

Tors' direction is most effective in this sequence, which isn't surprising considering 108 animals used were trained by him on his "Africa U.S.A." ranch near Palmdale.

Jim Davis and Dorothy Green are sympathetic as Jay's parents. Joyce Meadows, aide to Milner, has little to do except hand over hypos at proper times. Other roles are adequately filled.

Editing by Warren Adams was effective, and seems largely responsible for good pace of what could have been pedestrian footage of pedestrial script by Art Arthur. Warren Barker's score and Hal Hopper's title tune, sung by The Standells, have rocking beat appropriate for age group at which pic is aimed. Location for outmoded cramped zoo was well chosen—LA's own Griffith Park Zoo. *Hogg.*

Le Vampire De Dusseldorf
(The Vampire of Dusseldorf)
(FRENCH-FRANSCOPE)

Paris, March 16.
Rank release of Rome Paris Films-Benito Perojo production. Stars Robert Hossein; features Marie-France Pisier, Roger Duthoit, Paloma Valdes, Danick Patisson. Directed by Robert Hossein. Screenplay, Claude Desailly, Georges and Andre Tabet, Hossein; camera, Andre Levent; editor, Sophie Dubus. Previewed in Paris. Running Time, **90 MINS.**

| Peter | Robert Hossein |
| Anna | Marie-France Pisier |

Based on the same case that inspired Fritz Lang's famed German pic, "M," and the lesser American remake by Joe Loesy, director-actor Robert Hossein has wisely not tried to emulate the original. He sticks closer to the facts and comes up with an okay if cursory look at a twisted murderer of women whom love might have saved.

Hossein has as sidelights the growing Nazi terror and rise to power (takes place in 1930). The killer seems out of this politico angle and is a worker who dresses up as a middle-class type at night to haunt lowlife dives and look for women.

His murders come from sudden rages of need or refusal by women. But one day he finds a little, loose singer who seems to love him. She too goes the way of the others before he is caught. Hossein walks through this with grim, sickly detachment, but cannot suggest the battle within the man or the real psychological currents.

Marie-France Pisier, a pouting, callow young actress, is hard put to emerge a femme fatale who sings with whip and tights in the manner of Marlene Dietrich in "The Blue Angel" of Josef Von Sternberg.

Hossein obviously has seen and assimilated many of these pix and does not imitate but takes the ideas and aspects of the times. But this only a moderate suspense item, which may be an okay playoff item on its theme, with arty chances abroad chancey. *Mosk.*

Sommer i Tyrol
(Summer in Tyrol)
(DANISH-SONGS-COLOR)

Vienna, March 16.
Europa Film release of Merry Film (Henrik Sandberg) production. Stars Dirch Passer and Susse Wolt. Directed by Erik Balling. Screenplay, Balling, adapted from operetta, "White Horse Inn," by Ralph Benatzky and Robert Stolz; camera, (Eastmancolor), Jorgen Skov; music, Ralph Genatzky, Robert Stolz; editor, Erik Balling. At Kuenstlerhauskino, Viennese Fest of Gaiety. Running Time, 95 MINS.
Leopold .... Dirch Passer
Josepha .... Susse Wolt
Sigismund .... Ove Sprogoe
Clara .... Lone Hertz
Emperor Fr. Joseph ...... Peter Malberg

For the record, this is the fourth filmization of the Austrian operetta, "White Horse Inn," and the 100th film in which music by Robert Stolz is heard. The music by Stolz and Ralph Benatzky, who share composing credits, is the best thing about this Danish operetta film.

Pic is somewhat on the naive side yet amusing enough to please many filmgoers. "Summer in Tyrol" is a success in its home country because of its catchy music and some lovable characters including some pretty girls. Pic may succeed in some foreign markets. But it is nothing for the crix.

Funny thing about this is its title. The locale of the White Horse Inn is actually not Tyrol but Salzkammergut in Austria where film also was made.

The standout role of the waiter Leopold is played by Dirch Passer, Denmark's most popular cinema comedian. He's funny but could be better in a more demanding role. Two of the lovely girls are Susse Wolt and Lone Hertz, the former looking like promising talent. Even the old Austrian Emperor, Franz Joseph, played by Peter Malberg, shows up in this.

Erik Balling, director of countless Danish comedies, patterned this primarily for Danish taste. The camera cashed in on its many opportunities. There is a series of beautiful Austrian landscapes in this pic which was produced by Henrik Sandberg for about $200,000. *Hans.*

In Harm's Way
(PANAVISION)

Sea action-romantic drama set in Pacific immediately after Pearl Harbor. Big boxoffice.

Hollywood, March 30.
Paramount release of Otto Preminger production, directed by Preminger. Stars John Wayne, Kirk Douglas, Patricia Neal; features Brandon De Wilde, Burgess Meredith, Tom Tryon, Paula Prentiss, Henry Fonda, Dana Andrews. Screenplay, Wendell Mayes from book by James Bassett; camera (Panavision), Loyal Griggs; special photography, Farciot Edouart; special effects, Lawrence W. Butler; editors, George Tomasini, Hugh S. Fowler; music, Jerry Goldsmith; ass't. directors, Daniel McCauley, Howard Joslin, Michael Daves. Reviewed at Directors Guild of America, March 26, '65. Running Time, 165 MINS.
Capt. Rockwell Torrey ...... John Wayne
Commander Paul Eddington Kirk Douglas
Lt. Maggie Haynes .... Patricia Neal
Lt. (jg) William McConnel .. Tom Tryon
Bev McConnel .... Paula Prentiss
Ensign Jeremiah Torrey
                        Brandon De Wilde
Ensign Annalee Dorne .... Jill Haworth
Admiral Broderick .... Dana Andrews
Clayton Canfil ...... Stanley Holloway
Commander Powell ... Burgess Meredith
CINCPAC I Admiral ...... Franchot Tone
Comdr. Neal Owynn..... Patrick O'Neal
Lt. Comdr. Burke...... Carroll O'Connor
CPO Culpepper .... Slim Pickens
Liz Eddington........ Barbara Bouchet
Airforce Major .... Hugh O'Brian
CINCPAC II Admiral....... Henry Fonda
Ensign Griggs .... James Mitchum
Col. Gregory .... George Kennedy
Quartermaster Quoddy.... Bruce Cabot
Captain Tuthill.......... Tod Andrews
Lt. (jg) Cline .... Larry Wagman
Ensign Balch .... Stewart Moss
Lt. (jg) Tom Agar....... Richard Le Pore
Ship's Doctor .... Chet Stratton
Tearful Woman............. Soo Young
Boston .... Dort Clark
PT-Boat Skipper .... Phil Mattingly

While the framework of the plot is conventional in terms of characters and incidents, director-producer Otto Preminger has charged these basic elements with uncommon vitality and, moreover, has crowded the screen with rousing land, sea and air action that should make "In Harm's Way" a big winner.

That John Wayne dominates a cast of uniformly expert performers, including some doing bit roles who are accustomed to bigger assignments, should not be surprising either. This picture was tailored for Wayne. He is in every sense the big gun of "In Harm's Way." Without his commanding presence, chances are Preminger probably could not have built the head of steam this film generates and sustains for two hours and 45 minutes.

The title, incidentally, was inspired by John Paul Jones, "father" of the United States Navy: "I wish to have no connection with any ship that does not sail fast, for I intend to go in harm's way . . ."

Although the personal drama that unites and divides the lives of Navy people caught up in this dramatization of U.S. efforts to strike back within the year after the Pearl Harbor disaster won't win any prizes for creativity, Preminger uses it effectively to establish a bond between the characters and the audience.

It's a full, lusty slice of life in a time of extreme stress that Wendell Mayes has fashioned from the novel by James Bassett and which Preminger has artfully guided so that incidents of adultery, rape, suicide, opportunism and stupidity

in high command—not to overlook a couple of pungent but typically salty expressions—come across naturally, making their intended impression without battering the audience. This film is as good an example as any of what by now is an old Hollywood adage, "It's not what you do, but the way that you do it."

Romantic coupling of Wayne and Patricia Neal, as a Navy nurse, is the most natural stroke of *man and woman* casting in many a year. Both carry illfated marriage scars when they meet—Wayne with an opportunistic, still wet-behind-the-ears ensign son, who resents his father. The old seadog and the middleaged, still attractive nurse, are quickly magnetized, but conduct themselves with mature appreciation in having found a second chance for happiness within the shadow of ever present danger of quick, violent death.

Miss Neal brings to her role a beautifully proportioned, gusty strength and sensitivity, heightened by nuances of a woman desperately hoping to have and hold her man. By a curiously ironic turn of fate, Wayne, shortly after completing the picture, underwent a lung operation for cancer, but is now his old self again and Miss Neal suffered two major strokes that required brain surgery, but again, appears to be making remarkable recovery.

Though skillful blending of fact and fiction, Preminger provides, in the picture's action stretches, a highly suspenseful and, at times shatteringly realistic, account of an underdog U.S. Navy task force boldly seeking out and trading salvos with a superior in numbers and firepower—but not in spirit—Japanese group of ships. The sea battle sequences are filmmaking at its best. There is also a savage, starkly painful power to the sneak attack that virtually destroyed Pearl. Preminger doesn't spare the gunpowder or the props, and it should make for boff payoff.

There are some heroics that come out of a traditional mold and fall to Kirk Douglas to carry off as a hard-drinking exec officer, and buddy of Wayne, brooding the loss at Pearl of his double-timing wife. Douglas comes through rousingly in a broad and aggressive performance that gives off sparks. Henry Fonda, as the four-star boss of this Navy show, moves in and out of the story, hitting the mark every time.

Next to Wayne, Douglas and Miss Neal—the lead trio—Brandon De Wilde has the most footage; at least, it seems that way. As the ensign son, his character is the kind that invites a spanking, up to the point when he finally grows up emotionally and gets some of his old man's horse sense to boot. A nicely balanced job for De Wilde.

Indeed, the acting generally is first cabin. So for those whose contribution in footage may be on the smaller side, but nonetheless important to the cumulative effect, a well done to Jill Haworth, Dana Andrews, Franchot Tone, Stanley Holloway, Patrick O'Neal, Hugh O'Brian, Carroll O'Connor, Slim Pickens, James Mitchum, George

Kennedy and Bruce Cabot, among others.

Burgess Meredith has a meaty role as a Hollywood writer serving as an intelligence officer, a part that takes him pretty much through the picture, and handles it with his characteristic expertness. As a husband - wife combo, Tom Tryon and Paula Prentiss, individually and together, have several nicely turned sequences. However, it seems that in a reunion interlude, after Tryon had been believed lost in action, Preminger went a bit overboard in portraying the wife's longing to be left with child when the husband is summoned back to sea.

The director-producer might also be faulted for an aggressively sexy opening sequence, the night before Dec. 7, 1941, at a Pearl Navy bash where Barbara Bouchet (as the wanton wife of the absent Douglas) writhes and wiggles a Marine Corps major, (O'Brian) into a night on the beach that ends in disaster for both. There's nothing really objectionable for adults about these sequences, but there could be reservations about exposing to youngsters, whom the film should strongly attract with its action elements.

Much of the force of "In Harm's Way" comes from expert blending of technical skills which provide the magic that makes all things possible in motion pictures. A salute is appropriate for the Panavision photography by Loyal Griggs, Farciot Edouart and Philip Lathrop, second unit cameraman; special effects work by Lawrence W. Butler (miniatures of ships in battle are excellent except for one fleeting moment); production designer Lyle Wheeler; editors George Tomasini (since deceased) and Hugh S. Fowler; sound editor Don Hall Jr., and to Jerry Goldsmith for an appropriate music score, as well as to others behind the cameras.

Finally, whether or not the Mayes screenplay is faithful to Bassett's novel is a question this review will leave hanging. But on its own terms "In Harm's Way" is a compelling action-drama-romance. This is an accomplished work of picturemaking which should be gratifying to Preminger —just as it seems destined to please audiences generally. *Pry.*

The Sword of Ali Baba
(COLOR)

Arabian Night type escapism. For family trade in general runs.

Universal Pictures release of a Howard Christie production. No stars. Features Peter Mann, Jocelyn Lane, Peter Whitney, Gavin MacLeod, Greg Morris, Frank Puglia, Frank McGrath. Directed by Virgil Vogel. Screenplay, Oscar Brodney; camera (Eastman Color), William Margulies; editor, Gene Palmer; no music credits. Reviewed at Universal homeoffice, N.Y., March 19, '65. Running Time: 81 MINS.
Ali Baba .... Peter Mann
Amara .... Jocelyn Lane
About .... Peter Whitney
Hulagu Khan .... Gavin MacLeod
Prince Cassim .... Frank Puglia
Pindar .... Frank McGrath
Yusuf .... Greg Morris
Baba .... Frank DeKova
Captain of Guard ..... Morgan Woodward

Hoping that boxoffice lightning will strike twice in the same spot, this Universal loose remake of its 1951 "Prince Who Was A Thief" is meant to introduce new talent Peter Mann and Jocelyn Lane as the earlier film did Tony Curtis and Piper Laurie. While nothing great as a cinematic offering, "Sword of Ali Baba" is a pleasant trifle that should make an adequate showing in the general market.

Something of a mutation in that it borrows not only from the earlier "Prince" and the Arabian Nights but unabashedly from some of Universal's Maria Montez epics, "Sword" (which, technically, should be "Scimitar" as the setting is Baghdad) has a couple of refreshing variations on its earlier forms.

Yusuf, played in the 1951 "Prince" by character actor Everett Sloane as the foster-father of the prince-turned- thief, has now become a Negro slave and bodyguard to the Princess (Jocelyn Lane). As played by Greg Morris, he's a handsome young athletic type with plenty of opportunity to show off his athletic prowess which is on a par with titleroler Peter Mann.

Director Virgil Vogel had little to inspire him from Oscar Brodney's patchwork screenplay (whose original sources went as far back as the Arabian Nights) but has properly provided plenty of fast movement, fight scenes and only a touch of romance. William Margulies' camerawork was concerned more with matching recent footage with color work of stock shots used plentifully throughout the film, not always successfully. Although credited (but not on screen) as Eastman Color, process is too heavy on blue tones that make some scenes washed out. As first version was made in Technicolor, it must have been difficult to prevent visual conflict.

Among supporting cast, Gavin MacLeod's villain is helped more by his voice than by the very poor makeup. Colorful and outstanding enough to warrant him third billing, the 285-pound Peter Whitney brings both comic ability and physical impressiveness to part of Abou, a member of Ali Baba's gang of thieves.

Carefully slotted, film has adventure appeal to youngsters and adults who aren't too selective. Dramatically, it will likely do little to further anyone's career. *Robe.*

Il Momento Della Verita
(The Moment of Truth)
(SPANISH-ITALIAN—COLOR)

Rome, March 23.
Cineriz release of Federiz (Rome)— A. S. Film (Madrid) coproduction. Features Miguel Mateo Miguelin, Jose Gomez Sevillano, Pedro Basauri Pedrucho, Linda Christian. Directed by Francesco Rosi. Story and screenplay, Rosi, Pedro Portabella, Ricardo Munoz Suay, Pedro Beltran; camera (Technicolor), Gianni di Venanzo, Ajace Parolin, Pasquale de Santis; editor, Mario Serandrei; music, Piero Piccioni. At Adriano, Rome. Running time, 110 MINS.

With his latest film, director Francesco Rosi has managed a bright, colorful, dramatic and terrifying fresco of Spain today to serve as backdrop to a socially-keyed tale of a bullfighter's career. Pic looms a good money-earner here on word-of-mouth and content, with offshore slotting aimed at a more specialized clientele both in art and general circles.

Plot is straightforward, showing the wanderings of a Spanish village youth in an increasingly desperate search for a job in the big city, his turning to a bullfighting career as a way to a fast peseta, and the eventual breakdown under pressure. There is his ultimate, absurd death in an out-of-the-way hinterland corrida. But around this basic skein, Rosi has spun a vivid and frightening picture of exploitation and greed, of the seeming timelessness of an unchanging social structure persisting in Spain where—says Rosi by symbolic implication—a youth is forced into a dangerous profession if he desires to break out of a pattern of conformity. But even by doing so, he risks death daily, and eventually succumbs.

The director is in control all the way, eliciting positive performances from non-pros, pros and semi-pros alike. Mateo Miguelin, a bullfighter in real life, registers as the villager who becomes the celebrated matador. Linda Christian effectively limns a brief bit as a society gal who plays the corrida circuit.

Others in the vast, colorful cast lend bright backing. Special nods go to Gianni di Venanzo for his outstanding Technicolor-Techniscope lensing, often using shoulder-held cameras in documentary fashion, with telling effect and realistic impact. Piero Piccioni's music is similarly well-keyed to assist the picture's final effect.

Soundtrack with equal effect registers the sounds and echoes of the Spanish scene, the only jarring note being the Italian dubbing of principals, which disturbs otherwise uniform note of realism.

But in the final resume, it's director Rosi's hardhitting if not always smooth cinematic technique which makes this one of the outstanding films of the Italian year so far. His transposition into cinematic and entertaining terms of the age-old problems of Spanish traditionalisms, conformisms, and silent abeyance to century-old dominance of Church and State, provoke thought without resorting to the easier rabble-rousing tactics of less talented filmmakers.

Above all, from the spectator point-of- view, he manages ably to blend his polemics with his dramatic, entertainment values. *Hawk.*

La Vieille Dame Indigne
(The Unworthy Old Woman)
(FRENCH)

Paris, March 30.
UGC release of SPAC production. With Sylvie, Marika Ribovska, Etienne Bierry, Francois Maistre, Jean Bouise, Victor Lanoux. Written and directed by Rene Allio from a short story by Bertolt Brecht. Camera, Denis Clairval; editor, Sophie Coussein. Previewed in Paris. Running time, 90 MINS.
Old Lady .... Sylvie
Rosalie .... Marika Ribovska
Albert .... Etienne Bierry
Gaston .... Francois Maistre
Pierre .... Victor Lanoux
Alphonse .... Jean Bouise

Salutary fable concerns an old lady who finds a freedom in the last year of her life from family drudgery. More idea than deeper characterization, this still has a forthy gentle progression and inventiveness. It could be a specialized item, with some dualer playoff values also inherent in it.

A black-garbed woman is left alone when her old husband dies. Her sons and daughters gather and, after the burial, decide to give her a small pension. But she begins to get interested in life around her, meets some people she likes, sells all the old supposedly sentimental things and has a last year of freedom and change before dying.

Meanwhile some family members resent her seeming eccentric behavior and a grandson even has an affair with the young friend who has helped the old woman change beneficially before the end. But there is no preaching here, if the characters are familiar.

It is octagenarian actress Sylvie's blithe, gentle presence, with a hint of her inner resources, that carries the pic and gives it a gentle humor and an acceptable didactic ring. Her discoveries and reactions are always bright and sans artifice. Her flowering freedom is an achievement rather than any sort of crochety revolt.

Other characters revolve around her adequately. Rene Allio, as a set designer turning director for the first time, shows a flair for observation that is done more visually than in chatter.

Film still remains essentially thin and lacks the needed depth of the woman's change. But, as is, it is an engaging if fragile pic. This needs the right placement and handling for best results. *Mosk.*

Joey Boy
(BRITISH)

Some yocks, but this is a dated army comedy which will satisfy only the easygoing, despite the talent on parade.

British Lion presentation (through BLC) of a Sidney Gilliat, Leslie Gilliat, Frank Launder production. Stars Harry H. Corbett, Stanley Baxter, Bill Fraser, Percy Herbert, Lance Percival, Reg Varney; features Edward Chapman, Moira Lister, Derek Nimmo, Sean Lynch, Nora Nicholson, Eric Pohlmann, Thorley Walters. Directed by Launder. Screenplay, Launder and Mike Watts, based on Eddie Chapman's novel; camera, Arthur Lavis; editor, John Shirley; music, Philip Green. Previewed at Studio One, London. Running Time, 91 MINS.
Joey Boy Thompson......Harry H. Corbett
Benny Lindowski..........Stanley Baxter
Sgt. Dobbs .... Bill Fraser
Mad George Long........ Percy Herbert
Clarence Doubleday ..... Lance Percival
Rabbit Malone .... Reg Varney
Brigadier Chapman .... John Arnatt
Rabbit's Second Girl...... Yvonne Ball
General .... Basil Dignam
Anna .... Stephanie Beaumont
Signals Officer .... John Harvey
Sir John Averycorn........Lloyd Lamble
Lady Thameridge .... Moira Lister
Clancy .... Sean Lynch
Middle Aged Lady........Nora Nicholson
Lieut. Hope .... Derek Nimmo
Angie .... Toni Palmer
Italian Farmer .... Eric Pohlmann
Inspector Morgan .... John Phillips
R. A. Corporal ..... Norman Rossington
Ticket Collector .... Bill Shine
Bella .... Veronica Strong
Lt. Walther .... Ernest Walder
Colonel .... Thorley Walters

The experienced Frank Launder-Sidney Gilliat team has done much in the past to shape British film comedy, but this one is strictly oldhat. It garners a few easy and predictable laughs but is about 20 years out-of-date in plot and handling, despite plenty of talent having been recruited among technicians and actors. A safe enough booking for easygoing audiences, but it adds no lustre to the reps of its makers or of British films generally.

Based on a novel by Eddie Chapman, it tells of a bunch of layabouts who are drafted into the army (the alternative being the cooler) and continue their natural-born fiddling. For awhile they run a flourishing undercover gambling and liquor club for their army mates, exploit the black market and outsmart their officers and NCO's. Then they're shipped abroad, but keep up their fiddling and their malingering and are eventually after V-E Day permitted to start a social club to keep up the troops' morale. They build up a joint that is a near-brothel and are in trouble when a delegation of Members of Parliament pay a surprise visit. For an hour or so, they manage to pull the wool over the visitors' eyes but eventually it all comes into the open.

This untidy, thin storyline is merely the excuse for a string of predictable incidents and gags, variations of which have all been seen before. And Launder has not brought a great deal of ingenuity to his direction. The screenplay is stuffed with cliches in that the British private soldier is mostly represented as a malingering, boozing, womanizing jerk, the sergeant major is a loud-mouthed martinet, the officers are nimcompoops, and so on.

Technical credits are all okay. Launder has assembled some sturdy performers, notably using sound feature players in bit roles. Harry H. Corbett in the title role again goes through a routine which is merely a variant of his Steptoe's son character. It seems time this worthy actor broke away from this kind of stuff, which has been his main film contribution lately, without reaching the standard of the Steptoe character. Percy Herbert, Lance Percival, Reg Varney and Stanley Baxter are his varied buddies. They extract the most fun out of their adventures with the pack mules used on their Italian adventures. Bill Fraser, as a stentorian sergeant-major; Derek Nimmo, playing a dopey lieutenant; Thorley Walters, Eric Pohlmann. John Arnatt and Norman Rossington are among those who offer okay contributions in a large cast.

The script brings in plenty of opportunities for shapely dames in cameo roles. But Moira Lister, as a snooty member of Parliament; Anna Gilchrist, as Percival's girl friend, and Toni Palmer, in a bedroom bit with Corbett, are the only ones who slightly register except as easy-on-the-eye torsos. *Rich.*

Operation Crossbow
(PANAVISION-COLOR)

Rambling but sometimes suspenseful melodrama of British efforts to thwart Germany's building of giant rockets in World War II; okay where war films are accepted.

Hollywood, March 25.

Metro release of Carlo Ponti production. Stars Sophia Loren, George Peppard, Trevor Howard, John Mills, Richard Johnson, Tom Courtenay; features Lilli Palmer, Paul Henreid, Helmut Dantine, Richard Todd, Sylvia Syms, Jeremy Kemp, Anthony Quayle, Barbara Rueting. John Fraser. Directed by Michael Anderson. Screenplay, Richard Imrie, Derry Quinn, Ray Rigby; original Duilio Coletti, Vittoriano Petrilii; camera (Metrocolor), Erwin Hillier; music, R o n Goodwin; editor, Ernest Walter; asst. director, Basil Rayburn. Reviewed at Hollywood Paramount Theatre, March 24, '65. Running time, 118 MINS.

Nora	Sophia Loren
Lieut. John Curtis	George Peppard
Professor Lindemann	Trevor Howard
General Boyd	John Mills
Robert Henshaw	Tom Courtenay
Duncan Sandys	Richard Johnson
Wing Commander Douglas Kendall	Richard Todd
Constance Babington Smith	Sylvia Syms
Bradley	Jeremy Kemp
Bamford	Anthony Quayle
Frieda	Lilli Palmer
Flight-Lieut. Andre Kenny	John Fraser
Hanna Reitsch	Barbara Rueting
General Ziemann	Paul Henreid
General Linz	Helmut Dantine

"Operation Crossbow" is a sometimes suspenseful war melodrama said to be based upon British attempts to find and destroy Germany's development of new secret weapons—long - range rockets—in the early days of World War II. Ambitiously filmed in Europe and boasting production values which may seem to catch the spirit of the monumental effort, what the Carlo Ponti production lacks primarily is a cohesive story line. In present form script fails to maintain sustained interest because of a plethora of sketchy incidents, some of them unexplained. Properly exploited, however, and snapped up with some judicious trimming, feature should do okay in markets where war films are acceptable.

If the name of Sophia Loren, topbilled in stellar lineup, would indicate she has one of the top roles the spectator will be disappointed. Actress is in for little more than a bit, albeit a key character in one sequence. George Peppard plays the chief protagonist in this rambling tale of a British espionage mission, whose members impersonate German scientists believed dead, sent to locate and transmit information on the underground installation where Nazis are working on their deadly project.

Script by Richard Imrie, Derry Quinn and Ray Digby recounts the story of this massive piece of detective work (known to British government as Operation Crossbow). Narrative runs from the first clue—a mysterious object on an aerial photograph, where the first successful launching of early German buzz-bombs took place—until the final British bombing and total destruction of the German installation. This is made possible by the efforts of Peppard and another agent.

Michael Anderson's direction is forceful despite the loose continuity afforded him and he builds to an exciting climax. English subtitles are used for the German dialog spoken in many of the German sequences, adding to the realism, and care apparently was exercised in the selection of locations which strike an interesting note.

Film gets its most effective boost from the knowledable special effects devised by Tom Howard, responsible for particularly realistic bombing scenes of both London and the Nazi rocket plant. In these later sequences the art direction of Elliot Scott provides an effective backdrop. One of the most spectacular sequences is the German tryout of its first V. I flying bomb, when a suicide squad individually meets with disaster and finally a famous femme pilot in an act of extreme heroism locates a vital fault, paving the way for the buzz-bombing of London.

Peppard acquits himself satisfactorily although unexplained is his flawless command of German so he can impersonate a German scientist. Miss Loren, who portrays the estranged wife of this scientist — nearly upsetting the British plan when she arrives on the scene and discovers Peppard isn't her husband—plays a lacklustre role without much enthusiasm, coming to a violent end when Lilli Palmer, the underground contact for the British, shoots her so there's no possibility of a security leak.

Miss Palmer though briefly seen furnishes a fascinating interlude of glamour in a fairly suspenseful sequence which sees the German police arrest one of the British agents for a murder committed by the man he's impersonating. Tom Courtenay is convincing here, facing a firing squad rather than reveal he isn't the man he claims. Jeremy Kemp as the agent who gets to the bomb installation with Peppard also socks over his character.

Real-life people, who participated in the war operation, are generally s m o o t h l y portrayed. Richard Johnson plays the British official charged with bringing Operation Crossbow to a successful conclusion; Patrick Wymark appears as Sir Winston Churchill in a few scenes; Trevor Howard is an English scientist, John Mills a high Intelligence officer, Richard Todd a wing commander, Sylvia Syms the femme who first sees the mysterious object leading to the quest. On the German side, Paul Henreid and Helmut Dantine are generals, Anthony Quayle a high Intelligence officer, Barabara Rueting the German woman pilot.

Remaining technical departments are generally well handled. Edwin Hiller's color photography in Panavision is excellent except for his lensing of Miss Loren; Ron Goodwin's music score strikes the proper note. *Whit.*

Beach Blanket Bingo
(COLOR)

Comedy with music aimed at youth market. Filled with inane s u b p l o t s, sometimes amusing and with a few good performances. An exploitation film that features scantily-clad boys and girls and lots of rock-styled songs.

Hollywood, April 3.

American-International Pictures release, produced by James H. Nicholson and Samuel Z. Arkoff. Stars Frankie Avalon, Annette Funicello, Deborah Walley, Harvey Lembeck, John Ashley, Jody McCrea, Donna Loren, Marta Kristen, Linda Evans; features Don Rickles, Paul Lynde, Buster Keaton, Earl Wilson, Bobbi Shaw. Directed by William Asher. Screenplay, Asher and Leo Townsend; camera (Panavision and Pathecolor), Floyd Crosby; editor, Fred Feitshans, Eve Newman; music, Les Baxter; art direction, Howard Campbell; sound, James Nelson; asst. director, Dale Hutchinson. Reviewed at Lytton Center, L.A., April 2, '65. Running time, 100 MINS.

Frankie	Frankie Avalon
Dee Dee	Annette Funicello
Bonnie Graham	Deborah Walley
Eric Von Zipper	Harvey Lembeck
Steve Gordon	John Ashley
Bonehead	Jody McCrea
Donna	Donna Loren
Lorelei	Marta Kristen
Sugar Kane	Linda Evans
South Dakota Slim	Timothy Carey
Animal	Donna Michelle
Butch	Mike Nadler
Patti	Patti Chandler
The Hondells	Themselves
Rat Pack	Andy Romano, Allen Fife, Jerry Brutsche, John Macchia, Bob Harvey, Alberta Nelson, Myrna Ross
Big Drop	Don Rickles
Bullets	Paul Lynde
Buster Keaton	Himself
Earl Wilson	Himself
Bobbi	Bobbi Shaw

It is incredible how much director William Asher and his cowriter Leo Townsend have been able to fit into this newest bundle of beach tomfoolery. Every notion that might appeal to what the boxoffice has indicated is the current teenage taste is there. Not all of it is well done, polished, credible or even desirable in the normal sense of film development and construction.

If tunes with a beat, sloppy storylines with action and sentimental young romance and a bevy of half clad boys and girls with delicious looks are the points that satisfy, James H. Nicholson and Samuel Z. Arkoff will probably be again coining on a picture that strictly caters to the inanities of youth. It does nothing to lift their standards.

Basic story of "Bingo" is how girl (Annette Funicello) keeps boy (Frankie Avalon) when he reacts to the curves of cutie Linda Evans. To do it, they each go through daring feats of sky jumps, wild chases and softly "rough" and tumble bits until they, of course, fall back into each others arms. It's cute and precious.

Somehow, within the constant subplots, there comes a mermaid who falls in love with a nitwit played charmingly by Jody McCrea. And throughout are the Rat Pack, Harvey Lembeck's gang of idiot cyclists dressed in leather, stumbling all over themselves and looking like they should have stayed under a rock somewhere. Rats are joined by Timothy Carey as a satirical villain "Drunkard" style who has his own "Perils of Pauline" sawmill and gags it up with the girl about to get the blade. They do a lot of it in silent flicker speedup in a chase that has pure slapstick charge, moments of which are fun and funny.

No one can blame Nicholson and Arkoff for continuing a pattern that has made them money, but this is ridiculous. Are teenagers responding to such drivel as good natured satire of themselves rather than identifying with it? Let's hope so. But, not to lose a chance for a plug, producers tag the film with a credit line to "Watch for 'How to Stuff a Wild Bikini'," their next along these lines.

What is most pleasant about this frolic is the superb performance of Paul Lynde as the frothy, pushy talent manager whose major ambition is to get "pearls" for Earl Wilson. Wilson plays himself with the seriousness of a columnist who should never be an actor. Don Rickles, too, as the owner of the sky-diving school, works well in a role much like his nitery turn. He's a bundle of jolly grins and appealing mirth. And nothing could be better than Buster Keaton's gems of mime as a baggy-pants beachster running after scantly-clad Bobbi Shaw and ending with his great slapstick falls. Lembeck is so ridiculous he is funny as leader of the Pack, which also includes a gorgeous, statuesque b r u n e t t e named Myrna Ross whose "cool" performance makes her a standout.

Other than that, Miss Funicello's most noteworthy assets are the measurements she has developed since her "Mickey Mouse Club" days and Avalon is like a little boy who seems never to grow up. Pretty Donna Loren gets one song that kids may like and Deborah Walley and John Ashley are on for adequate scenes as another pair of jealous lovers.

Music with a beat is played by the Hondells and scored by Les Baxter, with lyrics by Guy Hemric, but dubbing of lyrics is badly off. Color, too, often seems washed out and dull. *Dale.*

The World Of Abbott & Costello
(Comedy Compilation)

Universal release of a Vanguard production. Bud Abbott and Lou Costello in scenes from films made for Universal. Produced by Max J. Rosenberg, Milton Subotsky; narration by Gene Wood, spoken by Jack E. Leonard; editorial direction, Sidney Meyer; music supervision, Joseph Gershenson. Reviewed at Universal h.o., New York, April 2, '65. Running time, 75 MINS.

Bud Abbott and Lou Costello, never as internationally successful as the Marx Bros. or as classic in their comedy style as Stan Laurel and Oliver Hardy, still managed a considerable span in motion pictures from the '40s through the early '50s.

From their big winner, "Buck Privates," through a series of films that provided varying backgrounds for their u n v a r y i n g routines, these alumni of burlesque pleased their following for a decade. It figures, then, that a film made up of scenes from several of their features should have some measure of appeal. With a short running time (75 mins.), "The World of Abbott and Costello" is evidently slated for second billing in most situations but might stand on its own if promoted and sold properly.

Producers Max J. Rosenberg and Milton Subotsky, faced with the task of which films to use (plus the fact that a few outside Universal features such as Metro's "A&C In Hollywood" and Warners' "A&C Meet Captain Kidd" would not be available), culled segments from 18 features. Sequences selected by editorial director Sidney Meyer are almost solid A&C, with other characters getting sparse film time. Nevertheless, a large assortment of familiar comedy faces flit through the various scenes, easily identifiable as Tom Ewell, Glenn Anders, Luis Alberni, Dorothy Grainger, Nat Pendleton, Thurston Hall, Lon Chaney, Bela Lugosi, Margaret Hamilton and others.

Connecting narration, written by Gene Wood and spoken by Jack E. Leonard, is properly sparse, merely enough to set the scene. Some animated titles by Gil Merit introduce A&C as cartoon characters to convey the few credits.

Although the order of sequence is not the same as that in which the films were released, all are similar enough to permit easy dissolves from scene to scene. Besides "Buck Privates," excerpts are used from "The Naughty Nineties," "Wistful Widow of Wagon Gap," "Hit The Ice," "Little Giant," "Mexican Hayride," "In The Navy," "Who Done It," "Go To Mars," "Lost In Alaska," "In The Foreign Legion," "Buck Privates Come Home," "Comin' Round The Mountain," "Ride 'Em Cowboy," "In Society," "Meet The Mummy," "Meet Frankenstein" and "Meet The Keystone Kops."

Rosenberg and Subotsky have only lightly tapped the source and have reservoir of unused features for a followup film should the success of this one indicate it. They still haven't touched "Rio Rita," "Pardon My Sarong," "The Noose Hangs High," "Africa Screams," "Meet Dr. Jekyll and Mr. Hyde," "Meet The Invisible Man" or "Meet The Killer." Then there's "Jack And The Beanstalk."

Besides the wonderfully silly drill scene from "Buck Privates," other choice bits included are their "Who's on first?" routine and a riotous sequence with Margaret Hamilton as a witch. A special item that could easily prove a winner. *Robe.*

Moi Et Les Hommes De Quarante Ans
(Me and The 40-Year Old Men) (FRENCH)

Paris, March 30.

Francoriz release of Franco London-Federiz-Eichberg production. Stars Dany Saval; features Michel Serrault, Michel Galabru, Paul Hubschmidt, Paul Meurisse. Directed by Jack Pinoteau. Screenplay, Paul Andreota, Philippe Bouvard, Pinoteau; camera, Raymond Lemoigne; editor, Borys Lewin. At Balzac, Paris. Running Time, 95 MINS.

Caroline	Dany Saval
Husband	Michel Serrault
Nicolas	Michel Galabru
Doctor	Paul Hubschmidt
Millionaire	Paul Meurisse

Comedy of a featherbrained but honest little sexpot trying to find a husband among settled 40-year-old men, before settling down with her own generation, is somewhat too laborious to have its telegraphed mixture of ribald, sentimental and situation comedy come off. It is mainly a local bet with only dualer uses abroad.

Dany Saval is somewhat vulgar and wide eyed. But she's an okay if scrawny looker. If without the charm to give a comedic balance to her innocence among the predatory middleaged men. There are three married men, a snobbish doc, a brash salesman and a millionaire who vie for her before she brushes them all.

Director Jack Pinoteau has given this workmanlike if uninspired mounting to have the comedy forced and the playing uneven. It may be an okay local bet. Film has a good production and technical envelope. *Mosk.*

Die Lustigen Weiber von Windsor
(The Merry Wives of Windsor) (AUSTRIAN—COLOR)

Vienna, March 23.

Elite Film release of Norman Foster production. Stars Norman Foster, Colette Boky, Mildred Miller, Igor Gorin. Directed by Georg Tressler. Screenplay, Norman Foster, based on opera of same name by Otto Nicolai; camera (Technicolor), Robert Hofer, Sepp Riff; music, Otto Nicolai; choreography, Rosella Hightower; editor, Paula Dvorak. At Kuenstlerhauskino, Vienna Fest of Gaiety. Running Time, 98 MINS.

Sir John Falstaff	Norman Foster
Mrs. Fluth	Colette Boky
Mr. Fluth	Igor Gorin
Mrs. Reich	Mildred Miller
Mr. Reich	Edmond Hurshell
Anna Reich	Lucia Popp
Fenelon	Ernst Schuetz
Dr. Caius	John Gittings
Spaerlich	Marshall Raynor

Norman Foster, an American opera baritone residing in Vienna, has been responsible for this Technicolor filmization of the famous Otto Nicolai opera, "The Merry Wives of Windsor," at the fifth "Festival of Gaiety" in Vienna. The Bostonian-born singer had the idea to make this film, he wrote the script and produced the pic, and played the leading male role, Sir John Falstaff. Film, which was made in German and English version, is nothing much for intellectual flimgoers but looks to be a commercial item. It benefits from beautiful color and costumes. All in all, it's a fast-running pic with a series of pleasant optical and scenic gags. Foreign possibilities seem strong.

Also this Austrian production may be termed an interesting document for it gives opera lovers in distant areas the opportunity to see a first-class opera production. In addition, it is something for future generations. The singers are excellent. In particular, this goes for Foster and Colette Boky. Latter, a Canadian soprano, is also an optical treat. It is a gay and dynamic opera filmization with singers who also can act.

Austrian Georg Tressler has contributed a competent directorial job within limits. The camera work deserves compliments, too. This Norman Foster production, incidentally, was given "the highest artistic distinction" by the Austrian film classification board. Understood that such a distinction hasn't been given in Austria for the last three years.

Ambitious Norman Foster intends to bring more opera filmizations to the screen. Bizet's "Carmen" is to be next. *Hans.*

Le Corniaud
(The Jerk) (FRENCH-ITALIAN-COLOR)

Paris, April 6.

Valoria release of Corona-Explorer Film production. Stars Bourvil, Louis De Funes; features Beba Loncar. Directed by Gerard Oury. Screenplay, Oury, Marcel Jullian, Georges and Andre Tabet; camera (Eastman-Color), Henri Decae; editor, Albert Jurgenson. At Mercury, Paris. Running time, 105 MINS.

Saroyan	Louis De Funes
Antoine	Bourvil
Ursula	Beba Loncar

Flippant title hides a breezy comedy that has some firstrate comics and enough inventiveness and perky progression to have this slanted for solid returns here, with commensurate foreign chances possible. Later chances seem best for arty houses if given the right sell. Word-of-mouth could help.

Pic mixes car chases, summery Italo feeling and two brilliantly juxtaposed funny men. All this makes it a generally entertaining film even though sometimes things tend to slow down. On the whole however, this is a refreshing surprise from France since it rarely does these pix so well.

It is obvious that this has been given a good production backing. Secondly, it has enough situation sequences to give its two leads an opportunity without making them seem forced. This should give comedians Bourvil and Louis De Funes some offshore mileage and recognition which they mainly have only at home these days.

De Funes, a wily, nervous gangster, picks Bourvil, a gentle, muddleheaded type, to drive a Cadillac loaded with dope, stolen goods and gold from Naples to Bordeaux. He feels that he looks so honest and dumb no customs men would suspect him. He also follows him in secret to see that all is well. But a rival gang is also in on the plot. So the chase goes on with Bourvil blithely feeling lucky and cheerful at his windfall.

De Funes is a middleaged, pugnacious man always on the verge of anger or beaming self esteem. His timing, facial contortions and blithe blending of the irascible and good heartedness makes his scenes all telling. Bourvil is more scatterbrained with an underlying peasant guile that also gets laughs.

These two thus complement each other well and get the most from the tightly paced, well plotted pic.

Film settles down to the chase of the unwitting Bourvil by both gangs, with some good car chases and gang fights and De Funes' tactics to keep from being seen by Bourvil. Some side bits with women hitchikers do not intrude and the final comeuppance of De Funes by Bourvil, when he finds out he is a fall guy, is well done.

Director Gerard Oury, an exactor, has heretofore made heavy-handed, bitter comedies stressing human pettiness. But here he manages to have a brighter, more easygoing flair. Of course, it's all helped by the comic lift of De Funes and Bourvil. Color is rightly mellow while the Italo countryside is also well captured by the camera. A good French comedy of this sort is rare, and it is clicking here. Supporting cast is tops. *Mosk.*

La Bonne Occase
(The Real Bargain) (FRENCH—FRANSCOPE)

Paris, March 23.

FOC release of CFC-Port Royal Films production. Stars Edwige Feuillere, Marie Jose-Nat, Jean-Claude Brialy, Jean-Louis Trintignant, Jacques Charrier, Francis Blanche, Darry Cowl. Directed by Michel Drach. Screenplay, Guy Bedos, Francois Billetdoux, Jean-Loup Dabadie, Rene Fallet, Albert Husson, Marcel Mithois, Rene De Obaldia, Jean Poiret, Michel Serrault; camera, Roger Fellous; editor, Genevieve Winding. At the Paris, Paris. Running Time, 90 MINS.

Gimmick here is a car that is owned by many people creating a link for a series of sketches. It also uses many widely-known pic, stage, screen and cabaret names. All does not mix well to keep this a sketchy, obvious and primarily local item.

But it does sum up something that symbolizes what is wrong with the film situation here. A young director who made two pix that had some personal flair and talent now tries to do an out-and-out commercial production—the others got only prestige but were not commercial successes.

But producer-director Michel Drach is not at home with the brash skepticism and vulgarity needed to bring off this type of comedy. Each comic situation is too well thought out and naturally losses impact.

Yarn shows an eccentric Countess who scares the daylights out of her secretary in wild ride in a new car and then sells it to an auto dealer. Plot then traces car from one owner to another.

Noted players offer okay silhouettes but the comedy is too obvious and is without the needed lift. It appears of limited export value and will only have so-so chances on its home grounds. *Mosk.*

Fluffy
(COLOR)

Light comedy about a friendly lion; escapist entertainment for dual situations.

Hollywood, April 3.

Universal release of Gordon Kay production. Stars Tony Randall, Shirley Jones; features Edward Andrews, Howard Morris, Ernest Truex, Jim Backus, Frank Faylen, Celia Kaye, Dick Sargent. Directed by Earl Bellamy. Screenplay, Samuel Roeca; camera (Eastmancolor), Clifford Stine; art direction, Alexander Golitzen, Walter Simonds; sound, Waldon O. Watson, Clarence Self; music, Irving Gertz; editor, Russell F. Schoengarth; asst. director, Phil Bowles. Reviewed at Academy Award Theatre, April 2, '65. Running time, 92 MINS.

Daniel Potter	Tony Randall
Janice	Shirley Jones
Griswald	Edward Andrews
Sweeney	Howard Morris
Claridge	Ernest Truex
Sergeant	Jam Backus
Catfish	Frank Faylen
Sally Brighton	Celia Kaye
Tommy	Dick Sargent
Bob Brighton	Adam Roarke
Dr. Braden	Whit Bissell
Mrs. Claridge	Harriet MacGibbon
Pete	Jim Boles
Police Captain	Parley Baer
Maid	Connie Gilchrist
State Trooper	Stuart Randall
Cook	Sammee Tong
Fireman No. 2	Barry O'Hara
Policeman	Sam Gilman
Tweedy Physicist	Milton Frome
Yokel	Doodles Weaver

"Fluffy" is a lightweight affair with all the fluff its title indicates. Some of the humor is pretty forced, but as strictly escapist fare the Gordon Kay production is laden with enough laughs to maintain nice momentum and qualifies as an entry for the nutty type of comedy. Star names of Tony Randall and Shirley Jones should spark chances at b.o.

Fluffy is a friendly lion who is the subject of a seven-year experiment by Randall, a biochestry professor at an institute of advanced science, to prove that everybody—even wild animals—can be nice if they're reared with proper training. When misinformed police move in with nets and tranquilizer guns to investigate reports there's a dangerous beast on the loose, Randall packs Fluffy into a car and checks into an apartment hotel across the state getting his lion upstairs without anybody realizing he's anything but a pet cat.

Sometimes it looks as though the director threw away the script and shot off his cuff as Fluffy's appearance created an uproar among the other guests, nub of most of the action which has Randall trying to convince everybody, including the police, that his lion loves people. Earl Bellamy's direction of Samuel Roeca's screenplay leans heavily upon sight gags, and there's the smacking, too, of old-time slapstick when anything went for a gag.

Randall gives a properly frenzied performance as he spends most of his time trying to find Fluffy, who has a habit of roaming and frightening people. Miss Jones, as daughter of the hotel owner whose apartment Randall rents, is a pretty foil, but there will be those who still prefer her blonde appearance rather than the dark brunette she now presents. She's a capable comedian, though, and patly fulfills demands of her part.

Kay, who backdrops his film with good production values, also has lined up a competent cast of comedians to support the two stars. Ernest Truex as Miss Jones' father, thought for a time devoured by the lion until it's discovered it's a venison leg Fluffy has been gnawing on, delivers another of his hesitant characters; Edward Andrews as the stuffy hotel manager amusingly underplays the role; Howard Morris has his moments as a drunk who owns a cat; Frank Faylen is Truex' buddy and Jim Backus a police sergeant. Fluffy is played by Zamba, well-trained and willing.

Technical credits are well handled by Clifford Stine, on color cameras; Alexander Golitzen and Walter Simonds, art direction; Irving Gertz, music score; Russell F. Schoengarth, editing. *Whit.*

La Fuga
(The Escape)
(ITALIAN)

Rome, March 30.
Dear Film release of a CINE 3 production. Features Giovanna Ralli, Anouk Aimee, Paul Guers, Enrica Maria Salerno, Carol Walker, Anita Sanders, Maurizio Arena, Jone Salinas, Guido Alberti. Directed by Paolo Spinola. Story and screenplay, Sergio Amidei; music, Piero Piccioni. At Ariston, Rome. Running time, 85 MINS.
Piera .... Giovanni Ralli
Luisa .... Anouk Aimee
Piera's husband .... Paul Guers
Psychiatrist ...... Enrica Maria Salerno

Paolo Spinola has tackled the controversial subject of lesbianism in this, his first pic effort. Despite an over-involved plot development, this touchy theme has been elegantly and tastefully developed, making this a thought-provoking, attention-getter for specialized outlets.

Told via an intricate web of flashbacks, dream sequences, and spoken commentary, the film tells of the sexual and emotional instability and dissatisfaction of a young married woman (Giovanna Ralli) who, after attempting in every way, to solve her quandries, is tempted into an unnatural relationship with an interior decorator (Anouk Aimee). Disgusted and confused, she commits suicide at finale.

Over-indulgent at times in its explanation of psychic disturbances, a bit too chopped up for smooth continuity, this nevertheless impresses via skillfull camera handling, adroit direction, especially of the two principles. It is most notable in the way it avoids any and all concessions to sensationalism implicit in its thematics and explicit in content of certain scenes.

Paul Guers and Enrico Maria Salerno are good as the two men; others backdrop neatly. Film boasts haunting music by Piero Piccioni and an outstanding lens job on colorful Italian locations.
Hawk.

3. November 1918
(3rd of November 1918)
(AUSTRIAN)

Vienna, March 30.
Neue Thalia Film release of Walfried Menzel production. Stars Erik Frey, Erich Auer, Walter Kohut. Directed by Edwin Zbonek. Screenplay, Franz Theodor Csokor, after his same-titled stage work; camera, Rudolf Sandtner. At Kuenstlerhauskino, Vienna. Running time, 90 MINS.
Oberst von Radosin.......... Erik Frey
Rittmeister Orvanyi .... Erich Auer
Oberleutnant Ludoltz......Walter Kohut
Oberleutnant Kaminski......Peter Weihs
Infantrist Josip .... Hugo Gottschlich
Leutnant Vanini .... Peter Matic
Oberleutnant Zierowitz..Wolfgang Gasser
Leutnant Sokal .... Hanns Obonya

Even if its outcome is not exactly convincing, this film can be classified as one of the more ambitious Austrian productions. Based on the stage work of same title, written by Franz Theodor Osokor, it deals with what happened to a group of Austrian officers at the end of the first World War. Pic may be interesting enough for the domestic market but foreign chances appear quite moderate. It's too much Austrian—which is one handicap.

The modest action takes place in a hospital for officers of the Austrian-Hungarian army somewhere up in the Austrian mountains. Snowstorms have disconnected the telephone line and the group up there is isolated from the outside world. The lineup of characters includes officers of several national descents for the then Austrian-Hungarian monarchy was not only composed of Austrians and Hungarians but also Serbs, Czech, Poles, Italians, etc. The end of the monarchy has inevitably come and talks center on such topics as heroism, discipline, faithfulness to the fatherland and future plans. Controversies of various kinds split the men, and their commander eventually commits suicide.

It's a rather talky film and one is always aware that this is originally a stage play. Also, one is always aware of film's modest budget (about $75,000) which, incidentally, was supplied by the Austrian educational ministry.

On the positive side Edwin Zbonek's direction is quite good. The cast was composed of Viennese stage actors. Zbonek, incidentally, has a good name as a Viennese stage director. "November 1918" is his sixth film. *Hans.*

Shenandoah
(COLOR)

Interesting Civil War drama with James Stewart, in strong offbeat role, to spark excellent boxoffice outlook.

Hollywood, April 1.
Universal release of Robert Arthur production. Stars James Stewart; features Doug McClure, Glenn Corbett, Patrick Wayne, Rosemary Forsyth, Phillip Alford, Katharine Ross, Tim McIntire, George Kennedy, Charles Robinson, Paul Fix, James Best. Directed by Andrew V. McLaglen. Screenplay, James Lee Barrett; camera (Technicolor), William H. Clothier; editor, Otho Lovering; music, Frank Skinner; sound, Waldon O. Watson; asst. director, Terence Nelson. Reviewed at Hollywood Paramount Theatre, March 31, 1965. Running time, 105 MINS.
Charlie .... James Ctewart
Sam .... Doug McClure
Jacob .... Glenn Corbett
James .... Patrick Wayne
Jennie .... Rosemary Forsyth
Boy .... Phillip Alford
Ann .... Katharine Ross
Nathan .... Charles Robinson
John .... James McMullan
Henry .... Tim McIntire
Gabriel .... Eugene Jackson Jr.
Dr. Witherspoon .... Paul Fix
Pastor Bioerling .... Denver Pyle
Colonel Fairchild ...... George Kennedy
Carter .... James Best
Lt. Johnson .... Tom Simcox
Capt. Richards .... Berkeley Harris
Jenkins .... Harry Carey Jr.
Mule .... Kevin Hagen
Abernathy .... Dabbs Greer
Engineer .... Strother Martin
Carroll .... Kelly Thordsen

"Shenandoah" centres, actually, upon one person, a sort of behind-the-scenes glimpse of one man's family in Virginia during the Civil War. Starring James Stewart in a character foreign to past appearances (perhaps Cary Grant started the offbeat - casting binge in "Father Goose"), the Technicolor film, despite a neuter title, packs drama, excitement and an emotional quality — particularly reflected in the climax — which should find better-than-average reception in the general market.

Under Andrew V. McLaglen's gutty direction the Robert Arthur production moves at quick tempo as James Lee Barrett's screenplay focuses on Stewart, a prosperous Virginia farmer in 1863 who completely ignores the strife raging around him. A widower, he has raised his family of six sons and one daughter to be entirely self-contained. Not believing in slavery, he wants no part in a war based upon it, providing the conflict does not touch either his land or his family. When his youngest, a 16-year-old boy whose mother died giving him birth and who therefore occupies a particular spot in the father's heart, is captured as a Reb by Unionists, the farmer then makes the war his own business.

Stewart, seldom without a cigar butt in the corner of his mouth, endows his grizzled role with warm conviction. He completely dominates the movement, which though not presenting him as a derringdo figure yet projects him as a man of action. He doesn't leave fighting to his willing sons, who though they may not always be in accord with his feeling about the war which has involved all their neighbors, still love and respect him. When government horse buyers order the sale of his prize mounts he starts his own free-for-all; he heads the search for his boy, setting up a blockade and burning a Northern prisoner train transporting Confederates to Union prisons.

Battle sequences are well integrated with the family's efforts to lead a normal life, and McLaglen, who also shows considerable sensitivity in his direction, is responsible for some rousing hand-to-hand action between the Blue and the Grey. There is one particularly dramatically-shocking interlude when one of the sons (left behind with his wife and baby to mind the farm while Stewart and the other hunt the boy) is murdered by a sword-wielding looter. Giving up the search as hopeless, on the way back home another of Stewart's sons is killed by a trigger-happy young Southern sentry, the same age as Stewart's missing son. A high degree of absorbing drama is touched in the return of his boy as Stewart and what's left of his family are attending church.

Strong support is afforted by a capable cast headed by Doug McClure, a Confederate called back to the colors as he is wedding Rosemary Forsyth, Stewart's daughter. Miss Forsyth gives a compelliing performance, as do Patrick Wayne, the murdered son, and Glenn Corbett, another son. As the youngest son whose capture motivates Stewart to action, Phillip Alford delivers impressively, and Katharine Ross also scores brightly as Wayne's wife, raped and murdered after her husband's death. Tim McIntire, George Kennedy, James Best, Paul Fix, George Kennedy and Charles Robinson lend further good assistance to plot unfoldment.

William H. Clothier's color photography head the list of top technical credits. Top-ranking, too, are art direction by Alexander Golitzen and Alfred Sweeney; Frank Skinner's unobtrusive but atmospheric music score; and Otho Lovering's fluid film editing.
Whit.

Primitive London
(BRITISH-COLOR)

Untidy documentary which hardly justifies its catchpenny title. Aimed presumably at peepshow market, but neither shocks nor titilates. Chancey bookings.

London, March 30.

Compton-Cameo Films (Arnold L. Miller, Stanley A. Long) presentation of a Troubadour Film. Features Ray Martine, MacDonald Hobley, Billy J. Kramer, Diana Noble, Vicki Grey. Written and directed by Miller; camera (Eastman Color), Long; narrator, David Gell; editor, Stephen Gross. At Windmill Theatre, London. Running Time, 80 MINS.

Compton-Cameo has struck a profitable seam of documentaries with angles calculated to intrigue a certain type of filmgoer by implied sensationalism. But the result does not always fulfill the promise, in terms of titillation. "Primitive London" is a ramshackle affair which looks as if the makers have gathered together a motley collection of odd-man-out sequences bearing little relation to each other and somehow strung them together under umbrella of a specious, narrative theme.

The script waffles along pur-

portedly describing the search for identity of a human being and, somehow, under the title of "Primitive London," manages to include scenes of the birth of a baby, nightclub sequences, a rowdy party, interviews with Mods, Rockers and Beatniks, a visit to a tattooist, striptease school and Turkish bath, judo lessons, a woman's hairdresser, a studio making a tv commercial, a youths' tailor shop, and even a visit to one of the most austere and famous men's hatters in the West End.

Editing is shaky, Eastman Color lensing variable and the commentary overgabby, and shuffled with verbal wind. Some of the sequences, taken independently, are directed by Arnold Louis Miller with perception and vitality, but and overall effect is one of a ragbag miscellany. TV commentator MacDonald Hobley, some singers from Churchill's night spot, pop vocalist Billy J. Kramer, and comedian Ray Martine appear briefly as themselves. David Gell puts over the commentary and does a sound professional job considering the verbiage with which he has to wrestle.
Rich.

The Golden Head
(Technirama-Color)
(HUNGARIAN-AMERICAN)

Naive, mildly diverting cops-and-robbers comedy. Pleasant to look at and okay for family audiences.

London, April 6.

Cinerama- Hungarofilms (Alexander Paal) presentation. Features George Sanders, Buddy Hackett, Jess Conrad, Lorraine Power, Robert Coote, Cecilie Esztergalyos, Denis Gilmore, Douglas Wilmer. Directed by Richard Thorpe. Screenplay, Stanley Goulder, Ivan Boldizsar, from Roger Pilkington's novel, "Neoomuk Of the River"; camera (Technicolor), Istvan Hildrebrand; editor, Frank Clarks; music, Peter Fenyes; theme song, music and lyrics by Mitch Murray. Reviewed at Coliseum Cinerama Theatre, London. Running time, 115 MINS.

Basil Palmer .... George Sanders
Lionel Pack .... Buddy Hackett
Michael Stevenson .... Jess Conrad
Milly Stevenson ,....... Lorraine Power
Braithwaite .... Robert Coote
Harold Stevenson .... Denis Gilmore
Anne .... Cecilia Esztergalyos
Det. Inspector Stevenson
                        Douglas Wilmer

Originally planned as "Millie Goes To Budapest" and skedded to star Hayley Mills, this co-production (Cinerama - Hungarofilm) filmed in 70m-Technirama (but with one long sequence shot with Cinerama's bugeye lens) is a naive, mildly diverting piece of cops-and-robbery which is not a strong entry for Cinerama houses. But it will pleasantly entertain the indulgent. Direction by Richard Thorpe is slow moving and unimaginative, and a more punchy script and brisker editing would have boosted the excitement. The hybrid cast, drawn from America, Britain and local sources ,is uneven in quality but has not overmuch into which to get its teeth.

There are some nice shots of Hungary which could give some pep to the tourist trade, but as a film for Cinerama audiences, now accustomed to such pix as "How The West Was Won," "Brothers Grimm" and "The Greatest Story,"

it can only be looked upon as a theatre stopgap.

Yarn concerns George Sanders and Buddy Hackett as a suave con man and stooge who try to lift the valuable Golden Head of St. Lazslo. But they are foiled by the amateur detective work of the children of a British police official who, with family, is in Budapest for a top level police conference. Events tend to meander along till the climax, which is a chase through Budapest involving the climbing of a suspension bridge, a speedboat dash on the Danube and a frenzied ride on a fire engine. But, with Thorpe's leisurely direction, even this finale doesn't add up to the pitch of excitement that might have been expected.

Sanders, though getting a shade the better for such rushing about, plays his role with a mixture of debonair tongue - in - cheek and amusing self consciousness. But the employment of Hackett as his dumb stooge fails to spark off much of a comedy team despite Hackett's determined mugging.

Major honors are copped by moppet Lorraine Power, as the little girl who unwittingly starts all the bother. She is a wideeyed youngster, who is not too cutely precocious, and who engenders much amusement by the way she handles the detective routine. Cecilia Esztergalyos and Jess Conrad handle the slight romantic stuff rather pallidly. But Denis Gilmore, who plays the Scotland Yard man with less aplomb than he is currently playing Sherlock Holmes on tele, is okay. Robert Coote gets a few yocks as a fatuous British Legation official.

The Hungarian Folk Dancers and the Hungarian Opera Ballet make brief, but colorful appearances, the first at a village wedding and the second at a special gala performance, but both incidents have no bearing on the story. They are merely brought in to add to tourist interest, as are visits to a nightclub.

The Technicolor shots are fine and art work and sound are also okay. But, overall, theatre patrons are less likely to be interested in whether or not Sanders gets away with his loot as whether or not Budapest and environs is likely to be a pleasant place for this year's vacation.
Rich.

The Bus

Documentary on one phase of the March on Washington. Subject matter will undoubtedly limit market.

Edward Harrison release of Haskell Wexler production; camera by Wexler. Editor, Conrad Bentzen; music, Richard Markowitz. Reviewed in N.Y., April 5, '65. Running Time, 62 MINS.

This feature-length documentary about the journey, by bus, of a group of San Franciscans, black and white, to the "March On Washington," is currently having its premiere booking at the Trans-Lux 49th Street Theatre, N.Y. Produced, photographed and personally financed by Hollywood cameraman Haskell Wexler ("America America," "The Best Man". and "The Loved One").

As most of the film is confined to the interior of the bus, there is considerable visual limitation that even Wexler's expert black and white camerawork can't overcome. For this reason, he introduces occasional stops to enable the passengers to move about and to introduce extra characters. Most of the interior filming was done by a modified Auricon camera which Wexler claims that he wore around his neck all the time. Only rarely does an individual indicate that he knows he's being filmed.

There is almost no background narration. The story, as such, is told by the passengers. After a short introductory speech by the family of Charles Franklin (father, mother, two daughters) who make up four of the white passengers, rest of film relies on conversations and some folk singing. A short stretch of film's ending, made in D.C., puts considerable emphasis on the March, but with the Frisco group continually featured.

Biggest drawback is the impression that, considering the events that have since ensued, all this is ancient history. Poor sound (seemingly via tape recording later added to film) and frequently erratic photography also work against sustained interest in film.

Scenes where picture does come alive include one, during stopover near Washington, where a young Negro who had been through some of the civil rights demonstrations in Gadsden, Ala., tells passengers what it was like. Impressive fact is that, despite the excitement and feeling in his voice as he recalls the actions taken by Alabama police against himself and his fellow demonstrators, he never lapses into pro-violent statements or illogical condemnation. This could have been result of training done by a nonviolence workshop.

Another scene, near end of trip, is when a heated debate breaks out among the bus passengers because of an apparent failure on part of some riders to support one-man demonstration of a male passenger while traveling through Maryland. They're oblivious to the fact that they're being recorded and filmed.

Evidently Wexler has attempted to express his personal feelings about civil rights. The film would have had greater dramatic emphasis with a better conceived format. Its appeal should be limited, even in areas where civil rights is a major concern.
Robe.

Mister Moses
(PANAVISION—COLOR)

Modernized Moses trek set in African veldt. Good for general market.

Hollywood, April 9.

United Artists release of Frank Ross production. Stars Robert Mitchum, Carroll Baker; features Ian Bannen, Alexander Knox, Raymond St. Jacques, Orlando Martins, Reginald Beckwith. Directed by Ronald Neame. Screenplay, Charles Beaumont, Monja Danischewsky; based on novel by Max Catto; camera (Technicolor), Oswald Morris; music, John Barry; editors, Phil Anderson, Peter Wetherley; asst. director, Colin Brewer; sound. John W. Mitchell, Bob Jones. Reviewed at Samuel Goldwyn Studios, April 8, '65. Running time, 115 MINS.

Joe Moses .... Robert Mitchum
Julie Anderson .... Carroll Baker
Robert .... Ian Bannen

Rev. Anderson ..... Alexander Knox
Ubi .... Raymond St Jacques
Chief .... Orlando Martins
Parkhurst .... Reginald Beckwith

The Biblical Moses, in a manner, has been undated for this Frank Ross production, switching the plot to an American diamond smuggler leading an African tribe to a promised land. Filmed in East Africa, picture stars Robert Mitchum and Carroll Baker. Rambling narrative would benefit from further editing but should qualify as a strong entry for the general market.

Director Ronald Neame has taken every advantage of fascinating African terrain lensed in Panavision and Technicolor, for his unusual adventure yarn scripted by Charles Beaumont and Monja Danischewsky from Max Catto's novel. The small cast is supported by natives lined up on location, and with the production values inherent in such locations there's a raft of authentic color. If the plot appears contrived this can be overlooked in the ensuing unfoldment, which sometimes reaches near-saga proportions.

Film takes its motivation from orders by the District Commissioner for a village, threatened by flood waters of a new dam being constructed, to evacuate. The religious-minded chief, who has heard the story of Moses from a missionary and his daughter who live with the tribe, refuses to take his people in helicopters to be provided for purpose, because the Bible says the children of Israel, when they went to their promised land, took their animals with them. No animals, no go.

Mitchum, a medicine-man who smuggles diamonds, is set down in this ticklish situation, a guy known as Dr. Moses from the inscription on his medicine-show wagon. He's plucked from the river, unconscious atop his floating half-submerged caravan after enraged Africans upstream tossed him in because his magic "muscle tonic" hasn't worked. The chief hails him as the true Moses who will lead them to a special government preserve. Refusing such a task, which would entail a trek of hundreds of miles across desolate waste, Mitchum finally agrees after Miss Baker, engaged to the District Commissioner, threatens to inform official of his smuggling if he doesn't save the tribe.

Neame captured considerable feeling in some of the episodes on the march, led by Mitchum in his wagon drawn by a village elephant which saved him from a deadly snake. There are vast panoramas of Africa seldom previously viewed, and color camera work by Oswald Morris is frequently spectacular. Plot takes on a routine character when son of a former witch doctor for the tribe and recently returned from a sojourn among the whites, tries to take over.

Mitchum delivers one of his regulation rugged performances and Miss Baker as missionary's daughter is okay in straight role. Alexander Knox handles the missionary well and Ian Bannen is effective in his brief appearances as the D.C. Orlando Martins is convincing as the chief, Raymond St. Jacques almost too smooth as the heavy and Reginald Beckwith is properly pompous as an over-offi-

cious engineer. The elephant, with the fancy handle of Emily, naturally steals all her scenes.

John Barry's music score, overtoned with African instruments, furnishes valuable background mounting. Editing by Phil Anderson and Peter Wetherley with few exceptions fulfills demands.
Whit.

Genghis Khan
(PANAVISION—COLOR)

Okay biopic of ancient Mongol leader is talky and short on spectacular action. Good cast help the sell. Moderate returns seen in general market.

Hollywood, April 13.
Columbia Pictures release of Irving Allen/CCC/Avala production. Stars Stephen Boyd, Omar Sharif, James Mason, Eli Wallach, Francoise Dorleac, Telly Savalas, Robert Morley, Yvonne Mitchell; features Michael Hordern, Woody Strode, Kenneth Cope, Patrick Holt, Gustavo Rojo, Roger Croucher, Don Borisenko. Directed by Henry Levin. Screenplay, Clarke Reynolds, Beverley Cross, from original story by Berkely Mather; camera (Technicolor), Geoffrey Unsworth; editor, Geoffrey Foot; art direction, Maurice Carter; music, Dusan Rudic; sound, George Stephenson, Hugh Strain; asst. directors, Buddy Coleman, Bluey Hill, Frank Wintersteln; second unit director, Cliff Lyons. Previewed at Columbia Pictures Studios, April 12, '65. Running Time, 124 MINS.
Jamuga .... Stephen Boyd
Genghis Khan .... Omar Sharif
Kam Ling .... James mason
Shah of Khwarezm .... Eli Wallach
Bortei .... Francoise Dorleac
Shan .... Telly Savalas
Emperor of China .... Robert Morley
Geen .... Michael Hordern
Katke .... Yvonne Mitchell
Sengal .... Woody Strode
Suhadoi .... Kenneth Cope
Massar .... Roger Croucher
Jebai .... Don Borisenko
Kuchiuk .... Patrick Holt
Chin Yu .... Suzanne Hsaio
Toktoa .... George Savalas
Genghis as child .... Carlo Cura
Altan .... Gustoavo Rojo
Ho Mum Tim .... Duran Vujisic
Fut Su .... Joyan Tesic
Chagedai .... Andreia Marcic
Jochi .... Thomas Margulies
Indian Girls .... Yamata Pauli, Linda Loncar
1st slave dealer .... Branislav Ragovic
2nd slave dealer .... Zvonko Jovic
Concubines .... Dominique Don,
Edwina Carroll, Carmen Dene, Sally Douglas, Nora Forster, Chieko Huber, Jatta Folke, Elke Kroger, Hannalore Meusel, Ursel Mumoth, Yvonne Shima, Lucille Soong, May Spils, Ester Anderson

"Genghis Khan" is an introspective biopic about the Mongol youth Temujin who unified Asia's warring tribes in the Dark Age. national cast delivers okay performances in occasionally trite script which emphasizes personal motivation rather than sweeping pageantry. Columbia release offers some good production values to relieve an essentially talky drama, and moderate grosses are likely in the general market.

The Clarke Reynolds-Beverley Cross screenplay, from story by Berkely Mather, hinges on continuing vendetta between tribal chieftain Stephen Boyd and Omar Sharif, once enslaved by Boyd but escaping to forge an empire that threatened western and eastern civilization some eight centuries back.

History is full of events that make poor drama because they seem unbelievable, but scripters' focus on people rather than events is only partially successful. Fact remains, unexploited in opening and closing narration, that millions of nomads still wander these Asian wastes, left alone by nominal Russian and Chinese Communist rulers, and a modern Temujin might affect future history. This might have been a better frame of reference, but still might be used to sell the Irving Allen production shot in Yugoslavia and Germany.

Withal, Sharif does a near-excellent job in projecting with ease the zeal which propelled Temujin from bondage to a political education in

China, and finally to realizing at death his dream of Mongol unity. Boyd is less successful as the brutish thorn in Sharif's side, being overall too restrained for sustained characterization despite flashes of earthiness.

Appearing to good advantage is Francoise Dorleac as Sharif's wife, whose kidnap-rape by Boyd cues recurring doubt as to fatherhood of couple's first-born son, and sparks final duel between the adversaries. Telly Savalas, Michael Hordern and Woody Strode (latter as mute giant) register okay in brief footage as Sharif's closer allies.

Most unusual characterization is essayed by James Mason, playing the neatly-contrasting urbane imperial counsellor who mentors political savvy. Mason is barely recognizable except for voice (that, too, oriental-accented), and his appearance may draw unwanted laffs, being initially too much a Charlie Chan-type. Fault lies in awkward intro, but he grows on the audience. Role is a key factor in plot, and Mason does a creditable job, forgetting the awkward lead-in.

Robert Morley plays the emperor as an English actor in Chinese togs, succeeding in repping a China long on culture but short on power, but always jarring with Mason. The effete but not-so-dumb emperor uses Sharif to repel Boyd's invaders, but keeps Sharif a virtual prisoner until latter crashes out via fireworks ruse to embark on Asian conquests.

The name Genghis Kahn, bestowed in China, is roughly translated to mean number-one conqueror, suggested by quick montages to climactic scenes during Sharif's march on Persia.

Eli Wallach makes a brief appearance, with shallow results, as a Persian potentate in uneasy alliance with Boyd to repel the Mongol leader. Obviously meant to contrast western indecision with Morley's eastern complacency, Wallach's role doesn't come off. All other players are okay, and Kenneth Cope stands out as one of Miss Dorleac's brothers, all of whom have joined Sharif.

Direction by Henry Levin is good, with some excellent staging in spots to suggest the pomp and pageantry which the script suppresses. Battle footage is skimpy but arrestingly staged in its moments. Geoffrey Unsworth's Panavision and Technicolor camera captures the vast and drab Asian wasteland, also the plush fat of Chinese palace life. Obvious attention to color values is seen in nearly black-and-white tones prevailing in exteriors, contrasting with vivid hues of imperial sequences. A few process shots look artificial.

Music by Dusan Radic is impressive. Geoffrey Foot's editing lends pace to film's 124 minutes, and conveys through reaction intercutting the explicit violence offscreen, at least in U.S. prints, ditto some concubine and bath scenes obviously removed for domestic sensibilities.

Excellent sound editing has reconstructed the live feel of the exterior scenes which predominate, and other technical credits spell quality.
Murf.

Horror Castle
(ITALIAN—COLOR—WIDESCREEN)

Inept horror pic. Rossana Podesta's looks and Christopher Lee's chillpix reputation don't save it. Grind house fate.

Hollywood, April 15.

Zodiac Films release of Gladiator (Marco Vicario) Production. Features Rossana Podesta, George Riviere, Christopher Lee. Directed by Anthony Dawson; English-language version directed by Richard McNamara. Based on novel "The Virgin of Nuremberg" by Frank Bogart; shot anamorphically in Eastmancolor; music, Riz Ortolani. Reviewed at Hollywood Theatre, L.A., April 14, '65. Running Time, **82 MINS.**

Mary .... Rossana Podesta
Max .... George Riviere
Erich .... Christopher Lee

Zodiac Films continues its no-tradeshow policy with a tedious and ridiculous English-dubbed Italian horror, teaming Rossana Podesta-Christopher Lee, and lowercased with "Dr. Terror's House of Horrors." Lip sync in "Horror Castle" is awkward and English dialog is not to be believed. Dimmest prospects even in least discriminating markets.

Every directorial device available has been used by Anthony Dawson (and Richard McNamara, credited with direction of English-language version) to follow Miss Podesta as she walks, and walks, and walks about the family castle in Germany owned by hubby George Riviere. Seems there's a monster afoot, called "The Executioner," who employs medieval tortures on helpless people, and wifey intends to find out despite sealed lips of palace crew.

Lee, a horror film favorite, is a war-scarred chauffeur who wanders about calling mysteriously to "mein herr." Turns out the monster is hubby's father, an anti-Hitler Nazi who was horribly disfigured as punishment for attempt on Hitler's life, and in demented state kills most of the household, tries to drown his son and torture latter's wife before an FBI agent (sic) and town doctor stop the show.

Riz Ortolani's full-bodied music telegraphs dozens of flop shock situations, accented further by zoom shots. Apart from a few murky scenes, color quality is fine. Technical credits are quite good, but the story premise was handled ineptly. Sample dialog, monster to victim: "modern science has developed new tortures, but the old ways are best."

All principals deserve better material. Producer Marco Vicario has not done well by his wife, Miss Podesta. *Murf.*

The Intelligence Men
(BRITISH—COLOR)

Spasmodically amusing debut of top tele and vaude comedians Morecambe and Wise. Spoof spy yarn does not fully get across, but should rate okay reception from comics' big following here.

London, April 13.

Rank Organization release of a Hugh Stewart production. Stars Eric Morecambe, Ernie Wise; features William Franklyn, April Olrich, Gloria Paul, Richard Vernon, Jacqueline Jones. Directed by Robert Asher. Screenplay, S. C. Green and R. M. Hills, from Peter Blackmore's story; camera (Eastmancolor), Jack Asher; music, Philip Green; editor, Gerry Hambling. Reviewed at Astoria, London. Running time, **104 MINS.**

Eric Morecambe .... Eric Morecambe
Ernie Sage .... Ernie Wise
Colonel Grant, M.I.5 .... William Franklyn
Madame Petrovna .... April Olrich
Gina Carlotti .... Gloria Paul
Sir Edward Seabrook ... Richard Vernon
Stage Manager .... David Lodge
Karin .... Jacqueline Jones
Reed .... Terence Alexander
Thomas .... Francis Matthews
Prozoroff .... Warren Mitchell
Laundry Basket Man .... Brian Oulton
Sinister Stranger .... Michael Peake
Phillipe .... Peter Bull
Seedy Schlect Agent ...... Tutte Lemkow
"Siegfried" Dancer .... Rene Sartoris
"Evil Owl" Dancer .... Graham Smith
Girl in Cinema .... Dilys Rosser
Boy in Cinema .... Johnny Briggs
Girl in Cucaracha .... Elizabeth Counsell
Carlos .... Gerald Hely
Conductor .... Joe Melia
Woman in Lift .... Marianne Stone
French Girl .... Jill Curzon
Rostov .... Alexis Checnakov
Ivan .... Laurence Herder

With Eric Morecambe and Ernie Wise riding high as British's top television and vaude double comedy act, their entry into feature films could not be long delayed. Their first film, while missing out on several cylinders, is an occasionally amusing spoof of current vogue for spy pix. M & W's formidable following here should ensure healthy returns at the wicket, at least in Britain. Their debut suggests a useful film career ahead of them, with care taken all round.

Snag with the current offering is that the comedians are best in small doses and they lack the experience to cover several passages where the inventiveness of director Robert Asher and of scriptwriters S. C. Green and R. M. Hills, who dream up most of Morecambe and Wise's material often lags. The writers have shrewdly dropped in two or three of the stars' popular routines and it is largely with them that they score the yocks.

For instance, a scene where an unwelcome corpse has to be got rid of in a hotel laundry basket; an episode where Morecambe, as a marked man, takes a hot seat in a cinema, byplay with glamorous femmes and parts of a finale at Covent Garden Opera House. In this last the funsters get involved as disguised dancers. Good humored mirth in their popular style is provided in all of these sequences.

The fact that the storyline is slim yet complicated is less important than the fact that the script is often flabby and the parody not sufficiently sharp. Sometimes, too, the comedians are forced out of their familiar character to the detriment of their well thought out image.

Plot involves sinister goings on with the mysterious agent, Tutte Lembow, concerning an Anglo-Russian trade agreement. There's the attempted dispatch of a Russian ballerina while she is dancing at Covent Garden. In this sort of yarn it doesn't much matter how or why these two amiable jerks become involved in the machinations.

Ernie Wise, the stooge of the act, has a role that consists of little more than appearing in a variety of easily spotted disguises and the gags are not over funny. Eric Morecambe, however, does get plenty of opportunity of exploiting his brand of throwaway tomfoolery. They are given conscientious support by William Franklyn, as the Secret Service chief; Peter Bull, David Lodge, Richard Vernon, Warren Mitchell and Terence Alexander. Distaff honors are taken mainly by April Olrich, as the ballerina, and Gloria Paul and Jacqueline Jones as a couple of spies. They are three well-assorted dishes and show up well in Eastmancolor.

Jack Asher has handled his camera well and artwork and locations are both okay, with Philip Green providing a useful but not obtrusive score. With Hugh Stewart producing, this is largely the team that has made many of the Norman Wisdom comedies. They, too, have had various teething troubles. It is probable that future Morecambe and Wise comedies will iron out the problems of "The Intelligence Men," thus satisfying an even larger audience than the comedians' present big and loyal following. *Rich.*

La Congiuntura
(One Million Dollars)
(ITALIAN)
(Color—Songs)

Rome, April 13.

Ceiad-Columbia release of Mario Cecchi Gori production for Fairfilm, Rome. Stars Vittorio Gassman; features Joan Collins, Jacques Bergerac, Hilda Barry. Directed by Ettore Scola. Screenplay, Ruggero Maccari, Scola; camera (Technicolor-Techniscope), Sandro D'Eva; music, Luis Enriquez Bacalov; editor, Marcello Malvestiti. At Metropolitan, Rome. Running time, **110 MINS.**

Don Giuliano .... Vittorio Gassman
Jane .... Joan Collins
Sandro .... Jacques Bergerac
Dana .... Hilde Barry
Grandfather .... Adolfo Eibenstein

Mario Cecchi Gori, whose Fairfilm set a trend in bitter-sweet comedies of the current Italian scene, has managed with his latest product to shape an internationally-angled tale with saleable general audience values in many world markets.

Perhaps inevitably, as a result, the pic lacks the claws which made previous laughs at local foibles so trenchant, as in "Il Sorpasso," also a Vittorio Gassman starrer. Whatever points it intends to make are diluted, and the humor remains principally on the surface. But conversely, most typically and topically Italian references are absent or are "explained," making the picture more accessible and understandable outside local frontiers.

Story is flim-flam excuse to set Vittorio Gassman, as an indolent but charming Roman nobleman, and Joan Collins, as part of a gang smuggling money to Swiss Bank safety, careening across the aptly-selected Italian landscape. Incidents occur along the way to provide laughs and suspense, until at the finale the hero lands both money and the (easily) reformed girl.

Script by Ruggero Maccari and director Ettore Scola is functional. At times it's witty and laugh-provoking. At others it lapses into oft-seen banalities. But generally, the tone is light and uninvolving, the people charming, the landscape colorful and the pace fairly sprightly.

Gassman is tailor-cast in his role as the nobleman whose conceit generally dims his wits. Miss Collins is nice to look at, though she frequently overacts, as his opposite. Jacques Bergerac registers in a short role as the brain behind the scheme, while there are some excellent characterizations by sideline characters, notably Adolf Eibenstein as Gassman's caustic and tradition-bound grandpa, and Hilde Barry, as a white-haired, man-chaser from whom Gassman hitches a hilarious ride in one of the funnier sequences. Noble's finale chase of Bergerac through the streets of a Swiss lake resort brings pic to a neat upbeat halt.

Physical trimmings are bright. Sandro D'Eva's Technicolor lensing properly reflects the beauties of Rome, the Riviera highspots and several Swiss settings. Luis Bacalov's music, including a brace of lightweight pop tunes, is similarly in the mood. *Hawk.*

She
(BRITISH—C'SCOPE—COLOR)

Fast moving and colorful remake of A. Rider Haggard novel. Solid programmer with exploitation possibilities.

Hollywood, April 8.

Metro-Goldwyn-Mayer release of a Seven Arts Hammer (Michael Carreras) Production. Stars Ursula Andress; features rest of cast. Directed by Robert Day. Screenplay, David T. Chantler, based on novel by H. Rider Haggard; camera (C'Scope-Metrocolor), Harry Waxman; supervising editor, James Needs, editor, Eric Boyd-Perkins; art direction, Robert Jones; music, James Bernard; sound, Claude Hitchcock; special effects, Howie Films Ltd.; asst. director, Bruce Sharman. Reviewed at Metro studio, April 7, '65. Running Time, **104 MINS.**

Ayesha .... Ursula Andress
Major Holly .... Peter Cushing
Job .... Bernard Cribbins
Leo Vincey .... John Richardson
Ustane .... Rosenda Monteros
Billali .... Christopher Lee
Haumeid .... Andre Morell

Current and fourth filming of H. Rider Haggard's fantasy adds color and widescreen to special effects, all of which help overcome a basic plot no film scripter has yet licked. Michael Carreras' Seven Arts Hammer production boasts lively direction and good performanaces. Metro release is a solid programmer for general situations, and combo of title and Ursula Andress' growing marquee lure could yield nice grosses in exploitation markets.

Miss Andress is sole-starred as the immortal "She," cold-blooded queen Ayesha of a lost kingdom who pines for return of the lover she murdered eons ago. In David T. Chantler's okay script, it turns out that John Richardson is the look-alike lover, footloose in Palestine after World War I with buddies Peter Cushing and Bernard Cribbins.

High priest Christopher Lee and servant girl Rosenda Monteros are emissaries who spot Richardson's resemblance, triggering a desert trek by the three men to Kuma land. Cushing and Cribbins keep their senses, while Richardson falls under Miss Andress' spell (some spell, too).

Director Robert Day's overall excellent work brings out heretofore unknown depths in Miss Andress' acting. Role calls for sincere warmth as a woman in love, also brutal cruelty as queen, and she convinces. Richardson's film debut is largely inanimate, but Haggard's character is little more than cardboard cut out of a seduced man anyway. Richardson's sensitive yet rugged looks will be better evaluated in stronger material.

All other players are good in routine roles, particularly Miss Monteros as the competing love interest who loses her man and her life. (In the 1935 b&w Merian Cooper-RKO version, Helen Mack wrested Randolph Scott from Helen Gahagan's regal wiles.) Christopher Lee is also effective as the loyal priest whom Ayesha kills when he wants to take the fire-bath which gives immortality. Climactic flame frolic between the lovers comes amid a slave rebellion, and Ayesha gets an overdose which causes decay into dust in a sock display of makeup and photographic craftsmanship.

Production values save the day, with crowd scenes and palace pomp worthy of far more expensive films. Day, art director Robert Jones, cameraman Harry Waxman and an uncredited costumer can all take a bow. James Bernard's score is sparse but full bodied, especially in crisp ceremonial passages.

Editors James Needs and Eric Boyd-Perkins have come up with a zippy 104 minutes, but a little trimming is needed in early desert scenes which flag the pace. Sound editing and mixing are professional in this British-lensed pic. Howie Films Ltd. did very good special effects work, including fire montages, little-used in recent years. Metrocolor values are consistently rich. Occasional Cinemascope pans are distorted.

Murf.

I've Gotta Horse
(BRITISH—COLOR)

Pop singer Billy Fury's name will attract local youngsters to an amiable, musical lark; just misfires on sparkle, but breezy exploitation should bring it in a winner.

London, April 13.

Warner-Pathe release of a Windmill Film (Larry Parnes-Kenneth Hume) from Anglo Amalgamated. Stars Billy Fury, Amanda Barrie, Bill Fraser, Michael Medwin; with John Pertwee, Fred Emney, The Gamblers, The Bachelors, Leslie Dwyer, Peter Gilmore, Marjorie Rhodes, Ann Lancaster, Sheila O'Neill. Directed by Kenneth Hume. Screenplay, Ronald Wolfe, Ronald Chesney, from an original by Hume & Parnes; camera (Technicolor), Ernest Steward; editor, Ernest Hosler; music & lyrics, David Heneker and John Taylor; choreography, Ross Taylor. Reviewed at Warner Theatre, London. Running Time, **92 MINS.**

Billy .... Billy Fury
Jo .... Amanda Barrie
Hymie Campbell .... Michael Medwin
Mrs. Bartholemew .... Marjorie Rhodes
Mr. Bartholemew .... Bill Fraser
Jock .... Peter Gilmore
The Gamblers .... Themselves
The Bachelors .... Themselves
Donkey Man .... John Kelly
Peter .... Michael Cashman
Costumier's Assistant .... Jon Pertwee
Lord Bentley .... Fred Emney
Lady Bentley .... Pauline Loring
Trainer .... Tom Bowman
Jockey .... Gareth Robinson
Woman Shopkeeper .... Ann Lancaster
Betty .... Sheila O'Neill

Billy Fury is a pop vocal favorite in Britain and he will be a marquee draw for this musical frolic, particularly with breezy exploitation aimed at the youth market. There are good tunes, some lively young people and an undemanding story. As "Wonderful Day" (its out-of-Britain monicker), it may face cooler audiences not presold on Fury. Its qualities, even for an unambitious pic, are just that mite less sparkling than are needed for a click musical. Still, Kenneth Hume, who directs the pic and is also partly responsible for both the original yarn and for production, has invested it with a disarming happiness and innocence. Film needs a shade tightening up and more sharpness.

Fury portrays himself, though he is, fortunately more professional in his attention to rehearsals and "pro" savvy than the film character suggests. Star of a seaside summer show, he causes headaches for his manager and producer by rehearsal tardiness due to his love for animals He clutters his dressing room with pet dogs and then acquires a racehorse which causes problems around the theatre.

Pic is geared to the acquiring of another horse (as Fury did in real life). This one runs in the Derby, persuading the entire cast to play hookey to visit the racetrack and only getting back to the theatre on the opening night just in time to go on in street clothes and wow the audience.

This type of tuner doesn't need a strong story, being mainly an excuse for some lively banter and cues for a song. Pity, though, that most of these ditty cues are remorselessly telegraphed and that the younger thesps tend to play too much to the camera. David Heneker and John Taylor, the tunesmiths, have produced some bright temporary fodder for the Hit Parade, but none of the numbers linger.

Hume has mainly directed with briskness and style, though falling down badly in a sequence in which The Bachelors meander through the countryside with planted figures (in duos) waving mechanical greetings.

Technical credits are all okay, with Ernest Steward's Technicolor lensing doing marvels, considering that instead ow the Riviera he had to cope with Great Yarmouth. Production scenes in a clothier's store and at a barbecue are bright but just lack that extra thing of inventiveness which separates the memorable musicals from the passables.

Fury sings well, within his range, and his likable personality compensates for a shortness on acting skill. Amanda Barrie, as his girl friend is pert and registers in one number, "Men," but is not given a chance to consolidate her growing rep as a bright little comedienne. Michael Medwir and Leslie Dwyer, as Fury's manager and dresser, both score through experience and several cthers make impact in brief cameo spots, notably Jon Pertwee as a mannered costumer and Fred Emney as a portly lord of the realm. Bill Fraser, as Fury's producer, makes his usual sound contribution in such explosive moments as he is allowed. Note one for the book. Sheila O'Neill, who plays the show's leading lady in the film. Miss O'Neill, currently playing in "Chaganog" in the West End, is a deft dancer and a witty comedienne. But director Hume and cameraman Steward might have played down a perpetual all-teeth-on-parade grin.

Rich.

The Secret Of Blood Island
(BRITISH)

Jap prison-camp actioner by Hammer should make good supporting dualer.

Universal release of Hammer Film production. Stars Jack Hedley, Barbara Shelley, Patrick Wymark, Charles Tingwell; features Bill Owen, Peter Welch, Lee Montague, Edwin Richfield, Michael Ripper. Directed by Quentin Lawrence. Screenplay, John Gilling; camera, Jack Asher; editor, Tom Simpson; special effects. Syd Pearson; music, composed by James Bernard. Reviewed at Universal h.o., N.Y., April 14, '65. Running Time, **84 MINS.**

Elaine .... Barbara Shelley
Sgt. Crewe .... Jack Hedley
Major Dryden .... Charles Tingwell
Bludgin .... Bill Owen
Richardson .... Peter Welch
Levy .... Lee Montague
O'Reilly .... Edwin Richfield
Lt. Tojoko .... Michael Ripper
Captain Jocomo .... Patrick Wymark
Captain Drake .... Philip Latham
Berry .... Glyn Houston
Mills .... Ian Whittaker
Leonard .... John Southworth
KEMPI chief .... David Saire
Red .... Peter Craze
Taffy .... Henry Davies

For some reason never explained, this Japanese prison-camp actioner was filmed in color but is being released in the U.S. in black and white. Indeed, Hammer has stressed color so long in its horror films, that it was something of a surprise to see this one unveiling in various shades of grey.

Producer Anthony Nelson Keys has provided situations that need short, action-filled supporting features with a suitable attraction. There's nothing pretentious about the film but several facets are so good that the more discerning filmgoer will be disappointed that more care wasn't taken throughout. A basically simple but good plot, generally well written by John Gilling, and several of the actors who bring much more to their roles than is demanded keep things moving along under the firm hand of director Quentin Lawrence.

The "secret" isn't one for long—a British female agent is shot down near a Jap prison camp in Malaya. The prisoners hide her and eventually help her to escape, not without some ensuing incidents that provide the necessary action. Barbara Shelley, only femme in the cast (other than a few native women), manages to fool the Jap guards into thinking she's just another male prisoner much more easily than she does the audience. But when she's supposed to look dirty and sweaty (and this attention to detail is due to meticulous work by the technicians on the film), she looks properly solied. Although obviously shot on a British film lot, none of the actors are ever seen out of character.

Besides Miss Shelley, very good performances are given by Jack Hedley and Charles Tingwell as the leaders of the British prisoners and Bill Owen, Peter Welch, Lee Montague and Edwin Richfield as other prisoners. Among the Japanese roles, however, there isn't one convincing performance in the group. Particularly bad as the commandant is Patrick Wymark (who played Churchill in "Operation Crossbow"), with ludicrous makeup that is of no help. Also limited are Michael Ripper as a sadistic Jap lieutenant and David Saire as the Japanese version of a Gestapo agent.

Gilling's screenplay has several logical loopholes but as the low-budgeter was never meant to be anything more than a programmer, these slips don't matter too much. Technical values throughout are generally excellent, especially Jack Asher's crisp photography. The music is routine.

Robe.

Masquerade
(BRITISH-COLOR)

Spankingly-paced, light cloak-and-dagger spoof; deft blend of comedy, intrigue and action suggests marquee value.

London, April 13.

United Artists release of a Michael Relph and Basil Dearden production. Stars Cliff Robertson, Jack Hawkins, Marisa Mell; features Michel Piccoli, Bill Fraser, Christopher Witty, Tutte Lemkov, Charles Gray, John Le Mesurier. Directed by Dearden. Screenplay, Ralph and William Goldman, based on Victor Canning's novel, "Castle Minerva"; camera (Eastmancolor), Otto Heller; editor, John Gutheridge; music, Philip Green. At Leicester Square Theatre, London. Running Time, **102 MINS.**

David Frazer .... Cliff Robertson
Colonel Drexel .... Jack Hawkins
Sophie .... Marisa Mell
Prince Jamil .... Christopher Witty
Dunwoody .... Bill Fraser
Sarrassin .... Michel Piccoli
Paviot .... Tutte Lemkow
Gustave .... Keith Pyott
El Mono .... Jose Burgos
Benson .... Charles Gray
Sir Robert .... John Le Mesurier
Ahmed Ben Ha'id .... Roger Delgado
Brindle .... Jerold Wells
Henrickson .... Felix Aylmer
King Ahmed .... Denis Bernard
Minister .... Ernest Clark
Photographer .... David Nettheim
Assistant .... Anthony Singleton
Bishop .... Norman Fisher
General .... Eric Blyth
James Mossman .... Himself

Michael Relph and Basil Dearden have had themselves a ball with "Masquerade," for once forgetting the sociological themes which they often blend with their dramas, and turning out a clever, tongue-in-cheek spoof of the cloak-and-dagger yarns. Result is a light, intriguing and action-packed vehicle which affords maximum entertainment.

Relph and William Goldman have jettisoned much of the earnestness of the Victor Canning novel, "Castle Minerva," retaining mainly the plotline and characters. They have deftly injected a wealth of twists, red herring and production highlights, used a cast that fully enters into the spirit of the thing and the end product will keep audiences on their toes.

Screenplay is ironic and amusing while Dearden's direction, plus shrewd editing by John Gutheridge, keeps the film moving at a fine pace. The story, mainly set in colorful Spain (to which Otto Heller's Eastmancolor lensing gives full value), involves kidnapping, disguised identity, macabre doings in a travelling circus, endless bumpings on noggins, gunplay, a mysterious Spanish girl, escape from an eerie castle, a fadeout running gun battle on a collapsing suspension bridge. The hero is in more sticky dilemmas (such as being locked up in a cage with a white headed vulture) than befell even Pauline at her most perilous. It is all laced together with the intriguing problem of who can be trusted and who is double-crossing who, and why.

The British Foreign Office hires Jack Hawkins and Cliff Robertson for a daring mission. Hawkins is an ex-war colonel and hero. In this film, he obviously relishes being able to spoof the sort of stiff upper lip roles that so often he has to play seriously. Robertson is an American soldier of fortune who is down on his luck. Their job is to abduct the young heir to the throne of a Near East State and keep him under wraps a few weeks until he comes of age and is able to sign a favorable oil concession to Britain. Kidnapping the youth is a pushover. Trouble starts when they try to keep him from being snatched back by other mysterious interested parties.

Then begins the chase, the treachery and the surprises, leading up to a slick, amusing payoff. Robertson is hardly in the Bond league, since he is on the receiving end of more trouble than he ever dishes out. But he gives a disarming, amusingly underplayed performance and also finds time for a slight romantic skirmish with Marisa Mell. Hawkins enjoys himself no end in a role that gives a surprise kick to the proceedings. There is an excellently icy, sinister performance by Charles Gray as a Foreign Office despot.

Bill Fraser, dependable as ever as an eccentric bird-recorder who turns out to be one of the heavies; Michel Piccoli, as a strong-arm leader of the travelling circus folk who are obviously up to hanky panky; Christopher Witty, Jerold Wells, Roger Delgado and John Le Mesurier all contribute in varying degree.

There are several big highspots, notably a dramatic and macabre sequence in which Robertson is lured into a circus ring and beaten up and kidnapped by crackling clowns to the delight of the unsuspecting audience, and a long chain of events in the dank castle.

Direction, writing, editing and artwork all contribute to a bright film which takes some sly cracks at other films and filmmakers but without treating it as a self-indulgent 'in' joke. Philip Green provides a suitably atmospheric score. *Rich.*

Marie Soleil
(FRENCH)
Paris, April 20.

Warner Bros. release of a Gueville production. Stars Daniele Delorme, Jacques Charrier; features Roger Blin, Christian Barbier, Genevieve Brunet. Written and directed by Antoine Bourseiller. Camera, Claude Beausoleil; editor, Sylvie Blanc. Previewed in Paris. Running Time, 85 MINS.
Marie .... Daniele Delorme
Axel .... Jacques Charrier
Therese .... Genevieve Brunet
Boss .... Roger Blin

A hopeless love affair between a bar girl and a young agronomist is told in a mannered, literary way by stage actor and director Antoine Bourseiller in this, his first

pic. It lacks sincerity in mood and the needed good acting to give it arty chances abroad. It has play-off opportunities, if well handled.

Bourseiller uses long walks and has his characters talking about themselves while sightseeing. Or has them posing as they make profound decisions. However there is a fluidity of visuals and dialog which keeps these scenes from becoming static.

The love scenes are done with tact and maturity. Daniele Delorme is spunky, touching and vital as the bar girl with a Negro child who has been kicked around until she can not quite accept the love offered by a younger man.

Jacques Charrier has the right rigidity and coolness for an ambitious young man caught up in a society-defying pattern for the first time. Director Antoine Bourseiller may borrow ideas, setups and even dramatic gimmicks (like the sound of a train and a swooping camera at a party) but uses them well.

This is technically good. Picture turns out to be offbeater with a highly personalized flair. It will be limited, at best, but has a definite tone, with specialized outlets indicated. *Mosk.*

Memetih
(The Flurry)
(RUSSIAN-COLOR)
Paris, April 13.

Mosfilm production and release. With Gueorgui Martyniouk, Valentina Titova, Oleg Vidov, Maria Pastoukhova. Directed and addapted by Vladimir Bassov from story by Alexandre Pushkin. Camera (Sovcolor), Sergueni Vronski; music, Youri Sviridov. At Kinopanorama, Paris. Running time, 80 MINS.
Bourmina .... Gueorgui Martyniouk
Maria .... Valentina Titova
Vladimir .... Oleg Vidov
Mother .... Maria Pastoukhova

Romantic Russo pic is more an illustration of a 19th Century Alexandre Pushkin story than a dramatic pic in its own right. But its simplicity, colorful period recreation and acting make it a visually rich item that could be of specialized use abroad.

After the War of 1812, a young officer is settled in the home of a widow and her beauteous daughter, located in a small town. Love grows but neither the soldier or girl can seem to admit it until a series of flashbacks by an omnipotent narrator straighten things out.

And a truly incredible coincidence smooths out their lives and leads to their confessions of love just before he has to leave. The countryside, the Russian winter and interiors of bygone days get fine renditions with color having the right look.

The serfs are not unduly miserable or horribly treated in this one. It is the mysteries of human nature and unrequited love that make up the core of this charmingly old-fashioned pic.

Acting is rightly posey with some feeling. Direction is academic but with a nice flair for capturing the problems of these bygone puppets. *Mosk.*

Be My Guest
(BRITISH)

Competently made second feature with some lively pop moments for younger beat patrons.

London, April 13.

Rank distribution of a Three Kings (Lance Comfort) production (in association with Harold Shampan and Filmusic). Features David Hemmings, Avril Angers, Joyce Blair, Jerry Lee Lewis, Thec Nashville Teens, The Zephyrs, Henry and the Wranglers, Niteshadas. Directed by Lance Comfort. Story and screenplay by Lyn Fairhurst; camera, Basil Emmott; editor, Sid Stone; music, Malcolm Lockyer. Reviewed at P.F.D. Theatre, London. Running Time. 82 MINS.
Dave .... David Hemmings
Ricky .... Stephen Marriot
Phil .... John Pike
Erica .... Andrea Monet
Herbert .... Ivor Salter
Margaret .... Anna king
Mrs. Pucil .... Avril Angers
Wanda .... Joyce Blair
Hilton Bass .... David Healey
Artie .... Tony Wager
Routledge .... David Lander
Matthews .... Robin Stewart
Dyllis .... Monica Evans
Stewars .... Douglas Ives

Designed as a second feature pic and to cash in on the still current vogue for the juve pop talent market, this one does its job adequately. Local patrons will enjoy an earful of some of the local groups, but nobody outside the United Kingdom will go overboard. Lyn Fairhurst's script reveals pro knowhow and Lance Comfort is a director with plenty of savvy. Result is an unambitious item that is a cut above many program film fillers.

Slim storyline concerns a London family taking over a seaside guest hotel, how it tries to put the guest house on the map, and how the son of the family, with a beat group, gets involved in a talent contest. Latter brings out some conventional double crossing (tidied up, eventually, by that good old standby, the tape-recorder). Situations and dialog are from hokumsville but there's plenty of opportunity for a few groups to put over some lively numbers.

Malcolm Lockyer's incidental music is bright and is interpolated by a number of songs, of which the title ditty, and "Somebody Help Me," look the likeliest to win honors. The Zephyrs, the Nashville Teens, Kenny and the Wranglers, The Niteshades and Jerry Lee Lewis all have the chance to do their stuff musically and are okay without starting any new breakthrough in the contemporary music field.

David Hemmings and Andrea Monet put over some calf love romance, somewhat self-consciously with Miss Monet showing her paces as a possible up-and-comer in the soubrette stakes, though a shade short on star sparkle. Ivor Salter and Diana King do their best in Mom and Dad roles, but have little opportunity in conventional situations. Avril Angers, as a battleaxe of a housekeeper, reveals a deft comedy attack.

Miss Angers, an experienced, local comedienne, currently playing in "Little Me" in the West End, is inexplicably overlooked in this pix. Other roles that stand out are David Healey, as a genial, egotistic

impresario; and, particularly, Joyce Blair, as his girl friend. Miss Blair, though now blonde instead of brunet, has two or three promising spots and proves herself a useful "blonde temptress" type.

Location work in Brighton has the right authenticity and artwork. Sound and lensing are all okay considering that this is a speedily made, inexpensive picture. *Rich.*

The Fool Killer

Post-Civil War drama of adventures of runaway boy has elements of suspense. Word-of-mouth should help.

Allied Artists release of a Landau Co.-Jack Dreyfus Jr. production. Stars Anthony Perkins; features rest of cast. Directed by Servando Gonzalez. Screenplay, Morton Fine, David Friedkin, based on novel by Helen Eustis; camera, Alex Phillips Jr.; editor, Juan Marino; music, Gustavo C. Carreon. Reviewed at New York, April 22, '65. Running Time, 100 MINS.

Milo Bogardus	Anthony Perkins
George Mellish	Edward Albert
Mr. Dodd	Dana Elcar
Dirty Jim Jelliman	Henry Hull
Mrs. Dodd	Salome Jens
Mrs. Ova Fanshawe	Charlotte Jones
Reverend Spotts	Arnold Moss
Blessing Angelina	Sindee Anne Richards
Old Crab	Frances Gaar
Old Man	Wendell Phillips

Ely Landau has invested as much time and care in putting on film Helen Eustis' 1954 novel about a runaway orphan's adventures in the period immediately following the Civil War as he did with "The Pawnbroker." However, "The Fool Killer" will take smart selling, as, with exception of Anthony Perkins, there are no big b.o. cast members. Careful build-up, making maximum use of favorable reviews and word-of-mouth, should create a good market for a good film. Elements of suspense and violence may be utilized although no actual scenes of violence are shown.

Production was turned over to David Friedkin, who also collaborated with Morton Fine on the screenplay. They have closely followed the plot and format of the novel, even using first-person narrative by the boy to fill in story background and motivations. The decision to use Mexican director Servando Gonzalez was based primarily on his treatment of another small-boy theme in his film, "Yanco." As Gonzalez is a director-writer, it can be assumed that he had some influence on the Friedkin-Fine script. Cameraman Alex Phillips Jr., who filmed "Yanco," repeats on the Landau film. Almost all of the filming was done in the environs of Knoxville.

Anthony Perkins, starred in symbolic title role, doesn't appear until a third of the film has elapsed. The main storyline concentrates on the boy, George (Edward Albert, son of Margo and Eddie Albert, making his film debut). A runaway orphan, his adventures in the adult world of impending danger, moral obligations and responsibility are his first difficult steps in growing up.

His first adventure is a funny and touching meeting with Dirty Jim Jelliman, a filthy, smelly old farmer (played superbly by Henry Hull with sly touches of Jeeter Lester). After sharing Dirty Jim's lazy life for a bit, George realizes that "doing nothing you don't want to" is as boring as adhering to a demanding schedule. Next he meets a strange young man, friendly yet anti-social, alternately moody and frolicsome, who both frightens and fascinates the boy. In his mind, he confuses Milo (Anthony Perkins) with the image of the Fool Killer, described by Dirty Jim as a legendary creature who seeks out and destroys

the fools of the world with his "chopper."

Milo, he learns, is a former hospitalized soldier who believes that other people, particularly the God-fearing, are his enemies. George talks him into attending a gospel meeting where the boy succumbs to the sin-condemning persuasions of the preacher (Arnold Moss). Milo disappears and when the preacher is found murdered, the boy connects him with the crime but says nothing. Taken in by a childless couple, the Dodds (Dana Elcar and Salome Jens), he quickly responds to his first "home." Milo returns to get him but George decides to stay. When Milo attempts to kill the Dodds he is stopped by the boy's pleas but plunges to his death from the rooftop.

While Perkins ably conveys the ephemeral moods of Milo, he somehow misses the needed suggestion of latent paranoia that he portrayed so beautifully in "Psycho" (and which may have been responsible for his casting). However, in a part that could have been flamboyantly melodramatic, he remains consistently in character. The demands on young Albert (almost never offscreen) have resulted in a sincere performance although he never quite meets the emotional demands of the more serious moments.

Other than Hull's brilliant vignette (big enough to remember when Oscar supporting choices come around) the more memorable cast members are Salome Jens as Mrs. Dodd and Sindee Anne Richards as a two-headed tyke, burdened with thick eyeglasses and the name Blessing Angelina, who helps George along his way. Dana Elcar, not given much opportunity as Mr. Dodd, is good in a pedestrian role.

While Gonzalez is apparently familiar with the American scene, even in this period setting, his use of primarily New York actors for principal roles, speaking in a variety of accents, puts the setting almost anywhere. Only explanatory dialog puts it in the South. Technically, the film is outstanding in every department, particularly Phillips' beautifully designed camerawork (except for an excess of closeups.) He keeps most of the action outdoors with some of the landscapes reminiscent of Andrew Wyeth . . . the boy racing across a field, one small dot of action against an impassive vista.

Gustavo Carreon's pleasant score is used primarily as incidental music, Gonzalez making a maximum use of natural sounds.
Robe.

Die, Die, My Darling
(BRITISH-COLOR)
Hollywood, April 19.

Horror story with expert thesping by Tallulah Bankhead should appeal to fright trade, and has b.o. potential with general audiences.

Columbia Pictures release of Hammer Films production. Stars Tallulah Bankhead and Stefanie Powers. Directed by Silvio Narizzano. Screenplay, Richard Matheson, based on novel "Nightmare," by Anne Blaisdell; camera (Eastman Color), Arthur Ibbetson; editor, James Needs;

music, Wilfred Josephs; sound, Ken Rawkins. Reviewed at Columbia Studios, Hollywood, April 19, '65. Running Time, 97 MINS.

Mrs. Trefoile	Tallulah Bankhead
Pat Carroll	Stefanie Powers
Harry	Peter Vaughan
Alan Glentower	Maurice Kaufmann
Anna	Yootha Joyce
Joseph	Donald Sutherland
Gloria	Gwendolyn Watts
Ormsby	Robert Dorning
Oscar	Philip Gilbert
Shopkeeper	Winifred Dennis
Woman Shopper	Diana King

"Die, Die, My Darling" should click with fright fans. Expert thesping by Tallulah Bankhead could cause the Columbia release to take off with general audiences the way other horror pix with veteran actresses have done. Stefanie Powers, victim of Miss Bankhead's violent obsessions, does highly creditable job.

Melodramatic script by Richard Matheson echoes with cliches from other stories set in sinister mansions on English countryside. But it provides Miss Bankhead with numerous chances to display virtuosity, from sweet-tongued menace to maniacal blood-lust, as religious-fanatic mother of Miss Powers' dead fiance.

Another standout in small cast of Hammer Film Production is Peter Vaughan, ne'er-do-well major domo of manse, who has roving eye for Miss Powers' trim figure and shapely legs, which are in sharp contrast to drabness of his housekeeper-wife, well-played by Yootha Joyce.

Story line has Miss Powers, modern miss, paying courtesy call to former fiance's mother, only to be held prisoner while the mother tries to cleanse her soul so she will be fit to meet the son in the hereafter. Escape attempts are violently thwarted by Vaughan, Miss Joyce and Donald Sutherland, who gives vivid portrayal of giant halfwit. Violent and illogical climax comes after Maurice Kaufman, who plays girl's current boyfriend with appropriate dash, comes to rescue.

Silvio Narizzano's direction is imaginative in catching interplay of Miss Bankhead's growing menace and Miss Powers' growing desperation and terror. Dialog generally is fresher than in most pix of its class and Narizzano's direction can be credited with giving dimension to the heroine, who often is cardboard character in such stories.

Arthur Ibbetson's Eastman Color photography captures spirit of production and creepy atmosphere of mansion. Music composed by Wilfred Josephs is appropriate to setting and James Needs editing is brisk and effective. *Hogg.*

Questa Volta Parliamo Di Uomini
(This Time Let's Talk About Men)
(ITALIAN)
Rome, April 13.

Magna Spa release of a Piero Notarianni production for Archimede-Chrono Film. Stars Nino Manfredi; features Luciana Paluzzi, Milena Vukotic, Margaret Lee, Patrizia de Clara. Written and directed by Lina Wertmuller. Music, Luis Enriquez Bacalov; editor, Ruggiero Mastroianni. At Adriano, Rome. Running Time, 90 MINS.

Man is somewhat of a monster, and appropriately it is Italy's only femme film director who sets out

to prove it with this four-episode item. Intelligently made, this pleases without being riotously funny. And this refusal to lower its sights, and cater to the public, will probably cost it an otherwise easy b.o. success. As is, the film needs all the sell it can get via the Nino Manfredi name.

Manfredi is one of major talents here, waiting for a breakthrough picture to hit the big time. His versatile limning of four vastly different roles is an achievement. He's seen first as a "Man of Honor" who doesn't disdain prodding his klepto wife into other hefts to save a bad business situation. Next, he's a broken-down sword thrower who sheds nary a tear even when he kills his longtime target. Then, he portrays a sex-sick professor in "A Superior Man." Finale finds Manfredi in the best item of the lot, the tale of a hard day spent doing nothing by an ever-complaining country hick.

The barbs tossed by the writer-director are sharp, the humor always grim and sometimes grotesque—perhaps overly so. Even at 90 minutes, some of footage drags in spots. Frame story is a mere pretense at linking plots, but manages some very amusing moments in which a naked Manfredi, soap in his eyes from a interrupted shower, gropes his way out into the apartment house hall and is of course locked out, with adventures following. Luciana Paluzzi and Milena Vukotic have their moments as two of Manfredi's women. Technically, the pic is plushly outfitted and elegantly shot. Luis Enriquez Bacalov's musical score is correctly tongue-in-check. *Hawk.*

The Naked Brigade
(U.S.-GREEK)

Wartime meller about German occupation of Crete needs hard sell approach. Plenty of girls in cast but no sex angle.

Universal release of a Box Office Attractions (U.S.) and Alfa Studios, S.A. (Greece) production. Stars Shirley Eaton, Ken Scott; features Mary Chronopoulou, John Holland, Sonia Zoidou, Eleni Zaferious. Directed by Maury Dexter. Screenplay by Alfred J. Cohen, A. Sanford Wolf, based on original story by Wolf and Irwin Winehouse; camera, A. Karides Fuchs; editor, El Siaskas; sound, Antony Bairaktaris; music, Theo Fanidi. Reviewed at Universal h.o., N.Y., April 10, '65. Running Time, 99 MINS.

Diana Forsythe	Shirley Eaton
Christo	Ken Scott
Katina	Mary Chronopoulou
Major Hamilton	John Holland
Athena	Sonia Zoidou
Sofia	Eleni Zaferious
Father Nicholas	Aris Vlachopoulos
Lt. Bentley	Patrick Kavanaugh
Corporal Reade	Clive Russell
Major Heilmann	N. Papaconstantinou
Professor Forsythe	Karl Nurk
Spyros Karrayiannis	Christ Himaras
Lefteris Karrayiannis	Socrates Corres
Yannis Karrayiannis	Zanino Papadopoulos
Stavros Karrayiannis	Gikas Biniaris
Manolakakis	Costas Balademas

This co-production between American producer Albert J. Cohen's Box Office Attractions and Greece's Alfa Studios was partially financed by Universal which is also releasing it. Presence of Shirley Eaton, girl who got the paint job in "Goldfinger," won't be much help in selling the pic. however, as she is kept under wraps throughout. Predictable spot for programmer is as support on an action double-bill.

Title evidently stems from the one good bit of action-suspense, near the end of the film, when Ken Scott, male leader of a female group of guerrillas on island of Crete during the Nazi occupation, takes his gals along on a ship demolition job. What starts off as a promising scene of group of lissome lasses stripping down to the buff proves disappointing. Much is promised but little is delivered. Scott needs them to spell him on task of carting a heavy marine bomb out to Nazi ship in harbor.

Miss Eaton, English gal stranded on Crete when her archaeologist father is killed during Nazi invasion, moves in with guerrilla group until she can be spirited off island by British sub. Scott makes a fast verbal pass early in film but is rebuffed and that's the end of the sex situation except for some mild outbursts of jealousy by his regular girlfriend Mary Chronopoulou (who gives the best performance in film—she was one of the prosties in the Greek Oscar nominee "Red Lanterns").

Cohen and A. Sanford Wolf's screenplay, based on an original story by Irwin Winehouse and Wolf, has more loopholes in its logic than in a prime Swiss cheese. In real life, none of the participants would have been alive at end of the first day of war, much less throughout the invasion. Scott, a well built lad with a limited acting range, might have come off better had there been a firmer hand at the directing but Maury Dexter was apparently as confused by the script as the audience will be.

Most of the war shots are obviously stock footage and, with few exceptions, there's little in the film to tell you that it was made in Greece. Performances, with exception of Miss Chronopoulou, are routine. Miss Eaton plays it too, too British. Only briefly, as in a scene where her best friend is killed alongside her while she's driving the guerrilla team's truck, does she show much emotion. Technical efforts are routine throughout with much use of night photography (to save on lighting bills?). *Robe.*

One Wish Too Many
(BRITISH)

Produced by Realist Film Unit for Children's Film Foundation. Screen adaptation by Mary Carthcart Borer from original story by Norah Pulling. Directed by John Durst. Reviewed in N.Y., April 15, '65. Running Time, 55 MINS.

Peter	Anthony Richmond
Nancy	Rosalind Gourgey
Ian	John Pike
Bert	Terry Cooke
Headmaster	Arthur Howard
Miss Mint	Gladyes Young
Mr. Pomfrett	Sam Costa
Mrs. Brown	Bay White
Mr. Brown	Frany Hayden
Barrow Boy	Paddy Joyce

Released by Sterling Educational Films, branch of Walter Reade-Sterling, this was winner of grand prize for best children's film at the Venice Children's Film Festival in 1956. Nine years have passed and time lag has not enhanced this one. Seen in 16m., sound is blatant, music intrusive, picture mostly murky and production is black & white kid's tale not only physically but script-wise.

Direction and story seem to talk down to children's audience. Anthony Richmond, who was young lad then, finds glass marble with all the properties of Aladdin's lamp, but no kibitzing genie. He uses it kidwise for toys and small revenges, but still gets into trouble, winding up with chase through East London dockside after he wishes toy steamroller up to giant size. The magic of screen effects is slightly hesitant and stilted, but possibly moppet audiences would not be too critical, although Disney has sharpened their tastes for good illusions. Kids in this one seem more natural than the grownups. *Levo.*

The Blind Bird
(RUSSIAN)

Mosnaoutch Films release of Boris Doline production. Directed by Doline. Features Zoia Fedorova, Volodia Agueev, Oleg Jakov, Alexei Gribov, Doline, Anatoli Jadan; camera (color), Yuri Berenstein. Reviewed at N.Y. International Children's Film Festival, April 16, '65. Running Time: 65 MINS.

(French Subtitles)

Although this nature film took a grand prize at the 1963 Venice Children's Film Festival, it is possibly too pastoral for the average American child's taste. Producer-director Boris Doline, a specialist in filming wildlife, certainly gets some rare shots of flocks of pelicans plus a bravura performance from the bird who has the title role, but the combination of straight nature shots and a story to fit the film footage is done infinitely better by Walt Disney.

A boy, helping his grandfather band pelicans before they fly south, finds one that is blind. He takes it home and protects it through the winter. One day, in a newspaper, he reads that a famous eye surgeon will be in Moscow. With the aid of a friend he manages to get the pelican to the city.

Much of the footage is taken up with his efforts in finding the surgeon in the big city and how he finally makes it. The operation, seemingly a failure, turns out to be successful and the boy releases the bird in time for it to fly south with the flock.

Yuri Berenstein's color photography is good when it deals with outdoor and closeup work with the pelicans and in some of the city shots but the color process used is poor and all interiors look distorted. Zoia Fedorova, as the boy, Vassia, is excellent, with a considerable emotional range that still manages to retain the perspective of a small boy. Too many purely atmospheric shots slow down the pace, but the film is refreshingly free of propaganda and could well have taken place in any country.

The reason for the French subtitles is that the print used was prepared for a children's festival in Montreal. The festival will need some sort of interpreting although the story is comparatively simple. *Robe.*

Skinny And Fatty
(JAPANESE)

Educational Film Exchange and Mingel Eiga Sha coproduction. Directed by N. Terao. Features Y. Kataoka, H. Sha, M. Shimojo, Y. Takano, S. Horie, Y. Omori, T. Naraoka, M. Saito. Screenplay, S. Yoshida, M. Wakasugi. Reviewed at New York International Children's Film Festival, April 16, '65. Running Time, 55 MINS.

Japanese entry in Jay K. Hoffman's week of children's films was a 1959 coproduction by the Japanese Educational Film Exchange and Mingei Eiga Sha. Simple tale centers about two small schoolboys, a well-to-do fat one and a small, poor boy, and their growing friendship.

Story is at its best when everyday incidents involving the entire school are shown, particularly an athletic competition. Print shown had no English subtitles and there were frequent periods where the average child viewer would lose the main storyline.

Particularly excellent is H. Sha as Kenkichi, the "Skinny" of the title, although it's a misnomer. He's a sturdy but quite small lad with plenty of personality. The "Fatty" is well-named, however, and some of the physical workouts he's put through seem much too arduous for such an extremely overweight child. Although aimed at ages 5-12, it's unlikely to hold the interest of the younger set.

Black-and-white photography is excellent as are other technical values. *Robe.*

Thomas L'Imposteur
(Thomas the Imposter)
(FRENCH)
Paris, April 27.

CCFC release of Filmel production. Stars Emmanuelle Riva; features Fabrice Rouleau, Sophie Dares, Rosy Varte, Michel Vitold, Jean Servais. Directed by Georges Franju. Screenplay, Jean Cocteau, Franju, Michel Worms, Raphael Cluzel; camera, Marcel Fradetal; editor, Gilbert Natot. Previewed in Paris. Running Time, 90 MINS.

Princess	Emmanuelle Riva
Thomas	Fabrice Rouleau
Editor	Jean Servais
Daughter	Sophie Dares
Nurse	Rosy Varte
Doctor	Michel Vitold

The late Jean Cocteau worked on the script of his early book with director Georges Franju several years ago. Put off often, it was finally made a year after Cocteau's death. This is a poetic film about a teen-age boy impersonating an officer during the First World War. It also embodies a gentle love story and a biting feel for war's horrors as well as its strangeness.

Pic has an atmospheric flair for the times. It hints that perhaps that war, after the still near destruction of the last one, and the A-Bomb, is the one that can still be treated on a personal basis and with the passage of time takes on an aura of a now almost costumed affair. Arty chances abroad are inherent in this absorbing tale.

A headstrong noble widow princess gets up a caravan to go to the front to pick up wounded men and bring them back to her chateau near Paris for treatment. Stymied by red tape, she is helped by a 16-year-old boy in an officer's uniform who says he is the nephew of a noted general. The name gets the papers and opens frontiers and military help for the group.

The boy becomes indispensable to the princess who feels a strange attachment for him. Her teen-age daughter falls in love with the lad, and the woman finally feels she has no place in the war. Also that it may be just a headstrong over-romantic affair on her part when she is faced by some of its true horrors. So she gives up her work. But the youth gets attached to a canteen on the farflung northern lines where he is finally killed one night on patrol.

The young girl commits suicide and her mother is confronted with complete loss. There is a mixture of commentary and visual narrative that give this a balance in its measured telling. The players fit the period. War's terrors are not blatant but shown in their useless waste as well as the so-called illusion of glory. Latter has made the young man believe in his impersonation till he dies with the false name on his lips.

Franju is true to the poetic, artful world of Cocteau but adds his own talent for imbuing the narrative with an underlying strangeness that makes it constantly eve filling and sometimes disturbing if always interesting. A horse running wildly through a street with its mane on fire, a priest giving communion to a dead soldier by prying his mouth open with a knife, a party with the Germans supposedly advancing on Paris, and other scenes build an offbeat, worldly commentary on war.

Casting is also excellent. Emmanuelle Riva, somewhat given to overdone dramatics is perfect here as the adventurous, worldly wise and touchingly courageous princess. Fabrice Rouleau, if seemingly gauche, has the right appearance as the audacious and helpful young man, who impersonates the nephew of an officer.

Illusion and reality are also constantly intermingled in this unusual pic. If the film may let down a bit in the second half, this still emerges pic with good arty chances abroad. But it needs careful sell for more selective audiences. A fine production dress and technical expertness also help make this strange costumer an important production here.

There is a possibility this may be a last-minute competing, invited pic at the coming Cannes Film Fest. *Mosk.*

Der Hexer
(The Squeaker)
(GERMAN)
Berlin, April 20.

Constantin release of Rialto Film production. Stars Joachim Fuchsberger, Heinz Drache, Sophie Hardy. Directed by Alfred Vohrer. Screenplay, Herbert Reinecker, adapted from novel of same name, by Edgar Wallace; camera, Karl Loeb; music, Peter Thomas; editor, Jutta Hering. At Zoo Palast, West Berlin. Running Time, 95 MINS.

Higgins	Joachim Fuchsberger
Wesby	Heinz Drache
Elise	Sophie Hardy
Warren	Siegfried Lowitz
Cora Ann Milton	Margot Trooger
Reverend Hopkins	Carl Lange
Maurice Messer	Jochen Brockman
Sir John	Siegfried Schuerenberg
Shelby	Karl John

The series of German filmizations of Edgar Wallace continues with "The Squeaker," probably the late English author's most prominent crime novel. Horst Wendlandt's Rialto production emerges as a routine mixture of thrill and violence plus wit and sex. These ingredients still spell coin in this country. Constantin has therewith another surefire domestic b.o. possibility at its disposal and this counts most. Certain foreign prospects loom.

There is, as per this Wallace filmization, a certain departure from the cliche inasmuch as screenwriter Herbert Reinecker has given the old plot a new twist: Although the original has been read by millions no cne will actually know who the "Squeaker" is in this vehicle. Reinecker has dreamed up a surprise ending and changed the plot accordingly.

This starts out with the killing of a secretary because she knew too much of her chief's dubious (traffic in young girls) enterprise. The evildoers here have not only to fear Scotland Yard but also the "Squeaker" who happens to be the brother of the murdered secretary. He comes from Australia to wipe out the entire gang much to the dismay of the London police who cannot accept this kind of justice. And once more the "Squeaker" manages to escape the police. This makes the way free for a sequel (already in production) to this Teutonic thriller.

This Rialto production employs more or less the same players who have been seen in countless other Wallace pix here. Cast is headed by Joachim Fuchsberger, as a Scotland Yard detective, and Heinz Drache, as an officer of the Australian crime department. While Drache's job still borders on the competent, it must be said that Fuchsberger puts Scotland Yard in a rather silly light. The inevitable sex is chiefly repped by French Sophie Hardy who shows a remarkable bit of flesh in this pic. The actor who plays the title role is not given to keep secret who the "Squeaker" really is.

Alfred Vohrer's direction displays technical knowhow. He sees to it that the confusion never ends and that the whole thing won't be taken too seriously. Karl Loeb's camera work on UltraScope and Peter Thomas' score are assets.
Hans.

N.Y. FEST

Miguelin
(SPANISH)

Arcadia Films, S.A. (Madrid) and Fundacion Espanola del Cine Infantil production. Features Luis Maria Hidalgo, Luis Dominguez Luna, Alberto Domarco, Rufino Ingles, Jose Luis Blanco, Francisco Jose Buetos, Crisanto Huerta, Rosa Fuster. Directed by Horacio Valcarcel. Screenplay, Valcarcel and Joaquin Aguirre Bellver; camera, Francisco Fraile; music, Manuel Garcia. Reviewed April 19, '65 at Museum of Modern Art, N.Y. (Spanish Film Week). Running Time, 63 MINS.

Perhaps most delightful film about children to come out of Spain since "Marcelino," this joint effort of Arcadia Films and the Spanish Foundation for Children's Films is a funny, often touching tale of a small boy's personal discovery of the rewards of faith and unselfishness.

Horacio Valcarcel, who directed and collaborated with Joaquin Aguirre Bellver on the script, shows great promise, having the rare gift of telling a story visually with simplicity and warmth. Shown as the first film on the Museum of Modern Art's Spanish Film Week (as a last-minute substitution for a previous entry that was being shown commercially), it was necessary to screen it without English subtitles. Although the interpretation of the dialog would have added to its appeal Valcarcel says so much through expression and movement that the storyline can be easily followed even without knowing Spanish.

Luis Maria Hidalgo, as the title character, is a serious boy whose personal war on poverty is to sell his precious mule and leave the money (he believes unobserved) in the church's poor-box. However, with the aid of the village priest and the other boys, the mule is recovered (just in time for the annual blessing of animals). The entire cast is excellent, although a small, uncredited towhead (who tags along after Miguelin until his devotion switches to a scrawny kitten) steals every scene he's in. Valcarcel has been lucky in having cameraman Francisco Fraile capture the daily life of the village and villagers on film.
Robe.

La Tia Tula
(Aunt Tula)
(SPANISH)

Eco Films, S.A. and Surco Films, S.A. (Madrid) production. Features Aurora Bautista, Carlos Estrada, Irene Gutierrez Caba, Laly Soldevilla, Mari Loli Cobos, Carlos Sanchez, Enriqueta Carballeira, Jose Maria Prada. Directed by Miguel Picazo. Screenplay, Miguel Picazo Dios, Luis Sanchez Enciso, Manuel Lopez Yubero, Jose Hernandez, based on novel by Miguel de Unamuno; camera, Juan Julio Baena; editor, Josefa Rubio Martos. Reviewed April 23, '65, at Museum of Modern Art, N.Y. (Spanish Film Week). Running Time, 118 MINS.

(English Titles)

If, as one program note states, it was director Miguel Picazo's purpose to capture on film a portrait of a woman bound to her beliefs, who does not even wish to discuss the matter, he has been very successful. That he has also eliminated the audience by having no character with which viewers can identify (at least no non-Spanish viewer), he has been equally successful.

Despite a bravura performance by Aurora Bautista in the title role which captures the tragic feeling of a misguided life, necessary relief the film should have had in making her victims less deserving of their fate is missing. Audiences look for some resistance, here there is none.

When the wife of a bank employee (Carlos Estrada) dies, his attractive sister-in-law (Aurora Bautista) takes over management of his and his children's lives, gradually usurping the privileges of a wife but not the responsibilities. As Spanish ideals concepts stress the behavior of the husband following the death of a wife, he is satisfied to go along with things as they are but becomes increasingly aware of the physical attractiveness of the sister-in-law. She dotes on his two children but spurns any effort on his part to be affectionate. At the same time, by criticism, keeps him from becoming interested in other women.

Part of the confusion undoubtedly stems from the script. Four writers receive credit plus the author of the original novel. Picazo's lack of sufficient control results in a static repetitiveness of dialogue and incident that makes the film seem much longer than the 118 minutes it takes. Some wholesale elimination might give a semblance of life to this too long, too talky effort.

Juan Julio Baena's black and white photography is good but the particular print shown in N.Y. was poor with frequent out-of-focus shots that proved very irritating. As other films in the series have been shown without mishap, the fault is probably in the printing.

Miss Bautista, too attractive and vivacious to be completely believable, gets across some tragic feeling of being spiritually or morally sick and refusing to accept it. Estrada, however, is weak in both characterization and demeanor. The initial sympathy is dispelled in the first 10 minutes. He probably realizes that he couldn't be helped because he doesn't really want to be.
Robe.

Dialogos De La Paz
(Dialogues Of Peace)
(SPANISH-ENGLISH TITLES)

Petruka Films, S.A. (Madrid) production. Features Nuria Torray, Angel Aranda, Manuel Gil, Juanjo Seoane, Maruchi Fresno, Antonio G. Escribano, Manuel Manzaneque, Carlos Munoz, Francisco Pierra, Ricardo Palacio, Amparo Pamplona. Directed and written by Jose Maria Font Espina and Jorge Feliu; camera, Godofredo Pacheco; editor, Jose Antonio Rojo. Reviewed April 19, '65, at Museum of Modern Art, N.Y. (Spanish Film Week). Running Time, 88 MINS.

The official Spanish entry at the 1965 Mar del Plata Film Festival, where actress Nuria Torray of its cast received the "best actress" award and the film was given the O.C.I.C. prize, this moody, slow-paced film may have an appeal for the fascinated-with-death Spanish but has almost no chance of successful release in the U.S.

Granted that its appeal for the need of "burying of the dead" by both sides following the Spanish civil war is for a worthy cause, this manner of telling it has resulted in a one-sidedness that may not be shared by the losing side of the struggle. Directors (and scripters) Jorge Feliu and Jose Maria Font Espina's use of frequent flashbacks gives some effect of movement but the excessive use of "spoken" thoughts of the protagonists gets tedious after a time.

A widow (Nuria Torray) of an officer (Manuel Gil) in the defeated army visits a former battlefield (along with many others) to seek her husband's body. There she is followed by a former friend (Angel Aranda) who became estranged because he believed in the opposite cause. Having long loved her, he asks her to remain in Spain. As they recall the life the three of them had together before the war, her convictions are shaken but she argues that she'll always be an "enemy" and insists on leaving. Before she crosses the border, however, she realizes that she's only taking her struggle with her and returns to "fight it out" for the sake of her child, and with the help of the friend.

Godofredo Pacheco's black and white photography is crisp and beautifully lit but a tendency to linger overlong on static scenes— a group looking at the battlefield, the heroine gazing from a window —adds only to the tedium—and most non-Latin viewers will object. Miss Torray's emotion-held-in-restraint style may be interpreted by many as lack of feeling. Feliu and Font Espina also introduce scenes or incidents that are sometime visually misleading. During the search of the battlefield, the camera returns frequently to a farmer plowing a near-by field. The implication is that, as the heroine has been unsuccessful in her search, the plow may momentarily turn up something. He doesn't. He speaks to the wife as one of the protagonists of "peace," with other characters also introduced for the same purpose. *Robe.*

Del Rosa . . . Al Amarillo
(From Pink To Yellow)
(SPANISH)

Impala, S.A. and Eco Films, S.A. (Madrid) production. Features Pedro Diez del Corral, Cristina Galbo Sanchez, Jose Vicente Cerrudo, Angelina Onesti. Directed and written by Manuel Summers; camera, Francisco Fraile; music, Antonio Perez Olea. Reviewed April 21, '65 at Museum of Modern Art, N.Y. (Spanish Film Week). Running Time, 94 MINS.

(English Titles)

Having won several prizes since its first showing at the 1963 San Sebastian Film Festival for both film and director, it is unusual that this sensitive, appealing, double love story hasn't been seen in the U.S. previously. Opportunity to see the work of new director Manuel Summers should be expanded beyond the one-time showing at the MMA's Spanish Film Week.

The two stories deal with very young love and very old love. Both are presented without mawkishness or precocity. Public appeal may possibly be greater for the younger half as the interest of the old in the young (as well as in themselves) is not always reciprocated. Fortunately, viewers exposed to both tales are doubly rewarded.

Summers' aproach to the possibility of love between the young— the boy, Pedro Diez del Corral, is several years younger than the girl, Cristina Galbo Sanchez, who must be all of 14—is dead serious. The boy, still in short pants, goes off the deep end and devotes himself entirely to the winning of the lovely lady who toys with his affections. His experiences are at once funny and near tragic, ambitious and fruitless. Convinced finally that she loves him, he returns from summer camp to find she has given her heart to another. His world crashes, but with the wonderful elasticity of the very young, he walks away, consoled somewhat by the fact that he's wearing his first long trousers.

The heartwarming tale of "old love" makes wonderful use of the motion picture camera to interpret human feelings. Two elderly inmates of a poor asylum (Jose Vicente Cerrudo and Angelina Onesti) carry on their romance by secret correspondence. As the "Poor house" policy is that of complete segregation of the sexes, they only see each other at close quarters once a week during church. Not once do they address each other directly. Hastily-scribbled "love letters," exchanged via a complicated series of hiding places, are read (in the off-screen voice of the sender) in the seclusion of their beds, or hastily amid the day's activities.

The old man, Valentin, sent on an errand to the city, returns aglow to report on the "wonders of the outside world" and tries to convince the old woman Josefa, to run away with him. Always timid and now afraid, she hasn't the courage to try and he decides to escape without her. But love overcomes even the need for personal liberty and as she looks next morning into the expectedly-empty courtyard, she sees him. They will go on, separated but together, in this fashion for the rest of their lives.

Francisco Fraile, who photographed "Miguelin," makes his camera move with the quick, impulsive actions of the energetic child in the first tale and with slow but stately grace in the second. *Robe.*

Ship of Fools

Profitable voyage looms for thoughtful "adult" drama with international star cast.

Columbia release of Stanley Kramer production, directed by Kramer. Stars Vivien Leigh, Simone Signoret, Jose Ferrer, Lee Marvin, Oskar Werner, Elizabeth Ashley, George Segal, Jose Greco, Michael Dunn, Charles Korvin, Heinz Ruehmann. Screenplay, Abby Mann from Katherine Anne Porter novel; camera, Ernest Laszlo; editor, Robert C. Jones; music, Ernest Gold; songs by Gold and Jack Lloyd; asst. director, John Veitch. Reviewed in Hollywood, April 22, 1965. Running Time, 148 MINS.

Mary Treadwell	Vivien Leigh
La Condesa	Simone Signoret
Rieber	Jose Ferrer
Tenny	Lee Marvin
Dr. Schumann	Oskar Werner
Jenny	Elizabeth Ashley
David	George Segal
Pepe	Jose Greco
Glocken	Michael Dunn
Capt. Thiele	Charles Korvin
Lowenthal	Heinz Ruehmann
Frau Hutten	Lilia Skala
Amparo	Barbara Luna
Lizzi	Christiane Schmidtmer
Freytag	Alf Kjellin
Lt. Heebner	Werner Klemperer
Graf	John Wengraf
Frau Schmitt	Olga Fabian
Elsa	Gila Golan
Lutz	Oscar Beregi
Hutten	Stanley Adams
Frau Lutz	Karen Verne
Johann	Charles de Vries
Pastora	Lydia Torea
Fat Man	Henry Calvin
Carlos	Paul Daniel
Woodcarver	David Renard
Ric	Rudy Carrella
Rac	Silvia Marino
Guitarist	Anthony Brand

Stanley Kramer's "Ship of Fools" appears headed on a profitable voyage for Columbia Pictures. The director-producer and scenarist Abby Mann, together with a cast of accomplished performers, have distilled the essence of Katherine Anne Porter's bulky novel, regarded by many as the author's magnum opus, in a film of two hours 28 minutes that appeals to the intellect and the emotions.

Some of Miss Porter's more dedicated admirers may fault Kramer for omitting incidents, truncating others and redrawing characters to more physically commercial film form. However, these are minor overall, considering the difficult job of dramatization. Moreover, for the millions who have not read the book but will see the picture this won't matter at all.

On its own terms as screen entertainment "Ship of Fools" is intelligent and eminently satisfying most of the time. The human cargo aboard the German ship Vera sailing from Vera Cruz to Bremerhaven (1933) is a conglomerate of society—a cross-section of mass humanity just as representative of the contemporary social order as that which a landlubber can encounter in any metropolis.

While Nazism was incipient at the time Miss Porter's story took place (she used the year 1931) and more reasonable Germans, including those of the Jewish faith, tended to shrug off its danger, this and other forms of racism are rampant today as well, thus giving "Ship of Fools" a pertinence that the passing of years and a devastating world war have not outdated. As a character in the film,

ironically a dwarf who is played by Michael Dunn with majestic resignation and cynicism, yet with a spark of faith, says in the opening scene, the passengers that comprise the ship of fools are the audience.

Like the book, the film does not have a neatly ordered story with beginning, middle and end. The voyage and confinement of shipboard provides the framework for a diverse series of character studies that are by turn tragic and amusing. Kramer has directed with keen appreciation of human elements and, no easy task, manages to maintain a flow of movement throughout the film, heightened at times by quick cuts for which director and editor Robert C. Jones can share credit. There is also a lively, physically punishing brawl among sugar field workers returning from Cuba to Spain who are crowded into the ship's hold like cattle.

All of the principals give strong performances from the aggressive interpretation by Jose Ferrer as a loathsome disciple of the emerging Hitlerian new order to Vivien Leigh as a fading American divorcee who gets her kicks out of leading on admirers and throwing cold water on their burning desires. Miss Leigh and Ferrer are indeed excellent in roles that in lesser hands and with less directorial understanding could easily have become lifeless stereotypes.

Of equal importance to the main stream of this drama, and also astutely attuned, are the contributions by Simone Signoret in the role of La Condesa and Oskar Werner as Dr. Schumann, the ship's doctor. The French star gives a finely balanced performance with shadings of pathos and lust for life as a dissolute middle-aged woman heading toward prison. Role of the doctor has been made younger than in the book, a concession to boxoffice no doubt, as they become romantically entangled. However, despite developing a most appealing, interesting portrait of a disturbed man and dedicated physician, Werner's attraction to a woman he knows is on drugs and who, while interesting, is physically unattractive, is hard to accept. There can be no doubt, however, that Werner is an actor of extraordinary talent and he should loom large as a fresh personality.

Also impressive and showing promise of bright futures are George Segal and Elizabeth Ashley as young lovers whose intellects and emotions seem to be always warring against the animal magnetism that draws them together. Lee Marvin, as a has-been baseball player with his mouth to the bottle and a lust for women, does a competent job on the whole, capped by a hilarious drunken scene when he attempts to illustrate for the dwarf how he could never manage to connect with an outside curve. It's a gem.

Other solid performances are turned in by Charles Korvin, captain of the ship, and Heinz Ruehmann. He plays a jew who is ostracized by "Pure" Germans, but can't conceive that there is a monstrous sickness corroding German hearts because he is first of all a German and loves his country. Jose Greco and his dance

troupe do expertly what comes naturally for them and also step out adequately in roles that require them to act. David Renard has a small role that stands out from the crowd of peasant workers as a woodcarver and uses his few moments most effectively.

Many people come before the camera, too many to be singled out individually, but among the more notable are Alf Kjellin, Christiane Schmidtmer, Lilia Skala, Stanley Adams, Olga Fabian, Gila Golan, John Wengraf, Charles deVries, Werner Klemperer and Henry Calvin.

Incidents not herein described, including facial by-play, or reaction, that gives significance to spoken and unspoken words heightens the impact of this film and, of course, redound to Kramer's credit as director. It is possible, however, that some viewers may find disturbing certain quick cuts from scenes which appear to be on the verge of reaching a higher point of drama. Yet Kramer uses this technique intelligently, creating sufficient continuity for attentive viewers. The photography of Ernest Laszlo is sharp and mobile; and Ernest Gold has provided a suitable music score, including two German songs for which Jack Lloyd wrote the lyrics, and production designer Robert Cratworthy created a realistic, seaworthy ship.

"Ship of Fools" is an "adult" picture, a meaningful observation of the joys, sorrows, frustrations, hopes, aspirations and cruelties of people. It also is a picture that contains a line of dialog not previously heard on the screen as the doctor, in examining La Condessa, inquires when she had her last period. It's a normal, natural medical question and it is asked with professional detachment, yet one wonders why. It doesn't contribute anything to the film, but it might needlessly cause adverse comment. *Pry.*

Kimberley Jim
(SONGS-SCANOSCOPE-COLOR)

Nice little South African import with country-western singer Jim Reeves to help chances in minor markets.

Hollywood, April 28.

Embassy release of Emil Nofal production. Stars Jim Reeves, Madeleine Usher, Clive Parnell; features rest of cast. Directed, story, screenplay by Nofal. Camera (Agfacolor), Judex C. Viljoen; art direction, Ian McLeod; editor, Harry Hughes; asst. director, Jans Rautenbach; sound, Bonne Ter Steege. Reviewed at Joe Shore Screening Room, April 28, '65. Running Time, 81 MINS.

Jim Madison	Jim Reeves
Julie Patterson	Madeleine Usher
Gerry Bates	Clive Parnell
Bert Patterson	Arthur Swemmer
Ben Vorster	Tromp Terre'blanche
Danny Pretorious	Vonk de Ridder
Punchy	Mike Holt
Jan le Roux	Dawid Van Der Walt
Eliza	June Neethling
Fred Parker	George Moore
Neels le Roux	Freddie Prozesky
Rube	Don Leonard
Max Bloom	Morris Blake
	and The Blue Boys

"Kimberley Jim," another of Joseph Levine-Embassy Pictures'

imports, is a minor entry but with the name of American country-western singer Jim Reeves for ballast and should prove fairly commercial in the market for which it's aimed. Reeves, making his screen bow in the South African production, socks over a half dozen or so tuneful melodies in his customary ingratiating style and producer-writer-director Emil Nofal has provided a story backdrop to allow good playoff of his talents.

Apart from Reeves and one of his co-stars, Clive Parnell (English), most of cast are South African, as well as those behind the cameras. Nofal himself is a 25-year old pro in the new film industry there. Film, lensed in Agfacolor and Scanoscope, lacks the finish of an American production but nonetheless is a lightly-flowing programmer which less discriminating situations should find agreeable.

Photographed in the Kimberley diamond area, narrative follows Reeves and Parnell, a pair of good-natured but larcenous gamblers who win a diamond mine in a crooked poker game. Then they arrive at the diggings and find both a pretty daughter of the man they've cheated, no diamonds—but expected any day now—and plenty of debts. There's a fight, dancing girls, comedy and plenty of music to keep film's 81-minutes active, and performances generally are satisfactory.

Reeves is pliable and likeable and his songs are intro'd naturally. Parnell, his partner, is his comedy relief, and Madeleine Usher, disports herself prettily in both song and acting as daughter of Arthur Swemmer, who lost his mine but regains it from the two strangers, with hearts of gold. Tromp Terre'-Blanche is an old-fashioned heavy, Vonk de Ridder, Dawid Van Der Walt and June Neethling standouts in support.

Camera work by Judex C. Viljoen is okay, as are balance of technical credits.   *Whit.*

The Woman Who Wouldn't Die
(BRITISH)

Part of suspense package, taut little thriller more than holds its own. No names but good script and direction evident.

Warner Bros. release of a Parroch-McCallum production. Features Gary Merrill, Jane Merrow, Georgina Cookson, Neil McCallum. Directed by Gordon Hessler. Screenplay, Dan Mainwaring, based on novel "Catacombs" by Jay Bennett; camera, Arthur Lavis; editor, Robert Winter; music, Carlo Martelli. Reviewed at Warner Bros. h.o., N.Y., April 30, '65. Running time **84 MINS.**
Raymond Garth .... Gary Merrill
Alice Taylor .... Jane Merrow
Ellen Garth .... Georgina Cookson
Dick Corbett .... Neil McCallum
Christine .... Rachel Thomas
Solicitor .... Jack Train
Police Inspector .... Frederick Piper

What could have easily been on of those quickie, murder-on-the-moors thrillers which the British seem to turn out over a weekend, this Jack Parsons production comes off something better than average because of a

very good performance by Georgina Cookson and taut direction by Gordon Hessler of Dan Mainwaring's spare but neat screenplay.

There are few surprises in the basically simple plot but the cast acts with more inventiveness than usually found in these programmers. Gary Merrill, an American married to a wealthy but also demanding and possessive English businesswoman (Georgina Cookson) takes on more frustrations when he finds himself physically attracted to his wife's pretty, young and very interested niece (Jane Merrow). Wife has a super efficient male secretary (Neil McCallum) whose services she insures through her possession of some forged checks he had tossed off in a moment of weakness.

When the two males team up to eliminate their nemesis she proves surprisingly durable and by no means as dead as they believe. The outcome can be predicted — more deaths. Miss Cookson dominates the film with an icicle-cold performance of a woman who combines an awareness of male weaknesses with a seldom-satisfied sexual hunger — an English countryside version of Craig's wife, Messalina and "She" combined.

Merrill's performance is lethargic until the physical demands of getting rid of the wife force him to show some response. McCallum is adequate as the secretary. Miss Merrow, as pretty as the young temptress she is poraraying, offers little beyond physical charms. Rachel Thomas is excellent in a small but important role of the maid who tips the plot.

Technical credits are generally better than would be expected from such a low-budgeter. Arthur Lavis' black and white photography is crisp and sharp except for the murky ending. With WB doubling the film with "Brainstorm" for a May thrill bill, returns should be satisfactory and "Woman" can stick around for quite awhile as good supporting fare on any suspense program.   *Robe.*

Le Majordome
(The Majordomo)
(FRENCH)

Paris, April 27.
Cocinor release of Marceau-Cocinor, Ceres Film production. Stars Paul Meurisse; features Genevieve Page, Paul Hubschmidt, Noel Roquevert. Directed by Jean Delannoy. Screenplay, Jacques Robert, Henri Jeanson, Delannoy; camera, Christian Matras; editor, Henri Taverna. At Colisee, Paris. Running Time, **90 MINS.**
Leopold .... Paul Meurisse
Agnes .... Genevieve Page
Chat .... Paul Hubschmidt
Lawyer .... Noel Roquevert

Here is a dinosaur of a pic. Old-fashioned tale of the suave valet of a noted criminal lawyer, who acts as an underworld law advisor and gets involved in a bigtime holdup is mixed with more modern holdup techniques and palaver made popular by the James Bond pix. The mixture does not jell too well.

Paul Meurisse, a specialist at playing gently smug, stuffy types involved in police or underworld activities, here overdoes things. He also is given some silly things to do which have him throwing off the comic potential of the role.

Add Jean Delannoy's stolid direction to quell most of the fun that could have been inherent in this underworld romp.

Meurisse gets mixed up with a noted crook in a plot to steal gold bullion. But he falls in love, and decides to hijack the hijackers. This is done, with a happy ending as the girl turns out to be a police-woman, and he gets off lightly.

Some ex-Foreign Legion men are dragged in but this is ambiguous.

Also there is a fairly punched-up holdup. But much of this comes too late to save this heavyhanded comedy.

However, this mixture of adroit plotting and lowdown underworld doings could give this a peg for playoff and specialized showing but it will need hard sell. Pic is technically okay. Supporting cast is fair with some okay gimmicks.
    Mosk.

Synanon

Well-made fictionalized yarn about the Santa Monica rehabilitation home for drug addicts, Synanon House. For selected market rather than general situations.

Hollywood, May 4.
Columbia Pictures release of Richard Quine production. Stars Edmond O'Brien, Chuck Connors, Stella Stevens, Alex Cord, Richard Conte, Eartha Kitt; features rest of cast. Directed by Quine. Screenplay, Ian Bernard, S. Lee Pogostin; story, Barry Oringer, Pogostin; camera, Harry Stradling; music, Neal Hefti; editor, David Wages; sound, Josh Westmoreland; asst. director, Carter DeHaven Jr. Reviewed at Academy Award Theatre, April 15, '65. Running Time, **105 MINS.**
Chuck Dederich ...... Edmond O'Brien
Ben .... Chuck Connors
Joaney .... Stella Stevens
Zankie Albo .... Alex Cord
Reid .... Richard Conte
Betty Coleman .... Eartha Kitt
Mary .... Barbara Luna
Chris .... Alejandro Rey
Hopper .... Richard Evans
Vince .... Gregory Morton
Arline .... Chanin Hale
Pruddy .... Casey Townsend
Bob Adamic .... Larry Kert
Pete .... Bernie Hamilton
Joe Mann .... Mark Sturges
The Greek .... Lawrence Montaigne
Carla .... Patricia Huston
And Residents of Synanon House
Arnold Ross, John Peterson, James Middleton, Anthony Daddio, Dan Spaccarelli, Herb Rosen, Candy Latson, William Crawford, Charles Haden, and Mathew Notkins.

"Synanon" is a fictionized semi-documentary of a rehabilitation home for drug addicts on the beachfront of Santa Monica, Calif., where almost miraculous cures are said to be achieved. As backdrop for a dramatic story it is grim, hard-hitting and sometimes shocking; as an outlet for plot unfoldment there may be some debate whether the overall qualifies as entertainment, but certainly it presents its story well and because of its honesty of purpose merits certain attention. Film will appeal more to the selected market, however, than to the general mass media.

Producer-director Richard Quine moved his cameras to the actual locale to ensure authenticity in this story of Synanon House, established by Charles E. Dederich, an ex-alcoholic, in 1958. The Ian

Bernard-S. Lee Pogostin screenplay blends clinical treatment of subject matter with personification of the project through the advent of a new applicant for help, and a documentary flavor is further pointed up by a realistic climax in which there is no compromise. Film ends on a note of hope for addicts who are willing to accept the help afforded them.

Edmond O'Brien enacts the character of Dederich (who acted as technical advisor), plagued by debts and civic opposition as he goes about his seemingly thankless task of trying to bring lives back from the brink. Already worried about a jail term he must serve on a zoning law conviction and the State's order for expulsion of parolees who are undergoing treatment, he finds further problems with the arrival of Alex Cord, ex-con hooked with the habit, who proves a non-conformist even while withdrawing from addiction. Latter romances one of the occupants, a prostitute, who is assigned to watch over his withdrawal, and generally upsets the routine of Synanon House. Leaving the haven after a fight with another occupant, Chuck Connors, Cord, returns to the needle and in an overdose dies in a cheap hotel room. The prostitute, who left Synanon House to follow him, returns after his death supposedly for a complete cure.

O'Brien's performance is smooth and convincing and lends strength to the character he portrays. Cord, a newcomer on the screen, registers decisively in an unsympathetic role, and Stella Stevens is persuasive as the hooker, with a great love for her five-year-old son in custody of her divorced husband but who cannot overcome her past profession. Connors' character of a parolee who has beaten the drug rap is more nebulous in form but he nevertheless delivers a good account of himself.

Richard Conte and Eartha Kitt play two real-life characters of Reid Kimball, second in command, and Betty Coleman, one of the regular workers at the house. Barbara Luna, Alejandro Rey, Richard Evans, Gregory Morton and Bernie Hamilton, among others, lend strong support. Some of the actual residents of Synanon House, undergoing therapy, appear as themselves.

Harry Stradling's photography makes interesting use of the various rooms of the house and is a potent asset, as is David Wages' expert editing. Neal Hefti's music score provides suitable background.
    Whit.

100 Briques Et Des Tuiles
(100 Million and Trouble)
(FRENCH)

Paris, April 27.
CFDC release of France Cinema Productions-RCM production. Stars Jean-Claude Brialy; features Marie Laforet, Sophie Daumier, Jean-Pierre Marielle, Albert Remy, Daniel Ceccaldi, Pierre Clementi, Michel Serrault. Directed by Pierre Grimblat. Screenplay, Clarence Weff, Grimblat from a book by Weff; camera, Michel Kelber; editor, Robert Isnardon. At Normandie, Paris. Running Time, **90 MINS.**
Marcel .... Jean-Claude Brialy
Ida .... Marie Laforet
Girl .... Sophie Daumier
Boyfriend .... Pierre Clementi
Justin .... Jean-Pierre Marielle

Etienne .... Albert Remy
Barman .... Daniel Ceccaldi
Elevator Man .... Michel Serrault

Picaresque pic, about an aborted holdup and comeuppances of sympathetic lowlife characters, just does not have the highflown invention, brisk progression and madcap zest to bring it off. This does have some far out yockful bits at the end but not enough to keep this uneven film from sagging much of the time. Mainly some dualer or tv interest for this abroad on its theme, with arty chances small.

A joy girl, her dim-witted panderer, a pro gambler and a couple of others decide to heist the till of a big department store just before Xmas. It comes off but money falls in glue before being picked up and there is an added complication when some teenage delinquents get the swag by mistake.

It finally comes back to the first gang who wash the money and hang it up to dry when a bull comes into the yard of their hideout followed by a horde of canewielding police, bullfighter style, trying to capture it. Here pic picks up and has some neat comic bits.

Players are all adroit comic pros and handle their assignments well. Director Pierre Grimblat has flashes of comic insight but not enough to bring off this one. But he shows promise. *Mosk.*

Alphaville, Une Etrange Aventure De Lemmy Caution

(Alphaville, a Strange Adventure of Lemmy Caution)

(FRENCH)

Paris, May 4.

Athos Films release of Andre Michelin production. Stars Eddie Constantine, Anna Karina; features Akim Tamiroff, Laszlo Szabo. Written and directed by Jean-Luc Godard. Camera, Raoul Coutard; editor, Agnes Guillemot. Previewed in Paris. Running Time, 98 MINS.
Lemmy .... Eddie Constantine
Natasha .... Anna Karina
Dickson .... Akim Tamiroff
Doctor .... Laszlo Szabo
Von Braun .... Howard Vernon

That most prolific of French filmmakers and ex-New Wavers, Jean-Luc Godard, has come up with an adventurous-philosophical pic with this one. He takes a popular actor and uses his screen personage in a new way. Film is somewhat disconcerting, and sometimes falls between action and art, making its use abroad difficult though worthwhile to appraise. With the right selling pattern, this could do well in arty spots. Also it has enough action for some playoff opportunities.

That Yank who became a star over here playing in parody G-Man pix, Eddie Constantine is shown here in some future city where human feelings have all but been done away with and where the powerful leader is a super computer.

Though supposed to be some city vaguely somewhere in this film (30 years hence), Godard has shot strictly on location in Paris. But he has managed to give it a depressing aspect in choosing grubby,

large tourist hotels as well as the canny use of many modern buildings. This builds up a sort of no-man's-land between totalitarian drabness and super-modern garishness.

Constantine is shown as a secret agent masquerading as a newsman authorized to bring back a scientist who has defected from the old American part of the universe termed Nueva York. He meets his daughter, now an automoton without much human feeling, who he makes feel again as he destroys the computer and takes off with the girl.

Godard again displays his camera virtuosity and insidy gags and commentaries and philosophical asides mixed with the action. This can sometimes be distracting albeit there is no gainsaying the disturbing quality of this dehumanized land which he creates.

The lack of communication, loss of human outlooks in automation and changing mores are familiar themes but Godard tries to weld them into a pseudo sci-fi actioner which does not always have these elements jell.

Constantine is the right choice for the intuitive, two fisted ladies' man agent caught up in a world where women with numbers on their back or forehead are ready for any man's use, and in which secret police are everywhere. He also displays a fine filmic presence.

Anna Karina has the right doll-like appearance as the robot who slowly feels long forgotten human feelings coming back. Akim Tamiroff is outstanding in one seg as an ex-agent who has been humanly destroyed by the system.

Here Godard again shows his uncompromising intellectual, unorthodox methods for a pic that is both piquant and sketchy. It has sound lensing by Raoul Coutard with a good musical score. Godard again establishes himself as one of the more original filmmakers in this pic. The Constantine name should help in European spots. *Mosk.*

Black Spurs

(COLOR-WIDESCREEN

Good oater script and performances, prospects ditto in action situations for Linda Darnell's final pic.

Hollywood, April 30.

Paramount Pictures release of A. C. Lyles Production. Stars Rory Calhoun, Linda Darnell, Scott Brady, Lon Chaney, Bruce Cabot, Richard Arlen, Terry Moore; features rest of cast. Directed by R. G. Springsteen. Screenplay, Steve Fisher; camera (Techniscope, Technicolor), Ralph Woolsey; editor, Archie Marshak; art direction, Hal Pereira, Al Roelofs; music, Jimmie Haskell; title tune, Haskell and By Dunham, sung by Jerry Cole; sound, Hugo Grenzbach; asst. directors, James Rosenberger, Dale Coleman. Reviewed at Paramount Studio, April 29, '65. Running Time, 80 MINS.
Santee .... Rory Calhoun
Sadie .... Linda Darnell
Tanner .... Scott Brady
Kile .... Lon Chaney
Henderson .... Bruce Cabot
Pete .... Richard Arlen
Anna .... Terry Moore
Clare Grubbs .... Patricia Owens
Sheriff Elkins .... James Best
Sam Grubbs .... Jerome Courtland
First sheriff .... De Forest Kelley
Sheriff Nemo .... James Brown
Swifty .... Joe Hoover

Manuel .... Manuel Padilla
Sadie's girls ....Sandra Giles,
Sally Nichols, Rusty Allen
Mrs. Nemo .... Jean Baird
Norton .... Chuck Roberson

A well-made oater from producer A. C. Lyles, "Black Spurs" depicts a bounty hunter's attempt to wreck a peaceful town. Good performances by vets and two younger thesps enliven an above-average script. Technicolor, widescreen and shoot-em-up directorial values make the Paramount release a good entry in action situations, also for lowercasing in the general market. Linda Darnell fans may be attracted to her last film.

Steve Fisher's screenplay gimmick has Rory Calhoun, top gun turned callous bounty hunter, trying to jazz up a quiet town so that partner Lon Chaney can divert a railroad franchise to his own diggings.

Recruited by Calhoun are bouncer Bruce Cabot, roulette sharpie Joe Hoover, and Miss Darnell's floozies, all joining Richard Arlen's saloon staff. Roles are stock but well filled, particularly by Hoover who displays promising talent. Miss Darnell's beauty and voice seem unchanged from her bigtime days, although role is that of a heavy. (She and her gals are honestly depicted as cold shills.)

Opposing change in town image are sheriff James Best, wife Terry Moore (former fiancee of Calhoun), and preacher Scott Brady (latter so identified only after brawl with Calhoun, a surprise plot turn). Ironic twist finds several townfolk nervous over Calhoun's presence, their guilty consciences unaware that he's not there on a bounty hunt. Patricia Owens and Jerome Courtland typify as common law couple who make it legal but fast.

Best gives standout performance among younger cast members as quiet sheriff whose tar-and-feathering by Cabot's heavies brings Calhoun to his senses. Also revealed is fact that latter is real father of Miss Moore's son, although hubby knew the score at marriage. Calhoun bows out of Chaney's scheme which has demoralized the town, forcing inevitable showdown. Order is restored and Calhoun discards his black spur killer trademark.

R. G. Springsteen directed a competent cast in good programmer fashion, keeping action going without excessive violence. With Ralph Woolsey's mobile camera, he has caught the cheap allure of saloon revelry, also the morning-after taste. Archie Marshak's editing is a major asset, although a little tightening might help in first 15 of film's 80 minutes, where overlong establishment of Calhoun's killer reputation uses too many montages.

Director has gotten effective underplaying of moral situations, thereby humanizing the old west so often glorified into black or white cliches that defy belief. Fisher's script of course set the tone.

Moppett named Manuel Padilla has an alert screen personality as guitar-strumming urchin. Jimmie Haskell's music lends good sup-

port, and Jerry Cole warbles okay title tune by Haskell and By Dunham over opening and closing credits. Other technical details bear Paramount professionalism.
Murf.

Jenseits von Oder und Neisse—Heute

(Beyond the Oder and Neisse —Today) (GERMAN—COLOR)

Columbia-Bavaria release of Hirsch Film production. Directed and written by Herbert Viktor. Camera (Agfacolor), K. W. Forbert; music, Bert Grund; editor, Doris Wissmach. At Adria-Lichtspiele, West Berlin. Running Time, 85 MINS.

This is a full-length documentary about the German lands on the other side of the Oder and Neisse Rivers (Pommern, East Prussia, Upper Silesia, etc.) which became Polish-controlled territory after 1945. Pic tries to give an honest answer to the question of what has happened to these parts of the former Reich within the past 20 years.

This documentary, of course, is primarily an item of interest for the Germans and especially those millions of refugees who once lived in these areas. Nostalgia and the fact that full-length documentaries have found their own specific audience in this country may make this production as essential boxoffice contender in this area. Columbia-Bavaria has it for distribution and there are certain releasing chances also outside the home market.

Herbert Viktor, winner of the Federal Film Prize for his documentary on Israel some years ago, had 76 shooting days at his disposal. Polish authorities gave him permission to film freely and without censorship within that period. To make this documentary more "appealing," he engaged a pretty young German girl and a young Pole, put them in a Volkswagen and let them drive through the Polish - administrated German lands. Eventually their talks on the subject and the conversation they had with people over there were put on tape. Bulk of patrons certainly won't mind this conventional trick.

Interesting about this first West German documentary on this subject is the gained knowledge that the Poles have done an amazing rebuilding job over there. Most of the bombed out areas have gone. It's noteworthy that the Poles rebuilt many historical German cities, such as Danzig, true to its old German pattern. Indeed an amazing achievement in view of Poland's postwar poverty.

The most sympathetic aspect about this documentary is its honest and objective approach. With regard to Germany's past, it doesn't mince matters. It's clearly said that the German tragedy is only the result of Hitler's brutal policy of conquest. Film has no political "message" and could, in this form, also be screened in Poland.

Technically, Herbert Viktor's work makes a fine impression. The color is very good and editing is tight. Film may make German patrons feel sentimental but hardly stir controversy for its attitude is just too honest and matter-of-fact. *Hans.*

Cat Ballou
(PATHE COLOR)

Spoof on Old West with strong women and weak men combines expected action with unexpected gags. Comedy more successful visually than as dialog, with Lee Marvin outstanding.

Hollywood, April 29.
Columbia Pictures release of Harold Hecht production. Stars Jane Fonda, Lee Marvin, Michael Callan, Dwayne Hickman, Nat King Co'e, Stubby Kaye. Directed by Elliot Silverstein. Screenplay, Walter Newman, Frank R. Pierson, based on novel by Roy Chans'or; camera, Jack Marta; music, Frank DeVol; songs. Mack David, Jerry Livingston; editor, Charles Nelson; asst. directors, Lee Lukather, Ray Gosnell. Reviewed at Academy Award Theatre, April 29, 1065. Running Time: 97 MINS.

Cat Ballou	Jane Fonda
Shelleen-Strawn	Lee Marvin
Clay Boone	Michael Callan
Jed	Dwayne Hickman
Shouter	Nat King Cole
Shouter	Stubby Kaye
Jackson Two-Bears	Tom Nardini
Frankie Ballou	John Marley
Sir Harry Percival	Reginald Denny
Sheriff Cardigan	Jay C. Flippen
Butch Cassidy	Arthur Hunnicutt
Sheriff Maledon	Bruce Cabot
Accuser	Burt Mustin
Train Messenger	Paul Gilbert

"Cat Ballou" spoofs the Old West, whose adherents take their likker neat and emerges middingly successful, sparked by an amusing way-out approach and some sparkling performances.

The Harold Hecht production could have received more inspired treatment—a requisite for this most difficult of all forms of cinematic art—and tighter editing could still snap up a sometimes-loitering tempo before color feature hits the turnstiles, but it looks to fare well in markets where comedy and outdoor subjects are favored. For added lure, there's Nat (King) Cole in his final film appearance. Word-of-mouth should also help.

Cat is a girl—Jane Fonda—and she's a young lady (educated to be a schoolteacher) vendetta-minded in Wyoming of 1894 when town baddies murder her father for his ranch. She turns a rootin', tootin', lovin' gunlady, rounds up a gang of devoted followers and stages a train holdup, getting away with a payroll fortune and holes up in the old Ho'e in the Wall outlaw lair. She kills an English lord who runs the town and is responsible for her parent's death; sentenced to the gibbet, she's rescued just as the trap drops.

Script by Walter Newman and Frank R. Pierson juggles the elements of the Roy Chanslor novel producing a set of characters who fit the mood natly. Elliot Silverstein's direction takes every advantage afforded him and does a generally creditable job in this swingover to features from television. A novel device has Stubby Kaye and the late Nat Cole, as wandering minstrels of the early west, telling the story of the goings-on via a flock of spirited and tuneful songs composed by Mack David and Jerry Livingston. The title tune is a natural.

Miss Fonda delivers a lively interpretation as Cat, who takes matters into her own hands in avenging her father's murder.

Lee Marvin doubles in brass, playing the gunman who shoots down her father and the legendary Kid Shelleen, a terror with the gun, whom she earlier called in to protect her father. In latter character, Marvin is the standout of the picture as he emerges from a drunken fumbler with a six-shooter to his past holy-terror status after being plied with additional drinks.

Michael Callan, young outlaw on the run, is the object of Miss Fonda's amorous pursuit, who doesn't want to be tied down, and another member of her gang is Dwayne Hickman, as Callan's preacher-pretending uncle who wields a mean gun and saves Cat from the hangman's noose. Both score decisively. Cole and Kaye add considerably, too.

Strong support also is offered by Tom Nardini, a Sioux Indian broncbuster who joins Cat's gang; John Marley is in briefly as Cat's father who thinks the Sioux is Jewish because he believes Indians are one of the lost tribes of Israel; Reginald Denny socks over his English lud with seduction in his heart. Jay C. Flippen, Arthur Hunnicutt, Bruce Cabot and Paul Gilbert lend conviction to small roles.

Color photography by Jack Marta is picturesque, Frank DeVol's music score provides melodic backing. Yakima Canutt is credited as second unit director. *Whit.*

The Art of Love
(COLOR)

Satire with commercial values based on Ross Hunter's production and femme appeal, along with Dick Van Dyke, Elke Sommer, Angie Dickinson. Too much slapstick and incredulity, but many excellent comedy performances.

Hollywood, May 1.
Universal release of Universal-Ross Hunter - Cherokee production. Stars James Garner, Dick Van Dyke, Elke Sommer, Angie Dickinson; features Ethel Merman. Directed by Norman Jewison. Screenplay, Carl Reiner, based on a story by Richard Alan Simmons, William Sackheim; camera (Technicolor) Russell Metty; music, Cy Coleman; editor, Milton Carruth; sound, Waldon O. Watson, Clarence Self; asst. director, Douglas Green. Reviewed at Village Theatre, Westwood, April 30, '65. Running Time, 99 MINS.

Casey	James Garner
Paul	Dick Van Dyke
Nikki	Elke Sommer
Laurie	Angie Dickinson
Madame Coco	Ethel Merman
Rodin	Carl Reiner
Carnot	Pierre Olaf
Chou Chou	Miiko Taka
Zorgus	Roger C. Carmel
Fromkis	Irving Jacobson
Janitor	Jay Novello
Mrs. Fromkis	Naomi Stevens
Pepe	Renzo Cesana
Prince	Leon Belasco
Judge	Louis Mercier
Prosecutor	Maurice Marsac
Fanny	Fifi D'Orsay
Executioner	Marcel Hillaire
Couchette	Dawn Villere
Margo	Nancy Martin
Yvette	Victoria Carroll
Betti	Sharon Shore
Cerise	Astrid De Brea

Ross Hunter's pic, directed swiftly by Norman Jewison and written by Carl Reiner from a story by Richard Alan Simmons and William Sackheim, starts out as pure film satire aimed only at light, bright comedy entertainment. With the addition of a wide variety of often zesty elements it grows into a garbled mixture of coquettish comedy that has side-splitting moments, some unusually fine character performances, but so much of everything it never once settles down to a consistent point of view.

There should be a sufficient box-office for this picture based on Hunter's record of clean, family entertainment and his proven appeal to female audiences who like the look of his pictures. There also is the benefit of Dick Van Dyke's growing popularity to general audiences and the attractiveness to men of beauteous Elke Sommer and Angie Dickinson, as well as the specialty attractions of Reiner and Ethel Merman.

Reiner's screenplay is filled with inanities. At moments one forgives them because they are genuinely funny at the time. But pieced together with an old hat formula storyline they turn into occasional jokes or slapstick action perched precariously on a theme that has been done before. It is clever and creative only within the picture, rather than as a whole.

Story is of would-be American artist Dick Van Dyke who gives up to return to the rich fiancee in America who is paying his bills—and those of his roommate, would-be author James Garner. Garner is so devastated at the loss of his meal ticket, he tries everything to keep Van Dyke in Paris, including a mock suicide that unwittingly backfires into what looks like the real thing. When Van Dyke reappears, he has to go into hiding because Garner has found a dead painter sells better than a live one so he's wheeling and dealing with Van Dyke's canvases—and, as it turns out, with his fiance. Dick goes along with the gag until Garner overplays his cards, then plants some clues that make the suicide look like murder and Garner the criminal. He plays the game until Garner sweats through a satirical trial and ends up with his head under the guillotine blade, then shows up in the nick of time.

Reiner and director Jewison went aground in this picture by allowing too many bits to fill their pot. The picture looks like one that kept changing as each member of the company suggested some new cute bit. And many of them are cute, like the satirical police inspector who is a takeoff on Peter Seller's Inspector Clouseau (and admits it in one line of dialog) or the Madame LaFarge character knitting and maniacally laughing at the guillotine ala "Tale of Two Cities." But there also are some outlandish areas, like Van Dyke's scarecrow race through town to save his friend from death, too many hairpulling and physical slapstick repeat jokes and tomfoolery that asks too much even of farce.

Talent, yes, in abundance. Van Dyke is inconsistently superb. He muggs, cavorts, plays and races pell mell all over the place in a physical performance that has frenetically funny bits but others that are ridiculous. One scene disguised as a old man is excellent and his overall ease and appealing mien is charming.

But the true charm is in the wealth of character comedians flavoring the atmosphere. There is Roger C. Carmel as a charlatan art dealer, an hilarious characterization; Irving Jacobson, wonderful as a Jewish delicatessen owner, and Naomi Stevens as 'his wife who cures all ills with chicken soup; Jay Novello as a janitor afraid Garner is going to kill him; Pierre Olaf, delicious as the comic inspector, and Reiner, himself, as a funny lawyer.

Garner plays like a romantic leading man who shouldn't be doing satire. Elke Sommer and Angie Dickinson are gorgeous to look at and fine for their roles. Miss Sommer emerges from the Seine after attempted suicide with nary a trace of makeup off, her eye shadow still intact and beautifully coiffed. Ethel Merman is loud, brassy and typically Mermanesque as a night club owner who really is a madame. Marcel Hillaire, Léon Belasco. Louis Mercier, rifi D'Orsay and Renzo Cesana are excellent in lesser roles and there is a bevy of eyecatching girls for pulchritudinal appeal.

True to his reputation, Hunter has mounted the production resplendently, particularly with Ray Aghayan's chic costumes, among them a gold trouser-gown worn by Miss Dickinson that will create a reaction from males and femmes alike, but for different reasons. Alexander Golitzen and George Webb's art direction, complemented by Howard Bristol and John Austin's sets, are handsome, and film editor Milton Carruth moves through the abundant material with a frequently-used, but effective, horizontal optical flip. Sound, by Waldon O. Watson and Clarence Self, was muddy in first part of film at screening caught. DePatie-Freleng titles are attractive.

Dale.

Karlek 65
(Love 65)
(SWEDISH)

Stockholm, May 4.
Europa Film release. Stars Keve Hjelm, Evabritt Strandberg, Ann-Mari Gyllenspetz, Ben Carruthers, Inger Taube, Bjorn Gustafson. Written and directed by Bo Widerberg. Camera, Jan Lindestrom. At Saga, Stockholm. Running Time, 95 MINS.
Keve .... Keve Hjelm
Evabritt .... Evabritt Strandberg
Ann-Mari .... Ahn-Mari Gyllenspetz
Ben .... Ben Carruthers
Inger Taube .... Inger Taube
Bjorn .... Bjorn Gustafsson
Kent .... Kent Anderson
Nina .... Nina Widerberg

Mostly tedious, "Love 65" is one of the most pretentious Swedish films to come out of the studios here, and has some of the most sensuous love sequences ever in Swedish films. Following his conviction that a film should not be carefully planned in advance, Bo Widerberg never seemed to discover what his film was going to deal with. Once stating that it is difficult to find a worthy subject, Widerberg let the film ramble on pointlessly.

"Love 65" is Widerberg's version of Fellini's "8½," but except for the love scenes, it is a far cry from the Italian film. Widerberg has made up Keve Hjelm to resemble himself. All the performers are referred to by their "real life" first names. In this film, Keve (Keve Hjelm) does not have a goal. And the people in film spend a good part of their time flying kites on the soft hills of southern Sweden.

Hjelm, who takes the atti-

tude of being a genius, is kept at a distance and never penetrated in this vehicle. Characteristic of the whole thing is the visit of Ben Carruthers, the American actor. Carruthers arrives to spend a couple of days working in Keve's films, but Keve continues to fly his kite and never discusses the film.

There is a rare beauty in some parts of the production. In many ways Widerberg shows remarkable improvement over his two previous feature pix. And the brilliant love scenes gain additional power from the background music. Despite this, on the whole, the film is tedious and irritatingly pretentious.

Fred.

Les Iles Enchantees
(The Enchanted Isles)
(PORTUGESE-FRENCH-COLOR)

Paris, May 4.
Antonio De Cunha Telles-Films Number One production and release. Stars Amalia Rodrigues, Pierre Vaneck, Pierre Clementi. Written and directed by Carlos Vilardebo from a story by Herman Melville. Camera (Agfacolor), Jean Rabier; editor, Sylvie Blanc. Previewed in Paris. Running Time, 80 MINS.
Hanila .... Amalia Rodrigues
Captain .... Pierre Vaneck
Pierre .... Pierre Clementi

A series of little tales about incidents among Pacific isles as recounted by an old sea captain from his log book (about his youth) during the 19th century, has nice color, good acting and a folksy feel. But it is somewhat slim and is mainly for special situation abroad.

There is a brief bit about a man put ashore for a crime who kills himself rather than stay alone on a deserted island, two officers who fight a duel and the main bit re a woman, her husband and brother who go from one island to another to gather turtle fat. The man and boy are drowned and the boat which is to pick them up never comes. The woman is left alone until a young French sailor arrives on the isle. The older woman and young boy have a simple idyll.

These sea stories make for a fairly sketchy film. However, new director Carlos Vilardebo does show a feel for atmosphere. Amalia Rodrigues has presence as the woman. Pierre Clementi is properly boyish as the youth while Pierre Vaneck effective as the storyteller.

Mosk.

Schuesse im ¾ Takt
(Shots in ¾ Time)
(GERMAN-AUSTRIAN-COLOR)

Berlin, May 4.
Noro release of Wiener Stadthallen production. Stars Pierre Brice, Heinz Drache, Daliah Lavi, Jane Brejchova; features Gustav Knuth, Charles Regnier, Walter Giller, Senta Berger as guest. Directed by Alfred Weidenmann. Screenplay, Herbert Reinecker; camera, Karl Loeb; music, Charly Niessen. At Gloria Palast, West Berlin. Running Time: 92 MINS.
Tissot .... Pierre Brice
Pierre Gilbert .... Heinz Drache
Irina Badoni .... Daliah Lavi
Violetta .... Jana Brejchova
Enrico .... Mario Girotti
Oberst .... Gustav Knuth
Burger .... Antony Diffring
Henry .... Charles Regnier
Renato Balil .... Walter Giller

This is a Teutonic attempt to cash in on the amazing James

Bond trend. The best about this Nora release is a superb trailer which could take care of special word-of-mouth. Film is technically very good but otherwise falls short of similar Anglo-American pix. Film's chances on the German-lingo market look very good while foreign prospects appear only so-so although this is a film beyond the current domestic average. However, it doesn't mean much internationally.

This follows the well-known James Bond pattern. It offers the conventional mixture of thrills, humor and sex. There are plenty of fights and victims along the 92 minutes to satisfy the patrons. What militates somewhat against the entertainment value is that the whole thing is marred by a rather confusing script. Confusion eventually seems allright for a vehicle of this calibre, but this kind of confusion probably was not intended. Plot concerns the disappearance of a newly-developed electronic steering apparatus for rockets. That's why Paris-based secret agent No. 11011 (Pierre Brice) has to break off his vacation for he has been chosen to get back that thing.

French Brice, who has made himself a big name as Winnetou, the apache chieftain in Karl May westerns in Germany, is the Gallic secret agent. His admirers will find him okay. Cast includes a good lineup of domestically prominent names and also has Czech Jana Brejchova and Israeli Daliah Lavi for sex interest.

Alfred Weidenmann, who knows how to follow all film trends, tried to direct this with a twinkle in his eye. Eventually he was let down by the script. Color and location footage in beautiful Vienna sometimes is very effective. *Hans.*

A King's Story
(BRITISH-COLOR)
Well-made, intriguing slice of British history. Active participation of Duke and Duchess of Windsor adds realism and marquee flavor; mature audiences, particularly, should respond to this with brisk wicket activity.

Columbia release through BLC of a Jack Le Vien production. With the Duke and Duchess of Windsor. Narrated by Orson Welles; voices of Flora Robson, Patrick Wymark, David Warner, Carleton Hobbs, others. Directed by Harry Booth. Screenplay, Glyn Jones, from Sydney Box' original screen treatment; narration, John Lord; research, Linda Metcalfe; camera (Color), Dick Bayley; editor, Alban Streeter; music, Ivor Slaney. Reviewed at Columbia Theatre, London. Running Time, 102 MINS.

London, May 4.
Jack Le Vien and his team have done a worthy job with "A King's Story," turning out an absorbing documentary slice of history which should intrigue most audiences, particularly the more mature. With obvious exploitation possibilities, this one sounds a brisker grosser potential even than its predecessor, "The Finest Hours."

Le Vien and director Harry Booth have coaxed some warm, human linking from the Duke and his wife, and the Duke reveals a nice sense of humor. Film is based

on the Duke's book. Le Vien not only had the advantage of the Duke's full co-operation, even to the extent of being able to select from nearly 13,000 feet of negative from his own private film library, as well as his physical presence in the film, but also his chief researcher was Linda Metcalfe, daughter of one of the Duke's closest friends.

But all this, plus newsreel material and a lot of up to the minute shooting, could have gone down the drain but for a screenplay and narrative that deftly blend a sense of history, drama, pageantry and, above all, destiny with fitting dignity and plenty of quiet humor. Those anticipating a pepped-up, peephole version of the most dramatic love story of a generation will be somewhat disappointed. About 70 of the film's 102 minutes pass before Mrs. Simpson is mentioned.

The fascinating preliminaries show the childhood days and the adolescence of the boy born to be king. The awesome figure of Queen Victoria dominates the early part of the vehicle. It shows the young prince at school and home, at work and play, being trained for the Navy and coached for the heavy responsibilities and duties ahead. It shows him as a young subaltern at war and then as the Prince Charming who became a world wide ambassador for Britain. It projects his staggering popularity. And scenes in Canada and America spotlight that popularity, and with much good humored amusement. It shows the Prince of Wales as a real right guy.

But, as an undertone, there is always his personal loneliness, which comes to a head following his accession to the throne for what was to be a reign of only 325 days. His meeting with Mrs. Simpson, and the realization that each day is bringing him nearer that time when he must make the agonizing decision between duty and loneliness and love and exile are firmly but calmly shown. Le Vien has introduced no "heavy" but the gathering political and religious intriguing and family concern is clearly shown. The film comes to its climax with the moving spectacle of the septuagenarian Duke re-reading with slight emotion the Abdication statement which shook and nearly split a nation.

Glyn Jones' screenplay, based on an original screen treatment by Sydney Box, covers a lot of ground but with the aid of Harry Booth's direction and Alban Streeter's editing there's no sense of hurry. John Lord's narration (put over without pomposity by Orson Welles) is wordy, but by no means oppressive. And the Duke's frequent and illuminating contributions as he sits in an easy chair in his garden in France add a relaxed note to the proceedings. Other voices are those of Patrick Wymark as Churchill. Carlton Hobbs, as the King George V; David Warner, as the Duke while a youth. Particularly impressive is the voice of Flora Robson as Queen Mary, in which she emerges even more as a mother than as a Queen.

Color, black and white and tint have been successfully juggled within Humphries' Laboratory and Dick Bayley's camerawork is vividly effective. Add to that a score by Ivor Slaney which aptly fits the various moods of the documentary.

Le Vien can take a bow for producing a human document and a worthy tribute to the Duke, without ever taking any sides. As a record, it cannot be faulted though many would have liked a greater attempt to answer some of the questions that arose at the time and which still linger in history. No camera-clicking tourist will ever take better pictures of some of the snippets of British pageantry that they find so fascinating. A looksee at the interiors of Buckingham Palace, Windsor, Sandringham and Osborne is notably worthwhile.

Whether the younger generation will go for it is a moot point. Perhaps, even though the Abdication and the love story that sparked it are only hazy memories for many and before the time of a lot of film-goers, they will be curious to see a first hand re-cap of a remarkable and moving story.
Rich.

I Saw What You Did

Well-made suspense-terror feature should appeal to both fright fans and general audiences attracted by Joan Crawford and two new teenagers. Entertainment values that could add up to good b.o.

Universal release of William Castle production, directed by Castle. Features Joan Crawford, John Ireland, Leif Erickson, Sarah Lane, Andi Garrett. Screenplay, William McGivern, from novel by Ursula Curtiss; camera, Joseph Biroc; music, Van Alexander; editor, Edwin H. Bryant; asst. director, Terry Morse Jr. Reviewed at Wiltern Theatre, L.A., May 7, '65. Running Time, **82 MINS.**
Amy Nelson .... Joan Crawford
Steve Marak .... John Ireland
Dave Mannering .... Leif Erickson
Kit .... Sarah Lane
Libby ....:... Andi Garrett
Tess .... Sharyl Locke
Ellie Mannering ...... Patricia Breslin
John Austin .... John Archer
Trooper .... John Crawford
Judith Marak .... Joyce Meadows

William Castle's "I Saw What You Did" is a well-produced, well-acted entry in the suspense-terror field. It has good b.o. possibilities, both with fright fans and with general audiences attracted by Joan Crawford's top billing and by engaging personalities of two teenage newcomers, Andi Garrett and Sarah Lane.

William McGivern's script has better-than-usual story line, which is helped by phone gimmick that could send youthful audience members rushing home to call numbers at random so they too can whisper, *"I saw what you did; I know who you are."*

Opening scenes are too matter-of-fact, with only Van Alexander's top-flight score revealing suspense is coming. But tension builds as the teenagers and Andi's younger sister (Sharyl Locke), who are alone overnight, begin the phone game. Inevitably, they get hold of John Ireland and whisper their message moments after he has killed his wife (Joyce Meadows). From that point on, it's a cat-

and-mouse story, with Ireland tracking down the girl he believes knows his guilty secret. Climax and last-minute rescue come in over-pat manner, but the terror created on the way is genuine.

Top-billing for Miss Crawford is justified only by making allowances for drawing power of her name. But her role as Ireland's shrewish, predatory lover is well-handled and vital to the story. Slightest gesture or expression of this veteran thesp conveys vivid emotion.

But the two teenagers are central figures, and virtually steal the show, with Andi the stronger of the two. Neither had had acting experience until Castle, who deliberately sought inexperienced girl without child-actress qualities, set them to work. Sharyl portrayed her less-demanding role in top fashion.

Ireland seemed wooden at times, but was vividly alive during terror scenes. As father of Andi, Leif Erickson had little to do except try to calm alarmed wife (Patricia Breslin). John Archer and John Crawford were okay in smaller roles.

Production values of the Universal presentation generally were good. Castle, who directed as well as produced, did top job with the girls. Art directors Alexander Golitzen and Walter M. Simonds and set decorators John McCarthy and George Milo provided appropriate settings. Edward H. Bryants editing showed no flaws. Photography by Joseph Biroc brought the right touch of mystery and suspense to scenes.
Hogg.

Brainstorm
(WIDESCREEN)

Smash suspenser with excellent performances and no physical violence. Strong unnecessary entry for general market and solid potential in exploitation situations.

Hollywood, May 5.
Warner Bros. release of William Conrad production, directed by Conrad. Features Jeff Hunter, Anne Francis, Dana Andrews, Viveca Lindfors. Screenplay, Mann Rubin, based on story by Larry Marcus; camera (PanaVision), Sam Leavitt; editor, William Ziegler; music, George Duning; sound, M. A. Merrick; art direction, Robert Smith; asst. director, Howard L. Grace Jr. Reviewed at Academy Award Theatre, May 4, '65. Running Time, **105 MINS.**
Jim Grayam .... Jeff Hunter
Lorrie Benson .... Anne Francis
Cort Benson .... Dana Andrews
Dr. E. Larstadt .... Viveca Lindfors
Josh Reynolds .... Stacy Harris
Angie DeWitt .... Kathie Brown
Dr. Ames .... Phillip Pine
Dr. Mills .... Michael Pate
Sgt. Dawes .... Robert McQueeney
Mr. Clyde .... Strother Martin
Clara .... Jean Swift
Butler ....,...... George Pelling
Julie .... Victoria Meyerink
Judge .... Stephen Roberts
Bobby .... Pat Cardi

"Brainstorm" is a smash suspenser with outstanding and inventive direction of excellent performances in story of a man who faked insanity becomes real. Producer-director William Conrad's third Warner Bros. exploitationer sustains interest through lively editing, no physical violence, and tension-relieving irony. Destined for pairing with "The Woman Who Wouldn't Die," film is strong enough for uppercasing in the general market.

Topping list of players (all names below title) is Jeff Hunter in excellent developing characterization of young scientist who aborts grade-crossing suicide try by Anne Francis, only to become romantically involved. Trouble is hubby Dana Andrews, who maintains vicious mental hold on her via their child. Miss Francis socks home the brittle gaiety of a bored and drinking wife.

Andrews delivers solidly as public angel-home devil who (discovering the affair) digs up employee Hunter's old nervous breakdown and rigs offbeat incidents to suggest instability. Kathie Brown registers great as floozy who accuses Hunter of obscene phone calls, but smart gumshoe Robert McQueeney clears him. Overall effect of incidents is to weaken department head Stacy Harris' confidence in him.

Hunter decides to capitalize on this by plotting Andrews' death, then copping credible insanity plea for later phony recovery. Pre-killing mastery of psycho jargon produces perceptible change. Is he or isn't he? Even analyst Viveca Lindfors doesn't know for sure in post mortem o.o. Latter underplays sympathetic role with inscrutable smile, overall a terrific return to Hollywood filmmaking.

Committed Hunter can't take asylum life, but Miss Francis won't confess the plot (she loves him, but not enough to face trial). Escape to Miss Lindfors precipitates breakdown. Mann Rubin's script (from Larry Marcus' story) keeps audience guessing, even to Hunter's final hauling off by asylum guards. All supporting players are fine.

Director Conrad has effectively transited space and time by cutting from physical objects and q&a dialog, and some Lubitsch touches mark party scene and boudoir aftermath. The violence is all mental (even when Andrews is shot to death at point-blank range, the camera replaces his weaving and blacking-out body). Economy of direction is abetted by editor William Ziegler and Sam Leavitt's Panavision camera, a reteaming of three pros.

George Duning has provided an appropriately sparse score which never intrudes in a film that impacts via picture and dialog alone. Other Warner technical credits are superior.
Murf.

Harlow
(ELECTRONOVISION)

First of Jean Harlow biopics to hit screen carries exploitation value but as a film is a run-of-the-mill affair.

Magna release of Bill Sargent-Lee Savin production. Stars Carol Lynley, Efrem Zimbalist Jr., Ginger Rogers, Barry Sullivan, Hurd Hatfield, Lloyd Bochner, Hermione Baddeley; features Audrey Totter, John Williams, Audrey Christie, Michael Dante, Jack Kruschen, Celia Lovsky, Robert Strauss. Directed by Alex Segal. Screenplay, Karl Tunberg; camera, Jim Kilgore; music, Al Ham, Nelson Riddle; asst. directors, Greg Peters, Johnny Wilson, Dick Bennett. Reviewed at National General Corp. screening room, May 7, '65. Running Time, 107 MINS.
Jean Harlow ...... Carol Lynley
Wm. Mansfield ... Efrem Zimbalist Jr.
Mama Jean .... Ginger Rogers
Marino Bello .... Barry Sullivan
Paul Bern .... Hurd Hatfield
Marc Peters .... Lloyd Bochner
Marie Dressler ...... Hermione Baddeley
Marilyn .... Audrey Totter
Jonathan Martin .... John Williams
Thelma .... Audrey Christie
Ed .... Michael Dante
Louis B. Mayer ...... Jack Kruschen
Marie Ouspenskaya .... Celia Lovsky
Hank .... Robert Strauss
First Fighter ,.......... Sonny Liston
Counterman .... James Dobson
Billy .... Cliff Norton
Waitress .... Paulle Clark
Stan Laurel .... Jim Plunkett
Oliver Hardy .... John "Red" Fox
Press Agent .... Joel Marston
Bern's Sec'ry. .... Miss Christopher West
Photographer .... Fred Conte
Wardrobe Woman ..... Catherine Ross
Al Jolson .... Buddy Lewis
Casino Manager ...... Danny Francis
Doctor .... Frank Scannell
Miss Larsen .... Maureene Gaffney
Second Fighter .... Nick Demitri
Asst. Director .... Ron Kennedy
Minister .... Harry Holcombe
Nurse .... Lola Fisher
Himself .... Fred Klein

As an exploitation project, and first-to-market, in light of all the publicity attendant upon the production of the Jean Harlow story by two different showmen, this biopic lensed in the quick-filming Electronovision process may reap profit. Its story, however, is strictly run-of-the-mill, peopled with a set of characters not altogether convincing and even the star part making small impression. Pic's appeal and ultimate success will depend upon what curiosity draw the name of the late star may exert, probably unfamiliar to many of today's audiences. Release is calculated to take some novelty edge off the Joseph Levine-Paramount more-detailed production which will follow within the next few weeks.

Trade interest will probably focus on the thesps playing the various roles, many of them based on real-life figures, although to the public most will go unrecognized. Carol Lynley, as the tragic, platinum-tressed queen of the '30s, who was a sex symbol of her time, tries valiantly but the outcome is not altogether a triumph. She has neither the personality nor the physical assets necessary for the character, at best one difficult to conceive for the screen. Several of the other parts seem more caricatures than characterizations, although a few carry certain persuasiveness.

The Karl Tunberg script follows the major points of the Harlow tradition although dramatic licenses are taken. The Paul Bern incident figures prominently, a dramatic hook utilized to mould the entire later character of the star. Hurd

Hatfield in the role of the producer writer who weds the sexy blonde and then commits suicide when he discovers he's impotent, delivers a sincere performance. Celia Lovsky's is another honestly-offered delineation, as Maria Ouspenskaya, the veteran actress to whom Jean goes for dramatic instruction after she temporarily deserts her film career.

Such real-life characters also figure as the star's mother, Mama Jean, enacted by Ginger Rogers, and her stepfather, Marino Bello, played by Barry Sullivan. Louis B. Mayer, Jean's studio boss and head of Metro, is undertaken for almost comic effect by Jack Kruschen, and Marie Dressler, to whom the star often went for advice, is played by Hermione Baddeley, but sans any conviction. Part of William Powell, who played a prominent influence in star's last years, is disguised in a character enacted by Efrem Zimbalist Jr., but in this role is also the Clark Gable character.

Technically, this third Electronovision production — preceded by "Hamlet" and "The T.A.M.I. Story" — and first to be shot under controlled conditions on a motion picture soundstage, still presents many problems for improvement. Photography continues to be a major difficulty, grainy and of general poor quality, and bad lighting heightens the effect of oldfashioned production. Filmed in eight days in the tv-type lensing process, picture very often looks it as action sketches the rise of the star, from the time she tested — and won — the part of femme lead in "Hell's Angels," until her untimely death while still a young woman.

Alex Segal's direction of the Bill Sargent production, produced by Lee Savin, is as good as the script and fast-filming process will permit. Miss Rogers is lost in her role of Mama Jean, a fault deflecting attention from some of the other parts. Other support roles are played by Lloyd Bochner, as an actor responsible for Harlow getting her first break; John Williams, director of "Hell's Angels" (Howard Hughes?); Audrey Christie, a hairdresser; Audrey Totter, as Bern's mistress who tries to warn star's mother of the writer's physical condition; Michael Dante, a Clover Club bouncer who romances star.

Music backgrounding film is a plus for Al Ham and Nelson Riddle, latter also arranging and conducting the score. On technical side, Jim Kilgore handled photography; Duncan Cramer, art direction; Harry Gordon, set decorations. *Whit.*

The Human Duplicators
(COLOR)

Sci-fi entry which keeps interest alive for program situations.

Hollywood, May 12.

Crest release of Hugo Grimaldi-Arthur C. Pierce productions, directed by Grimaldi. Stars George Nader, Barbara Nichols, George Macready, Dolores Faith; features Richard Kiel, Hugh Beaumont, Richard Arlen. No character names available. Screenplay, Pierce; camera (EastmanColor), Monroe Askins; editor, Don Wolf; asst. director, Juss Carrello. Reviewed at Iris Theatre, May 12, '65. Running Time, **80 MINS.**

"The Human Duplicators," paired with "Mutiny in Outer Space" as a scifi package presented by Woolner Bros., shapes as an okay entry in its field. Theme of earthlings being duplicated as androids, identical-appearing robots with an electrical brain, in a move by a master race of a far-off galaxy to take over Earth, isn't entirely new but as handled here generates enough interest to pass in minor situations. Topic carries exploitation value and color further helps.

Arthur C. Pierce screenplay, directed by Hugo Grimaldi and dup sharing producer credit, centers on arrival of a scientist from outer space who sets up a lab to create the androids. Involved, in addition to an American scientist whose lab spaceman takes over, and latter's blind niece, is a government agent who gets onto the scheme of setting up a colony of androids. There's the usual melodramatics in which the good guys nearly lose their lives, but right wins out and Earth is saved.

George Nader plays the detective, Richard Kiel the man from outer space who falls in love with the blind girl and George Macready the scientist who also is duplicated as an android. Dolores Faith is the sightless girl, Barbara Nichols is in as an undercover gal and Hugh Beaumont and Richard Arlen are law enforcement officers, entire cast up to demands of their roles.

Color cameras were handled by Monroe Askins and Don Wolf's editing is fairly fast. *Whit.*

Von Ryan's Express
(C'SCOPE-COLOR)

Suspenseful World War II prisoner - escape melodrama with thrills and names of Frank Sinatra and Trevor Howard to spark strong b.o.

Hollywood, May 7.

Twentieth-Fox release of Mark Robson (Saul David) production, directed by Robson. Stars Frank Sinatra, Trevor Howard; features Brad Dexter, Sergio Fantoni, John Leyton, Edward Mulhare, Wolfgang Preiss, Raffaella Carra. Screenplay, Wendell Mayes, Joseph Landon based on novel by David Westheimer; camera (DeLuxeColor), William H. Daniels; music, Jerry Goldsmith; editor, Dorothy Spencer; asst. director, Eli Dunn. Reviewed at 20th-Fox Studios, May 6, '65. Running Time, **114 MINS.**

Col. Joseph L. Ryan .... Frank Sinatra
Major Eric Fincham .... Trevor Howard
Gabriella .... Raffaella Carra
Sgt. Bostick .... Brad Dexter
Capt. Oriani .... Sergio Fantoni
Orde .... John Leyton
Costanzo .... Edward Mulhare
Major Von Klemment .. Wolfgang Preiss
Private Ames .... James Brolin
Col. Gortz .... John Van Dreelen
Battaglia .... Adolfo Celi
Italian Train Engineer .... Vito Scotti
Corporal Giannini .... Richard Bakalyan
Captain Stein .... Michael Goodliffe
Sgt. Dunbar .... Michael St. Clair
Von Kleist .... Ivan Triesault

Mass escape of 600 American and British prisoners-of-war across 1943 Nazi-controlled Italy lends colorful backing to this fast, suspenseful and exciting World War II tale which promises sturdy boxoffice potential. Mark Robson has made realistic use of the actual Italian setting of the David Westheimer novel in garmenting his action in hard-hitting direction and sharply-drawn performances and producer Saul David provides elaborate values in tome's picturization, lustily scripted by Wendell Mayes and Joseph Landon.

John Sturges' United Artists release of two years ago, "The Great Escape," which dealt with a mass breakout by Allied POW's during WW2 but in another theatre and under different circumstances, should not affect popular reaction to present film which shows smart production throughout.

Frank Sinatra and Trevor Howard co-star as leaders of the escape, who, under former's initiative, seize a freight train which is bearing prisoners for delivery to the Germans in Austria and divert it across Northern Italy in an attempt to find haven in Switzerland. Sinatra plays a hardboiled American Air Force colonel named Ryan, shot down by Italians and imprisoned in the camp where Howard, an equally tough British major, is senior officer.

By virtue of his rank, Sinatra becomes commanding officer. He immediately finds antagonism from Howard who resents his attitude to await what is expected to be early delivery by Allied forces instead of planning escape, and gains nickname "Von Ryan" when he commits two acts which the prisoners regard as throwing in with the enemy but performed actually for the POW's own good. Build-up of this introductory action might be accelerated, but is more than recompensed by the events taking place when the main incidents of escape aboard the prison train start.

Robson depends heavily on suspense and accompanying thrills after Sinatra and Howard take over the train by slugging German guards atop each car, capturing the Nazi officer in charge of the train and subduing the engineer. Some of the best moments of tenseful action occur when a Gestapo agent becomes suspicious after a British chaplain, masquerading as the Nazi commander of the train, beards the Nazis in a train stopover in Florence and succeeds in collecting the German's orders. A German troop train following the escaping freight furnishes another thrill, brought to a climax when suspicious Germans start pursuit in another train and German Messerschmitts attack and temporarily halt the escape only a mile or so from the Swiss frontier. A shocker scene is when Sinatra shoots an escaping Italian femme collaborator who has been aboard the train, so she won't betray the prisoners to the enemy. Yarn ends on an uncompromising but stirring note.

Sinatra socks over his character strongly and Howard is unusually convincing as the surly British officer champing to get back into the war after two years captivity. Sergio Fantoni scores brilliantly as the Italian administrative officer at the prison camp throwing in with the prisoners and helping their escape after Italy surrenders. In various supporting roles, Brad Dexter, as an American prisoner; Edward Mulhare, the English chaplain; John Leyton, a prisoner; Wolfgang Preiss, train commander; Adolfo Celi, camp commandant; Vito Scotti, the engineer whose knowledge of routes leads to the successful crossing of Northern Italy, are standouts. Raffaella Carra is only femme in cast, gunned by Sinatra.

Technical credits are particularly impressive. William H. Daniels' CinemaScope and DeLuxeColor photography is an artistic, outstanding achievement, and art direction by Jack Martin Smith and Hilyard Brown instills the necessary atmosphere. Jerry Goldsmith's stirring music score admirably backgrounds the unfoldment, tightly edited for the most part by Dorothy Spencer.

Top credit, too, goes to William Kaplan and Harold Lipstein, for second unit direction and photography, respectively. *Whit.*

Dingaka
(South African)
(C'SCOPE—COLOR)

From South Africa, a throwback to racial stereotypes. Interesting story, adequate production, with best chance in saturation bookings.

Embassy release of Jamie Uys Films production; direction and screenplay by Uys. Stars Stanley Baker, Juliet Prowse; features Ken Gampu. Camera, Manie Botha (Technicolor) and Judex C. Viljoen; editor, John Jumpson; music, Bartha, Egnos, Eddie Domingo and aBsil Gray; choreography, Sheila Wartski. Reviewd at Lincoln Arts Theatre, N.Y., May 13, '65. Running Time, **98 MINS.**

Tom Davis .... Stanley Baker
Marion Davis .... Juliet Prowse
Ntuku Makwena .... Ken Gampu
Mpudi .... Alfred Jabulani
Witch Doctor .... John Sithebe
Masaba .... Paul Makgoba
Judge .... Siegfried Mynhardt
Prosecutor .... Gordon Hood
Rurari .... Flora Motaung

In this South African import, the many Negro characters are seen as simple, superstitious souls who burst into song and dance on any occasion of joy or sorrow; noble withal, but vastly in need of help from the sympathetic white man. There's even a dance in the streets to the tune of "Shake yo' lazy bones."

Thus, this Embasy Pictures release revives racial stereotypes which have been pretty well banished from the U.S. screen. Some Americans defend the approach as true to reality in the area depicted, but it will be difficult for many to see it as anything but belittlement, or prevent it from dominating all other impressions of the film.

"Dingaka" offers a nod to cultural relativism and, in a courtroom speech by Stanley Baker, pays lip service to the idea that one code of law might be just as good as another. But the attitudes and traditions of black Africans are treated with scant respect: native religion tends to be mocked; and even the indigenous music and dance is treated with transparent fakery, to the extent that screen credit is given to *"original African music composed by . . ."* Only Ken Gampu, in what, despite billing, is the film's leading role, retrieves a modicum of humanity from it a!' — and this is achieved solely through his own personal dignity and acting skill.

Apart from all this, the basic plot is an absorbing one, concerning the murder of a young girl and the search for personal vengeance by her father (Gampu). And the central conflict, between tribal and "civilized" law is also viable. Thus, apart from the attitudes implicit in its treatment, the picture's future on the U.S. market may depend on its reception as an exotic adventure yarn.

Here, despite a certain technical amateurism (occasional flawed color values and lip movements out of sync with soundtrack in early sequences), and a few glaring inconsistencies in script (Gampu insists he must kill the murderer himself, then says he's been betrayed when state doesn't do it for him), writer-producer-director Jamie Uys has done a fairly creditable, if not very exciting job. And those who can agree with or ignore the social comment will have a reasonably good time.

Baker, as Gampu's Legal Aid attorney, is more than competent, and Juliet Prowse, as his wife, is okay in what amounts to a bit part. But adding to the cliches is their marital subplot, in which they don't have a child — after four years of trying — because he's not emotionally involved.

Gold.

Mutiny in Outer Space

Okay sci-fi with novel enough idea for program situations.

Hollywood, May 12.

Crest release of Hugo Grimaldi-Arthur C. Pierce production, directed by Grimaldi. With William Leslie, Dolores Faith, Pamela Curran, Richard Garland, Harold Lloyd Jr.; features James Dobson, Glenn Langan. No character names given. Screenplay, Pierce; camera, Arch Dalzell; editor, George White; asst. director, Jack Voglin. Reviewed at Iris Theatre, May 12, '65. Running Time. **80 MINS.**

Director Hugo Grimaldi takes his story to a space station some years hence, when interplanetary travel is no longer a novelty, for "Mutiny in Outer Space," a companion pic to "The Human Duplicators." There's some slight suspense as a creeping fungus which came from the ice caves of the Moon and being studied in a lab aboard the space station, proves to be a murderous instrument which kills as it spreads terror throughout SS X-7, and film stacks up as a suitable minor entry.

William Leslie is chief protagonist as an astronaut who carries the specimen picked up on the moon, to the space station. Richard Garland plays the station commandant who goes out of his mind and Dolores Faith and Pamela Curran are femmes working on SS. Grimaldi's direction of the Arthur C. Pierce script makes the most of the motivating idea which is novel enough to lend certain interest.

The Grimaldi-Pierce production was deftly lensed by Arch Dalzell and George White's editing is a plus.

Whit.

Mirage

Gregory Peck and good cast to help offset confusing overcomplicated plot.

Universal release of Harry Keller production. Stars Gregory Peck, Diane Baker; features Walter Matthau, Kevin McCarthy, Jack Weston, Leif Erickson, Walter Abel, George Kennedy, Robert H. Harris. Directed by Edward Dmytryk. Screenplay, Peter Stone, based on story by Walter Ericson; camera, Joseph MacDonald: music, Quincy Jones; editor, Ted J. Kent; asst. director, Terence Nelson. Reviewed at Chinese Theatre, April 27, 1965. Running Time: **108 MINS.**

David	Gregory Peck
Shela	Diane Baker
Ted Caselle	Walter Matthau
Josephson	Kevin McCarthy
Lester	Jack Weston
Major Crawford	Leif Erickson
Calvin	Walter Abel
Willard	George Kennedy
Dr. Broden	Robert H. Harris
Frances	Anne Seymour
Bo	House Jameson
Lt. Franken	Hari Rhodes
Benny	Syl Lamont
Irene	Eileen Baral
Joe Turtle	Neil Fitzgerald
Group Leader	Franklin E. Cover

"Mirage" starts as a mystery, unfolds as a mystery, ends as a mystery. There are moments of stiff action and suspense as the audience goes along with the buildup, but plot is as confusing as it is overly-contrived. While there is some feeble attempt to clarify the main story premise in closing reel the result is so shrouded in mist that the spectator is left in almost complete bewilderment. All the draw of Gregory Peck, who stars as an amnesiac trying to learn why he is the target for assassins, will be required to get this Harry Keller production off the ground.

Where the Peter Stone screenplay really misses is the clumsy attempt to link the past with the present as Peck struggles to grasp fleeting returns of memory. Emphasized story points need exposition and there is a general vagueness in treatment. Peck's position is scarcely ever clear, and this encompasses several of the other principals whose actions appear meaningless. Finale is inconclusive.

Story is about a man in N.Y. who suddenly discovers he cannot remember the past two years he has taken for granted, or, for that matter, any part of his past life. Returning to his apartment from a big office building which was suddenly without lights and where a prominent man plunged to his death from the 27th floor, he is confronted by a stranger holding a gun who informs him he's taking Peck to a man he has never heard of. Knocking the gunman out, he goes to the police to demand protection, only to discover he's a thoroughly confused man.

A psychiatrist, whom he visits, throws him out because the medico thinks he's in trouble with the police, and hiring a private eye to dig into his past results only in the fact he knows he's being sought by gunmen who pursue him through parks and buildings. It begins to look as though he had some connection with the dead man, an advocate of world peace.

Later he remembers he was in this man's office when latter tried to retrieve a paper which Peck was burning, and plunged out the window. Peck, a physio-chemist working for this man (played by Walter Abel) and whom he greatly admired, had discovered a formula eliminating the danger of radiation from nuclear explosions at their source. Disillusioned by Abel's order to turn his formula over to a business tycoon who planned to use it for personal gain, Peck touched a match to the document.

Edward Dmtryk in his taut direction keeps a tight rein on pace and manages vigorous movement in individual sequences, but cannot overcome script deficiencies. Peck's character is not clearly drawn but actor makes the most of what's offered him as a brooding man trying to save his life. Diane Baker, co-starred with Peck, flits in and out of plot as a mysterious figure whose true identity is never established.

Strong support is afforded by Walter Matthau as the detective, unaccountably murdered; by Abel, a key character but seldom onscreen; Jack Weston and George Kennedy, the gunmen; Leif Erickson, as the tycoon, but whose relationship with the world peace leader is nebulous; Robert H. Harris as the psychiatrist.

Joseph MacDonald's photography is well handled, and balance of technical credits competently performed.

Whit.

Girls on the Beach
(SONGS-COLOR)

Pleasant teenager entry with rock'n'roll action and plenty of pretty girls to assure nice reception in its particular market.

Hollywood, May 4.

Paramount release of Harvey Jacobson production. Stars Noreen Corcoran, Martin West, Linda Marshall, Steven Rogers, Anna Capri, Aron Kincaid; features Nancy Spry, Sheila Bromley, Lana Wood, Mary Mitchel, Gale Gerber, Peter Brooks, Linda Saunders, Lesley Gore, The Beach Boys, The Crickets. Directed by William N. Witney. Screenplay, David Malcolm; camera (PatheColor), Arch Dalzell; music, Cary Usher; editor, Morton Tubor; sound, John Bury Jr. Reviewed at Paramount Studios, May 4, '65. Running time: **82 MINS.**

Duke	Martin West
Selma	Noreen Corcoran
Stu	Peter Brooks
Beach Boys	Brian Wilson
	Michael Love
	Alan Jardin
	Carl Wilson
	Dennis Wilson
Crickets	Jerry Allison
	Jerry Naylor
	Sonny Curtis
Frank	Arnold Lessing
Cynthia	Linda Marshall
Brian	Steven Rogers
Arlene	Ann Capri
Wayne	Aron Kincaid
Mrs. Winters	Sheila Bromley
Emily	Mary Mitchel
Georgia	Gale Gerber
Patricia	Linda Saunders
Jenny	Mary Kate Denny
First Sorority Sister	Nan Morris
Bonnie	Lana Wood
Dancer	Pat Deming
Dancer	Michele Corcoran
Dancer	Larry Merrill
Guy I	Dennis Jones
Guy II	Bill Sampson
Dancer	Carol Jean Lewis
Second Sorority Sister	Joan Conrath
Parking Lot Attendant	Rick Newton
Lesley Gore	Lesley Gore
Betty	Nancy Spry
M.C.	Ron Kennedy
Pops	Bruno Vesota
Waitress	Lynn Cartwright
First Waiter	Richard Miller
Waiter No. 2	Leo Gordon
Contestant and Dancer	Helen Kay Stephens

Success of American International's romps-in-the-sand series ("Bikini Beach," et al) directed at the teenage market apparently cued Paramount to climb aboard the same bandwagon with release of this Harvey Jacobson production. Strictly for its intended market, where the names of Noreen Corcoran, singer Lesley Gore, The Beach Boys and The Crickets should pay off, it makes no pretense to be anything but light entertainment carrying youth appeal. Peopled with a pleasant cast and nicely photographed in color, with most of the cast spending most of their time in bikinis, it achieves its mark.

William N. Witney's direction of the David Malcolm script maintains a brisk pace as the slight plot follows the efforts of the officers of Alpha Beta sorority to raise $10,000 during Easter vacation at Balboa, Calif., to pay off the mortgage on their house. The sorority nest-egg which they were depending upon has been dissipated by the easy-for-a-touch house-mother, and it's up to the gals to replenish the kitty. They do this by winning various contests, and get themselves into a jam when a trio of lotharios tell them they can arrange for The Beatles to appear at a benefit show. Beatles never show up but lasses save the day anyway by giving a clever imitation.

Young Miss Corcoran, who has grown up after a moppet career to be quite a beauty, is the leading light as the prexy of the sorority who dreams up the way to rescue her house from foreclosure. She gets fresh support from Linda Marshall, Anna Capri, Gale Gerber and Linda Saunders, and male roles are handled well enough by Martin West, Steven Rogers and Aron Kincaid. Sheila Bromley is effective as the house-mother.

Lesley Gore warbles three numbers, including "I Don't Want To Be a Loser" and 'Leave Me Alone," in her usual easy style and The Beach Boys sock over several of their own numbers, as do The Crickets. Music by Cary Usher plays an important part in film's breezy atmosphere.

Technical departments are expertly handled, with Arch Dalzell on the cameras and Morton Tubor editing.

Whit.

The Party's Over
(BRITISH)

Downbeat drama of wild life among London beatniks. Some bright young thesping, but this glum pic is contrived and needs strong bally.

London, May 11.

Monarch Films release of a Tricastle Film (Anthony Perry) production. Stars Oliver Reed, Eddie Albert; features Clifford David, Ann Lynn, Catherine Woodville, Louise Sorel, Jonathan Burn, Mike Pratt, Maurice Browning, Roddy Maude-Roxby. Directed by Guy Hamilton. Screenplay, Mark Behm; camera, Larry Pizer; editor, John Bloom; music, John Barry. Previewed at Hammer Theatre, London. Running Time: **94 MINS.**

Moise	Oliver Reed
Carson	Clifford David
Libby	Ann Lynn
Nina	Catherine Woodville
Melina	Louise Sorel
Geronimo	Mike Pratt
Tutzi	Maurice Browning
Phillip	Jonathan Burn
Hector	Roddy Maude-Roxby
Fran	Annette Robertson
Countess	Mildred Mayne
Ada	Alison Seebohm
Almoner	Barbara Lott
Ben	Eddie Albert

There has been a two years' holdup of "The Party's Over," because of censorship problems. Maybe exhibitors will need this spot of controversial bally to help put over an arty, downbeat piece about life among London's young beatniks. Film to be exported differs only slightly from the trimmed domestic version. But the differences miffed producer Anthony

Perry and director Guy Hamilton enough to make them insist that their names be deleted from the home-version credits.

The tawdry yarn, loosely scripted by Mark Behm, concerns a young American girl, daughter of a tycoon, who comes to London and gets involved with a group of young Chelsea layabouts known as "The Pack," a disillusioned bunch which lives only for kicks. When her fiance arrives from the States to take her home, she realizes that she doesn't love him. She and the "Pack" go to endless and oafish lengths to prevent his meeting her.

Eventually the girl disappears after one of the wildest parties, and is found dead. How she met her death, the events leading up to it and immediately after, which involve a mock funeral, a hint of necrophilia and a young man's suicide all merge into a pseudo-psychological and phony finale.

The film catches the apathetic, desperately unhappy and dreary lives of these young iconoclasts. And this in itself leads to frequent bouts of tedium and dreariness in this film. The dialog varies from the highfaluting and wouldbe sophisticated to the naive, but Hamilton has kept direction moving as nimbly and understandingly as possible. Use of locations entirely, gives a sharp effectiveness to the film. Also Larry Pizer has done some good work with the camera.

Performances are mostly routine, but there are a few that show distinct promise, notably Oliver Reed, as the arrogant, womanizing young misfit leader of the "Pack," Clifford David, as a likeable American boy with a tricky role to which he brings a sense of humor, and Catherine Woodville, a standout as one of the few of the "Pack" with any decent instincts left. Ann Lynn, Maurice Browning, Roddy Maude-Roxby and Mike Pratt offer sturdy support, but Louise Sorel as the heroine is overly fey.

Editing and John Barry's music are okay, with Annie Ross doing a useful job with the title song.

"Party's Over" is a depressing picture which takes itself over-seriously in its attempts to shock. Instead, it tends only to leave a not very fragrant taste in the mouth, and a sense of some sort of message that's misfired. It is a poor advertisement for British youth and not much of a boost for British pix, either. *Rich.*

Two Left Feet
(BRITISH)

Flimsy, ill developed pic concerned with the turbulence of adolescence; disappointing and unlikely to make much of a mark at the boxoffice.

London May 11.
British Lion release through BLC of a Roy Baker-Leslie Gilliat production. Stars Michael Crawford, Nyree Dawn Porter, Julia Foster, David Hemmings; features David Lodge, Michael Craze, Michael Eipper, Bernard Lee, Dilys Watling, Cyril Chamberlain, Bob Wallis and his Storyville Jazzmen. Directed by Baker. Screenplay, Baker and Roy Hopkins, based on David Stuart Leslie's novel, "In My Solitude"; camera, Wilkie Cooper, Harry Gillam; editor, Michael Hart; music, Phil Green. Reviewed at British Lion Private Theatre, London. Running time: 93 MINS.
Alan Crabbe .... Michael Crawford
Eileen .... Nyree Dawn Porter
Beth Crowley .... Julia Foster
Ronnie .... Michael Craze
Brian .... David Hemmings
Mavis .... Dilys Watling
Bill .... David Lodge
Mr. Crabbe .... Bernard Lee
Miles .... Cyril Chamberlain
Ted .... Neil McCarthy
Peter .... Howard Pays
Joe .... Douglas Ives
Uncle Reg .... Michael Ripper
Mrs. Daly .... Hazel Coppen
Customer .... Peggy Ann Clifford
Policeman .... Anthony Sheppard

Whatever attracted producers Leslie Gilliat and Roy Baker in David Stuart Leslie's novel must have been lost in the transition to the screen because this is a very flyweight trite pic. It explores in only the most superficial terms the dilemma of a gauche youth whose ham-handed attempts to cope with his early sex problems are not highly satisfactory. Script by Roy Baker (who also directs) and John Hopkins is soft centered. Also the characters and their motivation are not sufficiently developed. It has been over two years getting to the screen and it is unlikely to strike gold after the long delay.

A callow youth is infatuated with a teasing waitress but his attempt to seduce her ends in disaster. She turns to brighter young men at a jazz club and he finds consolation in a naive young shop assistant. However, at the wedding of one of his buddies he gets mixed up again with the blonde siren which leads to a row with her new escort and a beating up. The lad turns back again to his more relaxing chick. And that's about size of it.

Undertones of homosexuality between two of the youths are only hinted at and the sex lark is more talked about than acted upon. An attempt to satirize an appalling suburban wedding party becomes more of a caricature. Director Baker seems to have been unable to pull together a limp script.

Nyree Dawn Porter plays the waitress with exaggerated sex appeal. But the performance is effective and she shows up as a provocative young dish. Michael Crawford, steadily gaining stature as a light comedian, handles the role of the gauche lad likeably. But much of dialog is out of step with the minus-confidence character he is playing. Julie Foster, as the simple, goodhearted wench with whom he feels at ease, is pleasant, but unexciting. David Hemmings and Michael Craze play the two other lads neatly enough.

Remainder of the trouping is routine, with David Lodge chipping in effectively as one of Crawford's more worldly-wise mates. Bernard Lee does a guest bit as his moralizing father in a trivial bedside scene. Dilys Watling, Hazel Coppen, Peggy Ann Clifford and a variety of others have minor chores. Michael Ripper as an overhearty "life - and - death - of - the-party" guest scores in an overlong sequence.

Technical credits are adequate. Bob Wallis and his Storeyville Jazzmen, Kenny Baker and others do some speciality music over and above Philip Green's nimble score. Tommy Bruce sings the title song which doesn't sound like Top Ten fodder.

It is difficult to pin down just what has gone wrong with "Two Left Feet," but with the exception of Miss Porter and, occasionally of Miss Porter and, occasionally, Crawford, it has the look of a very tired piece of old hattery. *Rich.*

Go-Go Bigbeat
(BRITISH-MUSIC-COLOR)

Programmer, strictly for the teenagers. A selling angle is inclusion of a ballet score by three of The Beatles, although latter don't appear in film.

Eldorado Pictures release of Kenneth Hume production. Directed by Hume and Frank Gilpin. Features Millie Small, The Animals, Lulu And The Luvvers, The Four Pennies, The Applejacks, The Merseybeats, The Hollies, The Wackers, The Cockneys, Brian Poole and The Tremeloes, The Migil 5, The Swinging Blue Jeans, The Tornadoes, Brian Matthew, Kent Walton, Alan Freeman, The Western Theatre Ballet Company, The Cheynes. Camera (Eastmancolor), Harry Orchard; music for "Mods And Rockers," Paul McCartney, John Lennon, George Harrison. Reviewed in N. Y., May 5, '65. Running time: 82 MINS.

British producer - director Kenneth Hume, realizing that his 1964 "Mods And Rockers" dance film wasn't long enough to hold down a program on its own, has preceded it with a dozen rock 'n' roll acts. Result is much singing and dancing and little else.

Aimed at teenager market with planned saturation bookings in N.Y. area in mid-June, pic's ultimate future is bottom half of double-bill.

Long string of acts making up first portion of film, directed by Frank Gilpin, ranges from such singles as Millie Small, a young Jamaican Negress whose squeaky voice reminds of Rose Murphy, to numerous farout combos including The Animals (who paid Stateside visit a few months ago), The Cockneys, and the Migil 5 (who look much older than other groups). Throughout there's much similarity in material and presentation although tunes are evidently those with which acts have made their reputations. A trio of emcees, Kent Walton, Brian Matthew and Alan Freeman, introduce acts but they may be replaced by illustrated titles before general release.

"Mods And Rockers" is, supposedly, a ballet to music by three composing members of the Beatles (group's only connection with film) but Peter Darrell's choreography is rarely ballet. His movements are extreme variations on dances popular today with teenagers. Company is divided between the black - leather - jacketed motorcycling Rockers and the Mods, whose trademark is their stylized Edwardian dress.

A weak carbon of "West Side Story" rumble, dance has two groups brought together by a dogooder vicar whose efforts to "reach" them includes wearing a leather jacket over his clericals and not interfering when the fighting starts. If there's any serious social comment, it is that British youth is rapidly becoming demasculinized because of addiction to extreme tastes in music, dress and deportment.

Hume's story would be innocuous had he not included a distaste-ful recurring shot of a young effeminate Negro youth, who never participates in the dancing, but lingers near an enormous statue of a naked male gladiator (this, in recreation hall-basement of an English church?) which he frequently gives admiring glances. At film's end, when all are departing, he leaves arm-in-arm with a motorcyclist. Editing shots out would be next to impossible as they're used throughout the dance film, while adding nothing to the choreography. Some particular parents may be offended even if the broaderminded teenagers are not. *Robe.*

Onkel Toms Huette
(Uncle Tom's Cabin)
(GERMAN—70M—COLOR)

Munich, May 10.
Nora release of Melodie-Avala production, starring O. W. Fischer, Mylene Demongeot, Herbert Lom, John Kitzmiller, Eleanora Rossi-Drago, Olive Moorefield, Juliette Greco, Thomas Fritsch. Produced by Aldo von Pinelli and Georg Reuther, directed by Geza von Radvany. Screenplay by Mr. Radvany and Fred Denger. Camera (MCS 70mm Superpanorama, Eastman Color): Heinz Hoelscher. Music: Peter Thomas. Reviewed at Munich's Matthaeser Palast. Running time: 170 MINS.

Uncle Tom .... John Kitzmiller
Saint Claire .... O. W. Fischer
Mrs. Saint-Claire .. Eleanora Rossi-Drago
Little Eva .... Gertrud Mittermayr
Harriet .... Mylene Demongeot
Dinah .... Juliette Greco
Haley .... Herbert Lom
Cassy .... Olive Moorefield
Eliza .... Catana Cayetano
Topsy .... Rhet Kirby
Singer .... Eartha Kitt
Dub voice .... Ella Fitzgerald

Europeans may take this version of "Uncle Tom's Cabin" as it stands, which is full of anachronisms and liberties with the Harriet Beecher Stowe hardy perennial melodrama. But for playoff in the U.S. itself there must be the wonder about audience reaction. It is a far cry from the story which has been done some four different times by American film companies and which toured with round actors for 80-odd years, from 1850 to 1930.

Coproduction retains nominal Dixie locale but the tone of the production is closer to the "westerns" which currently fascinate German film showmen. The German soundtrack is curiously untrue to the American original. What the English dubbing voices will be like, or how Yanks may react remains to be discovered.

Made in Yugoslavia there was the apparent problem of converting that country's cavalry from their familiar doubling as western rough riders into Southern plantation types. Nor are Serbian farm workers very convincing in their switch from redskins to blackface. They may just possibly push American audiences out of their cottonpicking minds with unintended amusement.

There are misrepresentations in other ways beside the "Western" tone. Washington's Lincoln Memorial is introduced but the customary location-identification shot directly preceding it shows the skyline of Manhattan. Shiningly green pastures depict Kentucky's rough winter. Right from this scenery, Eliza, in flight, jumps onto the ice floats drifting down the river.

"Independence Day" reads a streamer above a Fourth of July dance, was hardly meant as "archaic spelling." (This boner, however got vindication by some learned expert who belatedly proved there was a remote possibility that it could be spelled that way still at the time of the action.) The Mississippi steamer, shown is the cliche showboat of the musicals. Pseudo-Southern mansion inhabited by the Saint Claire family and Uncle Tom's shack strain credulity.

All of which may be dismissed as the "slips that will happen" in many, and even American, pictures. More serious is the innermost lack of veracity in about everything that purports to picture the American scene, e.g. the re-enactment of the Lincoln assassination, here included in the story. And when in the thin disguise of the slaying of Saint Claire the John Kennedy tragedy unfolds, followed by the lynching of a man totally innocent of the crime, many will resent not only the false detail but just everything.

More identified with the "subtle" school, director Von Radvany could not cope with the mass agitation and fighting scenes. Chases and barroom brawls come off, at best, as stereotypes from some American Western. Strange, however, that the creator of that poignant children's pic "Somewhere in Europe" (1949) could not prevent the sequences involving Little Eva (and Topsy, too) from turning icky.

If onetime German screen idol O. W. Fischer (Saint-Claire) intended to pick up the pieces of his career in a single performance, the purpose showed and thereby defeated itself. Sporadically though the viewer is reminded of the old, that is the young, Fischer thought a comeback in another and better picture might be still in the cards. Presentday glamour boy Thomas Fritsch (George Shelby) still shows nothing. Herbert Lom, in turn, delivers a highly creditable performance as archfiend Haley, the granddad of all fictional segregationists.

The late (U.S.) John Kitzmiller's Uncle Tom compensated through inborn power as a "native son" for what he was lacking in thespian gloss and skill. Convincing are Catana Cayetano (Eliza) and particularly Olive Moorefield (Cassy) who make beholder forget the synthetic screen world.

Eartha Kitt and Ella Fitzgerald could have contributed much more of that first-hand punch but somebody reduced Miss Kitt's appearance and song to a "medalion" inserted in the credits, and used Miss Fitzgerald merely as a dubbing voice.

Likewise, Juliette Greco's appeal and gifts were wasted. She did get a bit part as the cliche saloon hostess and a so-so chanson. She stooped to the task and conquered. Other white female headliners offered a heap of bad acting, with the possible exception of Eleanora Rossi-Drago whose beautiful frigidity happened to suit the character of Mrs. Saint Claire.

The music by German "Filmpreistrager" Peter Thomas does not match the original Negro spirituals it is interspersed with. Even

occasional helpings from Kern's "Old Man River" and Katchatourian's "Sword Dance" fail to lend it wings. If photography (Heinz Hoelscher) turns out excellent, main credit must go to the basically first-rate and with every new pic still further improving MCS 70m Superpanorama lenses which came through with flying (Eastman) colors. *Afka.*

Cannes Festival

The Knack
(BRITISH)

Offbeat comedy from Woodfall stable, with strong selective possibilities.

Cannes, May 14.
United Artists release of Woodfall-Oscar Lewenstein production. Directed by Richard Lester. Screenplay, Charles Wood, based on play by Ann Jellicoe; camera, David Watkins; music, John Barry. At Cannes Film Festival, May 13, '65. Running Time: 84 MINS.
Nancy .... Rita Tushingham
Tolen .... Ray Brooks
Colin .... Michael Crawford
Tom .... Donal Donnelly

There is, according to the theory expounded in "The Knack," quite a knack in the art of making it successfully with girls. And that about sums up the plot of this offbeat Woodfall production, which was justifiably invited to the Cannes festival. Pic has strong potentialities for selective situations, but may well encounter difficulties along the normal commercial route.

Oscar Lewenstein's production is almost successful, but just misses the bullseye in certain respects. There is considerable invention, but not quite enough; there are witty and amusing situations, but some are overstretched. Yet, on the whole, this is a mainly diverting lark likely to please more sophisticated tastes.

The expert exponent of the knack is played by Ray Brooks, and the immediate target is Rita Tushingham, a young girl just up from the country and hopefully setting off in search of the YWCA. The other two characters are both young men being instructed how to acquire the knack from the master. As Michael Crawford plays a schoolteacher, it is a neat trick to cut into schoolroom lessons with the same dialog as that used by Brooks to his two friends.

While the dialog is mainly easy to follow, there are a few Cockney expressions which may be beyond the comprehension of non-British audiences, but they are not important enough to hurt general acceptance. On the other hand, audiences with the knack of understanding Cockney dialect, will naturally derive additional fun.

Richard Lester (who directed the Beatles films) again shows a witty style, and has made a valiant stab at preventing the action from sagging. One scene, in particular, stands out, when Miss Tushingham believes she has been raped, and shouts it to the world; another,

when she follows directions to the YWCA and winds up outside Buckingham Palace.

The four performances are exceptionally good. Miss Tushingham's wide-eyed innocence is just right, and she plays with her familiar charm. Ray Brooks is superbly confident as the glamor boy with the knack, and Michael Crawford and Donal Donelly both hit the right mixture of eagerness and innocence. John Barry's sensitive score is another plus; and the originality of the final credit titles (though somewhat overlong) deserve to be kudosed.

"The Knack" was filmed entirely on location in London, David Watkin's sharp camera hypoes the backgrounds. *Myro.*

La Cage De Verre
(The Glass Cage)
(FRENCH-ISRAELI)

Cannes, May 18.
Telecinex-Eurodis-Noy Film-A.D. Matalon production and release. With Francoise Prevost, Jean Negroni, Georges Riviere, Dina Doron, Rina Ganor, Maurice Poli, Azaria Rapaport. Directed by Philippe Arthuys, J. L. Levi Alvares. Screenplay, Arthuys; camera, Georges Pessis; editor, Sylvie Blanc. At Cannes Film Fest. Running time, 87 MINS.

Helene .... Francoise Prevost
Pierre .... Jean Negroni
Claude ....Georges Riviere
Sonia ....Dina Doron
Tamar .... Rina Ganor
Antoine .... Maurice Poli
Newsman .... Azaria Rapaport

On the background of the Eichmann trial in Israel is unfolded a taut, knowing look at its effect on a group of people. If reminiscent of "Hiroshima Mon Amour," this is more incisive, penetrating.

Theme and treatment give this definite art and specialized chances abroad, with depth possibilities more limited. "Glass Cage" is, of course, the one Eichmann sat behind. But also it may be a symbol of the one surrounding many Israelis and people near them.

Film deals with a French deportee who had survived the camps and emigrated to Israel with his middle-class non-Jewish wife. Also a Jewish girl who had escaped the camp, a young girl who had never known either and her affair with a Frenchman, etc., etc.

The French-Jew has been fairly happy with his wife if there were certain things he had never confided. Things come to a head at the arrival of her first love, now a flippant newsman covering the trial. There's a confession as the Frenchman clears up a haunting thing in his own mind.

Director Philippe Arthuys, a musician, gives the pic a fluid mounting that carefully blends the various relationships without too much talk which could bog down a film like this. He is ably seconded by J. L. Levi Alvares who helped technically.

When the Frenchman is plagued and his memories are jostled, an elevator suddenly seems like a furnace that burned Jews. This works as do other quick inserts to give an estimation of the feelings of the characters.

It is well leased with a fine musical score by Arthuys also helping. Shots of Eichmann in his glass

cage and the courtroom make an effective counterpoint.

No preaching here, but it does intimate that both the victims and executioners had to face up to the horror and meaning of what had happened. Acting is well balanced.

Jean Negroni has the needed sombre, brooding quality as the Jewish man facing his past, with Francoise Prevost properly indecisive if compassionate as his wife. Dina Doron displays the right feeling of past suffering qualified by her new hopes. All the others are also fine with Rina Ganor expert as a girl who had been born in Israel, as is Georges Riviere as the newsman.

An offbeat, serious, intelligent pic, this may need hardsell but will be worth it on its fine handling of a difficult theme. *Mosk.*

Noite Vazia
(Night Games)
(BRAZILIAN)

Cannes, May 18.
Davis Films release of Kamera production. With Norma Bengell, Odete Lara, Mario Benvenuti, Gabriele Tinti. Written and directed by Walter Hugo Khouri. Camera, Rudolf Icsey; editor, Mauro Alice. At Cannes Film Fest. Running Time, 90 MINS.
Mara .... Norma Bengell
Christina .... Odete Lara
Luis .... Mario Benvenuti
Nelson .... Gabriele Tinti

With pressure groups getting fidgety over more and more outspoken films, this one will probably raise controversy and run into censoring trouble. This forthright look at some affluent Brazilian male specimens from Sao Paulo on a sex binge has probing non-leering honesty and a mixture of trim direction and fine acting. It could have strong arty chances abroad.

A rich young man (the money is mainly his wife's) prowls around at night looking for adventure and the so-called "different" woman who may change his life or give him new kicks. He is accompanied by a poor youth who is also mixed up. Latter hates these nightly sprees but is drawn along against his will.

The night of the film they pick up two deluxe call girls and go to the rich man's private apartment. There they begin to indulge in sex play, try to goad the girls into a lesbian exhibition, look at some blue films and end at dawn almost as empty and disenchanted as when they started.

But one of the girls is still capable of some normal feeling and does have an idyllic moment with the younger man. One of the merits of the film is its ability to paint boredom and lack of communication without being either tedious itself. It ably contrasts the humming vitality of the city to the still vague bumblings and disharmony of its characters.

Their night has self recriminations. There is always some hope that they may yet find something or someone to take them off their ceaseless nightly rounds.

Director-writer Walter Hugo Khouri may have been influenced perhaps by some New Wavers. The symbols of more human feeling and better people are also there.

Nudity is there along with some

fairly intimate love scenes, but they are handled with tact and taste. This may be reaching too far in trying to paint a whole society via a few people, but it does at times transcend its harrowing nighttime cavorting.

Norma Bengell has an expressive beauty and a comely face that hints inner strength, with some chance of getting off the eternal nightlife emptiness. Odete Lara has the right arrogance, hidden fear and bitterness as the more hopeless of the two joy girls. The men are also adroit in their delineations.

Film is also technically sound with a good musical counterpoint. This is a sophisticated production from Brazil reflecting themes of many European filmakers. But it has a personal note of its own. Somewhat too incisive for sexploitation use, where it may conceivably end up, and with censor raps in store. It might still be an art item for offshore if well hypoed.
Mosk.

Finnegan's Wake

A canny American indie, made in Gotham and Dublin, on the famed last book of Jame Joyce. Might create talk in literary circles but also filmic knowhow and offbeat aspects for arty chances.

Cannes, May 18.
Expanding Cinema production and release. With Martin J. Kelley, Jane Reilly, Peter Haskell, Page Johnson. Directed and adapted by Mary Ellen Bute from play by Mary Manning, based on James Joyce's "Finnegan's Wake." Camera, Ted Nemeth; music, Elliot Kaplan. At Cannes Film Fest. Running time, 92 MINS.
Finnegan .... Martin J. Kelley
Anna Livia .... Jane Reilly
Shem ....,........ Peter Haskell
Shaun .... Page Johnson
Commentator .... John V. Kelleher
Young Shem .... Ray Flanagan

Here indeed is a filmic rarity, the first feature made from one of the last works of that revolutionary literary (ever-exiled) Irishman James Joyce. And it is quite clear, warm, witty, churlish and even poetic. Pic seems filmic knowhow, plus the Joyce name, for specialized audiences. Hence, it may have good arty chances if well sold.

It is true that Joyce splintered the verb to give a free flow to the fibre of his characters. Here the image is jostled, mixed with animation, stock shots and races around in time and the sub-conscious. Film uses much of Joyce's difficult but flowery word formations.

Purists may carp that perhaps Joyce seems too clear here (there'll always be pros and cons on Joyce), but the film seems true in its way. It uses the legiter, "Finnegan's Wake," to give it an already rounded form. "Wake" never made Broadway but was an Off-Broadway show in N.Y.

Finnegan finds himself at his own wake, laid out in a coffin. Around him are the drinking Irish at one of their noisier wakes. He goes through things with his two sons and sees his daughter, as a youthful reincarnation of his wife.

There are barroom brawls, stage presentations to make certain points on love and the bright and sometimes bawdy puns of Joyce. The use of Irish players and production of part of the pic in Ireland insure

a true feeling for the basic characters.

Martin J. Kelley is bright, indulgent, fierce, politicking and dynamic as Finnegan. Jane Reilly is an attractive colleen, who can suggest purity or do a grind with the best of them in sideshow scenes. Peter Haskell and Page Johnson are fine as the two sons.

The director, American Mary Ellen Bute, has the right blending of real and unreal. Finnegan is depicted as having found something of himself in his wife's earthiness and is going forward to a new awareness of himself.

It may be dangerous to try to simplify Joyce, but judged as a film this is a deft, intriguing affair. Crix might help in arty spots. This is technically polished and well lensed, with music also a help. Here is an offbeater that will need special handling.

Made by an indie in the U.S., the producer wisely used suggestions from the James Joyce Society, to come up with the first pic from his more advanced works. *Mosk.*

Amador
(SPANISH)

Cannes. May 18.
Champs Elysees Productions-Jet Films production and release. Stars Maurice Ronet; features Amparo Soler Leal. Directed by Francisco Regueiro. Screenplay, Regueiro adapted by Angelino Fon, Manuel Lopez Jubero, Jean-Claude Lagneau; camera, Juan Julio Baena; editor, Pablo Del Amo. At Cannes Film Fest. Running time, 96 MINS.
Amador .... Maurice Ronet
Girl .... Amparo Soler Leal

Amador is an unbalanced Spanish thirtyish man who has a penchant for killing women. But film is neither a thriller nor even a morbid psychological drama. It concerns an oppressive atmosphere which in this case leads to blind killings.

Pic is an offbeater with certain pros and cons because of its seemingly lighthearted look at murder. It is intermittently successful in making the plot more symbolical than realistic. Thus, it's a pic mainly for arty outlets and chancey at that.

The man in question has been raised by a doting mother and aunt. He had an illegitimate child but not the strength to marry the mother. Pic depicts his effort to escape his home, a botched attempt to make up with the mother of his child and his murder of another woman and his aunt before a girl who loves him disarms him in another killing attempt.

French actor Maurice Ronet manages to keep the main character from being eerie and sickly. He is depicted mainly as a weak man whose killing is an almost involuntary reflex against his own human weakness.

The director, for a second pic, evidences a flair for mood and atmosphere. But he is not quite able to clarify this downbeat tale. It may have censor troubles in its own country and has dubious chances in the foreign field.
Mosk.

Hör Halevana
(A Hole In The Moon)
(ISRAELI)

Cannes, May 18.
M. Navon production and release. With Christiane Dancourt, Shoshana Lavi, Arieh Lavi, Shai K. Ophir, Uri Zohar, Avraham Heffner. Directed by Uri Zohar. Screenplay, Amos Kenan; camera, David Gurfinkel; editor, Gael Tomarkin. At Cannes Film Fest. Running Time, 80 MINS.
Mirage .... Christiane Dancourt
Starlet .... Shoshana Lavi
Sheriff .... Arieh Lavi
Samural .... Shai K. Ophir
Zelnik .... Uri Zohar
Mizrahi .... Avraham Heffner

Here is the first Israeli pic, at least seen by this reviewer, that has zesty, free wheeling and gutsy verve. It shows influence by the New York filmmakers, the New Wave, and there's a penchant for inside jokes and a showing off of film background. But this is coherent and original enough, with all its influences to give it specialized chances abroad.

Frozen images, going behind the camera or before it at will, jump cuts and a bleeding of many ideas are still clear in this raucous knowing pic. Film is a brash, fresh affair that emerges the first truly original Israeli production.

Two immigrants arrive and meet all different people of Israeli before each opens a lemonade stand along a seldom used road in the desert. Here they have hallucinations, see a city spring up, and are preparing to make a film into which all their ideas are welded.

There are takeoffs on oaters. monster pix and psychological dramas, but all have some bearing on the building of this new state. A Biblical figure with a bandaged hand is forever appearing to say "To Be or Not To Be," or walking on water. Then it fights age old monuments disastrously like Don Quixote and the windmills.

Some Arabs beg the director of one scene to be allowed to play sympathetic roles for a change.

Anyway, all this is cogently put together by director Uri Zohar to the witty, but canny script of Amos Kenan. Playing is of the broad character called for by the madcap carryings-on. Even the old pioneers are pointed up via a scene of two of them cavorting around the desert with a donkey rather than the self-sacrificing, sombre, people usually depicted.

This is a romp, a parody or comedy but has a tingling zest that keeps it constantly moving. It is that type of offbeat pic that will need special handling and placement for best results. It should do well on its own grounds. It is technically fine. *Mosk.*

Walkower
(Walkover)
(POLISH)

Cannes, May 18.
Polski State Film release of Syrene production. With Jerzy Skolimovski, Alexandre Zawieruzzanka, Krzysztof Schamiec. Written and directed by Jerzy Skolimovski. Camera, Antoni Nurzynski; music, Andrzej Trzaskowski. At Cannes Film Fest. Running time, 74 MINS.
Abdre .... Jerzy Skolimovski
Teresa ...... Alexandra Zawieruzzanka

The Polski title, which is supposed to mean being walked over or a push over, is as unusual as this film

is 2nd as ambiguous as the pic itself. Yet, this has a personal, quirky quality that gives it unusual force and emerges a strange picture of a certain type of Polish youth today.

Its being made in the regular way also shows surprising freedom allowed by the authorities. Whether it will be understood and appreciated by western audiences is another matter. This could well be something for dualer use in art spots or for more specialized bookings.

Director-writer Jerzy Skolimovski also plays the lead, a young man forced to fight in amateur boxing matches though he does not like them. Though schooled, he can not find a place he wants in industry and just seems to float about, selling hot watches and radios on the side.

During his wanderings he meets a pretty girl but it leads only to talk. It all ends with him trying to run out on a boxing match.

In the interim, background events also cast a sombre pall on life in Poland today. But all this has a taking air, Skolimovsky showing definite promise in writing, thesping and directing. Perhaps more coherence and less symbolism should have him a more potent force in the future. As is, his pic is uneven, but gives an air of disturbed and groping youth rare for an Eastern country pix. *Mosk.*

Le Chat Dans Le Sac
(The Cat in the Bag)
(CANADIAN)

Cannes, May 18.
Office National Du Film-Canada production and release. With Barbara Ulrich, Claude Godbout. Written and directed by Gilles Groulx. Camera, Jean-Claude Lebrecoue; editor, Roger Lamoureux, Marcel Carriere. At Cannes Film Fest. Running time, 74 MINS.
Barbara .... Barbara Ulrich
Claude .... Claude Godbout

Using the French language, this Canadian pic intelligently welds the cinema truth-type methods with real actors and spontaneous as well as planned scenes. Result is an off-beater that shows home insight into youthful rebellion as well as a touching young love. Looks mainly for specialized spots abroad on its knowing framework. Tele chances appear.

A young newsman and an actress are on the verge of breaking up their love affair. He is concerned with personal problems and his inability to find a place for himself and to cope with what he thinks is the corruption around him. She is a more earthy, Jewish girl who is interested in acting and the more tangible pleasures of life.

Barbara Ulrich and Claude Godbout are attractive and register in their intimate scenes. Their talk and his final decision to try to work things out alone for awhile bring their affair to a head.

Film ends inconclusively but it has given a good look at fretting French-Canadian youth. Production has a live, fresh look.

Director Gilles Grouix has taken hints from the cinema truth pix but also has added crisp editing and progression. It is a chancey item except for some arty spots. *Mosk.*

The Collector
(COLOR)

Highly dramatic and compelling suspense binge with William Wyler at his top best; word-of-mouth should help profitable outlook.

Hollywood, May 8.
Columbia Pictures release of William Wyler production, directed by Wyler. Stars Terence Stamp, Samantha Eggar; features Maurice Dallimore, Mona Washbourne. Screenplay, Stanley Mann, John Kohn; based on novel by John Fowles; camera (Technicolor), Robert L. Surtees (Hollywood), Robert Krasker (England); asst. directors, Sergei Petschnikoff (Hollywood), Roy Baird (England); music, Maurice Jarre; editor, 2d unit director, Robert Swink. Reviewed at Screen Directors Guild Theatre, May 7, '65. Running Time, 117 MINS.
Freddie Clegg .... Terence Stamp
Miranda Grey .... Samantha Eggar
The Neighbor .... Maurice Dallimore
Aunt Annie .... Mona Washbourne

William Wyler undertook a vastly difficult assignment, and carried it off with rare artistry, in bringing to the screen a solid, suspenseful enactment of John Fowles' bestselling novel. He has handled the unconventional theme with tact and imagination, while realizing his flair for the dramatic, and film's emotional overtones should capture response and unusual word-of-mouth attention. Like some of Wyler's top pix, "The Collector" will require specialized treatment, since it is a two-character play whose exponents are virtually unknown in this country; profitable returns, however, are indicated.

As a character study of two persons—an inferiority-ridden young Englishman with an uncontrollable sex obsession and the young woman he abducts and holds prisoner in the cellar of his secluded farmhouse—the Technicolor feature is adroitly developed and bears the stamp of class.

In certain respects, it is a shocker—one sequence drawing audible gasps from the preview audience—and fits patly in a school that has been growing via such filmmakers as Alfred Hitchcock. Where "The Collector" excels particularly is its maintenance of a tense mood of subdued excitement and uncertainty as narrative builds to an unexpected finish.

Director makes handsome use of the English countryside where he locationed for his Columbia Pictures release. The farmhouse itself lends an Old World atmosphere, and a certain section of London where the Englishman follows his unsuspecting quarry and overcomes in a deserted spot with a cloth soaked in chloroform, provides a fresh setting and adds to general interest. Jud Kinberg and John Kohn produced with Wyler, and the technical aspects are especially effective.

Color photography, in the hands of Robert L. Surtees in Hollywood and Robert Krasker in England, frequently is stunning, always of high quality, picture opening on a visually beautiful note as the leading male character, Terence Stamp, is introduced as a butterfly collector. The Stanley Mann-John Kohn screenplay expands on this premise; to his hobby of butterflies he broadens his collecting to girls. He falls in love with a young art student, and has an uncontrollable desire to force her to reciprocate his feelings. When he wins $200,000 in a British football pool, he buys an old farmhouse with an ideal cellar for what he has in mind.

This is to seize the girl and imprison her in the cellar which he furnishes with everything she may need, clothes to her measurements, classical records, art books. The girl, caught in a situation she finds unbelievable and frightening, tries every wile for the two months she has been told she must remain prisoner, to gain her freedom, but the man is impervious to her pleas and appeals to reason. He never makes any effort to touch her—he merely tells her he wants her to love him. This situation is built to a walloping climax as she attempts to escape and nearly kills him with a spade which Technicolor print shows in gory detail. Final denouement is totally surprising.

Both Stamp and Samantha Eggar turn in remarkably restrained performances under Wyler's guiding dramatic helpsmanship. Stamp makes his character of an insignificant London bank clerk, victim of a dormant imagination, entirely believable and carefully shades his characterization.

Miss Eggar, equally convincing, lends unusual force to the role of the terror-stricken girl who feels she will never leave her prison alive. It is strictly an acting role with no attempts at glamor or embellishment, a cinch for critical acclaim.

Only two other players have speaking lines. Mona Washbourne, as Stamp's aunt who comes to the bank with the news of his win, appears in two scenes; Maurice Dallimore, as a talkative neighbor who drops in on Stamp, is in a sequence which furnishes a good measure of suspense. Both are okay.

Further on the technical side, John Stoll's art direction is of superlative value in establishing atmosphere, and Maurice Jarre's score expertly points up the dramatic elements as pic unspools. Robert Swink's work as film editor and second unit director also is a decided plus.   *Whit.*

Stranded

Breezy Yank indie made in Greece and France by a new femme filmmaker Juleen Compton; might be useful for special and arty situations. Promises well for future pix if this one's commercial outlooks are only fair.

Compton production and release. With Juleen Compton, Gary Collins, Gian Pietro Calasso, Alkis Yanakis. Written and directed by Miss Compton. Camera, Demos Sakeyyariose; editor, A. Siaskas, Claude Plouganio; music, John Sakellarides. At Cannes Film Fest. Running Time, 90 MINS.
Raina .... Juleen Compton
Bob .... Gary Collins
Olivier .... Gian Pietro Calasso
Nicos .... Alkis Yanakis

A comely young American woman walks into the Adriatic near Arthens with her clothes on. Dog is left barking on the shore. She is pulled out by a Greek youth and goes off slowly. She finds her hat and says softly and almost mockingly, "I almost lost my hat." Then she is off to join two friends on a boat trip around the Greek islands.

So begins this pic made by Yank actress Juleen Compton. Throughout it possesses this combo of drama and comedy, and like some women, never makes up its mind. But that is one of the charming facets of this almost plotless film. It marks another femme encroachment into that domain of filmmaking—direction.

And it appears they can add something to pix. Most of them do not bother to find concise reasons for the actions of their characters or care too much about a clear-cut plot. At least Miss Compton does not.

There is a young handsome man who seems to be her boy friend but there is no inkling of anything sexy between them. Then there is a French homosexual artist whose hurts from virile Greeks she tries to assuage. Her one moment of love comes with a handsome Greek sailor on the boat when she slips off one night for a nude swim, and he follows her.

But there's nothing amoral here. There is a personal innocence that keeps this episode from being in any way scabrous. The group begins to fret and fight and takes a Turkish steamer back to France in steerage. Here they go to the French boy's chateau. She decides to stay on and clean up the spot while her American boy friend goes back to a career.

Thus there is no deep revelation about Americans abroad. She seems to have the means and is more interested in new adventures than in settling personal problems. That is about all there is to this skimpy pic. But in it are some gentle scenes of the three amusing themselves, sometimes awed by some of the ancient Greek sites, or her finding herself the only woman in a Greek bar and doing a solitary twist after the men have danced alone.

Film is well lensed with a sprightly helpful musical score. Miss Compton is guache, touching and refreshing as the energetic, motherly but domineering girl whose morality is personal. Gary Collins manages to keep the boy friend from being callow. Gian Pietro Calasso is cloying at times but never annoying as the effeminate painter.   *Mosk.*

The Amorous Adventures of Moll Flanders
(PANAVISION—COLOR)

Bouncy, bawdy tale of the Daniel Defoe heroine wanting to be a lady of quality—and what happens; promising grosses foreseen.

Hollywood. May 19.
Paramount release of Marcel Hellman production. Stars Kim Novak, Richard Johnson, Angela Lansbury, Vittorio De Sica, Leo McKern, George Sanders, Lilli Palmer; features Daniel Massey, Hugh Griffith, Peter Butterworth, Cecil Parker, Roger Livesey, Jess Conrad, Richard Wattis. Directed by Terence Young. Screenplay, Denis Cannan, Roland Kibbee; based on novel by Daniel Defoe; camera (Technicolor), Ted Moore; music, John Addison; production design, Syd Cain; editor, Frederick Wilson; asst. director, David Anderson; sound, A. H. Ross, Bob Jones. Reviewed at Beverly Theatre, May 18, '65. Running Time, 123 MINS.
Moll Flanders .... Kim Novak
Young Moll .... Claire Ufland
Jemmy .... Richard Johnson
Lady Blystone .... Angela Lansbury
The Count .... Vittorio De Sica
Squint .... Leo McKern
The Banker .... George Sanders
Dutchy .... Lilli Palmer
Grunt .... Peter Butterworth
Orphanage Supt. .... Dandy Nichols
Bishop .... Noel Howlett
The Mayor .... Cecil Parker
The Mayor's Wife ...... Barbara Couper
Elder Brother .... Daniel Massey
Younger Brother .... Derren Nesbitt
Elder Sister .... Ingrid Hafner
Younger Sister .... June Watts
Miss Glowber .... Judith Furse
Officer of Dragoons....Anthony Dawson
Drunken Parson .... Roger Livesey
1st Mohock .... Jess Conrad
2nd Mohock .... Noel Harrison
3rd Mohock .... Alex Scott
4th Mohock .... Alexis Kahner
A Lady .... Mary Merrall
Jeweler .... Richard Wattis
Draper .... Terence Lodge
Doctor .... Reginald Beckwith
Singer in Prison .... Lionel Long
Ship's Captain .... David Lodge
A Nobleman .... David Hutcheson
Prison Governor .... Hugh Griffith
Lord Mayor of London
                    Michael Trubshawe
The Ordinary .... Richard Goolden
Prison Doctor .... Leonard Sachs
Lawyer .... Basil Dignam
The Turnkey .... Michael Brennan
Convict Ship Captain .. Liam Redmond
Convict Ship Officer.... Neville Jason

"Moll Flanders" — the amorous adventures of — is a sprawling, brawling, gaudy, bawdy, tongue-in-cheek comedy that seeks to caricaturize an 18th Century London wench's desire to be a gentlewoman and her varying exploits thereof, mostly via a downy — or otherwise — couch. Starring Kim Novak in title role, it has sex and color, slapstick and lusty, busty characterization, action which is sometimes very funny and, again, equally unfunny.

Film is over-long, in need of frequent snap-up in tempo. Episodic nature sometimes tells against it and there may be those who will object to some of the more intimate details. Generally speaking, despite its many weaknesses, pic probably will appeal to audiences who found "Tom Jones" much to their liking two years ago.

The foreword slyly states: "Any similarity between this film and any other film is purely coincidental." However that may be, it was a natural that the success scored by the filmic translation of that early Henry Fielding time should be followed by a femme counterpart in another picture. This adaptation of Daniel Defoe's novel, as such, comes off almost as an excursion into ribaldry.

Catholic Legion of Decency has labelled it "morally objectionable in part for all," although it doesn't put its "condemned" mark on the Marcel Hellman production as was the case with Billy Wilder's "Kiss Me, Stupid." This, and the elaborate campaign which Paramount unquestionably will tailor to the lavishly-turned-out Panavision-Technicolor production, may help in boosting film into the sock money class, although still to be determined is femme star's draw in an enterprise of this sort.

There may be certain dispute

over Miss Novak's impersonation of Moll, who revelled in scandalous behavior (to her, completely natural) and bounced from one bed to another in her attempted stride upward, but there's an earthiness about actress which she utilizes to good advantage. She has no inhibitions, and is willing to enter into slapstick affray with fists and feet and whatever comes to hand to entice any man for gain, and she doesn't mind turning clown, if the occasion warrants it. She wears her flouncy costumes well, in all stages of dress and undress, and whatever may be lacking in her acting is more than recompensed by a gusty presence.

Director Terence Young seems constantly to keep in mind the comic potentialities of his subject and his helming is always broad, lavened with old-fashioned sight gags. He has the advantage of a good cast and a high budget, and accompanying production potential. The Denis Cannan-Roland Kibbee screenplay follows Moll as she goes to London after a brief unhappy marriage in the country, to seek her goal through a variety of affairs and marriages which culminates in a ceremony with a highwayman whom she mistook to be a wealthy landowner.

Richard Johnson (whom Miss Novak wed after pic ended) gives colorful and romantic enactment to the highwayman character and is a cinch for a repeat in leading roles. His attempted seduction of Moll in the captain's cabin of a ship he rents to prove his wealth is one of the funniest sequences in film.

George Sanders' portrayal of a rich banker wed to Moll who dies of a heart attack after he finds her in prison, thus leaving her a lady of wealth, is robust and comical. Leo McKern, as Johnson's outlaw henchman, also scores a comedy hit. Lilli Palmer shines as a fence who financially helps Johnson woo Moll, whom he thinks is a fine lady but actually is the maid masquerading the part. Angela Lansbury, as her employer who allows Moll to wear her clothes, is charming and Vittorio De Sica, her shiftless companion who goes on the make for Moll, lends gusto to the part of a bogus Italian count.

Strong support also is afforded by Daniel Massey, Moll's drunken first husband; Richard Wattis, a jeweler; Hugh Griffith, prison governor.

Technical credits generally are first-rate, with music score by John Addison particularly outstanding and atmospheric of the times as well as pointing up comedy scenes. Syd Cain handled production design, a thoroughly superlative credit; Ted Moore's color photography is splashy, although occasionally his closeups are harsh; and Frederick Wilson's editing is usually sharp. *Whit.*

Tabu No. 2
(ITALIAN-COLOR)
Rome, May 18.

Titanus release of a Guigo Giambartolomei production for Royal Film. Directed by Romolo Marcellini. Text, Giancarlo del Re, Ugo Guerra; camera (Eastmancolor), Rino and Angelo Filippini; music, Angelo Lavagnino; editor, Otello Colang-

eli. At Barberini, Rome. Running Time, 85 MINS.

Followup to director's previous "Tabu" item arrives on the market here when this type of film—conceived in the manner of "Mondo Cane"—has just about played itself out. Nevertheless, it contains enough colorful, shocking, interesting material, and has been shot with sufficient polish to make it stand out above the sleazier pix of this fertile skein. Its offshore chances are therefore to be considered good for the type of slotting this kind of film usually gets.

Basically, the pattern rarely wanders or varies. Principal targets of pic, as with many others, are Sweden, Hong Kong and India, though other areas are also touched upon. Dogs per usual have a hard time of it in various seqences, such as those showing professional dog fights or canine psychiatry. Attempt to show the world as topsy-turvy also has the usual dosage of exploitable nudity, sensation, blood, poverty, drugs and off-beat customs.

A man is shown eating a turtle —live; other males are seen doing the town-square washing in India; South American gauchos play a sort of basketball-polo combination with a live duck as the ball, etc. Some of more fascinating off-beat moments come from a demonstration of non-violent Chinese boxing and from a closeup glimpse of mating vampire bats. But basically, it's all very much like a stroll along the world's Bowery.

Text in the Italo version is excellent and frequently amusing and intelligent, a definite plus for this film. Also helping is the smoothly-cut color photography by Rino and Angelo Filippini, also setting this apart from others of the genre which frequently use blown up 16m or stock footage intercut with a few original bits. Angelo Lavagnino's musical backdropping is in the exotic tradition of this kind of pic. *Hawk.*

A High Wind in Jamaica
(C'SCOPE—COLOR)

Anthony Quinn turns buccaneer this time out, a slick characterization in an interesting picture with considerable family appeal.

Hollywood, May 18.

Twentieth-Fox release of John Croydon production. Stars Anthony Quinn, James Coburn; features Lila Kedrova, Gert Frobee. Directed by Alexander Mackendrick. Screenplay, Ronald Harwood, Denis Cannon, Stanley Mann; based on book by Richard Hughes; camera (DeLuxeColor), Douglas Slocombe; music, Larry Adler; are director, John Howell, John Hoesli; editor, Derek Yorke; sound, "Dickie" Bird. Reviewed at 20th-Fox Studios, May 17, '65. Running Time, 104 MINS.

Chavez	Anthony Quinn
Zac	James Coburn
Mathias	Dennis Price
Dutch Captain	Gert Frobe
Rosa	Lila Kedrova
Captain Marpole	Kenneth J. Warren
Mr. Thornton	Nigel Davenport
Mrs. Thornton	Isabel Dean
Margaret	Viviane Ventura
Alberto	Benito Carruthers
Pirates	Charles Hyatt, Dan Jackson, Trader Faulkner
Tallyman	Charles Laurence
Cook	Kenji Takaki
Curtis	Brian Phelan
Old Sam	Danny Williams
Mamie	Louise Bennett
Mrs. Fernandez	Marion Ward
Captain—Guardia Civile	Philip Madoc
Josephina	Maude Fuller
Nurse	Elsie Benjamin Barsoe
Judge	Gordon Richardson
Stunt Pirates	Joe Powell, Eddie Powell
Emily	Deborah Baxter
John	Martin Amis
Laura	Karen Flack
Harry	Henry Beltran
Rachel	Roberta Tovey
Edward	Jeffrey Chandler

Anthony Quinn's penchant for grizzled characterization gets a colorful boost in this picturization of Richard Hughes' 1929 best-seller, which projects him as a Caribbean pirate. British production turned out by John Croydon in effective CinemaScope and vivid DeLuxe Color for often spectacular treatment is a curious mixture of high melodrama and light overtones, the latter occasioned by presence of a flock of youngsters aboard a pirate ship. Film lends itself to an exploitation campaign to hit all classes of audiences, with emphasis figured for family trade.

Most of the action takes place at sea. Filmed on location around Jamaica, Alexander Mackendrick's direction keeps his movement alive within the somewhat limited confines of a schooner where Quinn, the Spanish pirate captain, is confronted with the disturbing question of what to do with seven children who unbeknownst to him have slipped from another ship he attacked and now are found in the hold of his own craft. Situation as developed in warm screenplay written by Ronald Harwood, Denis Cannon and Stanley Mann allows for a bizarre set of circumstances as pirate captain, a simple-minded but strong-willed individual, attempts to set moppets aboard a Dutch vessel and brings on a mutiny from his crew when he refuses to plunder the Dutchman.

Story builds to an ironic finale when Quinn and his men are sentenced to death in an English court for murder of the Dutch captain, act actually was performed by one of the little girls aboard who became frightened when she thought she was to be harmed and in desperation finished him off with a knife. What is still more ironic is that the child is one for whom the pirate had developed a vague feeling, a strange retribution. Children were on their way to England for education from their Jamaican home when their barque was pirated by Quinn. Stage for later events is set by the superstitious crew regarding youngsters as bad luck and wanting their captain to dump them overboard.

Quinn endows his role with a subdued humanness in which there is occasional humor. Part isn't as picturesque as some of his past characterizations but actor is no less adroit in catching the innerworkings of a man. Even in piracy he attracts certain sympathy and audience is with him all the way.

James Coburn, costarred with Quinn as his English mate, continues to command attention as an actor and socks over character in which he combines humor with dramatic strength. He's always handicapped, it seems, by being unable to understand the Spanish spoken by most of the crew and is

never quite certain what's going on, good for some laughs.

Deborah Baxter, 10, plays the moppet who kills the Dutch captain but in the English court becomes frightened and pins the rap on the pirate, who takes it philosophically. It's an uncolorful part but she handles it well. Lila Kedrova, this year's Oscar winner (supporting actress) for her role with Quinn in "Zorba the Greek," appears in one brief but flashy sequence as a Tampico bawdy house madam and owner of Quinn's ship, a part she enacts with exotic flair.

Strong support also is provided by a large cast. Tops here are Nigel Davenport and Isabel Dean, parents of the children; Gert Frobe, the Dutch captain, and Kenneth J. Warren, captain of the barque carrying the children to England; Dennis Price, the English prosecutor; Benito Carruthers, a pirate. Viviane Ventura is a pretty newcomer.

Color photography by Douglas Slocombe sometimes is fascinating, always an asset, and Larry Adler's music score similarly strengthens the overall effect. Derek Yorke's editing is compact and art direction by John Howell and John Hoesli sets an interesting backdrop. *Whit.*

Su E Giu'
(Up and Down)
(ITALIAN)
Rome, May 18.

Dino DeLaurentiis release of a Panda (Ermanno Donati-Luigi Carpentieri) production. Features Beatrice Altariba, Daniele Vargas, Lando Buzzanca, Antonella Lualdi, Paolo Ferrari, Alida Chelli, E. M. Salerno, M. Grazia Buccella. Eleonora Rossi Drago, Marc Michel. Directed by Mino Guerrini. At Galleria, Rome. Running Time, 90 MINS.

Episodes: (1) Questione di Principio (A Question of Principle), with Lando Buzzanca, Beatrice Altariba, Daniele Vagas. (2) Moglie d'Agosto (A Wife in August), with Paolo Ferrari, Antonella Lualdi, Alida Chelli. (3) Il Sogno (The Dream), with E. N. Salerno, M. G. Buccella. (4) Il Colpo do Leone (Once in a Lifetime), with Eleonora Rossi Drago, Marc Michel, Guido Alberti.

Quickie episoder by young director Mino Guerrini with modest playoff chances here and abroad. Though competently made and shot with some polish, pic lacks substance. Some of segments are merely puffed-up anecdotes with a tendency to deflation when the punch-line comes at blackout time.

Opener is a silly trifle played with ironic tongue-in-cheek about the shooting of the wrong man in a duel, replete with identity mixups and boudoir shennanigans. Item No. 2 is a rather explicit tale of a meandering husband who takes on more than he can handle in a young mistress, with his wife returning home early to double his dose of punishment. "The Dream" is an overextended daytime incident, in which a down-and-out salesman imagines a brief tryst—complete with ritual strip —with a comely passerby. Windup segment gets greater development, showing the way a penniless youth manages by bluff to worm his way into his boss' graces, thanks also to a major gambling coup. Card sequence gives the film a needed fillip of suspense.

with frequent lapses in taste. Ma-Guerrini's direction of this displays flashes of style interspersed terial at hand doesn't assist him much, and work of thesps is equally spotty and generally superficial. In short, the pic reflects effort, time and money put into it but stands to achieve its modest intentions probably more efficiently than some of its more expensive counterparts. *Hawk.*

Feu a Volonte
(Fire at Will)
(FRENCH)

Paris, May 18.
Comacico release of Spava Film-Cine Alliance-Epoca Film production. Stars Eddie Constantine; features Nelly Benedetti, Daniel Ceccaldi, Luis Davila, Laura Valenzuela. Directed by Marcel Ophuls. Screenplay, Jacques Robert, Ophuls; camera, Jean Tournier; editor, Louisette Hautecoeur. At Balzac, Paris. Running Time, 90 MINS.
Warner .... Eddie Constantine
Princess .... Nelly Benedetti
Girl .... Laura Valenzuela
Pablo .... Luis Davila
Stephan .... Daniel Ceccaldi

Usual Eddie Constantine parody undercover man vehicle is given a more Bonded look by adding offbeat gadgets and gimmicks plus breezy direction done by Marcel Ophuls on this, his second pic. But it remains mainly for filler or tv use abroad on its general action and pace sans the needed zesty fillip for more untoward chances. It should do okay on its own grounds.

Here Constantine is trying to find a young scientist who has invented a tiny electronic ring that can put people out for hours by contact. Also trying to find the boy is a Russian secret service man. He is being hidden by a bunch of amazon-like, good-looking women.

They are all working for a rich man who hides under a philanthropic cover. So after some hard plotting, fisticuffs and lovemaking, the boy is recovered. But he has lost his genius by falling in love.

All this is adequately tossed off and could have some value due to the tastes for such parodic actioners currently. Constantine is his usual phlegmatic self and walks through his familiar role with ease. *Mosk.*

The Monkey's Uncle
(COLOR)

Sequel to "Misadventures of Merlin Jones" should appeal to same trade with fair prospects in sight.

Hollywood, May 22.
Buena Vista release of Walt Disney production. Stars Tommy Kirk, Annette Funicello; features Leon Ames, Frank Faylen, Arthur O'Connell; Leon Tyler, Alan Hewitt, Norman Grabowski. Directed by Robert Stevenson. Screenplay, Tom and Helen August, based on story by Bill Walsh; camera (Technicolor), Edward Colman; music, Buddy Baker; editor Cotton Warburton; art director, Carroll Clark, William H. Tuntke; asst. director, Joseph L. McEveety; sound, Robert O. Cook. Reviewed at Academy Award Theatre, May 21, '65. Running Time, 90 MINS.
Merlin Jones .... Tommy Kirk
Jennifer .... Annette
Judge Holmsby .... Leon Ames
Darius Green III ...... Arthur O'Connell
Mr. Dearborne .... Frank Faylen
Leon .... Leon Tyler
Norman .... Norman Grabowski
Lisa .... Cheryl Miller
Mrs. Gossett ...... Connie Gilchrist

Professor Shattuck .... Alen Hewitt
College President ...... Gage Clarke

Walt Disney apparently was so intrigued with his Merlin Jones character, the brainy college student who dotes on tackling impossible scientific feats — limned previously in "Misadventures of Merlin Jones" (1964) — that he decided on another whirl with the screwball genius. "The Monkey's Uncle," like its predecessor, depends on gimmicks and some nutty situations, which provide mild amusement. Film is suitable chiefly for the family trade and teenage market where names of Tommy Kirk and Annette Funicello may attract. There's the magic draw, too, of the Disney tag.

Most of the same principals appear again, ditto director, scripters, original story writer, title song composers and technicians behind the camera. Tommy this time out is called upon twice to perform the impossible for Midvale College — first, to devise a method of "honest cheating" so a couple of star football lunkheads can pass their exams; second, invent a man-powered flight so school can win a $10,000,000 bequest.

Both experiments get audience response. First is accomplished by "sleep teaching," rigging a recorder to electronic hair-curlers, by which the two goons learn answers to the exam while they sleep. This, of course, leads to some entanglements with the prof when both students, and Tommy, come up with word-for-word papers.

Second is slightly more difficult, but Tommy comes through with a bicycle-driven prop job with which he flies like a bird — almost.

Tommy performs engagingly, and Annette reprises as his pretty co-ed girl friend who helps him with his experiments through some of her dumb questions. Film takes its title from Tommy being court-appointed The Monkey's Uncle when he tries to take out adoption papers on Stanley, his chimp.

Leon Ames again is the judge who has great faith in Tommy saving Midvale; Norman Grabowski repeats as the muscle-bound stalwart; and Alan Hewitt the professor out to ban football, all endowing their roles with proper schmaltz. Frank Faylen also scores as one of the regents still sore about not making the team when he attended Midvale; Arthus O'Connell lends just theright touch to the millionaire who wants to endow the college, then some keepers appear to take him back to the nut farm; and Leon Tyler is good for laughs as the other knucklehead whom Tommy uses in the first stages of his flying experiments. Cheryl Miller is a looker, as chimp's baby-sitter.

Robert Stevenson's direction of the Tom and Helen August screenplay, based on Bill Walsh's original story, is fair enough but he didn't have too much to work with. Edward Colman's color photography is excellent, and balance of technical credits are well handled, particularly the special effects by Robert A. Mattey and Eustace Lycett. Title song, rather catchy, was cleffed by Richard M. and Robert B. Sherman, which femme star

chirps with The Beach Boys. Ron Miller is credited as co-producer. *Whit.*

Three Hats For Lisa
(BRITISH—COLOR)

Modest, breezy musical, full of good humor. Slick direction and cutting and cheerful, young cast make this an above-average British tuner, a sound booking.

London, May 18.
Warner-Pathe release of a Seven Hills (Jack Hanbury) production from Anglo Amalgamated. Stars Joe Brown, Sophie Hardy, Sidney James, Una Stubbs; features Dave Nelson, Peter Bowles, Seymour Green, Jeremy Lloyd, Michael Brennan, Eric Barker. Directed by Sidney Hayers. Screenplay, Leslie Bricusse, Talbot Rothwell, from Bricusse's original story; incidental music, Eric Rogers; lyrics, music, Bricusse; camera (Eastmancolor), Alan Hume; editor, Tristram Cones; choreography, Gillian Lynne. Reviewed at Corner Theatre, London. Running Time, 99 MINS.
Johnny Howjego .... Joe Brown
Lisa Milan .... Sophie Hardy
Sid Marks .... Sidney James
Flora .... Una Stubbs
Sammy .... Peter Bowles
Signor Molfino .... Seymour Green
Miss Penny .... Josephine Blake
Guards Officer .... Jeremy Lloyd
Police Sergeant ...... Michael Brennan
Station Sergeant ...... Eric Barker

Recent British attempts to turn out musical pix with pop favorites as stars have scarcely set Film Row afire, but Seven Hills' "Three Hats For Lisa" has come off nicely. It's a bright, gay trifle the alert direction and editing, livey songs and some happy thesping helping it to hit its target effectively. There is not much marquee bait for America, but as a co-feature it will still bring some sunny fun to any program.

Leslie Bricusse's simple idea has been unpretentiously screenplayed by Bricusse and Talbot Rothwell. Bricusse also has provided a bunch of songs that are a cut above the obvious fodder aimed at the Top 10 by similar films. But it is Sidney Hayers' speedy direction and Tristram Cones' brisk editing that help "Lisa" most.

Bricusse's hero is a young Cockney working lad with a crush on Italian film star Lisa Milan (Sophie Hardy). When she visits London for her film preem he, his girl friend, another buddy and a cynical, warmhearted hackie find themselves involved in taking a truant Lisa for a day's sightseeing tour around London. The trip is complicated by a kinky hobby of the film star. She likes stealing headgear for her collection and has set her heart on a business man's derby, a Guardsman's bearskin and a cop's helmet. This gentle malarky is an excuse for a lightning trip around London, plenty of song and dance and some cheerful romping as the hats are lifted despite misadventures.

Hayers has directed at tremendous pace, thus glossing over occasional story frailties, and editor Tristram Cones and Alan Hume and his restless Eastmancolor camera are slick allies. Gillian Lynne's choreography is agile and mostly fits fluently into the action. A bonus, too, for Bricusse's songs which equally fit frequently into the locale and the action.

Some of the numbers may well hit the charts but there is no conscious attempt to make them do so. The cabby's paean of praise for his "hometown," a lusty piece of London called Bermondsey, is a neat piece of joshing, a Covent Garden song and another rather in the "Mack The Knife" idiom are nicely experimental. The running theme song is a bright ditty and even the conventional 'boy meets girl' type of love lyric seem to get out of a rut. Without overselling "Lisa," it's fair to say that it has much of the exuberance of "On The Town."

The young hero, Joe Brown, is a bouncy Cockney with an accent which makes Tommy Steele sound like Sir John Gielgud. His likeable, brash personality fits the role well. Una Stubbs, his girl friend is a pert lass, with educated legs and a chirpy sense of humor. Sophie Hardy, a French soubrette, without showing oversigns of thesping genius, bubbles happily throughout the action. The young blood also has the advantage of the presence of popular character actor. Sidney James who, as the taxidriver, adds a full quota of comedy savvy.

Dave Nelson, Peter Bowles, Seymour Green, Josephine Blake, Heremy Lloyd, Eric Barker and Michael Brennan, in effective bits, are useful support. Technical credits are okay. As an excuse for a swift o.o. of London on a summer's day is a lighthearted tonic. *Rich.*

The Battle Of The Villa Fiorita
(COLOR—PANAVISION)

Disjointed soaper piling juve comedy on parents' adulterous base. Marquee lure in Maureen O'Hara in offbeat role plus Rossano Brazzi. Well-mounted with okay prospects on duoble bills.

Hollywood, May 13.
Warner Bros. release of a Delmar Daves production, written and directed by Daves. Features Maureen O'Hara, Rossano Brazzi, Richard Todd, Phyllis Calvert. Based on novel by Rumer Godden; camera (Panavision, Technicolor), Oswald Morris; editor, Bert Bates; music, M. Spoliansky; art direction, Carmen Dillon; sound, Les Hammond, Len Shilton. Reviewed at Academy Award Theatre, May 12, '65. Running Time, 111 MINS.
Moira .... Maureen O'Hara
Lorenzo .... Rossano Brazzi
Darrell .... Richard Todd
Margot .... Phyllis Calvert
Michael .... Martin Stephens
Debby .... Elizabeth Dear
Donna .... Olivia Hussey
Charmian .... Maxine Audley
Lady Anthea .... Ursula Jeans
Father Rossi .... Ettore Manni
Travel Agent .... Richard Wattis
Emcee .... Finlay Currie
Celestina .... Celia Matania
Giuletta .... Rosi Di Pietro

"The Battle Of The Villa Fiorita" is a beautifully-photographed and well-mounted Delmer Daves production which falls short artistically by switching gears. Unusual casting of Maureen O'Hara as runaway wife whose new affair is broken up by her kids may be marquee lure, but Warner Bros. release is from sudsville.

Daves' script (from Rumer Godden's novel) propels Miss O'Hara into affair with Italian composer Rossano Brazzi when latter attends

English tunefest during one of hubby Richard Todd's frequent absences from home. Todd is on briefly when wifey confesses infatuation, and his surprise anger and acceptance register well. Then the lovers hie to Italian villa and set up housekeeping before her divorce action jells.

At this point concent shifts to attempts by her kids (Martin Stephens and Elizabeth Dear) to break it up, joined later by Brazzi's moppet, Olivia Hussey. Idea is played for laffs, from juves' trek from England through hunger strikes, faked illness and other gambits. Plot line becomes thin, and Miss O'Hara and Brazzi are reduced to mere reaction acting. Joke is dull at best even assuming that presence of offspring in parents' shack-up location is suitable base for comedy.

All names follow title, and top-featured Miss O'Hara looks appropriately shook up, but script does not permit much acting. Brazzi projects very well as lover, father and foil. Phyllis Calvert is on for seconds as gossipy English lady. The juves are good, especially Miss Dear, but script emphasis (and repetition of motivation and even dialog) makes them overly precocious at times. Ettore Manni makes a handsome village priest who publicly denounces lovers, but in context it is banal.

Inevitable victory of kids in the "Battle" follows climactic scene where kids get lost in boat during storm, only to be reduced by townfolk in soapy fashion. Lovers split up, Brazzi promising to be a better widower-father, while Miss O'Hara reluctantly returns with brood. Finlay Currie and other players are okay in stock meller bits.

Oswald Morris' Panavision and Technicolor camera paints an attractive backdrop, and director Daves drew a few lively moments from his uneven script. Pic's love theme by M. Spoliansky is good, but repeated too often. Obtrusive scoring and conducting during rescue scene only points up shallowness of what is on the screen. Editor Bert Bates did a professional job, as did all other technicians, including uncredited sound editors who reconstructed in fine fashion the many exterior sequences.

Murf.

China

Well-photographed but routine documentary of Red China by English writer-lecturer has only special-interests appeal.

A Felix Greene presentation, produced and written by Greene. Narrated by Alexander Scourby. Camera (Ektachrome), Greene and Hsu Chih-Chiang; editor, John Jeremy; sound, Walter Storey; music, Peking Symphony Orchestra and folk music. Previewed at N.Y., May 21, '65. Running Time, 65 MINS.

Britisher Felix Greene, with BBC prior to World War II, was able to travel in Communist China as a correspondent, was commissioned by British television, ATC-TV, to make a filmed report of every-day life of the Chinese. Result is this film which had its U.S. premiere May 25 at the Carnegie Hall Cinema. Commercial outlook for film is limited as it's too bland

a travelog for close students and the political-minded but contains too much "propaganda" for the escapist-minded.

Greene, who now lives in California, has tried to minimize political aspects of the film without losing the evident dramatic impact of the industrial growth in China since the end of World War II. As a result, he has been unsuccessful in both attempts. A'though he says that he has traveled over most of China, most of the film deals with two cities, Shanghai and Peking, both with heavy political overtones. The few rural or village shots could have been immediately outside either city. The bleak, cold Mongolian country is the only area which looks really different.

There is much of interest in the film if the viewer can ignore the uncomfortable feeling of being "sold" a message. This aspect will probably never change as the westerner will view the Communist Chinese with suspicion and hostility. That progress has been, and is being made, can't be denied when one sees the power plants, machine tool factories, massed demonstrations, and accelerated educational systems. Although no military might, as such, is shown, there are several displays of political leaders viewing student and other demonstrations.

Other than some old introductory black-and-white newsreel footage, Greene and an assigned cameraman, Hsu Chih-Chiang, did all the photography which is surprisingly clear and sometimes sweepingly impressive in scope. It contains none of the shock-intended material found in recent Italian travel films. Some footage is as recent as 1963, as indicated on banners carried in one of the parades.

References to religion, after a brief comment that the government is atheistic, shows both Buddhist and Catholic services. Comment on the latter, however, is that "the Catholic church in China has no formal relationship with Rome." Much industrial coverage deals with expansion of shipbuilding and airlines (latter to Burma, Pakistan, Japan and Russia). There is much interest in sports (basketball is national favorite).

Commentary, narrated by actor Alexander Scourby, although he gets no screen credit, was written by Greene, in a somewhat stodgy style. Occasional phrases linger, uncomfortably, such as "China" is determined to move forward into the modern world," which may have only been an unfortunate choice of preposition.

A short scene of the Peking Symphony Orchestra is mostly impressive because of the modern 10,000-capacity hall in which it performs. Music used through most of the film is modified folk music, plus many natural sounds. Peking Symphony is shown at greater length in a black-and-white short accompanying this feature.

Some of advertising for film is mild attempt to be controversial—"For the first time, the real China can be seen . . . for some, an artistic delight, to others, it may be as disturbing as the flight of the first sputnik." *Robe.*

Go Go Mania
(BRITISH—MUSIC—COLOR)

Screen bait for mod adolescents. Import has familiar rock 'n' roll tunes and full glimpse of Beatles.

American International Pictures release of a Hary Field production. Features The Beatles, Matt Munro, Susan Maughan, The Animals, The Honeycombs, The Rockin' Berries, Herman's Hermits, The Nashville Teens The Four Pennies, Billy J. Kramer and the Dakotas, The Fourmost, Sounds Incorporated, Peter & Gordon, Tommy Quickly & the Remo Four, Billie Davis, The Spencer Davis Group. Directed by Frederick Goode; choreography, Leo Kharibian; camera (Technicolor); no credit. Reviewed at RKO Palace, N.Y., May 20, '65. Running Time: 70 MINS.

Although selling pitch of this hodge-podge collection of British rock 'n' roll acts will evidently be based on inclusion of The Beatles, there's only a short bit with the group, used as introduction and close. Color and photography of the sequence, evidently made at a long-ago concert, clashes with the studio-shot remainder of the film.

Relative merits of the various acts would have to be decided by a musicologist, if that's the word. To adult ears they all sound alike after five or ten minutes. However, some of acts have had U.S. exposure for help in promotion.

AIP is pushing item as a "scream package," a bit more accurate description than most film advertising. After the first shocking appearance of Jimmy Savile, British disc jockey who emcees, sporting a bleached shoulder length thatch that outdoes Jayne Mansfield, there's little actual novelty in the noisome hour-plus bedlam.

An improvement in British dentistry is evident although the next major medical project for the Royal Society of Surgeons should be dermatology considering the frequent display of acne unfortunately spotlighted by the color camera's too frequent closeups. Oddly enough, most of the male voices sound closer to soprano or falsetto than the accustomed baritone or bass. Could this be Britain's answer to Italy's "white voices"? Certainly their addiction to coiffures that look like a wig-winder's nightmare doesn't refute this question.

Originally called "Pop Gear," a no-more meaningless title than the present one, "Go Go Mania" is being packaged with another social treatise — "Taboos Of The World" — something for the entire family. *Robe.*

What
(ITALIAN-BRITISH; COLOR)

Horror entry capitalizing on name of Daliah Lavi, which has top photography and good production values, should do well in its market with hard-sell ad and promo campaign promised by releasers.

Hollywood, May 19.
Futuramic Releasing release of Richard G. Yates presentation. Features Daliah Lavi, Christopher Lee, with Tony Kendall, Isli Oberon, Harriet White, Dean Ardow, Alan Colins, Jacques Herlin. Directed by

John M. Old. Screenplay, Julian Berry, Robert Hugo, Martin Hardy; camera (Technicolor) David Hamilton; editor Rob King; sound, Peter Jakson; asst. director, Julian Bery. Reviewed at Joe Shorr's screening studio, May 18, '65. Running Time, 90 MINS.

Novenka Menliff	Daliah Lavi
Kurt Menliff	Christopher Lee
Christian Menliff	Tony Kendall
Georgia	Isli Oberon
Kathia	Harriet White
Lomenko	Dean Ardow
Count Menliff	Jacques Herlin

"What" is a gimmicky title for a gimmicky story about murder and terror in gloomy castle, obviously designed by Italo-British co-production to capitalize on any exposure Daliah Lavi may have won through "Lord Jim." Technicolor photography by David Hamilton is superb, and hard-sell promotion planned by Futuramic Releasing could make it b.o. winner.

For sophisticated audiences, the Gothic-novel atmosphere and trappings of secret passages, muddy footprints from the crypt and ghost lover, probably will draw more laughs than gasps. But genuine suspense is maintained throughout story of "bad" brother who returns home from long absence and is murdered. Christopher Lee plays the heavy role in satisfactory fashion and makes admirable ghost after death. Miss Lavi, as one-time lover of Lee and now wife of "good" brother Tony Kendall, is decorative but barely adequate as emoter.

Lesser roles in small cast are handled in pro manner by British thesps. Isli Oberon is particularly good as housekeeper whose daughter killed self because she was seduced by Lee before his exile. Dean Ardow plays crippled manservant of castle and Jacques Herlin is the old Count, also murdered.

Script, credited to Julian Berry, Robert Hugo and Martin Hardy, has many preposterous lines, and is far too cluttered with cliches, such as screams in the night, hurried chases and mystery lights in the crypt. But John M. Old has directed it in workmanlike-fashion and Rob King's editing is competent, so action moves at good pace. Other production values are good, especially Jim Murphy's unobtrusive score, Peg Fax' 19th Century costumes, and Dick Grey's shadowy sets. *Hogg.*

Taboos Of The World
(ITALIAN—COLOR)

Compilation edited for U.S. with Vincent Price narrator. Hokum and Sadism mixture.

American International Pictures release of a Royal Films (Romolo Marcellini) production. Narration by Vincent Price. Directed by Marcellini; camera (Technicolor), Rino Filippini; editor, Otello Colangeli. Reviewed at RKO Palace, N.Y., May 20, '65. Running Time: 97 MINS.

This Italian import, which has been reworked by American International Pictures and an English commentary added, spoken by Vincent Price, follows in the footsteps of the other quasi-documentaries which have hit the American market. Like most of the others, it's colorfully photographed hokum, mixed with some routine travel shots given a suggestive tone by the not-always accurate commentary.

Although Vincent Price speaks the narrative in his best unctuous tones, it is as often as not his flippant remark that titillates the ear of the viewer and not what the eye is beholding.

Many scenes are variations of those shown in "Mondo Cane" and other earlier films of such ilk. Some are as innocent as a Fitzpatrick travelogue. All are distasteful, whether in appearance or description. The one real shocker is a member of a Japanese secret society slicing off his own finger as part of the initiation. Most scenes are Oriental, an area where, evidentaly, there's little chance of photographed individuals showing up later at AIP's door with invasion of privacy suits. The non-Oriental shots are almost entirely in one of the Scandinavian countries. There's a remarkable resemblance in several individuals who seem to appear in more than one sequence.

Price, thanks to his years indoctrination in the use of vapid screen dialogue, speaks most of his commentary with the proper hint of "double entendre" and oily confidence but even he gags on such phrases as "unusual pinnacle of euphoria." The Technicolor photography throughout is generally excellent, the one consistently outstanding quality of this type of film. The rest is rubbish. *Robe.*

Journal D'Une Femme En Blanc
(Diary of A Woman in White)
(FRENCH)
Paris, May 18.
Gaumont release of SOPAC-SNEG production. Stars Marie-Jose Nat; features Jean Valmont, Claude Gensac, Paloma Matta. Directed by Claude Autant-Lara. Screenplay, Jean Aurenche, Rene Wheeler from book by Andre Soubiron; Michel Kelber; editor, Madeleine Guy. At Colisee, Paris. Running time, 110 MINS.
Claude .... Marie-Jose Nat
Pascal .... Jean Valmont
Midwife .... Claude Gensac
Marietta .... Paloma Matta

Largely suds, drama about a female gynecologist who believes strongly in introducing contraceptive processes in France (which still forbids it) to do away with abortion. Then she finds herself pregnant and not ready to marry the father. Lacks the necessary feel for character to make this more than a surface affair with some exploitation value in its unfettered look at abortion consequences and birth.

However, it carefully refrains from showing any birth scenes and waters down its plea for contraception by having the heroine seemingly ready to have her illegitimate baby even if it will interfere with the one thing that matters to her, her career. Marie-Jose Nat is a touchingly vulnerable actress who gives her role more feeling than is inherent in the general treatment of the film.

This does have some good hospital footage and a well done scene of trying to save a girl there. But the meandering plotting, lacklustre direction and so-called social message aspects make this mainly a local bet.

Direction is stolid and film exudes an old fashioned air with its polemics not felt enough or powerfully reflected enough in the pic to make it either strongly controversial or poignant. It is technically acceptable. *Mosk.*

Cannes Festival

Kwaidan
(Ghost Stories)
(JAPANESE-COLOR)
Cannes, May 18.
Toho release of Ninjin Club production. With Rentaro Mikuni, Michiyo Aratama, Tetsuro Tamba, Katsuo Nakamura. Directed by Masaki Kobayashi. Screenplay, Yoko Mizuki from stories by Lofcadio Hearn; camera (Eastmancolor), Yoshio Miyajima; music, Toru Takemitsu. At Cannes Film Fest. Running Time, 125 MINS.
Samurai .... Rentaro Mikuni
Wife .... Michiyo Aratama
Michi .... Tetsuro Tamba
Warrior .... Katsuo Nakamura

Film is visually and physically stunning and its looks alone might make for a specialized arty house entry abroad. But its three tales of the supernatural are more intellectual than visceral. If there are a few jolts and awesome insights, it unfolds at leisure and this is more for selective audiences than for general distribution. However, the right selling and labeling of its exotic contents could make this worthwhile provided well handled.

Colors are subtle and used for dramatic effect with effectiveness. Production dress is another plus factor as is the brilliant but sometimes coldly analytical direction of Masaki Kobayashi. Playing has the right stylized flair and the general Kubuki classic traits are employed though absorbed filmically.

First story has a poor samurai leaving his wife to join a ruling clan and to marry again to a rich woman. But his love stays with his first wife and her image haunts him constantly. He returns to their home years later and finds her there still beautiful and forgiving.

A blind monk is taken by a spirit to unfold his story of a famous sea battle to the place where the clan was destroyed. This is the second tale. He does not know they are ghosts. His priest finds out and tries to save him by having holy scripture written all over him.

Third deals with a man who sees a reflection of someone in a cup of tea and drinks it. He has swallowed the man's soul and is then haunted by him. And then he tries to use brute force against them and goes down in defeat to madness.

All this is done in measured cadence and intense feeling. Certain sections seem repetitive. For all the tales have certain moral points pertaining to love, honor and the unknown. Excellent music and counterpoint sound effects help.

So this is a visually impressive tour-de-force that may still find hard going with ordinary western audiences because of its refusal to play for suspense and fright tactics.

There also was a fourth episode which was cut for the festival by the director himself on the suggestion it would be too long. *Mosk.*

Les Pianos Mechaniques
(The Player Pianos)
(HISPANO-FRENCH) (COLOR)
Cannes, May 18.
Prodis release of CICC-Films Borderie-Precitel-Francos Film-Standard Film-Tera-Explorer Film-Cesareo Gonzales production. Stars Melina Mercouri, James Mason, Hardy Kruger; feautres Didier Haudepin, Keiko Kishi, Renaud Verley, Sophie Dares, Karin Mosberg. Directed by Juan-Antonio Bardem. Screenplay, Henri-Francois Rey based on his book; camera (Eastmancolor), Gabor Pogany; music, Georges Delerue. At Cannes Film Fest. Running Time, 95 MINS.
Regnier .... James Mason
Janny .... Melina Mercouri
Vincent .... Hardy Kruger
Daniel .... Didier Haudepin
Serge .... Renaud Verley
Nadine .... Sophie Dares
Woman .... Keiko Kishi
Mistress .... Karin Mosberg

Main selling points for this internationally divided coproduction are the names of Melina Mercouri, James Mason and Hardy Kruger. But they can not do much with this surface melodrama. Even chances abroad look limited to playoffs on the marquee names or for specialized use on its would-be sophisticated theme of the decadent set in small Spanish sea resorts.

Juan-Antonio Bardem, Spanish director, has obtained a lot from the colorful small sea town used via nice color landscaping and the natural hues. But the story and characters are another matter. To the town comes a distraught young man, Hardy Kruger, trying to escape an inverted life in Paris.

He meets a worldly middleaged female nightclub owner who restores his masculinity. But their love is doomed because of their ages, outlook and the man's obvious concessions to his old life. There is also a noted writer down on his inspiration but big with young girls and in the eyes of his precocious little son.

All this gets posey and grandiloquent with cliche-ridden dialog, uneven acting and plodding plotting. The nitery owner ends up with the author, now ready to write, due to the machinations of the son. There are some side plots about the jetsam afloat during the vacation and the young people of the town corrupted by those who come to live there. But all are as sketchy and obvious as the main complications.

Melina Mercouri can not do much with the role of the worldly woman (nitery owner) trying for more love but finishing with compromise. She overplays rather than making the role breezy. James Mason floats through his role as the sodden Don Juanesque writer and Hardy Kruger underplays the ambivalent lover. Didier Haudepin comes through well as the conniving moppet if he is sometimes more precious rather than juvenile.

Film is technically good but this French book made by a Hispano director with Greek, German, British, French, Spanish and

Swedish thesps does not manage to congeal into a good picture. *Mosk.*

Paris Vu Par . . .
(Paris Seen By . . .)
(FRENCH-COLOR)
Cannes, May 19.
Films Losange-Barbet Schroeder production and release. With Stephane Audran, Claude Chabrol, Barbara Wilkind, Jean-Francois Chappey, Johanna Shimkus, Philippe Hiquily, Serge Davri, Micheline Dax, Claude Melki, Jean Michel Rouziere, Marcel Gallon, Nadine Ballot, Barbet Schroeder, Gilles Queant. Directed by Claude Chabrol, Jean Douchet, Jean-Luc Godard, Jean-Daniel Pollet, Eric Rohmer, Jean Rouch. Screenplay, Chabrol, Douchet, Godard, Pollet, Rohmer, Rouch; camera (Ektachome), Jean Rabier, Nester Almendros, Albert Maysles, Alain Levent, Etienne Backer; editor, Jacqueline Raynal. At Cannes Film Fest. Running Time. 95 MINS.
LA MUETTE
Husband .... Claude Chabrol
Wife .... Stephane Audran
ST. GERMAIN-DES-PRES
Katherine .... Barbara Wilkind
Jean .... Jean-Francois Chappey
MONTPARNASSE ET LEVALLOIS
Monica .... Johanna Shimkus
Roger .... Philippe Hiquily
Ivan .... Serge Davri
RUE ST. DENIS
Leon .... Claude Melki
Prostitute .... Micheline Dax
PLACE DE L'ETOILE
Jean-Marc .... Jean-Michel Rouziere
Victime .... Marcel Gallon
GARE DU NORD
Odile .... Nadine Ballot
Stranger .... Gilles Queant
Husband .... Barbet Schroeder

Enterprising 25-year-old producer Barbet Schroeder in this one has a six-sketch pic for $100,000, utilizing two noted ex-Wavers, one cinema truth innovator and three lesser known filmmakers. Done in 16m and blown up to 35m, it generally has enough good episodes and the Paris background pull to slant this for specialized or art playoff abroad. It lacks the overall physical values and eclat for more playoff possibilities. But Schroeder feels that some theatres especially geared to 16m could have this paying off, with 35m blowups for other situations. It remains to be seen if he can start this sort of operation.

Film color is sometimes uneven but passable. Each seg takes a part of Paris about which to build a small story or incident. In this, professionalism pays off and the most successful episodes are those by Wavers Jean-Luc Godard and Claude Chabrol and cinema truth man Jean Rouch. Others have some flair but are more fragile anecdotes.

Godard aptly calls his part action cinema. It follows a pretty young Canadian girl who thinks she has put two letters to two lovers in the wrong envelopes. So she has to confess to each. One is a scrap metal weld sculptor and the other a mechanic. And both work as she tries to explain and entice them to bed, and both end by throwing her out. Expert camera work, revealing movement and a probing little fable of the comeuppance of a little conniving woman, this is also well played and spouts clever dialog in the midst of much sound, movement and work. Gives this a sheen and bounce.

Claude Chabrol has a more gritty entry about a bickering couple in a fancy apartment who drive their son to using ear plugs. This keeps him from hearing his mother's screams when she falls down the stairs. It has a sharp satirical bent, and the right little jolt of drama to make this a short, but penetrating bit.

Jean-Daniel Pollet's tale of a jittery young worker who takes a prostitute to his room has the right balance of irony and restrained tenderness to keep out sentimentality or gross parody. Jean Rouch has a tour-de-force in his almost one shot tale, from a bickering couple to her run-in with a man who commits suicide when she refuses to go off with him. The excessive coincidence is acceptable as the stranger mirrors the wife's disenchantment with her sedentary husband and ordinary life.

Other segs have Jean Douchet cleverly showing how an audacious young American girl is taken in by a French masher and Eric Rohmer with a tale of a priggish salesman who thinks he has killed a man, finding out he has not.

So this has good and uneven parts but is generally a brisk roundup of sketches with an added plus in its Paris locales. It is an interesting attempt by a young producer and it may well pay off on its home grounds. Foreign chances are limited but possible if well placed. *Mosk.*

Clay
(AUSTRALIAN)
Cannes, May 25.
Ilford release and production. With Janine Lebedew, George Dixon, Chris Tsalikis. Written, directed, photographed and edited by Giorgio Mangiamele. At Cannes Film Fest. Running Time, 85 MINS.
Margot .... Janine Lebedew
Nick .... George Dixon
Chris .... Chris Tsalikis
Father .... Claude Thomas

Tale of an escaped con on the run, who finds fleeting love but then moves on, is somewhat too grandiloquent for much chance abroad except for a few arty spots.

Dialog is heavy and portentous rather than having any revealing personal potency. Acting also is stolid and unreal. It does not transcend its subject to make a more hip comment on humanity sought by writer-director Giorgio Mangiamele.

Grim atmosphere of a farm out in the Aussie wilds may seem like a good background for this tale but it does not get the life into the proceedings. Result is a plodding story despite its short length. Pic is technically good and has some okay conception. But it just does not have the needed fillip to make any of this convincing.

One of the few Australian films seen at a major festival, it intimates that filmmakers Down Under are still too static in ideas and hidebound in techniques for any untoward international chances for their films. Or at least judging from this one. *Mosk.*

Gorechto Pladne
(Torrid Noon)
(BULGARIAN)
Cannes, May 18.
Film Bulgaria production and release. With P. Slobokov, G. Vachtov, I. Spassov. Directed by Zako Heskia. Screenplay, Iordan Raditchkov; camera, Todor Stoianov; music, Miltcho Leviev. At Cannes

Film Fest. Running Time, 80 MINS.
General .... P. Slobokov
Boy .... I. Spassov
Mother .... G. Vachtov

A dramatic incident of a boy caught with his hand in a bridge piling one hot summer afternoon is the basis of an edifying look at collective behavior to save him from a rising river. Simple mounting, good visual asides and effective, little character vignettes keep this from being mawkish or untowardly sentimental.

However, its familiar outlook, action and treatment relegate this more for tele or some dualer use abroad than for any arty or playoff chances. The army, a stopped train and a group of peasants run to save the boy when his friends warn others.

The boy's mother, also comes running but the directory manages to make the scenes of her comforting the boy touching rather than soapy by subdued acting. It does make a point about youth being indispensable and paints the army a potent peacetime affair.

But this eschews obvious propaganda and shows that Bulgar pix can take a small subject and treat it with filmic finesse. It is technically good and promises Bulgarian films of western interest in the future. *Mosk.*

Eletbetancoltatott Lany
(The Girl Danced Into Life)
(HUNGARIAN-COLOR-SCOPE)
Cannes, May 18.

Hungarofilm release of Mafilm production. With Adel Orosz, Levente Harangozo and dancers of National Hungarian Ballet. Directed by Tamas Banovich from script by Banovich, with choreography by Miklos Rabai, Gyula Harangozo, Laszlo Seregi; music, Tihamer Vujicsics; camera (Eastman color), Ferenc Szecsenyi. At Cannes Film Fest. Running Time, 80 MINS.
Girl .... Adel Orosz
Boy .... Levente Sipeki

Magyar all-dance film has three episodes about a girl who puts on red shoes and cannot stop dancing. Based on the Hans Christian Andersen story, the only resemblance it has with the British pic, "The Red Shoes," is using the idea to put on three ballets in different eras up to the present.

Classic and modern are mixed as well as folk interludes. But this is difficult to give each part a definitive separateness or give the film a developing inventiveness. It gets repetitious. If it has good color, fine production and nice filmic ideas, this appears lacking the originality and depth to stand on its own for arty house use abroad. But it could be worth using for specialized dualers, if sheared, or for dance buffs.

First concerns a peasant girl who dons the red shoes from a sideshow tempter at a carnival to succumb, then a noblewoman in seemingly 18th Century times and then a modern girl who can take off the shoes and devote herself to her young man. So people are more emancipated today but this takes too much laboring in making point. Classis dances are colorful and a modern assimilation of Yank-type film. Stage numbers are adequate.

This is an ambitious production that should do well at home if exports will be more limited. *Mosk.*

Alksande Par
(Loving Couples)
(SWEDISH)
Cannes, May 18.
Sandrew Film production and release. With Harriet Andersson, Gunnel Lindblom, Gio Petre, Gunnar Biornstrand, Inga Landgre, Eva Dahlbeck. Directed by Mai Zetterling. Screenplay, David Hughes, Miss Zetterling from book by Agnes Von Krusenstjerna; camera, Sven Nykvist; editor, Paul Davies. At Cannes Film Fest. Running Time, 115 MINS.
Agda .... Harriet Andersson
Adele .... Gunnel Lindblom
Angela .... Gio Petre
Petra .... Anita Bjork
Jacob .... Gunnar Bjornstrand
Mrs. Landborg .... Eva Dahlbeck
Stellan .... Jan Malmsjo

Another femme filmmaker heard from here with actress Mai Zetterling, who has appeared in Swedish, Britain and American pix, now doing her first feature pic as director. It emerges a compendium of familiar Swedish themes and runs the gamut from "Miss Julie," servant rancors, through several Ingmar Bergman pix. If uneven, this has some forthright erotic scenes, is hardly ever gratuitous, and has some good acting and technical values.

However, its inability to give this tale of intertwined female lives of Sweden in the early 1900s some cohesion and form hurts. It vacillates from social drama, to farce and comedy of manners though seemingly speaking out against female exploitation by the bourgeois of the times.

It is perhaps meant to make a parallel to woman's still uncertain place in life and the private human in today's society. But this is somewhat blurred by the insistence on period prankishness. Film does have fine acting by a bunch of femme thesps though the men remain rather vapid and cardboard characters.

Three women in a maternity ward have their past lives revealed before their birthgiving. One is an orphan brought up by a spinster aunt impregnated by the man her aunt had loved and who has left her like he did the aunt. Another is a loose-living maid married off to an impoverished painter by a rich man whose child she is carrying. Last is a bitter maid who has a stillborn child.

Flashbacks set some characteristics of the women though they are often arbitrary and shed little light on the characters. Thus the orphan has had advances from a lesbo, the maid from an old lecher when she was a child and the last woman has always pined for a first love. But then the women's lives are mixed and the pic plays them out via an overnight party at an estate that interpolates expressionism, downright farce with boulevard and boudoir aspects.

Miss Zetterling does show a way with actresses and some sure techniques if direction seems too loose to really make its points about women remaining feminine, if attaining their liberty.

Harriet Andersson brings zest and warmth to her coltish freeloving character that keeps it from being downright stereotype, Gunnel Lindblom shows fierceness as

the love-hungry maid and Eva Dahlbeck a vixenish dash as the aging but still seductive women of the manor who has bedded most of the young swains.

This free-wheeling sexual romp may have exploitation pegs if it sometimes has unclear outlooks. But hypoing and good placing, pic could get some mileage out of this on its affinities with Ingmar Bergman pix and its wealth of inside feminine frankness. *Mosk.*

El Haram
(The Sin)
(EGYPTIAN)
Cannes, May 18.
Mounir Rafla production and release. Stars Faten Hamama; features Abdallah Gheiss, Zaki Rostom. Directed by Henri Barakat. Screenplay, Saad El Din Wamba from a story by Youssef Idris; camera, Ahmed D'a Eddin; music, Soliman Gamil. At Cannes Film Fest. Running Time, 95 MINS.
Azziza .... Faten Hamama
Husband .... Abdallah Gheiss
Guard .... Zaki Rostom

This film is a good cut above Egyptian pix usually showing up at international festivals. It tells its tale of peasant life in the days before land reform, without preachiness. This even manages to avoid melodrama in spite of its familiar tale of the tribulations of the poor.

However, it still looms mainly a local entry, with foreign chances only for a few language spots primarily. Pic just does not quite have the quality and deeper probing to give this the more timeless quality it needs.

A woman is raped by a guard when she goes into a field to get some potatoes for her sick husband. Pregnant, she hides it and finally has the child alone, and dies after having strangled it. But she becomes a symbol for the exploited migratory workers.

Faten Hamama has an expressive face, and does give some deeper delineation of her cheerful if downtrodden woman character. Pic has good observant qualities of the land, customs and activities of Egypt. Here is a director of some force and taste in Henri Barakat. He lifts Egypt above the usual ordinary films repping it at film fests. *Mosk.*

Obchod Na Korze
(The Small Shop on Main Street)
(CZECH)
Cannes, May 25.
Czech State Film release of Barrandov production. With Josef Kroner, Anton Brtko, Ida Kaminska. Directed by Jan Kadar, Elmar Klos. Screenplay, Jan Kadar, L. Grossmann; camera, Vladimir Novotny; music, Zdenek Liska. At Cannes Film Fest. Running Time, 125 MINS.
Tono .... Josef Kroner
Kolkocky .... Frantisek Zvarik
Rosalie .... Ida Kaminska

Racism is looked at deeply and provocatively in this revealing film. It has a balance of acting and dramatic punch which may make this worthy of specialized and arty use abroad. It has to be handled carefully with language, group and university showings.

During the last World War, a small Slavic town in Czechoslovakia was turned into a crucible Fascist state by the Nazis. Locals run everything and there are no Germans in sight. It concerns a not too petty and mean little man who harbors a resentment against the local Nazis though he does nothing about it.

His own brother-in-law is the town police head and he is given the right to take over the store of an old Jewish woman by his relative when plans for deporting the Jews are well developed. He is convinced by his wife to take it and goes off to do so. But here he runs into a headstrong but engaging old woman who can understand what he wants but is hardly aware there is a war on. She has lost her husband in the last war and her children are in America, and all that is left is this little drygoods shop.

The man lets her accept him as an assistant and he begins to fix the store and her apartment in the back. He becomes attached to her though she does treat him like a backward helper. When the deportations start she is somehow forgotten and he decides he will do something to hide her and make some amends for his inability to take a stand.

However, he has been petty enough to accept money from the Jewish community not to let her know what is really happening. Then he is goaded by his wife to get rid of her and turns on her, gets drunk and rushes to warn the old woman. But he finds her thinking he is in trouble, and she tries to hide him.

The deportees are lined up before the store and the end has him going through divided outlooks about what to do, both wanting to help her but fearing reprisals if he does, or being guilty after the war.

But this is all done with a non-rancorous flair sans any hysterical overtone. This makes it even more poignant. It becomes a statement on how anti-Semitism can be bred by oversight, plain laziness or general apathy.

Directors Jan Kadar and Elmar Klos have built this carefully, and have given a good feel of the times and personalities before the drama erupts. There is sometimes a tendency to overmultiply the meanness, smallness and saving decency of the main character's personality, but this is overcome in the growing potency of the pic as it shows the people in crisis.

This is technically excellent. Ida Kaminska, a noted Polish actress from the Warsaw Yiddish Theatre, has the right blend of charm and aging dignity. The timing and projection makes her character a well-rounded figure rather than any sort of symbol. Josef Kroner also gives life to the little man in his moments of decision.

Distance is also taken from the subject by small dream sequences that paint a world without hate and prejudice. *Mosk.*

Tokyo Olympiad
(JAPANESE-COLOR)
Cannes, May 19.

Toho production and release. Written by Natto Wada, Yoshio Shiraskawa, Shuntaro Tanikawa, Kon Ichikawa. Directed by Kon Ichikawa. Camera (Eastmancolor), Shigeo Hayashida, Kazuo Miyagawa, Juichi Nagano, Kinji Nakamura, Tadashi Tanaka; music, Toshiro Mayuzumi. At Cannes Film Fest. Running Time, 132 MINS.

It was a good idea to give the filming of the 1964 Olympics in Tokyo to a proven filmmaker, Kon Ichikawa. He gives it a balance, drama and realism to make this exciting in its own right as a documentary feature as well as an exemplary look at massive competing sports spectacle.

It is easy to understand that 164 cameramen were used. They have obtained close, long and medium shots that lay bare the competive dash, the human endeavor and the beauty as well as the underside of sweat, suffering and hurt.

First the torch being lit in Greece, the origin of the games; then being carried by plane, train, car and on foot to Tokyo to light up the fire that will burn throughout the 18th Olympic Games.

Naturally, with so many events not all could be included in full, but the most important are there. The races, the hurdles, pole vault, etc. get fine visual transference to the screen with slow motion enhancing an understanding of the beauty, tension, anguish and physical exhaustion of the athletes.

A rapid-fire volleyball game between femme Japanese and Russian teams is a highly suspenseful affair as are the swimming events and others. Intercut audience reactions are also knowingly used, and seldom overdone. The last event is naturally the marathon race and it brings this admirable pic to a glowing climax.

This seems easily the best film ever made on the Olympics and eschews lyric falsifying of happenings for their own sake. The many cameras patiently record and the footage expertly edited into a picture of a peaceful, competitive worldwide event.

This could be a fine worldwide playoff and arty item on its film knowhow. *Mosk.*

Javoronok
(Tank T-34)
(RUSSIAN)
Cannes, May 18.

Sovexport release of Lenfilm production. With Viatcheslav Gourenkov, Guennady Youkhtine, Valeri Pogoreltsev, Valentin Skoulme, Bruno Oya. Directed by Nikita Kourikhine, Leonide Menaker. Screenplay, Mikhail Doudine, Serguei Orlov; camera, Vladimir Karassov, Nicolai Jilline; editor, V. Isaacson. At Cannes Film Fest. Running Time, 85 MINS.

Driver .... Viatcheslav Gourenkov
Gunner .... Guennady Youkhtine
Boy .... Valeri Pogoreltsev
Frenchman .... Valentin Skoulme
SS Man .... Bruno Oya

Wartime heroism gets a racy going over in this adventurous tale of a group of Russian prisoners of war who manage to escape with a tank in Germany during the last World War, and have a series of funny and dramatic adventures until wiped out by a furious massing of German troops.

If the heroes are somewhat stalwart and one-dimensional, there is still no attempt to make them too heroic. And they have some human facets of fear, bad judgment and cockiness. Hence, this emerges a good actioner with some arty chances abroad with the right handling. There also is a possible slanting for specialized playoffs.

The Germans use Russian soldiers in their own tanks to practice a new anti-tank weapon. One crew concocts a plan that has them running off with the tank. They spread panic, tear down German war monuments and give some female slave laborers a moment of wild hope as they race through a field where they are working.

Made by two new directors, this sometimes has flurries of too planned and obvious lyrical moments and does not always escape the mold of these heroic pix on Russo soldiers. But pleasant playing, much inventive and breezy building of incidents keep this interesting. But some of the bigger moments are tipped by the advance planning and big scenes are overmilked.

However, there is a zesty quality and an eminently filmic theme in the tank's odyssey. The bravura gives this a good cut above the Soviet films of this kind. Rapid cutting is effective as it has starkly contrasted lensing. The directors have active visual outlooks if they sometimes overdo the tilted cameras' angles.

The pic's simple but bright scripting also slants this as something that could possibly be of remake interest for other countries. *Mosk.*

Prodossia
(Treason)
(GREEK)
Cannes, May 18.

Michaelides A. E. release of Damaskinos-Michealides-Konitsiotis production. With Petros Fyssoun, Elli Fotiou, Manos Katrakis, Dimitris Myrat. Directed by Costas Manoussakis. Screenplay, A. Alexandrou, Manoussakis from a story by N. Pergialis; camera, Nicos Gardellis; music, Christos Mourambas. At Cannes Film Fest. Running Time 95 MINS.

Karl .... Petros Fyssoun
Lisa .... Elli Fotiou
Victor .... Manos Katrakis
Doctor .... Dimitris Myrat

One of the more ambitious Greek films to come along in some time, at least since Michael Cacoyannis was making all-Greek pix before his "Zorba the Greek" (20th). This unfortunately is not too clear in intent, and, with a touchy theme of a Nazi in love with a Jewish-Greek girl in occupied Greece, therefore is a touchy foreign item.

However, it seems that the outlook is irreproachable but this still painful theme m_ not be taken as intended by _ll. The director has tried to show the nefarious almost theatrical pull of Nazism for a German romantic air officer. But it sometimes dwells too long on the pomp and after the point is made. Use of stock shots throughout is generally good.

The officer wants to marry the girl but turns her over to the Gestapo when she tells him she is Jewish. He only begins to feel remorse when he goes to the Eastern Front and first becomes conscious of Nazi atrocities. This, too, is a bit hard to swallow as iis the fact that the Jewish girl never questions his outlooks though she knows of them from an anti-Semitic speech he made, overheard by her uncle.

However the film is directed with tone. If somewhat laborious, it has passable character traits and some dramatically well-mounted scenes that are never overblown. Acting is acceptable and general production level is good.

So 2 years after, this is fairly lucid in most of its outlooks. But the pic overlooks too many points in its complications that do not give the complete, clear feel it needs. The regenerate German finally commits suicide. He is partly goaded into the act by a hangover post-war Nazi in Athens when he comes back hoping the girl may still be alive. *Mosk.*

Those Magnificent Men In Their Flying Machines
(TODD-AO-COLOR)

Crackerjack nostalgic comedy about a 1910 International air race between London and Paris when flying was young and hearts were bold.

Hollywood, May 28.

Twentieth-Fox release of Stan Margulies production. Stars Stuart Whitman, Sarah Miles, James Fox, Alberto Sordi, Robert Morley, Gert Frobe, Jean-Pierre Cassel, Irina Demick, Eric Sykes, Terry-Thomas; features Red Skelton, Benny Hill, Yujiro Ishihara, Flora Robson, Karl Michael Vogler, Sam Wanamaker, Tony Hancock. Directed by Ken Annakin. Screenplay, Jack Davies, Annakin; camera (DeLuxe Color), Christopher Challis; music, Ron Goodwin; production design, Tom Morahan; editor, Gordon Stone; sound, John Mitchell, Gordon McCallum; asst. director, Clive Reed. Reviewed at 20th-Fox Studios, May 27, '65. Running Time, 133 MINS.
Orvil Newton .... Stuart Whitman
Patricia Rawnsley .... Sarah Miles
Richard Mays .... James Fox
Count Emilio Ponticelli...Alberto Sordi
Lord Rawnsley .... Robert Morley
Colonel Manfred Von Holstein
.... Gert Frobe
Pierre Dubois .... Jean-Pierre Cassel
Courtney .... Eric Sykes
Sir Percy Ware-Armitage...Terry-Thomas
Brigitte, Ingrid, Marlene,
Francois, Yvette, Betty....Irina Demick
Fire Chief Perkins .... Benny Hill
Yamamoto .... Yujiro Ishihara
Mother Superior .... Flora Robson
Captain Rumpelstrosse
.... Karl Michael Vogler
George Gruber .... Sam Wanamaker
Neanderthal Men .... Red Skelton
French Postman .... Eric Barker
Elderly Colonel .... Fred Emney
McDougal, a pilot ...... Gordon Jackson
Jean, Pierre's Chief Mechanic Davy Kaye
French Painter ...... John Le Mesurier
Lt. Parsons, a pilot ...... Jeremy Lloyd
Sophia Ponticelli ...... Zena Marshall
Airline Hostess .... Millicent Martin
Italian Mayor .... Eric Pohlman
Waitress in Old Mill Cafe
.... Marjorie Rhodes
Assistant Fire Chief Norman Rossington
Tremayne Gascoyne....William Rushton
Fireman .... Graham Stark
Photographer in Old Mill Cafe
.... Jimmy Thompson
Niven, Lord Rawnsle.. 'de
.... Michael Trubshawe
Popperwell, an invent... ..Tony Hancock

As fanciful and nostalgic a piece of clever picture-making as has hit the screen in recent years, this backward look into the pioneer days of aviation, when most planes were built with spit and bailing wire, is a warming entertainment experience right down Pop Alley. Its subtitle, "How I Flew from London to Paris in 25 Hours and 11 Minutes," tips off content, a comical scanning of a period which is FUN spelled in capital letters. To go out as a roadshow attraction, the Stan Margulies production, bathed in breathtaking photography and color, can be ballyed into a top money entry with particular appeal for the family trade.

A newspaper circulation gimmick serves nicely as the story premise, with a London newspaper publisher offering a 10,000-pound prize to winner of an event which will focus worldwide attention on the fledgling sport of flying — circa 1910 — subsequently attracting a flock of international contestants. The Jack Davies and Ken Annakin screenplay is long on broad comedy as it simultaneously pays homage to those early stalwarts who dared the skies without any storehouse of technology to draw upon. Annakin's direction is inspired at times as

he catches uproarious comedy in presenting his subject, and if the footage sometimes devolves into a series of slapstick episodes these fit patly into a well-designed plan and help progress the movement. Film might be tagged a comic saga.

While there is naturally a plotline, and a nice romance, the planes themselves, a startling collection of uniquely-designed oddities, which actually fly, probably merit the most attention. They add immeasurably to the excitement generated as the fliers prepare for the race across the English Channel and the race itself, as some can't get off the ground, others crash, and still others are the stars of varying incidents. Recreated are such antiques of 1910 as the Antoinette, Demoiselle, Bristol Box-Kite, Avro Triplane, Eardley-Billings biplane and a Bleriot of the type which was the first plane to fly the Channel. Craft ascend several hundred feet.

Top characters are played by Stuart Whitman (only American principal), as an American entrant; James Fox, an English flier who interests publisher Robert Morley in the race to promote aviation; Sarah Miles, publisher's daughter understood to be the intended of Fox (arrangement with father) but beloved by Whitman. Terry-Thomas is a dastardly English lord not above the most abject skullduggery to win the race. Alberto Sordi as an Italian count with a worrying wife and immense family, Gert Frobe a German cavalry officer intent upon bringing glory to the Fatherland, Jean-Pierre Cassel, a whimsical Frenchman, are the chief Continental contestants.

One of the comedy highlights centers on a runaway plane which Mack Sennett would have been proud of as it is followed by a Sennett-type fire engine crew, then turns and chases the truck. There is a duel between the German and French fliers — balloons and blunderbusses in duplication of a famed duel which took place in 1870 at time of the Franco-Prussian War — which ends with the Italian's plane, which wanders in firing range, being hit and both duelists crashing. The scheming Terry-Thomas, flying low over a French railroad track, is overtaken by the Paris Express and when smoke from the locomotive envelops him the wheels of his plane become locked between two train carriages and a tunnel shears off his wings.

Good old-fashioned melodrama is provided in closing sequences as three finalists approach the finish line in Paris. The Italian's motor catches afire and Whitman sacrifices his own chance at winning by flying close over his rival's plane so latter can grab the under-carriage and pull himself to safety. The Englishman grounds first, but shares the purse with the American who (natch) wins the girl.

Players without exception sock over their roles in proper fashion, and principals get strong backing from those in support. Irina Demick is in for an amusing running gag, portraying half a dozen different sexpots of different nationalities for whom the French flier

is always falling. Eric Sykes as Terry-Thomas' henchman, Yujiro Ishihara the Japanese entrant, Zena Marshall the always-frantic Italian wife and Tony Hancock as a plane designer-pilot who finds himself going in the wrong direction, toward Scotland (a la Wrong-Way Corrigan), all scoring well.

Red Skelton is in for some amusing moments in a very funny prolog as a Neanderthal Man who participates in a series of early attempts at flying, each ending in fine failure.

Christopher Challis' color photography in Todd-AO is superb. He limns the English countryside most effectively and his flying shots frequently are thrilling. Tom Morahan's production design faithfully recreates the colorful era, and Osbert Lancaster's costumes furnish equal color and interest. Music score by Ron Goodwin lends a slick musical mounting for picture, tightly edited by Gordon Stone. Ronald Searle rates a particular plus for creating via cartoon the credit titles, giving flavor for what is to come.

Other credits go to Richard Parker for special effects; Don Sharp, second unit director; John Mitchell, Gordon McCallum, sound. *Whit.*

I'll Take Sweden
(COLOR)

Bob Hope as Tuesday Weld's pop in excellent comedy-romance with tunes. Prospects great in general situations.

Hollywood, May 29.

United Artists release of Superior Films (Edward Small) production. Stars Bob Hope, Tuesday Weld, Frankie Avalon, Dina Merrill. Features Jeremy Slate, Rosemarie Frankland. Directed by Frederick De Cordova. Screenplay, Nat Perrin, Bob Fisher, Arthur Marx, based on Perrin's story; camera (Technicolor), Daniel L. Fapp; editor, Grant Whytock; music, Jimmie Haskell, By Dunham; songs, Diane Lampert, Ken Lauber, Bobby Beverly, James Economides, Haskell, Dunham; art direction, Robert Peterson; sound, Al Overton; asst. director, Herbert S. Greene. Reviewed at Academy Award Theatre, May 28, '65. Running Time, 96 MINS.
Bob Holcomb .... Bob Hope
JoJo Holcomb .... Tuesday Weld
Kenny Klinger .... Frankie Avalon
Karin Grandstedt .... Dina Merrill
Erik Carlson .... Jeremy Slate
Marti .... Rosemarie Frankland
Bjork .... Walter Sande
Olaf .... John Qualen
Ingemar .... Peter Bourne
Hilda .... Fay De Witt
Greta .... Alice Frost
Ship's Captain .... Roy Roberts
Spinster .... Maudie Prickett
Electra .... Beverly Hills
Inter .... Siv Marta Aberg
Musical group .... The Vulcanes

Bob Hope returns to the theatrical screen in snug-fitting role of widower with teenage daughter problems. Excellent direction, performances and production values plus meaty script add up to brisk and tuneful comedy. Audience appeal for the Edward Small production ranges from teenage to medicare. Prospects look great for United Artists release in the general market.

Nat Perrin, Bob Fisher and Arthur Marx have fashioned Perrin's

story into a comic, yet literate look at juve vs. adult romance, American and Swedish style. Hope's role permits gagging it up as an out-of-touch adult, disapproving parent, and lover.

Pop doesn't dig the teen set, including Frankie Avalon as current heart-throb of daughter Tuesday Weld, a virgin on the verge. Avalon has three strikes against him: a motorcycle, behaviour and little dough. Helping to further convince Hope is raid on stripper joint where he has followed the pair (becoming en route part of Beverly Hills' peel turn), also daydream of their marriage (done in terrif silent-screen technique).

After wangling company transfer to Sweden and creating rift between lovers, Hope marvels at Miss Weld's switch to culture addict at the hands of suave playboy Jeremy Slate, an engaging young lecher who is building up to a "pre-honeymoon" pitch. Outraged at this, Hope summons Avalon from California, but latter won't intervene, being sidetracked quite understandably by Rosemarie Frankland (one of Slate's former flames).

Hope can't get any sympathy from Dina Merrill, with whom he himself has become romantically involved. Miss Merrill is a classy and gracious mature woman.

Hanky-panky on all sides brings everyone to a Swedish resort. The right people land in each other's arms, natch, although the other hotel guests involved in a hilarious room search might wonder.

Other standout appearances are by ship captain Roy Roberts, manhungry spinster Maudie Prickett, and dozens of bosom pals. Miss Frankland was Miss World of 1961. Avalon sings okay title tune by Diane Lampert and Ken Lauber in a zippy lakefront production number, also pair's "Would You Like My Last Name?" Both tunes are lightweight, as are fragments of four others.

Frederick De Cordova directed in firstrate fashion, obtaining believable depth and animation from Miss Weld and Avalon and utilizing handsomely the proven talent of other pros. Daniel L. Fapp's mobile camera enhanced the colorful proceedings. Grant Whytock edited to a nice 96 minutes. Music by Jimmie Haskell and By Dunham is an asset, along with all other technical work. Alex Gottlieb was associate producer.
Murf.

Cannes Festival

Tarahumara
(Always Further On)
(MEXICAN)

Cannes, May 27.
Matouk production and release. With Ignacio Lopez Tarso, Jaime Fernandez, Aurora Clavel. Written and directed by Luis Alcoriza. Camera, Rosalio Solano; editor, Carlos Savage. At Cannes Film

Fest. Running Time, 135 MINS.
Raul .... Ignacio Lopez Tarso
Corachi .... Jaime Fernandez
Belen .... Aurora Clavel
Tomas .... Eric Del Castillo
Romiali .... Alfonso Mejia
Celedonio .... Pancho Cordova

Under a deceptively familiar plot line, this is a penetrating look at Mexican Indians and their lives, problems with exploiting white men and the meshes that spring up when a sympathetic stranger enters into friendship with the Indians. However, this simple tale looks mainly for language houses or more selective situations in the U.S. It could stand some pruning for better chances abroad.

Writer-director Luis Alcoriza has mixed actors with the real Indians but it all comes off authentically. A sensitive white man thinks he has found something in this Indian life but ends up being killed by the men who fear he may ruin a lucrative land traffic they have in deluding the Indians.

The Indians at the hunt, their living habits and rituals make up the backbone of the pic and give it a fine ethnic ring. The ironic end has the white man perhaps helping in his own death.

Jaime Fernandez and Aurora Clavel as Indians, display the right dignified simplicity. There is not too much ado made about the Indians allowing friends to have access to their wives or becoming more civilized by finding perpetrators of rape.

Film is neatly lensed and well edited. However, some ritual scenes could be cut. Ignacio Lopez Tarso holds his own with the Indians as the sensitive do-gooder who becomes a victim. There's no preaching in the pic but a statement on changing Indian habits and their corruption. *Mosk.*

El Juego De La Oca
(The Goose Game)
(SPANISH)
Cannes, May 26.

Suevia Films release of Suevia-Cesareo Gonzalez-Benito Perojo production. With Jose Antonio Amor, Sonia Bruno, Maria Massip. Directed by Manuel Summers. Screenplay, Pilar Miro, Summers; camera, Francisco Fraile; editor, Pedro Del Rey. At Cannes Film Fest. Running Time, 110 MINS.
Pablo .... Jose Antonio Amor
Angela .... Sonia Bruno
Blanca .... Maria Massip

A banal situation about a young married man with three children beginning an affair with a girl in his office while his family is on vacation manages to escape sentimentality and boredom by some clever feeling for the situation and character. But it tries to blend arch comedy and deeper drama. If the film story does not come completely come off, it is generally entertaining with language theatre possibilities in the foreign market if not any arty chances.

Director Manuel Summers uses quick, speeded-up shots to mirror the thoughts of his characters which give this a piquant touch. The growing love and final consummation of the married man and the girl are done with taste and invention.

Film is left unresolved. It is somewhat long and could be cut down for offshore spots. Sonia Bruno emerges a warm, engaging

actress if others are not up to her standard. Chalk this up as a promising vehicle and directorial talent though it still has too many compromises. It does not quite attack the subject on an out-and-out satirical level or treat it in depth. Technically this is good if the editing is sometimes rough. *Mosk.*

Gill-Bill Starik So Staroukhoi
(There Was Once An Old Couple)
(RUSSIAN)
Cannes, May 26.

Mosfilm production and release. With I. Marine, V. Kouznetsova, G. Martiniouk, L. Maxomova, G. Polskikh. Directed by Grigori Choukrai. Screenplay, J. Dounsky, V. Frid; camera, O. Zgouridl, J. Gantman; music, A. Pakhmoutova. At Cannes Film Fest. Running Time, 110 MINS.
Old Man .... Ivan Marine
Old Woman .... Vera Kouznetsova
Nina .... Ludmilla Maxomova
Valentin .... Gueorgui Martyniouk
Galia .... Galina Polskikh

Grigori Choukrai, who made "Ballad of a Soldier," now looks at the life of an old couple. The sentimentality manages to avoid mawkishness, but it does aim for a cut above realism. Film does not quite achieve the needed poetic elan. Its asides on the human and political thaw in Russia are also somewhat dragged in. But well-pruned, this has taste in its dramatic aspects, and a colorful back-grounding. This gives it arty possibilities abroad as well as some more general chances on its theme.

An aging couple decide to visit their daughter in the North of the country when their house burns down. They arrive in a snowstorm to find the daughter has left her husband and child for a married man. But they settle down and take over the drunken husband and care for the child.

They straighten out things, see the husband take up with a local girl, find a place in this winterbound society with the old man even going further north to help check a reindeer sickness epidemic due to his past veterinarian work.

Director Choukrai sometimes gives this a heavy patronal air as the old man accepts a religious man as a human fellowman though he does not agree with his precepts. He also makes statements that Communism may eventually better man's way if it does not insist on the point to hit overstated propaganda. In fact, the latter is veiled and worked into the scheme of this picture.

Acting has the right measured but larger-than-life quality. The characters sometimes smack of the more complicated types of pre-Soviet literature than those usually treated in Russo pix today, at least in contemporary ones. It is extremely well lensed while direction soft-pedals the many lachrymose scenes.

This may be somewhat classic in its treatment and outlook but does possess a definite visual flair, and the pathos sometimes overcome the almost over-indulgent dramatics. Choukrai is a director with poetic traits but he has to remove the shackles of oversentimentality for best results; "Ballad" transcended these drawbacks in its concern for its characters. This does not. *Mosk.*

Padurea Spinzuratilor
(Forest of the Hanged)
(RUMANIAN)
Cannes, May 27.

Rom Film release of Bucaresti production. With Victor Rebengiuc, Liviu Ciulei, Stefan Gobotarasu, Gorgy Kovacs, Ana Szees, Gina Patrichi. Directed by Liviu Ciulei. Screenplay, Titus Popovici from book by Liviu Rebreanu; camera, Ovidiu Gologan; music, Theodor Grigoriu. At Cannes Film Fest. Running Time, 157 MINS.
Apostol .... Victor Rebengiuc
Klaoka .... Liviu Ciulei
Petre .... Stefan Gobotarasu
Von Karg .... Gorgy Kovacs
Ilona .... Ana Szeles
Roza .... Gina Patrichi
Varga .... Cziky Andrei
Maria .... Schaffer Emeric

A well thought-out film against war gets too much plotting and wordy exchanges which water down a potent theme. It has some exemplary performances, taut direction, but repeats itself too often for top impact. Extensive pruning could have this for specialized and lingo spots abroad. The probing, insight eludes it for arty chances.

The first World War's Rumanian front on the Austro-Hungarian Empire side is depicted here. Many nationalities mingle including a Rumanian. Pic concerns his realization of war's demeaning of mankind, after witnessing a hanging for desertion and a series of deceptions.

Direction has fluid visual know-how but finally begins to repeat and repeat to bog down a forthright, incisive first part. It shows Rumania as advancing in film production skill.

However, this is a stalwart, intelligent film somewhat denatured by too much talk even though much of it is good. *Mosk.*

The Pleasure Girls
(BRITISH)

Slim, superficial yarn about young femme problems amid the bright lights; familiar situations, but has some fair budding talent and occasional crisp direction of a routine pic.

Compton release of a Michael Klinger, Tony Tenser (Harry Fine) production. Features Ian McShane, Francesca Annis, Klaus Kinski, Mark Eden, Tonny Tanner, Suzanna Leigh, Rosemary Nicols. Written and directed by Gerry O'Hara. Camera, Michael Reed; editor, Tony Palk; music, Malcolm Lockyer; theme song, Bob Barrett, sung by The Three Quarters. Reviewed at Cinephone Theatre, London. Running Time, 88 MINS.
Keith .... Ian McShane
Sally .... Francesca Annis
Nikko .... Klaus Kinski
Prinny .... Mark Eden
Paddy .... Tony Tanner
Marion .... Rosemary Nicols
Dee .... Suzanna Leigh
Angela .... Anneke Wills
Cobber .... Coleen Fitzpatrick

This is about the nice, sensible girl who comes up from the country to become a model. She shares an apartment with some other bachelor girls who all have problems like men, and men and men. Since the action takes place in about 48 hours, screenwriter-director Gerry O'Hara cannot delve too much into the characters and their motivations. Result is a superficial, slick and conventional picture, relieved by some promising young thesping talent and occasionally crisp direction. It's a routine booking which is unlikely

to stir audiences very much in any direction.

Dialog is mainly of the flip, casual brand. A swinging party, a visit to a casino, a spot of mattress pounding, the beating up of a crook, a pregnant girl let down by a shiftless male, a touch of homosexuality and the heroine meeting up quickly with real love all slot inevitably into the picture. London locations and artwork are well enough depicted, but situations arise and then fizzle out and the characters mainly remain stock puppets.

Among the batch of young women, Francesca Annis has intelligent charm as the girl who falls quickly but won't compromise for a quick roll in the hay, Suzanna Leigh, who likes her comforts and goes around with a suave young foreigner who dabbles in slum property rackets and other dubious moneymaking businesses, and Rosemary Nicols, debutting as a girl who is rendered pregnant by an oafish liar and goodtimer, make most of the running. Anneke Wills and Coleen Fitzpatrick add to the pulchritude. The sextette should all do well with better chances.

Tony Tanner, as a warmhearted fairy, and Ian McShane, the lad with an eye for the birds who, despite himself, finds himself settling for the decent feet-on-the-ground newcomer, both produce credible characters. But Mark Eden's shifty swindler and Klaus Kinski, as the suave racketeer, have roles that are unconvincingly written and played necessarily with exaggeration. A familiar party sequence is well put over, but the film only flirts timidly with the sex angle.

Editing is adequate and Michael Reed's camerawork is sharp and alert. Malcolm Lockyer's musical score is pleasantly unobtrusive. Bob Barrett has come up with a title song, sung by The Three Quarters, which plugs the film's title but serves little other good purpose. *Rich.*

Fifi La Plume
(Fifi The Feather)
(FRENCH)
Cannes, May 25.

Films Montsouris production and release. With Philippe Avron, Mireille Negre, Henri Lambert, Raoul Delfosse, Martine Sarcey, Michel De Re. Written and directed by Albert Lamorisse. Camera, Pierre Petit, Maurice Fellous; Madeleine Gug; special effects, Henri Gruel, Georges Goetz. At Cannes Film Fest. Running Time, 80 MINS.
Fifi .... Philippe Avron
Girl .... Mireille Negre
Trainer .... Henri Lambert
Circus Chief .... Raoul Delfosse

Albert Lamorisse, who made that short, "The Red Balloon," which won an Oscar, now comes up with a feature pic in which he tries to repeat the same whimsy of the magical balloon. But here he refers the ability to fly at will to a human. It gets a bit repetitious and dragged out, sentimental and more a moppet pic for abroad than for most demanding arty spots.

Slight affair avoids complete mawkishness by Lamorisse's obvious sincerity. Actor Philippe Avron is an engaging petty thief who finds he can really fly when a chance job in a circus has him fitted for an act with wings which become part of him.

Off he wings to pick up clocks for a bareback rider he loves, straightening out a separated couple, bringing thieves around to the straight and narrow and defeating a jealous strong man and the police who think he is a big time thief. His wings are finally clipped and he settles down to raise little children.

Special effects of the flying are mainly good though the wires can be seen at times. Use of black and white robs this of the more demanding charm it might have had. Although a bit stretched out, this rosy-hued little pic might be of playoff value as well as tv airing.

Film just does not quite have the elan to weld the slapstick, sentimentality and gentle anarchism together. It escapes being purest mush but it's close. In these days of glib violence, harsh comedy and dramatic themes of non-communication, it might be some relief for those who want more lightweight fare. *Mosk.*

El Renidero
(The Amphitheatre)
(ARGENTINIAN)

Cannes, May 27.

Martin Rodriguez Mentasti production and release. With Fina Basser, Miryan De Urquijo, Milagros De La Vega. Directed by Rene Mujica. Screenplay, Sergio De Cecco, Martin Rodriguez Mentasti, Mujica; camera, Ricardo Aronovich; music, Adolfo Morpurgo. At Cannes Film Fest. Running Time, **80 MINS.**

Oreste .... Alfredo Alcon
Elena .... Fina Basser
Mother .... Miryan De Urquijo
Soliano .... Milagros De La Vega

Pretentious transposition of the Electra tragedy to the pretty underworld of Buenos Aires in 1915 is much too plodding and obvious to make any dramatic or filmic effect of worth. It is the kind of arty pic that just does not go over. This shows small chance for foreign spotting except possibly in a few language situations.

Director Renè Mujica just underlines each updated symbol and happening with talky precious facsimiles that fail to approach the lines of the tragedy or get anywhere near creating a good adventure tale.

A petty gangster head is murdered and his daughter suspects his friend and her own mother. Revenge is brought about by her and her own brother. Hence, the tragedy here is played out on a background of talk and heavy emoting.

But this is heavyhanded at best and posey acting does not help. Though the festival tried to discourage the pic, it was insisted on by Argentina and here it is. More endurance by the fest would have spared the pic getting rapped, and the fest a dead spot. *Mosk.*

Up From The Beach
(CINEMASCOPE)

Personal drama of post-D-Day operations. Good performances by lesser names. Natural tiein with "The Longest Day." Uppercasing or special handling for good returns.

Hollywood, May 27.

Twentieth Century-Fox release of Panoramic Pictures production, produced by Christian Ferry. Stars Cliff Robertson, Red Buttons, Irina Demick, Marius Goring; features Slim Pickens, James Robertson Justice, Broderick Crawford. Directed by Robert Parrish. Screenplay, Howard Clewes; additional dialog by Stanley Mann; based on novel "Epitaph For An Enemy" by George Barr; camera (C'Scope), Walter Wottiz; editor, Samuel E. Beetley; music, Edcar Cosma; art direction, Willy Holt; sound, Jacques Carrere, Max Olivier; special effects, Georges Iaconelli, Karl Baumgartner, Daniel Braunschwieg; asst. director, Michel Wyn, George Gradzenczyk, Andre Frederick. Reviewed at 20th-Fox Studio, May 26, '65. Running time, **98 MINS.**

Sgt. Edward Baxter .... Cliff Robertson
Pfc. Harry Devine .... Red Buttons
Lili Rolland .... Irina Demick
German Commandant ... Marius Goring
Artillery Colonel ...... Slim Pickens
British Beachmaster
James Robertson Justice
U.S. MP Major . Broderick Crawford
Mayor .... George Chamarat
Lili's Grandmother . Francoise Rosay
Dupre .... Raymond Bussieres
Barrelmaker .... Fernand Ledoux
Marie ....Louise Chevalier
Seamstress .... German Delbat
Widow Clarisse .... Paula Dehelly
Trombonist .... Gabriel Gobin
French horn player .. Charles Bouilland
Drummer .... Georges Adet
Field-keeper ...... Pierre Moncorbier
Postoffice clerk .... Nicole Chollet
Cobbler .... Raoul Marco
Cobbler's wife .... Charlotte Eizlini
Grocer .... Pierual
Grocer's wife .... Renee Gardes
U.S. Cpl. Evans .... Paul Maxwell
U.S. Pfs. Solly .... Ken Wayne
U.S. Pfc. Dinbo .... Brian Davies
S.S. Captain .... Robert Hoffman
S.S. Sgt. .... Michael Munzer
S.S. Cpl. .... Henri Kuhn
Resistance fighter
Jean-Claude Bervo
Picot, the boy .... Bibi Morat
grocer's assistant ...... Frawiev Becker
Colonel's driver .... Roy Stephens
Medic driver .... Jo Warfield
Other medic .... Rod Calvert
German pilot ...... Alexandre Grecq
Soldier in truck .... Tracy Wynn
Colonel in bunker .... Billy Kearns
Major in bunker .... Thomas Farnsworth

Lensed in France, "Up From The Beach" is a moderately-paced, reasonably successful attempt to humanize post-D-Day operations by focussing on a small group caught in a sidepocket of the action. Generally good performances by cast of lesser names are underplayed against properly drab backdrop of impending death.

20th Fox release opens with D-Day landing shots reminiscent of (or possibly from) "The Longest Day," Darryl F. Zanuck's smash which got the troops ashore. Following titles and transition to June 7, 1944, Cliff Robertson and remnants of his squad liberate a group of French villagers, assembled to welcome Allied troops but held in ditch capitvity by retreating Germans.

Based on George Barr's 1962 novel, script is screen-credited to Howard Clewes with additional dialog by Stanley Mann. Studio credits sheet, however, relegates Clewes to adapter, with Mann and Claude Brule named as scripters. Withal, plot turns on Robertson's transformation from unwilling overseer of war-weary civilians to good shepherd.

Grim irony finds NCO Robertson being shunted back and forth between beachhead area and village, result of customary lack of coordination between front-line and rear echelon points of view. Artillery colonel Slim Pickens typifies no-nonsense field officer who can't have townfolk in danger zone, so he orders Robertson to the rear and drops off Red Buttons as guard for Marius Goring, town's longtime Nazi commandant who was captured when villagers were liberated. Pickens is excellent.

At other end of the line, James Robertson Justice brightens continuity in excellent bit role as sympathetic but typically-harassed British beachmaster who, ironically, hasn't gotten the word about evacuating, and has his hands full moving troops and suppies forward from a beach with no room for civilians or a POW.

During repeated back-and-forth treks, Robertson's believable empathy with villagers emerges via interactions with Francoise Rosay, Irina Demick and Goring. Latter's role is perhaps most difficult to project, being herein a prewar lawyer and a believing (although not fanatical) Nazi who was hard but fair. In defeat he has remorse, but little shame.

Miss Rosay, most realistic of the villagers, describes Goring's kindness in releasing Gestapo hostages years earlier from church vault in which he is later killed by booby trap when assisting Robertson in during shelter for the group.

Encoring in role of slap-happy GI (this time a Jewish lad), Buttons comes across well as Goring's guard (with much nervous humor, perfect in context), only to be cheated of chance to imprison him in humane fashion. Miss Demick is adequate as resistance fighter who further softens Robertson, although romance is properly eschewed. Broderick Crawford delivers well in cameo as blustering MP Major who permits townfolk to steal some provisions.

Director Robert Parrish framed this personal drama with grim evidence of the surrounding death and destruction. Battlefield graves, marching regulars and other elements of war form a neat counterpoint. Some foreign dialog is interpolated without subtitles, but facial expressions are enough to convey the point.

Walter Wottitz' camera has captured the mood with full use of the black-to-white spectrum, while Samuel E. Beetley's sharp editing to 98 minutes lends pace to what otherwise might have become plodding chatter. Music by Edcar Cosma is full-bodied and used sparingly. Sound editing in most cases rebuild the exterior feel, and special effects work in explosives is noteworthy. *Murf.*

Io Uccido, Tu Uccidi
(I Kill, You Kill)
(ITALO-FRENCH—SONGS)

Rome, May 25.

Metropolis Film release of an Ettore Fecchi production for Metropolis (Rome)-Gulliver (Paris). Features Emmanuele Riva, Eleonora Rossi Drago, Tomas Milian, Franco Franchi, Ciccio Ingrassia, Marisa Pavan, Luciana Paluzzi, Giusi Raspani Dandolo, Paolo Panelli, Enrico Viarisio, Franca Polesello, Dominique Boschero, Jean Louis Trintignant. Directed by Gianni Puccini. Screenplay, Puccini, Ennio DeConcini, Ivo Perilli, from an idea by Philippe Saniust; camera, Silvano Mancini; music, Franco Salina, editor, Cleofe Conversi. At Moderno, Rome. Running Time, **130 MINS.**

(1) **Cavalleria Rusticana Moderna** (Modern Cavalleria Rusticana). With Franco Franchi, Ciccio Ingrassia, Franca Polesello.
(2) **La Danza delle Ore** (Dance of the Hours). With Enrico Viarisio, Paolo Panelli.
(3) **La Donna che Viveva Sola** (The Woman Who Lived Alone). With Emmanuele Riva, Jean Louis Trintignant.
(4) **Una Boccata di Fumo** (A Breath of Smoke). With Franco Franchi, Ciccio Ingrassia.
(5) **Giochi Acerbi** (Unripe Games). With Luciana Paluzzi, Marisa Pavan, Giusi Raspani Dandolo.
(6) **Il Plenilunio (Full Moon).** With Eleonora Rossi Drago, Tomas Milian.

Another in a long skein of Italo episoders, "I Kill, You Kill" is neither better nor worse than the others. It remains a saleable item on its names—at least in certain European markets—and the strength of some, not all, of its six segments. A few possess exploitation fillips.

Theme of all are killings or attempts at murder. Cavalleria Rusticana is spoofed to a fare-thee-well by comics Franchi and Ingrassia, with switch finding heroes alive and their women dead. In "Dance of the Hours," a broken-down nobleman desperate for an inheritance tries to speed an aging relative's departure by sending him a strip-teasing nurse. But the plot backfires when the uncle seduces his bedside assistant. In probably the best seg of lot, Emmanuele Riva falls in love with ne'er-do-well young neighbor to such a point that she saves his life by having herself killed to prove his innocence.

Next item is a tired local joke about a man addicted to cigarettes, played heavily for laughs by comics Franchi and Ingrassia. Fifth episode is a slightly over-extended reverse fairy tale in which some youngsters calmly and innocently murder several people in a castle haunted for all but them. Windup is a weirdie, nicely acted but sickly conceived, of a female werewolf who strikes during each full moon, makes love to, then kills her prey. Tomas Milian is good here as the Roman gigolo on the make who gets enmeshed in Eleonora Rossi Drago's thirsty coils.

Pace generally tends to lag under Gianni Puccini's straightforward direction, but occasionally, the pic has its moments. At over two hours, it's well overlong, however, and several okay gags lose impact after being played to death. Technically, the pic is well-fashioned and boasts a varied cast of well-known names and faces for the local mart, some in for actual bits. Couple of listenable tunes complete credits. *Hawk.*

The Hill
(BRITISH)

Uncompromising look at brutality and sadism in a British military prison. Sean Connery's marque appeal should help to boost b.o. returns.

Cannes, May 23.

Metro presentation of a Seven Arts-Kenneth Hyman production. Stars Sean Connery; features Harry Andrews, Ian Bannen, Alfred Lynch, Ossie Davis, Roy Kinnear, Jack Watson, Ian Hendry and Michael Redgrave. Director, Sidney Lumet; screenplay, Ray Rigby based on a play by Rigby and R. S. Allen; camera, Oswald Morris; music, Art Noel and Don Pelosi. At Cannes Film festival, May 22, '65. Running time: **125 MINS.**

Joe Roberts	Sean Connery
RSM Wilson	Harry Andrews
Staff Harris	Ian Bannen
George Stevens	Alfred Lynch
Jacko King	Ossie Davis
Monty Bartlett	Roy Kinnear
Jock McGrath	Jack Watson
Guard Williams	Ian Hendry
Medical Officer	Michael Redgrave

Kenneth Hyman's production of "The Hill" is a tough, uncompromising look at the inside of a British military prison in the Middle East during the last war. It is a harsh, sadistic and brutal entertainment, superbly acted by an all-male cast, and made without any concessions to officialdom. Sean Connery's current marquee appeal could help to give this picture the wide audience it deserves.

The "hill" of the title is a man-made pile of sand up and down which the soldier-prisoners have to run with full kit, often until they are physically exhausted, as part of a punishment designed more to break a man's spirit rather than provide corrective treatment. The film was the official British selection at the Cannes festival ("The Knack" and "Ipcress File" were invited entries) and the choice was well justified, though the subject matter may easily give rise to resentment in some quarters.

Sidney Lumet's forceful and authoritative direction gives added power to the production, and Oswald Morris's stark black and white lensing adds to the tough realism. The clipped military dialog may be difficult for some foreign audiences, particularly in the earlier sequences, but that's just a minor flaw.

Ray Rigby's screenplay puts the spotlight on a new bunch of prisoners, one of whom (Sean Connery) is a "busted" sergeant-major, and a natural target for the vindictive and sadistic treatment. Connery had apparently refused to obey an order to send his men into the front line because they had lost half their fighting equipment, and is immediately tagged a coward. Another is a Negro sent down for drinking three bottles of scotch from the officers' mess; the others are petty crooks, but they all suffer the same treatment.

One of the new intake is unable to stand up to the punishment and collapses in his cell, but when Connery calls for medical help, a staff sergeant orders the sick man to continue marching. A few moments later he collapses and dies, and that sparks off a mutiny, which is one of the most powerful and dramatic sequences of the pic. The clash between Connery and authority increases as he lodges a complaint against the staff sergeant, but it is only after he himself is beaten up that the camp medical officer, a weak character played by Michael Redgrave, actually takes action to halt the brutality.

The one weak spot of the screenplay is Rigby's cliche treatment of the Negro, played by Ossie Davis. It is he who is the only one with the guts to support Connery, and it is he who defies authority after he's called a "nigger." Davis takes off his uniform, and, dressed only in his underpants, announces that he has quit the service. Despite the tension the scene evokes, these sequences provide the only measure of light relief.

Breaking away from his 007 image, Connery gives an intelligently restrained study, carefully avoiding forced histrionics. The juiciest role, however, is that of the prison regimental sergeant major, and Harry Andrews does a standout job. Always a solid and reliable actor, he has never bettered this performance. Another top grade characterisation comes from Ian Hendry as the brutal staff sergeant who attempts to blackmail the medical officer to save himself from the inevitable.

A characteristic of the production is the all round acting quality. Each part is clearly drawn and has been exceptionally well cast. Michael Redgrave, in a comparatively minor role, at once suggests the weak M.O. whose conscience is eventually roused; Ian Bannen makes an effective staff sergeant with a sense of decency and fair play; Ossie Davis is fine as the West Indian, and Roy Kinnear, Jack Watson and Alfred Lynch give solid portrayals as prisoners.

"The Hill" may not be to everyone's taste, and certainly may have only limited appeal to femme audiences, but it is stamped with sinceritiy and expertise. *Myro.*

The Young Sinner

Low-budget teenage problem pic with some merit and appeal to mature juves. Marquee lure is Stefanie Powers. Lowercase item for young market.

Hollywood, June 3.

United Screen Arts release of T. C. Frank Production, produced, written and directed by Tom Laughlin. Stars Laughlin; features William Wellman Jr., Stefanie Powers, Robert Angelo. Camera, Ed Martin, Sven Walnum; editor, Don Henderson; music, Shelly Manne; sound, Charles Cooper, Leroy Robbins; asst. director, Herb Willis. Reviewed at Lytton Center of Visual Arts, L. A., June 1, '65. Running time, **81 MINS.**

Chris Wotan	Tom Laughlin
Ginny	Stefanie Powers
Priest	Robert Angelo
Tury	Linda March
Tury's Mother	Julia Paul
Tury's Father	Clint Gunkel
Mrs. Wotan	Dorothy Downey
Mr. Wotan	Charles Heard
Miss Meyers	Roxanne Heard
Head coach	John Burns
Football coach	Jack Starrett
Asst. coach	Ed Cook
Tury's Friend	Jane Taylor
Principal	Harry Zumach
Teacher	A. C. Pagenkoff
Miss Meyers' friend	Connie Van Dyke
Ginny's date	Richard Colla

Filmed three years ago in Milwaukee area, "The Young Sinner" is a low-budget offbeat story of a teenage loser. Some frank sex angles are handled well, and cast includes Stefanie Powers and other younger names who have gone on to bigger pix. Latter factors plus identity with teenage market partially overcome a substandard technical polish to the Tom Laughlin production.

Scripter Laughlin has placed star Laughlin in position of high-school athlete from unhappy home whose future education is threatened by hassle with a coach. Told in flashback Catholic Church confessional, story limns Laughlin's moral decay but ends on upbeat note.

Stefanie Powers does well as Laughlin's first sweetie whose love pales as he swings with rich-girl Linda March and teenage nympho Roxanne Heard. Story goes that Columbia Pictures was sold on Miss Powers from this role, and her basic talent is obvious. Miss Heard makes a believable amoral gal who drags Laughlin into a church loft, only to be rejected. Miss March is a bit wooden, but okay as spoiled brat out for kicks.

Charles Heard convinces as boy's sodden father who is too weak to help him, throwing family burden on Dorothy Downey's working mother. John Burns is okay as coach who puts Laughlin on the pan with principal Harry Zumach, but both roles are cliche. A. C. Pagenkoff is effective as teacher who has no sympathy with, or control over, his students, and most audiences will recall the type.

Jack Starrett is excellent as good-guy coach who tries to straighten out the kid, and brief footage with Heard and Laughlin is a dramatic highlight. William Wellman Jr., James Stacy, Dennis O'Flaherty, Chris Robinson and Bob Colonna are strictly background as Laughlin's buddies, but characters and dialog are believable. Other players are adequate in stock roles.

Robert Angelo excels as down-to-earth priest who hears Laughlin's story which includes latter's dramatic emotional outburst in empty church. This plot turn, plus use of a few salty expressions and other sex angles are handled with taste. Adults might wonder if teenagers live this way; many do, and those that don't, talk about it.

Director Laughlin has done a good job, aided by okay camera mobility of Ed Martin and Sven Walnum. Jazzman Shelly Manne's score is an assist, ditto Don Henderson's tight editing to 81 minutes. Sound looping and quality is poor and erratic. Other technical details are adequate. *Murf.*

McHale's Navy Joins the Air Force
(COLOR)

Another zany adaptation of pop teleseries to theatrical screen, this time without Ernest Borgnine but still showing coin potential.

Hollywood, May 25.

Universal release of Edward J. Montagne production. Features Joe Flynn, Tim Conway, Bob Hasting, Gary Vinson, Billy Sands, Edson Stroll, John Wright, Yoshio Yoda, Gavin MacLeod, Tom Tully, Susan Silo, Henry Beckman, Jacques Aubuchon. Directed by Montagne. Screenplay, John Fenton Murray; from story by William J. Lederer; camera (Technicolor), Lionel Lindon; editor, Sam E. Waxman, music Jerry Fielding, art direction, Alexander Golitzen, Russell Kimball; sound, Waldon O. Watson, Earl Crain Sr., asst. director, George Bisk. Reviewed at Wiltern Theatre, May 24, '65. Running time, **92 MINS.**

Capt. Binghamton	Joe Flynn
Ensign Parker	Tim Conway
Lt. Carpenter	Bob Hastings
Christy	Gary Vinson
Tinker	Billy Sands
Virgil	Edson Stroll
Willy	John Wright
Fuji	Yoshio Yoda
Happy Haines	Gavin MacLeod
General Harkness	Tom Tully
Smitty	Susan Silo
Colonel Platt	Henry Beckman
Lt. Wilbur Harkness	Ted Bessell
Madge	Jean Hale
Major Grady	Cliff Norton
Admiral Doyle	Willis Bouchey
Vogel	Berkeley Harris
Russian Seaman #1	Jack Bernardi
Russian Seaman #2	Norman Leavitt
Russian Seaman #4	Joe Ploski
Russian Seaman #3	Andy Albin
Tresh	Tony Franke
Lt. Wilson	Clay Tanner
Dimitri	Jacques Aubuchon

The high-rating "McHale's Navy" teleseries returns to the feature screen sans its skipper, Ernest Borgnine, this second time out for a theatrical release. Lt. Comdr. Quinton McHale, that hearty of the series who led his intrepid PT-boat crew into amazing adventure for the first feature adaptation last year, is missing here. Borgnine stepped out after coin disagreements. Joe Flynn and Tim Conway, regulars in the series and in the first feature, take on the top assignments in this one, turned out in the same zany formula but somehow missing the dominant personality of tv version's star to sparkplug and give balance to the action.

This is not to say, however, that "McHale's Navy Joins the Air Force" isn't riotously funny at times. It's purely escapist fare, as feathery in story line as its comedy is broad. With its built-in audience, pic should enjoy the same biz that its predecessor enjoyed, and there can be no quarrel with the script, which has one of the nuttiest closing sequences glimpsed in recent times. Mack Sennett might turn over in his grave at some of the sight gags and how they're worked but they tickle the risibilities and that's all that matters for the trade at which it's aimed.

Motivating premise of the John Fenton Murray screenplay, based on a story by William J. Lederer, revolves around Conway, the malaproptic Ensign Parker, assuming the identity of an Air Force officer in a uniform mix-up occasioned by a colossal hangover, and his misadventures thereof. Flynn, again in character of the flustered and frantic Navy Captain Wallace Binghamton, is forced to go along with the impersonation which leads finally to the sinking of the Japanese fleet and the blundering ensign being made a hero and called to Washington for an audience with President Franklin D. Roosevelt.

Edward J. Montagne, who again produces and directs, keeps his pace lively with accent always on corn. Flynn and Conway both turn in their customary type of performances, with most regulars of the teleseries reprising their roles. Jacques Aubuchon is amusing as a Soviet sailor. Tom Tully plays a hardnosed three-star general and Henry Beckman an Air Force colonel for good effect, and the distaff department is well handled by Susan Silo and Jean Hale. Bob Hastings gets laughs as Flynn's over-anxious aide.

Technical credits emerge first-rate. Jerry Fielding's music score furnishing melodic backdrop for Lionel Lindon's handsome color photography. Sam E. Waxman's editing is fast and Alexander Golitzen and Russell Kimball's art direction appropriate. *Whit.*

The Hallelujah Trail
(ULTRA PANAVISION-CINERAMA-COLOR)

Lusty, gusty western comedy with screwball situations; hefty grosses foreseen.

Hollywood, June 12.

United Artists release of John Sturges production. Stars Burt Lancaster, Lee Remick, Jim Hutton, Pamela Tiffin, Donald Pleasance, Brian Keith, Martin Landau; features John Anderson, Tom Stern, Robert J. Wilke. Directed by Sturges. Screenplay, John Gay, based on novel by Bill Gulick; camera (Technicolor), Robert Surtees; music, Elmer Bernstein; art direction, Cary Odell; editor, Ferris Webster; asst. director, Jack N. Reddish; sound, Joseph La Bella. Reviewed at Warner Hollywood Theatre, June 11, '65. Running Time, **152 MINS.** (without intermission).

Col. Thadeus Gearhart ... Burt Lancaster
Cora Templeton Massingale ... Lee Remick
Captain Paul Slater ... Jim Hutton
Louise Gearhart ... Pamela Tiffin
Oracle Jones ... Donald Pleasence
Frank Wallingham ... Brian Keith
Chief Walks-Stooped-Over ... Martin Landau
Sergeant Buell ... John Anderson
Kevin O'Flaherty ... Tom Stern
Chief Five Barrels ... Robert J. Wilke
First Brother-in-Law ... Jerry Gatlin
Second Brother-in-Law ... Larry Duran
Elks-Runner ... Jim Burk
Clayton Howell ... Dub Taylor
Rafe Pike ... John McKee
Henrietta ... Helen Kleeb
Interpreter ... Noam Pitlik
Phillips ... Carl Pitti
Brady ... Bill Williams
Carter ... Marshall Reed
Simmons ... Carroll Adams
Bandmaster ... Ted Markland
Bilkins ... Buff Brady
Horner ... Bing Russell
Simpson ... Billy Benedict
Mary Ann ... Karla Most
Loretta ... Elaine Martone
Mrs. Hasselrad ... Hope Summers
"A" Company Sergeant ... Carroll Henry
Hobbs ... Whit Bissell
Denver Bartender ... Val Avery
The Narrator ... John Dehner

It all begins with the burgeoning city of Denver facing the worst threat of its existence—becoming bone dry in 10 days in the approaching winter of 1867. This awesome situation (one of those "one jokes" you keep hearing about) paves the way for one of the nuttiest cinematic mishmashes you ever saw, in which thirsty miners, a worried U.S. Cavalry, a band of whiskey-mad Sioux, a crusading temperance group and a train of 40 wagons carrying 600 barrels of hard likker become so thoroughly involved that even the off-screen narrator has a hard time trying to keep track of them and their proper logistics. This whole concoction has been so expertly blended and with such consummate attention to utter chaos on the western plains that it emerges one of the broadest comedies of the year which should meet with appropriate reaction at the boxoffice, where it's headed for roadshowing.

Producer-director John Sturges has pulled every plug in spoofing practically every western situation known to the scripter, and the whole is beautifully packaged in eye-filling Ultra Panavision and Technicolor and released in Cinerama's single lens process. Screenplay by John Gay, in his adaptation of Bill Gulick's novel, approaches the situations straight; it's the treatment that counts here as each is reduced to cornpop potential and ultimately realized in this vein.

The Cavalry, coloneled by Burt Lancaster, is constantly threatened with breaching the articles of war and the Constitution itself by the demands of temperance leader Lee Remick. Sioux, leaving their reservation when they get wind of the approaching whiskey, can't be attacked by the Cavalry because they carry certain signed Government papers. Instead of the Indians circling a wagon train and coming in for the kill, they suddenly find they're in the closed wagon formation themselves and it's the Cavalry which is doing the circling.

These are only a few of the situations to which Sturges gives free-wheeling development. Probably the most amusing part of the picture is the off-screen explanations of the movement, accompanied by maps and sketches, designed further to orbit the spectator into a happy daze of calculated confusion and succeeding in fine manner. Performances, like situations, are played straight, and therein lies their beauty.

Lancaster, playing his first comedy role, does a bangup job as the harassed Cavalry colonel plagued with having to offer safe conduct to the whiskey train to Denver and also offer protection to the temperance ladies led by Miss Remick while simultaneously keeping them off the wagonmaster's neck. One of the funniest scenes in the entire unreeling is Lancaster's amazed question of why no one was injured, after Cavalry, Indians, the Denver miners who have arrived on the scene to escort the wagon train to Denver and the ladies themselves have shot millions of bullets in the worst duststorm known to man—without a single casualty.

Miss Remick is perky and charming as she decides she and her followers must halt and destroy the whiskey train, socking over a scene in which she nips "for medicinal reasons." Pamela Tiffin, pretty and fresh as a mountain violet, further impresses as Lancaster's daughter who throws in with the temperance femmes, and Jim Hutton gets good mileage out of his captain character, who finds the ladies a bit beyond him. John Anderson plays it all the way, too, for comedy as Lancaster's intrepid sergeant who frequently finds his superior's orders impossible to fulfill.

Donald Pleasance from Britain offers a fresh type of characterization as Oracle Jones, an old guide to whom the miners turn for one of his visions in helping them out of their dilemna. He's responsible for the wagons sinking in quicksand, after he's marked a passage which the ladies change. Brian Keith makes the most of the blustering wagonmaster.

One of the standouts in pic is Martin Landau, as Chief Walks-Stooped-Over, as deadpan as any Injun ever lived but socking over his comedy scenes mostly with his eyes. He's usually around as a symbol of good faith while attaching himself to the Cavalry during the many palavers. Robert J. Wilke, too, lends gusto to his Sioux chief role, figuring prominently in the sequence in which the Indians, trading off femme captives for wagons of whiskey, find they've acquired imported champagne instead and the liquid foams. Dub Taylor heads the miners and Tom Stern is amusing as a striking Irish teamster.

Technical credits are particularly noteworthy, especially Robert Surtees' magnificent color photography. Elmer Bernstein's music score builds the action as well as comedy with rare effectiveness, and editing by Ferris Webster, art direction by Cary Odell, costumes by Edith Head and special effects by A. Paul Pollard also add notably. Maps by DePatie-Freleng are cleverly worked out, and John Dehner's voice as narrator a masterpiece of understatement.

Whit.

Tickle Me
(PANAVISION—COLOR)

Lightweight Elvis Presley starrer which should run up customary good grosses.

Hollywood, May 14.

Allied Artists release of Ben Schwalb production. Stars Elvis Presley; features Julie Adams, Jocelyn Lane, Jack Mullaney, Merry Anders, Bill Williams. Directed by Norman Taurog. Screenplay, Elwood Ullman, Edward Bernds; camera (DeLuxe Color), Loyal Griggs; music, Walter Scharf; art direction, Hal Pereira, Arthur Lonergan; asst. director, Arthur Jacobson; sound, Hugo Grenzbach; Charles Grenzbach; editor, Archie Marshek. Reviewed at Hollywod Paramount Theatre, May 13, '65. Running Time, **90 MINS.**

Lonnie Beale ... Elvis Presley
Vera Radford ... Julie Adams
Pam Merritt ... Jocelyn Lane
Stanley Potter ... Jack Mullaney
Estelle Penfield ... Merry Anders
Deputy Sturdivant ... Bill Williams
Brad Bentley ... Edward Faulkner
Hilda ... Connie Gilchrist
Barbara ... Barbara Werle
Adolph (Chef) ... John Dennis
Mr. Dabney ... Grady Sutton
Mabel ... Allison Hayes
Ophelia ... Inez Pedroza
Ronnie ... Lilyan Chauvin
Donna ... Angela Greene
Jerry (Groom) ... Louie Elias
Henry (Gardener) ... Robert Hoy
Mrs. Dabney ... Dorothy Konrad
Pat ... Eve Bruce
Mildred ... Francine York

The substantial hold that Elvis Presley wields over his public will continue with this Allied Artists production, first time out for this studio with a film starring the singer-actor who previously has been associated mostly with Hal Wallis, Metro and 20th-Fox output. Ben Schwalb produced and Norman Taurog directed, both vets of the comedy field, who drew on their varied experience to provide present opus with more slapstick than Presley usually undertakes.

Screenplay by Elwood Ullman and Edward Bernds is wispy thin but allows singer to rock over nine numbers from past albums to good effect. He gets good comedy backing from a competent cast and a flock of young beauts cavorting in near-Bikini attire, and a wind-up finish, fast and corny, should tickle the palates of his natural audience as well as furnishing a field day for moppet specs.

Presley plays a rodeo rider who takes a temporary job as horse wrangler on an expensive Arizona dude ranch beauty spa while awaiting start of the rodeo season. Immediately, he's center of attention from all the glamour patrons who fall both for him and his singing.

Romance and sub-plot are offered in the shapely person of Jocelyn Lane, physical instructress on spread, who is continually the object of attack and attempted kidnap for the map of a hidden fortune in gold her grandfather willed her. Gold is finally found in a deserted hotel, restored by local historical society, with as wild a set of goings-on as any script and director could devise.

Presley takes his character in stride, giving a performance calculated to appeal particularly to his following. Some of the songs he warbles include "It's a Long, Lonely Highway," "It Feels So Right," "Easy Question," "Dirty, Dirty Feeling," "Put the Blame on Me," "I'm Yours," "Night Rider," "I Feel I've Known You Forever," "Slowly But Surely." His comedy timing is right for most of slapstick.

Miss Lane delivers a sharp enactment of the gal Presley falls for, and Julie Adams makes the most of her role as ranch owner. Jack Mullaney shines as a naive character. Merry Anders is an always-hungry ranch patron, and Edward Faulkner is in for a comedy part as swimming instructor. Bill Williams is a deputy sheriff masterminding plan to get the fortune map.

Technical departments are well handled, headed by Loyal Griggs' color photography, Hal Pereira and Arthur Lonergan's art direction, Archie Marshek's editing and Walter Scharf's music score.

Whit.

The Thrill Killers

Low-budget shocker with well-directed gore but poor script and acting. Exploitable lowercase entry in action situations.

Hollywood, June 8.

Hollywod Star Pictures release of a Morgan-Steckler Production produced by George J. Morgan. Features entire cast. Directed by Ray Dennis Steckler. Screenplay, Steckler, Gene Pollock; camera, Joseph V. Mascelli; editor, Austin McKinney; music, Henry Price; sound, Lee Strosnider; art direction and titles, Tom Scherman; asst. director, Don Russell. Reviewed at Lytton Center of Visual Arts, L. A., June 7, '65. Running Time, **89 MINS.**

Mort Click ... Cash Flagg
Liz Saxon ... Liz Renay
Joe Saxon ... Brick Bardo
Murdered lovers ... Carolyn, Brandt. Ron Burr
Gary ... Gary Kent
Herbie ... Herb Robins
Keith ... Keith O'Brien
Linda ... Laura Benedict
Erina Devore ... Erina Enyo
Dennis Kesdekian ... Atlas King
Motrocycle cop ... Titus Moede
Producer ... George J. Morgan

"The Thrill Killers" is a low-budget shocker depicting mayhem by a quartet of psycho cases. Inventive direction and good technical work by a group of young filmmakers convey impact in many scenes of raw violence. But script and performances are poor, causing weariness by final reel. Highly exploitable but strictly lowercase in less discriminating situations where there is a market for this type of film.

George J. Morgan's pic opens with murder of salesman Atlas King by hitchhiker Cash Flagg who encores after titles with hooker Erina Enyo. Latter's death-by-scissor is brutal but handled excellently by director Ray Dennis Steckler amid flashes of a neon sign. Miss Enyo is good in brief bit.

Gary Kent, Herb Robins and Keith O'Brien are a trio of escaped psychos who successively behead a rube landlord, then Ron Burr and sweetie Carolyn Brandt. O'Brien is the axe-man, Kent prefers fists, and Robins seems to emcee matters, and all are adequate within dimension of roles scripted by Steckler and Gene Pollock. Miss Brandt is also good in short role, and her aborted escape is visually interesting.

Laura Benedict scores the first point for society when she slips poison into Robins' coffee at roadhouse. Her cigar-smoking bit makes an okay character momentarily notable. Keith is subdued by Brick Bardo, playing an unsuccessful actor who has followed wife Liz Renay to the country. Latter is believable looking fading charmer, but thesping is confined in later scenes to screams and gestures which draw some unwanted laughs. Bardo is no actor.

Film falls apart in final trackdown of Kent and Flagg since audience is sated on gore and will pounce upon banalities in script and performance to relieve nervous tension. Further editing in final reel might overcome this to some degree.

Steckler has made two previous films, and his directorial talent is obvious. He defeated himself as scripter and as actor (Flagg). Joseph V. Mascelli's camera work is professional, ditto Austin McKinney's editing. Henry Price has provided an exciting score, and Lee Strosnider's sound is adequate. Title work by Tom Scherman is excellent. Film is being states-righted by Hollywood Star Films.   *Murf.*

Paris Secret
(FRENCH-COLOR)
Paris, June 15.

Rank release of Arthur Cohn and Pierre Roustang production. Directed by Edouard Logereau. Screenplay, Tom Rowe; camera (Eastmancolor), Roland Pontoizeau; music, Alain Goraguer. Previewed in Paris. Running Time, 85 MINS.

(*English Commentary*)

"Paris Secret" looks at the strange, off-the-beaten-track aspects of Paris rarely seen by tourists, or many locals for that matter. It may reenact incidents and stage others, but there is no attempt to shock or dismay. With the Paris pull, and a filmic compassion, rather than derision, for its contents, it appear good for arty and also playoff possibilities abroad.

If eccentrics and seamy things are looked at, the film accepts them and manages to have an affirmative nod towards its subjects. So a girl student, for money, has her backside tatooed to have the patch removed by a surgeon to sell to collectors of this sort of skin art.

A circus orphan has her confirmation party among a group of freaks who brought her up. But there's tact and no exploitation of the grotesque here. A mashers school is shown in action as members watch a newcomer, via field glasses, in action. He has a hidden tape reporter. This series of scenes is gently satirical of Gay Paree.

The sewers are shown and its rats, an upper class sport of old, which may be still indulged in, is acted out as women dress as birds, deer etc. and are chased through the woods by men. Commentator drily asserts that it is too bad if one snags one's own wife.

The perennial streetwalkers are shown plus the new motorized set. Amusing tidbit. reportedly based on the real thing, are two girls who operate with an ambulance. A bird lover who puts mucilage over nightingale eyes to have them sing during the day, an intern's ball with naked girls smeared with marmalade, various sects such as moon worshippers, naked girls praying to the moon and navel gazers also pass in review as well as a fanatic who allows bees to cover him entirely.

Pic winds up as a man leads a horse through the dawn of a new day in Paris.

Color is exceptionally good. Tom Rowe supplies an English narration that does not force the images and has a savory feel for life in spite of some of the eerie scenes.

Editing has rhythm and flow. This look at offbeat Paris manages to escape archness and shock for its own sake to seemingly have chances abroad in spite of the many documentaries of this type that have preceded it. And Paris comes out of it all alright with a catchy musical theme also helping.   *Mosk.*

Repulsion
(BRITISH)

Standout psychological horror pic, finely directed. Tough to sell in many situations, but absorbing for discerning audiences.

London, June 9.

Compton-Cameo release of Michael Klinger & Tony Tender (Gene Gutowski) production. Stars Catharine Deneuve, Ian Hendry, John Fraser, Patrick Wymark, Yvonne Furneaux; features Valerie Taylor, Renee Houston, Helen Fraser, James Villiers, Monica Merlin. Directed by Roman Polanski. Screenplay, Polanski and Gerald Brach; camera, Gil Taylor; sound, Leslie Hammond; editor, Alastair McIntyre; music, Chico Hamilton. Reviewed at Humphreys' Private Theatre, London. Running Time, 104 MINS.
Carol .... Catharine Deneuve
Michael .... Ian Hendry
Colin .... John Fraser
Landlord .... Patrick Wymark
Helen .... Yvonne Furneaux
Miss Balch .... Renee Houston
Bridget .... Helen Fraser
Madame Denise .... Valerie Taylor
John .... James Villiers
Reggie .... Hugh Futcher
Workman .... Mike Pratt
Mrs. Rendlesham....... Monica Merlin
Manicurist .... Imogen Graham

Highly acclaimed out-of-contest at Cannes Film Fest, and now entered for the Berlin Fest, "Repulsion" is a classy, truly horrific psychological drama in which Polish director Roman Polanski has drawn out a remarkable performance from the young French thesp, Catharine Deneuve. This absorbing British pic will need a heavy sell to tap all but discerning audiences. But its quality in the semi-arty field cannot be questioned.

Those with strong stomachs and keen imaginations who see it will have a gripping time. This pic draws but subtly, repels and fascinates, shocks and excites as it probes the way lust and repression take over a young girl's basically innocent mind. Polanski, who wrote the original screenplay with Gerard Brach, uses his technical resources and the abilities of his thesps to build up a

tense atmosphere of evil. He does it with the skill of an orchestra conductor and the imagination of a haunted artist.

There are a few seemingly loose and dilatory passages but they invariably whip up to sharp, stunning climaxes. With the help of cameraman Gil Taylor, every shadow plays its role in building tension.

A notable plus is Polanski's use of sound. There are two brief sequences, for instance, when the young heroine tosses in her bed as she listens to the muted sound of her sister and her lover in the next room. All the audience hears are the moans and ecstatic whimperings of the love act and it is a dozen times more effective and sensual than any glimpse of the lovers in bed. The occasional clanging of a bell from a nearby convent, the jarring sound of a telephone and other ordinary sounds all become part of a pattern, which highlight chilly silences.

Miss Deneuve is a youngster working in a beauty shop, a deliberately sharp contrast to the drab apartment which she shares with her flighty elder sister. The girl is sexually repressed, deeply attracted to the thought of men but at the same time loathing the thought of them. Her antagonism shows in her defensive attitude toward a clean. upstanding young man who is sweet on her but cannot get through to her. Then there's her keen disappointment of her sister's virile, earthy lover.

Her daydreaming grows into erotic sexual fantasies, and when her sister and boyfriend leave her for a few days while they go on an Italian vacation, her loneliness and imagination take hold and insanity sets in. She imagines time after time that she is being raped, that male hands are grabbing at her and that the apartment is beginning to crack up and collapse about her. Her frenzied imagination turns to madness but not before she brutally murders her admiring, shy young swain and her lecherous landlord.

The rape scenes and those where she sits in the disordered apartment crooning early to herself as she sews and irons, while one corpse is in the bloodstained bath and another behind an upturned divan are real chillers. It is a tribute to the hold that Polanski has over script. direction and cast that at the finale, when the sister and lover return from vacation to find this tragic shambles, there is no feeling of ridiculous exaggeration. The mood hangs on to the fadeout.

Miss Deneuve, without much dialog, handles a very difficult chore with insight and tact. John Fraser plays her would-be boyfriend likeably. Yvonne Furneaux makes a vivid impression as the casual sister and Ian Hendry gives another of his incisive studies of an attractive heel. Patrick Wymark handles a brief scene as a blustering landlord with lewd designs effectively. Valerie Taylor, Renee Houston, James Villiers, Monica Merlin and Helen Fraser cope adequately with minor roles.

London locations are authentic and the tawdry apartment adds to the brooding atmosphere. Chico Hamilton's music is used only briefly but always to effect. Taylor's lensing and Leslie Ham-

mond's sound all merit bows. But mostly, this is a fascinating amalgam between director, scriptwriter and leading lady which absorbingly lifts what might have been a mere horror meller to a much higher and more satisfying plane.   *Rich.*

San Simeon Del Desierto
(St. Simeon of the Desert)
(MEXICAN)

Luis Bonuel's Latest Hymn of Hate Against Religion. For Avant-Garde Situations.

Mexico City, May 28.

Gustavo Alatriste release and production. Directed by Luis Bunuel. Features Claudio Brook, Silvia Pinal, Hortensia Santovena, Jesus Fernandez Martinez, Enrique Alvarez Felix, Enrique del Castillo. Screenplay by Bunuel, additional dialog by Bunuel and Julio Alejandro; camera, Gabriel Figueroa; editor, Carlos Savage Jr. Reviewed at private showing at Periodistas del Cine Mexicana, Mexico City, May 27, '65. Running Time, 42 MINS.
St. Simeon .... Claudio Brook
Temptress .... Silvia Pinal
The Mother .... Hortensia Santovana
Dwarf Rabadan
                  Jesus Fernandez Martinez
Brother Matias ....Enrique Alvrez Felix
The Mutilated One .Enrique del Castillo
Priests........ Luis Aceves Castanada,
        Francisco Reiguera, Antonio
        Bravo Sanchez

Abrupt ending of this 42-minute film by Spanish director Luis Bunuel, which leaves the audience unsatisfied, is explained by producer Gustavo Alatriste in that it was originally intended to have two 45-minute sequences with two directors. Second half had originally been planned for Vittoria de Sica, then for Stanley Kubrick, neither of which materialized. Whether second half will be made is uncertain as are plans for possibly submitting this portion for the 1965 Venice Film Fest.

Film deals with temptations of fifth-century saint (Simeon Stylites of Antioch), who withdrew from the world to commune with God atop a pillar in the desert. Directorscripter Bunuel introduces figures of priests; a man whose hands, chopped off for robbery, are miraculously restored through Simeon's prayers; the inevitable grieving, silent mother; the Devil in the forms of a temptress and a priest; and a dwarf goatherd. They, in turn, represent superstition and mental blindness, ingratitude, suffering, confusion, evil and worldly vice.

Silvia Pinal, who played title role in Bunuel's "Viridiana," carries out his direction of her so precisely, as the temptress, that the effect is not altogether pleasing. As a little girl in a 19th-century dress and hat, rolling a hoop, she turns to reveal a worldly, wicked, grownup's face. Before the Saint's horrified eyes, she rips open her blouse to bare her breasts, an acton unlikely to set pulses pounding, and tasteless.

She is next seen transformed into what appears to be a Roman god with short beard, bearing a lamb in his arms. Puzzled audience failed to grasp this, although probably intended to represent a conventional 16th-century golden-haired angel. But why the Devil? To show that it is really the Devil? A discreetly-revealed cloven hoof would have made the point more effectively. With a vulgar move-

ment, she kicks the lamb away and we next see her atop the pillar, again in a female role, giving Simeon a rough time by tweaking his tattered beard, sticking out her tongue and tempting him to lewdness.

By an effort of will Simeon resists his tiresome visitor, who is then transformed into an hideous old hag, clad only in the sailor hat, with shrivelled breasts (role was reportedly enacted by a man in a rubber suit), who scuttles off, into the desert. Homosexuality in monastic life is suggested by the young monk, Matias. Simeon bids him begone and grow a beard. The dwarf, Rabadan, a fantastic misshapen figure, a non-believer, reveals bestiality with his goats. An evil priest tempts Simeon to worldly pleasures with fine food. Simeon rejects him also, reaching instead for a crisp lettuce leaf. Healthier, perhaps, if less sustaining, as the sadly ulcerated legs of the Saint-to-be show a shocking vitamin deficiency. War drums as background music are intended to show that wars continue to come and go.

Bunuel had earlier asserted that, in this film, he had no intention of mocking the worthy Saint whom he found a most interesting character, and whose life he had researched closely. One does not detect, however, any empathy between director and subject, although fun poked at the Saint is harmless, per se. Observing his own rotten tooth, Simeon automatically blesses it and, later, blesses an insect which settles momentarily upon his hand. He then looks around and ponders, "Let's see, now what can I bless? Oh, dear what am I saying?"

Claudio Brook plays the title role with dignity and manages to convey something of the heroism and fanaticism of the Saint who reputedly spent 27 of his 40 years atop a pillar, first in what became a vogue in pillar saints in his time (and with emulators as late as the 16th century in Russia and Ruthenia).

The message, if one can call it that, of the final scene is, in typical Bunuel manner, abrupt and shocking. Viewers are transported from the silence of the desert to 20th-century New York. There, the Saint, in a noisy Greenwich Village discotheque, is seated opposite the temptress who urges him to join in the frentic stamping, whirling and writing. Extras, purportedly U.S. high school students, and Gabriel Figueroa's roving camera combine marvelously to record this dizzying scene. Oppressed, ill at ease, aware of the unhappy, tense faces around him trying to forget their troubles, their sins, the emptiness of their lives and the uncertainties of their futures, Simeon wrenches himself away from his companion to leave. To his pillar? To isolation from the world which, per Bunuel, has not improved in 15 centuries.

Bunuel claimed, when he made this film (which was shot entirely on location, except for four days studio work at Churubusco), that it would be his last but has said this so often that it is not credited. Should it be true, however, he will have left a curious, at times brilliant, film to his memory. A Mexican resident for years, Bunuel is notoriously the atheist, constantly negative, incurably iconoclastic.

More sophisticated, discerning audiences appreciate Bunuel, a point which rarely, however, makes him a commercial success. He cares little about this and producer Alatriste has faith in him, gives him a free hand to express what he wants to say, which he does compellingly. One may disagree with his philosophy but cannot deny his talent. His style is of a harsh directness, lacking subtle shades of thought, emotion or tenderness. It seems to reflect the hard light and pitiless sun of the Extramadura of his native Spain.

Lucas.

Mitt Hem Ar Copacabana
(My Home Is Copacabana) (SWEDISH)

Cannes, May 21.

AB Svensk Filmindustri release and production. With Leila Santos De Sousa, Cosme Dos Santos, Antonio Carlos De Lima. Written, photographed, edited and directed by Arne Sucksdorff. At Cannes Film Fest. Running Time, **85 MINS.**

Lici	Leila Santos De Sousa
Jorghino	Cosme Dos Santos
Toninho	Antonio Carlos De Lima
Paulinho	Josafa De Silva Santos

Arne Sucksdorff is a Swedish documentary maker who has done some commendable pix on nature and foreign cities. But his mixing of fictional story and Rio De Janeiro backgrounding is uneven, somewhat repetitive and aimless. Camera looks at a group of homeless white and Negro waifs and their lives but does not take much stand and overdoes their escapades.

Children have a little house in the slum areas above Rio but are driven out by local gangsters. Kids make money by cutting kite strings of others by rubbing broken glass on their line, then selling the captured kites. They shine shoes, get involved with local shoplifters and pickpockets. One finally turns himself over to the police to go to reform school, away from physical misery and hunger of streets.

Sucksdorff obtained free and easy performances from his children in the pic but does not have artistic resources to achieve full feel and protest. "Picturesqueness" in poverty, Brazilian style, also somewhat waters down this overlong look at these fetching children in their rovings, wanderings and sufferings.

It is technically good and does have a few pointed and penetrating scenes that lay bare the mixture of opulence and poverty. But these are few and do not make up for the generally pedestrian, unformed pace and plotting.

Mosk.

Ski Party
(PANAVISION-COLOR)

Fast-paced and effective comedy-romancer with music and lively acting by young thesps in Sun Valley locales. Strong entry in youth situations.

Hollywood, June 11.

American International Pictures release of a Gene Corman production; executive producers, James H. Nicholson, Samuel Z. Arkoff. Stars Frankie Avalon, Dwayne Hickman, Deborah Walley, Yvonne Craig; features Robert Q. Lewis. Directed by Alan Rafkin. Screenplay, Robert Kaufman; camera (Panavision, Pathecolor), Arthur E. Arling; editor, Morton Tubor; music, Gary Usher; songs, Usher, Roger Christian, Bob Gaudio, Larry Kusic, Ritchie Adams, Guy Hemric, Jerry Styner, Marvin Hamlisch, Howard Liebling, Ted Wright; art direction, Howard Campbell; sound, Bob Post; asst. director, Dale Hucthinson. Reviewed at Academy Award Theatre, June 10, '65. Running Time, **90 MINS.**

Todd Armstrong (Jane)	Frankie Avalon
Craig Gamble (Nora)	Dwayne Hickman
Linda Hughes	Deborah Walley
Barbara Norris	Yvonne Craig
Donald Pevney	Robert Q. Lewis
Nita	Bobbi Shaw
Freddie Carter	Aron Kincaid
Gene	Steve Rogers
Bobby	Mike Nader
Ski boys	John Boyer, Ronnie Dayton
Arthur	Bill Sampson
Janet	Patti Chandler
Indian	Salli Sachse
Ski girls	Mikki Jamison, Mary Hughes, Luree Holmes
Themselves	The Hondells, James Brown and the Famous Flames, Lesley Gore

"Ski Party" is an entertaining teenage comedy romance in snow-country settings, with excellent direction of good satirical script ad fine performances by young thesps. Gene Corman production values are standout, and seven tunes enliven pace. Marquee lure of Frankie Avalon, Dwayne Hickman, Robert Q. Lewis plus wax names will appeal to young adults and teeners. American International release is strong uppercaser for the young market and very good programmer for general situations.

Robert Kaufman's script teams Frankie Avalon and Dwayne Hickman as loser-lotharios opposite Deborah Walley and Yvonne Craig, respectively. All the gals hanker for stuffy Aron Kincaid, and the two heroes engage in some female impersonation to find out why. Film is a sort of snowbound "Some Like It Hot" combined with "Tom Jones" asides to audience.

Director Alan Rafkin obtained relaxed and assured comedy acting from Avalon and Hickman as both stag and drag, while Miss Walley and Miss Craig are believable objects of pursuit. Kincaid stands out as the lightweight heavy who fights off femmes but goes after Hickman's "Nora."

Robert Q. Lewis is a very good pedantic ski lodge social director who can't cope with the heroes' switcheroo; his mother wanted a girl, and he believes she finally got her (s)wish. **Bobbi Shaw shines as the Swedish gal whom Avalon pursues, only to find she prefers romance American style.**

Bill Sampson has the lucky bit of necking with Annette Funicello, making unbilled brief appearance as college prof who discards her specs in night school. Other players contribute to the fun atmosphere. There's a scene by heated pool for those who remember the gang from the beachpix days.

Lesley Gore, James Brown and the Famous Flames and The Rondells each do a song, all okay. Title tune by Gary Usher and Roger Christian is rhythmic, while particular ear-catchers are "Lots, Lots More" (Ritchie Adams, Larry Kusic), and "Paintin' The Town" (Bob Gaudio). "We'll Never Change Them" (Guy Hemric, Jerry Styner) highlights a girls' dormitory pillow fight.

Rafkin kept a fast pace, abetted by Morton Tubor's editing zip which held pic to 90 minutes. Arthur E. Arling's Panavision-Pathecolor lensing brought both life and color to proceedings, also excitement to downhill ski slope antics. Other credits are firstrate.

Murf.

War-Gods Of The Deep
(BRITISH-COLOR-ANAMORPHIC)

Bright and tight sci-fi exploitationer. Good performances, excellent direction and special effects. Marquee lure in Vincent Price and other stars.

Hollywood, June 1.

American International Pictures release of a Daniel Haller production, exec-producer George Willoughby. Stars Vincent Price, Tab Hunter, David Tomlinson, Susan Hart; features John Le Mesurier, Henry Oscar, Derek Newark, Roy Patrick; with Anthony Selby, Michael Hevland, Steven Brooke, William Hurndell, Jim Spearman, Dennis Blake, Arthur Hewlett, Walter Sparrow, John Barrett, Barbara Bruce, Hilda Campbell Russell, Bart Allison, George Ricarde, Herbert the rooster. Directed by Jacques Tourneur. Screenplay, Charles Bennett, Louis M. Heyward; additional dialog, David Whittaker, based on poem by Edgar Allan Poe; camera (Pathecolor, anamorphic), Stephen Dade; editor, Gordon Hales; music, Stanley Black; art direction, Frank White; special effects, Frank George, Les Bowie; underwater photography and direction, John Lamb. Reviewed at Joe Shore's Screening Room, L. A., June 1, '65. Running time, **83 MINS.**

The Captain	Vincent Price
Ben Harris	Tab Hunter
Harold Tiffin Jones	David Tomlinson
Jill Tregellis	Susan Hart
Ives	John Le Mesurier
Mumford	Henry Oscar
Dan	Derek Newark
Simon	Roy Patrick
George	Anthony Selby
Bill	Michael Heyland
Ted	Steven Brooke
Tom	William Hurndell
Jack	Jim Spearman
Harry	Dennis Blake
1st Fisherman	Arthur Hewlett
2d Fisherman	Walter Sparrow
3d Fisherman	John Barrett
1st Woman Guest	Barbara Bruce
2d Woman Guest	Hilda Campbell Russell
1st Man Guest	Bart Allison
2d Man Guest	George Ricarde
The rooster	Herbert

"War-Gods of the Deep" is a brisk and colorful sci-fi exploitationer about lost underseas kingdom off British coast. Excellent direction and special effects, plus good performances, provide zip for standard plot. Daniel Haller production has marquee lure of Vincent Price, David ("Mary Poppins") Tomlinson and younger names, spelling very good prospects for American International release in its intended market.

The Charles Bennett-Louis M. Heyward script places Price in command of submerged kingdom of Lyonesse, leading small smuggler group which was driven underground by British sleuths a century before. Surviving in the dank atmosphere, they are plagued with an active volcano which threatens existence. Only hope is to kidnap earthquake experts.

Susan Hart is snatched from family home since she resembles Price's dead wife, and Tab Hunter with Tomlinson stumble into the depths in rescue attempt. Price convinces by underplaying two-sided role of tyrannical ruler with benevolent overtones. Miss Hart is up to demands of brief footage, and Hunter is believable as a rational young man who wants to scram captivity.

Standout performance comes from Tomlinson, initially a daffy artist (with pet rooster) who provides comedy relief and emerges as the more resourceful rescuer. John Le Mesurier is effective as one of Price's crew who assists in trio's escape via tricky undersea route that must be timed precisely to tidal changes. Final third of picture is the slow exit which includes increasingly destructive quakes, battles with sub-human creatures whom Price rules, eventual surfacing and latter's death-by-aging when he reaches sunlight.

John Lamb photographed and directed underwater sequences in top form, giving pace to inherently slow physical movement that could have bogged down proceedings. Abetting him here was Stanley Black's full-bodied music, also effective throughout. Frank George and Les Bowie concocted some excellent special effects work, ditto Frank White's art direction, adding up to realistic scenes of eruption, flood and destruction.

Director Jacques Tourneur rates special mention for drawing good performances and framing them adroitly, aided in the latter by Stephen Dade's inventive camera mobility. Gorden Hales edited to a tight 83 minutes. Vivid Pathecolors are an asset, also all other Pinewood Studio technical work. *Murf.*

Young Dillinger

The Dillinger name should help in program market, where exploitation chances are good.

Hollywood. June 10.
Allied Artists release of Alfred N. Zimbalist production. Stars Nick Adams; features Robert Conrad, John Ashley, Dan Terranova, Victor Buono, John Hoyt. Directed by Terry O. Morse. Screenplay, Arthur Hoerl, Don Zimbalist, from story by Zimbalist; camera, Stanley Cortez; music, Shorty Rogers; art direction, Don Ament; editor, T. O. Morse; sound, Harold Lewis; asst. director Robert Shannon. Reviewed at Pix Theatre, June 9, '65. Running Time, 99 MINS.
John Dillinger .... Nick Adams
Pretty Boy Floyd .... Robert Conrad
Baby Face Nelson .... John Ashley
Homer Van Meter .... Dan Terranova
Professor Hoffman .... Victor Buono
Dr. Wilson .... John Hoyt
Elaine .... Mary Ann Mobley
Parker (Federal Agent).. Reed Hadley
Baum (Federal Agent)... Robert Osterloh
Rocco .... Anthony Caruso
Warden .... Art Baker
Justice of Peace .... Gene Roth
J. P.'s Wife .... Ayleene Gibson
Watchman .... Frank Gerstle
Jergins (Detective) .... Emile Meyer
Floyd's Girl .... Beverly Hills
Van Meter's Girl ...... Helen Stephens
Nelson's Girl .... Patsy Joy Harmon

This is belatedly reviewed, having earlier played the RKO Palace in Times Square.

It is a rather old-fashioned gangster film, lacking in the type of violent action which characterized so many gangster pix but sufficiently actionful for the program market. Nick Adams stars as the young Dillinger, and the Alfred N. Zimbalist production purports to tell his story in his early days of crime, leading up through certain major operations but ending before he went down before FBI bullets in a Chicago alley.

Script by Arthur Hoerl and Don Zimbalist, based upon an original story by latter, is slow in starting and never makes the character a cold-blooded killer until closing reels. Impression is nearly given that an attempt is made to explain away his turning gangster with a whitewash brush, but ultimately his sadistic nature asserts itself. Plot follows his escape from a prison honor farm after being sent up for burglary of money so he can marry a girl, and his helping spring three young gangsters whom he later leads in the Dillinger gang.

Adams makes an okay impression in title role, and Mary Ann Mobley as his girl (not the Lady in Red) is convincing, remaining with him until she is shot and he is forced to leave her. Robert Conrad as Pretty Boy Floyd, John Ashley as Baby Face Nelson and Dan Terranova as Homer Van Meter, his gangster associates, also lend conviction. Victor Buono is a crime mastermind to whom the gang turns for big jobs, and John Hoyt a surgeon whom Dillinger kills after a fake face job.

Zimbalist has lined up atmospheric production values of the times, with a set of cars of the period, and Terry O. Morse' direction keeps a fast pace generally. Photography by Stanley Cortez is satisfactory, as is editing of T. O. Morse and art direction of Don Ament. *Whit.*

Harlow
(PANAVISION—COLOR)

Joe E. Levine's Jean Harlow story. Carroll Baker and expensive trappings potentially good grosser if sold strongly.

Hollywood. June 16.
Paramount release of Joseph E. Levine production, produced in association with Paramount. Stars Carroll Baker; features Martin Balsam, Red Buttons, Michael Connors, Angela Lansbury, Peter Lawford, Raf Vallone. Directed by Gordon Douglas. Screenplay, John Michael Hayes, based on book by Irving Shulman in collaboration with Arthur Landau; camera (Technicolor), Joseph Ruttenberg; art direction, Hal Pereira, Roland Anderson; editors, Frank Bracht, Archie Marshek; music, Neal Hefti; asst. director, Dave Salven; sound, Stanley Jones, Charles Grenzbach. Reviewed at Paramount Studios, June 15, '65. Running Time, 125 MINS.
Jean Harlow .... Carroll Baker
Everett Redman .... Martin Balsam
Arthur Landau .... Red Buttons
Jack Harrison .... Michael Connors
Mama Jean Bello ...... Angela Lansbury
Paul Bern .... Peter Lawford
Marino Bello .... Raf Vallone
Richard Manley .... Leslie Nielsen
Studio Secretary .... Mary Murphy
Mrs. Arthur Landau ...... Hanna Landy
Assistant Director of 30's.. Peter Hansen
Girl at Pool .... Kipp Hamilton
Director of 30's .... Peter Leeds

Second biopic of Jean Harlow — following on reels of Electronovision version released last month — is handsomely mounted. In what purports to be a true story of the platinum blonde's rise from extra to sex symbol of the screen covers a lot of ground. In the final analysis, however, this Joseph E. Levine production necessarily covers the same territory, more or less, as its hastily-made predecessor, and despite a new star, obviously more production and greater quality, it has the defect of coming to market second.

However, by virtue of all the publicity attendant upon the simultaneous making of the two films and perhaps new interest in the star of the '30s, additionally sparked by Paramount's big-budget exploitation campaign, film may reap satisfactory grosses. It is a return to glamour in picturemaking, lusciously caught in Panavision and Technicolor, with sets costing a fortune and costumes by Edith Head seldom duplicated in recent years. While the story line frequently flags, the color and lure of Hollywood are there for Gordon Douglas to build in his taut and comprehensive direction.

As the ill-fated Jean Harlow, Carroll Baker is a fairly reasonable facsimile although she lacks the electric fire of the original. Still, she delivers well, even resembling her namesake at times and all in all achieves probably as close a delineation as is possible to a personality still vividly recalled by many who knew the actress prior to her tragic death in 1937. Miss Baker is believable in the part; she communicates to the audience, and that's what counts.

Script by John Michael Hayes is based on the questionable (at least in Hollywood) biog by Irving Shulman, who wrote tome in collaboration with Arthur Landau, star's first agent. Whether by insistence on part of the authors or by design, the part of Landau is fashioned almost on a par with the star character herself in the open-

ing reels, past the needs of the story which essentially focuses on girl's rise to become one of the hottest properties in films of that era. Actually, the events leading up to her death are sketchy and much of the Harlow story is omitted but enough of the major points, including the Paul Bern episode, are present to qualify for pic's intended goal.

Several real-life characters are thinly veiled while parts of star's mother and stepfather are importantly projected. Angela Lansbury undertakes role of Mama Jean with quiet conviction, and Raf Vallone, in the Marino Bello-stepfather role, also lends a persuasive presence. Red Buttons is properly assertive as the smalltime agent (Landau) who has enough faith in Harlow to devote himself almost exclusively to getting her her big break, and Hanna Landy plays his wife.

Peter Lawford, as Paul Bern, Miss Harlow's husband who committed suicide shortly after the marriage, may be the most debatable casting in film. Friends of Bern may find little to recommend Lawford for the character, but he nonetheless turns in a good performance.

Martin Balsam, under the character name of Everett Redman, head of Miss Harlow's studio (here called Majestic Pictures) who gives her her chance at stardom, is the thinly-veiled Louis B. Mayer. Michael Connors as a film star probably is a composite of several thesps, among them Clark Gable. Leslie Nielsen as an indie producer who gives the ambitious young actress her first break is a way-off Howard Hughes, if the succession of thesp's rise is to be counted. In brief roles, Peter Hansen scores as an assistant director on the make, Kipp Hamilton looks well in a bathing suit and Peter Leeds rates as a director.

More impressive than the story are its physical values. Particularly outstanding are the sets as designed by Hal Pereira and Roland Anderson, which catch the opulence of Hollywood's more grandiose days. Edith Head's creations as worn by femme star similarly mark a return to the days when fashions figured so importantly in a picture.

Color camera work by Joseph Ruttenberg is artistic and fluid in painting a vivid scene. Neal Hefti's music score potently backdrops the action Frank Bracht and Archie Marshek hold fairly tight in their editing. *Whit.*

Pierwszy Dzień Wolności
(First Day of Liberty)
(POLISH—SCOPE)

Cannes, May 24.
Polski State Film release of Studio production. With Tadeusz Womnicki, Beata Tysziewicz, Mieczyslaw Kalenik, Mieczyslaw Stoor, Elzbieta Czyzewska, Tadeusz Fijewski. Directed by Alexandre Ford. Screenplay, Bohdan Czeszko from the play by Leon Kruczkowski; camera, Tadeusz Wiezan; music, Kazimierz Serocki. At Cannes Film Fest. Running Time, 95 MINS.
Jan .... Tadeusz Womnicki
Inge .... Beata Tysziewicz
Mikhail .... Mieczyslaw Kalenik
Luzie .... Elzbieta Czyzewska

A rather old fashioned study of mixed up outlooks and emotions near the end of the last war. Film insists too much on "expressionistic" and symbolical techniques which make it seem remote and without the insight into character and motives. So this looks more something for its own native play-off than for export.

A group of recently freed Polish soldiers hole up in a German town waiting to be repatriated. A German doctor has stayed to help people and one of his daughters has been raped by freed concentration camp internes. The Poles in one house take in the daughters to help the doctor.

But one of them feels that hate must pass before man can find himself again. Others think all Germans must pay. Back come the Germans and one of the girls is forced to fight alongside them and is killed by the man who abhors further fighting as the war nears its end.

Players are forced to be too talky and grandiloquent but the film does erupt into movement at times to make a potent point of war's futility and the need to understand before it can be laid to rest and man can take up other pursuits. But nothing new is said on the subject and, if it has some solid technical prowess, it all appears somewhat academic and preachy rather than incisive and probing.   *Mosk.*

What's New Pussycat?
(COLOR)

Mad Parisian farce which frequently goes overboard; grosses will depend upon names of Peter Sellers and Peter O'Toole.

Hollywood, June 19.

United Artists release of Charles K. Feldman production. Stars Peter Sellers, Peter O'Toole, Romy Schneider, Capucine, Paula Prentiss, Woody Allen, Ursula Andress; features Edra Gale, Nicole Karen, Catherine Schaake, Jess Hahn, Eleanor Hirt, Jean Paredes. Directed by Clive Donner. Screenplay, Woody Allen; camera (DeLuxe-Color), Jean Badal; music, Burt Bacharach; editor, Fergus McDonell; sound, William-Robert Sivel; art direction, Jacques Saulnier; asst. director, Enrico Isacco. Reviewed at Village Theatre, June 18, '65. Running Time, 108 MINS.

Fritz Fassbender	Peter Sellers
Michael James	Peter O'Toole
Carol Warner	Romy Schneider
Renee Lefebvre	Capucine
Liz	Paula Prentiss
Victor Shakapopolis	Woody Allen
Rita	Ursula Andress
Anna Fassbender	Edra Gale
Jacqueline	Catherine Schaake
Perry Werner	Jess Hahn
Sylvia Werner	Eleanor Hirt
Tempest O'Brien	Nicole Karen
Marcel	Jean Paredes
Philippe	Michel Subor
Charlotte	Jacqueline Fogt
Car Renter	Robert Rollis
Gas Station Operator	Daniel Emilfork
Jean, His Friend	Louis Falavigna
Etienne	Jacques Balutin
Emma	Annette Poivre
Beautiful Nurse	Sabine Sun
Fassbender's Children	Jean Yves Autrey, Pascal Wolf, Nadine Papin
Miss Lewis	Tanya Lopert
Durell	Colin Drake
Nelly	Norbert Terry
Nash	F. Medard
Fat Man	Gordon Felio
The Nutcracker	Louise Lasser

"What's New Pussycat?" is designed as a zany farce, as wayout as can be reached on the screen. It's all that, and more . . . it goes overboard in pressing for its goal and consequently suffers from over-contrived treatment. That there are laughs, sometimes plenty of them, there can be no denying, undeniable clever bits of business, and the windup is fast and crazy. Its success, however, will depend mostly upon the draw of its two top stars, Peter Sellers and Peter O'Toole.

The Charles K. Feldman production, given lush color packaging and filmed in Paris and the French countryside, is peopled exclusively by mixed-up characters. Sellers is a Viennese professor to whom O'Toole, editor of a Parisian fashion magazine, goes for psychiatric help in solving his women problems, which, to his unrestrained delight, keep piling up as he finds more pretty girls. He's in love with Romy Schneider, who teaches languages, but, as he explains to her, he isn't ready yet for marriage because he still has a lot of living to do. On his part, Sellers has his own problems, a jealous wife and a roving eye which keeps getting him into trouble.

Original screenplay by Woody Allen, who also enacts one of the principals — an un-dresser for strippers at the Crazy Horse Saloon and similarly afflicted with girl troubles—provides a field day for gagmen, who seldom miss a trick in inserting a sight gag. Clive Donner's direction is quick to seize upon a situation or possibility and makes best use of the crazy-quilt format offered him. Most monumental task of all probably was handed Fergus McDonell as editor, to try to make some semblance of continuity in his cutting. Very often, there is none, but this fits into the scheme of things.

Two top stars come off none too happily in their characterizations. Sellers' nuttiness knows no bounds as he speaks with a thick German accent, and O'Toole proves his forte in drama rather than comedy. Miss Schneider, however, is pretty and winsome as she keeps house for O'Toole, never at home, and she's his "Pussycat." So is every other gal O'Toole takes up with .

Trio of femmes who chase O'Toole have the proper looks and furnish as much glamour as any one man can take. Capucine is a beautiful neurotic whose icy exterior hides her passionate interest in men, O'Toole in particular. Paula Prentiss is a sensational stripper whom O'Toole takes home to listen to her poetry, always taking an overdose of sleeping pills. (Typical of picture is a remark made to O'Toole ",Will you excuse me, I'm going to the bathroom to take an overdose of sleeping pills"). Ursula Andress, a sex-mad parachutist, targets on O'Toole after she lands in his car from the sky ,and spends most of her time in a stunningly skimpy Bikini. The three, with Miss Schneider, complicate O'Toole's peace of mind considerably when he finds himself with them in a French country hotel where action becomes strictly bedroom farve.

Further contributions to senselessness of goings-on are made by Allen, the un-dresser; Edra Gale, Seller's would-be "Brunhilde" spouse; Nicole Karen, one of the many girls-at-large; Jean Paredes, Capucine's madly-jealous husband. Music score by Burt Bacharach superbly backs the action and Jean Badal's tint photography is luscious. Art direction by Jacques Saulnier, with Charles Merangel acting as set decorator, is outstanding, and costumes by Mia Fonssagrives and Vicki Tiel eye-filling. Richard Talmadge is credited as second unit director.   *Whit.*

Blood and Black Lace
(COLOR)

Okay Italian-made (in English) mystery, for double billing.

Hollywood, June 10.

Allied Artists release of Lou Moss production. Stars Cameron Mitchell, Eva Bartok; features Thomas Reiner, Arianna Gorini, Dante de Paolo, Mary Arden, Franco Ressel. Directed by Mario Bava. Story-screenplay, Marcel Fondat, Joe Barilla, Mario Bava; camera (Technicolor), Herman Tarzana; art direction, Harry Brest; editor, Mark Suran; music, Carl Rustic. Reviewed at Pix Theatre, June 9, '65. Running Time, 88 MINS.

Max Marlan	Cameron Mitchell
Christina	Eva Bartok
Inspector Silvester	Thomas Reiner
Nicole	Arianna Gorini
Frank Scalo	Dante De Paolo
Peggy	Mary Arden
Marquis Richard Morell	Franco Ressel
Taoli	Claude Dantes
Isabella	Lea Krugher
Marco	Massimo Righi
Zanchin	Guiliano Raffaelli
Clarice	Hariette White Medin

Produced in both Italian and English versions, the Woolner Bros. acquired latter for release in this country through Allied Artists. Film, handsomely produced by Lou Moss, is an okay mystery with a few chills here and there to keep the cash customers well enough occupied and qualifies for the double-bill market.

Title pretty well covers the subject, each of a bevy of pretty fashion models of a smart salon in Rome meeting a bloody end by an unknown assassin whose face is always covered by a stocking mask. Identity is a well-kept secret until closing sequences. Only names known to American audiences are Cameron Mitchell and Eva Bartok (latter the Hungarian actress), most of cast being foreign but well equipped for their respective roles. Script by trio of writers doesn't always bear analysis but generally progresses the plot.

Film, processed in Technicolor, is backgrounded by expensive sets which add a certain quality not always distinguishable in films of this sort. Harry Brest's art direction is tops, and color photography by Herman Tarzana takes advantage of his backdrops. Mario Bava's direction sets a grim mood never relinquished and music score by Carl Rustic maintains this atmosphere.

Mitchell's role, although playing a key character, is small, but well played, and Miss Bartok sometimes is luscious-looking as contessa-owner of the fashion salon. Glamor is provided by Arianna Gorini, Mary Arden and Lea Krugher, among the murdered models, and Thomas Reiner portrays an inspector.   *Whit.*

Ludwig von Beethoven
(E. GERMAN DOCUMENTARY)

Melbourne, June 15.

DEFA release. Directed by Jaap. Screenplay, S. Hermlin; camera, E. Nitzchmann. Reviewed at St. Kilda Palais, Melbourne Film Fest. Running Time, 92 MINS.

This is rather a wonderful documentary film sentered around existing documents and letters of and relating to German composer Beethoven. It was filmed against a background of the actual buildings in which he dwelt or visited, the streets he walked and countryside familiar to him. There is a commentary in English.

It is all fascinating material which is never boring, depending all the time on contemporary drawings and portraits of the famed composer, with a good slice of Napoleona. Personal side of Beethoven's life is barely touched upon, perhaps because too little is really known.

Interwoven through it all are the highlights of his music but in the background, and excerpts from his operas. This is a good fill-in on the composer, and well photographed. Only at the very end does it seem slightly at variance, when closeups of famous interpreters of his work are shown.   *Stan.*

Nirjan Saikate
(INDIAN)

Melbourne, June 15.

New Theatres (Exhibitors) Private Ltd. release. Stars Anil Chatterji, Sharmila Tagore. Written and directed by Tapan Sinha. Editor, Subodh Roy, camera, Bimal Mukerji; music, Kalipada Sen. Reviewed at St. Kilda Palais, Melbourne Film Fest. Running Time, 130 MINS.

Like most Indian pix seen in the Western World, this one proceeds at a leisurely pace, entertaining as it meanders along, even with the inclusion of a few songs and a dance sequence.

On a train bound for Puri, a young writer is befriended by four widows of varying ages and a young girl related to them who has been jilted. At Puri, he becomes more and more involved with the widows and the young girl.

Despite its length, this vehicle is never dull. The principal and supporting characters are all well drawn. They are interestingly presented with just a hint of Oriental mystery attached to them. Actual background of the young man himself is neither properly revealed nor how he gets his money to travel. But the film possesses such charm one doesn't think of this until later.

Many of the scenes are localled outdoors—some at the ancient temple of Konarak. Many of them are beautiful.

Most of the acting is sustained at a high level, although the actor playing the young writer could have been stronger. There are several outstanding cameo performances.   *Stan.*

Li Shuang-Shuang
(RED CHINA)

Melbourne, June 15.

China Film Distribution & Exhibition Corp. release of Haiyen Film Studio production. Features Chang Jui-fang, Chung Hsing-huo, Chung Wenjung, Liu Fei, Tsui Wen-shun. Directed by Lu Jen. Screenplay, Li Chun; camera, Chu Ching; music, Hsiang Yi. Reviewed at St. Kilda Palais, Melbourne Film Fest. Running Time, 104 MINS.

(English Subtitles)

This is a happy good-natured film in which the villians are pale grey and with little difficulty see their mistakes by the end of the pic. It shows the Chinese countryside and depicts clashes in a people's commune, particularly between a peasant and his wife, Shuang-Shuang. She is very outspoken and with the right Communist ideals wants to run the commune. In a nice way she points out faults to others, who, of course in the end see the wisdom of it all.

However, this causes a slight rift between Shuang-Shuang and her husband, but because they are in love, all is well at the end. The film moves at a leisurely pace, but the light humor is always near the surface. This seems to be a good sidelight on conditions in the countryside of modern day China. Acting is convincing with Chung Hsing-huo and Chang Jui-fang as the peasant and his wife respectively, especially good. Maybe at times this is all a little naive. Western audiences may not prove too guilable enough to swallow "the Party Line" that ultimately comes through. *Stan.*

The Family Jewels
(COLOR)

Mild comedy with Jerry Lewis playing seven roles. Performances, production and direction all good. Okay prospects in Lewis situations.

Hollywood, June 18.

Paramount Pictures release of Jerry Lewis Production, written (with Bill Richmond), produced, directed by Lewis. Stars Lewis; features Sebastian Cabot, Donna Butterworth. Camera (Technicolor), W. Wallace Kelley; editors, Arthur P. Schmidt, John Woodcock; music, Pete King; sound, Hugo and Charles Grenzbach; art dircteion, Hal Pereira, Jack Poplin; asst. director, Ralph Axness. Reviewed at Picwood Theatre, L.A., June 17, '65. Running Time, **98 MINS.**

Willard Woodward; Everett, James, Capt. Eddie, Julius, Bugsy, Skylock Peyton	Jerry Lewis
Dr. Matson	Sebastian Cabot
Donna Peyton	Donna Butterworth
Clown	Gene Baylos
Pilot	Milton Frome
Joe	Herbie Faye
Plane Passengers	Marjorie Bennett, Frances Lax, Ellen Corby, Renie Riano, Jesslyn Fax
Pool Hall Owner	Robert Strauss
Attorneys	Jay Adler, Neil Hamilton

"The Family Jewels" puts Jerry Lewis in multiple role of contenders for guardianship of moppet and her inherited fortune. Episodic script hits some highs in satire and low comedy. Players and direction are good, but film shapes up as comparatively mild entry even in dedicated Lewis situations, where okay returns seem likely for Paramount release.

The Lewis-Bill Richmond script focuses on precocious Donna Butterworth, cute nine-year-old orphan with $30,000,000 in trust to be administered by the uncle whom she picks. Jay Adler and Neil Hamilton make okay lawyers who explain provisions of late pop's will, triggering a visit to each uncle with family chauffeur Lewis.

Comic's tour de farce effort comes off unevenly. As sympathetic but bumbling chauffeur, he foils a bank-truck holdup avoids numerous murder attempts, and keeps plot thread together in good form. So-so bits include a San Diego ferryboat skipper, also a cynical and unpatriotic circus clown quitting the biz for Swiss tax haven.

More successful is his limning of crazy photographer who can't decide on setups. Standout is Lewis as screwy aviator who attempts to haul to Chi a group of five motorcycle-riding biddies, played well by Marjorie Bennett, Frances Lax, Ellen Corby, Renie Riano and Jesslyn Fax. Very good satire on in-flight pix involves Anne Baxter appearing in film clip from "Sustenance," a gag scene in which banquet guests, silverware and food slide about with aircraft motion.

Sebastian Cabot brightens as foil for Lewis' detective-uncle who gets hung up in zany pool game with Robert Strauss, while gangster-uncle bit is amusing. The little gal makes the right choice, natch. Lewis injects two clever inside plugs for son Gary Lewis (with latter's Playboys, current pop wax faves), surprise bits which are effective.

Director Lewis drew good performances from all thesps, and emphasized sight over sound in his many vignettes. Arthur P. Schmidt as editorial supervisor (also associate producer), and John Woodcock have trimmed to 98 minutes, with a bit more tightening possibly needed in Lewis' solo sequences. W. Wallace Kelley's Technicolor camera is mobile and visually interesting throughout.

Producer Lewis has coordinated well all other technical pros, including Hugo and Charles Grenzbach's sound and Edith Head's costumes. Tunesmith Pete King has bolstered audio interest with some character themes. *Murf.*

The Fascist
(Il Federale)
(ITALIAN)

Interesting, frequently funny, tale of an Italian Fascist whose small exposure to democracy is enough to humanize him.

Embassy Pictures release of an Isidoro Broggi-Renato Libassi production. Stars Ugo Tognazzi; features Georges Wilson, Mireille Granelli, Stefania Sandrelli, Gianrico Tedeschi, Elsa Vazzoler, Franco Giacobini. Directed by Luciano Salce. Screenplay gy Salce and Castellano-Pipolo. No other credits provided. Reviewed at New York, June 17, '65. Running Time, **102 MINS.**

(English Subtitles)

Italian import by Embassy Pictures, screened for the trades on June 16, opened next day at Embassy's Lincoln Arts Theatre. Apparently because of rush screening and booking, credits provided reviewers were incomplete and characters not identified. This happens frequently at the various distribs with imported product, plus fact that printed credits rarely match those shown on the screen. Inquiry in N.Y. into European background of the films more often than not is fruitless.

"Il Federale" (which has also been interpreted as "The Boondoggler") is an introspective look, with humor, at the political chaos that gripped Italy during World War II. While producers Isidoro Broggi and Renato Libassi are only surface critical of their country's Fascist past, they do at least deal with it in human terms that make their treatment dramatically acceptable.

Ugo Tognazzi and, to only a slightly lesser degree, French actor Georges Wilson (who's equally at home in Italian films) are the protagonists in a frequently funny, if logically inept, tale of a young Fascist, indoctrinated to the point of being a fanatic, who is given the mission of capturing and bringing in an elderly but politically dangerous anti-Fascist philosopher, Professor Bonafe (Wilson) who is a potential future president of Italy (if and when the Allies arrive). When Cpl. Arcovazzi (Tognazzi) is dispatched to capture him, he's told that, if successful, it may mean promotion to a Federale (a Fascist commissioned officer).

While possessing more spirit than intelligence, Tognazzi does capture his prisoner and the principal plotline deals with their adventures enroute to Rome. Their mishaps are more at Tognazzi's expense than Wilson's, making it hard for him to tell which is prisoner and which is guard. After being robbed by a young girl, they encounter German troops (who capture both men and turn Tognazzi into a one-man labor battalion).

Wilson engineers their escape but they almost get recaptured by two teenage Fascists. Tognazzi's cruelest blow, however, is finding that a Fascist poet, his teacher and idol during his political indoctrination, has chosen to pretend to be dead (while actually hidden in his own attic). The incongruous pair finally arrive in Rome on June 4, 1944. Tognazzi's disillusionment continues. Wearing a Federale uniform, sold him by the same teenager who had earlier stolen his clothes, he finds it a potential death sentence when they encounter some partisans. After he's brutally beaten, Wilson gets him away, gives him his own civilian clothing and turns him loose—still a Fascist but with his beliefs fast fading.

The two men are excellent contrasts. The virile Tognazzi, the epitome of Fascist conceit, obtuse and boorish, is still human enough to comprehend what is happening around him. Wilson, the idealist, also learns from his captor-companion. One of the best bits in the film is near the end. Passing American troops toss packages of cigarettes at their feet. Tognazzi's national pride makes him reject the gift. Wilson, understanding, hands over his last bit of paper, torn from a book of poetry which the two have been using for cigarette paper during their hazardous journey.

Other than a couple of minor incidents, played for laughs, there's no attempt to introduce sex into the plot although a thread of a romance is hinted at between Tognazzi and the niece of the defecting poet.

Luciano Salce, who directed as well as collaborated on the screenplay, contributes principally a series of plot fragments to his two able leads and lets them run with it. Frequent laughs are less the material than what Tognazzi does with it. *Robe.*

The Bounty Killer
(Color-Techniscope)

Off-trail Western brings back numerous oldtime actors from oaters of past era, and their presence plus Dan Duryea should help b.o., despite downgrading of action and downbeat ending.

Hollywood, June 16.

Embassy Pictures release of Alex Gordon-Premiere Productions; executive producer, Pat B. Rooney; producer, Alex Gordon. Stars Dan Duryea, Rod Cameron, Audrey Dalton; features Richard Arlen, Buster Crabbe, Fuzzy Knight, Johnny Mack Brown, Peter Duryea, Bob Steele, Eddie Quillan, Norman Willis, Edmund Cobb, Duane Ament, Grady Sutton, Emory Parnell, Daniel J. White, I. Stanford Jolley, John Reach, Red Morgan, Dolores Domasin, Dudley Ross, Ronn Delanor, Tom Kennedy, G. M. (Bronco Billy) Anderson. Directed by Spencer Gordon Bennett. Screenplay by R. Alexander and Leo Gordon; camera (Technicolor), Frederick E. West; music, Ronald Stein; editor, Ronald Sinclair; sound, Harry Lindgren. Reviewed at Joe Shore projection room, June 16, '65. Running Time, **93 MINS.**

Willie Duggan	Dan Duryea
Johnny Liam	Rod Cameron
Carole	Audrey Dalton
Ridgeway	Richard Arlen
Mike Clayman	Buster Grabbe
Luther	Fuzzy Knight
Sheric Green	Johnny Mack Brown
Youth	Peter Durysa
Red	Bob Steele
Pianist	Eddie Quillan
Hank Willis	Norman Willis
Townsman	Edmund Cobb
Ben Liam	Duane Ament
Minister	Grady Sutton
Sam	Emory Parnell
Marshal Davis	Daniel J. White
Sheriff Jones	I. Stanford Jolley
Jeb	John Reach
Seddon	Red Morgan
Waitress	Dolores Domasin
Indian	Dudley Ross
Joe	Ronn Delanor
Waiter	Tom Kennedy

Alex Gordon's "The Bounty Killer" is unusual western. Even though it brings back to screen many stars and featured players from era of Saturday matinee oaters, story is more akin to psychological westerns in vogue on tv several seasons ago. Hero's death makes for downbeat ending and action comes only fitfully. B.O. appeal rests with value of Dan Duryea's name on marquee and such attraction as may lie with once-familiar names of Johnny Mack Brown, Bob Steele, Richard Arlen, Fuzzy Knight, Buster Crabbe and numerous others.

Generally-imaginative script by R. Alexander and Leo Gordon has Duryea as mild-mannered Easterner who wipes out bandit gang by fluke, becomes pro bounty hunter and then drunken killer when sidekick (beardless Fuzzy Knight) is slain. During process he loses girl (Audrey Dalton) because of enmity of her father (Arlen).

Unusual casting twist has Duryea's son, Peter, portraying youth who kills him at end to launch own bounty-hunting career, but it's doubtful audience will be aware of relationship, because young Duryea's role is not identified in credits.

Elder Duryea handles thesping with usual competence and oldtimers play roles as if pleased to be back. Some of dialog echoes from past. Duryea, while vowing to get Knight's killer, grits, "I'll take them!" Miss Dalton shakes head sadly and comments, "You've changed, Willie." But greatest drawback results from scripters and director Spencer Gordon Bennett permitting long, talky stretches and generally unsatisfactory showdowns.

Production values, particularly Frederick E. West's Technicolor photography, are excellent in main. Art Director Don Ament's backdrop of mountain scenery, is too obviously painted, however. Editing by Ronald Sinclair has no lapses and Ronald Stein's score is properly dramatic. *Hogg.*

Saul E David
(Saul and David)
(ITALO-SPANISH)
(Color)

Rome, June 15.
S.P.F. release of a San Paolo Films (Rome)-San Pablo Films (Madrid) coproduction. Features Norman Wooland, Gianni Garko, Luz Marques, Eliza Cegani, Pilar Clemens, Virgilio Teveira, Anthony J. Mayans, Carlos Casaravilla, Marco Paoletti, Stefy Lang, Paolo Gozlino, Dante Maggio. Directed by Marcello Baldi. Screenplay, Baldi, Ottavio Jemma, Flavio Nicolini, Tonino Guerra; camera (Eastmancolor), Marcello Masciocchi; music, Teo Usuelli; editor, Giuliana Attenni. At Supercinema, Rome. Running Time, 118 MINS.

Saul	Norman Wooland
David	Gianni Garko
Abigail	Luz Marques
Akhinoam	Elisa Cegani
Mikol	Pilar Clemens
Abner	Virgilio Texeira
Jonathan	Anthony J. Mayans
Samuel	Carlos Casaravilla
David as boy	Marco Paolotti
Goliath	Stefy Long
Joab	Paolo Gozlino
Abdon	Dante Maggio

This Biblical spectacle is played straight, meaning it hews rather close to the Scriptures and eschews the usually inserted sex angles and fillips. Yet the pic contains some powerful performances, plenty of physical values, enough action for proper pace and other attributes to overcome these commercial weaknesses as well as lack of names. It shapes therefore as a general audience pic for all markets with ageless handling and content giving it staying power. Religioso market is another factor in the picture's future.

Slow to build, this tale concentrates on the agitated relationship between Saul and his young rival for the throne of Israel, David. Because of Saul's jealous obsession and fear, rivalry comes to a dramatic head with David exiling himself, Saul losing a vital battle with the Philistines and, unaided by David, committing suicide. Few dramatic highlights in Biblical story are left untold, from the slaying of Goliath by a youthful David to the brutal extermination —on orders from a half-crazed Saul —of the High Priests to the brilliantly staged final battle, a highlight in this pic and one of best seen in this kind of film.

The average cinemagoer may argue that nearly 2-hour pic contains too many dialogued scenes, and some trimming here and there would enhance its chances greatly. But the lines are intelligent, literal and ably tendered in the Italo-dubbed version seen (film was shot for the most part in English).

Also, some marquee lure would have helped pic along its commercial ways. But all thesps, from Norman Wooland's properly crazed Saul to Gianni Garko's strong, yet pensive David to other solid performances by Elisa Cegani (Akhinoam), Pilar Clemens (Mikol), Vigilio Texeira (Abner), Marco Paoletti (David as a boy) and Luz Marques move through their paces with determination.

Marcello Baldi has worked wonders in giving this physical stature on a limited budget (undisclosed, but reported at anywhere from £500,000 to $1,000,000). It certainly is on a par, if not often superior, to massively budgeted spectacles of the recent past. He has concentrated on drama, internal and external, in the physical and mental battle waged by the two tormented men, and often inserted, or highlighted, their symbolic and/or present-day significance. Nor has he avoided or toned down violence: the David-Goliath scene, the final battle, the slaying of the priests and other moments up to Saul's tragic suicide, leave nothing to the imagination in the explicit force with which they are portrayed.

A special nod must go to Marcello Masciocchi's splendid Eastmancolor lensing, much of it vividly catching the landscapes of Spain. Costumes, music, and other credits are in keeping with an impressively produced pic. *Hawk.*

Having A Wild Weekend
(BRITISH—MUSIC)

While strong on music in the Dave Clark Five fashion and some good chase scenes, film has little else to offer. Could carry its weight in teenage market.

Warner Bros. release of a David Deutsch production. Stars The Dave Clark Five (David Clark, Lenny Davidson, Nick Huxley, Mike Smith, Denis Payton); features Barbara Ferris, David Lodge, Robin Bailey, Yootha Joyce. Directed by John Boorman. Screenplay, Peter Nichols; camera, Manny Wynn; editor, Gordon Pilkington; sound, Ernie Cousins; background music by Dave Clark Five. Reviewed at the Garrick Theatre, N.Y., June 17, '65. Running Time, 91 MINS.

Steve	Dave Clark
Lenny	Lenny Davidson
Rick	Rick Huxley
Mike	Mike Smith
Denis	Denis Payton
Dinah	Barbara Ferris
Louis	David Lodge
Guy	Robin Bailey
Nan	Yootha Joyce
Zissell	David De Kayser
Whiting	Robert Lang
Duffle	Clive Swift
Beatnik	Ronald Lacey
Grey	Hugh Walters
Hardingford	Michael Gwynn
Mrs. Stone	Marianne Stone
Barker	Donald Morley
Officer	Michael Blakemore
Asst. Director	Julian Holloway

Apparently producer David Deutsch's idea was to try for the same success formula that made "A Hard Day's Night" more than just a film about a rock 'n roll group. He hasn't been too successful in trying to turn the Dave area of bod will.

Clark Five into actors but has, as cinematic insurance, packed enough action into his "chase" film to keep older members of the audience from squirming.

According to credits, "Weekend" is a first-time effort for screenwriter Peter Nichols, director John Boorman and several members of the cast, including the stars. This is very easy to believe although Deutsch's reason for using them, "young people should make a film about youth," is dubious logic. Why so? Inexperience is never superior to experience. He'd have been better served to have found a British version of George Abbott.

A more serious error in showmanly judgment, though, is his failure to properly supervise the poor editing and sound recording on his film. Gorden Pilkington's scissors have cut so erratically that one even hears characters answer questions that have been chopped out. Ernie Cousins' sound, which might have done a great service in covering up for the poorly-enunciated dialog, is also very poor. Many characters speak in such inaudible monotones that it is frequently impossibly to follow the storyline, as simple as it is.

Reported as having been made entirely on location (the exteriors are frequently lovely and always interesting), the soundtrack, other than the music, must have been recorded at the same time. Extraneous noises drown out conversations, characters mutter or speak with heads averted. On the other hand, the music, which must have been added later in a sound studio, comes over loud (too loud) and clear.

Title stems from an extended chase sequence that makes up most of the plot and provides the action. Barbara Ferris, a pretty blonde model, is bored with her career and talks Clark into escaping with her for a few days. The other members of the quintet, and, shortly thereafter, the rest of the cast, follow in quick pursuit. Her manager (David Lodge), the film's "heavy," tells the press that she has been kidnapped.

The pair, after losing their car, are picked up by a strange couple (Robin Bailey and Yootha Joyce) whose actions are never clarified (their lines being generally unintelligible) and with whom the youngsters attend a costume ball before the chase resumes. Tale ends with model resigning herself to the boredom of success while Clark and friends head for Spain (or a sequel?).

Other than the musical five, the cast is unknown, even for an English film. Selling will have to be done on strength of musicians' reputation with teenage market. The eight tunes they do as background music should have some success as a sound track album.

Cameraman Manny Wynn, who did some beautiful work on "The Girl With The Green Eyes," provides some fresh views of the English countryside although his camera tends to linger, occasionally, on a bit of architecture or scenery which, however photogenic, has nothing to do with the plot. His interiors are less successful, due, possibly, to difficulty of lighting actual locations. *Robe.*

That Funny Feeling
(TECHNICOLOR)

Glossy romantic mixup. Sound dualler with bright chances for Sandra Dee, Bobby Darin and Donald O'Connor.

London. June 18.
Rank release of a Universal-International picture Stars. Sandra Dee, Bobby Darin, Donald O'Connor. Features Nita Talbot, Larry Storch, Leo G. Carroll. Produced by Harry Keller. Directed by Richard Thorpe. Screenplay, David R. Schwartz; camera (Technicolor), Clifford Stine; editor, Gene Milford; music, Darin. Reviewed at Rank Private Theatre, London. Running Time, 93 MINS.

Joan Howell	Sandra Dee
Tom Milford	Bobby Darin
Harvey Granson	Donald O'Connor
Audrey	Nita Talbot
Luther	Larry Storch
Officer Broker	James Westerfield
O'Shea	Leo G. Carroll
Lennie	Gregory Shannon
Bartender	Robert Strauss
Bartender No. 2	Ben Lessy
Mr. Scruggs	Frank Killmond

This is a glossy, contrived, romantic comedy mixup which is running as a dualler in Britain and that's about its strength, despite some cheery performances by the stars. Sandra Dee, an aspiring young actress, works as a hired maid while waiting for a thesp break. Bobby Darin is a young publisher whose apartment is on Miss Dee's books, though they have never met. The two keep bumping into each other around New York and, striking up an acquaintance he insists on escorting her to her home. Reluctant to take him to the poky apartment she shares with a room mate, she takes advantage of the fact that she believes Darin to be away on a business trip (which, for plot purposes, has natch, been cancelled), and takes him back to his own luxury pad.

Introduced, he makes no sign of surprise, and Miss Dee and her girl friend move into his apartment, while he stays with his partner (Donald O'Connor). Latter is reluctant to become involved, but is worried about some valuable paintings that he has stashed away in Darin's apartment to avoid a handover in his pending divorce case. So, though he thinks Miss Dee is planning to steal the paintings, he is forced to keep mum under threat from Darin. This brief, inadequate outline of the situation indicates the tortuous contrivance of David R. Schwartz's screenplay.

Still, if not taken over seriously, it provides some fun and games. Miss Dee bubbles effectively, Darin handles an undemanding role well and O'Connor gives another of his easy, assured comedy performances. Best work, however, comes from Nita Talbot as Miss Dee's wry, dry, down-to-earth buddy, Larry Storch as a Method actor and a few bits from James Westerfield as a bewildered cop, Leo G. Carroll as a philosophical pawnbroker and Robert Strauss as an inquisitive bartender.

Richard Thorpe's direction is straightforward, interior sets are sleek and colorful and other credits are okay in an innocuous comedy that won't set any boxoffices alight but won't harm the week's take at most houses. *Rich.*

Una Pistola Per Ringo
(A Pistol for Ringo)
(ITALO-SPANISH-COLOR)
(Song)

Rome, June 15.

Cineriz release of an Alberto Pugliese-Luciano Ercoli Spanish-Italian coproduction for P.C.M. (Rome)-Balcazar Films (Barcelona). With Montgomery Wood (Giuliano Gemma), Fernando Sancho, Allie Amond (Lorella de Luca), Nieves Navarro, Antonio Casas, George Martin. Written and directed by Duccio Tessari. Camera (Technicolor), Francisco Marin; music, Ennio Morricone. At Rex, Rome. Running Time, 95 MINS.

Ringo .... Montgomery Wood
Sancho .... Fernando Sancho
Ruby .... Lorella de Luca
Dolores .... Nieves Navarro
Ruby's Father .... Antonio Casas
Sheriff .... George Martin

Capably fashioned oater, made in Italy and Spain by Italo writer-director Duccio Tessari, who also was involved on writing side of "Fistful of Dollars" the trend-setter of the booming local genre. Looks a financially sound entry on action and western spoof pegs for many world markets which still feel a desire for such fare.

Principally involved are an opportunist gunman, Ringo, who for coin helps justice triumph over a gang of Mexican-styled bandits, led by a rotundly villanous Fernando Sancho. There are plenty of cliche plot strings here and there, but generally these are played for chuckles via an exaggerated spoof approach which makes them acceptable. There's never a silent moment, with gunfire filling most of screen time and Ennio Morricone's lilting score the rest. Action, led by an acrobatic Montgomery Wood (Italo thesp Giuliano Gemma), is likewise in abundance to keep pace sprightly almost all the way.

What unfortunately lessens film's impact is generally dispersed character delineation and construction. For example, Wood is briefly introed, but only picked up much later, never really building into the author's intended stature as a character. Instead it's Spanish thesp Fernando Sancho, who—also thanks the actor's mugging ability—thefts most scenes.

Remainder of the cast is capable, from comely Allie Amond (Italo actress Lorella de Luca) to Antonio Casas, as her aristocratic father, to others in large and colorful cast. Tessari has also chosen his locations well. Apart from a few anachronisms and elements disturbing to attuned westernophiles, its physically a plushy outfitted pic, with Francisco Marin's Technicolor-Technirama camera providing a major assist.

"Angel Face" title song by Ennio Morricone, looks to sell locally, especially on the heels of the same author's hit, "Fistful" score.

Hawk.

The Eye of the Needle
(La Smania Andosso)
(ITALIAN-FRENCH)

Eldorado Pictures International release of MEC Cinematografica-Les Films Agiman production. Features Vittorio Gassman, Annette Stroyberg, Gerard Blain, by Marcello Andrei. Screenplay, G. Man-Nino Castalnuovo, Gino Cervi. Directed

gione, A. Bevilacqua, T. Dembi and Andrei, from story by G. Berto, D. Troizi; camera, Riccardo Pallottini; music, Carlo Rustichelli. Reviewed at New York, June 18, '65. Running Time, 97 MINS.

Lawyer Mazzaro ...... Vittorio Gassman
Rosaria .... Annette Stroyberg
Toto ....
Nicola .... Nino Castalnuovo
Lawyer D'Angelo .... Gino Cervi
Carmelina .... Mariangela Giordano
Don Salvatore .... Ernesto Calindri
Don Calo .... Leopoldo Trieste
Don Luigino .... Umberto Spadaro
Don Nene .... Ignazio Balzamo
Police Brigadier .... Alfredo Varelli
Za Santa .... Carla Calo
Za Rita .... Rina Franchetti

This import, which opened Monday (21) at New York's Cinema II, deals with that favorite subject of Italian filmmakers — the deflowering of Sicilian womanhood. As the filmmakers do not take the subject too seriously, it is doubtful that the average audience will, e i t h e r, although there's some question as to whether "Eye of the Needle" was intended to be a comedy or a social commentary.

Although Vittorio Gassman gets top billing in the film, his role of a lawyer defending one of the deflower-ers is actually a supporting part and his performance rather disappointing.

Gerard Blain and Nino Castelnuovo play the guilty pair of Sicilian males who compromise Annette Stroyberg and find themselves being pursued by both the shotgun-bearing f a t h e r of the maiden (Umberto Spadaro) and the local police (who get no help from the villagers who'd rather do things their own way, or the way of the Mafia). When the boys' parents bring in lawyers (Gassman and Gino Cervi) further controversy results.

The manner in which they're saved, the lady's honor restored and the Sicilian way of life left undisturbed (until the next film) is the principal story. Individually, no one in the cast is truly outstanding but director Marcello Andrei has, luckily, found character types who appear Sicilian to the core, or at least skin-deep. The ending fritters away in a series of loose ends but there are enough glimpses at an almost unbelievable way of life to keep the viewer interested. Not so much in whether the heroine will be avenged (she's much too pretty to leave little doubt) but whether the magistrate or the Mafia will come out on top.

Robe.

John F. Kennedy:
Years of Lightning,
Day of Drums
(COLOR)

Paris, June 22.

Paramount release of USIA-George Stevens Jr. production. Written and directed by Bruce Herschenson. Music, Herschenson; researched by Gene Evans. Commentary spoken by Gregory Peck. At Elysees, Paris. Running Time, 85 MINS.

USIA-compiled feature pic, detailing mainly the late President Kennedy's presidential character, with a few slants on his private life, already has played at two Continental film festivals, Cannes and San Sebastian. It opened commercially here via Paramount release.

Film finally obtained Congressional permission to be shown commercially in the U.S. despite

a ban on USIA pix for home consumption (on theory they may be too partisan), unless there is a consent of Congress. Now the film is free to play worldwide.

Besides its intrinsic appeal, via the Kennedy image, there are some more subjective aspects that have had some foreign critical antagonism. There appears, from here, to be a definite promise for this Government-produced vehicle on its homegrounds with some appeal abroad, due to the pros and cons on the production.

Bruce Herschenson has culled some good footage from the USIA archives, mainly centering around the so-called six points of the Kennedy presidency, the Peace Corps, the drive for Civil Rights, Communist containment, firmness on Cuba, Berlin commitment and the Alliance for Progress.

A six-way split screen has the late President making potent remarks on all of these subjects. Color is sometimes mixed with black and white. The funeral plays an ironic and poignant counterpart to the dynamic scenes of the President in action or returning to Ireland or at home with his children and wife.

There's no denying the Kennedy forcefulness, but the film sometimes is arch, grandiloquent or even too obvious in its commentary. But there is enough brittle sharpness to the talk, well delivered by Gregory Peck, to have it adequate. It is Kennedy delivering his own speeches that makes the top impact, especially his sharp, dynamic reiteration of American backing of Berlin at a speech there.

Music is somewhat too insistent but it shapes into a fitting testimonial backdrop to the tragically short Presidential term of the late President. Perhaps d o m e s t i c aspects are somewhat skimpy, except for Civil Rights, but this film apparently was aimed for abroad. So it paradoxically looks to perhaps score more profoundly at home than in foreign climes.

George Stevens Jr., USIA film director, gets production credit. He has given this scope and non-skimping time and r e s e a r c h chances that show in the general breadth in supporting imagery to its theme. Bruce Herschenson has done alright in his multiple writing, direction and music chores.

Mosk.

The Great Race
(PANAVISION-COLOR)

Whopping comedy headed for whopping grosses.

Hollywood, June 26.

Warner Bros. release of Blake Edwards production, produced by Martin Jurow. Stars Jack Lemmon, Tony Curtis, Natalie Wood; features Peter Falk, Keenan Wynn, Arthur O'Connell, Vivian Vance, Dorothy Provine, Larry Storch, Ross Martin. Directed by Blake Edwards. Screenplay, Arthur Ross; story, Edwards, Ross; camera (Technicolor), Russell Harlan; production design, Fernando Carrere; music, Henry Mancini; editor, Ralph E. Winters; sound, M. A. Merrick; asst. directors, Mickey McCardle, Jack Cunningham, Dick Landry. Reviewed at Pacific's Pantages Theatre, June 25, '65. Running Time, 157 MINS. (without intermission).

Professor Fate .... Jack Lemmon
The Great Leslie .... Tony Curtis
Maggie DuBois .... Natalie Wood
Mas .... Peter Falk
Hezekiah .... Keenan Wynn
Henry Goodbody .... Arthur O'Connell
Hester Goodbody .... Vivian Vance
Lily Olay .... Dorothy Provine
Texas Jack .... Larry Storch
Rolfe Von Stuppe .... Ross Martin
General Kuhster ..... George Macready
Frisbee .... Marvin Kaplan
Mayor of Boracho .... Hal Smith
Sheriff .... Denver Pyle
Baron's Guard .... William Bryant
Baron's Guard .... Ken Wales

"The Great Race" is a big, expensive, whopping, comedy extravaganza, long on slapstick and near-inspired tomfoolery whose tongue-in-check treatment liberally sprinkled with corn frequently garners belly laughs. Fitting patly into the current trend of big-budget funfests going into roadshow release (viz., "Those Magnificent Men in their Flying Machines" and "Hallelujah Trail"), the Blake Edwards production has already received big press coverage via Warner Bros. bringing 150 newspapermen from all over the country to Hollywood on a two-day junket, and should run up fancy grosses.

A certain nostalgic flavor is achieved, both in the 1908 period of an automobile race from New York to Paris and Edwards' broad borrowing from "The Prisoner of Zenda" tale and an earlier Laurel and Hardy comedy for some of his heartiest action. Characters carry an old-fashioned zest when it was the fashion to hiss the villain and cheer the hero. Slotting into this category, never has there been a villain so dastardly as Jack Lemmon nor a hero so whitely pure as Tony Curtis, rivals in the great race staged by an auto manufacturer to prove his car's worth. Their exploits as they vie across the world to be the first to finish under the Eiffel Tower provide the meat which the majority should find tasty and regard with word-of-mouth comment.

Handsome use is made of Panavision and Technicolor to backdrop to lavish sets and locations, many of the latter shot in Salzburg, Vienna and Paris. Edwards and Martin Jurow, who produced for Edwards, have inserted extravagant values right down the line which allow fine mounting for the daffy story-line. Extensive use of special effects, too, enable producers to insert thrills, particularly in the opening sequences when the rivalry between Curtis, as The Great Leslie, and Lemmon, Professor Fate, is established through a series of death-defying acts.

Strongly abetting the two male principals is Natalie Wood as a militant suffragette who wants to be a reporter and sells a N. Y. newspaper publisher on allowing her to enter the race and covering it for his sheet. When her Stanley Steamer breaks down on the western prairie, she latches on to Curtis for transportation, then back and forth between Curtis and Lemmon in varying aspects of the race, which she reports via carrier pigeon to her paper.

Two wondrous cars were built by studio craftsmen for the race. Curtis' is a gleaming white-and-brass phaeton, while Lemmon's appropriately is a villainous-looking square black monster which can be hoisted eight feet into the air from its six-wheel base and carries a cannon and equipment for laying down a smoke screen. To carry on the overall spirit, Curtis always is garbed in snowy white, Lemmon in black, a gent whose every tone is a snarl, who never speaks under a dirty should and whose laugh would put Woody Woodpecker to shame. Miss Wood, incidentally, in costumes designed by Edith Read, sports pink throughout, usually a vision to behold.

Tone of the picture is set by its opening, after a three-minute overture, on a series of old-fashioned credit slides. Edwards, directing from Arthur Ross' screenplay based on pair's original story, maintains this mood as the two rivals race westward from N.Y., across the Bering Strait into Siberia and thence on toward their Paris goal, with intermittent stopovers.

These include such waypoints as a western town, whose citizenry insist on delaying them for an honored-guest celebration; an ice floe in the Bering Strait; and the mythical kingdom of Carpania, where the principals participate in a "Zenda" plot. One of the wildest saloon donnybrooks ever staged (which could be trimmed considerably) highlights the stay in the western town, further highlighted by Dorothy Provine's singing of the catchy "He Shouldn't-a Hadn't-a, Oughtn'-a Swang on Me!" number.

One of the film's comedy highlights is the principals' discovery, after the two cars are snowbound next to one another in a blizzard, that they are actually adrift on ice floes and a polar bear has taken refuge in Lemmon's car. What probably stands as topmost in laughs, however, is the pie-throwing sequence in the palace kitchen, a fine Laurel and Hardy recollection of comics' "Battle of the Century," in which both Lemmon and Miss Wood are socked with dozens of pies in the face while literally thousands whiz around Curtis without a single one reaching its mark. Curtis remains untouched until a final one flung by femme star.

In the Carpania sequence Lemmon enacts a dual role, again a la "Zenda," standing in to be crowned in place of the prince who looks exactly like Professor Fate. Curtis takes over the Rassendyll character, fighting a duel vastly reminiscent of that between Ronald Colman and Douglas Fairbanks Jr., in "Zenda." Where Fairbanks jumped to safety from a window

into the moat below, Ross Martin, in a parallel character, crashes through a small boat into the moat for an additional laugh.

Finish of the race is a winner itself, and shouldn't be revealed here. Last few feet of film has Curtis and Lemmon starting another race, this time back to N.Y. This time Curtis is on his honeymoon with Miss Wood.

Lemmon's delineation is an event; he plays it dirty throughout and for huge effect. Curtis, of course, underplays for equally comic effect. For Miss Wood, the picture is a signal triumph; she pulls no punches in socking over her comedy and comes through on a par with the two male stars.

Nearing Lemmon in comic villainy is Peter Falk as his shifty henchman. Keenan Wynn, as Curtis' mechanic, is his duplicate in strength and honor. Scoring also in brief appearances are Arthur O'Connell as the publisher; Vivian Vance, his suffragette wife; Ross Martin, dashing as Curtis' dueling opponent; George Macready, as a Carpanian general; Larry Storch as a western badman. Miss Provine is immense in her singing role. Miss Wood also comes through shiningly with a song. "The Sweetheart Tree," both cleffed by Johnny Mercer and Henry Mancini.

Technical credits are standouts. Highly rating here are Russell Harlan's color photography; Fernando Carrere's production design; George James Hopkins' set decoration; Ralph E. Winters' editing; Danny Lee's special effects; M. A. Merrick's sund. Henry Mancini's music score is one of the best.
Whit.

Dani
(Time On Her Hands)
(YUGOSLAV)

Melbourne, June 22.
Avala Film production. Direction, script, camera, Alexander Petrovic. Music, V. Belosevic. With O. Vujadinovic, L. Samardzic, M. Dimitrijevic, E. Sinko. Reviewed at Melbourne Film Fest. Running Time, **90 MINS.**

(English Subtitles)
This film tells of an apparently well-to-do woman, Nina, trying to ward off boredom of a day when her husband is away. She idles her way around the shops and streets of Belgrade, visits an elderly aunt and has a chance encounter with a younger man.

Pic tends to drag a little, with no sign of a story line until the young man appears. He is very much taken with Nina, dispels her boredom, and by nightfall the encounter has taken on a deeper meaning. Eventually, she tells him she is married and the two part suddenly, both profoundly affected by their time together.

Direction is delicate and photography well above average with several unusual shots. Acting is firstrate and there is a lot of natural realism about the whole affair.
Stan.

The Sandpiper
(PANAVISION-COLOR)

Trite story of an affair between unwed nonconformist and married minister; names

of Elizabeth Taylor and Richard Burton will help at b.o.

Hollywood, June 17.
Metro release of Martin Ransohoff production. Stars Elizabeth Taylor, Richard Burton, Eva Marie Saint; features Charles Bronson, Robert Webber, Morgan Mason. Directed by Vincente Minnelli. Screenplay, Dalton Trumbo, Michael Wilson; adaptation, Irene Kamp, Louis Kamp, story, Ransohoff; camera (Metrocolor), Milton Krasner; music, Johnny Mandel; art direction, George W. Davis, Urie McCleary; sound, Franklin Milton; editor, David Bretherton; asst. director, William McGarry. Reviewed at Academy Award Theatre, June 16, '65. Running Time, 115 **MINS.**

Laura Reynolds	Elizabeth Taylor
Dr. Edward Hewitt	Richard Burton
Claire Hewitt	Eva Marie Saint
Cos Erickson	Charles Bronson
Ward Hendricks	Robert Webber
Larry Brant	James Edwards
Judge Thompson	Torin Thatcher
Walter Robinson	Tom Drake
Phil Sutcliff	Doug Henderson
Danny Reynolds	Morgan Mason

"The Sandpiper" is the story of a passing affair between an unwed nonconformist and a married Episcopalian minister who is headmaster of a private boys school attended by femme's nine-year-old son. Original by Martin Ransohoff, who produced, is trite and often ponderous in its philosophizing by the two principals, and picture is further burdened by lack of any fresh approach.

Doubtless as an exploitation gimmick, Elizabeth Taylor, who co-stars with Richard Burton, is frequently overexposed via lowcut sweaters and tops, and there is one scene where she is completely nude to the waist except for her hands barely covering focal points. Since there is no definite story point to be established by such cleavage many unquestionably will be offended by the poor taste evidenced by star. Certain stature is to be expected at the boxoffice, however, through the sock draw of the two stars, backed by quality production throughout.

Filmed in Panavision and Metrocolor in the Big Sur region of California, below Monterey, some of the most startlingly - beautiful coastline effects ever filmed lend a fascinating backdrop for yarn's unfoldment.

Under Vincente Minnelli's leisurely but dramatic direction, the Dalton Trumbo - Michael Wilson screenplay opens on Miss Taylor as a budding artist whose young son (whom she has taught herself in an attempt to keep him unsullied by outside influences) is taken away from her after lad's brush with the law and sent to the school run by Burton. Latter becomes interested in her, first as the mother of one of his charges, then all-out as a desirable woman, although ostensibly happily wed to Eva Marie Saint, mother of his twin teenage sons. Romance progresses to a realistic climax, after Burton confesses his part to his wife.

Burton probably comes off best with a more restrained performance, although Miss Taylor plays well enough a role without any great acting demands. Actor is more interesting in the opening phases of the affair as he displays a growing understanding of her philosophy and way of life, reduced to routine enactment as he becomes her lover. Femme, considerably overweight and not always showing to best advantage in

closeups, nonetheless imbues her part with intensity.

Eva Marie Saint gets the most out of a comparatively brief appearance, most of her drama confined to her reaction upon Burton's confession. Morgan Mason, son of Pamela and James Mason, makes a nice impression as Miss Taylor's son who surprisingly (to his mother) prefers school life to her teaching. Charles Bronson also scores as a beatnik sculptor, as do Robert Webber, a former lover of the artist, James Edwards as another of her beatnik friends and Torin Thatcher, the judge who orders the boy to Burton's school.

Color photography by Milton Krasner is for the most part outstanding. Art direction by George W. Davis and Urie McCleary is equally impressive, and Johnny Mandel's score is effective in maintaining mood. Richard Borden handled wildlife photography expertly, David Bretherton's editing is crisp and Irene Sharaff designed the costumes.
Whit.

Havou Banot Le'Eilat
(Girls For Eilat)
(ISRAEL)

Tel Aviv, June 17.
Carmel Films Ltd. release of Nathan Akselrod production, written and directed by Nathan Akselrod and Leo Filler. With Elisheva Michaeli, Shlomo Bar Shavit, Evva Li-on, David Ram, Yael Drouyanov, Ory Levi, Nahum Shalit and the special participation of Rephael Klatchkin. Camera, Haim Schreiber; editor, Laah Akselrod; sound, Haim Abish; music, Izhak Graziani. At Ben Yehuda Cinema. Running Time, **90 MINS.**

This local comedy, about the lack of girls in the Red sea port of Eilat, which is almost a counterpart of an American frontier-town in early pioneering days, has very little to offer to foreign audiences.

Its only merit is for a limited art cinema exposure, to people of Jewish origin, or relatives of beatniks who drifted through Eilat during the last decade. The wild beauty of the area surrounding this town is well caught, including the most southern Israeli desert and the site of King Solomon's Mines (capably shot, though in black and white only).

The plot, based on a comedy of errors, storyline, tells of an enterprising matchmaker (Rephael Klatchkin), who sees a chance to develop his trade in a city bursting with young, pioneering men—but not specially attractive to women. Elisheva Michaeli, as an energetic widow, being stood-up twice by the fellow she supposes would marry her, is hilarious, being mistaken, for an American tourst by a local gigolo.

Love interest is supplied by Evva Li-on, who was seen on Broadway as Leah in Habimah's recent tour of "The Dybbuk." It's naive and theatrical, even for Israeli patrons.
Rapo.

The Sons of Katie Elder
(PANAVISION—COLOR)

Actionful western starring John Wayne and Dean Martin; appropriate grosses indicated.

Hollywood June 22.
Paramount release of Hal Wallis production. Stars John Wayne, Dean Mar-

tin; features Martha Hyer, Michael Anderson Jr., Earl Holliman, Jeremy Slate, James Gregory, Paul Fix, George Kennedy, Dennis Hopper. Directed by Henry Hathaway. Screenplay, William H. Wright, Allan Weiss, Harry Essex; based on story by Talbot Jennings; camera (Technicolor), Lucien Ballard; music, Elmer Bernstein; editor, Warren Low; sound, Harold Lewis; art direction, Hal Pereira, Walter Tyler; asst. director, D. Michael Moore. Reviewed at Paramount Studios, June 21, '65. Running Time, 120 MINS.

John Elder	John Wayne
Tom Elder	Dean Martin
Mary Gordon	Martha Hyer
Bud Elder	Michael Anderson, Jr.
Matt Elder	Earl Holliman
Deputy Sheriff Ben Latta	Jeremy Slate
Morgan Hastings	James Gregory
Sheriff Billy Wilson	Paul Fix
Curley	George Kennedy
Dave Hastings	Dennis Hopper
Judge Harry Evers	Sheldon Allman
Minister	John Litel
Undertaker Hyselman	John Doucette
Banker Vannar	James Westerfield
Charlie Bob Striker	Rhys Williams
Charlie Biller	John Qualen
Bondie Adams	Rodolfo Acosta
Jeb Ross	Strother Martin
Storekeeper Peevey	Percy Helton
Doc Isdell	Karl Swenson

Hal Wallis returns to a field in which he particularly excels—the western (viz. "Gunfight at the O.K. Corral," 1957)—for his latest Paramount release. The John Wayne-Dean Martin starrer carries all the elements of a firstclass range drama, with lusty performances, fast gunplay and exciting action to attract and hold audiences and build to profitable returns.

The same gutty qualities that characterized the former entry are present in Talbot Jennings' story of four brothers—Wayne a notorious gunslinger, Martin a gambler—who return to their Texas home to attend their mother's funeral and remain to fight the town. Henry Hathaway's eventful direction takes full advantage of the Mexican locations (where troupe spent some weeks) to further color the moving William H. Wright-Allan Weiss-Harry Essex screenplay, and additionally sparks unfoldment with some unexpected comedy. Film moves smartly to a suspenseful climax.

Two stars are joined by Earl Holliman and Michael Anderson Jr., latter the kid brother, in family setup. The three older brothers are prodigals who left home years before and somehow forgot their mother, who always made excuses for them and pretended they were sending her money, while the youngest has been away at school. The mother is never shown, but her influence is felt throughout the film as the three seniors decide that the best monument they can erect for their mother is to send her last-born back to college, much against his wishes. Drama takes form as the brothers decide to stay long enough to learn who murdered their father six months previously, look into the situation of their mother losing her ranch to a townsman, and a grim young deputy sheriff learning Martin is wanted for murder and deciding to bring the brothers in.

Wayne delivers one of his customary rugged portrayals, a little old, perhaps, to have such a young brother as Anderson but not so old that he lacks the attributes of a gunman. He's in for one of the most sudden—and shocking—bits of action ever filmed, without a gun, he clobbers a hired gunman in the face with a club, bringing audible gasps from the preview audience which loved the moment. Martin, who plays his part with a little more humor than the others, is equally effective in a hardboiled characterization.

Holliman and Anderson both handle themselves well, the former killed in an ambush and latter badly wounded. James Gregory is the heavy, as the man who cheated the mother out of her ranch, hires George Kennedy to kill Wayne and is himself killed by Wayne in a fast climax. Both score, as do Dennis Hopper, Gregory's weak son who confesses his father's crimes to Wayne; Paul Fix, the sheriff who is murdered while trying to keep the peace; Jeremy Slate as his deputy. Martha Hyer upholds the distaff interest as a boarding-house keeper. Sheldon Allman, Rhys Williams and John Doucette contribute standout hits.

Technical departments rate highly, particularly Lucien Ballard's fluid color photograhpy. *Whit.*

A Very Special Favor
(COLOR)

Rock Hudson in another of his romantic comedies; usual response expected.

Hollywood, June 30.

Universal release of Stanley Shapiro production. Stars Rock Hudson, Leslie Caron, Charles Boyer; features Walter Slezak, Dick Shawn, Larry Storch, Nita Talbot. Directed by Michael Gordon. Screenplay, Stanley Shapiro, Nate Monaster; camera (Technicolor). Leo Tover; art direction, Alexander Goutzen, Walter Simonds; music, Vic Mizzy; editor, Russell F. Schoengarth; sound, Walter O. Watson. Corson Jowett; asst. director, Phil Bowles. Review at Hollywood Paramount Theatre. June 29, '65. Running time, 105 MINS.

Paul	Rock Hudson
Lauren	Leslie Caron
Michel	Charles Boyer
Etienne	Walter Slezak
Arnold	Dick Shawn
Harry	Larry Storch
Mickey	Nita Talbot
Mother Plum	Norma Varden
Pete	George Furth
Claude	Marcel Hillaire
Rene	Jay Novello
Bartender	Stafford Repp
Jacqueline	Danica D'Hondt
Desk Clerk	Frank De Vol
Dr. Lambert	John Harding

"A Very Special Favor" follows in the same groove as past Universal romantic comedies starring Rock Hudson and should attract the same type audiences as "Strange Bedfellows" and "Lover Come Back." It's a bit more contrived, and presses somewhat in its basic situation, but dialog often is sparkling, the action funny and generally it should run up satisfactory grosses.

Stanley Shapiro produced and Robert Arthur handled exec producer reins, same combo which turned out "Lover" and were associated on actor's "Come September." Michael Gordon, who directed Hudson in his successful "Pillow Talk," takes on same duties here with nice timing for comedy response.

The beautifully-mounted Technicolor feature draws its title from Hudson, an American oilman who bests French lawyer Charles Boyer in a Paris court case simply by romancing the femme judge, admitting to Boyer on a plane en route back to U.S. that he feels he owes him a favor by beating him at his own national sport, which he'll grant anytime latter requests.

Boyer, in N.Y. to see a daughter for first time in 25 years, sees in her, although a highly successful psychologist, a spinster with the spirit of an old maid, a woman nearly 30 who has never tasted the life her French father thinks every femme should know. He calls on Hudson to make good his offer; the favor: a romantic adventure with the daughter to help her discover herself as a woman.

Script by Shapiro and Nate Monaster develops along expected lines, with Hudson posing to Leslie Caron, the psychologist, as a man with a disturbing problem — he's irresistible to women who pursue him and he's a love toy. Consequent unfoldment becomes considerably complicated at times but winds on fulfillment of Boyer's dearest wish — marriage.

Hudson delivers one of his customary light characterizations. and Boyer as usual is suave. Miss Caron is up to demands of her part. Most outstanding work in pic, however, is contributed by Nita Talbot. a switchboard operator infatuated with Hudson, and Larry Storch, a hardboiled taxi-driver who gets drunk with Hudson en route to have it out with the psychologist, both these players scoring deliciously in smaller but effective comedy roles.

Dick Shawn, as Miss Caron's completely dominated fiance, has his amusing moments. Walter Slezak is Boyer's friend, proprietor of a restaurant where Miss Caron goes blank on champagne and is carried out by Hudson and taken to his flat. Norma Varden is in as Shawn's mother who sees Hudson lugging the unconscious femme into the elevator, good for a running gag as it's repeated.

Technically, the film is slickly turned out, with Leo Tover on color cameras, Vic Mizzy composing an appropriate music score to suit the action, Alexander Golitzen and Walter Simonds designing quality sets and Russel F. Schoengarth editing. Yves Saint Laurent created Miss Caron's smart wardrobe. *Whit.*

Dr. Who & The Daleks
(BRITISH-COLOR)

Sci-fi adventure based on popular BBC tele serial. Exploitation opportunities seem boundless and lively for juve patrons.

London, June 22.

Regal Films International release (through BLC) of an Aaru Films (Milton Subotsky-Max J. Rosenberg) production. Features Peter Cushing, Roy Castle, Jennie Linden, Roberta Tovey. Directed by Gordon Flemyng. Screenplay, Subotsky, from BBC television serial by Terry Nation; camera (Technicolor), John Wilcox; editor, Oswald Hafenrichter; music, Malcolm Lockyer; special effects, Ted Samuels. Reviewed at Studio One, London. Running time, 83 MINS.

Dr. Who	Peter Cushing
Ian	Roy Castle
Barbara	Jennie Linden
Susan	Roberta Tovey
Alydon	Barrie Ingham
Temmosus	Geoffrey Toone
Elyon	Mark Peterson
Antodus	John Bown
Ganatus	Michael Coles
Dyoni	Yvonne Antrobus

A slice of sci-fi for beginners which lacks the horror potential of many in this field, but, with its mechanical gimmickry, will ring the bell with the younger generation. There are boundless exploitation angles in this Techniscope-Technicolor pic. And in Britain, it will certainly be a big boxoffice money getter. It will be interesting to see how it stands up to stiffer Yank "sci-fi" competition, particularly since it lacks stellar pull.

Film is based on a click BBC children's tv serial, by Terry Nation and the Daleks, and this gives a presold impact on moppets. Many parents, themselves Dalek addicts, will not be loath to go along for the ride.

Absentminded professor Dr. Who (Peter Cushing) has invented Tardis, a Time and Relative Dimension in Space Machine, capable of lugging people to other worlds, in other eras. By accident. the prof. his grandaughters (Jennie Linden and Roberta Tovey) and Miss Linden's boy friend, (Roy Castle) are ejected from the earth and landed on a huge, petrified planet at a time many years back.

The planet is ravaged with radiation from a previous war and the quartet finds themselves in a struggle between the Daleks and the Thals. The Daleks, protected from radiation in an all-metal city and wearing mobile metal cones fitted with flame-guns, are determined to wipe out the gentle Thals. Dr. Who's party sides with the Thals and it has to face the threat of a neutron bomb and increased radiation. The Daleks are quashed within a comfortable 83 minutes and Dr. Who's party leave the Thals in peace ar.d set off back to the Earth.

A few more thrills and a rather more edged script (by Milton Subotsky) would have made "Dr. Who" a shade more acceptable to grownups. But the kids will revel in the fights and get kicks from the dangers facing Dr. Who and Co., from the Daleks and the threat of monsters. The Daleks are remarkably ingenious machines in the way they move and fight, though maybe they are given an excess of dialog, some of which is repetitious.

Gordon Flemyng has played his direction straight, without trying either to play down too much to the kids or to set it up for the adults. His chore would have been helped if the screenplay had had a little more bite and inventiveness.

Peter Cushing plays Dr. Who with amiable gravity. Jennie Linden is a pretty, routine heroine while Roberta Tovey is pleasantly cast as the little girl with scientific knowhow and commonsense. Roy Castle mugs and falls around a little too zestfully as the boyfriend with a fairly good sense of humor. Barrie Ingham is the stalwart leader of the Thals, a remarkable handsome bunch of stalwart young men and women decked up in wayout make-up. Yvonne Antrobus has one or two brief effective moments as his girl friend. It is only fair to say that the over genteel voice emanating from her, which raised an unwanted yock at the press preview, was dubbed and belongs to another, unidentified thesp.

Chief heroes among the technical crew are Ted Samuels, who has provided some slick special effects, and the team responsible for manipulating the Daleks with such mobility. The deep, growling voices used by the Daleks has sometimes defeated soundmixer Buster Ambler. Though much of the film's exterior footage smacks of studio, art director Bill Constable has done a commendable job. Malcolm Lockeer's score is useful and John Wilcox's Technicolor lensing is variable in color tone.

Rich.

The Incredibly-Strange Creatures Who Stopped Living And Became Mixed-Up Zombies
(COLOR)

Low budget shocker about carnival murders, visually interesting and well-directed. Exploitable for lowercasing in shock situations.

Hollywood, June 27.

Hollywood Star Pictures release of a Morgan-Steckler Production, executive producer George J. Morgan, produced and directed by Ray Dannis Steckler. Features entire cast. Screenplay, Gene Pollock, Robert Silliphant, based on story by E. M. Kevke; camera (Eastmancolor), Joseph V. Mascelli; editor, Don Schneider; music, Henry Price; songs, Libby Quinn; art direction, Mike Harrington, Patrick S. Kirkwood; sound, Lee Strosnider; asst. director, Don Russell. Reviewed at Nosseck's Projection Theatre, L.A., June 2, '65. Running time, 81 MINS.

Jerry	Cash Flagg
Madam Estrella	Brett O'Hara
Marge	Carolyn Brandt
Harold	Atlas King
Angie	Sharon Walsh
Madison	Madison Clarke
Carmelita	Erina Enyo
Ortega	Jack Brady
Stella	Toni Camel
Barker	Neil Stillman
Angie's Mother	Joan Howard
Nightclub m.c.	James Bowie
Nightclub owner	Gene Pollock
Dancer	Bill Ward
1st Policeman	Son Hooker
2nd Policeman	Steve Clark
Singers	Don Snyder, Carol Kay, Teri Randal

Already in release but not tradeshown, "The Incredibly-Strange Creatures Who Stopped Living And Became Mixed-Up Zombies" is a low-budget shocker about carny murders. Okay musical production numbers and good direction overcome weak script and performances. Excellent photography adds visual interest, and the Hollywood Star Pictures release has some strong exploitation value for lowercasing in appropriate situations.

Original story by E. M. Kevke as adapted by Gene Pollock and Robert Silliphant focusses on Brett O'Hara as an ugly carny palmist who disfigures enemies with acid, assisted by midget Jack Brady. Erina Enyo is her dancer-sister whose looks pay the bills and also lure beatnik Cash Flagg into palmist's hypnotic spell under which he embarks on killing spree.

Carolyn Brandt and Toni Camel are midway gals who get Flagg-ed down via interestingly staged knifings. Buddy Atlas King and girl friend Sharon Walsh participate in climactic cliff chase. All players are adequate in stock roles.

Interspersed with blood-letting are several chorus numbers staged well by Bill Turner and Alan Smith, with okay original tunes by Libby Quinn scored by Henry Price. Sequences are surprisingly good, and vary film's pace. Vocals by Don Snyder, Carol Kay and Teri Randal are okay. Bill Ward is effective in brief appearance as dancer.

Camera work is excellent, and a credit to Joseph V. Mascelli, who wrote the cinematographer handbook used by most industry lensers and obviously is a master of his craft. Exteriors were shot at Long Beach's amusement park and a roller coaster ride is an exciting bit. The cheap carny gaudiness has been captured effectively.

Don Schneider's editing to a tight 81 minutes is very good, ditto title work by Tom Scherman. Sound by Lee Strosnider is good but occasionally uneven. Director Ray Dennis Steckler rates an overall good, and his handling of production chores has derived much mileage out of shoestring finances. Film is being statesrighted. *Murf.*

The Little Ones
(BRITISH)

Modest, well-made second feature; useful family booking, though sans star bait.

London, June 29.

Columbia release through BLC of a Goldhawk (Fred Robertson) production. Features Dudley Foster, Derek Francis, Kim Smith, Carl Gonzales, Peter Thomas, Jean Marlow. Written and directed by Jim O'Connolly. Camera, David Holmes; editor, Henry Richardson; music, Malcolmn Lockyer. Reviewed at London Pavilion, London. Running Time, 66 MINS.

Jackie	Carl Gonzales
Ted	Kim Smith
Inspector Carter	Dudley Foster
Det. Sgt. Wilson	Derek Newark
Ted's Mum	Jean Marlow
Ted's Dad	Peter Thomas
Paddy	Derek Francis
Child Welfare Officer	Cyril Shaps
Lord Brantley	John Chandos
Peggy	Diane Aubrey

This modestly made, but pleasant second feature pic is something of a gamble for producer Fred Robertson. About two years ago he sank most of his capital into buying, re-equipping and reviving the flagging Goldhawk Studios. Now, with around $56,000, he has made his first pic. It is a second feature, but Robertson hopes that it will lead to more ambitious project.

This is unpretentious and not more than a useful program filler. But it is entertaining, produced and directed professionally, and has a stamp of sincerity which is engaging. Story, both written and directed by Jim O'Connolly, concerns two slum kids, one white, the other half-caste. The white child is bullied and ill-treated by his parents. The other is apathetically loved, but neglected, by his mother, a white prostie. They decide to run away, destination being Jamaica where they optimistically hope to find the lad's father, who walked out on the family two years earlier.

They vaguely remember that ships leave Liverpool Docks so they stow away in a furniture van and travel from London to the North. But tired, hungry and penniless they are tempted to lift a suitcase from a car and sell the contents to a fence. Owner is a local bigshot and they soon have the Liverpool police on their tails. Eventually, they are caught, given a mild lecture and jacked off home to London.

O'Connolly's script is often naive, and the characters of the white lad's parents are stridently overdrawn. But somehow the simple yarn works. His direction is straightforward and a nice blend of humor and atmosphere. Location scenes in London and Liverpool have been caught well. Other credits, including Malcolm Lockyer's score and Arthur Fell's sets, are okay within the simple limits of budget.

Carl Gonzales, as the half caste nipper, and Kim Smith, as his younger buddy are natural youngsters. Young Smith's thin voice is sometimes a strain on the ears. Dudley Foster turns in a sympathetic stint as a harrassed police inspector. There are effective bits by Cyril Shaps, as a welfare officer; Derek Newark, as a cop; Derek Francis, as a genial rogue, and John Chandos, as a pompous shipping magnate. As aforementioned, young Smith's parents are heavily over-drawn, and both Peter Thomas and Jean Marlow tend to pump up this exaggeration.

Rich.

Berlin Festival

Waelsungenblut
(GERMAN-COLOR)
Berlin, June 29.

Columbia-Bavaria release of Franz Seitz production. With Elena Nathanael, Michael Maien, Rudolf Forster, Margot Hielscher, Gert Baltus. Directed by Rolf Thiele. Camera (Eastmancolor), Wolf Wirth; screenplay, Erika Mann and Georg Laforet, adapted from novelette by Thomas Mann; music, Rolf Wilhelm. At Berlin Film Fest. Running time, 85 MINS.

Count Arnstadt	Rudolf Forster
Countess Isabella	Margot Hielscher
Beckerath	Gert Baltus
Siegmund	Michael Maien
Sieglinde	Elena Nathanael

"Waelsungenblut," Germany's official entry at this year's Berlin Film Fest, is the fifth Thomas Mann filmization. Pic's outcome is, as nearly expected, rather dubious. To make a screen version out of Mann's literature probably always will be a doubious enterprise. This Franz Seitz production has more or less the same as the previous Mann filmizations. It's too pretentious and neither fish nor fowl.

The pic has some dignity but it's all rather dull. And the characters are strange creatures. They never really come to life. Why they continue making Mann pix in this country is at best only a guess. "Waelsungenblut" (Blood of the Waelsungens) cost $300,000. One wonders if the money couldn't have been spent on more adequate screen material.

This film will have a tough time finding an audience. Admittedly one of the more ambitious German pix, this is not demanding enough to appeal to the more demanding customer. On the other hand, it's in a way too demanding for the average patron. Yet the subject of incest may create certain word-to-mouth and lure curio-seekers. Brother loves sister and vice versa, which hints an exploitable peg.

The whole thing takes place in Munich back in 1911. A young lieutenant feels attracted to the beautiful daughter of Count Arnstadt and he proposes to her. She's a conceited young thing. Her answer is that if he rides naked through the town, she will wed him. The young officer manages it to comply with this strange condition.

Yet he doesn't get her the way he wants because her heart belongs alone to her brother. Brother and sister. Siegmund and Sieglinde. ask the officer to grant them a farewell party. They go to the ópera to see Wagner's "Walkure." They become inspired by what they see on the stage, and passion overcomes them at home.

T'≏ f'm introduces Elena Nathanael, a breathtakingly beautiful girl of Greek descent, and Michael Maien. They portray the loving brother and sister. Miss Nathanael's looks may win her laurels. Cast includes vet player Rudolf Forster as their father who's the acting standout.

The best thing about this production is Wolf Wirth's colorful lensing. an optical treat. Director Rolf Thiele, Germany's specialist on "delicate" screen matters, once more reveals skill in many sequences. Yet it seems as though he again underestimated the difficulties furnished by the Mann material. Pic had been shown in various German cities before it came to Berlin. All in all, this is a rather controversial film. *Hans.*

Pajarito Gomez
(The Idol)
(ARGENTINIAN)
Berlin, June 29.
Jose A. Jiminez production. Stars Laurato Murua: features Hector Pellegrini, Maria Cristina Laurenz, Nelly Beltran, Maurice Jouvet and Beatriz Matar. Directed by Rodolfo Kuhn. Screenplay, Francisco Uranda, Carlos del Peral, Kuhn; camera, Ignacio Souto; music, Oscar and George Lopez Ruiz. At Berlin Film Fest, June 28, '65. Running time, 83 MINS.

In the light of the international impact of pop idols in all parts of the world, there is an interesting film theme in portraying the making and "selling" of such a personality. This Argentine pic. screened at the Berlin festival. is a valiant attempt, but doesn't quite make it. It has obvious potentialities as a dualer, and would also get by in Spanish lingo houses of the U.S.

Though its running time is held to 83 minutes, there are a number of tedious passages. But by and large, the subject is given realistic cinematic treatment. The private and public lives of Pajarito Gomez are neatly intermingled. The hysteria which accompanies his public performances are neatly dovetailed with his uneasiness when away from the stage and the adulation of his fans.

Easily the most fascinating part of the production is its climax, after the idol has been killed in a train accident. He is lying in state, as it were. in an open coffin, surrounded by sobbing fans, when one of his disks is played as a final tribute. Gradually, almost imperceptibly, the teenagers react to the music, enthusiastically responding to the rhythm via a lively rock display which wouldn't shame any discotheque.

Laurato Murua gives a lively and thoroughly believable display as

the bewildered idol. He sings well, and acts quite competently, and in most respects appears to have the qualities that make a present-day pop star. He's given brisk support by the featured cast. The whole thing is helped by a vigorous, rhythmic score. Direction and other technical credits are up to standard. *Myro.*

Siamo Italiani
(We Italians)
(SWISS)
(Documentary)
Berlin, July 2.
Seiler and Gnant production. Directed and scripted by Seiler, Gnant and June Kovach. Camera, Gnant. At Berlin Film Fest. Running Time, 79 MINS.

Presented in the information section of the Berlin festival, this feature-length documentary gives a closeup view of the Italians who migrate to Switzerland to live and work. There are half a million of them, representing about one in five of all the working population. and, according to this account, they have a rather rough time. The Latin temperament, it would seem, just doesn't mix with the Swiss coldness and aloofness. They're shunned socially, and are forced to live in homes which are barely fit for animals.

Basically, therefore, there is interesting material for an in-depth sociological documentary, but this Swiss-made film rarely takes more than a superficial look at the problem, and consequently misses its target. Using the cinema-verite technique to achieve some measure of spontaneity is a good idea, but doesn't work too well in this case. It often results in dull photographic images and uneven continuity.

The commercial hopes for theatrical release would seem to be extremely limited, but it could well find an outlet via television. *Myro.*

To
(Two People)
(DANISH)
Berlin, June 29.
Laterna Films (Copenhagen) production and release. Stars Jens Osterholm, Yvonne Ingdal. Directed by Palle Kjaerulff-Schmidt. Screenplay, Klaus Rifbjerg; camera, George Oddner; music, George Riedel. At Berlin Film Fest, June 28, '65. Running time, 89 MINS.
Niels .... Jens Osterholm
Lone ....Yvonne Ingdal
Esther .... Birgit Bruel
Fritz .... Peter Steen

As the title suggests, this modest Danish pic concentrates on two people one an irresponsible and unpredictable young man, the other a nice. steady young girl. It has a refreshing charm and is disarmingly spirited. which would suggest that its best chances would be within the Scandinavian countries and other European centres. Film shapes to have only limited hopes in more sophisticated areas such as the U.S.

The complete contrast in the two characters is in line with the principal of the attraction of opposites. He supposedly works as a cinema usher, but regularly sneaks out between performances, is not above petty theft and forgery, and dis-

plays a total lack of regard for the feelings of others. On the other hand, she is a hard-working laboratory assistant in a hospital. and tries to live a normal. decent life. Yet, the two are irresistibly attracted, though eventually she reaches the point of no return.

The production, directed at a lively pace, is dominated by the two stellar performances, both Jens Osterholm and Yvonne Ingdal acquitting themselves satisfactorily. He succeeds in being a thoroughly disagreeable type, and she inevitably commands full measure of sympathetic reaction. Two lesser roles are also competently filled. Birgit Bruel plays an old friend who, to her surprise and dismay, gets the brush. though she has shown her willingness by jumping into bed; Peter Steen is one of Miss Ingdal's better-type boyfriends, whose evening out is ruined by Osterholm's uncouth behavior. George Riedel's relaxed score matches the mood of the subject. *Myro.*

90 Degrees in Shade
(BRITISH-CZECH)

First Anglo-Czech coproduction emerges as a tautly-made study of weak woman under the spell of a cad; expertly directed and acted, this will need careful handl'ing.

Berlin, July 2.
Cinema V release (in U.S.) of Raymond Stross (UK)-Barrandov studios (Prague) production. Stars Anne Heywood, James Booth; features Rudolf Hrusinsky, Ann Todd, Donald Wolfit. Directed by Jiri Weiss. Screenplay, David Mercer, based on an original treatment by Weiss, Jiri Mucha; camera, Bedrich Betka; music, Ludek Hulan. At Berlin Film Fest, information section. Running Time, 90 MINS.
Alena .... Anne Heywood
Vorell .... James Booth
Kurka .... Rudolf Hrusinsky
Mrs. Kurka .... Ann Todd
Bazant .... Donald Wolfit

"90 Degrees in the Shade" is the first Anglo-Czech coproduction ever made, and therefore is something of a landmark between West and East. It was filmed at the Barrandov Studios in Prague, and and the story is set in that city, though it might just as well have been localed in any other capital. Background is quite incidental and irrelevant. What matters most is that the finished pic has quality, mainly because of the shrewd and observant direction by Jiri Weiss, who is probably the most internationally known and respected of all Czech directors.

It is largely thanks to this thoughtful direction that the film does not wind up as a trite, clicheridden piece of celluloid. but as a meaningful drama. in which emotion plays a larger role than reason in the life of a young and attractive woman. In less competent hands, this might well have been just a novelettish yarn, though some recognition is also due to David Mercer's sensitive script.

One thing, however, appears rather certain; "90 Degrees" is not going to have it easy at the wickets. It will need thoughtful selling. and the individual touch may count more than a massive campaign. Its natural home would appear to be better grade arty situations, though wider playoff possibilities are not to be discounted.

Cinema V has world rights outside Britain, the Commonwealth and Eastern Europe. and, of course, will be releasing it in the U. S.

From an original treatment by the director and Jiri Mucha, scripter Mercer has fashioned an interesting and often intriguing study of a nice. honest good-looking girl who falls under the spell of the manager of the shop where she works. He's married, of course, and that's a cliche the director couldn't lick. But he's also thoroughly unscrupulous. a petty thief and what the British would rightly term a cad. What's more, she is under no illusions and realizes he's no good for her.

As the story opens. there is a stock-taking check in the chain grocery and wine store where they both work. It starts at night and is then adjourned till 6 a.m. the following morning. so that the check can be completed before opening up for business. That just about gives the store manager enough time to replace some of the stock that he had stolen. but neither reckoned on a clumsy incident in which a bottle of cognac is accidentally broken, and it is realized that it is filled with tea. And so. also. are most of the other bottles. Both try to bluff it out, but when the manager suggests that the girl should take the blame—after all, he would get three years and she would be put on probation, she commits suicide.

While the main storyline is being unspooled, there are constant flashbacks to the happier days the lovers shared, and though these are occasionally confusing, they help to develop the relationship between the two principal characters. It was a passionate relationship, but rarely a satisfactory one, as the few love-making scenes testify.

Anne Heywood, an under-rated actress who usually fills glamour roles, gives a believable and penetrating study as the assistant manageress. .She's always dressed simply, uses little makeup and lives in fairly squalid surroundings. Yet she admirably suggests the girl who realizes there's no future in what she's doing, but can't stop doing it. James Booth, a talented actor, hits the right note as the scoundrel boss, always glib and persuasive, quietly confident that he will come out okay.

The one Czech player in a featured role is Rudolf Hrusinsky, and his performance is dignified and since. He's the stock checker who has discovered the discrepancy, and as a man who had always put duty first and human relations last, points the accusing finger at the girl, but after her suicide realizes his own failings. Ann Todd, as his drunken nagging wife, provides a standout bit, and her behavior helps in appreciation of her husband's moral stand. Donald Wolfit. another top-ranking actor, is a fellow stock checker with the reverse attitudes—he puts human understanding first.

In most respects, this is a competently made pic, and the technical credits are mainly up to Western standards. *Myro.*

Charulata
(The Lonely Wife)
(INDIAN)

Berlin, July 2.
R. D. Bansal production and release.
Features Soumitra Chatterjee, Madhabi
Mukherjee, Sailen Mukherjee. Directed
by Satyajit Ray. Screenplay, Ray; camera,
Subrata Mitra; editor, Dulal Dutta; music,
Ray. At Berlin Film Fest. Running Time,
117 MINS.
Amal .... Soumitra Chatterjee
Charu .... Madhabi Mukherjee
Bhupati .... Sailen Mukherjee
Umapada .... Shyamal Ghoshal
Mandakini .... Geetali Roy

Inexplicably rejected by the
Cannes Film Fest selection committee, "Charulata" adds lustre to
this Berlin festival, at which it had
an enthusiastic reception. Commercially, its prospects may well
be limited, but the director's name
will have special appeal for film
buffs. And in carefully selected
arty situations in the U.S. and elsewhere, it should earn its keep.

Possibly more relaxed and leisurely than most Satyajit Ray
films, "Charulata" nevertheless
has a graciousness and dignity
which impart an added sincerity to
the simple, yet thoroughly acceptable story. There are few directorial
tricks, but a sustained and honest
interpretation of a well-knit yarn,
in which simplicity takes rightful
precedence over sophistication.

There are times when it's felt
that the pace could be improved
by more determined editing, but
that would be out of keeping with
the director's mood and style. And
it is the style that counts as Ray
unfolds his story of a successful
publisher, whose main interest is
interpreting the political scene,
while his intelligent wife vegetates
by doing embroidery.

Eventually, he realizes his responsibility to the woman he sincerely loves but neglects, and invites his brother-in-law and wife
as house guests. Another visitor
is a handsome cousin, who is
urged to encourage the wife in her
creative talents. Inevitably, the
lonely wife and the handsome
cousin are drawn to each other,
but always maintain an appropiate
degree of restraint. The period,
after all, is 1879, and while the
husband is hoping that Gladstone
will defeat Disraeli at the polls,
the wife is torn between loyalty
and emotion.

The moment of crisis comes
when it is learned that the
brother-in-law has absconded with
funds entrusted to him. How could
someone in whom so much trust
had been placed behave so de-
spicably? And the handsome
cousin, feeling that a similar question could be asked of him, absconds in the night, leaving a bald
note for his hosts. The wife's
breakdown, not realizing that her
husband is within earshot, brings
the plot to its realistic climax.

Keeping to his traditional style,
the director keeps dialog down to
a minimum, allowing the camera
to be the main storyteller, and it
emerges as a typical example of
unhurried film making. Ray is well
served by his lenser, though editor
Dulal Dutta might have exercised
a little more authority to advantage.

The principal performances, are
universally good, Soumitra Chatterjee making a striking impression as the cousin. Madhabi and
Sailem Mukherjee add conviction
to the roles of wife and husband.
Shyamal Ghoshal and Geetali Roy
lend distinction to the roles of
brother-in-law and his wife.

Ray's script, based on a novel
by Rabindranath Tagore, is literate, and his music matches the
relaxed style of the picture. "Charulata" has deservedly won a number of Indian awards, including
the president's Gold Medal for
1964. *Myro.*

Das Haus in der Karpfengasse
(The House In Karp Lane)
(GERMAN)

Berlin, June 28.
Neue Filmform (Heiner Braun) release
of Independent Film production. With
Jana Brejchova, Edith Schultze-Westrun,
Frantisek Filipovsky, Ladislav Kriz,
Wolfgang Kieling. Directed by Kurt
Hoffmann. Screenplay, Gerd Angermann,
adapted from a novel by M.Y. Ben-Gav-
riel; camera, Josef Illik; music, Zdenek
Liska; editor, Dagmar Hirtz. Running
time, 110 MINS.
Bozena .... Jana Brejchova
Mrs. Kauders ..Edith Schultze-Westrun
Mr. Kauders ...... Frantisek Filipovsky
Emil Lauders .... Ladislav Kriz
Karl Marek .... Wolfgang Kieling
Olga Marek .... Rosl Schaefer
Lieutenant Slezak .... Helmut Schmid
Salomon Laufer .... Walter Traub
Mali Laufer .... Hanna Vitova
Ernst Laufer . ...Peter Herrmann

This is the German film which,
involuntarily, stirred such a hassle
some weeks ago. Cannes Film
Fest was responsible for it. The
festival there rejected the pic and
explained the turndown by terming
the film artistically not good
enough to appear at a worldwide
festival. The rejection shocked
German film circles. The whole
controversy naturally helped the
film, publicity-wise. It's now being
seen by more people than expected.
And consequently, it's making more
money than its creators originally
hoped for.

Ironically enough, foreigners at
festival had often shown surprise
that pix dealing with the Nazi past
were made everywhere but in West
Germany. In fact, few such pix
were produced in postwar West
Germany. Commercial failure gave
evidence of the fact that such product is boxoffice poison. Then came
this film.

Whether Cannes was right or not
"Karp Lane" looks like it would
have been able to compete at least
with some of the entries at Cannes.
Not a masterpiece, but it's an honorable film. "Karp Lane" has a big
subject but is only a little film
measured by international standards.

Film story depicts the Nazi invasion of Prague and shows what
happens to the Czech and Jewish
people living in an apartment house
in the town's Jewish quarter. There
is injustice, intolerance, opportunism, cowardice, Nazi arrogance and
brutality, resistance, and also love.
Fate of the Jewish people, of
course, is stressed. It's chiefly an
ensemble film, but nevertheless
some performers stand out. One is
Czech Jana Brejchova, a young girl
who joins a resistance group of
students. She encounters her first
love which becomes her last love
because the group is tracked down
by the Gestapo.

This is based on the same-titled
novel by M. Y. Ben-Gavriel, Israeli
writer, who, incidentally, revealed
that he was fully satisfied with the
film. It should be added that the
picture received the highest German distinction ("artistically particularly worthy") which means
considerable tax relief in this
country.

Kurt Hoffmann, the director,
handled the sensitive theme with
taste and feeling. However, the
film as a whole lacks certain directorial imagination needed to give
it the necessary excitement. Film
has many dull moments along the
way. Hoffmann seemingly intended
to make an anti-Nazi film without
showing Nazi atrocities. But he
does not seem to have reached his
goal.

"Karp Lane" was shown at the
Berlin festival outside of competition. A slightly different version
was on the West German tele three
months ago. Film received highest
praise by both the Catholic and
Protestant Churches here, and also
found special recognition by cultural and school authorities.
Hans.

The Glory Guys
(PANAVISION-COLOR)

Diverting Cavalry-Indian pic
with brawls, comedy and romance. No solid marquee
names. Good uppercase for
summer programs with sales
emphasis on action.

Hollywood, July 2.
United Artists release of Arnold Laven-
Arthur Gardner-Jules Levy production, di-
rected by Laven. Stars Tom Tryon, Harve
Presnell, Senta Berger. Screenplay, Sam
Peckinpah, based on novel "The Dice of
God" by Hoffman Birney; camera (De-
Luxe Color), James Wong Howe; editors,
Melvin Shapiro, Ernst R. Rolf; music, Riz
Ortolani; asst. director, Clarence Eurist.
Reviewed at Directors Guild of America,
L.A., July 1, '65. Running Time, 111
MINS..
Demas Harrod .... Tom Tryon
Sol Rogers .... Harve Presnell
Lou Woodard .... Santa Berger
Dugan .... James Caan
Gen. McCabe .... Andrew Duggan
Gregory .... Slim Pickens
Hodges .... Peter Breck
Mrs. McCabe .... Jeanne Cooper
Martin Hale .... Michael Anderson, Jr.
Beth .... Laurel Goodwin
Crain .... Adam Williams
Gentry .... Erik Holland
Marcus .... Robert McQueeney
Moyan .... Wayne Rodgers
Treadway .... Willaim Meigs
Mrs. Poole .... Alice Backes
Lt. Cook .... Walter Scott
Marxhall Cushman .... Michael Forest
Hanavan .... George Ross
Carl, the Gunsmith .... Dal McKennon
Gen. Hoffman .... Stephen Chase
Salesman .... Henry Beckman

"The Glory Guys" is an entertaining U.S. Cavalry-Indian conflict, sparked by an opportunist
Army general who sacrifices dedicated soldiers to his ambition.
Brawling fisticuffs, comedy and
romantic triangle mark a slightly
forced plot until an exciting climax of the Arnold Laven-Arthur
Gardner-Jules Levy production
featuring okay direction, production values and performances by
Tom Tryon, a non-singing Harve
Presnell and Senta Berger. Solid
supporting players bolster the
United Artists release which is
best sold on action values. Good
uppercasing prospects for the summer market.

Adaptation by Sam Peckinpah of
Hoffman Birney's novel, "The Dice
of God," finds Andrew Duggan
very effective as a general again
in responsible command despite
prior goofs based on political ambition. Prior to a major Indian
campaign, he rides herd on subordinate Tryon to train a batch of
raw recruits. Presnell will again
serve as scout although he, too,
knows Duggan's reputation for
expediency.

Miss Berger is an adequate but
voluptuous frontier woman with
an unspecified past, who provides
romantic interest as Tryon and
Presnell vie for her favors. Jeanne
Cooper is good as Duggan's vicious
and perfectly-matched wife who
never fails to insult Miss Berger.

Although Tryon is somewhat
wooden and Presnell too refined
for a frontier scout, director Laven
has drawn some fine performances
from supporting names. Slim
Pickens brings a new life to the
gruff humor and paternalism of a
cliche role as non-com. James
Caan makes a sharp impression

as the stubborn recruit in an amusing running battle with shavetail Peter Breck. When Duggan's disobedience of orders causes a mass slaughter, Caan buries nemesis Breck in a touching highlight.

Michael Anderson Jr. is okay in encore of "Major Dundee" role as a sensitive juve who matures under rigors of battle and barracks life, including a puppy-love affair with Laurel Goodwin who nurses him to recovery after one of several brawls. Michael Forest is effective in brief bit as marshal who permits soldiers to be abused by town toughs. Other players sustain the requirements of stock roles.

James Wong Howe's Panavision lensing is an asset, with a fine use of slow zoom which dramatically paints the battlefield odds against the Durango turf. DeLuxe Color was generally washed out, although very murky in spots of print caught. Riz Ortolani's score, at times overbearing, is full-bodied. Extensive dialog looping is generally successful, and recording by Alfred J. Overton and Rafael Esparza is up to standard. Melvin Shapiro and Ernst R. Rolf edited to 111 minutes for okay pace. Format Productions title work is interesting. *Murf.*

The Third Day
(PANAVISION-COLOR)

Fairly suspenseful yarn involving **a m n e s i a**; sturdy grosses indicated with name of George Peppard to spark chances.

Hollywood, July 7.
Warner Bros. release of Jack Smight production, directed by Smight. Stars George Peppard, Elizabeth Ashley; features Roddy McDowall, Arthur O'Connell, Mona Washbourne, Herbert Marshall, Robert Webber, Charles Drake, Sally Kellerman. Screenplay, Burton Wohl, Robert Presnell Jr., based on novel by Joseph Hayes; camera (Technicolor), Robert Surtees; editor, Stefan Arnsten; music, Percy Faith; asst. director, Victor Vallejo. Reviewed at Academy Award Theatre, July 6, '65. Running Time, 119 MINS.

Steve Mallory .... George Peppard
Alexandria .... Elizabeth Ashley
Oliver Parsons .... Roddy McDowall
Dr. Wheeler .... Arthur O'Connell
Catherine .... Mona Washbourne
Austin .... Herbert Marshall
Dom Guardino .... Robert Webber
Lawrence Conway ..... Charles Drake
Holly Mitchell .... Sally Kellerman
Lester Aldrich .... Arte Johnson
Logan .... Bill Walker
Preston .... Vincent Gardenia
Totti .... Janine Gray

"The Third Day" shapes up as an interesting and sometimes suspenseful drama revolving around a man fighting amnesia and faced with a manslaughter rap. The Jack Smight production, adapted by Burton Wohl and Robert Presnell Jr., from Joseph Hayes' novel, stars George Peppard and Elizabeth Ashley and should be a sturdy box-office entry.

Beautifully turned out in Panavision and Technicolor, the Warner release carries sound production values which Robert Surtees' fluid cameras point up in admirable fashion. A chief weakness lies in the lack of script development of how Peppard, who has lost all recollection of a 24-hour period during which a young woman meets her death, regains his memory, more successfully treated in the book. This lack may not seriously affect audience reception, however.

Where the book, too, carried a more legitimate climax, the picture engages in melodramatics to wind on an attempted sensational note, somehow striking an offkey. Smight's direction manages to overcome deficiencies to the extent that action flows evenly, and he gets strong performances from each of a capable cast.

Film opens on Peppard climbing a steep bank from a river into which he obviously plunged, but he cannot remember what happened or who he is. He learns he's married to a beautiful aristocrat whom he's about to lose because he's a drunk, and is about to be talked into selling the family business. Further, he's suspected of having been with a cocktail waitress, whom he is supposed to be romancing and found critically injured in the river, at the time of the accident. Or was it an accident? Narrative covers a three-day period in which Peppard moves through an uncertain world.

Peppard delivers an expert enactment and Miss Ashley, as his wife, lends a colorful note as she handles a well-played role. Roddy McDowall socks over a conniving character and a standout performance is offered by Mona Washbourne in a warm and understanding characterization, perhaps in the most memorable delineation of the picture. Sally Kellerman is persuasive as the tart who plays a part in Peppard's life; Robert Webber is effective as the District Attorney, and Arte Johnson scores as the tart's husband. Herbert Marshall appears as a strike victim who cannot speak or move, and Arthur O'Connell and Charles Drake likewise render valuable aid.

Edward Carrere's art direction is quality throughout, as is Ralph S. Hurst's set decorations, and Donald Brook's designing of Miss Ashley's clothes a particular plus. Stefan Arnsten's editing is crisp and music by Percy Faith provides suitable melodic backing. *Whit.*

Berlin Festival

Vereda da Salvacao
(The Obsessed of Catule)
(BRAZILIAN)
Berlin, July 3.
Anselmo Duarte (Rio de Janiero) production. Stars Raul Cortez; features Jose Parisi and Esther Mellinger. Direction and screenplay, Anselmo Duarte. Camera, Ricardo Aronovich; music, Diogo Pacheco. At Berlin Film Fest. Running Time, 100 MINS.
Joaquim .... Raul Cortez
Manuel .... Jose Parisi
Dolor .... Leila Abramo
Artuliana .... Esther Mellinger
Durvalina .... Margarida Cardoso

This Brazilian production is a strong, uncompromising story of a religious fanatic who dominates the ignorant peasants of a village, and who finally leads them to disaster. It's not the stuff of which boxoffice pictures are normally made, and it will be tough going to find a worthwhile commercial outlet beyond a few selected arties.

Anselmo Duarte, who has directed his own screenplay, is a forceful and provocative filmmaker who appears to be in love with his own technique. He uses a novel zooming effect powerfully in an early scene, but spoils it by repeating the gimmick again and again. He has directed the film with diligence, extracted a couple of extremely good performances from his cast, but is finally defeated by the subject matter. Boredom takes over long before the fadeout.

The central character is powerfully played by Raul Cortez who, as his mother says in one scene, really believes he's Jesus Christ. He certainly acts that way, relentlessly demanding unqualified support and allegiance not only from his followers, but from the "sinners" in the village. The principal sinners are also forcefully portrayed by Jose Parisi and Esther Mellinger, she having conceived out of wedlock; and under the preacher's orders both are brutally beaten up by the villagers.

Other roles are well filled. The crowd prayer scenes are superbly directed, though the overall effect is disappointing. *Myro.*

Shakespeare-Wallah
(INDIAN)
(English dialog)
Berlin, July 3.
Merchant-Ivory Productions presentation of an Ismail Merchant (Bombay) production. Stars Shashi Kapoor; features Felicity Kendal. Directed by James Ivory. Screenplay, R. Prawer Jhabwala and Ivory; camera, Subrata Mitra; music, Satyajit Ray. At Berlin Film Fest. Running Time, 125 MINS.
Sanju .... Shashi Kapoor
Lizzie .... Felicity Kendal
Tony .... Geoffrey Kendal
Carla .... Laura Liddell
Manjula .... Madhur Jaffrey

Flying the Indian flag at the Berlin festival, to which it was invited, "Shakespeare-Wallah" is officially designated an Indian-American coproduction, though the official credits do not name the U.S. associates, apart from the Californian-born director, James Ivory. It is an English language production, and though not justifying its running time of 125 minutes, might find a suitable outlet if judiciously trimmed.

It is the story of a touring theatrical company specializing in Shakespearean production which has seen better days. Now bookings are scarce and audiences sparse and unappreciative. And it's a struggle to keep the company going. It had been founded by Tony and Carla Buckingham, who still live in the reflected glories of past triumphs. They are totally dedicated, and expect the same from all around, and particularly from their daughter Lizzie, who is currently enamored of an Indian playboy, who is also indulging in some extra-curricular activities with an Indian actress in the company.

The pace of the production is always too leisurely, and some of the Shakespearean excerpts could advantageously be cut. Nevertheless, there is a naive charm to the production. Though far from distinguished, the pix is not without some merit. Technically, too, it's up to par, and Satyajit Ray (the distinguished director) has contributed a sensitive score.

There is also a very confident performance by Shashi Kapoor, as the Indian playboy. Felicity Kendal is a pert newcomer with an ingenuous style. Her dedicated and stern parents are nicely played by Geoffrey Kendal and Laura Liddell. Madhur Jaffrey ably completes the cast as the Indian actress. *Myro.*

Kabe No Nakano Himegoto
(Affairs Within Walls)
(JAPANESE)
Berlin, July 2.
Movie Haikyusha (Osaka) release of a Takashi Ito and Koji Wakamatsu production. Stars Yoichi Yasukawa; features Hiroko Fujino, Mikio Terajima, Yoichi Yasukawa. Directed by Wakamatsu. Screenplay, Yoshiak Otani and Wakamatsu; camera, Hideo Ito; music, Noboru Nyshiyama. At Berlin Film Fest. Running Time, 90 MINS.
Takeo Yamabe .... Norio Yoshizawa
Nobuko Yamabe .... Hiroko Fujino
Toshio Nagai .... Mikio Terajima
Kanju Uchida .... Michito Suzuki
Myio Uchida .... Aya Mine
Asako Uchida .... Kazuko Kanoo
Makoto Uchida .... Yoichi Yasukawa
Miyasko Tanaka .... Nobuko Maki

Japanese films usually have played a major part in lending artistic dignity to international festivals, but this entry can bring nothing but discredit. Pic can virtually be discounted outside Asian territories. It is, without doubt, one of the worst films ever to come out of that country, and its selection for such an event must remain an unresolved mystery.

According to a handout, the film was made on a shoestring and within a 10-day shooting schedule. Without being unnecessarily brutal, one cannot resist the observation that both the limited funds and the limited time could have been more profitably spent. It reeks of amateurism.

This is designed to be erotic and sensational, and it fails lamentably on both counts. It is the story, mainly, of a 16-year old youth, who prefers pinup books to school books, and when not looking at nudes in print, plays the role of a peeping tom by spying on his neighbors through a telescope.

And he finds that one married woman is having sex on the side while her husband is at work. So, having failed to rape his own sister (whom he has watched taking a shower), he has a try with the neighbor, and after some resistance, she suddenly becomes agreeable. But it all ends up in his stabbing her to death.

The festival audience showed its displeasure by giving the pic a rough reception, laughing in the wrong places, and protesting more vehemently at the final scenes. *Myro.*

Amanita Pestilens
(CANADIAN-COLOR)
Berlin, July 7.
Crayley Films Ltd., Ottawa, production. With Jacques Lebrecque, Huguette Oligny, Genevieve Bujold. Directed by Rene Bonniere. Screenplay, Bonniere; camera (Eastmancolor), Frank Stokes; music, Lawrence Crosley. At Berlin Film Festival. Running Time, 81 MINS.
Henry Martin........ Jacques Lebrecque
Louise .... Huguette Oligny
Sophie .... Genevieve Bujold

Simon .... Benisor Girard
Rose .... Roger Garveau
The mute man .... Blake James

A strange little film from Canada, shown at the Berlin film fest outside competition. It attracted a good number of curio-seekers for Canada is hardly known as a feature film producer on the Continent. Film has some appeal for its friendly atmosphere. It has dull moments but viewer always has the feeling that nice people must have created the pic. In that spirit, the film garnered some friendly applause after its screening.

It's the story of a man whose hobby is gardening. One day he discovers on his prize-winning lawn a poisonous mushroom. Although he employs all the measures of an experienced gardener, he cannot prevent the lawn from soon teeming with such mushrooms. It's said to be a tale of pride which is eventually followed by the fall. Here the man was badly neglecting his wife and daughter. Not a moral story, not an immoral, just a story, is film's attitude.

Direction by Rene Bonniere, who also wrote the script, displays imagination. The handling of the players is okay. Film borders very much on the cute side for which the generous colors are responsible too. In all, a little film somewhat out of the world in the true sense of the phrase. Again, its flaws couldn't be resented. *Hans.*

Una Bella Grinta
(The Reckless)
(ITALIAN)
Berlin July 4.
Ager Film (Giuliani G. de Negri) production. Stars Renato Salvatori and Norma Banguell. Directed by Giuliano Montaldo. Screenplay, Battistrada and Montaldo; camera, Erico Menczer; music, Piero Umiliano. At Berlin Film Fest. Running Time, **102 MINS.**

Ettore Zambrini ...... Renato Salvatori
Luciana Zambrini ..... Norma Benguell

Italy, which a couple of years back walked off with the grand prix at nearly every major international festival, has a lower-case entry for the Berlin festival with "Una Bella Grinta." It is a competently-made programmer, which is unlikely to do especially well at the wickets in its home territory, and export prospects must be rated minimal.

The screenplay puts the focus on a man with a load of problems. He's having difficulty raising the finance for a new textile factory which he is building, and at the same time his wife has left him and gone off with her lover. Eventually she returns to him, and insists it's all over, but when she makes a feeble excuse to go out, he tricks her into loaning him her car, keeps the date with her lover, and promptly kills him. Later he disposes of the other man's possessions, thereby believing he has wiped the slate clean.

In many respects, the script is inadequate, particularly as it fails to clarify and develop the relationship between the wife and her student lover. It also goes into too much detail about the problems confronting the husband in getting the coin to complete his factory. And this hardly makes for exciting

cinematic fare. Indeed, it is frequently downright dull to the observer.

Technically, however, the pic hits par. The two principal performances by Renato Salvatori and Norma Benguell, as husband and wife, are competent.

Incomplete credits circulated at the festival do not identify any of the feature players—not even the lover. *Myro.*

Klanningen
(The Dress)
(SWEDISH)
Berlin, July 4.
Omnia (Munich) release of Svensk Filmindustri (Stockholm) production. Stars Gunn Wallgren, Gunnar Bjornstrand, Tina Hedstrom. Directed by Vilgot Sjoman. Screenplay, Ulla Isaksson; camera, Sven Nykvist; music, Eric Nordgren. At Berlin Film Fest information section. Running Time, **85 MINS.**

Helen Furst .... Gunn Wallgren
Helmer .... Gunnar Bjornstrand
Edit .... Tina Hedstrom

A non-competitive entry at the Berlin festival, this Swedish pic tells an intriguing story of the effects of delayed puberty on a teenage girl. Omnia of Munich has picked up world rights from the producers, and it would seem that best chances would be as a dualer, rather than as an art house release.

There is a limited amount of nudity in the earlier sequences, but inexplicably Tina Hedstrom has her breasts partially covered by adhesive tape, which will probably help to eliminate any censor problems in the U.S. and elsewhere.

She's a girl with growing-up problems. She is a "Plain Jane," and knows it, but to breakaway from the teenage image, she insists on her mother buying her a model outfit, in which she "will look more naked than dressed." On the night she intends to wear the new dress, however, she has her first period (three years overdue). From that moment complexes set in.

It's not exactly a wholesome yarn, but this has a consistent script, the characters are thoughtfully etched, and it has been given sensitive direction by Vilgot Sjoman, one of Sweden's promising new directors. Film is also smoothly acted, with competent performances by the three principals. Miss Hedstrom is particularly believable as the mixed-up daughter. Gunn Wallgren makes a sympathetic mother who sacrifices her private life for the welfare of her daughter while the lover is convincingly portrayed by Gunnar Bjornstrand. *Myro.*

Moscow Film Fest

Father of a Soldier
(RUSSIAN)
Moscow, July 6.
Sovexport release of a Gruzia-Film (Geirgia) production. Stars Sergo Zakhariadze. Directed by Rezo Chkheidze. Screenplay, Suliko Zhgenti; camera, Lev Sukhov and Archil Filipashvili; music, Sulkhan Tsintsadze. At Moscow Film Fest. Running Time, **92 MINS.**

How wasteful is war, a favorite theme with filmmakers on both sides of the Atlantic, is again the moral underlying "Father of a Soldier," Soviet film which opened the Fourth Moscow Film Festival, in its way. Made in Georgia by Rezo Chkheidze, and starring Sergo Zakariadze, the film traces the adventures of a gnarled old Georgian wine-grower, who sets out to visit his son at a frontline hospital during the last phases of World War II. He gets caught up in the fighting, dons a soldier's uniform, and finally finds his son, only to lose him moments later to a German bullet.

Rezo Chkheidze's straightforward treatment of a straight-forward theme lends this essay on war a certain dignity absent from many more elaborate attempts in the genre. Sergo Zakhariadze as a dazed and stubborn old man, turns in a performance of unforgettable charm.

Remarkable here in Moscow as one of the few war films which avoids being pompous about war, "Soldier," with its sensitively filmed sequences, should prove as popular in the West as "Ballad of a Soldier" or "The Cranes are Flying." *Demi.*

Friends Are As Friends Go
(MONGOLIAN)
Moscow, July 7.

Sovexport release of a Mongolkimo production. Stars L. Lhasuren, G. Oyuun, D. Gunsendulam, N. Dagirans, G. Gotov. Directed by D. Hishie. Screenplay, C. Chimed; camera, O. Urtnasan; music, L. Mordorzh. At Moscow Film Fest. Running Time, **70 MINS.**

Mongolian films are hardly known in the West, but this Soviet republic has made vast strides in production technique over the last few years. And this is one of its better efforts. Though it is unlikely to have release outside the Eastern bloc, film is sincerely made, if on modest scale and offers an interesting glimpse of the countryside of this little known republic.

It is a vehicle with a moral, emphasizing that truck driving and vodka drinking don't mix. The yarn is told mainly in prolonged flashback, opening with a scene in which a driver refuses to imbibe with some of his mates when they meet on deserted wastelands, and is accused of being a goody-goody. The flashback explains why, leading up to the incident in which he wrecks his truck after taking too big a swig. Finally he's helped by an understanding militiaman.

Though it is naive and occasionally sentimental, the story is mainly credible. The private life of the driver and his fascinatingly attractive wife is handled with understanding. The performances are universally good, but the credits available at the Moscow festival do not identify the characters played by the cast, all of whom are unknown to Western viewers. *Myro.*

Storm of the Wild Kaiser
(AUSTRIAN)
Moscow, July 7.
Benesch Film (Austria) production. Stars Hans von Borsody and Alwy Becker. Direction and script, Edward von Borsody; camera, Walter Riml; music, Heinz Neubrand. At Moscow Film Fest. Running Time, **93 MINS.**

Had this been made in pure documentary form, it might well have proved a stirring account of man's determination to conquer one of the toughest peaks in the Austrian Tyrol. But the pic has been embellished — and consequently spoiled—by a fictional treatment, which is more a commercial for a mountain resort and its principal hotel.

There are some fine values in the tense climbing scenes, but the script shows these largely through the eyes of a ballerina who is watching the perilous ascent through a telescope on the balcony of her hotel room. It is extremely ingenuous and the film, which is certainly not worthy of a place in an international fest, would appear to have little chances outside the German language market. Acting and production values are fair. *Myro.*

Banished From Paradise
(UNITED ARAB REPUBLIC)
Moscow, July 8.
Societe General for the Production of Arab films presentation. Stars Gazid Chawki, Samira Ahmed, Nagua Gouad. Directed by Fatin Abdul el Wahab. Screenplay, Tewfick el Hakim and Aly el Zorokani; camera, Massoud Issa; music, Abdullah el Halim Nouera. At Moscow Film Fest. Running Time, **96 MINS.**

An amiable but extremely naive comedy, this UAR entry at the Moscow festival can hardly expect much exposure outside the Middle East territory, though it has the ingredients for a local success. It falls far short, however, of the standards expected of a major international event.

The central character is self-described as a man of God, but when he dies suddenly is shocked to find that he is refused entry into paradise. It is explained that never in his life had he gone out of his way to help his fellow man. He's sent down below to hell, but is also turned away because he has never sinned.

So he's given another chance to make good on earth, rises from his coffin and is determined to be both a dogooder and a sinner. His first bid to help another lands him in jail, and on his release gets a job as a bouncer at the Paradise night club where he readily succumbs to the overtures of a dancer. But it is all very contrived and there's no attempt at subtlety either in the writing, the situations or in the characterizations. The performances match the slender demands of the plot. *Myro.*

The Young Want to Live
(GREECE)

Moscow, July 7.
Stars Phedon Georgizis, Alexandra Ladicu, Sylvia Hadzigeorggiu, Notis Pergyalis. Direction and script, Nicos Dzimas. Camera, Georgos Kavachias;

music, Miki Teodorakis. At Moscow Film Fest. Running Time, 95 MINS.

There is warmth and sincerity in this Greek production, but they do not spell boxoffice. This is a pic which is mainly destined for local consumption where its theme will be more readily appreciated.

Director Nicos Dzimas' script deals with poverty, though not very realistically. And it's hard to believe that his characters are as poor as their dialog suggests. But the film's main weakness is the overly slow and painstaking style which the director has used and numerous scenes are extended interminably. But it has been made with heart, and therein lies its main virtue. There is also sincerity in the performances, and the production is technically up to average. *Myro.*

Hand in Hand
(JAPAN)
Moscow, July 9.
Dael Motion Picture Co. production and release. Stars Hideo Sato, Yuniko Hodzo. Directed by Susumu Hani. Screenplay, Mansaku Itami; camera, Sigekadzu; music, Toru Takeminu. At Moscow Film Fest. Running Time, 109 MINS.

"Hand in Hand" could almost be a commercial for the Japanese educational system because it deals solely with the teaching of a bunch of kids and its fadeout climax is the presentation of school certificates to youngsters who have qualified to pass on to high school. The material would have served as the basis for a modest-length, documentary type film, but certainly does not justify its feature status, particularly with a running time of 109 minutes.

There is virtually no plot in the accepted sense, but the script puts the focus on a couple of feuding youngsters who make the peace in the end after they have both graduated. It has some endearing qualities and an inherent charm, but does not have the ingredients which spell boxoffice in the Western world. Fortunately, the kids are not unduly precocious, and they act well without being self-conscious of the camera *Myro.*

Wedding Certificate
(BULGARIA)
Moscow, July 9.

Filmbulgaria production and release. Stars Nadeezhda Rancheva, Ivan Manev. Direction and Screenplay, Nikola Korabov. Camera, Konstantin Djidrov. At Moscow Film Fest. Running Time, 89 MINS.

A film which goes abruptly from one extreme to another, "Wedding Certificate" starts off as a gay, little trifle, and ends as sombre high drama. The ingredients don't mix too happily, and despite the modest length, this could be helped by thoughtful re-editing, especially in the first part where there is much repetitive material.

The first half depicts the gay informality of the wedding ceremony in present day Bulgaria. The scene is set in the Palace of Marriages, the brides are dressed in conventional white, the young couples are asked a few formal questions, and promptly declared man and wife. And that's followed by

singing, drinking, dancing (including the Twist), etc.

But then the clock is turned back 20 years to a batch of weddings that are taking place just before the grooms are due to be executed by the Nazis. The contrast is not just one of mood, but also of style; the orthodox ceremony, with all its hocus-pocus seems hundreds of years removed from the present day practice. It is a film of promise and possibilities, which, with re-styling, could have modest potentialities. *Myro.*

Such a Young Girl
(ALGERIA)
Moscow, July 9.
(No Credits Available). At Moscow Film Fest. Running Time, 95 MINS.

A last-minute entry at the Moscow festival, replacing the officially listed Turkish film, this is claimed to be the first truly Algerian pic to be made since that country won its independence. Technically and artistically, it is a very creditable job, and has an extremely macabre and unexpected ending. Its export hopes cannot be highly rated, but it may have some chance in a few selected territories.

It is the story of a bunch of kids in an orphanage who are divided into warring factions, some supporting the OAS and the others the FLN. Mostly the feuding is good-natured, but in the climax, an OAS kid is subjected to a mock trial, found guilty and then actually taken out and shot.

This is an intensely nationalistic and patriotic film, smoothly directed and with natural performances from most of the youngsters. Unfortunately, no credits were available at the Moscow festival. *Myro.*

Prometheus of the Island
(YUGOSLAV)
Moscow, July 8.
Yugoslav Film (Belgrade) presentation of a Jardan Film production. Stars Janez Vhrovec, Mira Sardoc, Dina Rutic. Directed by Vatroslav Mimica. Screenplay, Slavko Goldstein, Krunoslav Quien and Mimica; camera, Tomica Pinter; music, Miljenko Prohaska. At Moscow Film Fest. Running Time, 98 MINS.
Mate Bakula .... Janez Vrhovec
Lela .... Mira Sardoc
Vesna .... Dina Rutic
Bakula (young man)
.... Slobodan Dimitrijevic

Man's disillusionment when his fight for a better world is frustrated is the theme of this Yugoslav pic. But the overall effect is spoiled by confused plotting and too generous use of flashbacks. The confusion is confounded (in this case, particularly) by the language barrier. And a running translation which is always a couple of sentences behind is hardly a help.

The story begins in the present day, when the hero of the film is returning to his home town to attend a reunion with wartime colleagues. Then, through flashbacks, he recalls the days when he fought as a partisan, joined the Liberation forces and helped to defeat the invading Nazis. And, with the coming of peace, he recalls his de-

termination to create a better world, to bring employment to the town, and particularly to launch a power project which would help industrial development. But he's frustrated all along the line, and eventually is forced to throw in the sponge and seek his future in the big city.

Director Mimica has used the flashback technique not simply as a device but to analyze the man's feelings and to explain his behavior. It is, however, only partly successful. But he has succeeded in extracting some very worthwhile performances, notably from Janez Vrhovec and Dina Rutic, a dark-haired beauty who plays his first wife. She has a captivating personality to match her interesting features. Slobodan Dimitrijevic is a little too solid and earnest as the young Bakula. Mira Sardoc is an attractive blonde who has the colorless role of the second wife. Technical credits are up to normal standards. *Myro.*

Harvey Middleman, Fireman
(COLOR)

Offbeat entry for selected situations, will require hard selling.

Hollywood, July 8.
Columbia release of Robert L. Lawrence-Ernest Pintoff production. Stars Gene Troobnick; features Hermione Gingold. Direction-screenplay-music, Ernest Pintoff. Camera (PatheColor), Karl Malkames; editor, Hugh A. Robertson; asst. director, Roger Rothstein. Reviewed at Columbia Studios, July 7, '65. Running Time, 76 MINS.
Harvey .... Gene Troobnick
Mrs. Koogleman ..... Hermione Gingold
Lois .... Patricia Harty
Harriet .... Arlene Golonka
Dinny .... Will Mackenzie
Mother .... Ruth Jaroslow
Dooley .... Charles Durning
Barratta .... Peter Carew
Mookey ..... Stanley Myron Handleman
Cindy .... Trudy Bordoff
Richie .... Neil Rouda
Receptionist .... Gigi Chevalier
Librarian .... Stacy Graham
Mr. Koogleman .... Maurice Shrog

"Harvey Middleman, Fireman" has all the aspects of an experiment, an attempt at drollery in the story of a happily-married fireman who falls for a babe he rescues in a fire. Sometimes it is fairly successful in striking its tenor, but appears more like a laboratory exercise than a theatrical offering. There are moments when the thoughts and feelings of "an ordinary man" are well expressed, but the overall is offbeat and consequently probably will be accepted only in selected situations which cater to this type of film.

First full-length producer chore of Robert L. Lawrence, who swings over from many years in television, and marking Ernest Pintoff's entry into features as a director after a career in the animation and industrial film field, the Pathe Color film stars Gene Troobnick, with Hermione Gingold only name player in cast, featured. Script by Pintoff, who also composed the music score, recounts day-by-day Troobnick's life as he goes about his job as a N.Y. fireman.

He drives to work every morn-

ing, leaving his loving wife and two children: he discusses his job with fellow-firemen (he likes his job and feels a man shouldn't do a job he doesn't like). Then, one day he's off to a fire and carries out a young woman whom—unaccountably to him—he kisses after resuscitating her. For the first time in his life he's faced with a moral problem.

Troobnick gets the most out of his character, sometimes confiding into the camera how he feels about certain things. Miss Gingold, a psychiatrist to whom he goes with his problem, is lost in her part. Arlene Golonka is a happy choice as the wife and Patricia Harty is decorative as the girl with whom the fireman becomes infatuated. All in cast have been well chosen for their particular roles.

Karl Malkames' photography is interesting as action swings through various parts of N.Y., and Gene Callahan's production designing a well-filled assignment. Other technical credits are okay. *Whit.*

These Are The Damned
(BRITISH)

Finally being released in U.S., Joseph Losey film, outspoken on dangers of nuclear warfare, too well made to get second-bill treatment planned for it. A real make-you-think-piece.

Columbia Pictures release of a Hammer Film (Anthony Hinds) production. Stars Macdonald Carey, Shirley Anne Field, Viveca Lindfors, Alexander Knox. Directed by Joseph Losey. Screenplay, Evan Jones, based on H. L. Lawrence novel, "The Children Of Light"; camera, Arthur Grant; editor, Reginald Mills; sound, Malcolm Cooke; music, James Bernard. Sculpture by Frink. Reviewed at Harris Theatre, N.Y., July 8, '65. Running Time, 77 MINS.
Simon Wells .... Macdonald Carey
Joan .... Shirley Anne Field
Freya .... Viveca Lindfors
Bernard .... Alexander Knox
King .... Oliver Reed
Major Holland .... Walter Gotell
Capt. Gregory .... James Villiers
Ted .... Thomas Kempinski
Sid .... Kenneth Cope
Mr. Dingle .... Brian Oulton
Miss Lamont .... Barbara Everest
Mr. Stuart .... Alan McClelland
Mr. Talbot .... James Maxwell
Victoria .... Rachel Clay
Elizabeth .... Caroline Sheldon
Anne .... Rebecca Dignam
Mary .... Siobhan Taylor
Richard .... Nicholas Clay
Henry .... Kit Williams
William .... Christopher Witty
George .... David Palmer
Charles .... John Thompson

Released in England in 1963 as "The Damned" by American expatriate director Joseph Losey, this strange but fascinating film has been since shelved or shunted aside for reasons, possibly political, that will probably never be fully explained. Interest was renewed in it when it was shown at the 1964 Trieste Film Festival.

Produced by Anthony Hinds, with Anthony Nelson Keys as associate producer and Michael Carreras as executive producer, for Hammer Films, its subject or its director may have, in 1963, been considered too controversial. Meanwhile Losey, is now a director of international reputation on the strength of "The Servant" and "King And Country."

H. L. Lawrence's novel, "The Children Of Light," turned into a disturbing but compelling screenplay by Evan Jones, has been transferred by Losey into a film that deserves more specialized treatment than it is presently getting. Columbia is packaging the film, shortened by 10 minutes, with its bigger, colorful "Genghis Kahn." Although technically excellent, "Damned," by Hollywood standards, was not an expensive one and should easily regain its production costs.

A frequently-asked question is "What is a director's picture?" This one is. Although the cast is excellent, no one character dominates the action or overshadows the others. Losey's hand is so apparent that the film's considerable effectiveness must be accredited to him as must its few faults and the fearsome message it conveys. Much of the film's appeal is visual, although the dialog is a credit to the scripter. The only objection that may (and will) come up about the film, is in its failure to take a stand. Things happen in the film, and certain predictions are made. Will they really happen? Should they properly happen or can they be prevented? Losey poses the question but makes the viewer decide which of the two sides really represents "The Damned."

Macdonald Carey, Shirley Anne Field, Alexander Knox (particularly good), Viveca Lindfors and Oliver Reed have principal roles in the quasi-sci-fi story which centers on a group of children being exposed to radiation in preparation for the day predicted by Knox as sure to come—when global nuclear warfare will destroy all living things—except these few. All the principals are excellent, with Reed playing a Teddy boy and brother of Miss Field although his interest in her is strongly incestuous. Miss Lindfors' avant-garde sculptress is a most offbeat character although she sides with the wrong side, resulting in her death.

Arthur Grant's black and white photography of the photogenic setting (mostly sea, surf and barren cliffs) is more interesting than the routine interior shots. Reginald Mills' original editing, concise and sharp, is marred by some abrupt cuts, probably made in the U.S., that are particularly annoying as they occur at crucial moments. James Bernard's music, generally romantic, veers toward the electronic side for the sci-fi effects.

Robe.

Casanova '70
(ITALIAN-COLOR)

Mastroianni name and sex-weariness as farcical theme. Exploitable and promising.

Embassy Pictures release of Joseph E. Levine presentation of Carlo Ponti production. Stars Marcello Mastroianni, Virna Lisi. Directed by Mario Monicelli. Screenplay, Furio Scarpelli, Agenore Incrocci, Monicelli, based on story by Tonino Guerra; camera (color), Aldo Tonti; editor, Ruggiero Mastroianni; sound, Ennio Sensi; music, Armando Trovaioli; asst. director, Renzo Marigano. Reviewed screening room, N.Y., July 16, '65. Running Time, 113 MINS.

Major Andrea Rossi-Colombetti	Marcello Mastroianni
Gigliola	Virna Lisi
Noelle	Michele Mercier
Thelma	Marisa Mell
Count Ferreri	Marco Ferreri
Psychoanalyst	Enrico Maria Salerno
Monsignor	Guido Alberti
Dolly Greenwater	Margaret Lee
Chambermaid	Rosemarie Dexter
Addolarata	Yolanda Modio
Indonesian Airline Hostess	Seyna Seyn
Santina	Moira Orfei
Lion Tamer	Liana Orfei
Girl in Museum	Beba Loncar
Gen. Greenwater	Frank Gregory
Grocer's Wife	Luciana Paoli
Gigliola's Mother	Augusta Checcotti
Gigliola's Father	Mario Banchelli

(English Subtitles)

The sexual emancipation of modern women has made their physical conquest so easy that its no wonder a contemporary Casanova might only be aroused when finding some danger in the chase. That's the premise of this glossy, handsomely produced Italo import which labors mightily to realize the variations on its one basic joke. That it succeeds in getting laughs as often as it does (about half the time) is a credit to star Marcello Mastroianni and a generally fine cast including Virna Lisi and Marisa Mell and some of the loveliest women in all Europe.

Pic is a highly exploitable sex farce which, backed by the box-office power of the Mastroianni name, should rack up good grosses, particularly in lucrative summer playing time in the U.S.

In the title role, Mastroianni is seen as a jaded NATO officer who finds himself *toujours pret* only when the odds against his success are great. Thus, for example, his desire for his beautiful French mistress, Michele Mercier, can only be aroused by an elaborate charade in which he breaks into his own house in the guise of a burglar. Facing the possibility that his mistress might shoot him, he seethes with the sought-for passion. This opening sets the stage for the string of episodes which follow, some of which are little more than bawdy blackout skits and one or two of which might be eliminated for better pacing. There is evidence already that some footage has been eliminated because continuity is not always too clear.

Costars Virna Lisi and Marisa Mell highlight two of the longest (and best) episodes in the film. Miss Lisi, as a virginal beauty who enchants Mastroianni only until she decides to succumb, is a pure delight, funny and affecting, playing always with a straight sincerity that underlines humor. Miss Mell is almost as good as the wife of a nobleman whose murderous jealousy again arouses Mastroianni to magnificent heights of folly.

Interspersed between these segments are some others ranging from good to barely okay. One of the best concerns a Sicilian peasant girl whom Mastroianni seduces while posing as a doctor with her family waiting in the next room to learn whether or not she is "pure." One of the worst involves a visit to a crazy psychoanalyst who loathes women himself and confides to Mastroianni that he likes black lace stockings — that is, to wear.

Mastroianni inevitably must carry the burden of the film and if there are times when his performance seems overly arch, it is a reflection of the generally thin material provided by the writers, including director Mario Monicelli. They all run out of inspiration from time to time.

Producer Carlo Ponti has provided an exceedingly lovely physical production, with the color camerawork to match. The English subtitles are okay and, at times, appear to be in better sync than the Italo dialog, much of which apparently was post-dubbed.

Anby.

Rotten To The Core
(BRITISH)

Boulting Brothers' satirical knives not as sharp as usual in this bigtime crime spoof. There's a lack of stellar names but enough yocks.

London, July 14.

British Lion presentation through BLC of a (Roy Boulting) Boulting Brothers' production. Features Anton Rodgers, Eric Sykes, Charlotte Rampling, Ian Bannen, Avis Bunnage, Dudley Setton, Peter Vaughan, Kenneth Griffith, James Beckett, Victor Maddern, Thorley Walters. Directed by John Boulting. Story and screenplay, Jeffrey Dell, Roy Boulting, John Warren, Len Heath, from an idea by Warren, Heath; camera, Freddie Young; editor, Teddy Darvas; music and title song, Michael Dress. Reviewed at Rialto Theatre, London. Running Time, 89 MINS.

Hunt	Eric Sykes
Vine	Ian Bannen
Jelly	Dudley Setton
Lenny	Kenneth Griffith
Scapa	James Beckett
Countess	Avis Bunnage
Duke	Anton Rodgers
Sara	Charlotte Rampling
Anxious	Victor Maddern
Preston	Thorley Walters
Sir Henry	Peter Vaughan
Prison Governor	Raymond Huntley
Chopper Parsons	Ian Wilson
Inspector Hewlett	Richard Coleman
Mrs. Dick	Barbara Everest
The Admiral	Cameron Hall
The General	Basil Dignam
War Office Major	Robert Bruce
Guard Commander	Neil Hallett

Bigtime crime is the main target of the Boulting Brothers' latest piece of satirical joshing, with army and police figuring in the story. It provides a reasonable ration of yocks and amusing situations but these have to struggle against some dim passages. The Boulting Brothers' knives are less sharp than customary. This could be because four scriptwriters had a hand in the pic. However, it provides reasonable fun in the farcical cops-an'-robbers school.

Idea hinges on the recent appeal of Prime Minister Wilson to adapt scientific methods to 1965 big business and industry. And this the Boultings' have applied to the activities of a gang of crooks whose young boss (Anton Rodgers) has set his beady eye on hi-jacking an army payroll worth nearly $3,000,000. Rodgers, the leader, known as "Duke," assembles his gang under the front of running a health resort hospital near the army camp. Gang contains some of the dimmest-witted crooks ever to do a stretch, but The Duke remorselessly drills them along scientific lines and develops a foolproof plan for snatching the loot when it is being transferred from train to a security van. Unexpected arrival of a prominent NATO German officer to watch an army maneuver sends the plan crumbling at the showdown. The gang has to revert to strongarm stuff in a predictable, but fairly hilarious climax.

Also involved in the shenanigans are a private eye, and an insane army officer infatuated with the Duke's moll. Fumbling attempts of three minor crooks to operate without the guidance of The Duke, the vamping of the army officer, the hijinks when the German officer arrives at the same time as the payroll and the eventual capture of the gang provide some laughable situations. But the screenplay is spotty in its humor and largely lacks the characteristic keen eye and irreverence with which the Boulting Brothers have so successfully deflated pomposity and authority in high places in previous films.

Anton Rodgers (who's in U. S. company of "Pickwick," now in L.A.) shows versatility in four or five characterizations but it needed a comedy character actor to dominate the laugh sequences. Eric Sykes is largely wasted in the role of the private eye, a characterization which, though well intended, fails to jell, through script flabbiness. There's a nice performance by Thorley Walters as a fussy, hypochondriacal police chief. And among the various crooks, Dudley Setton, James Beckett, Avis Bunnage and Kenneth Griffith all contribute sound work when opportunity occurs. Ian Bannen is not well cast as the susceptible army lieutenant but is too good a performer not to score fairly well.

The Boultings have put their faith in an unknown girl (Charlotte Rampling) as the Duke's moll, a model from the provinces who is infatuated with "the easy life." It is Miss Rampling's first piece of acting and it has also earned her a seven year Boulting contract. But the Boultings seem to have taken an undue risk in handing her such a large role as a start. She is quite **easy on the eye but lacks the experience and the personality to make her register sufficiently even with a virtually all-male cast.**

With Roy Boulting producing, and being partly responsible for the script, directorial chores have fallen on John Boulting. His professional knowhow often makes the pic funnier than it really is on closer inspection. Filmed in Panavision, Freddie Young has done a sound job with the lensing as has Teddy Darvas in the editing. Michael Dress has done a lively score, played and sung by the New

Jazz Voices, and also scribed the "over-credits" song which is a tongue-twister affair sung by Pamela Michaels. *Rich.*

L'Arme a Gauche
(Arm at the Left)
(FRENCH)

Paris, July 13.
CCFC release of Cite Films-TC Productions-Intermondia-Agata-Vides production. Stars Lino Ventura, Leo Gordon, Sylva Koscina. Directed by Claude Sautet. Screenplay, Charles Williams. Fouli Elia, Sautet from a novel by Williams; camera, Walter Wottitz; editor, Jacqueline Thiedot. Previewed in Paris. Running Time, 100 MINS.

Captain	Lino Ventura
Morrison	Leo Gordon
Mrs. Osborne	Sylva Koscina
Pablo	Alberto Mendozo

The arm in the title is a firearm and this is an adventure-gangster pic that is a very big cut above average. It plays the game fairly but never forces the suspense or action. Production has finely felt characterization, neat scripting and adept playing and, above all, it has expert detailed direction.

Playoff looms for this abroad with some specialized and arty chances also via its knowing rendition of a familiar but still evergreen tale of an adventurer besting the bad guys in a tight spot. And love aspects are also held to an intelligent, acceptable minimium.

Director Claude Sautet obviously loves and knows that fine aspect of American lore, but adapts and assimilates to give a fresh, vital and acceptable pic of this genre on his own. He did his first pic about five years ago, "Classe Tous Risques" (Underwrite All Risks), also a gangster film raised above the average by a fine fee for friendship and a keen narrative style. Why he took so long to make another only reflects on the industry. His type of snap, precision and dash in direction is sorely needed here.

A French ship captain is called to some Caribbean isle to buy a ship. But it turns out it is for gun-runners and the ship is hijacked, and he gets blamed. The owner, a beauteous American widow, comes down and the captain agrees to help her find the ship when he is cleared. They track it down, and the captain finally gets the girl.

Lino Ventura, usually prone to overplaying his good guy roles here is wisely held down and has force and dignity as a wanderer who can not quite make it with society. Yank actor Leo Gordon, who has played many a heavy in Hollywood pix, is excellent as the head man who is brutal and menacing.

S y l v a Koscina is charmingly frisky as the woman in this production. Others are fine. But it is the men's world that counts in this as the work of shifting the load of guns to get the ship righted is rightly exploited.

This is crisply lensed and paced, has a neat counterpoint and dramatic music score. It is that kind of well-made pic that never gets banal or cynical, and emerges highly entertaining. In short, a nice filmic commodity which with proper handling, is sure to have this playing off profitably. *Mosk.*

Guerre Secret
(Secret War)
(FRENCH-GERMAN-ITALIAN)

Paris, July 13.
Gaumont release of Franco London Film-Eichberg-Fair Film production. Stars Henry Fonda, Robert Ryan, Mario Adorf, Bourvil, Vittorio Gassman, Annie Girardot, Georges Marchal, Peter Van Eyck, Jacques Sernas, Maria Garcia Buccela. Directed by Terence Young, Christian-Jaque, Carlo Lizzani. Screenplay, Jacques Remy, Christian-Jaque, E . Deconcini, Philippe Bouvard; camera, Pierre Petit; editor, Borys Lewin. At Colisee, Paris. Running Time, 120 MINS.

Kourlof	Henry Fonda
Bruce	Robert Ryan
Callagan	Mario Adorf
Petchatkin	Peter Van Eyck
Lalande	Bourvil
Monique	Annie Girardot
Ferrari	Vittorio Gassman
Glazov	Jacques Sernas

Serviceable sketch film uses that popular theme of spies, working in episodes along the Berlin Wall, Africa and Italy to bundle some okay international names plus two Yanks, Henry Fonda and Robert Ryan. It appears an okay playoff item though somewhat too pat to put into a high?gear gimmicky James Bond sphere or as a more serious and probing look at the spy world. Ely Landau has U.S. distribution and was also participant in the production. Release will be via Allied Artists.

This has three directors doing acceptable if not unusual work, and mixes languages without strain. Pic cannily strives for action, suspense and comedy and is thus an item that should fit present interest in Cold War background pix.

Robert Ryan, as an American Intelligence Corps General, is the link for the three tales. First Henry Fonda is on the lam from Russia where he had gone as a child as a future American plant. But a traitor gets him before he can give his important news.

But he manages to leave a clue which segues into the next part as comic Bourvil plays a canny French agent who unmasks a Red plot to wreck a Yank Polaris submarine. This group also leaves a clue about a meeting which brings in Italy via planting a ladies' man as a gangster. Latter is supposed to capture a noted scientist for the Chinese Reds.

Fonda is misplaced as a Russo type but acquits himself well. Vittorio Gassman overacts but gives some comedic kicks to the Italo seg. Bourvil is an accomplished comic who gives some relief to his obviously least real segment. This pic should have an okay career here with mainly dualer and tele values for abroad with an added plus in the Yank names.

Picture eschews aping James Bond, in spite of some scientific gimmicks, and is mainly a standard spy filler that has enough production dress to keep it out of the quickie class. It can cash in on the spy-action interest in most marts. *Mosk.*

Happy Games
(FINLAND)

Moscow, July 13.
JUULIA
Stars Pirkko Peltonen, Raimo Nenonen. Direction, screenplay and editing, Aito Makinen; camera, Heikki Katajisto; music, Pentti Lasanen.
STICK
Stars Riitta Elstela, Lasse Liemola, Etta-Liisa Kunnas. Directed by Esko Elstela. Camera, Heikki Katajisto; screenplay, Satu Waltari and Estela. At Moscow Film Fest. Running Time, 96 MINS.

This two episoder is mainly geared for the Scandinavian market, for its general air of unsophistication will have little appeal to mature audiences. There is no connecting link between the two items, one being a romanticised incident, and the other a broad comedy.

"Juulia" is described by writer-director Aito Makinen as a "cynical romance," but it emerges more as a closeup of an affair between a young couple, as narrated to a friend by the girl. It is extremely casually paced, and there is virtually no dialog other than the narration at the beginning and end. Pirkko Peltonen and Raimu Nenonen make an attractive team, but have slight opportunities to display acting skill.

"Stick" describes a family's weekend visit to grandma's in the country, the highspots of which appear to be such mirthful incidents as grannie adding salt instead of sugar when baking a cake, and getting a splinter in her eye when chopping firewood. It's all very simple and innocuous. And the performances are on a par with the undemanding nature of the script. *Myro.*

Arizona Raiders
(TECHNISCOPE-COLOR)

Audie Murphy in another quick-tempoed western which should do well.

Hollywood, July 16.
Columbia Pictures release of Grant Whytock production. Stars Audie Murphy; features Michael Dante, Ben Cooper, Buster Crabbe, Gloria Talbott, Ray Stricklyn, George Keymas. Directed by William Witney. Screenplay, Alex Gottileb, Mary and Willard Willingham; story, Frank Gruber, Richard Schayer; camera (Technicolor), Jacques Marquette; music, Richard LaSalle; editor, Grant Whytock; art direction, Paul Sylos Jr.; Grund, B. F. Ryan; asst. director, Jack C. Lacy. Reviewed at Columbia Studios, July 13 '65. Running Time, 90 MINS.

Clint	Audie Murphy
Brady	Michael Dante
Willie Martin	Ben Cooper
Capt. Andrews	Buster Crabbe
Martina	Gloria Talbott
Danny Bonner	Ray Stricklyn
Montana	George Keymas
Matt Edwards	Fred Krone
Eddie	Willard Willingham
Tex	Red Morgan
Quantrell	Fred Graham

Name of Audie Murphy should lend potency to b.o. chances of this fast-paced Columbia release which has star, an Arizona Ranger, posing as a member of a vicious gang of raiders to bring them to justice. Sound values are incorporated in the Grant Whytock production to give it polish, and there's competent acting, spirited direction and a script that keeps characters credible to parlay Technicolor film into good entertainment for the playdates at which it's aimed.

Murphy plays a young Confederate who with a pal (Ben Cooper) joins Quantrell, the guerrilla, immediately after the Civil War because he's driven from the South. Captured by Union soldiers headed by Buster Crabbe, pair are sentenced to 20 years at hard labor. When Crabbe later is appointed to captain the newly-formed Arizona Rangers, detailed to hunt down a band of former Quantrell killers who have been spreading a reign of terror throughout the territory, he arranges for pair's ostensible escape — upon a promise of unconditional pardon — so they may help him round up the outlaws.

Based on a story by Frank Gruber and Richard Schayer, director William Witney accords know-how development to the Alex Gottlieb-Mary and Willard Willingham screenplay, and also manages interesting photographic backgrounds via Jacques Marquette's fluid cameras. Murphy delivers one of his regulation gunman characterizations for plenty of gunplay, and a story twist has a tribe of Yaqui Indians — for once pictured as good guys, although they put the outlaws through some exquisite Yaqui cactus torture — helping star clean out the gang.

Cooper is strongly cast as Murphy's partner, murdered by the outlaw leader, Michael Dante, who handles his role in proper fashion. Buster Crabbe is convincing as the Ranger captain, and Gloria Talbott inserts distaff interest as the Yaqui chief's daughter. Ray Stricklyn, as Murphy's Ranger brother shot down by bandits, and George Keymas, a gunman whom Murphy shoots down, likewise contribute to action. *Whit.*

20 Hours
(HUNGARY)

Moscow, July 13.
Hungarofilm presentation of a Mafilm production. Stars Antal Pager, Yanos Gyorbe, Emil Keresh. Directed by Zoltan Fabri. Screenplay, Niclos Kyullvo; camera, Dyerd Iilesh. At Moscow Film Fest. Running Time, 114 MINS.

In a surprising way, "20 Hours" is frankly critical of the regime in Hungary, and particularly attacks the attitudes and behavior of party officials. But such self-criticism is obviously designed to serve as propaganda for home consumption, and can be of little interest in Overseas markets.

Zoltan Fabri, one of the best known Hungarian directors, has, unfortunately, used a clumsy device for telling the story, and the result is near utter confusion. The "20 Hours" of the title relates to the time spent by a newsman in a village ferreting out facts about past misdeeds, particularly in connection with the 1956 period. Communists are shown as cold-blooded assassins, but the ending points the moral of the progress that has been made since the Reds came to power. The principal players are sincere and intense. Technically the film is up to accepted standards. *Myro.*

Moscow Film Fest

Darling
(BRITISH)

Powerful and provocative portrait of an immoral and irresponsible girl. Hefty grosses predicted.

Moscow, July 16.

Warner-Pathe release of an Anglo-Amalgamated presentation, produced by A. Joseph Janni for Vic Films. (Embassy release in U.S.) Stars July Christie, Dirk Bogarde and Laurence Harvey. Features Jose Villalonga, Roland Curran and Basil Henson. Directed by John Schlesinger; screenplay, Frederick Raphael; camera, Ken Higgins; editor, James Clarke; sets, Pay Sim; John Dankworth. At Moscow Film Festivai, Kremlin Palace of Congress, July 15, '65. Running Time, 128 MINS.

Dina Scott .... Julie Christie
Robert Gold .... Dirk Bogarde
Miles Brand .... Laurence Harvey
Malcolm .... Roland Curran
Prince Cesare .... Jose Villalonga
Alec Prosser Jones .... Basil Henson
Felicity Prosser Jones .... Helen Lindsay
Billie Castiglione ...... Annette Carroll

The latest example of the maturity of British films, "Darling," is also a very provocative picture destined for hefty grosses. It has already been acquired by Joseph E. Levine's Embassy Pictures, and there can be little doubt that his showmanship flourish will take fullest advantages of the many sexploitation possibilities the subject offers.

In many ways, this Jo Janni production f o r Anglo-Amalgamated can be described as a British "Dolce Vita." Its central character is a lovely, young, irresponsible and completely immoral girl, who can see little wrong in jumping in and out of bed with a complete lack of discrimination, and who goes on a shop-lifting expedition in one of London's more famous stores, just for kicks.

While a fair slice of the credit must go to the three stars and to scripter Frederick Raphael, the lion's share is due to John Schlesinger, the documentary - trained director who has skillfully used that technique to give in-depth portraits to three principals. This analytical-style direction adds to the sophistication, but importantly makes the characters appear as real and credible people.

The screenplay, based on an idea by Janni and others, is a deft combination of tight writing, brittle dialog and adroit plot construction. Apart from an occasional lapse, each character is clearly drawn and every situation logically developed. And with that basic raw material, plus an excellent stellar trio, producer Janni and director Schlesinger have fashioned a powerful and often exciting motion picture.

Everyone calls Diana Scott (Julie Christie) "darling." She's that kind of a girl — gay, good-looking, amusing company. She is married to a young, immature man, and once she has met the more sophisticated Robert (Dirk Bogarde), a writer and television interviewer, there is little doubt that the marriage will go on the rocks. He, too, is married, and has a couple of kids, but finds her irresistible and leaves his family to set up house with her. But their unmarried bliss is short-lived, and no sooner has she met Miles (Laurence Harvey) the suave and influential PR man with a powerful organization, than she hops into bed with him, following it up with a trip to Paris, giving the excuse that she is to be screen-tested for an important role.

As he's suspicious and she is careless, it does not take Bogarde long to discover/her infidelity. He

leaves her and, very quickly recovering from the shock, she continues to play and sleep around, apparently enjoying life in her own gay and irresponsible way. In Italy, to make a commercial, she meets a wealthy prince with seven children, who follows her to Capri to propose but is rejected. Subsequently, however, without adequate explanation, she accepts him, but is soon bored and, on impulse, flies to London for another torrid night with Bogarde. But in the fresh light of day he rejects her, and sends her tearfully packing to her Italian prince.

"Darling" was conceived entirely in cinematic terms and this is reflected on the screen, with a few standout scenes hyping the plot. One, refreshingly, has a touch of comedy. When Julie Christie and Dirk Bogarde return from Southamton where he has been on an assignment (at a time when both are still married) they phone their respective spouses to explain that they have been delayed, she acting as operator for his call, and he for hers, thus creating the impression that they are speaking long distance. But when she tries that technique after her Paris jaunt with Harvey, it has a sharp touch of irony.

There are several other memorable scenes. In one, when she discovers she is pregnant by Bogarde, she first regards it as a "bit of a giggle," but soon realises it will affect her way of life and has an abortion. After the operation, she declares she wants nothing more to do with sex, adding significantly, that she didn't enjoy it very much anyway, an insight on her nymphomania. In another, after Bogarde has discovered the truth about her Paris escapade, he declines to take her in a taxi, declaring, "I don't take whores in taxis," and giving her a pound note while going down the escalator to a subway. Miss Christie, adopting a common Cockney accent, immediately begins shouting abuse, insisting a "pound ain't enough." That is one of the most character revealing sequences in the picture. Not quite as effective is a Parisian orgy scene, object of w h i c h is somewhat obscured, though it has its dramatic moments.

One of the features of the production is the high standard of thesping, not just from the three principals but also from the other members of the cast. Miss Christie almost perfectly captures the character of the immoral Diana, and very rarely misses her target. She has the looks, the personality and the vivacity the role demands, and these qualities are intelligently used. Dirk Bogarde again demonstrates his acting skill with a performance that is intelligent and always believable. Laurence Harvey is exceptionally good as the suave and cynical Miles; indeed, he has not bettered this performance for years. Among those who stand out in the supporting cast are Jose Villalonga as the Italian prince, and Roland Curran, Basil Henson, Helen Lindsay, Annette Carroll, among others.

A p p a r e n t l y some significant footage was cut from the picture for its showing at the Moscow

festival, including one scene in which Miss Christie strips off her fineries before leaving her Italian prince. Such deletions may be understandable in the circumstances, though are to be regretted. They will, of course, be fully restored for showing in the West. *Myro.*

Dosti
(Friendship)
(INDIAN)
Moscow, July 13.

Rajshiri Productions (Calcutta) presentation. Stars Sushil Kumar, Sudhir Kumar. Directed by Satyen Bose. Screenplay, Govind Moonis, from a story by Ban Bhatt; camera, Marshal Braganza; editor, G. G. Mayekar; music, Laxmikant and Pyarelal. At Moscow Film Fest. Running Time, 120 MINS.

Ramu .... Sushil Kumar
Mohan .... Sudhir Kumar
Sharmaji .... Nana Palsikar
Ramu's Mother .... Leela Chitnis
Headmaster .... Abhi Bhattacharya
Manju .... Baby Farida
Nandu's Mother .... Leela Misra
Nandu .... Master Aziz
Nurse .... Uma
Ashok .... Sanjay

A disarming and tender story of the friendship of two boys, one lame and the other blind, this is told in the typical leisurely style associated with most Indian pictures. Though it has ample feeling and sincerity to commend it, "Dosti" is a questionable bet for Stateside arties, and will find its best market in Asian territories.

There is a touching quality to the yarn, and the dependence of the two youngsters on each other is shown with just the right dash of sentiment. The screenplay is full of cliche situations. But they are part of the pattern and are mainly acceptable, thinks in large measure to the sincerity of Satyen Bose's direction.

The principal performances by the two boys are in the right key, Sushil Kumar, as the lame boy, and Sudhir Kumar, as the blind one, making an effective team. Supporting roles are mainly well filled, though there is something slightly grotesque about Baby Farida as a sick, rich child who befriends the two boys. Camera work is fair, and editing could do with a little more pace. *Myro.*

The Flower Market
(Color-Songs)
(ARGENTINE-COLOR)
Moscow, July 13.

Argentina Sono Films (Buenos Aires) presentation of a coproduction with Benito Perojo (Madrid). No other credits available. At Moscow Film Fest. Running Time, 125 MINS.

In style and technique, this Argentinian musical matches the old-fashioned operatta. It is coy, sometimes brash and invariably noisy. And it has neither the talent, the music nor the story to sustain its overlong running time. At best, it might get by in a few Spanish lingo houses catering for the most unsophisticated-type audience.

The plot, if you'll pardon the expression, involves a group of elegant ladies who conspire to enlist the aid of the mayor to demolish the local flower market, which they consider to be an eyesore. The flower girls, natch, fight back, predictably winning out in the end. Romantic angle is provided by the

mayor's playboy son and the godchild of a flower seller.

There is some visual appeal in the pic and a number of lookers in the cast. But the song and dance routines are dated and the music is strictly forgettable. The Eastmancolor print seemed unusually garish. *Myro.*

The White Moor
(RUMANIA-COLOR)
Moscow, July 13.

Romfilm production and release. Stars F'orin Piersis, C. C. Codrescu, S. Sever, Lica Gheorghiu, and I. Petrescu. Direction and screenplay, by Ion Popescu Gopo. Camera, (Eastmancolor), Grigore Ionescu; music, Dumitry Capoianu. At Moscow Film Fest. Running Time, 89 MINS.

A charming and thoroughly delightful fairy tale, this Rumanian entry at the Moscow fest is handsomely mounted and lensed in striking Eastmancolor. It has been directed with a fine sense of style and humor. If dubbed, this could be a potential asset in a program appealing mainly to kids, or on an appropriate tv time slot.

The story of the Emperor's son, known as the White Moor, embodies all the conventions of fairy tales, including the witch who turns into a beautiful woman, the super eater who could devour two oxen for breakfast, the super drinker who has a barrel of wine as a nightcap, the shivering man who turns the flames of a forest fire to ice by spitting. And, of course, the gorgeous princess.

It is done with considerable gusto and spirit, with plenty of comedy to help the story on its way. The White Moor, nominated by his father to succeed to the throne, is sent on a mission to his uncle. But on the way encounters a villain who takes his place and makes the real prince act as his servant. The subsequent adventures and the eventual defeat of the impostor are the basis for the better comedy sequences.

It is all acted with considerable flourish. There is a specially noteworthy performance by Florin Piersis as the handsome blonde prince who turns from coward to hero with remarkable facility. All other leading players enter into the spirit with obvious enthusiasm. *Myro.*

The Young Soldier
(NORTH VIETNAM)
Moscow, July 15.

Feature Film Studios (Hanoi) production and presentation. Features Hong Duc and Minh Duc. Directed by Hai Ninh and Duc Hinh; screenplay, Hai Ho; camera, Khanh Du and Phu-My. At Moscow Film Festival, Kremlin Palace of Congress, July 14, '65. Running Time, 90 MINS.

As there is not much commercial future in West for any film coming out of North Vietnam, this is a "for the record" review, but it is surprising to note that in the midst of guerrilla warfare the Vietnamese have the time and the resources to undertake feature film production. "The Young Soldier" is very immature by accepted Western standards, but technically it suggests the North Vietnamese are learning fast.

Expectedly, the yarn has strong propaganda overtones, and though it is a war story, it is not concerned with the present campaign against U.S. but with the bitter earlier struggle a g a i n s t the French when this was French-Indo-China. The hero is a dedicated graduate of the military school who is at first put to work on organizing provisions, but later gets his battle honors when he conducts a one-man vendetta against a tank.

Myro.

Tine
(Maid Tine)
(DANISH)

Moscow, July 14.

Rialto Film (Copenhagen) production and release. Stars Lone Hertz, Johannes Meyer, Joergen Reenberg, Ellen Gottschlach. Direction and screenplay, Knud Leif Thomsen; camera, Henning Kristiansen; music, Thorkild Knudsen. At Moscow Film Fest. Running Time, 110 MINS.

Based on a novel by Herman Bang, this Danish film has the Danish-Prussian war of 1863 as its background, and describes the love affair of a pastor's daughter with a lieutenant whose family has been evacuated from the battle zone. It is a modest production, but has integrity and an appealing performances by Lone Hertz in the title role. Its main appeal will be within Scandinavia and some European territories, but cannot be hopefully considered for the U.S. market.

Knud Leif Thomsen's direction responds to the leisurely pace of his own script, but is not without style. And the battle sequences are realistically staged. It is unrelieved drama, culminating with the death of the officer and the suicide of the girl.

Aside from Miss Hertz, the performances are sincere but heavygoing, but in tune with the theme. Thorkild Knudsen's score has unusual power while the sets and costumes capture the period.

Myro.

Three Steps in Life
(POLISH)

Moscow, July 14.

Film Polski presentation and release of three episode production directed by Jerzy Hoffman and Edward Skorzewski. Screenplay by Jerzy Janicki and Josef Kusmierek; camera, Wladyslaw Forbert; music, Vojciech Kilar. Cast: "Divorce—Polish Style" Ewa Wisniewska and Ludwik Pak. "Birthday" Tadeusz Fijewski and Irena Orska. "One Hour's Journey" Anna Ciepielewska. At Moscow Film Festival, Kremlin Palace of Congress, July 14, '65. Running Time, 100 MINS.

Not only has one of the Eastern bloc countries jumped on the bandwagon of multiple-episodic films, but even has a variation on one of the more popular Western titles in "Divorce—Polish Style," one of the three items in this Polish production. But there the crib ends, as otherwise it bears little or no relation to the more popular Italian film that was around a couple of seasons back.

Its human story notwithstanding, "Divorce—Polish Style" has a near documentary flavor as it outlines the procedure for ending a mar-

riage under present Polish laws. It is a diverting little item about a young couple who have never been able to have their own apartment, and even his landlord has objected when the young wife has spent the night with her husband. There is a neat, ironical ending when a likely reconciliation is foiled when they are cheated out of a flat by someone who had heard the judge rule in favor of divorce.

"Birthday" is an intriguing study of a retired official, whose natal day is remembered only by his wife. It is touching, but never sentimental and it is given the right flavor by the studied performances by Tadeusz Fijewski and Irena Orska as husband and wife.

Far more conventional is the third episode, "One Hour's Journey" in which a pediatrician is delayed by a pompous railway official while en route to save a dying child. It is stylishly made, however, and that helps to give it some artistic substance.

This three-parter may not have much of a chance in principal Western markets, but should conceivably do well within Eastern European territories. *Myro.*

4 x 4
(NORWAY-DENMARK-SWEDEN-FINLAND)

Moscow, July 14.

Svensk Filmindustri (Stockholm) release of a four-episode feature film coproduced by Laterna Film (Copenhagen), Kurvaara Filmi Oy (Helsinki) and Egil Monn Iversen (Oslo). At Moscow Film Fest. Running Time, 107 MINS.

THE STOP AT MURLANDET
(Swedish)

Svensk Filmindustri production. Stars Max von Sydow, Allan Edwall, Karl-Erik Flens. Directed by Jan Troell. Screenplay, Bengt Forslund and Troell; camera, Troell; music, Erik Nordgren.

THE SUMMER WAR
(Danish)

Laterna Film production. Stars Cristoffer Bro, Niels Barfoed, Yvonne Ingdal. Directed by Palle Kjaerulff-Schmidt. Screenplay, Klaus Rifbjerg; camera, Rolf Ronne; music, Bent Axen.

WHY
(Finnish)

Kurkvaara Filmi production. Stars Maj-Britt Seivala, Jaakko Ahvonen, Sinnikka Hannula. Direction, screenplay and camera, Maunu Kurkvaara; music, Usko Merilainen.

GIRL WITH WHITE BALL
(Norwegian)

Egil Monn Iversen production. Stars Kari Ohrn Geelmuyden, Ole Sorli, Anne Marit Jacobsen, Vegard Hall, Robert Broberg. Directed by Rolf Clemens. Screenplay, Sten Rune Sterner; camera, Finn Bergan; music, Egil Monn-Ivensen.

Although shown at the Moscow festival under the Norwegian banner, this episode film really comprises four short and unconnected stories contributed by each of the Scandinavian countries. It does not add up to very much in the way of boxoffice outside its native territories.

Of the four episodes, only the Swedish one, "Stop at Murlandet," has anything approaching artistic merit. The Danish contribution is passable, but the two others are aimless and pointless, thereby seriously hurting the overall potentialities of this pic.

The Swedish episode is highlighted by a standout study by Max von Sydow as a brakeman on a locomotive, who quits his job on an impulse to enjoy the fruits of nature for the first time in his life, roaming around the countryside at will and lapping up its

pleasures. His performance completely dominates the item, but sensitive direction is another plus.

"Summer War" is a trivial piece about an army unit on summer maneuvers. One soldier prefers to read poetry under a tree, and then hies off to a cafe to twist with one of the staff until picked up by the military police. Cristoffer Bro and Yvonne Ingdal make amiable leads.

The Finnish contribution is about a young art student who meets a French girl in a gallery just a few hours before she has to fly away, and they fall in love very quickly. "Why must you go?" he asks, and hence the title. It is casually directed and indifferently acted.

"Girl With a White Ball" is about a young girl who can best be described as a peeping Thomasina, and who spends her time eavesdropping on lovers in a park and elsewhere. It is dull and tedious to a degree. The girl's unchanging expression adds to the boredom. *Myro.*

The Assault
(CZECHOSLOVAKIA)

Moscow, July 16.

Czescoslovekly Film (Prague) presentation of a Barrandov Studios production. Stars Siegfried Loyca, Harry Studt, Radoslav Brzobohaty, Ludek Munzar and Josef Vinklar. Directed by Jiri Sequens; screenplay, M. Fabera, K. Piksa and Sequens; camera, R. Millic; sets, M. Vacek. At Moscow Film Festival, Kremlin Palace of Congress, July 15, '65. Running Time, 105 MINS.

Kral .... Radoslav Brzobohaty
Strnad .... Rudolf Kelinek
Vyskocil .... Antonin Mrkvicka
Klein .... Pavel Bartl
Vrbas .... Josef Vinklar
Heydrich ...., Siegfried Loyda
Canaris .... Harry Studt

The assassination of Reinhard Heydrich by Czech guerrillas, and the reprisals that inevitably followed, forms the plot of this production, which has been made in near-documentary style to give it an authentic historical flavor. It is a strong and tense entertainment, vigorously directed by Jiri Sequens, which has the qualities to justify limited presentation in the West, though would appear to be an unlikely prospect for more than modest grosses.

Working from a script that carefully reconstructs the assassination plot and the subsequent siege of the guerrillas in a disused church, the director has fashioned a forceful and well-paced picture, in which the heroes are presented as sincere patriots without any hint of mock heroics. The order from the commander when they are under siege to fight to the last bullet, and then to use that on themselves, is both believable and realistic.

The climactic siege sequence is both gripping and dramatic, and the defenders withstand smoke bombs and flooding of their hideout cellar as long as humanly possible. But they don't surrender, in spite of assurances that nothing will happen to them. There is always that last bullet to be used.

Production has all round vigor, which is matched by a number of first rate performances. The cast is consistently good, thus giving the fullest possible realism to the story.

Myro.

War and Peace
(Parts 1 and 2)
(RUSSIAN 70m—COLOR)

Magnificent and spectacular production and a major film by any standards. Final length will present serious exhibition problems in the West, but if overcome could be a boxoffice smash.

Moscow, July 17.

Sovexport (Moscow) presentation of a Mosfilm Studios production. Stars Lyudmilla Savelyeva, Sergei Bondarchuk and Vyacheslav Tikhonov. Directed by Bondarchuk; screenplay, Bondarchuk and Vassili Solovvov; camera, Anatolik Petritsky; sets, Mikhail Bogdanov and Gennadi Myasnikov; music, Vyacheslav Ovchinnikov. At Moscow film festival, Kremlin Palace of Congress, July 16, '65. Running Time: 218 MINS.

Natasha ..... Lyudmilla Savelyeva
Pierre Bezukhov ..... Sergei Bondarchuk
Prince Andrei Boikonsky
.... Vyacheslav Tikhonov
Bolkonsky .... Anatoly Ktorov
Prince Vasily .... Boris Smirnov
Countess Rostova.. Kira Ivanova-Golovko
Helene .. .. Irina Skobtseva
Liza Bolkonskaya .Anastasia Vertinskaya
Uncle ... . Alexander Borisov
Napoleon ...... Vladislav Strzheichik
Annette Scherer ...... Angelina Stepanova

More than three years in the making, and another year is expected to pass before it is finally completed, the first two parts of "War and Peace" are a mighty omen for the finished article. It is a sumptuous and lavish spectacular, making brilliant use of the 70m screen. But it has its faults and poses its own set of problems.

Sergei Bondarchuk, one of Russias great directors, is also on this showing one of the foremost filmmakers in the world. And he's a pretty good actor, too, but that's by the way for the moment. He has undertaken a mammoth project, with a budget which would be astronomical even by Hollywood standards, and kept to his intention of making a faithful filmization of Leo Tolstoy's famous novel That may have been a worthy decision, but not necessarily the wisest one, as the film suffers occasionally from being too "literary," which may please those who are familiar with the novel, though it may hinder the enjoyment of the mass of cinemagoers.

But the real problem has yet to be faced: how to present the finished production to audiences throughout the world—and there's no doubt that the world will want to see this film. The first two episodes run for more than three and a half hours, and there are two more parts yet to come. There is surely no theatre in the western world which would contemplate a feature lasting for some six or seven hours. It has been suggested that the exhibition pattern could follow that of Wagner's "Ring," but if that is acceptable in the Soviet Union, it is unlikely to be favored in the United States or in Europe. The ideal solution would obviously be to have a re-edited version for the West, lasting about half the final length, but such drastic cutting could involve delicate artistic and technical problems. And, in any event, it could destroy the director's original intention.

At its best, the production is superb. Bondarchuk is a master at controlling crowds, and the two great battle scenes in "1805" (the first part) are nothing short of breathtaking. In the Borodinov battle sequences there is an unforgettable moment as the rival Russian and French armies march defiantly towards each other, and the moment of impact is spectacularly exciting. Something like 10,-000 extras are used in these scenes, and as they crowd the large screen they bring a visual excitement rare in cinematic history.

Equally spectacular is the subsequent battle of Austerlitz, for which the Russians have changed sides and are fighting alongside their former enemies, the French, against their former allies, the Austrians. There is the same brilliant use of vast crowds, the same stunning visual excitement. Both are unsurpassed directorial triumphs.

But Bondarchuk errs from time to time, too frequently in fact for a director of his experience. In his determination to translate the novel literally, he tries also to be too poetic, and overdoes it with an endless succession of shots of clouds, trees and the countryside, while the story is being narrated over the picture. Enough would have been enough, but he uses this device over and over again, showing a surprising lack of self restraint.

On the other hand, he's not been afraid to use old-fashioned techniques where he believes it helps the picture, such as split screens and gimmicky camera angles. He has also used some fancy dissolves and wipes, but more fascinating is the prolonged fadeout, often leaving the screen dark for several seconds, between one scene and the next.

The spectacle, however, is not confined to the two battle sequences. In the second half, "Natasha," there is a superbly staged and photographed ballroom scene, and a magnificent hunt, which comes to a brilliant climax as the hounds grapple with the wolf. Closeup camera angles and standout editing makes this sequence another production highlight, as memorable as the battle scenes in the first episode.

One of the major problems with a production of this magnitude is the multiplicity of characters that have to be clearly established in the mind of the viewer, and this has been a tough nut to crack both for the writers and director. On the whole, this hazard has been surmounted, and in an English language version the average audience should have no serious difficulty in readily identifying the principals, and thus keeping up with the various threads of the plot.

From an audience standpoint, one of the major sources of pleasure will undoubtedly be in watching Lyudmilla Savelyeva, the Leningrad ballerina who plays the part of Natasha. She's an absolute find and a joy to behold. She's a beauty, and she can act. All the fresh, impetuous, eagerness of youth comes out in her performance, and it comes out naturally. Never does she appear to strain for effect, and there's an incandescent glow whenever she's on the screen. Her dance of joy

towards the end of the second part is as charming as it is sincere.

One of the surprises is Bondarchuk's own performance in the demanding role of the shy, tongue-tied Pierre. He may not look exactly right for the part, but he understands it and overcomes most of its problems. And his thesping range is quite remarkable, from a drunk scene with fellow officers in the opening stages of the film, to his embarrassed proposal to the beautiful Helene, down to the duel with another officer who has accused his wife of immorality. The actual duel scene itself is, perhaps, a little too theatrical and not up to the high overall standard which the director has set.

Another imposing performance comes from Vyacheslav Tikhonov as Prince Andrei Bolkonsky, who is wounded and missing after the Borodinov campaign, and eventually returns home as his wife is in labor. She shortly afterwards dies in childbirth. It is he who proposes to Natasha, and although she accepts overenthusiastically, he insists that she must wait for a year before giving her final answer. The proposal is a delicate and touching piece of filmmaking, truly in keeping with the character of the novel.

Though the aforementioned trio have starring status, they do not by any means dominate the story, and there are many other significant roles, all of which have been filled with utmost care and precision. They are all distinguished Soviet actors, and many have been recruited from the Moscow Arts Theatre, among them Anatoly Ktorov, who plays Prince Andrei's father, an old man who keeps his mind alert by working at a lathe; Boris ....ily and Kira Ivanov-Colovko as the Countess Rostova. Another beauty in the film is the blonde Irina Skobtseva, who is at first properly demure as Helene, but then changes character after lashing out at her husband's folly in challenging the other man to a duel. There is a tender cameo from Anastasia Vertinskaya as Prince Andrei's wife, and excellent support from Alexander Borisov as Natasha's uncle and Vladislav Strzhelchik as Napoleon, a ... ...rs.

It is not ... Bondarchuk and the cast, however, who merit the huzzahs, but also many of the highly skilled ... ... notably Anatolik Petritsky for his standout lensing. In spite of the previously mentioned gimmickry, his 70m lens has caught the magnificence and splendor of the major action scenes, as well as the intimacy of others. Credit also to the sound engineer (unnamed in the credits) who has not been afraid to use a deafening score where called for, but has also skillfully used his magnetic equipment to give full stereo effect to the battle scenes. The two art directors have also fullfilled a major assignment with distinction, and many of the authentic set decorations look impressive on the screen. The score, powerful at times, restrained at others, captures the mood with remarkable fidelity.

All told, a picture of remarkable merit which has almost lived up to

the word of mouth that has built up over the past three years.
Myro.

How to Stuff a Wild Bikini
(SONGS-PANAVISION-COLOR)

Latest entry in AIP's "beach" pix series for youth market lacks the go-go of past offerings but should do fair biz in intended outlet.

Hollywood, July 21.
American International Pictures release of James H. Nicholson-Samuel Z. Arkoff production. Stars Annette Funicello, Dwayne Hickman, Brian Donlevy, Harvey Lembeck, Beverly Adams, John Ashley, Jody McCrea, Buster Keaton, Mickey Rooney. Directed by William Asher. Screenplay, Asher, Leo Townsend; camera (Pathecolor), Floyd Crosby; music, Les Baxter; art direction, Howard Campbell; editors, Fred Feitshans, Eve Newman; asst. director, Dale Hutchinson; sound, Don Rush. Reviewed at Academy Award Theatre, July 20, '65. Running Time, 90 MINS.

Dee Dee	Annette Funicello
Ricky	Dwayne Hickman
B. D.	Brian Donlevy
Eric Von Zipper	Harvey Lembeck
Cassandra	Beverly Adams
Bonehead	Jody McCrea
Johnny	John Ashley
Animal	Marianne Gaba
North Dakota Pete	Len Lesser
Native Girl	Irene Tsu
Dr. Melamed	Arthur Julian
Khola Koku	Bobbi Shaw
Bwana	Buster Keaton
The Kingsmen	Theirselves
Puss	Alberta Nelson
J. D.	Andy Romano
Rat Pack	John Macchia, Jerry Brutsche, Bob Harvey, Myrna Ross, Alan Fife
Ad Men	Sig Frohlich, Tom Quine, Hollis Morrison, Guy Hamric, George Boyce, Charlie Reed
Patti	Patti Chandler
Mike	Mike Nader
Beach Girls	Lauree Holmes, Jo Collins, Mary Hughes, Stephanie Nader, Jeannine White, Janice Levinson
Beach Boys	Ed Garner, John Fain, Mickey Dora, Brian Wilson, Bruce Baker, Ned Wynn, Kerry Berry, Rick Jones, Ray Atkinson, Ron Dayton
Bookends	Salli Sachse, Linda Opie Bent
Chickie	Marianne Gordon
Secretary	Sheila Stephenson
English Girl	Rosemary Williams
Peanuts	Sue Williams
Italian Girl	Tonia Van Deter
German Girl	Uta Stone
Barberette	Toni Harper
Manicurist	Michele Barton
Shoe Shine Girl	Victoria Carrol
Peachy	Mickey Rooney

American International's latest contender in the youth market carries a catchy — if way out — title, but is a lightweight affair lacking the breeziness and substance of past entries. A nonsensical plot without enough happening and story line barely skimming the surface are further deterrents. So solid is the hold of company's beach pix on their particular market, however, that with such names as Annette Funicello, Dwayne Hickman, Frankie Avalon and Harvey Lembeck to spark interest the current opus should register fairly well.

Where James H. Nicholson-Samuel Z. Arkoff production shines is the presence of a flock of young lovelies bikini-clad, and several song numbers dished up by the femme star, The Kingsmen combo, and various others in cast, to provide welcome melodic interludes. They give gloss, but whole affair seems to have been given the once-over-lightly treatment.

Script by William Asher — who directs —and Leo Townsend is hit and miss, twirling around a myste-

rious redhead suddenly appearing to fill a bikini which has been floating in midair. Frankie, on duty in Tahiti with his Naval Reserve unit, enlists the services of Buster Keaton, a witch doctor, to determine whether his girlfriend back home — Annette — is being true to him. Then there's Mickey Rooney, a fast-talking pressagent, trying to promote a motorcycle race with femme stuffed in the wild bikini, and Hickman wooing Annette during Frankie's absence. Result: utter confusion.

Miss Funicello, usually with a bulk of the footage in these beach romps, obviously is enciente here (wrapups she wears, contrasting with scanty attire of other femmes, accentuates her condition), and aside from a couple of songs she has little to do. Avalon, too, has little more than a bit, but how he can overlook the charms of Irene Tsu, his little Tahitian playmate, is as mysterious as who Beverly Adams, gal stuffed in the bikini, really is. It doesn't matter, she's pretty. Hickman is in for a straight lead, Rooney plays his part broad, Harvey Lembeck appears again in his familiar Eric Von Zipper character, and Brian Donlevy is the race promoter. Flock of beach boys and girls are all comely as usual. A surprise single-shot appearance of a name tv actress in finale gives a belt.

Asher manages plenty of glamour in his direction and color camera work by Floyd Crosby is often a treat. Songs by Guy Hemric and Jerry Styner, and music score by Les Baxter, are nicely received.
Whit.

Dark Intruder

Satisfactory mellerdrama with horror touches should do well as second-bill fare.

Universal Pictures release of a Jack Laird production. Features Leslie Nielsen, Mark Richman, Judi Meredith, Werner Klemperer. Directed by Harvey Hart. Screenplay, Barre Lyndon; camera, John F. Warren; film editor, Edward W. Williams; sound, Robert Bertrand; music, Stanley Wilson; makeup, Bud Westmore. Reviewed at Riverside Theatre, N.Y.C., July 22, '65. Running Time, 59 MINS.

Brett Kingsford	Leslie Nielsen
Harvey Misbach	Gilbert Green
Nikola	Charles Bolender
Robert Vandenburg	Mark Richman
Evelyn Lang	Judi Meredith
Prof. Malaki	Werner Klemperer
Chi Zang	Peter Brocco
Dr. Burdett	Vaughn Taylor
Hannah	Harriet Vine

This short (59 mins.) feature, which Universal is packing with its current release, "I Saw What You Did," holds its own with its considerably more expensive companion.

While no great shakes as an example of cinematic artistry, "Intruder" is honest hokum, with some occasional flashes of excellent writing and should find many bookings because of its low cost, the satisfaction it will give its audiences and its convenient running time.

Producer Jack Laird's turn-of-the-century mellerdrama shows influence of and even copying from, earlier and better terror tales with same or similar settings. Evidently scripter Barre Lyndon was exposed to such films as "The Lodger,"

"The Body Snatcher" and other Victorian horror minor classics in the field of cinematic but at least he has been an attentive viewer. Occasional touches of humor, generally in the dialog, are his own contribution and welcome ones.

Leslie Nielson, as a San Francisco bon vivant whose flippant and frothy behavior is a cover for his real interest — as an amateur but, oh, so skilled, criminologist — is rather stodgy but it may be because he's forced to play second banana to both his dwarf valet, (Charles Bolender) and a dialogless but hypersensitive mandrake plant, the prop which inspires Lyndon's best lines.

Mark Richman is a socialite who finds that he has an evil twin brother who's something of an expert on transmigration and wants to change his hideous appearance (and he is ugly) for brother's pretty body. Judi Meredith, as Richman's fiancee, is pretty, rattle-brained and harmless. Werner Klemperer as a fortune teller and the link to the secret of the twin, is properly ominous but the only serious contribution to the minor mystery is Bud Westmore's make-up for the monster.

Peter Brocco as an ancient Chinese. Vaughn Taylor as the family doctor and Gilbert Green as the police inspector lend able support to the principals. John F. Warren's photography is over dark, many of the scenes occurring at night or in fog but it is still superior to Edward W Williams' editing which is disjointed, obvious and so choppy at times as to become annoying, unless the print seen was a particularly poor one. Music is routine.   Robe.

Morituri

Sometimes suspenseful World War II sea melodrama with names of Marlon Brando and Yul Brynner to boost chances of good reception.

Hollywood, July 16.
Twentieth-Fox release of Aaron Rosenberg production. Stars Marlon Brando, Yul Brynner; features Janet Margolin, Trevor Howard, Martin Benrath, Hans Christian Blech, Wally Cox. Directed by Bernhard Wicki. Screenplay, Daniel Tara-dash, based on novel by Werner Joerg Luedecke; camera, Conrad Hall; music, Jerry Goldsmith; art direction, Jack Martin Smith, Herman A. Blumenthal; asst. director, David Silver; editor, Joseph Silver; sound, Garry Harris, David Rockendorf. Reviewed at 20th-Fox Studios, July 15, 1965. Running Time, 118 MINS.
Robert Crain .... Marlon Brando
Captain Mueller .... Yul Brynner
Esther .... Janet Margolin
Colonel Slatter .... Trevor Howard
Kruse .... Martin Benrath
Donkeyman ..... Hans Christian Blech
Dr. Ambach .... Wally Cox
Branner .... Max Haufler
Milkereit .... Rainer Penkert
Baldwin .... William Redfield
Admiral .... Oscar Beregi
Nissen .... Martin Brandt
Kur .... Charles De Vries
Busch .... Carl Esmond
Wilke .... Martin Kosleck
Steward .... Norbert Schiller
German Crew Member....Robert Sorrells
Crew Member .... Rick Traeger
Lt. Brandt .... Ivan Triesault

"Morituri" — taking its title from the old Roman gladiator cry, "Those who are about to die salute you!"—is a World War sea drama of sometimes battering impact. Starring Marlon Brando and Yul Brynner, who should assure a

certain boxoffice lure, the Aaron Rosenberg production carries strong suspense at times and a brooding menace that communicates to the spectator.

In the narrative, however, there is confusion, and considerable dialog is spoken in such heavy accents that it often cannot be understood. Where the Daniel Tara-dash screenplay misses particularly is an over-abundance of attitudes and points of view, of ideologies, on the part of its principals. German director Bernhard Wicki nevertheless maintains his action forcefully and injects plenty of excitement despite the plot veering off in many directions in arriving at its climax.

Action takes place aboard a German blockade runner in 1942 en route from Yokohama to Bordeaux with a cargo of 7,000 tons of indispensable crude rubber for the Nazis, which the Allies also want. British put a man on the freighter with orders to disarm explosive charges by which the captain would scuttle his ship rather than allow capture. Allied naval units plan to intercept the vessel at a certain point, by which time it's figured British agent will have had time to disconnect all the charges.

Both Brando and Brynner contribute hard-hitting performances, Brando as the saboteur and Brynner as captain — despite the garbled characters they are called upon to play. Former, a German deserter threatened with return to Germany and certain death if he doesn't acquiesce to British demand, gives his impersonation almost tongue-in-cheek handling. Brynner, a German but not a Nazi, thinks Brando, posing as a high Nazi S.S. officer, has been put aboard to spy on him and refuses him the run of the ship, thus throwing up an unexpected hurdle. Wicki builds his suspense expertly as Brando goes about his mission.

In top support, Trevor Howard is in briefly as a British Intelligence officer, and Martin Benrath makes the most of his role as exec officer, a Nazi who takes over the ship when Brynner becomes raging drunk. Janet Margolin, sole femme in cast, is okay as a Jewish refugee put aboard by the Japanese. Others who stand out include Rainer Penkert and Hans Christian Blech, who plan their own seizure of ship: Wally Cox, doctor, and Oscar Beregi, a German admiral.

On technical side, Conrad Hall's black-and-white photography merits attention; Jerry Goldsmith's music score lends strong backing to action; art direction by Jack Martin Smith and Herman A. Blumenthal is effective.   Whit.

Help!
(BRITISH-COLOR)

The zany world of Beatledom rears its head again, this time in color. Many "with it" gags and giggles, and also many flat passages and near-misses. But with stellar draw, color and good songs it's a box-office bet.

London, July 27.
United Artists release of Walter Shen-son-Subafilms production. Stars The Beatles; features Leo McKern, Eleanor Bron, Victor Spinetti, Roy Kinnear, Patrick Cargill, John Bluthal, Warren Mitchell. Directed by Richard Lester. Screenplay, Marc Behm and Charles Wood, from Behm's original story; camera (Eastmancolor), David Watkin; editor, John Victor Smith; special effects, Cliff Richardson & Roy Wybrow; music, Ken Thorne; songs, John Lennon & Paul McCartney, George Harrison. Reviewed at Odeon, Leicester Square, London, July 27, '65. Running Time, 92 MINS.
John .... John Lennon
Paul .... Paul McCartney
Ringo .... Ringo Starr
George .... George Harrison
Clang .... Leo McKern
Ahme .... Eleanor Bron
Foot .... Victor Spinetti
Algernon .... Roy Kinnear
Superintendent .... Patrick Cargill
Bhuta .... John Bluthal
Doorman .... Alfie Bass
Abdul .... Warren Mitchell
Jeweler .... Peter Copley
Lawn Mower .... Bruce Lacey

With color, foreign locations, some typically lively Beatles' ditties and what started out, at least, to be a more ambitious storyline than that of their first pic, The Beatles' second effort is bound to be a resounding boxoffice click. It is peppered with bright gags and situations and throwaway nonsense. Richard Lester's direction is expectedly alert and the color lensing is a delight. But there are also some frantically contrived spots and sequences that flag badly. The simple good spirits that pervaded "A Hard Day's Night" are now often smothered as if everybody, from director, writers and artists to the technicians are all desperately trying to outsmart themselves and be ultra-clever-clever. Nevertheless, at 92 minutes, "Help!" is a good, nimble romp with both giggles and belly-laughs.

Story, which would have been a useful Marx Bros. vehicle, is by Marc Behm and Charles Wood and is a peg on which to hang special effects, songs and several bursts of riotous nonsense but it hasn't the wit and bite of Alun Owen's job for "Hard Day's Night." It concerns the efforts of a gang of Eastern thugs, led by Leo McKern to get hold of a sacrificial ring which has been sent to Ringo by a fan and which he is innocently wearing. Without it the Goddess Kali can hold no human sacrificial rituals. Also after the ring is a nutty, powerdrunk scientist who sees the ring as a key to world domination. With these two sets of hamhanded but desperate enemies (plus the almost equally risky police protection of Scotland Yard) The Beatles are given a heck of a runaround which takes them from London to Stonehenge, the Alps and the Bahamas.

There are some pretty funny sequences. Notably a roughhouse in a London Indian restaurant, a battle royal in The Beatles' opulent London apartment, a

tavern sequence with a stray tiger that can only be tamed to the strains of the "Joy Chorus" from Beethoven's 9th Symphony and which swells into community singing at a Wembley Cup Final, and some frisky frolicking in the Alps and Buckingham Palace. But there are also many misfires. An outstanding thud is a long, flat and unfunny sequence when the boys are recording on Salisbury Plain, protected by Army tanks and with their foe at their heels.

The Beatles prove more relaxed in front of the camera at this, their second attempt, and many of their throwaway gags are choice non sequiturs. But others are lost to the audience by the lads' mumbling accent. They have still to prove themselves to be actors, but as screen personalities they are good material and have a touch of the Marx Bros. in their similar irreverent flights of fantasy. Leo McKern, fine actor, is proving himself a stalwart comedians' laborer. He works energetically throughout, and with a string of grotesque disguises help to rocket the fun along. Victor Spinetti as the scientist also contributes a useful study, as do Roy Kinnear as his bumbling assistant. John Bluthal as McKern's aide, and Patrick Cargill as a Scotland Yard man, a role which looks to have been trimmed down somewhat. The only significant femme role is played by Eleanor Bron, as the Eastern princess who aids The Beatles' in their many hapless situations. This girl, who made a name in tv satire, is an adequate heroine but she is apparently bewilderedly out of her depth and it might have been better to have entrusted the role to a more experienced comedienne. Warren Mitchell, Peter Copley and Alfie Bass are others who chip in with fun bits. Lester's direction, as always, is imaginative and alert though sometimes a shade over-indulgent. It is clear that producer Shenson and Lester are The Beatles' guidng film angels. But every department gives the Liverpool lads sound support. Cliff Richardson and Roy Wybrow have a joyday with special effects and David Watkin's Eastmancolor lensing is superb in the Alpine sequences. Sometimes it becomes over-involved in intricacies and frills but the camerawork and the direction blend well to give the film a sharp, visual impact. Ken Thorne's score (which incorporates some classic composers as well as some of The Beatles' earlier songs) has apt gaiety and The Beatles have contributed several obvious winners in the songs, even though some have already been exposed on the air. The songs do nothing to help along the plot or situations but are agreeable for Beatles' fans particularly the title ditty. The singing action never palls because of the busy direction and camerawork. The fact, for instance, that a grand piano appears conveniently in the snowy Alpine wastes takes on its own particular brand of logic in the zany goings on.

Though it is difficult to assess the editing of John Victor Smith because of the inconsequential nature of the action it seems smooth enough. But it is obvious that large chunks of the film must have been tossed overboard. Ray Simm's art direction and the fore-and-aft color titles of Robert Freeman all help the atmosphere. There's a particularly neat "before titles" opening with the boys on a television set being pelted with darts by the High Priest Clang and his retinue, prevented from getting on with a human sacrifical ceremony by the absence of the ritual ring.

Best value of the film are the opening scenes in London. Those in the Alps have a fresh gaiety and irresponsible froth, but the Salisbury Plain and Bahamas shots are a disappointing waste. However, the film keeps nimbly on its toes for the main part and amusement comes from a constant wondering of what next cockeyed, irreverent and unexpected gag will be flung into the dialog or action. Use of deadpan subtitles, phoney intermissions and so on to bridge gaps in action are also amusing and not overdone.

Both producer Shenson and UA can await rich profits from "Help!" even though it's a much more costly job than was "Hard Day's Night." But The Beatles' film future is still not possible to assess. They are moneyspinners, but how they will develop as artists is a riddle. Perhaps their third will find a happy medium between the explosive anarchy and novelty of their first and the more conventional slapstick fun and games of this new offering.
Rich.

No Man's Land
(INDONESIAN)
Moscow, July 27.
P. T. Sanggabuana production. Stars Zainal Abidin. Direction and screenplay, Alam Surawidjaja; camera, Lukman Hakim; music, Den Garcia. At Moscow Film Fest. Running Time, 105 MINS.

The immaturity of Indonesia's film industry is all too amply demonstrated in "No Man's Land," made in 1963 and entered in the Moscow festival. And, inevitably, it deals with the "liberation" theme, though the enemies are not just the British, but also local citizens who indulge in banditry on the side.

Production values are substantially below par, which only underscore the naivete of the plot—a yarn about an ex-POW who returns to lead the guerrilla forces.
Myro.

Town Tamer
(WIDESCREEN-COLOR)

Dana Andrews and familiar-face cast in an okay western saloon action programmer.

Paramount Pictures release of A. C. Lyles production. Stars Dana Andrews, Terry Moore, Pat O'Brien; features Lon Chaney, Lyle Bettger, Bruce Cabot, Richard Arlen. Directed by Leslie Selander. Screenplay, Frank Gruber, based on his novel; camera (Technicolor, Techniscope), W. Wallace Kelley; editor, George Gittens; music, Jimmie Haskell; song, Haskell and By Dunham; asst. director, Howard Roessel. Reviewed at Beacon The-

atre, N.Y., July 19, '65. Running Time, 89 MINS.
Tom Rosser .... Dana Andrews
Susan Tavenner .... Terry Moore
Judge Murcott .... Pat O'Brien
Mayor Leach .... Lon Chaney
Riley Condor .... Bruce Cabot
Lee Ring; Marshal .... Lyle Bettger
Carol Rosser .... Coleen Gray
James Fenimore Feli....Barton MacLane
Dr. Kent .... Richard Arlen
Honsinger .... Richard Jaeckel
Sim Akins .... Philip Carey
Guy Tavenner .... DeForrest Kelley
Carmichael .... Sonny Tufts
Flon .... Roger Torrey
Davis .... James Brown
Kevin .... Richard Webb
Mary .... Jeanne Cagney
Vagrants ...... .Don Barry, Robert Ivers
Vigilante .... Bob Steele

Title-tells-all programmer with Dana Andrews cast in the unexpected role of a hired killer contains a cast-roll of familiar names and faces, from whom director Leslie Selander has wrested competent performances which partially disguise the plot contrivances. The release will suffice for duals and in its assigned task as western "action."

Adaptation by Frank Gruber from his own novel begins with the accidental killing of the wife of Andrews rather than himself. The rest of the story is two years later in another town where he traces down the assassin (Lyle Bettger) and the principal (Bruce Cabot) now installed as marshall and saloon owner, respectively. The denouement piles the saloon floor with more corpses than in the finale of "Hamlet."

Film has tempo, if inconsistencies, starting with the difficulty of wholly believing Andrews as an icy hired gun, especially as he is badly worsted several times and remarkably exposed as a target considering the bounty on his corpse. He is in and out of the saloon and the one local restaurant and his hotel room as the script strives for "movement" and suspense. As is now standard in vigilante situations the townspeople are on the weakling side, per Lon Chaney (mayor) and Richard Arlen (doctor) and Burton MacLane (realtor). The hashslinger (Jeanne Cagney) has rather more gumption and makes something of her bit.

Corruption runs to nervoustrigger thuggery in which the hates-himself marshall has an alter-ego sadist-aide played with convincing nastiness by Richard Jaeckel, whose fortune in films is his cocky strut and cold physiognomy. Roger Torrey's Flon is an over-size bully who wipes up the hashhouse floor with Andrews and gets away with it but later, coldbloodedly killing his (Andrews') horse just to rile him, gets a fatal attack of lead poisoning in the tummy.

W. Wallace Kelley's camera work in Technicolor and Techniscope is an asset to A. G. Lyles production via Paramount. George Gittens' editing helps director paper-over the cracks in the plot wall and Jimmie Haskell's score is helpful. Settings are colorful for the purpose of a western one-street burg as arranged by Hal Pereira and Al Roelefs. Sound recording of Hugo Grenzback is crisp and clean.
Land.

Furia a Bahia Pour O.S.S. 117
(Trouble in Bahia For O.S.S. 117)
(FRENCH-COLOR)
Paris, July 27.
Valoria release of PAC-PCM production. Stars Frederick Stafford, Mylene Demongeot; features Raymond Pellegrin, Perrette Pradier, Jacques Riberolles, Annie Anderson. Directed by Andre Hunebelle. Screenplay, Jean Halain, Pierre Foucaud from book by Jean Bruce; camera (Eastmancolor), Marcel Grignon; editor, Jean Feyte. At Normandie, Paris. Running Time, 115 MINS.
O.S.S. 117 .... Frederick Stafford
Anna Maria .... Mylene Demongeot
Leardo .... Raymond Pellegrin
Miguel .... Jacques Riberolles
Consuelo .... Perrette Pradier
Secretary .... Annie Anderson
Carlo .~............. Francois Maistre

The ersatz James Bond-type pic deals with an unruffled, athletic, Yank CIA man defeating some underground political group wanting to rule South America and then the world, and killing plenty to do it. None of the sleek Bond inventiveness or right ratio of parody and action is in evidence. Nor is there much knowing directional skill.

But Andre Hunebelle has successfully made two others like this film and is now at least putting more production coin into followup efforts. Accurate Brazilian locale, well-staged if overdone fights, and color and scope should have this okay on its home grounds with chances for dualer and tv use abroad as long as the Bond cycle continues to attract spectators to racy, spy pix.

Frederick Stafford has some dash if only one expression. But this helps give him the familiar mask of the ruthlessly efficient undercover operator. Women lack beauty and grace in this while the dialog is much too insipid for the needed gloss.

Director Hunebelle applies himself too literally to spelling out this tale of an underworld force trying to take over the world without the spirited tongue-in-cheek balance.

Taken from a bestselling series by the late, local writer Jean Bruce, his tales are also substandard Ian Fleming. But this series should go on here if its foreign chances are mainly in the playoff category.

As noted, production dress is bright. The battles, if they sometimes go on too long and lack humor, are stiffly planned and carried
Mosk. out.

Le Soldatesse
(The Camp Followers)
(ITALIAN-FRENCH-YUGOSLAV)
Moscow, July 27.
Morris Ergas presentation of an Italian-French-Yugoslav coproduction produced by Debora Film (Rome), Franco-London (Paris), Zebra (Belgrade). Stars Mario Adorf, Anna Karina, Marie Laforet, Lea Massari, Tomas Milian, Valeria Moriconi; features Aca Gavric, Rossana de Rocco, Milena Dravic, Guido Alberti. Directed by Valerio Zurlini. Screenplay, Leonardo Benvenuti, Piero de Bernardi; camera, Tonino Delli Colli; music, Flavio Nascimbene. At Moscow Film Fest. Running Time, 136 MINS.

Considerable talent and a great deal of heart has gone into making of "Le Soldatesse," and that's evident from what is seen on the screen. It is a moving document of one aspect of war—the recruiting

of girls to serve in military brothels and thus help satisfy the sexual impulse of their conquerers.

Though it is a theme that could easily lend itself to an overdose of emotion and pathos, these pitfalls have been neatly avoided via a thoughtful script and aggressive direction. Outside its domestic market, the pic seems destined for arty theatres, but its hopes could be improved by more vigorous editing. As it stands, there are a few slow and dull patches, and their elimination would be of enormous help.

The girls enlisted to satisfy the Italian soldiers are, as one would expect, a mixed bag. Some are professional and semi-professional prosties. Others have been lured by the temptation of regular rations and the chance to earn some money, both of which were in short supply after Greece had been overthrown by the Italian forces.

The 15 girls who have been recruited are being escorted to their destinations by a young lieutenant, and on the long truck ride, their backgrounds gradually emerge. One admits that she hasn't "done it for free" since she was 15, most are willing to please, but there is inevitably one exception. She explains her attitude to the lieutenant by telling him that she had a dream the previous night, in which a truckload of Italian girls were being escorted by her brother and "one of them was your sister."

The real drama is played out on the hazardous ride. Enroute, the lieutenant gives a lift to a Fascist major, and the clash of rank and temperament provides some dramatic fireworks. Then they encounter guerrillas, and the truck is blown up and several of them, including the sergeant truck-driver are injured. One girl, seriously wounded in the attack, is put out of her misery by the Fascist officer, and that leads to even more tension between the two officers.

The climax, somewhat drawn out but nevertheless moving, shows the eventual attraction between the lieutenant and one of the girls. After they have spent the night together, he encourages her to return to her own people, even though he regretfully realizes they will never meet again.

Valerio Zurlini's smooth and confident direction subtly captures the gradual change in mood. Ribald situations are avoided under his sensitive guidance, and the mounting tension and the personality clashes are clearly developed. The cast, too, is mainly first-rate, with some fine erformances by Anna Karina, Marie Laforet, Lea Massari, Valeria Moriconi, Rossana de Rocco and Milena Dravic as the enlisted girls. Matching portrayals by the males. include Mario Adorf, Tomas Milian, Aca Gavric and Guido Alberti. Technically, the production is up to accepted standards.
Myro.

El Arte De Vivir
(The Art of Living)
(SPAIN)
Berlin, July 27.
Eco Films and Fabra Films production. With Luigi Giuliani and Elena Maria Tejeiro. Directed by Julio Diamante. Screenplay, Julio Diamante and Elena Saez. Camera, Enrique Toran; mu-

sic, Adolfo Waitzman. At Berlin Film Festival. Running Time, 89 MINS.

Luis .... Luigi Giuliani
Ana .... Elena Maria Tejeiro
Julia .... Maria Carmen Abreu
Juanjo .... Jua Luis Galiardo

This film belonged to the also-ran category of the 1965 Berlin festival. There was nothing special about it to make it a serious festival contender. Story development and direction are on the old-fashioned side. Yet with regard to acting and situations there is something "sympathetic" about this modestly budgeted production. It has warmth and some amusing sequences. The Berlin audience reaction revealed that such humble film fare finds its clients, even at festivals. Yet a far cry from what the more demanding cinemagoer wants.

It's the simple yarn of a young rebel who dislikes his surroundings. He has a romance with a sweet young girl whom he eventually leaves for a society girl. He takes a fancy to the new life and wants to climb higher and higher, socially speaking. Even when his girl makes a suicide attempt, he's not inclined to give up his selfishness. He firmly believes that he has learned the art of living.

Elena Maria Tejeiro and Luigi Giuliani are the two principal players, both reveal acting talents. Miss Tejeiro is very lovely to look at. Pic contains some social criticism which, in this form, may be something special for Spain. But the whole thing looks somewhat outdated. Some of the problems touched here are actually those of yesterday. Nevertheless, the good will should be appreciated. *Hans.*

Acteon
(SPANISH)

Moscow, July 27.
X Films (Madrid) production and release. Stars Martin Lasalle, Pilar Clemens; features Juan Luis Galiardo, Claudia Gravy. Directed by Jorge Grau. Camera, Aurelio G. Larraya; music, A. Perez Olea. At Moscow Film Fest. Running Time, 75 MINS.

This Spanish entry at the Moscow festival is a pretentious example of "expressionist cinema," meaning that it is largely obscure and bewildering.. It rapidly emptied the large Kremlin Palace of Congress where it was being shown, and that's the clue to its ultimate boxoffice chances.

It is based on the legend of Diana, the Goddess of Love, and Acteon, the man who watched her bathe in the nude. Its significance, if any, is thoroughly obliterated by the treatment, and particularly by the ponderous direction. The cast hardly has a chance. Mercifully, it is short. *Myro.*

Un Dia En El Solar
(A Day in a Solar)
(CUBAN-COLOR)

Moscow, July 27.
Film Cubano production. Stars Sonia Calero; features Roberto Rodriguez, Tomas Morales, Assenneh Rodriguez. Directed by Eduardo Manet. Camera (Eastmancolor-Cinemascope), Ramon F. Suarez; music, Alberto Alonso. At Moscow Film Fest, Running Time, 88 MINS.

The best that can be said about this Cuban film is that it steers completely clear of politics, and is an attempt to portray a gay and light-hearted facet of life in Havana. It misfires badly, and even if relations with the West were friendlier, it wouldn't have much of a chance. As it is, outside some Spanish lingo territories, it must be considered a writeoff.

As a musical, it is years behind normal Western standards, though the Eastmancolor lensing in CinemaScope is okay. And there is a bunch of lookers to add color to the scene. But the songs are strictly routine, and there's nothing special about the choreography, either. The setting is an apartment compound and the simple script pinpoints the loves, hates, and petty jealousies of the inhabitants. Sonia Calero is a lively personality and looks good, too. Other thesps turn in average perfomances. *Myro.*

Love and Hate
(TURKISH)

Moscow, July 27.
Produced, directed and written by Turgut Demirag. No other credits available. At Moscow Film Fest. Running Time, 100 MINS.

Turkish production has always been mainly geared to the domestic and middle east markets. And this entry at the Moscow festival is no exception to this general rule. Nevertheless, it shows an advance over other productions from that country seen in recent years, and does attempt to break away from the naive format that has plagued most of its films.

In "Love and Hate," there is an attempt to develop a more sophisticated type sex drama, and despite the melodramatics of the plot, it partially succeeds. It is an involved yarn concerning two couples sharing a house. The wife of one of the men, who is crippled and confined to a wheelchair, wants a divorce to marry the doctor. The second wife wants to marry the cripple, but when that fails, finds solace in the bed of the chauffeur.

The acting is stereotyped and the direction somewhat casual. Other credits rate a modest nod. *Myro.*

Almodozasok Kora
(The Age of Illusion)
(HUNGARIAN)

Locarno, July 28.
Mafilm release of Studio 3 production. With Andras Balint, Ilona Beres, Judit Halasz, Kati Solyom. Written and directed by Istvan Szabo. Camera, Tamas Vamos; music, Peter Eotvos. At Locarno Film Fest. Running Time, 97 MINS.

Janos .... Andras Balint
Eva .... Ilona Beres
Gabi .... Judit Halasz
Annie .... Kati Solyom
Laci .... Be'a Asztalos
Matyl .... Laszlo Muranyi
Agi .... Cecilia Esztergalyos
Engineer .... Miklos Gabor

A gentle, wistful look at a group of youth and their coming of age has charm and insight. But it sometimes is too indulgent and skirts preciosity to leave this a chancey item for export. Film displays a budding filmic talent in Istvan Szabo for his first feature production after some good shorts.

Four young men and a girl graduate from engineering school ready to do big things and full of youthful enthusiasm. They are automatically against authority but find themselves dispersed, unable to do any traveling or adventurous things. Soon they are trying to fit themselves into life.

Film then picks out one more stubborn youth who drifts from girl to girl. Sketched in are well done looks at love, a certain political cutlook, notations on the war and 1956 uprising.

Communism is kidded, a girl asks the hero if he is a Communist and he answers that he is an engineer. There are vague feelings of wanting to travel, passionate affairs slowly going on the rocks and a melancholy in this youthful film made by a young man.

New Wave influences are evident via some stop action and a series of incidents to build a general feel for a period. Director-writer Szabo sometimes seems to be meandering and has not let this build to a true dramatic pitch.

But its feeling sans bathos, marks Szago as a man of some knowhow. He handles actors and actresses well if he sometimes overdoes little physical scenes. Technical credits are good as per usual from this country. *Mosk.*

Sci-Fi Fest

Frankenstein Meets Space Monster

Quickie Yank indie mixes stock footage horror and space aspects, but jells poorly; lower case cinema and tv use are its main chances.

Trieste, July 27.
Futurama release of Vernon-Seneca Films production. With James Karen, Nancy Marshall, Robert Reilly, Marily Hanold, Lou Cutell. Directed by Robert Gaffney. Screenplay, George Garret; camera, Saul Midwall; editor, Laverne Keating. At Trieste Sci-Fi Film Fest. Running Time, 75 MINS.

Adam .... James Karen
Karen .... Nancy Marshall
Frank .... Robert Reilly
Marcuzan .... Marilyn Hanold
Nadir .... Lou Cutell

Shoestringer mixes rocket space stock footage and monster angles to come up with a flat tale about a robot saving earth from outer space people. But this lacks the knowhow and production background to have this strictly for lower case use in some cinemas.

A robot-looking craft is sent into space but the ship is blown up by an enemy craft from another planet. Invaders are on their way to earth to capture female breeding stock since an atomic war is threatening their extinction. From there on, it's a lot more of the same.

He finally comes to grips with a grotesquely made up space monster and destroys it to save humanity. The robot on the rampage is fairly well done if the remainder is ludicrous. Flat acting does not help either. *Mosk.*

The Skull
(BRITISH—COLOR)

A cut above average horror pix with a more literate script; looms as good playoff material.

Trieste, July 27.
Paramount release of Amicus production. Stars Peter Cushing, Christopher Lee; features, Patrick Wymark, Jill Bennett. Directed by Freddie Francis. Screenplay, Milton Subotsky from story by Robert Bloch; camera (Technicolor), John Wilcox; editor, O. Hafferstern. At Trieste Sci-Fi Film Fest. Running Time, 90 MINS.

Maitland .... Feter Cushing
Collector .... Christopher Lee
Wife .... Jill Bennett
Marco .... Patrick Wymark

The occult and the malific are the themes of this classy shudder film. Script is sound except for dragging in some scenes for effect only and giving demoniac rather than psychological effects of the memory of the Marquis De Sade via his skull. A modern day occult researcher and author buys the skull of the Marquis. He is then subjected to visits of invisible demons from the skull which try to force him to kill his wife.

One scene of hallucinations has him dragged off to a court by two strange policemen and made to play Russian roulette before a mad looking judge and then pushed into a cell.

There are feeble sides to this pic but it has glossy pictorial qualities. The right ascetic approach is given by Peter Cushing as the determined collector. Dualer fare and smart playoff if given good publicity. *Mosk.*

Ziracena Tvar
(The Lost Face)
(CZECH)

Trieste, July 27.
Czech State Film release of Svabik-Prochazka production. With Vlastimil Brodsky, Jana Brejchova, Fred Delmare, Martin Ruzek, Jiri Vala, Zdenka Prochazkova. Directed by Pavel Hobi, Screenplay, Hobl, Josef Nesvadba; camera, Jiri Vojta. At Trieste Sci-Fi Film Fest. Running Time, 85 MINS.

Bartos .... Vlastimil Brodsky
Fiancee .... Jana Brejchova
Urban .... Fred Delmare
Marion .... Marie Vasova
Helena .... Zdenka Prochazkova
Rosen .... Jiri Vala

Broad satire, set in pre-war days, deals with a man who can change the faces of one human to another. It is fast paced and manages not to make its moral too blatant. However, its fairly obvious comedics limit this to specialized chances abroad.

A young doctor sincerely wants to help humanity but gets involved with a gangster on the run. He has perfected a way of transferring organs from one body to another. The killer makes him put on the face of a priest, who has been killed, and he becomes rich.

But he can't get a big clinic to adapt his work and he gets involved with the headman's daughter, and is sought by the police. Then after many chases he changes back to his old face.

The message here is simple but the pic uses many chases, familiar caricature and social hints to point up that in a corrupt society, decent acts may seem wrong. All this is acted with deft grace to sometimes lighten its heavyhanded symbolism. Film has fine production and art dress. But its old-fashioned theme, limits this in world markets. *Mosk.*

Siavash In Peresopolis
(IRANIAN)
Trieste, July 27.

Djam-Djam, Iran Film, Ashna Film production and release. With Minou Fabjad, Marva Nabili, Abbas Moayeri, Amir Farid, Ashgar Zolfaghari. Written and directed by Feydoun Rahnema from ancient Book of Kings. Camera, Palan. At Trieste Sci-Fi Film Fest. Running Time, 100 MINS.

Siavash .... Minou Fabjad
Soudabeh .... Marva Nabill
Kavous .... Abbas Moayeri
Afrassiab .... Amir Farid
Garssivaz .... Nader Koulkani
Rostam .... Ashgar Zolfaghari

A group of 13th Century characters wander around the ruins of a great ancient city talking of their past. Scenes are reenacted and they mix with visitors. Yet this preciosity seems to payoff and the theatrical rendering of ancient themes becomes effective if slow.

However, this film is slow and measured (in Oriental style) and it looks to have only specialized and language interest for abroad. The characters in this could be strolling players discussing their roles.

There is not the sombre, relentless and cold tragic beauty of the Greeks here, but more the human tragedy of power, wars and love in the Shakespearean tradition. This becomes an offbeat, slow and sometimes grandiloquent pic, with very limited theatrical chances. Flat photographically it does show a knowing filmed theatre flair via director Ferydoun Rahnema. Actors are properly stiff and declamatory. *Mosk.*

Dogora
(JAPANESE-COLOR)
Trieste, July 27.

Toho production and release. With Yosuke Atsuki, Yoko Fujiyama, Hiroshi Koizumi. Directed and scripted by Ishiro Hondo; camera (Eastmancolor). Haiime Koizumi. At Trieste Sci-Fi Film Fest. Running Time, 80 MINS.

Gangsters find themselves being beaten out in diamond robberies by strange phenomena from space. They float in as a viscous, glowing substance which cuts into safes and sucks up the diamonds. Mixture of gang warfare, sci-fi and special effects are par but this has a production value that could slant it for good playoff and dualer use abroad.

The "thing in space" is a mutant cell from atomic radiation. An old scientist finds that wasp venom can crystallize the thing and finally defeats it. The gangsters get their comeuppance from giant falling rocks.

Good looking girls, westernized gangsters and the fine effects keep this familiar affair racing along its fairly short course. Ishiro Hondo, the Japanese spcialist of this type of film, knows enough to let the formula work. He gives it good bolstering in deadpan seriousness. Color is good and scope is well utilizied. Actors are properly self effacing to Dogora, the space monster. *Mosk.*

Locarno Fest

Four In The Morning
(BRITISH)

A crisp, grim look at two emotionally stalemated couples; well acted with arty chances inherent but hardsell is needed.

Locarno, July 27.

West One Film Producers production and release. Stars Ann Lynn, Judi Dench, Norman Rodway, Brian Phelan; features Joe Melia. Written and directed by Anthony Simmons. Camera, Larry Pizer; editor, Fergus McDonnell. At Locarno Film Fest. Running Time, 94 MINS.

Girl .... Ann Lynn
Boy .... Brian Phelan
Wife .... Judi Dench
Husband .... Norman Rodway
Friend .... Joe Melia

There's no denying the spurt of filmic invention in style plus a forthright attitude toward emotion, showing up in British film festival entries this year. The usual restraint and quaintness seem out, with visual dazzle and probing at human problems apparent. After the free wheeling wit of the Cannes Film Fest top prizetaker "The Knack" (UA) and the look at an amoral femme in the Moscow entry "Darling," here is an indie with a grim tale of two couples destroyed by emotional sterility and the inability to act.

New writer-director Anthony Simmons, who has made several documentaries, shows two couples in crisis, tying them in with a gimmick, which works. There's an unidentified girl found in a river. Simmons gives the scene of the discovery and study of the drowned girl a metallic, sombre documentary flavor.

A seemingly rootless young man picks up a singer he knows after her work. He has known her awhile but neither can commit themselves on what they really feel for each other. At four in the morning they romp around the Thames shores, steal a boat, leave it, almost touch each other emotionally but part still uncommitted. Hints of the unstability of both are carefully and intelligently suggested by actions and subtle symbols.

A young married couple shows the woman waiting for her husband, out on-the-town with a bachelor crony. The baby cries and exasperates her. The growing incompatability of the couple is deftly outlined in bold, dramatic strokes.

First seg sometimes seems a bit arbitrary in its actions via a forcing of the inability of either to break out of their cocoons of past hurts. But the married episode has a more incisive dramatic edge of its crisis and irresolution.

Judi Dench has the right-checked hysteria for her role of the wife with a disposition towards love that make her poignant. Ann Lynn and Brian Phelan are also effective as the other couple with Joe Melia a pointed counterpoint to the married couple with his personal problems. Norman Rodway's husband is also an intelligent filming of a man who cannot cope with his feelings.

This film's unsparing downbeat look at the lack of human communication shows filmmakers taking up more modern themes. Picture's sharp, disturbing dramatic impact displays a solid, new British talent, fine new thesps and a growing maturity of British indie efforts. It is technically sound. Smart editing is also plus. *Mosk.*

The Organ
(CZECHOSLOVAKIAN-SCOPE)
Locarno, July 24.

Czech State Film release and production. With Alexander Brezina, Kamil Marek, Frantisek Bubik, Hana Maciuchova, Irena Bardyova. Directed by Stefan Uher. Screenplay, Alfonz Bednar; camera, Stanislav Szomolanyi; music, Jan Zimmer. At Locarno Film Fest. Running Time, 90 MINS.

Friar Felix .... Alexander Brezina
Guarian .... Kamil Marek
Bachnak .... Frantisek Bubik
Nela .... Hana Maciuchova
Wife .... Irena Bardyova

Made in the Slovak section of Czechoslovakia, this one shown at Locarno, Switzerland attests to that Eastern country's solid technical flair, feel for atmosphere and visual storytelling qualities. Film contains many allusions to the war days that may escape Western lookers. Also its ambivalent religioso aspects. Rather dramatically dense and too measured in telling. It looks mainly a home bet except for special situations abroad.

A Polish soldier on the run dons the clothes of a dead monk in the Slovak section of the country during the last war, area was then an independent Nazi state. Soldier is accepted into a monastery.

But his adeptness at the organ makes the old mayor, also the town organist, jealous, and it leads to him turning in the Pole, now ready to take the orders, and inadvertently bringing on the death of his own daughter. Allusions to the church and state differences are sometimes obscure as is the theme at times. Is it saying that clothes make the man? or that imposed government always leads to prosecution.

Still the director has a feel for unobtrusive symbolism. *Mosk.*

Acto Da Primavera
(Rite of Spring)
(PORTUGUESE-COLOR)
Locarno, July 24.

Manuel De Oliveira release and production. Written, directed, photographed, in Eastmancolor, and edited by De Oliveira and played by a small town in its annual Passion Play recital. At Locarno Film Fest. Running Time, 85 MINS.

Portugal, from time to time, reveals an interesting filmmaker at an international film fest. It is to the credit of the 1965 Locarno Fest to have had a retrospective of a Portuguese veteran director, Manuel De Oliveira, for his work exhibits definite personal talent and filmic prowess. This one, made in 1962, has a primitive force in freely filming and re-enacting a small town Passion Play for the camera.

There is a violent flair, not overdone, which communicates via this handed-down myth and religioso symbol a good classic and innocent aspect. First the townspeople are shown at their almost Biblical agricultural work and then the tourists arrive and one girl dons her

costume and the play is played out till it ends in a sudden rush of montage effects of the modern world. It somehow works.

The rugged faces, the singsong delivery and hueing to old Biblical and mythological moods give this a pageantry that is not hampered by the flimsy costuming and makeshift sets. The harsh, dry countryside of Portugal helps as well as the stolid countenances.

The usual Passion is done to the end. If there is a note of blaming the Jews for deicide of Jesus it does not harp on it in a defamatory way but is treated as something of the times that fell on all men and not one race, clan or religion. The montage of war and A-bomb explosions also makes a point that man is crucifying himself and his fellow man in various ways which may also be an interpretation of the Passion and not only as a religious spectacle.

However its subject, pared down treatment and ambivalent outlooks slant this primarily for institutional or school showings aboard with theatrical usage chancy. But it does unveil a definite filmic talent from this small country which makes a handful of pix a year. *Mosk.*

El Viente Distante
(The Distant Wind)
(MEXICAN)
Locarno, July 29.

Salomon Laiter production and release of three-sketch pic. At Locarno Film Fest. Running Time, 90 MINS.

EN EL PARCO HONDO

Directed and written by Salomon Laiter from story by Jose Pacheco. Camera, Sergio Vejar, Alex Phillips Jr.; editor, Carlos Savage.

Arturo .... Dario Asseo
Rafael .... Angel Dupeyron
Florencia .... Rosa Furman

TARDE D'AGOSTO

Written and directed by Manuel Michel from story by Jose Pacheco. Camera, Armando Carillo; editor, Carlos Savage.

Child .... Rodolfo Munoz
Julia .... Leticia Ortiz
Pedro .... J. Felix Guilmain

ENCUENTRO

Written and directed by Sergio Vejar from story by Sergio Magana. Camera, Alex Philips Jr.; editor, Carlos Savage.

Girl .... Elizabeth Dupeyron
Boy .... Jiminez Pons

It seems Mexico has closed filmmaker unions and it takes time for younger would-be directors or film-inclined youth to get into any pic branch. A young producer worked for three years as an architect to make this sketch pic, and a worthy effort it is. Three potential talents are unveiled.

Film did get help from an experimental contest organized by regular film technicians and will get release on its home grounds. Its simple, tenuous, if well observed themes of telling childhood and adolescent incidents; have this a likely playoff candidate for foreign spots as well as tele language houses and specialized use. It may not have the stamina for art houses, however.

But this does bode observant new talents in Mexico who should be heard from once they are making films regularly. Salomon Leiter, the producer, contributes one about a young boy living with a harridan aunt who is given the task of taking her beloved cat to a veterinarian. However, he and a friend decide to do away with it themselves only to have the cat escape. The boy suffers terror till he finds it dead on the doorstep. Second episode is about a 14-

year-old whose mother works and who has a crush on a beauteous 20-year-old cousin He is made to chaperon her one day with a suitor and it is here he feels his first emotional pain and realizes he is growing up.

Last one shows a 15-year-old youth who is brutalized by his father and who is smitten by a 14-year-old girl he sees in the streets. She has a brutal father who beats her and one day she runs off. She meets the boy and an idyll develops. He wants to bring her home but his father's reactions to his late arrival have the girl running off.

Influences of the noted Mexican filmmaker Luis Brunel and the French New Wavers are evident in a certain violence that is never exploited or jump cuts, frozen shots and interest in showing people at a variety of little pursuits. But these three filmmakers show they have assimilated all this and have a knowing way of telling their moody, atmospheric and emotional tales visually.

Mexico, at recent fests, has been showing a definite new flair in film subjects and rising talents. This pic adds to it. In spite of a limited budget, this one looks good and unskimping due to its fine handling of subjects familiar to these new directors, writers and technicians.

Mosk.

Uproar In Heaven
(RED CHINESE-COLOR CARTOON)
Locarno, July 14.
Shanghai Animation Studios release and production. Directed by Wan Lai-ming. Screenplay, Li Ko-jo, Wan Lai-ming; art direction, Chang Kuang-yu, Chang Cheng-yu; animation photography, Wang Shih-jung; music, Wu Ying-chu. At Locarno Film Fest. Running Time, **65 MINS.**

Based on 17th century folklore, this tells of a monkey king slighted by a heavenly court and how he wreaks more than adequate vengeance. Animation is good, if sometimes derivative of Disney in giving quaint personality facets to many characters, but mainly Chinese in design, tempo and tale.

It would take some doing to read Communist propaganda into the story via making the monkey king the people against exploiters. So it transcends this usual expectation and is mildly fine in some segments, especially a fight in the skies between the monkey head and a warrior as they change forms and turn the battle into a titanic affair. (Also used by Disney previously in "The Sword And The Stone.")

Otherwise cartoon feature is somewhat repetitious. There is some good color, sleek animation and enough invention for moppet showing abroad, for tv, or, if cut, as a supporting pic.

Red Chinese seem to be putting emphasis on animated pix and dance films which are mainly the ones seen at the Western and Eastern Fests they appear at.

Mosk.

Fraternelle Amazonie
(Fraternal Amazon)
(SWISS-FRENCH DOCUMENTARY)
Locarno, July 25.
Parkfilm. Julia Film release and production. Written, photographed in color, commentated by Paul Lambert. Editor, Henri Colpi. At Locarno Film Fest. Running Time, **80 MINS.**

Documentary has footage on the everyday lives, religious aspects and social outlooks of several primitive almost stone age tribes in the wilds of the Amazon section of Brazil. Commentary is somewhat too grandiloquent and patronizing. Track does not have progression, much insight or the kind of angles to make it a bet for U. S. art houses.

It appears more likely for lecture, tv or school use with some possibilities for short or medium length programs in houses if well pared. Commentator preaches about the plight of these people, the brutal doing away with them by hunters, oilmen, etc. and remarks they are on the verge of extinction.

All this could have been more incisive and moving if film had not tried to read classical purity into it all. They have dignity. But it is exploited for a fairly naive preachiness. But the handsome people shown do have grace and are photogenic and there is some okay footage if not enough to sustain smooth visual flow.

Color is acceptable and with a new commentary it can be used where it is fitted for.

Mosk.

Paskutine Atostogu Diena
(The Girl and the Echo)
(RUSSIAN)
Locarno, July 23.
Sovexport release of Lietouvos produc-tion. With Linute Braknyte, Valerijus Zubarevas, B. Babkauskas, K. Karmes. Directed by A. Zebriunas. Screenplay, J. Nagibinas, A. Cercenka; camera, J. Gricius; editor, V. Rimkevicius. At Locarno Film Fest. Running Time, **65 MINS.**
Vica .... Linute Braknyte
Roleas .... Valerijus Zubarevas
Vikos .... B. Babukaskas
Senelis .... K. Karmes

Slight but perceptive look at children at the end of a vacation benefits from unselfconscious acting. But the tale is mere anecdote, familiar moralizing at the end. Shorn a bit it could make a neat second item on selective bills.

A sprightly little girl, about 13, fills the loneliness of her grandfather during summer. Now she is waiting for her father to fetch her. She likes to swim nude and is not too conscious of it before a little male playmate. But some young bullies take advantage of it and she loses confidence in the boy. He tries to redeem himself to no avail.

That is about all there is to this quaint little film. The director shows feeling for the poetics of children at play or creating solemn renditions of the adult world. But he tries to stretch the symbolic purity of the girl and her ability to act to get echoes from a row of hills that nobody else can do.

There are moments of visual beauty, flashes of insight into the child's world which make this a work of promise since it is Zebriunas' first feature. It also marks the trend of Russia to now send films to Western Fests from many of its lesser Peoples' Republics.

Mosk.

Zycie Raz Jeszcze
(Back to Life Again)
(POLISH)
Locarno, July 27.
Polski State Film release of Syrena production. With Andrzej Lapicki, Tadeusz Lomnicki, Eva Wisniewska. Directed by Janusz Morgenstern. Screenplay, Roman Bratny; camera, Jerzy Wojcik. At Locarno Film Fest. Running Time, **95 MINS.**
Grajewski .... Andrzej Lapicki
Jakuszyn ....,... Tadeusz Lomnicki
Anna .... Eva Wisniewska
Journalist .... Edmund Fetting

A commendable anti-Stalinist theme comes a little late in this Polski pic. And the fairly stolid direction and various poitico angles make this primarily a local bet with foreign chances limited outside the Eastern belt.

A Polish flyer comes back from England after the war to his homeland. Here he finds outlaw bands of the army fighting against the new army after the Communist takeover. He goes along with the new rulers but is suspected and jailed. A girl tries to help him but the harsh Stalinist days find even good party people deposed and hounded.

After Stalin's death, things loosen up and the man is freed and the good Communist reinstated. If it does show the Party can be wrong and must change, this comes after many other films from Russia and other Eastern countries on the same theme. It is well acted but direction plods without much pace making little more than a politico curio affair. Technical credits are fine.

Mosk.

O Beijo
(The Kiss)
(BRAZILIAN)
Locarno, July 28.
Cia. Cinematografica Serrador produc-tion and release. With Reginaldo Faria, Nelly Martins, Jorge Doria, Xando Batista, A. Fregolente. Directed by Flavio Tambellini. Screenplay, Nelson Rodrigues, Tambellini from play by Rodrigues; camera, Tony Rabattoni, Amleto Daysse, Alberto Attili; editor, Lupe Luis Elias. At Locarno Film Fest. Running Time, **82 MINS.**
Arandir .... Reginaldo Faria
Selminha .... Nelly Martins
Mario .... Jorge Doria
Father .... Xando Batista

A man who kisses a dying man after an accident out of pity, and probably innocently, is dragged in by the police and hounded by a journalist as a probable homosexual. Let out of jail, his life is practically ruined and he is killed by his father-in-law, who, it seems, really loved him in an inverted way. But all this is done with such mannered, pretentious playing and direction that it exploits, almost absurdly, this idea instead of really coping with it.

Result is a pic played with eye-rolling acting and lush symbols and slow revelations that seem to evolve in a never-never land. The kiss that causes all the trouble is never seen.

The journalist suffered from not having tried to save his son from drowning which is given to explain his hysterical condemnation of the man. But this lacks both reality or a more incisive quality to give it any emotional probing.

Main chances abroad are for some arty spots catering to those looking for offbeaters. Chalk this up as a way-out affair with some good visual ideas at times but not the general balance to make it in any way successful. It is technically only fair.

Mosk.

Una Moglie Americana
(An American Wife)
(ITALIAN-COLOR)
Locarno, July 27.
Sadfi release of Sancro-Films Borderie production. Stars Ugo Tognazzi, Rhonda Fleming. Graziella Granata. Juliet Prowse, Marina Vlady; features Ruth Laney, Carlo Mazzone, Louisette Rousseau. Directed by Gian Luigi Polidoro. Screenplay, Rodolfo Sonego, Rafael Azcona, Ennio Flaiano, Polidoro; camera (Technicolor), Benito Frattari, Marcello Gatti, Enzo Serafin; editor, Eraldo Da Roma. At Locarno Film Fest. Running Time, **115 MINS.**
Ricardo .... Ugo Tognazzi
Oil Heiress .... Rhonda Fleming
Hostess .... Graziella Granata
Wife .... Juliet Prowse
Carole .... Marina Vlady
Girl .... Ruth Laney
Carlo .... Carlo Mazzone
Call Girl .... Louisette Rousseau

In his successful "To Bed or Not to Bed," Italo filmmaker Gian Luigi Polidoro had an Italo businessman trying to bed down Swedish beauties sans success, due to his ideas from Svenska pix. In this, he has a middleaged Italo visitor to the U.S. trying to marry an American in order to stay in that country. This makes for a surface if bracing parody of the so-called American Way of Life, and also the American Woman.

If this sometimes seems to have been based on American film myths, it has a bright new veneer because of the foreign-eye look at such obvious aspects of Americana as the emancipated woman, double standards of morality, affluence, eccentric Texas millionaires, brash Miami Beach and other familiar views of the American landscape seen by an Italian.

Rightly placed and played off, this breezy pic could ring okay boxoffice returns at arties and even other spots abroad. At home, its sprightly retooling of oft-done themes will help. So here are astronaut grass widows out for a good time, teenagers with marijuana, hot rods and dancing, the independent divorcees, rich heiresses indulging their whims, the vastness of the U S. and its many faceted sides and landscapes.

Of course, this comedy cannot be taken literally for it emerges a thickly packed series of adventures that have to be accepted by audiences before it can have the desired effect. A fortyish small town Italian teacher, engaged to an unprepossessing girl for many years, gets a chance to accompany a businessman to the U.S. as his interpreter.

On a weekend off, he meets an old friend who had married a rich, elderly woman to become an American and divorced her and remarried a rich young woman. But he is still a playboy. The newcomer feels he would like to stay in America and pic is the story of his hunt for a wife. If somewhat cynical, he still has some self-respect and can't bring himself to chase old woman and is always after the younger ones who always elude him.

From Miami Beach, he ends up at a Texas party. A brief affair with a rich femme oil well owner has him stranded, but revealing many more adventures as e treks across America back to N.Y. for a berating by his employer.

Ugo Tognazzi holds this episodic pic together by his perfect mixture of episodes. Rhonda Fleming has dash as the offbeat rich woman only using him for kicks, while Juliet Prowse is fine as a good-time grass widow. Marina Vlady is appealing as a self-sufficient divorcee brought back to her husband by Tognazzi's lauding of her virtues. Graziella Granata is beguiling as a double-standard girl who does not mind sex for its own sake while Ruth Laney is a kookie teenager with the right mixture of self-parody and naturalness.

Film is somewhat long with some ragged spots at the beginning Some pruning would help. It does underscore some American flamboyance, but also shows that both the marauding European and the direct American have something to give each other. It sometimes hits a note of seriousness, without any sentimentality, as it denotes the difficulties of adjusting at mature ages to other climes. But this also has the general human sameness that is getting more and more indivisible with the new worldwide communication.

This Italo comedy has some barbs in its look at the U.S. but it tries mainly for situation comedy rather than more depth. Film has nice color, and sometimes goes off on documentary sidelights. This is one of those earthy Italo comedies that laughs at its own failings as well as that of others. It is in the line of the gusty Italo comedies that have scored on world screens.

For commercial reasons several American girls are played by Europeans. But, on the whole, they are well dubbed and script manages to have reasons for them speaking Italian. This is a cursory, skin-deep rehashing of Americana modes and done mainly for entertainment. *Mosk.*

L'Amour A La Mer
(Love At Sea)
(FRENCH-COLOR)
Locarno, July 27.
Gilles production and release. With Daniel Moosin, Genevieve Therrey, Guy Gilles. Written and directed by Guy Gilles. Camera (Eastmancolor), Jean-Marc Ripert; editor, Noura Serra. At Locarno Film Fest. Running Time, 75 MINS.
Daniel .... Daniel Moosin
Genevieve .... Genevieve Therrey
Guy .... Guy Gilles

Perhaps, these days, charm and innocence are not enough to make a film a good bet in the more demanding international markets. This is a personal, simple tale of youthful disquiet before love and life and mixes some observation with well coordinated commentary. This makes it fetching if somewhat cinematically mannered little pic. It also denotes a definite new talent in writer-director-actor Guy Gilles.

Made quietly and sans the governmental Centre Du Cinema authorization, it was refused an official berth at the festival by French authorities and was shown in the commercial section. This seems a pity for it is the sort of offbeat, unusual pic that helps festivals. But it still got its fest airing which may help it to get release which has not been forthcoming on its home grounds for the last two years.

A sailor has an affair with a young secretary. However, he is still unsure of himself and his feelings. He finally breaks away to try to find his own way. In between are little vignettes of his and her daily lives, letters to each other, talks with friends and all sorts of deft sidelights that illuminate French youth and a certain ruthlessness.

Film's very personal qualities and New Wave tics of frozen images, spontaneous scenes and mixing color and black and white make it one of those pix that are mainly for arty house chances at best abroad. But it has a true and tender, probing sincerity that could slant this as worthwhile for some specialized spots. Players all ring true and their very gaucheness fits the easygoing but always revealing progression as it transcends its slight tale with insight into the needs and outlooks of its characters.

This is one of those newer pictures that has absorbed the new tendencies but is still somewhat too diffuse and rambling for broader circulation. *Mosk.*

En Este Pueblo No Hay Ladrones
(There Are No Thieves In This Village)
(MEXICAN)
Locarno, July 27.
Group Claudio production and release. With Julian Pastor, Rocio Sagaon, Graciela Henriquez, Luis Vicens, Luis Bunuel. Directed by Alberto Isaac. Screenplay, Isaac, E. Garcia Riera; camera, Carlos Carbajal; editor, Carlos Savage. At Locarno Film Fest. Running Time, 82 MINS.
Damaso .... Julian Pastor
Ana .... Rocio Sagaon
Ticha .... Graciela Henriquez
Barman .... Louis Vicens
Priest .... Luis Bunuel

A semi-delinquent, 20-ish young man lives with a woman almost twice his age, pregnant by him, and she supports him. But there's no social protest or preaching about morals here. Rather, the pic is a richly inventive look at life in a small town with any conclusions left to the audience. This film needs special handling and placement in selected arty houses for best results. It still looks chancy but critics and word-of-mouth might help.

The boy breaks into the local bar and billiard parlor, and, finding nothing, steals the billiard balls. This leads to a stranger being charged when he tries some pickpocketing in the local film house and a brooding boredom for the young, mostly non-working restless males, who find there's no place to relax sans billiards.

The young man finds out the balls are worth a lot and even envisages setting up a billiard ball gang to steal them in one town, replace them from another, etc. But the growing town restlessness and his own leads to his dallying with a local joy girl, getting into a fight and being charged with taking money that was not there. And so it ends.

The feel for revealing character and life in quick scenes and reactions plus good handling of the cast show Alberto Isaac as a Mexi-can filmmaker to watch. The pic is allowed to grow, make its statements and give an added fillip of irony that make it more effective than those that force issues. There is the general reflection of poverty and ignorance being nefarious influences.

An added plus for buffs is that Mexican filmmaker Luis Bunuel appears as a priest. This is a very specialized bet, but care in placement might make it a limited but worthwhile entry. *Mosk.*

Aarohi
(Ascent)
(INDIAN)
Locarno, July 26.
Goldwin Pictures release of Asim Pal production. With Kali Banerjee, Bikash Roy, Sipra Devi. Written and directed by Tapan Sinha from a story by Banaphul; camera, Bimal Mukherjee; editor, Subodh Roy. At Locarno Film Fest. Running Time, 120 MINS.
Arjun .... Kali Banerjee
Doctor .... Dilip Roy
Girl .... Sipra Devi
Zamindar .... Bikash Roy

Bengali feature tells of a peasant who determines to learn to read to better his lot in pre-war India. There is a nice feel for the times, land and characters, though work has a tendency to meander, talky and a bit too sentimental. Limited chances for this in U.S. despite surer visual narrative and perkiness than often found in India's output.

The peasant learns to read and teaches others and is an indispensable addition to the household of a doctor who had befriended him. He is sometimes irascible and tries to run other people's lives but only to help from his new found teachings. Script avoids preachiness and has some moving segments, a telling music score and the right larger-than life-acting.

Noted Indian director Satyajit Ray has clearly influenced Tapan Sinha's attempt to look at people in a direct, poetic way but sans the maturity, economy and air of Ray's greater films. There are dances and songs, but always justified and growing out of character and story. Pared down film might have more relevance for some specialized Western situations, but it is chancy at best in spite of its generally just tone and character insights. A gentle look at instruction, human rapports and ambitions and the passing of life in a little Indian town. *Mosk.*

Al Tarik
(Blind Alley)
(EGYPTIAN)
Locarno, July 25.
Dollar Films release of Cairo Cinema Co. production. Stars Chadia, Soud Hosni, Rouchdi Abaza, Tahia Carioca. Directed by Hossam El Dine Mostafa. Screenplay, Naguib Mahfaz from his own novel; camera, Ali Kheimina. At Locarno Film Fest. Running Time, 100 MINS.
Karina .... Chadia
Saber .... Soud Hosni
Husband .... Rouchdi Abaza
Girl .... Tahia Carioca

Not a cliche is missed in this tale of the comeuppance dealt a playboy whose mother was a brothel madame and father unknown. He is finally hung after murdering a beauteous woman though he has been having an okay time through it all. It smacks of the pre-war B pix and may have some grind or playoff or lingo chances on its movement and grab-bag familiar plotting.

The playboy is told his father is rich by his mother before she dies and he goes off to hunt him. In a hotel he seduces the voluptuous wife of the old owner. And she talks him into killing her spouse. However, he thinks she has used him and kills her before he is caught. He blames all on heredity as he is about to be hanged.

Acting is flamboyant and there is the pure girl who almost saves him. But the seeming seriousness of all this melodrama could give this unintended "camp" appeal if it were unreeled for giggles.

It is technically passable. *Mosk.*

La Donna Del Lago
(The Lady of the Lake)
(ITALIAN)
Locarno, July 24.
Telexport release of BRC-Manolo Bolognigni-Istituto Luce production. Stars Peter Baldwin, Salvo Randone, Valentina Cortese, Pia Lindstrom, Virna Lisi, Philippe Leroy, Franco Rossellini. Directed by Luigi Bazzoni, Franco Rossellini. Screenplay, Giulio Questi, Bazzoni, Rossellini from novel by Giovanni Comisso; camera, Camillo Bazzoni, Victor Hugo Contino, Roberto Biciochi, Leonida Bartoni; editor, Nino Baragli; music, Renzo Rossellini. At Locarno Film Fest. Running Time, 82 MINS.
Bernard .... Peter Baldwin
Father .... Salvo Randone
Mario .... Philippe Leroy
Irma .... Valentina Cortese
Adriana .... Pia Lindstrom
Tilde .... Virna Lisi

Absorbing psychological, sociological suspense drama marks two new directors of talent in Luigi Bazzoni and Franco Rossellini, nephew of Roberto. Pic has a canny probing atmospheric flair and, if it leaves some loose ends, is continuously taking and should do all right on home and foreign markets if its stray plot aspects would call for careful placement and sell.

A lake resort in the dead of winter lends itself to this exercise in memory, murder and invidious family secrets heightened by the fear of smalltown talk and disfavor. There is also the symbol of a desirable amoral girl who triggers all the mayhem, happenings and somber undercover feelings and characters of the people involved.

What on the surface looks like an old-fashioned expressionistic thriller gets heightened flavor and flair from the fine pacing, visual aspects, acting and progression of this shrewdly fashioned film. If the spectator might be left to deduce certain factors, this only adds to the interest and persuasive powers of the film.

A young writer, suffering a sort of moral crisis, goes to a lake resort he usually visits in winter. However it is also to see a beautiful maid at the hotel with whom he had had a passing idyll. But he finds she is dead and nobody will talk about it. Little by little he uncovers that she had died of a slashed throat and been thrown in the lake. Somehow covered up, the medical report also listed her as a virgin though he knew differently and some evidence pointed to her being pregnant.

The writer, a weak imaginative type, still enthralled by the memory of the maid, and whom he had once happened to see making passionate love to someone, slowly pieces things together with plenty of conjecture mixed with the so-called truth. Then the wife of the son of the owner of the hotel is found drowned and passed off as an accident, with a final murder of the father and son by the sister, a spinsterish half-crazed woman who seemingly could not live with the idea that both the father and son had been lovers of the maid.

It ends with frogmen dragging the lake for her as the writer leaves. Stark, heavily contrasted black and white lensing, with overlighting on flashback thoughts, are ample helps for this gripping tale as well as the dramatic musical score by co-director Franco Rossellini's father, Renzo. The facts of the killings are irrefutable but not all the real reasons are completely made clear since it is seen mainly through the writer's eyes.

Virna Lisi has the hard, brittle beauty, sexual aura and underlying amoral climbing aspects that make her only flashback appearances always vivid. Valentina Cortese is especially effective as the unbalanced woman who brings on a mad avenging series of harrowing murders. The men are all adequate in this closed in drama of hatred, love, desire and provincial narrowness.

Mood is kept throughout and the narrative flow is excellent in spite of its Pirandello-like mixture of reality, illusion and truth. This is a solidly carpentered affair but its very solidity and refusal to clear up all its leads, will make it more chancey in arties. But it still has the suspense for playoff, with right placement helpful all the way. It again underlines the generally high level of Italo pix, even on proven themes, and the growing numbers of talented new film practitioners.   *Mosk.*

Le Mystere Koumiko
(The Koumiko Mystery)
(FRENCH-COLOR-DOCUMENTARY)
Locarno, July 24.

Sofracima release of Sofracima-APEC-Service Recnerche ORTF production. With Muroako Koumiko. Written, directed, lensed and edited by Chris Marker on 16m color stock blown up to 35m. At Locarno Film Fest. Running Time, 45 MINS.

Chris Marker has made documentaries at home in France and aboard and has developed a distinctive style in a kind of cinematic essay. He mixes visual metaphor, intellectual comment, general musings, for a counterpoint of image and idea. Though sometimes mannered it usually escapes preciosity by a saving wit, generosity and urbanity.

Here he looks at Japan during the Olympics through a comely girl, one Muroaka Koumiko. The camera all but caresses her as an unseen man asks questions, shows her at liberty or wondering about life, situations and men. In between are smartly lensed looks at Japanese life, physical aspects, and, through it all, a sort of love affair with the girl.

Somehow it comprises a general comment on Japan's many facets; its aping of the West, that is now assimilated, its exotica and every-

day look and a generally clever, if surface, summing up of a charming but yet reserved and, finally, mysterious young girl whose faulty French and bland and innocent feelings are beguiling.

Short length of this feature documentary gives it some chance for pairing in U.S.   *Mosk.*

Who's Crazy?
Locarno, July 27.

Cinemasters International Reginald Kernan release and production. With Living Theatre Company. Directed by Allan Zion and Tom White from improvisations by players on a generally decided theme and series of happenings. Camera, Bernard Daillencourt; editor, Denise De Casabianca. At Locarno Film Fest. Running Time, 83 MINS.

Narrow gauge film expanded to 35m, this offbeat, inventive, semi-improvised feature is about a group of inmates from an asylum who escape from a bus and hole up in an old farm till police drive them out. It has some inadvertent clinical interest and some poetic, touching and funny moments. Presumably just for buffs and artsy-craftsy types. Shot in Belgium by Americans with the Beck couple's Off Broadway Living Theatre Co., now barnstorming around Europe.

Speech does not possess much coherence, but sudden shafts of insight do emerge. A mock wedding is both touching and visually brilliant. Film is sometimes repetitious, but its experimental nature supposedly excuses these flaws.

Blowup to 35m from the original 16m, is acceptable and the editing does give these disparate actions some cogency as they build from simple private doings to group cavortings. Invented musical score, built of percussion instruments and voices, is also fitting for this strangely made film that avoids exploiting madness for derision of risibility and yet finds some human echo in it.   *Mosk.*

Perlicky Na Dne
(Pearls Down Below)
(CZECHOSLAVAKIAN)
Locarno, July 28.

Czech State Film production and release. With Pavla Mersalkova, Milos Ctrnacty, Josefa Pechaltova, Vera Mrezkova. Directed by Jiri Menzel, Jan Nemec, Elwald Schorm, Vera Chytilova, Jaromil Jires. Screenplay, Bohumil Hrabel based on his own stories; camera, Jaroslav Kucera; editor, Miroslav Hajek, Jirina Lukesova. At Locarno Film Fest. Running Time, 105 MINS.

MR. BALTAZAR'S DEATH
Directed by Jiri Menzel
Mother .... Pavla Marsalkova
Father .... Ferdinand Kruta
Son .... Jan Pech
Baltazar .. .. Alois Vachek
THE IMPOSTERS
Directed by Jan Nemec.
Journalist .... Milos Ctrnacty
Singer .... Frantisek Havel
Barber .... Josef Hejl
THE HOUSE OF HAPPINESS
Directed by Elwald Schorm.
Painter .... Vaclav Zak
Wife .... Josefa Pechaltova
Agent .... Ivan Vyskocil
THE SNACK BAR
Directed by Vera Chvtilova.
Man .... Vladimir Boudnik
Wife .... Vera Mrezkova
Girl .... Alzbeta Lastovickova
ROMANCE
Directed by Jaromil Jires.
Gaston .... Karel Jerabek
Girl .... Dana Valtova

It is no secret that Czechoslavakia has been having a film renaissance both in talents and in the growing freedom of subjects and themes chosen. Economic, political,

social and personal themes abound, but, also important, is the filmmaking knowhow and vitality that have kept pace with the subject matter. This sketch pic, composed of five young filmmakers doing films based on the stories of one writer, shows a flurry of comic, dramatic and realistic bents that have an overall tone because of the central basis of the tales.

Sketch films usually are questionable boxoffice bets, for they mainly can't treat a subject thoroughly and have uneven segments. But this one has them all though this is mainly for more specialized possibilities abroad, on its bracing good humor and warmth.

First up is about a middle-aged married couple and and their senile father or father-in-law who love auto and cycle racing. They hie off to a race in an old car and are present at a fatal accident before they wend their way home. The right parodic qualities and pungent look at sport fanatics make this both witty, wry and generally amusing.

Follows two dying old men telling each other false tales about their respective careers which are fiction but help keep them alive. After their deaths, a barber holds forth that it is bad for society to be false and lie.

A real primitive painter, who has painted his whole house to leave to the state, is used as two insurance men try to sell him a policy. They are finally driven out ly the beguiling but eccentric painter and his witch-like mother. The only episode in color, this has a bright zany inventiveness. It pokes fun at State unimaginativeness and has the rhythm that brings the whole thing off.

In a sleazy snack bar full of seedy people, a girl has committed suicide. In comes a worker looking for his fiancee. It is not clear if the suicide is his girl. But he meets an abandoned bride, whose groom has been arrested. They go off into a stormy night and the bride ends up also seemingly suicidally inclined. The rich mixture of observation and elan give this a fine impact.

The last has a young boy meeting a sprightly, free-loving Gypsy girl and having a brief affair before she goes back to her people. If romantic in treatment, it has a feeling for its characters which remove any patronizing aspects.

It is hard to single out the top director among those of this pic but the gleam like a batch of pearls.

The technical prowess of the Czech technicians are also assets as well as the thesping. Here is a neat group of episodes which could do for specialized use or perhaps later used for its episodes on tv. But, as is, it makes a satisfying whole and could make an okay if limited career for it abroad.   *Mosk.*

Sergeant Deadhead
(COLOR-PANAVISION)

Above average space age comedy with tunes. Young thesps supported by vet film and tv names. Good prospects in the youth market.

Hollywood, Aug. 4.

American International Pictures release of a James H. Nicholson-Samuel Z. Arkoff production, co-produced by Anthony Carras. Stars Frankie Avalon, Deborah Walley, Cesar Romero, Fred Clark, Gale Gordon, Reginald Gardiner, Harvey Lembeck, Buster Keaton, Eve Arden, Pat Buttram; features John Ashley, Donna Loren. Directed by Norman Taurog. Screenplay, Louis M. Heyward, camera (Pathecolor), Floyd Crosby; editors, Ronald Sinclair, Fred Feitshams, Eve Newman; Music, Les Baxter; songs, Guy Hemric, Jerry Styner; art direction, Howard Campbell; sound, Ryder Sound Services, asst. director. Claude B'nyon Jr. Reviewed at Academy Award Theatre, Aug. 3, '65. Running Time 69 MINS.

Sgt. Deadhead, Pvt. Donovan	
	Frankie Avalon
Col. Lucy Turner	Deborah Walley
Adm. Stoneham	Cesar Romero
Gen. Rufus Fogg	Fred Clark
Capt. Weiskopf	Gale Gordon
Pvt. McEvoy	Harvey Lembeck
Pvt. Filroy	John Ashley
Pvt. Blinken	Buster Keaton
Lt. Cmdr. Talbott	Reginald Gardiner
Lt. Kinsey	Eve Arden
The President	Pat Buttram
Susan	Donna Loren
Tuba Player	Romo Vincent
Sgt. Keeler	Ted Windsor
Air Police	Norman Grabowski
	Mike Nader
Radioman	Ed Faulkner
Gilda	Bobbi Shaw
Patti	Patti Chandler
Sue Ellen	Salli Sachse
Luree	Luree Holmes
Ivy	Sue Hamilton
Gail	Jo Collins
Bellhop	Bob Harvey
Newsman	Jerry Brutsche
Marine MP's	Andy Romano
	John Macchia
WAFs	Mary Hughes, Astrid DeBrea, Jean Ingram, Peggy Ward, Stephanie Nader, Lyzanne Ladue, Janice Levinson, Alberta Nelson
Secretary	Sallie Dornan

"Sergeant Deadhead" is an entertaining space-age comedy with some younger thesps surrounded by vets who carry the load. Good direction and production values plus six tunes enliven a script that touches all bases. American International release is above-average formula fare for youth situations.

Louis M. Heyward's script concerns Frankie Avalon's switcheroo from bumbling airman to snooty, extrovert hero as the result of personality change during a space trip in a missile in which he took refuge following a guardhouse breakout. Eventual rehabilitation and clinch with patient sweetie Deborah Walley follows a series of lightweight complications via meddling military brass and a lookalike Avalon.

Eve Arden and Fred Clark are the comedy keystones, paired as WAF commander at a missile commanded by Clark, the latter his usual exasperated self while Miss Arden wanders throughout proceedings as his gal, foil, intermediary and advisor. It's good to see her back on the theatre screen, particularly essaying "You Should've Seen The One That Got Away," a number done in the WAF barracks and shower, and one of six okay tunes by Guy Hemric and Jerry Styner.

Cesar Romero, Gale Gordon and Reginald Gardiner are nicely teamed as a trio of inspectors who come to witness a missile shoot and wind up with an arrogant Avalon on their hands, threatening to expose the goof that sent him into space with a monkey.

Romero is good in a departure from his normal screen suavity, also Gordon as a daffy headshrinker. Gardiner has little to do, although his comment when a formation of towel-clad gals must come to attention and salute makes that scene.

Harvey Lembeck is also on briefly as the prisoner who forces Avalon and John Ashley into an escape, precipiating Avalon's missile trip. Crashout occurs during a gangster pic, a "George Raft Film Festival," one of the many esoteric throwaways. Buster Keaton does an okay firehouse bit, and Pat Buttram essays LBJ in a well-handled, mostly vocal, sequence.

Announcers John Heaston and Ed Reimers are paired in a Huntley-Brinkley takeoff that doesn't. Neither receives screen credit, although Dwayne Hickman does for far less. Other tunes go in and out of the ear, although "Let's Play Love," an Avalon-Walley duet, would make a good nitery-vaude showtune.

Director Norman Taurog did a professional job, aided by Floyd Crosby's sharp Panavision-Pathecolor camera. Ronald Sinclair, Fred Feitshams and Eve Newman edited to 89 minutes, with a bit more tightening in order. Other technical credits are pro, except the interpolation of b&w footage shot in older aspect ratio. James H. Nicholson and Samuel Z. Arkoff produced, with Anthony Carras billed as co-producer. As in vidpix, credits are split between opening and closing titles. *Murf.*

Crazy Paradise
(Det Tossede Paradis)
(DANISH—COLOR)

Sherpix release of Palladium production. Features Dirch Passer, Hans W. Petersen, Ove Sprogoe, Ghita Norby, Paul Hagen, Bodil Steen, Karl Stegger, Lone Hertz. Directed by Gabriel Axel. Screenplay, Bob Ramsing, based on novel by Ole Juul; camera (Eastman Color), Henning Bendtsen; film editor, Lars Brysesen; sound, Kai Larsen, Knud Kristensen; music, composed and directed by I. B. Glindemann. Reviewed at N.Y., Aug. 5, '65. Running Time **95 MINS.**

Angelus Goat .... Dirch Passer
Thor Goat .... Hans W. Petersen
Simon .... Ove Sprogoe
Edith Paste .... Ghita Norby
Vicar Paul Paste .... Paul Hagen
Foreign Minister Bertha Virginius .... Bodil Steen
Per Mortensen .... Karl Stegger
Greta .... Lone Hertz
Anne .... Lily Broberg
Ursula .... Judy Gringer
Ove Bierman .... Kjeld Petersen
Prime Minister .... Kai Holm
Von Adel .... Jorgen Ryg
Hjalmar .... Axel Strobye
Trommesen .... Gunnar Lemvigh
Editor Thomas Asmussen .. Poul Muller
Janus .... Valso Holm
Grocer Casper Cash . Keld Markuslund
Tripledick .... Arthur Jensen
Frederikl .... Hugo Herrestrup
Laurids .... Gunnar Stromvad
Jens .... Helge Scheuer
Borge .... Lotte Tarp
Karen .... Erik Paske
Betsy Buttock .... Elsbeth Larsen
Narrator .... Henning Moritzen

If Jean Genet had written "The Egg and I," the result might have been something on the order of this Danish sexport which Sherpix booked into the N.Y. New Embassy on Aug. 10 for its U.S. premiere. With Sherpix owned by art-theatre circuit chief Louis K. Sher, "Crazy Paradise" will undoubtedly be given as much exposure as are the actresses who figure in the so-called comedy.

Director Gabriel Axel has turned Ole Juul's novel of the same name into what may have been intended as ribald satire but comes off, as presented, as a vulgar, tasteless attempt to sell political satire with unadulterated sex. Principal gag is a "super-virility" supposedly imparted from eating raw eggs peculiar to a little island off the coast of Denmark.

Besides the egg bit, suggestiveness is heavily accented with byplay on the phallic symbolism of Pan, the god of goats, shown as a weather vane (and being reproduced in plastic as a publicity gimmick for the film). There's considerable borrowing from "Passport To Pimlico" and "The Mouse That Roared" for purposes of poking fun at idealist politicians, bureaucrats and graft. The egg-sex idea, with less repetition, might have been funnier, and with considerable editing, the overlong film (much of which will bore the sexploitation addicts) could still pick up pace.

What "Crazy Paradise" does have, with one exception, are several beautiful females. All voluptuous, in and out of costume, they'd look even better had cameraman Henning Bendtsen been more knowledgable about lighting and the proper use of Eastman Color. Film is generally murky and faded. The one exception, although she's the only funny one, is Bodil Steen as a femme Danish minister for foreign affairs who also succumbs to the island's sexy secret. Ghita Norby, as the vicar's wife, and Lone Hertz, Lily Broberg, Judy Gringer, Erik Paske and Elsbeth Larsen, as assorted island dolls, help to put across the film's message.

The entire male cast was evidently picked for funny-looking faces as they range from just plain to really ugly. Dirch Passer, Hans W. Petersen and Ove Sprogoe as leaders of the islanders, Paul Hagen as the vicar, and Karl Stegger and Gunnar Lemvigh as villainous types are unexciting in stereotyped roles. Other than the poor photography, other technical depatments are adequate. All this is of little importance if Sherpix sells the film on its "suggestive" theme as the promotion gimmicks suggest, although initial ads are rather subtle in the sex-sell — using a big-bosomed hen atop an egg with caption "something new and egg-citing." *Robe.*

You Must Be Joking
(BRITISH)

Breezy gagalog of mainly slapstick situations. Moves swiftly and employs excellent cast, and should raise the spirits and loot at the wickets.

London, Aug. 3.

BLC release of Columbia's presentation of a Charles L. Schneer production. Features Michael Callan, Lionel Jeffries, Denholm Elliott, Wilfrid Hyde White, Bernard Cribbins, James Robertson Justice, Leslie Phillips, Terry-Thomas, Gabriella Licudi, Lee Montayue, Patricia Viterbo, Irene Handl, Tracy Reed, Norman Vaughan, Clive Dunn. Directed by Michael Winner. Screenplay, Alan Hackney, from a story by Hackney and Winner; camera, Geoff Unsworth; editor, Bernard Gribble; music, Laurie Johnson. Reviewed at Columbia Theatre, London. Running time, **99 MINS.**

Tim .... Michael Callan
McGregor .... Lionel Jeffries
Foskett .... Terry-Thomas
Annabelle .... Gabriella Licudi
Sylvia .... Patricia Viterbo
Tabasco .... Denholm Elliott
Mansfield .... Lee Montague
Clegg .... Bernard Cribbins
Gen. Lockwood ..... Wilfrid Hyde White
Librarian .... James Robertson Justice
Parkins .... Richard Wattis
Bill Simpson .... James Villiers
Elderly Woman .... Irene Handl
Husband .... Leslie Phillips
Poppy .... Tracy Reed
Disk Jocky .... David Jacobs
Joe .... Norman Vaughan
Doorman .... Clive Dunn

Alan Hackney and Michael Winner's screenplay is not so much a story as a valid excuse for a bunch of accomplished and fairly well known comedians to plunge into a string of comedy situations, mostly slapstick. Directed by Winner at a nimble, goodhumored pace, they provide a lively enough brew. If some of the gags misfire, there are always others following hot on the trail to revive the proceedings. No strain on the brain, it provides fairly consistently amusing, light entertainment. Should do well at most situations.

Producer Charles H. Schneer has not skimped on his cast, in many cases employing biggish feature names for bit roles. So the pic has a good marquee pull, with Schneer playing all the names under title but flattering them with such tactful juggling as "starring," "guest star" and "introducing."

However, names are there, the gags are there and on the whole so are the laughs. The jape consists of a 48-hours army "initiative test" dreamed up by Terry-Thomas, as an eccentric army psychiatrist. The five competing soldiers are detailed to bring in a rare breed of rose, an electric hare from a dog-track, the mascot off the bonnet (hood) of a Rolls-Royce, a set of plaster flying duck wall ornaments, a lock of hair and a signed photograph of a Continental femme pop songstress and the much guarded and valuable Dutine Bell, pride of Lloyds.

Director and scriptwriters have managed to single the different escapades of the contestants niftily enough for them all to get a fair amount of the "fat," with frequent cutbacks to the sly humor of the General (Wilfrid Hyde White) and his staff. There is the inevitable frenetic chase sequence without which no modern comedy seems considered complete and a chaotic farcial finale.

The five hapless soldiers involved in "The Test" are suitably mixed. Denholm Elliott, rich, suave, unflappable Guards officer, pulls strings and conducts his campaign from his luxury West End hotel suite. He brings his usual cynical lazily detached brand of insouciance to the role. Hardest worked is Lionel Jeffries as a wild, wily Scottish sergeant major, complete with accent and kilt, who suffers a score of humiliations as he presses on. Michael Callan (presumably intro'd to boost American interest?) is pleasantly dashing as a Yank lieutenant. Lee Montague and Bernard Cribbins (the latter as a "running gag" character who never manages to get out of the Maze from which the contest starts) also have good moments.

White ambles nonchalantly through as a bland general, Terry-Thomas provides his own brand of lunacy to good effect and James Robertson Justice, Irene Handl, Richard Wattis, Leslie Phillips, Norman Vaughan, Clive Dunn and James Villiers are among those who make one-shot appearances as the action spreads, on location, through a mock up of Lloyds, a botanical garden a London club and hotel, a fruit market, greyhound track and the London streets. Gabrielle Licudi and Patricia Viterbo, two Continental actresses, also presumably introduced to pep up European interest in the pic, provide distaff interests. Miss Licudi scores as a very debutante young woman who plays Callan's girl friend. Miss Viterbo makes less impact as the pop singer. Tracy Reed also makes her mark again as Elliott's elegant sweetie.

Mostly filmed on location. Geoff Unsworth's lensing is sharp and vivid. Winner's direction though glossing over several loose ends, keeps pace with the breeziness of the slim yarn. He has mainly resisted an attempt to be arty, though some of the shots of characters frozen into 'still life' and then springing into action are a bit too arty and don't help any. Other technicalities are all sound. *Rich.*

Love And Kisses
(SONGS-COLOR)

Amusing young bride-and-groom comedy with good chances in family market; names of Ozzie Nelson and son Rick to gimmick exploitation.

Hollywood, July 31.

Universal release of Ozzie Nelson production. Stars Rick Nelson; features Jack Kelly, Kristin Nelson, Jerry Van Dyke, Pert Kelton, Madelyn Himes, Sheilah Wells. Direction-screenplay, Ozzie Nelson, based on play by Anita Rowe Block; camera (Technicolor), Robert Moreno; editor, Newell P. Kimlin; art direction, Alexander Golitzen, Frank Arrigo; asst. director, Carl Beringer; music, William Loose; sound, Waldon O. Watson, Frank Wilkinson. Reviewed at Picwood Theatre, July 30, '65. Running Time, **86 MINS.**

Buzzy .... Rick Nelson
Jeff Pringle .... Jack Kelly
Rosemary .... Kristin Nelson
Freddy .... Jerry Van Dyke
Nanny .... Pert Kelton
Carol .... Madelyn Himes
Elizabeth .... Sheilah Wells
Officer Jones .... Alvy Moore
Stage Manager ...... Angelo Brovelli
Dancers .. Betty Rowland, Nancy Lewis, Anita Mann

"Love and Kisses" snaps at the youth and family trade and should run up satisfactory response in situations catering to this type of product. Story of a pair of teenagers who suddenly get married and move in with groom's distressed parents is inclined to be a bit schmaltzy and sometimes lacks the professional touch but provides the kind of light comedy that plays well. Film additionally has the built-in benefit of the Ozzie Nelson name, moving over from tv as producer - director - scripter, and his son, Rick, stars, with latter's wife, Kristin, featured.

Nelson, apparently feeling he has caught the public pulse with his "Ozzie and Harriet" show, first on radio starting in 1944, on tv eight years later and still continuing as a standard, employs more or less the same technique in bringing his narrative to the screen. Based on the play by Anita Rowe Block, Nelson plays his situations for broad effect, sans subtlety and strictly for laughs, which he achieves in some measure.

Rick Nelson is billed as star but Jack Kelly, portraying his father, steals the show. As the doting parent who tries to untangle the love involvements of his son and new bride, and daughter about to get married to a stuffed shirt, he carries a load beautifully timed. Rick, with his wide tv following, is okay and gets a chance to sing three numbers, which juve spectators should appreciate.

Kristin Nelson, a regular on the Nelson tv show, registers a fine impression as the bride who brings with her a life-sized rabbit and otherwise isn't always grown-up. Madelyn Himes amuses as the groom's mother who keeps thinking of him as her "baby," and Pert Kelton gets a chance at some fancy comicking in her brief appearances as the family retainer. Sheila Wells as the daughter and Jerry Van Dyke her suitor lend further interest.

Technical departments are expertly handled, including Robert Moreno's tint photography, art direction by Alexander Golitzen and Frank Arrigo, editing by Newell P. Kimlin.   *Whit.*

Laurel & Hardy's Laughing 20's

Good compilation of lesser known Laurel & Hardy memorabilia. Well-produced. Needs handling for returns from film buff and selected dual situations.

Hollywood, Aug. 6.
Metro-Goldwyn-Mayer release, written and produced by Robert Youngson. Stars Stan Laurel, Oliver Hardy; features Vivian Oakland, Glenn Tryon, Edna Murphy, Anita Garvin, Tiny Sanford, Jimmy Finlayson, Charlie Chase, Viola Richard, Max Davidson, Del Henderson, Josephine Crowell, Anders Randolf, Edgar Kennedy, Dorothy Coburn, Lillian Elliott, "Spec" O'Donnell. Narration, Jay Jackson; music, Skeets Alquist; sound, Val Peters. Reviewed at Metro Studio, Aug. 4, '65. Running Time, **90 MINS.**

Robert Youngson has assembled some lesser known Laurel and Hardy silent shorts plus a few good samples of other comedy film work into a promising reprise. Unlike other recaps which combine too many brief clips, this 90 minute compilation permits situations to properly show. Commercial prospects for the Metro release look good for film buff and selected dual situations.

Jay Jackson effectively soft-pedals Youngson's script, itself a bit on the saccharine side but apparently thought necessary for juves. Early industrial film work of Laurel and Hardy is developed through five short clips, before giving them rein in five lengthy joint segments.

In latter group, "From Soup To Nuts," "Wrong Again," "The Finishing Touch" and "Liberty" are all standout, showing also the behind-camera talents of Leo Mc-

Carey and George Stevens. Edgar Kennedy makes several appearances, all to good effect, while Charlie Chase and Max Davidson get fine exposure in samples of their own work.

The eight-minute climactic reprise of more familiar Laurel and Hardy work includes a pie-throwing sequence (in which Margaret Dumont briefly appears), seed-bed for parts of Blake Edwards' current "The Great Race," which he has dedicated to the late comics.

Film quality is sharp and clear, and characters move at normal speed throughout. Herbert Gelbspan coordinated for Hal Roach Studios, and is credited as associate producer, along with Alfred Dahlem. Maurice Levy's optical work is excellent, including use of iris effects which still make an effective blackout.

Val Peters sound recording is pro, although the music is usually too loud in relation to Jackson's voice. Skeets Alquist composed an overly-busy score which becomes tedious in its mickey-mouse. Laurel and Hardy didn't need music then, and they don't need too much gimmickry now.
                     Murf.

Gente Conmigo
(People Like Me)
(ARGENTINIAN)

Locarno, Aug. 3.
Marcos Sanchez production and release. Written and directed by Jorge Darnell. With Violetta Antier, Albert Argibay, Fernanda Mistral. At Locarno Film Fest. Running time, **70 MINS.**
Woman .... Violetta Antier
Man .... Alberto Argibay
Friend .... Fernanda Mistral

A good theme of immigrants trying to adapt to a new life is ruined by overly declamatory imagery, soap-sudsy plotting and a theatrical rather than film air. So this appears to be mainly for some language situations abroad.

Pic starts in what is supposedly a poor Italian town where people moan about their relatives who have gone off to Argentina and forgotten them. Then a thirtyish woman goes and seems to find an okay life there in doing notary work and translating legal things from Italian to Spanish.

But helping others gets her into trouble with the law and a lover has her sign false papers, and then leaves her pregnant and losing her child to boot. She writes home from prison to tell her grandmother she is okay.

Rigid acting and posing, rather than allowing a feeling for the old and new countries to appear, make this a pretentious rather than probing look at people trying to adjust. Some good story ideas also go astray because of the treatment. Lensing is gray in keeping with the theme, as is the ordinary thesping.   *Mosk.*

Motor Psycho

Well - produced rape - murder drama loaded with violence and sex which finally defeats script. Good prospects in action-exploitation situations. Local bluenoses may be a problem.

Hollywood, Aug. 21.
Eve Productions Inc. release, written (with W. E. Sprague), photographed, produced and directed by Russ Meyer. Features Stephen Oliver, Haji, Alex Rocco, Holle K. Winters, Joseph Cellini, Thomas Scott. Editor, Charles G. Schelling, music, Igo Kantor; theme, Paul Sawtell, Bert Shefter; sound, Carl G. Sheldon; asst. director, George Costello. Reviewed at Pathe Labs, L.A., Aug. 11, '65. Running Time, **73 MINS.**
Brahmin .... Stephen Oliver
Ruby Bonner .... Haji
Cory Maddox .... Alex Rocco
Gail Maddox .... Holle K. Winters
Dante .... Joseph Cellini
Slick .... Thomas Scott
Harry Bonner .... Coleman Francis
Jessica Fannin .... Sharron Lee
Fisherman .... Steve Masters
Fisherman's wife .. Arshalouis Aivasian
Gas station man ...... F. Rufus Owens
Sheriff .... E. E. Meyer
Doctor .... George Costello
Ambulance driver .. Richard Brummer

"Motor Psycho" is a violent and highly-exploitable Russ Meyer production concerning three young bums on a rape-murder spree in a California desert town. Slick, well-made and initially absorbing, it features sex angles which kill the credibility of a script which itself is long on loose ends and short on moral compensation. No more promise. Not a nudie pic, it should recover its $38,000 negative cost several times over in action situations.

Stephen Oliver, Joseph Cellini and Thomas Scott are the vagrants who, within the first five minutes, have viciously beaten Steve Masters and raped his wife Arshalouis Aivasian. Holle K. Winters is then assaulted while hubby Alex Rocco is down the road resisting the advances of busty Sharon Lee.

At length, Coleman Francis is beaten and accidently killed when the gang moves in on his younger wife, played by a gal named Haji. Rest of pic concerns Rocco's trackdown of the trio, in which he is joined by Haji, left for dead after Oliver shoots her.

Scripters Meyer and W. E. Sprague have used the sex-and-sadism cliche by relating the guys to motorcycle riders, a timely though overblown concept which indiscriminately smears all bike riders. Major loose ends include a too-neat explanation of Oliver as an Army vet of Vietnam who flipped his lid, also Rocco's interest in Haji when his wife's tragedy plus his own snakebite would presumably cool the libido.

The major plot letdown is that, having piled outrage upon outrage, there is no welcome compensating violence as in John Sturges' "Bad Day At Black Rock" when Spencer Tracy finally beats up Ernest Borgnine to the vicarious relief of an entire audience. Instead, Oliver impulsively kills Scott, Haji knifes Cellini during a rape attempt, and Rocco blows Oliver to bits, but latter has by then become mentally unglued.

The gals are all lookers, and Oliver has promise of being developed into a screen name. To a lesser ex-

tent, so do Rocco, Cellini and Scott. Other thesps are adequate.

Meyer's direction is good, while his interesting and crisp camera work is excellent. Charles G. Schelling edited well, and Carl G. Sheldon's sound work is outstanding (nearly all exterior shots and no looping). Igo Kantor's score has the modern sound, and the Paul Sawtell-Bert Shefter theme is good. Eve Meyer was associate producer.   *Murf.*

Wild Wild World
(C'SCOPE-COLOR)

Poorly - filmed, low - budget sensationalism that will need hard sell, but should do okay in exploitation market.

Chicago, Aug. 11.
Sokoler Films Ltd. release of Alessandro Jacovoni (Ajace Productions Euro-International) film. Directed by Robert Sokoler. Narration, Eddie Bracken; music, Roberto Nicolosi. Reviewed at Town Theatre, Chicago, Aug. 6, 1965. Running Time, **80 MINS.**

"Wild Wild World" is another of the recent productions delving into the bizarre that is aimed at the exploitation market. The sequence of subjects covers a few of the macabre practices (not more or less stock from overexposure) that are peculiar to the Orient, such as certain tastes in food (dogs, snakes, etc.), and then for good measure displays the gore—with none of the drama—of a bullfight in Madrid and the frenzy of a cockfight in Manila. The majority of footage, however, is taken up by a long succession of dancing girls presented in various stages of undress.

Too often the camera is poorly focused and many of the outdoor scenes, as well as indoor, are soft. Changes of scene are usually rough and the suddenness is jarring. The preponderance of dancing women, placed in science-fiction and fantasy situations (as a moon-maiden, and an Arab chieftain with one of his harem girls) is both overdone and, in the main, dull.

Outstanding in the film is the Bayanihan National Troupe of the Philippines. The group performs a traditional dance ceremony and is superior to any other dancing troupe in the picture. Aside from this sensitive and beautiful sequence there is little else in the production that would make it acceptable for any kind of showing other than in theatres which are geared for this type of film.
                     Ron.

La Grosse Caisse
(The Big Swag)
(FRENCH)

Paris, Aug. 10.
Cocinor release of Cocinor-Marceau production. Stars Bourvil, Paul Meurisse; features Francoise Deldick, Roger Carel, Daniel Ceccaldi. Directed by Alex Joffe. Screenplay, R. Asseo, G. Gil, L. Charpentier, Joffe, P. Levy-Corti; camera, Louis Page; editor, Jacques Pluet. At Balzac, Paris. Running Time, **102 MINS.**
Bourdin .... Bourvil
Filippi .... Paul Meurisse
Angelique .... Francoise Deldick
Chef .... Roger Carel
Pignole .... Daniel Ceccaldi

Alex Joffe had the surprise sleeper of the year with his French-Israeli fantasy-parody, "Impossible on Saturday." Now he aims for a picaresque pic in the comedic line about an innocent caught up in a big holdup, but it does not manage to jell. This does sustain interest if the invention is feeble and the characterization rides against the well worked out big heist of a subway pay train in Paris.

With comics Bourvil and Paul Meurisee, and its twitting of duty versus gain, in the grandeur pattern of France it may have an okay career here, with foreign use more chancey. But there is a possibility for specialized or playoff spots on its theme.

This is a bit too pat and patterned to give the needed twists and acceptable satire to have it hold up throughout. Joffe's direction is solid but without the alert fillip to lift this out of its determined comedic rut.

Bourvil is a dim but engaging ticket puncher on the subway who writes a book about a holdup of the pay train. Every publisher turns it down. Then he tries to entice some crooks into doing the holdup so publishers will not say it is impossible. But he gets dragged into the plot to rob the train. It goes off well except for a few imponderables that have the crooks caught and he let off when the chief exonerates him.

Bourvil has the timing and human touches that make his fall guy acceptable while Paul Meurisse trots out his familiar suave underworld character. It is technically par with an okay cast and the subway locale giving it some added photo interest.

This is one of those tongue-in-cheek little man and underworld yarns that seems a bit displaced in these days of grim Bond-like, sadistically comic pix. But it does have an offbeat locale and is solidly if somewhat too predictably turned out. *Mosk.*

Merveilleuse Angelique
(Marvelous Angelique)
(FRENCH-COLOR-DYALISCOPE)
Paris, Aug. 10.

Prodis release of Francos Film-CICC-Gloria Film-Fonorama production. Stars Michele Mercier; features Claude Giraud, Jean-Louis Trintignant, Jacques Toja, Jean Rochefort, Noel Roquevert. Directed by Bernard Borderie. Screenplay, Claude Brule, Daniel Boulanger, Francis Cosne, Borderie from novel by Serge and Anne Golon; camera (Eastmancolor), Henri Persin; editor, Christian Gaudin. At Paris. Running Time, 102 MINS.
Angelique	Michele Mercier
Poet	Jean-Louis Trintignant
King	Jacques Toja
Innkeeper	Noel Roquevert
Lawyer	Jean Rochefort
Philippe	Claude Giraud
Nicolas	Giuliano Gemma

Sequel to a successful local costumer about an Amber-like girl's adventures in the picaresque and royal circles of 17th century France, this should follow suit here if somewhat too obvious and familiar for anything but playoff or tv chances abroad.

Continuing where the other left off, the film does not appear able to stand on its own without the first one. Pic was cannily shot at the same time as the first entry to cash in on sets and thesps. Here Angelique, a pretty wench of poverty-stricken nobility, has had her husband burned for witchcraft

and is saved by the king of the cutthroats of Paris, an old flame.

She becomes his mistress again but he is killed in a fight. She goes on to become a big business woman and takes various lovers to finally end up with a nobleman to restore her to court life.

Michele Mercier is fetching as Angelique and also does her few nude scenes with tact. But she does not have the needed depth and wronged innocence to make all this far-fetched romantic plotting palatable. Nor does Bernard Borderie's flatfooted direction help either.

However, production dress is good and it shapes up an old-fashioned film staple that just lacks the right winning parody and verve to give it more international chances. But the books, from which taken, have some sales here and will help put it across on its home grounds. *Mosk.*

Lorna

Sex angles dominate a weak straying wife plot. Technically excellent, but not quite out of the nudie theatre class.

Hollywood, Aug. 14.

Eve Productions Inc. release, produced, photographed, edited and directed by Russ Meyer. Features Lorna Maitland, Mark Bradley, James Rucker, Hal Hopper, Doc Scortt. James Griffith. Screenplay, Griffith, based on Meyer story; music coordination, Hopper, Griffith; song, Hopper, sung by Bob Grabeau; sound, Charles G. Schelling. Reviewed at Pathe Labs, L.A., Aug. 13, '65. Running Time, 78 MINS.
Lorna	Lorna Maitland
Fugitive	Mark Bradley
James	James Rucker
Luther	Hal Hopper
Jonah	Doc Scortt
Prophet	James Griffith

A sort of sex morality play. "Lorna" was Russ Meyer's first serious effort after six nudie pix which started with "The Immoral Mr. Teas." Still in slow playoff, film has a weak script nearly overpowered with sexploitation angles which will relegate it, in general, to houses which feature such product. Pic has successful, lengthy run at Times Square's Rialto, an exploitation house, earlier this year.

Meyer's story as scripted by James Griffith concerns Lorna Maitland as the buxom wife of James Rucker, a handsome young clod who each day joins Hal Hopper and Doc Scortt in commuting to work at a salt mine. (Latter is not the first Biblical overtone, since Griffith portrays a firebrand preacher-Greek chorus who greets audience via clever subjective camera intro with ominous foreboding of sin and payment therefor.)

Mark Bradley, escaped con and vicious killer, encounters Miss Maitland in the fields with predictable results, after which she takes him home for encores. Hubby's early return cues climax wherein wife and fugitive die violently. Such quick moral retributions following leisurely sensual dalliance are not new, Cecil B. DeMille having derived much mileage from same.

Miss Maitland has a sensual voice although vocal projection is her least asset. Bradley has rugged

looks, a voice to match, and a bigger future in films. His role requires expressions of fear, boredom, tenderness and amoral viciousness, and he is up to them all.

Rucker acts poorly. Hopper and Scortt convince as the slobs who bait Rucker about his wife until subdued in an exciting brawl. Griffith is a two-time loser, having overacted a trite part which he himself wrote.

Meyer's direction is good, considering talent and script, while his lensing and editing are excellent. Bob Grabeau sings Hopper's okay title tune, and other canned track music was well-selected. Charles G. Schelling's sound, unlooped throughout, is excellent. *Murf.*

Rope Of Flesh

Sexploitable but also dramatic yarn about a depression sharecropper. Well produced and directed. Good prospects in adult situations.

Hollywood, Aug. 14.

Eve Productions Inc. release, produced (with George Costello) directed by Russ Meyer. Features Hal Hopper, Lorna Maitland, Antoinette Cristiani, John Furlong, Stu Lancaster, Rena Horten, Princess Livingston, Sam Hanna, Nick Wolcuff, Frank Bolger, Lee Ballard, Mickey Foxx, F. Rufus Owens. Screenplay, Raymond Friday Locke, William E. Sprague; camera, Walter Schenk; editing, sound, Charles G. Schelling; music, Henri Price. Reviewed at Pathe Labs, L.A., Aug. 13, '65. Running time, 92 MINS.
Sidney Brenshaw	Hal Hopper
Clara Belle	Lorna Maitland
Hannah Brenshaw	Antoinette Cristiani
Calif McKinney	John Furlong
Lute Wade	Stu Lancaster
Eula	Rena Horten
Maggie Marie	Princess Livingston
Injoys	Sam Hanna
Sheriff	Nick Wolcuff
Brother Hanson	Frank Bolger
Sister Hanson	Lee Ballard
Thurmond Pate	Mickey Foxx
Milton	F. Rufus Owens

"Rope Of Flesh" concerns the mental decay of a jealous depression-era sharecropper, and its effects on his family and town. Some good acting by unknowns and lesser names enhance a script which is the strongest of three produced and directed by Russ Meyer since exiting the strict nudie sphere. Sexploitation elements exist, but in such a way that near-complete removal would still yield an acceptable and absorbing entry in the general adult market.

When California-bound John Furlong arrives at Missouri farm of Stu Lancaster after a prison stretch, his employment cues the declining sanity of Hal Hopper, wife-beating husband of Lancaster's niece Antoinette Cristiani. Latter projects very well as the loyal wife who takes all the punishment even after falling in love with Furlong in a tastefully-handled affair. Hopper is very good as the cheating, frustrated hubby who is variously taunting, remorseful, scheming, brutal and submissive. Top thesp honors go to Lancaster, the stolid landowner who wills his property to Furlong instead of Hopper, knowledge of which sends the latter into a final crazed spree of murder and barn-burning.

Interjected at intervals are Lorna Maitland and Rena Horten of the local bordello shanty run by toothless Princess Livingston whose cackles of derision wear

thin after a time. The babes are lookers, natch, and Miss Horten does well in a role which calls for her to play a deaf mute.

Frank Bolger is the film's Elmer Gantry, whose fire and brimstone talk is tinged with curiosity until Hopper corrupts him via a trip to the sporting pad. He helps Hopper turn the town against the latter's wife and lover until his own wife, Lee Ballard, is strangled by the unglued husband, then becomes the fanatic leader of a lynch mob over which sheriff Nick Wolcuff has no control.

The unusual climax finds a town full of embarrassed lynchers afraid to look at one another, Miss Horten shocked into speech, and an upbeat note for the young couple. Raymond Friday Locke and William E. Sprague scripted a Locke story which has some strong dramatic angles and salty dialog which is not out of place.

George Costello and Meyer allocated the $60,000 negative cost to good advantage. Latter's direction is excellent. Walter Schenk's camera is crisp. Editing and sound by Charles G. Schelling is also excellent, particularly the extensive recording achieved sans looping. *Murf.*

The Brigand of Kandahar
(BRITISH-COLOR)

Straightforward, hearty adventure yarn of bloodshed and intrigue on the Indian Northwest Frontier; sound dualer for average situations.

London, Aug. 10.

Warner-Pathe release and Associated British Picture Corp. presentation of a (Anthony Nelson Keys) Hammer production. Stars Ronald Lewis, Oliver Reed, Duncan Lamont; features Yvonne Romain, Catherine Woodville, Glynn Houston, Sean Lynch, Walter Brown, Inigo Jackson. Directed by John Gilling. Original story and screenplay, Gilling; camera (Technicolor), Reg Wyer; music, Don Banks; editor, Tom Simpson. Reviewed at ABC Cinema, Harrow Road, London. Running Time, 81 MINS.
Lieutenant Case	Ronald Lewis
Ali Khan	Oliver Reed
Colonel Drewe	Duncan Lamont
Ratina	Yvonne Romain
Elsa	Catherine Woodville
Marriott	Glynn Houston
Captain Boyd	Inigo Jackson
Rattu	Sean Lynch
Hitala	Walter Brown
Connelley	Jeremy Burnham
Serving Maid	Carol Gardner

Though rather too obviously studio manufactured, director John Gilling has contrived a good blood-and-thunder adventure yarn which will prove a useful bet as a dualer in most average situations. Spanking battle climax gives a lift to the action already peppered with bumpings off, minor skirmishes and a fine duel between Ronald Lewis and Oliver Reed.

Story concerns a half-caste officer in the British Army (Ronald Lewis) serving on the Indian Northwest Frontier who nurses a grudge against his harsh superior officer when the latter gets him tossed out of the Army on a framed charge. Lewis joins up with a fanatical local brigand (Oliver Reed) to fight the British. His split loyalties make him vulnerable on all sides.

The British Army eventually

wins out, with Lewis, Reed and Reed's sister all dead, but with the army colonel (Duncan Lamont) not showing up in any too favorable a light. Lewis and Reed make a hearty pair of adventurers. Duncan Lamont's sneaky colonel and Glynn Houston, as a tenacious Times war correspondent, also show up well.

Distaff side doesn't fare so brightly. Catherine Woodville in the puppet role of an officer's wife who causes the first downfall of Lewis seems unusually subdued. But Yvonne Romain, as the slinky, scheming petticoat influence among the brigands, scores.
Rich.

Montreal Fest

La Vie Heureuse de Leopold Z
(The Happy Life of Leopold Z)
(CANADIAN)

Montreal, Aug. 17.
Columbia Pictures of Canada release of National Film Board of Canada production. Written and directed by Gilles Carle. Camera, Jean-Claude Labrecque, Bernard Gosselin; music, Paul de Margerie. At Montreal Film Festival 1965. Running Time, 70 MINS.
Cast: Paul Hebert, Guy L'Ecuyer, Monique Joly, Suzanne Valery.

(In French)

Leopold, a plump, amiable happily-married man, drives a snowplow for the city of Montreal. It is Christmas Eve, the snow is falling heavily and between cleaning streets he runs around taking out a loan, buying his wife a fur coat as a present and taking care of his cousin, a nightclub singer, who has just arrived in the city. He finally gets his present to his wife at midnight mass. Throughout his long and tiring day he is watched by his foreman, who suspects he is up to other things.

Canadian wirters have long been considered the next worst thing to Siberia. For director Gilles Carle to make a comedy out of the subject is a considerable achievement. This is a lighthearted, deftly made and acted piece of whimsy, slight but entertaining, with a likeable and natural cast of players.

Made on a budget of around $60,000 this picture should have little difficulty getting its money back in Canada. With English subtitles it is possible on a double bill at second-run specialized cinemas. It won the Grand Prix here at the Third Annual Festival of Canadian films.
Prat.

La Neige A Fondu Sur La Manicouagan
(The Snow Has Melted on The Manicouagan)
(CANADIAN)

Montreal, Aug. 17.
Columbia Pictures of Canada release of National Film Board of Canada production (Marcel Martin). Written and directed by Arthur Lamothe. Camera, Gilles Gascon; music, Maurice Blackburn. At Montreal Film Festival 1965. Cast: Monique Miller, Gilles Vigneault, Margot Campbell, Jean Doyon.

(In French)

This is an atmospheric mood piece photographed in the snows of winter at the giant dam which Quebec Hydro is building in the northern wilds of the province. The slight story concerns the wife of a worker who is bored with her dreary existence in this wilderness of construction, walks around in the snow, recalls how she met her husband, and goes to the landing field to catch a departing plane. But she remains after all when her husband tells her how much his work means to him, even the winter snow.

This picture suffers from being neither one thing or the other: as impressionism it is tedious, as a drama it fails to bring characters or setting to life. It may do well in Quebec theatres on a double bill and on television, but has faint prospects elsewhere.
Prat.

Tjorven, Batsman Och Moses
(The Little Girl, The Dog and The Seal)
(SWEDISH-COLOR)

Montreal, Aug. 17.
Artfilm (Stockholm) production and release. Directed by Ollie Hellbom; scenario, Astrid Lindgren; camera, (color) Kalle Bergholm; music, Ulf Bjorlin. At Montreal Film Festival, 1965. Running time, 70 MINS.

This is one of two children's films shown at this year's fest at special morning performances. It's an unimaginatively told tale of children, dogs and a seal in the Swedish countryside—which looks remarkably like Canada.

The color is poor, but animals and children usually project some appeal no matter how indifferent the treatment. The children found it entertaining. It's reviewed here for the record and for program directors of special shows for kiddies.
Prat.

Mate Doma Lva?
(Do You Keep a Lion at Home?)
(CZECH)

Montreal, Aug. 17.
Ceskoslovensky Filmexport release and production. Directed by Pavel Hobl. Story & screenplay, Sheila Ochova & Bohumil Sobolka; camera, Jiri Vojta; music William Bukovy. At Montreal Film Festival, 1965. Running Time, 75 MINS.
Joe .... Ladislav Ocenasek
Johnny .... Josef Filip
Little girl .... Olga Machoninova
Painter .... Jan Brychta

This 1963 Czech film for children is a firstrate piece of humorous fantasy concerning the adventures of two little boys, who, finding their school closed for the day, roam around the town. They become policemen, meet a talking dog, go to the museum where a stuffed bear gives them roller skates, visit a wizard's palace, change dogs into musicians, go racing in an ancient car and meet ghosts in suits of armor.

In color and tinted tones, it moves quickly from place to place, is cleverly made with trick effects, nicely acted, and because it makes no concessions to adults and doesn't attempt to cater to everybody—succeeds in being entertaining for most audiences. *Prat.*

Once A Thief
(PANAVISION)

Fast-paced melodrama with crime background; Ann-Margret, Heflin and Palance for marquee.

Hollywood, Aug. 19.
Metro release of Jacques Bar production in association with Ralph Nelson, Fred Engel, directed by Nelson. Stars Alain Delon, Ann-Margret, Van Heflin Jack Palance; features John Davis Chandler, Jeff Corey, Tony Musante. Screenplay, Zekial Marko, based on own novel; camera, Robert Burks; music, Lalo Schifrin; editor, Fredric Steinkamp; asst. director, Erich Von Stroheim Jr. Reviewed at Academy Award Theatre, Aug. 18, '65. Running Time, 106 MINS.

Eddie Pedak .... Alain Delon
Kristine Pedak .... Ann-Margret
Mike Vido .... Van Heflin
Walter Pedak .... Jack Palance
James Sargatanas .. John Davis Chandler
Lt. Kebner .... Jeff Corey
Cleve Shoenstein .... Tony Musante
Frank Kane .... Steve Mitchell
Luke .... Zekial Marko
Kathy Pedak .... Tammy Locke
Drummer .... Russell Lee
John Ling .... Yuki Shimoda

"Once a Thief" packs both violence and young married love in unfoldment of its theme, aptly titled, about an ex-con trying to go straight, but constantly harassed by a vengeful cop. Exploitation values are apparent in presence of Ann-Margaret and first U.S.-made feature of French star Alain Delon. Film has plenty of suspense in latter reels, but essentially is only a stripe above an average well-turned-out cops-and-robbers piece.

Ralph Nelson, with such top entries under his belt as "Lilies of the Field" and "Father Goose," gives moving direction to the Zekial Marko screenplay on which he and Fred Engel were associated with Jacques Bar in producing. Bar, French producer, makes his American bow on this, in which Van Heflin, as a police inspector who thinks Delon once shot him, and Jack Palance, a gangster, also star. Picture's 106 minutes' running time would benefit by some judicious shearing. It gets away on a rock'n'roll note which adds up to nothing, before settling down to enactment of Delon's return to crime at the behest of his brother, Palance, after Heflin repeatedly has had him fired from jobs.

"Once a Thief" has a San Francisco setting, where lenser Robert Burks makes interesting use of Chinatown and North Beach locations to backdrop story of $1,000,000 platinum robbery and ultimate violent demise of each member of the five-man gang that pulled the job. Delon not too unwillingly is pulled into the plot when he finds his wife, Ann-Margaret, mother of their small daughter, working in a cheap nightclub so they may live.

Delon, whose only slight accent is explained by his hailing from Trieste, is an interesting young actor who delivers strongly and should earn wide popularity on the American screen. He's the romantic type who excels also in rugged action. Ann-Margret, too, is firstrate in her role.

Heflin, as Delon's nemesis, who carries as a pocket-piece a bullet dug out of his stomach as reminder of an unsolved crime, effectively plays the relentless police officer, and Palance, with less foot-

age, similarly scores. John Davis Chandler is okay as a killer who frames Delon — unexplainably — for a murder in opening reel. Tony Musante, Zekial Marko, Jeff Corey and Yuki Shimoda lend good support.

Technical credits are well handled. Lalo Schifrin's musical score lends a potent assist. Fredric Steinkamp's editing is fast and art direction by George W. Davis and Paul Groesse atmospheric.
Whit.

I Pugni In Tasca
(Fists in the Pockets)
(ITALIAN)

Locarno, Aug. 17.
Doria Cinematografica production and release. With Lou Castel, Paola Pitagora, Marino Mase, Liliana Gerace. Written and directed by Marco Bellochio. Camera, Alberto Marrama; editor, A. Margiatti. At Locarno Film Fest. Running time, 105 MINS.
Alessandro .... Lou Castel
Julia .... Paola Pitagora
Augusto .... Marino Mase
Mother .... Liliana Gerace
Leone .... Pier Luigi Troglio
Lucia .... Jennie MacNeil

Italy is blossoming out with fine, new creative directorial film talents. Here is a first pic about a tainted family and its downbeat tale always coherent, never brutal or horrific for its own sake. There is a compassionate but relentless narrative that shapes this mainly for arty situations abroad, its uncompromising subject limiting it for playoff.

There is a provincial family with some money living in a big house. Two brothers are epileptic, the mother is blind, the sister acting much more childish than her age, in the early twenties, and one normal, older brother who runs this strange household.

Brought up somewhat unaware of their condition, one epileptic, Lou Castel, seems sane but is somewhat twisted and apparently unconscious of social conditions and gives vent to his teenage feelings and frustrations without a necessary sane check on them.

He gets the idea that if the more unstable elements of the family are eliminated (his mother and a retarded brother), things would be better. He commits both crimes when the chance presents itself. This liberates him seemingly. He even seduces his sister who finally becomes aware of his crimes and is paralyzed in a fall.

Now he is even thinking of doing away with her and makes a sly pass at his older brother's girl. But alone in the house with his sister, he gets a fit, and dies in floundering agony. All this might sound horrific and forced, but it is not.

Director Marco Bellochio displays expert tact in first laying out this inbred sickly family in their daily unrestrained lives. The homicidal brother's strange childhood and affliction turns him into a killer whose brief moment finally leads to a solitary death.

Film is photographed with a sharp definition with acting extremely well balanced to keep this from falling into only the clinical or shocking. The unbalanced youth is not given commiseration or excuse if his state is echoed by his life and afflictions.

Lou Castel, a Swedish-Italo

youth, has the roughhewn looks to make his character always revealing, sometimes pathetic, disturbing but never gratuitous. Paola Pitagora is a lovely if slightly unbalanced beauty, fading in this humorless atmosphere except for her complicity with her brother. Others are also fine in this offbeat, sometimes shocking but never-forced look at an inverted family that engenders its own doom.

So this naturally needs careful handling. Things can be read into it as perhaps a study of a sort of fascist mind, if overboard, that can be bred by backwardness, stultifying growth and the freeing of adolescent needs in an airless social atmosphere. So it turns out to be a piercing pic, and unveils solid new talent even if its commercial chances are dubious.
Mosk.

Rapture
(C'SCOPE)

A touching child-woman story made tedious by length and gimmickry. No marquee names, but some good performances.

Hollywood, Aug. 12.
Twentieth Century-Fox release of Pan-Oramic Pictures (Christian Ferry) production. Stars Melvyn Douglas, Patricia Gozzi, Dean Stockwell, Gunnel Lindblom; features Leslie Sands, Murray Evans, Sylvia Kane, Peter Sallis. Directed by John Guillermin. Screenplay, Stanley Mann; camera, Marcel Grignon; editors, Max Benedict, Francois Diot; music, Georges Delerue; sound, Joseph de Bretagne; asst. directors, Louis Pitzele, Rik Wise. Reviewed at 20th-Fox Studio, Aug. 11, '65. Running Time, 104 MINS.
Frederick Larbaud .... Melvyn Douglas
Agnes Larbaud .... Patricia Gozzi
Joseph .... Dean Stockwell
Karen .... Gunnel Lindblom
Policemen .... Leslie Sands,
                          Murray Evans
Genevieve Larbaud .... Sylvia Kane
Armand .... Peter Sallis

Lensed on France's Brittany coast as a 20th-Fox European film, "Rapture" is a low key meller of a mentally retarded girl unable to cope with life and romance. Overlength and jarring direction make trite and tedious what could have been touching. With no hot names for the general market, the Christian Ferry production seems destined for artie situations.

Stanley Mann's script intros Patricia Gozzi at sister Sylvia Kane's wedding to Peter Sallis, where her infantilism is socked over by excellent dizzy camera action during a dance and later flight into town streets. Rescued by family maid Gunnel Lindblom, she returns to the loveless home of father Melvyn Douglas.

Her childish fantasy is disturbed by arrival of Dean Stockwell, on the lam from a jailbreak, at which point Miss Gozzi transfers her affection for a scarecrow to him. Miss Gozzi does a very good job in projecting the pitiable elements of love, jealousy, hate, anger and frustration, all inherent (sometimes within seconds) in a maladjusted person. (Very young thesp made her name as the sensitive, precocious child in French pic, "Sundays and Cybele.")

Douglas seems uncomfortable as a strict disciplinarian, initially insensitive but later revealed in talks with Stockwell as a disgraced ex-

judge. Withal, he is never sympathetic, even when shielding Stockwell from snoopy gumshoes Leslie Sands and Murray Evans, motivation being more a protest against stern law than a feeling for daughter and fugitive.

Miss Lindblom does well as the earthy maid and sole companion to Miss Gozzi who has an eye for men, including Stockwell. Her understandable exit from the plot comes after an exciting scene in which Miss Gozzi tries to kill her. (Swedish actress is Ingmar Bergman regular, most recently in the sexy "The Silence.")

Stockwell is good as the fugitive who comes to love Miss Gozzi, whom he eventually takes to Paris where he hopes to escape capture. Her mental condition is again displayed in a touching scene where she loses hubby's salary in a street panic. Subsequent flight home, and Stockwell's pursuit, cues the downbeat climax. Other thesps are adequate.

Director John Guillermin employed far too many gimmicks, including irritating jumps, bizarre setups and distracting camera mobility, which lends unreality to all characters and dilutes occasional effectiveness.

Marcel Grignon's camera caught the moody atmosphere, but Joseph de Bretagne's sound is uniformly too loud. Georges Delerue scored effectively, using a choral motif for Miss Gozzi's disturbed period. Editors Max Benedict and Francois Diot trimmed to 104 minutes, less than the studio production notes which indicated 133 minutes, with more tightening needed in final half hour.
Murf.

Le Lit a Deux Places
(The Double Bed)
(FRENCH-ITALIAN)

Paris, Aug. 24.
Dicifilm release of Cineurop-Metheus production. Stars Sylva Koscina, France Anglade, Margaret Lee, Dominique Boschero; features Jean Richard, Michel Serrault, Jacqques Charron, Carla Calo. Directed by Jean Delannoy, Francois Dupont - Midy, Gianni Puccini. Screenplay, Alfredo Giannetti, Darry Cowl, Jean-Loup Dabadie based on fables of La Fontaine; camera, Robert Lefebvre; editor, Henri Taverna. At Colisee, Paris. Running Time, 120 MINS.
Wife .... France Anglade
Carmela .... Margaret Lee
Colette .... Dominique Boschero
Giulietta .... Sylva Koscina
Albert .... Michel Serrault
Fiance .... Jacques Charon
Visitor .... Darry Cowl
Father .... Jean Richard
Mother .... Carla Calo

Film is an episoder that tries to bring in fairly rakish s'\: via slanting them all around a furniture store trying to sell a flock of beds that have stories connected with them. Each tale is then unfolded. But they are sans a true anecdotic fullness for the most part. Generally lagging and devoid of true bawdisness this is only a playoff item on its title and promise, mostly unfulfilled.

It is no use picking out the three directors for all contribute fairly cheerful looks at what goes on around these beds. Vet French director Jean Delannoy is especially heavy-footed in his two episodes of this five-part film.

First up is a hotel owner renting out everything and even part of his own room to two young men.

But one is the secret suitor of his daughter who is in a bed behind a curtain in the same room with the parents and the two boys. There's a lot of fairly innocent adventure that misses out.

Then a psychoanalyst, married to a young girl who will not have him, has himself taken for a sex maniac. An Italian couple have the man playing dead as she entices men in and has them pay before they run out when they see the dead man. This is the only one that has some wit if it is overworked.

A country bumpkin takes over a worldly model and a fiance gets worked over by the brother-in-law-to-be which breaks up the affair. All these are overlong and played with uneven results. Trying to cash in on the spate of earlier comedie Itala episoders, this French-Italo attempt does not have it.
Mosk.

Willy McBean And His Magic Machine
(COLOR)

Entertaining puppet cartoon with songs, well-written and produced. Good for juve market where satirical overtones will hold the more mature escorts.

Hollywood, Aug. 13.
Magna Pictures release of Videocraft International-Dentsu Motion Picture Co. production, written, produced and directed by Arthur Rankin, Jr. Features voices of Larry Mann, Billie Richards, Alfie Scopp, Paul Kligman, Bunny Cowan, Paul Soles, Pegi Loder. Songs, Edward Thomas, Gene Forrell, James Polack; associate producers, Jules Bass, Larry Roemer. Reviewed at Lytton Center of Visual Arts, L.A., Aug. 12, '65. Running Time, 94 MINS.

A puppet cartoon lensed in Japan by Dentsu Co. and dubbed domestically by Videocraft International, "Willy McBean And His Magic Machine" is a colorful, entertaining and well-produced juve pic. Comedy ranges from broad to satire, and is enlivened by good showtunes. Magna release seems a good prospect for kid situations where parental escorts will also be pleased.

Producer-director Arthur Rankin Jr.'s script focuses on mad professor Rasputin Von Rotton who has built a time machine by which he plans to scoop the achievements of Buffalo Bill, Columbus, Egypt's King Tut, King Arthur, and fire-discovering cavemen. His imprisoned pet monkey Pablo escapes with the plans to Willy McBean, who builds a dupe and, with Pablo, foils all the attempts before waking up from what has turned out to be a dream.

Episodic plot turns feature excellent stop-motion lensing in Eastmancolor which succeed in suspending disbelief. Characters and miniature sets seem real, with the effect heightened by firstrate dubbing by Larry Mann, Billie Richards, Alfie Scopp, Bunny Cowan, Paul Soles and Pegi Loder.

Edward Thomas, Gene Forrell and James Polack wrote the clever tunes which brighten each segment. Particularly good are Buffalo Bill's gone-showbiz number, the Round Table drinking song

(with King Arthur ignored by the preening knights), and the duet between Tut and his queen. All technical credits are topnotch.
Murf.

Murieta
(COLOR)

Okay programmer about bigotry and banditry in Gold Rush days of California. Overlong, sometimes talky, but diverting entry for dual bills.

Hollywood, Aug. 11.
Warner Bros. release of Pro Artis Iberica production, Jose Sainz de Vicuna executive producer. Features Jeffrey Hunter, Arthur Kennedy, Diana Lorys, Sara Lezana, Roberto Camardiel, Pedro Osinaga. Directed by George Sherman. Screenplay, James O'Hanlon; camera (Eastmancolor), Miguel F. Mila; editor, Alfonso Santacana; music, Antonio Perez Olea; songs, Paco Michael, sound, Enrique Molinaro; asst. directors, Stanley Torchia, Federico Vaqueda. Reviewed at Warner Bros. studio, Aug. 10, '65. Running Time, 107 MINS.
Joaquin Murieta .... Jeffrey Hunter
Captain Love .... Arthur Kennedy
Kate .... Diana Lorys
Rosita .... Sara Lezana
Three Fingers ...... Roberto Camardiel
Claudio .... Pedro Osinaga

"Murieta" concerns a young Mexican gold miner turned bandit by American intolerance in the Gold Rush days of California. Filmed last year in Spain and bought by Warners, pic is unpretentious and average action entertainment. Director George Sherman obtained okay performances from a Spanish-American cast. Film is a bit long and drags in the talky sequences, although shaping up as an okay entry for dual situations.

James O'Hanlon's script depicts the struggle of married couple Jeffrey Hunter and Sara Lezana against the bigotry of Gold Rush era Americans who forgot that the land recently belonged to Mexico, whence the pair had emigrated in search of a new life. Deputy marshal Arthur Kennedy can only sympathize and does not know of the subsequent boondocks rape-murder of the pregnant wife until a year later when Hunter has changed into a saloon card sharp on the alert for the three killers.

Hunter is properly immature in early scenes, becoming in turn quietly vengeful while stalking the killers whom he guns down in cold blood after Kennedy answers a hypothetical query which indicates that normal justice would not prevail. Ensuing jailbreak with cliche bandit type Roberto Camardiel and equally cliche comic sidekick Pedro Osinaga cues Hunter's unwilling career as gangleader.

Kennedy walks through an undemanding role with his usual underplayed competence, whether being freed by Hunter following a lawmen's slaughter, later freeing Hunter who promises to abandon lawlessness and finally tracking him down in film's climactic irony when the bandits are gunned down as Hunter leads them to what would have been peaceful surrender.

Diana Lorys is a better looker than actress in the role of wisecracking frontier woman who aids Hunter's jailbreak. Other thesps are adequate under direction of

Sherman, an old action pro, who diverts with some shoot-em-up business just when an audience is tiring of the chatter. Alfonso Satacana's editing to 107 minutes needs a bit more tightening to enhance Sherman's work.

Miguel F. Mila did a creditable camera job, although Eastmancolor hues were a bit irregular on the print caught. Scoring by Antonio Perez Olea is okay but busy in the early scenes. Paco Michel pinned two original tunes in good fashion.

Other technical credits are okay. English version is credited to Intersync, S.A. Jose Sainz de Vicuna was exec producer. *Murf.*

Le Gendarme De Saint-Tropez
(FRENCH-COLOR)

Paris, Aug. 17.
SNC production and release. Stars Louis De Funes; features Genevieve Grad, Michel Galabru, Christian Martin, Jean Lefebvre. Directed by Jean Girault. Screenplay, Richard Balducci, Jacques Vilfrid, Girault; camera (Eastmancolor), Marc Fossard; editor, J. Feyte. At Regent-Neuilly, Paris. Running Time, **95 MINS.**

Gendarme .... Louis De Funes
Nicole .... Genevieve Grad
Gerber .... Michel Galabru
Merlot .... Christian Marin
Fougasse .... Jean Lefebvre

This simple situation comedy has turned out to be one of the top grossers of the season here, and has even had a sequel, "Le Gendarme a New York," already finished. It also made a star of middleaged comedian Louis De Funes. Film seems somewhat sparse for any arty or good playoff chances abroad. But dualer possibilities are there on its fair comedic flair. Magna Pictures has it for U.S. release.

De Funes is the main asset with his cannily timed and conceived slow burns, harmless maliciousness and disarming selfishness. In short, he sums up the slightly distrustful French everyman, with an evident lack of spite. This is turning him into a big name here.

Pic is a series of okay scenes with an overplotted added bit about the gendarme's daughter trying to pass herself as a rich heiress and setting off a series of complications that end with her father, (De Funes) the local cop, becoming a hero and her getting her rich young man.

Direction is par with fair timing in some scenes, but it is mainly a passable comedy because De Funes, as the irascible gendarme, has more talent than his material. It is technically only passable with color uneven. Supporting players are okay. *Mosk.*

La Fabuleuse Adventure De Marco Polo
(Fabulous Adventure of Marco Polo)
(FRENCH - YUGOSLAV-COLOR)

Paris, Aug. 24.
SNC release of Avala, ITTAC, Pro-Di production. Stars H o r s t Buchholz, Anthony Quinn, Akim Tamiroff, Elsa Martinelli, Robert Hossein, Gregoire Aslan, Omar Sharif, Orson Welles; features Massimo Girotti, Folco Lulli, Lee Sue Moon. Directed by Denys De La Patelliere, Noel Howard. Screenplay, Jacques Remy, J. P. Rappeneau, Raoul J. Levy, De La Patelliere; camera (Eastmancolor), Armand Thirard; editor, Albert Jurgenson. At Ambassade - Gaumont, Paris. Running Time, **115 MINS.**

Marco Polo .... Horst Buchholz
Woman With Whip .... Elsa Martinelli
Kublai Khan .... Anthony Quinn
Nayam .... Robert Hossein
Old Man .... Akim Tamiroff
Teacher .... Orson Welles
Aliou .... Omar Sharif
Ahmed .... Gregoire Aslan

(In English)

After a change of director and star, bankruptcy and yet getting the pic finished (now in litigation with the Yugoslavs on Western Hemisphere rights), Raoul Levy has finished his costumer pic on Marco Polo, started in 1963. It emerges a not quite successful tongue-in-cheek affair with undertones of pontifical seriousness and with a James Bondish episode thrown right into the 13th Century.

But this film has such names to help as Anthony Quinn, Horst Buchholz and Omar Sharif for marquee value and a better-than-average production dress. Pic has the physical looks heralding okay playoff abroad, with its English version well-dubbed and playing here. It looks good for regular handling in more general depth distrib layouts in the U. S.

A commentary running throughout attests to the tortured career in making this film, and it sometimes explains things that should have been implicit in the actual footage. It pokes fun at the general goings-on but can't quite give this the epic or truly swashbuckling aspects needed.

Here is Marco being told he is ready to follow his destiny by an old Venetian teacher, Orson Welles, gotten up to look like Shylock. His father comes back from China and the Pope decides he will send him back with Marco as emissaries to the great Mongol Emperor Kublai Khan who rules all of China. They are to promise peace and Christian teachings.

But there are followers of the son of Khan who want war and try to stop the Polos. There is also a strange figure called The Old Man of the Mountain who wears a gold mask and has an underground palace, sculpted in desert caves. This Old Man has beauteous, slightly-clad girls and muscular warriors who help him run his evil kingdom with blasphemy and wiles and activities not unlike those of Goldfinger. Akim Tamiroff plays this headman for laughs and gives the film its one point of real parody.

He makes one of Marco's monk aides renounce his God by torture but turns the rakish Marco into a man of purpose and belief. Omar Sharif, a ladies' man sheik, befriends the Polos and saves Marco from the Old Man. Then come many hardships, and running into Elsa Martinelli as a woman with a whip in Samarkand, before he reaches the great Khan.

Quinn, with shaved head, plays it quite seriously as a man wanting peace. He is possessed of wisdom and understanding. He finally uses gun powder, heretofore employed only in fireworks, in bamboo rockets to defeat his own son who tries to overthrow him.

Marco stays on for 17 years before going back to tell his tales, which get him thrown into prison, where he writes his book on which the film is supposedly based.

Buchholz has the looks but lacks the flamboyant swashbuckling needed for the Marco Polo role. Others are acceptable, especially Quinn. Directors Denys De La Patelliere and Noel Howard have supplied some nice landscapes and some okay battle scenes. On-the-spot lensing in Africa, Asia and Yugoslavia give it some exotica, and costumes and sets are way above the standards for this kind of film.

Here is a rakish costumer that doesn't quite come off as parody, but has some good action spots and fine production dress to make it an acceptable playoff item. One of Levy's big scenes, made before the change of first director (Christian-Jaque), a gigantic chessboard made up of real people, does not figure in this version. Original title, "L'Echiquier de Dieu" (The Chessboard of God), had to be changed because of excision of this scene, although title was used during most of production period. *Mosk.*

Revenge Of The Gladiators
(TECHNISCOPE-COLOR)

Hollywood. Aug. 25.
Paramount release of Leone Films production. Features Roger Browne, Scilla Gabel, Giacomo Rossi Stuart, Daniele Vargas, Gordon Mitchell and Germando Longo. Directed by Michele Lupo. Story by Lionello de Felice and Ernesto Guida; camera (Technicolor), Guglielmo Mancori; editor, Alberto Gallitti; music, Francesio De Masi. Reviewed at Paramount Studios, Hollywood, Aug. 25, '65. Running Time, **100 MINS.**

Valerius .... Roger Browne
Cynthia .... Scilla Gabel
Fulvius .... Giacomo Rossi Stuart
Lucius Transone .... Daniele Vargas
Arminius .... Gordon Mitchell
Marcellus .... Germano Longo

"Revenge Of The Gladiators" is an inexpensive sequel to "Spartacus," marked by unconvincing script and wooden thesping. But dressed in Technicolor and Techniscope, with some impressive photography by Guglielmo Mancori, Paramount release may have b.o. possibilities, if properly exploited.

Original title was "Vendetta di Spartacus" (Revenge of Spartacus) and was evidently made back-to-back with Leone's "Seven Slaves Against The World," using same cast, crew and costumes, as well as basic plot incidents. Roger Browne and Gordon Mitchell are U.S.-ized names for Italo actors.

Script by Lionello de Felice and Ernesto Guida begins after Roman legions crush Spartacus' revolt, and follows the fortunes of the remnants of his slave and gladiator forces who regroup to carry on the fight. Complex plot has it they are puppets on the string of a Roman leader, protrayed by Daniele Vargas, who wants to keep the countryside stirred up so the Senate will name him dictator

He accomplishes this by subverting the rebel leader, Gordon Mitchell, who obeys orders from Rome while duping rebels into believing Spartacus is still alive.

Mitchell has the only role calling for subtlety, and he carries it off with proper cunning. Lead Roger Browne, as an ex-soldier drawn into the revolt after his family is slain, plays the part with clenched jaw and in muscular fashion that could spark interest with fans of toga epics. Scilla Gabel has little to do in the femme lead, nor have other featured players: Giacomo Rossi Stuart and Germano Longo.

Battle scenes are well-staged technically, but are preposterous in their outcome, with small slave bands handily defeating well-armed legions. *Hogg.*

Gunfighters of Casa Grande
(Los Pistoleros de Casa Grande)
(C-SCOPE-COLOR)

Fast western filmed in Spain; promising possibilities for American action market.

Hollywood, Aug. 27.
Metro release of Lester Welch production. Stars Alex Nicol, Jorge Mistral; features Dick Bentley, Steve Rowland, Phil Posner, Mercedes Alonso; Diana Lorys, Maria Granada, Roberto Rey, Aldo Sambell, Anthony Fuentes. Directed by Roy Rowland. Screenplay, Borden and Patricia Chase, Clarke Reynolds; from story by B. & P. Chase; camera (Metrocolor); Jose F. Aguayo, Manuel Merino; music, Johnny Douglas; editor, George A. Lee; asst. director, Manahen Velasco. Reviewed at Metro Studios, Aug. 26, '65. Running Time, **92 MINS.**

Joe Daylight .... Alex Nicol
The Traveler .... Jorge Mistral
Doc .... Dick Bentley
The Kid .... Steve Rowland
Henri .... Phil Posner
Maria .... Mercedes Alonso
Gitana .... Diana Lorys
Pacesita .... Maria Granada
Don Castellar .... Roberto Rey
Rojo .... Aldo Sambell
Carlos .... Anthony Fuentes

Metro is the latest major to snag domestic release of a western produced abroad. "Gunfighters of Casa Grande," a Spanish-U.S. coproduction, was filmed in Spain and emerges as a fast-paced actioner with the necessary ingredients to keep oater fans happy.

Hollywood know-how went into making of the Lester Welch production effectively filmed in Cinemascope and Metrocolor. Welch, former Hollywood producer now ensconsed in Spain, called in vet director Roy Rowland to helm screenplay by Borden & Patricia Chase and Clarke Reynolds, and cast ex-Hollywood thesp Alex Nicol to costar with Spanish actor Jorge Mistral. Result, backed by a sometimes-exciting music score by Johnny Douglas, is a smooth-sailing unfoldment of a story (originated by Chase duo) which builds to a stirring climax.

Nicol plays an American gunman, a killer, of the Old West who wins a Mexican rancho in a poker game and with his followers sets out to round up 15,000 head of cattle from his own and neighboring spreads, to drive north across the Rio Grande and make a fortune from the cattle-starved post-Civil War U.S. With the profits, he'll disappear without paying off the Mexican hidalgos who in good faith throw in with him. Complications set in when a Mexican bandit with several hundred men attack, and Nicol and Mistral, partners in the cattle drive, end their differences in a gun-blazing finale.

Acting honors go to Mistral in a sympathetic role. Nicol seems stiff and overacts, but is in for plenty of fast gunplay. As three members of Nicol's gang, Dick Bentley, Steve Rowland and Phil Posner score, and Aldo Sambell is picturesque as the menacing outlaw. Distaff interest is beguilingly taken care of by three charmers, including Mercedes Alonso, Diana Lorys and Maria Granada. Balance of cast are okay in colorful roles.

Photography by Jose F. Aguayo and Manuel Merino makes handsome use of the Spanish landscape, new to American audiences, and George A. Lee's editing is speedy.
Whit.

Venice Films

Good Times, Wonderful Times
(BRITISH)
Venice, Aug. 27.
Rogosin Film Productions release and production. Directed by Lionel Rogosin. Screenplay, Rogosin, James Vaughan, Tadeusz Makarczynski; camera, Manny Wynn; music, Chatur Lal, Ram Narayan, Ian Cameron; editor, Brian Smedley-Aston. At Venice Film Festival. Running Time, **70 MINS.**

Lionel Rogosin seems one of the most independent of the east coast U. S. film indies. He made his first pic, "On The Bowery," with family funds, his second "Come Back Africa," via subscription, and this 'third one ditto. All have deeply humane and social commitments sans any didactic or mawkish qualities but with strong outlooks and feeling. Though non-quota, pic is British entry at the Venice film fest.

In "Bowery" he used real alcoholics in a semi-fictionalized story which made a terse statement on the Bowery without preachiness, while with "Africa" he vicariously took a hard blast at apartheid in South Africa while ostensibly making a documentary on folk music there. Now he adroitly mixes specially shot footage and stock scenes to make an affecting commentary on war in general and World War II in particular.

Scenes made at a presentday British party and interviews with some very old retired soldiers are cannily, but commendably intertwined with footage on the havoc of the last war, its concentration camps, the A-Bomb results and the misery in its wake plus bald titled figures of its losses. It all works, due to the fine choice of footage, the taut visual blending, purely filmic metaphors and a pointed irony that is never condescending or forced.

Rogosin takes his time making a pic and he spent years tracking down the archives material he wanted. If some may have been seen by buffs, they take on a new strength meaning and weight in Rogosin's deft b a l a n c e that eschews patronizing or hindsight sagacity. The effect is stark and f o r c e f u l, but never grim or knuckle-rapping.

No commentary is used or needed with the party talk, or the old soldiers reminiscing of more romantic wars as counterpoint to the imagery of the wreckage, human anguish and waste in the last war plus its demoralizing of human values in the wake of Nazism and the terrible effects of the A-bomb.

At the party, some wined-up types discourse on various pseudo-intellectual things that segue into the potent and powerful footage that Rogosin collected from archives all over the world. A shot of female hair piled up in a warehouse at some concentration camp cuts to a girl's hair while dancing at the party that sums up the theme, and is never precious, banal or forced due to the fine balance, pace and rhythm of the film.

It appears slated mainly for specialized and art use but also has fine school, special showing and tv potential. Rogosin again shows he has a documentary flair that can be used for tellingly underlining a theme that is gripping and moving in its new filmic form. Excellent quality of the montage footage blends well with the new scenes of the party and the old soldiers' home.

This is an offbeat pic that tackles a much done theme with originality and new insights and should fare well, accordingly, if well placed, labeled and handled in selected houses. *Mosk.*

Kapurush
(The Coward)
(INDIAN)

Venice, Aug. 26.
R. D. Dansal production and release. With Soumitra Chatteriee, Madhabi Mukherjee, Premendra Mitra. Written and directed by Satyajit Ray. Based on story by Premendra Mitra. Camera, Soumenndu Roy. Music, Satyajit Ray. At Venice Film Festival. Running Time, **70 MINS.**

Karuna .... Soumitra Chatterjee
Amitabha Koy ...... Madhabi Mukherjee
Bimal Gupta .... Premendra Mitra

A fragile, sensitively-told triangle tale in the European manner by India's best-known filmmaker, Satyajit Ray, "The Coward" will probably disappoint all but the most rabid Ray fans used to deeper, more universal fare delivered by the director in his previous efforts. It may do for some special situations, but the outlook is tepid at best.

Simply constructed triangle finds two onetime lovers reunited by chance. She's now married to another man and apparently resigned to her present life. He's grown up since the time when he lacked the courage to marry her himself and face life head on. Now, behind her husband's back he tries belatedly to win her once again, but after coming close to success, loses her and once again remains alone.

Action is paced slowly by Ray as he lets his three principals interplay and the story develop by flashbacks in a leisurely manner.

With the exception of a few slightly overplayed sequences, most of the thesp work is muted in keeping with the story.

Principals deliver straightforward performances, and straightforward is also the word for the pic in general, devoid of directorial frills and business but also, with few exceptions, of some of the poignant and significant statements on human conditions with which Ray has left his mark in film history books. Technical credits are okay. *Hawk.*

Lasky Jedne Plavovlasky
(The Loves of a Blonde)
(CZECH)
Venice, Aug. 27.

Ceskoslovensky Filmexport release of Sebor-Barrandov Film Studio Production. Features Hana Brejchova, Vladimir Pucholt, Vladimir Mensik, others. Directed by Milos Forman. Screenplay, Forman, Jaroslav Papousek, Ivan Passer. Camera, Miroslav Ondricek. At Venice Festival. Running Time, **85 MINS.**
Andula .... Hana Brejchova
Milda ...., Vladimir Pucholt
Vacovsky .... Vladimir Mensik

This is a lightweight item with plenty of charm to overcome the basic fragility of its plot. Surprisingly for an Eastern block film, it has an exploitable nude scene, but its principle sales points remain some engaging acting, some keenly observed sequences, several humorous bits, and a general tongue-in-cheek air which should help make it, in its territories, a saleable entry.

Boy meets girl at a dance organized for factory workers. Couple falls in love and eventually goes to bed where the usual promises are exchanged. The day after, each returns to work, but the gal believes the boy and tracks him down at his surprised parent's home where, after hearing the boy dismiss her importance to his folks, the truth dawns on her and she returns to the factory with one more lesson in life learned the hard way.

Hana Brejchova and Vladimir Pucholt make a charming couple, with the boy especially good in his role. Standout however is thesping by an unbilled trio impersonating soldiers on leave who shyly try to contact some girls at a dance. Through the handicaps of subtitles, one would guess that the film's dialog is another major plus, as well as being frank and perhaps controversial.

Forman's direction shows promise, and his handling of nude scene between boy and girl is tasteful as well as humorous. Humorous observations on the human scene appear to be his forte. Technical credits are good. Pic is an official Czech entry.
Hawk.

A Falecida
(The Death)
(BRAZILIAN)

Venice, Aug. 26.
Production Cin. Meta Litda release and production. With Fernanda Montenegro, Ivan Candido, Wanda Lacerda. Directed by Leon Hirszman. Screenplay, Eduardo Coutinho, Hirszman; camera, Jose Madeiors; editor, Nello Melli. At Venice Film Fest. Running Time, **98 MINS.**

Zulmira .... Fernanda Montenegro
Husband .... Ivan Candido
Mother .... Wanda Lacerda

This anecdotal film has a neat structure and sudden twists that keep it from falling into the precious and overstrained. However its allusions and mixture of humor, social, delineation and irony make this a chancey art item.

Plot concerns a thirtyish woman who lives with her mother and her chronically unemployed husband who is mainly interested in soccer. She seems to have mystical overtones and decides she is dying and wants a marvellous funeral that will make stuck-up neighbors take note. She has checked and arranged the price of a big exit to the grave.

But the doctor finds nothing wrong and she slowly gets a cold, cavorts in the rain and actually dies. She asks her husband, before dying, to see a man who will help with the funeral. Passing himself off as a cousin, the husband hears that she had had an affair with this man.

He then demands the money for the funeral and gives her a very cheap one, stays away, and turns up at a soccer match yelling he has money to bet and then breaks down and sobs in the crowd as he loses the money.

Pic neatly avoids morbidity by cannily showing the woman discussing her impending d e a t h matter-of-factly and resigning herself to it as a great event. If some raps at Brazilian superstition and social backwardness are there, it is still mainly a smartly turned out film fable that is expertly played, especially by Fernanda Montenegro who exhibits both sly passion and strange fixations to make her figure a tricky bundle of female wiles, guilessness and simplicity mixed with the unpredictable.

Leom Hirszman displays a firm grip on this offbeat tale and avoids eeriness, cheapness or theatricality to denote promise when he sheds the more exotic for more straightforward subjects. It is technically good and is an offbeater with difficult chances, due to the ambivalence of its theme. But it's worth special handling and personal placement for possible returns via buff audiences. Pic is non-competing here.*Mosk.*

Below The Hill

Made via subscription by a New England Community Theatre group, this look at unemployment and personal problems is fairly adequate technically and with an underlying sincerity that could make this dualer or specialized fare.

Venice, Aug. 26.
L. T. Film Corp. release and production. With Ray Bernier, Lita Anderson, Roger Sorel, Suzanne Mannion. Directed and written by Angus Bailey. Camera, Eric Kollmar; editor, Nancy Lee. At Venice Film Fest. Running Time, **105 MINS.**
Alfred .... Ray Bernier
Marlene .... Lita Anderson
Ernie .... Roger Sorel
Claire .... Suzanne Mannion

This American independent film

was made under the auspices of Fall River, Mass., with the town as well as private subscription coming to $60,000. Looking at some economically impoverished conditions, via four people, it has an old fashioned and stereotyped ring if also a note of belief in its subject.

It is at times reminiscent of the Hollywood depression pix, except for a few modern, but without the depth, character portrayals, and transcending of the time to make it a general as well as a particular statement. It appears headed for dualer use in the regular film markets since it is adequately made, if it suffers from some amateurism in acting and conception.

The pic also has the forthright ring of sincerity, if not completely brought to fruition by its talents. It is an attempt to give a realistic portrayal of a school drop-out who can not quite understand his plight and confusedly rebels to end up in prison.

Hero, Ray Bernier, is from a Canadian-French immigrant family working since age 16 to support his family. Married and with a child he loses his job when one of the two local knitting mills closes down. He tries to live normally, but the slow sapping of his self respect change him into a drinking almost brutish type.

One day he slaps his wife out of sheer despair and frustration and she leaves him. He takes a friend's car innocently to visit a place where he was happy as a child, but the theft is turned in and he ends up in jail.

Around this plot are on-the-spot scenes that help give it an okay realistic envelope and acceptable if sometimes gauche characterizations. But the pic does not quite penetrate to the heart of the characters and leaves them mainly one-dimensional. However, Ray Bernier manages to express a decency buried in an almost inarticulate man.

Angus Bailey has directed with solidity if his script and handling rarely ever take a truly ironic compassionate or deeper tone. But its plotting, acting and plausibility are just too pat and flat to adequately achieve its purpose.

It was presented here by producer Leo Strickman who took part of his vacation from his regular job to attend. Pic was accepted sympathetically here, in a showings in the commercial section. *Mosk.*

Billie
(WIDESCREEN—COLOR)

Enjoyable but mild domestic comedy based on "Time Out for Ginger" legiter. Commercial success in youth situations hinges on Patty Duke's theatrical b.o. power.

Hollywood, Sept. 2.
United Artists release of Chrislaw-Patty Duke production, executive producer, Peter Lawford, Milton Ebbins in charge of production, produced and directed by Don Weis. Stars Patty Duke; features Jim Backus, Jane Greer, Warren Berlinger, Billy De Wolfe, Dick Sargent. Screenplay, Ronald Alexander, based on his play, "Time Out For Ginger," presented on stage by Shepard Traube; camera (Techniscope, Technicolor), John Russell; editor, Adrienne Fazan; music, Dominic Frontiere; art direction, Arthur Lonergan; sound, Harry Lindgren; asst. director, Dick Moder. Reviewed at Carthay Circle Theatre, L.A., Aug. 19, '65. Running Time, **86 MINS.**
Billie Carol	Patty Duke
Howard G. Carol	Jim Backus
Agnes Carol	Jane Greer
Mike Benson	Warren Berlinger
Mayor Davis	Billy De Wolfe
Coach Jones	Charles Lane
Matt Bullitt	Dick Sargent
Jean Carol	Susan Seaforth
Bob Matthews	Ted Bessell
Principal Wilson	Richard Deacon
Eddie Davis	Bobby Diamond
Ray Case	Michael Fox
Ted Chekas	Clive Clerk
Dr. Hall	Harlan Warde
Nurse Webb	Jean Macrae
Allan Grant	Himself
Mrs. Hosenwacker	Georgia Simmons
Mrs. Clifton	Arline Anderson
Miss Channing	Layte Bowden
Reporter	Mathew M. Jordan
Mrs. Harper	Shirley J. Shawn
Adele Colin	Maria Lennard
Mary Jensen	Breena Howard
Starter	Craig W. Chudy

Patty Duke returns to theatrical films as "Billie," the tomboy who complicates her family life before shedding athletic gear for maiden attire. Supporting players bolster domestic comedy which is on the mild side and reminiscent of pix from the innocent '30s. Editing and direction are good, enhancing thin production values. Biggest selling factor is Miss Duke, a home viewer fave. Okay prospects for United Artists release in youth situations.

Ronald Alexander adapted his "Time Out for Ginger" legiter of the early '50s, cutting some characters to focus on Miss Duke, the younger daughter of understanding Jane Greer and bumbling Jim Backus who shines in field meets via a mental gimmick. Coach Charles Lane uses her to goad his less proficient males, including Warren Berlinger to whom the gal eventually reveals her secret and gives her heart.

Complications, pat and unreal, include a mayoralty battle between Backus and Billy De Wolfe, wasted herein as a heavy who exploits pop's platform in terms of barbs at Billie and older sister Susan Seaforth, who is secretly married to, and pregnant by, Ted Bessell. Latter pair stand out, as does Berlinger. (Incidentally, DeWolfe and Berlinger were leads of London company of "How To Succeed.")

Backus is good in his now-standard characterization, while Miss Greed is radiant and charming in her return to pix. Miss Duke has an infectious personality which comes across. In okay solo warbling of two tunes she projects the frustrations of a young gal.

Don Weis, bowing as combo producer-director, obtained generally good performances from a large cast, keeping the predictable plot going via some good setups of John Russell's Techniscope - Technicolor camera. Adrienne Fazan's tight editing to 86 minutes is a big asset.

Scorer Dominic Frontiere injected a modern sound for the teen crowd, which Harry Lindgren recorded at a rather high level at times. Other technical credits are okay. *Murf.*

Hysteria
(BRITISH)

Hollywood, Sept. 3.
Metro release of Hammer Film Production. Features Robert Webber, Anthony Newlands, Jennifer Jayne, Maurice Denham, Lelia Goldoni, Peter Woodthorpe, Sandra Boize, Sue Lloyd. Produced and written by Jimmy Sangster. Directed by Freddie Francis. Camera, John Wilcox; editor, James Needs; music, Don Banks; sound, Cyril Swern; assistant director, Basil Rayburn. Reviewed at Metro Studios Sept. 1, '65. Running Time, **85 MINS.**
"Mr. Smith"	Robert Webber
Doctor Keller	Anthony Newlands
Gina	Jennifer Jayne
Hemmings	Maurice Denham
Denise	Lelia Goldoni
Marcus Allan	Peter Woodthorpe
English Girl	Sandra Boize
French Girl	Sue Lloyd

Although its cast list will not be of much marquee value, "Hysteria" is a well-made little shocker that should please audiences who catch it at the bottom of a double bill. Script contains many cliches of the genre, but production values are solid and Freddie Francis' direction is brisk and intelligent in this Hammer Film feature shot in Great Britain.

Lead role, of still another amnesia victim, is filled by Yank Robert Webber, whose face and name are fairly well-known, ("Sandpiper") via legit, tv and major studio assignments, before emigrating to England. He has rugged looks and build, along with acting ability that could take him somewhere eventually. He is well-cast as a roving American with his memory blotted out by an auto crash who leaves the hospital to move into the middle of sinister events.

Most important femme role is played by Italian thesp Lelia Goldoni, who is alternately lovable and sinister. More important billing goes to good girl, Jennifer Jayne, but she has little to do besides providing sympathy and getting knocked out once. Anthony Newlands is properly enigmatic as the psychiatrist treating Webber and Maurice Denham does well in a character part as a scruffy private eye who may or may not be helping the good guy.

Producer Jimmy Sangster must be charged with script cliches, since he also is credited as writer, which include mysterious voices that haunt the amnesia victim and a shower murder scene obviously inspired by "Psycho." But director Francis holds sinister glances and other cliches to minimum. John Wilcox' photography is effective but not obtrusive, and Don Banks' score blends effectively with action. Titles, credited to Chambers & Partners, are unusual but possibly not appealing to all, with their concentric circle motif. *Hogg.*

The Shepherd Girl
(CHINESE—COLOR)

Frank Lee International Films release of Shaw Bros. production. Produced by Run Run Shaw. Stars Julie Yeh Feng, Swan Shan; features Chu Mu, Chiang Kuang-Chao, Yang Chi-ching, Li Ting, Ouyang Sha-fei, Lin Feng. Directed by Lo Chen. Screenplay, Lo Chen; camera (Eastmancolor-Shawscope), Liu Chi; editor, Chiang Hsing-lung; sound, Wang Yung-hua; Songs — music, Wang Fu-ling, lyrics, Li Lo-young. Reviewed at 55th Street Playhouse, New York, Sept. 1, '65. Running Time: 1°5 MINS.

(English Subtitles)

Most of the Chinese films shown at the 55th Street Playhouse since its present cycle began several months ago have been in the costume-heavy action-war genre, easy to understand and accept, with only occasionally a switch to something lighter. "The Shepherd Girl" makes as complete a change as could be expected falling between operetta and filmusical.

Although production notes on film say that locations (islands near Hong Kong) represent present-day communities in Taiwan, to western eyes they look much the same as in any other Oriental costume film. What is evidently the main appeal of the film to Chinese audiences, however, is the biggest drawback to selling it to American viewers. Almost every word of dialog in the film is sung (in much the same manner as ''''''''''''''''''s "Umbrellas of '''''''''''''''''' ''') in the combination of Chinese music (which quickly grows monotonous to western ears) and the female voices, trained to sing everything at a high, nasal, sing-song pitch, loses any novelty appeal in a matter of minutes and becomes irritating long before the lengthy film ends. Strangely, the male voices are pleasant and although they eventually give the impression of singing different words to the same tune each time they give voice, they're not too hard to take.

Story is simple and easy to follow, even without the subtitles (which sometime begin and end offscreen, due to the projection).

A young shepherdess, beautiful but independent, falls in love with a visiting young boatman. Her father, however, a chronic loser at gambling, is heavily in debt to the town shopowner. When a rough and tough hunter sees the girl, he approaches the shopowner to act as matchmaker, paying him in advance. The girl is told she must marry the hunter unless her father can pay his debts. The boatman undertakes a dangerous voyage to earn the money, but fails to return. When the girl believes him lost at sea, she reluctantly goes through with the wedding but the hero returns just as the ceremony ends, fights the hunter for her, and wins.

Principle asset to the film is the firstrate Eastmancolor camerawork by Liu Chi, at its best when roving over the scenic sea and hills. Julie Yeh Feng, really a beauty, is excellent as the shepherdess (although her singing voice is ear-piercing). Her role calls for a wide range of emotions, all of which she handles well. Kwan Shan as the young boatman is also standout but Lin Feng's villainous shopowner is overacted, even for a musical. *Robe.*

Venice Films

Mickey One

Offbeat and occasionally obscure study in regeneration,
highlighted by dominating
stellar performance by Warren Beatty. Needs careful
nursing.

Venice, Sept. 2.
Columbia release of Florin-Tatira (Ar-
thur Penn) production. Stars Warren
Beatty; features Hurd Hatfield, Alexandra
Stewart, Teddy Hart, Jeff Corey, Kamatari
Fujiwara, Franchot Tone. Directed by
Penn; screenplay, Alan M. Surgal; cam-
era, Ghislain Cloquet; editor, Aram Ava-
kian; settings, George Jenkins; music,
Jack Shaindlin. At Venice Film Festival,
Sept. 1, '65. Running Time, 90 MINS.
Mickey One .... Warren Beatty
Castle .... Hurd Hatfield
Jenny .... Alexandra Stewart
Berson .... Teddy Hart
Fryer .... Jeff Corey
The Artist .... Kamatari Fujiwara
Ruby .... Franchot Tone

Invited to the Venice film festival as the sole representative of
the American motion picture industry, "Mickey One" is a strange
and sometimes confused offbeat
yarn which is going to need careful nursing if it is to make any
real impact at the .wickets. The
Arthur Penn production is dominated by a compelling, yet sometimes irritating, performance by
Warren Beatty which will certainly
attract attention and could help
stimulate boxoffice results.

"Mickey One" could be de-
scribed as a study in regeneration,
but Alan M. Surgal's screenplay
is overloaded with symbolic gestures which will inevitably puzzle
many audiences and which obscure
the main objectives of the plot.
But the main handicap of the story
is that the central character is
thoroughly unlikable, with few, if
any, redeeming features. He's bad-
tempered, violent and frequently
irrational, thus making it unusually difficult to obtain a sympathetic audience reaction.

Title character is a one-time top
nitery comic who has been leading
an extravagant life, getting mixed
up with dames and gamblers. In
a bid to get away from his past
and start afresh, he destroys all
his personal documents and assumes the identity of a Pole whose
name is conveniently abbreviated
to Mickey One. He sleeps rough,
takes a job as the garbage man
in a cafeteria, but gradually drifts
back to the world of night clubs,
and in a sleazy West Chicago joint
rediscovers the art of wowing an
audience.

To this point, the plot develops
reasonably smoothly and the few
touches of symbolism are not entirely unacceptable. Thereafter,
however, symbolism runs riot, occasionally to the point of pretentiousness, as Mickey One resists the
help of his agent and the en-
couragment of a sympathetic and
understanding girlfriend to return
to the big time. It is in the second
half, as the comedian finds he cannot lick his past, that the plot becomes obscure and confusing. The
climactic sequence, in which the
regeneration is apparently effected, is a masterpiece of vague
and almost incomprehensible symbolism.

Arthur Penn, as producer and
director, has concentrated his efforts on making Mickey One a compelling personality, yet he must
accept his share of responsibilty
for the confused style and bewildering nature of the more obscure sequences. But, in his main
intention he is powerfully backed
by Warren Beatty, who gives a
commanding, though highly mannered, performance; a consistently
dominating study of a man who
lives in fear of his past, but one
unlikely to evoke much audience
response.

In the only femme role of any
significance and, incidentally, in
her first Hollywood pic, Alexandra
Stewart makes a subtle impression
as the girl who shares her digs
with Mickey One, and asserts her
influence to help him back on to
the road of sanity and normality.
Hurd Hatfield gives reliable support as a night club operator who,
somewhat inconsistently, is determined to get Mickey One to
play his spot despite the comedian's irresponsible and unreasonable resistance. Teddy Hart shows
up well as a sympathetic agent,
Franchot Tone has a neat bit as
a bigtime gambler, and Jeff Corey
and Kamatari Fujiwara complete
the acceptble featured cast.

Production qualities are mainly
up to par, with smooth lensing by
Ghislain Cloquet and a forceful
score by Jack Shaindlin. *Myro.*

Akahige
(Red Beard)
(JAPANESE)

Venice, Sept. 1.
Toho production and release. Features
Toshiro Mifune, Yuzo Kayama, Yoshio
Tsushiya. Directed by Akira Kurosawa.
Story, Shugoro Yamamoto, camera, To-
moichi Nagai, music, Masaru Sato. At
Venice Festival. Running Time, 188 MINS.
Red Beard .... Toshiro Mifune
His assistant .... Yuzo Kayama

Take a season of "Doctor Kildare" tv skeins, throw in a half
dozen classic Hollywood hospital
perennials, but do them all up with
great taste and visual, cinematic
flair, and you have the latest Akira
Kurosawa pic, "Red Beard." It's
hokum lifted to the highest deno-
minator, the banal made into near-
art by great skill and craftsmanship by the Japanese master.

On a commercial judgment, the
over three-hour running time is an
undeniable but adjustable defect:
much of the film's initial footage
could be elegantly elided for major
effect. Here and there, too, a superfluous s e q u e n c e could be
trimmed to heighten the impact of
the many good ones which remain.

It's for specialized outlets, but
the aficionados could come running
if the print is properly reshaped.

The main plot is the old chestnut
about the enterprising young doctor
and the misunderstood old curmudgeon, in this case "Red Beard"
—Toshiro Mifune. Slowly, as Kurosawa interweaves several plots,
understanding for his methods
grows as human relations triumph
over sheer medical knowhow. Pic
in its various plot aspects also
marks a change from the Japanese
penchant for violence by highlighting love, warmth, and affection as
more important point-winners and
cure-alls.

Here and there, as noted, the plot

drifts into over-familiar waters, but
elsewhere it soars to stylistic and
heartwarming heights which show
that this is not just the routine
ward drama, but has higher scope
and targets. Kurosawa has blended
handkerchief elements with drama,
shock (there's a harrowing no-
anesthetic operation scene), humor
and lively action (a knock-down,
drag-out fight) for a neat parlay
which however needs plenty of
reshaping for workable audience
acceptance.

Thesping is uniformly good, with
Toshiro Mifune and Yuzo Kayama
standout in the two leads, but many
other uncredited players due for
encomiums. Lensing, music, and
other technical chores also deserve
a loud hand. *Hawk.*

Fedelta'
(Faithfulness)
(RUSSIAN)

Venice, Aug. 29.
Sovexportfilm release of Odessa Film
Studios production. With V. Cetverikov,
G. Polskih, A. Potapov. Written and di-
rected by P. Todorovski. Camera, V.
Kostromenko, L. Burlaka, V. Avloscenko;
music, B. Karamiscev. At Venice Film
Festival. Running Time, 87 MINS.

First feature effort by a young
director, Pietr Todorovski, the
pic officially repped the U.S.S.R.
at Venice. Film shows promise for
the director, but otherwise seems
a very dubious international entry,
which once again deals with the
last days of an army recruit before he sets off for the front lines.

Carefree barracks life, flirting
with a girl or two, and other
frivolous bits are played against
the still-distant but nevertheless
ominous sounds of approaching
war, which occasionally sober his
youthful buoyancy. Pic abounds
in cliche situations and sequences,
some of them brightly handled,
others easily predictable and patly
done. Long segments, notably a
semi-documentary showing a recruit moving up to front lines, are
merely descriptive. Occasionally,
they achieve a sort of minor poetic
quality, but more often than not,
the effect is spoiled by over-cute-
ness or banality.

Acting is in keeping with the
youthfully optimistic outlook of
the pic, and all the principals step
through their paces in lively
fashion. Camerawork is very slick,
Hawk.

Pierrot Le Fou
(Crazy Pete)
(FRENCH-COLOR-SCOPE)

Venice, Aug. 28.
SNC release of Rome-Paris Films-
Georges De Beauregard production. Stars
Jean-Paul Belmondo, Anna Karina; fea-
tures, Dirk Sanders, Raymond Devos,
Graziella Galvani. Written and directed
by Jean-Luc Godard. Camera (Eastman-
color), Raoul Coutard; editor, Francoise
Colin. At Venice Film Fest. Running
Time, 110 MINS.
Ferdinand .... Jean-Paul Belmondo
Marianne .... Anna Karina
Brother .... Dirk Sanders
Port Man .... Raymond Devos
Wife .... Graziella Galvani

Jean-Luc Godard has developed
a definite film style. There are the
insider jokes, the use of objects
to comment on a situation and a
mingling of the serious and comic.
He uses all of these devices here
but they do not completely work

out and the result is repetitive
and precious rather than inventive
and fresh. Pruning would help.

Cut down, this film might have
some chances abroad, although this
one appears too indulgent and uneven. Godard's first pic "Breathless" caused a stir in the U.S. and
his "A Married Woman" also
caught on while the others have
been more for buffs than regular
audiences. This one appears to be
a cross between the two.

A bored young man married to
a rich woman one night goes off
with the baby sitter after a boring
party. The party is typical Godard
with the emphasis on people living mainly on advertising influences and mixing pop art with
comments on the rising automation of life.

If he seeks a smple life with
the girl, he is soon immersed in
problems as a dead man is found
in her flat and they are soon on
the run. A car they escape in has
money hidden in it, but they lose
it during an accident. After an
idyllic time at the seashore they
get bored and hit the road and live
by stealing only to run into friends
of hers.

Two gangs, repping Arab gun-
runners and perhaps Israeli forces,
fight it out and he gets embroiled.
A cache of money is taken by the
girl who runs off with it and
her socalled brother. The hero
catches up, kills them, and then
wraps dynamite around his head
and lights the fuse. Trying to
change his mind it goes off.

There is a brilliant use of color
in spots to mark the mood. There
are also some seemingly spontaneous scenes of the two living
off the land that are topflight
Godard. But there is too much
padding, and interspersed songs
and fabricated scenes make up a
compendium of all his stylistic
tricks rather than a more coherent
off-beater.

Jean-Paul Belmondo has the
usual rugged verve as the bored,
but dynamic, young man who finally finds death inadvertently.
Anna Karina is delightful as an
unpredictable, beguiling but finally deadly female.

Godard does not yet seem ready
to kowtow to general taste and
goes his sprightly inventive way
mixing asides, story, atmosphere
and inventive insights. When they
jell they make firstrate films. Here
there is just too much self indulgence. But canny cutting could
put this pic into a more coherent,
rhythmic shape for chances abroad
with the Godard and Belmondo
names pluses for art and specialized situations. Playoff would be
more chancey. It is technically
fine. *Mosk.*

Mne Dvatsat Let
(I'm Twenty)
(RUSSIAN)

Venice, Sept. 1.
Sovexportfilm release of Gorkhi Studio
production. Features V. Popov, N. Gu-
benko, S. Ljunshin, M. Verzinskaia. Di-
rected by Marlen Kuzev. Camera, M.
Pilikina; music, N. Sidelnikov. At Venice
Film Festival. Running Time, 180 MINS.
Serghei .... V. Popov
Anja .... M. Verzinskaia

Nearly three hours is an un-
wieldly length for a film on youthful self-realization. But this one
has the mixture of characteriza-

tion, visual movement and a sense of place and time that makes it constantly revealing and eschews propaganda or undue unbeat sentiments. Cutting might well lose its fine proportions. This Russo pic appears likely for specialized spots, but could be worthwhile because of its frank look at Russian youth and the city of Moscow.

Three young men of 20 find it's time to face up to life. One marries, one tarries with a girl while a problem of her divorce holds things up, and one cannot quite adapt to the self satisfaction of his elders. All this is told against the changing of the seasons, the bustle of the city, and a series of well-coordinated incidents unravelling in the foreground.

Director Marlen Kuzev has control at all times and handles his young thesps expertly. One boy has a dream in which he sees his father killed at 21 during the last war. He asks how one is to live with disillusionment and the father notes that his son, 23, is older than he is. It ends with the familiar note that each generation must find its own solutions, but it is forthright, probing and visually paced to give it a feeling of reality. There is an ending indicating that Lenin's principles are the way which may be a censor sop. But it still denotes that not all are content and that Russian youth, like anywhere else, doubts, asks questions and has the hazardous task of personal, sensual and moral adaptation.

The old revolutionary song, "The International." is played wryly throughout. There are also poetry readings that reflect some problems and it generally delves into ordinary life in Moscow and thus Russia today. That is one of the highpoints of the film plus its fine blending of story, atmosphere and mood.

It is technically good and brimming over with life, incident and character. It is sometimes reminiscent of the 1920 and 1930 American pix. *Hawk.*

E Venne Un Uomo
(And a Man Came . . .)
(ITALIAN—COLOR)

Venice, Sept. 1.
Paramount release of a SOL Produzioni (Vincenzo Labella)—Harry Saltzman co-production. With Rod Steiger, Adolfo Celi, Rita Bertocchi, Pietro Gelmi, Antonio Bertocchi, Fabrizio Rossi, Alberto Rossi, Giovanni Rossi, Alfonso Orlando, Antonio Ruttigni, Giorgio Fortunato, Ottone Candiani. Directed by Ermanno Olmi. Screenplay and story, Olmi and Vincenzo Labella. Camera (Eastmancolor), Pietro Portalupi. Editor, Carla Colombo. Music, Franco Potenza. At Film Festival, Venice. Running Time, 90 MINS.
Mediator .... Rod Steiger
Monsignor Radini-Tedeschi Adolfo Celi
Mother of Angelo Roncalli Rita Bertocchi
Father .... Pietro Gelmi
Uncle Zaverio .... Antonio Bertocchi
Angelo at 4 .... Fabrizio Rossi
Angelo at 7 .... Alberto Rossi
Angelo at 10 .... Giovanni Rossi
Don Francesco .... Alfonso Orlando
Don Pietro .... Antonio Ruttigni
Secretary to Nuncio Roncalli
Giorgio Fortunato
Sinning priest in Venice Ottone Candiani

Two elements weigh heavily in favor of this novel if schematic filmization of the life of Pope John XXIII. There is great humility and taste with which this tribute to the late Pontiff's

memoirs was conceived and executed. Surely and perforce, it's a special entry for most marts.

Its principle targets are Catholic audiences around the world, with indefinite playoff potentialities offered by the religioso market. But also, the approach and subject matter offer the pic a chance at other audiences the world over, though a potent sales effort must be expended for full effect.

Of two possibilities offered him in depicting the life and thoughts of Pope John, director Ermanno Olmi has chosen to avoid the olio illustration mirroring the real thing (with physical approximation), by instead introducing the role of a "mediator"—Rod Steiger —to convey the Pope's thoughts, though not his actual physical presence, in the course of the story. Main differences of opinion on pic will lie in this choice, and for many, its success or failure will rest on this decision. On present evidence, it must be assessed an interesting, almost formidably difficult experience, which almost comes off.

Surely, the pic is at its most effective when Olmi is portraying young Roncalli's youth in his home village near Bergamo, with its earthy, basic upbringing a key to the future Pope's down-to-earth appeal and homespun, straight-to-the-heart charm and attraction beyond the borders of his faith.

Idea of depicting the grown-up Roncalli via a "mediator," a normally-garbed person to mouth his thoughts and words and go through the paces of his pre-Pontifical life, was naturally a gimmick to avoid the potential dangers in impersonating a figure so universally loved and respected, so soon after his death. On film, despite a valid, sometimes trenchant effort by Rod Steiger, the attempt comes through too mechanically at times, and one wonders, with dangerous hindsight, if a "straight" portrayal might not have been better.

Be this as it may from commercial standpoints, certainly Olmi is coherent in following through his approach, which touches on the late Pope's thoughts and actions with utter humility, taste, and underplaying.

Value of the pic therefore lies in its semi-documentary illustration of the thoughts and pronunciamentos of Pope John in his long and much-traveled pre-Pontifical career and, most importantly, in the lasting value and far-sightedness of these writings given widest projection via the cinema medium. It remains the picture story of a great man in his life and writings, brought vividly to life by acting by Rod Steiger, Adolfo Celi (as Monsignor Radini-Tedeschi), and a group of infant and grown-up onetime neighbors of Pope John in his native village of Sotto il Monte, with healthy assists from Pietro Portalupi's seizing color lensing job and other technical credits to match.

Multi-lingual versions are naturally planned, with Rod Steiger himself taking over the English-language chores of narration and dubbing, so fitly handled in the present Italo print by Romolo Valli. *Hawk.*

Double-Barrelled Detective Story
(SCANOSCOPE)
Yank oater indie spoof with the entertaining balance of parody and invention for playoff use.

Venice, Sept. 7.
Saloon Prod.-David Stone release and production. With Greta Thyssen. Hurd Hatfield, Jeff Siggra, Jerome Raphel. Written, directed and edited by Adolfas Mekas from a story by Mark Twain. Camera, Graeme Ferguson; music, M. Kupferman. At Venice Film Fest. Running Time, 90 MINS.
Archy .... Jeff Siggra
La Belle .... Greta Thyssen
Father .... Hurd Hatfield
Sherlock Holmes ...... Jerome Raphel

Adolfas Mekas, who did the far out Gotham-made comedy "Hallelujah the Hills," now comes up with an inventive film fantasy based on a Mark Twain tale with an oater background. The humor is muted, but amusing throughout, and the pic has the earmarks for playoff in the U.S. and abroad with specialized slotting.

The first half has the deceptively rustic humor of Mark Twain as a dastardly Northerner marries the daughter of a mellow Southern plantation owner. The man mistreats the girl to get revenge on the father. He even ties her to a tree with bloodhounds ripping off her clothes.

All this is done with the right use of mellow silent film techniques of obvious emoting, with the balance of mock seriousness, lampoon and sentiment sans slush. The old man is killed and the northerner runs off as a child is born who has the ability to sniff things out like a bloodhound.

A nice aside to Tom Sawyer is used during the boy's childhood and then, as a man, he's sent off to track down, torture and kill his vicious father. Pic then switches to the old west with wild shooting, quite harmless here, barroom shenanigans, the sexy but good-hearted femme saloonkeeper, all done up as an oater spoof.

Into this comes Sherlock Holmes on a trip and Twain's good natured chauvinism is brightly translated to the screen. Holmes saved from a mob and the boy's father is unmasked as the victim of his mistreated errand boy. There is the traditional happy ending.

This is a pleasant pic with an inventive first part. The sagebrush stuff is clever, but not up to its preceding invention and rustic but clever wit. Mekas again shows he has a way with parody and he gets disarmingly innocent performances from Jeff Siggra as the boy, Greta Thyssen as the sexy saloonkeeper, Jerome Raphel as a stuffy Holmes and Hurd Hatfield as the evil father. Mekas soft-pedals his visual tricks to have them pay off when used.

It is technically up to par with excellent, spirited music and some winning songs of the times. *Mosk.*

Viento Negro
(Black Wind)
(MEXICAN)

Venice, Sept. 1.
Producciones Yanco release and production. With Jose Elias Moreno, Devid Reynoso, Jorge Martinez De Hoyos. Directed by Servano Gonzales. Screenplay, Mario Martini; camera, Agustin Jiminez; music, Gustavo Carreon. At Venice Film Fest. Running Time, 130 MINS.
Manuel .... Jose Elias Moreno
George .... Devid Reynoso
Lorenzo .... Jorge Martinez De Hoyos

This film follows the much-blazed Hollywood trail of the '30s and '40s of rugged men at work. It emerges a stereotyped if solid adventure opus that has language market chances abroad. and even some dualer opportunity if pruned down from its excssive length for this most familiar tale.

A railroad is being built across a desert that is both freezing and melting and is prone to sudden storms called the black wind. A martinet work boss hides a soft heart under a brutal exterior and even makes it tough for his son till he proves himself.

There is the bosom buddy who is loud, sentimental and the only one to tell the rough hero his truths. Campfollowers give it a chance for some extra fights and some well-done sex bits that are not exploited. There is also the train wreck, an Indian who turns out better than most, the son's manhood, etc.

The acting is as one-dimensional as the story and direction. but it is done sans excesses and is a slick routine item.

The pic is technically good with on-the-spot desert lensing also a help. *Mosk.*

Salto
(The Dance)
(POLISH)

Venice, Aug. 27.
Polski State Film release of Kadr production. With Zbigniew Cybulski, Marta Lipinska, Jerzy Blok, Gustave Houlebek. Written and directed by Tadeusz Konwicki. Camera, Kurt Weber; music, Wojniech Kilar. At Venice Film Fest. Running Time, 100 MINS.
Kowalski .... Zbigniew Cybulski
Hela .... Marta Lipinska
Mayor .... Jerzy Blok
Father .... Gustave Houlebek

Tadeusz Konwicki is primarily a writer who is allowed to make a film when he wants to and has a script. This is his third and again uses a theme of the scars of the last war, physically as well as mentally and spiritually. But the picture also drags and remains more literary in its characterizations and progression than filmic. It is mainly an arty item at best.

A man hops off a train and comes to a small town where he claims he has been before. Another man takes him in and he proceeds to mark and change or bring out the covered inner feelings and beliefs of the inhabitants. A man who had hidden all during the war because he looked Jewish, even if he was not, takes on the mantle of a famed dead Jewish actor he resembles. Others also change only to stone him out of town when his wife turns up to claim him and point out he is always running off. He escapes at the end bent for another town.

All this is done in a fairly theatrical fashion as the personages overplay or try to fit the stereotypes who then can change. The town disappearing soon to industrialization is also hinted at ano there is a trio of femme nude bathers, hunting for buried treasures, exploding bits from the last war and oldtime scars still festering.

The title comes from a dance the intruder has the town folk do before he is unmasked. Zbigniew Cybulski plays this in a moody, proud, servile series of shifting moods that keeps him interesting if not clear. This mixture of appearances, illusion and imitations of truth appear pretentious rather than revealing due to a lack of fluid progression and insight and a tendency to be more precious than concise.

Konwicki's other pix were more clear and successful than his latest more ambitious, but less taking venture. There may also be a look at a regime that does not allow individuality and freedom of movement lurking in the film, but this is unclear as the other allusions.

Chalk this up as an offbeater with more buff than ordinary audience interest if it may say more to Polish audiences than to western patrons. *Mosk.*

Teni Zabytykh Predkov
(In the Shadow of the Past)
(RUSSIAN-COLOR)
Venice, Aug. 27.
Sovexport release of Alexandre Dovzhenko Studio production. With Ivan Nikolajciuk, Harisa Kadocnikova, Tatiana Bestaeva. Directed by Serghej Paradzhanov. Screenplay, Ivan Cendej, Paradzhanov from the book by M. Koziubinskij; camera (Sovcolor), Viktor Iljenko; music, Ja Skorik. At Venice Film Fest. Running Time, **95 MINS.**

Ivan .... Ivan Nikolajciuk
Maricka .... Larisa Kadocnikova
Palaghina .... Tatiana Bestaeva
Juko .... Spartak Bagascvili

Made in the studios named after the late famed Ukrainian director Alexandre Dovzhenko, this film has his influences all over it in its lyric flights, ties to the land and the past and an almost baroque blending of an old folk tale with fresh new film techniques. It is visually resplendent and could be of some art or specialized use abroad.

There's no real story here, but a sort of Romeo and Juliet legend taking place in the Carpathians during the early 1900s. One man kills another in a fight, but their respective children eventually grow up to fall in love. However she drowns in an accident and he marries almost against his will and then is fatally wounded to die near her grave and sees her come for him.

Beautiful costumes, a fine rendition of the times in a successful folklore fashion and, above all, the swooping camera, experimental color work and an overdone, yet graceful, progression weld this into a youthfully excessive, but filmically beguiling film in spite of its way out techniques. When the boy's father is killed a flash of blood flows across the screen and blood-red silhouetted horses leap over him as he dies. The boy and girl growing up in unselfconscious feeling and love

gambol through the woods with the camera ecstatically racing after them till they grow and the tragedy occurs.

The pic then goes to black and white as he listlessly marries with color again used for a brilliantly conceived wedding scene. He cannot shake the memory of the first girl and finally is mortally wounded by one of his wife's suitors. His wake has fervid dancing about him that make his body shake before he joins his beloved.

Pic won the direction and color prizes at the Mar Del Plata Film Fest in Argentina late last year and was shown here in the commercial section. *Mosk.*

Domingo A Tarde
(Sunday Afternoon)
(PORTUGESE)
Venice, Aug. 27.
Antonio Da Cunha Telles release and production. With Rui De Carvalho, Isabel De Castro, Isabel Ruth. Written, directed and edited by Antonio De Macedo from book by Fernando Namora. Camera, Elso Roque. At Venice Film Fest. Running Time, **100 MINS.**

Jorge .... Rui De Carvalho
Clarisse .... Isabel De Castro
Lucia .... Isabel Ruth

A doctor, specializing in incurable leukemia, is torn by his attitude towards his hopeless patients. One day he falls in love with one only to have to watch her die. The film tries to elucidate morality and scruples and is solidly made but keeps the characters too one-dimensional to lift this film a cut above a soapy medico pic.

Chances abroad loom mainly for language situations with some specialized possibilities.

This film within a film does have a truly diabolical, florid manner that makes it more interesting than the actual pic around it. Director-writer Antonio De Macedo does display a good sense of narrative and visual underscoring to make a growing talent in this country which yearly makes only a handful of pix.

A color segment is used when the girl begins to get blood transfusions, but this touch appears arbitrary. Hospital segs have a good clinical and documentary flair but is too much on the surface to delve deeply into its theme. However the film avoids morbidity and, if the theme remains evasive, it is also too obvious to give any new slants or insights. Playing is properly subdued and it is technically acceptable. *Mosk.*

Samyong
(SOUTH KOREAN)
(SCOPE)
Venice, Sept. 1.
Shin Film release and production. With Kim Jinkyu, Choi Enhee, Park Noshik, Do Kumbong. Directed by Shin Sangokk. Screenplay, Ra Dohyang; camera, Kim Jongnae. At Venice Film Fest. Running Time, **90 MINS.**

Samyong .... Kim Jinkyu
Oh .... Choi Enhee
Keagski .... Park Noshik
Daughter .... Do Kumbong

South Korea has had one or more pix at fests but only one director has made a mark, Shin Sangokk. In this he proves he is no flash-in-the-pan and contributes a touching folk tale about a mute servant in the feudal days of the '20s.

It is still familiar and naive, but

done with understanding, the right compassion and comic and dramatic leavening to make it a definite language entry with some specialized opportunities abroad if well placed, labeled and sold.

It is a charming pic that pleases and entertains. Film has a deaf servant being mistreated by the brutish son of his more gentle, older patron. One day the boy marries, but is as loutish with his wife, an aristocratic woman whom he feels is superior to him.

But the mute adores her and in a telling poetic scene even dreams he can talk to her. Incidents are piled high as he finds the husband sleeping with a maid and is himself accused of having been with the mistress of the house by town gossips. He saves the wife from hanging and is almost killed by the husband only to finally give his life saving the boor.

There's no preaching on the evils of feudalism; it makes its point in its tale, and shows good and bad on both sides. But it is more concerned telling a story and does it with fine comedic and dramatic dash. It is too slim for most foreign situations, but has the disarming simplicity of candor. Technically it is fine with good acting, if most characters are one-dimensional, while Kim Jinkyu adds stature with his mute portrayal. *Mosk.*

Bwana Toshi No Uta
(Bwana Toshi)
(JAPANESE-COLOR)
Venice, Sept. 2.
Toho release and production. With Kiyoshi Atsumi, Hamisi Sa'ehe, Tsutomu Shimomoto. Directed by Susumu Hani. Screenplay, Kunio Shimizu, Hani; camera (Eastmancolor), Manji Kanau; music, Toru Takemitsu. At Venice Film Fest. Running Time, **115 MINS.**

Toshi .... Kiyoshi Atsumi
Chief .... Hamisi Salehe
Aid .... Tsutomu Shimomoto

A tale of a Japanese worker sent to build a house in the African wilds of Tanganyika provides a fine groundwork for one of the most engaging looks at today's Africa. There's no condescending, patronizing or forced drama here, but a slow, if never faltering, story of two cultures learning and accepting each other. It's entertaining as well with its colorful and exotic backgrounds not overdone and they add to the overall success of the film.

Art and playoff chances would seem possible for this gentle yet incisive pic. Specialized, school and tv uses also appear indicated. Director Susumu Hani lightly balances the African climate in contact with a more developed brand of thinking.

The Japanese workman finds his contact gone and pushes on to the site where he is to build the house. Here he must recruit natives, but his bad Swahili has the natives thinking he wants a job handling cows till he makes himself clear. Then comes the building interspersed with homesickness, a meeting with a scientist studying gorillas and his final acceptance of, and being accepted by, the Africans and Africa.

The film makes bright use of

the animals without exaggeration and shows both the Japanese and the natives learning from each other without sentimentality, didactism or kowtowing. Color is exceptionally good as is the natural acting, especially Kiyoshi Atsumi as the harassed Japanese who runs the gamut from fear to homesickness to twinges of racism and despair before he adapts and learns a lesson from this old, if emerging, continent.

There are telling scenes of the Japanese being taken for a white man and a subsequent trial after striking a native intelligently makes the point of the silliness of racism and nationalism. It also shows a part of Africa rarely seen. Those involved abhor violence and only come to odds with the hero when he resorts to it. The film is a simple one that packs a much deeper insight and wallop than the story promises.

Another black mark against the fest was the refusing of this pic for competition and it was not even shown in the Film Palace out of competition. It underlines the fest penchant for mistaking artifice for art and not recognizing its simpler and more humane forms. *Mosk.*

The Agony And The Ecstasy
(TODD-AO—COLOR)

Outstanding film based on the Irving Stone biog of Michelangelo. Solid direction, thesping, production values and marquee names. Mighty b.o. from class and mass audiences.

Hollywood, Sept. 10.

Twentieth Century-Fox release of International Classics Inc. (Carol Reed) Production, directed by Reed. Stars Charlton Heston, Rex Harrison; features Diane Cilento, Harry Andrews, Alberto Lupo, Adolfo Celi, Venantino Venantini, John Stacy, Fausto Tozzi, Maxine Audley, Tomas Milian. Screen story and screenplay, Philip Dunne, based on the novel by Irving Stone; camera, (DeLuxe Color), Leon Shamroy; editor, Samuel E. Beetley; music, Alex North; choral music, Franco Potenza; production design, John de Cuir; art direction, Jack Martin Smith; sound, Charlton W. Faulkner, Douglas O. Williams; asst. director, Gus Agosti. Reviewed at 20th-Fox Studios, Sept. 9, '65. Running Time, (without intermission), 136 MINS.

Michelangelo	Charlton Heston
Pope Julius II	Rex Harrison
Contessina de Medici	Diane Cilento
Bramante	Harry Andrews
Duke of Urbino	Alberto Lupo
Giovanni de Medici	Adolfo Celi
Paris de Grassis	Venantino Venantini
Sangallo	John Stacy
Foreman	Fausto Tozzi
Woman	Maxine Audley
Raphael	Tomas Milian

Against a backdrop of political-religious upheaval during the Italian Renaissance, "The Agony And The Ecstasy" focuses on the personal conflict between sculptor-painter Michelangelo and his patron, Pope Julius II. Solid production values make an elegant but properly restrained setting for effective performances by a small cast of speaking players. Tastefully mounted by producer-director Carol Reed, the 20th-Fox release has a wide sales appeal, with prospects good for hefty hard-ticket returns in the world market.

Irving Stone's biographical tome covered all 89 years of Michelangelo's life, artistic highlights of which are displayed in a 13-minute, dramatically-lensed prologue which was written by Vatican scholar Vincenzo Labella and narrated in topnotch fashion by Marvin Miller. Scripter Philip Dunne, however, has zeroed in on a four-year span during which the painter labored on the ceiling frescoes for the Sistine Chapel.

The potent seeds in Dunne's excellent treatment are the artistic arrogance of Michelangelo and equally-stubborn mind of the soldier-Pontiff Julius. Neither Reed nor production designer John de Cuir have lost sight of their goal, and every facet of the Todd-AO lensing in DeLuxe Color contributes to their end—and that of Julius—that, come hell, high water, or artistic temperament, the ceiling of the Sistine Chapel is to be suitably adorned by Michelangelo, and by him alone.

Obvious temptations to inject spectacle for its own sake, and plot sidebars for relief, have been avoided. There's a lot of money showing on the screen, to be sure, but it all supports—as do the featured players—a battle of wills between two individualists.

Rex Harrison is outstanding as the Pope, from the moment of his striking entrance as a hooded soldier leading the suppression of a pocket of revolt, to his later scenes as an urbane, yet sensitive, pragmatic ruler of a worldly kingdom, who has of necessity turned warrior to hold the lands which he also rules.

The duality of the Papal throne, precisely explored by Dunne and brilliantly limned by Harrison, will surprise filmgoers unfamiliar with 16th Century history.

Another surprise is Charlton Heston, whose Michelangelo is, in its own way, also outstanding. Combination of austere garb, thinned face, short hair and beard, plus underplaying in early scenes, effectively submerge the Heston image fostered by his earlier epix.

Flushed with an early success as a sculptor in Florence under the patronage of the Medici family, Heston bridles under Harrison's commission which will mean a return to his earlier fresco specialty. The unspoken threat of Papal disfavor, and its effects on future jobs, cause him to relent.

Assisting Harrison's verbal whiplashes are the grandiose engineering plans of the architect Bramante, then engaged in building a new basilica of St. Peter. Harry Andrews excels in the role, while his protege, the painter Raphael, played by Thomas Milian projects very well as Heston's possible replacement. Harrison, however admiring he is of Raphael's promise, insists that Heston get on with the project.

Also serving as stimuli are Adolfo Celi, a Cardinal of the Medici family, and his sister, Diane Cilento, now married and at one time of distant romantic interest to Heston.

Although the latter has started the job—illustrated via interesting shots of the paper templating technique used—there is no inspiration, no concept. Heston destroys his early work (two Apostles), flees Rome and avoids capture by the troops of an enraged Harrison, but eventually discovers his motif in a poetically executed mountain scene in which mist and clouds shape his concept of an entire ceiling devoted to the Book of Genesis.

This scene closes the film's first half, after 61 minutes in which the divergent, yet complementary, points of view of the two men at last seem fused.

No so. The intermission is in reality a crossover, after which Heston's frenzied organization is contrasted with the now declining political fortunes of Harrison. Latter fears he'll never see the finished work, and becomes increasingly insistent, factor which again divides the pair since Heston refuses to accelerate, although he eventually works longer hours.

A subsequent accident, induced by exhaustion, brings Miss Cilento back into the plot as Heston's nurse, but her overt romantic overtures are not accepted. A period of self-pity follows, but Harrison again snaps Heston out of it. Following a military setback, a despondent and sick Harrison is himself squared away by his painter, and the ceiling is unveiled, after four years of work. Perception of the finished product is the "ecstasy," its creation having been the human "agony," on the part of both patron and artist.

Using the facilities of both the new Dino De Laurentiis studio and the older Cinecitta complex, both in Rome. Reed has done a superb job of staging both interior drama and panoramic exterior. The brilliant camera of Leon Shamroy has framed the Papal opulence with the mud of war, the privation of peasants, and, within the Chapel, the scaffolding used by Michelangelo. Art direction of Jack Martin Smith and Dario Simoni's set dressing pack a wallop.

Alex North's score, including a three-minute soundtrack epilogue, is robust and matches the appropriate mood. Alexander Courage's orchestrations are solid. Choral scoring by Franco Potenza heightens the solemnity of Chapel scenes.

Samuel E. Beetley's editing to 136 minutes (excluding intermission) is another big asset. Second unit director Robert D. Webb and lenser Piero Portaluni have enhanced the finished product. DeLuxe Color hues are firstrate. Carlton W. Faulkner and Douglas O. Williams recorded the always-clear and realistic sound.

An undertaking of this sort is not without its flaws. The interactions between Heston and Harrison are often touching, but, for example, their protracted battlefield discussion of the ceiling concept—carried on during enemy fire—is overlong, while the Pope's deathbed recovery after Michelangelo's rebuke is too telescoped.

Also, the display of the finished ceiling—via an upward pan, then a rotating camera, then a pan down, plus some isolated closeups —is a sparse exposition of a project that took eight man-years to achieve. The production stops could have been pulled out here without indiscretion.

Withal, it's a stirring film, inspiring and educational without being pedantic, with manifold selling angles, including the pre-sold readership of 11,000,000, the powerful combination of the two stars, the timeless interest in Renaissance art, all of which spell sock appeal to groups and individuals from all classes.

"The Agony And The Ecstasy" is a fitting climax to another renaissance, that of 20th-Fox since prexy Darryl F. Zanuck returned to executive leadership. With "The Sound Of Music" and "Those Magnificent Men In Their Flying Machines," company have completed its plotted 1965 release of three hardtixers, all of which have an appeal to all peoples of all age groups.   *Murf.*

New York Fest

Rysopis
(Identification Marks: None)
(POLISH)

Film Polski and Polish Film School production. Directed by Jerzy Skolimowski. Features Elzbieta Czyzewska, Jerzy Skolimowski, Tadeusz Mins, Jacek Szczek, Andrzej Zarnecki. Screenplay, Skolimowski; camera Witold Mickiewicz; music, Krzysztof Sadowski. Reviewed at N.Y. Film Fest, Sept. 12, '65. Running Time, 78 MINS.

Although Polish screenwriter-turned-director Jerzy Skolimowski impressed N.Y. Film Fest authorities enough to have them include two of his films in the current series, they would have done their ticket-buying public a favor by having skipped this one.

Skolimowski, who co-authored Roman Polanski's "Knife In The Water" and Andrzej Wajda's "Innocent Sorcerers" before trying his hand at directing, should have paid a bit closer attention to them. While his writing talents are evident in this study of modern Polish youth, his script too often provides situations he's unable to handle as a director.

Evidently the triple task of writing, directing and playing the male lead spread his talents too thin. However, the film, while beset with some dull passages despite its relatively short running time, evidences enough talent to credit the filmmaker with a good try and encouraged to try again (which he did with "Walkover," shown same day). There's little story line, being a running visual diary of a young man's actions during the few hours between his being called up for military service and his actual departure.

If typical of Polish youth today, the hero is beset with the same problems of insufficient self-identification, sense of frustration and lack of moral strength that is the lot of the modern male. Having avoided service for three years by working the college bit, he's finally driven into military service more by his own cynical outlook and economic utility than by any feelings of duty.

Skolimowski's lack of directorial experience shows itself most in a couple of poorly-conceived scenes which come across more as slipshod use of opportunity than as bad scripting. A fight scene is so poorly handled that it should have been omitted. A descent down the stairs of a building in which the hero lives, shot with a handheld camera, continues for so many floors that the suggestion of impulsive flight is destroyed and, instead, brings forth laughter when viewers start counting the stairs.
Robe.

A Rage To Live
(PANAVISION)

Unsatisfactory film version of John O'Hara's nympho novel. Dim b.o.

Hollywood, Sept. 10.

United Artists release of Mirisch (Lewis J. Rachmil) production. Features Suzanne Pleshette, Bradford Dillman, Ben Gazzara. Directed by Walter Grauman. Screenplay, John T. Kelley, based on the novel by John O'Hara; camera, Charles Lawton; editor, Stuart Gilmore; music, Ne'son Riddle; title tune, Ferrante and Teicher, lyrics, Noel Sherman; art direction, James Sullivan, sound, Alfred J. Overton; asst. director, Emmett Emerson. Reviewed at Academy Award Theatre, L.A., Sept. 10, '65. Running Time, 101 MINS.

Grace Caldwell	Suzanne Pleshette
Sidney Tate	Bradford Dillman
Roger Bannon	Ben Gazzara
Jack Hollister	Peter Graves
Amy Hollister	Bethel Leslie
Dr. O'Brien	James Gregory
Emily Caldwell	Carmen Mathews
Mrs. Bannon	Ruth White
Connie Schoffstall	Sarah Marshall
Emma	Virginia Christine
Brock Caldwell	Linden Chiles
Charlie Jay	Mark Goddard
Paul Reichelderfer	George Furth
Jessie Jay	Brett Somers
George Jay	Frank Maxwell

In this banal transfer from tome to film, the characters in John O'Hara's "A Rage To Live" have retained their two-dimensional unreality in a country-club setting. Nympho heroine goes from man to man amidst corny dialog and inept direction which combine to smother all thesps. Delayed a year in release, the Mirisch Corp.-Lewis J. Rachmil sudser has dim marquee lure and little exploitation value.

Vidscripter John T. Kelley fails in his feature debut to give contemporary life to characters. Dullsville dialog may draw unwanted laughs from far-hipper young audiences, while older film-goers will be insulted by the specious plot question: can a girl with a sex problem swing all over town without impairing community and domestic relationships?

Director Walter Grauman achieved little with the players, nor did he attempt to hypo visual interest via technical gimmicks. Charles Lawton's sharp b&w Panavision camera is mostly committed to dull medium shots, strung end-on for 101 minutes by editor Stuart Gilmore. Some below-the-line craftsmanship serves only to spotlight the flop script. Nelson Riddle's score is saccharine, and Ferrante and Teicher's theme is forgettable.

Thesps share the guilt. All names follow titles, and top-featured Suzanne Pleshette misses as the nympho who is dressed to the nines in an eye-catching Howard Shoup wardrobe. Her looks, voice and style are in the Anne Baxter manner, and she can be developed via better material. Ditto Bradford Dillman, the love in her life (as opposed to the men in her bed), whose Leslie Howard mien is wasted in Rover-boy lines. Ben Gazzara, the boy-who-worked-his-way-up, has little of the animal magnetism which is supposed to have rocked the pair's marriage boat. He's killed off in a police chase.

Mark Goddard reps the pre-martial playmates in some brief but effective bits, while Peter Graves seems to be the only one Miss Pleshette ever turned down. Ironically, she gets the blame for it when publicly bum-rapped by wife Bethel Leslie, the climactic plot turn that presumably points a moral. Linden Ihiles is a weak brother, family head after Miss Pleshette's promiscuity causes a stroke in widowed mom Carmen Mathews, who later dies while daughter is off in a sand dune tussle with a bellhop, unbilled.

Ruth White is Gazzara's mother who spitefully spills the post-mortem beans to Dillman. Medic James Gregory recites stock dialog, as do family friend Sarah Marshall, cook Virginia Christine. Dillman's buddy, George Furth, and Goddard's parents, Brett Somers and Frank Maxwell. Latter chews out his son, not for making it with Miss Pleshette (at the seven-minute mark), but for her jail-bait status. This started the preview snickers. In the background of a street scene, there's a one-sheet for "Kiss Me Stupid."   *Murf.*

Sytten
(Seventeen)
(DANISH-COLOR)

Copenhagen, Sept. 7.
Palladium production and release. Stars Ole Soltoft, Ghita Norby. Directed by Annelise Meineche. Screenplay, Bob Ramsing, based on novel by Soya; camera (Eastmancolor), Ole Lytken; music, Ole Hoyer. At Copenhagen Palladium. Running Time, **89 MINS.**

Jacob	Ole Soltoft
Vibeke	Ghita Norby
Professor	Haas Christensen
Uncle	Ole Monty
Young Doctor	Jorgen Kiil
Aunt	Bodil Steen
Cook	Lily Broberg
Maidservant 1	Susanne Heinrich
Maidservant 2	Lise Rosendahl
Girl in Train	Annie Birgit Garde
Pharmacist	Ingolf David

This film has more bawdy scenes of outspoken frankness than Denmark's controversial "A Stranger Knocks." Yet "Seventeen" is mostly a comedy, written and directed in the style usually confined to films for the family trade.

Artistically it's only so-so, but the picture is sure to reap a harvest at the Danish boxoffice and also do well abroad. However, it's hardly a U.S. prospect unless cut drastically.

"Seventeen" is a rather naively told story of an upperclass boy who in 1913 not only turns 17 but also turns man, almost to the point of a satyr. He clumsily makes love with his childhood sweetheart who feels rather disgusted.

But suddenly, all the young man's restless nights and days are over. In a matter of a week, he performs expertly in bed with several women of the domestic staff and also with a young girl he meets on a train. This almost sounds like daydreaming on the part of the author. However, it could be taken seriously by some filmgoers.

Much money and care has gone into a faithful reconstruction of provincial streets, dresses and attitudes of Denmark circa 1913. So much care that a certain stiffness ensues. Nevertheless, the film has its lyrical moments as well as several amusing ones.   *Kell.*

The Little Nuns
(ITALIAN-DUBBED)

Beguiling Italian comedy-drama about two nuns with a purpose; good chances for art and selected situations.

Hollywood, Sept. 10.
Embassy release of Ferruccio Brusarosco production. Stars Catherine Spaak; features Sylva Koscina, with Amedeo Nazzari, Didi Perego, Umberto D'Orsi, Sandro Bruni, Annie Gorassini, Alberto Bonucci. Directed by Luciano Salce. Screenplay, Franco Castellano, Giuseppe Moccia; camera, Erico Menczer; asst. director, Emilio Miraglia; editor, Roberto Cinquini; music, Ennio Morricone; sound, Franco Groppioni. Reviewed at Joe Shore's projection room, Sept. 9, '65. Running Time, **100 MINS.**

Sister Celeste	Catherine Spaak
Elena	Sylva Koscina
Livio Bertana	Amedeo Nazzari
Mother Rachele	Didi Perego
Spugna	Umberto D'Orsi
Damiano, the orphan	Sandro Bruni
Bertana's secretary	Annie Gorassini
Mr. Batistucchi	Alberto Bonucci

"The Little Nuns" could be a sleeper in art and selected situations. Should meet with good reception and word-of-mouth. Unpretentiously produced, yet turned out with an eye to the type of light values so often achieved by Italian producers, film is a charming comedy-drama in which natural fun is the most potent asset. Cast is almost entirely Italian, but English dubbing is excellent.

Its story is simple: jet planes, flying over an impoverished convent 35 miles from Rome, are destroying an ancient fresco of Saint Domitilla, for whom convent is named, and creating havoc among the orphans in its school. So two nuns go to Rome to convince airline officials to change the planes' route.

Producer Ferruccio Brusarosco takes this slight idea and beguilingly develops the situation of what happens, both en route to Rome in an old jalopy and after one of the sisters and the mother superior of the convent arrive in Rome intent upon their mission. In their naive, unworldly manner and unsophisticated stubbornness they accomplish many things besides their own goal, saving the airline director his job and talking him into marrying his mistress of many years.

As the younger nun, Catherine Spaak distinguishes herself in an outstanding performance which should gain her an American following (and quite a switch from her "Empty Canvas" sexpot). Didi Perugo, mother superior, knows her way through subtle comedy and also comes up with an engaging portrayal. Sylva Koscina is lovely as the airline exec's mistress and Amedo Nazzari socks over latter role. Sandro Bruni, an orphan who accompanies the nuns to Rome, and Umberto D'Orsi, convent handyman who wins a Judo contest to buy shares in the airline company so the nuns may participate in a stockholders' meeting, acquit themselves brightly.

Direction by Luciano Salce is inventive as he inserts human touches, and script by Franco Castellano and Giuseppe Moccia expertly devised. Erico Menczer's photography makes interesting use of Rome and Italian countryside backgrounds, and Ennio Morricone's music score gives melodic backing.   *Whit.*

Venice Films

Vaghe Stelle Dell'Orsa
(Of these Thousand pleasures)
(ITALIAN)

Grand Prix at Venice Fest a re-do of "Electra" situation of incestuous brother-sister. A hard sell in U.S. as "Sandra."

Venice, Sept. 4.
Columbia release of Vides Cinematografica (Franco Cristaldi) production. Stars Claudia Cardinale; features Jean Sorel, Michael Craig, Renzo Ricci, Fred Williams, Amalia Troiani, Marie Bell. Directed by Luchino Visconti. Screenplay, Visconti, Suso Cecchi D'Amico, Enrico Medioli. Camera, Armando Nannuzzi. Editor, Mario Serandrei. Music, Cesar Frank. At Venice Film Festival. Running Time, **55 MINS.**

Sandra	Claudia Cardinale
Andrew	Michael Craig
Gianni	Jean Sorel
Mother	Marie Bell
Gilardini	Renzo Ricci
Pietro Fornari	Fred Williams
Fosca	Amalia Troiani

A powerful, slickly-confectioned drama is director Luchino Visconti's latest pic. Primarily about an incestuous relationship it will need adroit salesmanship to help it win top favor beyond the arty fringe. Claudia Cardinale name plus the not-too-ambiguous brother-sister love theme may become sales points, as also points of moral attack.

An admitted steal from "Electra," Visconti's modernized story is set in a small Italian town where Sandra (the U.S. title) brings her new husband, Andrew, for a visit to the old family palazzo. Family's disintegration, not to say degeneracy emerges in rapid strokes, via an explicitly told tale of a far from chilled love affair between Sandra and her brother, Gianni, plus their mother's near-insanity, their father's mysterious death at Aushwitz, and the new and fairly sinister presence of their mother's second husband, Gilardini. The brother eventually commits suicide while Sandra presumably eventually rejoins Andrew, who has fled the unwholesome household.

Ambiguity prevails in many of Visconti's situation developments, and while this may irk some, it does confer an air of mystery and suspense on a feature which might otherwise be merely morbid. The brother-sister sex relationship is depicted as graphically as it has perhaps ever been on screen though actual seduction is left slightly ambiguous. Taste prevails throughout, however, and poignancy and power are in evidence as couple fight for and against their taboo love. Less clear are some of the sideline details concerning the mother and her second spouse: for example; did he or did they both conspire to speed the father's one-way trip to the crematorium? Other plot shadings have a like tendency—perhaps deliberate—to remain such in what is primarily a mood film, full of chiaroscuro notations.

Performances are up to Visconti's high standard. Claudia Cardinale makes a striking Sandra-Electra, rising to impactful heights in her near-finale scenes with Jean Sorel, whose limning of frere Gianni-Orestes should win him plenty of international attention as a new male lead.

Michael Craig's part as the husband is of more limited range, but he puts in an accomplished, sympathetic stint. Renzo Ricci is good as Gilardini, Fred Williams effectively plays a onetime suitor, while Marie Bell as the mother and Amalia Troianix as a housekeeper have relatively little to do. More than in the script itself by Visconti, Suso D'Amico and Enrico Medioli, film's force lies in direction which keys moods and action with the unity that only a dominant creator can give. Surely not an easy pic, but one which will rouse controversy and discussion, fruitful as attention-grabbing b.o. assists, as well as critical pegs for the aficionados.

Visconti's own musical selections, apart from some pop songs, consist mainly of a Cesar Frank potpourri, strangely effective in keying moods. Armando Nannuzzi's low-key lens work likewise adds to a strange and in many ways disconcerting film. *Hawk.*

Rekopis Znaleziony W Saragossie
(The Saragossa Manuscript)
(POLISH)

Venice, Sept. 6.
Polski State Film release of Kamera production. With Zbigniew Cybulski, Slavomir Linder, Franciszek Pieczka, Barbara Krafit, Leon Nemczek, Elzbieta Czyzewska. Directed by Wojciech J. Has. Screenplay, Tadeusz Kwiatkowski from the novel by Jan Poticki; camera, Mieczyslaw Jahoda; music, Krzysztof Penderecki. At Venice Film Fest. Running Time, 180 MINS.

Alfons	Zbigniew Cybulski
Van Worden	Slavomir Linder
Possessed One	Franciszek Pieczka
Camilla	Barbara Krafft
Avadoro	Leon Nemczek
Frasquetta	Elzbieta Czyzewska

Jack-in-the box pic with stories within stories, adult costumer follows a young 18th-century Spanish captain into a series of adventures while reason and magic strive for his soul. But length (180 minutes), complicated construction, and mixture of irony and philosophy make this primarily an "art" pic.

Though filled with trappings of 18th-century Spain, much derring-do and exotic and occult adventures, its appeal is more intellectual than swashbuckling.

A young captain wanders into an inn that appears deserted but he meets two Moorish beauties and is told he is a descendant of an important family and has many missions to fulfill before he has proven himself. Meetings with many people follow, whose stories have some bearing on him, or clarify an idea.

He meets a man possessed of demons, has trouble with the Inquisition, is subjected to many tales by a magician trying to win his soul while a rationalist also fight for it. No use looking for hidden modern allusions in this. They may be there but the film's main appeal is its expert stylization, visually clever and beguiling and imaginative period recreations and gusty playing by a big cast well coordinated by the inquisitive, bouncy and valorous Zbigniew Cybulski as the man on the quest. *Mosk.*

La Chasse Au Lion A L'Arc
(Hunting the Lion With Bow and Arrow)
(FRENCH-COLOR)

Venice, Sept. 5.
Films De La Pleiade-Pierre Braunberger release and production. Written, directed, lensed in 16m color and blown up to 35m, and commentary delivered by Jean Rouch; editor, Jose Malterossa, Jan Hoenig. At Venice Film Fest. Running Time, 70 MINS.

Ethnically interesting, and also visually fine, with incisive, clear commentary, this look at the disappearing lion hunters in some sections of West Africa is of school, tv and supporting fare interest.

Jean Rouch follows a group of lion hunters who track them down, maintain respect for their game and the ritual is exactingly but never listlessly repeated. The

for shepherds and herdsmen. They preparation of the arrows, the poison, the traps are shown and then the stalking.

The killing of the animals, already in a trap, is not sport. It gives a feel for the pitiless yet honorable work. The kills are shown and then the exorcism of the lion's soul by certain rites before the skinning, eating and tall tales of the hunt.

No forcing the affair or reaching for local color but a rigidly classical exposition of it all with fine feeling for the people, customs and country. An attack on a man was not filmed which attests to Rouch's excising of sensation. The blood is part of the life and, if it is some thing that is disappearing, it is effectively chronicled.

Color is good for a blowup and lensing effective with an added filmic flair that defeats any onus of dryness or didactics. *Mosk.*

Trois Chambres a Manhattan
(Three Rooms in Manhattan)
(FRENCH)

Venice, Sept. 5.
Cocinor release of Films Montaigne production. Stars Annie Girardot, Maurice Ronet; features, Otto Hasse, Roland Lesaffre, Gabriele Ferzetti, Genevieve Page. Directed by Marcel Carne. Screenplay, Jacques Sigurd, Carne from a book by Georges Simenon; camera, Eugene Schuftan; editor, Henri Rust. At Venice Film Fest. Running Time, 110 MINS.

Kay	Annie Girardot
Francois	Maurice Ronet
Hourvitch	Otto Hasse
Pierre	Rolande Lesaffre
Larzi	Gabriele Ferzetti
Yolande	Genevieve Page

Two emotionally drifting French people, an actor and an ex-countess, meet in New York and finally manage to fall in love after much soul-searching and fear of commitment for a happy ending. But all this lacks any depth in character and treatment to delve deeply into motivations and needs to keep this a bit surface and soapy if some adequate acting softens the pedestrian pace of the direction and writing.

Since it is familiar and does have some forthright love scenes it may have some playoff chances abroad but is not of the calibre for untoward art chances. Veteran director Marcel Carne displays an oldfashioned flat technique and melancholia not in keeping with the more incisive probings into the difficulties of the sexes and communication in many films today.

Annie Girardot shows a wry spark overlaying a craving, but not desperate need, for love that makes her character transcend the ordinary story and dialog. Maurice Ronet is good as the man with others fair except for Otto Hasse's glib limning of a vidpic producer. *Mosk.*

Marriage On The Rocks
(PANAVISION-COLOR)

Amusing marital comedy with names of Sinatra, Kerr and Martin to lend marquee voltage.

Hollywood, Sept. 14.
Warner Bros. release of William H. Daniels production. Stars Frank Sinatra, Deborah Kerr, Dean Martin; features Cesar Romero, Hermione Baddeley, Tony Bill, John McGiver, Nancy Sinatra, Davey Davison, Michel Petit, Trini Lopez. Directed by Jack Donohue. Screenplay, Cy Howard; camera (Technicolor), William H. Daniels; editor, Sam O'Steen; music, Nelson Riddle; asst. director, Richard Lang. Reviewed at Academy Award Theatre, Sept. 13, '65. Running Time, 109 MINS.

Dan Edwards	Frank Sinatra
Valerie Edwards	Deborah Kerr
Ernie Brewer	Dean Martin
Miguel Santos	Cesar Romero
Jeannie	Hermione Baddeley
Jim Blake	Tony Bill
Shad Nathan	John McGiver
Tracy Edwards	Nancy Sinatra
Lisa Sterling	Davey Davison
David Edwards	Michel Petit
Trini Lopez	Trini Lopez
Lola	Joi Lansing
Bunny	Tara Ashton
Miss Blight	Kathleen Freeman
Rollo	Flip Mark
Mr. Turner	DeForest Kelley
Kitty	Sigrid Valdis

"Marriage on the Rocks" is a marital situation comedy which both amuses and occasionally gets beyond its depth, but in the main qualifies as pleasant entertainment. Star names of Frank Sinatra, Deborah Kerr and Dean Martin will assure top bookings, where hefty boxoffice is strongly indicated.

Produced for Warner Bros. release by Sinatra's own company, the Cy Howard script focuses on a 19-years'-wed couple — Sinatra, hard-working head of a successful advertising agency, entirely complacement and taking his spouse for granted; Miss Kerr, bored, yearning for a divorce — who suddenly find their knot untied and the wife married to Martin, their closest friend and a perennial bachelor. Vet cameraman William H. Daniels — who also lenses — in making his producer bow is responsible for interesting Panavision-Technicolor values which lend class even when plot becomes overly-contrived.

Miss Kerr, in a change of pace far distant from her dramatic portrayal in "Night of the Iguana," helps give "Marriage" wacky overtones in a characterization allowing her to snap her bonnet. Screwball antics are developed particularly in a loony Mexican sequence in which Cesar Romero, an ambulance-chasing attorney who specializes in speedy marriages and divorces, seizes upon the couple as they arrive for a second honeymoon and fast-talks their change in marital status. Martin ultimately takes Sinatra's place as the serious family man and latter becomes the playboy.

Sinatra undertakes an entirely different type of role as the sober, middle-aged biz exec who has lost all rapport with his wife, daughter and young son. He, of course, delivers satisfactorily, but comes off second-best to the more sparkling delineations of his two co-stars, who benefit by comedy buildup of their roles.

Miss Kerr in an almost-zany character contributes immensely to the general fun as she wonders

constantly if she shouldn't have married Martin, her early beau, instead of Sinatra, whom she thinks has turned into a square. She's horrified to learn she is really Martin's wife, in a marriage ceremony conducted in Spanish neither understands — then sets her sights on getting Sinatra back. Martin, usually surrounded by a flock of luscious babes in abbreviated bikinis, plays his customary playboy role to the hilt.

In good support, Romero romps through an outlandish multi-faceted character; Nancy Sinatra — Frank's sprout — is his daughter who wants to leave home for her own style of living; Hermione Baddeley is Sinatra's whiskey-guzzling, bagpipe-skirling mother-in-law; Davey Davison a cafe a go-go dancer; John McGiver the family lawyer. Michel Petit plays the young son, Tony Bill, Nancy's boy friend, and Trini Lopez guestars with his own "Sinner Man" number.

Jack Donohue's direction, which sometimes presses for laughs, generally is on the light side. Technical credits are all plus, including Nelson Riddle's music score; LeRoy Deane's art direction: Sam O'Steen's editing. *Whit.*

Beach Girls And The Monster

Sex, sadism, and suspense come off in an adolescent way, but there's a nice jazz score throughout.

Hollywood, Sept. 16.
U.S. Films, Inc. release of Edward Janis Production. Features Jon Hall, Sue Casey, Walker Edmiston and Arnold Lessing, with Elaine DuPont, Read Morgan, Clyde Adler, Gloria Neil, Tony Roberts, Dale Davis, Carolyn Williamson. Directed by Jon Hall. Original story and screenplay, Joan Gardner; music, Frank Sinatra Jr., production manager, William Larkin. Reviewed at World Theatre, Sept. 15, '65. Running Time, 70 MINS.

Otto	Jon Hall
Vicki	Sue Casey
Mark	Walker Edmiston
Richard	Arnold Lessing

A surfside murder a go-go, this uneven quickie attempts to break into the Beach pix market, but black and white photography, small name cast, and skimpy production will make it hard going. There is some suspense, however, one cute music number, a few scenes of bikini clad lovelies gyrating on the sand, and a film clip of Hawaiian surfing.

Offbeat story should attract the young set as an inside joke since story shows two crazy mixed up parents, one of whom turns out to be the monster of the title. Plot is punctuated with monster clawing and killing two beauties on the beach, and then near the end two others in the small cast.

Story centers around oceanographer Jon Hall and his wish that son join him working at his lab. Son has other ideas and wants to live it up in Waikiki. Stepmother is a bored aging beauty who also wants to play around and gives some of her attention to her stepson's friend, a morose guy who had his leg mangled in a car accident.

Pic opens with girl on beach being accosted by mad monster and being killed. Some suspense is generated when Jon Hall, who lives with son and boy's stepmother in beach-house above on cliffs, tells the police that the surfing crowd is no good. Then there's the gimpy guy and he looks suspicious, too. As for the stepmother, she looks like she might be the Lady Macbeth of the piece.

The suspense, however, is soon broken, and with bad acting shining through, there's not too much to keep up interest. There's a wild car chase at the end, of course, and an interesting use of bongo music throughout, which is sometimes nicely synchronized to the action. The one tune of interest is "Monster In The Surf."

Sue Casey, as the stepmother deserves a better break; she does all right with her one dimensional role. Jon Hall is competent, but the juves in cast simply play it by seashell. *Dool.*

The War Of The Zombies
(WIDE SCREEN - COLOR)

A gaudy Roman epic, filled with special effects and battle scenes, but confusing story. Beautifully costumed and photographed, production value is good. Juves should find it mildly diverting.

Hollywood, Sept. 16.

American International Pictures release of Galatea production. Stars John Drew Barrymore, Susi Anderson, Ettore Manni and Ida Galli, features Philippe Hersent, Mino Doro, Ivano Staccioli, Matilde Calnan and Giulio Maculani. Directed by Giuseppe Vari. Reviewed at World Theatre, Sept. 15, '65. Running Time, **85 MINS.**

Aderbal	John Drew Barrymore
Tullia	Susi Andersen
Gaius	Ettore Manni
Rhama	Ida Galli

As a toga sci-fi spectacular, "War of the Zombies" boasts of a cast of thousands, not to mention a couple of thousand ghosts. Title is misleading, story line confusing, dubbing awkward, but film is colorfully mounted, packed with action, blood, gore and wild histrionics. It should provide the small fry with an imaginative Saturday afternoon away from it all.

An Armenian treasure is mysteriously hijacked on its way to Rome, a large number of Roman soldiers disappear and Roman agent 007, Gauis by name (Ettore Manni), is dispatched to investigate. He soon crosses paths with lively Ida Galli, but she's a Zombie of sorts. She belongs to a subversive cult headed by John Drew Barrymore which is collecting dead soldiers to do battle against Rome and rule the world. The cult has a one-eyed enormous gold goddess who performs spooky rites.

Plot thickens when it is revealed that Barrymore has duped Lutezius, the Roman ruler in the area, into believing the treasure will be turned over to him when the revolt succeeds. The Roman's wife has ideas of her own, which complicated things a lot more.

Film has some interesting special effects, suspenseful moments, many battle scenes and acting is creditable. Barrymore has a ball emoting like papa in the black high priest part; Manni as Gaius, exudes masculinity, and the two femmes, Susi Anderson and Ida Galli, are easy on the eyes.

Battle between Romans and the Zombie Romans at the end has a suspenseful buildup which doesn't pay off. Screen was simply covered with bluish splotches and the spectacle went on as usual, but the kids will probably dig the scene. *Dool.*

The Reward
(C'SCOPE-COLOR)

Tepid, fuzzy desert meller with some good acting and technical gloss.

Hollywood, Sept. 9.

Twentieth Century-Fox release of an Arcola (Aaron Rosenberg) Production. Stars Max von Sydow, Yvette Mimieux, Efrem Zimbalist Jr., Gilbert Roland; features Emilio Fernandez, Nino Castelnuovo, Henry Silva. Directed by Serge Bourguignon. Screenplay, Bourguignon, Oscar Millard, based on novel by Michael Barrett; camera (DeLuxe Color), Joe MacDonald; editor, Robert Simpson; music, Elmer Bernstein; art direction, Jack Martin Smith, Robert Boyle; sound, Jack F. Lilly, Elmer Raguse; asst. director, Joseph E. Rickards. Reviewed at 20th-Fox Studio, Sept. 7, '65. Running Time, **91 MINS.**

Scott	Max von Sydow
Sylvia	Yvette Mimieux
Frank	Efrem Zimbalist Jr.
Carbajal	Gilbert Roland
Lopez	Emilio Fernandez
Luis	Nino Castelnuovo
Joaquin	Henry Silva

"The Reward" for a fugitive and its effects on a group thrown together by fate comprise the theme of this moody, somewhat uneven, desert meller which marks director Serge Bourguignon's debut in American pix. Some good acting and excellent production values bolster a plot that fizzes out in final reel. Too slick and commercial for arties, the Aaron Rosenberg production shapes up as a moderate entry for 20th-Fox release in the general market.

Bourguignon and Oscar Millard adapted Michael Barrett's tome which crash lands crop-duster Max von Sydow in a boondocks Mexican town coincident with the passing through of Efrem Zimbalist Jr., latter on the lam from a murder rap and accompanied by Yvette Mimieux. Faced with pokey time for some plane-caused damage, Sydow cues police inspector Gilbert Roland to the price on Zimbalist's head, and the slow chase is on, leading to uneventful and unresisted capture.

About 40% of the film has elapsed before plot begins to move when brutal, sadistic police sergeant Emilio Fernandez finds out there's a reward and starts to dominate the group. Roland, malaria-weakened, cannot control his flunky, who also badgers younger cop Nino Castelnuovo and scout Henry Silva.

Latter does a good job as a sensitive Indian who helps Zimbalist and gal to escape, only to be killed by Fernandez whose performance is easily the standout.

Sydow gives a lethargic performance despite a role that is basically passive. He talks little, then in guttural tones, but mostly reacts sluggishly to events. Role is not clearly defined. Miss Mimieux looks dazed throughout, although she is pleasant to look at. Zimbalist has some good moments when he begs Roland to free him so he can escape a framed trial, but the sergeant eventually kills him.

Castelnuovo's death, never clearly explained, reduces the survivors to four. Roland remains in a ghost town while he sends Sydow and gal to a nearby fishing port. Fernandez is last seen chasing horses. Studio synopsis indicates some future action which would have achieved a grim irony, but it's not there on the screen. There can be no comparison with John Huston's "Theasure Of The Sierra Madre" or Erich von Stroheim's "Greed."

Bourguignon's direction is weak, but his visual sense is excellent. Joe MacDonald's crisp camera work is outstanding. Curiously, however, there are two sunset shots with intra-lens reflections which are jarringly artificial and add nothing to the drama of the moment. DeLuxe Color hues and sound values are excellent. *Murf.*

That Darn Cat
(COLOR)

Rollicking Disney comedy of a cat helping the FBI solve a case; excellent prospects for mass market, with names of Hayley Mills, Dean Jones and Dorothy Provine to attract.

Hollywood, Sept. 17.

Buena Vista release of Walt Disney production; co-producers, Bill Walsh, Ron Miller. Stars Hayley Mills, Dean Jones, Dorothy Provine, Roddy McDowall, Neville Brand; features Elsa Lanchester, William Demarest, Frank Gorshin, Richard Eastham, Grayson Hall, Ed Wynn, Tom Lowell, Richard Deacon. Directed by Robert Stevenson. Screenplay, Mildred and Gordon Gordon, Bill Walsh, based on book, "Undercover Cat," by The Gordons; camera (Technicolor), Edward Colman; editor, Cotton Warburton; music, Bob Brunner; art direction, Carroll Clark, William H. Tuntke; asst. director, Joseph L. McEveety; sound, Robert O. Cook, Dean Thomas. Reviewed at Academy Award Theatre, Sept. 16, '65. Running Time, **117 MINS.**

Patti Randall	Hayley Mills
Zeke Kelso	Dean Jones
Ingrid Randall	Dorothy Provine
Gregory Benson	Roddy McDowall
Dan	Neville Brand
Mrs. MacDougall	Elsa Lanchester
Mr. MacDougall	William Demarest
Iggy	Frank Gorshin
Supervisor Newton	Richard Eastham
Margaret Miller	Grayson Hall
Mr. Hofsteddwe	Ed Wynn
Canoe	Tom Lowell
Drive-in manager	Richard Deacon
Landlady	Iris Adrian
Graham	Liam Sullivan
Spires	Don Dorrell
Cahill	Gene Blakely
Kelly	Karl Held

Walt Disney comes up with a novelty charmer in this lilting translation of the Gordon's whimsical tale of a Siamese cat who helps the FBI solve a kidnapping case. Geared for mass appeal, it should receive warm welcome from both the adult and juve trade and for marquee voltage has names of Hayley Mills, Dean Jones and Dorothy Provine heading cast.

Script by Mildred and Gordon Gordon, adapting their tome, "Undercover Cat," in collaboration with Bill Walsh, allows some belly laughs of the sort all but forgotten these days, plus situations which titillate the imagination. Robert Stevenson's direction is light and airy as he develops the idea of FBI agents trying to follow a slippery feline who has brought home the only clue to a combo bank robbery and abducted lady teller the wristwatch she had slipped around his neck. Along the way are the goldangdest goings—on as D.C.—short for Darned Cat in family parlance — constantly eludes frantic Government eyes, but finally leads the way to the kidnappers' lair.

Hayley Mills, who lives with her elder sister, Dorothy Provine, discovers the watch around the family cat's neck as he returns from an evening's prowl and surmising its true meaning cues the action as she calls on the FBI for help. Continuing to show promise as one of the screen's most talented juve performers, Miss Mills socks over her comedy with a flair, but finds an equal in Miss Provine, who also knows her way through a comedy situation. They make a charming pair as sisters, and Dean Jones as the FBI agent allergic to cats assigned to the case handily performs his chores. D.C.—the cat—rates an Oscar, or at least, a Patsy.

Film is spotted with standout comic gems. Roddy McDowall, the fussy, mama's boy down the street; Elsa Lanchester, the nosy nextdoor neighbor, and William Demarest, her deaf husband; Tom Lowell, a surf nut who loves to eat at Hayley's house; Ed Wynn, a flustered pharmacist; Richard Deacon, a drive-in manager, al[l] deliver opulently. Neville Bran[d] and Frank Gorshin insert proper menace as the kidnappers, Grayson Hall is good as their victim and Richard Eastham is the FB[I] chief. Iris Adrian has a brief bi[t] as a suspicious landlady.

Disney and his co-producer[s] Walsh and Ron Miller, pack th[e] Technicolor picture with appro[priate] values. Bob Brunner['s] music score melodically underlines the action, which Cotton Warbur[ton]'s editing maintains at a bris[k] pace, and Edward Colman's pho[to]tography is superior throughout.

Richard M. and Robert R. Sher[man]'s title song is amusingl[y] sung by Bobby Darin, and Arthu[r] J. Vitarelli is credited as secon[d] unit director. William R. Koeh[ler]'s animal supervision is a wor[k] of art. *Whit.*

The Great Sioux Massacre
(C'SCOPE—COLOR)

Custer's last stand again, done up in excellent action and production values. Despite soft script, good bet for dual slotting.

Hollywood, Sept. 16.

Columbia Pictures release of an F. & F. Prods. (Leon Fromkess-Sam Firks) production, produced by Fromkess. Features Joseph Cotten, Darren McGavin, Philip Carey, Julie Sommars, Nancy Kovack. Directed by Sidney Salkow. Screenplay, Fred C. Dobbs, based on story by Salkow, Marvin Gluck; camera (Pathecolor), Irving Lippman; editor, William Austin; music, Emil Newman, Edward B. Powell; art direction, Frank P. Sylos; sound, John Bury Jr., Samuel Goldwyn Studio sound dept.; asst. director, Abby Berlin. Reviewed at Columbia Studios, Sept. 15, '65. Running Time, **92 MINS.**

Major Reno	Joseph Cotten
Capt. Benton	Darren McGavin
Col. Custer	Philip Carey
Caroline Reno	Julie Sommars
Libbie Custer	Nancy Kovack
Dakota	John Matthews
Sitting Bull	Michael Pate
Senator Blaine	Don Haggerty
Gen. Terry	Frank Ferguson
Mr. Turner	Stacy Harris
Crazy Horse	Iron Eyes Cody
Reporter	House Peters, Jr.
Tom Custer	John Napier
Miner	William Tannen
Presiding officer	Blair Davies
Mrs. Turner	Louise Serpa

"The Great Sioux Massacre" is

a firstrate programmer which depicts the background of Custer's last stand. Leon Fromkess production has some solid action sequences and production values worthy of far more expensive pix. A well-directed cast gives some depth to a slightly weak script, which, combined with lack of hot marquee names, will relegate the Columbia release to dual bills where it can, nevertheless, more than pull its share.

The Marvin Gluck and director Sidney Salkow story was adapted by Fred C. Dobbs to focus on Custer (Philip Carey), as seen through the subordinates Darren McGavin and Joseph Cotten. Latter is initially a boozy major, back in the Army after prior Confederate service in the Civil War. McGavin, junior in rank to other pair, endures Cotten out of respect for Carey, himself initially, a gruff, outspoken soldier friendly to Indians and down on politically-appointed and grafting Indian agents typified by Stacy Harris.

Recalled to Washington where his explosive charges of corruption lead to unofficial exile, Carey-Custer is embittered and ripe for U.S. Senator Don Haggerty's plan to build him up as political hero, providing he starts oppressing Indians. Reporter House Peters Jr. is assigned to Carey to dramatize the action for the eastern press.

Cotten and McGavin deliver good performances, while Carey falls short as Custer, although he does manage to suggest that the gruff, soldier-on-horseback image can be used for both good and evil. Michael Pate is very good as the stoic Sitting Bull, and his scenes logically spell out the exploding Indian resistance and the climactic slaughter of 251 troops headed by Carey who has jumped the gun on general Frank Ferguson in order to grab top honors.

Director Salkow has put a lot of sweep and action into many fast-moving situations, including the 15-minute climax which holds interest throughout. Femme interest rests in Julie Sommars, Cotten's daughter and McGavin's gal, and Nancy Kovack as Carey's wife. Both add to the scenery, all caught by Irving Lippman's versatile C'Scope and Pathecolor camera. John Matthews is effective as an Indian-hating scout who later becomes sympathetic as Carey hardens. Other thesps are good.

William Austin's editing to 92 minutes is a solid assist. Emil Newman and Edward B. Powell scoring is unobtrusive and adroit. The Goldwyn Studio sound department added a pro touch to the overall technical gloss. Told in brief flashback, "Massacre" ends on ironic note with military board of inquiry deciding nothing amiss has happened, the usual temporizing.   *Murf.*

The Unearthly Stranger
(BRITISH)

American International Pictures release of a Julian Wintle-Leslie Parkyn production. Stars John Neville; features Gabriella Licudi, Philip Stone, Patrick Newell, Jean Marsh, Warren Mitchell. Directed by John Krish. Screenplay, Rex Carlton; camera, Reg Wyer; editor, Tom Priestley; music, composed by Edward Williams, conducted by Marcus Dods.

Reviewed at Lyric Theatre, N.Y., Sept. 18, '65. Running Time, **88 MINS.**

Dr. Mark Davidson	John Neville
Julie	Gabriella Licudi
Prof. John Lancaster	Philip Stone
Major Clarke	Patrick Newell
Miss Ballard	Jean Marsh
Dr. Munro	Warren Mitchell

This 1963 British sci-fi import has sufficient interest thanks to a well-written screenplay and able acting, to more than hold its own on a double-bill.

Rex Carlton's screenplay takes place almost entirely within the confines of the offices of a space-connected research project. This presented some cinematic obstacles but director John Krish (this is his first feature effort) kept his small cast on the move within the limited area, cutting to occasional outside scenes for a change of pace. He is also helped tremendously by the ability of his three major actors to handle pseudo-scientific dialogue in a manner that makes it both interesting and dramatic. Special sound effects, which serve to replace the usual overdone 'creature from outer space, are also a great asset, backstopped by Edward Williams score, not particularly original but appropriate.

Shakespearean actor John Neville, who could have understandably coasted through this admittedly negligible role, gives it his complete attention and makes the principal scientist, who finds himself married to an unearthly creature (Gabriella Licudi) and besieged by the outer space powers that control her, a believable and sympathetic chaarcter. Miss Licudi, easy on the eyes, has comparatively little thesping to do, her voice evidently dubbed. On a par with Neville is Patrick Newell, particularly, as a deceptively jovial but suspicious security chief whose part has various "red herring" aspects that add some extra suspense, and Philip Stone as Neville's fellow scientist in the project, treated as the cold-blooded, "no funny stuff" counterpart of Neville's imaginative and romantic part.

The only attempt to go beyond the dialogue in tempting the viewer's imagination in the sci-fi aspects of the film is the use of the eerie sound effects and vanishing bits on the part of the wife and Neville's secretary (Jean Marsh), who becomes the human agent of the space powers when the wife is withdrawn.

Reg Wyer's black and white camerawork is excellent, considering that there's no opportunity to go beyond the realistic depiction of the every-day life of the cast. One good incident plays up Miss Licudi's realization that, although outwardly a beautiful female human, she has some limitations. When she stops by a schoolyard to watch the children, the latter gradually become aware of her and instinctively start to withdraw until finally all are fleeing, in panic, towards the schoolhouse.   *Robe.*

New York Fest

Nicht Versohnt
(Unreconciled)
(WEST GERMANY)

Straub-Huillet production, directed by Jean-Marie Straub. Features Henning Harmssen, Ulrich Hopmann, Heiner Braun, Heinrich Hargesheimer, Ulrich von Thuna, Carlheinz Hargesheimer, Martha Standner, Joachim Weiler. Screenplay, Straub and Daniele Huillet, based on Heinrich Boll's novel, "Billiards At Half-Past Nine"; camera, Wendelin Sachtler, Gerhard Ries, Christian Schwarzwald, Straub; sound, Lutz Grubnau, Willi Hanspach. Reviewed at N.Y. Film Festival, Sept. 18, '65. Running Time, **53 MINS.**

(English Subtitles)

"Nicht Versohnt" ist nicht guht. The very-short West German feature (possibly made originally for tv exposure) is a dull, plodding, self-conscious effort with no potential for U.S. release and a surprisingly bad choice at the New York film festival.

Programmed as a "free adaptation of Henrich Boll's novel dealing with the phenomenon of Nazism and its long-term effects on Germany," the result is that, if "Nicht Versohnt" is a fair example, the longest-lasting effect of the Nazi regime oh German filmmakers has been to stifle any creative ability among younger members of the industry.

The inept script, credited as the joint handiwork of director Jean-Marie Straub and writer Daniele Huillet, makes little sense and its so-called "cyclical narrative technique" consist of endless dialogues, delivered in a dull monotone by a series of what appear to be non-professional actors. Some speeches are so long, in fact, that after a fitful start, the subtitles just cease (implying that the rest of the conversation isn't worth translating).

With the exception of some crisp camerawork by a team of four, including Straub, the remainder of the film must be checked off as one more poor festival choice. One apt phrase used in the program notes is that "the film renders all the complexity and ambiguity of the German problem." That it does.
                    Robe.

Flaaden's Friske Fyre
(It's Nifty in the Navy)
(DANISH—COLOR)

Copenhagen, Sept. 14.
Dansk-Svensk Film production. Merry Film release of Merry Film production. Stars Dirch Passer, Ghita Norby, Ove Sprogoe, Poul Hagen. Directed by Finn Henriksen. Original story and screenplay, Carl Ottosen; camera, (Eastman Color), Henning Bendtsen; music, Svend Asmussen. At the Saga, Copenhagen. Running Time, **91 MINS.**

Valdemar	Dirch Passer
Svend	Ove Sprogoe
Knud	Poul Hagen
Hanne	Ghita Norby
Granddad	Hans W. Petersen
Kid brother	Jan Priiskorn Schmidt
Navy Commander	Carl Ottosen
Navy Captain	Prehen Marth
Signalman	Axel Stroebye

Comedian Dirch Passer has starred in a string of Merry Film productions about life in the Danish Army. Several of these pictures have also chalked up good boxoffice in Norway, Sweden and West Germany. Similarly, promising returns looms for "It's Nifty in the Navy," Merry's latest military farce.

A friendly little comedy, the film tries to avoid too much slapstick and wisely emphasizes the human interest touches. Passer, along with his usual comrades-at-arms. Poul Hagen and Ove Sprogoe, are professional fishermen who are drafted into the Navy.

It's a catastrophe for them since they owe considerable money on a trawler they just bought. Their problem is who will fish while they're away It appears that the new angler will be Ghita Norby, noted for her bounteous physical attributes in previous Danish pix. Assisting her in luring the finny tribe are Granddad and a kid brother.

Meantime, Passer and his mates blink messages with fishing hints through official channels to their angling craft. They also turn the destroyer to which they're assigned upside down. But they don't do it through the usual farcical landlubbers' ineptitude.

Passer scores in some excellent pantomime. Finn Henriksen's direction is fast paced while the editing is smooth. This entry won't stir up a tidal wave of laughter, but it will spark a fair share of chuckles. It also has a good potential in the foreign market.   *Kell.*

Cork Fest

El Nino Y El Muro
(The Boy and the Ball and the Hole in the Wall)
(MEXICAN-SPANISH)

Cork, Sept. 14.
Diana Films (Mexico) and J. Orduna (Spain) production. Stars: Daniel Gelin, Yoland Varela, Nino del Arco, Linda Christian, Karin Black, Carlos Pinar. Directed by Ismael Rodriguez. Screenplay, Henaghan, Herrero, Rodriguez; camera, Alfred Fraile; music, Alfred Waitzman. At Cork Film Festival. Running Time, **85 MINS.**

Exploitation of Berlin Wall problems through a child and its ball. Five-year-old child has a ball which is accidentally kicked by a man into Eastern sector. Child tries to recover ball but is stopped by Wall and can only see — through a hole — another child playing with it, an incident creating resentment and frustration for a youngster without playmates who it cannot have his own toy, nor share it with a neighboring child.

Film explores other problems of divided city including the Eastern guard who loves, through binoculars, a girl on the Western side of the Wall; and the frustrations of a working class family trying to save enough for a decent home in a supposedly affluent society.

Picture has fine human values and a sensitive style of expressing the problems of the divided city in terms of people rather than politics.   *Max.*

Beach Ball
(COLOR)

A fast moving surfing pic, with drag racing, deep-sea fishing and parachute jumping added, weaved together with rock 'n' roll renditions. Tailor-made for juve set.

Hollywood, Sept. 21.

Paramount release of Bart production. Features entire cast plus The Supremes, The Four Seasons, The Righteous Brothers, The Hondells and The Walker Brothers. Directed by Lennie Weinrib; screenplay, David Malcolm; assistant director, Gary Kurtz; production designer, Ray Storey; (Technicolor) camera, Alfred Taylor; editor, Karl Wald; music, Frank Wilson. Reviewed at Paramount Studio, Sept. 21, '65. Running Time, 83 MINS.

Dick	Edd Byrnes
Susan	Chris Noel
Bango	Robert Logan
Deborah	Gail Gilmore
Jack	Aron Kincaid
Augusta	Mikki Jamison
Bob	Don Edmonds
Samantha	Brenda Benet
Polly	Anna Lavelle
Mr. Wolf	James Wellman

A bouillabaisse of all the tried and true surfing ingredients, this loud, lively pic should prove a winner with the adolescent set. An innocuous plot, lots of bikini scenery, and endless rock 'n' roll featuring top selling recording personalities, assure boxoffice success. "Beach Ball" is a first outing for producer-director team of Bart Patton and Lennie Weinrib, who brought it in at $150, neg cost.

Laughs outdistance logic and action supplants motivation and the sweet life of surfing is thereby transplanted to near-fantasy, but clever camera work, good production value and a script pepered with humor and clean fun and some interesting plot twists, keep the "Ball" bouncing merrily along.

The story line is simple enough: Mr. Wolf is at the door. Four aspiring rock and rollers owe a grand on their instruments and the money lender, his name, so help us, is Wolf, wants the money or repossession.

In one try, Edd Byrnes approaches college credit manager, a staid girl played by Cris Noel. He persuades her to lend him and the other three $2,000, although he doesn't mention the fact that they are all dropouts.

Chris, and three other girls from the credit department decide to deliver the money in person, only to find a wild shindig going full swing at Byrnes Malibu pad. They later decide to return to the scene and get the boys to return to their books.

They are soon stripped to bikinis, jive lingo and surfing Mr. Wolf, all the while, has posted himself at the pad, but is continually outwitted in his attempt at repossession. In the final episode, with the boys set to appear at the Hot Rod and Musical Show, they are pursued by police and Wolf and finally appear onstage dressed in drag. With this unique long hair idea they walk off with the prize money, repay Wolf and decide to return to college.

Musical numbers include: "I Feel So Good," "Surfin Shindig," "Wiggle Like You Tickled," and "We've Got Money." the Supremes sing theme song "Beach Ball." Other groups that guest star are The Four Seasons, The Righteous Brothers, The Hondells and The Walker Brothers.

Director Len Weinrib keeps the pebblepic running at a fast clip, but the editing is sometimes abrupt and slightly jarring. Pic is well acted, which is to say that everyone is likeable, including Mr. Wolf, played by James Wellman. Chris Noel is especially attractive. Edd Byrnes and sidekicks, Robert Logan, Aron Kincaid and Don Edmonds, also act with ease. *Dool.*

Jeg—en Kvinde
(I—A Woman)
(SWEDISH - DANISH)

Copenhagen, Sept. 21.

A Nordisk Film A/S release of a Novaris production. Stars Essy Persson, Preben Marth. Directed by Mac Ahlberg. Camera, Ahlberg; screenplay, Peer Guldbrandsen; music, Sven Gyldmark. At the Nygade Teatret, Copenhagen. Running Time, 105 MINS.

Siv	Essy Persson
Mother	Tove Maes
Father	Erik Hell
Siv's fiance	Preben Koerning
Businessman	Preben Mahrt
Sailor	Bengt Brunskog
Surgeon	Joergen Reenberg
Tough Guy	Frankie Steele

A seldom interrupted string of bedside sex scenes are put within the framework of this thoroughly old-fashioned Danish-Swedish film. The film makes some pretense at attempting artistic photography and artful dialog, but as art it is a rather ridiculous affair.

This aims straight at the market for low - budget, second - feature films of quite dubious taste. However, "I—A Woman" is sure to sell tickets, especially in countries where the censors are as lenient as in Denmark, where the film has been passed without a single cut.

Story is about a young girl of strong sexual impulses who is about to cut loose from her namby-pamby fiance and from her strongly religious parents. She is a trained hospital nurse in a men's ward. She seems ready to take on all comers—patients and doctors inside the hospital, and chance acquaintances on the outside.

The young woman, in short, seems unable to get enough men. but the men cannot get enough of her. They all want her for keeps, she likes them only for the duration. And yet, she is no prostie. The script points her as just a woman; more honest than most and certainly less inhibited.

Mac Ahlberg, one of Sweden's finest black-and-white photographers, has directed. And direction he knows little or nothing about. He botches up even his own camera work. But the Peer Guldbrandsen script, with its dragged-out situations, absence of dramatic conflicts and its puerile dream-dialog is really what destroys what might otherwise have been a strong, honest film version of Siv Holm's bestselling "memoirs."

The stable of Swedish and Danish actors seem to have given up completely. They just stumble along, in and out of beds and dialog. Only Sweden's Essy Persson, who makes her bow in pictures with this one, seems happily unaware of the surrounding banality. She plays her role with vigor and talent, radiating sex and displaying an often-exposed body. *Kell.*

Secret of My Success
(PANAVISION-COLOR)

Uneven comedy meller, filmed in Portugal and England. Minor item for dual playoff.

Metro release of Virginia & Andrew Stone production. Stars Shirley Jones, Stella Stevens, Honor Blackman, James Booth; features Lionel Jeffries, Amy Dolby. Directed by Andrew L. Stone. Screenplay, Andrew L. Stone; camera (Technicolor), David Boulton. Previewed in New York, Sept. 24, '65. Running Time, 112 MINS.

Marigold Murado	Shirley Jones
Violet Lawson	Stella Stevens
Baroness von Lukenburg	Honor Blackman
Arthur Tate	James Booth
Inspector Hobart, Baron von Lukenburg, President Esteda, Earl of Aldershot	Lionel Jeffries
Mrs. Tate	Amy Dolby
Mrs. Pringle	Joan Hickson
Colonel Armandez	Robert Barnete
Pallazio	Nicolau Breyner

There are several capable players in "Secret of My Success," many of them from the British studios. But the screenplay Andrew L. Stone has whipped up is too much of a handicap, and what might have been a bright, little British comedy turns out to be neither comedy nor melodrama. Despite thespian values, directorial touches, three sexy looking femmes and massive sets, total never quite jells. Result is that four splendid portrayals by Lionel Jeffries, representing a tour de force, lose impact in U.S. as a career boost.

Three almost separate yarns are employed to trace the rise of a lowly English town constable to position of ruler in a mythical Latin-American country — and inheritor of a fortune. As James Booth, the lad who achieves wealth and fame, relates "the secret of my success," he points to his mother's guidance and unerring instinct "to do right" as the real secret. Actually, it is his mother's shrewd advice and uncanny conniving that pushes the lad up the ladder.

Initial episode details how his understanding of a comely, little village dressmaker, Stella Stevens, while only a town constable, wins a promotion to police inspector. The curvaceous, red-haired Miss Stevens, puts this across despite all its implausibilities, such as hiding the body of her slain husband.

Booth's first big job as police inspector shows him becoming involved with a Baroness. The most distasteful yarn of all three episodes, this little tale tells about the breeding of giant spiders until they become as big as over-sized bulldogs—and large enough to crush a man to death. Even though played somewhat with tongue-in-cheek, the battle between the spiders and Scotland Yard's experts and police is so absurd it becomes annoying. Even the presence of Honor Blackmang ("Goldfingess, fails to help.

Another sharp maneuver by his mother wins Booth the job of liaison officer to the president of Guanduria, Latin-American mythical land. By helping Shirley Jones, who is secretly plotting a revolution, he winds up as new ruler of this country. It seems that Miss Jones claims she wants to film a picture, with the plot concerning a takeover of the government. The filmmaking idea is a figment of the imagination but, by some quirk of the script, Booth is rated a hero.

And the venture prompts the Earl of Aldershot (Jeffries) to name him to his fortune.

Amy Dolby, the mother, nearly thefts the pic whenever given a chance but top acting laurels go to Jeffries and Booth. *Wear.*

One Way Wahini
(TECHNISCOPE-COLOR)

A surfing pix, this is not. Blond Joy Harmon, carries the show. Plot is neatly coiled around attempt to steal loot from two suspicious crooks. Problem is: is it the adolescent's cup of tea?

Hollywood, Sept. 24.

United Screen Arts release of Continental Pictures, Inc. Production, produced by Leon E. Whiteman. Stars Joy Harmon, Anthony Eisley, Adele Claire, David Whorf and Edgar Bergen; features Lee Kreiger, Ken Mayer, Harold Fong, Alvy Moore, Aime Luce and Ralph Nanalei. Produced and directed by William O. Brown. Screenplay, Rod Larson; editor, George White; camera (Technicolor), John Morrill; sound, Rod Sutton; second unit director, Don Laifer. Reviewed at Beverly Hills Hotel, Sept. 23, '65. Running Time, 80 MINS.

Kit Williams	Joy Harmon
Chick Lindell	Anthony Eisley
Brandy Saveties	Adele Claire
Lou Talbot	David Whorf
Sweeney	Edgar Bergen
Charley Rossi	Lee Kreiger
Hugo Sokol	Ken Mayer
Quong	Harold Fong
Maxwell	Alvy Moore
Tahitian Dancer	Aime Luce
Paulo	Ralph Nanalei

A slick comedy of errors, this kooky, offbeat production, basking in a Hawaiian locale, presents a frisky plot, workable comedic situations, subtle color and eager acting by unknowns, as well as some nicely photographed ethnic dancing (as opposed to ho-hum hula). Blonde newcomer Joy Harmon carries the weight of the show, but plot soon loses crazymixed-up girl approach to concentrate on robbing the robbers story. Film is neither purely for the juves nor for the older set, but film has snicker appeal.

Title refers to girls who buy one way tickets to Hawaii with hope of finding answer to their runaway problems. Joy Harmon, an American type Bridget Bardot, is two weeks on the island when she gets involved with two young guys who soon plot to steal money, which they believe to have been stolen, from two visiting Chicago boobs. The plan doesn't work out as expected, and Miss Harmon is near-raped in one long struggling scene.

Much of what is intended is circumvented in dialog but explicitly understood. The question will be whether this is a sophisticated item for juves or just in bad taste.

Producer-director William O. Brown has directed the Rod Larson screenplay subtly and with a flare for throwing in little hints of things that are to follow. Camera work is excellent and gives fine feeling of island living as it is and not totally romanticized. Particularly captivating are two Hawaiian dance numbers which actually present the dancing at its artistic best. The editing is also first rate.

Miss Harmon is irrepressibly alive and searching for people to correspond with her wave lengths.

She finds it on a level with the boozy beachcomber played by Edgar Bergen, and she also finds herself in all-out rock 'n' roll dancing, for which her ability is inexhaustive. But it's David Whorf who soon has her romantically as well as criminally involved in robbery plot.

Anthony Eisley and Adele Claire are other two who fall in for the ill gotten gain, and they all manage to hold up their end of the acting. Lee Kreiger and Ken Mayer play the Chicago foils and it's difficult to believe that they're not robbers after all. The whole thing ends happily. *Dool.*

Bunny Lake Is Missing
(BRITISH-PANAVISION)

Otto in Hitchcockland. Preminger's try at suspense comes off as worthy effort.

Columbia Pictures release of Otto Preminger production, directed by Preminger. Stars Carol Lynley, Keir Dullea, Laurence Olivier; features Noel Coward, Martita Hunt, Anna Massey, Clive Revill, Finlay Currie. Screenplay, John & Penelope Mortimer, based on novel by Evelyn Piper; camera (Panavision), Denys Coop; editor, Peter Thornton; sound, Jonathan Bates; music, Paul Glass; titles, Saul Bass. Opened Victoria Theatre, Oct. 3, '65. Running Time, **107 MINS.**

Ann	Carol Lynley
Steven	Keir Dullea
Newhouse	Laurence Olivier
Wilson	Noel Coward
Ada Ford	Martita Hunt
Elvira	Anna Massey
Andrews	Clive Revill
Doll Maker	Finlay Currie
Clerk in Shipping Office	Richard Wattis
Cook	Lucie Mannheim
Sister	Megs Jenkins
Taxi Driver	Victor Maddern
First Mother	Delphi Lawrence
Second Mother	Suzanne Neve
Dorothy	Adrienne Corri
Nurse	Kika Markham
Teacher	Jill Melford
Daphne	Damaris Hayman
Policeman	Patrick Jordan
Policewoman	Jane Evers
Finger Print Man	John Sharp
Police Photographer	Geoffrey Frederick
Policeman at Station	Percy Herbert
Rogers	Michael Wynne
Barman	Bill Maxam
Newscaster	Tim Brinton
Man in Soho	Fred Emney
Doctor	David Oxley
Attendant	John Forbes-Robertson
The Zombies	Themselves

Bunny Lake is about the only thing missing from Otto Preminger's exercise in suspense and the viewer is kept in uncertainty about her for most of the film. His first try at suspense since "Laura," Preminger doesn't really achieve that feeling as much as a "when will the other shoe drop?" tension which reaches its proper apex in the final moments.

His gimmick ultimatum that no ticketbuyers will be admitted after the film has started isn't that necessary to keep the plot's outcome from being disclosed (that is apparent early in the film) but it will be a big help in keeping the involved storyline and many characters (most of them unknown to American audiences) straight.

What Preminger has achieved, then, is no minor classic on the level of his own "Laura" but an entertaining, fast-paced exercise in the exploration of a sick mind. Evelyn Piper's 1957 novel dealt entirely with the unpredictable actions of a mother searching for her child (real or imaginary) who had disappeared. To this plot skeleton Preminger has added an equally important character whose predictable actions, engineered by an unconsummated incestuous compulsion, provides the search's principal obstacles.

John and Penelope Mortimer's screenplay uses only the main storyline of the Piper novel, the search for the child (but where the novel kept Bunny Lake's actual existence uncertain until the end, Preminger plants evidence (a la the envelope in "Charade") early in the film (but which most viewers won't notice). The New York setting has been changed to London, (allowing it to be made under the Eady Plan) and characters have been omitted, added or their identities changed. Carrying much of the film on

her shoulders, Carol Lynley, as the mother shoved into a state of near hysteria almost from the beginning, is outstanding. Bordering on exhaustion, she fights to find the strength to cope calmly (and, at the end, alone) with the dangers and uncertainties that beset her. Keir Dullea, as her brother (the character did not exist in the novel), is also cast as highly neurotic. Although he has become so over-identified with these parts as to be an expert in the ways of the wacky, he is, ironically, most effective in earlier scenes where he conveys the natural, if easily-aroused, anger of a devoted brother, resentful of what seems to be official indifference to his sister's plight.

Laurence Olivier's police inspector, a psychiatrist in the novel, is played in the manner of a psychiatrist. While nothing more than a routine role, Olivier does give it dignity and purpose and makes it a calm and restful contrast to the highly-strung emoting of Dullea and Miss Lynley. The Mortimers have given him some excellent dialog, not always relevant to the plot, which he delivers with relish and occasionally, with a touch of malice. One delightful line refers to Noel Coward (who plays Miss Lynley's and Dullea's lecherous and boozy landlord, who supplements his income by reading poetry on the BBC). Olivier asks, "Have you ever heard him read poetry? It's like a country parson gargling molasses."

Coward, whose role is not that important, is also given a curious scene in his apartment, hinting that his sexual tastes veer toward the bizarre. Preminger eschews any love interest in the story, making all the action a comment on the delaying or furthering of the child search. Martita Hunt, as a former teacher (kooky but wise in the ways of children — and grownups who act like children); Anna Massey, as head of the school from which Bunny has supposedly disappeared; and Finlay Currie, as an old dollmaker in whose shop the proper villain is revealed, are outstanding in short but colorful parts. Clive Revill, however, is wasted as Olivier's assistant and goes almost unnoticed.

The large cast isn't wasted, however, many being provided with plot-necessary lines. Although given feature billing, The Zombies, a rock 'n' roll combo, are only seen briefly on a pub's tv set and heard over a hospital radio. They add nothing but noise to the film. While some viewers may deplore the dropping of such characters as Miss Massey without explanation but Preminger's intent, evidently, is to always keep the viewer's attention on the two principals. This is as it should be. Miss Lynley and Dullea give the ending scene, a lengthy one, a chilling atmosphere that manages to avoid telegraphing the outcome.

Denys Coop's use of Panavision and sharply-detailed black-and-white photography to project the action against some scenic but unfamiliar London backgrounds, also helps maintain pace with tracking shots and occasional distortions. Peter Thornton's editing is also an important asset. Paul Glass' score combines music and electronic

sounds with latter used alone occasionally to step up tension. The simple but effective titles by Saul Bass will, as usual, carry over into the film's entire advertising and promotion campaign.
Robe.

Le Tonnerre De Dieu
(The Thunder of God)
(FRENCH-FRANSCOPE)

Paris, Sept. 21.
Comacico release of Films Copernic production. Stars Jean Gabin, Lilli Palmer, Robert Hossein, Michele Mercier; features Georges Geret, Paul Frankeur. Directed by Denys De La Patelliere. Screenplay, Pascal Jardin, De La Patelliere from book by Bernard Clavel; camera, Walter Wottitz; editor, Clauue Durand. At Mercury, Paris, Running Time, **95 MINS.**

Brassac	Jean Gabin
Marie	Lilli Palmer
Simone	Michele Mercier
Marcel	Robert Hossein
Roger	Georges Geret
Gendarme	Paul Frankeur
Priest	Daniel Ceccaldi

This film appears tailored for Jean Gabin's measure but is also a rote trotting out of his anarchic character full of anger and tirades. Somewhat talky, surface and soapy, this appears primarily a local entry because of many inside allusions. It should have some specialized chances abroad on the Gabin name and its outspoken, if synthetic, dealing with the regeneration of a joy girl and a reprobate.

Gabin is a noted veterinarian who is prone to long drunks. He brings home homeless animals, drunks, tramps and one day a prostie. Gabin at first does not know whether he wants her sexually or is attracted to her because of a hankering for a child.

After fighting off her pimp, the reformed joy girl falls for a neighboring farmer and Gabin rejoices. in becoming a grandfather.

All this is told solidly by director Denys De La Patelliere in a series of scenes which are more talky than visual. Its look at lowlife and country stuffiness remain skin-deep, and it all rests on the actors who are all adequate.

Gabin is his usual stormy self with a mite of self indulgence to rob the character of the depth and meaning it needed to give the pic more body. Lilli Palmer os adequate as his harassed wife who finally turns, as are Michele Mercier, as the reformed joy girl; Robert Hossein and Georges Geret. Pic is technically sound. *Mosk.*

Situation Hopeless— But Not Serious

"The Collector"—German style. Pleasant comedy, filmed in Germany but only thinly Teutonic, may have too much "gemutlichkeit" for the action fans. Needs special handling.

Paramount Pictures release of Gottfried Reinhardt production. Stars Alec Guinness, Michael Connors, Robert Redford; features Anita Hoefer, Mady Rahl, Paul Dahlke, Frank Wolff, John Briley, Elisabeth Von Molo, Carola Regnier. Produced and directed by Gottfried Reinhardt. Screenplay, Silvia Reinhardt, adapted by Jan Lustig, based on Robert Shaw novel, "The Hiding Place." Camera, Kurt Hasse; film editor, Walter Boos;

sound, Walter Ruhland; music, Harold Byrns. Reviewed at Paramount home-office, N.Y., Sept. 30, '65. Running time: **97 MINS.**

Herr Frick	Alec Guinness
Lucky	Michael Connors
Hank	Robert Redford
Edeltraud	Anita Hoefer
Lissie	Mady Rahl
Herr Neusel	Paul Dahlke
QM Master Sergeant	Frank Wolff
Sergeant	John Briley
Wanda	Elisabeth Von Molo
Senta	Carola Regnier

Everything is pleasant about this filmed version of actor-writer Robert Shaw's "The Hiding Place," filmed at the Bavaria Film Studios in Munich-Geiselgasteig and on German locations, and that may be the trouble with it.

It's a pleasant story, played by pleasant people and directed in a pleasant style. With the exception of two really funny scenes, however, there's a shortage of action and an overage of pleasantness. The problem of properly purveying this piece of gemutlichkeit will need some of Paramount's sharpest ad brains. His obvious effort to keep both sides of the Rhine happy has dulled the edges of producer-director Gottfried Reinhardt's satirical scalpel. Some of the fault may be in Silvia (Mrs. Gottfried) Reinhardt's screenplay, two-removed from Shaw's original story, being based on an adaptation by Jan Lustig.

The plot is simple but full of potential, with Alec Guinness playing a timid, lonely and rather eccentric German shopclerk into whose hands fall, literally, two American fliers (Michael Connors and Robert Redford). The Yanks take shelter in his cellar after parachuting into Germany, to find themselves trapped in an ironbound sanctuary, planned and outfitted by their host's dear, departed mother whose astrological gifts included prediction of the war and need for shelter, hence the cellar.

Guinness, a "good German," becomes so fond of his prisoners that he keeps them, until six years after the war has ended. This takes a bit of doing, naturally, and the Americans have some periods of uncertainty as to who's the nuttier, the jailer or the jailed. They do eventually find freedom, but only after going through a period of believing they're in a victorious Germany (giving the film one of its two hilarious moments). The ending is pat and predictable.

Because of the necessarily confined area, the three males dominate the film, with Guinness easily outshining the able but less-experienced Americans. Connors ably handles his role of a loud but likable sergeant and Redford, making his film debut, shapes up as a promising new face for the screen. This has already been recognized as he's set for the lead opposite Natalie Wood in "This Property Is Condemned."

While the supporting cast is given little opportunity, the film's best bit is shared by Guinness and Mady Rahl as a hostess-cum-madam whom he's trying to line up as a Christmas present for Connors, who has expressed a desire for a "dame." Guinness' description of his "friend," meant to prepare Miss Rahl for an unusual type, only succeeds in convincing

her that it is Guinness who is off his rocker. Other roles are well handled, particularly Anita Hoefer as a Hitler Youth type who winds up as the girlfriend of a Yank master sergeant (Frank Wolff); Paul Dahlke as Guinness' boss, who changes political affiliations faster than a chameleon changes colors; and Elizabeth von Molo as a screwball teenager the fliers encounter while escaping.

Kurt Hasse's excellent black and white camerawork blends scenic exteriors with studio shots and evades the static, confinde atmosphere one could expect of the **cellar area, letting his camera** roam about the intricate, highly ornate "junk" with which are director Rolf Zehetbauer has littered the set. Harold Byrns score begins with a spoof of the oompah-oompah German band and provides satiric undertones that help point up Reinhardt's gentle jabs at both Germanic and occupation force attitudes. *Robe.*

Murder In Mississippi

Sexploitation-slanted quickie on Mississippi civil rights killings more concerned with violence in assorted flavors and mixed races than justice, but will appeal to the mayhem market.

Tiger Production (Herbert S. Altman). Features Sheilla Britton, Sam Stewart, Derek Crane, Lou Stone, Martin St. John, John Steel, Wayne Foster, Dick Stone, Otis Young, Irv Seldin, Frank Philadelphia. Directed by J. P. Mawra. Screenplay, Altman; camera, Warner Rose; editor, Mawra; music, Joe Lesko. Screened in projection room, N.Y., Sept. 29, '65. Running Time: **85 MINS.**

About the only thing this film, made in and around Philadelphia but set in Mississippi, has to do with the slaying of civil rights workers in the southern state is the use of such an event as the basis for crowding as much violence and sex (and combinations of the two) into its 80-some minutes, as possible.

Producer Herbert S. Altman, who also takes responsibility for the script, has been successful in one thing. The events, as presented, are probably exploitable both north and south since he makes both sides equally guilty, at least morally. About the only territory he may have eliminated is Virginia as his heroine, played by Sheilla Britton, is named Carol Lee Byrd (that's double indemnity). She's written, and played, as a neurotic, involved in hysterical protest, or participating in various sex-situations, ranging from rape to romance.

The incidents that befall the three Negro and two white civil rights workers (only the two girls —one Negro, one white—come out of it alive) include beatings, shootings, kidnapping, rape, variations on sex (Negro boy-Negro girl, Negro prostitute-white boy), and, not quite consummated (Negro boy-white girl). To titillate the ear as well as the eye, during a ridiculous hearing, the white U.S. commissioner, a female, enunciates the word, "castration," with emphasis and frequency, accompanied by appropriate leers.

The one important contribution

this trash may contribute to the American film industry is to provide almost any group with censorship ammunition. Its sketchy tie-in with civil rights is more than diluted by the arbitrary characteristics of the roles as written. They're portrayed as uncertain about their cause, potentially violent (one Negro pulls a switchblade), and morally loose. White Southerners are also shown as crude, given to violence, and easily swayed by the possibility of material gain.

Even the one thing that is professional about the film works against it. All the voices are distinct, well-modulated and completely northern, even those of poor Negro sharecroppers. Acting ranges from plausible to unbelievably bad with the letter prize going to Dick Stone as the "movie star" brother of Carol Lee Byrd. No one is really good in film although John Steel, as a lethargic deputy sheriff, makes the best impression by just sitting still and not grimacing when on camera.

Warner Rose's camerawork is good when shooting outside scenes but is hampered by the poor lighting of interiors. Almost as offensive as the acting is Joe Lesko's music, poured on fortissimo and frequently drowning out the lines, a melange of every dramatic background cliche. Little to say about J. P. Mawra's "direction."

Distribution of the film will be via states rights handling. Advertising will evidently follow the pattern of the pressbook which plays up the sexual scenes. Stills shown include scenes evidently cut out of the finished picture. *Robe.*

Who Killed Teddy Bear

Exploitation entry for sex market; okay grosses indicated.

Hollywood, Sept. 30.
Magna release of Everett Rosenthal production. No character names. Stars Sal Mineo, Juliet Prowse, Jan Murray, Elaine Stritch. Others in cast Margot Bennett, Dan Travanty, Diane Moore, Rex Everhart, Alex Fisher Stanley Beck, Frank Campanella, Bruce Glover. Directed by Joseph Cates. Screenplay, Leon Tokatyan, Arnold Drake; story, Drake; camera, Joseph Brun; art direction, Hank Aldrich; editor, Angelo Ross; asst. director, Sidney Kupperschmid; sound, Charles Federmack; music, Charles Calello. Reviewed at L. A. screening room, Sept. 29, '65. Running Time, **94 MINS.**

Central character of this seamy exploitation offering is a sex psychotic who targets his desires on a virtuous young discotheque hostess in N.Y. Starring Sal Mineo and Juliet Prowse for name value, the action, designed strictly for shock appeal, includes violence, murder, rape, lesbianism, and may be ballyed for okay returns in its intended market.

Director Joseph Cates manages realistic feeling by shrewd use of Manhattan street backgrounds, well photographed by Joseph Brun, as well as sensational treatment which may find certain censorship problems. Leon Tokatyan-Arnold Drake script, based on a story by Drake, dwells almost clinically on Mineo's lust. Some of the footage of the Everett Rosenthal production, including

young pervert's emotions as he dreams of his quest and his indecent murmurings as he continually telephones her, is ultra frank and conceivably could run into group objections.

Mineo as the moody discotheque bus-boy who falls in love with Miss Prowse plays a downbeat role which probably won't progress his career but is convincing. Miss Prowse registers in a nicely restrained performance. Jan Murray, swinging from nitery-tv stand-up comic routines, is good as a police lieutenant with a compulsion to destroy every sex deviate, and Elaine Stritch, discotheque manager who accompanies the hostess home ostensibly to protect her, delivers well in a sharp-tongued role. Competent support is furnished by balance of cast, including Margot Bennett, Dan Travanty and Diana Moore.

Hank Aldrich's art direction, particularly of the club sequences, is excellent; Charles Calello's music score fits patly; Angelo Ross' editing tight. *Whit.*

The War Lord
(PANAVISION-COLOR)

Actionful 11th century costumer starring Charlton Heston and Richard Boone for name value; sturdy commercial potential.

Hollywood, Sept. 29.
Universal release of Walter Seltzer production. Stars Charlton Heston, Richard Boone; features Rosemary Forsyth, Guy Stockwell, Maurice Evans. Directed by Franklin Schaffner. Screenplay, John Collier, Millard Kaufman; based on play, "The Lovers," by Leslie Stevens; camera (Technicolor), Russell Metty; art direction, Alexander Golitzen, Henry Bumstead; music, Jerome Moross; editor, Folmar Blangsted; asst. director, Douglas Green; sound, Waldon O. Watson, William Russell. Reviewed at Academy Award Theatre, Sept. 28, '65. Running Time, **120 MINS.**

Chrysagon	Charlton Heston
Bors	Richard Boone
Bronwyn	Rosemary Forsyth
Priest	Maurice Evans
Draco	Guy Stockwell
Odins	Niall MacGinnis
Frisian Prince	Henry Wilcoxon
Marc	James Farentino
Volc	Sammy Ross
Piet	Woodrow Parfrey
Holbracht	John Alderson
Tybald	Allen Jaffe
Rainault	Michael Conrad
Dirck	Dal Jenkins
Boy Prince	Johnny Jensen
Chrysagon Man	Forrest Wood
Old Woman	Belle Mitchell

"The War Lord" digs back into the 11th Century against a Druid setting in ancient Normandy for unfoldment of its generally fast action. The type of adventure costumer that traditionally meets with favorable boxoffice reaction, sturdy commercial prospects should be realized, particularly with the name of Charlton Heston — who enjoys wide following for this sort of presentation— and flashy exploitation potential to spark its chances. Overall would benefit, however, by tighter editing to snap up tempo.

Producer Walter Seltzer has given his Panavision-Technicolor picturization of the Leslie Stevens' play, "The Lovers" — finely lensed by Russell Metty to lend realism and pictorial beauty—elaborate mounting and clash battle movement to attract global payoff.

Franklin Schaffner's direction, while not always overcoming deficiencies of convincing dialog and star's sometimes vacillating characterization, in the main projects the proper spirit of a derring-do, days-of-yore melodrama. His battle scenes, utilizing the weapons and tactics of the period and in which he was assisted by Joe Canutt as action coordinator (stunts), are particularly well handled.

Script by John Collier and Millard Kaufman presents Heston as war lord of the Duke of Normandy, detailed to oversee a primitive Druid village on a barren shore of the North Sea, whose inhabitants are constantly harassed by Frisian invaders from the north. With him are his brother, Guy Stockwell, and Richard Boone, his faithful aide in 20 years of warring. Plottage dwells on his mad passion for a village girl, claiming her on her wedding night according to custom of "droit de seigneur"—a lord's right of the first night: Plot twist: bride refuses to return to her enraged groom.

Heston is more convincing in his battle scenes than in romancing Rosemary Forsyth, but nevertheless delivers a hard-hitting performance. Boone scores effectively in a subdued but powerful role. Top acting honors, however, go to Stockwell, as the younger knight who turns against his brother in an exciting climax and is killed by Heston, whom he has tried to supplant in the Norman duke's graces. Part is film debut for Stockwell, son of Guy and brother of Dean, authough he's wellknown in Coast legit.

Miss Forsyth is pretty as distaff interest and Maurice Evans makes the most of a priest characterization whose charges are the villagers. Niall MacGinnis, Druid chief who is femme's foster father and father of James Farentino (also debuting) to whom girl has been betrothed since childhood, plays a sympathetic part and Farentino likewise is good as the vengeful husband who enlists aid of the Frisians against the Normans when his bride remains with the war lord. Balance of cast, including Henry Wilcoxon as the Frisian king, furnish hefty support.

Technical credits are mostly on the plus side, art direction by Alexander Golitzen and Henry Bumstead a particular standout. Suitable music score is composed by Jerome Moross. *Whit.*

Spaceflight IC-1
(BRITISH)

Futuristic space meller. Weak script, direction, and performances. Skimpy production values. Somewhat exploitable but strictly lowercase.

Hollywood, Oct. 1.

Twentieth Century-Fox release of a Lippert Pictures Ltd. production, produced by Robert L. Lippert, Jack Parsons. Features Bill Williams, Kathleen Breck, John Cairney, Donald Churchill, Jeremy Longhurst, Linda Marlowe, Margo Mayne, Norma West. Directed by Bernard Knowles. Screenplay, Harry Spalding; camera, Geoffrey Faithfull; editor, Robert Winter; music, Elisabeth Lutyens; sound, Jock May; art direction, Harry White; asst. director, Gordon Gilbert. Reviewed at 20th-Fox Studios, Sept. 24, '65. Running Time, **63 MINS.**

Mead Ralston .... Bill Williams
Kate Saunders .... Kathleen Breck
Steven Thomas .... John Cairney
Carl Walcott .... Donald Churchill
John Saunders .... Jeremy Longhurst
Helen Thomas .... Linda Marlowe
Joyce Walcott .... Margo Mayne
Jan Ralston .... Norma West
Griffith .... Tony Doonan
Capt. Burnett .... Andrew Downie
Dr. Garth .... John Lee
Webster .... Chuck Julian
Clown .... Max Kirby
Don .... Mark Lester
Michael .... Stewart Middleton
Robert .... Anthony Honour

"Spaceflight IC-1" is a modest budgeted b&w sci-fi programmer about a space ship en route some 50 years hence to establish a new earth colony. Made at England's Shepperton Studios, the Robert L. Lippert production is thin in the story, acting, directing and production value departments, thus negating a solid original basic plot premise which may, nevertheless, be used to sell the 20th-Fox release in lowercase slotting pected.

Harry Spalding's script had the germ of an excellent story of the genuine horror of a future civilization based on computer-programmed lives. Couples are selected for a space journey based on scientific parameters of health, blood and technical knowledge. They are permitted to procreate on a regulated birth control plan. There's no room for emotion or feeling in their world, nor for any physical deformity.

Under Bernard Knowles' routine direction, top-featured Bill Williams is adequate as the cold ship captain who takes his orders from a worldgovernment group known as RULE. Internal crisis is sparked when medic John Cairney's wife Linda Marlowe is discovered to have a serious illness, untreatable since the ship carries no insulin. Subsequent mutiny, various mild personality clashes and slightly upbeat climax conclude the brief footage which editor Robert Winter has held to 63 minutes, including prologue.

Combination of elements have defeated the impact of the film, including traditional British underplaying — okay in contemporary situations — which in futuristic melodrama simply amounts to flat throwaway of dialog and b&w lensing give little visual interest.

Technical credits are adequate. Film's length indicates more than a casual eye on eventual sale to television. *Murf.*

Village Of The Giants
(COLOR)

Teenage sci-fi exploitationer. Good special effects. Soft script, direction and acting.

Hollywood, Sept. 30.

Embassy Pictures release of a Bert I. Gordon production, directed by Gordon. Features Tommy Kirk, Johnny Crawford, Beau Bridges, Joy Harmon, Bob Random, Gail Gilmore, Tisha Sterling, Ronny Howard, Tim Rooney, Kevin O'Neal, Charla Doherty, Toni Basil. Screenplay, Alan Caillou, based on story by Gordon from H. G. Wells' novel, "Food Of The Gods"; camera (Pathecolor), Paul C. Vogel; editor, John Bushelman; music, Jack Nitzsche; songs, Ron Elliott, Frank Slay, Frederick A. Picariello, Nitzsche. Russ Titleman; sound, John Carter, Charles Grenzbach; art direction, Franz Bachelin; special effects, Gordon, Flora Gordon; asst. director, Jim Rosenberger. Reviewed at Paramount Studios, Sept. 29, '65. Running Time, **81 MINS.**

Mike .... Tommy Kirk
Horsey .... Johnny Crawford
Fred .... Beau Bridges
Genius .... Ronny Howard
Merrie .... Joy Harmon
Rick .... Bob Random
Jean .... Tisha Sterling
Nancy .... Charla Doherty
Pete .... Tim Rooney
Harry .... Kevin O'Neal
Elsa .... Gail Gilmore
Red .... Toni Basil
Chuck .... Hank Jones
Fatso .... Jim Begg
Georgette .... Vicki London
Sheriff .... Joseph Turkel
Singers .... The Beau Brummels, Freddy Cannon, Mike Clifford

Four teenage couples steal a chemical potion which enlarges physical size, thus turning small burg into "Village of The Giants." Bert I. Gordon production has some excellent special effects but little more. Script never delivers its promise, and adequate performances, at best, are the result of limp direction. Some tunes emphasize the monotony. Few thrills for solid exploitation push, although the Embassy release should recoup via fast saturation playoff in teenage situations.

"Village," first of 13 pix being made by Gordon for Joseph E. Levine in an equal partnership arrangement, is aimed at the youth crowd, but the scattershot concept will keep it from maximum market impact. Elements of television comedy, music, teenage rebellion, sex and fantasy compete in a hodgepodge through which only Gordon's special effects knowhow seems to stand out, but just slightly, since the inherent action and shock angles are never developed.

Alan Caillou's rambling script, based on a Gordon original drawn from an H. G. Wells' tome, focusses on eight hedonistic teenagers who drift into town after their car has been wrecked in an avalanche. **Beau Bridges, Joy Harmon, Bob Random, Tisha Sterling, Tim Rooney, Gail Gilmore, Kevin O'Neal and Vicki London comprise the octet which is introed in a sensual teen sequence staged in rain and mud.**

Tommy Kirk and Charla Doherty are the teenage lovers interrupted by latter's brother, Ronny Howard, a juve genius who has accidently invented some food that makes living things grow bigger. The eight stranded teeners steal the stuff, eat it, and get a superiority complex.

A submissive sheriff, Joseph Turkel, effectively surrenders the town to the giants with slightly more than a whimper. Johnny Crawford, Hank Jones and Jim Begg join Kirk in attempts to subdue the giants, all ineffective until the kid discovers an antidote. At regular intervals, The Beau Brummels, Freddy Cannon and Mike Clifford sing some forgettable tunes. Toni Basil, a redheaded looker, choreographed the terpery and personally displays her talents.

Director Gordon hasn't delivered enough of the potential action; the giants threaten, the others react, in both cases sluggishly. Potential of any thesp is nearly impossible to evaluate.

Special effects work is fine, including clever matching of blown up ducks, dog, cat and spider with life-size humans. Farciot Edouart's process photography is a big asset. Paul Vogel's camera, often buttocks-oriented, is crisp. John Bushelman has edited to a tight 81 minutes, long enough for this one.

Other technical credits are professional. *Murf.*

The Face Of Fu Manchu
(BRITISH—COLOR—SCOPE)

Slick production of first in series of Fu Manchu pix has proper combinations of suspense and corn to possibly spark renaissance.

Seven Arts Pictures release of a Hallam (Oliver A. Unger-Harry Alan Towers) production. Features Christopher Lee, Nigel Green, Howard Marion-Crawford, Carl Jannsen, Karin Dor, Tsai Chin, Walter Rilla. Directed by Don Sharp. Screenplay, Peter Welbeck, based on Fu Manchu character created by Arthur Sarsfield Ward (Sax Rohmer); camera (Technicolor-Techniscope), Ernest Steward; editor, John Trumper; sound, Fred Hughesdon, Ken Cameron; music, Christopher Whelen. Reviewed in New York, Sept. 29, '65. Running Time: **90 MINS.**

Fu Manchu .... Christopher Lee
Nayland Smith .... Nigel Green
Sir Charles Fortesque .... James Robertson Justice
Dr. Walter Petrie .... Howard Marion-Crawford
Lin Tang .... Tsai Chin
Carl Jannsen .... Joachim Fuchsberger
Maria .... Karin Dor
Professor Muller .... Walter Rilla
Professor Gaskell .... Harry Brogan
Lotus .... Poulet Tu
Hanumon .... Peter Mossbacher

While far short of the "class" horror flims put out by Britain's Hammer Films and American producer Roger Corman, this Hallam Productions venture into the market is a strong beginning. Producers Oliver A. Unger and Harry Alan Towers (latter gets screen credit but not in Seven Arts trade-review printed credits) have borrowed such basic ingredients of the Hammer and Corman pictures as strong use of colors, a pre-sold and internationally-known character (Fu Manchu, who isn't called Doctor in this epic, was created in 1911) and a mixture of international cast members.

Confident in success of this commercial effort, Hallam has second Fu Manchu feature starting production in November and third warming up in the "bull" pen. Seven Arts will peddle "Face" as top-half of double bill, spot it can easily fill. Film, shot entirely on location in and around Dublin, has Irish settings doubling for London, where most of action takes place, as well as China, an English coastal town and even Tibet.

Quibblers may note that most of the non-Orientals cast as Chinese, including title roler Christopher Lee, look something less than authentic (Gerry Fletcher's makeup being at fault), particularly in scenes with such real Chinese as Tsai Chin (Fu Manchu's daughter) and Poulet Tu as Nayland Smith's (Nigel Green) house servant. Smith is Fu Manchu's sworn enemy. As a concession to the international market, Germans Karin Dor, Joachim Fuchsberger, Walter Rilla and Peter Mossbacher are cast as the daughter of Prof. Muller, his assistant, the professor and Fu Manchu's lieutenant, respectively.

Nigel Green and Howard Marion-Crawford are excellent (and should be retained) as Nayland Smith and his assistant, Rohmer's answer to Sherlock Holmes and Dr. Watson. James Robertson Justice has a cameo role as the

director of the British Museum which plays a key part. Harry Brogan gets in a few good moments as an absent-minded scientist whose work is necessary to Fu Manchu's battle plans.

Christopher Lee's villain needs more work by the usually impressive actor who has played both monsters and Sherlock Holmes. His required dignity and slow movement put him at a disadvantage in the role as his only communication must be by voice and visually.

The plot is of little consequence as Peter Welbeck's screenplay allows Smith to dominate the film when it should, of course, be completely Fu Manchu until the last-minute rescue. Some of the sequences are first class—the drowning by Fu Manchu of a traitorous female servant in a glass-doored vault under the Thames and his destruction of an entire village.

Director Don Sharp gets sufficient pace into the admittedly cornball goings-on to prevent it from collapsing into comedy. He might have left a more suspenseful ending, however, had he ended the film after the mass escape from the underground vault rather than tack on a, by comparison, flat finish with the Tibetan trek. A red-herring pre-title sequence has Fu Manchu being beheaded so, presumably, the next one will start with his being blown up (this one's ending).

Ernest Steward's Technicolor camerawork, thanks to the authenticity added by the Dublin background and some carefully-researched props, is a major asset. Christopher Whelen's music, while not too original, does avoid the usual Oriental motifs.

Previous interpreters of the Oriental badman have included Warner Oland and Boris Karloff. Rohmer wrote 14 novels dealing with the character but only four have been filmed. Hopefully, Hallam Prods. will stick to the Rohmer properties and not veer off into such fantasties as "Fu Manchu Meets James Bond." *Robe.*

Ghidrah, The Three-Headed Monster
(JAPANESE—COLOR)

Three stooges of the monster world—Godzilla, Rodan and Mothra—team up to lick the new contender. This Honda vehicle is welcome addition to popular monster market.

Walter Reade - Sterling (Continental Dist.) release of a Toho Co. production. Stars Ghidrah, Godzilla, Rodan and Mothra; features Yosuke Natsuki, Yuriko Hoshi, Hiroshi Koizumi, Takashi Shimura, Emi Ito, Yumi Ito, Eiko Wakabayashi, Hisaya Ito. Directed by Inoshiro Honda. Screenplay, Shinichi Sekizawa; camera (Eastmancolor), Hajime Koizumi; editor, Ryohei Fujii; special effects, Eiji Tsuburaya; sound effects, Hisashi Shimonaga; music, Ikira Ifukube. Reviewed in New York, Sept. 30, '65. Running time: **85 MINS.**

(Dubbed in English)

Honda, to most Americans, may mean a motorcycle but to the Japanese and to all sci-fi film aficionados, it means Inoshiro Honda, Japan's master of the monster market. Although most of Honda's earlier unearthly eics have gone to American International, the

latest, and possibly the best, has been acquired by Walter Reade-Sterling's Continental Dist.

"Ghidrah," as the subtitle implies, is a three-headed monster (whose design is an unblushing copy of the dragon in Hiroshi Inagaki's "Nippon Tanjo") which invades Earth after depopulating Mars. As Honda never throws away any of his old monsters, Ghidrah comes to no good end when Godzilla and Rodan, sworn enemies, are conned into helping Mothra give the upstart invader his comeuppance.

Director Honda continues his policy of interlacing human action with that of the monsters without ever actually bringing them face to face. The movement of huge crowds of people is so expertly combined with the special effects footage, however, that the viewer is unlikely to quibble. A great help, of course, is the ability of special effects supervisor Eiji Tsuburaya to give his belligerent behemoths some human qualities, with Godzilla the walkaway champ in personality but Mothra the most sympathetic. When the viewer finds himself cheering on the trio of unlikely allies, it's a tribute to Honda's ability to capture an audience.

The humans concerned are only along for the ride and are never allowed to encroach on the activities of the monsters. They manage to provide plenty of action, however, with a subplot of assassins trying to kill a visiting princess. These films are now cast with some familiar (to art house patrons) faces including Takashi Shimura (who starred in Akira Kurosawa's "Ikiru") as a scientist and, although unbilled, Eiji Okada ("Ugly American" and "Hiroshima, Mon Amour" star) as a geologist. Emi and Yumi Ito, the twins from "Mothra," are also featured.

Hajime Koizumi's Eastmancolor camerawork is sometimes garish but fits the monster motif. Akira Ifukube's score is more western than oriental but never intrudes. The dubbing is, as usual, atrocious. *Robe.*

Marie Chantal Contre Dr. Kha
(Marie Chantal Against Dr. Kha)
(FRENCH—HISPANO—ITALO —MOROCCAN)
(COLOR)
Paris, Sept. 28.

SNC release of Georges De Beauregard, Dia, Mega, Maghreb, Uni Films production. Stars Marie Laforet, Francisco Rabal; features Roger Hanin, Serge Reggiani, Akim Tamiroff, Charles Denner. Directed by Claude Chabrol. Screenplay, Christian Yve, Daniel Boulanger, Chabrol, based on the character created by Jacques Chazot; camera (Eastmancolor) Jean Rabier; editor, Jacques Gaillard. At Ermitage, Paris. Running Time, 110 MINS.

Marie Chantal	Marie Laforet
Paco	Francisco Rabal
Dr. Kha	Akim Tamiroff
Ivanov	Serge Reggiani
Johnson	Charles Denner
Bruno	Roger Hanin
Olga	Stephane Audran

Putting a French snob into a James Bondish situation, but peppering it with suspense, some impertinent comedy and a fine balance makes this an entertaining pic that could cash in on the current tastes. Good local and in-

ternational prospects are in store for this perky production.

Marie Chantal is a haughty, rich French girl suddenly handed an important jewel by a French Secret Service man. He is killed and many people soon are after the gem, including the mysterious Dr. Kha, who wants to rule the world. Inept American and Russo undercover men and an idealist want to preserve the secret contained in the jewel.

It seems that a formula is locked into the gem that can give the one having it power over all mankind. All of this is not important, but the well-mounted adventures are. The stubborn Miss Chantal wants to hold onto the jewel and eventually outwits all those seeking it, including Dr. Kha, with the pic ending on hint that there may be a sequel.

Claude Chabrol, one of the first New Wavers, show he can turn his acerbic wit to fine results in a commercial pic. Having written a book on Alfred Hitchcock, he reveals he can use the master's suspense-comedic tactics with ease and personal finesse.

Murders in broad daylight, or in a club where a death battle is thought part of the show, have their impact. Equally exciting is a a chase through a Moroccan market of Marie Chantal by a razor-wielding henchman of Dr. Kha.

Good color and fine pacing in the mock adventures have this one of the better pix of this kind to come out of France. Miss Laforet makes her character stuffy and pouting but still manages some human warmth. This keeps her character from being stereotyped.

Others are fine, especially Serge Reggiani, as a harrassed Soviet agent, and Charles Denner, as a suave Yank Secret Service man. It all moves in colorful surroundings. Akim Tamiroff's limning of the sinister Dr. Kha has the right blend of satiric menace and self-indulgence to sum up the film's appeal. This shows that talent can make old formulas ingratiating and entertaining. *Mosk.*

The Loved One

Way out attempt at satire of funeral practices in California mortuary, cued by Evelyn Waugh's 1948 tome plus added Southern discomfort. Metro is selling it as film "with something to offend everybody." May stir lotsa dispute. Hard to sell.

Hollywood, Sept. 25.

Metro release of Martin Ransohoff production, produced by John Calley, Haskell Wexler. Stars Robert Morse, Jonathan Winters, Anjanette Comer; features Rod Steiger, Dana Andrews, Milton Berle, James Coburn, John Gielgud, Tab Hunter, Margaret Leighton, Liberace, Roddy McDowall, Robert Morley, Lionel Stander. Directed by Tony Richardson. Screenplay, Terry Southern, Christopher Isherwood; based on novel by Eve'vn Waugh; camera, Haskell Wexler; music, John Addison; editors, Antony Gibbs, Hal Ashby, Brian Smedley-Aston; production design, Rouben Ter-Arutunian; asst. director, Kurt Neumann. Reviewed at Metro Studios. Sept. 24, '65. Running Time, **119 MINS.**

Dennis Barlow	Robert Morse
Wilbur Glenworthy, Harry Glenworthy	Jonathan Winters
Aimee Thanatogenos	Anjanette Comer
Mr. Joyboy	Rod Steiger
General Brinkman	Dana Andrews
Mr. Kenton	Milton Berle
Immigration Officer	James Coburn
Sir Francis Hinsley	John Gielgud
Guide	Tab Hunter
Mrs. Kenton	Margaret Leighton
Mr. Starker	Liberace
D. J., Jr.	Roddy McDowall
Sir Ambrose Abercrombie	Robert Morley
The Guru Brahmin	Lionel Stander
Joyboy's Mother	Ayllene Gibbons
Assistant to the Guru Brahmin	Bernie Kopell
Secretary to D. J., Jr.	Asa Maynor
English Club Official	Alan Napier

"The Loved One," whatever its merits or demerits, is likely to become one of the most disputatious features of the year. Based on British author Evelyn Waugh's scathing satire of the mortuary business in California, the Martin Ransohoff production goes so way out in treatment — frequently beyond all bounds of propriety in an attempt at brilliance — that its appeal probably will be restricted to circles which like their entertainment weird.

At best, to touch even lightly a subject so emotional and so intimate to people in their most trying hour — arranging for the burial of a loved one — requires tact and great delicacy, exercised here with about as much finesse as a Main Street burlesque house. To reduce this further to a travesty, the producers can expect many to take offense, particularly since poor taste is prominent in the Terry Southern-Christopher Isherwood script.

Most of the subtlety of Waugh's approach is lost in an episodic screenplay bearing only a wavering story line and given often to sight gags. Tony Richardson in his direction (perhaps in fond remembrance of "Tom Jones") seems enchanted more with the idea of perhaps shocking the sensitivities with what seldom is satire but more often heavy-handed engagement of an offbeat premise, than dishing up fresh divertisement. Despite occasional flashes of humor, the fact remains such humor is usually gruesome and not conducive to expected word-of-mouth bally.

Story centers around the pomp and ceremony attendant upon the daily operation of a posh mortuary and a climaxing idea (not in the book) by a sanctimonious owner of a Southern California cemetery of orbiting cadavers into space—"to get those stiffs off my property"—so he can convert to a senior citizens' paradise for additional profit.

Within this fragile framework, characters have a field day as step-by-step funeral arrangements are completed for a Hollywood suicide; cemetery officials and Air Force brass toss an orgy in the casket room; a femme embalmer commits suicide by embalming herself after her romancing with an English poet and cemetery's chief mortician goes sour, and she becomes the first Loved One to go into orbit.

Robert Morse as the poet who falls in love with the lady cosmetician (later promoted to embalmer) while making arrangements for his uncle's interment, plays it light and airy, like a soul apart. He has one broadly funny sequence, when as an assistant at a pet cemetery he goes to pick up the carcass of a dog owned by Margaret Leighton and Milton Berle, both of whom score in brief but hilarious roles. Anjanette Comer, whose life is dedicated to her work and Whispering Glades Memorial Park — which many Southern California residents will recognize as a world-famous necropolis gradually surrounding Los Angeles—gives almost ethereal portraiture to her embalmer character.

Jonathan Winters appears in a dual role, shining both as the owner of Whispering Glades and his twin brother, who operates the nearby pet graveyard and is patron of a 13-year-old scientific whiz who invents a rocket capable of projecting bodies into orbit. Rod Steiger clothes his mortician part with oddball characteristics: when he thinks femme loves him, he prepares bodies — Loved Ones — with a smile on their face for her to make up; when her affections wane, their countenances are fierce.

A slick bit of casting has Liberace deserting his smile and sequined tails for the sombre role of casket salesman, which he fulfills with a flair. Dana Andrews is an Air Force general helping the Whispering Glades owner with his plan to rocket Loved Ones into space; John Gielgud, a member of the Hollywood British colony, who hangs himself after being fired by his studio; Robert Morley, the pompous colony leader; Roddy McDowall, studio head; Lionel Stander, a drunken advice-to-the-lovelorn columnist, all handling parts well. Tab Hunter and James Coburn are in for bits, and Ayllene Gibbons is Steiger's ravening mother who spends her time in bed gorging herself and watching tv food commercials.

Film, which lists John Calley and Haskell Wexler as producers with Ransohoff, carries expensive production values and technical credits are well executed. Wexler handles photography; Rouben Ter-Arutunian, production design; John Addison, music score; Antony Gibbs, Hal Ashby and Brian Smedley-Aston, editing. *Whit.*

L'Homme D'Istanbul
(The Man From Istanbul)
(FRENCH-SPANISH-COLOR)
Paris, Oct. 5.

CCFC release of EDIC-Isasi production. Stars Horst Buchholz; features Sylva Koscina, Perrette Pradier, Mario Adorf, George Rigaud. Directed by Antonio Isasi. Screenplay, Nat Wachsberger; camera (Eastmancolor), Juan Liar; music, Georges Gaverentz. At Paris, Paris. Running Time, 120 MINS.

Tony .... Horst Buchholz
Kenny .... Sylva Koscina
Liz .... Perrette Pradier
Bill .... Mario Adorf
CIA Chief .... Georges Rigaud
Brain .... Angel Picazo

(In English)

This is a fairly clever piecing together of a group of foreign talents into an English speaking pic with enough action and knowhow to slant it for good playoff chances in the U. S. and in most markets. The Horst Buchholz name may also help.

Picture is a mixture of pre-war U. S. anti-hero, adventure pix with Bondish gadgetry and spy sidelights thrown. Overloaded with fights, familiar borrowings from Hitchcock and rather familiar plotting all of these jell into a pic that wants to pay homage to its forerunners and entertain. The fact that it measures up a good part of the way is a pat on the back for Hispano director Antonio Isasi. Table has a shapely CIA girl going after a young adventurer in Istanbul when an atomic Yank scientist is kidnapped. He has been deported from the U.S.and runs a gambling room in a front club. Though not in on the scientists snatch, he becomes interested when he hears that $1,000,000 has been collected from the U. S. with a double given over instead of the real man.

Horst Buchholz, as the canny adventurer, plays both sides but finally does get back the scientist and absconds with the $1,000,000. Also he gets the comely Yank CIA agent. All this is harmless if the violence sometimes gets out of hand. But its pulled off with such blandness it keeps things moving.

There are the usual love scenes and some nudity if held to a minimum. Film has enough of action for playoff since it cleverly mimes the Bond type of brutal, suave and high-level spy material.

Buchholz has stamina and charm with others adequate. Sylva Koscina and Perrette Pradier, plus a bevy of bit part girls supply the pulchritude.

Pic is well dubbed into English with Buchholz doing himself. If script is familiar, it borrows from good things and unashamedly keeps things moving to gloss over any plot flaws. *Mosk.*

The Nanny
(BRITISH)

Fascinating duel in the menace market between Bette Davis and a knowing youngster. Sound booking for psycho-thriller addicts.

London, Oct. 6.

Warner - Pathe release of a Hammer Film production for Associated British Productions. Stars Bette Davis, Wendy Craig, Jill Bennett, James Villiers. Features William Dix, Pamela Franklin, Jack Watling, Maurice Denham, Alfred Burke, Harry Fowler. Produced by Jimmy Sangster. Directed by Seth Holt; screenplay, Sangster, from Evelyn Piper's novel;

cemera, Harry Waxman; editor, Tom Simpson; music, Richard Rodney Bennett. Reviewed at Warner Theatre, London, Oct. 5, '65. Running time; 93 MINS.

Nanny .... Bette Davis
Virgie .... Wendy Craig
Pen .... Jill Bennett
Bill .... James Villiers
Joey .... William Dix
Bobby .... Pamela Franklin
Dr. Medman .... Jack Watling
Dr. Wills .... Alfred Burke
Dr. Beamaster .... Maurice Denham
Mrs. Griggs .... Nora Gordon
Sarah .... Sandra Power
Milkman .... Harry Fowler
Susy .... Angharad Aubrey

It's not necessary to be an astute student to guess that Bette Davis as a middle-aged Mary Poppins in a fairly fraught household will eventually be up to no good. Which immediately sets the odds against screenwriter Jimmy Sangster and director Seth Holt. But, in fairness, the balance of power between Miss Davis, posing as a devoted nanny, and William Dix as a knowing youngster who hates Miss Davis's innards, is so skillfully portrayed and for so long that a sufficiently chilly and tense atmosphere of pending evil is built up to make "The Nanny" a superior psycho-thriller.

Miss Davis's reputaton, allied to a skilled cast, makes this a plus entry for most audiences who like a spot of arsenic mixed with their wine. It's an added plus to the pie that neither writer nor director teeters over the edge into hysterics, and the cast has cottoned on and helped to build up the suspense gently but with a steely pricking of the nerve ends. There are some melodramatic highlights, of course, but, with her usual professional knowhow, even Miss Davis plays comparatively pianissimo and wouldn't even get a malignant nod from Sweet Charlotte or Baby Jane. And it's all to the good of the film.

Yarn, briefly, concerns the relationship between Nanny Davis and Master Joey (young Dix) which is less than cordial. He comes out of a school for the unstable to which he has been sent when his baby sister is found drowned in the bath. He insists it was Nanny's fault, but, of course, the adults don't believe him. They don't believe him, either, when he accuses Miss Davis of trying to drown him, of poisoning his mother with a shot in her steak-and-kidney pie supper, or of bringing on the death of his aunt (Jill Bennett) who suffers from a weak heart. And, audiences will have to be alert for quite awhile deciding whether the moppet is the "heavy" or whether Miss Davis is craftily playing an undercover game.

Miss Davis handles her assignment with marked professionalism, and copes with plenty of knowhow competition. There's young Dix, playing his first screen role, after some tv commercial malarkey, with deft assurance. Miss Davis is also up against two of Britain's outstanding young femme thesps.

Wendy Craig is fine as a weak, fond young mama whose nerves are shot to pieces by the household happenings, and Jill Bennett is no less effective as her sister suffering from a weak heart (and, for once, two actresses really look and behave as if they could be sisters). James Villiers, playing Miss Craig's husband, copes excel-

lently with a dull, thankless role from which he escapes, mercifully for himself, by having to whip off to Beirut on a job. In addition, Maurice Denham, Alfred Burke, Jack Watling, Pamela Franklin and Harry Fowler handle lesser, but necessary roles in useful fashion.

But it is Miss Davis's restrained yet compelling peformance that makes the whole thing jell. Holt's direction is firm, as is Sangster's screenplay, except in one or two dithery moments when he provides flashbacks that are probably necessary to the evolution of the plot but are rather clumsily injected. (Evelyn Piper is also authoress of Otto Preminger's "Bunny Lake Is Missing.")

The mainly interior settings are all okay and other technical matters are smoothly unobtrusive. It could be that this film would have been improved with a little more imaginative screwing up of tension but it would have needed a Hitchcock to provide them, and those responsible have wisely stayed in their own backyard and refused to be lured out to play with the big boys. *Rich.*

Pleins Feux Sur Stanislas
(Spotlight on Stanislas)
(FRENCH)
Paris, Oct. 12.

Prodis release of CICC-Films de La Licorne-Caro Films production. Stars Jean Marais, Nadja Tiller; features Andre Luguet, Nicole Maurey, Bernadette Lafont, Billy Kearns. Directed by Jean-Claude Dudrumet. Screenplay, Michel Cousin, Dudrumet; camera, Pierre Guegen; editor, Armand Psenny. At Normandie, Paris. Running Time, 93 MINS.

Stanislas .... Jean Marais
Benedicte .... Nadja Tiller
Colonel .... Andre Luguet
Claire .... Nicole Maurey
Rosine .... Bernadette Lafont
American .... Billy Kearns
British Agent .... Edward Meeks
Russian Agent .... Clement Harrari

Adventures of a rich, suave French undercover agent, as played by matinee idol Jean Marais, seem to be turning into a series. First one did well here and this easy-going sequel also should do nicely though the verve and originality are not so self-evident. It has not too much chance abroad except for tele and perhaps dualers on generally okay action scenes and enough movement to bolster a confused story.

Marais wants to retire but is dragged into another case by his girl-chasing boss, head of the French Secret Service. Russians, Yanks, Britishers and a secret organization, maybe Chinese, are after secret plans hidden by a dying man found by Marais.

The chase ends with Marais getting the goods. That is about all there is to it but director Jean-Charles Dudrumet strikes the right flippant balance of suspense and okay fisticuffs, with Marais breezy and intrepid with okay supporting cast.

No gadgets and outlandish derring-do a la Bond, but more familiar caperings done with acceptable production dress. As long as public tastes go for these tongue-in-cheek adventure yarns, there is a place for this. However,

it lacks the more dynamic bombast and drive of its predecessors.
Mosk.

Quand Passent Les Faisans
(When the Pheasants Pass)
(FRENCH)

Paris, Oct. 5.

Gaumont release of Gaumont-International production. Stars Paul Meurisse, Bernard Blier, Jean Lefebvre; features Yvonne Cleche, Claire Maurier, Michel Serrault, Daniel Ceccaldi, Veronique Vendel. Directed by Edouard Molinaro. Screenplay, Albert Simonin, Jacques Emmanuel, Michel Audiard; camera, Raymond Lemoigne; editor, Robert Isnardon. At Paris, Paris. Running Time, 90 MINS.

Larsan	Paul Meurisse
Arsene	Jean Lefebvre
Yacinthe	Bernard Blier
Micheline	Claire Maurier
Jeanne	Veronique Vendel
Paterson	Yvonne Clech
Barnave	Daniel Ceccaldi

Picaresque comedy is sort of a fleecers - getting - fleeced fable, with final ending indicating it is starting all over again. This is fairly well mounted, wth a good collection of comedians, but belabors its point. Hence, it winds up as one of those slight comedies that is mainly for local use, with perhaps some specialized use abroad on its theme.

A petty crook cons a cop who has been fired for incompetence. The two join up after some chases and are picked up by a suave con man. They in turn put over a neat bit by convincing a rabid businessman that old Russian bonds will be repaid by the Soviets. In turn, they are taken in by a spurious rich widow.

Director Edouard Molinaro does not force things and keeps this moving if its telegraphed aspects soon lose some edge to the yarn. But the timing of Paul Meurisse and the fey qualities of Jean Lefevbre, plus the harassed limning of Bernard Blier, help keep this slim comedy within solid bounds.

It is technically neat and manages to avoid vulgarity if it does not achieve the finesse and disarming comedic values it needs to make all this underworld conniving above par.
Mosk.

The Bedford Incident

Firstrate sea drama based on little-known aspect of the Cold War. Excellent script and production values. Strong b.o. prospects in the general market.

Hollywood, Oct. 1.

Columbia Pictures release of Bedford (James B. Harris-Richard Widmark) Production, produced and directed by Harris. Stars Widmark, Sidney Poitier; features James MacArthur, Martin Balsam, Wally Cox, Eric Portman. Screenplay, James Poe, based on novel by Mark Rascovich; camera, Gilbert Taylor; editor, John Jympson; music, Gerard Schurmann; art direction, Arthur Lawson; sound, Leslie Hammond, Robert Jones; asst. director, Clive Reed. Reviewed at Academy Award Theatre, L.A.; Sept. 30, '65. Running Time, 102 MINS.

Capt. Eric Finlander, USN	Richard Widmark
Ben Munceford	Sidney Poitier
Ens. Ralston	James MacArthur
LCdr. Chester Potter (MC)	Martin Balsam
Seaman Merlin Queffle	Wally Cox
Commodore Schrepke	Eric Portman
Cdr. Allison	Michael Kane
Lt. Bascombe	Gary Cockrell
Chief Hospitalman McKinley	Phil Brown
Lt. Beckman	Brian Davies
Lt. Hacker	Edward Bishop
Lt. Berger	George Roubichek
Lt. Krindlemeyer	Michael Graham
Lt. Hazelwood	Bill Edwards
Radioman First Class	Laurence Herder
Hospitalmen	Donald Sutherland, Warren Stanhope
Seamen	Colin Maitland, Paul Tamarin, Frank Lieberman, James Caffrey, Burnell Tucker, Stephen Von Schreiber, Ronald Rubin, Eugene Leonard, Roy Stephens, John McCarthy, Shane Rimmer, Glen Beck, Paul Carson

"The Bedford Incident" is an excellent contemporary sea drama based on a little-known but day-to-day reality of the Cold War, the monitoring of Russian submarine activity by U.S. Navy destroyers. The James B. Harris-Richard Widmark production, made at England's Shepperton Studios, has salty scripting and solid performances, including one of the finest in Widmark's career. Excellent direction emphasizes human angles over technology. Strong b.o. likely for Columbia release in the general market.

James Poe's adaptation of a Mark Rascovich novel depicts the "hunt-to-exhaustion" tactic in anti-submarine warfare, whereby a sub contact is pursued until one side or the other either gives up or eludes. The battle is purely mental, the reward that of improved tactics. It happens regularly, to both U.S. and Russian subs.

Widmark stars as the skipper of the USS Bedford, a modern destroyer, equipped with tactical nuclear weapons, on patrol in the North Atlantic. Widmark's skipper is that rare breed (perhaps 10% of all commanding officers) whom the crew not only follows, but worships. The character of this sea dog is drawn out by the helicopter arrival of Sidney Poitier, also starred as a wise-guy magazine writer, and Martin Balsam, a Reserve medic back on active duty.

Poitier does an excellent job in both the light and serious aspects of his role, and manages to leave a personal stamp on his scenes. The part provides vital identity to civilian audiences since it lends exposition to certain aspects of Naval life, including the fact that some senior officers are best suited to fighting, while others are more adept on the social-political circuit.

Balsam neatly characterizes the World War II type who doesn't realize that modern sailors are often more interested in foreign language study and personal improvement than playing cards and goofing off. His unctuous use of modern psychological terms clashes with Widmark's no-nonsense approach, and pair's interactions are standout.

James MacArthur does well as the new Ensign earnings his spurs under Widmark's relentless prodding. Underscoring the yesterday's-enemy-today's-ally irony is Eric Portman, effective as the former Nazi sub skipper now a NATO consultant aboard the ship. Wally Cox provides some tragicomic moments as the sonar operator who maintains contact with the Russian sub until his collapse.

Poe's script has a genuine ending, entirely plausible, which makes the point that the technology of our time still depends on human beings. There are a few minor flaws in the writing, however. For one thing, Poiter's newshawk dialog is often cliche.

Also, when Widmark vents his frustration over being told by higher command to take no action when the Russian sub has violated some territorial waters, there is an unreality in his talking about being an oldfashioned patriot. Widmark's type never discusses patriotism: it's too deep in the bone marrow. This specious intro of melodrama obscures the pertinent issue: the age-old problem of an on-scene commander vs. the remote high command.

Director Harris has also obtained fine supporting performances from a large cast, framed by the artistic and mobile camera of Gilbert Taylor which makes full use of the black to white spectrum. John Jympson's tight editing to 102 minutes enhances the pace. Gerard Schurmann's score supports the mood. Other technical details are firstrate. Film was made sans U.S. Government cooperation, but few will catch the effects of this. Widmark co-produced and Denis O'Dell was associate producer.
Murf.

La Boheme
(ITALIAN-COLOR)

Herbert von Karajan turns film showman. Result is "musical treat" for discerning audiences. One of best "opera" filmings to date.

Warner Bros. special release of a Cosmotel (Herbert von Karajan) production. Stars Mirella Freni and Gianni Raimondi; features Rolando Paneria, Gianni Maffeo, Ivo Vinco, Carlo Badioli, Virgilio Carbonari, Adriana Martino, Franco Ricciardi, Giuseppe Morresi, Carlo Forti, Angelo Mercuriali. Artistic director and conductor, Herbert von Karajan; production designed and directed by Franco Zeffirelli. Opera in four acts by Giuseppe Giacosa and Lugi Illica, based on Henri Murger's novel, "Scenes de la Vie de Boheme," music by Giacomo Puccini. Camera (Technicolor), Werner Krein; sound, Guenter Hermanns; editor, Alice Seedorf. Reviewed in New York, Oct. 4, '65. Running Time, 107 MINS.

Rodolfo	Gianni Raimondi
Mimi	Mirella Freni
Marcello	Rolando Paneria
Schaunard	Gianni Maffeo
Colline	Ivo Vinco
Musetta	Adriana Martino
Benoit	Carlo Badioli
Alcindoro	Virgilio Carbonari
Parpignol	Franco Ricciardi
Sergeant	Giuseppe Morresi
Customs Official	Carlo Forti
Salesman	Angelo Mercuriali
Orchestra and Chorus of La Scala, Milan	

Warner Bros. should have no trouble filling the special engagements they've set for this filmed version of the La Scala "La Boheme." It comes off so well that it wouldn't be surprising if they later make it available for extended dates in qualified situations. Certainly it is going to be much sought by musically-inclined communities, schools and groups.

The honors for the film must be shared by both conductor Herbert von Karajan and director Franco Zeffirelli. It's the first opportunity for film audiences to view the handiwork of the latter who has created quite a stir in legit by his rejuvenation of some stale classics. He's also responsible for the overall design of this production.

Von Karajan, wanting to retain the operatic atmosphere of La Scala without adhering to the static staginess that works filmed in theatres or operahouses seem unable to avoid, found his solution by doing the actual filming in a Munich studio, using the La Scala settings, costumes and cast, and post-synchronizing the soundtrack later in Rome. This enabled him to give fluidity to the movement and much greater dramatic credibility to the action by not forcing singers to assume traditional postures in order to give voice. A good example is Rodolfo's tortured repeating of "Mimi! Mimi!" at the end which would have been completed muffled had he actually sung it with his head buried in the dying Mimi's shoulder as he's seen doing.

The slight occasional lapses in lip movement because of post-synchronizing won't be noticed by any but the most perceptive opera fans and is more than compensated for by the increased effort von Karajan has achieved. That he conducts beautifully, and inspires the La Scala orchestra to peak efforts, is to be expected, considering his international reputation.

The cast, completely Italian, is not well known to American audiences but two members soon will be. Mirella Freni, who sings Mimi, and Gianni Raimondi, the Rodolfo, made their debuts in these same roles at the Metropolitan Opera last week. Miss Freni, in particular, tops even that glowing performance. Her wonderfully expressive face is given full range by Zeffirelli with extended closeups during the most poignant passages, in which she avoids the facial distortions which operatic singing demands so often. Not really pretty, except for beautiful and expressive eyes, she's still a perfect Mimi, with no reservations.

Raimondi's Rodolfo repeats the success of his Met debut. He is stronger vocally, than dramatically, but capable enough in his portrayal to bring the audience close to tears with his wrapup of the ending. Other cast members, as could be expected, are overshadowed by the tragic lovers but, when given opportunities, make the most of them. Particular standout is Adriana Martino's Musetta, a lusty, big-bosomed blonde, who turns her Waltz into a paean to living life to the fullest. Likewise, as Colline, Ivo Vinco makes his "Coat Song," a brief but beautiful moment.

Rolando Panerai's Marcello and Gianni Maffeo's Schaunard round out the group of bohemians and they sing with richness and power. Carlo Badioli's Benoit and Virgilio Carbonari's Alcindoro make the most of their brief comedy scenes. The chorus seems more effective than is usual, because Zeffirelli keeps them in the background.

Where his staging really excels is in such hard-to-present scenes as the second act Cafe Momus setting. Instead of the usual outdoor cafe, always hard to believe, considering it's Christmas Eve, Zeffirelli divides the scene between the street filled with holiday crowds and the Cafe Momus interior, crosscutting between the two. The third act setting is so wintry and cold that it inspires shivers and makes Mimi's apparent illness the more effective.

Although the 108-minute running time lends itself to showing without intermission, the film is divided into the opera's four acts and Warners plans a short break after end of act two.

Werner Krein's Technicolor camerawork is restrained, given to brightness only in the Cafe Momus scene. The occasional dark areas may be due to difficulty of lighting the set. There's much to admire in this excellent film version of Puccini's "La Boheme" and very little to criticize. *Robe.*

Slalom
(ITALIAN-FRENCH-EGYPTIAN)
(Color)
Rome, Oct. 5.

Cineriz release of a Mario Cecchi Gori production for Fairfilm (Rome)—Cocinor (Paris), in collaboration with Copro (Cairo). Stars Vittorio Gassman; features Adolfo Celi, Beba Loncar, Daniela Bianchi, Emma Danieli. Directed by Luciano Salce. Screenplay, Castellano, Pipolo; camera (Technicolor) Alfio Contini; music, Ennio Morricone; editor, Marcello Malvestiti. At Adriano, Rome. Running time, 97 MINS.

Lucio Ridolfi	Vittorio Gassman
Friend	Adolfo Celi
Helen	Beba Loncar
Thea	Daniela Bianchi

Suspense and comedy are blended for good audience impact in this latest Mario Cecchi Gori production, which should easily keep his long string of b.o. hits intact. It has colorful locations, pretty girls, intrigue and humor for all but the most discriminating palates. Film looks a likely purchase both here and abroad.

Castellano and Pipolo's script blends various tried-and-true ingredients of the genre (reluctant businessman headed for rest cure who gets involved in heroically resolved international exploits) to good effect, despite frequent lapses in story logic.

Pace is fast, even confusing sometimes, as Vittorio Gassman becomes involved in an international battle between a gang of dollar counterfeiters (apparently serving the Red Chinese in an attempt to upset Yank economy by flooding the world with false notes) and the F.B.I. The affair finds him skiing in Northern Italy one day, sweating it out in the Egyptian desert the next; then back again for the happy ending. Gassman is practically a oneman show and is on-screen almost throughout. He makes the most of a meaty, (acrobatic) part. Beba Loncar walks winningly through a role as a mysterious blonde, with Daniela Bianchi somewhat sacrificed in a similar part. Adolfo Celi makes a good sidekick for Gassman, though his footage is limited, too.

Emma Danieli is briefly bright as Gassman's wife, and others in a large and truly international cast (pic was partly shot with Egyptian thesps and assistance) make for a colorful roster.

Director Luciano Salce has kept the pacing fast and maintained a touch light. A few sequences might have profited by more careful execution. Technical plaudits go to Alfio Contini for his Technicolor hues of Alpine and desert locations sites, and to Ennio Morricone for an aptly quizzical backdrop score. A special nod to

Rome's AU Studios for some strikingly designed credit titles. *Hawk.*

Je Vous Salue Mafia
(Hail, Mafia)
(FRENCH)
Paris, Oct. 5.

Fernand Rivers release of ITTAC-Film-studio-Raoul Levy production. Stars Eddie Constantine, Henry Silva, Jack Klugman, Elsa Martinelli, Micheline Presle. Written and directed by Raoul J. Levy from a book by Pierre Viel-Lescu. Camera, Raoul Coutard; editor, Victoria Mercanton. At Marbeuf, Paris. Running Time, 89 MINS.

Schaft	Henry Silva
Phil	Jack Klugman
Rudy	Eddie Constantine
Sylvia	Elsa Martinelli
Daisy	Micheline Presle
Secretary	Michel Lonsdale
Ruidosa	Karl Studer
Ben	Ricky Cooper
Hyman	Tener Riggs Eckelberry

(In English)

Raoul Levy, in spite of his financial woes with his "Marco Polo" pic, found time to write, direct and produce a neat programmer that is the usual tale of two killers on a job with enough twists to give it an added fillip for okay dualer chances abroad.

Made in English, it also looms good tv fodder for the U.S., with general playoff its main probability. Not much marquee value for the U.S. but okay for here via the Eddie Constantine name. However, the pic has two solid Yank thesps in Henry Silva and Jack Klugman, as the killers.

Not so crisp in getting under way, as the pic goes on a more assured flair takes over. The two killers are after a man who could be a witness against some highly-placed gangland officials in the U.S. He is hiding out in France, and they go after him. In the interim, the idea is changed but the killers cannot be stopped. An odd twist is that one of the killers has an elaborate plan to save the victim.

This misfires, and picture ends in mayhem and an excellent visually conceived gun battle. Levy shows some grasp of pacing and works up insight into the killers and their outlooks.

But the women run in for staple roles and the time lost in getting this moving militate against any specialized chances abroad. Silva, as a gunman who believes in his work, and Klugman, as the aging killer, etch incisive, standout performances. But Constantine does not have too much to do as the man on the run.

A big asset to the film is Raoul Coutard's expert camera work which gives clarity and depth. *Mosk.*

The Big Job
(BRITISH)

Offshoot of the "Carry On" stable, with several of the same characters in an earthy, cops-and-robbers comedy; plenty of mirth for the undemanding and sound b.o. for mass audience houses.

London, Oct. 5.

Warner-Pathe release of a Peter Rogers production from Anglo Amalgamated. Features Sidney James, Sylvia Syms, Dick Emery, Jim Dale, Joan Sims, Lance Percival, Edna Ronay, Deryck Guyler. Directed by Gerald Thomas. Screenplay,

Talbort Rothwell, from an original story by John Antrobus; camera, Alan Hune; editor, Rod Keys; music, Eric Rogers. Reviewed at Regal, Hammersmith, London. Running time, 88 MINS.

George Brain	Sidney James
Myrtle Robbins	Sylvia Syms
Booky Binns	Dick Emery
Dipper Day	Lance Percival
Mrs. Gamely	Joan Sims
Harold	Jim Dale
Sally Gamely	Edina Ronay
Police Sergeant	Deryck Guyler
1st Workman	Brian Rawlinson
Registrar	Reginald Beckwith
Judge	David Horne

This one is a slightly disguised, slightly more inhibited entry from the "Carry On" stable. With Peter Rogers producing, Gerald Thomas directing, Talbot Rothwell scripting and several of the "Carry On" stock company thesping, the formula of slapstick, double meanings, earthy vulgarity and simple situations will appeal to the many "Carry On" addicts. This provokes plenty of yocks for undemanding, mass audiences.

John Antrobus's original story has a familiar ring. It concerns a misfire of a bank raid and the subsequent return of the dim-witted crooks to pick up the abandoned loot of $140,000 after a prison spell. This has been hidden in a tree in the countryside. When the robbers are released from the cooler after a 15-year stretch they find that a new town has been built on the area near the scene of the crime. And the tree where the cash is hidden now is in the front yard of the local cop shop.

The bungling that makes the robbery go haywire is emphasized by the calamities that befall the ex-cons as they try to retrieve their swag by devious means which involve the use of the harpoon, wall scaling and tunneling. Thomas' direction is straightforward and as knowing as in his handling of the "Carry Ons" pix. This one might easily have been tagged "Carry On Stealing." Rothwell's script is easygoing fun and does not hamper itself with overmuch subtlety.

Technical credits are okay and inflict little strain on the crew's knowhow. Sidney James, as the misogynistic cluckhead who "masterminds" the robbery, is his usual highly competent performer in such situations. Dick Emery and Lance Percival are his stooges. Deryck Guyler and Jim Dale represent the law, which is depicted as a bunch of nincompoops. Joan Sims, as a landlady with a shady background; Edina Ronay, as her nubile daughter; and Sylvia Syms, as James' moll, who traps him into a marriage of convenience, look after the femme interests. All are okay, though Miss Syms, understandably, seems a little ill at ease in farcical surroundings foreign to her usual thesping.

Brian Rawlinson, Reginald Beckwith and David Horne are among those who chip in with effective cameos in an unpretentious comedy which is a safe booking for run-of-mill situations.

The Cincinnati Kid
(COLOR)

Suspenseful story of a stud poker game, with sex and excitement to further enliven festivities. Okay prospects seen.

Hollywood, Oct. 2.

Metro release of Martin Ransohoff production. Stars Steve McQueen, Edward G. Robinson, Ann-Margaret, Karl Malden, Tuesday Weld; features Joan Blondell, Rip Torn, Jack Weston, Cab Calloway. Directed by Norman Jewison. Screenplay, Ring Lardner Jr., Terry Southern; based on novel by Richard Jessup; camera (Metrocolor), Philip H. Lathrop; music, Lalo Schifrin; editor, Hal Ashby; art direction, George W. Davis, Edward Carfagno; sound. Franklin Milton; asst. director, Kurt Neumann. Reviewed at Hollywood Pramount Theatre, Oct. 1, '65. Running Time, 102 MINS.

The Cincinnati Kid	Steve McQueen
Lancey Howard	Edwrd G. Robinson
Melba	Ann-Margaret
Shooter	Karl Malden
Christian	Tuesday Weld
Lady Fingers	Joan Blondell
Slade	Rip Torn
Pig	Jack Weston
Yeller	Cab Calloway
Hoban	Jeff Corey
Felix	Theo Marcuse
Sokal	Milton Selzer
Mr. Rudd	Karl Swenson
Cajun	Emile Genest
Danny	Ron Soble
Mrs. Rudd	Irene Tedrow
Mrs. Slade	Midge Ware
Dealer	Dub Taylor

"The Cincinnati Kid" is the fast-moving story of a burningly-ambitious young rambling-gambling man who challenges the king of stud poker to a showdown for the champ title of The Man. Adapted from Richard Jessup's realistically-written novel, it emerges a tenseful examination of the gambling fraternity, what makes it tick, how big games are played. Embodied in its forceful enactment are such boxoffice elements as excitement, suspense and a liberal dosage of sex; such names as Steve McQueen, Edward G. Robinson, Ann-Margret, Karl Malden and Tuesday Weld to impersonate colorful characters. Even for those without knowledge of gambling the film should hold attraction, although there are moments when femme interest may be questioned.

Martin Ransohoff has constructed a taut, well-turned-out production in his latest bid to come up with something off the beaten path. In McQueen he has the near-perfect delineator of the title role. Robinson is at his best in some years as the aging, ruthless Lancey, Howard, champ of the poker tables for more 30 years and determined now to defend his title against a cocksure but dangerous opponent who believes he is ready for his big moment. The card duel between the pair is dramatically developed through grueling action, building in intensity as the final and deciding hand is played in what may well be the most suspenseful account of a poker game in film record.

Ring Lardner Jr., and Terry Southern have translated the major elements of the book to the Metrocolor screen in their script, changing, however, tome's St. Louis locale to a more picturesque New Orleans background. They have added a key situation, too, to point up the game—Malden, in part of Shooter, dealer for the game, is forced by another gambler holding his markers to slip cards to the Kid so he'll cinch his victory. The Kid, intent on winning on his own and proving he is the best stud player alive, senses what's going on and eases Malden from his post. Direction by Norman Jewison early establishes the rightful mood for the story and he draws top performances from his entire cost, which include some unusual types in bit parts. Even his staging of a cock fight, which distaff audiences may not particularly relish, adds a right note of realism, both in the fight itself and the reactions of the players. His tempo is aided by the sharp editing of Hal Ashby, whose shears enable quick change of scene, and Philip H. Lathrop's facile color camerawork contributes importantly to general interest.

McQueen's particular style of acting fits this role well, his mutterings and his sometimes-incoherency adding to the strength of his character, for which he is given occasional bursts of wry humor. Robinson is entirely believable as the old master at cards, and Malden is a standout as the ethical dealer caught in circumstances beyond his control.

Ann-Margret, playing his trampish wife and lushly photographed, displays plenty of cleavage and socks over a sex-laden portrayal, and Tuesday Weld likewise scores as McQueen's pretty girl-friend.

Joan Blondell, hands in a blowzy characterization as Lady Fingers, the dealer. Rip Torn as the gambler who puts Malden on the spot with his demand of dealing a crooked card; Jack Weston and Cab Calloway, who sit in on the early part of the game; and Midge Ware, as Torn's wife, register effectively.

Art direction by George W. Davis and Edward Carfagno is interesting, and Lalo Schifrin's music score nicely backdrops the footage. Ray Charles sings title song, with lyrics by Dorcas Cochran. *Whit.*

Pinocchio In Outer Space
(ANIMATED—COLOR)

Universal's Christmas release is pleasant cartoon with appeal to candy-counter customers but little for grownups. Heavy promotion as planned should help.

Universal Pictures release of a Swallow Ltd.-Belvision production. Produced by Norm Prescott, Fred Ladd; directed by Ray Goossens. Features voices of Arnold Stang, Conrad Jameson, Cliff Owens, Peter Lazer, Mavis Mims, Kevin Kennedy, Minerva Pious; Jess Cain, Norman Rose. Screenplay by Fred Laderman, based on idea by Prescott, from original story by Collodi. No other credits. Reviewed at Universal, N.Y., Oct. 11, '65. Running Time, **71 MINS.**

Although "Pinocchio In Outer Space" has the proper family fare ingredients of non-controversial content, technical gloss and a variety of exploitation approaches, all of which Universal expects to explore, the animated feature's appeal will be restricted to the under-12-years market and those doting parents who accompany their progeny to the theatre of necessity. Whether it will have the strength to carry on, once the lucrative holiday traffic has thinned, will depend on the selling momentum.

Taking a hint from Disney, not

only on the film itself, but how to sell it, Universal has already started a multi-faceted promotion campaign, using everything from advertising to toy merchandising. Producers Norm Prescott (who once worked for Joseph E. Levine in Boston and was a well-known disk jockey there) and Hank Ladd farmed out the animation work for the film to Belvision Prods., a Belgian company, enabling them to complete the feature faster and cheaper than believed possible in the U.S. Resultant work is good, if too derivative of Disney's style to garner much acclaim on its own. The occasional sci-fi sections (and a very good pre-title space sequence) are considerably better than the original character depiction. Indeed, there's too much contrast between the mittel-European town in which Geppetto and Pinocchio live and the ultra-futuristic space phases of the film.

Color process, as is Universal policy, is unidentified. Query as to process used (probably Eastman Color, with lab work by Pathe, as has been used in past), was answered, "Just say it's in color."

Ray Goossens direction of the Fred Laderman screenplay, which stems from an idea by Prescott based on the Collodi character, is simple, direct, and unimaginative. Prescott's variation on the original (which was filmed by Disney, also with variations) was to put Pinocchio into space adventures in order to again qualify as a real boy (his behavior having caused his reversion to a puppet). Most interesting new character is a Nurtle, a Twurtle from outer space, who accompanies Pinocchio to Mars to seek out and conquer Astro, a flying whale whose existence threatens the earth. Arnold Stang's voice is perfect for a Twurtle.

Other voices used, without character identification, are Conrad Jameson, Cliff Owens, Peter Lazer, Mavis Mims, Kevin Kennedy, Minerva Pious, Jess Cain and Norman Rose. All are appropriate although those used for Pinocchio and the Blue Fairy will seem affected to most grownups.

Possibilities of follow-ups are indicated by final comment that "you haven't seen the last of Pinocchio." Depending, obviously, on percentage of turnover at the ticket wicket. It is doubtful that Disney has any reason to worry. *Robe.*

Return From the Ashes
(PANAVISION)

Sometimes tense melodrama of a double murder, but misses as a thriller.

Hollywood, Oct. 12.
United Artists release of J. Lee Thompson production, directed by Thompson. Stars Maximilian Schell, Samantha Eggar, Ingrid Thulin; features Herbert Lom. Screenplay, Julius Epstein; based on novel by Hubert Monteilhet; camera, Chris Challis; music, John Dankworth; editor, Russell Lloyd; asst. director, Kip Gowans. Reviewed at Academy Awards Theatre, Oct. 11, '65. Running Time, **108 MINS.**
Stanislaus Pilgrin....Maximilian Schell
Fabiene .... Samantha Eggar
Dr. Michele Wolf .... Ingrid Thulin
Dr. Charles Bovard ...... Herbert Lom
Claudine .... Talitha Pol
Manager .... Vladek Sheybal
1st Detective .... Jacques Brunius
2d Detective .... Andre Maranne

Woman in Train .... Yvonne Andre
Man in Train .... John Serret
Mother in Train .... Pamela Stirling

"Return from the Ashes" does not always reach its mark as a thriller. The J. Lee Thompson production, filmed in England and presented by the Mirisch Corp., carries the makings of a suspenseful melodrama but in development is early contrived. There is, however, dramatic impact to hold the spectator and its teaser campaign pegged on the catchline, "No one may enter the theatre after Fabi enters her bath!" may help b.o. prospects.

The Julius Epstein screenplay based on a novel by Hubert Monteilhet builds around a plot for the perfect murder by an unscrupulous Polish chess master married to one woman and in love with her stepdaughter. Set in Paris at the close of World War II, when the wife, a Jewess, returns from tortured internment in Dachau to find her husband living with the younger woman, plottage concerns the Pole's passion for money as he does away first with one, then the other femme, to accomplish his goal. Film takes its title from wife's unexpected reappearance after being thought dead.

Thompson, who also directs, establishes a tense mood frequently, but level of interest suffers from character fuzziness which occasionally clouds the issue. Buildup of the crimes is given good exposition, then over-exposure in an unnecessary finale which lessens potency of the climax.

Maximilian Schell delivers strongly in a blackhearted role, lending credence to the character through constant underplaying his scenes. Samantha Eggar, who gained the attention of U.S. audiences through her work in current release of "The Collector," again displays dramatic aptitude as the amoral stepdaughter, Fabi, whose entry into her abth provides one of the highlights of the film. Ingrid Thulin's characterization of the wife lacks clarity but talent such as hers still permits good acting. Herbert Lom is quietly effective as the wife's old friend.

Technical credits are added assets, particularly the photography of Chris Challis, music score by John Dankworth and art direction by Michael Stringer. *Whit.*

The Eleanor Roosevelt Story
(DOCUMENTARY)

Well-made documentary on life of a memorable woman. Has interest for general audiences but will need special handling to achieve maximum results.

Landau - Unger Company release through Allied Artists of a Sidney Glazier production. Directed by Richard Kaplan. Narrated by Eric Severeid, Archibald MacLeish and Mrs. Francis Cole. Written by MacLeish; editor, Miriam Arsham; music, Ezra Laderman. Reviewed in N.Y., Oct. 18, '65. Running Time, **90 MINS.**

This film biography of Eleanor Roosevelt has been in the making for a long time, simultaneously through script by Archibald MacLeish and an enormous amount of research, followed by over a year

in the making, by producer Sidney Glazier. The result of their labors is a fascinating picture and word remembrance of this century's most memorable woman. Included is background on her early life that is, possibly, unknown to much of the world.

Glazier and MacLeish have not tried to make their film a flattering portrait of the wife and widow of Franklin D. Roosevelt, with uncomfortable details glossed over or ignored. While obviously made out of admiration for the late First Lady, they've not hesitated to show the ugly duckling side of her childhood and the conflicts in her adult life.

To prepare the film, much of the material was researched by Roberta Aarons, Eleanor Ferrar, Shirley Green, Jim Sage and Merle Worth, director and staff of the Franklin D. Roosevelt Memorial Library. Over 3,000 still photographs were obtained from both private and government files in 22 countries, some behind the Iron Curtain. Both Glazier and MacLeish were longtime associates of Mrs. Roosevelt, MacLeish having known her since her earliest days in the White House, and Glazier having served as executive director of the Eleanor Roosevelt Cancer Foundation for five years. The producer ended up with 24 hours of film footage which had to be cut down to 90 minutes.

The earlier part of the film, until the beginning of World War I, is told with stills. In sequences designed by Eckstein-Stone, using stop photography and zoom shots to give some semblance of motion, MacLeish's script tells the story of a very plain little girl, painfully shy, who lacked for nothing but love. Eric Severeid, MacLeish, but most particularly Mrs. Roosevelt herself and her first cousin, Mrs. Francis Cole, narrate the story. Mrs. Cole, now an elderly woman, is particularly moving as her voice is perfectly suited to the period she describes.

Once the use of motion picture film is introduced, the remainder of the film, with a few exceptions, is made up of a compilation of newsreel shots from, obviously, a variety of sources. Some of the scenes are important historically, particularly the two scenes of President Roosevelt's funeral and her own, with their concentration of dignitaries. One shot has past and present Presidents Truman, Eisenhower, Kennedy and Johnson alongside the Roosevelt grave at Hyde Park.

Glazier takes the biography beyond the President's passing, through the early years of the United Nations and Mrs. Roosevelt's personal triumphs with that assembly. Although sufficient comment is made of the divergence of attitudes toward both President and Mrs. Roosevelt, it is made without rancor or bitterness but as a historical fact. The film will open Nov. 8 at the Little Carnegie. Houghton-Mifflin's publication of the project in book form with MacLeish's text and profusely illustrated is scheduled to coincide with the motion picture release. The Roosevelt Foundation is working with Landau-Unger on promotion of group sales for the film, at least in New York. *Robe.*

Sálonica Fest

Blockade
(GREEK)
Salonika. Oct. 19.

A Kourouniotis Bros.-M. Petrolecas release of Giffilms productiom. Directed by Adonis Kyrou. With Costas Kazacos, Xenia Kalogueropoulou, Alexandra Ladikou, Yannis Fertis, Manos Katrakis, George Sarri, Yannis Kontoulis, Irene Koumarianou, Niki Tsigalou, Costas Bakas, Stavor Tornes. Screenplay, Guerassimos Stavrou; music, Mikis Theodorakis; camera, Georges Panoussopoulos, Gregory Danalis. At Salonika Film Fest. Running Time, 90 MINS.

This picture was expected to be the top prize winner of the Salonica Festival because Adonis Kyrou, a film director working in the French studios for many years, had a hot story based on a real-life incident. Far from being superior to Greek standards, however, his film turned out no better, even technically, than an average local pic.

Greatest disappointment is that the production did not touch anyone emotionally. Even young people, who had lived the hard and bitter years of the Nazi occupation in Greece, reacted badly. Result of director Kyrou's seemingly false approach to the war is a film lacking reality. Pic does not show the desperation and the desire for freedom that dominated and tormented the suffering people in Occupied lands.

After a short documentary preface showing the German atrocities in Greece, film opens on the wedding night of Kosmas, a young Greek, who had made some money in the black market. His bride, Myrto, is a member of the Underground movement. German soldiers blockade the district searching for suspects. All the male population is called to report in the central square. Myrto flees her house to advise the Underground committee.

Kosmas, not knowing the activities of his bride, is angered and upset by her strange behavior. Then he is forced by a traitor to inform on everyone he knew who was dealing with the Underground.

There is running and fighting in the streets between Greeks and Germans. Kosmas is brought to the square with his head covered so as not to be recognized. He is threatened with execution on the spot if he doesn't denounce the suspects among the people gathered. This he refuses to do. Instead he shoots the traitor who is trying to intimidate him, and is killed by German soldiers.

Among the many Greeks who lived through this incident, the feeling is that Kyrou presents an entirely false picture. Other out-of-place sequences are the private discussions among young people trying to solve their personal problems when everyone's life is at stake.

Costas Kazacos is good as Kosmas, the young racketeer. Xenia Kalogueropoulou delivers her usual fine performance as Myrto. Manos Katrakis is the underground leader.

Alexandra Ladikou also is good as the other girl wanted by the Germans. *Rena.*

Thou Shall Not Steal
(GREEK)
Salonika, Oct. 19.

Dimitri Dadiras production. Directed by Dadiras. With Takis Emmanouel, Guizella Dhalli, Demos Starenios, Koulis Stoligas, Georges Nezos, N. Constantopoulas, Theodoros Exarhos. Screenplay, Nicos Sphyroeras; camera, Stelios Damanis; music, Mikis Theodorakis. At Salonika Film Fest.

This is a swift-moving comedy that offers good entertainment. The many funny sequences are played superbly by the cast. It was one of the two best entries at the Salonika Festival, where it won an honorary distinction.

Set in a village of the Greek Island Naxos where there is a custom of stealing one's possessions just for the joke of it. Every day someone complains he had lost something the previous night without any chance of recovering it.

Village's priest and police agent are doing their best to stop all this, but in vain. When the cleverest thief of all dies, his two sons swear to carry on the family tradition and marry off their sister Megla to the most efficient thief of the village.

When couple has to face arrest by the police and the priest threatens to leave the village for good, they decide to become good citizens.

Screenplay by Nicos Sphyroeras is smart and full of gags. Directed by the producer himself, this has a good-humored pace which provides lively, light entertainment with no strain on the brain. However, some of the gags may not be appreciated by foreign audiences.

Guizella Dhalli and Takis Emmanouel are nicely teamed as the couple in love who plan to get married. Demos Starenios and several others are equally good but top laurels go to Theodoros Exarhos for his portrayal of the priest. He steals every scene in which he appears. *Rena.*

No, Mr. Johnson
(GREEK)
Salonika, Oct. 19.

An Anna Films release of James Paris production. Directed by Gregory Gregoriou. With Paris Alexander, Voula Zouboulaki, Titos Vandis, Nicos Rizos, Anestis Vlahos, Manos Christides, Despo Diamantidou, Lakis Skelas. Screenplay, Michael Gregoriou; camera, Aristidis Karydis; music, Yannis Marcopoulos. At Salonika Film Fest. Running Time, 100 MINS.

Greek American producer James Paris has made a comedy which is far superior to the average Greek standards. It could become strong as an international entry with big b.o. chances in most situations in and out of Greece. It is somewhat similar to "Never on Sunday." Male star, Paris Alexander, is excellent.

Story depicts the adventure of an American businessman who goes to Greece to promote the sale of a tomato juice. Wishing to live near the sea he rents a villa

nearby at an extravagant price from a fake owner while the real owners are away on a trip. His Greek driver Thanassis is trying to help him and protect him from any further misteps but it is not easy because Johnson can't adjust himself to the Greek mentality. So his misfortunes seem endless. The only good thing is that he falls in love with a nightclub singer, Heleni.

After these mishaps Johnson fails to promote the sale of tomato juice in Greece. He is about to be fired and then a thief steals all his money.

Heleni, with the help of her boss and Thanassis manage to get back his stolen money. When the president of the company arrives in Greece she is persuaded to import Greek wines into the States instead of trying to sell tomato juice in a country where tomatoes flourish.

Director Gregory Gregoriou did a far better job than on his recent previous pix while Alexander is excellent as the American salesman. Michael Gregoriou's screenplay won a prize at this Salonika Festival.

Greatest asset of the pic, is Alexander's portrayal of the American businessman. A Greek-American himself, he plays the role with natural ability. Voula Zouboulaki, as the nightclub singer, is very good. Same credit goes to Titos Vandis and Nicos Rizos, as owner of the club, and the Greek chauffeur respectively. Technical credits are also above average. *Rena.*

Return
(GREEK)
Salonika, Oct. 5.

Klearhos Konitsiotis production. Directed by Erricos Andreou. With Alecos Alexandrakis, Elli Photiou, Lambros Constantaras, Mema Stathopoulou. Written by Panos Kondellis, Antonis Samarakis; camera, Nicos Gardellis; music, Christos Mourabas. At Salonika Film Fest. Running time, 91 MINS.

Producer Klearhos Konitsiotis boasts that his only object is to produce b.o. pictures. Nevertheless he always tries to get into film festivals. This is the kind of film to show at a festival but it will certainly do well at the wickets.

The story, by Antonis Samarakis and Panos Kondellis, is almost the Greek version of "Waterloo Bridge," but placed in the last war. Valentis, a shipping tycoon, visiting his shipyards with his daughter remembers, in flashbacks, the tragedy that had wrecked his life. Back in 1940 on the eve of the Italian invasion of Greece, he was about to marry his girl, Anna, but he's drafted. After a few days, his plane is reported missing.

Anna, expecting his child, lives with a girl friend who becomes a tramp to support her and the baby. When Anna finds out about this, she decides to do the same job so that she and her child may live but not on her friend's expense.

When the war ends, Valentis, who had made a forced landing in Egypt, returns back and finds Anna. She does not tell him anything about the child but agrees to marry him. On her visit to the family mansion, however, she understands that her past will al-

ways be between them and kills herself.

The screenplay finds an easy solution to every problem in the life of the film's heroes. Director Erricos Andreou does fine job. Elli Photiou won first prize as best actress for her interpretation of the role of Anna.

Much of the footage has many talky sequences. It is slow paced and lacks ingenuity. Direction is below the usual standard of Andreou. Alecos Alexandrakis tries to do his best and Lambros Constantaras is his usual confident self. *Rena.*

Greece Without Ruins
(GREEK-DOCUMENTARY)
Salonika, Oct. 5.

Produced by Angelos Lambrou. Screenplay, Rose Macauley; music, M. Theodorakis, St. Xarhacos; camera, M. Grammaticopoulos, Angelos Lambrou. At Salonika Film Fest. Running time, 96 MINS.

Angelos Lambrou probably intended to present modern Greece and its people who live near the old ruins but who create new traditions and ways of living in this pic. And the production measures up, since the film gives a true picture of the Greek life as it is today.

Lambrou loves his country and everything he presents in this has been selected with tender care. One may object, perhaps, to the bull sacrifice in Mytilini since it seems rather out of place. Also the narration would have been better if there were not so many details. The excellent photography speaks for itself.

Color lensing is superb as is the musical score. Every thing in this pic makes it a grosser especially outside of the Greek borders. *Rena.*

The Fate of an Innocent
(GREEK)
Salonika, Oct. 5.

Anna Films release of James Paris production. Directed by Gregory Gregoriou. With Peter Physsoun, Pantelis Zervos, Heleni Annoussaki, Yannis Argyris, Niki Triantafyllidou, Anestis Vlahos, Christoforos Nazer. Screenplay by P. Kontellis based on a story by James Paris; camera, Ar. Karydis; music, Yannis Marcopoulos. At Salonika Film Fest. Running time, 90 MINS.

This last production of Greek-American producer, James Paris, set on his own native island, deals with the suppression of the weak by the wealthy tycoon. It's unusual, for a Greek film story, in its good, natural settings which should help the picture in the international market. Lack of a talented directorial handling is obvious.

In a small village on Mytilini Island, a middle-aged widower Ambarras has become the financial tyrant who thrives on the poor producers of olive oil who have neither the courage or the organization to get free of his claws. One after another their properties are auctioned and taken over by Ambarras because they could not meet his loans.

Whoever dares resist him is crushed. Only young Lefteris, returning from a two years' service in the army and finding the family property taken over by Ambarras, decides to fight him. He tries to persuade some other victims to wake up. But all-powerful Ambarras, used to years of submission, strikes back.

Lefteris is arrested for a slaying of which he is innocent. Ambarras pays the villagers to give evidence against him. Even his own brother is afraid to tell the truth. Only Ambarras' daughter, loving Lefteris secretly, hides him when he escapes. But he is finally shot to death. His death, however, awakens his fellow villagers, who swear to carry on his struggle for a better tomorrow.

This story in better hands would have turned out a fairly good picture but Gregory Gregoriou does not seem to take advantage of the plot or settings. Furthermore his technique reminds us of earlier pix.

Peter Physsoun, one of the best young Greek actors, delivers a fairly good interpretation as the young rebel while Yannis Argyris also is good.

Music by Yannis Marcopoulos won the prize in this year's festival for his musical score, *Rena.*

British Films

Hamile
(Hamlet)
(GHANA)

London, Oct. 12.
Ghana Film Industry Corp. (Sam Aryeetey) production and release. Directed by Terry Bishop. Adopted from play by William Shakespeare; camera, R. O. Fenuku; editor, Egbert Adjeso. At Commonwealth Film Fest, London. Running Time, **120 MINS.**

King (Claudius)	Joe Akonor
Hamile (Hamlet)	Kofi Middleton-Mends
Ibrahim (Polonius)	Ernest Abbeyquaye
Karim (Horatio)	Martin Owusu
Laitu (Laertes)	Kofi Yirenkyi
Abdulai (Rosencrantz and Guildenstern)	Gad Gadugan
Osuru (Osric)	Fred Akuffo-Lartey
Musa (Marcellus)	Jacob Gharbin
Banda (Bernardo)	Franklin Akrofi
Mahama (Francisco)	Kwame Adunuo
Awudu (Reynaldo)	Samuel Adumuah
Queen (Gertrude)	Frances Sey
Habiba (Ophelia)	Mary Yirenkyi
First Gravedigger	Auhofe Okuampa
Second Gravedigger	Shanco Bruce
Ghost	Sandy Arkhurst

Described as "The Tongo Hamlet," the action of Shakespeare's widely-traveled play now takes place in Tongo, home of the Frafra People, who live in the far, bleak north Ghana.

The dialogue is spoken in English and unaltered except where it would not make sense in a Frafra community or where an archaic word obscures the meaning. This film (although set outdoors in a simple native court in flat, open countryside) is based on the stage production performed by the students of the University of Ghana School of Music and Drama, under producer Joe de Graft.

Novelty value of the film makes it of interest to scholars and students, but as Shakespeare goes, it is all fairly tepid. The students speak their lines clearly and well, and may have been capable of better things under a director with some imagination.

Terry Bishop, however, has no camera sense and the whole is recorded in a dull and stilted way. There is no rhythm or movement, no feeling for the drama and no culminating sense of tragedy.

Only the ghost scene comes to life. It makes a good festival film, but its chances, even as a specialized booking in North America, are slight. *Prat.*

Funny Things Happen Down Under
(AUSTRALIAN-NEW ZEALAND)
(Color-Music)

London, Oct. 12.
Pacifi Films (Australia) production (Roger Mirams). Directed by Joe McCormick. With Bruce Barry, Howard Morrison, Suzanne Haworth, Tanya Binning. Screenplay, John Sherman; camera (Eastmancolor), Roger Mirams; music, Merv Moore. At Commonwealth Film Fest, London. Running Time, **90 MINS.**

Filmed on location at Mt. Macedon. Victoria, and at the Pacific Studios at Woodend, this comedy with music is described as the first Australian-New Zealand feature coproduction.

Mainly a film for children and cast in the earnest mould of a Children's Film Foundation pic, it concerns the furor caused in the little outback town of Wallaby Creek when a group of its children find a formula which enables sheep to grow colored wool.

It's all farcical and predictable, clean and jolly, but rather self-conscious in its American-styled dances and songs. The actors are likable, the children natural, and the music derivative. Mainly for children's Saturday morning shows. *Prat.*

Kalpana
(Imagination)
(INDIAN)

Cardiff, Oct. 12.
Produced, written and directed by Uday Shankar. Stars Shankar. Camera, K. Rammoth; editor, N. K. Gopal; music, Vishnudas Shirali. Reviewed at Cardiff Commonwealth Film Fest. Running Time, **122 MINS.**

(English Titles)
This 1948 film was the "discovery" of the Commonwealth Film Festival and may well be one of the most unusual films ever made in India. It's a marvelously entertaining mixture of comedy, drama, surrealism, sex and social criticism, combined with spectacle, songs, dances and dreams.

The frame for these elements is familiar enough: a writer goes to a film producer with a story. As he tells it, the scenes come to life together with moments from his own life. At the end, the producer has the writer thrown out, saying that his story has no popular appeal, no sex, no songs nor any spectacle. He has failed to see them because he refuses to depart from formulas. The picture ends with the writer making an impassioned plea for India to throw off its apathy and lack of imagination, not only in filmmaking, it seems, but in other aspects of life.

There are effects here worthy of Dali, Cocteau and Bunuel, conveyed with a sense of humor, good taste and cinematic skill. For Uday Shankar (who is Ravi Shankar's brother) this is practically a one-man film, but he acquits himself with distinction.

He would appear not to have received the recognition he deserves and the Indian government, apparently, is reluctant to have it shown abroad. Film societies and very

specialized cinemas will find it worth obtaining. *Prat.*

Woh Kaun Thi?
(Who Was She?)
(INDIAN)

Cardiff, Oct. 12.
A Prithvi Pictures presentation, produced by N. N. Sippy. Directed by Raj Khosla. Stars Sadhana and Manoj Kumar; features Pravin Chaudhari, K. N. Singh, Raj Mehra, Dhumal, Mohran Choti, Ratnamala and Helen. Story and screenplay, Dhruva Chatterjee; dialogue, Ehsan Rizvi; camera, K. H. Kapadia; editor, D. N. Pai; dance director, Satyanarayan and Surya Kumar; music, Madan Mohan. Reviewed at Cardiff Commonwealth Film Fest. Running Time, **140 MINS.**

(English Titles)
Apart from the films of Satyajit Ray, all Indian films appear to be alike—sentimental stories with songs involving unreal people both rich and poor upon whom fate heaps the most cruel blows. This picture is strikingly different, if no more real than the others.

It is actually an Indian Hitchcock, but with far more confusion than the master of suspense would permit. Expensively made, lavishly mounted, complicated in techniques and effects and artfully working in the inevitable songs and dances, it tells of a young doctor haunted by a woman who comes to him from different places, under different names, and almost drives him insane.

Is it a matter of hypnotism, spiritualism, madness or imagination? Not at all, only a devilish plot, calmly unravelled by the police inspector at the end, but where he got all his information is never revealed.

Stylistically, the film is fascinating. It doesn't look Indian at all. All the characters dress in Western clothes, the girls are as modern in fashions and hair styles as Fifth Avenue. And when they go to a nightclub they twist with more vigor, grace and enjoyment than any of our tired young set. The songs are attractive, the actors assured and the whole an unexpected change from the routine Indian festival film. *Prat.*

Saama
(CEYLON)

Cardiff, Oct. 12.
Kala Pela Cultural Society (G. D. L. Perera) production. Directed and written by Perera. Camera, N. A. Ratnayake; editor, T. A. Kumar; music, Amaradeva-Jayatissa-Devananda. Reviewed at Cardiff Commonwealth Film Fest. Running Time, **120 MINS.**

(English Titles)
Perera originally wrote this story as a play, which was successfully produced in 1960. When he suggested filming it, the idea was ridiculed. He persisted, however. And with members of the Kala Pela Society, who sold their cars, pawned jewelry and mortgaged houses, they rented equipment and every weekend traveled 15 miles into the countryside by car and bus to make this film.

His story is somewhat like Lester James Peries' "Gamperaliya." in that it attempts to show the changes taking place in village life in Ceylon. It is suggested here that the elders do not always know what is best for their children, as a young girl dies of a

broken heart when the old mother of the boy she loves prevents them from being married.

Otherwise, nothing much happens in the village or in the film. The narrative is quiet, leisurely, sincere and deeply felt. The young players are natural and engaging (there is no attempt to dramatize reality) and they merely tell what probably has happened many times. The enterprise has succeeded remarkably well considering the adverse circumstances under which it was made and the fact that it broke away from Ceylon's boxoffice pattern. *Prat.*

Sooterang
(PAKISTAN)

London, Oct. 12.
Eastern Films (M. A. Khayer-C. R. Chaudhry) production. Directed by Subhas Dutta. With Subhas Dutta and Kabori. Reviewed at Commonwealth Film Fest, London. Running Time, **100 MINS.**

A sentimental comedy-drama about a poor boy who falls in love with a rich girl. The father refuses to let him marry her until he has made a name for himself. Boy goes to the city, works hard, becomes wealthy, returns to the village only to find the girl's father has married her off to a wealthy but weak husband.

Extremely slow, with stagey sets and only average songs, this is strictly for the domestic (Pakistan) market. *Prat.*

Vermilion Door
(HONG KONG)
(COLOR-SCOPE)

London, Oct. 12.
A Shaw Brothers (SB) production (Run Run Shaw). Directed by Lo Chen. Screenplay, Chin Ko; camera (Eastmancolor), Liu Chi; editor, Chiang Hsingloong; music, Wang Ju-jen. Reviewed at Commonwealth Film Fest, London. Running Time, **120 MINS.**

Lo Hsiang-chi	Li Li-hua
Mei Pao	Ivy Ling Po
Chiu Hai-tang	Kwan Shan
The deaf maid	Hsia Yi-chiu
Chi Shao-shiung	Yang Chi-ching
Chao Eu-k'un	Chiang Kwang-chao
Yuan Pao-fan	Ching Miao
Shang Lao-er	Tien Feng
Lo Shao-hua	Ho Fan
Mrs. Meng	Woo Wei
Han Shao-wen	Chao Ming
Shiao K'ao-tse	Li Kwan
Old Man Han	Ruey Ming

(English subtitles)
The newest production from the wealthy Shaw Brothers empire of studios and cinemas, based in Hong Kong, this "Shawscope" melodrama is rich in color, trappings, sets, violence, tears and tragedy.

Set in the early days of "the Chinese Republic," it tells the story of young lovers torn apart by a lecherous army colonel, of clandestine meetings, of babies changed in their cradles, the lover whose face is scarred for life by a livid war lord, of a 17-year separation and a final reunion on the death bed.

Magnificently produced, directed with sweep and vigor and passionately played out by the popular stars, Li Li-hua and Kwan Shan, the Shaw brothers will make a fortune from it in Asia. And it should do good business in San Francisco. The second half drags, however, and by the time the end is reached western audiences may

well have tired of the suffering characters in their unreal world.
Prat.

The Lift
(BRITISH)

London, Oct. 12.
A Libra Film produced by Julius Rascheff. Written and directed by Burt Krancer; camera, Rascheff; music, Andre Hajdu. Reviewed at Commonwealth Film Fest, London. Running Time, **85 MINS.**

Margot	Helen Ryan
Mr. Maxwell	Alistair Williamson
Jane	Holly Doone
Joe	Job Stewart
Fanny	Shirley Rogers

This film poses a problem with regard to nationality. Described as "an independent Canadian feature," it was shot in and around London in two months on a budget of $60,000, by Julius Rascheff, a stateless Bulgarian who has applied for Canadian citizenship. Not even the money comes from Canada. And its young director is American.

This is the sort of film which took so much energy and resourcefulness to make by its team of struggling young makers that no one appears to have had time to think about the script. The story, farfetched and unconvincing, concerns a young man who tries to interest a tycoon in using his airplane for business purposes. He becomes involved with the man's two daughters, seduces them both, goes back to an early girl friend. But he doesn't know what to make of himself and ends up alone and with nothing. Absurd and chaotic it may be, yet oddly enough it is never boring, mainly because of Rascheff's lively use of his camera in some new and modern London locations. The cast does quite well with the badly defined characters, but cannot prevent certain scenes from being unintentionally hilarious. There is the usual nude scene, of course, quite harmless, but which most censors will remove.

Being so inexpensive, this picture may well find a place as second feature film. Rascheff and Krancer deserve to be encouraged.
Prat.

King Rat

Grim POW meller in which one hustling prisoner debases others. Performances, direction and production values strong. Impact lessened by overlength. Femmes may avoid, but good b.o. prospects in general situations.

Hollywood, Oct. 20.
Columbia Pictures release of Coleytown Production, produced by James Woolf. Features George Segal, Tom Courtenay, James Fox, Patrick O'Neal, Denholm Elliott, James Donald, Todd Armstrong, John Mills. Directed by Bryan Forbes. Screenplay, Forbes, based on novel by James Clavell; camera, Burnett Guffey; editor, Walter Thompson; music, John Barry; art direction, Robert Smith; sound, James Z. Flaster, John Cox; asst. director, Russell Saunders. Reviewed at Columbia Studio, Oct. 19, '65. Running Time, **134 MINS.**

King	George Segal
Lt. Grey	Tom Courtenay
Peter Marlowe	James Fox
Max	Patrick O'Neal
Lt. Col. Larkin	Denholm Elliott
Dr. Kennedy	James Donald
Tex	Todd Armstrong
Col. Smedley-Taylor	John Mills
Col. Jones	Gerald Sim
Major McCoy	Leonard Rossiter
Capt. Daven	John Standing
Col. Brant	Alan Webb
Capt. Hawkins	John Ronane
Chaplain Drinkwater	Hamilton Dyce
Dino	Joseph Turkel
Squadron Leader Vexley	Geoffrey Bayldon
Tinker-Bell	Reg Lye
Major Barry	George Pelling
Yoshima	Dale Ishimoto

Filmed near Hollywood but having the feel and casting of an overseas pic, "King Rat" is a grim, downbeat and often raw prison camp drama depicting the character destruction wrought by a small-time sharpie on fellow inmates at a Japanese POW site in the final days of World War II. James Woolf production has some fine characterizations and directions, backed by stark, realistic and therefore solid production values, which offset in part its overlength and some script softness. Subject matter and all-male cast may not attract femmes, but the Columbia release should hold its own in the general market.

Commercially speaking, the Military prison camp route has been traveled by many previous pix, and the b.o. potential of "Rat" could be missed unless selling emphasizes its unique gimmick, that of a con artist who, by virtue of fancy footwork, effectively manipulates the meagre goods and characters of other prisoners, most of whom have higher military rank. Amoral, insensitive and greedy, he's the Sammy Glick and Hud of POW life.

George Segal does an excellent job as U.S. Corporal King, the "Rat," properly top-featured (all names follow the title) as the pivotal heel. Director Bryan Forbes adapted the tome by James Clavell (himself an actual POW in the locale of the story), and Forbes has sharply etched his main character.

Ditto for Tom Courtenay, the young British officer trying to perform provost-marshal duties in the behind-the-wire hierarchy topped by weary, but worldly and practical John Mills, effective in brief footage. Courtenay reps the self-made lowerclass Briton whose hatred of Segal's wheeling and dealing is perhaps tinged with envy.

James Fox, another young British officer, registers solidly as he comes under Segal's influence and develops an affection for him, reciprocated only to the extent possible in Segal's nature. Patrick O'Neal stands out as another minion, as does James Donald's sympathetic medic and Reg Lye's Aussie promoter, counterpart to Segal. Other players make the most of various vignettes.

Forbes' sharp writing and direction eventualy work against the overall effect. In the overlong 134 minutes there is a tendency to pile on the raw incidents, effect of which, in view of the early character definition, is not to advance the plot but seems shock for shock's sake. When the war ends, Segal abruptly returns to his status, but this is not as effectively carried off as the earlier scenes when he debases the others, one by one.

Studio synopsis, compared with preview print, indicates some pruning, and more is in order by editor Walter Thompson.

Burnett Guffey's outstanding b&w camera lends solid assistance in capturing the steamy jungle atmosphere. John Barry's music has an appropriate eerie effect, and other technical credits are firstrate.
Murf.

Never Too Late
(COLOR-PANAVISION)

Excellent adaptation of the legit comedy success. Topnotch script, direction, acting and production. Excellent prospects in general situations.

Hollywood, Oct. 16.
Warner Bros. release of a Tandem Production, produced by Norman Lear. Features Paul Ford, Connie Stevens, Maureen O'Sullivan, Jim Hutton, Jane Wyatt, Henry Jones, Lloyd Nolan. Directed by Bud Yorkin. Screenplay, Sumner Long, based on his play; camera (Technicolor), Phil Lathrop; editor, William Ziegler; music, David Rose; title tune lyrics, Jay Livingston, Ray Evans; art direction, Edward Carrere; sound, Everett Hughes; asst. director, Bud Grace. Reviewed at Pacific's Pantages Theatre, L.A., Oct. 15, '65. Running Time, **104 MINS.**

Harry Lambert	Paul Ford
Kate Clinton	Connie Stevens
Edith Lambert	Maureen O'Sullivan
Charlie Clinton	Jim Hutton
Grace Kimbrough	Jane Wyatt
Dr. Kimbrough	Henry Jones
Mayor Crane	Lloyd Nolan

"Never Too Late" is excellent film comedy which shapes as a money picture. Outstanding direction and acting give full life to this well-expanded legiter about an approaching-menopause wife who becomes pregnant to the chagrin of hubby, spoiled-brat daughter, and free-loading son-in-law. Comedy ranges from sophisticated to near-slapstick, all handled in top form. Cumulative marquee lure touches all age bases. The Norman Lear production values are icing on a cake which should sweeten the Warner Bros. pot. Lotsa mileage and playing time in this one.

Sumner Arthur Long adapted his play which though essentially a one-joke affair he has filled out with exterior sequences which enhance, rather than pad. While the result is a family pie, it's not a pollyanna pot pourri of fluff. There's some meaty dialog for adults. Juves can identify with the younger players.

Paul Ford and Maureen O'Sullivan are smartly re-teamed in their Broadway roles of small town Massachusetts parents, settled in middle age habits until wife's increasing fatigue is diagnosed as pregnancy. Miss O'Sullivan has long been absent from the screen, and older audiences will only recall her in "Tarzan" pix and a few plush-mounted Metro oldies. She looks great and handles light comedy with a warm, gracious flair.

More familiar from videxposure and top-featured here (all names follow title), Ford carries the pic as the flustered father-to-be, saddled with the sly grins of neighbors, the incompetency of son-in-law Jim Hutton (which Ford has unconsciously fostered), and the domestic bumblings of daughter Connie Stevens who has never had to cook before mom's delicate condition.

Young players acquit themselves handily, with Miss Stevens showing excellent development in comedy under director Bud Yorkin's always-sure touch. Hutton adds to his reputation in light fun roles. Jane Wyatt, another theatre screen absentee, brightens proceedings as a family friend, wife of medic Henry Jones who monitors the baby show and also gives the young couple some good advice.

Lloyd Nolan, Ford's plot nemesis as the local mayor, gets the most out of broad comedy in an unusual but firstrate piece of casting. All players fully develop the many sub-plot interactions which lead to the expected climax, harmony and new-found maturity on the part of the kids.

Yorkin's direction is topnotch whether the action is in the kitchen, parlor, bedroom, street or bar, sites of solid vignettes. Phil Lathrop's perceptive camera is right in the groove, ditto William Ziegler's zippy editing to 104 minutes, although the Ford-Hutton tipsy scenes might be slightly clipped. Other technical credits are grade-A.

David Rose's score is good, but unfortunately the title tune gambit seems a misfire. Latter is a slow romantic ballad, snug over titles by Vic Damone, which makes for a tepid, overly-pastoral opening. Tune won't go anywhere. A brighter number would have set the right tone.
Murf.

Harum Scarum
(SONGS-COLOR)

Elvis Presley popularity will carry spoof that doesn't quite rate as firstclass scripting.

Hollywood, Oct. 21.
Metro release of Sam Katzman production. Stars Elvis Presley; features Mary Ann Mobley, Fran Jeffries, Michael Ansara, Jay Novello, Philip Reed. Directed by Gene Nelson. Screenplay, Gerald Drayson Adams; camera (Metrocolor), Fred H. Jackman; music, Fred Karger; art direction, George W. Davis, H. McClure Capps; editor, Ben Lewis; asst. director, Eddie Saeta; sound, Franklin Milton. Reviewed at Metro Studios, Oct. 20, '65. Running Time, **95 MINS.**

Johnny Tyronne	Elvis Presley
Princess Shalimar	Mary Ann Mobley

Aishah	Fran Jeffries
Prince Dragna	Michael Ansara
Zacha	Jay Novello
King Toranshah	Philip Reed
Sinan	Theo Marcuse
Baba	Billy Barty
Mokar	Dirk Harvey
Julna	Jack Costanzo
Captain Herat	Larry Chance
Leilah	Barbara Werle
Emerald	Brenda Benet
Sapphire	Gail Gilmore
Amethyst	Wilda Taylor
Sari	Vicki Malkin
Mustapha	Ryck Rydon
Scarred Bedouin	Richard Reeves
Yussef	Joey Russo

With anybody but Elvis Presley to gun possibilities this would be a pretty dreary affair at the boxoffice. Elvis, however, apparently can do no wrong — even if producers do manage — and "Harum Scarum," which suffers from a lack of imagination in providing star with a substantial showcase but enabling him to belt out eight song numbers, will probably meet with response similar to Presley's past entries.

Singer, portraying a Hollywood star attending the Middle Eastern preem of his latest opus, is set down in a modern Arabian Nights atmosphere in this Sam Katzman production. He's kidnapped by a band of assassins, involved in a palace intrigue in which he's supposed to kill the king and — natch— puts all in order finally to win the princess. Entire unreeling is designed as a spoof, but Gerald Drayson Adams' screenplay isn't always up to its intent.

Presley breaks out in song in unexpected places — viz., awakening from being drugged launches into a number while surrounded by a flock of bosomy beauts — but no matter, audiences will get the voice they love in the type of melody they've come to expect from him. One of the numbers, "Harem Holiday," is reprised, and "Go East, Young Man" carries a romantic flair. The Jordanaires are in for vocal backgrounds.

If Presley were any more relaxed, Perry Como and Bing Crosby would have to retire, but he gets into the general spirit of things and he's Elvis. Mary Ann Mobley is a pretty princess; Philip Reed as the king and Michael Ansara his plotting brother lend professional polish; and Jay Novello is active as a money-hungry rogue. Fran Jeffries torches up her femme heavy role, Theo Marcuse heads the assassins and Billy Barty is a midget purse snatcher. Dancing girls are comely as in their veils.

Gene Nelson's direction fits the mood and sets by George W. Davis and H. McClure Capps lavishly backdrop Fred H. Jackman's expert color photography. Other technical credits are on plus side, too. *Whit.*

Corrida Pour Un Espion
(Corrida For a Spy)
(FRENCH-SPANISH-GERMAN)
(Color)

Paris, Oct. 19.

Gaumont release of Oppenheimer Film-Transatlantic Production-Midega production. Stars Ray Danton, Pascale Petit; features Roger Hanin, Wolfgang Preiss, Helga Sommerfeld, Carl Lange, Horst Frank, Conrado San Martin, Manuel Gil. Directed by Maurice Labro. Screenplay, Claude Rank, Labro, Jean Meckert, Louis Velle from a book by Rank; camera (Eastmancolor), Roger Fellous; editor, Georges Arnstam. At Ambassade-Gaumont, Paris. Running Time, **105 MINS.**

Larson	Ray Danton
Chaton	Pascale Petit
Stewart	Roger Hanin
Captain	Wolfgang Preiss
Lina	Helga Sommerfeld
Scarred Man	Horst Frank
Luis	Conrado San Martin

Still another pic in the Bond-instigated cycle. This one also goes in for tripartite European coproduction with a mixed bag of Continental thesps including one Yank. With color and scope, and the usual mayhem and undercover work, it emerges one that could be an okay dualer item abroad.

A tough Yank CIA man, not above torturing his enemies, mostly Russian in this pic, breaks a secret Communist spying ring on U. S. bases in Europe. They use hidden cameras and are protected by atomic mines.

Involved is a Yank brainwashed turncoat who turns out okay at the climax and a pert French actress with whom the Yank can snuggle. After the usual fights, attacks, counterattacks and the use of gadgets the enemy is destroyed.

Production dress is adequate although direction lacks some spirit, the editing lacks keenness. There's also a failure to get the mock seriousness into the various roles.

Ray Danton has dash as the intrepid CIA man, but Pascale Petit seems dragged in to be on hand for the romantic moments as an assistant to the CIA man. Others acquit themselves professionally in the usual stereotype side roles. Script is average but the dialog is a bit flat. *Mosk.*

Il Compagno Don Camillo
(Don Camillo in Moscow)
(ITALO-FRENCH)

Rome, Oct. 19.

Cineriz release of Rizzoli Film (Rome)—Franco-Riz (Paris) coproduction. Stars Fernandel, Gino Cervi; features Graziella Granata, Gianni Garko, Saro Urzi', Leda Gloria. Directed by Luigi Comencini. Screenplay, Leo Benvenuti, Piero de Bernardi, from novel by Giovanni Guareschi; camera, Armando Nannuzzi; music, Alessandro Cicognini; editor, Nino Baragli. At Adriano, Rome. Running Time, **110 MINS.**

Don Camillo	Fernandel
Peppone	Gino Cervi
Peppone's wife	Leda Gloria
Nadia	Graziella Granata
Scamoggia	Gianni Garko

Time has considerably dulled the impact of the Don Camillo series, once guaranteed seasonal bestsellers locally. Latest item looks to fare well in depth here, especially in hinterland areas where its unsubtle humor will be most effective. In keys and for export, this is a chancy item which even its Russo angles cannot do much for.

This time out, Don Camillo (Fernandel), the battling red-belt priest, joins his perennial antagonist, Commie Mayor Peppone (Gino Cervi), on a junket to Russia —disguised as a member of the town's Communist council. Embarrassment of the Commie delegation at the presence of prelate, as well as by conditions and restrictions imposed on them in what they imagined their never-never land, produce a sizable number of laughs, predictable though they may be.

Interwoven is the usual east-west romance between a lens-hound and a Soviet girl guide, won over by his re-telling of the "Ninotchka" tale. Pace lags here and there, and some of the Russian "settings" have a home grown look about them. But Don Camillo fans will be satisfied that their hero is back for another go. Both Fernandel and Cervi could by now play their roles sans script. Graziella Granata is lovely as the femme guide, and others in colorful cast back ably. Armando Nannuzzi's lensing is occasionally murky. *Hawk.*

Three Weeks of Love
(C'SCOPE-COLOR)

Japanese love story filmed by American company in Orient. Tastefully made but of limited appeal so that bookings will be restricted to selective situatons.

Hollywood, Oct. 22.

Richard K. Polimer release of William E. Brusseau production. Stars Lane Nakano, Tamiko Aya; features Tony Russel, Tatsuo Saito, Roland Ray. Directed and original story by Brusseau. Screenplay, Harry Brown; camera (Eastman Color), Junichi Segawa; music, Calvin Jackson, Ralph Carmichael; editor, Warren Adams; art direction, Totetso Hirakawa; sound, Gene Garvin, Russ Malmgren. Reviewed at General Film Laboratory, Oct. 22, '65. Running Time, **75 MINS.**

Ken Okimura	Lane Nakano
Sumi	Tamiko Aya
Bud	Tony Russel
Mr. Yasuda	Tatsuo Saito
Captain	Roland Ray
Joe Young	Joe Yue
Mrs. Young	Miyako Morita
Sumi's Sister	Keiko Doi
Sumi's Friend	Reiko Okada
Girl in Hong Kong	Lucille Soong
Sumi's Mother	Kiyono Sasaki

"Three Weeks of Love" is a tragic Japanese love story produced by an American company and filmed in Hong Kong and Japan. As first feature production of documentary filmmaker William Brusseau beautifully and interestingly lensed in Eastman Color and tastefully turned out it carries certain attraction but lacks the ingredients necessary for mass appreciation. Consequently its limited appeal will probably restrict its exhibition to selected situations. Richard K. Polimer has acquired distribution rights and plans selling it either via territorial rights or through a major company.

Brusseau has captured the scenic charm of the Orient for his story background. Very frequently, film appears to be more a travelog than a regular dramatic feature, since interest focuses on the Chinese and Japanese settings and narrative provides only a means of parading these backdrops. Toward the close, however, accent is on the ill-fated romance between a Nisei seaman who becomes a ship's officer aboard a Dutch freighter and, a beautiful Japanese hostess in a smart Tokyo nitery. Considerable use is made of off-screen narration by the Dutch captain of the ship who acts as commentator for much of the action.

Lane Nakano, a real-life Hollywood Nisei, persuasively enacts the role of the seaman caught between his own and the world of old Japan which does not allow him marrying the Nipponese girl, who, though modern, still is bound by tradition. Tamiko Aya, a Japanese actress, is excellent in this role. Tatsuo Saito, as her father, scores heavily in his brief role, and Tony Russel is okay as the Nisei's American ex-GI friend who introduces him to night life. Roland Ray is well cast as the captain, and balance of supporting parts are well filled.

Brusseau functions in a triple role, also directing and as author of the original story. His helming of the Harry Brown screenplay is inclined to be over-leisurely at times but he scores his points. Color photography by Junichi Segawa is particularly outstanding. Don Yaka has choreographed two Japanese nightclub lines effectively, and balance of technical credits are strong assists. *Whit.*

The Crazy Quilt

Mannheim, Oct. 19.

A Farallon (Stinson Beach, Calif.) production. With Tom Rosqui and Ina Mela. Directed by John Korty. Screenplay, Korty, based on novel, "Illusionless Man and the Visionary Maid" by Allen Wheelis; camera, John Korty; music, Peter Schickele; commentary, Burgess Meredith; editor, John Korty. At Mannheim Film Fest. Running Time, **72 MINS.**

Henry	Tom Rosqui
Lorabella	Ina Mela
Noel	Ellen Frye
Cyrus, the actor	Harry Hunt
Jim, the fisherman	Calvin Kentfield
Dr. Milton Tugwell	Robert Marquis
Falbuck Wheeling	Doug Korty

This is the first full-length feature pic for 29-year old Californian, John Korty, who is not a stranger to European festival patrons. They have seen several Korty shorts; one, "Language of Faces," copping the Gran Premio at the Bergamo Fest four years ago. "The Crazy Quilt" was given its world preem here where it competed in the "first features of fomer short film makers" section. (Ed.— Film is also entry at Frisco Fest.)

Korty's initial feature film effort, on the positive side displays both technical and artistic knowhow. European critics have seen quite a number of such low-budgeted, independent American pix at this year's various festivals. But most of them were seen and forgotten. Korty's work makes at least a polished impression. It also benefits from competent acting. He produced, directed, lensed and edited "Quilt" and has done everything with real devotion. The result is a film which doesn't disappoint.

A good deal of controversy, however, stems from the plot and treatment of the subject matter. Film is based on a novel which might have justified a four-hour pic. Plot is generally simple. The whole thing was boiled down to 72 minutes and seems to have been cut at the expense of conviction. Story development is rather uneven. Time travels rather slowly during the film's first half and faster later. Much of film's second half remains too much on the surface. But also in this form this film could — if adequately dubbed — find its way into European releases. It would probably qualify best for tv programming. The narration, incidentally, is spoken by actor Burgess Meredith.

Plot revolves around two main characters. Henry, a carpenter, a man without illusions about what life concerns, and Lorabella, a good-natured girl who believes in the beauty of life. Although they completely differ from each other, they fall in love and get married. A miscarriage for which she makes her husband responsible leads to separation. Although he rejects a divorce, she leaves him and the following sequences see her hop from romance to romance, each ending with disillusion and disappointment. She falls for an actor but he turns out to be a thief. She falls in love with an elderly man but he emerges as a liar.

She finally returns to her husband who has become sick and she takes care of him. Eventually a daughter is born and they experience normal family life. A quarrel every now and then, but they live happily within the bounds of possibility.

Film's budget amounted to about $70,000 which Korty collected from 40 different persons. All in all, "Quilt" is certainly not a big hit. Yet it is a more memorable and better entry than many other Stateside contributions to this year's festivals. *Hans.*

I Complessi
(Complexes)
(ITALIAN)

Rome, Oct. 19.

Euro International release of Documento (Gianni Hecht Lucari) production. Music, Armando Trovaioli. At Metropolitan, Rome. Running Time. 100 MINS.
UNA GIORNATA DECISIVA
(A Decisive Day)
With Nino Manfredi, Ilaria Occhini, Riccardo Garrone. Umberto D'Orsi. Directed by Dino Risi. Screenplay, Risi, Maccari, Scola; camera, Franco Bruni.
IL COMPLESSO DELLA
SCHIAVA NUBIANA
(Complex of the Nubian Slave)
With Ugo Tognazzi, Claudie Lange. Directed by Franco Rossi. Screenplay, Leo Benvenuti and Piero Bernardi, from story by Age and Scarpelli; camera, Arturo Zavattini.
GUGLIELMO IL DENTONE
(Toothsome Guglielmo)
With Alberto Sordi, Professor Cutolo, Vincenzo Talarico, Franco Fabrizi, Gaia Germani, Edy Campagnoli, Nanny Loy, Romolo Valli. Directed by Luigi Filippo D'Amico. Screenplay, Sordi, Rodolfo Sonego; camera, Maurizio Scanzani.

Gianni Hecht Lucari has another saleable item in this latest documento episoder in a successful skein. In home territories, the Nino Manfredi, Ugo Tognazzi and Alberto Sordi names provide surefire marquee bait. Elsewhere, this should have a following with audiences which go for this type of segmentary film-flam. One drawback, compared to, i.e., the recent "Bambole" (from the same stable) is that while themes are universal, subject matter is less universally understandable among non-Italian general audiences. Full appreciation attracts these lingualers with some basic understanding of Italian manners and mores.

First seg spoofs timidity in showing gauche attempts by Nino Manfredi, a big-company employee, to win a longtime flame during a company excursion into the Roman countryside. Here he runs into the current suitor of the gal, a married man, but backs down when confronted by him. Thus, he takes the way out by switching his attention to an ugly but influential spinster. Manfredi is hilarious as the timid male. Ilaria Occhini, a looker with definite Stateside possibilities, is the target of his attentions. Riccardo Garrone is suitably brash as her lover while Umberto D'Orsi is fine as the prankish life-of-the-party. Dino Risi's direction, aided by a fine script by Maccari and Scola, has the proper bite alternating with risible moments.

Second episode is a bit confused and drawn out though it has its moments. Ugo Tognazzi is an Italo bigwig with important political-social ties which are endangered by his discovery that his wife once posed in the nude for a spear-and-sandals pic epic. Remainder of seg shows his frenzied efforts to find this film material and keep it out of the prejudicial public eye. Ironic twist, however, winds bit by having him accidentally caught in a morals raid. Tognazzi is good as the over-zealous moralist, but the material only occasionally does him justice. Authors have inserted some adroit barbs directed at film censorship.

Third part of vehicle, taking up half of its running time, is also a bit extended though Alberto Sordi fans won't complain. He has himself a field day with some fine scriptwork and a hilarious toothy makeup in depicting a self-confident applicant for a tele announcer spot. He makes the grade without inside aid and despite an un-telegenic mouthful of teeth.

It's practically a one-man show for Sordi, and he makes the most of it, with good assistance from Professor Cutolo, Nanny Loy (the pic director, playing himself). Romolo Valli, Franci Fabrizi, and Gaia Germani, last named a striking looker whose resemblance to Audrey Hepburn will certainly do her no harm in what could turn into a promising career if properly administered.

Technical credits are fine throughout, with Armando Trovaioli's musical backdropping functionally ironic. *Hawk.*

Le Chant Du Monde
(Song of the World)
(FRENCH-COLOR)

Paris, Oct. 19.

Cocinor release of Marceau-Orphee Productions production. Stars Hardy Kruger, Catherine Deneuve, Charles Vanel; features Marilu Tolo, Ginette Leclerc, Michel Vitold, Saro Urzi. Written and directed by Marcel Camus from the book by Jean Giono. Camera (Eastmancolor). Raymond Lemoigne; editor, Andree Felix. At Marignan, Paris. Running Time. 108 MINS.
Antonio .... Hardy Kruger
Clara .... Catherine Deneuve
Matelot .... Charles Vanel
Gina .... Marilu Tolo
Gina-La-Veieille .... Ginette Leclerc
Toussaint .... Michel Vitold
Carle .... Saro Urzi

Marcel Camus made that prize-winning pic. "Black Orpheus," some six years ago. Since then he has not been able to repeat his combination of romantic myth, color and exoticism. And he also falls down on this new entry about a rustic vendetta and love in a mountainous section of Southern France.

Mainly some possible playoff abroad loom on its action, but its old-fashioned air and literary ring limit this for any arty chances. Filmed in color on-the-spot, it does have some good production aspects. That is about all.

A traveling troubador sets out with a kindly old man to find his missing son. The son had run afoul of a ruthless family ruling most of the district over a girl. He is now hiding out with the girl and mortally wounds one of his pursuers. Film settles down into skirmishes between the two groups. But Camus has not been able to get a more fluid pace into this and it emerges a series of vignettes.

Hardy Kruger plays the traveling singer on a simple-minded plane. Catherine Denueve has nothing to do but look pretty as the girl while Charles Vanel adds some dash as the old man. Others are only adequate. This has some photographic flair and color rendition but not the depth to erase its plodding or talkiness. *Mosk.*

Der Vorletzte Akt—Brundibar
(Last Act But One—Brundibar)
(GERMAN)

Mannheim, Oct. 19.

Cineropa Film (Munich) production and release. Produced, directed and written by Walter Kruettner. Camera, Alois Nozicka; music, Hans Krasa; lyrics, Adolph Hoffmeister. At Mannheim Film Fest. Running Time. 62 MINS.

As per its contents, this German production, the first long film of Walter Kruettner, who created several prize-winning shorts, will stir considerable attention. It deals with a special chapter of Germany's most gruesome historical past: The Nazi concentration camp of Theresienstadt. It is especially dedicated to German-born Jewish composer, Hans Krasa, an inmate of this camp whose life ended in the gas chambers of Auschwitz. Kruettner's film, a documentary type of film, already has been sold to Israel. It is the type of cinema vehicle with which the critic feels inclined to put its moving contents above its artistic quality.

It was Krasa and Adolph Hoffmeister, a Czech writer, who created back in 1938 a children's opera. "Brundibar," in Prague. This couldn't have its premiere under normal conditions because of the Nazi invasion soon thereafter. The preem was held under unique circumstances in 1944 in the concentration camp of Theresienstadt where Heinrich Himmler, the SS chieftain, still permitted "cultural life" this camp being open to visits by the International Red Cross. Directed by adult inmates, Jewish children performed this opera and therewith honored its composer, Krasa, who later died with them in Auschwitz.

Some of the few survivors and eye-witnesses of this ghostly first performance of "Brundibar" in this film depict their experiences. They include Zdenek Ornest, a child at that time and only survivor of the opera's cast; Dr. Rudolf Franek, who rehearsed this opera performance; Dr. Norbert Fryd and Dr. Josef Bor, Czech writers, who witnessed the preem 21 years ago. Also heard is Adolph Hoffmeister, the opera's librettist and friend of Krasa.

Inserted in the film are excerpts from a new production of "Brundibar," performed by the Troja children's choir of Prague.

What Kruettner has brought to the screen, technically speaking, is a clean, good film job. With regard to the theme, he treated it with an objective, honest attitude. A special plus about this production is Krasa's delightful music. In fact, the music makes many listeners want to get a recording.

Critically speaking, it can't be overlooked that this is actually primarily tele material. The subject could, one feels. furnish the basis for a big-scale American film production for it is not only unique but also naturally draws emotional impact. It also poses the question of whether this unconventional documentary, which will have tough sledding on regular cinema circuits, could have been better. One feels that Krasa's music deserves a stronger frame. *Hans.*

La Metamorphose Des Cloportes
(Metamorphosis of Smalltimers)
(FRENCH)

Paris, Oct. 19.

20th-Fox release of Films Du Siecle production. Stars Lino Ventura, Charles Aznavour, Pierre Brasseur, Irina Demick; features Georges Geret, Daniel Ceccaldi. Directed by Pierre Garnier-Deferre. Screenplay, Albert Simonin, Michel Audiard; camera, Nicolas Hayer; editor, Jean Ravel. At Balzac, Paris. Running Time. 98 MINS.
Alphonse .... Lino Ventura
Edmond .... Charles Aznavour
Tonton .... Pierre Brasseur
Catherin .... Irina Demick
Roquemoute .... Georges Geret
Clancul .... Daniel Ceccaldi
Gegene .... Francoise Rosay
Leone .... Annie Fratellini
Lescure .... Maurice Biraud

This pic kicks around too many themes and rarely settles on whether it's a comedy, satire or ironic look at lowlife as a crucible of human pettiness. So this looks unlikely for arty chances abroad. However, it could do on a twin bill.

Some smalltime hoodlums talk a bigger gangster into backing a heist of some fine paintings. A mishap has only the big boy captured and the others run off with his money and let him languish in jail. Finally released, he comes out roaring for vengeance and knocks them all off. But he's put on the spot himself by a conniving girl. Director Pierre Garnier-Deferre does point up a film background in the use of symbols and creating the dreary, petty milieu. But the storyline seems to keep this from ever taking a firm footing. And the film winds up rather obviously.

Lino Ventura has the glowering weight to make the avenger acceptable but the others are more fragmentary in general thesping. Sometimes dreary, rather than truly pointed up in satire or irony, this still does have a severe underlying moralizing that does not quite come off. *Mosk.*

Les Tribulations D'Un Chinois En Chine
(Chinese Adventures In China)
(FRENCH-COLOR)

Paris, Oct. 19.

United Artists release of Ariane Films-Vides-UA production. Stars Jean-Paul Belmondo, Ursula Andress; features Jean Rochefort, Maria Pacome, Valerie

Lagrange, Inkijinoff, Jess Hahn, Darry Cowl. Directed by Philippe De Broca. Screenplay, Daniel Boulanger. De Broca based on the book by Jules Verne; camera (Eastmancolor), Edmond Sechan; editor, Francoise Javet. Previewed in Paris. Running Time, 110 MINS.

Arthur	Jean-Paul Belmondo
Alexandrine	Ursula Andress
Leon	Jean Rochefort
Suzy	Maria Pacome
Alice	Valeria Lagrange
Mister Goh	Inkijinoff
Cornelius	Jess Hahn
Biscotin	Darry Cowl

Philippe De Broca, who made the successful "That Man From Rio," tries to repeat in another madcap adventure yarn with engaging Jean-Paul Belmondo going through his acrobatic paces. It just accumulates gags and chases in exotic climes and emerges a staple in this growing genre, with probable solid business in store on its home grounds but foreign 'marts calling for some hardsell.

Story has Belmondo as a sad millionaire trying to kill himself. An Oriental friend tells him he needs to add some salt to his living and has him insure his life for millions to go to him and his fiancee's family. Then he says he will have him killed, secretly and unexpectedly. But he loses his money and then begins to resent the idea of being up to be killed.

Story opens in Hong Kong and then has him rushing off to the Himalayas to find his friend since he does not want to die that way. He finds out the friend was kidding just to give him a zest for life but his future in-laws try to get him and then hire a notorious Hong Kong gangster.

In the interim, he meets a beauteous stripper, Ursula Andress, who also builds up his desire to live. When all is reresolved, he finds he has not really lost his money and he begins to brood again. This skeletal updated Jules Verne story is only a peg on which to hang a series of zany chases, fights and adventures. It sometimes gets overcharged and some of the innocent verve of the earlier "Rio" seems missing.

With an impeccable valet following him as he dashes about Hong Kong, goes through the Himalayas, escapes a funeral pyre, gets back for more clashes, car pileups, escaping from an opium junk and finally marrying his stripper only to be saddened by his wealth again, it is sometimes reminiscent of "Around the World in 80 Days."

Belmondo shows his bouncing acrobatic dash. He disguises himself as a stripper in one scene and always keeps on the move as the pic does. The locations are colorful but shape as just a backdrop to a series of chases.

This is one of those saucy adventure takeoffs that at times gets repitious. Belmondo just tumbles his way through this while Miss Andress adds pulchritude. A few smaller roles supply a satiric dash such as Maria Pacome, as the fortune-hunting mother, and Inkijinoff as the inscrutable Oriental friend.

All this has big production values and careens along so fast it glosses over some weaknesses. Film has the foreign locale dazzle, movement, good humor to be able

to cash in on the tongue-in-cheek adventure cycle now proving so popular at world boxoffices.
Mosk.

Sands of the Kalahari
(BRITISH—COLOR)

Superbly photographed adventure tale should attract the action fans, although leaky plot occasionally swamps topnotch cast.

Paramount release of Joseph E. Levine (Cy Endfield-Stanley Baker) production, directed by Endfield. Features Stuart Whitman, Stanley Baker, Susannah York, Harry Andrews, Theodore Bikel, Nigel Davenort. Screenplay, Endfield, based on novel by William Mulvihill; camera (Technicolor-Panavision), Erwin Hillier, editor, John Jympson; special effects, Cliff Richardson; music, John Dankworth. Reviewed at Embassy Pictures h.o., N.Y., Oct. 25, '65. Running Time, 119 MINS.

O'Brien	Stuart Whitman
Bain	Stanley Baker
Grace	Susannah York
Grimmelman	Harry Andrews
Bondarakkai	Theodore Bikel
Sturdevant	Nigel Davenport

Excellent Technicolor and Panavision camerawork by Erwin Hillier and special effects by Cliff Richardson are two good reasons why producers Joseph E. Levine, Cy Endfield and Stanley Baker won't have any trouble peddling "Sands of the Kalahari," especially in the outdoor market.

Endfield, co-producer, director and scripter of the long film (made almost entirely on location in Africa—and utilizing the Eady Plan), wisely makes the camera as important as anyone in the cast, the Panavisioned blowup emphasizing the savagery that is throughout.

When a small group of players, however, are subjected to the continual emphasis on their actions that this big-screen effort does, it makes any slight tendency to overact seem greatly magnified. Although Endfield has been lucky with his casting, some members too quickly betray symptoms of scenery chewing. Even this isn't completely bad, as a bit of flamboyant style is required later, as the action mounts, but the evidence of too much, too soon, takes off some of the edge.

While the storyline is old hat, Endfield's variations, in terms of action, suspense and even terror, provide the film's best selling points. Early advertising indicates that this has already been recognized by Levine and Paramount.

A planeload of assorted types crashes in the desert and the rest of the film deals with their efforts to survive. It's some time before a villain is unveiled and, even then, the viewer's faith gets a few shakes. Whether any survive is part of the suspense and there's sure to also be some controversy as to whether the behavior of the individuals merits survival for any.

Susannah York, as the only female in the cast, gets plenty of exposure. Stuart Whitman, a gunhappy survivalist, and Stanley Baker, a nondescript loser, are the other main characterts, well supported by Harry Andrews,

Theodore Bikel and Nigel Davenport. Unbilled but colorful are assorted natives, animals and insects.

Any serious discussion of the illogical plot loses force since viewer finds himself forgiving flaws in the storytelling as he becomes engrossed in the next bit of action. Entertainment, pure and simple, was evidently what the filmmakers aimed for and that's the target they hit. The cameras, cleverly manipulated by expert hands, make inanimate objects narrate and animals sometimes outplay the humans. It's hard to believe that a band of baboons, important to the plot, were not trained.

Technically, the film couldn't have been done any better in a studio and the extra dramatic value of real locations is immeasurable. John Jympson's editing could allow for some additional scissoring but there are few slack periods. A bit more judicial snipping would have helped especially in a scene where Whitman fights a baboon barehanded. Some of the shots don't match. But the film's ending, with the baboons moving in on what may be their next meal, is superb, winding on a proper note of lingering goosepimples. John Dankworth's score, particularly at the beginning, has a delightful main theme that can stand exploiting. However, the music never intrudes when a minimum of background sound, or none, is indicated. *Robe.*

Giulietta de gli Spiriti
(Juliet Of The Spirits)
(ITALIAN-COLOR)

Fellini lets himself go in creating fantasy, life of an unhappy Italian wife of philanderer. Some confusion but big boxoffice foreseen.

Rizzoli Film Distributors release of Federiz production (Clemente Fracassi, exec producer), directed by Federico Fellini. Stars Giulietta Masina; features Sandra Milo, Sylva Koscina. Screenplay by Fellini, Tullio Pinelli, Ennio Flaiano, Brunello Rondi, based on an original story by Fellini and Pinelli; camera (Technicolor), Gianni di Venanzo; editor, Ruggero Mastroianni; music, Nino Rota. Reviewed in N.Y., Oct. 28, '65. Running Time, 148 MINS.

Giulietta	Giulietta Masina
Susy-Iris-Fanny	Sandra Milo
Sylva	Sylva Koscina
Valentina	Valentina Cortese
Giorgio	Mario Pisu
Giulietta as a child	Alba Cancellieri
Giulietta's mother	Caterina Boratto
Adele	Luisa Della Noce
Granddaughters	Sabrina Gigli, Rossella di Sepio
Grandfather	Lou Gilbert
Dolores	Silvana Jachino
Elena	Elena Fondra
Friends of Husband	Jose de Villalonga, Cesarino Miceli Picardi
Giulietta's maids	Milena Vucotich, Elisabetta Gray
Susy's grandmother	Irina Alexeieva
Susy's mother	Alessandra Mannoukine
Susy's chauffeur	Gilberto Galvan
Susy's masseuse	Seyna Seyn
Susy's maids	Yvonne Casadei, Hildegarde Golez, Dina de Santis
Russian teacher	Edoardo Torricella
Desperate friend	Dany Paris
Oriental lover	Raffaele Guida
Arabian prince	Fred Williams
Lynx-Eyes	Alberto Plebani
Lynx-Eyes' agents	Federico Valli, Remo Risaliti, Grillo Rufino
Bhishma	Waleska Gert
Bhishma's helpers	Assia Rubener, Sujata Rubener, Walter Harrison
Don Raffaele	Felice Fulchignoni
Psychoanalyst	Anne Francine
Family lawyer	Mario Conocchia
Headmaster	Fredrich Ledebur
Medium	Genius
Valentina's lover	Massimo Sarchielli
Dolores' models	Giorgio Ardisson, Bob Edwards, Nadir Moretti

Within a simple, naively romantic narrative frame concerning a wife's desperation over her husband's philanderings, director Federico Fellini ("La Strada," "La Dolce Vita," "8½," etc.) has put together an imperial-sized fantasy of a physical opulence to make the old Vincente Minnelli Metro musicals look like Army training films. "Juliet of The Spirits" first dazzles —and then boggles—the eye, but on the strength of the Fellini name as well as the comment it is bound to create, it shapes up as a big grosser in key situations.

In the freedom of its form and in its carnival of images, "Juliet" constantly recalls "8½." However, where the latter, at its core, summoned a kind of apocalyptic vision of modern man, "Juliet" pops out with a truism, seemingly directed exclusively to the upper middle class Italian housewife: to thine own self be true. The film thus adds up to something less than its individual parts, which are almost always fascinating and often quite funny, not only in their random comments on human relationships and contemporary society, but in the sheer splendor of the colorful, bizarre physical trappings. Indeed, there is the occasional feeling that had the director allowed the set or costume designer to add just one more piece of tulle, or even another ostrich plume, the entire production would have sunk beneath the surface of a sea called Precious.

This physical spectacle, photographed in brilliant Technicolor, may be the film's strength as well as its weakness. For while it amuses and delights, it also distracts to the point where the Viewer begins to forget that the film has, as its basic concern, the fate of desperately lonely and lost individual. In the title role, Giulietta Masina (Mrs. Fellini) is at first humble and appealing as she slowly drifts into a dream world to escape the hard facts of a crumbling marriage. But then as the Fellini fantasies grow increasingly more bizarre, her expressions seem to become more and more monotonous until she eventually pales into the background. There comes the realization that these are not so much the fantasies of an unhappy woman as they are those of an imaginative film director with a huge budget at his disposal.

Fellini has, apparently intentionally, stacked the cards against his heroine with whom, it's assumed, one is supposed to feel a certain amount of sympathy. She is a sweet but dull girl and many will be unable to blame the husband for looking elsewhere.

Once accepting these facts, however, the viewer may settle back and enjoy the three-ring circus Fellini has laid out. It is a non-stop show dominated by the secondary performers, particularly a magnificent specimen by the name of Sandra Milo, a female Presence seen here in three roles. In the most spectacular, she is a next-door demimondaine presiding over a non-stop orgy which Giulietta visits and flees. She also turns up as a rather ominous apparition and as a busty circus lady with whom Juliet's frisky old grandpa (Lou Gilbert) elopes in a flying machine. There are also Sylva Koscina, as Giulietta's scatterbrained sister, Valentina Cortese, a friend who introduces her to the spirit world, and a bevy of other dolls representing just about every conceivable type of womanhood.

The progression of scenes from real-life to fantasy and back again, builds swiftly to the point where there is little distinction between the two, which are equally wonderful as seen by Fellini. Thus a simple afternoon on the beach becomes just as weird an experience as a consultation with a grotesque Hindu mystic. Fellini can endow a straightforward scene of four women walking across a suburban lawn with a kind of terror, and then make a terrifying fantasy—Giulietta's memory of a school play, in which she was to be burned as a martyr—hilariously funny.

The huge cast performs ably enough, but it is clearly the director who is pulling the strings. The performers have not only great faces, but great bodies and costumes, and they exist only in the framework of the film: There are no personalities as such. Next to Fellini himself, art director Piero Gherardi seems the most important person on the production. As he has in the past, Fellini uses the rich, fulsome music of Nino Rota to counterpoint the screen images, usually to very good effect.

Anby.

Sette Uomini D'Oro
(Seven Golden Men)
(ITALO-FRANCO-SPANISH COLOR-WIDESCREEN)

Rome, Oct. 21.

Atlantica Cinematografica release of Marco Vicario production for Atlantica (Rome) — Paris Union Film (Paris) — AS Film (Madrid). Stars Rossana Podesta, Philipe Leroy; features Gadtone Moachin, Jose Suarez, Gabriele Tinti, Maurice Poli, Manuel Zarzo, Giampiero Albertini, Dario DeGrassi, Ennio Balbo, Renzo Palmer, Alberto Bonucci, Juan Cortes, Juan Luis Gagliardo, Renato Terra. Written and directed by Marco Vicario. Camera (Eastmancolor), Ennio Guarnieri; art direction, Arrigio Equini, Piero Poletto; music, Armando Trovajoli; editor, Roberto Cinquini. At Olimpico, Rome. Running Time, 90 MINS.

Giorgia .... Rossana Podesta
Albert .... Philipe Leroy

Production gloss, an inventive script, sprightly pace and a colorful cast headed by a comely Rossana Podesta and a suave Philipe Leroy contribute to making this pic an entry of major interest in world markets, especially in those areas where well-made chillers in the Bond-Topkapi tradition are most in demand.

True, the pattern of the tale is, when analyzed, updated elaboration of a bank heist blended with some of the ironic moral conveyed by "Sierra Madre." But in telling the intricately detailed sequence of events leading to the theft of a Geneva bank's gold cache by an International gang of pros headed by the Professor (Leroy) and his sometimes two-timing mistress (Miss Podesta), writer-director Vicario has shown an undeniable flair for invention, plus modern camera savvy and tongue kept firmly in cheek. This results in a frequently suspenseful, frequently humorous, always elegant and stylish morsel for most audience palates.

In this, Vicario also gets major assists from art directors Arrigo Equini and Piero Poletto, who presumably devised the fascinating and imaginative gimmicks which apply to the latest scientific wrinkles of radar, video, etc., in the art of bank robbery. Production in this sense is a visual delight, ably captured by Ennio Guarnieri's Eastman lensing.

Philipe Leroy is fine as the not-all-that-zany professor of crime while Miss Podesta is as pretty as always in orb-filling display of wardrobe or lack thereof. In a large number of up-front accessory roles, Jose Suarez, Gadtone Moachin, and a spate of French and Spanish thesps have a chance to shine via ably captured interpretations. Occasionally, their accents (in the Italo version) get in the way of the action—and comprehension.

Hawk.

La Communale
(The Public School)
(FRENCH)

Paris. Oct. 26.

Gaumont release of CAPAC-Gueville-Films De La Colombe production. Stars Robert Dhery, Colette Brosset, Yves Robert; features Fernand Ledoux, Jacques Dufilho, Didier Haudepin, Rene-Louis Lafforgue. Written and directed by Jean Lhote from his own book. Camera, Andre Dumaitre; editor, Eva Zora. At Ambassade-Gaumont, Paris. Running Time, 90 MINS.

Teacher .... Robert Dhery
Wife .... Colette Brosset
Henri .... Yves Robert
Inspector .... Fernand Ledoux
Peasant .... Jacques Dufilho
Pierre .... Didier Haudepin
Mechanic .... Rene-Louis Lafforgue

Quaint and anecdotal pic is really more a series of simplified episodes than a progressive story about smalltown school life in the 1930's. Slimness makes foreign chances skimpy except possibly for tele use on its homey aspects. Film has some dualer chances on the Robert Dhery name, who scored in the U.S. in the legit comedy revue, "La Plume De Ma Tante."

Dhery and his wife, Colette Brosset play a husband and wife teaching in a small beginner's school. Film mainly centers around Dhery's efforts to buy a car. Then the travels and problems that result when he uses it for a class in the country one day. All the students get lost, then there's a final trip to the sea.

Direction is simple and uninspired, placing the brunt of the pic on Dhery's shoulders. His charm and fine limning of a little middleclass man without much ambition does manage to keep things afloat. But he cannot pull this smug little pic out of the mediocre status.

Mosk.

Winter A-Go-Go
(COLOR)

Tepid teenpic with little plot. No marquee power. Padded with tunes and good Tahoe scenery. Prospects fair on lowercase in youth situations.

Hollywood, Oct. 23.

Columbia Pictures release of a Reno Carell production. Features James Stacy, William Wellman Jr., Beverly Adams, Anthony Hayes, Jill Donohue, Tom Nardini, Duke Hobbie. Directed by Richard Benedict. Screenplay, Bob Kanter, based on a Carell story; camera (Pathecolor), Jacques Marquette; editor, Irving Berlin; music, Harry Betts; songs, Howard Greenfield, Jack Keller, Steve Venet, Tommy Boyce, Bob Hart, Harry Betts, Toni Wine; art direction, Walter Holscher; sound, Earl Snyder; asst. director, Robert Vreeland. Reviewed at Columbia Studio, Oct. 22, '65. Running Time, 87 MINS.

Danny Frazer .... James Stacy
Jeff Forrester ... William Wellman, Jr.
Jo Ann Wallace .... Beverly Adams
Burt .... Anthony Hayes
Janine .... Jill Donohue
Frankie .... Tom Nardini
Bob .... Duke Hobbie
Dee Dee .... Julie Parrish
Jonesy .... Nancy Czar
Penny .... Linda Rogers
Dori .... Judy Parker
Roger .... Bob Kanter
Jordan .... Walter Maslow
Cholly .... H. T. Tsiang
Will .... Buck Holland
Themselves .... The Nooney Rickett Four, Joni Lyman, The Reflections

"Winter A-Go-Go" is a disappointing teenpic despite some occasional comic touches, good ski-country lensing, and talent glimmers among the younger players. Script doesn't take off until half-time, too late. Tunes and terp scenes flag what little pace exists. Reno Carell production is not up to standards of his earlier "A Swingin' Summer," and seems destined for lowercase Columbia release in youth situations.

Bunch of juves operate a ski lodge; end of Bob Kanter's script, predictable and thin. Jacques Marquette's color lensing has captured some exterior beauty of the Lake Tahoe area (although much of the film appears forced intro of ski slopes), and interiors focus on bouncing buttocks, in themselves not objectionable.

James Stacy handles his top-featured role (all names follow title) in fine fashion, showing comic and dramatic abilities. Buddy William Wellman Jr. is okay, better developed in more serious roles. Beverly Adams, Wellman's gal, is too wooden, poses like a model, and suffers from apparent uneasiness before the lens. Anthony Hayes, a heavy who eventually reforms, can be developed for straight drama. Jill Donohue plays a snooty chick, and show promise in sophisticated parts, either sympathetic or heavy.

Julie Parris projects animation. Tom Nardini is good as the likeable kid who can't make out with girls, although Judy Parker nicely keeps trying to get her message to him. Nancy Czar, a blond looker, has some very good comedy moments in a substantial part not indicated by her credit position. Other players are adequate.

Besides the surplus of padded exterior shots, music occupies a dominant position, all of it in the Columbia-Screen Gems music catalog, little of it of merit. Title tune, reprised often, does, however, create a bouncy mood and remains in memory. The Hondells sing it over titles. Harry Betts' score is telegraphed boom-chuck nonsense. The Nooney Rickett Four sings several tunes, joined by Joni Lyman for a number which, as the script says, is available on Colpix wax. The Reflections (4) do a slow tune. All music editing sounds canned and unreal.

Richard Benedict's direction, in the dialog portions, is adequate, but also excellent in a few funny highlights which are too few. Irving Berlin's editing to 87 minutes is satisfactory. Kay Carson choreographed the ensemble tunes, okay but unexploited in lensing except in the "Do The Ski With Me" sequence. Other technical details are standard.

Murf.

Madam White Snake
(HONG KONG-COLOR-SCOPE)

Frank Lee International release of Shaw Bros. (Run Run Shaw) production. Stars Lin Dai, Chao Lei. Directed by Yueh Feng. Screenplay, Ka Jui-Fan; camera (Eastman Color-Shawscope), T. Nishimoto; music, Wang Fu-Ling. No other credits. Reviewed at 55th St. Playhouse, N.Y., Oct. 21, '65. Running Time, 105 MINS.

Shaw brothers have stated frequently that they hope to make a dent in the international (preferably American) film market, but continue to do little to slant their films towards the tastes of non-Chinese audiences. "Madam White Snake," which had its N.Y. premiere Fri. (22) at the 55th St. Playhouse, distributor Frank Lee's Gotham showcase, isn't likely to advance their cause appreciably despite a few sequences that stand out. With the exception of Chinese-American audiences of considerable size in N.Y. and San Francisco, this highly-colored mixture of fairy tale, operetta and adventure won't appeal to many American markets.

Director Yueh Feng, whose "Last Woman of Shang" merited some attention last year, has made a token effort to seek outside help by using a Japanese cameraman, T. Nishimoto. Camerawork, in too-brightly-hued Eastman Color, however, gives the characters a porcelained look and suggests that Nishimoto had little actual control. In some fantasy sequences, also, his imagination is obviously restrained by the small studio sets used.

One gets the impression that the Shaw brothers' films seldom use outdoor locations, which may be due to their Hong Kong location. Certainly their approach to the wide screen, Showscope, is wasted on the tiny interiors. Ka Jui-Fan's script, based on "an old Chinese fairy tale," deals with a goddess (actually a 1,000-year-old white snake) who falls in love with an earthling (who had saved her in a previous life) and is punished, as is her mortal lover, although the idea of presenting Buddhist monks as villains would seem a touchy business, considering the religious angle involved.

When action is depicted, the whole thing turns into Chinese opera, Oriental euphemism for vaudeville. Rather than a display of prowess with a sword, the opponents try to outdo each other with tumbling routines. These are, admittedly, well done and provide a welcome change from the hokum of the plot. One area in which the Chinese must change, before the West is won, is in their film music. It is, to unaccustomed ears, shrill and monotonous, as are the female singing voices. Even the Japanese have westernized their film scores to make them aurally acceptable.

This feature has undoubtedly been cut considerably as the original credits gave it a running time of 124 minutes but even the 105 minutes shown could easily spare another half hour. Lin Dai, a stunning beauty, plays the title role with an impressive emotional range. If she just wouldn't sing. If they all just wouldn't sing.

Robe.

The Heroes of Telemark
(BRITISH-COLOR)

Tense wartime gripper with powerhouse characterizations by Kirk Douglas and Richard Harris. Shapes up as box-office gold.

London, Oct. 28.

Rank presentation and release of a Benton Films Panavision production. (Columbia release in U.S.) Stars Kirk Douglas, Richard Harris. Features Ulla Jacobsson, Michael Redgrave, David Weston, Anton Diffring, Eric Porter, Mervyn Johns, Jennifer Hilary, Roy Dotrice, Barry Jones, Ralph Michael, Geoffrey Keen, Maurice Denham, David Davies, Karel Stepanek, George Murcell, Gerard Heinz. Produced by S. Benjamin Fisz. Directed by Anthony Mann. Screenplay, Ivan Moffat, Ben Barzman; camera (Technicolor) Robert Krasker; art director, Tony Masters; editor, Bert Bates; special effects, John Fulton; music, Malcolm Arnold. Reviewed at R.F.D. Private Theatre, Oct. 28, '65. Running Time, 131 MINS.

Dr. Rolf Petersen .... Kirk Douglas
Knut Straud .... Richard Harris
Anna .... Ulla Jacobsson
Uncle .... Michael Redgrave
Arne .... David Weston
Major Frick .... Anton Diffring
Terboven .... Eric Porter
Colonel Wilkinson ...... Mervyn Johns
Sigrid .... Jennifer Hilary
Jensen .... Roy Dotrice
Professor Logan .... Barry Jones
Milssen .... Ralph Michael
General Bolts .... Geoffrey Keen
Doctor at Hospital .... Maurice Denham
General Courts .... Robert Ayres
Claus .... William Marlowe
Captain of "Galtesund" .. David Davies
Hartmuller .... Karel Stepanek
Mrs. Sandersen .... Elvi Hale
Erhardt .... Gerard Heinz
Sturmfuhrer .... George Murcell
Mr. Sandersen .... Russell Waters

This story of an heroic episode which may well have saved the free world stacks up as potential boxoffice gold, despite its $5,600,000 budget. Producer Benjamin Fisz and director Anthony Mann have made a motion picture that emerges as hefty, gripping and carefully made entertainment. Excitement builds up naturally and gradually to climax.

(Many of the Norwegians who played central parts in the gripping piece of Nazi-defiance are still alive and were used as technical advisers.)

Topleague performances throughout, some lively special effects and Robert Krasker's Technicolor camera gives an almost lyrical quality to the genuine Norwegian locations all add up to a film which, despite minor faults, is sure fire entertainment for all types, all ages, anywhere.

It's 1942 in Nazi-occupied Norway. The Germans are ahead of the Allies on atomic fission, as reports from the Norsk Hydro heavy water factory near Telemark reveal. It's the job of a tiny band of nine resistance workers to scotch the Nazi plans. The Vemork factory must be destroyed. Shall it be by bombing or by Commando raid? Both methods are tried and neither completely succeed. But the Nazis are forced to try and move the heavy water and factory equipment to Berlin and it's when the moveout is in progress on the railway ferry that the resistance heroes finally strike and win out. The exploit won those taking part a flock of decorations but, like many other great stories of the war, it is comparatively little known and this picture is a worthy tribute to their resource and bravery.

By keeping closely to the facts scripters Ivan Moffat and Ben Barzman have avoided pitfalls. Phony relationships between the characters have been largely avoided and the dialog rarely risks running into typewritten bathos. When, occasionally, the characters seem as if they are about to lapse into sentimentality or idealistic chatter the narrative crops up to bring them back to the action.

Mann's direction is taut and attention to detail is remarkably effective. A main snag is that the film appears to have been cut considerably and there are unexplained moments such as the glib way in which intelligence seems to reach the resistance workers. How, for instance, did the Norwegian leader get away from a Nazi-run hospital to rejoin his comrades? The relationship between the characters is also not always clearly defined. But this is not the fault of editor Bert Bates. Somewhere along the line the script must take the responsibility for such minor cavils.

Kirk Douglas, as the scientist drawn unwillingly into the exploit, and Richard Harris as the resistance leader, turn in powerhouse performances. They detest each other on sight (never satisfactorily explained) but learn to respect and grudgingly like each other during mutual danger. These two strong personalities, who clashed considerably on location, fight an honorable draw in the thesp stakes and their personal edginess gives an extra wallop to their screen relationship. Ulla Jacobsson, as Douglas' ex-wife, also fighting for the resistance, has a sketchy role but plays it with charm and conviction. Main flaw is the role of her uncle played by Michael Redgrave. The character seems unnecessary, is never fully delineated and, anyway, could have been played equally well by an actor of lesser stature than Sir Michael.

Maude Spector's casting has brought out a long string of first rate performances all down the line from experienced professionals. Ralph Michael as the undercover factory manager, Roy Dotrice as a Quisling and Jennifer Hilary have the most distinctive roles but people like Mervyn Johns, Eric Porter, David Weston, Geoffrey Keen, Maurice Denham, Karel Stepanek, Russell Waters and George Murcell are all in with bits that add greatly to the film's strength.

Malcolm Arnold's useful musical score is the more effective since much of the film is played sans music and often sans dialog. In fact, all technical departments rate nosegays. Both Mann and Fisz must be particularly grateful to cameraman Robert Krasker. His work over ice and snow-girt Norway is a joy and almost every frame becomes a rich picture in itself. Craftily he used Helge Stoylen, a Norwegian ski coach, to help out on some lensing. Stoylen held a Panavision camera between his legs for some of the graceful and gripping ski shots and whether this raised union problems or not it adds to the percentage of the pictorial beauty and fascination of the photography. Mann also roped in Egil Wexholt as second unit director and cameraman and Wexholt is a man who specializes in skiing and underwater camerawork. All this expertise shows up on the screen.

Final sequence when the ferry is timed to blow up and Douglas goes aboard to try and save the lives of the women and children, and particularly that of the widow and babe of one of his resistance colleagues, could easily have been played up more dramatically. But it is not blown up beyond natural tension and into phoney heroics and this is typical throughout one of the best British pix for a long time.

Rick.

Dr. Goldfoot And The Bikini Machine
(COLOR-PANAVISION)

Entertaining spy spoof, expensively mounted, well directed. Marquee strength in featured players. Not just another teenpic, has appeal to general audiences. Very good prospects likely.

Hollywood, Nov. 2.

American International Pictures release of a James H. Nicholson-Samuel Z. Arkoff production. Features Vincent Price, Frankie Avalon, Dwayne Hickman, Susan Hart, Jack Mullaney, Fred Clark. Directed by Norman Taurog. Screenplay, Elwood Ullman, Robert Kaufman, based on story by James Hartford; camera (Pathecolor), Sam Leavitt; editors, Ronald Sinclair, Fred Feitshans, Eve Newman; music, Les Baxter; title tune, Guy Hemric, Jerry Styner; art direction, Daniel Haller; sound, Vern Kramer, Ryder Sound Services; asst. director, Claude Binyon, Jr. Reviewed at Academy Theatre, Nov. 1, '65. Running Time, 88 MINS.

Dr. Goldfoot .... Vincent Price
Craig Gamble .... Frankie Avalon
Todd Armstrong ..... Dwayne Hickman
Diane .... Susan Hart
Igor .... Jack Mullaney
D. J. Pevney .... Fred Clark
Reiect No. 12 .... Alberta Nelson
Motorcycle Cop .... Milton Frome
News vendor .... Kaye Elhardt
Girl in nightclub .... William Baskin
Guard .... Vincent I. Barnett
Janitor .... Joe Ploski
Cook ....
Themselves .... Sam And the Ape Men, Diane De Marco
Robots . Patti Chandler, Salli Sachse, Sue Hamilton, Marianne Gaba Issa Arnal, Pam Rodgers, Sally Frei, Jan Watson, Mary Hughes, Luree Holmes, Laura Nicholson, China Lee, Deanna Lund, Leslie Summers, Kay Michaels, Arlene Charles

"Dr. Goldfoot And The Bikini Machine" is an amusing spy-spoof, aimed at the general market, which relies on a good script and performances and excellent direction to achieve its impact rather than on tunes. The expensive-looking James H. Nicholson-Samuel Z. Arkoff production runs the comedy gamut from high to low, with enough appeal for older audiences who can also enjoy the chases and the scenery. American International has a strong entry in the general market.

Elwood Ullman and Robert Kaufman scripted a James Hartford story which combines rather successfully the varied plot elements which have, individually, spelled commercial success in other pix. Mad medic Vincent Price manufactures femme robots in a weird lab equipped with computers and other modern trappings. The gals are deployed to seduce men of influence so Price can control the world. Avant-garde spy tools regularly appear. The whole package is wrapped up by the zesty Norman Taurog direction.

All names follow title, and top-featured Price is a genial menace, neatly paired with goofy assistant Jack Mullaney who scores in almost every scene. Susan Hart is very good in a role which demands several dialects, human warmth, and robot inanimity, often in rapid sequence. Her target is Dwayne Hickman, quite believable as the wealthy playboy and bewildered spouse. Foiling the nefarious scheme in spite of himself is Frankie Avalon, tyro secret agent working for Fred Clark, again the harassed and excitable bureaucrat, and enjoyably so.

As in most AIPix, unbilled cameos relate to past and future films, so sharp young eyes will catch Annette Funicello in a Pilgrim era punishment rig, Aron Kincaid as a sporty driver, and Harvey Lembeck draped in chains on a motorcycle. Film's ending leaves the door open for sequels.

With Sam Leavitt's versatile Panavision - Pathecolor camera, Taurog has staged some exciting chase scenes in and around Frisco: In particular, film opens with a terrif camera trip down a Frisco hill, unrelated to the plot but a sure attention - grabber. Taurog has been directing this type of comedy for years, and he hasn't lost the touch. Editors Ronald Sinclair, Fred Feitshans and Eve Newman trimmed to a tight 88 minutes.

Les Baxter's score punches the gags home to good effect, and title tune by Guy Hemric and Jerry Styner (sung by The Supremes) sets the right mood. A very brief appearance by a group called Sam And The Ape Men, with Diane De Marco, is the sole plot interruption. Recent b.o. data show juve audiences now hip to pix which are mere songalogs, a technique wisely avoided here.

Opening and closing titles, the work of Art Clokey and Butler-Glouner respectively, are cleverly done with the aid of human puppets and special photography, making for high visual interest. Other professional details were well-coordinated by co-producer Anthony Carras.   *Murf.*

Red Line 7000
(COLOR)

Sometimes-exciting auto racing melodrama okay for action market.

Hollywood, Nov. 1.
Paramount release of Howard Hawks production, directed by Hawks. Features James Caan, Laura Devon, Gail Hire, Charlene Holt, John Robert Crawford, Marianna Hill, James Ward, Norman Alden. Screenplay, George Kirgo; based on story by Hawks; camera (Technicolor), Milton Krasner; asst. director, Dick Moder; music, Nelson Riddle; editors, Stuart Gilmore, Bill Brame. Reviewed at Paramount Studios, Oct. 28, '65. Running Time, **110 MINS.**

Mike .... James Caan
Julie .... Laura Devon
Holly .... Gail Hire
Lindy .... Charlene Holt
Ned .... John Robert Crawford
Gabrielle .... Marianna Hill
Dan .... James Ward
Pat .... Norman Alden

Howard Hawks swings from fishing (viz., "Man's Favorite Sport") to stock car racing in this sometimes-actionful Technicolor melodrama about a flock of drivers and their romances. Cast is mostly unknown, the majority either making their film bows or having little previous screen exposure. Some of the characters become confused in the overly-complicated story line, leaving audience in state of uncertainty at windup. Hawks, however, manages some pretty fair thrills on the track as cars go into spills and crashes, and exploitation should help for the action market.

Producer-director apparently is making an attempt to bring fresh faces to the screen in "Red Line 7000," which he's done in the past,

although previously he's always had one or more names to head cast. Talent here individually give good accounts of themselves and several thesps display promise for the future.

Femmes particularly get a buildup through greater characterization than the men. Making excellent impressions are Laura Devon, Gail Hire and Marianna Hill, as girl friends of the three daredevils of the track who participate in the fast action. James Caan, John Robert Crawford and James Ward in these roles are effective. Miss Devon, from tv, plays her first top film part; the two other actresses undertake their first screen assignments. Crawford, too, from Broadway, debuts on screen. Caan has two previous pix under his belt while Ward has been featured four times before.

Hawks also has cast two principals from "Man's Favorite Sport?" Charlene Holt registers as the widow of a racer, and Norman Alden gets mileage from his role as boss of the three drivers. Singer Carol Connors is in briefly for teenage name value.

Script by George Kirgo, based on a story by Hawks, centers on three sets of characters as they go about their racing and lovemaking. Trio of racers are members of a team operating out of Daytona, Fla., their individual lives uncomplicated until three femmes fall in love with them. In a thrilling climax, one of the drivers, overcome with jealousy, causes another to crash but miraculously his life is saved.

Hawks is on safe ground while his cameras are focused on race action around such Southern courses as Daytona, Darlington, Charlotte, and Riverside in California. His troubles lies in limning his various characters in their more intimate moments. Title refers to an engine speed beyond which it's dangerous to operate a race car, perhaps symbolic of what Hawks wanted to achieve in the emotions of his players.

Second unit direction of Bruce Kessler, filming actual races at courses around the country, counts heavily in exciting aspects of track sequences, and Hawks otherwise has lined up top technical assistance. Milton Krasner's color photography is outstanding. Editing by Stuart Gilmore and Bill Brame allows fast movement, Nelson Riddle's music score is appropriate and Paul K. Perpae's special photographic effects and Farciot Edouart's process photography realistic.   *Whit.*

Coast of Skeletons
(BRITISH-SCOPE-COLOR)

Good action feature

Seven Arts release of Oliver A. Unger production. Stars Richard Todd, Dale Robertson, features Heinz Drache, Marianne Koch, Derek Nimmo, Elga Andersen. Directed by Robert Lynn. Screenplay, Anthony Scott Veitch from original story by Peter Welbeck, inspired by Edgar Wallace's "Sanders of the River"; camera (Technicolor-Technicscope), Stephen Dade; editor, John Trumper; music, Christopher Whelen. Reviewed at N.Y., Nov. 4, '65. Running Time, **90 MINS.**

One of several adventure features produced by Oliver Unger in

Africa, this actioner is being released by Seven Arts in the N.Y. market as a package with "The Face of Fu Manchu." While not strong on marquee names, the Techniscope - Technicolor background photography and an emphasis on action make it excellent second-bill material. In smaller situations, it should do very well on its own.

Only resemblance between Anthony Veitch's script and Edgar Wallace's famous adventure story, "Sanders of the River," is that the principal character, played by Richard Todd, is called Sanders and most of the action does take place in Africa. Film has already been released in Germany as "Sanders," as country is very fond of the Wallace stories. Lufthansa gets plenty of free screen space also.

International cast makes the villain (Dale Robertson) an American while both the British and the Germans involved are shown as noble characters, or weak characters who become noble. Deutsch frauleins Marianne Koch and Elga Andersen provide the romance angles although there's surprisingly little exposure (other than Miss Koch swimming through some murky water). Todd, a security officer, and his assistant (Derek Nimmo) oppose evil doings of Yank diamond dredger (Robertson). Robertson's ship captain, a former German naval officer (Heinz Drache), loses his wife (Elga Andersen) to his employer and his sister (Marianne Koch) to Todd, but holds on to his integrity.

Although Stephen Dade's interiors are murky and underlit, his exterior camerawork (much of it evidently made from a helicopter) includes car chases, ships at sea, aerial photography and even some underwater shots. Todd, who's no youngster, is evidently in excellent condition as he's easily recognizable in many of the fight scenes where a double could have been used. He has a double-handed rib-thrust in one scene that will probably be copied by every kid in the neighborhood. All technical aspects of the film are first-rate. Christopher Whelen's music is appropriate to the action.
            Robe.

Le Gendarme a New York
(FRENCH-FRANSCOPE-COLOR)

Paris, Nov. 9.
SNC release of SNC-Champion Films production. Stars Louis De Funes; features Genevieve Grad, Michel Galabru, Jean Lefevre, Christian Marin. Directed by Jean Girault. Screenplay, Richard Balducci, Jacques Vilfrid, Girault; camera (Eastmancolor), Edmond Sechan; editor, Albert Jurgenson. At Balzac, Paris. Running Time, **100 MINS.**

Gendarme .... Louis De Funes
Nicole .... Genevieve Grad
Gerbert .... Michel Galabru
Fougasse .... Jean Lefevre
Merlot .... Christian Marin
Adjutant .... Mario Pisu
Franck .... Alain Scott

This is a followup on one of the top sleeper comedy hits of the last few years "Le Gendarme De Saint Tropez." It has more comic trumps than its predecessor and should do solidly here helped by the Louis De Funes name. For abroad, it could have some playoff and dualer usage on its Frenchmen-in-

Gotham theme if it is a bit overcharged.

De Funes is a master of harmless irascibility and trots off to N.Y. for an international police meeting with his daughter stowing away when she can't go along. Plot has the various gimmicks of contacts with N.Y. life and the gendarme's chase after his daughter when he spies her. It all ends well.

Good New York exteriors are blended acceptably with a mixture of local exterior and interior shooting. If it stays surface in poking fun at Yank hygiene, French cuisine and imbroglios with language and fast U.S. ways, it rarely gets self-indulgent. It bowls along to overcome many of its overdone aspects like takeoffs on psychiatry, U.S. tele commercials and the melting pot aspects of the city.

Direction is adequate and playing in line with the situation madcap carryings on. This may turn into a series here. De Funes is now one of top comic boxoffice draws here.   *Mosk.*

Pigen og Millionaeren
(The Girl and the Millionaire)
(DANISH—COLOR)

Copenhagen, Nov. 2.
A Merry Film production and release. Stars Dirch Passer and Birgitte Price; features Paul Hagen. Axel Stroebye. Directed by Ebbe Langberg. Screenplay by Carol Ottesen and Peer Guldbrandsen; camera (Eastmancolor), Henning Bendtsen; music, Bent Fabric. At Saga, Copenhagen. Running Time, **98 MINS.**

Merry Film, which formerly turned out some of the flattest Danish farces and made a nice pile of money doing it, has changed its tune recently. Producers Henrik Sandberg and Dirch Passer now employ Eastmancolor, a widescreen and stories plus a good deal of money in an attempt to reach an international audience. With "The Girl and the Millionaire" the investment stands a fair chance of paying off.

The plot revolves around the old amnesia gag. The millionaire, played with inventiveness and charm by the comic actor Dirch Passer, gets a bump on the head and changes from playboy to hard-headed businessman. He also falls in love with his former wife, a concert pianist, played by Brigitte Price, an actress who has genuine talent in the modern vein. Everything is about to come up roses when Passer gets yet another bump on the head. That places him back in his true character.

Paul Hagen, who has exceptional talent in underplaying madness, helps things along nicely. Most surprising of all is the swift-moving direction and the freshness of the situation in an otherwise quite corny plot. The music by Bent Fabric oils the hinges, too. This film should please in many markets if it is subtitled properly.   *Kell.*

Piege Pour Cendrillon
(Trap For Cinderella)
(FRENCH-FRANSCOPE)

Paris, Nov. 2.
Gaumont release of Gaumont International-Jolly Film production. Stars Dany Carrel, Madeleine Robinson; features Hubert Noel, Jean Gaven, Rene Dary. Directed by Andre Cayatte. Screenplay, Sebastien Japrisot, J. B. Rossi, Jean Anouilh, Cayatte from book by Japrisot;

camera, Armand Thirard; editor, Paul Cayatte. At Colisee, Paris. Running Time, **115 MINS.**

Amnesiac, Dominique, Michele	Dany Carrel
Jeanne	Madeleine Robinson
Gabriel	Jean Gaven
Francois	Hubert Noel
Doctor	Rene Dary

Mixture of suspense and social contrasts do not mix well in this pic. It comes out soapsy, and even lesbian indications and scattered nudity do not heighten its possibilities. It appears something for playoff on its theme, with arty chances abroad chancier.

Ex-lawyer Andre Cayatte, the director, does not try for polemics or didacticism but is somewhat clinical in progression and the setting up of his yarn these are not able to imbue it with the mystery and drama it needs.

An amnesia victim finds she is a rich girl about to inherit a fortune. She was supposed to have been found near a cousin who had committed suicide. But a woman comes for her and tells her she is really the cousin and it was a plot to kill the rich girl. Then flashbacks unfold the tale and her hunt to find the real truth.

Dany Carrel does not quite have the ability to ring the subtleties of the three roles she plays—the rich girl, cousin and mixed-up amnesia sufferer. She shows improvement and looks to become a fine actress.

Twists are dragged in by outsiders who have seen things and then come in to sound off about them. But all this remains surface as do the intimations of lesbian activity by both cousins with the woman director of the inherited business.

Film tends to plod. This hybrid may do okay on its home grounds, however. Technically it is sound.
Mosk.

The Cavern
(ITALIAN-YUGOSLAVIAN)

Okay programmer

20th-Fox release of Edgar G. Ulmer production. Features Rosanna Schiaffino, John Saxon, Brian Aherne, Peter L. Marshall, Larry Hagman, Hans von Borsody, Nino Castelnuovo, Joachim Hansen. Directed by Ulmer. Screenplay and story, Michael Pertwee, Jack Davies; camera, Gabor Pogany; editor, Renato Cinquini; sound, Bruno Moreal; special effects, J. Natanson; music, Carlo Rustichelli, Gene di Novi. Title song, Caroll Coates, sung by Bobby Bare. Reviewed at Fox h.o., N.Y., Nov. 3, '65. Running Time, **83 MINS.**

(English Soundtrack)

Although the Fox credits for this import don't mention it, the film is evidently one made last year in Italy and Yugoslavia as an Italian-Yugoslav-U.S. coproduction. At one time Martin Melcher was reported to be a participant in the production. Much of the shooting takes place in caverns with the few fabricated interiors apparently done on an Italian soundstage.

Michael Pertwee and Jack Davies' script loses no time in putting the small cast in peril by having them, as the result of an aerial bombardment, trapped in a large cavern on an Italian mountainside. The polyglot crew is made up of a British general (Brian Aherne), a Royal Canadian Air Force officer (Peter L. Marshall), an American captain and private (Larry Hagman and John Saxon),

an Italian soldier (Nino Castelnuovo) and his girl (Rosanna Schiaffino), plus a German soldier (Hans von Borsody).

Producer-director Edgar G. Ulmer's biggest problem is to keep the confined action from becoming static. He does this with a combination of physical action (test trips down side tunnels and an underground river) and increasing emotional tension. What is hard to believe about the situation is how so many neurotics could have been found in each other's company, even by coincidence. Aherne and Hagman are alcoholics, Castelnuovo becomes jealous of Saxon's interest in Miss Schiaffino and the others also have their own problems.

Marshall (who's currently playing opposite Julie Harris in "Skyscraper" on B'way) is outstanding as the even-keeled Canadian who loses his life trying to escape. Von Borsody's fate ironically presented. The first one to find a way out, he's shot by Italian partisans before he can make his way back into the cavern. Hagman is drowned and Aherne, who goes berserk, blows up the cavern and, with his suicide, provides the means of escape for Saxon, Castelnuovo and Miss Schiaffino.

Evidently filmed with an English soundtrack, as lip movements fit the spoken dialog, there's enough of interest to hold the less discriminating filmgoer who's only looking for a little action. Gabor Pogany's camerawork is amazingly good considering the difficult lighting problems with which he must have been faced. Only occasionally does a background look fake and the authentic caverns photograph beautifully.

A good programmer that will need some push. The title, while appropriate, has no sales value in itself.
Robe.

Der Oelprinz
(The Oil Prince)
(GERMAN-YUGOSLAV)
(Color)

Berlin, Nov. 2.
Constantin release of Rialto Film Preben Philipsen Berlin-Jadran (Zagreb) production. Stars Stewart Granger, Pierre Brice, Harald Leipnitz. Directed by Harald Philipp. Screenplay, Fred Denger, Harald Philipp, based on novel by Karl May; camera (Eastmancolor), Heinz Hoelscher; music, Martin Boettcher; editor, Hermann Haller. At several West Berlin cinemas. Running Time, **89 MINS.**

Old Surehand	Stewart Granger
Winnetou	Pierre Brice
Lizzy	Macha Meril
The Oil Prince	Harald Leipnitz
Richard Forsythe	Mario Girotti
Frau Ebersbach	Antje Weissgerber
Campbell	Walter Barnes
Kovacz	Gerhard Frickhoeffer
Old Wabble	Paddy Fox
Hampel	Heinz Erhardt

There is, commercially speaking, nothing wrong with producer Horst Wendlandt's Karl May filmizations. The Berlin Rialto topper, who launched the Teutonic Karl May wave, collected another Golden Screen, a trophy given to films that draw more than 3,000,000 patrons in Germany within one year. This one was for "Among Vultures." Before that he was handed the award for three other Karl May Westerns.

For the record, "The Oil Prince" is Wendlandt's sixth Karl May Western made in collab with the Yugoslav Jadran Film. There is hardly any doubt that this one will

spell money in this country and, as with "Vultures," the first Stewart Granger starrer, the Granger name wil open a good number of foreign doors, too.

Plot concerns a group of settlers who head for the Golden West to start a new life there. They are joined by Old Surehand (Stewart Granger) and Winnetou (Pierre Brice), the Apache chief, who take care that peaceful contracts are made between the white men and the Indians who occupy the territory. Interfering with their good intentions is the badman, called the "Oil Prince." He wants the territory for his own benefit and doesn't hesitate to kill in getting it. Old Surehand, of course, knows how to get rid of such a character.

As usual with Wendlandt's Westerns, "Prince" offers an appealing mixture of colorful characters, beautiful landscapes, action plus comedy relief.

Cast is headed by Granger who is definitely a win for the German film industry. There is something sympathetic about Granger—he is the kind of hero who doesn't take himself too seriously. Pierre Brice, as Winnetou, is not very active this time but sticks to his traditional mild manners.

New to Karl May westerns are Harald Leipnitz and Heinz Erhardt. Leipnitz makes a competent villain while Erhardt supplies the laughs.

Supporting cast includes American Walter Barnes, a familiar face in these pix; German Antje Weissgerber, Italian Mario Girotti and a new face, Macha Meril. Smaller roles are played by Yugoslavs.

Technically, this film is okay. The score, however, is overly conventional. Composer Martin Boettcher leaves it too much to mere routine.
Hans.

The Second Best Secret Agent In The Whole Wide World
(BRITISH-COLOR)

Suitable second-bill programmer, with proper emphasis on the action scenes.

Embassy Pictures release of a S. J. H. Ward production. Features Tom Adams, Karel Stepanek, Veronica Hurst, John Arnatt, Francis de Wolff, Felix Felton. Directed by Lindsay Shonteff. Screenplay, Howard Griffiths and Shonteff; camera (Pathecolor), Terry Maher; editor, Ron Pope; sound editor, Terry Rawlings; music, Bertram Chappell. Reviewed at Embassy home office, New York, Nov. 12, '65. Running Time, **96 MINS.**

Charles Vine	Tom Adams
Henrik Jacobsen	Karel Stepanek
Julia Lindberg	Veronica Hurst
Rockwell	John Arnatt
Walter Pickering	Francis de Wolf
Walter Pickering	Francis de Wolff
Russian Commissar	George Pastell
August Jacobsen	Robert Marsden
First Russian Commissar	Oliver MacGreevy
Vladimir Sheehee	Paul Tann
Sadistikov	Tony Wall
Masterman	Peter Bull

Almost every film-producing country in the world has jumped aboard the spy-wagon since 007 turned out to be the magic number that turned on the boxoffice. Some of the imitations were made in such haste, however, that even Sean Connery wouldn't recognize them as carbons.

Producer S. J. H. Ward has taken no chances with this British import, which Embassy has acquired for distribution. Not only is the hero a close-as-possible Connery lookalike, his style is flagrantly imitative and there are thinly-veiled references to the Master Spy in the dialog.

Even the title is unoriginal although it won't cost Avis Car Rental any sleep. The unfortunate part of this attitude of "They're buying spy, given them spy — fast" is that this film does contain some moments of fun, even originality, and would imply that a reasonably good script, which needed more hours in the creative oven, has been turned into a hasty pudding.

Tom Adams, as the title character, is no James Bond. Nor is he a Harry Palmer, Sam Spade, or even a Charlie Chan. His Charles Vine is, really, a rather obnoxious character. Long on vanity, short on manners, he's a handsome face, impassive in demeanor, and only his voice has any life. Adams does handle himself well in the few scenes calling for physical action, but most of the time he relies on a flexible gun that starts as a revolver and turns into a machine gun. To make him appear human, he's also depicted as a terrible shot, using numerous bullets each time he's called upon to eliminate a member of the cast, which is fairly often.

Lindsay Shonteff's direction, as in his script (on which he collaborated with Howard Griffiths), is best when there's physical action involved. His characters are dull when forced to rely on conversation. Typical of the strained dialog is remark made by one of Vine's numerous femmes—"I met someone just like you in Florida. Said his name was James . . . something or other."

What there is of a plot suggests that two Danish scientists could successfully con both Great Britain and Russia into believing they had come close to perfecting an anti-gravity device. They not only sell both sides the plans (without their having been seen by a scientist on either side) but they almost get away with the double payment. Asking for American dollars should have been a tipoff in itself.

Vine is the agent assigned by the British to guard the one scientists, the other supposedly having been killed. Terry Maher's Pathe-color camerawork is first rate when shooting exteriors (extensive coverage of the London area is included), but the color process, during interior shots, is highly unflattering to the actors. Karel Stepanek as the scientist, Veronica Hurst as his assistant and John Arnatt as Vine's superior are better than their routine roles. Peter Bull, despite equal billing with Adams, is seen only fleetingly as a Russian contact. Most of the smaller roles are handled capably, a few being outstanding. One of the best scenes is the closing "duel" between Vine and the Russian assassin, Sadistikov (most impressively played by Tony Wall). This type of visual impact, more intelligently used, could have lifted the film out of its overall unimaginative rut.

Bertram Chappell's music is a real plus, particularly suited to the scenes where Vine is stalked by various agents. Sometimes a single instrument is used, sometimes only natural sounds. Since Embassy took over, a title song by Sammy Cahn and Jimmy van Heusen, sung by Sammy Davis Jr., has been added. *Robe.*

Chicago Film Fest

Saturday Night In Apple Valley

Extremely self - conscious attempt to satirize Hollywood and foreign films. Series of at times clever sight-gags that afford a few laughs, but in film becomes increasingly tiresome.

Chicago, Nov. 10.
Emerson Film release of an Empire Production. Features Phil Ford, Mimi Hines, Cliff Arquette, Shanton Granger, Joan Benedict, Marvin Miller, Anthony Dexter. Direction, screenplay and editing by John Myhers; music, Foster Wakefield; camera, Alan Stensvold; sound, Glenn Glen. Reviewed at the Carnegie Theatre, Nov. 9, '65. Running Time, 80 MINS.
Big Man .... Phil Ford
Mimi Madison .... Mimi Hines
Charley Weaver .... Cliff Arquette
Mama Coot .... Cliff Arquette
Beau Coot .... Shanton Granger
Poopsie Patata .... Joan Benedict

Film, which is supposed to be a spoof on motion picture styles and techniques, quickly bogs down into a series of sight-gags that accomplishes nothing more than becoming a vehicle for director-producer-writer John Myhers to demonstrate some clever visual humor and razzle-dazzle editing (he also edited). The pace, at times painfully slow, meanders down a rather dull path and seems to go nowhere other than to hit the audience over the head with the directors' satirical view of other filmmakers and their techniques.

The satire, obvious to the point of nakedness, soon loses any biting qualities that it might have accomplished with a more subtle approach, and, like a nude picture hanging over the neighborhood bar, quickly becomes uninteresting and eventually disappears into the surroundings. The romantic situation — satirizing the old Hollywood device of pairing a virginal school teacher and a tough guy — is a weak characterization at best and is even weaker in the satirical context of the picture.

Phil Ford as Big Man, and Mimi Hines as Mimi Madison, handle themselves reasonably well in a media in which they have had little experience. Cliff Arquette, playing dual roles, takes on both fairly well, but is hampered by the overly-complicated contrivance of his parts. The other members of the cast struggle along awkwardly and with little conviction.

The Fellini, Bergman spoofing, and the various symbolic goings on — from sex, per an almost pornographic miniature golf match, to a dream sequence of a bath in a tub — filled with money — has little or no meaning within the picture's frame-work, and the results are usually not worth the effort.

The film's final shot, showing the triumph of virtue, has a slot machine symbolically lying on its side as Big Man and Miami fly off to the promise of a new clean life. It would not have seemed inappropriate if the machine had registered lemons. *Ron.*

The Lollipop Cover

Gold Award Winner in the feature competition at the Chicago International Film Festival, with its Don Gordon winner of the Best Actor Award. Picture has a powerful, yet simple story that is supported by fine camera work, excellent performances, and creative direction.

Chicago, Nov. 13.
Continental release of International Productions' film, produced by Everett Chambers. Features Don Gordon, Carol Selfinger, Lee Philips, John Marley, David White, Midge Ware, George Sawaya, Bek Nelson, Bert Remsen, Annette Valentine, Cliff Carnell, Carolyn Hughes. Directed by Everette Chambers. Screenplay, Everett Chambers, Don Gordon on idea of Nancy Valentine; camera, Michael Murphy; editor, James Mitchell; music, Ruby Raksin. Reviewed at the Playboy Theatre, Nov. 12, '65. Running Time, 82 MINS.

A study in contrasts "Lollipop Cover" is the story of a disillusioned and bitter boxer named Nick Bartaloni and an abandoned nine-year old girl named Felicity. When Nick quits the ring he discovers that his sister, who was holding his savings, has committed suicide after giving his money away to a drug addict she was in love with. As he goes off to find the addict, who is living in California, he meets Felicity who has been deserted by her alcoholic father. The two, largely through the girl's efforts, join forces and begin to hitch-hike toward the coast.

Often moving, at times poignantly amusing, the two represent opposite ends of a simple philosophical position. Although both are destitute the girl clings to the beautiful world in her head. She's sure that life is good. The boxer however is bitter. He constantly tells Felicity what a simpleton she is. The girl uses a yellow cellophane lollipop cover to help her see beyond the colorless world that threatens to swallow her up.

As the two head West they encounter a variety of nasty, depraved people that serve to re-enforce Nick's belief that the world is a lousy place. Felicity however, refuses to give in and keeps urging Nick to look at the world through her beautiful lollipop cover.

At times the film threatens to become too precious, but manages to resolve satisfactorily. Don Gordon's rugged looks and deft handling of Nick's rough attitude is perfectly contrasted to Carol Selfinger's Felicity. Miss Selfinger charms with her innocence and successfully exhibits the sweet appeal that eventually draws Nick away from his dark, moody existence.

Symbolic religious touches are somewhat obvious, and rather unnecessary, but do not get in the way of the story. Effective camera angles and the occasional use of color to illustrate the sought after beautiful world work quite well. Everett Chambers' direction is excellent, always getting the most from every scene, and the score and editing are all of the highest calibre. Performances in support of the two main characters are all good. *Ron.*

Fog
(BRITISH-COLOR)

Excellent cast gives lift to this thriller-meller in which Sherlock Holmes is pulled in to solve the Jack The Ripper sex crimes; this gimmick should create boxoffice fillip.

London, Nov. 9.
Compton release (Columbia in Western Hemisphere) of a Compton-Sir Nigel Films (Henry E. Lester) production presented by Michael Klinger & Tony Tenser, produced by Herman Cohen. Features John Neville, Donald Houston, John Fraser, Barbara Windsor, Anthony Quayle, Robert Morley, Frank Finlay, Norma Foster, Adrienne Corri, Cecil Parker, Peter Carsten, Judi Dench, Georgia Brown, Barry Jones, Edina Ronay. Directed by James Hill. Screenplay, Donald & Derek Ford, based on Sir Arthur Conan Doyle's characters; camera (Eastmancolor), Desmond Dickinson; editor, Henry Richardson; music, John Scott. At Leicester Square Theatre, London. Running Time, 95 MINS.
Sherlock Holmes .... John Neville
Doctor Watson .... Donald Houston
Lord Carfax .... John Fraser
Doctor Murray ...... Anthony Quayle
Mycroft Holmes ...... Robert Morley
Annie Chapman ...... Barbara Windsor
Angela .... Adrienne Corri
Inspector Lestrade ...... Frank Finlay
Sally .... Judi Dench
Joseph Beck .... Charles Regnier
Prime Minister .... Cecil Parker
Saloon singer .... Georgia Brown
Duke of Shires .... Barry Jones
Chunky .... Terry Downes
Home Secretary .... Dudley Foster
Max Steiner .... Peter Carsten
Polly Nichols ...... Christiane Maybach
Cathy Eddowes .... Kay Walsh
Simpleton .... John Cairney
Mary Kelly .... Edina Ronay
Landlady .... Avis Bunnage
Mrs. Hudson .... Barbara Leake
P. C. Benson .... Patrick Newell
Liz Stride .... Norma Foster

A neat enough gag to weld a Sherlock Holmes adventure here with the Jack the Ripper legend. Though the mixture of fiction and fact doesn't entirely click, because of a mainly competent but not overinspired screenplay by Donald and Derek Ford, this provides a fair measure of amusement. An excellent cast gives the production full value. Dialog and situations sometimes teeter on the edge of parody (providing misplaced yocks), the fault resting mainly on the scripting and certainly cannot be blamed on the thesps or James Hill's conscientious helming.

John Neville, latest in the gallery of portrayals of the Baker Street sleuth, gives a stylish performance in full keeping with the Holmsian tradition. He gives plenty aid to the occasional humor of the role and also becomes a man of action when needed, particularly in the showdown in a burning tavern when, at the 11th hour he unmasks the Ripper. Typical Sherlock Holmes deduction enables him to solve the mystery that baffled Scotland Yard and, to this day, remains mere guesswork. Neville is particularly well supported by Donald Houston, as Doctor Watson, in the tradition of an unswervingly loyal friend who is in constant amazement at Sherlock's grey matter.

The scripters' theory about Jack the Ripper's background and motives for his sadistic murders of East End harlots clings to the now accepted belief that the crimes were the work of an educated man, with a surgical background, whose feud against prostitutes was prompted by revenge for a wrong that some harpy did to him or one of his f a m i l y . "A Study in Terror." original title and under which it will be shown in the U.K., provides some conjecture and red herrings; but only the least astute audiences will have much doubt about the identity of the quarry.

The mystery is not sufficiently profound and the surprises and horror not sufficiently sharp to make this more than an average thriller-meller. Storyline unfolds a tale of blackmail, a disinherited son, sinister goings on in a vice-tavern and misleading atmosphere in an East End doctor's surgery.

It is mainly set in the gloomy, sleazy background of the East End and Desmond Dickinson's camera-work is often hampered by the Eastmancolor which minimizes the dank dreariness of the back alleys and the shadows that are often great allies in building up suspense in this kind of yarn. The foggy sequences on the final, fatal night are also ill defined and lacking in menace. However, Henry Richardson's editing occasionally achieves some good shock effects, particularly in the immediate lead-ins to the several murders.

Apart from Neville and Houston, Anthony Quayle weighs in with a sound, strong performance as the East End doctor-surgeon who obstinately hangs on as long as possible to the key to the mystery. John Fraser handles a tricky part soundly and Peter Carsten fills the role of the blackmailing saloon keeper adequately. And several other male thesps are in with useful bits. Notable of these is Robert Morley in providing a short, choice cameo as Sherlock Holme's politician brother, Frank Finlay and Cecil Parker.

The femmes mainly have to make quick impact before getting their comeuppance. As prosties, Barbara Windsor, Norma Foster and Edina Ronay are killed abruptly with shrill squeals, with Miss Ronay having the most effective exit. Judi Dench is wasted in a colorless role. Adrienne Corri, as one of the girls, has a short key role and gives a performance marred only by the fact that her pleasant, well-trained voice is quite out of keeping with what the audience knows about the tart's background. Georgia Brown is also on hand to belt out a couple of songs as a saloon singer.

Artwork and location work smack of studio mock-ups and, apart from the pub scenes, the atmosphere provided, while vigorous enough, savors greatly of the old Hollywood conception of what Victorian Cockneys and the East End were supposed to be like. The pic is the first from the Compton stable to get a full circuit booking in U.K. In the U.S., where released as "Fog," it will have Columbia as its distrib. *Rich.*

All Men Are Apes

Out-of-town girl tramp takes postgraduate course in big city. Amoral, morbid, psycho. For fringe situations only.

Adelphia Pictures release of Barnard L. Sackett (Charles E. Mazin) production. Stars Stephanie De Passe; features Mark Ryan, Grace Lynn, Steve Woods, Steve Vincent, Bonny Lee Noll, Mia Marlowe, Ted Teschner. Walter Teague, Tom O'Horgan. Wendy Winston, Jeanine Costa, Brigitta Batit, Ceylon. Bob Worms, Frank Geraci, Joe Boatner's Ink Spots, Sandi Brown, Harry the Ape. Directed by J. P. Mawra. Screenplay, Charles E. Mazin and Sackett; camera. Richard E. Brooks; asst. camera, Charles Caffall; edited, J. P. Mawra: music. Irv Dweir; songs, Charles F. Nazin. Reviewed in New York Nov. 18, '65. Running Time, 85 MINS.

Reportedly produced in Philadelphia, this sexsational Barnard L. Sackett film for Stag Row situations is a hodgepodge of wierdies. The title suggests the exploitation come-on. All men are apes but the heroine leaps into their clutches. It's represented as comedy-drama, but is really a cornucopia of hankypanky involving a girl who comes to the corrupt city obviously well corrupted prior to arrival. Her first bit of promiscuity is to hav-hop with her mother's sailor, then to swing toward a hardly-vague lesbian.

A show biz career is foisted on her by a greasy agent. His aberation is a liking to have his back scrubbed in bathtub, Geisha style. Film "progresses" to a bacchanal as girl is introduced to people-in-the-know for career. Mixed in is female impersonating exotic dancer, Plum Girl. who has fruit heaped on her. Another, with lashmarks on back is Peacock Girl. She's auctioned off for the weekend.

Developing into a pro stripper, girl takes up with a smooth gangster whose first night of affection turns into a sadistic orgy. Disillusion sends girl back to old lesbian acquaintance. Restored once more stripper now takes job doing exotic dances with an ape. Success greets the new duo. Gangster seeks her out. Ape comes to her defense but is mistakenly shot by anxious stripper. Climax finds heroine and ape happily reunited.

Girl carries narration. She cues the other speeches. Over front credits a voice of authority exhorts on values of truth and understanding and non censorship.

Poorly acted. archaically filmed, childishly written and generally outside of professional quality, assumption is that this will find its market among the morbid, the slinky grey people of D. H. Lawrence's description. The complete amorality of the heroine and the odious types she encouters, and the fantasy of bestiality with the make-believe ape are all deliberately calculated to draw a certain kind of trade. It might be called unbelievable but on the other hand it is, regretably, all too believable in the present state of American society. *Arno.*

Die, Monster, Die
(BRITISH-COLOR-WIDESCREEN)

Routine sci-fi horror pic for exploitation market. Boris Karloff for marquee strength.

Hollywood, Nov. 19.

American International Pictures release of an Alta Vista Production, executive producers, James H. Nicholson, Samuel Z. Arkoff, producer, Pat Green. Stars Boris Karloff, Nick Adams; features Freda Jackson, Suzan Farmer. Directed by Daniel Haller. Screenplay, Jerry Sohl, based on "Colour Out Of Space," by H. P. Lovecraft; camera (Pathecolor, anamorphic), Paul Beeson; editor, Alfred Cox; music, Don Banks; art direction, Colin Southcott. Reviewed at Joe Shore's Screening Room, L.A., Nov. 19, '65. Running Time, 78 MINS.
Nahum Witley .... Boris Karloff
Stephen Reinhart .... Nick Adams
Letitia Witley .... Freda Jackson
Susan Witley .... Suzan Farmer
Merwyn .... Terence De Marney
Dr. Henderson .... Patrick McGee
Jason .... Paul Farrell
Cab Driver .... George Moon
Miss Bailey .... Gretchen Franklin
Pierce .... Sydney Bromley
Henry .... Billy Milton

"Die, Monster, Die" is a routine sci-fi horror programmer about a mad. Englishman and radioactive mutations, including people. Boris Karloff in for marquee value. Very good production values, but slowly paced in scripting and direction. Made at England's Shepperton Studios, the American International release will perform adequately in its intended market. (Initial domestic dates have it paired with "Planet Of The Vampires.")

Plot is a long time in taking off after initial interest in reason why Yank Nick Adams can't get transportation from an English burg to Karloff's heath manor: seems the villagers recall latter's brother as a devil worshipper, although this doesn't come out until much later. Daughter Suzan Farmer. easy on eyes, is Adams' girl, just returned from U.S. schooling.

Karloff is appropriately menacing as he wheelchairs about with servant Terence De Marney, both in on the secret of the radioactive meteorite which has been used to develop some plant mutations, and, along the way. some insect horrors. Radiation has taken its toll on humans, too, with wife Freda Jackson becoming disfigured. Parents blame troubles on ancestor.

Adams, up to script demands, precipitates fiery climax. Producer Pat Green has provided some below-the-line values. Daniel Haller directed with a good visual sense, caught by Paul Beeson's sharp camera, but principals walk through roles. Alfred Cox trimmed to 78 minutes, still overlong. Don Banks' score is good, ditto title work by Bowie Films. *Murf.*

Die Pyramide des Sonnengottes
(The Pyramid of the Sun-God)
(GERMAN-YUGOSLAV)
(COLOR)

Berlin, Nov. 16.

Gloria (Munich) release of CCC (Artur Brauner, Berlin) production in collab with Avala-Film, Belgrade. Stars Lex Barker, Rik Battaglia, Michele Girardon. Directed by Robert Siodmak. Screenplay, Ladislas Fodor, R. A. Stemmle, Georg Marischka, adapted from novel by Karl May; camera (Eastmancolor), Siegfried Hold; music, Erwin Halletz; editor, Walter Wischniewsky. At numerous West Berlin cinemas. Running Time, 92 MINS.
Dr. Karl Sternau .... Lex Barker
Count Alfonso .... Gerard Barray
Josefa .... Michele Girardon
Andre Hasenpfeffer ..... Ralf Wolter
Rosita Arbellez ... Alessandro Panaro
Captain Verdoja .... Rik Battaglia
Karja .... Theresa Lorca
Don Pedro .... Hans Nielsen

Robert Siodmak, 65-year-old German vet director with a U.S. passport, continues the German Karl May trend with "Pyramid of the Sun-God." the late author's 52d book. Siodmak's experienced hand is particularly obvious in the fight sequences. It's the latter which count most on the international action market. If this film does well in the foreign market, it's chiefly to Siodmak's credit. Omit the action scenes, and this is a rather naive type of adventure pic.

Fable concerns Mexico of 1864, at the time of French occupation and the population's u p r i s i n g against Emperor Maximilian. Terror and injustice sweep the country. Dr. Sternau (Lex Barker), a German medico, and a semi-funny type of German clock dealer (Ralf Wolter) are on the side of the proud Mexicans. Vicious characters want to take possession of the old treasure of the Aztecs hidden in the Pyramid of the Sun-God. But they are trying to reach their goal by the most reckless means. A certain Verdoja (Rik Battaglia) is the most dangerous one of the gang and it takes quite a while to liquidate him.

Barker, probably the best known of the ex-Hollywoodites filming for Germany these days, is not too active in this. More footage is given to Battaglia whose role is also more colorful. Wolter takes care of the comedy relief, and it's sometimes amazing how modest one can get with gags and jokes in Teutonic pix. Wolter and the late Hans Nielsen are the only Germans in the cast. Most of them are French, Italians and Yugoslavs.

Siodmak, as indicated, made the most of a not too imaginative script on which Hungarian-born American Ladislas Fodor, Austrian-born English Georg Marischka and German R. A. Stemmle worked. Erwin Halletz' score is an asset. Also the lensing by Siegfried Hold is generally quite good. Other technical credits are up to par. *Hans.*

Hallo, Amerika
(Hello, America)
(GERMAN-SWISS—COLOR)

Berlin, Nov. 16.

Globus (Munich) release of Helmut Stahl production. Directed, written and photographed by Helmut Stahl. Music, Roland Poeller; editor, Stahl; commentator, Alfred Bruggemann. Preemed at Adria-Filmbuehne, West Berlin. Running Time, 65 MINS.

Taking into account that long documentary pix lately have been doing quitely nicely here, "Hallo, Amerika" may be granted some commercial chances in the German-language market. Also, the title is attractive enough to stir interest. But a more critical viewer won't find much if any praise for it. There is absolutely nothing new or anything worth mentioning about this documentary about the U.S.A.

Dr. Helmut Stahl, a Swiss medico and his family. wife plus two youngsters, traveled around the U.S. for a couple of months and whatever "special" he saw he put on celluloid. But what the patron sees on the screen has been countless times before.

The best that can be said "Hallo, Amerika" is that it is the good-natured work of a seemingly nice man who with modest means tried to achieve something above modesty. It's actually more than an item for schools than for regular cinemas. The commentary is dry and conventional, and brings back old memories of geographical lessons given at school. Lensing, editing and other technical details often have the character of poor amateur work. *Hans.*

The Grand Substitution
(CHINESE-COLOR-SCOPE)

Frank E. Lee International Films release of Shaw Studios production. Stars Li Li-Hua, Ivy Ling Po, Yen Chun; features Li Ying, Ching Miao, Tung Di, Chen Yen-yen. Directed by Yen Chun. Screenplay, Chen E-Hsin; camera (Eastmancolor-Shawscope), Yu Tsang-Shan; music, Sian Hua, lyrics, Chen E-Hsin. Reviewed at 55th St. Playhouse, N.Y., Nov. 22, '65. Running Time, 116 MINS.

While true that this Hong Kong-made extravaganza won the Best Film award at the 1965 Asian Film Festival, the viewer shudders to think what the runners-up must have been like. Run Run Shaw has provided one more opulent, very lengthy and generally dull concoction which makes no concession to Western tastes.

As in the past efforts, the elaborate story is told in a combination of highly-exaggerated theatrics and a semi-operatic vocalizing that sounds to Western ears like an Yma Sumac recording played at the wrong speed.

Title deals with sacrifice of his own baby son by a patriot as substitution for an infant prince condemned to death by a tyrannical minister. Boy is reared to avenge slaughter of his father's people. While Li Li-Hua is beautifully appropriate as the princess-mother of the infant, the whole thing becomes ridiculous when the 15-year-old boy is played by a girl, Ivy Ling Po. Most of the rest of the cast emote in a like vein. Color photography is excellent but emphasizes fakeness of sets meant to be exteriors but look like window displays.

If Shaw wants to invade the Western film market, he'd be much wiser to find out first what the West is buying. This isn't it.
Robe.

Blessings Of The Land
(FILIPINO)

Okay meller about rural life of Filipino family. Some fine performances, but script is too sudsy for most contemporary English-speaking audiences. Primitive production values, but sufficiently interesting to be fair artie prospect.

Lyn Pictures Inc. production, produced by Manuel de Leon. Features Rosa Rosal, Tony Santos, Le Roy Salvador, Carolos Padilla, Marita Zobel, Carmencita Abad. Directed by Manuel Silos. Screenplay, Celso Carunungan; camera, Remigio Young; editor, Teofilo de Leon; music, Leopaldo Silos. Reviewed at Lytton Center of Visual Arts, L.A., Nov. 12, '65. Running Time, 109 MINS.

Hollywood, Nov 13.
Made at a reported $40,000 cost and showcased in shortened export form at the first Filipino film fest to be held here, "Blessings Of The Land" is a sentimental, often touching story of the married life of a Filipino couple. Some excellent performances overcome static direction, an over-sudsed plot, some primitive technical details and very poor English subtitles. An Asian Film Fest winner, it has a fair art house appeal in domestic situations.

Celso Carunungan's script focusses on Rosa Rosal and Tony Santos, top-featured as the couple whose marriage (in what appears to be a modern setting) encompasses over 20 years of village life, with the domestic triumphs and tragedies comprising the plot turns. Both thesps are excellent, Miss Rosal in particular, and their interactions project the tender and loyal love of unsophisticated people.

Story becomes saccharine from via plot turns of storm-ravaged crops, deaf-mute son, raped daughter, precocious moppet, prodigal son and vigilante justice. For audiences who dig suds, this Manuel de Leon production has it in spades.

Le Roy Salvador is very good as the mute son who eventually overcomes family coddling and becomes man of the house, after Santos is killed by the man who raped daughter Marita Zobel, herself properly adolescent and naive. Carolos Padilla is good as the second son who chucks his home chores to seek his fortune in Manila. The great disparity between rural Filipino village life and cosmopolitan Manila will appear unbelievable to those who have never visited the Philippines; it exists in the way it once did in the U.S.

All other thesps contribute to the overall effect, and film winds on an upbeat note with the harvest of a fruit crop, and the realization of a believably-aged Miss Rosal that the struggle has been worth it.

Manual Silos directed in a pedestrian fashion marked by endless medium shots from the boringly-anchored camera of Remigio Young. Time transitions are handled in okay fashion via falling leaves, tree carvings, etc. Teofilio de Leon edited to 130 minutes for the Asian audiences who reportedly like longer pix; print caught ran 109 minutes, long enough, since plodding pace is maintained.

English subtitles for the native (Tagalog) lingo are crude transliterations, often grammatically awkward. Lab processing is substandard. Music is sparse and adequate. Lyn Pictures produced, and Universal has reportedly acquired Latin American distrib rights.
Murf.

Mahapurush
(THE HOLY MAN)
(INDIAN)

Paris, Nov. 23.
Rajshri Productions-PVT. Ltd. production and release. With Charuprakash Ghosh. Directed by Satyajit Ray. Screenplay, Rajshekhar Bose, Ray; camera, Sumendy Ray; editor, D. Dutt; music, Ray. Previewed in Paris. Running Time, 67 MINS.
Holy Man .... Charuprakash Ghosh

The one Indian filmmaker with international renown, Satyajit Ray, noted for his probing looks at Indian life in his trilogy of "Pather Panchali" and "World of Apu," here displays a bright parodic vein and sense of humor. It is a tale of the debunking of a false holy man.

The bumptious "holy one" is adopted by a rich man who can not get the right sort of husband for his daughter. But a poorer swain shows up the bogus priest and wins the girl. The adoration of the man is given the right fillip of satiric humor and racy good nature as they take in his tales of talks with ancient greats since he seems to remember his former incarnations.

Pungent characters, crisp direction, well coordinated playing and a general maintenance of wit and observation throughout give this a robust air. It could be a good co-feature, because of its length, for special and art situations abroad. Good production values and fine technical aspects also help.

Now this was conceived as a companion piece to a 74-minute pic "Kaparush" (The Coward), which played alone at the Venice Film Fest this year. It takes a wistful look at an indecisive man who tries to make up for the cowardly desertion of a girl.

Each is mainly a sketch on human frailty and credulity. Together they make up a rounded, full film which will have difficulty in standing alone. They should be used together, as made abroad for best results in arty situations. Full title of the two pix is "Kaparush-O-Mahapurush" (The Coward and the Holy Man). *Mosk.*

Les Grandes Gueules
(THE BIG SHOTS)
(FRENCH-COLOR)

Paris, Nov. 16.
SNC release of Belles Rives-SNC-Allesandra Film production. Stars Lino Ventura, Bourvil; features Marie Dubois, Jess Hahn, Jean-Claude Roland. Directed by Robert Enrico. Screenplay, Jose Giovanni, Enrico from book by Giovanni; camera (Eastmancolor), Didier Parot; editor, Jacqueline Meppiel. At Marbeuf, Paris. Running Time, 130 MINS.
Laurent .... Lino Ventura
Hector .... Bourvil
Jackie .... Marie Dubois
Nenesse .... Jess Hahn
Nick .... Jean-Claude Roland

Overlong actioner deals with a sawmill that uses convicts on provisional release and the complications that ensue. If good natured, this lacks strength since there is not enough dramatic and character. Film is sketchy and surface.

Picture does have some fresh air, fairly well done fights and an okay if sometimes fuzzy progression. It should do well on its home grounds but would need shearing for foreign showings, with playoff and dualers its main chances.

Two ex-cons take up with a man who has inherited a lumber camp and talk him into using ex-cons on probation as workers. This leads to some troubles with them, fights with a rival gang, love and regeneration for the ex-con.

But all this lacks the fillip of growing action and character to keep it from sagging. Lino Ventura has his usual guttural role of a good, bad guy. Comedian Bourvil is somewhat miscast as the head of the sawmill who finally burns it down in frustration when the prisoners are carted back to prison due to too many fights.

American actor Jess Hahn scores as a fuzzy minded giant. The other cons are colorful types but the pic does not quite make up its mind as to whether it has a social point to make or is just a crazy adventure opus.

Mostly shot out-of-doors in the French wooded mountains, it has an airy plus in this. It might be close to an attempt at a sort of French oater and, as such, may get locals who go for this sort of thing, but it is not quite up to par for foreign marts. Color is good. This is a nice try in spite of some flaws. *Mosk.*

Das Geheimnis der Drei Dschunken
(The Secret of the Three Junks)
(GERMAN-ULTRASCOPE-COLOR)

Berlin, Nov. 9.
Constantin release of Arca (Gero Wecker) production. Stars Stewart Granger, Rossana Schiaffino; features Harald Juhnke, Paul Klinger, Sieghard Rupp. Directed by Ernst Hofbauer. Screenplay, Hans-Karl Kubiak and W. P. Zibaso; camera (Eastmancolor), Werner M. Lenz; music, Riz Ortolani; editor, Max Mellini. At several West Berlin cinemas. Running Time, 89 MINS.
Michael Scott .... Stewart Granger
Danny Dennis ..... Rossana Schiaffino
Smoky .... Harald Juhnke
Norman .... Paul Klinger
Blanche .... Margit Saad
Pierre Milo .... Sieghard Rupp
Harris .... Paul Dahlke

Overly familiar complications and situations make this only a so-so item for the action market. In fact, it would have been a rather boring vehicle if Stewart Granger was not in the cast. He is more or less the only plus point about this. Pic is just another of those not properly prepared, quickly made, international German pix which are quite common these days. For export, the Stewart Granger name can be an exploitation factor. Otherwise there is indeed not much to recommend about it.

Locale is Hong Kong. An international gang has been smuggling electronic material from there into Red China for many months. Local police authorities know some of the suspects but are unable to track them down. So Stewart Granger of the American Secret Service is sent in to clear up the case. Before he succeeds he has a narrow escape from death in several situations. Finale sees him happily paired with a beautiful girl who has been heroic in her own way. She had been one of the gangsters' secretary while working for the Secret Service.

While Granger is on the screen this is never dull. Others in the cast stand considerably in Granger's shadow although the players include a number of widely known local players. But the material they are given is just too thin.

Direction sticks to the oldest patterns. Technically, this film makes an uneven impression. Editing is all but smooth. The color ranges from mediocre to good. Film looks as though it was made in record time. *Hans.*

Les Bons Vivants
(The High Lifers)
(FRENCH)

Paris, Nov. 16.
Valoria release of Transinter-Corona-Sancro Film production. Stars Louis De

Funes; features Mireille Darc, Bernard Blier, Andrea Parisy, Jean Lefevre, Bernadette Lafont, Jean Richard, Frank Villard. Directed by Gilles Grangier, Georges Lautner. Screenplay, Albert Simonin, Michel Audiard; camera, M. Fellous, Robert Le Febvre; editors, Jacqueline Thiedot, M. David. At Marbbeuf, Paris. Running Time, 95 MINS.

Leon	Louis De Funes
Eloise	Mireille Darc
Charles	Bernard Blier
Lucette	Andrea Parisy
Crook	Jean Lefevre
Sophie	Bernadette Lafont
Friend	Jean Richard
Michel	Frank Villard

This sketch pic continues in two series of picaresque comedies here. This time prostitution is supposed to be funny. Though it has a solid cast, this film too often forces the issues and gets smirky. However, it remains photographically restrained. This could have some exploitation changes aboard with arty chances limited because of its lack of subtlety and its bawdy sequences.

First up is the closing of a French bordello after the laws in 1949. It has some piquancy as it tries to give the inmates a semblance of humanity. But its slyness rubs off and it finally just becomes gross.

Second portion is a too talky trial where all the ex-prosties and panderers show up after a robbery of one who has now become rich. This one seems too obvious and talky to perk up the pic.

Then an overlong final bit has a sanctimonious rich man help a lady of the evening one night and then allow her to stay with him. He seemingly accepts her and asks nothing of her.

But friends begin to flock in as she takes over his home and gets her sidekicks to help too. He soon becomes popular, leads a life of almost innocent pandering, as his friends take up with the girls. Finally one Xmas his home takes on the air of a house of ill repute when somebody puts a red lantern outside.

The actors here are better than their roles and keep this from being entirely tasteless. But it too often aims at tickling the grossness rather than the wit of an audience. Louis De Funes is his usual spluttery self with his fine comic timing helping put some life in the overlong last seg.

This may do neatly on its home grounds but would need a hardsell aboard. Its frank but overdone theme could give it some sexploitation legs if well hypoed.
Mosk.

La Dama De Beirut
(Woman from Beirut)
(SPANISH-FRENCH-ITALIAN)
(Color)
Madrid, Nov. 16.

Filmax release of Balcazar (Barcelona)—Intercontinental and Luxor (Paris)—Mediterranee (Rome) production. Stars Sarita Montiel; co-stars Giancarlo del Duca, Fernand Gravey, Magali Noel, Alain Soury; features Gemma Cuervo, Chonette Lauret, Carlos Casaravilla, Daniel Vargas. Directed by Ladislao Vajda. Original story by De la Loma, Alfonso Balcazar and Duccio Tessari; screenplay by Jesus Maria Arozamena and Ladislao Vajda; camera, Christian Matras; music, Enrique Garcia Segura. At Rialto Theatre, Madrid. Running Time, 95 MINS.

In the Spanish-language market, Sarita Montiel has lifted the long-laden soap opera to the realm of golden corn. Her latest vehicle, a bit more lavish in production values and bolder in theme and wardrobe, will enthuse her fans, loyal to the unchanged Montiel format and style with which she crashed to fame in "Ultimo Cuple" 10 years ago.

Not even a perceptive director like the late Ladislao Vajda (a cardiac victim three-quarters of the way through filming) succeeded in modifying the rigid melo formula punctured with slow chant that marked her previous bits.

Behind the glittering gowns, big musical heads and potpourri of past pop tunes, the writers concocted a cabaret warbler who dejectedly signs on for a Mid-East tour. It turns out to be a white slave lure. Barely escaping a harem-happy sheik, then trapped in a bordello, she is saved by an elderly French doctor, wins fame in Paris and ends up with the medico's son in a tragi-romantic finale under the Arc de Triomphe.

Actors are foils for the star. Despite the handicap, Fernand Gravey and Alain Soury, as medico and procurer, excel. Matras' color lensing is fine. Star's costumes are the best money can buy. Noteworthy are Juan Alberto Soler's sets and choice of exteriors. Enrique Garcia Segura's tune package and score fit the bill. Overall, a sad final exit for Ladislao Vajda.

Senjo Ni Nagareru Uta
(We Will Remember)
(JAPANESE-COLOR-SCOPE)
Chicago, Nov. 14.

Toho Company Limited Production. Produced by Sanezumi Fujimoto. Features Hasaya Morishige, Chang-Mei-Yao, Keiju Kobayashi, Daisuke Kato, Kon Omura. Direction and Screen Play by Zenzo Matsuyama, based on original story by Ikuma Dan; camera (Eastmancolor) Asaichi Nakai; music, Ikuma Dan; sound, Akira Saito. Reviewed at the Carnegie Theatre, Nov. 11, '65. Running Time, 134 MINS.

Kiyoshi Kodama	Hisaya Morishige
Yoichi Mashio	Chang-Mei-Yao
Masaya Nihei	Keiju Kobayashi
Akira Kubo	Daisuke Kato
Yoko Fijuyama	Kon Omura

A protest against war that makes its points through exposition rather than stark statements, "We Will Remember" is a personal glimpse into the lives of young Japanese men in an Army band near the end of World War Two. The men have joined the band, which is an accelerated eight-month course, to keep out of combat. The training and methods used to discipline them are similar to the hard nosed approach taken by any army that is preparing men for the hardships imposed by war.

Annoyed by the constant harassment, the men complain of the life that they must lead. The band completes its training and the men are sent to China to boost the morale of Japanese combat troops. As they move through China they witness the senseless destroying of people and land.

In one small town they are ambushed by Chinese bandits—guerrilla fighters—and the band is almost completely annihilated. Ultimately survivors are sent to Bagio in the Philippines where they are captured.

This film is big in scope, ambitious in its intent, it is technically excellent and artistically successful, with the humor and pathos coming from the reality that the events — which seemed outlandish —did and do happen.

There is no major leading role, but rather a number of fine, believable performances. Zenzo Matsuyama's splendid direction keeps the film moving at a swift pace without diminishing the absorbing adventure or weakening the strength of the characters. The picture won Best Color Cinematography in the festival for its color, which is as good as any 35m seen to date.

Literal translation of Japanese title is "The Song That Floats On The Battlefront." *Ron.*

Lady L
(COLOR)

An effervescent but erratic comedy. Some choice, witty writing and direction by Peter Ustinov; strong marquee value of Loren, Newman and Niven should pull in patrons, but reactions likely to be varied.

London, Nov. 30.

Metro presentation and release of a Carlo Ponti production. Stars Sophia Loren, Paul Newman, David Niven; features Claude Dauphin, Cecil Parker, Marcel Dalio, Eugene Deckers, Peter Ustinov. Directed by Ustinov. Screenplay by Ustinov, from Romain Gary's novel; camera (Eastmancolor), Henri Alekan; editor, Roger Dwyre; music, Jean Francaix. At Empire, London. Running Time, 124 MINS.

Lady L	Sophia Loren
Armand	Paul Newman
Dicky	David Niven
Inspector Mercier	Claude Dauphin
Gerome	Philippe Noiret
Lecoeur	Michel Piccoli
Sapper	Marcel Dalio
Sir Percy	Cecil Parker
Krajewski	Jean Wiener
Kobeleff	Daniel Emilfork
Koenigstein	Eugene Deckers
Beala	Jacques Duphilo
Agneau	Tanya Lopert
Pantoufle	Catherine Allegret
Prince Otto	Peter Ustinov

Experiment of starting and ending this pic with Sophie Loren as an 80-year-old, an alleged aristocrat with a somewhat simpering tedious voice, doesn't come off. Not till the Italian dish reverts to her own radiant, lush self will her followers settle down comfortably. David Niven is immaculately debonair and wittily amusing, but Paul Newman, though turning in a thoroughly competent performance, is not happily cast—his role calling out for the dependable mixture of solidity and lightness.

Still, the presence of this pulling trio, plus the nimble wit of Peter Ustinov as writer, director and, briefly, as actor, should insure brisk wicket activity. Audience reaction to this stylish but uneven mixture of high comedy, satire, farce, romance and drama may prove patchy.

Film, from Romain Gary's novel, was originally planned as a straight drama, but things misfired. Ustinov was later brought in to do a doctoring job. But, despite the cost, he took on the chore only on the proviso that he could wipe the slate clean and start afresh. His nimble brain and characteristics have since clearly shaped the entire project.

Story, set in Paris and Switzerland at the turn of the century (cut for some eyeworthy decor and costumes and some rich, warm lensing by Henri Alekan) has Miss Loren as an aging, allegedly aristocratic mystery woman recounting her life story for the benefit of a biographer (Cecil Parker). He finds that the details of her kinky life as an adventuress don't match up with her public image.

She begins as a laundress. While delivering the "whiter-than-whites" to a classy Parisian brothel (cover joint for a bunch of crooks), she becomes romantically involved with Newman, who is a hot headed thief, robbing the rich to help the poor. Dogged by the frustrated Paris police, the two are constantly on the run until Newman gets mixed up with a dim-witted bunch of anarchists who aim to bump off the senile Price Otto, for reasons inadequately explained. Miss Loren walks out on Newman and again becomes involved, this time with Niven, a British aristocrat, looking for a wife. He strikes a bargain. If she'll marry him, he promises to save her lover from the police.

The pic has Loren marrying Niven while he apparently complaisantly accepts her consorting with Newman. Ustinov's loose screenplay leaves a lot of these details to the imagination and he is content for the storyline to be a mere excuse for some amiable frolicking plus some witty dialog and amusing situations. But the whole thing is too erratically strung together to avoid some protracted, flattish passages.

Niven is typically suave in a lightweight, but well-written role. Miss Loren is at her best in the scenes with him. Her involvement with Newman creaks occasionally because the director never appears to know whether his writer (the "twin" Ustinovs) intend them to be played dramatically or for yocks.

Ustinov weighs in with a choice cameo as the doddering Prince Otto who is marked out for assassination by Newman and his dumb gang of petty anarchists (headed by Eugene Deckers). Claude Dauphin, as a frustrated chief of cops, while Jean Weiner, playing a Polish pianist whose recitals are invariably broken up by a heaved bomb, are fine foils. Cecil Parker plays the small role of the would-be biographer with his impeccably pompous dither.

Ustinov has brought a glinting comedy eye to a number of situations, notably the intended assassination, a piano recital in the bawdy house, chaos at a concert and the arrival back in Britain at his stately home of Niven and his wife. But the yocks are giggles and chuckles rather than sustained comedy. And he does not get nearly as much good-humored piquancy out of the excellent brothel setup as might be rightly anticipated.

Technically the pic is okay. There's been much attention to set and costume detail which will please the attentive. But, overall, the film jerks genteely rather than sweeps, through what could have been a still witty, but more boisterous and extravagant joke. *Rich.*

Johnny Nobody
(BRITISH)

Imported suspenser run-of-mill programmer despite stronger than usual casting.

Medallion Pictures release of Irving Allen-Albert R. Broccoli production. Features Nigel Patrick, Yvonne Mitchell, Aldo Ray, William Bendix, Cyril Cusack, Niall MacGinnis. Produced by John R. Sloan. Directed by Nigel Patrick. Screenplay, Patrick Kirwin, based on Albert Z. Carr story, "The Trial of Johnny Nobody." No other credits. Reviewed at Guild Theatre, N.Y., Nov. 24, '65. Running Time, 88 MINS.

Father Carey .... Nigel Patrick
Miss Floyd .... Yvonne Mitchell
Johnny .... Aldo Ray
Mulcahy .... William Bendix
Prosecuting Counsel .. Cyril Cusack
Defending Counsel.... Niall MacGinnis
Photographer .... Bernie Winters
Brother Timothy .... Noel Purcell
Landlord .... Eddie Byrne
Postman .... Jimmy O'Dea
Judge .... John Welsh
Tinker .... Joe Lynch
Supt. Lynch .... Michael Brennan
Caretaker .... J. G. Devlin
Father Bernard .... Christopher Casson
Tinker's Mother .... May Craig
Father Healey .... Norman Rodway

This belated British import (somewhat self-dated by presence in the cast of American actor William Bendix, who died in December 1964) has a cast that compares for talent with many bigger-budgeted and more ambitious efforts. And that's about the only thing it has going for it.

Actor Nigel Patrick in his second attempt at directing (he also helmed the underrated 'How To Murder a Rich Uncle' which may have been too early in the black comedy genre), has less success with this straight drama.

The quasi-controversial area of the story, which Patrick Kirwin has stodgily adapted from an Albert Z. Carr story, 'The Trial of Johnny Nobody,' is whether an individual can be accepted as an instrument of God. Presented in an insufficiently clear manner, it doesn't capture the viewer's interest, much less stir him with its controversy.

When a hard-drinking writer (William Bendix) defies God to strike him down as a blasphemer, a stranger (Aldo Ray) shoots him dead and says that he was forced to do so by a compelling force. The priest in the Irish village (Nigel Patrick), where the incident occurs, takes it upon himself to find a solution to the mystery, while the stranger, known only as "Johnny Nobody" awaits trial. Patrick uncovers evidence that Ray, in collaboration with his wife (Yvonne Mitchell) had planned the crime. Although Patrick is framed by the wife, who's also a reporter, he reaches the trial in time to see Ray acquitted. An ending that could be construed as the justice of Providence is tacked on for suspense but it's of little help.

Patrick, as an actor, as do the other principals, gives more to the script than it deserves. His directing, on the other hand, is generally uninteresting. The most logical market is among art situations which double-bill. *Robe.*

Compartiment Tueurs
(The Sleeping Car Murders)
(FRENCH)
Paris, Nov. 30.

20th-Fox release of PECF (Julien Derode)-7 Arts production. Stars Yves Montand, Simone Signoret; features Pierre Mondy, Catherine Allegret, Jacques Perrin, Michel Piccoli, Jean-Louis Trintignant, Charles Denner. Directed by Costa Gavras. Screenplay, Sebastien Japrisot; Gavras from a book by Japrisot; camera, Jean Tournier; music, Michel Magne. At Normandie, Paris. Running Time, 90 MINS.

Grazzi .... Yves Montand
Eliane .... Simone Signoret
Boss .... Pierre Mondy
Bambi .... Catherine Allegret
Daniel .... Jacques Perrin
Cabourg .... Michel Piccoli
Eric .... Jean-Louis Trintignant
Bob .... Charles Denner
Jean-Lou .... Claude Mann

Suspenser has a good gimmick but takes too many flashbacks that do not help keep up the interest. It does have the names of Simone Signoret and Yves Montand for some marquee weight and emerges a solidly made, if uneven, thriller that might be of dualer use abroad. Art chances are much more chancier.

A woman is found dead in a second class sleeping compartment when a train reaches Paris and all those who were in the car are systematically killed off. The use of that bit about what looks like a motiveless crime, to get somebody else who was in the car, is the main wedge of the pic. It has been used at least once before.

Montand is the police inspector with a cold, Marseilles accent, who solves the mystery. Miss Signoret adds a neat bit as a down and out actress with her own daughter, Catherine Allegret, playing a girl who was also present.

New director Costa Gavras gives this solid mounting if a bit more ruggedness and snap in the police routine scenes might have helped. It is reminiscent of the Yank investigation pix of this type but does not quite have the pungent character notations, pace and perkiness of those films. It is technically good. Gavras appears to be a needed craftsman who can put a pic together well. A better story and less insistence on acting cameos would help.

Montand is authoritative, with a good fillip of human outlook. Others are all adequate if the denouement is telegraphed and the ending is cluttered up with a chase. *Mosk.*

Boeing Boeing
(COLOR)

Comedy about bachelors and airline hostesses should fly high in general market. Tony Curtis teamed with Jerry Lewis topped for laughs by Thelma Ritter.

Hollywood, Nov. 11.

Paramount Pictures release of Hal B. Wallis production. Stars Tony Curtis, Jerry Lewis; features Dany Saval, Christine Schmidtmer, Suzanna Leigh, Thelma Ritter, Lomax Study. Directed by John Rich. Screenplay, Edward Anhalt, based on play by Marc Camoletti; camera (Technicolor), Lucien Ballard; editors, Warren Low, Archie Marshek; music, Neal Hefti. Reviewed in Hollywood, Nov. 11, '65. Running Time, 102 MINS.

Bernard Lawrence .... Tony Curtis
Robert Reed .... Jerry Lewis
Jacqueline Grieux ..... Dany Saval
Lise Brunner ....Christine Schmidtmer
Vicky Hawkins .... Suzanna Leigh
Bertha .... Thelma Ritter
Pierre .... Lomax Study

"Boeing Boeing" is an excellent modern comedy about two newshawks with a yen for airline hostesses. Firstrate performances and direction make the most of a very good script. Well-mounted Hal B. Wallis production should strike a responsive chord among adults and mature teeners, and strong b.o. is likely for Paramount release in the general market.

The fanciful dream of a dedicated bachelor—that of having a guaranteed supply of female companionship—is realized in Edward Anhalt's adaptation of a Marc Camoletti play in which Paris-based U.S. newsman Tony Curtis has three airline gals on a string.

In the dialog of Jerry Lewis, also starred above title, situation amounts to "one up, one down, and one pending." The gals' flight skeds make this possible.

Director John Rich has done a topnotch job in overcoming what is essentially (except for a few Paris exteriors) a one-set, one-joke comedy. Curtis is excellent and neatly restrained as the harem keeper whose cozy scheme approaches collapse when advanced design Boeing aircraft (hence, the title) augur a disastrous overlap in femme availability.

Rich has also brought out a new dimension in Lewis, herein excellent in a solid comedy role (sans a multitude of slapstick) as Curtis' professional rival who threatens to explode the plan. Curtis finds he needs Lewis more than he doesn't, and their interactions are solid.

The outstanding performance is delivered by Thelma Ritter, Curtis' harried housekeeper who, as one gal departs, makes the necessary domestic changes in photos, clothing and menu so that the next looker will continue to believe that she, alone, is mistress of the flat. Her sharp comments and asides hit the laugh jackpot every time, and the film derives much of its impact through her fortunate casting.

The three hostesses are well-played by Dany Saval, petite French chick, Christiane Schmidtmer, the self-sufficient German amazon, and Suzanna Leigh, the very-British type who, at length falling for Lewis, almost rescues Curtis from his predicament.

Boys will be boys, however, and at fadeout, they're busy setting up another deal with some female taxi drivers. Lomax Study rounds out cast in brief, effective bits as the translator in Curtis' office who doubles as informer and procurer.

Rich has kept the pace moving rapidly with the strong assist of Lucien Ballard's mobile technicolor camera and the tight editing (to 102 minutes) of Warren Low and Archie Marshek. Hal Pereira and Walter Tyler, with set decorators Sam Comer and Ray Moyer, have given much visual interest to the apartment interiors, while Edith Head's costumes help fix the eyes on the girls.

Neal Hefti's score is sparse and wisely unobstrusive. Per usual, associate producer Paul Nathan has contributed top class Wallis production touches and all other technical details are professional. *Murf.*

The Great Patriotic War
(RUSSIAN)
Leipzig, Nov. 23.

Central Studio for Documentary Films (Moscow) production. Directed by Roman Karmen, I. Venzher, I. Setkina. Written by Roman Karmen; music, Kara-Karayev; editor, Karmen. At Leipzig Film Fest. Running Time, 129 MINS.

As the title indicates, this full-length documentary depicts the fight of the Red Army against the Hitler forces in the last World War. Film is technically okay but has too much pathos and, at least for non-Russian ears, exaggerated glorification of the Soviet soldiers. This makes it primarily an item for the home market or, at best, Commie countries. Much if not most of the war footage has been seen in other documentaries before; hence, export chances look rather limited.

According to the commentary, the footage originates from the material lensed by 236 (mostly Soviet) cameramen of whom 40 were killed in action. The volume of this documentary is vast but only very few scenes appear new. It all begins in 1933 when the senile German Reich's president, Hindenburg, gave his blessing to this century's No. 1 madman, Adolf Hitler. Seen again are the big Nazi parades and the mass meetings at Nuremberg, the invasion of countries which, in 1941, included the Soviet Union.

The Stalingrad battle which was the turning point for the Soviet army naturally gets big coverage. Also included is the SS brutality of Soviet people, footage of Hitler's hell camps, the activity of resistance fighters in other territories, the Allied invasion in France, etc. The last part shows the advancing Soviet forces, the various battle defeats of the Germans, the fall of Berlin, Keitel signing the capitulation and finally the great Soviet victory parade in Moscow's Red Square.

This documentary gives impression that it was primarily the Communist forces which smashed Hitler fascism, and therefore it has the flavor of a dishonest enterprise. For instance, the American aid of arms which was certainly not secondary in those war years doesn't find mention at all. Repeatedly the commentator puts the question: Where is the promised second front? This question is imposed on the western Allied whose invasion of France was allegedly delayed. Also the Hitler-Stalin pact doesn't get the proper mention.   *Hans.*

A Thousand Clowns

Excellent comedy about a modern nonconformist. Marquee lure for sophisticates, and strong b.o. likely in urban keys. May need a hard sell in general market.

Hollywood, Nov. 24.

United Artists release of Harrell Inc. presentation, produced and directed by Fred Coe. Stars Jason Robards; features Barbara Harris, Martin Balsam, Gene Saks, William Daniels, Barry Gordon. Screenplay, Herb Gardner, based on his play; camera, Arthur J. Ornitz; editor, Ralph Rosenblum; music, Judy Holliday, Gerry Mulligan; asst. director, Dan Ericksen. Reviewed at Goldwyn Studios, Nov. 23, '65. Running Time, **117 MINS.**

Murray Burns	Jason Robards
Sandra Markowitz	Barbara Harris
Arnold Burns	Martin Balsam
Leo (Chuckles)	Gene Saks
Albert Amundson	William Daniels
Nick	Barry Gordon

"A Thousand Clowns" depicts a happy-go-lucky non-conformist who attains some maturity when a child welfare board threatens to take away his young resident nephew. Comedy performances throughout are slightly negated by overlength and overdone slam-bang cinematics which mar an otherwise excellent Fred Coe film. Very good b.o. prospects for initial United Artists release in sophisticated urban houses, but a hard sell (to overcome, among other things, a

blah title) will be needed in general situations.

Key personnel of the long-running 1962-63 Broadway legiter have followed through with the pic. They include playwright-adapter Herb Gardner, producer-director Coe, and Jason Robards, solo-starred as the ex-vidscripter living it up in a littered N.Y. pad while trying to prevent nephew Barry Gordon (also encoring) from becoming one of the "dead people," meaning conformists.

Terrif dialog to match Robards' scenery-chewing create a sock impact as he lectures the 12-year-old (a hip juve, wiser than unk), ignores the pleas of brother-agent Martin Balsam to return to work, and pierces the outstanding social worker bureaucratic shell of Barbara Harris and original cast member William Daniels, who've arrived to check the kid's home life.

Miss Harris falls for Robards, latter momentarily inspired to shape up, and after the inevitable spat, he actually returns to Gene Saks, the fretful, insecure host of a kiddie vidshow. (Coe delayed film's completion so that Saks could re-create the role.) All performances present three-dimensional, identifiable characters underneath the yocks.

Coe's capable direction ranges from intimate, moving scenes between principals to zesty satire on metropolitan life. Latter is captured by the zooming, always crisp camera of Arthur J. Ornitz, reinforced by the deliberately overdone (and well done) interpolation of marches, choral music and Dixieland into the score, and highlighted by the fast-paced editing supervised by Ralph Rosenblum.

Burr Smidt's sets, particularly the apartment, are outstanding. Sound recording by James Shields is firstrate. Rita Gardner chirps the title tune (heard so briefly as to be beyond recall or evaluation). Other N.Y.-based technical credits are topflight.   *Murf.*

The Common Fascism
(RUSSIAN)

Leipzig, Nov. 23.

Mosfilm production of full-length documentary. Directed by Mikhail Romm. Commentary by Romm; camera, German Lawrow; music, A. Karananof; editor, Michail Romm. At Leipzig Film Fest. Running Time, **130 MINS.**

There have been countless documentary films on Fascism in the years that followed the collapse of Hitler's Reich in 1945. This Soviet production which had its world preem at the just terminated 8th Leipzig Documentary Festival differs from the others as per a feature-type of mounting style and its narration which displays satirical wit. Also, it contains footage allegedly never seen before. Pic has considerable merit and could have been a highly recommendable item for the international market had director - writer - editor Mikhail Romm skipped the heavy anti-western propaganda stuff particularly in film's final chapter. But since the narration can be changed, the film's chances to get into western markets are okay. "Common Fascism," incidentally, has been acquired by West Germany, the country which is so heavily attacked by

this documentary for its alleged "new Fascism."

Romm, prominent Soviet feature film director, divided his documentary into 12 chapters and therewith utilized the same technique employed for his last pic. "Nine Days of a Year" which consisted of nine episodes. Viewing the film is like reading a book. The 12 chapters deal with Hitler's entire "career" and also concern such items as Fascist art, education and culture. Naturally, the persecution of the Jewish people by Hitler's henchmen and the Nazis' mad war of conquest find particular and substantial mention. Final chapter called "The Incomplete" shows contemporary footage: A series of events taking place in western countries which, according to Romm, have a striking resemblance with what went on in Hitler Germany.

The commentary (spoken by Romm himself) is mostly on the satirical side, sometimes sarcastic and occasionally genuinely funny. A smiling "Fuehrer," the bold heads of fat Nazi leaders or a conceitedly speaking Mussolini can naturally look very funny. But Romm also gets funny without intending to. For example, he pays big attention to the British (Sir Oswald Mosley) Fascist group which is hardly taken seriously in that country. He shows the military training of U. S. marines who are tabbed Fascist-type of soldiers. He shows rallies of East German refugees in West Germany—naturally new Fascists. And so forth. Eventually he says something like this: Men like Krupp and Thyssen, big West German industrial leaders, made a profit of about 100 Marks on every soldier that was killed in the last World War.

An interesting thing about the whole film is that some of the footage came from Goebbels' private archives. As long as the film dedicates itself to Germans and Germany under Hitler, it is certainly a well done production. But controversy is bound to come up when its creator calls the assemblies of vet soldiers rallies of Fascists who seek revenge.

There is, in West Germany, a radical rightist party called the Deutsche Partei. This one didn't get even the 5% needed to get into the Bonn Parliament. So, unfortunately. Romm's piece cannot escape being branded a propaganda film. This is deplorable, because his kind of montage (called "psychological montage" by him) is excellent. The editing is smooth and there's a fine score. Technically, "The Common Fascism" makes a solid impression.   *Hans.*

Planet Of The Vampires
(ITALIAN-COLOR-WIDESCREEN)

Sci-fi space fantasy that doesn't always make sense, but excellent production values and color photography make for good companion booking.

Hollywood, Nov. 23.

American International Pictures release of a Fulvio Lucisano production; associate producer, Salvatore Billitteri. Features Barry Sullivan, Norma Bengell,

Angel Aranda, Evi Marandi, Fernando Villena, Stelio Candelli, Massimo Righi, Mario Morales, Franco Andrei, Ivan Rassimov, Rico Boido, Alberto Cevenini. Directed by Mario Bava. Screenplay, Ib Melchoir and Louis M. Heyward, from Melchoir's story; camera (Pathe Color), Antonio Rinaldi; editor, Antonio Gimeno. Reviewed at Joe Shore Screening Room, L.A.; Nov. 22, 1965. Running Time, **86 MINS.**

Mark	Barry Sullivan
Sanya	Norma Bengell
Wess	Angel Aranda
Tiona	Evi Marandi
Karan	Fernando Villena
Mud	Stelio Candelli
Nordeg	Massimo Righi
Eldon	Mario Morales
Garr	Franco Andrei
Kell (Derry)	Ivan Rassimov
Keir (Key)	Rico Boido
Wan (Toby)	Alberto Cevenini

(English Soundtrack)

As out-of-this-world fantasy, Italian-made "Planet Af The Vampires" is pretty far out. Plot is punctuated with gore, shock, eerie music and wild optic and special effects that can be exploited by American International for okay biz in nabe spots. Color camera work and production value are smooth and first class. Acting is adequate but editing is often abrupt and confusing, while dialogue is also not up to snuff. Flash Gordon type story, however, should keep the young on the edge of their seats and the older set from falling asleep.

Heavy handed story involves two spaceships from a far off planet which land on another planet called Aura. The sleek, huge bat-like creations have been rigged with every scientific apparatus and it is this devotion to technical aspects which gives the pic a fantastic sense of realism, but also when pushed too far make for chuckles.

One group of spacemen, led by Barry Sullivan, become involved in a series of weird encounters once the ship lands. Other ship's crew are found dead, having clawed each other to death, which makes for gory close-up detail. Soon the dead arise. Seems whatever inhabits the place have a habit of taking over bodies for evil purposes. Nice suspense is generated by the unseen enemy which gradually kills the good space guys off with the attempt of taking over and returning to their home base.

Photography by Antonio Rinaldi, costumes by Gabriele Mayer and complicated spaceship set by Giorgio Giovanni are best part of film. Actors rush about with unrelieved solemnity and at times appear as confused as the audience at what is happening. Director Mario Bava has attempted to cram too much action into pic and continuity is unsmooth.

As a psychological thriller main premise pays off but ending is not to be believed. Leader Barry Sullivan and his Girl Friday, Norma Bengell, are only two left and orbit from planet. Without explanation, they have now been taken into possession bodily by the evil enemy and unable to get back to home base decide to land on another small planet, which through the zoom lenses turns out to be planet, Earth.   *Dool.*

When The Boys Meet The Girls
(COLOR-PANAVISION)

Mildly entertaining film version of "Girl Crazy." Many songs, predictable plot. Fair b.o. where dual-billed in youth markets.

Hollywood, Nov. 20.

Metro-Goldwyn-Mayer release of a Four Leaf (Sam Katzman) production. Features Connie Francis, Harve Presnell, Herman's Hermits, Louis Armstrong, Sam The Sham and the Pharaohs, Liberace. Directed by Alvin Ganzer. Screenplay, Robert E. Kent, based on musical "Girl Crazy"; camera (Metrocolor), Paul C. Vogel; editor, Ben Lewis; music, Fred Karger; songs, George and Ira Gershwin, Graham Gouldman, Louis Armstrong and Billy Kyle, Johnny Farrow, Karger, Ben Weisman and Sid Wayne, Jack Keller and Howard Greenfield, Liberace; sound, Franklin Milton. Reviewed at Academy Award Theatre, Hollywood, Nov. 19, '65. Running Time, 97 MINS.

Ginger	Connie Francis
Danny	Harve Presnell
Themselves	Herman's Hermits, Louis Armstrong, Sam The Sham and the Pharaohs, Liberace, Davis and Reese
Tess	Sue Ane Langdon
Bill	Fred Clark
Phin	Frank Faylen
Sam	Joby Baker
Kate	Hortense Petra
Lank	Stanley Adams
Pete	Romo Vincent
Delilah	Susan Holloway
Stokes	Russ Collins
Dean	William T. Quinn

"When The Boys Meet The Girls" is the third film to be based specifically on the 1930-31 legituner, "Girl Crazy." This Sam Katzman production is a spotty comedy film, loaded with often-extraneous tunes, also limited to some okay performances and gags. For commercial purposes, the Metro-Goldwyn-Mayer release shapes up as a fair dual-bill entry in youth situations.

Top-featured Connie Francis and Harve Presnell (seemingly cast more from contractual commitments than suitability) are adequate; she as the backwoods Nevada U.S. mail-woman saddled with pop Frank Faylen, a chronic gambler, while Presnell is the big-city playboy exiled to the boondocks to avoid a breach-of-promise suit by chorine Sue Ane Langdon.

Joby Baker is Presnell's buddy who eventually pairs with a rather mute Susan Holloway (who doesn't need to talk much, anyway), and Fred Clark is good as the neighboring rancher who (after Presnell persuades Miss Francis to turn the domestic digs into a dude ranch for divorcees) hitches up with Hortense Petra. Local gambler hoods are played by Stanley Adams and Romo Vincent, who cleverly talk and move about in unison.

The late Russ Collins is effective as Presnell's harried biz manager. Unbilled among the divorcees is Patti Moore (paired in vaude with Ben Lessy) who has a brief talking bit. Miss Langdon remains as the most impressive of the principals; she makes a firstrate shrew.

Among the 11 tunes spread over film's 97 minutes are five vintage Gershwin numbers, including "I Got Rhythm," subject of what is the big production number, effectively choreographed by Earl Barton. Presnell does "Embraceable You" in good fashion, better than "But Not For Me" when joined by Miss Francis.

Herman's Hermits essay a romantic pair, including "Bidin' My Time," while Louis Armstrong, Liberace and Sam The Sham and the Pharaohs each do a single. There's something for everyone in the tune department, although, conversely, theres little for anybody. Brightest number in the new batch is Miss Francis "Mail Call.' Fred Karger's surrounding score is okay. Comedy duo of Davis and Reese give pic a big boost after a slow start; they're corny but very good.

Director Alvin Ganzer has done a routine job, except for an exterior auto chase which is a real pip. Robert E. Kent is script-credited, many frames away from the source material, latter in type just exceeding notice that Four Leaf and Metro share the copyright. Paul Vogel's Panavision-Metrocolor camera work is excellent, and other technicals are okay, except for some interiors that look, and sound, artificial as all get out.

Murf.

Viva Maria
(FRENCH-COLOR-SONGS)

Bardot - Moreau - Hamilton names in lively comedy. Good prospects.

Paris, Dec. 7.

United Artists release of NEF-Artistes Associes-Oscar Dancigers-Vides Film production. Stars Brigitte Bardot, Jeanne Moreau; features George Hamilton, Claudio Brooks, Carlos Lopez Moctezuma, Gregor Von Rezzori, Paulette Dubost, Luis Rizo. Directed by Louis Malle. Screenplay, Jean-Claude Carriere, Malle; camera (Eastmancolor), Henri Decae; editor, Kanout Peltier, Suzanne Baron; music, Georges Delerue. Previewed in Paris. Running Time, 120 MINS.

Maria I	Jeanne Moreau
Maria II	Brigitte Bardot
Flores	George Hamilton
Rodolfo	Claudio Brooks
Magician	Gregor Von Rezzori
Rodriguez	Carlos Lopez Moctezuma
Strongman	Luis Rizo

Big Bertha pic looks geared for big business internationally with B.B. (Brigitte Bardot) in her best form since "And God Created Woman," and brilliantly matched by Jeanne Moreau. They are backed by a rollicking, comic adventure opus impeccably brought off by director Louis Malle. The American name is George Hamilton. Film's dialog is in English.

Here is a film that measure up to its advance publicity. It has the wit, scope and color for both arty and playoff or regular firstrun chances. It strikes the right note of larger-than-life adventure, uses sex in a delicious, rather than leering or over-exploited manner and deftly pays homage to the Yank films of this kind in its stable, good natured succession of gags, leavened with some frisky but never blue French humor.

Here is Miss Bardot as the daughter of a life-long anarchist who has spent her life blowing up bridges and police stations. She finds herself hunted in some Latino country in 1910 when she has to blow up papa and a bridge. She is taken up by Jeanne Moreau, a dancer in a traveling music hall cum circus. The two team up.

There follow some knowing take-offs on the songs of the era with Bardot unwittingly seeming to invent the striptease when her skirt falls off at one show. The tone of this allows big production suddenly to be worked into a moth-eaten bucolic theatre. One bit has them stripping with the last vestments suddenly having a cut.

The fine scripting takes advantage of the land, color, Panavision and outdoor shooting in Mexico as the tale gets the circus involved in a local revolution. Also neatly imbedded are the characters of the femmes, both named Maria. Bardot is an innocent who suddenly discovers love, approves of it, and just uses it like a pure little animal, an epitome of her sex-kitten shenanigans. Moreau is the more knowing and wry one who is still the more romantic and falls for a handsome revolutionary. She takes up his cause after his death.

Some big scale fight episodes are brought off with the right romantic violence and invention. A pigeon that drops grenades, Bardot handling a machine gun or swinging through the trees, Tarzan-like, to wipe out a cannon. The circus performers employ their acrobatic skill also in the fights. The gags spring naturally and are thus more effective.

None of the frenzied cutting, overloaded and forced comedics and leering attitudes towards sex get into this pic. It is a classic tale, set in a fresh, witty and zesty new mold. Production manages to keep up the pace, and rarely sags. The only love scene, of Moreau entering the prison of her hero, with the circus strongman bending the bars, is done with the right romantic flavor.

Color is right, supporting cast very strong and the comedy routines a delight. A local churchman tries to use old Inquisition torture tools on the girls but relents and apologizes when the things break down. As he puts it: "They have not been used in a long time."

Big scale extra scenes and mob fighting are also spectacular with bright gags interlarded. When a bank is blown up it rains gold coins. Exploding a statue of the tyrant has the monument falling among seated people and then a man frantically trying to ride the horse part.

It adds up to a bouncy, broad adventure opus that pays homage to its predecessors yet does not ape them. There should be a big worldwide career for this one in subtitled or dubbed forms. It can play arty and specialized spots easily too. The entertainment knowhow and comedy mix well to give this high b.o. potential.

Mosk.

The Early Bird
(BRITISH-COLOR)

Heavygoing, slapstick farce that should, as usual, hit the Norman Wisdom boxoffice target in those markets where he is established.

London, Nov. 30.

Rank presentation and release of a Hugh Stewart Production. Stars Norman Wisdom. Features Edward Chapman, Jerry Desmonde, Pattie ONeill, Bryan Pringle, Richard Vernon, John Le Mesurier. Directed by Robert Asher. Screenplay Jack Davies and Norman Wisdom, with Eddie Leslie and Henry Blyth; camera (Eastmancolor), Jack Asher; editor, Gerry Hambling; music, Ron Goodwin. Reviewed Nov. 30, '65 at Odeon, Haymarket, London. Running Time: 98 MINS.

Norman Pitkin	Norman Wisdom
Grismdale	Edward Chapman
Hunter	Jerry Desmonde
Mrs. Hoskins	Paddie O'Neill
Austin	Bryan Pringle
Sir Roger	Richard Vernon
Colonel Foster	John Le Mesurier
Fire Chief	Peter Jeffrey
Miss Curry	Penny Morrell
Woman in Negligee	Marjie Lawrence
Doctor	Frank Thornton
Demented Woman	Dandy Nichols
Commissionaire	Harry Locke
Nervous Man	Michael Bilton
Sir Roger's Secretary	Imogen Hassall
Pitkin's Horse	Nellie

Norman Wisdom's annual slapstick farce invariably hits the box-office with a wham and he is a popular, profitable property in world areas, except the States where he has yet to make impact. But the amiable and talented little comedian is not content. He is publicly on record as regretting that his screen image and comedy work is not taken seriously enough to garner worthwhile critical analysis. His latest pic will not help. Cast in his usual formula it turns out to be rather more witless, uninventive and exhausting than many previous efforts.

There is surely a limit to the number of yocks that can be milked out of constantly falling down stairs, physical indignities and ruthless wrecking of buildings and so on. With "The Early Bird" the regular Wisdom team (producer Hugh Stewart, director Robert Asher, and scriptwriter Jack Davies, abetted by Wisdom himself, Henry Blyth and Eddie Leslie) seems to have reached it.

Minimal story line has Wisdom as the milkman and general factotum of a small family dairy that is being taken over by a monopoly. On this is strung a batch of slapstick situations, mainly irrelevant, in which Wisdom as the small man stands up against the doublecrossing of the monopolistic bullies. Of the many long and telegraphed situations such as the wrecking of a pompous bigwig's garden, mayhem on a golf course and a frenetic finale whereby Consolidated's huge building is sabotaged by Wisdom and its fire brigade, none is given any real motivation or development. There is one scene which promised well, but fizzles out, a tenuous skit on the Shane film with Wisdom and a rival milkman doing the long, long walk down a deserted street. Wisdom's fun with his horse, which involves him getting the animal into bed, also comes out fairly strained.

Yet the comic works unflaggingly and with considerable knowhow in striving to produce the yocks. The material just isn't there—or, at least, not enough of it. Edward Chapman and Jerry Desmonde are hardworking stooges and Paddy O'Neill, a hefty femme newcomer to the Wisdom pix, gallantly subjects herself to considerable physical comedy punishment as the lovesick housekeeper of Wisdom's boss. Bryan Pringle, John Le Mesurier, and one or two pretty gals, such as Penny Morrell and Imogen Hassall, also circle around the star in brief incidents.

Innovation in this film is that it is the first Wisdom comedy in color, which enhances the sets and location shots under Jack Asher's camera. But neither Robert Asher's direction nor the editing and screenplay rate more than a so routine workmanship. There are also lively contributions from musicianman Ron Goodwin and some unnamed stuntmen and stand-ins. This is a safe enough booking for a large number of situations, but it doesn't stand up as a contribution from one of Britain's most reliable boxoffice stars. *Rich.*

The Ravagers

War drama, filmed in Philippines, is satisfactory entry for action market. Title is exploitable.

Hemisphere Pictures release of a Kane W. Lynn production. Features John Saxon, Fernando Poe Jr., Bronwyn Fitzsimons, Mike Parsons, Kristina Scott. Directed by Eddie Romero. Screenplay, Cesar J. Amigo, E. F. Romero; editor, Jovan Calub; sound, Demetrio de Santos; music, Tito Arevalo. No camera credits. Reviewed in N.Y., Dec. 3, '65. Running Time, **88 MINS.**

Capt. Kermit Dowling ...... John Saxon
Gaudiel .... Fernando Poe Jr.
Sheila .... Bronwyn Fitzsimons
Reardon .... Mike Parsons
Mother Superior .... Kristina Scott
Capt. Araullo .... Robert Arevalo
Cruz .... Vic Diaz
Capt. Mori .... Vic Silayan

Another action-war effort by producer Kane W. Lynn, made in the Philippines, this programmer, as did his previous "Intramuros" (Walls of Hell), successfully mixes American and Filipino talent with natural settings for a tale that has a familiar ring.

Although actor John Saxon gets top billing, and works hard to earn it, the distaff side of the audience is more likely to center on the romance between Filipino actor Fernando Poe Jr. and American Bronwyn Fitzsimons (if she looks disturbingly familiar, her mother is Maureen O'Hara, or two beautiful dames).

Cesar J. Amigo and E. F. Romero (latter is undoubtedly pic's director, Eddie Romero, who also helmed "Intramuros") have stressed action in their basically simple screenplay of Filipino guerrillas, led by Saxon and Poe, holding off a Japanese force trying to confiscate a gold bullion shipment hidden on one of the islands. When they become involved with a convent and its girl students, romance ensues as the battle rages on.

While the jungle settings are exotic, they're no cinematic match for the magnificent demolished fortress which provided "Intramuros" with a set that stole the picture. "Ravagers" should hold its own in the war-adventure-action area against similar fare. In New York, for example, it's playing across the street from "Walls of Hell." *Robe.*

A Patch Of Blue
(PANAVISION)

Firstrate film about blind girl befriended by a Negro. Racial angles tastefully handled but still forceful. Good b.o. prospects despite possible limited appeal in Dixie.

Hollywood, Dec. 2.
Metro-Goldwyn-Mayer release of Pandro S. Berman-Guy Green production, produced by Berman, directed by Green. No stars. Features Sidney Poitier, Shelley Winters, Elizabeth Hartman, Wallace Ford. Screenplay, Green, based on "Be Ready With Bells And Drums," by Elizabeth Kata; camera, Robert Burks; editor, Rita Roland; music, Jerry Goldsmith; asst. director, Hank Moonjean. Reviewed at Crest Theatre, Westwood, L.A., Dec. 1, '65. Running Time, **105 MINS.**

Gordon Ralfe .... Sidney Poitier
Rose-Ann D'Arcy .... Shelley Winters
Selina D'Arcy ...... Elizabeth Hartman
Ole Pa .... Wallace Ford
Mark Ralfe .... Ivan Dixon
Sadie .... Elisabeth Fraser
Mr. Faber .... John Qualen
Yanek Faber .... Kelly Flynn
Salina, age 5 .... Debi Storm
Mrs. Favaloro .... Renata Vanni
Mr. Favaloro .... Saverio LoMedico

"A Patch Of Blue" is a touching contemporary melodrama, relieved at times by generally effective humor, about a blind white girl, rehabilitated from a dreary home by a Negro. Expertly produced by Pandro S. Berman, film has very good scripting plus excellent direction and performances, including an exceptional screen debut by Elizabeth Hartman as the gal. A cinch for strong b.o. in sophisticated urban keys, the Metro release will need special handling in the mass market to overcome a marquee array presently only fair, a meaningless title, and — in Dixie — the inter-racial romance.

Director Guy Green adapted Elizabeth Kata's "Be Ready With Bells And Drums," and some long-memorial observers are certain to note similarities with Charles Chaplin's "City Lights" (1931), although here the greater emphasis is on the afflicted girl, and the ending, while positive, isn't sudsy. Miss Hartman gives a smash interpretation to the role, and progresses most believably from initial scenes as an uneducated, unwanted and home-anchored maiden, to an upbeat, firmer grasp on what is to be her sightless maturity.

Top-featured Sidney Poitier (all names follow the title) is excellent as he accidently encounters the girl in a park, becomes her first true friend, and gives her some self-assurance. She, of course, doesn't know he is Negro. The understated tolerance pitch is occasionally made explicit, and Ivan Dixon as Poitier's brother reps a Negro attitude towards whites, blind or otherwise, that is known as Crow Jim.

The domestic situation is grim, with Shelley Winters very good as Miss Hartman's sleazy mother who, with appropriately cheap Elisabeth Fraser, spends a lot of time in the sack with men, and (via flashback) often with daughter in the same room. She comes on strong, and early, thus negating some impact in later scenes.

Vet character actor Wallace Ford is Miss Winters' dad, also in the apartment as an aging drunk, and effectively blends personal frustration, shame and disappointment in his own daughter, and pity for Miss Hartman in limited footage. Other thesps lend solid support. Title derives from girl's memory of the world before being blinded in a domestic mother-father fight.

Green's dialog, often on the raw side (thus limiting audiences to mature teeners and up), also reveals in topnotch fashion now commonplace words can sting a blind person. His tasteful direction is excellent and includes many heartwarming touches. Robert Burks' crisp b&w Panavision lensing is a big plus, and all other technical credits are firstrate.

Rita Roland edited to 105 minutes, and another 10 minutes cut out would enhance the pace which flags somewhat in the last 45 minutes. The battle between Miss Winters and Ford, later extended to nosy neighbors, is true-to-life, but detracts emphasis from story. Also, some solo stree. maneuvers by Miss Hartman aren't worth all the footage. *Murf.*

Guests Are Coming
(POLISH)

Very good three-part Polish comedy, subtitled (and part dubbed) in English, with universal appeal. Good b.o. potential in selected houses if properly sold.

Hollywood, Nov. 27.
Mitchell Kowal Films release (in U.S.) of a Droga (Polish) production in three episodes. Features Mitchell Kowal, Paul Glass, Zagmunt Zintel. Directorial supervision by Antoni Bohdziewicz. Screenplay, Jan J. Szcepanski; camera, Stanislaw Loth; music, Stefan Kisielewski. Reviewed at Beverly Canon Theatre, L.A., Nov. 26, '65. Running Time, **109 MINS.**

(1) Directed by Gerard Zalewski
Peter .... Paul Glass
Uncle Konstanty....Kazimeriz Opalinski
Son .... Zenon Burzynski
Daughter in law.... Sylvia Zakrzewska
Blond woman........Wanda Koczewska

(2) Directed by Jan Rutkiewicz
Mike O'Rawiec .... Mitchell Kowal
Village priest .... Wladyslaw Hancza
Highlanders .... The Gorals

(3) Directed by Romuald Drabaczynski
Harry Kwasnick ...... Zagmunt Zintel
Truck driver .... Ryszard Pietruski

(English Subtitles)

"Guests Are Coming" is a three-part Polish comedy, subtitled in English, concerning the antics of three Polish-Americans on their first visit to their ancestral country. Very good scripting, performances and direction. U.S. actor Mitchell Kowal is handling U.S. distribution (because he couldn't take his performing salary out of Poland, but could have regional distrib rights), and fair to good b.o. prospects are likely in arties.

Jan. J. Szcepanski is credited with the entire screenplay which, in turn, focusses on skirt-chasing Paul Glass, wife-hunting Kowal and money-seeking Zagmunt Zintel, all of whom arrive in Poland on the same ship. The diverse humorous situations have a universal appeal, thus enhancing pic's booking chances.

Glass, delayed in Warsaw arrival by Wanda Koczewska and a few other lookers, is very good as the second-generation Yank en route to visit uncle Kazimeriz Opalinski, supposedly living comfortably with his own son Zenon Burzynski and latter's wife, Sylvia Zakrzewska, plus child.

As it turns out, uncle has been farmed out by his son to a senior citizen's home, so a hurried, and harried, reunion is set up to fool Glass. This, the most touching episode, was directed by Gerard Zalewski who, in the European fashion, presumably also supervised its editing to a tight 40 minutes.

Kowal is likewise very good as the middle-ager widower from Gary, Indiana, who has come to his pop's native town in search of a second wife. Wladyslaw Hancza is the village priest who heads up the unofficial committee to arrange the betrothal, with some side attempts at getting Kowal to leave some money in the town. Latter finally chooses the local barmaid who, until then, has been giving it away; she becomes a delightfully domineering wife. Jan Rutkiewicz directed this fast-moving 35-minutes, adroitly using some optical effects.

Zagmunt Zintel scores as the Chicago promoter who is digging up earth samples from Polish battlefields to sell to Polish-Americans as authentic historical souvenirs. Assistant Ryszard Pietruski makes explicit the point that Poland has been caught between so many power factions that it isn't very hard to find an authetic battlefield (including modern traffic routes).

Historical pix are satirized in one scene wherein a long-shooting film company (using the "Circorama" process) finds Zintel's station wagon amidst a horde of mounted Teutonic knights. Contemporary bureaucracy also gets the clever knock. Romuald Drabaczynski directed with a fine comedy flair.

Directorial supervision is credited to Antoni Bohdziewicz, and camera work, very good throughout, is that of Stanislaw Loth. Stefan Kisielewski's score is effective. Kowal's subtitling (and some English dubbing) is good.
Murf.

Seven Women
(PANAVISION—COLOR)

Stock melodrama about North China mission ravaged by Mongolian barbarians; for program market. but John Ford name to bally.

Hollywood, Dec. 1.

Metro release of John Ford-Bernard Smith production, directed by Ford. Stars Anne Bancroft, Sue Lyon, Margaret Leighton, Flora Robson, Mildred Dunnock, Betty Field, Anna Lee, Eddie Albert; features Mike Mazurki. Screenplay, Janet Green, John McCormick; based on short story, "Chinese Finale," by Norah Lofts; camera (Metrocolor), Joseph LaShelle; music, Elmer Bernstein; art direction, George W. Davis, Eddie Imazu; editor, Otho S. Lovering; asst. director, Wingate Smith; sound, Franklin Milton. Reviewed at Metro Studios, Nov. 29, '65. Running Time, 86 MINS.
Dr. D. R. Cartwright...... Anne Bancroft
Emma Clark .... Sue Lyon
Agatha Andrews .... Margaret Leighton
Miss Binns ....;.... Flora Robson
Jane Argent .... Mildred Dunnock
Florrie Pether .... Betty Field
Mrs. Russell .... Anna Lee
Charles Pether .... Eddie Albert
Tunga Khan .... Mike Mazurki
Lean Warrior .... Woody Strode
Miss Ling .... Jane Chang
Kim .... Hans William Lee
Coolie .... H. W. Gim
Chinese Girl .... Irene Tsu

"Seven Women" is a run-of-the-mill story of an isolated American mission in North China whose serenity is rudely shattered by a ravaging Mongolian barbarian and his band of cutthroats. John Ford-Bernard Smith production is set in 1935, when the Chinese-Mongolian border was a lawless, violent land dominated by bandits, and takes its title from the seven femmes trapped in mission and subjected to gross indignities. Anne Bancroft heads cast but absence of marquee strength and lack of anything new plotwise relegates Panavision-Metrocolor feature to the program market.

Ford directs from Janet Green-John McCormick's script based on a short story by Norah Lofts and manages regulation treatment. It's the theme itself that militates against any more than passing interest; back in program days this was a more or less stock subject and appears old-fashioned now.

While yarn attempts to tell the relationships of the septet — generally an uninteresting lot — most of the attention focuses necessarily upon Miss Bancroft, a recently-arrived doctor whose worldly cynicism brings her into conflict with the rigid moral concepts of mission's head, portrayed by Margaret Leighton.

Femme physician finds herself, immediately she is settled in an unfriendly atmosphere where her ways don't conform, with the pregnancy of an older woman who requires modern hospital facilities not available at mission; a cholera epidemic she puts down; and finally having to submit to the bandit leader to obtain her medical bag to treat the prospective mother. Miss Bancroft endows character with some authority, and Mike Mazurki is properly brutal as the huge barbarian.

Miss Leighton acquits herself well in an intolerant, self-righteous role, and Sue Lyon switches from past sexpots to an innocent, demure mission assistant. Betty Field plays the petulant pregnant wife of Eddie Albert, sole male assistant at mission, and Mildred Dunnock, Flora Robson and Anna Lee complete septet in various mission parts, all handicapped by t h a n k l e s s conceptions. Woody Strode is colorful as a bandit Mazurki kills in a fight.

Technical credits are all on plus side, including Joseph LaShelle's color photography, Elmner Bernstein's music score, George W. Davis and Eddie Imazu's Oriental art direction, Otho S. Lovering's editing.
Whit.

Where The Spies Are
(BRITISH-PANAVISION-COLOR)

Generally fast-paced spy meller with good exploitation prospects.

Hollywood, Nov. 24.

Metro release of Val Guest-Steven Pallos production, directed by Guest. Stars David Niven, Francoise Dorleac; features John Le Mesurier, Nigel Davenport, Eric Pohlmann, Paul Stassino, Ronald Radd, Cyril Cusack. Screenplay, Wolf Mankowitz, Val Guest; adapted from James Leasor novel, "Passport to Oblivion"; camera (Metrocolor), Arthur Grant; music, Mario Nascimbene; editor, Bill Lenny; asst. director, Eric Rattray. Reviewed at Metro Studios, Nov. 24, '65. Running Time, 113 MINS.
Dr. Love .... David Niven
Vikki .... Francoise Dorleac
Rosser .... Cyril Cusack
Macgillivray ....John Le Mesurier
Parkington .... Nigen Davenport
Farouk .... Eric Pohlmann
Simmias .... Paul Stassino
Jackson .... Noel Harrison
Stanislaus .... Ronald Radd
1st Agent .... George Pravda
Security .... Alan Gifford
Josef .... Richard Marner
Aeradio .... Bill Nagy
Assassin .... George Mikell
Lecturer .... Geoffrey Bayldon
2nd Agent .... Gabor Baraker
Duty Officer .... Derek Partridge
Sir Robert .... Robert Raglan
1st Taxi Driver .... Riyad Gholmieh
2nd Taxi Driver ...... Muhsen Samrani
Major Harding .... Basil Dignam
Inspector .... Gordon Tanner

Metro is latest to board the spy-melodrama bandwagon with this British import starring David Niven as a mild-mannered English doctor pressed into Middle East espionage. The Val Guest production carries suspense, after a slow and talky start, and action, even if a bit on the contrived side, is fast-paced once story gets underway. Locale is new to American viewers — Beirut — where troupe locationed to come up with interesting authenticity of background, and in the current cycle of a la James Bond releases film may be exploited profitably.

Based on James Leasor's thriller, "Passport to Oblivion," Guest, who also directs and collabed with Wolf Mankowitz on script, concentrates on the dangers confronting a secret agent. In this instance, Niven, who once figured in some fancy undercover work for British Intelligence, is sent from his English village practice to Lebanon to try to learn what urgent information the agent there had uncovered before he was bumped off by the Russians. After thwarting an assassination attempt upon a visiting pro-British ruling prince he's taken prisoner and packed off to Russia by a roundabout flight. British efforts finally rescue him in northern Canada, where Soviet plane is enticed to set down.

Niven delivers one of his customary competent performances, stuffy at times but able to cope with the melodramatic demands of the character who constantly is in trouble. Teaming with Niven as a French man'selle playing both sides as a secret agent and supposedly his contact is Francoise Dorleac, lushly effective. Nigel Davenport inserts the hazards of his profession as another British agent killed by Russians in an exciting knife-and-gun fight; Ronald Radd powerfully interprets a high Russian agent and John le Mesurier makes the most of his British Intelligence chief role. Eric Pohlmann and Paul Stassino also score in smaller parts.

Excellent production values have been lined up by Guest in association with Steven Pallos, and his direction once he's into story is firstrate. Particularly outstanding is Arthur Grant's photography in Panavision and Metrocolor, as is Mario Nascimbene's music score, one of the best in recent pix. John Howell's art direction contributes to the exotic settings, and Bill Lenny's editing for most is a definite asset.
Whit.

Othello
(BRITISH—COLOR— PANAVISION)

Sir Laurence Olivier's superb performance caught for cinematic history. Specialized fare but there's little doubt that it will do best biz yet for Warners' "special" film group. Acting far overshadows limitations of filming.

Warner Bros. release of a B.H.E. Production (Anthony Havelock-Allan, John Brabourne). Stars Laurence Olivier; features Frank Finlay, Maggie Smith, Joyce Redman, Derek Jacobi. Directed for screen by Stuart Burge, based on National Theatre Production staging by John Dexter. Continuity, Margaret Unsworth, based on play by William Shakespeare; photography (Technicolor-Panavision), Geoffrey Unsworth; editor, Richard Marden; music, Richard Hampton. Reviewed at Warner Bros. h.o., N.Y., Dec. 13, '65. Running Time, 170 MINS.
Othello .... Laurence Olivier
Iago .... Frank Finlay
Desdemona .... Maggie Smith
Emilia .... Joyce Redman
Cassio .... Derek Jacobi
Roderigo .... Robert Lang
Brabantio .... Anthony Nicholls
Duke of Venice .... Harry Lomax
Bianca .... Sheila Reid
Gratiano .... Michael Turner
Lodovico .... Kenneth Mackintosh
Montano .... Edward Hardwicke
Clown .... Roy Holder
Senate officers ..... David Hargreaves, Malcolm Terris
Duke's officer .... Terence Knapp
Senator .... Keith Marsh
Sailor .... Tom Kempinski
Messenger .... Nicholas Edmett
Cypriot officers .... William Hobbs, Trevor Martin

As theatre, this filmed version of "Othello" should be seen by every lover of fine acting. As proper use of film, however, it is inferior to Laurence Olivier's previous Shakespearean efforts.

What the eventual playoff of "Othello" will be is unknown. Warners will, undoubtedly, make maximum use of the areas previously served by the Richard Burton "Hamlet" and the Herbert von Karajan "La Boheme" but this could be extended as "Othello" shows greater commercial potential. British Home Entertainment, which produced the film, is a partner in Pav TV, British tollvision system which starts soon, and will undoubtedly make use of the film soon. The play runs 170 minutes without planned intermission.

The opportunity to see an internationally-known actor in one of the top roles of his career, plus the excellent groundwork done by the preceding "Hamlet," "Boheme" and "Royal Ballet" should enable "Othello" to not only surpass those markets but to lure back into theatrical circulation many "lost" patrons, so benumbed by a surfeit of inferior television fare that only such an exciting and stimulating theatrical adventure as this could break through their lethargy.

Cinematically, "Othello" is superior to the "Hamlet" and "Boheme." But, as the latter was a filmed opera, however excellent, this is a filmed play. The motion picture Technicolor camera is used, less as a creative force, than as an instrument for recording. Ineffective lighting obscures, but does not hide entirely, the stagy, unimaginative settings which are but a series of columns and bare playing areas, with entrances and exits made stage right and stage left as though still in a theatre.

What, then, makes "Othello" so important? First and foremost, to see and hear Olivier play "Othello." To see him create the tormented soul who "loved not wisely, but too well." To hear, as the ear is regaled by his incredible feat of turning the richly-embroidered lines into understandable conversation. As many phrases will fall strangely on the untrained ear of the listener and are, while dramatically imperative, couched in language that requires much concentration, the conversion, by masterful reading and timing, into easy to follow dialog adds much to the enjoyment. Olivier combines the many-faceted characteristics of "Othello" into a single, remarkable human being. Within him rages emotional storms unconceivable to the worldly Venetians. Outwardly Christian (he crosses himself and wears a crucifix), he sometimes reverts to a Muslim past with Mohammedan gestures and falling into a prayer-rug position, and even hints that the savage African is not completely stilled, in his animalistic display of torment at Iago's insinuations and his fondness for primitive jewelry. Need another reason for seeing "Othello"? To stake a claim for the future of having witnessed one of the great performances of our time.

Olivier is surrounded by a generally excellent company that, in a few instances, captures something of his magic. Maggie Smith's Desdemona is, by contrast to Othello, the most innocent of innocents, guileless and completely sympathetic. Joyce Redman's Emilia is not only impressive but brings forth viewers' tears when she dares defend Desdemona's honor before the jealousy-ridden Othello, thoughtless of her own safety ("Let heaven and men and devils, let them all, all, all, cry shame against me, yet I'll speak.")

More subdued (unfortunately, because of the role's importance) is Frank Finlay's Iago. Although older than the role ("I have looked upon the world for four times seven years"), this is no more amiss than are most Juliets. He loses some of the role's effectiveness in his not completely conveying the craftiness that (as written) enables him to gull not only the actually naive Othello, but his presumably more sophisticated fellow Venetians and, to some extent, his wife. His important lines come through clearly (fortunately, as Shakespeare has given him some of the play's best phrases ("Reputation is an idle and most false imposition; oft got without merit, and lost without deserving.")

Excellent as Cassio, Derek Jacobi's expressive face enables him to convey much, even when not speaking. A more important asset in film than on stage, perhaps, but it lends much to his performance. Other principals are uniformly good and the entire cast wears the beautiful costumes created by Jocelyn Herbert with ease and dignity.

Geoffrey Unsworth's Technicolor camerawork, restrained by the obscuring lighting, makes his muted portraits handsome ones. But one looks unsuccessfully for even a glimmer of the Wellesian gift that made that earlier filmed "Othello" a cinematographic masterpiece (if only lukewarm Shakespeare). Even Olivier's pain-wracked, throbbing voice cannot make the pre-slaying of Desdemona sequence as ominous as did Welles' snuffing the candle ("Put out the light . . .") and, continuing in total darkness, (". . . and then put out the light."). This was cinema.

Directing credits are difficult to apportion in this instance (as they were in the Richard Burton "Hamlet"). Screen credit is given to both original stager John Dexter and to Stuart Burge, but only one who had seen both the play and the film could tell where one began and the other left off . . . or, even, how much credit belongs to Olivier. Problem of direction in "Othello" is to create movement in a drama that is almost entirely dialog. For this, Dexter probably deserves the nod. But decisions as to camera angles and use of closeups (there are too many of these) are evidently Burge's contribution. Richard Hampton is given screen credit for the music which sounds like an arrangement of Elizabethan themes. While not of any great importance, it is lovely when used. *Robe.*

The Flight Of The Phoenix
(COLOR)

Robert Aldrich does superlative job in translating Elleston Trevor bestseller into a tenseful melodrama; wide general appeal.

Hollywood, Dec. 10.
Twentieth-Fox release of Associates & Aldrich Co. (Robert Aldrich) production. Stars James Stewart, Richard Attenborough, Peter Finch, Hardy Kruger, Ernest Borgnine; features Ian Bannen, Ronald Fraser, Christian Marquand, Dan Duryea, George Kennedy, Gabriele Tinti. Directed by Aldrich. Screenplay, Lukas Heller; from novel by Elleston Trevor; camera (De Luxe Color), Joseph Biroc; music, Frank DeVol; editor, Michael Luciano; art direction, William Glasgow; asst. directors, William F. Sheehan, Cliff Coleman, Alan Callow. Reviewed at Screen Directors Theatre, Dec. 9, '65. Running Time, 149 MINS.
Frank Towns .... James Stewart
Lew Moran ...... Richard Attenborough
Captn Harris .... Peter Finch
Heinrich Dorfmann ... . Hardy Kruger
Trucker Cobb .... Ernest Borgnine
Crow .... Ian Bannen
Sergeant Watson .... Ronald Fraser
Dr. Renaud .... Christian Marquand
Standish .... Dan Duryea
Bellamy .... George Kennedy
Gabriele .... Gabriele Tinti
Carlos .... Alex Montoya
Tasso .... Peter Bravos
Bill .... William Aldrich
Farida .... Barrie Chase

"The Flight of the Phoenix" is a grim, tenseful, realistic tale of a small group of men forced down on the North African desert and their desperate efforts to build a single-engine plane out of the wreckage of the twin job in which they crashed during a sandstorm. Robert Aldrich's filmic translation of the Elleston Trevor book is an often-fascinating and superlative piece of filmmaking highlighted by standout performances and touches that show producer-director at his best. Twentieth-Fox release which has James Stewart topbilled opens a pre-release engagement Dec. 15 at Warner Hollywood Theatre for a week's run to qualify for Oscar consideration and should have wide general appeal.

Aldrich had his work cut out for him in reducing most of action to the site of the wreck. Necessarily the story had to be strong enough to hold in this single situation without benefit of flashbacks or other devices. The Lukas Heller screenplay ably fulfills the task of concentrating interest on the motivating idea and various characters themselves, which Aldrich picks up to drive home point after point as days go by without any sign of rescue, rationed water grows short, men are weakened and the building of the plane must continue. De Luxe color photography by Joseph Biroc is a potent asset in painting the theme and Michael Luciano's editing forcefully limns the struggle against time.

Stewart, as the pilot of a desert oil company cargo-passenger plane who flies by the seat-of-his-pants, is strongly cast in role and is strongly backed by entire cast. There are no picturesque characters or delineations here — entire cast, seemingly hand-picked for the individual parts, are every-day persons who might either be employees of an oil company or business visitors. Stewart is particularly effective in underplaying his character, a man who takes the blame for the crash rather than passing the buck to his hard-drinking navigator who failed to check out a silent radio which might have warned of bad weather.

When a young aircraft designer, who had been visiting his brother at the oil camp, comes up with the extraordinary idea that a make-shift plane might be fashioned to fly the survivors to safety, Stewart is against the idea. The navigator, Richard Attenborough, is all in favor as a bare chance, and a doctor in the party, Christian Marquand, favors idea as a means of giving hope to the men. So work starts, and it is this endeavor in its various phases that makes the story.

Hardy Kruger delivers a sock portrayal of the German designer who goes all-out on his idea once it is sanctioned, a current of quiet strength underlying its enactment to add to its power. One of the outstanding scenes, leavened with a touch of wry humor, occurs when Stewart and Attenborough learn from his remarks that he actually is a model plane designer, and this is his first attempt at anything "real." The principle is the same, he argues, and finally wins his point.

Attenborough creates a fine impression as the navigator and Marquand's performance is smooth and sympathetic. Ernest Borgnine as a mental case being shipped home for treatment and who dies in the desert sands scores in what is a comparatively brief role. Peter Finch, a British officer who lives by the book and is murdered by Arab raiders who camp a short distance away when he goes to them for help, acquits himself with distinction. Others who rate mention include Ronald Fraser, Ian Bannen, Dan Duryea, George Kennedy, Gabriele Tinti.

Additional technical kudos go to Frank DeVol, for his music score; William Glasgow for art direction. Makeup of the men as the rigors of the desert begin to tell on them is effective, Ben Nye supervising this department. Connie Francis sings the theme song. Only femme role is vision of a dancer, played by Barrie Chase.

Following the closing credits of picture, Aldrich winds with an unusual testimonial to the man who handled the aerial sequences. This reads: "It should be remembered...that Paul Mantz, a fine man and a brilliant flyer, gave his life in the making of this film..." Mantz was killed on last day of shooting on location near Yuma. *Whit.*

Winter Kept Us Warm
(CANADIAN)

Engaging student film dealing with homosexuality and general campus life. Limited theatrical possibilities but should do well at film societies and universities.

Toronto, Dec. 6.
Varsity Films presentation of David Secter production. Features John Labow, Joy Tepperman, Janet Amos, Henry Tarvainen. Directed by Secter. Screenplay John Porter, John Clute and cast; photographer, Bob Fresco, Ernest Meersholk; editor, Michael Foytenyi; music, Paul Hoffert. Reviewed at Film House, Toronto, Dec. 7, '65. Running Time 81 MINS.
Doug .... John Labow
Peter .... Henry Tarvainen
Bev .... Joy Tepperman
Janet .... Janet Amos
Artie .... Iain Ewing
Nick .... Jack Messinger
Larry .... Larry Greenspan
Hall Porter .... Sol Mendelson
House Don .... George Appelby

"Winter Kept Us Warm," a University of Toronto student feature film is an appealing handling of a heavily implied but not activated homosexual relationship between a Big Man On Campus and a bookish, shy smalltown student. Its best moments are provided by the two main characters played by John Labow and Henry Tarvainen who plays the ill at ease, nervous, awkward, virginal freshman with his head in T. S. Eliot and his roots in a small-Ontario-town Finnish-Canadian home.

Cameramen Bob Fresco and Ernest Meersholk do well in scenes of downtown Toronto at night, a neon montage, the University campus in winter with the two main characters "horsing around" in the snow a la Beatles romp around in "A Hard's Day's Night," and most of the other outdoor scenes. Interior shots are stiff, and from a stationary view.

With its stilted dialogue and jumpy sound quality, "Winter Kept Us Warm," would be better shown at film societies and at universities. It lacks theatricality which would take it into general film houses. But it is a better than average campus film.

The homosexuality is carefully treated. Campus King takes shy one to a steam bath, rubs soap on his back in the shower shared by other males, learns a Finnish folk song, picks him up after a play rehearsal. Aggressor leaves his steady "chick" because he is more interested in the male friend.

Ending is a parallel night out with BMOC and his steady who finally make the hay and the shy student spending the night with a student actress. Big man rebels that the shy one has become a "man," punches him in the stomach and leaves his room. Their homosexuality is never verbalized.

Film has colorful student speech, goggle-eyed males watching a mock strip, eating at male residences and at their winter sports.

Producer-director David Secter has done his job with a ring of the truth but his effort is left with an awkward air. Title is from T. S. Eliot's poem "The Waste Land."

Adil.

Life at the Top
(BRITISH)

Sequel to "Room at the Top" 10 years later; fairly strong drama and excellent performances but lacks motivation of original; should do well in adult market.

Hollywood, Dec. 3.

Columbia Pictures release of Romulus (James Woolf) production. Stars Laurence Harvey, Jean Simmons, Honor Blackman, Michael Craig, Donald Wolfit; features Robert Morley, Margaret Johnston, Ambrosine Phillpotts, Allan Cuthbertson, George A. Cooper. Directed by Ted Kotcheff. Screenplay, Mordecai Richler; based on novel by John Barine; camera, Oswald Morris; editor, Derek York; asst. director, Kip Gowans; music, Richard Addinsell; sound, Norman Bolland, Bob Jones. Reviewed at Music Hall Theatre, Dec. 2, '65. Running Time, 118 MINS.

Joe Lampton .... Laurence Harvey
Susan Lampton .... Jean Simmons
Norah Hauxley .... Honor Blackman
Mark .... Michael Craig
Abe Brown .... Donald Wolfit
Tiffield .... Robert Morley
Sybil .... Margaret Johnston
Mrs. Brown .... Ambrosine Phillpotts
George Aisgill .... Allan Cuthbertson
Harry .... Paul A. Martin
Barbara .... Frances Cosslet
Hethersett .... Ian Shand
Graffham .... George A. Cooper
Mottram .... Nigel Davenport
McLelland .... Andrew Laurence
Psychologist .... Geoffrey Bayldon
Ben .... Dennis Quilley
Tim .... David Oxley
Oscar .... David McKail
Keatley .... Paul Whitsun Jones
Wincastle .... Charles Lamb
Newspaper Boy .... Michael Newport
Doctor .... Richard Leech
Stripper .... Ingrid Anthofer

Some of the gloss of "Room at the Top" rubs off on this follow-up, but the film—necessarily coming under comparative scrutiny—lacks both the motivation and rare subtlety which elevated its predecessor to one of the more notable releases of 1959. Nevertheless, the James Woolf production carries sufficient dramatic potency to rate among the year's better British imports. For marquee dressing, there are the names of Laurence Harvey—who starred in "Room" with Oscar-winning Simone Signoret—and Jean Simmons. The same type of campaign (updated) pegged on previous entry could be utilized to attract more mature audiences, for whom pic will have greater appeal than younger theatregoers.

Based upon a second novel by the same author, John Braine, the sombre, sometimes dreary but usually honest drama picks up its narrative 10 years later. The Mordecai Richler screenplay continues the story of the young, designing opportunist who rose to the top in social and business standing, but at loss of his self-respect, as limned in "Room." Now, however, after having enjoyed the position he sought for a decade, he is even more aware of the necessity of clinging to his ideals and tries to do something about a life he has found empty despite the presence of a wife and two children.

Woolf, who produced "Room" in association with his brother, John, goes solo here and has given production the same quality mounting. Direction is in the capable hands of Ted Kotcheff, who turns in a forceful job as he follows Harvey's rebellion and ultimate break with his element. Four of the same players repeat their original roles to lend added interest. Film is still on the adult level of its predecessor.

Harvey continues in the mood of his character in "Room," now sales chief of his millionaire father-in-law's woolen mills in a sooty Yorkshire town. He finds his position intolerable as he senses he is being given the brush-off both in business and otherwise. Elected to the town council, he defies his overbearing father-in-law's demands, voting on an important measure as his conscience dictates. He has an affair with a young television commentator, and after discovering his wife unfaithful and status at his office uncertain chucks the works and follows his young flame to London, where he is unable to find a job. Finale shows his return to his wife and the mill, which he now from all appearances heads but still with the feeling of being trapped.

Harvey, who played second fiddle to Miss Signoret for her Academy Award performance in "Room," tops interest here. Miss Simmons as his wife (replacing Heather Sears in original role) has a rather unsympathetic character which she nonetheless enacts persuasively. Donald Wolfit repeats his former success as the mill owner who controls the town, and the two others reprising their former parts are Ambrosine Phillpotts as his wife and Allan Cuthbertson, a councilman and widower of Simone Signoret, with whom Harvey had the affair in "Room."

Honor Blackman is well cast as the tv commentator who is Harvey's new romance, and Michael Craig does well with role of a family friend whom Harvey discovers is his wife's lover. Robert Morley registers briefly as a London businessman, Nigel Davenport as his assistant who conducts Harvey on a crawl through London strip clubs and Margaret Johnston as Craig's unhappy spouse.

Camera work of Oswald Morris is often interesting but he occasionally embarks upon unfortunate offkey lighting. Derek York's editing is tight and art direction by Edward Marshall creates the proper atmosphere.

Whit.

Har Borjar Aventyret
(Adventure Starts Here)
(SWEDISH-FRANSCOPE)

Stockholm, Dec. 14.

Sandrews production and release. Stars Harriet Andersson; features Claude Titre, Matti Oravisto, Goran Cederberg. Written and directed by Jorn Donner. Camera, Jean Badal editor, Per Krafft. Previewed in Stockholm. Running Time, 90 MINS.

Anne .... Harriet Andersson
Jacques .... Claude Titre
Toivo .... Matti Oravisto
Stig .... Goran Cederberg

For his third pic Jorn Donner, a Finn of Swedish origin working in Sweden, has come up with a modern item. It is a film that is fragmented in form, deals with a time of decision in the life of a woman, and the men in her life, but it has no definite denouement. Thus this appears mainly a specialized and arty pic for foreign spots but has good possibilities for more selective audiences.

Things are left wide open in this production. It is the interior feelings and emotions that are deftly blocked out by visual means. Their lives are reflected via images foreshadowing or underlining a thought, mood or outlook. The film is intellectual but never literary nor wordy.

Harriet Andersson (Donner's wife) is a woman in her mid-twenties who goes to Finland from Sweden on a buying job. There she meets a Finnish architect, with whom she has had a brief affair, and a former lover, a Frenchman, who comes up to make one last bid for her hand. The moods and characters are blocked out in a series of meetings, musings and talks, with the actual decision left ambiguous. Whether it is happy or unhappy ending, is a choice left open to the characters as well as the audience.

No Swedish physical lovemaking here. This has already been consummated. It is now the time of making personal adjustments. The film touches on the growing internationalism that is changing national barriers and outlooks if some still exist.

Miss Andersson breaks with the Frenchman who is easily consoled with other women and vacillates with the Finn who is also at a time of introspection and self discovery. He had been wounded in the war and recently had thought he was dying from an infection incurred in it. He is cured but still finds he has a sort of deception.

Miss Andersson is shown as independent and self-supporting but ready for a lasting relationship if it can come without her being submerged or subjugated. That is the core of this vehicle. It is all meted out with a sense of imagery that works in some revealing lensing and editing ideas. It infers perhaps, by its title, that adventure begins after this turning, and that it is not just smooth sailing.

Miss Anderson is beauteous with a placid exterior that is broken at times by her interior unrest. The Finnish architect also is still smarting from emotional war wounds. So both characters are composed of the past as well as the present.

Jean Badal has given the pic finely chiseled lensing, with deft editing also helping to give a clarity to this film.

Donner shows himself an extremely personal director, with a feeling for visual expression. It does show a departure from the Swedish brooding on sex and God in their pix. This embodies the newer, freer and more worldly approach to filmmaking.

Mosk.

The Slender Thread

Emotional drama based on true-life incident of efforts to save a woman who phones a Seattle clinic she has taken overdose of barbiturates and refuses help; Sidney Poitier and Anne Bancroft in sock characterizations.

Hollywood, Dec. 7.

Paramount release of Athene (Stephen Alexander) production. Stars Sidney Poitier, Anne Bancroft; features Telly Savalas, Steven Hill. Directed by Sydney Pollack. Screenplay, Stirling Silliphant; suggested by Life Magazine article by Shana Alexander; camera, Loyal Griggs; art direction, Hal Pereira, Jack Poplin; music, Quincy Jones; asst. director, Don Roberts; editor, Thomas Stanford; sound, John Carter, Charles Grenzbach. Reviewed at Paramount Studios, Dec. 6, '65. Running time, 98 MINS.

Alan Newell .... Sidney Poitier
Inga Dyson .... Anne Bancroft
Doctor Coburn .... Telly Savalas
Mark Dyson .... Steven Hill
Det. Judd Ridley .... Edward Asner
Marion .... Indus Arthur
Sgt. Harry Ward .... Paul Newlan
Charlie .... Dabney Coleman
Doctor .... H. M. Wynant
Patrolman Steve Peters .... Robert Hoy
Chris Dyson .... Greg Jarvis
Medical Technician .... Jason Wingreen
Mrs. Thomas .... Marjorie Nelson
Arthur Foss .... Steven Marlo
Liquor Salesman .... Thomas Hill
Al McCardle .... Lane Bradford
Edna .... Janet Dudley
Dr. Alden Van .... John Napier

"The Slender Thread," suggested by a Life Magazine article of an actual occurrence, is supercharged with emotion and dramatic overtones. As a showy vehicle for talents of Sidney Poitier and Anne Bancroft, past Oscar-winners co-starred here in particularly demanding characterizations, the Stephen Alexander production offers mounting tension, but good as the picture is it could have been improved through more lucid writing. General idea of premise is sufficiently intriguing to generate a high degree of interest which more mature audiences specially will find gratifying.

Story is of a distraught woman who has taken an overdose of barbiturates and phones a clinic. Film takes its title from the telephone line which suddenly becomes a slender thread by means of which Poitier, a college student volunteer who answers femme's call, must try to save her life without breaking the connection. While he holds her on the line for 54 minutes, vainly trying to learn her identity and whereabouts, rescue forces are marshaled to trace call and reach her in time.

Alexander, swinging over from tv to make his feature bow as a producer, based his subject upon an article written by his wife, Shana Alexander, tabbed "Decision to Die," in May 29, 1964 issue of Life. It reported a tragic experience of an unidentified Seattle woman who called 11 persons for help before taking an overdose of pills and phoning the clinic.

Stirling Silliphant developed situation into what in many respects is a dynamic script. However, his use of a multiplicity of flashbacks as the woman ramblingly recounts events she regards responsible for her action often is confusing and negates what had the makings of even greater dramatic effect.

Under the know-how direction of Sydney Pollack (also a swing-over from tv), action attains power and intensity as the minutes left remaining in the life of the phantom caller—as calculated by doctors—slowly dwindle. Poitier who remains on the telephone almost the entire unreeling of picture, delivers a compelling performance, matched by Miss Bancroft as the tortured wife and mother who attempts suicide when she sees her marriage of 12 years going down the drain after her husband discovers their son is really hers by a premarital lover.

Film is kept on a realistic level. The two stars never meet, their sole contact strictly telephonic. Most dramatic moments are played in the small clinic where Poitier is talking to Miss Bancroft, where effective use is made of latter's voice without her being constantly seen. Treatment is almost documentary at times as telephone employees, city police, Coast Guard and other agencies are mobilized for a desperate race against death. Lensed in the area of the actual incident, film aerial photography by Nelson Tyler of the World's Fair grounds and other parts of Seattle establishes an authentic opening.

The two stars have fine backing by Telly Savalas and Steven Hill, Savalas as head of the Crisis Clinic who helps Poitier marshal a rescue force and Hill as Miss Bancroft's seagoing husband. An outstanding bit is contributed by Edward Asner as a detective working on case, and Indus Arthur, a newcomer, shines in her brief offering as a clinic employee.

On technical side, Loyol Griggs' moving cameras help to maintain mood and Thomas Stanford's editing forcefully knits scenes. Quincy Jones' music score is also a potent assist and art direction by Hal Pereira and Jack Poplin excellent.
Whit.

The Spy Who Came In From The Cold
(BRITISH)

Firstrate Cold War spy meller, emphasizing human values and not technology. Strong in all departments, including world marquee allure and b.o. returns.

Hollywood, Dec. 10.
Paramount Pictures release of a Salem Films Ltd. (Martin Ritt-Paul Newman) production, produced and directed by Ritt. Stars Richard Burton, Claire Bloom, Oskar Werner; features Sam Wanamaker, George Voskovec, Rupert Davies, Cyril Cusack, Peter Van Eyck. Screenplay, Paul Dehn, Guy Trosper, based on the novel by John Le Carre; camera, Oswald Morris; editor, Anthony Harvey; music, Sol Kaplan; production design, Hal Pereira, Tambi Larsen; art direction, Edward Marshall; sound, John W. Mitchell, John Cox; asst. director, Colin Brewer. Reviewed at Paramount Studio, Dec. 9, '65. Running Time, 112 MINS.
Alec Leamas .... Richard Burton
Nan Perry .... Claire Bloom
Fiedler .... Oskar Werner
Peters .... Sam Wanamaker
East German defense a*t*v.
.... George Voskovec
Smiley .... Rupert Davies
Control .... Cyril Cusack
Mundt .... Peter Van Eyck
Asha .... Michael Hordern
Carlton .... Robert Hardy
Patmore .... Bernard Lee
Tribunal president .... Beatrix Lehmann
Old judge .... Esmond Knight
CIA Agent .... Tom Stern
German checkpoint guards
.... Niall MacGinnis, George Mikell
German guide .... Scot Finch
Miss Crail .... Anne Blake
Vopo Captain .... Richard Marner
Mr. Zanfrello .... Warren Mitchell
East German Judge .... Steve Plytas

"The Spy Who Came In From The Cold" is an excellent contemporary espionage drama of the Cold War which achieves solid impact via emphasis on human values, total absence of mechanical spy gimmickry, and perfectly controlled underplaying. Filmed at Ireland's Ardmore Studios and England's Shepperton complex, the Martin Ritt production boasts strong scripting, acting, direction and production values. International marquee strength plus pre-sold readership of the best-selling novel will boost the Paramount release to hefty b.o. in all markets.

No other recent film has so effectively socked over the point that East-West espionage agents are living in a world of their own, apart from the day-to-day existence of the millions whom they are serving; such people joust with one another, responding instantly to changing government policies and the corresponding change in friend-enemy status. It is a frightening fact of life, a deadly, vicious game of wits and chance, in which the toll on human spirits is indeed great.

Other modern fictional spies operate with such dash and flair that the erosion of the spirit is submerged in picturesque exploits and intricate technology. Not so in this Paul Dehn-Guy Trosper adaptation of John LeCarre's novel in which Richard Burton "comes in from the cold" — meaning the field operations — only to find himself used as a pawn in high-level counter-plotting.

Burton fits neatly into the role of the apparently burned out agent, British ripe for cultivation by East German Communist secret police as a potential defector. The route by which he attains that status includes British spy chief Cyril Cusack, the homosexual Michael Hordern, whose talent for picking up men fits in with recruitment of defectors by Robert Hardy to relay to Sam Wanamaker, thence to Oskar Werner, the Jewish second-in-command of East German forces who is fanatically jealous of his boss, Peter Van Eyck.

Gimmick is to discredit Van Eyck via play on Werner's jealousy, and Claire Bloom, sole femme principal, is another pawn, serving as a British Communist Party member enamored of Burton. An eventual Van Eyck-Werner confrontation cues a switcheroo climax which satisfies the demands of espionage, but leaves Burton and Miss Bloom literally out in the cold on the Berlin wall.

All thesps contribute solid and appropriate interpretations under the consistent braking direction of Ritt; effect of the underplaying is emotionally deafening. Only Werner, relatively flamboyant in dress and acting, breaks this mood at times.

Oswald Morris' terrif camera matches the changing plot loyalties with full use of the black-to-white spectrum, a complement to the Hal Pereira-Tambi Larsen pro-

duction design. Sol Kaplan's score is appropriately sparse and moody. Anthony Harvey edited to a good 112 minutes. The John W. Mitchell-John Cox sound is crisp, clean and thoroughly audible throughout. All other technical credits are professional. *Murf.*

Battle Of The Bulge
(CINERAMA-COLOR)

Cinerama's exciting and commercial war drama fictionalized from the World War II battle in Europe. Spectacle, plus strong thesping, overcome routine script. Hardticket outlook good. Excellent prospects for later release in general situations.

Hollywood. Dec. 16.
Warner Bros. Pictures release of Cinerama Inc. and Sidney Harmon (in association with United States Pictures Inc.) production, produced by Milton Sperling and Philip Yordan. Features Henry Fonda, Robert Shaw, Robert Ryan, Dana Andrews. Directed by Ken Annakin. Screenplay, Yordan, Sperling, John Melson; camera (Cinerama, Ultra-Panavision, Technicolor), Jack Hildyard; editor, Derek Parsons; music. Benjamin Frankel; song lyric, Kurt Wiehle; art direction Eugene Lourie; sound, David Hildyard, Gordon McCallum; asst. directors, Jose Lopez Rodero, Martin Sacristan, Luis Garcia. Reviewed at Pacific's Cinerama Theatre, L.A., Dec. 14, '65. Running Time (without intermission), 167 MINS.
Lt. Col. Kiley .... Henry Fonda
Col. Hessler .... Robert Shaw
Gen. Grey .... Robert Ryan
Col. Pritchard ..... Dana Andrews
Sgt. Duquesne ..... George Montgomery
Schumacher .... Ty Hardin
Louise .... Pier Angeli
F'ena .... Barbara Werle
Wolenski .... Charles Bronson
Gen. Kohler .... Werner Peters
Conrad .... Hans Christian Blech
Lt. Weaver .... James MacArthur
Guffy .... Telly Savalas

Based on the pivotal action which precipitated the end of World War II in Europe, but otherwise fictionalized, "Battle Of The Bulge" is a rousing, commercial battlefield action-drama of the emotions and activities of U.S. and German forces. Spectacular visual effects in Cinerama and outstanding special effects impart realism and audience participation in the overall well-mounted production which was lensed in Spain. Strong performances and direction enhance a routine script. Cinerama film (Warner Bros. release) has very good hardticket muscle, plus socko prospects for future general release in all markets.

Producers Milton Sperling and Philip Yordan collaborated with John Melson on a script which pits hard-charging German tank commander Robert Shaw against a U.S. military hierarchy topped by Robert Ryan, intelligence chief Dana Andrews, and latter's assistant, Henry Fonda, who is initially unpopular with the higher brass because he insists that the Germans are building towards a winter offensive. Fonda is top-billed among these principals, but after the title, in what is credited as a Sidney Harmon, in association with United States Pictures, production.

Shaw is outstanding in a multi-faceted role which demands he be a true war-lover, coolly rational under battle pressure and somewhat contemptuous of rear echelon chief Werner Peters (who, among other facilities, supplies the warm but brittle charms of Barbara Werle for some fast, fast relief (rejected by Shaw).

At the same time, he quite believably projects a properly limited compassion towards his longtime aide, battle-weary Hans Christian Blech. But most of all, he is terrific as the proud, resourceful and born leader of men, in this case a spirited but downy-cheeked bunch of youths — all that is left to the tank corps after five years of decimating warfare.

On the U.S. side, more interactions occur, and the script is flawed in the introduction of stock military types. Ken Annakin's direction and the adroit spacing of skirmishes minimize the script softness, exemplified by Fonda's character, whose solo sleuthing and tactical analysis strains credulity. Withal, Fonda is excellent in his warm, restrained underplaying which takes the edge off what otherwise could have become unbelievable derring-do.

Ryan provides strength as the general, and Andrews gives depth to the G-2 who is man enough to admit he was wrong. George Montgomery is very good as the professional NCO, saddled with a bumbling, but learning, shavetail James Macarthur. Charles Bronson impresses as the up-front infantry officer who must be sacrified to the advancing Germans as cover for the retreating Yanks.

Telly Savalas, projects in top form the earthy humor and simple tenderness of a likeable NCO sharpie. Pier Angeli, his partner in some black market operations, has an effective bit when they must end a sexless relationship which approached true love.

Among the Germans, Miss Werle, Blech and Peters offer strong portrayals, and also effective is Ty Hardin, playing the leader of the fake Yanks dropped behind U.S. lines to snarl communications. Large ranks of supporting players are good.

Cinerama prexy William R. Forman has said that the trade name Cinerama is properly called a star, and in this — the most contemporary story pic to date in the process — he is correct. Jack Hildyard's camera supervision (in which he was superbly assisted by aerial photographer Jack Willoughby and second unit lenser John Cabrera) has captured via Ultra Panavision lenses and Technicolor the grim sweep of advancing tanks and foot-slogging soldiers, plus the breathless pace of careening vehicles.

Added to the smash visuals are Alex Welson's (literally) boffo special explosive effects which give a fiery and bloody emphasis to the fact that this was a dirty, filthy, deathly war, not a high-level strategist's game. Capping these superior technical effects is the first-rate stereo sound recording by David Hildyard and Gordon McCallum of the topnotch sound editing by Kurt Herrnfeld and Alban Streeter, all of which gave an all-around live feel to the largely exterior scenes. Process work and Technicolor lab achievements are professional.

Eugene Lourie matched the mood with his fine art direction. Derek Parsons supervised editing to a good 167 minutes; as tradeshown, film breaks at the 105 minute mark for intermission.

Benjamin Frankel provided a full-bodied score, including a three-minute o v e r t u r e, which doesn't intrude during the action but effectively goes discordant at the fiery finale as the defeated Germans beat a confused retreat.

(On two occasions — the intro of Miss Werle and Savalas — it does, however, become ineffective gimmickry.) The "Panzerlied" song, lyrics by Kurt Wiehle and sung by Shaw's green troops, lends stirring plot development.

Title design, uncredited, is very good, ditto all other technical details. Brief opening voice-over is done by William Conrad, ex-radio actor now producer-director and in charge of a film unit at Warners, and who occasionally narrates. Fade-out narrative is banal anticlimax, should be cut or rewritten.
Murf.

Le Tigre Se Parfume A La Dynamite
(The Tiger Sprays Himself With Dynamite)
(FRENCH-ITALO-HISPANO)
(Color)

Paris, Dec. 14.
Gaumont release of Progefi, Dino De Laurentiis, Francisco Balcazar production. With Roger Hanin, Margaret Lee, Roger Dumas, Michel Bouquet, Michaela Cendali. Directed by Claude Chabrol. Screenplay, Antoine Flachot, Jean Curtelin; camera (Eastmancolor), Jean Rabier; editor, Jacques Gaillard. At Elysees, Paris. Running Time, 85 MINS.

Tigre	Roger Hanin
Pamela	Margaret Lee
Sarita	Michaela Cemdali
Vernorel	Michel Bouquet
Adjoint	Roger Dumas

Ex-New Waver Claude Chabrol has hit a fine commercial mine with his Bond-like takeoff pix. This, his third, looks to be his best. It has more menace and is full of parodical adventure, cruel fights and gadgets. But it lacks the right note of inventiveness and wit that the other pix had, so it appears mainly for offshore playoff on its okay action.

Undercover French agent Le Tigre seems invincible as he battles an organization of ex-Nazis bent on taking over the world through backing revolutions in many Latino areas. After a fierce flagellation scene the gang is broken and the Tigre has a girl, Margaret Lee, who looks like, and apes, the late Marilyn Monroe.

There's no denying Chabrol's dexterous knowhow. But here he just piles on fights and obscure story elements plus comic strip action without finding a balance between satire and the various illogical developments. He had managed to do this in his previous pix of this ilk. However, these films are all scoring here. Production is well lensed, moves crisply and is played adequately. Dualer and tv use abroad also appears likely.
Mosk.

Thunderball
(BRITISH-PANAVISION-COLOR)

Bangup James Bond meller with customary violence and romance; boff grosses seen.

Hollywood, Dec. 14.
United Artists release of Albert R. Broccoli-Harry Saltzman presentation, produced by Kevin McClory. Stars Sean Connery; features, Claudine Auger, Adolfo Celi, Luciana Paluzzi. Directed by Terence Young. Screenplay, Richard Maibaum, John Hopkins; based on original story by Kevin McClory, Jack Whittingham, Ian Fleming; camera (Technicolor), Ted Moore; editor. Peter Hunt;

production design, Ken Adam; asst. director, Gus Agosti; music, John Barry; sound, Bert Ross, Maurice Askew. Reviewing at Academy Award Theatre, Dec. 13, '65. Running Time, 130 MINS.

James Bond	Sean Connery
Domino	Claudine Auger
Emilio Largo	Adolfo Celi
Fiona	Luciana Paluzzi
Felix Leiter	Rik Van Nutter
"M"	Bernard Lee
Paula	Martine Beswick
Count Lippe	Guy Doleman
Patricia	Molly Peters
"Q"	Desmond Llewelyn
Moneypenny	Lois Maxwell
Foreign Secretary	Roland Culver
Pinder	Earl Cameron
Major Derval	Paul Stassino
Madame Boitier	Rose Alba
Vargas	Philip Locke
Kutze	George Pravda
Janni	Michael Brennan
Group Captain	Leonard Sachs
Air Vice Marshall	Edward Underdown
Kenniston	Reginald Beckwith
Quist	Bill Cummings
Mademoiselle La Porte	Maryse Guy Mitsouko
Jacques Boitier	Bob Simmons

Fourth time out for Ian Fleming's valiant British Secret Agent 007 should spell the same magical boxoffice figures that forerunners piled up. Ravages of time and past excursions of character into international espionage, rather than shading, seem to have enhanced lure of the derring-do, imperturbable undercoverman who approaches hazardous assignments with the same aplomb he displays in hopping into the hay with a covey of peeled sex kittens. "Thunderball" packs a wallop in its tongue-in-cheek treatment of agent-at-work.

Sean Connery reprises his indestructible James Bond in the manner born, faced here with a $280,000,000 atomic bomb ransom plot. Action, dominating element of three predecessors, gets rougher before even the credits flash on. Richard Maibaum (who coscripted former entries) and John Hopkins' screenplay is studded with inventive play and mechanical gimmicks. There's visible evidence that the reported $5,500,000 budget was no mere publicity figure; it's posh all the way, crammed with pop values, as company moves from France and England to the Bahamas.

Kevin McClory, who worked with late author Fleming on the original story (Jack Whittingham also sat in), is partnered with Albert R. Broccoli and Harry Saltzman in producer duties. Also, Terence Young, who helmed "Dr. No," first of series, and second, "From Russia, With Love," is back as director. Broccoli-Saltzman drew as well on same technical talents associated with their past Bond films; Ted Moore on color cameras, Peter Hunt as editor, John Barry, who composed music score for "Russia" and "Goldfinger"; and, of course, Maibaum on script. Result is a tight, exciting melodrama in which novelty of action figures importantly.

Yarn gets its springboard from theft of two atomic bombs, during a NATO training mission, by SPECTRE, the international crime syndicate, and threat to drop them on two English or American cities if $280,000,000 isn't paid by the British by a certain date. To Bond is assigned task of recovering bombs, which have been flown in a hijacked NATO plane to the Bahamas and sunk in the plane on the ocean's floor a short distance off-shore. His chief antagonist is the SPECTRE agent, Adolfo Celi,

whose villa and yacht figure as backgrounds for part of action.

One of highlight sequences is the underwater battle between U.S. Aquaparatroops, whom Bond calls upon after he locates the hidden bombs, and the heavies, both using spear guns for spectacular effect. Underwater weapon-carrying sea sleds provide an imaginative note, as does a one-man jet pack used by Bond in the opening sequence, reminiscent of the one-man moon vehicle utilized by Dick Tracy in the cartoon strip. A rocket-firing motor bike and a 95-mile-an-hour convertible hydrofoil are other thrill devices. Film winds with Connery and Claudine Auger, one of four beauts in pic, being snatched aloft from a rubber raft by a land-to-air rescue device, at 180-miles-perhour.

Connery is up to his usual stylish self as he lives up to past rep, in which mayhem is a casual affair. He has been given several priceless lines, one, "Do you mind if my friend sits this out — she's just dead," uttered to a couple at a table as he deposits femme heavy who has just been shot in the back on dancefloor by a bullet intended for him. If this be typing, every actor should have it so good.

Producers as usual have come up with their expected assortment of glamour, bikinis their favorite garb. Miss Auger (Miss France, 1958-59) as a European playgirl is chief charmer, but Luciana Paluzzi as an enemy agent is equally eyefilling. In lesser roles, Molly Peters as an English therapist and Martine Beswick a Bahaman agent are no less curvacious enchanting.

Celi brings dripping menace to part of the swarthy heavy who is nearly as ingenious — but not quite — as the British agent, whom, among other means, he tries to kill with man-eating sharks. Rik Van Nutter lends strong support as a CIA agent in the Bahamas, and Bernard Lee, British Secret Service chief, and Roland Culver, the Foreign Secretary, are suavely convincing. Paul Stassino is a key figure.

Terence Young takes advantage of every situation in his direction to maintain action at fever-pitch. In addition to outstanding technical credits listed above, underwater director Ricou Browning and cameraman Lamar Boren rate mention, as does Bob Simmons as stunt director. Anthony Mendleson's costume designing is all it should be to accentuate glamour and Ken Adam's production design and art direction by Peter Murton superb.
Whit.

Nick Carter Et Le Trefle Rouge
(Nick Carter and Red Club)
(FRENCH)

Paris, Dec. 14.
Columbia release of Chaumiane-Parc Films-Film-studio production. Stars Eddie Constantine; features Nicole Courcel, Jeanne Valerie, Jo Dassin, Jacques Harden, Jean Ozenne. Directed by Jean-Paul Savignac. Screenplay, Paul Vecchiali, Savignac from book by Claude Rank; camera, Claude Beausoleil; editor, Leila Biro. At Colisee, Paris. Running Time, 85 MINS.

Nick Carter	Eddie Constantine
Dora	Nicole Courcel
Lea	Jeanne Valerie
Jolas	Jo Dassin
Capitain	Jacques Harden
Professor	Jean Ozenne

After appearing in that offbeat sci-fi Jean-Luc Godard look at an eerie future, "Alphaville," Eddie Constantine appears to be taking things a bit too seriously in this return to his familiar parodic undercover man pix. Here it is played slowly. And the plot is not taut enough to bring it off.

Result is a rather plodding actioner with only dualer or tele use abroad on some okay fights, if not enough of them, and a tale of a new nuclear weapon. U. S. agent Carter (Constantine) goes to Antwerp where a new radioactive invention has been heisted. He finally tracks down the perpetrators after some fairly murky adventures, clues and complications.

Constantine is his usual phlegmatic self but does not seduce any girls though they appear to crave him. He hardly drinks either and a girl finds a picture of Humphrey Bogart in his wallet. A commendable ambition, but Constantine still seems to lack the wry character, bordered with rage that's wanted. New director Jean-Paul Savignac is too fussy and overloads rather than adds effect to this ordinary tale. However, he appears able to put a pic together and less embroidery could make him okay. *Mosk.*

The Tenth Victim
(La Decima Vittima)
(ITALIAN-FRENCH-COLOR)

Wacky but frequently chilling glimpse at la dolce vita in the next century. Marcello Mastroianni and Ursula Andress try to love each other to death in a pop art world. Crazy, but interesting.

Embassy Pictures release of C. C. Champion (Rome)-Les Films Copernic (Paris) production. Produced by Carlo Ponti; executive producer Joseph E. Levine. Stars Marcello Mastroianni, Ursula Andress; features Elsa Martinelli, Salvo Randone, Massimo Serato. Directed by Elio Petri. Screenplay, Petri, Ennio Flaiano, Tonino Guerra, based on short story by Robert Sheckley; camera (Technicolor), Gianni di Venanzo; editor, Ruggiero Mastroianni; sound, Ennio Sensi; no music credits provided. Reviewed at Embassy homeoffice, N.Y., Dec. 17, '65. Running Time, **92 MINS.**
Marcello Polletti ... Marcello Mastroianni
Caroline Meredith ... Ursula Andress
Olga ... Elsa Martinelli
Lawyer ... Massimo Serato
Professor ... Salvo Randone
Chet ... Mickey Knox
Cole ... Richard Armstrong
Martin ... Walter Williams
Victim ... Evi Rigano
Rudi ... Milo Quesada
Lidia ... Luce Bonifassy
Relaxatorium Girl ... Anita Sanders
Chinese assailant ... George Wang

What Jean-Luc Godard tried to do in "Alphaville," comes off with considerably more success in Elio Petri's satiric jibe at what faces humanity in the next century. To categorize "Victim," which must be seen from the beginning as the wrap-up ending is such a departure from the main storyline that it could take some of the edge off if not seen in proper sequence, the film is a mixture of hazardous adventure, even more hazardous romance, and unflattering social comment, made with enough humor to allay personal reaction.

Truly an international picture, as befits its theme of la dolce vita in what appears to be a pop art world, the soundtrack is a mixture

of languages, English when that tongue is called for, in Italian (with English subtitles) when more appropriate. Director Petri, who also collaborated with scripters Ennio Flaiano, Tonino Guerra Giorgio Salvione in adapting Robert Sheckley's short story, "The Seventh Victim" (upgraded in its transition to film by three victims), keeps the viewer suitably uncertain as to whether he's dead serious or playing it tongue-in-cheek in his depictions of mores in tomorrow's existence. The futuristic approach is made without resorting to far-out sets, utilizing a combination of natural Roman and New York settings, with some ultra-modern homes, to suggest the future.

Embassy's selling approach for this sometimes suspenser, sometimes wacky comedy, could be along, several lines. Certainly there's a wealth of exploitable material in the story, not to mention Mastroianni and Miss Andress. It's the Christmas period release for the Levine company, opening Dec. 20 at New York's Lincoln Art and Tower East Theatres.

Life, a la Petri, holds some surprises for any survivors who make it into the 21st century. War no longer exists but qualified international types are licensed for a period of 10 kills (half as hunters, half as victims). Survivors get $1,000,000, international notoriety and, apparently, unlimited political and moral privileges. What extra privileges could be added to the practices depicted or alluded to as standard is a matter for conjecture.

Ursula Andress, completing her fifth turn as a victim by shooting her Chinese pursuer with a bullet-firing brassiere, is assigned, by computer selection, Mastroianni as her fifth quarry. He, having completed his fifth round as a hunter, becomes a victim, alternately eluding Miss Andress and making love to her, whichever seems most appropriate at the moment. She has signed a deal with a tv company to perform the assassination as part of a tv commercial for a tea company. The problem is to get him to the spot where the tv cameras have been set up. He, alternately, has made a deal with an Italian tv producer to dump the demoiselle into a swimming pool where a grisly fate awaits her.

All this is played dead serious against a New York and Rome word where people go to a Gotham nightclub named Club Masoch (one -ism that will apparently be "in") or the Roman Hunt Club where the nitery show is a pair of gladiators fighting for real. Everything is pop art and op art influenced with furniture and buildings and everyday items stripped down to the barest essentials. For relaxation, Mastroianni goes to a club which provides a wide selection of female types, mood music, suggestively erotic sounds, all on credit.

Instead of a gymnasium he trains at a school for assassins whose professor (Salvo Randone), a former victim, has a body held together with leather, chrome, stainless steel and greed. Comic books are considered "classic" literature.

Although religion still exists (divorces are so hard to get that most

people just don't get married), Mastroianni moonlights as a priest for a cult of sunset-worshippers. As old people are turned over to the state for disposition, some sentimental Italians hide them away in specially built rooms, furnished with relics of the 20th century, as does Mastroianni with his parents.

Beside the two stars, who so dominate the film that most of the other cast members trail far behind, Elsa Martinelli is particularly effective as Mastroianni's mistress, who has waited 12 years for the church to annul his marriage to Luce Bonifassy, only to be rejected when Miss Andress, the shape of things to come, appears on the Roman scene. Also impressive are Massimo Serato, as Mastroianni's lawyer, Mickey Knox, Richard Armstrong and Walter Williams as the American tv types backing Miss Andress' project and, in smaller parts, George Wang, Evi Rigano and Milo Quesada.

Gianni di Venanzo, who also photographed "Red Desert" and "Juliet of the Spirits," handles his Technicolor camera like a paintbrush, using strong, brilliant colors to emphasize the Mondrian-like atmosphere of tomorrow. Giulio Coltellacci's costumes are generally uniform-like for the males but provide more range in the female area, from autumnal colors for the honey-blonde heroine to black-and-white Courregesian costumes for Miss Martinelli. Although no music credits were provided, the sound of tomorrow will apparently be predominantly electronic and progressive jazz with singing restricted to the scat genre. Weird but very effective. *Robe.*

Do Not Disturb
(COLOR-C'SCOPE)

Above average Doris Day comedy, strong on wardrobe and other production values. Good direction, performances, and b.o. prospects in general situations.

Hollywood, Dec. 16.
Twentieth Century-Fox release of Aaron Rosenberg-Martin Melcher production. Stars Doris Day, Rod Taylor; features Hermione Baddeley, Sergio Fantoni. Directed by Ralph Levy. Screenplay, Milt Rosen, Richard Breen, based on a play by William Fairchild; camera (DeLuxe Color), Leon Shamroy; editor, Robert Simpson; music, Lionel Newman; songs, Ben Raleigh, Mark Barkan, Bob Hilliard, Mort Garson; asst. director, Joseph E. Rickards. Reviewed at 20th-Fox Studios, Dec. 15, '65. Running Time, **102 MINS.**
Janet Harper ... Doris Day
Mike Harper ... Rod Taylor
Vanessa Courtwright ... Hermione Baddeley
Paul ... Sergio Fantoni
Simmons ... Reginald Gardiner
Claire Hackett ... Maura McGiveney
Culkos ... Aram Katcher
Langsdorf ... Leon Askin
Alicia ... Lisa Pera
Delegate ... Michael Romanoff
Reynard ... Albert Carrier
Mrs. Ordley ... Barbara Morrison
One-man band ... Dick Winslow

"Do Not Disturb" is a light, entertaining comedy, set in England but filmed in Hollywood, with Doris Day teamed with a new screen hubby, Rod Taylor. The Aaron Rosenberg-Martin Melcher production has class production values, including eye-catching femme styles, which support above average scripting, direction and per-

formances. Good b.o. prospects for 20th-Fox release in general situations.

Milt Rosen and Richard Breen adapted a William Fairchild play, and Miss Day and Taylor star as a Yank couple located in London, where hubby runs a woolen mill. European atmosphere permits a logical intro of some foreign sex mores, thereby lifting plot from the proverbial and predictable domestic situation comedy rut.

Stars play extremely well together, Miss Day as the loving, but slightly wacky wife who grapples with English currency problems, rescues a pursued fox, and never quite gets the home in order, while Taylor is busy getting his factory into the black.

Their lives diverge when Maura McGiveney becomes too much of an assistant to Taylor (not his doing, of course), and sales chief Reginald Gardiner spells out the key for biz success: getting on the good side of Leon Askin, big wool buyer who throws swinging parties, meaning no wives.

Action cross cuts from Taylor's problem to Miss Day, who, under the prodding of landlady Hermione Baddeley, becomes innocently entangled with Sergio Fantoni, antique dealer and a prototype Continental charmer. After the inevitable spat and a bedroom chase with amorous Askin gaining ground on Miss Day, story reaches its happy end.

Miss Baddeley has some solid non sequitur dialog, and Fantoni is very good. Miss McGiveney does very well in an unsympathetic role, her expressions and eyes particularly impressive as well as fine diction. Gardiner underplays effectively, while Askin's good-natured lechery is enjoyable. All other players give fine support.

Ralph Levy, directing his second feature after years in vidirection, has derived uniformly good results from players, and, with Leon Shamroy's facile camera, has staged effectively. Robert Simpson trimmed to a good 102 minutes. Ray Aghayan dressed Miss Day in a snazzy wardrobe, always a selling point in her pix.

Lionel Newman added to the comedy with a score which complements many gags. Ben Raleigh wrote the bouncy title tune which lingers in memory, and Mark Barkan's fine lyrics are warbled by Miss Day over the colorful De. Patie-Freleng title art. The "Au Revoir" ballad by Bob Hilliard and Mort Garson could catch on. Print, sound and all other technical credits are firstrate. *Murf.*

Curse of the Voodoo
(BRITISH)

Horror-suspense yarn limps through pastiche of stock footage, stale plot, wooden performances. Might help as programmer, but limited b.o. potential.

Allied Artists release of Galaworld Film-Gordon Films Production; produced by Kenneth Rive; stars Bryant Halliday; features Dennis Price, Lisa Danielly, Mary Kerridge, Ronald Leigh Hunt, Jean Lodge, Dennis Alaba Peters, Tony Thawnton, Michael Nightingale, Andy Meyers, and Louis Majoney. Directed by Lindsay Shonteff. Screenplay by Tony O'Grady with additional scenes and dialogue by Leigh Vance; camera, Gerald Gibbs, BSC; editor, Barry Vince; with music composed and conducted by Brian Fahey. Reviewed at Preview Theatre, N.Y.; Dec. 13, '65. Running Time, **77 MINS.**

Mike Stacy	Bryant Halliday
Major Thomas	Dennis Price
Janet Stacey	Lisa Danielly
Janet's Mother	Mary Kerridge
Doctor	Ronald Leigh Hunt
Mrs. Lomas	Jean Lodge
Saidi	Dennis Alaba Peters
Radlett	Tony Thawnton
Second Hunter	Michael Nightingale
Tommy Stacey	Andy Meyers
African expert	Louis Majoney
Barman	Jimmy Feldgate
Simbasa in London	Nigel Feyistan
Night Club Dancer	Beryl Cunningham
Night Club Band	Bobby Breen Quintet

With few real horror or suspense jolts, a cliche story, and only occasional action, "Curse of the Voodoo" stacks up in the substandard programmer category, despite injections of sexy scenes (now more available in standard product), stock footage and to-the-bones editing. Played straight, it lacks even the campy or unintended humor seen in many pics of the type. In the age of Bond, this genre has to fly way out to compete for the entertainment dollar. Suspense aspects, despite attempts to kettledrum each pregnant pause to life, are stillborn. For horror-suspense patrons, this kind of mild fare has low lure.

Routine story follows standard "darkest Africa" line with "voodoo curse" complications weaving around a white hunter, Bryant Halliday, who bags a lion on verboten native turf, despite companion's warnings of Simbasi vengeance, a local lion-worshipping tribe. After losing his native bearer, who had turned on him in a berserk Simbasi-inspired fit, and while recuperating from a claw wound inflicted by his close brush with the lion, Halliday, in one of the story's more alarming shifts, returns to London to patch up his failing marriage.

While there he is plagued by a baffling fever, an unhealing wound, hallucinations that Simbasi natives are pursuing him through Regent Park, and a dyspeptic mother-in-law. Worried by her husband's gradual disintegration, Lisa Danielly, consults an African expert who informs her that the curse can only be broken by killing his tormentor, the notorious M'Gobo, chief of the Simbas. Several inserts, cut into the action, reveal that M'Gobo is using Halliday's native bearer as live voodoo doll long-distancing the curse.

Robot acting by Halliday, Dennis Price, Lisa Danielly, and Mary Kerridge, done almost entirely in close-up presumably to mask slim budget locales, and unaided by cliche "natives are restless" dialog, approaches zombie level, as if entire cast is voodooed. Though Lindsay Shonteff's direction is tortoise-paced and generally actionless, Barry Elvin's cutting-in of stock lion footage into evidently polite English countryside locales almost approaches believability and economical trimming helps flip lagging story along. As horror, pic is less than mildly creepy. As suspense, flat acting and trite story add up to soggy thrills and as a shoestring production, it's pretty threadbare.

Near death, Halliday returns to Africa for a singlehanded show-down with M'Gobo. Finally expending ammo, he winds up running down native chief with jeep in a fairly exciting denouement. *Rino.*

The Ugly Dachshund
(COLOR)

Walt Disney story about a Great Dane which thinks he's a dachshund; lively entry for family market.

Hollywood, Dec. 18.

Buena Vista release of Walt Disney-Winston Hibler production. Stars Dean Jones, Suzanne Pleshette, Charlie Ruggles. Directed by Norman Tokar. Screenplay, Albert Aley; based on book by G. B. Stern; camera (Technicolor), Edward Colman; music, George Bruns; art direction, Carroll Clark, Marvin Aubrey Davis; editor, Robert Stafford; sound, Robert O. Cook; asst. director, Tom Leetch. Reviewed at Academy Award Theatre. Dec. 17, '65. Running Time, **93 MINS.**

Mark Garrison	Dean Jones
Fran Garrison	Suzanne Pleshette
Dr. Pruitt	Carlie Ruggles
Officer Carmody	Kelly Thordsen
Mel Chadwick	Farley Baer
Mr. Toyama	Robert Kino
Kenji	Mako
Judge	Charles Lane

Walt Disney, who knows his way with a dog as well as a family, has turned out a rollicking piece of business in this comedy about a Great Dane which thinks he's a dachshund. Possibilities are explored along hilarious lines and sum total adds up to firstrate family entertainment, not to mention as having definite appeal for dog lovers and audiences generally.

Dean Jones and Suzanne Pleshette are the two principals, a young married couple faced with the fancy cut-ups of four Dachs and a Dane raised with the low-slung pups. The Fritzels are hers, the Dane his, and actually the Albert Aley screenplay builds to trying to sell the Dane—named Brutus—that he actually is a Dane.

Action is light and airy as the couple go their own way with their respective pets, Suzanne insisting that Dean rid himself of the clumsy big-foot while her spouse stoutly maintains that his Dane has a rightful place in the household. Wife's insistance comes from several episodes in which the house is nearly demolished, the dachshunds having started the trouble but the Dane getting all the blame. Brutus finally comes into his own when he espies a lady Harlequin Dane at a dog show and proceeds to win best in breed and show.

Both Miss Pleshette and Jones turn in likable, swinging performances and Charlie Ruggles scores as the family vet who donates the Dane to Jones. Kelly Thordsen makes the most of a cop character treed by Brutus for a night, and Robert Kino, as a Japanese gardener hired to service a garden party tossed by couple gets laughs when he's panicked by Brutus, whom he thinks is a lion, as Dane makes shambles of the affair.

Winston Hibley co-produces with Disney and Norman Tokar's direction is geared for laughs. Color photography by Edward Colman is a definite asset, and George Bruns' music score is particularly apropos to the comedy unfoldment. Editing by Robert Stafford is fast, art direction by Carroll Clark and Marvin Aubrey Davis fitting. William R. Koehler and Glenn Randall Jr., who trained dogs, are specially befitting a hand. *Whit.*

Inside Daisy Clover
(PANAVISION-COLOR)

Hollywood - located drama about a young star and her problems. Episodic, often vague, but splashed with rich production values, Natalie Wood and showy musical numbers.

Hollywood, Dec. 14.

Warner Bros. release of Alan Pakula-Robert Mulligan (Alan J. Pakula) production, directed by Mulligan. Stars Natalie Wood, Christopher Plummer; features Robert Redford, Roddy McDowall, Ruth Gordon, Katharine Bard. Screenplay, Gavin Lambert, based on his novel; camera (Technicolor), Charles Lang; production designer, Robert Clatworthy; editor, Aaron Stell; music, Andre Previn; sound, M. A. Merrick; asst. director, Joseph E. Kenny. Reviewed at Pacific's Pantages Theatre, Dec. 10, '65. Running Time, **128 MINS.**

Daisy Clover	Natalie Wood
Raymond Swan	Christopher Plummer
Wade Lewis	Robert Redford
Baines	Roddy McDowall
The Dealer	Ruth Gordon
Melora Swan	Katharine Bard
Gloria Goslett	Betty Harford
Harry Goslett	John Hale
Cop	Harold Gould
Old Lady in Hospital	Ottola Nesmith
Cynara	Edna Holland
Milton Hopwood	Peter Helm

There will be those who may claim "Inside Daisy Clover" is based upon the true-life story of an actress who rose to shining blonde stardom. Alan J. Pakula and Robert Mulligan focus their sights upon a teenage beach gamin who becomes a Hollywood star of the 1930s. Covering a two-year period, the outcome, though splashed with rich production values, is at times disjointed and episodic as the title character played by Natalie Wood emerges more nebulous than definitive, sometimes difficult to fathom. Film ends on a puzzling note, perhaps clear to the producers but not to the audience. A smart exploitation campaign to which subject lends itself could help boost pic's chances at the box-office.

Miss Wood essays a change of pace as the 15-year-old, living with a near-demented mother in a drab trailer adjoining the Santa Monica amusement pier, who submits a recording of her voice to a studio searching for a new child star. She wins a contract, and immediately her life undergoes tremendous upheaval as she literally goes from rags to riches, finds her mother has been placed in a mental institution without her consent, completes her first film and tastes her first Hollywood party at her producer's home. Almost overnight she is a star.

Femme star seems to be eternally searching for the meaning of her role; she is almost inarticulate for long intervals and whoever is in a scene with her generally engages in a monolog since there is seldom dialog between them. The Gavin Lambert screenplay, based on his own novel, hop-skips through a brief romance with a screen idol, her one-day marriage, desertion and divorce; a nervous breakdown after the death of her mother. When she refuses to return to complete a picture the studio head threatens her with starvation.

Probably the outstanding parts of pic are two novel musical numbers, one in which the studio boss introduces his new star in a specially-made film shown at a party, in which special effects are ingeniously utilized, and second featuring her after she's reached stardom. Herbert Ross' choreography is spritely and both numbers have feeling. Dramatic tones are interrupted in closing reel with a comedy attempt at suicide, in which star's efforts to kill herself by placing her head in an oven are constantly interrupted by the doorbell and telephone.

Miss Wood is better than her part. Her co-star is Christopher Plummer, who gives polish and some stiffness to the sadistic studio head bound to build himself a star. As the mother, Ruth Gordon is immense in a vague character. Robert Redford makes as a glamour boy who constantly is flitting in and out of the star's life and who walks out on her after their first night in a bleak Arizona motel, and Katharine Bard delivers well as Plummer's wife who had an affair with Redford before young star enters the scene. Roddy McDowall is in as the studio head's yes-man, and Betty Harford plays Miss Wood's elder sister.

Mulligan in his direction is responsible for interesting inside-studio activity, one of his best moments the scenes in which Miss Wood breaks down while synching a song with her image on the screen. Like the cast, his work is hindered by the minimal plotline. Technical departments are strongly handled right down the line; rating highly are Charles Lang's color photography, Robert Clatworthy's production design, Andre Previn's music, femme star's costumes designed by Edith Head, John Hoffman's montage. *Whit.*

Doctor Zhivago
(COLOR—PANAVISION)

Meticulous and artistic David Lean film of the Russian Revolution, based on smuggled-out Boris Pasternak novel. Solid thesping by an international cast. Good hardticket prospects. Better in later general release.

Hollywood, Dec. 22.

Metro-Goldwyn-Mayer release of a Carlo Ponti production. Features (in alphabetical order) Geraldine Chaplin, Julie Christie, Tom Courtenay, Alec Guinness, Siobhan McKenna, Ralph Richardson, Omar Sharif, Rod Steiger, Rita Tushingham. Directed by David Lean. Screenplay, Robert Bolt, based on the novel by Boris Pasternak; camera (Metrocolor), Freddie Young; editor, Norman Savage; production design, John Box; music, Maurice Jarre; asst. directors, Roy Stevens, Pedro Vidal. Reviewed at Hollywood Paramount Theatre, L.A., Dec. 21, '65. Running Time (without intermission), **197 MINS.**

Tonya	Geraldine Chaplin
Lara	Julie Christie
Pasha/Strelnikoff	Tom Courtenay
Yevgraf	Alec Guinness
Anna	Siobhan McKenna
Alexander	Ralph Richardson
Yuri Zhivago	Omar Sharif
Komarovsky	Rod Steiger
Girl	Rita Tushingham
Sasha	Jeffrey Rockland
Yuri at age 8	Tarek Sharif
Bolshevik	Bernard Kay
Kostoyed	Klaus Kinski
Liberius	Gerard Tichy
Razin	Noel Willman
Medical professor	Geoffrey Keen
Amelia	Adrienne Corri
Petya	Jack MacGowran
Dam engineer	Mark Eden
Old soldier	Erik Chitty
Beef-faced colonel	Roger Maxwell
Delegate	Wolf Frees
Female janitor	Gwen Nelson
Katya	Lucy Westmore
Train jumper	Lili Murati
Political officer	Peter Madden

The sweep and scope of the Russian revolution, as reflected in the personalities of those who either adapted or were crushed, has been captured by David Lean in "Doctor Zhivago," frequently with soaring dramatic intensity. Director has accomplished one of the most meticulously designed and executed films—superior in several visual respects to his "Lawrence Of Arabia."

Some finely etched performances by an international cast illuminate the diverse characters from the novel for which Boris Pasternak won but did not accept the Nobel Prize. Carlo Ponti production is an excellent achievement in filmmaking, and seems destined for good hardticket action. Word of mouth, the burgeoning b.o. appeal of younger featured players, and the Lean reputation suggest even brighter prospects for later Metro release in general situations.

Robert Bolt, whose screenplay is itself a 224-page book just published by Random House, faced a major challenge in adaptation. The Pasternak novel turns on an introspective medic-poet who essentially reacts to the people and events before, during and after the Bolshevik takeover. The capacity, indeed the insistence, of the human spirit to survive and retain some measure of individuality is an essential story factor which must be cleverly balanced with, and related to, impersonal events. Bolt's adaptation is an effective blend.

At the center of a universe of nine basic characters is Omar Sharif as Zhivago, the sensitive man who strikes different people in different ways. To childhood sweetheart Geraldine Chaplin he is a devoted (if cheating) husband; to Julie Christie, with whom he is thrown together by war, he is a passionate lover; to Tom Courtenay, once an intellectual but later a heartless Red general, he's a symbol of the personal life which revolution has supposedly killed; to lecherous, political log-roller Rod Steiger he's the epitome of "rarefied selfishness"; and to half-brother Alec Guinness, the cold secret police official, he's a man who must be saved from himself.

Sharif, largely through expressions of indignation, compassion and tenderness, makes the character very believable. Miss Chaplin, in her English-language film debut. (She previously made an unreleased French film.) will be a "conversation piece" of casting.

Miss Christie is outstanding in a sensitive, yet earthy and full-blooded portrayal of a girl who, while not yet a woman, is used and discarded by Steiger, then marries Courtenay only to lose him to his cause. Her happiness with Zhivago (under the cloud of their adultery) also ends by his refusal to leave Russia.

Steiger, whose early lechery for Miss Christie later becomes a distant love and respect (a factor which precipitates the downbeat ending), capably handles a role which requires him to be callous and expedient without losing all warmth, and thereby, sympathy. Ralph Richardson and Siobhan McKenna are effective reps of the older generation which views the crumbling world of mannered society with quiet regret and considerable disgust.

Courtenay is an example of the "idealistic" liberal who will not compromise his principles, thus becoming cruel and vicious, totally dedicated to a philosophy which in time will no longer condone his excesses. His dress and manner in early scenes is immediately reminiscent of the student in Serge Eisenstein's "Potemkin," from which Lean drew a partial inspiration for a street massacre which is the first of many effective shock sequences. Lean also turns some familiar time transitions (swirling leaves, etc.) into artful, pictorial passages of high quality.

Guinness functions as occasional narrator for the bulk of the film, although the story is told in flashback as he gently questions Rita Tushingham, believed to be the daughter of Sharif and Miss Christie and whom he is seeking. Miss Tushinghm gives appropriate childlike simplicity to her role, and plays well opposite Guinness who neatly portrays a sometimes benevolent, always Party-line policeman. Effect of his underplaying is chilling.

On this, his third film in a decade, director Lean has devoted as much care to physical values as he has to his players. With John Box's terrif production design and Freddie Young's outstanding Panavision-Metrocolor camera, he has succeeded admirably in drawing the audience into the action. The bitter cold of winter (only section of film made out of Spain, these Finland settings are beautiful and foreboding at once), the grime of Moscow, the lush countryside, the drabness of life in a dictatorship, the brutality of war, and the fool's paradise of the declining Czarist era are forcefully conveyed in full use of camera, color, sound and silence.

His sure directorial hand appears to have slipped in the reentry of Steiger into the final action. Pace needs quickening at that point, but the mysterious stranger gambit, running for two minutes, in blinding snow far from civilization is on the meller side.

Effective symbolism—the gigantic hydroelectric plant, a supreme achievement of a materialistic society, and the ant-like laborers who toil thereon, also the baying wolves who precede the arrival of politico-military wolves at the door of Sharif and Miss Christie—complement the stark visual and aural contrasts. When the Moscow refugees, packed into freight cars like cattle, sweep the filthy straw from a moving train towards the camera, there is an instinctive drawing back by the viewer.

Maurice Jarre has composed and conducted a score which ranges from the brassy clash of men and ideas, to the intimate balalaika love theme, overall a first-rate achievement. His four-minute overture is stirring. Norman Savage supervised the sharp editing, and film runs (without intermission and overture) 197 minutes. Pic breaks at the 115-minute mark. (Time was shortened 15 mins. immediately following N.Y. showing.) Second part has less action, and could be tightened up here and there to accelerate the climax, since characterizations have already been well established.

Stereo sound recording and editing is crisp, but ran too loud at trade show; exhibs should watch the volume—its dramatic effect will not be lessened by lower decibels. Second unit director Roy Rossotti and his lenser Manuel Berenguer contributed solid support. All other technical work is top quality. *Murf.*

10 Little Indians
(BRITISH)

Second film version of Agatha Christie suspenser has built-in promotion gimmick. Technically excellent programmer.

Seven Arts Pictures release of a Tenlit Films production. Produced by Oliver A. Unger in association with Harry M. Popkin. Features Hugh O'Brian, Shirley Eaton, Daliah Lavi, Wilfrid Hyde-White, Stanley Holloway, Dennis Price, Leo Genn, Mario Adorf, Marianne Hoppe, Fabian. Directed by George Pollock. Screenplay, Peter Yeldham, based on a Dudley Nichols script, adapted by Peter Welbeck, from "Ten Little Niggers," play and novel by Agatha Christie; camera, Ernie Steward; editor, Peter Boita; music, composed and conducted by Malcolm Lockyer. Reviewed Dec. 10 at Seven Arts Pictures homeoffice, N.Y. Running Time, **92 MINS.**

Hugh Lombard	Hugh O'Brian
Ann Clyde	Shirley Eaton
Mike Raven	Fabian
General Mandrake	Leo Genn
William Blore	Stanley Holloway
Frau Grohmann	Marianne Hoppe
Judge Cannon	Wilfrid Hyde-White
Ilona Bergen	Daliah Lavi
Dr. Armstrong	Dennis Price
Herr Grohmann	Mario Adorf

Second film version of Agatha Christie's endurable variation on the old idea of putting a group of disparate characters into a confined situation and let them be killed one by one, this Seven Arts release of a Tenlit Films production shapes up as good suspenser with better than average possibilities due to a built-in promotion gimmick that will undoubtedly be given fullest exposure.

Producer Oliver A. Unger, in association with Harry M. Popkin, shot the film entirely in Ireland although the setting has been changed to what appears to be a solitary schloss in the Austrian Alps. There's quite a bit of really mountainous background scenery and it would appear that a second-unit, not credited, did some filming in the Alps or that stock footage has been inserted.

Director George Pollock, despite a script with complicated credits (screenplay by Peter Yeldham, based on a script by Dudley Nichols, and adapted by Peter Welbeck, based on the Christie novel and play, "Ten Little Niggers"), works quite a bit of suspense into the restricted action, successfully hiding identity of the tenth Indian without resorting to too many "red herrings." Filmgoers who remember Fox's 1945 "And Then There Were None," who think they've got the villain pegged will probably be surprised. Basically, all the characters remain the same as in that earlier version although, because of the switch in setting, former English housekeeping couple is Viennese (Mario Adorf and Marianne Hoppe). Other major switch, an unfortunate one, has the first victim, originally an eccentric prince, changed to an American rock 'n' roll singer (Fabian, in an embarrassingly bad performance).

No one rates star billing. Principal leads are taken by Hugh O'Brian and Shirley Eaton, with Daliah Lavi, Wilfred Hyde-White, Stanley Holloway, Dennis Price and Leo Genn rounding out the guest list. It's a bad situation for the tyro talent as Hyde-White, Holloway, Price and Genn, all first-rank character actors, effortlessly dominate all the scenes they're in. Miss Lavi, unflatteringly made up and out of character as a German actress, is unimpressive. O'Brian is quite good and Miss Eaton continues to show promise that she'll outlive that "Goldfinger" paint job.

Ernie Steward's chilly and foreboding black-and-white camerawork is an important asset to the suspense building and Peter Boita's editing is crisp without being choppy. What will create the most comment is a two-minute "whodunit break" inserted near the end when the action is suspended although the film continues, while the audience is encouraged to guess the murderer's identity. By inserting the "break" within the film, there's no problem of timing for projectionists to mishandle and no lapse in continuity for the viewer. While rapid, brief, still flashbacks to murders up to that point are shown, an animated clock ticks off the break. *Robe.*

Up Jumped A Swagman
(BRITISH-COLOR)

Easygoing musical geared to admirers of pop singer Frank Ifield who should go for it;

London, Dec. 21.

Warner-Pathe release of an Ivy (Andrew Mitchell) production presented by Elstree Distributors. Stars Frank Ifield, Annette Andre, Ronald Radd, Richard Wattis, Suzy Kendall; features Donal Donnelly, Martin Miller, Brian Mosley, Carl Jaffe, William Mervyn. Directed by Christopher Miles. Story and screenplay, Lewis Griefer; camera (Technicolor), Ken Higgins; editor, Jack Slade; music, Norrie Paramor. Reviewed at Warner Theatre, London. Running Time, **87 MINS.**

Dave Kelly	Frank Ifield
Patsy	Annette Andre
Harry King	Ronald Radd
Melissa	Suzy Kendall
Lever	Richard Wattis
Bockeye	Donal Donnelly
Jo-Jo	Bryan Mosley
Herman	Martin Miller
Luigi	Harvey Spencer
Analyst	Carl Jaffe
Phil Myers	Cyril Shaps
Wilkinson	Frank Cox
Docherty	Fred Cox
Mrs. Hawkes Fenhoulet	Joan Geary
Mr. Hawkes Fenhoulet	William Mervyn
Policeman	Ian Paterson
Pat	Paddy Joyce

"Up Jumped A Swagman" is one of those easygoing, harmless films that is geared successfully to the pop music public and particularly those with allegiance to Frank Ifield. As such, it should have reasonable success around Britain and certain points abroad. Lack of star names may militate against its U.S. click.

Ifield is an Englishman who spent most of his life in Australia before returning here and becoming a top disk and tele singer. This is his first film and he has obvious potential, being a virile goodlooker. It might have been a better idea, perhaps, to have allowed him to debut under the control of a more experienced director than Chirstopher Miles. Latter is one of the bright up-and-comers and he brings some neat touches of invention to this picture, but his previous work has been limited to shorts.

This one, not too tightly scripted by Lewis Greifer, employs Ifield as an Aussie singer who comes to London to try and hit the big time. He lives in a world that's half-real, half-fantasy, latter angle enabling Miles to indulge in some flights of fancy, some of which fail to click. As a kind of sub-plot, Ifield becomes unwittingly tangled with a boneheaded bunch of robbers and romances two girls, one of whom may or may not have been purely figment of his imagination. It's never quite clear. An audition in a music-publisher's office and a chase by the police which is a parody of a click BBC show, "Z-Cars," are two of the imaginative adventures that have their moments.

Ifield sings some 10 ditties, including the inevitable "Waltzing Matilda" and his popular "I Remember You." The songs, many penned by Ifield himself, serve their purpose, though failing to move the story along, being mostly mere interjections. He handles them well, though his yodelling trademark tends to pall. Pam Devis' choreography rises to the occasion without being memorable.

Of the two young dames in Ifield's screen life, one of them, Annette Andre, is down to earth and the other, Suzy Kendall, plays a dizzy deb type. Neither role is sufficiently defined to give much clue to the girls' capacity, but Miss Kendall, making her screen debut, looks promising. Ronald Radd, leader of the muddleheaded crooks, and his gang provide some simple yocks in the burglary scenes. Richard Wattis provides another of his "sourpuss" jobs as a music publisher.

Ken Higgins' lensing in Technicolor is okay. Art and sets are cheerful and sunny. Jack Slade's editing could be tauter but this can largely be attributed to the lack of sinew in the screenplay. As innocent fun and a launching pad for Ifield the film will pay off, but a little more tension, wit and offbeat thinking by the scripter, and sharper direction by Miles would have enhanced this one's prospects no end. He has settled too often for the completely conventional setup. *Rich.*

Dis-Moi Qui Tuer
(Tell Me Who to Kill)
(FRENCH-COLOR)

Paris, Dec. 21.

MGM release of Films Numbre One-Pierre Kalfon-Trianon-CIPRA production. Stars Michele Morgan, Paul Hubschmid, features Fiona Lewis, Daniel Ollier, Daniel Emilfork. Directed by Etienne Perier. Screenplay, Didier Goulard, Dominique Fabre, Maurice Fabre from book by Henri Lapierre; camera (Eastmancolor), Henri Raichi; editor, Monique Isnardon. At Elysees Cinema, Paris. Running Time, **85 MINS.**

Genevieve	Michele Morgan
Reiner	Paul Hubschmid
Pompon	Fiona Lewis
Machelin	Daniel Ollier
Li-Tchan	Daniel Emilfork
Galland	Yann Arthus
Federuci	Jean Yanne
Le Basta	Henri Rellys
Pitou	Dario Moreno
Fayard	Germaine Montero

This is a limpid programmer, about a youngster getting mixed up in adventurers while looking for Nazi loot in a sunken plane off the French coast. It lacks the dash or inventiveness to make it anything but mainly a playoff item here. Foreign chances are improbable despite the Michele Morgan name.

Youngsters get involved when a man takes over an old, unused hotel they want to employ as a club room and place for parties. Miss Morgan is after the treasure, too, but takes up with the other adventurer when the real murderer of a few people involved turns out to be someone dragged in for the purpose.

Inane dialog, mild direction and plodding pace also militate against finding the vein of situation adventure and suspense comedy sought for. Miss Morgan is hopelessly miscast as a worldly type, with Paul Hubschmid colorless as her male vis-a-vis. British actress Fiona Lewis displays some bracing presence and pulchritude. But the youth are mostly callow and the supporting players fallow. *Mosk.*

Five Gents' Trick Book
(JAPANESE—COLOR)

Toho release of Toho Co. Ltd. (Masumi Fujimoto) production. Stars Hisaya Morishige, Asami Kuji; features Keiki Koboyashi, Yoko Tsukasa, Daisuko Kato, Norihei Miki, Franky Sakai. Directed by Sayo Marubayashi. Screenplay, Ryozo Kasahara; camera (Eastmancolor), Takeshi Suzuki; music, Yosijuki Kozu. Reviewed at Toho La Brea Theatre, Los Angeles, Calif., Dec. 21, '65. Running Time, **95 MINS.**

Hisataro Iwato	Hisaya Morishige
Toyoko Iwato	Asami Kuji
Takashi Ishikawa	Keiki Koboyashi
Kyoko Ishikawa	Yoko Tsukasa
Tyuzo Togashi	Daisuko Kato
Benjiro Mamada	Norihei Miki
Tsuyoshi Kebanai	Franky Sakai
Chiyo Suzu	Junko Ikeuchi
Sumiko	Michiyo Aratama
Yuriko	Reiko Dan

(English Titles)

This Japanese comedy isn't an American spectator's dish but for Nipponese audiences "Five Gents' Trick Book" doubtless will have something to sell. Light plot deals with a Tokyo biz tycoon with a roving eye and a jealous wife, but though English titles sometimes are difficult to follow the unfoldment socks its theme across.

Hisaya Morishige, middle aged and somewhat portly, handles the tycoon character with a nice reserve, and Asama Kuji is okay as the wife. Norihei Miki is in for a comedy role and thesps generally handle themselves satisfactorily.

Sayo Marubayashi's direction is spirited in the Japanese manner and Masumi Fujimoto is responsible for satisfactory production values. Takeshi Suzuki's color camera work is artistic and Yoshijuki Kozu's light music score catches the proper spirit. *Whit.*

Die Hoelle von Manitoba
(The Hell of Manitoba)
(GERMAN-SPANISH-COLOR)

Berlin, Dec. 21.

Gloria release of CCC (Artur Brauner) production in collab with Midega-Film, Madrid. Stars Lex Barker, Pierre Brice; features Marianne Koch, Hans Nielsen, Wolfgang Lukschy. Directed by Sheldon Reynolds. Screenplay, Edward di Lorenzo, Fernando Lamas and Jerold Hayden Boyd, based on Boyd's novel; camera (Eastmancolor), Federico G. Larraya; music, Angel Artega. Daydating numerous West Berlin cinemas. Running Time, **83 MINS.**

Brenner	Lex Barker
Reese	Pierre Brice
Jade	Marianne Koch
Judge	Hans Nielsen
Bar man	Wolfgang Lukschy
Villaine	Gerard Tichy
Grande	Jorge Rigaud
Josh	Angel Del Pozo
Clerk	Victor Israel

The German western is getting tougher, judging from this pic which features fisticuffs, barroom brawls, gunfire display and dead bodies all along the line. Had the script and the acting been more polished, this Teutonic oater might have approached what Hollywood is doing. However, the names of Lex Barker and Pierre Brice will lure the local action fans. Yet foreign prospects seem little better than average.

Through the years the most popular German screen couples have been duos composed of a man and a woman. Here's a switch, the current No. 1 German screen couple is the combo of Yank Lex Barker and French Pierre Brice who have reached an amazing popularity in this country via their Karl May characters (Barker as Old Shatterhand, Brice as Winnetou) in German outdoor epics.

The two are teamed up again in "Manitoba." This time, however, they are not as good-natured as in their Karl May pix. Here they are hard-hitting lonely westerners always fast on the trigger. Separately they show up in a western spot called Glory City which has the reputation for staging thrilling gunfights. Barker is to duel with someone named Deakes. Since the latter has been killed in another fight, the "management" takes Brice as his substitute. Here's another switch: Barker and Brice don't like the idea of either of them getting killed and forget about the duel. But the thrill-minded crowd wants to see blood. This leaves Barker and Brice no other choice than to join forces and wipe out the most notorious of the duel-lovers.

Barker doesn't say much in this film. But he's active in handling his fists and guns and otherwise is mostly seen sipping whisky. Brice, mild in Karl May westerns, is super-masculine here. Marianne Koch supplies the inevitable romantic interest. In the supporting cast is the late German Hans Nielsen in one of his last roles.

Director Sheldon Reynolds, an American, has tried to give this the "Yank smell." He succeeded with regard to atmosphere helped by the Spanish landscapes and adequate sets. What militates against a satisfactory overall impression is a superficial script and too many of those cliche-type performances and situations. *Hans.*

White Rose of Hong Kong
(JAPANESE—COLOR)

Toho release of Toho Co., Ltd. (Masumi Fujimoto) production. Stars Chang Mei Yao, Tsutomu Yamazaki; features Akira Takarada, Kumi Mizuno, Kenjiro Ishiyama. Directed by Jun Fukuda. Screenplay, Ichiro Okeda; original story, Shinobu Hashimoto; camera (Eastmancolor), Sinsaku Uno; music, Sadao Bekku. Reviewed at Toho La Brea Theatre, Los Angeles, Calif., Dec. 21, '65. Running Time, **110 MINS.**

Yuli Rin	Chang Mei Yao
Shiro Matsumoto	Tsutomu Yamazaki
Susumu Uzuki	Akira Takarada
Yoshiko Nakao	Kumi Mizuno
Syozo Tabe	Kenjiro Ishiyama
Eidatsu Ki	Mar Chi
Chief Police named Jin	Yu Fiiki
Kiyoaki Hayashi	Eijiro Yanagi

(English Titles)

"White Rose of Hong Kong" is a well-produced Japanese import, perhaps long by American standards but handy for the Japanese trade who prefer lengthy offerings. Tale of efforts of a Tokyo detective to break up a dope ring, script is convincing. Of particular interest is the Hong Kong setting, which color cameras limned to often startling scenic effect.

Chang Mei Yao, a Chinese actress, is lovely and beautiful as femme star caught in the web of family involvement in the morphine-smuggling operations, and Tsutomu Yamazaki is properly authoritative as the detective. Akira Takarada is a persuasive heavy and balance of cast do well by their respective roles.

Masumi Fujimoto's production helming is strong, bringing values comparative to any Hollywood picture to backdrop the Ichiro Ikeda script. Direction by Jun Fukuda is strong, and both Sinsaku Uno's photography and Sadao Bekku's music score are specially valuable assets. *Whit.*

1966

Our Man Flint
(C'SCOPE-COLOR)

Whambang spoof of James Bond; fast, rugged, violent, with James Coburn knockout as a super super secret agent; boff grosses indicated.

Hollywood, Dec. 29.

Twentieth- Fox release of Saul David production. Stars James Coburn, Lee J. Cobb, Gila Golan, Edward Mulhare. Directed by Daniel Mann. Screenplay, Hal Fimberg, Ben Starr; based on story by Fimberg; camera (DeLuxe Color), Daniel L. Fapp; music, Jerry Goldsmith; editor, William Reynolds; asst. director, David Silver. Reviewed at 20th-Fox Studios, Dec. 28, '65. Running Time, 107 MINS.

Flint	James Coburn
Cramden	Lee J. Cobb
Gila	Gila Golan
Malcolm Rodney	Rodney Mulhare
Dr. Wu	Benson Fong
Leslie	Shelby Grant
Anna	Sigrid Valdis
Gina	Gianna Serra
Sakito	Helen Funai
Gruber	Michael St. Clair
Dr. Krupov	Rhys Williams
American General	Russ Conway
Wac	Ena Hartman
American Diplomat	William Walker
Dr. Schneider	Peter Brocco

James Bond may have met his match in Derek Flint. He's a resourceful sort of fellow who is the dangdest super secret agent probably ever to hit the screen. Perhaps he goes British Agent 007 one better because in this Saul David production, a dazzling, action-jammed swashbuckling spoof of Ian Fleming's valiant counterspy, he's given more tools and gimmicks to pursue his craft as he tracks down and destroys the perpetrators of a diabolical scheme to take over the world. In a cycle which sees virtually every studio clambering aboard the espionage bandwagon, indications point to blockbusting biz if film is properly exploited.

James Coburn takes on the task of being surrounded by exotically-undraped beauts and facing dangers which would try any man. But he comes through unscathed, helped by a dandy little specially-designed lighter which has 83 separate uses, including such items as being a derringer, two-way radio carrying across oceans, blowtorch, tear gas bomb, dart gun, you-name-it. He also has a one-man jet which orbits him in no time at all to Marseilles from the U.S. in search of a certain bouillabaisse which is a key to the assignment on hand.

This assignment comes to him when three mad scientists threaten the safety of the world by controlling the weather, and he's selected by ZOWIE (Zonal Organization on World Intelligence Espionage) as the one man alive who can ferret them out before their plan can put their final threatened plan into work. He doesn't need any organization behind him to assist him; he's the independent type, and goes his way alone, which leads to action that would be any stuntman's dream. Coburn seems to thrive on physical exertion, of the Karate kind, and script by Hal Fimberg and Don Starr tosses him into one situation after another where his ability to remain alive is no less than miraculous (courtesy of Fimberg's original story). Daniel Mann's direction is artful and thorough in realizing the full possibilties of his assignment.

For the most part, unfoldment is straightforward as Flint battles the wiles of a beautiful agent of Galaxy, organization beamed on world conquest, and efforts of other less lovely specimens of the underworld to write his name in the obituary columns. He's nearly blown to bits in a Marseilles bistro, imprisoned in a steel vault from which he escapes by using his trusty cig lighter.

Coburn plays with tongue-in-cheek seriousness. Character he portrays might make Bond blush for shame — Flint not only has four lovelies around his palatial N.Y. penthouse who shave, dress and otherwise take care of his wants, but a huge leaf-shaped bed built for five. Quartet — Shelby Grant, Gianna Serra, Helen Funai and Sigrid Valdis — figure in plot as well; they're kidnapped by Galaxy and Flint is faced with rescuing them from the island while destroying the elaborate setup which controls the weather. They're nice to look at.

Starring with Coburn is Lee J. Cobb, who has a field day as the exasperated American rep and head of ZOWIE who cannot keep Flint in line according to recognized standards for espionage, Gila Golan, Israeli actress borrowed from Columbia, serves as smart dressing as the Galaxy agent, a looker who could charm any counter-agent, and Edward Mulhare plays a suave but lethal Englishman who works with Miss Golan. Michael St. Clair is effective as a deadly would-be assassin whom Flint kills in an exciting washroom fight. The three scientists—Benson Fong, Rhys Williams and Peter Brocco—lend added menace.

Production has been expensively and handsomely mounted and Jerry Goldsmith's music score gives action terrific backing. Outstanding credit goes to Daniel L. Fapp for his color photography; Jack Martin Smith and Ed Graves for imaginative art direction; William Reynolds for expert editng. Nod also goes to Fred Harpman as production illustrator; L.B. Abbott, Howard Lydecker and Emil Kosa Jr., for special photographic effects; and Buzz Henry for special action sequences. *Whit.*

Wild, Wild Winter
(SONGS-TECHNISCOPE-COLOR)

Okay entry for youth market with flock of rock singers to bally.

Hollywood, Dec. 30.

Universal release of Patton - Weinrib (Bart Patton) production. Stars Gary Clarke, Chris Noel; features Steve Franken, Don Edmonds, Suzie Kaye, Les Brown Jr., Vicky Albright, Steve Rogers, Jim Wellman, Jay and The Americans, Beau Brummels, Dick & De Dee, The Astronauts, Jackie & Gayle. Directed by Lennie Weinrib. Screenplay, David Malcolm; camera (Technicolor), Frank Phillps; music, Jerry Long; editor, Jack Woods; asst. director, Thomas J. Schmidt. Reviewed at Universal Studios, Dec. 29, '65. Running Time, 80 MINS.

Ronnie	Gary Clarke
Susan	Chris Noel
John	Steve Franken
Burt	Don Edmonds
Sandy	Suzie Kaye
Perry	Les Brown Jr.
Dot	Vicky Albright
Benton	Steve Rogers
Dean	Jim Wellman
Fox	Val Avery
Stone	James Frawley
Rilk	Dick Miller
Danny	Mark Sturges
Bus Bit Girl	Anna Lavelle
Trisha	Linda Rogers
Jake McCloskey	Fred Festinger
McGee	Buck Holland
Bob	Darryl Vaughan
The Bear	Loren James
Larry	Paul Geary

Designed primarily for today's youth market, "Wild, Wild Winter" packs enough salable ingredients to be an okay entry for situations which like music with their entertainment. For marquee dressing, such rock singers as the Beau Brummels and Dick & Dee Dee, among other pop groups, should attract and the college setting, where major activities are skiing and romance, is ideal for this type of offering.

Producer Bart Patton and director Lennie Weinrib, under whose banner Techicolor pic was turned out for Universal release, have given satisfactory production mounting to film costarring Gary Clarke and Chris Noel. To whet eye appeal, a bevy of Bikini-clad babes prance on the Malibu beach, and another set of youthful pulchritude supplants them for the snow and college sequences where most of action unfolds.

Script by David Malcolm, thin and routine, concerns the efforts of members of a fraternity to thaw the standoffish attitude of a flock of sorority sisters who follow the lead of one of them who thinks men should neither be trusted nor dated. They send for a Malibu beach bum who has a reputation with women to work on femme, figuring if she can be humanized the other girls wil follow suit. It's a corncrop from here on in.

Gary Clarke handles himself well as the newcomer who poses as the son of a Hawaii millionaire, and Chris Noel is prettily effective in the hands-off department. Don Edmonds and Les Brown Jr., are the brothers who send for Clarke, Steve Franken as captain of the ski team and Miss Noel's prissy fiance, Suzie Kay and Vicky Albright, couple of college cuties and Jim Wellman, the dean faced with his college going into bankruptcy, are assets.

In addition to the two above-mentioned musical combos, Jackie & Gaye, The Astronauts and Jay & the Americans belt out typical r-r numbers.

Lennie Weinrib's direction nicely balances the action, and Jack Woods' editing is fast. Jerry Long's music is another plus, as is Frank Phillips' photography. *Whit.*

Judith
(PANAVISION—COLOR)

Sophia Loren in Israeli adventure yarn; strong b.o. prospects.

Hollywood, Jan. 7.

Paramount release of Kurt Unger production. Stars Sophia Loren; features Peter Finch, Jack Hawkins. Directed by Daniel Mann. Screenplay, John Michael Hayes; from story by Lawrence Durrell; camera (Technicolor), John Wilcox; music, Sol Kaplan; asst. directors, Gerry O'Hara, Yoel Silberg, Ivan Lengyel. Reviewed at Paramount Studios, Jan. 6, '66. Running Time, 105 MINS.

Judith	Sophia Loren
Aaron Stein	Peter Finch
Major Lawton	Jack Hawkins
Gustav Schiller	Hans Verner
Rachel	Zharira Charifai
Nathan	Shraga Friedman
Chaim	Andre Morell
Elie	Frank Wolff
Interrogator	Arnaldo Foa
Yaneck	Joseph Gross
Zeev	Roger Beaumont
Hannah	Zipora Peled
Lieutenant Carstairs	Terence Alexander
Dubin	Gilad Konstantiner
Arab Guide	Daniel Ocko
Aba	Roland Bartrop
Conklin	Peter Burton
Researcher	John Stacy

Israel in its birth pains backdrops this frequently-tenseful adventure tale realistically produced in its actual locale. The Kurt Unger production, beautifully caught in Panavision and Technicolor, combines a moving story with interesting, unfamiliar characters and the package emerges as strong entertainment both for general audiences and those with a flair for excitement.

Actually, the John Michael Hayes screenplay, based on an original by Lawrence Durrell, is two-pronged: the story of Sophia Loren, as the Jewish ex-wife of a Nazi war criminal who betrayed her and sent her to Dachau, intent upon finding him and wreaking her own brand of vengeance, and the efforts of the Haganah, Israel's underground army, to capture him. Formerly a tank expert with Hitler's Afrika Corps, this man now is helping the various Arab countries surrounding Israel to prepare for invasion of the new state. By seizing him, the Israelis hope to learn their enemies' strength and exact points of proposed attacks.

Under Daniel Mann's forceful direction, the two points are fused as femme finds herself obliged to throw in with the Israelis, who use her to track down the man they know is in the Middle East but do not know how to identify him. Unfoldment brings various fascinating highlights, one in particular the Israelis helping a shipload of illegal immigrants slip into the country by night under the very eyes of the British, who operate the country until the end of their mandate. Historical overtones of 1948, when this mandate was concluded, are woven tightly into the human story which shows a new national striving for independence, with most of action taking place in a kibbutz, a communal settlement in which all members share the labor and rewards.

Miss Loren, beautifully photogrpahed and sometimes fetchingly garbed, is excellent, turning here to a dramatic role from the light comedies in which she has lately appeared. It is a colorful role for her, particularly in her recollections of the young son she thought murdered until the Nazi finally captured, tells her he is still alive. Film winds on an uncertain note—former husband is killed before he reveals boy's whereabouts, but the kibbutz leader, Peter Finch, and one of the Haganah, assures her he'll be found.

Finch registers effectively and creates an indelible impression of what Israeli leaders accomplished in setting up their own state. As a British major, in charge of the area in which Finch's kibbutz is located and sentimentally inclined both toward the Israelis in overlooking their possession of guns, and Miss Loren, to whom he turns over the file on the Nazi, Jack Hawkins again portrays one of those rugged Englishmen in arms. Hans Verner is strongly cast in Nazi character, briefly seen but still outstanding.

Scoring in support are Zharira Charifai, nurse in the kibbutz, and such kibbutzniks as Shraga Friedman, Andre Morell, Frank Wolff, Arnaldo Foa.

Unger lined up an unusually competent array of technical aides. John Wilcox' photography is a particular asset, as are Wilfrid Shingleton's production designing, Sol Kaplan's music score, Peter Taylor's fluid editing. Special effects by Cliff Richardson and Roy Whybrow in the battle scenes between the attacking Syrians and Israelis often are spectacular, and Nicholas Roeg is credited with second unit direction and additional photography. *Whit.*

Rat Fink
(WIDESCREEN)

Hard-hitting story of a young man on the make for rock 'n roll fame introduces Schuyler Hayden, who brings a pulsating realism to this fast-paced, often - shocking psychopathic study.

Cinema Distributors of America presentation of a Genesis (Lewis Andrews) production. Stars Schuyler Hayden, Hal Bokar, Warrene Ott and Judy Hughes; features Don Snyder, Eve Brenner, Alice Rainheardt, Jack Lester. (No character list.) Director - script, James Landis; original story, Matt Cheney; camera, William Zsigmond; editor, Tom Boutross; music, Ronald Stein; assistant director, Hank Sheldon. Reviewed at Joe Shore Screening Room, Hollywood, Dec. 30, '65. Running Time, 80 MINS.

A remarkably effective low-budget film, "Rat Fink" suffers from only one thing, its title. It's apparent from this fact that distributor has decided to pitch pic for the teenage market, but this dandy little psychological drama deserves a wider showing and could well make it with the art houses if properly handled. Neatly and intelligently constructed, story is solid, technical aspects first rate and acting in all instances surprisingly convincing.

Yet "Fink" in the last analysis depends on actor Schuyler Hayden who is in almost every frame and who sustains an underpinning of title role with a rare and real acting ability. The first film role for the 24-year-old unknown actor, (he is reported to have personally put up a substantial amount of the $20,000 budget) he comes across with total believability as the King Rat Fink of them all who claws his way to the top as a rock 'roll singer.

He has a nice boyish smile that grates on the viewer since he is true-blue no good. Pic opens with him seducing a rural older woman and then cutting out with her purse money. In quick, successive steps he works his way to the Hollywood office of r&r manager and coldly calculates his way to overnight success as Mr. Big.

It's certainly not an uncommon plot but the style is brisk, often abrupt and totally unsentimental.

Camera work captures restless mood and inner anguish of a young man who "wants what he wants and aims to get it." Tom Boutross' editing also contributes to a mood of a man caged in by his own supreme ego. Music score by Ronald Stein also confines itself to atmosphere of the moment.

As the singer's manager, Hal Bokar doesn't have much demanded of him but does nicely with what he has; ditto for Warrene Ott, who play his wife, and Judy Hughes, as the teenager who gets in singer's way, has a natural and memorable charm.

James Landis' direction borrows a few pointers from others but he uses them to build a swiftly paced, often shocking story. He cleverly avoids the more brutal moments of seductions and murders by either panning away from the action or cutting them entirely. It is the rush of implicitly known events that gives the pic its suspenseful vertigo.

A balcony death scuffle between singer and manager's wife is frugally filmed for fierce impact; a drunk driving sequence and other montages manage the same. Wild beach sand parties are actually populated with kook beach types, and teenager at vet's for an abortion stands briefly before towering array of caged animals, and one immediately feels her anguish.

Production sets by Danny Toledo give pic an expensive look and pop songs introduced are above the screaming type and pic could well take its title from "My Soul Runs Naked," which in a way is what it is all about, and title under which it was made.

Screenplay by Landis never gets off its hard-hitting tract and dialogue is crisp, but it remains for Hayden to make it come to life and he does in what is one of the best hunks of acting by an unknown actor to be viewed in years. *Dool.*

Un Milliard Dans Un Billard
(A Million in a Billiard Table)
(FRENCH—COLOR)

Paris, Jan. 4.
Comacico release of Films Copernic-Atlas Films production. Stars Jean Seberg; features Claude Rich, Pierre Vernier, Elsa Martinelli, Elisabeth Flickenschild, Gunther Ungeheuer. Directed by Nicolas Gessner. Screenplay, Charles Spaak, Gessner; camera (Eastmancolor), Claude Leonte; editor, Jean Michel Gautier. At the Paris, Paris. Running Time, 95 MINS.

Bettina .... Jean Seberg
Bernard .... Claude Rich
Juliette .... Elsa Martinelli
Blondin .... Elisabeth Flickenschild

What hath Bond wrought? It seems like most French pix, even including the better ones, have some undercover, gangster or police angles these days. This one mixes gadgetry with a situation comedy format. Pic is too torpid and diffuse to come off and remains a fair entry for playoff and dualers in foreign climes with an added boost via the Jean Seberg name.

New director Nicolas Gessner lacks the comic punch or romantic elan. Result is that this plods most of the way despite a cast of

some charming players, nice color and a good, if familiar, story. Film is about a newcomer trying for one big robbery and how he outwits some pros. Happy ending smooth things out.

Claude Rich is the amateur who meets notorious thief Jean Seberg whose mother runs the gang. He lets them go through with a job, after finding out about it from her, and then he cops the swag. But he gives it all back for the insurance money.

Miss Serberg is highly photogenic and walks through her role with ease with Rich a good foil. Others are okay in this pic that just misses. *Mosk.*

The Ghost And Mr. Chicken
(COLOR-SCOPE)

Okay mystery - comedy. Don Knotts, established in tv, is sole marquee lure. Good bet for dual bills.

Hollywood, Jan. 8.
Universal Pictures release of an Edward J. Montagne production. Features Don Knotts. Directed by Alan Rafkin. Screenplay, James Fritzell, Everett Greenbaum; camera (Technicolor, Techniscope), William Margulies; editor, Sam E. Waxman; music, Vic Mizzy; asst. director, Phil Bowles. Reviewed at Pacific Picwood, West L.A., Jan. 7, '65. Running Time, 89 MINS.

Luther Heggs .... Don Knotts
Alma .... Joan Staley
Kelsey .... Liam Redmond
Beckett .... Dick Sargent
Ollie .... Skip Homeier
Mrs. Maxwell .... Reta Shaw
Mrs. Miller .... Lurene Tuttle
Simmons .... Phil Ober
Police Chief Fuller....... Harry Hickox
Whitlow .... Charles Lane
Mrs. Hutchinson .... Jesslyn Fax
Mrs. Cobb .... Nydia Westman
Judge .... George Chandler
Springer .... Robert Cornthwaite
Herkie .... James Begg
Loretta Pine .... Sandra Gould
Mr. Maxwell .... James Millhollin
Bailiff .... Cliff Norton
Miss Tremaine .... Ellen Corby
Billy Ray .... Jim Boles

"The Ghost And Mr. Chicken" is a silly, often funny, and entertaining mystery-comedy programmer tailored for the talents of Don Knotts, playing the rural tyro reporter whom nobody believes until . . . etc. Formula scripting is enhanced by generally good performances and direction. Lowbudget, but most money gets on the screen. Edward J. Montagne production will please Knotts fans, young and old. The particular type situation will dictate where Universal should spot it on a dual bill.

The James Fritzell - Everett Greenbaum script has a few sophisticated licks, but generally sticks to the homespun and predictable. Knotts is solo-featured (after title) as the bumbling typesetter, enamored of Joan Staley, girl friend of reporter Skip Homeier. Making good for Kansas town publisher Dick Sargent forces Knotts to prove that what he wrote was what he actually saw in Phil Ober's haunted house.

The first reel drags somewhat in its establishment of character, but just before the change, sympathetic but mysterious janitor Liam Redmond telegraphs part of the actual climax. In the meantime, remainder of large supporting cast serves as a backdrop for Knotts' facial and vocal antics.

Banker James Millhollin, henpecked by wife Reta Shaw, who's hung up on seances, landlady Lurene Tuttle and boarders Jesslyn Fax and Nydia Westman, lawyers Charles Lane and Robert Cornthwaite, judge George Chandler and vet teacher Ellen Corby offer good bits.

A nutty cop played by James Begg draws some big laffs to match Knotts' high points, also a sound - track "atta - boy" voice which is used with effective and surprising restraint. Unbilled for some reason, certainly not the length of the parts which at least matches the others, are J. Edward McKinley, the pompous mayor, and Eddie Quillan, a goofy elevator operator. Quillan appeared in many Universal programmers of two decades back, of which this one is strongly reminiscent, and he can still score.

Alan Rafkin's direction capably builds the pace after a slow start, and William Margulies' crisp Technicolor- - Techniscope lensing is a big assist. Of the younger players, Miss Staley's dimpled cheek, pleasant voice and expressive eyes promise more for the future. So does Rafkin's direction.

Vic Mizzy's score catches the mood and is a big plus value. Sam E. Waxman edited to 89 minutes, a bit too long, but his use of various types of transition is fine. The Cinefx titles hold the eye, and other technical credits are professional.

Tacked on at the end (after closing credits) is a plug for the Universal studio tour which reportedly has been standard for some months on release prints. Certain urban situations may prefer to kill the promo. *Murf.*

Le Bestaire D'Amour
(The Lair of Love)
(FRENCH—DOCUMENTARY—COLOR)

Paris Jan. 4.
Films De La Pleiade production and release. Directed by Gerald Calderon. Screenplay, Jean-Claude Cariere from book by Jean Rostand; commentary by Bertrand Poirot-Delpech spoken by Serge Reggiani, Nadine Alari, Rostand; camera (Eastmancolor), Jacques Duhamel, Jean-Louis Baucle; editor, Marguerite Renoir; music. Georges Delerue. Running Time, 70 MINS.

Nothing but lovemaking in this documentary from the lowest forms of animals to the highest, excluding man himself. Not a sexploiter but a sound, meticulously made and yet visually taking film. This should be a worthwhile supporting item for some arty spots or for more specialized use as well as in schools.

Based on a book by scientist Jean Rostand, Gerald Calderon has obtained some stunning imagery in the sex gyrations. Commentary is lucid and coherent. Fine editing also rates a nod in getting the most from several scenes. Man is noted as advancing to scientific attitudes towards sex that are seen often in animal forms.

This is one of those unique offbeat scientific documentaries with theatrical chances. *Mosk.*

Apache Uprising
(COLOR-TECHNISCOPE)

Fair lowercase oater shot down by dull story. Vet thesps offer some marquee lure.

Hollywood, Dec. 28.
Paramount Pictures release of A. C. Lyles production. Stars Rory Calhoun, Corinne Calvet, John Russell, Lon Chaney; features Gene Evans, Richard Arlen, Robert H. Harris, Arthur Hunnicutt, DeForest Kelley, George Chandler, Jean Parker, Johnny Mack Brown. Directed by R. G. Springsteen. Screenplay, Harry Sanford, Max Lamb, based on novel "Way Station" by Sanford, Max Steeber; camera (Technicolor), W. Wallace Kelley; editor, John Schreyer; music, Jimmie Haskell; asst. director, Dale Coleman. Reviewed at Paramount Studios, Dec. 27, '65. Running Time, 90 MINS.

Jim Walker	Rory Calhoun
Janice MacKenzie	Corinne Calvet
Vance Buckner	John Russell
Charlie Russell	Lon Chaney
Jess Cooney	Gene Evans
Capt. Gannon	Richard Arlen
Hoyt Taylor	Robert H. Harris
Bill Gibson	Arthur Hunnicutt
Toby Jack Saunders	DeForest Kelley
Jace Asher	George Chandler
Mrs. Hawkes	Jean Parker
Sheriff Ben Hall	Johnny Mack Brown
Henry Belden	Donald Barry
Young Apache	Abel Fernandez
Chico Lopez	Robert Carricart
Old Antone	Paul Daniel

"Apache Uprising" doesn't get much beyond het suggestion of large scale action, and the A. C. Lyles production emerges as a somewhat dull oater. Some vet thesps in switcheroo roles can help the sell, but propects look only fair for lowercase Paramount release.

The Harry Sanford-Marx Lamb script, based on novel "Way Station" by Sanford and Max Steeber, takes over a reel to get to the point. A stagecoach, bearing a woman-with-a-past, a vicious gunfighter and pal, a typical oater riding shotgun, and a corrupt stage line exec who is in cahoots with a criminal, arrives at a relay station where the gold theft plot is foiled and the proper people die. Dullsville dialog seems to pad the action and slow pace.

The players are up to script demands, including hero Rory Calhoun, and Corinne Calvet returns to pix as the shady lady who really isn't. Offbeat casting has John Russell as the mastermind criminal, Johnny Mack Brown as a sheriff who tries to put the make on Miss Calvet, and Lon Chaney as a jolly stage driver.

DeForest Kelley is good as the paranoid gunfighter who is shot down by the script long before a few Apaches nail him with an arrow. Gene Evans is very good as Kelley's sidekick. Richard Arlen plays a U.S. Cavalry officer who doubts Calhoun's fear of Indian trouble, a plot angle that fizzes out. Robert H. Harris has a good role as the fussy stage exec who is on the gold theft scheme. Arthur Hunnicutt makes the most of the grizzled scout part. Other players are adequate in stock characterizations.

The Lyles oaters all well-produced, and this is no exception. W. Wallace Kelley's crisp Techniscope-Technicolor camera maintains visual interest in the solid Paramount production elements. Jimmie Haskell's score is a big asset. But the story negates all these plus values.

John Schreyer's editing to 90 minutes is sluggish. Pic is half over before the stage starts its journey, and the inevitable climax is occasionally enlivened only by exactly how various people will die. Plot emphasis on one interior set and talky expo of ancient history make the affair a drag. Lyles has done better. *Murf.*

Lord Love a Duck

Hilarious entry for current way-out cycle; carries rich exploitation.

Hollywood, Jan. 14.
United Artists release of Charleston Enterprises (George Axelrod) production. Stars Roddy McDowall, Tuesday Weld, Lola Albright, Martin West, Ruth Gordon; features Harvey Korman, Lynn Carey, Howard Showalter, Martin Gabel, Donald Murphy. Directed by Axelrod. Screenplay, Larry H. Johnson, Axelrod; based on novel by Al Hine; camera, Daniel L. Fapp; music, Neal Hefti; editor, William A. Lyon; asst. director, Herman Webber. Reviewed at Samuel Goldwyn Studios, Jan. 13, '66. Running Time, 105 MINS.

Alan Musgrave	Roddy McDowall
Barbara Ann Greene	Tuesday Weld
Marie Greene	Lola Albright
Bob Barnard	Martin West
Stella Barnard	Ruth Gordon
Weldon Emmett	Harvey Korman
Miss Schwartz	Sarah Marshall
Sally Grace	Lynn Carey
Howard Greene	Max Showalter
Phil Neuhauser	Donald Murphy
Mrs. Butch Neuhauser	Judith Loomis
Dr. Lippman	Joseph Mell
Used Car Salesman	Dan Frazer
Inez	Martine Bartlett
Kitten	Jo Collins
Harry Belmont	Martin Gabel

Some may call George Axelrod's "Lord Love a Duck" satire, others way-out comedy, still others brilliant, while there may be some who ask, what's it all about. Somewhere in this wide breach lies the clue, dependent upon the viewer, but in this day when such offbeat effusions as "What's New Pussycat?" "Cat Ballou" and "The Loved One" are doing boff biz—and "Duck" fits into this category—it should reach its mark.

Whatever the reaction, there is no question that the film is packed with laughs, often of the truest anatomical kind, and there is a veneer of sophistication which keeps showing despite the most outlandish goings-on. Sometimes it would appear that Axelrod, in his thinking, had an over-exposure of the current crop of Bikini pix, but as the picture takes form there's no denying that some of the comedy is inspirational, a gagman's dream come true, and there is bite in some of Axelrod's social commentary beneath the wonderful nonsense.

The characters are everything here, each developed brightly along zany lines, topped by Roddy McDowall as a Svengali-type high school student leader who pulls the strings on the destiny of Tuesday Weld, an ingenuish-type sexpot whose philosophy is wrapped up in her words "Everybody's got to love me." His I.Q. is so high he knows what's in everybody's mind before they even speak.

He puts this handily little built-in gimmick to work as he makes possible all Tuesday's wishes, including 13 cashmere sweaters, a Balboa beach holiday, romance and ultimate marriage to the man of her choice and finally her goal as a movie star. Sometimes he'ls almost a mystic. But the spectator shouldn't inquire too sharply into some of the action, which may leave you on the confused end . . . if you care.

McDowall probably turns in the best performance of his career as the mastermind of the school, and he has a strong contender for interest in blonde Miss Weld in a characterization warm and appealing. Scoring almost spectactularly is Lola Albright as Tuesday's mother, a wack cocktail bar "bunny" who commits suicide when she thinks she's ruined her daughter's chances for marriage.

In these latter sequences the story becomes serious, but not for long, as Axelrod focuses on Martin West, the rich boy Tuesday weds, and his mother, Ruth Gordon. Miss Gordon provides one of the season's gemlike performances in an insane character who also becomes spellbound by McDowall's hypnotic influence, and West makes the most of his lunk inpersonation. He suffers, as does the picture, from forced comedy in the closing reel, when McDowall chases him with a bulldozer.

Standouts, too, in brief roles, are Harvey Korman, as the school principal who gives Tuesday a job as part-time secretary when she applies clad in a "Midnight a go-go" sweater; Max Showalter, femme's divorced father; Martin Gabel, the producer who "finds" Tuesday. Donald Murphy has some good moments as a minister who conducts a sex seminar, and also operates his own drive-in church, and Jo Collins might be Miss Bikini of 1970 as a fading starlet. Sarah Marshall makes the most of a psychiatrist role, as does Joseph Mell as a doctor and Lynn Carey in girlie role.

Axelrod, directing from a script in which he collabed with Larry H. Johnson (based on novel by Al Hine), never misses a trick in making the utmost of a situation. Sometimes there isn't any situation, merely a flock of beach lovelies in their scantiest, but otherwise Axelrod accomplishes good theatre. He has benefit of expert technical assistance, including Daniel L. Fapp's fluid lensing, Neal Hefti's most suitable music score, and Malcolm Brown's attractive art direction. William A. Lyon's editing fits the pattern of picture, and The Wild Ones chirp title song (lyrics, Ernie Sheldon) over the credits.

Mood of pic is set through clever stop-camera footage as it opens smartly. *Whit.*

The Money Trap
(PANAVISION)

Dreary con-gone-bad meller, inently written, acted and directed. Fair marquee lure for lowercase playing time.

Hollywood, Jan. 13.
Metro-Goldwyn-Mayer release of Max E. Youngstein Production, produced by Youngstein, David Karr. Stars Glenn Ford, Elke Sommer, Rita Hayworth, Ricardo Montalban, Joseph Cotten; features Tom Reese, James Mitchum, Argentina Brunetti, Fred Essler, Eugene Iglesias, Teri Lynn Sandoval. Directed by Burt Kennedy. Screenplay, Walter Bernstein, based on the novel by Lionel White; camera, Paul C. Vogel; editor, John McSweeney; music, Hal Schaefer; asst. director, Hank Monjiean. Reviewed at Stanley Warner's Wiltern Theatre, L.A., Jan. 12, '66. Running Time, 91 MINS.

Joe Baron	Glenn Ford
Lisa Baron	Elke Sommer
Rosalie Kenny	Rita Hayworth
Pete Delanos	Ricardo Montalban
Dr. Horace Van Tilden	Joseph Cotten
Matthews	Tom Reese
Detective Wolski	James Mitchum
Aunt	Argentina Brunetti
Mr. Klein	Fred Essler
Father	Eugene Iglesias

Daughter .... Terri Lynn Sandoval
——

A story of a policeman-turned-thief, "The Money Trap" is aptly named—but only as far as production coin is concerned. A cliche-plotted, tritely written script that is not to be believed could not be salvaged even by far better direction and performances than are evident in this routine Max E. Youngstein production. Some fair marquee bait, but the Metro release is headed for quick lower-casing.

Walter Bernstein's adaptation of a Lionell White novel has the kernel of a good drama about a contemporary problem, that of an underpaid gumshoe dazzled into dishonesty by the riches of the criminals whom he encounters. With the exception of some unwanted laughs from the audience at the preview, nearly all interest in this angle is snuffed out by extraneous, unbelievable subplots.

Specifically, Glenn Ford is the cop, husband of Elke Sommer (who appears in one revealing costume after another, her sole contribution to the pic). They live in a splashy pad made possible by her father's will and stocks. When the latter pass a divvy, hard times loom. Wife's idea to economize: fire the servants.

Ricardo Montalban is Ford's working partner, and, as film opens, they're hunting a man who has killed his wife for working in a brothel—to get money for their kid. Why was she hustling? They were Mexican-Americans, couldn't get a decent job, etc. This angle accounts for several needless minutes.

Add Joseph Cotten, a medic who supposedly works for the Syndicate. When he kills a junkie accomplice and reports it as self-defense from a supposed burglary, Ford gets the theft idea, keeps it from Montalban (who later finds out and wants in). Widow of the unbilled junkie is Rita Hayworth, a gin mill hash-slinger who—are you ready?—turns out to be an old girl friend of Ford. She is eventually murdered by Cotten's leg man.

The story creaks along to its eventual, predictable climax after a distressingly long 91 minutes. All thesps are shot down by their lines, their own acting, and the pedestrian direction of Burt Kennedy.

Picture might be helped if editor John McSweeney trimmed about 15 minutes from it. Technical credits are all good. Hal Schaefer's music has the modern sound, and, combined with the abbreviated opening credits, gets film off to a good start for a few minutes. David Karr and Youngstein produced. *Murf.*

The Great Wall
(JAPANESE—COLOR)

Lavishly-produced but ponderous adventure yarn with historic overtones; okay for double bills.

———

Hollywood, Jan. 12.

Magna release of Daiei (Masaichi Nagata) production. Stars Shintaro Katsu, Fujiko Yamamoto; Ken Utsui; features Hiroshi Kawaguchi, Ayako Wakao, Kohiro Hongo, Raizo Ichikawa, Ganjiro Makamura. Directed by Shigeo Tanaka;

Screenplay, Fuji Yahiro; camera (Technicolor), Machio Takahashi; music, Akira Ifukube. Reviewed at Academy Theatre, Jan. 12, '66. Running Time, 108 MINS.

———

"The Great Wall," story of the building of China's ancient barrier, is a lavishly-produced Japanese adventure melodrama with English dialog (dubbed) which has certain merit but becomes frequently ponderous and is over-lengthy. Historically, it has much to offer in focusing upon the great accomplishment of China's first emperor and for double bills rates as an okay entry.

Spectacle plays an important place here, both in the battle scenes in which thousands of soldiers appear and in the actual construction of the wall, which history records took more than a million lives. As the visionary emperor who welds the Chinese together for the first time, Shintaro Katsu is impressive, although occasionally his gruff tones are difficult to understand.

Fujiko Yamamoto is lovely as his bride who first tries to kill him for the death of her father, ordered by the monarch, and Ken Utsui scores as an enemy prince. A particular standout is Ayako Wakao as another bride.

Shigeo Tanaka's direction is expert and forceful and Machio Takahashi's color lensing is beautiful at times. *Whit.*

Dracula—Prince Of Darkness
(BRITISH-COLOR)

———

Well produced and mildly horrific entry from the Hammer stable; production values sometimes slipshod, but should do okay in its particular market.

———

London, Jan. 18.

Warner-Pathe release of a Hammer Production presented by Associated British-Pathe. Stars Christopher Lee, Barbara Shelley, Suzan Farmer, Charles Tingwell, Francis Matthews. Features Thorley Walters, Andrew Keir. Produced by Anthony Nelson-Keys. Directed by Terence Fisher. Screenplay, John Samson from an idea by John Elder based on Bram Stoker's characters; editor, Chris Barnes; camera (Technicolor), Michael Reed; sound, Roy Baker; music, James; Bernard special effects, Bowie Films Ltd. Reviewed at Warner Theatre, London. Running Time, 90 MINS.
Dracula .... Christopher Lee
Helen .... Barbara Shelley
Father Sandor ...... Andrew Keir
Charles .... Francis Matthews
Diana .... Suzan Farmer
Alan .... Charles Tingwell
Ludwig .... Thorley Walters
Klove .... Philip Latham
Brother Mark .... Walter Brown
Landlord ...... George Woodbridge
Brother Peter .... Jack Lambert
Priest .... Philip Ray
Mother .... Joyce Hemson
Coach Driver .... John Maxim

———

Dracula has been a film standby for years and Hammer's latest entry, "Dracula—Prince of Darkness," should please the following of this type of film and do all right at the wickets. Terence Fisher has directed it with his usual knowhow and the screenplay by John Samson is a workmanlike job which provides a useful number of mild thrills and little enough of the misplaced yocks that sometimes creep into this sort of pic.

The last Dracula film had the vampire count dead through crumbling into ashes but bringing the creature back to life presents little difficulty to a Hammer scriptist. Four inquisitive tourists are lured to Castle Dracula, met by a sinister butler and invited to dinner and to stay the night. The four treat this strange hospitality with incredibly bland acceptance. One of them (Charles Tingwell), wandering the castle at night, is killed and his blood used to reinfuse life into the Dracula ashes. Dracula then plunges his fangs into the neck of the corpse's wife, turning her into a vampire and the two are then arrayed against the other pair in the party. Of course, Right prevails over Evil. With the help of a cleric the two survivors manage to bump off Dracula in the nick of time—this time by drowning. But there's little evidence to show that this profitable boxoffice property has disappeared forever.

This simple yarn is played reasonably straight and the main snag is that the thrills are mainly ——————— in and do not arise sufficiently smooth out of atmosphere. After a slowish start some climate of eeriness is evoked but more shadows, suspense and suggestion would have helped. Christopher Lee, an old hand at the horror business, makes a latish appearance but dominates the film enough without dialog. Barbara Shelley, a beautiful and much underrated actress, who appears to be trapped in the horror business, makes a spirited vampire and Andrew Keir, Francis Matthews, Charles Tingwell, Suzan Farmer and others provide useful aid. This film has apparently cost rather more than its predecesssors and its color, sound and lensing are invariably okay. Pity that more care has not been given to cutwork values. The castle in the background is always the same back projected view. Typical British foliage has to make do also in Carpathia, and so on. But when Dracula's on the prowl at night (it's never quite nocturnal enough) the less pernickety audiences will not worry overmuch about such blemishes. *Rich.*

Kid Rodelo

———

Amateurish western filmed in Spain with American cast toppers; adequate for kiddie matinees.

———

Hollywood, Jan. 5.

Paramount release of Trident Films Inc. and Fenix Films (Jack O. Lamont and James J. Storrow Jr.) production. Features Don Murray, Janet Leigh, Broderick Crawford, Richard Carlson. Directed by Carlson. Screenplay, Jack Natteford; from story by Louis L'Amour; camera, Manuel Mering; music, Johnny Douglas; editor, Allan Morrison. Reviewed at Paramount Studios, Jan. 4, '66. Running Time, 91 MINS.
Kid Rodelo .... Don Murray
Nora .... Janet Leigh
Joe Harbin .... Broderick Crawford
Link .... Richard Carlson
Thomas Reese .... Jose Nieto
Balsas .... Julio Pena
Chavas .... Miguel Del Castillo
Cavalry Hat .... Jose Villa Sante
Gopher .... Alfonso San Felix
Warden .... Emilio Rodriguez
Perryman .... Fernando Hilbeck
The Doctor .... Roberto Rubenstein
Guard .... Billy Christmas

———

A juvenile oater, with a 10-gallon hatful of cliches, this made-in-Spain pic has little to recommend it except, perhaps, a primitive sense of improvisation. Name American cast appear not to be very serious about what they are doing and thus ham it up heavily. Script, on the other hand, is deadly, gunning down actors one-by-one, between situations that run gamut from corny to contrived.

Don Murray, as the Kid, is out of jail to get the gold hiked by fellow prisoners Broderick Crawford and Richard Carlson. Three others, including Janet Leigh, have the same idea, and by turns and spins, the rivaling groups pursue each other. There are also Indians in pursuit, and they ride beautiful horses.

Murray somewhere along the line loses his drawl, while Miss Leigh looks continually startled and Crawford grimaces and groans every chance he gets. Spanish actor Julio Pena actually appears to enjoy his work but the script by Jack Natteford doesn't allow him any dimension either.

Actor-director Carlson doesn't succeed in either role. Manuel Mering's photography captures the aridity of the Spanish landscape somberly, and background guitar music by Johnny Douglas is interesting but too repetitious.

Pic lists five producers: one exec. two associates and two other producers. It's apparent that there were many fingers in this goulash. For the kiddie matinees it will no doubt adequately fill the bottom of the bill. *Dool.*

Fantomas Se Dechaine
(Fantomas Tears Loose)
(FRENCH-COLOR)

Paris, Jan. 11.

Gaumont release of Gaumont International - PAC - Victory Film production. Stars Jean Marais, Louis De Funes, Mylene Demongeot; features Jacques Dynam, Robert Dalban, Olivier De Funes. Directed by Andre Hunebelle. Screenplay, Jean Halain, Pierre Foucaud from book by Pierre Souvestre and Marcel Allain; camera (Eastmancolor), Raymond Lemoigne; editor, Jean Feyte. At Ambassade-Gaumont, Paris. Running Time, 98 MINS.
Fandor, Fantomas........ Jean Marais
Juve .... Louis De Funes
Helene .... Mylene Demongeot

———

Sequel to a hit of two years ago, about an irascible, silly police inspector and an intrepid newsman against a master criminal out to rule the world, shapes up okay for local marts, with slimmer chances abroad except for playoff on some okay action stuff and production dress.

However, this lacks a real dynamic kick or the right note of parody with the lacklustre direction also a handicap. It is based on noted early 1900 stories that were made into popular pix episodes with the right mixture of derring-do. Updated, it now does not shape up to the Bond pix which it tried to ape.

Louis De Funes overdoes his dimwitted but relentless inspector while Jean Marais is dashing in the dual role of the reporter and the baleful underworld figure. Mylene Demongeot adds pert pulchritude to the yarn. Fantomas captures two scientists to make a weapon that will subjugate the world.

He is foiled but escapes thereby pointing to possibly more episodes.

Some gadgetry is okay, such as a car that turns into a plane, a pegleg that becomes a machine gun and loaded cigars that spray bullets. But this is not vintage in other ways and its mixture of old-style mistaken identity, since both Fantomas and the reporter are addicted to masks to impersonate others. And the slapstick only has this a routine effort but it should entice locals. *Mosk.*

Winnetou, Part III
(GERMAN-YUGOSLAV)
(Color)

Berlin, Jan. 11.
Constantin release of Rialto Film Preben Philipsen production, made in collab with Jadran Film, Zagreb. Stars Pierre Brice, Lex Barker; features Rik Battaglia, Sophie Hardy. Directed by Herald Reinl. Screenplay, Harald G. Petersson and Joachim Bartsch, based on novel by Karl May. Camera (Eastmancolor), Ernst W. Kalinke; music, Martin Boettcher; editor, Jutta Hering. At Zoo Palast, West Berlin. Running Time, **89 MINS.**

Old Shatterhand	Lex Barker
Winnetou	Pierre Brice
Rollins	Rik Battaglia
Sam Hawkens	Ralf Wolter
Governor	Carl Lange
Ann	Sophie Hardy

"Winnetou, Part III" puts an end to Winnetou that handsome, mild tooking chieftain of the Apaches gets shot in the 83d minute of this Rialto production. Remainder of the film is a tear-jerker for the many Winnetou fans. And never has one seen Old Shatterhand alias Lex Barker, Winnetou's lifelong friend, looking so serious on the screen.

There seems little doubt that this German-Yugoslav Karl May western will spell a lot of coin throughout the country. Also this one will sled into many foreign markets. Horst Wendlandt, the initiator and general supervisor of these Teutonic horse operas, has never had any complaints about their foreign sales.

The third and final part of the "Winnetou" films offers more fights, violence and blood than the previous Rialto productions. It gives clear evidence of the fact that the creators of this series have gained much knowhow about fisticuffs, saloon brawls and gunfights.

In brief, this shows once again Winnetou and his dear "white brother," Old Shatterhand, riding and fighting together versus vicious pale faces and ill-guided Indians. Winnetou knows that the white men and redskins could live peacefully together if there weren't those unscrupulous white settlers who try to squeeze the Indians out of their territory. Best of the good men, Winnetou, is killed by the meanest of them all. With the help of U.S. cavalry, the white evildoers are wiped out.

Frenchman Pierre Brice plays his Winnetou part in the manner which has made him an idolized screen hero with seemingly millions of native youngsters. Same goes for American Lex Barker who is "delightfully" robust with regard to handling his various opponents. Rik Battaglia scores as the prototype of an utterly vicious character in this pic. Ralf Wolter provides what is called "comedy relief." French Sophie Hardy contributes a bit of inevitable sex while Carl Lange turns in a competent portrayal of a justice-abiding American governor. Remainder of the cast, mainly composed of Yugoslav players, turn in okay performances.

Director Harald Reinl has found an appealing mixture of brutality, humor and sentiment which pleases large segments of the not too demanding Continental film patrons. He takes care that the whole thing remains very much on the romantic side. The beautiful Yugoslav landscapes help him. Ernst W. Kalinke's camerawork is very good.

One may wonder if Winneou is dead for the German screen. However, Karl May, even after the chieftain's death, wrote more novels dealing with the Apache chieftain's previous adventures. Hence, more Winnetou pix likely will be forthcoming. *Hans.*

The Big T-N-T Show

Wow poptune revue featuring 12 current teen faves. Big b.o. in the youth market.

Hollywood, Jan. 13.
American International Pictures release of a Henry G. Saperstein Production, executive producers James H. Nicholson, Samuel Z. Arkoff, Saperstein, produced by Phil Spector. Features Roger Miller, Joan Baez, Ray Charles and his Orchestra. Donovan, Petula Clark, The Byrds ,The Lovin' Spoonful, Ike and Tina Turner, The Modern Folk Quartet, The Ronettes, Bo Diddley, and guestar David McCallum. Directed by Larry Peerce. Camera, Robert Boatman; editors, Ronald Sinclair, Eve Newman; music coordinator, Spector; asst. director, Anthony Ray. Reviewed at Joe Shore's Screening Room, L.A., Jan. 12, '66. Running Time, **94 MINS.**

Featuring a mixed bag of poptune trends—blues, rock, folk, folk-rock and country music, "The Big T-N-T Show" spotlights 11 current personality acts, plus vidstar David McCallum, in a 94-minute songalog filmed before hundreds of screaming teeners at Hollywood's old Moulin Rouge nitery. The Henry G. Saperstein production, generally well-directed, has something for all teeners and many post-teeners. American International, which last year released the prototype "TAMI Show," will clean up in the youth market where much playing, and replaying, time is likely.

Director Larry Peerce has kept a neat pace by mixing up the tune styles, sometimes encoring an act in later reels to give the film more unity. McCallum, who makes an early entrance via okay gag reminiscent of his material on "The Man From U.N.C.L.E." vidseries, variously intros acts, conducts the Ray Charles band, and, on one occasion, pontificates too dramatically.

Roger Miller, Joan Baez, The Byrds, The Lovin' Spoonful, Charles (himself) Donovan, Petula Clark, The Ronettes, Bo Diddley, Ike and Tina Turner and The Modern Folk Quartet are spotted to good advantage throughout, singing the songs they made famous, as the saying goes.

Robert Boatman did a firstrate job as first cameraman, using facilities of Mark Armistead once called Electronovision (by William H. Sargent, who owns the handle), and now called Electrorama (but not so billed here). Pic is in 1.85:1 ratio, b&w, with a real live feel to the proceedings. Little distortion is evident in the electronic-film process.

Peerce, Boatman and editors Ronald Sinclair and Eve Newman rate a big nod for keeping high visual interest. Cuts and dissolves are appropriate to the mood of the music. Only in Donovan's overlong turn does the team falter, with some repetitious angles and cutting. One of his tunes should be eliminated for beter pace.

There's a consistent scream track (save for Miss Baez and Donovan) which becomes annoyingly obtrusive; the live crowds, while very enthusiastic, didn't maintain this obviously-phony background wail.

Technical credits (including Technicolor lab work) are excellent all the way down the line. Phil Spector coordinated the music and is credited as producer. Saperstein and AIP toppers James H. Nicholson and Samuel Z. Arkoff were exec producers. End title suggests another sequel next year. A print of each should be buried in a time capsule. *Murf.*

Moment to Moment
(COLOR)

Disappointing femme programmer about a once-unfaithful wife, her amnesia-stricken lover, and a forgiving headshrinker-hubby. Thin script and performances. Mervyn LeRoy's over-relaxed direction offset by costumes and Riviera locale. Fair dualer.

Hollywood, Jan. 21.
Universal release of a Mervyn LeRoy production, directed by LeRoy. Stars Jean Seberg, Honor Blackman; features Sean Garrison, Arthur Hill, Gregoire Aslan. Screenplay, John Lee Mahin, Alec Coppel, based on Coppel's story, "Laughs With A Stranger;" camera (Technicolor), Harry Stradling; editor, Philip W. Anderson; music, Henry Mancini; title tune, Mancini, Johnny Mercer; asst. director, Phil Bowles. Reviewed at Universal Studios, Jan. 20, '65. Running Time, **108 MINS.**

Kay Stanton	Jean Seberg
Daphne	Honor Blackman
Mark	Sean Garrison
Neil Stanton	Arthur Hill
DeFargo	Gregoire Aslan
Timmy Stanton	Peter Robbins
Mr. Singer	Donald Woods
Hendricks	Walter Reed
Travel Agent	Albert Carrier
Albie	Lomax Study
Givet	Richard Angarola
Louise	Georgette Anys

Mervyn LeRoy, who has tackled just about every type of film, returns to romantic melodrama in "Moment to Moment." an unabashed sudser aimed at the femme trade. A mild suspense story blending a wife's infidelity and amnesia, the film doesn't entirely jell for several reasons, mainly thin scripting, weak acting and LeRoy's own too-leisurely pace. With only light marquee lure, Universal will have a selling chore. Fair b.o. likely with judicious dualling in general situations, and better response in houses where middle-aged femme patrons like their drama on the teary side.

John Lee Mahin joined Alec Coppel in adapting latter's story about a happily-married Yank wife, increasingly neglected by headshrinker hubby who is on the lecture circuit all over Europe while she and the kid remain on the Riviera. A U. S. Naval officer has an affair with her, provoking a physical argument and a shooting.

Panicky wife and neighbor gal dump the body, believing it lifeless, but switcheroo has the guy later an amnesia victim, treated by hubby. Latter gets the picture but fadeout is marked by upbeat forgiveness.

In general, motivations of principals are weak and unclear, dialog is flat and LeRoy's relaxed direction backfires, since audiences have too much time to recall they've seen and heard it all before.

Jean Seberg lacks dimension as the wife, even allowing for the script.

In early scenes, an overly passive limning—which suggests jaded boredom instead of a well-adjusted spouse in a single fall from grace—robs the role of most sympathy. Later footage is too remorseful; she's merely sorry things didn't work out smoothly. Dressed to the nines (by Yves Saint-Laurent) a good sales angle—Miss Seberg often poses like Lana Turner, which isn't bad in one way, but further detracts from characterization.

Sean Garrison is lifeless in his pix debut as the officer, a stretcher case mama's boy who approaches the adulterous encounter in the manner of an adolescent, and, afterwards, is unable to handle the situation. Not without looks (which are far superior to his emoting), Garrison needs more dramatic development. He receives "intro" billing on screen, below title (rich-voiced actor was hired out of road company of "Camelot" and should be used in musicals.)

Honor Blackman, sharing above-title billing after Miss Seberg, gives the film some much-needed zip as the neighbor, although, in context, it's occasionally overdone. Still, she has life in her eyes, movements and speech, providing good relief, also occasionally humor.

Arthur Hill is saddled with the thankless role of the husband who can see everyone else's problems but not his own incipient domestic crisis, a valid point which is blunted by script and LeRoy's formula delivery.

Gregoire Aslan is the cop who knows Miss Seberg dumped Garrison's body, phoned the police on where to look, and arranged for Hill to be put on the case in order to prove it. He has a few highlight bits, although one ludicrous bit of writing has Aslan describing Garrison to Miss Seberg as "prepossessingly handsome."

Harry Stradling's Technicolor camera adds some dash and picture quality. Philip W. Anderson trimmed to a slow 108 minutes; nearly half the film is a flashback recap of the brief affair, the rest is the police and amnesia development. A good 20 minutes could be eliminated.

Henry Mancini's score is appropriate to the mood, and, again with Johnny Mercer, he has come up with a title tune. This one is serviceable if not memorable. It is reprised a bit too often, and receives a gauche plot plug. ("What is the name of that song? "Moment to Moment?" "Thank You.") Other technical credits are good, except some occasional grainy process work. *Murf.*

"Es"
(It)
(GERMAN)

Berlin, Jan. 18.
Atlas release of Horst Manfred Adloff production. Stars Sabine Sinjen, Bruno Dietrich. Directed by Ulrich Schamoni. Screenplay, Schamoni; camera, Gerald Vandenberg; music, Hans Possega; editor, Heidi Rente. Previewed at Academy of Arts, West Berlin. Running Time, **82 MINS.**
Hilde Pohlschmidt ...... Sabine Sinjen
Manfred Palm .... Bruno Dietrich
Claudia .... Ulrike Ullrich
Palm's employer ...... Harry Gillmann
Grandfather .... Robert Mueller
Old woman .... Tilla Dureieux
West German businessman
.... Bernhard Minetti

"It" is a German film hope. At least there is some justified hope that with 25-year old Ulrich Schamoni, a new, young native feature film creator has been found. This is his initial full-length feature pic and shows talent in several instances. Refreshingly enough, there is nothing esoteric about it. Unlike many other newcomers, Schamoni has handled a simple everyday yarn

the simple way, skipped symbolisms and let people be normal people. The outcome is a little, but good, clean film which, incidentally, has been nominated as Germany's entry in the upcoming Oscar derby.

Pic only cost something like $125,000 and Atlas, the most active and ambitious distrib in the land, already has secured enough bookings so it will break even in less than no time. Internationally, "It" may slide into some arty houses although censorship troubles must be taken into consideration. The young couple in this film leads to a "wild marriage" and "it" stands for abortion. But Schamoni tackled this subject with taste.

Against the actual backgrounds of today's West Berlin, this revolves around a young man and his girl. Both are very fond of each other and live together but they don't think of getting married. They enjoy their little private happiness and seemingly have no big problems until the girl becomes pregnant. She doesn't reveal this to her lover because she knows he's not keen on having a child. She goes from doctor to doctor to have an abortion. One finally does it. The film has practically no ending. It neither takes a pro nor an anti-abortion stand.

Ulrich Schamoni has tried to achieve something which may be termed a bridge between conventional film making and avant garde. There is nothing whatsoever confusing as per story development, treatment of subject matter and dialog. Direction which is kept at full speed, very tight editing and imaginative lensing are very modern. "It" makes a rather uneven impression but it's nevertheless a praiseworthy start for Schamoni.

Acting is uniformly right in style. Headed by Sabine Sinjen and Bruno Dietrich, who both have a number of impressive moments, the cast includes a number of locally top stage names such as 85-year old Tilla Durieux, Berlin's oldest active actress; Robert Mueller, also way above 80, and Bernhard Minetti. Also French pantomime Marcel Marceau, a friend of Schamoni, briefly shows up in this. Ditto several local personalities with a lineup of medicos playing themselves. All gave their services gratis. *Hans.*

Paris Au Mois D'Aout
(Paris in August)
(FRENCH)

Paris, Jan. 18.
CFDC release of UJC-Sirius-CFDC production. Stars Charles Aznavour, Susan Hampshire; features Alan Scott, Michel De Re, Daniel Ivernel, Helena Manson. Directed by Pierre Granier-Deferre. Screenplay, R. M. Arlaud, Henri Jeanson, Granier-Deferre; camera, Claude Renoir; editor, Jean Clavel. At Balzac, Paris. Running Time, **100 MINS.**
Henri .... Charles Aznavour
Pat .... Susan Hampshire
Peter .... Alan Scott
Neighbor .... Michel De Re
Painter .... Daniel Ivernel
Model .... Dominique Davray
Wife .... Etchika Choureau
Concierge .... Helena Manson

Simple slice-of-life film deals with a brief encounter between a little French worker, whose wife is on vacation, and a British cover girl. A deserted Paris backdrop in

August is the main factor since the characters skirt banality, direction is spiritless and characterization sometimes trite. But some good acting does give this a certain breeziness. Pic might have some specialized legs for abroad on its tale of a short love affair that ends in the unresolved love affair of the girl.

Charles Aznavour, the French singer, has a pleasant and beguiling screen personality but seems out of place with the head-taller British mannequin Susan Hempshire. However, it would have been acceptable if director Pierre Granier-Deferre had been able to get a true, observant feel into it. Instead, he opts for situation comedy, sentiment which sinks to bathos, and a love scene in which he tries to ape New Wave tactics but misses completely. The actual love scenes descend to vulgarity rather than the needed sentiments.

Side characters are mainly stereotypes or almost caricatures. Claude Renoir has given this a fine lensing envelope and Paris comes through well if the conventional tale does not quite have the sincere lift to bring it out of the ordinary.

Aznavour's underplaying does manage to make his role of the little man caught up in an almost unbelievable happening palatable. However, Miss Hampshire is comely but somewhat colorless and remains a mannequin. Aznavour even ends the film with himself singing a song about regrets and romantic encounters in Paris which is more sincere than the pic itself. *Mosk.*

The Plague Of The Zombies
(BRITISH-COLOR)

Well-made horror programmer for dual bills. Okay b.o.

Hollywood, Jan. 19.
Twentieth Century-Fox release of a Seven Arts-Hammer Film, produced by Anthony Nelson Keys. Features Andre Morell, Diane Clare, John Carson, Brook Williams. Directed by John Gilling. Screenplay, Peter Bryan; camera (De-Luxe Color), Arthur Grant; editor, James Needs; music, James Bernard; asst. director, Bert Batt. Reviewed at 20th-Fox Studios, Jan. 18, '65. Running Time, **90 MINS.**
Sir James Forbes .... Andre Morell
Sylvia .... Diane Clare
Clive Hamilton .... John Carson
Peter Tompson .... Brook Williams
Harry Denver .... Alexander Davion
Alice Tompson .... Jacqueline Pearce
Police Sgt. .... Michael Ripper
Martinus .... Marcus Hammond
Vicar .... Roy Royston
Policeman .... Dennis Chinnery

Filmed at Ireland's Bray Studios, "The Plague Of The Zombies" is a well-made horror programmer about strange happenings a century ago in a small town on the moors. Part of the Seven Arts-Hammer Film slate, being released outside of U.K. areas by 20th-Fox, the Anthony Nelson Keys production will, despite some overlength, satisfy horror fans and action audiences. It is being paired with "Dracula — Prince Of Darkness" in domestic release.

Peter Bryan is credited with the script which brings Andre Morell, a distinguished medic professor and daughter Diane Clare to the boondocks town where former pupil Brook Williams isn't having

much luck in his new practice. A dozen people have died mysteriously, and local squire John Carson won't permit autopsies. Jacqueline Pearce, Williams' wife, isn't looking too good, either.

The formula scripting involves about 55 minutes of seeding with various unexplained incidents, followed by an explanation of the diabolical forces involved (in this case, Carson and a group of young hoods are practicing voodoo in order to get workers for his tin mine). Then in the last 35 minutes, the demons are foiled. The relaxed pace wears interest; 10 less minutes in buildup, and five chopped from climax, would have made a tighter suspenser.

Director John Gilling has deployed his thesps to good advantage in some firstrate pictorial values from Arthur Grant's DeLuxe Color camera. Performers are all competent. Carson's voice is close to that of James Mason. Zombies bob up with regularity, and their striking makeup is the work of Roy Ashton.

The fiery climax finds the zombies turning on their brutal masters while the proper characters escape. James Bernard's full score adds punch at the right moments, and all other technical credits are topnotch. *Murf.*

When Tomorrow Dies
(CANADIAN)

Indie budget film lacks what it takes to move the wickets.

Vancouver, B.C., Jan. 25.
Laurence Kent production and release. Stars Patricia Cage, Douglas Campbell and Neil Dainard. Features Lanny Backman, Nikki Cole, Diane Filer, Francesca Long, Rex Owen, Louise Payne, Patricia Wilson. Directed by Laurence Kent; screenplay, Kent and Robert Harlow; camera, Doug McKay; music, Jack Dale; editor, Hajo Hadeler. At Lyric Theatre, Vancouver, B.C. Running Time, **91 MINS.**

Fledgling Canadian filmmaker Larry Kent's third full-length feature is, in a word, dull. The promise of his two earlier films, the raw campus production "Bitter Ash" and the much-praised story of teenage sex, "Caressed" (nee "Sweet Substitute") is quickly dissipated in the plodding opening sequences of "When Tomorrow Dies," which then slowly and painfully limps to a foregone conclusion. Story concerns a young mother of two who feels hopelessly trapped and increasingly lonely in a marriage that has lost its flavor as her husband has become busier and more occupied with his executive promotions.

Plot, as such, is humdrum, hackneyed stuff and to make a passing commercial grade would require exceptionally talented direction and acting to lift it. While a case might be made for some of the acting, Kent's direction is unequal to the challenge. His pedestrian pre-occupation with a style that rambles at times, jumps at others, and is quite derivative of Europe's avant films, never comes off.

As the central character, Patricia Gage demonstrates capacity to convey despair but in the absence of what appears to be properly directed motivation falls short of a performance of complete conviction. Miss Gage has an exceptionally expressive face, photographs beautifully and displays potential to warrant better opportunities. Douglas Campbell, as the inept husband, is miscast. Neil Dainard is excellent as a young university lecturer with whom the wife essays a brief and abortive affair.

Pic has considerable visual appeal, due to Doug McKay's stylish camera but suffers from graininess of print, blown up from original 16m. Sound also leaves something to be desired and film technically does not measure up to the $120,000 budget claimed for its production. This figure does not include the financial "co-operation" Kent received from acting and technical talent, equipment rental, location shooting, etc. which would come to an equivalent amount as the official budget. *Shaw.*

He Who Rides A Tiger
(BRITISH)

Smoothly competent crime meller with neat performances by Tom Bell and Judi Dench. Useful programmer but lacks marquee lustre.

London, Jan. 18.

British Lion release (through BLC) of a David Newman Film. Stars Tom Bell, Judi Dench, Paul Rogers. Features Kay Walsh, Ray McAnally, Jeremy Spenser, Peter Madden, Edina Ronay, Ralph Michael. Directed by Charles Crichton. Story and screenplay, Trevor Peacock; camera, John Von Kotze; music, Alexander Faris; editors, Jack Harris, John Smith. Reviewed at Columbia Theatre, London, Jan. 17, '65. Running Time, 103 MINS.

Peter Rayston	Tom Bell
Joanne	Judi Dench
Supt. Taylor	Paul Rogers
Mrs. Woodley	Kay Walsh
Orphanage Supt.	Ray McAnally
The Panda	Jeremy Spenser
Peepers Woodley	Peter Madden
Dept. Sgt. Scott	Inigo Jackson
Julie	Annette Andre
Anna	Edina Ronay
Ellen	Nicolette Pendrell
Carter	Ralph Michael
Mr. Steed	Frederick Piper
Flower Seller	Rita Webb
Det. Sgt. Crowley	Robin Hughes
Waiter	Jimmy Gardner
Prison Governor	Howard Lang
Lady Cleviand	Naomi Chance
Policewoman	Pat Shakesby
The Rapiers	Themselves

Legal and financial hassles upset the smooth production of this crime meller, but it does not show on the screen and emerges as a smooth and useful programmer. Trevor Peacock's screenplay might have benefited by a few more twists and the cast is not of star magnitude. But under Charles Crichton's seasoned directing the result is an entertaining enough 100 minutes.

Story concerns a young, nerveless cat burglar (specialty rocks from stately homes) with a split personality. Kind to children and animals, suave, good-mannered on the one hand. But this personable young guy is equally prone to violent outbursts of impatience and hot temper. Released from the cooler he sets out on a string of profitable crimes, with Superintendent Taylor (Paul Rogers) breathing down his neck.

He has a quick eye for the chicks but falls for a girl who does not realize that he is a crook, won't accept his money and with whom he spends most of his time at an orphanage where she works and where her illegitimate son lives. When she finds out that he is a criminal she first walks out on him, but then returns, her love for him too strong. But he won't accept the love, and instead goes off on a burglary to help an aging crook. This leads to tragedy and an ending which is rather too inconclusive.

Trevor Peacock's screenplay is crisp, and even in the love scenes and with the kids does not teeter overmuch towards the sentimental. Crichton directs with a sure touch and technically there is some fine location work, sound artwork and stylish lensing by John Von Kotze. Tom Bell as the anti-hero is one of the crop of young actors who emerged around the Finney, Courtenay, Lynch, O'Toole era. He's best known Stateside for "The L-Shaped Room." He has an easy style and diamond-hard personality which put him among the leading runners in this field.

Judi Dench, in a somewhat indecisive part, again shows her very bright talent and Paul Rogers is fine as the determined, disgruntled cop. Edina Ronay, as one of Bell's mistresses, Peter Madden and Jeremy Spenser as thieves and Ralph Michael as a shady crime organiser all contribute usefully. The scenes in the orphanage will have a distinct femme appeal. This straightforward film has much to commend it, particularly in its suspenseful moments but sometimes the action lags flabbily and has to be jerked back to its first and ultimate tensions.
Rich.

The Chase
(PANAVISION—TECHNICOLOR)

Sam Spiegel abandons foreign climes to take a look at sociological state of Texas. Name-studded cast and violence laid on with heavy hand should provide profitable grist for the exploitation mills.

Columbia Pictures release of a Horizon (Sam Spiegel) production. Stars Marlon Brando, Jane Fonda, Robert Redford, James Fox; features E. G. Marshall, Angie Dickinson, Janice Rule, Miriam Hopkins, Martha Hyer, Robert Duvall, Richard Bradford, Henry Hull, Diana Hyland. Directed by Arthur Penn. Screenplay by Lillian Hellman, based on novel and play by Horton Foote; camera (Technicolor), Joseph La Shelle; editor, Gene Milford; sound, Charles J. Rice; music, composed and conducted by John Barry. Reviewed at Columbia home office, N.Y., Jan. 20, '65. Running Time, 138 MINS.

Calder	Marlon Brando
Anna	Jane Fonda
Bubber	Robert Redford
Val Rogers	E. G. Marshall
Ruby Calder	Angie Dickinson
Emily Stewart	Janice Rule
Mrs. Reeves	Miriam Hopkins
Mary Fuller	Martha Hyer
Damon Fuller	Richard Bradford
Edwin Stewart	Robert Duvall
Jason Rogers (Jake)	James Fox
Elizabeth Rogers	Diana Hyland
Briggs	Henry Hull
Mrs. Briggs	Jocelyn Brando
Verna Dee	Katherine Walsh
Cutie	Lori Martin
Paul	Marc Seaton
Seymour	Paul Williams
Lem	Clifton James
Mr. Reeves	Malcolm Atterbury
Mrs. Henderson	Nydia Westman
Lester Johnson	Joel Fluellen
Archie	Steve Ihnat
Moore	Maurice Manson
Sol	Bruce Cabot
Slim	Steve Whittaker
Mrs. Shifftifieus	Pamela Curran
Sam	Ken Renard

Producer Sam Spiegel has turned away, briefly, from the more exotic climes of his earlier films to take a long, hard look at what makes people tick. The particular Texan examples with which he has peopled "The Chase" are not types one would want as neighbors (although one might have them). They are, however, colorful, uncomfortably identifiable and, hence, generally unsympathetic.

"The Chase," while far from being "Bridge On The River Kwai" or "Lawrence of Arabia," has enough going for it, plus a planned all-out promotional campaign, to make it one of Columbia's top grossers for 1966. Inadequacies in scripting are somewhat balanced by an interesting use of non-type casting. Superb technical work throughout provides "The Chase" with generally consistent dramatic excitement, topped by a violence-laden climax that leaves little to the imagination.

Only the framework of Horton Foote's novel (but little of his play, which preceded it), has been utilized by Lillian Hellman in her screenplay. The original plot centered on an escaped convict seeking revenge on the sheriff who had sent him up but Miss Hellman makes them only two of the many characters with which she has populated her sociologically sick Texas town.

Through introduction of various other types she manages to provide most of the social grievances which trouble the world today—injustice, bigotry, adultery, apathy, racial prejudice, the over-privileged rich and the undeserving poor, plus a bit of religious fanaticism that doesn't come off. The vapid efforts of Nydia Westman as a soft-spoken psalm-singing eccentric inspire laughter when none is intended. Her scenes, all distracting, should be excised from the over-long film. Miss Hellman gets across much of the melodramatic merit in the script but has left it with plenty of illogical loopholes.

Director Arthur Penn, a specialist in films about sick types, must share with Spiegel the credit for the film's merits and the blame for its occasional failures. The staging discipline and style that were vital elements in "Miracle Worker" are more relaxed here but Penn rules his large cast with a firm hand and gets, from most of them, interesting and even outstanding performances. He has cast some notably sexy screen types as plain to dowdy females and some good girls as bad ones, providing a point of interest which he fully utilizes.

Robert Redford, as the escaped convict whose impending return to his hometown gives many of its citizens the jitters, gives the film's best performance and the best, to date, of his still short screen career. He has an instinct for economy of dialog delivery and, alone on the screen during much of the earlier action and bypassed for lengthy sequences when the story deals with other plot elements, he so imprints his character on the viewer's mind that, upon re-entering a scene, his last-seen action is still clear to the memory. Even when he finally becomes involved with other cast members, his own performance dominates.

Marlon Brando, in the comparatively small but important role of the sheriff, has obviously given much time and study to the part, but such detailed preparation as a carefully-delivered Texas accent means little when other cast members read their lines with a mixture of regional accents. Underplaying during most of the film, the character doesn't really come alive until a beating scene when he undergoes a shellacking as if William Farnum and Tom Santschi had teamed up to work him over.

Jane Fonda, as Redford's wife and the mistress of wealthy oilman James Fox, makes the most of the biggest female role. While she still displays some awkward mannerisms and tends to blow up her emotional scenes, her overall impression is good and she has learned how to read lines. "I've waited all those years and all these years," spoken to Fox when he tells her Redford has escaped but pleads with her to stay with him, quickly sums up the lengthy frustration of awaiting Redford's release and the crossed emotions that enable her to love both men at once.

Fox, whose British accent melts believably into the soft tones of Texas, continues to add to his promise of becoming one of the screen's top young leading men. He combines the moral weakness of "The Servant" and the good-at-heart-edness of "King Rat" to make his well-meaning but spineless rich man understandable if not sympathetic.

Most of the other female roles are interestingly played, with it a toss-up as to which is the most outstanding. Angie Dickinson, plain and comfortable as Brando's wife; Janice Rule, as a held-in-check nympho married to the wrong man; Miriam Hopkins, as the self-deluding, c o n s c i e n c e-stricken mother of Redford and Martha Hyer, as an alcoholic wife, are all impressive. Diana Hyland is wasted, however, in a tiny part as Fox's wife.

The aforementioned Miss Westman and Jocelyn Brando, as Henry Hull's wife, have little chance to compete. Lori Martin and Katherine Walsh as two teenagers, yearning to be 21, are hardly noticed among the more professional adult cast members. Among the males, two in particular stand out. Robert Duvall, as Miss Rule's weak husband, makes his mouse of a man both pitifully weak and dramatically impressive. Also new to films, Richard Bradford, as the handsome, bored husband of Miss Hyer, is a welcome addition to the thinning ranks of younger character actors. E. G. Marshall, as Fox's doting but incompetent millionaire father; Henry Hull, as a bigoted, nosey real-estate dealer and Bruce Cabot as Miss Fonda's stepfather hold their own against the bigger parts of the others. Though uncredited, Eduardo Ciannelli is seen and heard briefly in a party scene.

An interesting contribution is made by actor Steve Ihnat, as one of the threesome responsible for the climactic violence. He doesn't have a line of dialog and is an unobtrusive type, but the viewer remains aware of him from the time he makes a late entry at a party given by Duvall until his unexpected Jack Ruby-like action at the end of the film.

One area approached but left unexplored by Miss Hellman's script is the racial attitude of the community towards Negroes. Although a few are seen briefly during the film and actor Joel Fluellen figures in an important key role, nothing much is said applicable to what must be on any southern city's social conscience today.

Joseph La Shelle's Technicolor and Panavision camerawork, particularly impressive in an excellent pre-title sequence which, though stylized and offbeat, quickly sets the atmospheric scene for the action that follows, also beautifully captures the wild rioting at the junkyard with its melange of fast action, noise, fires and explosions that backdrop the end of the chase. Gene Milford's editing, which could still find material for his scissors, manages to keep apace of the fast-moving happenings even when what is happening has little to do with the main storyline. John Barry's score, strong on melodic line, should provide a successful soundtrack album but contains no particular theme that lingers in the ear.

As a social treatise, a psychological study or just a thriller, there's much in "The Chase" that's open to question. As an example of action and good acting, it's outstanding, but there are dull passages just as there are brief, brilliant moments of cinematic excellence.

A panning shot of the townspeople looking on as three fellow citizens coldbloodedly try to beat their sheriff to death is one of the most impressive portrayals of civic apathy and non-involvement yet filmed. It should make most responsible citizens squirm in their seats when they recognize their own failures and shortcomings. Unfortunately, there will probably be even more possessed of that self-deluding talent, as common to the Bronx as to Texas, that enables them to see and condemn and never recognize themselves.
Robe.

The Rare Breed
(COLOR—PANAVISION)

Well-made cattle drama, with action, romance and comedy mixed in a script that sometimes wanders. Marquee bait in James Stewart-Maureen O'Hara tandem, plus fine acting by two newcomers and vets.

Hollywood, Jan. 25.
Universal release of a William Alland production. Stars James Stewart, Maureen O'Hara, Brian Keith; features Juliet Mills, Don Galloway, David Brian. Directed by Andrew V. McLaglen. Screenplay, Ric Hardman; camera (Technicolor), William H. Clothier; editor, Russell F. Schoengarth; music, Johnny Williams; asst. director, Terry Morse Jr. Reviewed at Universal Studios, Jan. 24, '66. Running Time, 97 MINS.
Burnett .... James Stewart
Martha Price .... Maureen O'Hara
Bowen .... Brian Keith
Hilary .... Juliet Mills
Jamie .... Don Galloway
Ellsworth .... David Brian
Simons .... Jack Elam
Harter .... Ben Johnson
Mabry .... Harry Carey, Jr.
Juan .... Perry Lopez
Alberto .... Larry Domasin
Taylor .... Alan Caillou

Based on the actual intro some 80 years ago of white-faced Hereford cattle from England to the U.S. western ranges, "The Rare Breed" is a generally successful fictionalized blend of violence, romance, comedy, inspiration and oater Americana. The well-mounted, colorful William Alland production has good scripting, direction and performances. James Stewart-Maureen O'Hara combo is solid marquee lure. Not a shoot-em-up, concentrating rather on personal conflicts, the Universal release has good-to-excellent b.o. prospects in general situations, particularly in family and action markets where Stewart's "Shenandoah" (also U) struck gold last year.

Ric Hardman's good—if overly wide-ranging—script takes as a point of departure the phasing out of the longhorn by the "rare" (circa 1884) Hereford stock from England. As the drama unfolds, rugged animal survival problems dissolve into human conflicts, including the character-stiffening of a broke down cowpoke, the resolution of a father-son impasse, and a pair of romantic involvements—one an adult triangle, the other a younger couple who reflect, and in turn affect, the viewpoints of elders.

For almost half of the 97-minute running time, the plot concerns the stubborn determination of widowed Miss O'Hara and daughter Juliet Mills to deliver a bull for breeding purposes. Op-posing factors include Stewart, initially a drifter who agrees, although reluctantly, to swindle the gals, via Alan Caillou's bribe, with two consiprators, Jack Elam and Harry Carey, Jr.

David Brian appears briefly, and well, as a smooth-talking beef buyer on the make for Miss O'Hara. Brian's role is somewhat extraneous, although it does provide added contrast of the delicate ladylike manners with a strange new environment. Ben Johnson, crippled cowpoke to whom Stewart gives away his bribe, is okay, although, again, Stewart's uneasy collaboration is otherwise evident.

Recurring fisticuffs between the latter and the Elam-Carey duo lead to Carey's brutal death by Elam's gun, and later to Elam's accidental death. The bull is delivered although Stewart's complicity is known, and he's on the outs with Miss O'Hara.

Second half of the film is virtually another pic, with quietly-stubborn Miss O'Hara pitted against Brian Keith in a sort of Anna-and-the-King-of-Siam byplay-Widower Keith, expatriate Scotsman, is virtually feudal lord in his domain, with no heart even for son Don Galloway. As Miss O'Hara softens him, she loses her spirit for the bull's survival while, by transference, Stewart has taken it up to unreasonable extremes. This is a valid point, for through her he has at last found something to believe in.

Miss Mills and Galloway play well together as their romance develops. Another member of the talented Mills family, she is charming yet spirited, and shows further progress as a versatile actress. This is her first Yank pic. Galloway, with less to project, has sufficent virility in both looks and voice to be developed further into more prominent casting. This is his first feature.

Keith's exaggerated mannerisms provide some comedy relief, although the over-written role is yet another digression from the mainstream. He restrains himself, however, and comes across well as the bluff range baron whose heart is not completely hardened. He's billed over title, after Stewart and Miss O'Hara.

Director Andrew V. McLaglen has derived uniformly fine performances from the cast, and has alternated the personal drama with some picturesque exteriors, captured faithfully by William H. Clothier's rich Technicolor and Panavision lensing. Whether depicting a brawl, a cattle stampede, a panoramic pastoral or a howling blizzard, the picture has an exuberant freshness.

Not intentionally saving the best for last, it should be noted that Stewart's somewhat offbeat role is handled in topflight fashion right down to the happy ending which, while predictable, is, more importantly, earnestly desired by average people, despite occasional externalizing to the contrary. Latter image is dictated more by cynical, hip fashion than basic inner human nature.

Miss O'Hara, still the titian charmer, again adds grace, warmth and gentle humor to another excellent characterization. Johnny Williams' score gives some zesty punch, and Russell F. Schoengarth's editing is good. Other technical credits all pro. *Murf.*

Walk In The Shadow
(BRITISH)

Parental religious authority theme. Excellent performances by leads could make this import one of season's "sleepers."

Walter Reade-Sterling (Continental) release of a J. Arthur Rank production. Produced by Michael Relph. Directed by Basil Dearden. Stars Michael Craig, Janet Munro, Patrick McGoohan, Paul Rogers. Screenplay by Janet Green, John McCormick; camera, Otto Heller; editor, John Guthridge; music, William Alwyn. Reviewed in New York, Jan. 27, '66. Running Time, 93 MINS.
John Harris .... Michael Craig
Pat Harris .... Janet Munro
Dr. Brown .... Patrick McGoohan
Hart Jacobs .... Paul Rogers
Mrs. Gordon .... Megs Jenkins
Teddy's mother .... Maureen Pryor
Mr. Gordon .... John Barrie
Mapleton .... Basil Dignam
Clyde .... Leslie Sands
Duty Sister .... Ellen McIntosh
Teddy's father .... Frank Finlay
Harvard .... Michael Aldridge
John's father .... Malcolm Keen
Ruth .... Lynn Taylor
Teddy .... Freddy Ramsey
John's counsel .... Michael Bryant
Crown counsel ..... Norman Woolland

This British import tackles an extremely disputatious subject as its theme—the right of a parent to invoke a religious belief when doing so would or might result in the death of a child. Evidently filmed on location in a British coastal town, "Walk In The Shadow" is a taut, well-made drama, blessed with some excellent acting, which could easily overcome the obstacles of lack of names and possible resentment to its story by proper exploitation of its many merits.

Basil Dearden has directed the original screenplay of Janet Green and John McCormick with no attempt to solicit the sympathy of the viewer one way or the other. It comes off, to a large extent, as almost a documentary. There are strong arguments presented but they're sufficiently free of prejudice to forestall any claims of favoritism on the part of producer Michael Relph or his scripters.

When the small daughter of Michael Craig and Janet Munro is injured in a boating accident and her only chance for survival is a blood transfusion, Craig forbids it as being against his religious convictions. Although his wife at first accepts his decision (although a former Anglican, she accepted his faith when they were married), she later returns and tells the doctor (Patrick McGoohan) to go ahead but it is too late. McGoohan, an agnostic, although the parents are cleared in an inquest, brings charges against Craig for manslaughter under a prevention of cruelty to children act, charging that the father's denial of vital medical help was tantamount to murder.

During the ensuing publicity and court proceedings, Craig finds that only his father (Malcolm Keen) and a Jewish lawyer (Paul Rogers) are on his side. His wife has returned to her parents, who've never really accepted Craig. Craig is acquitted, but admits his guilt as he was expecting a last-minute miracle to save his daughter's life. When he tries to commit suicide, he is prevented by McGoohan who tries to convince him that he must accept the responsibility for his act by living with it. The wife returns, realizing that he needs her, but the death of the child will always stand between them.

Craig gives a superb performance as the tragic parent, faced with a decision to which every individual must give his own answer if put to the test. His suffering is evident, his confusion and sense of loneliness compellingly present. Forced by the limitations on his emotions to do most of his acting with only facial expression he never lets the feeling of agony drop. Miss Munro is also outstanding. A very pretty woman who could have been tempted to hedge on the historionic demands on her, she lets her face go ugly when she cries as any grief-stricken mother would.

Patrick McGoohan's doctor will probably not be entirely pleasing to members of the medical profession since his actions seem personal rather than medical. While he's never guilty of maliciousness and makes his attempts to help Craig at the end as sincere as his fight to change Craig's mind at the time of decision, there's still a hint of vindictiveness in his portrayal.

Led by a fine job by Paul Rogers as the lawyer who turns down McGoohan's representation ("I'm a Jew and what you're doing smacks of persecution.") but takes on Craig's defense because he believes in the individual's right to personal religious convictions, the rest of the cast is uniformly excellent. Outstanding are Malcolm Keen as Craig's father, Michael Bryan as his counsel, Norman Woolland as the Crown counsel. Frank Finlay (Iago to Olivier's Othello) is unrecognizable as a neighbor.

The scripters have given their actors some intelligent dialog that doesn't hesitate to comment on many aspects of religious belief and the reluctance of public figures to publicly state whether there should be limitations on it. (In his chambers, but not in the court, the judge conducting the case remarks, "There should be a legal curb on parents' power.")

Otto Helle's black-and-white camerawork catches the dismal, unrelenting grayishness of life in the forbidding town, enlivened only by some handsome seascapes. Annoying changes in lighting during trade screening may have been result of faulty projection. If not the final release print should be corrected. Editing is tight and well handled. *Robe.*

Sky West And Crooked
(BRITISH-COLOR)

A hard sell on Hayley Mills' marquee value will be needed to put over this piece of amiable, but slightly old fashioned, hokum.

London, Jan. 25.
Rank release of a John Mills Production. Stars Hayley Mills. Features Ian McShane, Laurence Naismith, Geoffrey Bayldon, Annette Crosbie, Norman Bird. Produced by Jack Hanbury. Directed by John Mills. Screenplay by Mary Bell & John Prebble from Mrs. Mill's story; camera (Eastmancolor), Arthur Ibbetson; music, Malcolm Arnold; editor, Gordon Hales. At Leicester Square Theatre, London, Jan. 19, '65. Running Time, 102 MINS.
Brydie White .... Hayley Mills
Roibin .... Ian McShane
Edwin Dacres .... Laurence Naismith
Philip Moss .... Geoffrey Bayldon
Mrs. White .... Annette Crosbie
Cheeseman .... Norman Bird
Bill Slim .... Hamilton Dyce
Mrs. Moss .... Pauline Jameson
Grandma .... Rachel Thomas
Mrs. Rigby .... Judith Furse

It's a family affair with Hayley Mills starring, poppa John Mills doing his first directorial stint and his wife, Mary Hayley Mills, (who writes professionally as Mary Bell), sharing the screenplay with John Prebble from her own story. And, "Sky West and Crooked" turns out to be reasonably good family fare though it leans towards hokum in its concept. It should do okay at most wickets but will depend largely on the pulling power of young Miss Mills.

She is in transitional position. No longer a child star, but not yet developed into a mature young woman. But Mills has brought out of her unexpected qualities in this film. She still remains largely an undeveloped tomboy in the character dreamed up by her mother, but there are hints of depth and growing maturity.

Miss Mills portrays a village girl who is a misfit because of simplicity—the title is a novel expression for simplicity (Original title, "Bats With Baby Faces," was equally confusing). This is the result of an accident when a child which resulted in the death of her boy playmate and her own wounding. The adults around the village tolerantly regard her as slightly idiotic, with her morbid obsession with death which causes her to be at her happiest when playing in the local graveyard and in burying dead pets in consecrated ground. The meller develops to a point where she is saved from drowning by a gypsy lad which leads to her awakening and their subsequent nuptials.

This naive yarn is rescued from bathos by the evident sincerity of both star and director and by a very convincing portrayal of village life, highlighted by some excellent Eastmancolor photography by Arthur Ibbetson. Mills has played safe in his first directing experiment and the result, while often stodgy, suggests that he knows his way around a directorial chair.

Gordon Hales' editing is fluent and Malcolm Arnold has contributed an unobtrusive score. The village of Badminton, where most of the film was made on location, could hardly be bettered and minor roles are played with conviction, so that the village atmosphere rings true throughout.

Apart from the heroine who, as indicated, manages successfully to handle both tomboyish scenes and growing maturity, there is a thoughtful attractive performance by Ian McShane as the Romany lad who brings happiness to the girl. The only other significant role is that of the sympathetic

local vicar played in engagingly sprightly manner by Geoffrey Bayldon. Annette Crosbie as Hayley's gin-sodden mother, Laurence Naismith as a testy farmer, Norman Bird as the local undertaker and Pauline Jameson as the vicar's wife also etch in good work in a cast in which children predominate to plausible effect.
Rich.

Made In Paris
(COLOR—PANAVISION)

Weak comedy about Ann-Margret being chased by three wolves, none of whom have much bark nor any bite. Lush costumes amid Paris settings offer big selling angle. Fair dual entry.

Hollywood, Jan. 20.
Metro-Goldwyn-Mayer release of a Euterpe (Joe Pasternak) Production. Stars Ann-Margret, Louis Jourdan, Richard Crenna, Edie Adams, Chad Everett; features John McGiver. Directed by Boris Sagal. Screenplay, Stanley Roberts; camera (Metrocolor), Milton Krasner; eidtor, William McMillin; music, George Stoll; songs, Burt Bacharach, Hal David, Sammy Fain, Paul Francis Webster, Quincy Jones, Red Skelton; asst. director, Donald C. Klune. Reviewed at Crest Theatre, L.A., Jan. 19, '65. Running Time, 103 MINS.
Maggie Scott .... Ann-Margret
Marc Fontaine .... Louis Jourdan
Herb Stone .... Richard Crenna
Irene Chase .... Edie Adams
Ted Barclay .... Chad Everett
Roger Barclay .... John McGiver
Georges .... Marcel Dalio
Cecile .... Matilda Calnan
Denise Marton .... Jacqueline Beer
Attendant .... Marcel Hillaire
Elise .... Michele Montau
American Bar Singer ...... Reta Shaw
Themselves .... Count Basie and Octet. Mongo Santamaria and Band

A Parisian setting and some snazzy femme costumes provide the major props for this otherwise weak and formula comedy programmer. Sexy plot overtones are too protracted in scripting, and become boring via heavy-handed direction. Ann-Margret and Louis Jourdan top the list of adequate players, providing some marquee lure for the Joe Pasternak production. Fair b.o. prospects for Metro release on dual bills in general situations, although a hard fashion-show sell may boost returns in femme-oriented houses.

Stanley Roberts' dull script, strongly reminiscent of yesteryear Doris Day - Rock Hudson - Cary Grant plots (but less effective), finds fashion buyer Ann-Margret rushed to Paris from the lecherous arms of her employer's son, Chad Everett. Louis Jourdan is the French designer who, it appears, has had what is usually called an adult arrangement with Edie Adams, whom Ann-Margret has replaced. Richard Crenna is a foreign correspondent who bobs up from time to time.

Film gets off to a good start with a non-dialog sequence showing Ann-Margret and Everett at various stages of an evening out, ending after four minutes with the latter getting konked on the noggin for doing exactly what she all along has been silently telegraphing. Unfortunately, director Boris Sagal doesn't maintain the momentum.

Ann-Margret does not yet have the dramatic ability to acquit herself in comedy. Still a self-conscious sex kitten all the way, she is not believable here as the

knockout looker who really wants to settle down in a small (town) house with curtains, etc. Her emoting is strictly one-note. She would be far more effective as a femme fatale.

Everett has a certain flair which might be developed, although herein he is largely repped by static poses. Jourdan, who has polished his screen image as the Continental charmer to the highest degree, stands out above all others in the cast. Incidentally, he loses the girl. Miss Adams is okay in brief footage as the retired buyer now hitched to an unseen sugar daddy. Crenna misses as the cliche newsman. John McGiver is good as Everett's dad, and other thesps are adequate.

Plotting permits Ann-Margret to essay some wild terpery, which David Winters choreographed to the desired effect. Mongo Santamaria and band provide a solid beat for the bumps. Helen Rose's lavish wardrobe diverts the eye constantly, and is the biggest selling angle. Milton Kasner's Metrocolor-Panavision camera paints a good picture, ad editor William McMillin trimmed to an okay 103 minutes.

George Stoll's score lends some effective emphasis. Trini Lopez sings the Burt Bacharach-Hal David title tune over credits; Ann-Margret and Jourdan duet in Sammy Fain-Paul Francis Webster's "Paris Lullaby"; Red Skelton is credited with the "My True Love" instrumental recurring theme; and Quincy Jones wrote the material used by Count Basie and Octet in early brief footage. "Lullaby" fits the plot but doesn't linger in the ear. Other songs are competely forgettable.
Murf.

The Mermaid
(HONG KONG—COLOR-SCOPE)

Snail paced fish-tale operetta aimed at kiddie trade. Enhanced by naive charm, pastel tinting. Good, but ritualistic acting.

A Frank Lee release of a Runme Shaw production. Stars Ivy Ling Po and Li Ching; features Ching Miao, Au-yang Sha-fei, Yang Tse-ching, Chiang Kuang-chao, Yeh Ching, Feng I, Chen Yuen-hua, Tung Di, and Li Yuen-chung. Directed by Kao Li; screenplay by Chang Chien; assistant director, Yueh Cheng-chun; cinematographer, Tung Shao-yung; sound recording, Wang Yung-hua; film editor, Chang Shing-Loong; art direction, Chen Chi-ruey; set designer, Chen Ching-shen; make up, Fong Yuen; lyrics, Chang Chieh; musical score, Wang Fu-ling. Reviewed at 55th Street Playhouse, Jan. 24, '66. Running Time, 99 MINS.

If fantasy is enhanced by naivete, this pastel-tinted scope and color lotus blossom should glow with innocent charm for tots, but hardly in this jet age, when the kiddies are hip to Bond and Batman. Featureless pentatonic tuning, operetta-style, prosaic fairy-tale plot and molasses pace will prove ultimately boring to all but oriental insomniacs, despite its restful artlessness and delicacy.

Chinese puzzle box unfolds with the deliberate speed of a turtle. It's mermaid's hopeless-love-for-a-jilted poor-boy.

The poor-boy Chang, played, curiously enough, by exquisite topliner actress Ivy Ling Po, was betrothed before his birth to tne wealthy and beautiful Peony Chin, daughter of the local Prime Minister. Wily old Chin, however, has higher hopes for his daughter, and demands that Chang pass the tough imperial exams before nuptials, thereby hoping that the threadbare youth will tire of studying and exit. Chang, virtually held incommunicado in Chin's lakeside hut, warbles the seasons away in Grimm determination to win Peony's hand. Touched by the spurned suitor's plight, a carp-spirit rises from the lake magically transmogrified into Peony's twin. The pair plink and gong each night away serenading the moon.

Impetuous Chang, though, over-anxious about one evening's assignation, barges in on the real Peony, who spitefully turns him over to mean old Chin. The baffled Chang is banished, but is retrieved by the ersatz Peony, and is eventually caught by Chin traipsing around a local Dragon dance with the Peony look-alike.

At this point, the pic is reduced to an Oriental "To Tell The Truth," with the fake Peony summoning the aid of some lake-bottom goblins to duplicate the local Lord who is called in ask, "Will the real Peony Chin stand up." After some midly amusing horseplay involving a raft of doubles, old Chin calls in a sorcerer to work some wicked magic on the couple. A lake-bottom struggle ensues, with Chang, the carp-spirit and her piscatory buddies arrayed against a gang of celestial heavies until the goddess of mercy intervenes, offers the carp-spirit mortality, so she can marry Chang. Not so inscrutably, the pair live happily ever after.

Although production values are topflight in the color, sets, costuming and special effects categories, the pic is virtually bereft of such alleviating cinematics as close-ups, angles, and dramatic editing. Despite excellent acting in the oriental mode, especially by Ivy Ling Po, even the most frenetic land-based scenes are so stylistically studied they might have been shot 30 fathoms under water. *Rino.*

Deux Heures A Tuer
(Two Hours to Kill)
(FRENCH)
Paris, Jan. 25.

Inter-France release of GRK-Prodibel production. Stars Pierre Brasseur, Michel Simon; features Raymond Rouleau, Catherine Sauvage, Julie Fontaine. Directed by Yvan Govar. Screenplay, Bernard Dimey from the play by Vahe Katcha; camera, Pierre Levent; editor, Alix Paturel. At Lord Byron, Paris. Running Time, **80 MINS.**
Laurent .... Pierre Brasseur
Consigne .... Michel Simon
De Rock .... Raymond Rouleau
Diane .... Catherine Sauvage
Gabriel .... Jean-Roger Caussimon
Chief .... Marcel Peres
Lucien .... Paul Gay
Livia .... Julie Fontaine

A fine group of noted character actors could not do much with this would-be suspense film that remains talky and unresolved as to whether it is a thriller, comedy or drama. Ordinary, indecisive direction does not help. Chances abroad look mild because of the thesping, confined quarters and action in a railroad station in a small town. But it may be usable for tv.

A murderer has been killing women in a small town. A down-and-out reporter tries to solve things though he fails, he gets mixed up in a plot of a wife and her lover to kill a husband instead. All this—while waiting for a train. But he is killed and the woman-killer is unmasked in an unresolved surprise ending.

Pierre Brasseur is massive, wheeling and effective as the newsman with veteran actor Michel Simon funny but ill used as a station attendant. Others are adequate in this pedestrian-paced pic that reeks too much of studio and not enough of crispness in story and characterization. *Mosk.*

Spy In Your Eye
(ITALIAN—COLOR)

Confusing espionage meller hard to follow.

Hollywood, Jan. 25.

American International release of Fulvio Lucisano-Lucio Marcuzzo production. Stars Brett Halsey, Pier Angeli; features Dana Andrews, Gaston Moschin, Tanya Beryl. Directed by Vittorio Sala. Screenplay, Romano Ferraro; Adriano Bolzoni; camera (PatheColor), Fausto Zuccoli; music, Riz Ortolani; editors, Roberto and Renato Cinquini; asst. director, Stefano Rolla. Reviewed at Joe Shore screening room, Jan. 25, '66. Running Time, **88 MINS.**
Bert Morris .... Brett Halsey
Paula .... Pier Angeli
Col. Lancaster .... Dana Andrews

American and Soviet secret agents manage to confuse one another in their search for the formula of a death ray, but their confusion is nothing compared to the audience's in trying to follow the unreeling of this Italian-made film. American International release has a gimmick—the Soviets replacing a lost eye of an American colonel with an orb containing a powerful miniature television transmitter and sound transmitter—that might have been developed into a pretty fair espionage meller, but its effect is lost in the vast maze of perplexing events that seque across the screen.

Brett Halsey is cast as an American agent who finally catches up to the formula—tattooed on the skull of Pier Angeli, daughter of the dead scientist who secreted his secret there (and what the poor girl goes through). Dana Andrews plays the colonel who unwittingly is responsible for American secrets getting to the enemy when his every move and word is transmitted.

Vittorio Sala in his direction takes advantage of foreign locations, principally in Beirut and other European centers but frequently is lost in his story-telling. Color camera work of Fausto Zuccoli frequently is interesting. *Whit.*

Secret Agent Fireball
(ITALIAN—COLOR)

Okay Italian-made spy entry for minor market.

Hollywood, Jan. 25.

American International release of Mino Loy-Luciano Martino production. Stars Richard Harrison; features Dominique Boschero, Wandisa Guida, Alan Collins, James Clay. Directed by Martin Conan. Screenplay, Julian Barry; camera (Eastmancolor), Richard Thierry; asst. director, Charles Chelosi; editor,

Robert Quintley; music, Carlo Savina. Reviewed at Joe Shore screening room, Jan. 25, '66. Running Time, 89 MINS.
Robert Fleming ..... Richard Harrison
Liz .... Dominique Boschero
Elena .... Wandisa Guida

"Secret Agent Fireball" (packaged with "Spy In Your Eye") is an okay entry in the present espionage upsurge, but lacks the finish of most of its predecessors. It carries violence, femmes and interesting foreign scenes which combine to keep the audience moderately entertained and for less demanding situations should be well received.

Italian-produced and shot in Paris, Hamburg Beirut and way points, the Julian Barry script focuses on Richard Harrison, American intelligence officer assigned to locate microfilm of Russian military secrets stolen by two fleeing Russian scientists. Plot has so many facets the spectator is lost at times, but this is compensated for by endeavor which would keep even James Bond happy. With both American and Soviet agents seeking the film, there's an anti-climax which reveals the secret is the H-bomb, possessed by both countries.

Harrison plays his role well enough and enjoys interesting support by Dominique Boschero, a looker, and Wandisa Guida, femme fatale. Martin Conan's direction usually is competent and Richard Thierry's photography excellent. *Whit.*

Il Ritorno Di Ringo
(The Return of Ringo)
(ITALIAN: COLOR)
Rome, Jan. 25.

Cineriz release of an Alberto Pugliese-Luciano Ercoli production for P.C.M. Produzioni Mediterranee-Rizzoli Films. Stars Giuliano Gemma (Montgomery Wood); features Fernando Sancho, Lorella de Luca, Hally Hammond, Nieves Navarro, Antonio Casas, Pajarito, George Martin. Directed by Duccio Tessari. Story and screenplay, Tessari, Fernando di Leo; camera (Eastmancolor), Francisco Marin; editor, Licia Quaglia; music, Ennio Morricone. At Galleria, Rome. Running Time, **95 MINS.**

Ringo .... Giuliano Gemma
Esteban .... Fernando Sancho
Hally .... Hally Hammond
Rosita .... Nieves Navarro
Sheriff .... Antonio Casas
Myosotis .... Pajarito
Paco Fuentes .... George Martin

Fair-to-middlin' "eastern" shot in Italy and Spain with plenty to please action fans everywhere. Lack of names makes this a probable dualer on foreign circuits, but at home in Italy, the Giuliano Gemma name and the current vogue for locally-made westerns give it a surefire fillip which should pay off both in big-city subsequents and the hinterlands.

This is follow-up of "A Pistol for Ringo," which featured essentially the same cast of principals but, unusually, is better than first film. And also thanks to the rising star in pic, could top it at b.o. Duccio Tessari is again the scripter-director, and he keeps things lively, alternating action with humor, liberally sprinkling the prairie and saloons with bodies. True, the cliches are all there: the comic sidekick, the Mexican heel, the half-breed woman (who inevitably loses her man), the clean-cut prim Eastern gal, the cowardly sheriff, the hero who learns to shoot lefty when

his shootin' arm is knifed, etc. Also, there's a derivative influence of violence bordering on sadism. But despite these factors, this pic makes its points well, looks legit, is elegantly lensed and lushly produced. In Giuliano Gemma, who changed his name back to the McCoy after appearing as "Montgomery Wood" in the previous Ringo, thus furthermore has a sure bet for international action roles, even rating Yank attention thanks to the personality and physique, plus an ability for acrobatics, learned when serving with Rome's fire department.

As noted, technical credits are fine. Ennio Morricone, who won awards with previous scores for local westerns, this time tends to overstate his musical points, though the general effect remains pleasant. *Hawk.*

The Silencers
(COLOR-SONGS)

Slambang secret agent offering with Dean Martin and covey of gorgeous femmes to amuse and thrill; top prospects foreseen.

Hollywood, Feb. 4.
Columbia Pictures release of Meadway-Claude (Irving Allen) production. Stars Dean Martin, Stella Stevens, Daliah Lavi; features Victor Buono, Cyd Charisse, Robert Webber, Nancy Kovack, Arthur O'Connell, James Gregory, Roger C. Carmel. Directed by Phil Karlson. Screenplay, Oscar Saul; based on books, "The Silencers" and "Death of a Citizen," by Donald Hamilton; camera (PatheColor), Burnett Guffey; music, Elmer Bernstein; editor, Charles Nelson; asst. director, Clark Pavlow. Reviewed at Warner Hollywood Theatre, Feb. 3, '66. Running Time, **103 MINS.**

Matt Helm	Dean Martin
Gail	Stella Stevens
Tina	Daliah Lavi
Tung-Tze	Victor Buono
Wigman	Arthur O'Connell
Sam Gunther	Robert Webber
MacDonald	James Gregory
Barbara	Nancy Kovack
Andreyev	Roger C. Carmel
Sarita	Cyd Charisse
Lovey Kravezit	Beverly Adams
Domino	Richard Devon
Dr. Naldi	David Bond
Traynor	John Reach
1st Armed Man	Robert Philips
M.C.	John Willis
Frazer	Frank Gerstle
Radio Man	Grant Woods
Hotel Clerk	Patrick Waltz

Comes now another super-secret agent-dooper to out-Bond previous entries spilling like wildfire across the cinematic spy scene. Dean Martin — as Matt Helm, ace of the American counter-espionage agency, ICE — succeeds in a kind of lover-boy way in taking his place up there with such stalwarts as Sean Connery (007), James Coburn ("Our Man Flint") and David Niven ("Where the Spies Are"). "The Silencers," packed with gorgeous dames, electrifying moments and imaginative plottage, may be reckoned to hit top grosses, particularly with its built-in exploitation potential.

Produced by Irving Allen and directed by Phil Karlson, both utilizing shock technique, the fast-driving Oscar Saul screenplay is based on two of Donald Hamilton's Matt Helm books, "The Silencers" and "Death of a Citizen," and could rightfully presage a series on the character, who gets the glamour treatment in translation.

Plot focuses on a Chinese agent (Victor Buono) who masterminds a ring that plans to divert a U.S. missile so it will destroy Alamogordo, New Mexico, thus creating wide devastation and atomic fallout leading perhaps to global war. All Matt Helm has to do is halt this catastrophe.

Martin has a emperor-sized round bed is equipped with a rotary, a tv screen to show who he's talking to, et al, and pad rolls to a pool where it tips him into the suds by the side of a woo-woo secretary ready to execute his instant need. That's only his more intimate side; professionally, he sports a revolver that shoots backwards as anybody except him who appropriates it finds to his displeasure, and buttons on his jacket that can blow up the Bank of England.

He goes in, either, for just Judo or Karate, not he; he clobbers his foes with none other than Okinawa Te, which as anyone knows the ancient Okinawans learned from animals and reptiles when the Japanese took away their native weapons. Juveniles of all generations will respond.

Martin goes all out in a tongue-in-cheek enactment, even warbling a few songs for good measure. Action occasionally gets seriously melodramatic, such as when two enemy cars try to ram Martin's car between them on a winding mountain road, good for thrills. Climactic moments in the enemy's hideaway cave, where Martin wreaks havoc, is fast and bombastic.

Starring with Martin are Stella Stevens and Daliah Lavi. Miss Stevens does herself proud as a mixed-up living doll who can stumble over her own shadow. Miss Lavi is a femme fatale, Martin's ever-lovin' spymate who comes up with a big surprise for him.

The glamor department is further repped by Cyd Charisse as a dancer killed by the mob as she's dancing; and Beverly Adams. There's plenty of stripping in this picture.

Competent, too, are Buono as the chief menace who would rule the world; Roger C. Carmel, Arthur O'Connell and Robert Webber, three of his henchmen; James Gregory, **Martin's** boss always dreaming up fascinating new terrors to subject him to.

Top technical support is afforded by Burnett Guffey in his Pathe-Color photography; Joe Wright's imaginative art direction; Elmer Bernstein's appropriate music score; Charles Nelson's tight editing. Costumes designed by Moss Mabry are no less than sensational.
Whit.

The Last Chapter
(DOCUMENTARY)
Ben-Lar Productions (Benjamin and Lawrence Rothman) production. Narrated by Theodore Bikel. Directed by Benjamin and Lawrence Rothman. Screenplay by S. L. Shneiderman with historical research by Eileen Shneiderman. Postwar Poland scenes filmed by Victor Johannes; editor, Jacob Hameiri; choral selections, sung by Farband Culture Chorus. Screened in N.Y., Feb. 2, '65. Running Time: **90 MINS.**

This documentary - compilation film by Jewish theatrical producers-publicists Benjamin and Lawrence Rothman is an attempt to recreate something of the centuries of historical and cultural contribution made to Poland by its Jewish citizens; the country's treatment of them and their fate during and after World War II. Although frequently moving, and to be viewed with pride by those of the Jewish faith, it has a limited appeal in a market that has already been serviced with many somewhat similar films, both authentic and fictional. With considerable competition in its own genre, there's little commercial value to the offering.

Much of the film is devoted to a spoken commentary, read beautifully by folk singer-actor Theodore Bikel, of the contributions made to Poland by over 1,000 years of Jewish citizenry. This is narrated against a slim plotline of having a former Polish Jew return to the country of his birth and, through a combination of specially-filmed passages, excerpts from old newsreels and documentaries, still photographs and ancient records, invoke memories of the past. There's a static feeling, however, for non-Jewish viewers in watching the depiction of building after building, town after town, that have little meaning for him, with only the occasional dropping of a familiar name — Sholem Asch, Sholem Aleichem, etc.—to stir their interest.

The most effective portion of the film, as it must be with any reprise of the Nazi holocaust that left few of the country's 3,500,000 Jews alive, is the final compiled cinematic retelling of what happened, particularly in Warsaw, in those last dreadful days. Use of various film sources results, as is to be expected, in a hodgepodge of cinematic styles. Actual newsreel clips jar with apparent excerpts from newer motion pictures made about the period. Although the Rothmans would not reveal, beyond the screen credits, the source of their films, one of the acknowledged sources is the Polish State Film Company. Some of the clips are remarkably similar to such Andrzej Wajde films about the period as "Kanal" and "Sampson."

Writer S. L. Shneiderman's narrative is, actually, more outspoken than the film (with the exception of atrocity shots which are not used too often). He doesn't hesitate to condemn the reluctance of the Allies to be involved. "London was silent, no word came forth . . . from Washington, no protest was heard . . . from the Kremlin, nothing . . . no voice was raised in the Vatican . . . it was a silent and indifferent world. Every effort to get Allied help failed, even the obtaining of medical supplies."

An interesting excerpt for cinema buffs is the depiction of a Yiddish theatrical group in a play which stars Ida Kaminsky (the star of the much-acclaimed Czech film, "Shop on the Main Street," now showing in N.Y.). "The Last Chapter" has been booked into New York's Cameo Theatre, opening Feb. 21.
Robe.

The Battle of The Bulge
—The Brave Rifles

Interesting war documentary, but its 52-minutes' length poses booking problem.

Hollywood, Feb. 2.
Lawrence E. Mascott production (no release), written-directed by Mascott. Narrator, Arthur Kennedy; editor, Alan H. Presberg; music, Ruby Raksin. Reviewed at Lytton Center Theatre, Feb. 1, '66. Running Time, **52 MINS.**

Three years in the making, "The Battle of the Bulge — The Brave Rifles" was written, produced and directed by Laurence E. Mascott, himself a veteran of that critical World War II engagement whose story he purports to tell "from the point of view of the individual soldier." Running 52 minutes, it is a documentary consisting of clips from all manner of sources, lensed by both Americans and Germans as they accompanied their respective forces. Some of the German footage was acquired by Mascott from European film laboratory personnel.

Mascott has handled his subject well, but its comparatively-brief length may make booking difficult and the best he can hope for is lower half of double bills. His selection of scenes showing the Nazi attempted break-through in the Belgian Ardennes area is hypoed by a masterly narrative delivered dramatically by Arthur Kennedy, and atmosphere further is provided by realistic sound effects and an appropriate music score composed by Ruby Raksin.

Hitler's campaign of total terror in trying to crush American forces in reaching Antwerp in action centering on Elsenborn, St. Vith and Bastogne is graphically depicted. Attention frequently focuses on individual or historic bits of heroism by Americans, accompanied where possible by photographs of known servicemen. From these individual stories comes part of the title . . . these men created a new American legend, a legend as great as Valley Forge, or the Alamo, or Gettysburg, the legend of "The Brave Rifles."

There is a starkness to the unfoldment reminiscent of some of the better war documentaries of the past, and the grimness of war cloaks every moment of unreelment. Mascott's knowledge of the climactic battle shines through in his written narrative, and Kennedy's commentating punches up all its horror. Use occasionally is made of voices supposed to be American GI's as they talk about their part in the conflict.

Alan H. Presberg is credited as film editor.
Whit.

Faster, Pussycat, Kill! Kill!

Technically well-made sexploitationer from Russ Meyer. Weak script, loaded with violence, sex and some perversion angles. Too strong for general market, okay for male-oriented sex-action situations.

Hollywood, Feb. 4.
Eve Productions Inc. release, produced (with Eve Meyer), edited and directed by Russ Meyer. Features Tura Satana, Haji, Lori Williams, Susan Bernard, Stuart Lancaster, Paul Trinka, Dennis Busch, Ray Barlow, Mickey Foxx. Story, Jack Moran; camera, Walter Schenk; music, Paul Sawtelle, Bert Shefter; asst. director, George Costello. Reviewed at Pathe Labs, L.A., Feb. 4, '66. Running Time, **84 MINS.**

"Faster, Pussycat, Kill! Kill!" is a somewhat sordid, quite sexy and very violent murder-kidnap-theft meller which includes elements of rape, lesbianism and sadism, clothed in faddish leather and boots and equipped with sports cars. Some good performances emerge from a one-note script via very good Russ Meyer direction and his outstanding editing. Brought in at $44,000 and using California desert exteriors throughout, film is too strong for general situations, but should do good biz in houses which specialize in raw drama.

Jack Moran's story concerns a trio of bosomy swingers led by Tura Satana, her female lover Haji, and his ambiSEXtrous Lori Williams. Out for kicks, Miss Satana does in Ray Barlow via explicit karate, then kidnaps latter's chick, a petite Susan Bernard. Greed takes them to crippled widower Stuart Lancaster's desert diggings, where he dominates his retarded, but muscular son, Dennis Busch, also Paul Trinka, a more sensitive offspring. Latter and Miss Bernard survive the brutality, lechery and mayhem.

Although the technically well-made pic is, in its class, relegated to programmer status via the script melange, it is obvious that Meyer has a directorial talent which belongs in bigger and stronger films. His visual sense is outstanding, also his setups (executed by Walter Schenk's crisp camera). Meyer's editing has a zest and polish which, without being obvious post-production gimmickry, lends proper pace and emphasis. All he needs is stronger scripting and more adept performers.

Cast members have varying degrees of promise. Miss Satana has a mystic Oriental face which could be developed for better off-beat roles, while Miss Williams has a fresh, but sensual air that is promising in both heavy and sympathetic characterizations. Lancaster, no newcomer, is a fine actor who can project mature strength and nobility, as well as the deranged, self-pitying lechery required here. Miss Bernard, a bit unrestrained in the plot hysteria, is a pleasant ingenue. Other thesps are okay, including Mickey Foxx as a goofy gas pump jockey.

Paul Sawtelle and Bert Shefter have composed some good background themes, which music director Igo Kantor has blended into a full score. Charles G. Schelling's sound (no looping) is terrif.

Murf.

Make Like a Thief
(FINNISH-COLOR)

Interesting chase melodrama produced entirely in Finland by an American and with an American lead. Good possibilities in program market.

Hollywood, Feb. 4.
Emerson release of Palmer Thompson production. Stars Richard Long; features Ake Lindman, Pirkko Mannola. Directed by Thompson, Richard Long. Screenplay, Thompson; camera (EastmanColor), Kalle Peronkoski, Reijo Hassinen; music, Erkki Meloski; editor, Kari Uusitalo. Reviewed at National General Corp. theatre, Beverly Hills, Calif., Feb. 3, '66. Running Time, 79 MINS.
Burt .... Richard Long
Arvo .... Ake Lindman
Marja .... Pirkko Mannola
Toini .... Rosemary Precht
Weston .... Juhani Kumpalinen
Helvi .... Aulekki Tarnanen
Gunman .... Esko Salamen

The setting — Finland — where pic was produced, photographed and processed in its entirely, endows "Make Like a Thief" with values vastly superior to any which might normally have been associated with a regulation melodrama of this type. Project was conceived by Palmer Thompson, who produced and wrote story. He and Richard Long, star and co- director with Thompson, are only Americans in an otherwise all-Finnish company.

Such shrewd use has been made of the Finnish backgrounds, beautifully lensed in EastmanColor, that feature emerges a first-class entry for the program market.

Conceivably, it might do for Finland in attracting tourist travel what "Summertime" did for Venice and "Three Coins in the Fountain" for Rome.

This is the story of an American — Long — who has come to Finland to search for the master mind in a gigantic American swindle in which he was left holding the sack. He enlists the services of a personable mercenary who had turned him into the Helsinki police for a $5,000 reward. Dangling the lure of a $50,000 share if the informer helps him find the swindler, Long finally manages to catch up with his quarry, to the accompaniment of murder attempts and pursuits by the authorities.

Long cloaks his performance with a light touch and gets good backing from Ake Lindman, his somewhat reluctant associate, and especially from Pirkko Mannola, a little nightclub singer, who attaches herself to him and wants him to marry her. Rosemary Precht as Lindman's amour, and Aulekki Taarnanen, a conniving nitery operator, lend further distaff interest, while Juhani Kumpalinen is well cast as the swindler.

Direction by Thompson and Long is satisfactory and color photography by Kalle Peronkoski and Reijo Hassinen outstanding.

Whit.

La Vie De Chateau
(Chateau Life)
(FRENCH)

Paris, Feb. 8.
CFDC release of Ancinex-Cobela Films production. Stars Catherine Deneuve; features Pierre Brasseur, Philippe Noiret, Henri Garcin, Mary Marquet, Carlos Thompson. Directed by Jean-Paul Rappeneau. Screenplay, Alain Cavalier, Claude Sautet, Daniel Boulanger, Rappeneau; camera, Pierre Lhomme; editor, Pierre Gilette. At Biarritz, Paris. Running Time, 90 MINS.
Wife .... Catherine Deneuve
Jerome .... Philippe Noiret
Father .... Pierre Brasseur
Mother .... Mary Marquet
French Officer .... Henri Garcin
German Officer ...... Carlos Thompson

This slight, but bright situation comedy, manages to use a background of the imminent D-Day Landings, the Occupation and the Resistance during the last World War without being vulgar, irreverent or tasteless. Love is the theme, and if there is some quaintness for its own sake, and not enough character insight to bring it off entirely, this looks to click here. Its novelty as a war comedy give it some chances overseas if well sold and placed. But it seems a chancey item at best. Playoff and specialized bookings, rather than arty dates, appear called for in the foreign market.

A triangle develops when a Free French officer, parachuted into France to stake out ways of knocking out a shore gun before the Landing, falls for a comely, addlepated 20-year-old wife of the man who owns the local chateau. Also enamored of the flighty wife, who thinks only of going to Paris and feels her husband is a coward hiding away from the war, is a local Nazi officer.

It is a time, according to the

---

film's comedic bent, when the crusty mother of the chateau owner can keep out German billets by barking at any who show up. But the German moves in his men because of the wife while the Frenchman returns from a London trip, and is more involved in the girl than his mission. The husband turns out to be the real hero and wins back his wife. War rears its head at the end when Allied Commandos drop in and take the fortification, with some deftly used stock footage to lead into the Liberation of Paris.

Catherine Deneuve is fetching as the girl so much in demand, but lacks that spark and projection that would give her the appeal to have all these people forgetting wars for her. Pierre Brasseur is cranky as the girl's father, who is in the Resistance, while Philippe Noiret is effective as the stuffy husband.

Director Jean-Paul Rappeneau, a former scripter, on this his first pic, relies a bit too much on dialog, too much of ti theatrical, and not giving heft to the images. However, there are some okay visual comedic ideas.

This is a classically mounted pic with a stilted charm. It lacks the visual lightness and invention to give it a situation frothiness in its love tale.

Rappeneau may emerge an okay addition to the directorial ranks. Film will do okay on its home grounds. It could have some fair chances abroad, and some playoff rather for arty chances.

Film copped one of the oldest critic prizes here, Le Prix Louis Delluc, for the most promising and unique new talents. *Mosk.*

The Oscar
(COLOR)

Exploitable film about a Best Actor Award nominee; good performances right down the line with Stephen Boyd excellent in unsympathetic role.

Hollywood, Feb. 10.
Embassy release of Greene - Rouse (Clarence Greene) production. Stars Stephen Boyd, Elke Sommer, Milton Berle, Eleanor Parker, Joseph Cotten; features Jill St. John, Tony Bennett, Edie Adams, Ernest Borgnine. Directed by Russell Rouse. Screenplay, Harlan Ellison, Rouse, Greene; based on novel by Richard Sale; camera (PatheColor), Joseph Ruttenberg; music, Percy Faith; editor, Chester W. Schaeffer; asst. director, Dick Moder. Reviewed at Paramount Studios, Feb. 9, '66. Running Time, 172 MINS.
Frank Fane .... Stephen Boyd
Kay Bergdahl .... Elke Sommer
Kappy Kapstetter .... Milton Berle
Sophie Cantaro ...... Eleanor Parker
Kenneth H. Regan ..... Joseph Cotten
Laurel Scott .... Jill St. John
Hymie Kelly .... Tony Bennett
Trina Yale .... Edie Adams
Barney Yale .... Ernest Borgnine
Grobard .... Ed Beeley
Orrin C. Quentin ...... Walter Brennan
Sheriff .... Broderick Crawford
Network Executive ...... James Dunn
Edith Head .... Herself
Hedda Hopper .... Herself
Steve Marks .... Peter Lawford
Merle Oberon .... Herself
Nancy Sinatra .... Herself
Sam .... Jack Soo
Cheryl Barker .... Joan Hale

Joseph E. Levine's Embassy Pictures has an exploitable property in this Clarence Greene - Russell Rouse production based on Richard Sale's Hollywood novel of an unscrupulous Oscar nominee for Best Actor. Release is pegged to period of upcoming Oscar derby (April 18) and attendant publicity building toward that event should benefit film accordingly. Feature also is given certain additional authority by opening on an actual Academy Awards presentation and presence of Bob Hope as emcee, which sets the stage for what is to come via flashback technique.

This is the story of a vicious, bitter, firstclass heel who rises to stardom on the blood of those close to him. Without a single redeeming quality, part played by Stephen Boyd is unsympathetic virtually from opening shots of him as spieler for stripper at a cheap smoker.

Greene as producer and Rouse as director are unrelenting in their development of the character, in screenplay on which they collabed with Harlan Ellison, and they make handsome use of the Hollywood background as setting for a narrative some may accept as typical of the Oscar race and others may not accept at all.

Boyd is surrounded by some offbeat casting which adds an interesting note. Milton Berle switches from his usual comedic image to dramatic role as a top Hollywood agent, and Tony Bennett, the singer, portrays a straight character, Boyd's longtime friend victimized by the star in his battle for success. Bennett frequently acts, too, as off-screen narrator, a sometimes annoying device but in general serving satisfactorily to progress movement.

Actually, the story line builds to that single moment when name of the winner of the Best Actor award is announced by Merle Oberon, playing herself as presenter, from the stage. As Boyd sits in his theatre seat awaiting the great moment for which he has been n o m i n a t e d, his story is told through the eyes of his friend, Bennett; then action returns to the present and a surprise climax.

Boyd makes the most of his part, investing it with an audience-hate symbol which he never once compromises and turning in one of the best performances of his career. Elke Sommer, as his studio-designer wife who is another of his victims, is chief distaff interest in a well-undertaken portrayal. Eleanor Parker excels in the rather thankless role of a studio talent scout and dramatic coach who discovers Boyd in N.Y.

Joseph Cotten is lost as head of a studio who signs Boyd against his better judgment, but makes each scene count, and Jill St. John as the stripper is delectable in her brief opening - sequences appearance. Ernest Borgnine is effective as a double-crossing private eye with whom Boyd has some dirty dealings, and Edie Adams, cast as his divorced wife, stands out in a gemlike role. Jean Hale scores as a sexpot starlet, as does Peter Lawford as an ex-star reduced to employment as a maitre d' in a Hollywood restaurant.

An arresting impression is made by the late Hedda Hopper, playing herself. Also playing themselves are Edith Head, the designer, whose designs for picture fit the mood expected; Merle Oberon and Nancy Sinatra. Frank Sinatra is in for a single but meaningful scene. Jack Soo has a few good moments as a house boy, and Walter Brennan, Broderick Crawford, Ed Begley and James Dunn handle small roles well.

Technical credits are definitely on the superior side, including Hal Pereira and Arthur Lonergan's art direction, Percy Faith's music score, Joseph Ruttenberg's matchless photography, C h e s t e r W. Schaeffer's editing. *Whit.*

Per Qualche Dollaro In Piu'
(For a Few Dollars More)
(ITALO-GERMAN-SPANISH)
(Color)

Rome, Feb. 8.
P.E.A. release of a Produzioni Europee Associate (Rome) production in association with Arturo Gonzales (Madrid) and Constantin Films (Munich). Stars Clint Eastwood, Lee Van Cleef, Gian Maria Volonte'; features Mara Krup, Luigi Pistilli, Klaus Klinski, Josef Egger, Panos Papadopoulos, Benito Stefanelli, Robert Camardiel, Aldo Sambell, Luis Rodriguez, Mario Brega. Directed by Sergio Leone. Screenplay, Luciano Vincenzoni; camera (Technicolor), Massimo Dallamano; music, Ennio Morricone. Editors, Giorgio Ferralonga, Eugenio Aalabiso; at Supercinema, Rome. Running Time, 130 MINS.
Il Monco .... Clint Eastwood
Colonel .... Lee Van Cleef
Indio .... Gian Maria Volonte'

Hard-hitting westerns with upper-case values out of the busy Italo stable, this looks to top even impressive totals of director Sergio Leone's previous hit oater, "For a Fistful of Dollars," at local wickets. Pic is also a topnotch action entry for foreign markets although it's unlikely that it will approach the record-breaking pace it is setting in this territory, where it has such added pluses as the Clint Eastwood name, the rep of

Leone's previous pic, and the vogue for locally-made westerns riding in its favor.

Story deals with a race between two bounty killers, Eastwood and Lee Van Cleef, for reward money riding on head of a bandit, Gian Maria Volonte. First separately, then via a somewhat shaky and untrusting allegiance, the pair manage to set the stage for the killing of the bandido, called El Indio. In the finale, it turns out that Van Cleef's real reason for getting El Indio was not the coin involved, but vengeance for the death of a member of his family. As a result, Eastwood pockets all the cash and rides off a rich man.

Luciano Vincenzoni's script generally manages to avoid the cliche pitfalls traditional to the western, and his dialogue is literate and satisfying to the ear. But it's principally thanks to Leone's bigger-than-life style, which combines upfront action and closeup details with a hard-hitting pace reminiscent of the Bond pix, that this acquires its verile and impactful dimension. Audiences can laugh with it or at it, but they won't be bored.

Thesping is in keeping. Eastwood is fine in a tailor-made role of the squint-eyed opportunist who plays his cards right. Van Cleef etches a neat picture of his partner-rival. Gian Mario Volonte' makes a suitably villainous heavy (for an added fillip, script makes him a drug addict to boot). Others in the large and varied roster of players give pic in-depth characterization values. Incidentally, though frequently very violent, pic generally avoids pitfalls of previous Leone vehicles in eschewing excessive sadism.

Physical values are impressive, too. Spanish countryside and Italo studio interiors combine for realistic southwestern effect which should fool all but the expert into believing they're the real thing. Massimo Dallamano's Technicolor lensing is an added plus while Ennio Morricone's music, without measuring up to his previous efforts in the oater belt, is nevertheless pleasing.

Editors Giorgio Ferralonga and Eugenio Alabiso could have worked a bit more with their shears. Pic is somewhat overlong at 130 minutes. But the pace is generally just right, and then local patrons don't seem to be complaining about a film's length. *Hawk.*

Harper
(COLOR—PANAVISION)

Paul Newman as private eye in missing person meller. Fine performances and also direction of slick, but longish script. Colorful production values. Big marquee lineup promises warm b.o.

Hollywood, Feb. 8.
Warner Bros. release of a Jerry Gershwin - Elliott Kastner production. Stars Paul Newman; features (alphabetically) Lauren Bacall, Julie Harris, Arthur Hill, Janet Leigh, Pamela Tiffin, Robert Wagner, Robert Webber, Shelley Winters. Directed by Jack Smight. Screenplay, William Goldman, based on Ross MacDonald's novel, "The Moving Target"; camera (Technicolor), Conrad Hall; editor, Stefan Arnsten; music, Johnny Mandel; song, Dory and Andre Previn; asst. director, James H. Brown.

Reviewed at Pacific's Pantages Theatre, L.A., Feb. 4, '66. Running Time, 121 MINS.
Lew Harper .... Paul Newman
Mrs. Sampson .... Lauren Bacall
Betty Fraley .... Julie Harris
Albert Graves .... Arthur Hill
Susan Harper .... Janet Leigh
Miranda Sampson ...... Pamela Tiffin
Alan Traggert .... Robert Wagner
Dwight Troy .... Robert Webber
Fay Estabrook .... Shelley Winters
Sheriff .... Harold Gould
Claude .... Strother Martin
Puddler .... Roy Jensen
Deputy .... Martin West
Mrs. Kronberg ..... Jacqueline de Wit
Felix .. .. Eugene Iglesias
Fred Platt .... Richard Carlyle

"Harper" is a contemporary mystery-comedy with Paul Newman as a sardonic private eye involved in a missing person trackdown. Some excellent directorial touches and solid thesping are evident in the colorful and plush Jerry Gershwin-Elliott Kastner production, pair's first tandem effort. Abundance of comedy and sometimes extraneous emphasis on cameo characters make for a relaxed pace and imbalanced concept, resulting in overlength and telegraphing of climax. Newman and other players provide hot marquee lure, and very good prospects loom for Warner Bros. release in general situation.

In the current film market, loaded as it is with gimmick-laden, over-sexed super-spies submerged in international intrigue, "Harper" offers a change of pace in depicting the ramblings of a gumshoe among the jaded rich, proverbially blundering cops and some seamy characters. All are presented as specimens of Southern California living.

Ross MacDonald's novel, "The Moving Target," was adapted by William Goldman. Scripter's complicated plotting has Newman commissioned by Lauren Bacall to find her hubby (never seen until climax), although she has no love for either him or step-daughter Pamela Tiffin. Family counsel Arthur Hill got old pal Newman the job.

Complications i n c l u d e the spoiled Miss Tiffin, casual companion of family pilot Robert Wagner, himself hung up on Julie Harris, a piano bar entertainer also a junkie. Shelley Winters is the aging actress failure who has known the missing man, and is married to Robert Webber, brains behind a wetback smuggling ring run by religious nut Strother Martin.

Roy Jensen provides violent moments as a gin mill bouncer, while Jacqueline de Wit scores as Miss Bacall's patronizing housekeeper. Harold Gould and Martin West are the dub policemen. Janet Leigh is Newman's estranged wife.

Director Jack Smight has inserted countless touches which illuminate each character to the highest degree. In this he complements Goldman's sharp and often salty lingo. All principals acquit themseves admiraby, including Newman, Miss Bacall, Webber, and particularly Miss Winters, who makes every second count as the once-aspiring film star now on the high-calorie sauce.

While individual sequences are in themselves quite satisfying, the whole is less rewarding than the parts. The occasional violence

comes in rapid spurts(save for the Newman-Jensen shipyard fisticuffs), which are diluted by prolonged cameos. Miss Leigh accounts for perhaps 10 minutes of screentime, yet the character does nothing for the plot. Martin's mountaintop retreat adds a bizarre prop, but it serves only to intro the wetback angle—a lot of film to convey a minor point.

Then too, Hill's shy-guy overemphasis becomes thin. West's rookie fuzz bit is effective, but also pales in a lavatory scene with Newman which is as needless as it is tasteless. (Smight returns to the head when the missing man is at last discovered.) And the many eye-filling exteriors, in turn, are as picturesque as they are needless. Almost 20 more minutes could have been trimmed by editor Stefan Arnsten from present running time of 121 minutes.

Conrad Hall's lush Technicolor lensing in Panavision provides a neat picture. Johnny Mandel's score is exciting and appropriate, and his discotheque riff catches the ear. Dory and Andre Previn composed "Livin' Alone" for Miss Harris, an okay torcher which has the merit of being motivated by the script and logically introduced.

Good opener has Newman getting up in the morning under main titles. and the throwaway tag line (which leaves a few plots threads unresolved—such as manslaughter) is emphasized by stop-motion process, second consecutive Warner release—other was "Inside Daisy Clover"—to employ the gambit. Other technical credits are firstrate. *Murf.*

De Dans van de Reiger
(Dance of the Herons)
(DUTCH-GERMAN)

Berlin, Feb. 8.
Atlas release of a Fons Rademakers production made in collab with Atlas-Film, West Germany. Directed by Fons Rademakers. Screenplay, Hugo Claus and Rademakers; camera, Sacha Vierny; music, Jurrihan Andriessen; editor, Dick van der Maer. Previewed at Academy of Arts, West Berlin. Running Time, 90 MINS.
Edward .... Jean Desailly
Elena .... Gunnel Lindblom
Paul .... Van Doude
Mother....... Mien Duymaer van Twist

There may be some guessing about the sort of feature pic which Fons Rademakers, p r o m i n e n t Dutch film creator, directed and produced in collab with the German Atlas-Film. It's a mixture of burlesque, tragicomedy and modern marriage drama. Film looks like a good bargain for the arty houses. The names of Swedish Gunnel Lindblom (of "Silence") and Jean Desailly can be exploitation factors. Rademakers' fifth feature film looks like a good bet for this year's festivals.

Whole thing takes place near Dubrovnik on hte Yugoslav coast where Jean Desailly, a wealthy Dutch manufacturer, has rented a villa for the summer holidays. He's a middle-aged man, very conservative in all respects. His wife, 10 years younger, is just the opposite — temperamental, self-willed, modern woman. To make her husband jealous, she flirts with Van Doude, a Dutch tourist, whom she met on the beach. But her husband remains quiet. He cannot forget that, one year ago, she had been unfaithful to him. He won't forgive her and has never touched her since. It seems as though this "dark spot" in her past has torpedoed their marriage.

Eventually, Desailly tells his old mother who's holidaying with the couple that he has a mind to commit suicide. The mother suggests that he just pretend having committed suicide so that he can enjoy revenge on his wife. When his wife and Van Doude return one morning they find a "dead" husband. Yet the wife's reaction is just the opposite of the expected. She sees in his "suicide attempt" only proof of his deep love for her. She sends the tourist away and then both husband and wife realize that the dark past which separated them is over.

Rademakers' feel for atmosphere is excellent, as is his handling of the four players. Their acting is intentionally overly dramatic to give the whole thing a satirical bite. Gunnel Lindblom is perfectly cast as the vivacious wife. Desailly, as her husband, also turns in a brilliant performance. Although he's quiet most of the time, it's a delight to watch him work. Van Doude is the moustached tourist lover, while Mien Duymaer van Twist is the mother. Both do well.

Film benefits a good deal from competent black-and-white lensing and smooth editing. The intelligent score is a major asset. "Dance of the Herons" will maintain Rademakers' rep as Holland's top feature film creator. Atlas, which helped to finance the film, has world rights. The title, incidentally, is symbolically intended. The herons dance before they make love. Van Doude and Miss Lindblom come along with a suggestive dance in this, with folk music supplied by Yugoslav villagers.

Hans.

Promise Her Anything
(BRITISH-COLOR)

Good comedy-romance with tasteful handling of child care and nudie pix satirical angles. Well directed and acted, with appeal to young and old. Good marquee bait plus snappy sell equals neat b.o. in general situations.

Hollywood, Feb. 8.

Paramount Pictures release of a Seven Arts-Ray Stark (in association with Paramount) presentation, produced by Stanley Rubin. Stars Warren Beatty, Leslie Caron, Bob Cummings; features Keenan Wynn, Hermione Gingold, Lionel Stander. Screenplay, William Peter Blatty, based on story by Arne Sultan, Marvin Worth; camera (Technicolor), Douglas Slocombe; editor, John Shirley; music, Lyn Murray; title tune, Hal David, Burt Bacharach; asst. director, Ted Sturgis. Reviewed at Pacific's Picwood Theatre, West L.A., Feb. 7, '66. Running Time, **96 MINS.**

Harley Rummel .... Warren Beatty
Michele O'Brien .... Leslie Caron
Dr. Brock .... Bob Cummings
Angelo Carelli .... Keenan Wynn
Mrs. Luce .... Hermione Gingold
Sam .... Lionel Stander
Rusty .... Asa Maynor
Mrs. Brock .... Cathleen Nesbitt
John Thomas .... Michael Bradley
Mail-order film cast .. Warren Mitchell, Sydney Tafler, Mavis Villiers, Margaret Nolan, Viviane Ventura
Staff Doctor .... Michael Kane
Glue Sniffer .... Riggs O'Hara
Neighbors .... George Moon, Charlotte Holland
Vittorio Fettucini .... Ferdy Mayne
Clinic Mother .... Libby Morris
Pet Shop Customer ...... Bessie Love
Mrs. B.M. von Crispin .... Jill Adams

"Promise Her Anything" is a light, refreshing comedy-romance, set in Greenwich Village but filmed in England, which satirizes both child psychology and nudie pix in a tasteful, effective manner. Well-paced direction of many fine performances, generally sharp scripting and other good production elements add up to a satisfying comedy entry for most audiences. Stanley Rubin produced the Seven Arts-Ray Stark-Paramount presentation which, with the good marquee lineup augmented by a zesty sell, should garner bright b.o. in general situations.

An Arne Sultan-Marvin Worth story has been adapted and scripted by William Peter Blatty into what is basically a romantic triangle. Leslie Caron, with a precocious baby boy but no hubby, hopes to connect with her employer, child psychologist Bob Cummings who, in private life, abhors moppets. Miss Caron's neighbor, Warren Beatty, wants her, although he is careful to conceal his profession — making mail-order nudie films.

Director Arthur Hiller has overcome a basic problem; specifically, that Miss Caron and Beatty are not known as film comics. His fine solution has been to spotlight baby Michael Bradley in the first 30 minutes, when Miss Caron is establishing an easy audience rapport, while Beatty slides into a likeable groove via energetic tumbles and other manifestations of youthful enthusiasm. Bradley steals the show in this period and the kid has a good film future.

Hiller phases out comedy emphasis on the boy (although latter continues to figure in gags, but as a participant) as the principals begin to wham home their characterizations. Cummings, starred above title after Beatty and Miss Caron, remains the polished comedian in a role which permits him to be befuddled by his patients, defrosted by Miss Caron and prodded by his mother, Cathleen Nesbitt. Miss Nesbitt has some sharp lines, all delivered to wow response.

Complicating Beatty's life is Keenan Wynn, a mild-mannered pet shop operator who bankrolls Beatty's nudies on the side, and bugs him to come up with a new film gimmick. Also, landlady Hermione Gingold, who wants rent, not a picture career. Lionel Stander observes proceedings from outside crane as he builds a sign, plugging a European airline, which gets a trifle overplayed in final footage.

Spotted throughout are various nudie pix setups and satires, with Asa Maynor quite effective among these players. Good impact is derived all the way down the cast, including beatnik Riggs O'Hara, vet film thesp Bessie Love as one of Wynn's pet shop customers, and the George Moon-Charlotte Holland pairing as a goofy neighbor couple.

Stop-motion effects and zesty editing to 96 minutes by John Shirley keep things moving along, and Douglas Slocombe's fluid Technicolor camera captures the comedy highlights. This compensates for some trade gags which will be lost on general audiences, also for some throwaway lines not always heard, particularly through Miss Caron's dialect.

Lyn Murray's rhythmic score is a big assist. Hal David and Burt Bacharach wrote the title tune, heard at start and end via voiceover by Tom Jones, a current youth fave and a good sales angle. Opening titles, delayed five minutes, feature Bradley and are the work of Maurice Binder. Other technical credits of England's Shepperton Studios are firstrate.

Buffs and others may note that, although film is slugged as a Paramount "Picture" (not "Release"), sole copyright rests in Seven Arts Prods. Ltd. (U.K.).

Murf.

To Trap A Spy
(COLOR)

Elaboration of MGM-TV's "Man from U.N.C.L.E." pilot; weak entry for theatrical market.

Hollywood, Feb. 11.

Metro release of Norman Felton production. Stars Robert Vaughn; features Luciana Paluzzi, Patricia Crowley, Fritz Weaver. Directed by Don Medford. Screenplay, Sam Rolfe; camera (Metrocolor), Joseph Biroc; music, Jerry Goldsmith; editor, Henry Berman; asst. director, Maurice Vaccarino. Reviewed at Metro Studios, Feb. 10, '66. Running Time, **92 MINS.**

Napoleon Solo .... Robert Vaughn
Angela .... Luciana Paluzzi
Elaine May Donaldsen .. Patricia Crowley
Vulcan .... Fritz Weaver
Mr. Allison .... Will Kuluva
Ashumen .... William Marshall
Soumarin .... Ivan Dixon
Illya .. .. David McCallum
Gracie Ladovan .... Victoria Shaw
Lancer .... Miguel Landa
Alfred Ghist .... Eric Berry
Del Floria .... Mario Siletti
Nobuk .. .. Rupert Crosse

"To Trap a Spy" is an elaborated version of MGM-TV's "The Man from U.N.C.L.E." pilot, originally lensed in color but telecast in black-and-white to tee off series Sept. 23, 1964. Additional footage has been shot to bring total running time now to 92 minutes. "U.N.C.L.E." currently in its second season on NBC-TV, fits into the hour groove. Film is skedded to go out solo in some theatrical situations, while it will be dualed in others with "The Spy With My Face," also an extension of a segment in the same teleseries.

Patently released to cash in on current espionage mania, much of the new footage is devoted to build Robert Vaughn, the agent from U.N.C.L.E., into a glamour boy with a roving eye for beautiful femmes, and a few of such paradees. Whatever plot there is revolves around efforts to prevent the assassination of a visiting African dignitary, but the refurbished entry isn't much better than the original. This is for least discriminating audiences.

Vaughn tries hard and with some success through plot-holes, and gets capable support from Patricia Crowley, Luciana Paluzzi and Fritz Weaver. His sidekick in teleseries, David McCallum, is in only two scenes. Don Medford does as well with Sam Rolfe script as can be expected, Joseph Biroc's photography is okay and Jerry Goldsmith's familiar music score (from series) is consciously present. Norman Felton produced.

Whit.

La Dame De Pique
(The Queen of Spades)
(FRENCH)

Paris, Feb. 8.

CFDC release of Paris-Cite production. With Dita Parlo, Michel Subor, Simone Bach, Katharina Renn, Jean Negroni, Andre Charpak. Directed by Leonard Keigel. Screenplay, Julien Green, Eric Jourdan from story by Pushkin; camera, Alain Levent; editor, Andree Werlin. At Studio De L'Etoile, Paris. Running Time, **92 MINS.**

La Dame De Pique .... Dita Parlo
Lt. Herman .... Michel Subor
Lisa .... Simone Bach
St. Germain .... Jean Negroni
Husband .... Andre Charpak
Maid .... Katharina Renn

Aleksander Pushkin's story of the old countess who had the secret of winning at cards gets another screen round. After a Russo silent pic, a French pre-war sound film and the British 1949 version, this one appears a bit stilted and cold.

Instead of delving into the supernatural and psychological aspects of it all, director Leonard Keigel turns it into a series of tableaus that have little feel for the late 18th Century Paris and Russian times. This formalistic pic appears little suited for specialized and arty use abroad if its intime methods of progression could make this acceptable tele item.

The Russian countess, with a gambling mania, is saved from ruin in Paris when a mysterious man unveils a secret to win she can never divulge. When she does it, it leads to disaster for her source. A poor Russian officer tries to force this secret from her but kills her through fright.

After her death, he gets the secret but it leads to his madness. Dita Parlo, a pre-war actress, makes this comeback ill suited to her more zesty temperament as the Countess. Michel Subor is sober but one-dimensional as the the obsessed officer.

This is technically glossy with supporting players okay. But it is not up to its predecessors.

Mosk.

Io La Conoscevo Bene
(I Knew Her Well)
(ITALIAN)

Rome, Feb. 8.

Medusa release of Ultra Film production. Features Stefania Sandrelli, Mario Adorf, Jean-Claude Brialy, Joachim Fuchsberger, Nino Manfredi, Enrico Maria Salerno, with Ugo Toagnazzi, Karin Dor, Franco Fabrizi, Turi Ferro, Robert Hoffman, Franco Nero, Veronique Vendell. Directed by Antonio Pietrangeli. Story and screenplay, Pietrangeli, Ruggero Maccari, Ettore Scola; camera, Armando Mannuzzi; editor, Franco Fraticelli; music, Piero Piccioni. At the Arlecchino, Rome. Running Time, **115 MINS.**

Adriana .... Stefania Sandrelli
Publicity man .... Nino Manfredi
Onetime actor .... Ugo Tognazzi
Daddy's boy .... Robert Hoffman
Fraud .... Jean-Claude Brialy
Writer .... Joachim Fuchsberger
Boxer .... Mario Adorf
Press agent .... Franco Fabrizi
Friend of Adriana's .... Karin Dor
Starlet .... Veronique Vendell

One of the better Italian films of the year, this looms an okay grosser at home and an interesting arty entry abroad. But principally, it's a prestige item which is sure to show up at one of the year's festivals. A capsuled judgment might sum this one up as a pic on the Antonionian theme of lack of communication between human beings. But told without that Italian director's deliberately lengthy expositions and slow pace, it is at least for general audiences, more acceptable.

Briefly, the story is about a country girl caught up in the swirl and the temptations of the big city and its high life. It's all in her search for something solid .in the way of companionship and ideals, and her renunciation in suicide. The pattern is one of short, sometimes intercut, episodes which, by the film's end, fit together into a colorful if brightening mosaic.

Key character is Stefania Sandrelli, with entire plot, all characters and episodes introduced to provide the bits and pieces that make her an appealing, tragic young figure of today. Gal takes her love affairs lightly at first, then more intensely and desperately. But she never looks at the commercial and opportunistic side of things in her frantic quest for understanding and true affection.

With a few exceptions—Mario Adorf, as a pug-ugly pugilist who briefly instills what few rays of hope she ever gets—and Joachim Fuchsberger, as a writer who analyzes her, but treats her tenderly —most of the many men she meets are the here-today-and-gone-tomorrow variety. A bit overlengthy, and somewhat expected, her suicide scene is logical conclusion to what came before.

Miss Sandrelli is fine in the lead, displaying personality, unusual looks and temperament. Ugo Tognazzi shines in a cameo of a onetime star on the skids, and Nino Manfredi is likewise fine as a press agent of sorts. Adorf provides a poignant bit and others in very large cast measure up.

Technical credits are all on the plus side. There's sharp and mood-keying lensing by Armando Mannuzzi, neat choice of sets and locations by the director and Mario Chiari, and a lilting and equally effective backdrop (pop songs and original) chosen and written by Piero Piccioni. *Hawk.*

The Spy With My Face
(COLOR)

Confusing spy meller expanding a "Man from U.N.C.L.E." segment.

Hollywood. Feb. 11.
Metro release of Sam Rolfe production. Stars Robert Vaughn; features Senta Berger, David McCallum, Leo G. Carroll, Michael Evans, Sharon Farrell. Directed by John Newland. Screenplay, Clyde Ware, Joseph Calvelli; story, Ware; camera (Metrocolor), Fred Koenekamp; music, Morton Stevens; editor, Joseph Dervin; asst. director, E. Darrell Hallenbeck. Reviewed at Metro Studios, Feb. 10, '65. Running Time, **86** MINS.

Napoleon Solo	Robert Vaughn
Serena	Senta Berger
Illya Kuryakin	David McCallum
Alexander Waverly	Leo G. Carroll
Darius Two	Michael Evans
Sandy Wister	Sharon Farrell
Arsene Coria	Fabrizio Mioni
Kitt Kittridge	Donald Harron
Namana	Bill Gunn
Taffy	Jennifer Billingsley
Director	Paula Raymond
Nina	Donna Michelle
Doctor	Harold Gould
Wanda	Nancy Hsueh

Maggie	Michele Carey
Clerk	Paul Siemion
Waiter	Jan Arvan

"The Spy With My Face," new version of an old "Man From U.N.C.L.E." episode, is perhaps most garbled, plotwise, of any present entry on the current spy-melodrama cycle. Thrush, that band of murderous renegades that would rule the world and is constantly combatting U.N.C.L.E., fixes up one of its agents to be the exact double of Napoleon Solo, the goodguy , and nearly succeeds in its purpose—whatever that is.

Like with "To Trap a Spy," new footage has been added to the original tv segment hour's length to bring it up to 86 minutes for theatrical release. Scantily-garbed femmes are concentrated on in the updated version, so that Robert Vaughn in his familiar N. Solo character may vie with such stalwarts as Agent 007 and Our Man Flint in sexolo. At least they're diverting.

Film loses sight of story line, which has something to do with transporting a new combination to a vault in Switzerland containing a scientific secret of world import. Vaughn plays his double role straight, and Senta Berger is in as a beauteous she-spy. Femme honors, however, got to Sharon Farrell as a cute sexpot. David McCallum appears in his familiar sidekick role, as does Leo G. Carroll as U.N.C.L.E. topper, and Michael Evans is the smooth heavy.

John Newland's direction cannot cope with Clyde Ware-Joseph Calvelli's confusing s c r i p t, but technical credits are okay, including Fred Koenekamp's camera work and art direction by George W. Davis and Merrill Pye. Sam Rolfe produced. *Whit.*

Weekend Of Fear
A flop suspenser in every department.

Hollywood, Feb. 7.
JD Production, written, produced, edited and directed by Joe Danford. Features Micki Malone, Kenneth Washman. Camera, Saul N. Leyton; music, William H. Lockwood. Reviewed at Vagabond Theatre, L.A., Feb. 5, '66. Running Time, **63** MINS.

Judy	Micki Malone
Young Man	Kenneth Washman
Tom	Tory Alburn
Mrs. Harris	Ruth Trent
Connie	Dianne Danford
Jack	James Vaneck
Man In Car	Kurt Donsbach
Carol	Jill Banner

A maiden effort by Joe Danford, who scripted, edited, produced and directed, "Weekend of Fear" is an unsuccessful attempt at a suspenser-without-violence. Fair story gimmick isn't sufficiently developed—a ludicrous and redundant narration belabors the obvious, while blah thesping further dims the appeal. Tough sledding ahead, even for lowercasing, and dullsville b.o. likely.

Until final six minutes of the total 63-minute length—overlong at that, the question of why Micki Malone is being shadowed by deaf mute Kenneth Washman is not answered. Ruth Trent, middle-aged widow hung up on Miss Malone's fella, Tory Alburn, has ordered

Washman to rig a seemingly accidental death for the gal.

Miss Malone occupies most of the footage; her limited facial expressions are inappropriate to the mood of terror intended, and her narration is one-note, with unbelievably corny dialog. Washman evokes a measure of curiosity, but his plot business is not credible. Other thesps are substandard.

Two songs are introed in clumsy fashion. Saul N. Leyton's camera is static, matching the dreary directorial pace set by Danford, whose editing is routine. Other technical credits are standard.

Film's prospects might be enhanced by cutting most sound and letting the picture tell the story; it could then become an offbeat featurette for experimental situations. Danford's future efforts must start with a story line which can be strung with believable dialog. Good intentions aren't enough; what's on the screen is the only thing that counts. *Murf.*

Galia
(FRENCH)
Paris. Feb. 8.
Athos Films release of Speva Films-Cine Alliance-Variety Films production. Stars Mireille Darc; features Venantino Venantini, Francoise Prevost. Directed by Georges Lautner. Screenplay, Vahe Katcha, Lautner; camera, Maurice Fellous; editor, Michele David. At the Mercury, Paris. Running Time, **109** MINS.

Galia	Mireille Darc
Husband	Venantino Venantini
Wife	Francoise Prevost
Friend	Jacques Riberolles
Rich Man	Francois Chaumette

What starts out as an unfettered look at a free-living, career girl, a femme who picks up a man when she needs one, degenerates into a forced suspense item. It is short on motivation needed to make this a hybrid with mainly exploitation chances abroad on its uninhibited nude scenes and its look at a degenerate underside of Paris highlife. Arty chances are more limited:

Galia (Mireille Darc) is a lithe, comely girl from a smalltown who gets a good job as a window decorator in Paris. She has a lovely apartment, a car and seems fairly contented with her lot, if lonely at times. One day she pulls a woman out of the Seine and takes her home with her.

The woman has an oily, fortune-hunting husband. The girl decides to help her and goes out to meet the husband. But she falls for him and things become involved when she even thinks of killing the wife. But it is the wife who finishes off the husband, with Galia supposedly chastened.

Director Gerges Lautner has made a name for himself here with outsize gangster and undercover agent parodies. They usually have been local in appeal because their comedy has been forced buffoonery and a play on character pettiness. This sometimes clicks here but the pix are not too international in appeal. Trying for a more intensive mood, he fails because unable to draw the line between melodrama, realism and satire.

The ex-New Wavers did this better for their characters since they had bombast, and mirrored a kind

of youth that has grown up since the war. But here it is all watered down, with feeble orgy scenes and banal love scenes.

Miss Darc disrobes without quaintness but is nice to see. But she does not, in this, give an inkling of an inner strength to make her vulnerable character probing. Francoise Prevost has a steely rightness as the spurned wife while Venantino Venantini is empty as the husband. It is sleekly done with a classical dream sequence also thrown in. Mainly soap opera this, with some distaff appeal an added booster for foreign placement. *Mosk.*

The Gentle Rain
(BRAZILIAN-COLOR)

Final film of late Burt Balaban. Pictorially beguiling but overlong. Emotional conflict but not much plot.

Ft. Lauderdale, Jan. 10.
Comet Production for Allied Artists release. Produced by Bert Caudle Jr., coproduced and directed by the late Burt Balaban; screenplay by Robert Cream; music, Luiz Bonfa. Camera (Eastmancolor), Mario Di Leo; film editor, Fima Noveck. Premiered at Florida Theatre, Ft. Lauderdale, Jan. 10. Running Time, **110** MINS.

Bill Patterson	Christopher George
Judy Reynolds	Lynda Day
Nancy Masters	Fay Spain
Gloria	Maria Helena Dias
Harry Masters	Lon Clark
Girl Friend	Barbara Williams
Hotel Manager	Robert Assumpaco
Jimmy	Herbert Moss
Jewelry Girl	Lorena
Nightclub Girl	Nadyr Fernandes

Coproducers Bert Caudle and the late Burt Balaban shot Robert Cream's screenplay in Brazil. A Comet release via Allied Artists this feature has good aerial photography of the harbor and terrain around Rio de Janeiro. Add sensuous music and sensuality in a story of scant "plot" though some emotional conflict. There is lovemaking in the nude which might raise some reaction, though one bathroom tussle might perhaps pass as no more than good, clean fun.

The photography of Mario Di Leo is certainly a plus but the 110-minute feature drags somewhat and lacks action.

Lynda Day (only 17 when film was made) is cast as a "poor little rich girl, suffering from a parent-oriented marriage annuled because of frigidity. She has run away from New York ties, and is met at the airport by a family friend whose help and hospitality she refuses. But she seeks out a former college roommate and moves in with her. At a party she meets boy, an architect-in-hiding turned draughtsman, and resents his apparent rudeness until she discovers he is a psychotic mute. Their shared neuroses draw them together and they become lovers, until he rejects her as he can never fit into her social life. She counters that she would be willing to be wife and buffer if he would only see a psychiatrist, in an attempt to exorcise her trauma. This he refuses to do, so she takes off, and curtain leaves him trying agonizingly and futilely to use the telephone, whether to call her or the psychiatrist is not made clear.

It is a little hard to sympathize with them, as she quickly defrosted in her first session on his couch.

The directorial chores are Burt Balaban's swan song, as he died shortly after the film was in the can. He has shown a deft and gentle touch with the principals, but in other scenes the dialog is stilted and the action uneven. This may be due to inept cutting, although it could still be pared down to 90 minutes instead of its present 110.

Miss Day is an unusual, beguiling beauty and shows considerable talent which she uses sensitively and with a certain restraint. However, she has a coltish awkwardness and her diction is faulty. She recently appeared in a small role on Broadway in "The Devils" with Anne Bancroft.

Christopher George pantomimes the emotions of a mute convincingly, acting sincerely and from within. He is the strong, virile type and has since completed a pic with John Wayne, "El Dorado."

Fay Spain contributes a decorative and bright note as a pixieish lush, and Lon Clark makes the most of a small part as the family friend. Maria Helena Dies is exactly the type for a U.S.-educated Latin career girl, and like Hitchcock, producer Bert Caudle imprints his genial personality in a thumbnail bit as a party guest.

Barbara Williams, Robert Assumpaco, Herbert Moss, Nadys Fernandes and Lorena are well cast and adequate in the minor role. *Culm.*

Madame X
(COLOR)

Still a weeper; outstanding woman's picture with Lana Turner in a memorable performance and heavy b.o. assured.

Hollywood, Feb. 11.
Universal release of Ross Hunter production. Stars Lana Turner; features John Forsythe, Ricardo Montalban, Burgess Meredith, Constance Bennett, Keir Dullea. Directed by David Lowell Rich. Screenplay, Jean Holloway; based on play by Alexandre Bisson; camera (Technicolor), Russell Metty; music, Frank Skinner; editor, Milton Carruth; asst. director, Douglas Green. Reviewed at Directors Guild Theatre, Feb. 10, '66. Running Time, **99 MINS.**
Holly Parker .... Lana Turner
Clay Anderson .... John Forsythe
Phil Benton ...... Ricardo Montalban
Dan Sullivan ..... Burgess Meredith
Estelle .... Constance Bennett
Clay Anderson, Jr. ...... Keir Dullea
Christian Torben ... John Van Dreelen
Mimsy .... Virginia Grey
Michael Spalding ... Warren Stevens
Judge .... Carl Benton Reid
Clay, Jr., boy .... Teddy Quinn
Dr. Evans .... Frank Maxwell
Nurse Riborg .... Karen Verne
Carter .... Joe DeSantis
Combs .... Frank Marth
Sgt. Riley .... Bing Russell
Manuel Lopez .... Teno Pollick
Bromley .... Jeff Burton
Police Matron .... Jill Jackson

Latest time out for Alexandre Bisson's new-classic 1909 drama of mother love is an emotional, sometimes exhausting and occasionally corny picture which is assured wide femme reception. Lana Turner takes on the difficult assignment of the frustrated mother, turning in what many will regard as her most rewarding portrayal. Producer Ross Hunter draws generally on the original plot but has changed the locale from Paris to the U.S. for pic's opening and climaxing unfoldment. Some of the motivating circumstances, too, have been changed, and characters added to lend a more modern note. This may have been advisable, and conforms to the new plotline, but also has the effect of being old hat and melodramatic, reminiscent of countless film yarns in which the heroine has been turned out of her house to protect the family name.

For the femme star, pic is a triumph, particularly in the later reels when her ways become dissolute and she turns to drink and men. She follows such actresses in role as Gladys George in Metro's 1937 version; Ruth Chatterton in same studio's 1929 production; and Pauline Frederick in Samuel Goldwyn's 1920 silent entry. Miss Turner delineates character in her own style, giving legitimacy to her work, and while allowing herself to visually decay via some devastating makeup actually creates this illusion through the sheer force of sensitive acting.

Jean Holloway's screenplay now has femme star very much in love with her husband, instead of running away from her spouse, as in the original, to join her lover. However, following an affair with a rich playboy, who is accidentally killed while she is in his apartment, she is talked by her mother-in-law into disappearing in a phony drowning episode to save her politically-minded husband and young son from scandal. Balance of plot more or less follows the play, leading up to her shooting of a man who would blackmail her former husband and son, ultimate trial when her son, now an attorney, unknowingly defends his mother in his first case.

David Lowell Rich makes an excellent impression with his first feature directorial assignment, in swingover from television, and invests film with the type of values requisite for an outstanding woman's picture. Under his warm guidance, cast surrounding femme star contribute convincing performances, and mood is further enhanced by the know-how editing of Milton Carruth and background music of Frank Skinner.

John Forsythe excels as the husband, whose political career forces him to absent himself from home for long periods of time and thus lays the ground for his lonely wife's indiscretion. Where the original character was cruel and domineering, in the new version he is understanding and gentle. Ricardo Montalban is persuasive as the playboy who falls to his death, and Constance Bennett —in her last film appearance before her death—endows the mother-in-law role with quiet dignity and strength, seizing upon Montalban's demise and her son's wife's involvement to play upon the younger woman's fear and love of family to disappear.

Burgess Meredith is properly larcenous as the man Miss Turner kills, and Keir Dullea is fine as the son, unconsciously drawn to the woman known only as Madame X. John Van Dreelen is effective as a man who nurses Miss Turner back to health when he finds her unconscious on a street in Copenhagen, one of the cities she visits after leaving her husband. Plus performances also are offered by Virginia Grey, Warren Stevens, Karen Verne, Carl Benton Reid and Frank Maxwell in smaller roles.

Hunter as usual has brought in toppers for the technical end. Credit here goes to Russell Metty for his camera work; Alexander Golitzen and George Webb, art direction; Howard Bristol, set decorations; Jean Louis, gowns. *Whit.*

Una Questione D'onore
(A Matter of Honor)
(ITALO-FRENCH-COLOR)
(Color)

Rome, Feb. 15.
Panta Film release of a Mega Film (Rome)-Orphee Productions S.A. (Paris) coproduction. Stars Ugo Tognazzi; features Nicoletta Macchiavelli, Bernard Blier, Franco Fabrizi, Lucien Reimbourg, Tecla Scarano, Leopoldo Trieste, Sandro Merli, Franco Bucceri. Directed by Luigi Zampa. Screenplay, Zampa, Piero de Bernardi, Leo Benvenuti, from story by Enzo Giurace; camera (Technicolor), Carlo di Palma, Luciano Trasatti; music, Luis Bacalov. At Metropolitan, Rome. Running Time, **113 MINS.**
Efisio .... Ugo Tognazzi
Domenicangela ..Nicoletta Macchiavelli
Leandro Sanna .... Bernard Blier
Egidio Porcu .... Franco Fabrizi
Lawyer .... Leopoldo Trieste

With "A Matter of Honor," the Italian pic industry once again comes up with a tour-de-force. This is a hard-hitting item which attacks the age-old traditions and unwritten laws while remaining, basically, an amusing, all-stops-out comedy. While director Luigi Zampa's approach is more dramatic and brutal than Pietro Germi's "Divorce, Italian Style," both films have much in common in theme, setting (Sardinia instead of Sicily) and development. It looks a good bet on home grounds and a likely entry for selected foreign marts.

There are two basic plots. One deals with a longstanding and bloody island feud between two families. The second, brought in later, involves the "matter" of honor. Local man, Efisio (Ugo Tognazzi), who is working in Milan, is smuggled back onto Sardinia and into village to kill off a man for an affront. While he's back in Milan with his wife, however, someone else does the job, he's credited and, honor saved all round, so he remains mum. Only now, the wife's pregnancy becomes known around the neighborhood.

Though he knows he's the father of the unborn child, his "official" absence in Milan proves the contrary, and the villagers deride him as a cuckold. Finally exasperated, he takes the only action accepted by his people to save family honor, by shooting her. The story, especially at start, tends to be confused and confusing, and some of action drags during pic's 113 minutes. Trimming would help, and certain key plot points should also be cleared up.

Otherwise, it's a brutal, hard-hitting item, especially in hindsight, and small wonder that authorities in its home territory have raised objections. As with many finger-pointing pix, some situations tend to be exaggerated and exasperated, to make their points. But the basic elements of accusation still exist in retarded mentality of certain parts of this country obsessed by honor above all and in which, as pic repeatedly suggests, "what counts is not the truth but the appearances."

Tognazzi turns in a sterling stint as the harried defender of unsullied honor and hapless victim of outdated laws and traditions. Bernard Blier is solid as a key villager. Nicoletta Macchiavelli's strikingly unusual good looks are another asset of the pic which is chock-full of colorful types colorfully rendered.

Physical values, especially color lensing by Carlo Di Palma and Luciano Trasatti on unusual and well-chosen Sardinian locations, are definite assets. Also a lilting backdrop score by Luis Bacalov should get plenty of spins if properly exploited. *Hawk.*

10:32 In The Morning
(DUTCH)

Amsterdam, Feb. 11.
Gofilex release of N.F.M. production (J. M. Landre); producer, Bobby Rosenboom. Stars Linda Christian, features Bob de Lange, Eric Schneider, Wim de Haas. Directed by Arthur Dreifuss. Script, Dreifuss, Dity Oorthuys, based on an idea by Leo Derksen. Camera, Eduard van der Enden. Reviewed at Rialto, Amsterdam. Running Time, **90 MINS.**

This is the first time Linda Christian, born Blanca-Rosa Welter, of Dutch parentage, stars in a Dutch film. She speaks with slight accent, but this is explained in script by her being American wife of elderly lawyer. This lawyer is murdered and a young painter, found at the spot, is held by the police as the murderer, though he refuses to say anything in his defense. Actress in a long flashback accuses him of having murdered her husband, so that he can marry her. Police inspector doesn't believe this and in another flashback the real circumstances leading to the murder and murderer are explained.

Story is not very original but for the first part a willing viewer may experience some suspense though by half way everything is crystal clear. Psychological thriller can not bring enough that's new and exciting.

Director Arthur Dreifuss, who directed an American television series "Secret File U.S.A." in Holland 10 years ago, and also shot "The Last Blitzkrieg" here, does not rehabilitate himself with this film. Miss Christian is beautiful in the main part, but acting honors go to Bob de Lange as the inspector and Eric Schneider as the painter.

"10.32" (estimated time of murder) is being dubbed in English, though no release is set as yet. Film could find slot on television, or as second feature. Title may be altered as it creates confusion with Jules Dassin's production that starts twelve hours and two minutes earlier. *Saaltink.*

The Hopeless Ones
(HUNGARIAN)

Budapest, Feb. 16.

Hungarofilm release of Mafilm production. Features Janos Gorbe, Gabor Argardi, Tibor Molnar, Andras Kozak. Directed and screenplay, Miklos Jancso. Camera, Tamas Somlo; editor, Zoltan Farkas. Reviewed at Puskin Theatre, Budapest, Feb. 4, 1966. Running Time, 94 MINS.

Gajdor	Janos Gorbe
Lovas	Tibor Molnar
Son	Andras Kozak
Leather jacket	Gabor Argardi
First black-coat	Istvan Avar
Second black-coat	Lajos Oze
Veszelka	Zoltan Latino

Fable concerns Hungary of 1848, when the country's most notorious gang of highwaymen joined the war of independence sparked by Kossuth. After the defeat of the revolution, they became outlaws again, and even snowballed in strength. They had the sympathy of the villagers who looked upon the outlaws as fighters against the hated rule of the Austrian Hapsburgs and the rich.

Finally the government decided to exterminate the outlaws and turned over the job to Count Gedeon Raday, who swung into action, giving no quarter. It is at this point that Jancso's film takes up the story.

This is not a romantic adventure pic, crammed with galloping horsemen, wild chases and gunmen biting the dust. Action is pinned down to a single locale. Gendarmes pen up several hundred suspects in a stockade. They have proof that one of the men is guilty of a double murder, and promise him a pardon if he will finger a bigger fry. Scared out of his wits, Janos Gajdor makes a try.

This is a psycho pic. It focusses on the undertones in the battle between pursuer and pursued, the pitiless process of Power alienation. It is the anatomy of betrayal. Poor men, facing danger, slowly crumble. This psychic pattern is traced without needless trappings or action sequences. Long focussing and ingenious camera work build up tension.

Jancso proves to have a style of his own. If an anology were to be drawn, his work could be compared to the puritan, oversimplified approach of Robert Brassont. Janco, by the way, doesn't know Brassont's work since only one of latter's films has been shown here.

Closest thing to violence is a scene where girl runs the gauntlet of interrogators. But the impression here is rather psychic naturalism, which maybe gives it greater effect.

Janos Gorbe, who stood out in "Twenty Hours," is very good as Gajdor, the man who betrays his comrades out of fear. His jerky gestures, squinting, small eyes and sparse dialogue project Gajdor's mental fright in minute detail.

Interrogation scenes are well done, as the Black Coat powers that be compromise their victims by forcing them to face the tragic dilemma. Two interrogator characters are projected by the same methods in the brief playing of Istvan Avar and Lajos Oze.

Tamas Somlo's camera work is good, and he is a vet at black-and-white contrast. Emotional strength is given to the plot by the desolate horizon of the Hungarian lowlands, minus any natural beauty.

The pic's only background music is the Austrian anthem of the time and a couple of military marches. Otherwise, the director resorted to noise, din and clatter for his effects.

This is the only Hungarian film for several years with unadulterated Hungarian atmosphere and local color integrated with up-to-date film art. It probably won't gross a lot, but it should have production value on artkino programming. *Ban.*

La Sentinelle Endormie
(The Sleeping Sentinel)
(FRENCH—COLOR)

Paris, Feb. 15.

Prodis release of Le Film D'Art production. Stars Noel-Noel; features Pascale Audret, Michel Galabru, Francis Blanche, Jean Sobieski. Directed by Jean Dreville. Screenplay, Noel-Noel; camera (Eastmancolor), Pierre Petit; editor, Albert Jurgenson. At Marignan, Paris. Running Time, 100 MINS.

Mathieu	Noel-Noel
Mathilde	Pascale Audret
Florin	Michel Galabru
Nicolas	Jean Sobieski
Constant	Francis Blanche
Clemence	Micheline Luccioni
Sylvain	Alexandre Rignault
Villeroy	Raymond Souplex

Quaint costumer, in the "Napoleon Slept Here" vein, is too slight and anecdotal to make much impact as spectacle. And without the characterization or depth it has little for any action or art possibilities abroad. Only some playoff on its period and color appear in store for this offshore. Local chances also are only fair.

It is 1812 and a doctor is involved in a plot to kill Napoleon who's on his way to Russia. The medico is a decent family man but feels the Emperor is a tyrant. Chance has Napoleon stopping over in his very house with the doctor having a change of heart when he realizes his fellow terrorists would even kill innocents on their mission.

Little episodes fill out this stilted pic. Noel-Noel has assurance, the blend of irony and skepticism and reluctant humanity and sentimentality which have made him long a popular star. Others are adequate, especially Michel Galabru, as a fussy, talespinning servant. Production dress looks slim and pic takes place mostly in interiors. *Mosk.*

L'Uomo Che Ride
(The Man Who Laughs)
(ITALIAN—COLOR)

Rome, Feb. 15.

Metro release of Sanson Film (Joseph Fryd) production. Stars Jean Sorel; features Lisa Gastoni, Ilaria Occhini, Edmund Purdom. Directed by Sergio Corbucci. Screenplay, Corbucci, E. Sanjust, A. Issaverdens, A. Bertolotto, L. Ronconi, F. Bosetti; camera (Eastmancolor), Enzo Barboni; editor, Mario Serandrei; music, Piero Piccioni. At Galleria, Rome. Running Time, 94 MINS.

Lucrezia Borgia	Lisa Gastoni
Cesare Borgia	Edmund Purdom
Astorre, Angelo	Jean Sorel
Dea	Ilaria Occhini

With "The Man Who Laughs," Joseph Fryd has produced (Sergio Corbucci directed), a saleable actioner, neatly paced and lushly lensed in color. This should find ready openings on hungry world markets. Toned-down horror aspects in original story plus exploitable footage won't hurt either in luring the many patrons for this kind of fare.

Tale told is one of intrigue, passions and murder in the early days of Cesare Borgia and his sinister sister, Lucrezia. Involved in their rise to infamy are two youths, Astorre and Angelo, the latter deformed by scar which twists his face into a perpetual, horrible grin. Both are in love with a blind girl, Dea, and both, eventually, tangle with the Borgias, brother and sister. Angelo is seduced by Lucrezia and is later, thanks to a plastic surgery operation, substituted for Astorre, whom he resembles, to help along a political coup. Finale finds Astorre and healed Dea reunited, while Angelo saves the couple in a battle with the cruel Borgias.

Director Corbucci keeps things moving at a fast clip, at the same time leaving no one in doubt as to who's good and who's bad. Jean Sorel plays both Angelo and Astorre in dashing, charming fashion which should win plenty of femme attention. Lisa Gastoni makes a properly villainous—and beauteous—Lucrezia while Ilaria Occhini is suitably naive and pretty as Dea. Edmund Purdom's Cesare Borgia is likewise menacing in keeping with the spirit of this pic. This has been splendidly lensed in Eastmancolor on real castle and other locations in the country around Rome. Visual values are a decided plus.

Hawk.

The Group
(COLOR)

Assorted Malices in Wonderland from Mary McCarthy's uninhibited novel in somewhat inhibited screen version. Fascinating, if occasionally erratic, film provides a mass exposure of new femme talent in a polished production which should prove profitable for all concerned.

United Artists release of Famous Artists-Famartists (Charles K. Feldman) production, produced by Sidney Buchman. Directed by Sidney Lumet. No stars. Features Candice Bergen, Joan Hackett, Elizabeth Hartman, Shirley Knight, Joanna Pettet, Mary-Robin Redd, Jessica Walter, Kathleen Widdoes. James Broderick, James Congdon, Larry Hagman, Hal Holbrook, Richard Mulligan, Robert Emhardt, Carrie Nye. Screenplay by Buchman, based on Mary McCarthy novel; camera (DeLuxe Color), Boris Kaufman; editor, Ralph Rosenbloom; music supervision, Charles Gross, conducted by Robert de Cormier. Reviewed at Astor Theatre, N.Y., Feb. 24, '66. Running Time, 150 MINS.

Lakey Eastlake	Candice Bergen
Dottie Renfrew	Joan Hackett
Priss Hartshorn	Elizabeth Hartman
Polly Andrews	Shirley Knight
Kay Strong	Joanna Pettet
Pokey Prothero	Mary-Robin Redd
Libby MacAusland	Jessica Walter
Helena Davison	Kathleen Widdoes
Dr. Ridgeley	James Broderick
Sloan Crockett	James Congdon
Harald Peterson	Larry Hagman
Gus Leroy	Hal Holbrook
Dick Brown	Richard Mulligan
Mr. Andrews	Robert Emhardt
Norine	Carrie Nye
Mrs. Hartshorn	Philippa Bevans
Mrs. Prothero	Leta Bonynge
Radio Man's Wife	Marion Brash
Mrs. Davison	Sarah Burton
Mrs. MacAusland	Flora Campbell
Nils	Bruno di Cosmi
Mrs. Renfrew	Leora Dana
Bill, the actor	Bill Fletcher
Brook Latham	George Gaynes
Mrs. Bergler	Martha Greenhouse
Mr. Davison	Russell Hardie
Mr. Eastlake	Vince Harding
Nurse Swenson	Doreen Lang
Radio Man	Chet London
Mr. Schneider	Baruch Lumet
Putnam Blake	John O'Leary
Nurse Catherine	Hildy Parks
The Baroness	Lidia Prochnicka
Mrs. Andrews	Polly Rowles
Mr. Prothero	Douglas Rutherford
Mr. Bergler	Truman Smith
Mrs. Eastlake	Loretta White

The principal problem Sidney Buchman (who also produced) had to face in adapting Mary McCarthy's very successful college classmates novel to the screen was to transfer its colorful characterizations and storytelling without overloading his script with the mass of novelistic detail. His script did not completely solve this. While generally an excellent job of screen writing, he retained too much of the detail at the loss of much of the flavor.

United Artists will have little trouble, however, in selling the cinematic result which is one of director Sidney Lumet's best efforts to date and which introduces a talented covey of new actresses.

The original novel dealt with eight members of a Vassar graduating class (school is not identified in the film), with most of them getting close to equal coverage. This must have presented a next to impossible task to any screenwriter, and Buchman would have been wise to have dropped one or two of the weaker members of "The Group" (plus characters with whom they were involved) to concentrate more fully on the others. All eight, however, are used but some get trampled in the helter-skelter pace (and possibly in the editing) that Lumet had to maintain to get everything in. Although "The Group" is never slow, it is too long.

The entire film was made in New York and it was the intention from the beginning to use fresh talent. Shirley Knight is, possibly, the only cast member instantly recognizable to filmgoers, but another member, Elizabeth Hartman, who subsequently made "A Patch of Blue," received an Academy Award nomination for it, so she won't be a complete stranger.

There's little tampering with the original storyline but the filmscript concentrates on the story of Kay (Joanna Pettet), the first girl to be married and the one meeting the most tragic end. Throughout, she and Larry Hagman, as her philandering playwright husband, have the longest roles. However, if less important, the characters played by Joan Hackett and Jessica Walter, thanks to their performances, register as strongly as does Miss Pettet. Miss Hackett, particularly, is provided with a wide range of emotional changes.

Also outstanding are Shirley Knight and, to a lesser degree, Kathleen Widdoes. Miss Hartman's Priss (a natural redhead, she's going to have makeup problems with color film as she photographs too pale) may come across as sympathetic to female filmgoers (as, probably, will most of the female roles as written) but male reaction to her victimization by an overly aggressive, socially ambitious husband, may be less tolerant.

Biggest letdown, and doubly so because her few scenes are so effective and played so well, is the part played by Candice Bergen (daughter of Edgar Bergen). As Lakey, the ambisextrous leader of the Group (and the novel's most memorable character), her treatment in Buchman's script will puzzle the audience, as her few scenes at the beginning and at the end don't match with the billing and important promotion she receives.

Lumet's subtlety in casting the most beautiful member of the group as the one Lesbian would be more effective had Miss Bergen (a good an actress and a beauty) been given material to work with. There's indication, indeed, judging by the occasionally choppy editing, that the lengthy film (150 minutes) was trimmed down from a considerably longer version. As Buchman includes many of the stronger incidents from the novel and his dialog is completely adult, watering-down this role is both puzzling and disappointing.

The male characters, generally proficient, are only outstanding in a few instances, due, somewhat, to their original conception by Miss McCarthy. James Broderick's psychiatrist, who finally woos and wins Shirley Knight, and Robert Emhardt as her delightful but potentially manic father (a beautifully written and played part) contribute top performances, on a par with the principal femme roles. Hal Holbrook, as Miss

Knight's vacillating lover, just manages to keep a shallow role from becoming ridiculous. Mary-Robin Redd's Pokey is a nothing part that might have been wisely eliminated.

Larry Hagman's playwright, James Congdon's pediatrician, and Richard Mulligan's artist are played as unattractively as Miss McCarthy undoubtedly meant them to be. A very large cast of actors, recruited from Broadway, gives more depth to the myriad smaller supporting roles than some deserved but provides "The Group" with a more solid thespic background than found in most productions. The director's father, Baruch Lumet, is typical, being effective in a brief but important bit.

Lumet's use of actual New York backgrounds, beautifully photographed in DeLuxe color by Boris Kaufman, is another major asset. The task of making these modern settings convey an impression of the 1930s, presented a tremendous challenge which production designer Gene Callahan, set decorator Jack Wright Jr. and costume designer Anna Hill Johnstone all met beautifully. A too frequent reprise of the group's school song (the only music credits) is annoying and only occasionally appropriate, as at the very end.

"The Group" will be most rewarding to filmgoers who haven't read the McCarthy novel but even those who have will enjoy meeting some talented but unfamiliar actresses, most of whom should be very well known a year hence. *Robe.*

Johnny Reno
(COLOR-SCOPE)

Good oater programmer. Interesting yarn, well paced and refreshingly short. Strong dualler in general market.

Hollywood, Feb. 19.
Paramount release of A. C. Lyles production. Stars Dana Andrews, Jane Russell; features Lon Chaney, John Agar, Lyle Bettger, Tom Drake, Richard Arlen, Robert Lowery, Tracy Olsen. Directed by R. G. Springsteen. Screenplay, Steve Fisher, based on story by Fisher, Andrew Craddock; camera (Technicolor, Techniscope), Hal Stine; editor, Bernard Matis; music, Jimmie Haskell; title tune, Haskell, By Dunham; asst. director, Jim Rosenberger. Reviewed at Paramount Studio, Feb. 18, '66. Running Time, **83 MINS.**

Johnny Reno .... Dana Andrews
Nona Williams .... Jane Russell
Sheriff Hodges .... Lon Chaney
Ed Tomkins .... John Agar
Jess Yates .... Lyle Bettger
Joe Connors .... Tom Drake
Ned Duggan .... Richard Arlen
Jake Reed .... Robert Lowery
Marie Yates .... Tracy Olsen
Bartender .... Reg Parton
Indian .... Rodd Redwing
Wooster .... Charles Horvath
Ab Connors .... Dale Van Sickle
Indian Chief .... Paul Daniel
Bellows .... Chuck Hicks
Townsman .... Edmund Cobb

"Johnny Reno" is an above average A.C. Lyles oater about an ex-gunfighter turned lawman who cleans up another town during personal quest for an old heartthrob. Good scripting, performances, direction and production elements will keep action fans interested. Good marquee lure in Dana Andrews, quite active in

recent months, plus Jane Russell, absent from pix for some time. Paramount release is a strong lowercase for general situations.

Steve Fisher's script, based on his and Andrew Craddock's story, grabs immediate interest when Tom Drake and Dale Van Sickle, a pair of fugitives, bushwhack Andrews, a marshal who isn't really after them, but is heading for nearby town where ex-sweetie Miss Russell runs the gin mill. Andrews thus becomes involved in Drake's life—protecting him from sheriff Lon Chaney, flunky to mayor Lyle Bettger, while not entirely believing that Drake is innocent of the murder of an Indian.

Various plot turns are interestingly developed amid carefully-spotted fisticuffs. Director R. G. Springsteen has done an excellent job with a very competent cast. Tracy Olsen registers strongly as Bettger's irascible daughter who turns out to be a key story figure; her footage is limited, but she make the most of it.

John Agar, Robert Lowery and other players are good, including Richard Arlen, the most permanent member of Lyles' stock company. Andrews and Miss Russell, both listed over title, are effective. Andrews has been effective lately as a heavy, but herein proves he is still equally adept in projecting quiet strength. Miss Russell retains her good-natured earthiness.

Hal Stine's Technicolor-Techniscope camera maintains visual interest through versatile setups. Pic moves along very smartly, due in part to the fine editorial work of Bernard Matis who has trimmed to a neat 83 minutes. More ambitious and pretentious pix, using same story, would probably go another three or four reels, but with far less impact and pace.

Composer Jimmie Haskell again shows that a lowbudgeter can still boast an original, full-sounding score which avoids the oatune cliches. Jerry Wallace voices over credits the okay title tune by Haskell and by Dunham. Other technical credits are firstrate, including some exciting explosion effects. *Murf.*

The Singing Nun
(PANAVISION—SONGS—COLOR)

Routine entry fashioned around Belgian nun and her song, "Dominique"; with Debbie Reynolds toplining and dozen songs to attract, may be exploited for general market.

Hollywood, March 3.
Metro release of John Beck (Hayes Goetz) production. Stars Debbie Reynolds; features Greer Garson, Ricardo Montalban, Agnes Moorehead, Chad Everett, Katharine Ross, Ed Sullivan. Directed by Henry Koster. Screenplay, Sally Benson, John Furia Jr.; story, Furia; camera (Metrocolor), Milton Krasner; music, Harry Sukman; editor, Rita Roland; asst. director, Kevin Donnelly. Reviewed at Beverly Theatre, Beverly Hills, March 2, '66. Running Time 98 MINS.

Sister Ann .... Debbie Reynolds
Father Clementi .... Ricardo Montalban
Mother Prioress .... Greer Garson
Sister Cluny .... Agnes Moorehead
Robert Gerade .... Chad Everett
Nicole Arlien .... Katharine Ross
Himself .... Ed Sullivan
Sister Mary .... Juanita Moore
Dominic Arlien .... Ricky Cordell
Mr. Arlien .... Michael Pate
Fitzpatrick .... Tom Drake
Mr. Duvries .... Larry D. Mann
Marauder .... Charles Robinson
Sister Michele .... Monique Montaigne
Sister Elise .... Joyce Vanderveen
Sister Brigitte .... Anne Wakefield
Sister Gertude .... Pam Peterson
Sister Marthe .... Marina Koshetz
Sister Therese .... Nancy Walters
Sister Elizabeth .... Violet Rensing
Sister Consuella .... Inez Pedroza

"The Singing Nun," patently designed to cash in on the story of the now-famous Belgian nun, Soeur Sourire, and her song, "Dominique" (The Nun's Song), carries an expectancy not always realized. Fictionized approach to the true-life character — necessitated by agreement with Catholic church authorities not to make pictures autobiographical—resultantly loses in the transition, and while there are engaging musical interludes what emerges is slight and frequent slow-moving. Presence of Debbie Reynolds in title role, however, will assure popular reception and subject's natural exploitation potential may further help in the general market, particularly for the Catholic trade.

The John Beck production, co-produced by Hayes Goetz in effective Panavision and Metrocolor, unfolds mostly in the small Samaritan House, situated in a slum section of Brussels, where the young Dominican nun carries on her work with children and study preparatory to an African missionary assignment. In this role, femme star expertly warbles a dozen numbers to her own guitar accompaniment, some nine of the songs composed by the Belgian sister. The Sally Benson-John Furia Jr. screenplay, based on latter's original story, builds around the conflict between the nun's God-given gift of music and her duties as a servant of God, leading sometimes to commonplace and contrived situations.

Backing femme star, who gives a sturdy account of herself in both her reactions as a nun and her song delivery, is an effective cast headed by Greer Garson and Ricardo Montalban. Miss Garson is fine as the Mother Prioress of the settlement house. She is patient and understanding as the troubled young nun turns to her for advice.

Montalban also registers well as the priest who encourages the nun's musical career and is responsible for her recordings.

Chad Everett further impresses as junior partner of the recording company making femme star's albums. There's a suggestion of one-sided romance as he renews friendship with the convent-singer whom he knew previously when both attended the Paris Conservatory of Music. As the crotchety Sister Cluny, who finally comes to realize the hold music plays on the younger nun, Agnes Moorehead turns in another of her sharply-etched performances. Ed Sullivan plays himself, recreating the occasion of the real Belgian nun appearing on his tv show, several years ago when Soeur Sourire and her song first hit the front pages.

The character of Dominic, a small urchin of the neighborhood whom the nun befriends and is subject of her song, is in the hands of a cute little fellow with glowing eyes named Ricky Cordell. He gives part feeling under guidance of Henry Koster. The director, despite the deficiencies of screenplay endows his characters with warmth and otherwise turns in a good job. Also scoring in nun roles are Juanita Moore and and Monique Montaigne; Katharine Ross as Dominic's sister and Michael Pate as his father.

Beck has lined up able technical assistance right down the line. Music score by Harry Sukman makes excellent use of the familiar "Dominique" song, lacing passages continually through picture for background useage. Randy Sparks, who wrote English lyrics for "Dominique," also has put words to some of the other songs composed by Soeur Sourire, as well as writing several other songs. Color photography by Milton Krasner, art direction by George W. Davis and Urie McCleary and editing by Rita Roland are further assets. *Whit.*

Flame And The Fire
(DOCUMENTARY—COLOR)

"Sky Above And Mud Below" filmmaker repeats with first class documentary on rapidly vanishing primitives. Authentic, beautifully - photographed study of man.

Walter Reade - Sterling (Continental Dist.) release of a Vernon P. Becker & Mitchell R. Leiser production. Directed by Pierre Dominique Gaisseau. Commentary written by Charles Romine, narrated by Gaisseau; camera (Eastmancolor), Jens Bjerre, Jorgen Bitsch, James Bruce, Jean Fichter, Chris Hansen, Arvid Klemensen, Victor Petrashevic, Peter Rassmussen, Harald Schultz and Gaisseau; editor, Robert Farren; music, composed and conducted by Michael Colicchio. Reviewed at Baronet Theatre, N.Y., Feb. 28, '66. Running Time, 80 MINS.

Returning to the primitive tribes and aborigines of the type he dealt with in his successful "Le Ciel et La Boue" (The Sky Above, The Mud Below), French film documentarian Pierre Dominique Gaisseau has created a documentary that comes close to matching the earlier superb film and, indeed, provides a greater variety because

"Flame and the Fire" deals with rapidly vanishing tribes in Brazil, Australia and Africa as well as New Guinea.

Unlike some garish and distasteful shockumentaries that have been foisted on the filmgoing public in the past few years, this treatment of the primitives by Gaisseau seems completely authentic but told in a manner that skirts sensationalism. While there are many incidents that may prove shocking to the more narrow-minded viewers, such as completely unclothed natives and brutal (to civilized eyes) initiation and fertility rituals, Gaisseau includes such scenes as something completely natural and does not dwell on them.

While a large team of cameramen has been responsible for the extraordinary footage, much of it capturing scenes never seen before (and, tragically, some that will probably never be seen again), the Gaisseau touch is evident throughout the film, from his concise but clear descriptions to the occasional "first-person" inclusion of personal incidents, all of which make "Flame And The Fire" a pictorial and editorial comment on the incredible fact that Stone Age man persists in some remote areas of Earth, even while other Earthmen are probing outer space.

From the opening sequence dealing with the Suya tribe of Brazil's Matte Grosso, the male members of which wear six-inch wooden discs in slits in their lower lip, through various vanishing African tribes and a return visit to New Guinea and the surrounding Pacific area, to the closing visit to the Wailbri, Australian aborigines, there isn't a dull moment.

If some portions stand out, it is because the particular people being depicted are more colorful in personality (if not in body decorations, hairdresses and adornments or unusual customs) than others. The Masei, one of the most arrogant African tribes, are understandably so as they carry themselves with such an air of pride that one must admire them. The oddity of the Australian Wailbri is that they're born blonde and turn dark from the sun, whereas the general belief is that they're members of the black race. Gaisseau proves this isn't so.

The short running time (80 minutes) may make something of a booking problem but "Flame And The Fire" has plenty of general interest and should make an excellent impression wherever it is shown. As the space-ager might say, "Man, it's a Gaisseau!" *Robe.*

Blood Bath

Anemic script and tired thesping relegate this programmer to bottom of bill; will be packaged with "Queen of Blood."

American International Pictures release of a Jack Hill production. Directed and written by Hill and Stephanie Rothman. Features William Campbell, Marissa Mathes, Lori Saunders, Sandra Knight (no other cast names provided). Camera, Alfred Taylor; film editor, Mort Tubor; sound, Gary Kurtz; music, Mark

Lowry. Reviewed in N.Y., Feb. 25, '66. Running Time, 69 MINS.

Even the gore-and-guts market will be disappointed in this sad effort as its victims come through bloody but unboweled. An incoherent script that, as viewed, seemed to be made up of cutting room takeouts, might have come across better as a horror effort had it been filmed in color. American International will release it in a package with "Queen of Blood."

With the setting purportedly in Venice (and there's a mixture of non-U.S. type backgrounds with cheaply-shot interiors), the general theme is the hoary tale about the artist-vampire who lived on the blood of his victims. Jack Hill and Stephanie Rothman, who share blame equally for the direction and screenplay (while Hill bears the production burden alone), have inserted scenes inspired by "Ride The Pink Horse," "Mystery of the Wax Museum" and other more successful efforts.

William Campbell doubles as the daytime artist and the nocturnal plasma pursuer with Marissa Mathes, Lori Saunders and Sandra Knight as three of his victims. Although screen credits shown are extensive, these were only cast credits provided by AIP. Technical credits are on the par with those of the cast, most of whom could have used a transfusion of talent. *Robe.*

Africa, Addio!
(Africa, Farewell!)
(ITALIAN—COLOR)

Rome, March 8.
Cineriz release of Angelo Rizzoli presentation produced by Rizzoli Films. Conceived, written directed and edited by Gualtiero Jacopetti and Franco Prosperi. Camera, (Technicolor), Antonio Climati; music, Riz Ortolani. At Empire, Rome. Running Time, 138 MINS.

A shattering, unforgettable documentary filmed in Africa over the past three years by "Mondo Cane" maker Gualtiero Jacopetti. Too rich, too violent and bloody for many tastes, this thought-provoking and highly topical document of the so-called Dark Continent in the throes of change still makes a very saleable entry both for discerning audiences who can take its no-holds-barred frankness as well as the sensation seekers everywhere who can argue for months about the pros and cons of sadism on film. It needs very special handling, but should pay off handsomely.

While "Mondo Cane" often tickled the funnybone and titillated the senses, "Africa, Farewell!" is primarily a bitter, hardhitting one-purpose picture with few if any concessions to established audience patterns. As with its predecessors, it will, however, raise similarly violent reactions pro and con, as well as serve as "think" piece for some fairly agitated conversations. Many themes are touched, principal ones being the basic unpreparedness of many new African nations to cope with the legacies of colonialism and the problems of new independence. Also the fact that new dictatorships have risen from colonial ashes, cloaked by cries of freedom and democracy; the frightening

claim, amply documented by footage, that African wildlife is being brutally slaughtered by the whites and natives both; that violence, torture, death and blood are and will probably continue to be the accepted norm in all too many African areas until the current and future racial, ethnic, political and social upheavals cease.

The chances of this happening soon are painted as mighty grim and dim. And grim and dim are the words for most of the remainder of the Jacopetti-Prosperi footage, culled from miles of material lensed under trying, often dangerous conditions. There is nothing in this film of the tried-and-true safari saga or the bushmen vs. intrepid highlander regiment fiction. This is Africa, now. And a frightening, sobering picture it is, in its scenes of mass slaughter of animals with a sportsmanship-be-damned dependence on jeep and helicopter, in its up-front sequences of Congo executions, Angolan resistance fighting, and so on. Occasionally, the pic pauses for a respite, and one sees a baby zebra being helicoptered to safety by a wildlife preservation society fighting against impossible odds to save the "old Africa; a Boer trek against breathtaking scenic sunsets; ogling and ageing tourists snapping shots of lions trying to make love midst public clamor; or, in a more typically Jacopettian sequence, some bare-breasted native gals redressing, bras and all, after winding an "authentic documentary" sequence for a foreign film company. The material is rich, abundant, every shot trenchant and to the point. Again, as with "Mondo Cane," this is a yes-or-no picture. For those with it, its over-two-hour running time will seem short. For others, endless and probably unbearable.

Last but certainly not least in the credits is one of the most outstanding location lensing jobs ever by Antonio Climati and his crew, some as hauntingly beautiful as others are almost unbearably cruel. Riz Ortolani's moodful music is another major asset, and the uncredited sound effects, especially on six-track print seen here, are other major plusses in a picture which should prove an animated talking point for some time to come, wherever it is shown. *Hawk.*

Illusion of Blood
(Yotsuya Kaidan)
(JAPANESESCOPE-COLOR)

Kabuki ghost drama has blood and gore, some splendid acting and excellent color camerawork.

Hollywood, March, 1.
Toho Company Ltd. release of Tokyo Eiga (Ichiro Sato) Production. Costars Tatsuya Nakadai, Mariko Okada, Junko Ikeuchi, Kanzaburo Nakamura, Mayumi Ozora, Keiko Awaji, Eitaro Ozawa, Masao Mishima; features Yasushi Nagata, Kanjiro Taira. Directed by Shiro Toyoda. Screenplay, Toshio Yazumi; original story, Nanboku Tsuruya; camera (Tohoscope - Eastmancolor), Hiroshi Murai; music, Toru Takemitsu. Reviewed at Toho LaBrea Theatre, March 1, 66. Running Time, 109 MINS.
Iuemon Tamiya ...... Tatsuya Nakadai
Oiwa .... Mariko Okada
Osode .... Junko Ikeuchi
Gonbei Naosuke .. Kanzaburo Nakamura
Oume .... Mayumi Ozora
Omaki .... Keiko Awaji

Kihei Ito .... Eitaro Ozawa
Takuetsu .... Masao Mishima

"Illusion of Blood" is a blood-curdling Japanese ghost story, a hatchet-Hamlet, a What-Makes-A-Samurai-Run film set in the Nipponese Middle Ages. Lushly shot in Eastmancolor, drama vividly reiterates in painstakingly gory detail how an angry young soldier turns against those around him and chops them down with his samurai sword. The murdering in cold blood of a dozen or so characters is excessive to the point of being a bloody bore. Drama, taken from a 140 year old Kabuki play, is not for the faint-hearted and unlikely to appeal outside the special situations.

Interesting aspect of story is that the hot-blooded anti-hero played by Tatsuya Nakadai is totally believable and even sympathetic. Although he never looks back as he slashes the life out of father-in-law, first wife, second wife, her father, a houseboy, and so on, the feeling generated is that his circumstances an compulsion make his acts inevitable. There's a moral somwhere in this morality play. It may be that "hate conquers all."

Halfway through pic, Nakadai becomes haunted by the ghost of his first wife. With her recurrent apparitions, he is soon driven to madness and death.

The cast is uniformly fine. Nakadai especially registers bringing a determined discipline to the part of a man with massive emotions hell-bent on destruction. Mariko Okada as his first wife, Junko Ikeuchi as her sister, Mayumi Ozora as second wife, Masao Mishima and Kanzaburo Nakamura are all urgently alive and compelling.

Technical aspects, except for some abrupt cuts, are first rate. Hiroshi Murai's color camerawork captures the bizarre spirit of the story and on several sequences is used effectively to build suspense. Eerie, oriental, electronic music adds to the shock elements. Production and costumes also are high plus. *Dool.*

Le Dimanche De La Vie
(The Sunday of Life)
(FRENCH)

Paris, Feb. 22.

CFDC release of Sofracima production. Stars Danielle Darrieux, Francoise Arnoul; features Jean-Pierre Moulin, Oliver Hussenot, Hubert Deschamps, Jean Rochefort. Directed by Jean Herman. Screenplay, Olivier Hussenot, Georges Richar, Raymond Queneau from book by Queneau; camera, Jean-Jacques Tarbes; editor, Genevieve Winding. Previewed in Paris. Running Time, 95 MINS.

Julia .... Danielle Darrieux
Chantal .... Francoise Arnoul
Valentin .... Jean-Pierre Moulin
Paul .... Olivier Hussenot
Bourrelier .... Hubert Deschamps
Nanaette .... Berthe Bovy
Madame Bijou .... Paulette Dubost
Poucier .... Jean Rochefort
Didine .... Anne Doat
Jean Sans Tete .... Roger Blin

Jean Herman, who has made some notable documentaries on youth, does not quite bring off his ambitious first fiction pic. It's about a group of petty people and their mean ways, as the world heads towards the second World War, they are not perceived with enough compassion to make them of interest or enough pertinent observation to make them vile enough for true satire or ridiculous enough for true parody. Result is a meandering, forced comedy with mainly local chances but okay for specialized use abroad on its technical knowhow and controversial theme.

Done in a sort of larger than life manner, with the people types rather than real folks, it is a tale of an older woman who marries a dreamy younger man. They inherit a store and lead a simple life without much thought for others or world events for that matter. A brother-in-law profits from the imminent war via munitions work, and the wife finds she can foresee the future.

War breaks up this group as the young man goes off with the wife having a vision of his impending death. Danielle Darrieux has flair as the officious older wife with others adequate if not being able to overcome their caricatured roles. Herman obviously has something to say but adapting a book by a noted writer does not have him transcribing it acceptably to the screen.

If this hits at human foibles, it lacks a feel for the characters and sometimes goes off on some clever flights of technical fancy that do not give this the bite or pacing it needs. Chalk it up as an interesting if disapponting first try. But Herman may yet be heard from when he finds the right material. *Mosk.*

Tant Qu' On A La Sante
(As Long As You Are Healthy)
(FRENCH)

Paris, March 8.

CAPAC release of Films De La Colombe production. Stars Pierre Etaix. Directed by Etaix. Screenplay, Jean-Claude Carriere, Etaix; camera, Jean Boffety; music, Jean Paillaut. At Balzac, Paris. Running Time, 78 MINS.

Man .... Pierre Etaix

Pierre Etaix uses a comic idea and theme rather than any sort of story for his third pic. A look at a little man caught up in big city noise, crowds, traffic, and attempting to escape it all, make up the simple backing for a series of gag scenes. Many are successful and some are not so good. But, overall, Etaix shows he is an original film comic. And this pic should do well here, with specialized chances abroad, plus supporting playoff fare and tv use indicated.

Etaix plays a dandyish deadpan type at odds with a jackhammer that all but destroys his apartment and courtship. He is not funny by himself and does not create incidents. His is a character who comes into odds with all sorts of little harassing problems of life and tries valiantly to cope, only to escape to another predicament.

Around this Etaix adroitly builds a series of characters having the same troubles he has for the backbone and added developments around his own troubles. He has fine timing, inventiveness and comedic flair. Etaix has assimilated American slapstick themes but does not ape them. They are firmly planted in the French character and manage to be universal as well as sectional in the comedy of man's coping with modern life.

There is the doctor more harassed than his patients, a camping ground run like a concentration camp with everybody behind barbed wires, an attempt to go to a cinema but always losing a seat or having the usherette shining lamps in his face for tips (one tips in French film houses).

Even a final try at a desert island does not work. Etaix's first film had a comic line about a timid man trying to get married, his second dealt with two generations of clowns, and was more ambitious. Now he goes back to a series of gags. He is helped by his own good-natured character, his deft direction and a feel for comic balance in never forcing a gag. But the production does wear a bit thin and the variations on general minor problems of big city life are not enough to keep up the fun throughout.

Etaix now needs more depth in his character, more inventiveness in themes and more coherent emotional or progressive storylines to be able to make his obvious talents more lifesize and imposing. His technical backing is fine. *Mosk.*

Signore & Signori
(The Birds, the Bees, and the Italians)
(ITALO-FRENCH)

Rome, March 1.

Dear Film release of Robert Haggiag-Pietro Germi production for Dear Films-R.P.A. (Rome)—Les Films du Siecle (Paris). Features Virna Lisi, Gastone Moschin, Nora Ricci, Gigi Ballista, Olga Villi, Beba Loncar, Alberto Lionello, Moira Orfei, Alberto Rabagliati, Giulio Questi, Quinto Parmeggiani, Gia Sandri, Franco Fabrizi, Aldo Puglisi, Patrizia Valturri, Carlo Bagno, Virgilio Scapin, Gustavo d'Arpe, Ilia Gugliotto, Tity Carish, Giacomo Rizzo. Directed by Pietro Germi. Screenplay, Germi, Luciano Vincenzoni, Age, Scarpelli, from original story by Vincenzoni and Germi; camera, Ajace Parolin; music, Carlo Rustichelli; editor, Sergio Montanari. At Ariston, Rome. Running Time, 115 MINS.

Milena Zulian .... Virna Lisi
Oswaldo Bisigato .... Gastone Moschin
Gilda Bisigato .... Nora Ricci
Giacinto Castellan .... Gigi Ballista
Noemi Castellan .... Beba Loncar
Toni Gasparini .... Alberto Lionello
Ippolita Gasparini .... Olga Villi
Giorgia Casellato .... Moira Orfei
Giacomo .. .. Alberto Rabagliati
Franco Zaccario .... Giulio Questi
Lino Benedetti .... Franco Fabrizi
Mancuso .... Aldo Puglisi
Alda Cristofoletto .... Patrizia Valturri
Bepi Cristofoletto ...... Carlo Bagno
Scarabello .... Gustavo d'Arpe
Don Schiavon .... Virgilio Scapin
Nane Soligo .... Quinto Parmeggiani
Betty Soligo .... Gia Sandri
Bepi .... Ilia Gugliotto
Bianca .... Tity Carish
Egisto .... Giacomo Rizzo

Pietro Germi once again displays his upper-case filmic talent in this latest effort, set in the Italian north, far from the Sicily of "Divorce, Italian Style" and "Seduced and Abandoned," but nevertheless as searing in its denunciation of hypocrisy and face-saving as were those recent two pix. This should find ready eyes and ears with discerning filmgoers everywhere.

Though local-color aspects of his previous "Sicilian" pix gave them easier accessibility and built-in curio values, a proper (though by no means easy) foreign lingual version of this pic could help it to almost equal success. Above all, Germi's secret of success lies in his ability to put across biting, frequently cruel subjects and themes, by making them eminently accessible by pacing, vivid characterization, and the riotously funny manner in which they are conducted.

Lingual variation in Italo and English titles is, apparently, commercial pitch as simple "men and women" would have little appeal to U.S. audiences.

Dissection of life in a small north Italian town, Treviso, is conducted by Germi in three basic parts. In the first, the spotlight is on a doctor, his wife and the other man. Last-named is a patient of the doc's who feigns impotence to dupe the medic into believing he's not possibly his wife's lover. But when truth will out, the medico accepts situations to keep his rep. Number two sees henpecked spouse breaking out of home to live with a bar cashier, thus openly flounting town's false respectability. After a brief fling, he's forced back into the mold. Third item sees an under-age gal seduced by most of the eligible bachelors and married men in town until her father reveals her age and makes a federal case out of it. Town powers get to work and, after some touchy moments, papa is paid off and matter is put to rest. The town's "honor" is once again safe.

Actually, however, the stories **are mere pretexts for a worm's-eye view of the two levels on which township lives: the falsely proper, and the blatantly corrupt. And here Germi and his co-scripters Age, Scarpelli and co-writer Luciano Vincenzoni shine. Theirs is a no-holds-barred accusation told, to be sure, in highly amusing terms, but nevertheless uncompromising in its finger-pointing.**

And Germi has come up with an unusually vast gallery of characters, all vivid, all believable, enriched by career-topping performances by all concerned, without exception: from a different Virna Lisi, to a surprising Beba Loncar, a savvy Olga Villi, a wonderfully objectionable Gustavo d'Arpe, as the town bore, and many others, including surprising debuts by Patrizia Valturri, as the seduced teenager; Gigi Ballista, as the medico, and many others. Perhaps Gastone Moschin has the plum role as the bank employee on a sexual spree; it bids mightily for a bright future career. But all faces in this pic are memorable.

Remaining credits are topnotch. Ajace Parolin's location lensing is razor-sharp in carrying out the director's intent. Sergio Montanari's editing is tight, fast, perfect. Carlo Rustichelli's guitar-dominated score fits the bill. *Hawk.*

La Mandragola
(The Mandrake)
(ITALO-FRENCH)

Rome, March 1.

Titanus release of Alfredo Bini production for Arco Film (Rome)—Lux Cie. de France (Paris). Stars Rosanna Schiaffino, Philippe Leroy; features Romolo Valli, Nilla Pizzi, Armando Bandisi Toto, Jean Claude Brialy. Directed by Alberto Lattuada. Screenplay, Lattuada, Luigi Magni, Stefano Strucchi, from story by Nicolo Macchiavelli; camera, Tonino delli Colli; editor, Nino Baragli; music, Gino Marinuzzi, Jr. At Cola di Rienzo, Rome. Running Time, 100 MINS.

Callimaco .... Philippe Leroy
Lucrezia .... Rosanna Schiaffino
Fra' Timoteo .... Toto
Lucrezia's mother .... Nilla Pizzi
Nicia .... Romolo Valli
Ligurio .... Jean Claude Brialy

Based on the oft-banned classic by Niccolo' Macchiavelli, "La Mandragola" manages to touch on and recount explosively prurient material without being offensive or pornographic, thus making it an ideal subject of attention to both arty as well as an exploitation pic in many parts of the world. In Italy and France, it has the Schiaffino, Leroy, Brialy and Toto names to bank on. Rates Yank attention since special hardsell could pay off.

Philippe Leroy covets Romolo Valli's faithful wife. When he learns that her husband is desperate because he has failed to give him a child, Leroy devises a devilish scheme. Passing himself off as a French medico, he suggests that Valli give his wife a special potion made of Mandrake weed. The first man to lie with her will die within a few days, but her apparent sterility will be cured. Valli agrees and Leroy suitably disguised, plays the "victim" who is to cure the wife. The deed done, he reveals himself and Rosanna Schiaffino, the wife, falls in love with him. Both decide to continue fooling the husband, whose real thoughts appear to be with money and succession rather than his young wife's love and happiness.

Director Alberto Lattuada has given this pic polish and has managed to resolve even the most potentially objectionable scenes with taste. Film is frequently amusing though only rarely uproariously funny. Much of the humor is tongue-in-cheek, and emerges in a subtle production which may please the higher type audiences but may leave some of the average aisle-sitters rather cool.

Tasteful handling allows the film to get away with much near-nudity and sensuality, with Miss Schiaffino a major center of attraction. Acting honors go to Valli as the cuckolded husband, but Toto, Leroy and Jean Claude Brialy (as the go-between who makes the "exploit") possible also rate nods. Some trimming for pace might help this along for foreign audiences. All technical credits are firstrate. *Hawk.*

The Naked Prey
(COLOR-PANAVISION)

Raw yet touching story of a struggle for survival in South African bush lands. Artistically excellent, and very good prospects for exploitation could yield good b.o. results in class situations, also.

Hollywood, March 8.
Paramount Pictures release of Theodora Productions-Sven Persson Films coproduction, produced by Cornel Wilde and Persson, directed by and starring Wilde. Features Gert Van Der Berg, Ken Campu, Patrick Mynhardt, Bella Randels. Screenplay, Clint Johnson, Don Peters; camera (Eastmancolor, print by Technicolor), H. A. R. Thomson; editor, Roger Cherrill; music, Andrew Tracey; asst. director, Bert Batt. Reviewed at Paramount Studios. March 7, '66. Running Time, 86 MINS.
Man .... Cornel Wilde
Second Man .... Gert Van Der Berg
Warrior leader .... Ken Campu
Safari Overseer ..... Patrick Mynhardt
Little girl .... Bella Randels
Warriors Jose Sithole, Richard Mashiya, Eric Sabela, Joe Dlamini, Frank Mdhluli, Sandy Nkomo, Fusi Zazayokwe, John Marcus, Horace Gilman
Tribal chief .... Morrison Gampu

Filmed entirely in South Africa, "The Naked Prey" is a story of a white man's survival under relentless pursuit by primitive tribesmen. Told with virtually no dialog, the story embodies a wide range of human emotion, depicted in actual on-scene photography which effects realism via a semi-documentary feel. Film is an artistic achievement of which producer-director-star Cornel Wilde and associates can be justifiably proud. Scenes of raw violence and action make the Paramount release a very good prospect for exploitation selling, but the moving, often touching story is worth more than fast playoff. Special handling in certain situations to build word of mouth could turn this into a sleeper.

The basic story by Clint Johnson and Don Peters is set in the bush country of a century ago, where safari manager Wilde and party are captured by natives offended by white hunter Gert Van Der Berg. All save Wilde are tortured in some explicit footage that is not for the squeamish, while he is given a chance to survive — providing he can exist while eluding some dedicated pursuers.

Action then roves between the maroscopic and the microscopic; that is, from long shots of the varying bush country, caught in beautiful soft Eastmancolor tones by H. A. R. Thomson's Panavision camera and printed by Technicolor, where man is a spot on the landscape, all the way down to minute animal life, in which the pattern of repose, pursuit, sudden death and then repose matches that of Wilde and the natives.

For the greater part of the film, wherein only atmospheric native music and outstanding sound editing and recording are on the track, director Wilde has handled himself and other players in such a way as to present, economically and effectively, such abstract story aspects as suspense, comedy, nobility, sorrow, friendship,

love, fear and hate. And none of this is laid on with heavy-handed, deliberate symbolism. There are no heavies in the strict sense, only living creatures whose animal-spiritual codes create the conflicts.

At the same time, the film assaults the senses with appropriate audio-visual depictions of exhaustion, intense heat, repelling (but logical) brutality and starvation. Unlike the usual gimmicks of the bush country potboiler, not all plants are gourmet delights, either.

Ken Gampu, film and legit actor in South Africa, is excellent as the leader of the pursuing warriors. At the upbeat climax, when Wilde reaches safety — not a trite plot but instead something which the audience has been lead to want to happen, the two adversaries exchange brief glances of respect. Bella Randels registers well as the moppet girl who befriends Wilde. Other players come across in strong support.

Roger Cherrill has trimmed to a 96 minutes. Andrew Tracey, music advisor, has selected some dramatic, authentic rhythms to parallel the dramatic mood. Music cutter Archie Ludski, sound cutter Les Wiggins, and recordist James Chapman have done a firstrate job in enhancing what would be a very effective silent picture. Post production work was done in England.

Two minor flaws might be corrected. When Wilde speaks for the first time, his voice is too clear for a man who has for some days grunted from a parched throat. Also, his escape from a slave raid borders on sound-stage derring-do, long out of fashion. Overall achievement, however, is remarkable and proves, if a moral must be pointed out, that the difficulties of civilized life remain far superior to the primitive alternatives of insulated, elemental existence. *Murf.*

Una Vergine Per Il Principe
(A Virgin for the Prince)
(ITALO—FRENCH)
(Color)

Rome, March 8.
Ceiad release of a Mario Cecchi Gori production for Fairfilm (Rome)-Orsay Film (Paris). Stars Vittorio Gassman, Virna Lisi; features Philippe Leroy, Anna Maria Guarnieri, Vittorio Caprioli, Maria Grazia Buccella, Tino Buazzelli. Directed by Pasquale Festa Campanile. Screenplay, Campanile, Giorgio Prosperi, Stefano Strucchi, Ugo Liberatore; camera, (Technicolor) Roberto Gerardi; editor, Ruggero Mastroianni. At Mazzini, Rome. Running Time, 100 MINS.
Prince Don Vincenzo Gonzaga
.... Vittorio Gassman
Giulia .... Virna Lisi
Ippolito .... Philippe Leroy
Duke of Mantua .... Tino Buazzelli
Marquess of Pepara
.... Maria Grazia Buccella

Columbia, which has this for many territories, can look forward to okay results (depending however also on lingual versions—print seen had an Italo track) in this amusing and exploitable costumer. Though done with taste as the saying goes, both garb and situations and dialog could raise some censorship ire though none showed up in recently prudish Italy. Splendid color outfittings on lush settings plus the Lisi and Gassman names are added draw potentials.

Based on the letters of the 15th

Century which told of an actual such case, story boils down to the fact that a Prince Gonzaga must pass a pre-marital test to prove his virility before the father of the bride allows his daughter to wed the recently-divorced Prince. Elaborate buildup precedes the inevitable key scene, which must be witnessed, and the affair becomes a local issue even before it happens. The Prince's last-minute "success" brings the pic to an ironic climax, with everyone concerned celebrating.

Though equipped with some rather explosive material and situations, it must be said, that thanks to tongue-in-cheek (albeit rowdy) humor on the one hand, plus an elegant, typically exuberant performance by Vittorio Gassman on the other, most of the hurdles are successfully overcome. Though there are other valid backdrop performances, including Tino Buzzelli's fretting Duke of Mantua, this pic rests mainly on Gassman's shoulders. With the exception of some slow spots especially the climactic bedroom scene, milked for too many effects, he brings it off. Not so Virna Lisi, who gets by on undeniable beauty, suggestive garb and a sort of workmanlike approach to the part which is however completely lacking in verve. Not that Miss Lisi won't go over in a big way with the male contingent on visual values which, added to her b.o. draw, must have conditioned her choice for the role.

As per usual, Mario Cecchi Gori has given his production considerable gloss, his sets are opulent, as are Pier Luigi Pizzi's costumes. The location photography captures some splendidly scenic interiors and exteriors north of Rome, and in Tuscany. Festa Campanile's co-scripting is better than his direction, which bogs at times and could profit from trims here and there. In fact, opening half is far the best in its tongue-in-cheek, modern spoof of costume sagas and cliche phrases. When things get down to the serious sex stuff, the going is less elastic, more predictable, and only intermittently amusing. *Hawk.*

A Man Could Get Killed
(PANAVISION-COLOR)

Star names should help sell latest entry in wild undercover mellers.

Hollywood, March 11.
Universal release of Robert Arthur production. Stars James Garner, Melina Mercouri, Sandra Dee, Tony Franciosa; features Robert Coote, Gregoire Aslan, Roland Culver, Dulcie Gray, Cecil Parker. Directed by Ronald Neame, Cliff Owen. Screenplay, Richard Breen, T. E. B. Clarke; based on novel, "Diamonds for Danger," by David Esdaile Walker; camera (Technicolor), Gabor Pogany; music, Bert Kaempfert; editor, Alma Macrorie; asst. directors, Douglas Green, Robert Fiz. Reviewed at Wiltern Theatre, March 8, '66. Running Time, 97 MINS.
William Beddoes .... James Garner
Aurora-Celeste .... Melina Mercouri
Amy Franklin .... Sandra Dee
Steve-Antonio .... Tony Franciosa
Hatton-Jones .... Robert Coote
Doctor Mathieson ...... Roland Culver
Florian .... Gregoire Aslan
Sir Huntley Frazier ...... Cecil Parker
Mrs. Mathieson .... Dulcie Gray
Politanu .... Martin Benson
Zarik .... Peter Illing
Ship's Captain .... Niall MacGinnis

Inspector Rodrigues .... Virgilio Teixeira
Miss Bannister .... Isabel Dean
Osman .... Daniele Vargas
Abdul .... Nello Pazzafini
Lazlo .... George Pastell
Milo .... Arnold Diamond
Heinrich .... Conrad Anderson
Max .... Eric Domain
Carmo .... Pasquale Fasciano
Miss Nolan .... Ann Firbank

"A Man Could Get Killed" carries sufficient star voltage, headed by names of James Garner and Melina Mercouri, to rate b.o. attention. Skirting fringe of the current cycle of undercover whoop-de-dos, Panavision - Technicolor feature fits patly into the trend—if spectator isn't too demanding as to story clarity. Film unfolds a furious comedy approach to a search for smuggled diamonds. For further marquee dressing the Robert Arthur production has a second romantic team, Sandra Dee and Tony Franciosa, and with exteriors filmed entirely in Portugal the whole is given class mounting.

Richard Breen - T.E.B. Clarke script, based on David Esdaile Walker novel, "Diamonds for Danger," is set down in the spy atmosphere of Lisbon. Garner, an American businessman arriving to investigate investment possibilities for his bank, is instantly mistaken for a British secret agent, a firm belief he cannot shake as he becomes involved in a maze of intrigue. In essence, plot twirls around his recovery of the loot without losing his standing as an amateur, while objecting to the caper.

Before he knows it, the paramour of the murdered agent Garner sup. osedly is replacing transfers her affections to him, insisting he continue search for the missing jewels so she may share in the reward. Franciosa, another American who poses as a master Portuguese smuggler (with a beautiful accent) so he, too, may get his share, attaches himself to Garner and insists he help his unwilling compatriot in tracing the diamonds. Several groups of spies and smugglers watch his every move, to the accompaniment of some Mack Sennett-type chases. Meanwhile, all Garner's protestations that he isn't anything but what he calims are to no avail as he's whisked from one loony situation to another.

Garner registers well enough in one of his customary bewildered portrayals but to Miss Mercouri go any top honors which might accrue as the larceny-minded Aurore-Celeste glimpsed in various stages of dress and undress. Her comedy timing is better than ever. Miss Dee as a young American tourist who recognizes Franciosa as the man she—aged 11—was once madly in love with back in their hometown of Seattle, acquits herself with her usual distinction as she now sets out to prove the same feeling exists at age 20. Franciosa's performance is boff.

Highly capable support is offered by Robert Coote as a British embassy official; Roland Culver, ostensibly a respected English doctor who isn't all he seems; Dulcie Gray, his unsuspecting spouse; Cecil Parker, the British ambassador whose main interest is playing chess by mail with a friend in Pakistan; Gregoire Aslan, one of the spies. Niall MacGinnis lends spice to a sea captain character.

Producer made use of two directors on pic, Ronald Neame for the interiors filmed in Rome and Cliff Owen for the Portuguese locations, both handle their assignments nicely. Gabor Pogany's color photography is artistic, as is John De Cuir's art direction; Bert Kaempfert's music score displays quality, and Alma Macrorie's editing is fast. *Whit.*

Menage All'Italiana
(Menage, Italian Style)
(ITALIAN)

Rome, March 8.

Dino DeLaurentiis production and release. Stars Ugo Tognazzi; features Maria Grazia Buccella, Dalida, Romina Power, Anna Moffo. Directed by Franco Indovina. Screenplay, Indovina, Rodolfo Sonego; camera, Otello Martelli; music, Ennio Morricone; editor, Alberto Galliti. At Capranica, Rome. Running Time, **108 MINS.**

Alfredo .... Ugo Tognazzi
Giovanna .... Anna Moffo
Ulla .... Monica Siwers
Anna .... Dalida'
Erika .... Susanna Klemm
Carmelina .... Maria Capparelli
Egle .... Maria Grazia Buccella
Stella .... Romina Power
Erika's mother .... Gisa Geert
Stella's mother .... Rosalia Maggio
Momi .... Edoardo Arroyo
Virginia .... Mavie Bardanzellu
Dino .... Himself

Fairly amusing satire on Italian manners with a neat performance by Ugo Tognazzi and a varied cast of pretty females. Okay returns predictable on the home grounds, with some possibilities in the export market. Also this is noteworthy for a promising debut by Tyrone Power's daughter, Romina, as well as the equally interesting first pic stint by opera star Anna Moffo.

Loosely based on a real case of some years back, this deals with a man whose hobby is marrying women. An amiable, gregarious type equipped with a vivid imagination, he uses his traveling salesman job as a mobile excuse for excursions from woman to woman. For a while, he manages to avoid major conflicts, but at the end, he finds a good excuse in killing off his skirt-chasing career by assuming a drowned man's identity. His many wives and mistresses attend his funeral while he watches, temporarily relieved.

Film thus is comprised of partly intertwined episodes involving his various exploits, in few if any of which he's caught short. As rendered by Ugo Tognazzi, in one of his better stints, he's even basically a sympathetic sort of rogue. Two most interesting of these sweethearts are Anna Moffo, who displays looks and presence in her first pic role, as his first wife. Romina Power, the image of her late father, is also very winning in her role as another wife. Her talent is still rough-hewn, but she also has looks and youthful exhuberance which make her a youngster to be watched. Others in a vast cast provide able characterizations.

The Rodolfo Sonego-Franco Indovina screenplay provides some observant moments and some neat sequences. Thanks to the noteworthy performance by Ugo Tognazzi, the pic achieves some depth and projection despite repetition of motifs. Technical credits all rate bows, from Otello Martelli's lensing to Ennio Morricone's music to location selection by producer which add realism to a fantastic story. *Hawk.*

The Alphabet Murders

Agatha Christie's "A. B. C. Murders" whodunit gets travesty treatment with mildly diverting results.

Hollywood, March 10.

Metro release of Lawrence P. Bachmann production. Stars Tony Randall, Anita Ekberg, Robert Morley; features Maurice Denham; Guy Rolfe, Sheila Allen, James Villiers, Julian Glover, Grazina Frame. Directed by Frank Tashlin. Screenplay, David Pursall, Jack Seddon; based on Agatha Christie novel, "The A.B.C. Murders"; camera, Desmond Dickinson; music, Ron Goodwin; asst. director, David Tomblin; editor, John Victor Smith. Reviewed at Metro Studios, March 9, '66. Running Time, **90 MINS.**

Hercule Poirot .... Tony Randall
Amanda Beatrice Cross .... Anita Ekberg
Hastings .... Robert Morley
Japp .... Maurice Denham
Duncan Doncaster .... Guy Rolfe
Lady Diane .... Sheila Allen
Franklin .... James Villiers
Don Fortune .... Julian Glover
Betty Barnard .... Grazina Frame
"X" .... Clive Morton
Sir Carmichael Clarke.. Cyril Luckham
Wolf .... Richard Wattis
Sergeant .... David Lodge
Cracknell .... Patrick Newell
Judson .... Austin Trevor
Miss Sparks .... Alison Seebohm

Perhaps in keeping with today's filmic trend to spoof virtually everything relating to secret agents, spies, lawmen et al, this British translation of one of Agatha Christie's better-known whodunits, "The A.B.C. Murders," gets the broad comedy treatment. And not always for the best. There is, however, enough diverting action to keep spectator mildly engaged and name of Christie may help chances in the general market.

One branch of the Christie literary output deals with the little **Belgian detective, Hercule Poirot, who self-admittedly keeps drawing on his gray matter to solve crimes in his own peculiar method of sheer deduction. Instead of making him the epitome of shrewd ingenuity, however, a quality which has endeared him to millions of readers the world over, the David Pursall-Jack Seddon screenplay does a turnabout and projects him as inept and fumbling, albeit he bumbles his way to a successful solution of the mystery at hand.**

Much of the suspense of Agatha Christie writing is lost in converting to comedy, and result is no more than a parody of the original, insufficiently clever to be outstanding.

Tony Randall seems a strange choice for the Poirot role, which he clowns throughout. He introduces himself to audience in opening scene with remark, "I'm a Belgian snoop," thereafter proving he's just that. But he delivers a very definite characterization, even though it's not the original character, in making his way through the plot haze of a series of murders which has for its victims people with the initials A.A., B.B., C.C.

Lawrence P. Bachmann, who previously has brought to screen four Christie mysteries with Margaret Rutherford in the principal amateur sleuth part of Miss Marple, is responsible for excellent production values, making handsome use at times of London street backgrounds. Frank Tashlin's direction is attuned to the type of comedy intended and he has at his disposal an accomplished cast, as well as expert technical backing.

Robert Morley, as a British Intelligence (?) agent whose sole duty here is to see that Poirot remains unharmed while in England, like Randall clowns the part in a dippy sort of way. He throws in with the Belgian, apparently adding to general confusion, and turns in a gem of a hokum performance of a slow-witted Englishman. Anita Ekberg as a compulsive murderess, a schizophrenic obsessed with the alphabet, is mostly lost in her fleeting appearances bundled up in a trenchcoat.

Maurice Denham as the familiar Inspector Japp of Scotland Yard plays it straight, as does Guy Rolfe as the psychiatrist treating the mentally-disturbed Miss Ekberg. Sheila Allen, James Villiers, Julian Glover, Grazina Frame and Cyril Luckham further contribute key portrayals in okay fashion. Margaret Rutherford is in for a single scene.

On technical end, Desmond Dickinson's black-and-white photography interestingly limns movement and Ron Goodwin's music score catches the action appropriately. Editing by John Victor Smith is as sharp as script allows, and Bill Andrews' art direction is fresh. *Whit.*

Doctor In Clover
(BRITISH-COLOR)

Prescription as before, but with Arthur Haynes adding a touch of well-timed humor to the predictable, highly profitable corn.

London, March 8.

Rank release of a Betty E. Box-Ralph Thomas production. Stars Leslie Phillips, James Robertson Justice, Shirley Anne Field, John Fraser, Joan Sims, Arthur Haynes, Elisabeth Ercy; features Fenella Fielding, Jeremy Lloyd, Noel Purcell, Robert Hutton, Eric Barker, Terry Scott, Norman Vaughan, Ronnie Stevens, Alfie Bass, Suzan Farmer, Anthony Sharp. Directed by Thomas. Screenplay, Jack Davies, from Richard Gordon's novel; camera (Eastmancolor), Ernest Steward; editor, Alfred Roome; music, John Scott; title song and "Take A Look At Me," lyrics, Rick Jones; sung by Kiki Dee. At Leicester Square Theatre, London. Running Time, **101 MINS.**

Dr. Gaston Grimsdyke.... Leslie Phillips
Sir Lancelot Spratt
James Robertson Justice
Nurse Bancroft .... Shirley Anne Field
Dr. Miles Grimsdyke ...... John Fraser
Matron Sweet .... Joan Sims
Tarquin Wendover ..... Arthur Haynes
Tatiana Rubikov ..... Fenella Fielding
Lambert Symington .... Jeremy Lloyd
O'Malley .... Noel Purcell
Rock Stewart .... Robert Hutton
Professor Halfback .... Eric Barker
Robert .... Terry Scott
TV Commentator..... Norman Vaughan
Jeannine .... Elisabeth Ercy
Fleming .... Alfie Bass
Women's Ward Sister Anne Cunningham
Nurse Holiday .... Suzan Farmer
Grafton .... Harry Fowler
Len .... Peter Gilmore
Salesman .... Nicky Henson
Digger .... Bill Kerr
New Matron .... Justine Lord
Tristam .... Roddy Maude-Roxby
Publicity Man .... Lionel Murton
Dr. Loftus .... Anthony Sharp

Fat Woman Patient .... Dandy Nichols
TV Producer .... Ronnie Stevens
Sydney .... Robin Hunter
Beckwith .... Barry Justice

Over the last few years, the Betty E. Box-Ralph Thomas team has made half a dozen or so "Doctor" pictures, based on Richard Gordon's novels. It's been a profitable angle. This latest keeps to the familiar formula, the venerable storyline, designed merely to put over some predictable situations and gags which seem to be getting a shade bluer. Scripter Jack Davies has hardly extended himself on this one but nevertheless comes up with a few good wheezes and gags, though on both counts audiences will meet old buddies. Exhibitors will need no guidance about "Doctors in Clover." If previous Doctor pix have clicked at their houses, then this one will.

Storyline mainly concerns a flighty hospital doctor (Leslie Phillips) with a roving eye for the nurses and particularly for a shapely French physiotherapist. Somehow, from this situation evolves a hospital dance at which laughing gas is released, an operation which is televised, Phillips' attempts to become rejuvenated and a romantic tangle-bungle between the middle aged matron and the irascible house surgeon (James Robertson Justice).

Main boost for this comedy is the first star screen appearance of tv comic Arthur Haynes (he recently made his Hollywood debut as a hackie in "Strange Bedfellows"), as a belligerent patient who knows his rights and who even checks the medical routine from his own "Home Medical Encyclopedia." Haynes' withering look and his sharp timing lends funny point to several ribald lines: Haynes is a top-plus in a long cast most of whom are merely on parade for bits.

Justice, constant and sole survivor of the first "Doctor" pic back in 1953, again plays the peppery, formidable Sir Lancelot Spratt with the authority of his bulk. Phillips' light comedy technique is just right for the amorous hero. John Fraser, as his stolid cousin; Jeremy Lloyd, as another vapid young medico, and Joan Sims, dependable as ever as the matron, together with Shirley Anne Field, making minus impact as a nurse, are the main thesps.

The apparently necessary boost of introducing a Continental charmer in Elisabeth Ercy, a cool looker whose thesping seems unlikely to set either the Thames or the Seine afire. Of those brought in to give point to tiny cameos Fenella Fielding, in a bright wicked sendup of a ballerina, Suzan Farmer, Noel Purcell, Anthony Sharp and Ronnie Stevens get minor opportunities to shine.

Ernest Seward's Eastmancolor camerawork is fairly conventional but satisfactory. Editor Alfred Roome's chief task is to see that the comedy situations do not get too prolonged. Ralph Thomas milks Davies' screenplay of every possible yock but, in his direction, doesn't appear over-concerned at creating new phases of comedy. John Scott's music is okay, but the two ditties which he has penned with Rick Jones (sung by Kiki Dee) seem unlikely to cause congested queues among the Sinatras, Bennetts and Peggy Lees of the current disk scene. *Rich.*

Hold On
(COLOR-PANAVISION)

Good Sam Katzman teenpic featuring Herman's Hermits. Strong b.o. prospects in predominantly young situations, and okay on general duals.

Hollywood, March 5.
Metro-Goldwyn-Mayer release of Four Leaf (Sam Katzman) Production. Features Herman's Hermits, Shelley Fabares, Sue Ane Langdon, Herbert Anderson. Directed by Arthur Lubin. Screenplay, James B. Gordon; camera (Metrocolor), Paul C. Vogel; editor, Ben Lewis; music, Fred Karger; songs, Karger, P. F. Sloan, Noel Tay, Steve Barri, Sid Wayne, Ben Weisman; asst. director, Al Shenberg. Reviewed at Stanley Warner's Wiltern Theatre, L.A., March 4, '66. Running Time, 83 MINS.
Herman's Hermits ...Peter Blair Noone,
    Karl Green, Keith Hopwood,
    Derek Leckenby, Barry Whitwam
Louisa .... Shelley Fabares
Cecilie .... Sue Ane Langdon
Lindquist .... Herbert Anderson
Dudley .... Bernard Fox
Grant .... Harry Hickox
Mrs. Page .... Hortense Petra
Publicist .... Mickey Deems
Detectives .... Ray Kellogg, John Hart
Photographer .... Phil Arnold

"Hold On" is a comedy-tune vehicle spotlighting Herman's Hermits, one of the bigger wax names among youth, and in particular the leader, Peter Blair Noone. A diverting script, good direction, acting and pace are supported by fine Sam Katzman production values. Hard-core teen situations will garner strong b.o. from uppercasing the Metro release, while in the general market it's an okay supporting pic.

James B. Gordon's original script finds the Hermits, on a U. S. tour, shadowed by a space agency egghead because a nosecone is to be named after them. Object is to see if the boys are okay. Complicating the plot is an eager-beaver starlet out for publicity and a romantic interest. Eleven songs of varied tempo recur at regular intervals, and some daydream sequences strengthen via satire.

Noone is very good in both the vocal and mild acting department. He projects a likeable image. Shelley Fabares is okay as the sweet girl on whom Noone has a slight crush. Sue Ane Langdon registers quite strongly as the brassy babe who cons her way into headlines. She has a flair for this type role and, if desired, can specialize in it to long term success.

Herbert Anderson comes across well as the shy-guy scientist, underplaying in neat contrast to Miss Langdon, the Hermits and latters' manager, Bernard Fox, also good. Other players are handled in good fashion by director Arthur Lubin, who knows how to make light-weight, commercial fare.

Fred Karger's score has the modern sound and is a good production assist. All the songs, while not memorable, have a clean sound and rhythm. Paul C. Vogel's Metrocolor-Panavision camera is outstanding, particularly in an amusement park roller-coaster ride which has much of the excitement of the famous Cinerama prototype. Process work here is very good, also.

Wilda Taylor choreographed to good effect, and in the climactic tea party which becomes a swinging affair, there's an offbeat costuming gimmick—the girls in bikinis are paired with fully-clothed boys. Editor Ben Lewis has trimmed to 86 minutes, and assuming a teen-packed theatre, it's a good length with enough padding to cover laughs. More sedate or smaller audiences, on the other hand, may become aware of the gambit.

Franklin Milton's sound recording crew has turned in another professional job. In early scenes there is a scream track of such intensity that it's remarkable that the sound track striations don't leap over into the picture frame. One unresolved question remains: does hair stylist Sydney Guilaroff's screen credit cover the boys as well as the girls? *Murf.*

Une Balle Au Coeur
(A Bullet In the Heart)
(FRENCH—COLOR)

Paris, March 8.
Rank release of CMS-Lembessis Film production. Stars Sami Frey, Francoise Hardy; features Spiros Focas, Jenny Karezy. Directed by Jean-Daniel Pollet. Screenplay, Pierre Kast, Didier Goulard, Maurice Fabre, Pollet; camera (Eastmancolor), Alain Levent; editor, Denise De Casabianca. At Lord Byron, Paris. Running Time, 90 MINS.
Francesco .... Sami Frey
Anne .... Francoise Hardy
Carla .... Jenny Karezy
Nazara .... Spiros Focas

Unclear tale of a young idler, a nobleman done out of his inherited crumbling castle of a home by Sicilian bandits, and his attempt for revenge, is basically the man-on-run gimmick but done up with pretentious undertones. Lagging characterizations rob this of any depth and many entertainment values. Only possible playoff abroad is on its few scenes of mayhem with specialized chances chancier.

The nobleman is a brooder. And this spends most of its time playing on his face and the imbroglios he gets himself into. He goes off to Greece to find a man who can put the finger on the usurper of his home. But this man is killed and he wounded before he goes back alone and kills the gangleader.

He also manages to win the love of a pretty Greek bar girl, played with worldweary rightness by Jenny Karezy, and a naive French tourist done with gauche pouting by singer Francoise Hardy. Sami Frey does nothing but pose as the hero.

Sketchiness of the affair might have been acceptable with some knowing direction but firsttimer Jean-Daniel Pollet has digested New Wave techniques badly. He is not helped by the mediocre, aimless script and trite dialog. Color is good with some Greek backgrounds as assets. *Mosk.*

The Great St. Trinian's Train Robbery
(BRITISH-COLOR)

Another "St. Trinian's" comedy-farce with a topical twist. Juve 'horrors' in good form, plenty of topline British character comedians, hilarious train chase and overall a good bet for audiences out for a spree.

London, March 10.
BLC release of British Lion presentation of a Frank Launder-Sidney Gilliat production. Stars Frankie Howerd, Dora Bryan. Features George Cole, Reg Varney, Raymond Huntley, Richard Wattis, Portland Mason, Godfrey Winn, Terry Scott, Eric Barker. Produced by Leslie Gilliat. Directed by Launder and Sidney Gilliat. Screenplay, Launder and Ivor Herbert, based on Ronald Searle's characters; camera (Eastmancolor), Kenneth Hodges; editor, Geoffrey Foot; art director, Albert Witherick; music, Malcolm Arnold. At Studio One, London. Running Time, 94 MINS.
Alphonse Askett........Frankie Howerd
Gilbert .... Reg. Varney
Leonard Edwards..Desmond Walter Ellis
Maxie .... Cyril Chamberlain
Big Jim .... Arthur Mullard
The Voice .... Stratford Johns
The Minister .... Raymond Huntley
Bassett .... Richard Wattis
Butters .... Peter Gilmore
Culpepper Brown .... Eric Barker
Gore-Blackwood ....George Benson
Liftman .... Michael Ripper
Truelove .... Godfrey Winn
Amber Spottiswood .... Dora Bryan
Mabel Radnage .... Barbara Couper
Susie Naphill .... Margaret Nolan
Veronica Bledlow .... Elspeth Duxbury
Magsa O'Riley .... Maggie McGrath
Albertine .... Carole Ann Ford
Drunken Dolly .... Jean St. Clair
Flash Harry .... George Cole
Georgina .... Portland Mason
Marcia Askett ...... Maureen Crombie
Noakes .... Colin Gordon
Pakistani Porter .... Leon Thau
Chairman .... Meredith Edwards

Making one of their not-too-frequent film appearances, Ronald Searle's little schoolgirl demons from St. Trinian's are berserk again on the screen. This time Frank Launder and Sidney Gilliat have tailored a yarn with a topical twist, the Great Train Robbery. The fun often flags and is fairly predictable, but overall it keeps up a good level of slapstick comedy, garners plenty of yocks and should be a good bet for houses whose audiences demand no more than an evening's relaxation.

Having pulled off a $7,000,000 train robbery, the hapless gang of crooks stash the loot in a deserted country mansion. But when they go back to collect they find the St. Trinian's school has taken over, and they are completely routed by the hockey sticks and rough stuff handed out by the little she-monsters. When the gang returns on parents' day for a second attempt at picking up the loot they run into further trouble and complications and eventually get involved in a great train chase which is quite the funniest part of the film, having a great deal in common with the old silent slapstick technique.

Weakness of the film is that the St. Trinian's characters, particularly the school staff, have now been broadened tremendously, with the mistresses no longer even pretending to be anything but crooks and no-gooders themselves. However, this is offset by Launder and Gilliat having hired a long and splendid cast of well-tried British character actors and comedians, so that there are rewards all along the line.

Among the many performances which contribute to the gaiety are those of Frankie Howerd as a crook posing as a French male hairdresser, Raymond Huntley as a Cabinet Minister with amorous eyes on the St. Trinian's headmistress (Dora Bryan), Richard Wattis in one of his typical harassed civil servant roles and Peter Gilmore as his confrere. Dora Bryan is in good raffish form as Amber Spottiswood, the headmistress, with a hand-picked staff ranging from an all-in wrestler as games mistress to a strip-teaser as art-mistress. George Cole crops up again as Flash Harry, the school bookie, and among the shapely, gin-drinking, gambling sixth-formers appears James Mason's daughter Portland to good, eye-stunning effect. Leon Thau turns in a splendid cameo as a Pakistani porter, bewildered by the goings-on on the sleepy railway.

The well-known writer Godfrey Winn oddly appears in a small character role and Eric Barker, George Benson, Colin Gordon, Desmond Walter Ellis and the voice of Stratford Johns, the well-known "Z-Cars" police inspector, doing service as the unseen Brain of the gang, help along the action.

Kenneth Hodges' Eastmancolor photography is satisfactory and Geoffrey Foot's editing gives smoothness to an uneven script that tends to jump as erratically as an Alpine goat. *Rich.*

Angelique Et Le Roy
(Angelique And the King)
(FRENCH-ITALIAN-COLOR)
Paris, March 8.
Prodis release of Francos Films-Films Borderie-Gloria-Fono Roma production. Stars Michelle Mercier; features Robert Hossein, Sami Frey, Jacques Toja, Jean Rochefort, Estella Blain. Directed by Bernard Borderie. Screenplay, Alain Decaux, Pascal Jardin, Francis Cosne from novel by Serge and Anne Golon; camera (Eastmancolor), Henri Persin; editor, Christian Gaudin. At Paris, Paris. Running Time, 100 MINS.
Angelique .... Michelle Mercier
Peyrac .... Robert Hossein
King .... Jacques Toja
Desgres .... Jean Rochefort
Montespan .... Estella Blain

This is No. 3 in a successful series about the romantic, political and sexual imbroglios of a comely girl at the court of Louis XIV in 17th Century France. Simple in story, lavish in production, and disarmingly childlike in execution, this should please local audiences and there may be several more in the series.

Pic is a lacy answer to James Bond, and perhaps the French western. Angelique is quite often bedded down with different men though she remains true in heart to her first husband, supposedly dead. But he comes back but not before she takes a handsome Hungarian outlaw to bed and is almost seduced by a mad Turkish sheik.

Michelle Mercier is more sure of herself, and, if her acting is on the one-tone level of the tale, she wears the period robes fetchingly and does her few near nude scenes with aplomb. Court intrigues are brought into this as the King decides to make her one of his courtesans. But this

does not come off though she remains one of his favorites.

There is the throbbing music, outlandish adventure and romantic byplay reminiscent of the early Hollywood days. Although this does not have the saving naivete of its predecessors, this pic has the saving grace of playing it straight for the lush, soapy actioner it is.

This production looms as another hit here, and the others have caught on in various other countries. For the U.S., it appears mainly possible playoff fare on its hokum, lushness and movement, with firstrun and art chances out. *Mosk.*

L'Or Et Le Plomb
(Gold and Lead)
(FRENCH)
Paris, March 8.
Charles Mandel release of SIPAC-Louis Fleury production. Written and directed by Alain Cuniot, based on a story by Voltaire. Camera, Yann Le Masson; editor, Francine Grubert. Previewed in Paris. Running Time, 80 MINS.

Using a philosophical tale by the 17th Century writer Voltaire as a background, this mixes real interviews and re-enacted scenes to make a comment on France in particular and people in general. If at times arbitrary, pic has a flair for using fine visuals to make its points. And the tale of a man from another planet, sent to make a report on whether the earth is worth saving or not, never becomes too precious. This looks geared for some arty spots if well handled.

The envoy meets a composer in love with living. But then an old woman, who lives in abject poverty on a pension that in no way can fill her basic needs, changes his attitude.

He also attends a party given by a noted actress where free love and man's real feelings as opposed to his surface veneer is gone into. This one is a bit forced. Pic ends with a philosophical talk on liberty that is pertinent and well delivered if it remains a generalization.

This mixture of "cinema truth," social probing and surface, at times deeper which looks at various aspects of society, is done with tact and impact.

Director Alain Cuniot shows a visual flair and is aided by the expert lensing of Yann Le Masson. It is reminiscent of Chris Marker's "Jolie Mai." Not as all encompassing and talented, but a good showing for the first time out. *Mosk.*

Madamigella Di Maupin
(Mademoiselle de Maupin)
(ITALO—FRENCH—SPANISH—YUGOSLAV)
(COLOR)
Rome, March 8.
Unidis release of Silvio Clementelli production for Jolly Film (Rome)-Consortium Pathe' (Paris)-Tecisa (Madrid) in collaboration with Filmservis Lubjana (Yugoslavia). Stars Catherine Spaak, Robert Hossein, Tomas Milian; features Mikaela, Angel Alvarez, Ottavia Piccolo. Directed by Mauro Bolognini. Screenplay, Luigi Magni, freely adapted from the novel by Theophile Gauthier; camera (Technicolor), Roberto Gerardi; editor, Nino Baragli; music, Franco Mannino. At Olimpico, Rome. Running Time, 55 MINS.

Teodoro Maddalena ... Catherine Spaak
Alcibiade .... Robert Hossein
D'Albert .... Tomas Milian
Rosetta .... Mikaela
Mons. de Maupin....... Angel Alvarez
Ninon .... Ottavia Piccolo

Elegant and piquant costumer in the vein of "Tom Jones," tastefully exploitable, beautifully outfitted, this has story angles and other values to give it good foreign projection as well as nice Italo chances. In certain areas, the Spaak and Hossein names are plusses. It has built-in exploitation aspects for added impact.

Tale is about a heroine, Maddalena de Maupin, who briefly—for the length of the film—becomes a hero, Teodoro; to study the male of the species from a closer angle. That is, she dresses in male garb, joins an army of sorts, and otherwise becomes entangled in various male-female exploits imaginable once the premise is accepted. She falls for some males, notaby an officer, but can't display her affection as he thinks she is a man. Other gentler members of the male gender make obvious passes at her, while the one man who knows (D'Albert) and loves her can't do so openly because the situation, to say the least, would be misinterpreted.

So it goes, from barracks humor to bordello sequence, from one double-entendre to another, some fairly obvious, others very risible, but all generally diverting. There is also some very amusing spoofing of battles and other period business. Mauro Bolognini as always gets away with scenes that might otherwise be vulgar via taste, elegance, and discretion, and his period canvas is colorful, eye-appealing, and diffusedly romantic. There are moments when his script is wanting, and others where some scenes appear cut or rushed-through.

Catherine Spaak is a delight throughout, perfect in her piquant-boy-girlish characterization. One wonders why, after several years in Italian pix, this versatile as well as comely young actress has not yet been seized by U.S. filmmakers. Robert Hossein is fine as her officer love, while Tomas Milian, in a more limited part, shows continued promise. Italo and Yugoslav backdrops have been splendidly lensed in rich Technicolor hues by Roberto Gerardi. Franco Mannino's music is suitably period. *Hawk.*

Ich suche einen Mann
(I am Looking for a Man)
(GERMAN-COLOR)
Berlin, March 8.
Nora release of Franz Seitz production. Stars Ghita Noerby, Paul Hubschmid, Walter Giller. Directed by Alfred Weidenmann. Screenplay, Herbert Reinecker; camera (Eastmancolor), Wolf Wirth; editor, Inge Tschner. At Marmorhaus, West Berlin. Running Time, 89 MINS.
Barbara Schoenfelder.....Ghita Noerby
Dr. Pleskau .... Walter Giller
Ursula Bode .... Monika Dahlberg
Albert Bode .... Stefan Wigger
Helene Schmidt .... Brigitte Horney
Gregor .... Harald Leipnitz
Baron Federsen ..... Paul Hubschmid
Director Voss .... Sieghardt Rupp
A writer .... Jean Valmont
A teacher .... Gert Baltus
A hotel director ..... Rudolf Rhomberg
A student .... Claus Ringer

The biggest plus about this German comedy is Ghita Noerby. This

young Danish actress, a top star in the Scandinavian territory, is seen here in her first German pic. She brings some fresh wind to the Teutonic screen. Pic has enough entertainment value to please the bulk of native patrons. Foreign prospects appear limited but many foreign patrons will likely at least admit that Miss Noerby isn't a waste of time.

This is the story of an about 25-year-old woman who is charming, pretty and sexy enough so that she can't complain about lack of admirers. In fact, she has plenty of them. The trouble, however, is that everyone wants to play around with her and nobody feels inclined to marry. But she wants a husband. She finally applies to a matrimonial agency and is offered a wide selection of men. She encounters all sorts of suitors but the right one isn't among them. Naturally she finds one at last. It's her superior at the office where she works.

Miss Noerby steals the film. Her natural charm and gay sex are a full delight. Lineup of her partners includes many domestically familiar faces and there are several nice performances. This goes especially for Harald Liepnitz; ordinarily a villian in German pix, seen here as a shy lover; Paul Hubschmid, who is an elegant baron; Stefan Wigger, a fine stage actor, and Walter Giller, always dependable and sympathetic, the man who gets the lovely girl.

Alfred Weidenmann, who has already turned out a number of nice comedies, has directed with a light hand. There are quite a few amusing situations, and technically, the film makes a good impression. Wolf Wirth's lensing is especially good. *Hans.*

Born Free
(BRITISH-COLOR-PANAVISION)

Outstanding film version of pop book about British couple who train their pet lioness to return and survive in African bush. Special handling required.

Hollywood, March 11.

Columbia Pictures release of Open Road-High Road-coproduction, executive producer, Carl Foreman, produced by Sam Jaffe and Paul Radin. Stars Virginia McKenna, Bill Travers; features Geoffrey Keen, Peter Lukoye, Omar Chambati. Directed by James Hill. Screenplay, Gerald L. C. Copley, based on the books by Joy Adamson; camera (Technicolor), Kenneth Talbot; editor, Don Deacon; music, John Barry; technical adviser, George Adamson; asst. director, William P. Cartlidge. Reviewed at Columbia Studios, March 10, '66. Running Time, 95 MINS.

Joy Adamson	Virginia McKenna
George Adamson	Bill Travers
Kendall	Geoffrey Keen
Nuru	Peter Lukoye
Makkede	Omar Chambati
Sam	Bill Godden
Baker	Bryan Epsom
Ken	Robert Cheetham
James	Robert Young
Watson	Geoffrey Best
Indian Doctor	Surya Patel

"Born Free" is a heart-warming story of a British couple in Africa who, at the maturity of their pet lioness, educate the beast to survive in the bush. Executive producer Carl Foreman and producers Sam Jaffe and Paul Radin have executed an excellent adaptation of Joy Adamson's books which were as much photos as text with restraint, loving care, and solid emotional appeal that seldom becomes banal. The Columbia release is definitely not slanted towards juves, although latter will understand it. This outstanding artistic achievement will, however, require extremely sensitive selling techniques if full b.o. potential is to be realized since many adults will tend to shy away from sentimentality implications.

Animal pix seem to divide into two classes, Disney-type product which goes far at the b.o. on the combined strength of treatment, kid draw and the Disney name, and the remainder, usually overly-cute fluff aimed at infants and, at which, parental attendance is simply baby-sitting. "Born Free," however, fits into neither. Film buffs will have to go back to "Sequoia" to find a comparable film. While possessing the charm of Disney pix, it may suffer commercially from lack of the Disney endorsement.

Gerald L. C. Copley did a first-rate adaptation of the true story of Joy Adamson, who with hubby George, involuntarily domesticated several pet lions. They kept one, Elsa, until she was fully grown and then, to save her from Government-ordered zoo captivity, trained her to survive as a wild animal. The apparently childless couple, are portrayed in top form by real-life married couple Virginia McKenna and Bill Travers.

The wife's maternal affection for the lioness, and all pets, is handled by Miss McKenna and director James Hill with excellent taste and restraint. Man's affinity for pets is too basic in his nature to be cluttered up with the antiseptic verbiage of contemporary head-shrinking. Only occasionally do the two leads display a small degree of reservation towards Elsa.

Hill, known primarily for documentaries although bearing other feature credits, has succeeded admirably in effecting a balance of audience interest in the humans. Travers, also starred above title after Miss McKenna, is excellent. He's best known in the U.S. for "Wee Geordie." Pair's interactions cover the spectrum, from incidental humor to occasional strife, of genuine married love.

Geoffrey Keen is excellent as the friendly government commissioner who finally convinces them the lioness should be sent to a zoo or set free. Keen gives the role much depth via the humor engendered from his natural aversion to the lioness, balanced by his British reserve. Other players render fine support, especially Peter Lukoye as Elsa's "nursemaid."

Against the backdrop of Kenya, photographed on the spot by Kenneth Talbot's perceptive Technicolor-Panavision camera, the drama unfolds smoothly and logically, not showing the extremely-long shooting period needed. Don Deacon edited to an adroit 95 minutes. Peter Whitehead's animal supervision is outstanding, with George Adamson's technical advice a big assist. They interleave the lion footage with that of hundreds of wild beasts to underscore the point that the couple's lioness is a single exception to the rule of nature. There's a hilarious bit where the Adamsons try to play matchmaker with Elsa willing but the male too tired.

Foreman's production notes credit Jaffe and Radin with the idea for the film. Along with remarkable absence of the maudlin, there is an effectively-underplayed lesson in the triumph of human patience and courage, told with appropriate amounts of audio-visual humor. At the same time, there is no compromising of the fact that bush animals are, by nature, potentially dangerous.

John Barry's score adds solid emphasis and atmosphere. Post-production work was done at England's Shepperton Studios, and the sound team, recordists Claude Hitchcock and Robert Jones and sound editor Chris Greenham, rates a special nod for achievement. They have created (and recreated) a live, exterior feel.

Film was shown in London earlier this month as a Royal Command Performance, a prestige factor. *Murf.*

W.I.A.
(Wounded In Action)

War pic, made in Philippines, limited to second-billing due to lack of names but considerable hospital footage invites exploitation.

Myriad Productions Ltd. (Irving Sunasky, Samuel Zerinsky) production. Directed and written by Sunasky. Features Steve Marlo, Mauro McGiveney, Leopoldo Salcedo, Mary Humphrey, Albert Quinton. Camera, Enrique Rogales; editor, Gregorio Caraballo; music, Leopold Silos. Reviewed in New York, March 16, '66. Running Time: 87 MINS.

Pvt. Joe Goodman	Steve Marlo
Lt. Marietta Dodd	Maura McGiveney
Maj. Armando DeLeon	Leopoldo Salcedo
Lt. Joan Marsh	Mary Humphrey
Maj. Slater	Albert Quinton
Sgt. Roman	Victor Izay
Carmen	Bella Flores
Cpl. Bliss	John Horn
Pfc. Myers	Peter E. Deuel
Sanchez	Joe Sison
Capt. Ed Bill	Brennan Wood
Ruther	Romy Brion

While basically a war film, "W.I.A." (Wounded In Action), takes place almost entirely within the confines of a military hospital in the Philippines in 1945. Although filmed in the islands, the soundtrack is in English with exception of some scenes between Filipinos and many of these are in both Tagalog and English so there's no language difficulty for viewers.

Included in footage shot by producers Samuel Zerinsky and Irving Sunasky (as co-production with Filipino actor Leopoldo Salcedo) are clips from World War II combat films and apparently authentic hospital operations including the Caesarean delivery of an infant. While footage devoted to actors, some of whom were brought in from the U. S. by Sunasky, is routine, due to their limited thespic ability and Sunasky's pedestrian direction and writing, there are some charming moments in scenes played by the Filipino cast members plus some shudderingly realistic ones of wounds being dressed and operations performed.

Potential of film is probably limited to second-half of bill unless producers decide to push more gruesome aspects of footage. Salcedo, in small but key role, is shown as on point of having an affair with a nurse (Mary Humphrey) when she's ordered transferred. Another romance between enlisted man Steve Marlo and nurse Maura McGivency has, in one of their love scenes, a line of dialog meant to suggest amour but results in laughter—"Am I too heavy for you?" Minor roles which stand out are Bella Flores, John Horn, and Joe Sison. Enrique Rogales' camerawork is erratic, sometimes crisp and clear and as often murky and underlit. Newsreel footage used is also grainy and obvious.

Although an even shorter feature, "The Year Of The Horse," was screened at same time, with possibility of two being packaged, this would be a mistake as they're widely varying in content and audience appeal. *Robe.*

Gunpoint
(WESTERN-COLOR)

Adequate oater with stock horse opera plot, enhanced with color lensing, and plus marquee value in name of Audie Murphy.

Hollywood, March 16.

Universal release of Gordon Kay Production. Stars Audie Murphy; features rest of cast. Directed by Earl Bellamy. Screenplay, Mary and Willard Willingham; camera (Technicolor), William Margulies; music, Hans J. Salter; editor, Russell F. Schoengarth; rat direction, Alexander Golitzen, Henry Bumstead; assistant director, Phil Bowles; sound, Waldon C. Watson, Lyle Cain. Reviewed at Universal Studios, March 15, 1966. Running Time: 86 MINS.

Chad Luces	Audie Murphy
Uvalde	Joan Staley
Nate Harlan	Warren Stevens
Bull	Edgar Buchanan
Cap	Denver Pyle
Ode	Royal Dano
Nicos	Nick Dennis
Hoag	William Bramley
Ab	Kelly Thordsen
Mark Emerson	David Macklin
Drago	Morgan Woodward
Mitch	Robert Pine
Zack	Mike Ragan

"Gunpoint" is an adequate oater which should do satisfactory business in most action houses. Traditional western situations are generously sprinkled throughout a stock horse opera plot that is enhanced considerably by good color lensing. Another plus ticket selling factor is marquee value of Audie Murphy. Although Earl Bellamy directed film gets off to a slow start, the pace soon picks up via shootout with attacking Apaches and a stampede of wild horses.

Mary and Willard Willingham's script has Murphy as the sheriff of a small Colorado town on the border of the New Mexico territory shortly after the Civil War. Mountain country comes across beautifully in color camera work by William Margulies and provides good backdrop for badman Morgan Woodward and his gang, being pursued by Murphy and posse, after the heavies rob the train and kidnap dance hall dolly Joan Staley.

Location exteriors, near St. George, Utah, provide the best part of the whole thing. Art direction and sets add extra color, a definite asset.

Murphy comes through satisfactorily as the steely cool sheriff, who smiles little and means business. He might brighten his prospects, however, if he did occasionally smile. Miss Staley, the only femme in the outing, is adequate as the attractive dance hall gal.

Best performance of the lot is by vet oater scalawag Edgar Buchanan, who provides a brief touch of humor in the otherwise sober proceedings. Denver Pyle, as a vindictive deputy out for Murphy's job, has done better work—and leaves something to be desired in this one. Warren Stevens is competent as the saloon keeper-gambler.

Art direction by Alexander Golitzen and Henry Bumstead and sets by John McCarthy and Oliver Emert are capably handled in the Gordon Kay production. Editing by Russell F. Schoengarth is okay, but might have been strengthened in parts of the pic. *Mitt.*

Deathwatch

Photograph of talky Jean Genet play. Fine acting and photography. Limited appeal. Criminal minds ideas of prestige and sex.

Beverly Pictures release of Leonard Nimoy and Vic Morrow production. Stars Leonard Nimoy, Michael Forest, Paul Mazursky; with Robert Ellenstein, Gavin McLeod. Directed by Vic Morrow. Screenplay, Morrow and Barbara Turner from Jean Genet play; camera, Vilis Lapenieks; music, Gerald Fried; editor, Verna Fields. Reviewed at Metro Studios, March 17, 1966. Running Time, 88 MINS.

Jules LaFranc	Leonard Nimoy
Greeneyes	Michael Forest
Maurice	Paul Mazursky

Jean Genet's "Deathwatch" is a one-set stage play on film, marked by fine performances by the three principals and excellent black-white photography. Its presumed appeal will be to art house audiences. Limited potential in regular situations. There is little action in the story which evolves around the development of the three characters — their strongpoints and their failings—through a constant stream of dialog, punctuated by facial expressions.

Vic Morrow (of ABC's "Combat" series), directed film based on the stage play by Genet, which had a long run in Los Angeles. Picture was shot for about $120,000. Morrow and Barbara Turner wrote the screen adaptation.

Set in a prison, virtually all of Vilis Lapenieks' camera work—except for an introductory sequence in the prison yard and a couple of brief flashback scenes—was done on a single set, a prison cell occupied by three men.

One of the trio, Michael Forest, is a condemned murderer, Greeneyes, awaiting the guillotine who has achieved top status with other inmates because of the immensity of his crime. He is looked up to by his other two cellmates, Leonard Nimoy as LaFranc and Paul Mazursky as Maurice.

Nimoy is a loner, feeling a void because his only crime is that of a petty thief. He is constantly arguing and bickering with Mazursky—a thief and a homosexual—over the attention of Forest, while Mazursky is attempting to throw a wedge between Forest and his offscreen wife. His failure at this results in a strong final exchange with Nimoy, who strangles him. Nimoy then turns to Forest, who respects him completely.

Nimoy, who co-produced the film with Morrow, is excellent as the "outsider" not quite accepted by prison society, even though he has withstood extreme tortures in solitary confinement. Forest and Mazursky both give fine performances in respective parts as the king of the prison inmates and a weak homosexual.

Gerald Fried provided what little music there is, and it is used only on rare occasions to heighten the conflict. A score that does effectively what it is supposed to do. Verna Fields helps to put a sock into editing the well-knit yarn. James G. Frieburger's art direction provides good touch of realism in the primarily solo set of a French prison. *Mitt.*

Popioly
(The Lost Army)
(POLISH-SCOPE)
Berlin, March 15.

Atlas release of Film Polski production. With Daniel Olbrychski, Piotr Wysocki, Boguslaw Kierc, Beata Tyzkiewicz, Pola Raksa. Directed by Andrzej Wajda. Screenplay, Alexander Scibor-Rylski; camera (Cinemascope), Jerzy Lipman. At Academy of Arts, West Berlin. Running Time, 160 MINS.

The State-owned Film Polski has turned suddenly to big-scale, western-styled epics. "Popioly" and "Faraon" (Pharaoh) are the most noteworthy examples. Both pix have been acquired by Hanns Eckelkamp's West German Atlas-Film which owns global rights except in the Polish market.

This pic, previously titled "Ashes," is a whale of a production. This CinemaScoper is reputed to have cost around $3,000,-000, an enormous amount by Polish standards. Original run-

ning time was four hours. Atlas hopes to get "Popioly" into foreign markets and should do well there.

Although minus color, it is reminiscent of "War and Peace." Despite lack of color, there's compensation in part by the impressive black-and-white lensing and some of the roughest battle scenes seen on the screen. Occasionally it even seems as though the director, Andrzej Wajda, fell in love with violence. The mass scenes in this Napoleon era costumer are mostly spectacular and Wajda was certainly not economical on the utilization of extras either. He obviously had an abundance of the money-saving Polish army troops at his disposal.

Film shows how the wars swept over the unfortunate Polish country at the beginning of the 19th Century, and revolves around the Polish legion under General Dombrowski, who then fought on Napoleon's side hoping that with the latter's help they would regain their lost country. The production teems with situations. However, the various individual scenes contain enough tension to hold the viewer's interest. This production has love, seduction, society life, comedy, rape, dueling, fights with wild wolves and all sorts of carnage on the battlefield.

The acting is satisfactory. Editing and other technical credits display the necessary knowhow. It is, however, sort of a puzzle why this creator of genuine art films ("Ashes and Diamonds") devoted so much time and energy on a film which is mainly an item for general audiences and hardly anything for the crix and the more demanding cinema patron. His directorial talents are evident in several intimate scenes, but in the main this film is to satisfy the eye. *Hans.*

Mar Del Plata Fest

At Zije Republika
(Long Live the Republic)
(CZECH)
Mar del Plata, March 15.

Studios Barrendov production. Stars Zdenek Lstiburek; features Gustav Valach, Iva Janzurova, Vlado Muller and Josef Karlik. Directed by Karel Kachyna. Screenplay, Jan Prochazka; camera, Jaromin Sofr. At Mar del Plata Film Fest. Running Time, 123 MINS.

A film of rare beauty both in its pictorial values and poetic approach to the experiences of a Moravian child during the last days of the second World War, it has tenderness, humor and vitality. But some scissoring may be advisable to eliminate reiteration in incidents and meanings. Trimming done, its chances are good for the general market and certainly will be strong for arty houses, helped by the three awards as best picture which it won at the Mar del Plata festival.

The Moravian lad is in perpetual fight against other village boys who vex him because of his short stature. He has no friends other than a middle-aged, animal-loving man ruined by the greed of his neighbors.

He has no other love than his mother's. He endures almost daily beating by a senseless father, more interested in keeping his only horse away from military confiscation than in understanding his only son's problems. Olda, the son, is sent to hide the horse in the woods, where he loses it to German fugitives. Then he tries to steal another from a Russian camp. End of the war finds his father owning several stolen horses. The people, while welcoming the Russians, pursue and mercilessly kill his only friend.

The inner strength of a child struggling to overcome his physical handicaps, his astonishment when discovering cruelty in his elders and his own contradictory conduct when his need for affection clashes with his instinct for survival, are expressed without resorting to melodrama ties. The director and the screenplay he works with appeal to understanding. Only a few local angles might be confusing for the average viewer.

"Republic" has its own style, impregnated with the personality, feeling and true artistic creativeness that director Kachyna showed several years ago in "Lenka's Sorrows." He is more deeply human this time, his vision of the world and the miseries of war through a child's eyes more compassionate.

Outstanding performance is by child actor Zdenek Lstiburek, as Olda. There is a very good supporting cast. First-class camera work (mostly of beautiful Moravian valleys) is a solid contribution. Editing is technically sharp and helps sustaining a vivid pace but it has failed to get rid of some story reiterations. *Din.*

Castigo Al Traidor
(Punishment to the Traitor)
(ARGENTINE)
Mar del Plata, March 15.

Clase Films release of a Manuel Antin production. Stars Sergio Renan; features Marcela Lopez Rey, Miguel Ligero, Jorge Barreiro, Eva Donge and Enrique Thibaut. Directed by Manuel Antin. Screenplay, Andres Lizarraga, Antin, based on a short story by Augusto Roa Bastos; camera, Julio Lavera; music, Adolfo Morpurgo; editor, Jacinto Cascales. At Mar del Plata Film Fest. Running Time, 70 MINS.

Still attached to outdated early New Wave influences, Manuel Antin again displays the same esoteric cutting technique of all his previous pix without concealing the basic weakness of a thin story entirely told in dialogue and boringly illustrated with endless street walking. He has failed to fill the emptiness of the action with any kind of meaning.

In fact, Antin doesn't even suggest why a young man should pursue an old Peronist who caused his father's ruin. In the end, he says he is the pursued, not the pursuer. Perhaps the purpose was to stress the need for reconciliation in politically torn Argentina.

For the average cinema patron, this is a lifeless, obscure tale. In arty houses, the film may seem curious for those who have not seen other Antin pix. Some hand-camera shots are the only highlights in the technical department. *Din.*

Cast A Giant Shadow
(COLOR-PANAVISION)

Fictionalized biog of West Pointer, Col. Mickey Marcus, who assisted in the heroic establishment of Israel. Action, humor, romance, performances, direction and production help overcome length and some meller angles. Strong marquee lineup plus word of mouth indicate okay b.o. prospects.

Hollywood, March 19.

United Artists release of Mirisch Corp.-Llenroc-Batjac Production, produced and directed by Melville Shavelson; coproducer, Michael Wayne. Stars Kirk Douglas, Senta Berger; features Angie Dickinson, Frank Sinatra, Yul Brynner, John Wayne, James Donald, Stathis Giallelis, Luther Adler, Gary Merrill, Haym Topol. Screenplay, Shavelson, based on novel by Ted Berkman; camera (DeLuxe Color), Aldo Tonti; editors, Bert Bates, Gene Ruggiero; music, Elmer Bernstein; asst. directors, Jack Reddish, Charles Scott, Jr., Tim Zinnemann. Reviewed at Village Theatre, Westwood, L.A., March 18, '66. Running Time, 144 MINS.

Col. David (Mickey) Marcus	Kirk Douglas
Magda Simon	Senta Berger
Emma Marcus	Angie Dickinson
Vince	Frank Sinatra
Asher Gonen	Yul Brynner
Gen. Mike Randolph	John Wayne
Safir	James Donald
Ram Oren	Stathis Giallelis
Jacob Zion	Luther Adler
Chief of Staff	Gary Merrill
Abou Ibn Kader	Haym Topol
Mrs. Chaison	Ruth White
James MacAfee	Gordon Jackson
British Ambassador	Michael Hordern
Immigration Officer	Allan Cuthbertson
Senior Officer	Jeremy Kemp
Junior Officer	Sean Barrett
Andre Simon	Michael Shillo
Rona	Rina Ganor
Bert Harrison	Roland Bartrop
Mrs. Martinson	Vera Dolen
Gen. Walsh	Robert Gardett
First Sentry	Michael Balston
Second Sentry	Claude Aliotti
Belly Dancer	Samra Dedes
Truck Driver	Michael Shagrir
U.N. Officers	Frank Lattimore, Ken Buck'n
Aide to Randolph	Rodd Dana
Aide to Chief of Staff	Robert Ross
Officer	Arthur Hansell
Parachute Sgt.	Don Sturkie
Yaakov	Hillel Rave
Yussuff	Shlomo Hermon

"Cast A Giant Shadow" exemplifies the problems in contemporary film biography, particularly when the subject is less well known than the events which brought him honor. Some complete fiction and fuzzy composites melodramatize the career of an American Jew who assisted in the fight for the creation of the State of Israel. Melville Shavelson's overlong pic has some big marquee horsepower, exciting action highlights, fine production values and other assets which spell b.o. prospects for United Artists release in general situations.

Pic is billed, per increasing custom, as "a film by" Shavelson, who scripted from Ted Berkman's book, produced (with Michael Wayne as coproducer) and directed. The Mirisch Corp. presentation was shot mainly in Israel, with Rome interior lensing.

Story concerns Col. David ("Mickey") Marcus, West Point grad, N.Y. lawyer and cop, and participant in many facets of World War II, who, in the late '40s, is recruited to volunteer military help in the establishment of Israel, at that time still a dream subject to United Nations equivocation, militant Arab threats and uncertain world support.

Kirk Douglas stars as Marcus in a very good portrayal of a likeable, adventurous soldier-of-fortune who cannot get used to domestic inactivity even when wife Angie Dickinson is sitting by the hearth. Miss Dickinson does a good job in a role which calls for her to be a flip, sardonic chick, also an adoring wife.

Marcus' interior conflict was that of an American of Jewish ancestry who didn't yet have the nationalistic fire of Zionism, but gradually developed enthusiasm for it. Only then was he adjusted to participate in the bloody battles which eventually saw an established Israel. Douglas is able to project the subtle change from detached outsider to involved patriot.

Unfortunately for the overall impact of the film, it was found necessary to go into World War II flashbacks to establish the Marcus character. John Wayne, in one of three featured special appearances, is a composite of every superior officer under whom Marcus served in those days. A lot of good service humor emerges from the interaction, and pair's dialog is unusually salty, although understandable in context.

Senta Berger, also starred after Douglas above title, is an admitted fiction, a buxom fighter for Israel who provides some romantic interest and cues an ironic, tragic climax to Marcus' life. Yul Brynner and Frank Sinatra round out the featured cameos, former as an underground Jewish military leader, latter as a happy-go-lucky aviator. Sinatra is effective in brief footage, while Brynner, in a continuing role, projects a quiet intensity.

Luther Adler's role is that of a fictionally-named Israeli statesman whose manifold problems included international politics, warring Jewish internal factions, and actual warfare. Presumably patterned after David Ben Gurion, Adler is excellent. Haym Topol brightens pic as a friendly Arab, ditto Ruth White as Miss Dickinson's mother. All the humor is appropriate, both to the real-life incidents and people involved, and as an attention-keeping, tension-relieving device for pix audiences.

End result, however, of the extensive exposition and vignette is overlength — some 144 minutes, 95 minutes of which is virtually establishing footage prior to the lengthy action climax. Latter depicts the successful attempt to break the Arab blockade of an isolated Jerusalem via an old mountain path.

Shavelson has obtained effective performances from an unusually large and competent cast, and also shows a neat visual flair, one example of which is a lush, ripe wheat field which becomes, after a highlight skirmish, a blood-sodden pictorial canvas. Other interesting visuals, caught by Aldo Tonti's DeLuxe Color-Panavision camera, enhance the many stirring, tender and humorous moments with which the film is studded.

Elmer Bernstein's score adds solid emphasis, while in the technical department all credits are firstrate. Main title design, uncredited but executed by Pacific Title, is excellent, utilizing a b&w newsreel montage effect which gradually enlarges to fill the screen. *Murf.*

L'Ombrellone
(The Beach Umbrella)
(ITALO—FRENCH)
(COLOR)

Rome, March 22.

Interfilm release of an Ultra Film Production for Ultra-Les Films du Siecle-Altura. Stars Enrico Maria Salerno, Sandra Milo; features Daniela Bianchi, with Trini Alonso, Alicia Brandel, Pepe Calvo, Lelio Lutazzi, Raffaele Pisu, Leopoldo Trieste, Veeronique Vendell, Jean Sorel. Directed by Dino Risi. Screenplay, Risi, Ennio de Concini; camera (Eastmancolor) Franco Fraticelli; music, Lelio Lutazzi; editor, Danilo Marcani. At Olimpico, Rome. Running Time, 90 MINS.

Ing. Moretti ..... Enrico Maria Salerno
His wife ..... Sandra Milo
Sergio ..... Jean Sorel
Mrs. Dominici ..... Daniela Bianchi
Bellanca ..... Lelio Lutazzi
Teadier ..... Leopoldo Trieste

Lightweight item with okay chances in Italy but an iffy foreign entry because of abundance of local touches which limit its in-depth chances beyond the arty fringe. Locally, Sandra Milo and Enrico Maria Salerno names are help. Lush color trimmings and neat location work are plus factors.

Dino Risi is still in the "Easy Life" niche with this one, which is more expensive but has less impact. Once again, the director analyzes manners and mores of the dolce vita set along the Adriatic Riviera. While his sideline and backdrop notations are as sharp and biting as ever in their dissection of a certain aspects of modern society, it's the up-front story (philandering wife joined by philandering husband for beachside weekend), whcih is weakly developed, despite valiant efforts by Sandra Milo and especially Enrico Maria Salerno as the couple.

Perhaps inevitably, the "daymarish" happenings by the sea are more vivid, and more vividly portrayed, and spectator at end almost thinks he's been witnessing an episode film, colorful, intermittently amusing, but ultimately empty. Jean Sorel, Leopoldo Trieste, Lelio Lutazzi and others back colorfully, though Daniela Bianchi is wasted in silly minor role. Color lensing is lush, with busy soundtrack similarly used to counterpoint visuals, using many pops as backdrops. *Hawk.*

The Trouble With Angels
(COLOR)

Mild comedy about a Catholic nun who tames two upstart girls. Rosalind Russell and Hayley Mills provide marquee lure for okay b.o. prospects.

Hollywood, March 4.

Columbia Pictures release of William Frye Production. Stars Rosalind Russell, Hayley Mills; features Binnie Barnes, Gypsy Rose Lee, Camilla Sparv, June Harding. Directed by Ida Lupino. Screenplay, Blanche Hanalis, based on a novel by Jane Trahey; camera (Pathecolor), Lionel Lindon; editor, Robert C. Jones; music, Jerry Goldsmith; asst. director, Terry Nelson. Reviewed at Stanley Warner Beverly Hills Theatre, March 3, '66. Running Time, 111 MINS.

Mother Superior ..... Rosalind Russell
Mary Clancy ..... Hayley Mills
Sister Celestine ..... Binnie Barnes
Mrs. Phipps ..... Gypsy Rose Lee
Sister Constance ..... Camilla Sparv
Rachel Devery ..... June Harding
Sister Clarissa ..... Mary Wickes
Sister Liguori ..... Marge Redmond
Sister Rose Marie ..... Dolores Sutton
Sister Barbara ..... Margalo Gillmore
Sister Elizabeth ..... Portia Nelson
Sister Ursula ..... Marjorie Eaton
Sister Margaret ..... Barbara Bell Wright
Sister Prudence ..... Judith Lowry
Marvey-Ann ..... Barbara Hunter
Valerie ..... Bernadette Withers
Charlotte ..... Vicky Albright
Sheila ..... Patty Gerrity
Kate ..... Vicki Draves
Sandy ..... Wendy Winkelman
Ginnie-Lou ..... Jewel Jaffe
Priscilla ..... Gail Liddle
Ruth ..... Michael-Marie
Gladys ..... Betty Jane Royale
Helen ..... Ronne Troup
Brigette ..... Catherine Wyles
Mr. Gottschalk ..... Jim Boles
Uncle George ..... Kent Smith
Mr. Devery ..... Pat McCaffrie
Mr. Grissom ..... Harry Harvey, Sr.
Mrs. Eldridge ..... Mary Young

The trouble with "The Trouble With Angels" is hard to pinpoint. An appealing story idea—hip Mother Superior nun who outfoxes and matures two rebellious students in a Catholic girls' school —has lost impact via repetitious plotting and pacing, plus routine direction. William Frye's initial feature production is occasionally charming but overlong, and has some good performances. Names of Rosalind Russell and Hayley Mills are hottest selling angels. Okay b.o. likely for Columbia release in general situations.

Jane Trahey's novel, "Mother Superior," was adapted by Blanche Hanalis into an episodic screenplay. Simple plot premise, per usual in comedy, is not filled out with strong enough gag situations, over-abundance of which make the fault more glaring.

Story takes the extrovert Miss Mills and pal, sensitive, introverted June Harding (in a good feature debut), through three full years of school under the watchful eye of Miss Russell. Graduation finds Miss Mills in character switcheroo to which Catholic audiences will long since be alerted. Overall, she is believable.

Miss Russell, who has played almost every type of role, gives appropriate spiritual depth to her part, although eventually is shot down by excess chatter and exposition. Latter also affects two younger femme principals in achieving character development. All three are well established in about 15 minutes, after which an increasingly tedious pattern occupies most footage. Pattern consists of: (1) gals plot deviltry, (2) then do it, (3) are discovered, (4) then are chewed out for it. Few deviations are apparent.

The large supporting cast fares far better, simply from less exposure. Binnie Barnes (wife of Columbia world production chief Mike Frankovich) returns to pix in a good bit as the nun in charge of the band who wears ear plugs. Gypsy Rose Lee is okay as the gaudily-garbed terp instructor, and Camilla Sparv, photogenic in the extreme, registers okay as the young nun who plans to work with lepers. She, too, is making a feature bow.

Marge Redmond, the math-teaching nun whose death evokes an emotional response from Mis Russell, is charming, while swim-teacher Mary Wickes is her usual wacky, entertaining self. Portia Nelson also scores. Rest of the nuns and femme students are adequate prototypes. Kent Smith, another fine film-legit vet, has a brief moment as a globe-trotting relative, anxious to farm out his ward because of pressing business —meaning the blond looker waiting by his car. Jim Hutton, unbilled, brightens another cameo.

Director Ida Lupino, repped in vidpix credits since her last feature "The Bigamist" in 1953, maintained too leisurely a pace, even within the individual vignettes. A visual same-ness also tends in time to pale the charm of certain sequences. Entire concept of film, in fact,—scripting, direction and performances—seems oriented to convenient future televising.

Lionel Lindon's passive Pathecolor lensing is okay, and has captured the contrast between the dedicated nuns and younger, high-spirited gals intended by John Beckman's art direction and Sybil Connolly's clerical costume work. Jerry Goldsmith's score is good, and incorporates some adroit musical sound effects. Robert C. Jones trimmed to final 111-minute tradeshown version, overlong. DePatie-Freleng title animation is very good, and other technical credits are professional. Pic's copyright rests solely in Frye's indie. *Murf.*

Frankie And Johnny
(SONGS-COLOR)

Elvis money-winner, with singer toplining story loosely built around folk song, along with pretty girls and Technicolor.

Hollywood, March 23.

United Artists release of Edward Small production. Stars Elvis Presley; features rest of cast. Directed by Frederick de Cordova. Screenplay, Alex Gottlieb, based on story by Nat Perrin; camera (Technicolor), Jacques Marquette; music, Fred Karger; editor, Grant Whytock. Reviewed at Goldwyn Studios, March 22, '66. Running Time, 87 MINS.

Johnny ..... Elvis Presley
Frankie ..... Donna Douglas
Cully ..... Harry Morgan
Mitzi ..... Sue Ane Langdon
Nellie Bly ..... Nancy Kovack
Peg ..... Audrey Christie
Blackie ..... Robert Strauss
Braden ..... Anthony Eisley
Wilbur ..... Jerome Cowen
Earl Barton Dancers ..... Wilda Taylor, Larri Thomas, Dee Jay Mattis, Judy Chapman

"Frankie and Johnny" is a sure-fire boxoffice entry. It's Elvis all the way in a story built loosely around the classic folk song, coupled with a dozen or so tunes, pretty girls and Technicolor. Frederick de Cordova directed the Edward Small production, which hits the mark as pleasant entertainment, and is certain to be another Presley money-winner.

The Alex Gottlieb screenplay from a Nat Perrin story has Elvis and Donna Douglas, (the pretty one from CBS' "Beverly Hillbillies" in her first major film role) as entertainers on a Mississippi riverboat about 100 years ago. Elvis is Frankie, Donna is Johnny, and, like in the ageless song, they love each other. But Frankie gambles too much, losing all the time, until he finds a lucky redhead—Nellie Bly, natch—played by Nancy Kovack. The triangle figures into a song being written by Elvis' piano playing buddy Harry Morgan, and is built into a colorful, well turned production number.

The costume pic, however, proves to be nothing more than an hour and a half romp, providing a showcase for Presley's songs. He does 12 of them, including the title tune.

Elvis is Elvis. He sings and acts, apparently doing both with only slight effort. Presley does little hip swinging, no doubt in keeping with the period of the story, although he does get a chance to bounce out one number —"Shout It Out"—with Dixieland accompaniment. Fred Karger's scoring is pleasant and toe-tapping, built to the general entertaining theme of the film.

Miss Douglas and Miss Kovack endow pic with generous visual attractions, and the love interest for Elvis. Sue Ane Langdon gets a chance at a number of cute situations as the girl who is always edged out in the romance department. Harry Morgan and Robert Strauss come across well as the piano player and the boss' stooge, respectively. Anthony Eisley is adequate as the riverboat owner.

DeCordova's smooth direction, coupled with Grant Whytock's editing, gives a nice pace to the musical, helping to add to the easy-going relaxing mood of the whole thing. Jacques Marquette's camera work is good, especially on the Elvis songs and the "Frankie and Johnny" production number. *Mitt.*

Alfie
(BRITISH-COLOR)

Remarkably candid study of a young man with both eyes on main chance, especially with the femmes. Frank sex dialog, cheeky situations, mingled with humor, some pathos. Michael Caine and a flock of well-cast actresses should make this a curiosity draw all over.

London, March 29.
Paramount release of Lewis Gilbert Production. Stars Michael Caine; features Millicent Martin, Julia Foster, Jane Asher, Shirley Anne Field, Vivien Merchant, Eleanor Bron, Shelley Winters, Denholm Elliott, Alfie Bass, Graham Stark, Sydney Tafler, Murray Melvin. Directed by Gilbert. Screenplay, Bill Naughton, based on his own play; camera (Technicolor), Otto Heller; music, Sonny Rollins; editor, Thelma Connell. Reviewed at Plaza, London. Running Time, **114 MINS.**
Alfie .... Michael Caine
Ruby .... Shelley Winters
Siddie .... Millicent Martin
Gilda .... Julia Foster
Annie .... Jane Asher
Carla .... Shirley Anne Field
Lily .... Vivien Merchant
The Doctor .... Eleanor Bron
Abortionist .... Denholm Elliott
Harry .... Alfie Bass
Humphrey .... Graham Stark
Nat .... Murray Melvin
Frank .... Sydney Tafler

"Alfie," Britain's official Cannes Fest Film entry, produced and directed by Lewis Gilbert for Paramount release, pulls few punches in its candid exploration of the sex scene. With Michael Caine giving a powerfully strong performance as the woman-mad,

anti-hero, and with dialog and situations that are humorous, tangy, raw and, ultimately, often moving, the film may well shock. But behind its alley-cat philosophy, there's some shrewd sense, some pointed barbs and a sharp moral. It is based on Bill Naughton's play and looks to attract attention and brisk business whereever it plays.

One of biggest chances that the film takes is in its frequent use of the direct speech approach to the audience. This does not always come off in the picture as well as it used to do with Groucho in the old Marx Bros. films. But the device served well enough in the play, and does here. Caine developed the stage knack of talking confidentially to the customers, and yet appearing to play direct to the camera.

The screenplay, written with gusty humor and knowhow by Naughton himself, is something of a novelty in British films, since it effectively contrives to give the star a meaty role but it also gives good opportunities to a flock of femmes and at least three male thesps. Though only a couple of the distaff roles are developed in more than sketchy fashion, all the actresses have quick fire opportunities of making sock impact.

Story concerns a glib, cynical young Cockney whose passion in life is chasing dames of all shapes, sizes, and dispositions, providing they are accomodating. The film traces the promiscuous path of this energetic young amoralist as he flits from one to the other without finding much lasting pleasure. In fact, he finishes up as a somewhat jaded, cutprice Lothario, disillusioned but still on the chase. "Alfie" opens neatly with a lively sequence with Millicent Martin which aptly sets the mood of the picture and Alfie's character. She's a young married woman who once a week quits her dull husband in favor of a cheap thrill with Alfie in the front seat of his auto.

Apart from a few passing encounters with such as the manageress of a cleaning shop ("that way you get your suits pressed free, a well,") and various other chicks, the audience is mainly concerned with half a dozen key affaires. After Miss Martin comes Julia Foster, playing a dim young woman who wants Alfie's attention, but does not expect love or marriage. All's well till she gets pregnant and ups and marries a bus conductor, with Alfie more concerned at losing his son of whom he has become fond than the girl. He has no time to develop a romance with Eleanor Bron, playing the woman doctor, who packs him off to a sanatorium with T.B. But in the hospital he finds Shirley Anne Field to be a perky nurse prepared to do a lot that's not on the British National Health Scheme. Out of hospital, he comforts Vivien Merchant, playing the wife of one of the other patients and a three minute riverside interlude makes her pregnant and needing a seedy abortion which is the nearest thing to shaking Alfie's morale in the film.

He steals a lorry driver's girl

friend and lives with her, (Jane Asher), but finds her domestics binding, even though he is concurrently having boudoir gymnastics with a wealthy, voluptuous American (Shelley Winters), It's when she ditches him for a young guitar player and his original conquest (Millicent Martin) is not sure whether she wants to take up again where he left off, that Alfie begins to wonder whether the freewheeling, freelancing mattress play is worth the worry and the headaches.

By this time, the audience may have had enough of his amorous interludes but they will not have been bored. For, despite the undoubted sordidness of the story, there's a more serious intent beneath the apparent cynical bawdiness than is revealed on the surface.

Anyway, patrons in general will be held by the acting. Caine brings persuasiveness, and a sardonic thoroughly shabby and humorous charm to a role that gives him far more scope than either "Zulu" or "Ipress File." And it shows that he is not only a very deft actor but a valuable screen personality. The perky Miss Martin, the sad looking little Miss Asher, the ripe sexy extrovert, as played by Shelley Winters, Eleanor Bron's short, wise scene as the doctor and Shirley Anne Field's sketchy role as the nurse all carry weight.

But the two best performances among the women come from Miss Foster, becomingly wistful throughout, and Miss Merchant, Harold Pinkens' wife, in her first considerable screen role, as the married woman who suffers the abortion. This is a sad, grey and uncomfortably downbeat sequence, brilliantly played by Miss Merchant. Denholm Elliott is an unpleasant, unorthodox abortionist. Graham Stark, as the man who gets Miss Foster, and Alfie Bass, as Miss Merchant's husband, as well as Sydney Tafler and Murray Melvin, all help in minor but key roles.

Gilbert has directed with gusto and also a neat sense of balance between the out-and-out, brazen humor and the significant undertones, and he has resisted the inevitable bedroom scenes that are becoming film cliches. Otto Heller's Technicolor camera, Thelma Connell's neat editing and authentic London locations are invaluable plusses.

"Alfie" may shock some, and others will deplore its somewhat dingy theme. Many will miss its warning note. But none more likely to be bored. All in all, this frank study of cheap sex relations has a ring of uncomfortable truth which may even prove valuable. *Rich.*

Monnaie De Singe
(Funny Money)
(FRENCH-COLOR)

Paris, March 22.
CCFC release of Sud Pacifique Films-Capitole-Benito Perojo production. Stars Robert Hirsch; features Jean-Pierre Marielle, Sylva Koscina, Jean Yanne. Alberto Closas, Sylvie Breal. Directed by Yves Robert. Screenplay, Pierre Levi-Corti, Daniel Boulanger, Robert from a novel by Paul Chaland; camera (Eastmancolor-Techniscope), Edmond Sechan; editor, Monique Kirsanoff. At Mercury, Paris. Running Time, **95 MINS.**
Fulbert .... Robert Hirsch
Lucille .... Sylva Koscina
Baron .... Alberto Closas
Raymond .... Jean-Pierre Marielle
Felix .... Jean Yanne
Concepcion .... Sylvie Breal

Robert Hirsch, a thirtyish thesp at the state legit house the Comedie-Francaise, became a specialized comic star in the early Alec Guinness and Peter Sellers vein when he essayed eight roles in the sleeper French-Israeli hit pic, "Impossible on Saturday." Now he gets a solo star time out in one role in a pic that mixes situation comedy, slapstick and burlesque. It has some funny spots and moves briskly if it lacks some human warmth and is sometimes forced, with the humor skirting bad taste if managing to avoid it.

In color with the Hirsch name and some intermittently funny bits, this could loom for okay playoff use abroad with arty possibilities chancier. Hirsch plays a little sidewalk artist used by a swindler to make counterfeit money, unknown to him. His love for the man's mistress has him doing all this in innocence, if he gets imprisoned.

Then he is forced to escape and is sent in a hearse to Spain with the woman posing as a widow to make more money for them. Brunt of the comedy depends on whether Hirsch can be taken for a mousey little man and on comedic bits around keeping Hirsch in the coffin. Thrown in are a man who always sees him leaving it and a playboy following them because of the widow.

Film is patterned on the top hit of the year, "The Sucker," which had an innocent fall guy unwittingly smuggling contraband around Italy, and chased by gangsters. Using more backing and bigger production dress than usual, this vehicle is paying off here. This one also benefits from a bigger budget and good technical backing.

The countryside of Spain is eye-catching, and Hirsch gets a chance to show his versatility by getting mixed up in Spanish wedding and dancing, being embroiled in keeping out of sight as he often is caught out of his casket. He finally turns against crooks and gets the girl.

Hirsch has fine timing but is not a true comic figure. He cannot convincingly portray an inner oblivious world to the things around him, and most of the comedy comes from plot twists and good special effects. But Hirsch does have an underlying drollness despite his supposedly innocent character, that gives it some comic dash when he begins to revolt and trys to win the femme.

Director Yves Robert mixes farcical timing, special effects and some good gags into a comedy that has plenty of laughs but also too many dead spots since the comic logic is strained. Hirsch's turning at the end does not have the effect it would have had if he had been given a more humane feeling.

The color is fine, supporting roles good, with Jean Yanne, as the laconic hearse driver, and Jean-Pierre Marielle, as the fatuous playboy standout. This is another in the growing big budgeted situation comedies that should do well on their home grounds if calling for harder sell in foreign marts. But the vehicle could be used for depth distrib on its generally good production values and fair amount of successful comic moments.

Mosk.

La Religieuse
(The Nun)
(FRENCH-COLOR)

Paris, March 29.

Rome Paris Films-Georges De Beauregard production and release. Stars Anna Karina; features Liselotte Pulver, Micheline Presle, Francisco Rabal, Francine Berge, Yori Bertin, Catherine Diamant. Directed by Jacques Rivette. Jean Gruault based on book by Denis Diderot; camera (Eastmancolor), Alain Levent; editor, G. Durand. Previewed in Paris. Running Time, **140 MINS.**

Suzanne .... Anna Karina
1st Mother Superior .. Micheline Presle
2nd Mother Superior ... Liselotte Pulver
Catherine .... Francine Berge
Priest .... Francisco Rabal
Therese .... Catherine Diamant
Madame .... Yori Bertin

Though based on an almost 200-year-old classic book, this pic has had censor pressures against it by Catholic Film groups even before it was completed. Now that it is ready for release, it emerges a sort of episodic tale of a girl forced into a convent against her will and a series of adventures which end in her suicide. More a philosophic fable than realistic, film may have pull abroad on its theme, controversial aspects and generally absorbing, if overlong, treatment. Some pruning would help.

One convent has a too severe and almost vindictive Mother Superior who almost drives the reluctant nun to madness, while another has a frivolous one with lesbian tendencies. And the nun ends up escaping and going to her death when she can not face lay life. But there is no heavyhanded pamphleteering or leering in this pic.

Rather, the film tries to make a point that people within and without religious callings may have human weaknesses and that enforced religion is as bad as irreligion. It paints some human lacks on both sides. Thus this is not polemical but perhaps a too literal translation to the screen of a generally accepted and noted 18th Century novel by Denis Diderot. Novel has been done as a play and with excerpts on tele without any censorship problems until put into film form.

This underlines the fact that the mass appeal of film and its power make it more a target of censorship than most other media. Director Jacques Rivette, one of the early New Wavers and an ex-critic, is more academic in technique and careful in thespic handling and filmic form than is usual among the Wavers. Pressure from Catholic Film Office may result in title change for pic, with one choice "Suzanne Simonin, La Religeuse de Diderot."

One drawback in the production is its episodic quality as it deals with four segments in the girl's life. She is forced into a convent against her will because of her family's lack of dowry for her and the fact she has been sired by another besides her mother's present husband. She takes her vows in a sort of trance.

Trying to get out, she manages to get a courageous lawyer on her side. But the Mother Superior hounds her until she is almost driven mad and is finally sent to another convent because of the notoriety of the case even if she has lost it. Here the nuns seem to be from good families but may be court coquettes put there to be gotten out of the way. Anyway, they have lace ruffles on their nun's habits, live in sumptuous surroundings and the Mother Superior falls in love with her.

Escaping with a priest, who also says he was forced into religion, she flees him when he tries to make love to her. Finally she ends up a beggar and is then taken into a svelte household that turns out to be a bagnio. And of course, she leaps to her death. The director has not obtained any sort of conviction as to faith into his leading character and she emerges a victim who, if she feels she has no religious vocation, is too pure for some of the harsh, perverted and 18th Century life she gets into.

Anna Karina is comely and languishing as the victim with perhaps not enough inner projection and force to knot up this overlong pic. Liselotte Pulver is effective as the lesbian who is driven by desire over her wishes. Others are adequate in smaller roles.

The trouble is that the director has not taken a stand to make it truly polemical. Pic thus is a fairly solidly-made period piece that shows corruption in most walks of life and does suggest that the absence of choice can create a prison-like life This could be of interest for arty houses abroad on its theme. But for more general spots it looks chancey.

Mosk.

Made In Italy
(ITALIAN—COLOR)

Rome, March 22.

Ceiad release of a Gianni Hecht Lucari production for Documento Film. Features Sylva Koscina, Virna Lisi, Anna Magnani, Lea Massari, Catherine Spaak, Lando Buzzanca, Nino Castelnuovo, Walter Chiari, Peppino de Filippo, Aldo Fabrizi, Nino Manfredi, Alberto Sordi, Jean Sorel, Andrea Checchi, Giulio Bosetti, Rossella Falk, Claudie Lange, Fabrizio Moroni. Directed by Nanni Loy. Story and screenplay, Riggero Maccari, Ettore Scola; camera (Technicolor), Ennio Guarnieri; editor, Ruggero Mastroianni. At Astra, Rome. Running Time, **114 MINS.**

Anna .... Anna Magnani
Her husband .... Andrea Checchi
Virginia .... Virna Lisi
Renato .... Giulio Bosetti
Diana .... Sylva Koscina
Orlando .... Jean Sorel
Enrico .... Walter Chiari
Monica .... Lea Massari
Silvio .... Alberto Sordi
Erminia .... Rossella Falk
Mara .... Claudie Lange
Citizen .... Nino Manfredi
Signor Piras .... Aldo Fabrizi
Gavino .... Nino Castelnuovo
Carol .... Catherine Spaak
Gianremo .... Fabrizio Moroni

Vignette pic has been done up in color, with location backdrops, and boasting an impressive roster of Italo talent to boost its draw. Results, however, are uneven, humor is spotty construction of the film intricate. And the total effect suggests that a savvy revision could work wonders with basically valid material. In its present condition, chances appear more limited, especially for foreign marts where names alone won't do the trick, though the film remains an entertaining package.

Basically plotless, except in its generally satirical approach to things Italian, especially bureaucracy, which is repeatedly spoofed, this is hard to accurately describe. Some vignettes are mere blackouts, others are developed for human and/or humorous aspects. Some are trifles, others carry the weight of keen observation and just criticism, as in bit depicting Nino Manfredi's futile attempt to break through red tape and confusion to secure a vital document in a Rome office.

Another fine bit, splendidly acted by Anna Magnini, merely depicts the frustration of a Roman mother trying to cross a crowded traffic intersection to get her kids some ice cream. Okay also, but more superficial, are sequences such as one in which Alberto Sordi, caught in bed by his wife with a sometime mistress, talks himself out of the situation and turns the tables on her. Or another, in which Walter Chiari hurries through a bedtime rendezvous with a longtime friend to catch the last show at the local cinema. Or a fairly moving episode involving a janitor's daughter, Catherine Spaak, who's mistreated by her family while her rich suitor doesn't know of her modest origins. Virna Lisi is in one of more futile of the sequences, concerning a young widow who returns to a onetime fiance only to leave him when an older—but richer—man comes along. And so it goes, for many longer and shorter bits.

Director Nanni Loy also gets in some rather pointed attacks on the Church—one item supposedly shows a Monsignor directing major financial deals in the manner of an industrial tycoon. Elsewhere, he sometimes overdoes things in his juxtapositions of rich vs. poor, reaching for facile effects such as one in which a starving child brings his worker father his lunch bread, then sits there staring avidly as the father eats what the kid obviously hasn't been given.

This is an odd melange of situations, moods and themes, perhaps too many, and too varied. Yet audiences may find satisfaction here and there for there is something to satisfy almost anyone. Production values, as noted, are lush. Much (though surely not all) of the Italy on display is that stressed by Italian tourist offices. Other credits are tops.

Hawk.

Oggi, Domani E Dopodomani
(PARANOIA)
(ITALO-FRENCH)
(COLOR; BLACK and WHITE)

Rome, March 22.

Interfilm release of Champion Compagnia Cinematografica (Rome) — Les Films Concordia (Paris) coproduction. Stars Marcello Mastroianni; features Virna Lisi, Catherine Spaak, Pamela Tiffin, Luciano Salce. Directed by Marco Ferreri, Eduardo DeFilippo, Luciano Salce. Screenplay, Rafael Azcona, Isabella Quarantotti, Castellano, Pipolo, Salce, from stories by Marco Ferreri, Eduardo DeFilippo, Goffredo Parise; camera, Aldo Tonti, Mario Montuori, Gianni di Venanzo; editors, R. Lucidi, A. Novelli, M. Malvestiti; music, Teo Usuelli, Nino Rota, E. Bacalov. At the Mazzini, Fome. Running Time, **110 MINS.**

Mario (1st epis) .. Marcello Mastroianni
Michele (2d epis) Marcello Mastroianni
Michele (3d epis) Marcello Mastroianni
Dorotea .... Virna Lisi
Giovanna .... Catherine Spaak
Pepita .... Pamela Tiffin

Disappointing episoder which will have to ride on name values as otherwise it's uneven and thin. Presence of Marcello Mastroianni in all three segments is an undoubted help, though the material he's burdened with is not up to his recently satisfying par.

First episode, in black and white, is actually a trimmed-down version of a feature pic directed some time back by Marco Ferreri, but never released. It deals, rather pretentiously, with a Milan industralist obsessed by the bursting point of toy balloons. Completely disregarding his visiting mistress, he concentrates on his new hobby until finally, faced with failure of his theories, he kills himself by jumping out the window. It's a puzzling item with some valiant acting by Mastroianni and Catherine Spaak, but the impacts and/or significances are certainly not clear, with a drastic trimming job adding to the general confusion and tedium.

Item No. 2 is perhaps the most amusing. Shot in color with Eduardi DeFilippo directing, it has Mastroianni visiting an old friend who keeps his wife under control by shooting pistol blanks at her whenever she makes trouble or raises her voice. Every so often, he admits, he inserts a real bullet and fires it over her head—to keep her on her toes. In fact, as the seg finale shows, the system has been successfully adopted by entire neighborhood, which at certain critical hours echoes with pistol salvos. Virna Lisi and Luciano Salce are involved as husband and wife, but the joke is overextended.

Third seg has Mastroianni as harried husband who decides to sell wife Pamela Tiffin to a visiting Sheik whose hobby is collecting blondes. After a desert trek, tables are turned on Mastroianni by his supposedly dumb spouse who sells HIM into a male harem, while she drives off in a swank motor car. Again, this suffers from over-extension and, though intermittently amusing and with Miss Tiffin lovely to look at, it winds up in ho-hum tedium.

Except for the discrepancy between first non-color item and others, production is lushly outfitted, and technical credits are in keeping.

Hawk.

The Year of the Horse
(COLOR)

Very short but charming film about an elderly hansom cab-driver, a small Chinese-American boy and a horse.

Mildred Dienstag and Therese Orkin production. Associate producer, Jean Cantor. No distributor set. Written and directed by Irving Sunasky; story collaborator, Thomas Miller. Features Bradley Joe and Gabriel Mason, narrated by Mark Hubley. Titles and animation, John Hubley; creator and director of narration, Faith Hubley. Camera (Eastman Color), Morton L. Heilig; editor, Peggy Lawson. Reviewed in New York, March 16, '66. Running Time: **58 MINS.**

Michael Farrow .... Gabriel Mason
Richard Han Jr. .... Bradley Joe
Richard Han Sr. .... Alvin Lum
Mrs. Richard Han Sr. ... Mary Mon Toy
Tina Han .... Lorraine Wong
Han Grandparents .. Mr. and Mrs. Thom

Stewardess .... Mary Hui
Bachelor .... Peter Wong
Veterinarian .... Dick Hanover
Policeman .... Burt Harris

This entire film was shot on location in New York City with, apparently, a great deal of hand-held camerawork. The photography, done in Eastman Color by Morton L. Heilig, is a very plus factor in this slight and not too logical tale about a friendship between a 7-year-old Chinese-American boy (Bradley Joe) and an elderly hansom cab driver (Gabriel Mason) built on their mutual love for the driver's horse Molly.

Much of the film's charm depends on the ability of the young actor to deliver a visually impressive performance as there is no soundtrack, as such. The film is narrated, seemingly, by the boy, but the voice is actually that of Mark Hubley, son of John and Faith Hubley, animation team who've created the beautiful title credits and animated sequences. This isn't first narration job for young Mark who, with the other Hubley children, did a similar chore on their parents' animated feature, "Of Stars And Men." His voice is perfect and conveys the feelings of a serious type whose life revolves about the horse and its owner. For dramatic effect, director-scripter Irving Sunasky has the horse die and the boy getting the citizens of Chinatown to raise funds for a new one.

There's considerable photographic padding, recurring shots of Central Park, etc., which could be edited to make the film an easier-to-handle short subject, as present running time of 58 minutes is an awkward length for programming purposes. Although the New York setting could have utilized more familiar scenes, there are areas of the Central Park and Chinatown regions that have rarely been seen on film before, plus a fascinating sequence in which the first Molly is taken to Staten Island for burial. Some people may quibble about such illogical plotlines as the ability of a 7-year-old to negotiate the trips alone from Chinatown to Central Park and back, but this is quibbling and the tiny tale should be enjoyed as a delightful excursion into the world of a child.

The title is appropriate as 1966 is, in the Chinese calendar, the year of the horse. The market for the film, however, appears restricted to children's programs and non-commercial areas.
Robe.

Stop The World—
I Want To Get Off
(BRITISH-COLOR MITCHELL 35)

Brisk and entertaining filming of legit-style performance of the Anthony Newley-Leslie Bricusse musical. Topnotch credits in nearly all departments. No current marquee strength.

Hollywood, March 30.
Warner Bros. Pictures release of Bill Sargent production. Features Tony Tanner, Millicent Martin. Directed by Philip Saville. Stage director, Michael Lindsay-Hogg. Based on play by Leslie Bricusse, Anthony Newley, produced on stage by David Merrick; additional material, David Donable, Al Ham, Marilyn and Alan Bergman; camera (Mitchell 35, Technicolor), Oswald Morris; editor, Jim Sibley; music supervision, Al Ham; production design, Sean Kenny; asst. director, Robert Lynn. Reviewed at Pacific's Pantages Theatre, L.A., March 29, '66. Running Time, **98 MINS.**
Littlechap .... Tony Tanner
Evie, Anya, Ara, Ginnie..Millicent Martin
Susan .... Leila Croft
Jane .... Valerie Croft
Littlechap's son .... Neil Hawley
Father-in-law .... Graham Lyons

When Bill Sargent beat a strategic retreat after the "Harlow" biopix scuffles, he said he'd be back. And he is back, returning in probably the best possible way —with an excellent film. "Stop The World—I Want To Get Off" is an entertaining play-pic, that is, an essentially legit performance lensed with some film techniques added. The mood, comedy, drama and tunes from the Anthony Newly-Leslie Bricusse legituner are socked over by standout performances, direction, music supervision and production values. Absence of names indicates lots of trade and public sell is needed to emphasize the poptunes and fact that this is exceptional. Good b.o. prospects seem likely for Warner Bros. release in general situations. Its future is also assured as a pix-to-tv special.

"Stop" was filmed in England in two weeks and two days, with Philip Saville directing a legit staging by Michael Lindsay-Hogg. The film is the first to use Mitchell Camera's System 35, a multi-camera array employing some video aids. To dispel any notions that the result is a second-generation offspring of kinescope recordings, it will be noted that, while tv methods were used, the final 1.85:1 footage derives from raw stock exposed during shooting. Physically, then, the pic is original motion picture photography.

Artistically, "Stop" is a major achievement stemming in part from the outstanding performances of its principals, Tony Tanner and Millicent Martin. Tanner, who is now on Broadway, having replaced Tommy Steele in "Half A Sixpence," handles the original Anthony Newley role with an engaging style and flair as he traces the 35-year climb of a self-loving opportunist. Miss Martin, known in England for tv work, some pix, and now concurrently being introed to world theatre audiences by Paramount's "Alfie," makes an excellent impression as the hero's wife and various girl friends. She's an excellent comedienne.

The book is naughty, flip, sardonic while the lyrics often suggest Lorenz Hart. Youth could take it up as their own kind. There is an ultimate lesson in being unselfish which is smoothly presented via comedy and irony.

Tanner is the predominant thesp, and to him falls the burden of getting film audiences hip to the stagey atmosphere and the use of pantomime; these early minutes are the slowest, but once hurdled, the film rolls along with regular insertions of show tunes. Deliberate attempts to show that this is not a regular pic include audience inserts and some footage which shows backstage technical personnel. On some early tunes, a mitt track is used but disappears since audiences will tend to take up the applause for real, as on the public Coast tradeshow.

Saville has dotted the pic with many fine directorial touches, one of which is a gradual descent of camera in Tanner's continuing chats which an unseen father-in-law. Gimmick is a counterpoint to the character's own growth in stature, both figuratively and literally. Oswald Morris supervised the perceptive Technicolor lensing.

The score emerges as a robust and significant production assist under Al Ham's excellent supervision. Along with "What Kind Of Fool Am I?" "Gonna Build A Mountain," and "Once In A Lifetime" are other plot-oriented numbers which propel Tanner through the superficial phases of material and career progress until self-awakening.

Sean Kenny's production design is firstrate, as is its execution by all technical hands, except for a noisy sound level about 10 minutes before the end. Jim Sibley edited to a zesty 98 minutes. Tutte Lemkow rates a nod for directing the mime passages.

The legit concept in filming begins with opening titles, done in b&w against an eye-catching, documentary-style montage of production stills, ending after five minutes with players exiting dressing rooms for the curtain, at which time occurs the shift to color. Tunes are often reprised, and at finale, players bow and curtain falls with no end titling. Tanner yells 'Stop" at several points for some b&w speeches to the audience.

Warner Bros. has already cultivated some audience acceptance of play-pix via "Hamlet," "La Boheme" and "Othello." Unlike these, "Stop" is neither classic drama nor do plans call for it to go into the two-a-day release policy. *Murf.*

Io, Io, Io . . . E Gli Altri
(Me, Me, Me . . . and the Others)
(ITALIAN)

Rome, March 29.
Cineriz release of Luigi Rovere production for Rizzoli Film-Cineluxor. Features Gina Lollobrigida, Silvana Mangano, Walter Chiari, Vittorio DeSica, Nino Manfredi, Marcello Mastroianni, Sylva Koscina, Caterina Boratto, Vittorio Caprioli, Elisa Cegani, Andrea Checchi, Umberto D'Orsi, Graziella Granata, Marisa Merlini, Paolo Panelli, Mario Pisu, Salvo Randone, Luisa Rivelli, M. Grazia Spina, Saro Urzi', Franca Valeri. Directed by Alessandro Blasetti. Screenplay, Blasetti, Carlo Romano, in collaboration with Age, Scarpelli, Adriano Baracco, Leo Benvenuti, Piero de Bernardi, Lianella Carell, Suso Cecchi D'Amico, Ennio Flajano, Giorgio Rossi, Libero Solaroli, Vincenzo Talarico. From a story by Blasetti; camera, Aldo Giordani; music, Carlo Rustichelli; editor, Tatiana Casini. At Barberini, Rome. Running Time, **120 MINS.**

Vignette item is linked by theme and a main character. Marquee names in abundance signal good returns on the home grounds. Word-of-mouth and some of major names should help it in other non-Italian areas, too, but a specialized sell will be needed to give this upper-case projection. Some trimming to eliminate overly local connotations of some sequences could help. And in any case, topnotch lingual versions are called for maximum impact abroad.

Writer-director Alessandro Blasetti has typically not approached his subject the easy way. Nor has he conceded much to average or below-average aud tastes in order to exploit his ideas and subject matter. Result is a film which is more often tongue-in-cheek than hilarious, and which at times strives overly to make a barbed point, losing the purely entertainment-bound patron along the way. In short, for a comedy-satire, its humor is principally well above the belt, making it an oddity of sorts these days in which rather gross vulgarity is more the norm. And for this reason perhaps more difficult to sell. True also that the pic drags in spots, despite lively editing, generally, by Blasetti and Tatiana Casini.

Theme is selfishness in various facets of life today, as tipped early in the pic by a man eating in dining car who serves himself three healthy portions of cheese, leaving his three dinner partners with the crumbs. This and other related ideas are intertwined by writer-director as seen through eyes and musings of his hero, newsman Walter Chiari.

Principally involved are his wife, played neatly and piquantly by Gina Lollobrigida; the one unselfish friend he has, a nice cameo by Marcello Mastroianni; an unctuous VIP friend, portrayed by Vittorio DeSica; and an idealized would-be mistress, Silvana Mangano, whom Chiari abandons because involvement would mean complications. But many, many others help fill handsomely produced pic with oft-vivid characterizations, with names taking bits as a tribute to Blasetti. Technical credits are all solid. *Hawk.*

Cinerama's
Russian Adventure

Reedit with Bing Crosby narration added to Soviet Kinopanorama travelogs. Excellent family fare. U. S. Boxoffice outlook strong.

Chicago, March 30.
United Roadshow Presentation Inc. (J. Jay Frankel, Harold J. Dennis) release under the auspices of the Cultural Exchange Program, and distributed by arrangement with Soveportfilm. Stars Bing Crosby. Production supervisor, Thomas Conroy; original narration and prologue, Homer McCoy; Supervising music editor, William E. Wild. Direction, Leonid Kristy, Roman Karmen, Boris Dolin, Oleg Lebedev, Solomon Kogan, Vassily Katanian; cameramen, Nikolai Generalov, Anatoly Kolshin, Ilya Gutman, Vladimir Vorontzov, Sergei Medynsky, E. Yezhov, A. Missiura; original music, Aleksandr Lokshin, Ilya Schweitzer, Yuri Effimov. Reviewed at the McVickers Cinerama

Theatre, Chicago, March 29, 1966. Running Time, **145 MINS.**

This new release for Cinerama playoff results from USA-USSR cultural exchange and from a re-edit, with added Bing Crosby narration, of footage made entirely in and by Russia. Two films were exhibited some years ago at the DeMille in Manhattan under the titles, "How Wide Is My Country" and "Magic Mirror." Under the present arrangement the U. S. will send one U.S.-made Cinerama film to Russia, plus six other features, non-Cinerama.

Purpose of "Russian Adventure," and for that matter the Cultural Exchange Program, is to give the persons in each country the opportunity to see, and hopefully to better understand, the peoples, land, cities, aesthetics, et al., of a foreign culture.

The Russian offering is an opulent and ambitious production rich in the natural beauty of the impressive Soviet topography; filmic tapestry of the largest country on earth (Russia has no less than ten time zones) with its variety of geographical conditions is no small task. However, the film successfully captures the feeling, if not the totality, of the vast Russian landscape.

Particularly notable for their visual impact are the scenes photographed in the lush Taiga Forest and the rugged Taymyr Peninsula. Also, the underwater shots in the Sea of Okhotsk, and the log handlers on the Tisza River (on the Western and Eastern coasts respectively) proved to be especially engaging.

The film's piece de resistance, though, was the sequences taken in Moscow of the Bolshoi Ballet, the Moiseyev Dancers, and the Moscow State Circus. Except for witnessing actual performances, the 180 degree Cinerama screen would certainly seem to be the most effective way of reproducing the excitement, splendor and the high standard of excellence of the three organizations.

The segment on the Bolshoi Ballet skillfully captures the troupe's virtuosity and at the same time carefully illustrates that the results were gleaned from long and difficult preparation. The beguiling flair of the Moiseyev Dancers ,and the skillful acrobats and daring animal acts of the Moscow State Circus are presented in a similar fashion.

Except for an overly graphic segment of an Antarctica whale hunt and the subsequent skinning of the catch, the film makes for excellent family entertainment. Perhaps at times a trifle too deliberate in its desire to impress with the fact that the Russian citizen is a vigorous, fun loving individual, the film tends periodically to become self-conscious.

Moreover, the sequences dealing with the Russian at work do not include the day-to-day office worker that the average American might relate to, but rather places an emphasis on whale hunters and Soviet scientists doing research work at the North Pole. Majority of the film, however, shows the Russians at play.

The Soviets made good use of the wide screen's ability to transmit a feeling of depth and motion during such scenes as an exciting reindeer race and a rousing ride down a mountain road, exhibit a firm understanding of the uses of Cinerama techniques.

Bing Crosby, who handles the narration and appears briefly in the beginning to introduce the picture, turns in a firstrate job, easily projecting an affable aura around the entire production. ....

The several directors (6) and cameramen (7) score with a sure footed aplomb getting the most out of each scene, and the music is appropriate throughout.

Although shown in Chicago in the original three projector system, it is understood that all future releases will be in the 70m ture releases will be in the single-projector Cinerama process.

Ron.

Fumo Di Londra
(Thank You Very Much)
(ITALIAN-COLOR-SONGS)

Rome, March 29.

Rank Film release of Fono Roma production. Stars Alberto Sordi; features Fiona Lewis, Amy Dalby, Clara Bindi, Alfredo Marchetti. Directed by Alberto Sordi. Screenplay, Sordi and Sergio Amidei; camera (Technicolor), Benito Frattari; editor, Antonietta Zita; music, Piero Piccioni. At Metropolitan, Rome. Running Time, **118 MINS.**

Dante Fontana .... Alberto Sordi
Elizabeth .... Fiona Lewis
Duchess of Bradford .... Amy Dalby

Alberto Sordi in pleasant comedy along the lines of his Swedish-based "Il Diavolo," set this time in London. Despite good production values and several amusing moments, pic disappoints more than it pleases, especially considering precedents and the talent involved. Though he's had a hand in direction before, this is also Sordi's first officially credited stint behind the camera as well as before it. Foreign chances are spotty and in English-language areas dependent also on Anglo version which could—as well all thesps except Sordi mouth English lines in the copy seen here—prove better than the local one, if properly done.

In this one, Sordi is an anglophile Italian antique dealer who finally sees his longtime dream of visiting Britain come true. Remainder is principally exposure to the British scene and the British mode of life, spoofingly contrasted to the Italian. Star tangles with a duchess at auction, she invites him to her castle, and later her teen granddaughter leads him into British beat-land to see how the mod-and-rocker set lives, loves and thinks. Basically richer for his sobering experiences, Sordi heads back to Italy, wife and kids.

Though basically similar in construction to "Il Diavolo," this one lacks the latter's satiric, oft-bitter bite and its in-depth comment on the foibles of the Italian male on the make in territory where manners and mores are not familiar. There are plenty of stolen street shots to give this an authentic location flavor.

Benito Frattari's hued lensing of the British countryside is often breathtaking, but when the chips are down, many of the comedy effects are facile and stagey, even if Sordi gets away with the most thanks to his mugging and acting strength. Among many colorful sidelines role, Amy Dalby registers strongly as the Duchess, and Fiona Lewis makes a comely British gal befriended by the visitor. Production credits are excellent. Songs by Julie Rogers add to atmosphere of pic, especially "You Never Told Me," which looks a good spinner.

Hawk.

Du Rififi a Paname
(FRENCH—COLOR)

Paris, March 29.

Comacico release of Copernic production. Stars Jean Gabin, George Raft, Gert Frobe, Nadja Tiller; features Claudio Brook, Claude Brasseur, Marcell Bozzufi, Daniel Ceccaldi. Directed by Denys De La Patelliere. Screenplay, Alphonse Boudard, De La Patelliere from novel by Auguste Le Breton; camera (Eastmancolor), Walter Wottitz; editor, Claude Durand. At Ambassade-Gaumont, Paris. Running Time, **98 MINS.**

Paulo .... Jean Gabin
Binnagio .... George Raft
Walter .... Gert Froebe
Irene .... Nadja Tiller
Mike .... Claudio Brook
Lili .... Mirelile Darc
Noel .... Daniel Ceccaldi
Giulio .... C'aude Brasseur
Marque .... Marcel Bozzufi
Lea .... Dany Dauberson
Sergio .... Carlo Nell
Fille .... Christa Lang

This "Rififi" is a familiar tale of gang war and a planted undercover man that gets some added dash in making the gang international, some solid thespians and a good production dress. But its basically stolid direction and episodic progression slant this mainly for spinoff use abroad, where its okay action aspects could have it paying off. Jean Gabin and George Raft names could also help.

Gabin is again an aging lion of a gangster who has a code of honor. When the Italo Mafia and an American gang try to cut into his gold smuggling and selling spare parts to Cuba he fights back. A Yank government undercover man has wormed his way into Gabin's graces and proves his undoing.

In the interim, there are scenes in garish niteries and gun battles. Gert Froebe is good as usual as Gabin's partner while Nadja Tiller, Mireille Darc and assorted strippers add pulchritude and eye appeal to the proceedings.

Director Denys De La Patelliere has directed this tale of underworld action but rarely has been able to imbue a sense of life, character and crispness into it. Result is a slick affair that should do well here although its foreign chances need more hardsell and the right placement.

Gabin is his usual anarchic self with Raft fine in a cameo bit as the American gangleader. Claudio Brook is good as the Yank plant, with the women also helpful. It is technically solid, with a helpful color envelope.

Mosk.

Ghost In The Invisible Bikini
(COLOR—PANAVISION—MUSIC)

Another combination of comedy and spooks. Former "beach" types compete with old-hand comedians for laughs. Should do well in, by now, established market.

American International Pictures (James H. Nicholson and Samuel Z. Arkoff) production. Co-produced by Anthony Carras. Features Tommy Kirk, Deborah Walley, Aron Kincaid, Quinn O'Hara, Jesse White, Harvey Lembeck, Nancy Sinatra, Claudia Martin, Francis X. Bushman, Benny Rubin, Bobbi Shaw, George Barrows, Basil Rathbone, Patsy Kelly, Boris Karloff, Susan Hart. Directed by Don Weis. Screenplay, Louis M. Heyward, Elwood Ullman from story by Heyward. Camera (Panavision, Pathecolor), Stanley Cortez; film editors, Fred Feitshans, Eve Newman; sound, Ryder Sound Services; musical score, Les Baxter; songs (lyrics and music), Guy Hemric, Jerry Styner. Reviewed in New York, March 23, '66. Running Time, **82 MINS.**

Chuck Phillips .... Tommy Kirk
Lili Morton .... Deborah Walley
Bobby .... Aron Kincaid
Sinistra .... Quinn O'Hara
J. Sinister Hulk .... Jesse White
Eric Von Zipper .... Harvey Lembeck
Vicki .... Nancy Sinatra
Lulu .... Claudia Martin
Malcolm .... Francis X. Bushman
Chicken Feather .... Benny Rubin
Princess Yolanda .... Bobbi Shaw
Monstro .... George Barrows
Reginald Ripper .... Basil Rathbone
Myrtle Forbush .... Patsy Kelly
The Corpse .... Boris Karloff
The Ghost .... Susan Hart
Shirl .... Luree Holmes
Alberta .... Alberta Nelson
J. D. .... Andy Romano

Rat Pack: Myrna Ross, Bob Harvey, John Macchia, Alan Fife

Girls and Boys: Ed Garner, Mary Hughes, Patti Chandler, Frank Alesia, Salli Sachse, Sue Hamilton, Bobby Fuller Four

When the idea of combining the healthy specimens of their "beach" pictures with the denizens of their assorted terror tintypes was first conceived by American International toppers James H. Nicholson and Samuel Z. Arkoff, it sounded like a natural for gleaning more gold from the company's two best pay lodes. It started off very well with "Dr. Goldfoot And The Bikini Machine," and should do comparatively well with this ambitious effort. But the truth is, if better scripts aren't forthcoming, this cycle is going to fall apart.

Plus values apparent in the film are the presence of all those gorgeous girl-types, plus an even more gorgeous woman-type (Susan Hart) for the bigger boys; the usual Don Weis stress on action, even if it is frequently forced; heavy helpings of would-be slapstick, sometimes successful; and a large assortment of songs, played by the Bobby Fuller Four and sung by various cast members.

Disappointing are the waste of Susan Hart (who has earned a better vehicle by now than this carbon copy of more successful films). She's forced to conceal her charms in an unattractive blonde wig or in the special effect that makes her the title character: Louis M. Heyward and Elwood Ulman's inane script that is not only tired but borrows from such other sources as the curtain line of "Some Like It Hot." Almost all the girls are still good, Nancy Sinatra, Quinn O'Hara and Deborah Walley coming over best; but this year's crop of boys isn't up to the earlier "beach" cavaliers. Tommy Kirk, fresh from the Disney fold, (what appears to be dyed hair), lacks the kooky verve that made him fun to watch in the Disney epics; Aron Kincaid, who doesn't sing a la Frankie Avalon and hasn't the comedy promise of Jody McCrea, has still to find himself. Even Harvey Lembeck, whose spoof of the "Scorpio Rising" syndrome plus his one-man team of three stooges could always be relied on for a few giggles, is slowing down and his Rat Pack is of little assistance.

Outstanding among the older members are Jesse White as the shifty lieutenant of principal villain Basil Rathbone and, occasionally, Patsy Kelly. Boris Karloff and the other veterans are only along for the ride.

Guy Hemric and Jerry Styner's five tunes, "Geronimo," "Swing A-Ma-Thing," "Don't Try To Fight It, Baby," "Stand Up And Fight" and "Make The Music Pretty" are sufficient unto their purpose.

All other technical credits are excellent, particularly S t a n l e y Cortez' Panavision camera which makes good use of Pathecolor in exploring some still fascinating sets evidently left over from the Poe period, particularly a Chamber of Horrors used for a rousing but overlong free-for-all.

All in all, a good try but short on script and inspiration. Should do very well in its intended, non-demanding market. *Robe.*

Un Monde Nouveau
(A New World)
(FRENCH-ITALIAN)

Paris, April 5.
United Artists release of Harry Saltzman-Terra Films-Majestic Films production. Stars Nino Castelnuovo, Christine Delaroche; features Georges Wilson, Tanya Lopert. Directed by Vittorio De Sica. Screenplay, Cesare Zavattini, Ricardo Aragno; camera, Jean Boffety; editor, Paul Cavatte. At Colisee, Paris. Running Time, 82 MINS.
Anne .... Christine Delaroche
Carlo .... Nino Castelnuovo
Mary .... Tanya Lopert
Doctor .... Georges Wilson
Boss .... Pierre Brasseur
Woman .... Madeleine Robinson

Vittorio De Sica appears to have tried to renew ties with his neo realist days via a simple story and working with early scenarist Ceasre Zavattini. But all this emerges somewhat too schematic and a bit old-fashioned despite ringing in the question of abortion. Adequately played and done, this could show for specialized slotting abroad on its theme, with playoff possibilities also indicated if arty house chances appear slimmer.

Film appears to have been hacked up a bit since there are sudden outbursts or scenes that seem chiefly there to comment on the theme of the film, rather than move it along while others seem arbitrary. For example a pregnant girl snaps at her friend that she always thinks Negro men are following her and want her to mask a desire for them she will not admit,

Besides being a fairly platitudinous psychological gambit, it seems spurious here since there has been no inkling of it. This appears thrown in to titillate rather than make a true comment. Also, the girl involved has an episodic role that also makes this too obvious.

In fact, it appears like a gentle love story with the problem of pre-marital pregnancy that has been chopped up to fall in with newer film concepts and techniques that do not help it or make the theme more potent.

A young Italian from a good family, living in Paris as a freelance photographer, meets a provincial French student at a medical student ball. It is love at first

sight and he even dances her off the floor into a curtained alcove from where she soon emerges dishevelled and distraught.

She is soon pregnant. They meet again and love blossoms and then she tells him. He then vacillates and there are scenes to underline man's need to commit himself and make a choice. But he does not and picks up a rich woman to try to get money for an abortion.

De Sica uses stop action, here justified since the photog is taking pictures. But it shows New Wave influences and seems too obvious since it does not serve any purpose.

Christine Delaroche is a mousy, but pretty little girl who registers adequately for her first film. Nino Castelnuovo is charming though ambiguous as the boy. Tanya Lopert, in an episodic role, as the girl's roommate, shows a good feel for comedy and may be heard from in future pix.

There is some fine on-the-spot Parisian shooting, but this boy-meets-girl story is just too forced to make their affair winning.

Harry Saltzman produced through a French and Italo company for UA worldwide handling. And there is an inside wink via the photog hero trying to get a shot of Sean Connery at the opening of "Goldfinger" in Paris. Film appears well meaning but is not powerful enough. As teenagers show more maturity, and birth control spreads, the film's subject appears somewhat dated. This "New World" appears more like an older world pic tricked up with new flashier techniques.
Mosk.

Around The World Under The Sea
(PANAVISION-COLOR)

Imaginatively-made undersea thriller with good prospects in general market.

Hollywood, March 24.
Metro release of Ivan Tors production, producer-directed by Andrew Marton. Screenplay, Arthur Weiss, Art Arthur; music, Harry Sukman; camera (Metrocolor), Clifford Poland; underwater camera, Lamar Boren; editor, Warren Adams; asst. director, James Gordon McLean. Reviewed at Wiltern Theatre, March 23, '66. Running Time, 110 MINS.
Dr. Doug Standish ...... Lloyd Bridges
Dr. Maggie Hanford .... Shirley Eaton
Dr. Croog Mosby .... Brian Kelly
Dr. Phil Volker ...... David McCallum
Hank Stahl .... Keenan Wynn
Dr. Orin Hillvard .. Marshall Thompson
Dr. August Boren .... Gary Merrill

Ivan Tors, who stirred public imagination with underwater exploits in his successful "Sea Hunt" teleseries, returns to the mysterious and fascinating world below the ocean's surface for this unusual feature. He has taken the challenge of the deep and woven an arresting tale where beautiful underwater photography figures importantly as the protagonists embark on a hazardous mission. Excellent effects are achieved to lend an authentic note, and while in need of sharp editing to reduce over-footage the subject should hold attraction for both juve audiences and adults who flavor escapism.

Well-produced and directed by Andrew Marton for Tors and with

a competent cast headed by Lloyd Bridges, star of the four-year "Hunt" series, pic is premised on an intriguing idea. Motivated by an alarming number of violent underwater volcanic eruptions, a group of six scientists aboard a deep-sea submarine hydronaut plant a network of seismic warning devices on the ocean floor completely around the world to alert major cities and countries of impending earthquake disasters. While there is certain science-fiction flavor attached to the project the unfoldment is so legitimately handled that the whole takes on the aspect of fact.

Story line of the Arthur Weiss-Art Arther screenplay frequently is paper-thin and a fault lies in its episodic nature. These are more than compensated for, however, by events of the moment, excitement generated by the task at hand which includes an attack by a giant sea monster as long as the sub, and, again, the craft drawn by suction toward the crater of an underwater volcano. Other dangers of the deep are graphically depicted, as well as an amusing sequence of a dolphin trained to do errands.

Filmed partially in the waters of the Great Barrier Reef of Australia, where underwater effects are particularly spectacular, most of the location work with players was done in Nassau and Miami. Tors had the cooperation of the U.S. Coast Guard, the Miami Seaquarium, Marineland of the Pacific, Scripps Institute of Oceanography, Dept. of Defense and other agencies to assure realism.

Generally good performances are delivered by the cast. Assisting Bridges, who heads the expedition, are Brian Kelly, David McCallum, Keenan Wynn, Marshall Thompson and Shirley Eaton, only femme member of the party. As a specialist in marine medicine and biology, she's also in for romance with Kelly, Thompson and McCallum, which on one occasion nearly leads to disaster. Gary Merrill plays another scientist stationed on land who is in direct communication with the hydronaut.

Technical credits are outstanding. Clifford Poland's Panavision and Metrocolor photography is complemented by the underwater photography of Lamar Boren, and diving sequences were directed by Ricou Browning. Harry Sukman's music score serves to point up the melodramatic moments, and art direction by Preston Rountree and Mel Bledsoe is particularly imaginative. Warren Adams' editing, while the picture is far overlong, catches the realism of the project.
Whit.

Dateline Diamonds
(BRITISH)

Neat cheap-budget second feature, blending mild crime yarn with radio advertising pirate ship. Technically okay and a useful filler.

London, March 30.
Rank release of Viscount Films presentation. Features William Lucas, Kenneth Cope, George Mikell, Conrad Phillips, Patsy Rowlands, Vanda Godsell, Burnell Tucker, Geoffrey Sander, Peter Sander, Kiki Dee, Small Faces. The Chantelles, Mark Richardson, Kenny

Everett. Executive producer, H a r o l d Shampan. Produced by Harry Benn. Directed by Jeremy Summers. Screenplay, Tudor Gates, from an original idea by Shampan; camera, Stephen Dade; music, Johnny Douglas; editor, Sidney Stone. Reviewed at RFD Private Theatre, London, March 29, '66. Running Time, 70 MINS.
Major Fairclough ...... William Lucas
Lester Benson .... Kenneth Cope
Paul Verlekt .... George Mikell
Tom Jenkins .... Conrad Phillips
Mrs. Edgecombe .... Patsy Rowlands
Dale Meredith .... Burnell Tucker
Gay Jenkins .... Anna Cartaret
Mrs. Jenkins .... Vanda Godsell
Meyerhof .... Gertan Klauber
Asst. Commissioner .... Doel Luscombe
Spankharen .... Peter Sander
Army Officer ...... Geoffrey Lumsden
Garage Attendant ...... Ronald Bridges
Dock Policeman .... David Kirk
Guest Artistes, Small Faces, Kiki Dee, The Chantelles, Mark Richardson, Kenny Everett.

With a $90,000 budget, and delivered within six weeks of the cameras rolling, "Dateline Diamonds" is one of those competent little second features in which plenty of talent is involved. Its utility for the States lies in useful second-billing on duals. Exec producer Harold Shampan dreamed up the original simple idea which combines a straightforward crime yarn with the topicality of the Radio Pirate Ships situation in waters off Britain. Shampan has gathered a cast of good reliable thesps, and some bright, lesser-known pop stars and the result's a painless 70 minutes. But there are obvious signs of the pic having had to be cut down to size and in its short span there is insufficient time to develop either the plot angle or the pop atmosphere satisfactorily.

A cashiered sapper officer (William Lucas) master minds a series of daring diamond robberies and blackmails an ex-Army reformed criminal into assisting him. Played by Kenneth Cope, he is the manager of some pop groups, and the two use a publicity visit to a Radio Pirate ship, anchored outside British territorial waters, to transport the rocks to Holland. Patiently the cops build up clues and the climax comes at a teenage pop dance, followed by the inevitable car chase when the heavy is trapped.

William Lucas is a suave crook, Cope a plausible group manager, and George Mikell and Conrad Phillips first rate as diligent policemen. Pasty Rowlands turns in an amusing bit as a confused witness and Peter Sander, Vanda Godsell, Doel Luscombe and Anna Cartaret give useful aid, with Burnell Tucker showing promise as a goodlooking disk jockey. Tudor Gates' screenplay has some bright touches and is smoothly scribed but he hasn't much room to maneuver 70 minutes. Over much time is spent in the details of a jewel robbery (it's a kind of detailed 'Do It Yourself' demonstration of how to blow a safe) which might have been better spent in the novel Radio Pirate Ship atmosphere.

However, Jeremy Summers has directed without fuss and has intro'd some useful pop talent plausibly. The Chantelles, three goodlooking blonde chicks score with "I Think Of You," and Small Faces, Mark Richardson and Kiki Dee also give with neat ditties.

Johnny Douglas' perky score John St. John Earl's artwork and good sharp lensing by Stephen

Dade are a help to Summers' direction. In fact, technically, this unambitious pic has much to commend it, except that Sidney Stone's editing loses out on abruptness, through obvious trimming down to second feature length. *Rich.*

That Riviera Touch
(BRITISH-COLOR)

Video comics Morecambe and Wise in a robbery frolic on the Riviera. Several funny moments and brisk finale, but overall pic lacks pep and invention.

London, March 29.
Rank release of a Hugh Stewart Production. Stars Eric Morecambe, Ernie Wise. Features Suzanne Lloyd, Paul Stassino. Directed by Cliff Owen. Screenplay, S. C. Green and R. M. Mills, with Peter Blackmore; camera (Eastmancolor), Otto Heller; music, Ron Goodwin; editor, Gerry Hambling. Reviewed at Leicester Square Theatre, London. Running Time, **98 MINS.**
Eric .... Eric Morecambe
Ernie .... Ernie Wise
Claudette .... Suzanne Lloyd
Le Pirate .... Paul Stassino
Inspector Duval ...... Armand Mestral
Marcel .... George Eugeniou
Ali .... Peter Jeffrey
Coco .... Gerald Lawson
Pierre .... Michael Forrest
Renard .... Clive Cazes
Gaston .... Steven Scott
Hassim .... Paul Danquah

Second attempt by producer Hugh Stewart to put topline British tv comedians, Morecambe and Wise, on the film map has come off better than first pic, "The Intelligence Man." But though these likeable comedians are well occasionally in brief interludes the whole comedy plods somewhat and shows signs of strain. However, it builds up to a fast and funny finale and it is a pity that this punchy pace doesn't get infused earlier in the proceedings. Morecambe and Wise's many fans will enjoy this frolic, but it may rate a cagier reception in areas where they have not yet made their tv mark.

S.C. Green and R.M. Hills, regular tv scribes for Morecambe and Wise, have cleared up a conventional yarn in which the comedians go to the Riviera for a sunshine holiday and with nothing more on their minds than chatting up the bikini-clad chicks. But they quickly become unwittingly involved in a clash between rival gangs over a jewelry robbery which in turn lanhs them up to their eyebrows in killings and mysterious shenanigans in a gloomy old villa on the Cote D'Azur, with the chief heavy's girl friend (Suzanne Lloyd) playing both the lads for suckers. Some larks on the beach, Morecambe unwittingly breaking the Casino bank, some hamhanded Romeo work by Morecambe and the usual play on Tourist French, etc. offer some bright moments. But only the end really adds up to the kind of gusty slapstick needed for this sort of comedy.

This consists of Morecambe being whipped along on water skis behind a speedboat manned by the heavy, who is popping his gun off at the scared comedian. Meanwhile, Wise, the stooge, is hanging from a helicopter trying to rescue his buddy from his sticky situation. This, following a breakneck car chase along the winding Riviera coastline, will leave the audience cheerful.

Otto Heller's Eastmancolor camerawork makes the most of the lush Riviera scenery and sunshine, and editing by Gerry Hambling, art work by John Blezard and Ron Goodwin's chirpy score are all okay. Cliff Owen, the director, has wisely brought in several situations in which the comedians can give hints of their familiar techniques, but there are too many slack moments in between.

Supporting Morecambe and Wise are some useful performers. Suzanne Lloyd as the adventuress is a stunning looker and a sharp performer and Paul Stassino as the chief crook and Armand Mestral as a French gendarme both lend prominent aid. Attempts to put over Morecambe and Wise both as a personality twosome and as individual straight comedy actors sometimes clash in the result, but there's no doubt that the pair can be a useful asset to British comedy pix once the right blend of story and dialog is found. *Rich.*

Carry On Cowboy
(BRITISH-COLOR)

Latest "Carry On" slapstick comedy follows its usual well-tried formula of blueish gags, predictable situations and uninhibited performances by usual team. Should spin gold like its predecessors.

London, March 29.
Warner-Pathe release of a Peter Rogers' Production for Anglo Amalgamated. Stars Sidney James, Kenneth Williams, Jim Dale, Charles Hawtrey, Joan Sims, Angela Douglas. Features Percy Herbert, Bernard Bresslaw, Davy Kaye, Peter Butterworth, Sydney Bromley, Jon Pertwee, Edina Ronay, Lionel Murton, Peter Gilmore, Alan Gifford, Brian Rawlinson. Directed by Gerald Thomas. Screenplay, Talbot Rothwell; camera (Eastmancolor), Alan Hume; music, Eric Rogers; editor, Roderick Keys. Reviewed at Carlton, London. Running Time, **94 MINS.**
Johnny Finger .... Sidney James
Judge Burke .... Kenneth Williams
Marshall P. Knutt .... Jim Dale
Chief Big Heap ....Charles Hawtrey
Belle .... Joan Sims
Annie Oakley .... Angela Douglas
Charlie .. .. Percy Herbert
Little Heap .... Bernard Bresslaw
Josh .. .. Davy Kaye
Doc .... Peter Butterworth
Sam .... Sydney Bromley
Sheriff Earp .... Jon Pertwee
Dolores .... Edina Ronay
Clerk .... Lionel Murton
Curley .... Peter Gilmore
Fiddler .... Alan Gifford
Driver .... Brian Rawlinson
Kitikata .... Sally Douglas
Slim .... Gary Colleano

Producer Peter Rogers and director Gerald Thomas unabashedly continue their profitable way with the latest "Carry On," a Wild West spoof which might well be sub-titled "How The West Was Lost." Talbot Rothwell's story, though familiar nonsense, is less a string of irrelevant situations than usual, giving the team more Nevertheless, there's the usual opportunity for comedy thesping. ture of blue gags and slapstick situations, a blend that goes down well with its big following both in Britain and U. S., and even though some critics view the product with sniffs.

All the expected wild west characters and situations are lampooned. The bad man of Stodge City, the local ancient rancher, the tavern belle, the reluctant hero sent to clean up the place, the Injuns, the decrepit sheriff, the near-lynching, the pistol packing sweetie with revenge in her heart, the bath sequence, the brawl between jealous dames, are all taken for a ride by the irreverent Carry On gang. The result's vulgar but inoffensive fun in which a slap on the back is more dependable than a verbal riposte or wisecrack.

Stodge City is taken over by The Rumpo Kid (Sidney James), to the horror of Judge Burke (Kenneth Williams), who calls for a Marshal to clean up Stodge City. By error a sanitary engineer gets sent to the trouble spot, arriving on the same coach as Annie Oakley, daughter of the Sherriff who has been bumped off by the Rumpo Kid. What happens after that is all predictable and no strain on the brain, ending up with the sanitary engineer disposing of the Rumpo Kid in a spoof of the High Noon long walk along a deserted street, in which the bogus Marshal uses his knowledge of drains to good ingenious effect.

Jim Dale as the 'Marshal' proves himself a likeable and inventive comedian, Sid James is in good sound form as the Rumpo Kid, and Joan Sims, Kenneth Williams and Charles Hawtrey trot out familiar comedy. Angela Douglas is a pretty Annie Oakley and Jon Pertwee as the shortsighted sherriff, Edina Ronay as a local good-time girl and Davy Kaye, as the local undertaker, getting fun out of a running gag in which business booms every time Rumpo Kid strikes, all help the zany goings on.

Though actually filmed on a common in Surrey the "Wild West locations" are adequately authentic, and Alan Hume's color lensing gives an extra touch of class to this latest "Carry On." These films are not everybody's film fare by a long chalk, but they hit their modest targets confidently and provide same bawdy amusement for their indulgent public, and this new one is a distinct cut above some that have clicked in the series. *Rich.*

Morgan
(A Suitable Case For Treatment)
(BRITISH)

Eccentric artist's King Kong fantasies overwhelm his efforts to sabotage ex-wife's remarriage in zany tragi-comedy. Top acting, plus pranks, pratfalls and hip humor make artie entry b.o. prospects good. Could find commercial dates with special handling.

A Cinema V release of a British Lion Film and Quintra Film Production, produced by Leon Clore. Stars Vanessa Redgrave and David Warner. Directed by Karel Reisz; screenplay, David Mercer; edited by Tom Priestley; camera, Larry Pizer; music, Johnny Dankworth. Reviewed in N.Y. Running Time, **97 MINS.**
Leonie .... Vanessa Redgrave
Morgan .... David Warner
Napier .... Robert Stephens
Mrs. Delt .... Irene Handl
Mr. Henderson .... Newton Blick
Mrs. Henderson .... Nan Munro
Policeman .... Bernard Bresslaw
Wally .... Arthur Mullard
Counsel .... Graham Crowden
2nd Counsel .... Peter Collier
Judge .... John Rae
Best man .... Angus Mackay

"Morgan" follows the frequently funny, sometimes pathetic but relentlessly lunatic exploits of an eccentric artist of the Gulley Jimson variety, to his eventual, though not inevitable, incarceration in an insane asylum. Although it is established that the title character, played wih zest and skill by David Warner, was always engagingly dotty, his latest bizarre binge is triggered by his opposition to ex-wife's (Vanessa Redgrave) impending marriage to a sympathetic and likeable suitor.

Uninhibited hero's determined efforts to sabotage the union result in a series of hilarious pranks, ranging from wiring her house for the transmission of jungle sounds, to placing a bomb under her bed, and climax in a wildly abandoned scene in which Morgan literally lunges into a wedding reception disguised as King Kong, his hero and alter-ego. Audiences which flocked to recent comedies of the same genre, which usually combine the screwball elements of the Marx Bros. anarchy with situation comedy plots, could do the same for this British entry.

Despite the apparently lightweight marquee value of topliners David Warner (currently London's ranking "Hamlet") and Vanessa Redgrave (daughter of actor Michael Redgrave), they display such attractive film personalities and performing gifts that reviews and word-of-mouth should put them in the "discovery" category, usually a plus for artie appeal. Special handling could find a wider audience for the way-out pic, especially among the college set.

Spare, straight-line plot follows Morgan's misguided but amusingly slapstick attempts to win back his mate, Leonie, who, though displaying a tolerance and protectiveness bordering on the saintly, longs for a less frenetic and wearying life with a "normal" husband. To director Reisz's credit, the suitor, well played by Robert Stephens, is never cast as a villain.

Conflict develops basically out of Morgan's increasingly severe fantasies in which he identifies with liberated jungle creatures, notably "Tarzan" and "King Kong" (clips of the originals are skillfully woven into the action). Consequence, however, is that his behavior more resembles an ignoble savage crashing through life like a water buffalo in a china closet.

Denouement has Morgan, half-clad in his charred gorilla suit, exhausted and near collapse in a Thames-side dump, experiencing frightfully terrifying dream in which he paranoically imagines he is executed by the parade of previously revealed characters haunting his life, but now they are cast as tormentors. Herein lies the film's only major flaw, and unfortunately, it leaves a major scar in the sensibilities, and considerably blunts the witless humor which preceded it. By the expert hammering home of the insane images beleaguering Morgan viewers are now told that character traits which were formerly presented as, the accidents of a hapless, but engagingly eccentric character, were actually the symptoms of a dangerous and pathological schizophrenic.

The schizophrenia seems to have infected Reisz's direction also. Instead of providing the subtle gradually disintegrating character of Morgan, Riesz dwells on the comedic aspects of each prank, cunningly milked for maximum yaks, in the process ceding any hope of the observer taking Morgan seriously. Nor do any of the satellite characters contribute to the understanding of Morgan. His mother, excellently played by Irene Handl, is tossed in as a rabid but sentimental Marxist. Though her skittering in and out of several scenes provide some of the comic peaks in the film, her tough-Red cockney characterization bears little relationship to Morgan's illness and is consequently gratuitous. Schizoid directorial aspects are demonstrated by the abrupt shift in tone, from a comedic lighthearted style, to a heavy soddenly tragic climax. Problem is, Riesz attempted to juggle the two elements, always a delicate operation, and thuddingly dropped one. Ironically, it is apparent that he was too expert in handling both, but not deft enough to fuse them.

Top laurels go to technical credits, especially editing, while scripting must bear part of the blame for the disappointing denouement. Though the overall effect of the pic is dimmed by its unbalanced structure, most viewers will probably weight the sight gags as topflight, and be satisfied. *Rino.*

Jinrui Gaku Nyumon
(An Introduction to Anthropology)
(JAPANESE—SCOPE)
Tokyo, March 25.
Nikkatsu Production and release. Produced by Jiro Tomoda. Stars Shoichi Ozawa, Sumiko, Sakamoto. Directed by Shohei Imamura. From orginial by Akiyoshi Nozaka; camera, Masahisa Himeda; music Toshiro Mayuzumi. Running Time, 125 MINS.

Despite the title (Nikkatsu has added a running English-title, "The Amourist"), this is not a documentary. Rather, it is one of the funniest, blackest, most outrageous

Japanese films of recent years and should make itself a tidy art-theatre reputation shortly.

The work of Shohei Imamura (whose "Hogs and Battleships" and "Insect Woman" have had fairly wide U.S. showings), it is a straight - faced, but completely ironic, picture about a man who makes pornography not only his living but also his philosophy. He can get anything from 'stag-films through sex-drugs to pure virgins and is firmly convinced that he is a public benefactor.

Much of the rich humor in the film comes from his inability to understand the amorous lives of his two children, to the depravation of which he daily if innocently contributes. Most of the laughs come from deliciously - detailed take-offs on the actual making of stag films including a hilarious. pre-credit sequence where cameraman, director, and "stars" are out location-hunting.

Not so oddly, there is nothing at all objectionable about Imamura's film itself. His interest is in the humanity of his hero and though there is some sex, audience will be so busy laughing that there's no time for titilation. At the same time, the director knows that emotions have a darker side and, time and again, brings off the difficult feat of pushing us from . mirth into concern.

Beautifully filmed (entirely on actual locations in Osaka), usually using telescopic lenses, peering through windows, making the viewer a voyeur, this film seems a certain international prize winner in the event the industry decides to let it be shown at foreign film festivals. Though perhaps too long, and over talky, it contains laughter, compassion, and a great deal of humanity. *Nald.*

Das Bohrloch oder Bayern ist nicht Texas
(Drilling-Hole or Bavaria Isn't Texas)
(GERMAN)
Vienna, April 5.
Bavaria Atelier production and release. With Ludwig Schmidt-Wildy, Fritz Muliar, Fritz Strassmer, Konstantin Delcroix, Hans Fitz, Carl Baierl, Thomas Adler. Directed and written by Rainer Erler. Camera, Werner Kurz; music, Eugen Thomass; editor, Lilian Seng. At Vienna Film Fest, Vienna. Running Time, 80 MINS.

Rainer Erler, creator of several outstanding tv films and winner of the 1965 Ernst Lubitsch Prize (for his satirical "Transmigration of Souls," (originally a tv film), now comes along with another feature pic made both for tele and the cinema. This production, world preemed at the festival here, falls short of Erler's previous full-length efforts. But it looks okay for tv programming. However, this doesn't look essential enough to qualify itself for a successful theatrical run, and the absence of color is rated a handicap.

This tells the story of oil drilling in a Bavarian village. At first the villagers show an open dislike for such an enterprise. This, they argue, will ruin the beauty of the countryside, and, after all, Bavaria isn't Texas. Then they suddenly realize that oil can make them very rich. The drilling starts and it's soon found out that the soil

doesn't contain oil. However, mineral springs are discovered.

Pic shows the rivalry and intrigues among the villagers. Also, fun is poked at the ruling political parties in Bavaria.

As indicated, Erler's effort here isn't exactly crowned by success. For a parody, the wit remains too much on the surface. Erler, still a young (33) director, is regarded by some as one of this country's biggest directorial hopes. This film lacks imagination especially in its script. The basically funny story hasn't been exploited to best advantage. Also, the whole thing is perhaps too Bavarian to make it an item of more general interest.

Technically, the film doesn't make the best impression. But this may not be Erler's fault. The print which Bavaria sent to Vienna for the festival had its deficiencies. Especially the poor sound had its negative effect. *Hans.*

Butasagom Tortenete
(Story Of My Foolishness)
(HUNGARIAN)
Vienna, April 5.
Hungarofilm release of Mafilm production. Stars Eva Ruttkay, Lajos Basti; features Manyi Kiss, Krisztina Keleti, Laszlo Mensaros. Directed by Marton Keleti. Screenplay, Miklos Gyarfas; camera, Barnabas Hegyi; music, Szabolcs Fenyes. At Vienna Film Festival. Running Time, 90 MINS.
Kati Kabok .... Eva Ruttkay
Laszlo Merey .... Lajos Basti
Marika .... Krisztina Keleti
Forbath, author ...... Laszlo Mensaros
Aunt Gizi .... Manyi Kiss
Jacqueline Noiret ...... Irina Petrescu
An actor .... Zoltan Varkonyi

Hungarian films have gained considerable prestige at pix festivals in recent years. This one, a delightful comedy, had its right place at the recent Viennese festival which is dedicated to humorous films. It was one of the most applauded entries here. Film benefits much from experienced direction and, also the excellent acting of Eva Ruttkay, one of the more popular Hungarian stage and screen actresses. This East European film looks to slide easily into western markets. It provides fine entertainment down the line.

Yarn revolves around Kati Kabok (Eva Ruttkay), wife of a famous actor (Lajos Basti), who looks back on the 10 years of their marriage. She wanted to become an actress but became the wife of an actor instead. Now, after ten years, she's finally given the chance for her first stage appearance. She's afraid of her debut but scores a big success. Film tells via flashbacks episodes of her married life. There's love, jealousy and all the familiar marriage quarrels and troubles.

Marton Keleti, the director, has created a lovable marriage comedy and given it the right polish. A big compliment must be paid to Miss Ruttkay who has the same charm, beauty and intelligence which some western actresses such as Lilli Palmer or Danielle Darrieux used to display in their comedies.

Style of this Magyar production is indeed reminiscent of a good Gallic comedy. The script displays imagination and originality on situations and its dialog. Thesping is fine throughout but, in the main, it's Eva Ruttkay who wins the most kudos.

Technically, this film is fully

satisfactory. It isn't a big pic but one of those charming little comedies which have become so rare these days. *Hans.*

Bangkok No Yoru
(Night In Bangkok)
(JAPANESE—COLORSCOPE)
Tokyo, April 1.
Toho Productions release of Sanezumi Fujimoto production. Stars Yudo Kayama, Chang Mei-Yao, features Yuriko Hoshi and Praprapon Pureem. Directed by Yasuki Chiba. Camera, Eastman Color, TohoScope. Running Time, 100 MINS.

A sudsy star-crossed lovers' effort, partly redeemed by expert widescreen color lensing of Tokyo, Kyoto, Taiwan, and Bangkok. Story has young medical student (Yuzo Kayama, co-star of Kurosawa's "Red Beard") meet up with Thai girl (Hong Kong actress Chang Mei-yoo). with love-affair complications ensuing from Japanese girl-he-left behind and Thai starlet Praprapon Pureem.

Story is transparent, with plot lines leading nowhere and Bangkok does not come on the screen at all until after an hour of viewing time. No art-house bids here, and nothing for the neighborhood houses, ethnic theatres seem the only bet. One more in the long and sad decline of Yasuki Chiba, once one of Japan's most promising directors, whose excellent 1957 "Shitamachi" (Downtown) has had numerous American and European showings. *Nald.*

Hoyten
(Freezing Point)
(JAPANESE)
Tokyo, March 26.
Daiei release and production. Stars Ayako Wakao, Eiji Funakoshi. Based on a novel by Ayako Miura. Directed by Satsuo Yamamoto. Running Time, 100 MINS.

This well-made programmer, nicely sentimental through most of its length, turns sudsy eventually and thereby perhaps forfeits international-market showings. For local and ethnic houses, however, it makes a strong bid because the fame of Ayako Miura's best-selling novel will have reached there.

About a playgirl wife and her jealous doctor-husband, the script has their little girl murdered and then makes the father, from a macabre sense of vengeance, adopt the criminal's little girl, telling the mother nothing about it.

Truth out, however, and before long the mother is informing the now-grown girl. It all makes a horrible kind of sense to girl (she's already been tipped off when her "brother" announces his more than fraternal love) and she takes overdose of sleeping pills.

Until this point, veteran director Satsuo Yamamoto has, against these odds, made a consistently interesting picture. Now, however, plot takes over. Turns out the girl is not really daughter of criminal, after all, but daughter of a doctor. Picture suggests happy ending and inadvertently suggests that had she really been murderer's daughter, suicide would have been deserved.

The ending vitiates both film and chances of foreign distributors' attention. Production values up to Daiei's usual standard and performance of Eiji Funakoshi (hero of "Fires on the Plain") unusually fine. *Nald.*

Johnny Tiger
(COLOR)

So-so white-Seminole Indian yarn with little excitement, but names of Robert Taylor, Geraldine Brooks and Chad Everett may help in selected situations.

Hollywood, April 6.
Universal release of R. John Hugh production. Stars Robert Taylor, Geraldine Brooks, Chad Everett; features Brenda Scott, Marc Lawrence, Ford Rainey. Directed by Paul Wendkos. Screenplay, Paul Crabtree, R. John Hugh; original story, Hugh; camera, Charles Straumer; music, John Green; editor, Harry Coswick; asst. director, Max Stein. Reviewed at Universal Studios, April 5, '66. Running Time, 102 MINS.
Dean .... Robert Taylor
Doc .... Geraldine Brooks
Johnny .... Chad Everett
Barbara .... Brenda Scott
Billie .... Marc Lawrence
Sam .... Ford Rainey
Wendy .... Carol Setlinger
Randy .... Stephen Wheeler
Louise .... Deanna Lund
Shalonee .... Pamela Melendez

Universal has a mildly interesting attraction in its release of R. John Hugh's indie production dealing with the Seminole Indians of Florida and lensed in their tribal territory. Story set against age-old tradition and projecting Robert Taylor as a dedicated schoolteacher, Geraldine Brooks a femme medico and Chad Everett a half-breed destined to be the tribe's chief, lacks the spark which might have carried audience and footage is far overlength. Although a seemingly honest piece of film-making, feature is conducive more to selected situations than the general market.

Hugh, who authored original yarn and also scripted with Paul Crabtree, has attempted to catch the idealism of a fading race and transformation of a cold intellectual intent upon bringing knowledge into a man of compassion. Neither seems likely to intrigue today's audience, as presented here. Main premise of the feud between Taylor, who wants to teach the children, and the dying Seminole chief who resents white man's ways and wants his breed grandson to renounce white civilization and assume his rightful place next to him deep in the Everglades, is static and fails to generate any degree of excitement.

Taylor, fulfilling demands of his role, plays character in a grim manner, without tolerance. Miss Brooks is in for allure and suggestion of romance with Taylor in climax, and Everett delivers effectively as the grandson torn between Indian tradition and modern progress. Brenda Scott, a newcomer, likewise shows to advantage as Taylor's daughter who weds Everett. Ford Rainey as the chief and Marc Lawrence a rather whimsical medicine man do well with their respective characters.

Paul Wendkos' direction occasionally rises above script and he has benefit of excellent color photography by Charles Strau-

mer. John Green's music score provides good pacing for unfoldment and Dick Williams' art direction is another plus. *Whit.*

Maya
(PANAVISION-COLOR)

Well-made jungle picture produced by King Bros. in India; exploitation should help as handy entry for action market.

Hollywood, April 7.
Metro release of King Bros. (Frank and Maurice) production. Stars Clint Walker, Jay North; features I. S. Johar, Sajid Kahn, Jairaj, Sonia Sahni. Directed by John Berry. Screenplay, John Fante; adaptation, Gilbert Wright; based on story, "The Wild Elephant," by Jalal Din, Lois Roth; camera (Technicolor), Gunter Senftleben; music, Riz Ortolani; editor, Richard V. Heermance. Reviewed at Metro Studios, April 6, '66. Running Time, 91 MINS.
Hugh Bowen .... Clint Walker
Terry Bowen .... Jay North
One-Eye .... I. S. Johar
Raji .... Sajid Kahn
Gammu Ghat .... Jairaj
Sheela .... Sonia Sahni
Village Spokesman .... Ullas
Raji's Father .... Nana Palshikar
One-Eye's Daughter .... Uma Rao
Station Master .... Madhusdan Pathak

King Bros., who in recent years have been filming their product abroad, have a well-turned-out jungle melodrama in their latest Metro release, lensed entirely in India. Natural exotic beauties of the sub-continent lend themselves admirably to a story which achieves stark realism and excitement is generated in building to a climaxing battle between two Bengal tigers and an enraged mother elephant. Technicolor feature, effectively photographed in Panavision and adaptable to exploitation, carries both juve and adult appeal.

John Fante's screenplay takes on the aspect of a saga in its tale of a young Hindu boy charged by his dying father with taking a rare white elephant to a distant temple where it will be a sacred symbol. Based on a story by Jalal Din and Lois Roth, "The Wild Elephant," and adapted by Gilbert Wright, plausibility is given subject through John Berry's strong direction and persuasive performances of a cast headed by Clint Walker and Jay North, only Hollywood members of troupe otherwise peopled by Indian actors.

Plottage follows young North, an American boy of 13, who goes to India to join his father, Walker, a white hunter who was nearly killed by a man-eating tiger and lost his nerve. Disillusioned by Walker's apparent cowardice, lad runs away into the jungle where he meets a young Hindu his own age who cares for his father's mammoth elephant, Maya, and her white calf, a treasure beyond compare in India. After father's death, North encourages the Hindu to fulfill what latter believes a hopeless mission, due to the distance and dangers involved. Journey proves hazardous, not alone from wild animals but from men who would steal the white elephant, but finally is successful.

Script is uneven for first couple

of reels but when main story of the elephant trek starts it progresses smoothly and melodramatic punch is inserted via some stirring animal footage. Young North, nicely bridging the gap from playing title role in "Dennis the Menace" teleseries displays a lively presence in a straight dramatic part, and Walker, in a necessarily smaller assignment, is convincing. As the young Hindu, Sajid Kahn is particularly outstanding. Interesting menace is afforded by I. S. Johar, as the one-eyed heavy who tries to get away with the white calf and is killed by the mother elephant. Jairaj as Walker's Sikh gunbearer and Sonia Sahni his companion are interesting types.

Gunter Senftleben's color photography catches much of the fascination of India and art direction by Edward S. Haworth and Maurice King production gets additional offscreen values from a music score composed by Riz Ortolani and editing by Richard V. Heermance. *Whit.*

The Murder Game
(BRITISH)

Slowpaced British melodrama. Languid direction and lack of marquee names spells little commercial appeal.

Hollywood, April 7.
Twentieth Century-Fox release of Lippert Films Ltd. (Robert L. Lippert-Jack Parsons) production. Features Ken Scott, Marla Landi, Trader Faulkner, Conrad Phillips, Gerald Sim, Duncan Lamont, Rosamund Greenwood, Victor Brooks. Directed by Sidney Salkow. Screenplay, Harry Spaulding, from story by Irving Yergin; camera, Gerry Massey-Collier; editor, Robert Winter; asst. director, Gordon Gilbert; music, Carlo Marcelli. Reviewed at 20th Century-Fox Studios, April 6, '66. Running Time, 72 MINS.
Steve Baldwin .... Ken Scott
Marie Aldrich .... Marla Landi
Chris Aldrich .... Trader Faulkner
Peter Shanley .... Conrad Phillips
Larry Lindstrom .... Gerald Sim
Inspector Telford .... Duncan Lamont
Mrs. Potter .... Rosamund Greenwood
Rev. Francis Hood .... Victor Brooks

"The Murder Game" is a slowpaced British melodrama that is generally too wordy and lacking in punch. Languid stride melodrama as directed by Sidney Salkow plus lack of marquee names, spells little favorable commercial prospect for the film in U.S. aside from filling bottom half of a dual-bill.

Script written by Harry Spaulding from story by Irving Yergin concerns Trader Faulkner as a Britisher just back from his honeymoon with his new bride, Marla Landi. She and American heavy Ken Scott—to whom it's revealed she's still wed—plan his murder. He overhears the plotting, and devises a counter scheme—setting up his own murder and making it look like the two of them did the dirty work.

Pic, however, does have some good moments of suspense and a fine realistic round of fisticuffs, with black and white camera work by Gerry Massey-Collier showing to advantage.

Faulkner is a talented actor, who comes across as well as he

can under the circumstances. Miss Landi, an attractive brunet, is convincing as the scheming wife, but the storyline is lacking in an explanation of some of her past deeds that lead her to do in her new husband. Scott is capable enough, although he seems to be playing his part in a tongue-in-cheek manner.

In general, however, the film is ineffective, lacking in pace and fumbling along. *Mitt.*

Delka Polibku Devadesat
(Kiss Length 90)
(CZECH)

Vienna, April 5.
A Filmstudio Barrandov (Prague) production. Stars Dana Syslova, and Oldrich Vlach. Directed by Antonin Moskalyk. Screenplay, Irena Hofmanova, Ota Hofman, Moskalyk; camera, Josef Novotny; music, Lubos Fiser. At Vienna Film Fest. Running Time, 92 MINS.
Eva .... Dana Syslova
Jarda .... Oldrich Vlach
Svitacek .... Otomar Krejca
Chief nurse .... Vlasta Chramostova

Czechoslovakia is reputed to be one of the leaders of quality films today. But this Czech comedy is not very impressive. In fact, it proved a near disappointment at the Viennese festival. Foreign prospects appear slim.

This Barrandov production centers on two young people whose marriage is blessed by the birth of quintuplets. It's the first time such a thing ever happened in their country. The young couple gets the spotlight. Agencies and newspapers send their reporters, medicos rush to the scene, the government sets up a commission to watch the life of the five babies.

A big research starts on the question how can five babies be born at one time. Has the length of the kiss before the procreation had some function? All these investigations drive the husband crazy. He finally demolishes the furniture of the elegant villa which has been placed at the couple's disposal. It doesn't take long before his wife is again expecting. To general public disappointment, it's just one baby daughter this time.

The whole thing has a somewhat naive touch. It lacks pace and the necessary tongue-in-cheek humor. The so-called jokes are mostly thin. Yet there is something sympathetic about this little comedy: It pokes fun at so many unpleasant things in a Commie country such as socialist planning, spying among citizens, etc. In this respect, this film has a refreshingly liberal attitude. Incidentally, it's Antonin Moskalyk's first full-length feature pic. He has made a number of vidpix.

The acting in this is sympathetic, but no more. Technically, the film is good to average. The score is quite appealing. *Hans.*

Mi Primera Novia
(My First Girl Friend)
(ARGENTINE-COLOR)

Buenos Aires, April 5.
Argentine Sono Film release or GCL production. Stars Palito Ortega; features Evangelina Salazar, Dean Reed, Luis Tasca, Aida Luz, Tono Andreu, Norberto Suarez. Directed by Enrique Carreras. Screenplay, Sixto Pondal Rios from story by Pondal Rios and Carlos

Olivari; camera (Eastmancolor), Antonio Merayo; music, Lucio Milena; editor, Jorge Garate. Previewed at Monumental Theatre, B.A. Running Time, **93 MINS.**

The 1965 statistics on individual earnings by song writers and singers were topped by Palito Ortega, who also got the RCA Golden Disk for the third time in a row. A Palito single sells up to 200.000 copies in Argentina and his first two pix were winners. The juvenile idol—currently making an album at RCA's Nashville studios —makes his third film appearance in this tinter, a remake of the 1941 pic, "Adolescence." This pic already landed big coin in summer resorts and has started strongly on its run here.

Casting of Evangelina Salazar, who shot ahead on tv last year, is a b.o. plus for the domestic market. Selling to Spanish-speaking countries seem certain.

Story of a student who resorts to foul play when trying to keep his girl-friend away from a bit older, willing-to-wed suitor, has lost much of its original charm, heart and character observations in the process of being transformed into a musical. However, what remains of the plot and dialogue gets laughs from teenagers in between Palito's singing.

Acting and direction made no effort to go beyond routine entertainment, effective for this star's fans. Shot in and around suburban homes, its technical credits are standard. *Din.*

Operation Air Raid: Red Muffler
(KOREAN—COLOR)
Tokyo, April 1.

Snochiku release of a Shin (Korea) Productions film. Stars Yungkyoon Shin. Produced and directed by Sang Okk Shin. Camera, Eastman Color, Cinema-Scope. At Tokyo Gekijo, Tokyo. Running Time, **90 MINS.**

A well-made action drama, this Korean picture won the "best" award for Director Sang Okk Shin, actor Yungkvoon Shin, as well as for editing at the 1964 Asian Film Festival in Taipei. This first Korean effort to gain roadshow and national exhibition in Japan should offer America and Europe an interesting view of the Korean War, seen through Korean eyes.

A ROK Airforce group in 1951 is about to begin their hundredth sortie and the target is an important North Korean bridge. During the preparations and the final attack, flashbacks show the romantic triangle.

Though the situation is a familiar one (and film-goers may spot similarities to "The Bridges of Toko-Ri") the picture is put together with integrity and Director Shin knows how to polish up a cliche so that it retains some of its original luster. Consequently the film is fresh and sincere and there is no cynicism, no stereotyping. These people are reliving an important page of their history and are doing it with candor and integrity.

They are also doing it with a lot of style. This expertly-filmed motion picture has a finish and gloss to it that one associates mainly with American product. The color is excellent and wide-

screen is intelligently used. Final destruction of the bridge and the airfights that lead up to it are so well done that they seem like actual battle footage. *Nald.*

Berlin ist eine Suende wert
(Berlin Is Worth a Sin)
(GERMAN)
Berlin, April 5.

A Will Tremper production. Stars Eva Renzi, Harald Leipnitz, and Paul Hubschmid. Directed by Tremper. Screenplay, Tremper. Camera, Wolfgang Luehrse; music, Peter Thomas; editor, Ursula Moehrle. Previewed at Geyer Werke, West Berlin. Running Time, **97 MINS.**

Alexandra Borowski	Eva Renzi
Sigbert Lahner	Harald Leipnitz
Joachim Steigerwald	Paul Hubschmid
Timo, photographer	Umberto Orsini
Doctor	Rudolf Schuendler

This is Will Tremper's third feature film. Like the two previous Tremper pix, it had a modest (about $125.000) budget and employed players who don't think that a high salary is the thing as long as they are handled by an interesting director. In this respect. Tremper, the refreshing outsider among this country's film creators, enjoys a reputation of his own around here. Also his third opus was shot without a properly prepared script and against actual Berlin backgrounds.

Despite quite a few deficiencies, this looks like Tremper's best pic to date. Technically, he has learned a lot. There are many fine passages leaning not only on acting but also the scenes. What may militate against this film's commercial chances is a rather thin story.

However, the interesting lensing and the imaginative direction makes for an enjoyable film. Some may take a fancy to what goes on in this sex-loaded film which also tackles political themes. It looks okay for some special situations but chances for the big market appear limited.

It's all about 21-year old Alexandra, a pretty model, who sees a dream come true when she first visits Berlin, the native town of her father. She soon finds herself in the hands (and also beds) of many men. She hops from romance to romance and enjoys this kind of life, the more so as she's a down-to-earth gal who doesn't mince matters. Her partners vary with regard to age and mentality: There's a 48-year old successful architect (Paul Hubschmid), his 38-year old employee (Harold Leipnitz) and a 28-year old conceited star photographer (Umberto Orsini), all experts on sex matters.

Occasionally, this city's most topical building, the Communist wall which separates East from West Berlin, gets into the picture. Talk eventually centers on political subjects. End of film returns to what is called love.

There is no doubt that Tremper has obtained fine performances from his cast. This especially applies to Eva Renzi, a new find, and real talent. It's a treat to watch her. Supporting cast includes (typical of Tremper pix) many prominent Berlin people who are not professionals, such as Oestergard, top fashion designer here; Ricci, noted nightclub operator;

Zellermayer, famed hotelier, and some society people of Berlin.

Film's technical credits are very good. The score by Peter Thomas is excellent. Via its sexual, social and political ingredients, Tremper tried to give with his third opus an insight into today's West Berlin. He tried to avoid the cliche. *Hans.*

The Glass Bottom Boat
(SONGS-PANAVISION-COLOR)

Doris Day starrer with usual indications of okay reception; names of Rod Taylor and Arthur Godfrey to further attract.

Hollywood, April 14.

Metro release of Martin Melcher-Everett Freeman production. Stars Doris Day, Rod Taylor, Arthur Godfrey; features John McGiver, Paul Lynde, Edward Andrews, Eric Fleming, Dom De Luise, Elisabeth Fraser, Dick Martin. Directed by Frank Tashlin. Screenplay, Everett Freeman; camera (Metrocolor), Leon Shamroy; music, Frank De Vol; editor, John McSweeney; asst. director, Al Jennings. Reviewed at Pacific's Pantages Theatre, April 13, '66. Running Time, **110 MINS.**

Jennifer Nelson	Doris Day
Bruce Templeton	Rod Taylor
Axel Nordstrom	Arthur Godfrey
Ralph Goodwin	John McGiver
Homer Cripps	Paul Lynde
Gen. Wallace Bleecker	Edward Andrews
Edgar Hill	Eric Fleming
Julius Pritter	Dom De Luise
Nina Bailey	Elisabeth Fraser
Zack Molloy	Dick Martin
Mr. Fenimore	George Tobias
Mrs. Fenimore	Alice Pearce
Anna Miller	Ellen Corby
Donna	Dee J. Thompson

Doris Day enters the very modern world of rocketry and espionage in "The Glass Bottom Boat," an expensively-mounted Martin Melcher-Everett Freeman production in which she stars with Rod Taylor and Arthur Godfrey. Given frequently to sight gags and frenzied comedy performances, much of the humor of the Panavision-Metrocolor film is contrived in a loosely-developed plotline but builds into a slambang laugh ending.

Miss Day delivers one of her customary wide-eyed romantic portrayals as she's caught in a web of circumstances in which she's suspected of being a Russian spy. Some other comedy stalwarts, including Dick Martin (taking time out from his clowning with teammate Dan Rowan), add to the hilarious content. Frank Tashlin, who knows his way through every comedic situation, directs with an eye to milking each situation of possibility and has set a hectic pace in a chase finale which should have audiences screaming.

Original screenplay by Everett Freeman, who co-produced, fits into the current spy cycle and additionally attaches to the airspace pattern, elements to allow exploitation apart from star's name value. Bits of business are inventive at times, such as Miss Day glimpsing that Man from U.N.C.L.E. — Napoleon Solo, no less (in the person of Robert Vaughn) — leaning against a bar, but he's the man who isn't there when she does double-take. Liberal use is made of electronic gimmicks for several near-belly laughs, such as a dandy little kitchen cleaner that abhors dirt and loves to attack.

Star plays a conscientious public relations staffer in a space laboratory where Taylor, the engineering genius heading the facility, has invented a device both the U.S. government and the Soviets want. He falls for her and to keep her always by his side invents the idea of having her write a very definitive biography of him. She becomes a spy suspect because she has a dog named Vladimir, which she's always calling on the telephone so its ringing will give her pet exercise when she isn't there, and because she follows a standing order that every bit of paper should be burned. Windup has her in innocent possession of the equation for the sought-after device known as GISMO.

Miss Day gives part the works as she decides to play it cool and do some phony cloak-and-daggering. She chirps trio of songs, as well, including the title song, by Joe Lubin, "Soft As the Starlight," by Lubin and Jerome Howard, and the standard "Que Sera." with her usual know-how rendition. She collabs on first and third with Godfrey, who scores strongly in making his film bow as her father, operator of a glass-bottom sight-seeing boat at Catalina. Taylor lends his usual masculine presence effectively, both as the inventor and romantic vis-a-vis.

Standout support if offered, too, by Dick Martin, Taylor's partner and Pentagon contact; Paul Lynde, lab's security guard responsible for suspicion being directed at femme star; Edward Andrews, a general who insists she isn't what she seems; Dom De Luise, an inept hi-fi installer who fails miserably in spying; Eric Fleming, a CIA agent.

Leon Shamroy's photography is a work of art. The art direction by George W. Davis and Edward Carfagno and set decorations by Henry Grace and Hugh Hunt provide handsome settings. Other plus credits include Frank De Vol's music score, John McSweeney's editing. *Witt.*

The Night Of The Grizzly
(COLOR-SCOPE)

Dull programmer about the Old West and a town ravaged by a bear. Subplots, script, direction and performances all formula. Mostly video personalities among principals. Fair dual entry.

Hollywood, April 12.
Paramount Pictures release of a Burt Dunne production. Features Clint Walker, Martha Hyer, Keenan Wynn, Nancy Kulp. Directed by Joseph Pevney. Screenplay, Warren Douglas; camera (Technicolor-Techniscope), Harold Lipstein, Loyal Griggs; editor, Philip W. Anderson; music, Leith Stevens; song, Jay Livingston, Ray Evans; asst. director, Howard Roessel. Reviewed at Paramount Studio, April 11, '66. Running Time, 102 MINS.
Jim Cole .... Clint Walker
Angela Cole .... Martha Hyer
Jed Curry .... Keenan Wynn
Wilhelmina Peterson ..... Nancy Kulp
Charlie Cole .... Kevin Brodie
Hazel Squires .... Ellen Corby
Hank .... Jack Elam
Tad Curry .... Ron Ely
Duke Squires .... Med Flory
Cass Dowdy .... Leo Gordon
Sam Potts .... Don Haggerty
Cal Curry .... Sammy Jackson
Gypsy Cole....Victoria Paige Meyerink
Meg .... Candy Moore
Cotton Benson .... Regis Toomey

"The Night Of The Grizzly" is a disjointed drama about an ex-lawman who fights several men and one beast to retain his inherited homestead. Thin basic premise is overpowered by formula scripting, routine execution and non-essential vignette. The Burt Dunne production, with adequate below-the-line values, emerges as a tame, two-dimensional trifle. Cast is headed by Clint Walker, and includes other players known for tv work. Dullsville b.o. likely for Paramount release on general duals.

Warren Douglas is credited with a script, based on a Walker idea, which never really gets going in any one direction. The grizzly bear of the title doesn't even enter the plot for about 20 minutes, during which an overly lingering exposition introduces Walker, wife Martha Hyer, and family brood. Candy Moore is the orphaned niece whom they are raising, while Kevin Brodie, and Victoria Paige Meyerink play the teenage boy and moppet daughter, respectively.

Keenan Wynn is the land-greedy neighbor who wants the Walker acreage for his worthless sons, Ron Ely and Sammy Jackson. Wynn gives too much humor to the role, while Ely and Jackson are appropriately shallow. Latter, however, does start to fall for Miss Moore, although this plot turn is one of many that fizz out. Med Flory, Ellen Corby's shiftless son, makes bootleg whiskey for the local crowd, and is a buddy to Ely and Jackson.

Another sidebar is Nancy Kulp, of "The Beverly Hillbillies" vidseries and potato chip teleblurbs, who runs the general store. She gets off several comedy lines in her pursuit of Don Haggerty, Walker's partner. Haggerty gets killed by the bear, thus snuffing out Miss Kulp's raison d'etre, and she is seen no more. Jack Elam is the town bum who appears regularly with the precocious Miss Meyerink.

After about 66 minutes of running time, Leo Gordon enters as the former trigger-happy Walker aide whom the latter sent to prison. Remainder of film is their competition to kill the ravenging bear, whose forays wiped out local live stock. The humor then departs the pic, and footage is a tedious succession of slow-paced melodrama until the bear is killed.

Joseph Pevney directed a stock cast in stock fashion, with results adequate for the script. Walker is stiffly stolid, although action perks up when he dispatches with a few well-placed blows the weakly-motivated fisticuffs. Miss Hyer seems ill at ease as a frontier wife. Regis Toomey, the town banker, delivers a pro performance, ditto Miss Corby. Gordon leaves a good impression, suggesting a lot more talent than he is permitted to show. The title beast is rarely seen.

Loyal Griggs lensed the exteriors, shot at Big Bear, near Lake Arrowhead, and these Technicolor-Techniscope shots add a lush touch. Harold Lipstein took over when Griggs became ill. Setups are standard. Leith Stevens' score is routine, ditto a song, "Angela", by Jay Livingston and Ray Evans. Philip W. Anderson trimmed to a longish 102 minutes. Other technical credits are standard. *Murf.*

Svegliati E Uccidi-Lutring
(Too Soon to Die)
(ITALO-FRENCH)
(Color-Songs)

Rome, April 12.
Titanus release of a Joseph Fryd-Carlo Lizzani production for Sanson-Castoro Film (Rome)-C.I.P.R.A. (Paris). Stars Lisa Gastoni, Robert Hoffmann; features Gian Maria Volonte. Directed by Carlo Lizzani. Screenplay, Ugo Pirro, from story by Carlo Lizzani and Pirro; camera (Eastmancolor), Armando Nannuzzi; music, Ennio Morricone; editor, Franco Fraticelli. At Adriano, Rome. Running Time, 118 MINS.
Luciano Lutring ..... Robert Hoffmann
Candida Lutring .... Lisa Gastoni
Inspector Moroni....Gian Maria Volonte

Fast-paced, slickly outfitted and dramatically staged action drama on the short criminal career of Luciano Lutring, a headline-grabbing bandit familiar to this part of the world. A fine entry in the action market, with word-of-mouth a stronger builder-upper than the cast strength because the players are among many plus factors of a pic which is tailor-made for patrons of the genre. Its human and in-depth introspection give it extra-selling handles in general appeal.

Very loosely based on the real-life career of a fledgling bandido who was built into something bigger than himself in recent years thanks to an interested press buildup, film tells of his initiation as a car thief, his meeting his eventual spouse, her early but naive attempts to steer him clear, his inevitable snowballing into a crime name without the ability, brains or guts to back it. This winds up with Lutring chased to desperation by French police after almost everyone, including his wife and even a Milan police inspector, have tried to brake his misguided bent.

Opening half of pic is text-book in visual action pacing as it segues from one exploit to another with some neat editing, sharp lensing, and the always able and crisp direction by Carlo Lizzani. Pace slows a bit in second half as film's moral point is being made that Lutring is really being used by almost everyone, including the police, who build him into an underworld figure in order to trap other gangsters they feel more dangerous. In many ways, the pic harks back to great gangland pix of the U.S. in the 30's.

Lisa Gastoni walks off with thespic honors (as well as chirping some song originals in fine style) as Lutring's well-meaning wife. It's a rounded performance which should raise plenty of present and future attention. Robert Hoffman is physically perfect for role and brings it across ably despite the part's lack of range. Gian Maria Volonte' and a brace of French and Italian actors add solid backing, though the spotlight is generally on the principals.

Opulent physical trimmings and neatly-captured location footage in Paris, Milan, Nice, Amsterdam and other colorful spots are further production pluses, as is Ennio Morricone's haunting musical score. As noted, Franco Fraticelli's editing is outstanding, especially in the no-lag first half and breath-taking finale. For non-Italian auds, some trimming for pace conversely could be done in central stretch of pic, to make it fit the remainder of film's rhythm. *Hawk.*

Nouveau Journal D'Un Femme En Blanc
(New Diary of a Woman In White)
(FRENCH)

Paris, April 12.
Gaumont release of SOPAC-Gaumont production. With Danielle Volle, Michel Ruhl, Claude Titre, Josee Steiner, Bernard Dheran. Directed by Claude Autant-Lara. Screenplay, Jean Aurenche from book by Andre Soubiron; camera, Michel Kelber; editor, Madeleine Gug. At Marignan, Paris. Running Time, 115 MINS.
Claude .... Danielle Volle
Jacques .... Michel Ruhl
Doctor .... Claude Titre
Girl .... Josee Steiner
Agent .... Bernard Dheran

Sequel to a popular sudsy tale of a nurse who fought for abortion but then found herself pregnant and decided to have the child, "Diary of a Woman in White," again deals with an abortion. But this time, it's heightened by the fact that the baby probably will be deformed. Plenty of pious and forthright talk, but slim characterizations and melodrama show up in this drama.

It may do okay here but appears mainly for possible exploiter use on its subject abroad, with art chances dim. The nurse takes an alcoholic to a small town and stays to take care of him. Love blossoms as she gets mixed up with a pregnant woman.

Follows soul-searching on the right to do an abortion and the nurse finally going through with it and ready to face justice. Film is vague on its attitude towards abortion. Acting is generally phlegmatic. Director Claude Autant-Lara has used too many closeups to give this an even more static quality alongside its rather pompous people and palaver.

This emerges a fairly obvious medico pic. It is technically good but looms mainly a local item. *Mosk.*

Les Fetes Galantes
(The Lace Wars)
(FRENCH-ROMANIAN-COLOR)

Paris, April 19.
Gaumont release of Gaumont-Studio Bucaresti production. Stars Jean-Pierre Cassel; features Philippe Avron, Jean Richard, Genevieve Casile, Marie Dubois, Alfred Adam. Written and directed by Rene Clair. Camera (Eastmancolor), Christian Matras; editor, Louisette Hautecoeur. At Paris, Paris. Running Time, 90 MINS.
Joli-Coeur .... Jean-Pierre Cassel
Thomas .... Philippe Avron
Prince .... Jean Richard
Helene .... Genevieve Casile
Divine .... Marie Dubois
Allenberg .... Gyorgy Kovacs
Frederic .... Christian Barratier
Valda .... Jean Payen

Rene Clair now sits ensconced in the Academic Francaise and has many pre-war comedy hits to his name. But his latest film venture in over five years just lacks the delicate wit, balance and comedic wryness to bring it off. This look at the romantic wars of the 18th Century, when men stopped fighting for lunch, is too fragile and lacking in pace to have it come off.

Some special situations abroad may be in store on its color and intermittently comic scenes. But there are not enough of them to give this much chance for the more demanding arty spots. Clair has wanted to parody war by giving it an almost silly romantic air. All of this remains an old-fashioned romp with some production dress and okay playing but sans the needed punch to bring it off.

Jean-Pierre Cassel is an adventurer caught up in a war between two Dukedoms. He becomes the confidant of the Princess in a chateau being besieged. He goes between the lines to make her bid to the rival Prince so as to end the wars through an alliance. There are some okay fight scenes, trysts and an ironic ending as peace comes but with the Princess already making eyes at another. Co-production was made in Romania with okay color and dress. Acting is charming if somewhat wooden. *Mosk.*

A Big Hand for The Little Lady
(COLOR)

Outstanding comedy about a poker-game in the old West, with surprise ending. First-rate in all departments. Henry Fonda, Joanne Woodward, Jason Robards, Paul Ford head a powerful cast. Can be sold to all age groups for strong b.o. returns.

Hollywood, April 21.

Warner Bros. Pictures release of an Eden Production, produced and directed by Fielder Cook. Stars Henry Fonda, Joanne Woodward, Jason Robards; features Charles Bickford, Burgess Meredith, Kevin McCarthy, Robert Middleton, Paul Ford. Screenplay, Sidney Carroll, based on his teleplay, "Big Deal At Laredo"; camera (Technicolor), Lee Garmes; editor, George Rohrs; music, David Raksin; asst. director, Joe Kenny. Reviewed at Pacific's Pantages Theatre, L.A., April 20, '66. Running Time, 95 MINS.

Meredith	Henry Fonda
Mary	Joanne Woodward
Henry Drummond	Jason Robards
Benson Tropp	Charles Bickford
Doc Scully	Burgess Meredith
Otto Habershaw	Kevin McCarthy
Dennis Wilcox	Robert Middleton
Ballinger	Paul Ford
Jesse Buford	John Qualen
Sam Rhine	James Kenny
Toby	Allen Collins
Pete	Jim Boles
Jackie	Gerald Michenaud
Mrs. Drummond	Virginia Gregg
Old Man in Saloon	Chester Conklin
Mrs. Craig	Mae Clarke
Owney Price	Ned Glass
Mr. Stribling	James Griffith
Sparrow	Noah Keen
Fleeson	Milton Selzer
Celie Drummond	Louise Glenn
Arthur	William Cort

A big hand for "A Big Hand For The Little Lady," and for all hands involved in this outstanding comedy. Kid-glove casting, razor-sharp scripting, firstrate performances and topnotch direction add up to a totally entertaining Fielder Cook production, localed in the old West. Switcheroo ending makes for a brilliantly executed hoax, which will delight all age groups. A very strong marquee lineup, plus imaginative selling, should produce hot b.o. returns from Warner Bros. release in general situations.

For record purposes, pic is based on "Big Deal At Laredo," a 1962 Dupont tv special produced-directed by Cook, and written by Sidney Carroll, who adapted the 48-minute teleplay into a fully-integrated screen version which is packed with finely-etched characterizations and never suggests an over-inflated vidscript. Also, this is Cook's third feature, and first Hollywood-made pic — an impressive entry to Coast feature filming.

Story is cued by an iris shot of Charles Bickford, woman-hating and sardonic undertaker who is doing the Paul Revere bit in his horse-drawn hearse. Reason for the hurry is the rounding up of Kevin McCarthy, a suave lawyer who leaves a court case, and Jason Robards, who exits his daughter's wedding, in order that an annual high stake poker game can convene. Penurious John Qualen and gruff Robert Middleton complete the quintet.

Enter Henry Fonda and Joanne Woodward, traveling couple with child Gerald Michenaud, en route to new home in Texas. Fonda, a sucker for cards, blows the family savings, precipitating a heart attack for which town medic Burgess Meredith treats him. Miss Woodward, knowing nothing of poker, wins a big pot, aided by collateral-conscious banker Paul Ford who surprisingly accepts her card hand as security.

Cook never shows the cards, and audiences need not know a thing about poker. Emphasis instead is on the comedy values which exude from every major and minor character, all of whom are completely believable in expert delivery under Cook's sure directional hand. There is a fine economy in the sharp dialog which is enhanced all the more by a cast that knows how to act as well as to react.

Among supporting players, James Kenny scores as the bartender-game banker, and vet actress Mae Clarke has an effective one-line bit. Milton Selzer's officious bank teller is excellent, while William Cort registers solidly as Robards' prospective son-in-law. The (false) climax reveals the effect of Miss Woodward's courage on her fellow card players, while the real climax reveals that audiences have been taken on a hilarious trip up a garden path.

Lee Garmes' terrific Technicolor lensing complements the acting and direction, ditto David Raksin's full-bodied scoring which always fits the mood. Pacing is excellent, save for a bit of foot-dragging in the final few minutes. George Rohrs edited to a brisk 95 minutes. Robert Smith designed the production with a great eye for unobtrusive, but effective settings. Joel Freeman was associate producer. Other WB studio technical credits are excellent. *Murf.*

Rasputin—
The Mad Monk
(BRITISH—SCOPE—COLOR)

Hammer Films' global round-up of master villains had to get to Rasputin eventually. Excellent technical aspects help gloss over cornball plot. Should flourish in intended market.

20 Century-Fox release of a Seven Arts-Hammer production. Produced by Anthony Nelson Keys. Features Christopher Lee, Barbara Shelley, Richard Pasco, Francis Matthews, Suzan Farmer, Nicholas Pennell, Renee Asherson. Directed by Don Sharp. Screenplay, John Elder; camera (Cinemascope, DeLuxe Color), Michael Reed; editor, Roy Hyde; sound editor, Roy Baker; music, composed by Don Banks. Reviewed in N.Y., April 20, '66. Running time: 92 MINS.

Rasputin	Christopher Lee
Sonia	Barbara Shelley
Dr. Zargo	Richard Pasco
Ivan	Francis Matthews
Vanessa	Suzan Farmer
Peter	Nicholas Pennell
Tsarina	Renee Asherson
Innkeeper	Derek Francis
Patron	Alan Tilvern
The Bishop	Joss Ackland
The Abbott	John Welsh
Tsarvitch	Robert Duncan
Court Physician	John Bailey

This British import, to be released as top-half of a double bill with "The Reptiles," is a worthy entry, if not a classic, for the shocker market. As the screen peccadilloes of Russia's bad boy have, in the past, wound up in court, producer Anthony Nelson Keys had scripter John Elder take a somewhat fanciful (and unbelievable) approach to the subject. As a result, the dastardly villain has been given some attributes that are certainly colorful.

Actually, this Hammer Film effort's surface appeal, in its really first-class color photography, art direction and professional casting, makes the thin plot immaterial. Christopher Lee's Rasputin is completely in character — huge, deep-voiced, compelling stare — oh, he's a proper rascal—and this variation makes him also a dancer (not that one ever sees a long shot of dancing. It's usually his upper half, then cut to a real dancer's feet, then back. But it goes with the atmosphere and is, after the first shock, quite acceptable).

Religious aspects of l'affaire Rasputin are skimmed over, the only two dignitaries portrayed as colorless and dull. Of the Russian court, the Czarina (Renee Asherson) and the Czarevitch (Robert Duncan) are the only Romanoffs shown, the plot revolving (after the monk's entry into court affairs, accredited to his hypnotic influence over a lady-in-waiting) on a revenge plot by the would-be fiance (Nicholas Pennell) of the seduced lady-in-waiting (Barbara Shelley). His principal accomplices are an alcoholic doctor (Richard Pasco), and an Army officer (Francis Matthews), whose sister (Suzan Farmer) has been lined up as Rasputin's next victim.

Director Don Sharp wisely keeps everyone involved in a variety of situations that emphasize action, whether it's violence or seduction. The shocker mood is set early when the libertine holy man, fighting off a young assailant, chops off his hand with a scythe. After such ensuing action as flinging acid into Pennell's face, the climatic murder attempt is elaborated with the use of poison, stabbing and finally flinging Rasputin out a window, but not before he has polished off Pasco.

Keys and Sharp owe much credit to the work of production designer Bernard Robinson and art director Don Mingaye, who make what are certainly small sets take on the aspects of tremendous palace rooms, beautifully appointed and enriched by Michael Reed's excellent De Luxe Color and Cinemascope camerawork. Don Banks' score is also a big assist in underscoring suspense and action. *Robe.*

The Secret Seven
(ITALIAN-SPANISH-COLOR)

Greek adventure drama in color, story revolves around seven men who fight the ruling Spartan tyrant. Encounters and battle scenes predominate. Acting and technical aspects are only mediocre.

Hollywood, April 12.

MGM release of Columbus SPA-Atenea Films S.L. (Cleto Fontini and Italo Zingarelli) coproduction. Features Tony Russel, Helga Line, Massimo Serato, Gerard Tichy, Renato Baldini, Livio Lorgenzon, Barta Barry, Joseph Marc, Kris Huerta, Gian Solar, Frank Sorman, Emma Baron, Pedro Mari, Tomas Blance and Renato Montalban. Directed by Alberto De Martino. Screenplay, De Martino, Sandro Continenza; camera (Eastman-color), John

Bergame; music, Carlo Franci; asst. director, Jaime Bayarri; editor, Othello Colangeli. Reviewed at MGM Studios, April 11, '66. Running Time, 92 MINS.

Leslio .... Tony Russel
Lydia .... Helga Line
Axel .... Massimo Serato
Rabirio .... Gerard Tichy
Kadem .... Renato Baldini
Rubio .... Livio Lorgenzon
Baxo .... Barta Barry
Luzor .... Joseph Marc
Gular .... Kris Huerta
Nakassar .... Gian Solar
Aristograt .... Frank Sorman
Mother .... Emma Baron
Ario .... Pedro Mari
Panuzio .... Tomas Blance
Aristocrat .... Renato Montalban

A Greek sword and sandal adventure drama, this Italian-Spanish coproduction leans heavily on battle scenes, with seven heroes against the tyranny of Spartan rule. Color photography is good but other technical aspects only mediocre: lip sync is bad and dialogue is juvenile. Along with no name cast and only passable visual effects, lackluster sets and scenery, pic looks likely for lower bill slotting.

Plot evolves around two brothers and five ex-galley slave accomplices fighting off a 4th Century B.C. reign of terror. One brother, Leslio, takes up as resident architect at the palace of the ruling tyrant to counterspy military activities. He and sidekick continuously change clothes a la Batman and Robin to join brother, Axel, and other four in depleting segments of the enemy forces. Action skims from one encounter to another with all seven miraculously unscathed. In finale they loot gold from the palace vaults and leap thousands of feet into the sea.

Acting is static and occasionally embarrassing and attempt at Robin Hood-type camaraderie is overdone. Costumes by Antonelli-Baston are more Roman than Grecian and the sets look slightly dog-eared from use. Alberto De Martino's direction is servicable, while the camera work of John Bergame lacks inventiveness. Music score by Carlo Franci roars and rattles gustily, building suspense to visually unexciting scenes.

Of the seven heroes, only three look athletic enough to fit the demands of their parts. But the brothers, as played by Tony Russel and Massimo Serato don't cut the swordplay bit at all. *Dool.*

Son of a Gunfighter
(El Hijo de Pistolero)
(SPANISH-SCOPE-COLOR)

Fine shoot-em-up, loaded with excellent color and plenty of action.

Metro release of Lester Welch production (in association with Zurbano Films). Features entire cast. Directed by Paul Landres. Screenplay, Clarke Reynolds; camera (Metrocolor), Manuel Berenguer; music, Frank Barber; Sherman Rose; assistant director, Joe Ochoa. Reviewed at Metro Studios, April 19, '66. Running time: 92 MINS.

Johnny .... Russ Tamblyn
Fenton .... Kieron Moore
Ketchum .... James Philbrook
Don Fortuna .... Fernando Rey
Pilar .... Maria Granada
Morales .... Aldo Sambrell
Pecos .... Antonio Casas
Esteban .... Barta Barri
Sheriff .... Ralph Browne
Fuentes .... Andy Anza
Joaquin .... Fernando Hilbeck
Stagecoach Guard .... Hector Quiroga
Maria .... Carmen Tarrazo
Sarita .... Maria Jose Collado

"Son Of A Gunfighter" is a fine shoot-em-up, loaded with excellent color and plenty of action, emphasized by widescreen lensing in Cinemascope. Pace and direction are also in the plus category, and coupled with strong characterization of Russ Tamblyn as a rugged western type, makes this an above-average oater.

Spanish-locationed western does a good job of recreating the Mexican-American border country of the 1870's, and Paul Landres' direction of the Clarke Reynolds' script makes the story a believable yarn.

Strong adventure yarn has Tamblyn as an enigmatic man dedicated to one purpose — hunting down outlaw leader James Philbrook, because he killed Tamblyn's mother. Tamblyn is injured in a shootout, then nursed back to health on Fernando Rey's hacienda just across the Rio Grande. While recuperating, Rey's daughter, Maria Granada, falls in love with him, but he ignores her and continues his pursuit of Philbrook.

Eventually he meets up with the outlaw — an old gunfighter — and learns that Philbrook is really his own father. Hence, the title. Neither man will draw on the other. The two join forces and aid Rey in eliminating Mexican bandidos from harassing his hacienda. Philbrook is killed in the action, as are most of the bandits. The story ends with Tamblyn falling in love with the senorita.

Tamblyn comes across extremely virile and rugged as the hunter, and the part should spell more top action films for him. Philbrook is a believable heavy as the aging, but still-active gunfighter. Miss Granada is a delightfully attractive femme who convincingly provides the love interest for Tamblyn. Fernando Rey as the Mexican landowner, Kieron Moore as a deputy also hunting Philbrook, and Aldo Sambrell as the bandido leader all turn in good performances and aid the extensive action.

Landres' direction puts plenty of spirit into the pacing, helping to make the pic an interesting hour and a half. Cinemascope lensing by cameraman Manuel Berenguer provides a wide sweep of excellent scenery, adding a definite treat to the eyes.

Regarding the top musical backing by Frank Barber, based on the theme penned by Robert Mellin, of particular note is the use of a single flute in the musical arrangement, to denote Tamblyn in his solo search in the old west.

"Son of A Gunfighter" is a variation on an old western theme, but adds much with the Tamblyn performance, the Landres' direction and the photographic sweep of the Spanish countryside. *Mitt.*

Hikinige
(Hit-and-Run)
(JAPAN)

Tokyo, April 16.

Toho Productions Release. Stars Hideko Takamine, Yoko Tsukasa, Eitaro Osawa, Hisashi Nakayama, Toshio Kurosawa, Daisuke Kato. Directed by Mikio Naruse. Produced by Masumi Fujimoto. Script by Zenzo Matsuyama. Photographed by Rokuro Nighigaki. Music by Masaru Sato. TohoScope. Running Time: 100 MINS.

Veteran director Mikio Naruse is known in America for such subtle and restrained pictures as "When A Woman Ascends the Stairs." Scenerist Zenso Matsuyama wrote such slick tear-jerkers as "The Happiness of Us Alone" and "Could I But Live." The combination in this film is not propitious but the film has its values. The photography is, even for a Japanese picture, extraordinary; the music is by Kurosawa's favorite composer; Naruse's way with his actors is very persuasive; and Hideko Takamine, Japan's most popular actress, is given a very meaty role.

She is working-class mother whose only child is run over and killed by the philandering wife of a company president. He hushes the tragedy up but the mother takes a job in his house and aims to do in his young son, just the age of the child that was killed.

Borrowing from "High and Low," Matsuyama works out a heavily ironic plot but neglects interesting character facets (i.e., is the mother right, or even sympathetic in what she does? Rather, perhaps, is she not being corrupted by her own tragedy?) in favor of an ending which kicks the dead horse of the local traffic problem.

Still, there is enough in the film to hold interest. It is a solidly made programmer and will probably find ready audiences in U.S. Japanese-language houses. *Chie.*

Ride Beyond Vengeance
(COLOR)

Flat oater about prodigal Chuck Connors learning that "you can't ever go home again" the hard way. Thin production values, digressing plot. Some raw violence thrown in. Marquee lineup, of film and vidfilm faces, suggests more than is delivered but may help the sell. Fair b.o. on action duals.

Hollywood, April 8.

Columbia Pictures release of a Mark Goodson-Bill Todman, Sentinel and Fenady Associates Production, produced by Andrew J. Fenady. Stars Chuck Connors; features rest of cast. Directed by Bernard McEveety. Screenplay, Fenady, based on novel, "The Night Of The Tiger," by Al Dewlen; camera (Pathecolor), Lester Shorr; editor, Otho Lovering; music, Richard Markowitz; song, Markowitz, Fenady; asst. director, Lee H. Katzin. Reviewed at Columbia Studios, April 7, '66. Running time, 100 MINS.

Jonas Trapp .... Chuck Connors
Brooks Durham .... Michael Rennie
Jessie .... Kathryn Hays
Mrs. Lavender .... Joan Blondell
Bonnie Shelley .... Gloria Grahame
Dub Stokes .... Gary Merrill
Johnsy Boy Hood .... Bill Bixby
Elwood Coates .... Claude Akins
Hanley .... Paul Fix
Maria .... Marrisa Mathes
Vogan .... Harry Harvey, Sr.
Bartender .... William Bryant
Pete .... Jamie Farr
Mexican Boy .... Larry Domasin
Drunk .... William Catching
Census Taker .... James MacArthur
Narrator .... Arthur O'Connell
Aunt Gussie .... Ruth Warrick
Mr. Kratz .... Buddy Baer
Tod Wisdom .... Frank Gorshin
Hotel Clerk .... Robert Q. Lewis

Even by lowercase standards, "Ride Beyond Vengeance" is not to be believed. Chuck Connors, backed by his "Branded" vidseries production staff, stars in this confused, cameo-loaded, oater. Some action, violence and an anachronistic Freudian touch do not offset a dreary plot about unsympathetic principals. The thin-valued Andrew J. Fenady production looks like a padded tv film, and plays like one. If this is an example of tv-to-theatres product, forget it. Fair b.o.—at least enough to get off the low nut—looms for Columbia release in action situations.

Fenady adapted Al Dewlen's novel, "The Night Of The Tiger," into an episodic, double-flashback screenplay, so contrived it defies analysis. After the needless 10-minute prolog by bartender Arthur O'Connell and census-taker James MacArthur, story goes back to 1884 with Connors returning to his wife whom he abandoned 11 years earlier. Now he's got some dough, and just as he is about to reach home, all hell breaks loose, supposedly.

Booze-crazed Claude Akins and a pretty-boy Bill Bixby (who has a sado-masochistic streak which becomes more than evident in another plot-straying shock insertion) brand Connors on the chest, while passive town banker Michael Rennie watches. The basic idea—a returning prodigal finds out that the life and people he worked so hard for wasn't worth it—evaporates in all the sidebars.

It's hard to find a sympathetic character in the lot, except possibly for the ever-pro Joan Blondell, who registers the strongest as what appears to be a lady of easy virtue. Gloria Grahame is a playing-around wife, Frank Gorshin is her arrogant farm hand, and Gary Merrill is Connors' no-account dad who does come up with one saving action.

Paul Fix starts out as a likeable cattle hand, but it turns out he's been rustling on the side. His demise is violent. Ruth Warrick is a caricature of a mother, Robert Q. Lewis is okay as a desk clerk, and Marrisa Mathes is adequate as the down-trodden Mexican girl who, destitute after Bixby's self-imposed death, comforts Connors.

The obscured plot irony is Connors' wife, played by fashion model Kathryn Hays in her feature debut. She's a beautiful gal in an impossible role which forces her to try and be a loving wife, who, to overcome family objections to her marriage, fakes a pregnancy. Some way to start a married life. Later she fails to recognize Connors, but at fadeout tries to make amends. But Connors, by this time, has had it, a feeling which will have infected most audiences.

Bernard McEveety directed in routine style. Production has a sound stage look, all the more apparent from Lester Shorr's crisp Pathecolor lensing. Technical credits are standard. Richard Markowitz' score is okay, and Glenn Yarbrough warbles over titles "You Can't Go Home Again," which Fenady lyricized to Markowitz' melody, a flat effort which, nevertheless, sums up the obscured plot line. Film runs out after 100 minutes. *Murf.*

Gambara Tai Barugon
(COLOR—JAPAN)

Tokyo, April 17.
Daie Productions Release. Stars Kojiro Hongo, Kyoko Enama, Koji Fujima. Produced by Masayuki Nagata. Directed by Shigeo Tanaka. Scenario by Fumi Takahashi. Special Effects by Fumi Takahashi. Eastmancolor. DaieiScope. Running time: **100 MINS.**

A sequel to "Gambara" with which Daiei set out to rival Toho In making monster-films. Takahashi's special effects are not up to Tsurubaya's however, and Gambara (giant flying turtle which lives on atomic energy) does not have winning personality of the Toho stable, "Godzilla," "Radon," etc. Production values too (cheap New Guinea setting, unintentionally hilarious "Native Dance") are less than necessary.

Still, there is probably more monster-footage in the Daiei film than in most of Toho's where monsters are not often seen until past the halfway mark. Model-work in the picture (monster destroys Kobe and Osaka, having accounted for Tokyo in his first screen appearance) is average but again camera-angles poorly chosen, almost insist that all but the youngest identify title-lead as a man in a monster suit.

Plot has something to do with giant opal which turns out to be egg; with bad-guy who finally gets eaten by Barugon (big lizard with chameleon-like tongue); and with native-dancer Kyoko Enama. For exploitation position film needs some cutting — a dubbed version might do well at kiddy matinees or on the flea-house circuit. *Chie.*

Der Junge Toerless
(The Young Toerless)
(GERMAN-FRENCH)

Berlin, April 26.
Nora release of Franz Seitz (Munich) and Louis Malle (Paris) production. With Matthieu Carriere, Bernd Tischer, Marian Seidowsky. Directed by Volker Schloendorff. Screenplay, Schloendorff, after the novel by Robert Musil; camera, Franz Rath; music, Hans Werner Henze; editor, Claus von Boro. Previewed at Hasso, Munich. Running time, **85 MINS.**
Toerless .... Matthieu Carriere
Beineberg .... Bernd Tischer
Basini .... Marian Seidowsky
Reiting .... Alfred Dietz
Bozena .... Barbara Steele
Mrs. Toerless ...... Hanne Axmann-Rezzori
Mr. Toerless .... Herbert Asmodi
School director .... Fritz Gehlen
Waitress .... Lotte Ledl

It looks like there's a change within the West German film industry. At least a number of new young directors are bringing some fresh material to the Teutonic screen. One who rates special attention is 27-year old Volker Schloendorff. After having been assistant director to some noted French film creators, he now comes along with "Young Toerless," his first full-length feature. This is both artistically and technically a well-made film and certainly a very impressive directorial debut. It remains to be seen how the unconventional plot and treatment of subject matter will appeal to the audience. The pic qualifies definitely as an interesting item for the arty houses. Film has been invited to the Cannes Film Fest and will be the second German contribution to this French festival.

Story is laid in a boarding school of some six decades ago.

Central figure is the pupil Toerless, an intelligent but rather conceited outsider, who becomes the witness of a secret tragedy. One student has stolen money from a fellow inmate. The two leaders of the class, Beineberg and Reiting, blackmail and torture him to satisfy their sadistic interests.

Plot doesn't concentrate so much on the sufferings of the boy (Basini) but dedicates itself chiefly to the passive attitude of Toerless. The latter is not a weak character. He is fully aware of his obligations. He finally sees no other way out than to quit the boarding school. The viewer is confronted with the eternal "Who's wrong?" question. Film also shows how physical superiority and respective arrogance can lead to sadism and brutality. It therewith hints at the cruel things that happened years later during the Nazi era.

Helped by sensitive lensing, Schloendorff has caught the mood and atmosphere excellently. What he creates via his straightforward direction is a documentary type of realism. There is no comedy relief in this one. Pupils and teachers show unconventional faces. The absence of any warmth may scare off some patrons. It seems practicaly a matter of taste how this film will be judged.

"Toerless" stirred the interest of Hans Werner Henze, Germany's top longhair composer, who contributed the unconventional score. This Nora release is registered here as a German-French coproduction, with Franz Seitz being the German and French director Louis Malle, the Gallic producer. Whatever the commercial outcome, Schloendorff's initial opus is certainly a prestige item for those who backed this production. *Hans.*

Ganovenehre
(Crook's Honor)
(GERMAN-COLOR)

Berlin, April 19.
Atlas release of Inter West Film (Wenzel Luedecke) production. Stars Gert Froebe, Mario Adorf and Curt Bois; features Karin Baal, Helen Vita, Gretl Schoerg. Directed by Wolfgang Staudte. Screenplay, Curth Flatow, Hans Wilhelm, based on stage comedy by Charles Rudolph; camera (Eastmancolor), Friedel Behn-Grund; music, Hans-Martin Majewski. At Zoo Palast, West Berlin. Running time, **92 MINS.**
Paul .... Gert Froebe
Georg .... Mario Adorf
Nelly .... Karin Baal
Olga .... Helen Vita
Emil .... Curt Bois
Red Erna .... Gretl Schoerg
Edith .... Ilse Page
Max .... Robert Rober
Backe-Backe Kuchen....Juergen Feindt
Karl .... Matrin Hirthe
Arthur .... Gert Haucke

This is a remake of a German film which never was shown in German cinemas. "Crook's Honor" was directed by Richard Oswald in 1932. It was supposed to have its preem in the spring of 1933. But at that time the Nazis already had taken over the power in this country. They disliked such "decadence" as the portrayal of prosties and protectors with which this comedy has to do. And they disliked Oswald who was a Jew. The film was put on the "verboten" list.

"Crook's Honor" of 1966 is the first production of Wenzel Lue-

decke's Inter West since "The Endless Night" of three years ago. And it's the first German Gert Froebe starrer since "Three Penny Opera" which also dates back more than three years. Based on a legiter written by Charles Rudolph, "Honor" plays in a Berlin brothel of that era. It calls itself "a very frivolous film" and depicts pimps and prosties in a humorous way. Crix may find many faults with this production yet there is no doubt that such fare has mass appeal in this country. The name cast and the remarkably wide-open sequences (matters aren't minced) plus a lineup of very suggestive situations are exploitaton factors. However, this type of film will face considerable censorship trouble in many countries.

Central figure is Georg (Mario Adorf), a safe cracker who's just been released from a three year jail term. He finds shelter with his former love light (Karin Baal) who has joined the ranks of loose women in the interim. This brings Georg into a gang headed by Paul (Gert Froebe) which controls the prostie scene. George becomes a pimp. He doesn't like his job for he is more accustomed to what he calls physical work. Trouble seems certain. The gang sees no other choice than to liquidate Georg. The man assigned to do the liquidation job, by mistake, kills the wrong person. The finale is a comical funeral.

Wolfgang Staudte, creator of some of this country's best postwar pix and still one of the better German directors, has tailored this for mass appeal. General audiences may overlook what this film lacks —the light directorial hand. This pic should have had charm and esprit, both almost entirely missing. Sex and humor are overly robust and the gags often rather corny.

The most polished performance is turned in by Mario Adorf. He is always colorful and enjoyable. Further, he has a number of scenes which should make the most fastidious cric cheer. Froebe once again is a funny character although director Staudte allowed him to leave much to mere routine. Stage comedian Curt Bois, a fancyman in this, has a number of funny moments, yet, in all, he too could have been exploited to better advantage. Of the femmes, Helen Vita and Ilse Page come along with nice performances.

Production dress is quite appealing, and the music adds to the mood. Lensing is fine. *Hans.*

Le Coeur Vert
(The Green Heart)
(FRENCH)

Paris, April 19.
Raoul Ploquin Films-SODJR production and release. With non-pro players. Written and directed by Edouard Luntz; camera, Jean Badal; editor, Suzanne Sandberg. Previewed in Paris. Running time, **105 MINS.**

For a first film, Edouard Luntz, who has made some good shorts, shows a fine flair for utilizing non-pro thesps in this tale of semi-delinquents and big beat, long-haired boys and emancipated girls living on the outskirts of Paris. Familar and yet having a forceful insight, this should have some

fine arty and playoff possibilities abroad if well sold.

Luntz, who also wrote the script, does not go in much for story but rather a series of scenes concerning the lives of a gang or bunch of boys and the femmes in their lives. Family glimpses are pared down to only one which is an almost typical poor home. Film has some well-phased glimpses of the people involved.

Two are picked out for the story. One manages to get out of the aimless drifting and the other finally sinks to stealing and jail. There are the cafe squatting sequences, dances and fights and the endless gamboling around the hills where they live on the outskirts of Paris.

Women are used rather than accepted as peers unless they belong exclusively to one member of the group. The lack of schooling, training and money problems are sketched in, and the characters appear full-bodied, and ring true. There is a picking up of a lonely girl by one of the boys who leads her into a trap with most of the group profiting from her sexually.

Luntz punctuates his recitative with scenes of the group at violent play and suddenly abandoning themselves to exuberant byplay in a swimming pool. It sums up visually their pent-up need for action, play and excitement that is subverted by a life most of them can not cope with except through ignoring it completely.

These characters seem international in their strivings and addiction to big beat music, their own laws and delinquency.

Jean Badal's full bodied lensing is a real help. Luntz emerges as a director of sensitivity, and an ability to give a visual underlining of the delinquent world. Film needs special handling, but may be worth it. *Mosk.*

Hotel Alojamiento
(ARGENTINE)

Buenos Aires, April 19.
L. B. release of Aries (Fernando Ayala, Hector Olivera) production. Directed by Ayala. With Jorge Salcedo, Diana Maggi, Rodolfo Beban, Olinda Bozan, Jorge Sobral, Maria Aurelia Bisutti, Marilina Ross, Augusto Codeca, Gilda Lousek, Atilio Marinelli, Tincho Zaba'a, Fina Basser, Enzo Viena, Chico Novarro, Emilio Alfaro, Jorge Barreiro, Tono and Gogo Andreu, Marcos Zucker, Marcela Lopez Rey, Maria Concepcior Casar, Pepe Soriano. Screenplay, Gius, based on idea by Olivera; camera, Oscar Melli; editor, Atilio Rinaldi; music, Chico Novarro. At Trocadero, Buenos Aires. Running time, **108 MINS.**

With an unprecedented biz in first four days here, this sex comedy may hit a new alltime box-office high for the Argentina cinema. Word-of-mouth is strong because of the impact of several story angles. With smart selling and weaker episodes trimmed, it can be sold abroad. In the foreign-language markets chances may be enhanced by expert dubbing.

When attached to a hotel, the word alojamiento (meaning lodging) becomes in B.A. an euphemism identifying licensed places where couples can rent a room without showing documents nor worrying about police raids. Having mushroomed since they first appeared back in 1963, these sanctuaries of the flesh are regarded as a major source of revenue for the city treasure.

As the portenos (B.A.'s inhabitants) have in most instances no other choice than the hotel alojamiento when seeking where to enjoy pre and extramarital frolics, a pic spoofing the anecdotary of such collective love nests involves for many of them the premise to laugh at seeing mirrored either some thrilling personal mischief or the adventures of others that could (or would) happen to them.

Such potential "audience participation," as well as the rather lurid curiosity of the others has cleverly been kept in mind by scripter Gius when developing both the idea of coproducer Olivera and the research conducted by journalist De Dios. Local sex manners are depicted in 13 episodes. Some of these include a thief forgetting an imminent multi-million dollar robbery for a bed companion too luscious to be ignored; an engineer wishing to share with a distrustful prostie some refinements he has learned in Paris; four college pals determined to end the night of their annual meeting with a little orgy; a young couple caught red-handed by her parents; a suddenly scared man trying to delay an after-lunch performance when learning that a friend has just dropped dead; a housewife taking time off from marketing for an affair with a man who finds it impossible to ignite so early in the morning and in a garlic-scented room; a jet-set girl with a taxi driver; and two husbands betting on who first seduces the other's wife.

Producer-director Ayala chose a tongue-in-cheek a p p r o a c h and softened both pace and hilarity apparently not wishing to go beyond what was implicit in each sketch. He didn't squeeze many obvious possibilities for either jokes, slapstick or lustfulness, trying instead to give the pic a varnish of discretion, and perhaps even good taste. If he sought to avoid censorship troubles, he seems to have succeeded. Nevertheless, he could have done a brighter comedy with the same basic material.

As usual in omnibus pix, some segments (those of the thief, the engineer and the singers) are better than others, and at least one (that of the betting husbands) could have been suppressed for the benefit of the whole. Editing is uneven. Other technical contributions are standard. Actors do not always underline their ironic shade of the characters, making them hang between the broad and the clownesque. Exceptions are Jorge Sobral, Diana Maggi, Olinda Bozen, Augusto Coelca, Enzo Viena, Jorge Salcedo, Maria Aurelia Bisutti and Nathan Pinzon.

What "Hotel" may lack in both quality and wit is compensated by its star voltage, the effectiveness of many situations and the display of several nudes and semi-nudes to give it appeal. *Din.*

Arabesque
(PANAVISION—COLOR)

Names of Gregory Peck and Sophia Loren may see this foreign intrigue yarn through; shadowy plotline and confusing characters but strong production values.

Hollywood, April 27.
Universal release of Stanley Donen. Screenplay, Julian Mitchell, Stanley Price, Pierre Marton; based on novel, "The Cipher," by Gordon Cotler; camera (Technicolor), Christopher Challis; music, Henry Mancini; editor, Frederick Wilson; asst. director, Eric Rattray. Reviewed at Universal Studios, April 26, '66. Running time, 107 MINS.
David Pollack .... Gregory Peck
Yasmin Azir .... Sophia Loren
Beshraavi .... Alan Badel
Yussef .... Kieron Moore
Hassan Jena .... Carl Duering
Sloane .... John Merivale
Webster .... Duncan Lamont
Ragheeb .... George Coulouris
Beauchamp .... Ernest Clark
Mohammed Lufti .... Harold Kasket

"Arabesque" packs certain salable ingredients, such as the names of Gregory Peck and Sophia Loren and a foreign intrigue theme which fits into the current cycle, but doesn't always progress on a true entertainment course. Fault lies in a shadowy plotline and confusing characters, particularly in the miscasting of Peck in a cute role.

Stanley Donen, who produced films in England under his own banner for Universal release, has inserted plenty of hard-hitting punches in his dual function as director. He has taken advantage, too, of colorful London backgrounds and given production class mounting. Henry Mancini's music score is a particular assist to Donen's sometimes-violent treatment, and Christopher Challis' Technicolor-Panavision photography lends pictorial substance. Despite such plus factors, audience is never certain where it stands.

Based on the Gordon Cotler novel, "The Cipher," script by Julian Mitchell, Stanley Price and Pierre Marton projects Peck as an American exchange professor of ancient languages at Oxford drawn into a vortex of hazardous endeavor. He is called upon to decipher a secret message written in hieroglyphics, a document and its translation sought by several different factions from the Middle East. He is assisted by the paradoxical character played by Miss Loren, as an Arabic sexpot who seems to be on everyone's side. There are chases, murders and attempted assassinations to whet the appetite, as well as misuses of comedy.

Peck tries valiantly with a role unsuited to him, and Miss Loren displays her usual lush and plush presence. If her part is an enigma to Peck, certainly it is to the spectator, too, but she makes the most of certain disrobing scenes.

Menace is provided by Alan Badel and Kieron Moore, both trying to latch onto contents of the cipher and out to dispose of Peck. Carl Duering plays the Prime Minister of a Middle Eastern state who is to be murdered, and John Merivale and Duncan Lamont are among the baddies threatening Peck's life.

Further technical excellence is provided by art direction of Reece Pemberton, and sound by John W. Mitchell and C. Le Messurier. Frederick Wilson's editing frequently is fast. Miss Loren's wardrobe was created by Christian Dior. *Whit.*

Brigitte et Brigitte
(FRENCH-COLOR)

Paris, April 26.
Moullet production and release. With Colette Descombes, Francoise Vatel, Claude Melki, Michael Gonzales. Written and directed by Luc Moullet. Camera (Eastmancolor). Claude Creton; editor, Cecile Decugis. At Napoleon, Paris. Running Time, 95 MINS.
Tall Brigitte .... Colette Descombes
Little Brigitte .... Francoise Vatel
Leon .... Claude Melki
Jacques .... Michel Gonzales
Workman .... Joel Monteilhat
Pupil .... Gilles Chusseau
Sex Maniac .... Claude Chabrol
Samuel Fuller .... Himself

Luc Moullet was a disciple of the now absorbed New Wave. He remains way out, partial to inside jokes and gives an anarchic, free-wheeling but pleasant first film that has a morality of its own. It paints an original picture of modern youth and schools, rarely treated here.

Moullet opens with a 20-minute color segment on a backward part of France and then segues into black and white and the tale of two girls named Brigitte from this area who meet in a Paris school. They lose their accents and get caught up with Parisian high life and its intellectual fringes.

They discuss films, cheating at school, sex and cavort with boyfriends as Moullet goes in for a series of episodes, rather than a story, to take potshots at overcrowded schools, encroaching puritanism as well as the bright, zany or sometimes serious aspects of youth at play and work.

The players are all at ease. The two girls, playing the Brigittes are zesty, yet pleasing as well as definitely budding new thespic talents. Its complete personal qualities and treatment stamp this only for arty and specialized use abroad. It appears even more intimate than the first Wave pix, with regular and art playoff more chancey, and needing hardsell. *Mosk.*

Schonzeit fuer Fuechse
(No Shooting Time For Foxes)
(GERMAN)

Berlin, April 26.
Atlas release of Peter Schamoni production. With Helmut ' Foernbacher, Christian Doermer, Andrea Jonasson. Directed by Peter Schamoni. Screenplay, Schamoni and Guenter Seuren, based on Seuren's novel, "The Grating"; camera, Jost Vacano; music, Hans Posegga; editor, Heide Rente. Previewed in projection room, Munich. Running time, 92 MINS.
The young man ....Helmut Foernbacher
His friend Viktor ... Christian Doermer
Clara .... Andrea Jonasson
Lore .... Monika Peitsch
Clara's mother .... Edda Seippel
Viktor's father .... Helmut Hinzelmann
Viktor's mother .... Suse Graf
An uncle .... Alexander Golling
Hunting author .... Willy Birgel

The year of 1966 may mark a milestone in the history of the West German film industry. At least it gave birth to a series of attention - commanding unconventional feature pix directed by promising newcomers. "Foxes" is the first full-length feature of 32-year-old Peter Schamoni who has made good in the domestic short films field. He should be fully pleased with his first opus. Not only that it was given the highest distinction ("particularly worthy" which means considerable tax relief) by the West German film classification board, but

it also is to be a German entry at the forthcoming Berlin Film Fest. Moreover, Atlas, this country's most ambitious distrib, has "Foxes" on release. Domestically. "Foxes" will please a lot of critics and also large segments of the more demanding patrons. It also has enough entertainment value to appeal to less fastidious audiences. Foreign prospects are anybody's guess. The subject matter may be an exploitation factor in that market.

Schamoni has tried to give some insight into life and the feelings of young Germans who were still children when the last World War was over. The main characters are two young men, both around 30, who went to school together. One is a journalist who has to work hard to get his tasks done. The other is the son of a rich family.

Although they have different social backgrounds, they face more or less the same problems. Both feel misunderstood by the elder generation, dislike traditions, mistrust the adults and have practically no illusions any longer. They feel like young foxes who want to escape and finally realize that the "close time for Foxes" is over. While the journalist decides to stay and put up with the facts, his friend sees no other way than to go to a distant country (Australia), and try his luck there.

Schamoni has given a clearcut conception of the problems of young people. He gives "Foxes" enough depth without being esoteric. It should be noted that the young director avoided cliches, symbolisms and any sort of so-called avant garde ingredients. Although there is much dialog in this, it is never a "talky" film.

A special asset of this production is the acting. Schamoni has led the players to performances that ring true all through. Some of the younger players (Foernbacher, Doermer, Miss Jonasson) may be in for Federal awards. The cast includes a number of vet players (Birgel, Golling, Hinzelmann) repping the old, tradition-minded generation. They too feel right at home with their roles.

Technically, "Foxes" represents a high standard. The lensing and editing reveal care and devotion while the score is also very good. "Foxes" made a favorable impression here. It is noteworthy because first feature pix of newcomers often give an uneven impression. *Hans.*

A Fine Madness
(COLOR)

Far-out sex comedy-drama about a non-conformist, a sort of "Tom Jones" and "A Thousand Clowns" combo. Sean Connery and Joanne Woodward for the marquee. Strong selling should overcome some possible adverse reaction, particularly from femmes.

Hollywood, April 28.
Warner Bros. Pictures release of a Pan Arts (Jerome Hellman) Production. Stars Sean Connery, Joanne Woodward, Jean Seberg; features Patrick O'Neal, Colleen Dewhurst, Clive Revill, Werner Peters, John Fiedler, Kay Medford, Jackie Coogan, Zohra Lampert, Sorrell Booke, Sue

Ane Langdon. Directed by Irvin Kershner. Screenplay, Elliott Baker, based on his novel; camera (Technicolor), Ted McCord; editor, William Ziegler; music, John Addison; asst. director, Russell Llewellyn. Reviewed at Pacific's Pantages Theatre, L.A., April 27, '66. Running time, 104 MINS.

Samson Shillitoe	Sean Connery
Rhoda	Joanne Woodward
Lydia West	Jean Seberg
Dr. Oliver West	Patrick O'Neal
Dr. Vera Kropotkin	Colleen Dewhurst
Dr. Menken	Clive Revill
Dr. Vorbeck	Werner Peters
Daniel K. Papp	John Fiedler
Mrs. Fish	Kay Medford
Mr. Fitzgerald	Jackie Coogan
Mrs. Tupperman	Zohra Lampert
Leonard Tupperman	Sorrell Booke
Miss Walnicki	Sue Ane Langdon
Mrs. Fitzgerald	Bibi Osterwald
Chairwoman	Mabel Albertson
Chester Quirk	Gerald S. O'Loughlin
Rollie Butter	James Millhollin
Dr. Huddleson	Jon Lormer
Knocker	Harry Bellaver
Clubwoman	Ayllene Gibbons

"A Fine Madness" is offbeat, and downbeat, in many ways. Too heavyhanded to be comedy, yet too light to be called drama, the well-mounted Jerome Hellman production depicts a non-conformist poet-stud in an environment of much sex, some violence and modern headshrinking. Fine direction and some good characterizations enhance negative script outlook. Sean Connery and Joanne Woodward are chief marquee lures, and, with aggressive selling, the Warner Bros. release should attract adult-minded general audiences.

The sensitivity of an artist, by which he is able not only to create but also to perceive the shams of contemporary living, is tricky subject. Elliott Baker, who scripted "A Fine Madness" from his book, has instead taken an invective approach, spiced with some adulterous situations which are awfully wonderful, or wonderfully awful, depending on one's sense of humor.

Connery, in his third recent out-of-Bond role, is a virile, headstrong poet, hung up in a dry spell of inspiration. Absolutely nothing in the world means anything to him, except his unwritten masterpiece. He despises women in general, and to hammer home this point, all femme characters, except second wife Miss Woodward, are shrews, battle-axes, or shallow broads. Connery tolerates his wife in a domestic atmosphere of shrill argument and physical abuse.

Overdue back alimony cues an outburst, eventually leading Connery to psychiatric care, alternating with a running chase from the fuzz, and climaxed by a curiously ineffective brain lobotomy. A lot of sophisticated throwaway dialog is dispensed along with sight gag and slapstick. The social commentary is crisp, with modern woman and psychiatry taking it on the chin; yet the case for the artist as human being suffers from less exposition. Moral seems to be that Connery's type will never fit anywhere.

Director Irvin Kershner, schooled in documentary and lower budget documentary type pix, demonstrates a remarkable pictorial sense, translated by Ted McCord's ace Technicolor lensing into crisp and realistic imagery. Extensive N.Y. location work is evident in some great exteriors.

As for players, Kershner has drawn effective performances from Connery, who makes a good comic kook in a switch from the somnambulism of his James Bond roles, and Miss Woodward, almost unrecognizable in face and voice via a good characterization of the loud-mouthed, but loving, wife, done in the Judy Holliday style. Jean Seberg, bored wife of headshrinker Patrick O'Neal, is okay. She is the third of the above-title players.

Kershner's supporting players, mostly drawn from legit, are excellent. O'Neal gives depth and understanding to the cuckold hubby, almost in defiance of the author's apparent attempt to make the assorted medics ridiculous caricatures. Colleen Dewhurst is very under the poet's spell. Clive Revill, good as the femme doctor who falls the drooling lobotomist, and Werner Peters, on the make for Miss Seberg, also score.

Zohra Lampert, another Connery conquest, her older hubby Sorrell Booke and mom Kay Medford register well in a vignette which is not too clear until it is almost over. Sue Langdon, the secretary-chippy who is the film's first explicit seduction, again displays her neat talent as a brassy babe. Mabel Albertson has an outstanding bit as a clubwoman type, and among her crowd is hefty Ayllene Gibbons, perfect as the man-eating mom.

Gerald S. O'Loughlin bobs up regularly as the cop whom Connery regularly knocks breathless. When O'Loughlin finally gets his licks in, it is overdue and, as depicted, not a bad argument for a little police brutality in the right places. John Fiedler, attorney for the poet's first wife, is appropriately harried throughout. Jackie Coogan and Bibi Osterwald, the landlords, and agent James Millhollin are also effective.

John Addison's jazzy, often busy, score — including a theme not unlike those of the Bond pix — adds an adroit punch. William Ziegler trimmed to a good 104 minutes, and other Warner studio credits are at their customary professional excellence. *Murf.*

Masculin, Feminin
(FRENCH-SWEDISH)

Paris, April 26.

Columbia release of Anouchka Films-Sandrew Film-Filmindustri production. With Chantal Goya, Jean-Pierre Leaud, Marlene Jobert. Written and directed by Jean-Luc Godard from two stories by Guy De Maupassant. Camera, Willy Kurant; editor, Marguerite Renoir. At Publicis, Paris. Running time, 100 MINS.

Madeleine	Chantal Goya
Paul	Jean-Pierre Leaud
Elizabeth	Marlene Jobert
Robert	Michel Debord
Catherine	Isabelle Duport
Lavinia	Eva Britt Standberg
Man	Birger Malmsten

That prolific and inventive French filmmaker Jean-Luc Godard now takes a look at local youth in his usual personal style. Incidents, not story, inside jokes, despair, wit and a sort of mixture of cinema truth interview and sociological methods are intertwined in this offbeater that appears mainly for arty houses abroad.

But there is still no mistaking the Godard penchant for making asides, reading from his favorite sources and dovetailing meaningful insight with frivolous notations. Vaguely based on some stories by Guy De Maupassant, this soon becomes pure Godard as he looks at a callow youth and his affair with a comely, free living teenager bent on becoming a pop singer.

Between bouts of horseplay are sudden shafts of violence as Godard appears to make all human contacts temporary though sometimes allowing for tenderness and even notes on solitude and human distress. But the serious moods are set up by trips to the films with parodies on erotic pix seen, talks about Communism and democracy, surface jests and blasts at U.S. policy in Vietnam, discussions of birth control, homosexuality and other items of this ilk that seem to be the main penchants of Godard's young people.

Titles, sharply contrasted shooting and much use of closeups plus a lot of talk. This is definitely a Godard pic with his sometimes irritating side issues, quotations and observations.

The youth ends up either falling or jumping from a window as he inspects an apartment with his now pregnant little girlfriend. Godard shows the girls as much more mature, than his more romantic young men. There seems to be a wistful apology for these pint-size women.

Jean-Pierre Leaud has the right mixture of callowness and impulsiveness as the hero while Chantal Goya is a fetching little miss who uses love but is not ready to be tied down or annoyed by any possessiveness. Godard also finds a bevy of other young people who are photogenic and persuasive in this seemingly spontaneous documentary-like feature pic. The only concession to the Swedish coproducers is a supposed film (seen by the characters) which has two Svenska players doing a takeoff on an erotic Swedish pic.

Naive and knowing, irritating and engaging this is best for arty spots. *Mosk.*

Sleeping Beauty
(RUSSIAN—BALLET—COLOR)

A cinematically excellent, if truncated, version of the Kirov Ballet production.

Royal Films release of Lenfilm production, as part of U.S.-USSR cultural exchange program. Stars Illa Sizova and Yuri Soloviev. Features Natalia Dudinskaye and Irina Bazhenova. Music by Tchaikowsky; choreography by Konstantin Sergeyev after Marius Petipa; direction by Sergeyev and Appolinari Dudko; scenario by Dudko, Sergeyev and Iosif Shapiro; director of photography, Anatoli Nazarov. Running Time, 90 MINS.

Princess Aurora	Alla Sizova
Prince Desire	Yuri Soloviev
Wicked Fairy	Natalia Dudinskaya
Lilac Fairy	Irina Bazhenova
Bluebirds	M. Masakova, V. Panov

Any number of ballet films have been spoiled by failure to adapt the choreography to the film medium; this is the first within memory which could be faulted for sacrificing dance values to cinematic ones. In the first act Rose Adagio, for example, there are innumerable cuts back and forth from the dancers to the audience of fairyland courtiers, thus severely interrupting the musical-choreographic flow.

In the second act Vision Scene, all of the sumptuous lifts of the Kirov stage version are eliminated, and the final Aurora's Wedding pageant is cut beyond recognition. Of the many divertissements usually danced, only a snatch of the Puss 'n' Boots-White Cat duo and about a third of the Bluebird pas de deux are offered, and the final Grand Pas is cut in half and presented out of continuity. Leftover music is used for some pointless meandering in the woods (with dogs and horses) and for some very attractive trick shots of fairies appearing and disappearing in fields of artificial flowers.

One addition for the film, however, is the best thing in it. This is the transformation of the Wicked Fairy, usually mimed by a man in fairy's clothing, into a dancing role tailored for the Leningrad's now-retired principal ballerina, Natalia Dudinskaya. Close to 60, Dudinskaya whirls through the role with undiminished technical brilliance and with acting mastery that makes her the epitome of sinuous, clawing evil.

The two young principals, Alla Sizova, in the title role, and Yuri Soloviev, as the prince who awakens her with a kiss, are among the best on the Kirov roster, and they caused a sensation in the same roles when the company toured the U.S. a couple of years ago. On film they are somewhat less effective, Soloviev because he has so little dancing to do, and because no amount of excellent camera work can do justice to his fabulous elevation; Sizova because she seems a trifle too earthbound for this fantasy world, and because the close-up camera picks up the fact that, despite her overall technical wizardry, her turns are a wee bit off balance. As the Lilac Fairy, Irina Bazhenova is technically competent, but she has none of the requisite lyricism or authority.

Dancing aside, however, this is a film which is beautifully and imaginatively photographed. The sets and the costumes are lovely, the color is clean and appropriate, the trick shots add a lot to the fun, and the story line is as clear as it's ever likely to be in a film without dialogue or narration. Ballet buffs may be disappointed (though Dudinskaya alone is worth the price of admission), but the kiddies will love it. *Gold.*

Ne Nous Fachons Pas
(Let's Not Get Angry)
(FRENCH—COLOR)

Paris, April 26.

Gaumont release of SNE-Gaumont production. Stars Lino Ventura, Mireille Darc; features Jean Lefevbre, Michel Constantin, Jacques Sabor, Sylvia Sorrente. Directed by Georges Lautner. Screenplay, Michel Audiard; camera (Eastmancolor), Maurice Fellous; editor, Michele David. At Ambassade-Gaumont, Paris. Running time, 100 MINS.

Antoine	Lino Ventura
Eglantine	Mireille Darc
Leonard	Jean Lefevbre
Jeff	Michel Constantin
Vicki	Sylvia Sorrente
Colonel	Tommy Duggan

Film is one of those way-out comic, gangster tales, dressed up with color, scope, interludes and big production dress which the French make for the local market. If this has some okay action aspects, it is still too talky, and uneven to loom more than a play-off item for foreign markets.

Insistence is on human pettiness and wry shoulder-shrugging action as a retired gangster is forced back into business when he saves a small-time chiseler. Said chiseler is owed some money from a group of longhaired British delinquents headed by a sinister British ex-colonel. A fight develops between the gangster, aided by a friend and the small-timer, against the motorcycle-riding, rock playing gang. The former win and the ex-hood even gets the little man's wife.

Director Georges Lautner hops this up with wild gunfights, much explosives and a sort of fey fatalism as the gangs fight it out themselves with nary a policeman in sight. Michel Audiard's underworld jargon soon palls.

There is some color lensing. Lino Ventura is properly phlegmatic as the recalcitrant ex-underworld character with Mireille Darc decorative as the wife. Jean Lefevbre is cunning and still fairly appealing as the little man who sets off all the mayhem. It is just that the film does not balance its ruthless action with the right fillip of satire. Some Bond gadget bits, including underwater explosions and forays, are also worked into this situation comedy. Home chances look much brighter than foreign possibilities. *Mosk.*

L'Homme De Marrakech
(The Man from Marrakech) (FRENCH-COLOR)
Paris, April 29.

Prodis release of Europazur-Benito Perojo production. Stars Georges Hamilton, Claudine Auger; features Alberto De Mendoza, Tiberio Murgia, Daniel Ivernel. Directed by Jacques Deray. Screenplay, H. Lanoe, Jose Giovanni, Deray from the book by Robert Page Jones; camera (Eastmancolor), Henri Raichi; editor, Paul Cayatte; music, Alain Goraguer. At Marignan, Paris. Running time, **90 MINS.**
George .... George Hamilton
Lila .... Claudine Auger
Travis .... Alberto De Mendoza
Jose .... Tiberio Murgia
Engineer .... Daniel Ivernel

A slickly planned holdup that goes astray because of human cupidity is familiar, but this pic has some good exotic locale work in Morocco, neatly executed direction and the Georges Hamilton name for some indicated playoff abroad.

Director Jacques Deray has worked carefully and gleaned the most from the irony, fatalism and character slipups in this kind of shenanigan. It is just that the fillip of deeper character is not there to make it more than a good routine actioner.

Hamilton is a Yank adventurer who goes along with an Argentine playboy, an Italo garage mechanic, an attractive French girl and an aging engineer to heist a gold bullion, armored car in Morocco. All goes well until the Argentine tries to cut off the others. Hamilton is helped by the girl and they flee. But she is playing her own game and all the people involved,

except Hamilton, who is startled when he finds she is a doubledealer too, get their comeuppances.

This has good production dress and is carefully made, but not unusual enough to make it more than a well-made analysis of a holdup with inevitable ironic payoff. Color is fine and the Moroccan lensing a good backdrop plus a side trip to Lisbon. Claudine Auger is somewhat wooden as the girl. Alberto De Mendoza has dash as the doubledealer. Others adequately fill their well-worn characters. *Mosk.*

MODESTY BLAISE (BRITISH-COLOR)

Spy-spoof with Monica Vitti playing a femme James Bond. Includes slapstick, ace direction, some good performances, expensive production. Young sophisticates make up the most promising b.o. potential, elsewhere spotty unless sold strongly.

Hollywood, May 5.

Twentieth Century-Fox release of Joseph Janni production. Stars Monica Vitti, Terence Stamp, Dirk Bogarde; features Harry Andrews, Michael Craig, Alexander Knox. Directed by Joseph Losey. Screenplay, Evan Jones, based on a comic strip by Peter O'Donnell, Jim Holdaway; camera (DeLuxe Color), Jack Hildyard; editor, Reginald Beck; music, John Dankworth; songs, Benny Green, Evan Jones; production design, Richard Macdonald; asst. directors, Gavrik Losey, Claude Watson. Reviewed at 20th-Fox Studios, L.A., May 4, '66. Running time, **118 MINS.**
Modesty Blaise .... Monica Vitti
Willie Garvin .... Terence Stamp
Gabriel .... Dirk Bogarde
Sir Gerald Tarrant ...... Harry Andrews
Paul Hagan .... Michael Craig
Minister .... Alexander Knox
Melina .... Scilla Gabel
Nicole .... Clive Revill
Mrs. Fothergill .... Rossella Falk
Crevier .... Joe Melia
Walter .... Lex Schoorel
Pacco .... Sylvan
Hans .... Jon Bluming
Enrico .... Roberto Bisacco
Basilio .... Sara Urzi
Friar .... Giuseppe Paganelli

"Modesty Blaise" is one of ti nuttiest, screwiest pictures ever made. Not merely a spy spoof, based on a book and a British-American comic strip about a femme James Bond type, the colorful Joseph Janni production gives the horse laugh to many different film plots and styles. Sigh gags, production values, dialog and sound track strive to titilate audience comic sensibilities of all philosophical and moral persuasions. Fine direction and many solid performances are evident. A bit overlong, and lacking in powerhouse marquee line-up, film will need a strong sell. Best returns are likely in young sophisticated situations.

Evan Jones has concocted a wacky screenplay, most immediately derived from the English comic strip by Peter O'Donnell and Jim Holdaway, which propels Miss Blaise, played by Monica Vitti in her first English-lingo role, into a British government espionage scheme. Heading the opposition is Dirk Bogarde, an effete international criminal, while Miss Vitti is aided by longtime sidekick, bed-hopping Terence Stamp.

Nobody trusts anyone, and there is a stream of counterplot, subplot and vignette. The basic story is thin, so the treatment is the thing. Jones and director Joseph Losey, probably encouraged further by Janni and any other crew members who remembered some cliche cinematic bit, have loaded the film with innumerable comic touches.

Clive Revill, Bogarde's biz agent, keeps watching costs with the eye of a Poverty Row unit production manager. Another firstrate characterization is that of Harry Andrews, an outstanding actor who can do more with the flick of an eyebrow than many other thesp with a five-minute speech. Here he is cast as

the British agent who recruits Miss Blaise. Alexander Knox is excellent as a politician, undoubtedly from the Labor Party.

Miss Vitti's English is adequate for her part; her body English, however, transcends all language barriers. Stamp is good, and appropriately animated. Bogarde's jaded urbanity is very good, and all other players register in solid support.

Jack Hildyard's superior DeLuxe Color lensing captures the delightfully overdone production mounting — oversize goblets, bizarre surrealism and lush settings. Richard Macdonald pulled out all stops in production design. Film was made at England's Shepperton Studios, with some Amsterdam locations.

John Dankworth's score incorporates all types of music to add punch to proceedings. Scripter Jones and Benny Green wrote two songs which enhance the mood, one of them, "We Should Have," sounding like the sort of melody which Frank Loesser and Frederick Hollander used to turn out for Marlene Dietrich pix.

Losey's firm grip on everyone and everything is evident throughout. Pace drags a bit in the final 20 minutes, but editor Reginald Beck did a creditable job of trimming to 118 minutes. Other credits are excellent. **Murf.**

The Psychopath (BRITISH—TECHNISCOPE—COLOR)

Good script, standout performances and fine direction make this British nail-biter a top-grade shocker.

Paramount release of Amicus (Max J. Rosenberg & Milton Subotsky) production. Stars Patrick Wymark, Margaret Johnston, John Standing. Features Alexander Knox, Judy Huxtable, Don Borisenko, Colin Gordon, Thorley Walters, Robert Crewdson, John Harvey. Directed by Freddie Francis. Screenplay, Robert Bloch; camera (Technicolor). John Wilcox; music, Phil Martel; editor, Oswald Hafenrichter; assistant director, Peter Price. Reviewed at Paramount Studios, April 28, '66. Running time, **83 MINS.**
Inspector Holloway ....Patrick Wymark
Mrs. Von Sturm .... Margaret Johnston
Mark Von Sturm ...... John Standing
Frank Saville .... Alexander Knox
Louise Saville .... Judy Huxtable
Donald Loftis .... Don Borisenko
Dr. Glyn .... Colin Gordon
Martin Roth .... Thorley Walters
Victor LeDoux .... Robert Crewdson
Morgan .... Tim Barrett
Tucker .... Frank Forsyth
Mary .... Olive Gregg
Briggs .... Harold Lang
Reinhardt Klermer .... John Harvey
Cigarette Girl .... Greta Farrer

"The Psychopath" is a smoothly-done, suspense-filled shocker that should please its natural audience. Take the doll from "Baby Jane", multiply it by six, add some bright colors and extra violence and you've got all the ingredients of this socko British-made nail-biter. An excellent script, standout performances and fine direction make this a film that will be a real spellbinder, and should provide plenty of coin for exhibitors from the suspense crowd.

Robert Bloch's original screenplay has four men—John Harvey, Alexander Knox, Thorley Walters and Robert Crewdson—all knocked off early in rapid succession. Each is done in, in a different violent manner, and beside each body is found a small doll, dressed and fashioned in the image of the victim.

The awesome crimes create a puzzle for Scotland Yarder Patrick Wymark, until he learns that the dolls were included in a shipment of six similar ones sold to Margaret Johnston. She's a pathetic—sick—figure, widow of a bigshot German who was arrested for his wartime crimes after World War II. Confined to a wheelchair, she spends all of her time with her large collectiton of dolls.

The surprise ending wraps up all the loose ends and gives the audience a definite feeling of relief that the entire caper is finally buttoned down in believable fashion.

Freddie Francis' helming is a sharp job of putting the pieces of the puzzle into proper perspective and makes the whole narrative breeze along at a nimble pace, keeping the audience in the mood of not knowing exactly who the real culprit is. Francis, who has directed a number of adult horror pix in the past, has a sense of feeling for this sort of story.

Patrick Wymark is a talented and methodical actor well cast as the Scotland Yard inspector, who toplines the film and rightfully so. Miss Johnston injects plenty of life into the part of the crippled widow with the doll fixation and manages quite handsomely in getting the audience to both hate her and also feel sorry for her. John Standing, as the son, projects his part keenly and in a spirited manner, and should bring him bouncing back in other meaty parts like this one.

Alexander Knox is his usually capable self and the only cast name known to American audiences. Miss Huxtable is an attractive youngster, believable in the part, and Borisenko handles his lesser role with enthusiasm and ability.

John Wilcox's camera work helps considerably in putting in the shock values without resorting to actual on-camera scenes of mayhem. He does it deftly by implication. Oswald Hafenrichter's crafty cutting is adroit in sequing from one bit of suspense to another. It's all boosted along nicely by Phil Martle's scoring, implanted in the soundtrack at vital moments — and noticeably silent in other vital scenes to help provide the mood of the entire project.

"The Psychopath" is definitely an adult horror film and a credit to the team of Max Rosenberg and Milton Subotsky, who have turned out a number of this type of shocker. This one is top grade. *Mitt.*

Cannes Festival

La Noire De . . .
(The Negro Woman From . . .)
(SENEGALESE)
Cannes, May 9.
Domirev production and release. With Nbissine Therese Diop, Anne-Marie Jenelick, Robert Fontaine. Written and directed by Ousmane Sembene. Camera, Christian Lacoste; editor, Andre Gaudin.

At Cannes Film Fest. Running time, 60 MINS.
Maid .... Nbissine Therese Diop
Wife .... Anne-Marie Janelick
Husband .... Robert Fontaine
Fiance .... Momar Nar Sene
Mask .... Ibrahima Boy

This film might well be the first truly African work with its writer-director from there and its outlook and treatment only tempered by European or U.S. influences assimilated by its maker. It is a deceptively simple tale about a Senegalese girl brought to France where she serves as a maid to an ex-colonialist couple.

Film does lay bare an original outlook and shows an incompatability that is not always racist. Yet there is nothing sectional or inaccessible to all filmgoers in this. It would, of course, need adroit handling and coupling with a medium-length pic because of its own length, for best chances abroad.

The girl comes to Southern France expecting to take care of the children and see the country.

But she finds the kids away at school and herself almost a slave and forced to be a maid, feeling almost a prisoner. The woman of the house is overbearing and patronizing, and the husband well meaning but unable to really understand the imported maid.

She becomes morose and begins to withdraw into herself and finally, in a suddenly shocking move, commits suicide. The man returns her belongings to her home in Senegal and feels a sudden fear and uneasiness among her people. That is all, but it has well observed scenes in both Africa and France. Picture has a simple but well-constructed visual feeling for displaying character and insight.

It is not bitter but does show condescension, if almost unconsciously, as when a guest jumps to kiss the maid, fatuously saying he has never kissed a Negro woman before. The characters are schematic except for the spontaneous girl, well played by a lovely Senegalese actress. Director-writer Ousmane Sembene shows a budding film consciousness in Africa that may be heard from when and if production spreads there.

For a first African entry at a major film festival, this is viewable, handling a touchy theme well. *Mosk.*

Gyerekbetegsegek
(Children's Sicknesses)
(HUNGARIAN-COLOR)
Cannes, May 9.
Hungarofilm release of Studio Three production. With Istvan Geczy, Tunde Kassai, Emil Keres, Judith Halasz. Written and directed by Ferenc Kardos, Janos Rosza. Camera, Lanscoli Sandor Sara; music, Andras Szollosy. At Cannes Film Fest. Running time, 72 MINS.
Little Boy .... Istvan Geczy
Zizi .... Tunde Kassai
Rita .... Rita Baranyai
Uncle .... Gabor Lontay
Father .... Emil Keres
Mother .... Marta Mamusics
Mannequin .... Dori Banfai

Children, in their disarming cruelty, and their relations with adults, are treated with extremely comic yet discerning insight by two new young Magyar directors who should be heard from. Its gusty comedy and treatment of

children sans trying to ape them, but giving a parallel interpretation of their loves and family ties, make it good fun. Fine arty and playoff chances loom abroad.

It begins with a child being pompously told about his birth by his father and then bundled off to school. Follows a seeming documentary dealing with kids at school, about seven to eight years old, and then a sudden rushing freedom as they get out and cause mayhem via practical jokes and pranks. They heat a public phone to watch a user yelp, they change one way signs to cause accidents, touch big girls, run, and romp and see petty dealings around them.

It may sometitmes lag or get a bit precious but it is always revved up with fine scenes. Overall this is an extremely original pic about children and adults. It is a most promising start by a pair of new directors. Color is good, child players eschew all patronizing or cuteness and the adults are rightly ridiculous. Good chances for this on its sheer entertainment qualities even without the child psychology and symbols of Hungarian life today that may be imbedded in it. *Mosk.*

Bloko
(The Roundup)
(GREEK)
Cannes, May 7.
Griffifilms release of Hellas Films production. With Maria Xenia, Alexandra Ladicou, Janis Fertis, Manos Katrakis. Directed by Ado Kyrou. Screenplay, Kyrou, Jerome Stavrou, Jean-Paul Torok; camera. G. Panoussopoulos, M. Danalis; music, Mikis Theodrakis. At Cannes Film Fest. Running time, 85 MINS.
Myrto .... Maria Xenia
Antigone .... Alexandra Ladicou
Aris .... Janis Fertis
Ilias .... Manos Katrakis
Kosmas .... Kostas Kasakos

Ado Kyrou, a French highbrow critic with Greek origins, who has made some shorts, has been noted mainly for his books on surrealism in the cinema and his addiction to way-out themes of mad love. But here, in a return to his native land, he has made a taut, searing film about resistance in Greece during the last World War.

It deals with a German blockade of a small town where some resistance people are holed up, both Communists and others. Characters are picked out, as the Germans close in, who are either part of the underground, non-committed, traitors or people caught in the midst of it all.

Kyrou does not go in for any fancy effects but displays a mature control of the happenings that progress in an almost classic time sequence. A just-married man gets caught up in a German roundup and meets a traitor he knows. He is practically forced into staying with him and talked into naming names.

Playing is sombre, and there is an attempt to show good and bad on all sides. Though obviously done with a tight budget, there is a fine production dress.

It has strength, a fine feel for time and place, making its statement on man in war without any overstatement or overdone flourishes. Pic looms a possible arty

item abroad on its taste and jolting effect, with playoff also indicated via tactful handling. *Mosk.*

Le Pere Noel A Les Yeux Bleus
(Santa Claus Has Blue Eyes)
(FRENCH)
Cannes, May 4.
Anouchka Films production and release. With Jean-Pierre Leaud, Gerard Zimmerman, Henri Martinez, Rene Gilson. Written and directed by Jean Eustache. Camera, Philippe Theaudiere; editor, Antoine Bonfanti. At Cannes Film Fest. Running time, 50 MINS.
Daniel .... Jean-Pierre Leaud
Dumas .... Gerard Zimmerman
Martinez .... Henri Martinez
Photographer .... Rene Gilson

Rarely has a French film put small town life on view with such subjectivity and sans any forced comedics. If it is a bit grim, there is an underlying good humor among its youthful heroes that escapes grittiness. It makes its point on smalltown dullness and changing French youth. Only of medium length, film would fare best for an arty house use abroad.

The hero is a pale teenager who wears a hand-me-down coat. He exists by doing odd jobs and has a few attempted adventures with women. It is just a series of incidents but it builds a constantly incisive look at drifting small town types.

The title comes from a job the hero does one day posing as a Santa Claus while a photographer takes pictures of him with anybody who wants one. In his disguise, he finds himself able to parry and flirt with girls. He even gets a date with one only to have her dropping him soon when she sees him sans his disguise.

Jean-Pierre Leaud, who was the boy in Francois Truffaut's "The 400 Blows," is now a lanky, sallow teenager. And he does not force incidents or try for any excess drama or pathos. It is a simple, penetrating sketch of a fairly intelligent yet usually stymied young man who, it appears, will soon be leaving this small town to take his chances elsewhere, probably Paris.

Director Jean Eustache made this film on his own. He displays a fine feeling for his characters and place without forcing any issues. Thus it takes its own time, but is constantly amusing and revealing. This shows a side of French youth rarely seen in local films.

This is well lensed. Pic keeps up a lighthearted and even tender feeling. It marks Eustache a director of tact and with something to say about a subject he knows about. A group of non-actors surrounding Leaud are all laudable. *Mosk.*

Covek Nije Tica
(A Man Is Not a Bird)
(YUGOSLAVIAN)
Cannes, May 8.
Avala Films production and release. With Milena Dravio, Janez Vrhovec, Stole Arandelovic, Eva Ras, Boris Dvornik. Written and directed by Dusan Makavejev. Camera, Aleksandre Petrovic. At Cannes Film Fest. Running Time, 72 MINS.
Raika .... Milena Dravic
Jan .... Janez Vrhovec
Barbul .... Stole Arandelovic

Wife	Eva Res
Truckdriver	Boris Dvornik

Yugoslavia, the first to go it alone out of the Eastern Bloc, has lagged behind other Eastern countries in unusual themes and pix talents. But here is a frank, originally-made pic that does not hesitate to make a statement on grim aspects of things if love appears international.

A man comes to a town to install imported machinery in a factory. He takes up with a pretty, flighty young girl who is a barber and the daughter of the people he is boarding with. Love takes on as important a tinge as his work. And sidelights show some backward working conditions in a socalled worker state. And the direction is not backwards in drawing ironic parallels between reality and slogans.

The camera is hardly ever still, but it fits the harsh closeup of life and love in a small industrial town. A running counterpoint is a giant panel of worker hands to grace the hall when the work is finished and the machinery expert is to be given an award though no money.

The love scenes are done with a circling camera. The girl is young, lovely and seemingly content with things, if curious and with nagging desire to get away.

There is also a story of a drunken worker haplessly hemmed in by poverty who is sometimes held up as a model performer. All this is a deeply dramatic look at a few lives mixed up for a while.

A gray lensing quality also underlines the tale and nervous editing helps the sharp, probing camera style and obviously uncompromising tale. There is also lively wit and bounce in some scenes of everyday work and forthright talk. The hero is dedicated but has his own problems and is not crusading or starry-eyed. But it is the shrewd presentation of the pretty girl lost in a certain aimlessness that gives the films its most significant moments. *Mosk.*

O Desafio
(The Dare)
(BRAZILIAN)

Cannes, May 5.
Productora Cinematografica Imago-Mario Fiorani production and release. Stars Oduvaldo Viano Filho, Luiz Linhares, Hugo Carvana, Marilu Fiorani. Written and directed by Paulo Cezar Saraceni; camera, Guido Cosulich; editor, Ismart Porto. At Cannes Film Fest. Running Time, 90 MINS.

Isabella	Oduvaldo Visna Filho
Sergio	Luiz Linhares
Joel	Hugo Carvana
Gianina	Marilu Fiorani

Brazil is another country that has shown some promising new filmmakers and themes at festivals. Here is a brooding but well-made tale of a young man's trying to arrive at self-realization in his life, political outlooks and love. If showing influences of Antonioni and Godard, it still has these assimilated. This is a promising film with mainly arty possibilities abroad on its personal theme.

The young man works on a magazine, is having an affair with the wife of a rich industrialist and hopes to write a book. Or to make some sort of a move which would enable him to take his place in the changing Brazil.

The woman is tired of her husband's life. But suddenly she is faced with his work on visiting the factory and is torn between her attempted liberalism and realization that he may be doing something in employing all these people. Also she realizes her socalled liberal lover broods more than does anything even if he talks big.

Director Paulo Cezar Saraceni displays a good feel for visually translating the emotitons of his people. There are some talky spots and a bit too much philosophizing. But, on the whole, this is a most promising first pic. Film is forthright and courageous in its comments on Brazilian political changes and atmosphere as well as a perceptive love story of two unmatched people. Acting is excellent as is the technical quality. *Mosk.*

Fata Morgana
(The Fatal Woman)
(SPANISH-COLOR)

Cannes, May 10.
Jaime Fernandez production and release. With Teresa Gimpera, Marianne Benet, Antonio Ferrandis, Marcos Marti. Directed by Vincente Aranda. Screenplay, Aranda, Gonzalo Suarez; camera (Eastmancolor), Auerlio Larraya; editor, Emilio Rodriguez. At Cannes Film Fest. Running time, 90 MINS.

Gim	Teresa Gimpera
Miriam	Marianne Benet
Professor	Antonio Ferrandis
J. J.	Marcos Marti
Alvaro	Alberto Dalves

This is a way-out film to come from Spain. It mixes fantasy, expressionism and decorativeness to spin a tale of a lovely mannequin beset by rabid men and a mysterious professor plotting her death. Then there is a mad girl roaming around and killing people. There may be pilotico allusions in its suffocating atmosphere as well as mixing attitudes towards femmes and hinting at insidious underground groups.

All this will make it an offbeat item for foreign chances with mainly specialized use in store on its spirited progression. It seems to have tried to say too much and sometimes did too stylish tricks. Side plots are murky. But there is an exuberance and free wheeling attack not ordinarily seen from Spain.

The model has a giant picture of her stolen by young hoodlums. Then there is a professor who is predicting her death. And the mannequin can seem to trust only one rich man who has a strange girlfriend. The latter ends up killing him and going after the girl, missing her and then going on a murdering rampage.

Color is fine, the girls nifty looking, and this pic manages to make some points. There are classic Hispano characters like an evil blind man, who turns out to be the wily professor; young delinquents, sleek Latino lovers and the sun. Thus, it is an unusual pic with special handling and labeling called for to attain best results. *Mosk.*

La Longue Marche
(FRENCH-TOTALVISION)

Cannes, May 5.
UGC release of L. Jeffrey Selznick-Transatlantic production. Stars Robert Hossein, Maurice Ronet, Jean-Louis Trintignant; features Berthe Granval, Jean-Pierre Kalfon, Paul Frankeur. Directed by Alexandre Astruc. Screenplay, Astruc, J. C. Tacchella, acques Laurent Bost; camera, Jean-Jacques Rochut; editor, Claudine Bouche. At Cannes Film Fest. Running time, 90 MINS.

Carnot	Robert Hossein
Chevalier	Maurice Ronet
Philippe	Jean-Louis Trintignant
Girl	Berthe Granval
Druggist	Robert Dalban
Morel	Paul Frankeur

L. Jeffrey Selznick, son of the late David O., now a producer here (he's already done two commercial adventure pix), now has tackled a serious theme in the tale of a doomed resistance group in France during the last war. It is done simply and without excess. Pic emerges a taut actioner. Playoff abroad looks likely with arty chances needing harder sell.

A maquis group has an important but wounded man to send off to London. So the maquis highjacked a doctor (Maurice Ronet) who just wants to be left out of the war. There is the hot-headed, violent maquis head and a more reasonable young lieutenant, played by Robert Rossein and Jean-Louis Trintignant respectively. The doctor is saved from execution by Hossein for his good work but then Germans encroaching on the group have them kidnapping him, thinking he turned them in.

Film amply puts over the heroic aspects as well as the waste and grimness. It is all done sans frills to give the yarn authenticity, being helped by on-the-pot lensing in a rugged, mountainous country.

Actors are solid enough but the characterizations border stereotype and some high tone talk could have been done away with. But, on the whole, this is a fine film on a theme that is rarely treated in local films. Certain allusions may escape foreign viewers. But it is a terse, well-done war tale and could profit from worldwide market interests in the theme, with home chances high. Production dress is good, as are technical credits all along the line. *Mosk.*

Au Hasard Balthazar
(By Chance Balthazar)
(FRENCH)

Cannes, May 6.
Athos Film release of Parc Film-Athos Film - Svenskindustri - Institut Suedois production. With Francois Lafarge, Anne Wiazemsky, Phillippe Asselin, Nathalie Joyaut, Walter Green. Written and directed by Robert Bresson. Camera, Ghislain Cloquet; editor, Raymond Lamy. At Cannes Film Fest. Running Time, 90 MINS.

Girl	Anne Wiazemsky
Boy	Francois Lafarge
Father	Philippe Asselin
Mother	Natalie Joyaut
Friend	Walter Green
Tramp	J. C. Guilbert

Robert Bresson has always gone his own way, made films every few years, when he felt like it. His probings are marked by growing use of completely nonpro actors. Last few films were just tools of his tactics. Here he brings off a cool but poetic look at small town love and life that pierces deeply and dredges up a unique, offbeat pic which is mainly for art spots.

Shown in the market section of the unspooling Cannes Fest, it strongly merited inclusion in the competing fest. However it will likely grace another fest later this season and should be a contender for a prize somewhere. Around the life span of a donkey, Bresson has built a tale of country pride, young love, human frailty and strength and, in short, a parable on life that manages to bare humans in their weaknesses, strength, pettiness, cupidity and decency.

It begins with the donkey Balthazar's birth and ends with the animal's death. It is first used for hauling by a peasant and is usually beaten to run off one day. He is found by a man who runs a country estate for a rich man and given to his little girl. It grows up with the girl and seems to background her first trials and love and is successively used by a mystical, violent tramp, a young hoodlum and finally killed when employed for smuggling on the French-Spanish border.

Bresson does not overdo the parallel between human life and that of the animal. Rather it is just a non-thinking aspect that is thus used by the others and also reflects their actions without any twisting. It works as a link and helps raise the simple story to a poetic level.

The girl's awakening to love has her putting flowers on the donkey's head as the local town tough watches, hidden, and makes his first overtures to her that are finally accepted. Love is just physically shown and never rationalized or romanticized. The nonactors' very lack of expression makes what they say have deeper overtones and they also make effective characters if, at times, they may anticipate a movement or a blow. But this is rare.

So here is a personal, austere pic that would need personal handling for best results abroad. *Mosk.*

Kazdy Den Odvahu
(Courage For Every Day)
(CZECHOSLOVAKIAN)

Cannes, May 6.
Czech State Film production and release. With Jana Brejchova, Jan Kacer, Josef Abrham, Vlastimil Brodsky. Directed by Evald Schorm. Screenplay, Antonin Masa; camera, Jan Curik. At Cannes Film Fest. Running time, 90 MINS.

Vera	Jana Brejchova
Jarda	Jan Kacer
Borek	Josef Abrham
Editor	Vlastimil Brodsky

Here is a brilliant new director unveiled with a sharp incisive look at life and love among the young adults of today. Arty chances look possible abroad though its allusions and treatment make it more specialized and calling for more careful sell.

Filmmaker Evald Schorm deals with a popular young worker who begins to feel that the socialist dream is not being lived by the people. He begins to worry his lovely mistress when he tries to force friends to go to dull party lectures, goes around with a travelling show to m a k e outmoded slogan-laden speeches and begins even to be unable to carry on their relationship.

But there is no haranguing, but a well observed tale. There is a definite feel and value attached to life and love as well as finely etched main and side characters. Thus the boy and girl sneak into her room for their trysts.

The girl breaks out and attacks the boy for his meaningless despair and inability to give love or even voice exactly what ails him. He, in turn, gets drunk and is beaten up by p e o p l e he harrangues in a bar.

Acting is bright, richly textured and headed by Jana Brejchova as the lively, lovely and tender girl' who can not cope with the brooding problems of her lover. The red tape party tactics are tweaked. It is also technically impeccable and adds to the excellent Czech quality showing up at festivals in recent years. *Mosk.*

Le 17eme Ciel
(Seventeenth Heaven)
(FRENCH)

Cannes, May 7.
Comacico release of Copernic production. Stars Jean-Louis Trintignant, Marie Dubois; features Jean Lefebvre, Dalio, Maryse Martin. Directed by Serge Korber. Screenplay, Korber with dialog by Pascal Jardin; camera, Georges Barsky; editor, Marie-Claire Korber. At Cannes Film Fest. Running time, **85 MINS.**
Francois .... Jean-Louis Trintignant
Marie .... Marie Dubois
Dishwasher .... Jean Lefebvre
Head Waiter .... Dalio
Concierge .... Maryse Martin

Shown in the market section of the Cannes Fest, this is a gentle, romantic situation comedy about a young maid and a young window cleaner who try to pass themselves off to each other as a rich woman and a budding novelist, respectively. Quaint and somewhat skimpy in inventiveness and plotting, film still shows a fairly original filmic outlook via new director Serge Korber who may be heard from on the French film scene later judging from this first effort. The film, not entirely successful, is promising.

Showing dreams which parody James Bond and Richard Lester pix ("The Knack"), the youthful hero is set up as a sort of Walter Mitty. Cleaning windows one day he sees a maid sneaking a smoke on her boss' long cigarette holder and takes her for a rich girl. He follows her on a train one day.

She goes home to a castle that is a sightseeing affair run by her parents but he thinks she lives there. They meet and love blooms. They finally tell each other who they really are and go on in life from there. Some nice gags are strewn through the film such as his joyful bike ride to Paris to join her, working in a hotel with a tough headwaiter, and some trim scenes of their growing love.

But Korber has a tendency to be arch in his slim romantic interludes and it also shows knowledge of the pre-World War Yank comedies. But he has a way of gently parodying that is okay perhaps for a short but is too slim for the demands of a feature pic. In fact, Korber gained attention viz some shorts. If he gets meaty scripts,

Korber might well e m e r g e a needed, new comedy director here.

Lensing mixes grainy closeups and candid effects well. Jean-Louis Trintignant and Marie Dubois are charming players and manage to keep their rather dim characters from becoming banal. Supporting p l a y e r s are good, with Dalio doing a neat bit as the petty headwaiter. *Mosk.*

The Last Of The Secret Agents?
(COLOR)

Okay comedy about international art thief foiled by Marty Allen and Steve Rossi in their film debut. Nancy Sinatra's appearance and title tune will boost youth appeal. Okay general dualler.

Hollywood, May 7.
Paramount Pictures release, produced and directed by Norman Abbott. Features Marty Allen, Steve Rossi. Screenplay, Mel Tolkin, based on an Abbott-Tolkin story; camera (Technicolor), Harold Stine; editor, Otho Lovering; music, Pete King; songs, Neil Hefti, Lee Hazlewood, Bert Bacharach; asst. director, Francisco Day. Reviewed at The Beverly Theatre, BevHills, May 6, '66. Running Time, **92 MINS.**
Marty Johnson .... Marty Allen
Steve Donovan .... Steve Rossi
J. Frederick Duval .... John Williams
Micheline .... Nancy Sinatra
Papa Leo .... Lou Jacobi
Baby May Zoftig .... Carmen
Zoltan Schubach .... Theo Marcuse
Florence .... Connie Sawyer
Harry .... Ben Lessy
Enemy Agents .... Remo Pisani, Larry Duran
Prof. Von Koenig .... Sig Ruman
Belly Dancer .... Aida Fries

"The Last Of the Secret Agents?" (question mark included) is an often amusing, satire-slapstick comedy programmer about international art thefts. Marty Allen and Steve Rossi make their debut in pix as bumbling, but successful sleuths. The Norman Abbott production offers some good supporting players, situations and production values which add up to diverting entertainment. Nancy Sinatra's current platter popularity will help the sell. Paramount release shapes up as an okay dualler for youth-oriented hardtops, with better prospects likely in drive-ins.

Mel Tolkin scripted an original story, penned with Abbott, which has the flavor of spy comedies of two decades ago. Allen and Rossi are persuaded to join John Williams as latter moves in on Theo Marcuse, the wealthy, worldly and witty heavy. Williams heads an international ring which rescues famous artwork from thieves. Gimmicks, pratfalls and sophisticated dialog mark the predictable road to the triumph of good over evil.

This being the first Allen-Rossi pic, on a pact which, if fully exercised, will lead to two features per year for seven years, some comment is appropriate on the inevitable recall of Dean Martin and Jerry Lewis, who also entered pix via Paramount. But, there is no valid comparison.

Martin was, and remains, loose, casual, engagingly lethargic; Rossi is at present too stiff, trying too hard to be liked. Lewis has always clowned about, alternating with periods in which he evokes audience sympathy; Allen at present is too much like a man wearing a fright wig and rolling his eyes, while in quieter moments he conveys only a little comic petulance. The new pair so far make a better impression live and on tv; perhaps future pix will bring out greater depth and appeal.

If any comparison seems evident, it is to Bud Abbott and Lou Costello, if only from Allen's appearance and Rossi's relative stuffiness.

This, too, fails, since Costello, like Lewis, could evoke underdog empathy, and Bud Abbott never essayed the romantic image. In fairness, and all comparisons aside, it can be said that, at present, Allen and Rossi need more film warmth.

Producer-director Abbott, with a solid tv comedy background, has overcome the handicap of his top-featured players by mixing them sparingly in a rich broth of incidents sparked by other thesps. The pedantic Williams, the great Marcuse performance, and that of latter's companion, high-fashion model Carmen in her pix debut, hold audience attention.

Connie Sawyer and Ben Lessy register very well as U. S. tourists, while Remo Pisani and Larry Duran are good as the relentless agents of Marcuse. Sig Ruman has a fine bit as a daffy German scientist. Lou Jacobi does well as Miss Sinatra's nitery-operating dad, and gal herself makes a pleasant eyeful. She and Rossi pair off in romance.

Ed Sullivan has a brief cameo at finale which, if its ultimate gag payoff isn't sock, at least identifies the comics with their tv benefactor. Abbotts' direction is full of very fine touches, many of them satirical and effective. Harold Stine's Technicolor lensing is crisp and clean. Otho Lovering edited to 92 minutes, okay length although more tightening in some sequences would help. Pic opens with a slow five-minute sight gag which would have been more effective in three minutes.

Pete King's scoring adds punch in the right places. Rossi sings "You Are," unmemorable romantic ballad by Neil Hefti, and fragments of "Don Juan, Ole," by Bert Bacharach, also of minor interest. Big tune asset, however, is the title number, written by Lee Hazlewood who has penned Miss Sinatra's recent wax hits. She warbles it over titles, and it has a good sound. Other technical credits are strong. *Murf.*

Out of Sight
(MUSICAL-COLOR)

Another beach party pic, hypoed with five rock groups and bikini-clad cuties. Should go well in teen action market.

Hollywood, May 6.
Universal release of Bart Patton-Lennie Weinrib production. Features Jonathan Daly, Karen Jensen, Robert Pine, Carole Shelyne, Wende Wagner, Maggie Thrett, Deanna Lund, John Lawrence, Jimmy Murphy, Norman Grabowski, Forrest Lewis, Gary Lewis and the Playboys, Freddie and the Dreamers, Doble Gray, The Turtles, The Astronauts, The Knickerbockers. Directed by Lennie Weinrib. Screenplay, Larry Hovis (from story by Hovis and David Asher); camera (Technicolor), Jack Russell; music, Al de Lory, Fred Darian and Nick Venet; editor, Jack Woods; assistant director, Thomas J. Schmidt. Reviewed at Universal Studios, May 5, '66. Running time: **87 MINS.**
Homer .... Jonathan Daly
Sandra .... Karen Jensen
Greg .... Robert Pine
Marvin .... Carole Shelyne
Scuba .... Wende Wagner
Wipeout .... Maggie Thrett
Tuff Bod .... Deanna Lund
The Girl From FLUSH .... Rena Horten
Big D .... John Lawrence
Mousie .... Jimmy Murphy
Huh! .... Norman Grabowski

Mr. Carter .... Forrest Lewis
Mike .... Deon Douglas
M. C. .... Bob Eubanks
Madge .... Pamela Rodgers
Janet .... Vicki Fee
Tom .... Coby Denton
Midget .... Billy Curtis
John Stamp .... John Lodge

There's plenty to see—bikini-clad cuties, a souped-up jalopy and five top rock groups—for the teenage action market, but general adult audiences will probably be pretty cool to "Out of Sight." Bart Patton-Lennie Weinrib quickie production has all the ingredients (save a plausible plot) for a strictly commercial half of a double-billing.

Weinrib-directed pic moves along at a go-go speed, serving as little more than a pegboard to display the rock and roll groups, interspersed with the junior jet set continually dancing. It's all good clean fun, however, with the youngsters never getting any closer together than they do with the modern dance steps.

From the looks of things, there are no problems — nobody gets kissed, nobody even gets their swimsuit wet, and from all implications, the teens' biggest worry is finding a suitable band for the upcoming teenage fair. They just continue to dance away their thoughts to the big beat-sounds of Gary Lewis and the Playboys, Freddie and the Dreamers, The Turtles, The Astronauts and The Knickerbockers.

Rock groups are fitted into pic at regular intervals, and wrapped around them and the dancing is the Larry Hovis story (from an original by Hovis and David Asher), which has the heavy, John Lawrence, in a mish-mash scheme to eradicate Freddie and The Dreamers at the upcoming fair.

Teenager Karen Jensen overhears the plot and lines up a would-be secret agent, Jonathan Daly, to avert the disaster. Lawrence, however, is wise to Daly, and tosses problems in his path in the form of his secret weapons —luscious young things intent on getting Day's mind off the scheming. With such lovely diversions— blonde Wende Wagner, brunet Maggie Thrett and redheaded Deanna Lund—spectator might not quite understand why Daly didn't dally longer with the delightful dishes and leave the plot to falter on to its expected ending.

Jonathan Daly is oke as the bungling would-be secret agent, who never manages to do anything right. Miss Jensen looks good in a bikini and is believable as the innocent sweet young thing. Robert Pine is husky and handsome as Miss Jensen's boyfriend, but would have been better off to keep dancing on the beach and not open his mouth. Remainder of cast is capable.

Car buffs will like the looks of the souped-up secret agent's specially-built vehicle, tagged the ZZR. It looks like a glorified road grader to us, but, it's apparently a loose tongue-in-cheek burlesque of the famed "Goldfinger" gadgeted gas-buggy.

Each of the rock-roll groups gets a crack at a featured musical selection, and spotlighting of the varied aggregations should be the biggest attraction of this film.

Jack Russell's color camera work is generally good, although there are a few jumpy scenes that could have been replaced. Other credits are adequate.   *Mitt.*

Blindfold
(PANAVISION—COLOR)

Light Rock Hudson comedy fitting into current secret agent cycle; should hit same stride as star's past offerings.

Hollywood, May 4.
Universal release of Marvin Schwartz production. Stars Rock Hudson, Claudia Cardinale; features Jack Warden, Guy Stockwell, Brad Dexter. Directed by Philip Dunne. Screenplay, Dunne W. H. Menger; based on novel by Lucille Fletcher; camera (Technicolor), Joseph MacDonald; music, Lalo Schifrin; editor, Ted J. Krnt; asst. director, Terence Nelson. Reviewed at Universal Studios, May 3, '66. Running time, 102 MINS.
Dr. Bartholomew Snow ... Rock Hudson
Vicky Vincenti ...... Claudia Cardinale
General Pratt .... Jack Warden
Fitzpatrick .... Guy Stockwell
Detective Harrigan .... Brad Dexter
Smitty .... Anne Seymour
Arthur Vincenti .... Alejandro Rey
Captain Davis .... Hari Rhodes
Michelangelo Vincenti ...... Vito Scotti
Lavinia Vincenti .... Angela Clarke
Marlo Vincenti .... John Megna
Barker .... Paul Comi
Lippy .... Ned Glass
Homburg .... Mort Mills
Homburg .... Jack De Mave
Police Lieutenant .... Robert Simon

Outwitting the secret agents continues to be a popular endeavor for filmmakers and Rock Hudson now tries his hand at it. "Blindfold" carries its share of diversion as light escapist fare, and while overly-inventive at times provides a suitable entry for the general market where Hudson's name means turning wickets. Presence of Claudia Cardinale—the Italian sexpot who has been eliciting American interest—to more than competently handle femme values adds a nice plus to star's marquee voltage.

Scripters Philip Dunne and W.H. Menger, in their adaptation of Lucille Fletcher's novel, have approached their task with sights set on combining romantic comedy with tome's adventurous elements. Dunne, who also directs, follows through with this tenor in his visual exposition. Occasionally he lapses into a silly, such as Hudson running amok with a whip-cream dispenser to save himself from the clutches of a half-dozen baddies, but generally manages amusing unfoldment. Appropriate production values provided by Marvin Schwartz add a note of class. Robert Arthur is listed as executive producer.

Hudson plays part of a famed N.Y. psychologist treating a mentally-disturbed scientist sought by an international ring, who becomes involved in a plot to kidnap scientist from a top-secret hideout. Film takes its title from his being blindfolded whenever he is to visit his patient, held for self-protection by the government in a secluded spot in the swamp country of the South, where doctor is flown every night from N.Y. Later, when he's taken off the case he blindfolds himself and literally "feels" his way to the hideout where he saves the scientist from being transported by the ring, which captures and sells top brains to highest-bidding countries.

Hudson offers one of his customary light portrayals, sometimes on the cloyingly coy side, and is in for more physical action than usual. Miss Cardinale, who looks well either in or out of clothes, is the chorus girl-sister of the scientist displays plenty of appeal. Jack Warden, as an American general in charge of protecting the scientist and who hires Hudson to bring him out of his despondency, knows his way through a line and Guy Stockwell heads the ring. Capable support also is afforded by Brad Dexter as a dumb detective; Vito Scotti and Angela Clark as Miss Cardinale's parents; Alejandro Rey, the scientist; Anne Seymour, Hudson's wisecracking secretary.

Technical credits are all on the superior side, including Joseph MacDonald's tint photography, art direction by Alexander Golitzen and Henry Bumstead, music score by Lalo Schifrin, editing by Ted J. Kent.   *Whit.*

Lt. Robin Crusoe, U.S.N.
(COLOR)

Minor Disney entry, but with Disney name and Dick Van Dyke in title role probably will draw.

Hollywood, May 12.
Buena Vista release of Bill Walsh-Ron Miller production. Stars Dick Van Dyke, Nancy Kwan, Akim Tamiroff, features Arthur Malet, Tyler McVey, P.L. Renoudet, Peter Duryea, John Dennis. Directed by Byron Paul. Screenplay, Walsh, Don DaGradi; based on story by Retlaw Yensid; camera (Technicolor), William Snyder; music, Bob Brunner; editor, Cotton Warburton; asst. director, Tom Leetch. Reviewed at Walt Disney Studios, May 11, '66. Running time, 115 MINS.
Lt. Robin Crusoe ...... Dick Van Dyke
Wednesday .... Nancy Kwan
Tanamashu .... Akim Tamiroff
Umbrella Man .... Arthur Malet
Captain .... Tyler McVey
Pilot .... P. L. Renoudet
Co-pilot .... Peter Duryea
Crew Chief .... John Dennis
Native girls .... Nancy Hsueh, Yvonne Ribuca, Victoria Young, Bebe Louie, Lucia Valero

"Lt .Robin Crusoe, U.S.N." is one of Walt Disney's slighter entries. Intended as a wacky modern-day simulation of the Daniel Defoe classic, it might have borne up in reduced running-time but in its present far-overlength 115 minutes misses as sustained entertainment. Starring Dick Van Dyke as a Navy pilot bearing the celebrated name who is marooned on a South Pacific isle, there are laughs and some ingenious devising of counterpart situations but presentation never quite realizes on inherent values despite a multiplicity of gags and bits of business.

Disney himself wrote the story (under the credit of Retlaw Yensid, his name spelled backward) on which the Bill Walsh-Don DaGradi screenplay is based. Overall lacks the customary Disney label, but no doubt will draw on strength of his name and presence in title role of Van Dyke, who scored so strongly in producer's "Mary Poppins" and via his own tv series.

Also starring are Nancy Kwan as a spear-hurling native vixen out to win the castaway who has bedecked himself in typical Robinson Crusoe raiment, and Akim Tamiroff as her father, a shouting head-hunting chief who seldom can be understood and sets comicking back 20 years. Miss Kwan in her brief tropical clingies and there also are a bevy of island beauts — but so they are in every Bikini beach picture.

Yarn in Bill Walsh-Ron Miller production is told in flashback form as Van Dyke starts an 18-month overdue letter to his fiancee after a helicopter which has rescued him from his island lands him on the deck of a flattop. It all began during a routine mission off the carrier, when his plane caught fire and he was forced to parachute into the water . . .

For a good 35 miuntes Van Dyke appears solo as he sets up housekeeping on the island, narrating his actions off-screen until he chances upon a long-lost astrochimp named Floyd. Floyd he finds in the wreck of a Japanese submarine, which provides him with supplies, as well as sake for later tippling. Detecting footprints, he starts to follow them and comes upon Nancy, whose father has banished her to the island for refusing the man of his choice.

Arrival of a group of her sisters and cousins who have come to escape the tyranny of the chief allows Crusoe to launch on his theory of women's rights, and he organizes them into an all-girl army who address him as "Admiral-Honey." When the chief reaches the island he finds femmes in revolt, as well as Yankee ingenuity in warding off his attack.

Byron Paul maintains a sharp pace in his direction but cannot overcome the drawn-out aspects of script which causes frequent drag. Van Dyke's comedy is overly broad but he handles his assignment diligently for what it is. Miss Kwan charms in her role but Tamiroff is nothing less than silly, called on for the type of comedy long forgotten. The chimp, of course, takes practically every scene he's in.

Color photography by William Snyder is especially outstanding, and he makes the most of backgrounds afforded by location site, the Hawaiian island of Kauai. Bob Brunner's music score is effective as is art direction of Carroll Clark and Carl Anderson. Special effects by Peter Ellenshaw, Eustace Lycett and Robert A. Mattey are particularly noteworthy.   *Whit.*

Duel At Diablo
(COLOR)

Actionful cavalry - Indians meller with names of James Garner and Sidney Poitier.

Hollywood, May 13.
United Artists release of Fred Engel-Ralph Nelson production. Stars James Garner, Sidney Poitier; features Bill Travers, Bibi Anderson Dennis Weaver. Directed by Nelson. Screenplay, Marvin Albert, Michel Grillkhes; based on novel, "Apache Rising," by Albert; camera (Deluxe Color), Charles F. Wheeler; music, Neal Hefti; editor, Fredric Steinkamp; asst. directors, Emmett Emerson, Philip N. Cook. Reviewed at Samuel Goldwyn Studios, May 12, '66. Running time, 105 MINS.
Jess Remsberg .... James Garner
Toller .... Sidney Poitier
Ellen Grange .... Bibi Andersson
Willard Grange .... Dennis Weaver
Lt. McAllister (Scotty) .... Bill Travers
Sgt. Ferguson .... William Redfield
Chata .... John Hoyt
Clay Dean .... John Crawford
Major Novak .... John Hubbard
Norton .... Kevin Coughlin
Tech .... Jay Ripley

Casey .... Jeff Cooper
Nyles .... Ralph Bahnsen
Swenson .... Bobby Crawford
Forbes .... Richard Lapp
Ramirez .... Armand Alzamora
Colonel Foster .... Alf Elson
Chata's Wife .... Dawn Little Sky
Alchise .... Eddie Little Sky
First Miner .... Al Wyatt
Cpl. Harrington .... Bill Hart
Crowley .... J. R. Randall
Stableman .... John Daheim
Burly Soldier .... Phil Schumacher
First Wagon Driver..Richard Farnsworth
Second Wagon Driver .... Joe Finnegan

"Duel at Diablo" packs enough fast action in its cavalry-Indians narrative to satisfy the most avid follower of this type of entertainment. Produced with know-how by Fred Engel and Ralph Nelson and directed with a flourish by Nelson, the Deluxe-color feature is long on exciting and well-staged battle movement and carries a story that while having little novelty still stands up for good effect.

Based on the Marvin Albert novel, "Apache Rising," screenplay is by Albert and Michel Grilikhes. James Garner and Sidney Poiteir are starred, Garner as a scout, Poitier as a former trooper who now makes his living breaking in horses for the service. Rivalling them in interest and importance, however, is Bill Travers, a cavalry lieutenant who heads the column of raw recruits to a distant fort and is attacked en route by the Apaches. Suggested rather than played up is Garner's thirst for vengeance for the scalping of his Comanche wife, an insertion that carries no particular relation to the plot.

Garner is properly rugged and acquits himself handsomely, convincing as a plainsman who knows his Indians. Poitier tackles a new type of characterization here, far afield from anything he has essayed in the past. After spectator becomes a dominating figure in the various Indian skirmishes. Travers in a strong character part in vigorous and appealing and endears himself with his light and human touch.

Dennis Weaver scores solidly as a freighter, whose wife was once captured by the Apaches and later, after being rescued, returns to the tribe. He does yeoman service with a heavy role, and Bibi Andersson, U.S. film-bowing as the spouse who keeps running away, shows promise. John Hoyt is interesting as the attacking Apache chief and William Redfield is a standout in brief support.

Technical credits generally are superior, particularly the photography of Charles F. Wheeler and a superlative score by Neal Hefti for mood music. *Whit.*

Los Dias Calientes
(The Hot Days)
(ARGENTINE-COLOR)

Buenos Aires, May 14.

Pel-Mex presentation of a Sifa production. Produced, directed and written by Armando Bo. Stars, Isabel Sarli; features, Mario and Ricardo Passano, Claude Marting, Elcira Olivera Garces and Raul del Valle. Camera (Eastmancolor), Alfredo Traverso: editor, Rosalino Caterbeti. At the Normandie Theatre, Buenos Aires. Running Time, 97 MINS.

Isabel Sarli and her queenly endorsements are the only items that count in this tinter on a bosomy brunette that goes to the fruit plantations deep in the islands of the Tigre Delta to do plenty of swimming and waterskiing while seeking to revenge her brother's slaying and to collect her share of the latter's business.

Low-cut dresses, bikinis, mokinis and straight nudies help the gal to excite the appetites of all males in the area. In between there are some comments on how planters are plundered by unscrupulous, often criminal wholesalers, but these problems as well as other story segments are always a misty background for the lady's shape.

Scripting, direction and acting seem to have relied on the assumption that sensual patrons don't have a critical mind. *Nubi.*

Mohn ist Auch Eine Blume
(The Poppy Is Also a Flower)
(COLOR)

Vienna, May 10.

Wiener Stadthallen Film, Vienna release of Telsun Foundation Inc. production. With Senta Berger, Stephen Boyd, Yul Brynner, Angie Dickinson, Georges Geret, Hugh Griffith, Jack Hawkins, Rita Hayworth, Trevor Howard, Jocelyn Lane, Trini Lopez, E. G. Marshall, Marcello Mastroianni, Amadeo Nazzari, Anthony Quayle, Jean Claude Pascal, Gilbert Roland, Harold Sakata, Omar Sharif, Harry Sullivan, Nadja Tiller, Eli Wallach, Luisa Rivelli, Laya Baki, Silvia Sorrente, Howard Vernon, Marilu Tolo, Violette Marceau, Gilda Daheberg, Morteza Kazerouni, Bob Cunningham, Ali Oveisi. Directed by Terence Young. Screenplay, Jo Eisinger, after an idea by Ian Fleming; camera (Eastmancolor), Henri Alekan; music, Georges Auric. World preem at Wiener Stadthalle, Vienna. Running Time, 105 MINS.

Average cinema patron in German-language countries hardly connects the poppy with dope. It may be otherwise in other nations. But at any rate, the goal of this pic will be reached because good b.o. looms in the world market—and coin for the UN to fight dope peddling.

There's a lot of action, but even if a James Bond type of thriller it doesn't leave much for crix. Trevor Howard and E. G. Marshall are the top figures in trailing a dope ring from Teheran via Naples to Monte Carlo, winding up in a bloody fight on the "Train Bleu" from Paris to Marseilles. In the first half hour of the flicker, quite a number of persons are killed "in action," later the story turns more peaceful.

The fact that Terence Young, of Bond pix fame, directed and that the late Ian Fleming provided the idea for this story gives an idea. Film is as good as the average agent thriller.

Long line of stars should help the film draw. Each of the top players received one dollar as symbolic payment. Pic reputedly cost $1,800,000 of which $600,000 came from stateside Telsun. Profits will go to UNESCO.

Film, produced for ABC-TV exposure in U.S., was reviewed as tv special rather than theatrical release. ***Maas.***

Zato Ichi No Uta Ga Kikoeru
(I Hear Zato-Ichi Singing)
(COLOR-DAIEI SCOPE)

Tokyo, May 5.

Daiei Production (Masaichi Nagata). Directed by Tokuzo Tanaka. Script, Hajime Takaiwa, based on character created by Kan Shibozawa. With Shintaro Katsu, Maiyumi Ogawa, Kei Sato, Jun Hamamura. Camera (Eastmancolor), Kazuo Miyagawa. Running Time, 100 MINS.

The 13th in Daiei's top moneymaking series featuring the blind masseur, Zato-Ichi, this one boasts superlative camerawork by Kazuo Miyagawa (cameraman for "Roshomon" and "Gate of Hell") and the high production and entertainment values which characterize this series.

All of these Zato-Ichi films are distinguished by a coolness and a sense of fun that makes them quite comparable, despite pronounced differences, to the Bond series. The Japanese hero is a man with know-how, with superlative sword techniques, with innate knowledge of the "in" way to flick a kimono sleeve or sheath a sword. Filled with in-type jokes, and with comic-book-type spectaculars, the series is Japanese pop-art at its best. Few of the films have appeared on U.S. screens and with a minimum of cutting more could do quite well in the more sophisticated houses.

In this one the hero feels his way into a gang-controlled town and decides to clean it out. This is climaxed by a splendidly photographed and very beautiful fight-on-the-bridge which should really turn on art-house patrons. In Japan Zato-Ichi is beloved by kiddies and adults alike (for different reasons). Abroad, he would seem to be adult fare. ***Chie.***

And Now Miguel
(COLOR)

Good family entry; excellent acting and interesting story.

Hollywood, May 4.

Universal release of Robert B. Radnitz production. Stars Pat Cardi, Michael Ansara, Guy Stockwell, Clu Gulager; features Joe De Santis, Pilar Del Rey. Directed by James B. Clark. Screenplay, Ted Sherdeman, Jane Klove; based on novel by Joseph Krumgold; camera (Technicolor), Clifford Stine; editor, Hugh S. Fowler; music, Philip Lambro; asst. director, Phil Bowles. Reviewed at Universal Studios, May 3, '66. Running time, 95 MINS.

Miguel .... Pat Cardi
Blas .... Michael Ansara
Perez .... Guy Stockwell
Johnny .... Clu Gulager
Padre de Chavez .... Joe De Santis
Tomasita .... Pilar Del Rey
Pedro .... Peter Robbins
Gabriel .... Buck Taylor
Eli .... Edmund Hashim
Faustina .... Emma Tyson
Bonafacio .... Richard J. Brehm
Wool Buyer .... Hell F. Waters
Ranger .... James Hall
Shearer .... J. Scott Carroll
Priest .... Father Ralph W. Pairon
Sister .... Sister Katrina

"And Now Miguel" is the simple, homely tale of a young boy's yearning to grow up so he may shepherd the flocks his family has run for many generations. Based on Joseph Krumgold's Newberry Medal-winning novel of a present-day New Mexican family, the Robert B. Radnitz production, like producer's previous "Dog of Flanders," "Misty" and "Island of the Blue Dolphins," is welcome family fare with particular appeal for juve audiences.

Distinguished by good acting and interestingly color-lensed on the New Mexico range, Ted Sherdeman-Jane Klove's screenplay catches the spirit of the basic idea but devotes too much attention to unrelated incidentals. Consequently, film suffers from episodic treatment. Some trimming, particularly in the sheep-shearing and outdoor dinner sequences, would be beneficial. Yet, there is sufficient interest in the boy, warmly and convincingly portrayed by 12-year-old Pat Cardi, to hold attention generally and picture carries feeling which conveys to the spectator.

There is a wholesome quality about the lad's burning desire to gain stature in his father's eyes so he may go to the mountains in the summer time with the herd, and otherwise tend the sheep when the flock returns to the ranch for the winter. He believes he has nearly accomplished this when he falls into one of the 10-foot bags into which the wool is being packed and slows down the shearing operation. Suspense is provided in closing episodes when half a dozen ewes and their lambs wander away and the lad saves them from three attacking wolves.

James B. Clark directs sympathetically and draws persuasive performances from entire cast. Moppet star delivers one of the best juve enactments of the year, and Michael Ansara as his father and Pilar Del Rey the mother create excellent impressions. Peter Robbins as the younger brother is a standout whenever he appears. Guy Stockwell as an artist returned to his homeland, Clu Gulager, the shearing boss, Joe De Santis, the grandfather, and Buck Taylor, the elder brother, register well. Little Emma Tyson also is good in her brief moments as the young sister

Technical credits are superior, including Clifford Stine's photography, Phillip Lambro's music score, Alexander Golitzen and William D. DeCinces' art direction. *Whit.*

Seiki No Kando
(Sensation of the Century)
(EASTMANCOLOR — TOHOSCOPE)

Tokyo, May 11.

Toho release of Tokyo Olympic Film Committee production (Suketaro Taguchi). Supervisor, Nobumasa Kawanolo. Edited by Seishiro Matsumura, Kiyoshi Shinozuka, Akinori Hayashi. Music by Akio Yashiro. Reviewed, Tokyo, May 10. Running Time, 155 MINS.

This is the fifth film version of the Tokyo Olympic games. First was that masterpiece, the first Kon Ichikawa version, unseen by any but those fortunate enough to attend the first two press showings. Due to political pressure it was withdrawn and from it was cut the version which played all major Japanese theatres. From the original, however, Ichikawa made the International version which is at present playing in France, England, Italy, etc. not America, however. The U.S. distributor, one Jack Douglas, hacked up the International version, added a new sound track and is distributing it as the Ichikawa version—which it is not.

And this new "Seki No Kando" is no better. Though it purports to be a straight "documentary" it is nothing of the sort. Ichikawa's rejects are used plus whole sections lifted without acknowledgement from the Japan-released "Tokyo Olympiad." These are so good and the rest of the film is so bad that what advertises itself as a "correction" ends up a corroboration.

What the Olympic Film Assn. apparently wanted was not a document so much as a glorification of Japanese participation. As a whole the film is insular special pleading which verges on the jingoistic. The cutting is so inept, the pacing is so inexpert that the "inspiration of the century" comes out much less inspiring than it really was and infinitely less so than Ichikawa showed it to be. *Chic.*

Der Arzt stellt fest . . .
(The Doctor's Diagnosis)
(SWISS-GERMAN)

Zurich, May 10

Praesens-Film A. G. Zurich release of Praesens (Lazar Wechsler) CCC Fono-Film co-production. Features Tadeus Lomnicki, Sagine Bethmann, Franz Matter, Charles Regnier, Rene Deltgen, Fred Tanner, Margret Neuhaus, Elfriede Volker, Dieter Borsche, Margot Trooger, Vera Jesse, Peter Kummer, Beate Tschudi, Sepp Zuger, Ursula Heyer, Peter Oehme, Hermann Frick, Georg Wenkhaus and Gert Westphal. Directed by Aleksander Ford. Screenplay, David Wechsler, from a story by Walter M. Diggelmann; camera, Eugen Shuftan; music, Robert Blum. At Rex Theatre, Zurich. Running Time, 82 MINS.

(In German)

This Swiss-German coproduction by vet Swiss film producer Lazar Wechsler skims the surface of such topical questions as birth control, contraceptives, abortion, the anti-baby pill, premature sex relations, interrupted pregnancy, et al. Its best assets and, at the same time, most exploitable aspects are several documentary passages filmed, partly in color, at the Zurich Women's Hospital.

Included are such scenes as a normal as well as a Caesarean birth; the saving of a rhesus child by an exchange of blood; and the re-animation of a lifeless premature baby. While these authentic medical passages, shown in graphic detail and in color, may scare off sensitive viewers, they have definite curiosity value. And they are directly responsible for the film's boxoffice success here.

Otherwise, the picture offers little to recommend it. The story line built around the medical shots is clumsy and amateurish. It centers on the young chief medico of the Women's Hospital about to lose faith in his profession, but regaining it through various experiences with patients and their families. Direction by Aleksander Ford, from Poland, is oldhat and incoherent. The lensing by vet cameraman, Eugen Shuftan, is mostly unimaginative.

Acting by German and Swiss thesps as well as Polish actor Tadeus Lomnicki as the young doctor is negligible and, in some cases, downright bad. *Mezo.*

Don't Worry We'll Think of a Title

Collection of tired gags, bored performances and threadbare production. Bottom rung.

United Artists release of a Courageous-Kam Production. Stars Morey Amsterdam, Rose Marie and Richard Deacon. Features Tim Herbert, Jackie Heller, Joey Adams, Andy Albin, Michael Ford, January Jones, Carmen Phillips, Henry Corden, and Peggy Mondo. Directed by Harmon Jones; produced by Morey Amsterdam, Aubrey Schenck, executive producer. Screenplay, John Hart and Morey Amsterdam. Adaptation, George W. Schenck and William Marks. Cinematography, Brick Marquand. Edited by Robert C. Jones. Music, Richard De Salle. Reviewed at Preview Theatre, New York. Running Time, 83 MINS.

Charlie	Morey Amsterdam
Annie	Rose Marie
Mr. Travis, Police Chief	Richard Deacon
Seed, Samu	Tim Herbert
Mr. Big	Jackie Heller
1st Guy	Joey Adams
2nd Guy	Andy Albin
Jim Holliston	Michael Ford
Magda Anders	January Jones
Olga	Carmen Phillips
Lerowski	Henry Corden
Fat Lady	Peggy Mondo
Fat Man	Percy Helton
The Lover	LaRue Farlow
Mr. Raines	Moe Howard
Chinese Girl	Yau Shan Tung
Girl Student	Arline Hunter
2nd Student	Annazette
Boy Student	Gregg Amsterdam
Athlete	Darryl Vaughan

Cleverest element of this low-budget entry is the title. Otherwise, a compendium of wilted gags, tired repartee, and imbecile mishaps, "Don't Worry We'll Think of a Title" is so poverty stricken in imagination even the evidently half-embarrassed walk-ons by "name celebs" — Steve Allen, Milton Berle, Forrest Tucker, and others— can't rescue the stale comedics. Consequently, United Artists distribution of the film, via bottom-half slots in dualers, is probable pattern.

Plot follows standard mistaken identity gambit in which Amsterdam, playing a fumbling incompetent, is believed by a secret organization to be a defected cosmonaut hiding in the U. S. Most of the action revolves around a bookshop in a college town, which is suddenly infested with undercover agents, trapdoors, tunnels, etc., as the organization attempts to snatch Amsterdam. Negligible story line is merely used as a springboard for misfired gag scenes, most of them painstakingly contrived and painfully telegraphed.

Direction is standard video collection of two shots, stretched beyond their usual unendurable length. Script by John Hart and Morey Amsterdam reaches peak with such lines as "Girlie, girlie," he said, summoning the waitress. "Did you call me, sir?," she answered. "No I called you girlie," he snappily replies. From latter, the dialog skitters downhill. Performances by Morey Amsterdam, whose bug-eyed reaction to everything is apparently the limit of his style, and Rose Marie follow same walk-through pattern. Overall impression made is that performers seem to sense the inevitable audience yawns, and react accordingly. Production values O.K. *Rino.*

Fat Spy
(COLOR)

Not much to recommend this thinly scripted go-go pic. It's from dudsville and good name cast and endless pop singing do not make for even a mildly amusing pic.

Magna Pictures Distribution Corp. release of Phillip Productions Inc. and Magna Pictures Corp. coproduction, produced by Everett Rosenthal. Stars Phyllis Diller, Jack E. Leonard, Brian Donlevy, Johnny Tillotson, Jayne Mansfield, Lauree Berger and Jordan Christopher; features The Wild Ones, Lou Nelson, Toni Lee Shelley, Penny Roman, Chuck Alden, Eddie Wright, Tommy Graves, Tommy Trick, Linda Harrison, Deborah White, Toni Turner, Jill Bleidner, Tracy Vance, and Jeanette Taylor. Directed by Joseph Cates. Screenplay, Matthew Andrews; camera, Joseph Brun; music, Al Kasha, Joel Hirshhorn and Han Hunter; editor, Barry Malkin; assistant director, George Goodman. Reviewed at the Hollywood Academy Theatre. May 11, '66. Running Time, 75 MINS.

"Fat Spy" is overly long (one hour, 15 minutes). In it Phyllis Diller, Jack E. Leonard and Jordan Christopher make their screen debuts—more accurately screentests. But "Spy" will have to live off the fat of the teenage market. An endless trickle of pop songs, with everyone taking turns, meanders through this inane, underfed script. Technical aspects, with the possible exception of sound, are sophomoric and some cute editing—adding comic strip balloon titles throughout — only adds to the confusion.

For opening 10 minutes screen is occupied with singing and youths gyrating in swim suits. About every five minutes a song cuts into the nonexistent plot.

Leonard plays twin brothers, one with a hairpiece, and Miss Diller plays herself. Unfortunately they do not use their own material. Story erodes around a Florida island owned by lipstick manufacturer Brian Donlevy. Group of youths boat there to search for ancient treasure. Jayne Mansfield is sent to father Donlevy to help island "Fat Spy" curator Leonard to find what the kids are up to. Miss Diller wants to get on island to find the Fountain of Youth. At this point someone must have lost the script and cast is transferred to Cypress Gardens. The outcome is told in titles.

Miss Diller has few scenes in pic but handles them credibly, while Leonard is strapped with a larger share of this banal script. Christopher is handsome and youthful, he also sings well, but is not given a chance to act. As for Donlevy and Mansfield, they were hopefully only passing through. Lauree Berger is pretty and sings okay.

Joseph Cates is credited with the non-direction. Matthew Andrews with writing the script. *Dool.*

Mademoiselle
(FRENCH-BRITISH)

Cannes, May 17.

United Artists release of Woodfall Films-Procinex production. Stars Jeanne Moreau; features Ettore Manni, Keith Skinner, Umberto Orsini, Jeanne Beretta, Mony Rey. Directed by Tony Richardson. Screenplay, Jean Genet; camera, David Watkin; editor, Anthony Gibbs. At Cannes Film Fest. Running Time, 100 MINS.

Mademoiselle	Jeanne Moreau
Manou	Ettore Manni
Bruno	Keith Skinner
Antonio	Jeanne Beretta
Vieotte	Mony Rey

This film, though started before the French-British coproduction agreement, is the first to come out under this tag. It has two versions, one English and one French, since French star Jeanne Moreau is bilingual. Pic mixes Tony Richardson's free-wheeling style and the script of the controversial French writer-playwright Jean Genet.

This vehicle is somewhat excessive in its theme of ritual release of human problems, but it is absorbing, irritating and visually brilliant. It thus smacks more suited for arty houses where pro and con critical outlooks and its hothouse theme may make for solid interest. Playoff would need more careful attention, with exploitation use also in evidence.

United Artists has an unusual offbeat item, and its relentless violence and sexual forthrightness call for proper labeling. A small French farming town is the locale. Story is about an arsonist who is terrorizing the people. A poisoned drinking well, and opened irrigation ditches which flood the farms, finally lead to the populace to form a lynching mob.

The ingrained suspicion regarding a foreigner makes an Italian woodcutter, living in the town, the scapegoat. Although he is innocent, there is a link in his presence to the setting off of inhibitions which have made the prim local schoolteacher suddenly break out as a nymphomaniac and the pyromaniac who has been responsible for it all. If she goes scot-free, there is no flouting of morality here but an ironic comment of human actions.

However, this also underlines one of the flaws (the main one) of the film that keeps it from coming off.

The heroine is shown as perverse more than insane, and there is thus no direct link to her inhibitions that finally lead to her substituting fire and poison for love and identifying herself with Joan of Arc. But she does not remain virginal and finally meets up with the Italian for a mad night of love.

This is done with fervor, such as the woman licking the man's muddy boots. There are other nipups before she traipses back to town bedraggeled and tells the inflamed townspeople it was the Italian all along. He is hacked to death and seemingly buried as the town returns to normal.

The Italian's son has had a crush on the schoolteacher who has treated him cruelly once her passions were aroused. She had been nice before. Pic uses a high key flashback to show how her latent perversions and inhibitions are set off by the Italian.

There is a bit too much symbolism and explaining, but perhaps not enough bolstering of the character of the staid, matronly teacher to make her blowoff revealing enough. And the mixture of reality and the unreal are also not cohesive enough.

Jeanne Moreau's presence manages to make her schoolmarm character quite plausible in revealing her lurking lusts. The fire reflected in her eyes, her taking out her passions on the hapless boy and her defense of the Italian all get fine limning.

But the remainder is somewhat sketchy, even though Ettore Manni has the virility to bring on hatreds from the other men and finally his own demise. The script seemingly needed more depth and background to the characters. Either that or almost surrealistic playing and treatment.

Richardson has given this a fine

visual feel. He is helped by David Watkin's fine contrasty lensing and the sharp editing of Anthony Gibbs. It just appears that two temperaments have not quite jived. Richardson appears to want to chastise the townspeople for their pettiness and fears while the script seems to want no realistic blame.

At any rate, this is a controversial, offbeat item that might have solid art and specialized playoff in store. *Mosk.*

Cannes Festival

Zdrastovoui Eto Ia
(Hello, It's Me)
(RUSSIAN)

Cannes, May 10.
Mosfilm release of Armen Film production. With Armene Djigarkhanian, Polan Bikov, Amalia Fateeva, Marguerite Terekhova and Frounze Dovlatian. Directed by Frounze Dovlatian. Screenplay, Arnold Agababov; camera, B. Badalian; editor, G. Morisovkova. At Cannes Film Fest. Running time, 123 MINS.
Artiom .... Armene Djigarkhanian
Oleg .... Polan Bikov
Lussia .... Amalia Fateeva
Tania .... Marguerite Terekhova
Friend .... Frounze Dovlatian

Made in the old Armenian section of Russia (the Georgian area) pic is a series of tales woven together. The theme concerns wartime losses, waiting and the world of today. This is overlong and familiar. But it does have a feeling for character and incident that keeps up interest. However, its allusions, almost sudsy happenings and repetitive qualities relegate this mainly for the Eastern mart, with some language possibilities in the West on its general tenderness sans pathos.

A scientist loses his girl during the war, and never marries. His work is outlined as well as his lonliness. He meets a little girl who had brought him the news of his girl's departure during the war and who is now a young woman. Of course, love blossoms, and it is depicted as something to enhance one's life.

That this is not all platitudes is a tribute to the director who can make a muted dramatic scene play well. It also has a look at a more modern Russia, the individual sometimes lost in the mass, and the growing Westernization in gadgets. This has a place at a fest but more for producer marts or in non-competing slots than the coveted competing lineup. It is technically good and ingratiatingly acted.

It also shows the decentralization of Russo filmmaking and has a plus in its Armenian backgrounds. There is even a shot of a nude girl. Things are changing with the Russian producers. *Mosk.*

Con El Viento Solano
(In The Torrid Wind)
(SPANISH-COLOR)

Cannes, May 17.
Pro Artis Iberica production ano release. Stars Antonio Gardes; features Marie-Jose Alfonso, Vicente Escudero, Imperio Argentina, Maria Luisa Ponte.

Directed by Mario Camus. Screenplay, Ignacio Aldecoa; camera (Eastmancolor), Juan Julio Baena; editor, Pedro Del Rey. At Cannes Film Fest. Running Time, 100 MINS.
Sebastien .... Antonio Gardes
Fiancee .... Marie-Jose Alfonso
Dancer .... Vicente Escudero
Madame .... Imperio Argentina
Friend .... Maria Luisa Ponte

Color is lush and lovely, the summer Hispano countryside is beautiful. With such background, an oft-told tale about a hothead young rebel without a cause is unfolded. He mistakenly kills a cop and goes on the run. Consistently denied help, he finally gives himself up. Absence of more insight into the characters and modern Spain plus the telegraphed proceedings relegate this mainly to language spots abroad. There may be some playoff or lower case dualers via its color and theme.

Antonio Gardes has the fiery pride and hot headedness for the role of the delinquent on the run. Film may have more significance in Spain via its allusions to poverty, lack of ties of the characters involved and the absence of initiative of anyone when he demands help. But to outsiders it just remains an obvious tale heightened only by some nice flamenco interludes, the countryside and the fine tinting and lensing. *Mosk.*

Sult
(Hunger)
(DANISH-SWEDISH-NORWEGIAN)

Cannes, May 12.
Sandrews release of Studio ABC, Henning Carlsen, Sandrews, Filminstitutet production. Stars Per Oscarsson, Gunnel Lindblom. Directed by Henning Carlsen. Screenplay, Carlsen, Peter Seeberg from the book by Knut Hamsun; camera, Henning Kristiansen; editor, Anja Breien. At Cannes Film Festival. Running Time, 100 MINS.
Writer .... Per Oscarsson
Woman .... Gunnel Lindblom

First Scandinavian coproduction bodes well in its fine mixture of an adaptation of a book by a noted Norwegian writer, the long-dead Nobel prizewinner Knut Hamsun, two Swedish thesps and a Danish director and adapter. Pic is a taut tour-de-force affair about a time of hunger and near breakdown of a talented young writer in the Norway of the turn-of-the-century. Its relentless dwelling on anguish plus the brilliant playing of Per Oscarsson, keep this from ever being stilted or repetitive.

Oscarsson is a scrawny, black-clad young man waiting for a reaction of an editor on an article he has written. He is reduced to eating paper, pawning his things, succumbing to hallucination but still refusing to ask for help. His artist's pride never gets ridiculous or self indulgent. It stems from his need to believe in himself and keep some sort of face and also reflects the poverty and harshness of the times without being didactic or academic.

His giving of some money to beggars, dreams of fighting a dog for a bone, gnawing on raw bones

from a butcher, a brief stay in an overcrowded slum house are all heightened by his serious condition and give some insight into what it probably is he wants to say in his work. A brief interlude with a girl who spurns him for a silly reason puts the last touch on his resistance.

But he manages to get to a ship to go off somewhere towards another chance or another life. The saving quality of this unusual pic is the refusal to give way to despair or self-pity. The director, Henning Carlsen, holds a firm visual reign on the proceedings and creates the period, the mixture of hallucination and thought clearly and with probing strength and eschewing sentimentality and didactism,

It is a man's descent into near breakdown and its expert, fragmented capturing of his delirium, hopes and life force give this pic a potent envelope and flair. Its subject matter and refusal to go in for obvious dramatic effects and music may make this more difficult on foreign marts and it has to be handled carefully and personally for best results. Its solidity, grave progression and sometimes period allusions also mean art rather than playoff possibilities.

It is technically excellent. Gunnel Lindblom is enticing and unpredictable as the girl while Oscarsson's brilliant performance may win the acting prize of Cannes, 1966. *Mosk.*

Campanadas A Medianoche
(Chimes at Midnight)
(SPANISH-SWISS)

Cannes, May 10.
Harry Saltzman, Emiliano Pierda, Angel Escolano, Internacional Films Espanola production and release. With Orson Welles, Jeanne Moreau, Margaret Rutherford, John Gielgud, Marina Vlady, Alan Webb, Norman Rodway, Walter Chiari, Keith Baxter, Fernando Rey. Written and directed by Welles, based on several plays of William Shakespeare; camera, Edmund Richard; editor, F. Meuller. At Cannes Film Fest. Running time, 113 MINS.
Fals'--f .... Orson Welles
King Henry IV .... John Gielgud
Doll Tearsheet .... Jeanne Moreau
Hotspur .... Norman Rodway
Hal .... Keith Baxter
Tavern Keeper .. Margaret Rutherford
Lady Hotspur .... Marina Vlady
Shallow .... Alan Webb
Silence .... Walter Chiari

That American international journeyman filmmaker Orson Welles now surfaces with a Swiss-Spanish pic, coproduced by Harry Saltzman. It chronicles the story of Shakespeare's Falstaff. Taken from several plays, it details the last days of Falstaff's relationships with the Prince of Wales and the future King Henry V of England. A personal viewpoint, it mixes the grotesque, bawdy, comic and heroic, and does have a melancholy under its carousing and battles.

Welles has tried to humanize Falstaff in dwelling on his intimations of old age that make him accept a buffoonish part in the young prince's life. He contrasts this with the sombre reflections of the real father on whose uneasy head lies the new crown of England. The Prince finally has to choose

between an indulgent father figure, Falstaff, and the real adult father who means responsibility, dedication and adulthood.

The choice is the most moving part of this uneven pic as Falstaff is disdained by the new king at his coronation and sent off to die of a broken heart in exile. Here the stuff of tragedy peeps out after the bawdy play of Falstaff. Stylized recreation of the times is adequate if some Spanish exteriors seem too ornate for the more sombre England of the times. But the inns have the noisy swagger that is right.

However, it is the playing that counts. This is fairly consistent if some noted players falter in small roles. Welles himself is gigantically bloated and full of swagger that yet shows glints of lonely pride and fear of rejection under a pompous, exterior. John Gielgud, on the other hand, is sombre, suffering and stately as the new King Henry IV trying to sort out of the problems of the court and his vassals in order to unite his nobles.

The battle against the rebel Hotspur is the turning point as it tempers the fledgling Prince in combat, aided and abetted by a Falstaff imbedded in massive armor. Here there is a fury in the editing and a decided tempo of ebb and flow of battle that makes this one of Welles' most flashy and yet filmically taking segments of many a film.

Welles tries to veer from the theatrical in creating visuals that attempt to make many of the statements implicit in the text come over in an eyefilling as wel' as earfilling manner. He succeed: sometimes and at other times detracts from the language or replaces life and content by showiness and overdone angles.

Film looms mainly an arty house possibility for abroad on its Shakespearean backdrop and intermittent sparks of the state of loneliness and old age. At other times it does not blend the playing and times which make it repetitive and slow.

John Gielgud has the right poise as the King with Keith Baxter a right blend of youth and man as the young Prince. Jeanne Moreau is wasted as the strumpet Doll Tearsheet. Hence, this is another personal, showy but uneven pic from Welles who goes his own way and leaves his mark on films technically.

Lensing has the right contrasty edge, editing is exemplary and it adds up to an irritating, yet sumptuous, too personal, yet knowing, Shakespearean pic. *Mosk.*

Un Homme Et Une Femme
(A Man and A Woman)
(FRENCH-COLOR)

Cannes, May 11.
United Artists release of a Film 13 production. Stars Anouk Aimee, Jean-Louis Trintignant; features Pierre Barouh, Valerie Langrange, Simone Paris. Written, directed and lensed (Eastmancolor) by Claude Lelouch with Pierre Uytterhoeven collaborating on the script; music, Francis Lai; editor, G. Boisser. At Cannes Film Fest. Running time, 103 MINS.
Anne .... Anouk Aimee
Jean-Louis ...... Jean-Louis Trintignant
Husband .... Pierre Barouh

Wife .... Valerie Lagrange
Teacher .... Simone Paris

Claude Lelouch, 29, is the do-it-yourself French filmmaker. He has made several pix as director, writer and cameraman, and even produced via his own company. He now repeats with a little more ambition. Winning some directorial accolades abroad, he has yet to break through in France. This glossy production may manage to create prestige on his own grounds. Film itself needs nursing for foreign playoff.

Lelouch has practically no story. Ie seems influenced by Jean-Luc Godard, plus the cinema truth movement. He has mock scenes speculating on characters thinking, flash-forwards for hopeful consummation. There are practically non-stop car rides, and the inevitable love scene.

It concerns a widow who meets a racing car driver at the school where they board their respective offspring. He has a wife though he seems estranged. Love blossoms but is frustrated since she still seems too taken by the memory of her late husband. Ending implies she will finally forget spouse to live with the man who will divorce his wife, or shed his mistress, whichever.

Film misses puerility and coyness by Lelouch's seeming unfettered joy in filming his scenes. He overdoes every incident and it takes him a score of shots to get his hero into a sports car. Through constantly roving camera, and especially two charming actors, he redeems rough spots of repetition, archness and a general preciosity.

Two children are too patronized and winsome to ring true. Supposedly spontaneous dialog slights character insights. Sepia and tinted scenes are mixed with the regular color and are sometimes effective enough to give a mood to a scene that does not have it in its progression, talk or observation. Music is much too saccharine and insistent.

The flashes of the husband done to song bits and some parodic shots of all types of exploitation pix (he is an actor), do not mesh with the woman's sudden dedication to his memory.

Anouk Aimee has a mature beauty and an ability to project an inner quality that helps stave off the obvious banality of her character, and this goes too for the perceptive player, Jean-Louis Trintignant, as the man. There is nothing wrong in treating banal people and situations but some "information" is needed.

United Artists has the pic for the world except for the U.S. and Canada which was garnered by Allied Artists via a preproduction deal with Lelouch. *Mosk.*

La Guerre Est Finie
(The War Is Over)
(FRENCH-SWEDISH)

Cannes, May 10.
Cocinor release of Sofracima production. Stars Yves Montand, Ingrid Thulin; features Genevieve Bujold, Dominique Rozan, Michel Piccoli, Francoise Bertin, Jean Bouise. Directed by Alain Resnais. Screenplay, Jorge Semprun; camera, Sacha Vierny; editor, Eric Pluet. At Cannes Film Fest. Running time, 120 MINS.
Diego .... Yves Montand
Marianen .... Ingrid Thulin

Nadine .... Genevieve Bujold
Inspector .... Michel Piccoli
Ramon .... Jean Bouise
Yvette .... Yvette Etievant
Carmen .... Francoise Bertin
Chief .... Jean Daste

Alain Resnais, whose craftsmanship and mixture of weighty themes with love stories along with his novel techniques and experiments have made him a specialized name to conjure with in arty film houses, has made his most mature film to date. However, this demands some patience and attention from audiences and so this is mainly an arty bet abroad, with special situations also indicated. Good handling could also mean more depth.

The Yves Montand and Ingrid Thulin names are rated plus factors. It is the tale of three days in the life of a refugee revolutionary. He is Spanish but has been living in France since his childhood. He is part of a leftist group which still tries to control lead and join with revolutionary forces in Spain.

However, this is a general tale of any sort of revolutionary in exile, even if written by a noted refugee Hispano writer. The point is made that any change has to come from within and the outsiders are just constantly changing.

Resnais uses commentary, sudden shots that intimate fears. They are clear this time as compared to their use in previous films. This pic is understandable if there is a tendency to be too insistent on lyrical love scenes.

Yves Montand is subdued and patient. He finally is resigned to a return to his old country that may mean prison. The film points up the fact that these exiled revolutionaries are in many cases fighting a lost cause or something that has already been settled.

A French group of student terrorists who want to disrupt tourism by bombings is shown, but Montand castigates them about the uselessness of their efforts. There is nothing anti-Spanish in this. It just shows the lives of those people who in many cases are politically obsolete.

Ingrid Thulin has a luminous quality as the woman in Montand's life. Another femme, Genevieve Bujolds shows fetching, young beauty and poise that mar her an actress with a future. All the small roles are played with a deftness of tone that keep them from falling into stereotype. The finely-graded lensing is also a help as well as the intricate but smooth-looking editing that keeps this complicated tale coherent.

Film is measured and sometimes arbitrary in its refusal to allow its personages to relax into more familiar human beings. It thus makes them larger than life figures which makes this more a statement on a theme than a simple human tale. And it succeeds on this level. Resnais also has the ability to give this unforced suspense and even subtle comic notations.

Although this treats a political reality, the film transcends it. Film probably will thus have pros and cons on this score and in its measured progression. But this shows Resnais to be one of the most accomplished filmmakers here.

In "Hiroshima Mon Amour" there was a love story on the background of the Atomic Bomb and its consequences." This one again mixes political commitment and personal love. It is cleverer than its predecessors, and shows Resnais defining an outlook and themes that interest him. No concessions, however, and thus belongs to the arty circuits. *Mosk.*

Rascoala
(Winter in Flames)
(RUMANIAN)

Cannes, May 10.
Romania Films release of Bucaresti production. With Ilarion Ciobanu, N. Secareanu, Matei Alexandru. Directed by Mircea Muresan. Screenplay, Petre Salcudeanu; camera, Nicu Stan; editor, Evgeni Gorovei. At Cannes Film Fest. Running time, 100 MINS.
Peasant .... Ilarion Ciobanu
Lar downer .... N. Secareanu
Son .... Matei Alexandru
Teacher .... Ion Besiou
Daughter .... Adriana Nicolesco

Dignified but familiar tale of a peasant revolt against landowners takes place in Rumania at the turn-of-the-century. The need for land, the rumors of land grants and the aimlessness of the feudal upper classes and police finally set off revolts in many rural districts. This is the theme of this pic as it singles out one such revolt.

But it does not add anything to this event and the film uses the usual side events about the upper classes preying on lower class women. It even depicts a rape by a peasant of one of the rich women. It thus emerges a surface look at a bygone event that adds little new. It lacks the depth or filmic knowhow to make it in any way unusual. This remains academic and of limited possibilities in the foreign market, though probably a solid home item.

Not propagandist, pic does have a certain sincerity and soberness to help it avoid mawkishness and melodrama. It is just that everything is so obvious. Lensing is good, and acting balanced.
Mosk.

Stagecoach
(COLOR-C'SCOPE)

Excellent commercial remake, directed by Gordon Douglas. Strong scripting, direction, performances and production values.

Hollywood, May 12.
Twentieth Century-Fox release of Martin Rackin production. Stars Ann-Margret, Red Buttons, Michael Connors, Alex Cord, Bing Crosby, Bob Cummings, Van Heflin, Slim Pickens, Stefanie Powers, Keenan Wynn. Directed by Gordon Douglas. Screenplay, Joseph Landon, based on Dudley Nichols' screenplay of an Ernest Haycox story; camera (De-Luxe Color), William H. Clothier; editor, Hugh S. Fowler; music, Jerry Goldsmith; asst. director, Joseph E. Rickards. Reviewed at 20th-Fox Studio, May 11, '66. Running Time, 114 MINS.
Dallas .... Ann-Margret
Mr. Peacock .... Red Buttons
Hatfield .... Michael Connors
Ringo .... Alex Cord
Doc Boone .... Bing Crosby
Mr. Gatewood .... Bob Cummings
Curly .... Van Heflin
Buck .... Slim Pickens
Mrs. Lucy Mallory .....Stefanie Powers
Luke Plummer .... Keenan Wynn
Matt Plummer .... Brad Weston
Lt. Blanchard .... Joseph Hoover
Capt. Mallory .... John Gabriel
Mr. Haines .... Oliver McGowen
Billy Pickett ...David Humphreys Miller
Trooper .... Bruce Mars
Sgt. .... Brett Pearson
Woman .... Muriel Davidson
Ike Plummer .... Ned Wynn
Townsman .... Norman Rockwell
Sgt. Major .... Edwin Mills
Bartender .... Hal Lynch

New version of "Stagecoach" is loaded with b.o. appeal. Ten stars, repping a wide spectrum of audience interest, an absorbing script about diverse characters thrown together by fate, plus fine direction and performances are all wrapped up in a handsomely mounted Martin Rackin production. Comedy and action complement the basic human drama which, although set in the old U.S. West, is timeless. It is a remake of a John Ford Western of much buff renown with excellent b.o. prospects.

Rackin's pic, his first production for 20th, derives from a 1939 Walter Wanger production for United Artists, written by the late Dudley Nichols from a 1937 Collier's short story, by Ernest Haycox, "Stage to Lordsburg." Joseph Landon wrote the current version, providing some meaty dialog for the 10 basic interacting characters in a major script challenge, all the more significant since this is only his second oater effort.

Any film, regardless of its story origins, whether these be other forms of artistic expression or even prior pix, is still a self-contained, collaborative and creative effort which should be judged on its own merit and not on a comparative basis. Thus, apart from identifying Rackin's players with their counterparts in the Wanger-Ford version, no further comparisons will be made herein.

Film kicks off with a gory two-minute sequence establishing the brutality of Indians on the warpath, the menace which hangs over subsequent developments, after which the stagecoach starts loading its motley passenger crew. Ann-Margret, in the Claire Trevor role, is quite good as the saloon floozy bad-mouthed out of town under U.S. Army pressure by John Gabriel. Bing Crosby, the boozy medic originated by the late Thomas Mitchell, is a similar victim of Gabriel's incorrect evaluation of a drunken brawl.

Crosby projects eloquently the jaded worldliness of a down-and-outer who still has not lost all self-respect. Much humor evolves from his running gag with Red Buttons, the preacher-dressed and mannered, liquor salesman played earlier by the late Donald Meek. Slim Pickens fits neatly into the old Andy Devine role of the rough-and-ready stage driver who, although not overly enthusiastic about proceeding sans cavalry escort, adapts to the pressures which force them on.

Bob Cummings, the gutless bank clerk absconding with a large payroll, is excellent. Cummings delivers much depth, evoking pity and sympathy. He makes an excellent heavy. Burton Churchill played the part in Ford's pic. Van Heflin is outstanding as the underpaid but dutiful marshall; his virility and honor score throughout. George Bancroft did the earlier characterization.

Stefanie Powers is very good as the pregnant Army wife, en route to hubby Gabriel, an arresting plot irony providing a softening influence on Ann-Margret. Louise Platt was cast by Mr. Ford. Miss Powers' initial appearance is distracting, seeming more of a Quaker than a charming Virginia damsel, but her projection of quiet, solid strength—to the point of checking massacred corpses in order to spot her husband, possibly murdered—is excellent.

Michael Connors, in the old John Carradine role of the hardened gambler, delivers possibly the weakest characterization. As written, he must suddenly shift from card sharp to self-appointed watchdog of Miss Powers. In time it develops that he is the black sheep of a family from her environs, but the switcheroo is unbelievable for some reels, since the early warmth he delivers telegraphs some eventual enobling facet.

To Alex Cord, ex-rodeo stuntman in his second feature, goes the choice John Wayne role of Ringo, framed into prison by land-grabbing Keenan Wynn, latter doing the old Tom Tyler role. Cord underplays very well, and conveys the stubborn determination to avenge his dead father and brother, killed by Wynn, which sustained him during a sadistic incarceration from which he has escaped to join the stage. Cord also believably melts Ann-Margret's hard crust, and the lovers are joined after Cord has killed Wynn.

Wynn is excellent in projection of the sadistic father who, with sons Brad Weston and Ned Wynn, take delight in tormenting victims, thus insuring empathy with the Heflin-Cord confrontation. All other players render solid support.

Artist Norman Rockwell, who designed pic's logo and painted the perceptive talent portraits used in end titles and exploitation, appears briefly in an early saloon scene. Impact of his art might have been stronger if placed on opening titles, but, as is, the oils will halt a departing audience for an appreciative gander.

Director Gordon Douglas deserves a big credit for all performances; he is a vet pro craftsman, associated with a long string of well-made commercial product which has made his reputation within the industry, if not with aesthetes. But he is not alone in that regard. Assisted by second unit director Ray Kellogg, he has paced the film with several exciting chase sequences.

William Clothier's snazzy Cinemascope camera work has caught the dazzling natural beauty of the Colorado exteriors, printed in lush DeLuxe Color. Unlike many oaters which depict the old West as an arid landscape, Rackin's pic displays the rugged, spectacular greenery which also served to draw pioneers in search of a new life.

Jerry Goldsmith has provided a gutsy score which punctuates, but never overrides, the mood. Hugh S. Fowler trimmed to a zesty 114 minutes, and all technical credits are superior. End-title tune by Lee Pockriss and Paul Vance, sung by Wayne Newton, is a forgettable zero. Alvin G. Manuel, Rackin's longtime aide, was associate producer. *Murf.*

Secret Agent Super Dragon
(ITALY-FRANCE-MONACO; COLOR)

United Screen Arts release of Ramofilm-Fono Roma (Rome)-Film Borderie (Paris)-Gloria Film (Monaco) coproduction. Produced by Roberto Amoroso. Stars Ray Danton; features Marisa Mell, Margaret Lee, Jess Hahn, Carlo D'Angelo. Directed by Calvin J. Padgett. Screenplay, Bill Coleman, Mike Mitchell, Remigio Delgrosso and Amoroso from original story by Padgett; camera (Technicolor), Tony Secchy; scene designer, Arrigo Equini; music, Benedetto Ghiglia. Reviewed in New York, May 20, '66. Running Time, 95 MINS.
Bryan Cooper (Super Dragon)
    .... Ray Danton
Charity Farrell .... Marisa Mell
Cynthia Fulton .... Margaret Lee
Baby Face .... Jess Hahn
Fernand Lamas .... Carlo D'Angelo
Verna .... Adriana Ambesi
Professor Kurge ..... Marco Guglielmi
Elizabeth .... Solvi Stubing
Coleman .... Gerhard Haerter
Dumont .... Jacques Herlin

(Dubbed English Soundtrack)

For reasons known only to international film coproductions, this patchwork of Italian, French and Monagesque cinematic craft takes place in Amsterdam. Strictly a programmer, due to its leaden acting and deplorable dubbing, the slight germ of originality which peeps through occasionally only makes the viewer deplore such bungling.

Although producer Roberto Amoroso, director Calvin J. Padgett and their assorted scripters teeter back and forth between a straight secret-agent script and a spoof of the genre, the results are only confusing. Typical of wit is calling chief bad guy Fernand Lamas. What keeps one's interest from flagging entirely is the admittedly scenic background (smearily photographed in Technicolor), a bevie of beautiful birds (especially Marisa Mell) to watch, and some effort by lesser characters, particularly expatriate American Jess Hahn, to create something.

Ray Danton, like most of the lesser American actors lured into the foreign film scene, is so obviously bored with this assignment (with the exception of two or three good fight scenes) that his ennui quickly carries over to the audience. Hahn, as his brawny, ex-convict buddy, works to make the most of an asinine role. Gerhard Haerter as Danton's boss and Jacques Herlin as one of the "bad" men are impressive, despite deplorable dubbing. Technical credits are generally good but no more. Strictly for the second-half. *Robe.*

Lost Command
(COLOR-PANAVISION)

Well-made war actioner about French paratroops in Algerians' struggle for independence. Script falters in places but makes several strong points. Fine direction of an international cast headed by Anthony Quinn. Good pacing and other values spell warm b.o. on general deals.

Hollywood, May 20.
Columbia Pictures release, produced and directed by Mark Robson. Stars Anthony Quinn, Alain Delon, George Segal, Michele Morgan, Maurice Ronet, Claudia Cardinale; features Gregoire Aslan, Jean Servais. Screenplay, Nelson Gidding, based on the novel, "The Centurions," by Jean Larteguy; camera (color), Robert Surtees; editor, Dorothy Spencer; music, Franz Waxman; asst. director, Joe Ochoa. Reviewed at Academy Award Theatre, L.A., May 19, '66. Running Time, 129 MINS.
Lt. Col. Raspeguy ...... Anthony Quinn
Esclavier .... Alain Delon
Mahidi .. .. George Segal
Countess de Clairefons Michele Morgan
Boisfeuras .... Maurice Ronet
Aicha .... Claudia Cardinale
Ben Saad .... Gregoire Aslan
General Melies .... Jean Servais
Merle .... Maurice Sarfati
Orsini .... Jean-Claude Bercq
Verte .... Syl Lamont
Mavor .... Jacques Marin
DeGuyot .... Jean Paul Moulinot

"Lost Command" is a good contemporary action-melodrama about some French paratroopers who survive France's humiliation and defeat in Southeast Asia, only to be sent to rebellious Algeria. Filmed in Spain, the Mark Robson production has enough pace, action and exterior eye appeal to overcome a sometimes routine script. International casting provides flexible marquee bait. Warm b.o. prospects seem likely for Columbia release in general dual situations.

Jean Larteguy, French correspondent and novelist, fictionalized his experiences of the mid-1950s into a popular novel, "The Centurions." Nelson Gidding's adaptation conveys sufficiently the personal interactions of the principals against a backdrop of recent history. Early sequences depict the end of French influence in Asia, and, with the current Vietnam conflict, an exploitable sales angle results.

Anthony Quinn heads the list of six above-title players as the gruff, low-born soldier who has risen to field grade rank because of the attrition of Indo-Chinese guerrilla warfare which decimated the ranks of the French army. Independent, and as intolerant of professional incompetence in his subordinates as he is of the mannered politics of his superiors, Quinn lends a proper balance of ruthlessness and sensitivity to his performance.

Providing a two-way contrast, and exemplifying the extremes to which the Quinn character never extends, are Alain Delon and Maurice Ronet. Delon is the sensitive, quiet but effective assistant who, at fadeout, leaves military service, since fighting in itself has become meaningless, and the expediency of war is too erosive of character. His performance is very good.

At the opposite pole is Ronet, brutal, sadistic and callous, yet with enough fighting effectiveness to be needed in battle. Ronet gives a solid interpretation, which includes appropriate superficial warmth.

George Segal, in darker makeup and hair, registers strongly as the native Algerian, and one of the earlier Quinn group in Indo-China, who on return to strife-torn Algeria turns into a terrorist leader when his parents are killed. This very meaty and pathetic plot irony will strike some as underdeveloped, in that Quinn and Segal never effect a personal confrontation until latter is needlessly killed by Ronet, but by then it is too late.

Michele Morgan, gracious and charming, seems a victim of script which too rapidly forces her to turn from stuffy patrician to Quinn's lady friend (in bed and at military h.q.). Busty Claudia Cardinale, seen first as Segal's prim sister, later essaying a whore image, is an eye-grabber and, in addition, good in her part. She and Delon have an affair, and when he thinks she has used him, his slugging of her is motivated in believable fashion.

Other players respond under the very fine direction of Robson, who has staged both intimate scenes and panoramic battles with keen visual eye. Robert Surtees' Panavision photography is sharp and exciting, and ColumbiaColor print hues are excellent.

A neat recurring irony involves shots of Algerian juves who, literally under penalty of death, scrawl "independence" while older people are dying for it. Film winds on another ironic note—that of Quinn and crew being decorated for having slain a terrorist band, instead of receiving the promised censure if they had failed, while Delon ankles the fort and interprets the kids' scrawls as signifying his own independence.

Franz Waxman's score is often overpowered by the action noises, but, when heard, lends a full measure of support. Dorothy Spencer trimmed to 129 minutes, although film's smart pacing makes it seem less. Technical credits are outstanding, and comparable to those of a Hollywood-made interior-oriented pic. John R. Sloan was associate producer. *Murf.*

Un Printemps en Hollande/Een Ochtend Van Zes Weken
(A Morning Of Six Weeks)
(DUTCH)

Amsterdam, May 17.
DLS release of Cineurope (Dick Polak) production. Conceived and directed by Nikolai van der Heyde. Stars Anne Colette, Hans Culeman; features Lili van den Bergh. Camera, Gerard Vandenberg; music, Lasse Farnlof. Reviewed at the Leidspleintheatre, Amsterdam. Running Time, 80 MINS.

"A Morning of Six Weeks" is the first feature film of Nikolai van der Heyde, who already has two shorts to his credit. This also started as a short, subsidized by government, but the project expanded and financing was taken over by Heineken's Cineurope. It may prove a milestone in Dutch film history because "A Morning of Six Weeks" faces the facts of life. Dutch films can hardly break even on the home market. As Dutch feature films receive guarantees from the Production Fund, which requires the producer to put up 40% of the budget, filmmakers go ahead without too much risk of losing money.

Van der Heyde took into account that there is only a limited public for Dutch films and adjusted his budget accordingly. Technical staff and artists worked for minimum wages, literally for the love of working on this particular film and on Van der Heyde's team. He is the first of a new generation of Dutch filmmakers.

Bilingual title (Un Printemps en Hollande/Een Ochtend Van Zes Weken) is due to fact that picture itself is bilingual. Star Anne Colette is French. She plays a French model who comes to Holland to work for a short time and then stays on after meeting racer Hans Culeman. Both try to escape from themselves in their work, both love their freedom as their choice of profession indicates. There is a clash, and he especially can't completely adjust himself to the new feelings of love. At first he continues taking risks at the racetracks, even when she is with him, but later fear enters his mind and he has to give up racing.

This complex story of feelings is well-created by the author-director, who integrated the "modern professions" of photo model and racer in the frame work of his film. Visual aspects of film are very good, though the dubbing of two scenes is artificial, clashing with the poetic realism of the film. Although this pic may have possibilities outside Holland, it likely will be restricted to arty houses. Camera work by Gerard Vandenberg adds to the value of this film, as does the music of Lasse Farnlof. *Saal.*

An Eye For An Eye
(WESTERN-COLOR)

Oater, with unusual plot twist, may be too slow for the kids but merits attention from adult fans.

Embassy Pictures re'ease of a Circle Prod. (Carroll Case) production. Stars Robert Lansing, Pat Wayne, Slim Pickens, Gloria Talbott; features Paul Fix. Directed by Michael Moore. Screenplay, Bing Russell, Sumner Williams; camera (Pathecolor), Lucien Ballard; editor, William Austin; sound, Harold Lewis; music, Raoul Kraushaar. Reviewed at Embassy h.o., N.Y., May 23, '66. Running Time, **92 MINS.**

Talion	Robert Lansing
Benny	Pat Wayne
Ike Slant	Slim Pickens
Bri Quince	Gloria Talbott
Quince	Paul Fix
Trumbill	Strother Martin
Charles	Henry Wills
Jonas	Jerry Gatling
Harry	Rance Howard
Jo-Hi	Clint Howard

Carroll Case's independently-produced western, acquired by Embassy for distribution, begins as a hodgepodge of other western plots, seemingly a revenge tale a la "Nevada Smith," and winds up a la "Shane," but its principal storyline is nothing like any other western. Had a bit more care been taken with the casting, a tighter script, and the pace slightly accelerated, the result might have been a western sleeper.

Bing Russell and Sumner Williams' script has insufficient action, but plenty of dramatic content. Director Michael Moore, evidently not at home in the western genre, keeps his actors immobile for too long, and lets dialog take precedence over action. However, he gets excellent performance from his two principals despite the trying circumstances under which they have to operate.

Robert Lansing, a former bounty hunter whose wife and boy are murdered by Slim Pickens and two accomplices, takes up their trail to avenge himself. On the way he meets and joins forces with a young bounty hunter (Pat Wayne). At a trading post the pair meet the Quince family—Brian (Paul Fix), his daughter (Gloria Talbott) and young son (Clint Howard), who befriend them, unaware that they're bounty hunters (neither white nor black hats under the Western Code, but more of a dirty gray).

When the pair catch up with the murderers, the plot really changes. During the ensuing gunplay Pickens escapes (although his henchmen are slain), but first shoots Lansing in his pistol hand and grazes Wayne's skull, causing blindness. The pair decide to continue their search and combine skills, the blind youngster shooting at the crippled older man's command. Both Pickens and Wayne get killed in the windup gunfight and Lansing, Shane-like, rides away from the too-eager Miss Talbott.

Most of the cast are excellent, with Lansing and Wayne carrying the brunt of the plot (they're on the screen most of the time). Miss Talbott, Fix and especially the young Clint Howard provide strong support. Pickens and Strother Martin, as a derelict who peddles information to both sides, are too melodramatic compared to the slower-paced other cast members. Pickens' unpleasant voice is also out of place as he's supposed to be a resident of the valley but ranchers.

Lucien Ballard's superior color photography is a major assist and he makes the usually weak Pathecolor process come off like Eastman Color. The heavily-laid-on violence of the opening, however, makes the ensuing action snail-paced by comparison. Raoul Kraushaar's score is appropriately lonely, particularly effective at the beginning when Muzzy Marcellino whistles the main theme over the titles. The latter, incidentally, are poorly handled. Too bright yellow lettering, flashed off and on too abruptly, considering the pastels of the scenic background, hurts the eyes.

Exploitation will probably play up the violence and revenge (eye for an eye) motivation but a clever campaign could make better use of the more literal eye-for-an-eye relationship of the two bounty hunters, forced by fate into an unwilling partnership. *Robe.*

Nogiku no Gotoki Kimi Nariki
(You Are Like a Wild Chrysanthemum)
(COLOR — DAIEISCOPE)

Tokyo, May 21.

Produced by Daiei Motion Pictures Inc. Producer, Masaichi Nagata. Directed by Sokichi Tomimoto. Scenario by Keisuke Kinoshita. Photographed by Jyoji Obara. With Michio Yasuda, Hiroyuki Ota, Kaoru Kusuda, Jukichi Uno. Running time: **89 MINS.**

Expertly photographed remake of Kinoshita's fine 1955 film, based on the well-known Sachio Ito novel about an old man who revisits the scene of his first romance. He was 15 and in love with his 17 year-old cousin but the family misunderstood, sent him off to school, and her off to a marriage where she died in childbirth. He never recovered—hence the framing pilgrimage.

Daiei's production values are unusually slick in this film but, because of this, the poignancy and real pathos of the Kinoshita picture are not equalled. The "child" stars are, respectively, a young teen-age tv idol and a starlet the company is pushing, and are much too aware of their own importance to be convincing. Also story has been simplified and made obvious. It is sentimental which is something the 1955 picture avoided.

In Japan audience reacts instantly to this kind of easy emotional appeal and there were many wet eyes in the preview-theatre. In the U.S. the picture may prove a bore except for Japanese-language houses on the West Coast and Hawaii. Credits are slender, being mainly a fairly detailed examination of Japanese farm-life at the turn-of-the-century and photography which is never less than lovely and often fantastically beautiful. *Chie.*

La Seconde Verite
(The Other Truth)
(FRENCH-COLOR)

Paris, May 17.

Valoria release of Agnes Delahaie-Valoria Films-Explorer Films production. Star Robert Hossein, Michele Mercier; features Pascale De Boysson, Jean-Pierre Darras, Jean-Claude Roland, Jean Marchat. Directed by Christian-Jaque. Screenplay, Paul Andreota, Jacques Sigurd, Christian-Jaque from novel by Jean Laborde; camera (Eastmancolor), Pierre Petit; editor, Jacques Desagneaux. At Normandie, Paris. Running time, **90 MINS.**

Pierre	Robert Hossein
Nathalie	Michele Mercier
Secretary	Pascale De Boysson
Inspector	Jean-Piere Darras
Olivier	Jean-Claude Roland
Vadan	Jean Marchat

A sort of "Back Street" with suspense and ruminations on justice larded on to it, this is not helped by slanted camera angles or a plodding, talky script. However, old pro director Christian-Jaque moves this along. Also he has some okay thesps to have pic a playoff item abroad. It lacks the incisive insight into themes and character to make for any arty possibilities.

A successful, fortyish lawyer falls for a pretty girl who works at a discotheque at night to send herself through medical school. Her sumptuous apartment and dresses are not explained even if there is a rich, young swain. The lawyer is too weak to break with his wife and instead goes into gales of anger and public scenes with his mistress.

The rich suitor of the girl is killed, and the lawyer accused and acquitted. Then pic switches to his being hounded by those who will not believe he is innocent. It finally develops the girl did the killing in hysteria when she could not go through love with the rich admirer. She conveniently suicides.

Hence, too many themes and an excessive, seamy insistence re human pettiness make this a sudsy suspenser. Color is good and playing adequate within the stereotyped roles. *Mosk.*

The Russians Are Coming, The Russians Are Coming
(COLOR—PANAVISION)

Outstanding cold-war comedy about a Russian sub grounded off New England. Lacks solid marquee bait, but aggressive selling should produce hot b.o.

Hollywood, May 21.

United Artists release of a Mirisch Corp. presentation, produced and directed by Norman Jewison. Features Carl Reiner, Eva Marie Saint, Alan Arkin, Brian Keith, Jonathan Winters, Theodore Bikel, Paul Ford. Screenplay, William Rose, based on the novel, "The Off-Islanders," by Nathaniel Benchley; camera (DeLuxe Color), Joseph Biroc; editors, Hal Ashby, J. Terry Williams; music, Johnny Mandel; asst. director, Kurt Neuman, Jr. Reviewed at Directors Guild of America, L.A., May 20, '66. Running Time, **124 MINS.**

Walt Whittaker	Carl Reiner
Elspeth Whittaker	Eva Marie Saint
Rozanov	Alan Arkin
Link Mattocks	Brian Keith
Norman Jonas	Jonathan Winters
Submarine Captain	Theodore Bikel
Fendall Hawkins	Paul Ford
Alice Foss	Tessie O'Shea
Kolchin	John Phillip Law
Alison	Andrea Dromm
Luther Grilk	Ben Blue
Pete Whittaker	Sheldon Golomb
Annie Whittaker	Cindy Putnam
Lester Tilly	Guy Raymond
Charlie Hinkson	Cliff Norton
Oscar Maxwell	Dick Schaal
Mr. Porter	Philip Coolidge
Irving Christiansen	Don Keefer
Mr. Everett	Parker Fennelly
Muriel Everett	Doro Merande
Mr. Bell	Vaughn Taylor
Jerry Maxwell	Johnnie Whitaker
Polsky	Danny Klega
Brodsky	Ray Baxter
Maliavin	Paul Verdiar
Gromolsky	Nikita Knatz
Vasilov	Constantine Baksheef
Hrushevsky	Alex Hassilev
Lysenko	Milos Milos
Kregitkin	Gino Gottarelli

"The Russians Are Coming, The Russians Are Coming" is an outstanding cold-war comedy depicting the havoc created on a mythical Massachusetts island by the crew of a grounded Russian sub. Director Norman Jewison, bowing as producer in this handsomely mounted pic for Mirisch, has made expert use of all types of comedy technique, scripted and acted in excellent fashion by both pros and some talented newcomers to pix. An ultimate lesson in human relations on an international level is socked over. Hot b.o. prospects are in store for United Artists release in the general market.

Nathaniel Benchley's "The Off-Islanders" got its title from New

England slang for summer residents, herein top-featured Carl, Reiner (all names follow title), wife Eva Marie Saint, and their kids, Sheldon Golomb and Cindy Putnam. William Rose's hilarious adaptation was filmed almost entirely on location in Northern California, where the coastlines bears a similarity to the intended site of Nantucket.

Basically, story concerns aftermath of an accidental grounding of the Russian sub by overly curious skipper Theodore Bikel, who sends Alan Arkin ashore in charge of a landing party to get a towing boat. The wild antics which follow center around sheriff Brian Keith, sole resident who manages to keep cool except when arguing with Paul Ford, firebrand civil defense chief (self appointed) who arms himself to repel the "invasion" with a sword and an American Legion cap.

In the latter regard, it will be noted that much fun is poked at those U.S. residents who ride the crest of imagined Russian threats to super-patriot popularity. Film doesn't bear down on this too heavily, though, but a chilly reception may develop in U.S. areas where anything Russian is anathema. Some people, with no tolerance for satire, may even call it sugar-coated propaganda, and, if they are not careful in maintaining silence, their vocal protests could probably add a few more million to the gross.

For others, however, the pic is a delight, and with a strong campaign to sell the film as a whole, the lack of hot names will be overcome. Arkin, in his film bow after being established in legit, is absolutely outstanding as the courtly Russian who kisses a lady's hand even as he draws a gun.

John Phillip Law, who has made three Italo features, also registers in his home film debut as the shy young sailor who develops a puppy love romance with Andrea Dromm. Miss Saint's house helper. Miss Dromm, the gal in the National Airlines teleblurbs ("Is that any way to run an airline"), is good in a role which must convey suspicion, then compassion, then romance. Pair's interactions are fine, although in later reels they retard the pace to a slight extent.

English music hall vet Tessie O'Shea, also in film debut, is very good as the island's telephone operator who contributes to the spread of the "invasion" rumors, and her scenes with Reiner, in which they are lashed together and attempt to escape, is a comedy highlight; Keith is excellent, ditto Jonathan Winters, his flustered assistant, and also Ford. Reiner and Miss Saint play well together, and her comedy ability is good.

Unlike Arkin and Law, who often speak broken English between the all-Russian lingo (in terrif tutoring by Leon Belasco), Bikel and the other sailors converse only in native dialog. All the meaning comes through by their facial expressions and gestures. Bikel, in particular, has risen to a double challenge, since he must be both an amusing blunderer and a real menace. Latter facet shows in a serious climactic situation from which film's crea-.

tors extract themselves with amazing ability.

Jewison handles the varying comedy techniques with uniform success, obtaining solid performances all the way down the line. Ben Blue scores in a recurring bit as the town drunk trying to make like Paul Revere; the horse isn't having any until fadeout. Parker Fennelly and Doro Merande are teamed in a wow scene.

Climax has the sub leaving port under escort of small boats to inhibit an attack from U.S. Air Force jets, called by Ford. Air Force cooperation was obtained in the pic, but the U.S. Navy, apparently sensitive about an undetected Russian sub going aground in a work of comedy fiction, backed off.

On the production side, Joseph Biroc's superior Panavision lensing has captured not only all the fun, but also the seashore atmosphere, printed in soft DeLuxe tones that almost evoke a salt air scent. Johnny Mandel's fine score parallels the mock-heroic style, and also gives a new twist to some standard refrains by adding a Russian vocal flavor.

Jewison's prop man has gone so far as to get not only Mass. license places for cars, but also the Bay State's brake-light inspection sticker. Among the many subtle product plugs, however, he goofed on a brand of milk.

Editors Hal Ashby and J. Terry Williams trimmed to a neat 124 minutes. Intercutting of many running gags is excellent and helps maintain an effective, flexible pace. Nothing seems to be held too long. Only in the 80-100 minute period do things bog down a trifle. Arresting title work, using the U.S. and Russian flags, was done by Pablo Ferro, Inc. All other credits are pro. *Murf.*

Kiganjo no Boken
(The Adventure of the Strange Stone Castle)
(JAPANESE)

Tokyo, April 28.
. .Produced by Toho Motion Picture Co. Producer, Tomoyuki Tanaka. Directed by Senkichi Taniguchi. Scenario by Taoru Mabuchi. Photography by Kazuo Yamada. Music by Akira Ifukube. With Toshiro Mifune, Mie Hama, Tadao Nakamaru, Yumi Shirakawa, Tatsuya Mihashi, Makoto Sato., reviewed, Tokyo, April 28. Running time: 105 MINS.

.Colorful adventure - entertainment tied to the talents of Toshiro Mifune and lots of foreign location shooting. The location stuff (all done in Iran around Isfahan) is first-rate but rest of the film suffers by comparison. Story has Mifune as a shipwrecked sailor who meets up with a Japanese priest in search of Buddha's bones. He finds them but also discovers a castle full of heavies who try to do the pair in. Mifune cleans up, makes the king a better man, gives him a Japanese wife and departs.

Debits include silly juvenile story (good adventure stories are not childish), and the general sleeziness of Toho-lot "foreign" settings. Such attempts at oriental elegance are laughable by Western standards and betray Toho's strong Takarazuk ("all-girl opera") orientation. Thus the best bet for this picture in U.S. would be

dubbed as a kiddy film. Mifune's name might draw the art crowd but the film itself would send them away. Toho has optimistically alread given the film an English title "Adventure in Taklamakan." *Chie.*

Cannes Festival

Seconds

Offbeater that does not quite become a thriller, outright parable or complete suspense item. Tale of an older man made over young by a mysterious organization and his attempts to cope. Theme and Rock Hudson name for probably okay playoff, exploitation and specialized handling.

Cannes, May 20.
Paramount release of a John Frankenheimer-Edward Lewis production. Stars Rock Hudson; features Salome Jens, John Randolph, Will Geer, Jeff Corey. Directed by John Frankenheimer. Screenplay, Lewis John Carlino from the novel by David Ely; camera, James Wong Howe; music, Jerry Goldsmith; art direction, Ted Howarth. At Cannes Film Festival. Running Time, 106 MINS.
Tony .... Rock Hudson
Nora .... Salome Jens
Arthur .... John Randolph
Boss .... Will Geer
Ruby ....:..... Jeff Corey
Innes .... Richard Anderson
Charlie .... Murray Hamilton

U.S. suburbia boredom is treated in an original manner in this cross between a sci-fi opus, a thriller, a suspense pic and a parable on certain aspects of American middle-class life. Dispersal of emphases make this primarily a playoff and exploitation item plus the Rock Hudson name should be carefully booked and promoted.

A middleaged man has lost contact with his wife. His only daughter is married and gone. Even his work, which was his mainstay in life, seems to pall. Into this comes a strange call from a supposedly dead friend to come to a certain place. Man accepts though he thinks it is some sort of grotesque rib.

He finds himself in a sort of mysterious big business esthetic surgery corporation with some disquieting features of a room full of listless men. He is told he can be redone surgically to become a young man and start life over again. He decides to go through with it and after surgery wakes up as Rock Hudson.

He then finds a new life mapped out for him as a painter but somehow can not quite cope and relapses to his own self during a party and finds he is surrounded by more "reborns" of the strange company. He finally finds himself back with the listless men and being taken off to be used as a cadaver to substitute for other men who take this rejuvenation process since a corpse is needed to kill off the old figure.

So this has some intriguing aspects on the yearning for youth and a chance to live life over again by many men. But this Faus-

tian theme is barely touched on and the hero's tie with the past is also somewhat arbitrary. Film does not quite come off as a thriller, sci-fi adjunct or philosophical fable.

Director John Frankenheimer sets up a good mood at the beginning by expressing the man's loss of relatedness by using an extremely wide angle lens that distorts his world. But then the changeover and the revolt by wanting a choice rather than finding his life again ruled by convention and goals laid out for him, loses edge and point. It needed more insight into his life to make the next problem of maladjustment succinct or probing enough.

Some distorted set shots when he is put on drugs and makes advances to a girl as a sort of added inducement by the organization to make him try their methods, are effective if gratuitous. Perhaps a more expressionist style for the whole film might have been indicated. Hudson uses mainly a stricken look throughout though he manages to give urgency to the role while other players are adequate rather than able to give more body and depth to this offbeater.

Lensing is fine and the ending does have a jolt as Hudson is wheeled screaming to his death while a multi-denominational clergyman reads alongside him. But the rest of the film lags and an orgy sequence at a wine festival is somewhat too coyly shot to make its point of abandon or the inability of the newly young man to really be able to slough off his old ways and find a new life. All this is arbitrary and pic is a good idea gone astray which still has some unusual handles for specialized slotting with some word-of-mouth perhaps helping at home. Foreign chances look chancier. *Mosk.*

Lenin V Polche
(Lenin In Poland)
(RUSSIAN-POLISH)

Cannes, May 19.
Sovexportfilm release of Mosfilm-Polski State Film production. With Maxime Straukh, Illon Kuzmerskaja. Directed by Serge Yutkevitch. Screenplay, E. Gabrilovitch, Yutkevitch; camera, Yan Liaskovsky; music, A. Valitachinsky. At Cannes Film Fest. Running Time, 100 MINS.
Lenin .... Maxime Straukh
Oulka .... Illon Kuzmerskaja

Of course, Lenin is idealized and idolized in this tale of his stay in Poland just before the first World War. And if it hues to Lenin's party line, pic still has a neat feel for the period and mixes reminiscences, newsreel and simple story scenes to make this a fine biopic. Chances abroad are limited to special situations.

Lenin is shown in prison where he chafes as he feels that war is imminent. And he has things to do at home as the believer in a worldwide worker revolution and brotherhood. There is no dialog but a voice commenting all the incidents and his beliefs. Lenin is played with a human warmth and gentleness though the attitude is strictly that of honor and almost adoration.

The Russians naturally make Lenin larger than life and expound his beliefs repetitively. But it must be said the direction, acting and wealth of period incident make this an absorbing look at the work and outlooks of a pro revolutionary. But only one side is shown.

Film is technically fine and directed with a simple charm. This is a home product, primarily, even if its visual solidity had it coming in for okay acceptance at the Cannes Fest with nobody outraged by any propaganada aspects.
Mosk.

On
(The Island)
(SWEDISH)
Cannes, May 14.
AB Svensk Filmindustri release and production. With Per Myrberg, Bibi Andersson, Karin Kavli. Diirected by Alf Sjoberg. Screenplay, Bengt Janhsson, Sjoberg; camera, Lars G. Bjorne; music, Erik Nordgren. At Cannes Film Festival. Running Time, 115 MINS.
Count	Per Myrberg
Wife	Bibi Andersson
Countess	Karen Kavli
Teacher	Marian Grans

A talky tale of guilt and expiation on a little Swedish island that is to be evacuated and turned into an army gunnery range, film remains somewhat too obscure and uneven for much chances abroad. Mainly local or perhaps some art possibilities on the generally fine acting and cohesiveness of this otherwise symbolical affair.

The local nobleman feels alone and is accused of murder when the pastor disappears after they have an argument. But the latter is only hiding to try to regain his faith. He is finally routed out and the people of the island accept their coming banishment and most of the people have managed to make some adjustment during the crisis.

Director Alf Sjoberg has tried to give this a too portentous air to make its themes of quest and redemption somewhat literary rather than visual. But he is well served by luminous lensing, fine acting and a literate if somewhat arbitrary script. Too much seriousness, and too heavy and ominous a style to make the tale mesh with the state of man and his individuality versus his social needs that the film tries to bring off.
Mosk.

Faroan
(Pharoah)
(POLISH-COLOR)
Cannes, May 24.
Polski State Film release of Kadr production. With George Zelnik, Barbara Bryl, Krystyna Mikolajewska, Piotr Pawloski. Directed by Jerzy Kawalerowicz. Screenplay, Tadeusz Konwicki, Kawalerowicz based on novel by Boleslaw Prus; camera (Eastmancolor), Jerzy Wojcik; music, Adam Walacinski. At Cannes Film Fest. Running Time, 180 MINS.
Ramses XIII	George Zelnik
Kama	Barbara Bryl
Sarah	Krystyna Mikolajewska
Herbor	Piotr Pawloski
Pentuer	Leszek Herdegen
Thutmosis	Jerzy Buczacki
Nikotris	Wieslawa Mazurkiewicz
Mephres	Stanisla Milski

Poland appears to be the Eastern Bloc country vying with Russia in big scale epics. This sumptuous tale of the young Pharoah of Ancient Egypt fighting against the priests of the time, who are usurping temporal power, manages to be both personal and grandiose in its epic tale. But its running time

(3 hours) also has talky segments which are mixed with more spectacular battle scenes and those of ritual and pomp. Film appears a likely item for interest abroad for special situations because its staid and rigorous qualities make general playoff more chancey unless intelligently pruned, if then.

The young heir is a soldier, and brave, but also against the fact that the priests of the time have the right to direct military and even many governmental affairs since the old Pharoah is an honorary priest himself. He gives power to them when he is not present. The youth is marked by this when a canal is destroyed.

When he comes to power after the death of his father he openly defies the priests and the film details the struggle between the two factions. Whether this has a symbolical attachment to Poland today is swallowed up in the fine re-creation of the times. Perhaps language makes it sound less stilted and forced than many other spectacles of ancient civilization.

But the men are advanced in many ways and the use by the priests of an eclipse to strike terror into an aroused people (the young Pharoah realizes it is a natural phenomenon) is done with taste, visual brilliance and dynamic detail.

The massive sets in the middle of the desert, the battle scenes, the court pomp and the costumes all combine to give this a rich period flair. The intrigues sometimes get a bit involved but it has the potent mixture of human needs and implacable destiny to make for the tragic as well as the opulent.

Director Jerzy Kawalerowicz has handled this big-scale opus with control and a way of scaling pageants and court life into what look like friezes. So this is a cross between spectacle and parable. The playing has the solid, posey feeling necessary for the pageantry of the prelude. George Zelnik has the rigor and looks for the Pharoah role while the women in his life are lovely in their period dress.

This is an imposing if overlong fresco of Egyptian days. It is just that its refusal to be either spectacular spectacle or more realistic drama makes it a film needing special handling abroad. But it could pay off in some arty houses or for more general usage if cut sharply. Color, production, dress and style are tops.
Mosk.

Uccellacci e Uccellini
(Bad Birds, Good Birds)
(ITALIAN)
Cannes, May 17.
Arco Film (Alfredo Bini) production and release. Features Toto, Nino Davoli. Written and directed by Pier Paolo Pasolini. Camera, Mario Bernardo, Tonino delli Colli; music, Ennio Morricone. At Cannes Film Fest. Running time, 86 MINS.
Cournot	Toto
Ninetto	Nino Davoli

Offbeater which blends various ingredients into unusual film fare needing a specialized sell. In Italy, it has the name of country's top clown-comedian Toto', to ride on. Abroad, the new "Gospel According To St. Matthew" Pier Paolo

Pasolini cult should help it along in arty situations. Subject matter and mounting should inhibit more generalized release, and a special sell is indicated.

Phrased in parable-fabled form. pic symbolically spells out Pasolini's view of human survival via co-existence in the sense of the late Pope John, whose words are pointedly quoted. It's an odd pic overall, with little of the usual film format and structure—or plot for that matter.

While this will thrill the aficionados, it could well chill the average pic patron not captivated by Pasolini's worthy but unconventional presentation of the evils of the present world and its hope and salvation in peaceful co-existence and mutual understanding. Format, which appears shortened in locally shown version, deals with a man and youth who are harassed by a savvy talking crow whose preaching after a while bores them, despite rational and intelligent attempts to win them over to his ideology.

In the long run, and via a series of historical flashbacks, Pasolini seems to be saying that old-fashioned, party-line (and left wing) haranguing is passe, and that since Pope Paul a new understanding between the Left and the Church exists. Also that the new, modern approach can accomplish much more for worldwide rapprochement between opposite societies, ideologies and political ideals than adherence to text-book pamphleteerisms. Blended in, but perceptible only to Italo viewers, are many Italo "in" situations and hints, which, however, limit the film's general values or at least doesn't add to them.

Continuity is choppy, there is a fine performance by Toto' and a winning one by Ninetto Davoli, but the key is still in Pasolini's insistent dialogue. At times, it's alleviated by winning, humorous. intelligent notations, but at others, it's overly preachy; precisely one of the things the film is combating. Film's main titles, spoofily sung, are brilliant, and well worth the price of admission. Technical credits okay.
Hawk.

A Hora Et Vez De Augusto Matraga
(The Time and Hour of Augusto Matraga)
(BRAZILIAN)
Cannes, May 24.
Luiz Carlos Barretto production and release. With Leonardo Villar, Joffre Soares, Maria Ribeira, Mauricio De Valle. Written and directed by Roberto Santos from book by Joao Guimaraes; camera, Helio Silva; music, Geraldo Vandra. At Cannes Film Fest. Running Time, 105 MINS.
Matraga	Leonardo Villar
Bem-Bem	Joffre Soares
Quim	Mauricio De Valle
Wife	Maria Ribeira
Juminamamo	Flavio Miglacia

Brazil is the Latin American country that has been showing an interesting crop of new directors and some daringly themed pix at festivals in recent years. This parable on violence is vivid in its dramatic picturing of such but does not condone it. It is thus a subtle pic that may be unwittingly tagged an actioner. But it is not. Pic is a fascinating fable about Brazilian life which could have

some art and specialized legs abroad. It calls for personal and savvy handling. Playoff, for the wrong reasons, may also be inherent.

A brutish man terrorizes his townsmen. He takes women at will, lives with a woman by whom he has a child out of wedlock, and finally sobers up a bit when his woman leaves him. Going off for vengeance, he is practically beaten to death. But he is found by a devout peasant woman and begins to convalesce. It leads to his religious conversion.

He becomes a pious man trying to forget his previous life. But a group of bandits, the romantic Brazilian ones who preyed on the rich and only sometimes helped the poor, happen to visit him. The leader notes that he was obviously a man who had at one time liked the life of the outlaw and also liked a fight.

A strange friendship springs up to end when the now reformed man tries to save some hostages from the bandit head, who are holed up in a church. He takes on the gang and kills them all, mostly in the church, and outside finally does away with the chief and dies himself.

Film rises above reality and becomes a sort of romancero or folk fable about a violent man chastised in violence but being able to expiate himself. It appears against the things that bring on this sort of condition, like poverty, exploitation and violent conversion.

This is acted with ruggedness and romantic elan by the cast. It emerges still another unusual pic from Brazil. Perhaps its harshness and rugged reality, mixed with its fable-like qualities, underlined by songs on the sound track, may make this somewhat difficult for some audiences outside that country. But, again, the right labeling should make it something for specialized use.
Mosk.

Pogled U Zjenicu Sunca
(Looking Into the Eyes of the Sun)
(YUGOSLAVIA)
Cannes, May 19.
Jadran Film production and release. With Velimir Zivojinovic, Antun Nalis, Mladen Ladika, Faruk Begolli. Directed by Veljko Bulajic. Screenplay, Ratko Djurovic, Stevan Bulajic, Veljko Bulajic; camera, Kreso Grcevic; editor, Dusko Jericevic. At Cannes Film Fest. Running Time, 78 MINS.
Matija	Velimir Zivojinovic
Dukic	Antun Nalis
Gruiica	Mladen Ladika
Vidak	Faruk Begolli

A favorite Yugoslav picture theme since the last war has been about partisans. However, this differs in showing man in the brute state of survival and makes the dedicated party man somewhat lost in his slogans faced with reality. It is tautly done but still does not rise to the needed insights into human comportment. Hence, this is little more than something for the action or playoff marts abroad on its effective playing and direction.

Four men are lost in snowy mountain wastes and are suffering from typhus. They hallucinate, rage, regain some human perception but are finally wiped out one by one. Direction keeps the real and unreal in good focus. It is well played and does give off a virile feel of men in crisis. But this still does not escape stereotype and familiarity.

Film was turned down by the Cannes Fest selection committee though it was an official selection. But a rule can't allow this from countries with less than 50 pix per year. Actually, it ranked with some of the films accepted if it's not usual enough to give the festival a bad mark for refusal.

Mosk.

Dymky
(The Pipes)
(CZECH-AUSTRIAN-COLOR-SUPERSCOPE)

Cannes, May 16.
Czech State Film release of Barrandov, Constantin Film production. With Walter Giller, Gitte Haenning, Jana Brejchova, Richard Munch, Vivi Bach, Gerhardt Riedemann. Directed by Voltech Jasny. Screenplay, Jasny from stories by Ilya Ehrenbourg; camera (Eastmancolor), Josef Vanis; music, Svatopluk Havelka. At Cannes Film Fest. Running Time, 90 MINS.
George .... Walter Giller
Mary .... Gitte Haenning
Lady Mary .... Jana Brejchova
Lord Edward .... Richard Munch
Elsa .... Vivi Bach
Kurt .... Gerhardt Riedemann

The Czechs are not only content with winning an Oscar and making a name for growing new talents and forthright treatments of touchy political, social and moral themes. Now they show a flair for commercial-type pix in this sketch item about actor egos, British aristocracy and Teutonic romanticism.

Some allusions to Austrian cinematic fare may escape ordinary audiences abroad, and frothy wit and inventiveness sometimes skirts vulgarity but always avoids it by nuanced direction and comedics. Film is mainly for selective situations but good humor and surface fun should help.

First episode about an acting couple in the early days of the U.S. silent cinema. He is auspicious of another actor's attentions to his wife and finally mixes up his role in his film and the one in real life by really knocking off his rival. But until he is strapped into the electric chair he thinks it is still a film. It is partly paced with fine juxtapositions between the pic and the silent pic being made and the right innocent playing and catchy settings and simple story and emotions.

Next is a more obvious tale about an important old British Lord whose young wife ends up with the game keeper. Told without leering, or any deviations of taste, this takeoff on "Lady Chatterly's Lover" manages to keep from slipping into licentiousness or surface smuttiness.

Last episode is the most ambitious and funniest as a blonde peasant and her heavyhanded husband romp over the mountain countryside in an Austrian never-never land. When he goes off to the wars she takes a lover only to send him off when the husband comes back. This combines lovely scenery, gentle takeoffs on this Germanic schmaltz and a right parodic element throughout. It sends up its overromantic points to make for laughs and eyefilling aspects throughout. The pipes of

the title are props for the males in each seg and are also used for sight gags and symbols.

Playing is perky throughout with decoration eyecatching. In sum, a wispy but engaging pic with good general chances abroad provided it is rightly managed. Director Voltech Jasny shows a flair for lusty fun, clever parody and simple satire that manages to come off. *Mosk.*

Nevada Smith
(COLOR-PANAVISION)

Steve McQueen is principal marquee lure. Okay prospects in hardtops, better in drive-in dual situations.

Hollywood, May 24.
Paramount Pictures release, executive producer, Joseph E. Levine, produced and directed by Henry Hathaway. Stars Steve McQueen, Karl Malden, Brian Keith, Arthur Kennedy, Suzanne Pleshette; features Raf Vallone. Screenplay, John Michael Hayes, based on a character in "The Carpetbaggers," by Harold Robbins; camera (Eastmancolor), Lucien Ballard; editor, Frank Bracht; music, Alfred Newman; asst. directors, Daniel J. McCauley, Joseph Lenzi. Reviewed at Paramount Studios, May 23, 66. Running time, 131 MINS.
Nevada Smith (Max Sand)
.... Steve McQueen
Tom Fitch .... Karl Malden
Jonas Cord .... Brian Keith
Bill Bowdre .... Arthur Kennedy
Pilar .... Suzanne Pleshette
Father Zaccardi .... Raf Vallone
Neesa .... Janet Margolin
Big Foot .... Pat Hingle
Warden .... Howard Da Silva
Jesse Coe .... Martin Landau
Sheriff Bonnell .... Paul Fix
Sam Sand .... Gene Evans
Mrs. Elvira McCanles
.... Josephine Hutchinson
Uncle Ben McCanles ..... John Doucette
Buck Mason .... Val Avery
Sheriff .... Sheldon Allman
Jack Rudabaugh .... Lyle Bettger
Quince .... Bert Freed
Romero .... David McLean
Buckshot .... Steve Mitchell
River Boat Pilot .... Merritt Bohn
Bank Clerk .... Sandy Kenyon
Cipriano .... Ric Roman
Hogg .... John Lawrence
Storekeeper .... Stanley Adams
Paymaster .... George Mitchell
Doctor .... John Litel
Hudson (Bartender) ...... Ted de Corsia

In "Nevada Smith," a Joseph E. Levine oater, produced and directed by Henry Hathaway, a good story idea—boy avenging his murdered parents and maturing in the process—is stifled by uneven acting, often lethargic direction, and awkward sensation-shock values. Overlength serves to dull the often spectacular production values. Steve McQueen is biggest marquee lure. B.o. outlook for Paramount release is good but in less discriminating general situations.

John Michael Hayes scripted in routine fashion a story and screenplay, based on a character from Harold Robbins' "The Carpetbaggers." Hayes' yarn is not a sequel, but a predecessor work, in that it is centered on the Nevada Smith character who acted as guardian to Jonas Cord Jr., the youthful anti-hero of "Carpetbaggers." Plots are set in different generations, so the comparison is mainly for publicity value.

McQueen, heading the list of five above-title players, is the young half-Indian boy whose parents are brutally murdered by Karl Malden, Arthur Kennedy and Martin Landau. Vowing revenge, McQueen sets off to kill them all, a la "Monte Cristo." Brian Keith plays the elder Jonas Cord, then an itinerant gunsmith, who befriends the greenhorn and teaches him armed self-defense.

The above action takes 36 minutes, a clue to increasing torpor that ensues as McQueen hunts down Landau, Kennedy and Malden. Landau is dispensed with in a well-staged knife fight climax to a vignette that is marked by the first of some gauche inserts designed for the level of pimply high-school boys; some prosties and their cowboy bed partners. Janet

Margolin has an okay bit as an Indian gal gone wrong, who nurses McQueen to health.

Although excess footage is a prime heavy in film's impact, McQueen's erratic performance also detracts. Sometimes from setup to setup, he seems to be remembering that he is a teenager, while at other times lapsing into jarring, inconsistent maturity. He is known until final reel as Max Sand, the family name; Nevada Smith is a phony handle assumed in disguise.

After leaving Miss Margolin, McQueen traces Kennedy to a Louisiana prison, and he deliberately gets himself sent up the swamp to accomplish the second killing. This 41-minute segment spotlights Howard Da Silva as a brutal warden, Pat Hingle as the friendly trusty, and Suzanne Pleshette as a Cajun girl who helps McQueen escape. Although sex stress is bit heavy here, her rejection of his help as she's dying from snakebite because of his brutal slaying of Kennedy, is start of his adjustment from revenge obsession to something approaching normality.

McQueen's thesping becomes more assured following this sequence, and makes his later action regarding Malden plausible, if not completely logical.

En route back to California to find Malden, McQueen again sidetracks into a vignette with Raf Vallone, playing a rugged missionary priest. The gutsy casting is appropriate for the missionaries of the period, but the dialog is banal—Vallone was orphaned in an Indian raid, he has as much right to be bitter as McQueen, etc.

Malden is finally located, 19 minutes before fadeout, and, with more footage available than in the opening sequences, gives another of his intense readings. A gold heist cues McQueen's revenge, which amounts to shattering Malden's kneecaps, but—are you ready?—with a new-found maturity, he declines to kill him. McQueen rides off, according to synopsis, not final cut, to find Keith. Keith, incidentally, provides the only exciting and believable performance. A large supporting cast renders good support.

Hathaway's uneven direction alternates jarring, overbearing fisticuffs with exterior footage as spectacular in some cases as it is dull in others. Lucien Ballard's professional lensing captures panoramic beauty of setting but the Eastmancolor print seen at preview sometimes had poor registration.

Alfred Newman's routine score is brightened at one point by a stirring oater theme. Frank Bracht edited to 131 minutes—about 30 minutes longer than the plot properly sustains. Other credits are okay. Pic's copyright is split with Paramount, Levine's Embassy and McQueen's Solar Prods. *Murf.*

Les Sultans
(FRENCH-COLOR)

Paris, May 31.
CEDIC release of Jacques-Paul Bertrand-Cineurop-Mancori production. Stars Gina Lollobrigida, Louis Jourdan, Corinne Marchand, Philippe Noiret; features Muriel Baptiste, Daniel Gelin, Renee Faure. Directed by Jean Delannoy. Screenplay, Christine De Rivoyre, Jean-Loup Dabadie, Delannoy from the book by Miss Rivoyre; camera (Eastmancolor), A. Thirard; music, Georges

Gavarentz. At Marignan, Paris. Running Time, 95 MINS.

Gina .... Gina Lollobrigida
Laurent .... Louis Jourdan
Mireille .... Corinne Marchand
Michou .... Philippe Noiret
Kim .... Muriel Baptiste
Leo .... Daniel Gelin
Wife .... Renee Faure

Seems like updated version of that perennial tearjerker "Back Street," with an added dollup of French frankness. But its insights into behavior are slight and the characters fairly trivial, without depth as to social backgrounds. This might be a U.S. playoff item on its lush treatment, theme and Gina Lollobrigida and Louis Jourdan names for foreign spots.

Miss Lollobrigida is a fashion photographer who seems quite independent but also too vulnerable when it comes to her married lover, a youngish looking father of an 18-year-old and a successful businessman (Louis Jourdan). When he has to attend to his daughter's problems of being in love with a shallow woman-chaser like himself, Miss Lollobrigida takes his not being on time so hard that she never answers the phone and even tries suicide.

Reanimated through a giddy woman next door, who is kept by a boorish doctor who saves her, love blooms again only to be clouded when Jourdan rushes off to save his daughter who has run off. But it ends on an upbeat note as Miss Lollobrigida seems to realize that these sleek ladies' men are not worth taking that seriously.

Director Jean Delannoy gives this gloss and uses color well and gets okay performances if the tale seems forced and he can not get any comic warmth or acceptable pathos into it. A bit oldfashioned, in spite of workmanlike thesping, it appears headed for okay returns here and mainly playoff usage in other climes on its name values and luscious dress. *Mosk.*

The Wrong Box
(BRITISH-COLOR)

Period comedy has many yocks, but suffers from conflicting styles. Marquee names, plus Bryan Forbes' rep as director, ensures interest but result is spotty.

London, May 27.

Columbia Pictures release through BLC of a Salamander Film Production, produced and directed by Bryan Forbes. Stars John Mills, Ralph Richardson, Michael Caine, Peter Cook, Dudley Moore, Nanette Newman, Tony Hancock, Peter Sellers; features The Temperance Seven, Wilfrid Lawson, Thorley Walters, Cicely Courtneidge, Irene Handl, Gerald Sim, John Le Mesurier, Norman Bird, Tutte Lemkow, Vanda Godsell. Screenplay, Larry Gelbart and Burt Shevelove, suggested by a story by Robert Louis Stevenson and Lloyd Osbourne; camera (Technicolor), Gerry Turpin; music, John Barry; editor, Alan Osbiston. Reviewed at Columbia Theatre, London. Running Time, 110 MINS.

Masterman Finsbury ...... John Mills
Joseph Finsbury ..... Ralph Richardson
Michael .... Michael Caine
Morris .... Peter Cook
John .... Dudley Moore
Julia .... Nanette Newman
The Detective .... Tony Hancock
Dr. Pratt .... Peter Sellers
The Temperance Seven... Themselves
Peacock .... Wilfrid Lawson
Lawyer Patience .... Thorley Walters
Major Martha ..... Cicely Courtneidge
Mrs. Hackett .... Irene Handl
First Undertaker .... Gerald Sim
Dr. Slattery .... John Le Mesurier
Clergyman .... Norman Bird
Stranger .... Tutte Lemkow
Mrs. Goodge .... Vanda Godsell
Military Officer .... Peter Graves
First Rough .... Norman Rossington
Alan Fraser Scrobe .... Nicholas Parsons
Queen Victoria .... Avis Bunnage

Robert Louis Stevenson's macabre Victorian yarn has been impressively mounted by producer-director Bryan Forbes. He has lined up an impeccable cast of Britain's character comedian actors and brought his usual intelligent flourish to the film.

But it might have improved this Columbia release had he written the script for "The Wrong Box" himself, instead of using the uneven work of Larry Gelbart and Burt Shevelove. Forbes might then have been able to keep control of the picture instead of allowing it to meander into a maddening mixture of styles.

Film is occasionally funny (and when it is funny it is hilarious). Despite the sags, this shapes up as a possible hit for audiences who like their humor slightly offbeat.

Storyline concerns a macabre lottery in which 20 parents each toss $2,800 into a kitty for their children, the last survivor to draw the loot. Eventual survivors are two brothers who haven't seen each other for 40 years. One of them (John Mills) makes ineffective attempts to bump off his brother (Ralph Richardson), and their offspring take a more than casual interest in the proceedings.

Result is often baffling mixup of presumed deaths, switched bodies, juggled coffins, culminating in a Mack Sennett chase of hearses through a funeral. Although amusing, the film becomes farcical in a way not in keeping with the spirit of the well defined period comedy atmosphere.

First half of the picture is beautifully handled by Forbes. Ray Simm's excellent sets and artwork along with impeccable costumes by Julie Harris all contribute to the Victorian atmosphere, which Forbes also evokes by judicious use of silent film sub-titles. Cameraman Gerry Turpin's lensing is topdrawer.

But Forbes was unable to resist bringing in scenes which slow the action, though in themselves are funny. Also adding to the atmosphere, but not to the general movement of the film, is a superbly evoked Victorian "love affair" between Michael Caine and Nanette Newman, which subtly parodies the purity of respectable young love in that era.

Film opens smartly with a series of cameos showing how some of the other contenders for the inheritance come to sticky ends. Each vignette, though predictable, is yockworthy and employs the brief services of such accomplished performers as Nicholas Parsons, James Villiers, Jeremy Lloyd, Totti Truman Taylor and Avis Bunnage, among others.

Of the principals, John Mills amusingly hams his way through two or three sequences as one of the dying brothers. Ralph Richardson, as his brother, a bland, imperturbable old bore, is superb. He and Wilfrid Lawson, portraying a decrepit butler, virtually carry away the acting honors.

Peter Cook and Dudley Moore play Richardson's nephews and motivate most of the dirty work in the film since they are plotting throughout to land the cash. Their first important film roles prove that transition from the small tv screen to the wider demands of the cinema has its snags.

Thorley Walters as a bewildered lawyer, Cicely Courtneidge as a Salvation Army major, and, particularly Tony Hancock as a detective all contribute to the proceedings, as do a long list of supporting players.

"The Wrong Box" will absorb some filmgoers. But others will regret that a good idea should have frequently misfired because of a lack of taut control not usually associated with Forbes' expert work. *Rich.*

Der Kongress Amuesiert Sich
(Congress of Love)
(GERMAN-AUSTRIAN-70M-COLOR)

Berlin, May 24.

Nora release of Melodie-Film (Aldo von Pinelli and Peter Schaeffers) and Wiener Stadthalle production. Stars Lilli Palmer, Curt Jurgens and Paul Meurisse. Directed by Geza von Radvanyi. Screenplay, Fred Denger, Aldo von Pinelli and Geza von Radvanyi. Camera (MCS 70m Superpanorama, Eastmancolor), Heinz Hoelscher; music, Peter Thomas, Johann Strauss and Robert Stolz; settings, Otto Pischinger and Herta Hareiter; costumes, H. Reihs-Gromes and F. Sthamer. At Gloria Palast, W-Berlin. Running Time, 98 MINS.

Princess Metternich .... Lilli Palmer
Tsar Alexander .... Curt Jurgens
Prince Talleyrand ...... Paul Meurisse
Viennese guide .... Walter Slezak
Prince Metternich ... Hannes Messemer
Rosa, songstress .... Anita Hoefer
Stefan, Hungarian baron.. Bret Halsey
Napoleon's double ... Wolfgang Kieling
Sophie .... Bibi Jelinek
Stefan's father .... Gustav Knuth

This Nora release brings back old memories of the classical UFA pic ("The Congress Dances") of 1931 vintage. But the only thing both pix have in common is their central theme, the Viennese Congress of 1814-'15. Any other comparison would be nearly unfair. The new film lacks practically everything the old film had. Taking into account that there's a world-wide love for Vienna and Viennese music and that there's also a certain demand for such big-scale 70m productions on the part of international exhibitors, this "Congress" may be granted some commercial chances outside its homegrounds. Whether it will please the patrons is certainly another question.

This one starts out in a Viennese house of wax in 1965. An Austrian guide (Walter Slezak) is showing a group of tourists the great figures of Vienna's glorious historical past. When he reaches the famous Chancellor Metternich, that one suddenly becomes alive and the clock is turned back some 150 years. There is the Viennese Congress with all its trimmings and prominent characters. As the title of the film indicates, the members of the Congress don't dedicate themselves so much to politics but rather enjoy themselves. The viewer is confronted with a series of amorous escapades which mainly come on account of Metternich and the Russian Czar. The latter is a particularly woman-crazy character.

There is a certain plus with regard to this film's lavish production dress. But the best thing about it is the camerawork by Heinz Hoelscher. The (for domestic standards: rather expensive) MCS-70m-Super-Panorama system enabled him to catch a lineup of breathtakingly beautiful shots. But otherwise this is a rather meagre "Congress" which lacks the necessary charm and esprit to make it a worthwhile affair.

In the main, the scripting and direction must be made responsible for the pic's considerable shortcomings. Both lack a good deal of originality and imagination. This "Congress" gives the impression that its creators weren't given much leisure. The whole thing could have stood much polishing.

The musical score by Peter Thomas isn't exciting. He apparently left much to mere routine. Robert Stolz, the last grandseigneur of the great Viennese operetta school, contributed two songs which could have been two lovable contributions but they were practically "killed." There is nothing special about the acting. Hannes Messemer isn't a very convincing Metternich, Jurgens gives more the impression of a Siberian playboy, Lilli Palmer just turns in a routine performance and the same can be said of the others, except perhaps some supporting players. *Hans.*

L'Armata Brancaleone
(For Love and Gold)
(ITALO-FRENCH-COLOR)

Cannes, May 20.

Titanus release of Mario Cecchi Gori production for Fairfilm (Rome)-Les Films Marceau (Paris). Stars Vittorio Gassman, Catherine Spaak; features Gian Maria Volonte, Maria Grazia Buccella, Enrico Maria Salerno, Barbara Steele, Folco Lulli, Luigi Sangiorgi, Ugo Fangareggi, Alfio Caltabiano, Carlo Pisacane. Directed by Mario Monicelli. Screenplay, Monicelli, Age, Scarpelli. Camera (Technicolor-Widescreen) Carlo Di Palma. Music, Carlo Rustichelli. Editor, Ruggero Mastroianni. At Film Festival, Cannes. Running Time, 130 MINS.

Brancaleone .... Vittorio Gassman
Mathilde .... Catherine Spaak
Theophila .... Gian Maria Volonte'
Pecoro .... Folco Lulli
Widow .... Maria Grazia Buccella
Theodora .... Barbara Steele
Taccon .... Luigi Sangiorgi
Arnolfo .... Alfio Caltabiano
Abacuc .... Carlo Pisacane

This official Italo entry at the Cannes Fest provides rousing and riotously ribald screen fare for many of its 130 minutes. The amusing fillip provided by a specially invented brand of Italianate dialog, which provides added yoks in the original will serve as a challenge to lingual translators. An adroit effort will be needed to capture the spirit of the original, and much of pic's future may depend on it. Humor defies subtitling. Presumably there is boxoffice lure in ungarbed Catherine Spaak, Maria Grazia Buccella, and Barbara Steele. In Italy, the film is already cleaning up.

Though an offbeater in its totality, film is nevertheless derivative of several trends and ideas. Episodic tale concerns scraggily group of medieval Italian soldiers of fortune—or misfortune—and their adventures on the way to the Crusades. It seems sharply indebted to the violence of certain Japanese films such as "Seven Samurai," also to lengendary exploits as told by Sicilian puppet shows on the improvisation of the Commedia dell'Arte, or Don Quixote of Cervantes. But, to remain within the film context, its authors Age, Scarpelli, and writer-director Mario Monicelli have liberally cribbed and re-adapted the spirit if not the pattern of their well-known "Big Deal on Madonna Street" which also threw together a mismatched group of men heroically bent on impossible missions.

The plot is too filled with incidents to need detailing. Suffice to say that it pits group leader Brancaleone (Vittorio Gassman) and his brokendown gang against human and natural enemies along their lengthy trek to the sea. The gags are fast and furious, the humor often extremely far out. Some of point and counterpoint between sight and sound gags may be lost on foreign ears, but there's enough of the visual stuff to get people into the right mood pronto. To be sure, some of the effects are overmilked, and the pic would benefit from trimming for foreign release, especially towards end.

Vittorio Gassman is a perfect fit for the lead, and he plays it with apt gusto and ham. Three gals have little to do except look come-hitherly, which they all do with beauty and charged appeal. Gian Maria Volonte' makes a fine sidekick to Brancaleone, while Enrico Maria Salerno has some hilarious bits as a preach type. Folco Lulli, Carlo Pisacane, Ugo Fangareggi, Luigi Sangiorgi, and others lend weight and color in support.

Film's production values are other upper-case credits, from lavish use of colorful landscapes—almost all in exteriors—to Carlo di Palma's outstanding Technicolor lensing, which reaches heights in aiding and abetting the superb sets and costumes by Piero Gherardi, which hit and capture the eye in a seemingly never-ending sequence of "how-can-he-top-this-one?" efforts, of which the Byzantine court set, costumes, and thesp makeups must surely be rated one of the outstanding examples of this Oscar-winner's art. Carlo Rustichelli's rousing score and title song is in perfect keeping.

A tighter rein on pic, a greater effort in channeling its thematics and helter-skelter development, a less fractioned unfolding might have made this a truly outstanding film rather than merely a commercial entertainment. And there is still the risk that much of the film's built-in values may be lost on foreign audiences before — or unless—they are properly put into the spirit of this thing. *Hawk.*

Three On A Couch
(COLOR)

Jerry Lewis first for Columbia is same mixture as before. Should please Lewis cult, and distributor, but multi-character approach is wearing thin.

Columbia Pictures release of Jerry Lewis production, produced and directed by Lewis. Stars Lewis and Janet Leigh; features Mary Ann Mobley, Gila Golan, Leslie Parrish, James Best. Screenplay, Bob Ross and Samuel A. Taylor, based on story by Arne Sultan, Marvin Worth; camera (Pathe Color), W. Wallace Kelley; editor, Russel Wiles; sound, Charles J. Rice; music, Louis Brown. Reviewed at Victoria Theatre, N.Y., May 23, '66. Running Time, **109 MINS.**
Christopher Pride, also
Warren, Ringo, Rutherford,

Heather	Jerry Lewis
Dr. Elizabeth Acord	Janet Leigh
Susan Manning	Mary Ann Mobley
Anna Jacque	Gila Golan
Mary Lou Mauve	Leslie Parrish
Dr. Ben Mizer	James Best
Murphy	Kathleen Freeman
The Drunk	Buddy Lester
The Ambassador	Renzo Cesana
The Attache	Fritz Feld

Only the studio is new in this latest Jerry Lewis effort. Star, director, producer and, to a large degree, the script, remain the same. That means fun for Lewis fans, profits for Columbia, and some disappointment for the few who believed the promise that this would be a "more sophisticated approach to comedy." It isn't, although most Lewis addicts couldn't care less.

What started as a delightful experiment in "The Nutty Professor," playing multiple characters, and continued in "The Family Jewels," is used here also, but this time out, the extra characters are done without change of makeup (other than one drag bit), depending on voice and style variations. However, the idea has just about used up its potential and the multi-talented Lewis would be wise to spare his Roman horses.

One change is that the script, this time out, is not by Lewis but credited to an Arne Sultan-Marvin Worth story, expanded into a script by Bob Ross and Samuel A. Taylor. The plot, a slight one, has more dialog and less visual action than usually expected in a Lewis epic. With Janet Leigh as his psychiatrist-fiancee and Mary Ann Mobley, Gila Golan and Leslie Parrish as three of her patients, there's no paucity of pulchritude. All four get plenty of screentime in which to display their formidable (individually and collectively) talents. James Best is impressive in a Tony Randall-hero's-best-friend role though some may wonder why such a good-looking type doesn't try to take over one of the trio of beauties who appear ready and able. Kathleen Freeman is her reliable excellent self as Miss Leigh's receptionist. Other featured roles, cast better than they're written, (with exception of Buddy Lester's running gag of a congenial drunk) are broadly written, and played in a like vein.

All technical credits are excellent (as always in a Lewis production), with W. Wallace Kelley's color camerawork particularly outstanding. Process is credited to Pathe but, as is usually the case, it's probably Eastman Color, processed by Pathe. Louis

Brown's score s pleasant, as is Danny Costello's vocal rendition of "A Now And A Later Love."

With Lewis' peregrinations from studio to studio evidently halted, pro tem, with signing of his one-a-year Columbia deal, perhaps the oft-suggested transition of comedian into an actor who can play comedy will get underway. Mounting production costs of his films could be rationalized if the grosses mounted in the same proportion but with no evidence that they do (or can), a simplification of approach in production, direction and writing (with a more serious attitude towards acting), could at least enable Lewis to level off to the point of creating some really memorable films. That he has the ability, there's no doubt, but discipline is needed.

An incomparable clown, only recently "discovered" by the Cahiers du Cinema cult but recognized by American filmgoers right from "My Friend Irma," Lewis has proven over and over that he can make commercial comedies successfully. Now he should concentrate on making "great" comedies. Perhaps less "original" scripts and more well-researched literary or legit prop erties might be the answer
Robe.

Paradise, Hawaiian Style
(SONGS-COLOR)

New Elvis Presley tuner carries usual sales potential in slick production wrapping.

Hollywood, June 3.
Paramount release of Hal Wallis production. Stars Elvis Presley; features Suzanna Leigh, James Shigeta, Donna Butterworth, Marianna Hill. Directed by Michael Moore. Screenplay, Allan Weiss, Anthony Lawrence; original story, Weiss; camera (Technicolor), W. Wallace Kelley; editor, Warren Low; music, Joseph J. Lilley; asst. director, James Rosenberger. Reviewed at Paramount Studios, June 2, '66. Running Time, **87 MINS.**

Rick Richards	Elvis Presley
Judy Hudson	Suzanna Leigh
Danny Kohana	James Shigeta
Jan Kohana	Donna Butterworth
Lani	Marianna Hill
Pua	Irene Tsu
Lehua	Linda Wong
Joanna	Julie Parrish
Betty Kohana	Jan Shepard
Donald Belden	John Doucette
Moke	Philip Ahn
Mr. Cubberson	Grady Sutton
Andy Lowell	Dan Collier
Mrs. Barrington	Doris Packer
Mrs. Belden	Mary Treen
Peggy	Gi Gi Verone

Hal Wallis, who first brought Elvis Presley to the screen in 1956 and once before locationed in Hawaii ("Blue Hawaii," '61), returns singer to the island state in this gaily-begarbed and flowing musical. Seldom has the panorama and terrain of Hawaii been utilized to such lush advantage, beautifully caught in the finest tints of Technicolor and providing star with an atmospheric backdrop for the type of yarn he's best-suited for . . . girls and songs. It's a natural for Presley fans, who seem to be legion, and carries strong exploitation potential.

Star shares his vocalizing in several numbers with nine-year-old Donna Butterworth, herself rich in talent, who also scores solo with "Bill Bailey, Won't

You Please Come Home?" (in Hawaii, yet?). Presley's most impressive number is a production spread with about 70 native singers in a colorful South Seas ritual, effective and holding considerable eye-appeal. With Marianna Hill, Presley chants "You Scratch My Back," a routine he employs in talking a covey of young lovelies into drumming up trade for the helicopter charter service he and James Shigeta are partnered in.

Light script by Allan Weiss and Anthony Lawrence, based on former's original, serves more as a showcase for Presley's wares than as plottage but suffices to sock over the Presley lure. Star plays an airplane pilot with girl trouble, who loses one job after another when he becomes innocently embroiled. His troubles continue after he and Shigeta team up for their inter-island ferrying, with usual romantic entanglements, fights and outbursts of song.

Michael Moore, making his directorial bow after seven years with Wallis as an assistant, maintains a breezy pace and manages good performances from his cast. One particular sequence is a comedy gem: Presley loses control of his chopper while transporting six dogs of various breeds to a canine show on another island. Simultaneously, the helicopter stunting takes on a load of thrills, some of the best ever filmed for this form of locomotion. Nelson Tyler is responsible for heli photography, while A. Wallace Kelley admirably handles color cameras on picture proper.

Presley delivers one of his customary ingratiating portrayals, in usual voice and adept at comedy. Suzanna Leigh as the blonde secretary is nice to look at (particularly in a bikini) in main romantic role, and Miss Hill likewise establishes herself as a native charmer. Irene Tsu, Linda Wong and Julie Parrish spark further interest on distaff side, while Shigeta excels in a sympathetic role. John Doucette is an air official who has Presley grounded for 30 days after latter's crazily-flying chopper forced his car into a ditch.

Wallis as usual garments his film with top production values. Contributors here include Warren Low's editing; and direction by Hal Pereira and Walter Tyler; music score by Joseph J. Lilley; costumes by Edith Head; choreography by Jack Regas.
Whit.

Boy, Did I Get A Wrong Number
(COLOR)

Bob Hope in fast near-bedroom farce-type comedy with names of Elke Sommer and Phyllis Diller to further attract.

Hollywood, May 27.
United Artists release of Edward Small production. Stars Bob Hope, Elke Sommer, Phyllis Diller; features Cesare Danova, Marjorie Lord. Directed by George Marshall. Screenplay, Burt Styler, Albert E. Lewin, George Kennett;

original story, George Beck; camera (DeLuxe Color), Lionel Lindon; music, Richard LaSalle, "By" Dunham; asst. director, Herbert S. Greene; editor, Grant Whytock. Reviewed at Picwood Theatre, May 26, '66. Running Time, 98 MINS.

Tom Meade	Bob Hope
Didi	Elke Sommer
Lily	Phyllis Diller
Pepe	Cesare Danova
Martha Meade	Marjorie Lord
Schwartz	Kelly Thordsen
Regan	Benny Baker
Doris Meade	Terry Burnham
Telephone Operator	Joyce Jameson
Newscaster	Harry Von Zell
Larry Meade	Kevin Burchett
Plympton	Keith Taylor
Newsboy	John Todd Roberts

Public has come to expect a parade of nonsense in any Bob Hope picture, and this Edward Small production is no exception. Comic enters the realm of near-bedroom farce this time out as he finds a near-unclad film star on his hands in a lake cottage and his ever-loving spouse continually appearing on the scene to build up audience anticipation. If the action sometimes seems to get out of hand it really doesn't matter, for Phyllis Diller is there, too, to help him hide the delectable Elke Sommer from the missus.

Honors are three-pronged here, Hope having to take the brunt of Miss Sommer, as a Hollywood sex kitten who has disappeared and taken refuge in his Oregon town in an effort to escape from her boy-friend, director Cesare Danova, who keeps wanting her to take bubble baths for a picture.

For further keen competition, Phyllis Diller, in as a wise-cracking maid in the Hope manse, is a little nuttier-looking than usual with her wild hair standing every-which-way and her humor the kind that hits spectator right in the paunch. Original story by George Beck and screenplay by Burt Styler, Albert E. Lewin and George Kennett are tailor-made for their various talents, which shine brightly throughout.

Film takes its tab from Hope, a glib, fast-talking, enterprising Oregon real estate operator, attempting to reach his wife, Marjorie Lord, at the beauty parlor and being connected by mistake with Elke's hotel suite, where she's hiding out while the nation's headlines speculate on what has happened to her. She says she's hungry, and he raids the ice box at midnight to save her. Which leads, of course, to complications, including Hope trying to get her out of a bubble-filled bathtub after she has taken a sleeping pill, and the law entering to accuse him of murder when her car is found in a lake and blood on the carpet of the cottage.

Hope plays his role straight for the most part, making the most of the situation. George Marshall's direction sparks events in proper perspective, wisely allowing his characters to go their separate ways in their own particular styles. Miss Sommer, who knows her way through a comedy scene either with or without clothes, elects the latter state for most of her thesping, raimented mostly in a shirt. Miss Diller is immense as the nosy domestic responsible for the majority of the funny lines that abound throughout the fast unfoldment.

In briefer roles, Miss Lord is pretty as the wife and Danova effective as the lover-director who believes in permitting his star to blow off steam the temperamental way. As a pair of detectives investigating Elke's disappearance and "murder," Kelly Thordsen and Benny Baker are amusing. Terry Burnham and Kevin Burchett are okay as Hope and Miss Lord's teenage children.

Edward Small gives firstclass production values right down the line. Definite assets are provided by Richard LaSalle and "By" Dunham's clever music score; Lionel Lindon's color photography; Frank Sylos' art direction; Grant Whytock's fast editing.

Whit.

Incident At Phantom Hill
(COLOR-TECHNISCOPE)

A wild western with plenty of action, good production value, but storyline is weak and sometimes cliche riddled.

Hollywood, May 26.
Universal release of a Harry Tateman production. Features Robert Fuller, Jocelyn Lane, Dan Duryea, Claude Akins, Noah Beery and Linden Chiles. Directed by Earl Bellamy. Screenplay, Frank Nugent, Ken Pettus; asst. director, Michael Moder; camera (Technicolor), William Margulies; editor, Gene Milford; music, Hass J. Salter. Reviewed at Universal studio, May 25, '66. Runnisg time: 88 Mins.

Matt Martin	Robert Fuller
Memphis	Jocelyn Lane
Joe Barlow	Dan Duryea
Adam Long	Tom Simcox
Dr. Hanneford	Linden Chiles
Krausman	Claude Akins
O'Rourke	Noah Beery
General Hood	Paul Fix
First Hunter	Denver Pyle
Trade	William Phipps
Drum	Don Collier
Second Hunter	Mickey Finn

An action Western, this Technicolor-Techniscope pic is filled with guts and gore and should prove popular enough on a double bill. Technical credits are first-rate and action okay but story line as far as developing interesting characters attempts too much and too late. However, footage is peppered with enough visual excitement to hold attention.

Plot evolves around a group of men headed by Robert Fuller who work toward recovering $1,000,000 in gold. Money had been hijacked during an "incident" at Phantom Hill in the closing days of the Civil War. Dan Duryea participated in the attack on the Union Army and is forced to show whereabouts of the loot. Girl, Jocelyn Lane, also becomes part of the group, and story centers around interplay of characters in their quest for the gold.

Fuller is in command of group and has a determined air about all he does. Romance with Miss Lane is strangely elusive and this is one of those pix where there are no clinches. Duryea is good as the bad guy but is given little motivation and doesn't come off as a fully rounded villian. Other characters are okay but script by the late Frank Nugent and Ken Pettus doesn't really build suspense intended.

Earl Bellamy's direction keeps actors in motion and action scenes are expansively handled. Sets and scenery are first-rate as is the color camerawork of William Margulies. Music score by Hans J. Salter also is on the plus side.

Dool.

On a Vole La Joconde
(The Mona Lisa Has Been Stolen)
(FRENCH-ITALIAN-COLOR)

Paris, June 7.
Cocinor release of Liber Film-Marceau-Auerbach Films production. Stars Marina Vlady, George Chakiris; features Paul Frankeur, Jean Lefebvre, Margaret Lee. Directed by Michel Deville. Screenplay, Ottavio Poggi, Nina Companeez, Deville; camera (Eastmancolor), Massimo Dalla Mano. At Colisee, Paris. Running time, 98 MINS.

Nicole	Marina Vlady
Vincent	George Chakiris
Guard	Jean Lefebvre
Boss	Paul Frankeur
Titine	Margaret Lee

Film tightropes around a turn-of-the-century romantic tale mixed with gentlemen thieves and local color. If charming, this lacks the brio, dash and comedic flair to make it more than a fair prospect for playoff on its time, color and general entertainment values. But the needed briskness and more potent drive for arty houses are not adequate enough. Local chances look better than foreign ones, though the George Chakiris name could give it some marquee boost.

A suave, rich thief steals the Mona Lisa from the Louvre in Paris but falls hopelessly in love with a lovely little maid. She wants only a rich man and he can not reveal his identity. But some petty crooks follow her and the police follow them to start a long chase that is the backbone of this production.

Director Michel Deville gives this a classic comic facade as chasers get chased and then vice-versa for the final happy ending as the united couple become museum thieves together. Marina Vlady is lovely and with a good period bosomy, physical look. Chakiris is properly lithe and seductive, if a bit wooden, as the theif. Supporting comic players are good. Color and production dress are adequate.

Mosk.

Cul-de-Sac
(BRITISH)

Effectively absorbing pic which, with limited marquee draw, may need astute selling and nursing for mass audiences. Standout performance by Donald Pleasence.

London, June 7.
Michael Klinger & Tony Tenser presentation of a Compton (Gene Gutowski) production and Compton-Cameo release. Features Donald Pleasence, Francoise Dorleac, Lionel Stander, Jack MacGowran, William Franklyn, Robert Dorning, Marie Kean, Geoffrey Sumner, Renee Houston, Iain Quarrier. Directed by Roman Polanski. Original screenplay, Polanski and Gerard Brach; music, Komeda; editor, Alistair MacIntyre; camera, Gill Taylor. At Cuneo-Poly, London. Running Time, 111 MINS.

George	Donald Pleasence
Teresa	Francoise Dorleac
Richard	Lionel Stander
Albert	Jack MacGowran
Cecil	William Franklyn
Fairweather	Robert Dorning
Marion	Marie Kean
Christopher's Father	Geoffrey Sumner
Christopher's Mother	Renee Houston
Christopher	Iain Quarrier
Jacqueline	Jackie Bissett
Nicholas	Trevor Delaney

Though none of the leading players gets star billing and none is a notable marquee draw, performances give a great fillip to this always absorbing, offbeat comedy drama. The pic is already accoladed by being an invited entry to the Berlin Film Fest. Word-of-mouth on the performances, plus the record of producer Gene Gutowski and director Roman Polanski, should give it a ready following among discriminating audiences. However, it may need hefty selling and nursing to make it go in larger commercial houses.

"Cul-de-Sac" lacks the precise style of Polanski's "Knife in the Water" and the insidious bite of the same director's "Repulsion." But as a study in kinky insanity, the film creates a tingling atmosphere. This sags riskily at times when the director unturns the screws and does not keep control of his frequently introduced comedy.

However, Polanski shows complete rapport with his cast and with the dankly grey atmosphere of his location. And, although it's not so easy to define just what he is driving at in this pic, the result is a neat and edgy chiller.

Film was shot on location in and around a lonely castle on one of the remote Holy Islands off the North East coast of Britain. Gill Taylor's camera bleakly catches the loneliness and sinister background that sparks the happenings. Donald Pleasence, with steel-rimmed glasses and head completely shaven, is an obvious neurotic. A retired businessman, he is living like a hermit with his young, bored and flirtatious French wife (Francoise Dorleac), who is blatantly contemptuous of him. And it is never really established how the two ever managed to get married. Suddenly, two wounded gangsters on the run descend upon them. One of them is the huge, boisterous Lionel Stander; the other is Jack MacGowran, a shadowy character who quickly disappears when his wounds cause his death. From then on it's a battle of nerves, a cat-and-mouse psychological tightrope walk, as an uneasy truce develops between Pleasence and Stander, while the latter waits to be rescued by the boss of his gang, who never shows. Plenty of incident, but little definitive story unfolds. And it is largely due to Polanski's imaginative touches that interest keeps alive until, in the end, Stander is accidentally shot by Pleasence and the wife goes off with a visiting neighbor. Pleasence is left, half-crazy, babbling over the memories of his first wife.

Gangsters taking over a peaceful, scared household is not a new film angle. Usually, however, in such pix, the besieged household is rather normal. This one is far from that, which boosts the tension and the macabre flavor. Entry on a couple of occasions of dull but normal visitors (all quite oblivious to the sinister goings-on) also gives sharpened effect to the situation.

Some ruthless cutting could have helped the film a great deal. An early sequence needs drastic paring and there are moments in the middle when the tension slackens through over-exposure. But Polanski keeps audiences remorsely on the hook as they wonder what next he has up his sleeve. Pleasence pours some exaggerated but distinctive thesping into his pathetic role while Stander, obviously more flamboyant, blends nicely with him.

Stander also dies a death that may go down in film history as one of the more effectively embroidered exists. It's a collector's piece in "hammery," but Stander deserves the moment for he previously turns in a far more subtle performance of latent brutality, mixed with surface geniality, than the screenplay by Polanski and Gerard Brach may have promised. Francoise Dorleac as the budding, nympho wife has a hazy part and she gets away with it by turning on a slightly mocking, take-it-or-leave-it piece of coquettishness which fills the bill. Jack MacGowran, as the stooge gangster, has only short exposure, but plays the role with style.

The visitors to the castle, brought in to create a contrast of normality in the proceedings and thus heighten the sinister undertones, have only chances to grab at bits. But they're all proficiently played by William Franklyn, Robert Dorning, Renee Houston, Marie Kean, Iain Quarrier, Jackie Bissett and a youngster named Trevor Delaney. Finally, a bow to whoever located the island and the castle against which this edgy drama is played out. Clearly no place for a gay vacation, it turns out to be just right as a locale for a bleak meller. *Rich.*

Navajo Run

Half-caste Indian hunted down by paranoid prairie farmer. Tedious execution and dull impact. Okay filler on duals.

Hollywood, May 26.
American International Pictures release of Lorajon Production, produced and directed by Johnny Seven. Stars Seven, Warren Kemmerling; features Virginia Vincent, Ron Soble. Screenplay, Jo Heims; camera, Gregory Sandor; editor, Lee Gilbert; music, William Loose, Emil Cadkin; asst. director, John Irwin. Reviewed at Joe Shore's Screening Room, L.A., May 25, '66. Running Time, 83 MINS.

Matthew Whitehawk .....Johnny Seven
Luke Grog .... Warren Kemmerling
Sarah Grog .... Virginia Vincent
Jesse Grog .... Ron Soble

"Navajo Run" is a generally static story of anti-Indian prejudice and paranoia in the old West. The low-budget, four-character Johnny Seven production is thin in all creative departments, although it occasionally sparks interest. Despite its demerits, the unusual plot gimmick makes for satisfactory American International release as a contrasting or complementary filler item in less discriminating action-grind situations.

Jo Heims' script turns on the fate of a half-caste Navajo, played by Seven, who seeks medical aid for snake bite at the unhappy prairie home of Warren Kemmerling, vicious and sadistic husband of mail-order bride Virginia Vincent. Ron Soble is Kemmerling's brother, an emasculated and barely human clod. Their late brother was killed by Indians after he had raped an Indian maid, so Kemmerling's kicks are befriending Indians, then killing them. When

Seven arrives, 16 braves already lie in the cold, cold ground.

Film is more than half over when this angle becomes apparent, before which Kemmerling's nature is over-developed, while Miss Vincent's nature is under-developed. Overabundance of dull thesping, mugging and pallid pacing retards interest. Seven, driven out in the fields to be hunted down, eventually overcomes Kemmerling in a climactic knife-tomahawk fight which has some excitement.

Seven directed with a heavy hand. His acting is one-note, although the demands of the script that he be an educated Indian may have created the impression that he be erudite. In any case, effect is too passive. Kemmerling leers and sneers with a menace which, with meatier dialog and restrained direction, would be quite promising.

Miss Vincent is awkward in her tender moments, although in passive reaction she projects a measure of futility. Soble, who never speaks until fadeout, makes the most of a brutish mime.

Gregory Sandor's lensing is devoid of much excitement, and Lee Gilbert's editing makes for a slow 83 minutes. Other technical credits are standard. *Murf.*

Pimienta
(Pepper)
(ARGENTINE-COLOR)

Buenos Aires, June 7.
LB production and release. Stars Luis Sandrini, Lolita Torres; features Ubaldo Martinez, Selva Aleman, Guillermo Bredeston, Roberto Airaldi, Ricardo Lavie, Nelly Prince, Carlos Lopez Monet. Directed by Carlos Rinaldi. Screenplay, Abel Santa Cruz, from his own stage play; camera (Eastmancolor), Ignacio Souto; music, Tito Ribero; editor, Atilio Rinaldi. Previewed at Monumental Theatre. Running Time, 133 MINS.

Pimienta .... Luis Sandrini
Laura .... Lolita Torres
Cipriano .... Ubaldo Martinez
Lita .... Selva Aleman
German .... Guillermo Bredeston
Fernando .... Roberto Airaldi
Osvaldo .... Ricardo Lavie
Carolina .... Nelly Prince
Hariberto .... Carlos Lopez Monet

The producer-director-writer-star team that last year clicked with "Bicho raro" (Odd Insect) has turned out this tinter based upon a stage hit. The drawing power of Luis Sandrini here is coupled with that of singing star Lolita Torres. Pic is additionally reinforced with important tv and legit names such as Ubaldo Martinez, Selva Aleman and Guillermo Bredeston. All this and a fat budget hopes for a new blockbuster.

But it is not, although it looms a winner anyway in this city. If expertly trimmed, this could go well in Spanish-speaking markets.

The thin story concerns a redheaded, hot-tempered bachelor uncle who takes care of three nephews when his wealthy, divorced brother leaves for Europe with a young mistress. Troubles ranging from the boy's dislike for college to the older girl's pregnancy test his ability to inject a new spirit into those disenchanted young people. It's a task in which he is assisted by a woman doctor with whom he falls in love and eventually marries.

Long footage and too much talk hamper this yarn. But Sandrini's colorful personality and clever

acting do much to keep the viewers awake, and to make them laugh here and there. The sympathy of Lolita Torres also helps, as well as eye-catching sets.

Script allowed no chances for the other actors to score and the direction hasn't managed to enliven things, ditto the editing. It was shot mainly in and around a luxurious suburban house, and the photography is good. *Din.*

La Ligne
De Demarcation
(Line of Demarcation)
(FRENCH)

Paris, June y.
CCFC release of Rome Paris Films-Georges De Beauregard-SNC production. Stars Jean Seberg, Maurice Ronet; features Daniel Gelin, Stephane Audran, Jacques Perrin, Roger Dumas, Mario David, Noel Roquevert. Directed by Claude Chabrol. Screenplay, Colonel Remy, Chbrol; camera, Jean Rabier; editor, M. Gaillard. At Mercury, Paris. Running Time, 120 MINS.

Mary .... Jean Seberg
Pierre .... Maurice Ronet
Doctor .... Daniel Gelin
Wife .... Stephane Audran
Michel .... Jacques Perrin
Urbain .... Mario David
Passer .... Roger Dumas
Innkeeper .... Noel Roquevert

Claude Chabrol, one of the earliest New Wavers, here puts away many of his inside jokes, anarchic themes and characters to make a solid action drama on the divided France during the last World War. But its heroics, characters and plotting are a bit familiar, with mainly local pull in its look at a troubled time of Vichy France, with foreign chances primarily playoff on its theme and the added plus of the Jean Seberg name.

Story is set in a small town on the border of occupied France. It concerns people trying to get into so-called Free France as well as parachutists coming in to set up resistance webs and the reactions of the towns-people and their relations plus that with the Germans.

One man is an informer, another preys on unfortunates he promises to guide over the line but instead lets them fall into German hands and hides their goods. One nobleman believes that resistance is useless and another risks his life and family to help resistance plotter.

Chabrol smartly builds this into a solid if familiar mosaic of divided wartime loyalties, well defined characters but slips in making his two Gestapo men a bit too theatrically lugubrious rather than truly menacing. Jean Seberg is a Frenchwoman of English origins, to explain her accent, and etches a good picture of a dedicated woman ready to risk her life and yet accept her husband's weary resignation.

Others are solidly cast if sometimes stereotyped. This pic is an overlong but okay war entry, with an added notch in treating a subject that is only recently getting screen time here. That is the France during the resistance and occupation of the last war. Production aspects are good and on-the spot shooting in a small pro-

vincial town also helps give sweep to this tale of wartime heroics, cowardice, waste and history.
Mosk.

The Black Klansman

Exploitation pic about the KKK; bookings foreseen as spotty.

Hollywood, May 12.
U.S. Film release of Ted V. Mikels production, presented by Joe Solomon; director-editor, Mikels. Features Richard Gilden. Screenplay, John T. Wilson, Arthur A. Namew; camera, Robert Caramico; asst. director, Names. Reviewed at Joe Shore Screening Room, May 11, '66. Running Time, 88 MINS.

Jerry .... Richard Gilden
Andrea .... Rima Kutner
Rook .... Harry Lovejoy
Raymond .... Max Julien
Farley .... Jackie Deslonde
Lonnie .... Jimmy Mack
Carole Ann .... Maureen Gaffney
Wallace .... Wm. McLennan
Sawyer .... Gino De Agustino
Jenkins .... Tex Armstrong
Buckley .... Byrd Holland
Alex .... Whitman Mayo
Ellis Madison .... Francis Williams
Sloane .... Ray Dennis

"The Black Klansman" is patently aimed at cashing in on present Ku Klux Klan activities in the South and civil rights agitation which is sweeping the country. Film may be exploited for fair returns in less discriminating situations but subject matter probably won't appeal to mass audiences and bookings will be spotty.

Plot premise of the Ted V. Mikels production is fairly sound. A light-colored Negro learns in Los Angeles that his six-year-old daughter in Alabama has been killed by the Klan bombing a church, and he leaves immediately to find the killer. He is light enough to pass as a white man, and becomes a Klansman to help him in his search. Script by John T. Wilson and Arthur A. Namew brings in his white mistress, Negro gangsters from Harlem and the black Klansman remaining to help his people live peacefully with the whites.

Both direction and performances are static and sum total is of little importance. Mikels directs as well as edits, and Richard Gilden assumes title role. His bed scenes with Rima Kutner in femme lead role may be scissored in some areas. Harry Lovejoy as the Alabama community's Klan leader and Max Julien the imported Harlem mobster head supporting cast.
Whit.

Khartoum
(CINERAMA-COLOR-BRITISH)

Rousing action drama based on historical fact. Very good dramatic values, plus exciting Cinerama action effects. Charlton Heston and Laurence Olivier provide a mass-class audience marquee lure. Good hardticket outlook, with even better prospects in general release.

Hollywood, June 8.

United Artists release of Julian Blaustein production, presented in Cinerama. Stars Charlton Heston, Laurence Olivier, Richard Johnson, Ralph Richardson; features rest of cast. Directed by Basil Dearden; second unit direction, Yakima Canutt; prolog direction, Eliot Elisofon. Screenplay, Robert Ardrey; camera (Ultra Panavision, Technicolor), Edward Scaife; second unit camera, Harry Waxman; editor, Fergus McDonell; music, Frank Cordell; asst. directors, John Peverall, Bluey Hill. Reviewed at Pacific's Cinerama Theatre, L.A., June 7, '66. Running Time (excluding intermission), **124 MINS.**

Gen. Charles Gordon . Charlton Heston
The Mahdi . . . Laurence Olivier
Col. J. D. H. Stewart Richard Johnson
Prime Minister Gladstone
Ralph Richardson
Sir Evelyn Baring ..... Alexander Knox
Khaleel .. .. Johnny Sekka
Lord Granville ...... Michael Hordern
Zobeir Pasha .... Zia Mohyeddin
Sheikh Osman .... Marne Maitland
Gen. Wolseley .... Nigel Green
Lord Hartington .... Hugh Williams
The Khalifa Abdullah Douglas Wilmer
Col. Hicks .... Edward Underdown
Bordeini Bey .... Alec Mango
Giriagis Bey .... George Pastell
Major Kitchener .... Peter Arne
Awaan .... Alan Tilvern
Herbin .... Michael Anthony
Frank Power .... Jerome Willis
Dancer .... Leila
Lord Northbrook .. Ronald Leigh Hunt
Sir Charles Dilke ..... Ralph Michael

"Khartoum," named after the site of a major event in 19th century history of the British Empire, is an action-filled entertainment pic which contrasts personal nobility with political expediency. The colorful Julian Blaustein production builds in spectacular display, enhanced by Cinerama presentation, while Charlton Heston and Laurence Olivier propel toward inevitable tragedy the drama of two sincere opponents. Very good scripting, performances and direction add up to exciting all-age audience fare. Good prospects loom at the initial hardticket b.o., while subsequent United Artists release in general situations is even more promising.

Filmed in Egypt and finished at England's Pinewood Studios as an Eady Fund pic, the historical drama is the first to depict on film the events leading up to the savage death of Gen. Charles ("Chinese") Gordon, famed British soldier, as he sought to mobilize public opinion against the threat of a religious-political leader who would conquer the Arab world.

The brutal incident, avenged 15 years later by Kitchener, is perhaps less known outside of United Kingdom and Eastern Hemisphere areas, thus indicating that some extra ballyhoo emphasis on the real-life aspect will probably be needed in other locales.

Robert Ardrey, playwright-screenwriter and more recently involved in anthropological-historical writing, researched thoroughly with assistant Mary Bruce—a task made more complicated by contrasting opinions on Gordon. To a pragmatic politician, Gordon appeared as a loner, a mystic, an egotist, and a convenient scapegoat. To others he was a man of supreme principle, willing to die for it. Ardrey's finished script, while emphasizing the heroic qualities in Gordon, also gives depth and dimension of different points of view. This is perhaps the best that can be done with any real-life figure who rocks the boat.

There being no surprise in the climax, script properly unfolds from much initial exposition of characters, action being then soft-pedaled but gradually increasing in cinematic scope and dramatic emphasis. Basil Dearden directed with a fine hand which illuminated the personalities involved, while Yakima Canutt, second unit director given prominent screen credit, worked simultaneously to create much big-screen razzledazzle action, brought home to firstrun audiences in Cinerama.

Heston delivers an accomplished performance as Gordon looking like the 50-year-old trim soldier that Gordon was when picked to evacuate Khartoum of its Egyptian inhabitants, with no official British status on which to rely if the going got rough. The Bible-reading, booze-drinking, prayerful but practical idealist-realist is a challenge to an actor, and Heston meets it very well.

Olivier, playing the Mahdi, is excellent in creating audience terror of a zealot who sincerely believes that a mass slaughter is Divine Will, while projecting respect and compassion for his equally-religious adversary, Heston. Role calls for Olivier to have a darkened face, relative physical immobility and heavily-garbed body. Thus, through eyes and voice only, his impact is all the more noteworthy.

Richard Johnson strikes a neat balance between a protocol-minded Army type, sent to Heston as part adjutant, part Government watchdog, and a young soldier who is inspired with the merit of Heston's cause. Ralph Richardson, last of the above-title players, excels as Prime Minister Gladstone.

Supporting cast, all delivering good characterizations, includes Alexander Knox, sympathetic but realistic consul-general, Johnny Sekka, Heston's servant, Nigel Green, the British general who arrives too late to save Heston and Khartoum, and Peter Arne, the young Kitchener who in another decade would carve his own niche in history as the avenger of Gordon.

Edward Scaife was director of photography, achieving fine results in plot intimacy, when required, while Harry Waxman, in charge of second unit lensing, utilized to a great degree the opportunities for big-screen effects via 70m single-strip film, Ultra Panavision optics and Technicolor. The desert is a sea, with as many dramatic possibilities, and Waxman, under Canutt, has blended the waves of sand and hordes of tribesmen into an eye-filling canvas.

Pic is relatively short, the continuous running time being 134 minutes. Frank Cordell's full-bodied score sets the scene in a four-minute overture before the picture-start frame, and subsequently acts to punctuate the appropriate action. Intermission comes after 81 minutes. Fergus McDonell supervised the tight editing which has kept early action sequences short, so as not to dilute the impact of final scenes.

A four-minute prolog was directed by Eliot Elisofon, whose roving camera starts at dawn behind the pyramids and establishes the physical background for the ensuing drama. All technical credits are firstrate, including the stereo sound and also Richard Parker's special effects. Latter includes the flooding of a defensive trench which was built to isolate Khartoum from attack from the south. *Murf.*

Trois Enfants Dans Le Desordre
(Three Disordered Children)

Paris, June 10.

Gaumont release of Gaumont international production. Stars Bourvil, Jean Lefebvre; features Rosy Varte, Anne-Marie Carriere, Robert Dalban. Directed by Leo Joannon. Screenplay, Jacques Emmanuel, Joannon; camera (Eastmancolor), Henri Persin; editor, Robert and Monique Isnardon. At Marignan, Paris. Running Time, **95 MINS.**

Eugene .... Bourvil
Ferdinand .... Jean Lefebvre
Mother .... Rosy Varte
Woman .... Anne-Marie Carriere
Judge .... Robert Dalban

Pic is a mixture of slapstick, situation comedy and comedy of manners. These do not jell, and in spite of clever work by a group of comic actors this release impresses as mainly for French market.

Comic Bourvil is framed into prison by jealous business competitors where he adopts, sight unseen, three illegitimate children to save his business from being confiscated. But he is freed and then complications emerge as the three children and their mothers move in on him and give him trouble with a fiancee.

Far-fetched doings lack the ability to give them transcendent comic pungency and this is mainly rather coy, old fashioned and lacking a more forthright risible ruggedness and genuine far out comedy manner, or even yockful slapstick, to get it out of its good natured but lagging rut.

Bourvil and Jean Lefebvre make an okay comedy team but it needed the more classic timing, bombast and underlying finesse of the good old days of slapstick comedy. Here talk, explaining and generally lacklustre supporting roles rob this of its needed madcap pace and attitude. It is technically okay with color fair. *Mosk.*

This Property Is Condemned
(COLOR)

Handsomely - mounted elaboration on a Tennessee Williams play has sufficient slick production value to warrant commercial success, plus Natalie Wood name.

Hollywood, June 14.

Paramount Pictures release of a Seven Arts-Ray Stark presentation. Produced by John Houseman. Stars Natalie Wood; features Robert Redford, Charles Bronson, Kate Reid. Directed by Sydney Pollack. Screenplay, Francis Ford Coppola, Fred Coe, Edith Sommer, suggested by a one-act play by Tennessee Williams; camera (Technicolor), James Wong Howe; film editor, Adrienne Fazan; sound recording, Harry Lindgren, James E. Murphy; music, scored by Kenyon Hopkins; song, "Wish Me A Rainbow," music and lyrics, Jay Livingston, Ray Evans. Reviewed in Hollywood, May 31, '66. Running time: **110 MINS.**

Alva Starr .... Natalie Wood
Owen Legate .... Robert Redford
J. J. Nichols .... Charles Bronson
Hazel Starr .... Kate Reid
Willie Starr .... Mary Badham
Knopke .... Alan Baxter
Sidney .... Robert Blake
Johnson .... John Harding
Salesman .... Dabney Coleman
Jimmy Bell .... Ray Hemphill
Charlie Steinkamp ..... Brett Pearson
Tom .... Jon Provost
Hank .... Quentin Sondergaard
Max .... Michael Steen
Lindsay Tate .... Bruce Watson

"This Property Is Condemned" is a handsomely-mounted, well-acted Depression era drama about the effect of railroad retrenchment on a group of boarding-house people. Derived from a Tennessee Williams one-acter, the John Houseman production is adult without being sensational, and touching without being maudlin. Natalie Wood and Robert Redford head a strong cast. The Seven Arts-Ray Stark presentation is a trifle longish, but overall b.o. prospects look bright for Paramount release in general situations.

Francis Ford Coppola, Fred Coe and Edith Sommer are credited with the script, "suggested" (per credits) from an earlier Williams play in which two young kids chat about the past. In screen form, what is left of the play is contained in prolog and epilog. Williams' name was restored to screen credits after VARIETY publication of the curious absence, eventually explained by author's lawyer but only after an example of poor p.r. planning which could have been avoided. This should not affect an appreciation of a very fine film.

Miss Wood is solo-starred as the young Dixie belle, older daughter of Kate Reid, latter in her Hollywood film debut playing a sleazy landlady to some railroad men. Miss Wood dreams of another life while she flirts up a storm, acting as the shill for her mother, delivering a very good interpretation of what many believe, per play, was Williams' early development of the older Blanche Dubois, distilled into "A Streetcar Named Desire." Her drunk scene is an excellent piece of acting, and a highlight.

Redford, top-featured, should make a significant leap to stardom via his outstanding performance herein, as the railroad efficiency expert sent to town to lay off most of the crew. Plot-wise, the role is thankless and heavy, but Redford, through voice, expression and movement—total acting—makes the character sympathetic and rounded with depth and feeling, including a flair for light comedy. Under the excellent and sensitive direction of Sydney Pollack, Redford's eventual romantic involvement with Miss Wood illuminates his character as well as hers.

Charles Bronson is excellent as the earthy boarder, eyed by Miss Reid but with a hanker for Miss Wood, who marries him in spite, then rolls him to escape her environment. This is the fatal flaw which in time robs her of happiness with Redford. Miss Reid is outstanding in her projection of brittle warmth atop calculating cruelty. Mary Badham is the younger daughter who sets the stage for plot unfoldment in excellent fashion, giving warmth, dimension and appeal throughout. All other players render solid support.

Pollack, in his second feature film, shows a remarkable visual sense, executed by James Wong Howe's brilliant and versatile Technicolor camera. Players seem to come alive under Pollack's hand, becoming as real as the sets and other production artifacts which fit perfectly the mood of the moment. A fight scene, when the axed workmen take it out on Redford, has flash and excitement, in contrast with the very romantic, lyrical passages which evoke heartwarming response. One big atmospheric goof: if this is Mississippi, where are the Negroes?

Kenyon Hopkins' good score interpolates two old standards from the Paramount catalog, plus a traditional, and a newie by Jay Livingston and Ray Evans, "Wish Me A Rainbow." Latter has the required plaintive air, but gets overexposure; it is a show tune, nothing more.

Adrienne Fazan edited to 110 minutes, in flexible tempo per intent of Pollack. Pic is on the long side, made that way by a tendency to have Miss Wood keep on repeating her childish dreams while establishing an innocent selfishness. As always is the case, good early scripting and performances obviate reprise, and presence of same mars overall impact.

Also, after Miss Wood breaks away from home and reunites with Redford, plot does not advance for many minutes, over-telegraphing the eventual arrival of Miss Reid. Downbeat ending is suggested, and told in epilog, a proper plot economy. Other technical credits are excellent.
Murf.

Melbourne Fest

Nihon Retto
(A Chain of Islands)
(JAPAN)
Melbourne, June 6.
Nikkatsu production. Direction and script by Kei Kumai. Editing by Mutsuo Tanji. Photography by Masahisa Himeda. Music by Akira Ifukube. Leading players: Jukichi Uno, Hideaki Nitani, Mizuho Suzuki, Izumi Ashikawa. Black and white. Reviewed at Melbourne Film Festival. Running Time, 118 MINS.

(English Sub-titles)

Apparently based on fact, the setting is Japan in 1959, with the investigation a year after into the death of an American sergeant, found drowned in Tokyo Bay. The investigation uncovers a whole chain of black market dealings,

U. S. currency counterfeiting and related murders.

There's a constant flashing back onto other crime cases, until the gimmick becomes laugh-provoking, and although suspenseful at times, the film is far too rambling and needs drastic editing and tightening to approach anywhere near the Harry Lime or James Bond level of thriller. There's no real lead in the film to focus attention on and the nearest approach to this—the leading investigator—is killed some way before the end. A certain amount of anti-Americanism also could be read into the film.

Photography and direction are okay, without being outstanding, and performances in the main are competent enough although some of the actual film Americans—presumably actually Jap or other nationalities—are far from convincing. *Stan.*

Zero in the Universe
(U. S. A.)
Melbourne, June 6.
Jock Livingston production. Direction, editing by George Moorse. Script by Livingston and Moorse. No distributor. Photography by Gerard Vandenberg. Music by Donald Cherry. Leading players: Jock Livingston, George Bartenieff, Pamela Badyk, George Moorse, Henke Raaf. Black and white. Reviewed at Melbourne Film Festival. Running Time, 85 MINS.

If the intention of the makers of this film was to out-Dali Salvador Dali, then in this they've succeeded admirably. Its a mass of confusion and nonsense from beginning to end, though well photographed and seriously acted.

As far as one can make out its about two men, Zero and Steinmetz, who—along with Zero's secretary, Vivian, are always crossing each other's paths in improbable places, situations and guises. Many of the gimmicks beloved by avant garde and abstract filmmakers abound, but of real wit satire or even parody there is little evidence. It is a bore from beginning to end, give or take "symbolism" in many a shot. *Stan.*

Fireball 500
(COLOR-PANAVISION)

Good teenpic with plot substance. Auto racing and crime adds visual and dramatic excitement. Selling angle should emphasize more ambitious story line. Very good b.o. prospects in young adult and teen situations.

Hollywood, June 1.
American International Pictures release of James H. Nicholson-Samuel Z. Arkoff (Burt Topper) production. Stars Frankie Avalon, Annette Funicello, Fabian, Chill Wills, Harvey Lembeck, Julie Parrish; features rest of cast. Directed by William Asher. Screenplay, Asher, Leo Townsend; camera (Pathecolor), Floyd Crosby; editors, Fred Feitshans, Eve Newman; music, Les Baxter; songs, Guy Hemric, Jerry Styner; asst. director, Dale Hutchinson. Reviewed at Directors Guild of America, L.A., May 31, '66. Running Time, 91 MINS.
Dave .... Frankie Avalon
Jane .... Annette Funicello
Leander .... Fabian
Big Jaw .... Chill Wills
Charlie Bigg .... Harvey Lembeck
Martha .... Julie Parrish
Hastings .... Doug Henderson
Bronson .... Baynes Barron
Race announcer .... Sandy Reed
Joev .... Mike Nader
Herman .... Ed Garner
Prolog announcer .... Vince Scully
Farmer's daughter ...... Sue Hamilton
Herman's wife .... Rene Kiano
Man in garage .... Len Lesser
Jobber .... Billy Beck
Herman's Friend ..... Tex Armstrong
Themselves .. The Don Randi Trio
Plus One, The Carol Lombard Singers
Leander's girls .... Mary Hughes, Patti Chandler, Karla Conway, Hedy Scott, Sallie Sachse, Jo Collins, Maria McBane, Linda Bent

"Fireball 500" is an admirable attempt, realized to a significant degree, to add drama to what has become cliche teenpix fluff. A basic romantic complication is set against a backdrop of hopped-up racing cars, bootlegging, and morals. Exciting race scenes, generally good scripting, performances and William Asher direction make for a snappy pace that flags only in final minutes.

It will be recalled that Asher directed the AIPix which pioneered the bikini plots, since copied—and just about run into the ground—by all producers. Just as the early sound filmusicals were in essence just songalogs, so were the beachpix. And just as older musicals eventually began to flop until story content improved, it is time now for sturdier youthpix plots.

Frankie Avalon heads the list of six above-title players, delivering a credible performance as a cocky racer who initially competes with equally-cocky Fabian for the favors of Annette Funicello. Latter is daughter of Chill Wills, race promoter with an eye for the chicks. Harvey Lembeck is an unscrupulous sponsor of racers, and part-time moonshiner, in partnership with snooty young widow Julie Parrish.

The Avalon-Fabian rivalry carries over into the races, portrayed in exciting photography and zesty editing. Doug Henderson and Baynes Barron are two revenuers who enlist Avalon's aid in exposing Lembeck as the one who caused the death of Mike Nader, and near-death of Avalon. Latter winds up with a more mature outlook, and a more mature Miss Parrish. Fabian gets Miss Funicello.

Script has some holes in character motivations, but Asher's direction bridges the gap in many cases. Fabian occasionally is too mopey, and Miss Parrish's switch from swinger to nice gal is awkward, otherwise all principals are good. Nader shows promise. Big letdown occurs 15 minutes before fadeout, as Lembeck is unmasked. Event is terminated too abruptly, causing waning interest in final race, itself dull in comparison with all previous runs.

Guy Hemric and Jerry Styner wrote five songs, spaced adroitly, of which title tune, "Step Right Up" and "My Way" are ear-catching. Avalon and Miss Funicello are in good voice throughout. Les Baxter's score has the right sound. Floyd Crosby's Pathecolor-Panavision camera work is excellent, ditto process work by Jacques Marquette.

Fred Feitshans and Eve Newman executed the sharp editing to 91 minutes. Puppet sequences — prolog and epilog—were the clever

work of Clokey Films. All other technical credits are firstrate. Screen credit is given to various auto racing groups. Burt Topper co-produced with James H. Nicholson and Samuel Z. Arkoff.
Murf.

Who's Afraid of Virginia Woolf?

Powerhouse war of the sexes. Strong performances by Stellar cast. Click debut of Mike Nichols as director. Big.

Hollywood, June 20.
Warner Bros. Pictures release of Ernest Lehman production. Stars Elizabeth Taylor, Richard Burton; features George Segal, Sandy Dennis. Directed by Mike Nichols. Screenplay, Ernest Lehman, from play by Edward Albee; camera, Haskell Wexler; editor, Sam O'Steen; music, composed and conducted by Alex North; asst. director, Bud Grace. Reviewed at Pantages Theatre, Hollywood, June 20, '66. Running Time, 131 MINS.
Martha .... Elizabth Taylor
George .... Richard Burton
Nick .... George Segal

"Who's Afraid of Virginia Woolf?" was kept under wraps until the last moment before public preem, thus creating not only a tanta:izng suspense but also an artistic challenge to the talent involved. The suspense was worth it, and the challenge has been met—in spades.

The naked power and oblique tenderness of Edward Albee's incisive, inhuman drama have been transformed from legit into a brilliant motion picture.

Keen adaptation and handsome production by Ernest Lehman, outstanding direction by Mike Nichols in his feature debut, and four topflight performances score an artistic bullseye. This is adult stuff, and Warner Bros. has wisely adopted an under-18 nix on patronage. Elizabeth Taylor-Richard Burton combo will provide a major assist in propelling pic to a deservedly torrid b.o.

Albee's play contains words long familiar to legit, but the American screen has never until now employed such salty lingo. It was an uphill fight by Jack L. Warner to obtain, via appeal to the Motion Picture Assn. of America, the production code seal. The fight was justified, for the dialog, in context, is appropriate, not prurient, and on the credit crawl, in normal modest location, is PCA Seal No. 21074.

Miss Taylor, who has proven she can act in response to sensitive direction, earned every penny of her reported million plus. Her characterization is at once sensual, spiteful, cynical, pitiable, loathsome, lustful and tender. Shrews — both male and female—always attract initial attention, but the projection of three-dimensional reality requires talent which sustains the interest; the talent is here.

Burton, the sensitive history prof who is Albee's ringmaster in putting through the hoops not only his wife and himself but also the younger George Segal-Sandy Dennis couple, delivers a smash portrayal. He evokes sympathy during the public degradations to which his wife subjects him, and his outrage, as well as his deliberate vengeance, are totally believable, in the lingo of the play, he acts to "peel off labels" worn by all parties, including those of his wife, who dwells in a fantasy of a nonexistent child.

Provoking the exercise in exorcism is the late-night visit of Miss Dennis and Segal. Latter is the all-American boy type — the shallow cookie-cutter bright-young-man—who, in the course of one night, is seduced by his hostess, exposed by his host, but enlightened as to more mature aspects of love and marriage. Segal is able to evoke sympathy, then hatred, then pity, in a first-rate performance.

Miss Dennis makes an impressive screen debut as the young bride, nervously clutching her fur wrap, getting tight, then sick, on brandy, and finally pouring forth her unhappiness with the same emotional rhythm as her off-screen retching, her delivery is rounded with the intended subtlety of a not-so-Dumb Dora. It is not certain that she and Segal will learn from their shattering experience; that would be perhaps too pat a development. The elder couple, however, wind up at a new plateau of understanding, with an upbeat promise for the future.

Albee exalts the human spirit by taking to its logical conclusion the perversions of this spirit. Lehman, making his producer bow herein, has maintained Albee's point of view in adaptation, while expanding the action to some well-chosen, logical exteriors. Effect of this is to set a smart pace, sustained throughout by Nichols' imaginative eye, plus the versatile The b&w spectrum has a myriad of dramatic hues, rarely explored so fully.

The musty souls of the characters are matched by superb b&w lensing of Haskell Wexler, production design of Richard Sylbert, and Alex North's sparse score is a big asset. Sam O. Steen executed the editing to a tight 131 minutes (including the 90-second exit music) in which all character interactions have a self-contained, restrained unity which advances the overall movement. Sound recording by M. A. Merrick has a live, natural feel, another of the many fine touches which add up to an uncommon film achievement. *Murf.*

The Main Chance
(BRITISH)

Oldfashioned British meller, for least discriminating situations.

Hollywood, June 8.
Embassy release of Jack Greenwood production. Stars Gregoire Aslan, Tracy Reed, Edward de Souza; features Stanley Meadows, Jack Smethurst. Directed by John Knight. Screenplay, Richard Harris, based on novel by Edgar Wallace; camera, James Wilson; editor, Derek Holding; asst. director, Ted Lewis. Reviewed at Joe Shore screening room, June 8, '66. Running Time, 60 MINS.
Potter .... Gregoire Aslan
Christine .... Tracy Reed
Michael Blake ...... Edward de Souza
Joe Hayes .... Stanley Meadows
Ross .... Jack Smethurst

"The Main Chance" is a weak programmer, a British import released in this country by Embassy. Judged by today's standards, it belongs to the market of 20 years ago when anything went as a second feature. Despite its being based on a novel by Britain's one-time top mystery writer, Edgar Wallace, what emerges is about as exciting as last month's country newspaper. Pic was part of package acquired by Embassy for U. S. for release but being given some theatrical exposure first as filler fodder before tv.

Jack Greenwood production, lethargically directed by John Knight and turned out obviously on a greatly reduced budget, deals with doublecrossers who smuggle a cargo of diamonds from France into England. What's unbelievable is that any producer could think he could make a film out of such unimaginative activities.

Gregoire Aslan plays a wealthy operator, a nut on electronic devices, who hires Edward de Souza, a shady World War II pilot, to fly in the gems. Tracy Reed is Aslan's beauteous secretary who helps de Souza doublecross her employer and get away with the stones. *Whit.*

Rikugun Nakano Gakko
(The Army Nakano School)
(JAPAN-SCOPE)

Tokyo, June 7.
Produced by Daiei Films. Producer, Shusaku Watanabe. Directed by Yasuzo Masumura. Photographed by Setsuo Kobayaski. Music by Tadashi Yamauchi. With Raizo Ichikawa, Daisuke Kato, Maiyumi Ogawa, Sachiko Murase, Kiyosuke Machida. Reviewed, Tokyo, June 1. Running time: 95 MINS.

This tight and expertly made film about prewar activities at Tokyo's notorious "school for spies" is not only a first-rate "documentary" about spying techniques in 1939 (including such unlikely but presumably necessary courses as social dancing and the seducing of females)—it is also a bitter and intensely felt denunciation of the perversion of honest men into calloused agents.

Director Masumura (who made that astonishing comic antiwar film "The Hood:um Soldier" last year), never states this theme and here is one of the reasons it comes across so clearly. The reconstruction is immaculate, the feeling of reality is impeccable—the director's implication comes through the very restrained dialogue, the underplaying of all important scenes, the carefully drab photography, and a plot so cunningly wrought that the conclusion he desires—all patriots are monsters —is inescapable.

The transformation of plain, decent officers into spies, the chronicle of this murder of conscience, is powerfully paced with scenes of recalcitrant members forced to run themselves onto swords, and the hero's almost absent-mnded murder of the girl who loves him and has been waiting for him.

It is a frightening, depressing, and devastatingly honest picture. *Chie.*

Assault On A Queen
(PANAVISION-COLOR)

"Ocean's 6," or the rat pack goes to sea. Good actioner, given topdrawer production, should create b.o. action.

Paramount release of Seven Arts-Sinatra Enterprises (William Goetz) production. Stars Frank Sinatra, Virna Lisi; features Tony Francoisa, Richard Conte, Errol John, Alf Kjellin. Directed by Jack Donahue. Screenplay, Rod Serling, from novel by Jack Finney; camera (Panavision-Technicolor), William H. Daniels (also associate producer); editor, Archie Marshek; music, Duke Ellington; 2d unit director, Robert D. Webb; asst. director, Richard Lang. Reviewed at Paramount h.o., New York, June 6, '66. Running Time: 106 MINS.
Mark Brittain .... Frank Sinatra
Rosa Lucchesi .... Virna Lisi
Vic Rossiter .... Tony Franciosa
Tony Moreno .... Richard Conte
Eric Lauffnauer .... Alf Kjellin
Linc Langley .... Errol John
Captain .... Murray Matheson
Master-at-Arms .... Reginald Denny
Bank Manager .... John Warburton
Doctor .... Lester Matthews
Trench .... Val Avery
First Officer .... Gilchrist Stuart
Second Officer .... Ronald Long
Third Officer .... Leslie Bradley
Fourth Officer .... Arthur E. Gould-Porter
Junior Officer .... Laurence Conroy

After "Ocean's 11," it isn't surprising that Frank Sinatra would have welcomed another property that offered the same elements of suspense, action, and free-wheeling acting and dialog. If "Assault On A Queen," despite the tender, loving care applied to its production, doesn't match up to the earlier film, it still makes its mark as solid entertainment.

What "Assault" most lacks, perhaps, is the sense of morality that made the attempt of "Ocean's" motley crew to hold up a Las Vegas gambling casino sympathetic despite their criminal intent. Whereas a casino is more nearly fair game, there's little "humor" in trying to hold up an ocean liner by seriously threatening to torpedo it.

Rod Serling has avoided humor, almost entirely, in his adaptation of the Jack Finney novel but what would be, generally, a wise decision, has resulted in a script that asks for, and gets, little sympathy for the perpetrators. Their actions are exciting but their motives reprehensible and many will feel that their ultimate fate is better than they deserve.

Producer William Goetz has supervised a remarkable job of making plausible the admittedly wild-eyed adventures of an odd assortment of moral derelicts who salvage a submarine with the intent of robbing the Queen Mary (hence the title), Virna Lisi, Tony Franciosa and Alf Kjellin, on the hunt for a sunken treasure ship off the Bahamas, hire Frank Sinatra and his native partner, Errol John, who run a fishing boat business, to help them find the treasure. Sinatra, instead, finds a small sunken German submarine. Kjellin, a former German U-boat commander, talks the group into salvaging it and holding up the Queen Mary.

Most of the film deals with preparing the sub for the robbery attempt, and the ensuing conflict of personalities during this period. Sinatra becomes Franciosa's rival for the girl; Kjellin's stern leadership masks a suppressed desire to become again the Nazi sub commander; John, a Negro border-line alcoholic, stays on out of loyalty to Sinatra, despite Franciosa's open enmity. Richard Conte, a former associate of Kjellin's, is brought in, finally, because his mechanical skill is needed. Every member is at once essential to the caper, and a potential threat to it.

Director Jack Donohue keeps his cast moving, making the rehabilitation of the submarine such a backbreaking chore that it keeps the group too exhausted to plot, but not to hate. Art director Paul Groesse and set decorator John P. Austin do a superb facelifting operation on the sub which looks every bit the ten years it spent at the bottom of the Caribbean.

Oddly enough, Miss Lisi, one of the screen's most shapely craft (especially in a brief suggestion of a swimming suit designer Edith Head provides) looks both tired and unattractively made up during some early scenes. Actually, only Kjellin is able to create a well-rounded character and is outstanding as the apparently bland German, holding in control his diabolic intent. Sinatra and Miss Lisi are very good in roles that make few demands on their acting ability. John, while efficient in the tenser moments, seems inhibited in scenes where he must wax sentimental over his rehabilitation by Sinatra. Conte makes the most of an unsympathetic role.

There's a disagreeable air about Franciosa's performance, however, that can only be partially blamed on the part as written. A really obnoxious type, he projects this characteristic too quickly, making his relationship with Miss Lisi illogical. Other than a good set of teeth, there's nothing attractive about him and his demise will meet with audience approval, but one wonders what Miss Lisi saw in him in the first place.

For the short, fast scenes aboard the Queen Mary, Hollywood's entire British colony was seemingly signed. No one is particularly outstanding, though the group impression is excellent. Reginald Denny and John Warburton are seen, but not heard, as two of the ship's officers.

Although editor Archie Marshek doesn't allow the pace to slow much, he could still trim the 106 minutes down a bit, especially in such scenes as Conte's, brought in to put the sub in operation within a matter of hours, also being shown helping in such routine chores as chipping barnacles off the hull. Paramount's press book, incidentally, says "Six far-out fortune hunters stick up the Queen Mary in mid-Atlantic" whereas the action is pinpointed as the Caribbean near the Bahamas.

William H. Daniels, associate producer as well as cameraman for the film, uses Panavision and Technicolor to good advantage, with most of the intricate special process shots kept short and to a minimum, except for some rather obvious moments involving the finding of the sub, and the final raft scene. The underwater photography, which may be the work of Lawrence Butler and Paul K. Lerpae, is on a par with Daniels' excellent surface photography.

Duke Ellington's score, while not overly atmospheric, is most listenable and should be a big help in promoting the film. *Robe.*

Nippon o Shikaru
(Reprehensible Japan)
(COLOR-WIDESCREEN)

Tokyo, June 10.
Produced by Manzo Shibata Eiga Productions. Directed by Taijiro Tamura, Hirotatsu Fujiwara, and Yukio Sug Iura. Photographed by Shigenari Yoshida and Kiyoshi Koizumi. Distributed by Shochiku. Running Time, 80 MINS.

A "Mondo Cane" type exploitation picture of which there are numbers, the surprising thing about this one being that big Shochiku is distributing it. The formula is familiar: while pretending to censure, the film leers; the stern finger is waved, and the chops are licked.

Most of the material is about sex. The spectator is taken on long and badly photographed tours of various red-light districts viewed through the windshield; or he is shown innocuous couples petting in Tokyo parks and told that this is bad for youth; or he is made to look at ordinary people getting into ordinary taxis and informed that they are all off for assignation houses.

The strong voyeuristic-element may appeal to some but pious hypocrisy of the picture makes it difficult to take. In addition, production values are so primitive that many of the supposed raw scenes are (perhaps purposely) invisible. Shochiku's interest in such a cheap quickie can only be explained as trust in the directors (all of them Japanese TV "personalities") or as clutching at financial straws. *Chie.*

The Blue Max
(CINEMASCOPE-COLOR-BRITISH)

World War 1 air drama, told from German point of view, with lush, exciting production values and aerial lensing helping to relieve a negative, meller plot. George Peppard, James Mason, Ursula Andress the marquee lure. Prospects good for general release.

Hollywood, June 16.
Twentieth Century-Fox release of Christian Ferry production (executive producer, Elmo Williams). Stars George Peppard, James Mason, Ursula Andress, Jeremy Kemp, Karl Michael Vogler. Directed by John Guillermin. Screenplay, David Pursall, Jack Seddon, Gerald Hanley, based on novel by Jack D. Hunter, adapted by Ben Barzman, Basilio Franchina; camera (DeLuxe Color), Douglas Slocombe; editor, Max Benedict; music, Jerry Goldsmith; production design, Wilfrid Shingleton; asst directors, Jack Causey, Derek Cracknell. Reviewed at Directors Guild of America, L.A., June 15, '66. Running Time (excluding intermission) 154 MINS.

Bruno Stachel .... George Peppard
Count Von Klugermann .. James Mason
Countess Kaeti ... Ursula Andress
Willi Von Klugermann ... Jeremy Kemp
Heidemann ..... Karl Michael Vogler
Elfi Heidemann ...... Loni Von Friedl
Holbach .... Anton Diffring
Rupp .... Peter Woodthorpe
Kettering .... Harry Towb
Ziegel .... Derek Dewark
Fabian .... Derren Nesbitt
Field Marshall Von Lenndorf
.... Friedrich Ledebur
Crown Prince .... Roger Ostime
Hans .... Hugo Schuster
Pilots ......Tim Parkes, Ian Kingsley,
.... Ray Browne
Richthofen .... Carl Schell

"The Blue Max" is a World War I drama with some exciting aerial combat sequences helping to enliven a somewhat grounded, meller script in which no principal character engenders much sympathy. Elmo Williams was executive producer of the handsomely mounted Christian Ferry production. George Peppard, James Mason and Ursula Andress provide some international marquee bait. Overdone sex bits and other plot motivations, more valid and sophisticated, lift the 20th-Fox release out of the kiddie market. Initial hardticket b.o. is likely to be spotty, improving to good returns on later release in general situations.

Three scripters, two adapters and the original novelist are credited with the final version. Jack D. Hunter penned the 1964 tome, adapted by Ben Barzman and Basilio Franchina. David Pursall, Jack Seddon and Gerald Hanley are credited with the screenplay, title of which refers to the slang term used in Imperial Germany for the highest award to aviation war aces.

World War I is a meaty plot background, for it was, for the most part, the last clash of personal nobility in war leaders with the impersonal killing by machines; the latter was firmly entrenched by World War II. The emotional trauma of old-school warriors with the new breed, repped by aviators, suggests strong dramatic seeds, some of which are planted here.

In general, however, a downbeat air prevails in the drama. The hero, a lowerclass climber played by George Peppard, is a heel; his adversary in the ranks of an air squadron, also for the free affections of Ursula Andress, is also a negative character, played by Jeremy Kemp. James Mason, husband of Miss Andress, is looking for a propaganda symbol, finds it in Peppard, and eventually causes the latter's death. Only Karl Michael Vogler, the squadron commander, evokes any sympathy as a gentleman, but he, as the last of the above-title players, is literally swamped in the negative mire.

The National Catholic Office of Motion Pictures has already B-rated "Max" for the Peppard-Andress bedroom footage which is, indeed, rather torrid. It is not family stuff. Amour does not advance the plot, nor contribute to character illumination.

Given the story line, all players do a creditable job. Peppard is engagingly cold, while Mason can almost always give depth to a role with a few words and a gesture, as he does here. Miss Andress is an okay sexpot. Kemp is very good and Vogler is excellent. Among the strong supporting cast are Anton Diffring, Mason's efficient aide; Derek Newark, the typically harried squadron maintenance officer; Loni Von Friedl, Vogler's quiet wife, and Carl Schell, in a cameo as Baron Von Richthofen, real life German ace who is Peppards hero.

Filmed in Ireland, pic includes some beautiful Cinemascope photography, executed in ground sequences by Douglas Slocombe and in air shots by Skeets Kelly. Tony Squire directed the latter, while John Guillermin is responsible for remainder of the direction. The DeLuxe Color lensing is excellent throughout.

Guillermin, who derived the uniformly fine performances within the given plot frame, has at times an exciting visual sense. In one shot, the retreating German Army is the foreground for the advancing aircraft, en route to do battle with the by-now-advancing Allied forces. In another, Peppard's fatal aerobatics are shot through an observing crowd, thus giving film audiences an unusual, exciting participation effect. Battlefield action is appropriately grim and dynamic, all the more so against the lush pastoral greenery being defiled by war.

On the other hand, Guillermin's technique in more intimate sequences becomes obvious and mechanical: an overabundance of low-angle shots; also a repeated tracking shot which covers an arc of about 90 degrees while closing in on the action. Every director has a style, of course, but the object is to keep it from being formula.

Jerry Goldsmith's score, sometimes overpowered by action noise, is good. Wilfrid Shingleton did a firstrate job in production design, and the special effects by Karl Baumgartner, Maurice Ayres and Ron Ballinger are outstanding. Max Benedict edited. Film runs 154 minutes without intermish; first part runs 90 minutes. Overall pacing is smart. Other technical credits of Ireland's Ardmore Studios are excellent.

Selling the film appears to be somewhat of an uphill fight for several reasons: (1) segments of the world film audience are not receptive to picturing Germans—even pre-Nazi Germans—in a sympathetic light; (2) the leading characters inspire very little sympathy; (3) title is obscure in meaning. *Murf.*

Munster, Go Home
(COLOR)

Feature edition of "The Munsters' teleseries, with enough gimmicks, gags and ghoulish camp as well as some fine feature casting to make for a pleasant lightweight flick. The kids should especially dig it.

Hollywood, June 10.
Universal release of a Joe Connelly and Bob Mosher production. Features entire cast. Directed by Earl Bellamy. Screenplay, George Tibbles, Connelly, Mosher; camera, (Technicolor) Benjamin H. Kline; editor, Bud S. Isaacs; sound, Waldon O. Watson, Corson Jowett; music, Jack Marshall; assistant director, Dolph Zimmer; art directors, Alexander Golitzen, John Lloyd. Reviewed at the Picwood Theatre, Los Angeles, June 10, 1966. Running time, 96 MINS.

Herman Munster ...... Fred Gwynne
Lily .... Yvonne De Carlo
Grandpa .... Al Lewis
Eddie .... Butch Patrick
Marilyn .... Debbie Watson
Freddie .... Terry-Thomas
Lady Effigie .... Hermione Gingold
Roger .... Robert Pine
Cruikshank .... John Carradine
Squire Moresby ...... Bernard Fox
Joey .... Richard Dawson
Grace .... Jeanne Arnold
Millie .... Maria Lennard
Herbert .... Cliff Norton
Mrs. Moresby .... Diana Chesney
Alfie .... Arthur Malet
Hennesy .... Ben Wright

Producers Joe Connelly and Bob Mosher (who also wrote the screenplay with George Tibbles) have wisely transferred the scene of this feature based on the teleseries "The Munsters," from the haunted house home base to an opulent English estate. Pic holds up on its own, is well paced, has fine Technicolor lensing, and feature cast should make for brisk box-office biz, especially during the summer months. It's solid family entertainment.

Story revolves around Herman Munster (Fred Gwynne) and his friendly monster clan as they cross the ocean after being informed that his late uncle has willed him his estate and title of lord. The manor house is presided over by English relatives, Hermione Gingold, her son, Terry-Thomas, daughter Jeanne Arnold, and butler, John Carradine.

Lady Effigie (Gingold) attempts to scare the American relatives away, with the aid of the mysterious Griffin, in order to protect the secret of the manor house, where, it seems, coffins are carted off at regular intervals. Plot thickens when it is discovered by the Munsters that the house is a center of a counterfeit ring. Pic ends with a wild auto race through hills and dales with Herman in souped-up casket—shaped racing car pursued by a henchman of his inlaws.

Love interest is introduced when Marilyn Munster, played by Debbie Watson, (Pat Priest essayed the tv role) has a ship-board romance with Roger Moresby, Universal thespactee Robert Pine. The two are fine well groomed players and their scenes together are effective.

Gwynne, Yvonne de Carlo, Al Lewis and Butch Patrick as the Munsters have their roles worked to professional polish and everyone else has joined in the spirit and style of the comedy with just the right amount of intensity.

Earl Bellamy's direction allows his actors enough leverage to camp it up with personal bits. Costumes by Grady Hunt also contribute to the fey mood and visual effects are cleverly integrated throughout.

Jack Marshall's musical score adds an overall light touch, at times building outrageous crescendos, and Benjamin H. Kline's Technicolor camerawork is excellent.　　　　　　*Dool.*

The Endless Summer
(DOCUMENTARY-COLOR)

Independently-made documentary on surfing around the world has enough action and wit to make a dent in market with proper promotion.

Bruce Brown presentation. Produced, directed, written, edited, photographed and narrated by Brown. Features Mike Hynson, Robert August. Camera (color), Brown, R. Paul Allen, Bob Bagley, Paul Witzig. Musical theme written and played by The Sandals. Reviewed at Kips Bay Theatre, New York, June 14, '66. Running time: 95 MINS.

On the surface, a 95-minute film about surfing sounds like a great deal of time to devote to one subject. However, California surfer-filmmaker Bruce Brown has, after two years' work and a 35,000-mile journey around the world, successfully edited his nine miles of color film into a feature that will excite sports fans and should delight most other filmgoers.

Shot originally in 16m and blown up to 35m for theatrical exposure, the film's loose storyline has two young California surfers, Mike Hynson and Robert August, trying out the surf in various parts of the world. It figures that their own California

and the beaches of Hawaii get most of the footage but there are scenic and adventurous treks to Senegal, Ghana, Nigeria, South Africa, Australia, New Zealand and Tahiti. Their findings range from disappointingly mild waves (due partially to inadequate surf and partially to being on the spot out of season) to mountainous and dangerous waves off the north shore of Oahu in Hawaii.

Brown's own narration is, surprisingly, free of "inside" expressions. When he uses surfing terms he briefly explains their meaning. Although there's a touch of repetition in his commentary (his favorite word, apparently, is "ultimate" which seems to occur in every other sentence), he delivers it in such a flippant, spirited manner that the audience finds itself laughing at some pretty dated material.

The photography, in excellent color although type of film used and color process are not identified, is first class and frequently spectacular. The spray - spattered lens of the camera testifies to the risk of carrying any type of photographic equipment while riding a slippery surfboard through some wild, wild waves. Editing is crisp but some short "gag" shots should be expunged.

To kick off commercial run for the film, Brown leased the Kips Bay Theatre in New York (cash in advance) and is promoting it himself. A big boost in Gotham was sponsorship of premiere by city's Special Events Commissioner John (Bud) Palmer, a sports enthusiast, who had seen some of Brown's previous surfing film footage.

Only a shortage of available prints and necessary financing to properly promote the film should prevent it from having an excellent commercial run. Brown, for the time being, insists he doesn't want to turn it over to a major distributor but this depends presumably on the offers he gets. The rhythmic musical background provided by a group called The Sandals is proper for the mood the film conveys although it occasionally threatens to drown out the narrator.　　*Robe.*

Mara of the Wilderness
(COLOR)

Nice little actioner, with good appeal for moppets; should be helped by exploitation value of Adam West name.

Hollywood, June 8.
Allied Artists release of Unicorn (Brice Mark) production. Features Adam West, Linda Saunders, Theo Marcuse, Denver Pyle, Sean McClory, Eve Brent, Roberto Contreras, Ed Kemmer, Stuart Walsh, Lelia Walsh. Directed by Frank McDonald. Screenplay, Tom Blackburn, from story by Rod Scott; camera (DeLuxe Color), Robert Wyckoff; editor, Harold M. Gordon; music, Harry Bluestone; asst. director, Wilson Shyer. Reviewed at World Theatre, June 8, '66. Running Time, 90 MINS.
Ken Williams .... Adam West
Mara Wade .... Linda Saunders
Jarnagan .... Theo Marcuse
Kelly .... Denver Pyle
Dr. Frank Wade .... Sean McClory
Mrs. Wade .... Eve Brent
"Friday" .... Roberto Contreras
First Pilot .... Ed Kemmer
Second Pilot .... Stuart Walsh
Mara Wade (age seven) ...Lelia Walsh

"Mara of the Wilderness" is a

lively little actioner, which should nicely fill out the bottom half of a family dualer. Adventure yarn, shot in color on location in Alaska, has a pleasant pace due to Frank McDonald's direction, and with added exploitation value of name of topliner Adam West (in his pre-"Batman" years) should sell satisfactorily in moppet and action market.

Tom Blackburn's oke script of story by Rod Scott is a variation on the old plotline of an abandoned youngster being raised by wild animals. In this one, Linda Saunders is the grown-up child, who was raised by wild wolves. She's discovered by U.S. Fish & Wildlife man Adam West, but is also spotted about the same time by heavy Theo Marcuse, who wants to catch her and sell her to freak show. After assorted battles between the two, Marcuse is subdued, and West, as the pic ends, is given the pleasant task of civilizing the red-haired wild girl.

West turns in a good job, showing his ability in a different type role than most folks know him. Miss Saunders is a pretty young thing who essays a non-literate role (as Mara, she speaks no lines, only grunts, growls and howls in animal fashion) in an okay job. Marcuse as a mammoth sized heavy, comes across believable, and fully the nasty scoundrel. Only other principal in cast is Robert Contreras as Marcuse's tracker, who handles the lesser part adequately.

Robert Wyckoff's color lensing provides a nice bright look at attractive outdoor scenery in Alaska. Other credits are satisfactory.

Film was shown in a few southern locations last year, but not put into general release 'til this time.　　　　　　*Mitt.*

Destination Inner Space
(COLOR)

A spine-tingling sci-fi pic. Production values are top-grade and underwater sequences well-done.

Hollywood, June 2.
Magna Pictures Distrib. Corp. release of United Pictures Corp. (Earle Lyon) production in association with Harold Goldman Associates. Features Scott Brady, Sheree North, Gary Merrill, Mike Road, Wende Wagner. Directed by Francis D. Lyon. Screenplay, Arthur C. Pierce; camera (Eastmancolor), Brick Marquard; editor, Robert S. Eisen; music, Paul Dunlap; asst. director, Joe Wonder. Reviewed at Nosseck Projection Theatre, L.A., June 2, '66. Running Time, 83 MINS.
Commander Wayne ...... Scott Brady
Sandra .... Sheree North
Dr. Le Satier .... Gary Merrill
Hugh .... Mike Road

"Destination Inner Space" should go over big with the youngsters as well as provide solid entertainment for the adult sci-fi fans. Production and technical values are first class, story line is intelligently plotted and musical score of both electric and tonal sounds contribute to the erie excitement.

An underwater saga about oceanographers who discover an unidentified object, pursuit of "the thing" brings about a series of mysterious events, including an ugly sea monster. Suspense and surprise are neatly balanced and the underwater photography is at

all times authentic and visually fascinating.

Conflict between the various people involved gives a sense of dimension to this screenplay by Arthur C. Pierce and director Francis D. Lyon uses his actors well, sparring them off in a believable manner. Dialogue is to the point, shows intense research on oceanography and action sequences are briskly edited by Robert S. Eisen.

It's difficult at first to accept Sheree North as a doctor (of science) here but she competently brings it off; Scott Brady is brusque and interplay between him as Captain Wayne and Mike Road, as Hugh Maddox, is ruggedly handled. Road, handsome and brooding, also brings a strong masculine flavor to his role. Gary Merrill as the scientist, Dr. Le Satier, also contributes to the credibility of the plot. Wende Wagner is wonderful to look at and it would appear is an excellent underwater diver.

Although the title may seem misleading, ("inner space" apparently refers to the underwater reaches of the earth), there is plenty in this slickly made film to keep the whole family on the edge of their seats.

Music by Paul Dunlap, sound effects by Joseph von Stroheim and art direction by Paul Sylos also should be commended. *Dool.*

Walk, Don't Run
(PANAVISION-COLOR)

Very amusing housing shortage romantic comedy, set in Tokyo. Cary Grant outstanding as a mature matchmaker. Successful, updated remake of "The More The Merrier." Strong b.o. prospects in general situations.

Hollywood, June 17

Columbia Pictures release, and Granley Co. presentation, of Sol C. Siegel production. Stars Cary Grant, Samantha Eggar, Jim Hutton; features John Standing. Directed by Charles Walters. Screenplay, Sol Saks, based on a story by Robert Russell, Frank Ross; camera (Technicolor), Harry Stradling; editors, Walter Thompson, James Wells; music, Quincy Jones; asst. director, Jim Myers. Reviewed at Academy Award Theatre, L.A., June 16, '66. Running Time, 114 MINS.

William Rutland .... Cary Grant
Christine Easton .... Samantha Eggar
Steve Davis .... Jim Hutton
Julius P. Haversack....John Standing
Aiko Kurawa .... Miiko Taka
Yuri Andreyovitch..........Ted Hartley
Dimitri .... Ben Astar
Police Capt. .... George Takei
Mr. Kurawa .... Teru Shimada
Mrs. Kurawa .... Louis Kiuchi

"Walk, Don't Run" is a completely entertaining, often hilarious romantic comedy spotlighting as a matchmaker a deliberately mature Cary Grant at the peak of his comedy prowess. The fast-moving and colorful Sol C. Siegel production pegs its laughs on a Tokyo housing shortage during the last Olympics. Fine scripting, direction and performances — including a successful pace change for Samantha Eggar—invest the Columbia release with b.o. legs both strong and long.

Older filmgoers will detect a resemblance to "The More the Merrier," a smash George Stevens pic which Columbia released in 1943. Jean Arthur, Joel McCrea and the late Charles Coburn starred in that one, based on a story by Robert Russell and Frank Ross. "Walk" is, indeed, a remake, scripted in top fashion by Sol Saks, who shifted the locale from Washington, D. C., to Japan. Miss Eggar, Jim Hutton and Grant, all billed above title, are the respective counterparts in the new version.

Grant is outstanding as the middle-aged and distinguished English industrialist who arrives two days before his Tokyo hotel suite will be available. Noting an apartment-to-share sign, he finds it to be the diggings of prim, schedule-conscious Miss Eggar. She is engaged to a stuffy embassy functionary, played by John Standing, with whom Grant has already had a run-in.

Hutton, a member of the U.S. Olympic walking team (hence the title), is also awaiting quarters, so he, too, winds up in Miss Eggar's pad. Ben Astar is a comic Russian secret agent, spying on athletes including Ted Hartley, a Russian walking team member with whom Hutton has struck up a friendship. The simple plot complications call for a phony marriage, with Miss Eggar and Hutton winding up for real as newly-weds.

All three principals interact well together. Grant whams over every line with perfect timing. Two throwaway bits have him whistling title tunes from previous pix. His presence dominates every scene, including one long-shot—with only part of his face visible and but few words to speak—in which his magnetism draws the eye away from the predominant foliage. Miss Eggar becomes properly warmer and engaging as story unfolds, showing good comedy ability which will further impress those who caught her in William Wyler's "The Collector."

Hutton again shows his light comedy ability to good advantage. Standing is excellent as the stuffy bureaucrat. George Takei impresses as the urbane cop who helps unsnarl matters, and Hartley makes a good Russian. Miiko Taka comes across well as Miss Eggar's girl friend who, each day, finds more men in latter's pad. Teru Shimada and Lois Kiuchi have a good bit as Miss Taka's parents in a domestic scene of old Japanese manners competing with a tv set.

Charles Walters' direction is sure throughout. Harry Stradling's mobile Panavision-Technicolor camera is a big asset, whether in the confines of the apartment set or on the streets of Tokyo. Joe Wright's production design is first-rate, ditto the Quincy Jones score. Walter Thompson and James Wells trimmed to a good 114 minutes. Other credits are pro. *Murf.*

A Man Called Adam

Decline and fall of a Negro jazzman. Weak plot, but some of the thesping and direction hold interest. Sammy Davis Jr. and Louis Armstrong the main marquee lure. Okay dual prospects in general situations, better chances in specialty houses. Ike Jones first Negro to get a "producer" credit.

Hollywood, June 23.

Embassy Pictures release of Trace-Mark Productions, producers, James Waters, Ike Jones, executive producer, Joseph E. Levine. Stars Sammy Davis Jr.; features Louis Armstrong, Cicely Tyson, Frank Sinatra Jr., Peter Lawford, Mel Torme. Directed by Leo Penn. Screenplay, Les Pine, Tina Rome; camera, Jack Priestly; editor, Carl Lerner; music, Benny Carter; asst. director, Joel Glickman. Reviewed at Joe Shore's Screening Room, L.A., June 22, '66. Running Time, 103 MINS.

Adam Johnson ...... Sammy Davis Jr.
Willie Ferguson ...... Louis Armstrong
Nelson Davis .... Ossie Davis
Claudia Ferguson ...... Cicely Tyson
Vincent .... Frank Sinatra Jr.
Manny .... Peter Lawford
Himself .... Mel Torme
Theo .... Lola Falana
Martha .... Jeanette Du Bois
Les .... Johnny Brown
Leroy .... George Rhodes
George .... Michael Silva
Bobby Gales .... Michael Lipton

Filmed completely in the N.Y. area, "A Man Called Adam" stars Sammy Davis Jr. in a downbeat, somewhat uneven programmer about an embittered Negro jazz musician. Some good performances and direction sustain a certain amount of interest in the thinly-scripted Joseph E. Levine presentation. Principal thesps previously have not been as prominently cast, so marquee power is uncertain. Okay production values. Embassy release might be nursed along in special situations, otherwise okay dualler prospects are likely.

James Waters and Ike Jones produced for Davis' Trace-Mark Productions, indie's maiden effort in pix. The six-week shooting sked of director Leo Penn worked around the legit commitments of many principals. According to production notes, the Les Pine-Tina Rome original screenplay was once planned by the late Nat (King) Cole. Jones is the first Negro to receive a producer credit on a U.S. pic, and Waters, who heads Trace-Mark, was once Davis' biz manager.

The empathy of jazzmen, their music and their sympatico friends (not hangers-on) has yet to receive adequate exposition in any pic, "Adam" included, although periodic attempts have been made. Perhaps it can never be done. In any case, the usual result is a bunch of cats making with the hip jive talk, and interacting with stereotyped squares who snap their fingers on "one" and "three."

The plot is, however, compounded with a lot of other angles: a femme love interest who has a jail record for civil rights activities; a has-been musician who blows hot in a cool era; a white kid who gets mugged for interracial gigging; a white booking agent who freezes Davis out of work. These and other dramatic complications conceivably could challenge a protagonist, but in context, they serve to obscure, rather than illuminate, Davis' character.

Given the plotting, Davis registers quite well as the trumpet player, guilt-ridden from a booze-induced auto crash which, a decade earlier, killed his wife and child, and blinded Johnny Brown, still a member of his band. (Nat Adderly, incidentally, did the fine horn work for Davis' miming.) After a run of chicks, explicitly Lola Falana and Jeanette Du Bois, he meets Cicely Tyson, who gives an excellent performance as the plain-talking gal who falls for him. Louis Armstrong, in an unusually effective offbeat character casting, is her grandpop whom the musical world has passed by.

Ossie Davis is good as an old Davis buddy who loses Miss Tyson. Frank Sinatra Jr. does an okay job as the young trumpet star who learns from Davis. Michael Lipton is adequate as Davis' manager who finally drops him. Peter Lawford is good as the vindictive agent. Other players render good support, and Mel Torme is in briefly to sing an up tune, later reprised in slow rendition after Davis' death.

Penn's direction provided some thesp highlights, also some okay visuals, latter via Jack Priestly's lensing. Benny Carter's score is good, and Carl Lerner's editing to 103 minutes is okay. *Murf.*

What Did You Do In The War, Daddy?
(PANAVISION-COLOR)

Slight war comedy packed with bits of business and some good performances. Moderate returns indicated.

Hollywood, June 25.

United Artists release of Mirisch-Geoffrey (Blake Edwards) production. Stars James Coburn, Dick Shawn, Sergio Fantoni, Giovanna Ralli, Aldo Ray; features Harry Morgan, Carroll O'Connor. Directed by Edwards. Screenplay, William Peter Blatty; story, Edwards, Maurice Richlin; music, Henry Mancini; camera (DeLuxe Color), Philip Lathrop; editor, Ralph E. Winters; asst. directors, Mickey McCardle, Tim Zinnemann, Charles Scott Jr. Reviewed at Academy Award Theatre June 24, '66. Running Time. 115 MINS.

Lieutenant Christian.....James Coburn
Captain Cash .... Dick Shawn
Captain Oppo .... Sergio Fantoni
Sergeant Rizzo .... Aldo Ray
Major Pott .... Harry Morgan
General Bolt .... Carroll O'Connor
Kastorp .... Leon Askin
Benedetto .... Henry Rico Cattani
Romano .... Jay Novello
Federico .... Vito Scotti
Vittorio .... Johnny Seven
PFC Needleman .... Art Lewis
Cpt. Ninow .... William Bryant
German Captain ...... Kurt Kreuger
Cook .... Robert Carricart

"What Did You Do in the War, Daddy?" carries an engaging title but after dreaming it up the writers promptly forgot all about it and launched into a thinly-devised comedy without much substance. Blake Edwards production has lots of laughs but goes overboard in pitching for yocks and is sorely in need of trimming and snap. For the present market, attuned to broad comedy, film may do moderately well.

Edwards, who both produces and directs, also collabed on original story with Maurice Richlin. Set against a World War II backdrop—Sicily, 1943—the William Peter Blatty screenplay dwells on a single situation which holds promise but is never sufficiently realized.

Basic idea has a war-weary American company, commanded by a by-the-book officer, being detailed to take a town held by a large Italian force, and their welcome reception by the Italians who are agreeable to surrendering willingly. But first, they must hold their festival. No festival, no surrender.

Edwards has packed his action with a flock of individual gags and routines but frequently the viewer isn't too certain what's happening. Director draws good comedy portrayals from a talented cast headed by James Coburn, and Dick Shawn, both delivering bangup performances. Coburn plays a lieutenant wise to the ways of the army, continually coming to the aid of Shawn, the captain. Shawn, in another of his frantic comedy characters, is the commanding officer out for the first time on his own after being the general's aide, and louses up the works splendidly.

Sergio Fantoni lends certain lustre as the Italian officer only too happy to surrender if he can do it with honor—AFTER the wine festival, which leaves the entire company of GJs with the war's worst hangovers. As his girl-friend and out for Shawn, Giovanna Ralli displays sexpot tendencies and Aldo Ray is in there pitching as a dog-face. Harry Morgan as an American major who gets lost in the catacombs beneath the town; Carroll O'Connor as the general; Jay Novello, the mayor; and Kurt Kreuger, a Nazi officer, stand out in support.

Technical credits generally are first-rate. Philip Lathrop handled the cameras, Henry Mancini composed music score, Fernando Carrere did production design. *Whit.*

Juk Un Ja San Ja
(The Dead and the Alive)
(SOUTH KOREAN)

Melbourne, June 21.
Century Co. Ltd. production. Directed by Kangchon Lee. Screenplay, Keumdong Choi; editor, Choonam Yang; camera, Haksyung Kim; music, Choonsuk Park. Features Hyejyung Kim, Youngkyun Shin, Woong Kim, Yechoon Lee, Am Pak. Reviewed at Melbourne Film Fest. Running Time, **105 MINS.**

(English sub-titles)

As war spy films go, this is about average. But it has the advantage of seeming to have a more authentic background and atmosphere than most. And if at times this seems a little far-fetched, it's no more so than Western counterparts.

Time is January, 1951, when the UN forces are about to retreat from Seoul, following a successful Communist attack. Nam Hyangmi, a noted singer, pleads in vain for the life of her husband, who is shot on the orders of a Colonel Lee. With a small crippled son and an aged mother depending on her, Nam Hyangmi shoots Lee but only wounds him in the hand.

Sentenced to death (which is seemingly carried out) her escape is never really explained, although it's through Colonel Lee. He heads a spy ring and talks her into joining the ring as its chief female spy. With very little trouble, she soon becomes enamoured of Lee.

The spy ring passes on secrets Nam Hyangmi obtains from the Communist commander. whose mistress she becomes. Eventually the Communists suspect Nam Hyangmi and in a climactic episode she steals the commander's memo book, he is shot, and she staggers through the sewers with the entire Communist army chasing her. Before the memo book reaches hq., the Communists parade Nam Hyangmi's mother and child through the streets, knowing she will reveal herself. In the end Nam Hyangmi is tortured, and she and her family are to be shot. The South Koreans arrive to the rescue but not in time, the spy-singer being killed in the process.

Although contrived, this is well acted, particularly by Hyeiyung Kim as the singer-spy. It's noteworthy that in one sequence—when she sings for the Communist troops—what were originally Communist poster symbols on the stage have since been painted out on the film negative. *Stan.*

Cumbite
(CUBA)

Melbourne, June 18.
Production: Cuban Motion Picture Institute. Direction: Tomas Gutierrez Alea. Screenplay, Onelio J. Cardosa; camera, Jose Lopez; editor, Maro Gonzalez. Features Tete Vergara, Lorenzo Louiz, Marta Evans. Reviewed at Melbourne Film Festival. Running Time, **82 MINS.**

(Spanish-English subtitles)

The setting is the hamlet of Fonds Rouge, Haiti, 1940, where the countryside is absolutely devastated by a long drought. All the local inhabitants can do is to offer up sacrifices to their ancient gods, and other magical rituals. Into their midst comes Manuel, a young countryman who returns to his native village after having been in Cuba for 15 years as a cane cutter. With a divining rod

he is convinced he can discover water and so change the whole situation.

Manuel is greatly taken with a young girl Anaisa, but unfortunately there is a blood feud on between their two families so that the plot takes on a Romeo and Juliet aspect.

Manuel eventually discovers a source for water for the whole village, only revealing it to Anaisa. To channel the water to all areas it is necessary that the blood feud is forgotten and all work together. Everyone seems willing for this, except Anaisa's cousin. Gervelin, who, just as everything is going right, pounces upon Manuel in the darkness of night and mortally wounds him.

On his deathbed Manuel makes his mother promise not to reveal the details of his death, that there must be no more vengeance and that Anaisa—the only other person aware of the source of the water supply—shall reveal it, and all participate in its benefits.

Finely played by an all-Negro cast, photographed beautifully, this is an arresting film with a tale simply and leisurely told. There are three native highlights with the sacrificial ritual, Manuel's funeral and the procession and dancing that accompanies the first flowing of the water. *Stan.*

Zhoy
(Heat)
(RUSSIAN)

Kirgizfilm Studios production. Directed by Larissa Shepitko. Screenplay, Iosif Olshansky, I. Povotskaya, Shepitko, based on "The Camel's Eye" by Chinghiz Aitmatov; camera, Y. Sokol, B. Arkhangelsky. Stars N. Zhanturin, Shamshiev. Reviewed at Melbourne Film Fest. Running Time, **84 MINS.**

(English subtitles)

In Anarhai, of Kirghizia, an area of burning-hot steppes covered with prickly scrub, is a small farming community, miles away from anything. There's the owner and his wife, a couple of younger women, and two men, one of whom is middle-aged Akabir about whom there's some mystery. Apparently, Akabir, in the past, was a champion tractor driver. He is the hardest worker in the community, upon which he imposes his will in a rough but more-or-less kindly way.

To the community comes a teen-aged boy, Kemel, straight from farming school. First given the job of water carrier, he gradually rebels, and clashes with Akabir. His technical knowledge, gained from an agricultural school education, gradually shows signs of out-dating Akabir's long experience.

The two obstinately feud and in the final showdown, when Akabir declares one of them will have to leave, no attempt is made to oust the young boy. The film ends with Akabir, the best worker in the community, departing.

While performed in a sincere manner that seems to defy criticism, this provides no shattering experience. However, the film has charm and, at times, dramatic conflict. *Stan.*

Necesito Una Madre
(I Need A Mother)
(ARGENTINE)

Buenos Aires, June 21.
Argentina Sono Film release of G.S.L. production. With Teresa Blasco, Beatriz Bonnet, Fernando Siro, Guillermo Battaglia, Dringue Farias, Andres Mas, Diego Puente. Directed by Fernando Siro. Screenplay, Maria Elena Walsh, based on short story "The Escape," by Marta Lehmann; camera, Ignacio Souto; music, Lucio Milena; editor, Jorge Garate. At Iguazu, Buenos Aires. Running time, **82 MINS.**

Andres	Andres Mas
Boot-polisher	Diego Puente
The Father	Fernando Siro
The Mother	Beatriz Bonnet
The Servant	Teresa Blasco
The Drunkard	Dringue Farias
Night Watchman	Guillermo Battaglia

The pilgrimage of a boy through B.A.'s nightlife, after escaping from his careless parents, is depicted in this modest tale that seldom has the charm, pathos and poetic touches one may expect from the usually outstanding talent of writer Maria Elena Walsh.

A brisk initial sequence, at the boy's middle-class home, is followed by either uninspired or dull episodes that link him with another boy, a watchman, a drunkard, a prostie, several gamblers and seamen.

The best of Fernando Siro's direction lies in his handling of children actors Andres Mas and Diego Puente. But he has been unable to fill the gaps in the underworked script. Siro himself and Beatriz Bonnet, as the parents more worried about their fast-paced social life than their son's need for affection, head the able cast. Technical credits good. *Din.*

Every Day Is a Holiday
(SPANISH-COLOR)

Made-in-Spain pic has a pleasant little story about a girl who aspires to become a bullfighter on horseback. Color photography and background scenery are grand and Marisol is a delight on both eyes and ears.

Hollywood, June 20.
Columbia Pictures release of a Manuel J. Goyanes (Mel Ferrer) production. Stars Marisol; features everybody else. Directed by Mel Ferrer. Screenplay, Mel Ferrer, Jose Maria Palacio from original story by Ferrer; camera (Technicolor) Antonio L. Ballesteros; music, Augusto Alguero; editor, Rosa Salgado; asst. director, Manuel De La Cueva. Reviewed at Columbia Studio, June 20, '66. Running Time, **76 MINS.**

Chica	Marisol
Angel	Angel Peralta
Dancer	Rafael de Cordova
Impresario	Jose Marco Davo
Femme Fatale	Vala Clifton
Reventa (salesman)	Jesus Guzman
Gipsy	Jose Sepulveda
Servant	Francisco Camoiras
Hotel Employee	Jose Maria Labernie
Employee at Bull Ring	Luis Barbero
Boy	Toni Canal
American Father	Jack Gaskins
Manolo	Pedro Mari Sanchez

Petite Spanish singing gamin Marisol is starred in this cute, colorful story of a young girl who goes from rags to riches as a bullfighter on horseback. Pic should find appeal with the family trade, although the goring by bulls may not be considered proper fare for small fry by American parents. Scenes of ring encounters, however, are skillfully handled and are not played for sensationalism.

Produced, written and directed by Mel Ferrer, there are indications that pic has attempted to imitate the spirit of "Lili." But the flavor here is fully Spanish and there is fine authentic footage including the famed Feria de Sevilla, some charming flamenco songs as well as a ballet sequence.

Main drawback is believability that Marisol could pass for a boy, which she must do until the last scene. Story revolves around her being prepped as a boy matador although she has a crush on her mentor, handsome bullfighter Angel Peralta. He is totally unaware that she is a girl until fade-out. Situation could elicit comedy but little is in evidence.

Marisol is a fine young performer and especially registers in chirping throaty Spanish tunes. Pedro Mari Sanchez as her younger brother is also effective. Peralta essays his role with cool aloofness and Jose Marco Davo is fine as his manager.

Technicolor camerawork by Antonio L. Ballesteros captures the rich colors of the Spanish countryside as well as the streets of Seville and Madrid. The many bullfighting sequences add excitement to pic and are tightly edited by Rosa Salgado.

Ferrer's direction attempts to bring out the coy qualities of his young actors but is more successful with giving an earthy flavor to the overall production. Special mention should be made to the trained horses who must outdistance and outmaneuver the bulls in the ring. They should be given costarring billing. *Dool.*

The Cat
(COLOR)

A low-budgeted meller about a little boy in his quest to befriend a wildcat; pleasant little family film, should do okay at the neighborhood playhouse.

Hollywood, June 29.

Embassy release of World-Cine Associates production, produced and directed by Ellis Kadison. Screenplay, William Redlin, Laird Koenig; camera (Pathe Color) Monroe Askins; music, Stan Worth; editor, Jack Cornall; asst. director, Grayson Rogers. Reviewed at Joe Shore Screening Room, Hollywood, June 29. '66. Running Time, **87 MINS.**
Pete Kilby .... Roger Perry
Martha Kilby ...... Peggy Ann Garner
Walt Kilby .... Barry Coe
Toby .... Dwayne Redlin
Bill Krim ...... George "Shug" Fisher
Art .... Ted Darby
Jesse .... John Todd Roberts
Sheriff Vern .... Richard Webb
Mike, a Deputy .... Les Bradley

The oft-told tale of the boy who cried wolf once too often is given an added twist of excitement in this low-budget color meller and should make for brisk biz for the small fry as well as the family trade. Although suspense is unevenly sustained there are many moments that are chilling, and music score by Stan Worth adds to the overall effect. Production values are good, acting is fine, but camera work and editing at times lack a finished polish.

Barry Coe and Peggy Ann Garner, with eight-year-old son Toby, played by Dwayne Redlin, return from city living to the California ranch of Coe's brother, Roger Perry, which is being overrun by rustlers.

Enroute the family encounters old codger George "Shug" Fisher, who keeps a pet wildcat. The cat soon escapes and appears at the family cabin. The boy tells his parents he has seen the animal. They don't believe him and reprimand him for his continuous wild imagination.

Boy takes off with knapsack to find the beast and bring him back alive. In his search he encounters a fistfight between a rustler and a ranger who is brutally killed. After performing the act, rustler sees the boy looking on and begins to chase him. Boy escapes but he is soon approached by the lion. The boys loses his fear of the animal and is soon fast friends with the cat. For two days a searching party as well as the rustler search for the boy. Cat at the finale saves boy from rustler.

Largest slice of pic centers on moppet Redlin meandering in the wilderness. Redlin is a plucky young actor and reacts well to direction but much of the footage on his wandering becomes monotonous and tends to dissipate suspense of action scenes. Director Ellis Kadison has used great restraint and economy in getting good performances from his cast. Barry Coe manages to make the transition from callous father and husband to a more human being. Miss Garner, Perry and Fisher are okay in lesser parts.

Jack Cornall's editing (Douglas Robertson is credited as supervising editor) too often tends to hold too long on nature shots, such as sunrises and sunsets, while Monroe Askins' camerawork tends to be indecisive. *Dool.*

The Tramplers
(ITALIAN—COLOR)

Italian oater import with an international cast. Joseph Cotten, Gordon Scott and James Mitchum may prove a boxoffice pull and a couple of gunbattles are fun. Otherwise pic is from dullsville.

Hollywood, June 23.

Embassy release of Albert Band production. Stars Joseph Cotten, Gordon Scott, James Mitchum; features everybody else. Directed by Band. Screenplay, Band, Ugo Liberatore; from novel, "Guns of North Texas," by Will Cook; camera (Eastman Color), Alvaro Mancori, editor, Maurizio Lucidi; asst. directors, Franco Prosperi, Francois Dupont-Midy. Reviewed at Lytton Center of the Visual Arts, June 23, '66. Running Time, **105 MINS.**
Temple Cordeen ...... Joseph Cotten
Lon Cordeen .... Gordon Scott
Hoby Cordeen .... James Mitchum
Edith Wickett .... Ilaria Occhini
Charley Garvey .... Franco Nero
Bess Cordeen .... Emma Vannoni
Longfellow Wiley ...... Georges Lycan
Alice Cordeen .... Muriel Franklin
Jim Hennessy .... Aldo Cecconi
Pete Wiley .... Franco Balducci
Fred Wickett .... Claudio Gora
Paine Cordeen .... Romano Puppo
Bert Cordeen .... Dario Michaelis
Adrian Cordeen ...... Ivan Scratuglia
Mrs. Temple Cordeen ..... Carla Calo
Sheriff .... Dino Desmond
Hogan .... Silla Bettina
Emma .... Edith Peters

There is not much to recommend in this tedious Italian-made oater although it boasts a cast of three American actors, Joseph Cotten, Gordon Scott and James Mitchum. Story line plods along, camera work is murky and production values are only so-so. There is, however, one gun battle scene which should end all western gunfights for its hilarity. Although not intended to be funny, 10-minute scene has two men shooting down what appears to be a cast of thousands. No guns are reloaded and footage of some men falling is used twice.

Plot revolves around two sons and their longstanding feud with their father. It's after the American Civil War, the place is Texas and Big Daddy is a family tyrant (he keeps the women of the family upstairs, where they even eat their meals in private).

Sons, who disagree with father's views on the freeing of the slaves, as well as a daughter and her husband, cut out from the family homestead and rough it in the wilderness with a herd of wild cattle. Brothers and father (along with four bad guy brothers) and the cast of thousands fight it out in the end leaving one sole survivor.

Dialog is insipid and acting is wooden as a cigar store indian. Cotten merely rants and raves his way through while Scott and Mitchum attempt not to look too embarrassed.

Albert Band appears to have directed in slow motion and the camerawork by Alvaro Moncori is crude and often jumpy. No credit is given for the musical score and none is deserved. The kids will probably have a ball with "Tramplers" at the Saturday matinee. *Dool.*

Berlin Festival

Passionate Strangers
PHILIPPINES)

Berlin, June 28.

Michael J. Parsons (Manila) production. Stars Parsons, Valora Noland; features Mario Montenegro, Celia Rodriguez. Direction and screenplay, Eddie Romero; camera, Justo Paulino; music, Nestor Robles. At Berlin Film Fest in information section. Running Time, **101 MINS.**
Adam Courtenay ...... Michael Parsons
Margaret Courtenay .... Valora Noland
Roberto Valdez ...... Mario Montenegro
Lydia Trasmonte ...... Celia Rodriguez

Overtones of racial conflict between Americans and natives give a twist to this Filipino meller. Aside from that, however, it is a lowercase effort by modern standards. And with an absence of marquee values, would need substantial trimming to get by as a dualer in the U.S.

"Passionate Strangers" is largely made in the English language, though there are some relatively unimportant dialog exchanges in the local language (sub-titled for presentation at the Berlin festival information section). But when the natives speak in English, their style is careful and deliberate, and thus results in slowing-up the pace, never very marked at best.

Director Eddie Romero's screenplay has heavy melodramatic overtones, and little new to say on the subject of racial conflict. The murder of an important native by an American is the framework for the plot, the Yank having discovered that the Filipino was helping to protect his wife and her native lover. There are also involved side-issues concerning the negotiation of a new contract by American industrialists with the natives, which gives added scope to pinpoint the distrust of the locals for their Yank masters.

Though probably intended as a sincere contribution to the problem, the picture has little to commend it from a technical standpoint.

Both direction and camerawork are pedestrian, and there's little help from the cast. Michael Parsons, who also produced, gives a conventionally straightforward and uninspired study as the Yank charged with murder. Valora Noland, as his wife, looks quite beautiful, but offers little else. Mario Montenegro is a seriousminded lover. Celia Rodriguez adds little sparkle as a powerful but amorous Filipino. *Myro.*

La Caza
(The Chase)
(SPANISH)

Berlin, June 28.

Elias Querejeta (Madrid) production. Stars Ismael Merlo, Alfredo Mayo, Jose Maria Prada, Emilio Gutierrez Caba. Directed by Carlos Saura. Screenplay, Saura and Angelino Fons; camera, Luis Cuadrado; music, Luis de Pablo. At Berlin Film Fest. Running Time, **91 MINS.**
Jose .... Ismael Merlo
Paco .... Alfredo Mayo
Luis .... Jose Maria Prada
Enrique .... Emilio Gutierrez Caba
Juan ...... Fernando Sanchez Polack
Nina .... Violetta Garcia

"La Caza" is a harsh, grim,

black tale, told with considerable screen expertise by Carlos Saura, the Spanish director noted mainly for "Los Golfos." From a boxoffice standpoint, it has almost everything going against it. But it is a film with undeniable, though very limited appeal to film buffs, and might have a modest chance on the arty route.

As an official entry to the Berlin festival, it does credit to the Spanish film industry. But its humorless and relentless style must militate against its commercial prospects. Superficially, this appears to be a very ordinary story of four men, including one youngster, who spend a Sunday together shooting rabbits. The three older men in the party had fought on the same side during the Civil war, and the land on which the rabbit hunt takes place was the scene of heavy fighting. Gradually, their mood changes; bitterness succeeds cordiality, and after one of the men has deliberately killed a ferret, the three men pointlessly kill each other. The final scene is a vivid still shot of the youth, obviously bewildered and afraid.

Saura freely indulges in brutality, but not simply for shock effect. Instead, it's part of the symbolic pattern of the yarn which he co-scripted with Angelino Fons, and which has an undoubted link with post civil war reaction. Indirectly, the story is a commentary on the 30 years that have followed the start of that war, but only in an oblique way.

Aside from the director's forceful contribution, Luis Cuadrado's camera effectively captures the black mood of the story. The editor (uncredited) has done an excellent job in holding the final footage to a taut 91 minutes. There are fine moody performances by the principals. *Myro.*

O Fovos
(Fear)
(GREEK)

Berlin, July 5.

Th. A. Damaskinos and V. G. Michaelides (Athens) production. With Anestis Vlachos, Elena Nathanael. Direction and screenplay, Costas Manoussakis. Camera, Nicos Gardelis; music, Yannis Marcopoulos. At Berlin Film Fest. Running Time, **110 MINS.**
Chryssa .... Elli Fostiou
Anna .... Elena Nathanael
Stepmother ...... Mary Chronopoulou
Anestis .... Anestis Vlachos
Nico .... Spyros Focas
Canalis .... Alexis Damianos

All the fundamental elements of Greek tragedy are to be found in "Fear," a story loaded with brutality and violence. It's strong meat by most standards. Although well above the average standard of current Greek production, this may have a difficult passage at the boxoffice. While it has the ingredients for exploitation, best hopes may be in selected arty situations.

In directing his own screenplay, Costas Manoussakis has succeeded in translating into cinematic terms a story which has shock qualities, yet also has considerable integrity. There is a vicious rape scene which leaves little to the imagination, followed by a brutal and grimly presented murder of the victim. There's also a free-for-all battle and other scenes of violence, which are as grim as they are realistic.

Story is set in a remote village. The central character is a farmer's son who is a compulsive peeping tom, looking through keyholes, peering into parked cars, and even watching his sister strip nude for a swim.

Then he has a yen for the real thing. So he traps the family's domestic, a deaf mute, in the cowshed, rapes and then kills her. But he's caught by his stepmother while trying to conceal the body, and she in turn tells his father. Thereafter, the action is largely concerned with disposing of the body, shielding the son and keeping the police off the scent. It's during this period that the father sees his daughter being made love to in a cornfield, and the inevitable wedding scene that follows coincides with the discovery of the corpse.

Technically, the film has much to commend it. The camera sharply captures the countryside, the music has a distinctive quality and editing sustains the action at an even pace. Acting, on the whole, is generally very good, particularly the key performance by Anestis Vlachos, as the son. His final scene in which he dances solo at the wedding until he's dropping from exhaustion, has an unusual rhythm which hypoes the dramatic effect. Elena Nathanael is attractive as his sister and Elli Fostiou is pathetically charming as the mute. Other roles are up to standard. *Myro*.

Der Weibsteufel
(A Devil of a Woman)
(AUSTRIAN)

Berlin, July 5.
An Otto Duerer production. With Maria Emo, Sieghardt Rupp, Hugo Gottschlich. Directed by Georg Tressler. Screenplay by Adolf Opel, Georg Tressler, Wilhelm Sorger; camera, Sepp Riff; music, Carl de Groof. At Berlin Film Fest. Running Time, 92 MINS.
The woman .... Maria Emo
The gendarme .... Sieghardt Rupp
The woman's husband Hugo Gottschlich

Austrian feature pix have been a rarity at international film festivals in recent years. This one is, after quite some time, the first Austrian full-length entry at the Berlin festival. It received remarkably good to excellent reviews in its native country. But this hardly seems to be an item to compete internationally. Film looks strictly for home consumption, especially since the Tyrolese dialect is even hard to understand in German-language countries.

"Woman" was produced by a commission of the Austrian government. Somewhat surprising is the fact that Georg Tressler, undoubtedly one of the better Austrian directors, has created such old-fashioned film fare. It's remarkably old-fashioned in all departments·

Story is located high in the Tyrolese mountains. It concerns a young woman who's been taking care of her much older and sick husband for years. The old man makes money via smuggling things across the nearby border line. The police know about this but the clever old man knows how to fool the authorities. Then a young gendarme gets an assignment to start a romance with the young wife. The trap works but the young woman and the policemen actually fall in love. The old man is not willing to give up his wife and fights for her. It all ends tragi-

cally for the two men, gendarme stabbing the old man in self-defense, but the plot has it that this finishes the gendarme's career.

Title role is portrayed by Maria Emo, who displays real talent. Same goes for other two principal players. However, all are handicapped by a script which has lines that are often involuntary funny. The whole thing appears strictly for Austrian patrons. There are some nice shots of the Austrian Alps which, more or less, are the only assets of this festival entry. *Hans*.

Jakten
(Manhunt)
(SWEDEN)

Berlin, June 28.
Europa Film (Stockholm) production and release. Stars Halvar Bjork, Leif Hedberg, Lars Passgard. Directed by Yngve Gamlin. Screenplay, Per Olof Sundman; camera, Jan Lindstrom; editor, Wic Kjellin; music, Bengt Hallberg. At Berlin Film Fest. Running Time, 94 MINS.
Olofsson .... Halvar Bjork
Stensson .... Leif Hedberg
Desperado .... Lars Passgard

Apart from the initial establishing sequence prior to the main credit titles, there are only three actors in "Manhunt," which has been filmed mainly against the snowy wastes of the Swedish countryside. There is also comparatively little dialog. The director tries to develop the suspense visually, though it does not quite come off.

Of the three characters, two are on the side of the law searching for a killer on the run. When he is eventually trapped and shot in the leg because he refuses to surrender, the policeman and his teacher friend find that their real problems have only just begun. All three take shelter in a small hut, but comes the dawn, the desperado refuses to accompany them back to the base. For the first half hour or so, there is little action, as the two men head for the point where they expect to encounter the wanted man. There is, however, some excellent scenic camerawork, though it is impossible to conceal the monotony of the backgrounds. There is also some carefully observed detail showing how hunters cope with near-Arctic conditions, chopping down trees to provide temporary cover for the night as well as fuel for the fire.

Once the desperado is captured and taken to the hut, the tension gradually mounts but it mainly involves the cop and his companion, as they realize that they, too, are virtually trapped. There is an unusual twist to the ending as the prisoner, his boots and sweaters removed, is left alone in the hut, while the two men return to base for help.

Best performance comes from Halvar Bjork, as the policeman. There is also a useful contribution by Leif Hedberg, as his teacher-friend. Lars Passgard is a typical sullen and comparatively silent gunman. Other credits are up to standard. *Myro*.

O Padre e a Moca
(The Priest and the Girl)
(BRAZILIAN)

Berlin, June 28.
Joaquim Pedro de Andrade production. Stars Helena Ignez, Paul Jose; features Fauzi Arap, Mario Lago. Direction and screenplay by Andrade. Camera, Mario Carneiro; music, Carlos Lyra. At Berlin Film Fest. Running Time, 90 MINS.

A poverty stricken village, riddled with prejudice and ignorance, is the background to this heavygoing Brazilian drama. It's an unrelieved cinematic work, slow and laborious, with only minimal chances outside local territories. In any event, its theme would certainly fall foul of Catholic organizations in most parts of the world.

The title virtually tells the story. A young priest helps a village girl to escape from a would-be suitor, only to be pursued and trapped by the villagers themselves. There is little dramatic punch to the proceedings, largely due to the heavy-handed script and the slow, almost ponderous, direction.

The treatment gives little scope to the artists, though with a little encouragement, Helena Ignez could have been an animated heroine. Paul Jose gives a stolid and determined performance as the young priest. Supporting roles are in matching style. *Myro*.

Skrift i Snee
(Script in Snow)
(NORWEGIAN)

Berlin, June 28.
EMI-produksjon (Oslo) production and release. Stars Margit Carlquist, Jack Fjeldstad, Helen Brinchman, Kjetil Bang-Hansen. Directed by Pal Bang-Hansen. Screenplay, Odd Bang-Hansen; camera, Knut Gloersen; music, Egil-Monn-Iversen. At Berlin Film Fest. Running Time, 93 MINS.

Norway has only a modest film industry, and this production, a first directorial effort by show biz journalist Pal Bang-Hansen, is typical of that country's limited resources. Made on a tight $30,000 budget, the pic must look to the Scandinavian market to recoup most of its costs, though it may have some tv prospects for less discriminating European networks.

The naive story is sincerely presented, although obvious cliches in the script must necessarily evoke the wrong sort of response. The two central characters in the yarn are a middle-aged journalist, married with a family, assigned by his paper to cover the arrival of an attractive Israeli widow who is on a lecture tour. Inevitably, they fall in love, but she compels him to return to his family while she leaves to continue her tour in Copenhagen. The noveleitish theme is accented by some trite dialog, though the two principals, Margit Carlquist and Jack Fieldstad, play their roles with understanding. Helen Brinchman puts on a bold front as the neglected wife, and Kjetil Bang-Hansen (brother of the director) is okay as the bewildered son. Technical credits, within the budget limitations, are satisfactory. *Myro*.

How To Steal a Million
(PANAVISION-COLOR)

Boff comedy starring Audrey Hepburn and Peter O'Toole with unusually heavy grosses indicated. William Wyler at his best.

Hollywood, June 28.
20th-Fox release of William Wyler-Fred Kohlmar production, produced by Kohlmar, directed by Wyler. Stars Audrey Hepburn, Peter O'Toole; features Eli Wallach, Hugh Griffith, Charles Boyer. Screenplay, Harry Kurnitz; based on story by George Bradshaw; camera (DeLuxe Color), Charles Lang; music, Johnny Williams; editor, Robert Swink; asst. director, Paul Feyder. Reviewed at Academy Award Theatre, June 27, '66. Running Time, 127 MINS.
Nicole .... Audrey Hepburn
Simon Dermott .... Peter O'Toole
David Leland .... Eli Wallach
Bonnet .... Hugh Griffith
DeSolnay .... Charles Boyer
Grammont .... Fernand Gravey
Senor Paravideo .... Marcel Dalio
Chief Guard .... Jacques Marin
Guard .... Moustache
Auctioneer .... Roger Treville
Insurance Clerk .... Eddie Malin
Marcel .... Bert Bertram

"How to Steal a Million" makes like millions for its producers and exhibs booking the Audrey Hepburn-Peter O'Toole starrer which returns William Wyler to the enchanting province of his "Roman Holiday." Marking a sharp change of pace from director's product of recent years, particularly his last offering, the dramatically-absorbing shocker, "The Collector," this 20th-Fox release is an entertainment treat which should captivate every type audience and fits patly into the class category.

Film carries all the inspirational touches and bits of business the trade has come to expect from Wyler, who also produces with Fred Kohlmar. There is one particular sequence which probably will remain a classic. O'Toole, locked in a tiny closet with femme star, uses a large magnet to remove a key hanging outside on a hook, works it across a wall and around a corner to a position where he can insert it into the keyhole, via a further stroke of ingenious fiddling, and thus opens the door. Despite its rare comedic aspects, turn carries suspense seldom caught on the screen and sets the tone for the overall unfoldment.

Lensed in Paris in Panavsion and exquisite DeLuxe Color, advantageous use is made of the actual story locale to give unusual visual interest. Further eye appeal is provided by the handsome sets designed by Alexander Trauner. Charles Lang's fluid cameras create a canvas against whch the action under Wyler's sparkling direction flows in the same mood as the art masterpieces which spring-board the Harry Kurnitz screenplay.

Plot centers on a fraud in the art world via forging "masterpieces." Based on a story by George Bradshaw, the Kurnitz script twirls around Miss Hepburn, daughter of a distinguished French family whose father, Hugh Griffith, is a faker of genius. She has given up trying to reform him, continuing only to hope he won't get into too much trouble. O'Toole is a private detective who specializes in solving crimes in the world of art, but whom femme thinks is a burglar after she discovers him in the family home in the middle of the night apparently trying to make off with a canvas.

Action takes its motivation from Miss Hepburn hiring O'Toole to steal a small statue, regarded as a great piece or art but actually a fake perpetuated by Griffith's grandfather, also a forger Griffith has allowed the French government to exhibit it in a museum, then learns to his horror that he has signed an agreement which will permit its insurance for $1,000,000. Insurance investigators will test it, certify it a fraud. Femme decides the only way to prevent this is to spirit the sculpture from the museum, where it's all sorts of security devices, thus save her father.

Griffith is a particular standout as the elegant Parisian oddball with a compulsion to forge the greatest impressionistic painters although as a philanthropist he often makes gifts of classic works of art to important French museums. Charles Boyer, in briefly as a top French art dealer, scores, too, and Eli Wallach displays comedy form as a wealthy American also a rabid art collector. Lesser parts are suitably played for comedy by Fernand Gravet, Marcel Dallo, Jacques Marin and Moustache.

On the technical side, Johnny Williams' music score catches the spirit of the piece and Robert Swink's editing is fast and expert. Additionally, he's credited as second unit director. *Whit.*

Frankenstein Conquers The World
(JAPANESE-TOHOSCOPE-COLOR)

Another of Inoshiro Honda's monster pieces, plus an American name. Should do well in the macabre market.

American International Pictures presentation of a Toho-(Tomoyuki Tanaka)-Henry G. Saperstein Enterprise production. Stars Nick Adams. Directed by Inoshiro Honda; special effects, Eiji Tsuburaya; filmed in Eastman Color. No other technical credits supplied. Reviewed in New York, July 8, '66. Running Time, 87 MINS.
Dr. James Bowen .... Nick Adams
Scientist .... Tadao Takashima.
Woman Doctor .... Kumi Mizuno

What happens to a Japanese-made feature before it gets onto American screens is sometimes an odyssey that would make a good screenplay by itself. A I P's "Frankenstein Conquers The World" is apparently what started out as "Frankenstein Meets The Giant Devilfish," as the production, directing and cast credits are the same, but in the interim dat ol' debbilfish has disappeared.

With American actor Nick Adams to give a touch of international flavor, this coproduction of Toho's Tomoyuki Tanaka and Americans Henry G. Saperstein and Reuben Bercovitch is being marketed as a package with "Tarzan And The Valley of Gold." The results are about as complex as pablum and harmless to anyone except, possibly, the shade of Mary Shelley whose "Frankenstein" is irreverently dealt with in

this instance. Indeed, a film has finally been made in which the monster is called Frankenstein and the good doctor (patron saint of plastic surgeons) is nonexistent.

Although writing credits were not supplied, the storyline is straight out of the file used by director Inoshiro Honda in the past. Monster endangers Japan, scientist saves Japan. Acting is, as always, inconsequential, with most of the interest centering on the special effects. Using a human as the "monster" is a switch but the process photography necessary to let him work with another, but equally hideous, monster (a mutation mate of Honda's Godzilla, Rodan and friends) doesn't come off too well, but only jaded monster buffs will quibble. The title is completely meaningless.

Color photography is good, but that's an accepted fact with most Japanese films and Eiji Tsuburaya's special effects still manage to fool most viewers. All in all, a good programmer for monster market. *Robe.*

The Daydreamer
(ANIMAGIC-COLOR)

Charming retelling of four Hans Christian Andersen stories, combining live action, well-known personality voices, puppets and animation.

Hollywood, July 1.
Embassy Pictures release of Videocraft International Production, produced and written by Arthur Rankin Jr. Features Paul O'Keefe, Jack Gilford, Ray Bolger, Margaret Hamilton. Includes voices of Tallulah Bankhead, Gilford, Burl Ives, Victor Borge, Sessue Hayakawa, Boris Karloff, Cyril Ritchard, Ed Wynn, Patty Duke, Hayley Mills, Terry-Thomas. Directed by Jules Bass from original stories by Hans Christian Andersen. Live action camera (Eastman Color), Daniel Cavelli; Anamagic camera, Tad Mochinaga; music, Maury Laws; asst. director, Kizo Nagashima; Animagic sequences staged by Don Duga; live-action, by Ezra Stone. Reviewed at Joe Shore's Screening Room, June 29, '66. Running Time, 101 MINS.
Sandman .... Cyril Ritchard
Hans Christian Andersen..Paul O'Keefe
Papa Andersen .... Jack Gilford
Pieman .... Ray Bolger
Mrs. Klopplebobbler..Margaret Hamilton
Little Mermaid .... Hayley Mills
Father Neptune .... Burl Ives
Sea Witch .... Tallulah Bankhead
1st Tailor; Brigadier.....Terry-Thomas
2nd Tailor; Zebro .... Victor Borge
Emperor .... Ed Wynn
Big Claus .... Robert Harter
Thumbelina .... Patty Duke
Rat .... Boris Karloff
Mole .... Sessue Hayakawa

Blending live-action, Animagic telling of four Hans Christian Andersen stories, "Daydreamer" is skillful, inventive and charming. It should particularly appeal to a pre-teen audience but with a long list of well-known names voicing the fairy-tale characters, pic should also get good play from the older generations as well. It should especially do well at holiday bookings.

Story tells of a 13-year-old boy, Paul O'Keefe, who essays role of young Hans Christian Andersen. He daydreams and sets off for the legendary Garden of Paradise. During his dream adventures four

fables are dramatized with Animagic and animation. These are "The Little Mermaid," "The Emperor's New Clothes," "Thumbelina" and "The Garden of Paradise."

Color sequences are laced together with song and dance and most of it is cleverly executed. The use of easily recognizable voices does not distract from overall appeal but adds to the visual interest and the Animagic dolls in most instances are caricatures of the people whose voices are used.

Reported to have been produced in six countries.—the U.S., Canada, England, Japan, France and Denmark—the Arthur Rankin Jr. production has a universal flavor. Jules Bass' direction has balanced the live-action sequences well with those of Animagic. Bass also wrote the lyrics to the dozen songs by Maury Laws. There is also an entertaining live ballet.

Voices used are those of Tallulah Bankhead as The Sea Witch; Victor Borge, Second Tailor and Zebra; Patty Duke as Thumbelina; Sessue Hayakawa, the Mole; Burl Ives, Father Neptune; Boris Karloff, The Rat; Hayley Mills, The Little Mermaid; Cyril Ritchard, The Sandman; Terry-Thomas, First Tailor and Brigidier; and the late Ed Wynn, as the Emperor. Robert Goulet sings the opening "Daydreamer" theme song. *Dool.*

I Was Happy Here
(BRITISH)

Gentle pic with a tough underlying core. Standout booking for all but boisterous houses; will repay patient handling.

London, July 5.
Rank release of a Partisan Films (Roy Millichip) Production. Directed by Desmond Davis. Screenplay by Edna O'Brien and Davis, from an original story by Miss O'Brien; camera, Manny Winn; editor, Brian Smedley-Aston; music, John Addison. Stars Sarah Miles, Cyril Cusack; features Julian Glover, Sean Caffrey. Reviewed at Warner Theatre, London. Running Time, 91 MINS.
Cass .... Sarah Miles
Hogan .... Cyril Cusack
Dr. Matthew Langdon....Julian Glover
Colin Foley .... Sean Caffrey
Barkeeper .... Marie Kean
Kate .... Eve Belton
Gravedigger .... Cardew Robinson

This is the first film to be made under the new Rank-National Film Finance Corp. pact which aims to back worthwhile "indie" pix. It won the Golden Shell at San Sebastian this year. It has already been snapped up for the States. The film is by no means simply an item for arty houses, but it may need careful handling in some situations. "I Was Happy Here" is a wistful film that demands sympathy, imagination and understanding from the audience, and is well worth the effort.

Filmed entirely on location in County Clare, Eire, and London, the contrast between the peaceful, lonely sea-coast village and the less peaceful but equally lonely

bustling London is artfully wed by director, writer and lenser.

It provides Sarah Miles with her best opportunity in a long time. She plays a girl who escapes from the village to London, believing that her fisherboy sweetheart will follow her. He doesn't and Miss Miles, lonely and unhappy in the big city, falls into a disastrous marriage with a pompous, boorish young doctor. After a Christmas Eve row, she rushes back to the Irish village but is disillusioned when she finds that though the village has not changed, she has.

Her former lover is engaged to another girl and when her husband arrives to take her back to London she realizes that both her past dream and her present marriage are shattered. Desmond Davis, who directed "Girl With Green Eyes," from Edna O'Brien's story, finds an equally happy relationship with Miss O'Brien in this one. The story is told largely in flashback but Davis has skillfully woven the girl's thoughts and the present happenings by swift switching, which, occasionally, is confusing but mostly is sharp and pertinent.

The Irish scenes are beautifully handled by Davis and also superbly lensed by Manny Winn while the London sequences provide striking contrast, in that both offer an utterly different attitude to loneliness. Incidentally, the new Post Office Tower crops up frequently on the London skyline and this is likely to become the London screen cliche equivalent to the Eiffel Tower (Paris, France) and the Coliseum (Rome).

As first envisaged by Miss O'Brien, the femme lead calls for a rather older, more mature woman than Miss Miles. Nevertheless Miss Miles gives a most convincing performance, a slick combo of wistful charm but with the femme guile never far below the surface. Sean Caffrey makes his debut as her fisherman boyfriend and looks a promising bet. But Julian Glover makes heavy weather of his role as the girl's insufferable husband. This is largely the fault of the writing since the part is so loaded against him that it is difficult to believe that the heroine would ever have fallen for him in the first place. Cyril Cusack, as always, makes top impact as the Irish hotel owner who watches the proceedings with sympathy blended with cynicism. Marie Kean, as a barkeeper, Cardew Robinson, as a gravedigger, and Eve Belton, as Caffney's innocent colleen, chip in with effective bits. Miss Belton's slightly gawky shyness has a refreshing authenticity.

Here's a film that obstinately and rightly refuses to get on the bandwagon of gimmicks, speed and an event-packed script. It relies on visual appeal and complete sincerity of purpose, and comes off splendidly. *Rich.*

Berlin Festival

Georgy Girl
(BRITISH)

Gay, lightweight comedy, with standout stellar debut by Lynne Redgrave. Bright b.o.

Berlin, July 12.
Columbia release of a Robert Goldston-Otto Plaschkes production. Stars James Mason, Alan Bates, Lynn Redgrave; features Charlotte Rampling, Rachel Kempson, Bill Owen. Directed by Silvio Narizzano. Screenplay, Margaret Forster, Peter Nichols, based on the novel by Miss Forster; editor, John Bloon; camera, Kem Higgins; music, Alexander Faris; music for children's dance, Brian Hunter; title song, Tom Springfield and Jim Dale, sung by The Seekers. At Berlin Film Fest. Running Time, 100 MINS.
James Leamington ..... James Mason
Jos .... Alan Bates
Georgy Parkin .... Lynn Redgrave
Meredith .... Charlotte Rampling
Ellen .... Rachel Kempson
Ted .... Bill Owen

Invited to the Berlin festival, and selected for the closing night gala, dominated throughout by a topflight comedy performance by Lynn Redgrave. The Robert Goldston-Otto Plaschkes production, which received the Catholic Award at the fest although it has an "X" rating in Britain (barred to those under 16), shapes as a bright box-office prospect, and should notch healthy returns on either side of the Atlantic.

There are two significant debuts in this. Silvio Narizzano, who has had a distinguished career on tele, makes an impressive directorial bow, while for Miss Redgrave, it's the first time her name has been above the title, and it's obvious she had herself a ball in this newly-found starring status. The role of a gawky ungainly plain Jane, is a natural for her talents, and she frequently overwhelms her costars by sheer force of personality.

If taken seriously, which the Catholic jury hasn't, but the British censor has, it could be considered as highly immoral. But the featherweight style of the direction, the gay title song and frivo- and animation and giving a filmulous comedy situations are the standard bearers of an unabashed frolic. And in that light, it is intended to be accepted.

In the scene over the title song and preceding the credit titles, Miss Redgrave's character in the pic is clearly established. She's plain, and knows it, but attempts at sophisticated appearance misfire. She's sharing a slovenly apartment with an attractive, brittle and promiscuous girl friend. And whenever a lover is being entertained in the communal bedroom, Miss Redgrave takes herself off to the home of her parents' wealthy employer. Girl friend becomes pregnant, opts for marriage instead of another abortion, but when mother-to-be is in hospital, husband realizes he chose the wrong girl. After the birth, mother disowns child, and Miss Redgrave subs as wife and mother, until left in the lurch and marries her parents' boss.

On the whole, the script adroitly puts the emphasis on fun, but there are some unaccountable obscurities, particularly in regard to Miss Redgrave's occupation. There are some scenes, including an opening sequence, in which she's teaching a bunch of kids to dance in the top floor of the home in which her parents work, but these are not adequately explained. Nor is there any proper explanation of the fact that she has her own bedroom in this house, as she lives elsewhere. But these are relatively minor quibbles, and on the whole the script works extremely well.

James Mason, as the wealthy employer, attempts to adopt a father figure in relations to the girl, but is actually nothing more than a conventional old roue. At his 49th birthday party, when Miss Redgrave puts in a bizarre and outrageous appearance, he propositions her to become his mistress, complete with contract to protect her interest. When that fails, and after his wife's subsequent death, he settles for marriage, and that includes taking the baby along to the church.

Miss Redgrave has a pushover of a part, and never misses a trick to get that extra yock, whether it's her first passionate encounter with Alan Bates or her fielding of Mason's amorous overtures. She's consistently on target, and hits the bullseye all along the line. Mason adeptly displays that wealth is an important factor in getting one's girl. Bates makes a breezy scene and husband, though the scene in which he pursues his quarry through London, stripping on the way, is rather way out. Charlotte Ramplin is fine as the attractive, bitchy flat mate, Bill Owen and Rachel Kempson add effective contributions as the parents.

A lively score, brisk editing and excellent lensing, contribute to a well-made commercial picture.
Myro.

Myten
(The D.T.'s)
(SWEDISH

Berlin, July 5.
Svensk Filmindustri, Sandrews and Svenska Filminstitut production. Stars Per Myrberg, Evabritt Strandberg, Naima Wifstrand. Directed by Jan Halldorf. Screenplay, Stig Claesson; editor, Ingemar Ejve; camera, Curt Persson; music, Olle Adolphson, Lars Farlof. At Berlin Film Fest. (Information Section). Running Time, 80 MINS.
Holgersson .... Per Myrberg
Majken .... Evabritt Strandberg
Mrs. von Grun ...... Naima Wifstrand
Policeman, doctor, etc.. Bengt Ekerod
Guest .... Per Oscarsson

There's one hilariously funny scene in this Swedish surrealistic pic, which was an out-of-competition entry in the information section of the Berlin festival. But it takes more than just one scene to sustain a feature pic. And by that yardstick, "Myten" (literal translation, "The Myth") must be rated a miss, though it has some arty possibilities.

In general terms, and one can only generalize because the film has no specific plot, this is a story of a misfit who is searching for a way of life. It is full of surrealist and often very amusing symbolism:

like, for instance, when he picks a flower from under the nose of a policeman in a public park (forbidden fruit?) and is chased through the city. And another, when he brings momentary pleasure to an old lady, who loses her nurse in the subway, by escorting her home.

The comedy highlight, however, is the subsequent encounter between the man and the nurse in her apartment. She's strictly a no-nonsense gal, who partially strips for action without any prelim overtures and seizes the initiative by making an unabashed pitch. The man, slightly embarrassed that his feet are unusually dirty, asks to be excused, and attempts a cleanup job in the toilet. Unhappily, he gets one foot trapped in the pan, is rescued by the fire brigade, is taken to a hospital, and asks the nurse to direct him to a toilet.

There is also some fun to be derived from the scene with the old girl, a game lady who demonstrates that she's still adept at the tango, though it reduces her to a state of almost total exhaustion. But it is only such isolated incidents that hold interest, and the finished article is an uneven and partially unsatisfactory example of filmmaking.

The occasional ingenuity of the script is reflected in the direction. This is a first effort by a young man who obviously ought to be watched. Music, too, is interesting, and the acting by the principals is way above par. Per Myrberg is exceptionally good as the bewildered young man, and Evabritt Strandberg reveals a sharp sense of the ridiculous as the nurse. Naima Wifstrand is standout as the old girl, and supporting roles are first-rate.
Myro.

Een Ochtend Van Zess Weken
(A Spring in Holland)
(DUTCH)

Berlin, July 6.
Cineuropa (Amsterdam) production. Stars Anne Colette, Hans D. Culeman. Direction and screenplay by Nikolai van der Heyde. Camera, Gerard Vandenberg; music, Lasse Farnlof. At Berlin Film Fest. (Information Section). Running Time, 80 MINS.
Annette .... Anne Colette
Jimmy .... Hans D. Culeman
Stewardess .... Lili van den Bergh

The title of this pic (literally, "A Morning of Six Weeks") conjures up thoughts of tulips in Amsterdam. Not at all because this is a conventional story of a racing driver who falls in love with a model, and when she leaves him, tries his luck with another girl. It's a modest pic by any standards, but directed with almost outrageous pretentiousness by Nikolai van der Heyde. At best, it can only be regarded as a lower-case dualer.

Though much of the action takes place on the race track, there's very little in the way of action other than a couple of test runs; and that seems an opportunity missed. And the affair between the man and the French model is a very ordinary affair. It is illustrated via several bedroom sequences, but they're far from torrid and unlikely to raise the tem-

perature of even the most immature audiences.

Ann Colette is extremely attractive as the French model, and acts with sincerity. Hans D. Culeman is adequate as the hero; ditto Lili van den Bergh as the girl who temporarily takes over the role of his mistress. Editing has held the pic to a workable length, but is uneven. *Myro.*

Le Stagioni del Nostro Amore
(Seasons of Our Love)
(ITALIAN)

Berlin, July 5.
Gava Cinematographica (Rom) production. Stars Enrico Maria Salerno, Jacqueline Sassard, Anouk Aimee. Directed by Florestano Vancini. Screenplay, Elio Bartolini and Vancini; camera, Dario Di Palma, music, Carlo Rustichelli. At Berlin Film Fest. Running Time, 105 MINS.
Vittorio Borghi ...... Erico M. Salerno
Elena .... Jacqueline Sassard
The Friend .... Anouk Aimee

"Le Stagioni del Nostro Amore," which failed in its bid to get acceptance for Cannes, has shown up here as the official Italian entry. Though not without some merit, it hardly does justice to the flourishing and inventive Italian industry, and is not likely to make too much of a mark at the boxoffice, either in its home territory or in the major Overseas markets.

The screenplay, by director Florestano Vancini and Elio Bartolini, overdoes the flashback technique to present a portrait of a man at the crossroads of life. While not exactly confusing, it does not help ready acceptance of the plot, and is frequently irritating. A few prolonged flashbacks, rather than the frequent and short peeps into the past would have been more acceptable.

At the age of 40, Vittorio Borghi, an apparently successful journalist, finds his life crumbling before him. His wife torments him for his neglect of her and their child. At the same time his mistress decides that their association, happy though it has been, must come to an end. So in an attempt to get things into proper perspective, he goes back to his hometown, and finds that the friends of his youth have changed just as much as he has.

Most of the flashbacks cover the period of his return to his native village, and these include his relationship with his parents and frequent shots of Partisan Resistance to the Fascists during the war. There are also endless sequences showing his life together with his mistress, though hardly any with his family.

Under Vancini's slow and painstaking direction, the story hardly comes to life. There is very little sparkle to the script and the yarn is overly sentimental in its approach. And, presumably under director's guidance, Enrico Maria Salerno plays the mixed-up journalist in totally unrelieved style, with hardly a smile appearing on his countenance for the whole of the 105 minutes running time. There is, however, more shading to the characterizations by the two women in his life, Jacqueline Sassard and Anouk Aimee, the latter being particularly shining. Other credits are up to average standard. *Myro.*

Nayak
(The Hero)
(INDIAN)

Berlin, July 5.
R. D. Bansal and Saran Kumari Bansal production. Direction, screenplay and music, Satyajit Ray. Camera, Subrato Mitra. At Berlin Film Fest. Running Time, 120 MINS.
Arindam Mukherjee
.... Uttam Kumar Chatterjee
Aditi .... Sharmila Tagore

There are very few directors with Satyajit Ray's personal gift of a transforming a simple and leisurely told yarn into a work of cinematic importance. "The Hero" is a typical example of his art—a story without much incident or excitement which hold the attention, even though the director has been somewhat self-indulgent on this occasion.

The hero of this pic is a handsome young actor who has had to fight his way to the top. He as not exactly been ruthless in his ascent to stardom, but has always played it safe and has never taken a chance that might have offended his growing public. His image was all important.

A commonplace enough character, admittedly, but in Ray's sensitive treatment, he's an interesting and confusing personality who has learned that it can be mighty lonely at the top. The actor tells his life story to an attractive woman journalist whom he meets on a train to Delhi. And the main incidents in his life are told in flashback. It's in this area that the director has shown a tendency towards self-indulgence, as occasionally it makes for jerky development, though on the whole the method works admirably.

Surprisingly, also, the director has resorted to a typical Hollywood device in having his attractive heroine wear hour-rimmed specs to prove she's an intelligent gal, and only revealing her natural beauty when she removes them. But that's about the only concession to Western convention in a film which is absorbing, literate and always charming. It has been made in the director's familiar leisurely style. But some crix might suggest that some pruning might improve the end product.

Ray's relaxed direction invariably evokes excellent response from his cast, and this film is no exception. Uttam Kumar Chatterjee gives a beautifully observed performance as the star, blending a touch of arrogance and a suggestion of humility with his portrait of this stellar actor. Sharmila Tagore exudes charm and warmth as the journalist who finally tears up the notes of her interview as she feels it would be unethical to spill the story and destroy his image. All technical credits are up to standard.
Myro.

O Corpo Ardente
(Burning Body)
(BRAZIL)

Berlin, July 5.
Walter Khouri (Sao Paulo) production. Direction and screenplay, Khouri; camera, Rudolf Icsey; music, Rogerio Duprat. Stars Barbara Laage; features Pedro Hatheyer, Mario Benvenuti, Lilian Lemmertz. At Berlin Film Fest. (Information Section). Running Time, 78 MINS.

There seems to be little justification for the inclusion of this film in a festival program, even if confined to the non-competitive information section, particularly because Brazil also has an official entry. Its export chances are minimal.

Obviously something happened to the pic on the way to the fest, as the synopsis credits a running time of 100 minutes, whereas the lights went up after 78 minutes. There is ample evidence of erratic cutting which adds to the incoherency of a plot that relies for its unfolding in a series of flashbacks.

It's hard to make out what producer-director-writer Walter Khouri is aiming at. But the synopsis provides a clue by explaining it's a story of an unfulfilled woman who finds inner content and that the "symbol of her intense longing is a stallion." That's about it. Barbara Laage is sullen and moody throughout. Other members of the cast may be competent professionals, but have little scope for displaying any talent.
Myro.

Torn Curtain
(COLOR)

Okay Cold War spy drama, with chiller potential blunted by routine scripting, relaxed direction and overlength. Names of Alfred Hitchcock, Paul Newman and Julie Andrews will attract good summer dual b.o.

Hollywood, July 12.
Universal production and release. Stars Paul Newman, Julie Andrews; features Lila Kedrova, Hansjoerg Felmy, Tamara Toumanova, Wolfgang Kieling. Directed by Alfred Hitchcock. Screenplay, Brian Moore, based on his story; camera (Technicolor), John F. Warren; editor, Bud Hoffman; music, John Addison; asst. director, Donald Baer. Reviewed at Directors Guild of America. L.A. July 21, '66. Running Time, 126 MINS.
Michael Armstrong ...... Paul Newman
Sarah Sherman ..... Julie Andrews
Countess Kuchinska ..... Lila Kedrova
Heinrich Gerhard ... Hansjoerg Felmy
Ballerina ... Tamara Toumanova
Hermann Gromek ... Wolfgang Kieling
Prof. Karl Manfred .... Gunter Strack
Prof. Gustav Lindt ..... Ludwig Donath
Jacobi .... David Opatoshu
Dr. Koska .... Gisela Fischer
Farmer .... Mort Mills
Farmer's wife ...... Carolyn Conwell
Freddy ...... Arthur Gould-Porter
Fraulein Mann .... Gloria Gorvin

"Torn Curtain" is an okay Cold War suspenser with Paul Newman as a fake defector to East Germany in order to obtain Communist defense secrets. Julie Andrews is his femme partner. Alfred Hitchcock's direction emphasizes his earlier suspense and ironic comedy flair in a series of often intriguing scenes, but some good plot ideas are marred by routine dialog, and a too relaxed pace contributes to a dull overlength. Star and director names will probably carry the Universal release to very good b.o. returns on summer bills.

Brian Moore scripted from his original story about a top U.S. physicist who essays a public defection in order to pick the brains of a Communist wizard. Writing, acting and direction make clear from the outset that Newman is loyal, although about one-third of pic passes before this is made explicit in dialog. This early telegraphing diminishes suspense, and promises not much more than a series of incidents which will propel principals to their inevitable happy ending.

Hitchcock's reputation was built on artfully done chillers which suggested terror, but starting with "Psycho," he began a series of artfully overdone gory shockers. In "Curtain," he reverts to his earlier style, except for one five-minute sequence in which Newman and Carolyn Conwell, a peasant farmer's wife, proceed to knife, clobber and gas Wolfgang Kieling, Newman's secret police watchdog. The prolonged action here is amusing in a grim, embarrassing sort of way.

Elsewhere, Hitchcock freshens up his bag of tricks—a mysterious book, a mathematical symbol, his own silent bit in a hotel lobby with a baby on his lap, imminent violence and actual crowd panic in a cultural setting—in a good potpourri which becomes a bit stale through a noticeable lack of

zip and pacing. John F. Warren's Technicolor camera is a big asset. Film has a soft focus appearance. With the exception of many obvious sound-stage setups, pic's international supporting cast plus location exteriors give it a foreign-film flavor.

Newman gives a good underplaying to his role, while Miss Andrews' charming voice and appearance lend grace to a limited, but billed-over-title role. Pair's necking sequence at the start is tastefully sexy, reminiscent at times of "Rear Window." Lila Kedrova registers well as a daffy, but pitiable Polish refugee who assists the stars in their escape to the West after Newman has wrested a scientific concept from Ludwig Donath. Ballerina Tamara Toumanova, absent from pix for 12 years, is good as the star who nearly aborts the escape.

All other players lend fine support — security chief Hansjoerg Felmy, Kieling (who keeps using U.S. slang in brutish attempts at rapport), Gunter Strack, the quiet academic menace, femme medic Gisela Fischer and David Opatoshu, leader of an underground refugee unit which assists in stars' escape. Mort Mills is very good as the U.S. agent, masquerading with apparent success as a farmer despite an occasional cowboy twang in off-duty moments.

John Addison's score, somewhat obtrusive in some quiet moments, lends a good assist to the overall mood. Bud Hoffman handled the cutting chores, but the resulting 126 minutes is way too much. Edith Head's costumes for Miss Andrews are eye-catching, while properly restrained to the plot limits of femme's character, a femme scientist.

Hein Heckroth was production designer. Although film is in the 1.85:1 ratio, some of the apparent exteriors are held too long to disguise their artificiality. Sound recordists Waldon O. Watson and William Russell and unbilled sound cutters did an excellent job, particularly in a museum sequence in which footsteps create a significant momentary chill. Other credits are pro. *Murf.*

Duminica La Ora 6
(Sunday At Six O'Clock)
(RUMANIAN)

Bucharest, July 3.
Rumania Films release of Bucaresti production. With Irina Petrescu, Dan Nutu, Gratiela Albini, Eugenia Popovici. Directed by Lucian Pintilie. Screenplay, Ion Mihaileanu, Pintilie; camera, Sergiu Huzum; music, Radu Chaplescu. Previewed in Bucharest. Running Time, 75 MINS.
Anca .... Irina Petrescu
Radu .... Dan Nutu
Maria .... Gratiela Albini
Ancai .... Eugenia Popovici
Iona .... Catalina Pintilie

Though with a wartime background, pic is primarily a love story, albeit the romance is betrayed by the war and perils of resistance to the Rumanian anti-Commie faction of the time. A new director shows an awareness of changing techniques of narration plus a good feel for transposing emotions to visual terms. Tale is sometimes bit obscure in its allusions to the politics of the time, as well as use of three levels, memory, objective past and, switching, to present.

Film seems reminiscent of some of the more personalized Czech pix and the young French but it appears more an integrated influence than conscious aping. So a young man talks to a woman of a girl who has died with repeated highlighted flashbacks to a quick scene that finally becomes the place where she dies.

He had been in love with her before he found out she was to work with him in the resistance movement against the local Nazis shielded by the German occupiers. Their love is done in a series of dextrous scenes that measure their joy and growing awareness and closeness to the grimmer aspects of wartime life around them.

In fact, war stays in the background except when their convictions have it intrude on them by her arrest and then death at the hands of the police as they flee together after she is let out but followed. The boy realizes he is marked by her memory and yet may eventually forget her if it is not to be as he is betrayed on his next mission and captured and presumably killed by the Fascist police.

Irina Petrescu has a vulnerable warmth and charm and Dan Nutu the right youthful strength to make the lovers a pair who transcend the film to form a human and tragic duo.

Director Lucian Pintilie shows he can tell his tale visually and though he sometimes overdoes flashback shots that are not always clear, he has complete control most of the time and transforms a good script into a telling tale of love destroyed by war as well as etching insight into human relationships that are primarily filmic rather than literary, theatrical and academic in pic style, as most Rumanian pix seen tend to be.

It is also well lensed with a knowing moving camera to capture the fears and joys of the couple. Supporting cast is also fine and this may herald a more personalized, if socially slanted, cinema here as has happened in Poland, Hungary and Czechoslovakia among the smaller Eastern bloc countries.

This one marks Rumania pix as something director Pintilie as someone to be watched. Pic appears limited to specialized and art uses abroad due to its sometimes special allusions and offbeat delving into filmic time and space. *Mosk.*

Beau Geste
(TECHNISCOPE-COLOR)

Well-made revival of Foreign Legion tale. Hefty prospects indicated.

Hollywood, July 13.
Universal release of Walter Seltzer production. Features Guy Stockwell; Doug McClure, Leslie Nielsen, Telly Savalas; with David Mauro, Robert Wolders, Leo Gordon, Michael Constantine, Malachi Throne. Directed by Douglas Heyes. Screenplay, Heyes; based upon novel by Percival Christopher Wren; camera (Technicolor), Bud Thackery; music, Hans J. Salter; editor, Russell F. Schoengarth; asst. director, Terry

Morse Jr. Reviewed at Universal Studios, July 12, '66. Running Time, 105 MINS.
Beau .... Guy Stockwell
John .... Doug McClure
De Ruse .... Leslie Nielsen
Dagineau .... Telly Savalas
Boldini .... David Mauro
Fouchet .... Robert Wolders
Kraus .... Leo Gordon
Rostov .... Michael Constantine
Kerjacki .... Malachi Throne
Beauiolais .... Joe De Santis
Vallejo .... X Brands
Sergeant .... Michael Carr
Platoon Sergeant ...... George Keymas
Surgeon .... Patrick Whyte
Captain .... Ted Jacques
Legionnaire .... Jeff Nelson
Legionnaire .... David Gross
Legionnaire .... Hal Hopper
Legionnaire .... Chuck Wood
Legionnaire .... Duane Grey
Legionnaire .... Vic Lundin
Dancer .... Ava Zamora

Third time out for what was one of the most memorable silent films still packs hardy entertainment of the sort that is well received in both the general and action market, where smart exploitation should spell hefty grosses. The Walter Seltzer production is an expertly-made translation of Percival Christopher Wren's novel of the French Foreign Legion in a lonely Sahara outpost, distinguished by good acting, fine Technicolor photographic values and fast direction to maintain vivid impression.

Guy Stockwell delineates the title role previously enacted by Ronald Colman in the original 1926 Paramount version, and by Gary Cooper in the 1939 package. Telly Savalas undertakes the brutal sergeant, following Noah Beery and Brian Donlevy, respectively, in said character.

In this latest rendition, plot has been slightly changed. Beau and his brother, John, are now Americans instead of English, and the third brother, Digby, has been eliminated. While still a story of brother love under fire, this facet has been somewhat subordinated for a script-focusing on the savagery of the sergeant, a dominant point previously but accentuated even more in the present version.

Basic storyline has been little altered, Beau having joined the Legion after shouldering the blame for a crime he did not commit to save another from disgrace. Action centers chiefly on the sadistic sergeant, a Legion martinet, lusting for power and delighting in torture, whipping his soldierized riffraff into a desperate fighting machine to meet the onslaughts of the attacking Tuareg tribesmen. His life has been threatened in an unsigned letter and in trying to ferret out the man responsible he drives his Legionnaires to near-mutiny with his inhuman treatment. Beau is his chief target.

Topnotch performances are contributed right down the line. Stockwell handles himself creditably and convincingly. Savalas, in a switch from his usual light comedy or straight dramatic parts, delivers a hard, brilliant portrayal of the half-crazed sergeant who dominates the interest. Doug McClure, playing the brother previously limned by Neil Hamilton and Ray Milland, respectively, in two earlier adaptations, has little to do but does it well. Leslie Nielsen, as the lieutenant in command of Fort Zinderneuf, where all the Legionnaires but Beau meet their death, and actual author of the

letter to the sergeant, lends additional color.

Other hard-hitting characterizations are contributed by David Mauro, a mercenary who has re-enlisted; Robert Wolders, a dreaming Frenchman; Leo Gordon, former German army officer, and Michael Constantine, onetime Cossack; Malachi Throne, murderous Pole.

Douglas Heyes directed with a bold hand from his own screenplay. He tells his story in flashback form after a brief column arrives at the fort to find all the defenders massacred except Beau, and dead men at the wall gunports in grisly array. Technically, picture is excellent, and here particularly the color camera work of Bud Thackery stands out.

Hans J. Salter's music score is especially appropriate, making good use of martial themes; Russell F. Schoengarth's editing tight for the most part, and art direction by Alexander Golitzen and Henry Bumstead fitting. *Whit.*

The Wild Angels
(PANAVISION-COLOR)

Realistic leather-jacket delinquency yarn with plenty of shock value. Strong reception seen in exploitation market.

Hollywood, June 23.
American International release of Roger Corman production. Stars Peter Fonda, Nancy Sinatra; features Bruce Dern, Diane Ladd. Directed by Corman. Screenplay, Charles B. Griffith; camera (Pathe-color), Richard Moore; editor, Monty Helman; music, Mike Curb; asst. director, Paul Rapp. Reviewed at Nicholson Hilltop Theatre, June 22, '66. Running Time, 83 MINS.
Heavenly Blues .... Peter Fonda
Mike .... Nancy Sinatra
Loser .... Bruce Dern
Joint .... Lou Procopio
Bull Puckey .... Coby Denton
Frankenstein .... Marc Cavell
Dear John .... Buck Taylor
Medic .... Norm Alden
Pigmy .... Michael J. Pollard
Gaysh .... Diane Ladd
Mama Monahan .... Joan Shawlee
Suzie .... Gayle Hunnicutt
Thomas .... Art Baker
Preacher .... Frank Maxwell
Hospital Policeman .... Frank Gertsel
Nurse .... Kim Hamilton

The foreword to this well-turned-out Roger Corman production is its tipoff: "The picture you are about to see will shock and perhaps anger you. Although the events and characters are fictitious, the story is a reflection of our times."

For thematic motivation, Corman, who produces in almost documentary style, has chosen a subject frequently in the headlines. The marauding of the black leather set, a group of delinquents who in various localities like to boast the name of Hell's Angels, is topical and increasingly prevalent. Pinpointed here, the Angels, in vicious stride and without regard for law and order, operate in a Southern California beach community recognized as Venice, and it is upon this particular segment that Corman directs his clinical eye in dissecting their philosophical (?) rebellion. While not new in tone, treatment is sufficiently compelling to warrant strong exploitation.

The Charles B. Griffith screenplay carries shock impact of the sort that occasionally stuns. As

such, market is somewhat reduced. It is suitable mainly for the exploitation trade and situations which relish their action raw and violent, but lush take nonetheless is indicated.

Corman has developed his topic carefully and with an eye to values which pay off in sustained interest. He tackles assignment with realism, taking apart the cult and giving its members an in-depth study as he follows a gang headed by Peter Fonda in their defiance of common decencies. Added shock occurs in script focusing on black-jackets staging an orgy in a church after reducing it to a shambles when the minister tries to conduct funeral services for one of their members, and their lugging body for burial to a cemetery where they start a free-for-all with the townspeople.

Fonda lends credence to character, voicing the creed of the Angels in "wanting to do what we want to do" without interference, and is well-cast in part. Nancy Sinatra, present in cast for name appeal, plays his girl. Bruce Dern scores as one of the Angels who is mortally wounded by the police as he steals a patrolman's motorcycle. Diane Ladd is okay as his girlfriend, and Frank Maxwell has some good moments as the minister. Balance of cast stacks up satisfactorily.

Corman's direction carries conviction and he has the benefit of some exceptionally good technical assistance. Outstanding here is Richard Moore's color camera-work, catching some particularly interesting desert and outdoor backgrounds; Monty Helman's tight editing; Mike Curb's music score. *Whit.*

Batman
(COLOR)

Teleseries has been blownup to a widescreen, stereophonic sound, De Luxe color edition and employs every trick from the Batbook to make for a family funfest.

Hollywood, July 15.
Twentieth-Fox release of William Dozier production. Features entire cast of 16. Directed by Leslie H. Martinson. Screenplay, Lorenzo Semple Jr., based on characters created by Bob Kane; camera (De Luxe Color), Howard Schwartz; editor, Harry Gerstad; music, Nelson Riddle; asst. director, William Derwin. Reviewed at 20th-Fox Studio, July 14, '66. Running Time, 105 MINS.
Batman .... Adam West
Robin .... Burt Ward
The Catwoman .... Lee Meriwether
The Joker .... Cesar Romero
The Penguin .... Burgess Meredith
The Riddler .... Frank Gorshin
Alfred .... Alan Napier
Commissioner Gordon.... Neil Hamilton
Chief O'Hara .... Stafford Repp
Aunt Harriet Cooper .... Madge Blake
Commodore Schmidlapp Reginald Denny
Vice Admiral Fangschliester
.... Milton Frome
Bluebeard .... Gil Perkins
Morgan .... Dick Crockett
Quetch .... George Sawaya

With a big, opulent color feature production, "Batman" is now ready to take on the world. Pic is packed with action, clever sight gags, interesting complications and goes all out on bat with batmania: batplane, batboat, batcycle, etc., etc. Humor is stretched to the limit, De Luxe color is comic-strip sharp and script retrieves every trick from the highly popular tele-series' oatbag, adding a few more sophisticated touches. Pic should prove a big success although hour and 45 minutes length may prove too much of a dose for one sitting.

It's nearly impossible to attempt to relate plot. Suffice to say that it's now Batman and Robin against his four arch-enemies, Catwoman, The Joker, The Penguin and The Riddler. Quartet have united and are out to take over the world. They elaborately plot the dynamic duo's death again and again but in every instance duo escape by the skin of their tights. Antics soon to move to a United Nations level where the Security Council is dehydrated and—are you ready —bottled. The President of the U.S. is on the hot-line wishing Batman and Robin well in their attempt to bring the council back alive and the capitals of the world are also anxiously awaiting the outcome. At the height of the hushed proceedings Batman utters the world shattering words: "Turn on the faucet." Does Batman un-hydrate the Security Council? Tune into your local neighbourhood theatre and find out.

Production values are superior and inventive, giving entire pic a sense of style as reflected in art direction by Jack Martin Smith and Serge Krizman. Crisp color camerawork by Howard Schwartz also scores wham and music score by Nelson Riddle adds pow to the relentless action.

The acting is uniformly impressively improbable. The intense innocent enthusiasm of Cesar Romero, Burgess Meredith and Frank Gorshin as the three criminals is balanced against the innocent calm of Adam West and Burt Ward, Batman and Robin respectively.

Love interest is introduced between West and Catwoman Lee Meriwether, who understandably do not realize they are, when costumed—enemies. Some of their dialog takes on double meaning, but the Batman purists will no doubt overlook this. In chic nitery scene, on the other hand, he holds a large brandy snifter filled with milk.

Alan Napier, Neil Hamilton, Stafford Repp and Madge Blake repeat their teleseries roles and Reginald Denny essays Commodore Schmidlapp, a take-off on guess-who?

Funniest and best sustained scene in pic is Batman's attempt to get rid of a sputtering bomb. He is on a pier and runs wildly about, clutching bomb over his head, but everywhere he turns he is met with frustration.

Lorenzo Semple Jr., who wrote the Batman pilot, returns to script the feature and if his imagination seems to know no bounds, thank "Batman" for that. Perhaps, however, pic should be shortened, yet Harry Gerstad's editing is expert and keeps the action pace brisk. *Dool.*

The Uncle
(BRITISH)

Beautifully directed and acted drama from maker of "Girl With Green Eyes" and "I Was Happy Here." Changes made by producer without approval of director have neither improved nor hurt an overall successful film. Shapes as specialized fare.

Play Pix Film release of British Lion-Lenart production, produced by Leonard Davis, Robert Goldston (associate producers, Roy Millichip, Nancy W. Green). Directed by Desmond Davis. Features Rupert Davies, Brenda Bruce, Robert Duncan, Maurice Denham, William Marlowe, Ann Lynn, Christopher Ariss. Screenplay, D. Davis and Margaret Abrams, from book by Miss Abrams; camera, Manny Wynn; editor, Brian Smedley-Aston. Reviewed at Preview Theatre, N.Y., July 14, '66. Running time, 87 MINS.
David	Rupert Davies
Addie	Brenda Bruce
Gus	Robert Duncan
Wayne	William Marlowe
Sally	Ann Lynn
Tom	Christopher Ariss
Mr. C. Ream	Maurice Denham
Mary Ream	Helen Fraser
Emma	Barbara Leake
Jamie	John Moulder Crown

One reason why this excellent British film hasn't been seen earlier is the dispute which ensued after its completion between director Desmond Davis and producer Leonard Davis (no relation), because of editing and other changes made by the producer without the "permission" of the director. The producer's version, which opened in New York last Mon (18), at the Fine Arts, indicates that the changes were not sufficient to damage the film.

Director Davis has created a cinematic essay on the life of a seven-year-old who finds himself in a catastrophic situation. Totally unprepared for the position, he finds being an uncle of a nephew the same age presents many difficulties. The entire film is done from the attitude of the pint-sized hero. This has been attempted by other directors, mostly unsuccessful. The choice few, which "The Uncle" merits joining, include Kon Ichikawa's "Watashi Wa Nisai" (Being Two Isn't Easy), Manuel Summers' "Del Rosa al Amirillo" (From Pink to Yellow) and Philip Leacock's "The Kidnappers."

Most of "The Uncle" deals with the "loss of innocence" of a small boy, Gus (Robert Duncan), over one summer. At seven-and-a-half, he's set off from the other children by spotlighting his uncleship due to the difference in ages between his older sister, her son is the same age. His life suddenly becomes dominated by this fact. It's a subject for derision by the other children. When he approaches his parents for an explanation they fail to perceive the seriousness of the relationship and their surface attitude he interprets as indifference. He withdraws, gradually, from his family and his playmates, finding refuge in an abandoned house in the neighborhood.

Further intrusions on his private world are resisted. Gus attempts to explain things to himself by acting out fantasies, including the world of grownups. Jibes of the other children, such incidents as the sudden death of the village storekeeper, a revolting view of calves being castrated at his brother-in-law's farm—all these touch off his imaginative mind and he withdraws more and more. At his lowest point, Gus blames his father for having placed him in such a situation "by having a child late in life" and his resentment grows.

But, as things do in a child's life, explanations of sorts find their way into his world and he begins to adjust. When he finds himself siding with his nephew against the other children, their differences resolve themselves; his father comes close again when he explains the death of the storekeeper; his summer ends with his love for his father even stronger than it was the year before.

Although the firm control of director Davis is evident throughout, he has been fortunate in having a cast that is entirely excellent, particularly young Robert Duncan as Gus (only a British child could look so profound at seven) and Rupert Davies and Brenda Bruce as his parents. Christopher Ariss as Tom, the nephew, is as boisterous as Gus is gentle, all energy. William Marlowe and Ann Lynn as Tom's parents and Maurice Denham as Mr. Ream, the storekeeper, provide equally fine support. The large group of neighborhood children could be largely non-professional, never seeming affected or aware of the camera. Even their limited vocabulary, repeating phrases over and over seems natural. The film was shot almost entirely on location at Plymouth, England.

Manny Wynn's crisp black-and-white camerawork makes good use of the English countryside and some of the individual scenes are beautifully framed, especially a tracking shot of Gus and his father, walking along a boardwalk on a rainy afternoon, deep in serious discussion. Other technical credits are excellent although the editing, credited to Brian Smedley-Aston, is difficult to judge, because of the post-production dissension on the handling of the film.

According to one source, some short scenes have been eliminated and others have been moved about. The pre-title sequences were, supposedly, originally part of the main body of the film. As there is a tendency to cross-cut and rapidly, this could be easily believed, but the overall effect of the film is still great enough to warrant its being a very pleasant adventure for all filmgoers. Associate producer Roy Millichip is now teamed with Desmond Davis and their most recent effort, "I Was Happy Here," was the top winner at the 1966 San Sebastian Film Fest. They also worked together on "Girl With Green Eyes." *Robe.*

Valurile Dunarii
(The Danube Flows On)
(RUMANIAN)

Bucharest, July 2.
Rumania Films release of Bucaresti production. With Liviu Ciulei, Irina Petrescu, Lazar Vrabie. Directed by Liviu Ciulei. Screenplay, Francisc Munteanu, Titus Popovici. Previewed in Bucharest. Running Time, 80 MINS.
Mihai	Liviu Ciulei
Ana	Irina Petrescu
Toma	Lazar Vrabie

Film is a war actioner that has some okay segments though predictable characters. It does have a workable idea of a barge floating a shipment of German ammo and weapons to the mouth of the Danube and the fight between resistance workers to get it, the Germans protect it, plus the captain who is not quite taken up by any cause but opts for the resistants during the trip.

Mainly a local entertainment. Foreign playoff on its visually solid side and the okay action is moot.

Liviu Ciulei is both director and actor; he plays the captain. His thesping is sombre, solid and good, and his direction is sparse and tight to get the most from situation. *Mosk.*

To Homa Vaftike Kokkino
(Blood On The Land)
(GREEK)

Karlovy Vary, July 12.
Finos Films release and production. With Nicos Courcoulos, Mary Chroaopoulou, Yannis Voglis, Manos Katrakis. Directed by Vassilis Georgiades. Screenplay, Nicos Foscolos; camera, Nicos Dimopoulos. At Karlovy Vary Film Fest. Running Time, 120 MINS.
Odyssee	Nicos Courcoulos
Irena	Mary Chronopoulos
Rigas	Yannis Voglis
Father	Manos Katrakis

Greek tale of peasant and landowner fights over land partition laws in the early 1900s adds an envelope of melodramatic asides via two enemy brothers and a woman they fight over and some overlydone mayhem and violence. Neatly pruned, this could be play of possibility abroad on its social thematics with actioner mart showings also indicated. Arty possibilities are practically nil but the pic was up for the Oscar in the foreign film lineup this year.

Film paints its characters fairly black and white. There is one scene, the burial of a leftist who has tried to prime the peasants on their rights; that has one dramatic punch and social uplift, though pic is then again watered down as the melodramatics build up again. But it has a certain sincere naivete, mixed with obvious attempts to shore it up with exploitation aspects via the violence and sex. Acting is rightly flamboyant and this is a pic with okay production dress. *Mosk.*

Karlovy Fest

Nikto No Chotel Unirat
(Nobody Wants to Die)
(RUSSIAN)

Karlovy Vary, July 10.
Sovexport release of Lithuanian Film production. With Bruno Oya, Dontas Banenis, Algis Masyunis. Directed and written by Vitas Zhalskyavichyus. Camera Yionas Gritsyus; music, A. Apanavichyus. At Karlovy Vary Film Fest. Running Time, 105 MINS.

Russia follows its policy of sending pix from its many republics to film fests that filmmaking is decentralized there. Its not just Moscow and Leningrad studios turning them out. Lithuanian film turns out to be a tellingly made film of action and revenge in a small town with political backgrounding. It might be likened to a Western with its good guys, people are ready to go along with the takeover of the local Communists after the last war, and those of the last democratic regime, as well as collaborators with the Germans, who are fighting the Red takeover. But the political side is not gone into and the main aspect is the revenge of four sons on those killed their father, the head of the village.

Robust acting, fine lensing of the small town and the woods and sudden bursts of fighting between the two clans, as well as quieter moments of love, tenderness and mourning, give this a lyrical air at times. The four sons of the slain man put an ex-collaborator is as a head man who tries to change but its killed by the opposing forces. Then there is a fight and the routing of the fascists.

But it is the solidity of the characters. the poetic look of the village at dawn, the sharply drawn people and the right pegging in place and time that make this an action film with a deeper flair and feeling. It might be something for playoff abroad with some specialized use also indicated. Lithuania shows filmic knowhow and assimilated Russian and even American influences. *Mosk.*

Sposob Bycia
(Frame of Mind)
(POLISH)

Karlovy Vary, July 8.
Polski Film release of Rytm production. With Andrzej Lapicki, Lucyna Winnicka, Irena Szczurow. Directed by Jan Rybkowski. Screenplay, Kazmierz Brandys, Jerzy Markuszewski based on the book by Brandys; camera, Jerzy Lipman; editor, Gartena. At Karlovy Vary Film Fest. Running Time, 75 MINS.

Man	Andrzej Lapicki
Wife	Lucyna Winnicka
Mariola	Irena Szczurowska
Gorny	Leon Niemczyk
Bozenka	Barbara Wrzesinka
Leopold	Jerzy Skolimovsky

Polski pic seems reminiscent of the John Osborne play "Inadmissible Evidence" in that a man whose wife and child have left him reminisces about what led to it, his life and his outlook in general. But this lacks a truly probing and revealing manner and it soon begins to deteriorate into a self-pitying tirade.

Andrzej Lapicki shambles through his role that keeps him him perpetually on screen and sometimes does touch a comic or dramatic note as a sort of resigned little man who is not above cheating or lying to gain his ends. His concentration camp experiences have also marked him deeply and given him a wry rather than mature outlook.

All this is done with intercutting between thought and the present to finally lead o repitition and self indulgence rather than to the more

---

forceful and deeper exposition of a man who is almost down and out. Lensing has the right harsh and grainy texture to support this rather whining tale that needed candor or a more deft character in either a more forthright comic sight. *Mosk.*

Czar I General
(BULGARIAN—SCOPE)

Karlovy, Vary, July 6.
Filmbulgaria release of Bulgarofilm production. With Peter Slabakov, Naoum Shopov, Georgi Cherkelov. Directed by Vulo Radev. Screenplay, Lyuben Stanev; camera, Borislav Pouhcev; music, Simeon Pironkov. At Karlovy Vary Film Fest. Running Time, 75 MINS.

General	Peter Slabakov
Boris III	Naoum Shopov
Colonel	Georgi Cherkelov

More a political anecdote and shows a fine measure of visual knowhow as the execution of a Bulgar general, who wanted Bulgaria to side with Russia during the last war, is intercut with the events leading up to it. The Bulgarian king is prone to side with the Germans since he thinks this may be better for the fate of this little kingdom and also due to pressures from the local anti-Reds.

Pic does try to balance the outlooks of the two men and even attempts to humanize the monarch, though in a sort of theatrical self conscious manner. Of course, the Slav-oriented General is somewhat idealized. His moment with his wife, and the final execution with reverberating echos, since it is done in a subterranean stone hall, are expertly conceived with the right symbolical effects.

But this still remains somewhat skimpy and surface and appears mainly an item for Eastern Bloc countries sans the more full-bodied dash, characterization and clarity for Western art or playoff possibilities. Acting is good and it shows fine technical progress too from Bulgaria. *Mosk.*

Procesul Alb
(White Trial)
(ROMANIAN—SCOPE)

Karlovy, Vary, July 7.
Romania Film release of Bucaresti production. With Marga Barbu, Toma Caragiu, Iurie Darie, Gina Patrichi. Directed by Iulian Mihu. Screenplay, Eugen Barbu; camera, Aurel Samson; editor, Lucia Anton. At Karlovy Vary Film Fest. Running Time, 120 MINS.

Matei	Iurie Darie
Marta	Marga Barbu
Ana Maria	Gina Patrichi
Ciripol	Toma Caragiu
Dumitrama	Gheorghe Dinica
Constantin	George Constantin

Tale of a trial of two anti-Red policemen who killed a "resistance" man during the occupation of the last war unfolds on reminiscences of various people involved to then end with the trial. Fragmentation confuses things and too many allusions to the politics of the times makes it difficult for the outsider. Overblown direction and overdone thesping also detract from this overlong pic. Foreign chances are chancey.

A young Communist works with a chief who has married a girl he loved. But all is forgotten in the drive to beat the invaders and local non-Marxist group. He has a brief affair with an actress and

---

his chief is killed in a trap for which he is suspected. But he is absolved. Pic shows incidents in flashback and does not properly sort out underline or build the various versions to unfold into a cohesive form.

Result is confusion, stridency and a certain flatness of tone in spite of people playing at the tops of their voices. It is technically advanced over many other Romanian pix seen but too obscure for chances outside its home grounds. *Mosk.*

Menino De Engheno
(Boy of the Plantation)
(BRAZILIAN)

Karlovy, Vary, July 6.
MAPA release and production. With Geraldo Del Ney, Annecy Rocha, Rodolfo Arena, Savie Rolin, Antoine Pitanga. Directed by Walter Lima. Screenplay, Jose Lins Del Rego; camera, Raynaldo Barros; music, Pedro Santos. At Karlovy Vary Film Fest. Running Time, 88 MINS.

Carlinhos	Geraldo Del Ney
Marie	Annecy Rocha
Uncle	Rodolfo Arena
Maria	Savie Rolin
Grandfather	Antoine Pitanga

Nostalgic tale of boyhood experiences on a sugar plantation circa 1920 is somewhat too diffuse to bring the needed poetic and lyrical touch to pay off. Many of the allusions to the times and its social and political aspects will escape those unfamiliar with the Brazilian scene. But film does have some fetching insight into sensitive adolescence and, if it sometimes overdoes technique at the expense of content, it has a gentle, knowing feel for youth that should make this a nice language entry for abroad if not quite of the stature for art chances.

The boy goes to live with his grandfather when his mother dies. He is sensitive and marked by the violent death of his mother which he witnessed. He gets attached to his family but death, marriage and growth rob him of new friends till a first feeling of love matures him and he leaves all behind to go to school in the city with his background etched in his mind in a series of fast shots, mixed with his moving train at the end, that sum up the pic more forcefully than the actual film itself.

The boy is played without any preciosity and his first stirrings of sensual desire, meeting the romantic bandits of the time, the Congaceiros, who were both the thieves and revolutionaries, are well done if the pic sometimes overdoes an ancient already treated by little montages that repeat rather than enhance. But it shows a new, sensitive director and one who will probably be heard from for he displays a true lyric flair though still faltering narrative style. It is technically fine, with playing well controlled. *Mosk.*

Diplopenies
(Dancing the Sirtaki)
(GREEK)

Karlovy Vary, July 11.
Damskinos-Michaelides release and production. Stars Aliki Vouyouklaki, Dimitri Papamichael; features, Dionyses Papayannopoulos, Vassili Avlonitis, Rica Dialyna. Directed by George Scalenakis; screenplay, Alecos Sakellarios; camera,

---

Nicos Gardelis; music, Stavros Xarchacos. At Karlovy Vary Film Fest. Running Time, 75 MINS.	
Marina	Aliki Vouyouklaki
Grigoris	Dimitri Papayanno
Rita	Rica Dialyna
Friend	Dionyses Papayannopoulos
Boss	Vassili Avlonitis

Disarming little musical comedy is inspired by American pre-war musicals but wisely plays within its means sans attempting big-scale production numbers. It uses the popular Greek sirtaki music as background to a familiar love story. Its modesty slants this mainly for language situations abroad if it has the right simplicity and naivity, sans forcing for dualer use also.

A house painter gets a job as a singer and soon is a star and coveted by a rapacious rich woman. His wife rebels and becomes a star, too, and they break up only to make up again when she is pregnant. To keep her out of show biz he makes her many children for a happy ending.

Players are personable, the jangling, high pitched music agreeable and the dance interludes use the sunlit Greek landscapes well. The songs and dances also reflect the uncomplicated people and storyline, comment on it or move it ahead. So this manages to bring off a musical that is influenced by Yank patterns but well adapted to Greece. It is nicely lensed also.

Director George Scalenakis also displays some perceptive feel for comedic touches to make this oft-told unassuming little pic generally charming. *Mosk.*

Posledni Ruze Od Casanovi
(Last Rose From Casanova)
(CZECHOSLOVAKIAN-SCOPE)

Karlovy Vary, July 6.
Czech State Film release of Barrandov production. With Felix Le Breux, Milene Dvorska, Vladimir Brabec, Bohus Zaharaky. Directed by Vaclav Krska. Screenplay, Frantisek Daniel, F. A. Dvorak; camera, Vaclav Hanus; music, Vaclav Trojan. At Karlovy Vary Film Fest. Running Time, 90 MINS.

Casanova	Felix Le Breux
Valerie	Milene Dvorska
Wallenstein	Vladimir Brabec
Count	Bohus Zaharsky
Doctor	Ota Simanek
Matern	Valja Detrova

The idea is good. That famed lover Casanova, now an old man writing his memoirs via the charity of a Czech nobleman, is pitted against a young woman who wants to show him up. But film is bit heavyhanded on talk. Characters lack the knowing sophistication to give it bite. On its technical gloss and production dress it may have some specialized spot chances abroad.

Casanova bets he can seduce this independent creature, who believes only in emotion while he thinks that old world chivalry alone can win a woman, with his host. She, in turn, bets her husband she can show up Casanova. Each almost wins to end in a draw. There is some neat sensual fencing between the two if it does lack a neat, probing ease and insight to make its moral theme fetching or clear.

Some flashbacks to Casanovas early life are a bit precious and the theme of his coming age is also somewhat buried in the skimpy anecdote. But Felix Le Breux is

a properly grumpy old ex-libertine and Milene Dvorska is ardant and lovely as the new frisky woman, with others good in etching the residents of 17th century Mittel Europa. It is just that the right piquancy in dealing with its tale of sensuality vs passion is not quite incisive and revealing enough to keep this from being anecdotic and surface and thus lacking weight for a feature length pic.
Mosk.

Tri
(Three)
(YUGOSLAVIAN)

Karlovy, Vary, July 7.
Yugoslavia Film release of Avala production. With Bata Zivojinovic, Ali Raner, Senka Veletanlic-Petrovic. Directed by Aleksander Petrovic. Screenplay, Aontonije Isakovic, Petrovic from the book by Isakovic; camera, Tomislav Pinter; editor, Mila Milanovich. At Karlovy Vary Film Fest. Running Time, 70 MINS.
Milos .... Bata Zivojinovic
Man .... Ali Raner
Girl .... Senka Veletanlic-Petrovic
Soldier .... Voja Miric

Sharply made film zeroes in on three wartime anecdoes of ironic, heroic and useless death, always with a knowing pacifistic air though there is no preaching but an objective limning of the incidents. Its highly pitched camera work and driving force could make this eligible for specialized playoff abroad, shortness favors dual spotting possibly.

One man is the focus as he first is a hapless bystander of the killing of an innocent by hysterical people at the beginning of the war. The man does not have his papers and crowd insinuations goad things to a point where he is killed though the hero feebly tries to stop it. Next he is chased by Germans after a resistance raid into a swamp where he runs into another man. One will die and save the other since the Germans think there is only one man there.

Last is sad item as the man, now an officer in the Yugoslav army, is forced to sentence some collaborators to death one a young girl, though the war is nearing its end. Director Aleksander Petrovic keeps his camera perking and probingly moving throughout which fits the fragmentary but telling look at the hapless and hopeless face of war. Players have the right realistic look and this shapes a terse and taut offbeater.
Mosk.

Fantastic Voyage
(C'SCOPE—COLOR)

Excellent, entertaining, sci-fi suspenser about a trip into a living body by "miniaturized" scientists. Outstanding production values, exploitable for solid b.o.

Hollywood, July 20.
Twentieth Century-Fox release of Saul David production. Features Stephen Boyd, Raquel Welch, Edmond O'Brien, Donald Pleasence, Arthur O'Connell, William Redfield, Arthur Kennedy. Directed by Richard Fleischer. Screenplay, Harry Kleiner, based on a story by Otto Klement, Jay Lewis Bixby, as adapted by David Duncan; camera (DeLuxe Color), Ernest Laszlo; editor, William B. Murphy; music, Leonard Rosenman; asst. director. Ad Schaumer. Reviewed at 20th-Fox Studio, July 19, '66. Running time, 100 MINS.
Grant .... Stephen Boyd
Cora .... Raquel Welch
Gen. Carter .... Edmond O'Brien
Dr. Michaels .... Donald Pleasence
Col. Reid .... Arthur O'Connell
Capt. Owens .... William Redfield
Dr. Duval .... Arthur Kennedy
Jan Benes .... Jean Del Val
Communications Aide ...... Barry Coe
Secret Service .... Ken Scott
Nurse .... Shelby Grant
Technician .... James Brolin
Wireless Operator .. Brendan Fitzgerald

"Fantastic Voyage" is just that. The lavish Saul David production, boasting some brilliant special effects and superior creative efforts, is an entertaining, enlightening excursion through inner space — the body of a man. Relatively simple story line, with Cold War espionage overtones, is put over by good acting and direction. Very strong b.o. prospects are likely for 20th-Fox release in general situation.

The original Otto Klement-Jay Lewis Bixby story, adapted by David Duncan, has been updated and fashioned by Harry Kleiner into an intriguing yarn about five people who undergo miniaturization for injection into the bloodstream of a scientist. Latter has been wrested from Iron Curtain captivity to reveal his solution to the miniaturization problem; people and objects remain in shrunken form only one hour.

Thus, the five people, en route in a shrunken nuclear sub to repair some brain damage accessible only from within, have limited time to achieve their purpose. Action cross cuts from lifesize medics to the shrunken quintet who encounter, and are endangered by, the miracles of life. Adding to suspense is the suspicion that one of the five may be a traitor who will attempt to botch the expedition.

The competent cast of below-title principals is headed by Stephen Boyd, the U.S. agent who has brought scientist Jean Del Val to America, only to have a last-ditch attempt on latter's life — told in a four-minute pre-title prolog — cause the blood clot which necessitates the weird journey to come. Edmond O'Brien and Arthur O'Connell are top echelon officers in the Combined Miniature Deterrent Forces, name of the military service which shrinks fighting men and gear for quick transport.

Boyd is assigned to join the expedition under the command of Donald Pleasence, a medical specialist in circulatory systems, thus qualifying him as navigator for William Redfield's sub. Arthur Kennedy, the suspect traitor, is the doctor who will use a Laser beam to repair the brain damage, and his assistant, Raquel Welch, is included in the group. All principals acquit themselves handily. The cloud over Kennedy is a red-herring plot angle, becoming obvious too early in the game and constituting the major flaw.

Richard Fleischer's fine direction maintains a zesty pace thruout film's smart 100 minutes, edited in top fashion by William B. Murphy. Interest is sustained throughout, and remains after the film is over, by virtue of the military analogy between human struggle and the never-ending struggle for life that goes on inside the body. One of the characters voices a religious sentiment, certain to be already suggested in the minds of filmgoers (or at least a stupendous awe).

Leonard Rosenman's score is excellent, ditto the computer-age titles by Richard Kuhn and National Screen Service. Ernest Laszlo's outstanding DeLuxe color lensing brings out every lush facet in the superb production values. The color-less sets repping blood vessels and nerve fibre were painted with light in a degree reportedly never before attempted.

Over half of the disclosed $6,500,000 negative cost went into the special values which admit of extended sales exploitation. Art directors Jack Martin Smith and Dale Mennesy, set decorators Walter Scott and Stuart A. Reiss, technical advisors Fred Zendar and Peter Foy (latter for the flying shots), special effects lensers L. B. Abbott, Art Cruickshank and Emil Kosa, Jr., and researcher Harper Goff, who worked on the sub, have all turned in work which will endure as hallmarks of accomplishment.
Murf.

La Curee
(The Kill)
(FRENCH-PANAVISION-COLOR)

Paris, July 19.
Cocinor release of Marceau-Cocinor production. Stars Jane Fonda; features Peter McEnery, Michel Piccoli, Tina Marquand, Jacques Mondon, Simone Valere, Germaine Montero. Directed by Roger Vadim. Screenplay, Jean Cau, Vadim from book by Emile Zola; camera (Eastmancolor), Claude Renoir; editor, Victoria Mercanton. At George V, Paris. Running Time, 95 MINS.
Renee .... Jane Fonda
Maxime .... Peter McEnery
Alexandre .... Michel Piccoli
Anne .... Tina Marquand
Husband .... Jacques Mondon
Wife .... Simone Valere
Guest .... Germaine Montero

Roger Vadim, who introduced ex-wife Brigitte Bardot to the big time in "And God Created Woman," now has a pic with his present wife Jane Fonda starred. It appears to be a more gilded version of "God." This melodrama is sleek and elegant if sometimes short on motivation. It appears a solid exploitation and playoff item for abroad with arty chances needing more careful placement and handling. There is an English version which Columbia Films has taken for the U. S. and Canada.

With its exploitable handles and Jane Fonda name, it could be an okay item for abroad.

Updated version of an Emile Zola 19th century novel deals with a rich financier married to a very young woman (Jane Fonda). He also has a 22-year-old son, Peter McEnery. Love blossoms between this son and the young wife. This leads to the woman asking for a divorce which is granted. But the weakling son gives in to his father's need to have him marry the daugter of a banker in order to save his fortune.

Vadim has a glossy style that shows the aimless life of the bored wife and the drifting son that finally results in love only to be throttled by his weakness which ends in the woman's breakdown. Perhaps the updating loses this a bit of force since the recourse for misusing funds is different these days. And the father's strength is not adequately presented to dovetail with the shallow son's sudden weakness.

But it does delve into a self-indulgent, rich world that is recognizable if some of the denouement and effects are somewhat forced. Miss Fonda shows a solid drive and physical beauty. The so-called nude scenes are done with taste and tact if the love episodes are more precious.

The color is rich and Panavision cameras of Claude Renoir fill the screen with colorful settings. But the pic of decadence is somewhat arbitrary and stifling, a 19th Century rather than a modern feeling. So this appears a sudsy if tasteful melodrama that does not quite have the depth in character and insight to make its downbeat ending as touching as it should be.

But its surface sophistication and fairly consistent playing should give this some legs on the home grounds, and with good foreign possibilities if well hypoed and placed. A fine production dress also helps.

Peter McEnery is effective as the weak son while Michel Piccoli does not have the right sort of role to be able to limn a strong and overpowering father figure to overcome love and desired freedom.
Mosk.

Shokei No Shima
(Punishment Island)
(JAPAN-DAIESCOPE)

Tokyo, June 23.
Daiei release of Nissei Theatre productions. With Rentaro Mikuni, Shima Iwashita, Akiro Nitta, Kei Sato, Shin Kinzo. Directed by Masahiro Shinoda. Screenplay, Shintaro Ishihara, based on novel by Taijun Takeda; camera, Tatsuo Suzuki; art, Shigemasa Toda; music, Toru Takemitsu. Reviewed, Tokyo, June 23, '66. Running Time, 92 MINS.

Prime Festival material, an excellent art-house bet, this beautiful and disturbing film is both a first-rate action melodrama and a philosophically upsetting metaphysical thriller.

A young man returns to small island where he has apparently been before. Through extremely skillful flashbacks and very inventive inter-cutting we realize that he was imprisoned there as a child, that the island was during the war a jail for delinquents, the youngsters under the charge of a man of the most ferocious cruelty.

Bit by bit we also see that he was sent there because a member of the wartime military police murdered the rest of his family—the charge was anarchism—and had the child sent where he could not talk. We understand, through meetings with a now grown fellow-inmate (warden's favorite, now island bully), with an old schoolteacher, that—20 years later—this young man has returned for revenge.

He meets the daughter of his old tormentor—a girl he remembers as a child who simply stared at the tortures unable to believe that it was her father who was committing them. Though now grown, she still disbelieves. She tells him that her father has changed. He, living in his own past, does not believe her. He only remembers that this man, her father, threw him over a cliff and now believes him dead.

Having waited twenty years, having planned and schemed a revenge for a ruined childhood, the man races to meet his old tormenter. He comes face to face with him and finds . . . finds that life has gone on though he himself, consumed and sustained by his desire for revenge, has not changed at all, only he has kept the ghosts alive.

Faced not with terror or horror but with something much worse—the indifference of time itself—the young man pushes his plan through. He ascertains what he has suspected, that the brutal guardian and the military policeman are the same, and then confronts the old man whose fading memory yields that he too was (just like the boy) banished to this island for his military crimes, and that he remembers a boy who died . . . or was killed, it makes little difference which.

Baffled by the nature of the world, the young man decides to lets the old man live but makes him cut off one of his own fingers. This symbolic act completed, the young man grabs it up and, grimacing like a child, gleeful, runs down the mountain, gets on a boat, and the film suddenly ends —ends on a picture of the young man, his excitement, his satisfaction, and then, as he turns away from island, a new emotion: what will he do now?

The ending of the film asks its most important question, and throws everything that went before into doubt, and the true horror begins only as the houselights go up. For the real atrocity is that the young man has devoted his life to revenge, has lived for nothing else—not just his youth, but his entire life is a waste.

This upsetting conclusion turns conventional (eye for an eye or cheek for a cheek) upside down. It seems to indicate that the victim has no hope of redress, that revenge cannot be but hollow, and that evil remains evil simply because this is so. It is not that turning the cheek is a virtue: it is that turning the cheek is all that a human being can do and still continue to live. This film, which so successfully masquerades as a revenge-melodrama, reveals itself to be a metaphysical enquiry into the nature of evil. Multi-layered,

it can be seen as a singularly satisfying adventure film, as an allegory or—and this level reaches the emotions—a mysterious, disturbing, and truth parable.

Director Masahiro Shinoda makes all of this superlatively visible. Director of such films as the mysterious and disquieting "Pale Flower" and the beautifully elegiac "Of Beauty and Sorrow" (both Shochiku films) as well as that curious nouvelle - vague period-drama "Sasuke Sarutobi," Shinoda has here found a vehicle which perfectly fits the stunning visual style he has been evolving.

He has probably most been influenced in this by Antonioni. Thus, as in "L'Avventura," the natural backgrounds are used for character explication, the beauty of composition is used to enforce character motivation. The result is a very "cool" style but one which suits this heated story perfectly. Further, the combination of precise directorial control in conjunction (not with a story of indifference or despair—Antonioni's theme) with a story of violence, cruelty, and revenge makes for a combination which, perhaps paradoxically is strikingly reinforcing, one of the results of which is that compelling of the emotions, and that calm ideological logic which so orders the ideas, and which so distinguishes this picture.

Shinoda's camerawork is superb —it is by the man who photographed "Silence Without Wings," a new Toho film which contains some of the most amazing photography in recent cinema. The art work is by the man who did the spectacular "Kwaidan," and music is by the finest of contemporary Japanese composers, Toru Takemitsu, whose scores to "Harakiri," "Kwaidan," and "Woman of the Dunes" are now well-known.

Shinoda also gets remarkable performances from his actors. Rentaro Mikuni, it is true, is probably Japan's finest film actor (he was the lord in "Harakiri," the husband in the first section of "Kwaidan") but even he has never equalled this portrayal of a man completely cruel and therefore completely human. Keo Sato as the bully is infinitely better than he was as the man in "Onibaba;" and Shima Iwasita (hitherto a Shochiku ingenue) is for the first time memorable. The role of hero went to a stage actor, Akira Nitta of the Tokyo Actors' Theatre, and it is his portrayal which so rightly delineates the moral dilemma of the film. His is a superbly underplayed role: this is the kind of performance where you forget the actor is performing.

All in all this first Independent production by the Nissei Theatre is a great success. There have been just three first-rate Japanese films so far this year. Nikkatsu's "Introduction to Anthropology" now retitled "The Pornographer" and opening in Europe shortly is one; Susumu Hani's excellent but unreleased "Bride of the Andes" (a Toho picture) is another, and Shinoda's "Punishment Island" is the third. _Chie._

Zlata Reneta
(Golden Queen)
(CZECH)

Prague, July 19.

Czech State Film production and release. With Karel Hoger, Eva Limanova, Jiri Sedimayer, Ilja Prachat. Directed by Otakar Vavra. Screenplay, Frantisek Hrubin, Vavra from book by Hrubin; camera, Andrej Baria; editor, Karel Skvor. Previewed in Prague. Running Time, 80 MINS.
Man .... Karel Hoger
Mistress .... Eva Limanova
Friend .... Jiri Sedimayer
Boy .... Ilja Prachat
Girl .... Vera Tichankova

A rather diffuse series of flashbacks make up the backbone of this pic about a fiftyish man who goes back to the scene of his youth and thinks over his life. Arbitrary gimmicks, many allusions that may escape those not conversant with Czech recent history and a heavyhanded progression and acting make limited in foreign appeal.

It is a case of one of the older directors dealing with the war and Stalinist day memories in a more modern style of high key for thoughts, distortion and a tricky mixture of past and present. But it does not work out so well.

Like most Czech films this has fine lensing but here the easy entrance into everyday life and the heightening of it by visual revelations of tensions, unease or human needs is not deft or clear enough to have this tale of a wasted life jell.

Acting has a tendency to be too effusive and obvious to rob this of the subtleties needed to bring off statements about the various periods covered. Chalk this up as a Czech pic that does not quite come off. _Mosk._

Smoky
(COLOR—SONGS)

Interesting remake of Will James' classic story of a horse; good grosses indicated.

Hollywood, July 22.

Twentieth-Fox release of Aaron Rosenberg production. Stars Fess Parker; features Diana Hyland, Katy Jurado. Directed by George Sherman. Screenplay, Harold Medford; based on screenplay by Lillie Hayward, Dwight Cummins, Dorothy Yost; from novel by Will James; camera (DeLuxe Color), Jack Swain; music, Leith Stevens; editor, Joseph Silver; asst. director, Ted Schilz. Reviewed at 20th-Fox Studios, July 20, '66. Running time, 102 MINS.
Clint .... Fess Parker
Julie .... Diana Hyland
Maria .... Katy Jurado
Fred .... Hoyt Axton
Jeff .... Robert Wilke
Gordon .... Armando Silvestre
Manuel .... Jose Hector Galindo
Pepe .... Jorge Martinez De Hoyos
Abbott .... Ted White
Cowboys .... Chuck Roberson,
Robert Terhune, Jack Williams

Will James' story of "Smoky" still bears the makings of solid entertainment, particularly for the so-called family (and horse-loving) trade. Filmed twice previously — by Fox Films in 1933 with Victor Jory starred and by 20th-Fox in '46 as a Fred MacMurray starrer, both racking up good grosses — latest 20th version with Fess Parker topbilled for additional marquee lure should appeal to a new generation of theatregoers.

Producer Aaron Rosenberg has

invested the beautifully-lensed color film with type of values which pay off interest. The story unfolds naturally under the knowhow direction of George Sherman, at his best in this type endeavor, without any attempt at emotionalism despite its sentimental theme. Particular merit attaches to filming of picture on various locations in Mexico by Jack Swain, making handsome use of the scenery to enhance narrative.

The Harold Medford script, based on the 1946 screenplay of Lillie Hayward, Dwight Cummins and Dorothy Yost, actually stars the magnificent black stallion seen in title role. Parker helps considerably as the cowpoke who captures him on the range and trains him before he turns killer.

Events leading up to Smoky becoming a rodeo outlaw, later reduced to pulling a junk wagon and final ultimate return to his original master back at the ranch play well, although the situation of Parker going off to World War II and locating Smoky on day of his return is too contrived. Present edition runs 102 minutes as against '46's 86-minutes' running time and 33's 65 minutes, occasioned by building a past for Parker and conflict with Hoyt Axton. The folk singer makes his screen bow as the brother, a circumstance not particularly pertinent to plot.

Complementing story is Axton's singing of four of his own songs which fit into yarn. These include "Five Dollar Bill," "Smile As You Go By," "Trouble and Misery" and "Queen of the Rockin' R," serving as a suitable showcase for singer, who can act as well.

Parker brings his customary homely approach and creates a feeling of credibility in his role. Diana Hyland as the ranch owner who hires Parker is in for a hint of romance, delivering a sincere performance, and Axton also impresses. Katy Jurado as the cook, Jorge Martinez de Hoyos her husband and Jose Hector Galindo their son, handle themselves satisfactorily and Robert Wilke makes his work count as foreman. The horse, of course, steals every scene he's in.

Leith Stevens' music score is effective and Hank Thompson sings title song, written by Ernie Sheldon and Stevens, which has a haunting quality. Joseph Silver's editing is sharp and art direction by Jack Martin Smith and John M. Elliott registers. _Whit._

Pampa Salvaje
(Savage Pampas)
(ARGENTINE—SPANISH—70M—COLOR)

Buenos Aires, July 19.

Dasa release of Jaime Prades (Madrid) and Dasa (Buenos Aires) coproduction; producer, Prades. Stars Robert Taylor, Ron Randall, Marc Lawrence and Ty Hardin; features Mario Lozano, Rosenda Monteros, Fela Roque, Susana Mara, Angel de Pozo, Laura Granados, Milo Quesada, Hector Quiroga, Juan Carlos Galvan, George Rigaud and Isabel Pisano. Directed by Hugo Fregonese. Screenplay, Fregonese and John Melson, based upon an original story by Ulyses Petit de Murat and Homero Manzi; camera (Eastmancolor), Manuel

Berenguer; music, Waldo de los Rios. At Ocean, Buenos Aires. Running Time, **108 MINS.**

Capt. Martin .... Robert Taylor
Padron .... Ron Randall
Sgt. Barril .... Marc Lawrence
Carreras .... Ty Hardin
Santiago .... Mario Lozano
Rucu .... Rosenda Monteros
Camila .... Fela Roque
Lt. Del Rio .... Angel del Pozo
Carmen .... Laura Granados
Alfonso .... Milo Quesada
Pepe .... Hector Quiroga
Isidro .... Juan C. Galvan
Old Man .... George Rigaud
Lucy .... Isabel Pisano

This entertaining account on how the pampas were won is a remake of the 1946 Argentine hit "Pampa Barbara" and has gaucho flavor although it was lensed in Spain. An oater with plenty of action in well-staged cavalry-Indian clashes, it is however something more than a western in another dress because it arouses and sustains the viewer's attention via a truer than usual approach to historical facts. This way it stands up for good effect with its interesting, fast-paced depiction of seemingly genuine adventures in a remote land.

In Buenos Aires "Pampas" teed off to solid business in general release using color prints with monaural sound. Plans to roadshow it were dropped reportedly because a 70m. copy with six-track stereophonic sound wouldn't arrive from Paris in time for Independence Week. As this Prades-Dasa coproduction has entertainment values, names, some exoticism and first-class technical credits to lure international audiences, it seems a good b.o. bet everywhere. Special handling may enhance chances in some situations.

Story evolves around a tough, middle-aged army captain (Taylor), commander of an outpost circa 1880. His forces are decimated not in combat but in a subtler way: a renegade (Randall), linked with the Indians, offers a captive woman to each soldier who deserts the army to join his gang.

Taylor eventually convinces his superiors in Buenos Aires to let women go to the outpost. Actually they don't go; they are sent from prison and most of them are prostitutes. Their travel under military escort through hostile territory, their relationship with lonely men who have dreamed of the opposite sex for years but who are ordered not to put a finger on the females till the journey's end and the fighting in a little town where a huge renegade-Indian contingent surrounds them provides enough episodes to keep things vividly going.

Chases, duels and battle movement alternate with short scenes devoted to soldiers' troubles. Fregonese and Melson, rescripting the original story by Petit de Murat and Manzi, have developed a rather choral pic around the main theme instead of resorting to the traditional plot between a few central characters. They seem to have tried to attain a mass-appeal actioner but they have replaced the old-fashioned yarn with a somewhat adult approach to some characters and story angles.

They use the hero-villain cliche making a mild attempt to suggest that a hat with Freudian undertones link their lives. They go farther from formula in suppressing the sweet girl and the sentimentalities of romance. When Taylor likes an Indian girl he wastes no time talking; he simply throws her over his shoulder and ignoring her struggle carries her to bed; next day he trades one of the prosties for the girl, who by then seems to accept willingly her new master.

Action sequences are of the familiar type when cavalrymen engage with Indians, not quite so in personal duels thanks to some gadgets of the gaucho arsenal that are little known to international patrons. Wide use has been made of boleadoras, estacas, facones, etc., and this, added to settings and gaucho costumes, help to show something different to the viewer's eye.

Taylor, as the captain, is properly rugged, even brutal, while underlining compassion and understanding for his men. Ron Randall departs from the somber villain stereotype to play a laughing, screwball menace instead. Marc Lawrence injects comedy touches in his tough sergeant. Ditto Angel del Pozo to a young lieutenant coming fresh from the just created military academy. Ty Hardin is okay as a journalist accused of anarchism and sent to the desert in punishment. Rosenda Monteros impresses as the quiet Indian beauty. Fela Roque portrays a political prisoner taken from the original story but who serves no purpose in this remake. Mario Lozano, Susana Mara, George Rigaud, Isabel Pisano and Juan Carlos Galvan ably deliver brief cameos.

Fregonese has directed in a way reminiscent of the John Ford style, that is, sharp, virile, good-humored, with a gusto for the frontier saga and making the most to avoid visual dullness in an arid scenery. Excellent color lensing by Manuel Berenguer helps to attain this. Waldo de los Rios contributed a rich score which combines contemporary musical tendencies with the need to add punch to action and to be faithful to Argentine folklore. Editing is expert although trimming of some unnecessary footage (such as the one involving the political prisoner) may yield a tighter pic. Dialogue rarely interferes with action and contains some frank barracks talk that is appreciated by the audience.

Sex angles are given a comedy treatment and there is nothing fleshy besides a few low necks. Many horsemen were employed, specially in the last sequence. The prints seen in Buenos Aires have flaws reportedly because of some damage in the internegative; the obvious b.o. advantage of releasing "Pampas" in connection with the Sesquioentenary of the Argentine Independence apparently gave no time to solve problem. *Din.*

Kanchenjungha
(INDIAN-COLOR)

Edward Harrison release of a Satyajit Ray production. Directed and written by Ray. Features Chhabi Biswas, Karuna Banerji, Nilima Roy Chowdhury, Arun Mukherjee. Camera (Eastman Color), Subrata Mitra; film editor, Dulal Dutt; sound, Durgadas Mitra; musical arrangement, Ray. Reviewed at Bonded Film Storage, N.Y., July 20, '66. Running Time, **102 MINS.**

Indranath Choudhuri .... Chhabi Biswas
Labanya .... Karuna Banerji
Anil .... Anil Chatterjee
Anima .... Anubhe Cupta
Shankar .... Subrata Sen
Tuklu .... Indrani Singh
Monisha .... Nilima Roy Chowdbury
Bannerji .... N. Viswanathan
Jagadish .... Pahari Sanyal
Ashoke .... Arun Mukherjee
Shibsankar Roy .... Vidya Singh

Although "Kanchenjungha" is the first attempt at color by Indian director Satyajit Ray, it displays a command of tints that suggests much research before attempting an entire feature. Actually, the film was made several years ago and is only now being released in the U.S., as the primary attraction of a "Festival From India" at N.Y.'s Lincoln Center. It will then be put into general release by distributor Edward Harrison.

As the title suggests, the setting for Ray's film is in the foothills of the Himalayas, in the hill station of Darjeeling which has served as a refuge from the summer heat for the more affluent citizens of Calcutta for many years and is also a center of the tea-growing area of India. The tiny town, perched high above the tea plantations, is overshadowed by the surrounding Himalayan peaks, particularly Kanchenjungha, third highest in the world.

The entire action of the film takes place during one afternoon, during the last day of the stay of a wealthy Indian family. The summer is ending, mists creep up the mountainside and K. is more often than not wreathed in clouds. While the members of the family of Sir Indranath Choudhuri stroll about, hoping for a last glimpse of the great peak, their individual stories are enacted. Ray crosscuts back and forth, but easily and with no sense of interrupting a tale, from the father, a relic of the dominating, patriarchal, playing - at - God school, to his youngest daughter, committed by him to a marriage for which she has no heart; to the older daughter, already trapped in such a relationship and confronted with proof of adultery by her husband; to his son, a spoiled, aimless youth whose principal pastime is the pursuit of females.

Ray, ever the keen observer and reflective commentator on life in contemporary India, never creates as human portraits when he deals with the upper classes, however, as he did so beautifully in the Apu trilogy. This could be intentional, something of a comment in itself, but is too consistent a pattern.

Sometimes his political comment backfires. The father, a relic of British-rule days (his title, his defense of British customs, his "cricket" preference), is meant to be the villain of this sketch on changing Indian family life but, as portrayed by Chhabi Biswas, he's a delightful curmudgeon, an evident old opportunist who has twice the appeal of the gushy, independent example of modern youth (Arun Mukherjee) (God help India if this is tomorrow's leader), who falls in love with younger daughter (Nilima Roy Chowdbury).

Some story aspects get a bit mawkish — the strained relationship of the older daughter and her husband is patched up through their love for their small daughter; a "wiser, more idealistic" older man, brother-in-law of the industrialist, mostly beams, tsks-tsks, and stays out of the way. N. Viswanathan as Bannerji, man-most-likely-to-succeed and papa's selection for younger daughter, is excellent as a stuffy type who does want the girl but gets impatient at her indecisiveness. Just by seconds, he walks out on her before she drums up the courage to say no.

Ray's guidance and Subtrata Mitra's Eastman Color camerawork make the film a visual delight. The continuing perambulations of the family's various members enables the tracking camera to wander over the extremely photogenic village. Mists gather to turn the colors into subtle pastels, then drift away to allow the sun to highlight bright, but never vivid, pictorial settings. Always suggested, but never shown until the last few frames of the film, is the brooding dominance of K.

Within the framework of the versatile filmmaker's work (Ray not only directed and produced the film, he also wrote the screenplay from his own original story and, as usual, arranged the music), "Kanchenjungha" rates as, visually, one of his very best, if, dramatically, there's a coldness about it that isn't entirely mountain air. Effective, but at first a bit disconcerting, is his having the "upper class" Indians use a mixture of English and Hindi, sometimes in a derogatory sense, sometimes to express a thought not quite at home in the Indian mind.

Robe.

A Paty Jezdec Je Strach
(The Fifth Rider is Fear)
(CZECH)

Prague, July 26.

Czech State Film production and release. With Mireslav Machacek, Jiri Adamira, Josef Vinklar, Zdenka Prcohazkova. Directed by Zbynek Brynych. Screenplay, Hana Belohradska, Brynch; camera, Jan Kalis; music, Jiri Sternwald. Previewed in Prague. Running Time, **?5 MINS.**

Braun .... Mireslav Machacek
Vesely .... Jiri Adamira
Fanta .... Josef Vinklar
Policeman .... Jiri Vrstala
Mrs. Vesela .... Zdenka Prochazkova

This expressionist film captures the strange moody atmosphere of a city occupied by military forces, with deportation resistance and collaboration resulting from it. But this makes a generalized statement on the fear that can create heroism, cowardice or just plain withdrawal. This is slanted more for arty than general use abroad.

But its technical grasp again is a plus. The director is an established name and may sometimes show too much interest in brooding scenes and technical bravura but he has controlled to make a statement on people in crisis. There is also a Kafkaesque feeling of underlying tension and unseen menace tempered by some shafts of macabre comedy.

A doctor, who is forbidden to practice, works in an old synagogue used to house confiscated goods that have belonged to deported Jews. One day a wounded resistance man hides in his apartment house and he is forced to operate on him. He tries to find morphine and rambles through a mad house and a strange nightclub that caters to people facing deportation and who disport themselves with hysterical abandon. He is finally killed after having decided he can't withdraw from life or his responsibility as a doctor.

Director Zbynek Brynych has managed to bring off this offbeat film.

The stark, heavily contrasted lensing helps as well as the knowing editing and the larger than life playing that still does not hit exhibitionism. An unusual pic, despite a few macabre humor touches, it calls for specialized handling in the foreign market. *Mosk.*

Kocar Do Vidne
(Carriage to Vienna)
(CZECH)
Prague, July 19.

Czech State Film production and release. With Iva Janzurova, Jaromir Hanzlik, Ludek Munzar. Directed by Karel Kachyna. Screenplay, Jan Prochazka; camera, Josef Illik; music, Jan Novak. Previewed in Prague. Running time, 75 MINS.
Christa .... Iva Janzurova
Soldier .... Jaromir Hanzlik
Wounded Man .... Ludek Munzar

Vengeance is the main theme of this pic with a wartime setting. It is photographically outstanding but tends to try to make its simple tale a parable. But it is well meaning and nicely made and could have some special situation probabilities abroad.

A prologue states that a woman's husband has been killed for stealing a sack of cement from the Germans during the war in Slovakia. Two Germans commandeer her horses and wagon and she goes along with them vowing to kill them to appease her husband's memory. One is fatally wounded and the other is a young Austrian in the German Army who just wants to get back to Austria.

The film is the log of the trip as the woman slowly sheds weapons, compass and paraphernalia slyly till caught and driven off. But she trails the wagon. The wounded man dies and she has a chance to kill the young boy asleep but relents. They finally fall into each other's arms in mutual loneliness and need only to be surprised by partisans. He is killed and she is raped.

There are the scenes of the boy trying to just win some human warmth from her, showing her pictures of his family and trying to overcome her stoney hate. He does not know its origins.

The pic is implacable but misses true tragic depth or more acceptable characterization by being predictable. But the fine acting and the expert , if sometimes overindulgent, direction, keep this engrossing. *Mosk.*

Nikdo Se Nebude Smat
(No One is Going to Laugh)
(CZECH)
Prague, July 26.

Czech State Film production and release. With Jan Kacer, Stepanka Rehekova, Josef Chvalina, Hans Kreinanslova, Bohumil Vavra. Directed by Hynek Bocan. Screenplay, Pavel Juracek, Bocan; camera, Jan Nemecek; music, Villian Bukovy. Previewed in Prague. Running Time, 80 MINS.
Klima .... Jan Kacer
Klara .... Stepanka Rehekova
Josef .... Josef Chvalina
Wife .... Hans Kreinanslova
Labsky .... Bohumil Vavra
Jiri .... Radoslav Brzobohaty

Still another mark of the extraordinary blossoming of new Czech filmmaking talents. Using a comic tale of human foibles, this is also quite outspoken about some fringe individuals who cannot quite adapt to the system. The hero seems a sort of modern version of the wily Good Soldier Schweik, who confounded his superiors by being too effusive in following orders and rules, though he plays the game in another way by passing the buck or via evasiveness.

And he is neither a positive nor a competely negative type. An art critic, he gets involved with a pedantic man who has written a manuscript on an old Czech painter and wants the critic to help him get it published. He answers the letter by saying it is interesting and he wishes the man luck though he has not read it.

But along comes the little man to hound him and some-how he can not come out and tell him the truth. When he does find the manuscript and sees it is bad, he then avoids telling the truth until forced to. But meantime he loses a lovely girl, also is in the bad graces of the Party, and loses his job in the bargain. But there's no bitterness here. It is all told in a perky, comic manner.

A meeting of his apartment house group who chastise his character, his relationship with the girl, and his final decision to extricate himself from everything are done with excellent character notations.

This has wit, probing dramatic and character insight but would need special handling abroad where its mixture of comedy may have it too special for general foreign situations. Arty chances are more probable. Clear lensing and expert playing are also plus factors besides the brisk and personal direction of Hynek Bocan. *Mosk.*

KarlovyFest

Noi Gio
(Rising Storm)
(NORTH VIETNAMESE)

American tortures Northviet gal and is killed, frankly anti-Yank.

Karlovy Vary, July 17.

Hanoi Film Studios release and production. With Thuy Van, The Anh, Van Hoa, Dotcho Kossev. Directed by Huy Thanh, Le Huyen. Screenplay, Dao Hong Cam, Thanh, Le Huyen; camera, Nguyen Dang Bay; music, Hozng Van. At Karlovy Vary Film Fest. Running Time, 100 MINS.
Van .... Thuy Van
Phuong .... The Anh
Captain .... Van Hoa
American .... Dotcho Kossev

North Vietnamese pic is set in South Vietnam during the fighting between Saigon troops and the Commie-linked Viet Cong at time when American soldiers were only "advisors" attached to the Saigon troops. Openly partisan this one offers a Communist girl tortured by an American.

Yet film is well made and, in a sense, free of hysteria, though unabashed propaganda. A young man of the Northern sector is disowned

by his family when he joins the Southern Vietnamese army as an officer. His sister's husband has been killed as well as her little son. When she shows force against soldiers who want to fire on peasants she is arrested. Torture is to find out where her henchmen are hidden.

She resists even after the American has her hands bound with gauze and sets them afire. Her brother decides to join her and kills the American and joins the Viet Cong. Thus the plot is didactic, one-sided. Against that, sombre acting is surprisingly well controlled by direction and technical values.

Mainly of curiosity value since it would be nearly impossible to exhib in U.S. except on certain anti-State Dept. campuses. *Mosk.*

La Muerte De Un Burocrata
(Death of a Bureaucrat)
(CUBAN)

Delightfully urbane Cuban spoof at its own bureaucrats. Big Latin-lingo appeal forecast.

Karlovy Vary, July 17.

ICAIC release and production. With Salvador Wood, Silvia Planas, Manuel Estanillo. Directed by Tomas Gutierrez Alea. Screenplay, Alfredo Gueto, Gaspar De Santelices, Alea; camera, Ramon Suarez; editor, Pedro Orta, M. Logoello. At Karlovy Vary Film Fest. Running Time, 85 MINS.
Nephew .... Salvador Wood
Widow .... Silvia Planas
Bureaucrat .... Manuel Estanillo

Film is a pleasant surprise from the Cuban industry. It is a black comedy that deals in the bruising wastes that overdone bureaucracy can create. Could refer to any nation's bureaucracy. Besides kidding its own insistence on slogans, murderous paper work and the loss of humanity in the process film keeps up a sharp comedic dash throughout would seem fine prospect for Latino lingo houses with its entertainment values and social underpinning.

A worker who has perfected a machine to turn out busts of notables is given a big scale funeral by the Communist party. But it turns out his widow can not get a pension unless she can produce her late husband's work card. But the man had been so happy to receive it that the widow has buried it with him. Pic concerns her nephew's attempts to get the right to exhume the body and get the card since there is no other way to secure her pension.

He runs into all sorts of rules and finally in desperation gets some men to exhume the body. He retrieves the card but gets trapped with the coffin when a night watchman intervenes. He gets it home on a cart and tries the bureaucratic rounds agin until he runs amok and strangles a bureaucrat blocking the reburial. This solves everything.

Pic renders homage in its titles and in several scenes to Laurel & Hardy, Harold Lloyd, Ingmar Bergman and others. Ideas from these filmmakers are worked into the pic and emerge homges not copying. A fight in the cemetery is hilarious as well as the hero

trapped on a ledge atop a building.

Film has the right comic balance and deals with a little man caught up in red tape that finally destroys him. The mayhem and macabre comic touches are also neatly done such as buzzards hovering around the house, the ice used for the cadavre with a pan underneath to catch the dripping water and many other bright visual gags. It twists slogans, personality cults and also the anti-American posters. It looks like the Cuban films are perking up and forsaking propaganda for forthright comedy and dramas.

Direction is inventive and editing helps keep the pace with players all showing a sharp sense of comedy. The film has plenty of yocks as well as making a statement as all good comedies do. *Mosk.*

Aasman Mahal
(INDIAN)
Karlovy Vary, July 15.

Nana Sansar release and production. With Prithviraj Kapoor, Surekha Parkar, Dileep Raj. Directed by Khwaja Ahmad Abbas. Screenplay, Inder Raj Anand; camera, Ram Chandra; editor, Mohan Rathod. At Karlovy Vary Film Fest. Running Time, 110 MINS.
Aasman .... Prithviraj Kapoor
Saleem .... Dileep Raj
Salmah .... Surekha Parkar

Indian pic is about the last days of a fading Indian nabob. He represents the old order that the government decrees must pass. Pic treats him with dignity but the generally overdone acting, except for Prithviraj Kapoor as the nabob, the surface characters and obvious plotting limit this pretty much to homeland.

Son of the nabob is a drunken playboy who finally is brought around to leading a serious life by a young girl of the masses. The nabob refuses to go out into the new world or leave his moldering palace and even turns down millions from syndicate that would turn it into a hotel. Kapoor gives his scenes a dignity that create ironic undertones but still make him a sympathetic character who still must pass as times change.

So all this is well meaning but kept on a naive level. It is lensed with good and sharp definition and has a plus in its on-the-spot shooting in an actual moldering castle of the raj days. *Mosk.*

Hideg Napok
(Cold Days)
(HUNGARIAN-SCOPE)
Karlovy Vary, July 15.

Hungarofilm release of Mafilm production. With Zoltan Latinovits, Ivan Darvas, Adam Szirtes, Tibor Szilagyi, Margit Bara, Eva Vas, Iren Psota. Written and directed by Andras Kovacs from the book by Tibor Csendes. Camera, Ferenc Szecsenyi. At Karlovy Vary Film Fest. Running Time, 95 MINS.
Buky .... Zoltan Latinovits
Tarpataki .... Ivan Darvas
Szabo .... Adam Szirtes
Pozdor .... Tibor Szilagyi
Mrs. Buky .... Margit Bara
Edit .... Eva Vas
Betty .... Iren Psota

Taut and sometimes overelaborated film deals with an atrocity committed by Hungarian troops during the last war in Yugoslavia. Through four men, later arrested as part of it all, it tells its tale via their discussions and self-searchings in a cell. Story takes time to get going but then turns into a searing look at man's propensity for inhumanity. Grim and disturbing film has some selective chances in west.

Hungarian officer stirs up his troops by creating fake tales of patriotic activity and finally stages roundup of suspected people, mainly on an anti-Semitic basis. Series of massacres follow, victims are walked out to holes in the Danube River ice, shot and thrown in.

The four men tell how they were embroiled and even if some tried to help or stop it they all somehow went along with orders. The men talk and the scenes are seen and then they begin to overlap. It builds and blocks out its scenes of the horror that can be unleashed by hiding behind orders and the chances this allows for latent sadistic and brutal instincts.

Zoltan Latinovits is especially effective as a bookish, decent officer who finds his wife embroiled in the roundups and unable to help her or in any way quell the rising tide of brutality till it is too late. The others are also good. It may sometimes be too literary but the device finally pays off in building the various incidents into a driving coherent look at how incidents can lead to mass brutality and inhuman acts.

Andras Kovacs has given this a firm directorial drive and it has the stark lensing and sharp editing to help fit the pieces together and finally make a shattering statement on an infamous historical fact. It is based on a true happening. _Mosk._

Si Lange Leben In Mirist
(As Long As I Live)
(EAST GERMAN)
Karlovy Vary, July 18.
DEFA release and production. With Horst Schulze, Ludmila Kosjanowe, Rita Krips, Else Sonden, Michail Uljanov. Directed by Horst Brandt. Screenplay, Michael Tschesno-Hell; camera, Gunter Reisch. At Karlovy Vary Film Fest. Running Time, 110 MINS.
Liebknecht .... Horst Schulze
Wife .... Ludmila Kosjanowe
Daughter .... Rita Krips
Bride .... Else Sonden
Frowlov .... Michail Uljanov

Straitlaced, old fashioned biopic about a renowned German Socialist, Karl Liebknecht, who opposed the First World War and the German militarists. Film is mainly posed and in tableau form, and one-sided. There is a "feel of the times" and of the man's uncompromising attitudes.

Solidly mounted and played, net is yet too stolid, more a tract than a full political theme. It even indicates how backward is East Germany among the "satellite" countries in cinematic terms.

Production dress is good.
Mosk.

Hamida
(TUNISIAN)
Karlovy Vary, July 15.
DEFA release of SATPEC production. With Amor Aouini, Francis Lefebvre, Jean Davy, Christine Laszar. Directed by Jean Michaud-Mailland. Screenplay, L. Bost, Kh. Abdelwahab; camera, Otto Hanish, Jean Chiabaud. At Karlovy Vary Film Fest. Running Time, 85 MINS.
Hamida .... Amor Aouini
Renaud .... Francis Lefebvre
Owner .... Jean Davy
Mother .... Christine Laszar

One of the first Tunisian films, pic was directed by a Frenchman. It deals with some French colonialists in 1950 and centres on a friendship of the grandson of the owner of an estate and a little Arab boy, Hamida. It is well meaning and does castigate colonialism and displays an awareness of coming independence. But it is executed rather conventionally and its figures remain stereotypes rather than full-bodies to carry the rage, depth and dramatic pitch. Mediterranean playoff possibilities loom large.

The boys are not precious or mannered and their relations have some good observation and notations. Then the actions of the headstrong landowner and the Arabs on his land are blocked out. The little Arab boy dies due to neglect and the French boy ends with some awareness of the injustice if he appears to be set to follow in his grandfather's footsteps if he is not made more aware of conditions as he matures.

Film is well shot and locations help. Adult characters are a bit overplayed and the major good points of the film rest with the child players and their friendship that transcends the problems of exploitation and bad living conditions. _Mosk._

YUL 871
(Montreal Flight 871)
(CANADIAN)
Karlovy Vary, July 12.
Canadian National Film Board release and production. Stars Charles Denner, Andree Lachapelle; features, Francine Landry, Paul Buissoneau. Written and directed by Jacques Godbout with dialog by Jacques Languirand. Camera, Georges Dufaux; editor, Victor Jobin. At Karlovy Vary Film Fest. Running Time, 72 MINS.
Jean .... Charles Denner
Marguerite .... Andree Lachapelle
Girl .... Francine Landry
Antonio .... Paul Buissoneau

French Canadian film is a slight tale of a Frenchman in on a two-day business trip to Montreal who brings with him memories of his childhood, due to some relatives living there, and also finds a love interlude. But measured pacing and an oblique approach, leaving many things unresolved, plus its length, make this a chancey item for export. Perhaps okay video film.

The Frenchman thinks back to the war and his losing his parents at intervals as he searches for his relatives. He meets a little girl to whom he can talk as well as a big one with whom he has an affair. He confesses love as his plane wings off. Influences of the French New Wave and Michelangelo Antonioni are sometimes evident if director Jacques Godbout manages to give this a smooth envelope.

But it is just too skimpy to give a deeper insight into the characters, and also intimates suddenly that the Frenchman doesn't really want to link with the past by his relatives. Perhaps intending a pacifistic air, it still remains unclear. Montreal is a good backdrop to this slight, mannered but sincere little film. It is technically good with acting okay though not allowed much leeway in the constant flashbacks, short scenes and walk-

ing and car riding that take up a good part of the film. Flashes of gentle good humor help. _Mosk._

Kym Sa Skonci Tato Noc
(Before This Night Is Over)
(CZECH)
Karlovy Vary, July 18.
Czech State Film release of Koliba production. With Jane Gyrova, Jitka Zelenohorska, Stanislav Danciak, Marian Labuda. Directed by Peter Solan. Screenplay, Tibor Vichta; camera, Vincent Rosinec; music, Milos Jurkovic, Jaroslav Laifer. At Karlovy Vary Film Fest. Running Time, 85 MINS.
Olga .... Jane Gyrova
Mira .... Jitka Zelenohorska
Milos .... Stanislav Danciak
Balza .... Marian Labuda
Holub .... Vladimir Durdik
Betty .... Valentian Thielova

Action takes place entirely in a night club and deals with the interactions of a group of characters somewhat in the "Grand Hotel" pattern. There are obvious political allusions and some deft close-quarter work, but it's all a bit "surface" and repetitive. Obscure to those not aware of the interference.

Slovak part of Czechoslovakia makes eight films annually to the 32 from the Czechs. This one seems to bear influences of the more outspoken Czech pix on contemporary life. But the round of incidents does not quite have the relief, insight and more revealing character underpinnings of comedy of the better Czech features.

Two young men pick up two girls they think are foreigners but they turn out to be local working girls who save money for months for a five-day fling at a good hotel and bars. Man is spending money like a rich man, though he looks like a worker, and it turns out he has spent the payroll of his men from a construction site. He wanted to know how it felt to have money. Other related incidents make up the pic.

Playing is easeful and makes the most of people seen only in one habitat and during a night of trying to find entertainment and some sort of fulfillment. It may mirror a certain unrest, a desire for freer movement and unresolved problems of supply and demand. Well mounted and done, film does not quite have the dash, clarity and ability to make these internal problems more "international" in significance. But it bodes more interesting attempts and happenings in the Slovak films as well.
Mosk.

Fugefalevel
(Fig Leaf)
(HUNGARIAN)
Karlovy Vary, July 13.
Hungarofilm release of Nafilm production. With Laszlo Sinko, Judit Halasz, Ferenc Bessenyei, Zsuzsa Gordon. Directed by Felix Mariassy. Screenplay, Judit Mariassy; camera, Barnabas Hegyi; music, Imre Vincze. At Karlovy Vary Film Fest. Running Time, 88 MINS.
Csiki .... Laszlo Sinko
Ancsa .... Judit Halasz
Pattantyus .... Ferenc Bessenyei
Olgi .... Zsuzsa Gordon
Ilonka .... Zsuzsa Banky
Aunt .... Manyi Kiss
Lukacs .... Attila Nagy

Satiric comedy pokes small town prudishness and lackey qualities among the smaller Communist Party members. There is

also a two-faced, opportunistic hero. But all this is done in a fairly gentle situation comedy manner and does not develop much bite to extend interest beyond Hungary itself.

A journalist in a small town draws notice of young when he is inadvertently heard blasting the dreariness and conventionality of the town when he can't get anyone to open a toilet for him at a station. He is overheard on an open loud speaker. However, he is really a career-minded young man who even writes an editorial against a new public statue of a friend since it is felt a chance remark by a party official on the nudity of the statue was against it.

He also falls for his editor's girl who sends off an article of his for the statue to a big city paper. He manages to wiggle out of everything and be appointed to the big town even if he loses the girl who can not abide his duplicity.

Pic is deftly played and directed with charm if it lacks a drive under its thin comedic veneer to give it a more potent look and force. It is just a fair parodic film and may have greater appeal on its home grounds. _Mosk._

Birds Do It
(COLOR)

Soupy Sales' feature debut. Comedy about American missile program. Lot of good laughs, though bogs down unnecessarily near the end. Should provide family fare.

Hollywood, July 22.

Columbia Pictures release of Ivan Tors production.. Features Soupy Sales, Tab Hunter, Arthur O'Connell, Edward Andrews, Doris Dowling, Beverly Adams. Directed by Andrew Marton. Screenplay, Arnie Kogen, Art Arthur, based on story by Leonard Kaufman; camera, (Pathe Color). Howard Winner; music, Samuel Matlovsky; editor, Irwin Dumbrille; asst. director, James Gordon MacLean.. Reviewed at Columbia, July 21, 1966. Running time, 88 MINS.

Melvin Byrd	Soupy Sales
Lt. Porter	Tab Hunter
Prof. Wald	Arthur O'Connell
Gen. Smithburn	Edward Andrews
Ccng'woman Clanger	Doris Dowling
Claudine Wald	Beverly Adams
Sgt. Skam	Louis Quinn
Yellowcab Driver	Frank Nastasi
Devlin	Burt Taylor
Arno	Courtney Brown
Clurg	Russell Saunders
Prof. Nep	Julian Voloshin
Doorman	Bob Bersell
Curtis	Warren Day
Willie	Jay Laskay
Radar Operator	Burt Leigh

Feature starts out as stylized satire, hums along with sight gags and one-line jokes, has a wild Soupy Sales flying sequence, then suddenly gets grounded. With proper handling as mild-mannered family entertainment, pic should do okay. Name will help boxoffice draw.

Premise of pic is inventive. Sales arrives at Cape Kennedy as highly secretive agent. It is revealed that he is new janitor or "miniscule molecular particle surveillance monitor," as he is officially called, who has been assigned to see that no dust gets into missiles, since it has been proven that it is dust which has plagued the missile program causing a $5,000,000 rocket project to misfire.

Armed with special cleaning equipment, Sales sets to work. Counteragents, headed by Tab Hunter, attempt to undermine his activities but Our Man from Mr. Clean outwits them. Plot moves into high gear when Sales is negatively ionized and, as a result, defies gravity and begins to fly. Scripters Arnie Kogen and Art Arthur go all out in providing interesting sight gags: he effortlessly ascends to a hotel rooftop sign, holds onto a plant, a motorcycle, a car wheel, in order not to levitate, and in one long sequence to fly on his own power over city buildings and the ocean.

This particular sequence is deftly handled with Sales sailing through air, somersaulting, walking on water, ascending, flapping arms with the greatest of ease. However, halfway through inventiveness runs out and pic resorts to a cut to a screening room where film writers discuss what they should attempt next. Insert destroys the spirit of the improbable antics which have preceded and momentum of plot from this point is disrupted.

Despite this, director Andrew Marton has cleverly manipulated the visual aspects and extracted entertaining comic bits from his actors. Arthur O'Connell turns in a fine performance as a kooky scientist. Edward Andrews as the general and Doris Dowling as a Congresswoman are also fun people to watch, although their characters are not quite to be believed.

Beverly Adams, as the rebellious daughter of O'Connell, deports herself agreeably, while Tab Hunter is serviceable in a secondary part. Judi, woman astronaut, played by a chimpanzee, has a mind of her own and steals a number of scenes.

Howard Winner's photography is fine and special effects by Howard Anderson Company are expertly executed. Music score by Samuel Matlovsky is offbeat and nicely offsets action. Stanley Colbert produced for Ivan Tors Productions.

Sales, in his first topline role, shows a fine filmic presence, sustains his low-key comedy well and in flying segments, comports himself with eagle expertise. Too bad script let him down. *Dool.*

Namu, The Killer Whale
(COLOR)

Semi-documentary about real-life Namu, the killer whale. Good biz seen in right situations.

Hollywood, July 25.

United Artists release of Ivan Tors presentation, produced-directed by Laslo Benedek. Stars Robert Lansing; features John Anderson, Lee Meriwether, Richard Erdman. Screenplay, Arthur Weiss; camera (DeLuxe Color), Lamar Boren; music, Samuel Matlovsky; editor, Warren Adams; asst. director, Jack R. Berne. Reviewed at Academy Award Theatre, July 22, '66. Running time, 88 MINS.

Hank Donner	Robert Lansing
Joe Clausen	John Anderson
Lisa Rand	Robin Mattson
Deke	Richard Erdman
Kate Rand	Lee Meriwether
Burt	Joe Higgins
Nick	Michael Shea
Carrie	Clara Tarte
Charlie	Edwin Rochelle

"Namu, the Killer Whale" is an absorbing semi-documentary with enough novelty to rate good reception in selected situations. Based on the actual whale of this name which hit the nation's headlines several weeks ago when it finally drowned while attempting to escape from its Seattle mooring and became entangled in a net, the Ivan Tors presentation should benefit by its true-life aspects. Tors and Laslo Benedek, who produced and directed, have worked up a diverting film from Arthur Weiss' screenplay which will appeal specially to moppet audiences as well as nature lovers.

While fictionized, the story of Namu, the 25-foot killer whale captured in a British Columbia cove and transferred to Seattle, where it became both a number-one attraction and a pet of the city's children, is predicated upon fact. Step-by-step developments of Namu's training by Robert Lansing in the DeLuxe color film precisely duplicate the training methods evolved by whale's owner Ted Griffin, who bought the giant mammal for his Seattle Public Aquarium.

Picture carries suspense as Lansing tests the killer reputation of the whale which he has trapped by a net strung across a cove, and human interest after he learns it belies its reputation and is friendly, willing even to allow him to ride on its back and eat salmon out of his hand. For plottage, there's conflict between Lansing, in role of a naturalist doing foundation research on grey whales of the Pacific, suddenly afforded opportunity to study a killer whale, and the nearby towns-people who make their living as fishermen and try to kill his prize.

Photography, both underwater and surface shooting, of Lamar Boren is of the highest order and contributes immeasurably to the high interest which accompanies film's unfoldment. Of particular interest, too, are the whale's sounds, sometimes resembling the plaintive mewing of a kitten and again having a soft whistling effect, caught by sound mixer Al Strasser. Samuel Matlovsky's music score is a further atmospheric asset, as is Warren Adams' sharp editing.

Lansing plays his role convincingly, which must have taken a bit of courage due to his close contact with an actual killer whale. Richard Erdman as his boat handler and John Anderson as a fisherman intent upon the whale's demise are key characters, and Lee Meriwether is a beautiful addition to cast as owner of a store. Robin Mattson as her young daughter is an unusually pretty child. *Whit.*

The Idol
(BRITISH)

Mom's affair with son's friend may attract femme trade. Best suited to special situations.

Hollywood, July 27.

Embassy Pictures release of Leonard Lightstone production. Stars Jennifer Jones, Michael Parks; features John Leyton, Jennifer Hilary, Guy Doleman. Directed by Daniel Petrie. Screenplay, Millard Lampell; based on story by Ugo Liberatore; camera, Ken Higgins; music, John Dankworth; editor, Jack Slade; asst. director, Bryan Coates. Reviewed in projection room July 26, '66. Running time, 109 MINS.

Carol	Jennifer Jones
Marco	Michael Parks
Timothy	John Leyton
Sarah	Jennifer Hilary
Martin Livesey	Guy Doleman
Rosalind	Natasha Pyne
2d Woman at party	Caroline Blakiston
Lewis	Jeremy Bulloch
Barmaid	Fanny Carby
Man at party	Vernon Dobtcheff
Boy	Michael Gordon
Simon	Gordon Gostelow
Policeman	Ken Haward
Woman at party	Renee Houston
Rosie	Priscilla Morgan
Mrs. Muller	Edna Morris
Tommy	Peter Porteous
Laborer	Terry Richards
Laborer	Derek Ware
Police Inspector	Jack Watson
Landlady	Rita Webb
Dorothea	Tina Williams

Certain elements of plot, in which a matron surrenders to her son's best friend, may give this Embassy release a boost for femme interest but primarily it's suited for selective art house route. The Leonard Lightstone production is burdened with frequent static in its development of characters and a rambling narrative further reduces dramatic impact. On the plus side, however, is the name of Jennifer Jones for marquee dressing; also, there is sexploitation potential and of particular interest the London locations where black-and-white pic was lensed.

Millard Lampell's screenplay, based on Ugo Liberatore's original story, focuses on an irresponsible American art student in London, a disbeliever in everything except himself and his own talents. He has become friendly with a young man studying to be a doctor, completely under his mother's domination, and an English girl, also an art student. They form a romantic triangle, and later the mother, who at first takes a dislike to the brash young American, finds herself attracted to him. Yarn carries a tragic ending as aftermath of a fight between the two men, after the son learns his mother has gone to bed with his friend.

Lightstone has given impressive physical backing to his production, capturing the feeling of London, which Ken Higgins limns in his sensitive photography, but characters lack much interest. Daniel Petrie's direction registers as well as script will allow and cast performs satisfactorily.

Michael Parks as the art student impresses as an actor able to maintain a characterization. Miss Jones tries hard with an unsympathetic role but there is little to alleviate its dullness. John Leyton, as her son, is seen in varying moods, none too clear to audience, and Jennifer Hilary lends interest as the femme who lives with Parks. Guy Doleman appears briefly as Miss Jones' fiance, waiting for her to get her divorce. *Whit.*

Intimi Osvetlani
(Intimate Lighting)
(CZECH)

Prague, July 26.

Czech State Film production and release. With Vera Kresadlova, Zdenek Bezusek, Karel Blazek, Jaroslava Stedra, Jan Vostrcil. Directed by Ivan Passer. Screenplay, Vaclav Sasek, Jaroslav Papousek; camera, Josef Strecha, Miroslav Ondricek; music, Oldrich Korte. Previewed in Prague. Running Time, 70 MINS.

Stepha	Vera Kresadlova
Petr	Zdenek Bezusek
Bambas	Karel Blazek
Marie	Jaroslava Stedra
Grandfather	Jan Vostrcil
Grandmother	Vlastimila Vlkova
Druggist	Karel Uhlik

Another unusual Czech directorial talent is unveiled in this first film. It deals with a little incident that is probed for deeper revelations of human character and yet maintains a comic balance on human comportment. Smart handling here of a non-pro cast, which emerges larger than life. Pic is a diverting and extremely entertaining one, with foreign specialized and arty chances there. But this calls for a hard sell.

A classical musician and his modern girlfriend, much younger than himself, go to visit a school chum of his since he has a solo concert date in his village. Film takes place during this visit. It lightly deals with simple people but still have simmering tensions.

The friend, if content generally, feels a loss because of things he and the soloist and his girl have little spats.

A dinner at which the choice cuts are passed about turns into almost a slapstick affair. The two old friends get drunk together. It's all well fashioned and paced by Ivan Passer's deceptively simple direction.

No need here for flashy cutting, frozen shots and space continuity. It is a return to a well worked-out yet seemingly spontaneous situation comedy. The characters are allowed to grow and reveal themselves in little scenes that are never gratuitous. The clear camerawork, brisk editing and successful serio-comic relationships shed light on these ordinary people.

It is the comic observance without self-indulgence, the guileless playing and the directorial wit and comic drollery, that give this gentle comedy its risible effects. Its very simplicity calls for careful handling abroad for best results. *Mosk.*

Dama Na Kolejich
(Lady of the Rails)
(CZECH)
(Songs-Dances)

Prague, July 26.
Czech State Film production and release. With Jirina Bohdalova, Radoslav Brzobohaty. Directed by Ladislav Rychman. Screenplay, Vratislav Blazek; camera (Corwo Color), Josef Hanus; music, Jiri Bazant, Jiri Malasek, Vlastimil Hala. Previewed in Prague. Running Time, **80 MINS.**
Marie .... Jirina Bohdalova
Vaclav .... Radoslav Brzobohaty
Bedrich .... Frantisek Peterka
Katerina .... Libuse Geprtova
Marek .... Stanislav Fisar

Besides making dents with personal and outspoken pix, the Czechs also have been making neat commercial pix. This musical has a pleasant script, simple dances and songs. And it is done with taste and sparkle. Production dress is modest, with the ideas and charm the main ingredients. It appears a possible playoff item abroad, with dubbing indicated.

A woman tram driver sees her husband kissing a blonde. After a weeping spell, she draws out her savings and makes herself over into a woman of the world. A boxer comes into her life when she slaps him for hitting her husband. The husband trains to fight for her and when he is knocked out, she still raises her hand in victory because she loves him. This was a momentary dream or a comedic interpretation of what is to come because it ends as the pic began with her seeing him with the blonde.

Dance numbers spring from situation and are functional if not too inspired. Music is useful but not memorable. Jirina Bohdalova has spirit and a good comedic sense while others are more than passable. Color is only fair. This proves to be an amiable tale of a woman rebelling against male infidelity. It also has some nice parodic shafts at conformism. In all, a nice use of the tuner format. *Mosk.*

Souhvezdi Panny
(Constellation Virgo)
(CZECH)

Prague, July 26.
Czech State Film production and release. With Josef Cap, Jana Obermayerova.. Vladimir Pucholt, Jiri Wimmer. Directed by Zbynek Brynych. Screenplay, Milan Unde, Brynych; camera, Jan Kalis; music, Jiri Sternwald. Previewed in Prague. Running Time, **80 MINS.**
Standa .... Josef Cap
Jana .... Jana Obermayerova
Veleba .... Vladimir Pucholt
Rejman .... Jiri Wimmer
Augustin .... Jay Libicek

Director Zbynek Brnynch, who made his mark a few years before the new, exciting crop of Czech filmmakers, seems to want to use these new approaches but this does not quite jell. His dealing with young soldiers and a girl lacks the freshness and the inventive ease and insight into comportment that have made these new pix so charming. This tries too hard and does not come off.

A young soldier is waiting for his girl to visit him. They have not seen each other for sometime. But an alert keeps all the men on the base so some friends, with some officer connivance, smuggle in the girl. The girl takes offense when she finds herself locked in the infirmary and her boyfriend seeming only to want some lovemaking rather than to renew their fragile relationship.

There are complications when some men get drunk and try to get into the girl's room. But this is overdirected and does not allow the characters to unfold. Pic is so busy with effects that it loses its humor which would have made this entertaining rather than confused, as the film is now. There is a candid love scene but otherwise this looks difficult for foreign markets except possibly as an exploitation pic. *Mosk.*

Objectif 500 Millions
(Objective 500 Million)
(FRENCH)

Paris, July 26.
Imperia release of Rome Paris Films-Georges De Beauregard production. Features Bruno Cremer, Marisa Mell, Jean-Claude Rolland. Written and directed by Pierre Schoendoerffer. Camera, Alain Levent; editor, Armand Psenny. Previewed in Paris. Running Time, **92 MINS.**
Yo .... Marisa Mell
Reichau .... Bruno Cremer
Pierre .... Jean-Claude Rolland
Douard .... Etienne Bierry

Primarily about an unusual holdup in midair, this meller also works in lotsa underlying French political motivations and gambits that may be lost abroad. It may raise some interest on its home grounds but overseas prospects appear modest.

An army captain jailed for taking part in the uprising against France during the Algerian War gets out of prison. He is bitter and gets mixed up with a sexy cover girl. She has decided to hijack a plane that carries a $1,000,-000 pay load to Bordeaux from Paris every month.

Also in on the caper is a man who had fingered the captain to the French authorities and who also picked him out for the affair due to his commando talents. The captain at first desists but then goes along. He stows away the plane, then is supposed to parachute out with the money after

planting a bomb to remove the evidence.

Pic gets far-fetched when he spares blowing up the plane and jumps with a false sack. He ends up killing the man who turned him in and being shot down by the police.

But in trying to show a pro and almost fascist officer in a good light, the film also gets a bit mixed up in its psychology and romantic attachment to this bloodthirsty man. Perhaps he might have been able to readjust to life, as his men have done. However, it's implied that his betrayal has embittered him too much and he is good for nothing but fighting.

On the whole, "Objectif 500 Millions" is ambiguous and smacks of an uneasy reactionary outlook. Pic is mounted with style but characters remain somewhat surface and stereotyped. Marisa Mell is an almost risible femme fatale and Bruno Cremmer manages to acquit himself okay in the role of the older soldier gone wrong. *Mosk.*

Tanin No Kao
(The Face of Another)
(JAPAN)

Tokyo, July 26.
Toho release of Tokyo-Eiga Teshigahara production. With Tatsuya Nakadai, Machiko Kyo, Kyoko Kishida, Eiji Okada, Mikijiro Hira and Miki Irie. Directed by Hiroshi Teshigahara. Story and script by Kobo Abe. Camera, Hiroshi Segawa; music, Toro Takemitsu. Reviewed, Tokyo, July 10, '66. Running Time, 124 **MINS.**

This is the long-awaited new film by makers of "Woman in the Dunes"—same scripter, cameraman, composer; same two stars (Kyoko Kishida and Eiji Okada, though this time in minor roles) and same director.

Based on the latest novel by Kobo Abe (to appear in September via Knopf in E. Dale Saunders' translation), it is about a man whose face has been destroyed in a chemical explosion. Alienated, alone, repulsed by his wife (Machiko Kyo of "Rashomon" and "Gate of Hell" fame), and his associate (Eiji Okada of "Hiroshima Mon Amour" renown), he goes to a psychiatrist and plastic-surgeon (stage-actor Mikijiro Hira) who, with his nurse (Kyoko Kishida) constructs a mask that fools almost everyone.

Almost—the man successfully picks up his own wife but after their sordid little daytime affair discovers that she somehow knew all along. This is disturbing. He has been rejoicing in his new self and here is someone who remembers the old self. He wants to kill her but does not. Instead, and ironically, he kills the doctor (the only other who knows the "old" self) just after the treatment is completed and the doctor has "made a new man" out of him and has told him that "now you are perfectly free."

Like "Woman in the Dunes," both film and novel are existential allegory. By assuming a mask, the man (any man) becomes that mask which he has assumed, i.e. a man becomes whoever he chooses to become. The choice is mandatory but the choice of mask is arbitrary. There is no such thing as "self" and when this is realized "dreaful freedom" is fully appre-

hended. All of this is brilliantly delineated in the novel.

Not, however, in this often irritating, sometimes confusing, but at least consistently disturbing film. Abe's screenplay is loose and makes continual reference to the novel which most viewers will not have read. Further, Teshigahara, always a self-indulgent director, has apparently arbitrarily included scenes (those involving the wife (?) of the doctor in particular) which obtrude and irritate with their modish meaninglessness.

An example of this compounded is the treatment of the sub-story. In the novel the hero sees a film about a scarred girl from Nagasaki and is impressed by it. In the movie this seen-film is shown as a part of the "story" and the 'story' and the only indication is that its first scene is shown in small wide-screen size (though the Teshigahara film is otherwise standard). We follow her, baffled, as she does charity work, eventually gets her brother to make love with her, and then kills herself. Abe's novel-hero is much moved by this story; Abe's screen-hero is, naturally, not even aware of it. And we can only make the loosest connection between these two "faceless" folk.

As though to compensate for this, Teshigahara has made his production very slick. There is top lensing, art direction, and acting; the doctor's clinic is the current ultimate of chic, and the music-track is the electronic mishmash so modish at present. But the film is far too slick for its subject. Much better was the grubby little laboratory in the Abe novel where alone (there was no surgeon in the original) the hero feverishly worked, creating the mask he became.

This disconcerting combination of the arbitrary and the elegant does not make for empathy and, further, the "moral" is not (as in "Woman in the Dunes") dramatized. In addition, Tatsuya Makadai as the hero is his usual wooden self. The film is static and ice-cold, and it is just this combination which creates an interest which might be described as morbid; we are not in the least moved by these people but their actions —like those of certain insects— are occasionally fascinating. And this is, perhaps, all that the creators intended.

They have attended a powerful and personal statement and they have created quite successfully a philosophical mystery story. The film is scheduled for both the Venice and New York festivals this year. *Chie.*

Meandre
(Meanders)
(RUMANIAN)

Bucharest, July 26.
Rumania Films release of Bucaresti production. With Margareta Pogunat, Mihai Paladercu, Ana Szeles, Dan Nutu. Directed by Mircea Saucan. Screenplay, Horia Lovinercu; camera, Gheorghe Virel Todan; music, Tiberiu Olah. Previewed in Bucharest. Running Time, **90 MINS.**
Mother .... Margareta Pogonat
Architect .... Mihai Paladercu
Boy .... Dan Nutu
Girl .... Ana Szeles
Father .... Ernest Maftier

In this feature Michelangelo Antonioni, Alain Resnais and other western talents are all badly imitated. R e s u l t: pretension. Where clarity and concern are needed, obfuscation and obscurantism. Precious and overdone with mainly local chances in store and foreign bookings improbable.

Maker has obviously seen Antonioni's brooding tales of personal alienation, Resnais's literary attempts to deal with memory and the whole panoply of the French frozen shots, use of negative, held camera etc. But all this is trotted out to overstress a simple tale of adultery and a young man's vacillation as to what he will make of himself in life.

A woman carries on with a friend of her husband. Latter is an architect who feels he has botched his life and pic is mainly about his leavetaking of the woman and her adolescent son who has grown attached to him.

So there are long walks, repeated scenes, arbitrary bits of technique like a spinning bed during a love scene, and fairly aimless dialog that tries to be deep but ends up mannered. Actors appear hampered by this forced technical chopping up of a story that would have meant something if treated more literally, with more characterization and more of a tie with the country today rather than trying to foist Western techniques that are only affected on their home grounds and on their own problems.

Yet this self-conscious pic is interesting in foreshadowing more grasping and assimilation of techniques and opens Rumanian films. *Mosk.*

Ukamau
(And So It Is)
(BOLIVIAN)
Locarno, July 26.

Sanjines production and release with Nestor Cardenas Peredo, Benedicta Mendoza Huanca, Vicente Verneros Salinas. Directed and edited by Jorge Sanjines. Screenplay, Oscar Soria; camera, Hugo Roncal; music, Alberto Villapando. At Locarno Film Fest. Running time, 70 MINS.
Rosendo .... Nestor Cardenas Peredo
Andres ..... Vicente Verneros Salinas
Sabina ... Benedicta Mendoza Huanca

A first film from this small Latino country is familiar in treating the Indians, and deals with rape and revenge. But it has a firm feel for character and place and also denotes a director with filmic knowhow in Jorge Sanjines. It has tact and dramatic rightness, plus its ethnic aspects for Latino circuits with special chances also there if well handled and placed.

An Indian goes to sell his produce in town while a half-caste, who always buys his output, comes and finds the Indian's wife alone. At first he is angry but the wife says the market pays better. Then he becomes infatuated with the woman and makes advances leading to a fight in which the woman is killed.

The husband comes back and the wife gives the name of the culprit before dying. He does not seek revenge at once but waits. Finally, after the killer becomes rich, the Indian hunts him down and kills him in a fierce fight.

The customs are well mapped out and the rugged life and unusual characters of the Indians are also made clear and forceful to build this into a film with some dramatic punch. The acting is rigorous and acceptable and the technical credits are good. It is a simple tale, well told, with a wealth of colorful detail in the life and ways of these Bolivian Indians. *Mosk.*

Kdo Chce Zabot Jessii?
(Who Killed Jessie?)
(CZECH)
Prague, July 26.

Czech State Film production and release. With Jiri Sovak, Dana Medricka, Olga Schoberova, Karel Effa, Juraj Visny. Written and directed by Milos Macourek, Vaclav Vorlicek. Camera, Jan Nemecek; music, Savatopluk Havelka. Previewed in Prague. Running Time, 80 MINS.
Professor .... Jiri Sovak
Wife .... Dana Medricka
Jessie .... Olga Schoberova
Gunman .... Karl Effa
Superman .... Juraj Visny

Mixture of pop art ideas and sci-fi comes out an entertaining and amusing pic that also has some underlying more serious theme, making it worthwhile on playoff abroad. This lacks the production dress for some first-runs and is a bit too unassuming for arty houses. But the gimmicks are so well brought off that it would also be worthwhile for remake rights.

A middleaged couple, both scientists, have conceived a way of reading one's thoughts via a drug and headphones that turn the dreams or thoughts into images on a tele screen. But it is found that when this is done, it also makes the dreams real. So when the man dreams of some comic strip heroes, and his wife tunes in to see who it is he is dreaming of, they are around the next morning.

One is a beauteous girl, sparsely dressed, and the other a superman type, after her for the secret of magnetic gloves. It all ends with the superman and his sidekick and his wife infiltrated into a dog's mind.

Brainwashing gambits can be read into it, but it is mainly a clever comedy that needed color and more production dress to have made an unusual comedy contender in international marts. As is it has the right good looking people and simple but well done gags and special effects to make it entertaining if not unique enough for top chances offshore. *Mosk.*

Kino Kawa
(The River Kino)
(JAPAN-SHOCHIKUSCOPE)
Tokyo, July 26.

Shochiku release of Masao Shirai production. With Yoko Tsukasa, Shima Iwashita, Takahiro Tamura, Tetsuro Tamba, Sadaki Shamura, Chieko Higashion novel by Sawako Ariyoshi; yama. Directed by Noboru Nakamura. Screenplay, Eijiro Kuzaka, based on novel by Sawako Ariyoshi; camera, Toichi Narishima; music, Toru Takemitsu. Reviewed in Tokyo, June 12, '66. Running Time, 173 MINS.

This handsomely produced, extremely long chronicle-film stretches from 1900 to 1965 and covers the span from the heroine's marriage through her death. Based on a popular novel, it originally had great success as a

video serial and perhaps that and not the theatrical screen is the best vehicle for it. The problem is that, though the film is nearly three hours long (with a built-in intermission, five minutes of music on blank film) there is still not enough time to tell all. As a consequence viewers are rushed from marriages to funerals and are asked to feel the appropriate emotions—and cannot.

If you do not have the luxury of 52 installments (and here Lady Murasaki stole the march on tv in her "Genji Monogatari") then you do what a director like the late Yasujiro Ozu did. You restrict and let little stand for all and you make certain that your viewers feel deeply. This is the only way to keep the shoals of soap-opera and it is here that Nakamura (often excellent director) founders again and again. The picture becomes a bore and this seems to imply that life is a bore, and if that were so why make a chronicle-film at all?

Japanese have long (since the 10th century) been fond of the form. It is tre equivalent of the French 'roman a fleuve.' Whether the West finds the form entrancing is another matter. In the hands of an Ozu or a Naruse — yes. Anything less is apt to tire. Not that this Nakamura film does not have virtues. The camerawork is magnificent, the score (by the composer for "Kwaidan," "Harakiri," "Woman of the Dunes") is excellent, and the performances are never less than very good. The opening, for example, a bridal procession on boats in the river, is really lovely—just the sort of thing that the Japanese and only the J a p a n e s e can do—both mysterious and atmospheric; one **wants to like and understand this fragile bride.**

Then plot takes over and it remains in control up to the very quiet, flowing, fading end where it somewhat relinquishes its grip. This is not, then, the kind of picture that one can easily cut, plot ends would dangle. The only way to properly shorten the picture would be to take out the inessentials but these, as is so often the case with Japanese pictures, are precisely those places (the beginning, the end) that are the best. As it stands this handsome, expensive, and on the whole impressive film is in the West only a Japanese film-buff or a Nisei audience bet. And that's too bad. *Chie.*

Sedmikrasky
(The Daisies)
(CZECH-COLOR)
Prague, July 26.

Czech State Film production and release. With Jitka Cerhova, Ivana Karbandova. Directed by Vera Chytilova. Screenplay, Ester Krumbachova, Chytilova; camera (Eastmancolor-Or Wo Color), Jaroslav Kucera; music, Jiri Sust, Jiri Slitr; editor, Miroslav Hajek. Previewed in Prague. Running Time, 75 MINS.
Mary I .... Jitka Cerhova
Mary II .... Ivana Karbandova

Two zany young teenage girls are the focus of this extremely funny, witty and expertly-fashioned film. Through a series of scenes, the statement is made about the two fringe characters

who are anarchic, but never destructive, always inventive, sometimes despairing, but never desperate. They always are shown in a filmic manner that seems to sum up the various kinds of visual perceptiveness throughout film history. Here is no story but a series of sketches that have these two girls in various adventures.

The two gals seem to live on men, do not work and have no ties with society except as being an emanation from it. No pitch about their being drones or rebels, but in dealing with them director Vera Chytilova has them engaging but futile, completely free and therefore rebels or misfits who can never seem to fit into life.

Miss Chytilova displays a rare filmic background in this, her second feature pic, as she harks back to early silent comedies and displays a remarkable control of filmic language, special effects and rhythm and sight gags. This keeps this enticing and gay throughout with its jabs at inflexible society. Film is keenly national but international in spirit and treatment.

The episodes unfold with fantasy and charm. The two girls are introduced sitting on a beach and seem to be like puppets and manipulated like them. They are then seen at home in a mad pop art atmosphere of cutouts on walls, flower arrangements on their beds and strange eating habits. This is interlarded with their meetings with different types of men who are usually from out-of-town and whom they befuddle, amaze, belittle but enchant before they put them on trains back to their home towns.

They break up a night club act. They discourse on love and its lack of meaning. One even seems to try suicide and the other comes in, turns off the gas. They end up in a big hall where an enormous banquet is all set with nobody there. They turn it into a foray of smashing everything, having a pie fight and ending up swinging on an immense chandelier. It leaves them at the end back where they were originally. This emerges as a cannily brilliant foray into slapstick comedy that still has depth.

The two free-living madcaps never become annoying or silly because of the engaging treatment and playing. Color is subtle, pleasing and is mixed with sepia, tint and inventive special effects that help the mood and atmosphere.

This is cruel, compassionate but always full of taste and invention to mark Miss Chytilova the most talented among the crop of unusual new filmmakers in Czechoslavakia. The girls are beguiling and comely. Others are somewhat silly in the pic and the men impossibly self-indulgent.

This pic could partake of international appeal if rightly handled, placed and labeled abroad. It is technically impeccable with smooth editing and inventive filmically throughout. It will probably rep Czechs at the coming

Faust XX
(RUMANIAN-SCOPE)

Bucharest, July 26.

Rumania Film release of Bucaresti production. With Emil Botta, Iurie Darie, Jorl Voicu, Stella Popescu. Written and directed by Ion Popescu-Gopo. Camera, Grigore Ionescu, Stefan Horvath; music, Stefan Niculescu. Previewed in Bucharest. Running Time, 85 MINS.

Professor	Emil Botta
Wagner	Iurie Darie
Physician	Jorj Voicu
Emma	Stella Popescu
Margarete	Eva Krzyzewska
Father	Ion Ian-Covescu
Inspector	Nicolae Secareanu

Ion Popescu Gopo is the leading Rumanian maker of animated films but also makes feature pix. His first two, "Bomb Has Been Stolen" and "The White Moor," were fairly inventive fables and now he gets more ambitious in a comedy version of the Faust legend updated to today. But here he misses the needed inventive trickery to make it technically dazzling enough to forget the fairly primary and synthetic theorizing and philosophizing, or witty enough to make it a good comedy.

Pic should beguile on its home grounds. Possible playoff abroad roots in some fairly risible scenes or perhaps could be tv fodder. But it lacks the dash, depth and aplomb for art chances in Western countries. Popescu-Gopo has Faust an old professor and the Devil only an emissary who has evolved a way of putting the mind, which may also be the soul, into another body. The old body dies.

The change is made to the boyfriend of the professor and there are a lot of police mixups, a supposed nitery that is a gateway to Hell with a singer saying there is one more place and ending the song in suicide. But the effects are telegraphed, the message too obvious and the playing too diffuse to make for the charm, inventiveness and brightness that these type pix need. It is saved by a certain artless innocence but it sometimes falls into archness and self-indulgence. Popescu-Gopo appears better suited to the animated medium where this story might have appeared better. Players are hard put to do anything with their synthetic symbolical roles if lensing is bright and production dress good. *Mosk.*

Bloudeni
(Wandering)
(CZECH)

Prague, July 26.

Czech State Film production and release. With Jiri Pleskot, Jirna Jiraskova, Jaromir Hanslik, Jana Brejchova. Directed by Jan Curik, Antonin Masa. Screenplay, Masa; camera, Jan Curik, Ivan Slapeta; music, Jan Klusak. Previewed in Prague. Running Time, 80 MINS.

Father	Jiri Pleskot
Mother	Jirna Jiraskova
Michal	Jaromir Hanslik
Eva	Jana Brejchova

Film is a series of vignettes that deal with the relations between the two generations. Strokes are subtle and talk is important if the visuals also are expertly blended to underline the emotions, tensions and relationships. Thus, this is a pic that needs very careful

handling abroad and is only for arty houses or special situations. It may be worth it on its subtlety and filmic expertise.

A young boy feels lost with his father who seems well off though he has lost an important position. He runs off one day and film recounts various incidents and people he meets as well as dealing with the father who carries on little affairs and finally ends up being tied to a tree by some Czech beatnik types when he tries to seduce one of their girls.

The boy finds some rapport with various people and finally comes back if the relations do not seem any closer. There may be some references to Czech party aspects that may be obscure, but on a human plane and in its human relations it is clear, vital and universal. It again shows that ordinary human problems are recognizable everywhere and the clear treatment of their own contemporary world is making Czech pix viable for world marts.

The ease in acting, the fluid direction that keeps its rambling tale coherent and always pointed to build the characters and theme of adjustment, belie the fact that this pic is the work of two young directors. Another unusual Czech entry of the many. *Mosk.*

Love and Marriage
(ITALIAN)

Artful import deals with various aspects of infidelity. Diverting and with above-farce values.

Embassy Pictures release of Ermanno Donati and Luigi Carpentieri production. Features Sylva Koscina, Eleonora Rossi Drago, Ingeborg Schoener, Lando Buzzanca, Maria Grazia Buccella, Philippe Leroy, A'do Giuffre, Renato Tagliani. Directed by Gianni Puccini and Mino Guerrini. Screenplay by Bruno Baratti, Oreste Biancoli, Eliana De Sabata, Jaja Fiastri, Mino Guerrini, Gianni Puccini and Ennio De Conciini; camera, Gastone Di Giovanni, Maurizio Scanzani and Luigi Filippo Carlo; Music, Marcello Giombiini; editiors, Bruna Malaguti, Mario Forges and Davanzati; asst. director, Ruggero Deodato. Reviewed at Lincoln Art Theatre, N. Y. Running time, 106 MINS.

THE FIRST NIGHT

Concetto	Lando Buzzanca
Enea	Maria Grazia Buccella
Roro	Umberto D'Orsi
Lady on yacht	Luciana Angelillo
Baron	Gianni Del Balzo
Hotel clerk	Amedeo Girard

ONE MOMENT IS ENOUGH

Marina	Ingeborg Schoener
Giancarlo	Renato Tagliani
Parman	Sandro Moretti
Young man in cinema	Steve Forsyth
Andrea	Enzo Corra
Fisherman	Marino Mase
Don Eugenio	Armando Tarallo
Amelia	Flora Volpe

THE LAST CARD

Elsa	Eleonora Rossi Drago
Antonio	Aldo Giuffre
Gladys	April Hennessy
Ann	June Weaver
Linda	Ethel Levin
Manicurist	Gioia Durell
First man	Carlo Loffredo
Second man	Bruno Scipioni

SATURDAY, JULY 18

Diana	Sylva Koscina
Mario	Philippe Leroy

The four episodes of "Love and Marriage" are all about married couples in various stages of past, present and future infidelity, and apart from this the film is tied together by a tone of what might be called cheerful perversity. Each episode has the frame of what once was called the folk tale and nowadays has become the locker-room joke, and each has its moments of high humor. But there are fleeting glimpses of pathos or tragedy that bring the film as a whole above the level of the usual sex farce.

Best of the lot is the first episode, which brings a pair of charming, attractive Sicilian rubes to Naples for their honeymoon, and confronts them with temptation in the form of the local dolce vita. Director Gianni Puccini asks his actors to play very broadly indeed, and they come through handsomely, managing to be both hilarious and touching. A splendid future is predicted for Maria Gracia Buccella, who is not only a very deft actress but a luscious beauty in the style of (and with all the physical endowments of) Gina Lollobrigida. Lando Buzzanca, as the groom, is also more than okay.

Next best, again because of Puccini's ability to be outrageous without being unreal, is the final brief vignette, which spotlights Sylva Koscina as a wife on vacation in Capri and Philippe Leroy as the husband who's been looking forward with considerable relish to renewing his conjugal delights. It all leads up to a whammo, though not unexpected punch line, but the fun is in the waiting.

The first of two episodes

directed by Mino Guerrini has Ingeborg Schoener and Renato Taglioni as a couple engaged in a perverse little game whereby hubby follows his wife everywhere, even to the ladies' room, and she "invents" little tales about how she's managed to betray him in any case. Parallel with Puccini's first episode, which transforms itself from a sweet farce to a frightening little parable, this starts out as a gag and winds up almost a tragedy, except for an overextended and perhaps unnecessary gimmick at the end.

Weakest of the four has Aldo Giuffre as a retired soccer star whose wife cooks up a way for him to make money in retirement: rent himself out for the night to rich American ladies. That our hero can't go through with it provides some comic moments, but the happy ending doesn't quite come off.

Altogether, however, a charming little picture that should entertain audiences, providing lack of top stars and action gimmicks can drag them to the theatres initially. *Gold.*

Daleks Invade Earth 2150 A.D.
(BRITISH)
(Color)

Safe boxoffice magnet for juve audiences, though the plot seems a shade complicated for moppets.

London, Aug. 2.

British Lion release through BLC of an Aaru (Milton Subotsky, Max J. Rosenberg) production. Directed by Gordon Flemyng. Stars Peter Cushing, Bernard Gribbins, Ray Brooks, Jill Curzon, Roberta Tovey, Andrew Keir; features Geoffrey Quigley, Geoffrey Cheshire, Kenneth Watson. Screenplay, Subotsky, from BBC-TV serial by Terry Nation. Camera (Technicolor) John Wilcox; editor, Ann Chegwidden; music, Bill McGuffie. Reviewed at Studio One, London. Running Time, 84 MINS.

Dr. Who	Peter Cushing
Tom Campbell	Bernard Gribbins
David	Ray Brooks
Wyler	Andrew Keir
Susan	Roberta Tovey
Louise	Jill Curzon
Wells	Roger Avon
Conway	Keith Marsh

The Daleks films, offshoots of a pop BBC-TV series, have caught on with the youngsters, and current one should register strongly at boxoffice with them, though the plot and technical details may be a little too advanced for the main core of Daleks' followers. However, Ted Samuels has pulled off a lively job with the special effects and the Daleks themselves, mechanical monsters with voices rather like that of Andy Devine, are formidable heavies.

Dr. Who, in his time and space machine, arrives in London in 2150 A.D. to find it ravaged after a Dalek invasion. The earth's cities have been razed by meteorites and cosmic rays and human beings have been turned into living dead men called Robomen. Prisoners have been taken and forced to work in a secret mine as slaves. Objective of the Daleks, subsequently revealed, is to blast a metallic core out of the earth and the use the planet as a giant flying saucer. There's a small knot of resistance fighters holded out in London, determined to fight the Daleks. Dr. Who and his party join up with the resistance movement. After sundry narrow squeaks, Dr. Who's scientific knowledge enables them to outwit the invaders.

It is all fairly naive stuff decked out with impressive scientific jargon. Peter Cushing, as the professor; Jill Curzon, as his niece, and Roberta Tovey, as the granddaughter, have learned to play it with the necessary seriousness. Bernard Cribbins as the policeman provides some amusing light relief. Godfrey Quigley, Andrew Keir, Kenneth Watson and hSeila Steafel chip in with useful supporting performances.

But it is the clever way in which the cone-like Daleks are moved and juggled that gives the film its main kick. It's well-lensed in Technicolor by John Wilcox. Bill McGuffie's score is occasionally over heavy on the ear, but other credits, such as auditing by Ann Chegwidden, artwork and sound are efficient. *Rich.*

Fuzuzatsu No Kare
(A Complicated Man)
(JAPAN—COLOR—DAIEISCOPE)

Tokyo, Aug. 2.
Daiei release of Kiyoshi production. With Jiro Tamiya, Mariko Ko, Shuji Sano, Edith Hansen. Directed by Koji Shima. Screenplay, Kimiyuki Hasegawa from Yukio Mishima story. Reviewed, Tokyo, June 18, '66. Running Time, 90 MINS.

That this programmer is based on a Yukio Mishima story will generate an amount of interest. It will also be dissipated upon viewing this romantic girl's-mag-type vehicle about the heroine's love for a mysterious young man who turns out to be tattooed (polite indication of having once been a gang-member) culminating in unintentionally hilarious "Scarlet Letter" genre scene where he exposed his shame for all to see.

Either famous author Mishima nodded or else scripter Hasegawa and old-time director Shima did more than usual hack-work. Production values low with location work in Frisco and Rio clumsily attached to patent Japan-studio interiors, particularly noticable being a "Rio" night-club interior which is obviously the Daiei studio.

Color is good and Edith Hansen is as always excellent in her small role as the hero's foreign mistress. All in all, however, this picture will have a hard time holding its own even on the U.S. sukiyaki-circuit. *Chie.*

A Place Called Glory
(Spanish-German)
(WESTERN-TECHNISCOPE-COLOR)

Spanish-made oater manages some interesting characters, action and suspense. Has proved a moneymaker in European market.

Hollywood, Aug. 6.
Embassy Picture release of Midega Film-CCC Film coproduction. Produced by Bruce Balaban and Danilo Sabatini. Features Lex Barker, Pierre Brice, Marianne Koch. Directed by Ralph Gideon. Screenplay, Edward Di Lorenzo, Jerold Hayden Boyd, Fernando Lamas, from original story by Boyd; music, Angel Arteaga; camera (Pathe), Federico G. Larraya; art director, Enrique Alarco; asst.

director, Enrique Bergier; editor, Roberto Cinquini; sound, Renato Cadueri. Reviewed at Joe Shore's Screening Room, July 25, 1966. Running time, 92 MINS.
Brenner .... Lex Barker
Reece .... Pierre Brice
Jade Grande .... Marianne Koch
Seth Grande .... Jorge Rigaud
Jack Vallone .... Gerard Tichy
Homesteaders leader ... Angel Del Pozo
Mayor, Glory City .... Santiago Ontanon
Judge, Glory City .... Hans Nielsen

The ancient Roman gladiator story about two slaves who become friends and then are brought to face each other in mortal combat is given an Old West setting in this Spanish-German oater filmed in Barcelona. International cast: Lex Barker, American; Pierre Brice, Frenchman, and Marianne Koch, German, have appeared in European-made Westerns before and give creditable performances as three who oppose each other and become involved in a romantic trio. Pic has action, excitement and suspense and should receive good play in suburban and rural areas.

Story goes round the bush in unfolding, starting out with an impending gunfight-to-the-death, an annual event sponsored by Glory City officials. Barker and Brice meet on the plains, are first suspicious of one another, meet up again in Powder City and together assist each other to rid the town of evil hombres.

Miss Koch, the former girlfriend of Barker, has taken up with the saloon keeper, which makes Barker unhappy and at the same time Brice takes a fancy to her.

Main drawback to story is that the audience knows from the beginning that the two men will face each other in deadly combat but they remain ignorant of the encounter until they are face-to-face on the street. Outcome is in traditional bloody style with both Spartan heroes winning out.

Barker handles acting chores well, with a sinister smile that seems appropriate. Brice, as a cool cowboy from New Orleans, at first seems oddly cast. He has a heavy French accent, is darkly handsome, looking more like a Le Drugstore cowboy, but he soon proves rugged with his fists, as well as grimly disposed to life. It's an offbeat characterization and fascinating to watch. Miss Koch has a difficult role, pretending to be one thing when actually she's got a heart of gold. Rest of cast is okay.

Ralph Gideon has directed with an eye to getting at the individuality of his actors and also adds bright, inventive bits. Pathe color photog by Federico G. Larraya and film editing by Roberto Cinquini mesh well, while the music of Angel Arteaga gives the arid atmosphere of the pic a helpful boost. It's apparent that Spanish Western set was limited but art director Enrique Alarco does nicely with interiors. *Dool.*

Hakuchi No Torima
(Daytime Assailant)
(JAPAN)

Tokyo, Aug. 2.
Produced by Seizosha. Distributed by Shochiku. Producer, Masayuki Nakajima. Features Kei Sato, Sanae Kawaguchi, Akiko Koyama, Rokuhiro Tcura. Directed by Nagisa Oshima. Screenplay, Samu Tamura from the Taijun Takeda novel; camera, Yasuhiro Yoshioka; music, Hi-

kari Hayashi. Reviewed July 15, '66. Running Time, 100 MINS.

Director Nagisa Oshima came riding in on the Japanese "nouvelle-vague," with a sexy subject arted-up, fast-cutting, long-distance lens, stopped frames, etc.) several years ago, with pictures such as "The Sun's Burial" and "The Trap" (the latter shown at a few film festivals). He is again on a crest—at least he got Staid Shochiku to invest in this thoroughly (often irritatingly) arty little number which is, by Japanese standards, very way out indeed.

It is about a group of people who live on a farm (again the Tokyo intellectual's love-hate delineation of simple farm folk) and they get their sex life all mixed up. Eventually, one of them hangs himself along with the principal girl. She is cut down, however, and enjoyed while unconscious by the truculent laborer who has so far made up a fourth.

This confirms one of his bad habits: he likes to have sex with unconscious girls. Naturally, he goes too far, and is soon murdering left and right. The two women decide to save him, then to turn him in, the only motivation for their action being the favorite myth of the Japanese male: women just love being mistreated. Society and decency triumphs. They turn him in but to make amends (though why is not suggested) they go off to the woods to kill themselves and one succeeds.

This is the story, but the treatment is resolutely artistic from first to last. The camerawork is carefully over-exposed and usually (in the manner of "Cleo" white on white; the music is twelve-tone and electronic; the acting—particularly that of Kei Sato as the laborer (he was the man in "Onibaba") is studied Stanislavsky truculence, and Oshima cuts it all up, and then mixes it all together. The idea—splintered chronology—was apparently to emulate "Marienbad." Most of the time, however, it merely looks like "Tobacco Road" with the reels mixed up.

Not all the time, however, for Oshima loves film and he had made some very exciting sequences, particularly a night-time walk for the two girls which uses the jump-cut in a particularly sustained and forceful way. Of course, in this particular scene, the cutting happens to suit the subject. Most of the time it doesn't though it is quite refreshing to see a film which is really creatively edited.

Still, a picture is, after all, no better than its story and this feeble fable about the denigration of women is just too silly to bear all artistic icing piled so lavishly on top. Still—it will probably be widely seen. There are the festivals on one hand and the sexpits on the other and this is one film that seems to have successfully straddled both stools. *Chie.*

The Boy Across the Street
(ISRAELI)

Tel Aviv, Aug. 2.
Margot Klausner release of I.M.P.S.-Karnet Films Ltd. (Israel) production. Produced by Leo Filler, Avraham Roth. Stars Arie Elias, Shaul Shalhin. Direct-

ed by Joseph Shalhin. Screenplay, Shalhin and Edna Shavit, from Shalhin's story; camera, Marco Ya'acobi; editor, Jako Ehrlich; music, Mel Keller. Reviewed at Ben Yehuda Cinema, Tel Aviv, June 30, '66. Running time, 85 MINS.
David's father .... Arie Elias
David .... Shaul Shalhin
Tamar ....Hanna Shalhin
Tamar's mother .... Aviva Orgad
Tamar's father .... Baruch David
School nurse .... Betty Segal
Probation officer .... Amos Mokadi
Grocer .... Ya'cov Banai
and the pupils of Yavnieli School, Rehovot.

The oft-told drama of juvenile delinquency is main theme of this semi-pro film, conceived and directed by writer-director Joseph Shalhin, who has previously done only two privately-produced 16m films, about similar subjects (and shown mainly in schools and private clubs)—kids in trouble and the relations between healthy and crippled kids.

Yet Shalhin, using his own two children to play the leads and assisted by the professional know-how of I.M.P.S. (Israel Motion Picture Studios) at Hertzliya, has succeeded in projecting a sincere quality onto the screen. Together with Leo Filler's supervision and advice, the film works up to a really moving climax without losing its naive, direct appeal or quasi-documentary nature.

David, a boy of 12, lives with his drunkard father after his mother has deserted their humble dwelling in the immigrants' quarters of a small town. An invalid girl in his class is his only friend, except for a devoted dog. The boy tries unsuccessfully to resist the easy money offered him by his juvenile delinquent contemporaries, who ask him to be watchman during a "raid" on the local drugstore. The rest is obvious, including his running away, hiding, the search and happy ending when son and father make their peace and it is suggested that better understanding should bring the boy over to the safe side of the community.

Acting of Arie Elias as the father is touching and the two children (Shaul and Hanna Shalhin) give moving performances. Their beautiful eyes and handsome features make up for some clumsiness of direction and camera movement and helps convince the audience of the authenticity of the situation and the genuine feelings of the children. The background, a dilapidated newcomers' suburb in a small Israeli town, adds to the charm of this neo-realistic pic, which should have some appeal for special audiences abroad.

First favorable reactions from a showing at the Venice Children's Film Festival, just ended, point to such possibilities. *Rapo.*

O Slavnosti A Hostech
(Report On the Party and Guests)
(CZECH)

Prague, Aug. 2.
Czech State Film production and release. With Ivan Vyskocil, Jan Klusak, Jiri Nemec, Zdenka Skvorecka. Directed by Jan Nemec. Screenplay, Ester Krumbachova, Namec; camera, Jaromir Sofr; editor, Miroslav Hajek. Previewed in Prague. Running Time, 70 MINS.
Host .... Ivan Vyskocil
Rudolph .... Jan Klusak
Joseph .... Jiri Nemec
Eva .... Zdenka Skvorecka
Frantisek .... Pavel Bosek
Martha .... Helena Pejskova

Carl .... Karel Mares
Wife .... Jana Pracharova
Husband .... Evald Schorm

The fact that this film is still technically forbidden for export and local showing sheds some light on the paradoxes of the burgeoning film situation here. It also indicates, perhaps, why there are so many outspoken and unusual films allowed to be made. It is an offbeater that deals with morals, ethics and human responsibility but on a visual plane rather than realistically. So it appears mainly for special situations and arty spots abroad, needing careful labelling and placement. But it perhaps is worth it on the film's tour-de-force treatment.

It is usually felt that expression fares best during change. And in the last three years, the Czech authorities have eased up on film content. Reasons given for this are the need to have more unusual films for home consumption and in the foreign market.

This one, though banned, as noted, is allowed to be screened for foreign buyers and others. So it appears the pic has been nixed only for a while.

And since it is more a parable on human behavior than realistic, it also seems to predict that social realism is now completely out and ideas are allowed to be presented more abstractly if they may be contested. What is it all about? It concerns a strange garden party at which a practical joke by the host's adopted son brings on a flock of complications in which conformism is explored.

A group of men and women cavort at a picnic and talk mostly about selfish things. They eat, wash in a stream and then go off to a big outdoor dinner. But they are accosted on the way by a man and a group of strangers who herd them into a clearing and begin giving them orders. They obey meekly out of fear, habit or just plain absence of thought. Pic gives an inkling of what unawareness and unquestioning of actions can lead to, and inferences to fascism or other totalitarianisms can be inferred.

One man tries to object and is roughed up till the host appears. Then it seems it all has been a practical joke. Then they all go and sit down at a big outdoor table to eat. But one of the men, who has disapproved of the joke as dangerous, has disappeared. After a while the guests are goaded into rushing off to look for him because the non-conformist has to be brought to bay for the others to be at ease.

Using non-actors, director Jan Nemec deftly sets up a group of characters who become acceptable universal symbols of people but he does not try to fill in backgrounds or place. It is left up to the audience to do this and infer its meaning. But the hynotically clever notations, unfoldment and knowing parody, with deeper undertones, keep this engrossing.

It is technically expert, but its length, refusal to compromise and offbeat theme means arty use is the best for this unique pic.
Mosk.

The Man Called Flintstone
(CARTOON COMEDY-COLOR)

Video's "Flintstones" made into a widescreen feature has a pleasant, cleancut sense of humor and half a dozen delightful songs.

Hollywood, Aug. 6.
Columbia release of Hanna-Barbera Production, produced and directed by Joseph Barbera and William Hanna. With voices of Alan Reed, Mel Blanc, Jean Vander Pyl, Gerry Johnson, Don Messick, Janet Waldo, Paul Frees, Harvey Korman, John Stephenson, June Foray. Screenplay, Harvey Bullock, Ray Allen, with additional story material by Barbera, Hanna. Warren Foster, Alex Lovy; camera (Eastman Color), Charles Flekal, Roy Wade, Gene Borghi, Bill Kotler, Norman Stainback, Dick Blundell, Frank Parrish, Hal Shiffman, John Pratt; music, Marty Paich, Ted Nichols; editors, Milton Krear, Pat Foley, Larry Cowan, Dave Horton; art director, Bill Perez; animation director, Charles A. Nichols; sound, Richard Olson, Bill Getty; production supervisor, Howard Hanson. Reviewed at Academy Awards Theatre, July 9, 1966. Running time, 90 MINS.

Television's cartoon series, "The Flintstones," currently in its sixth season on ABC-TV, has been made with loving care into a full-blown, Eastman color, feature film that should please the small fry. Pic has a number of sophisticated touches, including a half dozen pleasant songs, which should appeal to adults as well. Technical credits are excellent and the visual stone-age scenery and machinery are mildly amusing and sometimes highly inventive.

Plot is pegged on secret agent gambit: Fred Flintstone becomes innocently involved in espionage and sets off to Paris with wife, Wilma, and neighbors, Barney and Betty Rubble, to encounter archenemy, The Green Goose. Flintstone, unaware that he is being mistaken for secret agent. Rock Slag, is pursued by S.M.I.S.H. agents while he attempts to contact double agent, Tanya.

Producers Joseph Barbera and William Hanna, scripters Harvey Bullock and Ray Allen carefully keep the action moving forward and cleverly spoof many of the fictional secret agent cliches. Basis of humor is to show prehistoric life in contemporary terms and although this can be fun—as in an airline sequence where fourth-class passengers are billeted on wings—but at other times wears thin, as with a stone Eiffel Tower and block stone fountains.

However, there are some lively musical numbers by John McCarthy and Doug Goodwin, and in these instances there is also a change of animation pace. Most successful of these is a nicely executed song, "When I'm Grown Up," which employs drawings in the manner of children's art. Sequence is entirely charming. Other pleasant tunes are "Team Mates," "Spy Type Guy," "The Happy Sound Taree" and "Tickle Toddle." Louis Prima also sings song "Pensate Amore."

Alan Reed, as the voice of Flintstone, and Mel Blanc (Barney Rubble) are uniquely suited to the cartoon characters, and a consistent style is also given by Jean Vander Pyl, Gerry Johnson, Don Messick, Janet Waldo, Paul Frees, Harvey Korman, John Stephenson and June Foray.

As a curious sidelight, there are no animals prominently involved in this pic, either talking, dancing, or otherwise, although they are used as beasts of burden for transportation, and somehow it seems a loss. No doubt the younger generation won't be aware of this absence.
Dool.

Kazdy Mlady Muz
(All the Young Men)
(CZECHOSLOVAKIAN)

Prague, July 26.
Czech State Film production and release. Pavel Landovsky, Ivan Vyskocil, Hana Ruzickova. Directed and written by Pavel Juracek. Camera, Ivan Slapeta; music, Karel Svoboda, Zaromir Vonacka; editor, Jose Dozzichovsky. Previewed in Prague. Running Time, 85 MINS.
Sergeant .... Pavel Landovsky
Private .... Ivan Vyskocil
Girl .... Hana Ruzickova

Fragmentary pic deals with general army conscript life. If a series of episodes, this has bright and witty inventiveness throughout which keeps it always perky. Its fine acting vignettes and clever parody and insights could give this good legs for foreign arties or even playoff since it seems draftees are about the same everywhere.

First, two soldiers come to a little town on a pass and spend a rather dreary time which only allows them to get to know one another. Laconic visual methods are used to block out their characters. Then there is a look at maneuvers and the usual army goldbricking and youthful patter.

Its alert satiric digs at army life, the wealth of character details in its short scenes and the mixture of visual and verbal gags have this a fresh and winning comedy. However, its skimpy story line and familiar though still risible tales of army life call for personal handling for best results. But it should be well worth it.
Mosk.

Waco
(WIDESCREEN-COLOR)

Low-budget oater, pic will have to depend on familiar names of actors, as well as a couple of sexy sequences. Otherwise its a run of the trendmill western.

Hollywood, Aug. 5.
Paramount release of A. C. Lyles Production. Stars Howard Keel, Jane Russell, Brian Donlevy, Wendell Corey and Terry Moore; features rest of cast, Directed by R. G. Springsteen. Screenplay by Steve Fisher, based on novel by Harry Sanford and Max Lamb; music, Jimmy Haskell; camera (Technicolor), Robert Pittack; art direction, Hal Pereira and Al Roelofs; asst. director, James Rosenberger, editor, Bernard Matis. Reviewed at Paramount Studio, Aug. 1, 1966. Running time: 111 MINS.
Waco ....Howard Keel
Jill Stone .... Jane Russell
Ace Ross .... Brian Donlevy
Preacher Sam Stone.....Wendell Corey
Dolly .... Terry Moore
Joe Gore .... John Smith
George Gates .... John Agar
Dep. Sheriff O'Neill ...... Gene Evans
Sheriff Billy Kelly ....Richard Arlen
Scotty Moore .... Ben Cooper
Patricia West .... Tracy Olsen
Bill Rile .... DeForest Kelley
Ma Jenner .... Anne Seymour
Mayor Ned West .... Robert Lowery
Pete Jenner .... Willard Parker
Kallen .... Jeff Richards
Ike Jenner .... Reg Parton
Telegraph operator.........Fuzzy Knight

The Old West has been spruced up in the sex department in this A. C. Lyles production. There's a rape scene and another sequence where three men are made to strip naked. Camera discreetly pans away from these sequences and they are done in good taste, but this "new hard look" at the Wild West may seem questionable fare for the entire family. However, pic does have a strong moralistic tone at the end and with list of well-known personalities should do fairly nice biz as a second bill.

Low budgeted pic has first rate technical production value but actors and script never seem to be on same footing. Except for action sequences pic just doesn't move in any particular direction and outcome is easily seen from the beginning.

Waco, an ex-con, played by Howard Keel, comes back to town and is made sheriff to clean up rowdy element. Ex-girlfriend, Jane Russell, has married minister Wendell Corey and gone straight. She, of course, gets ahankering for Keel all over again and he in the meantime has gotten religion. At one point it looks like he's going to go bad again, which upsets a lot of people, but he sticks by his good guns and cleans the town out in fine style. Near the fade-out Minister Corey conveniently gets killed off in attempt to stop gunbattle in the streets.

Story has occasional nice touches but style of acting is set by ex-singer Keel, who looks like but doesn't have the James Arness appeal. Dialogue by scripter Steve Fisher is pretty basic and actors Jane Russell, Brian Donlevy, Terry Moore, John Smith and John Agar didn't seem very happy with it.

Technicolor camerawork by Robert Pittack is okay, depending mostly on longshots and Hal Pereira and Al Roelof's art direction is unobtrusive. Editor Bernard Matis in a couple of instances reuses footage but for the most part does a serviceable job. R. G. Springsteen's direction attempts to get as much action out of situations as is possible and crowd scenes are handled well. Song "Waco" by Jimmie Haskell and Hal Blair, and sung over titles by Lorne Green, is fine.

It appears pic would have been more entertainment value if our hero went bad afterall. As it stands his character doesn't really have much dimension and results in the feeling of just plain bad acting.
Dool.

Locarno Fest

Tiempo De Morir
(Time to Die)
(MEXICAN)

Locarno, Aug. 2.
Alemeda Films and Cesar Santos Galindo production and release. With Marga Lopez, Jorge Martinez De Hoyos, Enrique Rocha, Alfredo Leal. Directed by Arturo Ripstein. Screenplay, Gabriel Garcia Marquez, Carlos Fuentes; camera, Alex Phillips; editor, Carlos Savage. At Locarno Film Fest. Running time, 90 MINS.
Juan ....Jorge Martinez De Hoyos
Mariana .... Marga Lopez

Pedro .... Enrique Rocha
Julian .... Alfredo Leal

Tale of vengeance is set in a classic oater mold as a man returns to his hometown after 18 years in prison for killing a man in a gunfight. Wanting to take up his life he finds himself faced by the avenging sons of the man he killed. Solidly made, this looks okay for Latin circuits, with its sagebrush form also slanting it for playoff. Lack of dimension makes any art chances abroad rather slim.

The man had killed his adversary fairly but the tale had been twisted by townspeople. He tries not to get involved with the two young men and then gets frightened.

Film is directed with firmness if lacking sufficient dramatic punch. It is well played but the tendency to go in for symbolism. This leads to portentousness. It is technically sound and does show a director, Arturo Ripstein, with a visual knowhow for a first film. *Mosk.*

Pingwin
(Penguin)
(POLISH)

Locarno, Aug. 2.
Polski State Film release of Kamera production. With Andrzej Kozak, Krystyna Konarska, Zbigniew Cybulski. Written and directed by Jerzy Stefan Stawinski. Camera, Stefan Matylaszkiewicz; editor, Miroslawa Garlicka, Irene Wron-Jasinska. At Locarno Film Fest. Running time, 85 MINS.
Pingwin .... Andrzej Kozak
Barbara .... Krystyna Konarska
Lucas .... Zbigniew Cybulski

Tale of a timid, lonely young man who faces up to corruption around him and takes a beating to protect the name of a girl he secretly desires, appears a bit skimpy for a feature pic. Tenuous theme may mean more on its home grounds. However, its ordinary direction and familiar tale makes this a chancey foreign item.

Called Penguin by others, the hero finds the girl he likes held up to public ridicule by a shady man she once loved who makes public her love letters. He gets them back and also foils a kidnap plot of the ex-lover and takes a severe beating before the girl begins to notice him.

The dealing with young delinquents and the abyss between generations may have repercussions on its home grounds, but it seems a bit skimpy for the foreign market. This is well played but direction is too static. Film emerges anecdotic rather than having a good dramatic flow. *Mosk.*

Ai No Kawaki
(Desire For Love)
(JAPANESE)

Locarno, Aug. 2.
Nikkatsu production and release. With Nobuo Nakamura, Ruriko Asaoka, Akira Yamouchi, Ikuko Kusunoki, Yoko Orono. Directed by Izen Kurahara. Screenplay, Yukio Mishima, Shigeo Fujita, Kurahara; camera, Yoshio Mamiya; editor, K. Chiba. At Locarno Film Fest. Running time, 98 MINS.
Etsuko .... Ruriko Asaoka
Yakichi .... Nobuo Nakamura
Saburo .... Tetsuo Ishitachi
Asako .... Yoko Orono
Kensuke .... Akira Yamouchi
Miyo .... Chitose Ko

Film has a clinical erotic depth in its look at a frustrated woman who turns her needs into the desire to suffer and have others do so with her. But it has a tendency to overdo atmosphere and twist characters a bit too much.

Apparently this pic means to take a blast at certain class pettiness. It is a sleekly-made tale that might have exploitation values abroad but the film's almost dogmatic theme makes it a more difficult bet for arties.

A woman whose husband has betrayed her and stifled her needs moves in with her old rich father-in-law. He takes her as a concubine but it is an affair without desire. She gets a fixation on a teenage gardener and, though it appears that she wants him as a lover, it finally develops she desired someone to share her suffering.

Pic cannily creates a sensual feeling in her reactions to the boy at work or killing chickens and breaking up his affair with a servant he has impregnated. When he finally tries to take her, she rebels and kills him with a hoe.

This tries to say more psychologically but gets caught up in too much expert atmospheric lensing, flashy direction and forcing the actions instead of letting it develop more freely.

There's no denying its powerful insights and its sexual brashness. But it may seem like an exercise in style rather than a more discerning study of sexual needs and a look at class differences in Japan today. Its sex scenes are not many and these are done with taste. But the richer development is not there even if it does have a knowing technical, thesping and directorial polish. *Mosk.*

Tero Nodim Parey
(Beyond Thirteen Rivers)
(INDIAN)

Locarno, Aug. 2
Ramdhana Films production and release. With Ganash Mukherjee, Priyam Hararaka, Narayan Chandra Mondal. Directed by Barin Saha. Screenplay, Nirmal Ghose, Saha from a story by Ghose; camera, Barin Saha; music, Gyan Prokash Grose. At Locarno Film Fest. Running time, 80 MINS.
Khamta .... Ganash Mukherjee
Ustad .... Priyam Hararaka
Moinak .... Nanda Adhikari
Director...... Narayan Chandra Mondal

This gentle Bengali pic deals with a scaled-down version of the old versus the new via a look at a small travelling circus. A clown holds out against dancing girls coming into his circus, though it is what people seem to want. It seems skimpy at first, but then settles down into a probing look at circus life. But its exotic aspect, simple and slow pacing make this a dubious arty house bet abroad.

It again shows that the Bengali films have more flair for characters and filmic tempo than is usually seen from India, with probably some influence from the noted Bengali filmmaker Satyajit Ray.

The clown becomes morose when a dancing girl is brought in. After a drunken accident it is she who nurses him and something appears to grow between them. It's the nicely done scenes of circus life and the girl's relationships that tag director Barin Saha someone to be watched.

Pic is well played but still a bit too special for demanding Yank arty chances. *Mosk.*

Yotsuya Kwaidan
(Illusion of Blood)
(JAPANESE-COLOR-TOHOSCOPE)

Locarno, July 29.
Toho release and production. With Tatsuya Nakadai, Junko Ikeuchi, Mariko Okada, Mayumi Ozora, Keiko Awaji. Directed by Shiro Toyoda. Screenplay, Toshio Yasumi, Namboku Tsuruya; camera (Eastmancolor), Hiroshi Murai; music, Toru Takemitsu. At Locarno Film Fest. Runing time, 107 MINS.
Iemon .... Tatsuya Nakadai
Oiwa .... Junko Ikeuchi
Samon .... Kanzaburo Nakamura
Oume .... Mariko Okada
Kohei .... Masao Mishima

Ghost story appears influenced by last year's Cannes prizewinning "Kwaidan." This one does not have the human insight and observation of the late Kenji Mizoguchi's "Ugetsu" nor the classical rigor of "Kwaidan." But it does have style and good acting, excellent color and avoids violence and horror for its own sake. Impresses as having some playoff chances in western markets.

It takes place during a past era that lacked any moral backbone. A jobless samurai feels he has been deposed by the aimless times and vows he will find another master and stoops to anything to achieve it. It leads to him killing his father-in-law, who knows he stole money from his last master, and doing away with his wife and others standing in his way to an advantageous marriage that will mean new status.

But his disfigured wife begins to haunt him and finally to drive him mad. There is plenty of flashing and slashing samurai sword carnage. *Mosk.*

Devojka
(The Girl)
(YUGOSLAVIAN)

Locarno, July 28.
Avala Film release and production. With Milena Dravic, Ljubisa Samardzic, Rade Markovic. Written and directed by Purisa Djordjevic. Camera, Branko Perak; editor, Vanja Bjenjas. At Locarno Film Fest. Running time, 80 MINS.
Girl .... Milena Dravic
Resistant .... Ljubisa Samardzic
SS Man .... Rade Markovic

Partisan activity in World War II still obsesses Yugoslav filmmakers. But the resistants are now treated more in depth and not just as cardboard, unsullied, politically right (because left) heroes. Here the plot tells of various reminiscences and characters. Process gets a bit tied up in technique. But reserved acting, and a concern with basic human characters helps. However dubious for export.

A girl falls for a resistant and he saves her from Germans when she is caught behind the lines wandering about after her family has been killed. They both get to the resistants and die together. There is a side look at an SS Man who seems to be the destiny symbol of the couple. *Mosk.*

Chevssurskaja Ballada
(Chevssur Ballad)
(RUSSIAN-SCOPE)

Locarno, July 27.
Sovexport release of Gruzia Film production. With S. Chiaureli, T. Archvadze, K. Deushvili. Directed by S. Managadze. Screenplay, G. Mdivani; camera, G. Chelidze; music, R. Legidze. At Locarno Film Fest. Running time, 80 MINS.
Mzekale .... S. Chiaureli
Imeda .... T. Archvadze
Mgelia .... K. Deushvili
Aluda .... D. Abashidze
Torgvai .... L. Pilpazni
Aparaeki .... I. Kapiyanidze

Russia's sending out features made in remote USSR republics, not just the Moscow and Leningrad studios. Present Georgian pic deals with a mountain people, the Chevssur, and spins a fairly conventional tale of love and folkways enriched by fine scenery, robust acting and a nice feel for past mores.

There is a perceptive, gentle pacing and stopping for songs, folkloric interludes and even delving into the methods of courting plus the central driving themes of the pic, love and vendetta. Forthrightness is lacking, and plot appears telegraphed. Still there is charm and mood.

A man who left this mountain country as a child in 1916 comes back to see his relatives as a man. The First World War and even the Soviet Revolution have hardly changed the place. He finds himself staying on and enamored of a girl who is desired by a local man. When he does not act the man forces him to fight and the former kills him. Then he flees with the girl to escape the dead man's family. She is killed by mistake and he stays on. *Mosk.*

The Pad
(And How To Use It)
(COLOR)

Excellent acting and good dialog make film version of Peter Shaffer's one-acter a firstrate vehicle for introducing new screen talent. Meaningless title no asset, however.

Universal release of Ross Hunter production. Features Brian Bedford, Julie Sommars, James Farentino, Edy Williams. Directed by Brian G. Hutton. Screenplay, Thomas C. Ryan, Ben Starr, based on Peter Shaffer's play, "The Private Ear." Camera (Technicolor), Ellsworth Fredricks; editor, Milton Carruth; music, Russ Garcia; music supervision, Joseph Gershenson; song "The Pad (And How To Use It)," words and music, Robert Allen, sung by The Knickerbockers; asst. director, Phil Bowles. Reviewed at Cinema II Theatre, N.Y., Aug. 11, '66. Running Time, 86 MINS.

Bob	Brian Bedford
Doreen	Julie Sommars
Ted	James Farentino
Lavinia	Edy Williams
Beatnik	Nick Navarro
Fat Woman on Bus	Pearl Shear
Waitress	Barbara London
Girl on Phone	Barbara Reid
Larry	Roger Bacon
Ralph	Don Conreaux

"The Private Ear," which made up one half of the Peter Shaffer play. "The Private Ear and The Public Eye," was a short but observant look at loneliness and the aborted effort of one shy male to communicate with the opposite sex. Ross Hunter's screen adaptation, thanks almost entirely to Shaffer's original dialog and the recreation by Brian Bedford of the shy young man he played in the New York production, recaptures much of the humor, compassion and wisdom of the legit production.

While the setting has been switched from an English flat to a Los Angeles rooming house, there, is, basically, little difference between the storyline of the play and the film. Necessary expansion shows scenes only referred to in the play and adds a few extraneous characters. With most of the credit going to Bedford, whose marvelously acted portrayal is the heart of the film, there is also first rate playing by Julie Sommars as the gauche girl he covets and James Farentino as the Lothario friend who wrecks the timid type's plans. Edy Williams is deliciously decorative as a "bird."

There's little for director Brian G. Hutton to do, however, but to call the cues and stay out of the way as what is good about the film was already in the play.

Indeed, the few awkward moments in the film are those added by scripters Thomas C. Ryan and Benn Starr, such as the banal dialog given a fat woman on a bus and an awkward scene at the Greek Theatre which quickly uses up the humor of the scene and could be edited considerably. While there is no attempt to explain Bedford's British accent, it is not obtrusive enough to lesson his characterization which grows continually throughout the film.

The ending has not been tampered with, fortunately, and is a gem of poignancy and identification with loneliness felt by everyone in the audience at one time or another. There are plenty of laughs in "The Pad" but never at the expense of the obvious outcome. One worries more, perhaps, that Bedford will be stuck with such an undeserving maiden, than whether she'll get away.

Although the locale and types of characters prevents Hunter from adding his usual brand of "souped-up glamour" to the setting, he has spared no expense in creating a believable and authentic atmosphere. There are shots made in L.A.'s "Whisky A Go Go," the Greek Theatre and other film capital spots which help scenically.

Ellsworth Fredricks' camera mutes its Technicolor tones in keeping with the middle-class setting, with only a couple of process shots showing Bedford and Farentino at work in a factory dispelling the illusion of realism. There's really no reason for having switched the setting to the U.S. and, quite possibly, something may have been lost. But it still winds up as an exceptionally well-acted film that should stimulate discussion among serious-minded filmgoers. Certainly, the title won't help, with its weak attempt to emulate "The Knack," a wrong move which is carried over into the farce-suggested advertising. Despite what might be considered similar themes, they're completely dicerent in treatment, and would not necessarily attract the same audiences. *Robe.*

The Sandwich Man
(BRITISH-COLOR)

Spotty pic with useful marquee value for local houses. But gags and situations do not add up to satisfactory comedy.

London, Aug. 9.

Rank release of Titan International (Peter Newbrook) production. Features Michael Bentine, Dora Bryan, Harry H. Corbett, Bernard Cribbins, Diana Dors, Ian Hendry, Stanley Holloway, Wilfrid Hyde White, Michael Medwin, Ron Moody, Anna Quayle, Terry-Thomas, Norman Wisdom, Donald Wolfit. Directed by Robert Hartford - Davis. Original story and screenplay, Bentine and Hartford-Davis; camera (Eastmancolor), by Peter Newbrook; editor, Peter Taylor; music, Mike Vickers. Reviewed at R.F.D. Private Theatre, Aug. 2, '66. Running Time, 95 MINS.

Horace Quilby	Michael Bentine
Mrs. De Vere	Dora Bryan
Stage-Doorkeeper	Harry H. Corbett
Photographer	Bernard Cribbins
Billingsgate Woman	Dina Dors
Motorcycle Cop	Ian Hendry
Park Gardener	Stanley Holloway
Rowing Coach	Ron Moody
2nd Billingsgate Woman	Anna Quayle
Scoutmaster	Terry-Thomas
Lord Uffingham	Wilfrid Hyde White
Father O'Malley	Norman Wisdom
Car Showroom Mgr.	Donald Wolfit
Steven	David Buck
Sue	Suzy Kendall
Girl in Plastic Mac	Tracey Crisp
Billingsgate Porter	Sydney Tafler
Chef	Max Bacon
Yachtsman	Alfie Bass
Drunk	Ronnie Stevens
Sir Arthur Moleskin	Fred Emney
Escapologist	Peter Jones

This is the second pic to be co-financed by the Rank Organization and the National Film Finance Corp. Tne combo will have to set its sights on to more nourishing fare if the scheme is to click. A big cast of star and feature names (though they are mostly in for bits) should attract curiosity and patronage at U.K. houses, but Overseas prospects seem glum. Main inspiration behind the film is Michael Bentine, whose zany sense of humor has worked well in his tele "Square World" series.

But he has tried an extended form of the technique in this film, and it doesn't jell. There are a couple of loosely running links but overall the film is merely a string of gag situations and occasional brisk quips.

Bentine, who wrote the screenplay with the director, Robert Hartford-Davis, seeks to give a picture of London and some of the wayout, curious behavior of its inhabitants through the eyes of a sandwich-board man who, wandering the streets, has a load of opportunity of observing, and of getting implicated. Not a bad idea and filmed on location entirely, it gives the director and cameraman Peter Newbrook a swell chance of bringing London to life. But in the countdown, a film has either got to be a feature pic or a "doc" primarily. "The Sandwich Man" is like a documentary in drag.

A loosely scribed romance between a young car salesman and a model, and the fact that on this day Bentine's prize racing pigeon is competing in an important race are the only two highly slim 'plotlines.' For the remainder, Bentine (dressed as a dude sandwich-board man) wanders around observing the odd things happening around him. These are often telegraphed in advance and are merely excuses to bring in names for what are often blackout situations.

Bentine has an amiable personality that deserves further screen exposure. Norman Wisdom's sequence as a boxing vicar is too long. For the rest a long string of names mainly make impact in a couple of minutes, Stanley Holloway, as a park gardener; Diana Dors, flashing across the screen as a Billingsgate shopper; Terry-Thomas, as an inane scoutmaster; Donald Wolfit, selling a car; Ron Moody, as a rowing coach; Suzy Kendall, as a model, etc.

Given more opportunity, Ian Hendry's surly traffic-cop, Dora Bryan's garrulous widow and Bernard Cribbons as a model-photographer might have developed even more amusingly. No names appear above title and the producers have played safe by naming 14 players in alphabetic under title order. What else can be done in a pic where Michael Chaplin, as a beatnik pavement artists gets as much exposure as John Le Mesurier or Jeremy Lloyd?

Hartford-Davis must have used much tact to bring ordinary Londoners as back-and-foreground of certain scenes so naturally, but direction, editing and screenplay are mainly uneven. Mike Vickers has turned in a lively enough score and Newbrook's Eastmancolor lensing makes London look a dream. *Rich.*

The Hostage
(MELODRAMA-TECHNICOLOR)

Low - budgeted independent production with plenty of suspenseful excitement and interesting plotting.

Hollywood, Aug. 15.

Heartland Prods. release of a Russell S. Doughten Jr. production. Directed by Doughten. Features Don O'Kelly, Dean Stanton, John Carradine, Danny Martins, Ron Hagerthy, Jenifer Lea, with Ann Doran, Raymond Guth, Nora Marlowe, Shirley O'Hara, Mike McCloskey, Dick Spry, Leland Brown, Pearl Faessler. Screenplay, Robert Laning, from the novel "The Hostage" by Henry Farrel; music, Jaime Mendoza; camera, (Technicolor) Ted Mikels; art director, Ray Storey; asst. director and editor, Gary Kurtz; sound, Lee Strosnider, Marvin Walowitz. Reviewed at Consolidated Film Industries, Hollywood, Aug. 11, 1966. Running Time, 83 MINS.

Low-budgeted meller, shot entirely in the Midwest, may have high potential as a sleeper. Not to be confused with the Brendan Behan legit of the same name, pic generates swift, chilling suspense through tight, unorthodox editing. Production values are fine and theme song written by Ronald Hanna and sung by Steve Smith could be exploited to sell pic. No-name cast, with exception of John Carradine, however, will hamper wide distribution.

Based on a Henry Farrel novel, screenplay by Robert Laning starts slowly and gradually picks up strong suspense momentum. Story centers around boy whose parents are in the process of moving. Movers arrive. One of them, Don O'Kelly, has committed a murder only the night before. He is a psychopath and takes his aggressiveness out on his helper, Dean Stanton.

Characters are well developed, plot then is unleashed. Boy is locked in moving van, witnesses burial of the dead man, is hounded by the psychopath and sidekick, and after a series of ordeals manages to survive. What gives pic a strong feeling of realism is the human idiosyncrasies of the characters involved which further the plot complications.

Parents, Ron Hagerthy and Jenifer Lea, are reluctant to call police; Carradine, as the bum last seen with the boy, bolts accidentally into a moving truck; an elderly couple give the boy over to the villain because of a sad attachment to a dead son of their own.

The innocence of youth, doing exactly the wrong thing because of inexperience, brings added excitement to the carefully wrought story. Des Moines locale also gives authenticity to the pic.

Producer - director Russell S. Doughten Jr. has got credible performances from his actors, especially from O'Kelly and moppet Danny Martins. Ann Doran and Nora Marlowe are also fine, etching nice cameos of frustration. Ted Mikels' Techni olor lensing is harshly low-keyed as if shot through a dimly lit mirror and Ray Storey's production design also contributes to the naked atmosphere.

Yet it is Gary Kurtz's curious editing that creates a vertigo pace. Scenes are cut just before a climax is reached and this is continuously repeated almost to the point of tedium. However, it works in generating emotional involvement.

"Hostage" is neither cute nor clever. It could be called an experiment, or better, an experience. *Dool.*

Movie Star, American Style, Or, LSD, I Hate You!
(COLOR)

Slapstick and satire about a sexy film star. Exploitable via LSD sequence. Mainly for specialty houses, but could be an offbeat dualler in some general situations.

Hollywood, Aug. 1.
Famous Players Corp. (Albert Zugsmith) production and release, produced and photographed by Robert Caramico. Features Robert Strauss, Del Moore, Paula Lane. Screenplay, Zugsmith, Graham Lee Mahin; editor, Herman Freedman; music, Joe Greene. Reviewed at L.A., July 30, '66. Running Time, 99 MINS.
Joe Horner .... Robert Strauss
Dr. Horatio .... Del Moore
Skippy Roper ...:....... T. C. Jones
Dr. Oscar Roscoe .... Steve Drexel
Barry James .... Steven Rogers
David Erickson .... Richard Clair
Miranda Song .... Jill Darling
Movie Queen .... Cara Garnett
Countess .... Sandra Lynn
Harvey Homantash ... Peter Van Boorn
Crash Dramm .... Ned York
Photographer Midget .....Frank Delfino
Miss Bee .... Juliet Picaud
Honey Bunny .... Paula Lane

Thinly-veiled impersonations of pix people plus the topicality of LSD give strong exploitation elements to "Movie Star, American Style, Or, LSD, I Hate You!" Occasionally sophisticated and also relying on some inside gags that would register only in Hollywood, the Albert Zugsmith film is basically an okay slapstick satire on contemporary sex symbols and psychiatry heightened by optical and musical gimmicks. Commercial prospects are mainly on the exploitation circuit, although the Famous Players release could hold its own in selected general situations.

In the European tradition of billing, now spreading in domestic circles, this is "a film by" Zugsmith who, besides appearing briefly as a director, is also credited with the script, along with Graham Lee Mahin. The producer of record is Robert Caramico, who also lensed, including the final 25 minutes which are in various hues to simulate the effects of LSD during the climactic group therapy. No one is billed as director.

The Zugsmith-Mahin script kicks off with the latest suicide attempt of Paula Lane, playing a film star whose looks, manners and voice are remarkably similar to the late Marilyn Monroe. Other key principals include top-featured Robert Strauss, Miss Lane's studio chief, and Del Moore, daffy headshrinker.

Running in and out of scenes at Moore's funny farm are T. C. Jones, the female impersonator who, herein, essays a swish designer, Steven Rogers as a leading man whose voice is one of the stock-in-trade items of any vocal impersonator, Richard Clair, an intellectual author who wears glasses, and Cara Garnett, femme fatale with a tendency to overeat.

Miss Lane's analysis is beset with a continuing parade of sight gags and throwaway lines, punctuated by stop-motion effects, as Strauss tries to get her back to work. Latter and Moore play it broadly all the way. The color-toned LSD trip, in which all characters seem to behave the way current literature describes such happenings, is appropriately bizarre. As a final irony, it is Miss Lane who has drawn the LSD placebo dosage.

Pic makes no lavish production pretense, and there are none. The LSD scene, while no great social commentary, is, in its own way, sufficiently offbeat to give an audience pause. This is because no one likes to appear the fool, but, to a turned-off person, another who is turned on is just that.

Herman Freedman is credited with the fast editing to 99 minutes, and Joe Greene composed and conducted an appropriate score, including a title tune sung by Jones. Caramico's lensing is good, ditto sound, although latter sometimes has a hollow tone.
Murf.

A Belles Dents
(Living It Up)
(FRENCH-GERMAN)
(Color)

Paris, Aug. 9.
SNC release of Chronos Film-SNC-Team Film production. Stars Mireille Darc, Jacques Charrier, Daniel Gelin, Peter Van Eyck, Paul Hubschmid. Directed by Pierre Gaspard-Huit. Screenplay, Gaspard-Huti, Will Berthold, Jean-Loup Dabadie; camera (Eastmancolor), Walter Lenz; editor, Louisette Hautecouer. At Colisee, Paris. Running Time, 105 MINS.
Eva .... Mireille Darc
Jean-Loup .... Jacques Charrier
Francesco .... Paul Hubschmid
Bernard .... Daniel Gelin
Peter .... Peter Van Eyck

Oldhat melodrama about a girl from the sticks who wants only love but ends up with only money. It's dressed up with the supposed modern trappings of rich cafe society. Sudsy pic looms only for sexploitation probabilities abroad on the casual nudity of star Mireille Darc and its hothouse plotting, synthetic orgies and laggard direction.

Half-French and half-German, the heroine is orphaned as a teenager and goes to Paris to seek her career. As an *au pair* girl she catches the eye of her boss, a noted photographer, and she ends up as a cover girl. She attains fame and what she thinks is true love with an architect. He turns out to be callow and wanting her for only a while. So she has two rich marriages which bring her luxury but not love. She is left with a thriving business but walks off into snowdrifts on her big estate as a voice intones the sad fate of her loneliness.

Miss Darc is a lithe, freckled and comely girl, and shows off her boyish build with abandon throughout. It has become her trademark. But here she does not have the poise to make her role convincing. Even as a sort of instinctively moral creature, giving herself only in love, there is a lack of the intensity needed. This Gallic-Germano pic is reminiscent of "Darling," but lacks the filmic snap so necessary. *Mosk.*

Carry On Screaming
(BRITISH—COLOR)

The 12th in the golden box-office series; rather less nimble than previous entries but still a certain winner.

London, Aug. 16.
Warner-Pathe release of a Peter Rogers production from Anglo Amalgamated. Features Harry H. Corbett, Kenneth Williams, Fenella Fielding, Joan Sims, Charles Hawtrey, Jim Dale, Angela Douglas, Peter Butterworth, Bernard Bresslaw, Jon Pertwee, Tom Clegg. Directed by Gerald Thomas. Screenplay by Talbot Rothwell; editor, Rod Keys; camera (Eastmancolor), Alan Hume; music, Eric Rogers. Reviewed at Warner Theatre. Running Time, 97 MINS.
Det. Serg't. Bung..... Harry H. Corbett
Doctor Watt .... Kenneth Williams
Valeria .... Fenella Fielding
Emily Bung .... Joan Sims
Dan Dann ....: Charles Hawtrey
Albert Potter .... Jim Dale
Doris Mann .... Angela Douglas
Det. Con. Slobotham..Peter Butterworth
Sockett.............. Bernard Bresslaw
Fettle .... Jon Pertwee
Odbodd .... Tom Clegg
Odbodd Jnr. .... Billy Cornelius
Mr. Jones .... Frank Thornton

This 12th and latest in the successful "Carry On" series puts the skids under horror pix and will undoubtedly click, though for sheer slapstick nonsense it doesn't match up to some of its predecessors. Snag is that most horror films themselves teeter on to parody and it is rather tough trying to burlesque a parody. But though some of the situations and patter are fairly heavygoing, the cast of old reliables buckle down to the task with their usual energy, and "Carry On" fans will get their full quota of yocks. Safe booking for those family houses that have previously benefited from the Peter Rogers - Gerald Thomas formula.

Abduction of a girl by a monster starts a trail of goofy adventures as henpecked Detective Sergeant Bung (Harry H. Corbett) and his bovine assistant (Peter Butterworth) try to unravel this, the latest crime of a series. Investigations lead to an eerie mansion, inhabited by a ghoulish doctor, who is dead but re-incarnated, his attractively-sexy, evil sister, a sinister butler and a couple of kidnapping monsters. There the brother-and-sister team ply their grisly trade of abducting girls, petrifying them and then selling them as shop dummies.

Before the yarn is wound up Harry H. Corbett & Co. endure some spooky indignities and the "Carry On" team, fed by screenplay writer Talbot Rothwell, dish out their usual assortment of double entendres, bangup vulgarity and irrelevancies which all add up to a well-tried, pop formula. "Carry On Screaming" has more than a touch of the Munsters about it though any screams will come from laughter rather than thrills.

Gerald Thomas' direction as usual is assured, though some of the gags and situations would be helped by speeding up via more ruthless trimming by editor Rod Keys. Alan Hume's Eastmancolor camerawork is effective and the music hits the mark. Corbett and Fenella Fielding, both debuting with the "Carry On" team, give it added strength. Corbett mugs a great deal but the role demands it and Miss Fielding as the grisly vamp glitters with an overdone seductiveness which is often funny.

Kenneth Williams, Joan Sims, Jim Dale, Jon Pertwee, Peter Butterworth, and Charles Hawtrey of the regulars, jump through their usual hoops energetically. Angela Douglas follows up her appearance in "Carry On Cowboys" attractively and a string of competent players make the most of the bit parts. *Rich.*

Lange Beine— Lange Finger
(Long Legs—Long Fingers)
(GERMAN—COLOR)

Berlin, Aug. 16.
Nora release of CCC (Artur Brauner) production. Stars Senta Berger, Martin Held, Joachim Fuchsberger; features James Robertson Justice, Irene von Meyendorff, Helga Sommerfeld. Directed by Alfred Vohrer. Screenplay, P. Lambda, Longrigg and Eberhard Keindorff; camera (Eastmancolor), Karl Loeb; music, Martin Boettcher; editor, Jutta Hering. At Gloria Palast, Berlin. Running Time, 90 MINS.
Dodo .... Senta Berger
Baron Halbach .... Martin Held
Robert .... Joachim Fuchsberger
Lady Hammond . Irene von Meyendorff
Sir Hammond . James Robertson Justice
Sarah .... Helga Sommerfeld
Sam Snapper .... Walter Wilz
The old Snapper .... Zeev Berlinsky
General .... Friedrich Schoenfelder
Emile Gavin .... Hanns Lothar

This CCC production shows what money can do for a pic. Artur Brauner spent something like $500,000 on this comedy, actually much too much for a German production to break even on its homegrounds. The film benefits from a rather lavish (for domestic standards) production dress and marvelous costumes. The general outcome is a nicely polished comedy that's sure to please the bulk of this country's film patrons. It also should find its way into foreign territories. Incidentally, part of film's exteriors were shot in Israel.

Plot concerns the elegant Baron Halbach (Martin Held) and his beautiful daughter Dodo (Senta Berger) who make a luxurious living by stealing jewelry. Both are extremely clever hotel thieves and their life would probably have continued the successful way had Dodo not suddenly fallen in love with a young Englishman who happens to be a barrister. Her love is so intense that she deserts her father and follows the man of her dreams to London.

Although her father uses all sorts of tricks to torpedo this romance, the two young people intend to get married. In order to raise money for the young barrister, she steals once more and is caught. The ending, however, is entirely happy — the barrister takes over her case and succeeds in having her acquitted. And her father and his father become business partners. As her father puts it: "Our way of being dishonest is outdated. There are now new methods of being dishonest the honest way." This refers to his new business partner who makes millions via dubious sales of arms to far away lands.

Alfred Vohrer directed this with a light touch. Taking into account that this is his first comedy, after having made mainly westerns within the past years, it's a remarkably good directorial job. And he led the players through fine performances. Top acting is turned in by Held which is actually no surprise since he is one of the leading stage actors here. Senta Berger is lovely to look at and wears beautiful robes in this pic. Joachim Fuchsberger enacts the young barrister, her lover.

Excellent support is given by James Robertson Justice and Irene von Meyendorff, as Fuchsberger's parents; Helga Sommerfeld, Zeev Berlinsky and Friedrich Schoenfelder. A brief but enjoyable performance is contributed by Hanns Lothar in the role of a celebrated and conceited fashion designer.

The color photography by Karl Loeb is outstanding. Score by Martin Boettcher is catchy and suits the swinging mood of this comedy. Though much money was spent on this production, this is a German comedy which its creators needn't be ashamed of. *Hans.*

The Fighting Prince Of Donegal
(BRITISH-COLOR)

Tame and cliche Walt Disney programmer about British-Irish troubles circa 1587. Modest production values, okay execution. Little appeal to grownups, not much more for the very young. No marquee strength beyond the Disney name. Okay for kiddie duals.

Hollywood, Aug. 20.
Buena Vista release of Walt Disney (Bill Anderson) production. Features Peter McEnery, Susan Hampshire, Tom Adams, Gordon Jackson, Andrew Keir. Directed by Michael O'Herlihy. Screenplay, Robert Westerby, based on book "Red Hugh, Prince Of Donegal," by Robert T. Reilly; camera (Technicolor); editor, Peter Boita; music, George Bruns; asst. director, David Bracknell. Reviewed at Academy Award Theatre, L.A., Aug. 19, '66. Running Time, 110 MINS.
Hugh O'Donnell .... Peter McEnery
Kathleen McSweeney..Susan Hampshire
Henry O'Neill .... Tom Adams
Captain Leeds .... Gordon Jackson
Clan leader .... Andrew Keir
Prison boy .... Maurice Roeves
Prisoner .... Donal McCann
O'Neill clan leader..... Richard Leech
Young girls .... Maire NiGhrainne,
Maire O'Neill, Fidelma Murphy

"The Fighting Prince of Donegal" is a tame and fictionalized slice of 16th Century Irish-British political life. Written, played and destined strictly for juves, pic shapes up as a minor Walt Disney effort even within its intended market. Bill Anderson coproduced at England's Pinewood Studios.

Robert Westerby has adapted Robert T. Reilly's historical novel, "Red Hugh, Prince of Donegal," into a semi-fictional screenplay revolving around Peter McEnery, young Irish nobleman who succeeds to the leadership of his clan in the period of the Spanish Armada threat to England. Heavy in the tale is Gordon Jackson, leader of the British troops sent to Ireland by Queen Elizabeth I.

Written in broad-brush, unsophisticated literary strokes, story is dotted with recurring personal combat, sight gag humor, and predictable situations. Perhaps the key flaw is that the final product is not sufficiently fanciful to charm the kids, nor sufficiently real to maintain the attention of babysitter escorts. In short, it is tedious.

Withal, McEnery is good as the young Irishman, ditto Jackson in the unsympathized lead role. Susan Hampshire provides the romantic interest. Tom Adams is an engaging swashbuckler type, and Andrew Keir and Richard Leech are good as clan leaders. Other players render okay support.

Michael O'Herlihy, brother of film actor Dan O'Herlihy, makes his feature directorial bow herein after piling up some U.S. vidpix credits. The direction is okay but often static. His big-screen potential cannot be evaluated from the pic, considering the modest production values made available, plus the confines of the script. Indeed, it would appear that the film was made with more than casual attention to possible tv exhibition in segmented, episodic form on a small screen.

Technical credits are pro, including Arthur Ibbetson's Technicolor camera and Peter Boita's relaxed editing to 110 minutes. George Bruns composed a good score. Hugh Attwool is credited as associate producer. *Murf.*

Two Kouney Lemels
(COLOR-SCOPE)
(ISRAEL)

Tel Aviv, Aug. 11.
Flying Matchmaker Co. presents (the late) Mordechai Navon film, a Geva Studios (Israel) Production. Stars Mike Bourstein, Jermain Unikovsky, Rina Ganor. Shmuel Rodensky, Rafael Klatchkin, Aharon Meskin, Elisheva Michaeli, The Twins Trio, Shlomo Vishinsky, Geta Louca, Ari Koutay etc. Directed by Israel Becker, from his own adaptation of the Avraham Goldfaden comedy, scripted by Israel Becker and Alex Maimon. Songs, Moshe Sahar; music, Shaul Perezovsky, arranged, orchestrated and conducted by Shimon Cohen; camera (Technicolor) Romulo Grounni and Adam Grinberg; sound, Fernando Pestacelli and Haim Avish. At Hod Cinema, July 31, '66. Running Time, 120 MINS.
Kouney Lemel, Max.... Mike Bourstein
The Matchmaker....... Rafael Klatchkin
His daughter....... Jermain Unikovsky
Reb Pinchas .... Shmuel Rodensky
His wife .... Elisheva Michaeli
His daughter .... Rina Ganor
Kouney Lemel's father..Aharon Meskin
Max' father .... Ari Koutay

This first Israeli musical film, in color and on wide screen, justifies all the excitement with which local audiences had been awaiting it. Israel Becker, himself born in Eastern Europe, an actor in the Yiddish theatre in Russia during the second World War and actor-director with the Hebimah Theatre since he came to Israel in 1948, has succeeded in capturing the naive, simple and funny air of the Jewish community as it had been mirrored in the theatre of that era, the middle of the 19th century. Becker, who directed the documentary feature about remnants of the concentration camps in Europe, in 1947, "Long Is The Way," proves himself a man of the cinema, both in his stylized adaptation of the old comedy, written almost 100 years ago by Avraham Goldfaden, and in his direction.

The story of the fresh breeze of "progress" and liberalism is manifested in the little community's life through love openly declared among the young generation, interfering with the age-old traditions of "The Matchmaker."

It tells of a match being arranged for the daughter of an illiterate, rich man with a stuttering, lame son, and of a respected family, which would never, otherwise, agree to marry into the rich butcher's family. The girl's boyfriend, a looked-down-upon cousin of the learned family, because of not living strictly according to the austere religious traditions, impersonates the stuttering bridegroom-to-be and the happy end comes when two weddings are being celebrated instead of the one scheduled, with the whole township benefiting from the event, singing and dancing, eating and drinking while the going is good, knowing that dreary, dull and poor days are ahead of them, as they had known in the past.

The humor, characters, situations and misunderstandings, the story and the music, are very much on a par with the very popular setting and background of "Fiddler on the Roof." Under direction of Becker the antic sight gags, as well as the nostalgia, don't top over the well-balanced performances by most of the participants, mainly Mike Broustein in the double role of Kouney Lemel and Max. This young actor, not unlike a younger Jerry Lewis, lights the bright-colored screen with his personality and charm, plus a pleasant singing voice and excellent timing.

The photography of Italian Romulo Grounni does wonders with the local landscape and the Israeli sun, and the recording of the music and songs (by Kolinor for a CBS—Israel Lp scheduled for September) are technically good. Performances by Shmuel Rodensky (local "Fiddler") and Aharon Meskin and Refael Klatchkin (among the luminaries of the Habimah) keep the film from tilting and going grotesque or melodramatic. The femmes (Michaeli, Unikovsky and Ganor) add charm and grace to the scene, which sometimes looks like a scene from "Seven Brides for Seven Brothers."

Film should enjoy special interest among specialized audience in the U. S. and elsewhere, what with the trend for Jewish humor and the success of "Fiddler," etc., as forerunners. Having been the most pretentious local effort (with an investment of close to $350,-000) to date, this film should do exceeding well locally and abroad. *Rapo.*

Bang, Bang, You're Dead
(COLOR)

Programmer that doesn't live up to its cast but should do well in the action-comedy market. Technical flaws and inept script hold down potential.

American International release of Ely Landau-Oliver A. Unger (Harry Alan Towers) production. Features Tony Randall, Senta Berger, Terry-Thomas. Directed by Don Sharp. Screenplay, Peter Yeldam; camera (Technicolor), Michael Reed; editor, Teddy Darvas; music, composed and conducted by Malcolm Lockyer; asst. director, Barrie Melrose. Reviewed in N.Y. City, Aug. 18, '66. Running Time: 92 MINS.
Andrew Jessel .... Tony Randall
Kyra Stanovy .... Senta Berger
El Caid .... Terry-Thomas
Casimir .... Herbert Lom
Arthur Fairbrother..Wilfred Hyde-White
Achmed .... Gregoire Aslan
George Lillywhite...John Le Mesurier
Jonquil .... Klaus Kinski
Samia Voss .... Margaret Lee
Hotel Clerk .... Emil Stemmler
Madame Bouseny....Helen Sanguinetti
Martinez .... Sanchez Francisco
Police Chief ......William Sanguinetti
Motorcycle Cop.......Hassan Essakali
Philippe .... Keith Peacock
Export Manager .... Burt Kwouk

One of the Landau-Unger features acquired for distribution by AIP, this spy spoof was filmed mostly on location in Marrakesh. Indeed, the original title of the film was "Marrakesh," since changed to "Bang, Bang, You're Dead," (although the screen credit has only one "Bang"). The reported hardships that belabored the crew during the shooting can be believed as the film is riddled with bits of bad photography and poor lighting, not to mention some technical mistakes that could have been avoided.

The strength of the film, such as it is, is in the cast which doesn't always work up a sweat but does provide occasional laughs and considerable suspenseful action. Most of the burden of Peter Yeldam's rambling script is carried by Tony Randall (who, too often, appears bored with the whole thing) and the beauteous Senta Berger. Short but happy lifts to the action are provided by Terry-Thomas as an Eton-educated sheikh and Gregoire Aslan as a wild Moroccan truckdriver.

Herbert Lom as the principal villain and Klaus Kinski as his assistant are good, but Margaret Lee (as Lom's girlfriend) is simultaneously saddled with the body of a Persian houri and a voice like Hayley Mills. Wilfred Hyde-White, John Le Mesurier and William Sanguinetti have very minor roles.

Although most of the film was made on outdoor locations in Marrakesh the photographic results are highly uneven, with many of the earlier scenes (important as establishing shots) looking dark and murky. Only the final third of the film, during the scenes at El Caid's oasis and some beautifully-made shots of what appears to be the remains of a castle makes up the ineptness of cameraman Michael Reed's earlier work which could have been that of second unit cameraman Egil Woxholt. Some very obvious process shots during two driving sequences are also distracting.

Director Don Sharp and producer Harry Alan Towers spent a great deal of time and effort in finding an exotic location for this film. It would have improved it if they'd devoted more effort to a workable script and reasonable shooting schedule. Most of their output so far has indicated considerable promise but, invariably, has fallen short of true excellence.

AIP should do well with this effort in the general market although it needs some second-spot support. The title is not much help as a selling point. *Robe.*

Ambush Bay
(COLOR)

Realistic U.S. Marines-World War II story with exciting action, tough performances, top production values; good entry for general market.

Hollywood, Aug. 27.

United Artists release of Schenck-Zabel (Aubrey Schenck-Hal Klein) production. Stars Hugh O'Brian Mickey Rooney, James Mitchum. Directed by Ron Winston. Screenplay, Marve Feinberg, Ib Melchoir; camera (DeLuxe Color), Emmanuel Rojas; editor, John Schreyer; music, Richard La Salle; asst. director, E. Read Killgore. Reviewed at Directors Guild of America Theatre, Aug. 26, '66. Running Time, 107 MINS.

First Sgt. Steve Corey	Hugh O'Brian
Sgt. Ernest Wartell	Mickey Rooney
PFC James Grenier	James Mitchum
Sgt. William Maccone	Pete Masterson
Cpl. Alvin Ross	Harry Lauter
Cpl. Stanley Parrish	Greg Amsterdam
Pvt. Henry Reynolds	Jim Anauo
Pvt. George George	Tony Smith
Capt. Alonzo Davis	Clem Stadler
Amado	Amado Abello
Midori	Juris Sulit
Max	Max Quismundo
Ramon	Bruno Punzalan
Miyazaki	Tisa Chang
Lt. Tokuzo	Buzz Fernandez
Capt. Kayamatsu	Joaquin Farjado
Man	Limbo Lagdameo
Soldier	Nonong Arceo

"Ambush Bay" packs the type of war action which is well received in both the general and outdoor market. Striking color photography and realistic treatment give meaning to this strong World War II melodrama which deals with mission of a nine-man U.S. Marines patrol in the Philippines. The Aubrey Schenck-Hal Klein production, lensed entirely in Luzon, is highlighted also by forceful acting and mounting tension which holds to its effective windup.

Hugh O'Brian, Mickey Rooney and James Mitchum star in the Marve Feinberg-Ib Melchior script and Ron Winston's dynamic direction is particularly praiseworthy as he builds his suspense. Vying, however, with the thesps in interest is the camera work of Filipino Emmanuel Rojas, a Manila University chemistry professor, whose skill and artistry in projecting the feeling of the story and its lush jungle locations match any topflight Hollywood lenser. Schenck, as executive producer, has lined up expert technical talent right down the line to lend quality to film as a whole.

Stirring plot deals with efforts of the Marines, landing secretly at night on a small Philippine island, to get through to a Nipponese-held village where they are to contact a Japanese who has important information concerning General MacArthur's planned invasion. They have only 96 hours to complete their mission and return. Instead of a swift passage through the jungle, as planned, they encounter Japanese resistance. When they finally reach the village they discover their contact is a Japanese girl from Long Beach, Calif., who has been acting as a spy.

Femme tells the Marines that the enemy has learned the exact route MacArthur plans to use in attacking the Philippines and have mined the area with a new kind of explosive anchored on the ocean bed and impervious to minesweepers. In one of the Japanese attacks on the Marines the radio they had hoped to use to transmit information is destroyed. Their only means of warning MacArthur gone, their only hope remains to make their way to a Japanese control center where the mines may be detonated prematurely. Action builds toward this climax.

Hugh O'Brian scores decisively as the Marine sergeant who takes over command of the small force after its leader, played by Lt. Col. Clement J. Stadler, USMC, Ret., is killed He delivers a sock performance in a hardboiled role, and Mickey Rooney, as another tough Marine vet, turns in another of his top enactments. James Mitchum does the best work of his career as the totally inexperienced Marine taken along on the mission because of his knowledge of radio after the man originally skedded comes down with malaria.

Tisa Chang is well cast as the American-Japanese contact finally killed when she attempts to delay a Japanese party so the two Americans remaining in the patrol can get to the coast. Among the Marines, Pete Masterson and Harry Lauter stand out; Amado Abello is excellent as a Filipino guerrilla guide and Buzz Fernandez is colorful as a Japanese officer.

Potent technical assistance is offered by John Schreyer, editing; Richard La Salle, music; Burdick S. Trask, sound; Charles Schulthies, special effects.

Whit.

An American Dream
(COLOR)

Film of Norman Mailer's novel starts off strong but fizzes out in flawed scripting. Salty lingo nixes juve trade. Okay prospects in mature general situations.

Hollywood, Aug. 24.

Warner Bros. production (William Conrad) and release. Stars Stuart Whitman, Janet Leigh; features Eleanor Parker, Barry Sullivan, Lloyd Nolan, Murray Hamilton, J. D. Cannon, Susan Denberg, Les Crane, Warren Stevens. Directed by Robert Gist. Screenplay, Mann Rubin, based on novel by Norman Mailer; camera (Technicolor), Sam Leavitt; editor, George Rohrs; music, Johnny Mandel; song, Mandel, Paul Francis Webster; asst. director, Sherry Shourds. Reviewed at Academy Award Theatre, L.A., Aug. 23, '66. Running Time, 103 MINS.

Stephen Rojack	Stuart Whitman
Cherry McMahon	Janet Leigh
Deborah Kelly Rojack	Eleanor Parker
Roberts	Barry Sullivan
Barney Kelly	Lloyd Nolan
Arthur Kabot	Murray Hamilton
Sgt. Leznicki	J. D. Cannon
Ruta	Susan Denberg
Nicky	Les Crane
Johnny Dell	Warren Stevens
Eddie Ganucci	Joe DeSantis
O'Brien	Stacy Harris
Shago Martin	Paul Mantee
Ganucci's lawyer	Harold Gould
Ord Long	George Takei
Freya	Kelly Jean Peters

"An American Dream" emerges, after an exciting start, as an okay meller of contemporary crime and punishment. Eleanor Parker is terrif as a psychotic rich shrew who gets murdered early. Stuart Whitman, Janet Leigh and others are less fortunate, remaining in a fuzzy script structure which eventually shoots them down. Based on Norman Mailer's novel, pic is the first of a diversified program under supervision of exec producer William Conrad. Much good direction and fine production values. Salty dialog is okay in context, but rules out family trade. Smart selling can reap okay b.o. for Warner Bros. release in more mature general situations.

Adaptation, credited to Mann Rubin, moves along smartly for almost 30 minutes as Miss Parker, disporting in bed with a male pickup (wisely kept out of focus), watches estranged hubby Whitman conduct his tv gab show. Latter comes to her penthouse and, after a violent fight and in a frenzy, he pushes her off a ledge for a 30-story drop. Under the direction of Robert Gist, making his feature debut after vidirecting, Miss Parker is completely hateful and drives all audience sympathy to Whitman. Her performance is excellent.

What the script does not do after this point is to focus sharply on a three-ply squeeze: Whitman under pressure from the police, from gangland boss Joe DeSantis, whose car has been wrecked in a traffic tie-up caused by Miss Parker's falling body, and from latter's father, Lloyd Nolan, a wealthy Catholic who, of course, cannot have his daughter buried under Church auspices if Whitman's suicide story is true. The dramatic seeds are there, but are dissipated and diluted as Whitman and Miss Leigh renew an old romance.

Barry Sullivan and J. D. Cannon, particularly the latter, are very good as the grilling gumshoes, while Les Crane and Warren Stevens make good hoods. Whitman and Miss Leigh try hard to make their dialog believable, but their romantic dalliance flags the pace and makes the plot holes more noticeable. Miss Leigh's character undergoes an abrupt change as she sells out her lover, a climactic irony which would have been neat had she not managed to convince an audience that she was really in love with him again.

Supporting players register quite well in brief footage — in particular, Murray Hamilton, Whitman's callous tv partner; Susan Denberg, Miss Parker's sexy maid; cop Stacy Harris and Kelly Jean Peters, in a nice bit as an embarrassed secretary.

On the technical side, Sam Leavitt's Technicolor lensing is firstrate, and George Rohrs trimmed to a good 103 minutes. Johnny Mandel's score is good, particularly in representation of traffic noise.

Murf.

The Liquidator
(BRITISH-COLOR)

Boysie Oakes, newest entry into comedy-adventure spy field, shapes up as a lively contender with sound box-office potential and marquee lure.

London, Aug. 30.

Metro release of a Leslie Elliot (Jon Penington) production. Stars Rod Taylor, Trevor Howard, Jill St. John; features Wilfrid Hyde White, Akim Tamiroff, Eric Sykes, Gabriella Lucidi, David Tomlinson. Directed by Jack Cardiff. Screenplay by Peter Yeldham from John Gardner's novel; camera (Metrocolor), Ted Scaife; editor, Ernest Walter; music, Lalo Schifrin; title song lyrics, Peter Callender, with music by Schifrin (sung by Shirley Bassey). Reviewed at Metro Private Theatre, London. Running Time, 104 MINS.

Boysie	Rod Taylor
Mostyn	Trevor Howard
Iris	Jill St. John
Chief	Wilfred Hyde White
Quadrant	David Tomlinson
Griffen	Eric Sykes
Sheriek	Akim Tamiroff
Corale	Gabriella Lucidi
Chekov	John Le Mesurier
Fly	Derek Nimmo
Young Man	Jeremy Lloyd
Janice Benedict	Jennifer Jayne
Frances Anne	Metty McDowall
Vicar	Colin Gordon
Jessie	Louise Dunn
Yakov	Henry Cogan
Gregory	Daniel Emilfork
Flying Instructor	Richard Wattis
Station Commander	David Langton
Flying Control	Tony Wright
Judith	Suzy Kendall

The flow of spy yarns, mainly spoofs in varying degree, shows no sign of dwindling. Latest in competition for public favor is Boysie Oakes, a creation of John Gardner, who has employed Oakes in three click assaults on the bestseller lists. "The Liquidator," which has been held up for awhile because of a legal squabble, may be a late starter but could well be up among the winners in the final count.

The Leslie Elliot production which is being released by Metro is overlengthy and from time to time runs into stodgy patches. But, without being gimmickry, brings in the necessary ingredients of the lush blond, goodlooking, sexy lasses; plenty of plot twists and firstrate thesping in smaller roles.

Riviera locale is an asset, too. Peter Yeldham's screenplay and Jack Cardiff's direction combine plenty of action and some crisp wisecracking. All in all, this pic should make for good wicket returns, unless audiences are now so bemused by all the scientific junk which screen spies currently use that they sniff at a hero who merely uses his fists and a gun and doesn't like doing either very much.

Where Boysie Oakes (Rod Taylor) is different from his counterparts is that he is neither a pro undercover agent nor an enthusiastic amateur with a flair. In fact, he is a vulnerable sort of guy who hates killing, is invariably airsick in planes but has an ever-roving eye for the girls. An ex-sergeant who accidentally saves Trevor Howard's life, he is conned into joining the Service by Howard (Security's No. 2) and is violently surprised and upset when he finds that he has been impeccably trained to become a kind of private executioner, expected to rub out security risks when ordered by his boss.

But he is hooked by the fringe benefits, the salary and the pleasures of the job. He compromises by hiring a professional killer to do the dirty work for him, an angle which had promise as a film plot. But this angle fairly quickly gets sidetracked and the pic reverts to the sinister outcome when Oakes takes "No. 2's" lush secretary for a dirty weekend in the Riviera. They get involved in a highly complicated rough and tumble with enemy agents which leads to him nearly being tricked into bumping off the Duke of Edinburgh, a wayout climax that builds up to a wild air sequence.

There are plenty of holes in the plot, but no matter. The vulnerable Oakes is played with plenty of charm and guts by Rod Taylor, though he hardly suggests a character with such fundamental failings and frailties as Boysie. Trevor Howard, as so often, makes his role as "No. 2" stand out as a ruthless, cynical getter of results without worrying about scruples. Jill St. John as Oakes' temptress who turns out to be the heavy looks smashing but her performance is marred by woodenness, and her habit of talking with computer-like inflexibility.

Where the film scores is in its long list of well-played lesser roles. Gabriella Lucidi is another attractive dame who does things to Boysie Oakes' blood pressure. Akim Tamiroff, as an incompetent, ham agent, produces a good, unctuous line. Colin Gordon, John Le Mesurier, Derek Nimmo, Betty McDowall, Jeremy Lloyd, Henri Cogan, Richard Wattis, Daniel Emilfork, Louise Dunn and Jenifer Jayne are all in with effective and varied cameos, with Nimmo, Emilfork, as a deadshot gunman; and Wattis making particular brief impact.

Eric Sykes, usually a light comedian, is cast out of character as an apparently seedy professional killer who assists Taylor, but Sykes builds it up as a small comedy role without tossing away its sinister implications. David Tomlinson splendidly plays a silly ass role which has more to it than meets the eye and ear.

Ted Scaife's Metrocolor photography makes snazzy use of the Cote D'Azur scenery. The artwork, costumes and decor all are richly easy on the eye. Coming in at 104 minutes, editor Ernest Walter might have wielded his scissors even more ruthlessly for the good of the production.

Lalo Schifrin has provided a lively score and also written a title song, with Peter Callender, which does nothing for the film. but which Shirley Bassey puts over through the credits in a way that should earn it a lot of airings. *Rich.*

Chamber of Horrors
(COLOR)

Oldfashioned chiller but with good prospects in program market.

Hollywood, Aug. 18.
Warner Bros. release of Hy Averback production, directed by Averback. Stars Cesare Danova, Wilfrid Hyde-White, Patrick O'Neal, Laura Devon, Patrice Wymore, Suzy Parker. Screenplay, Stephen Kandel; story, Ray Russell, Kandel; camera (Technicolor), Richard Kline, editor, David Wages; music, William Lava; asst. director, Sam Schneider. Reviewed at WB Studios, Aug. 17, '66. Running Time, 100 MINS.
Anthony Draco ...... Cesare Danova
Harold Blount ...... Wilfrid Hyde-White
Jason Cravette .... Patrick O'Neal
Marie Champlain .... Laura Devon
Vivian .... Patrice Wymore
Barbara Dixon .... Suzy Parker
Senor Pepe de Reyes .... Tun Tun
Inspector Strudwick.... Philip Bourneuf
Mrs. Ewing Perryman....Jeanette Nolan
Madame Corona .... Marie Windsor
Police Sgt. Albertson... Wayne Rogers
Judge Randolph ..... Vinton Hayworth
Dr. Cobb .... Richard O'Brien
Gloria .... Inger Stratton
Chun Sing .... Berry Kroeger
Dr. Hopewell .... Charles Seel
Barmaid .... Ayllene Gibbons

"Chamber of Horrors," originally skedded as a tv entry and built

into a feature via additional specially-shot footage, packs plenty of chills in its unfoldment but essentially an oldfashioned piece of melodramatics which had its day a generation or so ago on the screen. Nevertheless, it is suitable for the program market, where it may be exploited for satisfactory returns.

The Hy Averback production, marking tv producer's first assignment as a feature producer-director, carries one of those audience gimmicks designed to titillate the imagination.

"The motion picture you are about to see," a foreword states, "contains scenes so terrifying the public must be given grave warning." Both visual and audible warning signals are promised at the beginning of "each of the four supreme fright points."

Script by Stephen Kandel, based on his own and Ray Russell's original story, is reminiscent of WB's 1953- 3-D thriller, "House of Wax," which dealt with the same subject. The "fright points" referred to in present case occur as a sinister murdered, who has severed his right hand to escape from his guard en route to prison and execution—and now wears a steel claw—stalks his several victims to avenge his conviction.

The Technicolor production is accorded handsome physical and technical mounting, and flavor of its 1880 period in Baltimore is neatly caught in Art Loel's art direction and William L. Kuehl's set decorations. Averback's direction is attuned to his subject, and music by William Lava and fast editing by David Wages contribute further to the spirit.

Patrick O'Neal in role of the insane killer who terrorizes Baltimore with his crimes lends credence to part as a gaslight-acting figure, creating an aura of terror as he alternately replaces his claw with a razor-sharp scalpel and cleaver. Cesare Danova and Wilfrid Hyde-White as a pair of amateur criminologists who operate the House of Wax, a tourist attraction where history's most infamous murders are recreated in wax tableaux, share acting honors in firstrate characterizations of the period.

Laura Devon is beautiful and curvaceous as the sex-lure the killer uses to attract his proposed victims. Tun Tun, the Mexican shortie (3 ft. 9 inches), scores, too, as third partner in the museum, and other key figures are undertaken convincingly by Wayne Rogers, Philip Bourneuf, Jeanette Nolan, Marie Windsor and Vinton Hayworth. Patrice Wymore and Suzy Parker are lost in the shuffle. *Whit.*

The Street Is My Beat

Rise and fall of a streetwalker, suitable strictly for sexploitation trade.

Hollywood, Aug. 24.
Emerson release of Alan P. Magerman-Jack Paller-Irvin Berwick production, directed by Berwick. Stars Shary Marshall; features Todd Lasswell, John Harmon, Anne MacAdams, Susan Cummings. Screenplay, Harold Livingston, Berwick; camera, Joseph V. Mascelli; editor, Gerard Wilson; music, Harrose.

Reviewed at L.A., Aug. 23, '66. Running Time, 96 MINS.
Della Martinson ...... Shary Marshall
Phil Demarest .... Todd Lasswell
Mr. Martinson .... John Harmon
Mrs. Martinson .... Anne MacAdams
Johnny Gibson .... Tom Irish
Sally .... Beverly Oliver
McGruber .... Bob Brown
Cora .... Susan Cummings
Danby .... J. Edward McKinley

"The Street Is My Beat" is the story of a hooker. Plot centres on a bride framed by her pandering husband into prostitution, her rise and fall. What was intended to carry shock overtones emerges as a tepid tale with limited prospects in the sexploitation market.

Shary Marshall does well enough by a thankless star role and Todd Lasswell dittoes as the husband, finally sent to jail and thus paving the way for femme's rehabilitation. John Harmon and Anne MacAdams are her suffering parents and Susan Cummings has a few satisfactory moments as a street-walker who tries to get femme back on her feet when she goes on the skids.

Direction by Irvin Berwick, who also scripted with Harold Livingston and coproduced with Alan P. Magerman and Jack Paller, is stock, as are all departments. Marilyn Michaels sings title song over credits. *Whit.*

Igy Joettem
(This Was My Path)
(HUNGARIAN)

Budapest, Aug. 23.
Hungarofilm release of Mafilm (Studio IV) production. With Andras Kozak, Sergei Nikonenko. Directed by Miklos Jancso. Screenplay, Gyula Hernadi; camera, Tamas Somlo; music, Zoltan Jenei. Reviewed in Budapest. Running Time, 88 MINS.
The young Hungarian... Andras Kozak
The young Russian....Sergei Nikonenko

This one was directed by Miklos Jancso, creator of "The Hopeless Ones" which was rated one of the best Hungarian pix in recent years. "Path" does not have the good overall quality of "Ones" but may still be considered one of the better Hungarian films. Although the story borders occasionally on the naive, this has definite plus points, mainly the acting of its two principal players and technical credits. "Path" seems limited to home consumption, and foreign prospects are chancey.

Like many Magyar pix, this one deals with the last phase of the last World War. It concerns a 17-year-old Hungarian who flees the German - occupied territory and lands in Russian captivity. Along with a young Soviet soldier, he's ordered to tend the cattle. After some mistrust in the beginning, the two young people become real friends. The young Soviet soldier is still suffering from a severe wound he received in action and eventually finds himself in very bad shape. In his despair, his Hungarian friend puts on a Soviet uniform and forces a Hungarian medico to rush to his suffering partner. But help comes too late and the soldier dies. In the end, the young Hungarian, still wearing the Soviet uniform, is beaten up by Hungarians. Film makes a plea for friendship. *Hans.*

Hotel Paradiso
(COLOR)

Pleasant and glossy rendition of Feydeau farce proves routine entry with some theatre buff appeal and good cast values.

MGM release of Peter Glenville production, directed by Glenville. Stars Alec Guinness, Gina Lollobrigida, Robert Morley, Peggy Mount, Akim Tamiroff. Screenplay, Peter Glenville, Maurice Desvallieres; camera (Panavision and Metrocolor) Henri Decae; editor, Anne V. Coates; music, Laurence Rosenthal; associate producer, Pierre Jourdan; asst. director, Georges Pellegrin. Reviewed, New York, Aug. 31, 1966. Running Time, 100 MINS.
Benedict Boniface...... Alec Guinness
Marcelle Cot .... Gina Lollobrigida
Henri Cot .... Robert Morley
Angelique .... Peggy Mount
Anniello .... Akim Tamiroff
La Grand Antoinette .... Marie Bell
Maxime .... Derek Fowldes
Mr. Martin .... Douglas Byng
Duke .... Robertson Hare
Victoire .... Ann Beach
Inspector .... Leonard Rossiter
George .... David Battley
Turk .... Dario Moreno
Georges Feydeau ...... Peter Glenville

Film version of Georges Feydeau's turn-of-the-century "L'Hotel del Libre Echange" is a second generation production of Peter Glenville's recent legit revival of the French farceur in London. Unfortunately, despite its period charm, stylized performances and restful innocence, the dated gentility seems too remote for contemporary audiences. Boxoffice aide, however, could be forthcoming from the cast's marquee value.

Plot involves a complicated series of mishaps triggered by the 40-year-old "itch" of M. Boniface, played with wearily glossy perfection by Alec Guinness, for the wife of his next-door neighbor, Henri Cot, assayed with appropriate bluster by Robert Morley. Miffed by her neglectful husband, Mme. Cot, adequately acted by Gina Lollobrigida, succumbs to Boniface's suggestion that they rendezvous at the seedy Parisian assignation locale, Hotel Paradiso.

A concatenation of endless co-incidences, laboriously contrived for the better part of the film, conspire to relegate the rendezvous to farce. When it finally takes place, it is only after a parallel series of misunderstandings, misapprehensions and misguided actions cause the entire cast to converge on the place, including M. Cot, M. Martin (Douglas Byng), an acquaintance of Boniface and his four daughters, the maid, involved in her own liaison with Cot's nephew, assorted denizens of the hotel and ultimately the police.

Neatly halved, part one is devoted to wiring the plot mechanism, and part two to watching it unravel. An epilog, framed by "next day" device, witnesses the participants as they suffer the consequences of their escapade. With the hairsbreadth timing appropriate to farce, all somehow squeak through unscathed but wiser.

The play itself is framed by Glenville, in the role of Feydeau, observing the antics of his neighbors. The frayed device of Feydeau popping silently in and out of each scene like a Jack-in-the-Box is too cliche in an already stilted comedy.

Main problem with the film,

despite its excellent on-location lensing by Henri Decae and the professionalism of the cast, is a bloodless script. Glenville, in an attempt to infuse theatrical brio into the play, only succeeds in over-stylizing it. The focus is on a bewildering blur of activity, while the dramatic action, though admittedly slight, is lost in the scramble. Guinness slips into a by-now overfamiliar role with the bored ease of one donning a favorite smoking jacket, while Miss Lollobrigida seems to be attempting to revive silent film acting techniques by stacking her performance with impressions of wide-eyed surprise and frozen gestures of disbelief. Best performance is turned in by Peggy Mount, who delivers Mme. Boniface with the buzz-saw terror of a dominating wife. *Rino.*

Picture Mommy Dead
(COLOR)

A mildly entertaining melodrama with good marquee value name stars, pic should appeal to the teenage as well as family trade.

Hollywood, Aug. 31.
Embassy release of Bert I. Gordon production, produced and directed by Gordon. Features Don Ameche, Martha Hyer, Susan Gordon, Zsa Zsa Gabor, Maxwell Reed, with Wendell Corey, Signe Hasso, Anna Lee, Paule Clark, Marlene Tracy, Steffi Henderson, Robert Sherman, Kelly Corcoran. Screenplay, Robert Sherman; camera (Pathecolor), Ellsworth Fredricks; asst. director, Dennis Donnelly, editor, John Bushelman. Reviewed Hollywood, Aug. 29, '66. Running Time, **88 MINS.**
Edward Shelley .... Don Ameche
Francene Shelley ..:..... Martha Hyer
Jessica .... Zsa Zsa Gabor
Susan Shelley .... Susan Gordon
Anthony .... Maxwell Reed
Clayborn .... Wendell Corey
Sister Rene .... Signe Hasso
Elsie Kornwald .... Anna Lee
First Woman .... Paule Clark
Second Woman .... Marlene Tracy
3rd Woman .... Steffi Henderson
Father .... Robert Sherman
Boy .... Kelly Corcoran

Meller about a young girl who inherits a fortune from her mother and is mysteriously killed, has an opulent setting, name cast, and interesting shock situations that should draw well with the family trade. Fact that pic is the one for which Hedy Lamarr was to make a comeback also may work for exploitation value.

Pic, however, has a number of holes in the script by Robert Sherman and outcome, as to who killed "Mommy," appears to have been turned around and does not come off with plausability.

Outstanding feature is Greystone Mansion on Sunset Blvd., where most of the pic was filmed. The elegant old Doheny home gives pic a feeling of lushness, whereas the characters moving around before the cameras don't have much dimension.

Pic opens with flashback to Mommy unconscious on the floor beside burning bed. Daughter's hand reaches out and takes necklace from the body. It is soon revealed that under certain legal restrictions daughter gets bulk of mother's estate. Girl's stepmother and father have other ideas and there is also a cousin of the dead

woman who has an ax of his own to grind.

Suspense is very slow in building and only occasionally presents chilling moments, e.g., a hawk belonging to the cousin pursuing the girl and at another point crashing through her bedroom window.

Susan Gordon, as the poor little rich girl, gives a first rate performance and has been well directed by her father, Bert I. Gordon. Don Ameche as the father is fine and Martha Hyer as his second wife also acts agreeably. Zsa Zsa Gabor appears only in a few brief flashbacks and is on the screen for no more than a total of five minutes.

In cameo roles Wendell Corey, Signe Hasso and Anna Lee do nicely and Maxwell Reed, as the cousin, comes off strongly in a difficult role.

Ellsworth Fredricks' camerawork is crisp and John Bushelman's editing is expert. *Dool.*

Kaleidoscope
(BRITISH-COLOR)

Entertaining comedy suspenser. Little marquee power but mod styles give a selling angle. Needs nursing for word of mouth.

Hollywood, Aug. 18.
Warner Bros. release of Winkast (Jerry Gershwin-Elliott Kastner) production, produced by Kastner. Stars Warren Beatty, Susannah York; features Clive Revill, Eric Porter. Directed by Jack Smight. Screenplay, Robert and Jane-Howard Carrington; camera (Technicolor), Christopher Challis; editor, John Jympson; music, Stanley Myers; asst. director, Kip Gowans. Reviewed at WB Studio, Aug. 17, '66. Running Time, **102 MINS.**
Barney .... Warren Beatty
Angel .... Susannah York
Manny .... Clive Revill
Dominion .... Eric Porter
Aimes .... Murray Melvin
Billy .... George Sewell
Captain .... Stanley Meadows
Porter .... John Junkin
Chauffeur .... Larry Taylor
Receptionist .... Yootha Joyce
Exquisite Thing .... Jane Birkin
Johnny .... George Murcell
Leeds .... Anthony Newlands

Filmed in England, "Kaleidoscope" is an entertaining comedy suspenser about an engaging sharpie who tampers with playing card designs so he can rack up big casino winnings. The Jerry Gershwin - Elliott Kastner production has some eyecatching mod clothing styles, inventive direction and other values which sustain the simple story line. Marquee strength is weak, but careful nursing in initial dates for word of mouth can yield eventual good returns.

Robert and Jane-Howard Carrington's original screenplay turns on the exploits of Warren Beatty as he etches hidden markings on cards, wins big at various Continental casinos and, via an affair with Susannah York, comes under o.o. of her dad, Scotland Yard inspector Clive Revill. Latter forces Beatty to assist in capture of Eric Porter, British gambler who has overextended himself in various illegal commitments.

The relaxed progress of the story becomes, under Jack Smight's direction, more dynamic through his use of Christopher Challis'

mobile Technicolor camera. Subsidiary events and characterizations—Miss York's dress shop, her estrangement from Revill, latter's mechanical toy hobby, Porter's deliberate viciousness, climactic card game, chase, etc.—keep the pace moving. Final half-hour is all serious drama, while Beatty and the girl are trapped by Porter.

All performances are okay. Of the producing partners, Kastner is the producer of record, and pair's Winkast Prods. Ltd. holds pic's copyright. John Jympson trimmed to an okay 102 minutes, and Stanley Myers' music is adroit. The wardrobe, a plus factor for the femme trade, was done by Sally Tuffin and Marion Foale. Maurice Binder's title art fits in with the optical title theme, and cuts are kaleidoscopic. Overall, this modest little picture could prove a sleeper. *Murf.*

Venice Films

Nattlek
(Night Games)
(SWEDISH)
Venice, Sept. 2.
Sandrews production and release. Features Ingrid Thulin, Keve Hjelm, Lena Brundin, Jorgen Lindstrom, Naima Wifstrand, Monica Zetterlund, Lauritz Falk, Rune Lindstrom, Christian Blatt, others. Director, Mai Zetterling. Screenplay, Zetterling and David Hughes, from novel by Zetterling; camera, Rune Ericson; music, Jan Johansson, George Riedel; editor, Paul Davies. At Venice Film Festival. Running Time, **90 MINS.**
Irene .... Ingrid Thulin
Jan (grown up) .... Keve Hjelm
Jan (boy) .... Jorgen Lindstrom
Mariana .... Lena Brundin
Aunt Astrid .... Naima Wifstrand
Homosexual .... Rune Lindstrom

Likely to be the most-discussed film of the year—or of many a year—"Night Games" would appear to have an assured career open to it wherever it is, or can be, shown. Surely as a lure to prurient and sensation seekers, it has no peer, but since it is also a film of quality and of taste, wider b.o. horizons may be open to pic than the mere exploitation belt which girds the globe.

Axiomatically, exploitable product divvies into two major categories: the cheapie-quickie which skirts pornography, and the important film which contains similar material but treats it differently, copping critical plaudits and that sector of the audience (and indications are it's a notable and growing one) which would be ashamed to be seen entering houses showing the mere sexploitation pic.

"Night Games" is decidedly in the second group, in the great tradition of Scandinavian films. It also goes without saying, however, that since pic goes further than any of its ilk in displayed nudity, perversity, etc., it will have to wage pitched running battles with censors almost anywhere if a semblance of continuity is to remain and, it should be added, if its many qualitative factors — the scope of the film—are to remain recognizable.

The story: A man, whose sexual inhibitions have threatened to ruin his engagement and marriage, pauses, during a visit to the castle

home of his youth, to ponder the causes for his sexual distaste. In flashback form, intercut with the visit, audience is shown the perverted atmosphere which reigned at homestead years before, during which the 12-year-old boy witnessed orgies, rubbed elbows with his mother's lovers, and generally with his elders obsessed by topic number one. There is last but not least an incestuous mother-son relationship, carried to its early stages only, but graphic and eye-opening. With the help of his fiancee, the man finally is able to shake off his complexes, and after one final party at the castle, it is blown to bits, thus sealing his liberation.

For the record, the controversial sequences are herewith listed. There is a near-opening bit in which the boy's mother gives birth to a stillborn child during an orgiastic party at the castle and in full view of the guests and of her son. Surely this shocker is also the weirdest birth scene on film and, as with many others in pic, must be seen to be believed. In another, the boy sneaks under his mother's dress while she's kissing her lover and fondles her legs. In still another, the now-grown man's fiancee disrobes to the waist in an attempt to dispel his sexual inhibitions and arouse him, and remains nude, on camera, for the entire sequence.

Further on, there's the scene in which the young boy is sandwiched in bed between an old lecher and a saucy maid. And the two orgies: one the aforementioned opener, the other, complete with stag films being screened to spectators titillating themselves and others, held outside the grown boy and girl's wedding night bridal suite. Last but not least, the key scene and the most controversial one, in which mother and son share the same bed.

That much for the visually explosive scenes, but pic is also filled with far-out lines of dialogue, completely explicit and unbowing to cinematic convention.

All this said for the record, it would appear difficult to add—and win belief — that taste prevails, that the film is made with intelligence and determination and courage, and that femme director Mai Zetterling's primary intent was not to excite but to shock, to show many negatives to produce a positive. It's the old argument which will always emerge when a "Dolce Vita"-like pic is made: how many people in each audience will see (or are mature enough to see) the author's ultimate moralistic intentions, and how many others will see only the flesh 'n' sex display up front?

Be this as it may, and the argument could and will go on for years, it remains to be said that pic is well made, neatly acted by Ingrid Thulin as the mother, Keve Hjelm as the grown boy, Jorgen Lindstrom as the child, Lena Brundin as the fiancee and bride, and a large supporting cast for which colorful would be an understatement, especially Naima Wifstrand as the moppet's aunt and Rune Lindstrom as the homo house guest.

Sometimes, Miss Zetterling's

symbols, allegories and wh have you are a bit over-simplifie J, not to say naive, such as in the blowing up of the castle, supposedly symbolizing a corrupt and decadent Europe (world?) finally meeting its come-uppance, but generally, she has made a film of much interest and some importance, above and beyond the inevitable controversies and the violent pros and cons it will arouse everywhere. Technically, it's in the best Swedish tradition, with crisp photography, suitable music, settings, etc., throughout. *Hawk.*

La Battaglia di Algeri
(The Battle of Algiers)
(ITALO-ALGERIAN)

Venice, Aug. 31.
Magna Film presentation of an Igor Film (Rome)-Casbah Films (Algiers) co-production by Antonio Musu and Yacef Saadi. Features - Jean Martin, Yacef Saadi, Brahim Haggiag, Tommaso Neri, Fawzia el Kader, Michele Kerbash, Mohamed Ben Kaseen. Directed by Gillo Pontecorvo. Screenplay, Franco Solinas, from story by Pontecorvo and Solinas; camera, Marcello Gatti; editor, Mario Serandrei, Mario Morra; music, Ennio Morricone, Gillo Pontecorvo. At Venice Film Festival. Running time, 120 MINS.
Colonel Matthieu .... Jean Martin
Saari Kader .... Yacef Saadi
Ali la Pointe .... Brahim Haggiag
Capt. Dubois .... Tommaso Neri
Halima .... Fawzia el Kader
Fathia .... Michele Kerbash
Petit Omar...... Mohamed Ben Kassen

Graphic, straightforward, realistic re-enactment of the events that led to the birth, in 1962, of a free Algerian nation, pic is also the first feature film ever made in Algiers by Algerians — teamed here with Italian talent, notably director Gillo Pontecorvo and producer Antonio Musu. It's a dedicated effort with its importance as a "document," but one can't see it breaking b.o. records in many parts of the globe. A very special item due to theme and treatment, its sales points are political (with leftwing backing assured because of its paean to revolutions and revolutionaries) and as a suspense item of sorts, but it will need plenty of sell to move it into ampler fields.

Backdrop of documentary-like treatment of Algerian strife between 1954 and final liberation in 1962 is shown via restaging skillfully blended with newsreel clips. Grey reel quality gives pic an authentic flavor throughout, and adds to dramatic impact of many of its sequences. Up front, but not as spotlit as in usual pix of this kind, are some key characters drawn from life but guided here to heighten dramatic effect. Thus the chutist general whose all-out tactics make things tough for the Algerian rebels in the city, plus a handful of rebels themselves, stoically, heroically battling seemingly unbeatable odds. There are no stars and there is no glamor. Rebel ingenuity and heroism is stressed, but the enemy (in the growing recent tradition suggested by left-leaning films and pamphlets) is depicted as carrying out obviously misguided superior orders.

Non-pro thesps are all fine, all-location work is admirable, and other technical credits are top-notch. *Hawk.*

Chappaqua
(COLOR)

Unusual Yank indie on dope addiction. Personal and right handling could give this art legs as well as specialized chances at home and abroad.

Venice, Sept. 2.
Rooks release and production. With Conrad Rooks, Jean-Louis Barrault, William S. Burroughs, Paula Pritchett. Written and directed by Conrad Rooks. Camera (Eastmancolor), Robert Frank, Etienne Becker; music, Ravi Shankar; editor, Kenout Peltier. At Venice Film Fest. Running Time, 92 MINS.
Russel .... Conrad Rooks
Doctor .... Jean-Louis Barrault
Opium Jones.....William S. Burroughs
Girl .... Paula Pritchett
Messiah .... Allen Ginsberg
Sun God .... Ravi Shankar

For a first film, Yank indie Conrad Rooks has raised money, put in his own and made a personal film on the cure of a drug addict and alcoholic. It breaks new ground in telling it via hallucinations and a mixture of the real and the unreal. Its theme and the feeling of sincerity and revelation could give this fine art chances if well handled.

On the surface this may seem arbitrary and familiar in its mixture of fragments of shots that are kept together by commentary, association or even seem to have no connection at times. But this film gives a unity to the surfacing of the fantasies, ecstasy, misery and suffering of an addict. That is the film's main facet and it brings it off.

An American addict, played by Rooks, decides to go to Paris for a cure. He arrives and is taken in hand by a sinister chauffeur. At the clinic the amiable doctor, French actor Jean-Louis Barrault, seems to be replaced by an eerie-type known as Opium Jones who gives him shots when he needs it. Then film alternates with the hallucinations, treatment, escapes, returns, a dredging up of the inner life and a final cure which may or not lead to a relapse.

At one point the addict says he has been formed by American films, his mother and women. And these motifs also lend a coherence and edge to the film's structures. There are black comedics mixed up with the tale and the character may suddenly reenact bits from early pix and when, after an accident, the doctor sends for blood, it is a Dracula who comes up. An underpinning is the search for faith by the character who has studied with holy men in India, visited the Inca land in Peru and also met some self styled American gurus like poet Allen Ginsberg.

The eschewing of a controlled approach makes this a specialized pic and Rooks also underscores that it is a film by showing the technicians at times, or resorting to makeup in certain scenes that is out of keeping with what may be the real or even the unreal segments. So in the Commedia Del Arte makeup of a Pierrot, he talks to the doctor, or wears none at all during drunken or drugged forays in various bars or places in the world.

Associations have him telling of his childhood in the little New York town of Chappaqua which was an Indian burial place. There is also a recurrent image of a love-

ly woman who may be the needed loved one, mother or the female symbol as well as shots of his travels and his nightmares or more realistic moments of seeming withdrawal, rationality, effusiveness or near despair, which is always staved off.

Black and white is mixed with color and the lensing is sharp and atmospherically right throughout with expert double and more exposures that blend with the progress of the man's treatment. Barrault has understanding and charm as the doctor, William S. Burroughs, the writer, is properly baleful as the drug procurer with Paula Pritchett comely as the woman symbol. Rooks himself has presence and reflects the many sides of the addict and his manias with tact. Ravi Shankar's music is exemplary and brilliantly performed.

This appears one of those first films that dares to make far out associations and use a free wheeling approach usually uncharted by pros and more self-conscious beginners. It mainly works this time and Rooks also displays a fine visual flair. This could well be the filmic "Confessions of an Opium Eater."

So naturally most careful distrib handling is needed, but with the interest in drugs today and the film's offbeat and yet seemingly coherent approach, there may well be solid audiences for it. Critics' pros and cons should also help. *Mosk.*

La Busca
(The Search)
(SPANISH)

Venice, Aug. 31.
Surco Films production and release. Features Jacques Perrin, Emma Penella, Sara Lezana, Hugo Blanco, Lola Gaos, Luis Marin, Daniel Martin, Jose Maria Prada, Coral Pellicer, Fernando Polack, Candida Losada, Maria Basso. Directed by Angelino Fons. Screenplay, Fons, Juan Cesarabea, Flora Prieto, Nino Quevedo, based on novel by Pio Baroja; camera, Manuel Rojas; music, Luis de Pablo; editor, Pablo G. deAmo. At Venice Film Festival. Running Time, 105 MINS.
Manuel .... Jacques Perrin
Rosa .... Emma Penella
Justa .... Sara Lezana
El Bizco .... Hugo Blanco
Vidal .... Daniel Martin
Petra .... Lola Gaos
Leandro .... Luis Marin
Panadero .... Jose Maria Prada
Milagros .... Coral Pellicer
Tomas .... Fernando Polack
Leandra .... Candida Losada
Dona Camina .... Maria Basso

Hispano entry at Venice, period piece based on a w.k. novel by Pio Baroja, set in turn-of-century Madrid, emerges a well-made first pic by promising young (30) Spanish filmmaker Angelino Fons. On the markets, its main impact should be in the lingual circuits of North and South America as well as homegrounds, where novel's renown will help. Elsewhere, it's a chancy item despite its qualities, and very spotty returns are indicated.

Story is one of those items about the country youth who brings innocent candor to a big-city existence which is obviously not made for him. The breaks are all against him, be it in work or innocent love affairs, and he soon finds that the pace is just too fast—and the struggle for existence strictly a survival of the fittest. The influence of French novelists—Zola and others — is noticeable.

Finally caught up despite himself in a feud with a cutthroat thief, he kills him, then awaits police arrival.

Film's values are largely in a faithful rendering of period, unusually straightforward for a Spanish pic as well as explicit in depicting vices, depravities and down-and-out poverty of the times. Sets and costumes have a true feel about them, and pic in general has a realistic impact which at times is very effective and, as noted, unusual for country of origin. At same time, however, there is not always a similar audience participation in action, which at times is overly telegraphed. This may in part be due to thesping. Jacques Perrin has long specialized in these roles of the over-innocent youth caught up in big-city machinations ("Family Chronicle" is a very similar example, also based on a w.k. novel), and he does a good job though we rarely get an inside glimpse of him. Sara Lezana is a treat as his "nice girl" love, with Emma Penella dramatically limning the opposite type of sexual attraction. Hugo Blanco makes a distasteful heavy, while others in large cast cameo effectively. Manuel Rojas' camera works hand in hand with director in rendering the period feeling which is one of pic's main points of interest. Other credits okay. *Hawk.*

The War Game
(BRITISH-DOCUMENTARY)

Venice, Sept. 2.
British Film Institute presentation of a BBC-TV production. Directed by Peter Watkins; camera, Peter Bartlett. At Venice Film Fest, Sept. 1, '66. Running Time, 50 MINS.

"The War Game" was originally made by the BBC-TV for showing on tv, but Corporation brass had second thoughts after it had been completed, decided it was unsuitable for mass audiences, and ordered it to be kept off the airwaves. As a result of political and press agitation, it was eventually agreed to make it available for theatrical release through the British Film Institute. It was a prize-winner at the recent documentary fest here, and was rightly given a repeat in the main motion picture event.

A wholly imaginary picture of what could happen immediately before, during and after a nuclear attack on Britain, "The War Game" is grim, gruesome, horrific and realistic. It is not a pleasant picture to watch, but yet it is one that needs to be shown as widely as possible, as much in China and Russia, as in America, Britain or France. Although make-believe, it would give the general public, the army brass and even the politicians, some conception of what might happen if a nuclear war should ever be triggered off. It's frightening enough to make even the most rabid politico or general have (like the BBC) second thoughts.

The premise of this Peter Watkins production is of a Russian nuclear attack on Britain in support of a Chinese campaign in Vietnam. Civil defense preparations (sandbagging against nuclear bombs) evacuation of women and children, etc., are all grim reminders of the recent past. The attack itself is predictably grim, but the most telling part is the aftermath of the bomb — the severely burned are killed off and their bodies burned, and looters face the firing squad.

Watkins, who left the BBC in protest when it was banned, and who is now directing his first commercial picture, has done an excellent and imaginative job, based on considerable research. It is an effort that deserves to be rewarded by the widest possible presentation. *Myro.*

The Drifter

Freshly felt if somewhat tenuous first pic of a promising filmmaker.

Surfilms release and production. Stars John Tracy; features, Sadja Marr, Michael Fair, Jill. Written and directed by Alex Matter. Camera, Steve Winsten; music, Ken Laster. At Venice Film Festival. Running time 85 MINS.
Alan .... John Tracy
Renee .... Sadja Marr
Mike .... Michael Fair
Barbara .... Jill

First film, made in New York, eschews the usual youthful revolt, neurosis, violence and drugs. Instead is simple tale of rejection that leads to an inability to love and a drifting life that may or may not end with maturity. Sometimes over-indulged, this still shows a nice feel for portraying emotion, love and rueful tenderness sans mawkishness.

It shapes mainly for special situations on its charm and freshness though its still faltering ability to portray a growing dramatic climate and pitch has it sometimes meandering, like the central character himself, and with some scenes overdone and too underlined. Its sentiment does not fall into sentimentality but it skirts it precarously at times.

A young man is on the bum. Son of a concert pianist who prefers not to have him around, he is kept at bay by periodic handouts. Not working, he just floats around the country managing to have sundry affairs with nifty looking and willing girls. Then he moves on for he is unable to commit himself or truly accept any sort of human or spiritual ties, and politics are never mentioned.

He meets a girl he had one of his escapades with and follows her to Montauk Point on Long Island. He begins another affair with her and finds her small son is his. But though attached to the boy, he has to move on and it ends with him weeping on the beach and then going off. There are some influences of Federico Fellini, notably "La Strada," and a certain homage to the screen character of the late James Dean.

In fact, newcomer John Tracy sounds like Dean and mirrors many of his characteristics and even looks a bit like him. But the interior strength is missing. But Tracy has presence and should develop into an interesting thesp when he has absorbed the overleaning on tics.

Others are adequate but the film hangs on Tracy's vague and evasive course through life. There are some pleasantly hued scenes of playfulness and love but there is a tendency by writer-director Alex Matter to milk scenes. And lensing sometimes is too glycerine and arty for its own sake rather than bending to the dramatic pitch of the pic.

Actual top contribution is Ken Laster's perky, dramatically right and emotionally keyed music. Music could be used for pop songs too. *Mosk.*

La Soldadera
(The Female Soldier)
(MEXICAN)

Venice, Aug. 30.
Tecnicos Mexicanos-Productions Marte release and production. Stars Silvia Pinal; features, Jaime Fernandez, Sonia Infante, Pedro Armendariz Jr. Directed and written by Jose Bolanos. Camera, Alex Philips; music, Raul Lavista. At Venice Film Fest. Running Time, 85 MINS.
Soldadera .... Silvia Pinal
Juan .... Jaime Fernandez
Soldier .... Pedro Armendariz Jr.
Campfollower .... Sonia Infante

The Mexican Revolution is the background for this tale of a woman who follows her husband into it and becomes one of the female soldiers. It mixes comedy and drama, but does not strike the right balance. As it stands, it has fine possibilities for Latin circuits abroad.

Silvia Pinal is a popular actress but does not have the robust frame and dramatic presence needed for the part of a woman who follows her husband when he is inducted by government troops and then is taken by a peasant revolutionary soldier when he is killed. Miss Pinal plays it coyly and settled for quaintness rather than for a more straightforward character that grows or is affected by the events around her.

The director also overdoes scenes and still lacks a feel for pace, more succinct narration or the right blend of observation to have made this statement on an exciting time. There's the scene of seeing a film that ends with the peasants shooting up the screen, the femme soldiers raiding a rich house and the tearjerking ones of her return to a burned out home, the birth of her child or her trading her guns for food for the baby.

It does have some good battle scenes and sometimes the right note of the individual imbedded in sweeping events beyond them. Besides Miss Pinal's over-indulged, far-fetched girlish limning there is Pedro Armendariz Jr. who displays some of the dash of his late father but not the more robust presence and acting skill as yet. It is technically good and a pic that just misses due to wrong characterizations and the lack of a point of view. *Mosk.*

Les Creatures
(FRENCH-SCOPE)

Venice, Aug. 29.
Mag Bodard - Parc Films - Madeleine Films-Sandrews release and production. With Catherine Deneuve, Michel Piccoli, Eva Dahlbeck, Jacques Charrier, Ursula Kubler. Written and directed by Agnes Varda. Camera, Willy Kurant; editor, Janine Verneau. At Venice Film Fest. Running Time, 102 MINS.
Wife .... Catherine Deneuve
Writer .... Michel Piccoli
Hotel Owner .... Eva Dahlbeck
Young Man .... Jacques Charrier
Electrician .... Nino Castelnuovo
Vamp .... Ursula Kubler

One can understand what French filmmaker Agnes Varda is trying to do in this intellectually-slanted pic, but it is not always visually and dramatically effective. Its unfoldment on two levels, real life and an author's imagination while writing a book, that blends both, makes this somewhat overwrought and a bit pretentious and literary with patches of tedium. Mainly arty chances abroad on its theme and treatment which might create some curio and critical values. But playoff looks chancey.

An accident has a writer's wife left mute. They hole up on a little island, sometimes attached to the mainland at low tides, where he writes his book. But he begins to notice sudden strange actions of the inhabitants as he walks among them which he incorporates in his book. The real and imaginative get intertwined.

He spies on a recluse who he finds has a machine that allows him to make people act as their subconscious, rather than their conscious, demands at times of crisis or change. He gets into a sort of chess game with the man with the various characters as the pieces. A red-tinted screen marks when the characters are being manipulated from the game. The writer rebels and in a fight kills the man.

Then as his child is born and his wife regains her speech, he hears that an old recluse killed himself out of loneliness. It was the man in his imagination. So perhaps Miss Varda wanted to comment on creation, and keep it clear as it mounts, as well as showing how it also is an imaginative interpretation and twisting of reality to attain it.

But trying to get this on film does not quite work. It waters down both the real and unreal and finally neither makes a comment on the problems of artistic creation, nor can the film quite build characters out of the ambivalent nature of the two sets of actions.

It is well shot and does create a sort of clinical interest as the vanities, pettiness and sometimes violent underpinnings of small-town life are exposed and treated. But, finally, it appears affected rather than revealing, and somewhat cold and remote rather than truly entering the joy or anguish of creativity.

So this is an offbeater that would need extremely careful handling and placement abroad. It is technically fine and players are adequate. *Mosk.*

Mister Buddwing

Weak psychological suspenser about an amnesiac. Script thin, direction offbeat, performances good. Okay marquee lineup. Fair dualler for general mature situations. Needs selling hypo.

Hollywood, Sept. 8.
Metro - Goldwyn-Mayer release of a Mann - Laurence - Wasserman production, produced by Douglas Laurence and Delbert Mann, directed by Mann. Features James Garner, Jean Simmons, Suzanne Pleshette, Katharine Ross, Angela Lansbury. Screenplay, Dale Wasserman, based on the novel "Buddwing," by Evan Hunter; camera, Ellsworth Fredricks; editor, Fredric Steinkamp; music, Kenyon Hopkins; asst. director, Erich Von Stroheim Jr. Reviewed at Academy Award Theatre, L.A., Sept. 7, '66. Running Time, 99 MINS.
Mister Buddwing .... James Garner
The Blonde .... Jean Simmons
Fiddle .... Suzanne Pleshette
Janet .... Katharine Ross
Gloria .... Angela Lansbury
Shabby Old Man ...... George Voskovec
Mr. Schwartz .... Jack Gilford
1st Cab Driver .... Joe Mantell
Hank .... Raymond St. Jacques
Dan .... Ken Lynch
Policeman .... Beeson Carroll
2d Cab Driver .... Billy Ha'op
Counterman .... Michael Hadge
Printer .... Charles Seel
Tony .... John Tracy
Chauffeur .... Bart Conrad
Dice Players: Wesley Addy, Kam Tong, Romo Vincent, James O'Rear, Nichelle Nichols, Rafaael Campos, John Dennis, Pat Li, Rikki Stevens.

"Mister Buddwing" is an attempt, realized only in part, to convey the mental tortures of a temporary amnesiac via suspense situations and arty cinematics. Dale Wasserman's script, as directed by Delbert Mann, overemphasizes sub-plot vignette, thus weakening desired cliffhanger effect to a severe degree. Good production values accentuate the mood. Acting is generally competent, but, as a whole, film is not sufficiently strong. Sharp selling could yield good b.o. for Metro release on urban dual bills, but dimmer prospects loom in sabrum.

Evan Hunter's novel, "Buddwing" takes its name from a beer nickname and an airframe component, both sighted by central figure James Garner as he awakes in a N.Y. park unaware of his past. Wasserman's adaptation then takes him through a series of interactions with assorted characters until final recall.

Jean Simmons (in a return to pix after three years), Suzanne Pleshette and newcomer Katharine Ross are among those encountered by Garner. Each gal, via flashback, also reps his wife as the plot reveals the couple's inverse rags-riches, nobility-depravity progress under the pressures of contemporary life. Explicit references to abortion and bisexuality are made, neither of which seems adequately motivated. (Pic bears a Production Code Authority seal.)

Mann, co-producer with Douglas Laurence, has directed in New York with an eye to the offbeat, using subjective camera for the first four minutes before main titles, and jumping about in space and time by direct cuts. Latter are not confusing as much as they appear pretentious, to an unnecessary degree. Garner's real wife is never seen, as the three femme principals get across her past actions.

Despite a final running time of 99 minutes, executed by editor Fredric Steinkamp, pic seems overlong. This is due, in part, to the pallid dialog given Garner, which forces him repeatedly into the background as other players come (and go) with far stronger impact. He never really punches home the true agony of a man who cannot remember yesterday, and, in certain cases, his travail evokes unwanted laughs. Reactive facial expressions are not enough. Angela Lansbury's opening cameo is overdone.

The whole, then, is not the sum of its parts, for the three gals do very well, ditto hobo George Voskovec, beanery owner Jack Gilford, cabbies Joe Mantell and Billy Halop, and wife's uncle, Ken Lynch. Two particularly effective scenes involve cop Beeson Carroll, put upon by park hangers-on as he questions Garner, and the final main sequence in which gambler Raymond St. Jacques steers Garner and Miss Simmons to a no-limit crap game, zestily photographed and edited. But Garner gets lost in the shuffle, and pic thus loses proper audience interest.

Kenyon Hopkins' score has the modern jazz sound used for urban mellers, and Ellsworth Fredricks' stark b&w camera is excellent. Other technical credits are pro. *Murf.*

Texas Across the River
(TECHNISCOPE-COLOR)

Boisterous western spoof with belly laughs galore and Dean Martin. Top possibilities.

Hollywood, Sept. 10.
Universal release of Harry Keller production. Stars Dean Martin, Alain Delon, Rosemary Forsyth, Joey Bishop; features Tina Marquand, Peter Graves, Michael Ansara, Linden Chiles, Aldrew Prine. Directed by Michael Gordon. Screenplay, Wells Root, Harold Greene, Ben Starr; camera (Technicolor), Russell Metty; music, DeVol; editor, Gene Milford; asst. director, Terry Morse Jr. Reviewed at Grauman s Chinese Theatre, Sept. 9, '66. Running Time, 100 MINS.
Sam Hollis .... Dean Martin
Don Andrea .... Alain Delon
Phoebe .... Rosemary Forsyth
Kronk .... Joey Bishop
Lonetta .... Tina Marquand
Capt. Stimpson .... Peter Graves
Iron Jacket .... Michael Ansara
Yellow Knife .... Linden Chiles
Lt. Sibley .... Andrew Prine
Yancy .... Stuart Anderson
Morton .... Roy Barcroft
Willet .... George Wallace
Mr. Naylor .... Don Beddoe
Turkey Shoot Boss .... Kelly Thordsen
Emma .... Nora Marlowe
Gabe .... John Harmon
Medicine Man .... Dick Farnsworth

"Texas Across the River" is a rootin', tootin' comedy western with no holds' barred. It's a gagman's dream, an uninhibited spoof of the early frontier packed with a choice assemblage of laughs, many of the belly genre. With the name of Dean Martin for marquee voltage and a smart exploitation campaign to which the Harry Keller production admirably lends itself Universal may expect better than average grosses.

Writers Wells Root, Harold Greene and Ben Starr have de-

veloped a situation of a gallant Spanish innocent set down in a world he can never quite understand. That he is a nobleman, too, with courtly ethics, makes him all the more improbable, as a character who takes in stride wild Comanches and wilder longhorns, who finds in Martin, as a Texan, the most perplexing problem of all. Against this background unfolds slapstick, both sophisticated and unsophisticated humor and, in spots, romance.

Michael Gordon's direction exploits the laugh department as he juggles the misadventures of Alain Delon, in Spanish role, and Martin with a mission of transporting guns across Comanche territory and Delon on his hands. Both Indians and the cavalry are satirized with countless slick touches. Gordon likewise has at his disposal a clever set of pranksters who drain their roles of comic possibilities.

Martin delivers his trademark tongue-in-cheek approach to character and Delon scores strongly as the Spanish duke whose persistent gallantry leads to all manner of complications. Joey Bishop as Martin's Injun sidekick plays it straight for heightened humor, and Rosemary Forsyth is in for nice romantic interest as a Southern coquette.

In support, Tina Marquand, daughter of Jean Pierre Aumont and late Maria Montez, shines as an Indian maid whom Delon saves from death. Michael Ansara is immense as the Comanche chief who has a problem on his hands, his bumbling son, played hilariously by Linden Chiles, who doesn't seem able to do anything right, including accidentally setting his father's war bonnet on fire. Peter Graves is the cavalry captain who races his column through a hundred Indians without seeing them as he takes after Delon, wanted on a murder charge.

Technical credits are all first-rate, including Russell Metty's beautiful color photography, DeVol's music score, Gene Milford's sharp editing, Alexander Golitzen and William D. Cinces' art direction. The Kingston Trio sing title song cleffed by Sammy Cahn and James Van Heusen over opening credits. *Whit.*

The Appaloosa
(TECHNISCOPE-COLOR)

Loosely-made western with more directorial interest in camera angles than excitement.

Hollywood, Sept. 1.
Universal release of Alan Miller production. Stars Marlon Brando, Anjanette Comer, John Saxon; features Emilio Fernandez. Directed by Sidney J. Furie. Screenplay, James Bridges, Roland Kibbee; based on novel by Robert MacLeod; camera (Technicolor), Russell Metty; editor, Ted J. Kent; music, Frank Skinner; asst. director, Douglas Green. Reviewed at Universal Studios, Aug. 30, '66. Running Time, 98 MINS.
Matt .... Marlon Brando
Trini .... Anjanette Comer
Chuy .... John Saxon
Lazaro .... Emilio Fernandez
Squint Eye .... Alex Montoya
Ana .... Miriam Colon
Paco .... Rafael Campos
Ramos .... Frank Silvera
Priest .... Larry D. Mann

An interesting story premise is loosely developed in this 1870 Border western in which Marlon Brando, a man who has "killed and sinned," tries to recover the Appaloosa stallion which a Mexican bandit chieftain has stolen from him. Sidney J. Furie's direction appears overly concerned with unusual and sometimes grotesque camera angles. This seriously detracts in building excitement and slows action, a requisite for this type of film. As a result there is a shortage of thrills and a strange lack of color in the Brando character, which should have been more positive.

Alan Miller produced in beautiful Technicolor enrichment of scenes and Russell Metty's moving scenic photography is at its best. Based on novel by Robert MacLeod, the James Bridges-Roland Kibbee screenplay, in what may have been intended to characterize Brando, is over-leisurely at times and frequently misses out on the explosive qualities which Brando's introduction leads audience to expect. The driving purpose of star's quest seems long delayed in overcharacterizing him and his methods as he finds himself unable to rise above his difficulties.

Brando delivers a rambling performances, occasionally managing dynamic enactment of the man who crosses the Border into Mexico to beard the bandito in his village headquarters. He is the only member of cast who doesn't speak with a heavy Mexican accent.

John Saxon handles himself well in bandit role, as does Anjanette Comer, his woman. She helps Brando escape after latter is bested by outlaw in an Indian wrestling match and bitten by a deadly scorpion which awaited the one whose arm was forced to the table. Colorful support is provided by Emilio Fernandez, a bandit's aide, Alex Montoya, a murderous henchman, Miriam Colon and Rafael Campos, friends of Brando, and Frank Silvera, a goatherd.

Top technical assistance adds to quality of production, including Frank Skinner's music score, Alexander Golitzen and Alfred Sweeney's art direction and Ted J. Kent's editing. *Whit.*

Rat Pfink and Boo Boo

An off-beat low-low budget pix that occasionally presents some clever cinematic devices.

Hollywood, Sept. 7.
Morgan-Steckler Production, produced, directed, camera and original story by Ray Dennis Steckler. Features Carolyn Brandt, Vin Saxon, Titus Moede, George Caldwell, Mike Kannon, James Bowie, Keith Wester, Mary Jo Curtis, Romeo Barrymore, Dean Danger. Screenplay, Ronald Haydock; music, Henry Price; editor, Keith A. Wester. Reviewed at Esquire Theatre, Hollywood, Sept. 7, '66. Running Time, 72 MINS.
Cee Bee Beaumont .... Carolyn Brandt
Lonnie Lord/Rat Pfink .... Vin Saxon
Titus Twimbly/Boo Boo ... Titus Moede
Linc .... George Caldwell
Hammer .... Mike Kannon
Benjie .... James Bowie
Cowboy .... Keith Wester
Irma La Streetwalker .... Mary Jo Curtis
Ape Trainer .... Romeo Barrymore
Narration .... Dean Danger
Swinging Ape .... Kogar

As an experimental film, "Rat Pfink" has its interesting moments and cinematic devices. Unfortunately they are few and far between and not quite enough to keep the viewers attention fixed.

An intended humorous or better, satiric, takeoff on "Batman" and his likes, feature was actually filmed two years ago, before the Batman craze, according to filmmaker Ray Steckler. In light of the tv success of the "Batman" series, film might generate some offbeat excitement, but it doesn't have much weight as a spoof.

Best sequences are those in which a gang of three pursue and capture two women. Opening sequence painstakingly photographs one abduction and the second slowly builds in the center of the pix. By having camera concentrated almost exclusively on legs running and hands holding a chain and another, a hammer, along with skillful editing, a sense of animal inhumanity is economically presented.

Story line is either deliberately disjointed or just doesn't come off. Contrasted against the realism of brutality is rock & roll singer Lonnie Lord and a bumbling gardener. Lord, played competently by Vin Saxon, is boyfriend of the s cond abducted girl. Titus Moede, the gardner, who also has a sexual in.erest in the same girl, along with Lord merely wait for word from the abductors looking passive and almost unconcerned.

They spring to action as caped crusader and sidekick when they receive word of her whereabouts. After a series of so-so humorous mishaps they slug it out with the gang and after an added encounter with Kogar the Swinging Ape, all ends blissfully.

Black and white photog is not always crisp and camera often swivels at a vertigo pace. Sound is good and there are three agreeable r&r tunes that help stem the tide of trivia. Carolyn Brandt is toplined in the role of the abducted girl. It's evident that she can easily go on to bigger and better things.

Pic was made on a bare budget by Steckler and as an individual effort shows unlimited patience and persistence. Final result, however, seems to show that his energies have been misdirected. *Dool.*

They're A Weird Mob
(AUSTRALIAN—COLOR)

Melbourne, Aug. 27.
British Empire Films release of Williamson-Powell International Films (U.K.) Ltd. production. Produced and directed by Michael Powell. Stars Walter Chiari, Clare Dunne, Chips Rafferty; features Ed Devereaux, Judith Arthy, John Meillon, Slim de Grey, Alida Chelli, Gita Rivera, Doreen Warburton, Jeanne Drynan, Charles Little. Screenplay, Emeric Pressburger, based on novel of same name by John O'Grady; camera (Eastman Color), Arthur Grant; editor, Gerald Turney-Smith. Reviewed at Forum Theatre, Melbourne, Aug. 27, '66. Running Time, 109 MINS.
Nino Culotta .... Walter Chiari
Kay Kelly .... Clare Dunne
Harry Kelly .... Chips Rafferty
Giuliana .... Alida Chelli
Joe .... Ed Devereaux
Pat .... Slim de Grey
Dennis .... John Meillon
Jimmy .... Charles Little
Barmaid .... Anne Haddy
Fat Man in Bar........... Jack Allen

Texture Man	Red Moore
Newsboy	Ray Hartley

The first major Aussie film for a number of years, adapted from a bestselling novel Down Under, "They're a Weird Mob" is stirring hopes of a resurgence of a native motion picture industry. Such a goal, however, depends upon whether the so far indifferent federal government can be persuaded to subsidize it.

Picture is funny, entertaining and shows some aspects of life Down Under, although Australia and Australians as a whole shouldn't be identified 100% with the "Mob." The characters aren't as exaggerated as they may seem, but are as typical of the average Aussie as a cockney is of the average Englishman.

Italian import Walter Chiari scores in a role that seems tailor-made — an Italian journalist who emigrates to Australia to write for an Italian journal in Sydney edited by his cousin. He arrives very green, and much amusement is caused by his taking too literally some of the Aussie slang.

Chiari finds his cousin has fled. He left a very irate young lady, Clare Dunne, who has put money into the journal. Chiari gets a job as a bricklayer and ultimately makes the grade with his fellow Aussie workmen.

Determined to repay his cousin's debts in installments, Chiari seeks Miss Dunne on Sydney's beaches and elsewhere, but is rebuffed all the way. Arriving too late on the scene to propose to a girl from his own country, it is not surprising that he and Miss Dunne become romantically attached. He passes muster with her wealthy father and she with his brickie mates.

Apart from Chiari, Chips Rafferty (who gives an outstanding performance as Miss Dunne's father) and Ed Devereaux as the main bricklayer, most of the cast seems self-conscious before the cameras. Miss Dunne, although often looking stunningly beautiful, is cold and stilted with her work revealing obvious inexperience.

For the first half, the film strives too hard to be funny and concentrates too much upon the strange Aussie lingo. Once it settles down to telling a story and forgetting about this, it is stronger enertainment.

Obviously the film is angled for home screening. Overeas only Chiari and Rafferty would be known at the boxoffice while Devereaux is the only other actor likely to have a draw Down Under.

The color lensing is very good, and there are some excellent scenes of Sydney, its Bohemian King's Cross area and the beaches. The races and beer drinking—two great aspects of the Aussie way of life—are also introduced. Surprisingly, there's not one shot of the Harbour Bridge, nor the controversial upcoming Opera House.

One of the worst features of the film is an occasional background swelling music with vocal chorus declaring "Its a big big country"—which seems exactly like a cigaret commercial. At times, the recording seems to be of poor quality.

Doubtless the picture is going to be a big money-spinner Down Under, but for overseas it seemingly has limited appeal. But if cut somewhat, it might prove an acceptable supporting feature.

Stan.

A Tizedes Meg a Toebbiek
(The Corporal And Others)
(HUNGARIAN)

Budapest, Aug. 23.
Hungarofilm release of Mafilm (Studio III) production. With Imre Sinkovits, Tamas Major, Ivan Darvas. Directed by Marton Keleti. Screenplay, Imre Dobozi; camera, Istvan Pasztor; music, Istvan Sarkoezi. Reviewed in Budapest. Running Time, 90 MINS.

The Corporal	Imre Sinkovits
Albert	Tamas Major
Galay	Ivan Darvas
Szijarto	Gyoergy Palos
Soviet soldier	Lajos Cs. Nemeth
German officer	Laszlo Markus
German officer	Tivadar Horvath

Whatever Marton Keleti, the director of this pic, does he does it with knowhow and a sure hand. He is one of Hungary's vet directors. The oldtimer who used to be assistant director to the late Paul Fejos and Ladislao Vajda feels especially at home with comedies. "Corporal" is, subject-wise, a rather unusual comic vehicle inasmuch as it draws its funny situations from basically bitter happenings of the last World War. Although this is primarily an item for the home market, it has ingredients to amuse some segments of non-Magyar patrons as well.

Pic ridicules so many things that are Hungarian including bad habits and naive manners, but also pokes fun of the fact that this country, after all, was Hitler's last satellite. It plays during the last days of the war and centers around a Hungarian corporal who finds that, after all those bloody years, he has had it.

He flees his unit and finds shelter in an old castle where he joins a group of deserters. The upcoming situations see them involved with different dangers resulting from approaching Germans, Hungarian fascists or Red Army soldiers. Whatever the situation requires, they keep changing their colors and pretend being on the side which enters the scene.

Although the jokes are sometimes wild and bitter, there is a certain freshness about this film. As odd as it may sound, it makes fun of the cruel war in an almost charming manner. A definite advantage about this Magyar production is the splendid acting. This chiefly applies to Imre Sinkovits as the corporal. There is nice support all down the line. Technically, this represents an okay standard.

Hans.

Del Brazo Y Por La Calle
(Arm In Arm, Down the Street)
(ARGENTINE)

Buenos Aires, Aug. 30.
Argentina Sono Film production and release. Stars Evangelina Salazar, Rodolfo Beban; features Susana Campos, Enzo Viena, Luis Tasca, Javier Portales, Marupa Gil Quesada, Mirta Dabner. Directed by Enrique Carreras. Screenplay, Ariel Cortazzo, from a play by Armando Mook; camera Antonio Merayo; music, Tito Ribero; editor, Jorge Garate. At Monumental, B.A. Running Time, 94 MINS.

Maria	Evangelina Salazar
Alberto	Rodolfo Beban
Fernanda	Susana Campos
Jorge	Enzo Viena
Maria's Father	Luis Tasca
Maria's Mother	Maruja G. Quesada
The Fat One	Javier Portales
Draftswoman	Mirta Dabner

The social content of this meller is not intended to excite buffs but to attract femme trade. Pic tells of a young housewife whose marriage is almost on the rocks because of quarrels, lies and humiliating situations derived from her husband's shortage of money. Through her troubles, most female viewers see mirrored many of their own frustrations, dreams and missteps in a society plagued by inflation. At the same time, they enjoy an effective albeit old-fashioned tearjerker.

This, added to the drawing power of tele stars Evangelina Salazar and Rodolfo Beban, helped "Arm" to tee off to solid biz here. It may do well in lingo spots abroad if properly handled.

"Arm" was adapted from a two-character play written back in 1930 by Armando Mook. It has been enlarged to a multi-character script by Ariel Cortazzo, who sought to take the action away from the couple's little apartment as often as possible, within a flashback narrative scheme. Notwithstanding this effort, this is handicapped by too much talk, some repetition and by a rather conventional approach to a theme rooted in reality.

Miss Salazar's sensitive and convincing portrayal helps to rescue "Arm" here and there from its bi-dimensional look. Main credit for director Enrique Carreras lies this time in the way he took advantage of her sweet, yet strong, personality to enliven moments that presumably would have lacked verve. Rodolfo Beban goes no farther than lending his name for marquee dressing. Good cameos are contributed by Susana Campos, as a wealthy woman sharing her time between expensive shopping and dolce vita, and Enzo Viena, as a gentleman-type playboy.

Technical credits are okay, except for the outdated, long-optical effects.

Din.

Schornstein Nr. 4
(Chimney No. 4)
(GERMAN)

Berlin, Aug. 30.
Team release of Hans Oppenheimer production. Stars Romy Schneider, Hans Christian Blech and Michel Piccoli. Directed by Jean Chapot. Screenplay, Marguerite Duras and Jean Chapot; camera, Jean Penzer; music, Antoine Duhamel; settings, Willy Schatz; editor, Ginette Boudet. At Royal Palast, West Berlin. Running Time, 88 MINS.

Julia Kreuz	Romy Schneider
Werner Kreuz	Michel Piccoli
Radek Kostrowicz	Hans Christian Blech
Frau Kostrowicz	Sonja Schwarz
The boy	Mario Huth

Frenchman Jean Chapot, creator of several noteworthy short subjects, has directed his first full-length feature for German producer Hans Oppenheimer. This German production marks the return of Romy Schneider to the domestic screen after an absence of seven years.

Film's commercial prospects will largely depend on Miss Schneider's name. Otherwise, "Chimney No. 4" is far from being a commercial film. But it's the type of entry that may fit into special situations.

It is the story of a young wife who, prior to her marriage, gave away her fatherless infant son to unknown foster-parents. Now, after several years, she wants her child back. The law is on her side for the foster-parents have never legal-adopted the child.

The foster-father, an industrial worker of Polish descent, is not willing to return the boy and fights for him. Yet his mother insists and gets back her son through the help of the police. The desperate foster-father climbs a chimney and threatens to jump unless he gets back the boy.

The incident stirs wide interest, with the press, radio and tv covering it. Public opinion is on the side of the man up on the chimney. It takes the mother a restless night to realize that she can't keep her son.

What militates somewhat against suspense is the fact that the viewer hardly finds any sympathies with the boy's real mother (Miss Schneider). There is no inner conflict on the part of the viewer. This seems to be a fault of the script which should have patterned the role of the mother less hysterical. At times the dialog is implausible.

The players try hard to make the plot ring true. The most impressive performance is turned in by Hans Christian Blech in the role of the foster-father.

There's nothing glamorous about Romy Schneider in this film. One feels the utter devotion she puts into her portrayal. But it's so obvious that too often it's apparent that she's only acting. Same applies to Michel Piccoli (her husband here), if in another respect. He occasionally appears too quiet.

These deficiencies result both from the script and direction. Chapot's directorial abilities are evident but mainly in this film in technical respect. His first feature is best when it gives the impression of a documentary.

Hans.

Venice Films

Fahrenheit 451
(BRITISH-COLOR)

Cast and director provide needed marquee values for filmization of Ray Bradbury's bizarre peep into the future. Needs careful handling for maximum results.

Venice, Sept. 9.
Universal presentation and release of an Anglo-Enterprise Vineyard Film Production, produced by Lewis M. Allen. Stars Oskar Werner and Julie Christie; features Cyril Cusack, Anton Diffring, Jeremy Spenser and Bee Duffell. Directed by Francois Truffaut; screenplay, Truffaut and Jaen Louis Richard, based on the novel by Ray Bradbury; camera (Technicolor), Nicholas Roeg; editor, Thom Nobie; settings, Tony Walton; music, Bernard Herrmann. At Venice Film Feseetival, Sept. 7, '66. Running Time, 113 MINS.

Montag	Oskar Werner
Linda	Julie Christie
Clarisse	Julie Christie
Captain	Cyril Cusack
Fabian	Anton Diffring
Man With Apple	Jeremy Spenser
Book-Woman	Bee Duffell

Tv Announcer .... Gillian Lewis
Doris .... Anne Bell
Helen .... Caroline Hunt
Jackie .... Anna Palk
Neighbor .... Roma Milne

"Fahrenheit 451" is the first picture to come off the production line since Universal set up its own film making h.q. in London at the beginning of the year under the leadership of Jay Kanter, and marks an enterprising and courageous beginning. Ray Bradbury's bizarre peep into a totalitarian future has been intelligently adapted, and the stars and director should help it at the box-office, but it will need careful and specialized handling to make the maximum impact.

With a serious and even terrifying theme, this excursion into science fiction has been thoughtfully directed by Francois Truffaut (it's his first effort in the English language) and there is adequate evidence of light touches to bring welcome and needed relief to a sombre and scarifying subject.

In the author's glimpse into the future—time and place are unspecified—books are considered the opium of the people. They are evil things, reminders of a decadent past, and wield an unhappy influence on ordinary folk. Their possession is a crime and the state has a squad of firemen, thoroughly trained to detect secret hiding places, and to destroy the illicit literature with flame throwers. Fahrenheit 451, it is explained, is the temperature at which books are reduced to ashes.

The yarn develops just a handful of characters, emphasising the inevitable conflict between state and literate-minded citizens. One of the principals is Montag (Oskar Werner) an obedient and lawful fireman, who does his book destroying job with efficiency and apparent enthusiasm, while his equally law-abiding wife (Julie Christie) spends her days glued to the mural tv screen, soaking in the propaganda that is churned out through the day. A young probationary school teacher (also played by Miss Christie) whom Montag meets on the monorail while on the way to the fire station, plants the first seeds of doubt in his mind, and from then on he regularly steals the odd book which he reads secretly in the night.

It is at that point that the real conflict starts and the tension begins to mount, culminating in a situation in which the law-breaking fireman is finally sent to raid his own home after his nervous and frightened wife has informed on him. Montag's escape into the woods, where he joins up with a group of "bookmen" who have committed the classics to memory, is the hopeful indication that the struggle against totalitarianism will continue.

Throughout history, and particularly in more recent times, book burnings have been practiced by oppressive regimes, but Bradbury has extended the idea to its logical (or should one say illogical?) conclusion. It is certainly an offbeat idea, and not one which will command automatic popularity with cinemagoers, but it has been handled thoughtfully, even though it rarely achieves full emotional involvement. Too often the spectator is left on the sidelines and neither convinced by nor accepting what is projected on the screen.

Though the treatment can be faulted, there are no valid grounds for criticising the principal performances. Werner, in the difficult role of the once diffident and ambitious fireman who finally challenges authority, plays the part in low key style which adds to the integrity of the character, and Julie Christie is standout in her dual roles. As the wife, her long flowing blonde locks emphasize her looks and also her simpleminded acceptance of the official way of life; while the close crop she sports when playing the teacher complete transforms her appearance and character, and makes her thoroughly acceptable as the earnest and rebellious young woman. Cyril Cusack plays the fire station captain with horrifying dedication, and Anton Diffring is effectively cast as a heavy who has caught Montag in the book stealing act. Telling cameos are contributed by Bee Duffell (as a middle-aged woman who prefers to be burned with her books), Gillian Lewis as a tv announcer, and Jeremy Spenser, Anne Bell, Caroline Hunt, Anna Palk and Roma Milne. Among the long list of bookmen, Michael Balfour and John Rae stand out.

Surprisingly, there are few gimmicks, apart from a group of flying men kept in the air by small machines strapped to their bodies, and only one car (apart from the fire engines) is seen on the roads, the monorail apparently being the accepted mode of transport. But these effects are well done, while the architectural style of the future is imaginatively conceived by Tony Walton's designs, and put into effect by Art Director Syd Cain. Nicholas Roeg's color cameras are intelligently deployed, and Thom Nobie's editing and Bernhard Herrmann's music, are among the other plus credits.
Myro.

Mudar De Vida
(Change One's Life)
(PORTUGUESE)
Venice, Sept. 10.

Producoes Cunha Telles release and production. With Geraldo D'El Rey, Isabel Ruth, Maria Barroso, Joao Guedes, Constanca Navarro, Mario Santos. Written and directed by Paulo Rocha with dialog by Antonio Reis. Camera, Elso Roque; editor, Margareta Mangs. At Venice Film Fest. Running Time, 95 MINS.

Adelino .... Geraldo D'El Rey
Albertina .... Isabel Ruth
Julia .... Maria Barroso
Inacio .... Jose Guedes
Old Woman .... Constanca Navarro
Old Man .... Mario Santos

Paulo Rocha confirms his promise as one of the more individual among Portuguese filmmakers after his tale of a provincial trying to brave city life in "The Green Years" at the Locarno Fest last year. Here he handles love and life among poor fisherfolk with knowing insights into the emotions and lives and without undue didactics or forcing the issues. It is noted that things must change, both the people and their circumstances, but it also does it with a balance of form and content and, above all, the right blending of playing, visuals and tempo.

Perhaps there is a tendency to sometimes schematise the final decisions of the protagonists, but there is a tenderness towards the people plus a necessary concern. There is also a rightful probing of the conditions but it is done sans indulgence or overrighteousness. It thus appears a sure lingo item or for the Latin circuits abroad as well as a film worth specialized handling and showings if correctly placed and labeled.

A man comes back from military service in Angola, the Portuguese African possession in revolt, and a long stay afterwards. He finds his girl has married his brother after not hearing from him. She has changed and will not give into his advances and he finally goes off to meet a girl who wants out of the poverty by any means including stealing. It ends with his determination to try to stick it and work if it is not clear whether she will stay on.

The encroaching sea that tears down houses, the everyday work, the zesty humor of the people, even in their poverty, are also portrayed and it blends a compelling ethnic feeling with good characterizations and a forceful pacing.

This bodes some easing on censorship in that small pic producing country since it notes that changes are necessary and depicts a certain restlessness in its characters. It is technically good and the playing is sober and right. Perhaps the more epic flair and the fillip of deeper emotional breadth are not always there. But director Rocha displays a sure feeling for narration and should be heard from at future fests. *Mosk.*

Het Afscheid
(Farewells)
(BELGIAN)
Venice, Sept. 7.

Visie release and production. With Petra Laseur, Julian Schoenaerts, Senne Rouffaer. Written and directed by Roland Verhavert from the novel by Ivo Michaels. Camera, Herman Wuyts; At Venice Film Fest. Running time, 90 MINS.

Pierre .... Julien Schoenaerts
Wife .... Petra Laseur
Jessen .... Senne Rouffaer

Films from the Flemish section of Belgium are rare, but this is the second to show at a European fest this year. It is a rather grim but fairly arresting tale of an officer waiting to ship out on a boat that may be involved in troubles in the Congo. Fear theme is somewhat literary in trying to probe its effects sometimes arbitrarily and symbolically, on the characters.

One man finds it unbearable to keep saying goodbye to his wife each day as they get ready to leave but must be back every day to await shipping out. Another goes on drunks but finally decides to settle down before leaving. Each has strange adventures which are blended with thoughts and the omnipresent reality of the ship about to depart. So it is slow, a bit mannered, but does have some force in its quiet direction and growing tensions.

Its fairly surface characters, passable playing and poisness make this a chancy item for art chances but its concentrated playing and style might make this a tv possibility abroad. It, with the other Flemish pic seen, "The Man With the Shaved Head," of Andre Delvaux, seems to display a grim outlook of personal uneasiness, fears based on war scares, and a certain unassuaged desire in the main characters that seem to be the hallmark of both films. Though not a seeming renaissance, it does bode some interesting films coming from this linguistic part of this small country which may also reflect the tensions between the two different lingoed sections of the country.

It is technically good if the rhythm is too stilted and the tale too muted in symbols and intellectualism rather than with enough clearcut feeling and flesh and blood. *Mosk.*

Un Uomo a Meta'
(Almost a Man)
(ITALIAN)
Venice, Sept. 4.

Dino DeLaurentiis release of a Vittorio DeSeta Production. Features Jacques Perrin, Lea Padovani, Ilaria Occhini, Gianni Garko, Rosemarie Dexter, Pier Luigi Capposi, Francesca DeSeta, Kitty Swan. Directed by Vittorio DeSeta. Screenplay, DeSeta, Carpi, Gherarducci, from story by DeSeta. Camera, Dario di Palma. Music, Ennio Morricone. At Venice Film Festival. Running Time, 100 MINS.

Michele .... Jacques Perrin
Elen .... Ilaria Occhini
Marina .... Rosemarie Dexter
Ugo .... Pier Paolo Capponi
Michele's brother ...... Gianni Garko
Simonetta .... Francesca de Seta
Mother .... Lea Padovani

Strictly an art entry on strength of subject matter and handling, "Shadow" is nevertheless visibly the interesting, important product of an able and dedicated filmmaker, Vittorio DeSeta, whose second feature film it is. Deliberately slow pace and surface content will probably limit its audience to those geared to mood pix and introspective items a la Antonioni. (Pic is one of Italo entries at New York Film Festival.)

Story is about a young man, a writer, with an artistic and personal crisis. Unable to find happiness in love, incapable even of satisfying his girl, he becomes a voyageur and broods over his plight, at times skirting suicide. With flashbacks and flash-forwards, director DeSeta dissects his character, in turn showing him hurt by a callous, superficial girl, admiring his successful younger brother, escaping from an asylum where he's been subjected to electro-shock treatments, returning to the home of his youth and recalling his mother's dictatorial character. Finale finds him alone but presumably on the way to a self-satisfying solution to his woes. The plot however is not for the telling in this type of pic which is all mood and flashes of thoughts. Surely, the many seemingly static sequences may irk unprepared audiences to open rebellion while at the same time those "with it" will sing its praises highly. Certainly too, pic will need a hard sell, as on paper, it has little riding for it. While apart from the Antonioni influence it also has some Fellini-ish touches about it and is strangely un-Italian—almost Swedish—in "feeling" and cut of image, it is at the same time very Italian in basic concept.

Most of performances are mere flashes of director's impressions without development, but Jacques Perrin brings a new maturity and stature—after innumerable stints in significant Italo and French pix—to his role as the brooding writer. Unless stint proves a one-shot exception for young French thesps and is due to "use" by directors, Perrin could develop into an international personality in the wake and role niche of a Montgomery Clift, whom he resembles in this pic. Rosemarie Dexter and Ilaria Occhini are most easy on the eyes as two of Perrin's girls, while Gianni Garko lends youthful brashness to his role as the brother. Lea Padovani is wasted in a cameo as the mother, while others come through well.

Major nod must also go to Dario Il Palma's outstanding lens work, apparently all on actual locations, which does much to capture the mood or moods intended by De-Seta. Music by Ennio Morricone is effective. *Hawk.*

Abschied von gestern
(Farewell From Yesterday)
(GERMAN)

Venice, Sept. 6.
Constantin release of Kairos Film (Alexander Kluge) production, in collab with Independent-Film, Munich. With Alexandra Kluge, Guenther Mack, Eva Maria Meineke and Hans Korte. Directed and written by Alexander Kluge; camera, Edgar Reitz; settings, Bernhard Hoeltz; editing, Beate Mainka. Reviewed at Venice Festival. Running Time, 90 MINS.
Anita G. .... Alexandra Kluge
Pichota .... Guenther Mack
Mrs. Pichota ...... Eva Maria Meineke
Judge .... Hans Korte
Young man .... Peter Staimmer
Social worker ...... E. Kuntze-Pellogio
Disk chief .... Josef Kreindl
Mother .... Ursula Dirichs
Parachutists .... O. E. Fuhrmann
Gentleman .... Karl-Heinz Peters

Alexander Kluge, 34, a lawyer and writer, a teacher on films and creator of six intelligent s h o r t films, has his first full-length feature and expectedly it's very "cerebral." Perhaps too much. It will be a difficult sell to the regular trade. But, prestigewise, Kluge can be satisfied with the outcome of his opus at the Venice Festival of 1966. It shows (especially foreign) critics the continuation of the promising new German film trend which started not long ago with "It," "The Young Toerless" and "No Shooting Time For Foxes."

Some will feel feature is more a reportage than an entertainment. Occasionally it employs the silent film technique with lines projected on the screen, then it has the character of a modern documentary. But on the other hand its dialog sequences are utterly literary. There is much Jean-Luc Godard influence. Reactions will run from buffs' enthusiasm to some general boredom.

Story is extracted from Kluge's book, "Biographies," which was published in Germany four years ago. It revolves around a young girl who goes from East to West Germany hoping to find b e t t e r conditions of life. She steals something and gets involved with the law. She changes cities and has it tough to find her place in society. She becomes the mistress of her employer who lets her down. She is suspected of a theft which she hasn't committed. She becomes a r e s t l e s s wanderer. Kluge tries to explain how a hu-

man being can feel unable to get along even under changing regimes (in this case, the German Nazi era finds mention, then there is the confrontaion with the Commie system in E-Germany and finally the "capitalistic" system in W.-Germany) and become a victim of unfortunate conditions of life or society.

Stylistically, film is practically a montage of both facts and fiction. What militates against conviction is that the characters don't come to life. And the constantly changing form and period tend to lead to confusion. By all means, this is heavy meat for the ordinary viewer.

Nevertheless, pic has a lineup of definite advantages. One is, oddly enough, Alexandra Kluge, the director's sister and a medico in private life, who plays the central figure. There is something fascinating about her and primarily her face which can carry a scene. She delivers a gypsy-type performance which can't be measured the conventional way.

Lensing by Edgar Reitz is extremely good. (This is the official German entry at the Venice fest.) Positive value, too, is utilization of music which, to suit the atmosphere, doesn't hesitate to go from a schmaltzy Viennese waltz to a sentimental tango and then over to a hot rhythm.

Pic ends with this philosophy: "Everyone is guilty for everything but if everyone knew this we would have paradise on earth..." *Hans.*

Bride of the Andes
(JAPANESE-COLOR-TOSHO-SCOPE)

Venice, Sept. 7.
Toho release and production. Stars Sachiko Hidari; features, Ancermo Fukada, Koji Takahashi, Don Mateo, Takeshi Hika. Written and directed by Susumu Hani. Camera (Eastmancolor), Juichi Nagano; music, Hikaru Hayashi. At Venice Film Fest. Running Time, 108 MINS.
Tamiko .... Sachiko Hidari
Taro .... Ancermo Fukada
Sasaki .... Koji Takahashi
Quisquis .... Don Mateo
Takeshi .... Takeshi Hika

Picturesque pic about a Japanese bride who goes to Peru to wed a first generation Japanese, unseen. Film concentrates more on ethnic aspects and documentary treatment than on story and character. It has interest in its look at life there, and its treatment of the relations between the people and the newcomer. But the story sometimes gets bogged down in the focus on local color and history.

So it does not quite jell completely, but has interest in its subject and place that could slant this for playoff in special situations. The woman arrives with a child by a former marriage and finds her husband living with Indians in the Andes and doing archaeological work on Inca ruins.

First the squalor, strangeness and harshness of the life disconcerts and almost defeats her. But her attachment to her gentle husband, her son's adaptation and her own growing understanding of the people finally win her only to have things end tragically as her husband is killed excavating a treasure of Inca gold. The money received from the state is given

over to the village and she stays on to live.

Life in a Japanese colony, strange courting ways, with the Indian man fighting the woman, everyday life and the photogenic qualities of the country and ruins make up the backbone of the pic. *Mosk.*

Piervij Utchitelh
(The First Teacher)
(RUSSIAN)

Venice, Sept. 6.
Mosfilm release of a Mosfilm-Kirghiz-film production. Features Bolot Beishenaliev, Natalia Arinbascarova, others. Directed by A. Michailov-Kontcharovski. Based on story by Chingiz Aithmatov. Camera, G. Rerberg. Music, V. Ovchinnikov. At Venice Film Festival. Running Time, 90 MINS.
Teacher .... Bolot Beishenaliev
Altinay .... Natalia Arinbascarova

Modest Russo entry at Venice Film Festival is director's first feature effort and a rather old-fashioned way of telling an old-fashioned story. Interest lies mainly in unusual Kirghiz setting of tale, which is set in 1923, and use made of apparently local talent and non-pros, beginning with featured players. As a saleable entity, it has little hope of breaking through the lingual barriers, despite the naive charm it sometimes displays.

Tale is of a recently discharged Red Army man sent by the Komsomol to a remote village to win over its inhabitants to the Lenin cause. Most are still unequipped for education to the party line due to fear of landowners who still exert power behind the scenes. The aid and love of a poor orphan gal helps him, especially when the news of Lenin's death triggers a sort of local counter-revolution by the landowners.

After various adventures, the couple finally return to the village to begin their work anew, with inhabitants slowly but surely joining the common cause. Pic abounds with sheer propaganda, and hews the party line in describing the Red officer's missionary mission on behalf of the new men in the Kremlin. Yet at other times, it has some of elements and the cadence of a western in which the traditional patterns and allegiances have been replaced by social under- and overtones.

As an added fillip now introe'd into many eastern pix but previously taboo is a sequence in which the native gal takes a river swim in the buff, while her friend (but not the audience) turns his head away so as not to see. Gal, Natalia Arinbascarova, has a winning manner and smile, while Bolot Beishenaliev, who plays the teacher is convincing and a large number of locally recruited village types back colorfully.

Music and other credits okay. *Hawk.*

A Grande Cidade
(The Big City)
(BRAZILIAN)

Venice, Sept. 3.
Mapa Films release and production. With Leonardo Villar, Anecy Rocha, Antonio Pitanga, Joel Barcellos. Written and directed by Carlos Diegues. Camera, Fernando Duarte; editor, Gustavo Dahl.

At Venice Film Feest. Running Time, 85 MINS.
Jasceo .... Leonardo Villar
Luzia .... Anecy Rocha
Calunga .... Antonio Pitanga
Inacio .... Joel Baarcellos

This film is an ironic look at the socalled surface charms of Rio de Janeiro. Under the rich exterior are killers, slums, unhappiness as well as a zesty life force. But the pic is only intermittently ironic enough or spirited enough to bring off its familiar tale completely. It does have appeal for Latino circuits abroad with playoff and art spots limited.

A girl from the provinces comes to town looking for her lover who had promised to send for her. He is now a killer. She gets mixed up with two other men, a young boy longing to go back to the country and a dynamic Negro with a way of surviving. She is drawn in again with the murderer only to be killed with him in a trap.

The film has a nice framework with the Negro singing about getting along by understanding and coping until there can be a way of changing things. But the pic is sometimes a bit arch or slow to pick up tempo and bite in the scenes of the early carnival, the manhunt and the girl's attempts to find something in these three different men before the tragic end. It provides a picture of Brazil catching the old and new, poverty and riches, but does not quite have the depth, driving force and insight of some of the other Brazilian pix by newcomers unveiled at fests the last few years.

Carlos Diegues looms as a promising director if he has yet to find a better merger of form and content. Pic is technically adequate with thesps somewhat too loose and undisciplined. It does not detract from growing Brazilian picture activity, but does not add much lustre either. *Mosk.*

Not With My Wife, You Don't
(COLOR)

Outstanding romantic comedy about marital **problems** among U.S. Air Force personnel. Topnotch in all departments. Strong marquee bait in three stars. Solid b.o. prospects in general situations, with much playing time likely.

Hollywood, Sept. 14.

Warner Bros. Pictures release of a Norman Panama production, directed by Panama. Stars Tony Curtis, Virna Lisi, George C. Scott; features Carroll O'Connor, Richard Eastham, Eddie Ryder, George Tyne. Screenplay, Panama, Larry Gelbart, Peter Barnes, based on a story by Panama and Melvin Frank; camera (Technicolor), Charles Lang, Jr.; editor, Aaron Stell; music, Johnny Williams; song, Williams, Johnny Mercer; production design, Edward Carrere; asst. director, Jack Aldworth. Reviewed at Academy Award Theatre, L.A., Sept. 13, '66. Running Time, 118 MINS.
Tom Ferris .... Tony Curtis
Julie Ferris .... Virna Lisi
"Tank" Martin .... George C. Scott
Gen. Parker .... Carroll O'Connor
Gen. Walters .... Richard Eastham
Sgt. Gilroy .... Eddie Ryder
Sgt. Dogerty .... George Tyne
Doris Parker .... Ann Doran
Nurse Sally Ann........ Donna Danton
Lillian Walters .... Natalie Core

"Not With My Wife, You Don't!" is an outstanding romantic comedy about a U.S. Air Force marriage threatened by jealousy as an old beau of the wife returns to the scene. Zesty scripting, fine performances, solid direction and strong production values sustain hilarity throughout, marking an auspicious bow of Norman Panama as a solo producer. Tony Curtis, Virna Lisi and George C. Scott provide marquee bait. Initial b.o. should be excellent, with much staying and playing power evident for Warner Bros. release in general situations.

Panama and Melvin Frank, who formally split a year ago after 25 years as a team, wrote the original story, which sets up Curtis and Scott as old Korean conflict buddies whose rivalry for Miss Lisi is renewed when Scott discovers that Curtis won her by subterfuge. The amusing premise is thoroughly held together via an unending string of top comedy situations, including domestic squabbles, flashback, and an outstanding takeoff on foreign pix. Larry Gelbart and Peter Barnes worked with Panama on the meaty screenplay.

Curtis is excellent as the husband whose duties as aide to Air Force General Carroll O'Connor create the domestic vacuum into which Scott moves with the time-tested instincts of a proven, and non-marrying, satyr. Miss Lisi, who could just stand there and get a full measure of attention to her own looks, complemented by another snazzy Edith Head wardrobe, interacts neatly with her male stars. All three are billed above-title, and belong there. Scott delivers the outstanding performance.

Under Panama's sure direction, all players register strongly, particularly O'Connor as the gruff, cigar-chewing general: Eddie Ryder, Curtis' longtime non-com assistant, and George Tyne, Cur-

tis' partner in an Arctic survival test into which Scott has maneuvered him. Ann Doran, a consistently superior character actress, is teriff as O'Connor's wife; she embodies perfectly the glib, but warm, folksiness essayed by wives of military officers (and politicians) who have risen to prominence. In smaller roles, Richard Eastman and Natalie Core hit the right note as another top brass couple, while Donna Danton succumbs beautifully to the Scott-Curtis come-ons (to bed).

Overall impact is enhanced by an opening animation bit starring a green-eyed monster (jealousy), plus special visual effects, all wow work by Saul Bass, whose formal credit is for visual consultancy as well as for the deceptively simple title art. The arty pic scene, in which the three stars take on, in Miss Lisi's guilty eyes, the identities of the players, is a superb satire on foreign bedroom film frolics. Shot in b&w and printed on color stock, it looks just like something that finally cleared U.S. Customs.

These added effects, plus clip inserts from "Mighty Joe Young," 1949 RKO pic in the "King Kong" vein, a typical World War II films, and an actual Bob Hope clip from one of the comic's overseas troop entertainment treks, all prove that modern cinematics can add punch to an already strong script. Other contemporary pix, however, often rely on the gimmicks to cover the plot holes.

Aaron Stell executed the editing to a snappy 118 minutes, while Charles Lang, Jr. captured the humor in his mobile Technicolor camera. Paul Beeson is credited with the European lensing which provides some hair-raising, low-level flying around famous structures as well as natural terrain.
Murf.

The Eavesdropper
(El Ojo de la Cerradura)
(ARGENTINE)
(English Subtitles)

Royal Films International release of a Paul M. Heller production. Directed by Leopoldo Torre Nilssos. Stars Janet Margolin, Stathis Giallelis; features Lautaro Murua, Leonardo Favio, Nelly Meden, Ignacio de Soroa, Elena Tortesina. Screenplay, Beatriz Guido, Joe Goldberg, Mabel Itzcovich, Edmundo Eichelbaum and Torre Nilsson from original story by Beatrice Guido and Torre Nilsson; camera, Alberto Etchebehere; editor, Jacinto Cascales; sound, Juan Carlos Gutierrez, Juan Carlos Bertola; music, arranged and conducted by Lopez Furst. Reviewed at N.Y. Film Sept. 14, '66. Running Time: 102 MINS.
Ines .... Janet Margolin
Martin .... Stathis Giallelis
Hernan Ramallo .... Lautaro Murua
Santos .... Leonardo Favio
Lola .... Nelly Meden
Ramon Casal .... Ignacio de Soroa
Mariquita .... Elena Tortesina

Although Royal Films has had invested interest in this film since its production two years ago, it has never been released in the U.S. Major difference is, apparently, due to fact that Royal wanted film to go out in an English-dubbed version whereas producer Paul Heller and director Leopoldo Torre Nilsson wanted the Spanish-language, with English subtitles, version to go first. As result the film has only been seen in a few situations anywhere, including this year's Mar del Plata Fest. It was

requested by the New York Fest last year but Royal wouldn't go for the subtitling expense, according to Heller, who paid the costs, nearly $10,000, himself to make it eligible this year.

A first attempt by the Argentine director to use international names, there's little profit to the film in the performance of Greek actor Stathis Giallelis, miscast as the young university student whose political activities (which evidently require a good aim with a tar bomb on the city's myriad political statues) have necessitated him to "hide out" for a few days. A lecherous uncle suggests an old hotel in a no-longer fashionable area of Buenos Aires, now peopled principally by Spanish exiles and theatrical types.

Being a typical member of a typical Torre Nillson expose of upperclass Argentine society (he evidently refuses to admit that any other types exist), the boy talks a young society girl (Janet Margolin) into accompanying him on his enforced withdrawal from society. As sophisticated as the rest of her friends (plus an inferred incestuous loneliness for a just-married brother), she proves to be as sexually versatile as she is politically naive.

Although the girl becomes friendly toward, and even fond of, some of the hotel inmates, the boy, being a borderline paranoiac (a symbol of the paranoid Argentine society as seen by Torre Nilsson), becomes suspicious of a group of Spanish exiles whose activities are interpreted by him as a plan to assassinate a visiting Latin American dictator. He spends the rest of the film eavesdropping (hence the title) on the group, finally so misinterpreting their actions and conversations that he turns them in to the police. When they're proven innocent, they revenge themselves by mauling the boy and throwing him physically out of the hotel.

With the exception of some rather explicit sexual intercourse scenes and the beautifully-photographed Buenos Aires scenery, there's little excitement in the film. Performances, other than Giallelis,' which is quite bad, range from fair (Miss Margolin) to excellent, by several minor characters.

It is time for the director to find fresh material. He and Heller plan to work together on his next film.
Robe.

Let's Kill Uncle
(COLOR)

Producer - director **W i l l i a m** Castle has come up with a child's garden of intrigue and suspense. It's gauged for the young fry but entire family should find it entertaining.

Hollywood, Sept. 16.

Universal release of William Castle production. Features entire cast. Director, Castle. Screenplay, Mark Rodgers, based on novel by Rohan O'Grady; camera (Technicolor), Harold Lipstein; asst. director, Carl Beringer; editor, Edwin H. Bryant; music, Herman Stein. Reviewed at Universal Studio, Sept. 14, '66. Running Time, 92 MINS.
Major Kevin Harrison.... Nigel Green
Chrissie .... Mary Badham
Barnaby Harrison...... Pat Cardi
Sgt. Jack Travis....... Robert Pickering
Justine .... Linda Lawson

Ketch-man .... Reff Sanchez
Steward .... Nestor Paiva

If there ever was a film made for the 12-year-old audience this is probably it. Which is not to say that "Let's Kill Uncle" is an inept picture. Fact is, it has an innocent excitement that should appeal to anyone who enjoys or wishes to recapture those blissful years of youth.

"Uncle" has the ingredients of suspense, atmosphere and elegance going for it. Technical credits are slick and if the acting is forgetable, story plotline is offbeat enough to hold attention.

Pat Cardi essays role of a 12-year-old orphan, who has inherited millions from his father. He is brought to a small abandoned island by a police sergeant, (Robert Pickering,) and in transit by boat meets a girl his own age, Mary Badham, who is going to the island to visit her aunt, Linda Lawson.

There is a palatial home on the island which he has inherited and it is there that the boy is to rendezvous with his uncle, Nigel Green, a former SS war hero, who has since written a book on the art of killing.

Pic wastes a lot of time before uncle arrives and is slow to make its obvious point: uncle will attempt to kill the boy and inherit his late brother's money.

Once, however, pic gets down to business, plot romps along with childish glee. The boy allies Miss Badham and together they plot the demise of uncle. He, in turn, is intent on doing away with them. There's a creaky old abandoned hotel where a shark lives in the swimming pool and it is there that the three engage in attempting to have done with the other. All ends happily.

Cardi and Badham, for all their young years, have learned the art of mugging and work hard at stealing their scenes together from each other. Green camps it up in fine sinister fashion. Pickering and Miss Lawson bring in the romantic element and have little else to do but smile at each other.

Realistic questions about why Miss Lawson lives on the island alone or how uncle can land his plane there without an airstrip are gracefully unanswered.

Producer-director William Castle has carefully manipulated his people and plot in a filmic Robert Lewis Stevenson style. Harold Lipstein's camerawork is topgrade, often effectively holding on long shots and not moving.

Editing by Edwin H. Bryant takes advantage of cutting to various objects, causing added suspense, while art directors Alexander Golitzen and William DeCinces have come up with both bright and eerie sets. *Dool.*

Avec Le Peau Des Autres
(With the Lives of Others)
(FRENCH-ITALO-
COLOR-TECHNISCOPE)

Paris, Sept. 20.

Valoria Films release of Films Montfort, Fida Cinematografica production. Stars Lino Ventura; features Jean Bouise, Adrien Hoven, Wolfgang Priess, Marilu Tolo, Jean Servais. Directed by Jacques Deray, screenplay, Jose Giovanni; camera (Eastmancolor), Jean Boffety; editor, Henri Lanoe. At Marignan, Paris. Running Time, 90 MINS.

Agent	Lino Ventura
Anna	Marilu Tolo
Lawyer	Jean Servais
Chief	Wolfgang Preiss
Friend	Adrien Hoven

Espionage pic, taking place in Vienna, has a French agent licensed to kill and doing plenty of it. But since this is a bit confused, and lacks clarity, character flair and the more robust rhythm to give this a more adventurous air. it lags and is just an okay entry in the spy sweeps. Good production slants this for possible playoff or tv use.

Agent Lino Ventura is sent to Vienna to check a security leak. Here he runs into plenty of double agents and a mysterious spy, either Russo or Chinese, who is out to do away with the French ring. A French agent, bitter at headquarters and trying to make deals on his own, adds some interest to this otherwise ploddingly done and familiar spy opera.

Ventura is stolid; he does not have the brashness or spark of inner life to give some depth to his role of a murderous if dedicated undercover man. Others are adequate but direction is too sober to give this the fillip it needs. It is technically good. *Mosk.*

Venice Films

Atithi
(The Runaway)
(INDIAN)
Venice, Sept. 9.
Chayabani Private release of New Theatres Pvt.-S.N. Sircar production. With Partha Mukherji, Basabi Banerji, Mita Mukheri. Written and directed by Tapan Sinha from a story by Rabindranath Tagore. Camera, Dilip Basjan Mukherjee; editor, Subodh Roy. At Venice Film Fest. Running time, 105 MINS.

Tarapada	Partha Mukherji
Charushashi	Basabi Banerji
Sonamani	Mita Mukheri
Father	Salil Dutta
Mother	Smita Sinha

Bengal still seems the only part of India capable of turning out films worth film fest showing. This one seems influenced by the noted Bengali filmmaker Satyajit Ray in its tale of a young Indian and his ways. But it does not quite have the tangible tie with the land, and its poetics appear a bit arch rather than revealing and emotionally right.

Film does unveil a filmmaker with a nice feeling for mood, but it appears mainly of interest for specialized and language situations abroad since it is a bit repetitious. It concerns a young, poor boy who is always running off to adventures or just carried away by the life about him. He runs off with an opera company, then is adopted by a rich family and finally promised to their daughter only to run off in enchantment again as he sees a group of singers floating down a river in boats.

It is romantically overdone and the boy seems a bit too precious to give the romantic flair and outlook aimed at. But music has a zesty, jangling rightness, the playing is good and it does use the landscapes of the country to good

effect. It just does not quite have the poetic pulse or the true recreation of pre-war times to keep it from being a bit over-romanticized and finally precious rather than moving. *Mosk.*

La Prise De Pouvoir Par Louis XIV
(The Taking of Power by Louis XIV)
(FRENCH—COLOR)
Venice, Sept. 10.
Office Du Radiodiffusion Television Francise production and release. With Jean-Marie Patte, Raymond Jourdan, Silvagni, Katherina Renn. Directed by Roberto Rossellini. Screenplay, Philippe Erlanger, Jean Gruault; camera (Eastmancolor), Georges Leclerc. At Venice Film Fest. Running Time, 100 MINS.

Louis XIV	Jean-Marie Platte
Colbert	Raymond Jourdan
Mazarin	Silvagni
Queen Mother	Katherina Renn

Italo director Roberto Rosselini, who has left features to devote himself to tv, made this color pic for French tv. Presented in a non-competing slot the last night of the recent Venice Film Fest, it thus rates a review since it was shown on a big screen in public. Not surprisingly it emerges as best for the small tube. Didactic, intimate in manner it's a formalistic study of the anatomy of autocracy.

Color is good and Rossellini has cannily given a look of the 17th century court painting of the times. Groupings are somewhat static and talkiness prevails. Young King shrewdly disarms his nobles, turns the court into a ritual culminating in stunning pageantry of Versailles.

Jean-Marie Patte plays Louis in a flat manner with an emotionless way of talking that does help imply the inner strength and unpredictable aspects of him that fooled the court and helped him consolidate. It seems a convincing portrait. *Mosk.*

The Trap
(BRITISH—COLOR)

Rugged pioneer "romance" between a trapper and a mute in wildest Canada. Standout performances by Rita Tushingham and Oliver Reed give this 'meller' good potential. Strong Canadian support.

London, Sept. 14.
Rank release of a George H. Brown Production. Stars Rita Tushingham, Oliver Reed. Features Rex Sevenoaks, Barbara Chilcott, Walter Marsh, Linda Goranson, Jo Golland. Directed by Sidney Hayers. Original story and screenplay, David Osborn; camera, Robert Krasker; music, Ron Grainer; editor, Tristam Cones. At Leicester Square Theatre, London. Running Time, 106 MINS.

Eve	Rita Tushingham
La Bete	Oliver Reed
The Trader	Rex Sevenoaks
Trader's Wife	Barbara Chilcott
Trader's Daughter	Linda Goranson
Clerk	Blain Fairman
Preacher	Walter Marsh
Baptiste	Jo Golland
No Name	Jon Granik
Yellow Dog	Merv Campone
Captain	Reginald McReynolds

This Anglo-Canadian get together deals via producer George H. Brown with an earthy adventure yarn, a struggle for survival, an offbeat battle of the sexes, emotions which Brown figures can be

shared by world audiences. It may well prove a refreshing change from the current 'smart' cult. Strong sell to trade and public may be needed to give the film impetus. In Britain Rita Tushingham is respected as a fine growing talent, but her pulling power has yet to be established. Oliver Reed, also an up and coming talent, has not yet been recognized as a "star." The excellent band of Canadian players will likely have more meaning in the Dominion than elsewhere.

Where "The Trap" should sell is on its simplicity, several high peaks of adventure and the brilliantly lensed locations in primitive Columbia. Robert Krasker and his two second unit lensers, O. H. Borradaile and Bill Roozeboom, have brought a beauty to the screen which at times is awesome, whether it be in the dark towering forests, the vast placid lakes, the mountains, the skylines.

Story is set in the mid-90s when British Columbia was wild and untamed and only the strong came out on top. Jean La Bete (Oliver Reed), a huge, lusty French-Canadian trapper, returns to the trading post after three freezing winters, with a haul of furs and a bag of gold rich enough to buy himself a wife. But he is too late for the once-a-year 'auction' of harlots, thieves and femme riff-raff sent away from civilization for this purpose. So he settles for a young mute orphan, a servant in the trader's house, sold to him by the grasping wife. He hauls the protesting girl into a canoe and set off for the wastes. The girl is panic-stricken, stunned. She cannot escape. She cannot even speak. She's trapped. There follows an edgy Taming of the Shrew situation as the hunter tries to win her affection by cajoling, bullying, threatening, and occasionally sweet-talking. At the same time she is being forced reluctantly to learn the ways of the wild, how to trap, fish, shoot. How, in fact to exist.

Gradually the girl's hostility breaks down and at crisis time, when she is forced to amputate his leg to save him from dying (an over realistic sequence, this) she capitulates and they bed. As she hunts to keep both alive their relationship becomes tender and friendly, but when she realizes she is pregnant panic takes over again. She escapes in a canoe back to the settlement. Sometime later she is to marry the trader's clerk, but ditches him at the last minute to return to the primitive life and the man she's come to love.

There is Ron Goodwin's pleasant, evocative score to go with a story of David Osborn, who spent several years as a trapper in similar loneliness.

The script has several adventure highlights. There's a running battle between Reed, crippled after catching a foot in one of his own traps, and a pack of wolves which is sweaty in its excitement. Actor was reported badly mauled while doing the shot. Miss Tushingham (inevitably) canoeing herself over the rapids, a battle between Reed and two no-good Injuns who try to kidnap Miss Tushingham, the prowling animals, the girl's trek through deep snow in search of an Indian settlement to get medical

aid and then finding it full of dead, frozen Injuns. All these scenes have strong impact and, in fact, it is only one or two of the interior sequences that seem to lack the same authenticity. Though the pic is relentlessly tough it has plenty of raw humor especially in the earlier stages.

In a role which might have been custom built for Anthony Quinn, Reed, nephew of director Sir Carol, establishes himself as a virile type and the pic could be the turning point of his career. He is large-than-life as the crude, brawling trapper yet also has moments of great sensitivity with his co-star. Here is a hunk of man that Britain should promote, but fast. Miss Tushingham, sans benefit of dialog has to depend on her famous eyes, and wistful mouth to put over a tricky role embracing many emotions, from spitfire to waif, and she does marvels. Her fragility, matched with Reed's gutsy virility, makes a perfect combo for this pic. Among the Canadian assists come neat performances from Rex Sevenoaks as the trader, Barbara Chilcott, playing his shrewish wife, and Jon Granik, and Marv Campone as the sly Injun heavies. Linda Goranson, Jo Golland, Blain Fairman, Walter Marsh and Reginald McReynolds also contribute lesser aid.

Tristam Cones has edited cunningly, not letting the narrative hold up too much to allow the director or cameraman to linger overly on the scenic delights and Harry White has done an okay job with the artwork. Director Sidney Hayers' direction smoothly blends the various ingredients of adventure, romance, danger and suspense in a location that called for maximum stamina from entire cast and crew. Again a nosegay to the camera department. They have made British Columbia look a really exciting eyeful, but have also managed to keep the landscapes and waterscapes background to the narrative rather than dominating it. *Rich.*

The Bible
(COLOR—70M)

Unique, monumental film, brilliantly produced and executed. Hallmark of achievement.

Hollywood, Aug. 31.

Twentieth Century-Fox (in association with Seven Arts) release of a Dino De Laurentiis production; associate producer, Luigi Luraschi. Features entire cast. Directed by John Huston. Screenplay, Christopher Fry; camera (DeLuxe Color), Giuseppe Rotunno; editor, Ralph Kemplen; music, Toshiro Mayuzumi; asst. directors, Vana Caruso, Ottavio Oppo. Reviewed at 20th-Fox Studios, Aug. 30, '66. Running Time (excluding intermission), 174 MINS.

Adam	Michael Parks
Eve	Ulla Bergryd
Cain	Richard Harris
Noah	John Huston
Nimrod	Stephen Boyd
Abraham	George C. Scott
Sarah	Ava Gardner
The Three Angels	Peter O'Toole
Hagar	Zoe Sallis
Lot	Gabriele Ferzetti
Lot's Wife	Eleonora Rossi Drago
Abel	Franco Nero
Isaac	Alberto Lucantoni

The world's oldest story—the origins of Mankind, as told in the Book of Genesis, fountainhead of Jewish and Christian tradition—has been put upon the screen by director John Huston and producer Dino De Laurentiis with consummate skill, taste and reverence. Combining spiritual, natural and personal elements into a monumental tapestry, this epic film will endure for generations. "The Bible," subtitled "In The Beginning," is being distributed by 20th-Fox, in association with Seven Arts.

Christopher Fry, who wrote the screenplay with the assistance of Biblical scholars and religious consultants, has fashioned a straightforward, sensitive and dramatic telling, through dialog and narration, of the first 22 chapters of Genesis. Subjects of the interrelated episodes are Creation, the stories of Adam and Eve, Cain and Abel, Noah and the Flood, Abraham, the Tower of Babel, and the destruction of Sodom and Gomorrah.

A lavish, but always tasteful production—estimated to have cost $18,000,000, and involving shooting in Sardinia, Sicily, North Africa and at the De Laurentiis studio in Rome—assaults and rewards the eye and ear with awe-inspiring realism. Contemporary natural phenomena plus special effects are the stunning background for the unfolding of the personal, human drama. Painstaking, unhurried and meticulous attention are evident in every scene.

Huston's masterful direction elicits the entire spectrum of human emotions from his players, all of whom deliver believable performances. In addition, Huston's rich voice functions in narration, and he also plays Noah with heart-warming humility, compassion and humor.

Ernst Haas, commissioned to shoot footage for the sequence of Creation, spent 18 months in capturing actual natural phenomena, blended superbly into what is a spectacular 10-minute opening scene. The climax is the vivid representation of the creation of Adam, then Eve. Michael Parks and Ulla Bergryd project the proper innocence, enhanced by soft focus photography and a general mood of tranquility, and their nudity, far from being an exploitation gambit, is perfectly natural in context.

The seduction of Eve by the serpent, the latter well represented by a man reclining in a tree, cues a sudden shift of mood and pace. The expulsion of Adam and Eve from Eden and their later life is painted in stark hues, barren landscapes and violence. Richard Harris plays the jealous and remorseful Cain with a sure feeling, while Franco Nero's Abel conveys in very brief footage the image of a sensitive, obedient young man whose murder provoked a supreme outrage.

The 45-minute sequence devoted to Noah and the Flood is, in itself, a triumph in filmmaking. It plays dramatically and fluidly, and belies monumental logistics of production. Huston's Noah is, again, perfect casting. The gathering of the animals—real ones, including a pair of turtles who just make it aboard before the rains begin—the then torrential rains and the eventual calm all register with tremendous impact.

There is, in this sequence, the sole minor flaw in this epic—Huston as narrator, Huston as Noah and Huston as the voice of Almighty God make for slight, temporary confusion in a few spots. Apart from this, the Flood sequence is a stirring finale to the first half.

Following a three-minute overture to the second half (in contrast, the film opens properly with a silent 20th-Fox logo, then goes immediately into Creation), there, is a striking living genealogy tableau showing the increase in population and the passage of time. Stephen Boyd then emerges as Nimrod, the proud king, whose egocentric monument became the Tower of Babel where the languages of his people suddenly were changed.

The remainder of the film, which, excluding intermission, runs 174 minutes, is devoted to Abraham, played with depth by George C. Scott. Ava Gardner is very good as the barren Sarah who, to give her husband a male heir, urges him to conceive with her servant, Zoe Sallis. Gabriele Ferzetti is also very good as Lot, Abraham's nephew, whom the latter rescues from captivity.

Peter O'Toole is appropriately mystic as the three angels who rescue Lot and his family from Sodom, prior to its destruction by what in this era is conveyed effectively by a nuclear holocaust. Eleonora Rossi Drago is Lot's disobedient wife. Katherine Dunham choreographed the Sodom sequence in an outstanding pictorial representation of the never-ending sensual frustration inherent in the jaded and perverse.

The climactic sequence to this memorable film is Abraham's test of obedience as he prepares the sacrifice of his son Isaac, born after years of hope to an aging Sarah, and played here by Alberto Lucantoni. The sparing of Isaac from the flames of sacrifice is a brilliant and dramatic conclusion. All supporting players have been cast and directed with the same care as the principals, and all have contributed to the overall impact.

The world's greatest artists have, for untold centuries, used the tools of their craft to depict the events recorded in Genesis, and De Laurentiis and Huston have so marshaled their filmmakers to add to the archives this outstanding motion picture represention.

Toshiro Mayuzumi's full-bodied score, conducted by Franco Ferrara, highlights every mood. Giuseppe Rotunno's graphic cameras have recorded the sweep, as well as the poignancy, of the action, in 70m and color using Dimension-150 lenses. Method of projection has been the subject of litigation. Technicolor matched the outstanding camera work in its versatile color processing, while DeLuxe is handling release print work.

Mario Chiari's art direction is an achievement of note, as is the editing by Ralph Kemplen, the special effects by Augie Lohman, second unit direction by Haas, the sound recording by Fred Hynes and associates, and the scores of other fine craftsmen assembled by De Laurentiis and his associate producer, Luigi Luraschi.

The boxoffice prospects for "The Bible" are unlimited. It is a natural attraction for millions of people, including the religious, the atheist, the agnostic and the pagan. The Book of Genesis has penetrated many cultures, not just the Jewish and Christian tradition, hence the film is not limited to western civilization.

Repeat attendance is guaranteed. People will see it as children, as teenagers, later as parents taking their children. It can play on hard-ticket for years, and the 15 years in which 20th-Fox and Seven Arts have distribution rights seem just the beginning. Until home television or entertainment systems can present it in larger-than-life form, it belongs in theatres.

Uncluttered with commercially-oriented plot excursions, "The Bible" is a unique film achievement which will endure. It is a triumph of which De Laurentiis, Huston and Fry can be forever proud. *Murf.*

A Funny Thing Happened On The Way To The Forum
(COLOR)

Comedy blockbuster.

UA release of Quadrangle (Melvin Frank) production. Stars Zero Mostel, Phil Silvers, Buster Keaton, Jack Gilford, Michael Crawford; features rest of cast. Directed by Richard Lester. Screenplay by Melvin Frank and Michael Pertwee. Musical comedy book by Burt Shevelove and Larry Gelbart. Music and lyrics by Stephen Sondheim. Camera, (De Luxe) Nicholas Roeg. Production and costume design, Tony Walton. Music director, Irwin Kostal; asst. director, Jos Lopez Rodero; editor, John Victor Smith; choreography, Ethel and George Martin; 2d unit director, Bob Simmons; special effects, Cliff Richardson. Camera operator, Alex Thomson. Reviewed at United Artists screening room, N.Y., Sept. 13, '66. Running time, 99 MINS.

Pseudolus	Zero Mostel
Lycus	Phil Silvers
Erronius	Buster Keaton
Hysterium	Jack Gilford
Hero	Michael Crawford
Philia	Annette Andre
Domina	Patricia Jessel
Senex	Michael Hordern
Miles	Leon Greene
Gymnasia	Inga Neilsen
Vibrata	Myrna White
Panacea	Lucienne Bridou
Tintinabula	Helen Funai
Geminae	Jennifer and Susan Baker
Fertilla	Janet Webb

"A Funny Thing Happened On The Way To The Forum"—after the stage musicomedy of the same name—will probably stand out as one of the few originals of two repetition-weary genres, the film musical comedy and the toga cum sandal "epic." Flip, glib and sophisticated, yet rump-slappingly bawdy and fast-paced, "Forum" is a capricious look at the seamy underside of classical Rome through a 20th-Century hipster's shades. The amalgam of contemporary humor and the booty and culture plundering "greatness" of that historic empire yields a rare alloy, tarnished but nonetheless precious.

Curiously, the chemistry of both elements, under the masterful control of zesty scripting, imaginative direction and expert clowning by the principals, meld skillfully, producing, an unexpected meaty sidelight—exposing the remarkable resemblance between the "Great Society" and teaming, vulgar and grasping Rome. Whether or not the latter relation was part of the conscious intentions of its creators is most and probably academic, but the orgy of non-stop hilarity it produces will at least fulfill one of their palpable intentions—mining boxoffice gold. Aimed mainly at the growing body of "aware" audiences (and who isn't hip these days?) that have supported United Artists handsomely, the film could click like "What's New Pussycat?," with word-of-mouth seen as an important factor, since the cast, though enjoying legit celebrity, is not yet a local marquee magnet.

"Forum's" plot follows the efforts of a glib, con-man slave, Pseudolus (Zero Mostel), to cheat, steal or connive his freedom from a domineering mistress, Domina, and his equally victimized master, the henpecked Senex. Unwilling ally, through blackmail, is the timorous toady Hysterium (Jack Gilford), another household slave.

Early instrument of Pseudolus' plot is the callow Hero, who, smitten by one of the luscious courtesans peddled by Lycus (Phil Silvers), local flesh supplier, promises Mostel his freedom if he can finagle the "virgin's" purchase. Plot complications multiply like the film's pratfalls, however, and the winsome object of Hero's passion has already been sold to the egomaniacal Miles, a legion captain of legendary ferocity, who thunders onto the scene to claim the girl. Stalling to gain time for his gimlet brain to churn, Mostel claims she is a plague carrier, then contrives her funeral, with Gilford feigning the corpse. Predictably, the situation degenerates into one of director Richard Lester's fortes, the chase.

Interwoven through the plot is the presence of Erronius (Buster Keaton) who, searching for his lost children, unties the knotted situation by recognizing them in the "virgin" and Miles, now revealed to be brother and sister. Producer Melvin Frank coscripted with Michael Pertwee.

Though the story is soon submerged under the unburdensome

weight of production numbers, tricky visuals, sight gags and numerous bits, their expert· mechanics and overall cleverness excuse the interruptions. When consulted, however, it moves with speed appropriate to satirical farce.

Generally assayed with satirical thrust and on-target accuracy, almost all of the performances are top-rung and thoroughly expert. Despite the high level of competence, or partly because of it, the genius of Mostel and Gilford predominate. The former, who cavorts through "Forum" like an overstuffed Pierrot, reveals an improbable grace and nimbleness, marking the quirky character with the indelible Mostel stamp, while Gilford, as his subservient foil, bumbles and skitters with expertly continuously hovering on the nervous brink of a controlled pratfall. The comic artistry of the portrayals demand a reprise of the pairing, if a suitable script can be mustered. Phil Silvers, as the canny but eventually outs m a r t e d whoremaster, displays his usual skill as a needle-witted spy, while Michael Hordern's forlorn lechery, unevenly matched with the fire-breathing virago depicted by Patricia Jessel, expose the Roman "suburbanite" as a kind of seedy relation to video s i t c o m s. Though love-smitten youth is nearly a cipher role these days, Michael C r a w f o r d is adequate. In a takeoff on the robust masculinity of musical comedy baritones, Leon Green is superb. The late Keaton's deadpan trot about the Seven Hills of Rome, though brief inserts, summons nostalgia for the silent master, already assuring the film a slot in the archives. Annette Andre, as the "virgin," is appropriately desirable and blank.

Lester's direction, despite his operational mode which is somewhat akin to silent film lensing (each day's lensing must produce a completed "bit"), is finally approaching the ability to collect sight gags into a cohesive and structured whole. The strain h o w e v e r, sometimes s h o w s through, periodically degenerating into pastiche, obscuring script and performances. Within the integrity of each sequence, though, Lester's mastery of the form is dazzling. Plundering the whole paraphernalia of Roman culture, he exploits aqueducts for prancing cakewalks, temples for flash-cut positioning in production numbers. An overlong "finale" chariot chase, however, lacks the necessary pyramiding of action to justify its length.

One of "Forum's" great services is that it satirizes a "film-myth" culture, the Romans, too long buried under homogenized and idealized unreality of laundered togas and gleaming columns. The art direction is a grimy triumph of chipped friezes, crumbling plinths, sooty temples, and mud-stiffened togas. In short, Rome as it probably was, a sprawling, squawling collection of pimps, thieves, pickpockets and con-men.
Rino.

Le Chien Fou
(The Mad Dog)
(FRENCH)

Paris, Sept. 27.
SNC release of CEPC-Mat Film production. With Claude Brasseur, Dany Carrel, Jacques Monod, Olivier Hussenot. Written and directed by Eddy Matalon. Camera, Jean-Jacques Tarbes; editor, Agnes Guillemot. At Balzac, Paris. Running Time, 80 MINS.
Marc .... Claude Brasseur
Marie .... Dany Carrel
Parrain .... Jacques Monod
Fence .... Olivier Hussenot

Small budgeter, with little known actors, is the usual hoodlum-on-the-run tale. Modestly done, it works up little feeling for or against the young thief nor does it have the cynicism of Jean-Luc Godard's "Breathless," on which it appears patterned.

Claude Brasseur sees his friend dying after being wounded in a diamond heist. A partner will not call a doctor and, in a fight, Brasseur kills him and goes on the run. There are girls, all sorts of fence archtypes and his final demise at the hands of a rival gang whose actual job he and his friends had poached on.

Brasseur has a certain presence but can not do much with the dog eat-dog action and progression. Director Eddy Matalon, for his first pic, shows he can put a pic together but can not, as yet, breathe life, punch and dynamism into a proven tale of lowlife goings-on. Dany Carrel etches a nice portrait of a girl he picks up in his meanderings. Others are fair. So this might have okay filler use at home but is too thin for much foreign interest.
Mosk.

Moonlighting Wives
(COLOR)

Sexploitation film of a prostitution ring; okay for intended market.

Hollywood, Sept. 21.
Craddock Films release of Morgan Pictures production. Features Diane Vivienne, Joan Nash, John Aristedes, Fatima. Direction-screenplay, Joe Sarno. Camera (DeLuxe color), Jerry Kalogeratos; music, Stan Free; editor, Pat Follner. Reviewed at Pix Theatre, Hollywood, Calif., Sept. 21, '66. Running Time, 83 MINS.
Mrs. Joan Rand .... Diane Vivienne
Nancy Preston .... John Nash
Al Jordon .... John Aristedes
Belly Dancer .... Fatima

"Moonlighting Wives," story of a prostitution ring, is claimed to have its basis in the police files of an eastern city. An out-and-out exploitation picture, the Craddock Films release handles subject well enough, accompanied by the usual "recommended for adults only" tag, and should do okay for its intended market.

Joe Sarno wrote and directed the pedestrian yarn of a discontended housewife who hits upon the idea of enlisting pretty spouses who can use extra pin money by hiring themselves out for the evening. Her 'secretarial service" is an enlargement upon strictly office work, and she soon finds she's in a profitable operation. There's the usual business of getting femmes and party scenes, and the law finally stepping in. Plotline parallels an actual incident of a few years ago on Long Island.

Diane Vivienne heads cast, strictly of the wooden variety, Joan Nash is one of the girls who tips off the cops and John Aristedes the madam's partner.

Jerry Kalogeratos' color photography, while spotty at times, generally is good to head technical lineup. *Whit.*

Rings Around The World
(COLOR)

Circus feature made out of similar talent and with Don Ameche as on video's "International Show Time." Filmed in Europe. Spectacular stunts.

Hollywood, Sept. 16.
Columbia Pictures release of Gil Cates production. Stars Don Ameche; features top circus artists. Directed by Cates. Screenplay, Victor Wolfson; camera (Technicolor), Urs B. Furrer; music, Jacques Belasco. Reviewed at Columbia Studios, Sept. 15, '66. Running Time, 98 MINS.

Gil Cates, producer of the weekly NBC-TV spread, "International Show Time," which ran for four seasons with Don Ameche sitting in the audience as commentator spieling on circus acts lensed abroad, has come up with a 98-minute Technicolor extravaganza based on the same idea for theatrical release. Cates and his cameras skip about the various European circus rings for an interesting feature with particular appeal for the tanbark buff. Film should do okay in selected situations in general market.

Some of the acts, all of the headline variety, have been seen on Cates' teleseries, which leads one to believe, although there is no studio confirmation, that feature may be a compilation of the best of the tv outing. Whatever, there are plenty of thrills, occasional comedy, and some spine-tingling moments in close-up. A special impact, lightweight camera is said to have been constructed for some of the aerial artists to wear as they perform daring feats and effects achieved pay off sometimes in gasps. Presentation is a well-rounded panorama of the circus, both in and out of the ring, creating the impression spectator is on the spot.

Ameche again is commentator, this time worked into the slender plotline as a writer and circus authority who wonders what compulsion drives a performer to gamble his life in incredible feats of daring. Various acts are segued naturally into this backdrop as Ameche sees in his mind's eye the greatest in the circus world, each providing its own brand of excitement. Camera work under Urs B. Furrer's direction is responsible for projecting many of the thrills, and such moments are further implemented by frequent panning to rapt audiences reacting to the dangerous stunting.

With such an assemblage of top acts its for the theatre audience to choose which they find the most engrossing. Certainly one of the tops is Marco, who balances a sharp sword on the tip of a knife held in his mouth as he climbs a 20-foot ladder. The Tongas, high-bar specialists, generate genuine thrills, as do La Mara on her trapeze, Mendez & Seitz in a

high-wire act, the Laribles on the flying bars, Gunther Gebel Willims and his tiger.

Carl Sembach Krone, owner of the circus bearing his name in Kiel, Germany, where portion of feature was filmed, is in for an impressive trained horse act and his wife, Frieda, for elephants. Rudi Cardenas amazes with his juggling, and the Mascot Sisters for their balancing skill, one standing head to head as the other ascends a 12-foot ladder. Other thrills are provided by lion tamer Pablo Noel, The Flying Gaonas' trampoline act, Tarzan and his giant elephant. For laughs there are Fredy Knie Sr.'s white Lippiz ner going to bed and the Francesco Clowns.

The Flying Armors is a flying trapeze turn in the good old tradition, appearing at the Smethport County Fair in Pennsylvania, only act shot in this country. Cates, who handles his subject authoritatively, also photographed at circuses in Lausanne, Switzerland, Copenhagen, Stockholm and Madrid.

Victor Wolfson's screenplay is sufficient to get over the idea and John Oettinger's editing crisp. Music by Jacques Belasco is attuned perfectly to the action.
Whit.

One Spy Too Many
(COLOR)

Theatrical release of two-part tv "The Man From U.N.C.L.E." which ran on the tube as "Alexander The Greater." Diverting.

Hollywood, Sept. 12.
MGM release of Arena (David Victor) production. Features Robert Vaughn, David McCallum, Rip Torn, Dorothy Provine, Leo G. Carroll, Yvonne Craig, David Opatoshu, David Sheiner. Directed by Joseph Sargent. Screenplay, Dean Hargrove; camera (Metrocolor), Fred Koenekamp; music, Gerald Fried; editor, Henry Berman; asst. director, E. Darrell Hallenbeck. Reviewed at MGM Studio, Sept. 12, '66. Running Time, 1 1 MINS.
Napoleon Solo .... Robert Vaughn
Illya Kuryakin .... David McCallum
Alexander .... Rip Torn
Tracey Alexander ...... Dorothy Provine
Mr. Waverly .... Leo G. Carroll
Maude Waverly .... Yvonne Craig
Kavon .... David Opatoshu
Paviz .... David Scheiner
Princess Nicole ...... Donna Michelle
General Bon-Phouma .... Leon Lontoc
Colonel Hawks .... Robert Karnes
Claxon .... Clarke Gordon
Prince Phanong .... James Hong
Ingo Lindstrum .... Cal Bolder
Receptionist ...... Carole Williams
President Sing-Mok .... Teru Shimada
General Man-Phang .... Arthur Wong
Farrell .... Robert Gibbons

Expanded from a "Man From UNCLE" tv two-parter, "One Spy Too Many" zips along at a jazzy spy thriller pace and pulling power of video topliners, Robert Vaughn and David McCallum, along with some agreeable acting by Rip Torn and Dorothy Provine, add up to a diverting feature. Technical credits and production value are also toprate.

Action and gagetry are hung on a slender plot. Alexander, played by Torn, is out to take over the world in the fashion of his Greek namesake. He hoists from the U.S. Army Biological Warfare Division a tankful of its secret "will gas," leaving a Greek inscription in the lab.

International espionage agents Vaughn and McCallum begin to pursue Alexander and are joined in their efforts by his wife Dorothy Provine), who is attempting to reach her husband in order to have him sign her divorce papers.

In Athens they meet their foe and later are taken prisoner by him in a Greek underground temple, where they are left to die. They escape and follow their man back to America, continuing to engage in dangerous escapades.

Throughout, everyone maintains a stoic, unexcited ease, giving the impression that they have all read the last page of the script. Torn does manage to get a semblance of fanaticism into his role and Miss Provine cavorts with expert charm, displaying fine style as an actress. Rest of cast is competent.

Joseph Sargent has directed the whirlwind script by Dean Hargrove in whirlwind fashion. Fred Koenekamp's camera work and Henry Berman's editing are in the best Hollywood tradition. Sam Rolfe's music is also a plus.

"Too Many" borrows lavishly from the James Bond epics both in style and breeziness, except in the sex department. Under the vertigo sweep of events, the public will probably not notice the lack of that particular element.
Dool.

Sticcnik
(The Climber)
(YUGOSLAVIAN)
Venice, Sept. 20.
Avala Films productios and release. With Ljubisa Samardzic, Stanislav Pesic, Spela Rozin, Rade Markovic, Dusa Pockaj, Milhajlo Kostic. Directed by Vladan Slijepevic. Screenplay, Jovan Orilov; camera, Djord je Nikolic; music, Boajn Adamic. At Venice Film Fest. Running Time, 100 MINS.
Ivan .... Ljubisa Samardzic
Dragana .... Stanislav Pesic
Wife .... Spela Rozin
Vojin .... Rade Markovic
Woman .... Dusa Pockaj

Tale of an opportunistic climber who gets his comeuppance is familiar, but here it has more unusual undertones and interest in watching him push his way up ruthlessly in a socialist-communist country. It is also done with a good, brash outlook as to characters and pace. But its fairly surface treatment limits this for special situations mainly, with more chances in the Eastern markets.

A young provincial poet comes storming into Belgrade to try to make his way. His poems have been shelved by a publisher but his ambition is undiminished and pic depicts his harsh climb. At the university, he at first accuses the party group who run student affairs of neglecting rights and needs of others and writes editorials against them. Beaten up he joins them and begins to rise when he meets a middleaged woman who is a powerful publisher.

He becomes a journalist, marries for money and position but is finally made aware of his faults by his wife's suicide plus the realization that he may be pushed out soon. Film is briskly played and does not pull punches in stating certain aspects of Yugoslav frictions between the

generations, painting ruthlessness in politics or business.

This certainly has meaning and a reflection on the revisions in Yugoslav politics today, but it still remains surface in character though pic has a freewheeling visual style and is good in some individual scenes and its love sequences. However, this looks like Yugoslav pix are forsaking war themes for more modern themes. This film may foreshadow the rise of some new talents and outspoken films from this country.
Mosk.

Bolshoi Ballet 67
(COLOR)

Beautifully-produced Russian film on the Bolshoi Ballet with fascinating numbers; strong appeal for art house trade and balletomanes.

Hollywood, Sept. 20.
Paramount release of Mosfilm production. Features prima dancers of the Bolshoi. Direction-screenplay, Leonid Lavrovsky, Alexander Shelenkov, Leo Arnshtam. Camera (Technicolor), Shelenkov, Iolanda Chen; music, Tchaikowsky, Ravel, Rachmaninoff, Paganini, Prokofiev, Saint-Saens, Adan, Minkus, Krein. Reviewed at Paramount Studios, Sept. 19, '66. Running Time, 86 MINS.

"Bolshoi Ballet 67" is a must for every balletomane. It is ballet at its finest, sheer poetry of motion of the form most identified with Russia, a classic of its kind that should find wide response in every art house into which it will necessarily be booked.

The Bolshoi, one of Soviet top dance troupes, has made various tours in this country to enormous reception in metropolitan centers. Now, the Russian-produced Technicolor feature is to have an outing on American screens at prices nearer everybody's range.

As an undertaking to explain the Bolshoi, the 86-minute tinter achieves its mark. Expertly produced and directed by masters of the ballet, color plays a lively part, as does the particularly fluid cinematography. There is spectacle about the beauty and artful perfection of contemporary Soviet ballet. The music of some of the world's greatest composers, which provides sweeping motivation to the matchless choreography of veteran Leonid Lavrovsky, who also co-directed, is superbly played and recorded.

No full-length ballet is presented. Camera work and choreography are creatively combined to accent the remarkably-thorough training and daily rehearsals of dancers and choreographers; the spectator enters rehearsal rooms where solo artists and corps de ballet prep themselves after their years of practice. Then, one-act ballets and ballet pieces depict the fruits of the dancers labors in often spectacular enactment.

Most - sensationally - danced, perhaps, is the Spanish number set to Ravel's "Bolero," dramatic and forceful it builds in intensity. Danced here by Elena Kholina, Alexander Lavrenjuk and S. Radchenko, the huge Bolshoi stage in Moscow is utilized for a stairs routine where 42 performers are in motion, thrilling as audience reacts to the growing drum beats of the composition.

Tops, too, is the more classic 'Paganini' set to music by Rachmaninoff, starring Yaroslav Sekh (who has made several American tours) and Ekaterina Maximova. Prokofiev's composition, "The Stone Flower", colorfully backs a fast and rhythmic folk-dance number with interest focused on Raissa Struchkova, and A. Osipenko's dancing of Saint-Saens' "The Dying Swan" is lovely. Outstanding also are less spectacular (but no less lacking in technique) numbers: Ravel's "Waltzes," Adam's "Giselle," Krein's "Laurancis" and Minkus' "Don Quixote," performed by stars of the Bolshoi.

Production-wise, film is a masterpiece of values. Direction by Leonid Lavrovsky, Alexander Shelenkov and Leo Arnshtam, who collabed on script, is authoritative throughout; Shelenkov and Iolanda Chen's photography is beautiful and absorbing as it catches the full movement of the dancers. A. Parkhomenko's set design is simplicity itself, therefore more effective, and costumes by V. Ryndina for the "Paganini" ballet — eye-filling. Special music was composed and arranged by N. Yacovlev, and music was performed by the Bolshoi Theatre Philharmonic Orch, Bolshoi Symphony Orch of Radio and TV, and Violin Ensemble of the Bolshoi Theatre.

Ariane's narration in English of Sidney Carroll's commentary is interesting.
Whit.

Le Facteur S'En Va-T-En Guerre
(The Postman Goes to War)
(FRENCH—COLOR—SCOPE)
Paris, Sept. 27.
CCFC release of J. J. Vital-Alcinter-Regina production. Stars Charles Aznavour; features Daniel Ceccaldi, Maria Minh, Jacques Richard, Franco Fabrizi, Helmut Schneider. Directed by Claude Bernard-Aubert. Screenplay, Rene Hardy, Claude Accursi, Gernard-Aubert, Pascal Jardin, from the novel by Gaston-Jean Gauthier; camera (Eastmancolor), Marcel Grignon; editor, Gabriel Rongier. At Colisee, Paris. Running Time, 95 MINS.
Thibon .... Charles Aznavour
Cassagne .... Daniel Ceccaldi
Klein .... Jacques Richard
Vang .... Maria Minh
Maury .... Helmut Schneider
Jess .... Jess Hahn
Ritoni .... Franco Fabrizi
Clementine .... Doudou Babet

Singer-composer Charles Aznavour has concocted a screen image of a little, simple man who still has courage and ruses up his sleeve to get by. Here these traits are exploited in a familiar war tale. Though taking place during the French-Indochina War, it stays surface and uses stereotype characters. It borrows from many pix but has some fair battle scenes and looms only a dualer or playoff item for abroad.

Though made in Cambodia, this could have been done anywhere. Aznavour is an army postman who gets caught at a French outpost and is then made a prisoner, but not before he has a chance to have an affair with a pretty Combodian girl. Perky gags, battles and ironic escapes, just when the war ends, also show plenty of influences of "The Bridge on the River Kwai" plus other staple war pix.

Aznavour displays his usual presence in his usual role and others play their oft-seen parts acceptably with battle scenes not quite ringing true. It makes its pitches about the horror of war but plays it for laughs and the two are not quite jelled by the primarily pedestrian direction. Technical qualities are par.
Mosk.

De Man Die Zijin Haar Kort Liet Knippen
(The Man Who Got His Hair Cut Short)
(BELGIAN)
A Belgian National Ministry of Education Production with Senne Rouffaer, Beata Tyszkiewicz, Hector Camerlynck. Directed by Andre Delvaux. Screenplay by Anna de Pagter and Delvaux, from novel by Johan Daisne. Photography, Ghislain Cloquet; editor, Suzanne Baron; music, Freddy Devreese. At N.Y. Film Festival. Running Time, 90 MINS.
Govert Miereveld ..... Senne Rouffaer
Fran .... Beata Tyskiewicz
Professor Mato ......Hector Camerlynck

Though it ran roughly twice as long as "Simon of the Desert," with which it was paired at N.Y. Film Festival, this rarity, a Flemish-language film, was billed beneath the Luis Bunuel entry and was given a short shrift in the advance publicity.

This is as it should have been, since the film (translated on fest programs as "The Man With the Shaven Head"), was perhaps the least admired of the 28 entries, and it was roundly booed and heckled for at least its final half.

It's the story of a middle-aged, married schoolteacher who gets a crush on one of his students, but fails to tell her about it until he encounters her years later after she's become a famous chanteuse. It's also encrusted throughout with endless philosophical discourse and endless closeups of our hero in anguish, or walking hither and yon through the metaphysical void.

Some festival-goers seemed to think that it might be as profound as it comes on, and that its agonizingly slow pace made some sort of a point. This reviewer agreed with the majority, who seemed to think it was a pretentious bore from beginning to end, and that there was virtually nothing in the way of visual interest to keep one from dreamland during all the high-flown talk and pedestrian meandering. Indeed, one was grateful when the giggling started, since it was then possible to keep awake.

Otherwise, the only things of interest were Miss Tyskiewicz, who is a tasty dish, and two sequences: one a chilling autopsy (you don't see the body, but you do see the pathologists slicing and wrenching about) and the other, the haircut of the title (which was a sensual experience but didn't seem to have much to do with the rest of the picture). Senne Rouffaer's performance in the title role was more than adequate, considering the fact that most of the time he was required to adopt an attitude of trancelike misery. As for Andre Delvaux's direction, it has been adequately covered in the comments above.
Gold.

Hawaii
(COLOR-PANAVISION)

Excellent filming of a portion of James Michener's saga which concerns the commercial-religious development of Hawaii. Personal tragedy played off against the pitiable clash of civilizations. Production, acting, script and direction all topnotch, with Max Von Sydow terrif in pivotal role. Julie Andrews and Richard Harris also for marquee. Hardtix prospects very good, paving the way for excellent general playoff.

Hollywood, Oct. 1.

United Artists release of a Mirisch Corp. presentation, produced by Walter Mirisch; associate producer, Lewis J. Rachmil. Features Julie Andrews, Max Von Sydow, Richard Harris. Directed by George Roy Hill. Screenplay, Dalton Trumbo, Daniel Taradash; based on James A. Michener's novel; camera (DeLuxe Color), Russell Harlan; second unit camera, Harold Wellman; prolog camera, Chuck Wheeler; editor, Stuart Gilmore; music, Elmer Bernstein; song, Bernstein, Mack David; production design, Cary Odell; asst. director, Ray Gosnell; second unit director, Richard Talmadge; prolog supervisor, James Blue. Reviewed at Egyptian Theatre, L.A., Sept. 30, '66. Running Time (excluding intermission), **186 MINS.**

Jerusha Bromley .... Julie Andrews
Abner Hale .... Max Von Sydow
Rafer Hoxworth .... Richard Harris
Charles Bromley ...... Carroll O'Connor
Abigail Bromley .... Elizabeth Cole
Charity Bromley .... Diane Sherry
Mercy Bromley ..... Heather Menzies
Rev. Thorn .... Torin Thatcher
Rev. John Whipple .... Gene Hackman
Rev. Immanuel Quigley ... John Cullum
Rev. Abraham Hewlett ... Lou Antonio
Malama .... Jocelyne La Garde
Keoki .... Manu Tupou
Kelolo .... Ted Nobriga
Noelani .... Elizabeth Logue
Iliki .... Lokelani S. Chicarell
Gideon Hale ...... Malcolm Atterbury
Hepzibah Hale .... Dorothy Jeakins
Capt. Janders .... George Rose
Mason .... Michael Constantine
Collins .... John Harding
Cridland .... Robert Crawford
Micah Hale (at 4, 7, 12 18 years)
Robert Oakley, Henrik Von Sydow, Clas S. Von Sydow, Bertil Werjefelt

Based on James A. Michener's novel, which embraced centuries of history, the George Roy Hill-Walter Mirisch production of "Hawaii" focuses on a critical period — 1820-41 — when the islands began to be commercialized, corrupted and converted to Western ways. Superior production, acting and direction give depth and credibility to a personal tragedy, set against the clash of two civilizations. Julie Andrews, Max Von Sydow and Richard Harris provide international marquee allure for this exciting Mirisch Corp. presentation. Very good hardticket b.o. prospects are likely to become excellent in later United Artists general release.

Filmed at sea off Norway, also in New England, Hollywood, Hawaii and Tahiti, this vast production reps an outlay of about $15,000,000, including $600,000 for film rights, and seven years of work. Fred Zinnemann, originally set to produce-direct, worked four and one half years on it, after which Hill took over. Slippage in shooting sked, and a resultant budget overage of about 50%, brought Hill and Mirisch-UA to the mat, situation later resolved. Lewis J. Rachmil was associate producer.

Dalton Trumbo and original adapter Daniel Taradash are both credited with the screenplay, which develops Von Sydow's character from a young and overzealous Protestant missionary, through courtship of Miss Andrews, to their religious work in Hawaii. Harris, an old beau, turns up occasionally at major plot turns. The film ends with Von Sydow somewhat more mellow as a widower, separated from his children, abandoned by his Church, but devoted in his own way to his people.

The traditional origins of the Hawaiian peoples is told via brief opening narration over a beautiful prolog, supervised by James Blue and lensed by Chuck Wheeler. An eerie mood is effected by the absence of natural sound, with music alone underscoring the narration by Manu Tupou, who, after the ensuing titles, is finally seen as having been, in actuality, giving an address to fellow students at Yale Divinity School. This method of time-and-place transition is used frequently by Hill.

At fadeout, Hawaii is on the verge of the religious-commercial exploitation period which sparked the famous letter of Robert Louis Stevenson denouncing the hypocrisy of Honolulu merchants and missionaries. All this was yet to come, however, but the pic provides excellent exposition of the root causes. (As a sidebar, readers of William Bradford Huie's "The Revolt Of Mamie Stover" will recall his brief and excellent overview of Hawaiian history, expanded, of course, a thousand-fold by Michener.)

To understand the New England Protestant tradition — the hidebound, fire-and-brimstone Puritan heritage — is to understand Von Sydow's character. Repeated noble achievements of the mind and body are offset by as many acts of cruel, unforgiving behavior. Both were part and parcel of those times, and Von Sydow's outstanding performance makes the character comprehensible, if never totally sympathetic. A less competent actor, with less competent direction and scripting, would have blown the part, and with that, the film.

Miss Andrews, first of the three principals to follow the title, is excellent in a demanding dramatic role. From early scenes as a demure, charming young girl, through realistic seasickness and child birth, to her final appearances as a worn-out, devoted wife and mother, she is consistently appealing. Harris, colorful, virile, and forever in love with her, registers strongly in relatively brief appearances.

Uniformly strong performances are given by all supporting players, including the standout Jocelyne La Garde, in her film debut as the island queen who leads her people from happy paganism to uncertain futures under Western domination. Ted Nobriga, her consort, and Manu Tupou and Elizabeth Logue, her children, are very good. Much humor derives from the East-West conflicts as Von Sydow interacts with these people, serving to offset the tragedies.

Among the preachers, Gene Hackman is quite good as the medic-missionary who segues into biz affairs. Lou Antonio, likewise expelled from the ministry, garners sympathy, and John Cullum, repping the temporizing, increasingly worldly clergyman, is appropriately chilling. Torin Thatcher scores in early New England footage as he serves to illuminate the Von Sydow character. Carroll O'Connor and Elizabeth Cole handle with competence their roles as Miss Andrews' parents, while Malcolm Atterbury and Dorothy Jeakins (who did the excellent costumes — her usual forte outside of this acting bit) provide solid evidence of the foundations of the Von Sydow character.

George Rose is excellent as the ship captain who navigates an exciting passage through the Straits of Magellan. Michael Constantine, the old sailor who gets religion, then backslides, has a notable bit. Lokelani S. Chicarell is nice as the servant girl whom Harris carries off.

Hill's direction, solid in the intimate dramatic scenes, is as good in crowd shots which rep the major external events—the arrival at the Hawaiian island (with bare-breasted nudity okay in context), the preceding storm at sea, the burning of the town by irate sailors, the death of the queen and ensuing windstorm, the colorful pagan marriage ceremony and a measles epidemic which threatens to eradicate the native population. Russell Harlan's versatile DeLuxe Color and 35m Panavision camera work is outstanding, ditto second unit lensing by Harold Wellman under director Richard Talmadge.

Elmer Bernstein has provided a rich score, including about three minutes of overture before each segment. Stuart Gilmore supervised the editing to 186 minutes running time, of which 116 minutes are in the first part. Cary Odell's production design is superior. Various special effects are credited to Marshall M. Borden, Linwood G. Dunn, James B. Gordon, Paul Byrd and Film Effects of Hollywood, and their work is excellent. Other technical credits are firstrate. *Murf.*

What's Up Tiger Lily?
(COLOR)

Japanese crime meller re-edited and dubbed by Woody Allen for good, but erratic, comedy effect. Okay b.o. in youth situations.

Hollywood, Sept. 21.

American International Pictures release of a Henry G. Saperstein-Reuben Bercovitch production, based on a Toho Films (Japan) release. Stars Woody Allen; features rest of cast. Screenplay and dubbing, Allen, Frank Buxton, Len Maxwell, Louise Lasser, Mickey Rose, Julie Bennett, Bryna Wilson; camera (Eastman Color), Kazuo Yamada; editor, Richard Krown; music, The Lovin' Spoonful. Reviewed at Directors Guild of America, L.A., Sept. 20, '66. Running Time, **79 MINS.**

Narrator-host .... Woody Allen
Phil Moscowitz ..... Tatsuya Mihashi
Terri Yaki .... Mie Hana
Suki Yaki .... Akiko Wakayabayashi
Sheperd Wong ...... Tadao Nakamaru
Wing Fat .... Susumu Kurobe
Themselves .... The Lovin' Spoonful

Take a Toho Films (Japan) crime meller, fashioned in the James Bond tradition for the domestic market there, then turn loose Woody Allen and associates to dub and reedit in today's camp-comedy vein, and the result is "What's Up Tiger Lily?" The Henry G. Saperstein-Reuben Bercovitch production has one premise—deliberately mismatched dialog—which is sustained reasonably well through its brief running time. With Allen's name prominent in the sell, the American International release will appeal to youthful camp followers, particularly ozoner types, with okay or better b.o. likely on general duals.

The "production conception," per screen credit, is by Ben Shapiro. Film opens cold with over three minutes of straightforward Japanese meller and chase footage until Allen pops up, explaining the format to follow. The Samurai posturing, to the non-sequitur dialog, is relieved regularly by stop-motion and other effects, plus some interleavened footage of The Lovin' Spoonful, a contemporary rock group (and an effect in themselves) singing their credited, but sparse score, also title tune.

Allen's cohorts, both in writing and dubbing, are Frank Buxton, Len Maxwell, Louise Lasser, Mickey Rose, Julie Bennett and Bryna Wilson. Saperstein was exec producer, Allen associate producer. Colorful title work is credited to UPA, Murakami-Wolf, and Phil Norman. Richard Krown supervised the fast-paced editing to 79 minutes. Other credits are good. *Murf.*

Romeo And Juliet
(BRITISH-COLOR)

Surefire for ballet lovers..

Embassy Pictures release of Paul Czinner ballet film production. Stars Margot Fonteyn, Rudolf Nureyev; features David Blair, Desmond Doyle, Julia Farron, Michael Somes. Produced and directed by Paul Czinner; choreography by Kenneth MacMillan; camera (Eastman Color, printed by Pathe), S. D. Onions; editor, Philip Barnikel; sound supervisor, Edgar Vetter; scenery and costumes, Nicholas Georgiadis; music by Serge Prokofiev, played by Orchestra of the Royal Opera House, Covent Garden, conducted by John Lanchbery; asst. directors, A. Pearl, Peter Baynham-Honri. Reviewed in Hollywood, Oct. 3, '66. Running Time: **124 MINS.**

Juliet .... Margot Fonteyn
Romeo .... Rudolf Nureyev
Mercutio .... David Blair
Tybalt .... Desmond Doyle
Lady Capulet .... Julia Farron
Lord Capulet .... Michael Somes
Benvolio .... Anthony Dowell
Paris .... Derek Rencher
Escalus .... Leslie Edwards
Rosaline .... Georgina Parkinson
Nurse .... Gerd Larsen
Friar Laurence .... Ronald Hynd
Lord Montague ..... Christopher Newton
Lady Montague .... Betty Kavanagh
(Corps de ballet of the Royal Ballet.)

Following hard on the release of Paramount's "Bolshoi Ballet 67" comes this treat for balletomanes, "Romeo and Juliet," an Embassy release in color of London's Royal Ballet production based on Shakespeare's immortal love story. Produced and directed by Paul Czinner and starring Margot Fonteyn and Rudolf Nureyev, the 126-minute feature is an absorbing excursion into its particular art form, a beautifully executed and sometimes - spectacular attraction which carries must-appeal to every devotee of the ballet.

Photographed as a stage offering, with three acts and an intermission after the first act, ballet very often seems more like pantomime rather than dancing, ingredients are so subtly blended into choreographed drama.

Vying with the superb dancing of the two stars is the music by Serge Prokofiev, a wondrous symphonic experience played by the orchestra of London's Royal Opera House, Covent Garden. Kenneth MacMillan's choreography takes full advantage of its melodic sweep, and S. D. Onions' fluid cameras catch up the familiar story as it progresses swiftly and meaningfully.

The narrative follows the original faithfully and, unlike so many ballets, the audience is aware of every move. Preluding each of the three acts is a description of every scene, its locale, characters involved, its purpose and the action which is to follow. Consequently, greater appreciation is felt.

Major interest rests on the two principal dancers but scoring solidly also are David Blair as Mercutio, Romeo's friend; Desmond Doyle, the CCapulet nephew who is the heavy; Julia Farron and Michael Somes, Lady and Lord Capulet. There are many lesser characters.

Contributing heavily to the overall interest are the sets and costumes designed by Nicholas Georgiadis. As befitting the general tone of the story, both are in subdued shadings, the scenery mostly in dark blues, grays and black. Editing by Philip Barnikel is effective, too.

As in a stage performance, the feature ends in the principals taking bows, starting with the two stars. Then, after others in cast have had their moment, the stars come out individually and finally together. Miss Fonteyn presents her co-star with a rose after she is presented with the customary bouquet. *Whit.*

Utro
(Unfaithful)
(DANISH)

Copenhagen, Sept. 27.
Asa Filmudlejning A/S release of Astrid Henning-Jensen production. Stars Lone Hertz, Ebbe Rode, Anita Bjork. Directed by Astrid Henning-Jensen. Story and screenplay, Tove Ditlevsen; camera, Lars Bjorne. At Nygade, Copenhagen. Running Time, **95 MINS.**

Lots of controversy surrounded the making of this film by much-honored Astrid Henning-Jensen. The State Film Foundation refused it any production guarantee as the script was considered too weak. Financial backing was secured, however, and the shooting—entirely on location—was covered extensively by local and other news media.

As it finally emerges, "Unfaithful" fails exactly on its lack of script originality. The story is ultra-banal, the spoken-lines devoid of any freshness, the heavy-handed stressing of the director's and the scriptwriter's socio-political viewpoints run counter to any true artistic presentation of the non-plot and its resolution.

"Unfaithful" is, in spite of these drawbacks, not a total fiasco, but the negative sides must be expanded first. Story is about middleaged literary critic, with thwarted ambitions to write The Big Thesis, who meets and beds with dewy-fresh psychology student but fails to secure a roof over their bed while he takes refuge in his own frustrated home life with bitter wife and still-hopeful child: will Daddy come home more often and

play with their electric toy train?

Yes, Daddy comes home. It seems. And his young mistress gives painful, illegally provoked stillbirth to her child. She lets him know that as a father he has proved even less of a man than as a lover.

All the males in the film are drab cliches. And the women are pointedly described as strong, misled and let down, perhaps, but always strong. Strongest of the lot is the mistress, played by Lone Hertz, whose talent shines so bright here that it makes it worth most of the film's 95 minutes just to watch her. Her unconventional beauty and her richly faceted talent shine throughout. First foreign producer to pick her out of the rut of most Danish filmmaking. including ambitious mistakes like "Unfaithful," should be richly rewarded. She is star material. And the camerawork by Sweden's Lars Bjorne lives up to her. *Kell.*

Alvarez Kelly
(PANAVISION-COLOR)

Okay Civil War actioner about Confederate troops rustling Yankee cattle. Interesting plot peg diminished by tame script, uneven thesping and routine direction. Some exciting action scenes and good production values. William Holden and Richard Widmark for marquee.

Hollywood, Sept. 23.
Columbia Pictures release of Sol C. Siegel production. Stars William Holden, Richard Widmark; features Janice Rule, Patrick O'Neal, Victoria Shaw, Roger C. Carmel. Directed by Edward Dmytryk. Screenplay, Franklin Coen, Elliott Arnold, based on a story by Coen; camera (Eastman Color), Joseph MacDonald; editor, Harold F. Kress; music, John Green; song, Green, Johnny Mercer; asst. director, Frank Baur. Reviewed at Academy Award Theatre, L.A., Sept. 22, '66. Running Time, 110 MINS.
Alvarez Kelly .... William Holden
Col. Tom Rossiter....Richard Widmark
Liz Pickering .... Janice Rule
Maj. Albert Stedman....Patrick O'Neal
Charity Warwick .... Victoria Shaw
Capt. Angus Ferguson..Roger C. Carmel
Sgt. Hatcher .... Richard Rust
Capt. Towers .... Arthur Franz
Lt. Farrow .... Donald Barry
John Beaurider .... Duke Hobbie
Cpl. Peterson .... Harry Carey, Jr.
McIntyre .... Howard Caine
Capt. Webster .... Paul Lukather
Capt. Williams .... Robert Morgan
Prostitute .... Indus Arthur

Based on a true U.S. Civil War incident, "Alvarez Kelly" concerns successful cattle grab engineered by Southern forces and executed under the noses of Northern troops. Outdoor action sequences, including an exciting stampede, enliven a tame script, routinely directed and performed erratically. William Holden and Richard Widmark are the marquee bait for Sol C. Siegel's production, which looms as a spotty, but overall fairish b.o. bet for Columbia release.

Franklin Coen and Elliott Arnold scripted Coen's story, which pits Mexican-Irish Holden (hence, the title) against Confederate officer Widmark, eyeing Holden's cattle, delivered to Union forces, as food for a starving South. Film was shot in the Baton Rouge, La., area, with interiors at Columbia's Hollywood studio.

A lot of double-crossing takes place, with Victoria Shaw, mistress of a captured mansion, causing Holden's kidnapping by Widmark, who forces the former to teach his troops how to handle cattle. Janice Rule, Widmark's faithful sweetie, gives up her marriage hopes, and Holden helps her escape to N.Y. with Scottish sea captain Roger C. Carmel. Patrick O'Neal is the Northern officer who is depicted in unsympathetic hues.

Director Edward Dmytryk has achieved uneven response from his players, in part due to scripting which overdevelops some characters and situations, and underdevelops others. Dialog sometimes is excessive, and Dixie accents seem too cliche, and not always consistent. Holden seems too relaxed and refined for a man who has herded cattle for thousands of miles, while Widmark's dedication to duty is often expressed in unruly temper, not cold firmness.

Miss Shaw is quite stunning, while Miss Rule, a prime script victim, does not convince. O'Neal, a method Irishman, it seems, is saddled with an unclear character, shot down by unchecked, mannered thesping. Carmel is good as the skipper, and Richard Rust is quite effective as the non-com who hates Holden's guts. Donald (Red) Barry is good as one of the Widmark troop, and other supporting players are adequate. Indus Arthur shines in a brothel sequence as a daffy inmate whom Holden uses as a front for temporary escape.

Joseph MacDonald's Panavision-Eastman Color camera work is excellent, and the climactic stampede is a long overdue excitement. Harold F. Kress edited to a slow 110 minutes. John Green's score is flat, intrusive, and the title tune, words by Johnny Mercer and sung over titles by The Brothers Four, is a forgettable trifle. Sound editing and recording is excellent, considering the extensive outdoor footage. Color registration on preview print was uneven in one major scene. *Murf.*

Follow Me, Boys
(COLOR)

Topnotch Walt Disney drama with heavy family and general audience appeal.

Hollywood, Oct. 8.
Buena Vista release of Walt Disney-Winston Hibler production. Stars Fred MacMurray, Vera Miles, Lillian Gish, Charlie Ruggles; features Elliott Reid, Kurt Russell, Luana Patten, Ken Murray, Donald May, Sean McClory. Directed by Norman Tokar. Screenplay, Louis Pelletier; based on book, "God and My Country," by MacKinlay Kantor; camera (Technicolor), Clifford Stine; music, George Bruns; editor, Robert Stafford; asst. director, Terry Morse Jr. Reviewed at Academy Award Theatre, Oct. 7, '66. Running Time, 131 MINS.
Lemuel Siddons ...... Fred MacMurray
Vida Downey .... Vera Miles
Hetty Seibert .... Lillian Gish
John Everett Hughes....Charlie Ruggles
Ralph Hastings .... Elliott Reid
Whitey .... Kurt Russell
Nora White .... Luana Patten
Melody Murphy .... Ken Murray
Edward White Jr......... Donald May
Edward White Sr....... Sean McClory
P.O.W. Lieutenant .....Steve Franken
Mayor Hi Plommer ...... Parley Baer
Hoodoo Henderson (as a man)
                        William Reynolds
Leo (as a man)............ Craig Hill
Doctor Ferris .... Tol Avery
Judge .... Willis Bouchey
Ralph's Lawyer .... John Zaremba
Cora Anderson .... Madge Blake
Tank Captain .... Carl Reindel
Frankie Martin (as a man) Hank Brandt
Umpire .... Richard Bakalyan
Corporal .... Tim McIntire
Quong Lee (as a man) Willie Soo Hoo
Hetty's Lawyer .... Tony Regan
Artie .... Robert B. Williams
First P.O.W. Soldier....Jimmy Murphy
P.O.W. Sergeant ...... Adam Williams
Hcodoo Henderson .... Dean Moray
Leo .... Bill Booth
Beefy Smith .... Keith Taylor
Frankie Martin .... Rickey Kelman
Mickey Doyle .... Gregg Shank
Red .... Donnie Carter
Oliver .... Kit Lloyd
Tiger .... Ronnie Dapo
Jimmy .... Dennis Rush
Eggy .... Kevin Burchett
Duke .... David Bailey
Harry .... Eddie Sallia
David .... Bill "Wahoo" Mills
Quong Lee .... Warren Hsieh
Joe .... Duane Chase
Phil .... Mike Dodge
Ronnie Larsen .... Greger Vigen
Scout No. 1, Troop No. 1 Michael Flatley
Scout No. 3. Troop No. 1 Sherwood Ball
Scout at Cliff .... Colyer Dupont
First Scout in War Games
                        Dean Bradshaw
Second Scout in War Games
                        Chris Mason
Third Scout in War Games
                        Johnny Bangert

Walt Disney has a topnotch human interest feature in this warm adaptation of MacKinlay Kantor's novel, "God and My Country," which should strike a respondent chord with every audience regardless how sophisticated. Starring Fred MacMurray as a scoutmaster who becomes a legend in his small town, the Winston Hibler coproduction catches the spirit of rural America in the '30s with moving charm, blending comedy, drama and romance in buildup toward an emotionally-charged climax.

"Follow Me, Boys" is Disney at his best in this type of family entertainment. It is the touching story of an ordinary man, a saxophone player who, tired of his life as a travelling tooter, settles down in a Midwest hamlet and turns pied piper for a flock of kids to win the love of the town beauty, played by Vera Miles, MacMurray's co-star who eventually becomes his wife. Louis Pelletier's screenplay garments the unfoldment with a nostalgic flair for detail that will immediately touch home with spectators, and Norman Tokar in his discretion sets a mood which never ceases to hold attention. The drama of Kantor's tome as it dwells on Boy Scout movement gives excellent motivation to an honest narrative expertly turned out in every detail.

One of the highlights of Technicolor film is the appearance of Lillian Gish as a wealthy eccentric who isn't as addled as she sometimes appears to be. There is still the delicate beauty as remembered and when she's on-scene she captures the full interest of the moment.

MacMurray scores heavily as the scoutmaster whose life is centered in his avocation. He plays part with a light approach while basically underscoring its dramatic elements and comes up with one of the best performances of his long career. Miss Miles is lovely as his understanding wife and creates a lasting impression. Charlie Ruggles, fourth star, is on fleetingly as the store-owner who gives MacMurray a job when he decides to settle down, but delivers one of his usual heartwarming delineations.

In the large supporting case, Kurt Russell stands out as one of MacMurray's Scouts who is adopted by the leader and his wife to fill a void when it's learned the wife may not have any children. He makes substance of a difficult role, that of a boy bitter at the world who is handicapped with a loving alcoholic father, sensitively portrayed by Sean McClory.

Elliott Reid registers well as the heavy who sets out to prove in court that his aunt, played by Miss Gish, is incompetent when she presents valuable land to the Scout troop. Ken Murray is in briefly as leader of an aging collegians' jazz band which MacMurray leaves, and excellent bits are contributed by Donald May, Steve Franken, Luana Patten and Dean Moray, among others.

Technical credits as usual with any Disney production are tops. Rating mention are Clifford Stine's color photographer, Robert Stafford's editing, Carroll Clark and Marvin Aubrey Davis' art direction, George Bruns' music score. Title song by Robert B. and Richard M. Sherman is toe-tapping.
Whit.

Dead Heat on a Merry-Go-Round
(COLOR)

Good idea that misses in development; may be exploited for fair return with James Coburn ("Our Man Flint") name.

Hollywood, Oct. 1.
Columbia Pictures release of (Carter DeHaven - Bernard Girard production) written and directed by Girard. Stars James Coburn; features Camilla Sparv, Aldo Ray. Camera (Eastman Color), Lionel Lindon; editor, William Lyon; asst. director, William Kissel. Reviewed at Academy Award Theatre, Sept. 29, '66. Running Time, **107 MINS.**
Eli Kotch .... James Coburn
Inger Knudson .... Camilla Sparv
Eddie Hart .... Aldo Ray
Frieda Schmid .... Nina Wayne
Milo Stewart .... Robert Webber
Margaret Kirby .... Rose Marie
Alfred Morgan .... Todd Armstrong
Dr. Marion Hague ...... Marian Moses
Paul Feng .... Michael Strong
Miles Fisher .... Severn Darden
Jack Balter .... James Westerfield
George Logan .... Phillip E. Pine

The idea and the premise of "Dead Heat On a Merry-Go-Round" is okay but it doesn't jell, and the title, a deliberate attempt to be cute, is meaningless. What leads up to the comedy-melodrama O. Henry finale most likely was very funny in the producers' minds, but much of the action is so fragmentary and episodic that there is not sufficient exposition and the treatment goes overboard in striving for effect.

James Coburn, who made a name for himself as a distinctive type of private eye in "Our Man Flint," stars here in a character that puts him on the other side of the law. A con artist, he's out to rob a bank, which he does quite neatly.

First effort as a production team by Carter DeHaven — who produces—and Bernard Girard—who wrote original screenplay and directs—the unfoldment lacks cohesion and audience is required to use too much imagination through suggestion as to what is happening. This narrows appeal to sophisticated audiences rather than general public.

Coburn, who charms his way out of a prison into a parole via an affair with a femme psychologist (a nice trick if you know how to do it), has in mind the burglary of a bank at L.A. International Airport. Date set for the heist coincides with arrival of the Russian premier, when security will engage full attention of all arms of the law. First half is devoted to his raising $85,000 to pay for the plans of the bank, second half to the actual caper.

Coburn plays a rather sardonic character who, like his Flint, is capable of meeting every situation successfully and with what is given him comes through with a deft performance.

A new Swedish actress, Camilla Sparv, whom he weds and is an innocent accomplice, rivals him in interest, displaying a fresh note which communicates engagingly to audience. Aldo Ray is in as one of his confederates, and Severn Darden gets laughs as another pal. Nina Wayne scores, too, in brief bit as a maid whom Coburn romances, Marian Moses as the prison psychologist, and Rose Marie as another object of Coburn's affections. Robert Webber is government man in charge of protecting the arriving Soviet official.

Technical credits are all on plus side. Expert work is offered by Lionel Lindon on color cameras; William Lyon as editor; Walter M. Simonds, art director. *Whit.*

After The Fox
(COLOR)
(BRITISH-COLOR)

Peter Sellers' performance and Vittorio de Sica's direction (plus standout comedy from Victor Mature) keep this lively comedy bubbling. Good for most situations.

London, Sept. 29.
United Artists release of a Delegate A. G. and Nancy Enterprises Inc. production, produced by John Bryan. Stars Peter Sellers; features Victor Mature, Britt Ekland, Martin Balsam, Akim Tamiroff, Paolo Stoppa, Lydia Brazzi, Tino Buazzelli, Mac Ronay, Maria Grazia Buccelli, Lando Buzzanca. Directed by Vittorio De Sica. Screenplay, Neil Simon; music, Burt Bacharach; camera (Technicolor), Leonida Barboni; editor, Russell Lloyd. Title song (lyric, Hal David; music, Bacharach) sung by The Hollies and Sellers. At Odeon, Leicester Square, London. Running Time, 102 MINS.
Aldo Vanucci .... Peter Sellers
Gina .... Britt Ekland
Teresa Vanucci .... Lydia Brazzi
Pollo .... Paolo Stoppa
Siepe .... Tino Buazzelli
Carlo .... Mac Ronay
Tony Powell .... Victor Mature
Harry .... Martin Balsam
Okra .... Akim Tamiroff
Girl in Bikini... Maria Grazia Buccelli
Captain of the Guardia Lando Buzzanca
First Policeman .... Tiberio Murga
The Doctor .... Pier Luigi Pizzi
Raymond .... Enzo Fiermonte
Cafe Proprietor .... Carlo Croccolo

Peter Sellers is in nimble, lively form in this whacky comedy which, though sometimes strained, has a good comic idea and gives the star plenty of scope for his usual range of impersonations. In this one he crops up as a jailbird, a priest, a prison doctor, a tourist photographer, a member of the Italian constabulary and, most importantly to the plot, as a Fellini-type New Wave film director. The film has British, Italian and American roots but, filmed in Italy and with the majority of the supporting roles played by local players, the Continental flavor predominates, which gives added point to the parody of avant-garde filmmaking that's the crux of the pic.

Neil Simon's screenplay is uneven but naturally has a good quota of Simon wit, and Vittorio De Sica's direction plays throughout for laughs. The Fox is a quick-witted crook who nevertheless manages to find himself in the cooler seven times in nine years. But he's equally adroit at getting out. This time he makes the break (a) because he's worried about his sister who, he has a hunch, is getting into bad habits as a film starlet, and (b) to arrange for the smuggling into Rome of the loot from a $3,000,000 Cairo bullion robbery organized by Akim Tamiroff. He hits on the idea of pretending to make a film on an Italian beach and conning the local villagers and the police into landing the gold ashore as part of the "film script." But, of course, the scheme comes unstuck and Sellers lands up in jail again...till his next break.

Spoofing of Italian family life (his mother is a typical mamma mia) is neatly done. The filming parody is better in promise than when start of shooting is actually being made, but even these sequences are good for plenty of yocks. Much of this is created by Victor Mature, roped into the film within the film as an aging, corseted film star fighting the wrinkles and still living in the past (witness his determination to cling to the slouch hat and trench coat which were his trademarks in the 40's). It is a generous and delightful piece of self-parody and Mature blends well with Sellers and with Martin Balsam as his worried, cynical manager.

Britt Ekland (Mrs. Sellers) plays Sellers' sister, disguised with an Italian brunette wig, and shows up remarkably well in a small but pertinent role. She and Mature are both costarred, though their names appear under title.

Tamiroff gives his usual sound performance as the comedy heavy and various Italian thesps, such as Lydia Brazzi as Seller's mother, Lando Buzzanca as a starstruck chief of police, and Paolo Stoppa, Tino Buazzelli and Mac Ronay as Sellers' buddies, all chip in with useful work. Maria Grazia Buccelli, as Tamiroff's sister and object of Sellers' affections, is a stunning looker though she hasn't much scope in the pic.

Among the happy devices dreamed up by Simon, De Sica and Sellers are a sandstorm during a desert epic in which De Sica appears as the director and during which Sellers & Co. swipe the cameras and equipment; a miming sequence in which Tamiroff talks the crime plot over with Sellers with his guttural voice apparently coming from the lips of Signorina Buccelli, a bright opening jail sequence and sundry other visual gags.

With Sellers in such good form this is surefire entertainment throughout and it's backed by a lively score by Burt Bacharach. Sellers and The Hollies give with the over-titles theme song. Camerawork is okay, but Russell Lloyd's editing is sometimes a shade haphazard. *Rich.*

Return Of The Seven
(SPANISH-COLOR-PANAVISION)

Cliche sequel to "The Magnificent Seven," thin in all departments. Yul Brynner repeats earlier role for marquee value.

Hollywood, Oct. 5.
United Artists release of Mirisch Prods. (Ted Richmond) presentation. Stars Yul Brynner. Directed by Burt Kennedy. Screenplay, Larry Cohen; camera (DeLuxe Color), Paul Vogel; editor, Bert Bates; music, Elmer Bernstein; asst. director, Jose Lopez Rodero. Reviewed at Academy Award Theatre, L.A., Oct. 4, '66. Running Time, 95 MINS.
Chris ....Yul Brynner
Vin .... Robert Fuller
Chico .... Julian Mateos
Colbee .... Warren Oates
Manuel .... Jordan Christopher
Frank .... Claude Akins
Luis .... Virgilio Texeira
Lorca .... Emilio Fernandez
Lopez .... Rudy Acosta
Petra .... Elisa Montes
Priest .... Fernando Rey

Filmed in Spain by Mirisch, in association with C.B. Films S.A., "Return Of The Seven" is an unsatisfactory followup to "The Magnificent Seven," the 1960 John Sturges - Mirisch Corp. pic. Yul Brynner, sole holdover thesp, stars in a plodding, cliche-ridden script. Ted Richmond's routine production, thin in all departments, will have to be sold on the basis of star and earlier film. Fast saturation playoff appears mandatory before word of mouth relegates this dull United Artists programmer to lowcase status in lesser action situations. Theatrical playoff will not enhance by much a pix-to-tv sale, and it might as well go directly to the tube.

Larry Cohen's dreary screenplay reunites Brynner and two other members of the Sturges septet — Robert Fuller evidently in the old Steve McQueen part, and Julian

Mateos filling the former Horst Buchholz role — when the latter is dragooned by Emilio Fernandez, psychotic Mexican rancher who enslaves local farmers to rebuild a village. Four new characters are recruited — girl-chasing Warren Oates, brooding Claude Akins, suave Virgilio Texeira and juvenile Jordan Christopher, latter in a dim dramatic feature debut.

Under Burt Kennedy's limp direction, players walk through their predictable dialog while rescuing Mateos, and provoking the long-awaited showdown with Fernandez. Rudy Acosta plays latter's chief lieutenant, while Elisa Montes is okay as Mateos' wife, and Fernando Rey is competent in a thankless role of a prayer-mumbling priest. At fadeout, Brynner and Fuller ride away from an overproduced carnage, never to return, one hopes.

Elmer Bernstein, whose original "Magnificent" score reminded many of that by Jerome Moross for "The Big Country," has simply rescored — if that — for the current effort. Paul Vogels lensing in Panavision is excellent, but the De-Luxe Color release print work is obviously hampered by sub-standard Spanish negative professing. Bert Bates edited to an interminable 95 minutes. Other technical credits are adequate. *Murf.*

Le Voyage Du Pere
(The Father's Trip)
(FRENCH—COLOR—
FRANSCOPE)

Paris, Oct. 2.
Comacico release of Copernic-Gafer-Metropolis Films production. Stars Fernandel, Lilli Palmer, Laurent Terzieff; features Philippe Noiret, Michel Auclair, Madeleine Robinson. Directed by Denys De La Patelliere. Screenplay, Pascal Jardin, De La Patelliere, from novel by Bernard Clavel; camera (Eastmancolor), Jean Tournier; music, Georges Gavarentz. At Balzac, Paris. Running Time, 80 MINS.
Quantin .... Fernandel
Isabelle .... Lilli Palmer
Frederique .... Laurent Terzieff
Traveller .... Philippe Noiret
Man .... Michel Auclair
Madame .... Madeleine Robinson

Rubbery-faced comedian Fernandel has played serious roles before. He was a married man caught up in adultery in "Forbidden Fruit" and a mercy killer in "Murder." Now he is a peasant who goes to the big city to bring home his daughter and finds she has become a prostitute. Tale is old but told with reserve if it remains soapy and primarily a local item with some foreign playoff indicated on the Fernandel monicker if exploited on his change-of-pace role.

Fernandel's partner Jean Gabin played a crusty anarchist who puts a prostie on the right road last year in "God's Thunder" which turned out to be the sleeper of the season. Now the same director, actress, Lilli Palmer, and a similar tale are used and it may do well here. Fernandel and Gabin's company, Gafer coproduced.

Fernandel is a tender and simple man whose wife berates him for the lack of money and of opportunities for their daughters. The older one has lived in a big town for a couple of years but when she says she cannot come home for her sister's birthday, the father goes to get her. He is accompanied by a younger teacher who is in love with her but which is unrequited.

They find she has become a prostie and Fernandel's early anger and deep hurt are finally understood as he realizes she had been inundated with success stories and longings for material goods not so easy to come by in spite of growing affluence. Girl is never shown but the two men searching, and their reactions, make up the brunt of the tale.

If pic pays lip service to complacency, it is still somewhat surface in leaving too much to talk and neglecting a more visual forthrightness or firmer grip with life.

Fernandel has a canny ability to display disarray and hurt, though his character remains static. Laurent Terzieff is effective as the teacher with Miss Palmer making a gallant stab at a woman who is trying to make up for the things she lost through her daughters. But she is too graceful and fragile to give much body to a peasant woman. Color is good. This is only 80 minutes but seems a bit longer in its meandering treatment and sometimes contrived progression. *Mosk.*

Demain, La Chine
(Tomorrow, China)
(FRENCH-DOCUMENTARY)

Paris, Oct. 11.
Argos Films release and production. Directed and lensed by Claude Otzenberger; commentary, Christophe Berger; editor, Ragnar. At Racine, Paris. Running Time, 80 MINS.

Red China still packs curiosity interest and this is a fairly absorbing documentary that skims around the surface of that Communist country. It does not have an up-to-date look at the Red Guards, now pushing on the revolution, but it does deal with the myth and place of Mao Tse-tung, interviews people, and has enough new insights, good lensing and okay commentary to slant it for special usage or tv abroad.

Pic also deals with Formosa and is a bit cursory and surface in passing it off as a U.S. vassal. But its mainland excursions are more probing. There are the militia exercises, full of fanatical zeal, talks with students aghast at the idea that Mao could make a mistake, the paradoxical freedom of Catholic and Buddhist sects.

A Chinese Catholic priest says the local believers have broken with Rome because they backed the ex-colonialists and exploiters of China and adds that though Communism does not believe in God, it does not interfere with current religions. Novelist Han Suyin makes a good impression as she talks about China where she lives six months a year.

Film shows anti-American plays and children's games and school-teaching, but advanced students feel the American people are good and it is only the ruling class they are against.

Film had no access to any important political figures and filmmakers Claude Otzenberger could not go everywhere; many times he just lensed people at work or in the street or talked to them through interpreters. What emerges is a surface look, but because it is Red China it packs interest. If its attitude toward Formosa is clear, it is fairly objective on the Red China side and ends with a feeling that the country should try to be understood to be dealt with.

Commentary is usually clear and functional, if a bit precious at times in reading things into shots that do not call for musings on the future. *Mosk.*

Le Grand Restaurant
(FRENCH—SCOPE)

Paris, Oct. 1.
Gaumont release of Gaumont International production. Stars Louis De Funes, Bernard Blier, Maria Rodriguez, Noel Roquevert. Directed by Jacques Besnard. Screenplay, Jean Halain; camera, Raymond Lemoigne; editor, Gilbert Natot. At Ambassade-Gaumont, Paris. Running Time, 85 MINS.
Septime ... ... Louis De Funes
Inspector .... Bernard Blier
Secretary .... Maria Rodriguez
Minister .... Noel Roquevert
President .... Folco Lulli

Louis De Funes, a balding, middleaged, irascible comic, is popular here and now tries to carry a whole pic on his tics and risible timing. He is funny but cannot overcome a film that mixes a comic look at the workings of a fancy, high-toned Paris restaurant with Bondish-type undercover adventures. Result is a slim comedy with some dualer or playoff indicated on some of its madcap scenes, but with not enough body for specialized use abroad. Its chances look happier at home.

De Funes has a very popular eatery and, if he is terrified of his cooks, bears down on the other help. He spies on them, gives them lessons and seems resigned to this spleeny life until a visiting foreign dignitary is kidnapped in his restaurant. Then he is accused and tries to find the man to free himself. This is the excuse for madcap auto chases and one good one when a car turns over and goes careening down a snowy mountain, since it has skis strapped on top and can take a ski jump.

De Funes has a spluttering, beady, obsequious quality, underpinned by self-deprecation and selfishness, that gives his scenes savory flavor. But he needs a better script for he cannot bring it off all on his own. *Mosk.*

Tendre Voyou
(Tender Hoodlum)
(FRENCH—COLOR)

Paris, Oct. 4.
Prodis release of Sud Pacifique Films-Criterion-Foncrama production. Stars Jean-Paul Belmondo; features Nadja Tiller, Stefania Sandrelli, Mylene Demongeot, Robert Morley, Genevieve Page, Philippe Noiret, Jean-Paul Marielle. Directed by Jean Becker. Screenplay, Albert Simonin, Daniel Boulanger, Michel Audiard; camera (Eastmancolor), Edmond Sechan; editor, Monique Kirsanoff. At Mercury, Paris. Running Time, 90 MINS.
Tony .... Jean-Paul Belmondo
Baronne .... Nadja Tiller
Veronique .... Stefania Sandrelli
Mistress .... Mylene Demongeot
Edward .... Robert Morley
Wife .... Genevieve Page
Bob .... Jean-Paul Marielle
Bibi .... Philippe Noiret

Jean-Paul Belmondo has lately specialized in playing sympathetic young con men or madcap heroes. Here he mixes both for a pic that does not have enough script, directorial or comic inventiveness to keep him from being repetitious and a bit overbearing. Belmondo has charm, but needs a film around him too. So this appears a good local item with foreign usage more limited to dualers, on its fair amount of entertainment; art and specialized chances are risky.

Belmondo preys on women in this one but finally ends up surfeited after two nymphos and ends up running for his life from another one. In between he has a series of adventures via willing women. He goes to winter sports, Tahiti and then back to Paris before this tenuous pic is over. Along the way he tries to admit he is a phony to a girl he loves, but is repulsed.

Director Jean Becker relies on Belmondo too much. If the actor has flair and pluck, the cardboard characters around him, the slangy, forced dialog and the telegraphed proceedings swamp even him. There are some good actors and lookers wasted in small roles. It is technically okay. *Mosk.*

Martin Soldat
(Soldier Martin)
(FRENCH-COLOR)

Paris, Oct. 10.
CCFC release of Pierre Braunberger-Films De La Pleiade production. Stars Robert Hirsch; features Veronique Vandell, Walter Riller, Andre Weber, Georges Chamarat. Directed by Michel Deville. Screenplay, Maurice Rheims, Nina Companeez, Deville; camera (Eastmancolor), Claude Lecomte; editor, Nina Companeez. At Colisee, Paris. Running Time, 95 MINS.
Martin .... Robert Hirsch
Zuzu .... Veronique Vandell
General .... Walter Riller
Chauffeur .... Andre Weber
Director .... Georges Chamarat

Since Comedie-Francaise actor Robert Hirsch clicked in a sleeper Israeli-French pic "Impossible on Saturday" playing eight roles, locals have been trying to find the right vehicle to continue the good luck. But so far it has not carried over and this also looks like a miss, with mainly local chances.

Hirsch is an actor in a small traveling troupe who finds himself captured by the Americans when they land, since he had been rehearsing a play in a German uniform. He manages to get out of it and joins the Free French Army, only to be caught by Germans when he is wearing his General's uniform since his clothes had been taken by another. He then is used by the English for undercover work when he helps capture the Germans.

He gets involved with a plot to kill Hitler and finally winds up a hero and given an audition at the Comedie-Francaise, only to think it. Hirsch is clever at impersonations but is hard put to carve out a clear character in this ambling war tale that opts for comedics during D-Day, Gestapo torture and undercover work.

The needed invention, comic brashness to underline a lament on war, and more visual deftness are not always provided by director Michel Deville. It does appear a vehicle for the talented Hirsch, but there is not enough drive to bring it off. *Mosk.*

Hocuspocus
(GERMAN-COLOR)

Berlin, Sept. 29.
Constantin-Film release of Hans Domnick and Independent (Kurt Hoffmann) production. Stars Heinz Ruehmann, Liselotte Pulver; features Richard Muench, Fritz Tillman. Directed by Kurt Hoffmann. Screenplay, Eberhard Keindorff, adapted from the stage comedy of same title by Curt Goetz; camera (Eastmancolor), Richard Angst; music, Franz Grothe; sets, Otto Pischinger. At various cinemas, West Berlin. Running Time, 102 MINS.

Peer Bille	Heinz Ruehmann
Agda	Liselotte Pulver
Court President	Richard Muench
Public Prosecutor	Fritz Tillmann
Mr. Graham	Klaus Miedel
Amundsen	Stefan Wigger
Munio Eunano	Joachim Teege
Mrs. Engstrand	Kaethe Braun
Anna Sedal	Edith Elsholtz

Aside from the settings there is not much in this German "Hocuspocus" for which the more demanding critic can find praise. But it is the kind of production that makes for mass appeal, especially in Germany where the names of Heinz Ruehmann and Liselotte Pulver mean plenty.

This is (after "The House in Montevideo" and "Dr. Hiob Praetorius") Kurt Hoffmann's third filmization of a Curt Goetz work. And once again he produced it via his Independent in collab with Hans Domnick. This Goetz comedy (which, incidentally, has been brought to the screen a couple of times within the years) presents a murder trial with a difference. It concerns beautiful Frau Agda (Liselotte Pulver) who's accused of murdering her painter-husband by drowning him. All circumstantial evidence points to her guilt. Nobody gives her a a chance, with even her lawyer quitting because of the hopeless case.

Then, there is a switch. Another lawyer takes over her case and he is soon well on his way to proving her innocence. But suddenly there is another switch. After an interrogation of witnesses, this lawyer is being pointed as the lover of the accused. And finally another switch: The lawyer is nobody else but her husband. The whole thing is a case of mistaken identity and he let it go in order to stir attention for his paintings which are now suddenly in great demand.

There is no doubt that the original contains wit and imagination for which, after all, the late Curt Goetz was famous. The film, however, lacks a great deal of both. It is, in fact, a rather bloodless comedy without routine direction and acting. But with Miss Pulver and Ruehmann being practically an institution around here, the average native patron will hardly notice their mechanical performances. There is some nice support from Fritz Tillmann, Richard Muench and Joachim Teege. Cameraman Richard Angst did the lensing expertly and Franz Grothe contributed an adequate score. The best thing about this production is, as mentioned the pop-art type of settings which brought Otto Pichinger a Federal Film Award this year. *Hans.*

The Fortune Cookie
(PANAVISION)

Amusing but spotty satire about an attempted insurance fraud. Billy Wilder and Jack Lemmon are the marquee lures, but Walter Matthau makes things move. Good production values. Esoteric title needs clarifying sell. Good b.o. prospects in urban situations.

Hollywood, Sept. 13.
United Artists release of Mirisch Corp. presentation, produced and directed by Billy Wilder. Stars Jack Lemmon, Walter Matthau; features Ron Rich, Cliff Osmond, Judi West. Screenplay, Wilder, I. A. L. Diamond; camera, Joseph LaShelle; editor, Daniel Mandell; music, Andre Previn; asst. director, Jack Raddish. Reviewed at Academy Award Theatre, L.A., Sept. 12, '66. Running Time, 125 MINS.

Harry Hinkle	Jack Lemmon
Willie Gingrich	Walter Matthau
Luther Jackson	Ron Rich
Mr. Purkey	Cliff Osmond
Sandy	Judi West
Mother Hinkle	Lurene Tuttle
O'Brien	Harry Holcombe
Thompson	Les Tremayne
Charlotte Gingrich	Marge Redmond
Max	Noam Pitlik
Dr. Krugman	Harry Davis
Sister Veronica	Ann Shoemaker
Nurse	Maryesther Denver
Kincaid	Lauren Gilbert
Doc Schindler	Ned Glass
Prof. Winterhalter	Sig Ruman
Mr. Jackson	Archie Moore
Mr. Cimoli	Howard McNear
Intern	Bill Christopher
Specialists	Bartlett Robinson, Robert P. Lieb, Martin Blaine, Ben Wright
Nun	Dodie Heath
Maury	Herbie Faye
Locker Room Asst.	Billy Beck
Elvira	Judy Pace
Receptionist	Helen Kleeb
Ginger	Lisa Jill
Jeffrey	John Todd Roberts
Football Announcer	Keith Jackson
TV Director	Herb Ellis
Newscaster	Don Reed
Girl in Teleblurb	Louise Vienna
Man in Bar	Bob Doqui

Producer - director - writer Billy Wilder, in his first outing since "Kiss Me Stupid" two years ago, presents in "The Fortune Cookie" another bittersweet comedy commentary on contemporary U.S. mores. Generally amusing (often wildly so) but overlong, the Mirisch Corp. presentation is pegged on an insurance fraud in which Jack Lemmon and Walter Matthau are the conspirators. Lemmon and Wilder are the b.o. bait for a United Artists release which has a weak title. Prospects look good in the general market with adroit selling.

Original screenplay is by Wilder, paired for seventh time with I. A. L. Diamond, latter also associate producer with Doane Harrison. For record purposes, pic is the sixth Wilder-Mirisch-UA teaming. This time around. Wilder's plot turns on the complications following tv cameraman Lemmon's accidental injury at the hands of grid star Ron Rich. Matthau, shyster lawyer and Lemmon's brother-in-law, sees fancy damages in the injury, and ex-wife Judi West smells money in a fake reunion with Lemmon. Insurance gumshoe Cliff Osmond uncovers the fraud.

Actually a tragi-comedy, film is a too-leisurely excursion through Americana which even becomes boring when Matthau is not on screen. Properly billed above-title after Lemmon, he delivers the standout performance as the grousing legal scoundrel. Matthau and supporting players carry the "Cookie," a would-be low-key meller. (In 1944, incidentally Wilder co-scripted and directed an outstanding dramatic suspenser about insurance fraud—"Double Indemnity," a Paramount pic.)

Lemmon, confined perforce to sickroom immobility (bandages, wheelchair, etc.), is straddled most of the time with the colorless image of a man vacillating with his conscience over the fraud, and its effect on Rich, whose playing has deteriorated from remorse. Rich and Miss West, both in pix debuts, are okay. Miss West's part, as written and directed, is never sympathetic. Osmond gives some life to proceedings as the kookie private eye.

Besides the American penchant for litigation, Wilder also takes some gentle swipes at lawyer-types, telecasting of sports events (with the inevitable slow- and stop-motion replays of disaster), segmented tv programming (numbered and cleverly titled "parts"), doctors, teleblurbs and worthy causes. Pic goes very dramatic when Osmond deliberately provokes Lemmon's rage via some anti-Negro dialog about Rich. Lemmon squares Rich away in final scene, played at night on a darkened field.

Given his uneven satire, Wilder's direction is strong. Notable among the large supporting cast are Lurene Tuttle, Lemmon's hysterical mother, Harry Holcombe and Les Tremayne as two uptown lawyers, Noam Pitlik as Osmond's assistant, officious intern Bill Christopher (particularly good), and Louise Vienna, nitery chirp in a good feature debut starring in a teleblurb. Choreographer Wally Green has Miss Vienna gliding about linoleum in the best Loretta Young tradition.

Production credits are solid, topped by Joseph LaShelle's crisp b&w Panavision lensing, and Robert Luthardt's good art direction. Andre Previn's score is okay, and incorporates repeated use of Cole Porter's "You'd Be So Nice To Come Home To." Daniel Mandell executed the trimming to a slowish 125 minutes. Other technical credits are pro.

Most location work involved use of Cleveland Browns home field facilities there, and some footage shows prominently the use of CBS-TV gear, possible portent of where "Cookie" will land in the inevitable pix-to-tv. Title derives from a scene where Lemmon breaks a fortune cookie, only to find inside Abraham Lincoln's famous aphorism about fooling all/some people all/some of the time.

As a footnote. substitute "amuse" for "fool" and "Wilder" for "you" in Lincoln statement, and the result is a fair appraisal of the artistic and commercial merits of "Cookie." *Murf.*

Relax. Freddie
(DANISH-COLOR)

Copenhagen, Oct. 10.
Nordisk Film Kompagni production and release. Features Morten Grunwald, Ove Sprogoe, Erik Moerk, Hanne Borchsenius. Script: Bengt Janus, Henning Bahs, Erik Balling. Directed by Erik Balling. Camera (Eastmancolor): Jorgen Skov. Music: Brent Fabricius-Bjerre. Reviewed at Palads Teatret, Copenhagen. Running Time, 100 MINS.

Freddie	Morton Grunwald
Smith	Ove Sprogoe
Presto	Erik Moerk
Diana	Hanne Borchsenius
Mama	Clara Pontopoidan
The Boss	Asbjoern Andersen
Fettucino	Dirch Passer

Erik Balling's "Hit First, Freddie" (in the U.S., "Operation Love birds") was a front-runner among the spy-spoofs and enjoyed worldwide sales. This follow-up may come at the end of the spy run, but it seems assured of modest success anyway (it has already been sold for U.S. distribution). What Balling has done in "Relax, Freddie," is to take his tongue out of his cheek and instead thumb his nose at the entire *genre* instead. The result is not exactly sidesplitting, but it is certainly good for many a chuckle and even an occasional guffaw.

What sets Balling's spoof-on-spoofs apart from the rest of the flood is also his placing of international intrigue in a peaceful Danish landscape of cows, pastures and people like the unsuspecting Freddie, occupation salesman. The Danish word for salesman is agent and so, right away, Freddie is up to his sunny visage in an international gangland kidnaping of a Chinese statesman.

The Chinese is lugged about in Denmark in a wardrobe trunk with a special opening for feeding. Tough but beautiful Hanne Borchsenius, heading a gang of gungirls, takes care of the feeding and is rewarded with the sound of belching in Chinese. Later on, she is given custody also of agent-against-his-will Freddie, and is rewarded with a lesson in love, Danish country style which isn't Swedish but it ain't hay, either.

Although Freddie is played with gusto by big Morten Grunwald, tiny Ove Sprogoe is a constant scene-stealer as the official agent Smith who just has to solve the case or else his license-to-kill will be revoked. Sight-gags abound, but the dialogue is not without spice either. An English-speaking version of "Relax, Freddie" was made right along with the Danish version, but both retain nicely the very sweet and very Danish flavor of a joke otherwise worn to a frazzle. *Kell.*

Any Wednesday
(COLOR)

Outstanding film version of the legit comedy. Jane Fonda, Jason Robards, Dean Jones for good marquee spread. Solid entertainment for young and old. Word of mouth and a snappy sell will yield hotsy b.o.

Hollywood, Oct. 12.
Warner Bros. Pictures release of Julius J. Epstein production. Features Jane Fonda, Jason Robards, Dean Jones, Rosemary Murphy. Directed by Robert Ellis Miller. Screenplay, Epstein, based on the stage play by Muriel Resnik; camera (Technicolor), Harold Lipstein; editor, Stefan Arnsten; music, George Duning; song, Duning, Marilyn and Alan Bergman; asst. director, Victor Vallejo. Reviewed at Academy Award Theatre, L.A., Oct. 11, '66. Running Time, 109 MINS.

Ellen Gordon	Jane Fonda
John Cleves	Jason Robards
Cass Henderson	Dean Jones

Dorothy Cleves	Rosemary Murphy
Miss Linsley	Ann Prentiss
Felix	Jack Fletcher
Girl in Museum	Kelly Jean Peters
Milkman	King Moody
Nurse	Monty Margetts

Based on Muriel Resnik's popular legiter, "Any Wednesday" emerges in screen translation as an outstanding sophisticated comedy about marital infidelity. Adaptation and production by Julius J. Epstein is very strong, enhanced by solid direction and excellent performances. Jane Fonda, Jason Robards and Dean Jones provide diversified marquee bait, and sock b.o. prospects are in store from Warner Bros. release in general situations.

WB, incidentally, has been on a varied comedy kick all year. "A Fine Madness" and "A Big Hand for the Little Lady" came out earlier, and the year is ending with a solid, three-ply spread of "Kaleidoscope," "Not With My Wife, You Don't," and "Wednesday," the Christmas pic. Latter trio, in particular, have a long life in store, with word of mouth and entertainment values spelling thousands of extra playdates after the initial key city bookings.

Epstein's zesty adaptation of "Wednesday" wisely distributes the comedy emphasis among all four principals — Robards, the once-a-week philanderer; Miss Fonda, his two-year Wednesday date; Jones, whose arrival rocks Robards' dreamboat, and Rosemary Murphy, recreating in superior fashion her original Broadway role as Robards' wife. Robert Ellis Miller makes a standout bow as a feature film director.

Interactions between principals are uniformly strong, both in dialog and acting as well as in very effective use of split-screen effects. Action is not confined to one room, but spreads over some real N.Y. exteriors, makes a gag out of the blackout there, and unfortunately includes one very obvious and poor process shot. Time transitions are handled with simple ingenuity, using oil paintings and montage.

Miss Fonda comes across quite well as the girl who can't make up her mind, although she has a tendency to overplay certain bits in what might be called an exaggerated Doris Day manner. Her facial expressions are usually adroit, and her very crisp diction is a big plus factor in putting over the dialog. Jones continues to impress as a likeable comedy performer whose underlying dramatic ability gets a good showcasing here.

Robards is outstanding as the likeable lecher who winds up losing both his mistress and his wife. As the latter, Miss Murphy is terrif in her ability to combine the elements of a typical clubwoman, an understanding wife and a still-sexy femme into a charming, well-rounded characterization.

Supporting players shine in their brief appearances, notably Ann Prentiss, a goofy secretary who triggers the plot complications, and Jack Fletcher, the swishy aesthete from Decorator Row. Kelly Jean Peters again shows her strong character ability, herein as a museum attendant. King Moody is good as the bashful milkman, long curious about the Thursday a.m. cream order, and Monty Margetts

makes a hospital nurse come alive with one line.

Miller's impressive handling of his thesps is paralleled by effective use of Harold Lipstein's mobile Technicolor camera. George Duning's score is appropriate, and title tune is okay. Dorothy Jeakins' costumes heighten the visual impact. Stefan Arnsten trimmed to a fast-moving 109 minutes. Other technical credits are firstrate.

The only significant flaw results from a combination of scripting and a tv-induced production technique. At climax, Miss Murphy reads off Robards with what is a natural fadeout, but, as filmed, there is an unnecessary trailing-off scene. Latter effect is flattened further by a title format which places the creative credits at the start, and the rest on the end title.

Undoubtedly a convenience for the eventual pix-to-tv sale, this tube technique, in theatrical presentation, has the effect of washing out the impact of a climax, particularly the desirable blackout punch in comedy. Filmmakers of the '30s and '40s knew this, and most good cartoonists still do.
Murf.

Brigade Anti-Gangs
(FRENCH-COLOR-SCOPE)

Paris, Oct. 18.

Prodis release of FranCos Films-CICC-Films Borderie-Fono Roma production. Stars Robert Hossein, Raymond Pellegrin; features, Raffaele Trinti, Pierre Clementi, Carol Lehel, Michel Galabru, Philippe Lemaire. Directed by Bernard Borderie. Screenplay, Auguste Le Breton, Borderie, Francis Cosne; camera (Eastmancolor), Henri Persin; editor, Christian Gaudin. At Regent-Neuilly. Running Time, 90 MINS.

Le Goff	Robert Hossein
Roger	Raymond Pellegrin
Jobic	Raffaele Tinti
Pommes	Pierre Clementi
Maritine	Carol Lebel
Rondier	Philippe Lemaire
Larmeno	Michel Galabru

Either Paris detective brigades are unusually dense or this is a poorly plotted pic. Young thugs easily walk into Central Police headquarters in Paris to help someone escape and the police even release a killer because a soccer star has ben kidnapped and held in ransom for the killer's release. Even if plausible, this is done sans much character or snap and has only possible tv filler or duller grind use abroad on some okay action scenes and love interludes.

A tough detective is bent on breaking a payroll gang and suspects a man with a good front of a restaurant and family. He finally gets him but his own brother, a soccer champ, is kidnapped by young thugs who are involved by the head man through one's liaison with his daughter. All is finally arranged and crime does not pay.

Direction is ordinary and some good players cannot do much with stereotyped roles. It goes its predictable length and has color and scope plusses for home consumption but not the right snap, flair and suspenseful drive to give it the deeded foreign outlets. Production dress is adequate.
Mosk.

Safari Diamants
(Diamond Safari)
(FRENCH-COLOR-FRANSCOPE)

Paris, Oct. 18.

CFDC release of Chronos Film-Port Royal Films-Hans Oppenheimer production. Stars Marie-Jose Nat, Jean-Louis Trintignant; features, Helmut Lange, Horst Frank. Directed by Michel Drach. Screenplay, Albert Kantoff, Drach; camera (Eastman-color), Andreas Winding; editor, Geneviève Winding. At Regent-Neuilly. Running Time. 90 MINS.

Electre	Marie-Jose Nat
Raphael	Jean-Louis Trintignant
Alphene	Helmut Lange
Federico	Horst Frank
Pascal	Jean-Pierre Darras
Eric	Jean-Pierre Kalfon

Escapist theme is about a young man bored with his job who runs to get mixed up with a jewel robbery, a femme fatale, and death in the end. Some fanciful camerawork is imbedded in this conventional pic, but it is of only dualer or tv use abroad on fairly well done action segs.

Director Michel Drach tries to give this firmer outlining in making the hero a disillusioned ex-paratrooper. But is it the usual tale of a fairly decent hoodlum betrayed by a woman. The latter is played by actress Marie-Jose Nat who is winsome and fetching but sans any depth, pertinent presence and projection to make her doubledealing effective or meaningful.

Jean-Louis Trintignant is workmanlike as the adventurer who pays for his straying with his life. But it does not make up its mind whether to be a crisp action pic or a more detailed look at drifters caught up in crime inadvertently. It leads to plodding and cliche progression and emerges only as a fair programmer with mainly home chances.
Mosk.

Le Jardinier
D'Argenteuil
(The Gardener of Argenteuil)
(FRENCH—COLOR—SCOPE)

Paris, Oct. 17.

Comacico release of Copernic, Films Vertried-Roxy Film production. Stars Jean Gabin; features Liselotte Pulver, Pierre Vernier, Curt Jurgens. Directed by Jean-Paul Le Chanois. Screenplay, Francois Boyer, Alphonse Boudard, Le Chanois, from novel by Rene Jouglet; camera (Eastmancolor), Walter Wottitz; editor, Emma Le Chanois. At Balzac, Paris. Running Time. 85 MINS.

Martin	Jean Gabin
Hilda	Liselotte Pulver
Baron	Curt Jurgens
Nephew	Pierre Vernier
Albert	Jean Tissier
Dora	Mary Marquet

One of the bigger producer-distrib setups here, Comacico, is embarked, it appears, on trying to make family pix. But this skimpy attempt will probably not be it. Even the Jean Gabin name will not help much and foreign chances are very spotty.

Gabin is his usual anarchic self, but here a recluse who paints, gardens and for 50 years or so has been passing small denomination counterfeit bills to live. But a sudden tax bill means more money needed; and complications follow when his nephew and girl get on to it and have him do big bills to go in for the big life.

Gabin's heart is not in it. When they buy a villa on the Riviera, cars, etc., he wants out but says he will help them once more. A dotty rich man takes a liking to him and helps him win a fortune

in the casino. He leaves it to the nephew, without saying it is real and they burn it when police appear (though the gendarmes are chasing a lion).

This situation comedy just plods along. Gabin stands around looking old and is not even given a chance to do his stock anger scene. Others cannot do much against this attempt to make a so-called "surefire" commercial pic.

It is also indicative of the low level and bumbling look of the average commercial pix being turned out here. It even tries to knock the old new wavers with a character supposedly making a pic on happenings and in an arty way. But this only makes them, no matter how far out, appear better to anyone who bothers to compare.
Mosk.

Way . . . Way Out
(C'SCOPE-COLOR)

Moon story with Jerry Lewis up to his usual antics. Usual reception indicated.

Hollywood, Oct. 1.

Twentieth-Fox release of Coldwater-Jerry Lewis (Malcolm Stuart) production. Stars Jerry Lewis; features Connie Stevens, Robert Morley, Dick Shawn, Anita Ekberg, Dennis Weaver, Howard Morris, Brian Keith. Directed by Gordon Douglas. Screenplay, William Bowers, Laslo Vadnay; music, Lalo Schifrin; camera (DeLuxe Color), William H. Clothier; editor, Hugh S. Fowler; asst. director, Joseph E. Rickards. Reviewed at 20th-Fox Studios, Sept. 29, '66. Running Time, 105 MINS.

Peter	Jerry Lewis
Eileen	Connie Stevens
Quonset	Robert Morley
Hoffman	Dennis Weaver
Schmidlap	Howard Morris
General Hallenby	Brian Keith
Igor	Dick Shawn
Anna	Anita Ekberg
Ponsonby	William O'Connell
Esther Davenport	Bobo Lewis
Russian Delegate	Milton Frome
Deuce	Alex D'Arcy
Linda	Linda Harrison
Ted	James Brolin

Jerry Lewis goes to the moon at the turn of the century— next, not last—for his latest peregrination into fun and frolic. Comic plays a weathernaut at a lunar station in 1994 who combines his duties with honeymooning the bride he married exactly 45 seconds before blastoff, a "topical" backdrop if ever there was one. The Malcolm Stuart production for Lewis' own company carries the same type of values inherent in past Lewis comedies, smartly directed by Gordon Douglas, and should enjoy similar b.o. reception.

Title of the William Bowers-Laslo-Vadnay script is appropriate as a description of both locale and action. Lewis is up to his usual antics as a purveyor of slapstick although he's beginning to soften somewhat and there's a little less broad clowning in his performance. A seasoned supporting cast, all expert in the humor vein, adds a lively note to situations which have novelty and are sufficiently amusing to hold Lewis fans.

Lewis, a weathernaut in the training for 11 years—he's always found a way to stall leaving terra firma—is selected for the moon assignment after it's decided that instead of two men at the station a husband-and-wife team shall operate. The wife must be an astronomer, which narrows candidates to wear Lewis' ring down to three, and Connie Stevens is the femme selected. She can't be rushed into matrimony, however, finally agrees to go through with the whole operation only if she goes to the moon as Lewis' wife in name only until she can get to know him. When they arrive they're immediately plunged into the romantic plight of a Russian unwed couple who helm a similar weather station.

Dick Shawn delivers one of his insane frantic projections as the Russian weathernaut who finally weds Anita Ekberg only after he thinks she's pregnant, and actress turns on all facets of sex appeal. Miss Stevens is cute as usual and Lewis is Lewis. Robert Morley as director of the U. S. Weather Bureau, Lunar Division, Cape Kennedy, spends most of his humorous performance communicating with Lewis on the moon via tv.

Dennis Weaver and Howard Morris score as the two Americans whom Lewis and his bride replace, driven nuts by their stay, Brian Keith is an American general who directs Lewis to "secure the moon" when it appears there's to be war between the U.S. and Russia, then forgets all about it when the danger subsides and gets in a state after he learns Lewis has followed his order.

On the music end, Gary Lewis (Jerry's son) and his combo, The Playboys, sing title song and score by Lalo Schifrin lends melodic backing. Col. John "Shorty" Powers (of astronaut fame) acts as narrator. Technical departments are well handled by William H. Clothier, on color cameras; Jack Martin Smith and Hilyard Brown, art direction; Hugh S. Fowler, editing; L. B. Abbott, Emil Kosa, Jr., and Howard Lydecker, special photographic effects.

Whit.

El Greco
(ITALIAN-FRENCH; COLOR)

Italian-French film about a Greek in Spain who speaks English. Not "entertaining."

20th Century-Fox release of Produzioni Artistiche Internazionali - Arco Film (Rome)—Les Films du Siecle (Paris) (Mel Ferrer) coproduction. Directed by Luciano Salce. Screenplay, Guy Elmes; camera (DeLuxe), Leonida Barboni; asst. director, Emilio Miraglia. Reviewed at 20th-Fox homeoffice, N.Y., Oct. 6, '66. Running Time, **95 MINS.**
El Greco .... Mel Ferrer
Jeronima .... Rosanna Schiaffino
Francisco .... Franco Giacobini
Fra Felix .... Renzo Giovampietro
Cardinal Nino .... Mario Feliciani
Don Diego of Castile .. Nino Crisman
Don Miguel .... Adolfo Celi
Don Luis .... Angel Aranda
Maria .... Gabriella Giorgelli
Isabel .... Rosy di Pietro
Zaida .... Rossana Martini
Pignatelli .... Giulio Donnini
Prosecutor .... Andrea Bosic
Master of Arms ...... Giuliano Farnese
Leoni .... Ontanoni
King Philip II .... Fernando Rey

One of the headaches of coproduction between various countries is pointed up in "El Greco," filmed in Spain as a joint effort of Rome's Produzioni Artistiche Internazionali-Arco Film and Paris's Les Films du Siecle. With both Mel Ferrer and Alfredo Bini listed as producers and a trio of writers actually participating in the screen-

play, the decision was made to "divide the spoils" by apportioning credits to various individuals for various countries.

Thus, in English-speaking countries Ferrer is sole producer; in Italian and French-speaking countries, Bini gets sole credit; in Spain, Germany and Austria, they share billing (with Ferrer listed first). Also in the French countries, Les Films du Siecle is listed before the Italian production company. For writing credits, Guy Elmes gets sole screenplay credit in English countries; in Italian countries he gets sole story credit and shares screenplay with Luigi Magni and Massimo Franciosa. With all these decisions, the interested spectator might logically think that "El Greco" is a motion picture of magnificent proportions, a worthy competitor to "The Agony and the Ecstasy," at least. It isn't. It's a programmer and a not very exciting one, at that.

The lives of painters have always fascinated actors, sometimes to the profit of filmgoers. But Ferrer's Domenico Theatocopoulos ("El Greco") will never be rated with Charles Laughton's Rembrandt or Kirk Douglas's Van Gogh. One would suspect that research for the screenplay revealed that the Cretan painter who left such a lasting impression on Spanish art wasn't so exciting after all. To help things along, Elmes has introduced an Inquisition angle that would not be out of place in one of Roger Corman's early horror pix.

The English soundtrack gives Spanish grandees, the Cretan painter and his Italian man-servant similar accents. Ferrer's voice is, at least, his own, and one other is most appropriate. An effete fellow artist, well played by Giulio Donnini, speaks with a lisp. The screenplay also makes El Greco such an impulsive, obtuse, sour character that he comes off as irritating rather than sympathetic and most of the others seem costumed actors rather than 16th - century people. Rosanna Schiaffino is beautiful but wooden as Ferrer's love.

Italian director Luciano Salce has done such a variety of films in the past that he was, apparently, unable to decide on a style. As a result, his film has none and the technical credits are routine. The use of choral music as background comes off more as an attempt to convey the spirituality of El Greco's paintings that is not evident in the acting.

Robe.

10:30 P.M. Summer
(COLOR)

Torpid treatment of romantic trio makes for apathetic viewing. Talented cast chained to tedious script.

Lopert Pictures release of Jules Dassin-Anatole Litvak production. Directed by Dassin. Stars Melina Mercouri, Romy Schneider, Peter Finch; features Julian Mateos. Screenplay, Dassin, Marguerite Duras based on novel by Miss Duras; camera (Technicolor), Gabor Pogany; editor, Roger Dwyre; music, Cristobal Halffter. Reviewed in New York, Sept. 21, '66. Running Time, **85 MINS.**
Maria .... Melina Mercouri
Claire .... Romy Schneider
Paul .... Peter Finch
Rodrigo Palestra .... Julian Mateos

Judith .... Isabel Maria Perez
Rodrigo's wife .... Beatriz Savon

Jules Dassin's "10:30 P.M. Summer" is only 85 minutes long but seems longer. With the teaming of Melina Mercouri (Mrs. Dassin) and Dassin in the past, the screen was enlivened, embellished and generally enriched with colorful, carefree, dramatic and usually entertaining film fare. What could have happened to have taken all the life out of their cinematic efforts?

Dassin's direction is uncertain, frequently illogical and, for the most part, plodding; Miss Mercouri's thesping is in a similar vein. There's reason to believe that the major fault is in the script of Dassin and novelist Marguerite Duras and, beyond that, in the novella of Miss Duras on which the script is based. The thread of a plot (a married couple and a female friend, traveling together in Spain, are under a mounting tension that is touched off by an incident with a fugitive in a village) may have made a moody and effective short story but as the basis of an intelligent screenplay it is less than satisfactory.

There's some possibility of exploitation in the frankly erotic scenes of lovemaking between Romy Schneider (the reluctant guest) and Peter Finch (the husband), although Dassin never makes it clear whether it's really happening or only the figment of Miss Mercouri's alcohol-befuddled imagination. An even more grievous shortcoming is the absence of any explanation as to the reason for her condition. Alcoholism is, evidently, only a part of her tragedy, as is a suggested latent homosexual feeling towards Miss Schneider. Certainly, a scene in which the two women shower together can be interpreted in several ways, all sensual.

The "red herring" of a wounded wife-killer, played without dialog but with considerable facial expression by Spanish actor Julian Mateos, is another suggestive ploy that never materializes.

All the principals can be faulted for indifferent performances but several bit players, mostly unidentified, make greater and more lasting impressions.

Gabor Pogany's Technicolorful camerawork overcomes the necessary low-key lighting (most of the film takes place at night) to give a technical gloss to the proceedings. Indeed, during one afternoon shot, when the threesome stop at an inn to escape the hot sun, one can almost feel the heat pouring off the screen. Enrique Alarcon's art direction and Cristobal Halffter's sparse, lean musical score are also added assets.

With the release pattern aimed at the art houses, the film should have an initial success due to the lure of the Dassin-Mercouri combination but a lasting success is doubtful. Unfortunately for all, it's just a dull film. *Robe.*

Jack Frost
(RUSSIAN-COLOR)

A technically well-made children's pic that should both enchant and delight the small fry.

Hollywood, Oct. 14.
Embassy Release of Gorky Central Studios (Russian) production. Features Natasha Sedykh, Alexander Khvylya, Eduard Isotov, Yuri Millyar, Inna Churikova, Vera Altaiskaya, Pavel Pavlenko, Anatoly Kubatsky. Directed by Alexander Row. Screenplay, Mikhail Volpin, Nikolai Erdman; camera, Dmitry Surensky; music, Nikolak Budashkin. Reviewed at Joe Shore's Screening Room, Hollywood, Sept. 12, '66. Running Time, **79 MINS.**
Nastenka .... Natasha Sedykh
Jack Frost .... Alexander Khvylya
Ivan .... Eduard Isotov
Witch Baba Yaga .... Yuri Millyar
Marfushka .... Inna Churikova
Step-mother .... Vera Altaiskaya
The Old Man .... Pavel Pavlenko
Bandit Chieftain .... Anatoly Kubatsky

The cold war continues but if this Russian-made pic is an example of the current output from that country, it looks like competition between U.S. and Russian filmmakers is escalating into a "hot war." Neatly dubbed into English, the innoculously titled "Jack Frost," to be distributed matinees on weekends only by Embassy, is a captivating, technically clever and charmingly colorful Russian fairy tale that embodies everything from Cinderella to Sleeping Beauty.

Not that the film is perfect. Story starts out slowly and for a time doesn't seem cohesive. In its unfolding, it leaves a number of points unexplained, but this should not distract the small fry, since there are enough visual effects and trick camera work, as well as story book characters, not to mention pulsating Russian music, to keep their attention fixed.

"Frost" starts with Cinderella type, Nastenka, being forced by her harsh mother to finish knitting a sock for ugly duckling sister before dawn. Dawn arrives, but she has not quite finished. She importunes the barnyard chanticleers to hold back the dawn. The sun descends and when she is finished, re-ascends.

Story jumps to handsome young Ivan leaving home in another village. He is waylayed by bandits but escapes, then encounters a gremlin, Father Mushroom, later, in the forest, Nashtenka. Because of a dispute over slaying of a bear, Ivan's head is transformed into that of a bear.

Ivan must do a good deed to rid himself of his condition. After a series of attempts, he finally does so and again pursues the young girl, who by this time has been left in the wintry forest to die. Grandfather Frost (Russian title of film was "Morozhko," which translates as grandfather Frost) rescues her and takes her to his Arctic palace. The hunchback fairy has the girl frozen in ice, but Ivan brings her to life. The pic doesn't end there. Ugly sisted is deposited in woods in order to get a similar manly prize, but in humorous scenes returns alone in a low sled pulled by three fat pigs.

Natasha Sedykh is a wide eyed young actress of star quality, and Eduard Isotov as Ivan is a prince of an actor. Rest of the cast throw themselves into the spirit of the fantasy with high purpose.

Director Alexander Row has allowed no gimmicky sentimentality to blur the Mikhail Volpin and Nikolai Erdman screenplay and has kept a "Wizard of Oz" feeling to the entire production. Dmitry Surensky's Pathe Color camerawork has a warm filtered quality, while the musical direction of Nikolak Budashkin jauntily underscores with traditional Russian tunes. The music is so infectious, in fact, that one expects actors at anytime to bound into ballet steps.

Production designs by art director Arseny Klopotovsky are realistic replicas of Disney's animated "Snow White" world. The costumes (uncredited) are bright and add to the visual excitement.

"Frost" is the kind of film that children can proudly take their parents to see.   *Dool.*

Spinout
(COLOR-SONGS-PANAVISION)

Entertaining and tuneful comedy in which Elvis Presley dodges four femmes. Good in all departments, including b.o. prospects.

Hollywood, Oct. 13.
Metro release of Euterpe (Joe Pasternak) production. Stars Elvis Presley, Shelley Fabares, Diane McBain, Deborah Walley, Dodie Marshall; features Jack Mullaney, Will Hutchins, Warren Berlinger, Jimmy Hawkins. Directed by Norman Taurog. Screenplay, Theodore J. Flicker, George Kirgo; camera (Metro-Color), Daniel L. Fapp; editor, Rita Roland; music, George Stoll; asst. director, Claude Binyon, Jr. Reviewed at Academy Award Theatre, L.A., Oct. 12, '66. Running Time, 93 MINS.
Mike McCoy .... Elvis Presley
Cynthia Foxhugh ..... Shelley Fabares
Diana St. Clair .... Diane McBain
Les .... Deborah Walley
Susan .... Dodie Marshall
Curly .... Jack Mullaney
Lt. Tracy Richards ...... Will Hutchins
Philip Short .... Warren Berlinger
Larry .... Jimmy Hawkins
Howard Foxhugh .... Carl Betz
Bernard Ranley .... Cecil Kellaway
Violet Ranley .... Una Merkel
Blodgett .... Frederic Worlock
Harry .... Dave Barry

"Spinout" is an entertaining Elvis Presley comedy - tuner, in which four gals compete for his attention between nine new songs Well-produced by Joe Pasternak, and directed with verve by Norman Taurog, pic has Elvis as the leader of a touring rock-roll group. Racing car plot line adds another lure for the young market, while many subsid comedy situations maintain interest. Presley fans will rally to the b.o., and other drop-ins will likewise be diverted by this Metro release.

For record purposes, this is Elvis' 22d pic in 10 years, dating from 'Love Me Tender," a November, 1956, 20th-Fox release. Also, it is his seventh for Metro, his sixth for Taurog, and second for Pasternak. Hal B. Wallis has made most of the remaining pix for Paramount release. As usual, Col. Tom Parker is credited as technical advisor. "Spinout" is the Thanksgiving pic, in the current Parker-Presley film formula of three per year—Easter, summer and now. First two pix this year came out too close together, but many months have

passed, so Elvis is again a relatively fresh market entry.

Theodore J. Flicker and George Kirgo have penned a good script in which Elvis is played off against four femmes: spoiled brat Shelley Fabares, whose rich father, Carl Betz, connives for her and his auto racing interests; Deborah Walley, Elvis' drummer who finally emerges from tomboy status; classy, chic Diane McBain, whose speaking voice would turn on anybody, and Dodie Marshall, in briefly at the finale for minor potential love interest.

First three gals pair off at fadeout with Warren Berlinger (Betz' befuddled secretary), Will Hutchins (a gourmet cook and cop), and Betz, respectively. Jack Mullaney and Jimmy Hawkins provide laughs as other members of the Presley group. Taurog has obtained uniformly good performances, with Miss Walley particularly good as the prime comedienne. Cecil Kellaway and Una Merkel do nicely in brief footage as an old married couple.

Daniel L. Fapp's zesty Panavision-Metrocolor camera has enhanced the impact of the Presley production numbers and the racing exteriors. All nine songs, unbilled, have a good varied rhythm. The Jordanaires again render solid vocal support. Jack Baker staged the production numbers to good cinematic effect. George Stoll handled the overall score with competence. Rita Roland's brisk editing to 93 minutes is firstrate. Hank Moonjean was an effective associate producer. Other credits all pro.   *Murf.*

Goal! World Cup 1966
(BRITISH—COLOR —TECHNISCOPE)

Standout documentary of World Cup football series. Human, humorous and dramatic highlights skillfully blended.

London, Oct. 6.
Columbia Pictures release through BLC. Produced by Octavio Senoret. Directed by Abidine Dino and Ross Devenish. Commentary by Brian Glanville; narrated by Nigel Patrick; camera (Technicolor), Jean Jacques Flori, David Samuelson, Harry Hart; supervising editor, Jeanne Henderson; music, John Hawkesworth. At Columbia Theatre, London. Running Time, 108 MINS.

The World Cup football tournament, won by Britain, the 1966 host country, created a furore of interest, an unexpected slant being the surprise enthusiasm of femmes. Despite saturation coverage on television, this Techniscope, Technicolor documentary of the occasion should rate a big audience. Tint, size of screen, generous close-ups and occasional slow motion add new dimensions to what soccer buffs saw on tv. "Goal!" should hit the wickets hard in Britain and the other 15 countries represented in the tournament. Prospects in the States look rosy, too. Promised coverage of bigtime competitive soccer on CBS television when it begins in the States in a big way, pinponts Yank interest.

Technically "Goal!" is as well done as was "Tokyo Olympiad," though somewhat lacking in the rhythm and poetry that made "Tokyo" a standout. Also, "Goal!" is perhaps a share more repetitive since it is hinged on only one sport. These quibbles apart, it is a first-class 108 minutes of entertainment which should hold even those not feverishly sold on the game.

Chilean producer Octavio Senoret bought the rights to film the tourney for $42,000 against stiff competition. He used 117 cameras on the project, which cost $336,000, and four editors eventually cut down to 108 minutes material that would have run for nearly two days.

One of the two directors, Abidine Dino, did a rough shooting script but necessarily there was plenty improvisation. Final result is skillfully tailored to give a fair show to all competing countries and Brian Glanville's commentary is smooth, literate and not overladen with technicalities. In fact, less knowledgeable customers may justly think that a few more explanations would have been in order. But the narrative is neatly blended with sound effects and John Hawkesworth's lively score, plus razor-sharp editing, help to provide a word and visual commentary which is alert, exciting and often witty and gets the best out of both the playing events and the backstage stuff on the terraces. Nigel Patrick speaks the commentary vividly and points a number of amusing throwaway comments.

The script doesn't shirk occasional deflatory comment, though mostly the occasion calls for applause rather than knocks, but the action does not hesitate to show fouls, displays of bad temper and exhibitionism among the players as well as their skill, excitement, jubilation and chivalry. The "extras," that is, the supporters, add greatly to the atmosphere, for the revealing cameras have highlighted rare moments of suspense, pathos and drama.

Certain players inevitably emerge as characters, notably Nobby Stiles of England; Pele, Estuebo, Rattin (twice ordered off the field) and the German goalkeeper, all of whom get star exposure; and extra bonuses, for many are revealing glimpses of the Royal Family. It is a pity that some of the players' comments at moments of high drama, disappointment and frustration could not be heard on the peppy soundtrack, but anyone slightly versed in lip reading would rightly suspect that such a soundtrack would have been far too salty.

Technically all departments deserve to take bows—the camera team, headed by Jean Jacques Flori, David Samuelson and Harry Hart, and editors Jack Knight, Bill Butler and Michael Rabiger, supervised by Jeanne Henderson, in particular. For Senoret it was a bold project and it looks as if it will pay off handsomely.   *Rich.*

Is Paris Burning?
(Paris Brule-t-Il-)
(FRENCH—70M)

A global smash foreseen for Pine Par-7 Arts production.

Paris, Oct. 24.
Paramount release of Paramount Seven Arts-Ray Stark presentation of Transcontinental - Paul Graetz - Marianne production. Features Jean-Paul Belmondo, Charles Boyer, Leslie Caron, Jean-Pierre Cassel George Chakiris, Alain Delon, Kirk Douglas, Glenn Ford, Gert Frobe, Yves Montand, Anthony Perkins, Simone Signoret, Robert Stack, Skip Ward, Orson Welles. Directed by Rene Clement. Screenplay, Gore Vidal, Francis Coppola with additional dialog, by Marcel Moussy from the book by Larry Collins and Dominique Lapierre; camera, Marcel Grignon; music, Maurice Jarre; editor, Robert Lawrence; special effects, Robert MacDonald, Paul Pollard. At Elysees, Paris. Running time, 165 MINS.
Morandot .... Jean-Paul Belmondo
Monod .... Charles Boyer
Francoise .... Leslie Caron
Karcher ....Jean-Pierre Cassel
G.I. In Tank .... George Chakiris
Patton .... Kirk Douglas
Bradley .... Glenn Ford
Von Choltitz .... Gert Frobe
Bizien .... Yves Montand
Warren .... Anthony Perkins
Cafe Owner .... Simone Signoret
Sibert .... Robert Stack
Claire .... Marie Versini
G. I. with Warren .... Skip Ward
Nordling .... Orson Welles
Colonel Rol .... Bruno Cremer
Lebel ....Claude Dauphin
Parodi .... Pierre Dux
Hitler .... Billy Frick
Bayet .... Daniel Gelin
Pisani .... Michel Piccoli
Joliot-Curie .... Sacha Pitoeff
Ebernach .... Wolfgang Preiss
Leclerc .... Claude Rich
Serge .... Jean-Louis Trintignant
Gallois .... Pierre Vaneck
Chaban-Dalmas .... Alain Delon

With its origins in a documentary-like bestseller in most western countries, this contemporary historical and emotional happening, namely the Liberation of Paris, plus marquee names is boffo o.o. Ringing action, epic flavor, and fine production trappings give this French-made Yankbacked spectacle lucrative strength in the western world and especially lucrative on its homegrounds.

Film traces the uprising in Paris leading to the oncoming Allies changing their plans to invade Paris rather than bypass it, as intended. Underlying dilemma faces the German commander, General Von Choltitz who had been ordered to destroy Paris, if necessary or if it could not be held. The title is from Hitler's maniacal telephone demands to know if Paris was burning.

It is built on the premature uprising within the French resistance groups, and then the tensions as Paris is undermined with explosives and Von Choltitz hesitates as he realizes that Hitler is mad and that destruction of Paris will not help the German cause or the now hopeless Nazi war effort. Also involved are the men sent to try to get the Allies to change their minds which is finally done.

Since history already has given the answer, suspense is not the keyword for this pic. Director Rene Clement has wisely tried to give it a collective feeling to opt for the epic as it affects the people caught up in Liberation. Thus it would be the symbol of practically detonating Allied victory and also giving the French back face and self-respect after four years of Occupation.

It works well on this level since the people are only sketched simply and, in crisis or action, swept up in the overpowering event.

Of course there is the problem of the many international stars and name players essaying the roles. Most acquit themselves well albeit some appear just cast for name values.

But all this is accepted as the mounting action sweeps the French Le Clerc Deuxieme DB Tank Corps into a Paris on the verge of extinction and in the throes of resistance fighting. Most of the name thesps handle themselves acceptably, but it is the city of Paris and the surging action, the masses and the crescendo of unchained emotion that carries this pic along.

Orson Welles is rightly subdued as the harassed Swedish Consul who manages to effect a truce between the Germans and resistants for a while in order to save political prisoners. Leslie Caron does all right by a highkeyed look at a woman trying desperately to save her husband from deportation but bringing on his death by cracking.

Charles Boyer is a sympathetic resistant. Jean-Paul Belmondo finds himself requisitioning the governmental seat and being kowtowed to. Kirk Douglas has a bit as General Patton but his identification comes only after it is over and it is more a name appearance than a necessity. Glenn Ford is a quizzical but actionful General Bradley and other names also fit into small roles or sometimes have their personalities overshadowing them.

Gert Frobe has the pivotal part as Von Choltitz who is a career soldier and not above destroying Paris if a necessity. Perhaps his brief meeting with Hitler is not convincing enough of the latter's madness, but his reasoning that it would not help is more acceptable. He plays it with proper despair and does not overdo the sentimental aspect of the man. After all, Von Cholitz bombed Rotterdam and Sebastopol under orders and even referred to himself as the destroyer of cities.

Film does not go deeply into the complicated power struggle between the well organized French Communist Resistants and those faithful to De Gaulle's Free French. But it does show how one segment started things off too quickly and how the Gaullists tried to stave off the uprising till the Allied Forces were sure to come, and how the Communist seg wanted an arms drop to insure a secure city free of Germans before the arrival of the Allies.

But the Allied change of plan starts the film's main dramatic line as Le Clerc's division plows on towards Paris. The street fighting is done with fervor and dynamism and little cameos give an ironic, tender, dramatic, pathetic feel to the overall happening. It shows the ordinary man in the grip of an epic move and adds a balance to the bigger pronouncements and decisions of the men actually running or bringing on the events.

An old lady drinks tea as plaster falls around her, and some French soldiers use her window to knock out a German machinegun while an old man uses an old blunderbuss. Anthony Perkins is a G.I. bent on seeing the Eiffel Tower and dying within its sight. Simone Signoret is a tender bar proprietress helping emotionally speechless French soldiers call their parents as they are sweeping on towards Paris. Yves Montand is the first to die in Paris as he knocks out a German tank and is picked off by a sniper, etc.

Clement, one of the better French directors, was responsible for one of the best resistance films made, "La Bataille du Rail" (Battle of the Rails) (1946) about railroad worker resistance. Here he wisely does not try for arty effects or glib mounting. It is done with solid restraint but knowing tensions, and shows heroics, fears or dashing bits as part of a great, overwhelming happening.

All is well meshed. The agonizing betrayal of a group of young resistants and their murder by the Germans in the Paris parks is done with power sans forcing its moving relentlessness, as is a deportation scene at a Paris station. The well timed and powerful editing is an asset as well as Maurice Jarre's thematic music for the various factions plus the well done special effects and the knowing marshalling of these events by Clement.

Perhaps the political aspects have been watered down so as not to create any polemics.

A posthumous nod is due producer Paul Graetz who bought the book and pushed it through with needed American backing. He died during the last days of shooting.

Paris is as exciting visually as ever and the empty streets, for the fighting and Occupation, also denote the cooperation given by the people and the authorities during its making. Shots, like a German herding pigs down the empty Champs-Elysees, tank fights on the Place de la Concorde, the fights before the police headquarters taken over by the resistants, could never have been made any other way.

Film is in black and white but ends with color aerial views of a now gleaming and cleaned-up Paris and makes its point about how close this city that means so much to the world culturally, and for its sheer beauty, came to being destroyed. And what a loss and calamity it would have been.

A workable script was hauled out of the fact-filled book, but it is the directorial skill, sober playing and the city of Paris that have brought it off and made it a big b.o. pic contender.

General De Gaulle comes into it only at the end in well coordinated newsreel shots of his triumphal walk down the Champs-Elysees. Pic is in German, French and English here, with appropriate subtitles, but will be shown only in an all-English version in the U.S. *Mosk.*

O Psarovannos
(Fish-Kettle John)

Athens, Oct. 18.
A Millas Film production. Directed and written by Basile Mariolis, based on a novel by Takis Hatzianagnostou. Features Georges Foundas, Aleca Katseli, Maria Skountzou, Nicos Anagnostakis, Pavlos Liaros, Marina Michalopoulu; music, John Marcopoulos; camera, Costas Psarras. Reviewed at Salonika Film Festival. Running Time, 92 MINS.
Psaroyannos ....Georges Foundas
His wife ....Aleca Katseli
Katerina ....Maria Skountzou
Anthony ....Nico Anagnostakis
Stranger ....Pavlos Liaros
Younger daughter Marina Michalopoulou
Katerina's fiance ......Costas Diplaros

Based on a true story which happened on the island of Lesbos in the Aegean Sea many years ago, this picture depicts the dramatic end of a unique character who had his own beliefs in life and worshipped the freedom of body and soul above all else. It is a strange and powerful melodrama of love and revenge which will appeal to foreign audiences for the originality of story and settings.

A poignant drama, it is directed, however, at a slow pace and the lack of action is obvious. Some sequences are overdone, but the film is enhanced by the atmosphere it creates. The title character is much like "Zorba the Greek," especially in the last dance sequence which recalls ancient tragedy.

Georges Foundas' interpretation of the title role is outstanding and Aleca Katseli, as his wife, gives a forthright and moving performance. Black and white photography by Costas Psarras is excellent and music by John Marcopoulos is good. *Rena.*

I Deal In Danger
(COLOR)

Theatricalized translation of "Blue Light" teleseries; espionage theme will carry it in program market.

Hollywood, Oct. 12.
20th-Fox release of Rogo (Buck Houghton) production. Stars Robert Goulet; features Christine Carere, Horst Frank, Donald Harron, Werner Peters, Eva Pflug. Directed by Walter Grauman. Screenplay, Larry Cohen; camera (DeLuxe Color), Sam Leavitt, Kurt Grigoleit; music, Lalo Schifrin; editor, Jason Bernie; asst. directors, Ray Taylor, Hans Sommer, Wolfgang Von Schiber. Reviewed at 20th-Fox Studios, Oct. 12, '66. Running Time, 90 MINS.
David March .... Robert Goulet
Suzanne Duchard ......Christine Carere
Luber ....Horst Frank
Spauling ....Donald Harron
Elm ....Werner Peters
Gretchen Hoffmann ....Eva Pflug
Ericka von
Lindendorf ...Christiane Schmidtmer
von Lindendorf ....John van Dreelan
Richter ....Hans Reiser

Hard on Metro linking episodes of its "Man from U.N.C.L.E." teleseries for two theatrical features — "Spy With My Face" and "To Trap a Spy" — comes 20th-Fox to repeat the procedure with its now-defunct ABC series, "Blue Light," starring Robert Goulet. First three segments have been edited into a 90-minute theatrical entry, now tabbed "I Deal in Danger." Aimed obviously at the program market, its espionage theme will carry it although it is the old 1.33-1 ratio — standard before widescreen — which may militate against popular reception.

The Buck Houghton production

centers on Goulet who plays a double agent, an American spy posing as a traitor now working for the Nazis of World War II. Feature has handsome production values and manages a good straight melodramatic line as Goulet goes about convincing the Nazis he is strictly on their side. As in the vidseries, Goulet's actions aren't always explained, but for the lesser market the momentum is sufficient to build to a fast climax.

Goulet injects certain authority in his role, member of the Allied Forces' Blue Light organization, and has good support right down the line. Christine Carere is his fellow spy, Werner Peters a high Gestapo agent whom he eliminates, Eva Pflug a German scientist who helps him blow up a Nazi installation 200 feet underground where experiments are underway on a special type of submarine which is to be a secret weapon in conquering the U.S. Donald Harron is as a British secret agent-friend whom Goulet is supposed to betray and Horst Frank a security chief unable to block Goulet's plans to destroy the Nazi facility.

Walter Grauman, who with scripter Larry Cohen created the teleseries, gives sock direction to maintain certain suspense. Color photography by Sam Leavitt and Kurt Grigoleit is excellent in pointing up the assets of extravagant art direction and Jason Bernie's editing is superior in converting tv segments to feature. *Whit.*

Our Incredible World

(BRITISH-COLOR)
Technically well-made documentary, but subject matter of questionable entertainment value and taste.

London, Oct. 12.
Miracle Films presentation of a Harold Baim-Miracle production. Executive producer, Phil Kutner. Produced and written by Baim. Associate Producer, Scott Marshall. Directed by Edward Stewart Abraham. Commentators, Valentine Dyall, Franklin Englemann, David Gell, Kent Walton; camera (Eastman-color), Gus Coma; second unit cameras, Harry Orchard, Geoffrey Hermges; editors, Alan Brett, Eduardo Maclean; music, De Wolfe. At Cinephone Theatre, London. Running Time, 90 MINS.

Presumably an attempt to cash in on the "Mondo Cane" cult, this documentary misfires because of its content. Subject matter lacks the surprise and shock element of parts of the Italian doc pix and merely labors some conventional and heavygoing themes which are likely to revolt many and, in any case, add up to questionable entertainment for the average filmgoer. Technically this is a very competent job—director, cameramen, editors and writer of the score all doing okay jobs. But it is likely to attract only specialized audiences.

The title opens up possibilities that are not developed. Among the subjects explored are visits to a slaughter house, the removal of 12 piglets from a sow's uterus, extraction (in closeup) of a wisdom tooth, removal of the cornea of a dog's eye to aid human beings, a human eye operation, a visit to a Pest Infestation Laboratory and similar downbeat and not highly original themes. Inserted gratuitously and incongruously are such old hat stuff as a session at a discotheque, a trip on a roller coaster, a beauty contest, a waxwork exhibition.

The producers do not shirk revealing the most gruesome details of some of these subjects and each of them might hold up solo for the length of time devoted to them. Piled on each other for 90 minutes, the overall effect is downbeat rather than fascinating.

Four e x c e l l e n t commentators are employed and the charges of voice and pace of commentary are welcome. But Harold Baim's narrative (he also produced the pic) is marred by too frequently leading with its chin by overuse of the technique, "Many of you will not be able to watch the next sequence, but we bring it to you because it happens and is part of this incredible world." It speedily has the audience concurring with its self-depreciation.

De Wolfe has provided a jaunty score and the Eastmancolor photography is excellent. Alan Brett and Eduardo Maclean have edited with imagination but the shears could have been used more ruthlessly on several overlong sequences. The whole team shows a lively sense of how to put over a documentary. It's just that something went wrong in the blueprint stage when decisions were being made as to what the film was all about and what should be incorporated into it.   *Rich.*

Mannheim Fest

Ostre Sledovane Vlaky
(Sharply Watched Trains)
(CZECH)
Mannheim, Oct. 18.
Czech State Film production and release. With Vaclav Neckar, Jitka Bendova, Vladimir Valenta. Directed by Jiri Menzel. Screenplay, Bohumil Hrabal and Jiri Menzel, based on a novel by Hrabal; camera, Jaromir Sofr; music, Jiri Sust; editing, Jirina Lukesova. At Mannheim Film Festival. Running Time, 75 MINS.
Hrma ....Vaclav Neckar
Masa ....Jitka Bendova
Stationmaster ....Vladimir Valenta
His wife ....Libuse Havelkova
Hubicka, his adjunct.....Josef Somr
Railway worker ....Alois Vachek
Telegraph girl.......Jitka Zelenohorska
Zednicek ....Vlastimil Brodsky

This Czech production which saw its world preem at the Mannheim festival can easily be acclaimed as one of the wittiest and most original films that ever came from this East European country. Without being vulgar or tasteless, it mixes comedy, drama and the most delicate love sequences against the background of the German Occupation and the Czech resistance fighter who doesn't hesitate to spend a night with him. The end sees the young man blowing up a German ammunition train but he does it so clumsily that he becomes a victim of his own act of sabotage. He's blown up too.

Menzel registers a remarkable directorial debut which will make the critics watch his future work with special interest. His sense for witty situations is as impressive as his adroit handling of the players. A special word of praise must go to Bohumil Hrabal, the creator of the literary original, with whom Menzel wrote the script. Hrabal is a brilliant writer and it is understood that the many amusing gags and imaginative situations are primarily his.

The cast is composed of wonderful types down the line. The acting is competent and enjoyable, a first-class ensemble achievement. The general praise includes pic's technical credits. No doubt, this is another Czech triumph which will contribute much to prestige for that country's film industry.   *Hans.*

Charlie Is My Darling
(BRITISH)
Mannheim, Oct. 18.
Lorrimer Films Ltd. (London) production (no release as yet). Directed and written by Peter Whitehead. With the Rolling Stones (Mick Jagger, Keith Richard, Bill Wyman, Brian Jones, Charlie Watts); camera, Peter Whitehead; songs and incidental music, Mick Jagger, Keith Richard, Andrew Loog Oldham; editing, Peter Whitehead. At Mannheim Festival. Running Time, 60 MINS.

"Charlie," world-preemed at the just concluded Mannheim film festival, is the first pic on Britain's Rolling Stones. Technically, it demonstrates what its creator, 29-year-old Peter Whitehead, describes as "the method of direct cinema." Although reviews on the outcome of this unconventional documentary will be varied, there is hardly any doubt that "Charlie" will stir interest. After all, the Rolling Stones are "no nobodies." Film gives a good insight into the behind-the-scenes life of this idolized beat group, has a good number of interesting shots and some funny moments, and in a way reveals what price the Stones have actually to pay for their popularity. As much as they may want them, there don't seem to be any dull moments for them outside their homes.

It is said that it was the success of Whitehead's "Wholly Communion" (incidentally, this film was also at the Mannheim fest; it got one of the major awards there), a documentary on the recital of beat poetry before 5,000 people at London's Albert Hall last summer, which led to the invitation by Andrew Oldham, manager of the Stones, to make a film during the two-day tour of Ireland. The only conditions were said to be no tripods, no lights, one camera, two days, four concerts and on one knowing what would happen, film was as much a happening as the unforseen incidents that happen any day in the life of the Stones. Whitehead had only one assistant and one sound engineer at his disposal.

The direct cinema method, more or less like cinema verite, has a tendency to make a film rather jumpy and jerky, even to the extent of making the conventional viewer restless. As per the musical presentations in "Charlie," the conventional beat music lovers may find that this pic doesn't quite cover their expenses. But "Charlie" cannot be regarded as a conventional film. It is a departure from the cliche inasmuch as this is an honest film, at least in the sense that nothing was rehearsed or premeditated and the interviews were spontaneous. (Film's strength relies on the challenge it imposes on each individual Rolling Stone to display his "genuine" self behind the mask that every one of this group has to put on for his life in the public eye.) Their philosophy and kindred thoughts on life may not be very interesting, but it is certainly interesting what some of the hour's most cited and most idolized showbiz headliners think and what and how they talk. In this respect, film can be regarded as a welcome document even for those who normally don't go for beat music and teenage faves.

The title, of course, refers to Charlie (Watts), the tall, taciturn drummer of the crew.   *Hans.*

Jimmy Orpheus
(GERMAN)
Mannheim, Oct. 19.
Atlas release of Hanns Eckelkamp and Ernst Liesenhoff production. With Klaus Schichan and Orthrud Beginnen. Directed and written by Roland Klick; camera, Robert van Ackeren; music, Roland Klick; editing, Roland Klick. Reviewed at Mannheim Film Festival. Running Time, 52 MINS.
Jimmy Orpheus ....Klaus Schichan
Girl ....Ortrud Beginnen

Roland Klick, creator of a couple of prizewinning shorts, calls "Jimmy Orpheus" his first feature film. This is an exaggeration. What Klick has brought to the screen is just an overly long short film. It displays some sense for genuine atmosphere, but otherwise this opus, which competed in Mannheim's "first feature" section, is a near disappointment. More is expected of a festival entry. As a feature film director, Klick still has to prove himself.

The action takes place at night and early morning in Hamburg's St. Pauli district. It revolves around Jimmy, a poor harbor worker who has his bedstead in an asylum whose door he finds locked, so he spends the night strolling about the streets. He meets a girl, spends some time in shabby joints and intends to have an affair with the girl. Occasionally it looks as though his wish will see fulfilment, but he doesn't reach his goal.

It is the short story of a uselessly spent night. Its philosophy is that of senselessness, as senseless as the rubbish the two young people are talking throughout this film. The whole becomes rather stereotyped after a while and winds up as a bore.

The acting is okay and technically the film is satisfactory.   *Hans.*

Ursula oder das Unwerte Leben
(Ursula or the Unworthy Life)
(SWISS)
Mannheim, Oct. 19.
A television production Zurich (no releasing company as yet). Directed and written by Reni Mertens, Walter Marti; camera, H. P. Roth, R. Lyssy; editing, Lyssy; commentary, Helene Weisel. Reviewed at Mannheim Film Festival. Running Time, 90 MINS.

Although not exactly a festival film, "Ursula" can be regarded as one of the most important productions screened (outside the regular program) at the recent Mannheim festival. This has to do with handicapped children, a subject which fitted the festival's motto ("The Human Beings in Our Times") perfectly. This is a type of cinema presentation for which a reviewer feels inclined to put its moving and important subject above its artistic quality. This Swiss production should be given all possible assistance. Television might be best for exploitation.

The film concerns the treatment given to physically, psychically and mentally defective children in a Swiss institution. The number of such children is constantly growing everywhere, already explained by the fact that the death rate of newborns is constantly decreasing. Film makes a plea for understanding, tolerance and support for those unfortunate human beings and their plagued parents. It shows that much help is possible if the defective child is given the right treatment at an early age, and the earlier the better.

An example is given here via Ursula who, at the age of 8, seemed to be a hopeless case. According to her medico, she was blind, deaf, epileptic and idiotic. Even this girl could be led to a halfway normal life. The commentary spoken by Helene Weigel (the widow of Bert Brecht) said: "If a human being is very young...much is possible." This Swiss institution has apparently achieved amazing results along this line.

Both artistically and technically, film makes a good impression. But, as mentioned, it's the subject matter which counts most.   *Hans.*

The Professionals
(COLOR-PANAVISION)

Exciting rescue of an allegedly kidnapped woman in the Mexican upheavals of 1917. Burt Lancaster, Lee Marvin, Claudia Cardinale for the marquee. Particularly strong commercial outlook in action market.

Hollywood, Oct. 21.
Columbia Pictures release, written, produced and directed by Richard Brooks. Features Burt Lancaster, Lee Marvin, Robert Ryan, Woody Strode, Jack Palance, Ralph Bellamy, Claudia Cardinale. Based on novel, " A Mule For The Marquesa," by Frank O'Rourke; camera (Technicolor), Conrad Hall; editor, Peter Zinner; music, Maurice Jarre; asst. director, Tom Shaw. Reviewed at Directors Guild of America, L.A., Oct. 20, '66. Running Time, 116 MINS.

Dolworth	Burt Lancaster
Fardan	Lee Marvin
Ehrengard	Robert Ryan
Raza	Jack Palance
Maria	Claudia Cardinale
Grant	Ralph Bellamy
Jake	Woody Strode
Ortega	Joe De Santis
Fierro	Rafael Bertrand
Padillia	Jorge Martinez De Hoyos
Chiquita	Marie Gomez
Revolutionaries	Jose Chavez, Carlos Romero
Banker	Vaughn Taylor

"The Professionals" is a well-made actioner, set in 1917 on the Mexican-U.S. border, in which some soldiers of fortune rescue the reportedly kidnapped wife of an American businessman. Exciting explosive sequences, good overall pacing and acting overcome a sometimes thin script. Burt Lancaster, Lee Marvin and Claudia Cardinale are prime marquee lures for the colorful Richard Brooks production. Very good b.o. prospects loom for Columbia release in general situations, growing extra strong in action markets.

Brooks' adaptation of Frank O'Rourke's novel, "A Mule for the Marquesa," depicts the strategy of Marvin and cohorts, sent by gringo Ralph Bellamy into the political turmoil of Mexico to rescue his missing wife, Miss Cardinale, known to be secreted in the brigand village of Jack Palance. Latter only a few years earlier had achieved a transient victory in the Revolution with the help of Marvin and Lancaster.

Undertones of the inevitable disenchantment of both idealists and freebooters, plus pithy observations on human nature, are interpolated into scripting. But emphasis is on action, mixed with adroit amounts of broad comedy.

Main title is used to delineate characters, and Lee Marvin is the first to follow title (advertising order is different). Quiet and purposeful, Marvin underplays very well as the leader of the rescue troop. Robert Ryan, who loves animals, is in the relative background, as is Woody Strode, Negro-Indian scout and tracker. Lancaster is the most dynamic of the crew, as a light-hearted but two-fisted fighter.

Just after film is half through its 116 minutes, a plot switcheroo indicates that Miss Cardinale and Palance are lovers, and that Marvin's gang has been sent on a phony mission. Too late, however, to back out. As group race back to the U.S., story branches out into other areas — Miss Cardinale

trying to return to her lover, and Lancaster dropping back to buy precious time by fighting single-handedly Palance and Marie Gomez, a femme guerrilla. At fade-out, plot angles are resolved to the satisfaction of all hands, except Bellamy.

Director Brooks has obtained sharp performances from Marvin, Lancaster and Bellamy, and other players. Scripting - direction relegate other principals to reactive postures. Somewhere in Peter Finner's editing, supervised, of course by Brooks, there is an obvious break in physical logic: when the Marvin crew backs up a train, how, and why do they suddenly appear on horseback? Palance's men, in tandem pursuit, wonder about this as much as an audience will.

Pictorial values are excellent, since Conrad Hall's Technicolor-Panavision camera has caught the dusty mood of the Southwest. Maurice Jarre's score is brisk and effective. Willis Cook handled the explosive effects which add substantially to the excitement. Sound editing and recording are noteworthy in view of the exterior lensing in many desert and canyon areas. Other technical credits are all pro.   *Murf.*

The Swinger
(COLOR)

Jazzy cinematic tricks turn an amusing nudie mag satire into a zesty comedy. Ann-Margret, singing-dancing-acting, for the marquee. Solid production.

Hollywood, Oct. 27.
Paramount Pictures release of George Sidney production, directed by Sidney. Stars Ann-Margret, Tony Franciosa; features Robert Coote, Yvonne Romain, Horace McMahon. Screenplay, Lawrence Roman; camera (Technicolor), Joseph Biroc; editor, Frank Santillo; music, Marty Paich; title song, Andre and Dory Previn; asst. director, Daniel J. McCauley. Reviewed at Paramount Studio, Oct. 26, '66. Running Time, 81 MINS.

Kelly Olsson	Ann-Margret
Ric Colby	Tony Franciosa
Sir Hubert Charles	Robert Coote
Karen Charles	Yvonne Romain
Sgt. Hooker	Horace McMahon
Aunt Cora	Nydia Westman
Sammy Jenkins	Craig Hill
Mr. Olsson	Milton Frome
Mrs. Olsson	Mary LaRoche
Himself	Clete Roberts
Sally	Myrna Ross
Sir Hubert's Secretary	Corinne Cole
Police Capt.	Bert Freed
Jack Happy	Romo Vincent
Man With Fish	Steven Geray
John Mallory	Larry D. Mann
Warren	Lance Le Gault
Svengali	Diki Lerner
Blossom LaTour	Barbara Nichols

"The Swinger" is a very amusing original screen comedy which satirizes nudie books and magazines. The colorful, tuneful George Sidney production utilizes outstanding post-production skills to enhance impact of hip scripting and good performances. Ann-Margret and Tony Franciosa provide marquee bait. Title is highly exploitable, and this potential sleeper deserves a strong campaign. Commercial prospects look particularly hotsy for Paramount release in situations catering to younger and teenage audiences.

Pic's running time, at least in domestic version, is a relatively brief 81 minutes, but perfect here. Director Sidney, editor Frank

Santillo and cameraman Joseph Biroc have used some firstrate cinematic tricks to sock over an amusing comedy story, penned by Lawrence Roman. Result is a bang-up job.

Ann-Margret's best screen work derives from Sidney's direction, which herein spotlights her singing-dancing talents, and utilizes her dramatic abilities to best advantage. She is an aspiring mag writer who, unable to sell straight material, fakes her autobiog in the form of a mish-mash of lurid paperback plots. Franciosa, the editor, swallows the bait and ties to reform her, while nudie mag publisher Robert Coote seeks to exploit the gal.

Roman's plot development is along simple lines, effectively so, as individual characterizations carry the ball to touchdown results. There is actually a story moral which hits at the oversexed artificiality of modern life; thus justifying the sexy bits.

Prominent in their bits are Horace McMahon, the vice squad cop who paints on the side, and who stages a phony raid to impress Franciosa; also, Nydia Westman, Franciosa's hip aunt, L.A. newsman Clete Roberts, in a good satire of "in-depth" tv coverage, Romo Vincent, operator of a fast-turnover motel, and Barbara Nichols, head stripper in an L.A. peelery.

In lesser contributory roles are Yvonne Craig, Coote's daughter who eventually loses Franciosa to Ann-Margret, secretaries Myrna Ross and Corinne Cole, Milton Frome and Mary LaRoche, Ann-Margret's Minnesota parents, and harassed cop Bert Freed. Other players also register okay.

A two-minute terp scene by Ann-Margret, to a rhythmic title tune by Andre and Dory Previn, precedes main title. Uncredited, Bill Scott is responsible for the latter, a wow piece of work. Pic then opens with a hilarious tour of L.A., featuring non-sequitur narration by Coote to some jazzy picture editing. Editor Santillo has several opportunities to create a teleblurb effect, and all register strongly. Biroc's lensing is excellent.

Marty Paich's score has a solid modern sound which adds punch, while Paramount has reached down into its music backlog to give Ann-Margret three standards, by Johnny Mercer-Harold Arlen, Richard Rodgers-Lorenz Hart, and Billy Rose-Edward Heyman. Edith Head's lavish costumes complement the fine art direction of Hal Pereira and Walter Tyler. Other credits are pro.

David Winters choreographed the terp sequences, one of which is a rather sexy bit in which Ann-Margret, in a fake orgy, rolls about on canvas with her body covered with paint. Reportedly trimmed for domestic prints, it is quite sensual as is. Film has been in the can for months, after extensive post-production. Results count, however, and whatever was done, was done right.   *Murf.*

Taming of the Shrew

Converted to widescreen, 1929 Pickford-Fairbanks starrer, in combo with new docu on their careers, an interesting novelty.

Hollywood, Oct. 26.
Mary Pickford's reissue of "Taming Of The Shrew," in which she starred with the late Douglas Fairbanks in 1929, proves one point in shining clarity . . . couple richly deserved their longheld positions as top artists and could have held their own as personalities with any of today's stars.

Revised at estimated $100,000 refurbishing cost, which Pickford's Cinema Classics is packaging with newly-made 27-minute documentary, based on careers of Pickford-Fairbanks, new version is a novelty well worth seeing both by new audiences and oldsters.

Converted from original standard ratio to widescreen (1.85-1), new music score and new sound effects through optical printing give it an air of a more modern attraction although technically, both in calibre of photography and editing, it still appears old-fashioned. There will, necessarily, be comparison with Columbia's upcoming Taylor-Burton version.

As a comedy the barbs of the bard reach high level and both Pickford and Fairbanks sock over amusing characterizations with great artistry. Granted, Pickford particularly is inclined to be dated in thesping, but both display an awareness that is a joy to behold.

Matty Kemp, associated with Pickford in her company, still in existence, is responsible for more than 14 months of refurbishing work, a chore well executed. For art houses particularly, picture is a worthy attraction.

Film runs 63 minutes.   *Whit.*

Shiroi Kyoto
(The Great White Tower)
(JAPAN)

Tokyo, Oct. 15.
Daiei Motion Picture Co. production and release. With Jiro Tamiya, Eijiro Tono, Eitaro Ozawa, Osamu Takizawa, Takahiro Tamura, Eiji Funakoshi. Directed by Satsuo Yamamoto after the novel of Toyoko Yamazaki. Script by Shinobu Hashimoto; camera by Hajimeru Sakai; produced by Masaichi Nagata. Reviewed in Tokyo. Running Time, 150 MINS.

Satsuo Yamamoto's lambasting of the Japanese medical profession has been met with tacit protests from most of the major university hospitals and medical clinics. None would cooperate with the studio's request that it be allowed to film actual surgery. On the other hand, a group of interns and young doctors (the same which recently refused graduation and full degrees as a protest against the unpaid work that they are so notoriously forced to undertake in the hospitals) have pledged full support of the picture.

Things get off to a sardonic start when hot-shot young doctor Jiro Tamiya strides into the operating room and delivers a terse "Well, let's get started." Cut to the stomach of a patient. A hand holding a scalpel appears and begins the incision. It cuts straight down from sternum to navel, the layers of viscera appear, the bowels, the stomach itself is opened, and over it all the opening credits of the film appear.

Some hospital somewhere apparently cooperated to create this absolutely riveting opening and it is not really the fault of the film that (though there are more operations, mainly for that great Japanese killer—stomach cancer) it seems to run down after this sensational beginning.

Still, it is quite interesting. Tamiya is an opportunist, determined to get ahead. He is scalpel-happy and loves to have his handsome picture in the weeklies. Head surgeon Eijiro Tono is actually no better and his resentment is a combination of jealousy and moral indignation. His efforts to thwart the career of the young doctor splits the hospital and has far-reaching complications.

On his side Jiro gets Dr. Eitaro Ozawa and his own father-in-law. Tono gets Masao Shimizu and Tokyo big-wig Osamu Takizawa. The struggle begins, one faction against the other, and the patients are largely forgotten. Tamiya is indeed so taken up with politics that he errors in diagnosis (though dedicated - doctor Takahiro Tamura knows better) and the patient dies. This coincides with his appointment as head doctor and a trial is held. In the end Takizawa comes to bat and he is exonerated though the fault is most clearly his. Doctor Tamiya gets everything he wants, Dr. Tamura is exiled to the country, and the picture wryly concludes with the former (a moustache now added for dignity) being received as a very great medical authority indeed.

One thing the matter with this two and one-half hour film is that it is simple-minded. Author is naive to believe that doctors (subjected to many of the same pressures) should be any more altruistic than, say, lawyers or politicians. Writer, director, and scripter (Shinobu Hashimoto who also wrote "Rashomon") have "exposed" the situation but have neglected to say that is absolutely normal and always has been. One will presumably not change the medical profession without changing humanity   Chie.

All The Other Girls Do
(Tutte le Altre Ragazze lo Fanno)
(ITALIAN—FRENCH)

Harlequin International Pictures release of Saggitario-Tirso Films (Rome)-Dicifrance (Paris) production. Directed by Silvio Amadio. Features Rosemarie Dexter, Jacques Perrin, Folco Lulli, Magali Noel, Bice Valori, Arnoldo Foa, Alberto Bonucci, Mario Scaccia, Gina Rovere, Luisa Della Noce. No other credits provided. Reviewed in New York, Oct. 21, '66. Running Time, 98 MINS.

(English Titles)

The Italians have a new approach to filmmaking—dubbed sex! That is, substituting a pair of actors with less scruples than the featured team for those scenes in which the on-screen lovemaking has to be somewhat explicit.

The biggest fault with this Italo-French import, which Tommy Noonan and Chris Warfield are releasing under their Harlequin banner, is that it is obvious, when it gets down to bare facts, that the pair of actors used in the film's lengthy and lusty bedroom sequence is NOT the twosome who carry most of the slight storyline.

Harlequin plans to release both subtitled and dubbed versions of this minor effort which has little to offer other than the aforementioned sex bit. The film, originally titled "Oltraggio al Pudore" (The Outrage and the Shame), deals with misunderstood youth, saddled with parents whose stern measures lead to their illicit love adventure.

The youngsters, played by a very handsome pair, Jacques Perrin and Rosemarie Dexter, makes the mistake of telling their parents they've become engaged. The parents, mistakenly thinking that they'll tire of each other if allowed to remain betrothed, try every trick in the book to bring about the expected split. The boy's father (Folco Lulli) encourages him to get some experience first, while the mother of the girl uses the example of her older married sister (Magali Noel) to discourage her. Older sister, however, just encourages the maiden to take a chance.

When the young lovers finally get around to it, there's a very obvious cut to a different couple (their faces are never seen) who go through a rather explicit session seen on the screen only via their shadows. There are a few half-hearted attempts by director Silvio Amadio to make some satirical comments on European attitudes towards sex but they come off as belabored humor, the poorest being the closing piece of business when the young pair, following their rendezvous, happen to kiss while seated in an automobile and are arrested for "outraging public decency" but are released with a stern lecture.

The trailer for the film was also screened. It consisted entirely of scenes from the lovemaking sequences with an offscreen commentary that made it obvious that the film would be sold along the same lines as "Promises, Promises" and other Harlequin fare.

Strictly for the sex houses.
Robe.

Santa's Christmas Circus
(COLOR)

Indie production designed for kiddie matinees during holiday season. Has Whizzo the Clown, area television personality, for interest factor. Minimum production.

Kansas City, Oct. 11.

Mercury Film release of Gold Star presentation, produced by Byers Jordan. Features Frank Wiziarde, John Bilyeu; Directed by Wiziarde. Organ Music by Harry Jenks. Based on an idea by Jordan. Filmed at Horizon Studios, Kansas City. Reviewed at Centre Theatre, North Kansas City, Mo., Sept. 24. Running Time, 60 MINS.
Whizzo, the Clown .... Frank Wiziarde
Santa Claus .... John Bilyeu
Dancing Children .... Themselves

Out of his experience with holiday season kiddie films, Byers Jordan has come up with this entry as special matinee moppet fare. Essentially it combines the television show of clown Frank Wiziarde on KMBC-TV9 with a brief travelog of Christmas displays and shop windows and a smidgin of story. Picture is strictly a quickie with minimum production values, but should be sufficient to hold kiddie interest.

Circus idea is conveyed by 14 youngsters of the Johnny Miller Dance Studio doing turns as circus animals in Whizzoland, the clown's haunt. One little girl is pensive, however, and to cheer her up, and the others, Whizzo treats them all to a tour of Christmas lights and displays. Then he outdoes himself by taking them on a magic carpet right to Santa's haunt at the North Pole.

Santa gives them a quick tour of the toy shop with the elves at work, explains that Christmas is a spirit in the heart and thus is for everybody, and the sad little girl is cheered. Then via the fringed rug back to Whizzoland for the jolly finish. As such the picture is pretty much an extension of the program which Wiziarde has had for many years on Channel 9, K.C. He has well established popularity, and in the midwest makes the picture a good exploitation value where properly handled.

As manager of the Center Theatre, North Kansas City, of the Commonwealth circuit, Jordan has a head start and has booked the picture for over 30 matinees, mostly in others of his circuit and some in Fox Midwest Theatres. He has art and ads and press, and aims picture at other dates in the pre-Christmas season. Might rate for local video. Kids who haven't seen Whizzo before will make friends readily, and even an adult who may have to sit in with the kiddies may not have to squirm too much.   Quin.

Jinchoge
(Daphne)
(JAPAN-COLOR)

Tokyo, Oct. 10.

Toho Co. production and release. With Machiko Kyo, Haruko Sugimura, Reiko Dan, Yuriko Hoshi, Yoko Tsukasa, Yosuke Natsuki, Daisuke Kato, Akira Takarada, Makoto Sato, Tadao Takashima, Hiroshi Koizumi, Tatsuya Nakadai, Keiju Kobayashi. Directed by Yasuke Chiba. Produced by Masumi Fujimoto; script, Zenzo Matsuyama; camera (Eastmancolor), Choichi Nakai; music, Toshiro Maivuzumi. Previewed in Tokyo. Running Time, 170 MINS.

In these days of falling box-office receipts, the Japanese film industry continues to cast about to find a way to bring back the audience. Sex, monster, and war films having largely failed, Toho now comes up with a hopeful new formula.

Take a popular tv program (in this case "Haruya Haru") written by an acknowledged talent (Zenzo Matsuyama, a man who makes tribulation his business with such success that his excursion into the world of the deaf and the life of the paraplegics has already won him several Ministry of Education Awards); take a director (Yasuke Chiba) who, though once evidencing strong personal integrity ("O-Ban," "Shitamachi"), has now safely settled into formulated aways; mix in wide-screen and Eastman Color; decorate liberally with all of the stars that can be contracted; prepare an advertising campaign which costs almost as much as the picture; serve at once.

A mother (Haruko Sugimura) has a batch of daughters all named by a dead father after flowers—hence the title of the film. One (Reiko Dan), is already married and in the first reel the youngest (Yuriko Hoshi) is wed to a promising young man (Yosuke Natsuki) which relieves some of mother's burden, but she still has the eldest (Machiko Kyo) and second (Yoko Tsukasa). Both of these girls are occupied with their professions: Machiko is a dentist and Yoko is her assistant.

The cynicism of the film (not instantly evident in its spuriously warm-hearted plot) lies in its taking a mediocre tv home-drama and ruthlessly expanding it to almost three times its original length; in its lack of concern for real humans with real problems, which results in paper-thin characterization and the brutal excision of person after person from the plot, in a laxness of direction which allows and even encourages the actors to indulge in their favorite vice—impersonating themselves.

Nothing is all bad, of course, and there are several things worth viewing. Machiko Kyo is a fine actress and she carries the film in so far as it is carried at all.

The only purpose for such a film which so panders to a presumed public taste is to make money. Will it? This reviewer doubts it.   Chie.

Akai Tenshi
(Red Angel)
(JAPAN)

Nurse among defeated, sex-hungry Japanese soldiers. Grim, far-out yet handsomely produced.

Tokyo, Oct. 15.

Daiei Motion Picture Company production and release. With Ayako Wakao, Shinsuke Ashida, Yusuke Kawazu, Ranko Akagi, Ayaka Ikegami, Jotaro Senba, Daihachi Kita. Directed by Yasuzo Masumura. Produced by Ikuo Kubodera, original story by Yorichika Arima, screenplay by Ryozo Kasahara, photographed by Setsuo Kobayashi, sound by Kimio Tobita, lighting by Shozo Izumi, art by Tomo Shimogawara, music by Sei Ikeno, editing by Tatsuji Nakashizu. Previewed in Tokyo. Running Time, 105 MINS.
Nurse Nishi .... Ayako Wakao
Army Surgeon Okabe . Shinsuke Ashida
Private Orihara .... Yusuke Kawazu
Nurse Iwashima .... Ranko Akagi
Nurse Tsurusaki .... Ayako Ikegami

Director Yasuzo Masumura, who made "The Hoodlum Soldier" and a number of other fine films, here turns his attention to a novel by Yorichika Arima about Japanese army nurses during the latter years of the China campaign. Morale is very low, the war is being lost, the hospitals are packed. Nurse Wakao, fresh from training school, is immediately assaulted by a ward of sex-starved soldiers (very explicitly shown) and, perhaps because of this experience, comes to realize that her role of sister of mercy covers more ground than the medical profession usually imagines.

There is, for example, Private Kawazu, who has lost both of his arms and during his nightly rubdown asks the nurse for a very special favor indeed. She, having arms and hands, complies and then, feeling sorry for him, takes him off to a hotel where for an afternoon—hands or not—they enjoy themselves and he is given further reason to live. Just the opposite occurs, however. After this afternoon of bliss he kills himself and Nurse Wakao thinks it is her fault.

She does not let this deter her from her mission however. Next she turns her attentions to the head surgeon. She has asked him for a blood-transfusion for the soldier who originally raped her and he agrees to use the precious serum only if she will come to his quarters that evening. She agrees but is surprised that nothing whatever occurs to her. The reason is that he is a morphine addict and that this has unmanned him. At the climax of the film, however—during an enemy attack, with certain death looming, she pulls him to her, ties him up, and after he has come out of cold-turkey makes him prove to himself that he is indeed a man after all.

The Chinese are attacking during all of this, however, and they kill almost everyone. Almost because after the smoke has cleared Nurse Wakao gains consciousness, finds the bodies of her friends and lovers, and wanders away into the distance—and very probably into further sequals to this popular, criticized and money-making picture.

Films boast some very fine scenes. The general tone is dark and the general atmosphere is one of pain and suffering. The hospital scenes(amputations, chest probings, stomach wounds) are explicit, and the love scenes between nurse and armless soldier are done with restraint and candor. The sex (with its unconscious overtones of "Candy") works against general believability and there is calculated prurience in some of the sequences. Yet beyond the lurid sensationalism there is "sincerity."

Nurses organizations have protested. Indeed it is doubtful that the scene where the nurse provides manual-mercy could be shown in many countries.   *Chie.*

Tople Godine
(Hot Years)
(YUGOSLAV)
Mannheim, Oct. 20.
Yugoslavia Film release of Avala production. With Bekim Fehmiu, Ana Matic. Directed by Dragoslav Lazic. Screenplay, Ljubisa Kozomara, Goraidan Mihic; camera, Milorad Jaksic-Fandjo; music, Dusan Radic. At Mannheim Festival. Running Time, 68 MINS.
Mirko .... Bekim Fehmiu
Maria .... Ana Matic
Another girl .... Dusica Zegarac
Another man .... Milan Jelic

This is the first full-length feature of Dragoslav Lazic who has made himself a name in the shorts genre. "Hot Years," a contender in Mannheim's first-feature section, benefits from well-drawn atmosphere and a series of unconventional situations. Treatment of subject matter stirs some interest, but the plot itself is probably not interesting enough to give this pic special chances outside its homegrounds.

It is the story of two young people from the country in a big city. He is a worker and she a waitress. They are deeply in love but not happy. They long for the peaceful countryside and finally leave the city to start a new life in a quiet village.

Basic to this film is some criticism on the regime, which apparently concentrates too much on the cities and thereby neglects the

village. Obvious also is a plea for understanding for young people who want to escape banal everyday life and seek a way of their own which may give them a more profound outlook.

As in his shorts, director Lazic succeeds in giving this film a strong documentary sharpness. And once again he treats the problems with a nearly brutal frankness.

The acting is competent and technical credits satisfactory. As usual in Yugoslav pix, this one has excellent lensing.   *Hans.*

Qui Etes-Vous Polly Magoo?
(Who Are You Polly Magoo?)
(FRENCH)
Paris, Nov. 1.
Rank release of Robert Delpire-Club Des Producteurs production. With Dorothy MacGowan, Jean Rochefort, Sami Frey, Grayson Hall, Philippe Noiret, Alice Sapritch. Written and directed by William Klein; camera, Jean Boffety; music, Michel Legrand. At Lord Byron, Paris. Running Time. 100 MINS.
Polly .... Dorothy MacGowan
Gregoire .... Jean Rochefort
Prince .... Sami Frey
Publisher .... Grayson Hall
Commentator .... Philippe Noiret
Mother .... Alice Sapritch

William Klein, a longtime Paris Yank resident, has been a partner, a still and fashion photog, and documentary filmmaker. For his first feature he bundles all this into a pic that twits fashion models and pundits, satirizes tv and even stale governmental protocol as well as the French, slick mag sentimentalism and royal romanticism. It is a bit too much and pic is an overlong, overdone grab bag of ideas.

Pop and op effects abound, but its too insidey flavor may keep popularity limited. It emerges as a pic needing some pruning, and then mainly for some art usage abroad. Director Klein has gone astray in using New Wave and Cinema Truth methods sans truly opting for one or the other. Their mixture with far-out gags does not jell enough to provide comedy flavor.

A tv team interviews an American model named Polly Magoo. She patters about her life—at odds with preying men in the streets, an object of the love of a prince, at work in various garbs. Latter does have some showy aspects for good pictorial and visual gloss. Film also, at times, gets into the surface life of models.

Klein piles on smart gloss but too often loses his thread about the girl's life, her standing and emotions. Dorothy MacGowan, a real model, shows a pert presence and her unvarnished face does give a touching or fresh note to things. But too many spy spoof bits, tv takeoffs and the overdone scenes with the Prince Charming, who finally settles for any model, lose the unifying theme and the title is never answered.

Klein does show some fine ideas such as a weird fashion show with girls wearing aluminum dresses that sometimes cut them, and the interviews with the model. But the whimsy, irony and inventiveness too often get out of hand. It is well lensed and with its intermittent insights into the life of a model, could be a specialized art item.

With more discipline and more assimilation of the many styles he has picked, Klein may emerge a refreshing and original filmmaker on the scene here. But this one is perhaps too ambitious and too overlarded with many tricks to come off.   *Mosk.*

Daphnis Ke Chloe '66
(Daphnis and Chloe '66)
Athens, Oct. 18.
A Zygos Film production. Features Telis Zotos, Elisabeth Wiener, Charles Jarell, Jean Claude Sussfeld, Dominique Paturel, Alexandra Ladikou, Elli Romanou, Olympia Papadouca. Directed and written by Mica Zaharopoulou. Camera, Pierre Petit, Jaques Robin, Nicos Demopoulos: editor, Claude Bouheret; music, Notis Mavroudis. Reviewed at Salonika Film Festival. Running Time, 82 MINS.
Daphnis as boy .... Thanos Papas
Daphnisas, young man ...... Telis Zotos
Chloe as little girl ...... Elli Romanou
Chloe as young girl... Elisabeth Wiener
Sandra .... Alexandra Ladikou
Mitlton .... Charles Jarell
Yannis .... Dominique Paturel
Antigoni .... Olympia Papadouca

A modern version of the old legend, "Daphnis and Chloe" is the first long feature film of young Mica Zaharopoulou who had previously done only a short subject titled "Syantisis" (Encounter) and won a prize in last year's Salonika Festival. Set in Greece and in Paris with Greek and French actors who speak their own language (the foreign part is subtitled), it has a cosmopolitan appeal and should do well in European and other foreign markets. There are some sex scenes, treated with taste, which add commercial value.

Zaharopoulou is one of the new Greek directorial talents. His treatment in this picture is artistic from first to last and has some very exciting sequences, particularly in the first part. In the second part, however, the dramatic climax diminishes and the development of the story, with many flashbacks, is not clearly rendered.

The acting is good by all players and especially by little Elli Romanou, as Chloe in her early years, who gives a touching performance. The camera work is excellent in the first part of the picture, and adds to the charm of this film. The music and song by Notis Mavroudis is good.   *Rena.*

Sublokator
(The Lodger)
(POLISH)
Mannheim, Oct. 20.
Film Polski release of Kamera Film Unit (Warsawa) production. With Jan Machulski, Barbara Ludwizanka, Katarzyna Laniewska. Directed by Janusz Majewski. Screenplay Majewski; camera, Kurt Weber; music, Andrzej Kurylewicz. At Mannheim Festival. Running Time, 80 MINS.
Ludwik .... Jan Machulski
Maria .... Barbara Ludwizanka
Kazimiera .... Katarzyna Laniewska
Malgosia .... Magdalena Zawadzka

"The Lodger," first full-length feature by Janusz Majewski, a former documentary filmmaker, is an enjoyable comedy revolving around strange people. It has its dull moments but, in all, provides plenty of laughs. The fun stems from a series of odd situations and the peculiar behavior of the players. Film should especially please those who have a taste for macabre humor. It should be okay for release in Western countries.

Majewski displays a fine sense for the peculiarities of human beings. He also shows a sharp eye for detail. Eventually, especially in the middle, his first feature drags but that is inevitable when certain gags are carried too far. The acting in this surrealistic type of comedy is lovable. This applies in particular to Jan Machulski as the lodger, Barbara Ludwizanka who plays Maria, the widow, and Magdalena Zawadzka, the girl.

Technically, film shows competence in all departments. Incidentally, it was given the FIPRESCI Prize at Mannheim.   *Hans.*

San Francisco Fest

People on Wheels
(CZECH-COLOR-WIDE-SCREEN)
San Francisco, Oct. 26.
Cezkoslovensky Film Export release, directed by Martin Fric. Stars Emilie Vasaryova, Jan Triska, Jozef Kroner; features Martin Ruzek, Dana Medrick, Cestmir Randa, Josef Vetrovec. Screenplay by Antonin Masa and Martin Fric, based on Edward Bass' novel of same name; camera, Jan Statlich; music, Zdenek Liska; sets, Jan Zazvorka; sound, Emanuel Formanek. Reviewed at San Francisco Film Festival, Oct. 25, '66. Running Time, 87 MINS.
Nina .... Emilie Vasaryova
Vincet .... Jan Triska
Clown .... Jozef Kroner
Latvian .... Martin Ruzek
Latvian's wife........... Dana Medrick
Cripple .... Vlastimil Brodsky
Ringmaster .... Cestmir Randa
Reimann .... Ilja Parchar
Chonger .... Josef Hlinomaz
Wenzel .... Josef Vetrovec
Zhanda .... Jirina Stepnickova

(With English Subtitles)

"People on Wheels" is a pleasant bittersweet romance set in a one-ring circus touring Eastern Europe. Competently acted, directed and photographed in excellent color, it nevertheless lacks excitement or esthetics necessary to capture American audiences of foreign language films, although it offers a fascinating intimate view of the small European circus life far removed from the Big Top.

Jozef Kroner, lead of "Shop on Main Street," gives a touching performance as an aging clown, but it is a supporting role.

Main story concerns romance between two young bareback riders, Jan Triska and Emilie Vasaryova. Her parents have more ambitious plans for her than going around in sawdust circles. When Triska is drafted into the cavalry, they spirit the girl off to another circus heading for far off points.

On his dischage, Triska begins searching for the girl. He joins up with a touring wrestling troupe, a high wire act, and finally as assistant in a trained monkey act.

The romance of boy gets girl, loses girl, gets her again and finally loses her doesn't really evoke involvement. Miss Vasaryova is a stunning dark beauty, and Triska is sort of a young roguish Czech Jean-Paul Belmondo type, but he comes across more persistent than passionate.

As depicted here, circuses in

Eastern Europe are pretty dull affairs by American standards of sensation — consisting of unspectacular horseback riding, dog acts and one or two dreary clowns. Fric rather than develop the pathos and harshness of the life as in "La Strada," holds a romantic view, and the result is a lackluster entertainment.

The finale, with Triska taking over the clown act for the dying Kroner although, as they say, he's crying on the inside, just doesn't grab hold.

Pic was shown at San Francisco Film Festival as part of an afternoon tribute to Fric, a pioneer Czech director and current chairman of Czechoslovak Union of Sceen and Television Artists.
Rick.

Ride in the Whirlwind
(COLOR)

San Francisco, Oct. 24.
Monte Hellman-Jack Nicholson independent production with no distributor at present. Stars Cameron Mitchell, Jack Nicholson, Millie Perkins; features Tom Filer, Katherine Squire, George Mitchell, Rupert Crosse, Dean Stanton, and John Hackett. Directed by Monte Hellman. Screenplay, Jack Nicholson; camera (Eastman color), Gregory Sandor; music, Robert Drasnin. Reviewed at San Francisco Film Festival, Oct. 23, '66. Running Time, **82 MINS.**

Vern	Cameron Mitchell
Wes	Jack Nicholson
Otis	Tom Filer
Abby	Millie Perkins
Catherine	Katherine Squire
Evan	George Mitchell
Sheriff	Brandon Carroll
Indian Joe	Rupert Crosse
Blind dick	Dean Stanton
Hagerman	Peter Cannon
Sheriff's aide	John Hackett
Outlaw	B. J. Merholz

Monte Hellman's "Ride in the Whirlwind" was presented at the San Francisco Film Festival's afternoon New American Directors series under the mistaken notion that Hellman's lack of experience constituted a naturalistic style.

What unreels is a flat, woodenly acted western with mild suspense that never grabs. Part of the fault is with Jack Nicholson script, which is little more than a promising plot line rather than a fully developed scenario. Nicholson also plays the lead, but since Nicholson the writer has little to say, Nicholson the actor has even less.

At that Hellman never exploits the full potential of the situations. A trio of uncommunicative saddle tramps — Nicholson, Cameron Mitchell, Tom Fuller—stumble on a motley gang holed up in a mountain shack after a stage coach robbery. For reasons never adequately explained the one-eyed gang leader Dick Stanton is downright cordial to the cow pokes, inviting them to set down a spell and have a shot of redeye and some beans and biscuit. For unequally invalid reasons, this law abiding trio does just that, although they are mighty suspicious of the desperados, one of whom is wounded.

They even spend the night, and in the morning find themselves surrounded by a posse of vigilantes that is going to string them up first and ask questions later.

In the get away Filer is shot down and Mitchell and Nicholson have to climb up a sheer canyon. Now fugitives, they break into the cabin of a belligerent homesteader and hold his wife Katherine Squire and daughter Millie Perkins hostage.

Not one of the characters emerges from the flatness of the screen, and to a man they move and talk like animated cigar store Indians. When Mitchell is shot by homesteader George Mitchell, taking his horses to escape, and Nicholson in turn guns the family man down, there is no sense of tragedy in it. No one has been developed enough to care about. The most impressive thing in the film are the malevolently barren badlands of Utah where pic was shot entirely on location by Gregory Sandor, using the background to good effect.

Working on a rock low budget, Hellman successfully manages an authentic old west feel. However, there are a few lapses of reality like Nicholson and Mitchell, after supposedly spending days on the trail and climbing a cliff all night, being properly sweaty, only slightly soiled but clean shaven.

Film has minor marquee lure in Mitchell and Perkins, and some suspense and action suitable for play in general release as second feature on double bill. It does not stand alone.

"Whirlwind" is Hellman's second indie production. The first, another western, was "The Shooting."
Rick.

The Plastic Dome of Norma Jean

San Francisco, Oct. 25.
Privately financed film and without a distributor as yet, produced, directed and written by Juleen Compton. Stars Sharon Henesy, Robert Gentry, Marco St. John; features Samuel Waterston, Skip Hinnant, Arthur Hughes, Henry Oliver. Co-producer and editor, Stuart Murphy; music, Michel LeGrand; photography, Roger Barlow. Reviewed at San Francisco Film Festival, Oct. 25, '66. Running Time, **82 MINS.**

Norman Jean	Sharon Henesy
Vance	Robert Gentry
Bobo	Marco St. John
Andy	Samuel Waterston
Francis	Skip Hinnant
Chris	Arthur Hughes
Mayor	Henry Oliver
Announcer	Jack Murray
Spelunker	Jerry Serempa
Mrs. Meekas	Emma Coody
Chance Lawson	Gilbert Elmore
Johnny	Stanley Tiffany
Sheriff	Carl Wallace
Elmer	George Jackson
Finch	Roger Kreiger

"The Plastic Dome of Norma Jean" premiered at the San Francisco Film Festivals New Directors series and single-handedly justified the fest's existence as a showcase for new talent.

It is a film "by Juleen Compton." That is to say, she produced, directed and wrote it. It has no distributor as yet, its players are unknowns, the plot fits no standard category, yet specially handled pic could do well commercially in select situations. Word of mouth will be a big factor.

Title role, play by 15 year old ethereal blonde model Sharon Henesy in her first film exposure, is an innocent with natural powers of clairvoyance who falls in with a rock 'n roll band in the Ozarks. The slick young leader Marco St. John exploits her to draw publicity and crowds to the Plastic Dome, a mail order circus-tent structure that the kids have ambitions to turn into an entertainment center. It is symbolic of the blownup artificiality on which showbiz careers are often established.

With mixtures of surrealism & realism the story and conflicts are developed yet the weaknesses and blind alleys of Juleen Compton the writer almost lead the director astray.

The ending shown at the festival, abruptly killing the girl in a senseless, badly set-up accident, was a contrived cop out. Miss Compton also shot another ending in which the harmless old man who hides the girl when she runs away from the Dome, is killed instead and she rejoins the rock 'n roll group. This final corrupting of her innocence would be a more powerful ending than the girl's death itself.

There are several distracting side excursions that had nothing or little to do with the story. A parallel happening of a spelunker trapped in a nearby cave-in has only a symbolic and metaphysical relation to the plot. It could be cut out without altering the pic yet the scene of a TV reporter and would-be heroes at a disaster is sharply drawn. It is an example of the director succeeding with the writer's failure.

Sharon Henesy, despite her inexperience, carries the major dramatic load with naturalness and charm, as if she were living the role. Robert Gentry, as her brother vacillating between his desire to protect his sister and his own ambitions, is convincing although his part might have been more effectively written. Marco St. John is both attractive and menacing as the scheming leader of the rock group. Rest of cast is solid, especially Henry Oliver as the promotion-minded mayor. Background music contrasts as a lyrical score by Michel LeGrand and four original rock ballads performed by the Dupres and the Vacels. On the screen the actors fake it.

The music, which is dramatically integrated into story, could be used by itself for effective promotional tie-ins. Although a serious film artistically, it has great appeal to teen-age audiences.

Photography by Roger Barlow and tech credits are first rate.
Rick.

Incubus
(AMERICAN-ESPERANTO)

San Francisco, Oct. 26.
Independent production by Daystar, produced by Antony M. Taylor; directed and written by Leslie Stevens. Stars William Shatner, Allyson Ames; features Eloise Hart, Robert Fortier, Ann Atman, Milos Milos. Photography, Conrad Hall; editor, Richard K. Brockway; music, Dominic Frontier; associate producer, Elaine Michae; asst. director, Maurice Vaccarino. Reviewed at San Francisco Film Festival, Oct. 25, '66. Running Time, **78 MINS.**

Marc	William Shatner
Kia	Allyson Ames
Amael	Eloise Hardt
Olin	Robert Fortier
Arndis	Ann Atman
Incubus	Milos Milos

(With English Subtitles)
"Incubus" is the first feature film with the dialogue entirely in Esperanto, the invented language. It is a pretentious piece of hocus-pocus of evil demons vs. good in the mythical land of Nomen Tuum.

Esperanto is an artificial tongue that cultists have been trying unsuccessfully to promote as an international language since 1887. The strange tongue is used in the film with the intention of giving it a supernatural feel. It only succeeds in making the film unsuitable for a quick-buck via horror pix double bills. The use of subtitles underscores the absolute banality of the dialogue which sent the festival audience — those remaining from the general exodus — into laughter. Perhaps Esperanto loses something in translation.

It sounds like Latin recited in a Brooklyn classroom, which also pretty well describes the performances director-writer Leslie Stevens gets from the cast, which learned their roles by phonetics.

Actually the film is handsome visually. The fairy tale was shot entirely on location in Big Sur, and Conrad Hall's photography is brooding and impressive.

William Shatner looks competent in his role as the good man who is so hard to find, and once having found him the black spirits try to destroy. An incubus, incidentally, is a satyric demon who seduces women and claims their soul for the devil. The female counterpart, the succubi, is Allyson Ames, a fetching blonde with a believably wicked look in her eye.

She goes about in a black chin-to-ankle smock inviting men to come down to the beach and romp in the nude with her. It is symbolic of the film's completely unrealized possibilities that she never displays more than a knee.

Ann Atman, as Shatner's angelic sister, is also extremely attractive, but like the others she is destroyed by the dialogue.

Milos Milos is the incubus brought forth from the earth to rape Miss Atman in revenge for the succubi falling in love with Shatner. He plays the unbelievable the same way, unbelievably. The way Stevens stages the subsequent black masses and atrocities, they are actually laughable.

Perhaps, if producer Anthony M. Taylor re-edited, had the dialogue totally rewritten, and redubbed the pic in English, it might be salvaged. Otherwise, the land of Nomen Tuum is a total disaster area.

Apparently director-writer Stevens was trying to be like Ingmar Bergman but simply went too far out of his "Outer Limits." *Rick.*

The Romance of Aniceto & Francesca

San Francisco, Oct. 27.
Bresky-Achugar production, released by Brandon Films. Stars Elsa Daniel, Maria Vaner, Fedrico Luppi. Produced by Walter Achugar; directed and written by Leonardo Favio. Reviewed at San Francisco Film Festival, Oct. 26, '66. Running Time, **85 MINS.**

Aniceto	Fedrico Luppi
Francesca	Elsa Daniel
Lucia	Maria Vaner

This lackluster, brooding Argentine tragedy is directed, edited, written and acted in the style that is dreary to the point of total soporification. Prospects outside Latin America are nil.

"Romance" of title is a busstop pickup. Girl, Elsa Daniel, moves in with drugstore cowboy Federico Luppi.

He deserts Miss Daniel for Maria Vaner, who wears heavy eyemake to show that she is seductive. Luppi chain smokes and stares dully into camera to show he is troubled. Miss Daniel is lovely but wasted.

Writer-director Leonardo Favio is responsible. Editing ranges from lethargic to laughable, and story could have been told in half the time with same footage. *Rick.*

Penelope
(PANAVISION-COLOR)

Wacky comedy about a young wife whose hobby is larceny; well-made, abounding in laughs and excellent grosses foreseen.

Hollywood, Nov. 3.
Metro release of Arthur Loew Jr. production. Stars Natalie Wood; features Ian Bannen, Dick Shawn, Peter Falk, Lila Kedrova, Lou Jacobi, Jonathan Winters. Directed by Arthur Hiller. Screenplay, George Wells; from novel by E. V. Cunningham; camera (Metrocolor), Harry Stradling; music, Johnny Williams; editor, Rita Roland; asst. director, Terence Nelson. Reviewed at Wilter Theatre, Nov. 2, '66. Running Time, 94 MINS.

Penelope	Natalie Wood
James B. Elcott	Ian Bannen
Dr. Gregory	Dick Shawn
Lt. Bixbee	Peter Falk
Professor Klobb	Jonathan Winters
Sadaba	Lila Kedrova
Ducky	Lou Jacobi
Mildred	Norma Crane
Major Higgins	Arthur Malet
Bank Manager	Jerome Cowan
Honeysuckle Rose	Arlene Golonka
Miss Serena	Amzie Strickland
Sgt. Rothschild	Bill Gunn
Boom Boom	Carl Ballantine
Store Owner	Iggie Wolfington

"Penelope" is one of those bright, delightfully - wacky comedies that should get warm welcome from both trade and public— "cute" in the best-accepted use of the term. Starring Natalie Wood for marquee lure and featuring such slick back-up artists as Ian Bannen, Dick Shawn, Peter Falk and Lila Kedrova, it's got a good—if light—basic plot premise, plenty of glib laugh lines and situations, and an array of Edith Head creations likely to turn any femme spectator's head.

Final entry in Joe Pasternak's long tenure at Metro and produced with a lavish hand by Arthur Loew Jr., script by George Wells gives full sway to the story of a young wife whose hobby is larceny. Arthur Hiller's deft direction takes advantage of the intended spirit and seizes upon every opportunity for a romp, making full use of the rich, visual values of George W. Davis and Preston Ames' art direction. Pic carries a refreshing note which communicates to the audience.

Film opens with a little old lady holding up a bank and getting away with $60,000 a few hours after bank's official opening. She turns out to be femme star, married to the bank's prexy, Bannen, and disguised with a rubber mask which she doffs, along with a distinguishing yellow suit, in ladies' washroom. Besides being a femme "burglar," a term she likes immensely, she's the patient of a psychoanalyst, Shawn, who's in love with her. Shawn finally analyzes her as turning to crime because her husband neglects her for his duties at the bank. Part of footage is devoted to flashback sequences as she explains her forages into crime to her doctor, not always conducive to better continuity but no matter...the laughs are there.

Miss Wood does a nimble job and turns in a gay performance as well as being a nice clothes-horse for Miss Head's glamorous fashions. Bannen is properly stuffy as her spouse who cannot understand his wife's frequent whims and reasoning somewhat reminiscent of Dagwood's Blondie. As the psychoanalyst, Shawn is in his element in one of his zany characterizations and Peter Falk socks over his role as police lieutenant assigned to the bank case, who figures that his prey might just be the prexy's wife.

As operator of a fashion salon out to blackmail Natalie, Lila Kedrova plays it broad and she has a clever running mate in Lou Jacobi. Jonathan Winters' appearance is minimal, delineating a high school chemistry professor going on the make for femme star, then a sweet girl graduate, and succeeding in ripping off all but a tiny bikini in a fast comedy sequence.

Technical credits are of high grade. Besides those mentioned above, outstanding are Harry Stradling's color photography, Rita Roland's editing, Johnny Williams' music score, Henry Grace and George Gleason's set decorations. *Whit.*

Where The Bullets Fly
(BRITISH-COLOR)

Briskly directed tongue-in-cheek secret agent comedy-drama. Plenty of corpses and general mayhem and hokum. Solid entry for general light-hearted entertainment.

London, Nov. 3.
Golden Era release of Puck Film (James Ward) Production. Stars Tom Adams, Dawn Addams; features Sidney James, Wilfrid Brambell, Joe Baker, Tim Barrett, Michael Ripper, Gerard Heinz, John Arnatt, Michael Ward, Charles Houston, Heidi Erich. Directed by John Gilling. Original story and screenplay by Michael Pittock; camera (Eastmancolor), David Holmes; editor, Ron Pope; music, Ron Briges; title song (sung by Susan Maughan)—lyrics, Bob Kingston, music, Briges. Previewed at Prince Charles Theatre, London. Running Time, 90 MINS.

Charles Vine	Tom Adams
Fiz	Dawn Addams
Mortuary Attendant	Sidney James
Minister	Joe Baker
Angel	Michael Ripper
Train Guard	Wilfrid Brambell
Seraph	Tim Barrett
Thursby	Ronald Leigh-Hunt
Cherub	Maurice Browning
Carruthers	Heidi Erich
Celia	Sue Donovan
Air Marshal	John Horsley
RAF Sergeant	David Gregory
Michael	Michael Ward
Caron	Suzan Farmer
Verity	Julie Martin
Venstram	Gerard Heinz
Co-Pilot	Charles Houston
Harding	Peter Ducrow
Harding's Secretary	Barbara French
Rockwell	John Arnatt

Second adventure of secret agent Charles Vine, a kind of poor man's James Bond, is a tongue-in-cheek affair which should prove a lark to fairly self-indulgent filmgoers. Vine, played with rather conceited nonchalance by Tom Adams, made his bow in "The Second Best Secret Agent In The Whole Wide World" and he's up to his eyebrows in trouble again. (Embassy has release in U.S. and plans title-change to "Third Best, etc.")

A different screenplay writer, Michael Pittock, has been brought in and has dreamed up a yarn which John Gilling has directed at a swift pace, skating over the many confusions of the plot. It is difficult to sort out who's up against whom, but with so much ammunition and so many corpses biting the dust, it does not much matter. Sufficient that the action is vigorous and rarely flags from the credit titles when an attempt to blow up the Houses of Parliament is thwarted by Adams and his aides.

Germ of the plot is Adams' attempt to wipe out a sinister organization which is secretly double dealing with foreign powers. It aims to grab the plans and formulae of the Spurium Apparatus which enables a plane to fly by nuclear power from a unit lighter and smaller than anything conceived before. From then on the pic is a labyrinth of red herrings, double-crossings, intrigue and sabotage.

A long experienced cast responds enthusiastically to Gilling's handling of the way-out action. Michael Ripper is an urbane, slightly scatty semi-Oriental villain and Tim Barrett scores as his active assistant. Maurice Browning, Peter Ducrow, Gerard Heinz, Michael Ward, John Arnott (as Adams' boss), Tom Bowman, James Ellis and Ronald Leigh-Hunt all play smallish but key roles satisfactorily. There are three guestar bits of which the most successful is Sidney James as a lugubrious mortuary attendant on whose premises pseudo-cops fight out a battle which ends with a floor full of corpses to James' disgust. Joe Baker is victim of a silly role as a fatuous, exaggerated, dimwitted vulgarian of a Parliamentary Minister and Wilfrid Brambell has a brief scene as a lecherous train guard.

Dawn Addams, star distaff attraction, makes a late entry but registers well as an amorous WAAF officer who is romanced by Adams. Others who succumb to the kiss-and-run technique include Suzan Farmer, Heidi Erich, Julie Martin and Sue Donovan.

Editing is capable, film being trimmed to a reasonable 90 minutes and David Holmes' Eastmancolor lensing fares better outdoors than in the interior sequences. Musical score is adequate and there is a title song which, though belted out competently by Susan Maughan, is eminently forgettable. *Rich.*

Epihirissis Dourios Ippos
(Operation Trojan Horse)
(GREEK-U. S.)

Athens, Nov. 1.
A W. R. C. Film Production. Produced by B. Roumanas. Directed by Tredy Roumanas. Features Peter Fyssoun, Yannis Voglis, Anestis Vlahos, Phedon Georgitsis, Nicos Tsahirides, Christos Negas, Marianna Kouracou, Haritini Carolou, Costas Balladimas. Screenplay, Thanassis Valtinos; camera, Giovanni Variano; music, Manos Loizos. At Salonika Film Festival.

This picture is an attempt to show the disasters and stupidity of war. It is a Yank-Greek production financed by Greek-Americans of the W.R.C. company. On its battle sequences and top star values, it has good prospects for local and foreign audiences. As a matter of fact, six top Greek screen actors are playing the leading roles and this is the film's greatest asset for some local markets.

Set in a small island in the Aegean Sea, the story opens with a six-man commando unit arriving there on a mission to destroy the German base. With the help of a little boy they almost destroy the base. The boy and one of the commandos are killed and another is wonded. A girl finds the wounded man hidden in the cellar of her house. She nurses him and they make love. The next morning they are awakened by terrible gunfire. Three men who had not succeeded in reaching an appointed spot in time return to help their captain. Only one of them survives the terrible fight which follows.

This is the first picture of young director Tredy Roumanas who had done many short films for tv release in the States. In this pic he tries to express an anti-war message and succeeds, in a way, to make it believable to simple audiences. The film has some very good fight sequences and suspense, though the pace is slow for a war picture. Some other scenes are too overdone.

Thesping is good. Yannis Voglis, as the captain, plays heroically. Anestis Vlahos, as the wounded man, Peter Fysscun, Phedon Georgitsis and all others handle their parts we'l. A big asset is the black and white photography by Giovanni Variano. Music and all other technical values are good. *Rena.*

O Zestos Minas Augoustos
(The Hot Month of August)
(GREEK)

Athens, Oct. 31.
A Victoria Kapsaski production, written and directed by Socrates Kapsaskis. Features Peter Fyssoun, Betty Arvaniti; camera Demitris Papaconstantis; music, Stavros Xarhacos. At Salonika Film Festival. Running Time, 97 MINS.

This film does not have any artistic quality to justify its participation at a festival, but due to its action and suspense may have better chances at the b.o., albeit the screenplay is not clear enough in many sequences and audiences are left with some question marks.

The plot has suspense from the start. Phocas, a rich industrialist, hires a private eye in Paris, named Makris, to find out if his wife is unfaithful. Makris reveals his mission to the wife and she falls in love with him. They plot to kill Phocas but far from Athens, so they go to a Greek island. During the trip there the wife attracts young Philippou to use him as an accessory to the murder of her husband.

The plan fails, however. Phocas arrives on the island with his own plans. He kills his wife and Makris is wounded. Phocas frames young Philippou for the murder and he is arrested. But in the end Makris' innocence is proved, his alibi supported by the wife, and Phocas is arrested.

The plot works up in a very common way and the dialog is rather naive. The director has added some love and dramatic sequences to make it more commercial, but they hold up the action and slow the pace. The characters are false and generally the directorial work looks more amateurish than professional. *Rena.*

Steaua Fara Nume
(Nameless Star)
(RUMANIAN-FRENCH)

San Francisco, Oct. 31.
Rumania Film release of Bucaresti Studio Romanian-French co-production, directed by Henri Colpi. Stars Marina Vlady, Claude Rich; features Cristea Avram, Eugenia Popovici, Marcel Angelescu. Music, Georges Delerue. Reviewed at San Francisco Film Festival, Oct. 30, '66. Running Time, 85 MINS.
Mona .... Marina Vlady
Miroiu .... Claude Rich
Grig .... Cristea Avram
Miss Cucu .... Eugenia Popovici

This Rumanian-French co-production, the second by director Henri Colpi, is well acted and directed. "Nameless Star" is a bittersweet romance that is genuinely touching. Cast and director are relatively unknown to American audiences, and film has minor prospects unless word of mouth and reviews prove exceptional. (Frisco Fest very careless, incidentally, about screen credits, so above may be incomplete.)

Claude Rich is a shy eccentric bachelor who teaches math in a small Rumanian village. His passion is astronomy and by calculations he has discovered a new star, one that he cannot see and as yet has no name.

Expecting an expensive foreign book on astronomy to arrive by train, he goes to the station to wait. Off the train steps Marina Vlady, like some exquisite creature from another planet in an evening gown and a feather boa. After an argument with her lover at a distant gambling casino, she had impulsively jumped on the first train without any money, and the conductor threw her off at that stop.

The station master doesn't know what to do with this aloof, spoiled woman. The teacher, thoroughly awed by her, offers her his home, while he spends the night with a friend, an elderly music teacher.

Miss Vlady at first finds Rich, the prissy teacher-dreamy astronomer, ridiculous, then amusing, then endearing. The couple's transition from people worlds apart to lovers is accomplished with subtlety and humor. It is thoroughly believable and, that rarest of things, charming.

As the music teacher, who has written a symphony that the school orchestra cannot play, because it can not afford an English horn, Cristea Avram creates an exceptional vignette.

In the morning Miss Vlady's handsome, wealthy young lover Marcel Angelescu, roars up in an enormous sports car. The town is scandalized.

"I can't be jealous." says Angelescu. "This has nothing to do with our world."

In the end Rich realizes the girl is a star that has deviated from her orbit, and she goes off, leaving behind her name for his new star, not to mention very few dry eyes in the house. *Rick.*

Silence Has No Wings
(JAPAN)

San Francisco, Oct. 29.
Toho Film production, directed and written by Kasuo Kuroki. Features Mariko Kaga, Fumio Watanabe. Reviewed at San Francisco Film Festival, Oct. 29, '66. Running Time, 110 MINS.

"Silence Has No Wings" is the fascinating but bewildering account of a rare tropical butterfly traveling from the orange orchards of Nagasaki to northern Hokaido. The caterpillar attaches itself to several people involved in poignant, sharp-drawn vignettes ranging from a burlesque show to two lovers in Hiroshima living in terror of atomic sickness.

As the worm approaches metamorphosis to moth, the film's story and style abruptly change to a frantic fantasy ranging from Hong Kong to Tokyo involving smuggling and a government coup. The butterfly emerges in a burst of surrealism and symbolism.

The result is total confusion for the Occidental mind, although the program notes maintain it is all "a symbol of love, plagued by tradition and the desperation of modern Japanese urban life."

Fumio Watanabe is the boy who originally finds the butterfly, and Mariko Kaga is a lovely Japanese girl who appears as leitmotif throughout film.

Real star is meant to be director-writer Kazuo Kuroki, in his first feature. He uses a camera stunningly, and his first realistic scenes are gripping, before he runs amuck. One almost feels for the worm.

Nevertheless, allegory loses something in translation, and film is poor prospect for art circuit. *Rick.*

Le Deuxiene Souffle
(Second Wind)
(FRENCH)

Paris, Nov. 8.
Prodis release of Films Montaigne production. Stars Lino Ventura; features Paul Meurisse, Raymond Pellegrin, Paul Frankeur, Daniele Fabrega, Pierre Zimmer. Directed by Jean-Pierre Melville. Screenplay, Jose Giovanni, Melville, from the book by Giovanni; camera Marcel Combes; editor, Michel Boheme. At Colisee, Paris. Running Time, 150 MINS.
Gustave .... Lino Ventura
Inspector .... Paul Meurisse
Paul .... Raymond Pellegrin
Manouche .... Daniele Fabrega
Orlov .... Pierre Zimmer
Ricci .... Marcel Bozzufi
2d Inspector .... Paul Frankeur
Alban .... Michel Constantin

Director Jean-Pierre Melville has built a solid gangster opus influenced by some earlier American types but successfully transferred to the local milieu. It deals with an older gangster, escaping from prison, who finds that there is no longer honor among thieves —or policemen, for that matter.

Somewhat long, some pruning could weld this into an acceptable pic for dualer use abroad, with some specialized chances also inherent in it due to its objective insights and good workmanship.

A middleaged gangster escapes from prison and wants only to get away somewhere. But he finds his sister being blackmailed by some smalltime hoods and does them in, and then embarks on a last job to earn enough to retire to some tropical port. But double-crossing among the hoods, police

brutality and a final wiping out of the treacherous gang, and his own demise at the hands of the police, end this somberly-paced, but unflagging in interest, pic.

The cool attitudes and flip jargon, used both by police and hoods are reminiscent of Yank prototypes but jell well here. Lino Ventura has the right weight and honesty, albeit in a criminal way, and Paul Meurisse is a smooth, competent and ironically-tongued policeman who still shows he has some code of honesty compared with other policemen more prone to use torture to extract confessions.

Pic does not condone crime, but does offer look at the underworld as a twisted reflection of the norm. The self-justified torture scenes of the police will probably be cut here as current censor outlooks usually will not go for the besmirching of any official body.

This is an almost classical gangster film with Yank influences well assimilated. Played with intensity and gusto, with holdups done sharply, it has action and playoff legs and just that extra feel for milieu and character that could give it some art chances if well placed and if well cut. It is technically sound with the playing good down the line. *Mosk.*

Syntomo Dialima
(A Brief Intermission)
(GREEK)

Athens, Oct. 29.
An Hesperia Film Production. Produced by Marios Stavropoulos. Directed by Dinos Katsourides. Features Alecos Alexandrakis, Voula Zouboulaki, Alexis Damianos, Lavrentis Dianellos, Despo Diamantidou, Ketty Labropoulou. Screenplay by Michalis Gregoriou; camera, Aristides Karydis. At Salonika Film Festival.

An average picture with few good sequences, this should not have been selected for the Salonika Fest. Both director Dinos Katsourides and leading actor Alecos Alexandrakis have wasted their talents on an unworthy screenplay about the people of the theatre, their ambitions and activities behind the stage.

Katsourides could not do much to add value to a flat story. Alexandrakis does everything possible to save his role, while Voula Zouboulaki was awarded a prize as best actress at the festival for her performance in this picture.
Rena.

The Defector
(GERMAN—FRENCH—COLOR)

Montgomery Clift's last film—spy tale, but sans latterday flippancy. Topnotch cast bests flawed script.

Seven Arts Productions release of a P.E.C.F.—Rhein-Main Filmgeselschaft co-production. Produced and directed by Raoul Levy. Stars Montgomery Clift, Hardy Kruger, Macha Meril; features Roddy McDowall, David Opatoshu, Christine Delaroche, Hannes Messemer, Karl Lieffen. Screenplay, Robert Guenette and Raoul Levy, based on Paul Thomas novel, "The Spy"; camera (Eastman Color), Raoul Coutard; editor, Albert Jurgenson; sound, Jo De Bretagne; music, Serge Gainsbourg. Reviewed at 7 Arts h.o., N. Y., Nov 9, '66. Running Time: 108 MINS.
Prof. James Bower......Montgomery Clift
Peter Heinzman ....Hardy Kruger
Frieda Hoffman .... Macha Meril
CIA Agent Adam.......Roddy McDowall
Orlovsky ....David Opatoshu
Ingrid ....Christine Delaroche
Dr. Saltzer ....Hannes Messemer
The Major ....Karl Lieffen

The espionage film has been given such flippant treatment in the past few years, with a few notable exceptions, that when a serious treatment comes along and is done with some attention, it proves a welcome escape for the filmgoers who begin to tire of the agent who conducts most of his activities in, and from, the bed. "Spy Who Came In From The Cold" was such a "straight" film. "The Defector" is almost such a film.

The last motion picture made by Montgomery Clift prior to his death, "Defector" provides a part that allows him to substitute action of body and mind for the immobility of facial expression that clouded this fine actor's performances during his last years. His taut, troubled face is perfect for the role of a scientist, pushed into espionage by his own country and almost erased from it by enemy agents.

Producer-director Raoul Levy made "Defector" entirely in Germany as a German-French coproduction, a decision that gives him an international cast in a setting that has not yet been photographed to death. Indeed, Raoul Coutard's Eastman Color camerawork makes one of the greatest contributions to the element of suspense and danger that dominates the second half of the film, although he appears to have had frequent and considerable lighting problems in trying to match scenes. But the bleak, wintry landscape through which much of the action passes could never be mistaken for the San Fernando Valley and the architecture may be Munich passing for Leipzig but it is German.

The script, however, is something else. Levy and Robert Guenette's collaboration on an adaptation of Paul Thomas's "The Spy" has gone for "suspense" at the sacrifice of logic. There are also some political connotations that may upset a few delicate viewers although the most important, the murder of Kruger by the C.I.A., will escape anyone who doesn't catch the knowing glance between Roddy McDowall as a C.I.A. agent, and the truckdriver who has "accidentally" run down Kruger, at the film's end. Just plain logical loopholes also appear that, again, may escape most viewers but will disturb some.

Clift, a noted scientist, would be too intelligent to go into a strange country without a supply of medicine for a serious intestinal ailment he's supposed to have, or try to get such medicine in the first apothecary's shop he comes to, without a prescription. The incident, needed for the plot, should have been set up better.

Most of the intellectual byplay is between Clift, as an American scientist, and Kruger, as the German-born Russian agent given the assignment of getting Clift to defect. The physical action comes from Clift's evasion of the Security Police and his attempt to escape from East Germany. Kruger, at first hard to recognize because he's grown so plump, makes an excellent contrast, in his cool behavior, to Clift's nervousness. McDowall, who always manages to give a major performance, even in a minor role, is only in the pre-title and some other short sequences, but is important to the plot as the deus ex machina that starts Clift on his dangerous attempt to contact a defecting Russian scientist.

The supporting cast is, for the most, outstanding although French actresses Macha Meril and Christine Delaroche, who play German nurses, come across as French girls playing German nurses. David Opatoshu's Russian spy chief, Hannes Messemer's Jewish doctor and Karl Lieffen's army officer are controlled, impressive performances.

"Defector" should find its biggest market in the action-adventure field but could also be impressive in big-city serious-cinema theatres (those that used to be called "art" houses). Seven Arts evidently realizes this as the pic's New York premiere, Nov. 16, will be a three-house parlay at the Astor, Trans-Lux East and Murray Hill. *Robe.*

Gambit
(COLOR-TECHNISCOPE)

Topnotch suspense comedy-romance, expert in all departments. Shirley MacLaine and Michael Caine marquee bait for strong b.o.

Hollywood, Nov. 5.
Universal release of Leo L. Fuchs production. Stars Shirley MacLaine, Michael Caine. Directed by Ronald Neame. Screenplay, Jack Davies, Alvin Sargent, based on story by Sidney Carroll; camera (Technicolor), Clifford Stine; editor, Alma Macrorie; music, Jarre; song, Paul Godkin, Harper McKay; asst. director, Joseph Kenny. Reviewed at Village Theatre, Westwood, L.A., Nov. 4, '66. Running Time, 107 MINS.
Nicole .... Shirley MacLaine
Harry .... Michael Caine
Shahbandar .... Herbert Lom
Ram .... Roger C. Carmel
Abdul .... Arnold Moss
Emile .... John Abbott
Col. Salim .... Richard Angarola
Hotel Clerk .... Maurice Marsac

This particular "Gambit" will pay off. Shirley MacLaine and Michael Caine star in a firstrate suspense comedy, cleverly scripted, expertly directed and handsomely mounted by Leo L. Fuchs, bowing quite auspiciously as a producer. Comedy for the young and hip, eye - filling wardrobes for the femme trade, and entertainment for all spell hot b.o. action for Universal release in general situations.

Sidney Carroll's original story has been adapted in top fashion by Jack Davies and Alvin Sargent, resulting in a zesty laugh-getter as Miss MacLaine become Miss Malaprop in Caine's scheme to loot the art treasures of mid - East potentate Herbert Lom. An idealized swindle sequence lasting 27 minutes opens pic, after which the execution of the plan shifts all characterizations and sympathies.

Director Ronald Neame has obtained superior characterizations from all hands. Miss MacLaine, playing a Eurasian gal and garbed by Jean Louis in some dreamy attire, displays her deft comedy abilities after the opening segment, in which she is stone-faced and silent. Caine socks over a characterization which is at first tight-lipped and cold, then turning warm with human and romantic frailty.

Lom is excellent as the potentate, so assured of his security devices that audience sympathy encourages the machinations of Caine and Miss MacLaine. Arnold Moss, Lom's cool-headed aide, Roger C. Carmel, the amusing Arab functionary, and Richard Angarola, suave police chief, render solid support. John Abbott is particularly effective as Caine's accomplice in the plot, and at surprise fadeout, it is obvious that he has prepared to go it alone.

Fuchs, a former photographer, has turned loose a fine crew of artisans to dress his film to the nines. In addition to the Jean Louis clothes, art directors Alexander Golitzen and George C. Webb and set decorators John McCarthy and John Austin have provided a plush setting, quite appropriate to a potentate's way of life.

Clifford Stine's versatile Techniscope - Technicolor camera has captured the shifting moods. Pic was shot at Universal studios here (with some overseas location shots), thus making it Caine's first Hollywood film.

Alma Macrorie supervised the editing to a very neat 107 minutes, although the opening put-on sequence might have been trimmed a bit more for better pacing. Maurice Jarre composed-conducted a very good complementing score, and the sound recording and editing crew has produced a lifelike track with dimension and depth, unlike some other contemporary pix which sound antiseptic and artificial. *Murf.*

Dr. Goldfoot And The Girl Bombs
(COLOR)

Sequel to previous popular spy spoof has less to offer, with indicated limitation in appeal. Should do well in general market due to slick color and fast action.

American International Pictures release of a Fulvio Lucisano production. Stars Vincent Price, Fabian; features Franco Franchi, Ciccio Ingrassia, Laura Antonelli. Directed by Mario Bava. Screenplay, Louis M. Heyward, Robert Kaufman from story by James Hartford; camera (Technicolor), no credit. Musical score, Les Baxter; title song, music and lyrics, Guy Hemrick, Jerry Steyner. Reviewed in New York, Nov. 14, '66. Running Time, 85 MINS.
Dr. Goldfoot .... Vincent Price
Bill Dexter .... Fabian
Amateur Sleuths ...... Franco Franchi, Ciccio Ingrassia
Rosanna .... Laura Antonelli

This made-in-Italy attempt to repeat the formula that clicked for AIP in "Dr. Goldfoot and the Bikini Machine" proves, once again, that sequels rarely succeed. In almost every department this belabored spy spoof reprise suffers by comparison with earlier and much funnier original.

If this is typical of films being made for AIP through its Italian production set-up, the company might be wise to spend a bit more money and move back to England. The script by Louis M. Heyward and Robert Kaufman, based on a story by James Hartford, has no originality. As both Kaufman and Hartford were connected with "Bikini Machine," it was probably hoped that they'd strike paydirt again, but they've only repeated the basic formula of the first film.

Aimed at the general market, "Girl Bombs" should do satisfactory business because of its light-hearted approach, plenty of pretty girls, good color camerawork, frenetic pace that tires the audience long before it wears out the characters. Fabian, as the young American agent who continues to foil the nefarious Dr. Goldfoot, plays it straight and comes over as pleasant, attractive and sympathetic. Price, however, only slices the ham a bit thicker as the villainous title character, and makes one doubt that this could be the same actor who once played Albert to Helen Hayes' Victoria.

Laura Antonelli, the femme lead, is a pale parody on Pier Angeli and lacks the sexiness that she's forced to pretend.

Two Italian comedians, supposedly very popular in their own country, are the film's greatest drawback. Franco Franchi and Ceccio Ingrassia, or Franco & Ceccio as they're billed, are possibly the two least funny actors to be seen this side in years. Franco, a mugger, has no control over his part and the deadpan, by comparison, Ceccio, seems an ineffective straight man.

Technical aspects of the film are good, especially the Technicolor photography of Rome and its environs. The credits supplied the trade papers by AIP carried only the name of producer Fulvio Lucisano, director Mario Bava, writing credits and a musical score by Les Baxter, except for the title song, the handiwork of Guy Hemrick and Jerry Steyner. Considering the title, the tune team was licked before it started. *Robe.*

Gift
(Venom)
(DANISH)

London, Oct. 27.
Antony Balch presentation of a Nordisk Kompagni Production. Stars Soeren Stromberg, Sisse Reingaard, Poul Reichhardt, Astrid Villaume; features Judy Gringer, Grethe Morgensen. Produced by C. Bergesen. Directed and written by Knud Lief Thomsen; camera, Claus Loof; music, Niels Viggo Bentzon.

Reviewed at RFD Private Theatre. Running Time, 98 MINS.
Per .... Soeren Stromberg
Susanne .... Sisse Reingaard
Henrike Steen .... Poul Reichhardt
Mrs. Steen .... Astrid Villaume
Sonjo .... Judy Gringer
Frau Jacobsen ..... Grethe Morgensen

"Gift," which in Danish means both "Marriage" and "Venom," a statement as confusing as the objective of this piece, was the first Danish film to be completely banned by that country's censor, until required exclusion of scenes were made, not by cutting but by x-ing out most of "bad" footage. This evidently satisfied Danish censors. This "accolade" may help to stimulate its promotion, but the present version has been revised and given a thumbs-up by the censor which may lessen its potential titillation. It will need any sales help it can get, for, basically, it is a glib, pretentious pic that is less daring than it pretends to be and is often merely naive and even distasteful. It may well attract a limited audience in art theatres both in Britain and the United States, but seems unlikely to command a wider public.

It concerns the clash of two generations. A young, hedonistic boor saunters insolently into the family life of a frustrated real estate agent, seduces the man's daughter, tries to make his wife, humiliates the man with his sneering comments on life, religion and ideals and, when the father foolishly tries to prove that he is broadminded by inviting the youth into their home, involves the daughter in a pornographic film.

The sex and religious chat is on a fairly superficial level and the shock tactics (such as the young man arrogantly burning the family Bible at a party) are feeble. Writer-director Knud Lief Thomsen is trying to prove something, but his motivation is muddled. Direction is leisurely but camerawork and other technicalities are okay.

Best performances come from the more mature artists, such as Poul Riechhardt as the bewildered father and Astrid Villaume as his patient wife. (Pair also plays parents of girl who is starred in Disney's "Ballerina," also Copenhagen-filmed, indicating they're not discriminating as to tv parts taken.) Soern Stroemberg is overly flippant as the anti-hero and his thesping lacks bite and character. Sisse Reingaard is a looker as the willing seduced daughter and Judy Gringer registers as a maid with Hollywood aspirations. Grethe Morgensen impresses with a couple of neat bits as a wise, poised secretary. *Rich.*

Me Ti Lampsi Sta Matia
(With a Sparkle in the Eyes)
(GREEK)
Athens, Nov. 1.

A Georges Sterguiou production. Directed by Panos Glycofrides. Features Georges Foundas, Lavrentis Dianellos, Anestis Vlahos, Yannis Fertis, Xenia Kalogueropoulou, Ketty Papanica. Screenplay, Jacob Kampanellis, from novel by Panos Glycofrides; camera, Spyros Danalis; music, Christos Leontis. At Salonika Film Festival. Running Time, 100 MINS.

Manthos .... Lavrentis Dianellos
Dimitris .... Georges Foundas
George .... Anestis Vlahos
Nicolas .... Yannis Fertis
Lenia .... Xenia Kalogueropoulou
Maria .... Ketty Papanica
Mother of Lenio ...... Frosso Kokola
German Officer ...... Zoras Tsapelis
Priest .... Theodore Exarhos
Mayor .... Georges Economides
Teacher .... Georges Rois
Secretary .... Yannis Kounadis

This film was the surprise at Salonika, with an unexpected warm welcome from critics and audiences. It collected three prizes and an honorary citation. Its story is one of the many incidents during the German occupation in Greece, but though it is rendered melodramatically, the audience responded to its human antiwar message.

It opens with the killing of a German soldier by Greek guerrillas outside a small village. The Germans round up 30 Greek men to avenge his death, for execution the next morning. Among them are three brothers. A priest, the mayor, and the teacher of the village ask German officer to spare one of them, and he accepts. But the father must decide whom he wants saved. The unfortunate father, however, recalling his life, all night, with each of his sons, loses his senses and dies next morning in front of the execution posse.

Thanks to skillful handling by director Panos Glycofrides, film emerges better than its melodramatic story. It touches the heart by its simple characters and true dramatic situations. Of course, discriminating audiences may find the characters too monotonous and the film narration too flat.

Acting is good. Lavrentis Dianellos gives a strong performance in role of the father. Georges Foundas won the best actor prize of the festival for his performance, and Anestis Vlahos an honorary accolade. Christos Leontis was awarded a prize for his music. Camerawork is good. *Rena.*

The Quiller Memorandum
(BRITISH-COLOR)

Smoothly produced and directed topical spy drama devoid of gimmickery and with compelling performances. Good marquee value for all situations.

London, Nov. 10.

Rank distribution (National General in U.S.) of Ivan Foxwell Production. Stars George Segal, Alec Guinness, Max Von Sydow, Senta Berger. Features George Sanders, Robert Helpmann, Edith Schneider, Robert Flemyng. Directed by Michael Anderson. Screenplay by Harold Pinter, based on Adam Hall's novel; camera (Eastmancolor), Erwin Hiller; music, John Barry; editor, Frederick Wilson; sound, Archie Ludski; special effects, Les Bowie, Arthur Beevis. At Odeon, Leicester Square, London. Running Time, 103 MINS.

Quiller .... George Segal
Pol .... Alec Guinness
Oktober .... Max Von Sydow
Inge .... Senta Berger
Gibbs .... George Sanders
Weng .... Robert Helpmann
Rushington .... Robert Flemyng
Hengel .... Peter Carsten
Headmistress .... Edith Schneider
Hassler .... Gunter Meisner
Grauber .... Ernst Walder
Oktober's men .... Philip Madoc, John Rees

George Segal, playing a secret agent, goes through the entire action without even using a gun—a sure sign that this pic is not in the current spy film stable of "anything Bond can do I can do better." It relies on a straight narrative storyline, simple but holding, literate dialog and well-drawn characters. Based on a novel by Adam Hall (pen name for novelist Elleston Trevor) and with a screenplay by Harold Pinter, it has sufficient thesp marquee value to make it an acceptable entry in any situation.

"The Quiller Memorandum" provides producer Ivan Foxwell with a stroke of topical luck. It deals with the insidious upsurge of neo-Nazism in Germany and is released, fortuitously, around the time that just such a movement has had a shot in the arm through the Hesse elections. Unfortunately, the pic ducks anything but superficial surface-scratching of the political and ideological problems involved in the current disturbing situation. But on its own level of an intelligent, credible secret-service adventure it hits the mark entertainingly and effectively.

Set largely on location in West Berlin, it has Segal brought back from vacation to replace a British agent who has come to a sticky end at the hands of this new infiltrating group of Nazis. His job is to locate their headquarters. He does this in a lone-wolf way, refusing to be hampered by bodyguards. En route he has some edgy adventures. He is kidnapped, drugged, brainwashed, becomes romantically and dangerously involved, allowed to escape for mysterious reasons, tracked down by the Nazi chief's thugs and nearly blown up by a bomb before his mission is accomplished. But these are incidentals. The real tension is built up by implications.

The pic gets away in stylish start with Segal and the cold, witty fish who is in charge of Berlin Sector Investigations (Alec Guinness) meeting in the deserted stadium built for the Berlin Olympic Games. Other high spots are an equally witty exchange when Guinness is explaining spy strategy to Segal in a cafe with the aid of currant buns, the sinister and sweaty brainwashing sequence, an overlong but intriguing car chase and, particularly, a menacing sequence where Segal, on "parole" from his captors as a trap-tries to contact his own hq by phone but finds himself constantly enmeshed and outwitted in a circle of Nazi "tails."

Pinter's script is smoothly and capitally developed and his dialog has his usual economy and talent for making the most casual remark sound meaningful, sinister, provocative or pregnant with motive. Michael Anderson's direction falters at times in the middle of the film but overall keeps a firm grip on the surroundings, though the pace is sometimes over leisurely and sharper shearing by Frederick Wilson would occasionally have helped. John Barry has contributed an atmospheric score and makes effective use occasionally of harsh, unexpected sound to emphasize a highlight. Erwin Hiller's lensing of the Berlin scene cannot be faulted. The locations help a lot toward giving realism to the drama, as does the occasional use of German dialog without explanatory subtitles.

Segal plays Quiller with a laconic but likeable detachment, underlining the loneliness and lack of relaxation of the agent, who cannot even count on support from his own side. Nevertheless, Segal shows signs of certain mannerisms, not exactly Method, but which must be watched if he allows them to creep too persistently into his performances. Guinness never misses a trick in his few scenes. Every word, every gesture has clearly been thought out intensively and he builds up a shrewd, amusing study of a coldly ruthless, suave operator. Max Von Sydow plays the Nazi chief quietly but with high camp menace and he is surrounded by a bunch of henchmen who are obviously tough babies, but not caricatured as degenerate bullies or sadistic morons.

The femme side is mainly represented by a small, cool performance by Edith Schneider as a school headmistress and Senta Berger as one of her staff. Miss Berger looks attractive and provides a pleasantly shy romantic interlude which has a quiet sting in the climax. Robert Helpmann and George Sanders are credited as guest players, but their stints, as that of Robert Flemyng, are minor and irrelevant.

Foxwell, who does not plunge blindly into making a new film, has got himself a smooth vehicle in "Memorandum." There are few way-out kicks, but a strong building up of dramatic realities. At least the picture tackles something plausible that not only can happen but probably is happening some place. It does not deal with the fictional souped-up inspiration of a pulp-writer who pits his hero against a foreign organization craving power and wealth through some incredible invention or outlandish quirk of the writer's imagination. *Rich.*

Harold Lloyd's Funny Side Of Life
(COMPILATION)

Lloyd retrospective made up of clips from the 1920s and 1930s. Contains lots of first-rate sight gags and provides solid laughs.

Chicago, Nov. 6.
Janus release of Harold Lloyd production. Stars Lloyd in various examples of his silent films. Reviewed at Playboy Theatre, Nov. 5, '66. Running Time, 121 MINS.

Made up from selected film clips and the 1925 feature "The Freshman," "Harold Lloyd's Funny Side Of Life" constitutes a documentary of Lloyd's contributions to the sight gag genre. Both lively and engaging, the film is an outstanding example of a style and orientation that has all but disappeared from modern cinema techniques. Film was actually compiled by Lloyd for the retrospective of his works at N.Y.'s gallery of Modern Art and is now going into commercial release.

Since all the films used in the Lloyd retrospective were made during the silent era, a soundtrack has been added. It is, however, mainly supporting narrative with additional sounds, such as crowd cheers, music, etc., and never intrudes upon the visual values, which, of course, were the essence of those films.

Film begins with an introduction by Lloyd and the selected clips. After the bespeckled Lloyd character is firmly developed, "The Freshman" is presented in its entirety. In "The Freshman" Lloyd portrays a too eager new student of Tate College, which is described as a "large football stadium with a college attached." He dreams of being the most popular student at the school, and working toward that end invites everyone to "step right up and call me Speedy."

Lloyd, who selected the clips which make up the film, did an excellent job of editing. Picture afford plenty of laughs, and should be well received by both film buffs and devotees of the good fashion belly yocks. Ron.

Door-To-Door Maniac

Spotty exploitationer about a woman held hostage in an aborted bank heist. Hardsell and fast playoff for okay returns in action grinds.

Hollywood, Nov. 6.
American International Pictures release of James Ellsworth (Ludlow Flower) production. Directed by Bill Karn. Screenplay, M. K. Forester, based on story by Palmer Thompson, adapted by Robert Joseph; camera, Carl Guthrie; editor, Donald Nosseck; music, Gene Kauer; songs, Johnny Cash. Reviewed at World Theatre, L.A., Nov. 6, '66. Running Time, 74 MINS.

Johnny Cabot	Johnny Cash
Ken Wilson	Donald Woods
Nancy Wilson	Cay Forester
Ellen	Pamela Mason
Doris	Midge Ware
Fred	Vic Tayback
Bobby	Ronnie Howard
Max	Merle Travis
Pop	Howard Wright
Priscilla	Norma Varden

"Door-To-Door Maniac" is a clumsy, but exploitable suspense pic, in which a killer holds as hostage the wife of a bank exec who is planning to ditch her anyway. Limp dialog, below par acting and leisurely directing are somewhat overcome by a rape sequence, some taut editing and a switcheroo climax. Good sexploitation campaign will see it through to okay b.o. from American International release in action and grind situations.

Screenplay is by M. K. Forester, pen name of actress Cay Forester who plays the terrorized wife. Donald Woods is her spouse, two-timing with Pamela Mason. Johnny Cash debuts in top-featured role (all players follow title) as the cool-headed murders who muggs Miss Forester while Vic Tayback pressures Woods to hand over $70,000. Ronnie Howard is latter's precocious son.

Much of the dialog is trite, and on occasion incongruous. Cash, already known as a c&w wax performer, sings two songs, both his, "I've Come To Kill," the main-title tune, and "Five Minutes To Live," which underscores a climactic plot turn. The tunes, in context, are ludicrous, but at least provide a selling angle.

Bill Karn's direction is routine, although Carl Guthrie's facile lensing helps out where the plot development falters. Story actually could have been turned into a taut suspenser, and may yet in other hands. In any case, plot parallels "The Desperate Hours," with some inventive twists. Ludlow Flower was exec producer, James Ellsworth produced, and William Mace is billed as associate producer.

Mrs. Mason delivers a strong performance as the other woman, a restrained characterization that evokes audience sympathy. Norma Varden again delivers in a role she does well, the gabby matron. Moppet Howard is good. Merle Travis, who has a bit part, also did some sound track guitar work, while Gene Krauer supplied the other incidental music. Other players and credits are standard, at best, although Donald Nosseck's editing to 74 minutes is good. Final footage is an interesting stop-motion and still montage of plot highlights. Murf.

O Thanatos Tou Alexandrou
(The Death of Alexandros)
(GREEK)

Athens, Nov. 1.
A Dimitri Kollatos and Lia Karyotou production. Written and directed by and starring Kollatos. Features Arlette Bauhman, Dora Volanaki; camera, Aristides Karydes; music, Yannis Marcoopoulos. At Salonika Film Festival. Running Time, 78 MINS.

Alexandros	Dimitnis Kollatos
His Wife	Arlette Bauhman
His Mother	Dora Volanaki

This is the first long feature of Dimitris Kollatos, one of the most promising young Greek directors whose short, "The Olives," won a prize at the Salonika Festival years ago and aroused a good deal of controversial reaction for its realism. This year, Kollatos managed to present the most talked about picture of the festival. It is a story about a young man dying of leukemia, but Kollatos has brought this sad theme into the screen in a way that qualifies him as a mature and experienced director.

Film is not a pleasant picture to watch as the main point of interest is death. So it is a risky item despite its good qualities, and spotty returns are indicated, except perhaps for arty houses abroad.

Nevertheless, the film has an artistic style and some very good sequences. The atmosphere of approaching death is masterfully rendered, as is the grief of all around the dying young man. There are also two love scenes which caused much talk.

Kollatos handles acting chores as well, being perfect in the role of the ill-fated young man. Arlette Bauhman is touching in her performance as his wife (which she is in private life) and Dora Volanakis a silent dramatic figure as the tragic mother.

A top contribution to the picture is the excellent music by Yannis Marcopoulos. Other technical credits are top-grade. Rena.

Le Saint Prend L'Affut
(The Saint Lies in Wait)
(FRENCH-COLOR)

Paris, Nov. 15.
SNC release of Intermondia production. Stars Jean Marais; features Jess Hahn, Dario Moreno, Jean Yanne, Henri Virlojeux, Daniele Evanou. Directed by Christian-Jaque. Screenplay, Jean Ferry, Henri Jeanson, Christian-Jaque; from the book by Leslie Charteris; camera (Eastmancolor), Pierre Petit; editor, Jacques Desagneaux. At Normandie, Paris. Running Time, 90 MINS.

Saint	Jean Marais
Uniatz	Jess Hahn
Sophie	Daniele Evanou
Oscar	Henri Virlojeux
Fat Man	Dario Moreno
German	Jean Yanne

The Leslie Charteris character gets a comedic workout in this slapstick-type actioner. It is too skimpy in story, and fairly repetitive, to be anything but a dualer for foreign action marts.

Jean Marais is his jaunty self as the Saint who is after a cache of American dollars left over from a wartime undercover operation. It is also coveted by a bevy of foreign reps. Naturally, he finally gets it after the usual number of escapades, women and fights.

Jess Hahn, a locally-based Yank actor, is effective as the Saint's simple-minded sidekick. Others do nicely in this familiar chase affair that plods at times but does have enough comic touches and movement to emerge as a generally okay pic for supporting program chances. Mosk.

Eyewitness . . . North Vietnam
(BRITISH-DOCUMENTARY)

Rogosin Film Productions release of Report (London) production. Produced, directed, written and narrated by James Cameron. Camera, Malcolm Aird; assistant to Cameron, Romano Cagnoni. Reviewed in N.Y., Nov. 18, '66. Running Time, 43 MINS.

This short documentary by British journalist James Cameron of a visit (presumably recent) he made to North Vietnam, has been acquired by Lionel Rogosin for U.S. handling. Although no national distribution deal has been made, Rogosin is premiering the short (43 minutes) film at his Bleecker St. Cinema in Greenwich Village currently, on a bill with one of his own features.

As a documentary film, "Eyewitness . . . North Vietnam" (incidentally, the screen credits title as "Western Eyewitness in the North of Vietnam") has little to offer other than good black-and-white photography, presumably the handiwork of cameraman Malcolm Aird. It's a bit difficult to figure out the proper credits for the film as the screen credits differ from those provided at the trade screening. Cameron's assistant, Romano Cagnoni, gets credit as a cameraman in a printed release, but Aird gets sole screen credit.

Almost all of the footage is devoted to daily life of the North Vietnamese although most viewers won't be able to tell them from South Vietnamese except for Cameron's running commentary. As propaganda for the North Vietnamese, one must listen to the commentary as there's nothing shown that would alter one's political opinion of the country and its people. Cameron's insistence that the film was "untouched, uncensored and unseen" by the North Vietnamese conflicts with such obvious facts that his film shows nothing more startling than natives wearing weapons while going about their work, or an alleged air raid which consists of natives entering and leaving underground shelters but with no planes or bombs being shown. Only his soundtrack comment, "This is the sound of American planes over North Vietnam." They could have as easily been North Vietnamese, Russian, Chinese or a studio recording.

The brevity of the film and the skimming-over of incidents that could have been interesting (the opening and closing of a university, a gift from the Russians, or reference to an interview with Ho Chi Minh (unseen) also make the "uncensored" claim hard to accept. The locations on which the film is claimed to have been made are Hanoi, Hai Phong, Cam Pha and Than Hoa. The latter, described as "the most bombed area in North Vietnam," has no bombed-out areas shown.

There are some scenes of Cameron being photographed surrounded by Hanoi citizens and speaking directly into a hand mike. However, the overall soundtrack is too even and noise-free to have been done live, particularly some excellent music and singing which sounds like recordings. It is understood that the sound was done in Hanoi, but the lab work in London. Cameron calls the result a "humble" film. "Meaningless" would have been a better choice. Robe.

Prossopo Me Prossopo
(Face to Face)
(GREEK)

Athens, Oct. 29.
A Roviros Manthoulis production, written and directed by him. Features Costas Messaris, Heleni Stavropoulou, Lambros Constantaras, Theano Ioannidou; camera, Stamatis Trypos; music, Nicos Mamagakis. At Salonika Film

Festival. **Running Time, 90 MINS.**

Roviros Manthoulis was awarded the best director prize at Salonika for his work in this picture. He did a good and imaginative job and succeeded, in a way, with a mixture of sharp and scorching sarcasm and comedy. But somehow he did not strike the right balance.

The main character is a young teacher who undertakes to tutor a spoiled girl of a rich family in English. The girl is to become engaged to a rich Englishman. The teacher faces many unusual situations in rich surroundings empty of any moral value. Meanwhile, love is growing between him and his pupil. He is unhappy because he sees no way out. Everything around him is at variance with what he believes in. For the sake of his love, however, he tries to compromise and live in this sophisticated and false world, until he is deeply disappointed and revolts.

The director brought this story to the screen in a better manner than his own screenplay. He describes the empty life of the rich, modern Athenian society with a sharp sarcasm though in some sequences overdoes it. He builds the drama around the resistance of the young man to the false situations he faces, but his endeavor to seek smart items and a particular style harm the dramatic presence needed for the film.

The acting is monotonous, but Costas Messaris gives a sensitive portrayal of the young teacher. Lambros Constantaras overplays his role. The film is well edited by N. Papakyriacopoulos and the music by N. Mamagakis is good. Camerawork by Stamatis Trypos is first-rate. *Rena.*

Il Grande Colpo Dei Sette Uomini D'Oro
(Seven Golden Men Strike Again)
(ITALIAN—COLOR)

Rome, Nov. 9.

Atlantic Cinematografica production and release. Features Rosanna Podesta', Philippe Leroy, Gastone Moschin, Gabriele Tinti, Maurice Poli, Manuel Zarzo, Giampiero Albertini, Dario de Grassi, Enrico Maria Salerno. Written and directed by Marco Vicario; camera (Technicolor), Ennio Guarnieri; music, Armando Trovajoli. At Supercinema, Rome. Running Time, 103 MINS.

Albert, the Professor .. Philippe Leroy
Georgia .... Rossana Podesta'
Adolf .... Gastone Moschin
Dictator .... Enrico Maria Salerno
August .... Giampiero Albertini
Aldo .... Gabriele Tinti
Alfred .... Maurice Poli
Alfonso .... Manuel Zarzo
Antony .... Mario de Grassi

Marco Vicario looks to have another b.o. winner in this follow-up to his high-grossing "Seven Golden Men." Fans of first pic should join with new ones drawn by favorable word-of-mouth in pushing this prime example of escapist entertainment into healthy wicket business both here and abroad, especially if taken the rapid exploitation route before the audience demand for Bond-styled spoofs lags.

Story takes the "Seven Golden Men" in the "Professor's" perfectly-organized gang of big-stake thieves one step further than initial pic and into international political intrigue, which sees the group kidnapping a South American dictator for interrogation by a major power's military intelligence concerning vital hemispheric problems. At the same time, however, gang's more personal intent is to use atomic sub and other equipment furnished for above operation by the major power to bring off heist of a whole Russian shipload of gold bars. Coup and kidnapping both succeed, but windup is on ironic note with double twist, to good effect.

Pace is deliberately razzle-dazzle, and gag, gadget, and gimmick follow close one on the other, with audience panting to keep up with tongue-in-cheek shenanigans. At times, rhythm is even too fast, and some points and lines are lost in the shuffle. Also, with exception of Gastone Moschin's Adolf, the meatiest role of the lot via sometimes overplayed German accent, it's sometimes hard to distinguish one of "seven" from another, even physically. In the final analysis, however, it's the group effect that counts, and that comes off amusingly.

Philippe Leroy repeats as the British-styled gang chief and brain, while Rossana Podesta' lends ability and piquant beauty to a spoof of the sex symbol and Enrico Maria Salerno has a hilarious part as the love-hungry dictator. But the true stars of the film are the dozens (hundreds?) of gadgets ideated by Vicario which continuously delight the eye and tickle the risibilities. Production values are fine, color lensing slick, and other technical credits tops, including Armando Trovajoli's musical backdrop. *Hawk.*

The Navy Vs. The Night Monsters
(COLOR)

Okay exploitation picture aimed for specific market.

Hollywood, Nov. 16.

Realart release of George Edwards production. No character names. Stars Mamie Van Doren, Anthony Eisley; features Pamela Mason, Bill Gray, Bobby Van, Walter Sande, Edward Faulkner, Phillip Terry. Directed-scripted by Michael Hoey. Camera (DeLuxe Color), Stanley Cortez; editor, George White; asst. director, Dick Dixon. Reviewed at World Theatre, Nov. 16, '66. Running Time, 90 MINS.

"The Navy vs the Night Monsters" (packaged with "Women of the Prehistoric Planet") should do okay in its intended exploitation market. Narrative twirling about killer plants discovered in the Antarctic and transplanted to a Navy base in the South Seas en route back to the U.S. for study is imaginatively developed and should hold interest. While similar subjects of omnivorous vegetation have been done previously the George Edwards production stacks up as sometimes-exciting fare with certain mounting suspense.

Mamie Van Doren and Anthony Eisley costar, Miss Van Doren as a Navy nurse—would that service nurses were permitted to sport the sweater she wears on duty—Eisley as the officer left in charge of the island when his superior is called to Washington. Michael Hoey directs from his own script, and gets plenty of mileage from the idea of the plants threatening the entire island after killing several personnel.

Stars are well supported by Walter Sande, as a biologist; Pamela Mason, his assistant who is devoured by one of the creeping monsters; Bobby Van as a youthful ensign is also a victim. Bill Gray, Edward Faulkner and Phillip Terry lend further competent assistance.

Technical credits are all on the plus side. Stanley Cortez' color photography is interesting; George White's editing usually fast and art direction by Paul Sylos meets all demands. *Whit.*

A Midsummer Night's Dream
(BALLET—COLOR)

A stunning Yank ballet pic with b.o. potential.

Paris, Nov. 15.

Columbia and Richard David presentation and release of George Balanchine-Oberon Films production. With the New York City Ballet. Ballet conceived and choreographed by George Balanchine, from William Shakespeare's play. Directed by Balanchine, Dan Eriksen. Music, Felix Mendelssohn; camera (Eastmancolor processed Pathe Color), Arthur J. Ornitz; editor, Armond Lebowitz; art director, Albert Brenner; costumes, Karinska; main titles, Henry Wolf. Previewed in Paris. Running Time, 93 MINS.

Titania .... Suzanne Farrell
Oberon .... Edward Villella
Puck .... Arthur Mitchell
Hermia .... Patricia McBride
Lysander .... Nicholas Magallanes
Helena .... Mimi Paul
Demetrius .... Roland Vazquez
Court Dancers ..... Jacques D'Amboise,
Allegra Kent

Both ballet and film attain balance in this U.S. dance film, with neither betrayed. It is beautiful without sacrificing a full ballet to closeups, overcutting, etc., and yet is not static nor does it seem "filmed." This is due to George Balanchine's fine choreography, the expert terping, and sets that create mood and still leave room to dance sans seeming theatrical.

Dance fans should be a natural for attendance and it also has the visual flair for more general audiences, if rightly placed. It could also be a fine cultural Yank gambit abroad, with the production value and gloss for hardticket showings on its home grounds. Pic may preem at a gala benefit in Paris before bowing stateside, since it does have an international appeal on its pure dance and simple tale that is brilliantly moved from the theatre to ballet and film.

Producer Richard Davis is to be commended on the fine production dress of this Gotham-made production, plus the work of the technicians and the dancers. It is also a tribute to the overall effectiveness of the New York City Ballet.

Shakespeare's tale of the vagaries of love is clearly delineated in dance as two supernatural forest figures battle over a child and also having some humans become embroiled in it before all is straightened out.

A gnarled forest is the main backdrop for all the events except for a palace at the end. It had the right chiaruscuro and gleaming, or at times obscuring, backdrop to the terped tale. Arthur J. Ornitz's color cameras do admirably by the scenes and keep all in focus. Balanchine has adapted his choreography for the more minute pinpointing of the cameras without however, depriving it of an overall elan, robustness and grace. Although Balanchine directed the choreography and movement, Dan Eriksen, a new, young director provided the cinematic knowhow that allowed the merging of realism and fantasy that the story needs.

Arthur Mitchell is a vital, mischievous Puck. Edward Villella has drive as Oberon and Suzanne Farrell is ethereal as Princess Titania. Jacques D'Amboise and Allegra Kent are excellent in a court dance scene.

For once there is no hint of painted backdrops or stage imitations, although the entire film was made inside a far-from-large New York soundstage. But yet there is also no attempt to replace dance by visual tricks. It might be termed one of the few truly cohesive weddings of dance and film as it lays bare love's complications and does it with zestful dance, movement and an eyecatching blend of costume and sets.

All involved deserve kudos, including Henry Wolf for his inventive titles that roam about the forest and set the right mood and scene for the ballet. It is both an indelible record of a fine company at high mettle in a finely wrought ballet and a true balletic film. Right handling could have this touching regular audiences as well as dance buffs. *Mosk.*

Atout Coeur A Tokyo Pour OSS 117
(Heart Trump For OSS 117 in Tokyo)
(FRENCH-COLOR-FRANSCOPE)

Paris, Nov. 15.

Valoria release of PAC-Victory Film production. Stars Frederick Stafford, Marina Vlady; features Henri Serre, Inkijinoff. Directed by Michel Boisrond. Screenplay, Pierre Foucaud, Terence Young, Marcel Mithois, from the book by Jean Bruce; camera (Eastmancolor), Marcel Grignon; editor, Pierre Gillette. At Ambassade-Gaumont, Paris. Running Time, 90 MINS.

OSS 117 .... Frederick Stafford
Eva .... Marina Vlady
Wilson .... Henri Serre
Chief .... Inkijinoff

This is the fourth in a series about a Yank undercover man that seems to be the French answer to James Bond. In fact, the name of Terence Young, director of three of the Bond pix, is listed among the screenwriting credits. It is familiar, but has some okay derring-do and a plus in the exotic Japanese locale. Okay production dress may make this a useful dualer or playoff item abroad on its generally well done action segs, if the perky humor and inventive gadgetry of the Bond series are not up to that level here.

The agent, OSS 117, finds himself up against an undercover group, possessing small missile A-bomb warhead jobs, asking the U.S. for ransom not to blow up some of their Far East army camps. They destroy one after evacuation and the U.S. Army decides to pay the ransom, but the undercover man manages to destroy the illicit gang and save Uncle Sam a lot of dough.

Frederick Stafford is at ease in

his fight segs as the undercover man and also does okay in the female department. There is the inevitable Japanese bath with chattering females washing him down, a fight against a Samurai sword wielder and a very well done battle with a massive Japanese wrestler. There is also a man lassoed by a telephone cord and then knocked out a window to be hanged.

Marina Vlady is lovely but walks through her role of the romantic vis-a-vis and plenty of Japanese pretties also enliven the pulchritude department. It appears to have a good-sized production nut which pays off in the sets, color and neatly done car chases and action scenes so necessary in this kind of film. It appears headed for good local returns and is one of the few with definite foreign playoff possibilities. *Mosk.*

Ekdromi
(Excursion)
(GREEK)

Athens, Nov. 1.
A Costas Kanellopoulos production, directed by Takis Kanellopoulos. Features Lily Papayanni, Costas Karageorgis, Angelos Antonopoulos, Costas Lahas. Screenplay, Georges Kitsopoulos; camera, Syracos Danalis; music, Nicos Mamagakis. At Salonika Film Festival. Running Time, **90 MINS.**

Irene	Lily Papayanni
Captain	Angelos Antonopoulos
Sergeant	Costas Karageorgis
Corporal	Costas Lahas

Takis Kanellopoulos, one of the new Greek directional talents, refused to sign this picture when it was finished but later submitted it to the Salonika Festival expecting to win first prize. As a matter of fact, it was one of the best pictures shown in Salonika and, though it was not awarded a big prize, its director won a citation for "his contribution in raising the artistic level of the festival."

Film has beauty and poetry, despite its defects, and needs careful handling for bookings. But art houses abroad should welcome it.

The story involves an army captain who lives with his wife Irene in a small village near his base. He introduces his sergeant to her as his best friend and they fall in love. The two lovers are trying to find a way to escape this double life, but they find it impossible not to see each other.

During the war the captain is wounded on a dangerous mission and his sergeant lies to Irene, telling her he is dead. She believes him and tries to forget her husband in his arms. But comes the time when the captain returns home alive. The lovers decide to pass the frontier and get out of the country, but they are noticed and a posse is sent to capture the deserters. They are surrounded at the last moment but the sergeant shoots his beloved and kills himself, rather than surrender.

Director Kanellopoulos apparently could not avoid the many pitfalls this story has. It is full of improbable situations and of a lot of flashback sequences which do not add up. Many of the scenes are overdone and static.

Acting is good, especially by Lily Papayanni in the main female lead. Angelos Antonopoulos, Costas Ka-

rageorgis and Costas Lahas handling their roles well.

Actual top contribution is the excellent photography by Syracos Danalis which adds much to the beauty of the picture. He was awarded the prize for best photography at the Salonika Festival. The music by Nicos Mamagakis is emotionally and dramatically right, though much overkeyed in some sequences. Other technical credits are good. *Rena.*

Women of The Prehistoric Planet
(COLOR)

Minor entry on cosmic flight, to be packaged with "The Navy vs. the Night Monsters."

Hollywood, Nov. 16.
Realart release of George Edwards production. No character names. Stars Wendell Corey, Keith Larsen, John Agar, Paul Gilbert, Merry Anders; features Irene Tsu. Directed-scripted by Arthur Pierce. Camera (DeLuxe Color), Archie Dalzell; editor, George White; asst. director, Jack Voglin. Reviewed at World Theatre, Nov. 16, '66. Running Time, **90 MINS.**

Slotted for second half of the bill toplining "The Navy vs the Night Monsters," George Edwards' follow-up production, "Women of the Prehistoric Planet," is a handy entry about cosmic flight. Strictly in the B-category, enough novelty is displayed to maintain interest in less discriminating situations, despite considerable confusion in story line.

Wendell Corey heads cast as a fleet commander in deep space sometime in the future. His space ship has been out for six years as yarn opens. The Arthur Pierce screenplay, also directed by him, gets into trouble with the time element, in which months in space rep many years both on earth and on the planet on which one of Corey's ships has crashed. Much of the footage is devoted to Corey landing his craft on this unknown planet to search for survivors.

Capable backing is afforded Corey by Keith Larsen, an officer; John Agar as a doctor; Paul Gilbert in the comedy end; Merry Anders in communications. Probably most interesting figure is Irene Tsu, as a native of another planet who is aboard Corey's ship and who remains on the new planet after she falls in love with another native.

Archie Dalzell's color photography lends authority to the unreeling and Paul Sylos' art direction is suitable for subject which George White edits. *Whit.*

Don't Let It Get You
(NEW ZEALAND)

Auckland, Nov. 14.
Pacific Films release of John O'Shea production. Features Gary Wallace, Howard Morrison, Carmen Duncan, Normie Rowe, Herma Keil, Lew Pryme, Gwynne Owen, Kiri Te Kanawa, Gerry Merito. Directed by John O'Shea. Screenplay, Joseph Musaphia; camera, Anthony Williams; music, Patrick Flynn. Reviewed at Plaza Theatre, Auckland, N.Z., November 14 '66. Running Time, **80 MINS.**

A fast-moving, tuneful film, made with enough cinematic savvy to reflect, for the eye, the jumpy

rhythms that crowd the soundtrack. "Don't Let It Get You" is a coup for the director-cameraman team of John O'Shea and Anthony Williams. Locationed mainly in Rotorua, a New Zealand tourist mecca with geysers, boiling mud pools, and Maoris (the country's native Polynesian people) the pic, though shot in black and white, is an interesting eyeful from the opening frames. It reinforces the good visual impression registered by pair's earlier "Runaway," which otherwise came to grief by lame script and worse acting.

Cast of "Don't Let It Get You" is largely made up of Australian talent. Plot concerns antics of out-of-work drummer seeking job with a pop show and is essentially just a framework for the songs. These are mostly reminiscent of various hits of the day, and are almost all by Patrick Flynn, a composer-arranger-pianist better known for his serious work. But Flynn's score proves he has a good ear and knows the best models to imitate, and the film takes the audience along with considerable gusto and fun. Few will cavil about the soundtrack echoes.

Maori singer Howard Morrison, leading entertainer in Australia and New Zealand, has most of the songs and wrings them dry, scoring with title tune, where he is pursued by hand-held camera as he moves among audience in large auditorium, and a ballad, "I'm Home," sung while riding horseback over rolling sheep country.

None of talent on display will mean much on any but Australian-New Zealand marquees, but artists are cleverly indentified by intercutting of posters. Morrison shows up as personality of warmth and charm as well as a vital singer, though over-fast delivery of spoken lines may cause difficulty for any unused to area accents. Gary Wallace exploits talent for genial mugging to the full and handles drumsticks like a professional drummer, which is what he happens to be. *Dubb.*

Night Train To Mundo Fine

Totally inept meller, grim b.o.

Hollywood, Nov. 19.
Hollywood Star Pictures release of an Anthony Cardoza-Coleman Francis production, produced by Cardoza. Features entire cast. Written and directed by Francis. Camera, Herb. Roberts; editor, J. H. Russell; music, John Bath; title song, Ray Gregory. Reviewed at Encore Theatre, L.A., Nov. 18, '66. Running Time, **89 MINS.**

Griffin	Coleman Francis
Landis	Anthony Cardoza
Cook	Harold Saunders
Train Engineer	John Carradine
Joe	John Morrison
Cherokee Jack	George Prince
Ruby Chastain	Lanell Cado
Baylev Chastain	Tom Hanson
Sheriff	Julian Baker
Old Man	Charles Harter
Old Man's Daughter	Elaine Gibford
Newspaper Reporter	Bruce Love
Policemen	Nick Raymond, Clarence Walker
Priest, Jaime Russell	Richard Lance

"Night Train to Mundo Fine," tradeshown in 16m, is an awkwardly made low-budgeter (about $30,000), sub-standard in all departments. Plodding story line concerns an escaped convict who joins up with two drifters, thence to a

Cuban soldier-of-fortune incident, finally back to the U.S. for the convict's recapture. John Carradine sings the title tune, and appears in the first few minutes as sole marquee bait. Already grim and dim artistically and technically, absence of exploitable violence or sex augurs similar b.o. fate.

Coleman Francis wrote and directed what appears to have been a story about greed, and the depths to which it'll force men. Thin, cliche dialog plus static direction and overlength shoot down whatever merit the idea had. Performances are inept, but Francis, playing convict, and Tom Hanson, a fellow adventurer whom Francis abandons, could probably do better with stronger material.

Below the line, conditions are not any better. Herb Robert's b&w lensing is dull, largely immobile, and varying in light quality. John Bath's score sounds like a series of ill-chosen stock splicings, and Ray Gregory's title song is banal. "Mundo Fine" means end of the world, incidentally. J. H. Russell's editing to 89 minutes is flat, 'neffective.

Pic, in short, has all of the vices and none of the virtues which pop up occasionally in indie films, and its greatest liability — as always — is lack of a viable story line. *Murf.*

The Poppy Is Also a Flower
(UNITED NATIONS-COLOR)

Comet Film Distributors and Morin M. Scott release of Telsun (Euan Lloyd) production. Directed by Terence Young. Features, alphabetically, Senta Berger, Stephen Boyd, Yul Brynner, Angie Dickinson, Georges Geret, Hugh Griffith, Jack Hawkins, Rita Hayworth, Trevor Howard, Jocelyn Lane, Trini Lopez, E. G. Marshall, Marcello Mastroianni, Amedeo Nazzari, Jean Claude Pascal, Anthony Quale, Gilbert Roland, Harold Sakata, Omar Sharif, Barry Sullivan, Nadia Tiller, Eli Wallach. Screenplay, Jo Eisinger, based on story outline by Ian Fleming; camera (Eastman Color), Henry Alekan; music, composed by Georges Auric. Reviewed in N.Y., Oct. 16, '66. Running Time, **100 MINS.**

While it is the policy of VARIETY not to re-review a motion picture unless the circumstances under which it is released are markedly different from those under which it was first seen, it has done so on occasion. Such an instance was the current reissue of the Mary Pickford-Douglas Fairbanks' "Taming of the Shrew," which has been technically updated.

Another film, now being exhibited, which also merits such a second look, is "The Poppy Is Also a Flower." It was shown initially as a one-time television program as one of the projects financed by Xerox and made under the Telsun Foundation aegis for the United Nations. Since acquired for commercial theatrical release by Comet Films, a considerable amount of footage has been restored, giving the film a wider scope and dramatically changing it from its original version.

For the record, then, a second look.

From the opening shot, it is instantly apparent that director Terence Young never intended that this adventure-laden look at the international dope traffic should be limited to the small screen of a tv set.

The panoramic sweep of the badlands of Iran sets a visual pace that is met, and matched, frequently during the ensuing 100 minutes by cameraman Henry Alekan. It also needs the area provided by theatrical screens to really appreciate his Eastmancolor paintings of the entire Mediterranean area, from Iran to Geneva, with many stopovers in between.

Using a story outline by the late Ian Fleming, reportedly the last one written by the James Bond creator, screenwriter Jo Eisinger has fashioned an action-packed story that may not reform the world's dope addicts overnight but provides a fascinating insight into the international traffic in the poppy's deadly by-product and the types of characters who move in this morbid milieu. If an occasional lapse in logic occurs, or a particular character doesn't quite come off, these moments are rare and there's almost no let-up in the suspenseful scenario.

The 20-minutes-plus which producer Euan Lloyd and director Young restored after "Poppy's" solo showing on tv concentrates primarily on added characterization and violence-laden suspense that might have been considered too rough for televiewers. Theatregoers will be able to see such added moments as the ghastly shot of Trevor Howard's body after he has been worked over and drowned by minions of Gilbert Roland, the dope syndicate chief, or the prolonged fight between agent E. G. Marshall and villainous ship's captain Anthony Quayle aboard a train.

Fortunately, the big-name cast is uniformly able to restrain individual personalities sufficiently to make their brief roles believable, although the Lucky Luciano type played by Eli Wallach seems overly comic in such serious surroundings. Marshall is amazingly good as the middleaged agent, even in the obviously hazardous fight scenes, and Trevor Howard provides almost as fine a performance as his British counterpart.

Other bits that linger in the memory are Hugh Griffith's hammy Iranian sheikh, Rita Hayworth as Roland's dope-laden wife, Amedeo Nazzari's Italian police captain and a brief but brilliant scene between Yul Brynner and Jean Claude Pascal (as a rascally tribe leader). And always the excellent color photography. This one is much too good to let linger on the shelf of a tv film library and should have an excellent chance as a theatrical release once the word gets around. *Robe.*

The Christmas That Almost Wasn't
(Il Natale Che Quasi No Fu)
(ITALIAN—COLOR)

Childhood Production release of a Barry B. Yellen production. Features Rossano Brazzi, Paul Tripp, Alberto Rabagliati, Lydia Brazzi, Mischa Auer, John Karlsen, Sonny Fox. Directed by Rossano Brazzi. Screenplay, Paul Tripp; camera (Eastman Color), Alvaro Mancori; editor, Maurizio Lucidi; songs by Ray Carter (music), Paul Tripp (lyrics). Reviewed in New York, Oct. 31, '66. Running Time, **95 MINS.**
Phineas T. Prune .... Rossano Brazzi
Sam Whipple .... Paul Tripp
Santa Claus .... Alberto Rabagliati

Mrs. Santa Claus .... Lydia Brazzi
Jonathan .... Mischa Auer
Blossom .... John Karlsen
Department store owner..... Sonny Fox

(English soundtrack)

This slight children's tale, made in Italy but with an English soundtrack, may have some success in the children's market, particularly if given maximum exposure in the holiday period, but it will take some "doting" parents to sit through the entire film.

Although technically improved over some of Childhood Productions' earlier efforts, the film is sadly wanting in all departments as far as adult screen fare is concerned. Paul Tripp, who doubles from his role as scripwriter and lyricist, is actually the central figure whereas toplined Rossano Brazzi segues from directing to the role of the villain. He's responsible for much of the fun in the part of skinflint Phineas T. Prune who's about to toss Santa and wife out on their ear because they don't pay their rent. Had the rest of the cast followed Brazzi's outlandish melodramatics the results might have contained enough "spoof" to please adults instead of winding as a purely kiddie frolic.

Other than Brazzi, the cast is barely adequate although some of them, such as Lydia Brazzi (the director-actor's real life wife), had little demands made on them. John Karlsen's butler is a triumph of makeup over matter.

Scripter Paul Tripp doubles as the do-good lawyer of Santa Claus, who is physically perfect but woodenly played as portrayed by Alberto Rabagliati. Technical aspects of the film are average but will probably please the non-discriminating youthful ticketbuyer. *Robe.*

Rage
(El Mal)
(MEXICAN—COLOR)

Fairly suspenseful yarn about a doctor's race against time for Pasteur treatment; stellar names of Glenn Ford and Stella Stevens may help.

Hollywood, Nov. 22.
Columbia Pictures release of Cinematografica Jalisco (Gilberto Gazcon) production, produced in association with Joseph M. Schenck Enterprises Inc., directed by Gazcon. Stars Glenn Ford, Stella Stevens, David Reynoso. Screenplay, Teddi Sherman, Gazcon, Fernando Mendez; story, Jesus Velasquez, Guillermo Hernandez, Gazcon; camera (Pathe-Color), Rosalio Solano; music, Gustavo Cesar Carreon; editors, Carlos Savage, Walter Thompson; asst. director, Jesus Marin. Reviewed at Columbia Pictures Studios, Nov. 21, '66. Running Time, **103 MINS.**
Reuben .... Glenn Ford
Perla .... Stella Stevens
Pancho .... David Reynoso
Antonio .... Armando Silvestre
Blanca .... Ariadna Welter
Fortunato .... Jose Elias Moreno
Maria .... Dacia Gonzalez
Old Man .... Pancho Cordova
His Wife .... Susana Cabrera
Bus Driver .... David Silva
Pedro .... Quintin Bulnes
Jose .... Valentin Trujillo

"Rage", a joint Mexican-American production lensed entirely below the Border, is a moderately interesting story of a doctor's frantic race against time to reach a hospital for the Pasteur treatment against rabies. Starring Glenn Ford and David Reynoso for similar attraction in the Latin market, film is overlength in building to its major premise. Excellent performances and hard-driving direction nevertheless are afforded, as well as firstrate production values.

Produced by Cinematografica Jalisco S.A., in association with Joseph M. Schenck Enterprises Inc., film is the product of producer-director-writer Gilberto Gazcon. Richard Goldstone, acting as rep of Columbia Pictures, which distributes, was executive producer, working with Gazcon on script, casting and production problems. Color cameras were in the capable hands of Rosalio Solano, whose artistry is apparent in beautiful landscapes as well as the more intimate scenes.

The two Hollywood personalities are the only Americans in cast, balance recruited wholly from Mexican ranks. Although Mexican-made, pic was shot with English dialog, and in Latin American bookings will carry Spanish subtitles, somewhat of a switch.

Ford plays a guilt-ridden physician half-bent upon self-destruction, haunted by memory of the death of his wife and child, for which he blames himself. His base of operations is a construction camp practically in the wilderness, although he treats any one who calls upon him from miles around. He's constantly drunk, and drinking more.

Nipped by his pet dog, he finds later it has rabies, and by calculation figures he has only about 48 hours to reach a medical center where he may be treated. But before he can leave he's called upon to attend the pregnant wife of a laborer a long distance away, and the delay presents a serious time hurdle. In a jeep which finally breaks down, accompanied by the Mexican and Miss Stevens, a hooker who has been in the camp, he races thru desert and mountains in an attempt to reach the hospital before the rabies can take hold.

Good suspense is worked up in situation and Gazcon maintains mood realistically. He takes advantage of the varied locations to present additional handicaps for Ford in his mad dash for treatment. Script on which he collabed with Teddi Sherman and Fernando Mendez also allows him to turn to lighter moments in his direction, such as a bathing sequence in which Miss Stevens and six other femmes who have arrived from a border town to provide divertisement for the construction men, shower nude, good for exploitation. First half of film deals with femmes' arrival in camp and Miss Stevens staying on after she misses the truck back.

Ford etches a rugged characterization, particularly as panic begins to take hold in what appears to be a hopeless effort in reaching the hospital in time. Miss Stevens likewise is effective in a role which permits dramatic range as well as sexy approach. Reynoso similarly scores as the husband of the woman about to have a baby, who forces Ford at gunpoint to deliver his wife. In brief roles, Armando Silvestre, Jose Elias Moreno, Dacia Gonzalez, Quintin Bulnes and Ariasna Welter lend good support.

Technical credits are on the plus side, including music score by Gustavo Cesar Carreon and editing by Carlos Savage and Walter Thompson. *Whit.*

Nashville Rebel
(SONGS-TECHNISCOPE-COLOR)

Country music hoedown with top names; good returns indicated for its particular market.

Hollywood, Nov. 23.
American International release of Fred A. Niles production. Stars Waylon Jennings, Tex Ritter, Sonny James, Faron Young, Loretta Lynn, Porter Wagoner, Wilburn Brothers, Henny Youngman; features Gordon Oas-Heim, Mary Frann, Ce Ce Whitney, Cousin Jody, Archie Campbell. Directed by Jay J. Sheridan. Screenplay, Ira Kerns, Sheridan; original story, Click Weston; camera (Technicolor), John Eisenbach; music, Robert Blanford. Reviewed at Joe Shore's projection room, Nov. 23, '66. Running Time, **95 MINS.**
Arlin Grove .... Waylon Jennings
Tex Ritter .... Himself
Sonny James .... Himself
Faron Young .... Himself
Loretta Lynn .... Herself
Porter Wagoner .... Himself
Wilburn Brothers .... Themselves
Henny Youngman .... Himself
Wesley Lang .... Gordon Oas-Heim
Molly Morgan............. Mary Frann
Margo Powell .... Ce Ce Whitney
Cousin Jody .... Himself
Archie Campbell .... Himself

Country music buffs should have a field day with this musical which topbills some of the stars of the radio-created "Grand Old Opry" of WSM, Nashville, and specialists in their field. There are probably enough devotees of this stylized singing to show a good profit for the Fred A. Niles production, filmed in its actual Nashville locale for atmospheric effect, and color feature carries rich exploitation potential — for its particular market.

Script by Ira Kerns and director Jay J. Sheridan is built to showcase the singing wares of cast, with enough straight narrative to keep the ball rolling. RCA Victor artist Waylon Jennings makes his screen bow as an unknown singer whom an unscrupulous attorney builds into a star, then after an altercation proceeds to tear down. Set in Nashville, cameras go into the Grand Old Opry House for part of action, which permits a number of show's stellarites to appear.

Jennings displays a pleasant, ingratiating personality and sings five numbers, including title song. Others are "Green River," which he waxed for Victor; "Long Way from Home," "Nashville Bum" and "Silver Ribbons." Each is a standout.

Six "Opry" stars and groups appear with Jennings to give additional country music substance to unfoldment. Tex Ritter is on with "Hillbilly Heaven"; Porter Wagoner and his combo sock over "Country Music's Gone to Town"; Sonny James charms with "Do What You Do, Do Well"; Faron Young scores with "Sweet Dream of You"; The Wilburn Brothers and Loretta Lynn do "Christmas at the Opry" and Miss Lynn singles with "You Ain't Woman Enough," both outstanding in their class.

On the narrative side, Mary Frann pleases as Jennings' country bride who leaves him when his job keeps him away from her, and Gordon Oas-Heim handles himself well as singer's discoverer. Ce Ce Whitney lends a further assist as Oas-Heim's companion given job of taking some of the country out of the new discovery. Henny Youngman has a minute in a Chicago nitery as a wise-cracking comic.

Niles gives his feature appropriate production values and Sheridan's direction is okay, as are technical credits. *Whit.*

Persona
(Masks)
(SWEDISH)
Paris, Nov. 25.

Svensk Filmindustri release and production. Stars Bibi Andersson, Liv Ullman; features Gunnar Bjornstrand, Margareta Krook. Written and directed by Ingmar Bergman; camera, Sven Nykvist; editor, Ulla Nyghe. Previewed in Paris. Running Time, 85 MINS.

Alma	Bibi Andersson
Elisabeth	Liv Ullman
Husband	Gunnar Bjornstrand
Doctor	Margareta Krook

After two years of silence—since 'The Silence"—Swedish filmmaker Ingmar Bergman is back with a new opus, his 27th. It is not amusing, sometimes confusing, and he has veered from seeking an answer as to God's presence or silence and now looks directly at people. But big themes are still his forte, for here it is the very essence of a personality. Such questions as whether one can really be or only seem, and the duality of character and the interchangeability of fe-

male psyches, are also dealt with.

Bergman displays his usual rigorous style and now appears at the height of his technical mastery. But a return to his earlier pic styles that dealt in symbolic depictions of female traumas, thoughts and impasses, like "Thirst" and "Prison," seems somewhat too probing to make them always clear, and are often equivocal as to exact meaning. Certainly art can just display an experience, but here it is somewhat too weighted with talk, symbols and allusions to truly disturb, move or clarify life or womankind.

There is no denying the absorbing theme and the perfection in direction, acting, editing and lensing. It is hypnotic in its first part as a stark black-and-white imagery tells of a noted actress who has suddenly stopped dead during a performance of a Greek tragedy and has refused to talk since. She is tended by a nurse and they are finally sent off to a beach island house together under orders of a psychiatrist. Here the roles suddenly seem reversed for the nurse talks about herself, her attitudes toward her actions as opposed to her beliefs, and just about strips herself bare.

The patient listens, reacts and it is she giving solace; there is even a hint of love, not on a lesbianic plane but as a bare human need and love for another. Bergman keeps the first half intriguing by cannily right scenes of the women together, one listening and one talking, sharing things and then breaking into it by a sudden revelation to the nurse that the other, under her silence, is a bit patronizing of her.

There follows a sudden whiplash scene as the nurse abuses her out of pride and makes her say a word when she threatens to scold her. The nurse even lets her step on a piece of glass she has seen but not picked up. Here Bergman suddenly resorts to a Brechtian bit by showing it is a film through simulating a ripping of the pic and then a burning. The film seems misguided in these effects.

Garbled bits of soundtrack are also used as well as one scene in which the nurse tells the patient why she thinks she has withdrawn from life, which is then repeated exactly. He has also devised a shock pre-title scene of a hand being impaled by a big nail (does it mean his moving from religioso themes, or are both women crucified?) and quick scenes from early silent pix and film rushing through a projector, the arc lighting up, etc. At the end the arc is seen to go out on a projector and it is silence.

Bergman has devised a difficult but fascinating film that should raise pros and cons in critical circles. It looks like primarily an arty film needing right handling and good placing and followups on the lively reactions sure to be raised by this irritating, brilliant, beguiling and sometimes baffling filmmaker.

The two actresses are handled with the usual Bergman insight into women and are extraordinarily effective. Bibi Andersson's distraught, knowing, naive, helpful and then resentful performance of the nurse is a tour-de-force, and Liv Ullman's patient has the right luminous, questioning and sometimes impenetrable face and pro-

jection for the part of the beauteous but mute actress.

Whether dream, reality, pyschodrama or symbolical opus is not clear, but elements of all are there. The patient's husband turns up and is blind and makes love to the nurse. At the end their faces photographically are made up of half of each and fuse. The two actresses do look alike and this duality works visually and on a narrative plane.

A scene of the nurse telling of an orgy is one of the most explicit scenes of this kind ever heard. But it is never scabrous since it rings true as the women, at least the nurse, tell all that happened to them sans moral restrictions. Film is literary, in a good sense, in that talk is fused with visuals but gives a probing, revealing if a not always completely clear aspect of the women at all times.

Bergman has come up with probably one of his most masterful films technically and in conception, but also one of his most difficult ones. It is not that compassion is needed, but there has to be some outlook, some point. Bergman seems content to make both guilty and somewhat innocent as victims of the world's iniquities.

It appears mainly for special usage and arty spots abroad, with playoff doubtful. The title "Persona" comes from the masks used by the players in the classic Greek tragedies. It is Bergman coming back to probing people instead of the heavens. It is technically superior. *Mosk.*

White, Red. Yellow, Pink
(ITALIAN—PART-COLOR)

Four-part Italian import with too-far-out Italo humor for most American audiences.

Hollywood, Nov. 25.

Seymour Borde & Associates release of Francesco Mazzei production, presented by S. S. & B. Film Productions Inc. Stars Carlo Guiffre, Anita Ekberg, Agnes Spaak, Yoko Tani, Maria Grazia Buccella; features Sandro Dori, Giancarlo Cobelli, Marcella Ruffini, Claudia Gianotti. Directed by Massimo Midi. Music, Piero Umiliani. Reviewed at National Screen Service projection room, Nov. 22, '66. Running Time, 94 MINS.

"WHITE—'The Unkindest Cut'	
Albachiaria	Anita Ekberg
Vitaliano	Carlo Guiffre
The Mute	Sandro Dori
"RED"—'Veni, Vidi, Vici'	
Apollodorus	Carlo Guiffre
Poppaea	Maria Grazia Buccella
Nero	Giancarlo Cobelli
Sulpicia	Marcella Ruffini
"YELLOW"—'Suicides Anonymous'	
Brighenti	Carlo Guiffre
Enrichetta	Agnes Spaak
Mrs. Brighenti	Claudia Gianotti
"PINK"—'The First'	
Johnny	Carlo Guiffre
Yoko	Yoko Tani

(*English Subtitles*)

Italo film humor doesn't always parallel the American variety, and even for the art house trade this Italian import probably will have rough going. "White, Red, Yellow, Pink," a four-part excursion into Italian comedy, is described in the credits as "a multi-colored quartet of diversified comments on the many faces of love." What it boils down to is old-fashioned low comedy in the Italian manner with a few plot gimmicks aimed at tickling the spectator's funnybone.

English-dubbed dialog frequently is of poor quality.

The four sequences are entirely unrelated but each stars Carlo Guiffre who plays a far-removed character in each. In "White"— "The Unkindest Cut," he's a vet who falls in love briefly with a femme who castrates pigs; in "Pink"—"The First," he portrays a modern-day Casanova who gets involved with a Japanese babe and —hold on—he not only gets pregnant but has a baby. Finale in this sequence, which closes the pic, has the babe dragging him onto the pad again and his begging her not to make him pregnant again.

Three of the sequences are in black-and-white and the second, titled "Red"—'Veni, Vidi, Vici,' set in Rome in year 64 A.D., when Nero lit his bonfire, is in Technicolor. Remaining sequence, "Yellow"—"Suicides Anonymous," casts Guiffre as a wealthy industrialist with both a wife and mistress.

Anita Ekberg stars with Guiffre in "White" and Maria Grazia Buccella, playing Nero's Poppaea whom he meets in a milk bath, topbills with him in "Red." Agnes Spaak is the mistress and Claudia Gianotti the wife in "Yellow" and Yoko Tani, who does a strip job, is his dalliance in "Pink."

Francesco Mazzei is listed as producer and Massimo Midi's direction is about as subtle as a bop on the head. *Whit.*

Zoldar
(Green Years)
(HUNGARIAN)
Paris, Nov. 25.

Hungarofilm release of Mafilm production. With Benedek Toth, Virag Darab, Gabor Koncz. Directed by Istvan Gall. Screenplay, Imre Gyongyossy, Gall; camera, Miklos Herczenik; music, Andras Szollosy. At Ranelagh, Paris. Running Time, 95 MINS.

Marton	Benedek Toth
Bori	Virag Darab
Laszlo	Gabor Koncz
Eszter	Judit Meszlery

A timeless theme of a young man leaving the farm for the big city and the university is gently unfolded in this pic. But this is Hungary before the 1956 uprising, and its look at conditions has a deeper interest than most pix of this kind. Its known delineation of character and its forthrightness could have this of some interest for foreign spots.

However, this is still about another time and, if it foreshadows the discontent and corruption of the era, it still appears a bit remote and muted. The boy in question finds love but then a rebuff when he finds his girl has been, and is still, having an affair with an older man.

He is against her being chastened in public by the young school Communist group but leaves the girl anyway and then tries to help a friend, railroaded off to prison by what appears to be higherups when he tries to attack one of the leading university powers for misconduct.

The pic castigates Stalinist politics of the time and threats of the difficulty of finding one's own way under these conditions with a familiar tale that benefits from good acting and mounting. Direction is unassuming but sometimes a little too rambling. Some dramatic scenes need more insight. *Mosk.*

The Witches
(BRITISH-COLOR)

Competent thriller, but lacking the horror that "voodoo" suggests. Good performances with Joan Fontaine's name to sell.

London, Nov. 22.
Warner-Pathe release of Hammer Film (Anthony Nelson Keys) production presented by Associated British-Pathe. Stars Joan Fontaine, Alec McCowen, Kay Walsh; features Ann Bell, Ingrid Brett, Gwen Ffrangcon-Davies, Duncan Lamont. Directed by Cyril Frankel. Screenplay by Nigel Kneale, from Peter Curtis's novel, "The Devil's Own"; camera (Technicolor), Arthur Grant; editor, James Needs; music, Richard Rodney Bennett. At Warner Theatre, London, Nov. 21, '66. Running Time, 91 MINS.
Gwen Mayfield .... Joan Fontaine
Stephanie Bax .... Kay Walsh
Alan Bax .... Alec McCowen
Sally .... Ann Bell
Linda .... Ingrid Brett
Dowsett .... John Collin
Valerie .... Michele Dotrice
Granny Rigg ... Gwen Ffrangcon-Davies
Bob Curd .... Duncan Lamont
Dr. Wallis .... Leonard Rossiter
Ronnie Dowsett ...... Martin Stephens
Mrs. Dowsett .... Carmen McSharry
Mrs. Curd .... Viola Keats
Mrs. Creek .... Shelagh Fraser
Tom .... Bryan Marshall

Director Cyril Frankel and producer Anthony Nelson Keys have assembled a very professional cast for "The Witches." Despite that, this Nigel Kneale script doesn't spark off enough horror and tension to make the picture more than routine entertainment. Voodoo should be either highly horrific or incredible. Former is normally more effective.

' Joan Fontaine is a schoolmistress who endures a horrible traumatic witch-doctor experience in an African mission. She seeks a new, peaceful life in a British village as headmistress of the local school, but she runs into some odd situations. Two of her young pupils, great friends, are regarded with hostility by the local villagers. The boy (Martin Stephens) is suddenly struck ill, his father is found mysteriously drowned, dolls with pins in them are found on trees.

With memories of her African experience, Miss Fontaine realizes that the village is under some strange spell. But who is the guilty person? The young girl's sinister looking grandma? The two who run the school, who are an odd journalist woman and her brother who is posing as a clergyman? Miss Fontaine herself? So the character red herrings are neatly built up and lead up to a climactic devil-ritualistic orgy in which Miss Fontaine manages to save the potential victim.

All this keeps interest alive, but is fairly synthetic in atmosphere. Result is that there are some unintended yocks creeping into situations not designed for them. Frankel has directed the slightly phony script with skill, and Arthur Grant's Technicolor lensing of a typical country village is fine. There's also a quietly effective score by Richard Rodney Bennett.

But, mainly, it is the acting that keeps this pic alive. Miss Fontaine looks delightful and brings a sensitive air to her thesping, but there's not enough fiber in her role to give her full scope. Kay Walsh is excellent as the enigmatic journalist and Gwen Frangcon-Davies, making one of her rare screen appearances, is dominating as the grandmother. Alec McCowen, a fine actor but not a box-office personality, struggles with a dull, ill-defined part. The younger element emerges rather better. Brief appearances by Ann Bell as a junior schoolmistress are vivid, Ingrid Brett makes a striking debut as the ill-starred teenage victim of this village drama, and Michele Dotrice and Martin Stephens are also prominent in minor roles.

But this one has the air of a film that has lost its way. An amiable, but somewhat tepid drama where it could, and should, have been taut, tense and chillin' in its impact. *Rich.*

Once Upon a War
(Der var engang en krig)
(DANISH)

Copenhagen, Nov. 17.
Nordisk Film Kompagni production and release. Written by Klaus Rifbjerg. Directed by Palle Kjaerulff-Schmidt. Featuring Ole Busck, Jan Heinig Hansen, Yvonne Ingdal; camera, Claus Loof; in charge of production, Bo Christensen; music 1939-44 recordings of Leo Mathiesen, Chopin and Beethoven. Reviewed at Grand Theatre, Copenhagen, Nov. 16, '66. Running Time, 95 MINS.

With this third mutual effort, Klaus Rifbjerg and Palle Kjaerulff-Schmidt finally come into their own as major Scandinavian filmmakers. The writer-director team scored minor international hits with "Weekend" and "Two," but "Once Upon A War" seems sure to capture wider audiences even if, especially in the U.S., it will probably remain an art theatre item. The film's popular impact, however, would seem to be no smaller than, for instance, the new wave of Czech films.

"Once Upon A War" is not really a war film. There is no firmly defined plot, only a thin storyline about the dreams and actions of a 15-year-old boy living in suburban Copenhagen during the German occupation. The boy is no problem kid, but he has problems. He is in love with his older sister's 22-year-old girlfriend and dreams dreams of glory about rescuing her and all their friends from a German raid. He is more active in the attack—with sticks and shouts staged by himself and his playmates—on a remote shack where an unseen couple of lovers have sought refuge.

The boy's milieu is a protected one. His parents are not directly involved in the war. They are nice people, no less, and no more understanding of adolescence than most other parents. When confronted with real-life Germans, the boy sticks his tongue out at them—and dashes around the corner on his bike. All in all, the German presence and the war itself are more felt than seen throughout the film and throughout the thoughts and actions of the characters.

Kjaerulff-Schmidt has certainly not made heroes out of his Danes in "Once Upon A War," but he does not mock them, either. He uses the war years only as a background for reflecting a young boy's minor joys and conflicts, and he might just as well have chosen a mid-Victorian or other historical epoch to add local color in time and place.

Ole Busck, an amateur, performs magnificently as the young boy. Yvonne Ingdal, a proven young Danish actress, also gives a brilliant performance that is entirely fresh and unspoiled by theatrical attitudes. Claus Loof's camera follows the action and each chosen locale softly and discreetly. This is a sentimental film, but the sentiment is never contrived, always straight from the heart, and the heartbeat of "Once Upon A War" is a noble one. *Kell.*

La Nuit Des Adieux
(Nights of Farewell)
(FRENCH-RUSSIAN-70M-COLOR)

Paris, Nov. 29.
Cocinor release of Alkam-CICC-Cocinor-Lenfilm production. With Gilles Segal, Nathalie Velitchko, Oleg Strigenov, Jacques Ferriere, Nicolas Tcherkossov. Directed by Jean Dreville. Screenplay, Paul Andreota, Alexandre Galitch; camera (Sovcolor-Eastmancolor), Michel Kelber; editor, Claude Nicole. At Gaumont Palace, Paris, Running Time, 97 MINS.
Petipas .... Gilles Segal
Macha .... Nathalie Velitchko
Minkh .... Jacques Ferriere
Highness .... Nicolas Tcherkossov
Sister .... Sabine Lods
\

The 70m size and color have been used to make an oldfashioned biopic based on the life of the noted 19th century French dancer and choreographer who modernized the Russo St. Petersburg Ballet and is now considered the father of modern ballet.

Film is soapy and melodramatic, with only some token ballet scenes and Russian lensing plus factors. It appears mainly for European spots with U. S. chances slim.

A noted mime, Gilles Segal, who worked with Marcel Marceau, plays Marius Petipas, the young French dancer signed for the Russian Ballet. He can fake a few dance needs but is hard put to give a convincing picture of a man followed from youth to middle age. But Nathalie Velitchko, a dancer, has fresh appeal and some fetching dance segs before an untimely death.

Pic uses the conventional progression of commentary to fill gaps, lackadaisically done montages for the passage of time, and obviously planted tearjerking scenes and unimaginative narration. There are only a few dance segs, in spite of his profession, but some good views of old St. Petersburg, now Leningrad.

Picture makes a pitch for Soviet-French rapprochement via Petipas and Tchaikovsky teaming up to do the first truly modern ballet to mark the genius of each country. It looks like a political as well as business venture. *Mosk.*

Igy Jottem
(My Way)
(HUNGARIAN)

Paris, Nov. 24.
Hungarofilm release of Mafilm production. With Andras Kozak, Sergei Nikonenko. Directed by Miklos Jancso. Screenplay, Gyula Hernadi, from the book by Imre Vadasz; camera, Tamas Somlo; editor, Zoltan Farkas. At Ranelagh, Paris. Running Time, 100 MINS.
Student .... Andras Kozak
Kolia .... Sergei Nikonenko

Tale of a young student who strays into war's way near the end manages to avoid sentimentality or much overt propaganda, but does unfold slowly if always maintaining visual and character interest. It appears lacking in that extra fillip of human insight and dramatic intensity for art use abroad, although its knowing look at the human side of war may make it of interest for special situations.

A 17-year-old Hungarian boy is caught up in a Russian dragnet near the end of the last war. His youth has him spared execution and he is billeted with a young Russian who is based alone on the plains tending cows and supplying milk to the army, picked up at intervals. Though they cannot communicate, friendship and mutual esteem spring up.

They cavort among ruins, chase a naked girl when they find her swimming, and slowly evolve a true companionship. But the Russian is suffering from an old wound and becomes very ill. The boy tries to get help, but fails, and the Russian dies. He goes off in the Russian's uniform and is beaten up by some Magyar refugees.

It seems simple, but it does give a good deal of the different effects on people as the war nears its end. It is sensitively directed, eschewing sentimentalism, with nicely etched performances by the principals. It has a fine technical dress and also a subtle look at the ambivalent Hungarian attitudes toward the Russians. *Mosk.*

Grieche sucht Griechin
(Once a Greek)
(GERMAN—COLOR)

Berlin, Nov. 22.
Nora release of Franz Seitz production. Stars Heinz Ruehmann, Irina Demick; features Hannes Messemer, Hanne Wieder. Directed by Rolf Thiele. Screenplay, Georg Laforet (Seitz), based on comedy by Friedrich Duerrenmatt; camera (Eastmancolor), Wolf Wirth; music, Rolf Wilhelm; settings, Wolf Englert, Robert Stratil; editing, Inge Taschner. At Gloria Palast, West Berlin. Running Time, 93 MINS.
Archilochos .... Heinz Ruehmann
Chloe .... Irina Demick
Fahrcks .... Hannes Messemer
Georgette .... Hanne Wieder
Petit-Paysan .... Charles Regnier
President .... Walter Rilla

There is good reason to believe that "Greek" will emerge as a topflight moneymaker in this country. The Heinz Ruehmann name is still powerful enough to lure the masses. And there is Friedrich Duerrenmatt whose same-titled "prose comedy" furnished the basis for this Franz Seitz production. His name, too, means plenty. "Greek" should also do comparatively well outside its homegrounds.

This film shows that Rolf Thiele is still one of Germany's better directors. It is certainly not the best Thiele film and the performances by the central players cannot be called masterpieces. But pic shows directorial imagination in many instances and strong technical assets. Those are definite advantages, although the witty plot could have been exploited to better and more amusing advantage.

Ruehmann enacts the title role in the manner his many adherents expect, but the more fastidious viewer would have preferred to see less Ruehmann and more Duerrenmatt on the screen. The satirical and social-critical elements contained in the original remain too much on the surface in this.

It is the story of a middleaged bookkeeper of Greek origin living in an imaginary country which, however, can be easily described as Switzerland. A bachelor, he has never seen the land of his forefathers but has a soft spot in his heart for it. His wish is to marry someone of Greek blood. He takes an ad ("A Greek Is Looking For a Greek" which, incidentally, is the German translation of the original title) which brings him together with a beautiful Greek-born girl. He is extremely happy to find such a sweet creature and she is content with him. But the bookkeeper is set back when he suddenly discovers that his girl has a dubious past. The desperate bookkeeper is on the verge of committing suicide, but his love for the girl is bigger and so a happy end is only natural.

Ruehmann, as indicated, is once again Ruehmann. Of Irina Demick, a truly international beauty (a Russian-born Swiss national living in Paris and Rome) it can be said that she's truly a treat for the eye and is okay in her role. The best polished performances are turned in by a lineup of supporters, notably Hanne Wieder who helps Ruehmann to find his Greek-born woman, Walter Rilla as the president of the imaginery country in which the action occurs, Rudolf Rhomberg as Ruehmann's brother, and Franz Kutschera who contributes an amusing study of a bishop.

Technical credits are very impressive. This particularly applies to the excellent color lensing of Wolf Wirth. The score by Rolf Wilhelm is also an asset. The script, incidentally, was written by Georg Laforet, whose real name is Franz Seitz, producer of this Nora release. *Hans.*

Palaces of a Queen
(BRITISH-COLOR)

Absorbing documentary tour of the treasures of six British Royal Palaces, produced by Rank's "Look At Life" team by authority of the Queen. Should appeal to all who when touring like rubber-necking at historic show-places.

London, Dec. 1.
Rank release and presentation. Produced by George Grafton Green. Directed by Michael Ingrams; treatment, Alec Clifton-Taylor; commentary written by Christopher Hibbert and narrated by Michael Redgrave; music arranged and conducted by Michael Sargeant, featuring the Royal Philharmonic Orchestra; editor, Roy Drew; camera (Eastmancolor), Peter Cannon. At Odeon, Leicester Square, London. Running Time, **80 MINS.**

Many involved in the Coronation film, "A Queen Is Crowned," and the weekly Rank "Look At Life" documentaries have brought their expertise to this absorbing tour of six Royal Palaces, by authority of the Queen. In rich color and with searching cameras it shows beauties and treasures never before seen in such closeup detail, particularly in furniture, tapestries paintings and cartings. In addition to being a closer peek than would be possible on a real tour, it is less hard on the feet.

"Palaces of a Queen" should prove a real winner with the many who enjoy visiting ornate show-places, stately homes, art galleries and museums, and that includes people of all countries. In Britain it will be hitched with the new Cliff Richard film at the Odeon, Leicester Square. On release it will go tandem with "The Quiller Memorandum," a smartly contrasted double.

The six Royal Palaces featured in this dignified but lively doc, which cost around $168,000 to bring in, are Buckingham, Windsor, St. James's, Hampton Court, Kensington and Edinburgh's Holyroodhouse. Peter Cannon's Eastmancolor camera strays through stately halls, gardens and art galleries, many of which have never been seen before by the public and lingers lovingly on the accumulation of hundreds of years of history. Pic gets away to a slow but stirring start with excellent aerial views of the Thames, the river of palaces, thence to the Royal pads themselves. Producer George Grafton Green and director Michael Ingrams, though slightly handicapped by a lack of human beings in the film, have surmounted this by bringing vividly to life the subjects of paintings and statuary, and suggesting a sense of pageantry.

Helped considerably by advice from Royalty's experts, Alec Clifton-Taylor, art historian, has built up a packed-with-interest screenplay which Christopher Hibberd has embellished with an informative, dignified script that has a quiet vein of humor when needed and brings out the characteristics of past Royalty and their contributions to the treasures shown in the film.

Sir Michael Redgrave puts over the commentary professionally and with a sense of knowhow and af-

fection for his job. A skillful score arranged and played by Sir Malcolm Sargent with the Royal Philharmonic Orchestra and relying on music by such masters as Handel, Elgar, Bliss and Walford Davies, is a plus.

Roy Drew, the editor, might well have chipped 10 minutes or so from the running time with advantage, but with the wealth of material at the team's disposal he did a slick job in keeping it down to as little as 80 minutes.

This is the sort of prestige film that can and should be made from time to time and, handled with sagacity, it could pay off financially as well. *Rich.*

Der Brief
(The Letter)
(GERMAN—COLOR)

Berlin, Nov. 27.
A Peter Genee production, no release as yet. With Vlado Kristl, Mechthild Engel, Karin Fehler, Maria Fischer, Eva Hofmeister. Directed and written by Kristl; camera (Eastmancolor), Wolf Wirth; music, Gerhard Bommersheim; editor, Eva Zeyn. At Academy of Arts, West Berlin. Running Time, **83 MINS.**

Vlado Kristl, a Yugoslav working in Germany, specializes in pix of which the ordinary patron can make neither head nor tail. There is nothing conventional about his work, this even to the extent that the most imaginative professional critic feels puzzled or—this is certainly within the bounds of possibility — ridiculed. Kristl, a real wag around here, admits that he himself often doesn't know what he's driving at, and that there is no chance that the general audience will ever understand his pix. A plausible answer to the natural question why he is employing such a mass medium as the film has still to be given by him.

As with "The Dam," his first full length feature, "The Letter" has no chance for the regular circuit and can be classified as a waste of time, energy and celluloid. except perhaps for those few who go for the abnormal at any price.

What's worthwhile about "Letter"? Some sequences display a certain surrealistic beauty which, however, may have been accidental. As a gimmick for insiders, pic employs some faces known to the trade. For example, the four young men who carry Kristl's coffin (he "plays" the central figure in this) in the windup are the Schamoni Brothers—Viktor, Peter, Ulrich and Thomas—who all work in the native film biz.

Credit is given to Wolf Wirth, a prominent German cameraman, but one can take it for granted that it was Kristl who took care of the lensing. Same goes for the editing. *Hans.*

Der Bucklige von Soho
(The Hunchback of Soho)
(GERMAN—COLOR)

Berlin, Nov. 28.
Constantin release of Rialto-Film (Horst Wendlandt) production. With Guenther Stoll, Pinkas Braun, Gisela Uhlen, Eddi Arent. Directed by Alfred Vohrer. Screenplay, Herbert Reinecker, adapted from several Edgar Wallace novels; camera (Eastmancolor), Karl Loeb; music, Peter Thomas; editor, Susanne Paschen. Running Time, **92 MINS.**
Inspector Hopkins ...... Guenther Stoll
Allan Davies .... Pinkas Braun
Reverend .... Eddi Arent
Sir John ...... Siegfried Schuerenberg
Wanda Merville .... Monika Peitsch
Lady Marjorie .... Agnes Windeck
General Perkins . Hubert von Meyerinck
Mrs. Tyndal .... Gisela Uhlen
Gladys .... Uta Levka
The Hunchback .... Richard Haller

This is Horst Wendlandt's first Edgar Wallace filmization in color. Of the 21 Wallace pix turned out by Wendlandt's Rialto so far, this is one of the very best. Pic offers a well balanced mixture of suspense, horror and humor which in this form should find appreciation from the critics. Wallace pix are still going strong here. "Hunchback" should be a particularly stout b.o. contender here and is recommended for export.

Herbert Reinecker, vet screenwriter, utilized ingredients from several Wallace novels for this production. The plot concerns an American girl who comes to London for a huge inheritance. Some vicious characters kidnap her and put someone else in her place to collect the fortune. In view of the fact that there are so many dubious people involved, Scotland Yard has tough going. Justice, however, is given big help inasmuch as most of the evildoers wipe themselves out. There is a large number of corpses along the way.

Suspense plays a major role. The number of suspects comes to 19. The horror stems mainly from a hunchback in the service of the gangsters who looks like a medieval torturer. Comedy relief is supplied by a blockhead type of high-rank Scotland Yard official and a number of eccentric society people.

The acting is good. Guenther Stoll, rather new to the screen, enacts a Scotland Yard inspector and commands attention for his nonchalant way of handling dangerous situations. He is a sure win for the screen and should be a good bet for similar roles. Pinkas Braun and Eddi Arent, the latter in the guise of a clergyman, contribute some effective gangster portrayals. The whole cast is well chosen.

Director Alfred Vohrer shows that he has learned a lot in the thriller field. Film is never dull and shows more directorial imagination than most German pix of this type.

As usual with a production personally supervised by Wendlandt, this one makes a polished impression. Lensing by Karl Loeb and the score by Peter Thomas are also assets. In fact everyone concerned with this production displays much knowhow. Rialto's first Wallace tinter is a fine entry among the many cops-and-robbers pix that are made here and of which only a comparatively few stir critical interest. *Hans.*

The Offering
(CANADIAN)

Brightly - photographed but dully-scripted Canadian feature film set in Toronto. Playoff seen via the film society and campus. Film has freshness of youth and rarity of being Canadian.

Toronto, Nov. 26.
Private release of a Secter Film production. Executive producer, Samuel Roy. Directed by David Secter. Screenplay by Martin Lager, Secter, Iain

Ewing, Jan Steen, Gillian Lennox; camera, Stanley Lipinski; editor, Tony Lower; music, Paul Hoffert; costumes, Warren Hartman. Reviewed at the Odeon Danforth Theatre, Toronto, Nov. 25. Running Time, **80 MINS.**

Mei-lin	Kee Faun
Gordon	Ratch Wallace
Jung-ling	Ellen Yamasaki
Jack	Marvin Goldhar
Tien	Gene Mark

Clumsy and almost melodramatic best describe the plot of "The Offering," one of the few Canadian feature films ever made. Produced by 23-year-old former U. of Toronto student David Secter and given a commercial showing first in Toronto, "The Offering" is a hodgepodge of pseudo-political overtones.

Yet the film is brightly photographed by Stanley Lipinski and is set against the Toronto background using its new $30,000,000 City Hall, the city's modern airport, expressways, parks, Chinese restaurants and Royal Alexandra legit theatre at a socially accented first night.

The plot deals with a stilted relationship between a female member of a visiting Peking Opera troupe and a theatre stagehand. He pursues. She holds back in enigmatic Oriental fashion. He pursues again. She goes along, but the relationship is blocked finally at the end because she is a Red Chinese and has to return home where she isn't free.

The performers, all non-union, just stare or give off a blankness of expression most of the time, but even so there is a freshness about them and about the film's general bouncy pace that is often appealing.

The film still needs cropping to exclude irrelevant bits and characters that don't bear a relationship to the subject under review. There are bits of dialogue and scenes that are left dangling in midair.

Secter's film may be only for the film society and university campus box offices, but with some trimming it might scrape through in a few art houses. *Adil.*

Pondeljak Ili Utorak
(Monday or Tuesday)
(YUGOSLAVIAN-COLOR)
Paris, Dec. 4.

Jadran Film release and production. With Slobodan Dimitrijevic, Pavle Vujisic, Jagoda Kaloper, Olivera Vuco. Renata Freishon. Directed by Vatroslav Mimica. Screenplay Fedor Vidas, Mimica; camera (Owow Color), Tomislav Pinter. At Renalagh, Paris. Running Time, **75 MINS.**

Marko	Slobodan Dimitrijevic
Mistress	Pavle Vujisio
Wife	Jagoda Kaloper
Father	Olivera Vuco
Mother	Renata Freishon

Definite influences of Fellini, Antonioni and the French New Wave, with even a dash of the U.S. Underground Cinema abound in this look at a man's thoughts, outlooks and past during an ordinary day in his life. But this fragmented pic is handled knowingly by director Vatroslav Mimica, with the progression clear and the visuals telling in giving a picture of the times and the immediate past of this Eastern country.

The director is also an animator and this helps in his use of splintered scenes and the mixture of the real and unreal in a smooth flow of juxtaposition. In bed, things remind him of his youth, his father's murder during the war and his present mistress and ex-wife and his child. At work, his thoughts mix with his chores and the pic evolves as a look at a young disoriented journalist who longs for some sort of escape from the things he cannot cope with.

It does give a grim picture of bureaucratic dawdling and a life that seems to lack some polarity. The film sometimes gets repetitious and lacks a certain dramatic force, but makes up for it in fine observation, playing and photographic snap.

Its fairly subjective form makes this mainly for arty use abroad. There is a nice satiric and comic bite to it as well as a gentle melancholy as the man reacts to pettiness around him as well as the good things like children, love and his attempts to write or communicate more clearly with others.

Color is mixed with black and white and stock footage is also incorporated in this fairly way out study of a man and his inner self and remembrances. It is just that it relies a bit too much on external symbols to be able to make the characters come more to life and give a more human feel to the syncopated cutting style and direction. Picture was part of a Yugoslav Film Week in Paris. *Mosk.*

Ski-Faszination
(Ski Fascination)
(GERMAN—COLOR—ULTRASCOPE)
Berlin, Nov. 29.

Team Film release of Willy Bogner production. With Willy Bogner, Barbi Henneberger, Buddy Werner, Luggi Leitner, Heidi Biiebl. Directed and written by Willy Bogner; camera (Eastmancolor), Klaus Koenig, Ludwig Foeger, Willy Bogner; music, Benny Golson; editing, Beate Mainka. At Cinema Paris, West Berlin. Running Time, **50 MINS.**

"Ski Fascination" is a technically brilliant, artistically outstanding and highly imaginative and unconventional documentary on modern skiing. Its only problem may be its running time of 50 minutes, which makes it too long for a short and too short for a feature. ("Ski Fascination" is double-billed here with an hourlong documentary, "The Wild Horses of Glamador"). It has in Team Film a strong distributing outfit in this country.

Ski champ Willy Bogner, 23-year-old producer-director-author of this film, has done an amazing job which is the more remarkable since he regards filming merely as a hobby. He worked on this film for about two years and spent about $75,000 on it.

Bogner invited 27 of the world's best skiers who demonstrated the art of skiing high up in the Swiss mountains. The outcome was a delightful mixture of sports, grace, artistry and humor. The whole presentation can be termed a "ballet on skis."

The direction is fast-paced, and there are breathtakingly beautiful shots. The color is especially good. Editing and other technical credits are firstrate. The jazzy score by American Benny Golson is also a major asset.

In all, "Ski Fascination" is one of the best ski films ever made,

---

qualifying also as a genuine piece of cinematic art. *Hans.*

Bel Ami 2000—Oder Wie Verfuehrt Man Einen Playboy
(How To Seduce A Playboy)
(GERMAN-AUSTRIAN — COLOR)
Berlin, Nov. 24.

Constantin release of Intercontinental production. Stars Peter Alexander, features Antonella Lualdi, Linda Christian, Jocelyn Lane and Renato Salvatore. Directed by Michael Pfleghar. Screenplay, Klaus Munro and Pfleghar; camera (Eastmancolor), Ernst Wild; music, Heinz Kiessling; settings, Hertha Hareiter. At Zoo Palast, West Berlin. Running Time, **95 MINS.**

Peter Knolle	Peter Alexander
Boy Schock	Renato Salvatore
Vera	Antonella Lualdi
Anita Bionda	Scilla Gabel
Lucy	Helga Anders
Lucy's mother	Linda Christian
Ginette	Jocelyn Lane
Emile	Joachim Teege
Sokker	Joachim Fuchsberger
Coco	Elione Dalmeida

Obviously, an abundance (at least by German-Austrian standards) of money and energy went into this production. Director (mostly tv) Michael Pfleghar traveled with his players to such places as Paris, Rome and Tokyo to create something like a bigscale parody on sex. What he achieved is a thin-plotted gag, which lacks heart.

The plot, in brief, centers on a shy bookkeeper, singled out as "dream man of the year," due to the failure of a computer. A sex mag cashes in on that. The question is now who can seduce this involuntary playboy. A lineup of pretty faces aspire; naturally one emerges as the winner.

A presumed highlight occurs when principal player Peter Alexander, has to show himself naked (or nearly so), and is chased through the streets of Rome. Alexander, incidentally, is a multi-sided talent. A comedian-actor-singer-dancer-imitator he might go places if given the right material. He seems to be one of the most underestimated and perhaps neglected talents of the German-language film.

Film has a nice production dress. Colors and settings play a substantial role. Yet with the plot frivolous and the banal humor, it does not promise much in general playoff. *Hans.*

San
(The Dream)
(YUGOSLAVIAN)
Paris, Dec. 4.

Avala Film release and production. With Ljubisa Samardzic, Misa Janketic, Olivera Vuco, Neva Americ. Written and directed by Purisa Dordevic; camera, Mihailo Popovic. At Ranelagh, Paris. Running Time, **85 MINS.**

Girl	Ljubisa Samardzic
Boy	Misa Janketic
Soldier	Olivera Vuco
Heinrich	Neva Americ

Though this has the most popular theme in Yugoslav pix—partisans during the last war—it tries for a different twist by casting it in the form of a dream interspersed with realistic wartime fighting, partisan wrangling and suffering. It tries to say that the old myths have to be laid to rest, but is not always clear in its techniques, and it finally gets repetitious, mannered and loses its point.

Many allusions to partisan politics, the jumps in time from the past to today, and dead men coming back to life, tend to confuse at times instead of making a clear statement on war, resistance and human behavior under stress. It just gets a bit too ambitious and its comedy is sometimes too facetious. But it does have some well-manned battle scenes, tenderness sans mawkishness and an attempt to kill the partisan theme by showing up its academic aspects.

However, the film remains mainly a local item where all the allusions and points will be clearer than for more international audiences not always abreast of the history and meanings of many of the wartime and modern scenes. It is technically good. *Mosk.*

A Man For All Seasons
(BRITISH-COLOR)

Firstrate Fred Zinnemann filmization of the Henry VIII-Sir Thomas More conflict, adapted by Robert Bolt from his play. Paul Scofield recreates his legit role. Handsome production. For class situations using sophisticated roadshow sell.

Hollywood, Dec. 6.

Columbia Pictures release of a Highland Production, produced and directed by Fred Zinnemann, William N. Graf, executive producer. No stars. Features Paul Scofield, Wendy Hiller, Leo McKern, Robert Shaw, Orson Welles, Susannah York. Screenplay, Robert Bolt, based on his play; camera (Technicolor), Ted Moore; editor, Ralph Kemplin; music, Georges Delerue; production design, John Box; asst. directors, Peter Bolton, Al Burgess, Bill Graf Jr. Reviewed at Columbia Studio, Dec. 5, '66. Running Time, 120 MINS.

Sir Thomas More .... Paul Scofield
Alice More .... Wendy Hiller
Thomas Cromwell .... Leo McKern
King Henry VIII .... Robert Shaw
Cardinal Wolsey .... Orson Welles
Margaret More .... Susannah York
Duke of Norfolk ...... Nigel Davenport
Rich .... John Hurt
William Roper .... Corin Redgrave
Matthew .... Colin Blakely
Averil Machin .... Yootha Joyce

Producer-director Fred Zinnemann has blended all filmmaking elements into an excellent, handsome and stirring film version of "A Man For All Seasons." Robert Bolt adapted his 1960 play, a timeless, personal conflict based on the 16th century politico-religious situation between adulterous King Henry VIII and Catholic Sir Thomas More. Latter is played by Paul Scofield who created the legit role in London, later N.Y. William N. Graf is exec producer, utilizing Britain's Shepperton Studios and environs. Primary market is the class audience, with Columbia gearing its roadshow sell accordingly. Subsequent general playoff may be spotty.

Basic dramatic situation is that of a minister of the crown and his conscience being challenged by the imperious point of view which maintains that the lack of explicit support to an erring King is equivalent to disloyalty. This is the usual human dilemma whenever expediency confronts integrity. Bolt has adapted his legiter in a way that retains the illumination of diverse human natures, each in different degrees of honest and dishonest suport and conflict. The Common Man character, a solo Greek chorus stage device, has been eliminated, properly, in the screen treatment.

Scofield, in his first major film role, delivers an excellent performance as More, respected barrister, judge and Chancellor who combined an urbane polish with inner mysticism. Faced with mounting pressure to endorse publicly the royal marriage of Henry VIII to Anne Boleyn, but armed with legalistic know-how, More outfoxed his adversaries until "perjury" was used to justify a sentence of death. Scofield interprets in top fashion the interwoven loyalties of More to himself, his family, nation and religion.

Robert Shaw is also excellent as the king, giving full exposition in limited footage to the character: volatile, educated, virile, arrogant, yet sensitive (and sensible) enough to put the squeeze on More via subordinates, mainly Thomas Cromwell, played by Leo McKern. Latter's characterization, restrained and chilling at first, unfortunately becomes too broad, almost that of a jolly rascal, effect being to flaw the dramatic impact at times.

John Hurt registers strongly as the ambitious young man whose loyalties and integrity are overcome by material desires, furnished by McKern. The final battle, in which ambition crushes integrity, rages in Hurt's eyes, face and dialog. In contrast is Nigel Davenport, equally strong as the Duke of Norfolk, but a man who switches loyalties with few moral pangs. Both characters are prominent in More's final betrayal.

Wendy Hiller is brusque, but warm, as More's stolid wife, while Susannah York balances properly the youthful air of knowing innocence inherent in the daughter, always closer to her father. Corin Redgrave, of the theatrical family, is her suitor, headstrong and zealous as only an immature idealist can be, and he plays it well.

Orson Welles in five minutes (here an early confrontation, as Cardinal Wolsey, with More), achieves outstanding economy of expression. Colin Blakely is good as More's servant who makes the facile adjustment to prevailing winds, instinctive to lower classes.

With the single exception noted above, Zinnemann's direction of his players seems uniformly excellent. In addition, he establishes mood and contrast in brief shots—placid, then turbulent waters, bustling minions — which are heightened further by versatile use of Technicolor, toned to the dramatic needs of the moment. John Box did the outstanding production design, and Ted Moore's sensitive camera has caught all the nuances, including Zinnemann's international blanking of some frames to focus attention.

Zinnemann's overall pacing, as executed by editor Ralph Kemplin to a good 120 minutes, eliminates depiction of some obvious events, thereby creating a desired abruptness, while at other times it lingers appropriately over key personal interactions. Georges Delerue has provided a spare but effective score which complements the cinematics.

Other technical credits, including Terry Marsh's art direction and costumes by Elizabeth Haffenden and Joan Bridge, are excellent. There appears to be a minor technical flaw in the first reel, as tradeshown, where ambient noise levels vary with individual speeches.

Murf.

A Very Handy Man
(Liola)
(ITALIAN—FRENCH)

Rizzoli Films release of a Federiz-Film Napoleon (Nino Krisman) production. Stars Ugo Tognazzi, Giovanna Ralli Pierre Brasseur, Anouk Aimee. Directed by Alessandro Blasetti. Screenplay, Sergio Amidei, Elio Bartolini, Carlo Romano based on Luigi Pirandello play; camera, Leonida Barboni, Tonino Delli Colli, Carlo di Palma; music, Carlo Savina. No other credits provided. Reviewed in N.Y., Dec 12, '67. Running Time, 95 MINS.

Liola .... Ugo Tognazzi
Tuzza Azzara .... Giovanna Ralli
Simone Palumbo ...... Pierre Brasseur
Mita Palumbo .... Anouk Aimee

(English Subtitles)

This Italian-French coproduction made in 1963, is being released now on the U.S. market with no fanfare (it opened Dec. 14 at N.Y.'s Little Carnegie) although the cast is far from secondrate. Evidently the slight script, which makes little demands on the proven talents on view, and an attempt to get more Rizzoli product on the U.S. market, are responsible. Whatever the reason, it's a pleasant trifle that could be exploited on its sex angles but should make little impact on the art field.

Although the setting is not clearly defined, the behavior of the entire cast is cinema Sicilian. The women fight with each other over who's the current mistress of Liola (Ugo Tognazzi). Latter, as title says, is a very handy man—with his knowledge of mechanics during the day and willing wives at night.

The script, a pastiche by Sergio Amidei, Elio Bartolini and Carlo Romano, vaguely based on a comedy by Luigi Pirandello, is an antipasto of philandering females, honor-obsessed husbands, and a running battle between Tognazzi, a former mistress (Giovanna Ralli), an impotent landowner (Pierre Brasseur) and the latter's supposedly barren wife (Anouk Aimee). Most of the time the principals are rushing headlong up and down country roads, yelling about adultery (evidently close to being an obsession with Italian filmmakers).

Despite all the yelling, however, occasional moments, when the action slows down, permit the viewer to take an interest. The many minor characters, as impressive as the principals, were given no mention in the credits provided at the trade screening, but several look familiar. One of the five sons of Liola is played by Marietto, the tyke featured in "It Started In Naples."

Tognazzi is effective as the apparently only virile man in the village and Brasseur matches him as the egotistical, selfish landowner whose only thought is to sire a son (not unlike "Mandrigola" at times). Giovanna Ralli and Anouk Aimee, stunning to look at, make little impression in their limited roles.

The photography, credited to three chairmen, may have been done equally, but separately, by all three as outdoor scenes fail to match interior shots in definition or lighting, and the village square scenes were obviously filmed on a Cinecitta soundstage. *Robe.*

Funeral In Berlin
(BRITISH-COLOR-PANAVISION)

Excellent Cold War suspenser, full of surprises and adroit humor. Michael Caine returns as Harry Palmer in sequel to "The Ipcress File." Excellent b.o. prospects in general situations.

Hollywood, Dec. 10.

Paramount Pictures release, and Harry Saltzman presentation, produced by Charles Kasher. Stars Michael Caine; features Paul Hubschmid, Oscar Homolka, Eva Renzi. Directed by Guy Hamilton. Screenplay, Evan Jones, based on the novel by Len Deighton; music by Conrad Elfers; camera (Technicolor), Otto Heller; editor, John Bloom, production design, Ken Adam; asst. director, David Bracknell. Reviewed at Paramount Studios, Dec. 9, '66. Running Time, 102 MINS.

Harry Palmer .... Michael Caine
Johnny Vulkan .... Paul Hubschmid
Col. Stok .... Oscar Homolka
Samantha Steel .... Eva Renzi
Ross .... Guy Doleman
Mrs. Ross .... Rachel Gurney
Hallam .... Hugh Burden
Reinhart .... Thomas Holtzmann
Kreutzmann .... Gunter Meisner
Aaron Levine .... Heinz Schubert
Werner .... Wolfgang Volz
Otto Rukel .... Klaus Jepsen
Artur .... Herbert Fux
Benjamin .... Rainer Brandt
Monika .... Ira Hagen
Brigit .... Marte Keller

"Funeral In Berlin" is the second Harry Saltzman (solo) presentation of the exploits of Harry Palmer, the soft-sell sleuth, this time enmeshed in Berlin counterespionage. Michael Caine encores in the role that made him a star. Excellent scripting, direction and performances, plus colorful and realistic production, add up to surprise-filled suspense, relieved adroitly by subtle irony. Excellent b.o. prospects likely for the Charles Kasher production, via Paramount release in general situations.

Besides Caine, Saltzman and Kasher, pic also reunites from "The Ipcress File" (first Palmer pic. distributed by Universal and Rank) Guy Doleman, Caine's intelligence superior, and cameraman Otto Heller. This time out, Len Deighton's novel has been adapted by Evan Jones to a taut, economical screenplay, just right for the semi-documentary feel. Substantial Berlin location work is evident, and pic was polished at England's Pinewood Studios.

Unlike James Bond and his cinematic progeny, the Palmer character lives by instinct, not by gadgets, thereby creating audience identification. The Bond bunch, enjoyable as escapist entertainment, at times appear too unreal; Palmer, a small-time crook dragooned into intelligence work, suffers the same numbing shock as the man in the street when exposed to the insensitive, inhuman, cold-blooded regimen of undercover work. Thus, Palmer may outlive his competitors at the b.o.

Herein, amidst a clutch of running gags which never wear out their appeal, Caine is sent to East Berlin, where Communist spy chief Oscar Homolka is making the motions of trying to defect. Paul Hubschmid is the local British contact for Caine, and Eva Renzi, a newcomer with looks who also can act, pops up as an undercover agent for Israel, tracking down Nazis before statues of limitation run out.

Miss Renzi, who replaced Anjanette Comer when latter took ill, is, like Caine, under exclusive contract to Saltzman, and while this is her second film, the first, a German pic, is not yet in release. She indicates much promise.

This being a well-developed suspenser, few people are as they seem, including prissy-pedantic Hugh Burden, a secret documents clerk in Doleman's British spy group. Gunter Meisner is the expert in smuggling political defectors (the "funeral" in title is the

gambit) and is demanded by Homolka as the arranger of his own
escape, for wel-concealed reasons.
All supporting players are cast to
best effect.

The message conveyed so well
here is that espionage is a dirty
business in which basically decent
people must, from time to time,
become involved. While Miss Renzi and Caine have a romantic interlude, it is she who orders him
shot, then discovers that a mistake
has been made. Caine knows she
thought he was the gunned-down
man, and she knows he is aware
of it, too. In a few feet of silent
film, showing his eyes and hers,
the personal tragedy comes thundering off the screen.

Director Guy Hamilton, in a
change of pace from his earlier
direction of "Goldfinger," is equally at home with the Palmer character. Performances are uniformly excellent, and set off by Heller's graphic Panavision-Technicolor lensing. The bustling prosperity of Allied-controlled West
Berlin is in recurring counterpoint to the grim East Berlin
scene, still scarred with World
War II ruins. Color control is outstanding.

Production designer Ken Adam
and associates have exercised an
admirable and versatile restraint,
giving every scene—from an underground office to a nitery featuring femme impersonators—all
it deserved, but no more. John
Bloom's editing is sharp, zesty but
never jarring, and the 102 minutes move along smartly. Music
score is spare, effective when
used. All other technical credits
are pro, particularly sound editing and recording which combine
sound-stage clarity with an outdoor fee¹.   *Murf.*

The Brides of Fu Manchu
(BRITISH-COLOR)

Minor entry for the meller
market; name of title character should attract.

Hollywood, Dec. 8.
Seven Arts Pictures release of Hallam
(Oliver A. Unger-Harry Alan Towers)
production. Stars Christopher Lee,
Douglas Wilner, Marie Versini; features
Tsai Chin, Henrich Wilhelm Drache.
Directed by Don Sharp. Screenplay,
Peter Welbeck, based on Fu Manchu
character created by Sax Rohmer; cam-
era (Technicolor), Ernest Stewart; edi-
tor, Allan Morrison; music, Bruce Mont-
gomery; asst. director, Barrie Melrose.
Reviewed at Joe Shore's screening
room, Dec. 8, '66. Running Time, 93
MINS.
Fu Manchu .... Christopher Lee
Nayland Smith .... Douglas Wilner
Maria .... Marie Versini
Lin Tang .... Tsai Chin
Karl .... Henrich Wilhelm Drache

"The Brides of Fu Manchu,"
based on the Sax Rohmer character, is an old-fashioned piece of
melodramatics for the program
market. Follow-up to Oliver A.
Unger-Harry Alan Tower's previous meller, "The Face of Fu
Manchu," released last year also
by Seven Arts and with Christopher Lee again portraying the
evil Chinese Mandarin, in the present
age of advanced electronics the
Manchu hopes to dominate the
world seems antiquated. The acting and dialog aren't much better.

Fu Manchu goes about his plan
by kidnapping the daughters of
powerful political, industrial and
scientific figures in a dozen countries, whose forced collaboration
is thus accomplished. His principal
antagonist is his old arch-enemy,
Nayland Smith of Scotland Yard,
who finally thwarts the Oriental's
not-so-well-laid plans.

Lee capably undertakes the title
role, but his performance scarcely
equals those of the late Warner
Oland and Boris Karloff who delineated the Manchu character in
former American entries. Douglas
Wilner is talkative as the Scotland
Yarder and Marie Versini is in for
distaff interest as one of the
"brides." Best performance is offered by Tsai Chin, repeating her
part as Manchu's evil daughter.
Henrich Wilhelm Drache is okay
as Miss Virsini's fiance who helps
rescue her from Manchu's secret
headquarters in North Africa.

Screenplay by Peter Welbeck
is strictly pedestrian and out of
tune with the times, which Don
Sharp's direction cannot overcome.
Color photography by Ernest Stewart is competent, as are other technical credits.
                              Whit.

Murderers' Row
(COLOR)

Followup to "The Silencers"
with Dean Martin again at the
Helm. Mucho display of girls;
not mucho display of originality, but big boxoffice prospects.

Columbia Pictures release of a Meadway-Claude (Irving Allen) production.
Stars Dean Martin, Ann-Margaret, Karl
Malden, Camilla Sparv; features James
Gregory, Beverly Adams, Richard East-
hm. Directed by Henry Levin. Screen-
play, Herbert Baker, based on Donald
Hamilton novel, "Murderers' Row";
camra (Technicolor), Sam Leavitt; edi-
tor, Walter Thompson; sound, Charles
J. Rice; second unit director, James
Havens; special effects, Danny Lee; mu-
sic, Lalo Schifrin; songs, Tommy Boyce-
Bobby Hart, Lalo Schifrin-Howard Green-
field; asst. director, Ray Gosnell. Re-
viewed at Loew's 86th Street, N.Y., Dec.
13, '66. Running Time, 108 MINS.
Matt Helm .... Dean Martin
Suzie .... Ann-Margaret
Julian Wall .... Karl Malden
Coco Duquette .... Camilla Sparv
MacDonald .... James Gregory
Lovey Kravezit ...... Beverly Adams
Dr. Norman Solaris...Richard Eastham
Ironhead .... Tom Reese
Billy Orcutt .... Duke Howard
Guard .... Ted Hartley
Capt. Deveraux .... Marcel Hillaire
Miss January .... Corinne Cole
Dr. Rogas .... Robert Terry
Themselves.......Dino, Desi and Billy

It's a wise film producer who
knows his own successful formula.
About the only changes made by
Irving Allen in his sequel to the
successful "The Silencers" are in
scenery, girls and costumes.
There's a greater emphasis on
dancing and, possibly, a bit less
on the double-entendre lines that
were used to such profusion in the
first Matt Helm effort.

These changes aren't likely to
hurt the potential of this expensive carbon of the original pic,
and may even boost the market as
the slant now seems to be aimed
at a younger and less sophisticated audience (known to be very
large indeed). The addition of
Ann-Margret, for the consumer
market, is notable for some abandoned choreography and a chance
to use both of her expressions—
the open-mouthed Monroe imitation and the slinky Theda Bara
bit.

Let no one say that this picture
lacks class, though. It has it and
it's spelled Sparv. While the script
makes her the villainess and gives
her too little to do, Camilla Sparv
(who came on like thunder in
"Dead Heat On a Merrygoround")
continues to make a tremendous
impression. To paraphrase a line
of dialog from the pic, there's
more to her than meets the eye,
but what meets the eye isn't bad.
Beauty, plus class, plus a strong
suggestion of talent—who needs
Grace Kelly?

This time out, Dean Martin's
secret agent has to trek to the
Riviera to catch that bad old Karl
Malden who's about to blow up
Washington with a secret beam.
Most of the sexy lines are in the
first minutes of the film with
Helm, pursuing his cover-job of
photographer, using the Slaygirls
as calendar models, Beverly Adams,
on screen for a brief bit repeats
as his secretary, Lovey Kravezit,
and there's a heavy barrage of
laughs to fortify the viewer
(needed, when the switch is to
action primarily for the rest of
the film).

Best sight gag in the film (and
there are plenty) is the "wake"
held by the Slaygirls for Helm,
believed killed. It's held in a bar,
of course, with the femmes in
black trenchcoats and hats and
a tearful pianist pounding out
"Beer Barrel Polka."

Director Henry Levin's stress
on action (for which some credit
must also go to second unit director James Havens) takes the film
out of the comedy range at times.
Helm is, of course, given some
ridiculous special weapons; this
time, a delayed-reaction gun is
worked to death (no pun intended). But whenever the viewer begins to take things seriously, Levin
cuts back to a laugh bit (Martin
ripping off Ann-Margret's mini-
skirt which contains an explosive
and hurling it at a wall decorated
with Frank Sinatra's picture).
Followup film, "The Ambushers,"
is plugged at the end.

Herbert Baker's script, for some
odd reason, takes several cracks
at the French. While funny, they
may prove less so to les Francaise
and could possibly make Columbia persona non grata. They'd
be wise to alter the dialog
a bit for export to sensitive markets.

The technical aspects of the
film are excellent, typical of the
American film technician, with Sam
Leavitt's Technicolor camera making the most of the many and
varied scenic spots provided.
Danny Lee's special effects (one,
especially, of a distorted discotheque dance sequence) could
make him an Oscar contender.
Lalo Schifrin's music is riotous
although his best part is a ballad,
"I'm Not The Marrying Kind,"
which he and Howard Greenfield
provide for Martin. Martin's son,
Dino (who has a popular combo
—Dino, Desi & Billy)—is seen so
briefly that most viewers won't
get the parent-son wisecracks used.

Prospects, all in all, should be
very good for this one.   *Robe.*

Finders Keepers
(BRITISH-COLOR)

Easygoing musicomedy which
will well satisfy admirers of
pop singer Cliff Richard and
The Shadows. But more wit
and bite would have helped
a yarn that demanded a more
astringent approach.

London, Dec. 8.
United Artists release of an Interstate
Production. Stars Cliff Richard, The
Shadows, Robert Morley, Peggy Mount.
Features Viviane Ventura, Graham Stark,
Robert Hutton, Ellen Pollock, John Le
Mesurier. Produced by George H.
Brown. Directed by Sidney Hayers.
Screenplay by Michael Pertwee from an
original story by Brown; camera (East-
mancolor), Alan Hume; editor, Tristam
Cones; music lyrics, The Shadows;
choreography, Malcolm Clare, with
dances created by Hugh Lambert. At
Odeon, Leicester Square, London. Run-
ning Time, 94 MINS.
Cliff .... Cliff Richard
The Shadows ..... Bruce Welch,
        Hank B. Marvin, Brian Bennett,
                              John Rostill
Colonel Roberts .... Robert Morley
Mrs. Bragg .... Peggy Mount
Emelia .... Viviane Ventura
Burke .... Graham Stark
Mr X .... John Le Mesurier
Commander .... Robert Hutton
Junior Officer .... Gordon Ruttan
Grandma .... Ellen Pollock
Air Marshal .... Ernest Clark
Pilot .... Burnell Tucker
Priest .... George Roderick
G.I. Guard .... Bill Mitchell
Drunk .... Ronnie Brodie

George H. Brown's storyline a-
bout a minibomb dropped by accident from an American plane over
Spain and subsequent attempts by
various foreign "spies" to locate
it could have had a good astringent and satirical tang. The theme
is not only largely frittered away
but is hardly suitable for a relaxed, easygoing musicomedy designed to showcase a pop group such
as Cliff Richard and The Shadows.
Wit gets lost, and incidents are
held up, to make room for inevitable song, dance and fiesta. Still,
this is a sunny, pleasant entertainment which will satisfy Richard's
big following, offend nobody else
and is a suitable seasonable offering for most situations. Apart, perhaps, from Robert Morley there is
not much marquee value for the
U. S.

Richard and The Shadows hitch-
hike to a hotel in Spain and find
it deserted. The dropped bomb has
sent everybody scurrying away.
The lads, with the help of a local
charmer (Viviane Ventura), decide that it's in their interests to
find it and hand it over to the
U.S. troops who have moved in
on a similar mission. Mr. X, representing a foreign power, has the
same idea and blackmails the English manager of the hotel to do
the job. The hotel cook, for unexplained reasons, is also in on the
same racket. That's all.

Michael Pertwee's screenplay
does not build up much urgency
or suspense but provides opportunity for colorful fiesta, a gentle
romance between Richard & Miss
Ventura, some verbal dueling between Robert Morley the inept
hotel manager and Graham Stark
as his even more inept sidekick.
Richard, a pleasant young enter-

tainer, and The Shadows are more at home with the singing than the thesping. The Shadows have written the songs and music, none of them particularly memorable or helpful in pushing along the thin storyline, but all quite acceptable to the ear. Morley & Stark, allied to Peggy Mount as the belligerent cook, all work overtime to extract the maximum yocks from artificial roles. Robert Hutton keeps things on an even keel as the American army commander and Miss Ventura looks pretty enough but has little to do except to look at — and be looked at — by Richard in the cause of calf-love.

Ronnie Brody as a drunk, John Le Mesurier as the mysterious spy agent, Ellen Pollock as a Spanish-speaking grandma, Gordon Ruttan, Ernest Clark and George Roderick all contribute workmanlike cameos. One of the charms of the film is the sunny atmosphere of Spain which has been warmly captured by Alan Hume's camera. Sidney Hayers' direction is rather looser than could be wished but this may be because George H. Brown, the producer, and Pertwee, the scripter, have clearly tried to capture the best of two worlds, an innocuous, whiter-than-white musicomedy atmosphere allied to an up-to-date yarn. The two don't always jell. *Rich.*

You're A Big Boy Now
(COLOR)

Nutty comedy about a young male virgin; okay for selected situations.

Hollywood, Dec. 9.
Seven Arts Pictures release of Phil Feldman production. Stars Elizabeth Hartman, Geraldine Page, Julie Harris, Peter Kastner, Rip Torn; features Michael Dunn, Tony Bill, Karen Black, Dolph Sweet, Michael O'Sullivan. Directed, scripted by Francis Ford Coppola, based on novel by David Benedictus; camera (PatheColor), Andy Laszlo; music, John Sebastian; editor, Aram Avakian; asst. director, Larry Sturhahn. Reviewed at Fine Arts Theatre, Dec. 8, '66. Running Time, 96 MINS.
Barbara Darling .... Elizabeth Hartman
Margery Chanticleer.... Geraldine Page
Miss Thing .... Julie Harris
Bernard .... Peter Kastner
I. H. Chanticleer .... Rip Torn
Richard Mudd .... Michael Dunn
Raef .... Tony Bill
Amy .... Karen Black
Policeman Francis Graf ... Dolph Sweet
Kurt Doughty ...... Michael O'Sullivan

"You're a Big Boy Now," another in the rising tide of nutty pix, might be gauged a conversation piece in the selected-situation market for which this Phil Feldman production obviously is aimed. It is one of those films with a simple premise — this time a virginal young man growing into manhood, not so much through his own efforts as those about him — which has been expanded glowingly in a sophisticated approach. There probably will be those who object to development of the motivating idea, particularly as it relates to today's mores and morals — perhaps rightfully — but by the same token picture undoubtedly will be hailed by a certain section of the film-going public with enthusiasm.

There can be no doubt that the Seven Arts release is a director's picture. Francis Ford Coppola, ac-

cording to brochure of credits handed out at preview, wrote and directed "Boy" for his master's thesis at the UCLA Film School, as a student of its Theatre Arts dept. It is thoroughly professional, however, with a cast of top names and a budget said to be around the million-dollar mark, produced entirely in N.Y. Feature is packed with clever touches both in the gag field and in sustained sequences, and Coppola has drawn top-flight performances from his talented cast.

Credit is given in introductory titles to the cooperation of the N.Y. city fathers, along with expressed gratitude to Mayor John Lindsay and the N.Y. Public Library. One may wonder, as story unfolds on a collection of rara avis associated with the library (including the oddball curator of rare books and a booster-sniffing employee), why such cooperation was granted, since the institution citadel of respectability — backdrops much of the action, including young man's introduction to sex. Film runs the gamut of way-out story-telling, characteristic of much current screen humor.

Peter Kastner plays a roller-skating stack boy in the library, somewhat of a dreamer. Against the tearful protests of boy's mother, Geraldine Page, the father, Rip Torn, decides the best way for his son to grow up would be to move out of the family home on his own. Straightway, lad becomes ensconced in a rooming house run by Julie Harris, where the third floor is governed by a rooster belonging to landlady's departed brother and which doesn't like pretty girls.

With the help of his library, dope-inclined pal, Tony Bill, and a pretty library assistant, Karen Black, the boy is launched on his road to manhood, which takes him into the arms of a sexy, way-out, Greenwich Village discotheque dish, Elizabeth Hartman. Frequent laughs spark his career toward full-blossomed virility, with amusing bumps along the way.

Kastner turns in a slick portrayal, endowing role with just the proper emphasis upon youth in the wondering stage. Miss Hartman, who previously scored so heavily in "Patch of Blue," scores again in a vastly different type of role, to which she gives full conviction.

Both Miss Page as the mother and Miss Harris as the landlady go all-out in hilarious roles and Torn, too, delivers a sock performance as the father who has difficulty understanding his son. Miss Black offers a sensitive enactment of the girl in love with Kastner and Bill is arresting as the pal. Excellent support also is offered by Dolph Sweet as a cop in the rooming house, and Michael Dunn as Miss Hartman's friend.

Technical credits all rate high, standouts here Andy Laszlo's color photography, John Sebastian's music score, Vassele Fotopoulos' art direction and Aram Avakian's editing. *Whit.*

Press For Time
(BRITISH-COLOR)

Hearty slapstick comedy with Norman Wisdom milking the yocks energetically, Wisdom's

Broadway success could give this one a U.S. lift.

London, Dec. 8.
Rank release of an Ivy Production for Titan Films. Stars Norman Wisdom. Features Derek Bond, Angela Browne, Tracey Crisp, Noel Dyson, Peter Jones, David Lodge, Derek Francis. Produced by Robert Hartford-Davis and Peter Newbrook. Directed by Robert Asher. Screenplay by Wisdom and Eddie Leslie from Angus McGill's novel, "Yea, Yea, Yea"; camera (Eastmancolor), Newbrook; editor, Garry Hambling; sound, Ken Cameron; music, Mike Vickers. At New Victoria, London. Running Time, 102 MINS.
Norman Shields ...... Norman Wisdom
Wilfred Shields ...... Norman Wisdom
Sir Wilfred Shields...Norman Wisdom
Emily Shields .... Norman Wisdom
Major Bartlett .... Derek Bond
Eleanor .... Angela Browne
Ruby Fairchild .... Tracey Crisp
Mrs. Corcoran .... Noel Dyson
Alderman Corcoran ...... Derek Francis
Willoughby .... Peter Jones
Ross .... David Lodge
Liz .... Frances White
Ballard .... Alan Cuthbertson
Marsh .... Tony Selby
Sewerman .... Michael Balfour
Mrs. Doe Connor...Totti Truman Taylor
Nottage .... Stanley Unwin
Barman .... George Roderick

Though never the critics' loverboy, Norman Wisdom has built up a solid, profitable reputation as a slapstick comic with a certain wistful appeal, in Britain and in various other parts of the world. He has never yet, however, been able to crack the Yank market. "Press For Time", one of his best for some time, is in itself timely, as it coincides with his Broadway click, "Walking Happy," and shrewdly handled could well make its mark in the States. It will, inevitably, cash in in British theatres.

Wisdom, the little man who is disasterprone, but somehow manages always to win through ebulliently this time plays a goofy reporter on a smalltime seaside town newspaper. He's been landed on the paper by his embarrassed grandfather, the Prime Minister of England, who objects to the lad selling newspapers at a site near the Houses of Parliament. The paper's owner unwillingly takes on the encumbrance as a weapon for working himself into a Junior Ministership. Once on the paper Wisdom becomes embroiled in the skulduggery of local politics and finds himself in constant disaster.

A local council meeting and a beauty contest are just two situations brought into the screenplay (written by Wisdom and Eddie Leslie rather loosely from Angus McGill's novel, "Yea, Yea, Yea"). But everything that happens merely strings together a series of slapstick cameos in which Wisdom rates plenty of laughs from physical humiliation. He is an ingenious slapstick buffoon but also has a "little man" appeal which is often beguiling, especially in the ephemeral romantic incidents.

A final "love-everybody" homily which he puts over is an embarrassment. This is an error which has crept into Wisdom films before and he has clearly over-persuaded his new producers, Robert Hartford-Davis and Peter Newbrook. Wisdom also essays three or four other roles. He plays his suffragette mother & also his doddering old Prime Minister grandfather, both in his dotage and as a young man. The mother and grandfather cameos are over-hammed and mainly fail. Still, Wisdom

knows his market, is a far better actor than many people give him credit for and has a down-to-earth communion with his public which many a performer might envy.

Robert Asher has directed him in several previous films and the two have a successful rapport. Newbrook, as well as coproducing, handles the camerawork and makes good use of the authentic seaside backgrounds.

Though the comedy hinges mainly around the star, such very useful thesps as Noel Dyson, Derek Francis, David Lodge, Derek Bond, Michael Balfour, Peter Jones and Alan Cuthbertson offer good support. Stanley Unwin, who has made a name for himself on tv and radio with a doubletalk specialty, appears as the town clerk and provides some joyful minutes for specialists.

On the femme side, Angela Browne, as a snooty girl reporter, and Frances White, as the plain girl who wins the little man's heart, are excellent. Tracey Crisp, a real looker, is the most prominent of a bunch of lasses who make impact in the beauty contest sequences. Artwork, editing and music are all unobtrusively okay. *Rich.*

Echoes of Silence

A Yank "underground" pic from Gotham getting released abroad but still mainly for the specialized growing cult houses in the U.S. Arty and specialized usage indicated on some knowing insights and observations, if still too weak in dramatic flair and narration for regular outlets.

Paris, Dec. 12.
Goldman release and production. Written, directed, edited and photographed by Peter Emmanuel Goldman, assisted by Riva Freifeld, Michael Sheridan. With Miguel Chacour, Viraj Amonsin, Blanche Zelinka, Stasia Gelber. Previewed in Paris. Running Time, 76 MINS.
Miguel .... Miguel Chacour
Viraj .... Viraj Amonsin
Blanche .... Blanche Zelinka
Stasia .... Stasia Gelber
Jacquteta .... Jacquetta Lampson

Made in 16m, and blown up to 35m, this has a grainy look that fits its rambling, downbeat dealing with some drifting characters in New York's Greenwich Village. Splintered and fragmentary, it does not develop a dramatic line and contents itself with little vignettes on the lives of the characters. No talking and with only some Prokofiev music on the soundtrack, pic appears mainly destined for "Underground Cinema" devotees in the U.S. but does show some sensitivity, a flair for atmosphere and glimpses of mature observation by young Yank filmmaker Peter Emmanuel Goldman.

The characters are mainly drifters and somewhat alienated and not prone to much articulateness, making dialog unnecessary. Each little episode is clear and a simple subtitle sets the scene. There is no background, no attempt to give them character, depth or a try for any sort of growth in personality, meaning or outlook.

But there is a maturity in tone as one youth is followed in his endless rounds of picking up girls, a homosexual advance is detailed with tact and simple living incidents, sans artifice or mannerism, show a sincerity in purpose if not a corresponding ability to allow these people to grow in meaning. Still, it does give a surface impression of a certain kind of youth today and does not sentimentalize romanticize or get flippant or cynical about them. It thus has a certain interest on this score, but not enough depth, body or narrative flair or the more probing poetic needs for anything but extremely specialized use in the U.S. It has received critical pros and cons here. *Mosk.*

Made in U.S.A.
(FRENCH-
(COLOR-TECHNISCOPE)
Paris, Dec. 10.

Athos release of Rome-Paris Films, Anouchka Films production. Stars Anna Karina; features Laszlo Szabo, Jean-Pierre Leaud, Yves Alfonso. Written and directed by Jean-Luc Godard; camera (Eastmancolor), Raoul Coutard; editor, Agnes Guillemot. Previewed in Paris. Running Time, **85 MINS.**

Paula Nelson	Anna Karina
Richard Widmark	Laszlo Szabo
Donald Siegel	Jean-Pierre Leaud
David Goodis	Yves Alfonso
Doris Mizoguchi	Kyoko Kosaka
Marianne Faithfull	Herself

That prolific ex-New Waver and style innovator, Jean-Luc Godard, goes on doing his three pix a year. After a canny look at youth in "Masculin Feminin," here, in his first of two films made at the same time it appears he ran out of breath. It is a bit too obscure and slapdash for anything but arty spots abroad where buff attendance and the Godard name may help. Otherwise it looms mainly a local item where the political innuendos may help stir interest.

Why is it called "Made in U.S.A.?" Presumably because it is based loosely on a Yank detective yarn and also pays homage to that type of U.S. pic as well as having it take place in France in a place called Atlantic City. Otherwise the American influence is not clear save for character names like Widmark, Aldrich and others.

Now Godard's ex-wife Anna Karina is looking for a beau who may have been killed off by a mysterious organization. It seems he could be linked to the recent Ben Barka case about the Moroccan leftist abducted and presumably done away with here with local police compliance. But the name of a hood, killed or a suicide, is always blacked out by background noises.

This and other inside gags will not help clarify this talky affair for most audiences. Godard's flair for using literary quotations and asides and refusal to explain or do needed action scenes, do not jell in this plodding affair. Miss Karina floats through adventures and finally kills off a suspicious undercover type, then tries to explain what happened and gives some woolly comments on the shortcomings of left and right politics here.

All this is strained, overinflated and too meandering to give the dash, poetic asides and stylistic freshness that have beefed up his other pix. He appears to be imitating his other films without

their refreshing, zany candor and depth. However, it is shot with fine color rendering by Raoul Coutard. The actors do not have the spontaneous freshness and inventiveness of other Godard gangster adventures. *Mosk.*

Si J'avais Quatre Dromadaires
(If I Had Four Dromedaries)
(FRENCH—DOCUMENTARY)
Paris, Dec. 13.

APEC-NWDR release and production. Directed, edited, photographed and written by Chris Marker. Commentary by Pierre Vaneck, Catherine Le Couey, Nicolas Yimatov. Previewed in Paris. Running Time, **73 MINS.**

Film is made up of over 800 photographed stills done by filmmaker Chris Marker in many parts of the world. It is a tribute to Marker that he manages to create a witty, urbane style in the juxtaposing of the stills. The dry but never arch commentary keeps this of interest throughout much of its footage.

It finally begins to get a bit mannered and its private, personal outlook sometimes obscures its theme of trying to find hope, love and decency amidst a mixture of shots of man's inhumanity and humanity. That is, there are too precious descriptions and observations on photos that do not always support the cleverness, and there is a final flatness to the unmoving stills that do not always make up in composition, surprise and visual elegance for the lack of movement.

But the stills on many parts of the world and the generally fine underlining by the commentary have this an offbeater that could be good supporting art house fare with a companion medium pic. It also has the earmarks for tv use if a good English commentary worthy of the original could be concocted.

Marker is one of the more original filmic essayists here and brings off an intellectual trifle with grace and charm despite its slightness and sometimes pedantic qualities. *Mosk.*

The Sand Pebbles
(PANAVISION-COLOR)

Excellent Robert Wise pic based on the novel of gunboat diplomacy in China, circa 1926. Steve McQueen outstanding as marquee lure. Overlength negates impact of topflight production, acting and direction. Good roadshow prospects, improving in later playoff.

20th Century-Fox release of an Argyle-Solar production. Produced and directed by Robert Wise. Features Steve McQueen, Richard Attenborough, Richard Crenna, Candice Bergen, Marayat Andriane, Mako, Larry Gates. Screenplay, Richard Anderson, based on novel by Richard McKenna; camera (De Luxe Color), Joseph MacDonald; film editor, William Reynolds; special effects, Jerry Endler; sound, Bernard Freericks, Murray Spivack; associate producer-second unit director, Charles Maguire; music by Jerry Goldsmith, conducted by Lionel Newman. Reviewed in Hollywood, Dec. 20, '66. Running Time, **193 MINS.**

Holman	Steve McQueen
Frenchy	Richard Attenborough
Collins	Richard Crenna
Shirley	Candice Bergen
Maily	Marayat Andriane
Po-Han	Mako
Jameson	Larry Gates
Ensign Bordelles	Charles Robinson
Stawski	Simon Oakland
Harris	Ford Rainey
Bronson	Joe Turkel
Crosley	Gavin Ma-Leod
Shanahan	Joseph di Reda
Major Chin	Richard Loo
Franks	Barney Phillips
Restorff	Gus Trikonis
Perna	Shepherd Sanders
Farren	James Jeter
Jennings	Tom Middleton
Cho-Jen	Paul Chinpae
Chien	Tommy Lee
Mama Chunk	Beulah Quo
Victor Shu	James Hong
Haythorn	Stephen Jahn
Wilsey	Jay Allan Hopkins

Out of the 1926 political and military turmoil in China, a pot that still boils, producer-director Robert Wise has created a sensitive, personal drama. set against a background of old style U.S. Navy gunboat diplomacy. "The Sand Pebbles," based on the novel by the late Richard McKenna, is a handsome production, boasting some excellent acting characterizations. Steve McQueen delivers an outstanding performance. Overlong by at least 25 minutes, pic shapes up as a good 20th-Fox roadshow entry, with stronger b.o. prospects in later general release.

Although Wise is perhaps best known to filmgoers for "West Side Story" and "The Sound of Music," both filmusicals based on legit properties, he is no stranger to dramatic formats, as a perusal of his credits will make manifest. In "Pebbles," Wise has blended a series of conflicts, large and small, into a period drama that is, variously, exciting, tragic, stirring and romantic. Robert Anderson's generally excellent adaptation retains the flavor of McKenna's novel.

McQueen, who gets after-title billing, looks and acts the part he plays so well—that of a machinist's mate with nine years of Navy service . . . to have been a seagoing sailor is to understand the engineers, or snipes, as they are known. Cocky, independent, apparently surly, they live by their own rules in their overheated spaces, but when their captain wants speed or power, they always deliver.

Richard Crenna likewise is authentic as the gunboat captain, a young lieutenant, probably in his

first command billet, who speaks the platitudes of leadership with a slight catch in his throat, due to lack of practical experience. Such men were, and are, at any time liable to become involved in international incidents at some far-flung outpost, in the China of 40 years ago, when Communists and Nationalists were battling each other for power, as well as multinational foreign interests.

The title derives from a language perversion of San Pablo, formal name of the gunboat on Yangtze River patrol. Crenna's executive officer is greenhorn Charles Robinson, who matures under the pressure of events in an overall fine performance. Among the crew is Richard Attenborough, whose British accent is suppressed completely for a very believable role as a sailor who falls in love with newcomer Marayat Andriane in a tragic bi-racial romance. Her performance is sensitive.

Also in a good film debut is the Japanese actor Mako, playing the coolie whom McQueen trains, only to suffer brutal slashing before the entire ship's company in one of many local riots. Candice Bergen is appropriately sweet and charming as the school teacher for whom McQueen plans to desert. She and missionary Larry Gates are among the U.S. citizens whom Crenna must protect, even from themselves. Simon Oakland stands out as a brutal heavy in the crew, and vet Richard Loo has an important scene as a Nationalist Army officer.

The major drawback to the film as a whole is a surfeit of exposition, mainly in the second half. McQueen and Miss Bergen, for example, share a quiet interlude which, in two segments adding up to about 10 minutes, starts to flag the pace without substantial addition to plot. Also, as the ship is under siege while trapped by low river waters, some tightening could be done in the 15 minutes which lead up to an exciting near-mutiny.

The final 15 minutes, when Crenna and McQueen die while rescuing Miss Bergen, also tend to become lethargic. Every scene is in itself excellent, but unfortunately the overall dramatic flow of the pic suffers in the end. In addition, scriptwise, Crenna's temporary nervous collapse seems artificial, and McQueen's reaffirmed plan to desert seems at odds with his eventual acceptance by captain and crew.

Wise's otherwise expert direction is matched by meticulous production, from the outstanding exteriors, tinted towards the hues of a setting sun and the muddy waters, to the low-key interiors. Boris Leven's production design is superior. Joe MacDonald's first-rate Panavision-Deluxe color camera work is responsive to every mood, be it the touching intimacy of romance or the rousing action of hand-to-hand battle and street riot. Richard Johnson's second unit lensing for associate producer-second unit director Charles Maguire complements in top fashion.

Jerry Goldsmith's score, conducted by Lionel Newman, lends vigor and force as required, also subtlety. William Reynolds edited to 194 minutes total running time, sans intermish, including 98 minutes for the first part. Times include the two- and one-minute overtures for each portion. Sound editing and recording are first-rate, as are all other technical credits.

Main title bears a gag credit—"Diversions by Irving Schwartz"—put there by Wise in honor of a mysterious person, claimed to be unknown, whose letters proved a morale booster during trying location work in Taiwan and Hong Kong, where much of the film was shot. Production bogged down there due to weather and civil disturbances.

Film's copyright is shared by Wise, McQueen's Solar Prods. and 20th-Fox. *Murf.*

Soleil Noir
(Black Sun)
(FRENCH—COLOR—FRANSCOPE)

Paris, Dec. 20.

Comacico release of Films Copernic production. Stars Michele Mercier; features Daniel Gelin, David O'Brien, Michel De Re, Jean Topart, Valentina Cortese. Directed by Denys De La Patellierre. Screenplay, Pascal Jardin, De La Patelliere; camera (Eastmancolor), Armand Thirard; editor, Jacqueline Thiedot. At Triomphe, Paris. Running Time, **90 MINS.**

Beatrice	Michele Mercier
Guy	Daniel Gelin
Pilot	David O'Brien
Fat Man	Michel De Re
Bayard	Jean Topart
Maria	Valentina Cortese

Oldfashioned and quite hoary melodrama lacks the inventive bravura, brisk characterization and sharp direction to give it much chance overseas except for some dualer and grind possibilities on its African locale. Otherwise it is mainly a home item.

A rich girl goes to find an older brother lost in an isolated African desert town after the death of her father. The brother was a collaborator during the last war and has opted out of society. But the sister has promised the father to return him to civilization.

So off she goes and when she meets him and wants to talk to him, he takes her to his room to make a pass. She tells him she is his sister in time, and his remark is to the effect that it is too bad as he liked her. Though courted by a young American pilot, she pretends that she will give herself to a fat and unsavory local character who owns most of the hotels in this isolated hole.

This is to goad the brother back to life and he finally does rescue her from a fate worse than death, only to decide to stay with a desperate woman whose link to him has kept her alive. *Mosk.*

La Grande Vadrouille
(The Big Runaround)
(FRENCH—COLOR—PANAVISION)

Paris, Dec. 20.

Valoria release of Films Corona production. Stars Bourvil, Louis De Funes; features Marie Dubois, Terry-Thomas, Claudio Brook, Mike Marshall, Benno Sterzenbach. Directed by Gerard Oury. Screenplay, Oury, Marcel Jullian, Daniele Thompson, Georges and Andre Tabet; camera (Eastmancolor), Claude Renoir; editor, Albert Jurgenson. At Ambassade-Gaumont, Paris. Running Time, **130 MINS.**

Augustin	Bourvil
Stanislas	Louis De Funes
Captain	Terry-Thomas
Juliette	Marie Dubois
Peter	Claudio Brook
Colonel	Benno Sterzenbach
Hoteliere	Colette Brosset
Nun	Andrea Parisys

A big budget, two popular French comic stars and a free-wheeling slapstick trip around Europe made "Le Corniaud" (The Sucker), directed by Gerard Oury, one of the biggest hits here since the war. So the same trio repeat with a similar pic but with a wartime backdrop. Gags are more strained and World War II comedic shenanigans are a bit too drawn out, making it more obvious, telegraphed and less funny than its predecessor.

However, it looks good for sock results here if foreign chances appear slanted for fast playoff and spotty results, unless sheared down for more manageable future dualer use. It does have a helpful production dress and comics Bourvil and Louis De Funes do all right in their familiar roles of a bumbling but goodnatured fall guy and an irascible, mugging and overbearing, if harmless, type.

A crippled British bomber during the last war has to bail out its crew over Paris. One lands on the Opera, another in the zoo and one on Bourvil's scaffolding as he is painting a house. Pic concerns the attempts by Bourvil and De Funes, who gets mixed up with the flyers at the Opera, to get them to the Free France of that time.

Slapstick is the main ingredient which makes the Germans a bumbling, harmless batch. There is the stay at a hotel with the comedians unwittingly getting into German beds when a No. 9 on a door falls to make it a 6, a meeting at a steam bath and the main body of chases, captures and escapes till they make it away in a couple of gliders.

Bourvil and De Funes get sympathy here in their mixture of cowardice and bravado, but pic does not have the right ring of satire or true comedy depth. Terry-Thomas plays an English squad captain in a broad way and without enough comedy business or characterization to make him more than a stereotype.

Some romantic sidelights are brought in by Bourvil's infatuation with a French girl helping the group flee. But otherwise the pic rests on the two comics, who do manage to bring off some okay individual scenes even if the whole is bogged down by a tendency to overdo every gag. Lensing around France helps, as do production dress and good technical standards down the line. *Mosk.*

Triple Cross
(FRENCH—COLOR)

Paris, Dec. 20.

CEDIC release of Cineurop Films production. Stars Christopher Plummer, Romy Schneider, Trevor Howard, Gert Froebe, Claudine Auger, Yul Brynner; features Jess Hahn, Harry Meyen, Georges Lycan. Directed by Terence Young. Screenplay, Rene Hardy, William Marchant, Young, based on autobiography of Eddie Chapman; camera (Eastmancolor), Henri Alekan; editor, Roger Dwyre. At Normandie, Paris. Running Time, **140 MINS.**

Eddie	Christopher Plummer
Baron	Yul Brynner
Helga	Romy Schneider
Patricia	Claudine Auger
Chief	Trevor Howard
Colonel	Gert Froebe
Keller	Harry Meyen
Leo	Georges Lycan
Aide	Jess Hahn

(In English)

French pic made in English with an international cast has Warner Bros. handling it for the U.S. Though based on a true story of a British safecracker who worked as a double spy during the last war—Eddie Chapman—it is made in the standard spy pattern of having him a ladies' man, fast with his mitts, glib and shrewd, and with overloaded and obvious suspense bits thrown in to rob this of the verisimilitude needed to give it a more original fillip.

It has some good glossy technical aspects and a cast with some marquee value, but is still a spy opus that does not have the offbeat ring, original characterizations and treatment to give it more than okay playoff possibilities. Somewhat overlong, savvy shearing would help give it more punch for playoff spots. Indications appear fair if well hypoed and sold.

Terence Young, who has sworn off the James Bond films, here still plays this slightly tongue-in-cheek and it actually emerges as a sort of mini-Bond. Christopher Plummer is first seen cracking a series of safes and is finally arrested on the British Isle of Jersey. Along comes war and the Germans take over the island. He bluffs his way into getting a hearing with some top German undercover people.

He manages to gull them into letting him work for them and is tested, spied on, gets to bed down with a female operator and is finally entrusted with a mission. Once in Britain he goes to the British security people, finally convinces them and goes to work for them for a big sum and a promise to wipe out his criminal record.

Back again to Germany, he is first suspected of double agenting but finally gets a top German decoration and does get back to England again as the war ends. He also manages to get in a few romantic moments with a French underground lass.

Plummer walks through his role and does not quite have the impassive mask for the pro criminal or the needed lightness to give the romantic dash it calls for. But the ambivalence of the pic itself may have caused this, since it tries for gusty action and suspense.

Yul Brynner plays a brooding romantic German aristrocat who is really a pacifist, while Romy Schneider and Claudine Auger have nothing much to do but add some pulchritude to the show.

Gert Froebe is good as the persistent German colonel, an ex-policeman, who finally sees through Plummer's double dealing. Other support is adequate.

There are some good action scenes but too much of this supposedly true story has the usual spy trappings but set in the hot war of WW II rather than in the usual cold war.

The Private Right
(BRITISH—GREEK)

Paris, Dec. 13.

Onyx Films release and production. With Dimitris Andreas, Geaorges Kafkaris, Tamara Hinchco, Charlotte Selwyn. Written and directed by Michael Papas; camera, Ian Wilson; editor, Phil Mottram, Papas. Previewed in Paris. Running Time, **86 MINS.**

Minos	Dmitris Andreas
Tassos	Geaorges Kafkaris
Girl	Tamara Hinchco
Kypros	Cristos Demetriou
Waitress	Charlotte Selwyn

A Greek actor has come up with a highly mannered look at Cypriote revenge on an informer. It has some crisp action scenes at the beginning, but then bogs down into a fairly pretentious tale of tracking and eventual killing of the informer during the uprisings on that island which were put down by the British.

The overdone trick angles finally lose the interest generated in the film's early segs, and it turns into an overwrought suspenser that lacks the character insight and more subtle dash to sustain attention. But it does denote a highly colorful and inventive stylist in director Michael Papas, if only he can tone down his penchant for tricky camerawork, dragged-in love scenes and low-key lighting and hallucination scenes used too often for their own sake. The beginning has fierce gunplay and then a rugged torture scene as the hero is almost killed in a cell by the informer. Then after independence the former goes to London to find the traitor.

It has him trekking through colorful Cyprus and Greek sections of London till he runs across the man and tracks him down in a warehouse to gun him coldly to death. In the interim he makes love to a girl picked up at a party, goes in and out of restaurants and houses and through alleyways and narrow houses tracked by a ubiquitous camera.

Actors are mainly impassive except for the frightened, groveling traitor. Greek and Cypriote honor and dramatic tenacity are evident, **but treatment does not give the needed fillip of tragic inevitability and nobility.**

Film appears mainly an arty affair with some playoff on its well-done action parts. *Mosk.*

Tobruk
(TECHNISCOPE-COLOR)

Hard-hitting North African-World War II meller with names of Rock Hudson and George Peppard for marquee lure.

Hollywood, Dec. 14.

Universal release of Gibraltar-Corman (Gene Corman) production. Stars Rock Hudson, George Peppard, Nigel Green, Guy Stockwell. Directed by Arthur Hiller. Screenplay, Leo V. Gordon; camera (Technicolor), Russell Harlan; music, Bronislaw Kaper; editor, Robert C. Jones; asst. director, Terence Nelson. Reviewed at Chinese Theatre, Dec. 13, '66. Running Time, **107 MINS.**

Major Craig	Rock Hudson
Capt. Bergman	George Peppard
Colonel Harker	Nigel Green
Lt. Mohnfeld	Guy Stockwell
Sgt. Major Tyne	Jack Watson
Alfie	Norman Rossington
Dolan	Percy Herbert
Portman	Liam Redmond
Cheryl	Heidy Hunt
Sgt. Krug	Leo Gordon
Corporal Bruckner	Robert Wolders
Lt. Boyden	Anthony Ashdown
German Colonel	Curt Lowens
Corporal Stuhler	Henry Rico Cattani
Taureg Chieftan	Peter Coe
Italian Officer	Lawrence Montaigne
British Corporal	Robert Hoy
S.I.G. Bocker	Phil Adams
S.I.G. Schell	Ronnie R. Rondell

"Tobruk" reenters the cinematic World War II scene as a colorful, hard-hitting melodrama with plenty of guts and suspense to hold the action buff. Story-line of the Gene Corman production occasionally becomes over-complicated and femme audiences may blanch at some of the fighting but film generally stacks up as a suitable entry for its market, where a strong take is indicated.

Rock Hudson heads the four-name star roster but actually comes out third best as George Peppard and Nigel Green take precedence over him in point of interesting characterizations. Guy Stockwell, advancing steadily in his career, is fourth above title in a brief but authoritative role. Supporting parts are well-cast by Corman, who has packed his unfoldment with type of production values which pay off visibly on the screen.

Leo V. Gordon's screenplay has a serviceable plot twist as he projects his protagonists on a suicidal mission in the North African war of 1942. Daring plan calls for a British column of 90, composed of Commandos and German-born Jews who have come over to the Allies to form a special attack unit, to cross the Libyan Desert to Tobruk Mediterranean seaport in the hands of 50,000 German and Italian troops.

Once there, they are to hold its key fortified positions pending arrival of a British naval force, and blow up the gigantic German fuel bunkers upon which Rommel depends for his push to the Suez Canal. To reach their objective through the massive enemy lines, the German-speaking Jews are to masquerade as Nazis while bringing the Commandos through Axis checkpoints as prisoners of war.

Arthur Hiller's realistic direction makes the most of the premise, both in the eight-day desert trek and approach and invasion of Tobruk. On the desert, they nearly run into an Italian column which has set up camp a short distance away, and their position is further jeopardized by a large unit of the German Afrika Korps. By a ruse they make the two Axis forces think they are being attacked by one another as the British escape. At Tobruk, the enemy discovers the trick. Extensive use of flame-throwers heightens excitement.

Peppard scores heavily as leader of the Jews, delivering a finely-restrained performance, & Green is equally effective as the British colonel in command of the column. Hudson suffers from a role, in which he plays an English major, that allows him little opportunity for any more than a walk-through portrayal.

Standouts in support include scripter Gordon, as one of Peppard's men; Jack Watson as the sergeant-major; Robert Wolders & Henry Rico Cattani, two more of Peppard's group; Norman Rossington and Percy Herbert as Commandos. Liam Redmond is a German civilian spy.

Russell Harlan's color cameras lend high visual interest and Bronislaw Kaper's music score catches story mood. Balance of technical credits are well handled. *Whit.*

Arrivederci, Baby
(BRITISH-COLOR-
PANAVISION)

Silly sex farce with Tony Curtis as a modern Bluebeard. Scripted and played low for burley effect, sometimes tasteless. Rosanna Schiaffino adds to international marquee lure. Opulent production values. Okay b.o., but probably spotty.

Hollywood, Dec. 13.
Paramount Pictures release, in association with Seven Arts-Ray Stark, of a Ken Hughes production, directed by Hughes. Stars Tony Curtis, Rosanna Schiaffino; features Lionel Jeffries, Zsa Zsa Gabor, Nancy Kwan. Screenplay, Hughes, from a Hughes-Ronald Harwood story, suggested by Richard Deming's "The Careful Man"; camera (Technicolor), Denys Coop; editor, John Shirley; music, Dennis Farnon; second unit director, Richard Taylor; asst. director, Colin Brewer. Reviewed at Paramount Studios, L.A., Dec. 12, '66. Running Time, 100 MINS.

Nick Johnson	Tony Curtis
Francesca	Rosanna Schiaffino
Parker	Lionel Jeffries
Gigi	Zsa Zsa Gabor
Baby	Nancy Kwan
Fenella	Fenella Fielding
Aunt Miriam	Anna Quayle
Conte de Rienzi, Max	Warren Mitchell
Romeo	Mischa Auer
Capt. O'Flannery	Noel Purcell
U.S. Officer	Alan Gifford
German Officer	Joseph Furst
Butler	Monti De Lyle
French Inspector	Bernard Spear
Italian Dressmaker	Eileen Way
Headwaiter	Bruno Barnabe
Gypsy Baron	Gabor Baraker
Baby's Boyfriend	Tony Baron
Matron	Eunice Black
Radio Engineers	John Brandon, Windsor Davies
Romano	Franco DeRosa
Boy In Orphanage	John Fordyce
Maids	Iole Marinelli, Miki Iveria
Priest	Henri Vidon
Photographer	Raymond Young

"Arrivederci, Baby" is a silly sex comedy, as amusing at times as it is tasteless, in which Tony Curtis plays a contemporary Bluebeard. Colorful scenery and production values, plus tricky editing, give eye appeal. Individual performances and scenes have more merit than the ensemble footage. Younger audiences may go for the Paramount-Seven Arts-Ray Stark presentation, but overall b.o. outlook seems okay, if spotty, on general dual bills.

Producer-director Ken Hughes scripted, from a Hughes-Ronald Harwood story, in turn suggested by Richard Deming's "The Careful Man." Curtis stars as a gold-digging spouse-killer, who meets his match in Rosanna Schiaffino, a femme counterpart. Actual British and Continental locales give authenticity to the film, which was polished at England's Shepperton Studios. Richard McWhorter and Greg Morrison were associate producers.

Story attempts to make likeable a character who arranges the death of his femme guardian, her sailor suitor, later his first two wives and, unsuccessfully, Miss Schiaffino, bride-widow of an a.k. who expires in honeymoon excitement. Gimmick will repel those who do not find humor in explicit electrocution, drowning, etc., nor bedroom hanky-panky while a still-warm corpse reposes nearby. Implicit gore, seemingly a lost cinematic touch (even for Alfred Hitchcock), would have upgraded the comedy effect. As is, film suggests laterday burlesque, mortuary style.

Withal, Curtis does a very good job, plotting with Lionel Jeffries to do in Miss Schiaffino, whose knockout looks are heightened by Balmain gowns and recurring periods of undress, is by no means without acting ability, either. After 75 minutes, it finally becomes clear that she has worked the quick-marriage, sudden-death route before. They fall in love while plotting each other's demise, but have a change of heart and settle down at fadeout to Italian semi-poverty.

Script abounds in lecherous one-liners, ably put over by Anna Quayle, palpitating in the Marilyn Monroe manner as Curtis' guardian; Zsa Zsa Gabor, the non-stop gabber whom Curtis locks in a space vehicle at blast-off, and Fenella Fielding, the English heiress of robust appetites and bank accounts. Nancy Kwan also is good as Curtis' regular gal friend, who takes up with Warren Mitchell, eventual heir to the estate of Miss Schiaffino's short-lived hubby. Other players are equally competent.

Hughes' dialog includes a line which film buffs will recall instantly as spoken by Gloria Swanson from the Charles Brackett-Billy Wilder-D. M. Marshman Jr. script for "Sunset Boulevard," 1950 Paramount pic. Herein, Curtis talks about oil wells, "pumping . . . pumping . . . pumping."

Dennis Farnon's music is appropriately obtrusive, and The Plainsmen, as a Riviera rock-roll group, plus Tibor Kunstler's gypsy band, add further to the desired sound and fury. Denys Coop's Technicolor-Panavision camera lends opulence. Richard Taylor's second unit direction also is a big production asset. John Shirley edited to 100 minutes, a bit long because of the lengthy flashbacks to Misses Quayle, Gabor and Feielding, which alone take 32 minutes of screen time. Other technical credits are pro. *Murf.*

The Spy With A Cold Nose
(ENGLISH-COLOR)

Topnotch secret agent satire which should find response among all ages.

Hollywood, Dec. 15.
Embassy release of Associated London Films (Leonard Lightstone) production. Stars Laurence Harvey, Daliah Lavi, Lionel Jeffries; features Eric Sykes, Eric Portman, Denholm Elliott, Paul Ford. Directed by Daniel Petrie. Screenplay-original story, Ray Galton, Alan Simpson; camera (PatheColor), Kenneth Higgins; editor, Jack Slade; music, Ortolani; asst. director, Colin Brewer. Reviewed at Joe Shore's projection room, Dec. 15, '66. Running Time, 93 MINS.

Dr. Francis Trevellyan	Laurence Harvey
Princess Natasha Romanova	Daliah Lavi
Stanley Farquhar	Lionel Jeffries
Wrigley	Eric Sykes
British Ambassador	Eric Portman
Pond-Jones	Denholm Elliott
Russian Premier	Colin Blakely
Elsie Farquhar	June Whitfield
Belly Dancer	Nai Bonet
Disraeli	Himself
American General	Paul Ford
Professor	Peter Bayliss
Chief of M.I. 5	Robert Flemyng
M.I. 5 Commander	Robin Bailey
Night Club Hostess	Geneveve
Nurse	Norma Foster
Lady Blanchflower	Renee Houston
Braithwaite	Michael Trubshawe
Miss Marchbanks	Amy Dalby

One of the better British imports, "The Spy With a Cold Nose" is an ingeniously-contrived satire that should find wide response from all ages among appreciative American audiences. The "spy" in this case is an English bulldog presented by the English prime minister to the Soviet prime minister, surgically-inserted with a tiny transistor capable of transmitting conversation 2,000 miles. The chief protagonist in the witty espionage tale that fits admirably in the current trend is a bumbling British counter-intelligence agent who keeps a complete diary for his memoirs.

Leonard Lightstone has endowed his production with physical values, attractive people and amusing situations which Ray Galton and Alan Simpson in their original story and screenplay have developed into as clever material as seen in many a day. Daniel Petrie's direction never misses a card in taking advantage of the central theme and his touch is deft and blessed with true understanding. Art direction by Peter Mullins is a particularly strong asset in lavish sets and colorful London backgrounds.

Three genuine talents are starred. Laurence Harvey plays a fashionable London veterinarian to whom wealthy matrons bring their pampered pets for medical aid and more substantial solace for themselves. Daliah Lavi is an exotic Latvian princess working as a spy for the Soviet government. And Lionel Jeffries is the inept British agent who finally has a flash of genius and dreams up the plan for bugging the Kremlin by having implant the powerful mike-transmitter in the pooch which is to be a state gift to the Soviets. The smoothly-flowing narrative builds to droll finale with O. Henry overtones.

Jeffrie's timing is superb in his enactment of a role the perfect antithesis of James Bond, and Miss Lavi make Mata Hari look like a schoolgirl. Harvey's comicking is more on the broad side, but the character is amusing and strikes just the right tone. Eric Sykes as Jeffries' nitwit assistant, Eric Portman as the British prime minister and Colin Blakely his Russian opposite lend strong support, as does June Whitfield as Jeffries' missu. Paul Ford is in for a brief guest spot as an American general who has come under Miss Lavi's chams.

Technical credits rate highly. Kenneth Higgins' color photography is interesting, Jack Slade's editing fast, and music score by Riz Ortolani tuneful. *Whit.*

Juguetes Rotos
(Broken Toys)
(SPANISH)

Madrid, Dec. 4.
A Paraguas Films production distributed by P.E.F.S.A. Stars Paulino Azcudum, Nicanor Villalta, Guillermo Gorostiza. Directed by Manuel Summers; camera, Luis Cuadrado, Francisco Fraile. Running Time, 84 MINS.

This is the fourth film in as many years from young Spanish director Manuel Summers, one of the principals in his country's recent film resurgence. Like his earlier works it has opened to favorable reviews, since Summers can be counted on for interesting stories treated sincerely and in a consciously "arty" manner. And like "Del Rosa al Amarillo" (From Pink to Yellow), it explores a Summers preoccupation: the futility and loneliness of old age as contrasted with past youthful glories, here represented by three Spanish ex-heroes who are now forgotten—a champion boxer, a football star and a popular bullfighter.

Basically it is a collage—of old film clips of the stars in action, of faded still photographs, of scenes from pictures they made, of sequences of their present daily life—narrated by the protagonists and/or an interlocutor. The images are forceful, indeed often brutal (the photography is excellent, by far the best of any Summers film), but their arrangement is at times naive or overemphatic. Summers has a point of view — that old age is hell — which he beats a little too hard. Though always interesting, the film could and should have been shorter.

Will it interest an international audience? Probably not. Though the film presents a good general look at many of the customs and values of modern Spain, it is essentially too personal a vision, marred by sight gags, superficial asides and its anything-goes style. Even within Spain Summers has had trouble finding a distributor, and only in part because "the Spanish public just isn't prepared for this type of thing." "Los Tarantos" and "La Tia Tula," to cite two recent successful Spanish exports, treated areas just as narrow, but in a wider, more universal manner. Summers' film demands a much closer acquaintance with things Spanish than outside audiences are apt to have, and even then might seem superficial or labored.   *Lyon.*

Hallucination Generation

Routine programmer using LSD as shock gimmick. Made-in-Spain indie itself more sedative than stimulant.

Trans American Films release of an Edward Mann-Robert D. Weinbach (Herbert R. Steinmann) production. Features George Montgomery, Danny Stone. Directed and written by Edward Mann. Produced by Nigel Cox. Camera (with brief color segments), Francisco Sempere; editor, Fima Noveck; music, Bernardo Segall. Reviewed in N.Y., Dec. 14, '66. Running Time, **90 MINS.**

Eric	George Montgomery
Bill Williams	Danny Stone
Lise	Renate Kasche
Denny	Tom Baker
Carol	Marianne Kanter
Stan	Steve Rowland

This is first release by Trans American Films, recently-formed special film arm of American International Pictures, and judging by its content, "special" is evidently not intended to mean artistic, creative, or any of the other adjectives used by the art subsids of major distributors. Actually an acquisition, this independently-produced, filmed-in-Spain routine programmer properly belongs in the same department as AIP's "Wild Angels." It has already

opened in San Diego and is evidently to be rushed onto the market.

There's confusion as to production credits for "Hallucination," one-word title the film had until AIP's title-changing department took over. It's a Herbert R. Steinmann presentation, plus Nigel Cox producer, Robert D. Weinbach executive producer, and Jerome A. Siegel and Morton M. Rosenfeld, associate producers. As a motion picture, however, most of the handiwork is evidently that of Edward Mann, who wrote the story and directed it.

Despite the evident intention of plugging the film as a cinematic substitute for LSD, with the filmgoer promised something new in experiences, the disputed-as-to-danger drug is dragged in to juice up a thin tale of American beatniks in Spain and their aborted attempt **to pull off a robbery, resulting in a murder.** If the goings-on could have lived up to some excellent black-and-white camerawork by Francisco Sempere, they might have been something original but the screenplay provided by Mann, and his direction of it, plus uniformly poor acting by the entire cast, never let the film come to life. The potentialities of special effects and trick photography to shsow the psychedelic effects of LSD are ignored, with only a few amateurish color segments inserted that create laughter rather than interest.

George Montgomery's flatly-played character strongly suggests, in background, an American teacher who used his students in hallucinatory drug experiments (but where the real-life prof only lost his job, Montgomery gets pulled in with all the others as results of the murder). There's the usual disclaimer that the characters are purely fictional. Danny Stone as the principal subject of his experiments makes little impression, hampered by extensive mannerisms.

All the principals, despite the Spain locations, appear to be American or, in case of femme lead Renate Kasche, German. This may have been to avoid antagonizing the Spanish sensitivity but there are several bit roles, supposedly natives, that include streetwalkers, homosexuals, and a few police.

Technical aspects are average, other than aforementioned photography, but with an evidently small budget, Trans American should get its investment back quickly. With sufficent sexploitation and shock appeal of suggestive title, pic could arouse some prurient profits.   *Robe.*

Bariera
(Barrier)
(POLISH)

Paris, Dec. 11.
Film Polski release of Kamera Unit production. With Jan Nowicki, Joanna Szczerbic, Tadeusz Lomnicki, Zygmunt Malonowicz. Written and directed by Jerzy Skolimovski. Camera, Jan Laskowski; music, Krzysztof Komeda. Previewed in Paris. Running Time, **83 MINS.**

He	Jan Nowicki
She	Joanna Szczerbic
Doctor	Tadeusz Lomnicki
Eddy	Zygmunt Malonowicz
Manius	Andrzej Herder

A symbolical presentation of a young man's travels through the

Poland of today marks a more forthright thematic approach reappearing in Polski pix after a batch of historical specs and a few pix with the more touchy, probing look at their countries that has been appearing in Czechoslovakia and Hungary.

It is fairly far out in its approach to themes of youthful disillusionment, corruption in many walks of life, growing bitterness among youth and a generally grim picture of life in that country today. Yet there is no cynicism, and some true sentiment rather than sentimentality, plus a romantic dash that keeps this from being bleak or plodding.

Film appears mainly for arty spots abroad since many of its implications may be lost to those without some knowledge of the recent Polish films, country and politics. But it is also clear in its scenes of a young man's quest for some meaning and a substitution of outright material outlook for the now outmoded revolutionary ideals. The scenes give a clear look at the progress of this earthy pilgrim as he comes up against bureaucracy, aimlessness, lack of material goods or comfort or some coherent outlook, and finally finds some meaning in a relationship with a young femme streetcar driver.

Director Jerzy Skolimovksi imbues this with a series of impressionistic images that amply mirror the hero's progress sans trickery or archness or undue mannerisms. First he wins some group savings from other friends in a harsh game and decides to use it for himself rather than share it. From his father he gets an old sabre that symbolizes, perhaps, old Polish romanticism, and which he carries with him and sometimes uses in strange fights or forays.

Pic is a tantalizing offbeater that, while it may be strictly for arty chances abroad, manages to give a clear insight into some Polski youthful plaints about regimentation, plus shedding light on a growing individuality in that country. Film is technically topflight with the right use of thesps to convey symbolical as well as personal traits. It is an absorbing pic.   *Mosk.*

Blow-Up
(BRITISH-COLOR)

Archetypical Italo Avantegarde director Antonioni in full symbolism. Art houses for sure but average U. S. audiences likely to be puzzled.

Hollywood, Dec. 16.
Premier Productions presentation of Carlo Ponti production. Stars Vanessa Redgrave, David Hemmings, Sarah Miles. Directed by Michelangelo Antonioni. Screenplay, Antonioni, Tonino Guerra, in collaboration with Edward Bond; story, Antonioni; camera (Metrocolor), Carlo di Palma; editor, Frank Clarke; music, Herbert Hancock; asst. director, Claude Watson. Reviewed at Directors Guild of America Theatre, Dec. 14, '66. Running Time, **110 MINS.**

Jane	Vanessa Redgrave
Thomas	David Hemmings
Patricia	Sarah Miles

There may be some meaning, some commentary about life being a game, to 'Blow-Up' beyond what remains locked in the mind of its

creator, Italian director-writer Michelangelo Antonioni. But it is doubtful that the general public (anymore than this reviewer) will get the "message" of this film, shrouded as it is in shadings and symbols, in mysterious mummery and way-out treatment. As a commentary on a sordid, confused side of humanity in this modern age it's a bust.

Metro originally was skedded to release the Carlo Ponti production, which it financed. However, when a Code Seal was denied unless certain scenes were deleted and Antonioni refused any scissoring as his claimed right of artistic control, MGM decided to by-pass distribution under its corporate label. It now goes out as a "Premier Productions presentation of a Carlo Ponti production," through one of Metro's obscure releasing outlets.

Film will go into release sans the industry seal, which makes questionable any general release. At best, "Blow-Up" is for the most select of selected situations and an art house entry. Even with the liberalized Code it goes far beyond the limits of good taste, thru nudie action and play which undoubtedly will be found offensive by many.

Filmed in England and Antonioni's first English-speaking production, interesting use is made of London backgrounds. There also is certain sustained interest at times as the audience presses hopefully to piece together the significance of the story (?). What stumps the spectators is the avowed intention of the director, who also authored the original story(?) and coscripted with Tonino Guerra, as explained in a program: "he explores an exciting new area in his probing study of human nature and patterns, and individual's inability to distinguish certainty from fantasy, reality from the image."

Footage centers on a topflight London fashion photographer who learns of a murder through his secret lensing of a couple he sees embracing in a park. Through a series of blow-ups of the many exposures he snapped he finds indications of a murder, and visiting the park again discovers the body of the man whom he had been photographing. Then sequences are intriguingly developed by Antonioni.

Unreelment virtually is devoid of music score, and frequently there are long lapses of dialog as camera focuses on the photographer as he prowls London and its environs. Actually, this lack of anything but actual sound effects adds to reality, which occasionally reaches a high degree.

David Hemmings makes an interesting impression as the bulber whose studio is invaded by various femmes, and Vanessa Redgrave, as the woman involved in the park, projects another vivid impression. Sarah Miles, third member of cast, has little to do except appear in a snuggling scene which well might not pass the censors.

Ponti as producer has given lush production mounting and Antonioni establishes a mood in his direction for what he probably had in mind but seldom imparts to the audience. Carlo di Palma's color photography is an achievement and Ashton Gorton's art direction likewise is superlative. *Whit.*

Grand Prix
(CINERAMA-SUPER PANA-VISION-COLOR)

Stock characters but big action in Cinerama makes noisy ..automobiler likely b.o.

Hollywood, Dec. 21.

Metro-Goldwyn-Mayer release of a Douglas & Lewis Production, produced by Edward Lewis. Stars James Garner, Eva Marie Saint, Yves Montand, Toshiro Mifune, Brian Bedford, Jessica Walter, Antonio Sabato, Francoise Hardy. Directed by John Frankenheimer. Screenplay, Robert Alan Aurthur; camera (Metrocolor), Lionel Lindon; second unit camera, John M. Stephens, Jean-Georges Fontenelle, Yann Le Masson; editors, Frederic Steinkamp, Henry Berman, Stewart Linder, Frank Santillo; music, Maurice Jarre; production design, Richard Sylbert; asst. director, Enrico Isacco. Reviewed at Pacific's Cinerama Theatre, L.A., Dec. 21, '66. Running Time (excluding intermission), **179 MINS.**

Pete Aron	James Garner
Louise Frederickson	Eva Marie Saint
Jean-Pierre Sarti	Yves Montand
Izo Yamura	Toshiro Mifune
Scott Stoddard	Brian Bedford
Pat	Jessica Walter
N'no Barlini	Antonio Sabato
Lisa	Francoise Hardy
Agostini Manetta	Adolfo Celi
Hugo Simon	Claude Dauphin
Guido	Enzo Fiermonte
Monique Delvaux Sarti	Genevieve Page
Jeff Jordan	Jack Watson
Wallace Bennett	Donal O'Brien
Children's Father	Jean Michaud
Surgeon	Albert Remy
Mrs. Stoddard	Rachel Kempson
Mr. Stoddard	Ralph Michael
Sportscasters	Alan Fordney,
	Anthony Marsh, Tommy Franklin
Tim Randolph	Phil Hill
Bob Turner	Graham Hill
Journalist	Bernard Cahier

John Frankenheimer has given MGM a hot boxoffice runner in "Grand Prix." He also has placed a pace-setter for the Academy's technical awards sweepstakes. The roar and whine' of engines sending men and machines hurtling over the 10 top road and track courses of Europe, the U.S. and Mexico—the Grand Prix Circuits—are the prime motivating forces of this actioncrammed adventure that director Frankenheimer and producer Edward Lewis have, with able assistance from writer Robert Alan Aurthur, and an always capable, interesting cast of performers, interlarded with personal drama that is sometimes introspectively revealing, occasionally mundane, but generally a most serviceable framework.

The real stars of "Grand Prix," however, are the cameramen — Lionel Lindon and his second unit team consisting of John M. Stephens, Jean-Georges Fontenelle, Yann Le Masson—and the technicians behind them who worked out intricate business of running with the racing cars, all within the overall production design by Richard Sylbert. This emphasis on the technical is, in this instance, not meant to lessen appreciation for performances well done upon the part of the players. But "Grand Prix" is one of those rare pictures that draws its basic strength, excitement and interest-arresting potential through the visual (the pure art of cinema) and if it lacked brilliant virtuosity in the action department it would be just another filmflam.

With the oversized Cinerama screen to engulf the spectator in the action, the versatile Super-Panavision lenses and color to capture the flavor of the European courses and countryside, where most of the story takes place, the photography is more often than not a cause of wonderment. It is quite possible that for some viewers, director Frankenheimer might have gone one course too many, but it must be said that all of his meets, including those capsuled. are staged with tension and suspense. In fact, Frankenheimer starts the picture on a high note of excitement as the camera follows such principals as James Garner, Yves Montand, Brian Bedford and Antonio Sabato over the tight, winding Monaco road course, with Garner and Bedford figuring in a spectacular crash that sends them flying into the Mediterranean.

This is a pulse-stopper. One might easily jump ahead—a good two hours or more ahead—and say, "how's he going to beat that?" But top it Frankenheimer does, with the climactic death of the physically tired, emotionally tormented and drained champion, Montand. That Garner was able to swim away from the first accident might tax credulity more than the fact that Bedford was carried away, but the fact that he is breathing, considering the literal flight of the cars into the drink, is equally remarkable. But go along with Frankenheimer—it would be difficult not to be caught up in the spell that he weaves with overall sure instinct —and the senses respond with a fresh new assault upon the flaming disaster for Montand.

Whatever the reaction of auto racing aficionados, as far as the uninitiated goes, "Grand Prix" has the ring of authenticity over the roads and courses of the Riviera, Spa Franconchamps (Belgium) Nurburging (Germany) Clermont-Ferrand (France), Brands Hatch (England), Zandvoort (Holland), Rheims (France), Watkins Glen (New York), Mexico City and the climactic meet at Monza (Italy).

Frankenheimer has shrewdly varied the length and the importance of the races that figure in the film and the overplay of running commentary on the various events, not always distinct above the roar of motors, imparts a documentary vitality. The director, moreover, has utilized the mobility of camera via intercutting and frequently dividing his outsized screen into sectional panels for a sort of montage interplay of reactions of the principals — a stream of conscience commentary —that adroitly prevents the road running from overwhelming the personal drama.

There is a curious thing, however, about the exposition of the characters in this screenplay. Under cold examination they are stock characters. Garner, American competitor in a field of Europeans, is somewhat taciturn, unencumbered by marital involvement. Montand has a wife in name and forms a genuine attachment for American fashion writer Eva Marie Saint, a divorcee. Bedford is the emotionally confused Britisher competing against the memory of his champion-driver brother and whose compulsion to be a champion almost wrecks his 'marriage to whilom American actress-model Jessica Walter. Antonio Sabato, youngest of the drivers and Montand's team mate, is the only uncomplicated one in the bunch, a free-loving soul, convinced of his own immortality, who takes his fun where he finds it and has an enjoyable relationship with newcomer Francoise Hardy.

Stock characters, to be sure. Yet scenarist Aurthur, has invested these individuals with distinctive personalities that are brought to meaningful life by the performers. They are equally good in their respective roles, some of which are by circumstance of plot development more complexly involved. The romance between Eva Marie Saint and Yves Montand is poignant and beautifully expressive in mature terms. There is a brooding tempestuousness and immaturity, yet an abiding bond that withstands indiscretion, in the marriage of Brian Bedford and Jessica Walter.

As the team mate who comes between the two, when importuned by the wife, but within his own curious rationale of the code of morals, Garner communicates with quiet effectiveness the problem of a man who has to be a winner, no matter what. In many ways the richest, most refreshing role has fallen to Antonio Sabato and he gives off sparks like a shorted high tension wire. He could be the John Garfield of this age if properly handled. Although no real demands are made upon Francoise Hardy, she is to this youth generation born, handles herself with remarkable naturalness and indicates a strong potential.

Actually Aurthur has evolved a very busy plot and it is to Frankenheimer's credit that he has harnessed the many story offshoots and not permitted either them or the long race stretches to create an imbalance. He has juggled many elements with agility. Nor is "Grand Prix" without some meaningful observation about the compulsions that drive those involved.

Is it, for the drivers, the roar of the crowd, the chance at quick riches, the test of skill? Is it, for the spectators, the thrill, the thirst for blood, the balance between life and death? Or is it, as Garner expounds in a retrospective moment with Toshiro Mifune, the Japanese industrialist for whom he is driving in a chance to redeem himself in the big league, the certain brush with death that intensifies life for those who survive?

While some audiences will take away meaning from the story, chances are that the majority will respond to "Grand Prix" for its action and that, despite a tendency to lag here and there, should assure its boxoffice success.

To return to the contributions made by the technicians, natural sounds of revving motors and in racing motion are dramatically provocative and rate individual bows for sound editor Gordon Daniels and the recorders Franklin Milton and Roy Charman. The special effects and the racing camera mounts which made the exceptional photography possible, are the respective credits of Milt Rice and Frick Enterprises. Saul Bass was called upon as visual consultant and for the montages and titles and also did his job very well indeed. The Maurice Jarre score, which he also conducted, is effective but there is a recurring strain in the romantic theme which reminds too vividly of his brilliant score for MGM's "Doctor Zhivago." But the music is, by apparent design and final effect a secondary score, the primary one being the sounds of auto racing.

As with his principals, Frankenheimer has brought together an international cast of featured players. Among the more prominent in terms of roles, but all equally proficient, are Jack Watson, Claude Dauphin, Genevieve Page, Adolfo Celi, Rachel Kempson and Jean Michaud, who has a strong emotional role as father of a youth killed by Montand's car.

"Grand Prix," preceded by a short overture, runs two hours and 59 minutes, plus intermission. It could be trimmed beneficially for general release, but current length should not be a deterrent for initial hardticket outing.
Pry.

Thunderbirds Are Go
(BRITISH-COLOR)

Cinema bow of popular all-puppet sci-fi tv series to be seen soon in U.S. Feature, enhanced by color, makes good escapist entertainment for all ages.

London, Dec. 12.
United Artists release of Gerry Anderson production. Produced by Sylvia Anderson. Directed by David Lane. Screenplay by the Andersons; visual effects director, Derek Meddings; art director, Bob Bell; camera (Technicolor), Paddy Seale; editor, Len Walter; sound, John Peverell; music, Barry Gary. Voices by Miss Anderson, Ray Barrett, Alexander Davion, Peter Dyneley, Christine Finn, David Graham, Paul Maxwell, Neil McCallum, Bob Monkhouse, Shane Rimmer, Charles Tingwell, Jeremy Wilkin, Matt Zimmermann. At London Pavilion, London. Running Time, 94 MINS.

Ostensibly designed for children, a sci-fi television all-puppet series which started in Britain a couple of years ago also gained a quiet but enthusiastic adult audience. Now a color series may well be seen in the States, but meanwhile, "Thunderbirds Are Go" makes its theatrical feature debut in U.K. and, in Technicolor and Supermarionation, is enhanced in entertainment value by size and color, though at 94 minutes it may well be pressing its time luck.

Though not ready bet for the sophisticated adult cinemagoer, only the supercilious will not find some quiet amusement in watching it, particularly with children, who will certainly lap it up. Technically, it is a firstrate job in its puppetry, color and special effects. Story is occasionally stretched thin and leans a little toward

over-technical jargon, but it is briskly directed by David Lane and is crammed with futuristic flying gimmicks.

Jeff Tracy, millionaire ex-astronaut, and his five stalwart sons form International Rescue, dedicated to getting worthy people out of jams. In this instance, the plot is set in the 21st century and International Rescue successfully aids Zero X, the first space ship to Mars, twice sabotaged in its efforts to get to the planet. When it does, it finds the atmosphere hostile and needs the help of I.R. again to get safely back to earth. The slim plot provides plenty of opportunity for intrepid work by the heroes and thrills as they bring their monster futuristic planes into service.

The pace is kept up pretty briskly throughout and pauses only for breath for a couple of tongue-in-cheek nightclub sequences which permit puppets of Cliff Richard and the Shadows to sing a couple of songs. Dialog, when not too technical, is sometimes a shade naive, but not laughably so. Apart from all the special effects (well handled by Derek Meddings and his term, the big gimmick of this obvious potential boxoffice hit is the puppets themselves, created and built in the Anderson film factory, and heavily paying off in merchandising.

Though somewhat restricted in facial movement the puppets are remarkably lifelike and have been given distinct characterizations of their own, with big league wardrobes, and no detail has been spared to make them resemble humans. Only making the puppets walk realistically has so far eluded exec producer Anderson and his wife Sylvia, who not only produces, but supervises the creation of the dummies and also acts as one of the voices. The two have also have written the screenplay. Walking problem has been solved by use of mechanical devices that project the characters from X to Y logically, and by smooth editing.

Outstanding among the puppets are Lady Penelope (voice by Miss Anderson), a blonde, resourceful, aristocratic young lady and her Cockney manservant, "Nosey" Parker (voice David Graham), who has a touch of the Ned Sparks about him. These two provide some light relief by their upper-class way of life. The rest of the puppets are more down to earth and don't provide much humor, some more of which could be used to good effect.

United Artists is releasing this novelty film worldwide, and its technical gimmickry, allied with characters and storyline which could well serve any of the current vogue films of secret agents, etc., should repay enthusiastic ex-exploitation.
Rich.

Dutchman
(BRITISH)

Excellent, literal 55-minute filming of Le Roi Jones' racial stage drama. Strong lingo and petting scenes mark this for adult audiences in specialty houses, where good b.o. is

likely. Question mark on Dixie dates.

Hollywood, Dec. 19.
Gene Persson Enterprises production. Features Shirley Knight, Al Freeman Jr. Directed by Anthony Harvey. No screenplay, filmed from Le Roi Jones' stage play; camera, Gerry Turpin; music, John Barry; asst. director, Christopher Dryhurst; second unit director, Edward R. Brown. Reviewed at Los Feliz Theatre, L.A., Dec. 18, '66. Running Time, 55 MINS.
Lula .... Shirley Knight
Clay .... Al Freeman Jr.

"Dutchman" is a literal filming of Le Roi Jones' 1964 off-Broadway play, pitting a white slut against a middle-class Negro youth who is, in turn, seduced, disgraced and killed. Excellent direction and performances are enhanced by realistically grim production values. Salty dialog tags this taut Gene Persson production for mature audiences in specialty houses, where good or better b.o. prospects loom. Inter-racial theme may limit Dixie bookings, although, ironically, the down beat climax actually caters to "white supremacy" prejudice.

Producer Persson cast wife Shirley Knight and Al Freeman Jr. as the leads, actually a re-teaming since both starred in his 1965 L.A. and Frisco legit mountings of the property. Pic was filmed at England's Pinewood Studios, using three cameras on a six-day sked. With all principals on deferred percentage, film came in for $65,000, with Eady Plan qualification to boot. Persson has not yet filmed a distrib deal, and the L.A. run was booked direct for Oscar qualification.

Anthony Harvey herein makes his directorial debut after a long career as a film editor. It is a challenging debut, since there is no screenplay, only Jones' legit dialog, and the action is confined to a N. Y. subway car, except for some second unit subway lensing by Edward R. Brown. Withal, Harvey's work is impressive, in eliciting adroit performances, in camera setups, and in overall editing pace.

Miss Knight, a red-neck Jezebel if there ever was one, is outstanding as she deliberately debases Freeman, dragging him down from insecure middle class status to that of an embittered, violent youth. This having been done, she stabs him after he has chewed her out in an electrifying tirade against whites. At fadeout, she approaches her next victim. The salty dialog and sensual petting is proper in context. Moods vary from underplayed irony to very well restrained, but still effective, outbursts.

Gerry Turpin's grim b&w lensing catches the dingy atmosphere of a N. Y. subway, achieved by art director Herbert Smith. John Barry has composed a very spare score, used at natural brief breaks. Harvey supervised the editing to a trim 55 minutes, about 10 minutes longer than a legit presentation. Sound effects are excellent, as are all other technical credits.

Hy Silverman was associate producer.
Murf.

The Bubble
(3-D—COLOR)

Film introduces Space-Vision (Tri-Optiscope), improved one-camera, one-projector 3-D system. (Audience wears Polaroid glasses.) Plot, however, is weak science fiction adventure that will have to rely on 3-D novelty to score at the box-office.

Chicago, Dec. 22.
Arch Oboler release of Midwestern Magic-Vuers production. Produced, directed and written by Arch Oboler. Stars Michael Cole, Deborah Walley and Johnny Desmond; features Kassie McMahon, Barbara Eiler, Virginia Gregg, Victor Perrin, Olan Soule and Chester Jones. Camera, Charles Wheeler; music, Paul Sawtell and Bert Shafter; film editor, Igo Kantor; associate producer, Marvin Chomsky; asst. director, Richard Dixon; art director, Marvin Chomsky; sound, Alfred Overton and Carl Daniels. Reviewed at Woods Theatre, Chicago, Dec. 21, '66. Running Time, 112 MINS.
Mark .... Michael Cole
Catherine .... Deborah Walley
Tony .... Johnny Desmond

It has been about 13 years since former radio writer (Procter & Gamble) Arch Oboler introduced 3-D motion pictures to American audiences via "Bwana Devil," a process that never got off the ground because of eye-strain engendered by two projectors, the high cost of operating them, double printing costs, etc. Now, however, Obler bows Space-Vision or 4-D (Tri-Optiscope), an improved stereo system for films which utilizes one standard Mitchell camera equipped with newly developed lens, and can be shown with one projector outfitted with a special prism system set in front of it. New arrangement causes no noticeable eye-strain, and it can be produced with standard printing and standard negatives.

Oboler states that Space-Vision took some 14 years to develop, with the last five years of work being intensive. The camera lens alone took one and a half years to grind. It was apparently worked on with a sort of "Manhattan Project" secrecy, and during the actual filming of "The Bubble," only the production crew and the three leads knew that a three-dimensional film was being made. The new system was developed under the supervision of Col. Robert Bernier, the former head of 3-D film research for the Armed Forces.

As with the original process, Polaroid glasses must be worn by the audience. The results, however, are striking enough so that the visual dividend usually compensates for the physical investment. Ultimately, of course, the patrons will decide whether Space-Vision will be successful. If the boxoffice supports Oboler's faith in 3-D, the new system may well have a strong effect on the motion picture industry, especially since the lens may be used on wide screen cameras.

Besides adding depth to the screen, a somewhat startling bonus is available with the new method. By playing upon the psychology of the eye, the visual centre can be fooled into believing that objects are leaving the screen. In short, Space-Vision can bring images within inches of the audience when that aim is desired.

In the first film produced with Space-Vision, the process is clearly the major ingredient of the entertainment. Oboler's "Bubble" falls short of its engaging premise. Story concerns young married couple who had their mountain vacation interrupted when wife goes into we-weren't-expecting-it-so-soon labor. While returning in a private plane piloted by a fun-loving Korean vet, they are caught in a storm and land in a strange, unidentified town. Burg's citizenry is in some sort of zombie groove, mechanically moving about, refusing to answer questions and generally ignoring the new arrivals. The baby is successfully delivered by a doctor who has a similar affliction.

Trio soon discover that a huge chunk of real etstate is covered by an enormous clear dome or bubble, and they are trapped within. To their further distress they learn that about every seven days whatever has imprisoned the area hauls someone off into the blue yonder, presumable for study of homo-sapiens. Young husband Mark heads for the hills with spouse Catherine and baby, and they move into an old mill while he attempts to dig a tunnel under the bubble.

Pilot Tony gets a going over when he and Mark investigate a mysterious "station," a peculiar rock structure with an equally strange seat in the middle. Tony sits back and gets a shock treatment, which is accompanied by convulsions and a fantasy with faces of monsters swirling about him, and, utilizing Space-Vision's capacity to bring objects away from the screen and into the theatre, the audience. From that point on Tony's support is questionable, and he is eventually given the stellar boo kand flits off toward the top of the dome.

Mark manages to dig to the bottom of the bubble, and in an attempt to get help from the doctor, wrecks the shock seat, which it turns out also fed the community. The young couple were using canned food from a store, and with little remaining, the town, deprived of its source of food, begins to starve. Eventually they follow Mark and Catherine toward the mill, apparently to aid him in his bid to escape.

Film runs aground with a pace that's too ponderous to maintain interest in the action. Too, repetitious scenes of the town and the zombie inhabitants becomes increasingly dull, even with a boost from 3-D.

An underlying theme which questions whether humans would find a perfunctory Utopia agreeable is opaque to the point of being almost undetectable. With most of the explanation of what has happened coming from Tony's lengthy analysis of the situation, very little is left for the audience's imagination. Although the creatures that dropped the bubble over the area are not seen, there is never any indication given what they might be, thereby negating potential excitement from a possible encounter.

In his film debut, Michael Cole impresses as a promising new actor. Often, though, he had problems with stagy dialog. Deborah Walley's portrayal of the bewildered and frightened young wife is usually in key, however, she was also hampered by the awkward script. Johnny Desmond is suitable as affable Tony, but the role is one of stock extremes, and his character is never satisfactorily developed.

Oboler's direction is slow and repetitious, and although he kept razzle-dazzle effects at a minimum, he was apparently unsure of how to use Space-Vision in its initial outing. Camera work and music are okay throughout. *Ron.*

Operazione San Gennaro
(Operation San Gennaro)
(ITALO-GERMAN-FRENCH)
(Color)

Rome, Dec. 16.

Lyre (Paris)-Roxy Film (Munich) coproduction. Interfilm release of Ultra Film (Turi Vasile). Features Nino Manfredi, Senta Berger, Mario Adorf, Harry Guardino, Claudine Auger, Toto', Vittoria Grispo, Ugo Fangareggi, Jean Louis, Dante Maggio, Ralf Wolter. Directed by Dino Risi. Screenplay, Risi, Adriano Baracco, Ennio DeConcini, Manfredi, from story by DeConcini and Risi; camera (Color), Aldo Tonti; sets, Luigi Saccianoce; editor, Franco Fraticelli; music, Armando Trovaioli. At Metropolitan, Rome. Running Time, **96 MINS.**

Dudu	Nino Manfredi
Maggie	Senta Berger
Sciascillo	Mario Adorf
Jack	Harry Guardino
Don Vincenzo	Toto'
Concettina	Claudine Auger

Fast and furiously funny, "Operation San Gennaro" is one of the more riotously amusing pix to come out of Italy in some time, and its home-ground impact is more than assured. It should emerge as the sleeper of the year here. While the spoofy, intelligent script with which it comes equipped will lose much in translation from its current dialectic form, more than enough of the sound and amusing music of pic's Neapolitan lingo—plus its many visual values—should help tickle foreign risibilities as well for fine returns on offshore marts.

Basic plot sees a Yank gangster type (Harry Guardino) and his moll (Senta Berger) sweep into Naples with a near-sacrilegious plan: to heist the treasure of Naples' patron saint, San Gennaro. They enlist aid of a local operator (Nino Manfredi) and his would-be "gang" and, after a comedy of errors and unexpected twists, manage to make off with it until the surprise windup leaves them holding the (empty) bag.

Tale is told at a sizzling pace, many inventive plot twists, several colorful sequences neatly integrating story and its backdrop, namely the teeming, seamy, yet human world-of-its-own that is the city by the Vesuvius. There's little time to pause and quibble with some of strained plot incidentals, just as some of dialog and situational gems are also sacrificed to film's breakneck pacing. Suffice it to say there's nary a dull moment along the way, and that it's keyed to audience pleasure from start to finish.

Reading the credit sheet, top mentions must go—in order—to team of scripters, to director Dino Risi for his continued control of material, and to such thesps as Nino Manfredi, Toto', Mario Adorf and a number of uncredited backdrop players who populate and enrich each scene. Harry Guardino does well by his Yank ganglander role, Senta Berger is eye-filling as his gal, while Claudine Auger appears a bit sacrificed as Manfredi's constantly-jealous financee, with little chance to repeat her "Thunderball" impact.

Aldo Tonti's color lensing on Naples locations is a rich plus feature, as is Armando Trovajoli's lilting musical backdrop. Production values are outstanding. *Hawk.*

Le Roi De Coeur
(King of Hearts)
(FRENCH-COLOR-TECHNISCOPE)

Paris, Dec. 25.

United Artists release of Fildebroc production. Stars Alan Bates, Jean-Claude Brialy, Genevieve Bujold; features Pierre Brasseur, Michel Serrault, Micheline Presle. Directed by Philippe De Broca. Screenplay, Daniel Boulanger; editor, Francoise Javet. At Marbeuf, Paris. Running Time, **100 MINS.**

Peter	Alan Bates
Cocqulicot	Genevieve Bujold
Marquis	Jean-Claude Brialy
Eglantine	Micheline Presle
General	Pierre Brasseur
Hairdresser	Michel Serrault
Lady	Francoise Christophe
Major	Adolfo Celli

The theme that insanity, but of the gentle lunar kind, is better than war is generally accepted by most men of good will. This French film uses it to spin a repetitive, wispy tale of an incident in World War I that does not quite have the poetic flair, invention, performance and insights to bring it off. But its avoidance of excessive vulgarity and probably well intentioned, if overdone, theme may have it of art values abroad if well placed, hypoed and followed up with playoff inherent for dualer use.

The characters are extremely theatrical, from stereotyped broad Germans to irascible but simple Scotsmen, with a group of asylum inmates as harmless dreamers and not very recognizable human or symbolical counterparts of so-called normals. The inmates find the door open when people of a small French town leave upon hearing that retreating Germans have set explosives that will blow up the whole town when the British get there.

The mad people take over the town and dress up as a local bordello madam, a bourgeois couple, circus performers, generals, hairdressers and just, apparently, 19th century boulevard comedy types rather than even settling for counterparts, albeit alienated, of that era.

Into this comes a little Scot soldier sent to destroy the explosives when wind of it comes to the British troops. He gets mixed up with the mad ones and is elected their king. Film then tries to put emphasis on the finding of the explosives with the British and Germans waiting on each side. The Scotsman also finds a girl, a winsome, schizoid type, and finally manages to ward off the big blow-up.

But the theme is hammered home when the Germans come back, mistaking fireworks for a holocaust, and they slaughter each other, since the British are there. The mad people go back to their asylum and the little Scotsman decides to throw away his uniform and applies at the asylum, to be with his friends, stark nude.

Director Philippe De Broca, who did the madcap, freewheeling action slapstick sagas "That Man from Rio" and "Up to His Ears," here mixes this sort of thing with attempted poetics and more weighty themes. The mad people, fortunately, are not just figures of fun; but there is neither the effective ironic counterpoint to war, since both are treated in a broad comedic manner, nor a true feeling of war's madness and loss, especially when set in a never-never version of World War 1.

Alan Bates cannot do much with his role of the little Scot soldier, but does show dash and presence against his dialog which is one-dimensional. Others play their mad roles a la characters from old farces, with a certain bittersweet sense of loss or alienation only intermittently suggested.

Color is good and the use of a picturesque old town is also an asset. But uneven scripting and a repetitive storyline do not quite make it jell on a poetic level or as a parable on war. Still, its offbeat comedics and treatment might make this a contender for arty spots. *Mosk.*

The Family Way
(BRITISH-COLOR)

Hayley Mills hesitantly bridges the gap between adolescence and womenhood in a warm-hearted, earthy comedy handled with tact by the Boulting Brothers.

London, Dec. 22.

British Lion presentation through BLC of a Boulting Bros. production. Stars Hayley Mills, John Mills, Hywell Bennett, Marjorie Rhodes. Features Avril Angers, Wilfred Pickles, Liz Fraser, John Comer, Barry Foster, Murray Head. Produced by John Boulting. Directed by Roy Boulting. Screenplay by Bill Naughton and adapted by Roy Boulting and Jeffrey Dell, from Naughton's play, "All In Good Time"; music, Paul McCartney; camera, (Eastmancolor), Harry Waxman; editor, Ernest Hosler; sound, Christopher Lancaster. At Warner Theatre, London. Running Time, **114 MINS.**

Jenny	Hayley Mills
Liz	Avril Angers
Leslie	John Comer
Uncle Fred	Wilfred Pickles
Ezra	John Mills
Lucy	Marjorie Rhodes
Joe Thompson	Barry Foster
Mollie Thompson	Liz Fraser
Eddie	Andrew Bradford
The Vicar	Thorley Walters
Travel Agent	Colin Gordon
His Assistant	Robin Parkinson
Marriage Councillor	Ruth Trouncer
Housing Officer	Harry Locke
His Secretary	Maureen O'Reilly
Dora	Leslie Daine
Mrs. Bell	Hazel Bainbridge
Neighbors	Ruth Gower, Diana Coupland, Fanny Carby, Helen Booth, Margaret Lacey

Boulting Bros. have moved out of their usual groove of deflating authority, pomposity and institutions and the result is one of their best releases for some time. Based on Bill Naughton's warm-hearted play, "All In Good Time," and adapted by Roy Boulting and Jeffrey Dell, it's the story of an innocent young couple who marry and, because of the environment of the North Country home in which they live, are unable to consummate their marriage. It stars

Hayley Mills in an adult role, and also her father, John Mills, and they should provide adequate marquee bait in the States as well as in Britain.

Here's a film that could have turned out to be one big leer and a mock of a sensitive subject. But the Boultings, while not neglecting the chance of the occasional acid jab and some earthy, good-natured vulgar h u m o r, have shown tact in describing the problem of the young couple. Only the change of title seems to be an unnecessary error.

The youngsters (Hayley Mills and Hywell Bennett) marry and because of circumstances have to live with the lad's parents. Even the honeymoon is a disaster since a flyaway travel agent cheats them out of their package deal trip to the Continent. The wedding party grates on the sensitive young couple, with the usual robust cracks from guests and the practical joke which ensures that their bed collapses on the first night. An inability to communicate with his kindly but over-bluff father is only one of the pinpricks that get on Bennett's nerves and make him incapable of doing his duty as a husband. The story of his alleged impotence gets around the little North town community in a wave of gossip and the misery of the young couple grows. Of course, it all turns out with a happy ending but the building up is skilfully done and with an affectionate tact.

Hayley Mills gets away from her Disney image as the young bride, even essaying an undressed scene, but it looks as if she is going to have some difficulty in bridging the gap between adolescent and more mature adult roles. Bennett, a newcomer, is excellent as the sensitive young bridegroom and looks to have a potential, judging by this appearance. But it is the older hands who keep the film floating on a wave of fun, sentiment and sympathy.

John Mills is firstclass in a character role as the bluff father who cannot understand his son ("all that reading!") and produces the lower working class man's vulgarity without overdoing it. Avril Angers as the girl's acid mother and John Comer as her husband are equally effective, but the best performance comes from Marjorie Rhodes as Mill's astute but understanding wife. Murray Head, Liz Fraser, Colin G o r d o n, Harry Locke, Lesley Daine and Wilfred Pickles also contribute toprate cameos.

The film, directed by Roy Boulting and produced by his brother John, was filmed largely on location in Bolton, Lancashire, and this creates an authenticity which helps a lot. Played less farcically and more compassionately than on stage the film has the advantage of a neat, resourceful score by Beatle Paul McCartney and keen Eastmancolor lensing by Harry Waxman. Editing by Ernest Hosler is smooth and the 114 minutes does not appear excessive, though it probably is for the slight story. The shrewd observation in the tavern wedding reception sequence alone makes this film worth seeing, but overall it emerges as one of the best British productions of the year. *Rich.*

One Million Years B.C.
(BRITISH—COLOR)

Adventure hokum w h i c h should do wel'. Gives Raquel Welch a physical, if not thespic, boost.

London, Dec. 22.
Warner-Pathe release of a Hammer Production for Associated British-Pathe. Stars Raquel Welch, John Richardson. Features Percy Herbert, Robert Brown, Martine Beswick. Produced by Michael Carreras. Directed by Don Chaffney. Screenplay by Carreras, adapted from an original by Mickell Novak, George Baker, Joseph Frickert; special visual effects by Ray Harryhausen; music, Mario Nascimbene; editor, James Needs; camera (Technicolor), Wilkie Cooper. Previewed at Warner Theatre, London, Dec. 20, '66. Running Time, 100 MINS.
Loana .... Raquel Welch
Tumak .... John Richardson
Sakama .... Percy Herbert
Akhoba .... Robert Brown
Nupondi .... Martine Beswick
Ahot .... Jean Waldon
Sara .... Lisa Thomas
Tohana .... Malya Nappi
Young Rock Man........Richard James
Payto .... William Lyon Brown
1st Rock Man .... Frank Hayden
1st Shell Man ..... Terence Maidment
1st Shell Girl .... Micky De Rauch
Ullah .... Yvonne Horner

Biggest novelty gimmick of this likely click for unsophisticated situations is that, depite four writers on screenplay (including director Michael Carreras), dialog is minimal, consisting almost entirely of grunts. More saleable gimmick is that, at last, the nubile Raquel Welch is on view. Till more seen in stills than screened, Miss Welch here gets little opportunity to prove herself an actress but she is certainly there in the looks department.

Don Chaffey does a reliable job directorially, but leans heavily on the ingenious special effects in the shape of prehistoric animals and a striking earthquake dreamed up by Ray Harryhausen. Simple idea of the film is of the earth as a barren, hostile place, 1,000,000 years B.C., inhabitated by two tribes, the aggresssive Rock People and the more intelligent, gentler Shell People.

John Richardson plays a Rock man who is banished after a fight with his gross father (Robert Brown). Wandering the land, battling off fearful rubber prehistoric monsters, he comes across the Shell People and falls for Miss Welch, one of the Shell handmaidens. The two go off together to face innumerable other hazards. Then comes the earthquake. Then comes the end of the film and a better, more peaceable world with the two lovers still fighting for survival. But together.

The whole thing is good humored full-of-action commercial nonsense but the moppets will love it and older male moppets will probably love Miss Welch. Wilkie Cooooper, in Eastmancolor, has done fair justice to Harryhausen's effects and the only criticism that can seriously be made against the pic is that it is a pity that a full feature film has been made in which the cast, which includes Percy Herbert, Robert Brown, Marrine Beswick and several other reliable thesps, should have a minimal opportunity of doing some solid acting. *Rich.*

1967

A Countess From Hong Kong
(BRITISH-COLOR)

Three top names of Loren, Brando, Chaplin for the marquee will provide exploitation opportunities to achieve desired results.

London, Jan. 6.

Universal Pictures release of a Charles Chaplin presentation (Jerome Epstein, producer). Stars Marlon Brando and Sophia Loren; features Sydney Chaplin, Tippi Hedren, Patrick Cargill, Margaret Rutherford. Directed, written and scored by Chaplin; camera (Technicolor), Arthur Ibbetson; editor, Gordon Hales; sound, Michael Hopkins. At Carlton Theatre, London; Running Time; 120 MINS.

Ogden	Marlon Brando
Natascha	Sophia Loren
Harvey	Sydney Chaplin
Martha	Tippi Hedren
Hudson	Patrick Cargill
John Felix	Michael Medwin
Clark	Oliver Johnston
Captain	John Paul
Society girl	Angela Scoular
Miss Gaulswallow	Margaret Rutherford
Steward	Peter Barlett
Crawford	Bill Nagy
Saleswoman	Dillys Laye
Baroness	Angela Pringle
Countess	Jenny Bridges
Immigration officer	Arthur Gross
French maid	Balbina
Hawaiians	Anthony Chin, Jose Sukhum Boonlve
Girl at dance	Janine Hill
Hotel receptionist	Burnell Tucker
Purser	Leonard Trolley
Electrician	Len Lowe
Head waiter	Francis Dux
Taxi driver	Cecil Cheng
American sailors	Ronald Rubin, Michael Spice, Ray Marlowe
Photographer	Kevin Manser
Reporters	Marianne Stone, Lew Luton, Larry Cross, Bill Edwards, Drew Russell, John Sterland, Paul Carson, Paul Tamarin
Nurse	Carol Cleveland
Old steward	Charles Chaplin

In a personal note of explanation Charles Chaplin discloses that the story was inspired by a trip he made to Shanghai in 1931 but, though the period has been updated to the present time, the style of his screenplay and direction are obstinately reminiscent of the '30s. Nevertheless, "A Countess From Hong Kong" has several important factors going for it. There are three top names (Loren, Brando, Chaplin) to dress the marquee and they will provide the maximum opportunities for appropriate exploitation, which should stimulate enough activity at the wickets to make this a boxoffice success.

There are also other intriguing exploitation possibilities. His son, Sydney Chaplin, has a featured role, Chaplin himself has a momentary walk-on and other members of his family make brief, but telling, appearances. There is also a magnificent, though brief, cameo by Margaret Rutherford s an eccentric old lady confined to her bed on the cruise from Hong Kong to New York.

"Countess" is what may be described as a romantic comedy. It has a nebulous plot, slim characterizations and all the trappings of an old-fashioned bedroom farce. The moments of genuine hilarity are few and far between and there is little evidence of Chaplin's old directorial genius in his first film in almost 10 years, and the first since 1923 ("A Woman of Paris") which he directed and in which he did not star. "Hong Kong" is surprisingly,

and disappointingly, a pedestrian job of direction, which in many respects matches the style of his original story and script.

Sophia Loren who radiates an abundance of charm, plays a Russian emigree countess who, after a night out on the town in Hong Kong with Marlon Brando, stows away in his cabin with the intention of getting to New York. That's about it so far as the plot itself is concerned and is the basis for a succession of frantic scenes in which Miss Loren is dashing from one room to another, into the bedroom and bathroom, and into closets to avoid detection. Inevitably, Brando eventually finds her irresistible, but that's all part of the predictable nature of the plot.

There are, of course, ample embellishments to this bald outline. Sydney Chaplin, who is Brando's cruising companion, suggests as a possible solution that Miss Loren should marry Brando's valet and thus become an American citizen, but predictably, too, that doesn't work out according to plan.

Although the story barely taxes her acting resources, Miss Loren adds a quality to every scene in which she appears. She is stylish, classy and striking. Brando, on the other hand, appears ill at ease in what should have been a light comedy role, and plays it mainly on a one-note, heavy-handed style which throws the romantic comedy off key.

In the top featured role, Sydney Chaplin gives a thoroughly reliable performance, while Tippi Hedren, as Brando's wife, is superb in her few scenes at the tail-end of the picture. She registers just the right cool, icy note expected of a woman in the circumstances. Patrick Cargill makes a typical gentleman's gentleman and has one boisterously funny scene in Brando's cabin after his shipboard marriage.

In the long cast only two or three other characters have any chance to register. Michael Medwin makes a clear impression as a passenger who knew Miss Loren way back in Hong Kong, John Paul adequately plays the ship's captain, Oliver Johnston is okay as Brando's press agent and Angela Scoular has some amusing lines as a society girl who is always quoting "daddy."

Chaplin has relied on some crudities for his laugh effects. As one example, Brando belches loudly and often after taking an Alka-Seltzer; and the radio is deliberately turned on at full volume to drown the noise coming from the bathroom. There are, however, other moments of genuine humor and one typical Chaplin touch is when Sydney Chaplin steals a drink from under Medwin's nose at the ship's bar.

Whatever its faults "Countess" is stunning to look at. Bob Cartwright has designed a number of sumptuous sets, and although almost the entire action is confined to the ship, he has given the production a spacious and handsome appearance. These qualities are enhanced by Arthur Ibbetson's

lush Technicolor lensing. On the other hand, Gordon Hales' editing seems somewhat indulgent.

In addition to directing and writing, Chaplin also composed the score and though it's easy on the ear the background music is as reminiscent of the '30s as the film itself. *Myro*

Dama Spathi
(The Queen of Clubs)

Athens, Jan. 2.

A Th. Damaskinos-V. Michaelides & V. Papamichalis-A. Anastassatos production, directed by Georges Skalenakis. Features Helena Nathanael, Spyros Phocas, Theo Roubanis and Despo Diamantidou. Screenplay by Yannis Djiotis. Camera by: An. Anastassatos. Music by Yannis Marcopoulos. Reviewed at distributor's screening room. Running time: 105 MINS.

Helena	Helena Nathanael
Vassilis	Theo Roubanis
Alexandros	Spyros Phocas
Marianthe	Despo Diamantidou
Teacher	Demos Starenios
Doctor	Aris Malliagros

The producers' aim to attract all kinds of audiences is obvious in this picture. Hence, a lot of sex and nudity, sensual scenes, a leading lady of exquisite beauty. Throw in an anti-war message. Excellent photography helps. But somehow story fails to convey to audiences how boredom motivates modern people and turns them cynical. Which is supposed to be the message.

Screenplay is thin and uneven. It is based on a love triangle set in present day Greece. Helena, young and pretty, works as a model, is married to Vassilis, a sea captain who, returning home after a long voyage, takes her to a resort. During his absence Helena lived with an aunt, an unbalanced spinster under the obsession of a coming war.

Wife is drawn to a man at the resort who is aware of her desire and follows the married pair from a distance. Unable to control her passion for this stranger, wife confesses to her husband her weakness, asking him to take her away. He becomes furious, slaps her and leaves, alone, for Athens. Helena goes to her lover but later decides to return to her husband.

In the end her husband tricks and mocks her remorse.

Director Georges Skalenakis did not develop the characters fully. Only the unbalanced aunt is not flat as delineated by Despo Diamantidou.

Camera work is excellent especially in the outdoor sequences and music by Yannis Marcopulos is very good. Other technical credits are firstrate. *Rena.*

Warning Shot
(COLOR)

Excellent, well-made programmer about a cop accused of being trigger-happy. David Janssen and many cameo names for marquee. Very good uppercase potential in general situations.

Hollywood, Dec. 30.

Paramount Pictures release of a Bob Banner Associates Production, produced and directed by Buzz Kulik. Features David Janssen. Screenplay, Mann Rubin, based on "711—Officer Needs Help," a novel by Whit Masterson; camera (Technicolor), Joseph Biroc; editor, Archie Marshek; music, Jerry Goldsmith; asst. director, Howard Roessel. Reviewed at Paramount Studios, L.A., Dec. 29, '66. Running Time, 100 MINS.

Sgt. Tom Valens	David Janssen
Capt. Roy Klodin	Ed Begley
Sgt. Ed Musso	Keenan Wynn
Frank Sanderman	Sam Wanamaker
Alice Willows	Lillian Gish
Liz Thayer	Stefanie Powers
Mrs. Doris Ruston	Eleanor Parker
Walt Cody	George Grizzard
Calvin York	George Sanders
Perry Knowland	Steve Allen
Paul Jerez	Carroll O'Connor
Joanie Valens	Joan Collins
Orville Ames	Walter Pidgeon
Police Surgeon	John Garfield, Jr.
Judge Gerald Lucas	Bob Williams
TV Newscaster	Jerry Dunphy
Ira Garvin	Romo Vincent
Desigser	Vito Scotti
Dr. James Ruston	Donald Curtis
Rusty	Brian Dunne

"Warning Shot" is a very timely police drama, in which fine production, direction and performances overcome a sometimes-flawed script. David Janssen toplines as a cop accused of being trigger-happy. Multiple cameos use film vets for added flexible marquee lure. Buzz Kulik produced and directed the Bob Banner Associates pic, which has good b.o. prospects for Paramount release on the upper half of general duals.

Mann Rubin adapted Whit Masterson's novel, "711 — Officer Needs Help," in which a cop is accused of poor judgment in killing an apparently innocent medic. His superiors, the D.A. and the public turn on him, and only hope of vindication is proving the existence of a missing gun, and the discovery of evidence to prove the medic was breaking the law.

Filmed smoothly on L.A. locations, with technical assist from the Police Department here, pic has the immediacy of contemporary headlines about police brutality, irresponsibility, etc. Scripting incorporates some cliche, unnecessary angles which detract from a very viable story line; namely, that cops are fallible human beings who drink, smoke, make mistakes—just like everyone else. In context, plot tends towards a meller impact.

Kulik's handling of players and production largely overcomes this liability. Janssen, in a return to pix from "The Fugitives" videseries, is very effective as the accused police sergeant, although his apartment and buttermilk imbibing strain credulity. George Grizzard, newcomer to pix, makes an engaging, promising impression as the carefree pilot. He registers well on film. Police Capt. Ed Begley, fellow sergeant Keenan Wynn, secretary Stefanie Powers, and little old lady Lillian Gish are standout. Miss Gish, in particular, creates a memorable characterization.

Eleanor Parker, who electrified as the sodden dame in "An American Dream," again essays a similar unsympathetic role, certainly within her versatile acting range, but, hopefully, not to become impartial casting. Other fine cameos are handled by George Sanders, Steve Allen (playing a hypocritical, controversy-baiting telecaster), Joan Collins, as Janssen's estranged wife, Walter Pidgeon, Romo Vincent, and Vito Scotti, a swishy dress designer.

Broadcast and print journalism

takes it on the chin, plotwise, and for authenticity, Jerry Dunphy, of the local CBS o&o station, plays himself on camera. Sensation-seeking scribes is another over-played angle. Sam Wanamaker registers strongly as the cold-blooded D.A. out for Janssen's badge; it was, however, a major flaw to make him a cop-hater. John Garfield's son makes his film debut in another brief bit, and rest of cast renders solid support. Presence of multi-ethnic types in the cast gives an adroit touch of realism.

Kulik's direction also makes for visual interest in the many excellent point-of-view shots, and other solid setups of Joseph Biroc's mobile Technicolor camera. A tinted, slow-motion, and distorted fight sequence socks over the effect of violence with excellent economy. This is not Kulik's first feature, and, now ensconced at Paramount on a film pact, it won't be his last.

Many vidirectors who shift to features often appear shackled to boring medium shots, alternating with irritating camera movements as if they realized from time to time they they are in another medium; Kulik does not evince this tendency.

Jerry Goldsmith's score is excellent in lending mood, pace and emphasis with unusual orchestration. Edith Head's costumes again are firstrate, as are the excellent colorful production values, interior and exterior. Archie Marshek edited to a very good 100 minutes, another big asset. Tom Egan was associate producer. All other technical credits are superior.

Murf.

The Venetian Affair
(COLOR-PANAVISION)

Dreary spy meller for lowercase. Robert Vaughn, Elke Sommer and Boris Karloff for marquee.

Hollywood, Jan. 5.

Metro-Goldwyn-Mayer release of Jerry Thorpe, E. Jack Neuman production. Features entire cast. Directed by Thorpe. Screenplay, Neuman, based on a novel by Helen MacInnes; camera (Metrocolor), Milton Krasner; editor, Henry Berman; music, Lalo Schifrin; song, Schifrin, Hal Winn; asst. director, E. Darrell Hallenbeck. Reviewed at Pacific's Pantages Theatre, L. A., Jan. 4, '67. Running time, **92 MINS.**

Bill Fenner	Robert Vaughn
Sandra Fane	Elke Sommer
Claire Connor	Felicia Farr
Robert Wahl	Karl Boehm
Dr. Vaugiroud	Boris Karloff
Mike Ballard	Roger C. Carmel
Giulia Almeranti	Lucianna Paluzzi
Frank Rosenfeld	Edward Asner
Jan Aarvan	Joe De Santis
Russo	Fabrizio Mioni
Neill Carlson	Wesley Lau

"The Venetian Affair" is a tepid programmer about international espionage in Venice. Robert Vaughn, Elke Sommer and Boris Karloff provide some selling appeal. Pacing is tedious and plotting routine. The Jerry Thorpe-E. Jack Neuman production is enlivened by some actual footage of Venice. Metro release will find its best market in lowercase to a stronger companion pic.

Neuman adapted a Helen MacInnes novel into a routine script, dotted generally with prototype spy types. Vaughn, ex-CIAgent now a reporter, is sent to Venice after a diplomatic meeting has been bombed. Edward Asner, CIA boss there, once canned Vaughn because latter's then wife, Miss Sommer, was a Communist agent. Now she has disappeared.

Karloff is a political scientist who knows who blew up the meeting. Felicia Farr is another U.S. plant, Lucianna Paluzzi an Italo secretary at her best in lingerie, and Roger C. Carmel is another journalist. Karl Boehm is a spy who works all sides.

Pot boils slowly under Thorpe's casual direction. What was meant as an underplayed approach becomes awkward, meaningless pause, reinforced by dull dialog. For example, Asner's climactic comment is that spying is a stinking business, to which Vaughn's reply is "go to Hell." It's all been said and done before—only better on tv.

Performances are practically caricature, in a few cases leading to unwanted audience laughs. For record purposes, Miss Sommer, Miss Paluzzi and Carmel are killed off along the way, in Panavision and Metrocolor as dutifully recorded by Milton Krasner's camera which tries for fluidity. Enzo Serafin is credited for the Venice lensing, which gives an occasional visual lift. Other technical credits are standard.

Lalo Schifrin's score is creative, inventive. After a longish 92 minutes, as edited by Henry Berman, the title tune pops up under the closing credits. In one of the most ludicrous insertions of a film theme outside of deliberate satire, the romantic voice of Julius LaRosa croons—after the bloody murders, torture, etc.—"Our Venetian Affair is over . . ." Yecchh!

Murf.

Trunk To Cairo
(ISRAELI-COLOR)

Routine programmer, this Israel-U. S. coproduction with Audie Murphy has little new to say about the International intrigue gambit.

American International Pictures release of a Menahem Golan production. Stars Audie Murphy, George Sanders, Marianne Koch. Directed by Golan. Screenplay, Marc Behm, Alexander Ramati; camera (color), Mimish Herbst; film editor, Danny Shik; sound, Z. Naghtigal; art director, S. Zafrir; music, composed and conducted by Duv Seltzer; associate producer, Michael Kugan. Reviewed, New York, Jan. 7, '67. Running Time, **80 MINS.**

Mike Merrick	Audie Murphy
Prof. Schlieben	George Sanders
Helga Schlieben	Marianne Koch
Hans Klugg	Hans Von Borsodi
Capt. Gabar	Joseph Yadin
Yasmin	Gila Almago
Jamil	Eytan Priver

After the success of "Sallah," the next film by Israeli producer Menahem Golan was awaited with considerable interest but "Trunk To Cairo" will add little to his reputation, nor will it serve American International as more than a supporting feature on a double-bill. This was somewhat forecast in the long delay in releasing the Israeli-U.S. coproduction which Golan's Noah Productions made in 1965 and which is being exhibited in some spots well in advance of the January 19 trade-screening.

Perhaps the fault is not in Golan's ability as much as in his ambition. What "Trunk To Cairo" gains in internationally-known cast names, such as Audie Murphy and George Sanders, it loses in its stereotyped script and wooden directing. And producer (turned director for "Trunk") Golan forgot to add the major ingredient that made "Sallah" a minor masterpiece—Israeli actor Haym Topol. Although Marianne Koch does try to do more than look beautiful (as that's no effort), Murphy and Sanders come over in this secret agent-evil scientist effort like "The Bobbsey Twins at Sunset Beach."

Technical efforts throughout are good, but not outstanding, and even the Israel and Italy location work adds little that is new. A routine film.

Robe.

A Covenant With Death
(COLOR)

Uneven courtroom meller laced with some sex and prejudice angles. Okay for general duals.

Hollywood, Jan. 6.

Warner Bros. production and release, executive producer, William Conrad. Stars George Maharis, Laura Devon, Katy Jurado, Earl Holliman. Directed by Lamont Johnson. Screenplay, Larry Marcus, Saul Levitt, based on the novel by Stephen Becker; camera (Technicolor), Robert Burks; editor, William Ziegler; music, Leonard Rosenman; asst. director, Gil Kissel. Reviewed at Warner Bros. Studios, Burbank, Jan. 5, '67. Running Time, **97 MINS.**

Judge Ben Lewis	George Maharis
Rosemary	Laura Devon
Eulalia Lewis	Katy Jurado
Bryan Talbot	Earl Holliman
Judge Hochstadter	Arthur O'Connell
Col. Oates	Sidney Blackmer
Harmsworth	Gene Hackman
Dietrich	John Anderson
Rafaela	Wende Wagner
Ignacio	Emilio Fernandez
Parmalee	Kent Smith
Musgrave	Lonny Chapman
Digby	Jose De Vega
Chillingworth	Larry D. Mann
Bruce Donnelly	Whit Bissell
Dr. Shilling	Russell Thorson
Governor	Paul Birch
Willie Wayte	Erwin Neal

"A Covenant With Death" is a period crime and punishment meller, set in the American southwest of 40 years ago, in which an innocent, but worthless, man is vindicated of murder. Some adroit casting, performance and direction, plus good William Conrad production, overcome a desultory script which induces a halting pace and talky stretches. George Maharis, Katy Jurado, Earl Holliman and Arthur O'Connell provide some marquee versatility. Commercial prospects shape up as okay for Warner Bros. release on standard dual bills.

Stephen Becker's novel has been adapted by Larry Marcus and Saul Levitt into a patchy tale turning on Holliman, a small town libertine who is found guilty of the murder of his promiscuous wife. Maharis is a part-Mexican judge, pitted against older jurist O'Connell in a slight clash of judicial philosophy, also a jealous D.A. Miss Jurado plays the hen-pecking mother of Maharis, while Laura Devon and Wende Wagner are his romantic interests, in that order.

Holliman's plight — convicted, nearly executed on circumstantial evidence but rescued by a last-minute confession by Whit Bissell, and finally acquitted of a second murder, hangman Erwin Neal, dead from a scaffold scuffle—gets sidetracked at frequent intervals as a number of digressions occur.

Maharis' romance with a Nordic Miss Devon is aborted in a clash of temperament: she is the prim, white-cottage type, while he is fiery. Miss Wagner, a Latin, is more to his liking. What this all proves is moot. Also, prejudice against Mexicans and a cowtown blood lust receive an undue emphasis. Exposition ranges from well-integrated dialog to extended and forced chatter.

Director Lamont Johnson debuts herein in features after telefilm career. The story being what it is, evaluation of his ability is difficult. On the one hand, Holliman, O'Connell, Miss Jurado, and Miss Wagner (in particular) come across quite well, as do attorney Kent Smith and cop Gene Hackman. Maharis, saddled with the part, does well. But Miss Devon has little depth, while town patriarch Sidney Blackmer, prosecutor John Anderson and Emilio Fernandez, Miss Wagner's dad, are limned too broadly.

Johnson's visual eye is good, and at home in a large-screen environment. Robert Burks and his Technicolor camera provide mobility. A substantial, and rewarding, assist is the full-bodied score by Leonard Rosenman; it is a refreshing and welcome change of pace from contemporary scoring which often is little more than isolated riff gimmickry. William Ziegler edited to an okay 97 minutes, and two other credits are pro.

Since Conrad became exec producer a year ago on a slate of pix, two have been released, "An American Dream" being the first. Both, however, antedate Jack L. Warner's establishment of the Conrad unit, and files indicate a series of other persons who earlier were working up the properties. As with many inherited projects, the uneven quality of the finished pic is difficult to pinpoint.

Murf.

Red Tomahawk
(WIDESCREEN—COLOR)

Another Lyles western, this time with Indians. Cast and promises of action strongest selling points but it will all seem familiar.

Paramount Pictures release of an A. C. Lyles production. Stars Howard Keel, Joan Caulfield, Broderick Crawford, Scott Brady, Wendell Corey; features rest of cast. Directed by R. G. Springsteen. Screenplay, Steve Fisher, from story by Fisher, Andrew Craddock; camera (Pathe Color), W. Wallace Kelley; film editor, John F. Schreyer; sound, Harold Lewis, John Wilkinson; music, Jimmie Haskell; asst. director, James Rosenberger. Reviewed at Paramount h.o., New York, Jan. 9, '67. Running Time, **82 MINS.**

Capt. Tom York	Howard Keel
Dakota Lil	Joan Caulfield
Columbus Smith	Broderick Crawford
Ep Wyatt	Scott Brady
Elkins	Wendell Corey
Telegrapher	Richard Arlen
Bill Kane	Tom Drake
Sal	Tracy Olsen
Lieut. Drake	Ben Cooper
Bly	Donald Barry
3d Prospector	Reg Parton
Wu Sing	Gerald Jann
2d Prospector	Roy Jenson

Ned Crone ..... Dan White
Samuels ..... Henry Wills
Townsman ..... Saul Gorss

When it comes to getting maximum mileage out of a production dollar, there's probably no one to match A. C. Lyles. He continues to grind out, regularly, a series of good, if not great, outdoor pictures that provide the type of product frequently needed to bolster more expensive, but shakier, fare in the cities and, thanks to well-known cast names, can stand by themselves in the small towns and most drive-ins. Lyles comes so close, in fact, to making good westerns that one wishes that he'd loosen the budget strings occasionally.

With the teamwork he has organized through the use of such directors as R. G. Springsteen, who knows the value of action in a production where static scenes too often allow the penny-pinching to show, Lyles gives the audience "action by inference" much of the time. After a very brief but effective opening shot of the carnage wrought by the Sioux at the Little Big Horn, Indians seen for the remainder of the film never number more than six or eight at a time until the climactic, beautifully-staged, but again very brief battle that ends the film. Equally short location sequences are frequently interspersed with some obvious studio shots.

Although he provides excellent technical results, the principal weakness of this film is in the cliche - laden script of Steve Fisher and the less than inspired acting. Even a frequent familiar face doesn't hide the obvious fact that time marches on. Because he does use such known types as Broderick Crawford, Scott Brady, Wendell Corey, and Tom Drake in most of his films, Lyles has to cast some of them as "white hats" so there's no lone-riding, silent type hero here. There's also a waste of talent with Richard Arlen (looking twice as rugged as the lead males) seen in a bit part as a telegrapher and Donald Barry in briefly as an Army deserter. Drake has about four lines of dialog.

Unlike "Waco," which tried to sex things up a bit, "Red Tomahawk" reverts to the traditional western attitude towards women. Joan Caulfield is only slightly tarnished and then, it's blamed on the Indians. Yet most of these names are given star billing, indicating an exaggerated importance to the film.

W. Wallace Kelley's Pathe Color camerawork is excellent when turned to the action scenes (his pictorial composition during the river battle is outstanding) but the color process makes interior and studio - shot exterior footage murky. The stunt work is, as always in a Lyles western, very good and Keel, despite his size, handles himself beautifully in the close-in fight scenes. Jimmie Haskell's music is routine. *Robe.*

Shoot Loud, Louder . . . I Don't Understand

(Spara Forte, Piu Forte, Non Capisco)
(ITALIAN-COLOR)

An off-beat, far-out comedy made in Italy with English sub-titles, pic may become an 'in' item with the sophisticated art house audiences, but may seem too avant garde for the general public.

Hollywood, Dec. 28.

Embassy Pictures release of Master Film (Pictro Notarianni) Production. Directed by Eduardo de Filippo. Screenplay, de Filippo, Suso Cecchi D'Amico; camera (Pathe Color), Danilo Desideri; editor, Ruggero Mastroianni; music, Nino Rota; assistant director, Francesco Massaro. Reviewed at Joe Shore Screening Room, L.A., Dec. 20, '66. Running Time, **100 MINS.**

Alberto Saporito .. Marcello Mastroianni
Tania Mottini ..... Raquel Welch
Pasquale Cimmaruta .... Guido Alberti
Carlo Saporito ..... Leopoldo Trieste
Aunt Rosa Cimmaruta .. Tecla Scarano
Uncle Nicola ..... Eduardo de Filippo
Elvira Cimmaruta .... Rosalba Grottesi
Aniello Amitrano ..... Paolo Ricci
Mrs. Amitrano ..... Regina Bianchi
Chief Police Inspector .. Franco Parenti
Beautiful Woman ..... Angela Luce
Lieutenant Bertolucci .. Silvano Tranquilli
Matilde Cimmaruta .... Pina D'Amato
Marshal Bagnacavallo .... Carlo Bagno
Maid ..... Pia Morra
Luigi Cimmaruta ..... Gino Minopoli
Deputy Police Inspector .. Alberto Bugli
Carmelo Vitiello ..... Ignazio Spalla

(English subtitles)

A bizarre, surrealistic filmic jigsaw which whirligigs around fact and fantasy until both tumble and cascade together into a blurred third world, "Shoot Loud, Louder . . . I Don't Understand" will need special handling and will probably have its greatest appeal with "selective" house patrons. General interest will be limited by fact that dialog is in Italian with English subtitles.

Eduardo De Filippo coscripted, (with Suso Cecchi D'Amico) from his own play and also directed as well as playing role of Marcello Mastroianni's uncle, a man who has gone sour on the world, does not speak but communicates to his nephew by exploding firecrackers, which the nephew readily understands. The mute role is symbolic of the whole pic, since it's anybody's guess as to what it's all about.

"Shoot Louder" employs the same technique used by Fellini in "Juliet of the Spirits," never making clear what is the dream world and what is reality. There are indications that it is a spoof on the Fellini style of filmmaking. The point here seems to be that reality drives one to the world of illusion and illusion also impinges and makes its mark on what is real.

Mastroianni is wonderfully fey in the off-beat role of an antique collector and junk sculptor. He meets Raquel Welch, a girl of the streets, at the apartment of next door neighbors, where she is having her fortune told. He also talks to an unidentified older man. He later believes he sees the man murdered by the family, and goes to the police and tells about the killing. Although he is soon aware he may have dreamt the incident, a series of complications begin to tangle in Pirandello fashion. Pic ends with a fantastic fireworks explosion, which kills uncle, and Mastroianni and Miss Welch motoring away. They stop for a moment and Mastroianni shouts to the sky "Uncle, shoot louder, I don't understand you anymore."

Miss Welch, whose voice has been dubbed into Italian, is an actress of considerable charm and ability. Other members of the cast manage to shout at each other in almost operatic fashion.

Danilo Desideri's Pathe color camera work provides a lush flavor to the pic, while Nino Rota's music is generally restrained and appropriate. De Filippo's direction allows the actors wide latitude, which they take full advantage of and Gianni Polidori's art direction and set decor is intentionally and successfully theatrical. *Dool.*

Kiss The Girls And Make Them Die

(ITALIAN-COLOR)

Unsatisfactory spy spoof for dual bills.

Hollywood, Dec. 27.

Columbia Pictures release of a Dino De Laurentiis production. Features Michael Connors, Dorothy Provine, Raf Vallone, Margaret Lee, Terry-Thomas. Directed by Henry Levin. Screenplay, Jack Pulman, Dino Maiuri, based on a story by Maiuri; camera (Technicolor), Aldo Tonti; editor, Ralph Kemplen; music, Mario Nascimbene; title song, Nascimbene, Howard Greenfield; asst. directors, Giorgio Gentili, Gianna Cozzo; second unit directors, Alberto Pieralisi, Leopoldo Savona. Reviewed at Columbia Studios, L.A., Dec. 27, '66. Running Time, **105 MINS.**

Kelly ..... Michael Connors
Susan Fleming ..... Dorothy Provine
Mr. Ardonian ..... Raf Vallone
Grace ..... Margaret Lee
Lord Aldric, James ..... Terry-Thomas
Sylvia ..... Nicoletta Machiavilli
Karin ..... Beverly Adams
British Ambassador ..... Jack Gwillim
Ringo ..... Oliver McGreevy
Interpretor ..... Senya Seyn

Undoubtedly, there will be some people who will enjoy "Kiss The Girls And Make Them Die," but fact is that producer Dino De Laurentiis has made a limp, banal spy spoof, inept in all departments. Pace is plodding, dialog pallid, direction pedestrian, acting an embarrassment, and technical composition awkward. There is little marquee lure. Filmed in Italy and dubbed in English, the Columbia release might play well in another tongue; one hopes. A dullsville dualer that will need a far stronger playmate in less discriminating situations.

Jack Pulman and Dino Maiuri scripted, from latter's story about madman industrialist, Raf Vallone who wants to sterilize the world, keeping himself fertile along with some chicks whom he has placed in suspended animation. Other gal friends who are unfaithful are killed in bizarre ways.

Michael Connors and Dorothy Provine play U.S. and British undercover agents, respectively, with Terry-Thomas in a dual role, mainly as Miss Provine's chauffeur, a my-man-Godfrey type. All players take a form of refuge under the title.

Being a Bond-type pic (about 10 proof, however), there is an abundance of unusual mechanical and film effects. Far from being clever, they suggest the slapdash props of a '30s serial, but lack completely the curious suspension of belief which the latter engendered in its time.

Music alternates between two themes, each repeated endlessly until one is absolutely certain that the harmonica refrain derives from "Ruby," while the other mercifully stands on its own as an irritating nothing. Sound editing is gauche, sound mixing is just that, re-recording didn't help out a bit, and the dubbing is terrible. Camera work is of uncertain color registration—Technicolor is credited—but some exteriors, notably in Rio, are something to relieve the ennui.

Art direction is splashy, deliberately overdone, but it still looks cheap. Costumes, and the femmes which they barely cover, add another visual highlight. Pic runs 105 minutes, about 10-15 minutes too long. Re-editing might help via faster pacing. Film demonstrates the vagaries of the business: producer made "The Bible," and the editor trimmed "A Man For All Seasons." *Murf.*

Liselotte von der Pfalz

(GERMAN-COLOR)

Berlin, Jan. 2.

Constantin release of Independent Film (Kurt Hoffmann, Heinz Angermeyer) production. Stars Heidelinde Weis, Harald Leipnitz. Features Hans Caninenberg, Karin Huebner. Directed by Hoffmann. Screenplay, Johanna Sibelius, Eberhard Keindorff; camera (Eastmancolor), Richard Angst; music, Franz Grothe; settings, Otto Pischinger; editing, Claus von Boro. At Marmorhaus, W. Berlin. Running Time, **104 MINS.**

Liselotte von der Pfalz .. Heidelinde Weis
Duke of Orleans ..... Harald Leipnitz
King Louis XIV ..... Hans Caninenberg
Palatine ..... Karin Huebner
Ludwig von der Pfalz .... Erwin Linder
Lorraine ..... Robert Dietl

All that Kurt Hoffman, one of Germany's better known directors, had in mind with "Liselotte" was to provide good entertainment. Bulk of this country's average patrons may accept it as that. In a more demanding sense, however, one is inclined to say that he didn't reach his goal. A costume comedy like this should have charm and imagination in the first place. Both charm and imagination (which used to be this director's forte) are hardly evident in this production. Good thing that Hoffman had in Heidelinde Weis a delightful principal actress at his disposal. Miss Weis saves a good deal of an otherwise rather dull film. Nevertheless, films like this one find a receptive audience in this country. And the title has additional value around here.

"Liselotte von de Pfalz", treating of a historical figure (1652-1722), was the title of a highly successful and well remembered German pic of the 30s which starred the late Renate Mueller. This Kurt Hoffmann film which the director produced via his own Independent Film cannot be regarded as a remake. While the old pic had mainly to do with the destruction of Heidelberg by French troops in 1689, Hoffman's feature concentrates on the marriage of Liselotte of the Palatinate and the Duke of Orleans, a brother of French King Louis XIV. This was a political marriage. Film depicts the couple's squabblings, complications and intrigues which nearly lead to the murder of Liselotte. The Duke's dislike for his wife, which includes a loveless wedding night, is gradually turned into a big passion for her. The end sees them both as the happiest couple on earth.

Austrian-born Miss Weis enacts the title role which originally Liselotte Pulver was to play. There is no doubt that young and pretty Heidelinde Weis was a better choice, the more so since she had to play a 19-year-old girl which Miss Pulver could hardly have convincingly portrayed. Miss Weis is a delight. Not only is she lovely to look at, she can act. She is the film's major asset and most of this comedy's limited chuckles come on her account. Miss Weis has been acclaimed as one of the German-language's most talented young film actresses, and this pic gives clear evidence of it.

The others stand in her shadow. This applies to Harald Leipnitz, her starring partner, whose role is not exactly rewarding. The best polished supporting role is contributed by Hans Caninenberg as King Louis XIV. Most of the others are seen and forgotten.

Film's production dress is very much on the romantic side, with many beautiful castles and landscapes which give "Liselotte" the intended flavor of a historical fairytale. Veteran Richard Angst, an expert on colorful costume pix, did the lensing. *Hans.*

Way Out
(COLOR)

Gutsy probing of the lives of eight addicts with religioso ending. Pic is uneven but could probably register well with young audiences.

Hollywood, Dec. 28.
Premiere Presentations release of Valley Forge Film, produced and directed by Irvin S. Yeaworth, Jr. Features entire cast. Screenplay, Jean Yeaworth, Rudy and Shirley Nelson, based on legit, "The Addicts," by John Gimenez; camera, Thomas E. Spalding; editor, John Bushelman; music, Kurt Kaiser. Reviewed at Encore Theatre, L. A. Dec. 27, '66. Running Time, **102 MINS.**
Frankie .... Frank Rodriguez
Jim .... James Dunleavy
Anita .... Sharyn Jimenez
Jerry .... Jerry Rutkin
Stella .... Starr Ruiz
Fats .... Gilbert Mesa
Che Che .... Cecil White
Louie .... Louis Colon
Rudy .... Rudy Rosado
Pop .... John Gimenez
Harlem Man .... Eddie James
Anita's Mother .... Naomi Perez
Narco .... Eric Hutson
Snuffy .... J. R. Helton
Pusher .... Norman Yager
Policeman .... Chuck Painter
Guard .... Louis Sager

Obviously done as a labor of love, "Way Out"—not to be confused by the Jerry Lewis 20th-Fox release "Way . . . Way Out,"—takes a close harsh look, but not a very deep one, at the world of the dope addict. Ex-addicts who have never acted before play themselves and there is a religious message tacked onto the ending, with each of the eight actors addressing the audience and explaining that they had each found Christ and he is "The Way Out."

There are some frightening and startling scenes and one in particular during which one addict realizes his friend has died and he clutches at him, holds him, drags him to a chair and pours milk down the dead man's open mouth, all the while sobbing and struggling to hold onto reality. At another point another boy desperate

for a fix finally gets the stuff only to discover that instead of heroin, he has powdered flour and his outrage and hurt is totally compelling.

Produced and directed by Irvin S. Yeaworth Jr., who formerly produced and directed eight Billy Graham specials, pic has enough plot material for a dozen films. Story jumps from addict to addict, showing the ways and means that they go about stealing and robbing to pay for the habit. It balances the more brutal aspects of addiction with quiet romantic incidents, and the love scenes between Sharyn Jimenez and James Dunleavy are effective and played with sensitivity.

Some of the acting gets completely out of hand and even becomes embarrassing, as in a scene between Frank Rodriguez and John Gimenez, where father confronts his son and the two tumble in tears and with much moaning and groaning.

Thomas E. Spalding's photography is not always crisp and John Bushelman has attempted some unusual editing, some of which works very well. Kurt Kaiser wrote the score and it generally fits the mood of the pic.

"Way Out" should appeal to young audiences. Some adults may find it informative, but mature audiences likely will feel that the drama of the addict doesn't really get very deeply under the skin and into the bloodstream of the problem. Not only is their possibility of title confusion with the Fox comedy, the producing company is too similar in name to the Metro subsid, Premier Productions, which is handling the un-Sealed "blow-up." *Dool.*

Hotel
(COLOR)

Excellent film version of Arthur Hailey's book. Rod Taylor, Merle Oberon, Karl Malden and others provide marquee flexibility. Well written, directed and produced. Very good general b.o. outlook, with strong femme appeal.

Hollywood, Jan. 11.
Warner Bros. production and release, written and produced by Wendell Mayes. Features Rod Taylor, Catherine Spaak, Karl Malden, Melvyn Douglas, Merle Oberon, Richard Conte, Michael Rennie, Kevin McCarthy. Based on the novel by Arthur Hailey; camera (Technicolor), Charles Lang; editor, Sam O'Steen; music, Johnny Keating; asst. director, Mickey McCarthy. Reviewed at Warner Bros. Studio, Burbank, Jan. 10, '67. Running Time, **124 MINS.**
Peter McDermott .... Rod Taylor
Jeanne .... Catherine Spaak
Keycase .... Karl Malden
Trent .... Melvyn Douglas
The Duchess .... Merle Oberon
Dupere .... Richard Conte
Duke of Lanbourne .... Michael Rennie
O'Keefe .... Kevin McCarthy
Christine .... Carmen McRae
Capt. Yolles .... Alfred Ryder
Bailey .... Roy Roberts
Herbie .... Al Checco
Mrs. Grandin .... Sheila Bromley
Sam .... Harry Hickox
Mason .... William Lanteau
Laswell .... Ken Lynch
Morgan .... Clinton Sundberg
Kilbrick .... Tol Avery
Dr. Adams .... Davis Roberts
Elliott .... Jack Donner

"Hotel" is a very well made, handsomely produced drama about the guests and management of an old hostelry which must modernize or shutter. Uniformly strong performances, scripting and direction make for good pacing. Rod Taylor heads a cast which also includes Merle Oberon in a return to pix. Plush Wendell Mayes production values will appeal to femme audiences, while story will retain male attention. Very good b.o. prospects for Warner Bros. release in general situations.

In an impressive debut as a film producer, Mayes has dressed the pic with lush settings and wardrobe, while not neglecting scripting chores in adapting Arthur Hailey's novel. Basic premise—the diverse fates and fortunes of people temporarily in one place — is, of course, not new. But what makes the premise a satisfactory film is how well the writer and director juggle the themes to sustain interest. Herein, Mayes and director Richard Quine have succeeded.

In a neat economy of exposition, practically all plot lines have intrigued an audience within 15 minutes. Taylor, young and aggressive hotel manager, has his hands full with hotel owner Melvyn Douglas, who needs money to continue operation. Kevin McCarthy, a modern hotel magnate, eyes the property, as does Ken Lynch, union boss who sees an outright purchase as a way to satisfy longtime ambitions to organize the place. Douglas, of the old school, has pursued a no-union, and all-white guest, policy.

Merle Oberon, dripping in gems, registers well as the wife of Michael Rennie, whose hit-and-run driving cues a blackmail attempt by house gumshoe Richard Conte. Catherine Spaak, in her U.S. film debut, is charming and sexy as McCarthy's mistress who drifts to

Taylor. Carmen McRae pops up as the nitery chirp who, unfortunately for jazz fans, never gets to finish a tune.

Karl Malden has a choice role of a key thief who is frustrated at many turns by double-crossing accomplices. A comedy highlight is his tearful condemnation of credit cards, which means less cash in bedside wallets. Strong supporting cast includes Jack Donner and Clinton Sundberg, as McCarthy aides, desk clerk Roy Roberts, Tol Avery, the worried businessman who hikes his money loss, house dick Harry Hickox, police detective Alfred Ayder, and Davis Roberts, the paid Negro agitator used by McCarthy to blow the sale to Lynch.

Quine's direction is very good, and derives best efforts from all players. The climactic elevator crash sequence is handled in top fashion, and Quine's pacing is zesty, save for a couple of slow-downs, mainly in the Taylor-Miss Spaak interactions. Director's transitions are often neat, although an overuse of matched dissolves becomes obvious and contrived.

Charles Lang's fluid and exciting Technicolor camera is a big visual asset, capturing, at times by subjective usage, the ebb and flow of the human tide. Edith Head's lavish gowns, and Howard Shoup's opulent costume design, complement Cary Odell's lush art direction to provide surefire eye appeal. Sam O'Steen edited to 124 minutes, just a little bit too much of a good thing, with the romantic interludes involving Miss Spaak flagging the pace just after the half-way mark.

There is only one definite liability — Johnny Keating's score which intrudes at repeated intervals, particularly when Malden is pilfering hotel rooms. At such times, the orchestration is mood-shattering, both in loudness and in overuse of a jazzy refrain which in time becomes monotonous. Keating is a WB Records pactee, whose deal reportedly includes four pix scores. Miss McRae's brief vocalizing with her intimery band is very good. Other technical credits are firstrate. *Murf.*

The Reluctant Astronaut
(COLOR)

Don Knotts in follow-up to "The Ghost And Mr. Chicken," this time as an astronaut terrified of heights. Okay dual bill escapist pic.

Hollywood, Jan. 14.
Universal release, produced and directed by Edward J. Montagne. Stars Don Knotts. Screenplay, Jim Fritzell, Everett Greenbaum; camera (Technicolor), Rexford Wimpy; editor, Sam E. Waxman; music, Vic Mizzy; asst. director, Phil Bowles. Reviewed at Pacific's Picwood Theatre, L.A., Jan. 13, '67. Running Time: **101 MINS.**
Roy Fleming .... Don Knotts
Major Gifford .... Leslie Nielsen
Ellie .... Joan Freeman
Donelli .... Jesse White
Mrs. Fleming .... Jeanette Nolan
Plank .... Frank McGrath
Buck Fleming .... Arthur O'Connell
Blonde In Bar........ Joan Shawlee
Bert .... Guy Raymond
Aunt Zana .... Nydia Westman
Rush .... Paul Hartman
Cervantes .... Robert Simon
Moran .... Robert Pickering

"The Reluctant Astronaut" stars Don Knotts in an okay, but a trifle longish, space age comedy about a man, who cannot stand heights, suddenly involved in manned rocketry. Colorful production values and some good thesping provide undemanding escapism. Edward J. Montagne, who produced Knotts' sleeper of last season, "The Ghost And Mr. Chicken," encores, and this time has directed, too. The Universal release could duplicate the prior "Chicken" delight at the b.o., and in any case this will be a juve matinee staple.

Jim Fritzell and Everett Greenbaum scripted in routine fashion, with shy-guy Knotts dragooned into space program by dad Arthur O'Connell, a World War I vet who still exudes pride in his (supposedly) heroic service. Pert Joan Freeman is Knotts' eventual partner. Competent cast supports the action, which, in the middle third of footage, seems to slow down.

Knotts, of course, has his comedy delivery and mugging down to a science, and registers strongly. Forgetting the vocal timbre, it is remarkable how his timing, inflections and projection resemble the technique of James Stewart. Basic idea of the plot, incidentally, is credited to Knotts in studio production notes.

Montagne's direction elicits an excellent and dynamic performance by O'Connell, as well as some touching moments in the father-son relationship. Jeanette Nolan scores as Knotts' loving mother, Jesse White as his boss (the head janitor at the space center), also Leslie Nielsen, the astronaut hero, and family friend Frank McGrath. Joan Shawlee has a neat bit as a saloon floozy, Paul Hartman appears as another neighbor, and Nydia Westman again plays a nice little old lady.

A few comedy bits are run into the ground — the countdown airport loudspeaker, to name one — and Rexford Wimpy's Technicolor camera is often rooted in static setups. The climactic space fight, with a weightless Knotts floating about, is very amusing, but flawed slightly by holding too long, at least twice, on a shot which clearly shows the wires on his suit.

Vic Mizzy's score assists in the emphasia, and Sam E. Waxman edited to 101 minutes, a bit too long. Process work looks phony, and is underscored all the more by colorful sets, costumes and crisp lensing. Overall, pic will amuse the kids, but often will lose the attention of teenagers and older people. Other technical credits are pro. *Murf.*

The Chelsea Girls
(COLOR—BLACK AND WHITE)

No form, no substance, lots of deviation, limited but special audience.

Film-Makers' Distribution Center release of an Andy Warhol production, directed by Warhol. Features Nico, Ondine, Mary Might, International Velvet, Gerard Malanga, Ingrid Superstar, Marie Menken and Mario Montez. Reviewed at Regency Theatre, N.Y. Running Time, 210 MINS.

"The Chelsea Girls," perhaps the first Underground film to be accorded specifically non-Underground screenings, is a pointless, excruciatingly dull three-and-a-half hours spent in the company of Andy Warhol's friends. Film, nevertheless, has box-office potential as a curiosity item and a social phenomenon, and is scaled at the Brandt Regency at $2.50. Sexual deviations of the characters and the abundant four-letter dialog are possible exploitation angles. Appeal is necessarily limited to specialty houses in metropolitan areas, but even in these situations, after the initial voyeuristic interest fades, word-of-mouth is likely to be injurious.

Warhol has attempted to counter all conventional methods of film-making, and the result is an anti-film or, more accurately, a non-film. There is no plot-line. The single unifying device is that the film takes place in several rooms of a downtown hotel. Viewers are asked to spend a long, painful evening with various residents, almost all of whom are lesbians and homosexuals. Typical scenes include a blank-looking blond trimming and combing her hair, a lesbian bullying her roommates, another lesbian talking endlessly on the phone, a homosexual eating an orange, a middle-aged homosexual and a girl competing for the attentions of a half-nude male, a girl on LSD confessing to a homosexual priest!

There is no development or tension; each scene lingers on at irritating length. The characters chatter on and on, but no one really has anything to say or do. They just sit on a bed and talk or argue to no purpose.

The filmic technique is as ornery as the narrative structure. Warhol simply turns his camera on a scene and lets the camera run until there is no film left. Thus, there is no cutting. In place of conventional editing, Warhol lets his camera roam aimlessly around a room, zooming in portentously on an ash-try, remaining statically on a nose or a hand for minutes on end. At times the camera jiggles up and down or goes in and out of focus. Warhol is obviously playing with the camera and with the audience, and his game is the epitome of self-indulgence.

The only technical aspect which offers any interest at all is the split-screen device which is used throughout. Two scenes are shown simultaneously, one silent, the other with sound. Usually, the scenes take place in two different rooms with two different sets of characters, but occasionally there are two views of the same characters.

The result of all this free-wheeling experimentation is that the film is an endurance contest. Warhol is presumptuous in expecting viewers to be interested in his empty, bored characters. It is important to note that the film cannot be accepted as a reflection of the dislocation and degeneration of modern life. Warhol's work has no intellectual content, just as it has no form. It may indeed be an accurate transcription of a segment of society, but, in the absence of any selection, discrimination, or artistic discipline, the film is neither a coherent or meaningful statement. This is no "La Dolce Vita," nor is it a vision of a contemporary hell or a legitimate presentation of the lower depths. It is merely a hoax.

Performers are such "stars" of Underground cinema as Nico, Ondine, Ingrid Superstar, Mario Montez, Mary Might, International Velvet. They are not actors, but just some uninteresting people who sit in front of a camera and talk. There is no suggestion of performance. There is the feeling that it is all being improvised on the spot, without any preparation or direction whatsoever.

Production values are deliberately crude. Sound is scratchy, at times inaudible. Lighting is bleak. The color section is garish. There is no music. The sets consist of nothing more than chairs, a couch, and beds. It all has the look and quality of a home movie. *Hirsch.*

Syskonbadd
(My Sister, My Love)
(SWEDISH)

Paris, Jan. 10.

Sandrews release and production. Stars Bibi Andersson, Per Oscarsson; features Gunnar Bjornstrand, Jarl Kulle. Written and directed by Vilgot Sjoman; camera, Lars Bjorne. Previewed in Paris. Running Time, 96 MINS.

Sister	Eibi Andersson
Brother	Per Oscarsson
Husband	Jarl Kulle
Nobleman	Gunnar Bjornstrand

Swedish filmmakers have upset censors and film fests the last few years with such entries as "The Silence," "Loving Couples," "Night Games" and "491." Now the director of the latter comes up with a solidly made costume piece —placed in the 18th century—dealing with incest. The daring theme is handled with tact and persuasive taste. It will still have to be handled carefully abroad. It deals with a brother and sister love that is set off against a century that debased love and sex in a tawdry, almost vile, manner. Director-writer Vilgot Sjoman seems to be saying that real love, even if unlawful and socially forbidden, like incest, is truer than a hatred of it.

Film unfolds in a time of great social decadence that has led to perversions of love and yet great punishments are meted out to incest and other forms of premarital love. It is handled with such propriety and tenderness that it does not seem like a brother and sister affair at times.

To the girl it is something that comes out of a need for love in a tangled upperclass society of these times, whereas he is more fearful and not ready to sacrifice anything for this forbidden, illicit love. The sister is finally married and then admits to her husband, a cold aristocrat, that she is pregnant by her brother; yet he is ready to accept her. She is finally killed by a jealous young girl, but meanwhile with her baby delivered as she is dying.

There are some forced literary aspects such as the ending, and some academic handling of the period and times. But it is sober and manages to avoid being scabrous despite its theme. Sjoman says his source was the 17th century British tragedy on incest, "'Tis a Pity She's a Whore."

He has given this a scrupulous mounting, if it does lack a poetic fillip, and is sometimes heavy-handed in showing the sordid sex antics of the times. Yet the tender, luminous acting of Bibi Andersson as the sister, and the vulnerable, somewhat cowardly and yet truthful love of the brother, as intelligently limned by Per Oscarsson, who won the acting prize at the Cannes Fest last year for his work in the Danish-Swedish-Norwegian "Hunger" give this a tragic note.

Censorship troubles may be in store for this abroad and it is mainly an art house contender on its solid, knowing but at times stolid, direction. It manages to make a statement on incest; not condoning it but showing it as an aspect of love that can happen and is tragic but that bears dealing with its complications and results.

It is well-lensed and has a brooding if theatrical re-creation of the period, and the supporting players are well cast. Director Sjoman is a painstaking craftsman who can deal in extremely touchy subjects without exploiting them or cheapening them. But as in his "491," he shows one side of his theme and the people, and it is an extremely black one, at that. Yet it is sincere and not out to shock, albeit its subject matter makes it a hot potato for handling.

Its title literally means "Children's Bed," or "Brother and Sister Bed," and it has been called "My Sister, My Love" in Britain, where it has been released to generally good reviews and with not too much censoring, if allowed only for adult viewing. *Mosk.*

Come Spy With Me
(COLOR)

Inept spy comedy with songs. Grim b.o.

Hollywood, Jan. 11.

Twentieth Century-Fox release of an MPO-Futurama Entertainment-ABC Films production, presented by Arnold Kaiser; Alan V. Iselin, executive producer, Paul M. Heller, producer. Stars Troy Donahue, Andrea Dromm. Directed by Marshall Stone. Screenplay, Cherney Berg, based on a story by Stuart James; camera (DeLuxe Color), Zoli Vidor; underwater camera, Jordan Klein; editor, Hy Goldman; music, Bob Bowers; songs, William "Smoky" Robinson, Jr., J. Butler; asst. director, Charles Okun. Reviewed at 20th-Fox Studios, L.A., Jan. 11, '67. Running Time, 85 MINS.

Pete Barker	Troy Donahue
Jill Parsons	Andrea Dromm
Walter Ludeker	Albert Dekker
Larry Claymore	Mart Hulswit
Samantha	Valerie Allen
Augie	Dan Ferrone
Corbett	Howard Schell
Chance	Chance Gentry
Gunther Stiller	Louis Edmonds
Chris	Kate Aldrich
Pam	Pam Colbert
Kieswetter	Gil Pratley
Pantin	Georges Shoucair
Keefer	Alston Bair
Morgan	Tim Moxon
Karl	Eric Coverly
Brooks	Jack Lewis
Linda	Lucienne Bridou

Although a 20th-Fox release, "Come Spy With Me" is a slap-dash cheapie, awkward, clumsy, amateurish, inept and banal. Film exhibitor Alan Iselin is exec producer. Spy-song pic was tradeshown in the old 4:3 aspect ratio, leading to suspicion that it was shot in 16m, later blown up. Theatrical b.o. outlook is grim, even on lowercase, while pix-to-tv chances are strictly off-network, non-primetime. Sharing above-title billing with Troy

Donahue is Andrea Dromm. the former teleblurb gal whose famous line is subject to paraphrase: is this any way to make a motion picture? You bet it isn't.

Pic is an Arnold Kaiser presentation, and has been copyrighted by MPO, an eastern teleblurbery, and ABC Films. Futurama Entertainment Corp. is partnered with MPO. Paul M. Heller, MO prexy, is credited as producer. Marshall is credited as producer. Marshall Stone directed.

Cherney Berg scripted, working from an original story about spies in Jamaica as penned by Stuart James. Extensive, and corny, narration is used to cover the clumsy scripting, acting & direction. Cast regularly pauses for pool, party and terp scenes. Dialog is far beneath the status of top-featured Albert Dekker, but, at the same time, beyond the reach of Donahue, the one-note Miss Dromm, the cloying, overly-precious Valerie Allen, and a lot of others.

Zoli Vidor's DeLuxe Color camera, of uncertain focus, and Jordan Klein's better underwater lensing cannot make the Jamaican locations overcome the story and cast. Looping sound levels are uneven. Title tune is a zero, penned by William "Smoky" Robinson Jr., and sung (perhaps on the original sound-track single) by The Miracles. Bob Bowers' score, however, is okay. J. Butler's "The Shark" song is used in one of the terp scenes.

Hy Goldman edited to an interminable 85 minutes. Other credits are routine, at best, except Paul Petroff's title work which is clever. *Murf.*

In den Klauen des Goldenen Drachen
(In the Claws of the Golden Dragon)
(GERMAN-ITALIAN-YUGOSLAV-COLOR)

Berlin, Jan. 7.
Constantin release of Parnass (Munich) and Cinesecolo (Milan) production, jointly with Avala (Belgrade). Stars Tony Kendall, Brad Harris. Features Barbara Frey, E. F. Fuerbringer. Directed by Frank Kramer. Screenplay, Stefan Gommermann, Kramer, based on novel of same name by Bert F. Island; camera (Eastmancolor). Francis Izzarelli; music, Bobby Gutesha; editing, Edmund Lozzi. At Filmtheater Berlin, W. Berlin. Running Time, 92 MINS.
Inspector X .... Tony Kendall
Captain Rowland .... Brad Harris
Sybille .... Barbara Frey
Shabana .... Luisa Rivelli
Professor Akron ...... E. F. Fuerbringer
Stella .... Gisela Hahn
Benny .... Pino Mattei

Gangster pix which teem with sex and action sequences are still very much in vogue here. This one belongs to a series (German title: "Kommissar X") which tries to cash in on the current trend. It has all the conventional trimmings and should please those who don't mind seeing the same "stuff" over and over on the screen. It displays the usual car chases, fisticuffs, gunfire displays and a large contingent of what they call "sexy lookers" who eventually interfere with the heroes. One may classify this production as an okay filler with nothing special about it.

This vehicle, for which Theo Maria Werner's Parnass Film is responsible on the German side, once again has Jo Walker, alias Inspector X, a private detective, and his old pal, Capt. Tom Rowland of Manhattan's Homicide Division, teamed. Both have been sent to Singapore to protect a famous atomic physicist from a gang of unscrupulous blackmailers. Plenty of villains have to be wiped out before their task is done. Along their way it is amazing to see how easily the two heroes fall into a trap, especially if the one who ensnares them is a beautiful doll. They are nearly constantly involved with fisticuffs and occasionally beaten up, and it's incredible to see how quickly they recover. Pix like these can't and don't want to be taken seriously, of course, but even such films can benefit from imagination on the part of its creators. As far as imagination is concerned, this is a rather meager opus.

Tony Kendall and Brad Harris, familiar faces on the German screen, play the two heroes. Kendall here shows once more that he has a soft spot in his heart for the femmes. Harris does it more nonchalantly, and that nonchalance is sometimes refreshing if contrasted with the overly irresistible charm of his friend.

E. F. Fuerbringer is all right as the professor while the many girls are mainly of the seen-and-forgotten type. A compliment must be paid to the film's action scenes, which are very effective.

A good deal of the shooting was against the actual backgrounds of Singapore. ("Join the movies and you see the world" has long become also a slogan of German filmmakers.) Pic's lensing is fine and other technical credits are adequate. *Hans.*

Trans-Europ-Express
(FRENCH)

Paris, Jan. 10.
Lux release of Como-Film production. Stars Jean-Louis Trintignant, Marie-France Pisier; features Nadine Verdier, Daniel Emilfork, Charles Millot, Henri Lambert. Written and directed by Alain Robbe-Grillet; camera, Willy Kurant; editor, Robert Wade. Previewed in Paris. Running Time, 92 MINS.
Elias .... Jean-Louis Trintignant
Eva .... Marie-France Pisier
Singer .... Nadine Verdier
Frank .... Charles Millot
Agent .... Daniel Emilfork
Inspector .... Henri Lambert
Alain Robbe-Grillet .... Himself

Alain Robbe-Grillet is one of the so-called New Novelists more interested in description and external things than in the psychological mechanism of his characters. He wrote the hermetic "Last Year in Marienbad" and wrote and directed the even more static "The Immortal." Now he tries for a more adventurous and clearer pic but keeps it a bit equivocal and literary as he deals with an author discussing a script with a producer on a train and then having it acted out.

This Pirandellian method is not new in pix and here Robbe-Grillet himself is the author trying to dream up a story. It has a crisp approach and emerges as the usual tale of a criminal on the run and getting involved with a joy girl and a young boy who help him. But everybody has his own game as manipulated by the author.

It's a fairly amusing tidbit, though Robbe-Grillet too often uses forced erotic scenes that do not come off; for instance, the criminal who smuggles dope and who has some sadistic drives he takes out on the prostie; Marie-France Pisier, who's more a mischievous teenage type than one would associate with the more perverse scenes in which she is chained or raped.

While the whole pic seems ambiguous and overly glib, the author-director evokes some picturesque aspects of a train trip and he uses the gimmick of having everyone seem sinister, via close-ups and lingering shots.

This is mainly for specialized usage abroad on its tricky if familiar treatment. It is well photographed, played with some gusto by Jean-Louis Trintignant as the criminal hero, with others okay except for Miss Pisier's miscast femme fatale. *Mosk.*

Polizist Waeckerli in Gefahr
(Policeman Waeckerli in Danger)
(SWISS)

Zurich, Jan. 6.
Rialto-Film AG Zurich release of Kaegi-Film AG Zurich production. Directed by Sigfrit Steiner. Screenplay, Steiner, Schaggi Streuli; camera, Karl Wolf; music, Walter Baumgartner. Features Schaggi Streuli, Margrit Rainer, Fay Kaufmann, Rene Scheibli, Rainer Litten, Paul Buehlmann, Susy Lehmann, Joerg Schneider, Juliana Vonderlinn, Alfred Lohner, Liz Paspalis, Max Knapp, Elfriede Volker, Eva David, Elisabeth Schnell, Edy Huber, Valerie Steinmann, Ursula von Wiese, Ernst Stiefel, Megge Lehmann. Opened Dec. 16, '66, at Capitol Theatre, Zurich. Running Time, 109 MINS.

(In Swiss-German)

"Policeman Waeckerli in Danger," the first new Swiss feature film in almost two years, was made on location in and around Zurich, on a shoestring budget of $81,000. It is a sequel to a successful Swiss film based on a popular local radio series, "Policeman Waeckerli," of some years back.

It is doubtful whether this new entry, made in Swiss dialect, will repeat its predecessor's b.o. performance even in the local mart. Internationally, its chances are slight. A hackneyed script, unimaginative direction and stock performances will mar its chances. The slight story's pedestrian pace is an added liability.

The plot centres on a Swiss village policeman Waeckerli, a local stock character, his family problems and involvement with the murder—masked as a suicide—of an ex-convict returning to the village after a prison term based on false evidence. The real villain is finally revealed and brought to justice.

Performances vary from acceptable, locally-slanted portrayals by Schaggi Streuli (who also coscripted) and Margrit Rainer as the policeman and his wife to below-par ones. Technical credits are so-so. *Mezo.*

Bare en Tagsten
(A Bump on the Head)
(DANISH)

Copenhagen, Jan. 9.
Palladium production and release. Written by Bob Ramsing, based on a play by C. E. Soya. Directed by Annelise Meineche. Features Poul Bundgaard, Lily Broberg, Bodil Steen, Marianne Toensberg; camera (Eastmancolor), Aage Wiltrup; music, Ole Hoeyer. Reviewed at Palladium Theatre, Copenhagen, Jan. 8, '67. Running Time, 101 MINS.

Under a thin disguise of a period piece (1911) splendor and respected dramatist C. E. Soya's dialog, Annelise Meineche with this film uses hammy humor and clammy sex as her chief ingredients. Technically, she proves even more inept this time around than she did with her initial film efforts, "Sytten" and "Flagermusen." But like "Seventeen," "A Bump on the Head" may rake in good boxoffice on both the local and the German market.

Story is about the often-used bump on the head changing a man's life so radically that most everybody is relieved when still another bump brings him back to his senses, whatever they were. "A Bump" is this time administered to a dour middle-aged schoolteacher (Poul Bundgaard) who suddenly turns into practically the satyr of the Century. Or, if only he did. As put on the screen by Miss Meineche, the satyr remains too much the moron, and the occasional funny lines are blown up so as to appear like the balloon captions in a comic strip. *Kell.*

Monkeys, Go Home
(COLOR)

Light, entertaining Disney comedy. Maurice Chevalier and Dean Jones head competent cast. Good family b.o. outlook.

Hollywood, Jan. 21.

Buena Vista release of a Walt Disney Production, co-producer, Ron Miller. Features Maurice Chevalier, Dean Jones, Yvette Mimieux. Directed by Andrew V. McLaglen. Screenplay, Maurice Tombragel, based on the novel "The Monkeys," by G. K. Wilkinson; camera (Technicolor), William Snyder; editor, Marsh Hendry; music, Robert F. Brunner; song, Robert B. and Richard M. Sherman; asst. director, Tom Leetch. Reviewed at Walt Disney Studios, Burbank, Calif., Jan. 20, '67. Running Time, 101 MINS.

Father Sylvain	Maurice Chevalier
Hank Dussard	Dean Jones
Maria Riserau	Yvette Mimieux
Marcel Cartucci	Bernard Woringer
Em'le Paraulis	Clement Harari
Yolande Angelli	Yvonne Constant
Mayor Gaston Lou	Marcel Hillaire
M. Piastillio	Jules Munshin
Grocer	Alan Carney
Fontanino	Maurice Marsac
Sidoni Riserau	Darleen Carr

Set in France but filmed completely in Walt Disney's Studio, "Monkeys, Go Home" is an amusing comedy - romance in which Dean Jones, heir to an olive farm, provokes political and romantic complications when he decides to use chimpanzee labor. Maurice Chevalier heads the cast as a village priest. Co-produced by Ron Miller, film has the usual professional Disney blend of children, animals, humor and charm. Unpretentious, but well produced, pic shapes up as good family fare for Buena Vista release in general situaitons.

In adapting G. K. Wilkinson's novel, Maurice Tombragel has effected a subtle introduction of an implied cold war situation. Title is a play on the "Yankee Go Home" slogan, herein applied to Jones' monkeys who create a capitalist issue in a small French town. Conniving realtor Clement Harari and butcher Bernard Woringer plot to force Jones' exit; the former wants the land, the latter wants Yvette Mimieux, who has taken a fancy to the American newcomer.

Andrew V. McLaglen, in a shift froam oaters, shows another directorial facet in keeping the action going as plot lines coverage to an amusing climactic brawl scene involving the entire village. Miss Mimieux is pretty and lends charm to her role; her dramatic abilities have yet to be exploited fully, although herein she demonstrates a pleasant, kittenish air which registers well with an audience.

Jones, always a good underplaying comedian, reacts adroitly to the script demands that he be, variously, frustrated, angry and moon-struck, all the while remaining completely likeable. Chevalier, a showbiz legend, again scores in projecting a benign worldliness. Whether cast as a priest, as here, or else as an engaging man of the world, Chevalier never fails to project the image of a man who has lived fully, and learned something positive from every experience.

Other players all lend solid support, including the rascals Woringer and Harari, and the standout Yvonne Constant, recruited as Jones' fake relative, who radiates in a tippy sequence. Marcel Hilaire, Jules Munshin, Alan Carney and Maurice Marsac are good, and Darleen Carr, a new Disney protege, has a small part as Miss Mimieux's sister. Pic ends on an upbeat note of village co-operation, and the romantic ties are effected, natch.

The Gallic visual flavor in this 100%-studio pic is the excellent work of art directors Carroll Clark and John B. Mansbridge, and set decorators Emile Kuri and Frank R. McKelvy, assisted by matte men Peter Ellenshaw and Jim Fetherolf. William Snyder's Technicolor lensing is very good, and Marsh Headry edited to a good 101 minutes. Robert F. Brunner's score has an acceptable light rock-roll flavor, easy on the ears, and the "Joie De Vivre" song by Robert B. and Richard M. Sherman has a nice lilt. Other credits are firstrate. *Murf.*

Deadlier Than The Male
(BRITISH-TECHNISCOPE-COLOR)

Bulldog Drummond character returns to pix in an okay murder meller. Abundant sex and sadism may offend some audiences.

Hollywood, Jan. 18.

Universal release of a Sydney Box-Bruce Newbery Production, produced by Betty E. Box. Stars Richard Johnson, Elke Sommer, Sylva Koscina, Nigel Green; features Suzanna Leigh, Steve Carlson, Virginia North. Directed by Ralph Thomas. Screenplay, Jimmy Sangster, David Csborn, Liz Charles-Williams, based on an original story by Sangster; camera (Technicolor), Ernest Steward; editor, Alfred Roome; music, Malcolm Lockyer; title song, John Franz, Scott Engel; asst. directors, Simon Relph, Giorgio Gentili. Reviewed at Universal Studios, L.A., Jan. 17, '67. Running Time, 98 MINS.

Hugh Drummond	Richard Johnson
Irma Eckman	Elke Sommer
Penelope	Sylva Koscina
Carl Peterson/Weston	Nigel Green
Grace	Suzanna Leigh
Robert Drummond	Steve Carlson
Brenda	Virginia North
Miss Ashenden	Justine Lord
King Fedra	Zia Mohyeddin
Boxer	Lee Montague
Mitsouko	Yasuko Nagazumi
Sir John Bledlow	Laurence Naismith
Cerloggio	George Pastell
Chang	Milton Reid
Bridgenorth	Leonard Rossiter

There is no doubt that "Deadlier Than The Male" is loaded with colorful and exciting production values. Opinion thereafter is likely to divide, however, for the Sydney Box-Bruce Newbery production will strike some as okay dual bill escapism, and others as overly raw, offensive and single entendre. Sadism, sex and attempted sophistication mark this latest Bulldog Drummond pic, with Richard Johnson starred. Elke Sommer heads a long list of lookers. Femme audiences may be repelled by the abundant sadism, and b.o. prospects appear most promising for Universal release in male-oriented action situations. (Ed.—Also involved in production is Inflight Motion Pictures which coproduced, via film production subsidiary, with Universal and Rank.)

David Osborn, Liz Charles-Williams and Jimmy Sangster scripted the latter's original story, in which Miss Sommer and Sylvia Koscina are two cohorts of Nigel Green in his industrial deal-making. Green's modus operandum is simple: intervene in major deals and promise consummation, then kill off all opposition and collect the promised fee. Scripters had a major task in making brutal, explicit murder appear as nonchalant as taking tea, and they rarely achieve the goal.

Johnson enters the case at behest of industrialist Laurence Naismith. Only sub-plot involves Steve Carlson, Johnson's girl-chasing nephew, and their relationship is of the Jack Armstrong and Billy type — father-figure, etc. It is sometimes a clumsy plot line, as written, directed and acted. Virginia North is "introduced" herein as one of Carlson's playmates.

In the course of pic's longish 98 minutes, as edited by Alfred Roome, there are about nine explicitly gory episodes, plus a few that do not occur, although these are made deliberately obvious and are protracted to excess. Also, there are three major explosions which take human life. Adding up, it works out to one death-dealing event every eight minutes or so.

Director Ralph Thomas has done a routine job with script and players, although Ernest Steward's Technicolor - Techniscope camera provides lush eye appeal in sets, locations, wardrobe and femmes. A climactic chess game, in which Green and Johnson play by instructing a computer to move the life-size pieces, has insufficient impact, mainly because of low-angle shots which do not give dramatic perspective to the movements of the game.

Producer Betty E. Box, in short, has done a better job below the line than above. Malcolm Lockyer's score is okay, while John Franz and Scott Engel penned the title song, sung at main and end titles by The Walker Brothers. Tune is one of those contemporary de rigeur insertions which mean nothing. Final lyric line is "For the female of the species is deadlier than the male." It cannot really be called a love theme, per se. Other technical credits, executed at Britain's Pinewood Studios, are processional. *Murf.*

Nankai No Dai Ketto
(Big Duel In The North Sea)
(JAPANESE-COLOR)

Tokyo, Jan. 17.

Toho Co. production and release. With Akira Takarada, Toru Watanabe, Toru Ibuki, Chotaro Togane, Kumi Mozuno. Directed by Jun Fukuda. Screenplay, Sinichi Sekizawa; music, Masaru Sato; camera (Eastmancolor), Eiji Tsurubaya. Previewed in Tokyo. Running Time, 85 MINS.

This marks another return—the seventh or eighth, at least—of Japan's most beloved monster, Godzilla. By now he is so thoroughly tamed that he is anthropomorphic—plays soccer with bad monster Ebira, looks fondly at the heroine, has the whole cast rooting for him at the end, and escapes to swim off to another sequel.

In this picture he is awakened by a group of shipwrecked youngsters (well, Akira Takarada is not so young, but he acts it) and sets out to save them from the red plastic claws of Ebira, a giant shrimp, and the clutches of an unnamed group of badmen who are making secret atom bombs in their island hideout. At the end, Mothra (also a screen veteran, and one who has the good fortune to sleep throughout most of this entertainment) wakes up and moves the cast off the island minutes before the Toho special-effects department blows it up.

Since the setting is rural rather than urban, there is not much destruction in this film and the monsters are far too cute to appeal to most kids. Still, there is lots of aimless action and Ebira (this being his first screen appearance) is satisfactorily menacing. He does not fawn like Majin, or simper and brindle like Godzilla, nor flutter about self-importantly like Mothra. He is a really good, oldfashioned, unrepentant monster. *Chie.*

Ninja Bugelijo
(A Band of Ninja)
(JAPAN)

Tokyo, Jan. 18.

Oshima Productions Presentation released by Art Theatre Guild, Tokyo. Directed by Nagisa Oshima. Drawings by Shirato Sampei. Music, Hikaru Haiyashi. With the voices of Keo Sato, Hideo Kanze, Fumio Watanabe, Shoichi Osawa. Previewed in Tokyo. Running Time, 135 MINS.

"Ninja Bugelijo" is the title of a popular comic strip by Shirato Sampei, about Japan's 13-century civil wars and the activities of the "Ninja," military spies adept at the arts of water-walking, invisibility, castle-scaling, etc. Originally intended for children, the strip has recently become very popular with local intellectuals who follow it in the same way (though with less reason) that their opposite numbers follow "Peanuts" and "Pogo."

This is the background for the latest film of Nagisa Oshima, the first of the Japan "New Wave" directors several years ago, who skidded to a kind of fame with sex-cum-gore pix of the caliber of "The Sun's Burial." His idea was to make a kind of comic-strip which would please everyone, but, like most of his pictures, this one falls between stools. It isn't camp enough to be in nor involving enough to be out.

The technique (or lack of it) in the film is perhaps the biggest problem. Since Oshima and his staff decided against animation, there is drawing after drawing held in front of the camera while a completely realistic soundtrack (starring some of the big names in Japan's legitimate theatre) is supposed to supply the visuals. That this can work is attested by pictures as different as Chris Marker's remarkable still-film "La Jetee" and the reconstructed version of Andrzj Munk's film, "Pasazerka." But then, these films used photographs of real people and this one uses drawings done in a most unsettling style: half traditional

Japanese brush-and-ink, half early Betty Boop.

There is little hope for this film, even in Japan. Trimmed down, it might make some kind of short, though what kind is problematical since so much of the "action" emphasizes the most explicit black-and-white gore. As it is, asking an audience to sit through more than two hours of it is arrogance.
Chie.

The Vulture
(BRITISH)

Well-made horror-scifi meller with good chances in its intended market.

Hollywood, Jan. 20.
Paramount release of Lawrence Huntington production. Stars Robert Hutton, Akim Tamiroff, Broderick Crawford; features Diane Clare, Philip Friend. Direction-original story-screenplay, Huntington; camera, Stephen Dade; music, Eric Spear; editor, John S. Smith. Reviewed at Paramount Studios, Jan. 20, '67. Running Time, **91 MINS.**
Eric Lutyens .... Robert Hutton
Professor Koniglich ..... Akim Tamiroff
Brian Stroud ...... Broderick Crawford
Trudy Lutyens .... Diane Clare
The Vicar .... Philip Friend
Jarvis .... Patrick Holt
Ellen West .... Annette Carell
The Sexton .... Edward Caddick
Edward Stroud .... Gordon Sterne
Police Superintendent Wendell
.... Keith McConnell
Nurse .... Margaret Robertson

"The Vulture" is a well-developed chiller with sufficient mounting suspense to warrant good booking in its particular field. An English import, the Lawrence Huntington production stars Robert Hutton, Akim Tamiroff and Broderick Crawford for identification in the American market and has been soundly turned out with an eye to appropriate values.

Plot in screenplay by Huntington, who also wrote original story and directs, draws broadly on what is described as "atomic transmutation" in motivating action based on the curse of a Spanish sea captain buried alive in 1749 who swore to return and kill all living members of the family that interred him. Narrative unfolds in Cornwall, where the superstitious country folk believe the gruesome happenings are supernatural, but Hutton — a visiting American nuclear scientist — suspects it's a scientific experiment going awry.

It is his theory, which he proceeds to prove, that someone attempted to disintegrate a living human body by nuclear energy and reassemble it alive in the grave, without taking into his calculations a giant vulture which had been buried there with its Spanish master. A horrible fusion thus is achieved. The horrifying apparition, a huge black vulture-like bird with human hands and face, becomes the avenger of the long-dead Spaniard and causes the death of two of the three remaining members of the threatened family, and nearly kills the final descendant, wife of the American scientist.

Motivating theme has been evolved satisfactorily for scifi audiences and Huntington maintains a sharp tempo in building to his climax. Hutton persuasively enacts his character and Diane Clare does nicely as his wife. Tamiroff as an old antiquarian is a some-

---

what mysterious figure as he delves into the legends of the countryside, with a "fascination" for science, and Crawford plays a wealthy Canadian newspaper tycoon lately become a Cornish squire and first of the threatened family to be taken off by the giant bird. In lesser roles, Philip Friend, Patrick Holt, Edward Caddick and Gordon Sterne are effective.

Technical credits generally are firstrate, including Stephen Dade's fluid photography, Eric Spear's music score, John S. Smith's editing and Duncan Sutherland's art direction.
Whit.

Dai Majin Gyakushu
(The Return of Majin)
(JAPAN-COLOR)

Tokyo, Jan. 17.
Daiei Co. production and release. With Nideki Ninomiya, Shinji Hori, Shiei Iizuka, Muneyuki Nagatomo, Junichiro Yamashita. Directed by Isho Mori. Produced by Masaichi Nagata. Screenplay, Tetsuo Yoshida; music, Akira Ifukube; camera (Eastmancolor), Hiroshi Imai, Fujio Morita. Previewed in Tokyo. Running Time, **80 MINS.**

This marks the return of one of the more popular of last year's monsters, Japan's very own Golem, a big statuelike man in full armor who protects the innocent and good from clutches of the powerful and the wicked.

In this one he saves three little runaway boys and then wrecks the slave compound where badmen have been tormenting their relatives. The special effects, particularly at the beginning (earthquake, fire, flood) are better than usual, but Majin himself is obviously a man in a plastic and rubber suit carefully crunching expensive models.

One of the problems is that the camera angle always gives away the trick.
Chie.

The Deadly Bees
(BRITISH-COLOR)

A slow-paced shocker with a highly believable premise, pic also has a number of sustained suspense sequences and captivating presence of Suzanna Leigh.

Hollywood, Jan. 16.
Paramount release of Amicus (Max J. Rosenberg & Milton Subotsky) Production. Stars Suzanna Leigh, Frank Finlay, Guy Doleman. Directed by Freddie Francis. Screenplay, Robert Bloch, Anthony Marriott, based on novel, "A Taste of Honey" by H. F. Heard; camera (Technicolor), John Wilcox; music, Wilfred Josephs; asst. director, Anthony Waye; editor, Oswald Hafenrichter. Reviewed at Paramount Studio, Jan. 16, '67. Running Time, **123 MINS.**
Vicki Robbins .... Suzanna Leigh
Manfred .... Frank Finlay
Hargrove .... Guy Doleman
Mrs. Hargrove .... Catherine Finn
Thompson .... John Harvey
Hawkins .... Michael Ripper
Compere .... Anthony Bailey
Harcourt .... Tim Barrett
Coroner .... James Cossins
Doctor .... Frank Forsyth
Doris .... Katy Wild
Sister .... Greta Farrer
Secretary .... Gina Gianelli
Doctor Lang .... Michael Gwynn
Agent .... Maurice Good
Inspector .... Alister Williamson

"The Deadly Bees" is like "The Birds," only on a smaller scale. It boasts of uneven suspense, a plot long in unraveling and some gripping cinematic moments, pro-

---

vided by bees in deadly pursuit. Pic is not for the faint-hearted, but as a low-budgeted meller, should have appeal as an offbeat item for the teenagers, who no doubt will identify with Suzanna Leigh, playing a pop singer.

Plot is slow getting off the ground and becomes deliberately confusing, with final unreeling working out with unexpected conviction.

Miss Leigh has a mental breakdown from overwork and is sent to rest on a remote British island. The innkeeper, Guy Doleman, is a beekeeper. Miss Leigh soon stumbles across the chic cottage of Frank Finlay, who also keeps bees.

A swarm of killer bees soon attack Doleman's wife, and in a frightening realistic and chilling montage, she attempts in vain to ward them off and falls in a bloody heap, dead. Miss Leigh is later attacked by the deadly stingers while locked in her bedroom but escapes.

Suspense builds in a manner that viewer does not know which of the beekeepers is responsible for these bee-havings. Throughout, characters show little emotional involvement, except for Miss Leigh, who has command of all she does.

Finlay's reserve is an interesting piece of acting and helps keep the plot together. Doleman's role doesn't register well, but this is also the script's fault. Catherine Finn, as the wife, has nothing more to do than look bored.

Robert Bloch and Anthony Marriott's script is peppered with scholarly tidbits about the living habits of bees and manages to hold interest to the end.

Freddie Francis' direction is at times a little arty, with slow pans and other shots which seem to go on too long when nothing is happening. The bee-attacking sequences are in each instance cleverly done and also well edited by Oswald Hafenrichter. Music score by Wilfred Josephs contributes appropriately to the mood of the pic.
Dool.

Prehistoric Women
(BRITISH-SCOPE-COLOR)

A never-never land dominated by beautiful women, pic has a sick premise which gets worse as it goes along.

Hollywood, Jan. 18.
20th-Fox release of Hammer-Seven Arts Production, produced, directed by Michael Carreras. Features entire cast. Screenplay, Henry Younger; camera (color) Michael Reed; editor, James Need; music, Carlo Mantelli; asst. director, David Tringham. Reviewed at 20th-Fox Studio, Jan. 18, 1967. Running Time, **95 MINS.**
Kari (The Queen) ..... Martine Beswick
David Marchant ...... Michael Latimer
Saria .... Edina Ronay
A Slave-Girl .... Stephanie Randell
An Amazon .... Sally Calclough

A sadistic fantasy, "Prehistoric Women" may be of interest to the masochistic filmgoer, but as general entertainment fare it is dubious material, and parents should perhaps be warned to keep their children away from it.

Film is not only in questionable taste, it is pretty openly perverse. The fact that production values are good and the color camerawork generally excellent only calls attention to a lot of technically fine work that has gone into a mindless creative enterprise.

Made in Britain by Hammer-Seven Arts, this is the retelling of a kingdom of women in a dark garden of Eden. The men have been enslaved and kept in a dark chamber and the thousands of beautiful young girls in the kingdom are filled with venom for the entire species. The kingdom is in Africa, however, and a tribe of black natives supposedly protect the "wonderland" from outside influences. In repayment for this service, a ceremony of selection is periodically performed in which one of the virgins is turned over to the pleasure of the tribe and killed.

Film opens with an African safari guide chasing a wounded tiger into the forbidden kingdom of "the White Rhinoceros." He is taken prisoner and turned over to the white queen who throughout the film attempts to seduce him. In the end it is indicated that the hero — the queen's lechery is never realized — is given to believe that he has dreamed the whole thing. If this is true, he's psychologically a very sick man.

Although there is such visual excitement, this Henry Younger screenplay drains all sense of common decency from his inverted plot and one questions how the pic will have any appeal at all. Worse yet, the dialog is unbelievably infantile.

The acting is about as animated as the stone rhinoceros statue. Martine Beswick is the queen, Michael Latimer, the hunter. Fact sheet prepared by 20th-Fox, which is releasing pic, listed only three other actresses, Edina Ronay, Stephanie Randell and Sally Calclough no doubt in an attempt to save the rest of the large cast from embarrassment.

Michael Carreras produced and directed. Michael Reed provided the fine camerawork; Bob Jones, the serviceable settings. James Needs' editing is jumpy in spots, while Carlo Mantelli's music is unmemorable.
Dool.

Gohaku Muika
(JAPAN—COLOR)

Tokyo, Jan. 17.
Toei Production with Ikebe Rye Productions. Toei release. With Mako Midori, Kiyoshi Hitomi, Keizo Kawasaki, Yoko Isono. Directed by Yusuke Watanabe. Screenplay, Taro Kinoshita. Filmed in Eastman Color. Previewed in Tokyo. Running Time, **80 MINS.**

The title of this widescreen-color comedy refers to one of those travel plans of journey and five nights in hotels, all at package price. This is what two pairs of newlyweds (Mako Midori and Kiyoshi Hitomi; Keizo Kawasaki and Yoko Isono) sign up for. Consequently, they are together constantly and the trouble is that Mako and Keizo know each other, indeed had almost gotten married, and still long to bed down together.

This, despite their respective spouses, they do several times in this bright and irreverent little comedy made by Yusuke Watanabe for Ikebe Productions. Taro Kinoshita's script is balanced, formal (split screens and the like), and makes the most of all the parallel situations, and the theme-and-variations score underlines the humor apparent in such a purposely artifical situation.

Some of the laughs are too easy, some are too vulgar, but on the whole the film is light, bright and completely unpretentious. Nice touches are the violent and completely unrealistic double-takes (like those in Restoration comedy) when the lovers meet; fat Kiyoshi waiting for his fair bride to come out of the bathroom; Miss Midori trying to decide why she got married—and all the fine scenery of the Kii Peninsula through which these mixed doubles roam.

The film will bring a number of chuckles at the local language houses, but it probably isn't stylish enough for other locations.

Chie.

First To Fight
(PANAVISION-COLOR)

Okay U.S. Marine-World War II actioner for program market; excellent vehicle for Chad Everett.

Hollywood, Jan. 12.
Warner Bros. release of William Conrad production. Stars Chad Everett, Marilyn Devin, Dean Jagger, Bobby Troup; features Claude Akins, Gene Hackman, James Best, Norman Alden. Directed by Christian Nyby. Screenplay, Gene L. Coon; camera (Technicolor), Harold Wellman; editor, George Rohrs; music, Fred Steiner; asst. director, Victor Vallejo. Reviewed at Warner Bros. Studios, Jan. 11, '67. Running Time, **97 MINS.**
Jack Connell .... Chad Everett
Peggy Sanford .... Marilyn Devin
Lt. Col. Baseman........ Dean Jagger
Lt. Overman .... Bobby Troup
Capt. Mason .... Claude Akins
Sgt. Tweed .... Gene Hackman
Sgt. Carnavan .... James Best
Sgt. Schmidtmer .... Norman Alden
Sgt. Maypole .... Bobs Watson
O'Brien .... Ken Swofford
Hawkins .... Ray Reese
Karl .... Garry Goodgion
Adams .... Robert Austin
Sgt. Slater .... Clint Ritchie
Pres. F. D. Roosevelt...Stephen Roberts

"First to Fight" — watchword of the U.S. Marine Corps — is a regulation World War II South Pacific melodrama which should do okay in program centers but has little to set it apart for important bookings. Executive producer William Conrad has accorded film proper mounting and like most service pix it has saleable ingredients conducive to tub-thumping.

Script by Gene L. Coon, given vigorous direction by Christian Nyby, pinpoints a Marine Guadalcanal hero decorated with a Congression.1 Medal of Honor for outstanding bravery who loses his nerve in battle when he returns later to the Pacific theatre. This freezing as Marines hit the beach at Saipan and attempt to take a Jap-held objective is attributed to leatherneck's new status as a husband.

While there can be no exception taken to the legitimacy of

such a premise, point strikes a jarring note and is overly-prolonged in development, thus reducing dramatic impact. In the capable trouping of Chad Everett, however, the fear-bound Marine is a fairly convincing character and thesp should receive plenty of kudos for his general performance.

With the exception of Marilyn Devin, a blonde looker with a nice style who plays Everett's bride in stateside sequences after he returns from Guadalcanal to be decorated and is assigned temporarily as a training instructor at Camp Pendleton, cast is all-male.

Dean Jagger is effective as the colonel who promoted Everett from sergeant to lieutenant on the battlefield and later his commanding officer at Pendleton; Bobby Troup handles himself well as another medal-winner; James Best is likable as Everett's Guadalcanal buddy. Gene Hackman likewise makes a creditable impression as Everett's gunnery sargeant on Saipan who finally rouses him out of his panic.

Technical credits are plus right down the line. Standouts here are Harold Wellman's color photography; Fred Steiner's score, George Rohrs' editing, Art Loel's art direction. *Whit.*

Den Roede Kappe
(The Red Mantle)
(DANISH-SWEDISH-ICELANDIC-COLOR)
Copenhagen, Jan. 17.
An Asa Film Studio release of the Asa (Copenhagen) Movie Art of Europe AB, (Stockholm) and Edda Film, (Reykjavik) production. Written and directed by Gabriel Axel. Dialogue by Frank Jaeger. Featuring Gitte Haenning, Oleg Vidov, Gunnar Bjornstrand, Eva Dahlbeck. Camera (Eastmancolor) Henning Bendtsen. Music by Per-Noergaard. Reviewed at Kinopalaet Asa Bio, Copenhagen, January 16. Running Time, **105 MINS.**

The tragic story of Hagbard and Signe is an oft-retold Nordic tale of young love's fearful fate amidst a family blood feud on Iceland. Gabriel Axel (who hit it big for Palladium with the gross humor of "Crazy Paradise") was encouraged by Denmark's Asa Film Studio to aim for higher artistic stakes when filming his own version of the ancient saga as "The Red Mantle."

Denmark's heir apparent, Princess Margrethe, attended the world premiere of Axel's film, and so did Oleg Vidov, a leading young Soviet actor who had been enlisted for the role of Hagbard who has to revenge the killing of his two brothers by slaying the three brothers of his beloved Signe.

From Sweden came Gunnar Bjornstrand and Eva Dahlbeck, actors of international standing, who play Signe's royal parents in "The Red Mantle." Asa Film Studio had brought Swedish and Icelandic money into the production, but it still stands mainly as Danish cinema workmanship.

Workmanship is the word. The art is mainly missing, and the film got almost ferocious reviews from a bitterly disappointed Copenhagen press. "The Red Mantle," however, should stand a fair chance in international playoff.

Most of the footage was shot and

shot beautifully by cameraman Henning Bendtsen on Icelandic locations. The dramatic Nordic landscapes along with the particular Nordic lore should prove an evident attraction to many spectators, yearning for new vistas if not for new art.

Unfortunately, Gabriel Axel lacks power as a director of actors. He works mostly with frames and ideas and leaves the acting to the actors. A few of them come through anyway, especially the Swedish players and Russia's young James Dean-ish Vidov, but mostly players are "lost."

Horribly miscast as Signe is Denmark's young pop-singing star Gitte Haenning (who has a lot of cinema experience in B-grade German musicals). She is blond and perpetually babyish, even in a short, clumsy imposed-with-commercial-intent, nude scene. And her death by her own hand seems just a silly postulate.

Where Gabriel Axel and the film succeeds best is in the several gory fight scenes that have heads rolling in the Atlantic surf that is a most effective sound background through much of the action. But of action there is too little. Instead we get an earful of high-falutin' phony saga-style dialogue, spoken as by radio actors in 1930. But local voice dubbing might help considerably even though the film will remain an item more for the outer eye than for the inner mind.

Kell.

Night Of The Generals
(BRITISH-FRENCH-COLOR-PANAVISION)

Sam Spiegel's strong cast and production weakened by languid script. Needs vigorous selling.

London, Jan. 27.
Columbia Pictures release of Horizon-Filmsonor (Sam Spiegel-Anatole Litvak) production, directed by Litvak. Features Peter O'Toole, Omar Sharif, Tom Courtenay. Screenplay, Joseph Kessel, Paul Dehn, based on the novel by Hans Helmut Kirst, from an incident written by James Hadley Chase; camera (Technicolor), Henri Decae; editor, Alan Osbiston; music, Maurice Jarre; production design, Alexander Trauner; asst. directors, Tom Pevsner, Jean-Pierre Perier-Pillu. Reviewed at Odeon Theatre, London. Running Time, **148 MINS.**
Gen. Tanz .... Peter O'Toole
Major Grau .... Omar Sharif
Cpl. Hartmann ...... Tom Courtenay
Gen. Kahlenberge .... Donald Pleasence
Ulrike Gabler .... Joanna Pettet
Inspector Morand ..... Philippe Noiret
Gen. Gabler .... Charles Gray
Eleanore Gabler .... Coral Browne
Colonel Sandauer .... John Gregson
Otto .... Nigel Stock
Marshal Rommel...Christopher Plummer
Juliette .... Juliette Greco
Liesowski .... Yves Brainville
Doctor .... Sacha Pitoeff
Wionczek .... Charles Millot
Col. in War Room....Raymonde Gerome
Monique .... Veronique Vendell
Kopatski .... Pierre Mondy
Melanie .... Eleonore Hirt
Raymonde............ Nicole Courcel
Otto's Wife .... Jenny Orleans
Von Stauffenberg ..... Gerard Buhr
Hauser .... Michael Goodlife
Capt. Engel .... Gordon Jackson
Col. Mannheim .... Patrick Allen
Tanz's Driver .... Mac Ronay
Stupnagel .... Harry Andrews

With an important theme about the nature of guilt and the promise of a teasing battle of wits to establish it, Sam Spiegel's production, reuniting the stars of "Lawrence of Arabia," shaped as a big b.o. contender. But the result is an interesting feature that lets the tension runs slack, being afflicted with galloping inflation of its running-time. A 20-minute slice out of the middle would have worked wonders. As it is, hefty returns are indicated, and there's sufficient audience bait in the stars and the subject to override the inevitable disappointment.

Plot opens in Nazi-occupied Warsaw in 1942, with a prostie being brutally murdered and the killer being recognized as wearing the uniform of a German general. But that's the only clue for Major Grau (Omar Sharif), the Military Intelligence man in charge of the hunt, and he establishes that only three brasshats could have committed the crime, having insufficient alibis. One is Tanz (Peter O'Toole), a ruthless and devoted Nazi who destroys a quarter of Warsaw as an exercise in discipline. Another is Kahlenberge (Donald Pleasence), a cynical opportunist who has few scruples, but plenty ingenuity. And the third suspect is the pompous Gabler (Charles Gray), much henpecked by his bossy wife.

The background switches to Paris two years later, where all three suspects are gathered in the same place and Grau, who had been taken off the scent by a mysterious posting, doggedly resumes his sleuthing, having an innate belief in justice. Another prostie murder, carried out with similar brutality, is Tanz's doing, but he pins it on his orderly (Tom Courtenay) and shoots Grau, explaining that the latter is a traitor, involved in the famous 1944 plot- that failed to kill Hitler.

And the ironical comeuppance has Tanz, revered still in post war Germany and being used as a rallying-point for a Nazi revival, being uncovered by a French Interpol detective and shooting himself to evade disgrace.

A subplot, which distracts from the main theme, introduces a love note, the clinching being the affair of the orderly with a General's daughter and seeming a gratuitous sop to distaffers.

Adapted from Hans Hellmut Kirst's bitter novel, the story is told in flashback and the technique adds to the somewhat languid effect. The script, by Joseph Kessel and Paul Dehn, is worthy and lucid, but it has stilted passages that seem to betray translation and the characterization lacks depth. But the chief factor militating against conviction is the central performance by O'Toole, which lacks the firm savagery Tanz seems to require. He does convey the anguish of his neurosis, but he doesn't get close to the abhorrent principles which makes his disregard of human life, the main-spring of his personality, a convincing factor.

Omar Sharif is fine as the determined Grau, and Tom Courtenay wins sympathy for the fall-guy orderly, a musical pacifist unfitted for war. Donald Pleasence brings a steely fervor to Kahlenberge, and Charles Gray scores as the other flabby General suspect. And there's an outstanding cameo by Philippe Noiret, as the French resistance worker who helps Grau in his hunt and completes the work after the war, by unmasking Tanz at the rally.

Joanna Pettet brings charm to the thin role of Ulrike, the girl who falls for the orderly, and Christopher Plummer registers briefly as Rommel, brought in to show his connection with the General's plot. John Gregson, Nigel Stock and Coral Browne contribute to the acting strength, and there's a tiny appearance by Juliette Greco as a Paris cellar-club singer.

Anatole Litvak brings to the glossy production much helming competence, but he cannot fill out those middle reaches where the story loses its way in a side alley. The production is elegantly designed by Alexander Traumer, and the lensing of Henri Decae is superb, especially in his evocations of wartime Paris. In fact, all the technical credits cannot be faulted, and the soundtrack is musically embroidered by apt and sometimes poignant music from Maurice Jarre.

The film does convey a message of importance—that there's no moral difference between murder committed privately and mass killing perpetrated to government order. And that is its main asset.

But it lacks the final punch because Tanz, as conveyed by O'Toole, doesn't really come across as a complex human being, but as an unsmiling robot with strange sexual fantasies. He's shown inspecting Von Jogh's

self-portrait as if he's identifying himself with that painter's madness, but the parallel is mightily inexact.   *Otta.*

Three Days & a Child
(ISRAELI)

Tel Aviv, Jan. 24.
An S.Y.V., Tel Aviv production. Stars Odded Kotler, Germaine Unikovski, Illy Gorlitzky. Directed by Uri Zohar. Produced by Amatziya Hiyuni; camera, David Gurfinkel; made in Herzlia Studios.

Eli	Odded Kotler
Yael	Germaine Unikovski
Zvi	Illy Gorlitzky
Noa	Judith Soleh
Zeev	Misha Asherov

This is an arty arts film, sometimes beautiful and touching, about a student in Jerusalem (Eli) who agrees to take care, for three days, of the three-year-old son of his former girlfriend (Noa). The son could be his own—whether he is, is one of the things left unresolved. Uri Zohar's direction reflects various European influences: Scandinavian sex-scenes, a flashback in negative a la "Marienbad" and lingering "atmosphere" from Antonioni's book. Like the snake, which appears in the film (did its bite kill Zvi?), he was slow to digest what he swallowed. The thin borderline between art and artificial is too easily crossed.

Nevertheless, the film succeeds in creating a gripping mood, intruding into the viewers' equanimity with a bitter-sweet slice of life. Eli was Noa's lover for one night, while they both lived in a kibbutz. Eli left the kibbutz to become a student, Noa stayed on and married Zeev. Eli lives in a room in Jerusalem and takes up an affair with a co-ed, Yael. Eli's friend, Zvi, is in love with Yael and they create a triangle. Into this web of emotions an unusual caller cometh: Noa's little son. Eli wonders whether he is not his own. He develops a not wholly convincing love-hate relationship toward the little boy. Time and again he leaves him on the brink of disaster —in a busy street, on a roof, on a shaky seesaw, as if he wanted to see the boy killed. Probably taking some revenge on Noa. But what for? That is left unexplained. He even lets loose a snake in the room while the boy sleeps. But the snake bites Zvi, and (nearly?) kills him. One doesn't really know.

What really adds up in the film is the excellent acting. Two very intimate love scenes, between Eli and Noa and particularly between Eli and Yael, are as good as anything produced among the fjords. And Illy Gerlitsky plays the "third man" with tender humor.

Lapid.

Sweet Love, Bitter

Introduces Negro cafe comic Dick Gregory and return to screen of Diane Varsi. But plot is dreary self-torture in racial relations.

A Film 2 Associates release presented by Gerald Kleppel and Robert Ferman; produced by Lewis Jacobs. Features Dick Gregory, Don Murray, Diane Varsi and Robert Hooks. Written by Herbert Danska and Jacobs. Based on novel "Night Song" by John Williams. Music by Mal Waldron. Edited by Gerald

Kleppel. Camera, Victor Solow. Production supervised by Louis Kellman. Directed by Herbert Danska. Reviewed at Carnegie Hall Cinema, New York, Jan. 20, 1967. Running Time: 92 MINS.

Richie Stokes	Dick Gregory
David Hillary	Don Murray
Della	Diane Varsi
Keel Robinson	Robert Hooks
Candy	Jeri Archer

Despite the earnest hope that an independent film dealing with Negro-white relationships would succeed, especially at this juncture in U.S. history and even more especially since the subject is studiously avoided by the major producers, "Sweet Love, Bitter" must leave optimists crestfallen.

Assets include Dick Gregory and his attendant publicity, Don Murray, Diane Varsi (her comeback after several years voluntary exile) and newcomer Robert Hooks, due in Preminger's "Hurry Sundown"). But threadbare plotting and soggily sentimental breastbeating will curb critical reaction and word-of-mouth.

The one plus of "Sweet Love" however, is the debut of cafe comic Dick Gregory as a film actor. Assaying the role of a high flying jazz sax master, vaguely patterned after the late Charlie "Bird" Parker, on a skittering and doomed downslide oiled by the twin devastation of drugs and booze, Gregory turns in a vigorous and fascinating non-performance. Latter term isn't meant to trim the accomplishment, but it seems as if Grgeory's essential personal scrappiness and toughness nearly saves the melodramatics from sliding under the bathotic ooze of script and direction.

Plodding plot follows, desultorily, the human connection established between a nearly down and out college professor, played unconvincingly by Don Murray, and Gregory as jazz "great" on the bottom and determined to find the ultimate "freak out"—death.

Murray himself is self-tortured into a boozy decline because of his largely illusory guilt that he was responsible for his wife's death in an auto accident—a plot "twist" currently undergoing a revival on "Late, Late Show" reruns. Presumably because of Gregory's friendship, though motivation is never clearly suggested, the college professor is finally able to rescue himself from this slough of despondency and regain his old job at Nameless U.

Tangential to this relationship (which is, of course, resisted at first, because one is "Black" and the other "White") intersects that of Robert Hooks, playing an intelligent but bitter owner of a self-consciously multi-racial espresso emporium, who has appointed himself nursemaid to the aforementioned pair and his white girl friend, rather woodenly played by Diane Varsi (or perhaps it was faulty dubbing?), who is emotionally whipping herself for not being Negro, or perhaps, not having a white boyfriend. In any case she's continually upset about something, possible because the Hook character has difficulty "making it" with white chicks, so he says.

Actually more of a collection of supposedly critical incidents in this quadrangle than a designed plot, the randomness of the structure

might have succeeded had the scenes been more than glimpses and less object lessons in race relations. Despite the evidently sincere efforts of the able cast, none of them emerge from the opaque characterizations. The strain shows, almost embarrassingly, as they struggle for the breath of understanding absent from situation and dialog.

Pivotal point occurs after Murray has separated from his pals and is ensconced in the sanitized atmosphere of the college. Strolling with the dean of the college along one of its tree-lined streets, Murray is confronted by the spectre of a cop wantonly beating what appears to be a Negro vagrant. Recognizing the victim as his pal Gregory, Murray is tragically frozen by fear into inactivity. (Reminiscent of a scene of Sammy Davis' in "Man Called Adam," but in racial reverse.) In case the point is missed, the scene unrolls in slow motion, punctuated by freeze—frame closeups. Among the way to this clumsy climax, the loose ends of the Hooks-Varsi interaction are left dangling without resolution or further exploration. In the end, as expected, Gregory dies of an overdose of heroin and Murray is left with a new psychological albatross.

Directorial debut of Herbert Danska, though marked by occasionally interesting flashes, is doggedly academic and little imagination compensates for the shoestring budget. Final coup de gauche, on top of the direction and plodding script, is provided by the editing, which, despite baffling ellipses probably intended to abbreviate the dramatic lapses, manages to hobble the pace to a deadening effect.

Despite these creative tragedies, "Sweet Love, Bitter," could be considered a game try if sincerity was a substitute for artistry; or honest intentions, for dramatic excitement or pitch.   *Rino.*

The Deadly Affair
(BRITISH-COLOR)

Topflight espionage drama; excellent returns indicated.

Hollywood Jan. 6.
Columbia Pictures release of Sidney Lumet production. Stars James Mason, Maximilian Schell, Harriet Andersson, Harry Andrews, Simone Signoret; features Kenneth Haigh, Roy Kinnear, Max Adrian, Lynn Redgrave. Directed by Lumet. Screenplay, Paul Dehn, based on novel, "Call for the Dead," by John Le Carre; camera (Technicolor), Fred Young; music, Quincy Jones; editor, Thelma Connell; asst. director, Ted Sturgis. Reviewed at Columbia Studios, Jan. 5, '67. Running Time, 107 MINS.

Charles Dobbs	James Mason
Elsa Fennan	Simone Signoret
Dieter Frey	Maximilian Schell
Ann Dobbs	Harriet Andersson
Inspector Mendel	Harry Andrews
Bill Appleby	Kenneth Haigh
Virgin	Lynn Redgrave
Adam Scarr	Roy Kinnear
Adviser	Max Adrian
Samuel Fennan	Robert Flemyng
Director	Corin Redgrave
King Edward	David Warner
Gaveston	Michael Bryant
Lancaster	Stanley Leber
Young Mortimer	Paul Hardwick
Lightborn	Charles Kay
Matrevis	Timothy West
Gurney	Jonathan Hales
Nobles	William Dysart
Harek	Les White
First Witch	June Murphy
Second Witch	Frank Williams
Third Witch	Rosemary Lord
Stagehand	Kenneth Ives

Waiter	John Dimech
Head Waiter	Julian Sherrier
Daughter at Theatre	Petra Markham
Landlord	Denis Shaw
Blonde	Maria Charles
Brunette	Amanda Walker
Eunice Scarr	Sheraton Blount
Ticket Clerk	Janet Hargreaves
Barman	Michael Brennan
Businessman	Richard Steele
Businessman	Gartan Klauber
Mrs. Bird	Margaret Lacey
Stewardess	Judy Keirn

In a market already surfeited by secret agent spoofs this Sidney Lumet production, a soundly dramatic espionage entry, should strike a welcome chord. Filmed in London, lavish use of colorful backgrounds accentuates a suspenseful narrative which in turn lends itself well to exploitation. James Mason, Maximilian Schell and Simone Signoret add marquee lure, and Columbia may expect excellent returns from its release.

"The Deadly Affair" is based on "Call for the Dead," a first novel by John Le Carre, who later authored the best-selling "Spy Who Came In from the Cold." Shrewd and powerful development is given this tale of a British Home Office intelligence officer seeking to unravel the supposed suicide of a high Foreign Office diplomat. As drama builds in screenplay by Paul Dehn (he also scripted "Spy"), so does interest mount in its legitimate premise.

Lumet makes careful use of camera angles in recounting the story, although not obtrusively so. While his practice of flashing from one scene and sequence to the next without benefit of fades is occasionally vexing, this technique does quicken the tempo. Story emphasis is on quiet and thorough police work, rather than the usual theatrics of most spy mellers.

Mason is cast as an unromantic civil servant whose official problems are further complicated by his being wed to a compulsively sexual young woman who has many affairs on the side. His is a thorough acting job as he conducts his investigation in which he delivers one of his best performances.

Scoring in interest next to Mason is Harry Andrews, as a retired CIP inspector called in to assist the intelligence officer. He gives a rugged portrayal of police methods in dealing with criminals, which in this instance is a build-up to learning the identity of a foreign spy responsible for the death of the diplomat.

Schell handles his role completely but it's of brief tenure. Miss Signoret makes a fine impression as foreign-born wife of the diplomat, indirectly responsible for his murder, and Robert Flemyng in his few scenes as diplomat is convincing. Harriet Andersson lends credence to part of Mason's unfaithful wife.

In less demanding roles, Kenneth Haigh, Roy Kinnear, Max Adrian and Lynn Redgrave and Corin Redgrave stand out. David Warner as King Edward in the insertion of Marlowe's "Edward II" for a plot device in attaining climax delivers forcefully as do other members of the Royal Shakespeare Co. who appear in this sequence.

Lumet's production and directing are of high calibre and he has surrounded himself with top technical talent. Freddy Young's color photography is a particular asset. Topflight, too, are the music score by Quincy Jones, Thelma Connell's editing.

Whit.

Zatoichi Tekka Tasi
(Zato-Ichi's Gambling Travels)
(JAPAN—COLOR)

Tokyo, Jan. 15.

Daiei Co. production and release. With Shinataro Katsu, Shiho Fujimura, Yeshihiro Aoyama, Makoto Fujita, Eijiro Tono. Directed by Kimiyoshi Yasuda. Screenplay, Ryozo Kasahari; camera (Eastmancolor), Senkichiro Takeida. Previewed in Tokyo. Running Time, **90 MINS.**

Zato-Ichi, the blind masseur-swordsman, is now virtually a part of Japan's popular folklore. Though this is his 15th screen appearance, his popularity seems, if anything, augmented rather than diminished, and Daiei's making him the New Year's offering, traditionally lucrative, indicates the extent of the general approval.

At first sight he seems an unlikely hero. Plump, soft-looking and blind, he feels his way across Japan, outstretched hands often encountering the drawn swords of badmen, but occasionally the softer weapons of badwomen as well. It is then that Zato-Ichi reveals himself as the hero that he is. Not only is he an expert sworsman but also—and perhaps more important—he never loses his cool. This is indicated in his newest picture wherein he turns gambler, wins continually, places himself in the most hair-raising situations and still sits there with his pipe, laughing, smiling, polite, genial, until the moment when he will make mincemeat of them all.

As portrayed by Shinataro Katsu, Zato-Ichi is the epitome of the cool, the uninvolved, the certain, the sure. Even James Bond, even Napoleon Solo, even Modesty Blaise, have their moments of doubt—but Zato-Ichi, never.

Why some smart American distributor doesn't start these films going in low pop positions (where they still play westerns) is mystifying. They are filled with action a child could understand, so deft that they would delight adults, and they are as beautiful to look at as any films Japan now produces. If "Chushingura" can hit it in New York, Zato-Ichi ought to be able to sweep it in the provinces.

Chie.

The Busy Body
(COLOR-TECHNISCOPE)

A new kick for William Castle: more comedy and less gore. Sid Caesar and a host of other comics, plus Robert Ryan and Anne Baxter, for marquee. Talky suspense comedy, but okay dualler.

Hollywood, Jan. 24.

Paramount Pictures release, produced and directed by William Castle. Features entire cast. Screenplay, Ben Starr, based on the novel by Donald E. Westlake; camera (Technicolor), Hal Stine; editor, Edwin H. Bryant; music, Vic Mizzy; song, Edward Heyman, John Green; asst. director, Andrew J. Durkus. Reviewed at Paramount Studios, L.A., Jan. 23, '67. Running Time, **102 MINS.**

George Norton	Sid Caesar
Charley Baker	Robert Ryan
Margo Foster	Anne Baxter
Ma Norton	Kay Medford
Murray Foster	Jan Murray
Whittaker	Richard Pryor
Bobbi Brody	Arlene Golonka
Fred Harwell	Charles McGraw
Felix Rose	Ben Blue
Kurt Brock	Dom DeLuise
Archie Brody	Bill Dana
Mike	Godfrey Cambridge
Willie	Marty Ingels
Mr. Fessel	George Jessel
Cop. No. 1	Mickey Deems
Mr. Merriwether	Paul Wexler
Marcia Woshikowski	Marina Koshetz
Board Members	Norman Bartold, Mike Wagner, Larry Gelman, Don Brodie
Woman No. 1	Choo Choo Collins

"The Busy Body" is a diverting suspense comedy spoof of modern crime syndicates, murder and grave-robbing. Sid Caesar is top-featured among a slew of comic names as a stooge who is pursued by both cops and criminals. The amusing, if eventually talky, pic is a change of pace for producer-director William Castle, who herein emphasizes comedy rather than gore amid good production values. With okay b.o. outlook in store for exploitation playoff, the Paramount release shows extra life as a very serviceable lowercase entry in general subrun situations.

Film apparently is the second Castle-Caesar comedy teaming, but the first to be released. ("The Spirit Is Willing" was the first.) Thus, "Body" marks, as far as film audiences are concerned, a substantial shift in film concepts for Castle. He established his reputation some years ago for shock pix, lightly flavored with macabre humore. But everyone since has jumped on that bandwagon, so Castle is probably smart to shift gears. In the shifting, however, potential audiences may be confused, and particularly adroit selling is necessary to get the new program off the ground.

Ben Starr adapted the Donald E. Westlake novel to focus on Caesar, the natty syndicate member who becomes suspected of fleecing money by boss Robert Ryan and associates Charles McGraw, Norman Bartold, Mike Wagner, Larry Gelman and Don Brodie. The money was some bag boodle collected by Bill Dana, rubbed out for disloyalty. Dana's wife, Arlene Golonka, is a dizzy, color-blind, ex-stripper who selected the wrong garb for hubby's interment.

Result is a series of body-shiftings and murders, in which Caesar runs across undertaker Paul Wexler, hairdresser-turned-body dresser Dom DeLuise, conniving Anne Baxter and husband Jan Murray, as well as cop Richard Pryor. Marty Ingels, Godfrey Cambridge and Ben Blue are other hoods, while George Jessel has a self-satiric bit as a professional eulogist.

Castle's direction has elicited some strong performances from Caesar (now very slim and trim), Kay Medford, his doting Jewish mother, Miss Baxter (who scores a standout performance), Miss Golonka and Ryan. Pic starts off very well, but in time becomes drawn out and talky. Hal Stine's Technicolor - Techniscope camera is excellent, and the technical credits are very good.

Vic Mizzy's score is outstanding in adding comedy emphasis; title scoring is a soft-shoe shuffle, punctuated by machine-gun fire. Edward Heyman and John Green's "Out of Nowhere" gets a comic reprise when Miss Golonka demonstrates her strop routine. *Murf.*

Hot Rods To Hell
(COLOR)

Dullsville meller about teenage hot-rodders terrorizing a family. Needs help on dual bills.

Hollywood Jan. 19.

Metro-Goldwyn-Mayer release of a Four Leaf (Sam Katzman) production. Features entire cast. Directed by John Brahm. Screenplay, Robert E. Kent, from a short story by Alex Gaby; camera (Metrocolor), Lloyd Ahern; editor, Ben Lewis; music, Fred Karger; songs, Karger, Sid Wayne, Ben Weisman; asst. director, Maurice Vaccarino; second unit director, James Havens. Reviewed at MGM Studios, L.A., Jan. 18, '67. Running Time, **89 MINS.**

Tom Phillips	Dana Andrews
Peg Phillips	Jeanne Crain
Gloria	Mimsy Farmer
Tina Phillips	Laurie Mock
Duke	Paul Bertoya
Ernie	Gene Kirkwood
Jamie Phillips	Tim Stafford
Lank Dailey	George Ives
Wife At Picnic	Hortense Petra
Man At Picnic	William Mims
Policeman	Paul Genge
Little Boy	Peter Oliphant
Bill Phillips	Harry Hickox
Charley	Charles P. Thompson
Combo Leader	Mickey Rooney Jr.

Sam Katzman's reputation as a film producer is built on four factors: profitable pix, obtained via austere filming costs, about exploitable subjects, handled in the most superficial ways. "Hot Rods to Hell" is no exception. Dana Andrews and Jeanne Crain are featured as parents terrorized by some prototype juve delinquents. Over-acted, poorly-directed and cliche-ridden, the Metro release will find its best b.o. when paired with a stronger film.

Alex Gaby's short story, as scripted by Robert E. Kent, was originally made as "52 Miles to Terror," and a part of the features-for-tv slate for ABC-TV. Theatrical possibilities loomed, according to report, so here it is—full of the cardboard characters, inane dialog, vapid situations and flat impact.

Andrews and family—Laurie Mock and Tim Stafford are the kids—set out for the southwest, after an auto accident in New England has broken dad's back. En route to their new life as desert motel operators, Paul Bertoya, Gene Kirkwood and Mimsy Farmer nearly run them off the road in one of several brief drag-race inserts.

The three kids are hedonists—rather tame, by today's standards—and fear that Andrews will kayo the supposedly swinging proceedings at the motel if he takes over. As shown, the motel action would not turn on a 10-year-old. As usual, adults are portrayed in incredibly square light, but one which today's teenagers may not buy.

Andrews and family—Laurie's bright spot in the pic is when she deliberately engineers an auto crash for the two boys; by this time, anything out of the dull routine seems good. Miss Crain overacts as the teacherly mother, while the kids are adequate. Bertoya and Kirkwood could do better, and Mimsy Farmer has a few frantic moments as the town plaything, looking and acting too old for the teenage plot requirements. Other players are stock. The original idea of the story, by the way, is how dad regains his guts.

John Brahm, who directed "The Lodger" and "Hangover Square," both effective suspensers, started with practically nothing and did little more with it. Fred Karger's rock-roll score is routine, and Micky Rooney Jr. sings a song in the cafe scene. Lensing and other production credits are routine.
Murf.

Wilder Reiter GmbH
(Wild Rider Ltd.)
(GERMAN)

Berlin, Jan. 20.
CS-Cinema Service International release of Horst Manfred Adloff production. With Herbert Fux, Bernd Herzsprung, Chantal Cachin. Directed and written by Franz-Josef Spieker; camera, Wolfgang Fischer; music, Erich Ferstl; editing, Barbara Mondry; at Atelier am Zoo, West Berlin. Running Time, 90 MINS.
Kim .... Herbert Fux
Tanja .... Chantal Cachin
Georg .... Bernd Herzsprung
Whitey .... Rainer Basedow
Opera songstress .... Ellen Umlauf
Nun .... Marthe Keller
Uschi .... Karin Feddersen

"Wild Rider" marks the initial full-length feature of Franz-Josef Spieker, one of Germany's young "new wavers," who got into action last year with such pix as "It," "The Young Toerless," "No Shooting For Foxes," etc.

It is this group's first pic which tries to make the audience laugh. There are some rather unconventional facets about this modestly budgeted production and segments of this country's critics will appreciate Spieker's well-meant attempt to create "something different." Its native commercial prospects are still a guess. Internationally, it is probably not substantial enough to give it better than moderate chances.

"Rider" is a parody on show biz. Its style may be termed a mixture of the grotesque and satirical plus some sharp and aggressive ironical undertones. Central figure is Kim, a goofy American who lives in a shabby cottage in the woods outside Munich. His aim is to make a career as a pop singer at any price. With the help of a young "publicity manager," he does everything to stir attention and get his name into the papers. For example, he jumps into the bathtub of a striptease beauty in a nightspot; he "saves" a nun from drowning in the mud; he rides a horse across crowded squares and always has photographs lined up to take pictures of his stunts. His escapades make him a darling of the scandal sheets and popular with the crowd. And finally his records register big biz.

What Spieker had in mind was to poke fun at show biz and its heroes and all the dubious publicity often associated with them. The Kim characterization is full of basic flaws, and the idea that merely eccentricities plus publicity lead to success is somewhat banal. What is even more deplorable are the nearly complete absence of charm and the repeated utilization of corny gags. There's time-worn ridiculing of clergymen and politicians. And there are, of course, the familiar bed sequences, the usual "sweet life" ingredients, and

the rich American in a Cadillac who supplies the necessary coin. The script could indeed have stood some genuine wit and sophisticated touches.

The best that can be said about "Wild Rider" is that it is technically competent. It shows that Spieker, the creator of several noteworthy shorts and documentaries, knows his trade. And there are hints that he eventually could come along with a more convincing feature. This one meant perhaps too big a task for a directorial newcomer. And the creation of genuine comedy is one of the biggest tasks for any director.

With regard to the players, only Herbert Fux, who enacts the "Wild Rider," commands real attention. He has an unconventional, even interesting face and would make a good screen heavy or a psychopathic killer. To allow him to play the role of an idolized singer is too much.
Hans.

The Persecution and Assassination of Jean-Paul Marat as Performed by the Inmates of the Asylum of Charenton Under the Direction of the Marquis de Sade
(BRITISH-COLOR)

Photographed version of stage play. For strong stomachs. Probably will get both walkouts and repeats.

New York, Jan. 19.
United Artists release of The Royal Shakespeare Co. presentation of Peter Brook's film version of the original Broadway stage production. Produced by Michael Birkett. Features Ian Richardson, Patrick Magee, Glenda Jackson, Clifford Rose, Michael Williams, Susan Williamson, John Steiner, and Royal Shakespeare Company players. Directed by Peter Brook. Written by Peter Weiss. Music by Richard Peaslee. Production design by Sally Jacobs. Costumes by Gunilla Palmstierna-Weiss. A Marat Sade Production. Color by De Luxe. Previewed in New York, Jan. 19, '67. Running Time, 115 MINS.
M. Coulmier .... Clifford Rose
Mme. Coulmier .... Brenda Kempner
Mlle. Coulmier .... Ruth Baker
Herald .... Michael Williams
Cucurucu .... Freddie Jones
Kokol .... Hugh Sullivan
Polpoch .... Jonathan Burn
Rossignol .... Jeanette Landis
Jacques Roux .... Robert Lloyd
Charlotte Corday ..... Glenda Jackson
Jean-Paul Marat ...... Ian Richardson
Simonne Evrard ...., Susan Williamson
Marquis de Sade ...... Patrick Magee
Duperret .... John Steiner
Abbot .... Mark Jones
A mad animal .... Morgan Sheppard
Schoolmaster .... James Mellor
The Military Representative Ian Hogg
Mother .... Mark Jones
Father .... Henry Woolf
A newly-rich-lady .... John Hussey
Voltaire .... John Harwood
Lavoisier .... Leon Lissek
Patients .... Mary Allen,
   Michael Farnsworth, Maroussia Frank,
       Tamara Fuerst, Guy Gordon,
       Sheila Grant, Michael Percival,
       Lyn Pinkney, Carol Raymont
Nuns Heather Canning, Jennifer Tudor
Guards..Timothy Hardy, Stanton Trowell
Musicians .... Patrick Gowers,
   Richard Callinan, Michael Gould,
   Nicholas Moes, Rainer Schuelein

The stage play of this same 26-word titled work has now been photographed, largely in a single setting. It retains what the play had for audiences though the legitimate stage is something else and a film faces different strata of the population. Discriminating filmgoers may respond as did legit patrons but the release seems a special sell.

As a theatrical production in London and New York, the Royal Shakespeare Company's version, under Peter Brook's direction, of Peter Weiss' "Marat/Sade" has elements to make it impressive and stunning, also horrific and repellent. There were consummate performances, eye-filling spectacle, weighty natural verse, engrossing drama, burlesque (in its pristine sense), and, above all, startling originality. As a film directed and acted by the same director and cast, the result, after assessing the gains and losses encountered in its translation from one medium to another, is somewhat less.

Definitely for the discriminating filmgoer, the celluloid version will have to find its own audience since its essential novelty lifts it to the realm of the "unprecedented."

Initially, it will attract the cognoscenti who now form a sizable

portion of the public. Ultimately, enough discussion of the play has, and of the film will, stimulate attendance by the simply curious. In any case, it will either promote confusion and walkouts or excite multiple viewings, but will not fail to astonish. Given UA's modest (under \$500,000) investment, it should eventually enter the black in 16m distribution alone, if not in its preem engagement.

An integral part of Weiss's achievement in "Marat/Sade" is gained by his fusing of raw and unreconciled opposites. The tension of the play is derived not only by the clash of ideas and historical figures of Jean-Paul Marat and the Marquis de Sade, but from the collision of theatrical forms—the theatre of the emotions and the senses as envisioned by the French experimentalist.

Ostensibly "a play within a play," written by De Sade, story centers on a single action—the murder of the revolutionary leader Jean-Paul Marat by Charlotte Corday while he issued dictums to the people of Paris from his bathtub. The action, however, is hysterically performed by the inmates until their excitation reaches an intolerable pitch, and each segment of the action, is periodically aborted just short of pandemonium by lengthy arguments between the paranoiac Marat and the egomaniacal De Sade over their conflicting views of man vs. society and vice versa.

In the end, Marat is murdered, the action completed, and total mayhem ensues. The inmates assault their keepers and the audience and their barely supressed capacity for violence is released.

In the translation from stage to screen, despite Brook's virtuosity as a director in both meduims, there are, as aforesaid, gains and losses. Unfortunately the latter outweigh the former, but mitigating this is the fact that Brook did not rest content with merely filming his stage production but has attempted to translate the play into filmic terms.

Parodoxically, though film is supposed to be a more "intimate" medium, "Marat/Sade" is more remote on film. The gain, however, is that the viewer's attention is riveted on the speeches.

Performances are uniformly excellent. There are several moments in the film that make the hair bristle and the skin crawl. Whether or not this violent and stupefying emotional and intellectual assault finds favor among the critics and filmgoers outside of the larger cities is the question. United Artists shows courage in taking the gamble.
Rino.

Fruits Amers
(Bitter Fruit)
(FRENCH-YUGOSLAV-ITALO)

Paris, Feb. 7.
Rank release of Terra Film-Avala Film-Prodi Cinematografica production. Stars Emmanuelle Riva; features Laurent Terzieff, Roger Coggio, Beba Lancar, Rik Battaglia. Directed by Jacqueline Audry. Screenplay, Colette Audry, Jacqueline Audry, from play by the former; camera (Eastmancolor), Maurice Fellous; music, Joseph Kosma. At Lord Byron, Paris. Running Time, 108 MINS.
Soledad .... Emmanuelle Riva
Alfonso .... Laurent Terzieff
Paco .... Roger Coggio
Tita .... Beba Lancar
Sebastien .... Rik Battaglia

This is an example of coproduction gone wrong. Supposedly taking place in some unnamed Latino country that is harshly repressed and has a revolutionary group in action, it was made in Yugoslavia with French, Yugoslav and Italo players, a French director and based on a French play. It is talky, lifeless and badly dubbed and appears mainly for dualer use abroad on the name of Emmanuelle Riva and with tv use also possible on its theme.

Miss Riva is involved with the revolutionaries and captured by the head of the governmental police. She is mysteriously released; it appears her sister has been having an affair with the police chiefs, who gives in to her demands to help her sister. Suspected by her comrades, she shoots the man and then escapes with her sad but repentant sister.

All this is done in a plodding way. Miss Riva cannot do much with her role of the dedicated revolutionary, while others are fairly stodgy and one-dimensional. Direction is flat and insipid. Color is washed out. Film remains an attempt at mixing human needs and revolutionary ardors and sacrifices that do not jell well enough to get any insight into the characters or give a true picture of revolution in particular or in general.

Miss Riva does try to give her character some depth and poignance but cannot overcome a flatness in dialog and a laggard directorial pacing. Somehow this pic won the Grand Prix Du Cinema tag given every year for the film that gives French films a greater prestige. That it will not.

Mosk.

The 25th Hour
(ITALIAN-FRENCH-COLOR)

Odyssey of a Rumanian peasant caught up in war. Overlength negates some impact and mars the tragicomedy concept. Anthony Quinn and Virna Lisi for marquee. Needs special showcasing before general release.

Hollywood, Jan. 26.

Metro-Goldwyn-Mayer release of Carlo Ponti production. Stars Anthony Quinn, Virna Lisi. Directed by Henri Verneuil. Screenplay, Verneuil, Francois Boyer, Wolf Mankowitz, based on the novel by C. Virgil Gheorghiu; camera (Metrocolor), Andreas Winding; editor, Francoise Bonnot; music, Georges Lelerue; production design, Robert Clavel; asst. director, Claude Pinoteau. Reviewed at Pacific's Picwood Theatre, L.A., Jan. 25, '67. Running Time, **133 MINS.**

Johann Moritz .... Anthony Quinn
Suzanne .... Virna Lisi
Nicolai Dobresco .... Gregoire Aslan
Traian Koruga .... Serge Reggiani
Defense Counsel .... Michael Redgrave
Strul .... Marcel Dalio
Sgt. Apostol Constantin .... Jan Werich
Col. Miller .... Marius Goring
Prosecutor .... Alexander Knox
Father Koruga .... Liam Redmond
Abramovici .... Meier Tzelniker
Varga .... Kenneth J. Warren
Magistrate .... John Le Mesurier
Goldenberg .... George Roderich
Fourrier .... Jacques Marin
Joseph Grenier .... Albert Remy
Madame Nagy .... Francoise Rosay
War Minister's Aide ..... Jean Desailly
Nora .... Henia Suchar
Dr. Nagy .... Harold Goldblatt
Mrs. Koruga .... Dala Milozevic
Hurtig .... Victor Startic
Rosa .... Olga Schoberova
Marcou .... Stoian Decermic
Chitza Jon .... David Sumner
War Minister's Usher ... Raoul Delfosse

"The 25th Hour" is a poignant drama about the odyssey of a Rumanian peasant, shunted around for eight years as a political pawn during World War II. Anthony Quinn stars in another excellent performance, sharing top billing with Virna Lisi. The well-mounted Carlo Ponti production, filmed in France and Yugoslavia, is necessarily episodic, but loses some impact through overlength, which also occasionally overemphasizes the humorous aspects of what is properly a grimly ironic tragedy.

A clarifying, sensitive sell, to overcome a poor title, seemingly will be necessary. While Quinn's name will help put over this Metro release in the general market, pic should first be set up in more sophisticated situations.

A parallel may be drawn between "Hour" and "Doctor Zhivago," incidentally another Ponti pic, in that each turns on one human being, caught up in political and military turmoil, who tries to preserve and conserve his little corner of life while his world crumbles. "Zhivago" spotlighted a sensitive poet, however, while "Hour" depicts the travail of a poor peasant.

Director Henri Verneuil, Francois Boyer and Wolf Mankowitz adapted the 1950 novel by C. Virgil Gheorghiu to emphasize the Quinn character, and introduce some humorous aspects not in the book. Result is a heart-warming tale—too much so in parts—filled with delicate shadings of characters which all players convey in top fashion.

In a leisurely establishment of the plot, Quinn is seen as a Rumanian peasant, with wife Miss Lisi and family, on the eve of World War II. Lecherous village cop Gregoire Aslan falsely labels Quinn a Jew, and he is then conscripted for slave labor. Fellow Jewish prisoners do not believe Quinn when he protests he is a Christian, and, in an ironic switcheroo, Jewish refugee organizations later will not help him because he is not Jewish. There is a universality in Quinn's framing, specifically, that no one is safe from smearing in a police state.

Quinn is moved about Europe over the next eight years, from Rumania to Hungary, thence to Germany where he becomes a German soldier. Marius Goring, a German race specialist, circulates Quinn's photo as an example of pure-blood, so, when the war is over, Quinn then faces war crimes trial. Miss Lisi, meanwhile, has been raped (off screen) by the Russians, whose "liberation" of Rumania is little more than the German occupation has been. In climactic war trial, Michael Redgrave successfully pleads Quinn's cause, and latter is reunited with his family.

While the overlength—133 minutes, as trimmed by Francoise Bonnot—causes the tragicomedy to veer from the path via overdeveloped vignettes, Ponti and Verneuil have created an excellent pictorial canvas. Filmed at the Studios de Boulogne in Paris, and, via tie with Avala Films, in Yugoslavia, pic is a co-production of Les Films Concordia (Paris) and C. C. Champion (Rome). Simon Schiffrin was associate producer.

Andreas Winding lensed in versatile, adroit Metrocolor hues, using an anamorphic process called Franscope. Robert Clavel's production design is excellent, ditto the Georges Delerue score. All players turn in creditable jobs, including the deliberately deglamorized Miss Lisi (but, even in rags, she's a looker), and Quinn, just about the only actor today who projects a brutish, animal magnetism and sensitivity which is, at the same time, sympathetic, warm and completely likable.

The two drawbacks to this otherwise firstrate drama are, again, the title and the length. While retaining the book's title intuitively seems correct, for presell purposes, the tome is over 16 years old, and, moreover, the name suggests a mystery or futuristic sci-fi pic. As for the length, several episodes could be tightened, for an overall reduction of up to 20 minutes.

Murf.

The Cool Ones
(SONGS-PANAVISION-COLOR)

Okay entry for youth market; plenty of singing to appeal to jive crowd.

Hollywood, Feb. 1.

Warner Bros. release of William Conrad production. Stars Roddy McDowall, Debbie Watson, Gil Peterson, Phil Harris; features Robert Coote, Nita Talbot, George Furth, Mrs. (Elvira) Miller. Directed by Gene Nelson. Screenplay-story, Joyce Geller; camera (Technicolor), Floyd D. Crosby; editor, James Heckert; asst. director, Gil Kissel; music, Ernie Freeman. Reviewed at Warner Bros. Studios, Feb. 1, '67. Running Time, **98 MINS.**

Tony .... Roddy McDowall
Hallie .... Debbie Watson
Cliff .... Gil Peterson
MacElwaine .... Phil Harris
Stan .... Robert Coote
Dee Dee .... Nita Talbot
Howie .... George Furth
Mrs. Miller .... Mrs. (Elvira) Miller
Charlie Forbes .... Jim Begg
Manager .... James Milhollin
Uncle Steve .... Phil Arnold
Sandy .... Melanie Alexander

Also The Bantams, Glen Campbell, The Leaves, T. J. and The Fourmations.

"The Cool Ones" is a refreshing entry for the youth market. Loosely-constructed, story-wise, and frequently burdened with confusing continuity and some way-out characters, the William Conrad production still packs the type of ingredients acceptable to the juve crowd who compose much of today's audience Film should get good reaction in its intended goal.

Saga of a young rock'n'roll singer whose career has hit the skids and an ambitious chirp intent upon a career as a star, the Joyce Geller screenplay based on her own original is a combination of romance, songs and musical numbers and corny comedy.

Gil Peterson and Debbie Watson enact the two warbling roles, and Roddy McDowall and Phil Harris also topbill the lively piece that unfolds mostly in the Hollywood area. Mrs. Elvira Miller socks over a single song, "It's Magic," in her own particular style, and for additional possible marquee lure brief appearances are made by The Bantams, Glen Campbell, The Leaves and T. J. and The Fourmations.

Gene Nelson's direction establishes a wild pace as McDowall, screwball millionaire talent manager, takes over the task of boosting the two singers to stardom as a team. Action carries few surprises and telegraphs ahead, but it's pleasant enough as entertainment strikes a light note.

McDowall's impersonation is unbelievable but fits the general tone and Miss Watson, from the "Tammy" and "Karen" tv series, is pretty and vivacious and has a nice voice. Peterson is allowed to flounder in an indefinite part but displays an excellent voice, Phil Harris, in as a fast-talking tv show producer, is Phil Harris and in featured roles Robert Coote, Nita Talbot and George Furth are okay.

Technical departments generally are competently handled, including Floyd D. Crosby's color photography, LeRoy Deane's art direction and score by Ernie Freeman. Lee Hazlewood cleffed original songs.

Whit.

War Italian Style
(ITALIAN-COLOR)

Buster Keaton's last pic. So-so World War II comedy. Okay for duals.

Hollywood, Jan. 31.

American International release of Fulvio Lucisano production. Stars Buster Keaton, Franco & Ciccio, Fred Clark; features Martha Hyer. Directed by Luigi Scattini. Screenplay, Castellano and Pipolo, based on an idea by Lucisano; camera (Technicolor), Fausto Zuccoli; asst. director, Romana Fortini; music, Piero Umiliani; sound, Lodovico Scardella, Bruno Moreal; asst. director, Mauro Sacripante; re-recording director, Terry Vantell. Reviewed at Joe Shore's Screening Room, L.A., Jan. 30, '67. Running Time, **74 MINS.**

"War Italian Style" is a fair comedy programmer, set in World War II, which will attract some attention because it is the late Buster Keaton's last film. Keaton is a sympathetic, bumbling Nazi general, stationed in Italy just before the Allied invasion. Sight gags and low comedy are in less than effective abundance. Produced in Italy by Fulvio Lucisano, pic has Fred Clark and Martha Hyer for other marquee lure. Fair b.o. likely for American International release on general duals.

Producer's idea was scripted by the team of Castellano and Pipolo, and plotting alternates between several Keaton mime routines and the frenetic comedy of Franco & Ciccio, a duo whose impact may have been diminished in the English dubbing. Pair play two U.S. soldiers, deliberately permitted to escape by German femme spy Martha Hyer with what were to have been fake plans for the Allied invasion of Italy. They got the real plans, but no one will believe it.

Predictable situations are piled on, for overall dogged pacing. Keaton, in his own solo bits, displays much of the talent which made him a great silent film comic. Yet the very measured development of the pantomimes, once a delight, seems tame, protracted and old-hat by today's standards—and all the more so when combined with the Abbott & Costello, Martin & Lewis frantics generated by Franco & Ciccio, but not as effectively as the other teams.

Luigi Scattini directed in routine fashion. Camera work by Fausto Zuccoli is standard, in Technicolor and Techniscope, with interpolated stock footage showing its age. Clark plays the U.S. general with his usual fine exasperated air, and Miss Hyer adds some visual interest. Other players and credits are adequate. Film runs a brief 74 minutes. *Murf.*

Retsu-Go Waka Daisho
(Let's Go, Young Guy!)
(JAPAN—COLOR)

Tokyo, Jan. 15.
Toho Co. production and release. Features Yuzo Kayama, Yuriko Hoshi, Akira Takarada, Chocho Iida, Maida Bibari, Hoei Tanaka, To Man Rei. Directed by Katsumi Iwuchi; camera (Eastmancolor), Jo Aizawa; music, Kenjiro Hirose. Previewed in Tokyo. Running Time: 92 MINS.

Young Yuzo Kayama is just about the most popular personality in Japan. His records sell into the millions, his personal appearances bring in thousands, and his films are the only moneymakers now being made. "Let's Go, Young Guy!" (to give the company's English title) is the latest in the popular "Waka Daisho" series and was New Year's fare at all Toho theatres.

No one seems to know why he is so popular. He has been around the Toho lot for years and no one ever paid much attention to him except Akira Kurosawa, who gave him the lead in "Akahige" (Red Beard). Then, suddenly, there was a flurry in the fan magazines, an uproar in the record companies, and Kayama became the hottest thing in show business.

Some people say that the records (Kayama composes what he sings) did it and that the Japanese audience is still one which links films with records. Others say that he is synthetically successful, that his father (Ken Uehara, a former matinee idol) and lifelong Toho friends were right there when the Japanese films needed a new major star.

His one redeeming charm is that he is the boy next door with a modest voice and an average talent. He knows it and he doesn't care. Thus (as in this film) if he is called upon to sing, he may do it, and then carry on as though nothing has happened.

With such an attitude, he alone, of the entire cast, remains unencumbered by the sticky plot-lines of all the "Waka Daisho" films (and this is one is average), and unsullied by the cliches of which they are composed. He can reflect this kind of integrity, one guesses, because he is being so thoroughly himself. He is not acting.

This film is nonsense. It concerns a soccer-team captain who goes to Hong Kong for a match, meets a Chinese girl, is misunderstood by his Japanese girlfriend, but everything is straightened out on the soccer-field. The image of Yuzo Kayama—the way he handles himself, the natural dignity he displays, his appropriate modesty, his conventional and very Japanese behavior, his complete acceptance of himself—evidently grabs the spectator and must, indeed, create strong empathy. And that, indeed,

is what creates popular screen idols, at least in Japan.

How Kayama would fare abroad is another matter. He is a natural for the Japan-language houses on Hawaii and the west coast, however. *Chie.*

Ia wa Kokyo o Koite
(Love Beyond the Frontier)
(KOREAN)

Tokyo, Jan. 10.
Keuk Dong Production. Distributed and dubbed in Japan by Toei. Produced by Cha Tae Jin, with planning by Wa Mon Il. With Hwan Jong Soon, An In Sook, and a cast of amateurs. Directed by Kim Ki Duk. Screenplay, So Yun Sung, based on Kazu Nagamatsu autobiography; music, Lee Bong Joh; camera, Pyron In Jip, editing, Kwon Kyok Kyu. Previewed in Tokyo. Running Time, 105 MINS.

This Keuk Dong production won the special Eric Johnston Award at 1966 Asian Film Festival in Seoul. Though the Japanese distributor has cut the original running length of 135 minutes down to 105 minutes, and dubbed the whole thing into Japanese, it is still a well-made film, well worth seeing.

Not that it will appeal to all tastes. Director Kim Ki Duk and scenarist So Yun Sung, using Kazu Nagamatsu's autobiography as base, have made a humanism-filled film which is a real tearjerker. But it works. A rock could go see it and come out crying.

It is about Japanese woman (Hwan Jong Soon), early orphaned and raised in Korea, who has a number of adventures (cut out of Japanese version) and eventually decides to devote herself to taking care of the many homeless Korean children. Though desperately poor herself, she somehow manages to feed and clothe first five and eventually 16 children. They live in shacks in Pusan and Seoul, never have enough to eat, and still the woman keeps on going, feeding them, clothing them, sending them to school. Finally, during the graduation ceremony, the eldest girl (An In Sook) gives a speech in which she tells what her "mother" has done for her, and the film ends, but precisely how it ends cannot be foretold, because some will be blinded by tears and bawling so loudly they won't hear the soundtrack.

Despite the plot (a child killed, yet another major calamity) and Mama (played, one would suspect, by "the Joan Crawford of Korea"), a fine reality shines through, to an extent that may disarm cynicism.

There are things the matter with the picture, of course, all of them having to do with the question of sentimentality. What do you do with a film like this in a big American city? If the critics in unsure and cynical New York could call sentimental such a stern and terse picture as Kurosawa's "Akahige" (Red Beard), what mincemeat they would make of this lovable Korean item. There ought to be a public for a film like this, and there probably is; but there may not be a theatre for it. *Chie.*

La Grande Sauterelle
(The Big Grasshopper)
(FRENCH—COLOR)

Paris, Feb. 7.
Gaumont release of SNEG-Eichberg-

France Film production. Stars Mireille Darc, Hardy Kruger; features Maurice Biraud, Georges Geret, Francis Blanche, Venantino Venantini. Directed by Georges Lautner. Screenplay, Vahe Katcha, Michel Audiard, Lautner; camera (Eastmancolor), Maurice Fellous; editor, Michele David. At Colisee, Paris. Running Time, 100 MINS.
Salene .... Mireille Darc
Carl .... Hardy Kruger
Alfred .... Maurice Biraud
Marco .... Georges Geret
Gedeon .... Francis Blanche
Vladimir .... Venantino Venantini

Mireille Darc caught on as a free living, lissome girl in "Galia," and now she and the same director repeat in this pic about a drifting girl who lives by her senses and own morality. She gets mixed up with a petty thief who reforms through love. Somewhat mannered, skimpy and arch, this is more for exploitation on its love scenes and color than for art chances abroad.

Director Georges Lautner lingers long on Miss Darc's freckles, lithe and frequently undraped frame and her catching, if one-dimensional, movements, reactions and animal ardors. Without a true ability to make the relationship deeper, and with its dragging and lagging characterizations and story, it is more an excuse for closeups of Miss Darc than a pic with the needed character insight or more probing discernment of a so-called emancipated young girl.

Miss Darc roams about and either beds down with men she is attracted to or is helped by others out of friendship or for her own disarming, though surface, charms and warmth. She meets Hardy Kruger, who is tied up with two pals, and they are planning to rob a millionaire who plays for high stakes at the Casino in Beirut.

Kruger quits to take off on more adventures with Miss Darc as his two accomplices fail in their robbery. There is nice color and scenery and plenty of love scenes that finally bog down into preciosity and repetition, due to the lack of a true feel for relationships and overdone attempts at slangy dialog. But Miss Darc is emerging a winsome and winning personality, if her character seems one-dimensional and already stereotyped.
Mosk.

Hurry Sundown
(COLOR-PANAVISION)

Effective film version of the novel. Michael Caine leads the uniformly strong performances. Racial conflict treatment is tasteful, but strong enough to rule out kiddie trade. Big b.o. potential.

Hollywood, Feb. 7.
Paramount Pictures release of Sigma Production, produced and directed by Otto Preminger. Features Michael Caine, Jane Fonda, John Phillip Law, Diahann Carroll, Robert Hooks, Faye Dunaway, Burgess Meredith. Screenplay, Thomas C. Ryan, Horton Foote, based on the novel by K. B. Gilden; camera (Technicolor), Milton Krasner, Loyal Griggs; editors, Louis R. Loeffler, James D. Wells; music, Hugo Montenegro; production design, Gene Callahan; asst. director, Burtt Harris. Reviewed at Directors Guild of America, L.A., Feb. 6, '67. Running Time, 146 MINS.
Henry Warren .... Michael Caine
Julie Ann Warren .... Jane Fonda
Rad McDowell .... John Phillip Law
Vivian Thurlow .... Diahann Carroll
Reeve Scott .... Robert Hooks
Lou McDowell .... Faye Dunaway
Judge Purcell ...... Burgess Meredith
Lars Finchley .... Robert Reed
Sheriff Coombs .... George Kennedy
Rev. Clem De Lavery . Frank Converse
Thomas Elwell .... Loring Smith
Rose Scott .... Beah Richards
Eula Purcell ..... Madeleine Sherwood
Sukie Purcell .... Donna Danton
Prof. Thurlow .... Rex Ingram
Colie Warren .... John Mark
Ada Hemmings .... Doro Merande
Dolph Higginson ...... Luke Askew
Carter Sillens .... Jim Backus
McDowell Children .... Steve Sanders,
Dawn Barcelona, David Sanders,
Michael Henry Roth

In "Hurry Sundown," based on the novel, producer-director Otto Preminger has created an outstanding, tasteful but hard-hitting, and handsomely - produced film about racial conflict in Georgia, circa 1945. Told with a depth and frankness possible only today, story develops its theme in a welcome, straight-forward way that is neither propaganda nor mere exploitation material. Cast with many younger players, all of whom deliver fine performances, the Paramount release has excellent b.o. potential in situations catering to the mature young and adults, including large cities in Dixie.

There are myriad white attitudes towards Negroes, ranging from unequivocal acceptance through sincere, misguided paternalism, to outright hatred. Thomas C. Ryan and Horton Foote, working from the novel by K. B. Gilden (pseudonym for Katya and Bert Gilden) have fashioned an excellent screenplay which reflects these many shadings of opinion.

Michael Caine leads the seven stars, and delivers an excellent performance as the white social climber managing the Georgia land holdings of wife Jane Fonda. Two tracts block Caine's plans, those of distant relative John Phillip Law and Negro Robert Hooks, both just-returned war vets. Faye Dunaway and Diahann Carroll, respectively, provide some very sensitive, appealing romantic plot angles with their men. Burgess Meredith rounds out the stars as a corruptible judge.

Preminger fought successfully for a Production Code Seal (flagged for mature audiences, however) since there are three rather frank sex bits which, in context, are perfect exposition of Caine's coarse nature. They are not offensive, not sensational, and serve to contrast the other tender relationships. The physical movements of lust and love often are identical; the internal motivations determine their purpose. Preminger has, on film, socked over these varying motivations.

Caine is believable, showing no traces of an English accent, but a facility with his Dixie dialect. Miss Fonda, whose precise acting style often appears cold and mechanical in some of her U.S. pix, herein is excellent as the frustrated wife. Her conscience pangs block Caines court land-grab of Hooks' property, in the first of two climaxes.

Law, Hooks and Miss Dunaway, all relatively new in pix, earn their featured billing (Preminger alone is starred above title) in equally sensitive chaacterizations, as does Meredith, a Preminger regular. Entire cast is superb: lecherous sheriff George Kennedy; Beah Richards, Hooks' mother; Madeleine Sherwood, Meredith's dizzy wife (her lines evoke some laughs, which might tend to mask the genuine talent required to project a brassy, not-so-dumb Dora); Jim Backus, Hooks' lawyer; Rex Ingram, Miss Carroll's dad; Loring Smith, the callous businessman, and Steve Sanders, Law's eldest son who idolizes Caine.

There are two flaws, not enough to mar overall merit, but worthy of mention; Preminger is responsible for both, and one is overlength. Film runs 146 minutes, about 20 too much. Development of the Caine-Fonda loveless marriage, as contrasted with Law-Dunaway, is effected by direct cuts, and some fat could have been trimmed there, since exposition is achieved quite early. In final 26 minutes, between the court climax and Caine's coldblooded dynamiting of Law's house, more trimming for accelerated pacing would have helped. Louis R. Loeffeler and James D. Wells executed the editing orders.

Other flaw occurs as Hooks, standing firm when being apprehended by Kennedy on Caine's false charge that he caused the death of latter's retarded son John Mark, breaks out into the inevitable title song, assisted by a Negro chorale. While music is part of the Negro's culture, this scene is too much like the darkies-are-a-singin' discredited racial stereotype. Again, at fadeout, as all hands pitch in to help Law recover his flooded land, the shoulder-to-shoulder camaraderie is too forced.

Hugo Montenegro's first film score is an impressive debut, versatile, full bodied and melodic. Milton Krasner took over camera duties from Loyal Griggs, who became ill, and both have done a firstrate Panavision - Technicolor job which is perfectly toned to the natural hues of both elegance and poverty. Gene Callahan's production design is outstanding. Post-production work was done at MGM, since Paramount was full-up at the time, and latter's Harold Lewis and Metro's Franklin Milton head the excellent sound team.

Sound is so crisp and realistic that sound effects editor John Link 2d and music editor Richard Berres deserve separate mention. Willis Cook again shows his excellent ability to set up explosive effects sequences. *Murf.*

Les Compagnons De La Marguerite
(Friends Through Thick and Thin) (FRENCH)

Paris, Feb. 14.

CFDC release of Balzac Films-Le Film D'Art production. Stars Claude Rich, Francis Blanche; features R. J. Chauffard, Catherine Darcy, Michel Serrault, Jean Tissier. Directed by Jean-Pierre Mocky. Screenplay, Mocky, Alain Moury; camera, L. H. Burel; editor, Marguerite Renoir. At Balzac, Paris. Running Time, 85 MINS.

Matou	Claude Rich
Loulou	Francis Blanche
Patan	Michel Serrault
Chief	R. J. Chauffard
Francoise	Catherine Darcy
Martine	Paola Pitagora
Concierge	Jean Tissier

Satirical pic lacks the inventiveness and insight to bring it off, though it does have some laughs in its tale of a gentle little man outwitting the police and human bureaucracy via his talents as an artful forger. It shapes primarily as a local item with some dualer of playoff use abroad indicated on its theme, but limited, at best.

A gentle young man, who restores old manuscripts in the national library, is married to a cold, domineering woman. He decides he can be happy by switching wives, through the forging of public documents—if he can find another married couple to do it and provided the couples are fitted for each others' mates. So he advertises in a paper.

The police checks on it and one inspector goes along but finds his wife whisked from him, saddled with the other wife, and the forgery so good he is helpless. Rest of pic builds on this as police try to trap him at work, and meanwhile a whole movement grows as he helps others change wives or even become polygamous by making them Arab in public records.

Idea is good but the pic is directed a bit too stolidly to give this the needed graceful ease and acceptance.

Claude Rich has charm as the gentle and innocent forger, with Francis Blanche oily and offensive as the policeman who loses position and wife. But others are only adequate and there is too much padding to bring off this offbeat fanstasy. *Mosk.*

How To Succeed In Business Without Really Trying
(COLOR-PANAVISION)

Excellent film version of the legituner. Robert Morse's best pic to date. Many talented newcomers. Needs sharp selling to get word of mouth going. Very good b.o. outlook.

Hollywood, Feb. 11.

United Artists release of Mirisch Corp. presentation, adapted, produced and directed by David Swift. Features Robert Morse, Michele Lee, Rudy Vallee. From the stage play of Abe Burrows, Jack Weinstock, Willie Gilbert and the novel by Shepherd Mead; music and lyrics, Frank Loesser; camera (DeLuxe Color), Burnett Guffey; editors, Ralph Winters, Allan Jacobs; music supervision, Nelson Riddle; art direction, Robert Boyle; sound, Robert Martin; asst. director, John Bloss. Reviewed at Directors Guild of America, L.A., Feb. 10, '67. Running Time, 121 MINS.

J. Pierpont Finch	Robert Morse
Rosemary Pilkington	Michele Lee
J. B. Biggley	Rudy Vallee
Bud Frump	Anthony Teague
Hedy	Maureen Arthur
Benjamin Ovington	Murray Matheson
Smitty	Kay Reynolds
Mr. Twimble, Wally Womper	Sammy Smith
Bratt	John Myhers
Gatch	Jeff De Benning
Miss Jones	Ruth Kobart
Miss Krumholtz	Carol Worthington
Brenda	Janice Carroll
Receptionist	Lory Patrick
Media Man No. 1	Patrick O'Moore
Media Man No. 2	Wally Strauss
Johnson	Dan Tobin
Tackaberry	Robert Q. Lewis
Matthews	John Holland
Toynbee	Paul Hartman
Jenkins	Justin Smith
TV Announcer	George Fenneman
Mrs. Biggley	Anne Seymour
Mrs. Frump	Erin O'Brien Moore
Taxi Cab Driver	Joey Faye
Finch's Landlady	Ellen Verbit
Cleaning Woman	Virginia Sale
Newspaper Seller	Al Nessor
The President of the United States	Ivan Volkman
Narrator	Carl Prince
Elevator Operator	David Swift

"How To Succeed In Business Without Really Trying" is an entertaining, straightforward filming of the legituner, featuring many thesps in their stage roles. David Swift's production for the United Artists-Mirisch Corp. is generally fast-moving in tracing the rags-to-riches rise of Robert Morse within Rudy Vallee's biz complex. Colorful production values maintain great eye appeal. Lacking film names, the U. A. release will have to be sold inventively to spark word of mouth, which will be uniformly favorable, thus making for very good or better b.o. prospects in general situations.

Swift, besides producing-directing (and appearing briefly as an elevator operator), adapted the legit book by Abe Burrows, Jack Weinstock and Willie Gilbert, based on Shepherd Mead's novel. Result of his work is the best screen appearance to date by Morse, who made it first on Broadway, the opening up of film careers to Michele Lee, Morse's gal, and Maureen Arthur, a sexpot in the Judy Holliday genre, plus the establishment of former dancer Anthony Teague as a solid comedy performer.

Most of Frank Loesser's literate melodies have been retained, including "I Believe In You," "The Company Way," "Been A Long Day" and "Brotherhood Of Man." Loesser's Frank Productions was associated in the highly sucessful legit versions, as presented by Cy Feuer and Ernest H. Martin. Show won the legit Pulitzer Prize.

For film showmen unfamiliar with the plot, it concerns window-washer Morse who, by superior instinct for advancement and survival, becomes a top exec in Vallee's company in a matter of days. He has become so big that former well-wishers plot his downfall, but last-minute honesty only serves to propel him farther up the chain of command. In a remote way, story is not unlike "What Makes Sammy Run?"—although without any serious dramatic overtones. "Succeed" is pure escapism.

The pixie-like Morse is excellent, with both voice and facial expressions right on target all the time. Miss Lee shows the same uninhibited freshness and charm that made Doris Day a film star. Her vocalizing of "I Believe In You" is unfortunately too emphatic and exaggerated considering the intimacy of the film technique; on stage, fine, but blownup, the facial contortions and phrasing are overdone. Vallee is in top form as the big boss, his first pic in 10 years.

Miss Arthur's brassy babe is a delight. All key supporting roles are handled with dexterity—including Sammy Smith's mail-room boss, later board chairman; John Myhers' personnel chief; Jeff De Benning's exec personnel boss; Ruth Kobart, as Vallee's secretary; and Murray Matheson, the only exec not to fall for Morse's line, but whose fatal flaw is discovered anyway.

Burnett Guffey's versatile DeLuxe Color-Panavision camera has caught the prevailing moods of comedy, as underscored by Robert Boyle's art direction, Micheline's costumes, and the many talented set designers and decorators who have brightened every inch of the screen. Mary Blair is credited with color design.

Dale Moreda choreographed from Bob Fosse's legit musical staging, and shows a neat flair for film terpery. Nelson Riddle supervised the music contributes to the overall enjoyment. Virgil Partch, onetime Swift contemporary when working for Walt Disney on cartoons, is credited as visual gag man. Ralph Winters and Allan Jacobs edited to 121 minutes, just about enough of a good thing. Other credits are firstrate. *Murf.*

Oh Dad, Poor Dad, Mamma's Hung You In The Closet and I'm Feelin' So Sad
(COLOR)

Unsatisfactory film version of the off-Broadway play, gimmicked up in dim salvage effort. Campus houses might provide some b.o.

Hollywood, Jan. 28.

Paramount release of Seven Arts (Ray Stark-Stanley Rubin) production. Features entire cast. Directed by Richard Quine. Screenplay, Ian Bernard, narration, Pat McCormick, Herbert Baker, based on play by Arthur L. Kopit; camera (Technicolor), Geoffrey Unsworth; second unit camera, Skeets Kelley; editors, Warren Low, David Wages; music, Neal Hefti; asst. director, Mickey McCardle. Reviewed at Stanley Warner Theatre, BevHills, Jan. 27, '67. Running Time, 86 MINS.

Madame Rosepettle	Rosalind Russell
Jonathan	Robert Morse
Rosalie	Barbara Harris
Commodore Roseabove	Hugh Griffith
Dad, Narrator	Jonathan Winters
Airport Boss	Lionel Jeffries
Hawkins	Cyril Delavanti
Breckenduff	Hiram Sherman
Moses	George Kirby

Producers Ray Stark and Stanley Rubin have labored mightily to bring forth a mouse. "Oh Dad, Poor Dad, etc." is a meaningless trifle, based on, filmed, remade and otherwise tricked up from Arthur L. Kopit's off-Broadway legit comedy-drama, or whatever it is by genre. Richard Quine directed. High school kids might dig it, but older people are likely to find it slow, silly, and from nowhere.

Ian Bernard adapted, per credit crawl, with post-production narration inserts penned by Pat Mc-

Cormick and Herbert Baker. Rubin, per the trade grapevine, was upped to producer status with Stark from his remake efforts, which included expansion of the Jonathan Winters character from flashback to status of narrator and periodic commentator. The changes do not help much, final result being an uneven mix of low comedy and not-too-funny esoterica, destined to repel discriminating viewers.

Rosalind Russell is the emasculating mother of Robert Morse, sired by Winters who is dead, but stuffed and carried around by his widow as she and son travel about. Barbara Harris is the nymphet chippie who puts the make on Morse so successfully that he kills her in a psycho-substitution for his ma. Hugh Griffith is an aging lecher eyed by Miss Russell as her next victim.

Miss Russell in recent years has shown more professional guts than good judgment in accepting weird-for-her film roles, as this particular film again exemplifies. Despite multi-colored wigs and a game attempt, she falls flat. Morse has an appealing, winsome quality which certain film roles will fit, but not this one. Miss Harris does rather well, however, and Griffith is up to the demands of his role. Winters gets the best comedy material, but it clashes with the rest. Other players are competent.

Film was shot on Jamaica locations, which add color along with Phil Jeffries' art direction, all caught by Geoffrey Unsworth's Technicolor camera. To no avail, however. Carter De Haven Jr. was associate producer. Warren Low and David Wages are named as editors; whoever did it, pic seems overly longish despite running only 86 minutes, including the prolog. Neal Hefti's score has run out of life long before end titles. *Murf.*

Katz und Maus
(Cat and Mouse)
(GERMAN)

Berlin, Feb. 9.
Gloria release of Modern Art (Hansjuergen Pohland) production, in collaboration with Film Polski, Poland. Features Lars Brandt, Peter Brandt, Wolfgang Neuss, Claudia Bremer. Directed and written by Hansjuergen Pohland, adapted from same-titled novel by Gunter Grass; camera, Wolf Wirth; music, Attila Zoller; editing, Christa Pohland. At Atelier am Zoo, West Berlin. Running Time, 88 MINS.

Joachim Mahlke, the younger one .... Lars Brandt
Joachim Mahlke, the elder one .... Peter Brandt
Pilenz .... Wolfgang Neuss
Tulla .... Claudia Bremer
School director .... Herbert Weissbach
Mahlke's aunt ...... Ingrid van Bergen
German fighter pilot.... Michael Hinz
German Navy Lieutenant Helmut Kircher
Esch .... Hans-Peter Brandes

Due to its offbeat theme and principal players, Hansjuergen Pohland's "Cat and Mouse" stirred wide national attention long before it was completed. This had to do with Gunter Grass' novel of the same name, one of postwar Germany's most successful and controversial literary works, which furnished the basis for this production. And it had to do with the utilization of Lars and Peter Brandt, Willy Brandt's teenaged sons, both of whom portray the same role of the young school lad and later soldier in the German seaport city of Danzig which after the war became Polish Gdansk.

When the film was still in the making, Willy Brandt was "only" West Berlin's mayor. Meanwhile, Brandt has become this country's Vice Chancellor and Minister for Foreign Affairs. It stands to reason that this fact gives this film additional exploitation value.

There is reason to believe that if Brandt had known that he would climb up the ladder of political success that high, he probably would have been less liberal toward Pohland's attempt to get his two boys for this pic. The whole film has now assumed a rather delicate flavor.

As far as the two Brandt boys are concerned, it should be stated that this or that young actor could have turned in at least the same thesping job. So the whole thing looks like a matter of speculation. The producer will find it difficult to prove the opposite.

As it goes with so many films that have gained so much prebuildup, "Cat and Mouse" falls considerably short of expectations. Admittedly, it has its merits. For example, it offers rather interesting, if restless, camerawork and there is a demanding jazzy score by Attila Zoller, Hungarian-born composer living in New York.

But the number of deficiencies is bigger than a film of this type can actually afford. In the first place, it is a rather confusing film for those not familiar with the literary original. It eventually goes overboard with symbolisms. It lacks conviction and it lacks heart. What is especially deplorable about this production is that it cannot escape boredom. "Cat and Mouse" will have a difficult time finding a receptive audience. General patrons may deem it overly intellectual, while the greater part of the more demanding clientele will easily classify it as an item which doesn't make the grade—save, perhaps, those who regard the "message" as the most important thing in films.

Local reviews have been accordingly. While some critics see in "Cat and Mouse" a definite flop, there are others who have praise for Pohland's well-meant message, which leaves no doubt that the military trophy is a rather dubious thing.

The story is of Joachim Mahlke, a German highschool boy during the Third Reich. He is an outsider for which, at least partly, nature can be made responsible. Nature has "supplied" him with an unusually big Adam's apple. This gives him the idea that he must hide it and he begins to dream of a "Ritterkreuz," the higher distinction of a German Iron Cross, which he can wear around his neck. (The literary original makes a symbolic point that the military trophy is basically nothing more than the ambition to hide an inferiority complex.)

Mahlke eventually steals such a trophy from a war hero and is thrown out of school. Later he becomes a soldier, shows heroism in action and is awarded with such a Ritterkreuz. However, his old school director has not forgiven him .The disillusioned Mahlke goes back to his old favorite place, an old Polish wreckage, and never returns.

All this is told in a not exactly convincing manner. What adds to the confusion is the style of narration. Mahlke is shown as the school lad and later a soldier and escorted by Pilenz, his old schoolmate who, however, is now 20 years older. It is the latter who digs in memories. Past and present are told at the same time, in a style reminiscent of what Alain Resnais was doing in "Last Year At Marienbad." But Pohland's style borders on the chaotic. It is, in all, a strange mixture of realism, play with symbolisms, caricature which includes bits of grotesque acting, and some documentary footage which is woven in.

Film was shot in and around Gdansk with the assistance of Rytm, a production group of the Polish State Film. It cost only 750,000 marks, or about $188,000. Financial worries shouldn't exist, the more so as this production was granted a federal premium amounting to 300,000 marks ($75,000) which must be only returned if the pic scores at the boxoffice. Also, it is within the bounds of possibility that "Cat and Mouse" will make a lot of unexpected money. Reportedly, foreign interest looms big, and the current controversy may help.

Groups of German vet soldiers have come along with loud protests because of the alleged "ridiculing" of military medals in this pic. *Hans.*

Accident
(BRITISH-COLOR)

Boff item for buffs. Offbeat probe of sex motivations. Could develop b.o. momentum of same trio's 'The Servant.'

London, Feb. 9.
London Independent Producers release of Joseph Losey (Losey-Norman Priggen) production, directed by Losey. Stars Dirk Bogarde, Stanley Baker, Jacqueline Sassard; features Michael York, Vivien Merchant, Delphine Seyrig, Alexander Knox. Screenplay, Harold Pinter, based on Nicholas Mosley's book; camera (Eastman Colour), Gerry Fisher, editor, Reginald Beck; sound, Simon Kaye, Gerry Humphreys; art director, Carmen Dillon. Reviewed at Leicester Square Theatre, London. Running Time, 105 MINS.

Stephen .... Dirk Bogarde
Charley .... Stanley Baker
Anna .... Jacqueline Sassard
William .... Michael York
Rosalind .... Vivien Merchant
Francesca .... Delphine Seyrig
Provost .... Alexander Knox
Laura .... Ann Firbank
Bell .... Harold Pinter
Police Sergeant .... Brian Phelan
Plain Clothed Policeman..Terence Rigby
Man in Bell's Office..... Freddie Jones
Secretary .... Jill Johnson
Receptionist .... Jane Hillary
Ted .... Maxwell Findlater
Clarissa .... Carole Caplin
Hedges .... Nicholas Mosley

The team that turned 'The Servant' into a critical and b. o. success—director Joseph Losey, writer Harold Pinter and star Dick Bogarde—has come up with another offbeat and adventurous feature which, with shrewd selling, should click with more alert audiences and be a rewarding and provocative talking-point among film buffs.

Again they've taken a novel as their plot material—Nicholas Mosley's "Accident"—and jacked it into a haunting study in relationships, with Pinter's flair for spare, suggestive dialog getting full scope in an adaptation which stays remarkably faithful to the book, give or take the fusing of a character or two.

It starts with a car crash splitting that night air of the quiet countryside outside Oxford. A male student has been killed, and his female companion, a campus gal, is taken in to the neighboring mansion, occupied by the university teacher (Dirk Bogarde) who has been instructing them both in philosophy. The accident sparks the prolonged flashback that explores the tight-knit relationships of this enclosed community. For Bogarde, married to a heavily pregnant wife and feeling his age span, has hankered after the girl, and watched, with a mixture of envy and connivance, her affair with the boy.

But he has been preceded by a colleague, Charlie (Stanley Baker), another footloose husband, with a yen for skirts and the bottle. While Bogarde is away from his home, Charlie uses it to seduce the girl and pretends, as always, that it's top-carat love.

So a fine, sad complex of understated mistrust and mutual suspicion is created, and Pinter strings along it some sharply observed scenes that put it into focus. Bogarde's unsatisfying attempt to resume an affair with an old flame is one. Another is his return home to find his bed rumpled and the couple still in occupation, and it neatly captures the suppressed jealousy of his responses. And the climax, with Bogarde making pitiful love to the distaught girl after the accident, has a shocking pungency, and harshly pinpoints the story's despairing outlook.

Joseph Losey's helming is exact and sympathetic to the clipped nuances of the script. If it has a fault, it is too elliptical and some minor stretches of the development and character remain enigmatic. And he also errs in voiceovering the sequence between Bogarde and his former doxy (played by Delphine Seyrig, the girl from "Marienbad"), for this suggests it's all in the mind, and it's not. He's helped by superb technical credits, with Gerry Fisher's lensing making evocative use of subdued Eastman Color and Reginald Beck's editing enhancing the impact. John Dankworth's music soundtrack, using his own clarinet and a couple of harps, defines the moods in plaintive style.

A firstrate cast is headed by Bogarde, who wins sympathy for his superficially cold character, and his contained way with emotion is superbly right. But the main acting surprise is contributed by Baker, unusually bespectacled as the amorous Charlie, and wittily suggesting the man's self-esteem (he talks on tv about "anything") and his lonely search for horizontal satisfaction.

Jacqueline Sassard makes the most of a minimum of dialog, and produces the right air of a junior siren. Vivien Merchant (Pinter's wife) is first-rate as the don's wary spouse, and Michael York as the youth gets under the skin of his inability to comprehend these more adult neuroses. Next, minor cameos come from Alexander

Knox, and from Pinter himself as a tv producer. Original author Nicholas Mosley briefly appears; no thesp, he amusingly registers a yawnsome university man.

U shot is a brilliant exercise in offbeat drama, which may suffer in exposed situations by its generally down beat outlook and its cryptic way with people.

Otta.

The Corrupt Ones
(GERMAN—COLOR—TECHNISCOPE)

Crime meller with Robert Stack and Elke Sommer in Hong Kong. Old-hat plot, spiced with some sadism and sex. Okay dualler.

Hollywood, Feb. 14.
Warner Bros. release, produced by Artur Brauner; Nat Wachsberger, executive producer. Stars Robert Stack, Elke Sommer, Nancy Kwan, Christian Marquand. Directed by James Hill. Screenplay, Brian Clemens, based on a story by Ladislas Fodor; camera (Technicolor), Heinze Pehlke; editor, Fred Srp; music, Georges Garvarentz; title song lyrics, Buddy Kaye; asst. director, Frank Winterstein. Reviewed at Warner Bros. Studios, Burbank, Feb. 13, '67. Running Time, 92 MINS.
Cliff Wilder .... Robert Stack
Lily .... Elke Sommer
Tina .... Nancy Kwan
Brandon .... Christian Marquand
Pinto .... Werner Peters
Danny .... Maurizio Arena
Kua-Song .... Richard Haller
Hugo .... Dean Heyde
Chow .... Ah-Yue-Lou
Madame Vulcano .... Marisa Merlini
Jasmine .... Heide Bohlen

"The Corrupt Ones," filmed in its Hong Kong locale and also Berlin, is a routine crime programmer about the search for a long-lost Chinese treasure. Robert Stack and Elke Sommer head an adequate cast, inhibited by cliche scripting. Direction and production values give some life to the Artur Brauner production on which Nat Wachsberger is billed as exec producer. Pic is an old-fashioned meller, updated with overdone sadistic bits and a little sex. As such, it is, at least, a change of pace from spy product, a factor which may boost its booking chances. Okay dual bill outlook for Warner Bros. release in general or exploitation situations.

Once titled "Hell To Macao," pic has a new title which correlates indirectly with European translations of Stack's "The Untouchables" vidseries, still active in foreign markets. It is reported that the new handle is designed to cash in on that similarity. All of which may help it out in that territory; in the domestic market, title means nothing since it means just about anything.

Brian Clemens is credited with scripting Ladislas Fodor's original story, about professional photographer Stack caught up in the machinations of two criminal elements out to steal an ancient Emperor's burial treasure. Nancy Kwan is from a Tong, and Christian Marquand is an American who operates a gambling ship. Miss Sommer is Stack's romantic interest, after entry into plot as the wife of Maurizio Arena, killed for having stumbled onto the treasure trail.

There is no tongue in cheek, and the action is straightforward robbers - and - robbers material, but routine. Stack, for example, is necking with every dame he meets within 60 seconds; the plotting also is cliche in various menacing expressions. Werner Peters is a corrupt cop who joins Miss Kwan and Marquand for the unified search for treasure, but they later ace him out. Climactic irony: the five principals escape the underground tomb, only to find themselves in Red China. The right people die before fadeout.

James Hill, who also directed

"Born Free," has less interesting material with which to work, although his use of Stack and minor players is okay. Miss Sommer has one fixed expression, except when she is being tortured by Miss Kwan, herself changing from dead pan in these brief moments. Technical credits are very good, and the Technicolor-Techniscope lensing adds a lot of lush color.

George Garvarentz has written an often dynamic score.

Murf.

Le Vieil Homme Et L'Enfant
(The Old Man and the Boy)
(FRENCH)

Paris, Feb. 14.
Valoria release of P.A.C. production. Stars Michel Simon; features Alain Cohen, Luce Fabiole, Roger Carel, Paul Preboist, Jacqueline Rouillard. Directed by Claude Berri. Screenplay, Berri, Gerard Brach, Michel Rivelin; camera, Jean Penzer; editor, Sophie Coussein. Previewed in Paris. Running Time, 90 MINS.
Pepe .... Michel Simon
Claude .... Alain Cohen
Meme .... Luce Fabiole
Victor .... Roger Carel
Father .... Charles Denner
Mother .... Zorica Lozic
Teacher .... Jacqueline Rouillard
Raymonde .... Aline Bertrand

Tender and touching film is mainly about the friendship and love between a little boy of 9 and an old man. But in the background is World War II and one of the themes deals with anti-semitism. Film is takingly welded into a gentle, perceptive tale that should have wide appeal abroad in art situations as well as in regular channels. Right handling could make this a fine boxoffice contender both at home and in foreign markets.

Film also unveils a firm and needed new directorial talent in actor Claude Berri, who essays his first feature after copping an Oscar last year for his first short "Le Poulet" (The Chicken). His forte is the ability to treat delicate subjects as racism, childhood and love, with a sure taste and balance that avoid sentimentalism, mawkishness and over-indulgence.

The little boy is put with an old couple in the country to allow his parents to hide out during the last war. The boy is a Jew and his parents are on the run to escape deportation. He is housed with a crusty old retired man who is anti-semite. The boy has been schooled not to tell he is Jewish and even to use another name.

Being a child, he is still not conscious of the deeper meaning of events and comes to love the craggy old man. It seems his racism is based more on ignorance than true warped hate or meanness. It is in reaction to the war and events that surpass his understanding. The boy somehow seems to realize this and the film makes its statement on the silliness of racist theories by showing them clearly.

There is no gratuitous preachiness here. It is shown to be wrong by the very clarity of the story, the rightness and deftness of the characterizations and the boy's winning the heart of the old man, who always affirms he can "smell" a Jew anywhere. There is no confrontation scene and the old man never knows the boy is Jewish as

his parents come to claim him and they go off together.

To the child it becomes a game. He manages to avoid having the old man's wife wash him in his bath to escape detection of his Jewishness. He even baits the old man by having him trot out all his racist theories and then insisting the old man looks Jewish. Perhaps the avoidance of some more dramatic scenes, as the old man realizing the boy is Jewish, or the death of his loved old dog, rob this of a needed dramatic punch and drive.

But it also keeps this airy, graceful and full of fine human touches and notations on childhood and war's effects on those who are furthest from it. Film has a breezy decency that is never condescending. It is fresh and rare in these days of the absurd, violent, despairing and anguished that are the main themes of most filmmaker newcomers.

Berri displays a knowledge of films and there are scenes reminiscent of some past greats that are not imitative but show an assimilated influence. Old actor Michel Simon even has a scene when he shows his old World War I scars to the boy that is like a scene he did in a famous pre-war film "L'-Atalante" of Jean Vigo. There is also a feel for the country and its people, in a humanistic way, be they mean, decent, petty or fine, that reminds of some of Jean Renoir's films notably "A Day in the Country."

Simon gives credibility, charm and depth to the cantankerous old man. The boy's love for the old man is reasonable and acceptable and little actor Alain Cohen is handled with a delicacy that avoids preciosity and posiness. Their scenes together are vital and tasteful and the film makes a statement on a time and on racism without going overboard on breastbeating or didactics. And yet it shows up racist dottiness and still remains a film on childhood.

Film looks like one with sleeper potential and may be heard from during the coming film festival season. It tags Berri a perceptive new filmmaker. It is technically sound and also has a good cast around the excellent duo of Simon and Cohen. Georges Delerue's subtle and charming music is also an asset.

Mosk.

Three Bites of the Apple
(PANAVISION-COLOR)

Lightweight comedy with presence of David McCallum as possible lure but with magnificent foreign scenery; strictly for less discriminating situations.

Metro release of Alvin Ganzer production. Directed by Ganzer. Stars David McCallum; features Sylva Koscina, Harvey Korman, Domenico Modugno, Tammy Grimes. Screenplay, George Wells; camera (Metrocolor), Gabor Pogany; music, Eddy Manson; editor, Norman Savage; asst. director, Guiseppe Pollini. Reviewed at Warner Hollywood Theatre, Feb. 9, '67. Running Time, 98 MINS.
Stanley Thrumm .... David McCallum
Carla .... Sylva Koscina
Miss Sparrow .... Tammy Grimes
Harvey Tomlinson ..... Harvey Korman
Remo Romano ...... Domenico Modugno
The Doctor .... Aldo Fabrizi
Francesca Bianchini ... Mirella Maravidi
Croupier .... Riccardo Garrone
Gladys Tomlinson .... Avril Angers
Teddy Farnum .... Claude Alliotti

Gussie Hagstrom	Freda Bamford
Alfred Guffy	Arthur Hewlett
Peg Farnum	Alison Frazer
Bernhard Hagstrom	Cardew Robinson
Winifred Batterly	Ann Lancaster
Joe Batterly	John Sharp
Birdie Guffy	Maureen Pryor
The Yodeler	Edra Gale

As a travelog, "Three Bites of the Apple," as lightweight a title as most of the action, has certain merit; as a madcap comedy, its intended goal, hasn't. Perhaps the David McCallum name in star role is figured to help this Alvin Ganzer production filmed in Italy and Switzerland. What emerges is an unimaginative piece of film making suitable only for less discriminating situations where it may do okay biz.

The George Wells screenplay is based upon the flimsiest of premises. McCallum, a mildmannered tour guide, wins 1,200 pounds in a plush Italian gambling casino; then is faced with the question of how to save it from taxes so he'll be able to return to his native Britain with any more than a pittance. A pretty young adventuress, Sylva Koscina, out to get the coin for herself, sells him on allowing a "friend" help him in this matter.

Result—writer Wells and director Ganzer have created an inconsequential amount of tepid footage with only mild appeal. Foreign scenery, however, through the color lens of Gabor Pogany is frequently magnificent, but serves to point up the weaknesses of a narrative that doesn't jell.

McCallum seems to stumble through most of his appearance. Miss Koscina has a vapid look but is nice to look at. Tammy Grimes is lost in role of a man-hungry spinster on the tour who goes on the make for McCallum, and Domenico Modugno as Miss Koscina's former husband, brought into the case because he's "the only thief" she knows, is bombastic. Balance of cast doesn't matter.

Technical credits are on the plus side, Elliot Scott's art direction particularly interesting.

Whit.

The Mikado
(COMIC OPERA-COLOR)

D'Oyly Carte Opera Co.'s film presentation of the Gilbert & Sullivan classic, as British company has been doing it for many years; class offering.

Hollywood, Feb. 9.

Warner Bros. release of Anthony Havelock-Allan & John Brabourne production of Gilbert & Sullivan's "Mikado," as staged by D'Oyly Carte Opera Co. Features entire cast. Directed for screen by Stuart Burge. Based on stage production by Anthony Besch; camera (Technicolor), Gerry Fisher; editor, Alma Godfrey. Reviewed at Warner Bros. Studios, Feb. 8, '67. Running Time, 124 MINS.

The Mikado	Donald Adams
Pitti-Sing	Peggy-Ann Jones
Pish-Tush	Thomas Lawlor
Yum-Yum	Valerie Masterson
Katisha	Christene Palmer
Nanki-Poo	Philip Potter
Ko-Ko	John Reed
Pooh-Bah	Kenneth Sandford
Peep-Bo	Pauline Wales
Go-To	George Cook

D'Oyly Carte Opera Co.'s stage presentation of Gilbert & Sullivan's "The Mikado" is brought intact to the Technicolor screen in this transference with the same principals, costumes, etc., of the production which has become one of the top renderings of the British company. (Company plays U S. in repertory every few years. —Ed) Film producers Anthony Havelock-Allan and John Brabourne moved the troupe and properties from home base at the Savoy Theatre in London to a British motion picture studio for the filming under direction of Stuart Burge, and hired the City of Birmingham Symphony Orchestra to play the score.

(Another "Mikado" was released by Universal in 1939 with Jack Benny's then radio tenor, Kenny Baker, as Nanki-Poo amidst a British cast.—Ed.)

Warner Bros., which has acquired distribution rights, will play the comic opera in selected situations as a novelty. In Los Angeles, the 124-minute feature, bound to attract both Gilbert & Sullivan buffs as well as having wide appeal for groups, will be screened in a minimum of 21 theatres March 8-9, with two matinees and two evening performances. Other cities will get the same treatment.

"The Mikado" is more rewarding as a stage vehicle than as limned on-screen, due to the full sweep of the production as a whole always being visible. Camera is focused more on principals, in either semi-closeups or close full shots, in the picture, which somewhat detracts at first, or until audience becomes accustomed to manner of presentation. This is not merely a static filming of the opera, however; cameras move constantly and some fairly fast editing keeps principals in various aspects to side-step monotony.

As though to rectify the closer shots in what is the first of two acts—there will be no intermission—cameras pull back slightly in the second to get more out of the various numbers. It appears that the producers became aware of the limited first-act projecting and compensated for this in the second with greater attention to artistic values and staging of individual numbers.

Score and lyrics, substantially intact through the years, receive fine rendition and cast performs with the same style as on the stage. Standout is character of Ko-Ko, Lord High Executioner, adroitly undertaken by John Reed with nimble attention to the G&S feeling. Donald Adams scores spectacularly in title role. Kenneth Sandford as Pooh-Bah, the all-high everything, Philip Potter as Nanki-Poo; the Mikado's son; and Valerie Masterson as Yum-Yum colorfully parade their talents. Christene Palmer as the harridan Katisha and Peggy-Ann Jones as Pitti-Sing likewise are excellent.

Stuart Burge based his film direction on Anthony Besch's stage production, altering the traditional movement only for best camera effects. Peter Howitt's art direction, too, is based upon the stage settings by Disley Jones, Gerry Fisher's color photography is absorbing and Alma Godrey's editing superior.

Whit.

Just Like a Woman
(BRITISH-COLOR)

London, Feb. 9.

Monarch Film Corp. release of Robert Kellett (Dormar) production. Written and directed by Robert Fuest. Stars Wendy Craig, Francis Matthews, John Wood; features Dennis Price, Peter Jones, Clive Dunn, Miriam Karlin, Ray Barrett. Camera (Eastmancolor), Billy Williams; music, Ken Napper; sound, Kevin Sutton; art direction, Brian Eatwell. Reviewed at CEGB Theatre, London. Running Time, 89 MINS.

Scilla	Wendy Craig
Lewis	Francis Matthews
John	John Wood
Salesman	Dennis Price
Ellen	Miriam Karlin
Saul	Peter Jones
Fischer	Clive Dunn
The Australian	Ray Barrett
Isolde	Sheila Steaffel
TV Floor Manager	Aubrey Woods
Elijah	Barry Fantoni
Lewis's Girl Friend	Juliet Harmer

Shown for one night only at the 1966 Edinburgh Festival, this bright little feature has hung around waiting for a distributor. Now it's going out in support of Joseph Losey's "Accident" on full Rank release, and its sophisticated brand of gagging makes it an effective contrast with a discriminating public.

Made by the producer-director team, known to film buffs for the funny 40-minute "A Home of Your Own," it embroiders a skimpy situation, a marital breakup between a tv producer (Francis Matthews) and his slightly kooky wife (Wendy Craig). But, as writer, Robert Fuest evades the plot possibilities and it contributes neither conviction nor a backbone to the string of incidents festooning it.

What gives it survival value is the wit of some of its scenes, the lively style of Fuest's direction, and a collection of comic cameos dio with amusing extroversion. His uneasy relationship with the program topper makes for another spicy showbiz gag, and these episodes have a stylish zip that pleases.

So does the departed wife's search for a home of her own, eventually building a miniature astrodome in the middle of a field, with the help of a heavily Teutonic architect. And her bantering connection with a family friend leads to a few much-needed human touches.

Wendy Craig is adequate as the wife, but can't quite reach the wide-eyed pseudo-innocence required, and Francis Matthews has his moments, but is somewhat heavyhanded with the drunken rages. Most of the thesping pleasure comes from Peter Jones, as the wary tv boss, Miriam Karlin, as the tantrum-weary secretary, and especially from John Wood, firstrate as the pal scared of being forced too deeply into an emotional morass. Clive Dunn is okay as the architect with Nazi leanings, and Dennis Price is wasted in a pinhead role.

Sets (by Brian Eatwell) are a constant delight, and provide their own jokes, and American singer Mark Murphy contributes a couple of Ken Napper numbers in a nitery sequence, of which the title song has some commercial possibilities. The Eastman color lensing of Billy Williams is excellent, and the production has a modish, costly air about it, unusual on a small budget.

Otta.

The Taming of the Shrew
(BRITISH-ITALIAN-COLOR-PANAVISION)

Liz Taylor-Dick Burton in exciting boxoffice pillow fight in costume. Or boy beats girl.

Columbia Pictures release of a Royal Films International-F.A.I. Production presentation. Produced by Richard Burton, Elizabeth Taylor; co-produced and directed by Franco Zeffirelli. Executive Producer, Richard McWhorter. Stars Elizabeth Taylor, Richard Burton; features Cyril Cusack, Michael Hordern, Alfred Lynch, Alan Webb, Victor Spinetti, Michael York, Natasha Pyne. Screenplay, Paul Dehn, Suso Cecchi D'Amico, Zeffirelli, based on play by William Shakespeare. Camera (Technicolor), Oswald Morris, Luciano Trasatti; film editors, Peter Taylor, Carlo Fabianelli; sound, Mario Ottani, David Hildyard, Aldo de Martini; music, Nino Rota; asst. directors, Carlo Lastricati, Rinaldo Ricci. Reviewed at London, Feb. 27, '67. Running Time, 122 MINS.

Tranio	Alfred Lynch
Lucentio	Michael York
Pedant	Vernon Dobtcheff
Baptista	Michael Hordern
Bianca	Natasha Pyne
Katharina	Elizabeth Taylor
Gremio	Alan Webb
Hortensio	Victor Spinetti
Biondello	Roy Holder
Petruchio	Richard Burton
Grumio	Cyril Cusack
Priest	Giancarlo Cobelli
Curtis	Gianni Magni
Nathaniel	Alberto Bonucci
Gregory	Lino Capolicchio
Philip	Roberto Antonelli
Haberdasher	Anthony Garner
Tailor	Ken Parry
Vincentio	Mark Dignam
Widow	Bice Valori

Many of William Shakespeare's works have been screened over the years, some of them to substantial boxoffice response, though many of the releases required, and received, special handling. In the latest instance of "The Taming of The Shrew," Columbia Pictures secured the accolade of being the chosen offering at the Royal Film benefit, an annual event of much United Kingdom and world promotional value.

In general Columbia seems on safe ground with this production shot in Italy as a partnership of Richard Burton and the Italian stage director Franco Zeffirelli. It carries the boxoffice lure and budget burden of the married stars, but offering the interesting situation of Burton fictionally taming Elizabeth Taylor. Last similar instance presumably was Douglas Fairbanks versus Mary Pickford.

This newest version in color is a boisterous, often over-stagey frolic which will strike many as a fair compromise for mass audiences between the original Shakespeare and, say, "Kiss Me Kate."

Screenwriters have done neat job, infusing dialog and business without rocking Bard's memory over-much. The two stars pack plenty of wallop making their roles meaty and flamboyant with a larger-than-life Burton playing for plenty of sly laughs in the uninhibited wife-beating lark.

Miss Taylor tends to over-exploit an "earthy" aspect in early footage and switch to the subdued attitude comes too abruptly but against that she's a buxom delight when tamed. Comedy is sustained in witty wedding ceremony.

Shrewd casting of experienced players pays off with Michael Hordern, Victor Spinetti, Cyril Cusack, Alfred Lynch and Giancarol Cobelli standouts. Costume film introduces Michael York and Natasha Pyne as a secondary juve love interest. Though good-looking, pair proved insipid. Their inexperience conflicts with period mood.

Rich costumes by Irene Sharoff, Danilo Donati and Gloria Mussetta, incidentally, add greatly to film's air of gaiety. Zeffirelli's direction seldom lags and in general he succeeds in camouflaging spareness of the one-idea storyline. Photography, music and other details technically okay.
Rich.

Boudu Saved From Drowning
(Boudu Sauve des Eaux)
(FRENCH)

Pathe Contemporary Films release of a Michel Simon-Jean Gehret production. Directed and written by Jean Renoir from play by Rene Fauchois. Camera, Marcel Lucien Asselin; editor, Suzanne de Troyes; music, Raphaeal; asst. director, Jacques Becker. Reviewed in New York, Feb. 17, '67. Running Time, **84 MINS.**
Boudu .... Michel Simon
Monsieur Lestingois .... Charles Grandval
Madame Lastingois .... Marcelle Hainia
Anne-Marie .... Severine Lerczynska
Student .... Jean Daste
Godin .... Max Dalban
Vigour .... Jean Gehret
Poet on bench........ Jacques Becker

(English Titles)

Pathe Contemporary has acquired this early vintage (1932) Jean Renoir, never before released in the U. S. The acquisition, evidently, is in an attempt to build up its library of outstanding international directors (the retrospective has turned out to be a favorite item with film societies and college film groups, providing the packager can come up with a really good cross-section of the artist (usually a director being honored).

The commercial appeal for this quaint item, however, seems negligible even among the more intellectual film houses. Its value is only as an example of the early work of one of the screen's most outstanding directors. Viewed as a museum piece, it has some charm and a great deal of tripe, particularly in the acting of title-roler Michel Simon. His mugging and ridiculous style of moving offsets any momentary interest in the character he is portraying.

Renoir's small-scale "rites of spring" has Simon, as Boudu, saved from drowning in the Seine (where he has flung himself, despondent over the loss of his dog). A filthy, surly, ungrateful tramp, taken into the household of his rescuer (Charles Grandval) in an attempt to help him get started on the road to propriety, he nearly wrecks the house and lives of his benefactors. After seducing the wife (Marcelle Hainia), he wins a large amount of money in a lottery, marries the opportunistic maid (Severine Lerczynska) but at the last minute, rebels and returns to his tramp life—a free soul.

Renoir, despite the arch mannerisms of the time, manages to get in a few blows at the smugness of the middle-class French, the ambivalent attitudes towards sexual morality and the less-than-heroic actions of the average human being. Technically, the film is excellent if not judged by modern standards. Jacques Becker, Renoir's assistant on the film and later to become a director of note, also acts a brief vignette as a

kooky poet. What he may have learned from the master on this one must have been negligible, however.
Robe.

Peking Remembered
(COLOR DOCUMENTARY)
San Francisco, Feb. 13.

Butler-Hall independent production (no distributor as yet) directed by H. B. Butler; written by Bill Hall. Narrator, Paul Henreid; camera (color) Gordon Mueller; musical composition and direction, Andrew Belling. Reviewed at Butler Studios, San Francisco, Jan. 12, '67. Running Time, **60 MINS.**

Using creative animation techniques that breathe life into painstakingly dug-up photographs, paintings and Oriental objets d'art, independents H. B. Butler and Bill Hall have recreated the turmoil, history and atmosphere of Peking, the capital and hub of China, before the Communist take-over in an exceptional and timely documentary.

Short length (one hour) gives it some possible value alongside an overlength main feature. Strong prospect for pick-up for tv by either network or syndication.

Butler is filmmaker of the multi-festival prize copping "Death of Manolete," in which he similarly animated still photos to dramatically recreate death in the afternoon. Hall is ex-Sunday editor of the San Francisco Examiner. Paul Henreid narrates "Peking Remembered," and his mild Continental accent conveys the flavor of some exiled old China hand, nostalgic for the intrigues of the Forbidden City, the fetching singsong girls, and the exotic delights of Mandarin cuisine.

Hall's literate script avoids the soporific pedantry of most documentaries and is enlivened with anecdotes, court gossip, the nitty gritty of Peking life from the sex life of the Dowager Empress to the peasants who trained flocks of special pigeons to steal rice from the royal graineries.

Rather than spread the film thin over the enormous country, once an empire, the focus is within the walls of the capital. In ancient times, as today, all roads in China lead to Peking.

Butler's effects achieve the impression that the camera is actually moving through the old alleys, palaces and courtyards where the events happened, examining the people involved.

Location in San Francisco gave producers ready access to the local concentration of university and museum Oriental collections and records, which are believed greatest outside of China itself.
Rick.

Les Demoiselles De Rochefort
(The Young Girls of Rochefort)
(FRENCH — 70M — SONGS — DANCES—COLOR)
Paris, Feb. 28.

Comacio release of Parc Film-Madeleine Films-Seven Arts production. Stars Gene Kelly, George Chakiris, Catherine Denueve, Francoise Dorleac; features Michel Piccoli, Danielle Darrieux, Grover Dale, Jacques Perrin. Written and directed by Jacques Demy; music, Michel Legrand; choreography, Norman Mehn; camera (Eastmancolor), Ghislain Cloquet; editor, Jean Hamon. At Normandie, Paris. Running Time, **125 MINS.**

Delphine .... Catherine Deneuve
Solange ....~Francoise Dorleac
Andy .... Gene Kelly
Etienne .... George Chakiris
Bill .... Grover Dale
Maxence .... Jacques Perrin
Yvonne .... Danielle Darrieux
Josette ....,. Genevieve Thenier
Esther .... Pamela Hart
Judith .... Leslie North
Subtil .... Henri Cremieux

Jacques Demy, writer-director, and Michel Legrand, composer, who did the successful musical "The Umbrellas of Cherbourg," now reunite for a more ambitious pic that adds dance to a tale of small town life. It has charm, sustained human observation, mixed with catchy music, dances and songs to come up as a tuner with grace and dynamism. It is an elegant film fable that should have fine b.o. prospects in store for it worldwide.

As he did in "Cherbourg," Demy has his characters talk in song as well as break into them to comment on themselves, happenings or move things along. The dances, on the other hand, are more a way of getting an eyecatching backdrop to the smalltown streets or help maintain the larger-than-life treatment of recognizable but gentle characters. Yet there is a sadist who carves up a woman who will not have him, if he is twittery about carving a cake.

Into a sleepy little port town near a naval base comes a carnival used to advertise products. Two of the pitchmen lose their girls to sailors and ask two sisters, who give dance lessons and compose music, to put on an act for them. Also involved are the sisters' mother, who dreams of a lost love and runs a local cafe, a visiting American composer who falls for one of the girls, and an artist-sailor who has painted a portrait of his ideal woman who happens to look like one of the girls.

All this evolves mainly in the town square, a cafe in the middle of it and the girls' apartment and combo dance studio plus a white and gleaming music shop. As in "Cherbourg," the town has been repainted to look like a glowing and colorful little place and Rochefort will probably leave the pastel houses intact as Cherbourg did. And touristic sales of items based on the pic should also develop as it did in Cherbourg.

Demy is not concerned with cleaning up little towns but in continuing to put a sort of gentle, but never over-sentimental or mawkish, human comedy about ordinary mortals to song and dance. In his calm but incisive observation, right blending of the music and dance to underline his simple but emotionally beguiling interactions of his sweet but not saccharin characters, he has brought off a most ingratiating tuner.

Catherine Deneuve and Francoise Dorleac, real sisters, play twins with the right mixture of feminine guile, passiveness and stubborn aggressiveness when it comes to the men they want. Danielle Darrieux is fetching as their mother and she is the only one

who synched her own songs, at least in the French version.

Gene Kelly is trim, dynamic and both brash and winning as a visiting American who falls for one of the sisters, while George Chakiris has less to do as one of the carny men who loses out on the girls. But his and the Kelly names will help in stateside situations plus the sheer eye appeal and freshness of this musical. Though there is an English version, it might be a good idea to start off with the French one and then follow with the English lingoed item.

That is only an opinion, since, though a fairly classic musical reminiscent of earlier Yank tuners, it has a Gallic froth, tinged with unobtrusive melancholy and character delineation, that will need some more selective placing and perhaps aiming it at art audiences before general release. But critics and word-of-mouth should also help launch this deceptively simple and airy tintuner.

Legrand again comes up with sweet but never syrupy music with several earmarked for popular appeal. The album should also make a place for itself coincident with this disarming and delightful pic. Production values are fine and the cast is in harmony, with Michel Piccoli also an asset as the former lover of the mother, Henri Cremieux as the fusspot sadist, Grover Dale as a carny character, Jacques Riberolles as an unsuccessful suitor and Jacques Perrin as the dreamy sailor-artist.

Musicals were and are one of the indigenous American legit and screen creations along with oaters. But Italy has turned sagebrush sagas to hit camp takeoffs, and now Demy shows he has assimilated Yank musical ideas and used them in original transpositions to make comments on smalltown life and the growing moves to bigger cities, without undue sentimentality.

So it is a successful and original tuner that turns streets into pastel compositions with rapidly dancing passersby as the characters live out big decisions in their lives in three days. Norman Mehn has contributed simple but deft choreography and Demy again shows he is an original filmmaker who welds the same characters into all his films. But though this may be an extra sidelight for buffs, it does not detract from the elegant appeal of the film generally.

Seven Arts invested for Western Hemisphere and Japanese rights and has what could be a fine art and playoff entry. Color helming by Ghislain Cloquet is also an asset, as is the unobtrusive but knowing editing of Jean Hamon. Here is a wistful, but always witty and observant little tale set to songs and dance, with intermittent talk, that is easy on ears and eyes and has more body, human comment and gentleness, without being maudlin, than most tuners these days.
Mosk.

La Musica
(FRENCH)
Paris, Feb. 27.

United Artists release of UA-Raoul Ploquin production. Stars Robert Hossein, Delphine Seyrig; features Julie Dassin. Written and directed by Marguerite Duras, with codirection by Paul

Seban; camera, Sacha Vierny; editor, Christine Couve. Previewed in Paris. Running Time, 82 MINS.

Man .... Robert Hossein
Woman .... Delphine Seyrig
Girl .... Julie Dassin

"La Musica" tries to give a bittersweet, rhythmic, visual underlining to a lot of talk about lost love, alienation and the difficulties of communication. But the themes are treated in a static way and the film is verbose, stilted and precious rather than one capable of making a more coherent statement on these themes. It is a risky export item, except for arty spots on its theme and a fine bevy of players.

Marguerite Duras has done scripts for such prizewinning pix as "Hiroshima Mon Amour," "Such a Long Absence" and others, but her first attempt at directing shows that she has not learned much from her work with other directors. Codirector Paul Seban has helped in giving an okay technical flair to boring talkfest.

Robert Hossein comes back to a smalltown where his wife has just finalized their divorce. He meets her and they talk at length of how they tortured each other, how each cheated on the other, etc., etc.

Julie Dassin, daughter of director Jules Dassin, has a small but showy role as a young American tourist who gets mixed up with the morose man for a while. She displays a presence and offbeat looks that should have her heard from in other pix with more substance and clarity.

Delphine Seyrig is a fine actress but cannot do much to make her tortured wife anything but a rather forlorn and almost whining character.

Lensing has a good crisp finish, and on-the-spot shooting in a smalltown helps. But the intimate music of character revelation and dramatic pitch and statement elude Miss Duras both as director and scripter. It was adapted from a one-act play and still is too theatrical in its gab. *Mosk.*

The Hired Killer
(TECHNISCOPE-COLOR)
(ITALIAN)

Realistic actioner about an American killer in Europe which should do well in program situations.

Hollywood, Feb. 24.
Paramount release of Cinegai (F. T. Gay) production. Features Robert Webber, Franco Nero, Jeanne Valerie. Director-story-screenplay, Frank Shannon. Camera (Technicolor), Eric Menczer; music, Robby Poitevin; editor, Mark Sirandrews; asst. director, Jeffrey Darcey. Reviewed at Paramount Studios, Feb. 23, '67. Running Time, 96 MINS.
Clint Harris .... Robert Webber
Tony Lobello .... Franco Nero
Mary .... Jeanne Valerie
Secchy-Goldstein
         Jose Louis De Villalonga
Andrea Ferri .... John Hawkwood
Barry .... Michel Bardinet
Gastel .... Cec Linder
Lucy .... Theodora Bergery
Frank .... Earl Hammond

Superior production mounting is afforded in this Paramount release of an Italian import starring an American actor. A hard-hitting

and realistic actioner, pairing in top roles Robert Webber and European thesp Franco Nero (latter currently starred in Warners' "Camelot" as Sir Lancelot), it should do well enough in program situations where names do not necessarily count. For Frank Shannon, who triples in direction-story-screenplay, the 96-minute production beautifully lensed in Technicolor marks a decisive credit.

Title is the tipoff to the story. Webber portrays a rubout artist sent from N.Y. to Paris to erase a former member of a crime syndicate. He's accompanied by a young hood with proven ability as a tough guy, as an assistant Webber could very well do without. Trackdown of their quarry provides some mounting suspense carefully nurtured by Shannon, and Webber endows his character with plenty of authority.

Interesting use is made of Webber's methods in killing his quarries, both in an introlutory sequence in Gotham and later in Europe. Plotline occasionally becomes bogged down but treatment and acting are sufficient to overcome most of this deficiency.

Quiet menace is inserted by Webber in such a manner that his role is a standout. Nero, too, scores in a less definitive part, and Jeanne Valerie lends a nice degree of distaff interest murdered by the man Webber is seeking. Jose Louis de Villalonga in latter role socks over his few scenes effectively, and balance of player lineup is well cast.

F. T. Gay handles producer reins skillfully and is backed by a competent staff of technichians. Tops here particularly are the photography by Eric Menczer and music score by Robby Poitevin. Mark Sirandrews' editing and Hugo Nahier's art direction likewise are definite assets. *Whit.*

The Adventures of Bullwhip Griffin
(COLOR)

Excellent Walt Disney comedy spoof of the Gold Rush. First-rate direction, performances, production values and gimmicks. All-age appeal. Excellent b.o. likely.

Hollywood, Feb. 25.
Buena Vista release of a Walt Disney production; co-producer, Bill Anderson. Features Roddy McDowall, Suzanne Pleshette, Karl Malden. Directed by James Neilson. Screenplay, Lowell S. Hawley, based on the novel "By The Great Horn Spoon," by Sid Fleischman; camera (Technicolor), Edward Colman; editor, Marsh Hendry; music, George Bruns; songs, Bruns, Mel Leven, Robert B. and Richard M. Sherman; asst. director, John C. Chulay. Reviewed at Walt Disney Studio, Burbank, Feb. 24, 1967. Running Time, 110 MINS.
Bullwhip Griffin ...... Roddy McDowall
Arabella Flagg ...... Suzanne Pleshette
Judge Higgins .... Karl Malden
Sam Trimble .... Harry Guardino
Quentin Bartlett .... Richard Haydn
Irene Chesney ......Hermione Baddeley
Jack Flagg .... Bryan Russell
Capt. Swain .... Liam Redmond
Mr. Pemberton ...... Cecil Kellaway
Bandido Leader .... Joby Baker
Mountain Ox .... Mike Mazurki
Joe Turner .... Alan Carney
Chief Hangman .... Parley Baer
Referee .... Arthur Hunnicutt
Timekeeper .... Dub Taylor
Bandido ..... Pedro Gonzalez-Gonzalez

"The Adventures of Bullwhip

Griffin" is a lively, entertaining comedy spoof of the California Gold Rush era. Zesty direction, solid performances, firstrate production values and broad comedy angles make this Walt Disney production particularly strong for all-age audiences. The carnival-type ballyhoo campaign already evident seems perfect, with excellent b.o. prospects likely for Buena Vista release in general situations.

Lowell S. Hawley adapted Sid Fleischman's novel, "By The Great Horn Spoon," and the screen treatment is abetted further by Ward Kimball's gimmicks, such as screen titles reminiscent of silent pix, and a ricky-tick score. Bill Anderson coproduced, with Louis Debney as associate producer.

Proper Bostonian butler Roddy McDowall, with a yen for Suzanne Pleshette, young lady of the house, sets off in pursuit of Bryan Russell, her brother, when the kid lams it to California. A dead grandfather has left them nothing, and the lad has set out on his own. McDowall and Russell make the ocean trip, then have many adventures in gold country, until a happy fadeout with Pleshette, who also has made the trip and becomes a saloon chirp.

A very strong cast includes Karl Malden, genial villain who pops up in the right (i.e., wrong) places, ham Shakespearean actor Richard Haydn, ship captain Liam Redmond, Mexican bandit Joby Baker, bouncer Mike Mazurki and latter's boss, Harry Guardino. In earlier Boston scenes, Hermione Baddeley and Cecil Kellaway have bright moments. Unbilled, but easily recognizable, are many vet comedy players, such as Dave Willock.

James Neilson's direction is excellent. McDowall's straight-faced, straight-laced playing is very good, and Miss Pleshette—more often than not cast in kooky or bad-girl parts—proves (gratifyingly) that she need not be pigeonholed. Her saloon singing-dancing is a neat blend of ribaldry and dignity, which is what the part demands. McDowall's climactic fist fight with Mazurki is a choreographic and comedy delight. The Russell kid is very good.

Kimball's gimmicks—his screen credit is for "Titles & Things"—provide excellent transitions and mood-settings. The songs, by George Bruns, Mel Levens and the Sherman Bros., as well as Bruns' overall score, are perfect in context. Edward Colman's mobile and crisp Technicolor lensing is a big asset in capturing the splashy, also subtle, visual details. Marsh Hendry edited to a snappy 110 minutes. Special effects and matte work create the desired suspension of belief. All other credits are pro.

Murf.

Riot on Sunset Strip
(COLOR)

Okay exploitation or recent headlines. Youth appeal.

Hollywood, March 3.
American International release of Sam Katzman production. Features Aldo Ray, Mimsy Farmer, Michael Evans, Laurie Mock, Tim Rooney. Directed by Arthur Dreifuss. Screenplay, Orville H. Hampton; camera (PatheColor), Paul Vogel; editor, Ben Lewis; music, Fred Karger; asst. director, Donald C. Klune. Reviewed at Charles Aidikoff screening room, March 2, '67. Running Time, 87 MINS.
Lt. Walt Lorimer............ Aldo Ray
Andy .... Mimsy Farmer
Sgt. Tweedy .... Michael Evans
Liz-Ann .... Laurie Mock
Grady .... Tim Rooney

American International has an exploitable package in this Sam Katzman production based on youth riots on the Sunset Strip late last year which gained wide attention nationally. Producer's flair for handling topical events in his films is a proven commodity; here he has taken a routine story and inserted the type of values which pay off solidly, particularly in the younger market.

Lack of star-name dressing is inconsequential. Subject matter is sufficient to attract b.o. response, which may be further sparked by a smart campaign and lobby displays. The Orville H. Hampton screenplay covers theme by centering on Aldo Ray as head of the Hollywood police division, under whose jurisdiction the Sunset Strip and its multitude of beat activities lie, and a small group of which his daughter is a member.

Arthur Dreifuss' direction caters handily to the subject, and authenticity is afforded by footage shot of actual parading last fall on the Strip. A mod note is added via several musical combos blaring out their wares in Strip joints, one of which is Pandora's Box, a pop hangout which figured in the riots.

For added measure, last year's incident of a Los Angeles police officer, whose daughter was raped, shooting a suspect (no connection with Strip trouble) is drawn on for a similar episode revolving around a rape, but toned down to Ray using his fists instead of a gun. There may be censor trouble over one brief flash in a bedroom when Ray's daughter and a young beatnik are caught in act of copulation.

Ray delivers a straightforward performance and Mimsy Farmer as his daughter is properly appealing. Michael Evans in role of a police sergeant and Laurie Mock, Tim Rooney and Schuyler Hayden as juves also register effectively. The Standelles, Chocolate Watch Band and The Enemies are in for music.

Technical credits are firstclass right down the line, including Paul Vogel's color photography, Ben Lewis' editing, George Davis and Merrill Pye's art direction and Fred Karger's scoring. *Whit.*

Doctor, You've Got To Be Kidding
(PANAVISION-COLOR)

Amusing comedy for youth trade, with star names of

Sandra Dee and George Hamilton as lure.

Hollywood, Feb. 23.
Metro release of Trident (Douglas Laurence) production. Stars Sandra Dee, George Hamilton; features Celeste Holm, Bill Bixby, Dick. Kallman, Mort Sahl, Dwayne Hickman. Directed by Peter Tewksbury. Screenplay, Phillip Shuken; based on novel by Patte Wheat Mahan; camera (Metrocolor), Fred Koenekamp; music, Kenyon Hopkins; editor, Fredric Steinkamp; asst. director, Erich von Stroheim Jr. Reviewed at Warner Hollywood Theatre, Feb. 22, '67. Running Time, 83 MINS.

Heather Halloran	Sandra Dee
Harlan Wycliff	George Hamilton
Louise Halloran	Celeste Holm
Dick Bender	Bill Bixby
Pat Murad	Dick Kallman
Mr. Dan Ruskin	Mort Sahl
Hank Judson	Dwayne Hickman
Joe Bonney	Allen Jenkins
Judge North	Robert Gibbons
Policemen	Donald Mitchell, Scott White, Med Flory
Jenny Ribbock	Nichelle Nichols
Miss Reynolds	Charlotte Considine
Cigarette Girl	Allison McKay

"Doctor, You've Got To Be Kidding"—a catchy title fitting into the current cycle of way-out tabs is a comedy writer's dream which should click in the youth market. One thing it proves...in Sandra Dee, who already has demonstrated talented aptitude for this sort of performing, is a young comedienne who may be groomed to a top-flight niche in this little-tenanted orbit. The Douglas Laurence production carries good—if lightweight—motivation, plenty of glib laugh lines and players widely known to the younger crowd who should be strong marquee attractions.

George Hamilton costars with Miss Dee. She's a slightly wacky —and unwed—young woman who is being rushed to the hospital to have a baby as pic opens. She is accompanied by three young men anxious to marry her and be the father of her near-blessed event. Bill Bixby and Dwayne Hickman, from television, and Dick Kallman enact the swains.

Celeste Holm, a stagestruck mother who has had visions of her daughter being a star ever since she forced her to give singing auditions in an elevator when she was a little girl, plays Sandra's charmingly ambitious parent. For extra lure, Mort Sahl is in as an "intellectual" nitery owner who books Sandra and her act because he thinks turn is so terrible his patrons will vociferously dig it.

The Phillip Shuken screenplay, based on novel by Patte Wheat Mahan, utilizes the flashback technique in detailing Sandra's rise and ultimate pregnancy, a fact she refuses to believe. Hamilton enacts her stuffy boss, a business genius who knows everything but girls. Determined not to be a singer, when he calls her the dime-a-dozen variety after hearing her sing two notes, Sandra about-faces and seriously studies for a career.

Femme star warbles one song, "I Haven't Anything Better to Do," and mouths another, "Walk Tall Like a Man," which may strike favor with the younger crowd. The Wild Affair are on for a pair, "Talkin' Law" and "Little Girl," to give musical flavor.

Miss Dee socks over her role

under the deft direction of Peter Tewksbury and Hamilton competently handles the biz exec who romances his secretary. Bixby, Hickman and Kallman are lively protagonists and Miss Holm is a standout. Sahl does a fast-spieling character in his customary style and Allen Jenkins is good as a booking agent.

Excellent technical support is offered by Kenyon Hopkins on music score, Fred Koenekamp on color cameras, Fredric Steinkamp as editor, George W. Davis and Urie McCleary's art direction.
Whit.

Regreso Al Silencio
(Return to Silence)
(CHILE)
Santiago, Feb. 25.
Chilencine production, with direction and screenplay by Naum Kramarenco. Stars Humberto Duvauchelle, Hector Duvauchelle and Orietta Escamez. Features Nelson Villagra, Enrique Heine, Peggy Cordero, Roberto Parada, Mercedes Moral and Eliana Vidal. Camera, Andres Martorell. Music, Tito Ledermann. Running Time, 122 MINS.

Although more professional than other Chilean feature films, "Return to Silence" is still not very satisfactory. This story of a young American who returns to Chile to locate his stepbrother and gets involved with a smuggling plus black market gang that blackmails him, could have been made into an adequate suspense melodrama. But, at 122 minutes, the story is excessively drawn out and there are too many incidents that contribute neither to the plot nor to the general atmosphere.

It is Naum Kramarenco's third feature. He produced, directed, wrote the screenplay and even the lyrics of one of the songs. The film's basic flaws are a poorly developed screenplay (if properly tightened, it could have made a great difference) and sometimes stilted dialogue. Suspense is created far too late and the scenes at the beginning which were filmed in Miami contribute little to the plot, but have far too obvious puffs for the Chilean Airline.

The acting ranges from adequate to unimpressive. Most of the thesps have considerable legit experience but project far less effectively on the screen. Andres Martorell's photography is one of the plus aspects.

The outlook on the local market is favorable, as Chilean audiences tend to back up pix made in the country. Chances abroad are very limited.
Amig.

The Really Big Family
(DOCUMENTARY; 1.33-1)

Unusual family pic, with 18 children, nominated for feature documentary this year.

Hollywood, March 1.
David L. Wolper production (no release), produced-directed by Alex Grasshoff. Features Bill and Louise Dukes and their 18 children; Henry Fonda, narrator. Camera, Vilis Lapenicks; narration, Arthur Bramble; editor, John Soh. Reviewed at Columbia Pictures studio, Feb. 28, '67. Running Time, 51 MINS.

Originally made for television but never aired, this 51-minute feature copped a nomination in the documentary division for this year's Academy's sweepstakes and will go out first in theatrical release. Currently showcasing at the Tiffany Theatre on Sunset Strip bracketed with foreign "Loves of a Blonde," negotiations for a release are now being conducted by David L. Wolper, under whose banner Alex Grasshoff produced and directed with an eye to draining his subject of possibilities.

Title aptly refers to a Seattle family, Bill and Louise Dukes and their 18 children ranging in ages from 21 down to one. They were selected after UPI columnist Vernon Scott emblazoned news that Wolper was seeking a family with 18 offspring or more and Grasshoff personally interviewed 100 of the more than 300 families who answered.

The logistics of the Dukes' daily life is caught in a Niagara of noise, confusion and frequent crises as Grasshoff moved his 16m cameras into their small home and lensed them in various aspects of existence. Need for bargain buying both in food and clothing is particularly stressed as father's weekly salary ranging from $135 to $165—dependent on overtime — as a Boeing inspector must be stretched, and family relations likewise are pointed up. What comes out onscreen is often appealing and assaying rich in human interest.

Grasshoff has drawn uncommonly good performances from the entire family, the effect being there is no acting but that of the family acting naturally. Henry Fonda acts as narrator, appearing briefly at opening and windup. Whatever family dialog there may be seems to be spontaneous, as the occasion demands, which gives a realistic feeling to unfoldment. To foster certain motivation, preparations for the wedding of the eldest daughter, Bobbi, actually shown being married in a Catholic church, cue the later reels.

Vilis Lapenicks' photography is strictly on the documentary side; viz, he focuses on various family actions rather than striving for unusual or artistic camera effects, thereby accomplishing the realism subject requires. John Soh's editing also achieves its goal and narration written by Arthur Bramble sets a good tone.
Whit.

Le Mur
(The Wall)
(FRENCH)
Paris, March 7.
Procinex release of Procinex-Films Niepce production. With Michel Del Castillo, Denis Mahaffey, Mathieu Klosowsky. Written and directed by Serge Roullet, from the novel by Jean-Paul Sartre. Camera, Denis Clerval; editor, Denise Baby. Previewed in Paris. Running Time, 90 MINS.

Pablo	Michel Del Castillo
Peter	Denis Mahaffey
Boy	Mathieu Klosovsky
Doctor	Bernard Anglade
Gris	Rene Darmon
Concha	Maria Pacheco
Officer	Jorge Lavelli
Captain	Edgardo Canton

A Jean-Paul Sartre novella

written in 1937, about a group of men awaiting execution during the Spanish Civil War, is brought to the screen with telling observation, taste and knowhow by new director-adapter Serge Roullet. Sartre did the dialog himself and the pic looks to have art chances abroad, if somewhat too demanding for playoff. The Sartre name and the film's sombre but forceful qualities should help in university and special situations as well.

Near the beginning of the Hispano Civil War in 1936 a group of loyalists are rounded up by the Falangist forces who have taken over several towns. Three young men are sentenced to death and put in a cell together. They are Pablo, who had become involved in the loyalist cause through a friend, a young boy whose brother was a member, and an Irishman of the International Brigade.

As they are in a cell together with two soldier guards and a Belgian doctor, put in to study their reactions to impending execution, the film carefully watches how each faces his fate. Flashbacks are more like innermost thoughts as they begin to try to sort out their lives and face up to what is in store for them.

The characters are strong enough, the uncluttered direction and unmannered playing sober enough to make this film translate into an affecting human experience rather than in any way a pedantic or literary affair.

Using non-actors helps, and novelist Michel Del Castillo is extremely effective as Pablo. a man who cannot quite feel the great movement around him but is drawn into it by friendship. He manages to give the role an interior strength and a sheer human survival facet that make his actions, reflections and almost passive heroism right throughout. A man who was in a concentration camp as a boy, and wrote a telling book on it, "Child of the Century." his experiences help his presence and acting.

Others are also extremely well picked and used, and plus elements include a counterpointed musical background, appropriately stark lensing and excellent on-the-spot locations to simulate Spain in Southern France. All parts are spoken in Spanish, for greater authenticity, except for key passages in French between Pablo and the Irishman since it is the only language they have in common.

As with Alain Resnais' "The War Is Over," which dealt with modern Hispano refugees still fighting Franco Spain, and Fred Zinnemann's "Behold a Pale Horse" (Col), this pic will not get Spanish showing. But it transcends place and politics to make a statement on men facing death.

It should have art legs if well placed and carefully followed up elsewhere and at home, with critical outlooks and word-of-mouth sure to help. It shows a fine and subtle new director in Serge Roullet. While specialized at best, it is a pic of force and solid values that has to be handled most carefully for best release results. *Mosk.*

La Collectionneuse
(The Collector)
(FRENCH-COLOR)

Paris, March 7.
Rome Paris Films, Films Du Losange release and production. With Patrick Bauchau, Haydee Politoff, Daniel Pommbreulle. Written, directed and edited by Eric Rohmer; camera (Eastmancolor), Alain Levent. Previewed in Paris. Running Time, 85 MINS.

Adrien	Patrick Bauchau
Haydee	Haydee Politoff
Daniel	Daniel Pommbreulle
Sam	Gene Archer
Carole	Mijanou
Friend	Annik Morice
Boy	Denis Berry

The Collector of the title is a languid, pouting, teenage femme spending a summer with two dandyish young men. Film is too interested in aphorisms, literary narration and personal but over-indulged observation, and overlogged on talk, inaction and narcissism, to make much impact on a personal, social or emotional front. It's mainly for specialized use, abroad for this opaque tale.

Heroine is one of those pretty boyish-looking drifters showing up in French pix of late. She is sleeping around the Riviera and staying with an anti-social painter when the hero shows up. He is a fairly effete, remote type who is trying to sort out his life. He is attracted to the girl but tries to play it craftily; he finally loses her and decides to turn to another one who may be serious in his life.

Film unfolds through a series of scenes of vacation intrigues around Saint Tropez. It has nice color and the girl, Haydee Politoff, looks good and does have a cheeky appeal, if more work is needed in polishing her speech. Patrick Bauchau is rightly withdrawn and interior as the commentator and finally defeated would-be collector of sensations.

Writer-director Eric Rohmer remains somewhat too literary in letting talk carry the action and make points, and rarely has the visual observation take over and perk up the rather epigrammatic, self-indulgent and finally self-pitying actions of these drifters. Rohmer does display an insight into definite types, but cannot, it seems, make them more alive, spontaneous and meaningful in film form.

Mosk.

Maedchen, Maedchen
(Girls, Girls)
(GERMAN)

Berlin, Feb. 25.
Atlas release of Roger Fritz production. With Helga Anders, Juergen Jung, Hellmut Lange. Directed and written by Fritz; camera, Klaus Koenig; music, Safebreakers (Berlin combo) and Fatty George, with use of themes by Wilson Pickert; editing, Heidi Genee. At Atelier am Zoo, West Berlin. Running Time, 104 MINS.

Angela	Helga Anders
Junior	Juergen Jung
Senior	Hellmut Lange
Housemaid	Renate Grosser
Another girl	Monika Zinnenberg

The series of first feature pix contributed by W-Germany's young "new wavers" is continued with Roger Fritz's "Girls, Girls." The best that can be said about "Girls" is that it displays some beautiful lensing. In fact, there is some "optical chic" about this low-budget production which indicates that Fritz was a prize-winning-photo reporter before he joined the di-

rectoral ranks. He was Luchino Visconti's assistant director and then directed two short pix by himself.

Fritz calls his initial full-length film "a synthesis between artistic engagement and commercial consideration." Probably a well-meant ambition, but the outcome is just too thin to make an impression. It runs over 104 minutes but could have easily been trimmed to an hour. Fritz found it necessary to show certain scenes over and over again. Much too often his two young principal players, a pretty nymph and a handsome lad, undress themselves or put on "sexy" quarrels.

This may please segments of male customers and especially those who have a certain primitive taste for Lolita-type gals. (In fact, the first local showings saw young men primarily among the audience.) A patron with some demands in film entertainment may feel utterly bored after a while.

It is not easy to say what Fritz actually had in mind. The repetition of suggestive scenes and bed sequences make this film a sordid one. Also, the handling of the players is not exactly competent. Hellmut Lange, who enacts the role of Senior turns in a rather clumsy performance. Of Helga Anders, the nympho, it can be said that she is, optically speaking, a type that is in demand these days, but some of her scenes appear overly cute and border on the silly. The best performance is by Juergen Jung, the young lad, who shows genuine promise.

Technically, film represents a fine standard and reveals knowhow on the part of director Fritz, who may yet make his way. There should be no worries about this first feature's commercial side. It cost only 430.000 Deutsche marks (about $107,500) and shouldn't have it difficult to break even.

Hans.

Don't Lose Your Head
(BRITISH-COLOR)

Boisterous, uninhibited farce in the "Carry On" formula, which should draw the enthusiasts of previous pix in the series. That will mean boxoffice bonanza.

London, March 2.
Rank release of a Peter Rogers Production. Stars Sidney James, Kenneth Williams, Jim Dale, Charles Hawtrey, Joan Sims, Dany Robin. Features Peter Gilmore, Peter Butterworth. Directed by Gerald Thomas. Screenplay by Talbot Rothwell; editor, Rod Keys; camera (Technicolor), Alan Hume; music, Eric Rogers. Reviewed at Leicester-Square Theatre, London, March 1, '67. Running Time, 90 MINS.

Sir Rodney Ffing	Sidney James
Citizen Camembert	Kenneth Williams
Lord Darcy	Jim Dale
Duke de Pommfrit	Charles Hawtrey
Citizen Bidet	Peter Butterworth
Desiree Dubarry	Joan Sims
Jacqueline	Dany Robin
Robespierre	Peter Gilmore
Landlady	Marianne Stone
Henri	Michael Ward
Malabonce	Leon Greene
Captain of Soldiers	Richard Shaw

Peter Rogers' first film under the Rank banner, after a long association with Anglo-Amalgamated, is in format and spirit a "Carry On," despite the title. Though the series is beginning to show severe signs

of strain, this has happened before; the box-office has always responded well and there's no reason to expect any change. In America, too, the past successes of the "Carry Ons" should insure a useful repetition for this one.

The format is one of unabashed earthy vulgarity. No pun or double meaning seems too risque to throw into the script. Situations (as with the names of the characters) are designed largely to lead up to saucy gags and producer Rogers, director Gerald Thomas and screenwriter Talbot Rothwell have kept the boisterous brew bubbling with no concession to subtlety or logic. Previous pix have proved that there's an audience for a concoction of slapstick, camp humor and sex-and-lavatorial stuff.

"Don't Lose Your Head" is a wild parody of "Scarlet Pimpernel" adventures. Rogers has gathered most of his stock company of star, featured and bit-part thesps and let them loose in a crazy debauch of duelling, doublecrossing and disaster. The troupers jump through their wellknown hoops with agility. French actress Dany Robin, a looker, seems somewhat bewildered by her entry into this company but the rest approach their chore with no inhibitions and with apparent enthusiasm.

Sidney James and Jim Dale are the two bored English aristocrats who baffle Robespierre and his chief of police (Citizen Camembert — the Big Cheese) with their audacity. James, posing as "The Black Fingernail," turns up in a variety of disguises, none of which attempts to hide his homely features. He and Jim Dale, a somewhat neglected, very good actor, team up in sharp fashion. Kenneth Williams plays the police chief in his usual shrill style, which tends to pall when he is too heavily exposed in a film, and Peter Butterworth, Joan Sims and Charles Hawtrey valiantly cope with the passing nonsense in their usual capable manner.

The film takes full advantage of the costumes and furnishings of the period and Alan Hume's color lensing and Rod Keys' editing job with the guillotine keep the film going along at a lively pace. Eric Rogers' score, naturally, relies a great deal on familiar French themes.

"Don't Lose Your Head" has its flat spots (there is an all-out sword battle which is too long) and it is often just dirty, but audiences who have learned to know what to expect with these successful Rogers pix will get their full quota of breezy, rude amusement. *Rich.*

Ulysses
(IRISH-PANAVISION)

James Joyce's famous novel as film. May become test case for all time obscenity, as the dialog is complete, detailed and exquisitely spoken. An experience in aural voyeurism.

A Continental release of a Walter Reade Jr.-Joseph Strick production. Executive producer, Walter Reade Jr.; associate producers, Wilfrid Eades, Fred Haines. Produced and directed by Strick. Stars Milo O'Shea, Barbara Jefford, Maurice Roeves, T. P. McKenna, Anna Manahan. Screenplay, Strick and Haines from novel by James Joyce; camera, Wolfgang Suschitzky; editor, Reginald Mills; sound, Chris Wangler; art director, Graham Probst; music, composed and conducted, Stanley Myers. Reviewed at Baronet Theatre, N.Y., March 14, '67. Running Time, 140 MINS.

Molly Bloom	Barbara Jefford
Leopold Bloom	Milo O'Shea
Stephen Dedalus	Maurice Roeves
Buck Mulligan	T. P. McKenna
Simon Dedalus	Martin Dempsey
May Goulding	Sheila O'Sullivan
Haines	Graham Lines
Jack Power	Peter Mayock
Gerty MacDowell	Fionnuala Flanagan
Bella Cohen	Anna Manahan
Zoe Higgins	Maureen Toal
Josie Breen	Maureen Potter
Myles Crawford	Chris Curran
Mary Driscoll	Maire Hastings
Martin Cunningham	Eddie Golden
Blazes Boylan	Joe Lynch
Cyril Sargeant	Ruadhan Neeson
Cissy Caffrey	Biddie White-Lennon
Mrs. Mervyn Talboys	Meryl Gourley
Mrs. Bellingham	Ann Rowan
Nurse Callan	Rosaleen Linehan
Dr. Dixon	Robert Carlisle Jr.
Alexander J. Dowie	O. Z. Whitehead
John Henry Manton	Cecil Sheridan
The Citizen	Geoffrey Golden
Lt. Gardner	Tony Doyle
Pvt. Carr	James Bartley
Pvt. Compton	Colin Bird
Denis Breen	Jack Plant
Garrett Deasy	Dave Kelly
Joe Hynes	Des Keogh
Lynch	Leon Collins
Lenehan	Robert Somerset
Mrs. Yelverton Barry	May Cluskey
Bantam Lyons	Des Perry
Corny Kelleher	John Molloy
Florry	Claire Mullen
Kitty	Pamela Mant
Madden	Paddy Roche
Costello	Eugene Lambert
The Drinker	Danny Cummins
Bob Doran	Brendan Cauldwell

The trouble that the Walter Reade Organization has been having in securing bookings for its release of James Joyce's "Ulysses" is nothing compared to the trouble they're in for once it is in release. If ever a motion picture set itself up intentionally as a test case for obscenity, this one seemingly is it. And for the first time in the history of motion pictures, perhaps, the case for obscenity lies not in what is seen on the screen but what is heard on the soundtrack. (Film is playing off this week in three-day engagements at hard ducat scale.)

Joseph Strick, whose production of Jean Genet's "The Balcony" was also released by Continental, partially cleaned up that Krafft-Ebing exercise in putting it on the screen but, in so doing, didn't clean up at the boxoffice. Evidently he has figured that the Joycean flavor of "Ulysses," planted in Dublin dirt and nurtured over the years by censorship and exploitation, would only become a healthy transplant to the screen if brought along imbedded in a sizable portion of the ould muck and mire. This he has done.

"Ulysses" is a healthy, promising cinematic piece of flora, night-blooming and carnivorous, if healthy means that it retains all the obscenities of language, all the Hibernian schizophrenia about sex, religion and nationality, and the rich, fetid language that is, in truth, English but only as an Irish writer can compose it and Irish actors can speak it.

Filmed entirely in Ireland, with a cast almost entirely Irish (the leading lady is Canadian and at least one American is in the cast), the manner in which Strick has translated the rambling, unorthodox tale by Joyce of life among Dubliners (updated from 1904) by concentrating on the trio of primary characters — Leopold and Molly Bloom and student Stephen Dedalus. Although their tales overlap, the primary emphasis is on the two males during most of the film leaving the last 20 or 30 minutes to Molly's famous libidinous soliloquy.

Visually, there's little in the film to offend most adult viewers —an occasional bare buttock, a lingering view of an undraped statue, some brief action on the part of a character; but all this is underscored by dialog which turns even the most innocent scenes into comments against the marital state, religion, politics, prejudice, the war of the sexes and myriad lesser victims. The obscenity is in the speech, the ear is besieged with suggested phrases, propositions, descriptions, and regrets at lost opportunities. Even inanimate objects are used to comment—a cuckoo clock berates Bloom with its chirp of "cuckold, cuckold, cuckold." Some of the dialog is offensive in its very wording; much delightful in its apt description—"The weather is changing. It's as uncertain as a child's bottom."

But the irreverence towards everything—jokes are made in the graveyard; anti-Semitism is so evident that it begins to pall; English characters are made complete villains but this isn't weighed against a glorification of the Irish, they're generally portrayed as fools, bigots and suppressed sex maniacs.

The danger in "Ulysses" is not that it's obscene — that becomes quickly evident. The danger lies in that this obscenity of language is so beguiling. The Joycean dialog is spoken so beautifully by the entire cast, with such relish, that the viewer, while offended, catches himself listening with an intent that some may feel could better be given worthier fare. The film becomes an experience in aural voyeurism.

Casting is fine, Barbara Jefford's Molly is handsomely overblown, a wasted garden of a woman who yearns for a man with a passion that almost causes the screen to pulsate yet depriving Leopold of his marital rights because she so abhors another possibility of pregnancy. Milo O'Shea's Leopold Bloom is a realized example of the degraded, dejected husband — his dignity rapidly fading, but still capable of dreaming of lost sexual prowess; a Jew among the enemy, but an Irishman nevertheless.

Maurice Roeves' Stephen Dedalus might have been more impressive had some of the many flashbacks been used to better fill in his past—viewers are only told that he comes from an unhappy home, with a failure of a father. Outstanding among the lesser lights are T. P. McKenna as Mulligan, Stephen's domineering and evil fellow student; Joe Lynch, a caricature of an oversexed ladykiller; and Anna Manahan as Bella, the brothel keeper (straight out of "The Balcony"). American actor O. Z. Whitehead is seen briefly as a revivalist in one of Bloom's fantasies.

The technical credits are all outstanding. The crisp, black and white photography is always clear, even during numerous night scenes, and one longshot of Dublin, atwinkle with lights, is a beautiful landscape. Camera credits on the film are a bit difficult to pinpoint but Wolfgang Suschitzky is designated as lighting cameraman and Seamus Corcoran as camera operator. Chris Wangler's sound is some of the best recording on film, every voice as clear as a bell and an important part of the film's aural seduction.

Reginald Mills' editing is, likewise, excellent with no scene being allowed to linger beyond its stated purpose. There are occasional rough cuts that appear to be less the fault of the editor than that sufficient bridging shots were not made but, running 140 minutes, the film is certain to be subjected to some additional scissors work. Stanley Myers' music is adequate, not particularly Irish, and never allowed to overpower the spoken dialog, which takes in almost the entire footage.

If there is to be an argument for freedom of speech on the motion picture screen, the soundtrack of "Ulysses" has some powerful ammunition on its side but the only further step in freedom that can possibly be taken is to show what the characters freely talk about—and they leave practically nothing unspoken.

Robe.

Hombre
(COLOR-PANAVISION)

Handsome production about greed and survival in the old West. Paul Newman, Fredric March and Richard Boone head excellent cast. Big b.o. likely in general situations.

Hollywood, March 7.

Twentieth Century-Fox release, produced by Martin Ritt and Irving Ravetch. Stars Paul Newman, Fredric March, Richard Boone, Diane Cilento. Directed by Ritt. Screenplay, Ravetch, Harriet Frank, Jr., based on the novel by Elmore Leonard; camera (DeLuxe Color), James Wong Howe; editor, Frank Bracht; music, David Rose; asst. director, William McGarry; second unit director, Ray Kellogg. Reviewed at 20th-Fox Studios, L.A., March 6, '67. Running Time, 110 MINS.

John Russell .... Paul Newman
Favor .... Fredric March
Grimes .... Richard Boone
Jessie .... Diane Cilento
Braden .... Cameron Mitchell
Audra Favor .... Barbara Rush
Billy Lee .... Peter Lazer
Doris .... Margaret Blye
Mendez .... Martin Balsam
Steve Early .... Skip Ward
Mexican Bandit ...... Frank Silvera
Lamar Dean .... David Canary
Delgado .... Val Avery
Soldier .... Larry Ward
Apaches .... Pete Hernandez, Merrill C. Isbell
Mrs. Delgado .... Linda Cordova

"Hombre" is a well-executed Martin Ritt-Irving Ravetch production which develops the theme that socially and morally disparate types of people are often thrown into uneasy, explosive alliance due to emergencies. Paul Newman heads a uniformly competent cast of established and upcoming players. Excellent production values and authentic locations enhance the story setting—the late 19th century in the American west. Big b.o. prospects are likely from 20th-Fox release in general situations.

There is a consistent pattern in Ritt films: an unhurried, measured look at interacting human natures, caught up only for story purposes in a given situation. The characters speak truisms which, sometimes, are overdone platitudes. Ritt picks up people in some situation, stays with them for awhile, and as carefully removes his cameras from the scene as he first set them up, seeming to avoid intrusion on nature.

As a result, "Hombre" is no oater film; it is a conscious social commentary on greed, nobility, prejudice and resignation. For those who find such treatments lugubrious, this pic has the virtue of being brief—a well-edited 110 minutes, executed by Frank Bracht. For others, who wish to extrapolate the dialog and situations to life itself, the film has more than enough meat on which to chew.

Ravetch and Harriet Frank Jr. adapted Elmore Leonard's novel about an Apache-raised white boy who becomes the natural leader of a group in its survival against a robber band headed by Richard Boone. Literally, a "Stagecoach" full of personalities are involved.

Newman is excellent as the scorned (but only supposed) Apache. Fredric March, essaying an Indian agent who has embezzled food appropriations for his charges, also scores in a strong, unsympathetic — but eventually pathetic—role. Boone is very powerful, yet admirably restrained as the heavy. Diane Cilento, whose English accent has been completely submerged, exemplified a rugged frontier woman in a superior performance. All earn their above-title position.

Among the featured players, Barbara Rush is outstanding as March's prissy, unloving wife. As with March, the plot in time effects audience sympathy for her, when utilized as a pawn by Boone. And again, as with March, the sensitive direction and acting evokes that sympathy, while limited, because the earlier scenes have not been executed with a heavy hand. Miss Rush's dramatic spectrum is by no means fully exploited.

Professionals such as sheriff-gone-bad Cameron Mitchell and stage-driver Martin Balsam are totally effective in their smaller roles, while newcomers Peter Lazer and Margaret Blye (the unadjusted newlyweds) and David Canary, a very effective heavy, show much potential. Frank Silvera comes over strongly as Boone's bandit ally, and remainder of cast contributes effectively.

James Wong Howe's sensitive DeLuxe Color and Panavision camera records the dust, sweat and rugged natural beauty of the American West. David Rose's score is spare, muted and, in context, very effective and in tune with Ritt's concept. Long non-musical passages have, in effect, their own score—the absolute silence, or rustling natural sounds, as appropriate. Latter, as well as the live-sounding looping, are to the credit of sound editors and recorders. Uncredited title art is firstrate, ditto all other technical credits.

An apparent anachronism in dialog occurs when Newman, explaining to the others why they need his help, says he can "cut it." There is some doubt that the phrase meant "handle the situation" in the era of the film, and, as used to make a plot point, it sticks out. Generally, the truisms do not seem overly awkward platitudes, due to good scripting, acting and direction.

Murf.

Frankenstein Created Woman
(BRITISH—COLOR)

Technically-excellent programmer should be able to hold its own in commercial market. Exploitable title is also major asset.

20th Century-Fox release of a Seven Arts-Hammer Films production. Produced by Anthony Nelson Keys. Directed by Terence Fisher. Features entire cast. Screenplay, John Elder; camera (DeLuxe Color), Arthur Grant; film editor, James Needs; sound, Charlie Wheeler; art director, Don Mingaye; music, composed by James Bernard, supervised by Philip Martell. Reviewed at 20th Century-Fox homeoffice, New York, March 10, '67. Running Time, 92 INS.

Baron Frankenstein ...... Peter Cushing
Christina .... Susan Denberg
Dr. Hertz .... Thorley Walters
Hans .... Robert Morris
Anton .... Peter Blythe
Karl .... Barry Warren
Johann .... Derek Fowlds
Kleve .... Alan MacNaughton
Police Chief .... Peter Madden
Hans (as a boy) ...... Stuart Middleton
Prisoner .... Duncan Lamont
Priest .... Colin Jeavens
New Landlord .... Ivan Beavis
Police Sergeznt .... John Maxim
Mayor .... Philip Ray
Jailer .... Kevin Flood

Dr. Frankenstein's equipment for his do-it-yourself body construcstruction company hasn't improved much over the years (other than some hints at the use of nuclear energy) but the models he's turning out now are a vast improvement over his earlier Boris Karloff and Christopher Lee designs.

In the Hammer-Seven Arts produced "Frankenstein Created Woman," the title is, admittedly, a bit misleading. The good doctor, as usual, played by Peter Cushing, doesn't really create woman, he just makes a few important changes in the design. Considering the result is a beautiful blond Susan Denberg (who did a well-remembered walkon as the maid in Warners' "An American Dream"), most film fans would like to see the doctor get a grant from the Ford Foundation, or even the C.I.A.

This latest variation on the Frankenstein theme has the excellent technical assets which have come to be expected of the Hammer Film people. Production designer Bernard Robinson and art director Don Mingaye, aided by Arthur Grant's DeLuxe color photography, make the visual aspects of the film considerably superior to the script by John Elder which often seems overly influenced by other and better-written screen efforts. James Bernard's score, James Needs' editing and Charlie Wheeler's sound are also good if not particularly imaginative.

Frankenstein, this time out, dabbles as much as in transmigration of souls as actual patchwork surgery, capturing the psyche of an executed young man and instilling it in the body of a drowned young woman (Susan Denberg). The girl, originally a disfigured, shy maiden, is rejuvenated as a beautiful femme whose touch proves tres fatale when the male soul uses the female body to wreak vengeance on the trio of young wastrels responsible for his execution (Peter Blythe, Barry Warren, Derek Fowlds).

Cushing could walk through the Frankenstein part blindfolded by now but still treats it as seriously as though he were playing Hamlet. Thorley Walters, as his kindly, befuddled doctor assistant, is also outstanding. The remainder of the cast is uniformly superior to the roles they're playing but Miss Denberg often seems inhibited by all the clothes she's forced to wear (and playing much of the film with a horribly-scarred face). Duncan Lamont, seen briefly in the pre-title sequence as an executed murderer, is impressive in his short screen life. *Robe.*

In Like Flint
(COLOR-C'SCOPE)

Well-made sequel to "Our Man Flint," reuniting key thesps and production talent for sock eye appeal and good spy comedy spoofing. Bright b.o. prospects while the market lasts for this type of pic.

Hollywood, March 10.
20th Century-Fox release of Saul David production. Features James Coburn, Lee J. Cobb, Jean Hale, Andrew Duggan. Directed by Gordon Douglas. Screenplay, Hal Fimberg; camera (DeLuxe Color), William C. Daniels; editor, Hugh S. Fowler; music, Jerry Goldsmith; song, Goldsmith, Leslie Bricusse; asst. director, David Hall. Reviewed at 20th-Fox Studios, March 9, '67. Running Time, 115 MINS.

Derek Flint	James Coburn
Cramden	Lee J. Cobb
Lisa	Jean Hale
The President	Andrew Duggan
Elisabeth	Anna Lee
Helena	Hanna Landy
Simone	Totty Ames
Carter	Steve Ihnat
Avery	Thomas Hasson
Flint's Girls	Mary Michael, Diane Bond, Jacki Ray
Russian Premier	Herb Edelman
Natasha	Yvonne Craig
Austin	Buzz Henry
Cooper	Henry Wills
Russian Agent	John Lodge
Hilda	Mary Meade French
Amazons	Erin O'Brien, Ginny Gan, Eve Bruce, Inge Jaklyn, Kaye Farrington, Thordis Brandt, Inga Neilsen, Marilyn Hanold
Salon Clients	Pat Becker, Lyzanne La Due, Nancy Stone
Bill Lear	W. P. Lear Sr.

Girls, gimmicks, girls, gags and more girls are the essential parameters of producer Saul David's "In Like Flint", sequel to last year's "Our Man Flint" spy comedy spoof. With James Coburn encoring as the urbane master sleuth, also harried boss Lee J. Cobb this time getting greater comedy play, new pic turns on a femme plot to take over the world. Snazzy

production values, effects and sets enhance the visual impact over and above the built-in girl-watcher selling lure. In a flooded, possibly saturated, market of sleuth pix, this 20th-Fox release can more than hold its own in general situations.

Besides stars and producer, sequel also has Flint creator Hal Fimberg (this time solo-credited), as well as key special effects and action sequence technicians, all of whom lend a big hand. Dale Hennessy, Jack Martin Smith's creative art director associate on "Fantastic Voyage," is a new staffer, however.

As for the story, the tongue is best put way out in the cheek, since serious analysis would reveal it to flirt around with lesbian angles. To wit, Anna Lee, ever a charming and gracious screen personality, is part of a triumvirate bent on seizing world power.

Her femme troops, ranging from truck-driver types to nymphets, seem content in their own world. Coburn, it is suggested, is about the only man to keep his girls in heterosexual thrall. This script angle is in opposition to the James Bond plots, all of which are basically anti-feminine, in that the dames are strictly transient sex partners, possessing no individuality but only functional availability.

Miss Lee's plot in this film comes acropper when her male allies — corrupt General Steve Ihnat and cohorts, who have substituted an actor, Andrew Duggan, for the real U. S. President, also played by Duggan — move in to snatch the ultimate prize.

Coburn, natch, is the only man who can save the day, and, between other cultural and pulchritudinal pursuits, squeezes into his busy sked the rescue of civilization from the female of the species. With a fine pedantic urbanity, Coburn registers strongly.

Cobb, second-featured after Coburn (all names follow the title), gets an offbeat (for him) chance to show his comic talents, as the befuddled secret project supervisor who, in the Lee–Ihnat-Duggan machinations, is discredited via a badger game frame-up. Combining proper authority with high and low comedy angles (including a bit in femme attire), all in balance under the craftsmanlike direction of Gordon Douglas, Cobb is excellent.

Jean Hale, who has moved up from legit, vidshows & teleblurbs, has more looks than dramatic polish, as of now, but the former will tide her over nicely until the latter is more manifest. As is, she has a strong glamor-gal potential. Duggan, Ihnat and other players render very good support.

While the dialog scenes tend to be a mite sluggish, pace picks up regularly with slam-bang action sequences, Buzz Henry's work, and special photographic effects, by L. B| Abbott, Art Cruickshanck and Emil Kosa, Jr., both blended well with William C. Daniel's firstrate CinemaScope - DeLuxe Color lensing which extracts maximum value from sets, wardrobe (Ray Aghayan) and the beautiful girls. Hugh S. Fowler edited to 115 minutes, a little more than

optimum length but within good programming and plot bounds.

Jerry Goldsmith is back again with a zesty score, and the Flint theme eventually is sung over end titles. Leslie Bricusse supplied the serviceable lyrics. The psychedelic main title montage, a strong attention-getter, was done by Richard Kuhn and National Screen Service. Producer David, and associate producer Martin Fink, have selected a most professional film crew from top to bottom. *Murf.*

Le Voleur
(The Thief)
(FRENCH—COLOR)

Paris, March 5.
United Artists release of UA-Nouvelles Editions De Films-Comoania Cinematografica production. Stars Jean-Paul Belmondo; features Genevieve Bujold, Marie Dubois. Directed by Louis Malle. Screenplay, Jean-Claude Carriere, Daniel Boulanger, Malle, from the novel by Georges Darien; camera (Eastmancolor), Henri Decae; editor, Elisabeth Rappeneau. At George V, Paris. Running Time, 120 MINS.

Randal	Jean-Paul Belmondo
Caroline	Genevieve Bujold
Genevieve	Marie Dubois
Priest	Julien Guiomar
Roger	Paul Le Person
Uncle	Christian Lude
Renee	Martine Sarcey
Madame	Francoise Fabien
Sister	Marlene Joubert
Cannonier	Charles Denner

Tale of a turn-of-the-century thief and how he became that way and stayed one when he no longer had to, allows director Louis Malle to paint a partial portrait of the times. It also incisively pinpoints the mixture of revolt against the hypocrisy of the monied and political powers and classes of the era that sometimes led to criminality.

But picaresque tale eschews action and derring-do for its own sake. It is handled with tact and almost cold detachment as it chronicles the work of an amateur who begins to steal because of anger and revenge and becomes a professional who then must go on, for it has turned into his only way of living. Stealing has become a rite, a distorted form of action against a hated way of life.

Malle's treatment of only this facet of the man, with but a few glimpses of the times, gives this a slow if absorbing rhythm. It appears a film whose visual elegance and theme may have it in for art possibilities in more selective areas abroad, but depth chances appear more limited. Careful handling will also count in getting the most of this study of an almost detached, alienated modern-type man in the suffocating early 1900s.

Story is told in flashback as the hero is coldly and painstakingly ransacking a deserted villa. His childhood attachment to his pretty girl cousin who later rejects him, his guardian-uncle's attempt to inculcate disdain for poverty, and his self-indulgence and opportunism are blocked out, as is the boy's coming of age to find that his uncle has swindled him of his inheritance. He takes to a life of crime.

Aided by excellent color, fine costuming and expert thesping down the line, the rise of the thief is shown. He takes up with a corrupt priest who seems to be

putting his money in church works; a poet-thief, and various renegade bourgeois types who betray their own for needed kickbacks from the thieves by fingering empty villas.

The beginnings of fascist talk in politics by naming scapegoats, harsh police tactics and the sometimes mixed political anarchist and crime activities of the underworld are also etched in the background of the thief's progress. He gets back his cousin, gets revenge on his uncle, even picks up a woman companion when he finds a wife trying to break into her husband's safe as he comes to do it.

Pic does not condone crime but only delves into it as a way of life that can spring up through the inability to act in other ways. Belmondo gives a solid presence to the main role and a restrained violence that breaks out at times. He definitely shows himself one of the gifted young actors on the scene. Genevieve Bujold has a fragile prettiness that masks a fairly grasping nature, and Marie Dubois, as a twisted wife who takes to thievery, and Julien Guiomar, as the priest-thief, also add fine portraits. In fact, the thesping is extremely well handled by director Malle.

Malle shows himself one of the more talented young filmmakers here, if there is still a coldness in his work. Based on an anarchistic novel of the early 1900s, it is transcribed to film with a visual grace and finesse. It is a solid, intriguing pic full of topnotch production values, but it still needs careful handling, followup and placement for best results abroad. *Mosk.*

C'mon, Let's Live a Little
(SONGS-TECHNISCOPE-COLOR)

Tuneful entry for youth market with Bobby Vee and Jackie DeShannon.

Hollywood, March 8.
Paramount release of All Star Pictures-Hertelandy (June Starr-John Hertelandy) production. Stars Bobby Vee, Jackie DeShannon, Eddie Hodges; features Suzie Kaye, Patsy Kelly. Directed by David Butler. Screenplay, June Starr; camera (Technicolor), Carl Berger; editor, Eve Newman; music, Don Ralke; songs, Don Crawford; asst. director, Glenn N. Cook. Reviewed at Paramount Studios, March 8, '67. Running Time, 84 MINS.

Jesse Crawford	Bobby Vee
Judy Grant	Jackie DeShannon
Eddie Stewart	Eddie Hodges
Bee Bee Vendemeer	Suzie Kaye
Mrs. Fitts	Patsy Kelly
Rego	John Ireland Jr.
Tim Grant	Mark Evans
John W. Grant	Russ Conway
Wendy	Jill Banner
Melinda	Kim Carnes
Joy	Joy Tobin
Balta	Frank Alesia
The Beard	Ken Osmond
Jeb Crawford	Don Crawford
Spuko	Tiger Joe Marsh
Jake	Ben Frommer
An' Effel	Ethel Smith
Bo-Bo	Bo Belinsky
The Pair Extraordinaire	

There are enough song numbers and youthful movement in this modestly - turned - out musical to rate acceptance in its tended market. Bobby Vee and Jackie DeShannon names — both on the Liberty label — should attract the pop music trade who may also find the cavorting in light story line to their liking. A dozen numbers are whipped over for good effect.

The June Starr-John Hertelandy production takes its tab from a fast production number chirped by Suzie Kaye, standout in the picture which has a particular winner in Vee's rendition of "What Fool This Mortal Be." Vee plays an Arkansas country boy who is enrolled at a small college where Jackie De-Shannon is the president's daughter. Script by Miss Starr gets most of its motivation from a college senior (John Ireland, Jr.) using the boy from the country and his folk singing to cue his free speech movement.

Vee is ingratiating in his role and plays part naturally, scoring again particularly with "Instant Girl." Miss DeShannon's top tune is "Baker Man," doing better with her warbling than with her thesping. Eddie Hodges is the comic, Vee's dormitory roommate running for class prexy, and knows his ropes.

Suzie Kaye is cute and saucy as entertainer in night spot operated by Bo Belinsky, who is okay as an actor. He gets a laugh from the line, when Hodges tells him "we're taking you out"..."that's the story of my life." Patsy Kelly handles herself in her customary blatant manner as housekeeper of the school prexy, ably delineated by Russ Conway, and Ireland is good enough as the heavy. Mark Evans is a collegiate.

David Butler's direction is in the mood and he gets good technical backing right down the line. Credits here include Carl Berger on color cameras, Eve Newman's editing. Frank Sylos' art direction and Don Crawford's songs.
Whit.

Le Scandale
(The Scandal)
(FRENCH-COLOR-TECHNISCOPE)

Paris, March 7.
Universal Productions France release and production. Stars Maurice Ronet, Anthony Perkins, Yvonne Furneaux; features Stephane Audran, Annie Vidal, Suzanne Lloyd, Christa Lang. Directed by Claude Chabrol. Screenplay, Claude Brule, Derek Prouse, Paul Gegauff, from a story by William Benjamin; camera (Eastmancolor), Jean Rabier; editor, Jacques Gaillard. Previewed in Paris. Running Time, 107 MINS.

Paul .... Maurice Ronet
Chris .... Anthony Perkins
Christine .... Yvonne Furneaux
Jacqueline .... Annie Vidal
Blonde .... Stephane Audran
Evelyne .... Suzanne Lloyd
Denise .... Caterine Sola
Loukhoum .... George Skaff
Michele .... Marie Ange Anies

Universal made this suspenser here in two versions, French and English, and has a sleek pic with enough twists to keep it going its 107 minutes. With the Anthony Perkins name for stateside, it could emerge an okay playoff item in the U.S. and other spots.

Director Claude Chabrol has given this a satirical and tongue-in-cheek tang alongside its suspense aspects, plus a dash of sex, French high life and psycho underpinnings. Chabrol, long an admirer of Alfred Hitchcock, and who once wrote a book on him, shows some influences of the master but in a good assimilated sense and not in an aping way.

The murders are peremptory, people are not always what they seem, but the clues are there and even clear to those who may notice them.

A rich young man, who controls a champagne company, with a climbing woman married to an American gigolo, has a brain concussion when he is attacked in his car in a park while necking with a pickup.

He finds himself getting anonymous letters when he spends a drunken night with a prostie on a business trip to Hamburg. He passes out at a party, and another girl is lying dead beside him. Did he do it? His associate? Somebody else? The gigolo?

It all ends in a snake pit scene of the man, gigolo and culprit struggling as the camera comes up and shows them as specks cavorting about.

Maurice Ronet is charming as the would-be psycho and Anthony Perkins has his disarming boyishness, underspinned with menace, as the ladies' man, while Yvonne Furneaux is properly cold as the wife and Stephane Andran rightly menacing as a blonde who was along on the date in Hamburg when the first murder occurred and keeps showing up in strange spots.

Director Chabrol is sometimes too earthy in his gross satire of French monied classes but has a keen eye for decorative use of color, sudden shafts of menace and a solid narrative style. This is a shrewd murder yarn that should have okay playoff legs and good following in the action-suspense markets, though more demanding firstrün would need harder sell. It has fine production dress and a plus in having complete French and English versions.
Mosk.

Chafed Elbows

Another N.Y. film underground release for selected college and hip situations. 'Grownups' may hate it. Satire of wild themes, including incest.

Goosedown Production released through Filmmakers' Distribution Center, produced, written and directed by Robert Downey. Features George Morgan, Elsie Downey and Lawrence Wolfe. Photography by Stan Warnow. Edited by Fred Von Bernewitz, Robert Soukis. Reviewed at Bleecker St. Cinema, March 12, '67. Running Time, 63 MINS.
Walter Dinsmore .... George Morgan
All Women (12) .... Elsie Downey
Oliver Sinfield and 34 voices
                            Lawrence Wolfe

Despite all the current delirium and cooing critical response by several publications to the recurrently aborning so-called "New York film underground," that segment of U.S. production has produced little of note with the exception of some gangrenous peeks into the social underground of sexual perversion and artless chaos.

Count as an exception Robert Downey's zany "Chafed Elbows," not because it displays any tangible signs of maturity in "the movement" (no one really wants those cinematic gadflies to exhibit *that* tendency), but because its refreshing screwball irreverence and laudatory attempt to achieve technical faultlessness on a mini-budget (it can be seen, heard and generally understood—a rarity in the genre) is a welcome breath of air in the self-righteous and self-promoting "underground." Though "Elbows" has many evident faults, among them a proclivity for the scatological, its most salient virtue is that it doesn't take itself or any of its several hundred establishment and anti-establishment targets seriously.

The film is composed of about 80% photographed and angled still shots, and the balance actual "moving" pictures in color. The editing makes for ingenious construction.

Through constantly quipping and chattering voice-over narrative and dialog track, "Elbows" flips from episode to episode in the Oedipal life of its Candide-like hero Walter Dinsmore with deftly rapid pace.

Along the way Downey takes off after motherhood (Dinsmore's mother wears combat boots and attempts to lure Walter home with promises of French toast), the police (Dinsmore, disguised as a cop, fires two "warning" shots into the shoulder of another patrolman), advertising (an inserted commercial teasingly sings the virtues of "Kiss-Pruf" lipstick for virgins), civil rights (a "liberal" outlines his plans for a Southern Disneyland with mechanical reenactments of lynching as a money-making scheme), pornography (a slithering street shill attempts to sell Dinsmore an 8 x 10 glossy of Margaret Rutherford in the buff), pop music (Dinsmore records a disk entitled "Black Leather Negligee"), and even the underground cinema itself ("all the action is behind the camera," says Walter).

Downey, who cannot be faulted for subtlety, assails these and other contemporary neuroses with a spiked bludgeon, which is, despite his occasional lead-footedness, frequently hilarious.

Spare picaresque plotline generally follows Walter Dinsmore's episodic experiences during what he describes as his "annual January breakdown"—the aftermath of his exit from mother's pad. Pushing the cliche post-Freudian Oedipus complex beyond all previous reference to the syndrome, Downey has Dinsmore actually carrying on an affair with his mother ("so what if I'm robbing the cradle," she croaks, "it's my own"), and marrying her at the pic's finale. They settle down in the suburbs and live on welfare until he gets a job with Vogue magazine.

Major flaws of "Elbows" is its sometimes hair-raising excessiveness, which constantly strains the limits of the merely outrageous. Its slapstick humor, though, generally saves it from degenerating giddily into the unacceptably absurd. Tripping along at a frenetic pace, the film subjects the audience to a ceaseless barrage of gags, some unmercifully corny, others funny, and most of the sophomoric genre of collegiate humor.

It is this frenetic pacing, coupled with "Elbows" madcap outrageousness and generally on-target satire that will determine its audience. Though the film will probably be offensive to the older generation, with the proper handling it could do well in college and "hip" locale theatres, barring local censorship hitches.

Reminiscent of some of Nathan-iel West's early "black humor" tales ("The Dismantling of Lemuel Pitkin" and "The Dream Life of Balso Snell"), Downey's sense of the ludicrous approaches Rabelais filtered through Frank Tashlin and Pete Smith (of "Specialties" fame). Constantly hovering over the edge of tastelessness, and occasionally wallowing in it, his "Chafed Elbows" exhibits the beginnings of a so-called "commercial" talent, i.e., if it's controllable. Downey's especial claim, though, is his respect for technical polish which seems to be shunned by other subterranean filmmakers.

Though performances are difficult to gauge since most of the narrative is furthered by stills, George Morgan's expressions are apt as a latterday Candide. Elsie Downey (the director's wife) displays excellent comedic range as more than a dozen women, while Lawrence Wolfe's schizoid analyst and 34 different voices are consistently amusing.
Rino.

Ai No Kawaki
(The Thirst For Love)
(JAPANESE)

Tokyo, Feb. 14.
A Nikkatsu production and release. With Ruriko Asaoka, Tetsuo Ishidate, Nobuo Nakamura, Chitose Kurenai, Akira Yamanouchi. Directed by Koreyoshi Kurahara. Produced by Kanou Otsuka; screenplay, Shigeo Fujita and Kurahara based on novel by Yukio Mishima; camera, Yoshio Mamiya; music, Toshiro Mayuzumi. Completed, spring, 1966; released, Feb. 16, 1967. Previewed in Tokyo. Running-Time, 105 MINS.

An adaptation of a very early short novel of Yukio Mishima, "Ai No Kawaki" is a sometimes brilliant and always well-made film which, with tact and delicacy, delineates some of the most convoluted psychology to be seen on the recent Japanese screen.

So convoluted, indeed, that the film's showing has been delayed almost a year. Director Koreyoshi Kurahara, a young Nikkatsu staff director whose "Kuroi Taiyo" (Black Sun) was one of 1965's most unusual films, had been wanting to make the Mishima book into a film for some time. Upon completion it had a routine showing at the Nikkatsu studios where the president of the company happened to see it. The word went out that it was not to be released and the reason given was that the audience would not understand it.

This is not the first fine film that the industry has put into deep-freeze ("Rashomon" almost suffered that fate), but nowadays it costs almost as much to freeze a film as it does to make it and that is perhaps the reason it is now being released, a year later.

Actually, today's audience will understand it a lot better than the confections that are Nikkatsu's usual fare. For one thing, it is about problems that some of them are concerned with; for another, it treats these problems with insight and dignity.

A still young widow (Ruriko Asaoka) is living with her late husband's family and enduring the attentions of his father (Nobuo Nakamura). Lonely, caught, but wanting to live, she finds herself drawn toward one of the servants, a young gardener who is barely more than a boy (Tetsuo Ishidate). She does not let the youth know what she is feeling, but audience knows.

Yoshio Mamiya's camera lingers on flesh, caresses it; the image, purposely over-exposed, turning blazing white. Director Kurahara gazes at the heroine, capturing the tightness around her eyes, showing us her barely controlled desire, her all but uncontrolled despair, all the contradictory emotions of a woman in love despite herself.

When she learns that the boy has gotten one of the servant girls pregnant (Chitose Kurenai) she will not rest until she has made her get rid of the child. By this time the entire family is aware of her infatuation—the only one who does not know is apparently, the boy himself. In a ghastly but very funny dinner (with the first movement of Beethoven's "Fifth" thundering away on the phonograph), the brother (Akira Yamanouchi), drunk, tries to give her some advice, but she is no longer to be reasoned with.

That evening she commands the boy, as her mistress, to meet her at night in the greenhouse. He does so and she tells him what she did to his child. His relief shocks her, she who had built about him an ideal person which he in no way resembles—he is simply a healthy, animal-like youth. Ironically, it is her father-in-law who puts the weapon in her hands and she kills the boy just as heedlessly as she loved him.

This ironic, absurd, and disturbing tragedy has been brilliantly illustrated by Kurahara. He uses every cinematic technique that serves his purpose—flashcuts, almost subliminal frames of clor in a black-and-white context, negative shots, slow-motion. But more important, he has not concerned himself merely with technique—he wants to picture an emotion as clearly, strongly, and honestly as he can. And he succeeds.

Chie.

Easy Come, Easy Go
(COLOR-SONGS)

Very good Elvis Presley pic. Drive - In b.o. particularly bright.

Hollywood, March 15.
Paramount release of Hal B. Wallis production. Stars Elvis Presley. Directed by John Rich. Screenplay, Allan Weiss, Anthony Lawrence; camera (Technicolor), William Margulies; editor, Archie Marshek; music, Joseph J. Lilley; asst. director, Robert Goodstein. Reviewed at Paramount Studios, L.A., March 14, '67. Running Time, **95 MINS.**

Ted Jackson	Elvis Presley
Jo Symington	Dodie Marshall
Dina Bishop	Pat Priest
Judd Whitman	Pat Harrington
Gil Carey	Skip Ward
Schwartz	Sandy Kenyon
Capt. Jack	Frank McHugh
Madame Neherina	Elsa Lanchester
Cooper	Ed Griffith
Ship's Officers	Read Morgan, Mickey Elley
Vicki	Elaine Beckett
Mary	Shari Nims
Zoltan	Diki Lerner
Artist	Robert Isenberg

"Easy Come, Easy Go" is another well-made Hal B. Wallis production starring Elvis Presley, this time as an underwater demolitions expert who finds lost treasure. Good balance of script and songs, plus generally amusing performances by a competent, well-directed cast, add up to diverting entertainment. Commercial prospects are bright for Paramount release in general situations, particularly drive-ins.

This is the ninth Presley-Wallis pic, on which Col. Tom Parker is, natch, again screen-credited as technical advisor. Elvis now is in his 11th year as a film headliner, and this is his 24th pic. He began above the title in "Love Me Tender," a late 1956 20th-Fox release), and he is still there, rightfully so. Somewhat slimmer here than in recent pix, Elvis looks great and ageless, although his maturity shows in the acting department.

The word "formula" is too negative if applied to Elvis pix, although, to be sure, a given story line is simple, admitting of tune inserts, and assured of happy resolution. Anyone who has seen similar films recognizes the superior quality of Presley films: the story makes sense; the songs are better, and better motivated; cast and direction are stronger; production values are fistrate. A generation from now, Elvis pix will be film festival items, just as the Busby Berkely, Astaire-Rogers and Mae West pix are now.

Paul Nathan again has functioned very effectively as Wallis' associate producer. The Allan Weiss-Anthony Lawrence script (their third for Elvis, after "Roustabout" and "Paradise, Hawaiian Style") has star as a U.S. Navy demolitions man who, on mine-disposal chores off the California coast, discovers sunken treasure. Leaving the service, Elvis decides to claim the booty for himself.

Partnered with ex-biz partner Pat Harrington (who comes across very well as a bearded beatnik type), Elvis faces surmountable problems in the resistance of Dodie Marshall (an excellent young actress with appealing warmth and looks for meatier sympathetic roles), whose grandfather owned the sunken ship. The heavies are Pat Priest (excellent also as the

out-for-kicks, hardened rich dame) and her current beach-bum tagalong, Skip Ward (a bit stiff in some sequences, but overall okay for the part).

Frank McHugh has some good satirical scenes as the bathtub sailor (he was a tv kiddie show sailor) who overcames chronic seasickness. Elsa Lanchester shines in her bit as the kooky yoga instructor, and Diki Lerner sticks out as an effete artist with a flair for turning automobiles into mobiles. Rest of cast is good.

John Rich's direction is assured, although the two major underwater sequences run on too long before action develops. William Margulies' Technicolor camera has caught the splashy exterior-interior production values, including the colorful Edith Head wardrobe while Michael J. Dugan shot the underwater scenes. Uncredited songs (6) are easy on the ears, scored well by Joseph J. Lilley and choreographed in effective, and deceptive simplicity by David Winters. The Jordonaires, long-time Elvis backers, assist in the vocal department. Archie Marshek trimmed to a good 95 minute, a bit over optimum because of the underwater overlength. Other credits are pro. As usual, film's copyright rests in Wallis and partner Joseph Hazen.

Murf.

Quiere Casarse Conmigo?
(Would You Marry Me?)
(ARGENTINE-SPANISH-COLOR)

Buenos Aires, March 21.
Argentina Sono Film release of JCG (Argentina) and Suevia Films-Cesareo Gonzalez (Spain) coproduction. Stars Palito Ortega, Sonia Bruno; features Tono Andreu, Eddie Pequenino, Mariquita Gallegos, Aida Luz, Juan Carlos Altavista, Guido Gorgatti. Directed by Enrique Carreras. Screenplay, Abel Santa Cruz, adapted from his own comedy "Los Ojos Llenos de Amor"; camera (Eastmancolor), Antonio Merayo; music, Tito Ribero; editor, Jorge Garate. At Monumental, Buenos Aires. Running Time, **82 MINS.**

Tito	Palito Ortega
Chorus Girl	Sonia Bruno
Waiter	Tono Andreu
Sampognato	Eddie Pequenino
Mother	Aida Luz
Other Woman	Mariquita Gallegos

First of several new Argentine-Spanish coproductions aimed at far-reaching objectives, among them to enlarge markets by promoting Argentine names in Spain and Spanish ones in Latin America, this sitcom pairs young local warbler composer Palito Ortega, with Catalonian actress Sonia Bruno.

This remake of Abel Santa Cruz's play "Los Ojos Llenos de amor" (Eyes Full of Love) doesn't measure up to hopes largely because it depends heavily on the original legit play's dialogue. Its action seldom escapes the small apartment where a bachelor star reluctantly houses an ardent fan who had asked him to let her pretend to be his wife for one month, in exchange for having saved him from a jealous impresario. Occasional visual reliefs are provided by some locations forcibly introduced either to visualize the girl's dreams or to illustrate some half a dozen songs rather arbitrarily dragged into the comedy.

Further, Ortega is miscast as the foppish star, which forces director Carreras to resort to a direct, sometimes childish comic style. This is far distant from the sophistication that gave charm to the original play both on stage and in its first film version. However, some situations are still effective enough to make undemanding audiences laugh. This, added to names and color, may help in selling to Spanish lingo spots abroad.

Le Judoka Agent Secret
(FRENCH-COLOR)

Paris, March 14.
Gaumont release of France Cinema Production, Tigielle 33 production. Stars Jean-Claude Bercq, Marilu Tolo, Perrette Pradier, Patricia Viterbo; features Henri Garcin, Yves Brainville. Directed by Pierre Zimmer. Screenplay, Jacques Guymont, Zimmer, from book by Ernie Clerk; camera (Eastmancolor), Gilbert Sarthre; editor, Genevieve Vaury. At Mercury, Paris. Running Time, **90 MINS.**

Marc	Jean-Claude Bercq
Vanessa	Marilu Tolo
Dominique	Perrette Pradier
Catherine	Patricia Viterbo
Jacques	Henri Garcin
Chief	Yves Brainville

This is another newcomer joining the hordes of undercover agents who have sprung up on world screens since the advent of James Bond. This one uses judo and karate only, but that is his only distinguishing feature from the many who have preceded him. Listless tale, so-so direction and a lack of bite and bounce tag this mainly a local item with only dualler or playoff chances abroad, or on tv, on some well-done fight sequences and good color.

Agent comes up against an underworld group who are trying to abduct an atomic scientist. The judo man, called the Judoka, is with the French secret service and is soon tracking down the gang. He puts many away with his chops, judo and bombast and manages to find time to seduce one of the gang members who turns out to be a British agent.

Crisp dialog does not have the corresponding dash in direction, sharpness in characterization and originality of plot to keep this afloat and of interest. Jean-Claude Bercq is fine in action but a bit wooden as a man, and the girls do not have much to do. Comedy relief is by Henri Garcin who needs better material for his obvious good timing and presence. It's a standard entry in the spy stakes.

Mosk.

Y Manana ?
BELGIAN-SPANISH)

Brussels, March 10.
Progres Film release of L. Boogaerts production with Jacques Dufilho, Claudia Bremer. Written, directed, edited by Emile Degelin. Camera: Andre Goeffers. Music: Jos Mertens. Reviewed at Fine Arts, Brussels, March 9, '67. Running Time: **90 MINS.**

Jerome	Jacques Dufilho
Girl	Claudia Bremer

What could have been a pleasant trifle has, due to maker Emile Degelin's over-ambitious designs, become a bore. He seemingly wanted to express the vision of the world of loneliness of a simple-minded individual. Imagination, poetical insight, a touch of fantasy and the absurd were all called for but here sadly lacking. Degelin's previous directorial effort, "If the Wind Scares You," a story of incest, was perhaps more in his line, which does not mean it escaped heaviness and pomposity.

There is nothing funny in situations so old-fashioned that one gets the impression Degelin sat through hours of footage projection of Buster Keaton comedies of the heroic period. The initial situation falls flat.

It all concerns a Flemish gendarme stranded on a Spanish island. He tries in vain to get aboard the next Brussels-bound plane but has to wait for days, his dreams transplanted in reality. Lonely, he gets more and more disconnected; happier, too, apparently.

That's all. As played by French comic Jacques Dufilho, and as directed, one does not feel a bit concerned.

Claudia Bremer adds pulchritude as a recurrent vision. All the others play their very small roles much like silent era, namely, underlining everything at least twice.

Technical credits are good. There is very little dialogue, mostly in Spanish, as the film was made on Ibiza. *Flor.*

Tre Mand Frem For En Trold
(Three Men In Search of a Troll)
(DANISH-COLOR)

Copenhagen, Feb. 27.
A A/S Constantin Films release of Rialto Film/Preben Philipsen production. Written and directed by Knud Leif Thomsen. Features Joergen Ryg, Ebbe Rode, Axel Stroebye, Lone Hertz; camera (Eastmancolor), Lars Bjoerne, Henning Kristiansen; music, Thorkild Knudsen.; in charge of production, Leif Feilberg. Reviewed at Nygade Teatret, Copenhagen. Running Time, 96 MINS.

While the Swedes in their films are usually deadly serious about their sex, the Danes are apt to treat the subject as much less than a sacred cow. Too often, perhaps, they treat it more in a self-consciously farcical way, as if it were a gag about how to slip on cowdroppings. Knud Leif Thomsen, primarily a social critic of a rightish conviction, in "Three Men" folows the farce trend and does his own amount of slipping.

Thomsen, however, is much more of a craftsman than run-of-mill Danish farce directors, and his little tale about modern man's need of a belief in the supernatural and of his prompt commercial abuse of it once he meets it, has plenty of soft guffaws in between the loud and loutish humor.

Story is of a newspaperman's discovery of something that looks like a troll—a pagan forest being of Nordic mythology—based on a nature photographer's casual shot. Off go newspaperman Axel Stroebye, photographer Joergen Ryg, an outstanding Danish comic actor with more than a touch of genuine human, soft-spoken madness, and scientist Ebbe Rode into the woods of southern Sweden to prove or disprove the troll's existance.

One troll they do meet is Lone Hertz, who this time around is all sweetness and no spice as a charcoal burner's daughter with in-

clinations toward nocturnal bathing in the nude. She is also a sexy little wench, but in all her innocence nobody would suspect that she was invented by the man who currently is creating controversies with censors in many countries over his bitter, black and white sex-and-society treatise "gift" (Venom).

"Three Men" should make it nicely on those markets where Palladium's "Crazy Paradise" and "Soya's Seventeen" have been hits. But it is the first Knud Leif Thomsen film sure not to be accepted by any festival until they open one for junk pix. *Kell.*

Cinq Gars Pour Singapour
(Five Ashore For Singapore)
(FRENCH-COLOR)

Paris, March 6.
Rank release of Films Numbre One-Poste Parisien production. Stars Sean Flynn; features Marika Green, Terry Downes, Marc Michel, Denis Berry, Bernard Meusnier, Peter Gayford, Andre Ray, Jessy Greek. Directed by Bernard T. Michel. Screenplay, Michel, Pierre Kalfon, based on the book by Jean Bruce; camera (Eastmancolor), Jean Charvein; music, Antoine Duhamel. Previewed in Paris. Running Time, 105 MINS.

Art	Sean Flynn
Monica	Marika Green
Gruber	Terry Downes
Kevin	Marc Michel
Dan	Denis Berry
Angel	Bernard Meusnier
Brown	Peter Gayford
Tat-Chouen	Andrew Ray
Ten-Sin	Jessy Greek
Tchin-Saw	Trudy Connor
Captain	William Brix

Pierre Kolfon is an astute young producer on the local scene. Knowing that an actioner needs more markets than the local one, he has made two versions, in English and French, with Rank having already released in Europe and Britain and with Paramount probably taking it for the U.S. It is mainly a programmer in its mixture of old marine tactics and more James Bondish undertones.

If it lacks a more dynamic, disarming violence, with some of it brutish rather than done in romantic good spirits, it keeps moving along in spite of inadequate scripting and to many loopholes. It is all about Yank marines disappearing in Hong Kong and a CIA man and four marines sent out to find out why. The CIA bit may be an added hypo tag at that.

The group immediately starts tearing up the town. The reasoning seems to be that that will more easily lead to the kidnaping and get to the heart of the affair. So they break up a nightclub and are sure enough drugged and lugged off. But one wakes up ahead of time and only one is kidnaped. And so it goes till they find a madman with a Harvard background is keeping Yanks in deep freeze and then restoring them brainwashed. Presumably to sell to China, or is it the Viet Cong?

Direction is serviceable, if lacking sufficient tempo and wit. Playing is as broad as the tale with Sean Flynn crisp and dedicated as the CIA man. On-the-spot lensing helps and this may be an clay dualer for general programming abroad. *Mosk.*

Sales Temps Pour Les Mouches
(Bad Time For Squealers)
(FRENCH-COLOR)

Paris, March 21.
CCFC release of Jacques Roitfeld production. Stars Gerard Barray, Jean Richard; features Paul Preboist, Patricia Viterbo, Philippe Clay, Nicole Maurey. Directed by Guy Lefranc. Screenplay, Gilles Dumoulin, Guy Lionel, Michel Audiard from character created by Frederic Dard; camera (Eastmancolor), Didier Tarot; editor, Robert Isnardon. At Mercury, Paris. Running Time, 90 MINS.

San Antonio	Gerard Barray
Berrurier	Jean Richard
Pinaud	Paul Preboist
Felix	Philippe Clay
Eva	Nicole Maurey
Sylvie	Patricia Viterbo
Old Man	Jean Galland

Character of ladykiller, handsome French police inspector of special services, San Antonio, has been a popular tele, radio, book and comic strip figure. So it was only a matter of time before getting into a screen production. So here it is and it's a rather obvious and stolidly plotted affair. Film benefits from some well-handled fights and one original touch in a battle by two parachutists in free fall. Otherwise, this is standard action hokum, mainly for the French mart.

San Antonio makes believe he has turned renegade and manages to get into a gang kidnaping scientists for some unnamed Eastern power. He is fast on the draw and girls. And he manages to use many gimmicks. Otherwise, this pic falls into standard detective action folds.

There is the comic sidekick who in this case is also brutish and gluttonous. Role is played by Jean Richard in such a vulgar manner that it excludes the usual zest associated with these roles. Gerard Barray as San Antonio has wooden good looks but not the required dash for such a detective character. It appears in for good local returns but is somewhat heavy-handed for much foreign draw. *Mosk.*

Lenny Bruce

Photographic record of night club routine by the now-deceased disciple of verbal assault on Anglo-Saxon taboos.

Film-Makers Distribution Center release. Reviewed March 20, 1967 at W. 41 St. Theatre, New York. Running Time, 68 MINS.

Sociologists, moralists, critics and just plain curious folk have already exhausted themselves in a futile attempt to explain, dissect and properly catalog the weird phenomenon that was Lenny Bruce. Seeing him on a screen today, after his dismal final years and pathetic death, it is possible to recognize the stamp of doom on his countenance which, nonetheless, occasionally comes alive, as if fascinated by his own convoluted mental processes.

Because of the great interest in his career and the determined attempt of many to see him as a hero of some sort of necessary rebuke to gentility, it seems likely that this 68 minutes reprise of an actual performance in a nightclub (San Francisco) will have some commercial potential in hideaway sprocket parlors. It was unreeling from Palm Sunday (sic) onward at $2 top in a basement theatre off the garment district, where caught.

The flat-lighted camera picks up Bruce and never leaves him. The only action is his own stage business, now facing one way or another, sometimes giving his back to the lens. Working with a handmike he is sometimes unintelligible though mostly clear. This particular performance took the form of a semi-ad lib on one of the police summons, which he uses as an aide-memoir.

A defiant, unregenerate, physically-ravaged man nearing the end of his life, the question for the average person is not easily answered. This is funny? Witty rather than humorous, over-working the foul language not for its own sake but from lifelong habit (a distinction there!) Bruce keeps suggesting a barracks room "card."

Making capital of his own floor-show routine as picked up and converted into a legal charge of obscenity it is less interesting as a comic rebuttal than as an auto-biographical portrait of the artist in extremis. How boy-like the obsession with four-letter words seems! How monotonous, because ultimately incoherent, the semi-cerebral patter becomes! One is finally saddened for the man and his talent and his fixated postures of rebellion.

What Lenny Bruce proves, other than the pity of self-destructive tendencies, is far from clear, but at a guess he would have gotten nowhere without the filth. He needed it. In this he reeks of the worst of the burlesque comics and only a new generation would be confused by his Freudian vocabulary and air of education. *Land.*

The Honey Pot
(BRITISH-COLOR)

Lushly outfitted, elegantly sophisticated comedy but occasionally tedious, for discriminating audiences. Tends to overlength and burdened with basically misleading title. Marquee strength an assist for required strong sell.

London, March 22.
United Artists release of a Charles K. Feldman presentation written, produced and directed by Joseph L. Mankiewicz; based on the book by Thomas Sterling and play by Frederick Knott. Stars Rex Harrison, Susan Hayward, Cliff Robertson, Capucine, Edie Adams, Maggie Smith; features Adolfo Celi, Herschel Bernardi; camera (Technicolor), Gianni Di Venanzo; editor, David Bretherton; music, John Addison. Reviewed at Odeon, Marble Arch, London, March 21, '67. Running Time, 150 MINS.

Cecil Fox	Rex Harrison
Mrs. Sheridan	Susan Hayward
William McFly	Cliff Robertson
Princess Dominique	Capucine
Merle McGill	Edie Adams
Sarah Watkins	Maggie Smith
Inspector Rizzi	Adolfo Celi
Oscar Ludwig	Herschel Bernardi
Volpone	Hugh Manning
Mosca	David Dodimead

Joseph L. Mankiewicz's first film after a long hiatus emerges as an elegant, sophisticated screen vehicle for more demanding tastes, especially among big-city audiences in firstrun situations. Some trimming for pace, and proper pub-ad highlighting of its important cast roster could help it make a dent in subsequent sites as well, but a hardsell is indicated. For a pic which was previously billed as "Mr. Fox of Venice" and "Anyone for Venice?", its current handle, "The Honey Pot," does not seem the aptest in indicating content either, and this could prove an added sales burden.

Vaguely drawing its inspiration from Ben Jonson's "Volpone," film's updated plot centers around the fabulously rich Cecil Fox (Rex Harrison) who with the aid of a sometime gigolo and secretary, William McFly (Cliff Robertson), plays a joke of sorts on three one-time mistresses of his by feigning grave illness and gauging their reactions as they come flocking to his bedside in quest of the millions in his kitty.

There is the wisecracking hypochondriac, Mrs. Sheridan, played by Susan Hayward, who was Mr. Fox's first love, accompanied by her attractive nurse, Sarah Watkins (Maggie Smith), a seemingly remissive, selflessly devoted type. There's Princess Dominique, a glacially beautiful jetsetter played by Capucine. And there's the ebullient Merle McGill (Edie Adams) a Hollywood star without a care in the world—except for a massive debt to Uncle Sam. Harrison and Robertson watch with obvious relish as the women play into his hands and schemes in a frantic attempt to secure a spot in his will until a near-finale development unexpectedly brings the pic to a conclusion with a series of plot twists which helps bare each charader's true self.

While the sophisticated plotting may at times be too intricate, with the action—and audience attention- -bogging down dangerously as a consequence especially in the middle reels, the dialog (by Mankiewicz himself) is often a delight in its hark-back to the days when the turn of a phrase and the tongue-in-cheek were a staple of better Hollywood product. The puzzler which only general release can solve is whether or not present-day audiences more attuned to Bondian brashness than the innuendo will be prepared to accept —or welcome back—this sort of fare. It's a shame, too, that Mankiewicz' rich package hasn't been presented in a tighter, crisper form, an even-betted test of this argument.

The playing is all of a superior calibre, and the director has chosen his cast well and paced them properly to counterpoint his theses. Harrison is a natural as the scheming millionaire whose secret passion is to pirouette around his palazzo chambers to Ponchielli's "Dance of the Hours." Susan Hayward, Capucine and Edie Adams are fine as his vastly opposite onetime companions.

Cliff Robertson is surprisingly good in his offbeat role as the temporary righthand man, with Adolfo Celi lending solid support as a patient police inspector. But it is Maggie Smith as the nurse-companion who slowly, stealthily grabs the spotlight in a neatly-dosed performance which should deservedly give her even more international attention than she already commands.

Technically, the "Honey Pot" is a rich confection in every department, from the late Gianni de Venanzo's lush Technicolor lensing on set and Venetian locations, to John DeCuir's richly beautiful design work and John Addison's aptly Italianate musical backdropping. *Hawk.*

Seiki No Tsume Ato
(Scar of the Century)
(JAPAN—COMPILATION)
Tokyo, Feb. 28.
Chuo Eiga Production, distributed by Shochiku Co. Ltd. A newsreel compilation from Japanese, American, British and Chinese sources. (Names of director, editor, etc., not given.) Previewed in Tokyo. Running Time, 92 MINS.

This is a new newsreel collage of the Pacific phase of WW II, its causes and consequences. It advertises that it contains some new footage, hitherto unreleased, and so it apparently does. New, at least to local operators, is Japanese footage on the destruction of Manila, the ceremonies attending the Japanese delegation to Berlin, and a set of stills taken of bodies at Hiroshima just after the bombing; and American footage of the Battle of the Coral Sea, the destruction of Pearl Harbor, and an amazing air shot (perhaps formerly classified) of the bomb actually exploding over Hiroshima, a great growing ball of fire covering blocks and blocks.

The tone, too, is new. Heretofore, the Japanese-made collages (those of Toho and Daiei in particular) has been elegiac. Even the cutting has been such that any sense of outrage (on either side) has been muffled by an acknowledgement of the hopeless waste of war. In this new film, however, a frank reassessment is called for, if not given. The opening and end are devoted to the war-crimes trials and these serve as "present" in the film, the actually battle footage coming as "flashback." There are no atrocities (unless one counts Hiroshima) and none of the material on the rape of Nanking is used. But, on the other hand, neither does the compiler avail himself of the photographed records of Chinese atrocities.

Japan's military history is by no means glorified, but the audience is asked to remember that there was such a thing as the ABCD Line, and that the foreign boycott of Japan and its goods was quite serious. At the end of a fair and unbiased recounting of the war itself, the film returns to the trials and questions both their necessity and effectiveness, ending on Tojo's celebrated and near deathbed speech to the effect that in war it is never one side which is entirely wrong, that it takes two to be wrong.

Objective, and quite "historical" in tone, this picture is curious in that no listing of credits is given and Shochiku itself offers none. The music is a strange blending of Mahler, Respighi and Tschaikowsky, with the initial motif of the Bach D minor toccata sounding portentously during the trial scenes which — along with some very erratic cutting—indicates that perhaps the film was put togethter

in something of a hurry. As a document of changing attitude toward the Pacific war, it is perhaps more interesting than as a documentary of the war itself. *Chie.*

Sekishun
(Lost Spring)
(JAPAN—COLOR)
Tokyo, Feb. 28.
Shochiku Co. production and release. With Michio Aratama, Yoshiko Kayama, Mariko Kaga, Mitsuko Mori, Eijiri Tono, Mikojiro Hiro. Directed by Noboru Nakamura. Screenplay, Yumie Hiraiwa; camera (Eastmancolor), Hiroshi Matsumura. Previewed in Tokyo. Running Time, 95 MINS.

Noboru Nakamura, whose "Kii no Kawa" was named one of the 10 best Japanese film of 1966, is apparently becoming "the" traditional Japanese director, the one who follows the line of Kenji Mizoguchi, Yasujiro Ozu, and the still-alive but inactive Kozaburo Yoshimura. The mantle of these greats still fits a bit loosely, but Nakamura remains the only director at present interesting himself in the traditional Japanese film scene.

In "Sekishun" he tells the story of three sisters (Michio Aratama, Yoshiko Kayama and Mariko Kaga), daughters of a recently deceased traditional craftsman, a Tokyo thread and obi-ribbon maker. The one first marrying shall, according to the will, inherit the business, a manifestly unfair arrangement since Mariko is a modern girl who cares nothing for the past, and Yoshiko is self-seeking and cold, while Michio is the only one who cares for her father's work—and she cares violently. So much so, that when she is offered happiness in the person of obi-designer Mikijiro Hira, she hesitates to the extent that Mariko makes a try for him and Yoshiko (with the help of meddling stepmother, Mitsuko Mori) gets herself pregnant by one of the shop's employees and ends up mistress.

The opposition, as in so many good Japanese films (and perhaps best seen in Mizoguchi's great 1936 "Gion no Shimai"), is not so much between the oldfashioned sister and the modern one, as between the sister who tries to live by the fast-disappearing traditional virtues of self-abnegation, decorum, trust and goodwill, and the one who wants to live by such modern means as standing up for one's rights, taking what one wants, and living for herself alone.

This conflict usually splits the Japanese screen family in the most graphic fashion and in this film, too, one is allowed to see past the placid purpose and into the boiling center of the Japanese family offbalance.

Often, in conflicts of this sort, the "nice" traditional daughter is left to wander picturesquely, if miserably, off at the end. But director Nakamura and scripter Yumie Hiraiwa (who adapted this film from her own tv series, though it doesn't show) have something much better than that in mind. In a remarkable coda (the best part of the film) Michio does go off, but her destination is

the mountain workshop of a traditional Japanese potter. At the end she is sitting there in the sun, happy, watching his hands deftly form beauty, sure to try it herself, given time. It is a very wise ending to a very beautiful film.

Part of the beauty, aside from Nakamura's many subtle constructions and a gorgeously photographed excursion to Muro-Ji, is due to the performance of Michio Aratama as the eldest daughter. Always good, she has recently become extraordinary, and is probably the finest of all Japanese actresses. Her dignity, her goodness, her way of indicating the most complicated of emotions; the way she uses her hands, her eyes; the amount of feeling she can communicate without saying a word—all of this is a pleasure to see. Her performance in this quite good film illuminates it, makes parts of it unforgettable. *Chie.*

The Projected Man
(BRITISH-TECHNICOLOR-TECHNISCOPE)
Universal release of Protelco-M.L.C. production; executive producers Richard Gordon, Gerald A. Fernback; producers, John Croydon, Maurice Foster. Directed by Ian Curteis. Screenplay, John C. Cooper, Peter Bryan, based on original story by Frank Quattrocchi; camera (Technicolor), Stanley Pavey; editor, Derek Holding; special effects, Flo Nordhoff, Robert Hedges, Mike Hope; music, composed and conducted by Kenneth V. Jones, played by Sinfonia Orchestra of London; asst. directors, Derek Whitehurst, Tom Sachs. Reviewed in Baltimore, March 2, '67. Running Time: 77 MINS.

Prof. Steiner	Bryant Haliday
Dr. Pat Hill	Mary Peach
Dr. Blanchard	Norman Wooland
Chris Mitchell	Ronald Allen
Inspector Davis	Derek Farr
Sheila Anderson	Tracey Crisp
Latham	Derrick de Marney
Lembach	Gerald Heinz
Harry	Sam Kydd

One of a pair of British imports released without being tradeshown by Universal, "The Projected Man" is made with sufficient care and skill that it need not have been bypassed. Although billed second to the other film "Island of Terror," this pic is as good and in some ways better.

Bryant Haliday, whose experiments involve converting objects to energy and reforming them elsewhere, is in conflict with Norman Wooland, his superior at a Research Foundation. Latter is being forced by a third party to see that experiments fail. After an important demonstration is sabotaged, Haliday is told the project will be dismantled. Anxious to continue, he attempts to project himself into a visiting scientist's living room but an accident causes him to miss target, become facially disfigured and possessed with an electrical charge that is fatal on contact.

John C. Cooper and Peter Bryan's screenplay is a mosaic compiled from other films but the pieces hang together fairly well, though the origin and motives of the third party (Derrick de Marney) are never fully explained. Happily, the characters do not fall prey to all the usual cliches. Deformed scientist Haliday is "angry" but not "insane," and retains his human personality, killing only from fear or a sense of justice.

Acting is generally good, though Tracey Crisp's secretary is simply a sexy ingenue. No performances stand out but the money saved on names was better invested in the technical areas. Director Ian Curteis fills the Techniscope screen with compositions inspired by Sidney Furie's "Ipcress Files" style that keep the film visually lively without resorting to outright imitation. Lighting sharply selects or outlines objects and the costume and setting colors are chosen with an eye for subtle contrast. Stanley Pavey's photography and the naturalness of the characters add to the tension instead of sidetracking the viewer.

As with its partner film, "Projected Man" has its greatest weakness in the script but the result should put Planet Films into the same league as Hammer and Amicus. *Paul.*

Island of Terror
(BRITISH-COLOR)

Universal release of Protelco-Planet production; executive producers Richard Gordon, Gerald A. Fernback; produced by Tom Blakeley. Directed by Terence Fisher. Story and screenplay, Edward Andrew Mann, Allan Ramsen; camera (Eastmancolor), Reg Wyer; editor, Thelma Connell; special effects, John St. John Earl, Michael Albrechtson; music, composed and conducted by Malcolm Lockyer; electronic effects, Barry Gray; asst. director, Don Weeks. Reviewed in Baltimore, March 2, '67. Running Time, **90 MINS.**

Dr. Stanley .... Peter Cushing
Dr. West .... Edward Judd
Toni Merrill .... Carole Gray
Dr. Landers .... Eddie Byrne
Constable Harris .... Sam Kydd
Mr. Campbell .... Niall MacGinnis
Argyle .... James Caffrey
Bellows .... Liam Caffney

"Island of Terror," half of a British import package being sneaked to market by Universal without the usual tradescreening, is an exploitable and well-made thriller. In the modern vein of horror caused by science, rather than by supernatural force, the plot concerns a cancer-cure experiment that goes awry resulting in some impenetrable slug mutations. Scientific explanations are vague, but the situation is acceptable because much that surrounds it is believable.

Exteriors have apparently been shot on location and the usual villagers come in various realistic shapes and sizes. Male leads are scientists, of course, but the contrivance of each being the top man in his field is somewhat reduced by the amusing mock-pride they adopt in conversation. While Edward Judd seems a bit overweight for the role of an egghead ladykiller, Peter Cushing, whose performances in this type role are always above average, is properly brusque and has a wryly objective point of view. He also varies between heroism and cowardice, creating a character with natural, not exaggerated, fears and hesitations. Carole Gray, an easily-seduced rich girl, lends father's helicopter to the pair in exchange for being allowed to go along on their scientific trip. Other performers are fine, with Niall MacGinnis and James Caffrey outstanding.

Direction by Terence Fisher, once a big name at Hammer Films, is efficient in storytelling and creating tension but offers little of visual interest and originality. Good use is made, however, of overcast woods in the outdoor scenes.

It is too often true that the monsters in these films are not as convincing as the rest of the cast. In this case, the silicates designed by special effects expert John St. John Earl are adequate, but they move awkwardly in a series of jerks and boast a food-grabbing tentacle that no one ever tries to cut off. It might have been better had they flowed, gradually and inevitably, after their victims.

It is difficult to understand why "Island of Terror" was not tradescreened as, despite occasional weaknesses of a straining plot and casual pacing, it is tense, well-performed and not hysterical. *Paul.*

Thoroughly Modern Millie
(MUSICAL-COLOR)

Universal-Ross Hunter tuner spoofing flapper age. First half much better than second. Overall prospects good with Julie Andrews and Carol Channing as come-ons.

Universal release of Ross Hunter production. Stars Julie Andrews, James Fox, Mary Tyler Moore, Carol Channing; features John Gavin, Beatrice Lillie. Director, George Roy Hill. Screenplay, Richard Morris. Cameraman (Technicolor), Russell Metty; scored and conducted by Elmer Bernstein; arrangements and conducted by Andre Previn; songs, Jimmy Van Heusen and Sammy Cahn; musical supervision, Joe Gershenson; choreography, Joe Layton; editor, Stu Gilmore. Reviewed at Criterion Theatre, N.Y. March 22, 1967. Running Time, **138 MINS.**

Millie Dillmount .... Julie Andrews
Dorothy Brown ...... Mary Tyler Moore
Muzzy Van Hossmere....Carol Channing
Jimmy Smith .... James Fox
Trevor Graydon .... John Gavin
Mrs. Meers .... Beatrice Lillie
Number One .... Jack Soo
Number Two .... Pat Morita
Tea .... Philip Ahn
Miss Flannery .... Cavada Humphrey
Juarez .... Anthony Dexter
Cruncher .... Lou Nova
Baron Richter .... Michael St. Clair
Adrian .... Albert Carrier
Gregory Huntley .... Victor Rogers
Judith Tremaine .... Lizabeth Hush
Taxie Driver .... Herbie Faye
Singer .... Ann Dee
Waiter .... Benny Rubin

The first half of "Thoroughly Modern Millie" is quite successful in striking and maintaining a gay spirit and pace. There are many recognizable and beguiling satirical recalls of the flapper age and some quite funny bits. Unfortunately, after intermission, the whole thing goes to "plot" and it's as if the two halves were separate scripts. Overall, film should do okay.

In the first and more creative section the picture plays at "camp," intentional burlesque of itself, but cleverly done. Julie Andrews winks at the audience. Silent subtitles convey her thoughts. The creaky hotel elevator will move only if the passengers break into buck and wing. The laundry hamper used by the Chinese white slavers has seriocomic creaky wheels at every approach. The pretitle sequence in which Miss Andrews, on a first walk through the big city, first bobs her hair, then shortens her skirt, then contains her bosom in a tight brassiere so that the fall of her rope of pearls will not be thrown off straight-line is delightful.

The trouble after intermission is that the production forgets the mood it has created and breaks "camp" for crude, mindless chase. Theretofor film wasn't mindless but "aware" as when the rich girl, seeking a thoroughly middle class hotel, wants to pay her 35c taxi fare by check and then royally consents to a stranger, Miss Andrews, carrying in her luggage.

But if composed of two uneven parts the Universal-Ross Hunter production has the advantage of Julie Andrews after her "Poppins" and "Sound of Music" appearances have endeared her to the American public. It has perhaps the even greater advantage of Carol Channing who offers a powerhouse performance as a queen of hokum. Another who helps a great deal (but never sings) is the veteran Beatrice Lillie. She plays with wonderfully arch theatricality the role of a white slave supplier posing as manager of a hotel for sweet innocents, orphans preferred.

Liberties taken with reality, not to mention period, in the first half are redeemed by wit and characterization. But the sudden thrusting of the hero, played by James Fox in hornrimmed glasses, into a skyscraper-climbing, flagpole-hanging acrobat, a la Harold Lloyd, has little of Lloyd but the myth. This sequence is "forced" all the way, the comedy of terror cut to absurdity. It earns giggles from the easily-pleased at the cost of impatience and annoyance from others. Neither Fox nor Miss Andrews are suitable to this kind of slapstick.

Musically, "Millie" is a melange of the old and the new. Standards of yesteryear, per "Baby Face," "Poor Butterfly," "I'm a Jazz Baby" "Rose of Washington Square," and others, mingle with specials by Jimmy Van Heusen and Sammy Cahn. All is part of Elmer Bernstein's score, as arranged and conducted by Andre Previn, with a Joe Gershenson credit for music supervision. It would not be possible to speak confidently of anyone's contributions in such a galaxy. The film could, of course, re-popularize some of the standards.

Joe Layton's choreography is generally attractive, with the obvious liability that none of his principals are truly dancers. The film is well put together, professionally paced and the editing of Stu Gilmore firstrate.

After establishing Miss Andrews as a stenographer in search of a job she is abruptly introduced as a singer at a Jewish wedding. If this is mostly an excuse for her to do a number of Yiddish, possibly a boxoffice plus, the whole thing is rather affectionate in its unreality. A less tolerant report must be filed as to the Chinatown sequence, the opium den, the tied-up and gagged girls awaiting shipment in crates to the orient. One sign is addressed to the So-and-So Tart Shop, Pekin. (That's out of early Chaplin). The automobile escape predictably knocks the entire retail economy of Chinatown into total disarray. Contrived rather than funny, and drearily familiar, this stuff may draw giggles from elements of any audience. It will bore others.

Woven into Richard Morris' original screenplay are a number of sharp tidbits of characterization, notably Cavada Humphrey as a prissy office manager and Jack Soo and Pat Morita as the oriental menaces Morris and director. Hill also get a good deal of spoof out of John Gavin's "Arrow collar" with pipe profile poses. The sequence at Carol Channing's crazily splendid boozy Long Island estate will suggest nothing so much as Scott Fitzgerald's "The Great Gatsby."

The pity is that Hunter and Hill and the author have succumbed to the temptation of sheer "cinematic action" and been unfaithful to their own earlier and superior level of satire.

There are selling points in the aura and milieu of the 1920s, which vein of amusement and nostalgia the film works to exploit. Books by the likes of Mark Sullivan and Frederick Lewis Allen led the way. Various Broadway and off-Broadway satires brought it home in "The Girl Friend" and "Little Mary Sunshine." Interestingly Miss Channing herself made her first impact in "The Gladiola Girl" scene from the stage revue, "Lend An Ear" and Miss Andrews in "The Boy Friend."

Questions regarding the boxoffice prospects of "Millie" ride the age brackets. The very young may like it best. So that's strength. The oldsters capable of direct memory may also be beguiled for their own separate reasons. Where does that leave the in-between generations? At a guess, in-between.

Jean Louis who created the gowns of the period is naturally very much in the foreground of a critical onlooker's notice. The makeup of Bud Westmore and the hair styling of Larry German similarly stand out as important contributions to mood and illusion. Then, or perhaps first, comes the art direction of Alexander Golitzen and George Webb with set decorations by Howard Bristol.

Miss Andrews is very much like the leading lady of the story but hardly more than a bystander when Miss Channing commands the scene and at such times it is seldom that a star has been so static so long in a film. Mary Tyler Moore, who is billed above the title, along with Miss Andrews, Miss Channing and Fox, serves the plot in that she is essentially a prototype of a sweet, long curls and rather dumb rich girl of 40 years ago. Fox does okay but, as directed, is often more symbol than breathing reality. He is awkward when put in drag for a scene of uninspired recall of Jack Lemmon.

"Thoroughly Modern Millie" seemingly has its major investment in the lavish Hunter production, plus the salaries of Miss Andrews and Miss Channing. It is an uneven comedy but will probably do okay.

Land.

The Happening
(COLOR)

Wacky comedy a la mode, oddly mixed and only spasmodically effective.

New York, March 22.
Columbia Pictures release of Sam Spiegel-Horizon Pictures-Jud Kinberg production. Associate producers Robert Manchel, David Wolfson, Howard Jaffe. Features Anthony Quinn, George Maharis, Michael Parks, Robert Walker, Marthat Hyer, Faye Dunaway, Oscar Homolka, Jack Kruschen, Milton Berle. Directed by Elliot Silverstein. Screenplay by Frank R. Pierson, James Buchanan and Ronald Austin. Story by Buchanan and Austin. Edited by Philip Anderson. Assistant director, Ray Gosnell. Music by De Vol. Filmed at Ivan Tors Studios, Miami, Fla. Reviewed at Plaza Theatre, N.Y. March 21, '67. Running Time, 101 MINS.
Roc Delmonico .... Anthony Quinn
Taurus .... George Maharis
Sureshot .... Michael Parks
Herby .... Robert Walker
Monica .... Martha Hyer
Sandy .... Faye Dunaway
Fred .... Milton Berle
Sam .... Oscar Homolka
Inspector .... Jack Kruschen
O'Reilly .... Clifton James
First Cycle Officer .. Eugene Roche
Arnold ...... James Randolph Kuhl
Second Cycle Officer .... Luke Askew

Intriguing offbeat item, "The Happening," directed by Elliot Silverstein, attempts to blend various elements of kick-happy teenyboppers, melodrama, "pop culture," suburban tragedy, suspense, "in" gags, socalled "black humor," updated Keystone Kops, "Beach Party" pix, and alienation in the affluent society in a comedic potpourri, which, between expected laughs, seeks to offer satiric peeks at contemporary U.S. life and values.

Though sometimes telling and frequently funny, in this film, Silverstein has bitten off more than he can chew. He only pierces his thin-skinned subject-matter — the U.S. today, with the Eastern tinseltown, Miami, as paradigm — less than half the time.

Frenetically flipping all the above-named disparate elements, and others, too numerous to recount, Silverstein's timing is too faulty, as yet, in this juggling act to keep the Indian clubs airborne. Generally, "The Happening" doesn't really "happen," except for the too frequent clatter of misfired sight gags and dud one-liners.

Despite plethora of comedy-killing flaws, "The Happening" does contain enough zany elements peculiar to click comedies today to slip by general audiences as a really funny item, though discriminating audiences might bypass the technicolor satire.

Well-tempered plotline, with several corkscrew twists, follows the weekend hegira of four ennui laden but debauched Miami beachbums in search of some potent stimuli. They find it, albeit accidentally, by stumbling into an unlikely kidnapping.

The victim, temporarily, of their Ritz Brothers-like capers, is Roc Delmonico (Anthony Quinn), onetime Mafia hood now respectable hotel owner, who imagines he's been fingered by the mob and offers himself willingly into their clutches. From various picturesque sites in and about Miami Beach, Roc, under the quavering gun of an ineffectual gigilo malapropriately named Taurus (George Maharis), phones his wife, Martha Hyer, his partner Milton Berle, Mafia chieftain Oscar Homolka, and even his mother to raise the asked for $200,000 ransom. Their answer — keep him!—climaxes in one of the film's better touching sequences, with Quinn and kids realizing his worthlessness and consequently, bleak and wasted vistas of life.

First understandably dejected, then angered, Quinn wrests the pistol from Maharis and undertakes his own kidnapping. With verve, nerve and blackmail (he threatens to squawk to the IRS about the hotel's double ledgers, expose his wife's infidelity, and "tell all" about the Mafia "family" — not to the law, but who did what to whom in Chicago) he runs the ransom up to $3,000,000. Through a cleverly contrived airport sequence, the kids manage to snatch the suitcase full of cash from under the noses of the emassed strength of the FBI, the local and county police and the mayor. The cash lode, however, is marked, and therefore, worthless, like, it is suggested, the life of the hero and the yet-to-be-lived lives of the kids.

What is bothersome about this tragi-farce, is why it doesn't succeed, with all of the above and generally capable performers, going for it. Maharis, playing a bull without horns, whose main claim to existence is his power over bejeweled Miami matrons, is spotty but fine alternating swagger with weakness in his impersonation of a gigilo, while Michael Parks is less convincing but appropriately faceless as a blank-faced rich kid.

Newcomer Fay Dunaway, though stunning to view and essaying her role with eclan, is too womanly seductive for a teenybopper role. Almost totally wasted in the film is Robert Walker, whose virtually lineless portrayal of a "hanger on" relegates him to a cypher on the fringe of the action. Anthony Quinn, while ably capturing the punk with power aspects of his role, fails to find the right stance for the comedy sequences and overdoes it, trimming conviction.

Martha Hyer's range could have been better mined had her character been more shrill, but the dialog left her role again virtually empty, and dramatically actionless. Only Berle, whose broad comedic metier is well served in his role Fred the penny-scrimping partner who cuckolds Quinn on the sly, strikes the satiric bullseye upon which "The Happening" is supposedly built.

Main fault with the performances, and ditto, the film, is overdirection. Silverstein constantly reaches for "cute" effects, from use of outdated bebop chatter, contrived placement of actors, and even inclusion of distracting musicomedy elements and staging to make the film truly "different." Neglected along the way is timing, characterization and comedy rhythmics — all the gags seem to be surrounded by overlong pauses as if awaiting an unfound hilarity. "The Happening," overall, can be classed as a near miss, but close enough to rate praise as a game try. Production values, including frequently sparkling lensing, are topnotch.

Rino.

The Mummy's Shroud
(COLOR)

Routine chiller to fill out double bills.

Hollywood, March 23.
20th Century-Fox release of Seven Arts-Hamner Film production. Produced by Anthony Nelson Keys. Stars Andre Morell, John Phillips, David Buck, Elizabeth Sellars; features Maggie Kimberley, Michael Ripper. Direction and screenplay by John Gilling; camera (Color), Arthur Grant; editor, James Needs; music, Oon Banks. Reviewed at 20th-Fox Studios, March 22, 1967. Running Time, 90 MINS.
Sir Basil Walden .... Andre Morell
Stanley Preston .... John Phillips
Paul Preston .... David Buck
Barbara Preston ...... Elizabeth Sellars
Claire .... Maggie Kimberley
Longbarrow .... Michael Ripper
Harry .... Tim Barrett
Hasmid .... Roger Delgado
Haiti .... Catherine Lacey

Although macabre sequences create some tension and splash a lot of gore, dialog, characterizations and plot have little to recommend them. With lack of name marquee value, pic would seem to

have no place to go except bottom half of double bills.

Prolog reenacts palace coup against Egyptian Pharoh about four thousand years ago and subsequent burial of young prince by the faithful slave, Prem. Story deals with British excavation of the tomb in the 1920s and the vengeance of the mummy, Prem, against the members of the archaeological team. Much is of the abracadabra mumblings that bring the mummy to life and a laborious subplot that depicts the financier of the expedition as glory-hogging colonialist who has little regard for his family or his subordinates.

Michael Ripper does the best job as the harried, ineffectual stooge for the financier, John Phillips, and Roger Delgado and Catherine Lacey have a good time as the seedy mystics who invoke the maghis killing. Maggie Kimberley has an arresting face, but acting by her, Andre Morell, Phillips, David Buck and Elizabeth Sellars in the lead roles are unimpressive. Granted, they had little to work with.

John Gilling both wrote the screenplay and directed it, but showed little originality in either endeavor. Several crowd scenes did not disguise appearance that pic was on the low side of low budget scale.

Beig.

Maroc 7
(BRITISH-COLOR)

Smoothy mounted but brittle and slow-moving robbery and murder yarn. Gene Barry, Leslie Phillips, Cyd Charisse and a flock of models in this pic which is okay for easily amused.

London, March 21.
Rank release of a Cyclone Films presentation, produced by John Gale and Leslie Phillips. Stars Gene Barry. Elsa Martinelli, Leslie Phillips, Cyd Charisse; features Denholm Elliott, Alexandra Stewart, Angela Douglas, Eric Barker. Directed by Gerry O'Hara; original story and screenplay, David Mercer; camera (Eastmancolor) Kenneth Talbot; editor, John Jympson; music, Kenneth K. V. Jones; Party music and film theme, Paul Ferris. At Leicester Square Theatre, London. Running Time, 91 MINS.
Simon Grant .... Gene Barry
Louise Henderson .... Cyd Charisse
Claudia .... Elsa Martinelli
Raymond Lowe .... Leslie Phillips
Inspector Barrada ..... Denholm Elliott
Michele Craig .... Alexandra Stewart
Professor Bannen .... Eric Barker
Freddie .... Angela Douglas
Vivienne .... Tracy Reed
Suzie .... Maggie London
Penny .... Penny Riley
Alexa .... Ann Norman
Hotel Receptionist .... Lionel Blair
Police Officer .... Paul Danquah

This cops-and-robbers thriller, the first production of John Gale and Leslie Phillips, lacks the necessary for such a subject. Producers have no need to be unduly pessimistic for it has several credits which will satisfy the easygoing patron. But screenplay writer David Osborn and director Gerry O'Hara might well have injected more pace and highlights into the proceedings. It starts in an intriguing yet leisurely style and rarely whips up much urgency while the flip dialog is brittle and lacking in genuine wit.

Osborn's main ace is to make most of his leading characters suspect, although cinema goers will often be in doubt as to whether the characters are goodies or baddies and the answer never offers much of a kick. Performances are mainly smooth but do not engineer much excitement. On the other hand, the genuine Moroccan backgrounds give a colorful zest to the action. The film is peppered with gorgeous gals who wear an array of eye-popping duds that will enamour femme addicts.

Story has Cyd Charisse as a sophisticated editress of a fashionable magazine. Her frequent trips abroad with a photographic team and a bunch of leggy, photogenic models are ostensibly for magazine layouts, but actually are a front for daring jewel robberies. Her chief model (Elsa Martinelli) and her cameraman-partner (Leslie Phillips) are both in on the murky deals. Suspecting this, special cop Gene Barry poses as a thief, uses a blackmailing technique and forces Miss Charisse to let him tag along on her latest trip to Morocco, where she's got her predatory eye on a priceless medallion.

Arrival of the party in Morocco sparks off a long trail of murder, double-crossing and chicanery in which the local chief of police, his girl assistant, an eccentric archaeologist, and others all play puzzling roles. Early highlight of the film (in London) is a swinging, satirical party sequence. In Morocco, a slugging match between Barry and Phillips, ending in the latter's demise, are the main highlights, but they are not enough.

Barry lacks punch as the hero who might be either cop or cracksman but has an easy charm and light touch for throwing away lines. He is much in his element among the models, one of whom (Elsa Martinelli) he successfully romances. Miss Charisse also lacks the power which the role of the gang leader should generate, but her looks are a real delight and her poise is such that her role becomes credible and intriguing. Miss Martinelli is also a stunning looker, though her role is unsatisfactorily etched by the writer. Tracy Reed stands out among the other four elegant models. Angela Douglas makes a perky chief assistant to Miss Charisse, and Denholm Elliott, as the Moroccan chief of police, and Alexandra Stewart, as his girl assistant, and Eric Barker all give savvy performances. Phillips, normally a light comedian, is surprisingly cast as the ill-tempered, untrustworthy photographer-thug which he plays effectively.

Kenneth Talbot has used his camera splendidly to lush up the local backgrounds. John Jympson's editing copes well with the occasionally straggly screenplay. Director O'Hara's direction is competent, but somehow lacks the spark of audacity and dash which would have knitted together some of the loose ends of this workmanlike but brittle piece. *Rich.*

Thunder Alley
(PANAVISION-COLOR)

Run-of-the-mill look at stock car racing with stock characters and situations to go with the cars.

American International Pictures release. Executive producers, James H. Nicholson and Samuel Z. Arkoff; Burt Topper, producer; Richard Rush, director. Stars Annette Funicello, Fabian, Diane McBain, Warren Berlinger, Jan Murray, Stanley Adams, Maureen Arthur, Michael T. Mikler, Mike Bell, Kip King. Screenplay, Sy Salkowitz; camera (Color), Monroe Askin; art director, Danny Haller; film editor, Ronnie Sinclair; sound effects, Neison-Corso; assistant director, Jack Bohrer. Reviewed at Charles Aidikoff Screening Room, March 16, 1967. Running Time, 90 MINS.

"Thunder Alley" is an episodic string of inane, often banal and occasionally actionful cliches held together only by the film it's on. Heavy exploitation by AIP, emphasizing stock cars and the wild, younger generation, probably will enable pic to show a profit. Marquee value, except possibly for Fabian, is questionable.

Story concerns hotshot driver (Fabian), whose blackouts in times of stress on the track cause the death of another driver and his battle to regain his place in the racing fraternity—"What am I supposed to do, sling hash?" is how he memorably states his case.

There are about as many dents in the plot and characterizations as in the stock cars. Stanley Adams plays the owner of a small string of cars who won't hire Fabian, despite friendship, because of the blackouts. Yet, in the end, he does, saying Fabian seems to have improved, despite a just-completed practice race where he weaved all over the track. Jan Murray portrays a tight-fisted promoter who plays every angle for its dollar value. He really has the best lines in the pic, a fusillade of cynicisms that often are funny. Yet, it is ruined, near the end, when he tells his daughter (Annette Funicello) that he only has her interests at heart and she should fight to win Fabian. Murray goes through the whole speech as if setting up a great tagline, but it never comes, and one is left with undigestable feeling that audience is supposed to believe he has reformed.

Most startling, however, is the utter disregard by Fabian to his blackouts. He simply appears to be biding his time till the end of the pic so he can get back on the track and win the race. The fact that he caused the death of one driver and could easily cause other deaths is only shrugged at as an annoying detail that is preventing him from competing on the track.

To get away from the plot, which is probably the best thing to do with it, what is left are the individual scenes and the acting. Best of the scenes are a fun-n-games party—never mind the reason for it being there—and the stunt driving tricks. However, the regular stock car racing sequences, except for the spectacular accidents, were too logged with cars to allow any distinct duels or progression in the ranks to be distinguished.

As mentioned, Jan Murray has all the good lines and he cracks the jokes well. Maureen Arthur's dizzy redhead also stands out. Among the others, Diane McBain seems much too levelheaded and fresh to be a "track tramp." In many of the scenes, she is eating: coke, candy bar, apple, etc., as though that is a symbol of illicit sex, and occasionally yells "go, go, go" while at the track. But the inanity of that is made clear by Miss Arthur, who quizzes, "Go where?"

Fabian and Miss Funicello walk through their routine roles with routine effect, while Warren Berlinger, whose character is the only one that changes in the script, tries hard and is occasionally believeable.

Richard Rush catches the spirit of the party sequence, but otherwise direction is pedestrian to clumsy. Sy Salkowitz is the culprit for the script. Production values were good. *Beig.*

Welcome to Hard Times
(COLOR)

Unsatisfactory oater for bottom of grind bills.

Hollywood, March 18.
Metro-Goldwyn-Mayer release of a Max E. Youngstein-David Karr production. Stars Henry Fonda, Janice Rule. Written and directed by Burt Kennedy. Based on the novel by E. L. Doctorow; camera (Metrocolor), Harry Stradling Jr.; editor, Aaron Stell; music, Harry Sukman. Reviewed at Metro Studios, Culver City, March 17, '67. Running Time, 103 MINS.
Will Blue .... Henry Fonda
Molly Riordan .... Janice Rule
Zar .... Keenan Wynn
Adah .... Janis Paige
Ezra/Isaac Maple ...... John Anderson
Jenks .... Warren Oates
Jessie .... Fay Spain
Brown .... Edgar Buchanan
Man From Bodie .... Aldo Ray
Alfie .... Denver Pyle
Jimmy Fee .... Michael Shea
Mae .... Arlene Golonka
Avery .... Lon Chaney
John Bear .... Royal Dano
Jack Millay .... Alan Baxter
Mr. Fee .... Paul Birch
Bert Albany .... Dan Ferrone
Major Munn .... Paul Fix
Hanson .... Elisha Cook
China .... Kalen Liu
Flo .... Ann McCrea
1st Drinker .... Bob Terhune
Young Miner .... Ron Burke

"Welcome to Hard Times" is more than an oater title; it is a pretty fair evaluation of this Max E. Youngstein-David Karr production. Badly written, directed and acted, pic overemphasizes brutality at beginning and end, between which padded footage is devoted to indigestible social commentary and other hokum plot angles. Henry Fonda, Keenan Wynn and Aldo Ray offer some marquee lure for action fans, but their word of mouth soon will plummet this Metro release to its rightful place, artistically and commercially, at the bottom of dual bills in least discriminating situations.

Were B and C pix still being made—admittedly, that is, "Times" would be dismissed as part of the film block, played off under a solid feature as chaser material. Today, however, major company cheapies are palmed off on the public as uppercase material—available immediately thereafter for flat rental, in most cases. So, with indications that "Times" will be released as a top feature, it will be judged as such.

Burt Kennedy's direction is as inept as his script, an adaptation of E. L. Doctorow's novel about sadistic tough Ray who burns down a small western town. Ray's character is established in about two minutes, but the entire first reel is devoted to it, providing a clue to the padding to come. Cowardly (or is he?) Mayor Fonda inspires town to rebuild.

Janice Rule, billed with Fonda above the title, is unsatisfactory as the woman who taunts Fonda for a whole year, then cues a bloody climax which involves her own death. She plays it with an Irish accent, effect being a sort of Method school version of Maureen O'Hara. Script shares the blame for her erratic character definition

Keenan Wynn, with wife Janis Paige and three saloon babes, offer some low comedy relief. Edgar Buchanan comes off best as a territorial officer, while, among the newer faces, Dan Ferrone shows some screen potential. Presence of many pro names — Lon Chaney, Elisha Cook, Paul Fix, etc.—only serves to emphasize the lack of depth and perception in script and direction. Harry Sukman's score is adequate, ditto all technical credits. Aaron Stell executed the editing to 103 minutes, perhaps 20 minutes too much. *Murf.*

Bakuso
(Explosion Course)
(JAPAN-DOCUMENTARY)

Tokyo, March 21.
Teshigahara Production, distributed by Toho Co. Ltd. Directed by Hiroshi Teshigahara; camera, Touichiro Narushima; music, Kuranosuke Hamaguchi; commentary, Shoichi Ozawa. Previewed in Tokyo. Running Time, 74 MINS.

This documentary on the recent Indianapolis Race at Fuji, "Bakuso" (which might be translated as "Explosion Course"), is the latest film of Hiroshi Teshigahara, known for the international prize-winning "Woman in the Dunes" and for last year's "The Face of Another."

It is not his first documentary—that was the excellent half-hour "Jose Torres," and since then he has made an hourlong followup on Torre's boxing career, and done a short film on artwork of his famous father, Sofu Teshigahara. Nor is it, by any means, his best work, but it does show how a serious and talented director handles the reality from which the documentary must be made.

In a sense, of course, all of Teshigahara's films are documentaries. He retains the greatest respect for things as they really are, limits himself to close and near views but would not think of detracting from the photographed image by manipulating it or by choosing an angle or a tempo not in agreement with it. Watching the opening of this picture, a meticulous rendering of preparations for the Fuji race, one senses the director only in the restraint, only in the care lest a detail be lost. Like the well-bred British documentary-maker (now a vanished breed), he becomes a nameless, faceless reporter and if the facts are interesting, so is the report.

One admires this tact but (to this reviewer) racing cars are not very interesting in themselves and the director might well have allowed himself some of the free-swinging style seen to such advantage in John Frankenheimer's "Grand Prix." But this Teshighara did not want to do and so one must respect what he did want to do.

He wanted to make a well-tailored documentary, and this is what "Bakuso" became. The extent of his dedication is seen in the meticulous editing which does not seek to excite you (though Touichiro Narushima's camera-work sometimes does, the lenses seeming absolutely thirsting for a collision; and Kuranosuke Hama-guchi's score at times verges on hysteria; rather, he is meticu-lously concerned to keep separate all of the identical-seeming turns, all of those straight-track shots which seem so very similar. And he confines Shoichi Ozawa's narration to a factual report of things seen.

The disciplines of making such a film as this must have been enormous, particularly since the director's only direct comment is a juxtaposition (meaningless in context, unfortunately) of the car-happy habits of the younger generation in Tokyo. Otherwise it is sternly dedicated documentary-making of a high order. But, why, we wonder, did he want to do it? Of course, he has inherited from his father the greatest respect for craftsmanship, and his interest in the sheer car-pentry of filmmaking has always been great. Too, he much admires the "Tokyo Olympiad" of Kon Ichikawa (the structure of which contributed much to "Bakusho") and his interest in sport has been in evidence ever since the first Jose Torres film.

Well, for whatever reason, he has made what he wanted to and having made the perfect text-book documentary, one hopes he will go back to making motion pictures.
Chie.

Satsujinkyo Jidai
(The Age of Assassins)
(JAPANESE)
Tokyo, March 21.

Toho Co., production and release. With Tatsuya Nakadai, Reiko Dan, Hideo Anamoto, Hideo Tsunazuka. Directed by Kihachi Okamoto. Produced by Tomoyuki Tanaka and Kenichiro Tsunoda; screenplay, El Ogawa, Tadaki Yamazaki and Okamoto, from novel by Michio Tsuzuku; camera, Rokkuro Nihsigaki; music, Masaru Sato. Previewed in Tokyo. Running time: 99 MINS.

A kimonoed lady gets felt-up on a crowded train and the offender follows her to a deserted spot. Surrendering to his importunities, she turns, removes her eye-patch and — wham! — one dead sex offender.

In another part of the city, mad scientist Hideo Amamoto, secure in his art nouveau private asylum, is spouting away in German, remembering the good old days when Hitler was in power and the world's largest diamond was sewn into the body of an eight year-old Japanese boy in order to smuggle it out of the country. He now has one of the German guards in his power and is

torturing him. Slash, slash—sizzle, sizzle!

In Shinjuku, a near-sighted professor with a bad case of athletes foot (Tatsuya Nakadai) is approached by an agent for Committee for Population Control, a group which has a sound and simple solution in mind: kill more people. Killed by the toppling bust of the professor's dead but revered mother, the agent's place is promptly filled by another, curvy Reiko Dan, whose idea of protocol is to climb naked into the professor's bed and invite him to inspect the documents. "Where do I, ah, sign?" asks the man of letters lowering himself.

All of this and more, much more, makes up one of Japan's furthest out comedies, an occasionally wild and usually amusing spoof-piece. Based on the novel "Uetaisan" by Michio Tsuzuku, the script is a hokey mixture concocted by El Ogawa, Tadaki Yamazaki, and director Kihachi Okamoto (known heretofore as a maker of action pix, "Samurai Assassin" among them), which camps up the whole Japanese adventure-genre and which, at its best, is a wildly improbably collusion between "The Manchurian Candidate" and "The Wrong Box."

The idea is that the mad professor, though interested in solving the population problem is really hot for the diamond and that the dim-witted professor is really the little Japanische Jungen who went to Hitler's Berlin at the age of eight. This leads to a wild chase around Mount Fuji, in which the self-defense corps plays a thorough confusing role, a wholesale bombardment, and the unmasking of all the villains.
Chie.

Les Aventuriers
(FRENCH-COLOR-SCOPE)
Paris, March 21.

SNC release and production. Stars Lino Ventura, Alain Delon, Johanna Shimkus, Serge Reggiani. Directed by Robert Enrico. Screenplay, Jose Giovanni, Pierre Pellegri, Enrico, from the book by Giovanni; camera (Eastmancolor), Jean Boffety; editor, Jacqueline Neppiel. Previewed in Paris. Running Time, 112 MINS.

Roland .... Lino Ventura
Manu .... Alain Delon
Letitia .... Johanna Shimkus
Pilot .... Serge Reggiani

"The Adventurers" is about a youthful daredevil and an older, more settled inventor whose every attempt at moneymaking or evolving new cars or planes ends in failure. With a girl who latches on to them, they hunt and find buried treasure only to be tragically decimated by greedy and less scrupulous fellow adventurers. Brisk, perhaps a bit long, but good-natured and gentle without being too precious, it looms as a good local bet with foreign playoff indicated on its action, good playing and neat production dress, plus an added asset in the Alain Delon name.

Director Robert Enrico sometimes plays too deliberately on the bonhommie and innocence of his characters, which leads to a bit too much padding of their personalities and early adventures. Some tightening of the early segs

to segue more quickly into the treasure hunt and resulting reactions and adventures would make this more wieldy and palatable for foreign spots.

Delon and sidekick Lino Ventura build fast cars or try to make money on gambling, flying a plane under the Arch of Triumph or on other projects. All fail and they are joined by a pretty girl whose welded sculptures do not please the snobbish critics. They form a group of friends and any sex is subordinated to a joyous camaraderie. It is reminiscent of some of the Hollywood adventure pix in this groove.

When they find the treasure, a buried plane, they are beset by some ex-mercenary soldiers who knew about it and had watched their search. The girl is killed in the melee and the two friends try to find out who she was and help her relatives. But in come the heavies and Delon is killed, leaving a grieving Ventura to carry on alone in the trio's dreams of a tourist restaurant on a little island together.

Delon has the right blend of robust derring-do and gentleness, with Ventura fine as the more cantankerous older man and Johanna Shimkus fetching as the girl they both secretly love but cannot declare themselves to until tragedy strikes. It is an unusual French entry and may reflect the growing tendency of avoiding the more bleak and darker sides of people.

It is done with good humor and pictorial solidity and emerges a good, bright commercial adventure opus calling for some pruning of repeated character delineation for best results abroad. Color and production dress are good with only Serge Reggiani adding a more rounded human character to the gallery of more idealized people. Enrico emerges as a director with some force and pictorial flair for straightforward action pix—not too frequent on the local scene.
Mosk.

Double Trouble
(SONGS-PANAVISION-COLOR)

Extremely lightweight but sometimes-amusing Presley starrer; b.o. will depend on star's draw.

Hollywood, March 30.
Metro release of B.C.W. (Judd Bernard-Irwin Winkler) production. Stars Elvis Presley; features John Williams, Yvonne Romain, The Wiere Bros., Annette Day. Directed by Norman Taurog. Screenplay, Jo Heims; based on story by Marc Brandel; camera (Metrocolor), Daniel L. Fapp; music, Jeff Alexander; editor, John McSweeney; asst. director, Claude Binyon Jr. Reviewed at Academy Award Theatre, March 29, '67. Running Time, 91 MINS.

Guy Lambert .... Elvis Presley
Jill Conway .... Annette Day
Gerald Waverly .... John Williams
Claire Dunham .... Yvonne Romain
Wiere Bros. .... Themselves
Archie Brown .... Chips Rafferty
Arthur Babcock .... Norman Rossington
Georgie .... Monty Landis
Morley .... Michael Murphy
Inspector De Groote ...... Leon Askin
Iceman .... John Alderson
Captain Roach .... Stanley Adams
Frenchman .... Maurice Marsac
Mate .... Walter Burke
Gerda .... Helene Winston
The G Men .... Themselves

Hard on heels of Elvis Presley's current "Easy Come, Easy Go," comes another entry by the singing star, slated for early summer release. "Double Trouble" appears to have been whipped up to showcase a big-name without much thought of content other than to serve as footage to cash in on the star's draw. What emerges is the sketchiest of story-line and treatment which leaves spectator wndering what it's all about. Presley as usual however, gives a pretty fair account of himself despite what's handed him and the substantial hold he wields over his public should help reception.

Produced for Metro release by new team of Judd Bernard and Irwin Winkler, film permits Presley to belt out nine songs (some virtually drowned out by his backing) and there's a number of sight gags under Norman Taurog's vivid recollection which will delight slapstick aficionados. Taurog has helmed seven of the star's 25 pix and manages to inject good pace into the Jo Heims screenplay, based on story by Marc Brandel, which has a colorful European setting.

Presley plays an American singer touring foreign discotheques, and scene shifts from London, where two femmes enter his life, to Bruges and finally Antwerp. Intertwined in his travels, and femmes chasing him, are a couple of eccentric jewel thieves who have planted a fortune of diamonds in his luggage, mysterious attempts on his life and his arrest for allegedly kidnapping one of the kittens, who happens to be a rich heiress 17-going-on-18. Plottage seldom plays too important a part in Presley films but here is sheer confusion.

Excellent atmosphere is achieved through top art direction in hands of George W. Davis and errill Pye. Particularly effective is a festival sequence in Antwerp, although it should be trimmed somewhat to snap up action, which includes a murder attempt on the heiress. Color camera work by Daniel L. Fapp is interesting, too, giving the illusion of pic having been shot in actual locale whereas it was lensed at studio.

Presley delivers in customary style, entirely at home in his character. A young English newcomer, Annette Day, enacts the precocious teenage heiress who wants to marry singer, and Yvonne Romain is sultry as other femme on the make whose character becomes overly-contrived in final sequences. John Williams deftly portrays Miss Day's guardian who has been digging into her estate and Leon Askin has a few amusing moments as a police inspector holding Presley for assertedly kidnapping Williams' charge. The Wiere Bros. are up to their usual comedic antics as three confused detectives, and Chips Rafferty and Norman Rossington get laughs as jewel thieves who spend their entire time trying to recover their gems.

Music score is credited to Jeff Alexander and John Sweeney the editing chore. *Whit.*

The Great British Train Robbery
(GERMAN)

German-made, with British location work, this little programmer should please despite overlength and no U.S.-marketable cast names.

Peppercorn-Wormser Film Enterprises release of an Egon Monk presentation. Directed by John Olden and Claus Peter Witt. Entire cast featured. Story and screenplay, Henry Kolarz; additional dialog, Robert Muller; camera, Gerald Gibbs; film editors, Monika Erfurt Tadsen, Oswald Hafenrichter; sound, Horst Faahs; music, Heinz Funk. Reviewed in New York City, March 30, '67. Running Time, 104 MINS.

Michael Donegan .... Horst Tappert
Patrick Kinsey .... Hans Cossy
Archibald Arrow .... Karl Heinz Hess
Thomas Webster .... Hans Reiser
Gerald Williams .... Rolf Nagel
George Slowfoot .... Harry Engel
Andrew Elton .... Wolfran Schaerf
Ronald Cameron .... Gunther Tabor
Walter Lloyd .... Franz Mosthav
Alfred Frost .... Wolfried Lier
Arthur Finnegan .... Kurt Conradi
Twinky .... Horst Beck
Peter Masterson ...... Paul Edwin Roth
Inge Masterson .... Kai Fischer
Jennifer Donegan .... Grit Bottcher
Eileen Black .... Eleonore Schroth
Suzy Fast .... Sylvia Lydi
Dennis MacLeod ..... Siegfried Lowitz
Sergeant Robbins ..... Lotham Grutzner
Sergeant Davies ..... Dirk Dautzenberg
Montague .... Albert Hoerrmann
Mona .... Isa Miranda

(English Soundtrack)

Although far too long and with almost no familiar faces among the cast, this German-made film version of the British train robbery of recent memory is remarkably well constructed and holds the viewer's interest for most of its length.

While almost entirely a German production, only the interiors were done at Studio Hamburg. Much of the film is exteriors and required considerable location work in England, utilizing both countryside and urban sites. Producer Egon Monk and codirectors John Olden and Claus Peter Witt have rightfully followed a semi-documentary style and Gerald Gibbs' crisp black-and-white photography has a wellmade newsreel quality about it that is most appropriate.

Because of the many people involved in the almost-successful crime caper, and the necessity of depicting the extensive police work which resulted, Monk has had to utilize an exceptionally large cast, all of whom are key figures. Some cropping of family scenes (no female in the cast is of major importance except a short but important bit by Isa Miranda as the operator of a criminal talent agency). would improve the pace and eliminate some script embroidery.

The coolness of the planning and execution of the robbery, the absence of violence (a novelty in itself), and the human shortcomings of some of the gang members which provide the tipoffs needed by the police are matched by post-crime planning of the syndicate heads in springing some of the gang members from prison. Scripter Henry Kolarz also emulates the real-life action in leaving the ending hanging fire, with the possibility of further captures or further escapes, but manages to convey the impression that, despite the cleverness of the criminal brains involved, the magnitude of the robbery will insure that none of the gang will ever know a moment's peace.

All technical credits, with the exception of the need for further editing, are excellent. The German cast looks British enough, for the most part, to seem plausible and the English soundtrack, whether dubbed or post-synchronized, is excellent. *Robe.*

Mouchette
(FRENCH)
Paris, March 28.
Parc Film-Athos Film production and release. With Nadine Nortier, Marie Cardinal, Jean Vinenet. Written and directed by Robert Bresson from book by Georges Bernanos. Camera, Ghislain Cloquet; editor, Raymond Lamy. At Mayfair, Paris. Running Time, 85 MINS.
Mouchette .... Nadine Nortier
Mother .... Marie Cardinal
Mathieu .... Jean Vinenet
Arsene .... Paul Hebert

A 14-year-old girl, who is nothing but a drudge in an impoverished alcoholic peasant family, is the heroine of this brilliant film. Her sullen defiance, her failure to connect with life and a final opting out via suicide are treated with clear and uncluttered insight to make produce an uncompromising but shattering effect. Arty theatre chances appear in store but call for careful handling, followup and placements for best results.

Director-writer Robert Bresson has updated Georges Bernanos' pre-war book. But the theme is timeless and it is about a human calvary in a world that bottles her up so completely as to leave no other issue. But there are no usual melodramatics here or didactic accusations. Man's unawareness, charity without understanding and violence are handled so simply, forthrightly and probingly as to give a density, spirituality and bite of rare pitch.

Bresson's refusal to use professional actors also aids this treatment. They are creatures caught up in a series of actions to which they respond without any seeming premedlation.

A dying alcoholic mother is always telling her daughter to run away. Her father and brother use her to do all the house work and odd jobs for drinking money. At school, she is friendless and takes to heaving dirt at her classmates every time she gets out of school. Her only human contact comes through her rape, half consented to, by a local poacher after she has been found by him in the woods.

The death of the mother and the hypocritical piousness of her father and villagers, seem to be felt by this wild little girl.

Scenes of animal hunting around her do not unduly force a backdrop to her own hunted state and lack of understanding or pity from anybody. Bresson does not insist on any religioso trappings. He eschews any bid for emotion but it arises from the very coolness of the direction.

Everyday incidents take on an almost spiritual intensity in Bresson's manner of controlled and incisive direction and handling of the players. Nicole Nortier has the animal ferocity and gentleness needed for the role, and her one smile, as a boy flirts with her, lights up this otherwise terse, harsh but always clear-eyed film.

Bresson's pix have rarely made it stateside but changing art house patterns may give this pic a chance in the U.S. market.

The sharp but never prettied lensing, the unobtrusive cutting, the revelations of simple actions as counterpoints to life's various needs and meanings all combine to make this deceptively simple film a disturbing, poignant vehicle.

But the burgeoning art film distribution, more selective audiences, the breakthrough of "Blow-Up" may foreshadow that Bresson, after his eighth pic, may be ready to find his rightful niche on the art and special situation scene in America. *Mosk.*

Sept Hommes Et Une Garce
(Seven Guys And A Gal)
(FRENCH-ITALO-RUMANIAN-COLOR)
Paris, March 28.
Pathe release of Franco London Film-Dear Film-Rumania Film production. Stars Jean Marais, Sydney Chaplin, Marilu Tolo; features Guy Bedos, Serban Cantacuzino. Directed by Bernard Borderie. Screenplay, Mireille De Tissot, Cecil Saint-Laurent, Gerard Devries, Borderie; camera (Eastmancolor), Henri Persin; music, Paul Misraki. At Paris, Paris. Running Time, 100 MINS.
Captain .... Jean Marais
Adjunct .... Sydney Chaplin
Carlotta .... Marilu Tolo
Latouche .... Guy Bedos
Soldier .... Serban Cantacuzino
Lieutenant .... Ettore Manni

Adventure costumer during the Napoleonic Wars appears a parody of the genre. The usual fights, warring but gregarious French officers, and a bit of nudity are unfolded in this routine pic that has enough derring-do and acceptable tongue-in-cheek carryings-on for okay returns here, but it is mainly a tv or dualler item abroad.

Jean Marais and Sydney Chaplin are the scrapping pals who get separated from their outfit and mixed up with a capricious girl in the enemy camp. All ends well after some rough and tumble escapades. Good humor glosses over the fairly ordinary direction.

It was shot in Rumania, with production values adequate and color passable.

Marilu Tolo is in it mainly for some undraped scenes and Guy Bedos adds some comic relief as a stuttering, frightened foot soldier caught in the dash back to his own lines by the intrepid officers and their sexy hostage, who is both ally and enemy, as the mood strikes. *Mosk.*

Deux Ou Trois Que Je Sais D'Elle
(Two Of Three Things I Know About Her)
(FRENCH—COLOR)
Paris, March 28.
UGC release of Anouchka Film-Argos Film-Parc Film-Films De La Carosse production. Stars Marina Vlady; features Anny Duperey, Roger Montsoret. Written and directed by Jean-Luc Godard. Camera (Eastmancolor), Raoul Coutard; editor, Francoise Colin. At Marbeuf, Paris. Running Time, 85 MINS.
Juliette .... Marina Vlady
Marianne .... Anne Duperey
Robert .... Roger Montsoret
John .... Raoul Levy

That local filmic phenomenon Jean-Luc Godard is back on the scene with the second of two pix he made at the same time. It appears that more of his talents went into this one although it is still a fragmented mixture of vague story and social study cemented with a personal commentary on life in the French new housing projects today. It appears mainly for buffs with too much just surface patter. Specialized outlets abroad, at best, loom for this offbeater.

Godard uses some real actors mixed with non-actors to plow through his own attitudes towards the so-called affluent society, which, he feels, still outstrips its buying potential via ad comeons. It leads to some married women prostituting themselves during the day in these housing setups to buy the things they want which they can not truly afford as yet.

Director Godard has managed to work his personalized offbeat approach into the commercial setup with color and scope. He has a following here. He is shifting from his early themes of drifting youth to more direct statements on everything from morality, to leftist politics and Vietnam.

He uses actress Marina Vlady as a wife, who, though having affection for her husband and children, has drifted into parttime prostitution. She makes asides to the audience. Other characters also talk about themselves or their lives. Many times this method strikes a revealing chord.

His cameras capture the growing new suburbs with their superficial comforts still too dear for most pocketbooks leading to the need to sacrifice certain things for others and an unbalanced life. Godard himself makes his pamphlet-like comments on middleclass life today and still shows an unusual flair for capturing people in bewilderment before life's growing complexities.

But it still remains a surface and spongelike conglomeration of facts and people that rarely jell into more forceful and direct statements or offer a more cohesive palpable dramatic pitch. The players all have ease, and Miss Vlady manages to fit into this Godardian tract.

There are some true reflections of modern outlooks. It is just that Godard appears too surface, irritatingly pontifical and too full of private comments, readings and quotations to weld this whole fresco into a more clearcut vehicle statement. But there's no gainsaying his pictorial flair, aided by Raoul Coutard's expert color cameras.

Some of Godard's prolific output has clicked stateside, though rarely, and this one will be a difficult one for arty theatre chances and playoff. However, he seems to be mastering his style and appearing more certain about things he wants to say.   *Mosk.*

Winnetou und sein Freund Old Firehand
(Winnetou And His Friend Old Firehand)
(GERMAN—COLOR)
Berlin, March 28.

Columbia release of Rialto-Film production. Stars Rod Cameron, Pierre Brice, Marie Versini. Directed by Alfred Vohrer. Screenplay, David De Reszke, C. B. Taylor and Harald G. Petersson, based on novels by Karl May; camera (Eastmancolor), Karl Loeb; music, Peter Thomas; At Zoo Palast, West Berlin. Running time, 94 MINS.

Old Firehand	Rod Cameron
Winnetou	Pierre Brice
Ntscho-tschi	Marie Versini
Silers	Harald Leipnitz
Tom	Todd Armstrong
Ravenhurst	Viktor de Kowa

Whatever the crix may say about Horst Wendlandt's Karl May westerns (the local Rialto topper supervises these pix personally), they have at least to admit that they are made with remarkable care, at least as contrasted with the horse operas turned out by other domestic producers. Also this one has been shot in Yugoslavia and benefits from fine, and sometimes interesting outdoor lensing. And once again an American name heads the cast, Rod Cameron (his first Wendlandt western) this time. This western should still be able to chalk up at least satisfactory returns around here. It's a family type of outdoor thriller.

The simple plot sees Old Firehand (Rod Cameron), the old westerner, and his faithful pals ride to a border village named Miramonte. On their way they meet Winnetou, the handsome Apache chieftain, and his beautiful sister, Ntscho-tschi, who just had another narrow escape from death — the menace being this time the brutal white man, Silers, and his gang of badmen. The villagers of Miramonte are stricken with fear because the local sheriff has put the brother of Silers in jail. The greater part of this pic sees Old Firehand, Winnetou and all the good men fighting the attacking bandits. But eventually the picture changes and the bandits are pushed back on the defensive. There is the big final fight which sees few of the villians surviving.

As usual with these Teutonic outdoor epics, the cast is international. In addition to American Cameron, who turns in a sympathetic performance, there are the

French Pierre Brice and Marie Versini and the Germans Harald Leipnitz and Viktor de Kowa among the leading players. Remainder of the cast is composed of Italians, Yugoslav and French players. The inevitable "comedy relief" comes from Viktor de Kowa who enacts a Englishman siding with the good forces. He tries hard to be funny. Alfred Vohrer, one of Germany's busiest directors, shows again that he has picked up a good deal of western knowledge from his stateside colleagues. Technical credits are fully competent.   *Hans.*

After You. Comrade
(SOUTH AFRICAN-COLOR)
Continental Distributing release of Jamie Uys production, written and directed by Uys. Stars Jamie Uys, Bob Courtney, Arthur Swemmer; features rest of cast. Camera (Technicolor), Manie Botha; film editor, Dave Burman; backdrops and titles, Ian MacLeod, K. Dubinski; music, composed, arranged and conducted by Sam Sklair. Reviewed in New York, March 31, '67. Running Time, 84 MINS.

Igor Strogoff	Jamie Uys
Granger J. Wellborne	Bob Courtney
Tanya Orloff	Reinet Maasdorf
Johnny Edwards	Angus Neill
Ed Sloane	Joe Stewardson
Anzonia	Arthur Swemmer
Italian Mayor	Frank Gregory
Italian Butcher	Mimmi Poli
Hostel Matron	Marjorie Gordon
Television Announcer	Emil Mofal
Yugoslavian Mother	Sann De Lange
Austrian Farmer	Wilhelm Esterhuizen
Chief Russian Delegate	Victor Ivanoff
Chief American Delegate	Keith Stanners-Bloxam
Second Russian Delegate	Rickey Arden
Greek Sergeant	George Bertolis
Conference President	Bill Brewer

What is, probably, a major production for South African filmmaker Jamie Uys due to its large cast, color camerawork and the extensive location shooting across half of Europe, comes off as a pleasant, often refreshing, little comedy that is more original than professional. The general reaction of audiences will be a pleasant interlude but absence of recognizable players will require clever exploitation and selling.

Uys, one of those one-man-film-company types, has done a remarkable job of not allowing any one of his talents to overshadow the others. His original story idea, that a stalemate of an international committee meeting in Athens be resolved by a walking race between the American and Russian delegates (the principal stalematers), is the hook on which he hangs some excellent comedy and many lovely scenery shots as the course for the competition runs from Athens to Paris.

It is to the credit of Uys, who plays the Russian, and Bob Courtney, as the brash American, that they don't concede an inch to their magnificent scenic backdrops, frequently utilizing the very setting as part of their comedy connniptions. One could easily believe that the script, also by Uys, was intentionally left very loose in format to enable the pair to have as much license as possible for their fun.

The weakness of Uys' script is most noticeable in the meetings although some excellent jabs at international bureaucracy manage to shine through. Of course, the European location removes any necessity for mention of South African race relations which Uys

would not find so easy to satirize.

Most of the action revolves about the two delegates and Arthur Swemmer, as an Anzonian delegate who suggests the competition and keeps it perking. He's shown as both sincere do-gooder and mischievous meddler, with the ending categorizing him as a devil and an angel. Reinet Maasdorp as the pretty Russian aide to Uys and Angus Neill as Courtney's assistant provide the romantic interest, which is sketchy.

While considerable views of Greece, Yugoslavia, Austria, Switzerland and Italy are shown, France is only suggested as the ending of the race is delightfully crosscut with color newsreel footage of President De Gaulle receiving an important delegation in such a manner that le Grand Charles is made as ridiculous as the two contestants. This may possibly make it a bit tough to sell the film is in sensitive France. But they'll love it at the United Nations.   *Robe.*

Berenice
(FRENCH)
Paris, March 21.

CFDC release of CEPC production. With Anna Gael, Josee Destoop, Bernard Verlay, Jean Lescot, Marc Moro. Written and directed by Pierre-Alain Jolivet, from the tragedy by Racine; camera, Claude Beausoleil; editor, Claude Cohen. Previewed in Paris. Running Time, 90 MINS.

Berenice	Anna Gael
Titus	Bernard Verlay
Plautus	Jean Lescot
Friend	Marc Moro

Racine's 17th-century tragedy is played before modern buildings and interior. Neither a filmed play nor successful transposition, this rather arbitrary idea gets bogged down in rhetoric and appears an unlikely export item except for possible educational or specialized situation usage, and then mainly on the text rather than its laggard visual accompaniment.

To backgrounds of modernistic display halls, warehouses, and Paris streets of a few characters unfold the tale of the African Queen Berenice who loves and is loved by the Roman King Titus. But they are forced to part since Roman law will not sanction the marriage.

The rhymed speech is played out by the actors, whether escorted by French Republican Guards, substituting for the Centurions, or in an aquarium and other picturesque spots. But it does not work, for the intensity of the speeches gets only fair delivery, the modern backdrop does not attempt to transpose the play, and it is a rather arch and precious affair and with the use of negative and special double printing not helping much.

Pic got an advance on aid, presumably due to the Racine name in the credits. Otherwise it is hard to see how this got made under the regular commercial film setup here.   *Mosk.*

Un Idiot A Paris
(An Idiot in Paris)
(FRENCH—COLOR)
Paris, April 4.

Gaumont release of Gaumont International production. Stars Jean Lefebre, Dany Carrel, Bernard Blier. Directed by

Serge Korber. Screenplay, Korber, Jean Vermorel, Michel Audiard from book by Rene Fallet; camera (Eastmancolor), Jean Rabier; editor, Annie Maurel. At Paris, Paris. Running time, 95 MINS.

Goubi	Jean Lefebre
La Fleur	Dany Carrel
Boss	Bernard Blier
Mayor	Robert Dalban
Student	Philippe Avron
Girl	Bernadette Lafont

Tale of a backward village type adrift in Paris, of which he has long dreamed, is bogged down with fairly lacklustre adventures. These lack an element of inventiveness and surer taste to give it the needed pleasant comic edge. But it appears mainly a local item.

It seems that the idiot of this pic is a backward but good-natured rural worker who long has dreamed of going to Paris. One day some jokester truckdrivers load him into their van and take him to Paris where he proceeds to get lost, meets a big-hearted joy girl and a fellow orphan to go through a series of scrapes before heading home to the townspeople who now feel they have missed him. Also that they will be easier on the beguiling simpleton in the future.

Somehow this has an old-fashioned ring underlined by harsh and vulgar dialog. It does not jell with the attempt at winsome direction by newcomer Serge Korber. Jean Lefebre is properly winning as the idiot in question. The script is patronizing. Though okay as a local item, this has playoff or dualer possibilities abroad only on its okay color and rustic shenanigans.   *Mosk.*

The Young Warriors
(COLOR)

Technical excellence and outstanding camerawork overshadow cliche-ridden script and routine performances.

Universal release of Gordon Kay production. Stars James Drury; features rest of cast. Directed by John Peyser. Screenplay, Richard Matheson; camera (Technicolor), Loyal Griggs; film editor, Russell F. Schoengarth; sound, Waldon O. Watson, Clarence Self; art directors, Alexander Golitzen, Alfred Ybarra; no music credit; asst. director, Joe Kenny. Reviewed at Universal h.o., New York, April 7, '67. Running Time, **93 MINS.**

Sgt. Cooley	James Drury
Hacker	Steve Carlson
Guthrie	Jonathan Daly
Foley	Robert Pine
Riley	Michael Stanwood
Lippincott	Jeff Scott
Harris	Johnny Alladin
Fairchild	Hank Jones
Tremont	Tom Nolan
Sgt. Wadley	Norman Fell
Schumacher	L. E. "Buck" Young
Lieutenant	Kent McWhirter

The overall impression left by this programmer is that it was made as an exercise for many of Universal's younger contract talents and if sold for that reason alone — to introduce new faces — it could prove to be of benefit to both Universal and to exhibitors seeking good inexpensive fare. However, the technical side of the film, particularly Loyal Griggs' beautifully-handled camerawork, is so professional that the company may be tempted to handle it as an "A" film, which it is not.

Producer Gordon Kay and director John Peyser had two major obstacles to overcome in what was intended as an intimate look at the effect of warfare on the very young, hence the apt title. These obstacles, a screenplay ridden with just about every possible cliche and a cast that is collectively damp behind the ears, have proven too great for most of the people concerned.

On the other hand, being the product of a major studio which has some of the industry's best technical skills available, it has the surface appearance of a top-budget film. Paced by some beautiful camerawork by veteran cameraman Loyal Griggs, the film's technical aspects are worthy of a better project. Richard Matheson's screenplay, apparently, underwent considerable changes during the shooting as the film often hints at cancelled passages or sliced dialog. As a result, the actions of some of the characters, particularly the soldier played by Steve Carlson, are ill-defined.

Carlson, as a "young soldier who grows up in combat," has the most important role although James Drury, as a seasoned sergeant, has star billing and gives film's best performance. The rest of the youthful cast is a cross-section of stock war-film characters. Jonathan Daly, Robert Pine, Michael Stanwood, Jeff Scott and Tom Nolan have little chance due to the stereotype characters they play. However, a newcomer, Johnny Alladin, who reminds of a young Tony Curtis, could make a big impression on the teenage femme market despite the brevity of his role.

As the few interiors and more intimate scenes are played against obvious studio sets not too well designed they clash that much more with the bigger battle scenes that are either responsible for much of the budget expenditure or are borrowed from other films. A stunning pre-title battle-scape for instance has little to do with what follows.

All in all, a film worth playing if sold wisely, and Universal has evidently not completely decided how to sell it as the film goes into test engagements this week in the Dallas and Oklahoma areas.
Robe.

ABC Del Amor
(ABC of Love)
(ARGENTINE-BRAZILIAN-CHILEAN)
Santiago, April 12.

Continental Films release of Marcelo Simonetti (Argentine)-Saga Films (Brazil)-Jose Luis Contreras (Chile) coproduction. Features Susana Rinaldi, Federico Luppi, Hector Pellegrini, Jorge Rivera Lopez, Vera Viana, Reginaldo Farias, Cecilia Paez, Patricia Menz, Maria E. Cavieres, Miguel Littin. Directed by Rodolfo Kuhn, Eduardo Coutinho and Helvio Soto. At Cine Pacifico. Running Time, **110 MINS.**

The three stories of this pic were filmed separately and by different directors in Argentine, Brazil and Chile. It is the first time this type of coproduction has been attempted in South America. Its aim, to show three different aspects of love, but not from the boy gets girl angle, but rather to demonstrate how social mores condition relationships between man and femme.

This was only partially successful. Rodolfo Kuhn, the best known of the three directors, takes the story of a man from Buenos Aires who—the night before his wedding—backs out of marriage, not to face a lifetime of bourgeois respectability and routine. The story mostly visualizes his reflections during this night while he makes up his mind. Entertaining and well acted, but directed more for laughs than the depth and insight the subject called for.

Brazil's Eduardo Coutinho is a newcomer, but knows how to handle his actors and get them to display their characters well. He deals with a pair of adolescents: he tries to make the gal, while she conditions their sleeping together with a pact in which both engage to take lethal poison. Coutinho is a promising director, but he does not show enough of the girl's social background to make her quirks clearly understandable to non-Brazilians. Still, it is well narrated.

Helvio Soto's Chilean episode was a failure. It could be described as a tv director's "8½," but Soto is no Fellini. Amateurishly acted and with far too pretentious dialog, the story's intention simply does not come across with even a minimum of impact or intelligibility.

Boxoffice chances are only fair in Chile. In Argentine and Brazil, where "ABC" will be exhibited next, it will depend on audience's interest in the local director and actor's work. *Amig.*

Esto es Alegria
(This is Joy)
(ARGENTINE-COLOR)
Buenos Aires, April 4.

General Belgrano production and release. Co-produced by Jose Huberman and Ricardo Canto. Stars Tita Merello, Eduardo Rudy, Jorge Barreiro, Mercedes Carreras, Carlos Bala, Ubaldo Martinez; features Chico Novarro, Juan Carlos, Altavista, Tono Andreu, Luis Tasca, Nathan Pinzon, Dario Vittori and Chispita, Marisita and Quique Carreras. Directed by Enrique Carreras. Written by Carreras, Julio Porter and Tita Merello; camera (Eastmancolor), Antonio Merayo; music, Tito Ribero; editor, Jorge Garate. At the Atlas, Buenos Aires. Running Time, **100 MINS.**

CHILDREN'S COMMAND

Jimena	Mercedes Carreras
Gabriel	Jorge Barreiro

IDOLS AT HOME

Tita	Tita Merello
Eduardo	Eduardo Rudy

A ROUND ILLUSION

Cepillito	Carlos Bala
Comodoro	Ubaldo Martinez

Light entertainment, saleable in the Spanish-speaking markets, with several top Argentina names in the cast, this contains three episodes of different character, and appeal.

First, "Children's Command," looms effective for moppet audiences, with three nice kids (director Carreras' own children) influencing their widowed father, a tele executive, to rehire and eventually marry their favorite tv star (ably played by Carreras' wife). Fast action and colorful backgrounds strengthen this segment in which leading man Jorge Barreiro, who is rated No. 1 idol of teenagers in this country.

Second, "Idols at Home," depicts a middle-aged, semi-retired tango singer torturing her actor husand, still popular in the femme trade, with sarcastic references to his age and his apparently dead love for her. Sharp phrases, loaded with vitriolic humor, as well as funny observations of oldsters intimacy, keep patrons laughing till the sentimental end, somewhat weakened when an unnecessary song is dragged in.

Superb acting by Tita Merello and Eduardo Rudy greatly helps the impact attained by this episode.

Third, "A Round Illusion" disappoints local viewers by casting comic star Carlos Bala in a dramatic role. Besides, it is over-melodramatic and unconvincing. It ruins the pic's end. And it will help by spotting it either at the beginning or the middle for the foreign market. Technical credits are okay. *Nubi.*

Wild, Wild Planet
(I Criminali Della Galassia)
(ITALIAN-COLOR)

Metro-Goldwyn-Mayer release of a Joseph Fryd-Antonio Margheriti production. Features Tony Russell, Lisa Gastoni, Massimo Serato, Franco Nero, Carlo Giustini, Enzo Fiermonte. Directed by Anthony Dawson (Antonio Margheriti); original screenplay, Ivan Reiner; camera (Eastman Color), Richard Pallton; editor, Angel Coly; sound, Victor Massey; associate producers, Walter Manley, Reiner; art direction, set decorators, Piero Poletto; choreography, Archie Savage; music, Francesco Lavagnino; asst. director, Roger Godet. Reviewed at Metro h.o., N.Y., March 23, '67. Running Time, **93 MINS.**

Mike Halstead	Tony Russell
Connie	Lisa Gastoni
Nurmi	Massimo Serato
Jake	Franco Nero
Ken	Carlo Giustini
General	Enzo Fiermonte
Maitland	Umberto Raho
Hotel Agent	Isarco Ravaioli
A. G. Chief	Moha Tahi
De Lauty	Freddy Unger
Schneider	Lino Desmond
Jeff	Giuliano Raffaelli
Francini	Victoria Ziny,
A. G. agents	Kitty Swan, Rosemarie Martin, Annelise Stern
Claridge	Rodolfo Lodi
Detective	Renato Montalbano
Fryd	Aldo D'Ambrosio
Werner	Carlo Kechler
Edith Halstead	Margherita Orovitz
Dr. Delfos	Sandro Mondini
Dr. Delfos (dwarf)	Vittorio Bonos

(Dubbed English Soundtrack)

What the Italians lack in special effects skill they make up in athletic ability. With the decline in the previously popular 'sand and sandals' epics, the trend is changing to science-fiction but what the almost-identical casts previously gave to the undraped-torso efforts —lots of action and mucho display of muscles—has been carried over almost intact. Possibly the characters are now more fully clothed but the futuristic uniforms they wear are frequently tight enough to suggest the muscles beneath.

There are some old action hands in both acting and production credits of 'Wild, Wild Planet.' Coproducer Antonio Margheriti (who is also director Anthony Dawson) and cast members Tony Russell (an Italian actor despite the name), Massimo Serato and Enzo Fiermonte are well-known for their work in the Hercules-Ursus-Maciste-Samson field, which probably explains their teamwork in this opus insignificus. Ivan Reiner's script has some interesting angles but they're generally subjugated to the stress on action, of which there is plenty. Particularly outstanding is a free-for-all between some of the scientist-spacemen and some female agents of the villain. The girls, evidently well trained in judo and karate, give the big, husky males a real working over before they're subdued.

Franco Nero, who's now playing Lancelot in Warners' "Camelot," has little to do as a fellow officer of lead Tony Russell but Massimo Serato, playing his usual slick villain, makes the character almost sympathetic before the usual violent ending.

Technical credits are generally excellent with the exception of some of the miniature sets, evidently the work of scenery and set designer Piero Poletto. The life-size settings are too elaborate to be studio-made, so must have been filmed in some industrial plants. Interiors are ordinary until the windup action bit on space station Delphos which evidently took most of the production budget. Richard Pallton's Eastman Color camerawork is handsome but allowed little chance at exterior shooting. Francesco Lavagnino's score is surprisingly lush and romantic and not what one would imagine in the year 2015 when melody is usually prophesied as having disappeared.

A better-than-average programmer which should lend solid support to any adventure-action double bill and a natural for the matinee-kiddie crowd. *Robe.*

Die Nibelungen (Part I: Siegfried)
(GERMAN-YUGOSLAV)
(Color)

Berlin, April 4.

Constentin release of CCC (Artur Brauner) production made in collab with Avala-Film, Belgrade. With Uwe Beyer, Rolf Henniger, Maria Marlow, Siegfried Wischnewski. Directed by Harald Reinl. Screenplay, Harald G. Petersson, Harald Reinl and Ladislas Fodor, based on the Nibelungen story; camera (Eastmancolor), Ernst W. Kalinke; music, Rolf Wilhelm; editor, Hermann Haller. At City in Europa Center, West Berlin. Running Time, 91 MINS.

Siegfried	Uwe Beyer
Gunther	Rolf Henniger
Hagen	Siegfried Wischnewski
Kriemhild	Maria Marlow
Giselher	Mario Girotti
Gernot	Fred Williams
Volker	Hans von Borsody
Alberich	Skip Martin
Brunhild	Karin Dor

This one, involuntarily, brings back old memories of Germany's great film spoch. It was Fritz Lang who directed the two-part "Nibelungen" ("Siegfried's Death" and "Kriemhild's Revenge") as silents in 1922-'23 which marked the advent of this country's "classical" film era. But while the old "Nibelungen" pix made history and brought glory to their creators, the new filmization of the Teutonic saga will hardly stir more than average attention. It has to do with several facts and one of these is that the times have changed.

The success of the old Lang pix was based on their optical ingredients such as the outstanding masks of the players. There was no color lensing at that time and, of course, the films still had no sound. Lang was able to present his "Nibelungen" in spartanic style. Today such ventures must be spectacular. They require a lavish scenery, a big colorful cast and therefore lots of money. And therewith begins the dilemma for a German producer whose budget is rather limited in the big international sense. Artur Brauner's two-part "Nibelungen" reportedly cost about $1,750,000 which is an unusually big amount by native standards but obviously it was not enough to produce an extravaganza like "Nibelungen" with all its trimmings.

With such a limited budget, there was the choice of either concentrating on big sets or a gallery of name stars since both would have meant skyrocketing costs. Brauner concentrated on a lavish scenery at the expense of few names in his cast. The outcome is admittedly a lavish looking film and the expensive production dress is indeed this film's forte. Its weakness, however, is the cast. And this begins with the two principal players, Siegfried and Kriemhild (Uwe Beyer and Maria Marlow), two unknowns.

The 22-year old Beyer represents some marquee value. He's the winner of the bronze medal in hammer-throw at the last (Tokyo) Olympic Games and also is German champion. Physically, he's okay for the Siegfried role. Thanks to Harald Reinl, an experienced director, Beyer manages adequately. Karin Dor, actress-wife of the director, can hardly be regarded as an ideal Brunhild. She's just a beautiful femme in this. Even such a good actor as Rolf Henniger (King Gunther) fails to convince here. The most convincing performance is turned in by the sinister-looking Siegfried Wischnewski.

"Nibelungen" was ready to be remade in the 1930's here. But the then (Nazi) rulers nixed the project. It's said that they didn't like the plot's "Message." It poses the question whether heroism is paying off. *Hans.*

A Witch Without a Broom
(SPANISH-COLOR)

Made-in-Spain silliness with fair chances as dualer.

Producers Releasing Organization release of Sidney Pink production. Stars Jeffrey Hunter, Maria Perschy. Directed by Joe Lacy. Screenplay, Howard Berk; camera (Movielab color), Alfonso Nieva; editor, John Horvath; executive producer, Stan Torchia. Reviewed in New York, April 6, '67. Running Time, 86 MINS.

Garver Logan	Jeffrey Hunter
Marianna	Maria Perschy
Cayo	Gustavo Rojo
Octavia	Pearl Cristal
Don Ignacio	Reginald Gilliam
Wurlitz the Wizard	Al Muloc
Yolanda	Katharine Ellison
Necio	Felix Defauce
Valeria	Esperanza Roy
Chariot Master	John Clarke
Proprietor	Carl Rapp

Another link in Sidney Pink's chain of Spanish sausages for U.S. consumption, this one has Jeffrey Hunter as an American professor in Madrid who's the object of the affection of Maria Perschy, a 15th-Century apprentice witch.

Seems Maria has got a glimpse of Jeff in Daddy's bubbling cauldron, and after that there's no controlling her. First she projects herself into the present as a sort of high-fashion mirage. Then, when Pops has gone to the sorcerers' convention in London, she rubs madly away at a time-projection amulet — and she and Jeff are off on a tour of the Pink studio wardrobe. Stops include a 16th-Century castle, a caveman's soup kitchen, Rome at the time of Nero, and a nearly-depopulated 21st-Century wasteland. Everywhere they go, innumerable persons of the opposite sex find them irresistably attractive, and various hirsute (male) or anguished (female) mates find this too much to bear.

Dialog is archly inept for the most part with leads mouthing the prose in English, and most others — including non-linguistic cavemen — dubbed from Spanish. Synchronization is okay, but is off once in a while, even for the principals. With eventual tv market in view, camera work is exclusively close-in, including a chariot race.

Production values are fine, and even though that Roman street looks familiar, it seems to be holding up well. Color is good. The actors do the best they can. *Gold.*

The Sword Of Doom
(Daibosatsu Toge)
(JAPANESE-TOHOSCOPE)

Toho release of Sanezumi Fujimoto production. Directed by Kihachi Okamoto. Stars Tatsuya Nakadai, Michiyo Aratama, Toshiro Mifune. Screenplay, Shinobu Hashimoto, based on novel by Kaizan Nakazato; camera (Tohoscope), Hiroshi Murai; music, Masaru Sato. No other credits. Reviewed at 55th Street Playhouse, N.Y., April 10, '67. Running Time, 122 MINS.

Ryonosuke Tsukue	Tatsuya Nakadai
Toranosuke Shimada	Toshiro Mifune
Hyoma Utsuki	Yuzo Kayama
Ohama	Michiyo Aratama
Bunnojo Utsuki	Ichiro Nakaya

In an effort to stimulate attendance at his long-term-leased 55th Street Playhouse, Frank Lee has booked the first Japanese film into the small Manhattan house which has been trying to subsist on all-Chinese film fare, provided by the Shaw Bros. The trouble with Chinese films is that an hour after you've seen one, you're film hungry again.

A two-hour samurai effort from Toho, with two surefire marquee lures named Toshiro Mifune and Tatsuya Nakadai, should bring customers into this house for awhile but better efforts than this umpteenth remake of a tired story will be needed to bring them back again and again. The use of Mifune's name is something of a red herring, anyhow, as he's actually in briefly, although impressively, and leaves most of the work up to Nakadai.

Teaming these two is, to a samurai film, the equivalent of having John Wayne and Lee Marvin in the same cast. If the script is good, the result is a Nipponese variation on a John Ford western; if the script is fair, as in this instance, there's still plenty of action and enough gore to satisfy even a first-year medical student. Only color could have made it more impressive but Hiroshi Murai's black-and-white camerawork is skillfully used to make the wholesale mayhem acceptable.

Director Kihachi Okamoto's forte is mass violence (he followed up this one with "Age Of Assassins") and, despite the overlong unfolding of the story, rarely pauses for a rest. Besides a too-brief exhibit by Mifune (his sword arm has lost nothing of its prowess), there are frequent scriptcalls for Nakadai (as a brooding, fatalistic swordsman, doomed to bring tragedy into the lives of all with whom he comes in contact) to perform a highly-civilized form of butchery and wind the film with a lengthy, almost non-stop mad scene in which he takes on dozens of would-be assassins. Obviously dying, Nakadai is frozen in the final frame with sword arm still poised in mid-air.

When not busy with his cutlass, Nakadai is also called upon to seduce an opponent's wife, slay the opponent and, later, most of his relatives when they try to ambush him. A counterpoint story, as tender as the rest of the film is violent, has a young samurai (Yuzo Kayama) fall in love with a girl being prepared to be a courtesan. Masaru Sato's music, basically Western but with Japanese themes, manages to be both melodic and eerie.

At best a programmer, it's a relief from the sing-song Chinese efforts which have been the theatre's fare for too long. *Robe.*

Tell Me In The Sunlight

Offbeat romance, awkwardly made but sometimes touching. Steve Cochran's last pic, which he directed. Limited b.o. in certain situations.

Hollywood, March 31.

Movie-Rama Color Corp. release of Arnold Stoltz production. Features Steve Cochran, Shary Marshall. Directed by Cochran. Screenplay, Jo Heims, based on original story by Robert Stevens; camera, Rod Yould; editor, David Woods; music, Michael Anderson; title song, Cochran, Franz Steininger, Jack Ackerman; asst. director, Adrian Crossett. Reviewed at Lytton Center, L.A., March 30, '67. Running Time, 82 MINS.

Dave	Steve Cochran
Julie	Shary Marshall
Barber	Jay Robinson
Alex	Dave Bondu
Chata	Patricia Wolf
Tony	George Hopkins
Rocky	Rockne Tarkington
Dr. Franklin	Harry Franklin
Airport Attendant	Hamish Mackay
Princess Naga	Lucille
Pickpocket	George Roberts
Girl In Park	Jill Walden
Pepe	Oliver Nissick
Driver	Joseph Hardy

"Tell Me in the Sunlight," made by the late actor Steve Cochran in Nassau three years ago, has undergone some drastic editing. Despite its technical and artistic flaws, what is left is a sometimes touching account of two lost people who find happiness with each other. Acquired from Cochran's estate by Movie-Rama Color Corp., an indie distrib which will states right it, pic will either strike a responsive chord in certain semi-artie situations, or die at the b.o.

Title derives from the perpetual hope of strangers that their brief, nocturnal romantic encounters may develop into an enduring attachment. Jo Heims is credited with the adaptation of an original story by Robert Stevens. Cochran, who directed and starred, is a merchant seaman who, on shore leave, meets nitery stripper Shary Marshall.

Plot develops in rather slow fashion, incorporating what ordinarily would be called pure cliches —the inevitable misunderstanding, and the too-quick reconciliation, to name a pair of prime flaws. Curiously, however, there shines through the faults some genuine valid sentiment which will ring true in the hearts of the lonely. This one virtue overcomes to a measurable degree a host of acting, directing and lensing gaucheries.

Cochran's performance is okay, better than Miss Marshall's, but both get their message across. Rest of cast is barely adequate, although Jay Robinson's barber, Patricia Wolf's rough-tough stripper, and George Hopkins' buddy characterizations have some depth. Jill Walden, a pregnant girl befriended by Cochran in early footage, is good. Her character reportedly was developed more fully in the original Cochran cut, running over two hours, per Arnold Stoltz, who acquired pic and re-edited to 82 minutes with associate producer Jerald Cormier.

Cochran's direction is static, reflected in Rod Yould's fixed camera) often mismatched in cuts, where sound levels often vary, too). A possibly crushing irony is that this film ante-dates a current, successful foreign pic which deals with the same basic subject matter. Technical credits are on the primitive side, and title song, warbled over main title by Darlene Paul, is a trifle. *Murf.*

Fantomas Contre Scotland Yard
(Fantomas Against Scotland Yard)
(FRENCH-COLOR)

Paris, April 4.
Gaumont release of PAC-Gaumont International-Fair Film production. Stars Jean Marais, Louis De Funes, Mylene Demongeot; features Henri Serre, Francoise Christophe, Jacques Dynam. Directed by Andre Hunebelle. Screenplay, Jean Halain, Pierre Foucaud; camera (Eastmancolor), R. C. Forget; editor, Roger Dwyre. Running Time, 105 MINS.

Fantomas, Fandor	Jean Marais
Juve	Louis De Funes
Helene	Mylene Demongeot
Lady	Francoise Christophe
Lord	Jean-Pierre Caussimon
Andre	Henri Serre

Series based on a super-criminal and a madcap police inspector always after him, aided by an intrepid newspaperman and his girl friend, is now in its third time around. It still remains primarily a local item because of its stolid comedies, lack of a truly tongue-in-cheek adventurous spirit and its repetitive quality. However, its good production dress and campy outlook might have it okay for playoff and dualer use abroad.

Fantomas wears a gray rubber mask and also dons faces of others to trick the skeptical. fussy, self-indulgent inspector always chasing him. This time he goes after rich people, both respectable and in the underworld, and has them pay ransoms or be killed. The inspector follows him to a castle where there is some fun with ghosts, a fox hunt and the final escape of Fantomas. It means more sequels for this by-now threadbare series.

Nothing scary or imaginative in this, if there are some electronic gadgets. Louis De Funes is still funny in his slow burns but needs better material than this. Matinee idol Jean Marais dons the many masks of Fantomas and is also the newsman. Others are okay, production values good but direction is tepid.   Mosk.

Casino Royale
(BRITISH-COLOR)

All out wacky spoof on James Bond and spy stuff generally. Name-heavy cast, wagonload of gimmicks, frantic pace, should insure boffo b.o. returns despite too many cooks.

Columbia release of Famous Artists Production. Produced by Charles K. Feldma and Jerry Bresler. Features Peter Sellers, Ursula Andress, David Niven, Orson Welles, Deborah Kerr, Woody Allen, Daliah Lavi, Charles Boyer, John Huston, William Holden, George Raft, Kurt Kaznar, Jean-Paul Belmondo, Gabriella Licudi, Joanna Pettet, Bernard Cribbins, Duncan Macrae, Ronnie Corbett, Anna Quayle, Terence Cooper, Barbara Bouchet, Angela Scoular, Tracy Reed, Tracey Crisp, Derek Nimmo, Colin Gordon. Directed by John Huston, Ken Hughes, Val Guest, Robert Parrish, Joe McGrath; second unit directors, Richard Talmadge, Anthony Squire; additional sequences by Guest; screenplay, Wolf Mankowitz, John Law, Michael Sayers, suggested by Ian Fleming's novel, "Casino Royale"; camera (Technicolor), Jack Hildyard; additional photography, John Wilcox, Nicolas Roeg; editor, Bill Lenny; special effects, Cliff Richardson, Roy Whybrow; sound, Chris Greenham; titles and montage effects, Richard Williams; music, Burt Bacharach; lyrics, Hal David; title theme played by Herb Alpert and The Tijuana Brass; "The Look of Love" sung by Dusty Springfield. At Odeon, Leicester Square, London, April 14, '67. Running Time, 131 MINS.

Evelyn Tremble	Peter Sellers
Vesper Lynd	Ursula Andress
Sir James Bond	David Niven
Le Chiffre	Orson Welles
Mata Bond	Joanna Pettet
The Detainer	Daliah Lavi
Jimmy Bond	Woody Allen
Ransome	William Holden
Le Grand	Charles Boyer
McTarry	John Huston
Smernov	Kurt Kaznar
Himself	George Raft
French Legionnaire	Jean-Paul Belmondo
Cooper	Terence Cooper
Moneypenny	Barbara Bouchet
Buttercup	Angela Scoular
Eliza	Gabriella Licudi
Heather	Tracey Crisp
Miss Goodthings	Jacky Bisset
Frau Hoffner	Anna Quayle
Hadley	Derek Nimmo
Polo	Ronnie Corbett
Casino Director	Colin Gordon
Taxi Driver	Bernard Gribbins
Fang Leader	Tracy Reed
Inspector Mathis	Duncan Macrae
Cashier	Graham Stark
British Army Officer	Richard Wattis
1st Piper	Percy Herbert

Charles K. Feldman and Jerry Bresler set themselves a tricky task with their expensive, wacky comedy extravaganza, "Casino Royale," an attempt to spoof the pants off the James Bond. But the long run of spy films has already cashed in on almost every available wild gimmick, what with Matt Helm, UNCLE, Flint and the Bond films themselves, and it's difficult successfully to parody a parody. So the three-ring circus aspect is predominant and it will pay off.

The producers have spared no expense and have piled something like $12,000,000, five directors, at least three writers, endless special effects and a load of guest stars and supporting players into the picture. "Casino Royale" is a conglomeration of frenzied situations, "in" gags and special effects, lacking discipline and cohesion. Some of the situations are very funny, but many are too strained.

Nevertheless, the ballyhoo that's preceded the film, the subject and the names involved in it, plus the galaxy of gorgeous girlies, are bound to provoke audience curiosity and the gamble of Feldman, Bresler and Columbia may well pay off handsomely.

Based freely on Ian Fleming's novel, the story line of "Royale," as dreamed up by W f Mankowitz, John Law and Michael Sayers, seemingly with copious assistance from Woody Allen, the directors, Peter Sellers and probably everybody else who h: pened to be on hand, defies sane description. Sufficint to say that the original J. es Bond (David Niven), now knighted & living in eccentric retirement where he plays Debussy and breeds lions, is persuaded back into the Secret Service to help cope with a disastrous situation whereby SMERSH is gradually wiping out most of the world's secret agents.

To confuse the enemy it's decided that several other secret agents (including Ursula Andress, Sellers, Terence Cooper and Dahlia Lavi) should all be referred to as Bond 007. With SMERSH using a bunch of stunning dames to seduce Bond it is clearly necessary to start an Anti-Feminine League, with Terence Cooper, one of the pseudo Bonds, being trained to be immune to women's charms. Somewhere along the line Sellers, a skilled baccarat player, gets involved in a high-stakes gambling game with Orson Welles, one of the spy ring's top executives.

The action includes a crazy alcoholic orgy in a Scottish castle (presided over by Del rah Kerr, an agent who becomes a nun), lashings of scantily clad lasses, a visit to a "spy school" in Berlin, flying saucers, torture, Sellers posing in a variety of fancy dresses, Welles doing conjuring tricks and a fantastic punch-up t the Casino Royale as a finale which involves the French police, the Foreign Legion, a glimpse of the Keystone Cops and the assistance of United States Cavalry and a tribe of Injuns parachuting into the Casino.

That should be enough to indicate that the picture has been devised as a three-ring circus entertainment rather than a film and it will be up to every cinemagoer to decide which bits of the comedy non-sequiturs provoke him to giggle, a chuckle, a belly laff or a glum resistance to all the over-striving. It is virtually impossible to sort out which of the five directors, John Huston, Joe McGrath, Val Guest, Robert Parrish and Ken Hughes, has been responsible for which sequences, and Bill Lenny's editing has necessarily had to be confined more or less to spacing out various parts, rather than shaping a uniform whole.

The long cast, all featured below title, has Niven as Sir James Bond. Though he seems justifiably bewildered by the proceedings he has a neat delivery of throwaway lines and enters into the exuberant physical action with pleasant blandness. Sellers also has some amusing gags as the gambler, the chance of dressing up in various guises and a neat near-seduction scene with Miss Andress, but his role is strained in its effect. Then there's Woody Allen, playing a neurotic nutcase, nephew and chief foe of Niven, who is working on a scheme whereby all women will be made beautiful and all men over the height of four feet six will be destroyed. Of the other leading roles, Deborah Kerr lets her hair down amusingly as the widow of "M," with a rich Scottish accent and a surprising facility for slapstick, Orson Welles fits the role of the gross card-playing agent weightily and Miss Andress, as the richest spy in the world, is always easy on the eye.

Barbara Bouchet registers a nice line in sex appeal and Joanna Pettet has some good moments as Mata Bond, illegitimate daughter of Bond and Mata Hari. Duncan Macrae, Gabriella Licudi, Dahlia Lavi, Terence Cooper, Bernard Cribbins, Angela Scoular, Jacky Bisset, Anna Quayle, Ronnie Corbett, Tracey Crisp, Colin Gordon and Geoffrey Bayldon and John Wells in a neat sketch in which Sellers is fitted out in the secret service quartermaster's stores all make impact of varying dimension though tend to get lost in the line-up. In addition, there is a long list of capable feature actors and a highly curvaceous Bondwagon of assorted girl spies.

Feldman and Bresler have also brought in several names in "guest" spots, with William Holden and Charles Boyer as agents, Jean-Paul Belmondo as a French legionnaire, George Raft as himself and John Huston playing "M." They make only brief appearances and add little to the film, except as marquee bait. There is also one tiny "in" gag in which Peter O'Toole appears as a Scottish piper and cracks a gag with Sellers. This was a private joke sprung on Sellers and the director when O'Toole dropped into the closely guarded studio to watch the film's progress.

"Casino Royale" turns out to be a fiesta for special effects men Cliff Richarson and Roy Whybrow, while John Howell, Ivor Beddoes and Lionel Couch have provided some lavish artwork, much of which is destroyed in the frenzied action in a : ...er that must have caused the accountants to wince. Jack Hildyard has lensed the film in Technicolor very satisfactorily. Musical score is by Burt Bacharach and has a sufficiently jaunty lilt and he and Hal David have provided a so-so song which Dusty Springfield sings competently.

Film gets away with a neat and impudent scene before the titles in which Sellers and Macrae (playing a French police inspector with a thick Scottish accent) hold a conference in one of France's standup street gents' conveniences, and is followed by some jazzed up titles devised by Richard Williams. Second unit direction is in the hands of Richard Talmadge & Anthony Squire, with John Wilcox and Nicolas Roeg responsible for extra second unit photography.

While Sean Connery and the original James Bond associates will not lose much sleep over this joshing of their goldmine pictures, "Casino Royale" may easily find a profitable audience among those who see in it the ultimate in hectic screen spy gimmickry.   Rich.

Un Homme De Trop
(One Man Too Many)
(FRENCH-COLOR)
Paris, April 18.

United Artists release of Harry Saltzman-Terra Films-UA production. Stars Bruno Cremer, Jean-Claude Brialy; features Claude Brasseur, Gerard Blain, Jacques Perrin, Michel Piccoli, Julie Dassin. Directed by Costa-Gavras. Screenplay, Jean-Pierre Chabrol, Daniel Boulanger, Gavras from book by Chabrol; camera (Eastmancolor), Jean Turnier; editor, Christiane Gaudin. At Colisee, Paris. Running Time, 110 MINS.

Chief	Bruno Cremer
Jean	Jean-Claude Brialy
Friend	Gerard Blain
Catus	Claude Brasseur
Prisoner	Michel Piccoli
Boy	Jacques Perrin
Girl	Julie Dassin
Lucien	Pierre Clementi

French filmmakers have been going in for comic and heroic pix about the last World War. This one combines the first two in a tale of wartime resistance. It has a little too much of everything. It gets repetitious, lacks a true heroic and character edge and appears something mainly for the action mart or dualer use abroad on its fight sequences and production dress. But drastic pruning of this overlong actioner would help.

Director Costa-Gavras evidently has seen and liked Yank war pix and westerns. And the stereotyped characters abound in this pic, without the dash, and forthrightness of the Yank counterparts. Every move has to be explained in this and there are even some heady pacifistic angles in the midst of combat or executions that ring false.

A resistance group frees a bunch of French prisoners from the Germans but it seems there was one too many who may have been a German spy. Suspicion centers on one character and he is both watched and a bone of contention on whether he should be killed or not.

Direction keeps the camera moving, relies on closeups, and mixes smart action patter with rhetoric to lose the suspense needed. Too busy, and overdone, this has some brash action but not enough coherence and drive to keep it from sagging throughout its overblown length.

Actors cannot do much with their predictable characters. There is the chief, who reluctantly kills for his belief, the ladies' man, the old man caught up in events, the operation on a wounded man, some he-mannish patter, a bit forced, and the young boy who runs amuck after the death of a friend.

War bits do have some briskness and derring-do but this falls between a heroic suspenser, resistance tale and a look at men in action. Film has a bit too much of everything to settle down into a solid vehicle. So mainly playoff looks indicated for this in the foreign marts, but it may do well in France. *Mosk.*

Mahlzeiten
(Mealtimes)
(GERMAN)
Berlin, April 11.

Constantin release of Edgar Reitz production. With Heidi Stroh, Georg Hauke and Nina Frank. Directed by Edgar Reitz. Screenplay, Edgar Reitz; camera, Thomas Mauch; editors, Beate Mainka-Jellinghaus and Anni Giese. At Allegro, West Berlin. Running Time, 96 MINS.

Elisabeth	Heidi Stroh
Rolf	Georg Hauke
Irina	Nina Frank
Rolf's mother	Ruth von Zerboni
Ilona	Ilona Schuetze
Brian Leak	Peter Hohberger
Young editor	Klaus Lakschewitz
Young man	Dirk Borchert

"Mealtimes" is the first full-length feature of 34-year old Edgar Reitz who belongs to the lineup of this country's better known "young wavers." Reitz created a series of attention-commanding short features and was Alexander Kluge's cameraman when the latter directed his first feature, "Farewell From Yesterday," which won trophies. So it stands to reason that Reitz' first full-length effort was awaited with interest. The local trade put much hope in it.

However, it can't be regarded as a convincing first feature. Pic is technically competent but treatment of subject matter lacks conviction. What's worse, it cannot escape boredom. Put the blame on a thin plot.

Once again a modern marriage problem is tackled. A young medical student meets a young girl. They fall in love and soon the girl is expecting. They get married and soon she has another child. The young hubby has to give up his medical studies and to look for a steady income. The couple's problems grow when there is a fifth child. The husband eventually commits suicide.

The whole thing remains too much on the surface. In fact, the film has more the character of a family album. And just too many questions remain unanswered.

The performances are okay if nothing special. The film shows good and sometimes brilliant lensing. But this cannot be regarded as a special plus any longer for a first feature. It cost about $162,500, so financial worries don't exist for this low-budgeter.
Hans.

A Guide For The Married Man
(PANAVISION-COLOR)

A cram course for the would-be philanderer with the aid and comfort of some experienced friends. Title, plus comic-heavy cast, should make for big success. Will have "suggested for mature audiences" label.

20th Century-Fox release of Frank McCarthy production. Stars Walter Matthau, Robert Morse, Inger Stevens; features Sue Ane Langdon, Claire Kelly, Linda Harrison and numerous guest stars. Directed by Gene Kelly. Screenplay, Frank Tarloff; camera (De Luxe Color), Joe McDonald; film editor, Dorothy Spencer; music, Johnny Williams; title song, Williams (music) and Leslie Bricusse (lyric), sung by The Turtles; asst. director, Paul Helmick. Reviewed at Fox h.o., N.Y., April 14, '67. Running Time, 89 MINS.

Paul Manning	Walter Matthau
Ed Stander	Robert Morse
Ruth Manning	Inger Stevens
Irma Johnson	Sue Ane Langdon
Harriet Stander	Claire Kelly
Miss Stardust	Linda Harrison
Joselyn Montgomery	Elaine Devry
Maitre d'Hotel	Michael Romanoff
Mr. Johnson	Jason Wingren
Party Guest	Fred Holliday
Party Guest	Pat Becker

Guest Artists: Lucille Ball, Jack Benny, Polly Bergen, Joey Bishop, Sid Caesar, Art Carney, Wally Cox, Jayne Mansfield, Hal March, Louis Nye, Carl Reiner, Phil Silvers, Terry-Thomas, Ben Blue, Ann Morgan Guilbert, Jeffrey Hunter, Marty Ingels, Sam Jaffe.

When you stop to count, "A Guide for the Married Man" has a lot of things going for it. A highly exploitable title, super-slick technical attributes, attractive and popular leads and possibly the longest list of professional comics in bits since Stanley Kramer's "Mad World." Add to these a collection of the prettiest girls in one film within many years and the certainty that all exploitation stops will be out when it comes to selling the film.

Perhaps, then, the viewer could make excuses for the fact that, in writing and direction and acting, almost everyone concerned has done better work in the past. Taken only as escapism, "Guide" will appeal to a lot of people and, despite its "suggested for mature audiences" label, is unlikely to lead anyone astray.

Here and there, a small vignette by some of the guest players shines but most of them have no more than a one-liner or a short, short scene. Walter Matthau, as a married innocent, eager to stray under the tutelage of friend and neighbor Robert Morse, is reminiscent of Tom Ewell in Billy Wilder's earlier treatment of the human condition. But this long-married hubby is so retarded in his immorality (it takes him 12 years to get the seven-year-itch) that, between his natural reluctance & Mentor Morse's suggestions (interlorded with warnings against hastiness), he needs the entire film to have his mind made up.

Another attractive aspect of "Guide" is its return to the old, blessed idea that comedies should be short. The 89 minutes it needs to unspool are packed with action, pulchritude, situations and considerable (if not quite enough) laughs. Gene Kelly, moving over to Fox after a lengthy and unproductive stay at Universal, sparks the manipulations of his trio. Inger Stevens is beautiful as Matthau's wife, and so unbelievably perfect that it makes his reluctance most understandable. There are also inserted bits by well-known faces.

It is understood that originally Frank Tarloff's script was to include one or two guest names but evidently the idea got so carried away that half of Hollywood must have dropped in for a scene. They're introduced via a gimmick —as Morse's explanations to Matthau why such a gambit succeeded or failed. Two scenes are superb: Terry-Thomas and Jayne Mansfield, as a pair of philanderers, make the mistake of using his house for their trysting place. She is unable to find her brassiere and the horror of his wife's eventual discovery of it ages him overnight. In another item, Art Carney and Lucille Ball are happily married, but Carney strays occasionally. To be away overnight without arousing her suspicion he picks a quarrel and storms out of the house, changes into a dinner jacket from a cache he keeps in a bus station locker, has his rendezvous and calls wifey next morning from work that he's really ashamed of his being quarrelsome. He's forgiven.

Some of the guest talent have no more than one line (Jeffrey Hunter, Sam Jaffe), some are mimed (Wally Cox, Ben Blue) and others, such as the above, have several lines (Sid Caesar, Phil Silvers, Jack Benny, Hal March). A bevy of really beautiful types portray the various wives, mistresses, employees and customers of the meandering males.

The production gloss of the film is aided by the use of some 30 location sites in and around Hollywood which Joe MacDonald's color camerawork displays at their best. The numerous interiors, ranging from successful suburban to lavish love nest, plus a wild Africa-themed nitery, are a tribute to the handiwork of art directors Jack Martin Smith and William Glasgow and set decorators Walter M. Scott and Raphael Bretton. For all the svelte shapes available, Moss Mabry has provided a highly handsome group of gowns.

Johnny Williams' score, after a rather noisy start (his title song is lost, as are Leslie Bricusse's lyrics in the rock 'n' roll interpretation by The Turtles) settles down to a solid, if standard, job of underscoring the action. Producer Frank McCarthy pulls an old Warner Bros. bit in the opening scene (with Matthau in bed, reading). The book is Geoffrey Household's "Watcher in the Shadows," which is a future McCarthy project at Fox. *Robe.*

Chuka
(COLOR)

Excellent oater drama, solid in all departments. Rod Taylor, Ernest Borgnine and John Mills for marquee. Uppercase potential in action and general situations.

Hollywood, April 8.

Paramount Pictures release of Rodlor Production, produced by Rod Taylor, Jack Jason. Features Taylor, Ernest Borgnine, John Mills. Directed by Gordon Douglas. Screenplay, Richard Jessup, based on his novel; camera (Pathecolor), Harold Stine; second unit camera, Irmin Roberts; editor, Robert Wyman; music, Leith Stevens; asst. director, Howard Roessel; second unit director, Ray Kellogg. Reviewed at Paramount Studios, L.A., April 7, '67. Running Time, 105 MINS.

Chuka	Rod Taylor
Sgt. Otto Hahnsbach	Ernest Borgnine
Col. Stuart Valois	John Mills
Veronica Kleitz	Luciana Paluzzi
Trent	James Whitmore
He'ena Chavez	Angela Dorian
Maj. Benson	Louis Hayward
Pvt. Spivey	Michael Cole
Capt. Carrol	Hugh Reilly
Slim	Barry O'Hara
Baldwin	Joseph Sirola
Hanu	Marco Antonio
Lt. Daly	Gerald York
Indian Girl	Herlinda del Carmen
Stage Driver	Lucky Carson

Flawed only by a prolog which blows the climax (but which could be eliminated), "Chuka" is a well-paced period oater about an Indian massacre of U.S. soldiers. Rod Taylor heads a uniformly competent cast in a gutsy and very effective change of pace. Scripting, prolog apart, is excellent, and production values, though modest, are solid. Direction by Gordon Douglas is outstanding. A model programmer and definite uppercase material, the Para..10unt release has big b.o. chances in general situations.

Richard Jessup adapted his novel into a topnotch screenplay, in which every personal interaction serves to advance the plot with new developments. Elements of courage, cowardice and humor are interleaved in firstrate fashion, along with two-fisted action and properly - motivated violence. Not one scene is repetitious or boring. The flashback prolog telegraphs the downbeat finale; had it been cut, genuine audience surprise and regret would have enhanced the pic's many assets.

Taylor, of late confined to contemporary, sometimes r e a c t i v e, roles, gives an excellent title-role performance as the bearded, rugged, totally virile saddle-tramp who enters a Western fort on the eve of its annihilation by starving Indians. John Mills, himself in a change of pace, plays a martinet with complete assurance, evoking eventually pity and a measure of sympathy. Ernest Borgnine is Mills' devoted sergeant. The fort is staffed by rejects from the Army.

Douglas has framed both overall and individual plot developments with a sure eye for exposition through economy. Harold Stine's Pathecolor lensing, and that of second unit director Ray Kellogg and I'min Roberts, adds versatility and zest throughout the tight 105-minute running time, as edited by Robert Wyman.

Taylor and partner Jack Jason, under the former's Rodlor banner, have assembled a great cast of both pros and new faces: Luciana Paluzzi, an old Taylor love interest who is reunited with him just before death; Angela Dorian, her younger traveling companion; James Whitmore, a boozy, likeable scout; Louis Hayward, back in pix after 10 years but retaining a suave polish, herein as a coward.

Also, Marco Antonio, Indian chief who honors an earlier Taylor favor; Lucky Carson, quiet stage driver who hates war because it destroys horses (an angle usually overlooked by writers, as well as audiences); and Michael Cole, whose wise-guy soldier, although a trifle Method-ical, marks him for bigger parts. Other players are equally strong.

A two-minute fist fight to exhaustion between Borgnine and Taylor is one of the most effective brawls in recent years. It is justified by the plot, and completely arresting. Leith Stevens has composed an unusually fine score, effectively and imaginatively orchestrated by Nathan Van Cleave and Herbert Spencer. Other technical credits are excellent.

With a bigger budget and somewhat more detailed elaboration of the principals' pasts, pic would have been a shoo-in for the big money and top playing time. As is, however, there is enough going for it to turn out as a very pleasant surprise at the b.o. Taylor, Jason and Douglas have made a pic which has lots of booking and exploitation mileage in it. *Murf.*

Le Vicomte Regle Ses Comptes
(The Viscount Settles Accounts)
(FRENCH-ITALIAN-SPANISH COLOR)

Paris, April 11.

Lux release of Criterion Films-DIA-CCM production. Stars Kerwin Mathews; features Sylvia Sorrente, Jean Yanne, Armand Mestral. Directed by Maurice Cloche. Screenplay, Georges Farrel, from book by Jean Bruce; camera (Eastmancolor), Henri Raichi; editor, Raymond Leboursier. At Ermitage, Paris. Running Time, 100 MINS.

Le Vicomte	Kerwin Mathews
Lili	Sylvie Sorrente
Assistant	Jean Yanne
Claude	Armand Mestral
Marco	Fernando Rey
Barone	Folco Lulli

A special investigator Le Vicomte, who has electronic gadgets, gets girls easily and works for insurance companies. This seems earmarked for a series here. But this first one is strictly a programmer with its quota of undraped girls, fights and obvious plotting. Color and scope help but there is a lack of crisp direction and some wooden acting, making this mainly for playoff use on its general mayhem.

The Vicomte tracks down robbers who have grabbed a batch of drugs hidden in a French bank strongbox. It ends with two gangs wiping each other, as he walks off with the insurance company payment to other adventures. Better scripting, direction and playing will be needed if this series is to have the needed staying power.

Kerwin Mathews is a bit stilted if okay in action segs with Sylvie Sorrente more effective in a strip number at a Paris strip boite than in her scenes where some emoting is needed. Folco Lulli and Fernando Rey are the heavies and the remainder of the cast is used mainly for knockabout. Production dress is fair as are technical aspects. *Mosk.*

Gamera Tai Gyaos
(Gamera vs. Gyaos)
(JAPAN—COLOR)

Tokyo, April 11.

Daiei Co. production and release. With Kojiro Hongo, Kichijiro Ueda, Hisayuki Abe, Reiko Kasahara. Directed by Noriaki Uyasa. Camera (Eastmancolor), Akira Uehara, Kazufumi Fujii; music, Tadashi Yamaguchi. Previewed in Tokyo. Running Time, 87 MINS.

This new film marks the return of a favorite monster, because **Gamera has been around for some time. He is the one which looks like a fanged, rubber turtle and spits flame. Gyaos, his playmate, appears to be a needle-toothed, rubber flying-fox.** He shoots laser beams out of his mouth. Otherwise, however, he seems singularly ill-equipped for a monster. He cannot stand light and must retire before dawn (which occasions his downfall, Gamera keeps him up all night), hates water (which is turtle-like Gamera's natural element), and is afraid of fire.

His liabilities are precise, however, because it is clear from the start that he is going to lose. The reason is that our chubby little hero (played by chubby Hisayuki Abe, a child-actor) has this unreasonable passion for Gamera—requited it would seem, though their tenderer moments are forever being spoiled by the short-tempered Gyaos. Anyone who likes kids

cannot be too monstrous, however. And, sure enough, at the end (accompanied by chorus, sunrise, and little Hisayuki's t e a r - c h o k e d "Sayanora, Gamera"), the youngster drags bad Gyaos up the slopes of Fuji and dumps him in.

At least this short-lived and irritable monster is true to his own nature, which is more than one can say for the now thoroughly domesticated and completely, undignified Gamera. Perhaps it is because the man inside the newer rubber suit swooping on wires or carefully crunching Nodels of Nagoya, is a born actor. Gyaos exhibits a strong sense of timing, a good deal of projection, and consequently generates an amount of empathy—he is obviously a Stanislavsky monster.

The film ought to do fairly well playing whatever U.S. locations these pix usually play. *Chie.*

Dai Kyoju Gappa
(Gappa—Triphibian Monster)
(JAPAN—COLOR)

Tokyo, April 11.

Nikkatsu Corp. production and release. With Tamio Kawaji, Yoko Yamamoto, Tatsuya Fuji, Koji Wada, Yuji Odaka. Directed by Haruyasu Noguchi. Screenplay, Iwao Yamazak and Ryuzo Nakanishi; camera (Eastmancolor), Muneo Ueda; music, Seitaro Omori. Previewed in Tokyo. Running Time, 90 MINS.

Nikkatsu's creation, Gappa, a real credit to his grandparents, King Kong and Godzilla, makes an auspicious debut and reveals himself as "best monster" so far. Very large, he behaves with complete dignity, often showing a striking profile. Although fierce, he is also capable of the finer sentiments and even a few tears. He is amazingly talented—can walk, swim and fly.

Director Haruyasu Noguchi has shown him off to best advantage in a technically superior film which blends horror and hokum, cataclysm and camp in just the right proportions. Taking not only pages but whole chapters from "King Kong" and that British-made thriller, "Gorgo," he has created a thoroughly anthropomorphic monster whom one may love at first sight.

This is because, as in all firstrate monster films—it is humans who are the real monsters. Tamio Kawaji, Koji Wada, Tatsuya Fuji and Yuji Odaka are the not-too-bright scientists who go to the distant tropical isle to gather strange animals for the new Playmate Land which an insufferable company-president type is creating in the suburbs of Tokyo. They are all dreadful people messing around in things they ought not to.

They come upon the egg of a baby Gappa and, after it hatches, kidnap him to Hakone where his Playmate Land indoctrination is to begin. What they don't know, but soon discover, is that Papa and Mama Gappa are fast in pursuit, intent upon rescuing their baby. And in the end that is just what they do. All of the Self-Defense Force, lots of devices for under water detonation, rocks and bombs galore—all of them fail. Japanese know-how is finally defeated and the Gappa family, tearfully reunited, flies home.

As one may infer from the plot, someone had his tongue-in-cheek at Nikkatsu, and while this fact never become too apparent, there is

an amount of objectivity about the film which is most enjoyable after this long parade of compulsive and self-absorbed Guilalas, Gyaosus, and Gameras. This is particularly apparent in the Gappa family's choice of where first to go in Japan. Naturally, on a family trip to Atami Spa.

Destruction of Atami is one of the delights of the pic. Others include a great tidal wave on Lake Kawaguchi, much stomping about, getting rid of industrial Kawasaki; and a wonderful detail when a wedding party getting its photograph taken at the Nikko Shrine is disturbed.

Most of these effects are well done, a few superb. There is a magnificent shot of an Atami geisha party in full swing when one of the Gappas steps on it, a fine scene during the Kawasaki destruction, and misty photography of the island jungle sequences.

There are also a few wires visible and lots of bad camera angles. But, on the whole, the film is carefully done. And the Gappa family is completely endearing. These are the only Japanese monsters one might like to see again. *Chie.*

Belle De Jour
(Beauty of the Day)
(FRENCH-COLOR)

Paris, April 18.

Valoria release of Paris Film Production-Robert and Raymond Hakim-Rive Films production. Stars Catherine Deneuve; features Jean Sorel, Michel Piccoli, Genevieve Page, Pierre Clementi. Directed by Luis Bunuel. Screenplay, Bunuel, Jean-Claude Carriere from book by Joseph Kessel; camera (Eastmancolor), Sacha Vierny; editor, Louisette Hautecoeur. Previewed in Paris. Running Time, 102 MINS.

Belle De Jour	Catherine Deneuve
Pierre	Jean Sorel
Husson	Michel Piccoli
Renee	Macha Meril
Michel	Pierre Clementi
Hippolye	Francisco Rabal
Amais	Genevieve Page
Client	Francis Blanche
Catherine	Francoise Fabian
Girl	Marie Latour

Luis Bunuel, Mexican filmmaker of Hispano origin, who has made several pix here, now does his latest under local aegis. He comes up with a crackling look at a supposedly well-married, comely girl who begins to give way to masochistic leanings working by day in a sporting house, if a good wife by night. Yet there's no moralizing or explaining here. Sharp insights, wit and a solidity slant this for arty or even specialized chances abroad.

The correct sell is indicated. Playoff would need extra cautious handling. But despite its theme, this is never scabrous. It suggests rather than shows. This gives it an even more powerful impact. And it keeps this look at a woman and a marriage intriguing and finally disturbing. But no clinical study this. Rather it transcends its isolated case to make a statement on senses and emotions, human comportment and perversions, without ever for their own sake.

Bunuel eschews any false moralism. Dreams, or elements of obsession, mix with life and are finally replaced at the end by an intimation regarding her future life since she is now taking care of a now crippled and almost blind husband. And the dreams are not exactly dreams. They sometimes clarify or underline a sentiment or hint at an early happening in her life that is also involved in her present actions.

Catherine Deneuve has the fine, luminous features to help make her heroine always coherent, rigorous and forthright enough to clarify the dual life. Jean Sorel is properly attractive and weak as her husband. Michel Piccoli is an outspoken friend who sees through the heroine as effectively as the many perverted clients in her bagnio life.

The color photography is also an asset as is the production dress and the well-done editing. Miss Deneuve has been married for a year and feels deeply for her husband but yet not completely in a sensual way. Pic starts in a jolting manner as she is riding with him in a carriage in the woods. He gets angry with her when she is lethargic in responding to him. He has his coachmen stop, string her up, strip her, whip her and then begin to make advances. This was all in her mind.

It is later, when the dandyish friend talks of clandestine houses and even drops an address of one he used, that she finds herself looking up the place, and finally beginning to work there.

Then she goes every day but at night lives with her hard working husband. She becomes almost happy and even seemingly balanced though leading this double life. A Japanese with intimated strange desires, a man, who likes to be whipped, a petty gangster who falls for her and others in her house of ill fame life are as real as her husband.

As censor barriers are pushed back, this pic should be another to cater to the adult audiences. Censor problems do not appear excessive.

Emotional and sensual love are dissected with canny clarity but without any double entendre or cheapness. It is an estimable work. Bunuel is one of the noted buff names in the arty film field. This should be another Bunuel pic for more selective audiences. "Belle De Jour" is the name the married woman uses while working at the joy house during the day.

Bunuel holds this taut, always engrossing and expressive by his seemingly simple but revealing direction which even imbues objects with meaning.

Here is an unfettered look into human comportment with neither insistence on sordid details nor trying to justify the happenings. Word-of-mouth should be good.
Mosk.

Other World Of Winston Churchill
(Color-Documentary)
(BRITISH)

Short, neatly contrived documentary based on Sir Winston's Churchill's paintings, with narration by Oscar-winner Paul Scofield. Possibly limited interest, but sound boxoffice for discriminating audiences.

London, April 18.
Gala release of a Jack Le Vien production. Features Viscount Montgomery, Merle Oberon, Sian Phillips, Lady Birley, Paul Maze. Directed by Lou Stoumen. Script by Caryl Brahms, based on Sir Winston Churchill's book, "Painting For Pleasure"; narrator, Paul Scofield; Churchill's voice (except when spoken himself), Patrick Wymark; camera (Eastmancolor), Hone Glendenning; editor, Alan Streeter; research, Linda Metcalfe; music, Carl Davis. At Continentale Cinema, London. April 12, 1967. Running Time, 51 MINS.

This color doc of Jack Le Vien's may well fall between two categories. Those not interested in painting as a hobby or as therapy will not get much kick out of it, even though it's based on the paintings of such a distinguished character as the late Sir Winston Churchill. Expert artists will probably find it over-simplified since it never explores Churchill's technique or explains how he became such a prolific artist. It merely expounds on the reasons that prompted him to take up the hobby.

However, Churchill's name, the value of Oscar winner Paul Scofield's voice as the narrator of Caryl Brahms' sound, straightforward and not fulsome script, and the presence of such people as General Eisenhower, Viscount Montgomery and Merle Oberon, should make it a safe booking for spots having discriminating audiences.

Churchill turned to painting, completely unfledged, as therapy when he was in the political wilderness. He quite genuinely found it a considerable solace in his moments of stress and between his bouts of high pressure work and responsibility.

He turned out a tremendous number of canvases and many of these are shown in this film, with anecdotes on how the subjects came to inspire Churchill. The layman may not regard his pictures as being all that hot, particularly noticeable when compared with a Constable in the pic but they have certainly become collectors' pieces. Miss Brahms, in writing the script, has drawn considerably on Churchill's book, "Painting As a Hobby" with Patrick Wymark excellently simulating the statesman's voice in direct quotes from the book. There are interviews with artists such as Paul Maze and Lady Birley, who kept Churchill stimulated in his painting in its early days, and with people like Montgomery and Miss Oberon, who give revealing sidelights on Churchill as the artist.

Familiar war scenes and other newsreel coverage on aspects of Churchill's career are woven into the footage quite adroitly by director Lou Stoumen and editor Alan Streeter. The color lensing of Hone Glendenning does full justice to the paintings.

In comparison with Le Vien's "Valiant Years" and "The Finest Hour," this documentary is small beer, but since it runs only 51 minutes, it is unlikely to cause any yawns, though noticeably lacking in both humor and drama. *Rich.*

Eight On The Lam
(COLOR)

Diverting Bob Hope comedy. Phyllis Diller and Jonathan Winters for added marquee lure. Family trade entry, with okay b.o. on duals.

Hollywood, April 14.
United Artists release of a Hope Enterprise Production, associate producer, Bill Lawrence. Features Bob Hope, Phyllis Diller, Jonathan Winters, Shirley Eaton. Directed by George Marshall. Screenplay, Albert E. Lewin, Burt Styler, Bob Fisher, Arthur Marx, based on a story by Fisher and Marx; camera (DeLuxe Color), Alan Stensvold; editor, Grant Whytock; music, George Romanis; asst. director, Frank Baur. Reviewed at Samuel Goldwyn Studios, L.A., April 13, '67. Running Time, 107 MINS.
Henry Dimsdale .... Bob Hope
Golda .... Phyllis Diller
Jasper Lynch .... Jonathan Winters
Ellie Barton .... Shirley Eaton
Monica .... Jill St. John
The Children .... Stacey Maxwell, Kevin Brody, Robert Hope, Glenn Gilger, Avis Hope, Debi Storm, Michael Freeman
Mr. Pomeroy .... Austin Willis
Marty .... Peter Leeds

Bob Hope, surrounded by seven kids, teased by babysitter Phyllis Diller, and chased by cop Jonathan Winters, plays in "Eight On The Lam" a bank teller suspected of embezzlement. Amusing comedy, well produced, is a diverting entry for the family and youth market. Generally good b.o. is likely from United Artists release on general duals.

Bob Fisher-Arthur Marx story, adapted by them, Al Lewin and Burt Styler, presents Hope as a widower with large family. Plot angle permits Shirley Eaton to be his eventual second wife, after clearing himself of the bank heist charge. Hope's boss, Austin Willis, really juggled the books in order to keep Jill St. John, again playing a dumb, buxom party girl.

Winters and Miss Diller provide the most comedy spark. Some good slight gags include the leisurely opening title, during which Hope gathers his brood, plus hound, into the family Volkswagen, and also a freeway traffic jam. Spoof of a w.k. detergent blurb is interpolated to a good effect. Kids are played by Stacey Maxwell, Kevin Brody, Robert and Avis Hope, Glenn Gilger, Debi Storm and Michael Freeman.

Director George Marshall handled his players in good fashion. Miss Eaton has limited footage, but she has charm, and, at fade-out, a remark by one of the kids causes her to break up in a delightful way. Miss Diller's fans will not be disappointed by her antics.

Bill Lawrence is billed as associate producer, but no producer is credited for the Hope Enterprises pic. All players follow title. All technical credits are okay. Music is by George Romanis, whose relaxed score does not always enhance or sustain a comic mood; with a cast like this, music should have punch. *Murf.*

Good Times
(SONGS—COLOR)

Sonny & Cher starrer for readymade audience.

Hollywood, April 17.
Columbia Pictures release of Motion Picture International (Lindsley Parsons) production. Stars Sonny & Cher; features George Sanders, Norman Alden. Directed by William Friedkin. Screenplay, Tony Barrett; story, Nicholas Hyams; camera (DeLuxe Color), Robert Wyckoff; editor, Melvin Shapiro; music, Sonny Bono; asst. director, David Salven. Reviewed at Columbia Studios, April 6, '67. Running Time, 92 MINS.
Sonny & Cher .... Themselves
Mordicus .... George Sanders
Warren .... Norman Alden
Smith .... Larry Duran
Tough Hombre .... Kelly Thordsen
Garth .... Lennie Weinrib
Brandon .... Peter Robbins
Mordicus' Girls .... Edy Williams, China Lee, Diane Haggerty
Lieutenant .... James Flavin
Solly .... Phil Arnold
Kid .... Hank Worden
Proprietor .... Morris Buchanan
Telegrapher .... Charles Smith
Gangster .... John Cliff
Wrestlers ..Herk Reardon, Bruce Tegner
Peddler .... Richard Collier
Old Timer .... Howard Wright
Bartender .... Joe Devlin
Deputy .... Mike Kopach

"Good Times," marking Sonny & Cher's bow on the screen, packs ready-made audience appeal calculated to pay off profitably in pic's intended market. Popularity of rock pair—husband-and-wife combo in real life who are one of top acts in their field with a dozen or more boff recordings—should attract wide response particularly among the young.

Initial production of Steve Broidy's new indie company, formed after he exited Allied Artists, film is a well-handled takeoff of the two singers in a story tailored strictly to their talents. Producer Lindsley Parsons displays a showmanship approach to subject, which has couple playing themselves and Sonny wanting to expand their activities by taking on a film career while Cher is quite content with things as they are as a singing team known to millions. Sonny signs a contract for pair with George Sanders, a powerful film tycoon, and immediately complications arise.

Each of the nine musical numbers is well staged, one particularly, in which Cher plays a western bar singer, carrying spectacular treatment. Color camera work is unusually good, credit going to Robert Wyckoff as director of photography and Farciot Edouart responsible for process work. Songs, seven sung by pair and two by Cher solo, are all originals, cleffed by Sonny under his own name of Bono.

Sonny and Cher are natural enough in their acting, but expectedly excel in their song numbers which they sock over in their customary style. Sanders has little to do, but does it with his usual suavity. Balance of cast in the Tony Barrett screenplay are meaningless, interest centered on two stars.

William Friedkin's direction keeps action at a lively pace and he's aided in dance sequences by Andre Tayir's choreography.
Whit.

Valley Of Mystery
(COLOR)

Tv retread has enough going for it to make pleasant addition to programmer list.

Universal release of a Harry Tatelman production. Features Richard Egan, Peter Graves, Harry Guardino, Joby Baker, Lois Nettleton, Julie Adams, Fernando Lamas. Directed by Joseph Leytes. Screenplay, Richard Neal, Lowell Barrington from story by Neal and Larry Marcus. Color by Technicolor. No other credits. Reviewed at Universal, N.Y., April 20, '67. Running time: 94 MINS.

One of the projects originally created as a pilot (sales come-on) for a television series and reworked as a theatrical release, this Harry Tatelman production was converted so quickly that no credits other than producer, director, featured cast and writing credits were available at the trade screening. One market that must be bypassed, however, is the inflight entertainment field as the plot involves a spectacular aircrash. Film is scheduled for a June national release.

Considered simply as a programmer, or what used to be called a "B" picture, "Valley of Mystery" is a satisfactory minor effort that won't bore most grownups and will be popular with the younger, less discriminating market. This is due, probably, to the fact that its technical values are excellent in color photography, editing and an uncredited, but very melodious, score as well as the surprisingly strong cast lineup, some of whom are cast out of type.

The simple story, which borrows freely from aircrash classics such as "The High And The Mighty," has pilot Richard Egan landing a jetliner, damaged in a hurricane, in a South American jungle. A novelty of the crash is that no one is hurt other than a policeman escorting murderer Fernando Lamas back to be executed (and his demise is due to Lamas, not the flying).

The polyglot passenger list includes novelist Peter Graves who's searching for a sister married to a missionary; Lois Nettleton (usually cast as a plainjane) as a sexy liquor saleswoman; Julia Adams (as a neurotic schoolteacher), Joby Baker (as a pop singer), Harry Guardino (as a comedian trying to overcome alcoholism) and Lamas. While Egan works towards getting the passengers rescued, Graves and Miss Nettleton get involved with some bloodthirsty natives while Lamas gets involved with Miss Adams, then gets himself killed.

Richard Neal and Lowell Barrington have left loopholes of logic in their script big enough to fly a Boeing 707 through (they mention the fact that there are 130 passengers aboard but you never see more than 15 or 20 people at the most; or what's behind Miss Adams' neurosis) but director Joseph Leytes knows that action is everything and seldom lets his cast stand still, much less sit down. Not "High And The Mighty" but not bad, at all. *Robe.*

Peau D'Espion
(A Spy's Skin)
(FRENCH-GERMAN-ITALO)
(Color)
Paris, April 18.

Gaumont release of Gaumont International, Eichberg Film, Franca Film production. Stars Louis Jourdan, Senta Berger, Edmond O'Brien, Bernard Blier; features Maurice Garrel, Fabricio Capucci, Gamil Ratib. Directed by Edouard Molinaro. Screenplay, Jacques Robert, Molinaro; camera (Eastmancolor), Raymond Lemoigne; editor, Robert Isnardon. At Helder, Paris. Running Time, 87 MINS.

Charles	Louis Jourdan
Sandra	Senta Berger
Commandant	Bernard Blier
Harry	Edmond O'Brien
Cecil	Fabricio Capucci
Scientist	Maurice Garrel
Professor	Gamil Ratib

Spy caper is about a disillusioned professional soldier and writer caught up with foiling the defection of a French scientist to Red China. Slick but predictable, film gets through its short length with interest sustained in spite of this. This is because of sharp, if cold, direction and okay playing. However, its pedestrian plot makes this just passable in the spy sweepstakes with playoff or dualer usage abroad on its okay production dress and names of Senta Berger, Louis Jourdan and Edmond O'Brien.

Jourdan looks rightfully tired and bored as he gets caught up in the affair by an old comrade in arms now a French undercover man. He gets picked up by Senta Berger, married to a smooth Yank operator who sells scientists to the East—in this case China. Jourdan is used to fooling both sides since the gang knows he is working for the French and that he will kill the scientist.

Fights, colorful backdrops and the usual tired and laconic patter of these disenchanted undercover men backup the plot that has some twists but not enough to give this an edge in the plethora of pix of this type. Color is nicely hued and technical credits fine with Edmond O'Brien rightly tough, as the head man, and Miss Berger, good as the wife almost betrayed by love for Jourdan. *Mosk.*

The Jokers
(BRITISH—COLOR)

Excellent comedy with suspense about theft of Britain's Crown Jewels. Made by young people for that market. Special handling for very good b.o.

Hollywood, April 19.
Universal release of Gildor-Scimitar Production, produced by Maurice Foster and Ben Arbeid. Stars Michael Crawford, Oliver Reed, Harry Andrews. Directed by Michael Winner. Screenplay, Dick Clement, Ian La Frenais, based on a story by Winner; camera (Technicolor), Kenneth Hodges; editor, Bernard Gribble; music, Johnny Pearson; asst. director, Kenneth Softley. Reviewed at Universal Studios, L.A., April 18, '67. Running Time, 94 MINS.

Michael	Michael Crawford
David	Oliver Reed
Marryatt	Harry Andrews
Col. Gurney Simms	James Donald
Riggs	Daniel Massey
Sir Matthew	Michael Hordern
Eve	Gabriella Licudi
Inge	Lotte Tarp
Harassed Man	Frank Finlay
Lennie	Warren Mitchell
Mrs. Tremayne	Rachel Kempson
Mr. Tremayne	Peter Graves
Sarah	Ingrid Brett
Catchpole	Brian Wilde
Lt. Sprague	Edward Fox
Lt. Col. Paling	Michael Goodliffe
Brigadier	William Devlin
Uncle Edward	William Mervyn
Maj. Gen. Jeffcock	William Kendal
De Winter	Kenneth Colley
Camilla	Charlotte Curzon
Capt. Browning	Mark Burns
Capt. Green	Brook Williams
Speedcop	Brian Peck
Bank Manager	Basil Dignam
Solicitor	John Kidd
Mrs. Pervis	Freda Jackson
Mrs. Jeffcock	Nam Munro

In telling a story of today's youth, who do things for the sake of the doing and without regard to the consequences, "The Jokers" should strike a responsive chord in the young market. Made in England by some very talented filmmakers and featuring many relatively new faces, film is basically a suspense comedy, blending some valid tragic overtones in the aftermath. Optimum initial bookings will be in smaller specialty houses, near the campus, from which Universal can gauge a careful later playoff in general situations.

Pic has the supreme virtue of portraying young people as they are, without patronizing or exploiting them: restless, somewhat disenchanted, privately aware of their immaturity, and with a tendency to rush needlessly into action with a later psychological hangover in many cases. Director Michael Winner created the original story, scripted in often hilarious fashion by Dick Clement and Ian La Frenais. Maurice Foster and Ben Arbeid produced.

Although a trifle pretentious at times in his camera angles—one more shot through foliage and cracks would make audiences feel like voyeurs, winner has a zesty visual feel for contemporary life, as the many actual location shots (with related sound quality) will attest. A large cast is directed in uniformly fine performances.

Michael Crawford and Oliver Reed are starred as two brothers, the former just expelled from still another college for a practical joke, the latter the author of that scheme. Together, they plan and execute a national outrage—theft of the Crown Jewels, with no intent to keep them, just to carry off the theft. Harry Andrews, also above title, is the Scotland Yard gumshoe assigned to the case.

Sight gags and underplayed British throwaway gags are interleaved neatly with the growing suspense over whether the guys will succeed. Then, a switcheroo: Crawford, all his life brow-beaten by Reed, fakes innocence when the plot is discovered, and resolution of this takes the final footage. There remains an ambiguity: did Crawford pretend so as to be solely responsible for the climax of the heist, or did the plan of Reed and Andrews force him to own up? The ambiguity is appropriate in context.

Andrews' footage is limited, but very effective and he belongs above the title. Crawford and Reed, latter a gutsy leading man, will enhance their careers herein. James Donald is top-featured as the publicity-seeking demolitions expert who holds the lantern while others de-fuse the various decoy "bombs" placed by the brothers as they rehearse their plot. Donald's performance is equally excellent.

Daniel Massey registers strongly as a photographer who figures in the denouement. Michael Hordern, Rachel Kempson, Peter Graves and other fine actors enhance this pic with surefire characterizations.

Kenneth Hodges' mobile Technicolor camera responds to Winner's demands of the moment, whether those be for illuminating intimate shots, tv-type news coverage, documentary or home-movie flavor. Bernard Gribble edited to a tight 94 minutes. Johnny Pearson's music underscores the comedy to good overall effect. Remaining technical credits are pro.

Favorable word of mouth can be established by deliberate, but not overdone, promotion of the pic in smaller theatres catering to students. It could become a sleeper on this circuit, after which careful nursing in more general, but still small, houses would expand the market. *Murf.*

The Ride To Hangman's Tree
(COLOR)

Western peopled with Universal contract players, with no message other than action entertainment.

Universal release of Howard Christie production. Features Jack Lord, James Farentino, Don Galloway, Melodie Johnson, Richard Anderson. Directed by Al Rafkin. Screenplay, Luci Ward, Jack Natteford, William Bowers, from story by Ward, Natteford; camera (Technicolor). Gene Polito; editor, Gene Palmer; asst. director, Joe Kenny. Reviewed at Amsterdam Theatre, N. Y., April 20, '67. Running Time, 90 MINS.

Guy Russell	Jack Lord
Matt Stone	James Farentino
Nevada Jones	Don Galloway
Lillie Malone	Melodie Johnson
Steve Carlson	Richard Anderson
Jeff Scott	Robert Yuro
Sheriff Stewart	Ed Peck
Corbett	Paul Reed
Ed Mason	Richard Cutting
Keller	Bing Russell
Teressa Moreno	Virginia Capers
Blake	Robert Sorrells
T. L. Harper	Robert Cornthwaite
Indian	Fabian Dean

A western, which would have been called a low-budgeter in the old days, but with much better technical values, provides an excellent opportunity to showcase some of the younger talent on hand. The resulting film is a natural for the family and action market although the leading lady's nude swimming scene may stir up a few yelps of protest.

Switch in script is making the three major leads (Jack Lord, James Farentino, Don Galloway) outlaws but likable types. When the trio split, Farentino goes it alone until he meets an old buddie (Robert Yuro), supposedly gone straight (practicing law instead of breaking it) and the pair start a stagecoach holdup routine that pays off. Back into his life ride Lord and Galloway and a dancer-singer (Melodie Johnson), Life becomes more interesting if increasingly dangerous.

The trio of males are played off against each other with Galloway providing the comedy touch. Farentino decides to give himself up after an unsuccessful holdup but, remembering Miss Johnson, decides he can do it as well next morning.

All technical credits are okay and it's all good exposure for talented young players. *Robe.*

The Double Man
(BRITISH-COLOR)

Competent mystery-thriller with the old double-identity gimmick working quite neatly. This Yul Brynner starrer should do steady business in everyday houses.

London, April 25.

Warner-Pathe release of an Albion (Hal E. Chester) production, presented by Warner Bros. Stars Yul Brynner; features Britt Ekland, Clive Revill, Anton Diffring, Moira Lister, Lloyd Nolan. Directed by Franklin J. Schaffner. Screenplay by Frank Tarloff and Alfred Hayes, from Tarloff's screen story based on Henry S. Maxfield's novel, "Legacy Of A Spy"; camera (Technicolor), Denis Coop; music, Ernie Freeman; editor, Richard Best. At Warner Theatre, London. Running Time, **105 MINS.**

Dan Slater) Kalmar(	Yul Brynner
Gina	Britt Ekland
Frank Wheatly	Clive Revill
Berthold	Anton Diffring
Mrs. Carrington	Moira Lister
Edwards	Lloyd Nolan
Max	George Mikell
Gregori	Brandon Brady
Anna	Julia Arnall
Miller	David Bauer
General	Ronald Radd
Police chief	Kenneth J. Warren
Halstead	David Healy

The double-identity gimmick usually causes some plot confusion but in "The Double Man" it crops up rather late in the proceedings. Although producing momentary puzzlement 'as to motive and who's who, it certainly adds to the taut suspense of a good, average thriller which should have steady wicket appeal among regular cinema patrons. At least, "The Double Man," though involved in international intrigue, sticks to a straightforward routine and does not strive after the effects of the current wayout espionage parodies.

Frank Tarloff and Alfred Hayes have tailored a solid screenplay from Henry Maxfield's novel, "Legacy Of A Spy," in which Intelligence Agent Dan Slater (Yul Brynner) is plunged into strange problems when he goes to the Austrian Alps to investigate the death of his son on a ski-slope. The police write it off as an accident. Brynner suspects murder.

The film builds up an intriguing sense of tension with the motives of various people rating suspicion, Brynner being tailed by obvious enemy agents and a big payoff when he is confronted with his double, Kalmar.

Plastic surgery has worked the "miracle" and Slater Two is to be planted for the real Slater in Washington. Showdown comes in a scrap between the two in which one unguarded remark by the fake agent causes his death.

Atmosphere of mystery and menace is slowly but skillfully built up. Brynner gives a strong, taciturn portrayal of a ruthless, determined man to whom duty is far above human relationship. Overall, it's a pokerface performance but fits the bill perfectly.

Clive Revill, an ex-agent pal of Brynner's, though not fully trusted by him, also turns in an interesting show as an honest but weak, indecisive character who rallies at the critical moment. Anton Diffring is a suave enemy scientist and David Bauer does excellent work as an agent detailed to bring Brynner back to Washington. Lloyd Nolan, Ronald Radd, George Mikell, Brandon Brady and Kenneth J. Warren all turn up trumps with sound-backing roles.

Britt Ekland gets perhaps her biggest chance in this pic as a young woman involuntarily involved with the investigations. As well as looking delightful, she tackles one or two tricky scenes with unexpected assurance. Moira Lister amusingly fluffs through the part of her flighty employer and Julia Arnall, for some time an absentee from the screen, returns in the minor role of Revill's wife. With minimum opportunity she reminds one of her grace and sure touch.

Franklin J. Schaffner has directed this Hal Chester production without frills and has paced out his dramatic highlights usefully. Inevitably, though, the pic lacks real humor, an always useful blend with dramatic proceedings.

Denis Coop's camera has produced some engaging Technicolor shots of the Austrian Alps, particularly a night race, with the skiers illuminated with flares. Use of sombre greys and startling white in the color also adds to the authenticity of the location. Other technical credits stand up well, particularly an unobtrusive score by Ernie Freeman. *Rich.*

The Sailor From Gibraltar
(BRITISH)

Dreary tale of nympho seeking her lost youth—the title character.

Lopert Pictures release of a Woodfall (Oscar Lewenstein) production. Directed by Tony Richardson. Stars Jeanne Moreau, Ian Bannen, Vanessa Redgrave; features Zia Mohyeddin, Hugh Griffith, Orson Welles. Screenplay by Christopher Isherwood, Don Magner, Richardson based on novel by Marguerite Duras. Camera, Raoul Coutard; editor, Anthony Gibbs; sound, Andre Hervee, Gerard Maneveau; no music credits; asst. director, Christian de Chalonge. Reviewed at U.A., N.Y., April 19, '67. Running time: **89 MINS.**

Anna	Jeanne Moreau
Alan	Ian Bannen
Sheila	Vanessa Redgrave
Noori	Zia Moyheddin
Legrand	Hugh Griffith
Louis of Mozambique	Orson Welles
Postcard Vendor	Umberto Orsini
Eolo	Erminio Spalla
Carla	Eleanor Brown
Girl at Dance	Gabriella Pallotta
Man on Train	Arnold Foa
Jeannot	Claudio de Renzi
Captain	Fausto Tozzi
John	John Hurt
Theo	Theodor Roubanis
Brad	Brad Moore
Massimo	Massimo Sarchieilli
Guglielmo	Guglielmo Spoletini
Wolf	Wolfgang Hillinger

This Tony Richardson effort was, reportedly, shot back-to-back with his 'Mademoiselle' and although with a better-known and more interesting cast than that effort, can only be checked off as a failure for the British director-producer. A major fault is that too many talents have had a hand in what must have been a very slight project.

The novels of Marguerite Duras are frequently no more than lengthy short stories — and not too strong on the narrative side. With such interpreters as Christopher Isherwood and Richardson (neither famous for clarity of intent) plus Don Magner, the ensuing screenplay is replete with repetitive sequences that make the 89-minute running time seem endless. Such dialog as "I've been in Africa so long one white man looks like any other" doesn't help.

There also seems to have been considerable uncertainty on the part of Richardson and producers Oscar Lewenstein and Neil Hartley as to how best to end the pic. The synopsis provided has the film ending with the African native sequence but, as seen, this portion of the film precedes the closing Alexandria incident, a possible switch to provide a finale with action.

The sympathy of the viewer is never won by any of the characters involved, and the acting of the three principals is frequently overshadowed by the minor roles. Zia Mohyeddin contributes more by his very liveliness than do most of the others.

A Britisher (Ian Bannen) and his mistress (Vanessa Redgrave) are on an Italian holiday which quickly becomes evident will be their last. She's still hungry for him but he can't stand her but isn't brave enough to send her away. When a mysterious woman on a yacht (Jeanne Moreau) crosses their path, his greed (both sexual and practical) provides the impetus to ditch his mistress and make a fast pass at the yachtswoman. This sick chick, a wealthy widow, is sailing the seven seas looking for her lost youth — a young sailor from Gibraltar she once saved, wooed and lost. Not one to waste time, she's also bedding down with most of the men she meets along the way.

Bannen joins the harem and search which takes them to Greece (where a gas station attendant is a near-miss), to Alexandria (where a postcard vendor almost produces the sailor), and to Ethiopia (where the only clue is a native gal left behind by the always-elusive sailor). In the meantime, Moreau's falling in love with Bannen (although why is never made clear, as he's pure clod from the begining and her entire yacht crew is younger, handsomer and less demanding).

Orson Welles is wasted on a brief bit as an information peddler and Hugh Griffith is only slightly better as a white hunter and guide. Umberto Orsini as the tough postcard vendor, Arnold Foa as a man Bannen meets on a train, and Mohyeddin give the most believable portrayals in the film. Miss Redgrave is touching and believably irritating in her brief role although so unattractively photographed that she resembles a middle-aged Twiggy. The rest of the cast, Bannen and Miss Moreau in particular, walk through their parts like somnambulists or camp a la Welles and Griffith.

Raoul Coutard's inventive camerawork is a major waste but he does manage to convey the muggy, humid atmosphere of Italy although too-numerous seascapes get eventually monotonous. The art house market will get considerable play on the strength of the Richardson-Moreau-Redgrave names but there's little holdover strength and no evidence of commercial appeal. But perhaps Coca Cola can make up the difference. The film is studded with ads for the drink. *Robe.*

Mord und Totschlag
(A Degree of Murder)
(GERMAN—COLOR)

Berlin, April 18.

Universal release of Rob Houwer production. With Anita Pallenberg, Hans P. Hallwachs, Manfred Fischbeck. Directed by Volker Schloendorff. Screenplay, Volker Schloendorff; camera (Eastmancolor), Franz Rath; music, Brian Jones; editor Claus von Boro. At Constantin screening room, Berlin. Running Time, **88 MINS.**

Marie	Anita Pallenberg
Guenther	Hans P. Hallwachs
Fritz	Manfried Fischbeck
Hans	Werner Enke

This Rob Houwer production marks the second full-length feature of 28-year-old Volker Schloendorff whose first opus, "The Young Toerless," was an official German contender at last year's Cannes Festival where it won the FIPRESCI (International Film Critics' Assn.) prize. This second feature pic, "A Degree of Murder," is repping West Germany at this year's Cannes Fest. Contributing to prestige for this director is the fact that his Dutch-born German producer, Rob Houwer, 29, has sold "Murder" to Universal, which is handling film's world rights except the German - language market which is taken care of by Constantin, top German distrib. There is hardly any doubt that "Murder" will benefit from these evident distributing advantages and sled into many markets. Scholendorff, incidentally, has been given a six-year, non-exclusive contract by Universal.

It has been repeatedly said that Schloendorff who had been assistant director to several noted French film creators is the technically most advanced of all the new young German directors. This production gives clear evidence of this fact. It's technically a first-rate pic which displays directorial knowhow in every sequence.

Unlike Schloendorff's first opus ("Toerless"), which dealt with the sadistical happenings in a boarding-school some five decades ago, his second pic presents the current times.

It's a simple story which Schloendorff, who also write the script, picked from the daily press. A young waitress has killed her long-time friend in sort of a self-defense when he was about to enforce a last intimate affair which she, however, was not willing to grant. The desperate young girl hires the services of two young workers to carry away the dead man. They do this at night and manage it so that their actions are not witnessed. The viewer sees that the corpse is discovered but the film leaves open whether the young people are caught and face punishment.

There is evidently neither a moral issue nor a message about this film. It's the type of vehicle whose content plays a secondary role—all that counts here is how it is made. Yet despite the common plot and the apparent absence of any message, "Murder" gives a feel and a reflection of present times via the dialog sequences and the attitude towards life on the part of the individual players. "Murder" is somewhat reminiscent of the good U.S. films of the 1930s which, despite simple plots, even today give a good insight into life and problems of society.

The best thing about this film is its technical side. It is the work of a real professional. Also the directorial handling of the players is noteworthy. The two young men are highly convincing all through. Of Anita Pallenberg, the girl who is shown in every scene, she is undoubtedly a type who may go places if she gets some additional acting chores. Her performance holds interest throughout.

Film may face objection on the part of those who find a moral issue necessary. But somehow or the other "Murder" deserves credit for what it conveys. There is an additional asset, the score, which was contributed by British Brian Jones of the Rolling Stones. Brilliantly lensed, the film's budget amounted to about $225,000.

Hans.

A Mother's Heart
(RUSSIAN)

Paris, April 25.

Mosfilm release of Gorki Studios for Children Films production. With Elena Fadeeva, Danili Sagal, Guennady Tchertov, Nina Minichkova, Rodion Nakhapetov. Directed by Marc Donskoi. Screenplay, Z. Voskresenskaia, I. Donskoia; camera, M. Iakovitch; music, R. Khozac. At Ranelagh, Paris. Running time, 95 MINS.

Mother	Elena Fadeeva
Oulianov	Danili Sagal
Anna	Nina Menichkova
Alexandre	Guennady Tchertov
Vladimir	Rodion Nakhapetov
Olia	Nina Vikovskaia
Dmitry	A. Bogoslavsky

The mother's heart in the title belongs to Lenin's mother. But no pedantics or didactics here, but a poetic and lyrical romantic film about turn-of-the-century Russia and the stirrings of revolt and the mother's reactions to the outlooks of her two sons and a daughter involved in the ferment of the times.

Foreshadowing the future of Lenin, the protagonist is still the mother. This is played with reserve and interior poise. Elena Fadeeva has a face that can mirror emotion, resolve and resignation without any false bravado or overplaying. It keeps the film on on even keel and brings off its lyrical look at pre-revolutionary Russia.

Lenin's father is a pedagogue trying to bring schooling to the peasants. His older brother and sister are arrested in a plot against the Czar, with the brother hung and the sister exiled. Lenin himself is put under surveillance after an impassioned defense of workless peasants as a young lawyer. It ends with him going off to his destiny and the big city with his mother.

Vet filmmaker Marc Donskoi, who did the trilogy based on the life of writer Maxim Gorki, uses his scope cameras to capture the times and also a background of the unrest, oppression and the passing of seasons. Family life is counterpointed to the future of one of the members of this group, namely Lenin.

Young actor Rodion Nakhapetov is cannily made up as a young Lenin with gestures to match. But his coming limelight is only sketched in his one courtroom sequence, his studies and fervent talks with young revolutionaries.

Film otherwise is content to give a colorful epic feel to the Russian winters, people, and country as well as city life. This is counterpointed by the mother's attempts to save her children and finally accepting their views.

This has some legs for specialized playoff abroad on its sheer filmic knowhow and solid but never stolid look at family ties. Perhaps a bit academic in its careful shooting, scripting and playing, it transcends it by its poetic notations, touching but never mawkish sentiments. Generally fine production dress and helpful music, settings and acting all helps.

Mosk.

Two for the Road
(BRITISH-PANAVISION-COLOR)

Breezy trip through married life via various vehicles, one of fastest of which is the script. Audrey Hepburn's superb performance carries stodgy costar most of trip.

20th-Century Fox release of Stanley Donen production, directed by Donen. Stars Audrey Hepburn, Albert Finney; features Eleanor Bron, William Daniel, Claude Dauphin, Nadia Grey, Georges Descrieres. Screenplay, Frederic Raphael; camera (De Luxe Color), Christopher Challis; editors, Richard Marden, Madeleine Gug; dubbing editor, Sharpe Ludski Enterprises; art director, Willy Holt; aerial cameraman, Guy Tabary; special effects, Gilbert Manzon; music, Henry Mancini; asst. director, Jacques Corbel. Reviewed at Fox h.o., N.Y., April 26, '67. Running time, 112 MINS.

Joanna	Audrey Hepburn
Mark	Albert Finney
Cathy Manchester	Eleanor Bron
Howard Manchester	Wililam Daniel
Maurice Dalbret	Claude Dauphin
Francoise Dalbret	Nadia Grey
David	Georges Descrieres
Ruth	Gabrielle Middleton
Caroline	Kathy Chelimsky
Michelle	Carol Van Dyke
Simone	Karyn Balm
Palamos	Mario Verdon
Gilbert, Comte de Florac	Roger Dann
Yvonne de Florac	Irene Hilda
Sylvia	Dominique Joos
American lady	Libby Morris
Joanna's touring girl friends	Jackie Bisset, Joanna Jones, Judy Cornwell, Patricia Viterbo, Olga George Picot, Sofia Torkeli, Clarissa Hillel
Police Inspector	Yves Barsacq
Madame Solange	Helene Tossy
Boat Officer	Jean-Francois Lalet
Customs' Officer	Albert Michel

The combination of producer-director Stanley Donen and actress Audrey Hepburn has proven boxoffice magic before, which may be the reason this latest effort has been tapped by Radio City Music Hall. As far as producer, director, femme lead and screenwriter are concerned, this attempt to visually analyze the bits and pieces that go into making a marriage, and then making it work, is successful. If it drags a bit here and there, blame it on the stodgy performance of actor Albert Finney who is unable to convey the lightness, gaiety and romanticism needed. (Music Hall ads feel obliged to parenthetically identify him as star of "Tom Jones"—Ed.)

What must have been a tremendous challenge to producer-director Donen is the script dreamed up by Frederic ("Darling") Raphael which has the same married couple, making basically the same trip, from London to the Riviera, at three different stages of their life with continual crosscutting and flashing backwards and forwards from one period to the other. The credibility of the changes in periods is left, except for changes of costume and vehicular equipment, to the two leads. Finney remains the same throughout but Miss Hepburn is amazing in her ability to portray a very young girl, a just-pregnant wife of two years, and a beginning-to-be-bored wife of five years. Helped partially by variations in her hairdos but mostly by her facial expressions, she's completely believable, lovable and totally delightful.

Finney, who doesn't help things much with some very bad imitations of Humphrey Bogart, comes over as such a boor that the viewer sympathizes completely during his wife's moral slip (the charmer with whom she dallies is limned smoothly and with enviable assurance by Georges Descrieres). However, the viewer doesn't really blame Finney too much for his episode with a gorgeous creature (Karyn Balm) whom he meets on a solo business trip (played without dialog but with an offscreen narrative that has him writing home to wifey that the trip is a bore without her).

Raphael pieces out his repeated treks (all captured in gorgeous scenic shots by Christopher Challis' color camera) by including some of the friends and acquaintances met by the pair. The highspot for laughs is a joint journey made with another married couple (Eleanor Bron and William Daniel), doomed by the couple's obnoxious offspring (Gabrielle Middleton). Figuring importantly in the plot, but given little opportunity or dialog with which to create their characters in depth, are Claude Dauphin and Nadia Grey as wealthy French benefactors of Finney, who socially monopolize him.

An unintended laugh is provided by the film's credits for Miss Hepburn's clothes. Usually gowned by Givenchy, she wears, this time out, clothes right off the hook and credited "to Ken Scott, Michele Rosier, Paco Rabanne, Mary Quant, Foale and Tuffin, and others." Evidently the "others" provided the blue jeans she wears in one scene.

Another major asset is the score by Henry Mancini, one of the most romantic he's done to date and sure to show plenty of legs as a soundtrack album. A refreshing change is that there's no title tune sung during the credits.

Scheduled for June release nationally, "Two For the Road" has plenty of general appeal, although it's going out "Suggested For Mature Audiences Only," which may have some effect on its overall boxoffice pull.

Robe.

Devil's Angels
(PANAVISION-COLOR)

Quickie cyclist film made to take advantage of the "Wild Angels" success.

American International Pictures release of Roger Corman (Burt Topper) production; executive producers, James H. Nicholson, Samuel Z. Arkoff. Stars John Cassavetes, Beverly Adams, Mimsy Farmer. Directed by Daniel Haller. Screenplay, Charles Griffith; camera (Pathecolor), Richard Moore; editors, Ronald Sinclair, Kenneth Crane; music, Mike Curb; title song, Curb, Guy Hemric, Jerry Styner; asst. director, Dale Hutchinson. Reviewed in New York, April 28, '67. Running Time, 84 MINS.

Cody	John Cassavetes
Lynn	Beverly Adams
Marianne	Mimsy Farmer
Joel-the-Mole	Maurice McEndree
Louise	Salli Sachse
Tonya	Nai Bonet
Sheriff Henderson	Leo Gordon
Royce	Russ Bender
Billy-the-Kid	Marc Cavell
Gage	Buck Taylor
Rena	Marianne Kanter
Roy	Kip Whitman
Karen	Mitzi Hoag
Funky	Buck Kartalian
Leroy	George Sims
Grog	Wally Campo
Bruno	Dick Anders
Robot	John Craig

Although there's about as much originality in the making of 'Devil's Angels' as any other hastily put together carbon of a successful film, the very inclusion of the same ingredients that went into producer Roger Corman's "Wild

Angels" will undoubtedly garner the film a fair measure of boxoffice success. There's little doubt that it will be aimed at the same market, with the same selling gimmicks, and as its potential audience is not particularly discriminating, will probably be accepted in a like manner.

Trouble with this one is that AIP has settled for second-team work all the way around. Burt Topper's producing for Corman and Daniel Haller directing for Corman and a lesser-known pair of leads than Peter Fonda and Nancy Sinatra have provided a considerably watered-down version of the earlier "protest" film and is likely to hasten the end of this particular genre a bit faster than originally planned.

While scripter Charles Griffith hasn't hesitated to borrow sequences from both "Wild Angels" and "Wild Ones", such sequences have begun to pall because of their very familiarity. A usually excellent actor, John Cassavetes, who once also had ambitions about directing, shows little of the promise indicated in "Edge of the City." He mumbles through the male lead with a watered-down "method" approach to the role. Even less impressive is Beverly Adams who seems more concerned with not smearing her makeup or losing one of her artificial eyelashes (all the motorcyclists' women are too pretty and far too clean to appear credible).

The motorcycle "gang" is made up of the usual stock characters, carried over intact from earlier, similar efforts. An interesting angle is that the few characters who do convey some degree of credibility are all members of the small-town citizens with whom the motorcyclists come in contact, and conflict. Leo Gordon as the sheriff of such a town is the only admirable character in the plot, his fellow citizens being exaggerated (evidently in some script attempt to explain the antagonism of the cycle beatniks towards law and order).

It appears obvious that AIP is going to have a much shorter money run with its protest-type films than they did with the previously successful comedy-terror and beach features. It may be that the generation of filmgoers they're seeking is growing up faster than the people who make their films. Technical credits throughout are run-of-the-mill. *Robe.*

Up The Down Staircase
(COLOR)

Valladolid, April 22.

Warner Bros. release of a Pakula-Mulligan production. Stars Sandy Dennis, Patrick Bedford, Eileen Heckart, Ruth White; features Jean Stapleton, Sorrell Booke, Ray Poole, Florence Stanley. Directed by Robert Mulligan. Screenplay, Tad Mosel, based on novel by Bel Kaufman; camera (Technicolor), Joseph Coffey; film editor, Folmar Blangsted; sound, Dennis Maitland; music, Fred Karlin; art director, George Jenkins; asst. director, Don Kranze. Reviewed at the XII International Week of Religious and Human Values Cinema at Valladolid, Spain. Running Time, **120 MINS.**

Sylvia Barrett .... Sandy Dennis
Paul Barringer .... Patrick Bedford
Henrietta Pastorfield.... Eileen Heckart
Beatrice Schracter .... Ruth White
Sadie Finch .... Jean Stapleton
Dr. Bester .... Sorrell Booke
McHabe .... Roy Poole
Ella Friedenberg ..... Florence Stanley
Joe Ferone .... Jeff Howard
Alice Blake .... Ellen O'Mara
Jose Rodriguez .... Jose Rodriguez
Ed Williams .... John Fantauzzi
The Mother .... Vinnette Carroll
Miss Gordon .... Janice Mars
Social Studies Teacher.. Loretta Leversee
Mr. Osborne .... Robert Levine
Nurse Eagen .... Elena Karam
Charlotte Wolf...... Frances Sternhagen
Linda Rosen .... Candace Culkin
Harry A. Kagan .... Salvatore Rosa
Lou Martin .... Lew Wallach

Based on the novel of the same title by Bel Kaufman, "Up the Down Staircase" concerns troubles of a beginning teacher in a tough city high school. And it is very good, almost in spite of itself. With only one major star (Sandy Dennis) and virtually a single setting, this pic is nevertheless thoroughly cinematic in its treatment and completely engrossing. This is mainly because it is well acted, carefully scripted and directed and finely photographed. Warm and human perhaps best describe a picture of this nature, especially in the context of a film festival of "religious and human values." Yet director Robert Mulligan has for the most part avoided sentimentalism and presented his story honestly and directly.

It may not delight intellectuals or thrill-seekers — it is not consciously "arty" or sensational—but if presented intelligently should do good general business, especially with the backing of Miss Dennis' recent Oscar.

As pretty young Miss Barrett, fresh from a purely theoretical college training as an English teacher, she is plopped into impersonal Calvin Coolidge High School, a multi-racial institution where most of the teachers feel they are successful if they manage to keep their classrooms fairly civilized. Many of her students are hostile Negroes and Puerto Ricans with no inclination toward the joys of English literature, and she is discouraged by her inability to get through to them.

Even after she does make some progress, an inopportune advance from the handsome class thug sours her on the job. She decides to quit at the end of the term. But then, after she realizes her students really appreciate her efforts, she changes her mind. She will stay on, even though it is difficult.

Though many of the characters are familiar stock ones—the heartless disciplinarian, the scatterbrained librarian, the inadequate guidance counselor, the "love" obsessed teenage girl, the dropout, the withdrawn student—their treatment is generally successful. The mood of a large school, with its stumbling bureaucracy, and less paperwork and lack of communication, is well evoked, although perhaps occasionally ever so slightly over-emphasized.

The scene at the school dance, with its groping, tentative encounters between students and teachers, is especially excellent. In spite of a fragmented, episodic script, there is an overall smoothness and unity. And it is heartening that the heroine was confined to her school and no attempt made to develop a love interest or show her at home. While the film might be faulted on its happy ending, the optimism has been generally well prepared in advance.

As noted, much of the credit must go to the excellent acting. Miss Dennis is nearly perfect as the harried newcomer although at times one wishes scripter Tad Mosel had made her a bit more decisive in handling the students. Patrick Bedford, a cynical teacher and unpublished novelist who would like to court her, is also very good, as are Eileen Heckart and Ruth White in lesser roles as teachers. Whether professionals or untrained, the students are all very convincing. Direction of this group is a strong point which could easily have been weak.

Production values are first-rate. Joseph Coffey's subdued Technicolor photography is natural and forceful without ever being garish. It's especially good in his handling of the dance and the several street scenes. Sets are all authentic. The musical score is generally subtle and effective, only occasionally obtrusive. The editing is crisp and economical. One gets the impression that a smoothly trained team —producer, director, scenarist, actors and technicians—worked carefully and happily on a project for which they had great affection. *Lyon.*

Gunfight In Abilene
(COLOR)

Average western with added marquee lure of Bobby Darin name: with extra push, could take off.

Universal Pictures release of Howard Christie production. Directed by William Hale. Stars Bobby Darin; features Emily Banks, Leslie Nielsen, Donnelly Rhodes, Don Galloway, Frank McGrath, Michael Sarrazin. Screenplay, Berne Gilber, John D. F. Black, based on novel by Clarence Upson; camera (Technicolor), Maury Gertsman; film editor, Gene Palmer; sound, Waldon O. Watson, Frank H. Wilkinson; art directors, Alexander Golitzen, William D. Decinces; music, Bobby Darin; asst. director, Joseph Kenny. Reviewed in New York, March 15, '67. Running Time, **86 MINS.**

Cal Wayne .... Bobby Darin
Amy Martin .... Emily Banks
Grant Evers .... Leslie Nielsen
Joe Slade .... Donnelly Rhodes
Ward Kent .... Don Galloway
Ned Martin .... Frank McGrath
Cord Decker .... Michael Sarrazin
Leann .... Barbara Werle
Loop .... Johnny Seven
Frank Norton .... William Phipps
Ed Scovie .... William Mims
Nelson .... Robert Sorrells
Scrague .... Don Dubbins
Smokey Staub .... James McCallion
Frobisher .... Bryan O'Byrne

Reviewed for the record. This is one of the films which Universal originally planned to release without tradeshowing but about which it changed its mind. Most male actors eventually want to try their hand at an action film but the "cowboy" film is one of the toughest to carry off successfully. As they rarely continue in this type of film, such experiments are generally forgotten. So it isn't likely that Bobby Darin's jump will stir up much fuss among the western fans.

The kicker, however is that Darin has a considerable following among the music fans and their interest in any film he might make could stir up enough interest to get "Gunfight in Abilene" moving at the boxoffice. He also composed the music for the film, a possible first in the western field.

"Gunfight" is, generally, a rough and tough actioner with enough talent in the cast to put some meaning into William Hale's direction. Darin, as an ex-Confederate officer who is gun-shy as the result of his unintentional killing of a friend, is offbeat casting but is quite acceptable. He's supported strongly by Leslie Nielsen and Donnelly Rhodes as the villains and a plethora of young faces in the cast including Michael Sarrazin, who's moved over to a star role in 20th-Fox's "Flim-Flam Man." Technical credits are first-rate. *Robe.*

Tammy and The Millionaire
(COLOR)

Tiresome tv pilot fails to recover from operation to theatricalize it. Brief spurt of hope when "river pirate" Jeff York appears but too late.

Universal Pictures release of Dick Wesson production. Features Debbie Watson, Frank McGrath, Denver Pyle, George Furth, Donald Woods, Dorothy Green, Jeff York. Directed by Sidney Miller, Ezra Stone and Leslie Goodwins. Screenplay, George Tibbles, based on "Tammy Out of Time" and "Tammy Tell Me True" by Cid Ricketts Sumner; camera (Pathe color), John F. Warren, Robert Wyckoff, Enzo A. Martinelli, Bud Thackery; editor, Larry D. Lester; sound, Waldon O. Watson, Earl Martin Madery; music, Jack Marshall; asst. directors, George Bisk, John Clarke Bowman. Reviewed at Universal h.o., N.Y., April 27, '67. Running time, **87 MINS.**

Tammy .... Debbie Watson
Uncle Lucius .... Frank McGrath
Grandpa .... Denver Pyle
Dwayne Whitt .... George Furth
John Brent .... Donald Woods
Lavinia Tate .... Dorothy Green
Peter Tate .... David Macklin
Gloria Tate .... Linda Marshall
Steven Brent .... Jay Sheffield
Dewey Maine McKinley ... Teddy Quinn
Sybelline Tate .... Bella Bruck
The Mailman .... Andy Albin
Billy Joe Morgan .... Craig Hundley
Governor Alden .... Roy Roberts
Grundy Tate .... Jeff York

The advertisers, or Universal, decided not to go ahead with this pilot of a planned tv series. Understandably, an entire generation would never have forgiven them and the view of the South the film presents could still bring on Civil War II.

This minor disaster needed three directors. What was once a successful "drippin'" with mo-lasses and good intent" idea, as initiated by Ross Hunter in the 1957 "Tammy and the Bachelor" with Debbie Reynolds, has deteriorated into the same cinematic drivel that finally killed off the Ma and Pa Kettle series.

Briefly, but only so, there's a touch of real comedy when Davy Crockett's old river pirate crony, Jeff York, makes an appearance as an unbelievably dirty and larcenous "poor relation" of the rich females, who're trying to land the local millionaire. As he's as great a threat to the acting of the leads as Mercutio was to Romeo, he's gotten rid of quickly. Most of the audience will want to sail on down the river with him.

Technical credits are fine — good color photography, handsome sets, nice music; but script and acting are only tol'able. *Robe.*

Made In Italy
(ITALIAN-FRENCH-COLOR)

Royal Films release of a Documento Film (Gianni Hecht Lucari) production. Directed by Nanni Loy. Features entire cast. Screenplay, Ettore Scola, Ruggero Maccari, Loy; story, Scola, Maccari. Camera (Techniscope, Technicolor), Ennio Guarnieri; editor, Ruggero Mastroianni; sound, Claudio Maielli; art director, Luciano Spadoni; no music credits. Reviewed at 34th Street East Theatre, N.Y., April 30, '67. Running Time, 102 MINS.

Bored Diner	Marina Berti
Renato	Gullio Bosetti
Giulio	Lando Buzzanca
Enrico	Walter Chiari
Wronged Wife	Rosella Falk
Bored Diner's Husband	Claudio Gore
Diana	Sylva Koscina
Other Woman	Claudie Lange
Virginia	Virna Lisi
Anna	Anna Magnani
Citizen Lamporecchi	Nino Manfredi
Monica	Lea Massari
Rosalia	Yolanda Modio
Gianremo	Fabrizio Moroni
Another Diner	Lionello Pio Di Savola
Errant Husband	Alberto Sordi
Orlando	Jean Sorel
Karol	Catherine Spaak

(*English Subtitles*)

An even better title for this hurried, but frequently funny and touching look at Italian ways, would have been "Made All Over Italy." Director Nanni Loy, best known in the U. S. for his memorable "Four Days In Naples," filmed exteriors in Rome, Taormina, Catanina, Amalfi, Naples, Venice, Turin, Milan, Florence and a closing bit in Stockholm.

Although his intent, and that of producer Gianni Hecht Lucari, was to capture on film "the mind, heart and soul of the Italian people of today," the episodic nature of the telling tries to cram too many ingredients into the pizza. The result is two excellent segments, two or three good ones with the remainder ranging from unexciting to dull. Some of the incidents are extended (although none are very long), others no more than blackouts; some will seem familiar to Italian film buffs.

The cast contains an assortment of top-level Italian film names, with Anna Magnani providing the funniest bit as a mother of three children trying to move them, her unemployed husband and his mother across a death-by-traffic Roman street to buy some ice cream. After a harrowing trip they make it only to find the store has run out but the clerk suggests they try a new drugstore—across the street.

Nino Manfredi also has a wonderful skit with which everyone who has run into the red tape of bureaucracy will identify. Trying to obtain an identity card he is shuttled back and forth from one department to another until finally an electronic computer comes to a final decision—he does not exist. Asking the clerk why, then, he gets his tax bills, the answer is "no doubt a postal error."

There are some rather caustic comments on "habits and customs," one of the sections into which Loy has divided his film. Others are "work," with a laborer returning home, groggy with fatigue, to be greeted by a tv commercial for a do-it-yourself exercise kit; "women," with the usual approaches to infidelity; "citizens-state-church," with a crack at the affluence of the Church which would delight Bishop James Pike;

"family," with the Magnani sequence; and a recurring bit with four Italian laborers on their way to Sweden to find work.

Technical qualities of the film are generally good although the Technicolor camerawork could have been improved and the pace quickened by the excision of two or three of the minor bits. For the specialized market. *Robe.*

L'Horizon
(FRENCH—COLOR)

Paris, April 27.

International Cinevision production and release. With Jacques Perrin, Macha Meril, Rene Dary, Monique Melinand. Directed by Jacques Rouffio. Screenplay, Georges Conchon, Rouffio from book by Conchon; camera (Eastmancolor), Raoul Coutard; editor, Monique Herran. At Cannes Film Fest. Running time, 100 MINS.

Antonin	Jacques Perrin
Girl	Macha Meril
Father	Rene Dary
Mother	Monique Melinand
Max	Felix Brizard
Jerome	Jean-Pierre Honore
American	Steve Gadler

Color costumer unfolds behind the lines during the first World War. It has well conceived characters and a forthright theme of war weariness and pacifism. It has deceptively simple progression and some of its allusions to the events and politics of the time. This could make the pic more difficult for playoff abroad but it hints good arty chances.

A young man comes home on furlough in 1917 after being wounded. He falls in love with the widow of a cousin living with his family and is torn between finding a way of not going back to the war or giving in. Into this are woven his love affair, his father's decision to keep him out of more fighting at all costs, patriotism be hanged and a suggestion about the growing horror and waste of the war. He finally goes back to the front.

Jacques Perrin has the right mixture of callowness and sensitivity as the boy. Also, there is his will to live for his love. Macha Meril is glowing as a suffragette female of the times while Rene Dary and Monique Melinand etch strong portraits as the parents. The subtle color work of Raoul Coutard is an asset in getting the plush feel of the times in Paris as contrasted with the starkness of the war scenes.

This is an offbeater here since there is a touchiness about themes that may not follow the line of French grandeur and prestige. It remains to be seen if this may run into censor problems.

Pic is technically fine and director Jacques Rouffio shows a good narrative style for his first production. *Mosk.*

Cannes Festival

A Ciascuno Il Suo
(To Each His Own)
(ITALIAN—COLOR)

Cannes, May 2.

United Artists release of Cemofilm production. Stars Gian Maria Volonte, Irene Papas, Gabrielle Ferzetti; features

Mario Scaccia, Leopoldo Trieste, Laura Nucci, Luigi Pistilli. Directed by Elio Petri. Screenplay, Elio Petri, Ugo Pirro from book by L. Sciascia; camera (Technicolor), Luigi Kuveiller; editor, Ruggero Mastroianni. At Cannes Film Fest. Running Time, 99 MINS.

Paolo	Gian Maria Volonte
Luisa	Irene Papas
Rosello	Gabriele Ferzetti
Rascio	Salvo Randone
Mother	Laura Nucci
Antonio	Franco Tranchina
Arturo	Luigi Pistilli
Rosina	Luciana Scalise

Sicily, with its shimmering charm and almost tropical ease, underlined with a sort of menace is still a place for dramas, tales of passionate crime and the underworld. Here, all this is welded into a probing film of suspense and mounting tension that builds to organized mayhem. This transcends its cadre rather than just having it a tale of the Mafia or localized crime.

Director Elio Petri shows a flair for sharp observation, crisp progression and acceptable visual metaphors. All this makes for a solid comment on man's latent violence that can be used by secret organizations. A sort of lovesick innocent, a loner and a teacher, is the victim in this seemingly complicated tale of anonymous letters and murders for love.

The man, Gian Maria Volonte, has two friends killed after one has been receiving anonymous letters threatening him. They are killed on a hunting trip. But it seems that the letters were a coverup to get a friend whose wife is coveted by a local bigwig. There is even a hint the wife of the man getting the anonymous letters might have been glad to get rid of her husband.

The professor falls for one of the widows and becomes entangled to be finally done away with when he gets too close to things. It ends with a big wedding of the widow.

This may have some difficult sidelights for ordinary audiences, but has the ruggedness and clarity in dealing with the meshes of organized violence to give it arty theatre chances. Playoff is indicated on its well sustained narrative.

Fine color helps this pic. Gian Volonte has presence and growth as the man finally outpaced by his growing awareness and betrayal. Greek actress Irene Papas is excellent in her dark brooding joys, woes and final sellout activities to the widow. A moody and dramatically counterpointed music score also helps.

Scripting is always economical and robust. Direction gives this a heightened awareness combining actioner and social comment. UA has a solidly-made film that needs the right to sell. But it should snare critical interest and word-of-mouth. *Mosk.*

Tizezer Nap
(The Ten Thousand Suns)
(HUNGARIAN)

Cannes, May 2.

Hungarofilm release of Mafilm production. With Tibor Molnar, Gyongyi Buros, Andras Kozak, Janos Kaltai. Directed by Ferenc Kosa. Screenplay, Sandro Csouri, Imre Cyongyossy, Kosa; camera, Sandor Sara; music, Andras Szollosy. At Cannes Film Fest. Running Time, 112 MINS.

Istavan	Tibor Molnar
Wife	Gyongyi Buros
Son	Abdras Kozak
Fulop	Janos Kozak

The last 30 years of shifting history, changes and wars in Hungary are seen via a small village and mainly three men. It does try to say a lot and succeeds mainly by a firm control of pace and an epic elan. But perhaps some is not too clear to those not familiar with Hungaro history. And there is sometimes a too academic approach.

But this does have a visual drive and robustness. The poverty of the peasants, their harshness, brought on by their conditions, as well as their rugged humanity, are neatly etched on the background of changing years and outlooks by new director Ferenc Kosa. A Communist and a man who can not understand it are friends in a small town. It has them looking back over the highlights of their lives today. Also the reactions of the son who is ready to go back to his big city schooling. The peasants, who are bought and sold, strikes, the war, the Communist takeover and the 1956 uprising all have their repercussions.

Pic does not spare Stalinist prisons and repression, but is firmly for the system if it notes that it has to be made to work yet. Expert lensing that captures the mists and beauties of the land. Earthy but never overdone acting and a compelling directorial dash give this film strength though it appears too special in intent and outlook for anything but arty use abroad. But for a first film, it marks Director Ferenc Kosa a definite new Magyar talent to watch. *Mosk.*

Ljubavni Slucaj ou Tragedija Sluzbenice P.T.T.
(Affair of the Heart or Tragedy of a Postal Worker)
(YUGOSLAV)

Cannes, April 28.

Avala Film production and release. With Eva Ras, Slobodan Aligrudic, Ruzica Sokic. Written and directed by Dussan Makaveiev. Camera, Aleksander Petkovic; editor, Katarina Stojanovic. At Cannes Film Fest. Running time, 75 MINS.

Isabelle	Eva Ras
Ahmed	Slobodan Aligrudic
Friend	Ruzica Sokic
Seducer	Miodrag Audric

Unselfconscious nudity and a sly witty moralistic fable about love, betrayal and marriage comes from Yugoslavia via this pic. So film themes seem to be changing there. This clever film might have some specialized chances abroad if its length slants it mainly for arty houses.

A bright, earthy girl of Hungarian background is living in Belgrade and working in a post office. She meets a man and they are attracted and begin to live together with marriage rarely mentioned. But the film is built on a plot regarding the girl's body found in a well and her trip to the morgue plus the police inquiry and flashbacks re her love and death.

Director Dusan Makavejev shows a fine feel for clever blending of comedy and a sharp observance of human conduct to turn this into a smartly paced moralistic look at man and woman relationships. Even asides to the audience are handled in the right mood and help keep this bright comedy moving.

The man is content to just coast while the girl yearns for marriage. But, if he seems to be quite open-minded, he turns out to be unable to forgive her a misstep. While he is away on a trip she is seduced and finds herself with child.

This is one of those smartly done comedies with a layer of more pungent dissection of human motivations. The acting is winning, the technical quality fine, and the pic has taste and ironic but never glib serio-comic undertones. *Mosk.*

Mord Und Totschlag
(Death and Homicide)
(WEST GERMAN—COLOR)

Cannes, May 2.
Universal release of Rob Houwer Film production. With Anita Pallenberg, Hans P. Hallwachs, Manfred Fischbeck, Werner Enke. Directed by Volker Schloendorff. Screenplay, Schloendorff, Gregor Von Rezzori, Niklaus Franz, Arno Boyer; camera (Eastmancolor), Franz Rath; music, Brian Jones; editor, Claus Von Boro. At Cannes Film Fest. Running time, 87 MINS.
Marie .... Anita Pallenberg
Gunther .... Hans P. Hallwachs
Fritz .... Manfred Fischbeck
Hans .... Werner Enke

The last two years at film festivals has definitely shown a renaissance in West German film talents, plus more forthright themes and subject matter. This tale of youth does not preach or moralize but is handled with tact and taste to emerge another German pic with foreign potential. The relentlessness slant this for arty situations with playoff possible on its theme. A certain sort of almost amoral youth is not new, but this adds a dimension in just showing their comportment in the context of an accidental murder.

The girl, Anita Pallenberg, works in a cafe, is pretty and free living. But late one night, she kills her fiancee in a fight over a revolver he has given her. She enlists the aid of a young man by promising money and he, brings in a friend to help. They wrap the body in a rug and leave it in a hole on a big roadway under construction. But a bulldozer unearths the body at the end as the girl is thinking of going off with a young man to Greece. So there's' no denouement or retribution here. One weakness of the pic is trying so hard not to take sides that some of the reactions may seem gratuitous. Are they rebels of a sort? But there is not enough of a relationship with others, and especially older people, to clarify this. So it may give a slightly distorted view of a certain kind of youth.

But they do reflect a definite reality. And director Volker Schloendorff shows a sure hand in dealing with these drifting youngsters who display a hatred of the so-called German virtues of work, tidyness and self-contentment.

Miss Pallenberg has the angular frame, pert face and restrained emotion that befits her seeming callousness and repressed hysteria at the accidental death of her fiancee. Color is rightly subdued, pace is well maintained and playing good all down the line. The stirrings of a new West German film renaissance now seems a fact and this adroit, incisive pic about

untethered youth may be too objective to give a deeper insight into their motives and lives.

But on its own level, this is absorbing, direct and should get some attention abroad on its theme and theatment. Schloendorff can be added to such other recent German filmmakers as the Schamoni Brothers and Alexandre Kluge. *Mosk.*

L'Inconnu De Shandigor
(The Unknown of Shandigor)
(SWISS)

Cannes, May 2.
Frajea Film production and release. With Marie-France Boyer, Ben Carruthers, Daniel Emilfork, Jacques Dufilho, Howard Vernon, Serge Gainsbourg. Directed by Jean-Louis Roy. Screenplay, Roy, Gabriel Arout; camera, Roger Bimpage; music, Alphonse Roy. At Cannes Film Fest.. Running time, 90 MINS.
Sylvaine .... Marie-France Boyer
Manuel .... Ben Carruthers
Von Krantz .... Daniel Emilfork
Yank .... Howard Vernon
Russian .... Jacques Dufilho

Swiss spy and undercover pic mixes sci-fi, sinister underworld organizations and national spy undercover outfits revolving around a scientist who has found a way to make atomic weapons unworkable. It is fairly slick and works the usual familiar roads in this type of pix. But it has enough craftsmanship and the right tongue-in-cheek for okay dualer use abroad.

The scientist holes up in a villa where his daughter is kept practically a prisoner. But outside are American and Russian agents and then a mysterious Asian organization all seeking the secret. The scientist is finally devoured by some sort of sea monster he keeps in his pool and his daughter escapes to find love with a mysterious stranger.

Film has nice production dress, plenty of mayhem and does not get too far out. But the road it travels becomes predictable and pic finally becomes a bit like Bond films. Director Jean-Louis Roy, however, has a crisp hand and keeps things moving. The cast is workable and pic is a neatly-made commercial opus which could find programmer and tv niches on world marts. And, if not of fest calibre, it still was not amiss on its action flair and found buyer interest and audience acceptance. *Mosk.*

The Bell
(JAPANESE)

Cannes, April 27.
Aoshima production and relase. With Keitaro Miho, Keisuke Ishizu, Katsuhito Matsura, Mari Tashibana. Written and directed by Yukio Aoshima. Camera, Tadashi Sato, Mitsuo Nakagawa, Tomomi Kamata; editor, Rikuo Shirae. At Cannes Film Fest. Running time, 60 MINS.
First Boy .... Keitaro Miho
Second Boy .... Keisuke Ishizu
Third Boy .... Katsuhito Matsura
Fourth Boy .... Mari Tashibana
Girl .... Yosuke Kondo

Most Japanese films to reach the West are usually either costume or classic tales, actioners and sometimes a situation comedy. But rarely has a visual gag comedy come through. Hence, this one truly has a filmic flair that has assimilated U.S. slapstick and given it a Japanese feeling. Film still has international flavor and feeling.

Pic is only an hour long so is mainly something that could serve

with another medium length pic in arty and even playoff situations abroad. It has freshness and tang. Also this has no talk and needs no subtitles. It is done without forcing.

Four young men and a sultry, good looking girl are off to the beach in a jeep. On the way they taunt drivers, siphon off gas, tussle with coke machines and generally deport themselves as rowdies but are rarely mean. But there is a definite revolt against conventions here.

A love romp is done off camera and there are moments of repose that make a good counterpoint to the general roughhouse or animalistic good spirits. The bell of the film's title is found submerged by one boy as he skin-dives. Much of the pic is concerned with their ways of hoisting it up.

The timing here is almost impeccable. Echoes of Buster Keaton, Harold Lloyd and Chaplin are prevalent.

Players are fresh but always likable. There is comic verve and talent in newcomer Kazuo Kuroki. Sustained gags and quick sight jokes are fused well into this wild weekend at the beach. *Mosk.*

Le Regne Du Jour
(Duration of the Day)
(CANADIAN)

Cannes, April 30.
Canadian Film Office production and release. Conception, direction and editing by Pierre Perrault. Camera, Bernard Gosslein, JeanClaude Labrecque. At Cannes Film Fest. Running time, 118 MINS.

Canadian film follows an old couple of French Canadians in their first trip to their ancestral home in France. It intercuts with their meetings and reactions to their reliving it at home with friends. Pic builds a touching if repetitive look at two brisk and fetching old people. But its very nature limits this for special showings abroad with more tv and school usage indicated than for arty houses.

The director has a knowledge of and affection for these rural people in northern Canada and has already made a pic on them in their own habitat "Pour La Suite Du Monde" (For the Future of the World). Now he shows they have accepted him and hardly seem aware of the camera. Director Pierre Perrault has some lively bits as they discuss things with fellow rural French people.

However, this type of film has a tendency to include too much and can stand a good deal of pruning. It does not always seem to take a more compelling distance in making a statement on the lives and outlooks of these people.

But no gainsaying the workmanship and dedication in this kind of pic which make important historical footnotes and sometimes revealing films. This is uneven but one of the better so-called cinema-truth pix. *Mosk.*

Theatre De Monsieur Et Madame Kabal
(Mr. and Mrs. Kabal's Theatre)
(FRENCH)
(Animation-Color)

Cannes, May 2.

Cineastes Associes production and release. Written, edited animated and directed by Walerian Borowczyk. Camera (Eastmancolor), Guy Durban; music, Avenir De Monfred. At Cannes Film Fest. Running time, 80 MINS.

Working in France, Walerian Borowczyk, the Polish animator says in his titles this is an animated feature for adults. It mixes some live action and objects with a look at a strange couple Mr. and Mrs. Kabal, that may embody a look at mankind generally, or be just an inventive tale of a harridan and a meek man. Or it is just a beguiling, but always comic animated film that breaks new ground. Above all, it unveils a brilliant animation talent.

Borowczyk is known for his prizewinning shorts, but here he fills this out to full-length without ever failing. This is a very special pic and needs extremely sensitive handling for best results. Small arties and specialized, university and even special programming scene most likely.

No use trying to tell the story. Imaginative line drawings set up a crisp humor that can sometimes be even alarming but always delving into a new and private world that is rewarding in its asides.

It may sometimes seem difficult but this does set up a new experience in animation. The gags are all visual and the witty music plus blending of real objects and the systematic examination of human relations on a poetically comic plane give it depth. This may be rated an unusual film experience that naturally needs extremely right sell to reach more demanding audiences. Pic was given a special showing under the auspices and backing of the Cannes Critic section. *Mosk.*

Jeu De Massacre
(Killing Game)
(FRENCH-COLOR)

Cannes, May 2.
Inter France Distribution release of Francinor-A. J. Film production. Stars Jean-Pierre Cassel, Claudine Auger; features Michel Duchaussoy, Eleonore Hirt, Anna Gayor, Guy Saint-Jean, Nancy Holloway. Written and directed by Alain Jessua. Camera (Eastmancolor), Jacques Robin; editor, Nicole Marco. At Cannes Film Fest. Running time, 95 MINS.
Pierre .... Jean-Pierre Cassel
Jacqueline .... Claudine Auger
Bob .... Michel Duchaussoy
Mother .... Eleonore Hirt
Ado .... Guy Saint-Jean
Nancy .... Nancy Holloway
Lisbeth .... Anna Gaylor

Pop art backgrounds this comedy about truth and illusion and the final subduing and calming of a disturbed rich boy. It has sharp comic touch and does balance its dual look at life and questions if it were affected by the comic strip world. Hence, this solidly-made pic needs careful handling abroad but has selling points on its pop aspects.

However, the right placement is needed because it does not opt for an easy and broad comic flair. Instead, it rings in subtle notations. A bright color envelope and some good thesps also help to keep this from falling apart. So this is an item that may well have offshore and local legs if properly sold.

Director-writer Alain Jessua deals with a writer of pulp fiction and comic strips who is visited by a rich youth who says he has lived many of the adventurers he's read about in his books. He finally intrigues the writer and his wife, and they end up being his house guests at his posh Swiss villa.

It appears that the rich lad is leading a rather aimless life by preying on women. The writer begins a comic strip based on his desired adventures which suddenly begins to be acted out by the youth. He mistreats women, even stripping one nude, and almost seduces the writer's wife. But he is brought back from his dream life after a stretch in prison.

Jessua brings off many subtle notations on this seemingly broad satire. Michel Duchaussoy has the right mixture of ingenuousness and menace while Jean-Pierre Cassel shows lightness and charm and keeps the writer from emerging a cynic.

Claudine Auger is decorative as the wife with Eleonore Hirt rightly disturbing as a rather lascivious-minded mother. So on the surface, this comedy is sometimes obvious but has the subtle shafts of insight to make a statement on the effect of pulp stuff.

Careful handling could make this okay for arty theatre usage. A jangling big beat musical score is also a plus factor.   *Mosk.*

Warrendale
(CANADIAN)
Cannes, May 1.
CBC release of Allan King Associates production. Directed and conceived by Allan King. Camera, William Brayne; editor, Peter Moseley. At Cannes Film Fest. Running time, **105 MINS.**

This pic is a shattering documentary look at a home for disturbed children and adolescents in Canada. It deals with a group of young, dedicated workers who stay with these emotionally mixed-up youngsters and emerges an engrossing, stark film. It is in English.

The people involved seem unaware of the camera except when the filmmaker is mentioned by one of the workers. Aim of the home is to try to keep the inmates from falling into trances.

It is the treatment in this institution that is the thing in this well-made and incisive truth pic. Death of a beloved cook is one of the main segs of the film as it details the reactions of the patients who had become attached to her.

The workers display almost superhuman patience but it is their work and never sentimentalized. Its relentless theme make this mainly a specialized item for commercial use, but arty houses might be attracted to it. It is a natural for colleges.

Psychologically absorbing, well-made and edited, it is another of the Canadian documentary films treating with aspects of ordinary life. It could come in for some theatrical interest in France. "Warrendale" is the name of the institution.   *Mosk.*

Frank's Greatest Adventure
(COLOR-TECHNISCOPE)

Chicago - made indie that spoofs American film myths,

could be taken as far out satire. Well-made with good technical qualities and a filmmaker to be watched in Phil Kaufman.

Cannes, April 29.
Jericho Film, Inc., production and release. With Jon Voight, Monique Van Vooren, Joan Darling, Severn Darden. Written and directed by Phil Kaufman. Camera (Technicolor), Bill Butler; editor Aram Boyajian, Luke Bennet. At Cannes Film Fest. Running time, **83 MINS.**

Frank .... Jon Voight
Plethora .... Monique Van Vooren
Doctor .... Severn Darden
Lois .... Joan Darling
Boss .... Lou Gilbert
The Cat .... Ben Carruthers
The Rat .... Dave Steinberg
The Stranger .... Ken Nordine
Needles .... Nelson Algren
Screnose .... David Fisher

In the guise of a far-out tale of a superman and a manmade monster, gangsters and scientists is intended to be a disarming spoof of the American myths as embodied in its films. This indie pic, made in Chicago, also benefits from fine color, scope and technical solidity. At time reviewed, however, no major U.S. company had picked it for distribution. the symbolical ribbon. This comes had picked it for distribution. (Paramount looked at it in N. Y. some months ago and decided to pass—Ed.)

Film adroitly lines up all those secret sentimental dreams that have made up the backbone of some Hollywood films. So harmless underworld types, an optimistic hick with charm to overcome the so-called intellectuals and city slickers, women of the world who succumb to his charms and the panoply of big city life versus the small town all get a going-over in this simple pic.

That is the trouble. Some may just read another wacky comic adventure yarn with fantastic overtones. But it surpasses all this in its humor, shredding of myths and generally shrewd timing and downright enjoyable shenanigans.

Phil Kaufman, who was co-director of another Chicago-made comedy "Goldstein," goes it alone as director. Perhaps he is too slack in the second half of this and at times overworks a gag. But, on the whole, he shows a fine grasp of filmic comedy.

It is in the Chicago Second City vein, with a host of individual scenes setting up the targets and nicely plinking away at them with air rifle precision rather than using a slapstick blunderbuss. Frank, a hayseed, is shown in his city adventures, in Chicago, of course.

Plot has Frank awakening as a superman after apparently having been slain by gangsters.

Little-known players all etch neat performances, with Monique Van Vooren just right as the pulpy moll who has time to warble some songs. Pic may be difficult for arty chances on its surface-like simplicity and would need careful placement in special houses.

Perhaps Kaufman now needs less pop and more hep material, but he is a filmmaker with verve and knowhow. He uses his group of thesps well. Jon Voight has the healthy blonde openness that lends itself to the dual characters whether as a good one or an evil character. Joan Darling is both

urchin and then a demanding female as the good doctor's daughter. Severn Darden etches neat linnings as the two doctors. Lou Gilbert and Ben Carruthers are fine as the boss and one of his henchman. Smart musical scove is also an asset.

Pic was shown in the Cannes Fest Producer Section with a special nod from the Critic Section who recommended it. Color is bright, production values solid, and this is a most beguiling offbeater for playoff or arty chances.   *Mosk.*

Trio
(ITALIAN)
Cannes, April 28.
IDI Cinematografica production and release. With Marisa Galvan, Walter Vezza, Mariella Zanetti. Written and directed by Gian Franco Mingozzi. Camera, Ugo Piccone; editor, Domencio Gorgolinu. At Cannes Film Fest. Running time, **105 MINS.**

Herself .... Marisa Galvan
Enzo .... Walter Vezza
Anna .... Mariella Zanetti
Maurice .... Maurizio Bonuglia

A look at three young people is intertwined in this knowing first pic that shows a mastery of clarity and character. Gian-Franco Mingozzi makes a fine impression in his initial feature film after several shorts and documentaries. Film's theme and firstrate handling might give this a good chance in foreign arties and it should make a dent in Italy.

A young girl, who wins a pop singing contest, an introverted youth and a bachelor, who tries to live freely, are the three protagonists of this skillfully made Italo pic.

The pop singer is seen at her triumph, her simple reaction to it and then her rise and work as a singer. The youth takes to spying on the bachelor across the way who leads a lonely life that somehow seems almost settled to the boy. At one time he decides to rob him because he notices him always fingering bills.

He can't go through with it and finally feels he needs this man to show him some way to cope with his own feelings. The girl, who takes lovers and leaves them sans any remorse is shown free and yet unable to find a balance in her own life.

Director Mingozzi ties up his various scenes with a forward impetus. In this way, it is a refreshing pic and has a solid mixture of almost documentary segments of the youth world and the more personal acts and adventures of its trio. It also reveals a new director who can handle people and make his dramatic statements in a good visual style.   *Mosk.*

Joszef Katus
(DUTCH)
Cannes, May 2.
Scorpio Film-Pim De La Parra Jr. production and release. With Rudolf Lucieer, Etha Coster, Shireen Strooker. Directed by Wim Verstappen. Screenplay, Pim De La Parra, Verstappan; camera, Wim Van Der Linden; editor, Rob Van Steensel. At Cannes Film Fest. Running time, **100 MINS.**

Katus .... Rudolf Lucieer
Girl .... Etha Coster
Friend .... Shireen Strooker
Wife .... Barbara Meter
Man .... Els Mes

This film deals with a refugee

Hungarian who has lived in Holland and then traveled around Europe, and is now back in the country. It treats with wanderings, loves and attempts to join the revolutionary youth of the country, without actually making any true human or social contacts. Then there is his mysterious death at the hands of a man who follows him throughout the film.

Made on a shoestring, and blown up from 16m. film, this looks fair technically. It does show the influence of French New Wave and Cinema Truth pix in its fragmented scenes and lack of attempting any coherent narrative. But there is a consistency in the playing by the main character. A frisky camera and some shafts of insight, are plus factors.

But this is mainly too repetitive and rather unformed to be anything but specialized fare abroad.   *Mosk.*

The Perils of Pauline
(COLOR)

Funny cornpop that should meet with okay reception in laugh market.

Hollywood, May 3.
Universal release of Herbert B. Leonard production. Stars Pat Boone, Terry-Thomas, Pamela Austin; features Edward Everett Horton, Hamilton Camp, Doris Packer, Kurt Kasznar. Directed by Leonard, Joshua Shelley. Screenplay, Albert Beich; suggested by story by Charles W. Goddard; camera (Eastmancolor), Jack A. Marta; music, Vic Mizzy; editor, Sam E. Waxman; asst. director, Joseph E. Kenny. Reviewed at Universal Studios, May 2, '67. Running Time, 98 MINS.
George .... Pat Boone
Sten Martin .... Terry-Thomas
Pauline .... Pamela Austin
Casper Coleman ..Edward Everett Horton
Thorpe .... Hamilton Camp
Mrs. Carruthers .... Doris Packer
Consul General .... Kurt Kasznar
Frandisi .... Vito Scotti
Commisar .... Leon Askin
Vizier .... Aram Katcher
Prince Benji .... Rick Natoli

"The Perils of Pauline" (named for the serial of 1915) is one of the nuttiest comedies of the season. It should do good biz in situations where patrons aren't too demanding about the laugh material quality. A spoof of oldtime melodrama, the heroine is subjected to more harrowing tribulations than Pearl White ever encountered. What comes out is novelty escapism of the wildest sort. Project originally was intended as pilot of a proposed teleseries, but midway through its making decision was reached to expand it into a theatrical feature.

There are overtones of Belle Poitrine—sans her promiscuity—in the starry-eyed innocence of title character in this cornpop starring Pat Boone, Terry-Thomas and Pamela Austin. For Miss Austin, known on tv as the Dodge Rebellion Girl, the Herbert B. Leonard production is a minor triumph as she develops hamminess into little less than a definite art form.

Boone as the shining pure hero, richest man in the world who was raised in a foundling home with Pauline and has rented Venice for their honeymoon, and Terry-Thomas, a dastardly heavy who keeps poping up in all manner of places to harass the two lovers who somehow never seem to get together, play their respective roles in the same tenor.

Treatment is what sets picture apart. A series of amusing cardtitles to herald certain subsequent action and a music score by Vic Mizzy atmospherically attuned to the goin's-on particularly lending a rollicking air. Two directors are given credit, the producer and also Joshua Shelley, so it's anybody's guess who is responsible for what. But what really counts is the final tally, which adds up to corn and laughs.

The Albert Beich screenplay, suggested by a story by Charles W. Goddard, follows Boone as the boy who promised to make a millin dollars and return to the orphanage to marry Pauline, only she's left to be a schoolteacher to a prince in Arabia. He follows her to Africa, where white pygmies try to reduce her 34-17-34 measurements to their own size; tries to follow her when she's swept into a N.Y. sewer; freezes himself for 25 years when he learns she's been frozen for a similar span; nearly catches up to her on the Riviera after both have been prethawed; finally gets to Venice after all.

Handy support is afforded by Edward Everett Horton, as the 99½-year-old second richest man in the world who wants Pauline for his grandson, aged one year (so he freezes her to wait for infant to grow up). Equally helpful are Hamilton Camp, Boone's knowall male secretary; Doris Packer, orphanage mistress; Kurt Kasznar, a Russian consul-general who has Pauline sent into space as an astronaut. Vito Scotti is in for a funny bit as an excitable Italian film director who can't find an innocent girl until he espies Pauline and promptly falls in love with her. Pauline given to saying 'G'osh' in most of her situations, goes through film saving herself for George, who happens to be Pat Boone.

Technical departments are all firstclass, standouts here are Jack A. Marta's color photography and Alexander Golitzen and John T. McCormack's art direction. Whit.

Privilege
(BRITISH-COLOR)

Acid, but confused look at the 'pop' scene's effect in the immediate future. Will need shrewd exploitation but marquee curiosity should be sparked by names of director Peter ("War Game") Watkins, singer Paul Jones and model Jean Shrimpton.

London, April 28.
Rank Release (Universal outside U.K.) of a World-Film Services—Memorial Enterprises production for U. Stars Paul Jones, Jean Shrimpton. Features Mark London, William Job, Max Bacon, Jeremy Child, James Cossins, George Bean Group. Produced by John Heyman. Directed and narrated by Peter Watkins. Written by Norman Bogner from an original story by John Speight, with additional scenes and dialog by Watkins; editor, John Trumper; camera (Technicolor), Peter Suschitzky; music, Mike Leander; lyrics, Mark London. At Warner Theatre, London. Running Time, 103 MINS.
Steven Shorter .... Paul Jones
Vanessa Ritchie ...... Jean Shrimpton
Alvin Kirsch .... Mark London
Andrew Butler .... William Job
Julie Jordan .... Max Bacon
Martin Crossley .... Jeremy Child
Professor Tatham ...... James Cossins
Marcus Hooper ...... Frederick Danner
Freddie K .... Victor Henry
Leo Stanley .... Arthur Pentelow
Bishop of Essex .... Michael Barrington
Bishop of Cornwall .... Edwin Finn
Bishop of Surrey .... John Gill
Bishop of Hersham .... Norman Pitt
Bishop of Rutland .... Alba
Rev. Jeremy Tate ...... Malcolm Rogers
Miss Crawford .... Doreen Mantle
Timothy Arbutt .... Michael Graham
The Runner Beans..George Bean Group

The Rank Organization admits that it has a problem on its hands with this one and are trying it out in certain picked situations before deciding pro or con a circuit release. It's a film made by new young talent, director, producer, writers, cast, key technicians are all mainly less than 30, but ironically the more youthful element among filmgoers may well feel that they've been sold down the river. "Privilege" takes an acid swipe at the "pop" industry, its admirers and its possible effect on British life in the near future and some of its best ideas mercilessly criticize those to whom pop music is a way of life.

Vital new young director Peter Watkins, Oscar'd for his bitter-about-bomb film "The War Game," has slashed at so many issues that he has blurred the vision and misses several of his targets. Looked at with utter detachment it's possible to admire a great deal of the pic but without becoming involved or necessarily believing its confused message. Watkins visualizes a time when the power of pop music and its performers is such that a Coalition Government and the Church will conspire to manipulate the business so blatantly for its own ends that nearhysteria may set in. This seems an over-reach, since the general opinion is that pop music's influence and those of its purveyors is, if anything, on the wane.

Watkins has chosen his usual technique of near-documentary, with a commentary of his own coolly put over in mock-interviews. The blend is not entirely successful since it strives to bring an air of realism to obvious fantasy. Still, "Privilege" provides plenty of thoughtful moments and, with shrewd exploitation, could well repay the work and ideas put into it by its youthful team, headed by producer John Heyman in his film debut.

A Coalition government encourages the violence of the act of pop idol Steve Shorter (Paul Jones) as a means of guiding the violence of Britain's youth into controllable channels. Then, cynically, it's decided that his image must be changed and he is taken from the ordinary scene of putting over national-interest commercials and selling consumer-goods to his worshipping fans and exploited by the Church as a kind of Godlike hot gospeller. In the end, manipulated on all sides, the lad revolts and his popularity becomes ashes overnight after blasting his fans and the whole messy business on tv.

Shock opening shows the singer doing his act, manacled and in a cage, while police sadistically watch over him and his fans respond to his melancholy singing appeal "Free Me." The other big production highspot is when he appears at an open-air revivalist meeting. Watkins swings his full production guns on to this scene, with blazing crosses in the sky, faithhealing mass hysteria and the lot. Crowd scenes are manipulated well but nevertheless smack too much of trained extras, though, in fact, ordinary youngsters and adults of Birmingham were used.

But the best angles of the pic are those which turn a cynical and only too accurate searchlight on the pop music scene and those who batten on a minimal talent, plus the gullibity of the fans. John Speight, the author of the yarn, Norman Bogner who has done the screenplay and Watkins himself have come up with some revealing dialog and a cast of comparative unknowns shine. Particularly apt and alert is Mark London as an oily, sharp, hip press agent-cum-exploit manager, Max Bacon as a bland, wily music publisher, William Job as a suave, ruthless boss of the investors putting over Steve Shorter Enterprises, Victor Henry as an obnoxious bandleader and Malcolm Rogers as one of an assortment of unctuous clerics.

The producer is less lucky in the choice of the two principals though, ironically, these are likely to sell the ducats. Paul Jones, erstwhile singer with the Manfred Mann Group, makes his acting debut. Maybe it's the fault of writer, director or both but Jones plays the role of the bewildered, disillusioned singer on one note of unanimated distaste. True he brings out the idea of the lad being trapped and helpless but sometimes even a pop idol must occasionally show some verve to account for his popularity. Model Jean Shrimpton, the only character in the film who engenders any sympathy, plays a young artist who recognizes the fate of the singer and tries to steer him from the leeches. Miss Shrimpton is a lush looker, but her acting ability, on this evidence, is tiny and her equally tiny voice is monotonously projected.

Peter Suschitzky's Technicolor camerawork is lively and colorful and John Trumper has edited the piece to give the somewhat frenetic effect that this type of film is seeking. Mike Leander's score is embellished by London, who plays the aforementioned flack, with one or two neat lyrics and Vanessa Clarke's costumes and Bill Brodie's artwork are all satisfactory.

Trouble with "Privilege" is that it cannot make up its mind whether it's a crusading film for the intelligentsia or a snide, "withit" comedy (as during the filming of a hilarious tv commercial designed to make Britain all eat more apples to stamp out a glut) in which the sponsor is played briefly and well by Michael Medwin, whose expierence shines through.
Rich.

Nissei Keiji
(False Policeman)
(JAPAN)
Tokyo, April 28.

Daiei Co. production and release. With Shintaro Katsu, Jitsuko Yoshimura, Daisuke Kato, Yunosuke Ito, Michiko, Sugata, Jutaro Hoju. Directed by Satsuo Yamamoto. Screenplay by Hajime Takaiwa; camera (widescreen) Setsuo Kobayashi; music by Masanobu Higure. Previewed in Tokyo. Running Time: 89 MINS.

Satsuo Yamamoto is one of the few Japanese directors still making "Shakai-Mono," films which are about social problems and usually offer an amount of criticism. Formerly left-wing and still firmly anti-establishment, Yamamoto has previously attacked politics in "Kizudarake No Sanga" (A Public Benefactor), hospital corruption in "Shiroi Kyoto" (The Great White Tower), big-business, "Senso To Heiwa" (War and Peace), and the legal conception of justice, "Nippon Dorobo Monogatari" (The Burglar Story). In "Nissei Keiji" (False Policeman), he returns to the latter subject with the story of a policeman (Shintaro Katsu) who loses his job and, no longer a representative of law and order, gets caught in the often humanly impersonal mechanics of the law itself.

He defends a girl (Michiko Sugata) attacked by young hoods but she is injured in the scuffle and he feels responsible no matter what father (Daisuke Kato) or sister (Jitsuko Yoshimura) say. Then when one of the little boy pupils in Miss Sugata's kindergarten is kidnapped on his way to the hospital to see her, everyone feels responsible and Shinataro sets out to capture the criminals himself even though his former police chief (Yunosuke Ito) has forbidden him to. Sure enough, the underlings are the hoods that he originally encountered when protecting Miss Sugata. The criminal (Jutaro Hoju) is caught, and the child returned.

But the boy's father is arrested because, working in a bank, he stole some documents in order to raise the ransom money, and Shintaro is in jail because the original hoods are suing him and because he impersonated an officer during the fight to get the boy back.

Yamamoto is a good director but he is never any better than his material and here he has been badly served by Hajime Takaiwa who wrote both the original and the screenplay for this film. With its distinct echoes from two good "Shakai-Mono," Kurosawa's "Stray Dog" and "High and Low," and its all but deafening reliance on the most melodramatic of constructions, the scenarist continually undercuts the director's intentions.

The director's best points, given the inadequacy of the script, tend to be minor ones. The changing attitude of the police force toward the hero (friendly and smiling when he's on the legal side; absolutely glacial when he is trying to do the human thing, despite the law) is brilliantly delineated; the lack of any kind of social responsibility in the country is beautifully indicated in the behavior of the crowd when the girl is attacked—it is quite realistic, no one does anything except gape or hide behind magazines; the essential inhumanity of the police, made so by inhuman laws, is quietly and devastatingly shown in the "got to do my duty no matter how I feel" attitude of an essentially "nice" man, the police chief.

Also, Yamamoto, always good with actors, helps that fine actor Shintaro Katsu give a beautiful performance as the baffled false cop who follows his heart more than his judgement, and who innocently believes that the law works is on the side of human justice. Most famous as the creator of the title-role in the Zato-Ichi series, Katsu is the personification of trusting good humor, of human warmth. That we feel something, however, is due to the art of Yamamoto and of Katsu himself. *Chie.*

Sons and Daughters
(DOCUMENTARY)
American Documentary Films production and release. Direct handling, U.S.; Rogoson, Europe. Narrated by Janet Pugh. Directed and written by Jerry Stoll; camera, Stephen Lighthill; written narration, David Cearlto; editors, Sally Pugh, Stoll, Lighthill; music composition and performances, Jon Hendricks, Virgil

Gonsalves, The Greatful Dead. Viewed at Palace Theatre, San Francisco, April 21, '67. Running Time, **98 MINS.**

This dramatic feature-length documentary on the anti-Vietnam War protest movement that culminated in a march from the University of California to the Oakland Army Terminal last year will find little acceptance in general run houses, but will make its mark in close-to-campus situations and for special group bookings. A unique non-profit organization, American Documentary Films has set up own distribution apparatus to tap just this market with both a 35m theatrical version and 16m prints.

Like its historical predecessor, the social protest film of the 1930s, "Sons and Daughters" tells its story from a definite point of view. In this case it is a currently unpopular one, that of the young protesting the war. The film, however, is primarily a sensitively photographed and edited work of documentary art, not propaganda.

The San Francisco Bay area is probably the area in the country most intimately concerned with the Vietnamese War. It is through here that the troops and supplies leave and the casualties returns. The ties with the Orient are the most sensitive, and the defense industries and military bases are powerful segments of the economy. Opposition to the war is not an abstract argument, but a face-to-face encounter. It has its strongest base in the university community, the young people of "Sons and Daughters." This is the fabric of the film.

Director-writer Jerry Stoll intercuts with disturbing wire service footage from Vietnam that has not been shown on tv. Student Janet Pugh narrates the film in a young, artless voice that is much more effective than any professional actor's.

The film is overly long, unabashly slanted, contains a completely unrelated and extraneous segment on the Hunter's Point race riots, and uses some obviously faked news broadcasts to score a sardonic point. However, where television documentaries create a vacuum and call it objectivity, "Sons and Daughters" honestly portrays how a great hunk of our young people view the Vietnamese controversay. To dismiss it is to dismiss them.

As a narrow gauge work print, it has already had nearly 200 group and campus bookings. First-run at the Palace Theatre in San-Francisco has begun, with others set for New York, Honolulu and Los Angeles. Rogoson Films, Ltd., has European distribution. ADF plans to use same setup for a series of documentaries on controversial contemporary subjects.

Folk - rock background music composed and sung by Jon Hendricks backed by the Grateful Dead is highly effective. Title song will be useful in promotion. *Rick.*

Historien om Barbara
(Story of Barbara
(DANISH)
Copenhagen, April 25.
A/S Nordisk Film Kompagni production and release. Stars Yvonne Ingdal, Peter Steen. Directed by Palle Kjaerulff-

Schmidt. Written by Klaus Rifbjerg; camera, Claus Loof; music, Ole Schmidt. Reviewed at Nygade Teatre, Copenhagen. Running Time, **84 MINS.**

Graduating into the ranks of major Scandinavian filmmakers with last year's "Once Upon A War,'" the writer-'director team of Klaus Rifbjerg and Palle Kjaerulff-Schmidt this time tells "The Story of Barbara" as more or less a followup to their initial effort of six years ago, "Weekend." Which is rather a pity since their too private little world of young Danish semi-intellectuals just is not world enough to insure universal interest over so long a stretch of creative work.

Barbara (played with tenderness, intelligence and humor by Yvonne Ingdal) is a young actress caught in self-doubt before any love-affair drained the juices of artistic ambition. One lover (Peter Steen) seems made of stuff to build stronger things than dreams on. But one day, probably he also will want to take as much as he gives.

What happens? An adequate answer might have been the story, but we are not told what happens. The film has no story. It has sensitively "hinted" moods, discreetly "hinted" character motivations, and it has a lot of cool, up-to-date acting, all caught with perfect control by Claus Loof's camera. There are spots of dry humor, too, and of trapped love, mostly expressed in quiet desperation.

This pic has been accepted as Denmark's official entry at this summer's Berlin Film Fest. It seems worthy of that honor although hardly a winner either there or at boxoffices aside from more dedicated art houses. *Kell.*

Erbinka
(ISRAEL)
Tel Aviv, March 30.
Erbinka Ltd., Tel Aviv, distribution of an Ephraim Kishon production. Directed and written by Kishon. Stars Haym Topol. Camera, Alex Thomson; editor, Dany Shick; music, Dubi Seltzer. Running Time, **104 MINS.**

Erbinka	Haym Topol
Ruti	Gila Almagor
Yossi	A. Hizkiyahu
Weinreb	Shraga Friedmann
Morice	Yosef Banai
Police sergeant	Shai K. Ophir
Liz	Edna Fiidel

Evidently as a result of his success as director of Noah Films' "Salach Shabati," released in the U. S. as "Sallah." Ephraim Kishon turned producer and scripter as well for this follow-up to the 1964 effort which also toplined Haym Topol. The latter's appearances in "Sallah" and Melville Shavelson's "Cast a Giant Shadow" will help in American bookings as will his casting as Tevya in the London production of "Fiddler On The Roof" be an assist in Britain.

Dealing with a young Israeli vagabond, Erbinka will be compared with Sallah as the two characters have much in common. However, while Sallah was a loafer by tradition, Erbinka, younger and native-born, is a loafer by conviction. His dream is to win the national lottery.

When this doesn't materialize he robs the lottery headquarters with the help of the police (he dupes

them by pretending to be shooting a commercial for the lottery). In a series of funny but loosely-connected episodes Erbinka crashes bar mitzvah parties to get food: charges for parking in a lot he doesn't own an even seduces the policeman who arrests him.

Although the film has both Kishon & Topol from the earlier effort it is less consistent and incisive, but just as funny, as "Sallah." Alex Thomson, who photographed "Darling," uses the Israeli sunshine to give "Erbinka" a happy glare.

Topol is excellent as the carefree lad, light years away from the dedicated Israeli youth usually projected but none-the-less sympathetic. He is well supported by A. Hizkiyahu in a role that makes him Sancho Panza to Erbinka's Don Quixote. *Lapid.*

Sasaki Kojiro
(JAPAN—COLOR)
Tokyo, April 15.
Toho Co. production and release. Features Kikunosuke Onoe, Yuriko Hoshi, Toko Tsukawa, Isamu Nagato, Yoshio Tsuchiya, Nakadai Tatsuya. Directed by Hiroshi Inagaki. Produced by Keiichiro Tsuno, art direction by Hiroshi Ueda, script by Yoshio Shirasako, Kendo Matsuura, Hiroshi Inagaki, photographed by Tako Saita, music by Goichi Sakide. Previewed in Tokyo. Running Time, **165 MINS.**

Toho is celebrating its 35th anniversary and director Hiroshi Inagaki his 100th and something film, with this big, long, star-studded "thrilling entertainment," "Sasaki Kojiro." While it is neither entertaining nor thrilling, it does offer the non-Japanese a big, long look at Japanese "Chambara" at its most typical.

Those to whom the mystery of "sword-fight" entertainment is as yet complete could do no better than avail themselves of the opportunity because it is not often in these days of changing cinematic syntax that a "chambara" as unspoiled as this one arrives. It is in all ways but its use of color precisely like the sword-fight films of 50 years ago—which was about the time that Director Inagaki was beginning the career he is now celebrating. It has all the same old tried and true plot complications, all the same tested heroes—even the dialogue is typical.

Kojiro (played by Kikunosuke Onoe, tv player and son of a Kabuki actor), is so good with the sword that the samurai hate him and he has to leave. Followed by his girlfriend (Yuriko Hoshi), he goes out into the world and at once becomes involved in the current trouble between the Toyotomi and the Tokugawa. Befriended by many a nubile maiden (including Okinawan princess, Yoko Tsukasa), many a bold warrior, many a nimble spy (tv comic Isamu Nagato); attacked by many a ruthless killer, many an ancient enemy (Yoshio Tsuchiya): he cuts his way through both ranks, and at the end prepares himself for the great duel of all—that with Miyamoto Musashi.

This is the part that always thrills the "chambara" fans because now his identity is disclosd. He is the "other" one—the famous foe of the great Miyamoto, beloved of every schoolboy in Japan. Of course, being fans they knew it all along—but one of the many curiosities of "Chambara" is that pre-knowledge never prevents thrills, if anything it seems to encourage them.

For this reason sword-fight-films move at great pace from one highpoint to the next with little or nothing in between. This is very confusing to the foreigner who expects a story, but the fan already knows the story and connecting material would only get in the way. When Inagaki's 1954 "Miyamoto Musashi" was bought by an American firm it had to be recut so that some sort of story, arbitrary though it was, could be constructed. Japanese audiences, however, do not mind the sudden jumps and breaks in continuity because they always lead directly into yet another famous and beloved scene.

It would follow, naturally, that there is no character development as such, none of Kojiro and neither of anyone else. The audience already knows the characters very well—that is why they are in the theatre. Too, if any of these well-loved heroes said or did anything "out of character," the audience would probably resent it. Consequently dialogue of an exquisite triteness, of an amazing banality.

In the west fans laugh when the cowboy says "He went that'a-way," or the detective climbs into a taxi saying "follow that car." In Japan, however, this does not occur. First, a cliche is considered reassuring rather than insulting; second, the Japanese audience only laughs where it is meant to. Obviously then such patrons are ideal for all Japanese entertainments, from "Kamishibai" to the Kabuki, but they are particularly right for the traditional "chambara." Chie.

Cannes Festival

War and Peace Part III
(Voina i Mir)
(RUSSIAN-70M-COLOR)

Cannes, May 4.
Mosfilm release and production. Features Ludmilla Savelieva, Sergei Bondarchuk, Viatcheslav Tikhonov, Boris Zakhava. Directed by Bondarchuk. Screenplay, Vassili Soloviev, Bondarchuk, based on novel by Leo Tolstoi; camera (Sovcolor), Anatoly Petritsky; music, Viatcheslav Ovtchinnikov. At Cannes Film Fest. Running Time, 85 MINS.
Natacha .... Ludmilla Savelieva
Pierre .... Sergei Bondarchuk
Prince Andre......Viatcheslav Tikhonov
Koutouzov .... Boris Zakhava
Rostov .... V. Stanitsyne

When parts one and two of this massive Russian film were reviewed in VARIETY (July 28, '65) from the 1965 Moscow Film Festival, they copped the grand prize. Now part three bows, and there is still one more to be seen (which director Sergei Bondarchuk recently finished shooting). While the first two films ran over three and a half hours, this one, almost all of which is devoted to the battle of Borodino, runs only 85 minutes.

Part III deals with the death of

Prince Andre's father; Pierre's visit to the young Natacha and his visit to the battlefield of Borodino, where he wanders amidst the carnage, bombast and explosiveness of hand-to-hand combat and its skirmishes, cannons and the mingling of flesh, horses, earth and sky.

The film remains posey, conventional and more often opting for tableaus, rather than the more personal and interpretive look at the Napoleonic wars and their effect on the Russian people and country. But its sheer size soon casts a spell; that, and the dinning sound of battle. The camera will suddenly zoom up from the field, disclosing thousands of scurrying men, horses and battlegear, or it will watch one character face death near a sizzling bomb, or climb dizzily among the trees.

Bondarchuk has stayed completely with the Tolstoy novel and translated it ambitiously to the screen. It sometimes, therefore, appears literary but has an epic drive that manages to overcome its academic trappings. In the first two sections, the more complex relationships between the main characters were inked in heavily. Here it is war, and mainly the battle that disseminated Napoleon's army and finally led to his disastrous retreat from Moscow.

Bondarchuk also lends massive presence to the role of Pierre and his wanderings and final involvement with the battle creating a good gambit for isolating it and reacting to the clash of professional soldiers. The almost tintype-garish colors help, since the approach is academic, but in a good sense. A man's leg shot off, and his quizzical look as awareness dawns; horses hurtling off their feet; cannons exploding; men rallying, running, withdrawing, going on again. All this begins to take on a hypnotic quality and somehow, the logistics of battle are clear. Napoleon, in the midst of hundreds of bodies, brooding, is the final shot as a series of frozen stills front for a stentorian voice extolling the victory of the Russian moral drive over the French will of conquest.

The costuming, sheer manpower and the rattling din of violence overpower most critical reservations on this immense film. A scene of hundreds of soldiers running into a stream for a swim before the battle and small personal vignettes counterpointed by the overall sweep give a rhythm to its predictable but always eye-filling spectacle. It also manages to avoid an exhilaration in battle, if that, too, is an unfortunate part of man's constant fighting with man.

A savvy compilation of the first three parts and the last three and still-to-come film should make a strong, big-gun spectacle for foreign playoff, with the pre-sold name of the pic and its sheer, staggering size, if it sometimes gets overweight in its stodgy but firm direction, are also plusses.
Mosk.

Elvira Madigan
(SWEDISH-COLOR)

Cannes, May 1.
A. B. Europa Film release of Janco Film production. Stars Pia Degermark.

Thommy Berggren; features Cleo Jensen, Nina Wilderberg. Written and directed by Bo Widerberg. Camera (Eastmancolor), Jorgen Persson; music Ulf Bjorlin. At Cannes Film Fest. Running time, 95 MINS.
Elvira ....Pia Degermark
Sixten .... Thommy Berggren
Friend ....Lennart Malmen
Girl ....Nina Widerberg
Cook .... Cleo Jensen

Based on a true story of a doomed turn-of-the century love affair, this film opts for the poetic, timeless and lyrical and succeeds right down the line. It is delicate but always in control, and there should, and must, be a fine place for this pic in foreign art and general situations. But its simplicity and fragile rightness call for delicate handling. Returns should well repay care in placement and followup.

Softly-hued color and a well chosen classical background of Mozart music envelop the tale of the love affair of a young Swedish army officer of noble lineage and a young girl from a circus who is a noted tightrope walker. Film begins with them together and then his desertion and her foregoing the circus and their idyll until an inability to make any sort of contact with society lands to their suicide pact.

But a joyous tenderness is the main note of the film, for it is a hymn to love and life, not a social tract or a story of alienation, difficulties of human communication etc. The social bigotry, the waste of enforced militarism are only background.

Pia Degermark has the luminous elan and delicacy, underpinned by the strength of her show background, to make her role of the girl always pleasing to the eye and revealing in her feelings, moods and interior and exterior life. Thommy Berggren is a perfect counterpoint as the man who gives up all for love and is not defeated but ends it rather than allow it to be destroyed by their outcast status.

Director Bo Widerberg shows a sure hand throughout and never wavers in pace, revelation or the right notations of love, human rapports and the life around them that finally makes it impossible to cope. If man cannot live by bread alone, he can not live on love alone either. The metaphors and symbols are always deftly worked in and are consistent with the style of the film which is slanted to reveal the spirit and keep its almost legendary qualities rather than go for realism.

And the visual charms are never for their own sake or mannered. It reflects the love and things around it that do not undermine it but make it almost impossible to exist without concessions, renouncements or desertions. So this is one of those poetic films that is rare in these days when neurosis, perversion, anguish, incommunicability, cruelty, etc. are the main thematic forces of films on love.

The film should be heard from internationally and looked like the pic to beat as the Cannes Fest went into the final round.
Mosk.

Hotel Pro Cizince
(Hotel For Strangers)
(CZECHOSLOVAKIAN)

Cannes, April 30.
Czech State Film release of Novotny-Kubala production. With Petr Cepek, Tatana Fischerova, Marta Krasova, Vladimir Smeral. Written and directed by Antonin Masa. Camera, Ivan Slapeta; music, Svatopluk Havelka. At Cannes Film Fest. Running time, 103 MINS.
Petr .... Petr Cepek
Veronika ....Tatana Fischerova
Rosicka .... Marta Krasova
Blech ....Vladimir Smeral
Marie ....Jirina Jiraskova

This pic is a bit more symbolic, far out and comedic than many of its Czechoslovakian predecessors. It appears a modern treatise, cloaked by a turn-of-the-century setting. Though not always clear, the visual inventiveness, offbeat and menacing background and downright charm suggest art playoff abroad. Drawback is "mannerism" for its own sake. But such are minor faults to a generally clever and probing pic.

The term "Kafkaesque" will probably be used on the sinister backgrounding to what appears to be a parable on manners and life that adds sudden tragedy to comedy. The hero, a gentle poet, comes to a Gothic old hotel where he hopes to meet a girl he is enamored with. Strange characters and personnel abound. He finally meets, eternally loses his girl and ends in a mysterious death.

Is it the individual submerged in paternalism? The drowning of humanity in bureaucracy? Pic captures the feel of early silents in smart use of speeded up action, sharply contrasted lensing, and exaggerated acting. There is a fat cook with homosexual leanings, sinister clerks and waiters, violent valets etc.

Peter Cepek projects vulnerable innocence as the doomed poet-hero and other players are able. Film shows Antonin Masa a most unusual new talent who ought to avoid piling on cleverness and effects sans plot need.

Technically fine, though could use a little tighening on time.
Mosk.

Sreo Sam Cak I Sreene Cigane
(I Even Met a Happy Gypsy)
(YUGOSLAVIAN-COLOR)

Cannes, April 29.
Jugoslavija Film release of Avala Film production. With Bekim Fehniu, Olivera Vuco, Bata Zivojinovic, Gordana Jovanovic. Written and directed by Aleksander Petrovic. Camera (Eastmancolor), Tomaslav Pinter; editor, Milo Mica. At Cannes Film Fest. Running time, 86 MINS.
Bora .... Bekim Fehmiu
Lence .... Olivera Vuco
Mirta .... Bata Zivojinovic
Tissa ....a.......Gordana Jovanovic
Pavle .... Mija Aleksic
Nun .... Rahela Ferari
Peasant ....Severin Bijelic

Poverty-ridden, rough and tumble, paganistic life in a section of Yugoslavia inhabited by gypsies gets colorful treatment in this inventive, constantly moving film. No messages or overdone folklore or ethnic angles. Rather a richly textured tale of life that leaves audience to draw own conclusions.

The smooth colors do not mask the poverty but create a balance between the highly dramatic and simple actions of the characters. The hero travels to get out of his rundown hut filled with kids and an aging wife. His work is buying goose feathers from peasants. He falls for a young girl whose stepfather marries her off to a 12 year old boy to really have her for himself.

He gets the girl away, loses her and finally kills the stepfather and disappears into the Yugoslav plains. And writer-director Aleksander Petrovic has a highly mobile camera that still captures the volatile actions and characters of these people without any undue esthetics. In fact, it heightens the robustness, primary but natural outlooks, actions and elans and angers of these people.

A fight in a pile of feathers, gypsy songs, brutal love, a marriage ceremony by a raffish Orthodox Church priest, and the daily life, work, play and anguish and compensating freedom and "naturalness" of these people are all finely combined into a fetching and colorful pic that does not (a) falsify customs, (b) make a pitch for reform or (c) condemn society.

Instead it leaves thoughts in the mind of character's plight and their problems in trying to integrate them and their own attempts at coping without any undue propaganda or didactics. Thus, this is a colorful pic that could well be a good art, specialized, lingo or even playoff entry, if rightly hypoed and followed up, abroad. Director Petrovic made the pic "Three" that was up for the Oscar as best foreign film this year. New pic adds to his stature as a knowing director who may sometimes get carried away by sheer camera gymnastics, but, on the whole, dominates his subjects.

The fact that real actors are not easy to tell from the many actual gypsies in the pic attest to his knowing handling of pros and nonpros. Fine indigenous music, color, brisk editing and, above all, a communicative feel for his subject make this entry that should be around comes prize time at the presently unrolling Cannes Film Fest. *Mosk.*

J'Ai Tue Rasputine
(I Killed Rasputin)
(FRENCH—COLOR)

Cannes, April 27.

Comacico release of Copernic Films-CGC production. Stars Peter McEnery, Gert Frobe, Geraldine Chaplin, Robert Hossein; features Ira De Furstenberg, Ivan Desay. Directed by Robert Hossein. Screenplay, Alain Decaux, Claude Desailly from book by Prince Youssopov; camera (Eastmancolor), Henri Persin; editor, Jacqueline Thiedot. At Cannes Film Fest. Running Time, **102 MINS.**

Rasputin	Gert Frobe
Youssopov	Peter McEnery
Mounia	Geraldine Chaplin
Princess	Ira De Furstenberg
Grand Duke	Ivan Desay
Serge	Robert Hossein

Rasputin again takes a lot of killing off in this fifth pic version of the tale. Reportedly based on the story of the man who actually did it, and is now living in Paris, Prince Youssopov, film still remains a bit too surface to give a true background of the times and concentrates mainly on the preliminaries to the murder.

Nice production dress helps, but this remains somewhat too detached to give new insight into this oft-told tale and appears mainly of some use in playoff abroad on its name actors, the theme and a final slambang murder after a cursory buildup.

Director Robert Hossein has barely suggested that Rasputin, the Monk who had a hold on the Czar and his family during the First World War and while the Revolution was brewing, was a debaucher. The glowering, bearded Rasputin, holding forth in a red plush room surrounded by black-garbed girls who dance for him, is more a man with some pungent tastes and cashes in on his position, but hardly a monster.

So this called for more insight into the times and intrigues than the film goes into. It does try to show a sort of begrudging admiration for the unkempt peasant monk by his future murderer Prince Youssopov, played by Peter McEnery. But this too is more suggested than firmly gone into.

Intimations that Rasputin might have been a German spy, and the vague political motives of the crime to remove the man who might lose Russia to the Germans, are also subordinated. Picture looks at the surface of the times, and the final murder that turns into butchery as Rasputin almost appears unkillable for a while.

Gert Frobe, hidden behind a big beard, has presence if not much more than a figurehead to be cut down. McEnery is effete, weak and properly indecisive as the assassin. Geraldine Chaplin does not have much to do as a girl under Rasputin's sway while Ira De Furstenberg has even less. But the showy colors, nice surface rendition of the times, and the final butchery, as Rasputin downs poisoned cakes and is shot many times before succumbing, might put this costumer in line for okay playoff possibilities. There is an English version. *Mosk.*

The Plank
(BRITISH-COLOR)

Cannes, May 3.

Associated London Films production by Jon Penington and Beryl Vertue. No release set. Stars Eric Sykes, Tommy Cooper; features Jimmy Edwards, Roy Castle, Graham Stark, Stratford Johns, Jim Dale, Hattie Jacques, Jimmy Tarbuck. Written and directed by Sykes. Camera (Technicolor), Arthur Wooster. Music, Brian Fahey. Editor, John Pomeroy. Previewed at Cannes Film Festival. Running Time, **58 MINS.**

Larger Workman	Tommy Cooper
Smaller Workman	Eric Sykes
Policeman	Jimmy Edwards
Man in Garbage	Roy Castle
Amorous Driver	Graham Stark
Station Sergeant	Stratford Johns
House Painter	Jim Dale
Barman	Jimmy Tarbuck
Woman with Rose	Hattie Jacques

Eric Sykes and his producers, Jon Penington and Beryl Vertue, have shaped themselves what should be a profitable bundle of laughs in this short but highly diverting comic feature. As a saleable package, its only possible fault may lie in its in-between (58 minutes) running time, which may make for a problem in pairing.

Consists almost entirely of visual gags in rapid succession, with not a single line of dialogue vital to the plot or to understanding. It thus becomes immediately accessible—as were and are the silent comedies—to audiences in all climes and age brackets.

Story is simple yet involved, dealing mainly with the trip of a plank of wood from warehouse to building site, and with the many accidents it falls prey to—and causes—along the way. Mainly involved are two workmen, Erik Sykes and Tommy Cooper, who ineptly and humorously wrestle with the chore of hauling the single plank through a London suburb, and with the many characters who get involved in the action along the way. Among these is a harassed cop (Jimmy Edwards), a man (Roy Castle) who falls into a garbage truck and makes odorous sorties through the rest of the picture, Jim Dale as a befuddled painter, Graham Star as a truck driver with love on his mind, and many others in for major and minor bits but all contributing to the general levity.

Pic in its present state is not entirely faultless. Some gags are 100% clicks, others only 80%, but the general batting average is high. There is however a notable lag at the start before things really get going. A neat trimming job here can sharpen the timing and pace, and immediately prep auds for the legless stretch of laughs to follow.

Technically, effort is first rate, with color, music and (with the noted exception) editing all working together towards a continually chucklesome and very often hilarious effect. *Hawk.*

Incompreso
(Misunderstood)
(ITALIAN-FRENCH-COLOR)

Cannes, May 4.

Francoriz release of Rizzoli Film, Institut Luce, Franco London Film production. With Anthony Quayle, Stefano Colagrande, Simone Gianozzi, John Sharp, Georgia Moll. Directed by Luigi Comencini. Screenplay, Leo Benvenuti, Piero Di Bernardi, based on the novel by Florence Montgomery; camera (Technicolor), Armando Nannuzzi. At Cannes Film Fest. Running Time, **104 MINS.**

Andrea	Stefano Colagrande
Milo	Simone Gianozzi
Duncombe	Anthony Quayle
Will	John Sharp
Judy	Georgia Moll
Governess	Graziella Granata
Luisa	Adriana Facchetti

Determinedly old fashioned Italo assault on the tear ducts deals with a misunderstood boy who is finally reconciled with his distraught father on his, the boy's, deathbed. But one can't gainsay its efficacy. It made tears flow even among the hardboiled Fest audience. So this seems mainly a playoff item for abroad if it should ring the bell in its home markets.

Based on a turn-of-the-century novel, it is updated to modern Rome and concerns a British Consul whose wife has just died. He breaks it to his older son but not to the younger one. The older boy is being constantly mistreated by the father who is too deep in his own grief to notice that of his son.

Film does handle the two children well and there are a few neatly observed scenes of the children at play, plotting or just existing with naturalness. But pic insists on evading any true ties to modern life and substituting sentiment for more potent characterization.

Anthony Quayle is remote as the father but the two boys are generally fetching in their battles with an ogress governess. Ending pulls out all stops as the older boy is hurt and dying and his father finds that he had misjudged him and tries to make up to the boy as he expires. Color is good, direction polished but uninspired, and this sudsy opus may find its audiences on its unabashed, simple, relentlessly sugary treatment of growing pains and a child's plight before adult incomprehension and mortality. *Mosk.*

Terra Em Transe
(Land In a Trance)
(BRAZILIAN)

Cannes, May 3.

MAPA release and production. With Jardel Filho, Paulo Autran, Jose Lewgoy, Glauce Rocha. Written and directed by Glauber Rocha. Camera, Luis Carlos Barreto; editor, Edouardo Escorel; music, Sergio Ricardo. At Cannes Film Fest. Running Time, **106 MINS.**

Paulo	Jardel Filho
Porfirio	Paulo Autran
Felipe	Jose Lewgoy
Sara	Glauce Rocha
Julio	Paulo Gracindo
Silvia	Danuza Leao

A frenetically baroque, convoluted film that is both didactic and impassioned, "Land In a Trance" draws a bead on the mixture of the exalted and the clearheaded in Latino politics and ideals. It is thus not an easy film for those unacquainted with Brazilian politics or Latin American mores, methods. Result suggests limited playoff abroad. Against that the film has in young filmmaker Glauber Rocha a talent who must curb his almost staggering visual strivings.

Seemingly not in sympathy with any of his characters, Rocha deals with a poet torn between a reactionary politician who has brought him up and a "progressive" man who promises reform. But both betray him and youth dies in a futile gesture of revolt. Brazil's backwardness, susceptibility to old influences of original European conquerors, mixed in African mysticism and religiosity, forms the background.

Rocha shows the poet abandoning ideals for sensual abandon. His demise is not meant to be noble but ironic.

Film remains top heavy in trying to say perhaps too much about too many things and only intermittently succeeding. It mixes song, legend, symbolism and polemics and sometimes is shattering in the revelations of man's need to make a stand, but too often obscures point to the point of the grotesque or the pedantic.

Forcefully lensed with an editing flair. *Mosk.*

Monday's Child
(ARGENTINE-U.S.)

Cannes, May 1.

Andre Du Rona release and production. Stars Arthur Kennedy, Geraldine Page; features, Deborah Reed, Gracilea Borges, Roberto Parilla, Jose De San. Directed by Leopoldo Torre Nilsson. Screenplay, Beatriz Guido, Torre Nilsson, Noelle Gillmour from an original subject by Andre Du Rona; camera, Alex Phillips Jr.; editor, Carl Workman. At Cannes Film Fest. Running time, **85 MINS.**

Argentine director Leopoldo Torre Nilsson is a festivalier via made-in-Argentina films but this one was made in English in Puerto Rico with U.S. indie backing and name players. Theme concerns a catastrophe. Somewhat superficial in observation, film appears mainly a playoff item on Arthur Kennedy and Geraldine Page names. Specialized situations may respond.

A weakling father who has overindulged his daughter, an unsatisfied mother and a spoiled hysterical daughter are the Yank types involved. The father has taken a good job in Puerto Rico and the mother had even had the remains of her son, killed some 12 years ago, sent for reburial to Puerto Rico.

Pic starting point is the mother giving away a favorite doll of the daughter to a relief collection for flood victims. The girl's almost psychotic tantrum has them going off to find the doll which brings them in contact with a poorer, now homeless, batch of people.

Girl's hysteria grows, mother becomes more selfish, unkempt and self-pitying. Father finds a certain self-realization through his weakness and realization of neglect in taking cognizance of the misery around him.

Story ends downbeat. Family is hopelessly disintegrated by self indulgence, smulness and a sort of isolation from realities. Girl is heading for a whacking neurosis.

Though basis holds interest, the pic remains obvious in characterization and somewhat too general in bringing its special Americans into focus. Knocks at tv commercials, automation and isolationism are knowing, but needed insight into the characters is another matter.

Geraldine Page achieves a middleaged woman falling into blowsy self-indulgence due to a refusal to accept responsibility. Arthur Kennedy is convincing as the weak husband. The girl is somewhat too one-note and horrendous. Comes through as almost insane bratishness.

Release is technically neat.
Mosk.

Rondo
(YUGOSLAVIA)

Cannes, April 28.
Jadran Film production and release. With Relja Basic, Milena Dravic, Stevo Zigon. Written and directed by Zvonimir Berkovic. Camera, Tomislav Pinter. At Cannes Film Fest. Running time, **90 MINS.**

Mladen	Relja Basic
Neda	Milena Dravic
Fedja	Stevo Zigon

"Rondo" is a very well observed comedy-drama about a married couple and a friend which is almost broken up by counter attractions. Fine acting, incisive visual notations and a rightness in characterization make this a film with some specialized and arty possibilities abroad. It would need proper handling.

Its subtleties and soft-pedaled narrative events soon take one into a series of well notated scenes between three people. A young judge takes to visiting an artist friend every Sunday. He is unmarried, more prone to quick affairs and yet conscious of a void in his life. The friend is an artist who has compromised as an illustrator. His wife is a student.

Chess games, talks and shared personal tastes make these Sundays which had been rather dreary before, important weekly events. Then there is some sort of attraction that springs up between the friend and

the wife. They fight it, give in, but finally renounce it.

But now the camaraderie is broken and in its place is an edginess that will finally lead to a dissolution of this friendship, the couple going their way and the friend his.

This Communist country displays a subtle flair in putting individual psyches and psychology on film.

The acting also helps in this production, but above all, it's the knowing and intelligent direction of newcomer Zvonimir Berkovic that combines to make this a delicate but telling pic.

Film also has fine technical aid with soft-toned lensing, a helpful musical score and tight editing. Yugoslavia is another Eastern country beginning to make a name for itself at festivals. *Mosk.*

Le Vent Des Aures
(Winds of the Aures)
(ALGERIAN)

Cannes, May 5.
Office Des Actualities Algeriennes release and production. With Keltoum, Mohamed Chouikh, Omar Tayane, Hassan Hassani. Directed by Mohammed Lakhdar Hamina. Screenplay, Hamina, Tewfik Fares; camera, Hamina; editor, Sylvie Blanc. At Cannes Film Fest. Running Time, **95 MINS.**

Mother	Keltoum
Son	Mohamed Chouikh
Father	Omar Tayane
Friend	Hassan Hassani

The first Algerian feature film shows a surety in technique and a desire to delve into the country's recent tribulations during its war of independence. However this one dotes more on folklore and anecdote rather than going more directly into the theme and deals with ordinary people who were caught up in the debacle. It is somewhat slow and measured and appears suited mainly for language spots and abroad without the more cohesive insight for more general chances. But it does show a budding talent in writer-director-lenser Mohammed Lakhdar Hamina.

It treats with peasants living in poverty among their rocky plains and has a probing feel for outlining their everyday lives. Nearby are rebels who are constantly being harassed by the French. During an air raid a farmer is killed and his son is later arrested for supposedly helping the underground movement. The film is mainly about the mother's attempt to find her son.

She tracks him down in a detention camp and every day comes and sits before an electrically charged fence to watch him. One day he is no longer there and she finally throws herself against the fence to die. The scenes of her vigil are done with fine observation, tact, and build to a true poignancy.

It just does not quite have the as yet rightness of tone, pace and insight to keep from being uneven. But it is technically fine, with acting sober, and it is a most promising and well made pic from the emerging North African countries and should promise more at future festivals. *Mosk.*

Special Servicer
(AUSTRIAN)

Vienna, April 25.
A Karl Lackner production. With Heinz Trixner, Otto Ambros, Rudolf Blahuvec, Carlo Boehm, Fritz Hackl. Directed by Georg Lhotzky. Screenplay, Peter Loddynski, Georg Lhotzky; camera, Walter Kindler; music, Johannes Martin Duerr. World preem at Vienna Film Fest of Gaiety. Running Time, **60 MINS.**

This experimental type of film is said to be the first attempt to start something like "a new wave" in Austria. It has been shot for both cinema and tv utilization and its relatively short running time of just one hour is explained by the fact that "Special Servicer" has been made for participation in the forthcoming Montreux Tele Fest where regulations don't allow the participation of contenders running longer than 60 minutes.

To begin with, the ordinary viewer will hardly be able to make head or tail of this. Credits are given to two writers but the whole thing looks as though writers never existed. What adds to the confusion is the complete absence of any dialog sequences and what is heard are either strange sounds or the roar of a crowd.

Eventually one may guess that this is a parody on publicity. Central figure is a young man who is chasing all day after something. He's representing kindred characters ranging from top-rank politicians to common beggar. The creators of "Special Servicer" termed it a grotesque type of documentary feature pic on all the nonsense of our times. It is said to poke fun at nothing and everything. It tries to explain that too much if not everything is taken overly seriously.

This one can't be taken seriously. Quite apart from the confusing contents, if there are any contents, it has no merits in technical respect either. Film looks as though it was made in a great hurry. It lacks polish all down the line. A pleasant thing about this pic is the score by Johannes Martin Duerr. It includes a series of appealing motifs and rhythms. Cast is headed by Heinz Trixner who belongs to the famous Viennese Burgtheater ensemble. Director Lhotzky may have had a basically good idea but what he has achieved comes dangerously close to being wasted celluloid. *Hans.*

Bonditis
(SWISS—COLOR)

Vienna, April 25.
A Turnus Film production. With Gerd Baltus, Marion Jacob, Christiane Ruecker. Directed by Karl Suter. Screenplay, Karl Suter; camera (Technicolor), H. P. Roth; music, Werner Kruse. World preem at Vienna Film Fest of Gaiety. Running Time, **100 MINS.**

Frank Born	Gerd Baltus
Hata Sari	Marion Jacob

There is increased film activity in Switzerland. There are new names and there are some successes. Walter Marti and Reni Mertens' "Ursula Or the Unworthy Life" has emerged as a genuine

moneymaker around here. "Bonditis," a full-length parody on James Bond pix which saw its world preem at the terminated Vienna film Fest of Gaiety, is the most recent example of the upbeat in Swiss pic activity. It's at least technically a well-made film. Commercial prospects are still anybody's guess.

"Bonditis," whose full title is "Bonditis Or the Horrible and Terrible Adventures of a Nearly Normal Human Being" (English translation of original title) pokes fun at the current spy and agent film trend. Central figure is a young man who can't help dreaming of James Bond all the time. Whenever he falls asleep it is this screen hero who enters the scene. His doctor tells him that he's suffering from a new sickness called "Bonditis" and advises him to seek recreation in a peaceful and idyllic mountain village.

But this village turns out to be everything but peaceful. In fact, it teems with agents from all countries who watch the negotiations that happen to take place here between the representatives of a young but important African state. Both the Americans and Russians want to be the first ones when it comes to giving financial aid to this country. The young man is thought a spy and gets involved with all sort of complications and intrigues. And there are the familiar sex and violence sequences.

The best thing about this film is its technical side. It benefits from attractive Technicolor and TechniScope camera work. The score is quite catchy and the acting is generally okay. Even if the screenplay furnishes a series of funny situations, it can't be overlooked that the subject matter has not been exploited to best advantage. There are definite shortcomings on the script as well as direction. The whole thing gives the impression of a stretched-out cabaret sketch. Repetition of certain scenes lead to a series of dull moments. This could and should be trimmed down quite a bit. Whenever a good joke is prolonged or carried too far, it's bound to lose something. This also applies to "Bonditis." *Hans.*

Tango Pre Medveda
(Tango For a Bear)
(CZECH)

Vienna, April 25.
Czech State Film release of Ceskoslovensky Film Bratislava production. With Villiam Polony, Walter Taub, Olga Salagova, Frantisek Gervay, Otto Hlavacek and Hana Slikova. Directed by Stanislav Barabas. Screenplay, Ivan Bukovany, camera, Viktor Svoboda; music, Zdenek Liska. At Viennese Film Fest of Gaiety. Running Time, **88 MINS.**

Czech pix are currently enjoying a better reputation with Continental critics. This is only a little film but, nevertheless, even this modestly budgeted production has many good things to offer. It has an amusing tale, enjoyable acting and a series of witty situations. Also, it has something to think about inasmuch as it pokes satirical fun at such things as bureaucracy, tourism and the Czech interest in getting foreign currency into their land. The sympathetic, warm-hearted pic had its world preem at the Vienna Film Festival of Gaiety.

In the main, this one benefits from the Czech filmmakers' skill in observing human beings the way they are and present them on the screen with a twinkle in their eye. There's quite a bit of tongue-in-cheek in this production which, for western standards, has its slow moments but still has enough entertainment value to hold the viewer's interest.

Film centers around the director of a zoological garden who feels miserable because the government has turned down his request to place at his disposal foreign currency with which he had in ,mind to buy exotic animals. Moreover, his most valuable creature, a rare bear, has fallen deadly ill. This gives the desperate man the idea to let an ardent foreign hunter shoot the bear and to collect money (foreign currency, of course) for it. The foreigner eventually finds out that he has been cheated, but everyone is happy at the end because everyone gets what he wants.

There is nothing cynical about this satirical comedy. The humor is skillfully balanced so that no one can feel offended. Direction is smooth and technical credits are fully competent. Film may quickly be forgotten but it's the type of feature production which hardly anvone will classify as a waste of time.   *Hans.*

The Caper of the Golden Bulls
(COLOR)

Topnotch crime yarn set against running of the bulls in Pamplona, Spain; colorful and suspenseful with S t e p h e n Boyd name to draw.

Hollywood, May 11.
Embassy release of Joseph E. Levine presentation of Clarence Greene-Russell Rouse production, produced by Greene, directed by Rouse. Stars Stephen Boyd, Yvette Mimieux, Giovanna Ralli; features Walter Slezak. Screenplay, Ed Waters, David Moessinger; from novel by William P. McGivern; camera (PatheColor), Hal Stine; music, Vic Mizzy; editor, Chester Schaeffer; asst. director, Danny McCauley. Reviewed at Paramount Studios, May 10, '67. Running Time, 105 MINS.

Peter Churchman	Stephen Boyd
Grace Harvey	Yvette Mimieux
Angela Tresler	Giovanna Ralli
Antonio Gonzalez	Walter Slezak
Francois Morel	Vito Scotti
Philippe Lemoins	Clifton James
Paul Brissard	Lomax Study
Canalli	Tom Toner
Bendell	Henry Beckman
Ryan	Noah Keen
Carlos	Jay Novello
Mr. Shahari	Arnold Moss
Morchek	Leon Askin

Pamplona, the Spanish town where bulls annually race through the streets in the Fiesta of San Fermin on their way to the bullring and most of the male population, to show their manhood, try to outdistance them, makes a colorful setting for this tale of a fantastic jewel robbery. Clarence Green-Russell Rouse production packs an intriguing plot in a tense and absorbing unfoldment, reminiscent somewhat of "Topkapi" as a master crime is planned and perpetrated. It's the type of feature that when well done meets with favorable b.o. reaction, further sparked with a high exploitation potential.

Stephen Boyd is the chief protagonist as he's blackmailed into returning to his earlier career as a skillful bank robber, long since renounced for honest respectability. Femmes are Yvette Mimieux, in effective romantic interest, and Italian Giovanna Ralli, latter a former associate holding his past over him so she may come into another fortune to satisfy her extravagant tastes. Walter Slezak also is in prominently as a Spanish police chief who harasses Boyd in a good-natured but sinister manner.

As a production, pic is rich in pictorial effects and mounting suspense. Greene as producer and Rouse as director shot during the entire seven days of the Fiesta in Pamplona, catching the mood of the Mardi Gras-type event to backdrop the crime as Boyd and three past partners set about robbing the bank—directly across the street from the police station—where a fabulous fortune in jewels is deposited. The jewels, of untold value, have been brought in to adorn the Virgin statues from many parts of Spain during the religious procession at the height of the fair.

Script by Ed Waters and David Moessinger, based on the novel by William P. McGivern, centers on Boyd and his partners' split-timing their almost impossible task of breaking into the bank right under the noses of guarding police during the very few minutes

the bulls are dashing through the streets and past the bank itself. Rouse has handled situation forcefully in working it into the festival action and has come up with an imaginative narrative well enacted by entire cast.

Boyd is convincing as the ex-robber who enters the new robbery unwillingly and is relieved when through a fluke the jewels are returned, even though he has accomplished his task successfully. Miss Mimieux is sparkling on the romantic end, never prettier, and Miss Ralli acquits herself charmingly as the heavy who forces Boyd into his new crime. Slezak as usual fulfills every demand of character.

As his three past associates who are called in to help Boyd in breaking into the bank, Henry Beckman, Tom Toner and Noah Keen is dapper in a sinister character. Clifton James and Lomax Study are similarly okay.

Hal Stine's color camerawork is always arresting in getting the full effect of the festival and Vic Mizzy's music score is a particular standout. Art direction by Hal Pereira and Arthur Lonergan is expert, as is Chester Schaeffer's fast editing and Edith Head's costumes are eye-filling.   *Whit.*

The Way West
(COLOR—PANAVISION)

Dull oater, badly adapted from the A. B. Guthrie Jr. novel. Performances, direction limp, but sharp production values. Kirk Douglas, Robert Mitchum and Richard Widmark star. Okay b.o. if well-mated on action duals.

Hollywood, May 13.
United Artists release of a Harold Hecht production. Stars Kirk Douglas, Robert Mitchum, Richard Widmark. Directed by Andrew V. McLaglen. Screenplay, Ben Maddow, Mitch Lindemann, based on the novel by A. B. Guthrie, Jr.; camera (DeLuxe Color), William H. Clothier; editor, Otho Lovering; music, Bronislau Kaper; title song lyric, Mack David; asst. director, Terry Morse. Reviewed at Academy Award Theatre, L.A., May 12, '67. Running Time, 122 MINS.

Sen. William J. Tadlock	Kirk Douglas
Dick Summers	Robert Mitchum
Lije Evans	Richard Widmark
Rebecca Evans	Lola Albright
Preacher Weatherby	Jack Elam
Johnnie Mack	Michael Witney
Sam Fairman	Stubby Kaye
Mercy McBee	Sally Field
Amanda Mack	Katherine Justice
Brownie Evans	Michael McGreevey
Mrs. McBee	Connie Sawyer
McBee	Harry Carey, Jr.
Mrs. Fairman	Elisabeth Fraser
Michael Moynihan	William Lundigan
Mrs. Moynihan	Anne Barton
Masters	Roy Barcroft
Mrs. Masters	Eve McVeagh
Turley	Paul Lukather
Mrs. Turley	Peggy Stewart
Tadlock, Jr.	Stefan Arngrim
Big Henry	Hal Lynch
Middle Henry	Timothy Scott
Little Henry	John Mitchum
Saunders	Roy Glenn
Col. Grant	Patric Knowles
Calvelli	Nick Cravat
Paw-Kee Mah	Gary Morris
Sioux Chief	Michael Lane
Sioux Braves	Eddie Little Sky, Michael Keep
Caleb Greenwood	Clarke Gordon
Hank	Ken Murray
Barber	Paul Wexler
Indian Boy	Mitchell Schollars
Cattlemen	Jack Coffer, Everett Creach, Jim Burk, Gary McLarty

"The Way West," Harold Hecht's first production since "Cat Ballou," is a disappointing meller about

pioneers on the Oregon Trail, circa 1843. Cluttered scripting, routine characterizations and tame directions smother some firstrate exterior scenery and production values. Kirk Douglas, Robert Mitchum and Richard Widmark provide marquee power. Overlong at two hours plus, the United Artists release will need a sturdy lowercase companion for fair b.o. on action duals.

A. B. Guthrie Jr. wrote the Pulitzer Prize novel on which Ben Maddow and Mitch Lindemann based a rambling screenplay. Story takes a group of Missouri farmers, under martinet Douglas, to the promised land of Oregon. Mitchum is the trail scout who leads them despite fading eyesight, and Widmark an irascible member of the party.

Project probably looked good on paper, but washed out in scripting, direction and pacing. Incidents do not build to any climax; excepting the first and last reels, any others could be shown out of order with no apparent discontinuity. A lot of time, money and logistics—including use of national parks for some terrif location work—makes the final result all the more disappointing.

The three male stars all could have phoned in their acting. Douglas, the stern disciplinarian, at one point orders Negro slave Roy Glenn to whip him; this incident, as written, is crude, and instead of indicating a Spartan attempt at self-control, it comes across as unmotivated masochism. Mitchum, evidently aware of the script vapidity, didn't try too hard; Widmark, evidently unaware, gave it the college try to no better results.

Vignettes make the trip West a rough one for audiences, too. Sally Field, "introduced" in billing, is a teenbopper of the time, teasing Michael McGreevey (good as Widmark's son), and seducing Michael Witney, just-married to a frigid Katherine Justice, latter also "introduced" in credits.

Witney is a wooden actor, herein, and victimized by script. When he accidentally shoots an Indian boy, hiding under a wolfskin, he never even explains the incident, and calmly permits himself to be hanged for the offense. Man, that's guilt for you.

Miss Justice, the frigid wife, remains so after hubby's death, when she bobs up now and then with glassy stare, and eventually causes Douglas' death; he was supposedly the last to descend a steep cliff, but she (presumably) went unnoticed in the airlift, and cut the line. Miss Field and McGreevey eventually marry and both are adjusting to each other at fadeout.

Lola Albright is Widmark's wife, object of some suspicious stares by Douglas in a sidebar that never got off the (cutting room) ground; synopsis indicates more plot than appears. Miss Albright is a very good actress; she is one of the few thesps. Jack Elam is an itinerant preacher who evokes laughs, even when there should be none. Huge supporting cast includes William Lundigan, Patric Knowles (both sighted in bits) and Ken Murray, listed but not seen. All are okay in stock roles.

Andrew V. McLaglen has directed actioners before, and in

better style. He has a good eye for oater spectacle, and in intimate action bits he also has a flair. But between those extremes lies a vast spectrum of necessary exposition and dramatic rhythm, missing herein. Neither McLaglen, Hecht nor editor Otho Lovering have effected any mounting suspense, or sustained audience interest. Pic runs a longish 122 minutes.

William H. Clothier's Panavision-Deluxe Color lensing is excellent. Score, by Bronislau Kaper, is full-bodied, as conducted by Andre Previn. A titlesong, lyrics by Mack David, is sung by The Serendipity Singers, a contemporary folk group. This tune is well-placed—about 10 minutes after the start of pic, as the pioneers set off in exuberance. Other credits are pro. *Murf.*

Caprice
(COLOR—C'SCOPE)

Dull Doris Day comedy about industrial espionage. Richard Harris for added marquee lure. Tepid b.o. on duals.

Hollywood, May 11.
Twentieth Century-Fox release of an Aaron Rosenberg-Martin Melcher Production. Stars Doris Day, Richard Harris; features Ray Walston, Jack Kruschen, Edward Mulhare. Directed by Frank Tashlin. Screenplay, Jay Jayson, Tashlin, based on a story by Martin Hale and Jayson; camera (DeLuxe Color), Leon Shamroy, editor, Robert Simpson; music, Frank De Vol; title song, Larry Marks; asst. director, David Silver. Reviewed at 20th-Fox Studios. L.A., May 10, '67. Running Time, **97 MINS.**
Patricia Fowler .... Doris Day
Christopher White ..... Richard Harris
Stuart Clancy .... Ray Walson
Matthew Cutter .... Jack Kruschen
Sir Jason Fox .... Edward Mulhare
Madame Piasco .... Lilia Skala
Su Ling .... Irene Tsu
Inspector Kapinsky ..... Larry D. Mann
Auber .... Maurice Marsac
Butler .... Michael Romanoff
Mandy .... Lisa Seagram
Barney .... Michael J. Pollard

"Caprice" is one of those occasional pictures about which it can be said fairly that it could have been better than it is. A timely and inventive plot—industrial espionage,—is never fully developed in either writing, acting or direction. Doris Day and Richard Harris star in this so-so Aaron Rosenberg-Martin Melcher production. Plush production values do not cover the story gaps, only to serve to accentuate them. Tepid b.o. likely via 20th-Fox release in general dual situations.

Frank Tashlin has done a flat job in direction, also in scripting, with Jay Jayson, a story by the latter and Martin Hale. Miss Day and Harris are double-crossing double agents working, variously, for U.S. cosmetics king Jack Kruschen. British counterpart Edward Mulhare, or Interpol. Ray Walston plays Kruschen's inventive genius, although it turns out that Lilla Skala, Walston's mother-in-law in Switzerland, is the creative brain. Elements of comedy, murder, satire and psychology are blended uncertainly in the never-boiling pot.

Kruschen and Mulhare try too hard to be funny, and rarely succeed. What is most frustrating is that the plot elements could have been shaped into a zesty comedy which offered a change of pace from the James Bond gang to the reality of industrial spying, exciting in its own right. As a word, "Caprice" means a whim or freak; so it seems.

It is getting more difficult with each pic to see much of Miss Day; she is far too invisible via exaggerated hair styles, concealing hats and wardrobe (again by Ray Aghayan) and long shots. In addition, Tashlin, an expert in broad comedy setups, has laid it on too thick here. Miss Day going from one slapstick bit to another. Harris and Tashlin both are responsible for his mannered posturing.

Walston almost succeeds in being the nutty cosmetics genius. In final scene, where he is revealed as the murderer of Miss Day's secret agent dad, she utters an unbelievable, unmotivated and overly-pat bit of abnormal psychology: a man who likes to be around girls is basically transvestite!

On the plus side, but not plus enough, are the exciting down-hill ski scenes and other eye-catching CinemaScope-Deluxe Color setups by lenser Leon Shamroy: Nelson Tyler's aerial photography: the Jack Martin Smith-William Creber art direction; and the outstanding pop-art title work by National Screen Service, which has gotten many a recent pic off to a great start.

Frank De Vol's score is okay, and Larry Marks' title tune—sung by Miss Day as she attends a local theatre playing this pic—is nothing. Robert Simpson executed the editing to 97 minutes; production notes indicate 103 minutes, probably an earlier count; end result still is sluggish. Other credits okay.

Miss Day has one more 20th pic to go. *Murf.*

Africa—Texas Style

Exciting meller filmed in Kenya; thrills abound in sequences of two Texas cowboys going to Africa to rope wild animals; good prospects for action market.

Hollywood, May 10.
Paramount release of Ivan Tors production, produced-directed by Andrew Marton. Stars Hugh O'Brian, John Mills; features Nigel Green, Tom Nardini, Adrienne Corri, Ronald Howard. Screenplay, Andy White; camera (Eastman-Color), Paul Beeson; music, Malcolm Arnold; editor, Henry Richardson. Reviewed at Paramount Studios, May 9, '67. Running Time, **110 MINS.**
Jim Sinclair .... Hugh O'Brian
Wing Commander Hayes .... John Mills
Karl Bekker .... Nigel Green
John Henry .... Tom Nardini
Fay Carter .... Adrienne Corri
Hugo Copp .... Ronald Howard
Sampson .... Charles Malinda
Mr. Oyondi .... Honey Wamala
Veterinary .... Charles Hayes
Peter .... Stephen Kikumu
Turk .... Ali Twaha
Witch Doctor ..... Mohammed Abdullah

Ivan Tors, who has "Cowboy in Africa" coming up as a teleseries, to be lensed in its actual East Africa locale, precedes this project with a motion picture feature which might be tabbed a theatrical pilot for the home series. Originally carrying the same tag but now bogged down with the heavy-handed "African — Texas Style" handle, film is a slick and exceptionally well-turned-out piece of adventure picture-making, its title the only weight of heaviness about it. For action houses particularly and the general market where exotic backgrounds, wild animals and fast excitment are popular, feature stands a good chance for big play.

Produced and directed for Tors by Andrew Marton, picture was shot entirely in Kenya. Marton, scripter Andy White and cameraman Paul Beeson have thoroughly caught feeling of Africa in pic's speedy 110-minutes' unfoldment. They make effective use of the African terrain as an atmospheric setting and thousands of animals of all descriptions to lend authenticity to a narrative which is both topical and interesting. Danger, romance, humor and magnificent scenic backdrops are blended to maintain audience attention.

Story twirls about the subject of game ranching, the domestication and breeding of wild animal life in Africa as a potentially huge source of meat and as a means of preserving many of the Dark Continent's rapidly vanishing species of wild beasts. Premise is given punch via its human story of rancher John Mills importing Texas cowboys Hugh O'Brian and his Navajo pal Tom Nardini to rope and corral as many animals as they can ride down. (Chuck Connors will take over the O'Brian role in teleseries).

O'Brian realistically undertakes his character, and Mills delivers strongly as the rancher intent upon saving animal life from decimation in what has become a popular practice in Africa. Credible support are contributed by Nigel Green, as a cattle rancher who opposes Mills' idea; Nardini who rides with O'Brian; Adrienne Corri as distaff interest; Ronald Howard as a naturalist. Charles Malinda, a small native boy, is particularly outstanding. *Whit.*

The Fastest Guitar Alive

Fair Civil War oatuner comedy to showcase singer Roy Orbison. Okay b.o. in the country music belt, fair dual entry elsewhere.

Hollywood, May 3.
Metro-Goldwyn-Mayer release of a Four Leaf (Sam Katzman) Production. Features Roy Orbison, Sammy Jackson, Maggie Pierce, Joan Freeman. Directed by Michael Moore. Screenplay, Robert E. Kent; camera (Metrocolor), W. Wallace Kelley; editor, Ben Lewis; music, Fred Karger; songs, Karger, Kent, Orbison, Bill Dees; asst. director, Donald C. Klune. Reviewed at MGM Studios, Culver City, May 2, '67. Running Time, **87 MINS.**
Johnny .... Roy Orbison
Steve .... Sammy Jackson
Flo .... Maggie Pierce
Sue .... Joan Freeman
Charlie .... Lyle Bettger
Max .... John Doucette
Stella .... Patricia Donahue
Rink .... Ben Cooper
Indian Chief .... Ben Lessy
Joe .... Douglas Kennedy
Deputy .... Len Hendry
1st Indian .... Iron Eyes Cody
1st Expressman .... Sam The Sham
Emily .... Wilda Taylor
Margie .... Victoria Carroll
Tanya .... Maria Korda
Carmen .... Poupee Camin

"The Fastest Guitar Alive," which marks the film debut of Nashville-sounding Roy Orbison. Is a hybrid; a Civil War comedy with songs and kooky Indians. Produced by Sam Katzman to showcase Orbison's songs, pic is occasionally amusing, more often silly, but well-made trivia. Hard sell in the country belt will produce good b.o., at least in relation to investment, but elsewhere, the Metro release will need a sturdier running mate on less discriminating dual bills.

Robert E. Kent's routine, and somewhat anachronistic script features Orbison and partner Sammy Jackson as two Confederate soldiers who steal gold from the Frisco mint to help the South. Enroute, they latch on to Maggie Pierce and Joan Freeman—part of a medicine show femme troupe—for the romantic interest. General Lee's surrender makes their mission fruitless, and reduces them to thieves. They foil the bad guys, seeking to steal the loot, and everyone, who should, winds up happy.

Seven tunes by Orbison and collaborator Bill Dees, plus one by scorer Fred Karger and Kent, pop up at regular intervals. All are good, easy listening, and rhythmic. The tie-in record album should do very well. Karger's overall music supervision is an excellent production value, as is Wilda Taylor's simple choreography.

Director Michael Moore, recently graduated from first assistant ranks has done a fair job, within the low-budget bounds imposed, but there is a static, formula impression created on a viewer. W. Wallace Kelley lensed well in Metrocolor.

Of the featured players (all names follow title), Jackson and Miss Freeman are most at ease and competent, showing ability far beyond this script. Orbison, a far better songwriter-singer than actor, is covered nicely to register okay. Among the supporting cast, Lyle Bettger, Ben Cooper, Douglas Kennedy and Ben Lessy (as a goofy Indian chief) turn in professional readings. Ben Lewis trimmed to 87 minutes, and other technical credits are pro. *Murf.*

Cannes Festival

Batouk
(FRENCH DOCUMENTARY)
(Color)

Cannes, May 10.
Images Distribution release of Dalhia production. Directed by Jean-Jacques Manigot from an original idea by Calros Paez Vilaro. Camera (Eastmancolor), Gilles Bonneau, Andre Persin, Jean Fichter, Alain Boisnard; commentary by Leopold Sedar Senghor, Aime Ceasire, spoken by Andre Maurice; editor, Andre Delage; music, Michel Magne. At Cannes Film Fest. Running Time, **66 MINS.**
Dancer .... Judith Jamison
Runner .... Lamine Sy

Overblown but mercifully short documentary on Africa looks like a mass of stock footage that the makers have tried to give a significance to via foisting some poetic writings placed on the sound track. Pic rarely jells and gives a forced view of a primitive side of Africa intercut with an African girls in mod clothes dancing in a studio or on the Eiffel Tower and a constantly running marathoner.

There are some good shots of animals now and then but intercutting jazz, mod dancing and modernism with primitive rites is just too arch to have this work out. Pic looks to have little arty use abroad and only some supporting fare possibilities on some okay animal work. *Mosk.*

Tvarbalk
(Rooftree)
(SWEDISH)
Cannes, May 10.

Sandrews production and release. Stars Harriet Andersson, Ulf Palme; features Gunnel Brostrom, Ernst-Hugo Jaregard. Written and directed by Jorn Donner from a book by Sivar Arner. Camera, Rune Ericson; editor, Donner. At Cannes Film eFst. Running Time, 90 MINS.

Noomi	Harriet Andersson
Leo	Ulf Palme
Magnus	Ernst-Hugo Jaregard
Inez	Gunnel Brostrom

In a taut look at two couples who interchange, Jorn Donner has woven an engrossing film that backs talk and inner life with a knowing visual counterpoint and constant rigid character revelation. It manages to make big statements via the look at seemingly ordinary human comportment and decisions. It appears slated for specialized use mainly on its refusal to play for obvious drama. But its control and fine acting should find this a place in more demanding arty house situations abroad.

A Jewish girl who had been in a concentration camp and then found refuge in Sweden, still finds her past something that cannot as yet be erased even though she is now fully grown. She is with a painter who is having an affair with a friend's wife. The friend falls for the girl and divorces his wife to be with her.

That is the surface look of this production, but director-writer Jorn Donner delves deeply into the affairs of this foursome. The wife is more interested in living than being loved, the husband finally finds a person to love, and the girl begins to feel a chance to live if her broken body and past are still menacing her reason at the end.

Donner weaves a pungent insight into the refugee who is sometimes used by people to allay their own senses of guilt. The adult and penetrating look at love in its physical as well as motional and romantic sides is always revealing here. The dialog is welded well with the knowing imagery. Film emerges a penetrating one about people in crisis.

Harriet Andersson is poignant and forceful as the girl still weighted down with her past, with Ulf Palme helping via sensitivity as her lover. Gunnel Brostrom adds a revealing limning as the older but physically rapacious wife. This makes a searing statement on one of the most horrible incidents in man's recent history in showing the effects that still linger in the people who lived through it. It's no easy pic but has forceful pace, intelligent writing and solid editing. *Mosk.*

Ultimo Encuentro
(Last Meeting)
(SPANISH)
Cannes, May 10.

Uniespana release of Elias Querejeta production. Stars Antonio Gades; features Maria Cuadra, Daniel Martin. Directed by Antonio Eceiza. Screenplay, Elias Querejeta, Eceiza; camera, Luis Cuadrado; editor, Pablo G. Del Amo. At Cannes Film Fest. Running Time, 90 MINS.

Antonio	Antonio Gades
Juan	Daniel Martin
Rocio	Maria Cuadra
Dancer	La Polaca

Hispano drama deals with a successful flamenco dancer who looks back on his life when a tele show does a sort of "This Is Your Life" show on him. But situations are predictable and the main plus is the dancing of Antonio Gades. Hence, this is mainly for Spanish-language cinemas abroad on its music and dynamic terp segs. There is not enough dramatic punch for much playoff potential.

Film does give a backdrop to a certain tension that seems to be present in the country. But this is rarely developed and the pic intercuts past and present as the dancer meets old friends and family on the tv show, thus thinking back on his past as it is contrasted with his present life.

He had taken a friend's girl but now he is married. But the simmering thing between him and his old friend finally breaks out after these many years. Pic shows the hard rise of a poor boy to a venerated dancer. But Gades is more effective as a dashing dancer than actor. Vehicle wends its way sans surprises. It is technically good and moves crisply if familiarly. *Mosk.*

Mon Amour, Mon Amour
(My Love, My Love)
(FRENCH—COLOR)
Cannes, May 10.

Cocinor release of Les Films De La Boetie, Les Films Marceau production. Stars Jean-Luis Trintignant; features Valerie Lagrange, Annie Fargue, Michel Piccoli, Anna Katerina Larsson. Written and directed by Nadine Trintignant. Camera (Eastmancolor), Willy Kurant; editor, Nicole Lubtchansky. At Cannes Film Fest. Running Time, 94 MINS.

Vincent	Jean-Louis Trintignant
Agathe	Valerie Lagrange
Friend	Michel Piccoli
Jeanne	Annie Fargue
Marilou	Anna-Katerina Larsson

Nadine Trintignant is the wife of actor Jean-Louis, and was an editor and made some shorts before essaying her first feature pic. All this background has not helped her avoid a patchy film. Too much unassimilated influences, a fragmented style trying to encompass the beginning and end of a love affair and inside gags just do not give this the needed life and charm to escape a laggard pace.

There are the seemingly banal story, constant walks, car rides, etc., and the flash forwards and backwards. There is a rather insistent girlishness that is arch rather than bright.

An architect is having an affair with a girl trying to become a pop singer. She is pregnant but never tells him as they drift apart. It is left up in the air whether she goes through with an abortion or that it was all in her head.

Old New Wave influences also float rather than take on their own

life here. Overdone camera angles do not help the rather overblown love scenes. Posing rather than acting is also a drawback. This rambling pic substitutes prettiness for taste and visual garrulity for tact.

There is a fair color envelope, nudie scenes and general attempt to be fashionable and this may give the pic some playoff legs abroad. It looms as a chancy arty entry.

It does not look like Mrs. Trintignant will add to the many femme newscomers in films unless she develops a narrative style. A flashy but empty pic, it will need hardsell for best returns. *Mosk.*

Le Depart
(The Departure)
(BELGIAN)
Cannes, May 10.

Elisabeth Films production and release. With Jean-Pierre Leaud, Catherine Duport, Jacqueline Biz, Paul Roland. Directed by Jerzy Skolimovski. Screenplay, Andrej Kostanko, Skolimovski; camera, Willy Kurant; editor, Bob Wade; music, K. T. Komeda. At Cannes Film Fest. Running Time, 89 MINS.

Marc	Jean-Pierre Leaud
Michele	Catherine Duport
Woman	Jacqueline Biz
Friend	Paul Roland
Boss	Leon Dory

Jerry Skolomovski is a Polish filmmaker who has gained some renown at festivals. This his fourth pic has been made in Belgium. It is an extremely self-indulgent tale of a young anarchist. This appears mainly ripe for specialized use abroad if more generalized art and playoff call for harder sell.

Pic is about a young worker in a beauty parlor who is concerned mostly with autos. It leads to him borrowing his boss' car at night and working out deals to try out motorcar dealer models via various ingenious subterfuges. He finally goes off in his boss' car with a young girl and there he discovers love for the first time.

Skolimovski is extremely inventive. But overall this shows a personal talent that should make a bigger impact when he is more selective and pays more attention to narrative.

The hero is a French thesp, Jean-Pierre Leaud. He has the proper callow outlook, underlined by offbeat, far-out shenanigans, to make his character of a vulnerable if unpredictable young man always engaging. He is seduced by a rich woman before going off with a young girl.

Film shows the desires of lesser endowed youth for the trappings of affluent society. It has wit and builds up a series of adventures that are usually beguiling if some are sometimes overdrawn.

Skolimovski has cannily created a sort of Polski picaresque quality though he has made the film in Belgium. The sharp lensing, brittle editing and easy playing keep this potent most of the time. But no denying the frothy invention and definite talents. *Mosk.*

L'Immorale
(The Immoralist)
(ITALIAN)

United Artists release of Robert Haggiag, Delphos, Dear Film production. Stars Ugo Tognazzi; features Stefania Sandrelli, Gigi Ballista, Renee Longarini, Grazia Carmassi. Directed by Pietro Germi. Screenplay, Germi, Alfredo Giannetti, Tullio Pinelli, Carlo Bernardi; camera, Aiace Parolini; editor, Sergio Montatnari. At Cannes Film Fest. Running Time, 97 MINS.

Sergio	Ugo Tognazzi
Marisa	Stefania Sandrelli
Giulia	Renee Longarini
Adele	Maria Grazia Carnassi
Michele	Gigi Ballista
Colasanti	Sergio Fincato
Masini	Marco Della Giovanna

Pietri Germi has made comedies castigating outmoded divorce laws and courting outlooks in Sicily and the middleclass hypocrisy in Northern Italy. Here he sets up a more soft-pedaled pitch for tolerance in love. It's on a far-out premise about a man with a wife and three children who has two other women with children he is also supporting. But there's no smirking in this. Germi is sometimes too gentle to make for some fine comedic stretches. Finally he has to kill off the loving hero to end the problem.

On a hot Rome day he sees off his family and then tells a priest friend about his complicated life. It seems he has two children by another woman (not his wife) and is expecting a child by another girl, the two extra-curricular women know about the wife but not about each other.

Ugo Tognazzi has the requisite charm with the gentle timing and the right blending of this tale to keep it churning long after the p'c has become a bit repetitive. Whether it is just a whimsical pic ploy about the sheer logistical problems of a too-full love life or a potshot at the rigid Italo divorce laws, is not too clear.

It sets out to show that a man who can't resist love has to be almost a superman. The women in his life all have some traits that may not always appear together in one woman. The wife, Renee Longarini, is understanding, quietly sensual. One mistress is voluptuous and loving. The other one is a younger and more demanding one.

Pic resolutely plays this for laughs and garners many sans ever being crude. It thus appears a likely candidate for fine playoff possibilities if rightly handled abroad on its spicy, offbeat but always tactful qualities. Arty legs also are indicated by the general witty tenure of the affair. It is fairly brisk but some pruning, to make the second half move a bit faster, would help. *Mosk.*

Katerina Izmailova
(RUSSIAN-COLOR)
Cannes, May 10.

Sovexport release of Lenfilm production. With Galina Vichnevskaia, A. Inozemtzev, N. Sovolov. Directed by Mikhail Shapiro. Screenplay, Dimitri Shostokovitch based on his own opera from the story by N. Leskov; camera (Sovcolor), R. Davydov, V. Ponomarev. At Cannes Film Fest. Running Time, 116 MINS.

Katarina	Galina Vichnevskaia
Serguei	A. Inozemtzev
Zinovi	N. Sovolov
Boris	A. Sovolov

The opera of Dimitri Shostoko-vitch was banned by Stalin in 1936, after it gained significance and success abroad, since it ex-tolled man's right to choose his own way. Since rehabilitated, it is now well adapted to the screen if it remains primarily for music buffs since a filmed opera though its visual adaptation has sweep.

In the 19th Century Russia, a rich but bored woman takes a farm laborer as a lover on the property owned by her husband. She poi-sons her father-in-law and then has her husband killed before she and her lover are apprehended and sent to Siberia. There he takes up with another woman and it ends in tragedy.

Big 70m screen is used to under-line the fine music of Shostoko-vitch but it remains more opera than film. Thus some filmgoers may be disturbed by the singing in full voice that are supposed to be whispered. But those that ac-cept it and its classical filmed opera mold will be beguiled by its expert music, fine singing and photographic illustration. It is pri-marily for music buffs but may be useful in some specialized spots. Chances for more commercial playoff and art usage appears limited.

Singing is exemplary and music sublime. Acting is also topnotch and the 70m lensing is bright. *Mosk.*

Pedro Paramo
(MEXICAN)

Cannes, May 10.
Clasa Films Mundiales, Produccciones Barbachano Ponce production and re-lease. Stars John Gavin, Ignacio Lopez Tarso, Pilar Pellicer; features Narciso Busquets, Julissa, Graciela Doring. Di-rected by Carlos Velo. Screenplay, Car-los Fuentes, Carlos Velo, Manuel Bar-bachano Ponce from book by Juan Rulfo; camera, Gabriel Figueroa; editor, Gloria Schoeman. At Cannes Film Fest. Run-ning Time, 110 MINS.
Pedro .... Jean Gavin
Fulgor .... Ignacio Lopez Tarso
Bartolome .... Narciso Busquets
Susana .... Pilar Pellicer
Ana .... Julissa
Damiana .... Graciela Doring
Juan .... Carlos Fernandez
Toribo .... Roberto Canedo

Overblown fantasy depicts the search of a young man for his father in a seething Mexico of the early 1900s. It appears everybody in it is dead or a phantom, and the boy himself is finally swallowed up by his mother's grave. This parable is just too flashy to get any true point into its rambling look at stereotyped figures from old time Mexican pix. Mainly Span-ish or some lingo spots for this abroad.

Flashbacks abound as scenes of the Mexican Revolution, excessive killing and hot blood are poured out. All this is lensed in a heavy manner and played flamboyantly. John Gavin looks good in the earthy father role if he can't do much with the gusty character. Pic may have some significance on its home grounds, but the stereotyped direction, playing and outlandish symbols do not jell into a palatable allegory on Mexican life and its division between European, Indian,

rational and mystical influences. It should be a nice home item if its offshore future is doubtful. *Mosk.*

Barefoot In The Park
(COLOR)

Outstanding film version of Neil Simon's legit comedy. Robert Redford, Jane Fonda, Charles Boyer for marquee. Slow playoff probable best strategy.

Hollywood, May 9.
Paramount Pictures release of a Hal B. Wallis production. Stars Robert Red-ford, Jane Fonda, Charles Boyer, Mildred Natwick. Directed by Gene Saks. Screen-play, Neil Simon, based on his play; camera (Technicolor), Joseph La Shelle; editor, William A. Lyon; music, Neal Hefti; title song, Hefti, Johnny Mercer; asst. director, Howard Grace. Reviewed at Directors Guild of America, L.A., May 8, '67. Running Time, 104 MINS.
Paul Bratter .... Robert Redford
Corie Bratter .... Jane Fonda
Victor Belasco .... Charles Boyer
Mrs. Ethel Banks...... Mildred Natwick
Harry Pepper .... Herbert Edelman
Aunt Harriet .... Mabel Albertson
Restaurant owner .... Fritz Feld
Delivery Man .... James Stone
Frank .... Ted Hartley

"Barefoot In The Park" is one howl of a picture. Adapted by Neil Simon from his legit smash, re-taining Robert Redford and Mil-dred Natwick from the original cast, and adding Jane Fonda and Charles Boyer to round out the principals, this excellent Hal B. Wallis production is a thoroughly entertaining comedy delight about young marriage. A cautious initial playoff, to build word of mouth, will be needed to guarantee the Paramount release the smash b.o. which it merits.

Release pattern and publicity is the major hurdle for "Park," as seen from an analysis of the com-edy market for the past couple of years. Many excellent comedies, ac-knowledged as such within the trade and in reviews, caught on too late in first release. While these pix remain staples in sub-run playoffs, they missed the top money. In all cases, word of mouth, while favorable, was slow in building. Only feasible solu-tion outside of "Park's" Radio City Music Hall showcasing in N.Y. is to give it several weeks in a small house, let the word get around, then cash in with multiple bookings.

Film version of "Barefoot" is excellent in all departments. Redford is an outstanding actor, particularly adept in light com-edy, whose performance and con-tribution herein justify his first position over the title. He should have a successful film career for decades, the logical follow-on to Cary Grant. He recreates his role of newlywed hubby to Jane Fonda, who has taken over the Elizabeth Ashley legit role.

Gene Saks, who has never be-fore directed a pic, makes a sock debut. Miss Fonda is excellent, ditto Miss Natwick, her mother. A genuine surprise casting is Boyer, as the Bohemian who lives in the attic above the newlyweds' top-floor flat. For the first few minutes of Boyer's screen time, many audiences will be distracted by the offbeat role (for him), and hence miss the full impact of his topnotch comedy delivery; once adjusted, viewers will find him delightful.

Simon's adaptation of his play sparkles throughout the spectrum

of comedy. Telephone man Her-bert Edelman, also from the orig-inal cast assembled by producer Arnold Saint-Subber for stager Mike Nichols, whams over his part, as does James Stone, the delivery man whose out-of-breath bit is but one surefire develop-ment of a basic gag—those five flights of stairs, plus front stoop. Mabel Albertson, Fritz Feld and Ted Hartley are fine in brief scenes which, wisely, have been added to expand the action from one interior set.

With only one slight flagging pace—about 30 minutes from the end, when Redford and Miss Fonda have their late-night squabble—pic moves along smart-ly through its 104-minute running time, as edited by William A. Lyon. Joseph La Shelle's respon-sive and mobile Technicolor camera enhances both character-izations and production values.

Production elements again were expertly supervised for Wallis by associate producer Paul Nathan. Neal Hefti's score is on the subdued side, adroit for the unfolding of the plot, but it makes for a pallid main title, where, in a comedy, there should be some punch. Johnny Mercer penned title tune lyrics. Other credits are pro. *Murf.*

Psycho-Circus
(BRITISH)

Okay mystery meller for smaller program market.

Hollywood, May 5.
American International release of Harry Alan Towers production. Stars Christopher Lee, Leo Genn; features An-thony Newlands, Heinz Drache, Eddi Arent, Skip Martin. Directed by John Moxey. Screenplay, Peter Welbeck; cam-era, Ernest Steward; editor, John Trum-per; music, Johnny Douglas; asst. di-rector, Barry Melrose. Reviewed at Charles Addikoff projection room, May 4, '67. Running Time, 65 MINS.
Gregor .... Christopher Lee
Elliott .... Leo Genn
Barberini .... Anthony Newlands
Carl .... Heinz Drache
Eddie .... Eddi Arent
Manfred .... Klaus Kinski
Gina .... Margaret Lee
Natasha .... Suzy Kendall
Sir John .... Cecil Parker
Mason .... Victor Maddern
Mario .... Maurice Kaufmann
Manley .... Lawrence James
Jackson .... Tom Bowman
Mr. Big .... Skip Martin
Red .... Fred Powell
Negro .... Gordon Petrie
Hotel Porter .... Henry Longhurst
Armoured Van Guard....Dennis Blakely
Fourth Man .... George Fisher
Speedboat Men .... Peter Brace,
Roy Scammel
Security Men .... Geoff Silk,
Keith Peacock

"Psycho-Circus," ineptly titled for America and bogged down with a confused story line, still car-ries sufficient action to rate as an okay entry for the smaller program market. British-produced, only name familiar to American audiences is Leo Genn, who plays a London police inspector at-tempting to unravel the robbery of an armored truck. Scene moves from the London riverfront, where film opens effectively as heist of a fortune in bank notes is execut-ed, to winter quarters of a cir-cus, where some of the money is traced.

Unfoldment is peopled with various circus characters: an animal trainer who wears a black hood to hide the scars he claims to have received; the circus owner who cooperates with police; a jealous knife-thrower and his sexy girlfriend who has a roving eye; a black-mailing dwarf; a ringmaster who joined circus to await arrival of a man who killed his father, whom he knows someday will show up. Plotline in script by Peter Welbeck frequently gets out of hand as mysterious characters move about and two murders take place.

Genn handles his part with his usual aplomb and Christopher Lee, who co-stars with him, is the animal trainer. Anthony Newlands does well as circus owner, as does Heinz Drache in ringmaster role, and Maurice Kaufmann and Margaret Lee are the betrothed couple.. Cast generally acquit themselves well under John Maxey's direction.

Technical credits in the Harry Alan Towers production are adequate.   *Whit.*

La Loi Du Survivant
(Law of Survival)
(FRENCH — COLOR — TECHNISCOPE)
Paris, May 17.
SNC release of Stephan Films-SNC production. With Michel Constantin, Alexandra Stewart, Jean Franval. Written and directed by Jose Giovanni from his own book. Camera (Eastmancolor), Georges Barsky; music, Francois De Roubaix. At Ermitage, Paris. Running Time, **100 MINS.**

Manu	Michel Constantin
Helene	Alexandra Stewart
Friend	Jean Franval
Charles	Roger Blin

Jose Giovanni has been responsible for numerous adventure and gangster scripts adapted from his books. Now he turns director and adapts a book of his own for vehicle. Result is a solid adventure love story with good possibilities in France and (maybe) playoff in general foreign markets.

Giovanni goes in for stories of honor, either among thieves or adventurers, and adheres to patterns of the Hollywood heyday but well assimilated and adapted to France and especially to his native Corsica, where this one takes place.

Hero is a good-hearted drifter who has struck it rich via finding buried treasure. Ready to help a lady in distress, this one seemingly held prisoner in a big villa, he decides to assist her escape. He does so after being attacked by vicious dogs. It appears she is afraid of animals and of about everything else, and he helps her overcome them as love blooms. But up turn the people who had sequestered her and it seems she had been responsible for turning a man who loved her over to the Germans during the last war.

She commits suicide after being found out and is buried by the grieving hero, Michel Constantin, a craggy thesp with good presence if he lacks personal dash. Giovanni wisely retrains from love scenes and gives this a classical mounting highlighted by a rugged duel with revolvers, gentle scenes of getting to know each other, and the by now overworked, but still brought off, scene of a bullet being removed from the man's carcass.

Alexandra Stewart has freshness

and elan as the girl with a past and others fill out the heavy roles adequately. Perhaps lacking gusto and sometimes a bit stilted in direction, pic still has a genuine feel for its people, a rugged flair for showing men with codes without being mawkish, and a nice backgrounding by the Corsican scenery. Giovanni brings some needed fresh air and simplicity into pix here if he still needs to let action take over from explaining and a greater ease in direction.

But it is a good start and he adapted the pic from a section of his book "The Adventurers" which has opened here in a version by Robert Enrico. Giovanni used a seg not used by Enrico and this has become a talking point among critics and is helping both pix off to a good start besides their own disarming and generally good commercial looks and treatments.   *Mosk.*

Le Plus Vieux Metier Du Monde
(Oldest Profession in the World)
(FRENCH—ITALIAN—GERMAN—COLOR)
Paris, May 17.
Athos Film release of Films Gibe, Francoriz, Rialto Films production. Stars Michele Mercier, Elsa Martinelli, Jeanne Moreau, Raquel Welch, France Anglade, Nadia Gray, Anna Karina, Marilu Tolo. Directed by Franco Novina, Mauro Bolognini, Philippe De Broca, Michael Pfleghar, Claude Autantlara, Jean-Luc Godard. Screenplay, Ennio Flaiano, Daniel Boulanger, Georges and Andre Tabet, Jean Aurenche. Godard. Camera (Eastmancolor), Pierre Lhomme; music, Michel Legrand. At George V, Paris. Running Time, **115 MINS.**

THE PREHISTORIC ERA	
Girl	Michele Mercier
Older Man	Enrico Maria Salerno
Younger Man	Gabriel Tinti
ROMAN NIGHTS	
Girl	Elsa Martinelli
Man	Gaston Moschin
MADEMOISELLE MIMI	
Girl	Jeanne Moreau
Young Man	Jeane-Claude Brialy
Older Man	Jean Richard
THE GOOD OLD DAYS	
Girl	Raquel Welch
Older Man	Martin Held
TODAY	
Woman	Nadia Gray
Girl	France Anglade
Young Man	Jacques Duby
Visitor	Francis Blanche
Older Man	Dalio
ANTICIPATION	
Girl	Anna Karina
Friend	Marilu Tolo
Young Man	Jacques Charrier

Series of sketches about joy girls through the ages. Approach is gamey, mainly farcical. Treatment avoids vulgarity but too many bits are skimpy. Production dress and some name values could help for foreign dates.

It all begins with an anachronistic prehistoric bit about a cave girl who finds that inventing makeup and making men give her things to be with her is a worthwhile new trend. Michele Mercier is lacking in needed comedic wit and timing to give much bite to this "birth" of the oldest profession.

Skip to ancient Rome. A bored Emperor finds his wife in a bawdy house. But she says it was to trap him. But she was working the place all the time. Lackadaisical Roman reconstructions and listless playing do not give this seg much punch.

Things pick up a bit with Jeanne Moreau as a cheeky hire girl during the French Revolution. Taken in by a young man who promises her power and a name when he

inherits the goods of his beheaded uncle. Promise is a gimmick to have her for free. Miss Moreau has the preening smugness of her type plus womanly wiles that manage to contribute some style.

A turn-of-the-century bit has Yank sex purveyor Raquel Welch as a shrewd and lusty bar girl who lands an old and simple banker by playing on his vanity. It has nice production zip and Miss Welch does a clever sort of frilly strip tease.   *Mosk.*

Teenage Rebellion
(DOCUMENTARY)

Compilation of foreign-made and U.S. items on what makes teenagers tick. Quality varies according to ability of various directors. Exploitable.

Trans American release of an Unger Productions presentation. Produced, directed and written by Norman Herman. Foreign sequences directed by Jorn Donner (Sweden), Eriprando Visconti (Italy), Jean Herman (France), Walt Sheldon (Japan). Narration by Burt Topper. Music, composed by Mike Curb, Mike Summers. No other credits. Reviewed in N.Y., May 8, '67. Running Time, **81 MINS.**

It must have been a temptation to Trans American (the "special" film subsidiary of American International) to call this one "Mondo Teeno," as it cuts back and forth from one country to another in its discovery that, aside from language barriers, kids the world over are faced with the same difficulties and usually come up with the same answers.

Although the printed credits provided for this compilation would have it appear that Norman Herman produced, directed and wrote the entire film, the screen credits include the names of four foreign directors, three of whom are well-known. Jorn ("To Love") Donner is responsible for the Scandinavian sequences; Eriprando ("Una Storia Milanese") Visconti (nephew of Luchino Visconti) did the Italian sequences; and Frenchman Jean ("Le Dimanche de la Vie") Herman handled the French insertions. What Herman has done is to take these, plus Japanese sequences filmed by Walt Sheldon and interspersed them with his own or other uncredited footage.

As the screen also reads "produced and directed in England, in association with James Garrett & Partners Ltd.," the actual country of origin is in some doubt. However, the resulting documentary does manage to catch much of the movement without purpose and action without meaning of the dozens of teenagers shown.

There's little originality in the scenes shown, including the now familiar Scandinavian permissive not to say eager attitudes towards pre-marital relations, the obsession of American youth with "pot" parties and LSD experimenting, the trend towards teenage prostitution of the Italian and Japanese.

The interest maintained by any particular sequence is usually dependent on the ability of the particular director involved. Visconti provides some of the most interesting footage, dealing with schoolgirl prostitution and the increasingly open action of Italian homosexuals but some of his visual imagery is

vitiated by the producer's allowing individuals to make lengthy speeches in Italian with neither subtitles nor running commentary by narrator Burt Topper, who comes in at the end for a brief, less than satisfactory wrap-up of the scene shown.

While there are attempts to "shock" occasionally, these are immediately apparent in their staginess. The film ends, however, with an on-screen birth as the tagline for an unwed mother sequence. The subject matter indicates it will need a strong sell but is highly exploitable for specialized audiences. The musical background is, as expected, rock 'n' roll.   *Robe.*

The War Wagon
(COLOR-PANAVISION)

Excellent oater. Powerful John Wayne-Kirk Douglas teaming. Lush exterior production.. Strong b.o.

Hollywood, May 17.
Universal Pictures release of a Batjac Production, produced by Marvin Schwartz. Stars John Wayne, Kirk Douglas. Directed by Burt Kennedy. Screenplay, Clair Huffaker, based on his novel, "Badman"; camera (Technicolor), William H. Clothier; editor, Harry Gerstad; music, Dimitri Tiomkin; title song lyric, Ned Washington; second unit director, Cliff Lyons; asst. director, Al Jennings. Reviewed at Directors Guild of America, L.A., May 16, '67. Running Time, **100 MINS.**

Taw Jackson	John Wayne
Lomax	Kirk Douglas
Levi Walking Bear	Howard Keel
Billy Hyatt	Robert Walker
Wes Catlin	Keenan Wynn
Pierce	Bruce Cabot
Lola	Joanna Barnes
Kate	Valora Noland
Hammond	Bruce Dern
Hoag	Gene Evans
Strike	Terry Wilson
Shack	Don Collier
Snyder	Sheb Wooley
Felicia	Ann McCrea
Calita	Emilio Fernandez
Bartender	Frank McGrath
Brown	Chuck Roberson
Early	Red Morgan
Hite	Hal Needham
Wild Horse	Marco Antonio
Rosita	Perla Walter

"The War Wagon," marking John Wayne's return to Universal under a multi-pix pact, is an entertaining, exciting western drama of revenge, laced with action and humor. Strong scripting, performances and direction are evident in this Marvin Schwartz production, enhanced by terrif exterior production values. Kirk Douglas also stars in an excellent performance. Gutsy b.o. in store in action situations.

The coming summer market has three ambitious oaters in tandem competition: "Wagon," Howard Hawks' "El Dorado" (a Paramount pic starring Wayne and Robert Mitchum), and Harold Hecht's "The Way West" (United Artists pic starring Douglas, Mitchum, also Richard Widmark). This coincidental spread of three pix, in which Wayne, Douglas and Mitchum are paired in two films, presents possible problems of audience confusion.

Adroit promotion on all pix could overcome an apparent surfeit, and stimulate a three-way want-to-see.

Clair Huffaker's novel, "Badman," has been adapted by the author into a very fine screenplay which is a neat blend of always-advancing plot, the right amount of good-natured grousing, and two-fisted action, all building to a strong climax and switcheroo fadeout. Burt Kennedy directed with an eye for panorama, as well as intimate, personal interaction.

Wayne, framed into prison by Bruce Cabot who then seized his land to make a fortune in gold, returns for revenge. He teams with Douglas, a hired gun used earlier by Cabot. Together they plan a heist of Cabot's armored gold wagon (hence, the title, although not the best one), and recruit Howard Keel, playing an Indian in a good change of pace, Robert Walker, Keenan Wynn, and an Indian chief, Marco Antonio.

Nicely intermixed in the planning of the heist are illuminating sidebars. For Douglas, the role offers him the chance to be an appealing, ambivalent rascal, whose extrovert antics set up a hilarious finale. Wayne's familiar screen personality again registers strongly, this time as an underdog seeking to recover stolen goods.

Walker is very believable as the booze-inclined young punk, who is a demolition expert when sober. Cabot, only occasionally in pix, does a firstrate job in the heavy role. Joanna Barnes, a very sexy gal, makes the most of her saloon dame part. Wynn again scores in an unsympathetic role, and his death sets up Walker's future with Valora Noland, Wynn's bartered bride. Rest of cast lends effective support.

William H. Clothier's superior Panavision - Technicolor lensing makes for a never-boring canvas, underscored by Dimitri Tiomkin's full-bodied, but wisely spare, music. Ed Ames sings the okay title tune, lyrics by Ned Washington. Harry Gerstad executed the trim editing to a well-paced 100 minutes. Second unit director Cliff Lyons rates a nod for his contribution. Other credits all topnotch. *Murf.*

Cool Hand Luke
(COLOR—PANAVISION)

Paul Newman as rebel-hero in a Dixie chain gang. Downbeat, but well-made. Very good b.o. prospects, although femmes may not dig it.

Hollywood, May 25.
Warner Bros. Pictures of Jalem Production, produced by Gordon Carroll. Stars Paul Newman; features George Kennedy, J. D. Cannon, Lou Antonio, Robert Drivas, Strother Martin, Jo Van Fleet. Directed by Stuart Rosenberg. Screenplay, Donn Pearce, Frank R. Pierson, based on the novel by Pearce; camera (Technicolor), Conrad Hall; editor, Sam O'Steen; music, Lalo Schifrin; asst. director, Hank Moonjean. Reviewed at Warner Bros. Studios, Burbank, May 24, '67. Running time, **126 MINS.**

Luke	Paul Newman
Dragline	George Kennedy
Society Red	J. D. Cannon
Koko	Lou Antonio
Loudmouth Steve	Robert Drivas
Captain	Strother Martin
Arletta	Jo Van Fleet
Carr	Clifton James
Boss Godfrey	Morgan Woodward
Boss Paul	Luke Askew
Rabbitt	Marc Cavell
Blind Dick	Robert Donner
Tattoo	Warren Finnerty
Babalugats	Dennis Hopper
Boss Kean	John McLiam
Gambler	Wayne Rogers
Tramp	Dean Stanton
Boss Higgins	Charles Tyner
Alibi	Ralph Waite
Dog Boy	Anthony Zerbe
Dynamite	Buck Kartalian
The Girl	Joy Harmon
Steepy	Jim Gammon
Fixer	Joe Don Baker
Sailor	Donn Pearce
Stupid Blondie	Norman Goodwins
Chief	Charles Hicks
John Sr.	John Pearce
John Jr.	Eddie Rosson
Patrolman	Rush Williams
Wickerman	James Jeter
Jabo	Robert Luster
Negro Boys	James Bradley Jr., Cyril "Chips" Robinson
Sheriff	Rance Howard

Paul Newman is "Cool Hand Luke," another in his series of "loner" roles. Technically well made, the Jalem (Gordon Carroll) production depicts the social structure of a Dixie chain gang. Versatile & competent cast maintains interest throughout rambling exposition to a downbeat climax. Newman pix usually do well, and this Warner Bros. release will be no exception in the general market.

Jalem is Jack Lemmon's indie company, veepee of which is Carroll, who has served as exec producer on two previous films but now is billed as producer. Stuart Rosenberg herein bows as a feature director after a long vidirecting career. "Luke," obviously supposed to be the South, but without specific location, was shot near Stockton, Calif., where the desired flat land, occasionally broken by gentle rolls, makes for an effective physical backdrop. Carter DeHaven Jr. was associate producer.

In this case, it is a chain-gang compound, ruled by some patronizing, sadistic guards, to which Newman will not conform. Donn Pearce adapted (with Frank R. Pierson) his novel into a screenplay which is as arresting in its parts as it is obtuse in getting to its point.

Theme is, at least, commercial: one man's rebellion against rules, imposed and perpetuated by flunkies. The unsatisfying aspect of such protests is that all the fury goes into the act of protest, after which the rebels succumb to, or are subdued by, the particu-

lar Establishment. Goals represent wasted effort.

Withal, Newman gives an excellent performance, assisted by a terrif supporting cast, including George Kennedy, outstanding as the unofficial leader of the cons who yields first place to Newman. Strother Martin's camp chief is chilling, a firstrate characterization. His goon squad likewise delivers strong performances: Morgan Woodward, Luke Askew, Robert Donner, John McLiam, Charles Tyner, Clifton James, the burly building overseer, is appropriately warmer.

Among the disparate prisoners, citified J. D. Cannon, hero-worshipper Lou Antonio, Richard Davalos and dog-lover Anthony Zerbe leave good impressions. The barracks life is conveyed with subtle force by entire cast, and enhanced by production values which include an apparent attention to realistic Technicolor hues, caught by Conrad Hall's sensitive Panavision camera. Cary O'Dell's art direction and Howard Shoup's adroit costuming help create the desired mood.

There are only two femmes in cast—Jo Van Fleet, who has a good cameo as Newman's mother, and Joy Harmon, who teases the cons while washing a car in a very sensual, non-speaking scene. Latter, directed and edited in superior fashion, practically leaps off the screen and, in its saturated sexual symbolism, will move male audiences as it does the drooling prisoners.

Rosenberg has made a good shift from tv to the big theatre screen, although there are a few too many tricky setups, inspired no doubt from habit. What is effective on a 21-inch tube is not necessarily so on a 21-foot screen; the human eye needs more time to adjust to changing perspective in a theatre, and, if that time is not provided, the artificiality of photography can often dispell a dramatic mood. Luckily, such instances are few herein.

Sam O'Steen edited to a leisurely 126 minutes, although the montage epilog seems unnecessary after Newman's death. The use of dissolves—long by today's standards—is gratifying, and only demonstrates that what is an old technique is not, per se, ineffective. Lalo Schifrin's score is spare, wisely so, but punchy, full-bodied and inventive. Interpolation of a few folk airs, sung by the cons, is a realistic touch. Other credits are firstrate. *Murf.*

Kopfstand, Madam
(Headstand, Madam)
(GERMAN)

Berlin May 23.
Cinema Service release of Dumont production. With Miriam Spoerri, Herbert Fleischmann, Heinz Bennent. Directed by Christian Rischert. Screenplay, Christian Geissler, Alfred Neven Dumont and Christian Rischert; camera, Fritz Schwennicke; music, Carlos Diernhammer, Manfred Niehaus, Otto Weiss; editor, C. Rischert. At Cinema Paris, West Berlin. Running Time, **104 MINS.**

Karin Hendrich	Miriam Spoerri
Robert, her husband	
	Herbert Fleischmann
Ulrich, her friend	Heinz Bennent
Another husband	Lutz Berks
Another wife	Helga Toelle

Christian Rischert is another of West Germany's young directorial talents. His first full-length feature, "Headstand, Madam," displays marked promise. What makes Rischert a standout among his colleagues is the adroit handling of the players. For a change, and refreshingly enough, Rischert is not one of those young domestic directors who want to be "progressive." His first opus displays a sympathetic modesty. One may term it an appealing combination of old and new cinema recipes. His low-budget pic only cost about $112,500, which means that about half a million people will have to see it to break even. This figure should be reached.

There is nothing new about the plot of "Madam." It is the form which counts. There are only three principal players: A hard working middle-aged engineer, his 30-year old wife, and a young bachelor to whom the wife of the engineer feels attracted. The overly busy husband has primarily had in mind to improve the standard of living of his family which includes a little daughter. But being so busy means that he had to neglect his wife. The latter feels lonesome and she does what eventually comes naturally: She seeks the company of another man and betrays her husband.

It is an everyday plot which is somewhat reminiscent of what Jean-Luc Godard was doing in "The Married Woman." But while the French pic was more of extravagant calibre, Rischert's film is more on the conservative side. This has its advantages and drawbacks: The plot has an old-hat flavor. But whatever is said and done in it comes very much like genuine life. The people in Rischert's film are real people and talk like real people.

What practically all the first pix of this country's "new wavers" have in common, this one shows excellent lensing. As per the acting, the three players, all still unknowns, owe much to Rischert. Their performances are praiseworthy and convincing all through. Miriam Spoerri enacts the neglected wife, a beautiful portrayal which makes one wish to see this actress soon again on the screen. Herbert Fleischmann plays her quiet husband and he too should be welcome back on the screen. Heinz Bennent, Miss Spoerri's illegal lover, rounds out this trio of talented thesps.

In all, this film marks a fine debut for Rischert. His future work deserves to be watched. *Hans.*

The Bobo
(COLOR)

Topflight sophisticated farce with general appeal and Peter Sellers to exploit in one of his cleverest portrayals; sex build-up possible for Britt Eklund (Mrs. Sellers) in standout character.

Hollywood, May 25.
Warner Bros. release of Jerry Gershwin-Elliott Kastner production. Stars Peter Sellers; features Britt Eklund, Rossano Brazzi, Adolfo Celi. Directed by Robert Parrish. Screenplay, David R.

Schwartz; based on his play, "The Bobo," and novel, "Olimpia," by Burt Cole; camera (Technicolor), Gerry Turpin; editor, John Jympson; music, Francis Lai; asst. director, Gus Agosti. Reviewed at Warner Bros. Studios, May 24, '67. Running time, 103 MINS.

Juan Bautista..............Peter Sellers
Olimpia Segura..........Britt Ekland
Carlos Matabosch.......Rossano Brazzi
Francisco Carbonell........Adolfo Celi
Trinity Martinez..........Hattie Jacques
Silvestre Flores..........Ferdy Mayne
Pepe Gamazo ....Kenneth Griffin
Eugenio Gomez........Alfredo Lettieri
Luis Castillo ....John Wells
Pompadour Major.......Marne Maitland

"The Bobo"—illuminatingly explained as coming from an old Gypsy proverb. "A Bobo is a Bobo"—is a clever, sophisticated and charming farce which sheds new light upon Peter Sellers as one of Britain's most adept comedians. Replete with the type of light touches and bits of business which delight the average audience, particularly the class trade, film's locale of Barcelona, where exteriors were lensed, affords colorful backdrop for an amusing fable imaginatively developed and skillfully turned out in every department.

Sellers is teamed here with a new screen sexpot, one Britt Eklund, who just happens to be Mrs. Sellers. She delivers surprisingly and should be in line for offers on her performance as the most beauteous, capricious, frivolous and difficult femme in all Barcelona.

As a golddigger to stop all golddigging she is at once endowed with childlike naivete and a witchiness that makes her the focal point of the entire male population. Which, of course, makes all the more beguiling the challenge offered Sellers—a matador who sings, or a singer who is a half-baked torero, take your pick—of possessing her within exactly three days by a stopwatch if he is to receive a week's enagement at the city's biggest teatro.

The Jerry Gershwin-Elliott Kastner production has been handsomely mounted and Robert Parrish's direction of the smooth-playing David R. Schwartz screenplay establishes a racy spirit, sparked by performances that come across. Based upon scripter's play, "The Bobo," and the Burt Cole novel, "Olimpia," basic idea, not altogether new, is fresh enough to lend certain enchantment & fits into today's type of pop etertainment.

Sellers undertakes a change of pace as the impoverished but self-confident bullfighter from the provinces who arrives in Barcelona determined to make his debut as a singer and meets stubborn opposition from impresario Adolfo Celi. In a gemlike performance, Celi finally acquiesces to Sellers' brash siege for a week's stand if latter will conquer Olimpia (Miss Eklund), to whom the essentials of life are fabulous apartments, expensive furs and a Maserati. Sellers plays with magnificent aplomb, adding another notch to his list of cinematic accomplishments.

Miss Eklund, clad enticingly in a series of mini-skirts which set off lush gams, score decisively as the femme who gets but never pays. Her costumes deserve a high credit mention for the designer,

---

not listed. Her Olimpia is a character deserving of a repeat in a possible sequel, as is Sellers' Juan Bautista, the freewheeling matador whom Olimpia ducked in a tub of blue dye guaranteed fast for two years when she discovered he used her to get himself a job.

Rossano Brazzi is in for a few scenes as a millionaire whose new Maserati Olimpia appropriates, and Kenneth Griffith as a lovesick youth whose apartment Olimpia takes for herself. Both roles are well handled. Hattie Jacques as femme's suspicious maid, Alfredo Lettieri a barkeep and Ferdy Mayne, who learns to his financial sorrow Olimpia is under-age after he has romanced her, contribute brief standout portrayals. A femme Flamenco dancer in an overly-long sequence also is outstanding.

Technical credits are superlative, including Gerry Turpin's Technicolor photography, John Jympson's deft editing, Elven Webb's art direction and music score by Francis Lai.

Whit.

Al Diablo con Este Cura
(To Hell With This Priest)
(ARGENTINE-COLOR)

Buenos Aires, May 23.
Brava production and release. Stars Luis Sandrini; features Ubaldo Martinez, Elizabeth Killian, Iris Marga, Virginia Lago, Ricardo Bauleo, Eduardo Rudy, Enzo Viena, Diana Ingro, Maria Luisa Robledo, Roberto Airaldi, Ricardo Castro Rios, Francisco de Paula, Alita Roman and Cristina del Valle. Directed by Carlos Rinaldi. Screenplay, Ulyses Petit de Murat; camera (Eastmancolor), Ignacio Souto; music, Tito Ribero. At Sarmiento, Buenos Aires. Running time, 97 MINS.

Priest ....Luis Sandrini
Bishop ....Ubaldo Martinez
Nun ....Elizabeth Killian
Mrs. Solares ....Iris Marga
Servant ....Virginia Lago
Financier ....Eduardo Rudy
Artemio .... Enzo Viena

Two years ago, "Odd Insect" launched a new successful stage in the long career of vet comedian Luis Sandrini, who attained film stardom back in 1933. Last year, Sandrini did another moneymaker, "Pepper," and currently he is hitting the jackpot for third time with this comedy on a down-to-earth priest, engaged in a socially-minded struggle against insensitive people living in a highclass neighborhood.

His is a rather verbal fight, forced by a script with more talk than action, but Sandrini enlivens it with his colorful personality and his ability combine humor and melodrama. Director Carlos Rinaldi took advantage of his star's appeal to keep undemanding audiences entertained in spite of the unimaginative story treatment and the oldfashioned clash between evil millionaires and kind have-nothings.

But this basically true conflict has been approached in more demagogic than dramatically convincing terms, such as that expressed by Pope Paul VI in his last encyclical, somewhat rescue it from its own faults. It has sympathy instead of insight.

Good cameos are provided by an all-star cast assembled to support Sandrini. Technical credits are okay. Production is lavishly

---

mounted by Brava's topper Celestino Anzuola. *Nubi.*

L'Homme Qui Trahit La Mafia
(The Man Who Betrayed the Mafia)
(FRENCH-COLOR)

Paris, May 30.
CFDC release of Filmatec, Mercurfin production. Stars Robert Hossein; features Claude Mann, Claudine Coster, Jose Luis De Villalonga, Carl Studer. Directed by Charles Gerard. Screenplay, Giles Duvernier, Lise Fayolle, Gerard; camera (Eastmancolor), Patrice Pouget; editor, Andre Delage. At Balzac, Paris. Running time, 90 MINS.

Bianchini ....Robert Hossein
Lambert ....Claude Mann
Valia..........Jose Luis De Villalonga
Wife ....Claudine Coster
Gangster ....Carl Studer
Chief ....Robert Manuel

The Mafia tag seems dragged in because this pic is primarily a familiar cops-and-robbers item that seems to lean heavily on Yank counterparts. It is brisk, but does not have the acceptable core of reality to give it much chance for foreign spots except for playoff on its subject, okay action and color.

A shady lawyer tries to back out of a gang he fronts for when he realizes that he cannot use American methods in France. But he is finally gotten by the gang as an intrepid French special investigator wipes out the gang single-handed with a sawed-off rifle.

Dope-running is the focal point of this piece which rings in hand-held cameras, much riding in fast autos and Yank gangsters and the inevitable triumphing of justice through violence. Playing is acceptable if the characters are stock ones. Direction tries to be sharp but appears mainly stilted. The hardboiled dialog just does not jell in French. Tag this as a programmer with some possible tele usage later on. *Mosk.*

Stranger In The House
(BRITISH-COLOR)

Lack of communication between youth and parents is hub of this smooth murder yarn with good marquee pull of James Mason, Geraldine Chaplin and Bobby Darin. Bold handling should insure results.

London, May 23.
Rank release of a De Grunwald Production. Stars James Mason, Geraldine Chaplin, Bobby Darin; features Paul Bertoya, Ian Ogilvy, Pippa Steel, Bryan Stanyon, Clive Morton, James Hayler, Lisa Daniely, Moira Lister, Megs Jenkins, Yootha Joyce. Directed and written by Pierra Rouve, from original story by Georges Simenon; camera (Eastmancolor), Ken Higgins; editor, Ernest Walter; music, Patrick John Scott; Ain't That So," written by Vic Briggs and Scott, and sung by Eric Burdon & The Animals. At Leicester Square Theatre, London. Running time, 104 MINS.

John Sawyer...........James Mason
Angela Sawyer........Geraldine Chaplin
Barney Teale.............Bobby Darin
Jo Christophorides........Paul Bertoya
Desmond Flower...........Ian Ogilvy
Peter Hawkins...........Brian Stanyon
Sue Phillips.............Pippa Steel
Colonel Flower...........Clive Morton
Harry Hawkins...........James Hayler
Mrs. Christophorides......Megs Jenkins
Diana ....Lisa Daniely
Girl at Shooting Range.....Yootha Joyce
Mrs. Flower..............Moira Lister
Inspector Colder...........Ivor Dean
Brenda ....Marjie Lawrence

This yarn once again pinpoints the complete misunderstanding and lack of communication between many of the flip generation and their middle-aged parents. It is sparked by the suspicious, coldly antagonistic attitude of Geraldine Chaplin to her middle-aged father (James Mason), who was once a brilliant barrister.

About 15 years earlier his flighty wife walked out on him and since then Mason has become a recluse, wallowing in memories, music and alcohol.

The idea is woven into a smooth, holding murder mystery, based on a story by Georges Simenon, scripted and directed by Pierre Rouve and produced with polish by Dimitri de Grunwald. Names of Mason, Miss Chaplin and Bobby Darin insure marquee lure and the pic should prove a staunch booking in most situations.

The plot is melodramatic but it has one very useful gimmick apart from literate writing and good performances. It is not set, in the usual film cliche fashion in the swinging circles of Mayfair, Soho and Chelsea, but in a small, good-class county town not far from Southampton. The locations are fresh and authentic.

Miss Chaplin plays one of a small, live-it-up discotheque and coffee-bar set that gets its kicks from way out expressionism, whoop-it-up parties and drugs. A predatory, slightly nutty and blandly sinister young American ship's steward (Bobby Darin) infiltrates the group and he's found murdered in the Mason home.

One of the gang accused is a Cypriot lad who is tolerated by others of the bunch because Miss Chaplin is sweet on him.

The case intrigues Mason and he agrees to defend the boy. Outcome is predictable but the Mason method of putting over the climax has an intriguing and unexpectedly angled touch which is imaginative and which, of course, brings him and his daughter together again.

Atmosphere of the wild, young set is put over in lively and often amusing fashion. And a party sequence contrasted with a stuffy party held by the adults adds to the flavor.

Scene in a Southampton strippery, a scrap between Darin and the Cypriot lad and, particularly, the first police court hearing on the charge of murder in which Mason ostensibly makes a bumbling ass of himself plus a sinister "joke" perpetrated by Darin, which indirectly leads to his death, are worthwhile highspots.

Mason's' firstrate performance holds the pic together and it is a fine study of disillusionment, self-disgust and sly humor. The role's well-written and well-observed by the thesp even to a convincing limp which must have inconvenienced him, but which somehow adds to the portrait.

Miss Chaplin ranges from mischief to pathos neatly enough and Darin is okay as the brash, superficially amusing but patently obvious heel.

Of the others in the Chaplin group, newcomer Ian Ogilvy scores as the spoiled, young man who turns out to be the heavy because of jealousy caused by impotence (a tack deduced rather over-glibly by Mason).

Pippa Steel chips in decoratively and Paul Bertoya makes a good impression as the pleasant, but somewhat prickly young Cypriot.

Marjie Lawrence, as a stripper; Megs Jenkins, as the accused lad's bewildered mother, Danvers Walker, Moira Lister, Yootha Joyce, Bryan Stanyon, James Hayter, Clive Mortan and Lisa Daniely are all in with lesser roles which stack up nicely around the central characters.

Smooth Eastmancolor lensing by Ken Higgins, Tony Woolard's stylish artwork and controlled editing by Ernest Walter provide technical polish with a film main fault of which is that it tends to jump from serious drama to "meller" with snatches of comedy brought into mix the moods rather mechanically.

Individually some of the characters are implausible but they brew into a strong acceptable concoction around Mason's sterling performance.

Eric Burdon and The Animals give with a catchy ditty called, "Ain't That So," a favorite expression of Darin when he's holding forth with his acolytes in the film. *Rich.*

Mini Weekend
(BRITISH)

Slight sex fantasy, set in seamier side of "Swinging London." Shapes up as a sub-supporter.

London, May 23.
Tigon Pictures- Global Productions release of a Tony Tenser production. Stars Anthony Trent, Veronica Lang, Anna Palk. Directed by Georges Robin. Screenplay by Robin and Tenser; camera, Stanley A. Long; editor, Roy Nevill; music, De Wolfe. Reviewed at Anglo Private Theatre, London. Running Time, 79 MINS.

Tom	Anthony Trent
Sandra	Liza Robers
Jenny	Veronica Lang
Mother	Connie Frazer
1st Dream Sequence	Vicky Hodge
Supermarket Girl	Jane MacIntosh
Cafe Sequence	Patti Bryant, Avril Gaynor
Tube Sequence	Rosalind Elliot, Kathleen Southern
Boutique Sequence	Maria Hauffer, Lucy Swain
Old Hag	Eve Aubrey
Girl in Cinema	Anna Palk

Screen scripters Tony Tenser and Georges Robin have saddled producer Tenser and director Robin with a Walter Mitty-like sex fantasy theme which rarely gets off the ground,

Stanley A. Long has made frequent use of roving and practically anonymous cameras in a tourist's eye safari through the "Wild West Jungle" of swinging London, but comes up with little new about King's Road, Chelsea, and the peeleries, back alleys and pubs of Soho.

Yarn concerns an East End, sex-starved youth who is obsessed with pinups and romantic dreams about chicks. He has only to gander a girl in the street or bus and he imagines himself rolling in the hay with her. On a weekend roam around the West End, he is snubbed whenever he tries to pick up a mini-skirted young dame, but gets his kicks out of daydreaming about sharing their nights. His real-life encounters and his dreams are somewhat untidily mixed up in the script.

Against this trite territory the film gives a chance for a number of young actresses to go through their paces. But few can rise above the leaden script with its adolescent innuendos. Worth noting are Anna Palk, who plays a ritzy young deb who brushes off the young hero in a cinema after giving him the come-on; Nina Dwyer, Vicky Hodge and Valarie Stanton. These suggest that given the right opportunity they could make a mark. But the likeliest bet is Veronica Lang, who makes big impact as the girl who in one of the lad's fantasies, gives him a perfect night of sexy pleasure. This is about the only scene that has any real emotion or imagination and Miss Lang handles it with distinct promise.

It also gives Anthony Trent his most solid opportunity, for though he gets plenty of screen exposure he can hardly expect to shine much with a role of such monumental silliness.

Camera, sound, music and other technical credits are okay. *Rich.*

The Gnome-Mobile
(COLOR-SONGS)

Okay Walt Disney comedy-fantasy about forest gnomes. Walter Brennan in dual role. Production, songs, acting all good. Geared for the juve market. Good b.o. for such.

Hollywood, May 27.
Buena Vista release of Walt Disney Production; coproducer, James Algar. Features Walter Brennan, Matthew Garber, Karen Dotrice. Directed by Robert Stevenson. Screenplay, Ellis Kadison, based on the novel, "The Gnomobile," by Upton Sinclair; camera (Technicolor), Edward Colman; editor, Norman Palmer; music, Buddy Baker; songs, Robert B. and Richard M. Sherman; second unit director, Arthur J. Vitarelli; asst. director, Paul Cameron. Reviewed at Academy Award Theatre, L. A., May 26, '67. Running Time, 84 MINS.

Mulrooney, and Knobby	Walter Brennan
Jasper	Tom Lowell
Rodney Winthrop	Matthew Garber
Elizabeth Winthrop	Karen Dotrice
Rufus	Ed Wynn
Ralph Yarby	Richard Deacon
Horatio Quaxton	Sean McClory
Dr. Conrad Ramsey	Jerome Cowan
Dr. Scroggins	Charles Lane
Male Nurse No. 1	Norman Grabowski
Gas Station Attendant	Gil Lamb
Katie Barrett	Maudie Prickett
Violet	Cami Sebring
Etta Pettibone	Ellen Corby
Charlie Pettibone	Frank Cady
Male Nurse No. 2	Hal Baylor
Paul	Karl Held
Airport Attendant	Charles Smith
Hotel Clerk	Byron Foulger
Airline Stewardess	Susan Flannery
Nell	Ernestine Barrier
Second Secretary	Dee Carroll
Chauffeur	William Fawcett
Twin Oaks Attendant	Robert S. Carson
Manson	Jack Davis
Night Watchman	John Cliff
Bellboy	Mickey Martin
Doorman	Mark Allen
Gas Station Mechanic	Alvy Moore
Uniformed Guard	Dale Van Sickel
Voice of Owl	Parley Baer
Voice of Raccoon	Jimmy Murphy
Voices of Bluejays	Jesslyn Fax, Dee Carroll

"The Gnome-Mobile" is an amusing, if somewhat uneven, Disney comedy-fantasy with songs, involving Walter Brennan in a dual role, as a lumber baron and, via outstanding special effects, an old forest gnome. Production values are strong, and a near-climactic car chase is one of the best. As plotted and played, pic is geared strictly for juves, with spotty interest for adults. James Algar co-produced the Buena Vista release which has generally good b.o. prospects. To be paired in first release is a 48-minute documentary featurette, "The Legend Of The Boy And The Eagle."

It will surprise many people that California social reformer Upton Sinclair wrote the novel, "The Gnomobile," from which Ellis Kadison has penned a good script.

Brennan, in what is called his first dual role, takes his grandchildren Matthew Garber and Karen Dotrice (from the "Mary Poppins" cast) on a motor trip through northern California's lush forests. En route, Miss Dotrice discovers the gnomes — Brennan, and Tom Lowell—and the three humans set out to relocate the gnomes to areas where others of their kind may exist. Sean McClory, a villainous side-show owner, kidnaps the gnomes for his troupe.

Richard Deacon, Brennan's biz aide, has him committed to a sanitarium for the assumed sanity lapse when talk of gnomes is brought up. Kids rescue Brennan, leading to the outstanding car chase sequence, after which script detours for its final 15 minutes to an overlong anti-climax in which Lowell is mated with Cami Sebring. The late Ed Wynn, in his last pic role, plays a goofy gnome in this sequence.

Director Robert Stevenson has gotten solid performances from the entire cast, which includes vets such as Ellen Corby, Jerome Cowan, Byron Foulger and Gil Lamb. McClory makes a very good hiss-able heavy, perfect in context. Moppets come across well, and Brennan handles both parts with warmth and assurance. Arthur J. Vitarelli's second unit direction is a big production asset. Forest lensing and other scenes were shot in Technicolor by Edward Colman, and edited by Norman Palmer to an okay 84 minutes.

Special effects are terrif in the matching of figures, also in the completely life-like automated animal figures which talk. Buddy Baker's score is adroit, and the songs, by the Sherman brothers, are good production numbers. Other credits are pro.

As a footnote, it is observed that, while certain ethnic stereotypes are practically forbidden on threat of civil rights protest (though Chinese figure in "Modern Millie"), usage of the Irish stereotype continues. Brennan-the-gnome is pure Pat-and-Mike. But then, the Irish, may not fret too much about such things or perhaps enjoy them. *Murf.*

Lightning Bolt
(Operazione Goldman)
(ITALO — SPANISH — TECHNI-COLOR — TECHNISCOPE)

Another dubbed Italo spy meller, with usual gimmicks; fair dualer for its market.

Woolner Bros. release of Seven Films production. Features Anthony Eisley, Wandisa Leigh, Diana Lorys, Ursula Parker, Folco Lulli. Directed by Anthony Dawson. Screenplay, P. C. Balcazar; music, Riz Ortolani. No other credits provided. Reviewed at Harris Theatre, N.Y., May 24, '67. Running time, 96 MINS.

(English Soundtrack)
Following Clint Eastwood, Burt Reynolds and others, former tv thesp Anthony Eisley has now attempted the Cinecitta route to stardom, with "Lighting Bolt," spy caper with American background, as his first effort. Actor's hair is now blonded and he is sans the moustache of his "Hawaiian Eye" days. Presence of Eisley—hardly a name on either side of the Atlantic—indicates that producers had American tv market clearly in view as pic's eventual and most profitable playoff. Actor makes a more than adequate hero, fighting and womanizing in the accepted post-Bond manner as a secret agent sent to Florida to locate saboteurs of U.S. space program.

Film's incredible plot premise has no fewer than nine U.S. moon rockets having been destroyed by explosion in mid-air shortly after take-off at Cape Kennedy. Eisley and his superior, female agent played by Wandisa Leigh, are sent to Miami following the disappearance of a key space scientist. Trail eventually leads to well-designed underground city run by power-mad Folco Lulli. Unfoldment is professional and rapid, if still standard and uninspired spy fare.

Through careful avoidance of daylight street scenes, etc., Miami is believably simulated, though scripter P. C. Balcazar seems under the impression that the city is right next door to Cape Kennedy. Chase sequences, rescue operations and final fiery climax come off excitedly if predictably, with Eisley being rescued at the end from the sea via helicopter a la "Thunderball."

Direction by Anthony Dawson (sometime nomiker for Antonio Margheriti) is adequate. Score by Riz Ortolani (spelled "Ritz" on the main titles!) is an unusual departure for him, since it abandons his usual lush style for the poignant trumpet sounds made popular by Ennio Morricone's music for the "Dollar" films. All other technical credits are okay. *Byro.*

Divorce American Style
(COLOR)

Firstrate comedy about U.S. marriage mores, including tragic overtones. Excellent in all departments. With Dick Van Dyke, Debbie Reynolds, Jason Robards, Jean Simmons, Van Johnson. Hot b.o. prospects.

Hollywood, June 2.

Columbia Pictures release, and Natl. General Production, of Tandem (Bud Yorkin-Norman Lear) film, produced by Lear. Stars Dick Van Dyke, Debbie Reynolds, Jason Robards, Jean Simmons, Van Johnson. Directed by Yorkin. Screenplay, Lear, based on a story by Robert Kaufman; camera (Technicolor), Conrad Hall; editor, Ferris Webster; music, David Grusin; production design, Edward Stephenson; asst. director, Rusty Meek. Reviewed at Academy Award Theatre, L.A., June 1, '67. Running Time, **109 MINS.**

Richard Harmon	Dick Van Dyke
Barbara Harmon	Debbie Reynolds
Nelson Downes	Jason Robards
Nancy Downes	Jean Simmons
Al Yearling	Van Johnson
Lionel Blandsforth	Joe Flynn
David Grieff	Shelley Berman
Dr. Zenwinn	Martin Gabel
Dede Murphy	Lee Grant
Pat Collins	Herself
Farley	Tom Bosley
Fern Blandsforth	Emmaline Henry
Larry Strickland	Dick Gautier
Mark Harmon	Tim Mathieson
Jonathan Harmon	Gary Goetzman
Eunice	Eileen Brennan
Jackie	Shelley Morrison
Celina	Bella Bruck
Judge	John J. Anthony

Comedy and satire, not feverish melodrama, are the best weapons with which to harpoon social mores. An outstanding example is "Divorce American Style," which pokes incisive, sometimes chilling, fun at U. S. marriage-divorce problems. Written, acted, directed and produced in top fashion, the Bud Yorkin-Newman Lear production for National General Productions shapes up as solid popular and class entertainment. Dick Van Dyke, Debbie Reynolds, Jason Robards, Jean Simmons and Van Johnson score in offbeat starring roles. Strong b.o. outlook for Columbia release in general situations.

Jet-set social pressures, combined with the inequities of some divorce laws, are the basis for an excellent Robert Kaufman story, scripted in versatile comedy form by producer Lear. Yorkin directed a competent cast in a fluid manner which socks over broad, sight-gag comedy, as well as sophisticated satire. Pic is a hefty argument for reinstating an Academy Award for comedy direction, discarded after Oscar's first year (1927-28).

Trade press showing less than a month prior to release—a practice usually reserved for nervous pix—is in this case inexplicable. For "Divorce" is by no means a chancy item. It is socko social commentary about American life today, delivered by American filmmakers with none of the putdowns evident when foreign talent takes up similar cudgels. This makes pic a nifty export item, since self-criticism is far more effective abroad than subsidized propaganda.

Amidst wow comedy situations, story depicts the break-up after 15 years of the Van Dyke-Miss Reynolds marriage, followed by the economic tragedies exemplified by Robards and Miss Simmons, caught in a vicious circle of alimony and remarriage problems. Johnson, a possible recruit to marital ranks to alleviate the woes, plays a used-car dealer, Southern California style, in an adept manner which should renew his film career.

Supporting cast includes Joe Flynn, hubby to Emmaline Henry, and a man who feels sincerely that paid-for sex, without emotion, is not cheating. Lee Grant, a swinger-for-hire, has a terrif bit to highlight Flynn's philosophy. Shelley Berman and Dick Gautier, two chummy lawyers, spotlight the occasional feeling by litigants that their personal problems are secondary to the games attorneys play.

Martin Gabel has a good recurring part as a marriage counselor, and real-life radio-tv marriage counselor John J. Anthony, in a switcheroo casting (incidentally his first film role), is an irate judge who awards an inequitable divorce settlement against Van Dyke. Hypnotist Pat Collins, re-creating her nitery turn, is worked logically into plot when the couple patch things up—only to start bickering again at fadeout.

Three highlight scenes among many will linger in memory. Opening title setup has a symphonic conductor leading the discord of suburbia from a hilltop podium. Yorkin's next scene, that of Van Dyke and Miss Reynolds silently steaming in their bedroom, is hilarious silent comedy, reminiscent of George Stevens' staging of a scene between Jean Arthur and Joel McCrea in "The More The Merrier," a 1943 Col pic.

Finally, in a yard sequence, Miss Reynolds, with escort Tom Bosley, witnesses a frantic scramble of three inter-divorced parents and their multi-conceived children. It starts out as a funny bit, but in seconds, without one iota of preaching, becomes a tragedy of confused kids, uncertain of where they will visit today. There is an emotional wallop that hits right in the gut: children are the literal debris of divorce. Offspring of wild animals mercifully forget abandonment after a time; human offspring never do.

Contributing to the overall excellence are Conrad Hall's responsive Technicolor cameras, David Grusin's spare, puncy and versatile score, Edward Stephenson's outstanding production design, Bob Mackie's eye-catching wardrobe, and the snappy editing by Ferris Webster to 109 minutes, perhaps a bit too much in view of a slight limp in pace in last half hour. There is one glaring blemish: not one, but two dialog mentions of a real-life femme apparel shop, followed by a shot of its storefront. What price tie-in?

National General, the divorced 20th-Fox National Theatres circuit, formed National General Productions as a packaging subsid, and "Divorce" actually was the first project although "The Quiller Memorandum" was the first to reach the market, however.

Between the two, it is obvious that NGC's desire to create more quality product, of a diversified nature, has been realized. Advertising billing has this pic as a Col. in association with NGP, presentation; on the screen, NGP alone presents, and pic's copyright rests in NGC and Tandem.
Murf.

Fort Utah
(TECHNISCOPE—COLOR)

Okay western programmer with names of John Ireland, Virginia Mayo and Scott Brady to draw.

Hollywood, May 19.

Paramount release of A. C. Lyles production. Stars John Ireland, Virginia Mayo, Scott Brady; features John Russell, Robert Strauss, James Craig, Richard Arlen, Jim Davis. Directed by Lesley Selander. Screenplay, Steve Fisher, Andrew Craddock; camera (Technicolor), Lothrop Worth; music, Jimmie Haskell; editor, John F. Schreyer; asst. director, Ralph Axness. Reviewed at Paramount Studios, May 18, '67. Running time, **84 MINS.**

Tom Horn	John Ireland
Linda Lee	Virginia Mayo
Dajin	Scott Brady
Eli Jonas	John Russell
Ben Stokes	Robert Strauss
Bo Greer	James Craig
Sam Tyler	Richard Arlen
Scarecrow	Jim Davis
Harris	Donald Barry
Britches	Harry Lauter
Cavalry Lieutenant	Read Morgan
Rafe	Reg Parton
Shirt	Eric Cody

"Fort Utah," latest A.C. Lyles production for his Paramount western program, is a loosely-constructed and over-talky range drama which does considerable rambling but nevertheless suffices for its particular market. Most of the requisite elements are there ...Indians, wagon train, badmen, fights, a slight tinge of romance and a hero who is supposed to be a gunman. Only more often than not he misses. But he gets his gal, wearing a fright wig.

Lyles as usual peoples his action with tried-and-true vets who may be depended upon to turn in good performances. John Ireland stars with Virginia Mayo and Scott Brady, backed by John Russell, Robert Strauss, James Craig, Richard Arlen and Jim Davis. Script by Steve Fisher and Andrew Craddock focuses on Ireland, a drifter who gets involved in Indians on the warpath, and Strauss, an Indian agent intent upon trying to round up his charges as well as capture a mystery badman, played by Brady.

Lesley Selander's direction is standard and Lyles gives production suitable mounting. Lothrop Worth's color photography makes the most of interesting scenic backgrounds.
Whit.

Rush to Judgment
(DOCUMENTARY)

Mark Lane's "brief for the defense" of Lee Harvey Oswald in visual form. Seemingly sober pic is effective propaganda for the Warren Report dissent.

Impact Films release of Judgment Films Production, produced by Mark Lane and Emile de Antonio; directed by Antonio. Commentary and narration by Lane, based on his book; camera, Robert Primes; editor, Daniel Drasin. Reviewed at Carnegie Hall Cinema, N.Y., June 2, '67. Running Time, **122 MINS.**

Lawyer Mark Lane, whose "brief for the defense" of Lee Harvey Oswald, whom the Warren Commission called the lone assassin of President Kennedy, was in the No. 1 non-fiction best-seller position for several months, has now converted his apparently exhaustively researched material into a film of the same name, "Rush to Judgment." For many it will seem a surprisingly convincing pic, opening up severe doubts anent the thoroughness and even integrity of the Commission members, and leaving the firm impression that this incredible murder has not yet been solved, as some think Lincoln's assassination was never fully explained.

While Warren Report defenders have often pictured Lane as a wild and impetuous figure, he has had the tact (or showmanship) to present himself on the screen as the very image of concern and restraint. "Rush to Judgment" is sober and unexcited, making its points with quiet and controlled definiteness, sans hysterics or frenzied accusations. Lane and collaborators Emile de Antonio (a familiar figure on the N.Y. film scene whose documentary on Senator Joseph McCarthy of a few years back, "Point of Order," operated on the same principle) have let their material present itself, utilizing wryness as their main weapon to sow seeds of doubt.

One wise decision on Lane's part was to concentrate almost exclusively on points which could be illustrated filmically. This, of course, also has its drawbacks. The famous bullet dispute, wherein it is alleged that the fragments removed from Governor Connally's wrist were too heavy to have emanated from the "retrieved" bullet, is mentioned only in passing. It is a key point, but since little photographic or filmic material is available, Lane cannot and does not dwell upon it. Likewise the suppressed autopsy photos (they are now in Government hands, but still not open to inspection) are not even mentioned; nor is the purely verbal discrepancy between earlier and later FBI autopsy reports.

Instead Lane and Antonio base their case on evidence that seems meaningful on the screen. Opening section (except for brief and morbidly-fascinating rehash of events of November 22-24, '63 from television stock footage) is a series of interviews with assassination witnesses in Dallas. Lane appears to demonstrate that the overwhelming preponderance of eyewitness testimony is that three shots came from the so-called "grassy knoll," rather than from the Texas School Book Depository building. Interviewees were stationed all around Deeley Plaza on the fateful day, yet many who were in the position to survey the whole scene, Lane is keen to point out, were not called as witnesses by the Warren Commission.

The familiar story that Oswald was not a crack shot is given by one of his old Marine buddies, and there is an intriguing disquisition by Lane on the fate of four key assassination photographs, one of which was apparently lost by the Commission, another cropped. It's heart-stopping to see again the well-known photo of an "Oswald-like" face amongst the crowd in front of the Depository building at the very moment of the assassination. It certainly looks like the socalled killer, and not like another Depository employee with whom the FBI attempted to identify the face.

Final section goes farthest afield, dwelling on the subsequent murder in Dallas of officer J. D. Tippitt and on Oswald-murderer Jack Ruby's intimate ties to the city's police. Although never stated in so many words, pic clearly implies that all the incidents of the three days may very well have stemmed from one great conspiratorial plot, and that the investigation should certainly be reopened. One particularly fascinating interview takes place with a man who claims that he rode in the same police car with Tippitt and Ruby several weeks before the assassination. He was never called by the Warren Commission. He seems a sane, rational man who is telling what he clearly believes to be a truth.

Although much background is carefully explicated, film still leaves impression that it is intended mainly for those who have some knowledge of the burgeoning controversy. A few of the witnesses in the opening "grassy knoll" section might have been removed in favor of an extended prolog. As it is, pic does become somewhat tiresome in this segment, as it lingers over yet another on-the-scener well after point has been made. But this is only real quibble generated by a fine piece of propaganda which its makers never pretend is objective.

Robert Primes maintains a steady camera, eschewing distracting zooms and other tricky set-ups of of the "new" documentarists. Daniel Drasin, who hasn't been heard from since he made the pioneer cinema-verite short "Sunday" six or seven years ago, had done yeoman editing service, mixing stock footage with the interviews in masterly fashion. Bill Mielche's sound is impeccable, especially impressive considering complete lack of studio conditions. Lane himself narrates in a professional manner.

Point of the film is neatly summed up by one interviewee, a track and signal supervisor for the Union Terminal Railroad: "The Warren Commission, I think, had to report in their book what they wanted the world to believe...It had to read like they wanted it to read. They had to prove that Oswald did it alone." *Byro.*

The Drums of Tabu
(U.S.-SPANISH-COLOR)

Made-in-Spain South Seas meller strictly for less discriminating situations.

Producers Releasing Organization (PRO) release of F.I.S.A.-Splendor Films coproduction, produced by Sidney Pink. Features James Philbrook, Seyna Sein, Frank Moran, Frank Fantasia, Beny Deus. Directed by Javier Seto. No other credits provided. Reviewed at Liberty, N.Y., June 1, '67. Running Time, 91 MINS.
Bill .... James Philbrook
Ananhita .... Seyna Sein

Yawata .... Frank Moran
Padre Lorenzo .... Frank Fantasia
Charlie .... Beny Deus
Bruno .... Chick Cicarelli
Comandante Duras ..... Carl Taberlani
Taaroa .... John Sutton
Ling .... Joseph Han

There's hardly anything to recommend in "The Drums of Tabu," a tedious South Seas adventure drama which is part of Sidney Pink's made-in-Spain package of quickies for tv via Westinghouse. Like the rest, pic is being allowed a brief theatrical release first via newly-formed Producers Releasing Organization. Story line drags in cliche after cliche, photography is grainy and production values are skimpy.

In terms of plot, character development and dialog, pic reminds of nothing less than an American meller of 1915. Especially reminiscent of early silents is the Yellow Peril heavy played by Frank Moran. When asked whether he is Malaysian, he shifts eyes and replies, "In part. Let's just say I'm Asiatic." Sessue Hayakawa used to specialize in such roles.

James Philbrook is the American sailor who has taken to drink on a small island in the Fiji Archipelago. He returns to womanizing when a native girl, Seyna Sein, appears. After establishing a romance, it develops that she has escaped from totally evil nightclub owner Moran, who regards her as his slave. When the "Asiatic" comes for her, she thinks she murders him, so the scene shifts to her native Samoan island wherein the loving couple takes refuge from the police. He.e it turns out that the girl is regarded as "tabu" and there are more complications before the final fiery climactic battle between Philbrook and Moran's forces.

Direction by Javier Seto is inept, and dialog is wooden. Philbrook is saving grace of pic, rendering a natural performance in he-man role. Miss Sein is insipid, as are Frank Fantasia and Benny Deus in lesser roles. Film is strictly for the program in least discriminating situations. *Byro.*

Sullivan's Empire
(COLOR)

Last of the '67 crop of Universal tv pilots expanded for theatrical release. Miscasting tells the tale of tube failure. Brazilian adventure yarn is okay dualer.

Universal release of Frank Price production. Features cast. Directed by Harvey Hart and Thomas Carr. Screenplay, Frank Chase; camera (color), Hal A. McAlpin; editor, Robert F. Shugrue; music, Lalo Schifrin; asst. director, Thomas J. Schmidt. Reviewed at New Amsterdam Theatre, N.Y., May 31, '67. Running Time, 85 MINS.
John Sullivan .... Martin Milner
Patrick Sullivan .... Linden Chiles
Kevin Sullivan .... Don Quine
Juan Clemente .... Clu Gulager
John Sullivan, Sr. .... Arch Johnson
Doris .... Karen Jensen
Amando .... Bernie Hamilton
Rudi Anduiar .... Lee Bergere
Inspector Huante .... Than Wynn
Miss Wingate .... Jeanette Nolan
Driver .... Miguel de Anda
Clerk .... Ken Renard
2d Girl .... Marianne Gordon

3rd Girl .... Eileen Wesson
Boy .... Mark Miranda
Carlos .... Ruben Moreno
Ramona .... Nadine Nardi
Chico .... Robert De Coy
Bartender .... Pepe Callahan
Pilot .... Peter Pascal

Seeing "Sullivan's Empire," one of the projects Universal originally filmed as a pilot for a television series and which has been refashioned for theatrical release, brings back Alfred Hitchcock's remark that his 1942 espionage pic "Saboteur" was a failure because its hero, Robert Cummings, had a "comedy face" totally out of kilter with film's serious thriller style. Problem with 'Empire' as a tv come-on at bottom lies in such vulgar fact: all three of the talented players cast as sons of an American mogul who has put together a personal domain in the Brazilian interior seem to have faces made for comic, or perhaps romantic, relief.

Arch Johnson is the proud, strong-willed senior Sullivan. It is a stock figure for tv, though perhaps not for films, and basically similar to the Sam Jaffe character in "Ben Casey" or the Dan O'Herlihy character in "The Long, Hot Summer." Viewer is expected to believe that although he abandoned his three sons when they were tots, they have retained enormous respect for him — "*because one thing you taught us was that our name is Sullivan*" — enough at least for them all to leave their lives in various parts of the world in order to seek their father out in the jungle after his plane is reported missing.

Frank Price production, entirely shot on the Hollywood lot, is stockshotsville, as directors Harvey Hart and Thomas Carr vainly try to simulate Brazilian environment. Plot has three brothers fighting Izo head-hunting Indians, handling attacking wild beasts and otherwise displaying expertise with firearms without indicating anything in their backgrounds which would equip them for such tasks. In effort to find father, they become involved in an embezzlement which has as conspirators a rich partner of the father and a guerilla revolutionist. Needless to say, film is scandalously naive on the motives of such Castroite types.

Martin Milner, seemingly intended as star of the series, is most possessing of a "comedy face," making him unconvincing as the racing-car driver brother. Baby-faced Don Quine is the surfer in the brother team, and Linden Chiles, who ironically has the facial makings of a hero, provides most of the comedy relief as the gambler brother. Clu Gulager puts in best job as the hypocritical Fidel-type, and bozomy Karen Jensen is in for a brief romantic stint. The technicians do their best under the close-up, tv-style circumstances. *Byro.*

You Only Live Twice
(PANAVISION—COLOR)

Back to the bona fide Bond. Deadly cool Sean Connery defies all probabilities for a probable boxoffice mop-up.

United Artists release of Eon (Albert R. Broccoli-Harry Saltzman) Production. Stars Sean Connery. Directed by Lewis Gilbert. Screenplay, Roald Dahl, based on a novel by Ian Fleming; camera (Technicolor), Freddie Young; editor, Thelma Connell; music, John Barry; production design, Ken Adam; asst. director, William P. Cartlidge. Reviewed at DeMille Theatre, N.Y., June 12, '67. Running Time, 117 MINS.
James Bond .... Sean Connery
Aki .... Akiko Wakabayashi
Tiger Tanaka .... Tetsuro Tamba
Kissy Suzuki .... Mie Hama
Osato .... Teru Shimada
Helga Brandt .... Karin Dor
Miss Moneypenny .... Lois Maxwell
"Q" .... Desmond Llewelyn
Henderson .... Charles Gray
Chinese girl .... Tsai Chin
"M" .... Bernard Lee
Blofeld .... Donald Pleasence

First the prediction: big playoff. Then the reservation: can it go on indefinitely? This, the fifth Albert R. Broccoli-Harry Saltzman James Bond film, is bigger and more expensive ($9,500,000) than previous entries in the Ian Fleming-sired sexy superspy cycle. As entertainment it compares favorably in quality and is replete with as many fights, gadgets, and beauties as its predecessors, "Dr. No," "From Russia With Love," "Goldfinger," and "Thunderball." It should live twice in first playoff and reissue.

United Artists Bond cycle has seen increasing b.o. success with each succeeding film. Whether "You Only Live Twice" will surpass "Thunderball's" domestic rental take of $26,000,000 is perhaps open to question, since the market has lately been flooded with the likes of Matt Helm and Derek Flint. Has the spy by now come in from the gold? Fortunately for United Artists, such public desertion seems unlikely for some time to come and very, very big biz can be anticipated for "You Only Live Twice."

Hint of trouble in keeping pace with Bond's imitators, many of whom have plundered unfilmed Ian Fleming stories for gimmicks, is screen credit for "additional story material by Harold Jack Bloom." Seams do not show in Roald Dahl's slick screenplay, however, and all seems authentic Fleming. (Dahl, w.k. as a writer of macabre short stories, replace series-scripter Richard Maibaum without any loss in awful puns.)

Film begins with a prolog in which a U.S. astronaut's spacewalk is interrupted by another spacecraft that, crocodile-style, opens its jaws and swallows the capsule. U.S. government is peeved at what it assumes to be a Russian attempt to foil space exploration, and 007 is assigned by helpful British intelligence to locate the missing rocket before full-scale war breaks out between the two nuclear powers.

Film's title refers to Bond's "murder," which precedes the credits. Ensconced with the first in a long line of Japanese beauties ("I'll be sorry to go," he whispers in her well-nibbled ear), he is abruptly gunned down and pronounced dead in her bed by officials ("*Well, at least he died on the job; he'd have wanted it this way"*). Needless to say, death and resultant burial at sea are merely a cover to give him a wider latitude in finding the enemy powers bent on destroying the world (what less?).

As usual, 007's antagonists are implausibly unwilling to kill him by simple, direct methods. Two dozen Japanese henchmen assault him with waterfront weaponry, a redheaded villainess (who gets hers eventually via piranha fish) bolts him down in a plane from which she parachutes prior to its crash on the ground, four helicopters chase him in an airborne version of "Goldfinger's" Aston-Martin, not to mention endless karate fights, gun battles, and an attempted stabbing by an aspiring samurai.

Bond remains invincible through the holocaust, never losing his obligatory cool in the face of villain or voluptuary. His well-documented reputation as bon vivant is here extended to his having placed first in Oriental languages at Cambridge and knowing that saki should correctly be served at 98.4 degrees Fahrenheit. Audiences obviously relish these Superman qualities, the stuff on which mass daydreams and UA b.o. millions are made.

Sean Connery plays 007 with his usual finesse, though he does look a bit older and more tired (as who wouldn't be?). Interesting sideline to UA's ad campaign—"Sean Connery Is James Bond"—is fact that "You Only Live Twice" is last in five-pic pact between Connery and Eon Productions. Presumably next Bond entry plugged at end of "Twice," namely "On Her Majesty's Secret Service," will have to go it without Connery unless he can be wooed back to the mint.

Rest of cast is strictly secondary, although Akiko Wakabayashi and Tetsuro Tamba register well as Bond's Japanese cohorts. Donald Pleasance makes a suitably menacing German heavy who appears in film's final scenes. Lois Maxwell and Bernard Lee briefly repeat from earlier pix as Miss Monneypenny and "M," respectively.

Technical credits are on a par with previous 007 pix, a real tribute to producers Broccoli and Saltzman since most of the current staff is new to the Bond films. Lewis ("Alfie") Gilbert was hired to direct, with results that do not perceptibly differ from those previously obtained by directors Terence Young and Guy Hamilton. Peter Hunt, whose editing of the other Fleming adaptations helped establish a faster cutting style in commercial films, has moved up to second-unit director, suggesting that he may follow fellow Britisher Anthony Harvey's move from editor to director (of "Dutchman"). Cameraman Ted Moore is also absent from the Bond crew for the first time.

Freddie Young's color photography is okay, but not up to his own high standards as revealed in "Lawrence of Arabia" and "Doctor Zhivago." As with earlier Bonds, color sometimes seems almost greasy. Thelma Connell's editing is snappy and makes running time pass quickly. Production designer Ken Adam again scores with extravagant but authentic looking sets, as opposed to the Miami

Beach baroque hideaways of villians in the Flint and Helm films.

John Barry's score is more subdued and romantic than his past 007 music, and a title song (with lyrics by Leslie Bricusse) warbled under the credits of Nancy Sinatra could catch on, especially given UA's typical intensive promotional assist.

One minor quibble: in so expensive a film containing such elaborate special effects work (by John Stears), process photography should be comparably sophisticated. At one point Connery and Miss Wakabayashi are driving in a sportscar pursued by villains, and several closeups show them sharply enveloped in a wiggly purple haze that a great number of today's knowing filmgoers will recognize as studio fakery.

Withal, this is a smooth piece of entertainment that wisely doesn't overdo the elbow-nudging, winking self-parody of so many of its imitators. The mass audience has to go for it. *Beau.*

Klimaks
(Climax)
(NORWAY)

Melbourne, June 6.
Norsk production (Egil Monn-Iversen) and release. Directed by Rolf Clemens. Screenplay, Sten-Rune Sterner; camera, Knut Gloersen; music, Arne Nordheim; editor, Clemens. Stars Per Jansen, Rut Tellefsen and Lars Nordrum. Reviewed at Melbourne Film Fest. Running Time, 87 MINS.

This film centers around 18-year-old Kirster, an only son, described by his father as an amateur psychoanalyst, who has an alternating attraction and revulsion towards his father's mistress.

Apparently she committed suicide, but later it would seem to have been murder not perhaps on the part of the father, as at first intimated.

This, basically, seems to be the plot unfolded by director Rolf Clemens, although relying mainly on English sub-titles. Hence, it perhaps would be possible to get another impression of the happenings—sans such titles.

It seems all too heavily dramatized. Although the film mostly holds one's attention, and is intriguingly mysterious, a good deal more outright suspense could have been created.

The film is well photographed and directed and both Per Jansen as Kirster and Rut Tellesfsen as Nina turn in firstrate performances.

Even for the Film Festival, the Australian Censor has made certain cuts in the film *Mosk.*

To Sir, With Love
(BRITISH-COLOR-SONGS)

Long-delayed release. Negro teacher of white class in London. If smartly showcased should build.

Hollywood, June 9.
Columbia Pictures release of James Clavell production, adapted, and directed by Clavell; executive producer, John R. Sloan. Stars Sidney Poitier. Based on the novel by E. R. Braithwaite; camera (Technicolor), Paul Beeson; editor, Peter Thornton; music, Ron Grainer; songs, Don Black, Marc London, Toni Wine,

Carole Bayer, Ben Raleigh, Charles Albertine; asst. director, Ted Sturgis. Reviewed at Directors Guild of America, L.A., June 8, '67. Running Time, 104 MINS.

Thackeray	Sidney Poitier
Denham	Christian Roberts
Pamela Dare	Judy Geeson
Gillian	Suzy Kendall
Barbara Pegg	Lulu (Marie Lawrie)
Mrs. Evans	Faith Brook
Potter	Christopher Chittell
Weston	Geoffrey Bayldon
Clinty	Patricia Routledge
Moira Jackson	Adrienne Posta
Florian	Edward Burnham
Mrs. Joseph	Rita Webb
Miss Phillips	Fiona Duncan

"To Sir, With Love" is a well-made, sometimes poignant, drama about a Negro teacher, working in a London slum, who transforms an unruly class into a group of youngsters better prepared for adult life. Sidney Poitier stars in an excellent performance. James Clavell adapted, produced and directed. Columbia release will have an appeal to the young market, where maximum b.o. returns will be realized via careful showcasing in specialty houses before general release.

Film is the second example, in as many months, of a bizarre Columbia screening policy. Many exhibs saw pic a year ago; production notes are dated six months back; practically all consumer mags already have published reviews; finally, just prior to openings, tradepaper screenings are held. Policy is usually a manifestation of fear on the part of a distributor who either has a dud on his hands, or doesn't know what to do with a good film. "Sir," which is a good film, thus goes to market under the disadvantages of held-back trade evaluation.

John R. Sloan was exec producer for Clavell's adaptation of the 1959 E. R. Braithwate novel, in which Poitier is presented as a native of British Guiana who has knocked about in the U.S.; this justifies for plot purposes his accent.

Although Warners' new "Up The Down Staircase" has a ghetto school theme (in the U.S.), a far more interesting comparison is to Metro's "The Blackboard Jungle." In just 12 years, Poitier, as an actor, has gone from a role of slum trouble-maker, in conflict with his teacher, Glenn Ford, to the role of the teacher himself. And although in "Sir," there is a very dramatic, but brief, plot point involving racial prejudice, Poitier's character is simply that of a teacher who, incidentally, is Negro.

Poitier scores strongly as the teacher who, after gauging the rebellious mood of his class, scraps the formal agenda and institutes what he rightly calls "survival training." Casting of students relies on relative newcomers — Christian Roberts, very good as the natural class leader, Judy Geeson, a looker who gets a crush on teacher, Christopher Chittell, another reformed punk, and Lulu (stage name for Marie Lawrie), an engaging personality who shows substantial acting ability.

Among the other teachers, Suzy Kendall is quite good as the bespectacled, shy gal; Faith Brook registers very well as down-to-earth type; Geoffrey Bayldon is convincing as the cynical pedant,

and Edward Burnham as the deliberately remote principal. Rita Webb socks home a bit as a slum market clerk. Rest of cast, particularly the students, is competent.

Clavell, who got his first chance in pix from Robert L. Lippert and has not forgotten it, has penned a tight screenplay, in the hip-flip style which will grab young audiences. His direction is strong, although final cut of pic suffers from the use of direct cuts: the time-compression is never too clear, and the effect — that is, the transformation of Poitier's class— is too sudden. Peter Thornton executed the editing to 104 minutes.

George White is credited with a montage sequence, in which Poitier's class takes a museum trip. Scene is a good break from the drab classroom atmosphere, and offers good sight-gag comedy relief in still shots of gawking kids and works of art. End title presents action stills of featured players for identification—a good idea for audiences as well as casting personnel.

Paul Beeson's Technicolor lensing is excellent in capturing both human emotion and the pervading slum atmosphere. Ron Grainer's score has the mod sound. Four songs are billed — a dreary, wailing title bleat, sung by Lulu & arranged by Mike Leander, which is heard not once, but three times for numbing effect. Don Black wrote the awkward lyrics, to Marc London's melody.

Only other tune to get any prominence is "It's Getting Harder All The Time," which is a very good song, lyricized by Ben Raleigh from a Charles Albertine melody. A group called The Mindbenders is heard and seen. Other technical credits, from Pinewood Studios, are good. *Murf.*

Hells Angels On Wheels
(COLOR)

Still another turn of the motorcycle, with usual ingredients wasted on excellent color photography. Drive-in and double bill fodder.

U.S. Films release of Fanfare Film (Joe Solomon) Production. Features Adam Roarke, Jack Nicholson, Sabrina Scharf. Directed by Richard Rush. Screenplay, R. Wright Campbell; camera (Eastman Color), Leslie Kovacs; editor, William Martin; sound, LeRoy Robbins; music, Stu Phillips; song, "Study In Motion No. 1," by Chuck Sedacca, Stu Phillips; sung by The Poor; asst. directors, Willard Kirkham, Bruce Satterlee. Reviewed in New York, June 2, '67. Running Time, 95 MINS.

Buddy	Adam Roarke
Poet	Jack Nicholson
Shill	Sabina Scharf
Abigale	Jana Taylor
Jock	John Garwood
Bull	Richard Anders
Pearl	Mimi Machu
Gypsy	James Oliver
Bingham	Jack Starrett
Moley	Gary Littlejohn
Justice of Peace	Bruno Vesota
Artist	Robert Kelljan
Lori	Kathryn Harrow

The most depressing thing about this latest adventure of the Rover Boys is that such first-rate color camerawork was thrown away on such trivia. Either cameraman Leslie Kovacs is a still undiscovered film talent or he's careless about where he points his lens. Beyond the cinematography, which even manages to give over-photographed California highways a new and interesting look, there's little to recommend in this tedious treatment of what makes motorcyclists tick.

Director Richard Rush, no stranger to the action scene ("Thunder Alley"), knows enough to keep his cast moving. Producer Joe Solomon evidently has tossed this conglomeration of stock story and sick situations together to grab a bit of the action market stirred up by AIP's "Devil's Angels," but the script provided by R. Wright Campbell consists of the now-expected attributes of the cycling syndrome—much footage on cycle riding, mass raids on service stations and small towns, the conflict with police and town people, and through it all, fights, sex and fights. The abrupt ending, on an illogical note of violence, gives the impression that the script and budget both gave up at the same time.

The sketchy storyline is padded out (too much so) by the incessant riding of the cycles over California and Nevada highways. There's a credit nod to the Hells Angels of Oakland, Richmond, Daly City and the Nomads of Sacramento but they're evidently only used in the long road shots as the number of actors viewed on the highways. Hells Angels' president Sonny Barger is also credited as technical advisor, very likely his only contribution to the film, which has some insertions of irrelevant material, such as a hill-climbing race, which could be stock footage.

Acting by the entire cast is only average with Jack Nicholson's contribution as the non-conformist made up mostly of variations on a grin. As is now expected of these cycling pix, the girls are too clean and too pretty. One new gimmick is the suggestion of perversion among both the cyclists and their girls. Stu Phillips' score is pleasant, often melodious but never intrusive. Other technical credits are routine. *Robe.*

Toutes Folles De Lui
(All Mad About Him)
(FRENCH-COLOR)

Paris, June 13.
Prodis release of Sud Pacifique Films production. Stars Robert Hirsch; features Sophie Desmarets, Maria Latour, Jean-Pierre Marielle, Sylvie Breal, Julien Guiomar. Directed by Norbert Carbonnaux. Screenplay, Didier Goulard, Maurice Fabre, Michel Audiard, Carbonnaux; camera (Eastmancolor), Edmond Sechan; editor, Monique Kirsnaoff. At Mercury, Paris. Running Time, 80 MINS.
Mathieu .... Robert Hirsch
Lili .... Maria Latour
Melina .... Sylvie Breal
Helene .... Sophie Desmarets
Father .... Julian Guiomar

Comedie Francaise actor Robert Hirsch clicked in the Israeli-French sleeper "Impossible on Saturday" in which he essayed 13 roles. Since then multiple part-type pix have been tried for him. Now he is a prissy little man who inherits an international call girl empire and only runs amuck when he is fed American pep pills.

But Hirsch is not a true comic actor. He can play a nervous little man but creates no comedic aura about him and pic is too obvious

and heavy-handedly suggestive to give the comic drive it needs. So it has some lowdown suggestiveness, unclad girls, color and scope which may slant it for some playoff. But arty legs are stunted.

Hirsch practices yoga and is engaged to a snobbish girl whose father is really a retired bagnio operator. His inheritance has him taking for granted the cover of his lupanars such as cleaning stores, private ambulances, etc. It leads to his narrow escapes from his own workers till the pills have him becoming a great lover and cynically giving in to the business.

Sans the needed ingenuity to keep this bubbling along, it lapses into forced slangy lingo, leering comedics and listless sex shenanigans. But it has some exploitation pegs which will have to be hit hard for chances for this beyond this country. *Mosk.*

Vali
(DOCUMENTARY—COLOR)

Okay study of recluse painter Vali Myers for specialty spots.

FilmMakers' Distribution Centre release of a Sheldon Rochlin production. Produced by Rochlin, in collaboration with George Plimpton and Mark Lawrence. Directed by Rochlin. Commentary written and narrated by Vali Myers and Rudi Rappold; camera (color), Rochlin; editors, Rochlin and Diane Rochlin; sound, Mark Dichter. Reviewed at Bleecker St. Cinema, N. Y., May 31, '67. Running Time, 65 MINS.

Although promoted as an "underground" feature, this short study of Australian-born painter Vali Myers is nothing more than a cinema-verite documentary in a well-established mode. While apparently well-known to a coterie of library and art intellectuals, Vali has always refused to sell her paintings, which naturally precludes knowledge of her by the general public. This, plus documentary form, pegs "Vali" for specialty spots, at best.

Pic was financed for $30,000 by Paris Review editor George Plimpton, who gave Vali her first publicity via articles in his mag. At that time, 1958, she was described as "at once the symbol and plaything of the . . . milieu that haunted . . . the Left Bank." After an abortive suicide attempt, she married Rudi Rappolid, an Austrian, and they now live in a primitive existence in Italy, in a hut near Positano where they raise animals and rarely see neighbors.

To judge from pic, Vali is a strange creature indeed, a believer in witchcraft who dresses in bizarre clothes and is entirely free in her speech and way of life. Film gives a reasonable compendium of her activities—preparing a meal, putting on makeup, tattooing a friend, writing and drawing in the "blackbook" where she collects her thoughts, dancing for a small gathering of friends in Naples, etc.

Director Sheldon Rochlin has done a capable if academic job employing Vali's voice-over thoughts against silent images at times, at others using direct synch. Pic would be helped by title card or brief narration giving artist's background. As often happens with these bottom-budget proj-

ects, the sound, credited to Mark Dichter, is incomprehensible half the time. Rochlin and his wife Diane have edited to a brisk 65 minutes. There is no original music. *Byro.*

El Dorado
(COLOR)

Topnotch oater drama, with comedy, starring John Wayne and Robert Mitchum. Excellent Howard Hawks production. Hot b.o. and sturdy subrun potential.

Hollywood, June 6.
Paramount Pictures release, presented, produced and directed by Howard Hawks. Stars John Wayne, Robert Mitchum. Screenplay, Leigh Brackett, based on the novel, "The Stars In Their Courses," by Harry Brown; camera (Technicolor), Harold Rosson; editor, John Woodcock; music, Nelson Riddle; song, Riddle, John Gabriel; asst. director, Andrew J. Durkus. Reviewed at Paramount Studios, L.A., June 5, '67. Running Time, 126 MINS.
Cole Thornton .... John Wayne
J. B. Harrah .... Robert Mitchum
Mississippi .... James Caan
Maudie .... Charlene Holt
Doc Miller .... Paul Fix
Bull Thomas .... Arthur Hunnicutt
Joey MacDonald ...... Michele Carey
Kevin MacDonald ...... R. G. Armstrong
Bart Jason .... Edward Asner
Nelse McLeod .... Christopher George
Maria .. .. Marina Ghane
Pedro .... John Gabriel
Saul MacDonald ...... Robert Rothwell
Milt .... Robert Donner
Matt MacDonald .... Adam Roarke
Jared's Wife .... Victoria George
Jason's Foreman .... Jim Davis
Mrs. Saul MacDonald .... Anne Newman
Mrs. Matt MacDonald .. Diane Strom
Luke MacDonald ...... Johnny Crawford
Gunsmith .... Olaf Wieghorst
Dr. Donovan ... . Anthony Rogers

Technical and artistic screen fads come and go, but nothing replaces a good story, well told. And Howard Hawks still knows how to tell a good story. "El Dorado" stars John Wayne and Robert Mitchum in an excellent oater drama, laced with adroit comedy and action relief, and set off by strong casting, superior direction and solid production. The Paramount release will strike it rich at the firstrun b.o., and stout coin looms later from its inherent subrun potential.

Completed a year ago, shown to exhibs six months ago, but in another example of inexplicable distrib "thinking," not shown to tradepress until days before release, film is based on a Harry Brown novel, "The Stars In Their Courses." Leigh Brackett, a woman, has adapted it into a very good screenplay, male-oriented but with an appeal to all audiences. Arizona locations were used for 36 shooting days, followed by nine weeks of interior lensing at Par's Hollywood studio. Paul Helmick was Hawks' associate producer.

Hawks, in a translation of an interview published years ago in France, observed that his oaters were, basically, a love story between two men. The love he was referring to is the fraternal bond between longtime associates and partners which transcends passing incidents. Pattern is followed here, with Wayne a hired gun, dissuaded from working for landgrabber Edward Asner by Mitchum, a reformed gunslinger now a sharplooking, disciplined sheriff.

Story unfolds in about five logical segments. First one, about 25

minutes, establishes the Wayne-Mitchum relationship, and seeds the later conflict between Asner and R. G. Armstrong's large family, whose control of water rights blocks Asner's plans. Second portion, occurring after a time jump of six months, intros Christopher George (in his pre-"Rat Patrol" tv days), as Asner's next choice as killer, and also James Caan, top-featured as a light-hearted drifter who latches on to Wayne and provides some welcome comic interludes.

Next comes Mitchum's rehabilitation, by Wayne, Caan and deputy Arthur Hunnicutt, from an extended bender which has cost him the respect of the town. Asner's arrest then sets the stage for the final shoot-out with George and his crew, and the amusing fadeout of the two stars, both semi-crippled for the time being.

All performances are adept, particularly those of Wayne, Mitchum (especially good), Hunnicutt, and—among the younger thesps—Caan and Michele Carey, latter one of Armstrong's daughters. Miss Carey's part is a showcase for her talents. Charlene Holt, the saloon owner and longtime friend of both Wayne and Mitchum, is restrained by a reactive part, which she delivers in okay, throaty style. George, well made up (by Wally Westmore) with facial scar, projects neatly the uneasy camaraderie between hired guns.

Atop his sure handling of players, Hawks has eschewed the very wide (anamorphic) screen ratio. Yet, even in the latterday standard 1.85:1 ratio used, it becomes apparent that his framing essentially is based on the old 4:3 screen ratio. He appears to be saying that the original frame size still can be used effectively to tell a story, in both its intimate and panoramic aspects. What's more, he's right. Too many other films rely on the razzle-dazzle of screen acreage to mask a far-weaker story. The faddish zoom shot, overworked by newer directors, is used by Hawks in the context of a reaction to a blow on the chin, a completely valid gambit which makes artistic use of the dizzying sensation always inherent in that artificial technique.

Harold Rosson's facile Technicolor camera work is excellent. John Woodcock executed the editing to 126 minutes, a bit too much in view of a relaxed final two reels but not a substantial defect. Nelson Riddle's score is an asset while the title song, sung over titles by George Alexander and The Mellowmen, is an okay production element. Artist Olaf Wieghorst did the attractive paintings used in the eye-catching main title. Other technical credits are topnotch.

Pic has been held back for the big summer biz, where it will be competing with two other major oater projects—Universal's "The War Wagon" (with Wayne and Kirk Douglas), and United Artists' "The Way West" (with Mitchum and Douglas). The two Waynes will snag top b.o. *Murf.*

Red-Dragon
(A-009 Missione Hong Kong)
(ITALO-GERMAN-AMERICAN — TECHNICOLOR - TECHNISCOPE)

Spy caper rises above expectations, thanks to excellent thesping by Stewart Granger and Rosanna Schiaffino. Still, at best a classy dualer in Stateside market.

Woolner Bros. release and production. Features Stewart Granger, Rosanna Schiaffino, Horst Frank, Suzanne Roquette. Directed by Ernest Hofbauer. Music, Riz Ortolani. No other credits provided. Reviewed at Harris Theatre, N.Y., May 24, '67. Running time, 98 MINS.

(English Soundtrack)

Although at bottom just another entry in the recent European spy film sweepstakes, this Italian-German-American coproduction, apparently partially-financed by the Hollywood-based Woolner Brothers, shapes up as a better-than-average actioner for the U.S. market, thanks largely to the accomplished professionalism of Stewart Granger and Rosanna Schiaffino, plus some tongue-in-cheek direction by Ernest Hofbauer. Well-mounted film features extensive Hong Kong locations, and probably served adequately as a top feature in European situations, what with names coupled with current spymania. Pic shapes best here as a classy dualer, with enough pizazz to shore up a weak top-of-the-biller.

Plot has Granger, an FBI agent, sent to the Chinese port city to locate a clandestine supplier of smuggled electrical parts to the Reds. Miss Schiaffino, another agent, works as a teletype operator for the gang suspected by the FBI to be involved in the smuggling operation. Problem is to find the "Mr. Big" behind it all, and here film falls down as the solution is predictable.

Earlier sections of the pic are often amusing, however, with much facetious give-and-take by Granger and Miss Schiaffino. At one point, Granger is saved by the lady via her sharp karate blow to his assailant, and his look of surprise at this female's feat brings comedy to an otherwise standard action set-up. Pic indicates that Granger, who is returning to Hollywood product with Par's "The Last Safari," has lost none of his finesse during his recent European foray.

Hofbauer moves the pic smartly, bringing in colorful locations, adequate fisticuffs and gunplay and a soupcon of sex. Riz Ortolani has supplied one of his more standard scores, but it is quite suitable for action framework. All technical credits are fine. *Byro.*

Don't Look Back
(DOCUMENTARY)

Bobby Dylan, Joan Baez & entourage photographed on tour of Britain. Good for young buff crowd

San Francisco, June 2. Production and release of Leacock Pennebaker Inc., (Albert Grossman, John Court). Photographed by D. A. Pennebaker with Jones and Howard Alk. Features Bobby Dylan, Joan Baez, Donovan, Alan Price, Albert Grossman, Bob Neuwirth, Tito Burns, Derroll Adams. Concerts recorded by J. Robert Van Dyke. Reviewed at Presidio Theatre, San Fran-

cisco, June 2, '67. Running Time, 96 MINS.

Without fanfare, a narrow gauge print of "Don't Look Back," a cinema verite documentary by D. A. Pennebaker of Bobby Dylan's spring, 1965, concert tour of Britain, premiered at the 788-seat Presidio art house here. It immediately matched the hardticket "Throughly Modern Millie," which opened the same week at the 1,381-seat Orpheum, as the largest grossing picture in town.

Pennebaker, with Jones and Howard Alk, has fashioned a relentlessly honest, brilliantly edited documentary permeated with the troubador-poet's music. Its appeal to the young people, for whom Dylan is a folk deity, is obvious.

"Tell it like it is'" is the battle cry of thep resent highly probed and publicized population of sub-25 year olds, and the film does just that. During, the month-long tour, Dylan was accompanied by Joan Baez, haunted by the rival reputation of Donovan, and badgered day and night by the press, teenieboppers and hangers on. Pennebaker shot some 20 hours of film, and edited it chronologically to the present hour-and-a-half revealing a portrait. That is not always flattering.

There is Dylan, faintly hostile, "putting on" the press. In one scene destined to become a classic, he tells a Time magazine reporter exactly where Time and its readership are at, and if his outburst lacks tact, it seems to the point. In a hotel room party Dylan gets into a childish, bullying argument about who threw a glass out the window. The exchange is petty, the language foul.

In one unique sequence Dylan's manager Albert Grossman and agent Tito Burns wheel, deal and bluff the British Broadcasting Co. playing them against Granada-TV to double the price for a Dylan appearance. It will pass as a remarkable view of actual behind-the-scenes show biz haggling.

Grossman, with his chubby cherubic face, spectacles, bald head and long hair, looks like Ben Franklin, and curses hotel managers with courtly obscenity. His less flattering vignettes and Dylan's are all the more remarkable for their "honesty" as he is one of the film's producers, along with John Court, Richard Leacock and Pennebaker. They are also distributing the film independently.

Alternating with the back stage scenes are the concert appearances with Dylan singing "Gates of Eden," "It's All Right Ma," "Hattie Carroll," and "Dont Think Twice." Without losing a beat, Pennebaker cuts directly from Dylan on stage singing "The Times They Are A-Changing" to the song on a car radio as he travels between engagements. The deejay give the song rising number on the charts.

In another transition the music continues as the picture dissolves from one concert hall to a tired Dylan riding the train to the next one, and the applause at the end of the number becomes the rumble of the wheels. J. Robert Van Dyke is credited with the music recording, and it is excellent.

As Dylan types in his hotel

room, Joan Baez strums a guitar and beautifully sings "Turn, Turn Again." Later Dylan finally meets Donovan at a party, and the latter entertains with "To Sing For You." Dylan takes the guitar and sings "Baby Blue." It is all natural and unstaged, entertainers casually playing for each other for the pure joy of it.

In only staged bit, a humorous intro before titles, audio plays the ear-bending "Subterranean Homesick Blues" while Dylan stands slouching in a alley dropping flash cards with the key words.

Narrow gauge print currently being shown here is muddy and contrasty, but the 35m blow-up being prepared for general release is reportedly much improved.

The film has no formal narration, but the press conferences and conversations make all the commentary necessary. Enroute to an appearance, Dylan reads a distorted newspaper account to Baez and Grossman, and remarks, "God, I'm glad I'm not me."

The camera zooms in on a London reporter in a phone booth calling in his story, ". . . The times they are a-changing period. They are when a poet and not a pop singer fills an auditorium period."

And when documentaries about them fill a movie house and gross $42,000 in two weeks. *Rick.*

The Fickle Finger of Fate
(U.S.-SPANISH-COLOR)

Tab Hunter excellent in charming comedy thriller for top supporting slots.

Producers Releasing Organization release of L. M. Films-Westside International coproduction, produced by Sidney Pink and J. Lopez Moreno. Stars Tab Hunter. Directed by Richard Rush. Screenplay, Jim Henaghan; camera (color by Movielab), Antonio Macasoli; music, Gregory G. Segura; editor, John Horvath. Reviewed at New Amsterdam Theatre, N. Y., June 7, '67. Running Time, 91 MINS.

Jerry	Tab Hunter
Winkle	Luis Prendes
Estrala	Gustavo Rojo
Fuentes	Fernando Hilbeck
Jaffee	Ralph Brown
Paco	Pedro Maria Sanchez
Inger	Elsa Skolinstad
Pilar	Patty Sheppard
Maria	Alejandra Milo
Maika	Andrea Lascelles
Jane	May Heatherly

Probably because the comedy thriller is less rigid in its conventions than the straight adventure drama, "The Fickle Finger of Fate" emerges as the best so far among the Sidney Pink program of made-in-Spain low-budgeters going out through Producers Releasing Organization. Pic has pace, some good acting and direction, and a hard-edged '60s feel lacking in producer's other features to be released here.

Cast and production values probably limit "Finger" to program booking in the U.S. But it should be reserved for top second-feature slots, where strong support is needed or where a top-quality draw demands relatively adult fare on the rest of the bill. Smaller locations might well try the pic on its own.

Plot has Tab Hunter, an American engineer on assignment in

Madrid, prevented from leaving for home when a priceless church art object, one of two candlesticks known as the Fickle Fingers of Fate, is found in his suitcase. He is forced to stay in Spain and to help find the candlestick's match and the thieves who stole both figures. When his suspicions fall on five beauty contest winners, both criminal and romantic complications ensue. But solution to the mystery is pat and predictable from the start.

Hunter is the major surprise, and his timing and momentum are mainly responsible for the film's fluid pace. More relaxed and charming than he's been for years, he seems to have conquered the stiffness so awkwardly projected in his Warners contract days. "The Fickle Finger of Fate" might do for Hunter what "The Pink Panther" appears to have accomplished for Robert Wagner in reactivating his career.

American Richard Rush handles the broad Spanish character actors in secondary roles with greater subtlety than has been displayed by some of the native directors Pink has previously used. Luis Prendes as a wearisome hanger-on, Ralph Brown as a pressagent, and Fernando Hilbeck as an inspector are effective in these parts.

Antonio Macasoli's photography is grainy, but all other technical credits are fine. Two curiosities: Jim Henaghan's screenplay credit is found in pressbook but there is no script credit at all on main titles; also, as in other of his Spanish films, producer is listed as Sidney W. Pink on main titles, without the middle initial on posters and in pressbook. *Byro.*

Le Soleil Des Voyous
(Hoodlums' Sun)
(FRENCH)
(Color)

Comacico release of Copernic-Fida Cinematografica production. Stars Jean Gabin, Robert Stack; features Margaret Lee, Jean Topart, Suzanne Flon. Directed by Jean Delannoy. Screenplay, Alphonse Boudard, Delannoy from the book by J. M. Flynn; camera (Eastmancolor), Walter Wottitz; editor, Henri Taverna. At Ambassades-Gaumont, Paris. Running Time, 100 MINS.

Denis	Jean Gabin
Jim	Robert Stack
Betty	Margaret Lee
Wife	Suzanne Flon
Henri	Jean Topart

This fairly slick gangster suspenser is about the aging hoodlum, now a respected businessman, going in for one last job, but this time just for the kicks. It has good production dress and is predictable. This is a suitable playoff item abroad if not having enough crispness, dash and unusualness for arty usage. The Robert Stack name also could help in foreign playoff as is noted old-time French thesp Jean Gabin.

Director Jean Delannoy has given this a stolid but well-mounted look though lacking the more individual character flair and insight to make it more than routine. nicely done, holdup caper. Gabin is settled with an intellectual wife, is rich, but yearns to get back to underworld days since he is bored as an accepted biz tycoon.

He gets his chance when thugs begin to work him over for crimping dope peddling in one of his restaurants. He is helped by an old buddy, a Yank adventurer played by Robert Stack. They decide to rob a bank together. The usual preparations are minutely shown but this does have some new twists.

In fact, Gabin gets a symbolic sendoff via being trapped in a bank vault where he has gone to get money for a getaway and finding himself behind the bars of the bank's safety deposit vault as the police come for him. He is his usual crusty self and still wields a solid film presence. Stack has fashioned a name for himself here via his tele series, "The Untouchables." This is his third starring role in French pix. He does alright if he is somewhat wooden as the Yank adventurer who inadvertently leads to foiling a perfect job by his yen for a two-timing girl played flamboyantly by British actress Margaret Lee. Latter has okay pulchritude. *Mosk.*

Gunn
(COLOR-SONGS)

Okay transplant of the Peter Gunn tv series by creator Blake Edwards. Craig Stevens encores in title role. Surprise climax. Henry Mancini score.

Hollywood, May 30.
Paramount Pictures release of Blake Edwards by (Owen Crump) Production, directed by Edwards. Features Craig Stevens, Laura Devon. Screenplay, Edwards, William Peter Blatty, based on story and characters created by Edwards; camera (Technicolor), Philip Lathrop; editor, Peter Zinner; music, Henry Mancini; songs, Mancini & Leslie Bricusse, Ray Evans & Jay Livingston; production design, Fernando Carrere; asst. director, Mickey McCardle. Reviewed at Directors Guild of America, L.A., May 29, '67. Running Time, 94 MINS.

Peter Gunn	Craig Stevens
Edie	Laura Devon
Jacoby	Edward Asner
Fusco	Albert Paulsen
Samantha	Sherry Jackson
Mother	Helen Traubel
Daisy Jane	M. T. Marshall
Tinker	J. Pat O'Malley
"The Bishop"	Regis Toomey
Leo Gracey	Dick Crockett
Lazlo Joyce	Charles Dierkof
Corwin	Jerry Douglas
Capt. Brady	Ken Wales
Harry Ross	Gary Lasdun
Archie	George Murdock
Barney	Frank Kreig

Blake Edwards has transplanted his three-season "Peter Gunn" NBC-TV series to the theatre screen in "Gunn," a well-made, but a trifle longish, programmer. Craig Stevens returns in a very good title-role thesping. Episodic scripting, as befits a murder suspense comedy, is combined with solid Owen Crump production supervision, Henry Mancini music, and a surprise ending. As with Warners' "Harper," this Paramount release offers a refreshing change of pace from far-out, gimmick-ridden sleuth pix, and commercial prospects look good on general dual bills, with exploitation selling.

Basic characters were created by Edwards, joined for screenplay by William Peter Blatty. For those who recall the vidseries which began in the 1959-60 season, policeman Jacoby is not Herschel Bernardi, but Edward Asner, and Gunn's gal, once Lola Albright, is

essayed herein by Laura Devon, who gets to chirp two tunes. Helen Traubel is cast as Mother, the saloon owner. Ken Wales and Dick Crockett were film's associate producers.

As with other recent pix, Richard Kuhn and National Screen Service have created a jazzy, psychedelic main title, which follows a prolog murder of a top-dog gangster. Albert Paulsen, successor to the gangland throne, is the natural suspect. M. T. (Marion) Marshall, a seagoing madame, hires Stevens to prove Paulsen guilty. Eventually, Paulsen forces Stevens to prove him innocent.

Popping up at intervals are Miss Devon, Gunn's occasional dame, Sherry Jackson, in a standout sexpot part, J. Pat O'Malley, excellent as a boozer informer who plays it like Alfred Hitchcock's old tv show intros, and skid-row topster Regis Toomey. The associate producers have bits, including Wales in a good satire of the helicopter traffic reporter for a tv station.

Violent scenes are effective, and alternate with exposition which may be faulted for overly-relaxed pace. The jazzed-up cinematics of pix and teleblurbs have definitely not rendered exposition obsolete (contrary to some opinion), but they have succeeded in conditioning audiences to expect a stepped-up rhythm. Edwards' direction thus alternates in somewhat uneven fashion. An extremely close-up necking scene is more irritating than sensual.

Phil Lathrop's Technicolor camera has caught the very good production values—also the sets of twins who work in Miss Marshall's boat-bordello—arising from Fernando Carrere's excellent production design.

Climax, which from out of nowhere introduces a homosexual-transvestite plot angle, is indeed a surprise, although Miss Jackson's repeated presence (visually, not unwelcome) telegraphs some raison d'etre. But, disappointingly, she turns out to be the dead hood's daughter, just like her counterpart in dozens of other pix. As long as Miss Marshall, in the script, is not what she seems, and as long as scripters have dragged in the drag angle, Miss Jackson might well have had some relation to Gary Lasdun, Miss Marshall's roommate.

Mancini's score, which includes a reprise of his famed series theme, leads adroit atmosphere. A new song, "I Like The Look," lyrics by Mancini's new semi-regular partner Leslie Bricusse, is good, as is a reprise of "Dreamsville," lyrics by Ray Evans and Jay Livingston. Peter Zinner edited to 94 minutes, and other technical credits are pro. *Murf.*

Mamaia
(FRENCH-COLOR)

Paris, June 13.
Films 13, Cite Films, Films De La Pleiade production and release. With Adriana Bogdan, Cristea Avram, Jean-Pierre Kalfon, Pascal Aubier, the Jets (4). Directed by Jose Varela. Screenplay, Serge Ganze, Varela; camera (East mancolor), Patrice Poujet; editor, Brigitte Dornes. At the Napoleon, Paris. Running Time, 89 MINS.

Nana	Adriana Bogdan
Stephane	Cristea Avram
Baltahzar	Jean-Pierre Kalfon
Manager	Pascal Aubier
The Jets	Themselves

This pic won the top award at the Hyeres Young Film Festival at that Mediterannean resort town before Cannes. And it is young in its rambling look at a brief affair between a French beatnik type and a disgruntled Rumanian girl about to be married. Shot in Rumania, it is still a French pic. Mamaia is actually a sea resort spot.

The trouble is this sort of theme and treatment is getting about as familiar as a western or a musical. Influences of Claude Lelouch's "A Man and a Woman" and Jean-Luc Godard abound. In fact, Lelouch was one of the coproducers. So there is much car riding, much big-beat music and four characters are a local r&r band, the Jets. Isolated scenes of talk, wanderings and final ending of the idyll with the girl going sagely back to her fiance and the beat wandering on to other lands.

However, director Jose Varela does have some insight into inarticulate love and a few inventive interludes of youthful horseplay. But the girl is already familiar from her Western counterparts. Though this seems to say that East and West, that is the politico division, may not meet yet, there does not seem much difference, judging from this film.

The fiance is a committed student. And Jean-Pierre Kalfon gives some inner intensity and even a sinister underlining to the beatnik who changes money on the black market, fights off any true feelings and even denies his own budding love for the girl. He is a thesp on the local scene to be watched.

Adriana Bogdan has musky good looks and is at ease as the feckless girl who finally returns to her fiance after a brief idyll and brush with Western youth. Varela does avoid pretentiousness but too much is strained and padded.

The color is fresh and mixes the usual sepia scenes for indoor dance segs. This is another look at youth that may have some foreign chances, but it calls for right placing and finding its way to youthful audiences. *Mosk.*

The 1,000,000 Eyes of Su-Muru
(COLOR-TECHNISCOPE)

Lightweight meller should draw fair in nabe spots.

Hollywood, May 29.
American International release of Harry Alan Towers production. Stars Frankie Avalon, George Nader, Shirley Eaton; features Wilfrid Hyde-White, Klaus Kinski, Ursula Rank, Marie Rohm. Directed by Lindsay Shonteff. Screenplay, Kevin Kavanagh, from original story by Peter Welbeck, based on books and characters by Sax Rohmer; camera (Technicolor), John von Kotze; music, Johnny Scott. Reviewed at Charles Addikoff Projection Room, May 29, '67. Running Time, 95 MINS.

Tommy Carter	Frankie Avalon
Nick West	George Nader
Su-Muru	Shirley Eaton
Colonel Baisbrook	Wilfrid Hyde-White
President Boong	Klaus Kinski
Louise	Patti Chandler
Mikki	Salli Sachse
Erna	Ursula Rank
Zoe	Krista Nell
Helga	Marie Rohm
Inspector Koo	Paul Chang
Kitty	Essie Huang
Colonel Medika	Jon Fong
Su-Muru Guards	Denise Davreux, Mary Cheng, Jill Hamilton, Lisa Gray, Christine Lok, Margaret Cheung, Louisa Lee

"The 1,000,000 Eyes of Su-Muru" in this lightweight meller refer to the many femmes enlisted by power-mad gal committed to dominating all influential men in the world. Handled half tongue-in-cheek and half seriously, entry should draw four in nabe spots but will need heftier co-feature.

Although Frankie Avalon toplines (obviously just for name), he still doesn't know how to handle a gun and most action and story movement falls to George Nader, as a CIA-agent vacationing in Italy with Avalon, American playboy Tommy Carter who just happens to be on the scene. Nader delivers some unfunny comic lines in a way that they are not completely lost and Avalon poses, moves and talks like a nightclub entertainer.

The pair find themselves in deep trouble when one of Su-Muru's female guards is sent to an untimely death by the great lady for failing to capture Nader and Avalon while investigating women's hideout on assignment by British secret agent Wilfrid Hyde-White. Su-Muru, deftly played by Shirley Eaton, arranges for a body to pop up in Nader's room.

Hyde-White hustles them out of Italy to Hong Kong where Su-Muru and her bevy are trying to do away with President Boong (Klaus Kinski) by sending her latest neophyte to assassinate him after she has blackmailed Nader into arranging the introduction. Neophyte Helga, played by Marie Rohm, chickens out and joins forces with Nader, Avalon and Hyde-White and helps the trio destroy Su-Muru's bastion on island just outside Hong Kong. Whether Su-Muru dies is not definite, leaving opening for possible sequel.

Director Lindsay Shonteff and writer Peter Welbeck let story get out of hand from time to time. The best comic lines, based on subtle references to old jokes and cliches, are delivered as throwaway gags that won't be missed if they're not understood.

Heavy reference to Lesbianism is somewhat disconcerting and denouement is unclear when it is learned Avalon has all along been British secret service agent and "found it difficult to sustain this American accent!"

Technical credits in the Harry Alan Towers production are proficient. *Edwa.*

Woman Times Seven
(COLOR)

Episodic comedy-drama, with Shirley MacLaine excellent as seven types of modern woman. Well directed, by Vittorio De Sica, and handsomely produced. Good b.o. potential. Peter Sellers and Michael Caine also help come-on.

Hollywood, June 16.

Embassy Pictures (20th-Fox, overseas) release of Arthur Cohn production, in seven episodes; executive producer, Joseph E. Levine. Stars Shirley MacLaine, Alan Arkin, Rossano Brazzi, Michael Caine, Vittorio Gassman, Peter Sellers. Directed by Vittorio De Sica. Screenplay, Cesare Zavattini; camera (Pathe Color), Christian Matras; editors, Teddy Darvas, Victoria Spiri-Mercanton; music, Riz Ortolani; asst. director, Marc Monnet. Reviewed at Joe Shore's Screening Room, L.A., June 16, '67. Running Time, 99 MINS.

"FUNERAL PROCESSION"
(8 MINS.)

Paulette .... Shirley MacLaine
Jean .... Peter Sellers
Mourner .... Elspeth March

"AMATEUR NIGHT"
(15 MINS.)

Maria Teresa .... Shirley MacLaine
Giorgio .... Rossano Brazzi
Jeannine .... Catherine Samie
2d Streetwalker .... Judith Magre

"TWO AGAINST ONE"
(15 MINS.)

Linda .... Shirley MacLaine
Cenci .... Vittorio Gassman
MacCormick .... Clinton Greyn

"SUPER SIMONE"
(14 MINS.)

Edith .... Shirley MacLaine
Rik .... Lex Barker
Dr. Xavier .... Robert Morley
Woman in Market ..... Elsa Martinelli

"AT THE OPERA"
(15 MINS)

Eve Minou .... Shirley MacLaine
Henri Minou .... Patrick Wymark
Mme. Lisiere .... Adrienne Corri

"THE SUICIDES"
(16 MINS.)

Marie .... Shirley MacLaine
Fred .... Alan Arkin

"SNOW"
(16 MINS.)

Jeanne .... Shirley MacLaine
Young Man .... Michael Caine
Claudie .... Anita Ekberg
Victor .... Philippe Noiret

"Woman Times Seven" means a seven-segment showcase for the talents of Shirley MacLaine, playing in tragicomedy and dramatic fashion a variety of contemporary femme types. International names in starring support lend marquee versatility for the handsome Arthur Cohn production, made in France. Vittorio De Sica directed with an economic, but telling eye. Inherent promo flexibility will aid the sell in various situations. Overall good b.o. potential, if spotty, via Embassy release in the domestic market, 20th-Fox elsewhere, where mature audiences should be the prime sales target.

Joseph E. Levine, exec producer, has taken what appears to be a good gamble with De Sica's concept of Cesare Zavattini's original screenplay. Although Miss MacLaine appeared in various guises in 20th-'s "What a Way To Go," that Arthur P. Jacobs production was geared primarily for general audience laughs. Here, Miss MacLaine is spotted in many different adult situations, and largely convinces with each switcheroo.

With Peter Sellers, she is the bereaved widow, trailing her late husband in funeral procession, as Sellers puts the make on her. At fadeout, she and Sellers, totally engrossed, miss a turn in the march and drift away. Some sight-gag relief is thrown in via convenient mud puddles, and a touch of the macabre enters when De Sica shoots the pair from atop the coffin.

Then as a wife who surprises hubby Rossano Brazzi in bed with a neighbor, Miss MacLaine shifts to the enraged female, determined on revenge This takes her to a park inhabited by streetwalkers, where an amusing discourse on the economics of prostitution is conducted by Catherine Samie and Judith Magre.

Miss MacLaine is not up to it, however, and when a pimp flattens Brazzi, who has pursued her, the couple is reunited.

Switching to a poker-faced modern hippie, Miss MacLaine then enters a fantasy world of T.S. Eliot poetry and cocktail-party small talk nonsense, along with Vittorio Gassman and Clinton Greyn competing for her charms — that night. As a fantasy sex world often becomes the norm, she, and they, succumb.

Hack writer Lex Barker, obviously not a stranger to neighbor Elsa Martinelli, spellbinds Miss MacLaine, his adoring simpleton wife, into desiring to be like the empty femmes about whom he writes. Her far-out antics, funny at first, become pitiable when he, with lawyer Robert Morley, plots a fake insanity rap. Touching, although ambivalent fadeout is a highlight.

In an overdone caricature of a rich selfish woman, Miss MacLaine becomes incensed when Adrienne Corri is known to be wearing a similar dress to the opera opening. A small bomb — to induce "terror," not death — is planted to thwart Miss Corri's entrance. The plan is doomed, for a third woman shows in identical costume. Heartbroken Miss MacLaine — a Left Bank Craig's Wife — is reduced to hysterics as Miss Corri and hubby, blackened but determined, scramble into the theatre.

The major tour de force segment finds Miss MacLaine and Alan Arkin alone in a flophouse room, plotting suicide together. The sort of routine that Mike Nichols and Elaine May did so well, but herein steeped in blacker comedy, it runs out of substance to telegraph the climax; both chicken out and flee, independently.

Final episode is solid, bittersweet romance, with Miss MacLaine and Anita Ekberg as two wives who shop, perhaps at times for some extra-marital sex. Both eye Michael Caine, outstanding in a totally silent part as an apparent street swinger. Miss MacLaine gets him to follow her home, where, it turns out, hubby Philippe Noiret actually has hired Caine to follow wifey. Assured via a telephone report that her account of the day is accurate he is tenderly, contritely caressing her at the window, as she, oblivious of Caine's identity, smiles as latter walks away, secure that she can get a man.

Miss Ekberg herein gets to mouth some contemporary morality: as to Caine's possible educational status, "The less they know, the better they go." Also as to his preference between the two, she says he may dig "both of us, if he's modern." This sort of philosophy, regardless of its merit, is one of many which indicates a somewhat mature audience is needed to appreciate the film.

DeSica's direction is on target, and Christian Matras has lensed with a generally fluid Pathecolor camera. Riz Ortolani has supplied what cannot be called a score, rather musical effects, sometimes repetitious. His main themes begin with the subtlety of a needle suddenly dropped onto a phonograph record. Ortolani is not alone in this era of filmusical gadgetry. Other technical credits are pro.

Murf.

The Dirty Dozen
(BRITISH—COLOR—70M)

Exciting film version of the book. Lee Marvin heads excellent cast. Overlong, but hot b.o. likely, including femme audience appeal despite all-male principals.

Hollywood, June 13.

Metro-Goldwyn-Mayer release of Kenneth Hyman production. Features Lee Marvin, Ernest Borgnine, Charles Bronson, Jim Brown, John Cassavetes, Richard Jaeckel, George Kennedy, Trini Lopez, Ralph Meeker, Robert Ryan, Telly Savalas, Clint Walker, Robert Webber. Directed by Robert Aldrich. Screenplay, Nunnally Johnson, Lukas Heller, based on the novel by E. M. Nathanson; camera (Metrocolor), Edward Scaife; editor, Michael Luciano; music, Frank De Vol; songs, De Vol, Mack David, Sibylle Siegfried; asst. director, Bert Batt. Reviewed at Grauman's Chinese Theatre, L.A., June 12, '67. Running Time, 149 MINS.

Maj. Reisman .... Lee Marvin
Gen. Worden .... Ernest Borgnine
Jos. Wladislaw .... Charles Bronson
Robt. Jefferson .... Jim Brown
Victor Franko .... John Cassavetes
Sgt. Bowren .... Richard Jaeckel
Major Armbruster .... George Kennedy
Pedro Jiminez .... Trini Lopez
Capt. Kinder .... Ralph Meeker
Col. Breed .... Robert Ryan
Archer Maggott .... Telly Savalas
Samson Posey .... Clint Walker
Gen. Denton .... Robert Webber
Vernon Pinkley .... Donald Sutherland
Milo Vladek .... Tom Busby
Glenn Gilpin .... Ben Carruthers
Roscoe Lever .... Stuart Cooper
Cpl. Morgan .... Robert Phillips
Seth Sawyer .... Colin Maitland
Tassos Bravos .... Al Mancini
Pvt. Gardner .... George Roubicek
Worden's aide .... Thick Wilson
German Girl .... Dora Reisser

"The Dirty Dozen" is an exciting World War II pre-D-Day drama about 12 condemned soldier-prisoners who are rehabilitated to serve with distinction. Lee Marvin heads a very strong, nearly all-male cast in an excellent performance. Robert Aldrich directed the well mounted, grimly realistic Kenneth Hyman production. Despite some rough edges, both technical and artistic, solid b.o. returns are likely from Metro release in general, and foreign roadshow, situations.

E.M. Nathanson's novel was careful to disclaim any truth to the basic plot, for, if ever pressed, the U.S. Army apparently can claim that no records exist on the subject. Still, Nathanson's book, as well as the very good Nunnally Johnson-Lukas Heller screenplay, has a ring of authenticity to it.

Marvin again delivers a top performance probably because he seems at his best in a role as a sardonic authoritarian. Herein, he is a Major, handed the task of selecting 12 hardened, stockaded punks, training them for a guerrilla mission with just faintest hope of amnesty. Seeds of official conflict are sewn into plot: Marvin & Robert Ryan do not get along—but later they must; Ernest Borgnine and Robert Webber, as two generals, do not like Marvin's flip attitude.

In selecting his dozen men—they get "dirty" later under his discipline during training, Marvin is assisted by Richard Jaeckel, excellent as a sergeant and one of Jaeckel's strongest screen roles in years. Ralph Meeker, a liaison officer and psychiatrist, assists Marvin, against his better judgment. Meeker sees the group as completely anti-social; Marvin sees a natural leader among the crew.

That leader is John Cassavetes, who in recent years has maintained a reputation by what he has not done, rather than what he has done. Here, he is firstrate as the tough Chicago hood who meets his match in Marvin, later becoming a model soldier, when it counts. Charles Bronson, a very capable actor, stands out as a Polish-American who, once affixing his loyalty, does not shift under even physical brutality.

Jim Brown, former pro-football player for the Cleveland Browns in his second pic role (after "Rio Conchos"), is terrif as the Negro prisoner, who has a natural conflict with Dixie-dialected, & Bible-toting Telly Savalas. Brown has a strong acting future. Savalas, playing the only eventual Judas among the con apostolate, walks the fine line between colorful characterization and overdone thesping; he does not always appear surefooted.

Clint Walker, a mountain of a man, is spotlighted less prominently as an American Indian. Donald Sutherland appears to good advantage as a likeable kid. Rest of the dozen includes Trini Lopez (in screen debut), Tom Busby, Ben Carruthers Stuart Cooper, Colin Maitland & Al Mancini. Latter six render strong, but minor support. George Kennedy, usually a heavy, essays a good sympathetic part as an officer of Borgnine's staff.

Director Aldrich, while obtaining neat performance all around, has fallen down in the final editing. How, for example, does Ryan know that Marvin, as a sort of graduation present for his troops, brought in some girls for them? (The dozen previously has shown obedience to orders for absolute secrecy.) Also, some scenes, which now are incidental transition, obviously were meant to be much more, but as compressed, effect an awkward plot acceleration.

Aldrich obviously had to trim the pic, and its final form is 149 minutes, executed by Michael Luciano. A natural intermission break for foreign roadshowing occurs just after Ryan is captured in a war game. Domestic audiences, unfortunately, will be rushed into the final, 45-minute guerrilla mission, and a tedious element, also limping pace, will be introduced. Plot-wise, the men are shaped up in a well-paced initial 66 minutes; the Marvin-Ryan conflict takes the next 35 minutes and climax the final 48. Running time for continuous performances is overlong.

Technically, the 70m firstrun print is only fair. Aldrich shot in 1.85:1 aspect ratio, and decision to blow up to 70m (flat) involves.

by the basic geometry of frame size, a more than doubling of width, also a chopping off at top/bottom of about 15% of pic. Latter is not as obvious as the grainy look evident in some shots but in every dissolve.

Craft credits are very good—Edward Scaife's great lensing (printed in Metrocolor), art direction by W.E. Hutchinson, and outstanding special effects supervision by Cliff Richardson, who planned the finale explosive scenes. *Murf.*

Don't Make Waves
(PANAVISION—COLOR)

Mildly amusing comedy with Tony Curtis, Claudia Cardinale, Edgar Bergen, Mort Sahl.

Hollywood, June 15.
Metro release of Filmways-Reynard (John Calley-Martin Ransohoff) production. Stars Tony Curtis, Claudia Cardinale; features Robert Webber, Joanna Barnes, David Draper, Mort Sahl, Edgar Bergen. Directed by Alexander Mackendrick. Screenplay, Ira Wallach, George Kirgo; adaptation, Maurice Richlin; based on novel, "Muscle Beach," by Wallach; camera (Metrocolor), Philip H. Lathrop; music, Vic Mizzy, editors, Rita Roland, Thomas Stanford; asst. directors, Carl Beringer, Erich von Stroheim Jr. Reviewed at Metro Studios, June 14, '67. Running Time, 100 MINS.
Carlo Cofield .... Tony Curtis
Laura Califatti .... Claudia Cardinale
Malibu .... Sharon Tate
Rod Prescott .... Robert Webber
Diane Prescott .... Joanna Barnes
Harry Holland .... David Draper
Sam Lingonberry .... Mort Sahl
Madame Lavinia .... Edgar Bergen
Millie Gunder .... Ann Elder
Ted Gunder .... Chester Yorton
Fred Barker .... Marc London
Henderson .... Douglas Henderson
Ethyl .... Sarah Selby
Seamstress .... Mary Grace Canfield
Electrician .... Dub Taylor
Monster .... Reg Lewis
Helen .... Julie Payne
Myrna .... Hollie Haze
Pilot .... Paul Barselow
Newspapermen .... George Tyne,
David Fresco, Gilbert Green
Decorator .... Eduardo Tirella

"Don't Make Waves", a title probably holding little meaning to most minds, is small help to this John Calley-Martin Ransohoff production, mildly amusing film which never gets off the ground in its intended purpose of wacky comedy. Based on Ira Wallach's novel, "Muscle Beach," film stars Tony Curtis & Claudia Cardinale and has names of Mort Sahl and Edgar Bergen also in cast as well as sometimes enticing femme shots.

Script by Wallach and George Kirgo has a Southern California setting, mixing romance, infidelity, beach antics and sky diving with utter confusion as Curtis plays a frantic young man and Miss Cardinale a peppery import with an accent. Plot(?) gets underway as femme's car causes Curtis' Volkswagen to plunge down a hillside and burn, during which Curtis' pants and all his worldly possessions also go up in flames. Driving home with femme to look at her insurance policy, Curtis finds himself involved in her romance with a swimming pool operator, cheating on his wife.

Alexander Mackendrick's direction seldom rises above his script but Philip H. Lathrop's color photography is superior. Balance of technical credits are standard.
Whit.

In The Heat Of The Night
(COLOR)

Sidney Poitier and Rod Steiger team to solve a Dixie murder amid ironic racial conflict. Some script and directing flaws, but strong production. Hot b.o.

Hollywood, June 10.
United Artists release of Mirisch Corp. presentation, produced by Walter Mirisch. Stars Sidney Poitier, Rod Steiger; features Warren Oates, Lee Grant. Directed by Norman Jewison. Screenplay, Stirling Silliphant, based on the novel by John Ball; camera (DeLuxe Color), Haskell Wexler; editor, Hal Ashby; music, Quincy Jones; song lyric, Marilyn and Alan Bergman; asst. director, Terry Morse Jr. Reviewed at Grauman's Chinese Theatre, L.A., June 9, '67. Running Time, 109 MINS.
Virgil Tibbs .... Sidney Poitier
Bill Gillespie .... Rod Steiger
Sam Wood .... Warren Oates
Mrs. Colbert .... Lee Grant
Purdy .... James Patterson
Delores Purdy .... Quentin Dean
Eric Endicott .... Larry Gates
Webb Schubert ...... William Schallert
Mama Caleba .... Beah Richards
Harvey Oberst .... Scott Wilson
Philip Colbert .... Jack Teter
Packy Harrison .... Matt Clark
Ralph Henshaw .... Anthony James
H. E. Henderson ...... Kermit Murdock
Jess .... Khalil Bezaleel
George Courtney .... Peter Whitney
Harold Courtney ...... William Watson
Shagbag Martin .... Timothy Scott
City Council .... Michael LeGlaire,
Larry D. Mann, Stewart Nisbet
Charlie Hawthorne .... Eldon Quick
Dr. Stuart .... Fred Stewart
Ted Ulam .... Arthur Malet
Arnold Fryer .... Peter Masterson
Engineers .... Alan Oppenheimer,
Philip Garris
Henry .... Jester Hairston
Deputy .... Clegg Hoyt
Young Toughs. Phil Adams, Nikita Knatz
Baggage Master .... David Stinehart
Conductor .... Buzz Barton

An excellent Sidney Poitier performance, and an outstanding one by Rod Steiger, overcome some noteworthy flaws to make "In The Heat Of The Night" an absorbing contemporary murder drama, set in the deep, red-necked South. Most production elements are well coordinated by producer Walter Mirisch, and enhanced by an excellent cast. Norman Jewison directed, sometimes in pretentious fashion, an uneven script. Nevertheless, hot b.o. prospects are likely from United Artists release in general situations.

Novelist John Ball has written three books about a Negro gumshoe named Virgil Tibbs, "Heat" being the first. Stirling Silliphant has adapted it into an erratic screenplay which indulges in heavy-handed, sometimes needless plot diversion, uncertain character development and a rapid-fire denouement. As a matter of fact, suddenness of climax suggests that the creative team went dry. Pic clearly is a triumph over some of its basic parts.

Intriguing plot basis has Poitier as the detective, accidentally on a visit to his Mississippi hometown where a prominent industrialist is found murdered. Arrested initially — and ironically — on the assumption that a Negro, out late at night must have done the deed, Poitier later is thrust, by his boss in Philadelphia, his own conscience, and a temporary anti-white emotional outburst, into uneasy collaboration with local sheriff Steiger.

Steiger's transformation from a diehard Dixie bigot to a man who learns to respect Poitier stands out in smooth comparison to the wandering solution of the murder. En route, assorted characters include policemen Warren Oates, sexpot Quentin Dean & her brother, James Peterson, Lee Grant, as the murdered man's widow, unreconstructed manor lord Larry Gates, glib mayor William Schallert, town abortionist Beah Richards, sleazy greasy-spoon clerk Anthony James, and petty criminal Scot Wilson.

Script emphasis on James in early reels telegraphs something, and indeed that occurs. But the explanation of the murder takes only several seconds and many audiences will have to discuss the matter before reaching agreement; even a fast synopsis reading leaves some questions. Jewison's direction of his cast is excellent, particularly the relationship between the two above-title stars, although some dialect is obscure.

Exactly why Gates' scene is there is unclear — perhaps the face-slapping bit with Poitier was considered daring, although incorporation could have been smoother. Exactly why Poitier seeks out Miss Richards — for that matter, the details of his entree there — are unclear. These flaws, and others to follow, are noteworthy in view of their substantial, obvious presence.

Miss Dean, Patterson, Wilson and James are "introduced" herein, and each has a distinct potential. Oates and Miss Grant, topfeatured, are just right, and rest of cast supports in solid fashion.

Jewison's presumed influence on final editing is not up to his dramatic direction. In an early scene, for example, Wilson is pursued by hounds to a large bridge, over which lies another state — and freedom. What could have been a compelling and ironic frustration becomes a tedious intercutting of a long zoom, then Steiger sitting in a patrol car, waiting for his prey, Steiger driving at speeds which process work indicates must be about 80 m.p.h., then Wilson shuffling along with the car behind, and finally a long-shot which ends it all. Scene does not play; it fizzes out completely.

Then, too, the subjective camera, used several times, gets a little old. Wilson's flight through underbush is overemphasized by dizzying shots; frames, not feet, of film can convey the desired impression. Also a peeping-tom view of some hoods getting into a car for the climactic confrontation is needlessly obscured by foliage — and the obscured characters only confuse who's who.

On the peeping tom bit, Oates' voyeuristic o.o. of Miss Dean, a nubile, fullbreasted nifty to be sure, is followed by a long-held shot for audience voyeurs; again, too much of a good thing — cinematically, that is. Perhaps there is no door-screen, or convenient strut in the foreign version.

Haskell Wexler's DeLuxe lensing captures the desired drabness of the locale for mood-enhancement, but in several scenes it intrudes. Must auto departures so regularly start from a tail light? Only a nearby tire thief would ever see it that way. Difference, for its own sake, is pretension.

An excellent score has been provided by Quincy Jones whose title tune is sung by Ray Charles to good effect. Hal Ashby, also billed as assistant to the producer executed editing to 109 minutes, overall very good with exceptions as noted. Sound recording is excellent, as are other production credits. Out-of-focus title effects are credited to Murray Naidich, who did a firstrate job; UA might include an alerting note to boothmen however, to insure a smooth opening.

Jewison had, after switch from tv, directed five programmers before The Mirisch Corp. sponsored his "The Russians Are Coming The Russians Are Coming," which landed him firmly on the film map, and extended his ties with Mirisch for five more pix, including "Heat."
Murf.

Melbourne Fest

Knight Without Armor
(Rizar Bes Bronja)
(BULGARIAN)

Melbourne, June 13.
Bulgaria State Enterprise release of Feature Film Studio Production. Directed, Borislav Sharaliev. Script, Valeri Petrov; camera, Atanas Tassev; music, Lazar Nikolov. Leading Players: Oleg Kovachev, Maria Roussalieva, Tsvyatko Nikolov. Reviewed at Melbourne Film Festival. Running Time, 85 MINS.

This somewhat naive film centres around a small boy, Vanio, brilliantly played by Oleg Korachev, who succeeds in twisting around his little finger most of the adults with whom he comes into contact. There is very little in the way of a real plot, being more a series of minor episodes—the first ride in his parents' car, a street fight with other children, the shadowing of a woman described by the other children as a "spy" who turns out to be Vanio's own mother, a day spent in his favorite uncle's company.

Photographed in monochrome it is all pleasing, although many may find the child's behaviour at times obnoxious. The film is well directed and photographed, with suitable performances from all concerned. It would be ideal as a support film.
Stan.

The Happiest Millionaire
(COLOR-SONGS)

Outstanding Walt Disney film version of book and play, with original new music. Handsome production, excellent cast. Appeal to all age groups.

Hollywood, June 21.

Buena Vista release of Walt Disney (Bill Anderson) production. Features Fred MacMurray, Tommy Steele, Greer Garson, Geraldine Page. Gladys Cooper, Hermione Baddeley, Lesley Ann Warren, John Davidson. Directed by Norman Tokar. Screenplay, A. J. Carothers, based on book and play by Kyle Crichton and Cordelia Drexel Biddle; camera (Technicolor), Edward Colman; editor, Cotton Warburton; music, Richard M., Robert B. Sherman; asst. director, Paul Cameron. Reviewed at Academy Award Theatre, L.A., June 20, '67. Running Time (excluding intermission), 164 MINS.

Anthony J. Drexel Biddle	Fred MacMurray
John Lawless	Tommy Steele
Mrs. Cordelia Biddle	Greer Garson
Mrs. Duke	Geraldine Page
Aunt Mary Drexel	Gladys Cooper
Mrs. Worth	Hermione Baddeley
Cordy Biddle	Lesley Ann Warren
Angier Buchanan Duke	John Davidson
Tony Biddle	Paul Peterson
Livingston Biddle	Eddie Hodges
Rosemary	Joyce Bulifant
Sgt. Flanagan	Sean McClory
U.S. Marines	William Wellman Jr., Jim McMullan, Jim Gurley
Walter Blakeley	Aron Kincaid
Charlie Taylor	Larry Merrill
Aunt Gladys	Frances Robinson

"The Happiest Millionaire," last major live-action production of the late Walt Disney, is a family comedy, blending creative and technical elements, scripting, excellent casting, direction, scoring, choreography and handsome, plush production for "happy" b.o. prospects. Fred MacMurray heads the cast, which includes Britain's Tommy Steele in his U.S. film debut as an Irish servant in 1916 Philadelphia. Bill Anderson coproduced for Buena Vista release. Film has good hardticket potential, providing momentum for later mop-up in extended general playoff.

Cordelia Drexel Biddle and Kyle Crichton collaborated on a book and a 1956 legiter, starring Walter Pidgeon, which concerned Miss Biddle's father, Anthony J. Drexel Biddle, the millionaire of the title. Wealthy, eccentric (alligators for pets, a boxing fetish) but still a father, Biddle is essayed here by Fred MacMurray in the A. J. Carothers screenplay. Richard M. and Robert B. Sherman have added a large score, making film an original screen musical.

Disney organization enters the roadshow field with the pic, and results will be of trade interest. Hardtix pix mean advance planning by patrons, yet a typical Disney audience unit—a carload of juves with parents—might be more properly considered an impulse-type of attendance. When all the arguments and counter-arguments are given, however, fact remains that 20th-Fox's "The Sound Of Music," a Robert Wise production, struck gold in the family market on roadshow.

MacMurray, snug in an excellent characterization, is well teamed with Greer Garson, long absent from the screen, as the Philadelphia parents. Lesley Ann Warren, introduced herein, plays the teenage daughter with charm and radiance. Paul Peterson and Eddie Hodges are her brothers, with little footage. Of immediate appeal to young audiences is Miss Warren's growing desire to lead her own life, later a marriage to John Davidson, also new to pix, playing the N.Y.-bred heir to the Duke tobacco fortune.

Complications ensue when Geraldine Page, Davidson's mother, is convinced that Philadelphians are hicks. Miss Page is outstanding in her role, highlight of which is a terrif song duet with Gladys Cooper, MacMurray's indomitable aunt. Running through the light-as-air-no-message plot is Steele, a song and dance "butler."

Decision to open pic with Steele's song-and-dance to "Fortuosity" is showmanly: it satisfies curiosity about him (this is his first major pic), thereby permitting him to become part of the ensemble. Steele has an expected appeal to moppets, teens and adults; his talents are many, and not just mechanical; he projects warmth, good will with right amount of deviltry.

The other newcomers—Miss Warren and Davidson—act very well, and provide images with which the young can identify. Their frequent vocals, duet and solo, indicate an occasional uncontrolled tremolo, lack of sustaining power and unsure pitch, at times. These flaws, however are somewhat overcome by the firstrate musical staging of Marc Breaux and Dee Dee Wood, and the excellent orchestrations of Jack Elliott. Latter has given the score the desired World War I licks.

Norman Tokar's comedy direction is competent, from the sophisticated scenes of Miss Page to the broad, sight-gag antics of Steele, housekeeper Hermione Baddeley and the rest of the very competent cast. Joyce Bulifant socks over her minor role as Miss Warren's roomate, pair sharing one of many excellent production numbers which enhance plot. Sean McClory plays an Irish cop in a saloon donnybrook, a highlight sequence.

The Sherman brothers are responsible for 13 songs, all of which are perfect in context, although none, at first hearing, seem destined for longtime outside popularity except in the nitery-vaudeo field. "Fortuousity," "There Are Those" (the Page-Cooper number), "Let's Have A Drink On It" and "I'll Always Be Irish" should be around for years, however, as basis for specialty staging. "Detroit," a duet between the young lovers, is marred by a set of banal, predictable lyrics, as far below par as the words to "There Are Those" are above average.

Edward Coleman's Technicolor lensing is outstanding, capturing what appears to be nearly every penny spent on some handsome production values. Art directors Carroll Clark and John B. Mansbridge, set decorators Emile Kuri and Frank R. McKelvy, costume designer Bill Thomas, costumers Chuck Keehne and Neva Rames are among those responsible for the strong visual interest. Alan Maley's title art, employing moving photography of sketches, is topnotch. Other technical credits are pro.

Cotton Warbuton executed the editing. Overture runs just over two minutes before the 95-minute first segment; a shorter overture precedes the final part, which runs 65 minutes. Total time, sans intermish but with overtures, is 164 minutes, a bit long, although no particular scene seems at fault. But five minutes out of the first part wouldn't hurt, though.

Pic has a summer-long pre-release booking in L.A. at the Pantages before breaking in many keys in the late fall. It is a natural for group sales. In order to cater to impulse attendance, it might be well to let the public know that some seats are available at the window.

Murf.

Spree
(SONGS-COLOR)

Minor Las Vegas exploitation film; names of Vic Damone, Jayne Mansfield, Juliet Prowse may carry through program market.

Hollywood, June 23.

United Producers release of Carroll Case-Hal Roach Jr. production. Stars Vic Damone, Jayne Mansfield, Juliet Prowse; features Mickey Hargitay, Constance Moore, Clara Ward Singers, Rozana Tapajos, Barklay Shaw. Directed by Mitchell Leisen, Walon Green. Screenplay, Sydney Field; camera, (PatheColor), Alan Stensvold; asst. director, Bill Forsythe; editors, Ray Livingston, Ed Biery; music, Remo Usai. Reviewed at Hollywood Theatre, June 23, 1967. Running Time, 80 MINS.

Vic Damone warbles two songs, Juliet Prowse toe-dances and clowns pair of terp numbers and Jayne Mansfield strips in this exploitation film which makes a pitch via sensational display ads for current local engagement. Film also carries a no-admission-to-minors label. What comes out on screen in poor color and static handling is a pseudo-travelog through Las Vegas casinos, niteries, party places et al, without any of the spectacular overtones promised. It's okay for smaller program houses where quality doesn't matter.

Feature obviously was produced several years ago. Carroll Case and Hal Roach Jr., coproduced and Mitchell Leisen and Walon Green shared directing chores, neither of the assignments displaying much imagination. Considerable footage is shot of the Folies Bergere in action at Tropicana Hotel and "Vive Les Girls" at Dunes, with plenty of nudity in low house lighting, plus entertainment in other night spots.

Shown are clips of various entertainers at work. Additionally bulwarking the overall proceedings are Constance Moore piping a couple of numbers, Clara Ward Singers in a revival routine, cute singer Rozana Tapajos and Barklay Shaw with his puppet. Mickey Hargitay does a minor dance number with his then-wife, Miss Mansfield, which gives an indication of film's date.

Alan Steesvold is credited with color photography. Ray Livingston and Ed Biery had their work cut out as editors. *Whit.*

The Big Mouth
(COLOR)

Typical Jerry Lewis starrer, likely headed for hefty reception among comic's aficionados.

Hollywood, June 16.

Columbia Pictures release of Jerry Lewis production, produced-directed and starring Lewis. Features Harold J. Stone, Susan Bay, Buddy Lester, Del Moore, Paul Lambert, Jeannine Riley, Leonard Stone, Charlie Callas, Frank DeVol. Screenplay, Lewis, Bill Richmond; story by Richmond; camera (PatheColor), W. Wallace Kelley; editor, Russel Wiles; music, Harry Betts; asst. director, Rusty Meek. Reviewed at Columbia Pictures Studios, June 15, '67. Running Time, 107 MINS.

Gerald Clamson	Jerry Lewis
Thor	Harold J. Stone
Suzie Cartwright	Susan Bay
Studs	Buddy Lester
Mr. Hodges	Del Moore
Moxie	Paul Lambert
Bambi Berman	Jeannine Riley
Fong	Leonard Stone
Rex	Charlie Callas
Bogart	Frank DeVol
Gunner	Vern Rowe
Lizard	Dave Lipp
Fancher	Vincent Van Lynn
Detective No. 1	Mike Mahoney
Detective No. 2	Walter Kray
F.B.I. Agent	John Nolan
Specs	Eddie Ryder

Character established long ago by Jerry Lewis, that of a nitwit bordering on a halfwit with occasional bursts of sanity, has resulted in his being one of the top money stars of the screen. "The Big Mouth," marking his 36th film appearance and perhaps a little more way-out than usual, is strictly of the Lewis pattern, which implies substantial grosses.

Current outing not only stars the comedian, but was both produced and directed by him, as well as coscripted with Bill Richmond, who authored the original story. What comes out is frequently bewildering, but that's the story. The Columbia Pictures release limns the oft-bewildering trails of an eccentric fisherman who hooks a frogman and is entrusted with a map and some mumble-jumble about diamonds and a hotel with a yardarm just as a gang descends to dispatch the bleeding victim to happier hunting grounds.

Lewis draws on his customary zaniness and facial expressions as he tried to get someone to listen to his story, then is on the receiving end as two sets of crooks who pursue him for the stones.

Proceedings are narrated intermittently by Frank DeVol, who assures audience that what they are about to see was taken directly from the files of the Treasury Dept.'s "roughest cases," and "everything is true." Sandwiched between his being chased and encounters with various hoodlums Lewis indulges in a romance with Susan Bay, a newcomer playing an airplane stewardess who tries to help him out of his difficulties. Cost, most of whom are portrayed as slightly frantic-minded, is headed by Harold J. Stone, gangster leader, his three henchmen, Charlie Callas, Buddy Lester and Paul Lambert, and Del Moore, a hotel reception clerk. Jeannine Riley is in for sexpot purposes.

W. Wallace Kelley's color photography is effective. Production design by Lyle Wheeler, music by Harry Betts and editing by Russel Wiles are on plus side.

Whit.,

Der sanfte Lauf
(The Soft Course)
(GERMAN)

Berlin, June 17.
Constantin-Film release of Haro Senft production. With Bruno Ganz, Verena Buss and Wolfgang Buettner. Directed by Haro Senft. Screenplay, Haro Senft and Hans Noever; camera, Jan Curik; music, Erich Ferstil; editing, Thurid Soehnleim. At Bellevue-Lichtspiele, West Berlin. Running Time, 88 MINS.
Bernhard Kral .... Bruno Ganz
Johanna Benedikt .... Verena Buss
Richard Benedikt .. Wolfgang Buettner
Gertrud Benedikt .... Lia Eibenschuetz
Wolf Kamper .... Hans Putz
Susanna Kamper .... Dany Mann
Stefan .... Jan Kacer
Vera .... Nina Diviskova
Professor Koenig ...... Vladimir Hlavaty

Haro Senft has with "The Soft Course" (originally titled "Career") directed a first feature after 15 short pix. It's an adroitly made film though somewhat late to market. Had it been the first—or at least one of the first—German "new wave" pix, the overall impression might have been stronger. There is now regrettably too much cliche connected with it.

Film tackles the generation problem. There is a young man, a common employee who works in the dispatch department of a medium-sized company, who is actually a bright boy and he would have been seen in a higher position had he not been, for some reason, thrown out of a university. Yet he makes a career nevertheless. Responsible for it, at least indirectly, is his romance with the daughter of a wealthy businessman. The latter takes care that his daughter's friend gets an influential and well paid job. The young man still shows his grudge against the older generation and revolts against its "empty society"—but only for a while. He gradually loses this aggressive attitude and finally opts for the "soft course." Although he preserves some sort of irony, he too becomes materialistic-minded.

There is hardly any doubt that this is the creation of an intelligent director. But the whole thing is too much on the dry side and too "familiar."

Hans.

Those Fantastic Flying Fools
(BRITISH—PANAVISION— COLOR)

Named-studded cast help thin plot in this funny, if derivative, spoof of man's inventiveness and villainy.

American International Pictures release of a Harry Allan Towers production. Features Burl Ives, Troy Donahue, Gert Frobe, Hermione Gingold, Lionel Jeffries, Daliah Lavi, Dennis Price, Terry-Thomas. Directed by Don Sharp. Screenplay, Dave Freeman from original story by Peter Welbeck, inspired by writings of Jules Verne; camera (Pathe Color), Reg Wyer; music, John Scott; art director, Frank White; no other credits. Reviewed in New York, May 31, '67. Running Time, 92 MINS.
Phineas T. Barnum .... Burl Ives
Gaylord Sullivan .... Troy Donahue
Prof. Von Bulow .... Gert Frobe
Wayward Girls Custodian
                        Hermione Gingold
Sir Charles Dillworthy .. Lionel Jeffries

Madelaine .... Daliah Lavi
Duke of Barset .... Dennis Price
Warrant Officer .... Stratford Johns
Grundle .... Graham Stark
Capt. Sir Harry Washington Smythe
                        Terry-Thomas
General Tom Thumb .. Jimmy Clitheroe
Bulgeroff .... Joachim Tege
Queen Victoria..Joan Sterndale Bennett
Anna .... Renata Holt

If imitation is the sincerest form of flattery, then producer Harry Allan Towers has, at least, picked some first-rate originals to copy in "Those Fantastic Flying Fools" (of which even the title is derivative). Intended as American International's big summer release, it holds up better than fair as a colorful, frequently hilarious and never boring piece of funfare. The cast alone should insure bookings in better houses and an initial good impression on the comedy market.

While Dave Freeman's script contains more than token portions of previous Jules Verne stories (and the granddaddy of science fiction is given a fast credit for his inspiration), it isn't the lack of originality in theme that more than once make the film bog down. The dialog is something less than right, so much so that even excellent actors like Burl Ives and Gert Frobe are unable to salvage it.

The appeal of "Fools" is a visual one and here it holds up. A hilarious pre-title sequence (which is never reached again in the plot proper) makes a splendid opening for the foolishness that follows. It also establishes Lionel Jeffries as the world's most unsuccessful inventor (with Joan Sterndale Bennett as a deadpan Queen Victoria making a perfect straight-woman).

Director Don Sharp's experience as a comedy director helps him to gloss over the story's rough spots and he wisely gives his cast their heads as much as possible. Burl Ives is surprisingly subdued in the role of con man Phineas T. Barnum who has left the U.S. one jump ahead of the law but he holds up well against such skilled farceurs as Jeffries, Terry-Thomas and Dennis Price. Gert Frobe's German "mad" inventor is a bit heavy-handed at times but is ideal in the rich pre-title portion. There's almost nothing of Hermione Gingold as a briefly-seen custodian of a home for wayward girls.

Troy Donahue and Daliah Lavi provide the romantic interest, playing their scenes in the Victorian style used in "The Wrong Box." They make an attractive team. The rest of the cast is equally commendable, as is Reg Wyer's color photography which makes maximum use of the scenic Irish countryside where most of the location filming was done (although setting is Victorian England).

John Scott's score is melodious but not particularly original, continuing the Victorian spoof motif. Frank White's contribution as art director is one of the film's major assets and should be seriously considered come Oscar time, particularly the rocket ship which comes off as an outer space version of one of Lucius Beebe's private railroad cars.

A welcome change from the violence of the "protest" films AIP has been concentrating on lately, and with the widest appeal to the family market, "Fools" should be able to rack up some sizable business for the company.

Robe.

Jiouchi
(Rebellion)
(JAPANESE)

Tokyo, June 20.
Toho release of Mifune production. With Toshiro Mifune, Tatsuya Nakadai, Tsukasa Yoko, Go Kato, Michiko Otsuka, Katsuyoshi Ebara, Tatsuo Matsumura, Shiberu Koyama, Etsuko Ichihara. Directed by Masaaki Kobayashi. Screenplay by Shinobu Hashimoto, based on novel by Yasuhiko Takiguchi; Kazuo Yamada; music, Toru Takemitsu. Previewed in Tokyo. Running Time, 125 MINS.

Unless something better turns up, Massaki Kobayashi's "Joiuchi" (Rebellion), will probably turn out to be the year's best adult Japanese film. Written by Shinobu Hashimoto (who also wrote "Rashomon" and "Harakiri"), with music by Toru Takemitsu and directed by the man who created "Harakiri" and "Kwaidan," this Toho-Mifune production represents all the best in the Japanese period film.

At the end of the 18th Century, a middle-aged court official stationed in the North (Toshiro Mifune), married into the house of a virtuous harridan (Michiko Otsuka), discovers that the local daimyo (Tatsuo Matsumura) is demanding back an ex-wife (Yoko Tsukasa), who has since become married to Mifune's elder son (Go Kato). The reason is that she bore a child to the daimyo whose eldest boy has just died of illness in Edo. Hence, for appearances sake, the mother of the daimyo—apparent must be returned to the court.

Mifune has seen that his son and daughter-law love each other and love is something which he himself has never known. He therefore questions the authority of, first, his wife's family, then the family council, and finally that of the court secretary (Shigeru Koyama) and the daimyo himself. Though he believes that there is a purely private matter, it soon becomes apparent that he is questioning the entire feudal concept of government. But even he can do nothing for his friend once the entire feudal machine is set into motion against Mifune.

At first there are various attempts at intimidation and blackmail. When this does not succeed comes the daimyo's order for Mifune and Kato to kill themselves. Mifune does the unheard of; he refuses. Instead he barricades his house and awaits the worst. It occurs. The husband is killed. Mifune, however, kills soldiers and Koyama, and then taking his son's infant child, rushes to the barrier to get to Edo so as to state his case. His friend, Nakadsi, cannot let him through. Mifune must kill him and then he, the master swordsman, is killed by an ambusquade of muskets.

If this seems involved, it is only because the pic is extraordinarily convoluted. The film is very talky most of the time. Nothing happens, except talk, for the first hour and 40 minutes, and the screen explodes into the most slashing chambara since "Harakiri:" And there are many resemblances to this film.

The film is so absolutely hope-less and is also depressing. The major portion of this is carefully claustrophic and the spurting sword-play at the end brings no relief. Rather, the letting of blood does not purify nor is it intended to.

But showing waste as waste and the hopeless as hopeless indicates a startling honesty. This has long been Kobayashi's strongest virtue as a director, and Hashimoto's as a scripter. Unlike the Kabuki, the films of Kobayashi never once settle for the sentimental isn't-it-all-too-bad. Instead, the feudal philosophy (still as lively as ever in contemporary Japan) is attacked head-on and if the hero cannot win, then he makes a grand display of his immolation.

Chie.

Flame Over Vietnam
(SPANISH)

Okay but oldfashioned Spanish drama on French-Indo-Chinese War.

Producers Releasing Organization (PRO) release of Westside International (Sidney Pink) production. Features Elena Barrios, Jose Nietos. Directed by Joe Lacy. Screenplay, Ralph Salvia, Lacy, John Hart, from story by Salvia; camera, Miguel F. Mila; editor, Felix Suarez; music, F. Garcia Morcillo; song, "Mon Amour, Mon Amour," by Camilo Murillo Genero; sung by Maria Martin; asst. director, August Felonnar. Reviewed at Lyric Theatre, N.Y., June 14, '67. Running Time, 88 MINS.
Sister Paula .... Elena Barrios
Lazlo .... Jose Nietos
Brother Bartholomew ... Manolo Moran
Father Elias .... Nicholas Perchicot
Selma .... Rosita Palomares
The Driver .... Vincente P. Avila
Ellison .... Felix Dafauce
Angela .... Maria Martin

(Dubbed English Soundtrack)
This dubbed black-and-whiter from Sidney Pink's Spanish program of low-budgeters for PRO (theatrical) and Westinghouse (television) is not, as might be expected, filmdom's first fictional foray into the current Southeast Asian conflict. Brief narration at pic's beginning indicates that the French-Indo-Chinese War is involved. But in fact, except for one reference to Saigon and a few to "the French," film could be taking place anywhere in Asia. For instance, the foe is never called "the Communists" or "the Viet Minh" but simply "the enemy."

"Flame Over Vietnam" has many angles which make it a strange addition to Pink's package, which otherwise consists of color pix in which most of the main characters speak (or at least mouth) English. Much internal evidence suggests that it was not "produced" by Pink (although such a credit is found in ads, there is no producer's credit on film's main titles, where Pink is merely the "presentor"), but picked up by him with the explosive new title in mind.

Costuming, lighting and 1:33-1 aspect ratio all seem to indicate production date of some years ago. In addition, leading man is an older, moustachioed type common to films aimed purely to a Latin market. This, plus lengthy religioso passages anent mission in Indo-China suggest that feature emanates from an earlier era when Spain had domestic rather than international market in view.

Although ostensibly a war film, "Flame Over Vietnam" is solely concerned with civilians caught up in the conflict. Jose Nietos is the gun-running hero who is reformed by the efforts of the Spanish nun played by Elena Barrios. He arrives at her mission after being wounded by the French following one of his smuggling operations. In return for her tender loving care, he helps the sister and the orphans she tends leave country when the going gets rough, but he is himself killed in final moments.

Script by Ralph Salvia, Joe Lacy and John Hart from story by Salvia holds the interest, and Lacy's direction actually succeeds in keeping bathos and sentimentality to a minimum. Film can be programmed at most spots and its title can be counted on to attract.

Miss Barrios and Nietos essay leading roles adequately, but the famous Spanish broadness is all too evident in Manolo Moran's friar, Vincente P. Avila's truck driver and Maria Martin's nitery singer. The last-named warbles one French ditty amiably.

Extensive use of opticals by editor Felix Suarez is another indication of datedness. F. Garcia Morcillo's music is surprisingly modern, while Miguel F. Mila's photography, as suggested above, has the muted grey tones of the '50s.
Byro.

Warkill
(COLOR)

Somewhat standard heroic war film told "like it is," viewpoint heightening dramatic values. Hardhitting contemporary version of South Pacific action. With George Montgomery, Tom Drake. Good b.o. prospects in multiple release.

Hollywood, June 12.
Balut Productions presentation, in association with Centaur Ltd., produced, written and directed by Ferde Grofe Jr. Stars George Montgomery, Tom Drake. Camera (DeLuxe color), Remegio Young; editor, Phillip Innes; music, Gene Kauer, Douglas Lackey; assistant director, Ricardo Velasco. Reviewed at Lytton Center of Visual Arts, L.A., June 9, '67. Running Time, 103 MINS.
Col. John Hannegan .George Montgomery
Phil Sutton .... Tom Drake
Pedrini .... Conrad Parham
Dr. Fernandez .... Eddie Infante
Willy .... Henry Duval
Mike Harris .... Paul Edwards
Major Hashirl .... Bruno Punzalan
Sgt. Johnson .... David Michael
Max .... Joaquin Fajardo
Dr. Namura .... Bert La Fortesa
U.S. Major .... Claude Wilson

Initial feature of Balut Productions and Ferde Grofe Jr. is somewhat standard heroic war film presented from viewpoint similar to hippies' "tell it like it is," as if television cameras were following action of Filipino guerrillas in South Pacific during WWII. New angle heightens dramatic values of film which should have good draw as top half of double bill in multiple release.

Film is contemporary version of historical events near end of war when handful of Filipinos led by American officer roamed island still in partial control of scattered Japanese troops. Group seeks and smokes out small groups of Nipponese.

George Montgomery as Col. John Hannegan epitomizes the blood-and-guts warrior who uses whatever means is at his disposal to conquer the enemy—ethics be damned. He has been made a hero by correspondent Phil Sutton (Tom Drake) who has written several books about the colonel's exploits even though he has never met the man.

Sutton parachutes into the jungle to meet his ideal and write from firsthand experience and is warned that the soldier is not exactly what Sutton has pictured him to be. The correspondent's idea of war is not as ugly as it really is and his sensitivity is run over roughshod when he witnesses action of the colonel "who never takes a prisoner."

From time of the meeting, story is conflict between ideals of the two men; Hannegan's attitude of the hardened warrior and Sutton's compassion for the enemy. Montgomery deftly portrays implacable iron man and Drake gives credence to less empathetic role of fainthearted idealist. Grofe has wisely not drawn any conclusions from either attitude, neither favoring nor condemning horrors of war.

Film sets mood before credits with scene of Japanese soldier pursued by dogs trained to flush out enemy who are quickly dispatched by guerrilla guns. First half shows for shock value techniques used to kill off foes which turn Sutton's stomach and manage to do same for some of audience, i.e., half-starved giant rats are released in deep caves to attack Japanese who run out into volley of guerrillas' fire.

Action and drama heighten as Hannegan schools Sutton in nuances of guerrilla fighting. He explains, without apologizing, "In every man there is a beast and it's only this war that makes us animals." After the two are alienated completely, group comes upon results of Japanese atrocities and Sutton begins to understand.

Weakest scene in movie is when Sutton tells Hannegan he wants to go on "hunt" of concentrated Japanese forces, but what follows is excellent oater-type action, replete with ambushes, counterambushes, retreats, attacks, etc., which lead up to Alamo-type ending with suspense sustained through climax of arrival of reinforcements (cavalry).

Grofe has underplayed to achieve a hardhitting film which should keep war action fans on edges of seats. Acting is good throughout and camera work better than run-of-mill—overhead shot in opening scene used to good advantage and remainder filmed in proper perspective. Erratic march-tempo music nicely spaced for impact by coming in as camera pulls back from closeup of action scene. Special effects well-handled and locationing on monotonous jungle terrain offers no scenic beauty, just endless miles of jungle. *Edwa.*

The Sorcerers
(BRITISH-COLOR)

Boris Karloff as main marquee bait in straightforward thriller slanted to 'horror' addicts.

London, June 20.
Tigon Pictures release of Tigon-Curt-wel-Global production; executive producer, Arnold Miller. produced by Patrick Curtis and Tony Tenser. Stars Boris Karloff; features Elizabeth Ercy, Ian Ogilvy, Victor Henry, Catherine Lacey. Directed by Michael Reeves. Screenplay by Reeves & Tom Baker from John Burke's original idea; camera (Eastmancolor), Stanley Long; editor, Ralph Sheldon; music, Paul Ferris. Previewed at Hammer Theatre, London, June 12, '67. Running Time, 86 MINS.
Professor Monseratt ...... Boris Karloff
Estelle .... Catherine Lacey
Mike .... Ian Ogilvy
Nicole .... Elizabeth Ercy
Alan .... Victor Henry
Audrey .... Susan George
Laura .... Dani Sheridan
Inspector Matalon .... Ivor Dean
Detective .... Peter Fraser
Snack Bar Owner ..... Meier Tzelniker
Constable .... Bill Barnsley
Tobacconist .... Martin Terry
Customer .... Gerald Campion
Ron .... Alf Joint

Boris Karloff brings his familiar adroit horror touch to the role of an aging somewhat nutty ex-stage mesmerist who aims to complete his experiments by dominating the brain of a young subject. Karloff himself is dominated by his wife (Catherine Lacey) who was his stage assistant. The ripe experience of the two thesps is neatly blended with some promising younger talent such as Ian Ogilvy, Elizabeth Ercy and Victor Henry and Michael Reeves, a young director who also co-scripted the yarn, has done a commendable job in turning out a film which, without being remarkable, will stand up as a useful dualler in most situations.

Karloff persuaded Ogilvy, who plays a feckless, slightly moody youth, to become the subject for his experiments. Initial experiments work well as Karloff sees in the youth a tool who may be able to benefit mankind under his influence. But Karloff's wife, motivated by greed, insists that the lad should work for their benefit for awhile. She persuades her husband to let her take over the experiments. She commands the young man to rob a store to provide her with a fur coat. This leads to further demands on her part. The professor is anxious to bring the boy back to normal. But his wife, now flushed with power, eggs the lad on to violence and murder and the short film ends up in tragedy.

The screenplay is competent and effective, Eastman color lensing by Stanley Long makes good use of several London locations and Paul Ferris' score is pleasantly unobtrusive. Karloff handles his role with notable professionalism and Miss Lacey adds to the macabre atmosphere with a role that could easily have been hysterically overplayed.

Featured players chip in neatly and both Ogilvy who scored recently in "Stranger In the House," and Henry look to be more than useful entries in the young leading man stakes. *Rich.*

Jo-En
(Ardour Aflame)
(JAPANESE)

Tokyo, June 20.
Shochiku release of Gendai Eigasha production. With Mariko Okada, Isao Kimura, Etsuji Takahashi, Yoshie Minami, Shinako Shimeni. Directed by Yoshihige Yoshida. Screenplay, Yoshihige Yoshida after novey by Masaaki Tachihara; camera, Manji Kanao; music, Shigeru

---

Ikeno. Previewed in Tokyo. Running Time, 99 MINS.

This well-made existential parable, written and directed by Yoshihige Yoshida, is one of the most interesting Japanese films of the year.

Using a completely contemporary cinematic vocabulary (telephoto, lenses, over-lapped dialog tracks, variable focus, widescreen composition, fractured chronology), the director is not so much concerned with the story as he is with reflecting the totality of that single shattering experience suggested by the title, "Ardour Aflame."

A young woman (Mariko Okada) has a very loose mother (Yoshie Minami). She tries to break up her affair with a sculptor (Isao Kimura). Years pass. The woman becomes an unhappy wife and her younger sister (Shinako Shimeni) becomes very wild, eventually sleeping with her mother's final lover (Etsuji Takahashi), a laborer. Mariko, fighting against not only the emptiness of her own life, throws herself in the arms of the laborer, breaks with her husband, and seduces the sculptor. She has become, as she says, just like her mother.

The acting is excellent (particularly that by Mariko Okada who is on the screen almost continuously). The visuals are brilliant and the soundtrack is extraordinary. The film itself is moving, depressing, brilliant, sometimes erratic, and spendidly honest. The sex (there's a lot of it, even for a Japanese film) is amazingly candid. At the same time it's shown with a kind of dignity absolutely foreign to the kind of sexy-cheapies which this picture (because it is an independent production) might unfortunately become confused with.
Chie.

San Sebastian Fest

La Ragazza E Il Generale
(The Girl and the General)
(ITALIAN-COLOR)
MGM release of Carlos Ponti production. In Italian with Spanish subtitles. Stars Virna Lisi, Rod Steiger, Umberto Orsini. Directed by Pasquale Festa Campanile. Screenplay, Festa Campanile, Luigi Malerba; camera, Ennio Guarnieri; music, Ennio Morricone. Reviewed at International Film Festival at San Sebastian Film Fest. Running Time, 113 MINS.

This film's two scriptwriters were evidently a comic and a straight man. Basically a minor comedy of wartime errors (Italians vs. Austrians, 1914-18), it is marred by too many rotting soldiers bodies and too much pocket philosophizing on the evils of war. In the last reel the two lovers are killed by a land mine, leaving the audience to wonder just why so much laughter preceded their tragic demise. In less demanding general situations, the disparities of theme and treatment may go unnoticed, and the Lisi-Steiger names plus good production values should be enough to make money for this pic.

The General of the title is Rod Steiger, an Austrian captured by hayseed trooper Umberto Orsini. Orsini figures if he can get his prize back to the Italian lines, he will collect a fat reward and a medal. On the way Steiger escapes, but Orsini runs into peasant girl Virna Lisi, who makes a deal to help recapture the general for an equal share of the prize money. After numerous misadventures, most of them played for laughs, Steiger finally does reach the Italians, but his captors, whom he has come to like, die before they can claim their reward.

As the general, Steiger is good, alternately resigned to his fate and kind to his amateur captors. But for much of the picture he just plods along stoically. Virna Lisi is adequate as the earthy peasant, but her encounter with some Austrian soldiers who make her disrobe in exchange for some food is out of place and in bad taste.

Better than both is Umberto Orsini as the sleepy, hungry, love-starved soldier. Whether falling asleep just after Miss Lisi has agreed to bed down with him or extracting a potato from her bosom, he is completely natural. It is a shame all three did not have a better leader for their odyssey; as either comedy or tragedy (but not both), this pic would have been more successful.

Lyon.

Zwie Wie Wir
(Two Like Us)
(GERMAN)

Karl Hamrun Film production, with Spanish subtitles. Stars Susanne Beck, Thomas Piper. Features Hartwig Schindowski, Max Eckardt, Konrad Georg, Angelika Feldtmann, Walet Jokisch and Maria Paudler. Screenplay and direction by Hamrun; camera, Wolfgang Fischer, Klaus Engel; music, Irmin Schmidt. Reviewed at San Sebastian Film Fest. Running Time, 105 MINS.

"Two Like Us" is the first feature film by Karl Hamrun, a young German director. With the very best of intentions, he presents the platonic liaison between two adolescents in Hamburg—a naive, spoiled, rich girl who has run away from home to look for her boyfriend, and a lower class beatnik with whom she takes up instead.

What begins as an engaging, almost convincing relationship eventually becomes slightly ridiculous. Though utterly poor, their bliss is complete; though living in one room, they never even kiss. When the girl's parents come to take her away we cannot fully sympathize with the lovers' grief.

In spite of a modern, comparatively accomplished technique, Hamrun's story is too innocent and romantic to be believed. The two protagonists are adequate, at times almost fighting against the absurdity of the script. The other characters are stock ones, the gossiping women in the building, the drunken family man, over-zealous police inspector, bourgeois parents and avaricious landlord. It just might happen this way sometimes, but by avoiding any confrontation with a sexual, deeper relationship, Hamrun weakens his point of view. *Lyon.*

Szevasz; Vera
(Hello, Vera)
(HUNGARIAN)
San Sebastian, June 15.
Mafilm Production. With Spanish subtitles. Stars Maria Nemenyi; costars Tamas Balint, Teri Horwath, Laszlo Mensaros. Directed by Janos Herski. Screenplay, Isuzsa Biro and Hersko, based on novel by Magda Soos; camera, Janos Zsombolyai; music, Emil Petrovics. Reviewed at San Sebastian Film Fest. Running Time, 110 MINS.

Though socialism is a fact of Hungarian life, films from this part of Europe are inevitably suspect as propaganda vehicles. In this story of a maturing 17-year-old girl, director Janos Hersko has attempted a realistic look at his country's society and changing values, yet has refrained from political overtones in favor of a more "universal" approach. Lacking a familiarity with Hungarian life and the novel upon which this film is based, it is hard to measure the accuracy of his reflection of this culture. He has admitted that the film's vision of national life provoked fierce debate at home. On a purely cinematographic level, the picture is thoroughly engrossing, although its original, almost documentary style suggests any foreign playoff be limited to arty and specialized situations.

The yarn is about Vera, a young girl who decides to spend her summer at a university work camp while her parents and younger brother vacation elsewhere. Injured in a fall from a bicycle, she is sent to a hospital where she meets Terus, a middle-aged woman. By chance they meet again on a train and go to the wedding of Terus' daughter, where Vera meets a young guitarist. Repulsing his advances, she hitchhikes to meet Gyurka, an old boyfriend. Separated from him, she returns to her family. Uncertain of her relation to her elders, her little brother and her contemporaries, these few brief days of having to decide things for herself have been crucial in Vera's maturity.

The technique is modern — a telegraphic style with frequent improvization by the actors and the continued use of a zoom lens and hand-held camera. While this approach is successful in the village wedding sequence, beautifully capturing its intimacies and frantic merrymaking, it is at other times less appropriate. Despite the beauty and richness of the images, one feels the director was not always in complete control and perhaps relied too heavily on an overly inventive cameraman. At the beginning of this film, the technique is even less controlled, with a too fast, constant dialog and little pacing.

"Hello, Vera" is nevertheless convincing. Its dominant tone is freshness and sincerity—that what one sees really is happening for the first time. The acting, even in translation, is good. The casting of Maria Nemenyi as Vera is especially apt, although this appears to be her first and last picture. Though often excessive, the photography is first-rate. This is an interesting film that might repay a modest investment for foreign arty situations. *Lyon.*

Yovita
(POLISH)
San Sebastian, June 20.
Syrena Film Unit production. Stars Daniel Olbrychski; co-stars Barbara Kwiatkowska, Zbigniew Cibulski, Kalina Jedruski. Directed by Janusz Morgenstern. Screenplay, Tadeusz Kowicki, based on novel, "Disneyland," by Stanislaw Dygat. Camera, Jan Laskowski; music, Jerzy Matuskiewicz; editor, Wieslawa Otooka. Reviewed at San Sebastian Film Fest. Running Time, 100 MINS.

The director of this attractive film has joined sex, mystery, psychology, athletics, social comment and philosophy in an almost perfect combination. Story of the amorous, spiritual gropings of a young Polish athlete is modern and intense. Though understated and by no means a masterpiece, this pic is as good as some of the recent Polish works seen in the West, without the excesses of many of them. With intelligent publicity, it could do business in foreign arty spots.

The hero is Marek, a young architect and track star whose sports career has made him a national hero. Tall, handsome, he glides through life with a bemused naturalness. He is a supreme egotist and is tremendously successful with women. He believes happiness and greatness in both his careers are tangible and within his grasp. But he is dissatisfied. His life is without real meaning and he feels he is responsible for the suicide of an elderly friend.

At a costume ball he meets a masked girl with beautiful eyes who calls herself Yovita. In a brief, mysterious encounter he feels she is the one he is destined to love. But Yovita disappears, and he takes up with Agnieszka, who occasionally refers to the mysterious girl as a friend who has had to leave the country.

Now Marek is frantic. Tired of athletics, he wants to quit but his coach will not let him. He wants to find Yovita again, with whom he has identified his salvation. He is reluctant to leave Agnieszka. Attempting to expiate the guilt he feels over the death of his friend, he attacks his friend's lover, a prostitute, and is sent to jail. Here Agnieszka visits him to say she is marrying another man. As she turns to go she tells him that she was Yovita; he had her all the time!

The acting is first-rate. Especially good is the late Zbigniew Cibulski as the coach. Morgenstern's technique is always modern, but never excessive. It is "classic" and sober in its economy and arrangement of shots, yet fluid and penetrating. The photography is realistic yet subtle. This is a balanced, even elegant film, and probably the best of the festival. *Lyon.*

Una Historia de Amor
(A Love Story)
(SPANISH)

San Sebastian, June 20.
Estela Films, S.A., production. Stars Simon Andreu, Serena Vergano, Teresa Gimpera; features Yelena Samarina, Felix de Pomes, Jose Franco, Adolfo Marsillach. Directed by Jorge Grau. Screenplay, Grau, Jose Maria Otero, A. Castellon; camera, Aurelio G. Laraya; music, Antonio Perez Olea. Reviewed at San Sebastian Film Fest. Running Time, 100 MINS.

The best description of "A Love Story," both in theme and treatment, is its title. Director Jorge Grau has taken the eternal triangle, but has been unable to add very much new to it. His situations are by now cliches and his treatment, though sincere, is often more melodramatic than dramatic. Although the acting and production values are good, the story is predictable.

Daniel is a young novelist in Barcelona who supports himself and his pregrant wife by working on a newspaper. When her sister Sara comes to stay with them to help out, she and Daniel are mutually attracted. Not wanting to hurt the wife they are reluctant to carry their flirtation farther than a few passionate embraces, which the wife discovers. On New Year's Eve she has her baby, and the sister, finally realizing she must not continue, leaves them.

Unfortunately, the story does not seem to merit the length and grandness of its widescreen treatment. Grau gives it more importance than it deserves, when the peccadillo for the husband is little more than understandable and passing fancy and a frivolous flirt for the sister. Things end completely naturally, but with little choice by the characters of their fate. Although this is a smooth film, it takes rather long developing and the photography never becomes more than purely functional. *Lyon.*

Vrazda Po Cesky
(CZECH)
San Sebastian, June 21.
Barrandov Film production. Stars Rudolf Hrusinsky and Kveta Fialova; features Vaclav Voska, Vladimir Mensik, Vera Uzelacova, Libuse Svormova, Vjaceslav Irmanov. Directed by Jiri Weiss. Screenplay, Weiss and Jan Otcenasek; camera, Jan Nemecek; music, Zdenek Liska; editor, Miroslav Hajek. Reviewed at San Sebastian Film Fest. Running Time, 86 MINS.

For the first half of "Vrazda Po Cesky," director Jiri Weiss masterfully presents a timid clerk, his search for love, his pointless marriage and the realization that he is a cuckold. Only after the clerk begins to plot his rival's murder (it is his boss) does the picture lose some conviction and interest. Abandoning the initial mood of realistic satire for one of unbridled fantasy, Weiss plays camera and chronological tricks on the spectator but without equalling the film's strong beginning. From a good director, this is a disappointing picture.

Frantisek is a fat, aging clerk with little future. He plods through his job and life demanding and getting very little. One cinema, one concert and one good meal a month are his only pleasures. Winner of a week's vacation at his company's country hotel, he meets a clerk in the central office of the same government bureau. After a brief courtship (encouraged by his boss) they are married, even though they can only see each other on weekends.

When Frantesek discovers he is being deceived, he kills his wife and her lover. He smothers his wife instead, than changes his mind, begins again to commit suicide. But when he views his own funeral he decides to blackmail his boss for a better job and ignores his wife's infidelities. The last sequence has them happily driving down a highway together (a color insert); when they come to a traffic jam their car takes off into the air to avoid it. *Lyon.*

The St. Valentine's Day Massacre
(PANAVISION-COLOR)

Excellent semi-documentary about the 1929 gangland shoot-out. Jason Robards heads solid cast. Socko production, direction, scripting. Exploitation bonanza.

Hollywood, June 28.
Twentieth Century-Fox release of Corman Co. production, produced and directed by Roger Corman. Features Jason Robards, George Segal, Ralph Meeker, Jean Hale. Screenplay, Howard Browne; camera (DeLuxe Color), Milton Krasner; editor, William B. Murphy; music, Fred Steiner, conducted by Lionel Newman; asst. director, Wes Barry. Reviewed at 20th-Fox Studios, L.A., June 27, '67. Running Time, 100 MINS.

Al Capone	Jason Robards
Peter Gusenberg	George Segal
Bugs Moran	Ralph Meeker
Myrtle	Jean Hale
Jack McGurn	Clint Ritchie
Sorello	Frank Silvera
Weinshank	Joseph Campanella
Scalisi	Richard Bakalyan
Frank Gusenberg	David Canary
May	Bruce Dern
Frank Nitti	Harold J. Stone
James Clark	Kurt Kreuger
Narrator	Paul Frees
Charles Fischetti	Paul Richards
Guzik	Joseph Turkel
Adam Heyer	Milton Frome
Schwimmer	Mickey Deems
Dion O'Banion	John Agar
Josephine Schwimmer	Celia Lovsky
Newberry	Tom Reese
Willie Marks	Jan Merlin
Aiello	Alex D'Arcy
Patsy Lolordo	Michele Guayini
Hymie Weiss	Reed Hadley
Rio	Gus Trikonis
Salvanti	Charles Dierkop
Bobo Boretto	Tom Signorelli
Albert Anselmi	Rico Cattani
Diamond	Alex Rocco
Heitler	Leo Gordon

Producer-director Roger Corman has come up with a slam-bang, gutsy recreation of "The St. Valentine's Day Massacre", a 1929 gangland sensation of Chicago. Well-written, and presented in semi-documentary style, pic features Jason Robards as Al Capone. Salty dialog and violence are motivated properly, and solid production values recreate a by-gone era. Torrid b.o. potential evident via 20th-Fox release in general situations. Treatment permits a hard exploitation sell, but in certain markets an emphasis on the timeless sociological aspects of organized crime might be effective.

Howard Browne, credited by production notes as being an expert of the Capone era, has fashioned a hard-hitting original screenplay, climax of which is the brutal slaying of seven hoods of the Bugs Moran gang, then competing with the Capone mob. There is no attempt to glorify the hoods; they were bum trash, pure and simple, as are their grey-flannel counterparts today who flourish because society and payoff permits them to. Very good occasional narration by Paul Frees documents the backrounds, and the final destiny, of the criminals.

The horrendous premise, properly understated, is that, in the minds of bigtime criminals, society is composed of suckers who deserve to be fleeced. The sole problem, then, is carving up the business franchises. With such a mentality, perhaps a fist in the face, or worse, is the only meaningful argument; it is the only logic criminals understand among their own kind, apparently.

Robards is excellent as Capone, and Ralph Meeker, as Moran, is equally chilling. A large cast also spotlights George Segal, who with brother David Canary, act as Meeker's ace gunmen. Clint Ritchie, playing in very good fashion the ever-smiling, dapper Jack McGurn, one of Capone's key aides, is placed by his boss in charge of eliminating Moran and his mob. Latter — through a stroke of fate — escaped the bloodbath, and Capone was never proven the man behind it all.

Recurring use of ethnic vulgarisms, today frowned upon, is perfect in context. Frequent gun deals — expertly staged by Corman and edited in terrif fashion by William B. Murphy — hold strong interest in the way that people cannot help being both repelled and attracted by disaster and atrocity. While both violence and dialog make pic a doubtful item for the very young, such elements are motivated properly in the dramatic sense, thereby escaping any charges of cheap exploitation of brutality for its own sake.

Under Cormans excellent direction, entire cast delivers on-target performance. Jean Hale, while in limited footage, comes across superbly as the kept woman of Segal; pair's fight over a fur coat is a highlight, and one can feel her well-placed knee in the gut. Frank Silvera scores as an immigrant who fits into Ritchie's plan for the rub-out.

Milton Krasner's photography, in Panavision and DeLuxe Color, is crisp and clean, also fluid. Art directors Jack Martin Smith and Philip Jefferies and set decorators Walter M. Scott and Steven Potter, have exercised a lavish hand in outfitting people and places. In two Robards flashbacks, a deliberate color-toning of release prints, effect of which is a rotogravure look, was a showmanly gambit.

Fred Steiner composed the main-and end-title music excerpts, conducted by Lionel Newman. Remainder of music derives naturally from plot as nitery bands, records and radios play contemporary songs. Overall pacing of the 100-minute pic is excellent, and makes clear the events leading up to the massacre. End title footage — the wall where the massacre occurred — is a solid switcheroo from the earlier gore; so powerful is the impact that the blood can be seen with the mind's eye. All other credits are pro. *Murf.*

The Naked Runner
(BRITISH—COLOR—SCOPE)

Poorly written spy drama, shot down further by inept direction. Frank Sinatra cannot save it. Dull dual bill prospects in less discriminating grind situations.

Hollywood, June 23.
Warner Bros. Pictures release of a Sinatra Enterprises Production. Stars Frank Sinatra. Directed by Sidney J. Furie. Screenplay, Stanley Mann, based on the novel by Francis Clifford; camera (Technicolor), Otto Heller; editor, Barry Vince; music, Harry Sukman; asst. director, Michael Dryhurst. Reviewed at Academy Award Theatre, L.A., June 22, '67. Running Time, 104 MINS.

Sam Laker	Frank Sinatra
Slattery	Peter Vaughan
Col. Hartmann	Darren Nesbitt
Karen	Nadia Gray
Ruth	Toby Robins
Anna	Inger Stratton
Cabinet Minister	Cyril Luckham
Ritchie Jackson	Edward Fox
Joseph	J.A.B. Dubin-Behrmann
Patrick Laker	Michael Newport

The entire b.o. burden of "The Naked Runner" will have to be shouldered by Frank Sinatra, who receives little help from other elements of this dreary Sinatra Enterprises programmer, produced by Brad Dexter. Script premise is dubious, plotting lacks suspense, and climax is unsatisfying. Sidney J. Furie directed in pretentious fashion. Made in England at an obvious price, the Warner Bros. release will need a fast playoff, on dual bills, in general situations.

From a Francis Clifford novel, writer Stanley Mann has fashioned a dullsville script, based on premise that British Intelligence—with its vast facilities so obvious in story development—cannot assign one of its own to murder a defector to Russia. Instead, Sinatra, a World War II spy now a businessman-widower, is dragooned into service, and by events, deliberately staged, is goaded into killing the defector. Not only British Intelligence, but anybody's intelligence, is likely to be affronted by this potboiler.

Sinatra, whose personal magnetism and acting ability are unquestioned, is shot down by script; his limning suggests awareness of futility of the story. Peter Vaughan overacts part as the British agent who stages a deception for Sinatra's benefit; latter's son, Michael Newport, ostensibly has been kidnapped by alleged East German agent Derren Nesbitt, in reality a British spy. Nadia Gray, Toby Robins and Inger Stratton play femmes who somehow get involved.

There is no suspense engendered, for audiences know, from the first reel, that Sinatra is a patsy.

Furie's direction is inept. Possessed professionally by a low-angle and furniture fetish, he relegates his audiences to the floor in nearly all setups, and characters are seen in the background behind telephones, a coffee cup and other physical claptrap with which Furie junks up his imagery. Towards the end of pic, human faces are rarely seen at all.

Harry Sukman's musical excerpts are justified in awkward fashion: phonographs in some scenes. Otto Heller's lensing indicates that he did what he was told to do. The Techniscope-Technicolor images look grainy and inferior, even from the back row of a large theatre; pity the down-fronters. Barry Vince executed editing to an interminable 104 minutes. Other credits are routine. *Murf.*

Banning
(COLOR-TECHNISCOPE)

Dreary sudser about country-club set. Topnotch production values cannot salvage bad script, blah direction. Lower-case entry in tear-jerker situation.

Hollywood, June 27.
Universal release of a Dick Berg production. Features Robert Wagner, Anjanette Comer, Jill St. John, Guy Stockwell. Directed by Ron Winston. Screenplay, James Lee, based on a story by Hamilton Maule; camera (Technicolor),

Loyal Griggs; editor, J. Terry Williams; music, Quincy Jones; song lyric, Bob Russell; asst. director, Edward K. Dodds. Reviewed at Universal Studios, L.A., June 26, '67. Running Time, 102 MINS.

Banning	Robert Wagner
Carol	Anjanette Comer
Angela	Jill St. John
Linus	Guy Stockwell
Chris	James Farentino
Cynthia	Susan Clark
J. Pallister Young	Howard St. John
Kalielle	Mike Kellin
Tommy Del Gaddo	Gene Hackman
Tyson	Sean Garrison
Doc	Logan Ramsey
Stuart Warren	Edmon Ryan
Sen. Brady	Oliver McGowan
Maggi Andrews	Lucille Meredith
Tony	Bill Cort

"Banning" is one of those sex-laden sudsers, all talk and no action, and loaded with two-dimensional cardboard country-club characters, which once titillated matrons at matinees. Billed as the feature debut of ex-tv producer Dick Berg, meller is handsomely produced and features a slew of younger players, none of whom can rise above a zero script and pedestrian direction. Title, which might suggest action-adventure, is merely top-featured Robert Wagner's last name in the plot — and even that name is a phony. Dullsville b.o. likely on Universal lower-case release.

A Hamilton Maule story has been adapted by James Lee into a lifeless script, in which all characters, nearly, engender absolutely no sympathy. Tale is about jaded rich people who enjoy forced frolic at a country club where Wagner cons a job as assistant golf pro. Guy Stockwell, who once ruined Wagner's career by false charges of dishonesty, is having an affair with Anjanette Comer. His wife, Susan Clark, is tycoon Howard St. John's daughter. Jill St. John is a combination sexpot and queen bee character who has eyes for Wagner.

James Farentino is an ambitious ex-caddy who yearns for Wagner's job, and thereby plays into Stockwell's hands. Sean Garrison has a minor part, and Mike Kellin plays a hood whose demands for a gambling debt payoff provide the basis for what action there is. Most of the dialog has a superficial bite to it—that is, smart rejoinders that have no meaning but sound awfully chic — but the story is a sorry potboiler.

Some of the players come off well: with better script, Wagner would have been more impressive; Stockwell is okay; Farentino is very good, Kellin and Hackman excellent. Howard St. John overdoes the tycoon bit. Among the femmes, Miss St. John is in the groove, and Miss Clark shows promise in better roles which demand graciousness. Miss Comer, however, is stuck with a measured, rote delivery. It is difficult with scripts such as this to apportion credit or blame. Ron Winston herein directing his third feature (according to production notes), shows little imagination.

Plot vapidity is only underscored by superior, lavish production. Art direction, by Alexander Golitzen and Henry Bumstead, the Jean Louis gowns, and Bud Westmore's makeup contribute excellent visuals, caught by Loyal Griggs' Technicolor-ful lensing.

Universal de-emphasizes Tech[illegible] usage in ads (light-face type) and titles (separate card from the color process). Techniscope, as has been said before, looks fine on exteriors, but interiors tend to be grainy.

Quincy Jones wrote good score including a love theme. Latter, lyrics by Bob Russell and sung — twice — by Gil Bernal, is further overemphasized in background, and by the end of 102 minutes, it definitely sounds like a combination of the theme from "An Affair To Remember" and "Face To Face" Tune is plugged in the dialog, a bit too obviously, when Miss Comer comments on it to Wagner. Other credits are pro.

Murf...

The Tiger and The Pussycat
(Il Tigre)
(ITALIAN-AMERICAN)
(Color)

Rome, June 27.

Fair Film coproduction with Joseph E. Levine's Embassy Pictures. Stars Vittorio Gassman, Ann-Margret, Eleanor Parker; features Fiorenzo Fiorentini, Antonello Steni, Luigi Vannucchi, Caterina Boratto. Directed by Dino Risi. Original screenplay, Age and Scarpelli; screenplay, Age, Scarpelli, and Dino Risi; camera, Sandro D'Eva; editor, Marcello Malvestito; music, Fred Bongusto. At the Bernini, Rome. Running Time, 105 MINS.

Francesco Vincenzini	Vittorio Gassman
Carolina	Ann-Margret
Esperia Vincenzini	Eleanor Parker

Combination of Vittorio Gassman, director Dino Risi and producer Mario Cecchi Gori has put into release pix like "Easy Life" which often have brushed aside all competition—foreign and domestic—to run in the clear at the head of Italy's top grossers. "The Tiger" goes one step further and adds the marquee names of Ann-Margret and Eleanor Parker in a bid to topple marks set by "Easy Life."

An example of the rich, slick film entertainment, "Tiger" is a sophisticated comedy (all Italiano), filmed in English and dubbed somewhat defectively in Italian. Though the shoe is on the other foot, Italo audiences spend less time worrying about inaccurate lip synch and more time enjoying the salty bedroom situations and bold dialog.

Screenwriters Age and Scarpelli, with a script assist from Risi himself, take a timeworn three-point relationship, bulwark it with many physical gag situations and flash comic inserts. But they depend on the more basic cleavage between parents and offspring to underscore the extra-marital fling between a middle-age captain of industry (Vittorio Gassman) and a 20-year-old Bohemian ball of fire (Ann-Margret). Eleanor Parker plays the abused wife with suave dignity.

For about two-thirds of the film "The Tiger" is a swiftly-paced romp of gay deceit for the male partner and a purposeful drive for sexual plentitude on the distaff side. Slowdown occurs with Gassman's dilemma. Prodded by his young mistress to give up wife and family (his career by this time is practically shot anyway), the charm and tempo slacken while Gassman weighs a choice that distills the joy of a seven-inning stretch. Risi also attempts to comment on the bruising conflict between the older and younger generations and, if he makes a point, it is the almost imperceptible suggestion to resist crossing the tracks.

Vittorio Gassman is on the scene almost every minute of the film. It's an unfair load to bear with such a slight story in support but he's first-rate until the action sags. Eleanor Parker is standout as the attractive, understanding wife and mother of two grownup children. Her top portrayal often adds a note of implausibility to Gassman's foray. The role will certainly lead to many others. Ann-Margret is many things. While she has the physique and sexy stare, she is not a modern-day continental Bohemian. Inexplicably her beat dance number at the Piper Club was edited down to a brief terp appearance with quick fade just as the number of starts to grow on the eye. Technical credits are on par with Hollywood standards.

Werb.

The End of August at the Hotel Ozone
(Konec Srpna V Hotelu Ozon)
(CZECH)

Czechoslovak Army Film Studios production, featuring Ondrej Jariabek, Betta Ponicanova, Magda Seidlerova. Directed by Jan Schmidt. Screenplay, Pavel Juracek; camera, Jiri Macak; editor, Miroslav Hajek; music, Jan Klusak; asst. director, Milan Jonas. Reviewed at Festival of New Czechoslovak Cinema, Museum of Modern Art, N.Y., June 18, '67. Running Time, 87 MINS.

The Old Man	Ondrej Jariabek
The Old Woman	Betta Ponicanova
Barbara	Magda Seidlerova
Theresa	Hana Vitkova
Clara	Jana Novakova
Judith	Vanda Kalinova
Magdalen	Natalie Maslovova
Anna	Irina Lzicarova
Martha	Jitka Horejsi
Eva	Alena Lippertova

This offbeat fantasy-cum-scifi from young director Jan Schmidt is only one of the 12 pix at N.Y.'s current Festival of New Czechoslovak Cinema which has not been previously reviewed in VARIETY. It proves a strange admixture of arty and traditional commercial elements. "The End of August at the Hotel Ozone" emerges as unsuitable for either market in the U.S.

Scripted and directed in another manner, story of a group of wild girls who kill and forage in order to survive 15 years after an atomic war has destroyed most of the world might have served splendidly as a subject for Roger Corman a few years back, and it still could do as a basis for a Hammer-style programmer now. But Schmidt and screenplay writer Pavel Juracek have chosen to present tale in a somber, slow "festival style."

Juracek's idea, which seems more Hobbesian than Marxist, evidently was that a group of girls brought up in this kind of environment would be wild, impetuous, amoral figures, not too different in manner than the femalekind in such features as "Prehistoric Women," "One Million Years B.C.," and like that. Result is that arty audience assembled at Museum of Modern Art this week often giggled at incidents on screen, though director's serious intention was recognized and there was some applause at the end.

The girls find food any way they can, killing all sorts of animals in cold blood. Story develops quietly until they find an old man living alone at a deserted hotel—the first male they have ever seen. But despite his implorations, the girls travel on after their leader, an old woman beautifully played by Betta Ponicanova, dies. Idea seems to be that mankind will survive, even, in this uncivilzed fashion. Before moving on, the girls shoot the old man in order to steal his gramophone.

The American Society for the Prevention of Cruelty to Animals, which has raised objections to previous Eastern European pix, may well be shocked anew at viewing this one. In long takes, with no faking apparent, a snake and a dog are killed on camera.

The girls are given little individual characterization, being primitive beasties all, but young Czech actress Magda Seidlerova scores as second-in-command of the group. Jiri Macak's camerawork is uneven at times, while Jan Klusak's music has an electronic, modern feel. All other technical credits are pro.

Byro.

The Shuttered Room
(BRITISH-COLOR)

London, June 27.

Warner-Pathe release of Seven Arts (Troy-Schenk) production. Features Gig Young, Carol Lynley, Oliver Reed, Flora Robson. Directed by David Greene. Screenplay, D. B. Ledrov, Nathaniel Tanchuck; camera (Technicolor), Ken Hodges; editor, Brian Smedley-Aston; music, Basil Kirchin. Reviewed at Warner Cinema, London. Running Time, 99 MINS.

Mike Kelton	Gig Young
Susannah Kelton, Sarah	Carol Lynley
Ethan	Oliver Reed
Aunt Agatha	Dame Flora Robson
Zebulon	William Devlin
Tait	Bernard Kay
Emma	Judith Arthy
Luther Whateley	Robert Cawdron
Aunt Sarah	Celia Hewitt

With a good quota of shudders and a neat suggestion of evil throughout, this is an efficient entry in a somewhat oldfashioned vein of melodrama. The main credit for its tension goes to director David Greene, who uses his cameras with versatile effect, occasionally making them represent the spooky presence that haunts the story, so that the thesps fearfully retreat from them with skin-prickling effect. Although supposedly taking place in New England, the locations are blatantly British scenery to the local eye but may convince the uninitiated.

Susannah Kelton (Carol Lynley) has inherited an old millhouse on a remote island, and turns up there with husband Mike (Gig Young) to take possession. A prologue already has warned that there's a mad dame locked up in an upper story, and so Susannah is greatly puzzled by the insistence of the natives that she should stay away. Ethan (Oliver Reed), who heads a mischievous gang of layabouts, surveys her with a morose and lascivious eye and chases her to the end of a jetty, where she is rescued from a damp rape in the nick of time. Aunt Agatha (Flora Robson), a sturdy old lady in need of a hair-do, also insists that the pair should return to Manhattan forthwith. And other inhabitants are rather discouraging.

Ethan gets his followers to set upon the husband and tie him up, thus making possible further pursuit of the distraught Susannah. And one of his girl friends is alarmingly killed by an unseen assassin. The whole thing rises to an uninhibited climax, with Ethan falling to his death and dropping his torch, which starts a fire, frying the mill and its crazy occupant. She is Susannah's long-lost sister, of whom she had been wisely kept in ignorance.

The script (from D. B. Ledrov and Nathaniel Tanchuck) is adequate in the plotting but feeble in the dialog department, sparking off untoward laffs in the wrong places. Carol Lynley is competently scared throughout. And Oliver Reed brings a brooding touch of lechery to the over-excited Ethan. Dame Flora Robson has little to do but look woeful, but does it with expected force. Of the minor thesps, Judith Arthy makes an impression as Ethan's local girl, who must endure much unbuttoning of the blouse. Gig Young has the undemanding role of the solicitous husband and treats it with indifference.

All technical credits are up to par, with fine Technicolor lensing from Ken Hodges and brisk editing from Brian Smedley-Aston. It adds up to medium entertainment for the not-too-selective, with an extra touch of class in Greene's helming. *Otta.*

Berlin Festival

The Penthouse
(BRITISH—COLOR—SONG)

Taut, gripping, horrific thriller, splendidly written, directed and played, with great sleeper chances; sales push needed to speed word-of-mouth and overcome marquee weakness.

Berlin, June 27.
Paramount release of Tahiti-Twickenham Film Studios production for Compton Intl. Stars Suzy Kendall, Terence Morgan, Tony Beckley, Norman Rodway, Martine Beswick. Written and directed by Peter Collinson. Based on C. Scott Forbes' play "The Meter Man." Camera (Eastmancolor), Arthur Lavis; music, John Hawksworth; song, "World Full of Lonely Men," by Hawksworth and Harold Shaper, sung by Lisa Shane; editor, John Thumper. Reviewed at Berlin Film Fest. Running Time, 90 MINS.

Barbara	Suzy Kendall
Bruce	Terence Morgan
Tom	Tony Beckley
Dick	Norman Rodway
Harry	Martine Beswick

Paramount (and Rank, which has this pic for a few areas including France) have themselves a trim entry in the horror-thriller stakes with this neatly written, directed and acted item. It's one of those happy commercial films in which the money invested comes out many times multiplied thanks to a simple but often absent ingredient: talent. If properly sold, it should overcome such obvious hurdles as lack of international names and go on to make itself a tidy little bundle in most areas. It's deliberately strong, heady contents might, if handled differently than here, have irked some and especially a censor or two. But under

the current more liberal outlook on films, this shouldn't hit too many snags.

Story is one of those claustrophobic items which find hero and heroine trapped in an isolated apartment with a pair of deranged hoodlums alternating physical and mental bouts of sadism as they break down the couple's resistance. But it's not what goes on but how it's developed that raises this item above the level of other orgy-chiller entries. Peter Collinson's script and direction work hand-in-hand like a precision watch in milking a situation or line to the utmost before seguing, after a pause for breath, to the next crescendo build-up.

Admittedly, there's plenty of very sick stuff around. The sexual characteristics of the two, and ultimately three intruders are to say the least blurred, and there are at least two open references to "real" cigarettes that help people "fly," as well as some rather over-graphic symbol sin. And there's some nudity, too, albeit tasteful, on the part of Miss Kendall, which shouldn't hurt the film's chances any.

But, apart from fact that the pic, especially in its two closing plot twists, makes some telling points about human frailty and selfishness, it's as noted the quality of the lines and their subtle yet powerful impact of their contents, plus the superbly controlled delivery by the cast, that makes this a compelling—if at times inevitably distasteful—glimpse at some of the seamier characteristics of the human being.

Tony Beckley and Norman Rodway make up as sinister a pair of menaces as seen onscreen in some time, with Beckley contributing a chilling seven-minute monologue about alligators (and people?) caught in sewage pipes that stands as a classic of its kind. Both are outstanding.

Martine Beswick adds menacing good looks to a briefer stint, coming across very strongly. Terence Morgan has the most sacrificed role, strapped to a chair for most of the pic, but brings it off convincingly, especially in the degraded last moments. In her first sizeable part to date, Suzy Kendall displays great promise and personality in a well-modulated performance as the harassed target of the men's attentions, which augurs well for this talented young looker's future.

Technically, the production is tops, with Arthur Lavis' caressing lenswork especially effective in its abundant use of closeups and in its chiaroscuro pattern of growing menace. Song by John Hawksworth and Harold Shaper, "World Full of Lonely Men," is tacked on over the finale, ostensibly to underline pic's message about the frail of the human being. *Hawk.*

Il Conigliaccio
(The Strange Night)
(ITALIAN)

Berlin, June 27.
Independent release of Angal Film-Mancori Prodn. Features Sandra Milo, Enrico Maria Salerno, Giulio Platone, Lydia Alfonsi, Massimo Serato, Ettore Manni, Giorgio Capecchi, Evi Maltagliati, Antonella Steni, Adriano Micantoni,

Elvira Cortese, Gino Rochetti, Ugo Fangareggi, Adria Ramacci, Ettore Ribotta, Franco Fiorini, Anna Maria Checchi, Sandro Quasimodo, Paolo de Bellis. Directed by Alfredo Angeli. Screenplay, Angeli, Marco Guglielmi, Bruno Rasia, from story by Guglielmi; Added dialogue, Angeli, Giulio Paradisi; camera, Marcello Gatti; music, Benedetto Ghiglia; editor, Giulio Paradisi. Reviewed at Berlin Film Fest. Running Time, 110 MINS.

Debra	Sandra Milo
Grao	Enrico Maria Salerno
Aldo	Giulio Platone
Erika	Lydia Alfonsi

Strange and overlong, with some amusing interludes here and there, this first pic effort by Alfredo Angeli never really makes up its mind what it wants to be, turning rapidly from farce and satire (its strongest ingredients) to whodunit melodrama and social commentary, and then back again. Result is a ultimately unsatisfying item with slim chances in non-Italian marts. This does, however, show a decided if undisciplined flair for filmmaking by Angeli, whose background is advertising films, which could mature into a substantial career. One suspects, also, from the unevenness of this film, that all was not smooth sailing along the way. Nevertheless, this does not excuse the disjointed and often far-fetched story line.

This deals with a last-fling night on the town by a Roman father (Giulio Platone) who expects his wife and kids back from vacation the next day. At one point, he's picked up by an elegantly dressed mystery woman (Sandra Milo), who promptly commits suicide on him in his flat after first having conversed at length with an otherwise unknown man called Rossano. Remainder of pic details his efforts to get help and rid himself of the body without compromising his family life, but friends, chance acquaintances and strangers all fail him and he'll presumably have a lot of explaining to do to the police, who find the body in his place just as his wife's arriving.

Giulio Platone is excellent in his picture debut as the harassed husband. All other performances, including a rather static one by Sandra Milo and an overly agitated bit by the usually reliable Enrico Maria Salerno, are uneven. Pic boasts some flashy lensing by Marcello Gatti and a rather obsessive music track by Benedetto Ghilia. *Hawk.*

Het Gangstermeisje
(A Gangstergirl)
(DUTCH)
(SONG)

Berlin, June 21.
Unset release of Jan Vrijman-Cineproductie (Amsterdam) production. Features Kittie Courbois, Paolo Graziosi, Asta Weyne, Gian Maria Volonte, Joop Van Hulzen, Walter Kous. Director Frans Weisz. Screenplay, Weisz; Remco Campert; camera, Gerard Vandenberg; editor, Astrid Weyman (Asta Weyne). Reviewed at Berlin Film Fest. Running Time, 100 MINS.

Karen	Kittie Courbois
Wessel Franken	Paolo Graziosi
Leonie Franken	Asta Weyne
Jascha	Gian Maria Volonte
Danny	Joop Van Hulzen
Max	Walter Kous

Diffuse, dedicated and ambitious pic (which, for the record, may travel under a fuller title: "Illusion is a Gangstergirl"), all the worthier because it comes from a small country with a limited number of cinemas (and thus fewer

guaranteed outlets). Item is nevertheless not one to raise foreign temperatures by many notches — at least on the general audience level. It is, despite its many Riviera and Roman location sequences, basically nordic in mentality and concept, factors which will partly restrict its impact in other areas.

Films about struggling, tormented young writers, who have reached a critical point in their career, have been a filmic staple for ages. And this differs little from the pattern. Uncertain about his ability and his married life, Wessel Franken (Paolo Graziosi) leaves Holland for sunnier Cote d'Azur climes to hack out a pic script based on his own bestseller. Only partially distracted by a homosexual relationship between his Riviera host and latter's longtime majordomo pal, Franken segues to Rome and an affair with the film's leading lady. But, he soon tires of the artificial local film-flam and heads back to the Dutch homestead he once thought he abhorred.

Two things stand out in an otherwise overlong and unexciting pic: some imaginative sequences showing the scribes intercut thoughts as his future pic script takes visual form; and a very sensitive, unsensationalized treatment of the homo relationship, nicely underplayed by Walter Kous (the ageing host) and Joop Van Hulzen (the young majordomo).

There are some good performances, too, by Kittie Courbois and Asta Weyne (who under her real name, Astrid Weyman edited the pic as well) as the two women, and by two Italo thesps, Paolo Graziosi and Gian Maria Volonte.

Technically, this has been lavishly mounted and has some topnotch lensing by Gerard Vandenberg, with other credits in kind. An uncredited song, "Tag und Nacht" (Day and Night) is inserted to underline a pic point close to the finale, and is sung over action. *Hawk.*

Taetowierung
(Tattoo)
(GERMAN-COLOR)

Berlin, June 29.
Eckelkamp-Verleih release of Rob Houwer production. With Helga Anders, Christof Wackernagel, Rosemarie Fendel, Alexander May. Directed by Johannes Schaaf. Screenplay, Johannes Schaaf and Guenter Herburger; camera, Wolf Wirth; music, Georg Gruntz; editor, Dagmar Hirtz. At Berlin Film Fest. Running Time, 87 MINS.

Gaby	Helga Anders
Benno	Christof Wackernagel
Frau Lohmann	Rosemarie Fendel
Herr Lohmann	Alexander May
Lohmann's brother	Tilo van Berlepsch
Sigi	Heinz Meier
Auctioneer	Heinz Schubert
Simon	Wolfgang Schnell

"Tattoo" is the first feature pic of 34-year old Johannes Schaaf who has already achieved some native prominence via the legit and television, both as an actor and director. Whatever may be said about the contents of this Rob Houwer production, there is no doubt that it displays remarkable directorial talents. It is an outstanding directorial debut and Schaaf is one of the most impressive among this country's young and new film creators. If handled with care, "Tattoo" should be in for at least satisfactory returns within its homegrounds.

Also, it should be able to stir foreign attention. However, it requires a receptive audience since the type of film that can easily be misunderstood.

Direction is fast, fluent and imaginative all down the line. Yet there may be some controversy regarding film's moral issue. But even this may help it inasmuch as the viewer is always aware of the fact that this is the work of a serious-minded director who wants to say something. The ending of "Tattoo" will force patrons to think. The film's central figure, a young lad, shoots his stepfather without apparent reason, and even looks happy about it. It's a thoroughly unconventional e n d i n g which has its meaning. It is the revolt of a young human, a victim of our society.

The film starts out in a home for juve delinquents. The first scenes show him being tortured by his fellow inmates for he is not willing to tell them where he has hidden a gun which he has stolen. This scene makes a point that he's alone in the world. He then is given the chance to live in what is called better surroundings. His stepfather takes him home and he has the privileges of being a member of a family that has no financial worries and he could lead a normal life with so many a material advantage. But he can't take a fancy to it. Not only that he has a dislike for his babbit type of stepfather there is also the big gap between: him and **the older generation evident. He** feels that there is so much false and empty talk on the part of the adults. Everything on both sides seems to lead nowhere. The hopelessness of his situation leads to self-destruction when the boy kills his stepfather.

Much of this rings true. Eventually there are symbolisms but, fortunately enough, Schaaf doesn't go overboard with them. He keeps them under control. What may stir special controversy is the utilization of the Commie wall that separates West from East Berlin. There are some scenes associated with the world's "most ugly building" and which is shown here as a pure tourist attraction. The fact that this is basically a sad wall gets, involuntarily, another meaning here.

Director Schaaf deserves praise for his adroit handling of the players. All the performances come close to being lifelike. In 16-year-old Christof Wackernagel, the "hero" in this, one may even congratulate Schaaf. In him he found the most ideal casting imaginable. A brilliant piece of acting is also turned in by Alexander May.

The entire film had been shot against actual Berlin surroundings. This gives "Tattoo" a highly authentic flair. Wolf Wirth's Eastman-color lensing shows discipline despite its fastidious ambitions. Editing and other technical credits are firstclass.   *Hans.*

La Noche Terrible
(The Terrible Night)
(ARGENTINIAN)
Berlin, June 27.
Marcello Simonetti production and release. Features Susana Rinaldi, Jorge Rivera Lopez, Maria Luisa Robledo, Hec-

tor Pellegrini. Directed by Rodolfo Kuhn. Screenplay, Kuhn, Francisco Urondo, Carlos del Peral, C. F. Moreno, from story by Roberto Arlt; camera, Juan Jose' Stagnaro; music, Oscar Lopez Ruiz; editor, Antonio Ripol. Reviewed at Berlin Film Fest. Running time, 47 MINS.
Julia .... Susana Rinaldi
Ricardo .... Jorge Rivera Lopez
Julia's mother .... Maria Luisa Robledo
Paco .... Hector Pellegrini

Taking a page or two from some recent Italian satires, especially those of Pietro Germi, Argentine director Rodolfo Kuhn has fashioned an amusing, stinging comedy which should ride along nicely on worldwide Latino circuits. Beyond this fringe, it is handicapped by a local cast (though they play very well) and by so-so production values. Might make a good lightweighter if transposed to Yank setting with an English-language cast.

Story, parts of which have a dejavu quality about them but still work admirably here, concerns the pre-wedding qualms of a man on the eve of the ceremony. Via flashforwards, he imagines what would happen if he bowed out of wedding, went ahead with it, or how things might stand if he'd taken a more honest straightforward approach to his fiancee and her family. Much of this is told in a zany blend of burlesque, black and white humor, political barbs, plus some racy lines and rather graphic bed and bedroom scenes abundantly laced with nudity. Latter, however, is played for laughs, not leers.

Jorge Rivera Lopez and Susana Rinaldi, especially the former, are fine as the intended couple. And there's some rather good backing throughout by a large cast, headed by Maria Luisa Robledo, who plays the scheming mother-in-law. Production values of pic (especially the lensing), as noted, tend to lessen the impact of pic which, if dressed up a bit, might have helped the films horizons.   *Hawk.*

Largo Viaje
(A Long Journey)
(CHILE)
Berlin, June 30.
Enrique Campos Menendez and Alfonso Naranjo Urrutia production. Directed by Patricio Kaulen. Screenplay, Patricio Kaulen, Javier Rojas; camera, Andres Martorell; music, Gastone Lefever; editor, Carlos Piaggio. At Berlin Film Festival. Running Time, 83 MINS.
The boy .... Enrique Kaulen
The husband .... Emilio Gaete
The wife .... Eliana Vidal
The lover .... Fabio Serpa
Boy's father .... Ruben Uberra
Boy's mother .... Maria Castiglione

With only three feature pix produced in 1966 and maybe five this year, the Chilean feature film production is apparently still in its infancy. Patricio Kaulen's "A Long Journey" is rated as one of this Latin American country's better productions and even regarded as a milestone in Chilean filmaking. Pic was submitted to the Berlin Festival and accepted here as an entry for the so-called "Film Show of the Countries," a frame program w i t h i n the festival. Foreign chances are probaby very slim but it has possibilities for tele exploitation inasmuch as it gives an interesting insight into life, habits and problems of this South American country.

Although it fails to make an impression on the more demanding

patron, this film displays a good deal of ambition on the part of its director. This is certainly not a superficial production. In addition to a series of interesting scenes there is also an impressively realistic death-bed sequence woven in. This one is the highpoint of the film. Pic contains strong social criticism and its respective attitude can be both on the Marxist and Christian side.

According to the belief of the Chilean country population, a child who dies after birth is called "a little angel" which results not only in sadness but also in a joyful celebration because the "the little .angel" gets into heaven. Central figure here is a boy who has always been wanting a brother to play with. His mother gives birth to a brother but he dies after birth. Film depicts the dilemma of the boy. Quite a number of themes are tackled such as juve delinquency, adultery, prostitution, aristocracy, superstition, etc. It has very much the flavor of a documentary but is not exactly such type of presentation because the boy walks through nearly all the scenes and there is quite a bit of dialog along the line.

The boy, incidentally, is enacted by the director's son, Enrique Kaulen. It's a nice moppet performance. Film's technical credits are okay.   *Hans.*

The Flim-Flam Man
(PANAVISION-COLOR)

Outstanding comedy about an aging con man and his younger partner. George C. Scott heads great cast. Direction, script, production tops. All-age appeal. Hotsy b.o.

Hollywood, June 29.
Twentieth Century-Fox release of a Lawrence Turman production. Stars George C. Scott, Sue Lyon. Directed by Irvin Kershner. Screenplay, William Rose, based on the novel, "The Ballad Of The Flim-Flam Man," by Guy Owen; camera (DeLuxe Color), Charles Lang; editor, Robert Swink; music, Jerry Goldsmith; asst. director, William Kissel; second unit director, Yakima Canutt. Reviewed at 20th-Fox Studios, L.A., June 28, '67. Running Time, 104 MINS.
Mordecai .... George C. Scott
Bonnie Lee Packard .... Sue Lyon
Curley .... Michael Sarrazin
Sheriff Slade .... Harry Morgan
Mr. Packard .... Jack Albertson
Mrs. Packard .... Alice Ghostley
Deputy Meshew .... Albert Salmi
Jarvis Bates .... Slim Pickens
Lovick .... Strother Martin
Tetter .... George Mitchell
Market Manager .... Woodrow Parfrey
Customers .... Jay Ose, Ray Guth

"The Flim-Flam Man" is an outstanding comedy starring George C. Scott as a Dixie drifter. Socko comedy-dramatic direction by Irvin Kershner makes the most of a very competent cast and a superior script. Handsome exterior production values spell an impressive debut of Lawrence Turman as a solo producer. Michael Sarrazin, as Scott's fellow-traveler, makes an impressive feature film bow. Subject matter lends itself to zesty promotion, with correspondingly snazzy b.o. prospects likely via 20th-Fox release in general, all-age situations.

Guy Owen's novel, "The Ballad of The Flim-Flam Man," has been adapted by William Rose into a finely balanced screenplay which exploits inherent comedy situations while understating, appropriately, the loneliness of a rootless man. A series of flim-flams are pulled off only on people who seemingly deserve to be stiffed, thus minimizing any complaint that lawlessness is being made attractive.

Scott delivers a superior performance as the aging sharpie. Sarrazin, who was loaned out from Universal for the part of the younger partner, will return to that studio leagues up the professional ladder. Identification with younger audiences is achieved as he works out his own destiny. Sue Lyon, billed above title with Scott, provides romantic interest for Sarrazin, and sparks latter's second thoughts about leading a carefree, wandering existence.

Among the greedy suckers, taken in ingenious fashion by Scott and Sarrazin, are Slim Pickens, Strother Martin, George Mitchell, Woodrow Parfrey, Jay Ose and Ray Guth. Each of them registers a bulls-eye, all the more impressive because of the brevity of their vignettes. Jack Albertson and Alice Ghostley bring life to the parts of Miss

Lyon's parents, and each has good opportunity to show comedy talents. Harry Morgan, top-featured, is excellent as the long-suffering sheriff. Albert Salmi is his able deputy.

One of the best comedy car chase scenes in years—six minutes of total hilarity as Scott and Sarrazin practically wreck a town—is the work of Kershner and second unit director Yakima Canutt. This scene is most reminiscent of Fields, while the interaction between Scott and other principals conjures up memories of Tracy.

Spotting of chase scene, less than 30 minutes from start of pic, was rather daring, in light of possible anti-climax of what follows. Thanks to scrip, actors and direction, there is no letdown in entertainment throughout the 104 minutes of running time, as edited in fine fashion by Robert Swink.

Photography, in Panavision and DeLuxe Color, by Charles Lang is firstrate. Jerry Goldsmith has provided a very good score, with a rhythmic, citified country and western flavor prevailing. Music enhances the desired comedy effect without ever being heavy-handed. Other technical credits are superior, except in a brief ferry scene where sound recording is fuzzy. *Murf.*

A Rose for Everyone
(Una Rosa Per Tutti)
(ITALIAN—COLOR)

Claudia Cardinale cheering up a host of sad males in Brazil. Sexploiter.

Royal Films International release of Vides Film, produced by Franco Cristald. Stars Claudia Cardinale; features Nino Manfredi and Mario Adorf. Directed by Franco Rossi. Screenplay, Eduardo Borras, Ennio de Concini, Franco Rossi, Nino Manfredi, based on play by Glaucio Gill; camera (Technicolor), Alfio Contini; editor, Giorgio Serralonga; music, Luis Enriquez; asst. directors, Mario Forges Davanzati, Maurizio Rotundi, Nello Vanin. Reviewed at Little Carnegie, N.Y., July 2, '67. Running Time, 107 MINS.

Rosa .... Claudia Cardinale
The Doctor .... Nino Manfredi
Paolo .... Mario Adorf
Basilio .... Akim Tamiroff
Lino .... Lando Buzzanca
Silvano .... Luis Pellegrini
Sergio .... Milton Rodriguez
Nino .... Oswaldo Loureiro
Floreal .... Jose Lewgoy
Ze Amoro .... Grande Othelo
Nilse .... Celia Bilar
Donna Natalia .... Laura Soares

This Italian import, which opened without much fanfare at N.Y.'s Little Carnegie, tries to do for Brazil what "Never on Sunday" did for Greece. It succeeds in promoting South American tourism but is only fair as entertainment. Limited art-house runs seem likely before pic is dubbed for sexploitation bookings.

Directed and coadopted by Franco Rossi from a play by Glaucio Gill, film depicts sexual and romantic adventures of warm-hearted Rosa (pun of Italian title is lost in literal English translation used in advertising). Besides haphazardly dispensing drug samples to her friends in Rio de Janeiro, Rosa gives herself freely to a wide variety of male admirers. She explains her promiscuity to a stiffly proper doctor bent on converting her by saying, "Most men are sad, and after they've been with me they're happy for a while." Point is carefully made that Rosa receives no money for her favors, just the joy of seeing others happy.

Many viewers are likely to distrust this ingenuous alibi for loose morals. Were this accomplished with charm and humor, fine, but unfortunately Rossi frequently strains for laughs Result is an overlong pic with too many moments of attempted pathos to score as comedy and too much superficial silliness to qualify as drama.

Miss Cardinale does well as Rosa, showing more spunk and appeal than usual. If something can be done about her scratchy voice, she might join the forefront of screen comediennes. Nino Manfredi, an excellent comedian and pleasing personality, is again wasted as the doctor. With the right roles, Manfredi could become an international star, but instead he continues to squander his talents in innocuous pix. Reminder of cast, especially Mario Adorf and Lando Buzzança, is colorful and loud.

Technically "A Rose for Everyone" is quite slick. Alfio Contini's color photography is bright, although overuse of interior lighting effects becomes tiresome. Film could profitably lose 15 of its 107 minutes running time, but otherwise editing is okay. Luis Enriquez' music is effective except for some overly melodramatic throbbing in the final reels. A song, "Rosamor," written by Enriquez and Jose Chavez, is in the "Man and a Woman" groove and could conceivably catch on. *Beau.*

My Hustler

Underground homo feature is something for the boys, though big-city and college-town hipsters of all sexes may dig its closeup look at deviate squabbling.

Produced, photographed, directed, and distributed by Andy Warhol. At Hudson Theatre, N.Y., July 10, '67. Running Time, 79 MINS.

Blond hustler .... Paul America
Bald man .... Ed Wiener
Second hustler .... S. P. Farry
Beach girl .... Jeanne Vieve

Andy Warhol's ascension from the N.Y. underground will provoke many responses—annoyance, indignation, amazement, not to mention some high-pitched "male" tittering—but one thing it will not do to audiences is bore them. Considering the unprecedented tedium of Warhol's last pic, "The Chelsea Girls," this is high praise indeed. **In today's anything-goes market, it is difficult to predict b.o. future of such a pic, but film could repeat the special situation and college-town success of "Chelsea."** One thing's for sure—it'll never make the circuits.

"My Hustler" looks no more professional than Warhol's previous excursions into filmmaking. The camera still remains stationary for long stretches (one static take lasts a full 30 minutes), and what motion Warhol does employ consists of headache-inducing zooms and wobbly pans. The sound reproduction is so poor as not to deserve the epithet "amateur": volume level suggests an aural rollercoaster, about a third of the dialog is muffled, and lip sync is off for most of the film.

Still, for all the technical blunders, "My Hustler" possesses some narrative fascination for those with sufficiehtly strong stomachs and/or psyches. A young boy, hired for the weekend by a wealthy Fire Island homo through the "Dial-a-Hustler Service," is fought over by the aging deviate, a girl from next door, and another hustler well past his prime. What makes the film morbidly absorbing is not this tenuous storyline—which, in the best N. Y. underground tradition, is never resolved—but the considerable detail with which the "gay" life is documented. At show caught, audience seemed predominantly homosexual, but more liberal heterosexuals may find the bitcheries, the clawing, and the implicit sadness of this vacuous life of some sociological interest.

As underground pix go, this is surprisingly well acted by a cast that seems to be improvising its way through the 79 minutes with little screenplay and less directorial guidance. Ed Weiner, as the petulant and waspish older man, hits the right note of overdrawn malevolence and strained witticism. S. P. Farry, deinitialized in the pic and called *"The Sugar Plum Fairy,"* scores as the pathetic mid-30s hustler and neatly satirizes (if unintentionally) the guy's obsessive narcissism. Jeanne Vieve seems unsteady as the next door neighbor. As for Paul America (no kidding!), he may well become Warhol's inverted answer to Monica Vitti.

For the record, the current version of "My Hustler" includes some totally extraneous footage not included when first shown in January, '66, at the Filmmakers' Cinematheque. At several points in the film, the story is interrupted for irrelevant montages of male-to-male kissing, fully displayed genitals, and the like.

The film seems sufficiently scandalous without these gratuitous inserts, but credit Warhol with a firm knowledge of his "specialized" audience and its entertainment requirements. *Beau.*

King's Pirate
(COLOR)

Okay pirate meller for escapist market.

Hollywood, July 6.

Universal release of Robert Arthur production. Stars Doug McClure, Jill St. John, Guy Stockwell; features Mary Ann Mobley, Kurt Kasznar, Richard Deacon, Torin Thatcher. Directed by Don Weis. Screenplay, Paul Wayne, Aeneas MacKenzie, Joseph Hoffman; story, MacKenzie; camera (Technicolor), Clifford Stine; editor, Russell F. Schoengarth; music, Ralph Ferraro; asst. director, Phil Bowles. Reviewed at Universal Studios, July 6, '67. Running Time, 100 MINS.

Brian Fleming .... Doug McClure
Mistress Jessica Stephans Jill St. John
John Avery .... Guy Stockwell
Patma .... Mary Ann Mobley
Zucco .... Kurt Kasznar
Swaine .... Richard Deacon
Captain Cullen .... Torin Thatcher
Molvina MacGregor...... Diana Chesney
Cloudsly .... Ivor Barry
Captain Hornsby .... Bill Glover
Gow .... Woodrow Parfrey
Sparkes .... Sean McClory
Collins.............. Michael St. Clair
Captain Mission .... Emile Genest
Captain McTigue .... Ted De Corsia
Caraccioli .... Alex Montoya

Universal, which two decades ago concentrated on derring-do mellers for big reception at box-office, has a suitable entry for its intended market in this reprise of the cycle which made stars of Turhan Bey and late Maria Montez. Starring Doug McClure, Jill St. John and Guy Stockwell, the Robert Arthur production, turned out with tongue-in-cheek treatment, is filled with the type of escapist action favored by program trade.

Madagascar, circa 1700, backdrops the Paul Wayne-Aeneas MacKenzie-Joseph Hoffman screenplay which twirls around efforts of the British to halt piracy of the rich trade route to India. McClure, playing a Colonial American, volunteers to silence the guns of the pirate port of Diego Suarez and in regulation style accomplishes his mission. If the plot and dialog creak a bit, ingredients are still there to suffice as an okay buccaneer yarn in the spectator doesn't take it too seriously.

McClure smiles through most of his performance, and Miss St. John dons some beguiling attire sometimes more exciting than the action. Stockwell is the pirate first mate out to get the hero. Mary Ann Mobley as the daughter of the emperor of India and Kurt Kasznar, leader of an acrobatic troupe which helps McClure, add their talents to brighten the unfoldment.

Don Weis' direction is fast but tighter editing would benefit. Clifford Stine's color photography is handsome. Technical credits are mostly on plus side. *Whit.*

Born Losers
(COLOR)

Sock Hell's Angels meller with topical theme; hefty grosses seen in its particular market.

Hollywood, July 1.

American International release of Donald Henderson (Delores Taylor) production. Stars Tom Laughlin, Elizabeth James, Jeremy Slate, William Wellman Jr.; guest star, Jane Russell; features Jeff Cooper, Robert Tessier, Edwin Cook, Paul Prokop. Directed by T. C. Frank. Screenplay, E. James Lloyd; camera (PatheColor) Gregory Sandor; editor, John Wineld; asst. director, Paul Lewis. Reviewed at screening room, June 27, '67. Running Time, 114 MINS.

Billy Jack .... Tom Laughlin
Vicky Barrington ...... Elizabeh James
Mrs. Shorn .... Jane Russell
Danny Carmody .... Jeremy Slate
Child .... William Wellman Jr.
Cue Ball .... Robert Tessier
Gangrene .... Jeff Cooper
Crabs .... Edwin Cook
Tex .... Tex
Speechless .... Paul Prokop
LuAnn Crawford .... Julie Cahn
Linda Prang .... Susan Foster
Jodell Shorn .... Janice Miller
Sheriff .... Stuart Lancaster
Deputy .... Jack Starett
District Attorney .... Paul Bruce
Mr. Crawford ....Robert Cleaves
Mrs. Prang .... Ann Bellamy
Jerry Carmody .... Gordon Hobal

Third in American International's spread of Hell's Angels pix is dramatic and topical, carrying shock impact and exploitation potential which should garner fast playing time in the wide market that caters to subject. Following "The Wild Angels," which launched cycle as a minor blockbuster, and the more hastily-contrived "Devil's Angels," put together to cash in on forerunner's success, "Born Losers" carries the mark of authority and has been well made throughout. Pic, started as an indie, was acquired by AIP during shooting.

The Donald Henderson production is even more frank than its two predecessors in pointing up the ruthlessness of an outlaw motorcycle gang which takes over a community. There is greater violence, more outspoken scenes of the gangs depredations against society. Premise of the E. James Lloyd screenplay, too, is a more legitimate pinpointing of a topical situation which sees peace officers stymied in steps to curb lawlessness by reluctance of the public, through fear, to testify against those who have committed crimes.

Shortcomings of the law are graphically depicted as several young girls are raped by members of a gang headed by Jeremy Slate. Efforts of lawmen to prosecute, even arrest, the offenders, are continually balked by lack of evidence, created by the gang threatening their victims if they should testify against them. Only hand raised against them is by a part-Indian, Tom Laughlin, who launches a one-man crusade and finally is successful, climaxing in his killing the leader. He is mistakenly killed by the sheriff's deputy.

Director T. C. Frank builds mounting tension and suspense and draws sock performances from his entire cast, in which Jane Russell appears as a "guest star," the mother of one of the raped girls. Topical overtones are apparent throughout, and as such the film deserves social attention for touching on one of America's sore spots today. For weak stomachs there is perhaps an overdose of violence, but it fits the tenor of the theme and is not objectionable.

Laughlin delivers a firstrate performance in an underplayed portrayal and Slate scores strongly as leader of cutthroats out to terrorize the community. Elizabeth James also delivers a superior delineation as one of the raped teenagers, a college girl who becomes innocently involved and is made a virtual prisoner by the gang. William Wellman Jr., and Jeff Cooper are standouts among the gang members, both excellently cast, and Paul Bruce is good as the frustrated District Attorney.

Technical credits are decided assets, including particularly Gregory Sandor's color photography, John Winfield's realistic editing, Rick Beek-Meyer's' art direction.

Whit.

What Am I Bid?
(COLOR-TECHNISCOPE)

Entertaining original musical-romance, aimed at country-western market. LeRoy Van Dyke, Al Hirt for marquee. Story thin, production thinner, but hot b.o. in c&w areas.

Hollywood, July 6.

Emerson Film Enterprises release of Liberty International (Wendell Niles Jr.) production. Features LeRoy Van Dyke, Kristin Nelson, Stephanie Hill, Bill Craig. Written, directed, words, music by Gene Nash. Camera (Technicolor), Ralph Woolsey; editor, Terry O. Morse; music conducted by Ernie Freeman; asst. director, Jim Myers. Reviewed at Lytton Center of Visual Arts, L.A., July 5, '67. Running Time, **92 MINS.**

Pat Hubbard	LeRoy Van Dyke
Beth Hubbard	Kristin Nelson
Maggie Hendricks	Stephanie Hill
Mike Evans	Bill Craig
Bus Ticket Clerk	Leland Murray
Tractor Salesman	Andy Davis
Concert Fan	Muriel Landers
Fenster	Sid Rushakoff
Publisher	J. B. Towner
Clem	Bill Benedict
Hal Cook	Jack McCall
Darrell	Darrell McCall
Secretary	Lea Marmer
Themselves	Al Hirt, Tex Ritter, Johnny Sea, Faron Young

The first production of Liberty International, a partnership of Wendell Niles Jr. and Atlanta developer Hue R. Lee, "What Am I Bid?" is an entertaining original screen musical. LeRoy Van Dyke, already established in the country-western tune field, makes a promising film debut. Also in a film bow, Gene Nash scripted and directed in good fashion, and composed 10 of the 11 new songs, all arranged and conducted by Ernie Freeman. The (Joe) Emerson Film Enterprises release, with cameo appearance by Al Hirt, Tex Ritter, Johnny Sea and Faron Young, has strong uppercase potential in its basic market, plus very good dual bill strength in all general situations.

Nash, a onetime vaude hoofer, in later years has become a songwriter and talent manager, among whose clients are Van Dyke (no relation to Dick or Jerry) and Sea. It is Nash's 1st screenplay which, although basically fictional, includes some actual career highlights of Van Dyke: Young, for example, first got him on a performing stage; Ritter got him a tour; and Hirt booked him into his New Orleans nitery. Presence of all three adds b.o. potential.

Story is uncomplicated: Van Dyke is pursued by magazine writer Stephanie Hill, on a c&w assignment, and by Bill Craig (actually a Nashville d.j.), a hard-up waxery man, both of whom want him to turn pro. Kristin Nelson, Van Dyke's sister, shares his initial reluctance to do so, based on unhappy childhood when their dad abandoned his family for such a career.

Expected romantic ties develop, then get hung up on misunderstanding, settled before fadeout, between Craig-Miss Nelson and Van Dyke-Miss Hill. Final scene is aboard a U.S. Navy carrier, where Van Dyke sings a patriotic number, "We've Got The Best There Is", including a simple, but effective, dance sequence, staged by George Jack, and involving 10 sailors and guitars.

Van Dyke has a likeable screen personality, and, over and above his excellent singing voice (the diction will remind many of the late Buddy Clark), can be promoted further in film roles. He himself, with Buddy Black, penned "Auctioneer," a remarkable test of vocal versatility. Among the other songs, "Don't Look Back," "I'll Make It Up To You," and the title song are excellent. Sea's one number, "When A Boy Becomes A Man," will reach young people particularly.

The Misses Nelson and Hill, also Craig, are adequate in their roles. Supporting bits, all of which come off well, feature ticket-clerk Leland Murray, tractor salesman Andy Davis, c&w buff Muriel Landers, record label chief Sid Rushakoff, publisher Stuart Randall and hayseed Bill Benedict. Nash's direction is straightforward, free of pretentious angles. Montages are okay, but two superposition sequence look awkward. Physical production values are thin; pic came in under $400,000, and was shot at the Goldwyn Studio.

With a song coming along every eight minutes or so, prime attention will be paid to the music. Freeman and Nash recorded the entire score before cameras rolled. It has the "Nashville sound" evident in all current pop music. Besides songs already nabed. Ritter's "I Never Got To Kiss The Girl" is an amusing look back at his pix roles, and Hirt's trumpet solo on "Too Late, Too Soon" has a nice romantic melancholy. Other numbers are pleasant.

Below the line, Ralph Woolsey's Technicolor-Techniscope lensing is okay, and Terry O. Morses editing makes for a fast-moving 92 minutes. Coast publicist Phil Paladino was associate producer. Exhibs in key non-Dixie cities, where large audience ratings exist for radio stations which feature c&w music, will book and exploit pic accordingly.

Murf.

Round Trip
(COLOR)

N.Y. Negro model snubs Harlem; French painter dotes on Negro folkways. It's hard going.

Continental release of Chablis (Mitchell Leiser) Production. Features Venantino Venantini, Ellen Faison, Larry Rivers. Directed by Pierre Dominque Gaisseau. Screenplay, William Duffy; camera (color), Victor Petroschevitz; editing, Sidney Katz. Previewed in N.Y., June 30, '67. Running Time, **88 MINS.**

Marc Daumel	Venantino Venantini
Ellen Tracy	Ellen Faison
Larry	Larry Rivers
Diana Evremont	Joan Thornton
Clarice	Clarice Rivers
Jacques	Jacques Kaplan
Sheila	Sheila Clarke
Silverstein the Loft King	
Silverstein the Loft King	Himself
Drama coach	Melinda Lasson
Travis (playwright)	Henri Abehsera

Of the many English-language pix made by w.k. foreign directors in this era of international film-making, "Round Trip" is possibly the worst. The Continental release can expect only meager returns in the U.S. General ineptitude rules out successful art-house runs, while its lack of names and touchy theme (miscegenation) preclude general playdates in all but the hungriest markets.

Pierre Dominique Gaisseau has previously been repped in this country by three documentaries, the Academy-Award-winning "The Sky Above—The Mud Below," "Only One New York," and "The Flame and the Fire." This background shows in his first fictional effort, with its sociologically slanted tour of Harlem and other N.Y.C. points of interest. Trouble with these Manhattan views is they impede development of a story that never does gather any momentum.

William Dufty's screenplay tells of romance between a French painter recovering in N.Y. from a broken marriage and a Negro fashion model. Conflict arises out of overly pat contrast between his enthusiasm for Negro folkways and her desire for the finer things like minks, cars, and classical music. Eventually he returns to Paris to care for his injured daughter, while she remains behind, wistfully aware that "neither time nor love ever return."

Dialog throughout relies heavily on cliches ("I don't want to get involved again . . . at least not right now"). Exposition is clumsy, e.g., the exchange in which she asks him about his ex-wife ("Was she dark like Sophia Loren or blonde like Brgiitte Bardot?") and he replies, "Not exactly: my daughter tries to look like Brigitte Bardot, but she's only six years old." The non sequitor, needless to say, is designed to advance the plot.

The model's running narration elaborates thoughts and emotions that a better director would have conveyed visually ("He finally said 'I love you' in French . . . it sounds so nice, but what does it mean?"). Furthermore, the subjective point of view is sometimes violated by including events she could not have witnessed and yet describes in detail.

Acting is on a par with the writing, although Venantino Venantini (recently seen here in "Galia") possesses sufficient charm and finesse to register well in a better written and directed film. Same cannot be said for newcomer Ellen Faison, a beautiful but completely wooden actress. She reads dialog three or four words at a time, with awkward pauses and no discernible emotion. Rest of the cast, including avant-gardist Larry Rivers as himself, is equally amateur.

Beau.

Satogashi ga Kawareru Toki
(When The Cookie Crumbles)
(JAPANESE—COLOR)

Tokyo, July 4.

Daiei Co., production (Masaichi Nagata) and release. With Aiyako Wakao, Eiji Funakoshi, Takash Shimura, Masahiko Tsugawa, Jun Fujimaki, Takahiro Tamura, Hisako Hara, Jun Negami. Directed by Tasadhi Imai. Screenplay, Sugako Hashida, after novel of Aiyako Sono; camera, Yoshihisa Nagagawa. Previewed in Tokyo. Running Time, **96 MINS.**

One of the most interesting Japanese films this year is the new Tadashi Imai picture, "Satogashi ga Kawareru Toki" (almost literally "When the Cookie Crumbles"). Based on a novel by Aiyako Song and scripted by Sugako Hashida, it reminds one of the life of Marilyn Monroe. Or perhaps it is the latest interpretation of the myth of Marilyn Monroe, the sweet girl whom lousy civilization did in but who remained, somehow pure, untouched to the very end.

At the beginning (in this Japanese version), Aiyako Wakao is just another pretty and ambitious actress. She is completely honest. This attribute wins the love of an important older producer (Takashi Shimura) but he shortly dies and leaves her alone. In the meantime, the company has heard about her posing for nude calendar photos, and is furious. She throws up her career, makes friends with a girl who later becomes her secretary (Hisako Hara), again the very delicately understated hint of a more than ordinary affection. She decides to improve her mind by going to school.

Where, however, she attracts the

attention of a professor (Eiji Funakoshi) and endures his advances simply because she does not know what else to do. She enjoys her platonic friendship with a newspaper reporter (Masahiko Tsugawa) very much but when introduced to a star baseball player (Jun Fujimaki), she suddenly and paradoxically decides to get married.

It is no good. From the first innocent and hilarious conversation (which side do you sleep on at night?) to the full horror of an evening at home with his baseball friends, the marriage is wrong. Divorced, she turns to a bespectacled, pipe-puffing intellectual playwright. He writes a script for her (same title as this film) but her emotional demands get in the way of the script. And after her dismay at discovering she cannot have a child, and that he is writing a play about their relationship, she divorces him, too. She fights with her girl-friend, and takes her too many sleeping pills.

All this is shown with a candor and a delicacy rare in Japanese films. *Chie.*

Manana Sera Otro Dia
(Tomorrow's Another Day)
(SPANISH-COLOR)

Fairly effective try to escape Spanish filmic stereotypes. Probable Festival entry.

Madrid, July 4.
Mercurio Films release of a Tibidabo Films production. Stars Sonia Bruno and Juan Luis Galiardo; features Ines Alma, Sergio Mendizabal, Alberto Berco. Directed by Jaime Camino. Screenplay by Roman Gubern, Marta G. Frias and Jaime Camino; camera (Eastmancolor Techniscope), Luis Cuadrado; music, Victor Capblanguet. Reviewed at Cine Callao, Madrid, June 3, '67. Running Time, **101 MINS.**

Though a flawed film, with obvious debts to Antonioni, Godard and Lelouch, this second pic by Jaime Camino is important as an attempt by a Spanish filmmaker to break away from stock themes —flamenco, bullfights, Spanish Honor, etc.—toward a more universal, European concept of cinema. Solidly arty, with good acting and exquisite color photography, "Manana" is currently being considered as a Spanish representative at one of the major film festivals, where its reception would be a strong indication as to possible success on the international market.

The story is both personal and social. Paco and Lisa, an attractive unmarried couple, leave Madrid in a stolen car for the promise of Barcelona. Once there, they seek work in films and modeling, though their experience in these fields is minimal. Living from day to day in a cheap hotel, they eventually become established — she as a model and he as man Friday to the leader of a local racketeering group. But their hours conflict and each comes to doubt the other's love; she leaves him. Later reunited, they take off for Torremolinos and Spain's gold coast, again in a stolen car. Even though they have no set plans, tomorrow will be another day.

Though thoroughly modern, Camino's treatment is formalist and rather distant. At times he seems more concerned with the richness of the photography than a deep revelation of the protagonists' fate, and though the two lead roles are well acted they seemed at times too removed for complete sympathy. The girl's brief interlude as a prostitute, though sensitively handled, is unprepared. And surely there must be a pictorially better way to express her love for the boy than "Paco, I love you" scrawled melodramatically across a mirror in lipstick.

In spite of these weaknesses Camino's film is an important step toward a truly "international" Spanish cinema, not one that relies on the cliches and "typical Spanish" themes of most Iberian exports. Though his story has been done before and better in other parts of Europe, he has had the courage to say that, within Spain, there are adventurers, that some people actually do live together out of wedlock, that there are prostitutes and homosexuals, that some business methods are suspect. For Spain this is heady stuff. *Lyon.*

Berlin Festival

The Whisperers
(BRITISH)

Great performance by Dame Edith Evans in appealing tale of solitude and old age. Somewhat special and will need adroit sell to let word-of-mouth build among discriminating audiences.

Berlin, July 4.
United Artists release of a Seven Pines (Michael S. Laughlin, Ronald Shedlo) production. Features Edith Evans, Eric Portman, Nanette Newman, Gerald Sim, Avis Bunnage, Ronald Fraser, Harry Baird, Robert Russell, Kenneth Griffith, Claire Kelly. Written and directed by Bryan Forbes. Based on novel by Robert Nicolson; camera, Gerry Turpin; music, John Barry; editor, Anthony Harvey. Reviewed at Berlin Film Fest. Running Time, **103 MINS.**
Mrs. Ross .... Edith Evans
Archie .... Eric Portman
Girl upstairs .... Nanette Newman
Conrad .... Gerald Sim
Mrs. Noonan .... Avis Bunnage
Charlie .... Ronald Fraser
Earl .... Harry Baird
Andy .... Robert Russell
Mr. Weaver .... Kenneth Griffith
Prostitute .... Claire Kelly

United Artists has a good prestige entry for discriminating markets in this British-made entry, which boasts a finely chiseled performance by Dame Edith Evans and other quality production facets. Downbeat theme of old age loneliness will, however, prove a challenge to drumbeaters and sales departments, especially outside the art belt, but it could build via word-of-mouth. (Dame Edith won "Best Actress" award at Berlin Fest—Ed.).

Low-budgeter centers around an old woman, estranged from her husband, who lives alone in a broken-down, tiny flat in a slummy outskirt of a British town. Her life consists of daily putterings about the place, plus visits to the local pension office for assistance, the free library to read a daily (and warm her toes), and other by-the-clock routine chores. Her imaginary dream of sudden riches due her from a relative unexpectedly comes true one day when her son hides the haul of a robbery in her spare room, and she finds it.

Her life changes, but she soon draws too much attention, is drugged by a neighbor and robbed, winds up in hospital. After a slow recovery, a social worker tries to reconcile her with her no-good, sotty husband. But after some pathetically unhappy days together, he also is involved in a theft, runs off with the money, and once again leaves her alone in her musty flat with her noises, quiet obsessions and memories.

Few other films, except Vittorio DeSica's vintage "Umberto D.," have attacked the unglamorous but poignant and unfortunately ever-topical theme of old-age loneliness with such understated feeling and un-"sentimental" taste and discretion. It has in Edith Evans' great performance an invaluable asset. Her portrayal of the ageing woman, now living on the near edge of insanity but unbowed by other physical hazards, determinedly struggling ahead in her waning fight for life, but head high, without complaints, makes the film. And it is difficult to see anyone else doing it so well, so believably, so un-actingly. She conveys warm humor, especially in the opening sequences which establish her normal life pattern. But she turns ably to a restrained, muted portrayal of instinctive courage in the more dramatic middle and near-final passages.

It's obviously her picture all the way, but there is a very neat bit by Eric Portman as her callous and selfish husband, also played just right. Also there are some fine contributions by Gerald Sim, as the understanding welfare official who, within the limits of his duties—and budget—helps out the old lady, and very briefly, by Ronald Fraser, as her wayward son Charlie. Nanette Newman makes an attractive neighbor. Avis Bunnage has her moments as the woman who steals from the oldster, and others do well in smaller roles.

Throughout, Bryan Forbes holds a tight rein as director-writer, and adds almost everywhere small, neatly-timed notations, comments, ironies that add much to the central theme. It is his matter-of-fact, basically unsentimental, yet not overly cruel portrayal of the problems of the over-age in contact with today's world which does much to make this a believable film. If the pic is to be faulted on artistic grounds, it is perhaps for a slight fragmentation in mid-pic, where, for a while, one loses sight of the old lady to follow her husband.

Forbes obviously has had full support from his production team, and everything about its work, from Gerry Turpin's location lensing to Anthony Harvey's editing and John Barry's subdued score, is in keeping. *Hawk.*

The Road That Has No End
(TURKISH)

Berlin, July 4.
A Gen-Ar Film production, Istanbul, Turkey. Directed and written by Duygu Sagiroglu. Camera, Orhan Cagmag; music, Arif Erkin; editor, Duygu Sagiroglu. At Berlin Film Fest. Running Time, **96 MINS.**

It was a Turkish film which, three years ago, created the biggest sensation at a Berlin Film Festival. Not because of its quality (admittedly quite good by Turkish standards) but because of the simple reason that it copped the Grand Prize of this fest. Decision of the jury and the adjoining scandal contributed to "popularize" Turkish pix around here.

Current film festival has this Turkish film within its "Film Show Of the Countries," a frame program. According to its producer, Kocatas Muhtar, this is a pic that had been banned by the Turkish Censor Board since 1965 and only was released recently by a high court order.

This production seems to be one of this country's better ones. Story centers on a young man who decides to go to the big city of Istanbul and try his luck there. But life is tough and jobs hard to find. Pic shows the misery that unqualified workers have to face. And then there's a love affair which ends tragically.

Some of the scenes are involuntarily funny. Film lacks pace according to western standards. Acting can't be measured by western standards, either. Whether pic will get into western markets is very problematical. *Hans.*

Alle Jahre Wieder
(Every Year Again)
(GERMAN)

Berlin, July 4.
Constantin release of Peter Schamoni production. Stars Ulla Jacobsson, Sabine Sinjen, Hans-Dieter Schwarze. Directed by Ulrich Schamoni. Screenplay, Michael Lentz and Ulrich Schamoni; camera, Wolfgang Treu; editor, Heidi Genee. At Berlin Film Fest. Running Time, **88 MINS.**
Hannes Luecke...Hans-Dieter Schwarze
Lore .... Ulla Jacobson
Inge .... Sabine Sinjen
Spezie .... Johannes Schaaf
Dr. Meneke............. Hans Posegga
Mother .... Hertha Burmeister
Andreas Luecke ....Andreas Lentz
Monika Luecke...........Marina Lappe
Brother .... Hermann-Josef Kuepper

"Every Year Again," official German entry at the 1967 Berlin Film Fest is the second feature film of 28-year old Ulrich Schamoni who, in early 1966, started the new German surge with "It," his first feature pic, which has shown at numerous festivals. About this second feature it shows that this young director has especially improved in technical respects. Also, it has its artistic merits but some objections must be granted. Commercially, this Constantin release should fare well in the native market. It will be given mass release in West Germany in September. Film was given the "particularly worthy" distinction by this country's classification board which means considerable tax relief. It also has definite foreign chances because containing human problems that should be generally understood.

Produced by Peter Schamoni, the director's elder brother, this brotherly liaison can be regarded as a happy one. While Ulrich Schamoni, the director, is evidently gifted with a light hand, Peter is undoubtedly the more serious-minded of this twosome.

Plot starts in Muenster, a medium-sized town in West Germany, and concerns a bunch of 40-year-old Germans who are all, more or less, good fellows. Most of them are married. All seem to be quite successful with their jobs. They have their problems, too, but they master them with sort of a take-it-easy attitude. But the patron easily finds out what the director want to show: That there is much dishonesty about these newly-rich men.

Central figure is Hannes Luecke (Hans-Dieter Schwarze) who, at Christmas time, pays a visit to his family and his old pals. It's just a routine visit ("Every Year Again," as explained by the pic's title). He's still married for the sake of his two children but is living somewhere else and has a regular girl-friend. Film pokes fun at the Babbitt types of relations that surround his legal wife.

The dialog furnished by Michael Lentz and Ulrich Schamoni ring true in many instances. And there are the prototypes of Babbitts and the newly rich folks. The language they use may be called authentic. It is easy to show and to criticize the narrow-minded bourgeoisie. And Schamoni does it, unfortunately, the easiest and also the most superficial way via showing stupid faces and ridiculing the German sentimentality. He just shows things, but doesn't go deeper. Much is pure corn about this cinematic offering. And, unfortunately, there are quite a few repetitive and superfluous scenes. Those are film's definite deficiencies.

Strictly on the plus side, however, is the acting. There are some top-flight performances especially those turned in by Hans-Dieter Schwarze and Swedish-born Ulla Jacobsson who enacts his estranged wife. Both walked off with this year's Federal Film Prizes for best acting. Both Sabine Sinjen, Schwarze's girl-friend, and Johannes Schaaf, a hotel owner and one of his old buddies, are hardly less effective. And there's excellent support all down the line. Ulrich Schamoni's direction is very self-conscious, perhaps too self-conscious. This chiefly contributes to giving this film a flair of conceit on the part of its creator.

Technical credits are very good. Lensing, as usual with the new German pix, is excellent. In all, certainly not a bad film. It has interesting ingredients but one may say that Schamoni has made it himself a bit too easy. This, however, won't militate against its commercial prospects. On the contrary, a film in this form is easier to reach a bigger audience.
Hans.

Livet Ar Stenkul
(Life's Just Great)
(SWEDISH—SONGS)
Berlin, July 2.
Rank release of AB Svensk Filmindus-

tri production. Features Inger Taube, Mai Nielsen, Keve Hjelm, Bengt Ekerot, Lars Hansson, Thomas Janson, Stig Toernblom, Leif Claesson. Directed by Jan Halldoff. Screenplay, Halldoff, Stig Claesson; camera, Curt Persson, Peter Fischer; music, Fabulous Four; editor, Wic Kjellin. Reviewed at Berlin Film Fest. Running Time, **78 MINS**.

Britt	Inger Taube
Maj	Mai Nielsen
Roland	Keve Hjelm
Grannen	Bengt Ekerot
Kent	Lars Hansson
Thomas	Thomas Janson
Jan	Stig Toernblom
Bauer	Hanny Schedin
Klein Roland	Leif Claesson

Lightweight item with plenty of pace and humor of the sort that youthful audiences could go for, especially due to uncompromising insight into teen-age mind displayed. Proper channelling could make this an entry in certain foreign slottings catering to the young set.

Though he somewhat disjointedly tells a fragment of a tale, and though he refuses to really take any teen stand, director - writer Jan Halldof has plenty going for him in this perceptive insight into the young mind of today and into the actions that it triggers. Basically, it merely tells of two girls' entanglement with a trio of beatnik types with only two cares in the world: avoiding work, and having fun doing it. Live today, as the message goes, and forget about tomorrow.

Film depicts series of adventures about the group as it steals, rabble-rouses and otherwise makes a nuisance of itself until, finally, it goes too far and has a murder on its hands. The style and content are derivative of earlier Italian ventures into this field, but theres' a different, fresher, zanier—though none less dangerous—spirit here. Few pictures have as clearly as this one illustrated the complete fracture existing not only between generations, but also between various age-groups of the same generation.

Focus on this is sharpest when it treats the case of a young divorcee with a growing child who, free again, suddenly finds herself hard-put to catch up with others almost her own age but can't because the few years of marriage have left her far behind in today's fast-changing times. There are several other perceptive and eye-opening bits showing the interplay of the divorced couple, its child, the friends, a neighbor and a number of others unwittingly involved in the gang's short-lived activities. Had the director and writers knotted the whole thing together better, and expressed an outlook, the hurried downbeat ending would have been more acceptable.

There are some bright faces and performances in the "group." Among those to be commended are the girls — both lookers — Inger Taube and Mai Nielson, as well as Lars Hansson, Thomas Hanson and Stig Toerblom as their playtime companions. Keve Hjelm is fine as the rejected husband, and there's a nice bit by the apartment neighbor, played by Hanny Schedin. Camerawork, much of it in locations, is aptly atmospheric, and the Fabulous Four contribute several appropriate beat songs in catchy fashion.
Hawk.

Paranoia
(DUTCH)
(Song)
Berlin, July 4.
Parnasse Productie (Gijsbert Versluys) production and release. Features Joseph Guilty, Mimi Kok, Ton Vos, Pamela Rose. Directed by Adriaan Ditvoorst. Screenplay, Ditvoorst, Willem Frederik Hermans, based on novel by Hermans; camera, Jan de Bront; music, Marco Klein; song: "Love Me, Please Love Me" sung by Michel Palnareff; editor, Jan Bosdriesz. Reviewed at Berlin Film Fest. Running Time, **102 MINS.**

Arnold Cleever	Joseph Guilty
Anna	Pamela Rose

Offbeater in which a strange blend of styles go into a downbeat tale of growing paranoic tendencies culminating in suicide of a young man. It fails to convince or jell, and its outside chances appear limited, with even a long nude sequence dragged in and not really adding commercial fodder for the effort.

Shocked by a wartime battle experience, Arnold Cleever on his return home becomes more and more obsessed by the fear that he may be an escaped SS man sought by police. Even his fiancee can't help him out of this and other traumas, and, after shooting the landlord, who wants to evict him, he jumps to his death from his attic window.

There's little conviction in the acting, writing and directing. The result is merely a jumble of sequences with predictable development and facile use of bizarre, juxtaposition to give the looney effect needed for main character. For the collectors, there's one of the longest—and unsexiest—nude scenes in which Cleever locks his nude girl friend in a bare room overnight. Pamela Rose is the actress who spends most of her footage running about in the buff while Joseph Guilty is the harassed mental case.

Pic is technically okay. There's a solo stint on the soundtrack by Michel Palnareff, who sings "Love Me, Please Love Me." *Hawk.*

Budjenje Pacova
(The Rats Wake Up)
(YUGOSLAV)
Berlin, July 4.
A Filmska Radna Zajednic (Belgrade) production. With Velimir Bamberg, Slobodan Perovic, Dusica Zegarac, Severin Bijelic, Mirjana Blasokovic, Mica Tomic. Directed by Zivojin Pavlovic. Screenplay, Gordan Mihic, Ljubisa Kozomara; camera, Milorad Jaksic-Fando. At Berlin Film Fest. Running Time, **86 MINS.**

This was Titoland's second feature film entry at the Berlin festival. It emerged as a strange presentation, but managed to keep the viewer's interest because of its interesting characters and situations. Pic is very much on the tristesse side, with some humorous bits plus, every now and then, a "delicate" sequence concerning nude or half-nude females. Technically well-made this benefits in the main from good direction. Commercially it's perhaps too much of a departure from the normal program to stir the interest of foreign buyers. But it perhaps deserves being noticed.

The action centers around a lonely middle-aged man who has been disillusioned by life. He still pays attention to what he wears but otherwise doesn't care much

about things that surround him. Film makes a point that he, once interested in politics and even active in this respect, has also lost interest in political changes. The only aim he still has is to make and save money for his sick sister so that she can be sent to the seashore for recuperation.

Then he meets a girl, falls for her and believes it is mutual love. Temporarily he feels happy. But all that the girl has on her mind is to steal the money he has saved. And eventually she disappears with his savings. The good man falls back to resignation and his grey life starts all over again.

This is Pavlovic's third feature film. He shows a fine feel for the atmospheric detail. And once again it can be confirmed that Yugoslavia has fine actors who make one forget that they're merely acting. Velimir Bamberg, who enacts the main role, is a fine example. Technical credits are exceptionally good. The whole thing is perhaps a bit too gloomy for the western market. But there's a realistic approach which rings true. *Hans.*

Il Fischio Al Naso
(The Man with the Whistling Nose)
(ITALIAN—COLOR)
Berlin, July 3.
Cineriz release of an Alfonso Sansone-Enrico Chroscicki production for Sancro International. Stars Ugo Tognazzi; features Tina Louise, Olga Villi, Franca Bettoja, Alicia Brandet, Gildo Tognazzi, Gigi Ballista, Marco Ferreri, Riccardo Garrone, Alessandro Quasimodo. Directed by Tognazzi. Screenplay, Tognazzi, Giulio Scarnicci, Renzo Tarabusi, Alfredo Pigna, Rafael Azcona; adapted from "I Racconti," by Dino Buzzati; camera (Eastmancolor), Enzo Serafin; music, Teo Usuelli; editor, Eraldo da Roma. Reviewed at Berlin Film Fest. Running Time, **106 MINS.**

Giuseppe Inzerna	Ugo Tognazzi
Immer Mehr	Tina Louise
Anita	Olga Villi
Gloria	Alicia Brandet

After a sparkling start, which promises an amusing session with one of Italy's top actor-comedians, Ugo Tognazzi's first self-directed starring vehicle rapidly skids into an only intermittently amusing string of increasingly grim and morbid sequences of would-be humor. Taken wholly, it's an oddball item which gets by, but only just, on eye and name appeal. But even Tognazzi's recognized acting ability can't help this one out. It looks a very chancy export item. (Film is to be called "The Seventh Floor" in the U. S.)

Tognazzi is a dynamic, gadget-ridden industrialist whose business and personal contacts are perjudiced by a disturbing affliction: a seemingly incurable nose whistle which starts at unpredictable moments and resists all attempts to stop it. He finally decides to visit a clinic, where specialists take over, rapidly and Kafka-like turning his relatively minor affiliction into a series of increasingly serious and variously diagnosed disturbances. This keeps him moving upwards, floor by floor, in the clinic, apparently a symbol of life, until he reaches the top, or death.

While a spoof on hypochondria and related diseases of the mind, the gags and twists are soon too heavy-footed and grim. Picture's more horrific elements, such as the hibernation sequence, are too tamely handled to appeal to chiller fans, and pic lands between genres. All in all, it lacks, with very few exceptions, the imaginative talent that went into Fedrico Fellini's "8½," which it somewhat resembles in content.

Lead, in his now-usual role of the doomed human male, does his best with an involved and unsatisfying script and is at times very funny or moving. Others in large cast walk busily through their roles, but without real conviction. Technical outfitting is lush.

Hawk.

Zeugin Aus Der Hoelle
(Witness Out of Hell)
(GERMAN-YUGOSLAV)

Berlin, July 4.
Rank release of a CCC Filmproducktion GmbH-Avala Film (Belgrade) co-production. Features Irene Papas, Heinz Drache, Daniel Gelin, Werner Peters, Jean Claudio, Alice Trell, Hans Zesch-Ballot, Branco Tatic, Radmilla Gutesa, Petar Banicevic. Directed by Zita Mitrovic. Screenplay, Frieda Filipovic, Michael Mansfeld, from an idea by Frieda Filipovic; camera, Milored Markovic; editor, Katarina Stagarovic, Ursula Karlband. Reviewed at Berlin Film Fest. Running Time, 83 MINS.

Lea Weiss .... Irene Papas
Hoffman .... Heinz Drache
Petrovic .... Daniel Gelin
Von Walden .... Werner Peters
Carlo Bianchi .... Jean Claudio
Frau von Keller............... Alice Treff
Dr. Berger .... Hans Zesch-Ballot

Grim but frequently gripping suspenser about a onetime concentration camp tenant whose past continues to come back to haunt her, this pic also has a strong anti-Nazi message which becomes a real shock element towards the finale as story details are slowly revealed. Rank has the film for German-speaking areas, but this might make it as filler material elsewhere if properly exploited.

Irene Papas, the onetime c-camp inmate, is being sought as the only surviving key witness needed to nail down guilt of the camp's doctor, who's still living scot-free in Western Germany. German police enlist the aid of a Yugoslav newsman who once knew her. Finally, after a long chase and repeated attempts to convince the blackmailed woman to talk, they succeed; only to have her commit suicide in continued fear of ever-present Nazi persecution.

Zita Mitrovic's direction is rather pedestrian, but he manages to milk his more dramatic moments well, especially during some of the more telling, near-finale sequences in which gal's sobering camptime reminiscences take on a horrific note as her fear grows.

Irene Papas is good, but rarely has a chance to let her dramatic talent emerge. Daniel Gelin is somewhat wooden and miscast as the newsman, while Heinz Drache makes an okay policeman. Others, especially Werner Peters, as a diehard Nazi lawyer, contribute some effective backing.

Technically, the pic is okay if somewhat oldfashioned in lensing and sets.

Hawk.

Har Har Du Ditt Liv
(Here You Have Your Life)
(SWEDISH)

Berlin, July 4.
Rank release of Svensk Filmindustri production. Features Eddie Axberg,

Signe Stade, Gunnar Bjornstrand, Max von Sydow, Allan Edwall, Ulla Sjoblom, Per Oscarsson, Ake Fridell, Ulf Palme, Holger Loewendaler, Bengt Ekerot. Written, photographed, edited and directed by Jan Troell. Script collaborator, Bengt Forslund. Based on novel by Eyvind Johnson; music, Erik Nordgren. Reviewed at Berlin Film Fest. Running Time, 145 MINS.

Olof .... Eddy Axberg
Olivia .... Ulla Sjoblom
Lundgren .... Gunnar Bjornstrand
Smalands-Pelle .... Max von Sydow
Larsson .... Ulf Palme
Stepmother .... Gudrun Brost
Mother .... Ulla Akelson
Older brother .... Bo Wahlstroem
2nd Brother .... Rick Axberg
Kristiansson .... Holger Loewenadle
Olsson .... Goeran Lindberg
Lund .... Tage Sjoegren
Linus .... Tage Jonsson
Johansson .... Jan-Erik Lindkvist
August .... Allan Edwall
Dream woman........Anna Maria Blind
Maja .... Catarina Edfledt

For about two-thirds of this lengthy Swedish entry, based on a novel by Eyvind Johnson, the spell binds. even though the pace is slow as it unfolds the growing pains, turmoils and adventures of a youth. Then it slips, for a while, into convention in telling of the youngster's love affair with Marxism and the Swedish workers movements, until a poetic finale once again comes through on a human level.

Sprawling pic is chockfull of production values, tells a poetic story, boasts a cast of internationally recognized Swedish players. Yet it's difficult to predict a particularly rich future for the film in the general market, to which it apparently aspires, outside the specialized runs for which, instead, it seems more indicated.

Director Jan Troell, whose first feature pic effort this is, has obviously been given a free rein in guiding script, images and actors. He has done so with understanding and a fine feeling for the travails, both physical and mental, of a down-to-earth youngster of some ambition who's determined to make it on his own. Pic follows the hero, Olof, from his working start in a Swedish logging camp on the other jobs in various fields, his first love affairs with girls and literature.

This boasts superb lensing, some leisurely editing, a few repetitive passages, a few confusing ones, but generally is a consistently fine production. A couple of color sequences are inserted for poetic effect. The acting, from Eddy Axberg's understanding up-front limning of the youngster to a very colorful and adept performance by Ulla Sjoblom, as a sometime gypsy aquaintance, is excellent. It includes some telling cameos by May Von Sydow, Per Oscarsson, Gunnar Bjornstrand, Ulf Palme and other Swedish thesps. Other credits are firstclass. *Hawk.*

Den Onda Cirkeln
(The Vicious Circle)
(SWEDISH)

Berlin, July 4.
Ufa International release of an A-Produktion (Stockholm) production. Features Gunnel Lindblom, Erik Hell, Gio Petre, Mathias Henrikson, Marie-Louise Hakansson, Heinz Hopf. Directed by Arne Mattson. Screenplay, Elsa Prawitz; camera, Lasse Bjorne; editor, Carl-Olof Spettsell. Reviewed at Berlin Film Fest. Running Time, 90 MINS.

Maria .... Gunnel Lindblom
Father .... Erik Hell

Inger .... Gio Petre
Sten .... Heinz Hopf
Eva .... Marie-Louise Hakansson
Man .... Mathias Henrikson

Morbid, weird tale from Sweden which once again has sex and other basic instincts asserting themselves among the inhabitants of—and one visitor to—an isolated boarding house on a Scandinavian coast. Not sexy per se, item nevertheless contains some pretty heady scenes which certainly won't hurt its chances in the arty and semi-arty release niches for which pic is intended. Here and there, an encounter with a bluenose is to be expected, despite the transposed Greek tragedy pattern on which the pic is based.

A lonely, disoriented woman who has attempted suicide, returns to the scene of her childhood rape at the hands of a rooming house owner twenty years after the event which has made shambles of her life. Slowly, almost inevitably, a pattern of revenge emerges as she acts as catalyst to a series of sexual upheavals in the visited household. The old lecher again makes a pass at her, as does his son, but she violently repulses both. Then the grown daughter displays a lesbo leaning which turns out to have been caused by her witnessing the original rape, thus conditioning her hatred for men. The innocent victim of the inbred circle of violence is the youngest daughter of the house who is in turn raped by a peeping tom neighbor. All meet their comeuppance at curtain time except the visitor and the little girl, who leave the sick scene together.

As noted the story development and direction avoid its coming through pruriently, but there are some graphic scenes involving titillation, masturbation, child-rape, and violence, which defy description here and which have rarely been paralleled. Pitty of the film is that while in no sense a cheap exploitationer, despite its way-out content, pic also isn't as notable an artistic achievement as some of director Arne Mattson's previous successes or, to name one more, of even the more controversial Ingmar Bergman's. It's instead somewhere in between, and this makes it less defensible than others both in its fight with the censor and in potential inroads on the higher-brow arty mart.

Lensing is a bit murky throughout, adding to atmosphere but otherwise depressing. Acting is first-class, with all hands rating a nod, from Gunnel Lindblom, as the visitor; Erik Hell, as the ageing rapist, Gio Petre', as the lesbo; to Marie-Louise Hakansson as the victimized moppet, and Mathias Henrikson, as the demented neighbor. *Hawk.*

The Face of Medusa
(GREEK)

Berlin, July 3.
Finos Film release of Finos-Minos Film production. Features Hara Angelousi, Phanis Hinas, Alexis Manthakis, Phillippos Vlacos. Screenplay, Kondouros, Vangelis Goutas; camera, Karlheinz Hummel; music, Yian Markopoulos. Reviewed at Berlin Film Fest. Running Time, 88 MINS.

This tediously slow and studied

updating of a Greek legend is too labored and cryptic to allow for easy audience acceptance. But it does have a b.o. incentive in the abundantly displayed nudity of its attractive star, Hara Angelousi, who makes her screen debut here. Could have limited runs on the strength of this factor in arty houses.

As explained in the synopsis—but not, sufficiently, in the film—pic re-tells the story of Perseus who lands on an island to conquer the formidable Medusa, whose mere look according to age-old legend used to turn men to stone. In this pic, the latter is a pretty young girl who's living on the isle with two other men. After various maneuvers, the modern Perseus manages to lure the girl aboard his boat and there breaks Medusa's spell with his love.

It's all very slowly developed, with a minimum of dialog and a maximum of stationary scenes in which the actors stare at one another or at the landscape. And, at least in the locally glimpsed sub-titled version. the dialog has many unwitting laugh lines. It's also difficult to tell much concerning the ability of the four-man cast on this evidence. with Phanis Hinas, Alexis Manthakis, and Philippos Vlachos turning in workmanlike performances as the three men while Hara Angelousi is easy on the eyes as the target of their attention.

Director Nikos Kondouros, who won a prize here some years back for "Young Aphrodites," is consistent in his stylistic attempt to switch periods on the Medusa legend, and in playing it dead slow. But it's not likely that general audiences will be grateful to him for the lethargic results.
Hawk.

The Magnificent Two
(BRITISH-COLOR)

Potentially Britain's best comedy duo, Morecambe and Wise, have their third picture stab here. Better than the other efforts but this one still doesn't quite click, though it raises a lot of yocks; good booking for easygoing audiences.

London, July 6.
Rank release of a Hugh Stewart production. Stars Eric Morecambe, Ernie Wise; features Margit Saad, Virgilio Texeira, Cecil Parker, Martin Benson. Directed by Cliff Owen. Screenplay by S. C. Green and R. M. Hills, with Michael Pertwee and Peter Blackmore, from a Pertwee story; camera ((Eastmancolor), Ernest Steward; music, Ron Goodwin; editor, Gerald Hambling. At Leicester Square Theatre, London. Running Time, 100 MINS.

Eric	Eric Morecambe
Ernie	Ernie Wise
Carla	Margit Saad
Carillo	Virgilio Texeira
British Ambassador	Cecil Parker
Juanita	Isobel Black
President Diaz	Martin Benson
Manuelo	Michael Godfrey
President's children	Sue Sylvaine, Henry Beltran, Tyler Butterworth
Armandez	Sandor Eles
Juan	Andreas Melandrinos
Drunk Soldier	Victor Maddern
Doctor	Michael Gover
Assassin	Charles Laurence

Morecambe & Wise, probably Britain's best comedy duo, jell like eggs-and-bacon on television. But in films they haven't entirely clicked because the screenplay writers don't use them enough as a double act. Eric Morecambe, the affable, moonfaced, bespectacled lad gets most of the fat. His partner, perky Ernie Wise, is the stooge. They are at their best when they are together, sparking each other.

"The Magnificent Two" is their third film. It is also their best, but it still is not good enough. In this pic they play a couple of British commercial travellers who, for the purposes of plot, arrive in a little South African town triying to sell miniature toy soldiers.

They find themselves up to their necks in a revolution, with Morecambe, to save themselves from execution, having to pose as the late president's son, until the revolution is won. Not a bad idea for a screen comedy. Snag about this film, which will do okay with easygoing audiences, is that it is labored, and lacking in wit as distinct from robust humor. It makes no attempt to use the two principals as characters instead of puppets.

There is a funny sequence in which Moracambe, posing as the new president, does a tele speech in which he promises the natives the earth. It takes a few minutes, but funny though it is this merely adds up to a short, amusing tele skit.

Cliff Owen has directed with verve and pace but is clearly hampered by a paucity of material from four writers, who are the Morecambe and Wise regular writers, S. C. Green and R. M. Hills, plus Michael Pertwee (his original story) and Peter Blackmore. Maybe too many cooks spoiled the broth.

Filmed locally, this still manages to have a distinct breath of foreign parts. Ernest Steward's color lensing is excellent. Cecil Parker turns up in a cameo "guest" role as a British ambassador, and

Virgilio Texeira, as the leader of the rebels. Margit Saad, Martin Benson and Isobel Black all contribute handsomely to the pic, which is amusing in spasms, innocuous and a near-miss. *Rich.*

Surfari
(DOCUMENTARY-COLOR)

Surfing epic tries to ride on success of "Endless Summer," but just seems endless.

Don Brown release of American Sports Films (Brown) production, produced and directed by Milton Blair. Commentary written by Brown, spoken by Hal Buckley; camera (Eastmancolor), Brown; editor, Brown; music, The Blazers. Previewed at Kips Bay Theatre, N.Y., July 13, '67. Running Time, 90 MINS.

With "The Endless Summer," Bruce Brown's documentary on surfing, having already hit a smash $1,000,000 in U.S. net rentals, it was inevitable that other pix would try to follow up its surprise success. But "Surfari" looks like it was put together by Don Brown (no kin) solely for this reason. It lacks the wit, pace, beauty and excitement of the earlier pic, although it may generate some b.o. action on the strength of the similarity of subject matter. There's obviously an audience for surfing, but whether it will embrace pix as poor in quality as "Surfari" remains to be seen.

If "Endless Summer" seemed at times almost a film poem on surfing, this new one is nothing but an extended travelog. There are constant interruptions for "cute bits" (children falling off boards, etc.) avoided in the earlier film. Structure seems contrived, photography is grainy, and narration is laughable ("*This day will be rerembered as one of the most dramatic in California surf history*").

Film follows a group of real surfers—Ricky Grigg, Greg Noll, Sue Peterson and others—as they meet the waves in California, Hawaii and Australia. There's some interesting footage of surfboard shops—but far more of irrelevant matters such as bathing suit contests, dancing and even, incredibly, a skiing vacation supposedly taken by some of the surfers (they are not recognizable and it looks like stock skiing footage).

On the whole the impression is of a group of home movies stretched out interminably to feature length. To employ the sport's own lingo, "Surfari" is a wipeout. *Byro.*

The Spirit Is Willing
(COLOR)

Speedy ghost spoof; William Castle digs again into the supernatural, this time tongue-in-cheek; good for general market.

Hollywood, July 11.
Paramount release of William Castle production, directed by Castle. Stars Sid Caesar, Vera Miles, Barry Gordon; features John McGiver, Cass Daley, Jill Townsend. Screenplay, Ben Starr; based on novel, "The Visitors," by Nathaniel Benchley; camera (Technicolor), Hal Stine; music, Vic Mizzy; editor, Eddie Bryant; asst. directors, Danny McCauley, Nat Holt Jr. Reviewed at Paramount Studios, July 10, '67. Running Time, 94 MINS.

Ben Powell	Sid Caesar
Kate Powell	Vera Miles
Steve Powell	Barry Gordon
Uncle George	John McGiver
Felicity Twitchell	Cass Daley
Miles Thorpe	Ricky Cordell
Gloria Tritt	Mary Wickes
Fess Dorple	Jesse White
Ebenezer Twitchell	Bob Donner
Felicity's father	Nestor Paiva
Booper Mellish	Doodles Weaver
"Mother"	J. C. Flippen
Jenny, Priscilla Weems, Carol Weems	Jill Townsend
Dr. Frieden	John Astin

With spy spoofs current on every screen in America, comes now William Castle with a spoof on ghosts. Well done, amusing and in Castle's now-familiar area of the supernatural, "The Spirit Is Willing" should attract in the general market, particularly with audiences who like their entertainment in light vein.

Sid Caesar, Vera Miles and Barry Gordon star, but it is Gordon's picture straight through as the others' problem son who lacks communication with his distraught parents. Action takes place in the haunted house of a New England village which Caesar and his wife have rented as a vacation retreat, only to find it inhabited by a trio of wildly violent shades who perpetrate all sorts of pranks on the mere mortals. Clever and imaginative special effects enhance the theme, further embellished with a crackling atmospheric music score by Vic Mizzy.

Based on the novel, "The Visitors," by Nathaniel Benchley, late Robert Benchley's son, screenplay by Ben Starr traces the family's encounter with the spirits, which only the son seems able to see. Ghosts are a mid-1850 bride who finds her bridegroom ensconced in the arms of a servant girl, and in the process of killing them meets her own death. They continue to dwell in the house, and after the renters arrive create a series of complications for young Gordon and his parents.

Gordon, playing role of a youngster going-on-16 who knows he can't get through to his parents, who in turn are certain their son hates them, has the benefit of sparkling lines and a characterization which allows broad comedy. Caesar and Miss Miles patly fill roles of his parents and John McGiver scores roundly as Miss Miles' wealthy and impossible Uncle George. Cass Daley, who parades through entire picture in a red nightgown and bed-bonnet, is the bride-ghost and Bob Donner and Jill Townsend play her victims. Miss Townsend also undertakes two sister roles in the present, for three portrayals in all, acquitting herself charmingly in each. In briefer roles John Astin, J. C. Flippen, Mary Wickes and Jesse White lend additional laughs.

Castle in his dual role of producer-director handles latter assignment with a facile hand calculated to best project the goofy elements of the action. He is backed with expert technical assistance, particularly by special effects of Lee Vasque, special photographic effects of Paul K. Lerpae and process photography by Fairciot Edouart, while Hal Stine's color cinematography is interesting. Eddie Bryant's editing is tight

and art direction by Hal Pereira and Walter Tyler handsome. *Whit.*

The Sea Pirate
(Surcouf, Le Tigre Des Sept Mers) (FRENCH-SPANISH-ITALO—COLOR)

Inept swashbuckler for bottom half.

Paramount release of Edic (Paris), Balcazar (Madrid) and Arco (Rome) co-production, produced by Georges de la Grandiere. Features Gerard Barray, Antonella Lualdi, Terence Morgan, Genevieve Casile. Directed by Roy Rowland. Screenplay, Grandiere, Jack Severac, G. Farrel; camera (Eastmancolor), Juan Gelpi; editor, Jean-Michel Gautier; music, Georges Garvarentz. Reviewed at RKO 86th St. Theatre, N.Y., July 7, '67. Running Time, 83 MINS.

Surcouf	Gerard Barray
Margaret Carruthers	Antonella Lualdi
Lord Blackwood	Terence Morgan
Marie Catherine	Genevieve Casile
Nicolas	Frank Oliveras
Captain Fell	Armand Mestral
Kernon	Gerard Tichy
Garneray	Alberto Cevinini
Napoleon	Giani Esposito
The Jailer	Fernando Sancho

This poor swashbuckler, of which Paramount never acknowledged the existence until it suddenly opened on lower of half of N.Y. circuit bill with "El Dorado" ((resulting in hastily-called screening the morning of opening), is so full of meaningless and incredible action in the current European mold that it hardly seems the work of an old Hollywood hand like Roy Rowland. And indeed some question of directorial credit is raised per the fact that "The Sea Pirate" showed all around Europe last fall with one Sergio Bergonzelli listed as director and Rowland in a "supervisory" capacity.

An explanation is suggested in that although version seen here is all-too-obviously post-synchronized, the entire multi-national cast mouths its lines in English. Was Rowland merely on hand to reshoot each scene in English, with goal in mind to enhance pic's value for U.S. theatres and television? Or was Rowland the "real" director, with another having to be listed for subsidy reasons (just as Anthony Mann's "El Cid" appeared in Italy under the name of the native director)?

Neither Bergonzelli nor Rowland at any rate megged at least 20 of the shots, which are lifted from "The Son of Captain Blood," also made in Spain (in '64), and also, coincidentally, distributed here by Paramount. Sean Flynn and Walter Barnes, featured in earlier film, are easily distinguishable.

In this one, Gerard Barray is a French corsair (e.g. pirate working for the state) during the Napoleonic wars. After freeing an island in the Indian Ocean from British blockade, he faces romantic problems when his fiancee (Genevieve Casile) is kept from him by a rival suitor. Dalliance with an American girl in Paris, played by Antonella Lualdi, is followed by a return to plundering on the high seas and his eventual reunion with his first love.

This kind of thing is done often with dash and brio, but here everything is sacrificed to romance and action in a thoroughly schematic manner. Barray is simply cocky and fearless and the rest of the characters are similarly one-dimentional.

Far more careful scripting was needed too as issues are left dangling or as farfetched coincidences intrude. Ridiculous stunts in battle scenes rival the shootouts in recent Italo westerns.

Entry obviously had to be cut for U.S. program market but it could have been better handled. One crucial plot point—whether Barray's crew will share in the booty of a British ship they have captured—is completely abandoned at midpoint and never resumed in Stateside version.

Reason for sudden acquisition by Par of this seems apparent. Company's entire backlog of second features consists of A.C. Lyles westerns and it needed something else to go with "El Dorado," another oater. *Byro.*

Moscow Film Fest

Quien Sabe
(Who Knows?)
(ITALIAN-COLOR)

Moscow, July 9.
M. C. M. release of Bianco Manini production. Features Gian Maria Volonte', Klaus Kinski, Martine Beswick, Lou Castel, Jaime Fernandez, Carla Gravina, Andrea Ghecchi. Directed by Damiani Damiani. Screenplay, Salvatore Laura, Franco Solinas; camera (Eastmancolor), Tony Secchi; editor, Roberto Cinquini; music, Luis Bacalov. Reviewed at Moscow Film Fest. Running Time, 120 MINS.
Chuncho .... Gian Maria Volonte'
Boy .... Lou Castel
Adelita .... Martine Beswick
Don Felipe .... Andrea Checchi
His wife .... Carla Gravina

Another in a long line of Italian oaters, this a bit off the beaten track thanks to its Mexican revolutionary content, and a certain attempt at reasoning out its social-political implications. It is this which ultimately weighs down the action and rates this many cuts below par for the genre. With considerable trimming, it might do okay as a filler in general situations, but is more than likely to be lost in the shuffle of an inflated skein of ersatz westerns.

An itinerant Yankee (Lou Castel) is caught in the crossfire of a Mexican revolutionary-cum-bandit leader (Gian Maria Volonte') when the latter attacks a train. This ends up following him about through various adventures, mostly involving killings of government troops and theft of weapons to carry on the "just" cause. Much of this, right up to the bloodspattered finale, is repetitious. And several scenes come dangerously close to being parodies (or were they meant to be?). But some may relish Volonte's hammy all-out performance as the near-demented bandit chieftain with his own strange concept of what the word revolution means.

Lou Castel is overrigid as the observer from north of the border, and Martine Beswick has little to do except look pretty as a gang spitfire. Others lend some colorful support, thanks to liberal doses of sweat-caked makeup and oddball Mexicali grab. In keeping, too, is Luis Bacalov's rousing musical scoring while (at least in the print viewed) lensing by Tony Secchia

is generally washed out and loses location values. *Hawk.*

Un Dorado de Pancho Villa
(A Faithful Soldier of PanchoVilla)
(MEXICAN-COLOR)

Moscow, July 7.
Centauro production and release. Features Emilio Fernandez, Soria Amelio, Maricruz Olivier, Carlos Lopez Moctezuma, Jose Eduardo Perez. Written and directed by Fernandez. Camera (Eastmancolor) Jose Ortiz Ramos; music, Manuel Esperon; editor, Carlos Savage. Reviewed at Moscow Film Fest. Running Time, 102 MINS.

Stereotyped, generally overlong and telegraphed story of a Mexican revolution loner who eventually ends up in trouble when he tries to fit back into his hometown pattern once the battles are over. Okay for Latino markets, but disappointing entry from the director who made Mexican pic history some years back with a series of internationally acclaimed films. If pruned down, could also serve as tele fodder thanks to okay production values and color. But needs re-pacing.

One of Pancho Villa's faithful henchmen returns to his village to find his girl married to the local bigwig, despite her promise to wait for him. Boss tries to have him jailed, but is eventually killed by his wife, whom he murders at the same time. The major, who's about to leave town to rejoin Villa, is charged with the murder, and after a long chase, is massacred in the town square by the gendarmes.

For Fernandez aficionados, it has almost all his favorite ingredients: sunset silhouette shots, very long shots framed by nearby bushes, fences alternating with pore-riddled closeups, small wayside chapels, black-shawled peasant girls, trumpet fanfares to accompany and backdrop scenes, etc. But here, unfortunately, these stylistic quirks have a pretentious quality due also to their endless repetition and staticness. Acting is similarly over-emphatic, especially in case of the two women, though Fernandez himself plays his usual role of the strong silent hero without much effort and some nostalgic effect.

Eastmancolor lensing by Jose Ortiz Ramos is often breathtakingly beautiful. Other production values are on a very elaborate scale. *Hawk.*

No Stars in the Jungle
(PERUVIAN—COLOR)

Moscow, June 7.
Roberto Wangeman Co. production and release. Features Ignazio Quiroz, Jorge Montero, Jorge Aragon, Susana Pardahl. Written and directed by Armando Robles Godoy; camera (Eastmancolor) Jorge Pratz; music, Enrique Panilla. Reviewed at Moscow Film Fest. Running Time, 101 MINS.

Neatly made low-budgeter (though high for country of origin) with good production values, a dramatic story sustained to the end and some ruggedly fascinating jungle locations in South America's Amazon region. This has a modest niche in the exotic-adventure markets for undemand-

ing audiences, especially if given a good trimming job.

Story tells the partially flashbacked adventures of an adventurer's quest for a gold cache belonging to the white queen of an Amazon tribe. Also of his struggle to get the heavy booty out of the dangerous area, ending ironically and tragically. Interspersed are some reflected thoughts about the hero's city life and loves and other bits and pieces to either lighten or heighten the tension. Some of the fight scenes are played too broadly for comfort, but chances are that fans of the genre won't mind overly. Also adding to interest are some nicely integrated sequences of native customs.

Performances, as noted, are in keeping with action, while true production values emerge in hued lensing by Jorge Pratz and generally good technical level of this unusual production. *Hawk.*

The Detour
(BULGARIAN)

Moscow, July 8.
Sofia Film Studios production and release. Features Nevena Kokanova, Ivan Andenov. Directed by Grisha Ostrovski, Todor Stoyanov. Screenplay, Blaga Dimitrova; camera, Todor Stoyanov; music, Milscho Levnev. Reviewed at Moscow Film Fest. Running Time, 80 MINS.

Interesting item from Bulgaria, indicating a thaw in previous ideological story lines, with some penetrating insight into some youthful stirrings as well as a neatly developed and underplayed love story. Very limited and mainly for the student, but promising for the future, if followed by others like it.

Man is forced via a detour to pass near an archeological excavation site where by chance he finds his erstwhile longtime fiancee. Both are now married, but as they return together years before.

It's an adult story, underemphasized throughout in intelligent development, and is made more charming and believable by two pleasant performances by a pretty Nevena Stoyanov and a burly Ivan Andenov. Some of it is longwinded, at other times there's some perhaps deliberate fogging of the main story line, but generally it comes off effectively.

Most interesting facet, however, is portion of the pic devoted to student debates concerning such controversial subjects as what caused Majakowski's suicide, love or politics. Also a rather frank, outspoken plea in favor of sex as a social interest over party-line preoccupations, indicating a stirring in the ranks as well as a welcome possibility of depicting such doubts and cracks in previously rigid leftwing conformisms. The effect was not lost on local audiences.

Pic is technically well-fashioned, and other roles are nicely played. *Hawk.*

Khan El Khalili
(EGYPTIAN)

Moscow, July 7.
Cairo Film production and release. Features Emad Hamdi, Hassan Youssef, Samira Ahmed. Directed by Hatef Salem. Screenplay, Mohamed Mustafa Sami; camera, Abdel Aziz Fahmi; music, Fuad El Zaheri. Reviewed at Moscow Film Fest. Running Time, 110 MINS.

Soapy, overlong and slow item with appeal limited to Arab areas. It deals with a middleaged man's infatuation for his pretty nextdoor neighbor. She's interested until his son comes along and steals her away until it's discovered that he's suffering from TB. And after a protracted, overmilked illness, he dies plunging everyone into gloom except, possibly, the spectator who's waited all too long for the moment to make a dash for the exit.

Performances are in keeping, and pic is technically rather primitive. *Hawk.*

O Caso Dos Irmaos Naves
(The Case of the Naves Brothers)
(BRAZILIAN)

Moscow, July 9.
MC release of an MC-Lanper Production. Features Anselmo Duarte, John Herbert, Juca de Oliveira, Leila Abramo, Sergio Hingst, Cacilda Lamoza. Directed by Luiz Sergio Person. Screenplay, Person, Jean Claude Bernadet, based on book by Joao Alamy Filho; camera, Osvaldo de Oliveira; editor, Glauco Mirko Laurelli. Reviewed at Moscow Film Fest. Running Time, 92 MINS.

One of those tales, taken from life, of a miscarriage of justice, pic is viewable and has its dramatic moments. But this is generally limited both by modest production values and by an overdose of sadistic cruelty.

An apparently honest man disappears from a remote Brazilian village with a large amount of cash. A zealous police lieutenant soon decides a scapegoat is necessary and invents and then constructs a case against two brothers, forcing them by torture to admit to being accessories to the murder and theft. Despite the absence of the body and the stolen money, the two are batted about from court to court despite the valiant defense of a young lawyer. One eventually dies in pail, the other is finally freed when some 25 years later the man who originally stole the cash shows up. He also dies soon afterwards.

Story, apparently a big case in Brazilian history, is straight-forward and similar to others of its unfortunate kind. But the director has sought to heighten his criticism of police brutality by some of most violent portrayals of torture ever seen on the screen.

Film is perforce frequently talky, and picture quality is very uneven and frequently murky, but performances are generally good. *Hawk.*

Spring Flood
(MONGOLIA)

Moscow, July 6.
Mongolkino production and release. Features N. A. Krutchkov, S. Genden, Ch. Dolgorsuren, B. Datitcha. Directed by Dedjidin Jigjid. Screenplay, S. Udval and Dorjoidorj; camera, M. Duinhar; music, L. Movdorj. Reviewed at Moscow Film Fest. Running Time, 89 MINS.

Okay if somewhat primitive straightforward actioner set in Mongolia before the Russian revolution. Strictly local in outlook and chances to sell.

Story deals with the early stirrings of communism in Mongolia, with natives caught between White Army brutality and needs of the clandestine Red movement, especially in running arms and men across a river. It is filled with betrayals, prison horror and a number of instances depicting purported Czarist savagery.

Has the sort of unsubtle approach of the vintage western, and is technically rough-hewn, though undoubtedly an achievement for the country of origin.   *Hawk.*

Tyomiehen Paivakirja
(The Diary of a Worker)
(FINNISH)

Moscow, July 9.
Elokuvaosakeyhtio Filminor production and release. Features Elina Sanc, Paul Osipow. Directed by Risto Jarva. Screenplay, Jarva, Jaako Pakkasvirta; camera, Autti Peippo. Reviewed at Moscow Film Fest. Running Time, **90 MINS.**

The French new wave stylization has now reached Finnish shores with a liberal dose of social comment and rationalization added, as in this modernly designed exposition of the age-old problem of career ambition vs. duty and devotion to wife and home. It's all rather heavy going, however, and should not travel too far abroad.

Divided into various parts, with "chapter" headings it deals mainly with a battling worker's achievement of house and spouse, his acceptance of a better position at a distant factory, a tempting side affair with another girl, and eventual return to the homestead a soberer person. There are some sensitive notations here and there, but there's an oppressive overdose of union chatter in the factory sequences and a likewise overlong bit showing the plight of the lonely wife at home.

Performances by two leads are likeable, there's an abundance of location lensing around Finland, and the film is technically slick.
     Hawk.

Jeudi On Chantera Comme Dimanche
(Thursday We Shall Sing Like Sunday)
(FRANCO-BELGIAN)

Moscow, July 8.

Les Films de la Toison D'Or (Bruelles) —Andre Tadie'—Les Films de L'Hermine (Paris coproduction. Features Marie France Boyer, Bernard Fresson, Etienne Bierry, Francis Lax, Francoise Vatel, Herve Jolly, Raymond Aveniere, Simone Durieu, Jean Rovis, Liliane Vincent. Directed by Luc De Heusch. Screenplay, De Heusch, Hugo Claus, Jacques Delcorde; music, Georges Delerue; camera, Fernand Tack; editor, Suzanna Baron. Reviewed at Moscow Film Fest. Running Time, **98 MINS.**

Nicole .... Marie France Boyer
Jean .... Bernard Fresson
Devos .... Etienne Bierry
Marc .... Francis Lax
Francine .... Francoise Vatel

Strange, slow-paced pic from Belgium, overburdened with symbolisms and the problems of the everyday, with limited chances outside a very modest French-language area.

Several story ingredients are blended here into a mishmash of rather unexciting sequences. It's mostly about a truck driver and his shopgirl fiancee who dream of security but never quite make it until the finale, which sees them off to relative bliss. Along the way, the gullible hero is taken in by a con man who sells him an old

---

truck and otherwise gets him and others into endless trouble.

Enmeshed are stories about strikes and strike-breaking, social and social security problems, and other minor points, but few of these are properly integrated. Couple, played by Marie France Boyer and Bernard Fresson, are a likeable pair, but their efforts to appear sincere only rarely break through a rather cold, over-involved and calculated script.

Some nicely lensed exteriors and a very pleasant musical score by Georges Delerue brighten things a bit.   *Hawk.*

Luv
(COLOR)

Filmization of Broadway hit loses in transference to screen but name of Jack Lemmon will help spark potential.

Hollywood, July 21.
Columbia Pictures release of Martin Manulis production. Stars Jack Lemmon; features Peter Falk, Elaine May, Nina Wayne, Eddie Mayehoff. Directed by Clive Donner. Screenplay, Elliott Baker; based on play by Murray Schisgal; camera (PatheColor), Ernest Laszlo; music, Gerry Mulligan; editor, Harold F. Kress; asst. director, David Salven. Reviewed at Directors Guild Theatre, July 20, '67. Running Time, 93 MINS.
Harry Berlin .... Jack Lemmon
Milt Manville .... Peter Falk
Ellen .... Elaine May
Linda .... Nina Wayne
Attorney Goodhart ..... Eddie Mayehoff
Doyle .... Paul Hartman
Vandergrist .... Severn Darden

As a play, Murray Schisgal's "Luv" was a hit comedy which ran more than two years on Broadway. Many of the beguiling qualities are lost in its transference to the screen. Where the legiter was wildly absurd and deliciously outlandish much of the humor of the picture is forced, proving that a sophisticated stage comedy isn't always ideal fare for the screen. A saving grace is marquee name of Jack Lemmon to attract, and while his performance in part fits into the character of the play its way-out qualities probably won't get to the more general film audiences.

There can be no denying that the Martin Manulis production is a daffy lampooning of love—or luv—as was the original, but the expanded Elliott Baker screenplay, while sometimes funny, more often than not is humorless. Perhaps it is the elusive nature of the play that cannot be caught in sectional transition. Manulis has lined up a top cast, albeit small, to support Lemmon, each of whom perhaps is allowed to acquit himself more notably than the star.

Four characters people the plot, the fourth only mentioned in the stage piece. Opening on Manhattan Bridge, where Lemmon, a self-proclaimed failure, is about to commit suicide, story takes form as Peter Falk, a self-proclaimed success, comes along and saves him. Falk recognizes in Lemmon an old school friend and takes him home to meet his wife, whom he immediately tries to palm off on Lemmon so he can get a divorce and marry the girl of his dreams, a gymnasium instructor named Linda. Each of the characters is loaded with neuroses which assert themselves in different ways as yarn builds for a climactic return to the bridge.

Clive Donner's direction fits the frantic overtones of unfoldment, but in this buildup occasionally goes overboard for effect. Lemmon appears to over-characterize his role, a difficult one for exact shading. Falk as a bright-eyed schemer scores decisively in a restrained comedy enactment for what may be regarded as pic's top performance. As the wife, who leaves Falk to wed Lemmon, only to find herself still love-starved, Elaine May proves herself a talented comedienne. Nina Wayne displays an arresting presence as the sexpot whom Falk marries, a welcome scenic addition to film

---

merely talked about in play. In gemlike support, Eddie Mayehoff, Paul Hartman and Severn Darden score.

Technical credits are definite assets right down the line, including Ernest Laszlo's color photography, Gerry Mulligan's music score, Harold F. Kress' editing, Al Brenner's production design.   *Whit.*

The Swan Lake
(COLOR)

A multi-camera filming in Munich of the Rudolf Nureyev-choreographed full-length Tchaikovsky ballet. Technically excellent and visually exciting, with the fame of Nureyev and Dame Margot for sell.

Hollywood, July 20.
Henry G. Saperstein release of United Productions of America-Seven Arts Productions presentation. Features Rudolf Nureyev, Dame Margot Fonteyn and the Vienna State Opera Ballet. Directed by Truck Branss. Camera (EastmanColor), Gunther Anders; editor, Marina Runne. Reviewed at BevHills Hotel Projection Room, July 19, '67. Running Time, 111 MINS.

Filmed on soundstages in Munich last February, this full length (complete four acts) of Tchaikovsky's ballet utilized a three camera technique, a cast of 80, including 60 dancers of the Vienna State Opera Ballet, and the Vienna Symphony Orchestra conducted by British John Lanchbery. Cost of production is reported at nearly $1,000,000. Henry G. Saperstein's United Productions of America & Seven Arts Productions picked up the tab. Saperstein will release here on a special college circuit — with theatrical and tv rights going to Seven Arts.

Production values are toprate, with lush and well coordinated costumes, imaginative & impressive sets, both designed by Nicholas Georgiadis, and the Eastmancolor camera work by Gunther Anders adding brisk dimension to film ballet.

Unlike many ballets which have been filmed on stage with a static center camera, "Lake" here has been photographed at various angles, high, low, and overhead, and a number of close-ups have been utilized. Tight, smooth cuts by editor Marina Runne, give a visual excitement to the dancing not found in viewing stage versions.

Naturally, Nureyev choreographed in a style that permits both himself and partner Dame Fonteyn to display their highly accomplished skills to advantage. Together and separately they perform with brilliant technical finesse and engage in some of the most difficult leaps, beats and pirouettes with virtuoso ease and poise. Pic should well enhance their reputations while trading upon them.

There is also fine dancing by two boy and girl dancers from the Vienna State Opera Ballet, but they do not receive billing. The large corps de ballet does not always dance in unison but their sequences have been choreographed and filmed in a manner that minimizes this, to American eyes, drawback.

Overall effect of pic is that of people who are dancing for the pure joy of it. In this respect Nureyev has not allowed the "Swan" to take on a heavy or arch style, but is primarily concerned with giving the classic ballet a visually dramatic impact, and in this respect he never allows the dancing to predominate for its own sake.

He has changed the ending to some extent, adding billowing purple silk, which raises and falls to symbolize rough waters, while he attempts to reach his fleeting swan as she appears to glide away. The sequence is theatrically effective.

John Lanchbery underscores the dancing with a quiet, vigorously skillful baton. All in all, this filmization of "Swan Lake" should please the general balletomane and serve to introduce those unfamiliar with ballet to enjoyment of its many visual delights.
Dool.

Fathom
(PANAVISION-COLOR)

Somewhat complicated but fast meller with names of Raquel Welch (and figure) and Tony Franaciosa for b.o. bait; carries good exploitation for program market.

Hollywood, July 21.
Twentieth-Fox release of John Kohn production. Stars Tony Franciosa, Raquel Welch; features Ronald Fraser, Greta Chi, Richard Briers, Tom Adams, Clive Revill. Directed by Leslie Martinson. Screenplay, Lorenzo Semple Jr.; from novel by Larry Forrester; camera (DeLuxeColor), Douglas Slocombe; music, John Dankworth; editor, Max Benedict; asst. director, David Tringham. Reviewed at Academy Award Theatre, July 21, '67. Running Time, 100 MINS.
Peter Merriweather .... Tony Franciosa
Fathom Harvill .... Raquel Welch
Douglas Campbell ...... Ronald Fraser
Jo-May Soon .... Greta Chi
Timothy .... Richard Briers
Mike .... Tony Adams
Serapkin .... Clive Revill
Mr. Trivers .... Reg Lye
Mrs. Trivers .... Ann Lancaster
Ulla .... Elizabeth Ercy
Mehmed .... Tutta Lemkow

"Fathom," lensed on location in various parts of Spain to take full pictorial advantage of scenic backdrops, is a melange of melodramatic ingredients personalized by the lush presence of Raquel Welch, who can qualify as "Miss Sexpot" of year. Femme, in role of an American sky diver competing in Europe, is set down in a maze of cops-and-robbers done up in a complicated plot but which nevertheless provides entertainment for the program market. With Miss Welch as natural exploitation lure, in sensational garb in virtually every scene, film carries enough ballyhoolecs to assure hefty returns.

Actress stars with Tony Franciosa in this John Kohn production, highlighted partially by some exciting parachute scenes and more particularly the Welch chassis. Script by Lorenzo Semple Jr., based on the Larry Forrester novel, is obviously triggered by the real-life incident of an American H-bomb accidentally lost off the coast of Spain couple years ago. Miss Welch's services, as a parachute jumper, are enlisted to help

recover what is described as an electronic device which will fire the bomb, now in the possession of certain "evil" forces, and which was not retrieved at the time the bomb itself was salvaged.

Femme, who sports name of Fathom (first letter for each of six wealthy uncles), enters search in the belief she is aiding the British government. She soon learns that the device, called the "Fire Dragon," is actually a priceless piece of jewelry of the Ming Dynasty stolen in China, and three sets of characters are after it. Latter sequences are devoted to her attempts to unravel who's the good guy, who's the bad guy, something audience is interested in discovering, too. It makes for fast action, despite perplexing elements, and director Leslie Martinson keeps his cast on the move.

Miss Welch is fascinating to watch and Franciosa, mebbe a good guy, mebbe a baddie, handles himself with competency. Ronald Fraser plays the Scotsman and Clive Revill is called upon to overplay a mysterious character named Serapkin, one of those out to get the Fire Dragon. Richard Briers, Greta Chi and Tom Adams lend able support.

Technical credits are exceptionally well executed, particularly the parachute sequences devised by Ken Vos and filmed by Jacques Dubourg. Regular photography by Douglas Slocombe is interesting, as is art direction by Maurice Carter, and Max Benedict's editing is fluid.

Music score by John Dankworth furnishes melodic backing.*Whit.*

Hostile Guns
(COLOR-TECHNISCOPE)

Loosely - put - together melo about prison wagon. Okay for western fanatics.

Hollywood, July 11.

Paramount release of A. C. Lyles production. Stars George Montgomery, Yvonne De Carlo, Tab Hunter, Brian Donlevy. Directed by R. G. Springsteen; story, Sloan Nibley, James Edward Grant; camera (Technicolor), Lothrop Worth; editor, John F. Schreyer; music, Jimmie Haskell; asst. director, Ralph Axness. Reviewed at Paramount Studios, July 11, '67. Running Time, 90 MINS.
Gid McCool ...... George Montgomery
Laura Mannon ...... Yvonne De Carlo
Mike Reno .... Tab Hunter
Marshal Willett .... Brian Donlevy
Aaron .... John Russell
Hank Pleasant .... Leo Gordon
R. C. Crawford .... Robert Emhardt
Angel Dominguez
                Pedro Gonzalez Gonzalez
Ned Cooper .... James Craig
Sheriff Travis .... Richard Arlen
Uncle Joe .... Emile Meyer
Johnson .... Donald Barry
Buck .... Fuzzy Knight
Jensen .... William Fawcett
Bunco .... Joe Brown
Chig .... Reg Parton
Tubby .... Read Morgan
Alfie .... Eric Cody

A. C. Lyles has dashed off another oater for Paramount, loosely based on a historical slice of the old west and loosely put together with players from an earlier era of Hollywood western. Many ends dangle in story of dangers of transporting prisoners to penitentiary. Appeal is to moviegoers who can suspend disbelief. It should fit in nicely as supporting feature in double bill,

for nabes or as topline of kiddies' Saturday matinees.

George Montgomery as U. S. Marshal assigned task of taking load of prisoners to Huntsville, walks through the role. Tab Hunter, as a rebellious young man conned into riding rifle for Montgomery, tries to cooperate with his role but dialog makes it tough. Most of his action scenes are obviously handled by a double.

Yvonne De Carlo, only female in cast, is dancehall hostess who shot a man who done her wrong and creates conflict between Montgomery and Hunter. She emotes far more than the role demands and in scene in which she tries to con Hunter into letting her escape from prison wagon, she almost becomes laughable rather than lovable.

Character roles are most strongly performed by Leo Gordon as the child killer; Robert Emhardt, railroad commissioner whose crime is graft; Pedro Gonzalez, goat stealer who sees prison as a place to learn a trade; and John Russell, brother of the murderer and leader of the gang who tries to bushwhack the prison wagon and free the prisoners.

Cameo roles by Richard Arlen, Brian Donlevy, Donald Barry, Fuzzy Knight and William Fawcett are okay.

Flimsy story deals with Montgomery's prison wagon, which leaves small Texas town in 1860's and picks up "passengers" along the way. From time it starts out to shortly before it arrives at destination, bad guys are stalking it hoping to ambush all involved, kill Montgomery and Hunter and let prisoners go.

Miss De Carlo, of course, attracts Hunter, who Montgomery thought would not cause trouble and his falling for her, of course, causes trouble. Not until chips are down do we learn Montgomery and Miss De Carlo had once had a thing going and she still loves him. Hunter winds up as Montgomery's prisoner when he tries to let Miss De Carlo go and not until bad guys return with reinforcements, and only as Miss De Carlo confesses that she was just putting Hunter on, does he get out of his shackles and help Montgomery wipe out all the crooks.

At one point in proceedings, Gordon, the killer, breaks out of his handcuffs (no one knows how) and makes a futile attempt to bash Montgomery's head open with ball at end of his chain. Hunter is involved in no less than four furious fistfights but blood appears on his face only once whereas opponents always wind up bloody wrecks.

Meat of story is interrelation of prisoners but writers Sloan Nibley and James Edward Grant pushed "human element" too far, resulting in overlong and repetitious dialogue in scene justifying Miss De Carlo's crime. Opening music and recurring theme were pleasant but not enough was heard. Background music in love scene droned more like a dirge. Camera work static and unimaginative, sets

too obviously staged and editing okay.

Other credits passable.
Edwa.

A Coeur Joie
(With Joyous Heart)
(FRENCH-BRITISH)
(Color)

Paris, July 18.
Comacico release of Francos Film-Films Du Quadrangle-Films Pomereu-Kenwood Films production. Stars Brigitte Bardot, Laurent Terzieff; features Jean Rochefort, Mike Sarne, James Robertson Justice, Carole Lebel, Annie Nicolas. Directed by Serge Bourguignon. Screenplay, Vahe Katcha, Pascal Jardin, Bourguignon; camera (Eastmancolor), Edmond Sechan; editor, Jean Ravel. At Colisee, Paris. Running Time, 95 MINS.
Cecile .... Brigitte Bardot
Vincent .... Laurent Terzieff
Philippe .... Jean Rochefort
Photographer .... Mike Sarne
Friend .... Annie Nicolas
Model .... Carole Lebel
Laird .... James Robertson Justice

Serge Bourguignon won an Oscar with his sentimental French pic "Sundays and Cybele," then made a Hollywood pic "The Reward" (20th), somewhat too ambitious and uneven, and now for his third film essays a vehicle for "aging" sex kitten Brigitte Bardot as a French-British coproduction. He tries to merge a lyrical melodramatic love idyll with situation comedy and it does not quite fuse well enough to give this either a good dramatic pitch or a more flip comedic zest.

Since Miss Bardot's pix in late years have fared so-so abroad, this one also looks headed for spotty chances in foreign climes unless given a hard sell on its neatly etched love scenes and Miss Bardot's ease in almost playing her own public image, albeit she is a top cover girl in this and not a pic star. She is living with an understanding rich man but is not at ease with herself or her life.

Pic deals with her trip to London for a noted fashion photog and how she meets a young Frenchman, Laurent Terzieff, and how they fall in love, have a rich and desire-ridden affair but then part ironically as she misses a plane he has beseeched her to take with him as her boyfriend is on his way to London.

Film overplays the lachrymose side. It is hard to imagine that Miss Bardot can not take the next plane after him. True, story paints her as a creature of whim but of sensitive instinct. However she can not quite cope with her own needs to be free and is bound by physical, rather than any sort of deeper, attachment. So the pic forces its poetics on a background of so-called "swinging London" with its photogs, birds, discotheques, miniskirts etc.

But under this modern dress is a well worn tale of a "brief encounter" love affair, plus the girl torn between two loves, one promising more emotional security and the other merely physical and that may or may not last. Miss Bardot looks good and is spontaneously girlish, pouting and frisky as usual. Nudity is sparingly used until a climactic love scene at the end that is brought off with tact.

Terzieff has charm and offbeat good looks to give his fairly routine role of the new man in her life a nice edge. But the dash and inventiveness, to paint character and give the early segs a polish and point, are somewhat blurred and the ensuing love affair becomes fairly precious and sentimentalized rather than growing from a well observed and revealing context. *Mosk.*

Don Giovanni in Sicilia
(Don Juan in Sicily)
(ITALIAN)

Rome, July 25.

Interfilm release of an Adelphia Cinematografica production. Stars Lando Buzzanca, Katia Moguy; features Katya Christine, Carletto Sposito, Pino Ferrara, Ewa Aulin, Rosanna Martini, Grazia Di Marza, Stefania Carredu. Directed by Alberto Lattuada. Screenplay by Attilio Riccio, Sabatino Ciuffini and Alberto Lattuada, based on Vitaliano Brancati's novel of same title; camera, Roberto Gerardi; editor, Roberto Perpignani; music, Armando Trovaioli. Previewed in ANICA screening room. Running Time, 105 MINS.

Giovanni	Lando Buzzanca
Ninetta	Katia Moguy
Francoise	Katya Christine
Scannapieco	Carletto Sposito
Muscara	Pino Ferrara
Wanda	Ewa Aulin
Sisters: Rosanna Martini, Grazia Di Marza, Mary Mizar, Stefania Carredu.	

There is something of a Boccaccio in Alberto Lattuada. The talented Italian film director has a way with libertinage that is both daring and disarming. He can get audiences to accept **sex** as pleasantly as sipping malted milks.

In "Don Giovanni in Sicilia," (or "Sex alla Siciliana"), he presents a free, slightly caricatural adaptation of the people who inhabit a bit more grimly the pages of Vitaliano Brancati's post-World War I novel. Each in his own way, Lattuada and Brancati situate the Sicilian lover boy within the Island's moral and immoral traditions.

Foreign femmes are fair game for rapid, total conquest. Sicilian belles are governable but altar bent. Lando Buzzanca mistakes a blonde Sicilian (Katia Moguy) for a Nordic and gets trapped to the tune of wedding bells and disgruntled bewilderment of his dame-baiting cronies.

Settling in Milan, our Don Juan finds his virility diminishing to the point of impotency with his simultaneous rapid success in industry. Payoff is a frustrated attempt to bed his Lolita-like mistress at an all-work trade congress in the northern lake country. So he throws wife and belongings into a fast car and, like a homing pigeon, races back to the erotic climate, aromas, food and pad of his native, paceless Catania.

Lattuada's comic style, cheery satire, penchant for carnal delights and eye for unclad beauty are all evident in this sprightly, madcap and low-budget comedy. Film confirms newcomer Lando Buzzanca's' welcome thesp potential at a time when Italo stars under 40 are hard to come by. Expressive eyes and handsome features are big camera assets.

Lattuada's flair for picking up new talent (often to keep budgets low) again pays off with Katia Moguy's fresh, new face and the debut of luscious 17-year-old Ewa Aulin of Sweden.

Producer's decision to film in black and white is hard to explain. Color contrast between Sicily and Milan is part of the story and could have been a major selling point, considering the long weeks Lattuada spent on exteriors both north and south.

But there is a place for "Don Giovanni" on foreign screens as a solid sex exploitation comedy, if nothing else. To help this along are the many first-rate comedy performances of supporting artists and Armando Trovaioli's music. Other technical credits okay.
Werba.

Det er Ikke Appelsiner, Det er Heste
(They Are Not Oranges, They Are Horses)
(DANISH-COLOR)

Copenhagen, July 18.

Rialto Film/Preben Philipsen production and release. Stars Morten Grunwald, Jesper Langberg, Judy Gringer. Directed by Ebbe Langberg. Screenplay, Peer Guldbrandsen; camera (Eastmancolor), Claus Loof; music, Soeren Christensen. Reviewed at Imperial Biografen, Copenhagen. Running Time, 88 MINS.

Three young artists despair of ever gaining fame and fortune. Then one fakes a suicide and right away everybody fights to get in a bid on his pictures. A strange girl steps in and claims to be the late genius' fiancee and while her imagination may run_ wild, her salesmanship is great. She makes a mint—and leaves it to the painter's friends to squander. Then the suicide returns home to claim his share of the loot.

The story, based on Mark Twain's "Dead or Alive," is gently milked for its many possibilities, including barbs at the welfare state's often color-blind aiding of young artists as well as the general public's equally color-blind attitude towards contemporary art in general.

Ebbe Langberg's direction mostly soft-pedals its way through situations that might easily be overplayed or stressed too much. But the script grows weaker and interest lags all along. However, the spoof is better than average Danish funfare. Judy Gringer, as the fiancee, puts in a memorably comic performance. *Kell.*

Moscow Film Fest

The Journalist
(RUSSIAN)

Overlong tale of Soviet newspaperman set in Moscow, small Ural mountain town and capitalist country assignments. Will have special interest for Westerners because of insights.

Moscow, July 17.

Sovexport Film release of Gorki Studio production. Features Yuri Vasiliev, Galina Polskik, Ivan Lanikov, Sergei Nikonenko, Nadejda Fedosova, Tamara Makarova, Sergei Gerasimov, Anatloi Krishanski, Tania Miasina, V. Telichina. Written and directed by Sergei Gerasimov. Camera, Vladimir Rapoport; music, P. Checkalov. Reviewed at Moscow Film Fest. Running Time, 205 MINS.

Yuri Aliabiev	Yurl Vasiliev
Djura Okaemova	Galina Polskik
Reytof	Ivan Lanikov
Pistovoitov	Sergei Nikonenko
Anikina	Nadejda Fedosova
Kolesinkov	Sergei Gerasimov
Barton	Anatoli Krishanski
Lanina'	Tamara Makarova
Michele Aubrey	Tania Miasina
Valya	V. Telichina

This vast, sprawling three-and-a-half hour item of epic intentions, which served as official USSR entry at the Moscow event, is a well-made and very interesting film to emerge at this time from a still-hesitant Soviet pic industry. It is bulky and rather unwieldy, with some very uneven stretches, notably a great contrast—a wanted one perhaps—between the first and second parts. From an audience point of view, it has some warm lyric and human moments which have a universal impact built in, others that are too local and parochial for worldwide interest. In its present form, it must be assessed an interesting art entry, but certainly no world-beater. Drastic trimming can only help.

Notably, especially in view of the fact that it was made by a Soviet filmmaking vet, Sergei Gerasimov, it is a surprisingly modern film—one of the most modern of recent Russian product—both in content and style, while retaining, at times, some (good) elements of classic tradition.

Story concerns a young newsman who's been stuck at a letters-to-the-editor desk for three years, and is finally sent on his first out-of-town assignment to a small burg in the Urals. There he gets a feel of provincial journalism and of small-town-ness in the form of a gossipy poison penster, but also meets Djura, a solid, unflighty, unspoilt country girl with whom he falls in love. When, close to his departure time, she rejects his advances, he's first angered, but soon realizes her strength and ultimate hold. Reassigned to Geneva and then Paris, he next gets a glimpse of the western world in its various facets and gets to meet a Yank reporter whom he befriends and who shows him the capitalist ropes in a fair, balanced way. Pic winds with our man's return to Moscow and later his trip to the Ural town to bring home the girl, who meanwhile has been brutally ostracized by the smalltowners because of her link with the man from Moscow.

Pic is chock full of interesting notations, especially for western observers, and it goes a long way to try to be objective and truth-telling in its observations of the current Russian and European scene. There are some tongue-in-cheek glimpses of provincial stage efforts, some rather frank views of Soviet newsgathering efforts and methods, and a very interesting, if uneven, portrayal of a Yank newsman (well played by a Soviet newsman. A n a t o l i Krishanski). Last, if somewhat of a liberal (and in one scene criticised by some fellow-Yanks for some apparently over-leftish articles), is with only a few exceptions not caricatured. Though he is shown as somewhat glib and talky, and though this facet is contrasted discreetly with the Russian's silent strength, he does add a positive note both to the pic in general and to the Soviet newsman's baggage of formative experiences. Their relationship is a nice realistic one in the main, and it is to be hoped that

in it, the film's makers have symbolized understanding between nations to a like degree. In this framework it is significant that it's the Yank newsman who opens the Russian's eyes as to his girl's true worth and helps him attain manhood in deciding to win and marry her. But these are only a few of the facets in a generally absorbing film which Gerasimov develops much too slowly at times, in an attempt at the epic. This doesn't come off due to the fragmentation in the European sequences, in which the viewers linearity and consistent development, with the principals always up front, gives way to a talky, choppy pot-pourri sampling of the West by the newsman, who with the few exceptions provided by his talks with the Yank, rarely participates. The French sequences are seen with only a little implied criticism, more as statements of facts about the western way of life and love, and one feels them more to be used to enrich the Russian's background as well as to show him, by implication, that things are not really so much different, in good and bad, at home.

Acting is good in every sector. Yuri Vasiliev makes a handsome lead, more in the western than the Soviet tradition of massive hero figures. Galina Polskik is a winning blonde and perfect foil for him. Other notable characterizations are by Anatoli Krishanski, as noted, in the role of the Yank newsman, Nadejda Fedosova as the village gossiper, Sergei Nikonenko as the small town reporter, and many others, including director Gerasimov, who plays a journalist in the Paris sequences as does Tamara Makarova. There are bits by such guest stars as Annie Girardot, singer Mireille Mathieu, and others, also in the Paris footage. V. Telichina adds a gem of a cameo as a dumb blonde secretary type rather hopelessly on the cultural learn. Pic is splendidly photographed by Vladimir Rapoport, there is discreet use of music here and there, and all other facets in the ambitious production are first rate.
Hawk.

Nguyen Van Troy
(NORTH VIETNAMESE)

Moscow, July 18.

Hanoi Film production and release. Features Tzan Kiem, Le Thanh Duc. Directed by Bol Dinh Hac, Ly Thai Bao. Screenplay based on "The Way He Lives," by Tran Dinh Van; camera, Luu Xuan Thu, Nguyen Xuan Chan; music, Do Nhuan. Reviewed at Moscow Film Fest. Running Time, 90 MINS.

This crudely made, out-and-out propaganda film, reviewed only for the record, is a rabble-rousing no-holds-barred anti-American film without even a minimum of filmic worth to justify its presence at an international film event. Whether the point is appreciated or not, it will be to the everlasting credit of festivals in western countries that films of this kind, regardless of the ideological or political targets of their gross offensiveness, have always been turned down not only by festival regulations (forbidding the screening of films offensive to participating nations), but merely from common sense standpoint.

As stated in the film's preamble,

It is "based on documents put down during the early days of U.S. aggression to Saigon" and, per a signed and reproduced title letter by Ho Chin Minh, is "to serve the valiant fight against American imperialism." That much cleared away, this proceeds to tell the story of the Viet Cong guerrilla who attempted to blow up a bridge over which Defense Minister McNamara was to cross, and was arrested. It then segues into a set of scenes in which man is tortured by grotesque means explicitly depicted (nails driven through fingers, etc.) to get him to reveal his collaborators, with mental torture also inflicted on his wife. After a long spell in jail, he's briefly released, then jailed again before being executed.

Film is filled with references to "American dogs" and "American imperialism," and in one torture scene, one of instruments depicted is visibly marked "U.S. Army Property."

No trick is missed is making this into a standard, for-the-masses propaganda item, from the mentioned torture scenes, to tear-pleading ones involving wife and husband, to plea-copping use of winningly smiling moppets, to ire-rousing outbursts of anti-U.S. speech. Film winds up with widow of Nguyen joining guerrilla forces in march through jungle to South Vietnam, midst song and slogans. Only person of "opposition" depicted with any favor of sorts is a South Viet prison guard who at one point sneaks into a cell to salve the wound of a North Viet victim. Film quality is expectedly rough, and acting is in keeping with content, played broadly and heroically. Action takes place in Saigon, and some of footage appears to have been shot there and sneaked out for backdropping purposes on Hanoi-filmed material. *Hawk.*

Westerplatte Resists
(POLISH)

Moscow, July 18.

Film Polski release of a Rytm Filmmaking unit production. Features Zygmunt Hubner, Arkadiusz Bazak, Andrzej Zaorski, Jozef Novak, Tadeusz Plucinski, Tadeusz Schmidt. Directed by Stanislaw Rozewicz. Screenplay, Jan Josef Szczepanski; camera, Jerzy Wojcik; music, Wojciech Kilar. Reviewed at Moscow Film Fest. Running Time, 97 MINS.

Major Sucharski .... Zygmunt Hubner
Captain Dabrowski .... Arkadiusz Bazak
Lt. Kregielski .... Andrzej Zaorski
Sgt. Buder .... Jozef Novak
Cpl. Grudzinski .... Tadeusz Plucinski
Lt. Gryzman .... Tadeusz Schmidt

Hard - hitting straightforward battle epic, based on a true event which took place on the Polish coastline during the first days of the German invasion in 1939. Film has been directed with plenty of dedication and drive and, thanks also to some sober underplaying by a very capable cast, emerges a good entry of its kind. Lack of names known for the West however, will make its chances of release in other areas iffy.

The Westerplatte of the title is the name of a fort set in a strategic north Polish position, which held out for over seven days at the start of the last World War though only supposed to last for 6-12 hours at most. Pic runs from pre-war tension to battle proper on to qualms by fort commander about how long to hold out, and the use of its fall in the tragic bigger picture complexion of the lightning Polish invasion by Nazi forces.

Some interesting psychological problems are touched on here above and beyond the muted heroics of the "episode" per se, and it's in these parts, and in truly outstanding action sequences, this rises above the norm for such films. The battle sequences are among the best of their kind, neatly directed, cut and lensed. Acting and other credits are good. *Hawk.*

Apa
(Father)
(HUNGARIAN)

Moscow, July 18.

Hungarofilm release of Mafilm Studio III (Budapest) production. Features Miklos Gabor, Klari Tolnay, Andras Balint, Dani Erdelyi, Kati Solyom. Written and directed by Istvan Szabo. Camera, Sandor Sara; music, Janos Gonda. Reviewed at Moscow Film Fest. Running Time, 95 MINS.

Father .... Miklos Gabor
Mother .... Klari Tolnay
The son .... Andras Balint
Son as child .... Dani Erdelyi
Anni .... Kati Solyom

A warm, sensitively made film, this second feature pic for young Hungarian director Istvan Szabo, almost but regrettably not quite has the universal qualities needed to achieve worldwide impact. It nevertheless is interesting in giving a valuable insight into current filmmaking trends in the East, as well as serving as an enjoyable example of new stirrings both in content and style to be seen in long-arid production areas.

The growth of a youth into manhood is explored here via the use of real and imaginary flashbacks to life with father, a doctor who died just after the end of the last World War, leaving his young son with a number of confused memories. As he grows, the child becomes slowly obsessed by the father's continuing influence on his life, and he unconsciously begins inventing war time exploits with the partisans and other exaggerated achievements to further the hero image which, he finds, rubs off on him with his fellow-pupils. Eventually, however, he begins to realize that he must "make" life on his own. The picture winds with his initial attempts to find himself and his own personality and status in life and society.

Szabo is especially good in his brief, sketch-like notations, either real or imagined, in which the boy recalls or constructs his father's past. This is real, solid, moving yet unsentimental stuff, and it's beautifully illustrated as well by Sandor Sara's camerawork, with its nostalgic glimpses of the past.

Pic also avoids no issues, thorny or not, and its integration of the 1956 Hungarian uprising is apt and honest, as are such other topics as early befuddlement with Marxism or the problems of a Jewish minority in Budapest. Director also displays skillful technique in handling, i.e., of a nighttime chase between partisans and Germans, and is definitely a talent to be reckoned with in the fast-blooming talent pool emerging these days in some Eastern countries.

Acting is uniformly good, with Miklos Gabor lending his personality to the role of father. Andras Balint is able in the role of the youth which Dani Erdelyi is winning in earlier scenes as the child. *Hawk.*

L'Occhio Selvaggio
(The Savage Eye)
(ITALIAN—COLOR)

Moscow, July 18.

George Marci-Paolo Cavara Film production and release. Stars Philippe Leroy; features Delia Boccardo, Gabriele Tinti, Giorgio Gargiullo, Lars Bloch. Directed by Paolo Cavara. Screenplay, Cavara, Tonino Guerra, in collaboration with Alberto Moravia; from story by Cavara, in collaboration with Fabio Carpi and Ugo Pirro; camera (Technicolor), Marcello Masciocchi; music, Gianni Marchetti. Reviewed at Moscow Film Fest. Running Time, 98 MINS.

Paolo .... Philippe Leroy
Barbara .... Delia Boccardo
Cameraman .... Gabriele Tinti

A strange, sometimes exciting but generally disconcerting behind-the-scenes glimpse of a feature-documentary maker at work which at times falls prey to the very footage it wants to attack and debunk, namely the out-of-context glimpses of exotica and erotica in various lands, or the re-staging—with apt exaggeration—of sensation-rousing things and events. Though it falls short of its ambitious scope, and though it doesn't even scrape the surface of a potentially very powerful story, this does have a certain fascination and uneven effectiveness. Therefore it might get an interested offshore reception. Its exact audience target is similarly hard to define, as the pic falls rather in between such varied genres as art, feature-doc and general audience fare.

Cynical hero of this tale is Paolo, an Italian feature documentary maker who'll do anything for a "realistic" sequence for his new feature. This includes marooning himself and his friends—and, of course, a camera — in mid-desert for days to film their suffering, until, as arranged, they are "saved" just as film is running low.

Similarly, after seducing a friend's wife and running off with her to make her the target of his lens in cynically observed glimpses of drug addicts being beaten in a Far Eastern "clinic," deaf-mute prosties plying their trade in gestures, and so on. He turns the lens on himself after he's savagely beaten up by a group of North Viet terrorists whose exploits he was filming. In another sequence, he re-arranges a Viet execution so that the light is right when the victim hits the dust, and in the climax, he grabs footage of a bomb explosion in a Viet nightclub, about which he's heard via a bribe, without warning the future victims of their pending doom. In the explosion, his girl is killed, and, of course, he turns the lens on self and on her for the fadeout.

The intentions are good, but Cavara and his many co-scripters have confused more than one issue, and never clearly defined his variout characters nor plowed them with any depth. The picture could and should have been much more brutal and hardhitting, given the subject, even thought it does spring to life occasionally, notably in the staging of the Viet execution.

Philippe Leroy has the physique for his role, and occasionally gives it the depth it should have throughout. Delia Boccardo is a looker used mainly to highlight the hero's synique, while Gabriele Tinti, Giorgio Gargiullo, and others suitably go through their paces. The lensing by Marcello Masciocchi is outstanding, and Gianni Marchetti has composed a lush musical backdrop, very similar to that of the many doc-features this film is lashing into. *Hawk.*

Romance Por Kridlovku
(Romance for Bugle)
(CZECH)

Moscow, July 18.

Ceskoslovenski Film release of a Barrandow Studio Prague (Bohumil Smida-Ladsislav Fikar Proda Group) production. Features Jaromir Hanzlik, Julius Vasek, Jaroslav Rozsival, Janusz Strachocki, Zuzana Ciganova, Stefan Kvietik, Miriam Kantorkova. Directed by Otakar Vavra. Screenplay, Vavra, Frantisek Hrubin; camera, Andrej Barla; music, Jiri Srnka; editor, Antonin Zelenka. Reviewed at Moscow Film Fest. Running Time, 85 MINS.

Vojta as student ...... Jaromir Hanzlik
Vojta as headmaster ..... Julius Vasek
Vojta's father .... Jaroslav Rozsival
Vojta's grandfather....Janusz Strachocki
Terina .... Zuzana Ciganova
Tonka .... Miriam Kantorkova

Otakar Vavra's latest is a warmly glimpsed, charming love story, and another feather in the cap of an ever-more-accessible Czech film industry. It's strictly for the arties, but might make it on the strength of recent pro-Czech work of mouth as well as its own merits.

Story is a fragile one of the flashbacked love interlude of two men for the same girl. One is a young student, the other a fairground shooting gallery boss. Both fall for the girl with the carousel, Terina. For the student, it's a first, life-shaping affair; for the other, older man, it's more of a routine thing designed to lead to a marriage of convenience. After a brief, lyric interlude, the youngsters are separated by circumstances, and she drives off with the older man, only to die soon after of diphtheria aggravated by the loss of her loved one. It's not a tale for the telling, however, and Vavra has composed a ballad of a youth's crucial days: the one in which he becomes a man.

It's slow, atmospheric, pausing frequently to close in on a detail of nature, but the youngster's budding world is seen with affection, warmth and spontaneity. There's a neatly limned bit by a lusty, busty older woman who tries to seduce the youth by swimming naked in a stream. There is a macabre yet strangely moving scene in which the youth alone in his home washes and dresses the body of his grandfather, whom he's taken care of after a stroke, in preparation for the funeral. In fact, the whole reluctant but patient and tender relationship between crippled oldster and the boy are another highlight of pic, as are the brief, almost unstated attempts to make love to the girl.

Jaromir Hanzlik is very good as the boy. And there's an outstanding performance by Janusz Strachhocki as the granddad while all others fill their roles well. Andrej Barla's camerawork is in the high Czech tradition while Jiri Srnka's music, especially the plaintiff leitmotif on the cornet, is apt throughout. *Hawk.*

El Amor Brujo
(SPANISH-COLOR)

Moscow, July 18.
Films R. B., S. A. production for Exclusivas Floralva release. Features Antonio Gades, La Polaca, Rafael de Cordova, Morucha, Nuria Torray, Jose Manuel Marin, Fernando Sanchez Polack. Directed by Rovira Beleta. Screenplay, Rovira Beleta, Jose Antonio Medrano, J. Caballero Bonald; camera (Eastmancolor), Gabor Pogany, Francisco Marin; music, Manuel de Falla, adapted by Ernesto Halfter; dances, Alberto Lorca. Reviewed at Moscow Film Fest. Running Time, 110 MINS.
Antonio .... Antonio Gades
Candelas .... La Polaca
Diego .... Rafael de Cordova
Lucia .... Morucha
Soledad .... Nuria Torray
Lorenzo . ...Jose Manuel Marin
Candelas Father
                     Fernando Sanchez Polack

With some trimming and other polishing jobs on this rushed-to-completion pic (to make the local deadline), it could think of denting a specialized foreign market of sorts, on the heels of director's preceding pic, "Los Tarantos," which had a modicum of showings in various areas. Also going for it is the DeFalla name and title. But at least in the print seen, it must be assessed as strictly a hardsell item for specialized viewing.

This is a potpourri production which blends dance, music, story and suspense, basing it on the various movements of the De-Falla original. Result is a melange which really doesn't fully satisfy fans of any of the genres in such setup. Terp aficionados will find the dance numbers, group and solo, too few for full satisfaction; the story line, kernel of which is the haunting, tragically impossible love of a girl for a one-time lover, and the involvement of an okay No. 2 suitor, is similarly over-stretched. There are seemingly interminable sequences bridging dramatic highlights, in which principals are seen running to and fro, up narrow streets, across beaches, etc., escaping from or running towards each other.

Condensation of these might spotlight the generally effective central scenes highlighting the girl's obsessions and fears or the savage fights between her two suitors. There's also an imaginative under-titles dance sequence which perhaps better than any other shows what the film could have been like if given a stylistic unity, one way or another, and the other terp numbers here and there are imaginative and exciting to ear and eye.

La Polaca, except for some over-stressed, starry-eyed dramatic moments here and there, fits the bill well as the obsessed girl. Antonio Gades is effective as her "good" suitor while Rafael de Cordova is properly sinister as the evil influence. Morucha backs capably as a spell-casting gypsy. Others in busy cast all do their share with dedication.

Production values are excellent. Gabor Pogany's and Francisco Marin's color lensing on Spanish locations are among the film's highlights and sales points. Remainder of all-location production work is visibly nonskimping nature. Importantly, DeFalla's music aptly punches through to one from the clear soundtrack.
Hawk.

The Dawn
(TUNISIAN)

Moscow, July 18.
Omar Khlifi production and release. Features Ahmed Hamza, Habib Chaari, Tahar Haouas. Directed by Omar Khlifi. Screenplay, Khlifi, Mokhtar Hachicha; camera, Ezzedine Ben Ammar. Reviewed at Moscow Film Fest. Running Time, 85 MINS.

This Tunisian entry is an example of the pitfalls of such fests as Moscow which accept national entries with (almost) narv a turndown. Seemingly, its only reason for being here is its revolutionary theme, for pic fails on all other counts.

Story of first individual, then mass uprising which led to Tunisian independence from French rule, is told in the most rudimentary, often unwittingly risible way. Basically, it relates the familiar story: modest heroics by modest underdogs against superior forces; police brutality; messages and slogans of hate for the oppressor, and so on, all taking place in an Arab world in which good men don't speak French or guzzle wine, which the gullible Gallic forces, depicted here, invariably do.

But every facet of this film is incredibly amateurish, though conceivably much effort went into its making. Direction is mostly at fault, but editing is choppy and inept, and the acting stiff and, self-conscious. Even the many chase and battle scenes, abounding in this, result in unwanted laughs on more than one occasion.
Hawk.

The Enchanted Forest
(CAMBODIAN-COLOR)

Moscow, July 20.
Khemara Pictures production and release. Features Norodom Sihanouk, Monique Sihanouk, H.R.H. Princess Bopha Devi, Madame Visakha Tiulong, Bruno Forsinetti, Tim Dong. Written and directed by Norodom Sihanouk. Camera (uncredited color), Som Sam Al; music, Sihanouk. Reviewed at Moscow Film Fest. Running Time, 106 MINS.

Strange, much-heralded (it was once intended for Cannes) pic by the current ruler of Cambodia, Norodom Sihanouk, this item emerges as a gauche yet fascinating attempt at filmmaking. It has some curio value to go by on the names involved in its creation, but nothing further to recommend it for subsequent exposure, despite some colorful dance sequences and some glimpses of local folklore.

Like a home-pic shot in 35 instead of 16m, this pic has an amateur flavor from start to finish as it tells of a dream-like visit to the mid-forest palace of a prince by a group of hunters. They are shown the beauties of the place, the surrounding country and its workers, product and folklore, and a generous sampling of native dances and songs, before they return to their home bases. Action is stiff, dialogue obvious and naive, pace tedious and camerawork flat.

There remains the curiosity of a visit to Sihanouk by Sihanouk, in which a strange blend of narcissism and sincerity emerges as he flaunts his prowess at the piano, singing his own song, or embraces his happy peasants in the fields. Or he explains dances staged by another member of the family and performed by still other presumably near or distant relatives, to

name just a few of the pic's "features." The director-prince has blended in some standard gag items, mostly comedy bits by inept servants, as well as several unconscious moments of humor such as one showing a (male) guest soaping himself in a palace bathtub or others where workers toiling in fields drop their implements to cheer their ruler.

Proceeds from film, Sihanouk revealed here, would go to "victims of savage bombardments of our frontiers by American imperialists and their accomplices in Saigon and Bangkok." *Hawk.*

Subteranul
(The Subterranean)
(RUMANIAN—SCOPE)

Moscow, July 18.
Romania Film release of Bucarest Film Studio production. Features Lurie Darie, Leopoldina Balanuta, Viorica Farcas, Stefan Ciobotarasu, Emil Botta, Toma Garagiu, Mircea Basta, Constantin Codrescu, Geo Barton, Dem. Radulescu, Dumitru Rucareanu, Monica Ghiuta, Elena Caragiu. Directed by Virgil Galotescu. Screenplay, Ioan Grigorescu; camera (Cinemascope), Costea Ionescu, Tonciu Raducanu; music, Theodor Mitache. Reviewed at Moscow Film Fest. Running Time, 93 MINS.

Well-made but familiar story of oil drillers at work, complete with explosion, fire and eventual last-minute flame cut-off, here mixed with battle between two engineers over validity of new drilling procedure. It's a straightforward tale with some suspense and some very good photography, but generally not a subject of interest to non-Rumanian audiences in its present form.

A young engineer returns from a business trip to find that his project, an old drill done with a new caulking method for speed, has literally blown its top, vindicating his enemies and prejudicing his rapidly ascending career. He races to the scene and after some doubts (and several flashbacks to backdrop the tension) manages to extinguish the fire which, it turns out, was attributable to accidental causes anyway.

Involved as well are two women, a wife and a former mistress, for some usual triangular highjinks. There's some surface tension in the long sequences dedicated to fire and explosion, and a certain mystery intrigue about how it got started in the first place. Acting is competent, and the fire sequences have been very vividly lensed by Costea Ionescu and Tonciu Raducanu.

Other credits good. *Hawk.*

The Love-Ins
(COLOR)

Good exploitation film of San Francisco's hippie movement.

Hollywood, July 26.
Columbia Pictures release of Four Leaf (Sam Katzman) production. Stars Richard Todd, James MacArthur, Susan Oliver; features Mark Goddard, Carol Booth, Marc Cavell, Joe Pyne. Directed by Arthur Dreifuss. Screenplay, Hal Collins, Dreifuss; camera (PatheColor), John F. Warren; music, Fred Karger; editor, Ben Lewis; asst. director, Donald C. Klune. Reviewed at Columbia, July 25, '67. Running Time, 85 MINS.
Dr. Jonathan Barnett ..... Richard Todd
Larry Osborne .... James MacArthur
Patricia Cross .... Susan Oliver
Elliot .... Mark Goddard
Harriet .... Susan Oliver
Mario .... Marc Cavell
Lamelle .... Janee Michelle
Bobby .... Ronnie Eckstine
Joe Pyne .... Joe Pyne

"The Love-Ins" is producer Sam Katzman's latest coup. Getting there first with solid, if standard, story, fringed in fine style with love-ins and hippie happenings, he has given Columbia a surefire b.o. success, both with fast initial playoff and later reissue should the hippie movement continue to flower.

Story concerns professor (Richard Todd) at a mythical San Francisco college who resigns his position in protest to administration's dismissal of students James MacArthur and Susan Oliver, editors of an "underground" newspaper. Todd is hailed by the hippies as one who understands, but adulation soon subverts his initial sincere belief in their way of life into moneymaking scheme that raises him as leader of a cult.

Essence of Todd's preachments is "Be More, Sense More, Love More," with the underlying formula that unrestricted use of LSD is the way to attain such behavior. Along the way, a fantasy sequence involving Miss Oliver, who has taken too much LSD and goes on a far out trip, is well done, but presumably (a) does not capture how LSD affects the mind, (b) does not really capture the intensity and rapidity of impressions and emotions of the user. Still (c) it does hint at it.

MacArthur soon reverses his regard for Todd and becomes a solitary outcast as he uses his paper to crusade against him. Miss Oliver, his sweetheart, turns her affections to Todd until he tells her to get rid of the baby she is carrying because it would ruin his image. Cop-out ending has MacArthur, acting very rationally throughout, shooting Todd at a big rally, thus, as he immediately admits, making a martyr out of him.

Perhaps the only major flaw in story treatment is the theme that one man could dominate the hippie movement to extent that Todd is represented as doing. While parallel to a certain "doctor" seems obvious, a unique aspect of the hippie movement is that there is no fountainhead for it. Otherwise, screenplay by Hal Collins and Arthur Dreifuss provides a revealing, though superficial study of the hippie way of life. What is stressed throughout is that the one thing hippies detest and want to overcome is the hypocritical attitude in human relations as they believe adults practice it. Statements and scenes in support of this are well done. Also caught is thoughtlessness of hippies in a scene where they invade a park where well-scrubbed young adults are playing football.

The death of a hippie, under LSD influence, as he tries to stop the ensuing fight between hippies and footballers by jumping from a second story window, was not convincing, his act explained by exposition by the principals rather than from within the suicide himself.

Todd gives a good performance as the sincere idealist whose sincerity is twisted into fanaticism. MacArthur appears a bit too old and stodgy as the freewheeling student-editor. (The newspaper scenes were the most amateurish part of the pic) while Susan Oliver also appeared too mature as a student and hippie. In lesser roles, Mark Goddard, Carol Booth, Marc Cavell, Janee Michelle and Ronnie Eckstine, were well cast, with Miss Booth very good in her scene with her father. In a cameo role, Joe Pyne did quite well with a hammed-up script.

George Davis and Charles Hagedon's art direction and sets by Henry Grace and Jim Berkey were slick and colorful. But the constant reference by adults to filth that hippies lived in was seldom in evidence on the screen. Dreifuss moved pic along at very good pace and other credits were pro.
Beig.

La Vie Normale
(Normal Life)
(FRENCH)
Paris, July 25.
Moc Mahon release of Jeune Cinema Theatre De France production. With Monique Lejeune, Victor Lanoux, Denise Gence. Directed by Andre Charpak. Screenplay, Charpak, Anna Langfuss from book by Micheline Maurel; camera, Marcel Weiss; editor, Francine Grubert. At Studio De L'Etoile, Paris. Running Time, **80 MINS.**

Laurence .... Monique Lejeune
Jean .... Victor Lanoux
Mother .... Denise Gence
Tom .... Marc Joannes

The theme of a girl who had been in a concentration camp trying to adapt to so-called normal life after the war is worthy but somewhat too schematically treated to give this the density and dramatic depth it needs. So it looms mainly for specialized use abroad on its theme and some adequate acting without the mounting to give it much art legs.

The girl, Monique Lejeune, goes to London to find a friend of the resistance days but comes across him married. She drifts, harassed by her camp memories and shaky health, until she meets a young French intern studying in London. But a love idyll is shattered by his callowness and selfishness and her return to normal life is via betrayal.

New director Andre Charpak comes from legit and has a tendency to explain too much. He's not quite able, as yet, to transpose the narrative to more visual terms. But he does give the love scenes

a fresh feeling and is helped by the restrained emotion and offbeat good looks of Miss Lejeune, as the girl.

Victor Lanoux has the right self indulgence as the selfish but honest young doctor. Film pads a bit via repetitive scenes and overdone posing. However, it does integrate stock footage on the camps effectively. This is an estimate first work with an ambitious theme that does not quite come off entirely.
Mosk.

O Beautiful Istanbul
(TURKISH)
Bordighera, Aug. 1.
A Be-Ye film production, Istanbul. Directed by Atif Yilmaz from screenplay by Sefa Onal. Features Ayla Algan, Sadri Alisik. At Festival Hall in Bordighera. Running time, **94 MINS.**

How "O Beautiful Istanbul" slipped into the Festival of Comedy Films at Bordighera-San Remo is a mystery. More than anything it is a sentimental love story that takes place on the banks of the Bosphorus.

In contest screening at Bordighera indicates growing confidence of Turkish filmmakers and an increasing effort on their part to place product outside the home market. Of further significance is the obvious technical knowhow in turning out "B" films on a shoestring budget.

The story reflects sweeping Europeanization of Turkey's traditional folk ways. In it, a Bohemian noble, who has unloaded a family fortune on loose dames and gaming tables, falls in love with a waterfront waif, Ayse. Music publishing friends get him to blend Turkish melodies with the modern beat. Ayse (Ayla Algan) successfully warbles the songs at a port side cafe and becomes an overnight pop music star. She goes the road to fame, disillusionment and attempted suicide, finally taking the ferry back to her Bohemian lover.

The story contrasts new and old Istanbul in human terms. Both leading players are surprisingly real. The supporting cast is equally believable.

Atif Yilmaz directed with a sure hand, a good sense of mood and a neat touch for human values. He and the cast offer evidence of the progress Turkey's filmmakers are beginning to show. Missing is screenplay material that rises above local color.
Werb.

Beach Red
(COLOR)

Sincere anti-war pic defeated by vague screenplay and lethargic pace. Weak b.o. likely in most situations.

United Artists release of a Theodora (Cornel Wilde) production. Stars Wilde; features Rip Torn, Burr DeBenning, Patrick Wolfe, Jean Wallace. Directed by Wilde. Screenplay, Clint Johnston, Donald A. Peters, Jefferson Pascal; from novel by Peter Bowman; camera (DeLuxe Color), Cecil R. Cooney; title theme, Elbey Vid; music arrangement, Col. Antonio Buenaventura; editor, Frank P. Keller; asst. director, Derek Cracknell. Previewed at United Artists screening room, July 21, '67. Running Time, 105 MINS.

Captain MacDonald ....Cornel Wilde

Sergeant Honeywell........ Rip Torn
Egan ....Burr DeBenning
Cliff ....Patrick Wolfe
Julia MacDonald........ Jean Wallace
Colombo ....Jaime Sanchez
Captain Sugiyama ....Genki Koyama
Goldberg ....Gene Blakely
Nakano ....Norman Pak
Mouse ....Dewey Stringer
Lieutenant Domingo ..... Fred Galang
Michio ....Hiroshi Kiyama
Tall girl ....Linda Albertano
Susie ....Jan Garrison
Captain Kondo.........Michio Hazama
Colonel's wife ....Masako Ohtsuki

"Beach Red" unfortunately falls between two stools and will probably suffer as a result. Action audiences are likely to complain about its insistent pacifism and lack of the usual heroics, while more serious-minded patrons will object to dialog banalities, vacant characterizations, stylistic inconsistencies, and slack pacing. Boxoffice future of the Cornel Wilde production looks shaky, although pic's apparently low budget may facilitate recoupment.

In contrast to many professedly anti-war films, "Beach Red" is indisputably sincere in its war-is-hell message. Except for brief reveries of civilian life, the film focuses entirely on a single dreary campaign by an American unit out to take a Japanese-held island in the Pacific. (Although obviously set in World War II, the film mentions no specific date.) Notably absent are the usual stereotypes: the tough-talking sarge with the heart of gold, the frightened kid who becomes a man in combat, the wise-cracking cynic who ultimately turns hero and saves six buddies at the cost of his own life.

The trouble with the screenplay, adapted from Peter Bowman's 1945 novel by Clint Johnston, Donald A. Peters and Jefferson Pascal, is that little is substituted for these wisely-avoided cliches. The central characters are spokesmen for differing points of view, not real, full-bodied people. The acting quality suffers as a result.

The captain (Cornel Wilde) loves his wife and hates war (regarding the many deaths suffered in a battle: "I'll have a lot of letters to write...I'd rather get shot, I think"). The sergeant (Rip Torn) derives sadistic pleasure from the war ("That's what we're here for—to kill—and the rest is all crap"). An 18-year-old minister's son (Patrick Wolfe) remembers his girl back home and inarticulately echoes the captain's pacifism ("There's gotta be some other way, there's just gotta be, or what's the point?"). His Southern sidekick (Burr DeBenning) is a hearty illiterate for whom the armed forces is a haven ("I ain't seen my folks since I was four ...that sits just right with me").

In marked contrast to the script's trite theatricalism and skimpy development, Wilde has directed the battle scenes with unrelenting realism. Not only does he show a severed foot floating in the water, an arm blown off, a thumb shot off, even a needle being stuck in his own arm, but the forcefully underscores the boredom and fatigue of battle.

There is little respite from the grim setting, little humor to lighten the apprehensive mood, little variation in the combat maneuvers. With a more sharply dramatized screenplay, this atmospheric honesty could have contributed to a good film. The irony of "Beach Red," however, is that Wilde's unyielding versimilitude only reinforces the tedium of the script.

In addition to these conceptual flaws, there are minor weaknesses, some of which could be corrected before the film goes into general release. Color processing is uneven, making some of photographer Cecil R. Cooney's generally good work look like stock footage. Sound recording is inconsistent: conversations and inner monologs have identical aural quality in early scenes, then are sharply differentiated later.

The musical score, arranged by Col. Antonio Buenaventura from a haunting title theme by Elbey Vid, shifts uneasily from a tinnily reproduced band to full symphonic orchestra. Some of Wilde's subjective camerawork is arbitrarily inserted without clear reference to the camera "I."

Editor Frank P. Keller could have trimmed at least 15 minutes off the running time and lessened the lethargy and redundancy of several sequences. Two unmatched close-up inserts in the closing scene might well be removed. Since most of the stop-action inserts (of family and home or of earlier battle action) are silent, the screams accompanying one montage are jarring. There also seems little reason for Wilde's totally inflectionless readings in the flashbacks recalling his wife, played reasonably well by Jean Wallace (a usually unconvincing actress who debuts as a singer under the well-designed credits and reveals a strikingly androgynous voice).

"Beach Red" is worthy in its theme and honest in its presentation. Its pacifist plea might conceivably draw favorable editorial comment from those willing to overlook its faults. (However, its bare-breast footage may encounter censorship trouble.) But lacking any femme appeal and the quality to go the art-house route, it will need a very hard sell to approach the b.o. success of Wilde's last film, "The Naked Prey." *Beau.*

Sedmi Kontinent
(Seventh Continent)
(YUGOSLAVIAN—COLOR)
Trieste, July 25.
Yugoslavia Film release of Jadran Film, Kolba Film production. With Iris Vrus, Tomica Pasaric, Andulaj Seck. Directed by Dusan Vukotic. Screenplay, Vukotic, Andro Lusicic; camra (Eastmancolor), Karl Krska; music, Tomica Simovic. At Trieste Sci-Fi Film Fest. Running Time, **80 MINS.**

Boy .... Tomica Pasaric
Girl .... Iris Vrus
Negro Boy .... Andulaj Seck
Mother .... Hermina Pipinic
Father .... Demeter Bitnec

A first film by a noted and prizewinning Yugoslav animator Dusan Vukotic appears to be trying a bit too hard to appeal both to moppets and grownups alike. It does not quite bring it off but abounds in some ingenious ideas. Film has enough charm to make it something for specialized use abroad though it is not cohesive and firm enough in story, outlook and direction to give it arty or more general playoff legs.

Two moppets, overlooked by grownups on a ferry trip, slip off to sea in a little plastic boat. After disturbing a cruising submarine, they land on an island where they proceed to plant cutouts of plants and trees from a map. Then they find they can see others by looking through the map and soon have enticed plenty of moppets to their children's paradise.

The good use of children and some inspired bits of animation give the first part a fresh tang. But then the grownups get hysterical and begin beseiging the police for their children. Here some rather used cliches of adult life and political takeoffs are filtered in, and the film loses its early charm.

Too much has been tried by filmmaker Vukotic and direction sometimes is too schematic to get the right blending of fable and satire. But it is promising, and a firmer script should have Vukotic a needed maker of unusual children's pix, with enough insight perhaps to entice adults. This is technically good.   *Mosk.*

Sei No Kigen
(The Origin of Sex)
(JAPAN)
Tokyo, July 25.
Shochiku release of a Kindai Eiga production. With Taiji Tonoyama, Nobuko Otowa, Hideki Haaiyashi, Wioko Akaza, Kaiyo Matsuo, Hideo Kanzai, Minoru Chiaki. Written and directed by Kaneto Shindo. Camera, Kiyomi Kuroda; music, Hikaru Haiyashi. Previewed in Tokyo. Running Time, 100 MINS.

Director Kaneto Shindo, noted for "The Island" and "Onibaba," has completed the second film in what seems to be a series of pictures about sex. The first was last year's "Honno" (variously called "Impotence" and "Lost Sex"). This Kindai Eiga Kyokai production, written and directed by Shindo himself, is about an older man (Taiji Tonoyama), somewhat disturbed, who, during a stay in a hospital, tries to kiss the young girl (Kaiyo Matsuo) in the bed next to his wife (Nobuko Otowa). She understands, but his son (Hideki Haiyashi) and daughter (Mioko Akaza) are scandalized. The boy sets out to apologize but ends up seducing the girl (a simple accomplishment), the father dies, and the home is broken up.

That is all there is to the story. It is simply a vehicle for the personal, social, and moral observations of the director. That society is excessively, if perhaps necessarily hypocritical is the first. The nocturnal kiss of a sick old man is not going to hurt any young girl, particularly one s loose as Miss Matsuo. Further, the reason for his intrusion is a very human one, a sense of death. Sick, alone in the hospital, Tonoyama hears of the death of a friend's wife and though he was not apparently particularly close to her, the annihilation of someone he knew sets him to thinking about himself and the

kiss as a symbolic act, an affirmative gesture, an indirect prayer to the life we experience in love and/or sex. Society (the son and daughter, girl's father and the head doctor) does not understand this. Society sees simply a dirty old man.

Another observation is that sex is properly understood only by adults. While the son is making out with the girl, the mother and father go on a trip, and Shindo cuts between the two couples— the youngsters unloving, guilty, furtive; the oldsters romping about naked in the sea, lying on the sand, unashamed, enjoying themselves. But the kids get away with it and a nasty village cop breaks up the married couple's holiday— an irony that needs no further comment. And, once more, sex as a life affirming force is denied.

There seems little hope, the director seems to say, that such necessary and essential truths ever will be realized. That one understands this is due to Shindo's intensity, single-mindedness and skill in this film.   *Chie.*

Smukke-Arne and Rosa
(Pretty-Boy and Rosa)
(DANISH-COLOR)
Copenhagen, July 26.
Teatrenes Film Kontor release of Saga Studio production. Features Morten Grunwald, Judy Gringer. Written and directed by Sven Methling. Camera by Ole Lytken; music by Ole Hoeyer. Reviewed at Saga Bio. Running time, 90 MINS.

The off-beat lovebirds of Sven Methling's "Five Men and Rosa," a successful film comedy of 1965, were Morten Grunwald and Judy Gringer as the good-natured, loud-mouthed safecracker and his chesty, gun-toting gal. The director and his stars are back now, this time in color, with "Pretty-Boy and Rosa."

Story and treatment hum along nicely on the once-stated formula. This time, Pretty-Boy and his girl are enlisted to break into a bank and steal $2,000,000 contraband U. S. dollars. The money belongs morally to the Danish State, but cannot, for some red-tape reason, be seized officially.

Pretty-Boy stages the bank robbery by setting up what looks like the shooting of a robbery sequence by a local film company. The gullibility of everybody looms as soon as a chance appears for them to be involved in this scene. This probably has been done before in a film production, but in Methling's hands, it comes off well. There are plenty of laughs. As a crook comedy, this is not in the big league class, but it's okay for a small league.   *Kell.*

The Long Duel
(BRITISH—COLOR)

Trite dialog in true but tall yarn relieved by plenty of stimulating physical action, colorful backgrounds by topnotch performances by Trevor Howard and Harry Andrews; with Yul Brynner starred this

should do satisfactory box-office.

London, July 25.
Rank production (Ken Annakin) and release. Stars Yul Brynner, Trevor Howard; features Harry Andrews, Andrew Keir, Charlotte Rampling, Virginia North, Laurence Naismith, Maurice Denham. Directed by Ken Annakin. Screenplay by Peter Yeldham, based on story by Ranveer Singh; orginally adapted for screen by Ernest Borneman; addition material, Geoffrey Orme; camera (Eastmancolor), Jack Hildyard; music, Patrick John Scott; editor, Bert Bates; special effects, Dick Parker. Reviewed at Odeon, Marble Arch, London. Running time, 115 MINS.

Sultan	Yul Brynner
Young	Trevor Howard
Stafford	Harry Andrews
Gungaram	Andrew Keir
Jane	Charlotte Rampling
Champa	Virginia North
McDougal	Laurence Naismith
Governor	Maurice Denham
Tara	Imogen Hassall
Jamadar	Paul Hardwick
Gyan Singh	David Sumner
Abdul	Shivendra Sinha
Ram Chan	George Pastell
Colonel	Patrick Newell
Crabbe	Jeremy Lloyd
Major	Terence Alexander
Hardwicke	Edward Fox
High Priest	Bakshi Prem

Produced and directed by Ken Annakin at Pinewood and on location in Granada, Spain, this is an ambitious actioner which has plenty of punch in its physical situations, crowd sequences and bitter massacres, horse-riding and hand-to-hand fighting. But the yarn, though based on fact, unfolds with little conviction and is repeatedly bogged down by labored dialog and characterization in Peter Yeldham's screenplay.

Still, with Trevor Howard, Yul Brynner and Harry Andrews as leads, backed by some solid feature players and convincing native players, the film should stir up some sound business for Rank in Britain and Paramount, who will handle distribution elsewhere.

Rank, incidentally, gives the pic an interesting sendoff. For the first time the organization will show a film in two West End cinemas simultaneously, hardticket at the Odeon, Marble Arch, and continuous performances at Leicester Square Theatre.

Story is set on the Indian Northwest Frontier during the 1920's and basically hinges on the uneasy relationship and lack of understanding between most of the British top brass and the native tribes. Trevor Howard, an idealistic police officer is very conscious of the need for tact and diplomacy when handling the touchy natives.

When he is ordered to track down the Bhanta tribe leader (Yul Brynner), who is trying to lead his people from the bondage of the British, Howard recognizes Brynner as a fellow idealist and an enemy to respect. Howard's chivalrous methods of tracking down and attempting to trap Brynner cause him to clash with government officials and his immediate superior (Harry Andrews). But Howard obstinately insists that his methods are necessary if bloodshed and hatred is to be avoided and India is ever to be given a break.

So the long duel between the two begins and produces some exciting highlights. The raiding and burning of the police barracks by Brynner and his men, a forest battle, Brynner and a dancing girl escaping from the

police by a precarious rope bridge over a ravine, a couple of massacres and a final payoff when the two adversaries meet for the last time are all good filming.

Whenever the film is operating outdoors, this is lively enough. It is in the local officers' club and in the office of the governor that the film gets overloaded with talk. As is customary, both Howard and Harry Andrews turn in strong, dominating performances as two policemen diametrically opposed in their views. Brynner also has a meaty role which tends to pall since it is played by him with his usual impassive expression and without a gleam of humor.

Laurence Naismith is sound as the District Collector, as is Maurice Denham as the governor. Among the many good performances by local actors are those of Shivendra Sinha and Baksi Prem while Andrew Keir, as Brynner's fiery right-hand man; George Pastell & David Summers effectively simulate Indians.

Apart from a handful of dancing girls, only three actresses have proper roles. Imogen Hassall disappears fairly promptly in the early stages. She plays Brynner's young wife and dies in pregnancy. Virginia North registers attractively as Champa, a dancing girl who, under torture reveals Brynner's whereabout to the police. She does a nifty belly dance in a nightclub scene.

Charlotte Rampling, one of Britain's most promising young thesps, draws a pallid role in this. She plays Andrews' daughter who goes out to India from school & learns to respect Howard's point of view and fall in love with him.

Jack Hildyard's Eastmancolor photography sweeps splendidly across the Indian mountain landscape. Bert Bates has edited to an overlength of 115 minutes. Further bows should be taken by special effects man Dick Parker.   *Rich.*

Chudy I Inni
(Skinny and the Others)
(POLISH)
Warsaw, July 25.
Polski State Film release of Syrena production. With Wieslaw Golas, Franciszek Pieczka, Ryszard Filipski, Marian Kociniak. Directed by Henryk Kluba. Screenplay, Wieslaw Dymny; camera, Wieslaw Zdort. Previewed in Warsaw. Running Time, 95 MINS.

Skinny	Wieslaw Golas
Scythe	Franciszek Pieczka
Bull	Mieczyslaw Stoor
Partyman	Marian Kociniak
Ewa	Krystyna Chmielewska
Small	Wieslaw Dymny

Poland, which led the Eastern Bloc countries in forthright themes, talents and filmic breakthroughs at Western film fests in 1957-58, has taken a pic backseat for some time now as other Eastern partners made the world scene. Taken to big scale epics, comedies (mainly local) and exporting talents, not many Polski Films gained international attention lately. But this one marks a newcomer with pictorial flair and robust outlook and potential.

Whether it hints a Polski revival is not clear. Though it does show itinerant workers talking outspokenly about outlooks towards the omnipresent party, it, above all, spins a good adventure yarn. It sometimes forces things in the script, but does not flatter in characterization.

This takes place on a dam and bridge site where a group of part-time workers come and are working. They all are mainly individuals out to make a small bundle and move on except for a party newcomer, who is all ideology and self-sacrificing. But even the latter thaws as they finish their work.

Sharp camerawork, brisk editing and good acting give this a bright actionful look which may have it a playoff item abroad. A telling last episode has them all deciding to throw away their hard-earned money to show they care more for their friendship than it. But only the party members heaves away his coin. The others chip in to help him as they go off to another job.

This may not be revolutionary but it does look at the individual and collective spirit. And notes that both have to be found a place. Playing is also a help in its refusal to replace character by color and personal tics. It marks a director to be watched. Perhaps it is a forerunner of more unfettered and more unusual films from Poland. *Msok.*

Daraku Suru Onna
(A Fallen Woman)
(JAPAN)

Tokyo, July 25.
Shochiku release of a Kindai Eiga Kyokai production. With Miyuki Kuwano, Takahiro Tamura, Etsushi Takahashi, Mitsuko Mito, Toshiyuki Hosogawa. Directed by Kimisaburo Yoshimura. Screenplay, Kaneto Shindo, after the novel by Junichiro Tanizaki; camera, Masamichi Sato; music, Sei Ikeno. Previewed in Tokyo. Running Time, 95 MINS.

Kindai Eiga Kyokai's production of "Daraku Suru Onna" (A Fallen Woman), is based on a Junichiro Tanizaki short novel and is directed by veteran Kimisaburo Yoshimura, the last of the Mizoguchi disciples. Yoshimura has done some excellent pictures. But this picture (scripted by Shindo Kaneto) is not among them if interesting.

A well-born girl (Miyuki Kuwano), daughter of a Prime Minister, is being gently wooed by a young teacher (Takahiro Tamura) whose suit is also being pressed by her mother (Mitsuko Mito) and brother (Etsushi Takahashi). She, however, falls in love with a thoroughly bad boy (Toshiyuki Hosogawa of the Bungakuza Dramatic troupe). No matter how badly he treats her, which is considerable, she always goes crawling back.

Tanizaki's theme is both simple and profound. There are some people who find fulfillment in degration and who discover their greatest pleasure in pain. The film too finally gets around to making that statement. But until then it is aimless and contradictory.

Part of the trouble is Yoshimura. Having heard that there is a new cinematic style, he attempts it: lots of overexposure, off-the-cuff

acting, Zooming-lenses and symbolism. The last is extreme: the belt he is beating her with turns into a snake. Sometimes all of this decoration is functional (he lets grains of sand shower from his fist and cut her under a shower), but most of the time it is what the German's used to call "expressionismus."

The other part of the trouble is Kaneto Shindo. While elevating sex in all of his recent works, he cannot rid himself of a certain middle-class snobbism about it. Certainly, since he wrote the script, it must have been his idea to so confuse Tanizaki's very simple statement with endless plot complications. And certainly the melodrama is Kaneto's and it is that kind of melodrama which arises when one has not the wit and courage to deal originally with the original truths.

Finally, something must be said against young Hosogawa of the stage. He is a firstrate ham with such public breast-beatings.

Apart from this, the film remains interesting because of its theme, clumsily expressed though it is. The story is true, important, and not said nearly often enough. *Chie.*

Enter Laughing
(COLOR)

Spasmodically-funny light entertainment for less demanding situations.

Columbia Pictures release of Acre-Sajo (Carl Reiner-Joseph Stein) production, directed by Reiner, screenplay, Stein, Reiner, based on play by Stein, adapted from novel by Reiner, Stars Jose Ferrer, Shelley Winters, Elaine May, Jack Gilford, Reni Santoni, Janet Margolin; features David Opatoshu, Michael J. Pollard, Don Rickles, Richard Deacon, Nancy Kovack. Camera (PatheColor), Joseph Biroc; music, Quincy Jones; editor, Charles Nelson; asst. director, Kurt Neumann. Reviewed at Academy Award Theatre, July 13, '67. Running Time, 112 MINS.
Mr. Marlowe .... Jose Ferrer
Mrs. Kolowitz .... Shelley Winters
Angela .... Elaine May
Mr. Foreman .... Jack Gilford
David Kolowitz........... Reni Santoni
Wanda .... Janet Margolin
Mr. Kolowitz .... David Opatoshu
Marvin .... Michael J. Pollard
Harry Hamburger .... Don Rickles
Pikes .... Richard Deacon
Miss B .... Nancy Kovack
Mr. Schoenbaum .... Herbie Faye
Clark Baxter .... Rob Reiner
Spencer Reynolds .... Danny Stein
Policeman .... Milton Frome
Theatregoer .... Lillian Adams
Subway Rider .... Mantan Moreland
Butler .... Patrick Campbell
Lawyer Peabody .... Peter Brocco

"Enter Laughing," a spasmodically-funny stage play, is just that as a motion picture. There are occasional outbursts of genuine hilarity, while again the humor is strained. As light film entertainment it's okay for less demanding situations, and particularly the family trade.

Some delightful talent in clever bits of business highlight the transference of the Joseph Stein play which had more than a year's run on Broadway and which in turn was based on Carl Reiner's nostalgic account of his own entry into show biz. Col release was coscripted and coproduced by pair, with Reiner handling direction. They succeed in garmenting storyline with certain warmth and a gay spirit which fits the premise.

Reni Santoni, from the "Merv Griffin Show", plays the young Reiner character in his first major film appearance, nicely capturing the mood intended of the stage-struck apprentice in a two-man machine shop who is accepted as a paying trainee at a small, run-down theatre operated by Jose Ferrer, a seedy, gin-guzzling ham.

Ferrer, in a role which permits him to run the whole if familar gamut of hamminess, is colorful addition who milks part of laughs and Elaine May, as his leading lady daughter who prevails upon her father to accept the strictly-no-talent aspirant, is witty and competent. Shelley Winters scores particularly as Santoni's Jewish mama who wants her son to go to school and be a respectable druggist.

Jack Gilford creates an aura of amusement with his own brand of comedy as Santoni's boss who cannot understand his young employee. As the girl friend, Janet Margolin is appealing and pretty, a decided asset, and David Opatoshu is equally effective as Santoni's father who never dares to cross his wife in the rearing of their son. Nancy Kovack is brief standout as a sexpot, Don Rickles panics, and both Michael J. Pollard and Richard Deacon are excellent in support.

Technical credits are all on plus side, including Joseph Biroc's color photography, Quincy Jones' lilting music score, Charles Nelson's apt editing, Walter M. Simonds' art direction. *Whit.*

Mondo Hollywood
(COLOR)

Documentary-type approach to what portends to be a Mondo Hollywood; may be exploited for okay returns in selected market.

Hollywood, July 25.
Hollywood International Productions release of Robert Carl Cohen; directed, photographed (PatheColor) and edited by Cohen. Music, Mike Curb. Reviewed at Pathe Laboratories, July 25, '67. Running Time, 88 MINS.

Takings piled up by flock of foreign-made, often-slammed films with similar titles ("Mondo Cane," "Mondo Pazzo," "Malomondo," etc.) undoubtedly was the inspiration for this Robert Carl Cohen production which trains its lenses on the Hollywood scene and some of its people, particularly the way-out hangers-on. Said to be 18 months in preparation and edited from more than 120,000 feet of color film, what comes out is series of clips wrapped up with specially-shot footage. Occasionally dull, it nevertheless probably will be exploitable for okay returns, cashing in on the "Mondo" tag which in past has had some bite.

Cohen, with such documentary credits as NBC's "Inside Red China" plus "Inside East Germany" and Inside Castro's Cuba," calls feature a "flippy, trippy psychedelic guide to Hollywood," which he sets out to prove. Flip approach settled on as screen seen, each claims to be the real article—who acts, speaks, cavorts

— some a genuine part of Hollywood with their accomplishments. To this footage, Cohen flashes on many screen names, such as celebs attending first-nights, etc. Some off-color language might well be deleted, but may be considered desirable "realism", and film would benefit by wholesale cutting to speed action and give it better continuity.

Not all the characters are oddball. Topic of LSD is given attention through shots of Dr. Richard Alpert, dismissed from Harvard for his experiments with the drug; sculptress Valerie Porter is limned as she practices her art; and Rudi Gernreich, who invented the topless fad, is shown at a parade of his attire for moppets. There are others, too, but Cohen focuses primarily on what he sees as the Hollywood the public does not know. For what is one of the first times on the screen Cohen takes his cameras into a topless joint where waitresses are serving bare to the waist.

Productionwise, film is virtually a one-man project. Cohen handles quadruple chores of producer - director - photographer - editor, and also the music editing. Most of the technical aspects are expertly executed. Interesting free-fall photography of a parachute sequence is done by Doyle E. Fields and Mike Curb does job with musical direction.

Narration is handled by various characters seen on-screen, and there are 19 song numbers socked over by 12 singles and combos for background music. *Whit.*

Ski On The Wild Side
(DOCUMENTARY—COLOR)

Colorful and lighthearted ski film could follow up "Endless Summer" biz with sports fans with some additional editing.

Sigma III release of a Warren Miller production. Produced, directed and narrated by Warren Miller. Camera (Eastman Color), Don Brolin, Rod Allin, Warren Miller; music, Billy Allen. Reviewed at Festival Theatre, New York, July 25, '67. Running time, 104 MINS.

Evidently what the sports-on-film business needed to catch on with filmgoers was a large helping of levity. It worked with "Endless Summer" and should probably repeat with Warren Miller's "Ski On The Wild Side." Doing the global bit with a pair of skis, as Bruce Brown did with a surfboard, Miller has collected some beautifully-photographed footage on a cross-section of the world's top skiing grounds. He narrates with a comic sense that will be appreciated by most audiences, if broad enough at times to make super sophisticates wince.

What the film really needs in its present state is more expert editing as the 104 minutes (plus a 10-minute intermission) has the defect of being repetitious in some sequences.

The emphasis, of course, is on American ski spots and some of these, such as the Squaw Valley sequence, could be considerably shortened. All the vistas are beautiful, several being breathtaking in their scope, such as the

Tasmanian Glacier in New Zealand with probably the world's longest ski-run (14 miles) over snow that is frequently 800 feet deep.

Besides Miller, an expert skier who's seen in several sequences, the footage includes an enormously talented international group of ski addicts—Nancy Greene, Jean Claude Killy, Marielle Goitschel, Sue Chaffee, Joan Hannan, Stan Tomlinson, Roger Staub, Annie Famose, Karl Schranz, Jimmy Huega, Alf Engen, Art Furrer and Junior Bounous. With most footage devoted to Yankee spots such as Squaw Valley (Calif.), Vail and Aspen (Col.), Mt. Snow (Vermont), and Jackson Hole (Wyom). Miller also takes in New Zealand; Val D'Isere and Courchevel, France; Planecia, Yugoslavia; Mt. Zoa, Japan; and Itkol in Russia. The latter is no spot to attract any but the most dedicated ski bums although beautiful in its barren setting.

Miller's commentary varies between technical description, identification of locale and skiers and straight narrative to some humorous comments on the "types" who frequent the locales visited. There's more than a trace of snobbery in his voice towards the "weekend" visitor to Squaw Valley and other resorts, overrun by hopelessly awkward beginners. He describes one hotel as "sleeping 400 people ...in 37 rooms" and, commenting on his departure from one such spot, says "we spent the next 13 hours in an 86-mile-long parking lot."

The color camerawork of Don Brolin, Rod Allin and Miller gives 'Ski On The Wild Side" a visual beauty that will, if anything, only increase the pilgrimage of would-be skiers to these areas. The stay-at-homers will have to satisfy themselves with the on-screen performances of those captured by Miller. *Robe.*

Nueve Cartas a Berta
(Nine Letters to Bertha)
(SPANISH)

Madrid, July 25.
Eco Films and Transfisa production. Stars Emilio G. Caba; features Elsa Baeza, Antonio Casas, Mary Carrillo, Jose Maria Resel, Lepe, Fernando Sanchez Polack, Josefina Serratosa. Directed by Basilio M. Patino. Camera, Luis Enrique Toran; screenplay, Patino; music, Carmelo Alonso Bernaola; editor, Pedro del Rey. Reviewed at XV International Film Fest at San Sebastian. Running Time, 90 MINS.

The treatment accorded this pic, about a maturing university student in provincial Spain, is typical of the problems facing many young directors here. In spite of an award at last year's San Sebastian film fest, it was pre-judged a bad risk by distribs and exhibs.

And wasn't released here until a few months ago, when it did big b.o. in two Madrid firstruns. Since then, it has gone on to play successfully in other Spanish cities.

But what is good for Spain is not necessarily fit for foreign consumption; this must be the least universal product of what is coming to be called the "new Spanish cinema."

Although a brave attempt to say something meaningful about Spanish life, especially as the younger generation sees it, the film has met with some strong criticism, much of it from this younger generation itself.

For Spain, a notable effort toward something new, but a picture which demands a much greater knowledge of things Spanish than foreign audiences are likely to have.

The hero (Emilio G. Caba) is a student at the ancient university of Salamanca. He lives with his parents, a bourgeois couple with most of the prejudices of the Spanish provincial and little of the dignity and simplicity of the rural version. Caba gets a gentleman's rating, has a girlfriend and is very analytical about himself and those around him. Recently he was in England, where he met Berta, the daughter of exiles.

The film is a series of nine "letters" to Berta, each narrated by Caba and separated from the others by a Roman numeral and a medieval tapestry design. In his letters we see Caba with his fellow students, his girlfriend, a visiting lecturer, his family, on a trip to Madrid, and on vacation.

He tells Berta of his doubts, his longings, his urges to break with life in the provinces and look for something bigger and more challenging.

Althouh episodic, the story flows smoothly enough. The technique is modern, at times even polished. And there is a strong feeling of what it must be like to live in a stifling provincial capital.

But the production is too long and at times repetitious. "Five Letters to Bertha" would have been a better title. Neither is director Patino's intent always clear, as when, in a quiet garden beside a babbling fountain, a wordy young priest attempts to bring his message to the "new" generation.

The treatment is so sincere and naive as to be almost satirical. In the end, Caba disappoints us by marrying his fiance and opting for a safe life in the country. If this Spanish youth, with all his liberal leanings and awareness, could not break away, which one can? *Lyon.*

Leg er Sgu Min Egen
(I Belong to Me)
(DANISH-COLOR)

Copenhagen, July 25.
A/S Nordisk Film Kompagni production and release. Stars Daimi, Caesar, Peter Steen, Ove Sprogoe, Paul Bundgaard. Directed by Erik Balling. Story and screenplay, Klaus Rifbjerg; camera, (Eastmancolor) Joergen Skov; music, Bent Fabricius-Bjerre. Reviewed at Palads Teatret, Copenhagen. Running Time, 94 MINS.

Starring Daimi, a comedian loved by every Dane, "I Belong to Me" is a rather dubious item for the international market. Daimi looks like a Barbra Streisand run over by a half-hearted steamroller. She sings in her own, strongly personal way; jazzy now, healthily sentimental at other times.

Klaus Rifbjerg's script is built around this particular personality. Story tells of a wayward girl, on parole from an institution. She comes to wicked Copenhagen and conquers everybody, including a lecherous and wildly religious

baker, a timorous playboy and a poor folksinger. She marries the rich young man so that society can wash its hands of her. But on the wedding night she opens the bedroom window and listens to the folksinger down in the garden. She decides she belongs to herself and really to nobody else.

As a musical, this film has obvious faults. Balling halts the action to make room for the song-and-ance numbers instead of incorporating them in the natural stream of the plot. And there is not too much action to begin with. Much of the fun is too local and too much of the internationally-aimed fun just is not up to the standards of a Hollywood musical.

Still, this may appeal to foreign audiences because a Danish pic. The director is the creator of "Relax, Freddie," one of the first all-spy spoofs and a solid seller. The music is definitely ear-catching. It was penned by Bent Fabricius-Bjerre, the composer of "Alley Cat." *Kell.*

The Monster of London City
(Das Ungeheuer von London City)
(GERMAN-SCOPE)

More Edgar Wallace. No chills, no thrills in mild German film about a mad killer who stalks the British capital. A possible dualer.

Producers Releasing Organization release of a CCC Film (Arthur Brauner) production. Features Hanjorg Felmy, Marianne Koch, Dietmar Schonherr. Directed by Edwin Zbonek. Screenplay, Robert A. Stemmle, from a story by Bryan Edgar Wallace; camera, Siegfried Hold; music, Martin Bottcher; editor, Walter Wischniewski; asst. director, Lucie Berndsen. Reviewed at Selwyn Theatre, N.Y., July 16, '67. Running Time, 87 MINS.
Richard Sand .... Hanjorg Felmy
Ann Morlay .... Marianne Koch
Dr. Morel Greely .. Dietmar Schonherr
Dorne .... Hans Nielsen
Betty Ball .... Charikila Baxevanos
Sir George .... Fritz Tillman
Horrlick .... Walter Pfeil
Teddy Flynn .... Peer Schmidt
Maylor .... Kurd Pieritz

(Dubbed English Sountrack)
Despite an ad campaign which challenges patrons to "Take the Terror Test!" there are few thrills and chills in this mild German updating of yesteryear Edgar Wallace story, which generates less fright than a typical segment of such former vidseries as "The Twilight Zone" or the Hitchcock hour. Packaged as a combo with "The Phantom of Soho" by Producers Releasing Organization, "Monster" at best has only dualer possibilities in the U.S.

Though simulation of London in a German studio is believable, Wallace's story has not been updated sociologically. It unreels like the conventional earlier era version of Jack the Ripper though mad killer who goes around modern-day London murdering prosties is contemporary. The familiar relationships presented are too Victorian to jibe with today's "swinging London."

"Monster" still might have general audience possibilities if it engendered the teeniest amount of fright. It does not. The acting by the largely unfamiliar to U.S. German cast is only adequate, running to the hammy in some

instances. Hanjorg Felmy as the actor suspected of the killings has an interesting bearing, but he deserves more colorful material than this.

Pic has been dubbed in an okay manner, but English-language inserts have not been prepared so that letters, signs, newspaper headlines, etc. are all in German. Some footage of above-the-waist female nudity is included in one scene, but is not lengthy enough to suggest possible sexploitation value. Film has not yet been rated by National Catholic Office for Motion Pictures.

Edwin Zbonek's direction of Robert A. Stemmle's script indulges in numerous "red herrings" to cast suspicion on innocent parties. They come off crudely. All other technical credits are standard.

Seemingly, Germans have always been fascinated by stories of killers who terrorize an entire city, and what still remains the most famous German sound film had this idea as subject. But it's been a long, long time since Fritz Lang's "M" (1931). *Byro.*

The Phantom of Soho
(Das Phantom von Soho)
(GERMAN-SCOPE)

Labored, confused German mystery pic based on Edgar Wallace story; fails to generate real suspense. Top dubbing job by France's Jacques Willmetz.

Producers Releasing Organization release of a CCC Film (Arthur Brauner) production. Features Dieter Borsche, Barbara Rutting. Directed by Franz Josef Gottlieb. Screenplay, Ladislas Fodor, from story by Bryan Edgar Wallace; camera, Richard Angst; music, Martin Bottcher; no other credits provided. Reviewed at Selwyn Theatre, N.Y., July 16, '67. Running Time, 92 MINS.
Hugh Patton .... Dieter Borsche
Clarinda Smith .... Barbara Rutting
Sir Philip .... Hans Sohnker
Hallam .... Peter Vogel
Corinna Smith .... Helga Sommerfeld
Dr. Dalmar .... Werner Peters
Lord Malhouse .... Hans Nielsen
Gilard .... Stanislav Ledinek
"Liver-spot" .... Otto Waldis
Captain .... Hans W. Hamacher
Daddy .... Emil Feldmar
Charlis .... Harald Sawade
Joanna Filati...Elisabeth Flickenschildt

(Dubbed English Soundtrack)
West German producers have long been on an Edgar Wallace kick but this kind of German mystery pic is usually used to fill out a television syndication package in the U.S., and in the case of "The Phantom of Soho" it's hard to find what prompted the newly-formed Producers Releasing Organization to envision much theatrical potential. The inclusion of some crude horrific elements does not make up for lack of any real suspense in a confusing and labored adaptation from long-ago Wallace. It's about a series of strange murders in London. Dualer possibilities in general situations are further vitiated by lack of color.

When several prominent Londoners are killed in a similar manner, chief inspector Patton (well-played by Dieter Borsche) identifies them all as passengers on an African sea voyage of a few years previous. He catches murderer by setting a trap which takes film through some exotic sections of the city, including Soho strip joints, morgue, airport terminal, etc. Though apparently entirely shot in German studio, film looks plausibly like Britain.

Largely this is due to excellent dubbing job, credited to Les Films Jacques Willmetz in Paris. Voices are expertly matched to physiques and nuances of British speech are cannily caught in dialog. Charges by some American dubbers against socalled "cheap" European counterparts seem unfounded after "Phantom,' which completely lacks a "dubbed feeling."

As noted above Borsche is excellent as the inspector, but rest of acting is uninspired. One thesp, Werner Peters, has been seen in "36 Hours" and other Yank pix. The stripper scenes are realistic and viewer sees no less than a real customer would. National Catholic Office for Motion Pictures has yet to speak on this bare-breast footage.

Direction by Franz Josef Gottlieb is standard, as is lensing by Richard Angst. Other technical credits are pro. *Byro.*

Moscow Film Fest

Las Aventuras De Juan Quin Quin
(The Adventures of Juan Quin Quin)
(CUBAN)

Esoteric treatment of a hero as pixilated revolutionary robber and village cutup. Not for most westerners but has curio value in illuminating Castro Cuba's film biz.

Moscow, July 25.
Cuban Institute of the Arts and Cinematography production and release. Features Julio Martines, Erwin Fernandez, Adelaida Ramat, others. Directed by Julio Garcia Espinosa. Screenplay, Pedro Garcia Espinosa; camera, Jorge Haydu; music, Leo Brower. Reviewed at Moscow Film Festival. Running Time, 113 MINS.

This Cuban entry is a strange hodgepodge, half fairy tale or ballad, half adventure epic, which tells oft-serious things about man and—inevitably—revolution but in tongue-in-cheek manner which often forgets about unity of time, place and style. It's a weirdo, not without curio value, but otherwise overlong and, to audiences not regularly tuned in on the Havana wavelength, ultimately unsatisfactory.

Story flashes back to the early peacetime pre-revolutionary days in which a current hero, Juan Quin Quin, was only a priest's reluctant helper with the buddings of an anti-church, anti-authority attitude already evident. Later, on his revolutionary way which is lined with sneering police chiefs and greedy landowners, he meets a girl who joins his "forces" and gets himself a lieutenant of similar political leanings. Rest of pic is a series of chopped episodes, mainly of battles with police, some told straight, as military training films on, for instance, how to raid a village for arms. At points, the hero speaks in comic-strip "balloons" instead of dialogue. In all, he's characterized as a sort of zany, athletic, pixyish type somewhere between "Fanfan la Tulipe" and "Don Quixote" who stages village

raids as easily as he sets up an impromptu humorous corrida with the town bull.

Inevitably too, the caricatured Yank moneyman arrives near finale, to give the signal for the final rebellion which is to sweep the country.

Apart from the jump continuity and basic absence of a solo plot line, which instead is linked merely by the main characters, pic is well acted, in the broad manner desired, and boasts some okay production values, including slick lensing . Further nods must go to a nice set of main titles and especially to some rousing music backdropped by Leo Brower. *Hawk.*

The Princess
(SWEDISH)

Moscow, July 25.
Europa Film (Stockholm) production and release. Features Grynet Molvig, Lars Passgard, Monika Nielsson, Thor Lyndhol, Brigitta Walberg. Directed by Ake Falk. Screenplay, Falk, Lars Wilding, based on novel by Gunnar Mattsson by same name; camera, Mac Alberg, Ralph Evers; music, Harry Arnoldt; editor, Ake Falk. Reviewed at Moscow Film Fest. Running Time, 105 MINS.

The Princess .... Grynet Molvig
Gunnar Mattsson ...... Lars Passgard
Pirjo .... Monika Nielsson

Finely tooled little picture based on a much-translated novel which in turn was based on fact, about a woman being cured of a certain cancer of the blood cells thanks to her love for and marriage to a man who takes her despite her dooming affliction. The difficult but successful birth of their child apparently results in medically unexplained elimination of her illness. And, as in the fairy tale parallel which gives pic its title, they live happily on.

It's the sort of film the Swedes seem to bring off so beautifully and uniquely, making even the most controversial and/or unpleasant passages not only palatable, but believable and appealing. It is not, however, an easy film to sell, for despite handling and upbeat ending, it rarely strays from its central theme and subject matter. Worth an arty looksee, however, and should elicit distaff interest.

Love as the best therapy is warmly demonstrated by Grynet Molvig and Lars Passgard, as the couple. Both, but especially the girl, are very good, and there's a nice cameo by Monika Nielsson, as the other woman, who wants to save the man from an unhappy doomed splice.

'But above all, this is a director's film, and Abe Falk has made it a very personal effort. Among the highlights are a winning scene in which the onetime athlete husband celebrates the child's birth by performing at an empty stadium to —him at least—cheering crowds, expressing his inner joy in terms he knows best. And also a lovemaking scene between husband and wife which, finally, adds something to a cliche situation too often abused and mishandled. Lastly, the entire near-finale hospital birth sequence, though graphically rendered, is of great realism and, thanks also to the acting, it's hard to believe, at the end, that the whole thing has not really been a documentary and that the couple are not man and wife and parents of the child.

The fact that the story told is a true one merely adds a fillip to a warm, affectionate and tasteful effort. Camerawork is outstanding, among other firstclass production values. *Hawk.*

Escandalo en la Familia
(Scandal in the Family)
(ARGENTINE-SPANISH)
(Color)

Moscow, July 18.
G.S.L. release of G.S.L. (Argentina)-Benito Perojo (Spain) coproduction. Features Nini Marshall, Pili, Mili, Angel Garasa, Yaco Monti, Vicente Rubino, Alberto Olmedo, Fidel Pintos, Lalo Malcon. Directed by Jorge Velasco. Screenplay, Julio Porter, Norberto Aroldi; camera (uncredited color process), Americo Hoss; music, Lucio Milena; editor, Jorge Garate. Reviewed at Moscow Film Fest. Running Time, 102 MINS.

Flyweight musical comedy with some surface amusement, okay number of songs and musical numbers, all giving it good playoff possibilities in the Latino markets, but more limited chances elsewhere.

Plot skein is the familiar one about two' separated twin sisters whose father and mother haven't seen one another for some time, and who are brought together, via an infinity of hoary plot twists, via a beauty contest run by a tele station. Various story lines spin off here and there via gals' romances, the father's political ambitions, etc. until the upbeat happy (and musical) ending sets things straight for all.

Jorge Velasco has kept his action rapid, and writers Julio Porter and Norberto Aroldi have embroidered some risible plot angles to help maintain pace throughout. Some of the musical numbers (especially in the opening street ballet) are reminiscent of some Yank originals, are arbitrarily inserted to give dancers or singer Yaco Monti (latter a very good voice) a chance to shine. But it's all in keeping with the lightweight flavor maintained throughout.

Acting is in similar broad style. The twins, Pili and Mili, are easy on the eyes and perform zestfully both on and offstage. Color, uncredited on local print, is good but at times uneven. Lucio Miena deserves a nod for his musical supervision. Production boasts some unusually fine femme costume design. *Hawk.*

Bonnie And Clyde
(TECHNICOLOR)

Warren Beatty as producer-star in tale of stupid-brutal pair on crime spree. Taken from real-life. Rough stuff but boxoffice. Opener at Montreal Film Fest.

Warner Bros.-Seven Arts release of Tatira-Hiller Production. Stars Warren Beatty, Faye Dunaway, Michael J. Pollard, Gene Hackman, Estelle Parsons. Produced by Warren Beatty. Directed by Arthur Penn. Screenplay, David Newman and Robert Benton; camera (Technicolor), Burnett Guffey; editor, Dede Allen; special effects, Danny Lee; music, Charles Strouse; Flatt & Scruggs' "Foggy Mountain Breakdown"; asst. director, Jack N. Reddish. Reviewed at Academy Award Theatre. Aug. 1, '67. Running Time: 111 MINS.

Clyde Barrow .... Warren Beatty
Bonnie Parker .... Faye Dunaway
C. W. Moss .... Michael J. Pollard
Buck Barrow .... Gene Hackman
Blanche .... Estelle Parsons
Frank Hamer .... Denver Pyle
Ivan Moss .... Dub Taylor
Velma Davis .... Evans Evans
Eugene Grizzard ...... Gene Wilder

Hollywood, Aug. 1.
Warren Beatty's initial effort as a producer, "Bonnie and Clyde," incongruously couples comedy with crime, in this biopic of Bonnie Parker and Clyde Barrow, a pair of Texas desperadoes who roamed and robbed the southwest and midwest during the bleak depression days of the early 1930's. Conceptually, the film leaves much to be desired, because killings and the backdrop of the depression are scarcely material for a bundle of laughs. However, the film does have some standout interludes, and with a hard sell exploitation campaign should do big. Beatty and Faye Dunaway are the only cast names of any established marquee value. (Feature was opener at Montreal Film Festival last Friday (4).—Ed.)

The David Newman-Robert Benton screenplay depicts the Parker-Barrow gang as clowns and good-natured oafs most of the time, even during some of their holdups. Characterizations are, in the main, inconsistent and confusing. When Bonnie Parker, in a moody moment, as she senses the end is near for them, asks her lover, Barrow, what he would do differently if he could start all over again, he drawls unhesitatingly, that he would rob banks in states other than the one in which he lived.

Thus it is for the entire film. Scripters Newman and Benton have depicted these real-life characters as inept, bumbling, moronic types, and if this had been true they would have been erased in their first try. It's a picture with conflicting moods, racing from crime to comedy, and intermingling genuinely moving love scenes between Faye Dunaway as Bonnie and Beatty as Clyde. Bonnie is a sexy, lusty, beautiful femme, and discovers with deep frustration that Clyde is impotent, but stays with him. Late in the film, it is inferred that he becomes a man in every sense of the word.

These are sensitive and well-executed scenes, yet made all the more incongruous against the almost slapstick approach of much of the picture. When the gang heists a bank and kills someone, they barrel off in their car, to accompaniment of a soundtrack which is built-in for laughs, music which seems to be right out of "The Beverly Hillbillies."

This inconsistency of direction is the most obvious fault of "Bonnie and Clyde," which has some good ingredients, although they are not meshed together well. It has a lot of violence, climaxed with the killing of Bonnie and Clyde by lawmen who pour many bullets into them in an ambush.

Like the film itself, the performances are mostly erratic. Beatty is believable at times, but his characterization lacks any consistency. Miss Dunaway is a knockout as Bonnie Parker, registers with deep sensitivity in the love scenes, and conveys believability to her role. Michael J. Pollard and Gene Hackman are more clowns than baddies as gang members; Estelle Parsons is good, as Buck Barrows' wife, and there is some substantial support from Denver Pyle, Dub Taylor and Evans Evans.

Arthur Penn's direction is uneven, at times catching a brooding, arresting quality, but often changing pace at a tempo that is jarring. Color camerawork by Burnett Guffey is excellent. Music by Charles Strouse is in the hillbilly comedic vein, seems out of tune for an outlaw yarn. *Daku.*

Rough Night in Jericho
(TECHNISCOPE—COLOR)

Dean Martin plays the heavy in fast, violent western which also stars George Peppard and Jean Simmons for marquee bait; okay grosses seen.

Hollywood, July 25.
Universal release of Martin Rackin production. Stars Dean Martin, George Peppard, Jean Simmons; features John McIntire, Slim Pickens. Directed by Arnold Laven. Screenplay, Sydney Boehm, Marvin H. Albert; based on novel, "The Man in Black," by Albert; camera (Technicolor), Russell Metty; music, Don Costa; editor, Ted J. Kent. Reviewed at Universal Studios, July 25, '67. Running time, 102 MINS.

Alex Flood .... Dean Martin
Dolan .... George Peppard
Molly .... Jean Simmons
Ben Hickman .... John McIntire
Yarbrough .... Slim Pickens
Jace .... Don Galloway
Torrey .... Brad Weston
Ryan .... Richard O'Brien
Claire .... Carol Anderson
Simms .... Steve Sandor
Harvey .... Warren Vanders
McGivern .... John Napier

Most unusual aspect about this Martin Rackin production is offbeat casting of Dean Martin as a heavy, without a single redeeming quality. George Peppard is the hero. Both are embroiled in as bloody and violent a western as has played the screen. Femme audiences probably will recoil from the brutality but film should find hefty response from the males. With the star names for marquee dressing, including Jean Simmons, Universal has an attractive money package here.

Plotwise, "Rough Night in Jericho" frequently carries a nebulous story line, particularly in limning the actions of Martin, onetime lawman turned vicious town boss. Screenplay by Sydney Boehm and Marvin H. Albert, in adaptation of Albert's novel, "The Man in Black," is lacking in the suspense one expects from a big league

western but regulation action is there in good measure. Arnold Laven's direction maintains fast movement throughout to hold audience attention.

Peppard plays a former deputy U.S. marshal who becomes involved in the affairs of the town of Jericho—and Martin—when he arrives with John McIntire, onetime marshal whom he once served under. Latter has come to help Jean Simmons save her stage line, coveted by Martin, who also wants its femme owner. Peppard, now a gambler who figures the odds on everything, realizes the percentages are against femme and wants no part of what he knows is to come but remains to help his friend. They clean up the town and in the climax Peppard and Martin have it out in the bush, former badly wounded and Martin with a bowie knife in his heart.

Peppard endows his performance with quiet strength, participating in an unusually brutal fight with Slim Pickens, who has deserted his customary comedy for a heavy part. One wonders, however, at the thinking in casting Martin in his role, which does not add stature to the image he long has established for himself. He does a good job and inserts plenty of menace in a not-always-believable town-boss character.

Miss Simmons is excellent as a western woman fighting against odds to retain her business. A drinking sequence between herself and Peppard is amusing. McIntire is up to his usual competence. Pickens, Don Galloway and Brad Weston lend strong support.

Color photography by Russell Metty is a decided asset, as is Don Costa's music score. Balance of technical credits is in kind. *Whit.*

Brot und Rosen
(Bread and Roses)
(EAST GERMAN)

Moscow, July 26.
Defa Film production and release. Features Guenter Simon, Harri Hindemit, Eva Maria Hagen. Directed by Heinz Thiel. Screenplay, Gerhart Bengsch, Thiel; camera, Horst E. Brandt; music, Helmut Nier. Reviewed at Moscow Film Fest. Running Time, 103 MINS.

Elaborately produced and carefully shaped but basically sterile, dull, and oldfashioned tale of a man's climb up the (East German) socialist ladder until, along with car, home and family, he achieves that ultimate status symbol, party membership. Pic is a very doubtful traveler, especially in these days when even Eastern cinematographies are at grips with more accessibly mundane and more daringly outspoken things.

The problems and preoccupations of East Germany yesterday, today (and tomorrow?) are very much up front in this, with the human aspects of man's existence serving as mere storyline pretexts, and only here and there felt. Most of the dramatics are in the commentary and dialogue about varied but always politically pegged topics concerning Marxism, German reunification, plant efficiency and premiums, and so on.

Hero makes it by slow degrees via study and diligence. Dramatic highlights are a spat with wife and mother-in-law, and another with his plant manager over in-

efficient methods. But it all winds up in conformity as he joins the party and, presumably, heads for an upwards and onwards future, as one of the builders of a new (East) Germany.

Guenter Simon is somewhat wooden as the hero. But other acting is capable, as are pic's technical facets, which are smooth and fairly elaborate. *Hawk.*

Locarno Fest

Navrat Ztraceneho Syna
(Return of Prodigal Son)
(CZECH)

Locarno, Aug. 2.
Czech State Film release of Barrandov production. With Jan Kacer, Jana Brejchova, Jiri Menzel. Directed by Evald Schorm. Screenplay, Sergej Machonin, Schorm; camera, Frantisek Uldrich; music, Jan Klusak. At Locarno Film Fest. Running time, 96 MINS.

Jan .... Jan Kacer
Jana .... Jana Brejchova
Jiri .... Jiri Menzel
Olga .... Dana Medricka
Doctor .... Milan Moravek
Nurse .... Jirina Trebicak

This starts with the main character trying to commit suicide. But this probing Czech pic is not about that subject but rather the need to cope with life. It shows that the individual needs for self realization and finding a place in society are being treated in Eastern pix also. This angle could make the film of interest abroad. But its many allusions to Czech realities as well as its wandering subject matter make this primarily for arty usage.

A young architect, supposedly having good means, a beautiful wife who loves him, and a child, tries to take his own life. Then it deals with him in a sanatorium that lets him leave at times but always bring him back.

Director Evald Schorm delves into the maze of the man's mind and problems and sometimes gets a bit too involved with side issues and symbols. It is acted with perceptiveness by a well-selected cast and has the usual expert Czech technical polish.

This is an absorbing pic for more selective audiences and another affirmation of the continuing Czech forthrightness and daring in handling touchy themes. *Mosk.*

Mucednici Lasky
(Martyred Love)
(CZECH)

Locarno, Aug. 3.
Czech State Film release of Barrandov production. With Petr Kopriva, Marta Kubisova, Hana Kuberova, Jan Klusak. Directed by Jan Nemec. Screenplay, Ester Krumbachova, Nemec; camera, Mioslav Ondricek; music, Jan Klusak, Karel Mares. At Locarno Film Fest. Running time, 70 MINS.

THE MANIPULATOR
Manipulator .... Petr Kopriva
Girl .... Marta Kubisova
NASTENKA'S DREAM
Nastenka .... Hana Kuberova
Doctor .... Jan Klusak
Singer .... Karel Gott
Tramp .... Vladimir Preclik
ADVENTURES OF RUDOLF THE ORPHAN
Rudolf .... Josef Konicek
Girl .... Denisa Dvorakova

Unusual, offbeat Czech films are now regular events at film festivals. Here is one that takes the

luxury of fashioning a sort of homage to oldtime films, and especially American silent comedies, with salutes to all sorts of cinema greats thrown in. If it may regale buffs, its comedic graces might not be too evident to regular audiences. So specialized and arty possibilities, at best, for this sketch film abroad.

Director Jan Nemec certainly shows he has a fine film background, but he does not imitate but rather goes in for witty adaptations of old techniques to modern filmmaking. This makes for a strange stylized air as he situates his films in past eras and deals with little people whose dreams of love, human companionship or a place in life are usually shattered or hopeless.

But this is played for comedy and not pathos. A little clerk, who never takes off his derby hat, sees everybody coupled off around him. One night he takes his savings and goes on the town but cannot connect until a girl invites herself and her girlfriend and another man to his flat. But this has his girl falling asleep on him and finding himself taken for a lecher the next day, and hounded out of his job.

Next is about a young serving girl's dreams of finding the Prince Charming that always ends in her awakening. The last sketch is about a grownup lonely orphan who stumbles on a drunken rich family which takes him in, mistaking him for somebody else. The family accepts him and makes him happy. He is invited to come back but he can never find the house again.

Film keeps a unity of tone in its three sketches, but sometimes the comedy is a bit too dragged out to have all the sketches come off. However, there is an inventive airiness to much of it. *Mosk.*

Niejnosti
(Tenderness)
(RUSSIAN)

Locarno, Aug. 1.
Mosfilm release of Ouzbekfilm production. With M. Sternikova, R. Nakhapelov, R. Agrenenov, M. Maichmoudova. Directed by Elior Ichmoukhamedov. Screenplay, E. Ugrudtiot; camera, I. Louin; editor, Loldan Bagden. At Locarno Film Fest. Running time, 75 MINS.

Lena .... M. Sternikova
Sandjar .... R. Nakhapelov
Timour .... R. Agrenenov
Girl .... M. Maichmoudova

The lives of two young men and two girls are intermingled by chance meetings in this charming and disarming pic that tries, and succeeds most of the way, to delve into individual reactions in relationships. Delicately done, and possessing knowing observations, this might capture critical and regular patron fancies abroad if given personalized selling.

Made in the Ouzbekistan part of the Soviet Union near the city of Tashkent, it bubbles over with simple warmth without falling into mawkishness or undue sentimentality. But its fragile theme and sudden doses of tragedy at the end call for careful hypoing for best results. It shows a neat, new talent in 23-year-old director Elior Ichmoukhamed...

Youthful cast also displays ease. This concerns a young boy who floats about a town river along with friends. He spots a lovely girl one day. She is Russian, evacuated during the last war, and he is from Tashkent, seemingly a mixture of Oriental Arabic and Caucasian peoples. He takes to her and invents all sorts of dreams. She tells of a man who writes to her.

This all ends in a carnival as the principal characters cavort in spite of their hurts. It is the happy wedding of talk and action that gives this film a chance. However, the second part has a tendency to ramble a bit.

This shows that more pix from the farflung parts of the USSR should be sent to festivals as they display other facets of Soviet film attitudes outside the more mature and too often propagandist Moscow and Leningrad pix. *Mosk.*

Panna Zazracnica
(Miraculous Virgin)
(CZECH)

Locarno, Aug. 2.
Czech State Film release of Koliba production. With Jolanta Umecka, Ladislav Mrkvicka, Otakar Janda, Rudolf Trun. Directed by Stefan Uher. Screenplay, Dominik Tatarka, Uher; camera, Stanislaw Szomolanyi; music, Ilja Zeljenka. At Locarno Film Fest. Running time, 95 MINS.
Anabella .... Jolanta Umecka
Tristan .... Ladislav Mrkvicka
Havran .... Otakar Janda
Rafaj .... Rudolf Trun
Vilo .... Stefan Bobota

An attempt at creating a surrealistic film about man's fear of death during wartime, or substituting needed inner illusion for reality, does not come off in this too literally-made offbeater. Instead of seeming to reflect instinct, it smacks of labored preparation. Its effects do not ignite, and it becomes repetitious and finally tedious. Mainly for home use, where its allusions to war days may be clearer, but only for some arty spots abroad on its fine technical merits. It just does not live up to film's aims.

The Slovak part of Czechoslovakia makes only a few films a year.

This production obviously is aimed at showing the stifling atmosphere of the times in an unreal way. Because men tried to escape into dreams without any overt resistance or attempts to fight the pocket Nazi regime. So the pic deals with a group of artists who suddenly find all their desires and instincts aroused by a girl who comes to the town.

She is supposedly a refugee, sans papers. But only an anguished sculptor tries to help. The others just use her as she wakens all their frustrated sexual desires and also their guilts. She is supposedly killed, but it seems she is not mortal. The sculptor sends her death mask to the men who betrayed her to make them suffer.

This does have a brooding visual quality but not the inventiveness to give the film its needed lift and more powerful clarity. The casting also is weak, with Jolanta Umecka not possessing the needed qualities of a woman who is all things to all men. But technical mastery is shown in this. *Mosk.*

Ombres Et Mirages
(Shadows and Mirages)
(SWISS-DOCUMENTARY)

Locarno, Aug. 2.
Moritz De Hadeln production and release. Directed and edited by Moritz De Hadeln. Commentary by De Hadeln, E. Von Dem Hagen; camera, Richard Clifton-Day, De Hadeln. At Locarno Film Fest. Running time, 52 MINS.

This documentary deals with the underside of Paris tourism that is the life of young girls who come to Paris looking for adventure or a new life plus the world of the international beatniks. It sometimes does have an overdone commentary, but this somehow gives the imagery a good underlining and almost makes it a takeoff on a certain French penchant for flowery studies of subjects that might also have disturbing undertones.

Director Moritz De Hadeln has probed with his camera into re-enacted scenes of girls who drift about Paris and adventures that may befall them. Though based on real happenings, they are redone for the camera and so constitute a sort of dramatic edge mixed with on-the-spot looks at youthful street carousings and beatnik life.

This pseudo-documentary is an uneven but fairly unusual mixture of fancied documentary. It could be used for supporting fare in arty houses abroad or for tv. Blown up from 16m, the technical qualities are acceptable. There are German and English versions of this available. The French one was shown at this festival. *Mosk.*

La Lune Avec Les Dents
(The Moon By One's Teeth)
(SWISS)

Locarno, Aug. 1.
Arado Film production and release. With William Wissmer, Noelle Fremont, Michel Fidanza. Written and directed by Michel Soutter. Camera, Jean Zeller; editor, Eliane Heimo. At Locarno Film Fest. Running time, 80 MINS.
William .... William Wissmer
Noelle .... Noelle Fremont
Michel .... Michel Fidanza

One of the more offbeat Swiss films, this looks like an unassimilated grab bag of New Wave influences about the maladjusted young man living on life's outskirts, reading, shouting, having an occasional girl and finally running into a mysterious policeman who tries to kill him.

This might be trying to reflect some youthful feeling re smothering in the so-called affluent and self-righteous Swiss society. But there are too many repetitive scenes of violence and vague relationships with girls to give this any coherent progression and thus enable it to swallow the padded scenes of interviews, aimless talks and cinema truth bits.

An added handicap is that this was blown up from 16m. It is technically passable except for some grainy sequences. It is pointed out that Jean-Luc Godard is of Swiss origin. But it is not enough to be Swiss and try to emulate the French master because one has to have talent too. Director Michel Soutter does not display enough to make the pic jell. But it is an unusual film from staid Switzerland. *Mosk.*

A Derrota
(The Defeat)
(BRAZILIAN)

Locarno, Aug. 1.
Fiorani Filmes production and release. With Luiz Linhares, Glauce Rocha, Italo Rossi, Oduvaldo Viana Filho. Written and directed by Mario Fiorani. Camera, Mario Carneiro; editor, Renato Neumann. At Locarno Film Fest. Running time, 75 MINS.
Man .... Luiz Linhares
Woman .... Glauce Rocha
Chief .... Italo Rossi
Clerk .... Oduvaldo Viana Filho

A grim, harrowing tale of secret police torture is spun out in this tale of an arrested man interrogated, tortured, running amuck and killing and finally hung. A look at political secret police, and an almost hopeless affirmation of man's inhumanity to man are meted out in this relentless pic.

This has a tendency to use violence for its own sake and bogs down in a ritual of kill or be killed. It is not bolstered by any insight into character or to give a more-controlled look into the uses of cruelty. But too much is repeated or telegraphed without compensating tones of inevitability or clear progression to eventually rob this of its intent and purpose.

A man is questioned, his wife or mistress is brought into the rundown house that serves as a prison to succumb to the brutal headman and tell all to supposedly try to save her man. But his near escape and bloodbath of killing has him betrayed by her as she wants to survive while he has already gone too far to remember what he stood for as he sinks to the level of his inquisitors.

But there is no denying the powerful progression and definition in detailing probable firsthand experiences down in Brazil. But the outlook is lost as brutality becomes a thing for both sides without a true clarification of what anybody stands for. Acting is rightly larger than life and the film is completely made in interiors to add to the grisly tone. Some special situations abroad are likely on its obsessive theme but sans the redeeming clarity of tone to make this of arty house pro ortions. *Mosk.*

The Trip
(COLOR)

An attempt at a psychedelic experience through film, pic depends mostly on editing gimmicks and cross cutting, but should do boffo boxoffice biz with the youth market.

Hollywood, Aug. 4.
American International release of a Roger Corman Production. Features entire cast. Produced-directed by Corman. Screenplay, Jack Nicholson; camera, (color) Arch Dalzell; music, American Music Band; asst. director, Paul Rapp; editor, Ronald Sinclair. Reviewed at the home of James Nicholson, Aug. 3, '67. Running Time, 85 MINS.
Paul .... Peter Fonda
Sally .... Susan Strasberg
John .... Bruce Dern
Max .... Dennis Hopper
Glenn .... Salli Sachse
Lulu .... Katherine Walsh
Flo .... Barboura Morris
Alexandra .... Caren Bernsen
Cash .... Dick Miller
Waitress .... Luana Anders
Al .... Tommy Signorelli
Wife .... Mitzi Hoag
Nadide .... Judy Lang
Helena .... Barbara Renson

As a far-out free floating LSD freak-out, "The Trip" should provide enough psychedelic jolts, sexsational scenes and mind-blowing montages and optical effects to prove a boxoffice magnet for the youth market. No story line in the conventional sense, pic mainly depends on cinematic gimicks to grab the viewers attention and also dabbles in Bergman and Fellini symbols and techniques.

Main problem in viewing "Trip" is trying to guess the intent. Is producer-director Roger Corman simply exploiting a new horror avenue or is this an honest attempt to reproduce by film an actual hallutionary experience?

Jack Nicholson script opens with Peter Fonda, a director of tv commercials, shooting on a beach and being confronted by wife, Susan Strasberg, who is about to divorce him. Distressed by his personal life, he goes off with friend Bruce Dern to the hippie, wierdly painted house of a pusher, played by Dennis Hopper, to buy LSD.

Guarded by Dern, Fonda's trip begins. Scenes rapidly cut from Fonda climbing lofty sand dunes, being chased by two black hooded horsemen through forests, as well as beeing the sacrificial victim at a dark medieval rite in a torch-lit cave. Unconnected scenes begin to spin off the screen with increasing speed and with no attempt at explanation.

At one point Fonda fears he is about to die. He is shot from the rear, fully nude, struggling with Dern to gain his breath. Later visualizing making love, he and girl twist and turn in bed, covered only by psychedelic lights while camera continuously cuts to various parts of their naked flesh. Montages of a painted topless dancer are also flashed through film.

When Fonda escapes from Dern's keeping, he wanders the Sunset Strip and the eye-splitting, split second cutting continues. It all ends abruptly with Fonda discovering that the hooded horsemen pursuing are symbolically his wife and girlfriend.

Fonda comes across very well, establishing the various moods needed to further the visual effects. Miss Strasberg is on only briefly, and Hopper is okay, except in dream sequence in which he plays a wierdo high priest, but that whole scene is sophomoric. In lesser roles Salli Sachse, Katherine Walsh, Caren Bernsen and Barboura Morris deport themselves creditably.

Arch Dalzell's color photography is crisp, frequently using camera optics effectively. Dennis Jacob is credited with creating the montage sequences and Ronald Sinclair, with editing. At final cut who was responsible for what would be difficult to say.

Music score was composed and performed by the American Music Band and contributed unobtrusively to the atmosphere.
Dool.

The Christmas Kid
(U.S.-SPANISH—COLOR)

Jeffrey Hunter in tight little made-in-Spain western with excellent dualer possiblities.

Producers Releasing Organization release of Westside International-L. M. Films coproduction, produced and directed by Sidney W. Pink. Stars Jeffrey Hunter; features Louis Hayward. Executive producer, J. Lopez Moreno; screenplay, James Henaghan, R. Rivero; camera (color by Movielab), Manolo Hernandez San Juan; F. Garcia Morcillo; editors, Anthony Ramirez, John Horvath; asst. directors, Paul Gonzales, Philip Pink. Reviewed at New Amsterdam Theatre, N.Y., Aug. 13, '67. Running Time, 90 MINS.
Joe Novak .... Jeffrey Hunter
Mike Culligan .... Louis Hayward
Mayor Louis Carrillo ..... Gustavo Rojo
Marie Lefleur .... Perla Cristal
George Perkins .... Luis Prendes
Dr. Fred Carter .... Reginald Gilliam
Jud Walters .... Fernando Hilbeck
John Novak .... Jack Taylor
Percy Martin .... Eric Chapman
Luke Acker .... Dennis Kilbane
Pete Prima .... Russ Stoddard
Sherriff Anderson .... Carl Rapp
Karl Humber .... Guillermo Mendez
Burt Froelich .... Alvaro De Luna
Marika Novak .... Alejandra Nilo

One of the better entries in Sidney Pink's program of made-in-Spain features going out through Producers Releasing Organization (theatrical) and Westinghouse (television), "The Christmas Kid" is an offbeat western with good chances as a dualer in its intended market. Jeffrey Hunter offers some marquee allure in the title role of a hero-villain who is presented mostly as a "mixed-up kid," and the package has been neatly put together by producer-director Pink.

Film does offer some sociological aspects unusual in even big-budget oaters. Progress of a town from poverty into saloon-infested gambler's paradise is believably presented. Hunter's motivation in becoming a "bad man" (temporarily) are seen as purely psychological in a somewhat modern way.

Discovery of copper in Jasper, Arizona brings in heavy gambling in the form of ruthless promoter Louis Hayward. Hunter, a town troublemaker whose father became a drunkard after his wife died in childbirth, joins Hayward as a hired gun. After Hunter's girl (Perla Cristal) is killed by another Hayward henchman, he returns to the side of law. Hayward's subsequent framing of Hunter on a murder rap leads to a fairly suspenseful climax.

The script by James Henaghan and R. Rivero is more of a character study than a western in the traditional sense, and better casting and production values might have produced a top feature. As it is, Hunter, Hayward and Gustavo Rojo (as the town mayor) are fine but other thesps are mediocre. The tinny post-synchronization common to all of Pink's Spanish films infects all players.

Pink directs the film fluidly, concentrating on dialog and character relationships, as there is little fast action. Photography by Manolo Hernandez San Juan is fine except for the all-too-obvious day-for-night scenes in which a light blue sky shines during supposed p.m. hours. Other technical credits are pro, and there is a nice atmospheric score by F. Garcia Morcillo. *Byro.*

Topo Gigio I La Guerra Missile
(Topo Gigio and the Missile War)
(JAPANESE-ITALIAN-COLOR-C'SCOPE)
Paris, Aug. 8.

Towa release of Towa-King production. Directed by Kon Ichikawa. Screenplay, Maria Perago, Ichikawa. Camera (Eastmancolor), Y. Asayana. Previewed in Paris. Running time, 90 MINS.

Japanese director Kon Ichikawa is known in the West for his expertise in diverse and mainly deep themes, plus his extraordinary documentary, "Tokyo Olympiads." Now he comes up with a pic blending an animated tv mouse, popular in Italy and Japan, Topo Gigio, mixed with live action. The little mouse is also familiar on Ed Sullivan's U. S. teveer. It has gloss, expertise and is generally diverting though perhaps Ichikawa's extremely brilliant direction has robbed it of a simplicity and charm it needs for moppet audiences. As is, it may have some specialized and playoff use, especially in Italy and Japan, but lacks the overall punch for more extended foreign playing or the ease for wide kiddie shows.

Ichikawa has used black backgrounds to hide the man manipulating the foam rubber or plastic mouse character which gives it mainly night settings but also an unusual visual aura. The mouse is first introed being knocked out of bed by a car crash and his fumbling as a maladroit little man, or mouse, character has some well timed gags and okay personalizing of the easygoing, good-natured but unsuspectingly canny mouse.

Then, on a walk, he gets mixed up with a bunch of criminals trying to break into a government safe to steal missile plans. He helps outwit them after plenty of fights, action and also a red balloon that follows him about.

But there is enough action, pathos when the balloon dies, some songs sung by the mouse, and fine color and blending of hand animation and live action to insure this some notice, if rightly handled for specialized and even school spotting. Long-held shots of Alitalia Airline posters, Coke bottle and a certain brand of toothpaste suggest tie ins for this Japanese-Italo coproduction.

It is true Ichikawa started as a cartoonist and animator and did situation comedies before his more renowned pacifistic pix with war backgrounds, "Fires on the Plains," "The Burmese Harp," his look at obsession in "Conflagration" and his probing tale of erotic meanderings in "Kagi," not to mention his brilliant documentary on the Olympics. But his now finely honed techniques are a bit wasted on this simple pic and he would do better to stick to his weightier pix though he seems to have enjoyed making this judging by its care and intermittently brilliant gags, with leavening of emotion. It is technically exemplary. *Mosk.*

Boxer
(POLISH)
Paris, Aug. 8.

Polski Film release of Start production. Directed by Julian Dziedzina. Screenplay, Bohdan Tomaszewski, Jerzy Suszko; camera, Mikolaj Sprudin; editor, L. Romanis. Previewed in Paris. Running time, 96 MINS.
Antoni .... Daniel Olbrychski
Manager .... Tadeusz Kalinowski
Walczak .... Leszek Drogosz
Girl .... Malgorzata Wlodarska

A rather familiar tale, of a young boxer reliving his life in flashbacks before a main bout, is given a good mounting and some solidly staged fight scenes. It does not have much depth in character and plays it for surface observation to make it in line for some playoff on its fairly well made aspects if not having enough edge and depth for art use abroad.

The young boxer of the title studies with a kindly, knowing manager who grooms him for the Olympics. He gets on the outs with the lead boxer, has a brief fling and gets jailed when he beats up a group he feels are mocking him during a drunken spree. But he is rehabilitated and Poland's desire for a good Olympic showing gets him a crack at it which he wins.

A girl in his life is only sketched in as are most of the characters. But Daniel Olbrychski has presence and a dynamic charm that comes across and helps bridge the fairly pedestrian progression and flashbacks. He also is acceptable as a fighter. He should go further than this well made, well meaning but academic pic on the amateur fight game. Direction just does not have that extra perceptiveness and pace to lift it out of the ordinary of sport-themed pix.

A sidelight is that the man he beats in the big fight is a Russian. The fight is good and both are game, but the Russians have not bought the film as yet according to some Polski film reps. Others will not be as touchy and it has the makings of an okay playoff pic for action marts on its well done fight scenes and generally good playing and okay technical credits right down the line. *Mosk.*

Pula Festival

Jutro
(The Morning)
(YUGOSLAV)
Pula, Aug. 8.

A Dunav-Film (Belgrade) production. With Milena Dravic, Ljubisa Samardzic, Mija Aleksic, Neda Arneric, Ljuba Tadic, Jelena Zigon. Directed by Purisa Dordevic. Screenplay, Purisa Dordevic; camera, Mihajlo Popovic. At Pula Film Fest. Running Time, 91 MINS.

"Jutro" was one of the filmic highpoints at this year's Pula Festival. It's a highly intelligent feature pic which centers around war returnee and the new conflicts imposed on him in peace time. Film has many plus points and gives an excellent overall impression. This interesting subject qualifies itself for export. Incidentally, it will rep Yugoslavia at the forthcoming Venice Film Fest. It certainly will please many crix.

This is the third part of a trilogy which was started with "Girl" and continued with "Dream" which both dealt with war themes and which also were directed by Purisa Dordevic. This pic revolves around a Serbian partisan who returns to his home after four war years. Warfare has left its traces and there is still much misery and confusion but, after all, it's peace. But is it really peace for him? He still has to straighten out some things which include settlements with fellow people who collaborated with the Germans and the shooting of a traitor. He has to realize that he's actually still at war. And what will tomorrow bring? There's always war in the air. Or isn't war all the time? Human beings have to struggle day by day. Film makes the point that war is "senseless" but one feels the unholy fact that "no more war" is practically an illusion as long as there are human beings on earth.

This is a demanding film. And it is not easy to follow the director's intentions, the more so because there are a number of flashbacks which occasionally lead to confusion. Repeatedly persons who have been seen dead are again alive on the screen.

Pic is not easy to classify. It contains much fun in addition to the tragic elements. In fact, this starts out as a comedy and then goes tragic. The intelligent direction led the players to give very good performances.

Technically, the film reaches a high peak. The fine lensing is a credit to Mihajlo Popovic who is 70 and the oldest active film cameraman in the land.

This Dunav production walked off with the second highest trophy.
Hans.

Iluzija
(Illusion)
(YUGOSLAV)
Pula, Aug. 8.

A Jadran production. With Slobodan Dimitrijevic, Marija Lojk, Vanja Drah. Directed by Krsto Papic. Screenplay, Krsto Papic, Zvonimir Majdak; camera, Kreso Grcevic; music, Miljenko Prohaska. At Pula Film Fest. Running time, 82 MINS.

There is nothing special about this feature pic which centers around the old-hat plot of two brothers being in love with the same woman. Film is well made and easy to understand therefore it should be good enough to make its rounds within its own market. Foreign prospects appear more than slim because of the absence of real exploitation factors.

In this, a young man leaves his

small native town and goes to the big city, Zagreb here, where he has a reunion with his considerably elder brother who has left his wife and child and started a new life with a pretty young girl. As every patron will expect, the young brother soon falls for the girl and a romance develops between the two. Their affair, of course, leads to complications between the two brothers. The elder one feels cheated and his already existing grudge against the younger generation becomes even more radical.

Acting is generally competent and direction shows some intelligence which is evident in the details of the film. But the whole thing is nothing much more than an average production. Lensing, as usual in Yugoslav pix, is good. Other technical credits are allright. *Hans.*

Fraznik
(The Feast)
(YUGOSLAV)
Pula, Aug. 7.

A Cine Club Belgrade production. With Jovan Janicijevic, Anka Zupanc, Dusan Janicijevic, Bata Zivojinovic, Janez Vrhovec. Directed by Dorde Kadijevic. Screenplay, Dorde Kadijevic; camera, Alexander Petkovic. At Pula Film Fest. Running Time, 90 MINS.

This is the first feature film by Dorde Kadijevic and it is a promising debut as a director. This has interesting ingredients although many sequences don't ring exactly true. Some are confusing. But Kadijevic's directorial abilities are evident. Foreign prospects appear slim for this. Had the story been told in a more common manner, international chances might have been better.

Story shows a Serbian village in 1943 when the country was occupied by the Germans. Two American flyers, crew members of a plane that has been shot down, get into this village which is run by the Chetniks who side with the Germans. At first the Chetniks welcome the Americans but then fear the Germans who are searching for the two Americans. The latter manage to escape and the Chetniks now feel that they are in a tough spot if the Germans show up. They kill two of their own men and put them in American uniforms and hand their corpses over to the inquiring Germans. But the Germans already have caught the real Americans. End of pic sees a revolt of the villagers against the ruthless Chetnik leader.

Technically, film makes a good impression and there are some beautifully lensed scenes of local landscapes. The two Americans can hardly be taken seriously. One of them speaks like a Britisher while the other, a Negro, seems to hail from some African country. Their voices should have been dubbed by real Americans. The way they act and talk makes one occasionally smile. *Hans.*

Breza
(The Birch-Tree)
(YUGOSLAV-COLOR)
Pula, Aug. 2.

A Jadran Film (Zagreb) production. With Manca Kosir, Bata Zivojinovic, Fabijan Sovagovic. Directed by Ante Babaja. Screenplay, Slavko Kolar, Ante Babaja, Bozidar Violic; camera (Eastmancolor), Tomislav Pinter; music, Andelko Klobucar. At Pula Film Fest. Running time, 100 MINS.

This Jadran production has a number of assets but tops is undoubtedly the brilliant and beautiful lensing by Tomislav Pinter, rated one of Yugoslavia's best cameramen. The beauty of the scenes can make "Birch-Tree" even a special item for export although it can't be denied that this film is, per its plot and mentality, chiefly something for the home market. It contains some sort of Serbian sarcasm and sentiment which most foreign patrons may find strange.

Film's central figure is a girl, named Janica, who because of her beauty and slenderness is an optical standout among the village girls. She's called "a birch-tree among beech-trees" by the villagers. But it so happens that the villagers find a beech-tree more useful than a birch and she's therewith made an outsider. Yet there is an old forester who appreciates her beauty and he talks his gamekeeper, a handsome fellow named Marko, into marrying her. There is a short happiness for Janica. But then she's confronted with this life's sadness. Her baby dies soon after birth, she falls ill and soon thereafter she dies too. Had are numerous flashbacks throughout the film.

Film combines tragedy with humorous elements. In fact, it's occasionally a peculiar mixture of many things that range from poking fun at peasants' life to plain socialistic sarcasm. Film appears overly long, and there is an abundance of sentiment. It has, besides its topflight lensing, definite plus points such as the acting and the lively accompanying music. *Hans.*

Kaja ubit cu te
(Kaja, I'll Kill You)
(YUGOSLAV—COLOR)
Pula, Aug. 9.

Jadran Film (Zagreb) production. With Zaim Muzaferija, Ugljesa Kojadinovic, Antun Nalis, Izet Hajdarhodzic, Jolanda Dacic. Directed by Vatroslav Mimica. Screenplay, Vatroslav Mimica, Kruno Quien; camera (Eastmancolor), Franco Vodopivec. At Pula Film Fest. Running time, 75 MINS.

Although this is a relatively short feature pic, there is real boredom in the film. One has the feeling that the whole thing could have been told in half an hour Most of the scenes seem stretched out. This is an experimental type of production which emerges as an anti-film. And it's not easy to make head and tails out of it. The director's ambition to create something different may be appreciated but it's the type of cinematic offering in which both fastidious and average patrons will find little to please them.

The socalled action takes place in a small Mediterranean Dalma-

---

tian town at a date which could be any time. The story of this town has it that no human being has been killed here for many centuries. Then, suddenly, a war breaks out and friends become enemies. Brutality dominates the scene and there are hints or indications that the events depicted here are based on real happenings during the Occupation time. But all that is intended doesn't come off.

What adds to the confusion is the lineup of strange characters who remain on the static side. What's good about this offbeat presentation is the camerawork but fine camerawork is nothing special for Yugoslav pix. *Hans.*

Cetvrti Sputnik
(The Fourth Companion)
(YUGOSLAV)
Pula, Aug. 10.

A Production Unit, Zagreb, and OHIS, Skopje, film production. With Mihajlo Kostic, Renata Frajskorn, Ilija Dzuvalekovski, Mira Zupan. Directed by Branko Bauer. Screenplay, Slavko Goldstajn, Bogdan Jovanovic, Branko Bauer; camera, Tomislav Pinter. At Pula Film Fest. Running time, 80 MINS.

Vet director Branko Bauer still rates as one of Yugoslavia's better film creators and he's had many good films in recent years. "The Fourth Companion" isn't one of his best efforts. It shows directorial knowhow but, apparently, too much is left to mere routine in this production. A rather conventional film, this deals with politics and bureaucracy as well as love. It's primarily an item for the home market. Foreign buyers are not apt to be interested in this.

Story centers around the building of a recreation centre in a Yugoslav town with many interests involved. Central figures are a young secretary of the municipal committee, then a political figure with personal ambitions, and a young female professor who's to get an assignment at the recreation centre. The latter becomes the mistress of the ambitious politico and some of the complications stem from the fact that she had once been romantically tied up with the secretary. There are quarrels and misunderstandings until the recreation centre is completed.

Branko Bauer's handling of the players is okay. And he is able to create a number of interesting sequences. Technically, the film sets to a good standard. But, all in all, it isn't exactly a memorable film. It belongs more in the seen-and-forgotten category. *Hans.*

Protest
(Protest)
(YUGOSLAV)
Pula, Aug. 9.

Viba Film (Ljubljana) production. With Bekim Fehmiu, Ilija Dzvalekovski, Boris Buzancic, Nada Subotic. Directed by Fadil Hadzic. Screenplay, Fadil Hadzij; camera, Ivija Rajkovic. At Pula Film Fest. Running time, 85 MINS.

"Protest" is one of the more impressive films seen at this year's Pula Festival. It shows that a common worker can become the victim of social injustice also in a Commie country. Pic has strong plus points with regard to acting and

---

atmospheric details. Even if commercial prospects seem limited, this production should be able to sled into western markets.

This centers around Ivo Bajsic (Bekim Fehmiu), a manual worker, who committed suicide by jumping from a skyscraper. Pic tells via flashbacks the last phases of his life. The question is put why this physically robust man took his life. The viewer finds out that he was a tough guy, it's true, but he just was unable to accept any false friendship and superficial cordiality. His superiors hated him for his open attitude and he had constant trouble with them. When also his best friend let him down, he found life senseless and committed suicide.

"Protest" stars Bekim Fehmiu, one of Yugoslavia's popular actors these days. As a hardly ever smiling rough worker who just can't stand injustice and superficial friendliness, he's very impressive in this production. An interesting and colorful personality, Fehmiu should also be a good bet for western producers. Also the support is good in this one. As usual in Yugoslav pix these days, there are some frank sex scenes in this. But they add to the mood and are not tasteless. The adequately directed film reps a good technical standard. *Hans.*

Nemirni
(The Naughty Ones)
(YUGOSLAV)
Pula, Aug. 8.

A Production Unit FRZ (Belgrade) production. With Spela Rozin, Milena Dravic, Marko Todorovic, Dusica Zegarac, Janez Vrhovec. Directed by Kokan Rakonjac. Screenplay, Dusan Savkovic; camera, Branko Perak; music, Zoran Hristic. At Pula Film Fest. Running time, 70 MINS.

The best thing about this little film is a series of episodic roles which makes Milena Dravic a standout. Her portrayal of a talkative blonde brought her a best-actress trophy at this Pula festival. Lineup of players includes Spela Rozin, one of Titoland's best-known young actresses. Acting is noteworthy in this pic but otherwise it is too modest a film to make any special impression. Consequently, it has modest export possibilities.

What happens in this production has been picked from the newspapers. It concerns a traffic accident which was caused by the driver of a stolen car. Witnesses say that a girl was driving the car but, strangely enough, she's not found in the car.

The police start a search for the missing girl. Film could have been told in a more plausible manner. Developments get mixed up after a while. Main good about it is a series of highway sequences which often have documentary sharpness. The performances, even if only episodic roles, are the most noteworthy things in this. Direction is average while technical credits are generally okay. *Hans.*

Diverzanti
(The Demolition Squad)
(YUGOSLAV)
Pula, Aug. 10.

A Bosna-Film (Sarajevo) production. With Rade Markovic, Bata Zivojinovic,

Ljubisa Samardzik, Jovan Janicijevic, Husein Cokic. Directed by Hajrudin Krvavac. Screenplay, Vlata Radovanovic, Hajrudin Krvavac; camera, Ognjen Milicevic; music, Bojan Adamic. At Pula Film Fest. Running time, **80 MINS.**

They still shoot Partisan pix in the Titoland. And to shoot those "Yugoslav westerns" appears justified inasmuch as the films still have a big following in this country. This Bosna production probably was the pic that found the biggest applause on the part of the Pula crowd. Somewhat naive and overly heroic this may be faulted by crix but it is a very entertaining film. Having no dull moments, and much action, it also has some fun moments. Pic will probably become a stout moneymaker in Yugoslavia. Despite its conventional ingredients, this "Demolition Squad" should also be able to get into foreign markets.

This one concerns partisan units which have been surrounded by the Germans. They manage to resist the Teutonic forces successfully but what bothers them more is the German Luftwaffe. Hitler's pilots are giving them a rough time via bombs and machine-gun fire. So the leader of the partisans decides to send out a demolition squad of eight men to the German airport and destroy the menacing planes. Naturally, they reach their goal but all are killed carrying out this task.

There are funny (and sometimes involuntarily funny) moments galore in this. The players obviously enjoyed their work. The Germans in this film are different—they talk and act so silly they hardly can be taken seriously. This is an enjoyable film which has a number of plus assets. There is exciting camerawork and there is a catchy score by Bojan Adamic, one of Yugoslavia's most active film composers. *Hans.*

Na avionima od papira
(On Paper Planes)
(YUGOSLAV)
Pula, Aug. 8.

A Viba Film (Ljubljana) production. With Snezana Niksic, Polde Bibic, Stanislava Pesic, Dare Ulaga, Stefka Drolc. Directed by Matjaz Klopcic. Screenplay, Matjaz Klopcic; camera, Rudi Vavpotic; music, Joze Privsek. At Pula Film Fest. Running time, **75 MINS.**

This is a poetic love film. Director Matjaz Klopcic dedicated some obvious devotion to his intention to create a demanding type of feature pic, but his good intentions were not exactly crowned by success. The outcome is too much on the pretentious side. It smells too much of Godard, pseudo-Godard in this case. It may do well within its home grounds but has only limited foreign possibilities.

This revolves around an about 30-year old photographer who has fallen for a beautiful ballet dancer. Although he doesn't make the impression of a faithful character, she falls for him too and believes it's big love. In fact, she is so much in love that she is willing to marry him. Her mother tries to convince her that marriage would be a foolish thing. Yet she doesn't realize that to marry this man who himself admits that he's leading a senseless life would be a mistake. Film makes a point that both will soon become members of just an

average crowd, with all illusions gone.

As per its dialog sequences, there is much poetry about this film and the photography follows this pattern. Unfortunately, many scenes are somewhat banal. Snezana Niksic turns in a fine performance as the loving ballet dancer. Technically, this film is very good and there is also a fairly good score. *Hans.*

Kuda posle kise
(Where To After the Rain?)
(YUGOSLAV-COLOR)
Pula, Aug. 8.

A Vardar Film (Skopje) production. With Stanislava Pesic, Ali Raner, Ilija Dzuvalekovski, Olga Spiridonovic. Directed by Vladan Slijepcevic. Screenplay, Jovan Cirilov; camera, Kiro Bilbilovski; music, Tomo Prosev. At Pula Film Fest. Running time, **105 MINS.**

Treatment of this film's subject matter makes this an interesting film. It gives some good insight into today's Yugoslav life and thinking as well as its problems. Film benefits from imaginative direction and some good performances. Although it is not fully convincing, it is the type of cinematic offering which may force some meditation.

Film only employs a handful of characters. The most substantial role is played by Stanislava Pesic, a comely, romantic-minded girl who is very much on the aggressive side when it comes to talking with her parents whom she finds of "small-town mentality." The parents belong to their country's upper class and are both financially and politically well off. The girl's fiance used to share her "progressive" way of thinking but, as he grows older he too forgets his youthful ideals. Finally she also loses her aggressive attitude and the film makes it clear that she's adjusting to her Babbitt-type parents. *Hans.*

Locarno Fest

Le Grand Dadais
(The Big Softie)
(FRENCH-COLOR)
Locarno, Aug. 8.

Prodis release of Films Borderie, Films De La Licorne, Rialto Film production. Stars Jacques Perrin, Eva Renzi, Daniele Gaubert; features Yves Renier, Yvonne Clech. Directed by Pierre Granier-Deferre. Screenplay, Bertrand Poirot-Delpech, Granier-Deferre from book by Poirot-Delpech; camera (Eastmancolor), Andreas Winding; editor, Emma Lechanois. At Locarno Film Fest. Running time, **85 MINS.**

Alain .... Jacques Perrin
Patricia .... Eva Renzi
Emmanuelle .... Daniele Gaubert
Germain .... Yves Renier
Mother .... Yvonne Clech

Soft-ribbed pic has flaccid direction and listless playing. It's a tale of a mother's boy off on a fling with a pretty model. The trite dialog and limpid progression have this pic just too surface to make its points.

The boy, who also lives on handouts from an aunt, becomes enamored of a free-living German model and leaves all for a summer idyll with her. But they soon tire of each other and it ends with her going back to an old flame.

Told in flashback during the trial, this lamely makes its way from situation to situation without breathing any life into the callow personages or giving the proceedings any pertinent dramatic flair. So it appears mainly a home item with perhaps some playoff abroad on dualers. Some love scenes and a few haute couture interludes may help in selling this. *Mosk.*

Szyfry
(The Enigma)
(POLISH)
Locarno, Aug. 8.

Polski Film release of Kamera production. With Jan Kreczmar, Zbigniew Cybulski, Irena Eichler, Barbara Krafft. Directed by Wojciech Has. Sceenplay, Andrzej Kijowski; camera, Mieczystaw Jaroda music, Krzyshtof; Penderecki. At Locarno Film Fest. Running time, **88 MINS.**

Tadeusz ....Jan Kreczmar
Maciek .... Zbigniew Cybulski
Zofia .... Irena Eichler
Jadwiga ....Barbara Krafft

A complicated tale encompasses still live aftermaths of the last war in Poland. Through a search for a boy lost during the war revealing effects that still last are uncovered as well as the irony of it being gone and buried for most people, those who shared any guilt or not. It is intensely personal and has a sharp pacifistic content. But it has too many references that may not be easily deciphered by those unaware of Poland during the war years.

This shapes a specialized entry, at best, abroad. It is too stringent for any arty or much playoff in Western spots. But it marks director Has as a subtle filmmaker in command of his medium. He is able to keep a complicated tale absorbing.

A Polish officer, who had managed to flee to London and stayed there during the war, comes back when he hears his wife is ill and has never recovered from the disappearance of their 12-year-old boy during the war.

He uncovers facts of the boy's mysticism, which even seemed to be spellbound by the Germans and that his wife had been with a partisan who the boy may have turned in.

Pic manages to make its literary script visually forceful, helped by some fine acting. The late Zbignew Cybulski, as the living son, is a loss in his fine sensitive limning of a young man who was not able to rise from the war's effects. It has fine lensing, editing and a notable musical score. Here is a specialized pic that delves into Polish war wounds. But it's too rigid and elusive for much foreign chances. *Mosk.*

The Circle
(CANADIAN-DOCUMENTARY)

National Film Board of Canada production and release. Produced by John Kiemeny; directed and written by Mort Ransen; features Don Franck and the Gilles Gascon; sound, John Knight; editor, Mike McKennirey. Reviewed at NFBC office, N.Y., Aug. 18, '67. Running Time, **60 MINS.**

The miracles of group therapy, rather than the horrors of dope addiction, is the strong point of National Film Board of Canada documentary, filmed in its entirety at Day Top Village, the Staten Island self-cure center for narcotics addicts. None of the gruesome details of withdrawal are shown and the language of the residents of the center, while strong, is proper for the situation so there should be no qualms on the part of educational institutions or even tv stations or theatres about showing the film.

Although most of the NFBC's projects are concerned with Canada and its citizens, it does go outside the geographical limits of the country to make films if the subject matter seems important enough. "The Circle" was made in cooperation with the Canadian Broadcasting Corp. and, in Canada, will have its first showing on that network. Distribution in the U. S. will be handled by McGraw-Hill, with the 16m prints being leased or sold to schools and similar institutions although any indication of interest on the part of theatres or tv will be welcomed

Mort Ransen's working script has Canadian actor Don Franck enter the group as a dope addict wishing to be cured. The policy at Day Top is the complete withdrawal, or "cold turkey," system and it is understood that the residents there, all former narcotics users, do not accept the usual interpretation of complete withdrawal as being the hallucinatory nightmare that the public imagines. However, they more than recognize the importance of their problem and find strength, as a group, that they all lack as individuals.

Franck's acceptance by the residents (who were aware of the filming, but may have had the impression that he was a former addict) is fascinatingly depicted. No concession is made for him. He's given the same responsibilities and censured for the same faults as the others. He tends to underplay as he's supposed to be an anti-social, withdrawn type who resists the necessary involvement on which the entire concept of the center is based.

The therapy, generally, is to bring the new resident down to the basest emotional level, assigning him (or her, as there are some 18 females among the roughly 100 residents) to demeaning labor, forcing him to constantly expose his inner feelings through frequent group discussions, and more often than not goading reluctant types into angry (but usually honest) declarations. Above all, the new member is forced into involvement, either through drawing out his interest or by needling him into participating.

It is difficult to tell how much of the film was actually scripted by Ransen (evidently most of Franck's scenes) but some dialog heard during the numerous meetings has an original flavor, such as "I have a real groovy family situation . . . they all hate me."

If there is a certain softness to the film, a lack of violence in an atmosphere where the threat of it must be ever present, it's not really an important fault. There's some suspicion that producer John Kiemeny and director Ransen picked the more attractive and photogenic inmates (most of the girls are goodlooking and one is beautiful, while several of the men are above average in looks) but the result justifies this, if so. Gilles Gascon's camera work is excellent, considering the physical limitations of the setting and the need to not intrude on any of the unrehearsed action. Editing and sound are adequate although the soundtrack during a few of the group scenes has too much reverberation.

As is typical of NFBC productions, there's no cut and dried ending to the film. The viewer is left to decide for himself whether the character played by Franck has been cured. The reaction at a Day Top screening of the film was about 50% either way   *Robe.*

The Viking Queen
(COLOR—BRITISH)

Fast spectacle of Roman occupation of Britain okay for general market.

Hollywood, Aug. 25.

Twentieth-Fox release of Hammer-Seven Arts (John Temple-Smith) production. Stars Don Murray, Carita; features Donald Houston, Andrew Keir, Niall MacGinnis, Patrick Troughton, Adrienne Corri. Directed by Don Chaffey. Screenplay, Temple-Smith; camera (DeLuxe color), Stephen Dade; music, Philip Martell; editor, Peter Boita. Reviewed at 20th-Fox Studios, Aug. 25, '67. Running Time, 90 MINS.
Justinian .... Don Murray
Salina .... Carita
Maelgan .... Donald Houston
Octavian .... Andrew Keir
Tiberion .... Niall MacGinnis
Beatrice .... Adrienne Corri
Priam .... Wilfrid Lawson
Fergus .... Sean Caffrey
Talia .... Nicola Pagett
Catus .... Percy Herbert
Tristram .... Patrick Troughton
Dominic .... Bryan Marshall
Boniface .... Jack Rodney
Benedict .... Patrick Gardiner
Nigel .... Brendan Mathews
Dalan .... Paul Murphy
Fabian .... Gerry Alexander
Osiris .... Denis Shaw

Ancient Britain, during the Roman occupation and the warring Druids, provides a colorful background for this spectacle produced in Ireland by Hammer-Seven Arts for 20th-Fox release. Script by film's producer, John Temple-Smith, focuses on the Druid queen, in love with the Roman governor-general, who takes up the sword when the invaders massacre her people. Feature, in lush DeLuxe color, should be an okay entry for the general market which goes for historical yarns.

Don Murray is the only American actor in the cast, starring with a new Finnish actress, Carita, who makes her screen bow. Subject allows many hand-to-hand encounters between the Romans and the Britons, early Druid rites, & a smash climax in which the queen charges the Roman legions in her knife-hubbed chariot with devastating effect.

Murray acquits himself vigorously. Carita, as daughter of a dying king who places the mantle of responsibility for his country's future upon her, also the daughter of his Viking queen, handles role well enough. Spirited support is afforded by Andrew Keir, Roman second-in-command; Patrick Toughton, faithful retainer of royal house; Adrienne Corri, queen's elder sister; Donald Houston, Niall MacGinnis and Sean Caffrey.

Don Chaffey's direction is sufficiently rugged to maintain the intended spirit of spectacle and Stephen Dade's color photography is a beautifully-executed assignment. Editing by Peter Boita is fast, Philip Martell's musical supervision fills the bill and John Furniss' costumes, particularly on distaff side, are effective.   *Whit.*

I, A Man
(COLOR)

Another Andy Warhol entry, with usual technical inadequacies and with even more elements of "sexploitation." But it contains many elements of genuine cinematic interest, including a penetrating and honest view of its characters.

Andy Warhol production, written, directed and photographed by Warhol. Stars Tom Baker; features rest of cast. Reviewed at Hudson Theatre, N.Y., Aug. 24, '67. Running Time, 99 MINS.
Tom .... Tom Baker
Girl In Bed .... Cynthia May
Girl In Bedroom......... Ivy Nicholson
Girl on Table .... Ingrid Superstar
Girl on Balcony ...... Stephanie Graves
Girl on Staircase .... Valeria Solanis
Girl in Bed .... Bettina Coffin

"Do you mind the fact that I don't have any clothes on? Does it turn you on?", asks Tom Baker of Bettina Coffin, the last of five girls he "makes out with" in this picture. "Well," she says after a moment of silence, "music would turn me on."

Does this sound silly? Or prurient? Or dull? It's probably all of these things, but one thing it isn't is unbelievable—not if you're willing to credit Andy Warhol with the ability to get real people to act like themselves. Some folks may never have met any girls like these, of course, but some who have might be in Warhol's debt if he gets them to stop pretending they haven't.

All the girls are pickups for the night, and Baker is generally cast as "straight man" for their hang-ups. Ingrid Superstar, for example, hopes her breasts won't become "runny eggs," and might like to make more than spiritual contact with, as Baker puts it, "a beautiful, blond-haired, bisexual madman" like the dead James Dean. Ivy Nicholson feels scorned and rejected, but doesn't know why; Stephanie Graves is kept in a mod apartment but would like "chairs that look unmistakably like chairs" and has "an awful feeling that you like his taste better than mine." Valeria Solanis (with whom Baker doesn't make out even though she pinched him in an elevator) has instincts that "tell me to dig chicks—why should my standards be lower than yours?" And Miss Coffin has endless fights with her husband about whether or not to kill the cockroaches.

Warhol has tried cutting in this one, to the accompaniment of pointless bleeps and flashbulb effects; the sound is impossible at times; the color photography, with a few attractive exceptions, is static and fuzzy. The mostly-improvised conversations go on beyond reason; and Baker is simply not an actor. But the girls, even those who watch the camera for awhile before warming up, are real people, and their lives are pathetically interesting.

Oh yes, there are endless shots of bosoms, with Baker fondling them; there are closeups of Baker's crotch (clothed) and rear end (bare); there are glimpses of male and female genitalia; and there is an explicit sequence involving intercourse. It would be too bad if judgments of this basically honest film are made on the basis of these ingredients alone.   *Gold.*

Yoko Ono Film No. 4
(BRITISH-DOCUMENTARY)

Inane, pretentious doc which lenses 365 twitching bare bottoms. Thumbed down by British censor, but okayed for limited showing by local London authorities. Any anticipated titillation swamped in utter boredom.

London, Aug. 22.

Connoisseur Films release of a Yoko Ono production. Produced, directed and edited by Miss Ono and Anthony Cox; sound and camera, Cox. Reviewed at Hammer Theatre, London. Running Time, 80 MINS.

Japanese actress-director-producer Yoko Ono and her husband Anthony Cox have compiled a documentary film which considers itself a piece of avant-garde filming that would "strike a blow for world peace." Through an ad in a newspaper she persuaded 365 people to have their bare behinds photographed while they walked on a kind of moving platform. Posteriors belong to actresses, actors, writers, critics, celebrities and nonentities, and might be called a remarkable assortment of such.

Result of this utterly ludicrous piece of pretentiousness is complete boredom. Behind the nonstop, 80 minutes kaleidoscope of nude buttocks is a kind of wild track of comment from those taking part and these comments range —in lensed context—from the unconsciously funny, the even more unconsciously bawdy to the utterly stupid and pompously self-conserious. (Black and white raw stock cost $168, the set was a borrowed apartment and the "cast" was unpaid.)

The British Board of Film Censors turned down this film as "unsuitable" but the licensing committee of the Greater London Council issued it an X certificate for showing in certain theatres. The first booking is the Jacey-Tatler here.

Miss Ono and her husband should not be rapped for turning out a pornographic picture. It is not that. But they should be rapped for having the effrontery to clutter up a West End cinema with such trash.   *Rich.*

Un Choix D'Assassins
(A Choice of Killers)
(FRENCH-ITALO-COLOR)

Paris, Aug. 22.

Gaumont release of Rome Paris Film, SEPIC, Cinegi production. Stars Bernard Noel, Duda Cavalcanti; features Robert Dalban, Marcel Lupovici, Corinne Armand, Mario David. Directed by Philippe Fourastie. Screenplay, Remo Forlani, Fourastie from book by William P. McGivern; camera (Eastmancolor), Alain Levent; editor, Armand Psenny. At Madeleine, Paris. Running Time, 90 MINS.
Sephan .... Bernard Noel
Dany .... Duda Cavalcanti
Inspector .... Robert Dalban
Lopez .... Marcel Lupovici
Dominic .... Guido Alberti
Jennifer .... Corinne Armand
Gunman .... Mario David

It's hard to classify this French pic, based on a Yank adventure-gangster book. An alcoholic, maddened by the death of his mistress in a car accident, gets embroiled with gunrunners and foils their plot and seems to be salvaged by a little girl. But there is a lack of moral fibre, brisk direction and knowing thesping to make this fuse.

Film rambles along with direction by newcomer Philippe Fourastier having a tendency to play this off the cuff without firm pacing. Result is a mixture of exotic atmosphere in Morocco and a supposedly hard-boiled tale that remains a bit loose. One example is that of a police inspector talking to a girl about gangsters while standing in the middle of a crowded street, with only their voices heard.

Bernard Noel is unable to imbue the character of the drifter with much semblance of inner hurt or drive. Duda Cavalcanti is a heavyset looker who fails to register in an episodic role as beatnik helper and lover of the drifting hero whose desire for death makes him a useful addition to a gang of gunrunners.

Idea and storyline are good. Film's color and theme might make this an okay dualer for foreign use. But it lacks the drive necessary for more demanding firstruns or arty spots. However, it is technically good. *Mosk.*

Zatoichi Royaburi
(Zatoichi Breaks Out)
(JAPANESE)

Tokyo, Aug. 22.

Daiei production and release. With Shintaro Katsu, Rentaro Mikuni, Akira Nishimura, Toshiyuki Hosokawa, Yuko Hamada. Directed by Satsuo Yamamoto. Screenplay, Takehiro Nakajima, Koji Matsumoto, Kiyokata Saruwaka; camera, Kazuo Miyagawa; music, Sei Ikeno. Previewed in Tokyo. Running Time, **95 MINS.**

This is about the 16th appearance of the cool, skilled, and very human blind masseur. Usually these films are among the most entertaining Japan is making at present. Ichi, though both blind and poor, is an expert swordsman, and can lay out dozens of his attackers without, well, turning an eye. In this one, however, something has happened.

He has been given a big name director, Satsuo Yamamoto, and a known co-star, Rentaro Mikuni, and a big story with a message. The idea was to make "Zatoichi" important. But he was already important in his own way, and this attempt makes an inflated film which is, by comparison with the others, not very entertaining. Ichi goes into a town where the peasants are groaning under the double-yoke of gangsters and a corrupt government. The local lordlings are, in fact, hand in glove with the hoodlums. Naturally, it is up to Ichi to save the poor, oppressed farmers.

The message comes through loud and clear. It is Director Yamamoto's usual message. It is the tired, impractical, do-gooding of the professional leftist—we must somehow "save the masses" from exploitation, etc. Neither life nor economics are that simple but this never dismays directors like Yamamoto.

Under the circumstances Shintaro Katsu's usually glorious impersonation of the blind Ichi is much subdued, as perhaps befits the "importance" of the occasion, and that fine actor, Mikuni, can make little of a ridiculous role (first he's good, then he's bad) which should never have been written and which he, as a fine actor, should never have taken. *Chie.*

Point Blank
(PANAVISION—COLOR)

Extremely violent gangster meller. Lee Marvin for marquee. City b.o. prospects very good.

Hollywood, Aug. 24.

Metro-Goldwyn-Mayer release of Judd Bernard-Irwin Winkler production, produced by Bernard and Robert Chartoff. Stars Lee Marvin. Directed by John Boorman. Screenplay, Alexander Jacobs, David and Rafe Newhouse, based on the novel "The Hunter," by Richard Stark; camera (Metrocolor), Philip H. Lathrop; editor, Henry Berman; music, Johnny Mandel; song, Stu Gardner; asst. director, Al Jennings. Reviewed at Metro Studios, Culver City, Aug. 23, '67. Running Time, **92 MINS.**

Walker	Lee Marvin
Chris	Angie Dickinson
Yost	Keenan Wynn
Brewster	Carroll O'Connor
Carter	Lloyd Bochner
Stegman	Michael Strong
Reese	John Vernon
Lynne	Sharon Acker
Gunman	James Sikking
Waitress	Sandra Warner
Mrs. Carter	Roberta Haynes
First Citizen	Kathleen Freeman
Carter's Man	Victor Creatore
Car Salesman	Lawrence Hauben
Customer	Susan Holloway
Penthouse Lobby Guards	Sid Haig, Michael Bell
Receptionist	Priscilla Boyd
Messenger	John McMurtry
Roommates	Ron Walters, George Strattan
Carter's Secretary	Nicole Rogell
Reese's Guards	Rico Cattani, Roland LaStarza

"Point Blank" is a violent, dynamic, violent, thinly-scripted film. Lee Marvin stars as a double-crossed thief seeking vengeance, only to find he has again been used. Director John Boorman's first Hollywood pic is a textbook in brutality and a superior exercise in cinematic virtuosity. Marvin's name and a hard sell should create urban b.o. turmoil for the Metro fall release. Violence-conscious censor boards in some areas may induce cuts. Pic, incidentally, is one of the four National Assn. of Theatre Owners October specials.

Besides Britisher Boorman, other relatively new faces (either in billets or in U.S. pix) include the (now-dissolved) production team of Judd Bernard and Irwin Winkler, producers Bernard and Robert Chartoff, Canadian thesps John Vernon and Sharon Acker, and N.Y. art director Albert Brenner, working under Metro's George W. Davis.

Richard Stark's novel, "The Hunter," is the basis for the screenplay by Alexander Jacobs, David and Rafe Newhouse, in which first five minutes recap Marvin's betrayal by best pal Vernon and wife, Miss Acker. The space-time jumps are lucid, effective, inventive, fluid—and repetitive. A hurry-and-wait sensation grows on a viewer as, once transposed from one scene to another, a dramatic torpor ensues at times, except for the hypo of choreographed brutality.

Used by Keenan Wynn, who at fadeout emerges as the man who seeks to take over a crime syndicate, Marvin stalks his betrayors, and their associates. When he has not near-maimed his adversaries, he precipitates their death, although he seems never to have actually been the direct cause of death. The futility of revenge is exemplified by the cyclic pattern of Marvin's movements, and Boor-

man's frequent cuts to the past overmake the point.

Marvin's dialog is spare, and while the role is no big deal, it sustains his image as a gruff figure of power. Were he to have been a wronged honest man, stronger identification might have resulted. A panorama of hoods bumping off hoods is not too gripping.

Angie Dickinson, playing Miss Acker's sister, provides the right mixture of beauty and bewilderment as she assists Marvin. A romantic future for the pair is barely suggested; indeed, Marvin's blackout at the end leaves a big question mark.

Of the Canadian actors, Vernon is stiffly virile, perhaps because most principal characters project a zombie-like air, suitable as bad-dream atmosphere which appears to be deliberate. Miss Acker does well in limited footage.

Exceptions to the limbo-like characterizations occur in the case of Carroll O'Connor, a flesh-and-blood accountant who pursues his criminal career with as much businesslike detachment as his counterpart in any corporation; because of this, his scenes with Marvin lend grim humor, also get Marvin thinking about the futility of his vendetta.

In addition, greasy car dealer **Michael Strong** is very good in projecting the sweaty-palmed two-timer who wants to be in, and yet not in, the thick of shady doings. A highlight scene occurs when Marvin takes him for a ride, and turns a car into a deadly vehicle of torture; the effect is black slapstick, possibly a redundant phrase since slapstick always has sadistic overtones. Other performances are adroit.

The real star of the film is the film itself—the uptight assemblage of footage, meticulous over-recording of sound, the complementing Johnny Mandel score which is deliberately, and effectively, mechanical in sound, and assorted visual effects. Phil Lathrop's Panavision and Metrocolor lensing has vitality, ditto Henry Berman's editing to 92 minutes.

Withal, Boorman has a distinct cinematic flair, and Bernard-Winkler-Chartoff can produce. Use of Frisco Bay's former Alcatraz Prison, L.A. freeways, and other locations is a big asset. *Murf.*

The Hellbenders
(U.S.-ITALO-SPANISH-COLOR)

Fair Italo western with Joe Cotten name to bally.

Embassy release of Aiba Cinematografica (Rome)-Tecisa (Madrid)-Albert Band coproduction. Stars Joseph Cotten; features Norma Bengell, Julian Mateos, Gino Pernice, Angel Aranda. Directed by Sergio Corbucci. Screenplay, Band, Ugo Liberatore, from original treatment by Virgil C. Gerlach; additional dialog, Louis Garfinkle; camera (Eastmancolor by Pathe), Enzo Barboni; music, Leo Nichols; editor, Nino Baragli. Reviewed at New Amsterdam Theatre, N.Y., Sept. 1, '67. Running Time, **92 MINS.**

Jonas	Joseph Cotten
Claire	Norma Bengell
Ben	Julian Mateos
Jeff	Gino Pernice
Nat	Angel Aranda
Kitty	Maria Martin
The Beggar	Al Mulock
Pedro	Aldo Sambrell
Commander of Fort Brent	Enio Girolami
Sheriff	Jose Nieto

Although "The Hellbenders" has a plot line typical of made-in-USA westerns, it does not rise above the majority of European oaters because of indifferent direction, uneven color quality and heavy-handed acting. With Joseph Cotten's name for the marquee, it should, however, have a better-than-average career as a programmer and should end up doing okay biz in its intended market.

Script by Albert Band and Ugo Liberatore has Cotten as a former Confederate officer who dreams of "saving the cause" if he can find the cash. After he and his sons massacre a Union convoy, netting almost $1,000,000 in greenbacks, they must transport the money through desert terrain filled with posses searching for the killers. They hide the money in a coffin which they claim contains the remains of Cotten's son, and get away with the trick until a final—and unconvincing—O.Henryesque climax.

Cotten gives one of the weakest performances of his career precisely because he is expected to register continual stubbornness and strength. The result: one shrill pitch throughout which produces more than a few risible moments. Norma Bengell offers film's best playing in role of bereaved "widow," but Julian Mateos' beachboy face is wrong for the role of Cotten's halfbreed son who eventually becomes Miss Bengell's paramour.

Sergio Corbucci's direction is almost completely undisciplined in re the staging of the action, and he has a habit of indulging in dizzying zooms and pans when a simple cut would be more effective. Something went wrong somewhere with the photography, credited to Enzo Barboni; color correction seems never to have occurred as the sky is a deep blue one moment and a pale white the next. There are the usual violent scenes in the familiar European manner, but one fight scene in a bar ranks with the least lucid action segments ever filmed.

As is often true with Italo westerns, major honors go to the musical score. Leo Nichols has written poignant tunes for trumpet, piano and guitar which rank with the best work of his countryman Ennio Morricone of the "Dollars" series.

"The Hellbenders" is one of three Embassy programmers released this summer which were not trade-screened. The other two consist of the British horror combo, "The Terrornauts" and "They Came From Beyond Space," which has already had some dates. *Byro.*

Our Mother's House
(BRITISH-COLOR)

Very good Jack Clayton film about seven children who conceal their mother's death until Dirk Bogarde destroys their fantasy. Not a juve market item, but for sophisticated situations in careful playoff.

Hollywood, Aug. 29.

Metro-Goldwyn-Mayer release of Heron/Filmways (Martin Ransohoff) production, produced and directed by Jack Clayton. Stars Dirk Bogarde. Screenplay, Jeremy

Brooks, Haya Harareet, based on novel by Julian Gloag; camera (Metrocolor), Larry Pizer; editor, Tom Priestley; music, Georges Delerue; asst. director, Claude Watson. Reviewed at Metro Studios, Culver City, Aug. 28, '67. Running Time, **104 MINS.**

Charlie Hook	Dirk Bogarde
Elsa	Margaret Brooks
Diana	Pamela Franklin
Hubert	Louis Sheldon Williams
Dunstan	John Gugolka
Jiminee	Mark Lester
Gerty	Sarah Nicholls
Willy	Gustav Henry
Louis	Parnum Wallace
Mrs. Quayle	Yootha Joyce
Miss Bailey	Claire Davidson
Mr. Halbert	Anthony Nicholls
Mother	Annette Carell
Bank Clerk	Gerald Sim
Doreen	Edina Ronay
Girl Friend	Diana Ashley
Mr. Moley	Garfield Morgan
Woman Client	Faith Kent
Man Client	John Arnatt
Motorcyclist	Jack Silk

"Our Mother's House," a film about children but not to be considered in any way a kiddie pic, is a well-made look at family life and parenthood by seven destitute moppets. Dirk Bogarde stars in an excellent performance as their long-lost legal father, who is not the total heel he seems; nor, for that matter, are the kids all angels Producer-director Jack Clayton's absorbing pic, filmed in London in partnership with Martin Ransohoff's Filmways for Metro release, will show greatest b.o. strength in semi-artie situations with thoughtful nursing. Exposure as a British entry at current Venice Film fest will help attract the class trade and assist in later general playoff.

Julian Gloag's novel has been adapted by Jeremy Brooks and actress Haya Harareet into a good screenplay which develops neatly the accelerated maturing of children after the death of their long-ailing mother, Annette Carell. Latter, object of adulation, is buried in the back yard, eldest child Margaret Brooks imposing her belief on others that this will eliminate orphanage fears. To all except eldest son Louis Sheldon Williams, she conceals existence of a father, Bogarde.

In pic's first 50 minutes, during which the burial scheme is hatched and daily visitations to a makeshift shrine occur, emphasis is on the kids as they project various traits having exact counterparts in adults: fear, submission, overemotionalism, misguided nobility, and the like. The child is, indeed, father to the man. Only Yootha Joyce, mom's former housekeeper, discharged by Miss Brooks, gives a clue that Miss Carell was not exactly perfect.

Arrival of Bogarde changes the household. In a superior performance, this versatile actor charms the kids with a gruff tenderness which they have never known, having been under the constant spell of mother's puritanical moralizing. He steals the kids blind, brings women to the home, but only Miss Brooks objects, and her obstinance is rooted more in jealousy at being superseded as top dog. Miss Joyce, who smells a rat, forces her way back into things.

Pamela Franklin, who has played unusual children before, is unfortunately saddled with the most awkwardly drawn character: an emotional girl who becomes the family mystic, then succumbs mentally to Bogarde's charm as she is torn asunder by the combo of stirring womanhood and abhorrence of sex, and finally clobbers him fatally when, in an outstanding scene, she exposes the dead mother as a nymphomaniac. The progression of the character is certainly consistent, but the execution here is not smooth.

For Bogarde, however, the climactic scene makes for an outstanding acting achievement. Far from being a cold-blooded con man, he is revealed as a long-suffering hubby to a nympho, who finally deserted her. The seven kids are all illegitimate, so why, as a knockabout, should he care about them at all? Why indeed? Miss Franklin's impulsive manslaughter restores Miss Brooks to leadership, and, shocked into the inevitable disclosure of events to the outside world, she takes the brood to a doctor.

Clayton's direction is with tender, loving care—perhaps a bit too much in the first 45 minutes, although the desire to orient an audience to a kid's-eye view of life may have precipitated deliberate overexposition here. Other juves who deliver good performances are Sarah Nicholls, the extrovert who has her hair trimmed for riding on a motorcycle with Jack Silk; stuttering Mark Lester, John Gugolka and Gustav Henry. Parnum Wallace has a good brief scene as a shy boy brought home to stay by Lester, but teacher Claire Davidson explains the meaning of kidnap. Other performances are just right. A plaintive music score to point up appropriate scenes is provided by Georges Delerue, with Peter Katin billed as pianist. Lowkey lensing in Metrocolor by Larry Pizer accents the low-income physical mood, as well as the dramatic undertow. Tom Priestly trimmed to an okay 104 minutes, and other credits are pro. *Murf.*

Peppermint Frappe
(SPANISH—COLOR)

Offbeat Geraldine Chaplin starrer has strong art house potential.

Madrid, Aug. 12.
Elias Querejeta production. Stars Geraldine Chaplin, Jose Luis Lopez Vazquez, Alfredo Mayo. Directed by Carlos Saura. Screenplay, Saura, Angelino Fons, Rafael Azcona; camera (Eastmancolor), Luis Cuadrado; music, Luis de Pablo; editor, Pablo G. del Amo; art director, Emilio Sanz de Soto; production chief, Primitivo Alvaro. Reviewed in Madrid, Aug. 10, '67. Running Time, **94 MINS.**

This impressive, offbeat pic about the obsessions of a provincial Spanish doctor marks the artistic maturity of young director Carlos Saura. His fourth feature film, it is modern and engrossing throughout, casting a weird, almost diabolic spell. With careful handling of Geraldine Chaplin plus the publicity of his previously seen in America "The Hunt" (same producer, cameraman, director of music and one of the same stars), it should do excellent art house business and might even have a market in more general situations.

The story is rather intricate and regional: Julian is an aging provincial doctor, a bachelor with little to look forward to other than his practice and solitary life. Though basically a good, sensitive person, he is introverted and timid, the victim of an antiquated, inhibited attitude toward women. In large part his obsessions about them are due to an overly severe sexual and religious upbringing.

Then his brother Pablo, a playboy-businessman also getting on in years but attempting to disguise it, comes to town and things go haywire. Pablo has brought his young bride Elena (Miss Chaplin), a frivolous blond foreign girl with very modern ideas about love and marriage, and Julian is immediately drawn to her. He thinks he saw her once in a rural Holy Week celebration where it was the custom of the villagers to play drums until the skin between their thumbs and forefingers was raw and bleeding, leaving an almost permanent scar. Elena has such a scar.

Convinced that Elena is the love of his life, Julian tells her his story and tries to lure her away from Pablo, but she only makes fun of him, partly leading him on, partly ridiculing him. Meantime, Julian, struck by the physical resemblance between Elena and his virginal peasant nurse Ana (also played by Miss Chaplin) has converted Ana into her likeness, seducing her, dressing her in modern clothes, making her wear a blond wig, even obliging her to play a drum until her hands are raw.

At the end again rejected by Elena (and by Pablo, too, to whom she has revealed Julian's obsession), Julian pushes them and their car off a cliff, killing them. At the finale, he and Ana ("Elena"), who has decided to cast her fate with this strange man, dance fetishly to the sound of the drum.

In spite of its uniqueness, the story line and basic premise of the film never seem artificial or contrived, at least to anyone familiar with Spain.

Much of the credibility of the film is owed to its director. Saura's story is strongly, often brutally told, but always fascinates. Several scenes — the upsetting dance by Julian, Elena and Pablo; their tormenting of him on a bridge; Julian and Ana's bizarre encounter at the end—are masterful. Throughout there is a careful sense of pace. Saura's camera is always in complete control, polished and modern at the same time. Though a private and perhaps limited version of life, it always convinces.

He is helped in large measure by the three principals. Miss Chaplin is excellent in the dual role, demonstrating great range. As sophisticated Elena she is alternately innocent and childlike or cruel and calculating. As the nurse she is at first shy, later seductive. If her transformation in this second role seems perhaps too rapid, it is due only to a momentary and minor weakness in the script.

As Julian, Jose Luis Lopez Vazquez is totally convincing. This is surprising, because in his dozens of previous films he has always played comic parts. His performance is particularly sensitive, capturing the humor, pathos and obsessions of the character. Alfredo Mayo in the lesser role as Pablo is firstrate.

Technical credits are all pro. Luis Cuadrado's color lensing is exquisite throughout, especially subtle and convincing in the scenes at the ramshackle country estate. Extremely varied musical themes, some by Luis de Pablo, are integrated forcefully and unobtrusively. This is a careful, complete film—very Spanish in its theme and treatment yet expressive of a deeper, social problem common to many places. Saura dmonstrates that he is a director to be reckoned with. *Lyon.*

Young Americans
(SONGS-COLOR)

Interesting semi-documentary on the teenage singing group of same name; recommended for family trade particularly.

Hollywood, Aug. 25.
Columbia Pictures release of Robert Cohn production. Features The Young Americans and Milton C. Andersen. Directed and written by Alex Grasshoff; camera (Technicolor), Richard Moore; editor, David Newhouse; music, Billy Byers. Reviewed at Academy Award Theatre Aug. 24, '67. Running Time, **103 MINS.**

In this day of hippie groups, LSD and the raft of weird cults perverting the American scene, there stands out a troupe of clean-living teenagers known as The Young Americans who are maintaining the decency expected of youth through their common bond of love of music. Founded by former Los Angeles school teacher Milton C. Anderson to show that the average teenager is not the hip or psychedelic way-out person he so often is pictured in mass demonstrations throughout the country, this group both here and abroad has done much to prove that youth today generally has a normal outlook upon life.

The Young Americans' story has now reached the screen via as pleasant a novelty semi-documentary as has been seen in recent years. Alex Grasshoff, who previously made "The Really Big Family"—a graphic truelife feature of a Seattle family of 18 children—has taken this talented group of 36 teenage high-school and college boys and girls who have been touring the country since 1962 as a major singing attraction and developed a warm screen recital which should find favor particularly with the family trade.

Produced by Robert Cohn as a Columbia Pictures release, after he and Grasshoff got together and were mutually impressed by the spirit generated by The Young Americans when they saw them at a charity benefit, the Technicolor film is reported to have cost around $500,000.

In certain respects it is almost a travelog as the Young Americans, headed by Anderson, visit by chartered bus such widely divergent locations as Boston, N. Y. City, Washington, D. C., several Illinois towns, the desert regions of California and other localities. These backdrops, however, serve actually to pinpoint the activities and personal reactions of the youngsters in their close association with one another.

Good as the picture now stands,

it would benefit by less emphasis upon their frolicking and more on their singing. Highlight of film is group's appearance at the Illinois State Prison at Menard, when the thousand and more inmates watch the performance and a dramatic mood is established as the prisoners respond to the entertainment. Particularly effective here is one of the group, Ken Prymus, a young Negro, singing "The Whole World in His Hands," which gets to the prison audience as well as the theatre spectator.

There is no particular script dialog, most of the spoken lines extemporaneously uttered in the manner of a documentary and much of the action apparently unrehearsed. Few of the Americans are identified by more than first names, a few of the so-called principals including Judy Thomas, who actually composed one of the song numbers, "The Road Ahead of Us," sung by group on steps of the Jefferson Memorial.

Color photography by Richard More is inexpert, David Newhouse' editing is excellent and Billy Byers' music score fits subject perfectly. *Whit.*

Shijin No Ai
(Love for an Idiot)
(JAPAN—COLOR)

Tokyo, Aug. 29.
A Daiei Production and Release. With Shoichi Ozawa and Michio Yasuda. Directed by Yasuzo Masumura. Based on novel by Junichiro Tanizaki; screenplay, Ichiro Ikeda; camera (Color) Setsuo Kobayashi; music, Naozumi Yamamoto. Previewed in Tokyo. Running Time, **95 MINS.**

One of the most interesting Japanese films of the year, Yasuzo Masumura's "Shijin No Ai" (Love for an Idiot), is based upon Junichiro Tanizaki's novel about a perfectly ordinary man who falls in love with a girl no better than she should be.

Shoichi Ozawa is a very serious man. Unmarried, steady on the job, he doesn't drink or smoke. But he has one human weakness. This is Michio Yasuda, a lower-class Galatea and every day after work he rushes home to play a passionate Pygmalion. Determined to make something of her, he forces her to take piano lessons, English instruction, is forever buying her new clothes, taking her picture, and trying to make her into a real dream girl. The problem is that she isn't. She's just an ordinary little working-class girl whose only aspiration is to have a good time. This she accomplishes by lying, and eventually sleeping around with younger men.

The film, detached and wry, shows this and makes occasional ironics asides. He goes to her mother to formally ask for her daughter's hand once he has decided to marry her only to be told "I thought I gave you her hand a year ago"; the girl sends him off to work, helping him on with his coat like every good Japanese wife, the difference being that two young men are awaiting for her back in bed). Pic makes sure that the audience feels something for these two unhappy people.

So, if this film is not one for the entire family (sex scenes are, even for a Japanese picture, astonishingly outspoken), it is certainly

a picture for thinking and feeling adult. It is a bold, funny, moving and honest love story. *Chie.*

Venice Films

U Toszezon
(Late Season)
(HUNGARIAN)

Venice, Aug. 29.
Hungarofilm release of Studio No. 1 Mafilm production. With Antal Pager, Klari Tolnay, Janos Lajos Basti. Directed by Zoltan Fabri; screenplay, Peter Szasz from book by Gyorgy Ronay; camera, Gyorgy Illes; music, Szabolcs Fenyes. At Venice Film Fest. Running Time, **125 MINS.**
Kerekes	Antal Pager
Mrs. Szilagyi	Klari Tolnay
Szilagyi	Janos Zath
Hohl	Lajos Basti
Woman	Noeml Apor
Laufer	Sandor Kumoves
Sodits	Janos Rajk
Bonta	Karoly Kovacs
Chauffeur	Samu Balazs
Zorkai	Joszsef Szandro

Man's individual and collective guilt and its various ramifications are handled in this massive film with a surprising envelopment of grotesque comedy that turns to stark drama. It is controlled and, overall, jolting. Since it calls for concentration, it is mainly for possible art or specialized foreign usage.

A sincere ring keeps this generally absorbing and it can be tagged a denouncement of man's complicity in mass murder. A group of retired old men meet every week for drinking beer, storytelling and almost childish ribaldry though many were once responsible figures. This part is treated in farcical stop motion, speeded up shots and seems to be setting the scene for a zany comedy on old people. But they decide to play a joke on an absent member of their group.

It is the time of the Eichmann Trial in Israel and they somehow call the friend and pretend he is wanted at a police station. This man, Antal Pager, reacts with fear and distress at the call and goes off to his old hometown followed at a distance by the old jokers. He is in search of something that happened during the war and the film slides into a suspenseful, sociological and psychological treatment.

Hallucinations, old events in which he stays his own age, plus the zany inspections of the following friends are blended as his secret is played out. It seems he once expressed the opinion to a policeman friend that the druggist couple he worked for were Jewish. He gets the store from his friend and the couple are deported. He tries to find if they are dead or alive and gets embroiled with a woman who also seems to have some past guilt. But she is facing the death of her son from illness.

He finally has himself tried by his friends and is found guilty. He bungles a suicide attempt and ends with his remorse still apparent as life goes on. There may be a superficial resemblance to the noted Czech Oscar-winner "The Shop on Main Street," but this one is more cerebral than emotional.

Now this is still a touchy theme.

VARIETY carried a story from Tel Aviv April 23, spotlighting Antal Pager as the weak denouncer in the film for he is identified as a Nazi who denounced people during the war and played in a notorious anti-Semitic film of the time. The Hungarian delegation was asked about this and director Zoltan Fabri replied that Pager "made mistakes" and did appear in this film but did not do all the things stated in the VARIETY dispatch from Israel.

This has yet to be verified, but, if true, it does bring up the question of using a player in a film purporting to castigate the very thing Pager is accused of. So this aspect has to be resolved since the film deals with the most horrendous of man's inhumanities to man.

The film seems to take a stand on the actual crimes and also the crime of standing by and not doing anything about it. It is extremely well acted. sometimes loses its thread but always comes back to taking its stand of showing the guilt of those who both participated in or condoned by silence the terrible genocide of World War II.

The disparate styles sometimes clash or bring in a comic innuendo at the wrong time. But, on the whole, it manages to come off even if there are slow spots. Pic always builds up again to telling dramatic pitch. *Mosk.*

Head Of The Family
(Il Padre Di Famiglia)
(ITALO-FRENCH)
(EASTMANCOLOR)

Venice, Aug. 30.
Ultra Film presents an Ultra Film-MN-C.F.C. (Rome) - Marianne Productions (Paris) coproduction for Paramount distribution. Stars Nino Manfredi, Leslie Caron; co-stars Claudine Auger; features Mario Carotenuto, Antonella Della Porta, Evi Maltagliati, Marisa Solinas, Sergio Tofano, Elsa Vazzoler, Ugo Tognazzi; directed by Nanni Loy from his original screen story with screenplay by Loy, Ruggero Maccari; camera, Armando Nanuzzi; musical score by Carlo Rustichelli. At Venice Festival Hall. Running Time, **115 MINS.**
Marco	Nino Manfredi
Paola	Leslie Caron
Anarchist	Ugo Tognazzi

"Head of the Family" won its place as a contender for Venice honors on the premise that it corresponded to the festival's program accent on theme and point of view. Anticipated was a devastatingly ironic Nanni Loy film blasting at the constant sag in heroic idealism with Italy's push toward progress and affluence during the past two decades.

What emerged was a clever sentimental comedy, delightfully at odds with the Lido film meet's art and fulm culture pretensions.

Culprit behind the decline and rupture of Marco's (Nino Manfredi) happy marriage with Paola (Leslie Caron) is not society but an old time life force know as childbirth. Too many kids around the house can dim, even cripple a human being's natural drive for sex and accomplishment, Loy is saying. Even his tribute to the wife-mother as principal pivot and buffer in any home, doesn't detract from his warning that a big brood is a short cut to marriage on the rocks.

Attempt is made to say a bit more about the young couple of

strong-minded student architects thrown together from opposite ends of a post-war political riot into blissful wedlock. Their big social vision (she is willing to share his) has a beginning and finale resurge but no middle. It gets lost under a torrent of diaper pins and neo-realistic breast feeding.

What's left is a bitter-sweet comedy with pregnant box-office potential—in Italy at least. Yank audiences have yet to vote on the recent wave of similar product rolling off the coparticipation mill. Leslie Caron's name and standout performance will lend solid support to foreign campaigns. Nino Manfredi is at ease in his role as the child haunted backsliding idealist and Ugo Tognazzi clicks as a hobo-anarchist.

Technical credits, particularly color lensing, are first-rate
Werb.

Noe Novesty
(Night of the Bride)
(CZECH—CINEMASCOPE)

Venice, Sept. 5.
Czech State Film release of Barrandov production. Directed by Karel Kachnya; screenplay, Jan Prochazaka, Kachnya; camera, Josef Illik; music, Jan Ncvak. At Venice Film Fest. Running Time, **80 MINS.**
Missy	Jana Brejchova
Amborse	Gustav Valach
Picin	Minislav Hofman
Priest	Josef Kemr
Klara	Libuse Havelkcva
Skovajs	Cestmir Randa
Sabatka	Josef Elsner
Philipa	Valerie Kaplanova

Film is a strange one to come from Czechoslovakia, for it mixes mysticism and bucolic drama at the time when the country was painfully trying to collectivize its farms in the early 1950s. It does have a curious flair and offbeat theme but its overripe dramatics slant this mainly for arties abroad.

A Communist official is shown exhorting suspicious peasants about the greatness of the farms to come which will have them wallowing in grain and practically swimming in milk. They go reluctantly and one man shoots all his cows and himself rather than turn over his chattel to the state. The others comply grumpily, until home comes a novice nun whose father has just killed himself.

Here film shifts to a more mystical plane as she becomes an embodiment of peasant rebellion against the new order. But she is somewhat fanatic and treats Christmas Eve as a sort of actual and almost erotic wedding to Christ. She gets the people out to a forbidden midnight mass and tries to get the chalice from the priest, practically blaspheming, before she is driven out into the snow where she dies.

A condemnation of Stalinism perhaps, but its unreal treatment has this practically transcending its subject to one of a misguided religioso vocation. Jana Bejchova has a dignity and drive as the forceful novice and others play their peasants and party men in stylized manners. Lensing has the sharp contrasts and inventive angles and polish usual in Czech pix.

Surprising aspect is an almost reactionary tinge to this pic, and reports are that it is in trouble on

its home grounds though it was allowed to come to the Venice fest.
Mosk.

O Salto
(The Leap)
(FRENCH)

Venice, Aug. 27.
United Artists release of Fildebroc-UA production. With Marco Pico, Ludmilla Michael, Antonio Passalia. Directed by Christian De Chalonge. Screenplay, Roberto Bodegas, De Chalonge; camera, Alain Derobe; music, Luis Clia. At Venice Film Fest. Running Time, **85 MINS.**

Antonio	Marco Pico
Dominique	Ludmilla Michael
Claudio	Antonio Passalia

A grim tale of the plight of clandestine Portuguese workers in France is the basis of this first pic. It tries to be a reenacted documentary which gives it a cold, distant air and robs it of a true indignation or even a more incisive insight into the problem. So pic appears of interest for language or specialized showing abroad plus tv use and even school showings. But it appears chancy for art and playoff use.

A pre-title scene shows a boy leaving home via a promise of a friend to help him settle in France. He leaves to get out of army chores and also for needed money. The trip is depicted in short brisk scenes until his arrival in France. Here his friend's absence has him wandering in Paris and meeting other Portugese and being sluffed off by a girl he met when she vacationed in Portugal.

Marco Pico plays the hero in a puppy dog fashion, always trying for sympathy and companionship and retreating like a whipped dog when he does not get it. It does not help give the pic a more robust air and are just too many scenes of his endless walkings. They may have been intended to show his solitude and loss in a big cold city, but, sans some more telling insight into his character, they become repetitious and finally unnecessary padding.

The French are just indifferent or exploit him and his friend also turns out to be parasitic in demanding a cut of his wages when he finds him a job. Christian De Chalonge, for his first pic, shows a concern for his characters and an attempt to treat a timely theme. But it stays on surface and ultimately appears academic and a bit old-fashioned in its treatment.
Mosk.

Le Regard Picasso
(The Picasso Look)
(FRENCH-COLOR-
DOCUMENTARY)

Venice, Aug. 28.

Cythere Films production and release. Directed, conceived and with commentary and editing by Nelly Kaplan. Camera (Eastmancolor), Francois Bogard. At Venice Film Fest. Running Time, 52 **MINS.**

The Picasso name alone could insure this documentary a place as a supporting medium - length pic in specialized art programs besides tv, school and lecture use. It helps in that it is well done and delves into his work via the recent massive exposition of his paintings, sculptures and drawings in two museums and a public library in

Paris last year to mark his 85th birthday.

Nelly Kaplan does not try too hard to classify and give an insight into Picasso's many styles. She does select well and stays mainly on the paintings. Color is good and it gives a feel of the amazing prolific qualities of the painter and his range of subjects without trying to pigeonhole him or be pedantic about it all. It can thus serve as a general sumup of the impressive exposition that may never be able to repeated again in any other country.

As an exhib memento, and a restrained cataloging of the immense output of the Hispano artist living and working in France, it is a worthy asset to art films and could have commercial values if rightly handled.
Mosk.

Spur Eines Madchens
(Trace of a Girl)
(WEST GERMAN)

Venice, Sept. 5.
Ehmck Film Germania production and release. Directed by Gustav Ehmck; screenplay, Ehmck, Susanne Jordan, Egon Mann; camera, Egon Mann. At Venice Film Fest. Running Time, **89 MINS.**

Hanna	Carola Weid
Friend	Gunther Lagarde
Man	Rainer Basedow

A West German new wave has been touted at fests for some time now and Venice itself had three first pix from there. All delve into youthful disorientation and this is about an alienated girl who sinks into breakdown from a seeming surfeit of self satisfaction and self indulgence around her. But her revolt seems surface and pic lacks any insights to give this drive and clarity.

In a series of scenes of the girl at school, at home, making love or with friends, she has a spate of crises that are too arbitrary. But pic has a good photographic quality even if there is too much frilly and fast cutting.

The German new school goes on being promising rather than having broken through with any major new works as yet. But there is an interest in putting personal outlooks on film and the newcomers may yet come up with more pertinent pix in the near future.
Mosk.

Ciao

N. Y.-made indie about a middleaged couple facing up to the return from the hospital of a semi-paralysed husband. Sincerity and taste could slant this for some specialized use, though limited.

Venice, Aug. 31.
Daval Productions Ltd. release, written and directed by David Tucker. Camera, Gardner Compton, Paul Glickman; music, Ed Summerlin. At Venice Film Fest. Running Time, **85 MINS.**

Sophia	Corina Magureanu
Husband	Henry Nemo
Claudia	Cheryl Morgan
Boy	Nowi Milly

The impending return of a semi-paralyzed fruitstore owner to his wife is the basis of this New York-made indie. In flashbacks it blocks out the frustrated lives of this couple who have still managed to bring up three children. But

this is done with fairly surface characterization and lacks the fluidity, insights and the perceptive acting to ward off a melodramatic, telegraphed and sketchy air. Possibilities are mainly for dualer use on its obvious sincerity which its execution does not equal.

David Tucker directs placidly but does not seem able to erase a feeling of self-consciousness in some of the actors or overcome the essential weakness of a sketchy script. The retailer, played on notes of garrulousness and anger by Harry Nemo, has never been able to make a true go of it and is in dire straits from supermarket competition when he has his stroke.

His wife, thesped too stridently by Corina Magureanu, has reached an age of frustration and despair at the things she feels she has missed, and tries to run off before his homecoming from the hospital. She is shepherded back by a niece and takes up her duties to help her needy husband.

It is technically passable but lacks the deeper insight, controlled building drive to give it the dramatic bite and statement it needs.
Mosk.

Johnny Yuma
(ITALO—COLOR)

Most violent Italian western to date to be released in U.S. Blood-drenched programmer is for less discriminating markets.

Clover release (distributed by Atlantic Pictures) of West Film-Tiger Film (Italo Zingarelli) production. Stars Mark Damon, Lawrence Dobkin; features Rosalba Neri, Louis Vanner, Fidel Gonzales, Gus Harper, Leslie Daniel. Directed by Romolo Guerrieri. Screenplay, Scavolini, Simonelli, DiLeo, Guerrieri; camera (Eastmancolor), M. Capriotti; music, Nora Orlandi; title song, Paul and Nora Orlandi; sung by the Wilder Bros.; editor, Sidney Klaber; asst. director, Jim Gregory. Reviewed at New Amsterdam Theatre, N.Y., Sept. 7, '67. Running Time, **99 MINS.**

Johnny Yuma	Mark Damon
L. J. Carradine	Lawrence Dobkin
Samantha	Rosalba Neri
Pedro	Louis Vanner
Sanchez	Fidel Gonzales
Henchman	Gus Harper
Thomas Felton	Leslie Daniel

Word from abroad that the most recent Italian westerns make "A Fistful of Dollars" seem like a nursery tale can now be confirmed. "Johnny Yuma" is the most violent oater yet, an unending series of beatings, blood-lettings and brutal gunfights. Plot, a weak tale about a fight between relatives over a ranch, is little more than a peg on which to hang sadistic elements calculated to appeal to the most undiscriminating patrons.

This first film by director Romolo Guerrieri also includes numerous "comic" episodes of a most heavyhanded kind, including a tiresome fight in a bar and the presence of a Mexican servant right out of pre-WW II Hollywood days. A kind of crypto-Fascism is suggested in the hero played by Yank actor Mark Damon. At the climax, he first unarms the villain before shooting him several times, with each shot calling out the name of a previous victim.

That Louis Vanner, playing the evil Pedro, has been most villainous is undeniable. In full view of the camera, he has bashed in the head of a little boy and has performed a kind of medieval "test" on Damon which also draws lotsa blood. He's equalled in viciousness, if not in sadism, by Rosalba Neri, his sister and the "brains" behind the operation.

Acting is inept, direction stagy and photography undistinguished. The music by Nora Orlandi is an imitation of the "Dollars" scores.

It should also be pointed out that its distributor claims that "Johnny Yuma" has already had some successful second - feature playoffs in the U.S., including being programmed in large cities with such as "Divorce American Style" and "You Only Live Twice."
Byro.

Tarzan And The Great River
(PANAVISION—COLOR)

Tarzan name will probably sell this one, but for the less discriminating market.

Hollywood, Aug. 29.
Paramount release of Sy Weintraub production. Stars Mike Henry, Jan Murray; features Manuel Padilla Jr., Diana Millay, Rafer Johnson. Directed by

Robert Day. Screenplay, Bob Barbash; story, Barbash, Lewis Reed; camera (EastmanColor), Irving Lippman; editors, Anthony Carras, Edward Mann, James Nelson; music, William Loose; asst. director, Mario Cisneros. Reviewed at Paramount Studios. Aug. 29, '67. Running Time, **88 MINS.**

Tarzan	Mike Henry
Capt. Sam Bishop	Jan Murray
Pepe	Manuel Padilla Jr.
Dr. Anna Phillips	Diana Millay
Barcuna	Rafer Johnson
Professor	Paulo Grazindo

Tarzan goes into upper reaches of the Amazon for his latest escapades, marking the first time that this location has been utilized for the Apeman series — based on the Edgar Rice Burroughs character. Beautifully photographed against striking and often magnificent scenery, the Sy Weintraub production is strictly run of the mill in story content, often clumsily scripted. For less discriminating markets it is an okay entry with Tarzan name to bally b.o. chances.

Mike Henry is the umpteenth thesp to portray the little character, his physique is better than his acting, but he's doing well enough by the few demands of the role. In Rio de Janeiro, he's called upon to break an ancient killer cult which has been revived in the jungle by a vicious native leader, and with his pet lion, which has been in the city zoo, and Cheeta, his chimp, arrives on the scene. He accomplishes his mission by killing the cult leader, in a spectacular fight.

Weintraub has given often interesting production values to his indie pic which Paramount is releasing. Zoologists probably will be a bit startled to learn that African maned lions roam the Brazilian jungles, as well as hippos who splash in the Amazon. Robert Day's direction is as good as the Bob Barbash script will permit and Irving Lippman's photography is exceptional.

Starring with Henry is Jan Murray, as a convincing river skipper in for too much out-of-place comedy, but handling assignment competently. Manuel Padilla, Jr., plays his small Indian charge, who travels up and down the river with him, and Rafer Johnson is the native leader. Diana Millay portrays a doctor who wants to help the natives, looking like she just stepped out of a beauty parlor.

Whit.

Eye Of The Devil
(BRITISH)

Dreary diabolical doings with David Niven and Deborah Kerr. Flat script, performances, direction. Once titled "13," needs help on duals.

Hollywood, Aug. 26.

Metro-Goldwyn-Mayer release of Filmways (Martin Ransohoff and John Calley) production. Stars Deborah Kerr, David Niven, Donald Pleasence, Edward Mulhare, Flora Robson, Emlyn Williams. Directed by J. Lee Thompson. Screenplay, Robin Estridge, Dennis Murphy, based on novel, "Day Of The Arrow," by Philip Loraine; camera, Erwin Hillier; editor, Ernest Walter; music, Gary McFarland; asst. director, Basil Rayburn. Reviewed at MGM Studios, Culver City, Aug. 25, '67. Running Time, **88 MINS.**

Catherine	Deborah Kerr
Philippe	David Niven
Pere Dominic	Donald Pleasence
Jean-Claude	Edward Mulhare
Countess	Flora Robson
Alain	Emlyn Williams
Odile	Sharon Tate
Christian	David Hemmings
Dr. Monnet	John Le Mesurier
Grandec	Michael Miller
Rennard	Donald Bisset
Jacques	Robert Duncan
Antoinette	Suky Appleby

There is a hex on "Eye Of The Devil" that has nothing to do with the black-mass and diabolical spirit angles of the plot. Forced direction, lethargic pacing and routine acting complement a dull script. Made in England by Martin Ransohoff and John Calley, Filmways pic has Deborah Kerr and David Niven for marquee value. Metro release needs inventive selling for okay dual bill rturns.

Originally titled "13" and yanked suddenly from last fall's release schedule, film has a production history far more interesting than the final cut. From files, names of Julie Andrews and Kim Novak appear, latter forced out, after production started almost two years ago, by an accident, and replaced by Miss Kerr.

Script-wise, "Day Of The Arrow," a Philip Loraine novel, went from Terry Southern (unbilled) to Robin Estridge, who shares screen credit with Dennis Murphy, engaged just before shooting. The directorial montage includes Sidney J. Furie, Arthur Hiller and Michael Anderson, latter dropping out on medic's orders, with J. Lee Thompson taking over reins. Title was changed only last May.

The faddish tv commercial technique used before titles intercuts arrows, train tracks, a dinner party and religious cult rites for a lively opener. This is the fastest action in all of the 89 minutes.

Niven, a vineyard manor lord, is called back to his property because of another dry season. Miss Kerr, against his wishes, follows with their children, Suky Appleby and Robert Duncan, latter acting mysteriously at start and finish. At the gloomy ancestral home, characters include Donald Pleasence, the local "priest," butler Donald Bisset, Flora Robson, Niven's aunt who knows (and finally tells) what is going on, and Emlyn Williams, Niven's father who faked a sudden death in apparent conformity with a family tradition. For his pains, Williams has spent years hiding in a corner of the castle.

Sharon Tate (to have been "introduced" in pic, but, with delayed release, has already appeared on screen) and David Hemmings loom as paper threats who speak deadpan dialog about the goings on. Miss Kerr is our only touch with reality, and she tries to carry the pic, to little avail. Still, garbed in Julie Harris clothes, she is, as ever, a delight to watch.

Edward Mulhare has brief footage as a family friend who rescues Miss Kerr. Juve Duncan, however, has been contaminated by the evil mystique, and in some future time, he will return for the black-mass sacrifice. Audience knows Niven's determination to be sacrificed long before Miss Kerr gets the picture.

Thompson's direction is ineffective, despite resorting to a lot of tricks to mask the plot. Some flashy editing bits and overly-mobile camera work (by Erwin Hillier) fail in attempts to substitute physical motion for plot action. While other production credits are pro, those, plus the known talents of the principal players, prove only that there must be a viable story line. Film is enough to put the Devil out of business. *Murf.*

Nippon No Ichiban Nagai Hi
(The Emperor and a General)
(JAPAN)

Tokyo, Aug. 31.

Toho Production and Release. With Toshiro Mifune, So Yamamura, Chishu Ryu, Seiji Miyaguchi, Rokko Toura, Yoshio Kosugi, Takashi Shimura, Takao Nakamaru, Toshio Kurosawa, Ushio Akashi, Takeshi Kato, Koji Mitsui, Yoshio Tsuchiya, Shogo Shimada, Daisuke Kato, Jun Tazaki, Akihiko Hirata, Nobmuo Nakamura, Ryuji Kita, Eisei Amamoto, Mokoto Sato, Kenjiro Ishiyama, Susumu Fujita, Yunosuke Ito, Kaiju Kobayashi, Ichiro Nakaya, Yuzo Yayama, Koshiro Matsumoto. Directed by Kihachi Okamoto; produced by Sanezumi Fujimoto, Tomoyuki Tanaka; screenplay by Shinobu Hashimoto; photography by Hiroshi Murai; art directed by Iwao Akune; sound recording by Shin Tokai; lighting by Tsuruzo Nishikawa; music by Masaru Sato. Previewed in Tokyo. Running Time, **158 MINS.**

Shortly after midnight on Aug. 14, 1945, the government met with the Emperor in the palace air-raid shelter where it was decided that the Potsdam Declaration be accepted. There were some dissident views but the Emperor's desire to end the war carried the day and the famous recapitulation speech was recorded. Among a group of young Army officers, however, there was much discontent over this decision and they attempted a coup d'etat. Failing, a number of them died, the war minister killed himself, the message was broadcast and the second world war came to a close.

This is the content of the new Toho film, based on Shoichi Oya's best-selling book. The company spared itself no expense, got together every star and near-star on the Toho lot, hired Japan's best screen-writer Shinosu ("Rashomon") Hashimoto gave the director Kihachi Okamoto unprecedented time and money, and the result is a handsome black-and-white widescreen film.

It is also the kind of picture that takes two hours and 38 minutes to unfold a plot which, as you see, fits nicely into the single paragraph which opens this review. Toho has chosen to make a film about an incident which is neither filmic nor epic; the event itself is important but not dramatic; decisions were made through talk, not action, and there is certainly a lot of talk. It takes half an hour of talk to recap into the main titles and then there is an hour and a half more of talk until the young officers revive us with a fancy bit of swordsplay (rolling heads) and the rather subuded Harakiri scene of the war minister.

And though there are miles of dialog, the talk is by no means restricted to what the actors say. There are written titles all over everything: each new person on the screen gets his title and name given; place names are given with each new sequence; papers and documents are identified when viewed; even the various kinds of airplanes get titled. And on top of everything else, like gravy, is a relentless commentator, explaining the obvious, indicating the apparent, who is ubiquitous throughout the first half of film, sporadic during the second.

One recognizes the genre. This is an "official" film presenting "official" history. Though its surface is "documentary" (a keeping track of minutes worthy of "Dragnet," clips of actual newsreels including some new and horrible material from Hiroshima and Nagasaki, a careful "emotionless" delivery), the intentions of the film are, not.

They are nothing less than an elaborate rationale for Japan's having lost the war. This has been needed now for 22 years, and is still as necessary as it was in 1945. A national 'failure' is very hard to live with. Oya, Hashimoto, and Okamoto have built up a perfect brief accounting for Japan's surrender.

It goes this way. Prime Minister Chishu Ryu (a marvelous actor, Ozu's favorite, and almost never better than in this film) receives the Potsdam Declaration and Foreign Minister Seiji Miyaguchi (another fine actor — the sword-master in Kurosawa's "Seven Samurai") is of the opinion it should be accepted. This occasions some difference of opinion between War Minister Toshiro Mifune (lending enormous dignity to a difficult role) and Navy Minister So Yamamura. Others enter the argument, Information Chief Takashi Shimura (hero of Kurosawa's "Ikiru") among them, but overriding all of these objections are the wishes of the emperor (played by Koshiro Matsumoto, the Kabuki actor, but you'd never know it because you never see his face, this being, remember, an "official" film.) In effect, the diety-emperor becomes the scapegoat but since he is, after all, a diety as well as an emperor, he escapes all onus while, at the same time, bearing all responsibility.

Seen this way the coup d'etat and the firebrand officers are quite beside the point. This, however, is the only visible drama in the film (their attempts to get the recorded speech of the emperor before it is broadcast) and, further, though wrong-headed, they are brave, and so their exploits are to be included in the rationale. Too, as in all myths, the god-king needs an adversary,

(It is interesting that those on the "good" side are directed with fluency and respond with fine performances. Those on the "bad" are sloppily directed and the actors are encouraged in every excess. The only restraint among the officers is that fine actor Tadao Nakamura who makes perfect sense of his part.)

The Emperor assumes full responsibility. Since he is a "god" his acts becomes acts of god and no one is responsible. He has saved everyone's face and if more saving of face is necessary there is always Harakiri.

The argument is both sound and logical, a tribute to all concerned who kept their heads in treating this still emotion-fraught subject, and if the film is neither believable (how could it be with all those stars—and when the NHK announcer comes on, who is it? Why it's Yuzo Kayama, Japan's own Mr. Coca-Cola). Nor, actually very interesting, still, it is an "official" film and, as such, it could have been, oh, so much worse. *Chic.*

Ola & Julia
(SWEDISH-COLOR)

Stockholm, Aug. 30.
Svensk Filmindustri production and release. Features Monica Ekman, Ola Hakansson; directed by Jan Halldoff; screenplay, Stig Claesson, Bengt Forslund, Jan Haldoff; camera (Color) Gunnar Fischer; music, Claes af Geijerstam; editor, Siv Kanaelv. Reviewed at China, Stockholm. Running Time, 87 MINS.

Julia	Monica Ekman
Ola	Ola Hakansson
Janglers	Claes af Geijerstam, Ake Eldsaeter, Leif Johansson, Johannes Olsson
Thomas	Thomas Janson
Max	Bengt Ekerot
Lasse	Lars Hansson
Nisse	Lars Lind

"Ola & Julia" is a well handled Romeo-and-Juliet story in contemporary Sweden.

Romeo is pop band vocalist Ola Hakansson, who plays himself. Juliet is a young actress. She is touring Sweden in the female lead—in a garbage can—in Samuel Beckett's "End Game." He is touring with his band, Janglers, attracting swarms of young girls everywhere.

She is 21. He is 19. Their meetings and their subsequent romance develop as their tours cross in various small towns.

The theatrical group and the Janglers get annoyed by the romance as Ola and Julia skip rehearsals and slip out on their respective groups to meet. Because of the disturbing effects, the groups demand that the romance come to an end.

It is a contemporary saga about two young people whose love is not disturbed by their families, but by their potential careers and by the people with whom they work. The film refrains from satirizing the pop band world. It succeeds in catching some of the moods that surround touring in provincial Sweden, where each town is the same for persons who spend only one night.

Perhaps Swedish films are entering a new era of romanticism. During the spring Bo Widerberg told the tale of Elvira Madigan, a Romeo and Juliet story set some 70 years ago.

Being modern youngsters in Sweden, Ola and Julia are independent of their families and need not revolt against them. They believe in love, but they do not believe that it can be experienced with only one person. When this romance ends, there will be another sometime in the future.

Sex is played down when compared with many recent Swedish films. The couple naturally go to bed, but rather little is made of their love-making or nudity.

If handled with care, "Ola & Julia" should have good potentials. *Fred.*

Venice Films

Festival

Well made documentary Yank indie on the Newport Folk Song Festival that surpasses its subject and gives an insight into folk songs and their meaning to performers, audiences and even more distant observers.

Venice, Aug. 31.
Patchke production and release. Directed and conceived and camera by Murray Lerner. With Stanley Meredith, Francis Gruman, George Pickow; editor, Howard Alk. At Venice Film Fest. Running Time, 80 MINS.

Murray Lerner probed the Newport Folk Song Festival for three years, 1963-66, and has edited his footage into a solid slice of folk singing and performer revelation and audience ideas, for a documentary that carries both specialized and even art playoff use if rightly handled and placed. It's a natural for tv and schools.

No tricky scripting here; just a forthright look at singers in action. Most of the toppers are seen, with particular emphasis on Joan Baez, Peter, Paul & Mary, and Bob Dylan. Many and various types of folk tunes and dances, from protest through ethnic, regional and inherited types, plus the blues, pass in review. Audience reactions and the asides and opinions of the performers themselves are recorded.

As someone remarks, maybe folk was pop some years ago, and many young practitioners note it is easy and also a way of expression that can be shared most effectively. Miss Baez's fine projection, poise and wit are here in her talk as well as her songs, and her spoken truths have the ease and sincerity to erase any self-indulgence. Dylan sings more than he talks, as ditto Peter, Paul & Mary.

But there are arresting asides on the blues and other folk facets. Pic is put together to overcome any rote or just a seeming series of acts. Lerner has been objective and not flashy and come up with an incisive picture of the folk scene in its festival guise. Its color, freshness and communal air are there as well as the personal element. Blown up from 16m, it is technically fine. *Mosk.*

La Chinoise
(The Chinese Girl)
(FRENCH-COLOR)

Venice, Sept. 7
Athos Film release of Anouchka Films, Productions De La Gueville. Parc Film, Simar Film production. With Anne Wiamensky, Jean-Pierre Leaud, Juliet Berto. Written and directed by Jean-Luc Godard; camera (Eastmancolor), Raoul Coutard; editor, M. Renoir. At Venice Film Festival. Running Time, 95 MINS.

Veronique	Anne Wiamensky
Guillaume	Jean-Pierre Leaud
Henri	Michel Semeniako
Kirlov	Lex De Bruijn
Yvonne	Juliet Berto

That fecund French filmmaker Jean-Luc Godard, in his second feature of the year, has not run out of ideas. He is still following his last few pix in essay-like political-social themes made up of readings, simulated discussions, cinema verite interviews and a bare schema of action and characterization.

This makes his films a bit irritating and repetitive at times and present one does not escape these flaws. But here he delves into a sort of Marxist-Leninist-Maoist cell of five young people who shut themselves in an apartment for a summer to sort out their leftist philosophies. This gives Godard a chance to go in for plenty of his aphorisms. He hits at the French left, American policy in Vietnam and Russo revisionism while showing the Chinese Red Guard's basic terrorism.

Hard to say if Godard has any sides, and he appears to try to give a convoluted serio-comic look at all aspects of youthful leftist thinking. The characters here are constantly calling for action and sounding off against intellectualism, while the film is mainly quotations and often a sophomoric probing of leftist politics. Inside knocks at French politics will escape ordinary foreign patrons. As usual, Godard has come up with a saucy, provocative but self-indulgent pic for arty and specialized audiences.

One girl, who is a Red Guard-type, finally decides to kill a visiting Russian as a step against revisionism. But she kills the wrong man and then goes back to get the right one, all done in a girlish manner. Godard does not define his own position for he just gives all sides. He castigates leftist lackadaisical policies at home, and rants against so-called imperialism, but he has nothing to offer in their place.

The girl is played by his new wife, Anne Wiamensky, granddaughter of noted conservative, Catholic, Gaullist writer Francois Mauriac. Her upper-class manners and voice also give a piquant air to her terroristic leanings. Godard gives a zest to the talk. There is a revealing dialog between the girl and a philosopher, who was on the Algerian side during the last war. He deals with the girl's attempt to apply principles of another culture and setup to actual French ways.

Color is tangy and players do not attempt to give characterization but have a headstrong, zany, sometimes touching mixture of youthful candor and searching amidst the half-digested politico patter. Godard's fast work, reasonable budgets and controversial themes have built him a following in his own country and with buffs abroad. *Mosk.*

Sikator
(Deadlock)
(HUNGARIAN)

Venice, Sept.
Hungarofilm release of Mafilm Studio 2 production. Directed by Tamas Renyi; screenplay, Akos Kertesz, Renyi; camera, Otto Forgacs; music, Geza Berki. At Venice Film Fest. Running Time, 89 MINS.

Gabi	Mari Torocsik
Vince	Gabor Koncz
Miklos	Sandor Horvath
Feri	Istvan Degi

A tender tale of an aborted love affair is unfolded without falling into mawkishness in this muted film. However, its refusal to go in for more drama makes this a specialized item for foreign market.

But it has fine performances, revealing insights and a provocative feeling for simple misunderstandings and decisions that can lead to tragedy. It reveals the plight of a divorced woman, with a child, who is torn between a young man who cannot make up his mind and an unwanted, insistent suitor.

Mari Torocsik has looks bolstered by inner strength and a fine presence. Her role of the bereft woman is a telling portrait and gives the film its force.

Director Tamas Renyi shows a flair for mood helped by a simple but well modulated script. It just misses that added fillip of more dramatic punch to give it a more dynamic framework. It has fine visual mounting. *Mosk.*

Edipo Re
(Oedipus Rex)
(ITALIAN-COLOR)

Venice, Sept. 12
Euro International Films release of Arco Film-Alfredo Bini-Somafis production. Stars Silvana Mangano, Alida Valli, Franco Citti. Written and directed by Pier Paolo Pasolini; camera (Technicolor), Giuseppe Ruzzolini; editor, Nino Baragli. At Venice Film Fest. Running Time, 110 MINS.

Giocasta	Silvana Mangano
Edipo	Franco Citti
Merope	Alida Valli
Tiresia	Julian Beck
Creonte	Carmelo Bene

Pier Paolo Pasolini made two naturalistic pix on the plight of the Roman sub-proletariat in "Accatone" and "Mamma Roma," then this Communist writer made a surprisingly objective tale of Christ's Passion in "The Gospel according to Saint Matthew" and a fable about Communist and Catholic outlooks coexisting or clashing in "The Hawks & The Sparrows." Now he turns to Greek tragedy in "Oedipus Rex" with an attempt to give it a Freudian ring with a modernistic envelope. Pasolini here used the exotic Moroccan desert and sandstone castles for the ancient Greek sites.

Japanese music, at times, is used and Silvana Mangano, as the mother Oedipus unwittingly marries, is made up in chalky white, while others have natural skin tones. Franco Citti does not quite have the stature for Oedipus. There is no inexorability about this. It has more of an illustrative quality with some pretty pictures of the colorful countryside but rarely invokes the grandeur of the old Greek tragedy

Pasolini wants to give this eternal implications by a prolog, set in the 19th century showing the birth of Oedipus to an officer and his wife and the latter's suspicion of the child. Then it segues into the ancient tragedy in which Oedipus rips out his eyes when he realizes he has killed his real father and married his own mother.

Pic has Oedipus as a child abandoned when his father is told by an oracle he will be killed by his own son. The man who is supposed to kill him cannot do so and he is found and brought up as their son by a childless couple. Then he goes off to adventure when he is grown and consults an oracle who predicts he will kill his own father and marry his mother. He decides not to go home and in his wanderings refuses to budge before a chariot which leads to a fight in which he kills unknowingly, his real father, a king.

He defeats the Sphinx and is married off to his own mother. But plague hits the city due to the unsolved murder of the King. Oedipus starts the investigation, which finally discloses that he was guilty. He blinds himself after the revelation and his mother-wife commits suicide. But even if the tragedy is followed fairly closely, pic does not strike a true mythical air and has a tendency to bog down in self indulgent scenes of lovemaking and shouting. It is a sort of tableau-like affair with fine lensing.

Pic appears mainly an arty house entry. Playoff seems chancey since it is just a bit too stilted and watered down.

Lensing is pretty enough and Miss Mangano is a lissome figure as the incestuous mother. Using Japanese music and tunes about Lenin, may mean something to director-writer Pasolini, but adds a further lack of cohesion to the pic.

Incidentally, Sophocles, who wrote the original tragedy, is given no billing. *Mosk.*

Desert People
(AUSTRALIAN-DOCUMENTARY)

Venice, Sept. 1.
Australian Commonwealth Film Unit release and production. Written and directed by Ian Dunlop. Camera, Richard Howe Tucker; technical consultant, Robert Tonkinson. At Venice Film Fest. Running time, 55 MINS.

Beseiged by flies, two families are observed in their nomadic haunts in the Australian desert. They are the remnants of Aborigines who have practically all been moved to government compounds. Seemingly oblivious of the camera, they go about their practically prehistoric, everyday activities.

Mainly, it's an item for ethnic, school and specialized use, with educational tv also indicated on its solid techniques.

The families go to various camp sites depending on the water and food available. Each unit usually has several wives, one man and several children. Food is the major occupation. The women forage for grass seed of which they make flour and mix with water for a doughy cooked affair. Lizards, fruit, animals and grubs are the dietary mainstays.

The pic is absorbing, depicting the activities of man at practically his most primitive form existent today. Commentary is judicious and simple. It is a well lensed and telling anthropological documentary and record. *Mosk.*

Jaguar
(FRENCH — COLOR — DOCUMENTARY)

Venice, Sept. 3.
Films De La Pleiade release and pro-

duction. Written, directed, filmed (East-mancolor) and edited by Jean Rouch. At Venice Film Fest. Running Time, 100 MINS.

Jean Rouch here gives a sprawling documentary look at Nigeria before and during its independence via a recreated trek of three native friends from their provincial home to the big city. It has a tendency to go off on tangents, but does give a picture of Africa. It could have interest for school showings, though being somewhat too diffuse for more demanding commercial use.

The people in question decide to see their country one day and take off to find jobs. They prosper and then decide to go home. They give away their money and take up their old places in shepherding, hunting, and, in one case, as a sort of local ladie's man called "Jaguar."

It is well filmed in a candid way and the 16m color, blown up to 35m, is effective. *Mosk.*

Soy Mexico
(I Am Mexico)
(FRENCH — COLOR — SCOPE—DOCUMENTARY)

Venice, Sept. 2.
Capricorne release and production. Directed and filmed (Eastmancolor) by François Reichenbach. Commentary, Carlos Fuentes, Jacqueline Lefevre; editor, J. B. Lubtchansky. At Venice Film Fest. Running Time, 95 MINS.

Film roams about Mexico delving mainly into its Indian heritage, past and present. It does have some unusual footage but pic remains a bit diffuse. It touches on too many remote Indian aspects of the country, skirting the so-called unfinished revolution. It needs a more coherent visual pattern before it can emerge a possible art item abroad.

However its ethnic content and a direct commentary by Mexican writer Carlos Feuntes do pull the diverse scenes together a bit to indicate specialized school possibilities plus tv usage. Film races around the country with interspersed scenes of native ceremonies, of Mexico City, Acapulco and bullfights.

One strange section shows a group of Indios who had destroyed their Spanish missionaries long ago, but keep up an adapted version of the Christ story. The destruction of Indian ways by the Conquistadores and the North America impact add an interesting footnote to this surface look at the country. Lensing is good but editing needs more pacing. *Mosk.*

Games
(TECHNISCOPE-COLOR)

Okay low-key suspense drama of murder and double-cross. Simone Signoret prime lure for class audiences. Uneven b.o. prospects in specialty situations.

Hollywood, Sept. 13.
Universal release of a George Edwards production. Stars Simone Signoret, James Caan, Katharine Ross. Directed by Curtis Harrington. Screenplay, Gene Kearney, based on a story by Harrington, Edwards; camera (Technicolor), William A. Fraker; editor, Douglas Stewart; music, Samuel Matlovsky; asst. director, Hal Polaire. Reviewed at Universal Studios, L.A., Sept. 12, '67. Running Time, 100 MINS.

Lisa	Simone Signoret
Paul	James Caan
Jennifer	Katharine Ross
Norman	Don Stroud
Harry	Kent Smith
Miss Beattie	Estelle Winwood
Nora	Marjorie Bennett
Dr. Edwards	Ian Wolfe
Winthrop	Antony Eustrel
Celia	Eloise Hardt
Terry	George Furth
Holly	Carmen Phillips
Count	Peter Brocco
Baroness	Florence Marly
Arthur	Carl Guttenberger
Pharmacist	Pitt Herbert
Detective	Stuart Nisbet
Bookseller	Kendrick Huxham
Masseur	Richard Guizon

"Games" is a low-key suspenser with more appeal to the intellect than to the emotions. Simone Signoret stars in the first major-studio effort by ex-indie filmmakers, producer George Edwards and director Curtis Harrington. Colorful production values add a visual hypo to the apparently deliberate underplaying of a fairish script, leisurely directed. Despite lack of strong marquee power, the Universal release will have general playoff prospects in direct proportion to want-to-see generated in initial exclusive runs, where overall good, if spotty, b.o. may be expected.

The Harrington-Edwards story, with screenplay by Gene Kearney, concerns a modern couple, played by James Caan and Katharine Ross (both above title, also), who supposedly live in a hedonistic atmosphere. Miss Signoret, an immigrant reduced to peddling door-to-door cosmetics, becomes a house guest. A series of practical jokes leads to the murder of Don Stroud (Universal contractee moved to pix from tv work), and Miss Ross eventually loses her mind. Caan and Miss Signoret are revealed as secret plotters to this end, and a double-cross occurs at fadeout.

Harrington's evident attempt was to create a quiet terror, long on slow-building suspense and short on blatant shock values; the attempt was admirable, the achievement less so. For in the process, audiences, whose adrenalin flows on but a few occasions, have too much time to think.

And too much thinking can spoil "Games." Miss Ross, for example, is too sympathetic to be materialistic wife, and yet takes in a stranger at the door. Caan's dialog and emoting in the first half hour do not establish even his superficial image. Miss Signoret's entrance is too forced. Her subsequent interaction is somewhat inconsistent: she caroms between

a former lady of elegance to a sleazy housefrau (usually with cigaret but without ash tray), with recurring diversions into astrology and mysticism.

Although Miss Signoret and Caan are apparently at odds, and their secret plot adequately concealed, some sort of plot against Miss Ross emerges by default. Is it a supernatural agency? Hardly, for Miss Signoret's carny-like evocations of the unknown are unbelievable. Are human beings at work? Of course, for, with the two heavies physically separated from Miss Ross, yet with tangible evidence that someone is prowling around, who's left? Stroud. That growing suspicion, plus title, telegraphs something.

First climax, played in near silence, finds Miss Ross deranged at the frame-up; second climax loses impact as soon as Miss Signoret serves the drinks. An effective suspenser can, indeed, be a total fraud put over by razzle-dazzle which becomes obvious in hindsight. But when the story begins to fall apart in the telling, less impressive results obtain.

Despite script, three stars are competent, also featured players Stroud, family lawyer Kent Smith, dizzy neighbor Estelle Winwood, medic Ian Wolfe and rest of cast. Harrington's direction is professional, at times routine, often interesting in visual transitions. Visual consultant Morton Haack and art directors Alexander Golitzen-William D. DeCinces went all-out in the far-out interior trappings of the house, caught in Techniscope and Technicolor by William A. Fraker's sluggish camera.

Samuel Matlovsky's score, conducted by Joseph Gershenson, adds a good, spare note of impending trouble, and long periods of silence sometimes are effective. Douglas Stewart edited to a tepid 100 minutes, and other credits are pro. *Murf.*

It
(BRITISH-COLOR)

Roddy McDowall gets himself a Golem, a statue which does his bidding, and he has a wild time of it. Well-photographed suspense story should do well in general runs.

Hollywood, Sept. 12.
Warner Bros.-Seven Arts release of Gold Star Production. Written, produced and directed by Herbert J. Leder. Camera (Technicolor), Davis Boulton; editor, Tom Simpson; asst. director, Bill Snaith; music, Carlo Martelli. Reviewed at Warner Bros.-Seven Arts Studios, Sept. 12, '67. Running Time, 98 MINS.

Arthur Pimm	Roddy McDowall
Ellen Grove	Jill Haworth
Jim Perkins	Paul Maxwell
Professor Weal	Aubrey Richards
Harold Grove	Ernest Clark
Trimingham	Oliver Johnston
Inspector White	Noel Trevarthen
Wayne	Ian McCulloch

Also: Richard Goolden, Dorothy Frere, Tom Chatto, Steve Kirby, Russell Napier, Frank Sieman, Brian Haines, Mark Burns, Raymond Adamson, Lindsay Campbell, John Baker, Alan Sellers.

Production values on this color suspense thriller are excellent and Roddy McDowall has a grand time going mad after he discovers the secret of how to bring an indestructable stone statue to life. Story is "believable" and logically developed. Pic will be released as top-half of bill with "Frozen Dead," which was also written, produced and directed by Herbert J. Leder in Britain, and should have a good run in multiple house releases and neighborhood theatres.

Plot is based on the legend of a lost ancient Hebrew statue said to come alive when a gold scroll is placed in its mouth. The statue, being shipped to a London museum, is the only object left undestroyed when a warehouse burns.

Three persons mysteriously die when in the presence of the statue. Museum curator Roddy McDowall, who in "Psycho" or Faulkner fashion lives with the decomposed remains of his mother, learns through the Jewish inscriptions, the location of the scroll and sets about to use the Golem for destructive ends, including murder and wrecking a London bridge.

Curator does this with the hope of impressing his girlfriend, Jill Haworth, but she has eyes for an American, Paul Maxwell, who has arrived to inspect the authenticity of the statue for an American museum interested in purchasing it.

McDowall, with his sense of power mounting, becomes increasingly deranged and he manages to make the role seem plausible. Near the end he abducts Miss Haworth and with the Golem and his mother's coffin in the back of a hearse takes them to a country hideaway. The army moves in, attempts to bombard the statue, finally resolves to attack it with a small nuclear bomb.

Pic has the advantage of authentic museum settings and crisp camerawork by Davis Boulton. Tom Simpson's editing is also an asset, and the Carlo Martelli music, which evolves from a heartbeat tempo, adds to the overall suspense.

Cast disports itself with fixed solemnity, and the English actors have a way of making even the most trivial line seem important. Miss Haworth is very clever at not showing any emotion, while Maxwell supplies a scholarly concern throughout.

There are some unintended funny lines, but for the most part producer-director Leder has kept the proceedings under stiff-lip control. *Dool.*

Matchless
(ITALO-COLOR)

Above-average lower-half fare that may merit some top-half bookings.

United Artists release of Dino De Laurentiis (Ermanno Donati and Luigi Carpentieri) production. Features Patrick O'Neal, Ira Furstenberg, Donald Pleasence, Henry Silva, Nicoletta Machiavelli, Howard St. John, Sorrell Booke. Directed by Alberto Lattuada. Screenplay, Dean Craig, Jack Pulman, Luigi Malerba, Alberto Lattuada; camera (Deluxe), Sandro D'Eva; editor, Franco Fraticelli; music, Ennio Moricone and Gino Marinuzzi Jr.; asst. director, Antonio Brandt. Reviewed at United Artists homeoffice, N.Y., Sept. 18, '67. Running Time, **104 MINS.**

Perry "Matchless" Liston .... Patrick O'Neal
Arabella .... Ira Furstenberg
Andreneanu .... Donald Pleasence
Hank Norris .... Henry Silva
Tipsy .... Nicoletta Machiavelli
General Shapiro .... Howard St. John
Colonel Coolpepper .... Sorrell Booke
Hogdon .... Tiziano Cortini
Hypnotizer .... Valeri Inkijinov
O-Chin .... Andy Ho
O-Lan .... Elizabeth Wu
Li-Huang .... M. Mishiku
O'Chin's doctor .... Jacques Herlin

If audiences are not yet satiated with spy spoofs, United Artists' "Matchless" may get an appreciative reception from the action market. The Dino De Laurentiis production has a kinky sense of humor that staves off a feeling of deja vu until the final reels, when pic's straight-faced pitch for suspense casts a pall over the entire film. Its lack of names may consign the film to bottom-half bookings, but it could prove more popular than many upper-case pix it supports.

The original screenplay concerns a New York journalist mistaken for a spy by the Red Chinese. While imprisoned between torture sessions, he is given a ring by an ancient prisoner that, when rubbed, renders him invisible for a short period of time. He escapes a Chinese firing squad only to land, via a voluptuous Oriental double agent, in the equally disreputable arms of the American military. He agrees (for reasons never made clear) to assist the U.S. intelligence forces in recovering a formula and samples of a chemical substance (exact powers never revealed) in the possession of a sinister gangster (nationality never stated).

Fortunately the film doesn't take itself too seriously and makes some clever gibes at the expense of military and intelligence powers of all nationalities. It is well paced by director Alberto Lattuada (best known in this country for "Anna," "Mafioso" and "Mandragola"), and the gags lightly season rather than suffocate the generally absurd action.

Uneven acting and technical credits hamper the film's chances of rising above programmer status. Patrick O'Neal, a fine character actor, is not sufficiently suave to enter the 007 sweepstakes. As for the long-publicized screen debut of Princess Ira Furstenberg, she has sexpot potential if she can learn to move less awkwardly, but assessment of her vocal talents must be deferred. (Although the film was presumably shot in English, her dialog has clearly been dubbed.) Donald Pleasence, fresh from "You Only Live Twice," **makes a charmingly comic villain, and Howard St. John and Sorrell Booke register adequately as two Army officers. The usually reliable Henry Silva overplays an American traitor to embarrassing results.**

Despite evident skillful lensing by Sandro D'Eva in various New York and European locations, color quality is generally grainy and unattractive. (While the credits distributed by UA cite Color by Technicolor, the print viewed contains a credit for Color by Deluxe. European prints for "Matchless," like many other UA pix, were probably processed by the former lab, while U.S. prints were handled by Deluxe.) Other technical credits are okay, although Forquet's costumes for Miss Fursteriberg border on the grotesque. *Beau.*

The Tiger Makes Out
(COLOR)

Uneven blowup of Murray Schisgal's one-acter, "The Tiger." Spotty b.o.

Hollywood, Sept. 19.

Columbia Pictures release of George Justin production. Stars Eli Wallach, Anne Jackson. Directed by Arthur Hiller. Screenplay, Murray Schisgal, based on his play, "The Tiger"; camera (Pathecolor), Arthur J. Ornitz; editor, Robert C. Jones; music, Milton (Shorty) Rogers; song, Rogers, Diane Hilderbrand; production design, Paul Sylbert; asst. director, Burtt Harris. Reviewed at Directors Guild of America, L.A., Aug. 17, '67. Running Time, **94 MINS.**

Ben .... Eli Wallach
Gloria .... Anne Jackson
Jerry .... Bob Dishy
Leo .... John Harkins
Mrs. Kelly .... Ruth White
Mr. Kelly .... Roland Wood
Beverly .... Rae Allen
Miss Lane .... Sudie Bond
Mr. Ratner .... David Burns
Pawnbroker .... Jack Fletcher
Mrs. Ratner .... Bibi Osterwald
Registrar .... Charles Nelson Reilly
Lady on Bus .... Frances Sternhagen
Receptionist .... Elizabeth Wilson
Toni Songbird .... Kim August
Neighbor .... Alice Beardsley
Rosi .... Mariclare Costello
Housing Clerk .... David Doyle
Hap .... Dustin Hoffman
Waitress .... Michele Kesten
Pete Copolla .... James Luisi
Housing Guard .... Remak Ramsey
Red Schwartzkopf .... Sherman Raskin
Toni's Escort .... John Ryan
Old Man .... Edgar Stehli
Policeman .... Oren Stevens

Beware of the one-act play with apparent screen possibilities. "The Tiger Makes Out" has been adapted by Murray Schisgal from his 1963 two-character comedy-drama, "The Tiger," into a distended, uneven pic. Filmed in New York, the George Justin production stars Eli Wallach and Anne Jackson, encoring their legit roles. Good performances, production and yeoman directorial effort by Arthur Hiller buoy up interest. In certain specialty situations (near-campus theatres, urban arties, etc.), b.o. prospects are okay.

There is a bit of the tiger in all of us—a restless spirit, striking out against the real or imagined injustices of life. Such an attitude, within bounds, has an efficacious tension-relieving effect; unchecked, it can lead to mighty bizarre behavior. Schisgal, in expanding his play, has simply added a string of vignettes (many good) which, in time, pall because the plot has barely moved.

The play concerned the (offstage) kidnapping of Miss Jackson, a suburban housefrau, by fraustrated mailman Wallach, after which some genuinely tender dialog brings together the two spirits, and, at curtain, future meetings are assured. The kidnapping itself is not detailed; on film, however, it is, and, while necessary, the act itself is not a laugh-getter. Also, the fadeout has far less heart-warming implications than the legit curtain.

Withal, Wallach is excellent as he rages against a slew of modern situations, and interacts with a variety of neatly-cast cameo performers: Ruth White and Roland Wood, the landlord couple who become his spiritual parents at fadeout; bureaucrats Sudie Bond and David Doyle; neighbors David Burns and Bibi Osterwald, also Alice Beardsley; pawnbroker Jack Fletcher; Frances Sternhagen, the lady on a bus owes her bosom to air, not to silicones.

Other scenes with Wallach also involve Kim August, the femme impersonator who finds a boyfriend in John Ryan; beatnik lovers Mariclare Costello and Dustin Hoffman; cops Oren Stevens and Remak Ramsey; casual acquaintance James Luisi; Sherman Raskin, a property owner; and elderly Edgar Stehli, who figures in a standout scene about urban government bureaucracy.

Miss Jackson, whose rich voice and expressions hold attention throughout, has a problem in hubby, Bob Dishy, who with neighbor John Harkins engage in a running discussion about wife and family swapping. Her pal is played by Rae Allen, who gives strong comedy effects to the role of a man-crazed divorcee in the best Geraldine Page style. Receptionist Elizabeth Wilson and school registrar Charles Nelson Reilly highlight Miss Jackson's academic pursuits.

Hiller's direction heightens the impact of the many cameos, and the perceptive lensing by Arthur J. Ornitz elicits character in desired economy. The Pathecolor hues are generally consistent. Production designer Paul Sylbert had a field day in depicting the material claptrap which clutters our lives. Milton (Shorty) Rogers' score adds a strong contemporary feel. Robert C. Jones trimmed to a fair 94 minutes.

Given the talent involved, it is regrettable that, instead of expanding the play from its kernel, Schisgal's screenplay in essence tacks on a long preceding act, and an artificial quickie closing bit. *Murf.*

The Frozen Dead
(BRITISH)

A cold and calculated study of a German doctor attempting to thaw Nazi soldiers who were frozen alive, pic is a neatly-made low-budget meller of questionable taste.

Hollywood, Sept. 12.

Warner Bros.-Seven Arts release of Gold Star production. Written, produced and directed by Herbert J. Leder. Features Dana Andrews, Anna Palk, Philip Gilbert, Karel Stepanek, Basil Henson, Alan Tilvern, Ann Tirard, Edward Fox, Oliver MacGreevy, Tom Chatto, John Morre, Charles Wade. Camera, Davis Boulton; editor, Tom Simpson; asst. director, Doug Hermes; music, Don Banks. Reviewed at Warner Bros.-Seven Arts Studios, Sept. 12, '67. Running Time, **95 MINS.**

Dr. Norberg .... Dana Andrews
Jean Norberg .... Anna Palk
Dr. Roberts .... Philip Gilbert
Elsa Tenney .... Kathleen Breck
Lubeck .... Karel Stepanek
Tirpitz .... Basil Henson
Essen .... Alan Tilvern
Also: Ann Tirard, Edward Fox, Olver MacGreevy, Tom Chatto, John Moore, Charles Wade.

This low-budgeted, English-made production is a skillfully contrived, clinically ghoulish pic that should keep the young set riveted to their seats. Plot maintains suspense and shock impact pounces off the screen in a regular and re-

volting manner. Faint-hearted parents should be advised to stay comfortably at home watching tv.

Title refers to 12 top Nazi officers who were frozen alive 20 years ago and are being brought back one by one,—but in a cretin state — by German doctor Dana Andrews. There are 15,000 other frozen Nazi dead and intention is to bring them back and resurrect the Hitler regime.

The doctor determines to find a living brain to study and an associate abducts a girlfriend of the doctor's niece and they sever her head from her body and keeping it alive, through scientific apparati, place it in a lab box. An American scientist assists in studying the head, which focuses its eyes with venom at the two. The niece all the while doesn't believe, as she has been told, that her friend has simply decided to leave the house of her uncle.

Remainder of pic involves the severed head's attempting to transmute to the doctor's niece the fact that she has been mutilated and that the doctor's niece is in danger of death because she has become suspicious of what is really going on.

The senses cringe at the realism of the presentation and it can only be wondered if this morose subject can be considered entertaining. In the end the head cries, "Bury me. Bury me." Hopefully this will not be the boxoffice response to this project of producer, writer, director Herbert J. Leder.

Andrews' talents lend a special credence to this ugly presentation and Anna Palk's passive appeal as the niece, encourages continuing curiosity in regard to what ability she will have to accept the outcome of her friend.

The film works hard at being amoral and because it succeeds in this to an extraordinary degree one can only wonder at one's own moral viewpoint.

The dark photography of Davis Boulton shrouds the murky tale in a low key manner and the music by Don Banks underscores the activities of the inhuman machinations with devious success. Technically other credits are good.
Dool.

Venice Films

Jutro
(Morning)
(YUGOSLAVIAN)
Venice, Sept. 14.
Jukoslavija Film release of Dunav Film production. With Milena Dravic, Ljubisa Samardzic, Mija Aleksic, Neda Arneric. Written and directed by Purisa Dordevic. Camera, Mika Popovic; editor, R. Risim. At Venice Film Fest. Running time, 80 MINS.

Mila	Ljubisa Samardzic
Janja	Milena Dravic
Alessandra	Neda Arneric
General	Ljuba Tadic
Captain	Mija Aleksic

Director Purisa Dordevic has been building a human comedy with a war background in his pix. In "The Girl" and "The Dream" he mixed past, present and future to draw a complex but pacifistic look at war. Here he goes a step

further and again has war as background to a firmer understanding of his characters marked by it and tempered by it.

Film is personal and mixes farce, tragedy and comedy. It has its private aspects which may not always be clear to foreign audiences. This makes it a specialized item for offshore usage. The players walk through their war experiences and can suddenly take part in a little bittersweet charade to make a point. Then it goes off on a controversial Pete Seeger song course, and peace and rebuilding begin to make their demands.

Splintered and episodic, this still has a coherence in the directorial use of war as a sort of symbol of human distress and experience. It is well shot and acted with ease by a well-honed cast. The director seems to have had his say on war in his triology of pix. No denying the control, visual finesse and originality in this film.
Mosk.

The Stranger
(Il Straniere)
(ITALO—FRENCH—COLOR)
Venice, Sept. 6.
A Dino De Laurentiis Italo-French co-production from Master Film (Rome), Marianne Productions (Paris) and Casbah Film (Algiers) for Paramount release world-wide, less Italy. Starring Marco Mastroianni and Anna Karina; featuring George Wilson, Bernard Blier, Pierre Bertin, Jacques Herlin, Bruno Cremer and Algred Adam. Director: Luchino Visconti; screenplay by Suso Cecchi D'Amico, Luchino Visconti, Georges Cochon and Emmanuel Robles based on the novel by Albert Camus. Photography: Giuseppe Rotunno; music: Piero Piccioni; art director: Mario Garbuglia. World premiere, Venice Festival Palace. Running time, 104 MINS.

Arthur Meursault	Marcello Mastroianni
Marie Cardona	Anna Karina
Judge	George Wilson
Defense Attorney	Bernard Blier
Raymond	George Geret
Priest	Bruno Cremer
Trial Judge	Pierre Bertin

Fully aware of the pitfalls in attempting to bring the novel of Nobel Prize winner Albert Camus, "The Stranger," to the screen, the author's widow, after long hesitation, finally agreed to make rights available to producer Dino LeLaurentiis with the proviso that Luchino Visconti direct. Final result, despite Visconti's labor of love and Marcello Mastroianni's performance, falls short of expectations.

A stylist of recognized virtuosity, Visconti hewed too close to the print word instead of creating an interpretive mood that would both express the anguish of the novel's basic philosophy and capture the story of man's indifference to the absurdity of his daily lot and incommunicability with his fellow man. Film director's literal transposition often labors surface details and fails to record the inner resonance of Camus' titular hero. It builds slowly to unload its charges mistakenly on an ironic miscarriage of justice and one man's disbelief in God.

Side-tracked in doing the screen version with the distinction Camus' book still enjoys in the world of contemporary letters as an origin of the individual's detachment from existential folly, Visconti has given Paramount a well-made commercial film in which Mastroianni, Anna Karina and a number of fine character actors often break through with telling effect.

Story essentially belongs to the title star. Mastroianni, a pied noir in Algeria during the late '30s, buries his mother and makes love to his mistress with equal detachment that barely situates him but leaves him unencumbered of the day-to-day habits, tastes, prejudices and passions surrounding him. He begins to evaluate his role in the universe when brought to trial for the cold-blooded murder of an Arab boy—a murder he cannot motivate except to blame it on the sun at high noon. He takes stock during the trial. A roster of witnesses and courtroom reactions demonstrate that the Arab's death is in itself insignificant compared to the defendant's crimes of sending his mother to a home for the aged, tearlessly attending her burial, indulging his sex drive right after the funeral, associating with a procurer and generally comporting himself as a social misfit—a stranger.

Condemned to die on the guillotine, Mastroianni as Arthur Meursault builds a judical blunder into a dim appraisal of existence itself and in a dramatic debate with the prison chaplain, denies God and after life as solutions for terrestial emptiness and absurdity.

A running offstage commentary reflecting Meursault's thoughts are straight from the novel. But other aspects are missing. Famous for his scrupulous reproduction of time and place, Visconti does not quite achieve the climate and detailed background of pre-WW II Algiers. French-Arab juxtaposition is omitted. Period dress is not consistent.

Intensity of color and light are variable and tints do not come up to Visconti standards. Shining eboy of Meursault's prison walls distract and irritate. Music is not inspired.

It all comes back to conception rather than talent. The artistic striving of Visconti is readily evident, but in conceiving "The Stranger" as a limpid translation of the book, he restricted his own imaginative resources and ended up with an above-average motion picture instead of the distinctive film he so ardently desired to make.
Werb.

China Is Near
(La Cina E Vicina)
(ITALAN—Black & White)
Venice, Sept. 1.
A Vides film produced by Franco Cristaldi for Columbia release. Cast: Glauco Mauri, Elda Tattoli, Paolo Graziosi, Daniela Surina and Pierluigi Apra. Directed by Marco Bellocchio from his own screen subject. Script by Marco Bellocchio and Elda Tattoli. Photography, Donino Delli Colli, art director, Elda Tattoli; music, Ennio Morricone. Shown at Venice festival palace. Running time, 110 MINS.

Vittorio	Glauco Mauri
Elena	Elda Tattoli
Carlo	Paolo Graziosi
Giovanna	Daniela Surina
Camillo	Pierluigi Apra

Marco Bellocchio stirred wide interest recently at Venice with his out-of-contest screening of "Fists in His Pocket." In contest this year, as a favorite in competition with Luis Bunuel, Jean Luc Godard and Pier Paolo Pasolini, his "China Is Near" unqualifiably confirms the promise revealed in his debut effort. At 27, it's a heady start.

To reach the bitter conclusion that humanity is practically a dead loss guided only by the craving for wealth or power, Bellocchio inflates a provincial microcosm with a generous dose of raw sex, character comedy and needling satire to come up with thought-provoking entertainment that should clean up in Italy, please moviegoers in Europe and find a profitable art house nest in America.

Timeliness of theme is a helpful factor in this regard. Author and director reserve an opportune spot for a group of wild-eyed pro-Maoists as a device to stress the barren political climate and decimate the governing powers that be. Bellocchio was nurtured among the left fielders for whom he reserves most of his pellets. But the parallel between Maoism in Peking and hinterland red guard hysterics lifts the film beyond boot country barriers and gives it an international, if not universal, theme.

In the small town swamp of opportunism, landed gentleman and professor Vittorio (Glauco Mauri) wants first to ride into municipal power on the Socialist ticket and then bed down his secretary (Daniela Surina). Sister Elena (Elda Tattoli) rules the patrimony with an iron hand and wide-open boudoir. Young brother Camillo is a red guard seminarist whose opposition violence and sexual mayhem at night help sustain his daytime bible studies.

Young socialist leader Carlo (Paolo Graziosi) yields his own politicial goals to become Vittorio's campaign manager to get at his candidate's sister and her family fortune. Whereupon the Secretary (Carlo's mistress) heads for her patron's bed chamber as an almost welcome relief from love-making on party hall benches. Big brother and sister are birth-trapped by their lower-class lovers (Carlo actually fertilizes both femmes) and even accommodate to the new family ties forced upon them.

In achieving this sardonic picture of sub-human relations and political debauchery, Bellocchio authentically sets the film a la Germi in the Italian provinces. With a sure, well-paced film author touch, he balances comedy and emotional conflict without letting his theme and story falter for a moment.

Franco Cristaldi's brilliant mounting belies Bellocchio's modest budget. Tonino Delli Colli lensing is brilliant. Glauco Mauri and Elda Tattoli give full-depth performances and lick the suspicion of caricature. Others come through strongly as well.

It is a hopeful sign for the film industry when at least one capable film author turns to pix that not only carry their weight in ideas and intent but can also be marketed commercially. As such, pic is also a credit to Franco Cristaldi and Columbia.
Werb.

Egy Szerelem Harom Ejszakaja
(Three Nights of Love)
(HUNGARIAN COLOR-SONGS)
Venice, Sept. 8.
Hungarofilm release of Mafilm Studio I production. With Benedek Toth, Vera Vemczel, Imre Simkovits, Zoltan Latinovits, Ivan Darvas, Philippe Fourquet. Di-

rected by Gyorgy Revesz. Screenplay,
Miklos Hubay from stage musical by
Hubay, Vas and Ranki; camera (East-
mancolor), Tamas Somlo; music, Gyorgy
Ranki. At Venice Film Fest. Running
time, **100 MINS.**

Poet .... Beeαek Toth
Julia .... Vera Venczel
First Magi .... Imre Simkovits
Second Magi .... Zoltan Latinovits
Third Magi .... Ivan Darvas
Gilbert .... Philippe Fourquet

Film is a muted musical because
using some songs in a sad tale of
two lovers parted by war. It is
sentimental sans bathos. Pic does
manage to build a charm and grace
despite its story. Music is mainly
instrumental in underlining moods
with a few songs. Primarily this is
done by a trio who sort of comment on the story. Some ditties
have bite and flavor.

A young man is called up to his
regiment and has three nights of
love with his girl before he leaves.
But he deserts and goes back to
her only to have her disappear. It
turns out she had been a Communist agent and when hounded
by police he manages to bring off
a confrontation with her, and
denies that he knows her.

Film is told via flashbacks. At
times, there is a poetic finesse to
the pic but it just does not quite
bring off the blending of the music,
story and atmosphere completely.
Result is a slow-moving first part
which then is bolstered up by a
growing tension, mood and dramatic pitch.

This is an interesting offbeat
musical attempt but appears
limited to special situations only
abroad. It has fine lensing and
some good acting. Director Gyorgy
Revesz does give this a good pace
and ironic edge if the right blending of its elements is only intermittently successful. *Mosk.*

Les Patres Du Disordre
(Pastures of Disorder)
(FRENCH-GREEK)

Venice, Sept. 14.
Lenox Films production and release.
Written and directed by Nico Papatakis
with non-pro actors. Camera, Jean Boffety, Christian Guillouet; music, Pierre
Barbet. At Venice Film Fest. Running
time, **125 MINS.**

Nico Papatakis is of Greek
origin but has lived in Paris for
more than 25 years. He owned the
famed Rose Rouge nitery in the
early Existentialist days, backed
some pix, notably the Yank indie
"Shadows," and then made his
first feature pic in France "Les
Abysses" (The Depths). Now he
has made a film in Greece — a
baroque tale of rustic doings that
purports to be a sort of symbolical
look at the country.

It is a strange, overblown tale
about a young shepherd who wants
to emigrate to Australia. Involved
are the problems of illiteracy,
hysterical class hierarchy, poverty
and superstition that seem to
haunt the provincial populace. The
shepherd is falsely accused of robbery and becomes the object of a
manhunt, thus releasing the re-
pressions of a number of characters.

The daughter of the rich farmer,
betrothed to another, tries to help
the shepherd but it turns out to
be from pride and then revealed as
a hidden desire for him.

They run off and finally are
hunted down by the whole pop-

ulace. Made just before the recent
military takeover, and finished
about then, the pic brings in references to the revolt. It is filled with
fine contrasty tones. The acting
has the right ring of larger-than-
life figures of mock tragedy.

Papatakis has mixed the baroque, grotesque and symbolic.
However, the first part takes a bit
too much time in setting up the
characters, story and theme. Too
many scenes do not quite seem to
have a point until the manhunt
gets this into the right high-
pitched and tragi-comic mood that
was probably sought.

There's no denying that Papatakis has something to say, tackles
offbeat themes and has a filmic
strength and dash. He only needs
a bit more coherence in style. Pic
may be of interest for language
spots abroad on its allusions and
insights into the Greek dilemma,
with some specialized usage indicated. Some careful pruning
would help this uneven but
notable film. *Mosk.*

Far From the Madding Crowd
(BRITISH-COLOR)

**Good b.o. potential in story,
production and names, though
slightly ponderous in execution; needs vigorous assist in
sales department to stress actual and implied values.**

London, Sept. 26.
Metro-Goldwyn-Mayer release of a Joseph Janni production. Stars Julie Christie, Terence Stamp, Peter Finch, Alan
Bates; features Prunella Ransome, Fiona
Walker. Directed by John Schlesinger.
Screenplay by Frederick Raphael from
novel by Thomas Hardy; camera (Metrocolor), Nick Roeg; music, Richard Rodney Bennett; editor, Malcolm Cooke.
Previewed at Odeon, Marble Arch, London. Running Time, **169 MINS.**

Bathsheba Everdene .... Julie Christie
Sgt. Troy .... Terence Stamp
Boldwood .... Peter Finch
Gabriel Oak .... Alan Bates
Fanny Robin .... Prunella Ransome
Liddy .... Fiona Walker
Henery Fray .... Paul Dawkins
Andrew Randle ...... Andrew Robertson
Joseph Poorgrass .... John Barratt
Jan Coggan .... Julian Somers
Mrs. Tall .... Pauline Melville
Mark Clarke .... Vincent Harding
Laban Tall .... Lawrence Carter
Maryann Money .... Margaret Lacey
Temperence .... Harriet Harper
Soberness .... Denise Coffey
Matthew Moon .... Brian Rawlinson
Cainy Hall .... Freddy Jones
Pennyways .... John Garrie
Mrs. Coggan .... Marie Hopps
Bold Smallbury .... Owen Berry
Laborer .... Michael Beint

Metro has a lush, lavishly outfitted effort going for it in this
latter-day version of the Thomas
Hardy tome. It reeks with atmosphere and has milked the utmost
from an obviously and visibly
open-pursed location production
budget which allows it to roam
splendidly throughout the "Hardy
country" in Britain's Southwest
and thus capture its richness and
flavor frame by frame. And as capable a cast as could be imagined
has been recruited to give body
and substance to the vintage tale.

Yet despite these over and
under-the-line attributes, plenty of
sales effort will have to be expended, and certain slightly over-indulgent passages crisped and tensed
up, if the waiting public is to be
expected to come through with the
kind of cash outlay which is expected of this pic — and which,
in many ways, it deserves.

Literary classics or semi-classics
traditionally provide pitfalls in
adaptation, and "faithfulness" can
often prove a double-edged sword,
especially in adaptation to a new
medium. In this case, scripter Frederick Raphael has perhaps hewn
too closely to the original. Thus
he has allowed director John
Schlesinger only occasional—and
principally mechanical — chances
to forge his own film. In outline,
and unfortunately also (with few
exceptions) on the screen, the
Hardy tale is populated with basically cliche characters acting out
an almost inevitably predictable
story.

Through years of palpable or
pulp fiction since this original
made its literary dent in 1874, the
story of Bathsheba Everdene's multifaceted love for the three men
in her life, Sergeant Troy, Gabriel
Oak and Boldwood, has been seen
so often and in so many different
guises that it now no longer shocks
of interests or surprises one. Troy
is the classic dashing handsome
heel in uniform; Boldwood the
rich, aging and dull landowner ob-

sessed with the only thing, or person, his money can't buy; and
Gabriel Oak is, from the first
frame or chapter on, the faithful,
patient, always-present winner by
default of the rather self-centered
heroine who thinks she's better
than the lot of them.

Burdened, rather than aided, by
such a hoary outline, Schlesinger
has done wonders in lightening
the pace, in diverting the eye, ear
and senses in general with some
of the most thrilling atmospheric
footage seen on the screen in some
time. His visual asides, in which for
example he perfectly captures a
mood by a rapid — or protected—
backdrop shot of a child making its
way across a sun-splattered field,
are among the picture's joyful moments of creation, though (or
because?) they are in part digressions from the main storyline.

Similarly, and ironically, the
sequence which most convinces
and strikes is one in which the
on-screen principals, Bathsheba
and Troy, meet by the sea, their
lines drowned out by the crashing surf. The director is also adroit
in keying moods by the first shot
of a given scene, working hand in
hand with editor Malcolm Cook
in acute choice of juxtaposition.

But these are mainly audio-
visual experiences. And though
the dramatics are in most capable
hands, and Julie Christie, Peter
Finch, Terence Stamp and Alan
Bates are variedly handsome and
have their many effective moments, there is little they can ultimately and lastingly do to overcome the basic banality of their
characters and, to a certain degree,
their lines. Miss Christie has few
real opportunities to branch out
of her rather muted and pouty
lead. Peter Finch struggles man-
fully against his role, but never
really defeats it by convincing one.
Stamp is the cocky, sneering Sergeant to the part born, but there's
nary a glint of anything more.
Nor does Alan Bates have more of
a chance as the ever-reliable Oak.

In fact, it's in some of the many
supporting parts that some true
subsurface warmth comes across,
notably in handsome and most
promising Prunella Ransome's film
debut portrayal of Fanny Robin,
Troy's ill-starred mistress, and in
Fiona Walker's warmly etched
Liddy. The literally dozens of
smaller cameos are also neatly
limned.

At least for the most discriminating viewer, therefore, the main
story line generally fails to convince, especially in the increasingly mellerish (and sometimes
frankly mawkish) later segments,
which also in their speeded-up
tempo lose any feeling gained at
the start.

Yet there's no gainsaying its
potential hold on the less sophisticated masses which could find
pic's scope, authenticity and possibly even its leading characters
just the thing for a rainy afternoon.

As noted, there should be nothing but praise for Nick Roeg's lensing, while other technical facets
in the Joseph Janni production are
all of the highest order, coming
across strongly in their contributions to the physical outfittings of
a film which, if it were blessed
as well with heart, could have been
a worldbeater rather than merely a big and important picture.
Hawk.

Who's Minding the Mint?
(COLOR)

Zany comedy with flock of topnotch comics; properly exploited, good grosses seen.

Hollywood, Sept. 22.
Columbia Pictures release of Norman Maurer production. Stars Jim Hutton, Dorothy Provine, Milton Berle, Joey Bishop, Bob Denver, Walter Brennan; features Victor Buono, Jack Gilford, Jamie Farr. Directed by Howard Morris. Screenplay, R. S. Allen, Harvey Bullock; camera (PatheColor), Joseph Biroc; music, Lalo Schifrin; editor, Adrienne Fazan; asst. director, Bud Grace. Reviewed at Academy Award Theatre, Sept. 21, '67. Running Time, 98 MINS.

Harry Lucas	Jim Hutton
Verna Baxter	Dorothy Provine
Luther Burton	Milton Berle
Ralph Randazzo	Joey Bishop
Willie Owens	Bob Denver
Pop Gillis	Walter Brennan
Captain	Victor Buono
Avery Dugan	Jack Gilford
Mario	Jamie Farr
Samson Link	David J. Stewart
Doris Miller	Corine Cole
Imogene Harris	Jackie Joseph
Maxwell	Bryan O'Byrne
Grayson	Robert Ball
Bertha	Dodo Denney
Jess	Luther James
Drunk	Mickey Deems
Man in Window	Lennie Bernian
Woman in Window	Cordy Clark
First Guard	Thom Carney
Second Guard	Khalil Bezaleel

"Who's Minding Mint?" is a nutty, imaginative, zany, laugh-provoking dish of fun that with specialized promotion should ring up happy grosses for producer Norman Maurer and Columbia Pictures. Film is in the novelty comedy class and should be treated as such. Word of mouth should help chances.

Maurer's years with the Three Stooges, during which he dreamed up story ideas and also produced and directed a couple of their fests, apparently gave him a taste for the insane which now pays off in a more legitimate outlet, although some of the same type of thinking still is apparent. He invades the U.S. Bureau of Engraving and Printing — the Mint — in Washington, to backdrop his tale of foolishness that revolves around a young Mint employee who accidentally destroys $50,000 in new bills—and phonies—rally around to help him.

Script by R. S. Allen and Harvey Bullock is long on inventive action, a gagman's holiday. When Jim Hutton, the Mint money checker, inadvertently takes home the 50 grand in a bag of fudge presented him by his girl friend, and sees it go down the garbage disposal, he calls upon Walter Brennan, a retired Mint employee who wants to get back in action. His plan is that they sneak into the Mint in dead of night and, with Brennan operating his beloved presses, run off 50,000 and replace the money. It's not stealing, Hutton argues, just replacing.

There's one hitch, the engraving plates, for which they'll need a safecracker to open the safe. This leads to a raft of other "assistants" in various occupations to finally get through the sewer and into the basement of the Mint. If the spectator doesn't indulge in logic and accepts merely what meets the eye — the fast unfoldment will be a rib-tickling treat.

Hutton scores as the would-be playboy who comes under his boss' suspicion when he lives like a millionaire through a raft of lux-

ury items — limousines, furniture, clothes — which he keeps on-approval for 60 days, then returns. His character, however, isn't entirely consistent, since without any particular reason he turns from the pinnacle of honesty to dishonesty when he decides to run off a million dollars in bills for himself, along with the million he has finally promised each of his aides, up from his original $2,000 offer.

Dotty portrayals are turned in by all these aides. Dorothy Provine, in love, plays a Mint money cutter whose services are needed to clip the sheets as they come off the press; Brennan insists upon taking along his pregnant beagle expecting any moment. Jack Gilford is the safecracker, best in the business but deaf, so they buy a hearing aid from Milton Berle, a pawnbroker, who sells them on his being their manager on the project. Joey Bishop is the sewer expert, always broke from playing the horses, who knows the sewer system; Victor Buono builds a boat needed to navigate the sewer; Bob Denver an ice cream truck operator who keeps a sexy brunette away from a window overlooking the manhole the party goes thru. Jamie Farr is Bishop's Italian cousin who doesn't speak a word of English, hired as lookout.

Howard Morris in his direction keeps his cast in order, despite their constant bunching together in many sequences, and comes thru with an expert job. There is little relief, at times, from laughs, but generally these are paced for best effect. One of the most novel points of the film is the opening credits, when names are flashed on Treasury bills of every denomination from $1 to $100,000.

Technical departments also are expertly handled, including Joseph Biroc's color photography; Lalo Schifrin's light music score; John Beckman's art direction; Adrienne Fazan's tight editing; Nelson Tyler's aerial camera work. Whit.

L'Homme Qui Valait Des Milliards
(Man Who Was Worth Millions)
(FRENCH-COLOR)

Paris, Sept. 26.
Gaumont release of France Cinema Production, CVM Produzione Cinematografica production. Stars Frederick Stafford, Raymond Pellegrin; features Peter Van Eyck, Anny Duperrey, Henri Czarniack, Jess Hahn. Directed by Michel Boisrond. Screenplay, Michel Lebrun, Annette Wademant, Boisrond; camera (Eastmancolor), Raymond Lemoigne; editor, Claudine Bouche. At Ermitage, Paris. Running Time, 90 MINS.

Jean	Frederic Stafford
Novak	Raymond Pellegrin
Muller	Peter Van Eyck
Girl	Anny Duperrey
Hank	Jess Hahn
Agent	Henri Czarniack

Jailbreak is mixed with a planted U.S. Treasury Dept. agent and a hunt for Nazi counterfeited dollars hidden since the war. Film is told a bit stolidly while the fights are a bit wanting in true punch. This appears mainly for lower case or tele use abroad via some colorful locale and fair if routine mounting and playing.

The agent breaks out with a man who knows the whereabouts of the

cache but oldtime Nazis intercede and the chase is on to end in Morocco where the phoney money is burned. The agent wins a girl, and all is over. Playing is fair, color good. This is a filler fare that lacks the ease adventurous dash to make it more than a routine adventure opus. Mosk.

Live for Life
(Vivre Pour Vivre)
(FRENCH-COLOR)

Yves Montand and Candice Bergen in new Lelouch film which may open well but falter on disappointing substance and photography.

Lopert (UA) release of Films Ariane, Vides Films, Artistes Associes production, produced by Alexandre Mnouchkine and George Danciger. Stars Yves Montand, Candice Bergen, Annie Girardot. Directed by Claude Lelouch. Screenplay, Lelouch, Pierre Uytterhoeven; camera (Eastmancolor), Lelouch, Patrice Pouget; editor, Claude Barrois; music, Francis Lai; song, Raymond Le Senechal, Pierre Barouh. Reviewed at United Artists homeoffice, N.Y., Sept. 21, '67. Running Time, 130 MINS.

Robert Colomb	Yves Montand
Candice	Candice Bergen
Catherine Colomb	Annie Girardot
Mireille	Irene Tunc
Maid	Uta Taeger
Jacqueline	Anouck Ferjac
Waiter	Jean Collomb
Photographer	Jacques Portet

Claude Lelouch's previous "A Man and a Woman" copped first prize at the Cannes Film Festival, won Oscars for best foreign-language film and original screenplay, and has thus far earned a phenomenal $3,000,000 in U.S. rentals. His new pic, "Live for Life," is very similar in subject matter and style but must rate a big disappointment. It lacks the lyric sweep and charm of its predecessor and even falters technically despite a sizable budget. While it should do well in initial dates here and in Europe on the strength of its director and cast, probable critical reception and word-of-mouth may hamper its staying power.

Why does "Life" fail where "M&W" succeeded? Part of the reason lies in the unappealing quality of two of the pic's three protagonists. The hero; a married man whose ritualized adulteries unexpectedly culminate in a serious love affair, is self-absorbed and emotionally sterile. The young American girl whom he loves is equally immature, much given to pouting and aimless tear-ridden sessions in which she berates him for not leaving his spouse. Since both of these characters lack depth or warmth and since their love for each other does not stem from clearly defined emotional needs, it is hard to see their romance as anything more than a rather shabby and silly extramarital dalliance.

Also responsible for the film's weakness are the performances of Yves Montand and Candice Bergen in these two roles. Montand's acting generally consists of who-cares shrugs, downturned mouth, eyebrows raised in a perpetual state of boredom, and tired line readings. Miss Bergen has seemingly been asked to improvise many of her scenes, but she lacks

the spontaneity and experienced self-confidence to carry such moments. In acting as well as writing, this romantic duo is a long way from the subtleties and complexities of the Aimee - Trintignant relationship in "M&W."

Much better is Annie Girardot in the hazily defined role of Montand's long-suffering wife. The best moment in the entire pic is the sustained close-up of her face when she learns of her husband's affair, a beautifully controlled and moving piece of acting. With little apparent help from Lelouch, Miss Girardot makes the wife an authentic human being for whom one genuinely cares. Unfortunately, this imbalance in audience sympathy makes the film resemble tv afternoon sudsers pitched to unloved housewives.

Lelouch selects colorful vocations for his heroes apparently to justify flamboyantly pictorial divertissements. This worked beautifully in "M&W," where the suspense of the racing scenes mirrored the inner tensions of the characters. In the current film the hero is a tv reporter whose job takes him to Africa, Vietnam, and other inflamed sections of the world. Trouble is that these side-trips don't connect to the narrative or develop the main theme but seem entirely gratuitous.

The inclusion of mini-documentaries of worldwide violence, French mercenaries' training in the Congo, and the Vietnam War within this syrupy context may strike some viewers as an offensively superficial deployment of serious world problems. Most debatable, insofar as taste is concerned, is a sequence near the film's end: Montand in a realistically bloody Vietnam battle, Miss Girardot watching tv, and Miss Bergen walking through wintry Central Park are crosscut to the accompaniment of a vapid love ballad.

This inventory of disappointments is nothing compared to the inferior pictorial quality of the film. The color lensing is below even minimal professional standards. Shots are often badly framed, with portions of bodies or heads awkwardly lopped off and with an abundance of "white spaces" on the screen. Depth-of-field focus is nonexistent: foreground and background figures alternately assume focal attention and the intended juxtaposition of two visual planes doesn't come off. Even relatively uncomplicated shots are fuzzy, while the use of a hand-held camera is often irritating and irrelevant.

Irrelevance, in fact, is the key word for Lelouch's many "cinematic" effects. One sequence, for example, consists of a single take from outside a hotel room, the camera shooting through the window. Although the distorting effect of the glass is "interesting," it serves no dramatic purpose. (Later in the film, the same gimmick is employed on a scene of almost contradictory tone and meaning.) Lelouch also cannot resist meaningless montages of rock 'n' roll sessions, boxing matches, animal hunts, and the like.

What little emotional impact "Live for Life" has derives from the vibrant musical score by Francis Lai. Many conversational scenes are played with music but without recorded dialog, perhaps a wise decision in view of the generally tepid dialog that is heard. Other sequences feature throbbing, almost melodramatic music supporting trivial daily actions and abundant tourist views of Paris, Kenya, Amsterdam, New York and the French Alps. After seeing the film, one feels more like buying the soundtrack album than reseeing the pic.

Just as there was a small minority that found "A Man and A Woman" maudlin and insincere, so "Live for Life" will undoubtedly have its ardent partisans. Still, most viewers are likely to rate the film a big letdown and become impatient with its 130 minutes of largely repetitive love scenes,flora and fauna inserts, and extraneous skimmings of world events. United Artists (and artie subsid, Lopert), which lost profitable U.S. returns on "M&W" to Allied Artists but acquired foreign rights, has "Life" for all markets. They may be one picture too late, in re probable U.S. boxoffice results.

Beau.

Hell On Wheels
(SONGS-COLOR)

Hodgepodge stock racing entry with Marty Robbins.

Hollywood, Sept. 20.
Crown-International release of Robert Patrick production. Stars Marty Robbins, John Ashley, Gigi Perreau; features Robert Dornan, Connie Smith, The Stonemans. Directed by Will Zens. Screenplay, Wesley Cox; camera (Technicolor), Leif Rise. Reviewed at Admiral Theatre, Sept. 20, '67. Running Time, 97 MINS.

Marty	Marty Robbins
Del	John Ashley
Sue	Gigi Perreau
Steve	Robert Dornan
Connie Smith	Herself
The Stonemans	Themselves
Moonshiners	Robert Faulk, Frank Gerstile

"Hell on Wheels," ostensibly a stock car racing picture, tries to incorporate too many divergent plot elements to emerge as anything more than a hodge-podge of picture-making. With Marty Robbins, the recording artist, as its star, footage veers from the race track to his singing five songs, to the Federal government cracking down on mountain stills, and mother love. For the younger market, however, packaged with "The Wild Rebels," film should meet with mild response.

Story line by Wesley Cox presents Robbins as a racing champ by day, a nitery entretainer at night. Conflict is built up between Robbins & his kid brother, John Ashley, a mechanic who built Robbins car to the powerhouse it is and is jealous of the admiration of the crowd accorded champ. Latter goes it alone in an attempt to beat his brother on the track, and inadvertently becomes mixed up in a moonshine ring.

Plenty of track thrills caught by Leif Rise's color cameras and Will Zens' direction spark the action occasionally, but the multitude of story facets usually retards pace. Robbins acquits himself in okay fashion, and scores particularly with his singing, which includes "No Tears Milady" and "Fly But-

terfly Fly." Music end is further bolstered by country singer Connie Smith and The Stonemans combo.

Ashley does well enough as the belligerent brother and Gigi Perreau is pretty as his girl-friend.

Whit.

The Chkid Republic
(RUSSIAN)

Paris, Sept. 19.
Sovexport release of Lenfilm production. With Sergei Yourski, Youla Bouryguina, Pavel Louspelaiev. Directed by Guennadi Poloka. Screenplay, Leonid Panteleiev, G. Bieleikh; camera, D.mitri Dolinine, Alexandre Chetchouline: music, Sergei Slominski. At Theatre Maringy, Paris. Running Time, 100 MINS.

Viksinor	Sergei Yourski
Elanlian	Youla Bouryguina
Kostalmel	Pavel Louspelaiev
Yankel	Lev Vaynstein
Goga	Viktor Perevalov
Tolia	Violetta Ioukhimovitch
Tizgane	Anatoli Podchivalov
Mamotuchka	Sacha Kavalerov

This pic at first bows as a refreshing takeoff on the usually serious, dramatic and edifying pix on World War One and Russo revolutionary orphans who roamed the countryside and their rehabilitation in special schools. But it soon falls into sentimentality and patronage. However, its early verve and good nature could give this a few specialized chances in the U.S. if the rather mawkish ending could be pruned down.

It is 1920, the Revolution is over, and the Soviet state is just being built as an upper-class man takes over one of the institutions for thieving orphans. The usual stereotyped but fairly colorful crew first rebels but finally they are tamed by the knowing teacher, to become good young Communists.

Early spoofing of slogans and comedic bits on the war between authority and the youths have freewheeling wit. But this soon falls into rote and repetition. Pic does show a beginning of tongue-in-cheek attitudes toward old Russo filmic warhorses. It is well shot and acted.

Mosk.

The Wild Rebels
(SONGS-COLOR)

Minor entry for Hells Angels market but should click with trade.

Hollywood, Sept. 20.
Crown-International release of Comet production. Stars Steve Alaimo; features Willie Pastrano, John Vella, Bobbie Byers, Jeff Gillen. Directed and written by William Grefe. Camera (Technicolor), Clifford H. Poland Jr., Harry Walsh; music, Al Jacobs; editors, Julio C. Chevez, Robert Woodburn; asst. director, Ronald Walsh. Reviewed at Admiral Theatre, Sept. 20, '67. Running Time, 90 MINS.

Rod	Steve Alaimo
Banjo	Willie Pastrano
Jeeter	John Vella
Linda	Bobbie Byers
Fats	Jeff Gillen
Lt. Dorn	Walter R. Philbin
Detective	Robert Freund
Walt Simpson	Seymour A. Eisenfeld
First Man	Phil Longo
Bartender	Milton Smith
1st College Boy	Kurt Nagler
2d College Boy	Steve Cellar
3d College Boy	Gary Brady
Nori	Nora Alonzo
The Band	The Birdwatchers
Driver	Dutch Holland
Gunshop Owner	Art Barker
Bank Teller	William P. Kelley
Bank Guard	Cosmo Lloyd
1st Sheriff	Tom Frysinger
2d Sheriff	Emil Dealon
Policeman	Jamie Hickson
Policeman	Aaron Deaton

Policeman	Nick Bontempo
Policeman	Edward Wanisko
Policeman	Dennis French
Policeman	Bob Sparks

Comes still another entry based on the leather jacket set which should find acceptance in the same market that made "Wild Angels," "Hell's Angels on Wheels" and "Born Losers" money pix at boxoffice. Released by Crown-International as upper half of a package which includes "Hell on Wheels", this Comet production, while lacking some of the merit of its predecessors and not engaging in the same type of wild riding and thrills, draws on similar violence for exploitation purposes.

Starring Steve Alaimo, new recording personality, in his first picture, script by William Grefe, who also directs, focuses on a trio of brutal Satan's Angels who commit bank holdups and other crimes strictly for kicks. Alaimo — a race driver who has had to retire when fire destroys his machine — joins them as a police undercover man. He's to drive their getaway car, since they do not want to draw attention to themselves on their bikes.

Grefe establishes a suitable atmosphere and proper gang menace as Alaimo becomes involved, inserting some good production values both on the race track and later in climax. Star creates a favorable impression as an actor, as well as sings a couple of songs, including one of his recordings, "You Don't Know Like I Know."

As the three ruthless Angels, John Vella — the leader, Willie Pastrano — former world light heavyweight champ, and Jeff Gillen satisfactorily sock over their characterizations. Bobbie Byers is in for distaff interest, a member of the gang who stays on also for kicks.

Technical credits are generally well handled, including Clifford H. Poland Jr., and Harry Walsh's color photography, editing by Julio C. Chevez and Robert Woodburn, music score by Al Jacobs.

Whit.

N.Y. FEST

Funnyman

First half quite funny but San Francisco-made indie feature of no marquee strength fails to realize promise. Gags give it some commercial chance.

Korty Films Inc. of San Francisco production (Hugh McGraw, Stephen Schmidt) featuring Peter Bonerz. No release set. Directed and photographed by John Korty. Screenplay by Korty and Bonerz; editor, David Schickele. Reviewed Sept. 23, 1967 at N.Y. Film Festival, Lincoln Center. Running Time, 102 MINS.

Perry	Peter Bonerz
Sue	Sandra Archer
Sybil	Carol Androsky
Roger	Larry Hankin
Molly	Barbara Hiken
Mahlon	Gerald Hiken
Jan	Nancy Fish
Vogel	Budd Steinhilber
Vera	Ethel Sokolow
Sid	Marshall Efron
Advertising Executive	George Ede
Girl in bikini	Jane House
Watson	Herb Beckman
Heidi	Manuela Ruecker

Lester	Roger Bowen
Phil	Mel Stewart
Zach	Dick Stahl

"Funnyman," independently produced in San Francisco and premiered at New York Film Festival, examines the vaudeville bits and skits, and the private discontent of a coffee house comic in that burg. Film starts off beguilingly and remains amusing while the protean impersonations and patter of Peter Bonerz hold out. The first half affords whatever commercial playoff chances it may have. In the end, the story is too long and not sharp enough. But the film's worst flaw is the photography, especially the interiors, which tend to washed-out whites and faded brownie snaps as if from an old album.

The cast introduces a number of quite deft performers but mostly it's Bonerz's picture, his contribution being the more significant when it is considered that he is also co-scripter with the director, John Korty. Korty has managed many subtle, understated comments on the present times, on advertising, on talent and the elusive nature of humor. But he shoulders the blame for the camera work since he did that, too. Give him special marks for some clever animation inserts but it still won't square the ill-lit photography.

This "Funnyman" is fairly likeable human being, precisely because he worries that he is not. Though obsessed with the sameness of his routines professionally and the monotony of his too-easy bedmates, he is not always "on" as might be expected. Nothing much happens actually. Most of the laughs come from floor show material and very little from plot complication, per se.

On a soul-searching vacation, which is too prolonged for the best interests of the film's pace, the comic encounters an extremely likeable Japanese family and a model with whom he seems to form his first wholesome relationship. It is impossible to dislike anybody, but at the same time hard to become thoroughly engaged. What is the story saying? That a layabout, bumming existence, even if talented, and no fixed ties induces a growing loneliness? Sure.

The interesting point perhaps is that an indie film from San Francisco is as good as this one is, despite final disappointment.

Land.

Black Natchez
(DOCUMENTARY)

Powerful documentary of the failure of a civil rights drive in a small Mississippi town. For 16m and educational market.

Ed Pincus-David Neuman production for the Center for Social Documentary Films. Directed and photographed by Pincus, Neuman. Commentary, James Jackson; editor, Michael Goldman. At New York Film Fest. Running Time, 60 MINS.

This compelling look into the efforts to integrate Natchez, Mississippi in the summer of 1965 achieves a national significance largely because of events since then: By showing how two civil rights groups, the National Assn. for the Advancement of Colored People and the Freedom Democratic party, came into sharp conflict over tactics, "Black Natchez" demonstrates why many Negroes have come to favor "black power" organizations. While maintaining apparent objectivity, the film nevertheless leads to the conclusion that "moderate" tactics are no weapons against an implacable foe —in this case a small-town Southern white power structure which turned down every reasonable demand presented by the town's Negroes.

Charles Evers (brother of the slain Medgar), the NAACP's state field secretary, speaks against marching and more physical acts of protest throughout the brief drive. Even after a committee of middle-class Negro businessmen fails to bring about the slightest change, Evers still warns against possible "bloodshed." And since he has repeadedly stated that "this is an NAACP project and no other group should butt in," the reps of FDP are reluctant to speak out. When they finally do, the Negro community has become numbed by its failure:

Film is done in a familiar cinemaverite style. While structure of the narrative is fine, the camerawork itself is remarkably unsteady and a very inexpensive film stock seems to have been used. Voice of James Jackson, a local resident who fails in his attempts to set up a chapter of the gun-wielding "Deacons" (a kind of Negro Ku Klux Klan), sometimes narrates a sequence. "Black Natchez," which has already been shown on "NET Journal," is a powerful demonstration of Negro frustration and hope. If of little value to commercial theatres, it deserves a healthy career in the 16m and educational market.

Byro.

Home For Life
(DOCUMENTARY)

Extraordinarily moving study of a home for the aged. Utilizes 'cinema-verite' techniques to greatest advantage.

Films, Inc. release of a production for Drexel Home, Chicago. Writer-director: Gerald Temaner; cameraman-editor: Gordon Quinn; sound: Richard Vorisak. Seen as part of Social Cinema in America program at N.Y. Film Fest. Running Time, **80 MINS.**

This extraordinary document was made as a promotional film for a home for the aged serving Jewish families in Chicago, and was rejected for that purpose —not because it fails to show that Drexel is a remarkably well-run place of its type, with a wealth of psychological, physical rehabilitation and social services, but because its searching camera was unable to conceal a truth: that old age, in a society which finds the majority of its elders "useless" as their physical and mental powers begin to deteriorate, is a painful, confusing and frightening business.

"Home for Life" follows two new residents from the time of their admission through their

first weeks of "adjustment" to the new setting, principally as they are subjected to a deluge of examinations and introduced to the available forms of institutionalized activity and entertainment. Only obliquely are the between-times moments of stagnation suggested, but this unseen background becomes increasingly important as the film's protagonists wage their hopeless battle for dignity and "settle down" to wait for death.

One of these people, a twice-married man, has carted all his belongings with him, and is concerned with ordering them neatly in a room "the size of my bathroom at home." He reluctantly agrees to part with his cash, ignoring as best he can the fact that he's being treated "like a child." Crippled with arthritis (he needs help just to tie his shoes), he's aware that "I can't take care of myself anymore" and has made his own decision about "the best solution for the balance of my life." He, at least, is able to find a guilty solace in his memories of the "good woman" who shared her last years with him.

But the central figure is a gentle, good-humored little lady who cannot escape from the present, from a round of "gas pains" and bunions and memory lapses that provoke the patronizing impatience of her juniors and peers. Her choice was made by her bumbling, balding son and not-a-pin-out-of-place daughter-in-law, and perhaps the most revealing sequence in the film is a "first visit" in which these two—chattering, wheedling, bickering, demanding —are sorting out the old lady's laundry, while she drifts dazed between them.

It is hardly possible to describe the poignant, even agonizing, impact of such a scene. But one thing becomes apparent from this and some of the other "cinema verite" efforts seen as part of N. Y. Film Festival's Social Cinema series: the new hand-held camera, zoom lens and minimal lighting techniques have made it possible for sensitive, imaginative documentarians to approach the level of cinematic "inner reality" heretofore possible only with actors.

It may be difficult for "Home to Life" to gain theatrical release and even then it might be impossible for it to attract an audience. But if screen art is defined as that which offers the Aristotelian experience of "pity and terror," t h e r e can be few "art films" which have included anything so devastating as a single scene in this film. An old woman is asked to think about the fact that she's on the second, not the sixth floor of Drexel Home. She answers simply, "I don't think anymore."

Gold.

Puss & Kram
(Hugs and Kisses)
(SWEDISH)

Reversal of husband-and-butler in wife's affections. Swedish item dubious bet for U.S.

Sandrews (Bo Jonsson) production, produced by Goran Lindgren. No U.S.

distrib set. Features Agneta Ekmanner, Hakan Serner, Lena Granhagen, Sven-Bertil Taube. Directed and written by Jonas Cornell. Camera, Lars Swanberg; editor, Ingemar Ejve; music, Bengt Ernryd. Reviewed at the New York Film Festival, Sept. 23, '57. Running Time, **93 MINS.**

Eva .... Agneta Ekmanner
John .... Hakan Serner
Hickan .... Lena Granhagen
Max .... Sven-Bertil Taube

This Swedish sex comedy is an eccentric mixture of Noel Coward and Harold Pinter. While it is rather charming much of the time by virtue of fresh performances, it finally becomes a routine exercise in facile role-reversal a la "The Servant." Lacking insightful wit or names, it seems a dubious bet for stateside release, even in peripheral art houses.

A young married couple adopt a derelict author as a house guest-butler. The three spend a good bit of time gamboling together, but the menage a trois is upset when the newcomer invites a blonde to share his guestroom. Both the wife and husband are jealous of this new addition and contrive to get rid of her. One night they send the blonde out to a film and then arrange to have the guest make love to the wife for his girlfriend's displeased notice. The plan works and the blonde leaves, but the charade has unexpectedly aroused the wife's interest in their protege. When the husband comes home one evening, he discovers the two of them making love and resignedly goes to the guestroom, where he will undoubtedly be sleeping henceforth.

It is hard to know how debuting director Jonas Cornell wishes his fable to be viewed. If it is intended as a light sex romp, its many turgid moments and a dissonant, almost electronic musical score must be counted a minus. If it is to be taken more seriously, it must be faulted for a tricky narrative device that seems imposed upon rather than growing naturally out of the characters, none of whom are drawn very sharply.

While overly schematic and predictable, "Puss and Kram" does have moment of wayward charm due to an appealing and attractive quartet of actors. Agneta Ekmanner is a strikingly attractive brunette in the Dana Wynte. mold who cannot quite overcome the sketchy outlines of her role. She undoubtedly will be heard from in the future. Hakan Serner (the guest) is blessed with a face comic even in repose, and his physical grace is also an asset that should serve him well in future assignments. In lesser roles, Lena Granhagen (the blonde and Sven-Bertil Taube (the husband) also do very well.

On the basis of this first film, Cornell is an uncertain talent whose ideas seem more verbal than visual. His pic does have a surface sheen that is remarkable for a beginner, and with a less derivative subject and a less talky script he may well make a film of some stature. *Beau.*

Lay My Burden Down
(DOCUMENTARY)

A look at the poverty-stricken life of Negro tenant farmers. Made-for-tv docu has telling moments.

National Educational Television production. Producer-director-writer: Jack Willis; associate producer: Catherine Clarke; camera: Robert Elfstrom; editor; Howard Milkin. Shown as part of Social Cinema in America program at N.Y. Festival Sept. 21. Running Time, **60 MINS.**

Originally seen on television as part of the remarkable NET Journal series, "Lay My Burden Down" takes a look at the life of the Negro tenant farmer in the south, particularly in the area of Selma, Ala., where 1955 civil rights marches took place.

Valuable for its straightforward dissatisfaction with the fact that the march didn't change much, that the Southern Negro still does "the white man's dirty work," and that much is needed in the way of Federal action, the film is hampered by its inability to get footage that illustrates many of its points. Thus, compared to most of the festival documentaries (and others in NET series) it has an "old-fashioned" reliance on voice-over narration.

Nevertheless, there are such things as a telling visit with a family of 10 that subsists on less than $1,000 a year; which has never been able to borrow more than $50 at a time "cause that's the way the white man set it up a long time ago and that's the way it still is"; and whose young mother, smiling in the security of her religious faith, chooses, among all the things in the world, for only just enough to keep her children from going naked and hungry.

There's also a poignant interview with a farmer who's about to be kicked off his land for refusing to turn his government check over to his landlord; a look at a railroad gang ("See the white man; he's the boss. He's just standin' around, but says we're lazy"); and, perhaps most revealing of all a session with a group of whites who use a grinning, shuffling, "yessuh-boss" old man to prove that "We take care of our nigras." *Gold.*

The Day The Fish Came Out
(COLOR)

Comedy-cum-allegory, thanks to top technical attributes, manages to stay afloat in a sea of pretentiousness.

International Classics release of a Michael Cacoyannis production. Produced, directed and written by Michael Cacoyannis. Features entire cast. Camera (Deluxe), Walter Lassally; sound, Mikes Damalas; no editing credits; art direction, Spyros Vassiliou; music composed and conducted by Mikis Theodorakis; choreography, Arthur Mitchell; asst. director, Tom Pevsner. Reviewed at 20th Century-Fox homeoffice. N.Y., Sept. 28, '67. Running Time, 109 MINS.

Navigator	Tom Courtenay
Elias	Sam Wanamaker
Pilot	Colin Blakely
Electra	Candice Bergen
Peter	Ian Ogilvy
Dentist	Dimitris Nicolaidis
Goatherd	Nicos Alexiou
Mrs. Mavroyannis	Patrick Burke
Fred	Paris Alexander
Frank	Arthur Mitchell
Goatherd's Wife	Marlena Carrere
Mr. French	Tom Klunis
Man in Bed	William Berger
Manolios	Costas Papaconstantinou
Travel Agent	Dora Stratou
Director of Tourism	Alexander Lykourezos
Mike	Tom Whitehead
Base Commander	Walter Granecki
Policeman	Demetris Ioakimides

Tourists: Lynn Bryant, James Connolly, Assaf Dayan, Robert Killian, Derek Kulai, Alexis Mantheakis, Raymond McWilliams, Michael Radford, Peter Robinson, James Smith, Grigoris Stefanides, Peter Stratful.

Fortunately for International Classics, the 20th Century-Fox subsidiary which is handling "The Day the Fish Came Out," this only fair film has some highly exploitable gimmicks.

Considering that even though the young Greek director, Michael Cacoyannis, who provided Fox with "Zorba, The Greek" with very happy results, had exhibited such a diversity of talents, the men who held the production strings should have kept tighter reins on the film. Not only did Cacoyannis produce, direct and write "The Day The Fish Came Out," for some reason known only to his vanity, he also designed the costumes. As a screenwriter he's only passing fair but as a designer he's an untalented poseur.

What the Greek has tried to do, with only fair success, is to mount an allegory or a personal political comment (against war and the careless use of atomic power) in the form of a wild comedy, resulting finally in a tragic ending that is his personal comment. Inspired by what might have happened, as the result of the accident at Palomares, Spain, he has two atomic bombs and a mysterious box (later proven to contain highly radioactive material) scuttled on a small Green island when the plane carrying them develops engine trouble. The pilot (Colin Blakely) and navigator (Tom Courtenay) swim ashore and spend the remainder of the film, clad only in their underpants, trying to find a way to telephone the accident to the proper military authorities.

The latter, however, become aware of the accident almost immediately and dispatch a team, headed by Sam Wanamaker, to find and secure the dropped items. To maintain secrecy, they pose as hotel experts scouting the island for a possible future site. This subterfuge, in turn, sets off a wave of interest in the island which is soon invaded by tourists, including some archaeologists. These include a young assistant (Candice Bergen) who heads into a fast affair with one of Wanamaker's team (Ian Ogilvy).

Actually, the only logical explanation of her presence is to provide the means of opening the box (via a chemical she uses in her work) for the goatherd (Nicos Alexiou) who finds and hides it in his hut but whose attempts to open it are unsuccessful until he chances upon the chemical.

The dramatic tension engendered by Alexiou and his wife (Marlena Carrere) is played against the farcical antics of Blakely and Courtenay (whose almost nude state makes them daytime hideouts, nearly starving and yet unable to ask for help) and the highly-charged pitch made by Miss Bergen to the shy young Ogilvy (they may well be the skinniest pair of lovers in film history).

Director Cacoyannis keeps things moving, making full use of the colorful setting, but screenwriter Cacoyannis often falls apart, with logical loopholes one could walk through, and forced to dig deep for plot explanations. Sporadically, his dialog is clever, but his basic plot, handled by a more efficient screenwriter, might have resulted in an original treatment. The principal failure of his script is in keeping the three areas — comedy, romance and suspense — in proper balance, often dispelling a mood by cutting away from it too quickly. No editing credits are provided, indicating that Cacoyannis may have handled this department also.

Of the large cast, few of them known to American audiences, Alexiou's goatherd is most effective and moving in his frantic, frustrating search for a means to open the box which may provide the means to raise his station in life (he even steals a dentist's drill). His disappointment in finding only a few odd egg-shaped objects, which he disgustedly throws into the sea, is believably portrayed. Almost all of the Greek characters speak Greek on the soundtrack with English titles provided.

When, as a result of his act, the harbor starts filling with dead fish, the ensuing tragic ending mounts, played against a background of funseeking tourists, carousing in a waterfront cafe. While Blakely and Courtenay will add no laurels to their acting careers with these roles, they are sometimes funny, but both Wanamaker and Miss Bergen are limited in their slight roles and provided, too often, with banal dialog.

Walter Lassally's color photography, a major asset, gives even the barren island used for the film an attractive look. He balances the professional faces with some beautifully-caught shots of natives, their naturalness arousing the viewer's fullest sympathy when their undeserved fate is fully realized. Mikis Theodorakis (now in prison in Greece as a political prisoner) has provided a variety of Hellenic airs that, to the non-Hellenic ear, quickly sound repetitious but are appropriate for the wild dances dreamed up by New York City Ballet dancer Arthur Mitchell (also seen briefly as one of Wanamaker's team).

Whatever boxoffice success the film rates will depend on the manner of selling it. As an International Classics release, a semi-art policy is indicated. *Robe.*

La Desordre A Vingt Ans
(Disorder Is 20 Years Old)
(FRENCH-DOCUMENTARY)

Paris, Oct. 3.
Pathe release of Argos Films, Pathe production. Directed, conceived and commented by Jacques Baratier, with additional commentary by Alain Vian. Camera, Etienne Becker, Patrice Wieus; editor, Marie France Thomas. At Git-Le-Coeur, Paris. Running Time, 70 MINS.

Saint-Germain-Des-Pres is only a crossroads section in Paris with several cafes and boites in depth. But after the war it was the Paris offbeat, esoteric spot from whence came many talents, the birth of Jean-Paul Sartre's Existentialism and emergence of a tourist mecca place to watch the new free-living fauna. It has since simmered down and this pic looks at its history via new footage and old.

But this is likely to appeal mainly to the tourists and insiders who knew the old Saint-Germain days. It is a bit too insidey and specialized for those sans a smattering of the meaning and appeal of the spot. Thus this medium-length documentary appears more for specialized and supporting fare plus tv use if given a clear exposition.

Director Jacques Baratier drew on one of his early shorts as well as showing the section today, and interviews and footage done by others. It shows the early postwar youth and intellectuals discovering the section and turning an all-night worker cafe into the first famed Existentialist nitery, Le Tabou.

But the pic mainly looks at a few people who seemed to sum up the time. Philosopher Jean-Paul Sartre himself is only in a few shots. Film mainly focuses on the late Boris Vian, songwriter, writer and jazz critic and player to give an idea of the rather witty and non-violent early attempts to cope with the new freedom and changing ways.

Some scenes are missing and especially the whole saga of the noted Rose Rouge nitery which gave many theatrical talents to the scene today. This has some offbeat appeal in documenting the noted Paris section. Tight editing and atmospheric music also help. *Mosk.*

The Jungle Book
(COLOR-CARTOON FEATURE)

New Disney animated pic, based on Rudyard Kipling stories. Strong production and excellent vocal casting enhance a pastoral story line. Good b.o. prospects.

Hollywood, Sept. 30.
Buena Vista release of a Walt Disney Production. Directed by Wolfgang Reitherman. Screenplay, Larry Clemmons, Ralph Wright, Ken Anderson, Vance Gerry, based on the "Mowgli" stories by Rudyard Kipling; directed animators, Milt Kahl, Ollie Johnston, Frank Thomas, John Lounsbery; layout, Don Griffith; background, Al Dempster; editors, Tom Acosta, Norman Carlisle; music, George Bruns; songs, Robert B. and Richard M. Sherman, Terry Gilkyson. Reviewed at Academy Award Theatre, L.A., Sept. 29, '67. Running Time, 78 MINS.

Bear's Voice	Phil Harris
Panther's Voice	Sebastian Cabot
Ape King's Voice	Louis Prima
Tiger's Voice	George Sanders
Snake's Voice	Sterling Holloway
Elephant's Voice	J. Pat O'Malley
Boy's Voice	Bruce Reitherman
Other Elephants	Verna Felton, Clint Howard
Vultures	Chad Stuart, Lord Tim Hudson
Wolves	John Abbott, Ben Wright
Girl	Darleen Carr

"The Jungle Book," based on the "Mowgli" stories by Rudyard Kipling, is Disney's first animated feature in four years, the 17th such film from the studio, and the last under Walt Disney's personal supervision before his death. Superior animation, production values, vocal casting and direction make for colorful melodic entertainment which, though never reaching peaks in either drama or comedy, will strike a responsive chord in the intended market. Buena Vista release is set for the peak year-end period, in tandem with a live-action animal documentary feature, "Charlie, The Lonsome Cougar."

Filmed at a declared cost of $4,000,000 over a 42-month period, story has been constructed from Kipling sources by Larry Clemmons, Ralph Wright, Ken Anderson and Vance Gerry. Full directorial credit is given to Wolfgang Reitherman, a 35-year Disney vet. Reitherman is one of several "Jungle" hands who worked on Disney's first animated feature, "Snow White And The Seven Dwarfs," which bowed just 30 years ago and is in current reissue.

(Incidentally, with pix-to-tv and other selloffs in most major film companies, "Snow White" qualifies as the oldest blockbuster classic still in regular and successful wide theatrical rerelease under the control of its original production company.)

Friendly panther, vocalized by Sebastian Cabot, discovers a baby boy in the jungle, and deposits him for upbringing with a wolf family, John Abbott and Ben Wright. At age 10, boy, looped by Clint Howard, is seen in need of shift to the human world, because man-hating tiger, George Sanders, has returned to the jungle. Story wends its way through an episodic 78 minutes until Howard is caught up into civilization by the demure looks and voice (Darleen Carr) of a village gal.

Encounters along the way include a friendship with a devil-may-care bear, expertly cast with the voice of Phil Harris. The standout song goes to Harris, a rhythmic "Bare Necessities," extolling the value of a simple life and credited to Terry Gilkyson. Robert B. and Richard M. Sherman wrote five other songs, best of which is "Wanna Be Like You," sung in free-wheeling fashion by Louis Prima, vocalizing the king of a monkey tribe.

Other characters, all of whom are drawn in harmony with their vocal counterparts, include sinister serpent Sterling Holloway, Col. Blimpish elephant J. Pat O'Malley and his wife, Verna Felton, and four hippie-like vultures looped in engaging fashion by Chad Stuart (of Chad & Jeremy) and deejay Lord Tim Hudson.

Story development is restrained —the potential dangers are suggested and there is an overriding upbeat end in sight from the beginning—so moppet audiences may squirm at times. Animation execution, supervision and editing thus are on the purely pastoral side although lush throughout. George Bruns penned a very fine score, particularly main title theme which, in counterpoint to beautiful Technicolor hues, hints at potential dramatic situations. In the entapping beat. All technical credits are first rate.

Murf

Zosya
(RUSSIAN-POLISH)

Paris, Sept. 26.

Sovexport release of Maxim Gorki Studio production. With Pola Raksa, Youri Kamorny, Nikolai Merzlikin. Directed by Mikhail Bogin. Screenplay, Vladimir Bogomolov, Andrei Tarkovsky; camera, Jerzy Lipman; music, Raphale Khozak. At Theatre Marigny, Paris. Running Time, 88 MINS.

Zosya	Pola Raksa
Lieutenant	Youri Kamorny
Friend	Nikolai Merzlikin
Mother	Waclawa Mazurkiewicz
Father	Zygmunt Tzintel

A simple tale of a brief rest by a group of Russian soldiers on a Polski farm during the last World War is the basis of this unassuming pic. It does have some gentle observation and a hint at unspoken feelings between a Polish girl and a Russian officer. But it appears somewhat too restrained for much chance abroad.

Direction keeps this naive story always visually taking with good acting staving off some banality. The early segs measure the violence of war, but it stays in the background during the idyllic stay on the farm. The love affair never gets started nor does the pic.

But this does peg an emerging new director and one who needs a bit more meaty scripts to give his obvious gifts of timing and pace greater sway.

Mosk.

Si J'Etais Un Espion, (ou Breakdown)
(If I Were a Spy or Breakdown)
(FRENCH)

Paris, Sept. 26.

CFDC release of Pathe, Sirius, UGC, CFDC production. Stars Bernard Blier, Bruno Cremer; features, Suzanne Flon, Patricia Scott, Claude Pieplu. Directed by Bertrand Blier. Screenplay, Antoine Tudal, Jean-Pierre Simonot, Jacques Cousseau, Philippe Adrien, Bertrand Blier; camera, Jean-Louis Picavet; editor, Kanout Peltier. At Marbeuf, Paris. Running Time, 95 MINS.

Doctor	Bernard Blier
Agent	Bruno Cremer
Woman	Suzanne Flon
Daughter	Patricia Scott
Friend	Claude Pieplu

An ordinary little neighborhood doctor is caught up in underground spy operations because of a patient he is treating. Pic is directed solidly, with good acting, but keeps on a muted note without a more dramatic drive needed to lift it above a competent but not unusual spy entry.

The beginning has a nightmarish air as the doctor goes to answer a patient's call and gets embroiled with people following him. It turns out he innocently met this man on a trip to Poland and is moved in on by a secret service man with his daughter also imperiled.

For some stretches, this has an offbeat tenseness as the doctor succumbs to panic and his shadow slips away. Director Bertrand Blier, for his second film, displays a good feeling for mood but can't get enough tension and excitement into his tale. It becomes repetitive and finally plodding.

Story does not allow for fuller insights into the doctor's character and does not stave off disbelief. Bernard Blier manages to portray mediocrity sans falling into stereotype while Bruno Cremer is a good vis-a vis as the undercover man who comes to like the squat medico.

Film has the simple progression that might slant it for tv. It does not quite have the tensions and dramatic insights for arty use abroad. Bertrand Blier may emerge a needed new director here with more original scripts.

Mosk.

Lamiel
(FRENCH-COLOR)

Paris, Sept. 26.

Warner Bros. release of Rome Paris Films Film Copernic production. Stars Anna Karina, Robert Hossein, Jean-Claude Brialy; features Michel Bouquet, Claude Dauphin, Denise Gence, Pierre Clementi, Alice Sapritch. Directed by Jean Aurel. Screenplay, Cecil Saint-Laurent, Aurel from book by Stendhal; camera (Eastmancolor), Alain Levent; editor, K. Peltier. At Ambassade-Gaumont, Paris. Running Time, 95 MINS.

Lamiel	Anna Karina
Valbert	Robert Hossein
Count	Jean-Claude Brialy
Doctor	Michel Bouquet
Duke	Claude Dauphin
Woman	Alice Sapritch
Countess	Denise Gence
Young Man	Pierre Clementi

Costumer version of Stendhal's early 19th Century unfinished book is not quite clear in its outlook. Tale of an amoral girl's climb to social heights, from orphanage to a noble name and ironic death in Paris high life, vacillates between irony, comedy-drama, libertine escapades and satire. Result is an uneven pic with mainly exploitation possibilities on its theme and sexploitation usage because of its tastefully handled love scenes dotted with nudity.

Anna Karina is more pert than possessing the needed voluptuousness to help right the film's mixture of styles. It applies inserted titles, modernistic thought and a rapid style that does not give the film a period feel. Pic also hasn't enough wit, character insight and pace to keep it afloat through the heroine's odyssey from peasant hut to Paris town house.

A country doctor takes the pretty peasant in hand and tries to live through her and attain the top social pinnacles and experiences denied him. He insinuates her into a noble household where she first pays a worker to make love to her to find out about it, seduces the son to get to Paris, and marries a down-and-out Count for his title.

A thief steals into her boudoir one day and true love extricates her from a life of boredom to end in tragedy as she is killed in flight with him. Elegant color costumes and good production dress help, but this stylized period piece is somewhat skimpy in mood and atmosphere. It lacks the needed romantic dash and more robust visual inventiveness. But its theme and cynical love romping are assets on its home grounds with hard sell called for abroad.

Mosk.

Robbery
(BRITISH-COLOR)

A cleverly-spun suspense story with authentic British locale shooting, pic should do well at the boxoffice.

Hollywood, Sept. 26.

Embassy release of a Stanley Baker-Michael Deeley production. Directed by Peter Yates. Features Stanley Baker, Joanna Pettet, James Booth. Screenplay, Edward Boyd, Yates, George Markstein; camera (PatheColor), Douglas Slocombe; editor, Reginald Beck; music, Johnny Keating; asst. director, Derek Cracknell. Reviewed at Charles Aidikoff Screening Room, Hollywood, Sept. 25, '67. Running Time, 114 MINS.

Paul	Stanley Baker
Kate	Joanna Pettet
Langdon	James Booth
Robinson	Frank Finlay
Frank	Barry Foster
Dave	William Marlowe
Jack	Clinton Greyn
Ben	George Sewell
Don	Michael McStay
Freddy	Patrick Jordan
Seventh Robber	Ken Farrington
Squad Chief	Glyn Edwards
Detective Inspector	Anthony Sweeney
Constable	David Pinner
Prison Contact	Frank Williams
Car Lot Owner	Barry Stanton
School Teacher	Rachel Herbert
CID Chief	Michael David
Chief Constable	Martin Wyldeck
Delta One Observer	Malcolm Taylor
Night Club Deb	Linda Marlowe

This precision-tooled suspense thriller turns many of the traditional ingredients that usually go into this kind of film inside out and manages to come up with a tight, well paced, highly entertaining pic. The big chase episode opens the film rather than closes it and although there is display of violence and brutality, there are no guns seen or fired in this British-made Joseph E. Levine Embassy presentation. "Robbery" is an unusually fine cinematic departure from the usual cops and robbers story and if so billed in ad-pub campaigns should garner heavy response from both general as well as sophisticated audiences.

For a brisk start there's a car robbery and the maneuvers of the robbers in London streets consume the first 20 minutes, during which there is no dialog but a thumping good score by Johnny Keating which add to the unexplained incidents. The cleverly executed theft is followed by a roller-coaster car chase.

Peter Yates directed with a sense of authenticity and detail, allowing arm's reach of the actors involved, arms reach of the actors involved, which makes the viewer both detached and increasingly curious concerning the various incidents involved in blueprinting and executing the robbery of 3,000,000 pounds from a British mail train.

The screenplay by Edward Boyd, Yates and George Markstein deliberately puzzles the action and gives inventive and unexpected twists to the plot which add to the overall suspense. Dialog is minimal, used only when absolutely necessary.

This technique surprisingly backfires in the film's one romantic scene in which Joanne Pettet appears at home with her husband, the mastermind of the hoist, played by Baker. The camera angles and abrupt cutting seem all wrong and the terse conversation carries no emotional interest, although Baker is attempting to get her back to bed.

Overall, the incidents have much greater impact than the individual characters involved. Miss Pettet appears only briefly, Baker and the rest of cast perform generally without facial expression, which is what the script demands.

Much of the film's effectiveness is due to Reginald Beck's crisp editing as well as skillful camerawork of Douglas Slocombe. The sound recording of Dudley Plummer particularly catches background audio effects. Keating's score is introduced sparingly, and with long sequences of complete silence, is all the more helpful in underscoring the action.

Also on the plus side are the use of the real Scotland Yard facilities as well as prisons and other British government buildings.

Dool.

Waterhole No. 3
(TECHINSCOPE-COLOR)

Okay, but uneven satire, made by newcomers under Blake Edwards' sponsorship. James Coburn stars. Needs strong pre-selling and special handling.

Hollywood, Sept. 23.

Paramount Pictures release of a Blake Edwards production, produced by Joseph T. Steck; executive producer, Owen Crump. Stars James Coburn. Directed by William Graham. Screenplay, Steck, R. R. Young; camera (Technicolor), Robert Burks; editor, Warren Low; music, Dave Grusin; song lyric, Robert Wells; asst. director, Daniel J. McCauley. Reviewed at Grauman's Chinese Theatre, L.A., Sept. 22, '67. Running Time, 95 MINS.

Lewton Cole	James Coburn
Sheriff Copperud	Carroll O'Connor
Billee Copperud	Margaret Blye
Sgt. Foggers	Claude Akins
Hilb	Timothy Carey
Deputy	Bruce Dern
Lavinia	Joan Blondell
Capt. Shipley	James Whitmore
Ben	Harry Davis
Doc Quinlen	Roy Jenson
Clerk	Robert Cornthwaite
Cpl. Blyth	Jim Boles
Soldiers	Steve Whittaker, Ted Markland
Prince	Rupert Crosse
Bartender	Jay Ose
Cowpoke	Buzz Henry

"Waterhole No. 3" is a slow-building, deliberate oater comedy blending satire, slapstick and double entendre dialog for laughs. James Coburn, Joan Blondell and James Whitmore provide some marquee diversity for the Blake Edwards production, produced by Joseph T. Steck with Owen Crump as exec producer. William Graham's direction is competent, but overall pacing is sluggish and film falls short of true sleeper calibre. With adroit cultivation of the intended market, Paramount release can look to good if uneven b.o.

Immediate impression is that "Cat Ballou," a 1965 Harold Hecht production for Columbia release, fathered this pic. While "Cat" exploded at the b.o., to the surprise of many, "Waterhole" conveys the uneasy feeling that it is too consciously patterned in the same groove. Withal, the original screenplay, by producer Steck and R.

R. Young, has some solid guffaw nuggets which stand out despite a lack of zip in final editing.

Until initial reviews tell audiences that film is a comedy, many viewers will not be sure what to do in the first reel. Although Roger Miller's tongue-in-cheek vocalizing of title tune, by composer Dave Grusin and Robert Wells, hints at what is to come, first reel dialog could pass for softsell irony, appropriate to drama as well as to comedy. But after sheriff Carrol O'Connor and deputy Bruce Dern are locked in their own jail, and forced to strip, by Coburn, show gets on the road.

Distended story line turns on two gags: gold heist by crooked Army sergeant Claude Akins, grounting outlaw Timothy Carey and unwilling hostage Harry Davis; and casual seduction by gambler Coburn of O'Connor's daughter, Margaret Blye. O'Connor is far more interested in Coburn's theft of a prize horse, and this gag is milked for all it is worth. Joan Blondell has a bright role as a madame, ditto James Whitmore as a cliche frontier Army officer.

Having graduated from vidfilms, Graham shows ability in feature direction despite thin production values and accompanying limitations. Coburn, O'Connor and Miss Blye (whose voice and projection are perfect) handle their roles in very good fashion, while rest of cast offers good support. The seduction scene and the finale shootout in Miss Blondell's pleasure dome are highlights. Action expert Buzz Henry stands out in a scene as a drunken cowboy.

Onetime attorney-biz manager Steck, also in his maiden major pic effort, assembled a good crew, including Techniscope-Technicolor cameraman Robert Burks and composer Dave Grusin, whose score adds adroit punches. Transitional reprises of title tune occur too often in early reels. Warren Low trimmed to a tepid 95 minutes; jazzier optical effects would have helped. Other technical credits are pro. *Murf.*

The Subversives
(I Sovversivo)
(ITALIAN)

Venice, Sept. 26.

Ager Film production. Directed by Paolo and Vittorio Taviani from their own original screenplay. With Ferruccio De Ceresa, Lucio Dalla, Giorgio Arlorio, Giulio Brogi, P. P. Capponi, Marija Tocinowsky, Fabienne Fabre. Camera, Gianni Nazisi, Giuseppe Ruzzolino; music, Giovanni Fusco. Running Time, 105 MINS.

Ludovico	Ferruccio De Ceresa
Ermanno	Lucio Dalla
Sebastiano	Giorgio Arlorio
Ettore	Giulio Brogi
Muzio	P. P. Capponi
Giulia	Marija Tocinowsky
Giovanna	Fabienne Fabre

Paolo and Vittorio Taviani have a decade or more behind them of tight collaboration in making films with sharp insight into Italy's political and social scene. Writing, directing and editing together with a fused vision, they have again presented a political commentary, "The Subversives." Agitated camera and situations contrasting starkly with their focus on a stolid political machine in an embryo stage of disintegration, gives the film leeway for specialized release on some foreign screens.

The Tavianis narrate four separate stories connected only by the death of Italy's communist chief Palmiero Togliatti and the three-day mourning period ostentatiously mounted by the party for their defunct leader. Flashbacks to the party mausoleum is a necessary structure to keep the spectator abreast of the interwoven yet unrelated episodes. The characters are human material set in motion to express the decline of revolutionary romanticism and the beginning of policy pacification as the party adapts non-violently, unheroically, to the new phase of power struggle in a social welfare democracy, mainly preoccupied with material well-being.

Four parts are divorced from political doctrine and develop human beings as prone to submersion by their individual problems as they are to ideological despair and doubt by the first big political shock to come along. The Bolognese party bureaucrat becomes an abject figure when his wife meets an old girlfriend and succumbs to her lesbian ploy while he is out to mourn.

The radical Venezuelan spends a final amorous spree with his bourgeois girlfriend in a shabby four-poster. When he comes up for air, it is only long enough to voice diminishing enthusiasm for the struggle at home between party forces and guerrilla revolutionaries. At plane takeoff time, his attitude is "right or wrong, I must go back and help the cause."

Pop singer Lucio Dalla plays a young philosophy student. Togliatti's death for him is the moment to kick over the traces of party discipline to become a social lone wolf rebel, violently maladjusted to any mass action, though a good candidate for a small, select and hippie clan.

The film director is the most caricatural of the four-parter, victim of a chronic malady, obviously suffering from a mother complex and excessively tempermental as a film pro. Purpose of this segment seems hinged to the character of Leonardo da Vinci in the pic within a film to highlight artist's pessimism in the dwindling years of his life.

Film authors' intent is not always accessible, as the four stories intercut in free-wheeling fashion and always at high speed. But the film is a provocative one, very much in keeping with the "E finita la revoluzione" spirit prevailing among the cinematic left.

Dalla, as the student rebel, and Fabienne Fabre, as the lesbian wife, both score in a cast hard-put by brevity and technique to give anything like rounded performances. Dalla is particularly good in off-beat comedy situations.

Use of newsreel footage is no impediment to black and white lensing of Gianni Nazisi and Giuseppe Ruzzolino. Giovanni Fusco's musical score is better than adequate. *Werb.*

Hour of The Gun
(PANAVISION-COLOR)

Talky followup to "The Gunfight At The O.K. Corral." James Garner, Jason Robards, Robert Ryan for marquee. Good b.o. prospects in saturation playoff.

Hollywood, Sept. 28.

United Artists release of Mirisch Corp. presentation, produced and directed by John Sturges. Stars James Garner, Jason Robards, Robert Ryan. Screenplay, Edward Anhalt; camera (DeLuxe Color), Lucien Ballard; editor, Ferris Webster; music, Jerry Goldsmith; asst. directors, Thomas Schmidt, Robert Jones. Reviewed at Grauman's Chinese, L.A., Sept. 27, '67. Running Time, 101 MINS.

Wyatt Earp	James Garner
Doc Holliday	Jason Robards
Ike Clanton	Robert Ryan
Octavius Roy	Albert Salmi
Horace Sullivan	Charles Aidman
Andy Warshaw	Steve Ihnat
Pete Spence	Michael Tolan
Virgil Earp	Frank Converse
Morgan Earp	Sam Melville
Anson Safford	Austin Willis
Thomas Fitch	Richard Bull
John P. Clum	Larry Gates
Dr. Goodfellow	Karl Swenson
Jimmy Ryan	Bill Fletcher
Frank Stilwell	Robert Phillips
Herman Spicer	William Schallert
Curly	John Voight
Turkey	Lonnie Chapman
Sherman McMasters	Monte Markham
Texas Jack	William Windom
Doctor	Edward Anhalt
Billy Clanton	Walter Gregg
Frank McLowery	David Perna
Tom McLowery	Jim Sheppard
Latigo	Jorge Russek

"Hour Of The Gun," produced-directed for Mirisch by John Sturges under earlier title of "The Law And Tombstone," continues the story of Wyatt Earp after "The Gunfight At The O.K. Corral," a 1957 Sturges film for Hal B. Wallis-Paramount. James Garner, Jason Robards and Robert Ryan star. Genuine zip and interest in first half eventually dissipates into talky, telescoped resolution, perhaps from final editing. A sell based on "Corral" is being used, and wisely so. Fast playoff by United Artists should produce good b.o. returns, after which pic will be a serviceable, if longish, supporting item on duals.

Edward Anhalt, using Douglas D. Martin's "Tombstone's Epitaph," has fashioned a heavily-populated script which traces Earp's moral decline from a lawman to one bent on personal revenge. Unfortunately, for any filmmaker, probing too deeply into the character of folk heroes, reveals them to be fallible human beings—which they are, of course—but to mass audiences, who create fantasies (and have fantasies created for them, to fulfill inner needs), such exposition is unsettling. Reality often makes for poor drama.

Sturges this time has apparently aimed at both the action-loving, plot-disinterested filmgoer, as well as the more sophisticated audience. He has missed both targets, to land in an uneasy twilight zone. First five minutes reprise the famed shootout, a sharp opener, after which a courtroom sequence sustains interest of the literate. Subsequent absence of slam-bang events (instead, a series of individual killings between talky setups) will tire the action fan, while class audiences may regret the curious script duality.

Garner, nicely strengthened in appearance here by a moustache, essays the Burt Lancaster "Corral" role, while Robards and Ryan, respectively, replace Kirk Douglas as Doc Holliday, and Lyle Bettger, as Ike Clanton. Robards and Garner play well together, the former supplying an adroit irony in that he, an admitted gambler as much outside the law as in, becomes more moral as Garner lapses into personal vendetta. Ryan is a perfect heavy.

Larry Gates, Charles Aidman, Austin Willie and Thomas Fitch essay some upstanding citizens who support Garner. Their later decline from righteousness to bribery is conveyed in dialog between other characters, a major script flaw. Ryan's crew includes Bill Fletcher (who registers strongly as a corrupted lawman, prosecutor Albert Salmi, Robert Phillips, Michael Tolan, Steve Ihnat and Jon Voight.

Other Earp family members are Frank Converse and Sam Melville, both savagely gunned down by Ryan's troops. Karl Swenson appears briefly as a frontier medic, and William Schallert excels as a judge whose sympathies, and ruling, are cleverly concealed in solid thesping of keen writing. Anhalt, incidentally, appears as a medic in the sanitorium where Robards repairs to die. At fadeout, Garner says he is through with the law, and rides off, having killed off Ryan and four others.

Jerry Goldsmith's score is a very potent asset.

On the technical side, superior production comes across as result of excellent Panavision-DeLuxe Color lensing by Lucien Ballard, using Mexican locations. Editing, to sluggish 101 minutes, was by Ferris Webster, and other production credits are firstrate. *Murf.*

The Last Challenge
(PANAVISION-COLOR)

Handy entry for the western market with Glenn Ford name for marquee potency.

Hollywood, Oct. 3.

Metro release of Richard Thorpe production, directed by Thorpe. Stars Glenn Ford, Angie Dickinson, Chad Everett; features Gary Merrill, Jack Elam. Screenplay, John Sherry, Robert Emmett Ginna; based on novel, "Pistolero's Progress," by Sherry; camera (Metrocolor), Ellsworth Fredericks; music, Richard Shores; editor, Richard Farrell; asst. director, Erich von Stroheim Jr. Reviewed at Metro Studios, Sept. 28, '67. Running Time, 96 MINS.

Marshal Dan Blaine	Glenn Ford
Lisa Denton	Angie Dickinson
Lot McGuire	Chad Everett
Squint Calloway	Gary Merrill
Ernest Scarnes	Jack Elam
Marie Webster	Delphi Lawrence
Pretty Horse	Royal Dano
Frank Garrison	Kevin Hagen
Outdoors	Florence Sundstrom
Sadie	Marian Collier
Harry Bell	Robert Sorrells
Turpin	John Milford
Ballard Weeks	Frank McGrath

A standard western plot undergoes high polish in this Glenn Ford starrer which comes off as good entertainment for the playdates at which it's aimed. Satisfactory performances, sound direction and a screenplay that keeps its characters credible combine to hold audience interest.

Richard Thorpe, who handles dual chore of producer-director, maintains a fast pace for the John Sherry - Robert Emmett Ginna script, based on Sherry's novel,

"Pistolero's Progress." Ford plays a town marshal, the most deadly hand-gun man in the Southwest, who is the object of a young pistolero from the Deep South who aspires to hold Ford's distinction. Idea is developed logically and with enough suspense to build to an okay windup.

Ford underplays his role throughout. He doesn't particularly wish to meet the challenge because he understands the younger man's feelings and sees in the youth his own self during his rising years as a gunman. Chad Everett delivers well as the brash youngster who finally meets Ford in a blazing climax. Angie Dickinson is in as a saloonkeeper in love with Ford, Gary Merrill enacts a cheating card sharp gunned down by Everett and Jack Elam a blackmailer hired by Miss Dickinson to dry-gulch Everett so he cannot meet Ford.

Metrocolor lensing by Ellsworth Fredricks achieves some smart pictorial values, while editing by Richard Farrell, music score by Richard Shores and other technical credits rate accordingly. *Whit.*

Cork Fest

Cry In The Wind
(GREEK)

Cork, Sept. 26.

Huntsman, Ltd. (Vaduz) production. With Flora Robson, Yannis Yoglis, Dimitra Voglis, Anna Tzanis, Takis Emanouil, Christopher Nezer, Dimos Starenious, Despo Diamantidou, Zannino, Anna Bratsou, Vasilis Andronidis. Directed by Leonard Schach; Anthony Heller. Screenplay from original short story by George St. George; camera, A. Heller; music, Christos Leontis at Cork Film Fest. Running Time, 87 MINS.

Anthony Heller's "Cry In The Wind" is likely to be remembered chiefly for the ear-splitting screams from labor pains which lasted through most of the final sequence.

Filmed in the peace and heat of the beautiful, primitive island of Skyros between Greece and Turkey, and with participation by the swarthy-faced and rigid islanders, this is high emotional drama against a background of traditions of honor and revenge.

It's the story of Kosta, an orphan seaman who on his wedding night has to leave his bride, Anna, and go back to the sea. He plans to save enough money to buy a shop in Athens so that they may never be parted again. He saves what he earns and goes back after 11 months of absence to find her heavily pregnant and thrown out of the ancestral home by his grandfather who is bitter at the loss of the good name of his family. She is befriended by Anastasia, the local medicine woman but when he finds her he is ready to kill her until he learns that eight months earlier she had been raped. In spite of this, he can no longer look on her with love.

Eventually, out of this welter of emotional conflict caused by the ridicule of the neighbors, rejection by his family and physical attraction to the local prostie, he re-discovers his old love for her during the long, drawn-out labor. While their reconciliation is taking place, the entire community assembles outside the door as the child is being born. A dark birthmark under the child's ear is exactly like that on Kosta.

Even with good photography, interesting landscape and a biting humor plus some wonderful acting by secondary players, it is hard to see this reaching a market outside its own native country. Flora Robson, veteran British actress, who has her lines dubbed in Greek, made the most of her role. But for newcomer Dimitra Voglis, who is shown pregnant throughout, this was no easy debut. *She.*

A Scent of Almonds
(BULGARIAN)

Cork, Sept. 26.

Bulgarian Cinematography, Sofia production. With Nevena Kokanova, Georgi Georgiev, Iskra Hadjieva, Stefan Danailov, Dorotea Tontcheva. Directed by Andre Thomas. Camera, Jules Beschoff, Claude Francois; music, Pierre Bartholomee. At Cork Film Fest. Running time, 78 MINS.

"Scent of Almonds" looks not to be the most successful of the Cork entries. The idea behind it is not easy to follow. Plot has two separate threads that were meant to knit but just missed.

One part concerns a lonely little hairdresser, mistress of a married man for six years. Longing to be his real wife and urged by an older colleague to give him up, she tells him to get out and stay out. His wife is waiting outside, willing to take him home and help her rear their children and use his fatherly influence on them. But he can't take it, and takes poison as a way out.

The other theme is about the youngish wife of a dim, doting professor who wants to have a last fling with a brilliant young student assistant. He has no time for such intrigue—he's more interested in intellectual debate on the computerized man. But the student is young, the little sister is young and they end the debate with a kiss in the rain. This is not clear enough to make it generally acceptable. Despite an excellent cast and good lensing, it left no bite in the memory. *She.*

N.Y. FEST

Far From Vietnam
(Loin de Vietnam)
(FRENCH—COMPILATION—COLOR)

Anti-American film put together by five French and one American director in Paris. Unbashed propaganda but some commercial prospects.

Slon production of Paris. No U.S. distributor yet. Directed by Alain Resnais, William Klein, Joris Ivens, Agnes Varda, Claude Lelouch, Jean-Luc Godard. Edited by Chris Marker. Reviewed at N.Y. Film Festival, Sept. 30, 1967. Running Time, 110 MINS.

Previously unreeled in early August at the Montreal Film Festival but not then reviewed, this film is frankly intended by its six directors, including the American William Klein, to "express solidarity with the people and government of North Vietnam". It comprises film culled from American and Hanoi sources, plus editorialized sequences in Paris, assorted borrowed or specially made footage, some in color.

The soundtrack presents many different voices, sometimes fairly straight, sometimes passionately denunciatory and at one point a rather fascinating monolog on history, wars in general, the Americans as ex-idols of a liberated France, and the perversity of the human species.

In one sense "Loin de Vietnam" is the old 1915 atrocity film genre using updated cinematic compilation technique and streaked with intellectual irony. It is remarkable for (a) the glorification of Fidel Castro, recently supposed more embarrassment than asset to the Communist world and (b) open approval of the Che Guevara mission of revolution throughout Latin America. The main target is America, President L. B. Johnson, and the whole U.S. foreign policy. There is no pretense of impartiality or a balancing of viewpoints. Washington is tried and found guilty on all counts.

In light of the foregoing there are naturally many pertinent business questions. For some American localities this film would be a risky booking. No great effort of the imagination is required to foresee pickets and opposition. On the other hand, the film says what a lot of Americans at this time fervently wish to have said. Some commercial potential must be presumed.

Close students of propaganda will dissect the content and trace the ideology of this film. Indeed, the promoters could probably sell 50 prints forthwith to university and government analysts. Not that there is anything subtle or secretive. Uncle Sam is drenched in scorn. Americans are the new Nazis, the enemy of the poor everywhere, the architects of death. Americans, and Americans alone, are evil, given to aggression and terror.

All because, goes the argument, John Foster Dulles pulled a con game by which the Vietnamese were tricked out of their victory over and expulsion of the French some 10 years ago. A secondary thesis is that since then U.S. failure to abort the Cuban revolution of Castro has led Presidents Kennedy and Johnson to favor a policy of stopping revolution anywhere and everywhere. There is extended glorification, some by Castro himself, of guerrilla warfare. So, too, there is advocacy of starting many "new Vietnams".

The film does have a certain unity of feeling as edited by Chris Marker. However, some segments are markedly superior to others and more leisurely reviewers will undoubtedly identify in detail. The U.S. film trade will be intrigued by the direct remarks of Jean-Luc Godard that he feels a prisoner of the world power of Hollywood films. His actual language would be worth reproducing, if only that it reveals somuch about Godard and perhaps the core of Parisian cinematic intellectuals.

Minor points arise. Was the American footage pirated? Was the Hanoi footage "staged" for the cameras? One clip of a South Vietnamese soldier knocking over a bound and kneeling captive is repeated again and again. The commentary also reserves some special sneers for Korean soldier allies.

There is insight aplenty in many of the sequences, proof anew, if any is needed, that film is the great communication medium of the 20th Century. Few Americans will have viewed in such detail the shots of the several separate demonstrations in Manhattan which either opposed or supported the war. By artful selection and sequencing, and cross-cuts, the "patriots" are made to seem pretty primitive. However, the emotionalism of the crowds on both sides and the fierce vulgarity of the street discussion has educative value.

Partisans will hardly care for the questioning of whether the film is not too long for its own propaganda ends. It grows tedious, The debate reduces to tribal chant, hysterical heckling and the intermingling of other tensions in American society only indirectly involved with Vietnam. "Black Power" has a prominent feature role.

This film is a shrieker and its gives an abundance of support for the idea, important to Hanoi, that America is divided about the Vietnam war. The viewpoint is never in doubt and what is said, and with a few exceptions the method of statement, are predictable. So considered, it is more of all-too-familiar debating points.

It would be impossible to predict ultimate impact, though the film must make things harder for the Pentagon and the State Department. But the literary critic, Alfred Kazin, has recently doubted that "anger in the arts" will move the "arrogance of our leaders," as he puts it.

"Loin de Vietnam" landmark in propaganda, in political activism by talent, in French intervention in American (as recently in Canadian and Polish) politics will be debated with much heat.

One-sided, but often clever, demagogic while cerebral in its accents, preaching to the converted, turning G.I. kindness to the natives into Freudian guilt complexes, piling on abuse, vehemence raised to the nth power, "Loin de Vietnam" will draw responses predictable according to prior political conditioning of those who see it. Some will be edified, others infuriated. Who will be enlightened? And will the French resistance to Washington later develop separate complications?

In short, a fascinating, disturbing, gripping, sometimes outrageously unfair motion picture. *Land.*

Portrait of Jason
(DOCUMENTARY)

Feature-length interview with Negro male prostitute is more sociology than art, and pretty superficial sociology at that. Could score in offbeat houses.

Film-Makers' Distribution Center release of a Shirley Clarke production. Di-

rected and edited by Shirley Clarke. Photographed by Jeri Sapanen. Reviewed at the N.Y. Film Festival, Sept. 29, '67. Running Time, 105 MINS.
Jason .... Jason Holliday

"Portrait of Jason" was photographed entirely during one 12-hour drink-and-pot marathon last winter by indie filmmaker Shirl- Clarke ("The Connection," "Cool World") and focuses exclusively on a Negro male prostitute. By forsaking all traditional cinematic techniques in favor of a calculatedly ragged visual style, Miss Clarke obviously hoped to penetrate beneath the surface of her "star" to learn some unvarnished truths about the role of the "loner" in our society, be he Negro, homosexual, or whatever.

Judging from audience response upon her ... lm's conclusion at Lincoln Center, many viewers will agree that the interview was an "extraordinary" experience, and word-of-mouth among today's hip young filmgoers could stir up good business in houses specializing in such underground fare. A great many more will object to the sensational subject matter and verbal vulgarities, however, and censorship difficulties may be encountered in some situations.

Jason Holliday (ne Aaron Paine) is a would-be nightclub performer who has used sex as a means of escaping the nine-to-five treadmill. For a while the film entertains because he is an undeniably funny, even charming raconteur of raunchy stories. Even when he indulges in female impersonations (Mae West, Butterfly McQueen, Pearl Bailey) that are strictly Paste Box Revue, he is mildly amusing in the manner of a drunken "life-of-the-party."

Unfortunately, as the evening wears on and Jason gets progressively more turned on, he turns somber and starts recounting his unhappy childhood and his degrading adulthood. Since he has earlier told the camera, "When I do my pathetic bag, I'm really pathetic," it is hard to see these moments as more than the exuberant excesses of an emotional exhibitionist. Even this psychological sham would have merit had Jason less obviously been an attentive student of the collected oeuvres of LeRoi Jones, Douglas Turner Ward and James Baldwin on the one hand and John Rechy, Gore Vidal and James Baldwin on the other. Jason's experiences have already been recounted, with considerably more passion and art, in the mushrooming litterature of the "outcast."

Reviewing such a film requires more psychoanalytic than critical skill, but one extra-cinematic point should be made. Miss Clarke, in her off-camera remarks to Jason, comes across like a Freudian lion tamer. She impassionately eggs him on, taunts him, lacerates him, attacks him. "You should be lonely," she barks out to him, obviously hoping the needle will finish what the joint and the bottle began. Miss Clarke has unattractively been exploiting Jason, but to his credit her efforts don't succeed. Nothing of the man, the non-performer, has been revealed.

It is impossible to discuss the film's technical achievements, because it doesn't have any. The photography is often out-of-focus (an intentional affectation, perhaps), and at several points the picture is lost completely. Since Jason is not developing a particularly valuable idea at these points, one wonders why a little cutting wouldn't have been in order, but c'est la verite, apparently.

If the film were 45 minutes shorter, it might be a tolerably perverse record of a nightclub act, which is where one suspects Jason hoped the film would land him.

Beau.

The Titicut Follies
(DOCUMENTARY)

Sensational and horrifying but in some ways morally ... tionable documentary on an in... man prison for the criminally insane in Massachusetts. Could be a "succes de scandale" in commercial playoff.

Titicut Follies Distributing Co. (Grove Press) release of Bridgewater Film Production, produced, directed and edited by Frederick Wiseman. Camera, John Marshall. At Social Cinema in America series. N.Y. Film Fest. Running Time, 85 MINS.

Despite its similarity in structure and technique to other cinema verite pix at the 1967 New York Film Fest's "Social Cinema in America" sidebar event, Frederick Wiseman's "The Titicut Follies" differs from them commercially: Its four-letter words and prolonged views of male genitalia completely eliminate television as a potential market. Already notorious before the fest, the vain efforts of the Attorney General of the State of Massacusetts to prevent its showing last week guarantees that the newly-formed film distribution arm of Grove Press has an art house moneymaker in "Titicut." It should prove a sensation wherever it can play.

There's no doubt that "The Titicut Follies" is sensational: One scene in the present version features a man masturbating—genitalia and all. But the film is also frightening, horrifying, pulverising—a cry and a plea to a society that can tolerate such brutal, inhuman treatment of some of its members.

The state institution for the criminally insane at Bridgewater, Mass. emerges as nothing less than a hellhole in Wiseman's film. Prisoners are kept in completely bare cells and are not allowed to wear clothes in them. They are stripped of all dignity by guards who tease and hound them to points of "insane" rage. They are "treated" by psychiatrists mostly interested in a raw description of sexual behavior. Their physical ailments are misdiagnosed, causing unnecessary deaths.

Death, in fact, almost appears as an escape from such a place. This especially is brought home via a contrast Wiseman draws between some of the younger prisoners—who though acutely paranoid at times are most often rational and who might be cured with the right

treatment—and the older ones who are completely "gone." To herd these two types together does no good, as an impassioned plea by one young man to a prison board makes abundantly clear. (His cries that "This place is doing me harm" are met with a prescription for "more tranquilizers.")

Against this Dickensian intensity on the part of the filmmaker must be placed, however, another impulse. Knowing from the beginning that he would need theatrical distribution in order for his film to be shown at all, Wiseman has included some titillating scenes which appear merely gratuitous and do not advance the social argument one whit. There is, for example, a scene of an old man singing a song against the counterpointing background of an operating television set; "artistic," but nothing else. Shots of a prisoner giving a disconnected political discourse which sounds right out of "Waiting for Godot" are repeated at film's end when they serve no purpose whatsoever.

Much of this suggests that along with his social motive, Wiseman also saw the possibility of making his film a kind of true-life "Marat-Sade." In this he is guilty of an offense only slightly less serious than that of the authorities who permit places like Bridgewater to exist—he is exploiting the men for his own "artistic" ends.

Well...as far as art goes, Wiseman needs as much as he can get. Even by usual 16m amateur standards, "Titicut" is badly photographed. The editing is clumsy, Wiseman indulging in outdated montage experiments which do not come off. For example, shots of a prisoner being forcefed are intercut with those of his embalming after he died three days later. The "statement" that emerges—that he was treated better in death than in life—smacks of the very subjectivity Wiseman claims to be avoiding by eschewing narration. Only an Eisenstein or a Pudovkin in any case, could do this kind of thing with elan.

Title derives from a show put on by the inmates, excerpts from which—in Brechtian fashion—begin and end the film. *Byro.*

The Other One
(L'Un et L'Autre)
(FRENCH—COLOR)

Rene Allio's followup to "Shameless Old Lady" is a disappointing Pirandellian exercise about an actress's identity probems. For the arties, and chancey even there.

Continental Distributing (Walter Reade) release of Ancinex (Nichole Stephane) Production. Stars Malka Ribovska. Features Philippe Noiret, Marc Cassot, Christian Alers, Francoise Prevost, Claude Dauphin. Directed by Rene Allio. Screenplay, Allio; camera, Jean Badal; music, Serge Gainsbourg; editor, Chantal Delattre. At New York Film Fest. Running Time, 81 MINS.
Anne .... Malka Ribovska
Andre .... Philippe Noiret
Julien .... Marc Cassot
Remoulin .... Christian Alers
Simone .... Francoise Prevost
Serebriakov .... Claude Dauphin

French director Rene Allio's second film rates as a disappointment, coming as it does after the

international success of "The Shameless Old Lady." Ostensibly a Pirandellian study of the relationship between art and life, with focus on an actress trying to alter the course of her existence, "The Other One" emerges as a flat, unrealized exercise. Walter Reade's Continental Distributing has pic via a pre-production deal. Its commercial outlook is chancey at best, even in its intended artie market. However, with color lensing as lure, it should fit into a television feature package.

Malka Ribovska (the director's wife, and the reformed prostitute in "Shameless") works with a Parisian repertory company. She feels herself stifled and her creative vitality ebbing as long as she continues living with a talented photographer (Marc Cassot) who has "sold out" to the advertising market. Lacking the courage to have it out with him she hits upon the scheme of impersonating her sister (whom he has never met) for the final confrontation. This doesn't work but the very act of having tried for the charade give her the gumption to disclose to him her true feelings.

Problem is that nothing in the pic has been defined with an exactitude which would be meaningful on the screen. The sterility of the affair in question has to be taken on faith: If not ideal, it hardly seems near a crisis stage. Moreover, it is not clear just what would be gained for the woman in a new situation—what freedoms, talents, potentialities would be unlocked.

Excerpts from Marlowe and Chekhov presented on stage and from Max Ophuls in a film theatre are at once too obvious and too vague. Two of them reflect the heroine's concern with onrushing old age and the struggle to maintain creative energies in the face of it. Yet Allio seems to be aiming for more—for some comment on the relationship between faces and masks, between appearance and reality. If so, it remains on a surface level, with deeper meanings elusive.

Miss Ribovska as the heroine is at times interesting, but does not achieve the promised "Garbo-like intensity." Other performances are perfunctory, with Marc Cassot's as the lover running somewhat against the sense of the character. Technical credits are unexceptional. *Byro.*

Tonite Let's All Make Love in London
(BRITISH — DOCUMENTARY — COLOR)

A smashing time is had by all in swinging London. Brash, colorful entry has good commercial chances.

Peter Whitehead production, directed, photographed and edited by Whitehead. Music: The Pink Floyd, Immediate Records, The Rolling Stones, Eric Burdon and the New Animals, Chris Farlowe, The Small Faces, Marquis of Kensington. Participants include Michael Caine, Edna O'Brien, Vanessa Redgrave, Andrew Loog Oldham, Julie Christie, David Hockney, Lee Marvin. Reviewed at press screening of N.Y. Film Festival, Sept. 26, 1967. Running Time, 70 MINS.

Subtitle for this film is "Pop Concerto for Film," and that's as good a description as any of its form and content, since it's not a documentary in any ordinary sense but rather an impressionistic view of "the land of mod" as seen by a sympathetic participant.

Overture and postlude for the concerto is montage, jazzily shot, edited and scored, and in-between are seven "movements" covering such aspects of swinging Britain as pop music and painting, political protest and love (or the local equivalent).

It all begins tongue-in-cheek with "the way it used to be" as represented by the changing of the guard (there's a brilliant bit of camp cinema involving a trombone player and a zoom lens), and the giggles continue with some views of London young ladies including not-so-young novelist Edna O'Brien ("most thinking people are decadent," "marriage is such a handicap").

Then things get a bit more serious: Vanessa Redgrave sings off-key for Castro, the Rolling Stones get philosophical, Julie Christie confesses her need for "close relationships" and Michael Caine thinks the new society might be trading "our morals for a mass of cultural pottage." Director Peter Whitehead has stopped making fun of his subjects and is taking them at their own valuation.

But most of all it's fast-paced fun, illustrating in film terms what most of its subjects seem to be looking for: Pleasure, and Miss Christie's thesis that the cornerstone of the New London is "a good time much easier had by all." It's for this reason, combined with Whitehead's bangup technical virtuosity (and the brief on-screen moments of some of the era's most idolized mortals) that the film has a fairly strong chance of succeeding in the commercial marketplace.

Some, of course, will see it as a sociological document, heralding the fact that (as Allen Ginsberg says, voice over, in the postlude) "a new kind of man has come to his bliss." More likely it's what one of the pop painters refers to as "absolute ephemera." But either way it's a good show.   *Gold.*

The Benefit of the Doubt
(BRITISH—DOCUMENTARY—COLOR)

Principal appeal is for theatre buffs, but has added interest as an individual British view of the Vietnam war. Unlikely for theatrical market.

Peter Whitehead, Carol Weisweiller, Dominique Antoine production for Lorrimer-Saga. Directed and edited by Whitehead. Photography: Whitehead, Louis Wolfers, Richard Mordaunt. Excerpts from the play "US" directed by Peter Brook, designed by Sally Jacobs. Music and lyrics by Richard Peaslee and Adrian Mitchell. Original material by Denis Cannan. With Eric Allan, Mary Allen, Jeremy Anthony, Hugh Armstrong, Roger Brierley, Noel Collins, Ian Hogg, John Hussey, Glenda Jackson, Mark Jones, Marjie Lawrence, Joanne Lindsay, Leon Lissek, Robert Lloyd, Ursula Mohan, Pauline Munro, Patrick O'Connell, Mike Pratt, Clifford Rose, Morgan Sheppard, Jayne Sofiano, Barry Stanton, Hugh Sullivan, Michael Williams, Henry Woolf. Reviewed at New York Film Festival press screening, Sept. 26, 1967. Running Time, 70 MINS.

A fair sampling of scenes from the Royal Shakespeare Company's stage production of "US" is offered in this film, intercut with black-and-white interviews with director Peter Brook and some of his actors, who discuss the political and artistic framework of the presentation.

A substantial portion of the potential audience, if reaction at N.Y. festival showing is an indication, will find this dull, but for Americans interested in current theatrical trends it could be a must, since it's their only current opportunity to see one of the most adventuresome and controversial stage productions of the past few years. A discussion of its merits as theatre may be outside the scope of a film review, so suffice it to say that viewers are treated to glimpses of such events as the on-stage burning of a live butterfly, the portrayal of the Vietnamese nation by a writhing near-naked actor, and a rousing song about how, in Brook's words, "The Americans are able to blow the legs off children and then, with true, deep conviction, sew them back again."

It may be that "The Benefit of the Doubt" fails as a film precisely because "US" is so specifically a theatre piece, and it might have been wiser for Peter Whitehead to acknowledge the presence of a proscenium and simply seat his camera in the front row. Instead, he makes an effort to get inside the action, and the results are seldom "cinematic."

The title of the play is deliberately ambiguous, Brook explains, meaning not only "U.S." but "us," the British, and its purpose is to reveal the nature of Great Britain's responsibility for and involvement in the Vietnam war. To this end, a great deal of research was done, and much of the script was taken verbatim from documentary materials.

Curiously, it is this objectivity which has provoked the greatest criticism, since it seems to expose both the United States and North Vietnam as exploiters of the Vietnamese people. The point of view is clearly opposed to the war, to American policy there, yet not "anti-American" or pro-Cong. So the film can't be even as a propaganda pic, the most that even its most native audience is likely to say for it is that it's "interesting"—a description which may serve to bar it from theatrical release.   *Gold.*

The Holy Ghost People
(DOCUMENTARY)

Okay cinema-verite report on a West Virginia holyroller church with some occult practices. Best for tv and 16m.

Thistle Films (Blair Boyd) Production. No distrib set. Direction, camera and editing by Peter Adair. Sound, Jon Zimmerman, Steve Reich. At Social Cinema series, N.Y. Film Fest. Running Time, 53 MINS.

"The Holy Ghost People," a cinema-verite report on a holy-roller church service in rural West Virginia, illustrates a key point about the effects of the new lightweight cameras and sound equipment: As long as an offbeat and ritualized "event" takes place—whether it be a church service, protest meeting, or whatever—it is now possible for almost anyone with the requisite apparatus to make a "structured" film of it.

This is not to say that documentarian Peter Adair did not have to exercise skills of compression and selection in shooting and editing "The Holy Ghost People" — only that his basic problems were solved by the fact that what he filmed was already formed and theatrical. He needed but to be there when it happened and get it on film — which he has done in a relatively superior manner.

There's no doubt that the stuff is sensational in impact. This particular cult of worshippers — one of many in Appalchia — takes its rites from a passage in Mark which, they think, commands the devout to handle serpents and drink poison as signs of faith. During the service rattlesnakes are clutched like so many strands of twine, usually in the midst of a trance characterized by writhing and "speaking in tongues." There are hymns performed for the congregation by excellent amateur hillbilly singers, and a collection taken up for a destitute family which reminds that this area is a key target in the War on Poverty.

Pic stands as a good journalistic demonstration that despite easy middle-class assumptions about "modern" U. S. chruchgoing, American Christianity still remains strikingly diverse—and, in pockets, startlingly fundamentalist. Cut down to about 20 minutes it might do as a theatrical short for arties. As it is, best prospects are for television and the 16m-educational market.   *Byro.*

Huelga
(DOCUMENTARY—COLOR)

Well - photographed film of the migrant workers' strike against Northern California's grape growers has a stirring revolutionary form which does not jibe with the event's history as pic tells it.

King Screen Production, produced by Mark J. Harris. Directed by Skeets McGrew. Commentary written by Harris, spoken by Paul Herlinger; camera, John Haney, Richard Pearce, Carol Burns; music, Augutin Lara; editors, Dick Gilbert, McGrew; sound, Gilbert. At Social Cinema in America series, N.Y. Fest. Running Time, 53 MINS.

As a viewing experience, "Huelga," a color documentary which was given a showing at the New York Film Fest's sidebar "Social Cinema in America" series prior to its airing this fall on educational television's "NET Journal," is a very moving thing. Its subject is the continuing strike of Mexican-American migrant workers against 35 grape growers in the San Joaquin Valley town of Delano, Calif., an event which has received nationwide attention.

As filmed by Mark J. Harris and Skeets McGrew, "Huelga" has more than its share of emotion-filled, tearjerking moments: the intense, dignified face of a woman who has been fired by a grower for "not thinking like us" after working for him for 24 years; a march to Sacramento, with flags of the National Farm Workers Assn. (AFL-CIO) unfurled; the convincing of a foreman and his crew to leave the fields and join the strike by a group of microphone-wielding organizers; most of all, a Christmas rally featuring impassioned singing of "Solidarity Forever" and "We Shall Overcome."

The problem with the pic arises when the known history of the strike is compared with the superstructure imposed on the film. Perhaps inspired by early Eisenstein, Harris and McGrew see the strikers as representing a force of ever-rising momentum leading to inevitable victory — and the film has been edited to reflect this. One curtain-line (prior to a fadeout for commercial interruption) has a strike leader saying about the Sacramento march, "We knew then that we would win."

It turns out, however, that the strike is now entering its third year with only three out of the 35 growers having recognized the union. Though Harris and McGrew admit this via narration at the end of the pic, they do not seem to realize that it calls into question the entire emotional thrust of "Huelga," which was shot during the walkout's first year. Has art triumphed over truth?

It would appear, for instance, that the growers have been able to go through two seasons with substitute labor—that the strikers' success in discouraging "scabs" has been much less than the film has earlier implied. Do the growers have more credible economic justification for their actions than the film shows? Is this subjective, at time, racist ("Are you with your race—the Mexicans—or with the landowners?" the strikers shout at the scabs) view of the situation the whole story?
    Byro.

Memorandum
(DOCUMENTARY—CANADIAN)

Contemporary Films release of a National Film Board of Canada production. Directed by Donald Brittain and John Spotton; screenplay, Donald Brittain; camera, John Spotton; editor, John Spotton; sound, Roger Hart; music, Karl Duplessis. Narrated by Alexander Scourby. Reviewed at the New York Film Fest, Sept. 25, '67. Running time: 60 MINS.

Built around the framework of a visit in 1965 of a group of former inmates of Belsen concentration camp, now American and Canadian citizens, to the German scene, this documentary by the National Film Board of Canada adds little to the already heavy dossier on film of the Nazi genocidal attempts.

Perhaps because of the lack of new material, an inadequate script or the usual policy of not taking a stand, the Film Board has excellently photographed and recorded an event that only infrequently moves the viewer. If there is any comment at all it is that complacency has largely settled on both sides of the issues. The visiting Jews bring along their sons, but the latter are unable to respond to something that happened to their parents, two decades before, in a time and place that is no longer identifiable. The Germans who participated "want to quietly live out their time."

Interspersed with newsreel and film library footage of the activities in the camps (others than Belson are shown briefly), there's little similarity to today's Belsen, a beautifully landscaped and carefully tended monument. The viewer who lived through World War II can induce his own shudders by conjuring up the thought that such carefully preserved places are ready made for the next world holocaust. A grimmer view, because it hasn't changed in the interim. Is the footage on a Polish concentration camp, abandoned and remote, little changed since the days when, as narrator Alexander Scourby says, it served as the extermination grounds for thousands.   *Robe.*

Marie Tudor
(FRENCH)

L'Office de la Radio-Television-Francaise production. Stars Francoise Christophe, Marc Cassot. Directed by Abel Gance. Screenplay, Gance, from the play by Victor Hugo. No other credits available. At N.Y. Film Fest. Running Time, 210 MINS.

This most recent work by Abel Gance, a version of Victor Hugo's play made in 1965 for the French state-run television network, was listed as the concluding entry in the New York Film Festival's Gance retrospective but sans informing festgoers that it was not, as might be expected, 60 or 90 minutes long, but three and a half hours! Consequently, most of the audience last Friday (22), including the VARIETY reviewer, was forced to depart before the showing was half over.

Another film for French tv made by a distinguished director, Roberto Rossellini's "Rise of Louis XIV," made a transition to theatre and is at main event of N.Y. Fest, but "Marie Tudor" cannot hope for such a career. To judge from its first part, it is a literal filmization of the play done on a few sets. The talk is majestically paced in Gance's best romantic style, but it is all talk. This can come off okay in tv's close-up medium, but to be of value on the big screen much more action is required. Cut down drastically and subtitled, there might be some chance in the educational market, though even this is doubtful. The acting, as indicated, is slow and beautiful, with Francoise Christophe scoring as the Bloody Mary of 16th-Century Britain. Some of the sets are patent mock-ups, another unsuitable factor for theatres.   *Byro.*

Paradis Perdu
(Paradise Lost)
(FRENCH-SONGS)

Taris Film (Joseph Than) Production. Stars Fernand Gravey; fetures Micheline Presle, Robert Pizani, Robert Le Vigan, Gerard Landry, Alerme, Jean Brochard, Edmond Beauchamp, Plau, Elvire Popesco, Jane Markin, Monique Rollan, Gaby Andreu. Directed by Abel Gance. Screenplay, Gance, Than, Steve Passeur; camera, Christian Matras; music, Hans May; editor, Leonide Azar; art director, Henri Mahe. At New York Film Fest. Running Time, 88 MINS.

Reviewed for the record. The literature on Abel Gance supports

a conclusion arrived at by noting that his 1939 comedy, "Paradis Perdu," was not reviewed from Paris in VARIETY and was not imported for even the limited art market in the U.S. (Despite the imminent war, both activities were continuing apace.) That conclusion is that the film created but a faint stir in France and was soon forgotten, only to be rediscovered by a new generation of Gance enthusiasts fifteen years later.

That its recognition was so delayed can only be seen as a pity, for "Paradis Perdu" is a light, charming and even moving film. As an attempt by Gance to imitate the "comedie a l'americaine" which had been admired by French cinephiles since "It Happened One Night," it totally succeeds. Perhaps because it is more like a Frank Capra, Leo McCarey or Frank Borzage effort rather than any French film, it was not properly appreciated in its home country.

A painter - turned - couturier shares an ideal love with a dressmaker's assistant. After they are married, he goes off to the Great War and she dies in childbirth. His despair after the war ends when he agrees to raise the child and returns to his profession. Years later, his daughter prevents him from persuing a romance with a girl her own age. Film concludes with the daughter marrying happily.

It mixes humor, romance and sentimentality in equal doses (the very technique admired by the French in the '30s U.S. comedies), and succeeds in drawing laughs and tears. If still too "commercial" an effort for even the 16m-college-film society market today, it may yet find its audience if and when Gance achieves a reputation with Yank film buffs.

Fernand Gravey is charming and witty as the hero and Micheline Presle (in her screen debut) is lovely in dual roles of wife and daughter. Together, they make an attractive pair. The still-active Christian Matras ("Woman Times Seven") contributes some ravishing photography. "Paradis Perdu" is one of Abel Gance's less personal works, but perhaps one of his most entertaining.   *Byro.*

La Dixieme Symphonie
(The 10th Symphony)
(FRENCH)

Le Film d'Art Production, produced by Abel Gance. Features Severin-Mars, Jean Toulout, Emmy Lynn. Directed by Gance. Screenplay, Gance; camera, L. H. Burel; editor, Marguerite Beauge. At 1967 New York Film Fest. Running Time, 80 MINS.
Enric Damors .... Severin-Mars
Frederick Ryce .... Jean Toulout
Eve Dirant .... Emmy Lynn
Marquis de Groix St.-Blaise Andre Lefaur
Claire Damors .... Elizabeth Nizan

Reviewed for the record. This 1918 opus by Abel Gance opened the retrospective of his films at this year's New York Film Festival. It was his second feature-length pic and first commercial success, and if the fest series succeeds in rescuing Gance's reputation here as it has already been rescued in Europe, "La Dixieme Symphonie" could have some value on the 16m film society circuit. It reveals his characteristic themes, techniques, obsessions and beliefs at an early

point in his career when they were in a relatively "pure" state.

Story is a romantic meller straight from 19th-century theatrical tradition. A woman of quality is innocently implicated in the suicide of her lover's sister. The lover, a familiar cad type, then blackmails her first into supporting him and, later, into keeping her thoughts to herself while he courts her sister-in-law. The famous composer to whom the lady is married misinterprets everything, thinking his wife romantically involved, and writes his greatest symphony as a record of his grief. All ends with a gunfight as a result of which justice and true love triumph.

Obviously what matters here is not the basic plot but what Gance did with it. The psychology and characterization of the leading protagonists are strikingly modern, and a tension is achieved which is still involving. There is a grace and rhythm to the film which is not "campy" but a true expression of an older morality. Most of the director's efforts went into the film's most famous sequence — the playing of the symphony and its effect on the composer's wife, who feels the piece is expressing her own emotional conflicts. Her swoons and ecstasies are old-fashioned but do not seem amusing even today, mostly due to the stunning performance by Emmy Lynn.

Severin-Mars and Jean Toulout are also excellent as the two leading men, and the photography and editing stand up well too. "La Dixieme Symphonie" lives up to its billing as a key work in the Gance canon.   *Byro.*

Reflections In A Golden Eye
(PANAVISION—COLOR)

Uneven John Huston film version of the novel about latent homosexuality. Elizabeth Taylor and Marlon Brando hot marquee bait. Obtuse scripting. Strongest b.o. likely in urban areas.

Hollywood, Oct. 4.
Warner Bros.-Seven Arts release of Ray Stark production. Stars Elizabeth Taylor, Marlon Brando; features Brian Keith, Julie Harris. Directed by John Huston. Screenplay, Chapman Mortimer, Gladys Hill, based on Carson McCullers' novel; camera (Technicolor), Aldo Tonti; editor, Russell Lloyd; music, Toshiro Mayuzumi; production design, Stephen Grimes; asst. director, Vana Caruso. Reviewed at Academy Award Theatre, L.A., Oct. 3, '67. Running Time, 109 MINS.
Leonora .... Elizabeth Taylor
Maj. Penderton .... Marlon Brando
Lt. Col. Langdon.......... Brian Keith
Alison Langdon .... Julie Harris
Pvt. Williams .... Robert Forster
Anacleto .... Zorro David
Stables Sgt. .... Gordon Mitchell
Capt. Weincheck .... Irvin Dugan
Susie .... Fay Sparks

The recently demised Carson McCullers' novel, "Reflections In A Golden Eye," about a latent homosexual U. S. Army officer in the pre-World War II period, has been turned into a pretentions melodrama by director John Huston and producer Ray Stark. Stars Elizabeth Taylor and Marlon Brando, who can be counted upon to draw, alternate in mannered thesping. Filmed in Italy, the Warner Bros.-Seven Arts release may well encounter erratic b.o. response. Urban audiences already are accustomed to sturdier, more direct treatments, and rural audiences could possibly miss the point completely. A pre-conditioning sell of the sex situation is indicated.

Adaptation, by Chapman Mortimer and Gladys Hill, features six disparate characters: Brando, the latent homosexual; his wife, Miss Taylor, a practicing heterosexual —practicing with Brian Keith, whose own wife, Julie Harris, once cut off her breasts with scissors after unfortunate childbirth; Robert Forster, young fetichist and exhibitionist; Zorro David, Miss Harris' fey houseboy. Also prominent are a host of sex symbols, and some salty expressions.

Instead of building to what could have been a literate exposition of latent homosexuality, film is more accurately a succession of scenes thrown to individual players. Brando struts about and mugs as the stuffy officer, whose Dixie dialect is often incoherent. Miss Taylor, again tongue-clucking and shrewish in the "Virginia Woolf" groove, is plot appropriately unaware of appropriately unaware of her husband's torment. Her dialect also obscures some vital plot points.

The most outstanding and satisfying performance is that of Brian Keith. This versatile actor is superb as the rationalizing and insensitive middle-class hypocrite. Avoiding the excesses, Keith often dominates ensemble scenes with the stars. Miss Harris, a prime script victim, tries hard and succeeds to an extent in projecting her pitiable character. Her death is a deus ex machina gaucherie, handled poorly in near-finale dialog.

Forster, making his film debut

after a Broadway legit bow last season ("Mrs. Dally Has A Lover"), cannot be evaluated fairly, for his part is practically silent. He rises and suns buttocks bared on a mare (Miss Taylor has a stallion), and creeps into latter's bedroom at night to fondle her undergarments. At the same time, he teases Brando. Considering part as written, he does well.

David, the Filipino houseboy, also is in his screen debut. Role has him an effeminate servant who brings some happiness to Miss Harris, while at the same time, providing a very strong contrast with Keith's character. Other players, whose sexual aberrations are mercifully unprobed, render okay support.

At length, film climaxes with Brando fully expecting Forster to come to his room, but when latter goes to Miss Taylor's separate bed, Brando kills him. Fadeout is a back-and-forth series of pans between the dead soldier, a screaming Miss Taylor, and Brando.

Huston's direction of players is erratic, although his visual sense is intact. Panavision lensing by Aldo Tonti is moody, an effect heightened by desaturated Technicolor printing (which gives a roto or sepia tone to all colors except flaming scarlets — which show as pale pink). Huston in 1956 achieved similar effect in "Moby Dick." Opinions will vary as to merit of such color printing, although it does give a period flavor. (Yet the script has some anachronisms.)

Production designer Stephen Grimes has captured garrison environs, and Toshiro Mayuzumi's spare score adds a good dramatic undertone. Only the Italo-looking inmates of Miss Harris' sanitarium give away the setting of principal photography — the Dino De Laurentiis Studios in Rome (one U. S. locale was used for prize-fight sequence).

Soundtrack is on the noisy side —a lot of grass evident on trade-show print, in which desaturated hues also were uneven between shots. Russell Lloyd edited to a fair 109 minutes. Other credits are okay.

Murf.

The Violent Ones
(COLOR)

Actor Lamas directs himself in a static tale of Gringo-Yanqui race bias.

Feature Film Corp. of America release of Madison Productions presentation in association with Harold Goldman Associates, produced by Robert W. Stabler, directed by Fernando Lamas. Stars Lamas, Aldo Ray and Tommy Sands. Screenplay, Doug Wilson and Charles Davis; story, Fred Freiberger and Herman Miller; camera, Fleet Southcott; editor, Fred W. Berger; music, Marlin Skiles; art direction, Paul Sylos, Jr.; sound, Ryder Sound Service; asst. director, George Fenaja. Reviewed at Tiffany, L.A., Oct. 3, 1967. Running time: **84 MINS.**

Manuel Vega .... Fernando Lamas
Joe Vorzyck .... Aldo Ray
Mike Marian .... Tommy Sands
Lucas Barnes .... David Carradine
Dolores .... Lisa Gaye
Juanita .... Melinda Marx

Best prospects for "The Violent Ones" appear to be the bottom half of double bill bookings. Fernando Lamas directed as well as starred in this low-budget, out-of-date treatment of the old lynch-mob routine, written by Doug Wilson and Charles Davis from a story by Fred Freiberger and Herman Miller.

Lamas turns up as the grim, noble peace officer of Mexican ancestry forced to contain his dislike of gringos long enough to shield his three Mexican-hating, Yankee suspects (David Carradine, Tommy Sands and Aldo Ray) from certain hanging by an aroused Mexican-American community.

For openers there is a rape scene. The Mexican-American rapee, portrayed in standard style by Groucho Marx's daughter, Melinda (will those pretty young things never learn to pull down their window shades before stripping?), has just time enough to reveal her attacker's national origins before death. From then on, the plot plods predictably.

Lamas pleads with the townsfolk for a fair trial, in the name of justice. The girl's blue-haired father swears revenge and incites his buddies. Lamas sneaks his prisoners out of town, only to be followed by papa and his posse, who do not want them to make it over the dry hills to the safety of the Silver City jail. During the long chase, with everyone now afoot or ahorse, the murderer-rapist reveals himself, and all four chased men learn that racial prejudice is bad.

Lamas takes the whole thing seriously. The other principal actors—especially the stylish David Carradine — seemingly know better, and have a grisly sort of fun putting on everyone.

Static direction, uninspired photography, and over-dramatic scoring by Marlin Skiles help roast the corn. *Esse.*

The Hills Run Red
(ITALIAN-COLOR)

Enough action in this Italian-made oater to fill three pix, but film carries on the European tradition of shooting up everyone in sight. Limited boxoffice appeal.

Hollywood, Sept. 27.

United Artists release of Dino De Laurentiis production. Directed by Lee W. Beaver. Screenplay, Dean Craig; camera, (Technicolor), Toni Secchi; music, Leo Nichols; Reviewed at Goldwyn Studios, Sept. 26, 1967. Running time **89 MINS.**

Jerry Brewster .... Thomas Hunter
Mendez .... Henry Silva
Getz .... Dan Duryea
Ken Seagull .... Nando Gazzolo
Mary Ann .... Nicoletta Machiavelli
Hattie .... Gianna Serra
Tim .... Loris Loddi
Horner .... Geoffrey Copleston
Stayne .... Paolo Magalotti
Federal Sergeant .... Tiberio Mitri
1st Gambler .... Vittoria Bonos
Sancho .... Mirko Valentin
Pedro .... Guglielmo Spoletini
Burger .... Guido Celano
Soldier Mitch .... Mauro Mannatrizio
Carson .... Gian Luigi Crescenzi

Another of what is apparently an endless supply of European-made blood and gut oaters, "Hills" has good guy Thomas Hunter pitted against incredible odds and a cast of a thousand bad men and he slugs, shoots and scowls his way through this action packed adventure yarn in such an incredibly naive manner that he should be nominated for the Nobel Peace Prize for acting.

The Dean Craig script has the hero, recently released a five-year prison stretch, searching for Seagull, former partner in crime who has taken stolen loot and disappeared. He finds that his wife has been killed by Seagull who is now extremely wealthy. You seen it before, you think?

Plot centers around the endless attempts of Seagull's band of desperados to kill the hero. There are barroom fights, fights by a river, barn fights, gun fights and a dozen others, all with Hunter overwhelmingly outnumbered. There are also some well photographed outdoor action sequences, including one in which firery branches are pushed from cliffs to stampede thousands of wild horses.

In the finale Hunter, aided by Dan Duryea, manages to wipe out hundreds of attackers with dynamite sticks and a pistol which miraculously doesn't need reloading.

Hunter endures every brutalizing incident with a ninexhaustible seeming energy, while the rest of the cast appears to be in a hurry to get to the next setup. Dan Duryea apparently didn't take a moment of it seriously and Henry Silva is given a number of chances to laugh sardonically at the screen. Nicoletta Machiavelli is very pretty and Geoffrey Copleston is pretty awful as a leader of a town of cowards. Nando Gazzolo is the villain, Seagull.

Lee W. Beaver (who's really Italo director Carlo Lizzani) directed and the Leo Nichols music was serviceable. There is an uncredited ballad, "I Know A Girl With Golden Hair," sung over the opening shots and fade-out that has a nice lilt. Original Italian title was "Un Fiume di Dollari" (A River of Dollars). *Dool.*

Charlie, The Lonesome Cougar
(COLOR)

Semi-documentary about a cougar that refused to believe he wasn't a human, and some humans who taught him otherwise.

Buena Vista release of Cangary Ltd. production, produced by Winston Hibler, Lloyd Beebe, Charles L. Draper, Ford Beebe, with cooperation of Potlatch Forests Inc., Weyerhaeuser Co. Features entire cast. Directed by Hibler. Screenplay, Jack Speirs, from story by Spears and Hibler. Narrator, Rex Allen. Camera (Technicolor), Lloyd Beebe, William W. Bacon 3d, Charles L. Draper; editor, Gregg McLaughlin; sound, Robert O. Cook; animal supervision, Marinho Correia, Dell Ray; music, Franklyn Marks, orchestrated by Wayne Robinson; song, "Talkin' About Charlie," Speirs, Marks. Reviewed in New York, Oct. 2, '67. Running Time, **75 MINS.**

Jess Bradley .... Ron Brown
Potlatch .... Brian Russell
Jess's fiance .... Linda Wallace
Farmer .... Jim Wilson
Mill manager .... Clifford Peterson
Chief engineer .... Lewis Sample
Mill hand .... Edward C. Moller
Charlie .... Himself

Usually, the short subjects that Disney packages to go out with his animated features run about a half-hour or so but this one, which will go out with "The Jungle Book," has almost the same running time as the animated feature. It properly belongs in the category of the Disney "True-Life Adventure" series rather than the fictional film genre as the "feeling" is that of a documentary, albeit a staged one with professional actors and a prepared script.

Shot against the background of the lumber country near Sequim, Washington, its cameramen also had to cover a 110-mile log drive down the Clearwater River to the Potlatch Lumber Mill at Lewiston, Idaho The river run is as exciting as the considerably longer footage given to Charlie, a cougar rescued in infancy by a forester and brought up by him in the atmosphere of a lumber camp.

Although Charlie, once he reaches full size, is too sleek and potentially dangerous to inspire the love that Joy Adamson's Elsa evidently did, he does portray some very human traits. While under the strict supervision of some skilled animal trainers, there's nothing of this evident in the reactions of the human actors who have to work in close quarters with the beautiful animal. The storyline is simple and makes little demands on the actors other than requiring them to assume a friendliness for the big cat that they may not necessarily have felt.

Lloyd Beebe, William W. Bacon 3rd and Charles L. Draper's Technicolor camerawork resists the temptation to dwell on the gorgeous scenery and sticks close to the conniptions of the cougar and his human buddies. The film has enough legs to stand on its own, once its usefulness in support of "Jungle Book" has passed, and is a natural for the Disney periodic reissue pattern.

Robe.

A Pistol Shot
(RUSSIAN-COLOR)

Paris, Oct. 3.

Sovexport release of Mosfilm production. With Mikhail Kozakov, Youri Iakovlev, Ariadna Chenguelaia. Directed by Nikolai Trachtenberg. Screenplay, Nikolai Kovarsky from story by Alexandre Pushkin; camera (Sov-color), S. Chenine; music, Karen Katchatourian. At Theatre Marigny, Paris. Running Time, **80 MINS.**

Silvio .... Mikhail Kozakov
Count .... Youri Iakovlev
Countess .... Arianda Chenguelaia
Blekine .... Oleg Tabakov
Enseigne .... V. Bariatinski
Colonel .... V. Davydov
Kuzka .... B. Novikov

A story of Alexandre Pushkin is screened with reverence for the great poet's work. But its theatrical, static quality, uneven color and stilted playing make this mainly a home item. There could be some specialized use on faithfulness to its subject and its fairly taking quality despite its filmic ineptitudes.

A morose man lives in a garrison town in the early 19th Century. It seems he had once been humiliated in a duel by a dashing Count and had refused to take his turn after the other grazed him. Now, after years of brooding, he is ready to take his pistol shot since the man is now married and may care more for his life.

Pushkin's offended, painfully thin-skinned hero finally cannot do it and joins a revolutionary movement in Greece. Old Russia has a seemingly tintype recreation of some resemblance if in a literary rather than realistic manner. The Russians appear to venerate their classics too much to give them a better filmic adaptation. *Mosk.*

Carmen, Baby
(YUGOSLAV-GERMAN-U.S COLOR-ULTRASCOPE)

Latest Carmen variation. It's well - photographed. Trash about a tramp. Strictly sexploitation.

Audubon Films release of an Amsterdam Film Corporation (Radley Metzger) production. Stars Uta Levka, Claude Ringer, Carl Mohner. Directed by Metzger. Screenplay, Jesse Vogel, based on Prosper Merimee story; camera (Eastman Color), Hans Jura, no other technical credits. Reviewed in New York, Sept. 29, '67. Running time: 90 MINS.

Carmen .... Uta Levka
Policeman .... Claude Ringer
Medico .... Carl Mohner
Dolores .... Barbara Valentine
Baby Lucas .... Walter Wiltz
Misty .... Christiane Rucker
Magistrate .... Michael Munzer
Darcy .... Doris Pistek

There's at least one improvement in the sexploitation film, the photography. Now, if they'd do something about the writing, the acting and the direction!

Radley Metzger's variation on Prosper Merimee's Carmen tragedy doesn't venture far afield in the story line—she's a waitress in an unidentified port, Don Jose is a policeman, and Escamillo is Baby Lucas, a rock 'n' roll singer. Where Metzger really does experiment is in the sexual connotions of his fatalistic heroine. This kitten believes in anything goes.

Within the loose framework of the Carmen story, adapted by Jesse Vogel (whose idea of dialog is "She was a witch. Her kisses poisoned me but I couldn't have enough of them.") Metzger loads his film with pad scenes that inventories most of the handbook approaches to sex, conventional and otherwise. There's titillation for any type of voyeur—except bestiality.

The people involved are uniformly handsome. The girls, particularly lady Uta Levka, are well endowed physically if not histrionically. And Walter Wiltz, despite his ridiculous "Baby Lucas" label, is a truly sexy male type. Which can't be said for Claude Ringer, the unfortunate cop who gets fatally entangled in Carmen's web. Michael Munzer, as magistrate who holds orgies, and Carl Mohner as a businessman who shares his bed and his wife with Carmen, are also highly presentable.

Booked into both the Rialto and the 72d Street Playhouse, Audubon is evidently aiming for a quick return from both the Times Square sexploitation crowd and the East Side art fans who occasionally buy such fare, hoping to repeat the previous success of "I, A Woman." Some of the scenes may prove a bit strong, however, for even the sophisticated East Siders.

Handsomely mounted, and photographed in Eastman Color by Hans Jura (his exteriors are on a par with much more expensive films and make the most of the Yugoslavian exteriors), Audubon has a very commercial and, very likely, profitable bit of cinematic trash. *Robe.*

Sadismo
(SHOCKUMENTARY—COLOR)

Still another tired compilation of imported and/or staged sequences (mostly Japanese), with principal theme man's inhumanity to animals and, to lesser degree, man's inhumanity to man. Limited appeal.

Trans American release of Salvatore Billitteri production. Narrated by Burt Topper and Terry Telli; commentary, Philip Marx; editors, Fred Feitshans, Billitteri; music, Les Baxter, supervised by Al Simms. No other credits provided. Reviewed at Selwyn's 42d St. Theatre, N.Y., Oct. 6, '67. Running Time, 81 MINS.

This latest contribution to the shockumentary field must have put the producer to a lot of trouble as the Japanese portions weren't enough to make a feature and were padded out with odd bits of newsreel and stock footage plus a ridiculous opening sequence that Roger Corman may have inspired but would never have acknowledged.

The film, being released by American International Pictures' "special films" subsidiary, Trans American Films (how that name must annoy United Artists' parent company), ran into trouble even before it hit the market because of its "cruelty to animals" scenes which have caused protests from the Human Society to the Motion Picture Assn. of America.

Trans American is playing it cautiously, even for the usual taken-for-granted New York release, teaming it with AIP's "Devils Angels" in one 42d Street house, whereas "Devils Angels" is playing 28 other Gotham area houses, but with "Riot On Sunset Strip" as the other half.

While the ordinarily hard to upset 42d Street audience, at the showing caught for this review, reacted to most of the film with its usual nervous titters, outright laughter and occasionally caustic comment (one voice was heard yelling "Show de uddah pickchuh!"), it fell completely silent during a brief sequence near the end, of footage showing Nazi concentration camps and the thousands of emaciated, tortured bodies (this, they knew, wasn't faked). That couldn't be said for much of the film which includes many semi-familiar shots (the snake skinning, the plastic surgery, the Caesarian operation, the pseudo-festivals)—many scenes probably innocent but with the commentary slyly suggesting that "beneath this seeming innocence, all is evil."

What happens to humans in "Sadismo" is no worse than what has been in previous films of this genre —and tame compared to "Mondo Cane" or "Africa Addio"—but the animal sequences deserve condemnation. A dogfight that goes on interminably, feeding baby chickens (live) to a giant lizard, and other repellent indignities are not for the kiddies. The scenes being used in the ads, however, are 100% faked and deserve the laughter with which they're greeted.

Cinematic trash that will, it is hoped for the good name of show biz, quickly use up its sick market. *Robe.*

Castle of Evil
(COLOR)

Rudimentary horror-cum-mystery programmer, okay for duals. Virginia Mayo excellent.

United Picture Corp. release of World Entertainment Corp. presentation of a National Telefilm Associates production, produced by Earle Lyon; executive producer, Fred Jordan. Features Scott Brady, Virginia Mayo, David Brian, Lisa Gaye, Hugh Marlowe. Directed by Francis D. Lyon. Screenplay, Charles A. Wallace; camera (Eastman Color), Brick Marquard; music, Paul Dunlap; editor, Robert S. Eisen; asst. director, Joe Wonder. Reviewed at New Amsterdam Theatre, N.Y., Oct. 5, 1967. Running Time, 80 MINS.

Matt Granger .... Scott Brady
Sable .... Virginia Mayo
Carol Harris .... Lisa Gaye
Robert Hawley .... David Brian
Dr. Corozar .... Hugh Marlowe

Television has revitalized Hollywood's Poverty Row, as this poor horror-cum-mystery item, which bears the copyright of film-package syndicators National Telefilm Associates, reveals once again. (It has not, however, yet been on tv.) Reminding of tube pyrotechnics are the small amount of sets, the underrehearsed acting, the totally uninvolved direction, the art director's realiance on few primary colors, etc. Still, as a 42d St. grind audience demonstrated, there are enough chills in the last 20 minutes to make "Castle of Evil" an okay programmer in its market.

Plot has five people brought together to a famous chemist's castle on a remote Caribbean island. They had all been present when his face was disfigured by some phosphorous salts. Now he is dead, but his "spirit" announces that the five will not share in his wealth until the guilty one is discovered among themselves and killed. There is an unexpected plot development midway which explains the mechanics of the supposed supernatural happenings and so the spectacle of the group eliminating one of their member is avoided.

Audience found some appearances of the mechanical monster near the end thrilling, though this will not be shared by more sophisticated viewers. Some of the dialog in Charles A. Wallace's script will more likely be appealing to this element ("You must think I'm a crazy old man." "No, but I think you've got some pretty savage ideas.").

Acting, like most technical credits, is way below par, especially for such an experienced cast. They sound like they had learned their lines not a moment before shooting each scene with no time for the slightest modulation or interpretation. None of this applies, happily, to Virginia Mayo, who deserves better than her current career in lowbudgeters. *Byro.*

Bike Boy
(COLOR)

Latest peepshow from the Warhol factory. Strictly for yawns.

A film produced, directed, written and photographed (Eastman Color) by Andy Warhol. Reviewed at the Hudson Theatre, N.Y., Oct. 5, '67. Running Time, 96 MINS.

Motorcyclist .... Joe Spencer
His buddy .... Ed Wiener

Fellow cyclist .... Vera Cruz
Older woman .... Ingrid Superstar
Another older woman....... Ann Wehrer
First salesman .... George Ann
Second salesman .... Bruce Ann
Also, Bridget Parker, Clay Bird, Viva!, Bettina Coffin.

Underground films began as a reaction against the "impersonally" manufactured Hollywood product but have quickly degenerated into the most predictable and tedious "formula" pictures now being made. Andy Warhol's latest, "Bike Boy," is indistinguishable from his previous "I, a Man" in plot (what little there is), dialog, acting and visual style. Considering the earlier opus has yet to get a date outside New York, it seems reasonable to doubt the commercial success of the new pic even in its highly specialized market. You can bore some of the people some of the time, et cetera.

Say this for Warhol's theatrically released stag films; they don't separate the men from the boys. Although his male performers typically receive more lustful attention, there is sufficient bare-breast footage to counterpoint the displays of male genitals and buttocks. Only diehard voyeurs of either sexual persuasion are likely to tolerate the tedious loquacity for these brief views of flesh, however.

"Bike Boy" tells of a motorcycle moron's escapades with a variety of young women, all of whom are intensely interested in his sexual skills. A few of the encounters yield scattered laughs, particularly an interlude with Viva, Warhol's latest "discovery." Most of the amateur players' improvisations are merely vulgar and pointless, ultimately making the frequently inaudible soundtrack and fuzzy color photography blessings in disguise. *Beau.*

Gentle Giant
(COLOR)

Pic which spawned the current CBS-TV series. So-so story about boy and pet bear. For the very young, on duals.

Hollywood, Sept. 27.
Paramount Pictures release of an Ivan Tors Production; executive producer, Stanley L. Colbert. Features Dennis Weaver, Vera Miles, Ralph Meeker, Clint Howard. Directed by James Nielson, Screenplay, Edward J. Lakso, Andy White, based on the novel, "Gentle Ben," by Walt Morey; camera (Eastancolor), Howard Winner; editors, Warren Adams, Peter Colbert; music Samuel Matlovsky; asst. director, Buddy Nadler. Reviewed at Paramount Studios, L.A., Sept. 26, '67. Running time, 93 MINS.

Tom Wedloe .... Dennis Weaver
Ellen Wedloe .... Vera Miles
Fog Hanson .... Ralph Meeker
Mark Wedloe .... Clint Howard
Dink .... Huntz Hall
Mike .... Charles Martin
Tater .... Rance Howard
Charlie .... Frank Schuller
Swenson .... Robertson White
Mate .... Ric O'Feldman

The title "Gentle Giant" is a contrivance to eliminate confusion with the new "Gentle Ben" CBS-TV series, although the Ivan Tors feature film in fact served as a sort of pilot. Affection of a boy for a black bear is told in a bland and padded script, produced and directed in routine, low-budget fashion. Animal sequences, technically clever, bog down in the chatter. Filmed at Tors' Miami studios and other Florida locations, the Paramount release needs a strong dual bill mate for satisfactory returns in situations catering to the very young. In addition, release after related vidseries has already begun may hinder b.o. action.

Edward J. Lakso and Andy White adapted Walt Morey's "Gentle Ben" novel into a talky screenplay. Clint Howard, seven years old but five years in the acting profession, plays a lonely boy who finds companionship with a bear cub. Dennis Weaver and Vera Miles are his parents. Ralph Meeker, ex-Dead End Kid and Bowery Boy Huntz Hall, and Rance Howard (Clint's real-life dad, incidentally) play the heavies of the piece.

As written, acted and directed, Meeker and pals are limmed with the subtlety of a sledgehammer. Their fishing boat is scroungy; so are they. They drink beer, and smoke. The good guys are pure as the unsmogged snow. Such broad-brush treatment ill prepares young people for their later years. In contrast, Walt Disney scripts usually are more "sophisticated."

Family film producers presumably should be alert to fact that tolay's sub-teeners are far more hip than their kind used to be. Accordingly, pollyanna pix face a shrinking market, unless scripts begin to show the grays of this world, and not reflect the blacks and whites of 19th century melodrama.

Ralph Helfer, Tors' partner in Africa, U.S.A., is credited with animal work supervision. Scenes between young Howard and the bear are genuinely touching. But even the very young will begin to squirm at distended dialog which flags the predictable pace. Weaver is good, Miss Miles is charmingly reactive, as required, and other thesps render stock support. Samuel Matlovksy's harmonica-oriented score lends a good assist.

Pic has the low-budget look—erratic color tones between shots (one of them, a fishing-boat bit, very grainy), simple set-ups, etc. James Neilson, a pro at this type of film, was apparently unduly handicapped by budget. Howard Winner's camera (color process uncredited), and Edmud Gibson's second unit lensing, depict the Florida backwaters. Other credits are standard. In the tv series, Weaver and the Howards are regulars. *Murf.*

They Came From Beyond Space
(BRITISH—COLOR)

Routine sci-fi tale, not up to Freddie Francis' usual level, but adequate bottom-half support for Embassy package.

Embassy Pictures release of an Amicus production. Stars Robert Hutton, Jennifer Jayne, Zia Mohyeddin, Bernard Kay. Produced by Max J. Rosenberg, Milton Subotsky. Directed by Freddie Francis. Screenplay, Subotsky, based on novel, "The Gods Hate Kansas," by Joseph Millard; camera (Pathe Color), Norman Warwick; editor, Peter Musgrave; sound, Clive Smith; art directors, Don Mingaye, Scott Slimon; special effects, Bowie Films; music, composed by James Stevens, conducted by Philip Martell; asst. director, Ray Corbett. Reviewed at New Amsterdam Theatre. New York, Oct. 1, '67. Running Time, 85 MINS.

Temple	Robert Hutton
Lee	Jennifer Jayne
Fargo	Zia Mohyeddin
Arden	Bernard Kay
Monj	Michael Gough
Mullane	Geoffrey Wallace
Stilwell	Maurice Good
Girl Attendant	Luanshiya Greer
Bill Trethowan	John Harvey
Mrs. Trethowan	Diana King
Rogers	Paul Bacon
Doctor (Street)	Christopher Banks
Peterson	Dermot Cathie
Dr. Andrews	Norman Claridge
Guard	James Donnelly
Blake	Frank Forsyth
McCabe	Leonard Grahame
Williams	Michael Hawkins
Doctor (Office)	Jack Lambert
Maitland	Robin Parkinson
Bank Manager	Edward Rees
Girl In Street	Katy Wild
Commentator	Kenneth Kendall

Even Freddie Francis, who gives routine sci-fi scripts considerably more than they deserve, isn't able to help this tired tale. Certainly not helped by some abysmal color photography, this one might as well have been made in black and white.

Perhaps the switch from a Kansas location to Britain was too much for Milton Subotsky, who not only adapted Joseph Millard's novel, "The Gods Hate Kansas," but also coproduced with Max J. Rosenberg. The plotline is familiar, the investigation of meteorites and the projection of outer space "things" into the bodies of humans.

Robert Hutton, immune to the spacemen's efforts because of a silver plate in his skull, is thus free to carry on the investigation that every sci-fi fan knows will eventually bring the fugitives to justice. What is disappointing in this particular effort, as much as the obvious plot, is the lack of special effects of any importance.

Hutton, Jennifer Jayne and Geoffrey Wallace as Hutton's assistants, East Indian actor Zia Mohyeddin (familiar to Broadway audiences) as a scientist friend, and Michael Gough as the Leader of the Spacemen, are very good within the confines of their limited parts. All technical aspects of film are good, but not outstanding, with exception- of color, which is very bad. Film is being released as package with "The Terrornauts," by Embassy. *Robe.*

Operation Kid Brother
(ITALIAN—COLOR)

Latest 007 imitation ineptly funny. Campy ad campaign may save it.

United Artists release of a Dario Sabatello production. Stars Neil Connery, Daniela Bianchi, Adolfo Celi; features Agata Flori, Bernard Lee, Anthony Dawson, Lois Maxwell, Yachuco Yama. Directed by Alberto Demartino. Screenplay by Paul Levi, Frank Walker; camera (Technicolor), Alejandro Ulloa; music, Ennio Moricone, Bruno Nicolai; song, Nohra-Nicolai, Moricone; editor, Otello Colangeli; asst. director, Carlo Moscovini. Previewed at United Artists home office, Sept. 21, '67. Running Time, 104 MINS.

Neil Connery	Neil Connery
Maya	Daniela Bianchi
Thair	Adolfo Celi
Mildred	Agata Flori
Commander Cunningham	Bernard Lee
Alpha	Anthony Dawson
Max	Lois Maxwell
Yachuco	Yachuco Yama
Kurt	Guido Lollobrigida
Juan	Franco Giacobini
Ward Jones	Nando Angelini
Gamma	Mario Soria
Lotte	Anna Maria Noe

Of the many gimmicks used to justify a semingly endless succession of spy pix, casting Sean Connery's younger brother Neil as mankind's latest sexy savior must represent a new "reaching." The film resulting from this brainstorm is so unbelievably inept that many viewers may find it hilarious fun. United Artists realizes the pic's camp potential, as ads will self-kiddingly proclaim that "'Operation Kid Brother' is too much for one mother." At best the film deserves bottom-half bookings, however, and even in this slot may irk patrons lacking a sense of the ridiculous.

The plot has Neil Connery cast as a plastic surgeon blackmailed by the Allied powers into helping smash an international criminal conspiracy. Besides being the younger brother of 007, he also has the powers of truth-compelling hypnosis and lip-reading. (Considering that most of the lips are mouthing Italian while the voices are speaking dubbed English, it's hard to see how the latter talent is very helpful.) Needless to say, he rescues the world from these unsavory megalomaniacs and makes a few girl friends along the way, albeit in perfunctory sexual interludes.

In a film rife with laughs, perhaps the most memorable moment occurs when Connery comes upon a body lying on the floor with a knife stuck through the heart, bends down to check the pulse, and then provides his informed medical opinion: *"I think he's had it."* Technical mistakes, like the clearly visible driver in a car supposedly propelled by radar, also contribute to the fun.

Production notes quote the tyro Connery as saying: "The first week before the cameras I was ready to pack my bags and head back to the peace and serenity of Scotland. It seemed to me that if B. B. C. wa ted to make one of their funniest films, all they had to do was to turn their cameras on me." None of the other cast members is on record as possessing similarly astute self-perception.

Alejandro Ulloa's color lensing makes the film look like a blow-up of an 8m print, while Franco Fontana's art direction is decidedly budget-conscious. Otello Colangeli has edited to a lethargic 104 minutes, a b o u t 30 minutes too much of a bad thing. Ennio Moricone and Bruno Nicolai's music tries hard to agitate the film to life but may instead only agitate viewers. *Beau.*

Midaregumo
(Scattered Clouds)
(JAPANESE — COLOR)

Tokyo, Sept. 29.

Toho production and release. Produced by Masumi Fujimoto, Shoso Kankeo. Directed by Mikio Naruse. Features Yuzo Kaiyama, Yoko Tsukasa, Daisuke Kato, Nobu Tsuchiya, Mitsuko Mori, Mitsuko Kusabi, Yuniiko Iida, Nadya Kusakawa. Screenplay, Nobuo Yamada; camera (Eastman Color), Jo Minezawa; art director, Satoru Nakano; music, Toru Takemitsu. Previewed in Tokyo. Running time: 110 MINS.

The film director, like any other artist, sees the world from his own angle. If this partial view is meaningful and consistent, it is spoken of as the director's style, meaning both his prospect and his interpretation.

The style of Mikio Naruse, Japan's leading senior director, is one of the most consistent, and one of the least comforting. Heinosuke Gosho at least permitted his people to hope; Yasujiro Ozu left his people each other; but Naruse shows us that there is no hope at all and that other people are but one of the mirages in this hopeless world.

"Scattered Clouds" (Midaregumo) is the latest, and in some ways, the best of his films. A young husband (Nobu Tsuchiya) and wife (Yoko Tsukasa) are getting ready to go abroad when he is killed in a car accident. The driver of the vehicle (Yuzo Kaiyama), though the trial finds him innocent, insists upon paying a monthly sum to the widow. Hating him as the murderer of her husband, Yoko is prevailed upon by his sister (Mitsuko Mori) to take the money, because the dead man left her very little.

Naruse gives himself a problem of considerable complexity. He begins with two people as estranged as is possible to get, and moves them toward each other and into the false u n i t y which is love. He must make the entire maneuver believable, and does it brilliantly.

The film is splendidly made, beautifully acted, most accurately observed, and sad, even depressing, to an extraordinary degree. Yet it is saved, both from easy pathos and from black despair, by the degree to which Naruse feels for his people. If he did not, this would not be such a rich film but, more, the faint aura of hope which illumines even the ending, would not be there. That Naruse shows up these depressing truths, that he so truthfully indicates to us the state of his world, and perhaps ours, reveals a chink in that massive wall which is life, and through it we see light. *Chie.*

Separation
(BRITISH)

Sorrento, Oct. 1.

Bond Films presentation. Stars Jane Arden and David Kayser. Producer and directed by Jack Bond. Based on a story by Jane Arden. No other credits available. Screened at Sorrento Film Festival, Sept. 30, '67. Running time: 92 MINS.

"Separation" collared a certain amount of international notieriety when it was yanked from the Cork festival program about 10 minutes ahead of screening time. It is, therefore, having its world preem during the British film week at Sorrento. A fast summation: Cork was right, Sorrento blundered.

There is certainly a place, even perhaps a need, for avant garde films and filmmakers, but Jack Bond and his colleagues have just run riot. Maybe they know what it's all about, but for the audience (as the King of Siam would have said) it's a puzzlement. It is not just that the story line is obscure; that's fairly commonplace nowadays. But "Separation" is without shape or form, has no inherent or logical continuity, is self-indulgent and obviously derivative.

One of its more irritating features is the habit of repeating the dialog at irregular intervals throughout the film; that would have been bad enough in any circumstances, but when the script is dull and witless in the first place, repetition only adds to the boredom.

Jane Arden has credit for the original subject, and the best that can be said of her contribution is that she has penned a fat part for herself, as she's on screen throughout almost the entire footage. Her story is presumably a study in mental breakdown, and that allows the opportunity to display a certain amount of conventional histrionics. David Kayser as her husband is barely adequate. A couple of gratuitous nudie sequences will hardly help at the boxoffice.

Jack Bond's direction adds to the confusion, and the editing (with the action jumping forwards and backwards in time) increases the obscurity. Black and white photography, with many location backgrounds, is okay, but occasional insets seem pointless.

Myro.

Clambake
(SONGS—TECHNISCOPE— COLOR)

Elvis Presley at his best in well-motivated yarn; good entry for general market as well as for Presley trade.

Hollywood, Oct. 12.
United Artists release of Jules Levy-Arthur Gardner-Arnold Laven production. Stars Elvis Presley; features Shelley Fabares, Will Hutchins, Bill Bixby, James Gregory, Gary Merrill. Directed by Arthur H. Nadel. Story-screenplay. Arthur Browne Jr.; camera (Technicolor), William Margulies; music, Jeff Alexander; editor, Tom Rolf; asst. directors, Claude Binyon Jr., Bill Green. Reviewed at Samuel Goldwyn Studios, Oct. 12, '67. Running Time, 100 MINS.

Scott Heyward	Elvis Presley
Dianne Carter	Shelley Fabares
Tom Wilson	Will Hutchins
James Jamison III	Bill Bixby
Duster Heyward	James Gregory
Sam Burton	Gary Merrill
Ellie	Amanda Harley
Sally	Suzie Kaye
G'oria	Angelique Pettyjohn
Gigi	Olga Kaya
Olive	Arlene Charles
Mr. Hathaway	Jack Good
Doorman	Hal Peary
Race Announcer	Sam Riddle
Cigarette Girl	Sue England
Lisa	Lisa Slagle
Bartender	Lee Krieger
Crewman	Melvin Allen
Waiter	Herb Barnett
Bell Hop	Steve Cory
Barasch	Robert Lieb
Ice Cream Vendor	Red West

Elvis Presley has the benefit of superior mounting throughout in his latest "Clambake," carrying such a title because of a fast and colorful musical production number. The Jules Levy-Arthur Gardner-Arnold Laven production is one of singer's top offerings to date, backed by a legitimately-premised story line, melodic songs, acceptable acting and winding with a spectacular water race. Film has all the makings of being one of Presley's heaviest grossers.

Star plays a rich boy here, a level-headed kind of guy who doesn't want any of his father's money to help him win success, or boost him with the gals, either. So he changes identities with Will Hutchins, whom he meets at a snack bar, and takes his place as the new water ski instructor at a swank Miami Beach hotel. Hutchins is ensconced meanwhile in the Presidential suite and lives it up under the millionaire's name.

Such familiar overtones are sparked in the Arthur Browne, Jr., screenplay to come out as refreshing fare, with enough novel twists to keep interest at a high level. Plottage builds to Presley making an arrangement with a local speed boat designer, Gary Merrill, to rebuild his boat that blew up in last year's race and enter in the upcoming Orange Bowl Regatta classic. Lenser William Margulies is responsible for exciting race footage, some of the best done for such an event, and Arthur H. Nadel forges good suspense in his direction.

Presley is surrounded by a competent cast and delivers a better acting job than usual, as well as having eight song numbers for excellent effect. One of these, "Confidence," is a delightful sequence with a flock of youngsters on a swing; each is logically inserted.

Shelley Fabares provides pretty distaff interest, a gal posing as wealthy in an attempt to snag a moneyed husband, and Bill Bixby

enacts a playboy who has won the race classic for past three years, on the make for femme who finally sez no-thank-you. Hutchins and Merrill both acquit themselves satisfactorily and James Gregory is sufficiently bluff as Presley's tycoon father who finally sees the light.

Technical credits are all first rate, incuding Lloyd Papez' lush art direction, Tom Rolf's fast editing, Jeff Alexander's appropriate music score. *Whit.*

Undertaker And His Pals

Extremes of Gore and Psycho sadism laughed off at finale when all come alive. Sure to shock adults. Dubious market.

Louisville, Oct. 11.
Howco release of Eola Pictures production, produced and directed by David C. Graham. Stars Robert Lowery, Ray Dannis, Warrene Ott. Screenplay, T. L. P. Twicegood. Reviewed at West End Theatre, Louisville, Ky. Running Time, 60 MINS.

Filmed in black and white, exteriors are obviously of the Los Angeles area, with occasional studio scenes. Film opens on a night scene, usual city lights and neon signs, while camera follows three motorcyclists cruising streets, which seemed almost deserted—few cars or pedestrians. One cyclist parks his motorbike and enters a phonebooth to make a call. He then comes out, mounts his bike, and the three take off with mufflers open, and speed away. The riders are masked, and wear crash helmets.

Next scene shows a shapely femme, scantily clad, and obviously living alone in her apartment. The three hoods enter the apartment, threaten her with long knives. Next a loud scream from the femme, and cameras come in for a close shot of the woman, with the audience left with the suggestion that the hoods cut off her leg. Gal's name was Susie Lamb.

Next scene switches to an undertaker's parlor (sic), where the bereaved mother, a portly emotional woman, enters with her husband, to the accompaniment of loud wailing and crying. Undertaker, taken unawares, hurriedly switches off the rock 'n' roll music being played by his tape recorder, segueing to funereal, doleful music, as the couple enters the room where their daughter is laid out. The parents discuss payment of the bill, which the undertaker told them will be $1,200. The father remonstrates, saying that the undertaker had told him total cost of the funeral would be $149.98 "with the possibility of some extras which might be added to the total cost." Father becomes quite argumentative with the undertaker, saying his price is too high, and besides he quoted him a price of $149.98. Sign outside the establishment said, "We give trading stamps." While the father is arguing with the undertaker, the mother is stuffing long sheets of trading stamps in her purse.

Music background is mostly drums, and a horn. Indie film made in Hollywood, has borrowed every

gimmick from horror and macabre comedy films, with a resultant mish-mash which is difficult to appraise viewer-wise. Some will be disgusted—others might be tuned to the comedy slant, as were several in the audience at show caught. *Wied.*

The Girl and the Bugler
(Zvoniat, Otkroyte Dver) (RUSSIAN)

Pallid morality tale about 12-year-old girl's first crush on an older boy. A hard-sell in this market.

Artkino Pictures release of a Mosfilm Studios production. Directed by Alexander Mitta. Screenplay, Alexander Volodin; camera, A. Panasyuk; music, V. Basner. Previewed in New York, Oct. 13, '67. Running Time, 76 MINS.

Tanya	Lena Proklova
Bugler	Rolan Bykov
Petya	Victor Belokurov
Girl-friend	Lena Zolotuhina

Also, Vitya Kosykh, S. Nikonenko, Olya Semyonova, Vitya Sysoyev.

This old-fashioned, slowly paced story of a 12-year-old girl's crush on her Young Pioneer (a Soviet co-ed scouting group) leader won the Gold Lion at last year's Venice Children's Film Festival. This award may mystify most American audiences—young and old alike. Pic has little charm, wit or style to engage adults. Its spoon-fed moral to kids is about serving the public interest as well as one's personal interest. (This is "Say not what your country can do for you" stuff, stressed by JFK.)

Tanya, played in moderately appealing fashion by Lena Proklova, is being looked after by her neighbors in the absence of her mother who is visiting Tanya's father in a distant location where he has been temporarily asigned to work. Child's infatuation with the Young Pioneer leader ends when she sees him ice-skating affectionately with "an older woman." In the meantime Tanya has learned a few truisms from the bugler-father of a friend, who addresses an assembly of Young Pioneers and steals the show with his trumpet-playing and his heart-felt sentiments

Many viewers are likely to remember such earlier Soviet kiddie pix as "A Summer to Remember" and "My Name Is Ivan" and conclude that this one is minor league. Technical credits are mediocre, with soft-focus black-and-white lensing making many of the exteriors look like process work.

Film will be briefly spotlighted in upcoming Russo fest at N.Y.'s Cinema Village. U.S. bookings beyond that showing look highly unlikely. *Beau.*

The Terrornauts
(BRITISH—COLOR)

Inexpensive but well-handled sci-fi actioner, which should be able to handle itself well in the exploitation market, altho coupled with dull supporting piece.

Embassy Pictures release of an Amicus Production. Stars Simon Oates, Zena Marshall, Charles Hawtrey. Produced by Max J. Rosenberg, Milton Subotsky. Directed by Montgomery Tully. Screenplay, John Brunner, based on novel, "The Wailing Asteroid" by Murray

Leinster; camera (Pathe Color), Geoffrey Faithful; editor, Peter Musgrave; sound, Laurie Clarkson; art director, Bill Constable; special effects, Ernest Fletcher-Bowie Films; music, composed by Elizabeth Lutyens, conducted by Philip Martell; asst. director, Tom Walls. Reviewed at New Amsterdam Theatre, N.Y., Oct. 1, '67. Running Time, 75 MINS.
Burke .... Simon Oates
Sandy .... Zena Marshall
Yellowlees .... Charles Hawtrey
Mrs. Jones .... Patricia Hayes
Keller .... Stanley Meadows
Shore .... Max Adrian
Burke as a child .... Frank Barry
Danny .... Richard Carpenter
Nick .... Leonard Cracknell
Robot Operator .... Robert Jewell
Uncle .... Frank Forsyth
Gendarme .... Andrew Maranne

───

John Brunner, using Murray Leinster's novel, "The Wailing Asteroid," has fashioned a tight little sci-fi programmer that holds the interest. Director Montgomery Tully has wisely spiced the action with comedy, ably handled by veterans Charles Hawtrey as a prissy accountant and Patricia Hayes as a Cockney charwoman.

Producers Max J. Rosenberg and Milton Subotsky have been luckier in their casting in "The Terrornauts," than in companion piece, "They Came From Beyond Space." Male lead Simon Oates makes a good impression and lends credence to trade talk that he's a hot contender for the James Bon' parts being vacated by Sean Connery.

Zena Marshall is a photogenic dish, her principal requirement for the role, but displays more than physical attraction in her role as Oates' assistant. Legit actor Max Adrian, he of the immaculate diction and resonant tones, is outstanding as the near-villain of the piece, playing Oates' superior.

Geoffrey Faithful, although not helped much by the color process used, provides crisp and attractive photography. The special effects are not elaborate but exceptionally well handled, especially a robot provided with its own personality (a la Metro's "Forbidden Planet"). Tightly edited by Peter Musgrave, "Terrornauts" could hold its own on any sci-fi program. It's coupled with "They Came From Beyond Space" as a packaged release from Embassy.
Robe.

───

Yowake No Kuni
(Dawning Nation)
(JAPAN-COLOR)
Tokyo, Oct. 10.
Towa release of Twanaim Eiga (Takeji Takamura) production, produced by Takeji Takamura; directed by Toshie Tokieda. Camera, Hidehiko Fujise, and Shigeharu Watanabe; music, Akira Miyoshi. Previewed in Tokyo. Running time, 110 MINS.

Producer Takeji Takamura of the Iwanami Eiga Company first approached the Chinese People's Overseas Cultural Friendship Association to get permission to make a documentary back in 1959. Negotiations were repeatedly pursued by Iwanami over the years and, finally, last year, permission was granted to film in Peking and northeast China. A camera crew and femme director, Toshie Tokida, completed this color one-hour 50-minute feature pic in seven months.

The result is "Yowake No Kuni" (Dawning Nation). It is relatively unbiased, often strikingly beautiful, and quite well carpentered.

But it is also sometimes a bit dull and always politically naive.

The dullness is, in part, due to the team's being confined to one of the least interesting sections of China. Indeed, what is there to see in Changchun but the fertilizer plant; in Anshan but the iron works; and in Fushun the main sight would naturally be the big open-air coal mine. Though there are some Peking shots (mostly the area around the Teinan Gate), the film spends most of its time at such places as the Harbin Happiness People's Commune.

Still, director Tokieda puts in enough people so that her film does not always resemble an industrial documentary. There are crowds bathing on the banks of the Sungari, workers having conferences, medical teams at work. and, this being a Japanese film, lots of children. Also the Japanese eye for nature is clearly in evidence and there are lovely single shots of fields, trees and the flat, placid country of north China.

There is also lots of Mao. The man's image and influence has thoroughly saturated the country. There are oleographs, pastels, drawings and photographs of those familiar features everywhere. And almost everyone seems to be carrying the little red book which contains the man's stujefying banalities. Posters are on every wall, inside every home; slogans are everywhere and the tiniest country road has its own, spelled out in separate signs like the old Burma slave highway ads.

The picture that emerges is of a civilization so entirely materialistic as to make that of America seem almost mystical by comparison. Perhaps people still look at the moon or read books (other than the little red one) but there is no evidence of this. It is a sobering, sad, and eventually depressing picture.

Concerning this, however, director Tokieda and producer Takamura make no comment. As documentary-makers they apparently felt that their duty was merely to show and not to interpret. Still, to show the Red Guard (a small group on a walk to Yenan, following the footsteps of Mao Tse-Tung) and offer no explanation of their activities except that they are "patriotic," is decidedly naive. No indication of their political purpose or their less peaceful activities is given. As they march off into the distance at the end of the picture and the commentator speaks hopefully of a "dawning nation," one knows that one has not been shown enough.

We have witnessed the spiritual collapse of a state and not the emergence of one. With its godking, its double-think, its indoctrination of the young, its presumed tyranny of the mass, China has become barbaric—it is a civilization which has lost its humanity because this society is now frankly inhuman.

For China-watchers, however (and who isn't?), the film is very interesting.
Chie.

───

Akamegumo
(Sunset Clouds)
(JAPAN)
Tokyo, Oct. 10.
Shochiku release of Shinoda Productions film. With Shima Iwashita, Tsutomu Yamazaki, Mayumi Ogawa, Kei Sato. Directed by Masahiro Shinoda. Screenplay, Takayuki Suzuki, after Tsutomu Minakami's novel; camera, Masao Kosugi; music, Toru Takemitsu. Previewed in Tokyo. Running time, 105 MINS.

Masahiro Shinoda (who made "Pale Flower," "With Beauty and Sorrow," and "Punishment Island", has become one of Japan's finest directors. Certainly, in this day of the slip-shod production, he is one of the few to retain a respect for his craft, to exercise himself in the fine carpentry that is also filmmaking. Also, working slowly, about one film a year, the young director chooses his script with care, and works over their realization with a rigorous attention to detail, matching camera with emotion to a degree that is now rarely seen.

"Sunset Clouds" is a very good example of his art. Based on the Tsutomo Minakami novel, scripted by Tadayuki Suzuki, it puts together two of Shinoda's favorite themes: man alone, trying unsuccessfully to escape authority (the theme of "Pale Flower," and "Punishment Island") and both the beauty and the weakness of love (theme of "With Beauty and Sorrow").

Tsutomu Yamazki is AWOL from the Army, a serious offense in 1937, and goes to a small town on the Japan Sea to begin again. There he meets a young girl working as a maid at an inn (Shima Iwashita) and helps her to get a better job. Later, he visits her. She is already half in love with her benefactor but his proposition startles her. For a certain amount of money and to help him with his job, will he agree to sleep with an older colleague of his? That she eventually does is a measure of her gratitude, her simplicity and her need for money.

Her country-Geisha friend (marvelously played by Mayumi Ogawa) is shocked, mainly perhaps because the price for her virginity was so low, and when the secret police officer (Kei Sato, of "Onibaba") inevitably appears, it is she who tells what the escaped soldier has done. Sato tricks the wronged but completely trusting girl into leading him to Yamazaki's hideout, and then the MP's close in—not, however, before boy and girl have finally gotten together. So much for the story, but not where the virtues of this particular film lie.

They are first, in the way that Shinda conveys its atmosphere of 1937. With just a few details, so rigorous and so right, Shinoda creates the whole world of 1937, its frivolity, its uneasiness; the tawdry summer gaiety of a provincial hot-spring resort; and that vague sense of foreboding.

Shinoda does this (with the help of Masao Kosugi's discreet but brilliant photography) in a number of ways, but mainly through selection of detail (light on tile roofs, a single rising-sun flag, the way a girl puts up her hair), and incisively apt use of camera move-

ment and an extraordinary ability to get the best from actors.

This last is perhaps the most difficult part of the director's art, particularly in Japan where acting often means over-acting. Yet here, Shinoda gets superlative performances, even from Sato (usually a bit hamming) and certainly from Shima Iwashita (in real life, Mrs. Shinoda), whose delineation of the young girl, so trusting as to be almost stupid, so loving as to be almost absurd, is one that will not be forgotten for a time.

An example of what Shinoda can do with actors is seen in the performance he gets out of Mayumi Ogawa. Formerly but one in the Daiei stable, one of the older of the "new faces" girls, she played bar-hostesses and badwomen with no style and less distinction. Here, her performance is electrifying.
Chie.

───

The Further Perils of Laurel & Hardy
(COMPILATION)

Another Youngson compilation. Nostalgic in appeal and a gasser for those who like this sort of stuff.

Hollywood, Oct. 11.
Twentieth-Fox retrospective of Robert Youngson, continuity written by Youngson. Principals: Stan Laurel, Oliver Hardy, Jean Harlow, Charley Chase, Edgar Kennedy, Jimmy Finlayson, Snub Pollard, Billy West, Charlie Hall, Tom Kennedy, Noah Young, Charlotte Mineau, Tom Dugan, Charles Rogers, Bryant Washburn, Viola Richard, Edna Murphy, Dorothy Christie, Kay Deslys. Reviewed at 20th-Fox Studios, Oct. 11, '67. Running Time, 99 MINS.

Laurel and Hardy's past is again caught by producer-writer Robert Youngson in this second filmic excursion into their two-reelers. Following producer's previous cavalcade of clips focusing on yesteryear filmic tomfoolery, "Laurel and Hardy's Laughing 20s," released in 1965, this present edition is in the same line and mood and should attract similar audiences.

Slapstick is no more, but every time one of these novelty features reprising such insanity reaches the theatres its appeal is re-demonstrated. "Further Perils" carries a nostalgic kick for oldtimers. It is easy to forecast young audience reaction, particularly the Saturday matinee trade. Film also makes the case for the gagman, unseen hero who plotted the frantic action.

Pic marks Youngson's sixth cinematic gander into the comedy of the past, the first four general in tone as he drew on most of the celebrated comics of the day. Like "Laughing 20s," "Perils" pretty much confines its footage to the two comedians in the title, although several of their compatriots, such as Charle Chase, Billy West, Jimmy Finlayson, Snub Pollard and Edgar Kennedy, are in for good footage. Jean Harlow, before Howard Hughes found her, and cast her in "Hell's Angels," appears, too, in a sequence with onetime silent star Bryant Washburn.

Youngson has found footage dating back to 1918, long before the two comics teamed up. Most of film projects them as a team, but in these earlier clips of them solo each demonstrated the particular talent that was to boost them to stardom. Jay Jackson's narration weaves the pattern linking the more than 25 clips together, in which he inserts the proper punch and establishes just the right mood.

Half a dozen longer sequences in closing half give substance to the quality of the two comics' clowning, where each could do more with a look, a quick bit of business, than the majority of writers can capture today in a whole sequence. "The Great Mud Fight," like their "Battle of the Century"—later, the one about the pies—is among these; "The Great Water Fight," with Edgar Kennedy, another.

Filming, which showed the crudity of those past days, still is of sufficient quality to be acceptable without complaint. Music score by John Parker is inclined to be over-loud at times. Good sound effects have been inserted and feature comes off as a well-done piece of editing and production. *Whit.*

Des Garcons Et Des Filles
(Boys and Girls)
(FRENCH-BELGIAN)
(Color)

Paris, Oct. 10.
Rank release of Planfilm, Spiralfilm production. With Francois Leccia, Nicole Garcia, Francois Duval, Jean-Christophe Maucorps. Directed by Etienne Perier. Screenplay, Dominique Fabre; camera (Eastmancolor), Henri Raichi; editor, Sophie Coussein. At Lord Byron, Paris. Running Time, 95 MINS.

This film starts out with a cinema red herring via an interview with a young man that indicates the pic may be an attempt to put an actual youth outlook on film. But it then spins a wholesome yarn about a group of young students and workers who take over a house and try to live communally. Good-natured and well-meaning, it is somewhat too obvious, with mainly stereotyped characters, to give any sort of insight into modern youth.

Boy scoutish bit has them setting up house and sharing chores and having affairs, parties and some would-be intellectual discussions before drama strikes in an attempted suicide and a premature birth by an unwed mother. Destruction of the house has them going their own ways, presumably more mature.

But obvious comedics do ont get much depth into the film. The comedy is a bit familiar via the various types, that is the ladies' man, the dedicated but almost cynical artist, the poor little rich girl, the more easygoing, zesty working girl, etc. But it is a change-of-pace from the more violent youth pix and may have some family trade legs here with. Perhaps, it may have some corresponding use abroad.

But this lacks the more spirited depth in character and pace to give this much arty or specialized chances abroad. New group of young thesps are pleasing if no outstanding talent is unveiled. Direction is easygoing in conjunction with a routine script. *Mosk.*

Le Grand Meulnes
(FRENCH) (COLOR) (SCOPE)

Paris, Oct. 10.
CFDC release of Madeleine Films, AWA Films production. With Brigitte Fossey, Jean Blaise, Alain Libolt, Alain Jean, Marcel Cuvilier, Juliette Vilar. Directed by Jean-Gabriel Albicocco. Screenplay, Isabelle Riviere, Albicocco from book by Alain Fournier; camera (Eastmancolor), Quinto Albicocco; editor, Georges Klotz. At Imperial, Paris. Running Time, 110 MINS.

Meulnes	Jean Blaise
Yvonne	Brigitte Fossey
Francois	Alain Libolt
Franz	Alain Jean
Teacher	Marcel Cuvilier
Girl	Juliette Vilar

"Le Grand Meulnes" has become a romantic literary classic in France and been reprinted in most parts of the world. It deals with the attachment of a young friend to a more dashing and older fellow student whose lyrical imbroglios seem to take the place of his own lack of adventure as the son of a private school director in turn-of-the-century provincial France. This looks like the director has been extremely literal, and unfortunately somewhat too literary in transcribing it to the screen.

Result is a rather glossy, sentimental opus that too often uses prettiness in imagery for its own sake and a mixture of styles to have this lachrymore drama fairly staid and uneven. But its surface, glycerined good looks, arty interpretation and intentions could draw arty attention abroad. Its mannered mounting calls for a hardsell.

"Le Grand Meulnes" of the title is an older boy who infatuates the more timed son of the schoolmaster. It seems that Meulnes has once met a girl at a ball but can't find her again. He spends time searching and then gives up and goes to Paris where he meets a girl who was once the fiancee of the brother of the mysterious girl. If this sounds involved, it is. And so is what follows—unbelievably so, if one has the patience to try to figure out what is happening and why.

The film overdoes use of vaselined lenses or shooting through smeared glasses to finally blur what reality there is in this. This appears a long, stylishly lensed but haltingly directed pic with the acting also uneven.

Brigitte Fossey has the right quality as the dream symbol, but the pains of adolescence, idealism and youthful coming-of-age are somewhat lost in the maze of pretty images. *Mosk.*

Cork Fest

Unconsecrated Earth
(Ongewijde Aarde)
(NETHERLANDS)

Cork, Oct. 10.
Production by Skelfilm of Hoorn. Script and direction by Jef van der Heyden. Photography by Jan Oonk and Fred Tammes. Music by Enrico Neckheim. With Shireen Strooker, Tom Lensink, Leo Derijeks, Harry van Airtum, Wim van der Huevel. Reviewed at Cork Film Festival. Running time: 65 MINS.

Made entirely on location on a three week shooting schedule this

hort feature cost only $44,000 and was mainly financed by its director, he young Dutchman who showed "The Blue Lamp" at last year's Cork Film Festival.

It recounts the story of a gay orphan, Birgitte, who escapes from a convent and gets herself a house in a village where she earns a living by making artificial flowers. She falls in love with Louis, a handsome young showman at the local fair but he has a bigger problem on his mind. Because his father committed suicide, the parent is not buried in consecrated soil and Louis won't rest until he is re-interred. He repeatedly begs the local priest for permission to move the body to the official graveyard but always the priest says only over his dead body.

The priest dies and at dead of night Louis goes to the prepared grave, deepens it, lightly covers it with earth. Next day it is the priest's coffin which is under that of the suicide's. By the graveyard Louis raises his voice in a light-earted "Amen" and then himself and Birgitte go laughing and loving away in their caravan. For he funeral sequence shots of an uthentic funeral of a priest were sed with the result that the film was banned for screening in the Catholic part of Holland.

It is original, it is merry and entertaining but it would be more effective if it ended at the cemetery and if its pace was more even. Still, entertaining, though he situation is outside the ken f many of today's irreligious. *She.*

The Yellow Robes
(Ran Salu)
(CEYLON)

Cork, Oct. 10.
Production of Chameekara Producers Ltd., Colombo. Directed by Lester J. Peries. Script by P. K. D. Seneviratnefl Photography by Sumitta Amerasinghe; Music by Amaradeva. With Punya Heen-Jeniya (Sujatha) Tony Ranasinghe (Cyril) Anula Karunatillak (SaroJini) and Dayananda Gunawardene, J. B. Gunasekera, Iranganie Meedeniyat, Suhasini Athukorale, A. P. Gunaratne, Somi Meegama, Shanti Lekha, Kithsiri Perera and S.A. James. Reviewed at Cork Film Festival. Running Time: 108 MINS.

This picture from Ceylon is a airly successful attempt at translating a Buddhist morality play nto modern setting. The heroine, Sujatha, belongs to a wealthy, upper-middle class family, still conservative in its way. She is engaged to Cyril, a young barrister who comes back from Europe and s impatient and critical of the ld traditions of his country. He becomes the lover of Sarojinia, he lively and uninhibited friend f his fiance but abandons her when she bcomes pregnant. Both girls eventually escape from their roblems and find peace of mind s Buddhist nuns.

It was well directed, with intelligent, sensitive and sparse dilogue. Easily one of the best of he Far East films of recent years. Perhaps the religious and moral one of "goodness" is a bit naive o western experience but it is o well done otherwise that this ault is easy to forgive.

Such films are often prone to emotionalism and hgih histrionics

but not so here. This is well controlled.

A pleasant, interesting pic, reealing of what Buddhist belief an mean to the Cingalese. Fine acting all around. *She.*

Harvest, And So Ye Shall Reap
(La Cosecha)
(ARGENTINE)

Cork, Oct. 10.
Production of Imago S.R.I., Buenos Aires. Directed by Marcos Madanes. Script by Ezequiel Marrinez Estrada, photography by Adelqui Camusso. Music by Virtu Marango. With Pedro Buchardo, Guerino Marchesi, Hector Carrion, Margarita Corona, Elsa Berenguer, Lola Palombo. Reviewed at Cork Film Festival. Running Time, 78 MINS.

There were better-made features than this at the recent Cork Film Festival but this is one which sticks in memory. Its beginning was tedious, its camera work and effects were not remarkable, yet, sequence by sequence and almost against its defects it involved the audience in the frustrations and exasperations, the loneliness and the sheer helplessness of one honest-to-God man against the crippling machinery of the State.

The film presents 24 hours in the life of Don Aparacio Fuentes who has the best wheat harvest of his life. All his neighbors have theirs home and dry but he cannot cope with his. The Board of Cereals will give him only a fourth of the bags he needs; his machinery breaks down and he cannot get a replacement; his laborers quarrel and desert him; his family is indifferent and go off to a festival.

A friendly trader who might have helped him falls ill and begs to be taken to a doctor. The screw tightens as the sick man dies in his car; the hospital won't accept the body; the police are too concerned with breakers of "public morality" to heed or to help him. He reaps only despair.

Despite its limitations this film on the social conflicts in Argentina with their crushing effects on the unfortunate individual had something worthwhile to say and it said it with an anger that was perhaps too controlled to make the impact that Madanes' script and Buchardo's acting deserved.

Should get sympathetic audiences in farming belts, anywhere. *She.*

Camelot
(MUSICAL—COLOR—PANAVISION)

Big, beautiful, emotionally full musical telling of the King Arthur-Lancelot-Guenivere triangle. Must be one of season's roadshow smashes.

Warner Bros.-Seven Arts release of Jack L. Warner production. Features Richard Harris, Vanessa Redgrave, Franco Nero, David Hemmings, Lionel Jeffries. Directed by Joshua Logan. Screenplay and lyrics by Alan Jay Lerner; from T. H. White's "The Once and Future King; music by Frederick Loewe, conducted by Alfred Newman. Camera (Technicolor), Richard H. Kline; costumes and scenery, John Truscott; sound, M. A. Merrick and Dan Wallin; editor, Folmar Blangsted. Reviewed at Warner Theatre, N.Y., Oct. 23, 1967. Running Time, 179 MINS.
King Arthur .... Richard Harris
Guenivere .... Vanessa Redgrave
Lancelot .... Franco Nero
Mordred .... David Hemmings
King Pellinore .... Lionel Jeffries
Lady .... Estelle Winwood
Merlin .... Laurence Naismith
Dap .... Pierre Olaf
Girl .... Sue Casey

On the sumptuous face of it, "Camelot" qualifies as one of Hollywood's alltime great screen musicals. While most big musicals have fine production, dazzling costumes and all that, what gives "Camelot" special value is a central dramatic conflict that throbs with human anguish and compassion. It might be termed a woman's picture cast in the form of a thoughtful legend. There is something else that is uncommon nowadays, an investigation of infidelity that ponders its destructive aspects.

Tracing back, the story strength of "Camelot" throws the spotlight again upon those three canny men of the Broadway legitimate theatre, Alan Jay Lerner, Frederick Loewe and the late Moss Hart. Again, as with "My Fair Lady" where they borrowed from Bernard Shaw's play "Pygmalion," they borrowed from a minor classic of this century, T. H. White's novel, "The Once and Future King." And so the lesson emerges a second time that a musical with fully developed characters in a durable situation, has that needed plus.

"Camelot" never need resort to the more obvious kind of added "action." Indeed whole sequence involving derring-do by Lancelot has been stripped away to keep the focus on the three mentally-tortured people, the cuckolded king, the cheating queen, the confused knight.

All of this is against the often exquisite sets and costumes of John Truscott, the creative use of research that is constantly visible. Add the fine camera work of Richard H. Kline in Technicolor and Panavision. The clever screenplay of Lerner, the singular appropriateness to time and place of the Loewe score as lovingly managed by Alfred Newman are all major contributions. So, too, the "big" roadshow sound of M. A. Merrick and Dan Wallin.

The editing of a film running 179 minutes with an alternation from populated but rural England to the intimacies of an obsessive castle love affair leaves questions as to who did what. Say that Folmar Blangsted presumably worked directly under director Joshua Logan on the editing and that it is part of the overall production strategy of Jack L. Warner.

Logan surely rates extraordinary tribute for the performances he has elicited from Richard Harris as King Arthur and Vanessa Redgrave as Guenivere. But as both players have previously demonstrated professionalism that may be less an accomplishment than taking an unknown Italian youth of 25, Franco Nero, and managing him for conviction as the knight whose idealism succumbs to passion. He is presented, true to the story, as a Frenchman. David Hemmings is rather too modern, not to say "mod" for the role of Mordred but many may regard that as a quibble. A quite remarkable job of fullscale eccentric, half soft in the brains, is offered by Lionel Jeffries.

A musical with wit proved its boxoffice case in "My Fair Lady." A musical with wisdom, which says and demonstrates so much about human belligerency and the slow nature of "progress," is now moving to market. It must generate a great deal of discussion of its substance and not alone its means. The means are magnificent. The heart is beneath the trappings of knighthood. This is especially a great picture for Harris whose performance is rich in nuance and heartbreak, abounding in the kind of nobility which has temporarily gone out of fashion in fiction.

Finally "Camelot" may be Logan's finest cinematic achievement even though for a moment, when Lancelot is first discovered, he seems about to camera-rape the male body in the hokey style of "Picnic." Land.

Fleur D'Oseille
(Sorrel Flower)
(FRENCH-COLOR)
Paris, Oct. 17.

CCFC release of Speva Films, CCFC production. Stars Mireille Darc; features Maurice Biraud, Anouk Ferjac, Henri Garcin, Renee Saint Cyr. Directed by Georges Lautner. Screenplay, Michel Audiard, Marce Jullian, Jean Meckert, Lautner from book by Jean Amila; camera (Eastmancolor), Maurice Fellous; editor, Michele David. At Balzac, Paris. Running Time, 110 MINS.
Catherine .... Mireille Darc
Marite .... Anouk Ferjac
Jo Le Frejus .... Henri Garcin
Man .... Amidou
Directress .... Renee Saint Cyr

Mireille Darc caught on here, as a free living, loving girl in "Galia." Here, she and the same director, Georges Lautner, do a serious comic gangster opus. This time, she is the unwed mother of a dead gangster's child. Satire, mayhem and brisk modernity are mixed but with the usual conventions and telegraphed qualities that have this mainly a local item with only some dualer use abroad, intimated.

She and another unwed mother go off to find her lover's buried swag, followed by two gangs, the police and a snoopy neighbor. After some shoot-em-up scenes all is worked out and the money goes to the police. She accepts her child. Lowdown slang is used throughout, plus an ironic commentary on the proceedings. But this fails to develop more easy characterizations to help the familiar proceedings out of the usual rut. No love scenes here, but Miss Darc, a spindly but sexy and nonchalant young girl, has plenty of tasteful nude scenes. This may give it some exploitation handles, the only things appropriate for this gangster comedy. Mosk.

Kiss Me, Kiss Me, Kiss Me

William Mishkin release of Extraordinary Film (William Mishkin) production. Directed and photographed by Andy Milligan. Stars Natalie Rogers, Don Williams. Screenplay by Josef Bush, based on story by Mishkin; music, Harry Huret. Previewed in New York. Running Time, 81 MINS.
Jean Bernowski .... Natalie Rogers
Stan Bernowski .... Don Williams
Ed .... Peter Ratray
Ellen .... Joy Martin
Lurlene .... Anjela Peters
Mrs. Bernowski .... Esther Travers
Dominick .... Matt Baylor
Ray .... Gerald Jaccuzzo
Sal .... Nick Orzel
Jimmy .... Sean Martin

William Mishkin, distributor of sexploitation pix, is making his debut as film writer and producer with this contribution to the perennial erotica sweepstakes. Pic is a promising initial effort, being not as improbably lustful as recent entrants in this genre. Of course Mishkin aims mainly for the male trade, where it should "satisfy."

Unlike so many glandular pix, this has a real plot, the usual sequence catering (a) to those who are not happy unless the femmes are man-handled or (b) the male gentry get their cumuppance. The boudoir scenes call for no laboring of the imagination. Twist here is the male trying to get his sister involved, though not successfully. The whole thing ends in a shocking tragedy, almost unheard of in this type of film.

Camera work by Andy Milligan (who also directed) is above par. Background music is unusually perky as supplied by Harry Huret. Acting is not exactly overwhelming but good enough to tell this rather familiar story. Whole production was made in New York City. Plot concerns a sexy wife, who feeling neglected, strays afield.

Of the routine cast, Natalie Rogers looks best as the wife while Don Williams is okay as the husband. Joy Martin is unusually excellent as the sister. This original Mishkin effort looks like a moneymaker despite not being as explicitly raw as some recent sexploitation releases. Wear.

How I Won The War
(BRITISH—COLOR)

Tepid satire on militarism, which needs hefty ballyhoo. Richard Lester's directorial gimmicks do not overcome flaws. Spotty b.o.

San Francisco, Oct. 21.

United Artists release of Richard Lester production, directed by Lester. Features Michael Crawford, John Lennon. Screenplay, Charles Wood, based on the novel by Patrick Ryan; camera (DeLuxe Color), David Watkin; editor, John Victor Smith; music, Ken Thorne; asst. director, Pepe Lopez Rodero. Reviewed at San Francisco Film Festival, Masonic Auditorium, Oct. 20, '67. Running Time, 109 MINS.
Goodbody .... Michael Crawford
Gripweed .... John Lennon
Clapper .... Roy Kinnear
Transom .... Lee Montague
Juniper .... Jack MacGowran
Grapple .... Michael Hordern
Cowardly Musketeer .... Jack Hedley
Odlebog .... Karl Michael Vogler
Spool .... Ronald Lacey
Drogue .... James Cossins
Dooley .... Ewan Hooper
American General ..... Alexander Knox
British General .... Robert Hardy
Mrs. Clapper's Friend ...Shiela Hancock
Flappy-Trousered Man .... Charles Dyer
Paratrooper .... Bill Dysart
Skipper .... Paul Daneman
Staff Officer .... Peter Graves
Toby .... Jack May
Old Man at Alamein .. Richard Pearson
Woman in Desert ..... Pauline Taylor
Operator .... John Ronane
Soldier at Alamein ... Norman Chappell
Reporter .... Bryan Pringle
Mrs. Clapper .... Fanny Carby
1st Old Lady .... Dandy Nichols
2d Old Lady .... Gretchen Franklin
Large Guild .... John Junkin
Driver .... John Trenaman
1st Replacement .... Mick Dillon
2d Replacement .... Kenneth Colley

Richard Lester's latest film is an uneven, forced black comedy in which liabilities outweigh assets. John ('The Beatles') Lennon has some marquee value, but his part is small. Made in Britain and serving as Lester's producer debut, pic has spotty potential in special situations, and satisfactory subrun dual chances.

Although already running in London, film had its first U.S. showing as kickoff attraction at the 1967 San Francisco Film Festival, where reception ran from fair to cool. Advance ballyhoo had pic as a stinging satire on militarism, with jolting rattles of contemporary heroes, but precious little of this is on the screen. Pacifists may be embarrassed by the film, and militarists may be embarrassed for the pacifists.

Charles Wood adapted Patrick Ryan's novel into a screenplay which, as directed by Lester, substitutes motion for emotion, reeling for feeling, and crude slapstick for telling satire. Film opens at a superficial level of fast comedy, but never develops further. After a while, it begins to bore.

Michael Crawford, an able and acrobatic actor who can play comedy, is top-featured (all names follow title) as a gee-whiz British Army officer whose unthinking ineptitude kills off, one by one, all members of his unit. Lennon, whose billing far exceeds his part, and contribution, plays one of the crew.

Lee Montague is the inevitable seasoned Army vet who tries to cover Crawford's mistakes. Roy Kinnear, a fat, wife-worried inductee. Jack MacGowran the (overspotlighted) platoon buffoon, gunshy coward Jack Hedley, Ronald Lacey, James Cossins and Ewan Hooper round out the unit.

Episodic treatment cross-cuts between plot turns, and actual footage of World War II battles, latter tinted in different hues. Idea was to have one of Crawford's men die in action parallel to a real death, they have the "dead" man continue in plot but dressed head-to-foot in the color of the excerpt. Conception was good, but gets old after a time.

Recurring throughout are appearances by Michael Hordern, excellent as a Col. Blimp type, and Karl Michael Vogler, who also excels in what is one of the film's few assets—a satire of the "nice" Nazi who was just obeying orders. But this, too, has been done before, and better.

A prominent flaw which inhibits pic is incomprehensible dialog; the cockney slang may be authentic in content and delivery, in which case film may kill 'em in London nabes. Rest of the world is something else again. But, judging from what can be understood (sound recording, incidentally, is crisp, therefore presumably blameless), nothing much is missed.

Some effective satirical bits include "Lawrence Of Arabia" overtones (complete with Maurice Jarre's theme), and "Bridge On The River Kwai" recollections. Winston Churchill, it is assumed, is the platitudinous puppet worked by MacGowran to dullsville impact. Alexander Knox plays a Dixie-accented U.S. general to same effect. Best that can be said is that punches were pulled. No real-life counterparts need worry, whether or not they deserve gibes.

Lester, it must be said, even kids the cinematic school of which he is considered an adherent: the probing, intrusive camera which demands entree even to scenes of personal injury and tragedy. Film supposedly was made with military cooperation.

Denis O'Dell was Lester's associate producer, and production values, also other credits, are good. *Murf.*

Jack of Diamonds
(PANAVISION-COLOR)

Fast-paced cat-burglar yarn with enough suspense to rate good acceptance in general market.

Hollywood, Oct. 18.
Metro release of Sandy Howard production. Stars George Hamilton, Joseph Cotten, Marie Laforet, Maurice Evans; features Wolfgang Preiss, Carroll Baker, Zsa Zsa Gabor, Lilli Palmer. Directed by Don Taylor; Screenplay, Jack DeWitt, Sandy Howard; camera (Metrocolor), Ernst Wild; editor, Hans Nikel; music, Peter Thomas; asst. director, Wolfgang Glattes. Reviewed at Metro Studios, Oct. 17, '67. Running time, 107 MINS.
Jeff Hill .... George Hamilton
Ace of Diamonds .... Joseph Cotten
Olga .... Marie Laforet
Nicolai .... Maurice Evans
Von Schenk .... Wolfgang Preiss
Helmut .... Karl Lieffen
Brugger .... Alexander Hegarth
Geisling .... Eduard Linkers
Carrol Baker .... Herself
Zsa Zsa Gabor .... Herself
Lilli Palmer .... Herself

Some of the suspenseful elements of "Topkapi" and "To Catch a Thief" are incorporated in this latest cat-burglar melodrama to give impetus to what emerges as generally fast-paced entertainment for the general market. Built around an attempt to pull off a multi-million-dollar jewel robbery,

the Sandy Howard production, lensed mostly in Europe, carries straightforward action well directed and enacted and good exploitation potential.

George Hamilton plays title role, a gentleman-thief who takes over the mantel formerly worn by Joseph Cotten, his mentor now-retired and once known as the Ace of Diamonds, tops in his profession. Premise of the Jack DeWitt-Sandy Howard screenplay twirls around a daring plan to steal a fabulous diamond necklace, known as the Zaharoff diamonds and valued at $5,000,000, from a believed-impregnable Paris bank and then substitute fakes before jewels are transferred to a museum. A crucial step is the theft of the combination of the safe in which diamonds repose, from Paris Police Headquarters.

Script is well-developed and Don Taylor's direction cleaves to a line which makes best use of the idea, building good suspense as Hamilton enters the bank and evades various burglar alarms until a fluke brings the police. For added marquee dressing, Carroll Baker, Zsa Zsa Gabor and Lilli Palmer portray themselves, as their victims of Hamilton in his dizzy cat-burgling before his chef-d'oeuvre is undertaken.

Hamilton is a good choice for his character and Cotten, in only briefly, lends an interesting presence. Marie Laforet enacts a femme cat-burglar in on the job which her stepfather, Maurice Evans and former partner of Cotten, master-minds, both okay. Wolfgang Preiss handily delivers as a jewel-recovery detective.

Technical departments generally are top-grade, including Ernst Wild's color photography, Peter Thomas' music score, Lutz Hengst's art direction and Hans Nikel's editing. *Whit.*

Wait Until Dark
(COLOR)

Excellent Mel Ferrer-produced suspenser, based on the play. Audrey Hepburn's performance superior. Strong, and durable, b.o. prospects.

Hollywood, Oct. 17.
Warner Bros.-Seven Arts release of Mel Ferrer production. Stars Audrey Hepburn, Alan Arkin, Richard Crenna. Directed by Terence Young. Screenplay, Robert and Jane-Howard Carrington, based on play by Frederick Knott; camera (Technicolor), Charles Lang; editor, Gene Milford; music, Henry Mancini; title song lyric, Jay Livingston, Ray Evans; asst. director, Jack Aldworth. Reviewed at Academy Award Theatre, L.A., Oct. 16. '67. Running Time, 107 MINS.
Susy Hendrix .... Audrey Hepburn
Roat .... Alan Arkin
Mike Talman .... Richard Crenna
Sam Hendrix ...... Efrem Zimbalist Jr.
Carlino .... Jack Weston
Lisa .... Samantha Jones
Gloria .... Julie Herrod
Shatner .... Frank O'Brien
Boy .... Gary Morgan

"Wait Until Dark," based on Frederick Knott's legit hit starring Lee Remick, emerges as an excellent suspense drama, effective in

casting, scripting, direction and genuine emotional impact. Audrey Hepburn stars as the not-so-helpless blind heroine, in a superior performance. Producer Mel Ferrer coordinated adroit production elements for sure-fire direction by Terence Young. The Warner Bros.-Seven Arts release has hot firstrun b.o. potential, plus durability in extended subrun booking combinations.

Fred Coe mounted the 1966 N.Y. legit presentation, under direction of Arthur Penn. Film rights were acquired by Wb in pre-production deal for $350,000 minimum, up to $650,000, plus film profit participation. Robert and Jane-Howard Carrington are responsible for a literate, intriguing screenplay. (Knott incidentally, wrote "Dial M For Murder," filmed for WB in 1954 by Alfred Hitchcock.)

As in "Murder," "Wait" turns on a supposedly hapless femme protagonist, in this case an accident-blinded Miss Hepburn. Hubby Efrem Zimbalist Jr. has, sometimes at the expense of immediate compassion but for long-range benefits, made his wife self-sufficient and reasonably able to fend for herself in their apartment home. Regime pays off when Zimalbist accidentally plays into the hands of heroin-smuggling Samantha Jones (N.Y. fashion model in good film debut), who plants a dope-loaded doll in his possession. Alan Arkin, also billed above-title along with Richard Crenna, disposes of Miss Jones, then hires Crenna and Jack Weston to intimidate Miss Hepburn into surrendering the doll.

Strategy is to lure away Zimbalist, while Crenna poses as an old Marine Corps buddy, Weston fakes a cop, and Arkin, in a few unnecessary disguises (a point made by Broadway legit critics), pretends to be several persons supposedly suspecting Zimbalist of wife-stealing. The trio of hoods has a falling out, Arkin emerging the survivor only to be overcome in an exciting climax.

Aided by the generally strong script, Miss Hepburn conveys superbly the combination of helplessness and sense acuity sometimes found in the blind. Film is refreshing in that it engenders solid rapport for the underdog (instead of glorifying the criminal), and even sophisticated audiences will find themselves gasping, cheering and clapping.

Climax is firstrate, aided at tradeshow by killing houselights for added effect to the black film; idea should be made formal part of firstrun showings. Crenna and Weston give very fine shadings to diverse criminal characters, and Arkin (although a bit unrestrained at times to point of sounding like Jerry Lewis) projects appropriate sadistic overtones. Julie Herrod, repeating her legit role, is very good as the wilful youngster who helps Miss Hepburn.

Besides the unnecessary disguises for Arkin as he plays different fake parts, only other noteworthy flaw lies in the Zimbalist character: at fadeout, he remains too aloof to his wife's understandable near-hysteria. Writing here jars an audience which, through Zimbalist, would just as soon rush

up to Miss Hepburn and comfort her. Given the writing, Zimbalist does a smooth, professional job.

Director Young's achievement is aided by the just-right nervous energy in Charles Lang's fluid Technicolor camera. George Jenkins' art direction provides a comfortable backdrop. Editing to a good 107 minutes was executed by Gene Milford. Henry Mancini's excellent score, which is deceptively simple, conveys underlying drama via a dissonant bass. The obligatory title song, mercifully held for end titles, may be dismissed, forgiven, and forgotten. Other credits are tops. *Murf.*

Doctor Faustus
(BRITISH-COLOR)

Strong marquee values in the Burton-Tayor combo, backed by an insightful performance by Burton, for very specialized appeal and related curio values which must be suitably hypoed to milk maximum returns from this offbeater.

London, Oct. 17.
Columbia Pictures release of a Richard Burton-Richard McWhorter production. Stars Richard Burton, Elizabeth Taylor; features Oxford University Dramatic Society. Directed by Burton and Nevill Coghill. Screenplay, Nevill Coghill, adapted from original by Christopher Marlowe; camera (Technicolor), Gabor Pogany; music, Mario Nascimbene; editor, John Shirley. Reviewed at Cameo-Poly, London, Oct. 16, '67. Running Time, 92 MINS.
Doctor Faustus .... Richard Burton
Helen of Troy ...... Elizabeth Taylor
Mephistopheles ..... Andreas Teuber
Emperor .... Ian Marter
Empress ..... Elizabeth O'Donovan
Lucifer .... David McIntosh
Belzebub .... Jeremy Eccles
Valdes .... Ram Chopra
Cornelius ...... Richard Carwardine
First Scholar .... Richard Heffer
Second Scholar ...... Hugh Williams
Third Scholar ...... Gwydion Thomas
Cardinal .... Nicholas Loukes
Knight .... Richard Durden-Smith
Wagner .... Patrick Barwise
Pope .... Adrian Benjamin
Attendant .... Jeremy Chandler
Rector Magnificus .. Angus McIntosh
First Professor ...... Ambrose Coghill
Second Professor .. Anthony Kaufmann
Third Professor .... Julian Wontner
Fourth Professor ... Richard Harrison
Fifth Professor ...... Nevill Coghill
Good Angel .... Michael Menaugh
Boy-turned-into-Hind .. John Sandbach
Idiot .... Sebastian Walker
Pride .... Nicholas Loukes
Lechery .... Gwydion Thomas
Envy .... Anthony Kaufmann
Avarice .... Ambrose Coghill
Wrath .... R. Peverello
Sloth .... Maria Aitken
Idleness .... Valerie James
Gluttony .... Bridget Coghill,
Petronella Pulsford, Susan Watson
Dancers .... Jacqueline Harvey,
Sheila Dawson, Carolyn Bennitt
Nun, Court Lady .... Jane Wilford

Probably one of the most desperately non-commercial enterprises in motion picture history, this version of "Doctor Faustus" derives from the Burton-Taylor foray into Oxford last year to join the university dramatic society in a production directed by Burton's former tutor, Nevill Coghill. It was then decided to film it in Rome, with Richard Burton, in addition to repeating his performance at Faustus, helming it in collaboration with Coghill.

The result is a curio unlikely to recover its negative cost. Firstly, Christopher Marlowe's 400-year-old play is no great shakes in construction, its principal virtues belonging to the theatre and its chief glory being its flashes of poetry. Secondly, Burton is, as yet, too inexperienced as a director to translate it with confidence to celluloid. And, though there are some suitably sombre and flickering episodes (with evocative lensing by Gabor Pogany), the rhythm and momentum necessary to carry one along with the plot are entirely lacking.

What remains is an oddity that may have some archive appeal, for at least it records a performance by Burton that gives an insight into his prowess in classical roles, even more than his Petruchio in the "Shrew." He is obviously captivated by Marlowe's verse, and speaks it with sonorous dignity and sense.

The story concerns the medieval doctor's attempt to master all human knowledge by selling his soul to the devil, who dangles before him such delights as nights with Elizabeth Taylor, who flits through the film in various undraped poses as the Helen of Troy siren promising a fate worse than death. Finally, the devil redeems his contract, and Faustus meets his fate in the everlasting bonfire, beckoned down an escalator by Miss Taylor.

One surprise is the general adequacy of the Oxford amateurs, with a good performance in any terms from Andreas Teuber as Mephistopheles. But the impersonation of the seven deadly sins is hardly likely to send good men off the rails.

The asset of the Burton-Taylor combo on the marquee, and the success of the "Shrew," work in the film's favor, but its future looks confined to the more esoteric art houses. *Otta.*

Tom Thumb
(Pulgarcito)
(MEXICAN—COLOR)

Dubbed entry for the kiddie-matinee market. Hopefully the pre-school set won't mind its totally amateurish look.

Childhood Productions release of a Clasa Films Mundiales, S.A. (Armando Orive Alba) production. Directed by Rene Cardona. Screenplay, Cardona and Adolfo Lopez Portillo, based on a story by Perrault; camera, Jose Ortiz Ramos; music, Paul Lavista; editor, Jorge Bustos. Previewed in New York, Oct. 19, '67. Running Time, 85 MINS.
Fairy Princess .... Maria Elena Marques
Ogre .... Jose Elias Moreno
Tom Thumb .... Cesareo Quezadas

Childhood Productions specializes in dubbed kiddie pix skedded for weekend matinee playoff and has no illusions about the adult appeal of its product. This 1958 Mexican pic may have trouble pleasing more cerebral tots nursed on the relative professionalism of tv. Nonetheless, lack of (morally) offensive material may encourage Parent-Teachers Assns. and similar groups to support the film, thus hypoing b.o. in this specialized market.

Visual fantasy is not "Tom Thumb's" forte. Apart from a few shots of Tom's romping beside oversized furniture and of the giant ogre's hovering over midget trees, Tom looks like any other short five-year-old and the giant resembles a red-bearded wrestler. The ogre's wife, an ex-fairy princess gone to seed since her marriage, is uglified via black enamel

on a front tooth and a purple floor mop for hair. Very few kids will be amazed by her physical transformation via magic wand at pic's end.

The really magical transformation is the conversion of a charming children's story into a tract about cleanliness. Tom extols the life of soap and water to the ogre and his ogress-daughters, thus breaking the behemoth's bad habit of eating children. Parents may applaud this hygienic lesson, but some kids are likely to be turned off by the detergent preachment. They get that aplenty on video.

Technical credits, like Tom, are minuscule. The color looks like smudgy crayons, with a predominance of ugly blues and purples. The dubbing is okay on lip-synch but bad on syntax (Tom says things like "I suggest we hurry back to the house as fast as our feet will take us"). Paul Tripp's narration is arch and condescending ("Ogres have a very good sense of smell; let's hope he doesn't pick up their scent or all will be lost").

Music is syrupy, with two lower case songs awkwardly thrown in for bad measure. *Beau.*

La Route De Corinthe
(The Road to Corinth)
(FRENCH-COLOR)

Paris, Oct. 17.
CCFC release of Films De Boetic, Compania Generale Finanzaria Cinematografica, Oscar Films production. Stars Jean Seberg, Maurice Ronet; features Michel Bouquet, Christian Marquand. Directed by Claude Chabrol. Screenplay, Claude Brule, Claude Rank, Daniel Boulanger; camera (Eastmancolor), Jean Rabier; editor, Jacques Gaillard. Previewed in Paris. Running Time, 100 MINS.
Shanny .... Jean Seberg
Dex .... Maurice Ronet
Robert .... Christian Marquand
Sharps .... Michel Bouquet
Kalhides .... Saro Urzzi
Killer .... Antonio Passalia
Josio .... Paolo Justi

Spy spoof has Jean Seberg trying to track down her husband's murderers in sunny Greece. He was a Yank undercover man killed by unidentified spies lousing up NATO missiles and radar. Pic has some wit, some okay tongue-in-cheek mayhem and good photographic backing. But there is not enough invention to give this more than playoff possibilities abroad.

However, a full English version was made alongside the French one and it could emerge an okay dualer on the Jean Seberg name and as a fairly-well sustained chase pic. Miss Seberg plays the innocent but redoubtable American girl caught up in the bloodshed. Others in the cast are mainly foils to her spreading havoc among both the chased and chasers.

Director Claude Chabrol's wry ways work in her being picked up by a lecherous rich man addicted to blue films, and being pursued by fake priests and finally her dead husband's friend. So this ambling mock adventure pic brings off some Hitchcock-like broad daylight murders and suspense. It also dawdles a bit and begins lamely to get in some clever spy shenanigans near the end.

Color is good and the Greek landscape okay. Film should get

some good results if properly placed and finding its right market in the thriller groove. *Mosk.*

An Uncommon Thief
(Beregis Automobilyi)
(RUSSIAN)

Amusing but low-powered Soviet comedy with little chance in competitive U.S. art market. Famed thesp Innokenti Smoktunovsky superb in comic role.

Artkino Pictures release of a Mosfilm Studio Production. Stars Innokenti Smoktunovsky, Oleg Yefremov. Directed by Eldar Ryazanov. Screenplay, Emil Braginsky, Ryazanov; camera, Anatoli Mukasei, Vladimir Nakhabtzev; music, Andrei Petrov; sound, Valeri Popov. Previewed in N.Y., Oct. 20, 1967. Running Time, 93 MINS.
Detochkin ..... Innokenti Smoktunovsky
Maxim Podberezovikov ... Oleg Yefremov
Also, Lubov Dobrzhanskaya, Olga Aroseva, Andrei Mironov, Anatoli Papanov, Tatyana Gavrilova, Georgi Zhenov, Eugene Evstigneyev, Sergei Kulagin, Victoria Radunskaya.

This mild, if often charming, Russian comedy about an automobile thief who only steals from black-marketeers and others he considers as having gotten their vehicles through shady dealings, moves well and calls forth many chuckles. It's a look at a more typical, perhaps more local-oriented Soviet product rarely seen in the West. Unfortunately no other fate in the U.S. can be foreseen for it other than its getting lost among all the art house blockbusters of more immediate interest to U.S. fans. There's simply not enough depth, hilarity or strangeness to it and its bookings will be sharply limited.

It's reportedly the first comedy role for the USSR's supposedly best actor, Innokenti Smoktunovsky of "Hamlet" fame. His portrayal of a meek clerk who nevertheless manages the ingenious car thefts is a rich and detailed one, reminding of Alec Guinness in "The Man in the White Suit" and "Situation Hopeless But Not Serious." Like Guinness' performances it impresses with breathtaking technique—a theatrical density so remarkable that its lack of real spontaneity is forgiven.

The film is quite fluid and swift, with some nice visual jokes and a pace that never lags in its mild, low-keyed way. There's an extended inside joke as the character played by Smoktunovsky gets to play title role in "Hamlet" in an amateur theatrical production. This calls for especial dexterity on the actor's part, since he must play Hamlet not as he, but as the character, would. It comes off beautifully.

"An Uncommon Thief" is really of more sociological than cinematic interest to Yanks, presenting intimate views of Russian highways, policemen, detectives, stores, new high-rise buildings, etc. Most Russo pix which have had wide playoff here, strangely enough, have been either historic or "provincial" in nature. Since film is in a way a study of the affluence of a certain class, the "western" attitudes often expressed are only slightly surprising. Photographers Anatoli Mukasei and Vladimir Nakhabtzev give the pic a quite modern look, and Eldar Ryazanov,

directing from a script by himself and Emil Branginsky, turns in a credible job. *Byro.*

Ithele Na Guini Vassilias
(He Wanted To Become King)
(GREEK)

Athens, Oct. 15.
Angelo Film production. Directed by Angelos Theodropoulos. With Theodoropoulos (lead role), Anna Iassonidou, Lycourgos Kallerguis, Athena Michaelidou, Guicas Biniaris. Screenplay, Yannis Ioannides from Shakespeare's "Hamlet"; camera, Takis Venetsanacos; music, Christos Mourbas. Reviewed at Salonika Film Fest. Running Time, 88 MINS.
Alecos .... Angelos Theodoropoulos
Philitsa .... Anna Iassonidou
Venos .... Lycourgos Kallerguis
Sophia .... Athena Michaelidou
Guerolymos .... Guicas Biniaris
Petros .... Dinos Karydes
Nicolas .... Stavros Farmakis
Leader of Workers .. George Velentzas

If director-actor Angelos Theodoropoulos would pick up another and better story, he would surely emerge with a stronger pic. Many directorial and acting abilities are obvious in this, which is an attempt to present a modern version of "Hamlet." Apparently, the task was too heavy for the fragile shoulders of this young director. Result is just a picture with good intentions. Nevertheless, this has certain exploitation values and possibly would be better off in small, arty situations.

The central character in this picture is a young man, Alecos, who comes back to Athens after hearing that his father was accidentally drowned. His mother is married to the ex-partner of his late father and he now controls the factory. Alecos calls him a "king," and pretends to be mentally unbalanced because he wants to find out about his father's death and to unmask Guerolymos his new "father," who is conspiring against him at the factory.

But when his father's will is read, he is the only heir. Then his step-father tries to get away with as much money as he can from the company's safe but is killed in an auto crash.

Theodoropoulos could not overcome the weakness of a script which is loaded with too much dialog. This and the heavily theatrical tone throughout the film hurt this screen effort.

Theodoropoulos, as the main character, gives a particularly good performance in a role that demonstrates great range. However, he is not helped much by Miss Loassonidou, whose performance, as Philitsa, is inadequate. Other members of the cast are mostly up to standard.

Black and white photography by Takis Venetsanacos is good. Other production values are adequate. *Rena.*

De Verloedering van de Swieps
(The Whipping Cream Hero)
(DUTCH)

Mannheim, Oct. 19.
A Bob du Mee production. Directed by Erik Terpstra. Screenplay, Heere Heeresma; camera, Mat van Hensbergen. At Mannheim Film Festival. Running Time, 93 MINS.
Manuel .... Ramses Shaffy
Jan-Hein Swiep .... Wies Andersen

This is the first feature pic of Erik Terpstra, a 30-year-old Dutchman, who has some short pix to his credit. His "Whipping Cream Hero" was screened, outside competition, at the Mannheim Festival. Although it fails to make the grade, it was not exactly the worst initial feature film shown at the festival. Had the subject matter and the characters been treated in a more convincing manner, this might have some limited commercial chances. In this form, "Hero" is too much on the offbeat side to interest general buyers and just not good enough to make it an item for arty houses.

In this odd comedy, the central figure is Manuel, a tall, longhaired, fancy-dressed beatnik, who is given a lift by a good-natured office employee. Generosity extends to the latter is more than just remarkable — inviting the hitch-hiker to his neat home and providing all he wants. Story development has the Beatnik turning everything upside down. Not only does he do a great deal of drinking and uses vulgar language, he also makes passes at his friendly host's young wife. He turns this house into an uproar.

The whole thing borders on the silly. It's hard to believe that such a dangerous looking chap like Manuel would "just like that" get invited into a decent family's home. And as per the chaos on the screen, complete with orgies, the creators of this went overboard in practically every respect. Less chaos would have helped.

What is, in particular, robbing this of any conviction is a rather flat character motivation. The performances remain too much on the surface. Film makes an overly schematized impression.

Some good technical qualities, including nice lensing, can't save much. A fairly good theme has been wasted due to exaggeration and lack of competent performances.   *Hans.*

Ah! Afti I Guineka Mou
(Oh! That Wife of Mine!)
(GREEK)

Salonika, Oct. 15.
Th. Damaskinos & V. Michaelides production. Directed by Georges Skalenakis. With Aliki Vouyouklaki, Dimitris Papamichael, Yannis Mihalopoulos, Despina Stylianopoulou, Spfo Notara. Screenplay, N. Tsiforos and Pol. Vassiliades from their own stageplay; camera, Nicos Gardellis; music, Mimis Plessas. Reviewed at Salonika Film Fest. Running Time, **96 MINS.**

This is a musical comedy of manners portrayed by one of Greece's most popular screen and stage teams, Aliki Vouyouklaki and Demetris Papamichael. This should support it primarily in the local market but foreign buyers may not be interested because it has little to offer in originality.

Screenplay written by N. Tsiforos and Pol. Vassiliades is based on their successful stageplay. It is loaded with dialogue which is rather dull. Director Georges Skalenakis also added unnecessary dance sequences for his femme star in hopes of making it stronger at the b.o. However, many of the films situations seem improbable and its narration spasmodic.

The story concerns a young lady looking at a new car which her husband promises her if he wins a promotion at his office. Death of the manager of his company leaves a post open. His boss has two weaknesses only: women and good food. So Demetris invites him home for dinner. But due to a misunderstanding, he is forced to present his wife as their maid. The boss falls for the "maid" and the situation becomes quite embarassing for the young couple. Finally all misunderstandings are cleared up and the husband gets his promotion while his wife gets the auto.

Aliki Vouyouklaki and Demetris Papamichael, husband and wife in real life, deliver their usual good performances as the young couple. They are colorfully supported by Yannis Mihalopoulos and Despina Stylianopoulou, as the "merry widow."

The score by Mimis Plesses is excellent.   *Rena.*

Rosie
(TECHNISCOPE—COLOR)

Female "King Lear," with Rosalind Russell victimized by greedy daughters. Drama with comedy, based on two legit plays, well cast and handomely produced. Careful selling for general situations.

Hollywood, Oct. 27.
Universal Pictures release of Ross Hunter presentation, produced by Jacque Mapes. Stars Rosalind Russell; features Sandra Dee. Directed by David Lowell Rich. Screenplay, Samuel Taylor, based on the play, "A Very Rich Woman," by Ruth Gordon, from "Les Joies de la Famille," a play by Philippe Heriat; camera (Technicolor), Clifford Stine; editor, Stuart Gilmore; music, Lyn Murray; title song, Johnny Mercer, Harry Warren; asst. director, Joseph Kenny. Reviewed at Directors Guild of America, Oct. 26, '67. Running Time, **98 MINS.**

Rosie Lord	Rosalind Russell
Daphne	Sandra Dee
Stevenson	Brian Aherne
Mildred	Audrey Meadows
David	James Farentino
Edith	Vanessa Brown
Cabot	Leslie Nielsen
Mae	Margaret Hamilton
Patrick	Reginald Owen
Nurse	Juanita Moore
Mrs. Peters	Virginia Grey
Willets	Dean Harens
Lawyer	Richard Derr
Detectives	Harry Hickox, Eddie Ness
Telephone Man	Hal Lynch
Old Lady	Ann Doran
Psychiatrist	Than Wyenn
Judge	Walter Woolf King
Pianist	Ronald Chisholm
Sedalia	Doris Lloyd
Taxi Driver	Ron Stokes
Joseph	Eugene Roth
Secretary	Kathleen O'Malley
Florist	Doodles Weaver

Handsomely produced, adroitly cast and well directed, "Rosie" stars Rosalind Russell as a daffy rich woman whose two daughters and son-in-law plot her legal insanity in order to get the family fortune. Essentially a drama with establishing comedy overtones, the Universal release could be called "Whatever Happened to Auntie Mame?" A bit overlong, film release has a certain appeal to young (in heart) audiences. Careful selling will be needed for maximum impact in general situations, where good b.o. prospects are indicated.

Philippe Heriat's Play, "Les Joies de la Famille," was adapted by Ruth Gordon into "A Very Rich Woman," as unsuccessful, 28-performance legiter of the 1965-66 season in N.Y., staged by Garson Kanin. Samuel Taylor in turn has fashioned an often-sharp script for pic, on which Jacque Mapes makes a good producer debut herein. David Lowell Rich, the director, has obtained some fine performances from his cast.

Miss Russell, although identified mostly with screen and legit comedy, is an actress of some dramatic depth. Her full range is exploited herein, ranging from the madcap first reel to an outstanding tour de force scene, played sans make-up, when locked up in a dreary sanitarium cell.

Transition, incidentally, from a zany "Mame" mood to melodrama is, at the same time, film's basic artistic asset and potential commercial liability. Greedy offspring have, indeed, resorted to contrived legalistics to control money, and that story is worth telling. On the other hand, film's campaign should not be restricted to selling fun angles, for subsequent word of mouth might hurt it. Some middle ground, hinting at tragi-comedy and eventual triumph of a youthful spirit, seems indicated.

Rallying to Miss Russell's side in plot is Brian Aherne, an excellent actor of sophistication and depth, playing her lawyer. Also, Sandra Dee, top-featured, displays a refreshing maturity and sensitivity which should help her escape from the rut—rightfully or wrongfully ascribed—of the cardboard, unreal teenager. James Farentino, one of Aherne's legal assistants, gives a superior performance which spotlights his acting, and reacting, talent.

Heavies are played in chilling, sardonic fashion by Audrey Meadows and Vanessa Brown, Miss Russell's daughters, Leslie Nielsen, Miss Brown's gutless hubby, sanitarium chief Dean Harens and attorney Richard Derr. Solid supporting cast includes maid Margaret Hamilton, butler Reginald Owen, nurse Juanita Moore and legal secretary Virginia Grey.

Rich's direction is sure, only lapse worth mentioning is when Miss Dee goes into tears at one point; this is her only lapse into overplaying.

Production values are snazzy. The well-illuminated Techniscope-Technicolor visuals are caught by Clifford Stine's fluid camera. Lyn Murray's spare score, supervised by Joseph Gershenson, adds punch, and title tune, by Harry Warren and Johnny Mercer, sets the right opening mood of gayety. Sound is excellent, and other credits are firstrate.   *Murf.*

The Comedians
(PANAVISION—COLOR)

Tedious meller, based on Graham Greene's book and screenplay, about current politics in Haiti. Marquee lurre of Richard Burton, Elizabeth Taylor, Alec Guinness and Peter Ustinov may make for fair b.o.

Hollywood, Oct. 10.
Metro-Goldwyn-Mayer release, produced and directed by Peter Glenville. Stars Richard Burton, Elizabeth Taylor, Alec Guinness, Peter Ustinov. Screenplay, Graham Greene, based on his novel; camera (Metrocolor), Henri Decae; editor, Francoise Javet; music, Laurence Rosenthal; asst. director, Jean-Michel Lacor. Reviewed at Directors Guild of America, L.A., Oct. 9, '67. Running Time, **156 MINS.**

Brown	Richard Burton
Martha	Elizabeth Taylor
Jones	Alec Guinness
Ambassador	Peter Ustinov
Smith	Paul Ford
Mrs. Smith	Lillian Gish
Henri Philipot	Georg Stanford Brown
Pierre	Roscoe Lee Browne
Mrs. Philipot	Gloria Foster
Dr. Magiot	James Earl Jones
Michel	Zakes Mokae
Joseph	Douta Seck
Concasseur	Raymond St. Jacques

The despair of people living under a despot may, indeed, be a sort of living death. It may be depicted well in a novel, such as Graham Greene's short tome, "The Comedians." But that in itself does not make exciting, or moving, film material. Producer-director Peter Glenville's pic, scripted by Greene, is a plodding, low-key, and eventually tedious melodrama. Stars Richard Burton, Elizabeth Taylor, Alec Guinness and Peter Ustinov give good, if routine, performances.

Filmed in Africa and France, Metro release will have to depend on marquee pull, with b.o. prospects generally just fair.

Project was a filmmaking challenge from the start, since "Papa Doc" Duvalier, considered a despot in his latterday rule of Haiti, remains in power. For a dramatist, problem was to take a real situation, still unresolved, and inject a note of hope at the end. But impact of the film is that present regime has emasculated all hope, and that any change will be at the whim of the rulers. Even that could be told well cinematically, but it is not.

Greene's screenplay rambles on through a seemingly interminable 156 minutes, unbroken in domestic engagements by any intermission. Drastic pruning certainly would improve pacing. Production values are good and realistic, but film as a whole does not jell.

Not the least of film's flaws is the role played by Miss Taylor, wife of South American ambassador Ustinov, who has a recurring, deteriorating affair with hotel-owner Burton. The Burtons rendezvous with clock-like regularity, and this may please matinee matrons, although in context, scenes are strictly sudser inserts.

The very poorly-made story point is that Burton gradually, finds something to live for, in his eventual flight to join mountain rebels, pitiably equipped and pitilessly portrayed. Guinness is a society-type arms promoter who fakes a military background. In a climactic scene where he confesses the fraud to Burton, Guinness excels. After latter's death, Burton takes his place.

Ustinov, the betrayed husband, effects an urbane, knowing bewilderment in another badly written part. Paul Ford and Lillian Gish, featured players, brighten their few scenes as two not-so-ugly, not-so-quiet Americans—something of a switcheroo for Greene, it might be noted.

Other highlights include a fine scene in which Gloria Foster expresses outrage at government interference in the burial of her husband, driven to death by the dictator. Effete journalist Roscoe Lee Browne, idealist-turned-guerrilla Georg Stanford Brown, medic James Earl Jones, and heavies Raymond St. Jacques and Zakes Mokae render good support.

Glenville cannot rise above the screenplay, although an "A" for effort might be accorded were it not for the fact that professionals may be assumed to exert best efforts. Indicated credits in other departments are good. *Murf.*

Mannheim Fest

Kristore Roky
(The Age of Christ)
(CZECH)

Mannheim, Oct. 17.
A Feature Film Studio (Bratislava-Koliba) production. With Jiri Sykora, Jana Hernova, Vlado Mueller, Miriam Kantorkova. Directed by Juraj Jakubisko. Screenplay, Juraj Jakubisko, Lubor Dohnal; camera, Igor Luther; music, William Buborg. At Mannheim Film Fest. Running Time, **100 MINS.**

Juraj	Jiri Sykora
Jana	Jana Hernova
Andrej	Vlado Mueller
Marta	Miriam Kantorkova

Title of this Czech pic is misleading. This is neither a film about Christ nor a religious film. "Age of Christ," a Czech expression, refers to men between the age of 30 and 33. This makes a point that these years are possibly the most difficult in life. At about that age, they often face personal and inner conflicts. They then are already too old to be young but still too young to feel old. This brings up the complications. "Christ" is the first feature pic of 31-year-old Juraj Jakubisko and had its world preem at this festival. It made, despite its flaws, an outstanding impression. Commercial chances seem limited and it's probably, at best, an item for the arties. But this is another prestige item for young Czech filmmakers.

Considering that this is Jakubisko's first feature venture, this young director deserves high praise. It displays artistic, technical knowhow. His film tends to be uneven at times and some of the funny situations seem far-fetched. But nevertheless it's still a very good production.

Central figures here are two brothers, Juraj and Andrej. The former has just recently finished his studies at an art academy but already starts doubting the sense of living. Both a sensitive and cynical artist (painter), he also doubts his artistic abilities. His brother, Andrej, seems to be the opposite. But he has his problems too—an unhappy marriage. Eventually Jana, Juraj's girl, falls in love with him. But Jana goes back to Juraj when Andrej has to leave. Then Andrej is killed in a car accident and his death kills the romance of Juraj and Jana.

This has many funny situations in the beginning and later gets more serious. Much looks conventional, but the inner conflicts of the two men are competently explained. There is indeed much that rings true in this film. *Hans.*

David Holzman's Diary
(U.S.)

Mannheim, Oct. 19.
A James McBride production. With L. M. Kit Carson, Penny Wohl, Louise Levine, Michael Levine, Robert Lesser, Fern McBride, Jack Baran. Directed and written by James McBride. Camera, Michael Wadley; editor, James McBride. At Mannheim Film Fest. Running Time, **74 MINS.**

David Holzman	L. M. Kit Carson
Penny	Penny Wohl

This film captured the Grand Prize (best first full-length feature) at the Mannheim festival. It's a surprise winner. According to James McBride, the producer-director-writer-editor of "Diary," this cost him $2,500 to shoot. Nevertheless, it is still amazing to see what McBride, a 27-year old New Yorker, was able to "achieve" with such a ridiculously small sum. Genuine commercial chances are hardly within the bounds of possibility, but the winning of Mannheim's Grand Prize will probably stir interest among film buffs. So it may slip into special situations.

There is admittedly a certain freshness about this film. The shortage of coin may have forced him to use all his imagination. There is no denying that "Diary" contains quite a number of imaginative and amusing sequences. It also has some ironical wit to offer. In all, "Diary'" was termed as "a film beyond expectations" at the Mannheim festival.

The plot concerns David Holzman, a young filmmaker, who takes along his camera wherever he goes. And shoots whatever he finds important. The camera makes him become a truth fanatic. No matters are minced. The whole thing covers nine days. In view of the small monetary investment, naturally, there are deficiencies. Some sequences seem rather stretched out.

One may add that the dialog is often very much on the vulgar side. An interview with a "street goddess" is particularly frank, but rates as a highpoint. All in all, McBride can be more than pleased with the outcome of his initial feature. It won the top prize and therewith nosed out the Czech "Age of Christ." *Hans.*

Herbst der Gammler
(GERMAN—DOCUMENTARY)

Mannheim, Oct. 17.
A Peter Fleischmann production. Directed and written by Peter Fleischmann. Camera, Klaus Mueller-Laue; editor, Fleischmann. At Mannheim Film Fest. Running Time, **65 MINS.**

This was the best West German entry at the Mannheim Festival. Also, it was this country's only contribution handed a prize. It's a far cry from being a masterpiece but at least it's technically well made and has something to say. Documentary is chiefly if not entirely an item for tv utilization. Inconvenient length and absence of color will limitt film for theatrical release.

This production centers around the socalled "Gammlers," those longhaired German beatnik types that stroll about this country's big cities, often doing nothing and earning nothing. Gammlers are various calibres, ranging from typical good-for-nothings to victims of unfortunate circumstances. There are aggressive as well as real nice ones.

Writer-director Peter Fleischmann joined the Munich Gammlers for several weeks in order to get an authentic insight into their way of life and attitudes. Many viewers feel that the film gets tiresome after a while, the more so as the cinema verite style tends to make listeners restless for much that is said on the screen can't be understood. Also, it's certainly not to everyone's taste to listen to pseudo-philosophical bla-bla for an hour. Of special interest are the remarks made by "normal citizens."

For German standards, this qualifies as a documentary above average. *Hans.*

Grajski Biki
(Stronghold of Toughs)
(YUGOSLAV)

Mannheim, Oct. 18.
A Viba Film (Ljubljana) production. With Kole Angelovski, Hana Brejchova, Janez Rohacek, Miki Micovic, Miha Baloh. Directed by Joze Pogacnik. Screenplay, Primoz Kozak, after a novel by Peter Kavalar; camera, Janez Kalisnik; music, Zoran Hristic. At Mannheim Film Fest. Running Time, **88 MINS.**

This Yugoslav first feature entry is a distinct disappointment at the Mannheim Film Fest largely because Titoland had submitted a good number of quality pix to international festivals during the year. It's not totally a bad film. This has some good sequences at the start and near the middle, but the general deficiencies and the worse than mediocre fadeout have just too many negative effects. Subject-wise, film could have been of foreign interest. In this form, however, it will hardly stir the necessary interest.

This one has its action in a reform school whose inmates are mostly war orphans. There is the big gap between the educational personnel and the young people who show an open dislike for the adults. One of the juvenile main characters in this is Danny, a real tough guy who gives the impression that a man has to be tough in order to survive. He organizes a breakout and becomes the victim of his own toughness. Pic contains a good deal of violence and some sex sequences which have become so popular in this country's films.

Most of the shortcomings stem from a rather confusing script. In his obvious attempt to create a "demanding" film, the director goes overboard, especially towards the end. The result is an odd mixture of cliches, exaggerated sequences plus some scenes which are hard to understand. On the plus side, the acting is often quite good. And there is some fine lensing. *Hans.*

Navajo Joe
(ITALO — SPANISH — TECH-NISCOPE—COLOR)

Lowercase western lensed in Spain. Okay for minor action market.

Hollywood, Oct. 27.
United Artists release of Dino De Laurentiis Cinematografica, Roma-C.B. Films Barcelona (Ermanno Donati-Luigi Carpentieri) production. Stars Burt Reynolds; features Aldo Sanbrell, Nicoletta Machiavelli, Tanya Lopert, Fernando Rey, Franca Polesello, Lucia Modugno, Pierre Cressoy. Directed by Sergio Corbucci. Screenplay, Dean Craig. Fernando Di Leo; story, Ugo Pirro; camera (Technicolor), Silvano Ippoliti; asst. director, Deodato Ruggero. Reviewed at Goldwyn Studios, Oct. 26, '67. Running Time, **89 MINS.**

Joe	Burt Reynolds
Duncan	Aldo Sanbrell
Estella	Nicoletta Machiavelli
Maria	Tanya Lopert
Rattigan	Fernando Rey
Barbara	Franca Polesello
Geraldine	Lucia Modugno
Lynne	Pierre Cressoy
Chuck	Nino Imparato
Sancho	Alvaro De Luna
Honor	Valeria Sabel
Clay	Mario Lanfranchi
Jeffrey	Lucio Rosato
Monkey	Simon Arriaga
El Gordo	Cris Huerta
El Cojo	Angel Ortiz

Reagan .... Fianni Di Stolfo
Blackwood .... Angel Alvarez
Bandit .... Rafael Albaicin

"Navajo Joe" is a blood-letting western jointly produced by Italian and Spanish producers and filmed in Spain for the American market. Apart from Burt Reynolds, in title star role, cast is composed entirely of Europeans. What comes out is okay for minor action situations which do not demand either top quality or any particular novelty of them.

Reynolds kills more people with his knife and rifle as he tries to help a town save itself from complete annihilation by a murdering outlaw gang than half a hundred heavies in previous oaters. Seems that this is his whole purpose in life, avenging himself for some unexplained reason on the bandit leader and his men. Before he's finished he wipes them out entirely, perhaps himself as well in a final showdown with the outlaw chief, who shoots him and leaves audience wondering if it's for real.

Script by Dean Craig and Fernando Di Leo, from story by Ugo Pirro, allows fast movement which director Sergio Corbucci handles well enough. Color lensing by Silvano Ippolitti is interesting. Reynolds makes the most of his role and Aldo Sanbrell's interpretation of the outlaw is a return to heavies of old. Supporting cast means little. (Tanya Lopert is daughter of UA's Ilya Lopert—Ed.) *Whit.*

Oscar
(FRENCH—COLOR)
Paris, Oct. 24.

Gaumont release of Gaumont International production. Stars Louis De Funes; features Claude Rich, Claude Gensac, Mario David, Dominique Page. Directed by Edouard Molinaro. Screenplay, Jean Halain, Molinaro, De Funes from play by Claude Magnier; camera (Eastmancolor), Raymond Lemoigne; editor, Robert and Monique Isnardon. At Mercury, Paris. Running Time, 85 MINS.
Bertrand .... Louis De Funes
Christian .... Claude Rich
Wife .... Claude Gensac
Maid .... Dominique Page
Masseur .... Mario David
Valet .... Paul Prebcist

Louis De Funes is a balding, middleaged comedian with an underlying human exasperation that keeps him from being obnoxious. He is funny, even in this rather tepid farce about disappearing suitcases and wrong meetings. He manages to get some laughs by his sheer selfish frenzy that seems to delight local audiences who find him a sort of French everyman. But it may not travel well for foreign chances. (Not to be confused with Joe Levine's "The Oscar.")

Here, De Funes finds an employee descending on him who demands his daughter's hand in exchange for money he has embezzled from the firm. But it seems his girl just used the daughter's name. And so the plot builds as the daughter is finally married off to Oscar, the chauffeur, and everybody gets their just due.

Talky and somewhat laggard, film does pick up a bit at the end. But this is stage farce that does not get the right timing, deftness and clockwork pacing to give this silly tale of human pettiness much comedic insight. Direction mis-takes loudness for point and stereotype as characterization. Only De Funes get some spirit into this forced farce by his sheer madcap shenanigans. *Mosk.*

The Beautiful Swindlers
(Les Plus Belles Escroqueries du Monde)
(FRENCH—ITALO—JAPANESE—FRANSCOPE)

Much-delayed U.S. release of four-part anthology pic is tepid entry in the international sweepstakes. Limited bookings foreseen.

Jack Ellis Films release of a Ulysse Productions-Primex Films-Lux C.C.F.-Vides Cinematografica-Toho Films (Pierre Roustang) production. Reviewed at Apollo Theatre, N.Y., Oct. 22, '67. Running Time, 90 MINS.
AMSTERDAM
Directed by Roman Polanski. Camera, Jerzy Lipman; music, K. Komeda; editor, Rita von Royen. Features Nicole Karen, Jan Teulings.
NAPLES
Directed by Ugo Gregoretti. Camera, Tonino Delli Colli; music, Piero Umiliani. Features Gabriella Giorgelli, Guido Guiseppone, Beppo Mannaluolo.
PARIS
Directed by Claude Chabrol. Camera, Jean Rabier; music, Pierre Jansen; editor, Jacques Gaillard. Features Jean-Pierre Cassel, Catherine Deneuve, Francis Blanche, Sacha Briquet, Jean-Louis Maury.
TOKYO
Directed by Hiromichi Horikawa. Camera, Asakazu Nakai; music, Keitaro Miho. Features Mie Hama, Ken Mitsuda.

This four-part anthology pic has had a curious and confusing history. Walter Reade's distrib subsid, Continental Distributing, picked up the film in a preproduction deal when it was known as "World's Greatest Swindles." Herman G. Weinberg was signed in October, 1964, to provide English subtitles, but the pic remained in the can stateside. Although Continental is still nominally releasing the film (its logo appears on the end-titles), current engagements are being handled by subcontractor Jack Ellis, to whom Reade passed the film.

The Reade homeoffice has no credits or info on the film save a circular describing a four-part film, one episode of which is a Tokyo section directed by Hiromichi Horikawa that differs completely in plot outline from the Horikawa episode in the version caught. Originally a fifth episode was shot by director Jean-Luc Godard with a cast headed by Jean Seberg, Charles Denner and Laszlo Szabo. This episode, not described in the aforementioned circular, was dropped from the version that preemed Aug. 14, 1964, in Paris and was instead released as a short subject later that year under the title, "Le Grand Escroc" ("The Great Swindle").

The film recently obtained two bottom-half bookings, one at New York's Apollo Theatre and the other at Chicago's Monroe Theatre, but otherwise it remains the black sheep in the Reade fold. If not quite as bad as this checkered career might indicate, the film certainly is a pallid item that might well never have invaded the U. S. market. For film buffs it has the dubious merit of displaying the worst work of noted directors Roman Polanski and Claude Chabrol. For less devout (or masochistic) filmgoers, the film has little to offer.

The first episode by Polanski is a shapeless anecdote about a young Parisienne in Amsterdam who cons a middle-aged Dutchman into paying for an extravagant diamond necklace, only to trade her acquisition for a parrot being sold by an uneducated waterfront type unaware of the necklace's value. Presumably a comment on flip young people who will do anything for a kick, the episode has a superficially jazzy look that ill conceals its flabby content.

Next comes a Neapolitan joke about a pimp's elaborate plan to marry off his hard-working girls to doddering old men to evade an Italian law permitting municipal police to evict prosties as undesirable citizens. The plan predictably backfires with heavy-handed irony, and Ugo Gregoretti's drab visuals and ambling pace further dull a reasonably sharp comic idea.

Claude Chabrol's contribution is a silly variation on the whiskered gag about selling the Eiffel Tower to a nutty German. Some effective camera tricks can not resuscitate this old wheeze, however, and overplaying by a cast headed by Jean-Pierre Cassel only augments the tiresomeness.

After three such mediocre segments, it takes a real directorial master to come up with something worse. Credit Horikawa with this dubious distinction, as he wavers from desperate humor (old man chasing a Japanese B-girl around the bed) to truly laughable serious moments (the old man's death via strangulation while eating noodles is accompanied by *sturm und drang* music). The episode ends with an hysteric scene by young actress Mie Hama that is an acting lesson by negative example. *Beau.*

The Last Safari
(BRITISH—COLOR)

Good, if long, programmer about personal conflicts in contemporary Africa. Stewart Granger major marquee lure. Two new acting talents spotlighted by Henry Hathaway. Okay dual bill prospects.

Hollywood, Oct. 25.
Paramount Pictures release, produced and directed by Henry Hathaway. Features Kaz Garas, Stewart Granger, Gabriella Licudi. Screenplay, John Gay, based on the novel, "Gilligan's Last Elephant," by Gerald Hanley; camera (Technicolor), Ted Moore; second unit camera, John Coquillon; editor, John Bloom; music, John Dankworth; second unit director, Richard Talmadge. Reviewed at Paramount Studios, L.A., Oct. 24, '67. Running Time, 110 MINS.
Casey .... Kaz Garas
Gilchrist .... Stewart Granger
Grant .... Gabriella Licudi
Jama .... Johnny Sekka
Alec Beaumont .... Liam Redmond
Refugee .... Eugene Deckers
Chongu .... David Munyua
Rich .... John De Villiers
Game Warden .... Wilfred Moore
Mrs. Beaumont .... Jean Parnell
Commissioner .... Bill Grant
Harry .... John Sutton
Gavai .... Kipkoske
Village Chief .... Labina
Dancers........Masai Tribe Wakamba Tribal Dancers

"The Last Safari" is a good programmer, filmed by Henry Hathaway in Kenya, in which personal conflicts are resolved against the backdrop of an Africa experiencing growing pains. Stewart Granger is featured with two promising younger talents. Excellent location production values help sustain interest against a somewhat distended script. Good to okay b.o. prospects on general duals, and reasonably durable subrun legs.

Gerald Hanley's novel, "Gilligan's Last Elephant," has been adapted by John Gay to spotlight the conflict between Granger, a disillusioned white hunter plagued by guilt over the death of a friend, and Kaz Garas, typical U.S. tourist type. Each helps the other attain greater maturity. Gabriella Licudi plays a half-breed safariparty girl, hired by Garas.

Very strong first reel establishes interest in all principals. Garas, determined to follow Granger into the back country, develops the more positive sides to his character. External conflicts are interwoven for good irony: artificial national boundaries of new nations upset a balance of nature which has prevailed for centuries; and race prejudice—on both sides —is seen as the ludicrous thing it really is.

According to a Hathaway associate, Garas was signed from a tv pilot which was screened for an o.o. of a potential femme lead. She wasn't hired, but he was, in one of those showbiz ironies. Currently under contract to Hal B. Wallis (who has the knack of prospecting talent), Garas shows here, in his first pic, a very good combination of ruggedness and sensitivity, and an Aldo Ray huskiness of voice which certainly can be developed.

Miss Licudi, already featured in some recent pix, has good acting-reacting ability which can be exploited further, particularly in the good bad-girl groove. On a few occasions, however, both thesps get a bit unrestrained. Granger delivers a good performance. Episodic script, and lack of pruning in final reels, introduces a serious letdown which mars overall impact.

With the exception of what appear to be some bad process shots, producer - director Hathaway has invested pic with some excellent exterior shots: the endless bush country, animal stampedes and grazing, etc., set an adroit mood. Ted Moore's Technicolor lensing is excellent, ditto second unit camera work of John Coquillon under director Richard Talmadge. John Dankworth's score, which is particularly good on opening titles, sometimes gets too cute for the later dramatics.

John Bloom edited to an okay 110 minutes. Other credits are strong. Film was made by Par's overseas arm, Paramount Film Service Ltd. Kenyan government cooperation was used to good advantage.
Murf.

Pretty Polly
(BRITISH—COLOR)

Smoothly confectioned item with distaffers as primary target; Trevor Howard, Hayley Mills and exotic settings are added lures.

London, Oct. 24.
Universal release of a George Granat-Universal production. Stars Hayley Mills, Trevor Howard, Shashi Kapoor. Di-

rected by Guy Green. Screenplay, Willis Hall and Keith Waterhouse, based on Noel Coward's original; camera (Technicolor), Ron Robson; music, Michel Legrand; editor, Frank Clarke. Previewed at Astoria Theatre, London. Running Time, 102 MINS.

Polly	Hayley Mills
Robert Hook	Trevor Howard
Amaz	Shashi Kapoor
Mrs. Innes-Hook	Brenda de Banzie
Rick Preston	Dick Patterson
Lorelei	Kalen Lui
Critch	Peter Bayliss
Miss Gudgeon	Patricia Routledge
Mrs. Barlow	Dorothy Alison

Beamed straight at distaffers, this slick slice of romantic confectionery marks another step in the emancipation of Hayley Mills, who is now ready to be quizzed about the state of her virginity and to clinch with handy males. However, the liberation hasn't gone so far as to shock her young fans, for Miss Mills retains the puppy appeal that established her and is far more :ice than naughty.

She (as Polly) goes on vacation with a rich, disagreeable aunt to Singapore. Frumpish, bespectacled and lumpily dressed, she timidly obeys her aunt's constant demands for attention and looks suitably badgered. But the relation dies from taking a swim too soon after a heavy lunch, and this sparks off the transformation scene. Polly is encouraged by an Indian acting as guide and helpmate to have her hair done, exchange her glasses for contact lenses, and indulge in a riot of makeup. She emerges as a siren.

So she decides to stay on in Singapore, having buried her aunt, and meets up with a rakish and dissolute uncle (Trevor Howard) who has a Chinese chick as mistress and a raffish air of not caring about convention. She encourages the Indian to make love to her, and the main emotional pull of the tale is in this transitory affair, doomed to break up when Polly takes off to return home. This is what predictably happens, with a hint of pathos in the parting.

Derived from a Noel Coward short story — itself written in the vein of Somerset Maugham—the script (by Keith Waterhouse and Willis Hall) goes all out for sentiment, and, on its undemanding level, achieves it. Guy Green makes effective use of Singapore locations — especially of seaboard sunsets, where the couple canoodle, and of colorful st.eet scenes in the redlight district. The whole thing has the oldfashioned air of glossy romance in a woman's magazine idiom. That should be its strength at the b.o.

Hayley Mills is pert and pleasant, but doesn't strike the right contrast between the depressed Polly and the stunning recreation, so that her newfound efficiency and tinge of ruthlessness (she hocks her dead aunt's jewels and pockets the proceeds) don't register strongly. Shashi Kapoor, an Indian actor first noticed in "Shakespeare Wallah," is agreeable as the guide, but the role needs more definition from the script, leaving uncertainty as to whether he is really as unscrupulous as others hint.

Trevor Howard is wasted as the raffish Uncle Bob, but, as always,

gives a sturdy performance. Lesser thesps are well cast, but their roles are stereotypes and the feature pic encourages a vein of overplaying (principally by Brenda de Banzie, who caricatures the role of the aunt) that destroys conviction.

It's a film that would gain from extra sharpness and irony in the telling. But its soothing escapism should find an audience amongst distaffers and Mills fans.

Otta.

Jag Ar Nyfiken-Gul
(I Am Curious-Yellow)
(SWEDISH)

Stockholm, Oct. 27.
Sandrew production and release. Stars Lena Nyman, Peter Lindgren, Borje Ahlstedt. Written and directed by Vilgot Sjoman; camera, Peter Wester; editor, Wic Kjellin. Running, Time, 110 MINS.

Under the guise of making a film about the young generation which lives in the present, Vilgot Sjoman, known for his earlier films ("491" and "My Sister, My Love") that abounded in sex, has tried to portray how the welfare state in Sweden has not fulfilled its political aims. Instead Sjoman has devoted most of his attention to fornication.

Using the film-within-the-film gimmick, the characters more or less portray themselves. Lena Nyman, the main character, is presented as Sjoman's mistress who is anxious to become a star in Sjoman's film.

In the film-within the-film, she is a curious young girl who participates in protest demonstrations outside the U. S. Embassy and goes around with a taperecorder asking trade union officials why they have not demanded better measures; asking Swedes, just returned from vacation in Spain, what they thought of Franco, and whether they had not been disturbed by touristing in a dictatorship; and asking draftees why they were not pacifists.

Miss Nymen, however devotes most of her time boudoiring with Borje Ahlstedt, a married salesman out to get the most possible out of life and not the least disturbed by the political issues that involve Lena.

Both spend a good deal of the film slipping out of their clothes, and playing, fighting and making love in the nude. Even though men have appeared in the nude before in a Swedish film, viz., "Together with Gunilla," they have never been exposed to the same extent as Borje. As for Lena, Ripley or not, she is filmed in a closeup that is as explicit as one can get in or out of a stag film.

In his glorification of the sexual act, Sjoman has placed his main characters making love in an oak tree, with a religious group in sight; on the ·balustrade of the sight; on the balustrade of the Royal Palace, in view of a guard; and a number of other places when they get too impatient to wait (and they never have any thought of waiting).

Despite the abundance of sex, "I am Curious-Yellow" is mostly a rather boring one. As the couple start making love suddenly with-

out any love play, they leave their audiences way behind.

The film also has political pretensions but it has no political viewpoint. It jabs at certain Swedish attitudes and has a good many in-jokes, but really takes no stand.

It seems unlikely that "I Am Curious-Yellow," which is supposed to be followed by "I Am Curious-Blue" in about a month, will be shown outside of Sweden in an uncensored version. When the censors get through with it, there probably won't be much left.

Artistically, "I Am Curious-Yellow" is a minor film. It may well come to play a more important role in film censorship.

Fred.

I Spheres Den Guyrizoun Pisso
(Bullets Don't Turn Back)
(GREEK)

Athens, Oct. 24.
Finos Film production. Directed by Nicos Foskolos. Stars Costas Kazacos, A. Antonopoulos, Spyros Kalaguerou, Mema Stathopoulou. Screenplay by Foskolos; camera, Nicos Demopoulos; music, Mimis Plessas. Previewed at Salonika Film Fest. Running Time, 118 MINS.

Tsacos	Costas Kazacos
Stathis	A. Antonopoulos
Peye	Mema Stathopoulou
Leader of outlaws	Spyros Kaloguerou
Outlaw	Paul Liaros
Outlaw	N. Lycometros
Jail's warden	Costas Bacas
His mistress	Betty Arvaniti

This is really a film off the beaten track of the usual melodramatic stories in Greek films— a story loaded with violence set high in the Greek mountains. It's strong meat by all standards and has all the ingredients of exploitation, with best chances with action-lovers.

Plot starts with Stathis returning home from the funeral of his wife, accompanied by his sister Peye and his two boys. Stopping to get water from a river, he is arrested and charged with murder and robbery. Because the body of one of the real robbers was found nearby, but the stolen money can't be found. No one believes his innocence, and he winds up with a life imprisonment sentence.

After a few months' stretch, he manages to escape, helped by the warden's mistress. They send another convict, Tsacos, after him. Tsacos having been born in the mountains, knows every path and hiding place. He tracks down Stathis, and both start back for the prison. On their way, Stathis, saves Tsacos' life. Finally Stathis joins the good men, and all the robbers are killed.

This is the first directorial work of Nicos Foskolos, one of the most popular and successful screen Greek writers. He tells his story violently but effectively, although he uses many clinches.

Costas Kazacos lends an excellent performance as Tsacos. Some colorful support also is given Antonopoulos, Kaloguerou and Mema Stathopoulou.

Nicos Demopoulos captured the beauty of the mountainous landscape with his camera. Music of Mimis Plessas won a prize at this fest. Other technical values are good.

Rena.

MIFED Fest

Sayarim
(The Patrol)
(ISRAELI)

Milan, Oct. 20.
An Eli Gil production. Directed by Micha Shagrir. With Illy Gorlizki, Leor Yani, Zeev Revah, Elli Cohen, Yossi Ohana, Assi Dayan, Jack Cohen. From an original story by Avraham Heffner; screenplay, Orna Spector, Micha Shagrir; camera, Yachin Hirsch; editor, Tova Biran; music by Sascha Argov, in cooperation with Vladimir Kusma. At MIFED Film Fair, Milan. Running Time, 98 MINS.

Zevi	Illy Gorlizki
Ya'al	Leor Yani
Elli	Zeev Revah
Nussi	Elli Cohen
Soubhi	Yossi Ohana

Newspaperman and film critic Micha Shagrir set out in "The Patrol" to defuse the warring spirit existing between Israel and its Arab neighbors by deplicting the life in uniform on both sides of the border as one of mankind's necessary evils. His impressive debut as film director will probably receive less attention than it merits. Because the film's anti-heroic viewpoint ran afoul the recent Israel-Arab war which erased human nuances and reduced the Middle Eastern powder keg to stark black and white truisms.

Story of an Israeli commando raid on an enemy border town to capture and bring back alive the Arab leader of a sabotage ring is limited to five principal characters who play against the barren expanse separating the two countries. Two of the commandos are army vets, one is an ex-commando on temporary military duty, and the fourth a trained recruit on his first mission.

The saboteur is captured as planned, but a subsequent outpost alarm forces the Israeli unit to seek a desert escape route on foot. This trek occupies almost half the footage and leaves the outcome unresolved after a dramatic skirmish in which the Arab prisoner kills one of the commandos and attempts escape.

"The Patrol" generates tension from the first title and the narrative is packed with action. Brief but concise moments are spared to clarify relationships between the men and individual ties with places and people left behind — all intelligently weaved into the action without fracturing the narrative texture. Weariness and landscape emptiness slow film's tempo in final reels without diminishing the story's outcome.

Illy Gorlizki and Leor Yani (particularly the former) as army vets give first-rate performances. Sascha Argov provides an effective musical score. The black and white photography by Yachin Hirsch aids the film's spectacular sobriety.

Director Shagrir has achieved a far bigger film than the sparse ingredients that go into it. It will not be welcome screen entertainment for those in Israel and abroad who under the stress of history do not believe that the time has come to philosophize about the war situation in the Middle East. Grave situation does not alter Shagrir's bright career starting with this production. *Werb.*

The Flying Matchmaker
(ISRAELI—COLOR)

Milan, Oct. 24.
Geva Films release of Mordekhay Navon production. Stars Mike Burstein; costars Germaine Unikovski, Rina Ganor; features Raphael Klatzkin, Shmuel Rudensky, Aaron Meskin, Elisheva Michaeli. Directed by Israel Becker. Screenplay, Alex Maimon and Becker; based on a musical play by Abraham Goldfaden; camera, Romulo Garroni; editor, Nelly Bogor; music, Shaul Brezovsky. At MIFED Film Fair, Milan. Running Time, 104 MINS.

Max/Koony Lemel	Mike Burstein
Caroline	Rina Ganor
Libaleh	Germaine Unikovski
Shalom Munio	Aaron Meskin
Reb Kalman	Rafael Klatzkin
Pinchas'l	Shmuel Rudensky
Rivka	Elisheva Michaeli

Israel condenses in a population of little more than 2,000,000 probably the richest collection of folklore in the world. One aspect of this heritage is the literature and music cultivated by Jewish communities in Eastern Poland and Western Russia.

Film director Israel Becker was born in this region and was influenced by the folk culture flowering there. At 15, he joined the Goldfaden Theatre of Traveling Players, named after a folk writer-composer who contributed among other works, "The Flying Matchmaker," to Jewish folklore. With almost three decades behind him as a member of the Jewish Municipal Theatre in Kiev, the Theatre of Liberated Jews (sponsored by UNNRA) and actor-director with the Habimah National Theatre, Becker now adds to the growth of Israel's frenetic little film industry with a labor-of-love screen recreation of Goldfaden's "Flying Matchmaker."

Film falls short of a brilliant, balanced libretto a la "Fiddler On The Roof," but compensates with style and performance that gives Israel's costliest film production to date a genuine note of comedy, fantasy, and original melody. This sets it apart in the long tradition of stage and screen folk musicals.

Reb Kalman (Rafael Klatzkin) is a hustling matchmaker who has brought more couples together than a harvest moon, but can't seem to marry off his own daughter Libaleh (Germaine Unikovsky). Caroline (Rina Ganor) loves her tutor Max (Mike Burstein) but her wealthy father Pinchas'l (Shmuel Rudensky) wants her to mate a young man of pedigree. Koony Lemel (Mike Burstein), the stammering game-legged son of a scholar in another town is the matchmaker's choice. Max doubles as Koony and a mish-mash of double identity ensues until the big song and dance finale in which the young lovers wed and Koony stutters his way to the canopy with the matchmaker's daughter.

In his twin role, Burstein fares better as Koony Lemil than he does as Max. The two girls — one resisting the matchmaker's code — the other embracing it — complement each other throughout. All other supporting performances follow the broad lines of ancient lore

and long standing theatrical convention.

Becker directed his own adaption (in collaboration with Alex Maimon) with great affection and respect for the Goldfaden original. In fact, this explains the over-length, but scissoring down is no problem. Becker's treatment of "Matchmaker" starts off as a folk tale, picks up tunes and size along the way and closes like a flamboyant Broadway musical. This might peeve folk culture buffs but gives the Mordekahy Navon production a bigger specialized audience to play with.

Shaul Brezovsky's score dresses several folk tunes into pop chart possibles. Romulo Garroni's color lensing heightens the films tableau quality. *Werb.*

Samurai (Part 2)
(Zoku Miyamoto Musashi)
(JAPANESE—COLOR)

Sequel to Hiroshi Inagaki's Oscar-winning "Samurai" finally seen in New York after delay of more than a decade. For hardcore samuraddicts only.

Toho International release of Kazuo Takumura production. Stars Toshiro Mifune; features Koji Tsuruta, Sachio Sakai, Akihiko Hirata, Yu Fujiki, Daisuke Kato, Eijiro Tono. Directed by Hiroshi Inagaki. Screenplay, Tokuhei Wakao, Inagaki, from novel "Miyamoto Musashi" by Eiji Yoshikawa; camera (Eastman Color), Asushi Atumoto; music, Ikuma Dan. Reviewed at 55th St. Playhouse, N.Y., Oct. 22, 1967 Running Time, 102 MINS.

Musashi Miyamoto	Toshiro Mifune
Kojiro Sasaki	Koji Tsuruta
Matahachi Honiden	Sachio Sakai
Seijuro Yoshioka	Akihiko Hirata
Denshichiro Yoshioka	Yu Fujiki
Toji Gion	Daisuke Kato
Baiken Shishido	Eijiro Tono
Old Priest Nikkan	Kuninori Kodo
Jotaro	Kenjim Iida
Otsu	Kaoru Yachigusa
Akemi	Mariko Okada
Oko	Mitsuko Mito
Yoshino	Michiyo Kogure

To judge from the packed house this second part of Hiroshi Inagaki's "Samurai" trilogy of 1954-56 had this weekend at N.Y.'s 55th St. Playhouse, there would seem to be an impression in the U.S. that it is some sort of Japanese "classic." Nothing could be further from the truth. A purely commercial effort, it is barely mentioned in the standard histories of the Nipponese cinema, and Inagaki never developed an artistic reputation of any real note.

First part of this trilogy opened in the U.S. a dozen years back and was reviewed in the Nov. 11, 1955 VARIETY. Though it won the Academy Award as best foreign-language film that year, it is only now that its two sequels are being unspooled in New York. The trilogy would seem to have its greatest appeal to the Yank equivalent of those Europeans who think the best westerns are those told most "purely"—the most *western* westerns. In like manner, many samurai-film fans appear not to realize that the best examples of their favorite genre are those which both honor and work against the tradition to express the personal viewpoints of their directors.

"Samurai (Part 2)" has no personal point of view other than a tendency towards meaningless ac-

tion and theatrical romantic scenes. It recounts the education of a young wandering samurai as he learns that along with strength and swordsmanship a warrior must show mercy and kindness. He is pursued by no fewer than three women but rejects them all, preferring martial to marital life.

The staging is static and unfortunately Asushi Atumoto's excellent color photography has the ironic effect of making everything even more picture-bookish. Toshiro Mifune give an indifferent performance in 'the title role; more and more, this Japanese star seems a one-director (Akira Kurosawa) actor. Particularly annoying is the very western music of Ikuma Dan, which is as loud and insistent as that in any grade B action-adventure film. *Byro.*

Les Arnaud
(The Arnauds)
(FRENCH—COLOR)

Paris, Oct. 31.
SNC release of Belles Rives, SNC, Flora Films production. Stars Bourvil, Adamo; features Christine Delaroche, Marcelle Ranson, Michel De Re. Directed by Leo Joannon. Screenplay, Joannon, Jacques Robert; camera (Eastmancolor), Willy Cricha; music, Adamo, Franck Pourcel. At Elysees, Paris. Running Time, 95 MINS.

Arnaud	Bourvil
Andre	Adamo
Tina	Christine Delaroche
Landlady	Marcelle Ranson
Antique Dealer	Michel De Re

Sudsy pic suffers from plodding direction and smug, patronizing characterizations and plotting. It has black and white characters, and a forced script. All of which relegates this to little chance abroad and small possibilities here in spite of sporting some marquee values in comedian Bourvil, playing a dramatic role, plus popular pop singer Adamo in his first film.

Adamo has a lispy speaking voice that does not help make his part of a determined poor boy trying to become a lawyer very believable. He does manage to deliver a song in the titles that shows he is better on stage or wax than on celluloid. Bourvil has charm as a big-hearted magistrate who helps the boy when he is caught up in a murder rap. All this is done with flagrant homilies on youth needing its chance.

Color is uneven while the story is forced. Production dress is fairly skimpy. Mainly a local item on its names and okay pitch for youth emerging triumphant. *Mosk.*

Kill a Dragon
(COLOR)

Hollywood, Oct. 31.
United Artists release of Aubrey Schenck (Hal Klein) production. Stars Jack Palance, Fernando Lamas, Aldo Ray. Directed by Michael Moore. Screenplay by George Schenck and William Marks; camera (DeLuxe Color), Emmanuel Rojas; editor, John Schreyer; music, Philip Springer. Reviewed at Goldwyn studios, Oct. 25, '67. Running Time, 91 MINS.

Rick	Jack Palance
Patral	Fernando Lamas
Vigo	Aldo Ray
Tisa	Alizia Gur
Win Lim	Kam Tong
Ian	Don Knight
Jimmie	Hans Lee
Chunhyang	Judy Dan

Put the theme of "The Magnificent Seven" in and around Hong Kong, surround it with a cliche

script, routine performances and direction and a small budget, and it adds up to a low-quality pic that may have a short run in the nabes as lower half of a double bill before being sold to tv.

Plotline of nice, tough guy Jack Palance helping some Chinese peasants claim some salvage of cargo of explosives in a junk that beached on their island away from the owner, bad, tough guy Fernando Lamas, is believable only because it's so familiar.

It provides the framework for several fight scenes, with fists, karate, automatic weapons and explosives. Palance and his four friends win them all, without even sustaining a loss except when the junk they are trying to rebuild collapses on Hans Lee. Although it appeared as if it had crushed entire lower half of his body, there he as the next day, jumping and prancing around, good as new.

Lamas, on the other hand, allegedly a feudal baron type with a small army of men, loses virtually all of them, singly and in bunches during course of the picture, yet is goodtime Charley at the end, bringing Palance a bottle of champagne while the latter is again in bed with Alizia Gur. As if it were just a game they had been playing.

Palance and Aldo Ray seem to take it all seriously and work hard, but a menacing Lamas is not very stock, and roles are performed that way, though Don Knight, as Ian, shows a bit of style. But the film doesn't. *Beig.*

More Than A Miracle
(ITALIAN—FRENCH—
(COLOR—FRANSCOPE)

Tepid Cinderella story, shot down by heavy-handed political tract. Sophia Loren and Omar Sharif star. Dubious art house or lowercase potential in domestic situations.

Hollywood, Oct. 26,
Metro-Goldwyn-Mayer release of a Carlo Ponti production. Stars Sophia Loren, Omar Sharif. Directed by Francesco Rosi. Screenplay, Tonino Guerra, Raffaele La Capria, Giuseppe Patroni Griffi, Rosi; camera (Metrocolor), Pasquale De Santis; editor, Jolanda Benvenuti; music, Piero Piccioni; title song lyrics, Larry Kusik, Eddie Snyder; asst. directors, Camillo Teti, Dante Brini. Reviewed at Metro Studios, Culver City, Oct. 25, '67. Running Time, 102 MINS.

Isabella	Sophia Loren
Prince	Omar Sharif
Queen Mother	Dolores Del Rio
Monzu	Georges Wilson
Brother Joseph	Leslie French

"More Than A Miracle," formerly titled "Happily Ever After," is a real curiosity: labelled in production notes as a "fairy tale for adults," the Carlo Ponti production tells a Cinderella story, with some rather heavy-handed anti-clericalism and anti-monarchism thrown in. Stars Sophia Loren and Omar Sharif provide marquee bait. Metro release faces an uphill b.o. battle, with fair outlook in special situations, but limited lowercase potential in general runs. Overseas, film may have longer legs.

Director Francesco Rosi was one of four scripters who labored to limited success. Rosi's direction often is exciting, and film has a crisp, clean look. It was made in Franscope, a French anamorphic process frequently used of late by Metro, and Metrocolor.

Although the fairy tale approach is evident—the stock Cinderella, handsome prince, witches, next-to-closing tragedy but fadeout bliss, script defeats itself in part by going too far into reality. Sharif, therefore, is not only handsome, but arrogant, wilful, brutal to his servants; also, the beautiful Miss Loren, looking a bit uneasy and out of place in peasant weeds, eventually berates Sharif publicly for oppression of the lower classes.

Furthermore, Leslie French, a benevolent monastic Brother who flies, literally, later, after death, aids Miss Loren and cautions her against listening to pap which implores resignation to fate, etc. He, too oviously, is the "good" cleric, in contrast to all the others.

Dolores Del Rio, still a striking woman of grace and beauty, plays Sharif's mother with a bemused air. Palace chef Georges Wilson is appropriately effete. The witch who follows Miss Loren is played by Italo comic Carlo Piscane in drag, who is very funny. Other players are routine. Pleasant title song, performed by Roger Williams and chorale, is spotlighted before titles by running over out-of-focus opticals. Piero Piccioni's score, emphasizing harpsichord, enhances the fantasy mood.

Pic's fatal flaw is vacillation between pure make-believe, which would have gone over to some degree, and corny political tract which is what one would imagine "Snow White" to be if produced by Russian filmmakers. Production credits are good. Made in Cinecitta Studios in Rome, pic legally is a partnership between C. C. Champion (Rome) and Les Films Concordia (Paris).

Murf.

San Francisco Fest

Sofi

San Francisco, Oct. 27.
Robert Carlisle, (John F. Meyers) Production, directed by Carlisle. No release set. Stars Tom Troupe. Screenplay by Don Eitner, Troupe; camera, Albert Taylor; editor, Robert Grant; music, Allyn Ferguson. Reviewed at San Francisco Film Festival New Directors Series, Oct. 27, 1967. Running Time, **97 MINS.**
Madman .... Tom Troupe

For his first feature film producer-director Robert Carlisle has simply photographed the one-man drama "Diary of a Madman" based on Nicholai Gogol's short story, and as such it is an impressive 97 minute solo tour de force for actor Tom Troupe, who recreates the Los Angeles stage play. Production is polished and reeks of integrity; it should have a modest payoff in art houses, campus situations, and possible sale to expanding public television.

Title was changed to "Sofi" because United Artists used original for a Vincent Price horror flick. Sofi is the daughter of the boss of an impoverished, bullied, neurotic clerk, who is obsessed with her while she is hardly aware of his plagued existence. When Troupe learns of her engagement to an army officer, he disintegrates into paranoia and delusions of grandeur. Troupe is a fascinating young actor to watch, as he

transitions f r o m an introverted neurotic to the final screaming lunacy of imagining himself Ferdinand VIII, the fugitive King of Spain.

The audience itself may suffer from claustrophobia, as all the action takes place in the clerk's dreary room, moving only at the end to an even drearier madhouse cell. Carlisle has r e s i s t e d the temptation to "open up" or get tricky, using the oppression of one set to great effect, but still keeping it visually interesting. Albert Taylor's photography is faultless; and Allyn Ferguson's original score contribute heavily to the emotional intensity.

For dramatic variety, Troupe and Carlisle m i g h t have developed more of the black laughter of the clerk's madness, for certainly there is humor in a man who converses with puppets, reads letters written by dogs, and struts about with a broom as the royal mace. But that is a matter of interpretation.

Rick.

Vancouver Fest

The Funniest Man In The World
(DOCUMENTARY)

Vancouver, Oct. 20.
Darer Corp. (N.Y.) release of Funnyman Inc.-Polara Organization Inc. production. Produced by Vernon Becker and Mel May. Direction and script by Vernon Becker. Editing, William B. Dalziell. Music composed by Albert Hague; arranged and conducted by Johnny Douglas. Sound by Recording Studio Inc. Narrated by Douglas Fairbanks Jr. Reviewed at Bay Theatre, Vancouver Film Festival, Oct. 20, '67. Running Time, **102 MINS.**

"The Funniest Man in the World," given its global premiere at the Vancouver Film Festival, is, a warm frankly nostalgic tribute to Charles Chaplin. It's on the artist and not the political controversy that the film concentrates. Perhaps, like Chaplin's own recent autobiography, this film will disappoint those who are looking for insights beyond surface aspects.

The people it will not disappoint — and the audience Becker and May must have had in mind when they initiated this project — are the millions of Chaplin fans the world over. Film achieves its purpose in a most entertaining way, a documentary treatment of Chaplin's artistic development from a London music hall child through his first U.S. shorts.

While film is not just a compilation of selected Chaplin scenes, Becker and May have provided a massive array of such clips. And the laughs still are there. Many early Chaplin capers, fairly familiar because of continued tv exposure plus some previous film attempts to present the Chaplin story, are included of course, but given a revitalized treatment that keeps them hilarious. And film producers have also come up with what appears to be fresh film clips, or at least less familiar.

Film, via stills and stock footage, begins with story of Chaplin's early London days, traces his poverty-ridden life as a youngster, notes his start as a child stage actor, and brings him to America with the Fred Karno vaudeville

company and his success in the sketch, "A Night in an English Music Hall." It is from this performance that Chaplin catches the attention of Mack Sennett as a replacement for the departing Ford Sterling. Excerpts from this period include Chaplin's first film, "Making A Living"; "Kid Auto Races"; in which his tramp character is first seen; "Mabel at the Wheel"; "Caught In A Cabaret"; "The Masquerader"; "His Trysting Place"; "Dough and Dynamite," his first big popular success; and "Tillies Punctured Romance," the screen's first full length comedy.

Now with Essanay and his own director, Chaplin begins to be more sure of himself and to put his unique creative comedy ideas to work, noted in clips from "His New Job"; "Police"; "A Night Out"; and "The Tramp", in which Chaplin introduces pathos to his comedy for the first time and thus initiates what is to become his characteristic ' trademark. Three years after Chaplin leaves Essanay they release "Triple Trouble," made up from unused and discarded scenes from his earlier films, including the unreleased "Life." Clips from these "outs" are still boff as are the shots from Chaplin's next series of films for the Mutual company, "The Rink"; "The Immigrant"; "Easy Street"; and a series of unused out-takes from "The Count."

Shots of Chaplin imitators and a parade of Chaplin song hits, Charlot story books, comic strips and an animated cartoon point up the fact that at age twenty-seven, just three years after his screen debut, Charlie Chaplin is now hailed as "The Funniest Man in the World," and at a salary of $10,000 a week, plus a bonus of $150,000, he is the highest paid film star in the universe. With U.S. entry into World War One Chaplin teams with Douglas Fairbanks, Mary Pickford and Jack Dempsey to help sell Liberty Bonds, produces his own film, "The Bond" at his own expense, to further this effort.

At war's end Chaplin, Fairbanks and Pickford join with director D. W. Griffith to form the United Artists film company ("the lunatics are now running the asylum," notes the head of another studio).

Shaw.

Tony Rome
(PANAVISION—COLOR)

Frank Sinatra excellent as private eye. Fast-moving suspenser relying heavily on burley comedy. Topnotch production values. Strong, and long, b.o. legs.

Hollywood, Oct. 19.
Twentieth Century-Fox release of an Arcola-Millfield (Aaron Rosenberg) production. Stars Frank Sinatra. Directed by Gordon Douglas. Screenplay, Richard L. Breen, based on a novel, "Miami Mayhem," by Marvin H. Albert; camera (DeLuxe Color), Joseph Biroc; editor, Robert Simpson; music, Billy May; songs, May, Randy Newman; title song, Lee Hazlewood; asst. director, Richard Lang. Reviewed at 20th-Fox Studios, L.A., Oct. 18, '67. Running Time, **110 MINS.**

Tony Rome	Frank Sinatra
Ann	Jill St. John
Lt. Santini	Richard Conte
Rita	Gena Rowlands
Kosterman	Simon Oakland
Boyd	Jeffrey Lynn
Rood	Lloyd Bochner
Turpin	Robert J. Wilke
Sally	Virginia Vincent
Fat Candy	Joan Shawlee
Donald Pines	Richard Krisher
Langley	Lloyd Gough
Oscar	Babe Hart
Mrs. Schuyler	Templeton Fox
Packy	Rocky Graziano
Irma	Elizabeth Fraser
Catleg	Shecky Greene
Lorna	Jeanne Cooper
Ruyter	Harry Davis
Sam Boyd	Stanley Ross
Diana	Sue Lyon

"Tony Rome," is a flip gumshoe on the Miami scene, and a very commercial blend of tasteful and tasteless vulgarity. A busy, heavily-populated script, zesty Gordon Douglas direction, and solid Aaron Rosenberg production values add up to a potent first-run b.o. package. Also, the 20th-Fox release will have extended subrun strength.

Marvin H. Albert's novel, "Miami Mayhem," was scripted by the late Richard L. Breen into a fast-moving whodunit which, per se, is far less intriguing than the individual scenes en route to climax. By fadeout, few will particularly care about the mystery angle, for the eye and ear is bedazzled with vignette. Credit Sinatra's excellent style, and the production elements, for pulling it off.

Apart from some inside gags, including an overplugging of the beer with which Sinatra has a blurb tie-in, there is an abundance of double-entendre dialog which in reality can be taken only one way. Script is not exactly that of a stag smoker, but portions will be considered cheap and crass, even though amusing in an embarrassing sort of way.

Story peg is Gena Rowlands' gems, which she switched to glass to pay off blackmail. Second Hubby Simon Oakland, drinking daughter Sue Lyon, party-girl Jill St. John, detective Richard Conte, unlicensed medic Jeffrey Lynn, dope-pusher (and, apparently, homosexual) Lloyd Bochner, toughs Lloyd Gough and Babe Hart, gunman Shecky Greene (comic's first dramatic role), mongoloid Stan Ross, shady jeweler Harry Davis, lesbians Deanna Lund and Elizabeth Fraser, hooker John Shawlee, and others are involved.

Action specialist Buzz Henry aided director Douglas in certain scenes; in others, Douglas did his customary professional job in exacting strong performances amid interesting camera setups Sinatra is excellent. Miss St. John gives a warmth to her role which adds depth to the character and others give sturdy support. Rocky Graziano and Mike Romanoff appear in bits. Miss Shawlee is outstanding in her brief scene, and the lesbian sequence, for all its deliberate tawdriness, is far more compelling in its subject treatment than all of "Reflections In A Golden Eye."

Billy May's score is good, although one of the two songs for pic is relegated to use in an overdone, and cliche, running gag about newlyweds. Lee Hazelewood composed a title tune. for warbling by Nancy Sinatra, which is a good production song. Moss Mabry's colorful fashion eye is a superior asset. On the technical side, Joseph Biroc's Panavision-DeLuxe Color camera is outstanding, as are other credits.

Robert Simpson edited to a good 110 minutes. *Murf.*

House of 1,000 Dolls
(BRITISH - GERMAN - SPANISH TECHNISCOPE-COLOR)

Okay whiteslavery entry from Harry Alan Towers, with good exploitation potential.

Hollywood, Nov. 3.
American International Pictures release of Constantin Film (Munich)-P. C. Hispamer Films (Madrid) (Harry Alan Towers) production. Stars Vincent Price, Martha Hyer, George Nadel; features Anne Smyrner, Wolfgang Kieling, Sancho Gracia, Maria Rohm. Directed by Jeremy Summers. Screenplay, Peter Welbeck; camera (Technicolor), Manuel Merino; music, Charles Camilleri; editor, Allan Morrison; asst. director, Juan Estelrich. Reviewed at Charles Aidikoff Screening Room, Nov. 3, '67. Running Time, 78 MINS.
Felix Manderville .... Vincent Price
Rebecca .... Martha Hyer
Stephen Armstrong .... George Nadel
Marie .... Anne Smyrner
Inspector Emil .... Wolfgang Kieling
Fernando .... Sancho Gracia
Diane .... Maria Rohm
Paul .... Louis Rivera
Ahmed .... Jose Jaspe
Salim .... Juan Olaguivel
Abdu .... Herbert Fuchs
Madame Viera .... Yelena Samarina
Liza .... Diane Bond
THE DOLLS
Andrea Lascelles, Ursula Janis, Monique Aime, Marisol Anon, Jill Echols, Loli Munoz, Lara Lenti, Sandra Petrelli, Kitty Swan, Karin Skarreso, Carolyn Coon, Francoise Fontages.

American International Pictures has a satisfactory exploitation entry in this German-Spanish co-production about a European white slave ring which abducts beautiful young femmes. Vincent Price, Martha Hyer and George Nader are the names pegs and plottage, while routine, has the melodramatic i gredients to carry it through to okay b.o. prospects in program market.

Script by Peter Welbeck has Tangier for its locale, where exteriors were lensed for excellent photographic effect. Film takes its title from the name of the luxurious establishment the syndi-

cate uses to attract the wealthy to the Casbah, where femmes are brought from all over the world. Jeremy Summers' direction is long on fast action while inclined to static exposure during some of the more intimate scenes, and manages to make the best out of his undraped cast of dolls.

Price delivers suavely as the illusionist who uses his profession to find "talent" for the ring and Miss Hyer is beautiful as his mental telepathist partner in act, once one of the girls. Nader is a young American visiting Tangier with his wife, Anne Smyrner, both of whom are caught in the net of the syndicate.

Technical credits are well enough handled. *Whit.*

Blood Beast From Outer Space
(BRITISH)

Strange avoidance of a suitably action-packed climax makes this otherwise well-made British sci-fi pic questionable for program audiences.

World Entertainment Release of Harris Associates presentation of a New Art (Ronald Liles) production. Directed by John Gilling. Screenplay, Jim O'Connaly, from novel, "The Night Callers," by Frank Crisp; camera, Stephen Dade; music, John Gregory; editor, Philip Barnikey; sound, John Cox. Reviewed at New Amsterdam Theatre. N.Y., Oct. 29, 1967. Running Time, 84 MINS.
Jack Costain .... John Saxon
Professor Morley ......Maurice Denham
Ann .... Patricia Haines
Army Major .... John Carson
Thorburn .... Jack Watson
Supt. Hartley .... Alfred Burke

The problem with "Blood Beast from Outer Space" is that it is simply too well-made for its own commercial good. As a British sci-fi programmer it is far above average of its kind, but it eschews a standard action-adventure climax in favor of a "philosophical" one. A 42d St. grind audience recently showed its displeasure quite volubly after this sputtering finale—and this in spite of the fact that there were audible gasps to be heard during the earlier part of the pic. Vet director John Gilling provides some suspenseful moments indeed in the first half.

But Jim O'Connaly, scripting from Frank Crisp's novel "The Night Callers," gives Gilling little to work with for the important final moments. Story has a visitor from one of Jupiter's moons kidnapping young girls to take back with him. He is a half-man, half-beast kind of monster and explains that this is a result of nuclear war on his planet many eons ago. Now they must have the girls in order to normalize things again via procreation, so he says. This explanation serves in lieu of the battle with the London police for which the audience has been prepared.

Though John Saxon is embarrassing as a young scientist whose investigation of a strange transmitting orb sets off the mystery (his real forte, as "The Appaloosa" proved, is character acting), some of the other players are good, particularly Maurice Denham, an older professor who is one of the monster's first victims. Stephen Dade's black-and-white lensing is superb

in exteriors, just routine in interiors.

John Gregory's music is fair, and other credits are acceptable. *Byro.*

The Incident

Very good drama of urban alienation and indifference. N.Y.-made pic mixes new and established talents, well directed. Far above exploitation calibre, needs showcasing in special situations.

Hollywood, Nov. 2.
Twentieth Century-Fox release of Moned (Monroe Sachson-Edward Meadow) production. Directed by Larry Peerce. Screenplay, Nicholas E. Baehr; camera, Gerald Hirschfeld; editor, Armand Lebowitz; music, Terry Knight; asst. director, Steve Barnett. Reviewed at 20th-Fox Studios, L.A., Nov. 1, '67. Running Time, 99 MINS.
Joe Ferrone .... Tony Musante
Artie Conners .... Martin Sheen
Pvt. Teflinger .... Beau Bridges
Pvt. Carmatti .... Bob Bannard
Bill, Helen Wilks .... Ed McMahon,
                          Diana Van der Vlis
Tony .... Victor Arnold
Alice .... Donna Mills
Also, Bertha Beckerman, Jack Gilford, Thelma Ritter, Harry, Muriel Purvis, Mike Kellin, Jan Sterling, Douglas McCann, Gary Merrill.
Kenneth .... Robert Fields
Arnold, Joan Robinson .... Brock Peters,
                                  Ruby Dee
Susie Wilks .. Eileen and Kathleen Smith
Derelict .... Henry Proach

Strong casting, impressive direction and generally sharp writing (from an old tv script) make "The Incident" a very fine episodic drama about two toughs who intimidate passengers on a N.Y. subway train. Some overexposition and relaxed editing flag the pace, but, overall, the Monroe Sachson-Edward Meadow production is a candid indictment, in situation and in dialog, of contemporary alienation, and is definitely not an exploitation item. Showcasing in smaller situations is mandatory for maximum b.o. yield. Urban prospects are particularly strong.

Historically, Nicholas E. Baehr's original teleplay was a David Susskind production, "Ride With Terror," for the Dupont "Show Of The Month," directed by Ray Winston. A Susskind-Joseph E. Levine film adaptation never came off, and lapsed film rights later were acquired by the Sachson-Meadow team. Canadian backers pulled off. Richard D. Zanuck came to the rescue, and film was completed for about $790,000.

Baehr's screenplay spotlights Tony Musante and Martin Sheen, out-for-kicks pair, who terrorize 16 train riders. Latter include soldiers Beau Bridges and Bob Bannard, middle-class couple Ed McMahon and Diana Van der Vlis (with child), elderly marrieds Jack Gilford and Thelma Ritter, unhappy Mike Kellin and berating wife Jan Sterling, and a Negro couple, Brock Peters and Ruby Dee. Other victims are alcoholic Gary Merrill, homosexual Robert Fields, derelict Henry Proach, a pair of young lovers, Victor Arnold and Donna Mills. The two toughs lay bare the weaknesses in all characters.

The powerful, and emotionally disturbing, aspect of story is that most audience segments can iden-

tify with one or more victims, scorn the others, yet find that, ultimately, no one is safe from irrational scum bent on violence. Peters' sequence is particularly moving: an impatient Negro, very anti-white, he digs the degradation of the others, but when his turn comes, he is no better than the rest.

Director Peerce, whose earlier feature work was "One Potato, Two Potato," shows superior ability in eliciting character nuances through striking, but uncluttered and unpretentious, camera setups; this facility alone is noteworthy and admirable. Performers all register very strongly, through excellent camera work by Gerald Hirschfeld.

Stories of this genre always are helped by physical momentum generated by a space-and-time movement, in this case a subway ride. This factor helps overcome a levelling off of plot. The 10-minute prolog, in which the Musante-Sheen characters are established, eventually works to the detriment of film as a whole, because the early physical violence precedes the verbal lashings to come.

In addition, although all characters are introduced in good fashion, it takes 50 minutes of screen time (out of 99 total) to get the main story going. Prolog pruning, and a tightening up in first hour, would have enhanced the pace. Armand Lebowitz edited.

Terry Knight's contemporary, and spare, score helps establish the mood, and all other credits are very good. *Murf.*

The Longest Night
(BULGARIAN)

Paris, Nov. 7.
Films Bulgaria production and release. With Victor Rebenchuk, Nevena Kokanova, Georgi Gergolev, Georgi Kaloyanchev. Directed by Velo Radev. Screenplay, Vesselin Branev; camera, Borislav Pounchev; music, Simeon Pironkov. At Arlequin, Paris. Running Time, 100 MINS.
Fugitive .... Victor Rebenchuk
Doctor .... Nevena Kokanova
Juggler .... Georgi Kaloyanchev
Father .... Georgi Gergolev
Old Man .... Ivan Bratanov
Boy .... Oleg Kovachev

It appears that staple Bulgar film fare is mainly academic as it looks at the last war and simple heroism, cowardice and decisions in crisis. Here, an escaped British prisoner, hiding on a train during the last war, sparks reactions in a cross section of a group of characters. Telegraphed and obvious, this still has firstrate workmanship and denotes a knowing director in Velo Radev who just needs more original scripts.

Expert camerawork and back projection keep the mainly interior train sequences alive and brisk as the parade of stereotype characters react to the desperate British flyer trying to hide out from alerted Germans and Bulgar police during the last war.

It ends with an American air raid on the train that resolves things for many but leaves the fate of the airman ambiguous. This Bulgar pic is adroitly made, solidly played but obvious in its sentiments, action and progression. Mainly local chances for this. *Mosk.*

Herrliche Zeiten im Spessart
(Glorious Times In the Spessart)
(GERMAN-COLOR-SONGS)

Berlin, Oct. 31.
A Constantin release of Independent-Film (Kurt Hoffmann, Heinz Angermeyer) production. Stars Liselotte Pulver, Harald Leipnitz; features Willy Millowitsch, Tatjana Sais, Hubert von Meyerinck. Directed by Kurt Hoffmann. Screenplay, Guenter Neumann; camera (Eastman-color), Richard Angst; music, Franz Grothe; settings, Werner and Isabella Schlichting; editor, Gisela Haller. At Gloria-Palast, West Berlin. Running time, 105 MINS.

Anneliese	Liselotte Pulver
Frank Green	Harald Leipnitz
Consul Muemmelmann	Willy Millowitsch
Frau Muemmelmann	Tatjana Sais
Max	Rudolf Rhomberg
Toni	Hans Richter
Hugo	Joachim Teege
Katrin	Kathrin Ackermann
General Teckel	Hubert von Meyerinck
Johanna	Hannelore Elsner
Rosalinde	Vivi Bach

This is Kurt Hoffmann's third "Spessart" (a chain of mountains in Southwest Germany) film. Commercially speaking, the continuation of this series seems justified. The first two "Spessart" pix proved topflight moneymakers. It looks as though the third opus will also chalk up fine returns, at least in the German-lingo markets.

While the two previous films played in the past, this one has to do with modern times. The robbers of the preceding films now show up as astronauts. There are rockets and space ships. Also the NATO finds mention in this one. The story is thin, but this shouldn't be too much of a handicap.

Liselotte Pulver, who also was starred in the first two Spessart pix, is seen here as a German Consul's daughter who is about to marry a rocket specialist (Harald Leipnitz). But just a few steps from the altar, the young man has to dash off on NATO orders. For some not so plausible reasons, film then makes a long ride through the centuries.

Hoffmann shows via several sequences that he is still the possessor of a light hand. But, quite obviously, he was let down by the material furnished by the script. It's sort of a puzzle to see how a once-lauded writer (Guenter Neumann) apparently has lost the knack of dreaming up a competent script. The jokes border too much on the banal side.

Miss Pulver and Harald Leipnitz enact an okay couple. The best performance is contributed by 71-year old Hubert von Mayerinck, German vet stage and screen player who already has more than 300 pix to his credit.

This Constantin release has other assets. One is songs (sung by Leipnitz), a melodious ballad could become a real hit. Laurels also should go to Werner and Isabella Schlichting for their imaginative settings. Had director Hoffmann had a more imaginative script, his third "Spessart" opus probably would have gained much. But this one should spell money, nevertheless. *Hans.*

Pyretos Stin Asphalto
(The Asphalt Fever)
(GREEK)

Salonika, Oct. 31.
Finos Film production. Directed by Dinos Demopoulos. Screenplay by Nicos Foscolos. Stars Georges Foundas, Jenny Roussea, Phedon Georguitsis; camera, George Arvanitis; music, Mimis Plesas. Reviewed at Salonika Film Fest. Running Time, 100 MINS.

Police officer	Georges Foundas
His wife	Jenny Roussea
Lunatic	Phedon Georguitsis
His girl	Nora Valsami
Blood donator	Spyros Kaloguerou

This is the second film which this oldest producing company of Greece (Finos Film) presented this year at the Salonika Film Fest. It copped many of the prizes.

This is a social drama. Plot while weak, has all the melodramatic ingredients for doing well at the wickets. In addition, it has an excellent performance by the male star which makes it even more worthwhile.

The central character is an officer of the Flying Squad of Athens whose wife is expecting a child. Both are looking forward to this happy event because there were many unhappy miscarriages before. But on the day of the baby's arrival, the police officer being on duty, is advised that the life of his wife and child is in danger and a blood transfusion is needed. The hospital hasn't the type of blood needed. So a dramatic search starts to locate a bottle of the needed blood. When he starts with it to the hospital, he is ordered to go after a lunatic who's got on board a school bus full of children. The police officer does not know what to do, whether to run to his wife or to save the 15 children on the bus. His loyalty to duty prompts him to speed to the bus as he sends the blood to the hospital via his men. He makes the lunatic go back to the asylum, and saves the children. But his own baby dies. His wife can't forgive him for this.

Director Dinos Demopoulos was awarded the prize as best director at the festival. Action is even and the flashbacks skillfully woven into the narration. In this, he is greatly helped by the performances, especially that by Georges Foundas who turns in an impressive portrayal as the police officer. He copped the prize as best actor. Georges Foundas and Phedon Georguitsis carry the emotional burden of this film. Other good performances are turned in by Spyros Kaloguerou and Jenny Roussea.

The photography is good and the music by Mimis Plessas is effective. Production values are solid. This pic was awarded the prize as the best production at the Salonika Fest. *Rena.*

Estouffade A La Caraibe
(Stew In the Caribbean)
(FRENCH—COLOR)

Paris, Oct. 31.
Valoria release of PAC CMV production. Stars Frederick Stafford, Jean Seberg; features Maria-Rosa Rodriguez, Serge Gainsbourg, Paul Grauchet, Mario Pisu. Directed by Jacques Besnard. Screenplay, Pierre Foucard, Marcel Lebrun from book by Albert Conroy; camera (Eastman-color), Marcel Grignon; editor, Gilbert Natot. At Regent, Paris. Running Time, 100 MINS.

Morgan	Frederick Stafford
Colleen	Jean Seberg
Estella	Maria-Rosa Rodriguez
Clyde	Serge Gainsbourg
Valdes	Paul Grauchet
O'Hara	Mario Pisu
Kosta	Vittorio Sanipoli

On the surface this pic almost seems timely, what with a guerrilla and political revolt on a tropical isle. Adventurers join in to help but mainly to get a part of the loot from the island dictator. But the treatment turns this into a stereotyped programmer with mainly actioner or dual usage abroad. It should be helped by the Jean Seberg name for some marquee bait.

Albert Conroy, of course, is one of pseudonyms of U. S. novelist-screenwriter Marvin H. ("Tony Rome") Albert, one of four nomo-de-plumes actually.

An ex-safe cracker, gone straight, is lured aboard a boat by Miss Seberg and hijacked. He wakes up to see an old racketeer from the U.S., Miss Seberg's daddy, offering him money to help crack the safe of the island despot. He finally goes along and even gets imbued with patriotic fervor along with love for the girl.

There are some fair battle scenes and the obvious suspense of the safe cracking ploy. Production dress is okay. But this rather turgid tale neither reaches the heights of a gusty tongue-in-cheek actioner or a melodramatic politico adventure opus. Frederick Stafford is the ladies' man crook turned patriot while Miss Seberg does as well as one can expect in a familiar role of a good girl saddled with a gangster dad. *Mosk.*

La Permission
(The Pass)
(FRENCH)

Paris, Oct. 31.
Opera production and release. Stars Harry Baird, Nicole Berger; features Christian Marin, Pierre Doris. Written and directed by Melvin Van Peebles from his own book. Camera, Michel Kelber; editor, Liliane Korb. Previewed in Paris. Running Time, 87 MINS.

Turner	Harry Baird
Myriam	Nicole Berger
Hotelman	Christian Marin
Peasant	Pierre Doris

(*Under title "Story of a Three-Day Pass" this film unreeled recently at the San Francisco Film Festival.*)

On the surface, this is a familiar romantic tale of a love affair between a Yank (on a pass to Paris) and a French girl. What was felt true love was only a fleeting thing. But there is a difference here—the GI is a Negro and the pic was directed by an American Negro filmmaker.

But, wisely, there is no straining for a racist theme here. It is mainly a simple, perhaps too simple, love story. Still, the soldier's captain is a bit too patronizing to him and he realizes it is because he supposedly knows his place. Plot says the captain would demote him if he knew he was out with a white girl.

That, and a rather forced scene of violence when he thinks he has been insulted by a singer in a nightclub, are the main bows to the color problem. But being abroad changes things if it can not completely change the soldier, his past and his attempts at trying to be true to himself.

But writer-director Melvin Van Peebles mixes a bit via too much speeded-up motion and stop motion with romantico daydreams and situation love comedy aspects. It is true the hero, Harry Baird, is a simple, direct type and his early daydream thoughts of winning a girl are acceptable. But his final meeting with the girl and their trip to the seashore, growing love and then his realization it was temporary do not quite get the right balance.

Love scenes are done with tact. Nicole Berger has a simple directness as a sickly girl who appears to find love and reveals that her sickness is mainly mental. This film is technically good. Its theme could call for more specialized and playoff use abroad although Peebles still needs more cohesion in theme, story and character delineation.

But he displays good ideas and should be heard from when he develops more ease and filmic flair.

Its main plus is transcending any forced problem pic aspects and didactics, and keeping this simple, albeit at times, a precious little story of a GI love affair. *Mosk.*

Le Samourai
(The Samurai)
(FRENCH-COLOR)

Paris, Nov. 7.
Prodis release of Filmel-CICC-Fida Cinematografica production. Stars Alain Delon; features Nathalie Delon, Francois Perier, Jacques Leroy, Cathy Rosier. Written and directed by Jean-Pierre Melville from book by Joan McLeod. Camera (Eastmancolor), Henri Decae; editor, Marguerite Bonnot. At Colisee, Paris. Running Time, 105 MINS.

Jeff	Alain Delon
Inspector	Francois Perier
Girl	Nathalie Delon
Pianist	Cathy Rosier
Gunman	Jacques Leroy
Wiener	Michel Boisrond

Jean-Pierre Melville has made parts of two of his films in the U.S. and has a great knowledge and fondness for Yank pix, especially gangster items. Here he uses an American book on a hired killer and transposes it to France for a curiously hybrid pic. This appears a bit too solemn to inject all the suspense, action and characterization he seeks.

It almost seems to be an American film dubbed into French with some strange effects in altering the French scene to appear American in such things as night clubs, sordid little hotels, police lineups and the general comportment of the personages. It is intermittently successful. Without a true French gangster core that would breed this sort of automation killer, Melville extends it to try to compare him to the Japanese Samurai dedicated to the military codes.

Gangsters may have gotten folk hero status in some societies, but appear forced in a French setting. Melville conducts this with solid seriousness and maintains interest even if using the familiar happenings in tales of hired killers.

Alain Delon has the empty agate eyes, cold demeanor and implacable presence for the glacial killer. Killer manages to spark love in a part-time kept woman, and becomes the prey of a dedicated unswerving police inspector. Melville does wring some suspense as the killer tries to gun down his ex-employers and is also being hounded by the police.

He is killed on his final job. But it seems he has had some heart for he walks into the trap wittingly and without a true desire to kill his next victim.

Nathalie Delon is somewhat too frigid as the killer's mistress while Cathy Rosier has presence and poise as the comely pianist. Francois Perier, a comedian, is cast against type as the almost fanatical inspector but manages to acquit himself acceptably. Film has tempo but could be cut a bit.

There's no denying Melville's admiration for this kind of pic and his assimilation to local terms. But this one doesn't come off completely. It appears a likely play-off item abroad if tightened and using the hardsell. *Mosk.*

Los Caifanes
(The Outsiders)
(MEXICAN-COLOR)
Paris, Nov. 7.
Estudios America S.A. Cinematografica Marte S.A. production and release. With Julissa, Enrique Alvarez-Felix, Sergio Gimenez, Oscar Chavez. Directed by Juan Ibanez. Screenplay, Carlos Fuentes, Ibanez; camera (Eastmancolor), Fernando Colin. At Ranelagh, Paris. Running time, 95 MINS.
Paloma .... Julissa
Jaime .... Enrique Alvarez-Felix
Mazacote .... Sergio Gimenez
Azteca .... Oscar Chavez
El Gato .... Ernesto Cruz
Estilos .... Edouardo Lopez

An upper class couple get mixed up in a wild night on the town with a group of lower class semi-delinquents. It leads to the dissolution of the couple as well as a look at class, race and social setups in Mexico today. But a fairly laggard directorial pace keeps this perky script from coming off or delving more deeply into character. More for playoff, on its brashness in some language situations stateside than arty theatre possibilities.

The couple are a comely girl and a well-mannered young man on the verge of engagement. But a rainy night sans a car has them picked up by a gang of Indian types and they go along with them to visit various clubs, on escapades, petty larcenies and finally a break up of the couple when the girl realizes their differences.

The script has some literate notations on Mexican tensions and delinquency. But direction opts for obvious lowlife color and does not have the pace and telling visual flair to give this any depth.

Script potentials go unrealized with sensationalism getting the upper hand over character and social insight. Some exploitation usage is also indicated. *Mosk.*

Las Piranas
(The Piranhas)
(ARGENTINE—SPANISH)
Buenos Aires, Oct. 31.
Argentina Sono Film release of its co-production with Cesareo, Gonzalez (Madrid). Stars Rodolfo Beban, Sonia Bruno; features Lautaro Murua, Osvaldo Miranda, Ana Maria Compoy, Marilina Ross. Directed by Luis Garcia Berlanga. Screenplay, Berlanga and Rafael Azcona; camera, Americo Hoss; music, Astor Piazzolla; editor, Jorge Garate. At Atlas Theatre, Buenos Aires. Running Time, 98 MINS.
Ricardo .... Rodolfo Beban
Carmen .... Sonia Bruno
Carlos .... Lautaro Murua

Martinez .... Osvaldo Miranda
Mrs. Fuentes....... Ana Maria Compoy
Pity .... Marilina Ross
Mariano .... Juan Carlos Altavista
Doctor .... Dario Vittori
Bank employee .... Javier Portales
Future husband....Juan Carlos Calabro
Mrs. Martinez............Paula Maciel

This witty, sarcastic probe on people caught by the whirlwind of contemporary big-city life, marks the comeback of noted Spanish director Luis Garcia Berlanga after a self-imposed vacation of three years. Taking advantage of a cleverly-built script, he entertains ordinary patrons with a seemingly light comedy material intended more for tongue-in-cheek than laughs.

But his is an author's film with an individual stamp, not a standard product. Thus it is better understood by selective audiences that, while enjoying its biting observations and often black humor, get Berlanga's point on the substitution of true feelings with prefabricated sensations in a world that has lost pace with nature. Dubbing will enhance its chances.

Story penned by Berlanga and Rafael Azcona, somewhat centers around a young man playing the field after just one and a half year of having married a seemingly charming creature. When his mother-in-law tells him his wife will die within few months from an incurable illness, he abandons his model girl friend, quits auto-racing, neglects his business and devotes his life to appeasing her demands, caprices and abuses.

Thinking only of making her last days happy, he willingly agrees to stepped-up marital bed games, incurs heavy debts to give her luxury and even ignores her adultery with a mutual friend.

When he discovers his wife neither is nor has ever been ill, that it all was a trick, he plans to murder her. But at the crucial moment he is killed in an accident. Soon after that, another young man approaching the mini-skirted widow, is told the same story about the supposed illness and the lad believes it as the one in the grave did.

Berlanga neither seeks an inside story within the glamorous set he depicts nor restricts himself to ironic glances at its dazzling vacuum.

Rodolfo Beban plausibly plays an antihero endowed with an animal sympathy but he is immature, irresponsible, lacking moral landmarks that may have him realize when he is doing dirty things. Sonia Bruno, as his wife, subtly portrays one of those dolls lovely to look at, but sinister inside. Lautaro Murua in a character of refined cretinism and Osvaldo Miranda is a businessman who can't see beyond his interests. Ana Maria Campoy as the unsuspectedly cynic mother-in-law, and Marilina Ross as the proletarian teenager, are all good.

A more-white-than-black photography by Americo Hoss, a modern score by Astor Piazzolla, luxurious settings, and okay editing deserve mention among production values.

Some minor technical flaws are attributable to Berlanga's insistence on lensing every scene in a single master shot to let the actors submerge completely into it.

'Las Piranas" is the best effort from the growing coproduction setup between Argentina and Spain so far. *Nubi.*

Los Traidores de San Angel
(The Traitors of San Angel)
(ARGENTINE-U.S.-COLOR)
Buenos Aires, Oct. 31.
Contracuadro release of Andre Du Rona (New York) and Leopoldo Torre Nilsson (B.A.) coproduction. Directed by Nilsson. Screenplay, James Lewis, Beatriz Guido and Nilsson, adapted from story by Du Rona; camera (Eastmancolor), Alex Philips Jr.; music, Sergio Mihanovich; editor, Carl Workman. At Opera, Buenos Aires. Running Time, 90 MINS.
Nick Thomas .... Ian Hendry
Fonseca .... Lautaro Murda
Marina .... Graciela Borges
James Keefe .... Maurice Evans
Rodriguez .... Enrique Lucero
Consuelo .... Esther Sandoval
Jail Director .... Jose de San Anton

Intracontinental coproduction involving one or more South American countries is widening its scope. Argentine, U. S., Mexican, Puerto Rican and Chilean elements, not to mention British actor Ian Hendry, have joined forces in filming this bilingual story concerning a Trujillo-style Latin American dictatorship that succeeds in crushing a plot aimed at overthrowing it.

As an account of rebels' underground activity, it contains sparse suspense and thrills. As study of a disillusioned man finding through love of a guerrilla girl a cause to die for, it doesn't quite jell.

The rather erratic script presumably sought to mix intrigue and other entertainment ingredients for ordinary patrons with a meaningful approach to a Latin American political tragedy. But it failed to integrate the story material.

Nevertheless, this has some interesting angles, beginning with its background. Albeit representing an unidentified Central American nation, Puerto Rican people and locations provide a documentary-like attraction because it covers a much-talked-about region rarely seen on screen. Contradictory attitudes from Catholic priests facing tyranny—from conspirational involvement to quiet acceptance—also draws attention. Ditto some abuses of the dictator with people around him. These are the picture's more saleable points for specialized situations.

Good performers are unable to go beyond the possibilities of bi-dimensional, sometimes conventional characters. Ian Hendry plays a smuggler, formerly a Kenya settler whose family was killed by Mau-Maus. Captured by the dictator's police, he is offered freedom and money if he disguises as a priest to enter a convent where conspiracy is suspected. Graciela Borges portrays a girl pretending to be a prostie to be admitted into a jail where she could contact political prisoners. Lautaro Murda is the ruthless, illiterate tyrant; Maurice Evans, a priest linked with the underground forces, and Enrique Lucero the strongman's police chief.

In the print seen here, some of the actors' lip make-up is so strong that it weakens the male look,

introducing a remarkably false note in several scenes. Other credits are good. *Nubi.*

Silouettes
(Silhouettes)
(GREEK)
Athens, Oct. 31.
Malte Film production. Written and directed by Costis Zoes. Stars Pery Poravous, Nikiforos Naneris. Camera, St. Trypos; music, N. Mamagakis. Reviewed at Salonika Film Fest. Running Time, 82 MINS.
Husband .... Nikiforos Naneris
Wife .... Pery Poravous
Fisherman .... Christos Tsagas
Woman tourist .... Martine Marshall
Boy .... Panos Guiocas

Reputedly a Greek version of "A Man and a Woman," this is a story of divorce, and the emptiness and loneliness it leaves the people involved. This is the initial feature film of Costis Zoes, a young Greek director, who had previously made only one short film, "The Horse," but had won a prize with it last year.

However, this film emerges a top winner again, getting first prize as the best artistic film entered at this festival in 1967.

Though the story is different one cannot help but recall the film, "A Man and Woman" while the film is being screened. Many sequences have a striking similarity and one is inclined to say that it is a Greek version of the Lelouch pic. Because it hardly can be compared with that Gallic drama, this remains an arty attempt and as such, its prospects will be best in selected arty situations.

Story opens with a young woman trying to cope with everyday chores in a small house of a Greek provincial town while her 10-year-old son is still asleep. Her expression shows a bitterness and sorrow beyond description because it's the day that her ex-husband is due in Athens to take the boy into his custody. She tries to enjoy the last hours left with her boy.

On the other hand her ex-husband, on his way to meet them, gives a lift to a foreign tourist and spends a few pleasant hours with her. But he, too, can't avoid remembering his ex-wife and his child.

In flashbacks, the lives of the couple before and after the separation are revealed. When the boy leaves with his father, his mother tries to forget her sorrow in the arms of a fisherman. But the emptiness is still there and even greater.

Zoes wanted to express that loneliness is the greatest enemy of all people. The heroes of his film are longing for happiness and understanding, but the cruel reality of life lands them in every day routine.

This is done with directorial knowhow but lacks the deeper insight which would give his film a more dramatic bite. Some of the dialogue between the man and the tourist is in English with Greek subtitles, which if they are not good, do not harm the film.

Pery Poravous' performance is very good and won a prize as the best actress at this festival. Other players are adequate. Camera work by St. Trypos is excellent and won the photography prize at the fest. Music by N. Mamagakis has a distinctive quality and other production values of the film are fairly good. *Rena.*

Custer of the West
(U.S.-SPANISH-CINERAMA-COLOR)

Another filming of Custer legend. Visual values hold up disappointing story line. Seems good bet for action market, and especially less discriminating youth.

London, Nov. 10.
Cinerama release of a Louis Dolivet and Philip Yordan presentation of a Security Pictures Inc. film. Stars Robert Shaw; features rest of cast. Directed by Robert Siodmak. Screenplay, Bernard Gordon, Julian Halevy; camera (Technicolor), Cecilio Paniagua; music, Bernardo Segall; editor, Maurice Rootes; asst. director, Jose Maria Ochoa. Reviewed at Casino Cinerama Theatre, London, Nov. 7, '67. Running Time, 143 MINS.
Gen. George Custer .... Robert Shaw
Elizabeth Custer .... Mary Ure
Lieut. Benteen .... Jeffrey Hunter
Major Marcus Reno .... Ty Hardin
Lieut. Howells ...... Charles Stalnaker
Sgt. Buckley .... Robert Hall
Gen. Philip Sheridan .. Lawrence Tierney
Cheyenne Chief .... Kieron Moore
Goldminer .... Marc Lawrence
Mulligan .... Robert Ryan

The heart-in-mouth thrills of Cinerama lensing are meshed with the legend of Custer's last stand in this Spanish-shot Western. Result is capable, audience-involving adventure on the visual level, with some tinge of disappointment about the storyline, which doesn't rise to the epic stature but is content to resume the "facts" about the Seventh Cavalry without taking a coherent attitude to them. The aird, rock Spanish vistas stand in okay for old Indian territory—especially for those not overly familiar with them— and promising grosses should en sue, due to film's direct appeal to the young who like their Westerns direct and uncomplicated.

At the end of the Civil War, Custer is assigned to tame the Cheyenne, whose rights under government treaty are being whittled away by white depredations. He is at first content with his commission, and carries out his orders with zest and zeal. Conscience is represented by one of his junior officers, who looks mighty anxious about the moral probity of this constant onslaught on the Indians. In this plot Custer himself loses his command when he accuses government toppers of finagling the profits that come from opening up the new territories. He has failed to prevent the destruction of a new railroad, and is put into temporary retirement. But he returns for a final encounter with his old opponents, sees his hoop encircled and arrowed down by an outnumbering host of Indians, and his own fate seems a comment on the policy towards the Cheyenne. An attempt is made to represent Custer as a victim of outdated ideas.

(This film bypasses all the charges that Custer was a glory-seeker, that while strict with others he was himself militarily careless and that he met death while defying orders. Custer has been the theme of about 12 previous films, many books, radio series and so on. He's never gone out of fashion with kids.—Ed.)

Robert Shaw gives Custer a simple forthrightness and dash that is effective, despite its naive context. But the script takes an undecided view of his character. It points out his ruthlessness as a disciplinarian, with a scene showing him browbeating his soldiers into shape. When one deserts to rummage for gold, Custer has him shot, and he is generally displayed, in the first half, as a rigid martinet who obeys cruel orders without questioning them. Thereafter he softens up, and sympathy is requested for his doubts about the opening up of the West at the Indians' expense. He is then put forward as a soldier out of touch with progress, preferring horses to armour-plated tanks. The portrait, however starkly Shaw puts it across, doesn't acquire a clear focus.

Other thesp. support is adequate within its straightforward idiom, with Jeffrey Hunter and Ty Hardin contrasting neatly as the troubled and dedicated junior officers respectively, Mary Ure dispensing coffee and sympathy as Custer's nebulous wife, and Robert Ryan guesting as the deserting gold-hungry soldier with a forceful cameo.

But the main bait will be the Cinerama tricks of eye involvement, well carried out by director Robert Siodmak and cameraman Cecilio Paniagua. Sequences with an out-of-control train, a similarly undirected wagon, a soldier escaping down rapids—all these have the queasy stomach appeal of those early Cinerama travelogs. The fighting, too, makes great play with arrows going through necks and other assorted mayhem, and the action sequences are appropriately noisy and lethal. *Otta.*

The Witnesses
(Le Temps du Ghetto)
(FRENCH—DOCUMENTARY)

Frederic Rossif's documentary about the Warsaw Ghetto is unworthy of its subject matter. Foresee minor b.o. attention.

Altura Films International (Clem Perry) release of a Les Films de la Pleiade (Pierre Braunberger production. Directed by Frederic Rossif. Commentary written by Madeleine Chapsal, narrated by Viveca Lindsfors and Michael Tolan. Camera, Marcel Fradetal; editor, Suzanne Baron; music, Maurice Jarre. Previewed in N.Y., Nov. 3, '67. Running Time, 82 MINS.

(English soundtrack)

Frederic Rossif's 1962 documentary of the Warsaw Ghetto is finally making its U.S. commercial bow, as a probable result of the b.o. success stateside of his later "To Die in Madrid." But on any level—historical, intellectual, emotional, esthetic or commercial— "The Witnesses" must be counted a failure.

Admittedly the long delay in release unfairly puts Rossif's film at an unfair disadvantage. In the past five years, a flood of other material (in films, tv and print) on Nazi persecution of the Jews has inundated the American public, lessening the impact of Rossif's documentary footage. (Even in 1962, however, much of his visual material must have seemed redundant after the similar and better-organized documentaries, "Night and Fog," "Mein Kampf" and "The Black Fox.")

The English-language version, prepared by the film's U.S. distributor, Altura Films International, also vitiates the original's effect. Testimonials by the few remaining survivors of the Ghetto, which alternate with the wartime footage, are sterilized by the American translations flatly voiced over the dimly heard French of the "witnesses." The narration of Viveca Lindfors and Michael Tolan only underscores the cheap irony in Vince Pereira's English translation of Madeleine Chapsal's original text. ("What's the hurry?" asks Tolan of people crowding into a cattle car bound for a crematorium. "Stop pushing. There's plenty of room for everyone in death.")

"The Witnesses" remains historically superficial and naive, almost as if Rossif thought we were hearing about Naziism for the first time. Questions of any greater historical subtlety or complexity are not even raised, let alone answered. How did Hitler persuade the Germans to follow his mad lead? Why didn't the Jewish people learn earlier of their impending fate? What reason was given for the formation of the ghetto, so as to prevent an immediate insurgence of Jewish rebellion? One would think that even a hasty overview of the Warsaw Ghetto would be obliged to deal with these and similar matters, but Rossif betrays little historical knowledge of his subject.

Hitler's slaughter of the Jews has occupied many of the world's finest philosophical minds for the past 20 years, perhaps most notably Jean-Paul Sartre. Not only have these men pondered the causes of Hitler's fanaticism and the seeming predisposition of the German people to cling to a paternalistic figure and to self-aggrandizing dogmas, but they have also raised the question of Jewish inculpation in their own destruction.

In Rossif's interviews with the witnesses, he could have tried to evince their feelings about these matters. Instead, he has settled for an easy recitative of tortures.

What is needed today is not another compilation film of wartime atrocities. No matter how well done, they all trigger a protective mechanism within us that stifles our reaction to horror on such a frighteningly grand scale. Instead, the memory of the nearly 600,000 Polish Jews who were killed by the Nazis deserves a memorial fashioned of art, a film that will induce empathy for just one Jew or one German and awaken us to the always-present possibility of inflicting or enduring similar suffering. *Beau.*

The Fearless Vampire Killers
(BRITISH-PANAVISION-COLOR)

Dracula-and-vampires spoof with Mack Sennett overtones; may go in specialized situations.

Hollywood, Nov. 9.
Metro release of Martin Ransohoff-Roman Polanski production, produced by Gene Gutowski. Stars Jack MacGowran, Roman Polanski; features Alfie Bass, Sharon Tate, Ferdy Mayne. Directed by Polanski. Story-screenplay, Gerard Brach, Polanski; camera (Metrocolor), Douglas

Slocombe; music, Christopher Komeda; editor, Alastair McIntyre; asst. director, Roy Stevens. Reviewed at Metro Studios, Nov. 8, '67. Running Time, **91 MINS.**

Professor Abronsius....Jack MacGowran
Alfred, his assistant....Roman Polanski
Shagal, Innkeeper............Alfie Bass
Rebecca, his wife..........Jessie Robins
Sarah, their daughter......Sharon Tate
Count Von Krolock.........Ferdy Mayne
Herbert, his son ....Iain Quarrier
Koukol, Hunchback........Terry Downes
Maid .... Fiona Lewis
Village Idiot .... Ronald Lacey
Sleigh Driver .... Sydney Bromley
Woodcutters .... Andre Malandrinos, Otto Di Amant, Matthew Walters

"The Fearless Vampire Killers," which carries the sub-title, "Pardon Me, But Your Teeth Are in My Neck," might be even more aptly titled, "Mack Sennett Among the Vampires," or, "Mr. Sennett Meets Count Dracula." Metro release is a Martin Ransohoff-Roman Polanski coproduction lensed in Europe which outdoes the legendary slapstick comedy impresario in corn and antics. Designed as a spoof on the Dracula theme, outcome is furious Central Europe comedy but for American audiences its reception is more moot. Film may go with specialized selling for the specialized trade.

Polanski is in project on a quadruple assignment. His Cadre Films unit produced with Ransohoff's Filmways, and he directed, collabed on story and screenplay with Gerard Brach and costars. Ransohoff acted as executive producer, and Gene Gutowski, Polanski's partner in Cadre, handled actual producer reins. Brach and Polanski wrote script in French and piece then was traslated into English by Gillian and John Sutro, giving international tones to the overall, which some may find old-fashioned in this jet age of sophisticated comedy.

(It should be emphasized that this version under review is the Ransohoff cut to which Polanski objects and asks removal of his credit.—Ed.)

Plotline (?) deals with an old professor (who resembles Andy Clyde, acts like him, sports his huff) and his assistant who arrive at a Central Europe inn in dead of winter on a crusade to hunt down and destroy the chilling mystery figures of generations of legends, the dreaded vampires who stalk Slovania. They reckon they have reached their proper destination when they see great bunches of garlic on every beam, which of course indicates that the villagers live in deadly fear of a local resident vampire (and which, as everybody knows, helps ward off the depredations of the vampires' fangs).

Sennett might have taken it from there, as the two searchers after truth see the marks of the vampire who has attacked a young woman in her bath. They meet Count Von Krolock (which is just another name for Dracula) in his castle and witness a score of vampires leaving the coffins they have rested in during the day for the night's frivolities. They barely escape with their lives, taking the young woman who was victim of the vampire's attack, and you'd be surprised what she does to the young assistant in the sleigh, leaving the good professor the only simon-pure of the lot who unknowing is to spread the evil throughout the world.

Jack MacGowran cavorts as the nimble oldster and Polanski plays his somewhat-dimwitted assistant, both up to the demands (?) of their roles. Ferdy Mayne is the menacing Dracula (pod'n, Von Krolock), and Sharon Tate, lady in question, looks particularly nice in her bath. Alfie Bass, the innkeeper; Iain Quarrier as the count's effeminate son, who has some fangs all his own; Terry Downes, the toothy hunchback castle handyman (who might be Quasimodo returned), and Jessie Robbins, innkeeper's spouse, lend proper support.

Polanski's direction fits in with his subject and he has benefit of interesting technical assistance. Douglas Slocombe's photography is artistic, Wilfrid Shingleron's production design atmospheric and Christopher Komeda's music score is melancholy, as befitting the theme.

Film opens with a long animated sequence, with Andre Francois credited with title design.

Whit.

O Thekatos Tritos
(The Thirteenth Man)
(GREEK)

Athens, Nov. 7.

A James Paris production. Directed by Dimitris Dadiras. With Yannis Voglis, Helena Nathanael, Paris Alexander, Theodoros Exarhos. Screenplay by Panos Kontellis from story by James Paris; camera, Dimitris Papaconstantis; music, Yannis Marcopoulos. Reviewed at Salonika Film Fest. Running time, **100 MINS.**

Lucas .... Yannis Voglis
Dimitris .... Paris Alexander
Maria .... Helena Nathanael
Thanassis .... Theodoros Exarhos

This is a dramatic incident of the last World War and the German Occupation of Greece. Its story is loaded with action, passion and suspense, set in an original background with fair prospects in many situations.

Yarn opens with a young girl returning to her native island, Lesbos, to attend the unveiling of a statue dedicated to a war hero, Dimitris, a young officer who came over from Middle East during the German occupation and supposedly blew up a German fort full of ammunition. The girl, being in love with Dimitris, knew what really happened. Visiting his father, he reveals to him the truth via flashbacks of the incident.

It seems that Dimitris had landed on the island with a mission to blow up the German fort, filled with ammunition which was destined for Africa. He was found wounded on the mountain by a poor shepherd, Lucas. Lucas tried to take care of him, though, being in love with Maria, he hated him before. He called Maria and both tried to save Dimitris, keeping his being wounded secret from even his own father. Dimitris, feeling that he could not make it, had asked Lucas to accomplish his mission instead of him. He agrees, and with the help of his dog and Dimitris' instructions succeeded in blowing up the fort while Dimitris died in his mountain hut.

The Germans arrested 13 men the next morning. Among them was Thanassis, Dimitris' father. On their way to the execution place, Thanassis managed to escape. The German soldiers arrested Lucas, who happened to be passing by. He was nabbed to be executed as the 13th man. Thanassis realizes that the real hero was Lucas, the poor outcast of the village, who finally gave his life to save another man.

Screenplay by Panos Kontellis, based on an idea of producer James Paris, won a prize at the festival. Though it has some weak points, it is well narrated and has strong b.o. elements.

Director Dimitris Dadiras transferred this story in good cinematic terms, depicting the atmosphere of oppression and fright that swept the country during the German Occupation as well as the resistance of the people. But somehow he fails to bring out the inner conflicts of his characters. Hence, his picture has not the deep dramatic effect the story needed.

Yannis Voglis and Theodoros Exharhos turned in good performances and fairly supported by the remainder of the cast. Camera work is very good especially the night shots. Music by Yannis Marcopoulos underscores the dramatic effects.

Rena.

The Devil's Daffodil
(Das Geheimnis der Gelden Narzizzen)
(BRITISH-GERMAN)

Six-year-old British thriller on the drug trade as Edgar Wallace imagined it, circa 1920. Barely suitable even for program slots.

Goldstone Film Enterprises release of Omnia Films (London)-Rialto Films (Hamburg) coproduction, produced by Steven Pallos and Donald Taylor. Features Christopher Lee, Marius Goring, Penelope Horner, Ingrid Van Bergen, William Lucas. Directed by Akos Rathony. Screenplay, Basil Dawson, Donald Taylor, from novel, "The Daffodil Mystery," by Edgar Wallace; camera, Desmond Dickinson; music, Keith Papworth; editor, Peter Taylor; asst. director, Tom Pevsner; sound, Bob Jones, Bert Ross; art director, William Hutchinson. Reviewed at Selwyn Theatre, N.Y., Nov. 6, 1967. Running Time, **86 MINS.**

Ling Chu .... Christopher Lee
Oliver Milburgh .... Marius Goring
Anne Rider .... Penelope Horner
Gloria .... Ingrid Van Bergen
Jack Tarling .... William Lucas
Raymond Lyne .... Albert Lieven
Peter Keene .... Colin Jeavons
Superintendent Whiteside..Walter Gotell
Jan Putek .... Peter Illing
Katya .... Dawn Beret
Trudi .... Bettine Le Beau
Charles .... Jan Hendriks
Sir Archibald .... Campbell Singer
French Gendarme ...... Lance Percival
Detective .... Frederick Bartman
Mrs. Rider......Grace Denbeigh-Russell
Sluttish Woman .... Nancy Nevinson
Max .... Martin Lyder
Chinese Girl .... Edwina Carroll
Hotel Receptionist ..... Gundel Sargent
Maisie .... Irene Fradcr

This 1961 version of Edgar Wallace's 1920 novel "The Daffodil Mystery" was shot in London in simultaneous English and German versions by director Akos Rathony (there's a "von" in his name in the German-language prints). The German version, called "Das Gaheimnis Der Gelben Narzissen," had Joachim Fuchsberger, Sabine Sesselmann and Klaus Kinski essaying roles played in English by, respectively, William Lucas, Penelope Horner and Colin Jeavons; otherwise the two casts were the same, with lotsa dubbing presumably having gone on to prepare the Teutonic prints.

It can only be assumed that Rathony worked more forcefully in his native tongue, for, among numerous other ineptnesses, "The Devil's Daffodil" displays the directorial hand of someone quite obviously unfamiliar with the rhythms of conversational English. The actors all talk and act as if they had been numbed by some of the heroin which, the film proposes, is being shipped into Britain from Hong Kong in the stems of daffodils.

If this sounds like yellow-press interpretation of the drug traffic, that's absolutely right. The Mafia and its attendant Middle Eastern, Sicilian and Corsican connections might never exist, according to this film which takes Wallace's lurid and dated assumptions about the Oriental origins of heroin and transfers them bodily to the 1960's.

Factual inaccuracy is not balanced by artistic achievement.

Marked by indifferent photography, flat direction and busy sound. Latter is especially disconcerting as traffic noises, music, even the sounds of actors' own footsteps are continually drowning out important speech. The plot is incredible not only in essense but in detail.

Byro.

Revolution D'Octobre
(The October Revolution)
(FRENCH)

Paris, Nov. 14.

Paramount release of Tele-Hachette production Conceived, directed and edited by Frederic Rossif; commentary, Madeleine Chapsal. Running time, **95 MINS.**

Though primarily a compilation pic, done fairly objectively, about the Russian Revolution, this is timely because of the 50th anni celebrations of the event now in progress. Fine selection of footage and a half hour of new film shot for the occasion are well blended by Frederic Rosiff, who also made one on the Spanish Revolution, "To Die in Madrid."

This one does not have the moving punch of "Madrid" but makes up for it in a coherent, linear look at that critical historical time from the crowning of Czar Nicholas II to the death of Lenin in 1924. Perhaps some of the more controversial characters, such as Trotsky and Stalin, are little seen. This might explain the Russian acceptance of the pic.

But this tries to be as straightforward as possible and succeeds in making this period clear in its many conflicting loyalties, moves and complications until Lenin took and kept the upper hand. Early shots, made practically at the beginning of projected film, are extraordinarily clear and corrected to remove the usual jerkiness and show the early Russian court clearly and not as doll-like comic figures.

From the autocracy of the early revolts the First World War and the final Revolution all is actual newsreel footage sans any recourse to fiction film. Only early documentarist Dziga Vertov has some actual scenes imbedded in it. Rossif's own footage tries to give a timeless feel of the sprawling land.

Rossif went through the archives of many countries and received Russian cooperation with accounts for much that has not been seen before or very often. Scenes of the terrible Russian famine after the first World War are searing and handled with tact. A fine commentary, expert editing and a clarity of tone make this worthy for specialized handling abroad plus tv and school showings. It has built-in, timely handles. *Mosk.*

Samurai—Part III
(Ketto Ganryu Jima)
(JAPANESE-COLOR)

Windup of tri-part Hiroshi Inagaki film on woes of a wandering samurai.

Toho International Films release of a Kazuo Takimura production. Directed by Hiroshi Inagaki. Stars Toshiro Mifune; features Koji Tsuruta, Kaoru Yachigusa, Michiko Saga, Takashi Shimura, Mariko Okada, Kenji Iida. Screenplay, Tokuhei Wakao and Inagaki from original story by Eiji Yoshikawa; camera (Eastman Color), Kazuo Yamada; music, Ikuma Dan. No other technical credits. Reviewed at 55th Street Playhouse, N.Y., Nov. 10, '67. Running Time, 102 MINS.
Musashi Miyamoto ...... Toshiro Mifune
Kojiro Sasaki .... Koji Tsuruta
Otsu .... Kaoru Yachigusa
Omitsu .... Michiko Saga
Akemi .... Mariko Okada

'The third portion, and windup, of Hiroshi Inagaki's 1955-56 lengthy tale of a Japanese "Cool Hand Luke" (although this troubled type does manage a happy ending) in a lengthy, colorful buildup to the big gunfight (or sword, in this instance) at the Ganryu Corral. The similarity of the classic western and the classic samurai story is so consistent that any faithful follower of horse opera can figure out the next samural ploto turn with little diffi-, culty.

Although director Inagaki and script collaborator interpolate such sidebar stories as the two maidens who pursue Musashi (Shane) Miyamoto, plus sundry comic bits and colorfully-depicted comments on Nipponese feudalism, it all leads up to the final confrontation between the two master swordsmen, Miyamoto and Kojiro Sasaki.

The latter, indifferently played by Koji Tsuruta, never strikes the creative spark that young Jap actor Tetsuya Nakadai always manages in scenes with Toshiro Mifune. Most supporting parts are good and that superb character actor, Takashi Shimura, (Kurosawa's "Ikirn" hero), is seen briefly as a court official.

The film, made in 1956, was preceded by the 1955 "Miyamoto Musashi," which as "Samurai," won an Academy Award for best foreign film. Part Two, "Zoku Miyamoto Musashi" (Duel at the Ichijoji Temple), and Part Three, although made at the same time, were never released in the U.S. until now (as parts of the triple feature). It's a commercial attempt, and as such, it's successful. *Robe.*

Indomiable Angelique
(Untamable Angelique)
(FRENCH-GERMAN-ITALIAN)
(COLOR)

Paris, Nov. 14.
Prodis release of FranCos Film, CICC, Gloria Film, Fono Roma production. Stars Michele Mercier, Robert Hossein; features, Roger Pigaut, Renato De Carmine, Bruno Dietrich. Directed by Bernard Borderie. Screenplay, Pascal Jardin, Francis Cosne, Borderie from book by Anne and Serge Golon; camera (Eastmancolor), Henri Persin; editor, Christian Godin. At Ambas-
sademont, Paris. Running time, 82 MINS.
Angelique .... Michele Mercier
Peyrac .... Robert Hossein
Pirate .... Roger Pigaut
Captain .... Renato De Carmine
Mate .... Bruno Dietrich

Unendable rather than untamable appears to be the name for Angelique, that intrepid, adventure-prone 17th century heroine, who goes from the Court of Louis XIV to the underworld, pirate ships, etc. from film to film. This, the fourth in a series, now no longer even tries to be a complete pic in its own right, but ends as a cliffhanger with come-on shots from the fifth film which was made at the same time as this one.

Angelique loves only one man, a scarfaced, limping romantic who is her husband and is fighting against the King and for liberty. Hence, he is always on the run. This leaves poor Angelique a prey to rape, side love affairs, in which only her body not her heart is involved, and other adventures in her constant search for her elusive husband.

In this, she finds he has become a pirate fighting the King's ships and goes after him. But not before she is captured by a naughty pirate who rapes her, throws her into a cell full of hungry cats or sex starved galley slaves and finally seils her in a slave mart in some African country. But she is bought by her husband.

After a night of bliss, he has to run to save his burning ship, in spite of his limp, and she is captured and whisked off by some covetous Arabs. Pic ends with shots of her being whipped and admonishing the audience to follow her further adventures. These pix have done well here and in Europe generally if mainly lacking a true tongue-in-cheek edge for much U.S. chances.

However, some of the earlier episodes did have a more romp-like flair and the piling up footage might be cut into a playoff dualer or even a grind production via its nudity, far out action and color. Michele Mercier is comely girl but lacks the voluptuous qualities to make all the desire for her appear credible.

But Miss Mercier does not spare herself In undraped scenes. Robert Hossein has the requisite sullen and tortured looks for her freedom-fighter husband.

Direction is workable if uninspired and its period feel makes "Forever Amber" seem to be a serious historical document compared to this. But locals seem to like the cardboard characters. And it is shaping as a sort of lowdown French oater equivalent. *Mosk.*

Hogy Szaladnak a Fak
(The Sack)
(HUNGARIAN)

Pecs, Hungary, Nov. 7.
A Hungarofilm release of Mafilm Studio 2 (Budapest) production. Directed by Pal Zolnay. Screenplay, Peter Modos, Pal Zolnay; camera, Ferenc Szecsenyi; music, Zsolt Durko. At Pecs Film Fest. Running Time, 89 MINS.
Simon .... Istvan Iglodi
Aunt Lina .... Manyi Kiss
Misa .... Janos Koltai
Judit .... Eva Papp

"The Sack" is a good film in the every sense of the word. It tells a simple story in a simple manner but it has depth and dignity. And, like so many recent Maygar films this has much warmth. Perhaps this has too much Hungarian to grant it special export possibilities although it would deserve them. There seems little doubt but that this pic makes a fine impression.

This touches on a problem with which Hungary also is confronted: The migration of country people into towns. The plot revolves around a young historian who has just recently left the university. While having a vacation he returns to his old village. All that he has in mind is to say hello and take it easy there for a couple of days.

But he finds a new world there. His old friends have left for the big cities, and it seems as though only old people are still around the village. His old aunt Lina is there but she has a grudge against him because he has become "unfaithful" to the village. The young man starts contemplating and all his childnood memories return.

Pal Zolnay has directed this with sensitive care. He manages to hold the viewer's interest although not too much happens. This also has definite merit on its acting, especially that of Manyi Kiss, as the old aunt, who turns in a stellar performance. Incidentally, she was honored as best actress at the Pecs Festival. Also 23-year-old Istvan Iglodi, as her nephew, deserves mention. It's his first big screen role. Lensing and other technical credits are good. Film's English title doesn't seem to be the best choice. One can only guess what is meant. *Hans.*

Nyar a Hegyen
(Summer On Mountain)
(HUNGARIAN)

Pecs, Hungary, Nov. 7.
A Hungarofilm release of Mafilm Studio I (Budapest) production. Directed by Peter Bacso. Screenplay, Peter Basco and Peter Zimre; camera, Janos Zsombolyai; music, Szabolcs Fenyes. At Pecs Film Fest. Running Time, 105 MINS.
Doctor .... Laszlo Mensaros
Komora .... Josef Pecsenke
Mari .... Katalin Gyoengyoessy
Veszell .... Nandor Tomanek
Sari ....-.. Terez Varhelyi

Although "Summer On the Mountain" is primarily an item for the home market, its theme is interesting enough also to stir non-Hungarian interest. It concerns the victims of the Stallnistic era (before 1956) in this country. Even if only the fate of one victim finds mention here, film succeeds in giving a competent insight into a period that made many Hungarians suffer, the period of the "person's cult" which sacrificed both Communists and non-Communists.

Film has not much of what is termed "entertainment value" in the conventional sense. Direction is overly deliberate, the lensing is mostly rather static, and there is an abundance of dialog. This is a rather talky film. Film is an honest attempt on the part of its young creators to tackle a both difficult and unpleasant subject.

Story starts with a group of people whose central figure is a young painter. He's very interested in a deserted camp located on a mountain outside the village. He thinks this would be an ideal working place. With the exception of a girl, the group is not keen on lingering around here because this place used to be a concentration camp for political prisoners in the early fifties when the Stalinistic "person's cult" was still in vogue.

Later, a middle-aged man joins the group and the girl learns that he once was an inmate of this camp. This leads to many dialog sequences. Film makes a point that the young painter is uninterested in what has happened in those years. He doesn't care about politics and all that counts for him is his own individual life. There's a certain climax when a group of visitors arrives, one of them being the former commander of this camp. The two people, the camp boss and the former inmate whom he then treated badly, meet again. But the former inmate has no feelings of revenge and after some discussions, there is understanding and some sort of reconciliation.

Film's plot is not easy to follow for the greater part of it is mere dialog. "Mountain" shows that young Hungarian filmites are willing to touch on difficult themes.

Acting is generally convincing. The lensing shows discipline and avoids any effects to maintain the intimate character of the action. Film has a good score. If pic appears stretched out at times this likely reflects the mentality in Hungary. They still have somewhat more leisure time in the East. *Hans.*

Billion Dollar Brain
(BRITISH—COLOR)

Credulity overstretched in least of the Len Deighton spy frolics. Slow start and hard-to-follow plot. Hard going foreseen.

London, Nov. 15.
United Artists release of Harry Saltzman production. Stars Michael Caine, Karl Malden; features Ed Begley, Oscar Homolka, Francoise Dorleac. Directed by Ken Russell. Screenplay, John McGrath, from Len Deighton's novel; camera (Technicolor), David Harcourt; music, Richard Rodney Bennett; editor, Alan Osbiston; asst. directors, Jack Causey, Jim Brennan. Reviewed at Leicester Square Theatre, London, Nov. 13, '67. Running Time, 111 MINS.
Harry Palmer .... Michael Caine
Leo Newbigin .... Karl Malden
Anya .... Francoise Dorleac
Colonel Stok .. .. Oscar Homolka
General Midwinter .... Ed Begley
Colonel Ross .... Guy Doleman
Dr. Eiwort .... Vladek Scheybal
Basil .... Milo Sperber

Third of the Len Deighton spyworks from the Harry Saltzman stable, "Billion Dollar Brain" shows a decided falling-off in impact, though fair grosses will be garnered from followers of the Michael Caine impersonation of Harry Palmer and from addicts of the general cult. But indications are that this particular vein of reluctant syping has been mined to rock-bottom, and few nuggets remain to be unearthed.

Part of the trouble is that the plot takes too long to get moving, and when it does it is quite incredible and hard to follow. Palmer is instructed to take a package containing mysterious eggs to Finland by an electronic voice over the phone, and when he arrives to collect his fee of $560, he meets up with a former American CIA man, Ed Newbigin (Karl Malden), whose life he has saved in the past.

Palmer, whose mission is known to his previous M.I.5 employers, pretends to join the organization, which turns out to be controlled by a crazy American General (Ed Begley) with a Senator McCarthy attitude re Commies and a determination to defeat them by formenting revolution in satellite countries and attacking with his own private army. The General administers his worldwide machinations through a mammoth computer, into which messages are fed and immediate answers obtained.

After making a strange foray into Latvia, considered ripe for rebellion, Palmer visits the General's headquarters in Texas, and the climax comes with a foolhardy attack across the Arctic ice, with the General's forces drowned in the cracks.

It doesn't matter so much that the storyline offends belief—so do the Bond gambols—but it is deployed by director Ken Russell with such abrupt speed that it doesn't make immediate sense in its own frivolous terms. It transpires that Newbigin is feeding the General false information about the number of agents in Latvia, by inventing them and pocketing the money sent to support them. But this ingenious twist is also largely lost in the general confusion.

Michael Caine, playing deadpan, repeats the familiar Palmer line of uninterested nonchalance, and John McGrath's script, overfaithful to Deighton's original novel, doesn't give him much chance to develop it. So the flavor that gives this skein its touch of difference is largely missing. Karl Malden and Ed Begley, always reliable, do what they can with roles conceived as stereotypes of greed and fanaticism respectively, and the late Francoise Dorleac introduces a touch of glamor as an agent who might be working for anybody, and so contributes to the besetting plot fog. Oscar Homolka is his chortling self as the Russian Colorel Stok.

Ken Russell, who has acquired a merited tv reputation, errs in taking the story too fast, so that each incident piles on the other without transition. Visual assets are some offbeat winter locales near Helsinki and in the frozen regions, though these are somewhat vitiated by a Latvia that's strictly musicomedy and a Texas that consists of a hoedown.

Production has virtues of gloss and some agreeably oddball interiors from designer Bert Davey. The music track, from Richard Rodney Bennett, has above-average qualities, using a piano concerto-style. But the surface can't disguise the lack of inner impetus, and the excitement is minimal. *Otta.*

Un Homme a Abattre
(A Man To Kill)
(FRENCH—SPANISH—COLOR)

Paris, Nov. 21.
Lux release of Ulysse Production, Intercontinental Films, Carlton Continental, Urania Film production. Stars Jean-Louis Trintignant, Valerie Lagrange; features Andre Oumansky, Luis Prados. Directed by Philippe Condroyer. Screenplay, Philippe and Marietta Condroyer, J. B. Rolland; camera (Eastmancolor). J. B. Penzer; editor, Renee Lichtig. At Marbuef, Paris. Running time, 85 MINS.
Raphael .... Jean-Louis Trintignant
Girl .... Valerie Lagrange
Georges .... Andre Oumansky
Julius ....:...... Luis Prados

The man to be killed in this suspense opus is an ex-SS man living in Spain. It is not clear whether the would-be-killers are Israeli agents or in the employ of a man bent on revenge but still somewhat unsure of his conscience. But the pic evades making any stand and is somewhat thin in suspense and surface in characterization. It appears mainly for playoff use on its theme and fair execution, with tele also indicated on its close quarter work.

Film starts explosively with the killing of a man who is an accomplice of the shadowed suspect when he discovers a camouflaged truck used for filming the man's various treks and outings. It is thus hard to accent the vacillation in the killing of the suspect when it is clear he is probably an ex-Nazi, if perhaps not the one in question.

This would be acceptable if motives were clearer. Direction is fluid and clear but the bungling of the group after their clever spying, in luring the man to an old house, appears as padding as a side flirtation of one of the would-be killers.

Theme is interesting and the spy tactics are absorbing. But the refusal to clarify things and the imbalance of dedication and amateurism give this rather uneven pace. Dialog is also somewhat colorless. *Mosk.*

Guilt
(Tillsammans med Gunilla Mondag Kvall och Tisdag)
(SWEDISH)

Crown International release of AB Svensk Filmindustri production. Directed and written by Lars Gorling. Stars Sven Bertil Taube, Helena Brodin, Tina Hedstrom. Camera, Lars Goran Bjorne; music, Ulf Bjorlin; no other credits provided. Reviewed in New York, Nov. 17, '67. Running Time, 90 MINS.
Hans .... Sven Bertil Taube
Gunilla .... Helena Brodin
Inga .... Tina Hedstrom

About the only improvement Crown International has made in this 1965 Swedish import has been to change the unwieldy original title, "Tilsammans med Gunilla Mandag Kvall och Tisdag" (With Gunilla on Monday Evening and Tuesday) to the shorter and more exploitable "Guilt." Although it would seem apparent that the film will be exploited for its few sex scenes (which are, admittedly, quite graphic despite their briefness), the main storyline conceived by Lars Gorling, who both scripted and directed, does deal with the growth of guilt in the mind of an individual after he has become involved in an accident.

The thin plot deals with the hit-and-run slaying of an individual by a young man who's just had a not completely satisfactory session with his girl. Obeying his first impulse, he runs away and the couple spend the night and all the next day rationalizing, in their own minds, how their actions, including the accident, were influenced by their physical relationship.

Gorling, who did the screenplay for Vilgot Sjoman's delinquent youth-themed "491" (which has had a delayed entrance into the U.S.), made his directorial debut with this effort and one wonders how much of the film is fact or fiction, considering that Gorling committed suicide last year.

A plodding, repetitious and never moving film, the two principals are played, on the part of the male, with such coldness and superficiality, and by the heroine, in a tired, almost bored manner, that the viewer, whose sympathy has never been aroused, also loses interest. The complete nudity during the sex scenes (although the action itself is only implied) will encourage a certain attendance but once the word gets around that nothing much follows this scene, there may be a mass exodus in the middle of the film.

As a sexploiter, it's briefly successful; as a serious piece of filmmaking, it's a drag. *Robe.*

Pop Game
(FRENCH)

Paris, Nov. 21.
Lerol production and release. Written and directed by Francis Leroi. With Gaetane Lorre, Daniel Bellus, Christian Baux, Bernard Leonard. Camera, Leroi. At Studio 43, Paris. Running time, 85 MINS.
Poupee .... Gaetane Lorre
Patrick .... Daniel Bellus
Friend .... Christian Baux
Lover .... Bernard Leonard

A young filmmaker has made a film on his own about teenage youth. It is candid without being coy and observant sans self consciousness. This is a refreshing if still surface film. It needs careful placement abroad. The seeming familiarity, through deceptive, and just passable technical look have this mainly a specialized entry.

A girl and a boy have left their provincial town and live mainly holed up in a bare apartment in Paris with only a fairly rich boy as a friend. They go off on shoplifting benders, go to films, and lead a sort of anarchic but innocent life. However, society has its reflections in their dress and final breakup, and then reunification as each has apparently lived a little.

Perhaps the true appearance of maturity is not indicated, but there is a subtle change as an awareness of self and others begin to impinge on this fairly gentle, innocent but outsider trio. The girl has an affair with a younger writer who is not much help when she is pregnant. She throws herself in front of a car, and miscarries.

There are definite influences of Jean-Luc Godard and Francois Truffaut in the use of jump cuts, anecdotic segments and asides, readings from books and fragmentation rather than a more cohesive progression. But newcomer Francis Leroi displays a notable flair for reflecting youthful obsessions.

The acting is fresh, direct and generally appealing. There is a vulnerability as well as a strength in these youngsters that keeps this from becoming just another mixture of cinema truth tactics and shallow shenanigans. True, it sometimes mixes irrelevance with rationality and is sometimes gauche and repetitive.

But this manages to get over these pitfalls on its sheer ingenuity and is helped by a genuine feel for the milieu and an incisive insight into youthful behavior and unpredictability that gives it charm. To have made this for a reputed $6,000 is a feat in itself. Blown up from 16m, it is quite acceptable technically. *Mosk.*

The Nude Restaurant
(COLOR)

Most accomplished (and most sexually exposed) of Warhol's recent studies of boy-girl relationships. Stars Viva, perhaps his most talented "discovery."

Andy Warhol production and release. Stars Viva; features Taylor Mead, Louis Waldron, Julian Burroughs. Directed, written, photographed and edited by Warhol. Reviewed at Hudson Theatre, N.Y., Nov. 13, 1967. Running Time, 100 MINS.

Prophesying the b.o. potential of Andy Warhol's recent efforts is difficult as long as the filmmaker continues his present limited distribution. As far as is known, he makes no effort to set up out-of-town dates, and is apparently able to recoup the costs of his bottom-budget pix via the moderate returns from New York dates. In any case, the audience for these latterday modest pix would seem to be large enough only in a half-dozen U.S. burgs (the kind of "notoriety" surrounding the epic "Chelsea Girls" being absent from recent Warhol). And probably a temporarily idle out-of-the-way house like the Hudson would have to be found in each town.

"The Nude Restaurant" is the most accomplished of the Warhol trilogy of boy-girl relationships which began with "I, a Man" and continued with "Bike Boy." As opposed to the strictly realistic (if perverse) rendering of events presented in the previous two pix, "Restaurant" introduces fantastic elements but in a thoughouly natural context. Everyone is semi-nude in the main restaurant scene, yet the people act no differently than if they were wearing clothes. The result can perhaps be termed metaphorical: by "neutralizing" the flesh and making it the matter-of-fact stuff of the earth, the sexual candor of the dialog is robbed of its strangeness and is heard in its natural, confessional state.

The film has been designed as a showpiece for Viva!, (exclamation hereafter dropped) the latest Warhol "discovery" and probably his most important one ever. Her admixture of dumb-blonde bluntness, absentminded pixilation, and caustic wit reveal her an excellent comedienne whose future beyond the Warhol Factory and underground cinema should develop. Though different in kind, she has an inadvertent quality and comedic timing that suggest an American Rita Tushingham or Lynn Redgrave.

There's a curious view of the U.S. sexual war that is promulgated in Warhol's last three pix. His men seek always soft, warm love but they always come up against women with acute urban identify hangups. One could say that in "I, a Man" the hero spent the entire film verbalizing these feelings in a jaded, defensive manner while in "Bike Boy" there was a more two-sided view of the situation. "Nude Restaurant" really completes the cycle in that a typical Warhol woman has become the prime subject. The men she meets seem to w nt nothi g more than a selfless all-embracing love but she rejects this via her incessant chatter.

The first such encounter takes place in Viva's bathtub as she prepares to go to work at the restaurant. A boy suddenly appears out of nowhere (another fantastic element) and joins her in the tub. He seems quite high on marijuana and stares sheepishly at her while engaging in some elementary foreplay which will only remain that as Viva chitchats about the scientific aspects of sex. Even Warhol's trademark exposure of sexual organs may have a point here precisely because no real sex ever develops as Viva harangues on. Incidentally, there is more and longer exposure in this film than in any previous U.S. pic.

Later Viva goes through a long kissing scene with a customer at the restaurant (she is a waitress) which is a Warhol steal from a Troy Donahue-Connie Stevens bit in "A Summer Place." Film ends with a long monolog on the girl's part which is twice as interesting as anything in "Portrait of Jason."

Warhol has a habit of adding new material to his films and subtracting some other footage while they are in the midst of their runs at the Hudson. He always makes sure that the running time remains the same. At show caught (13) there was a second bathtub scene featuring a different boy as well as two other girls, This has since been replaced by an extension of the restaurant scene in which Viva describes her adventures with a most uncelibate priest.
Byro.

Csillagosok, Katonak
(Internationalists)
(HUNGARIAN—RUSSIAN)
Budapest, Nov. 14.
Hungarfilm release of a Mafilm-Mosfilm co-production. Directed by Miklos Jancso. With Krystyna Mikolajevska, Tatjana Konjuhova, Mihail Kazakov, Gleb Strizhenov, Andras Kozak, Jacint Juhasz, Jozsef Madaras. Screenplay, Miklos Jancso, Gyula Hernadi, Georgij Mdivani; camera, Tamas Somlo. Reviewed at Puskin Theatre, Budapest. Running Time, 92 MINS.
Olga	Krystyna Mikolajevska
Matron	Tatjana Konjuhova
Red Commander	Mihail Kazakov
Hungarian Commander	Jozsef Madaras
Hungarian soldiers	Andras Kozak, Jacint Juhasz, Tibor Molnar
Colonel	Gleb Strizhenov

Theme of Miklos Jancso's new pic, the first Hungarian-Soviet co-production, is an episode in the 1918-1922 civil war in Russia. Several films already have been made about revolutionary struggles, starting from similar stories made by the Russian film industry. But this vehicle is basically different from many of the others. It is not a historic pic in the usual sense. There are no heroes and its main topic is not based on one outstanding event. Somewhere in Russia, two forces fight each other: a unit of the Red Army, which also includes Hungarian Internationalists, and a group of White Guards, mainly former Tsarist officers. It seems that there is only one aim, to liquidate the other side.

Jansco concentrates his message on the philosophical problem of life and death. Unknown and nameless men enter history in a given moment and after some time they step out of the scene with their death. With the study method of behaviour psychology, excerpts of the events bring flashing glimpses of these characters to the screen.

Another question which interests Jancso—the relationship between men and women receives a similar simplified treatment. Attraction and repulsion are depicted in an extreme concentration and this results in highly exaggerated tension. The most characteristic example of this used by Jancso to the most beautiful sequence of the film.

In a remote hospital, a dozen nurses look after the wounded soldiers, both Whites and Reds. A White Guard unit arrives. They take all the nurses by coaches to a woods. The tension of this scene increases the underlying fear that the nurses will be executed. Instead, in the forest, the eight nurses, dressed in evening gowns, have to dance to the music of a military orchestra. They dance the waltz as if they were at a ball of the aristocrats. The light movement of the dancing girls indicates nostalgia of these officers for their former life.

The "Internationalists" is a merciless film. It is as merciless as the necessity which activates history. With this lack of pathos, Jancso's new work seems to differ from any pic on a similar topic. There is no stirring spectacularity in it. His dialogues are limited almost to military commands.

His technique, supported by the outstanding camera work of Tamas Somlo, organically serves his object. The camera moves without ceasing. Various shots most accurately point out the significant momentum of the scenes. This continuous movement and the continuity of internal cutting, creates a strong tension. Jancso's technique almost excludes careful rehearsals and requires constant improvisations suitable to the situation. Consequently, the choice of types is the most important factor in the cast, and cast here fills this requirement.

Jancso's is doubtlessly the most outstanding and the most original figure of Hungarian film art. Perhaps one might call this the outstanding creation of the Hungarian film industry.
Ban.

Woman and Temptation
(La Tentacion Desnuda)
(ARGENTINE)

Zero as art, but the talents of the buxom Isabel Sarli make this a top sexploiter entry.

Prentoulis Films release of Armando Bo production. Stars Isabel Sarli; features Armando Bo, Victor Bo, Oscar Valicelli, Juan Jose Miguez. Directed by Armando Bo. Screenplay, Armando Bo; camera, Alfred Traverso; music, Eligio Ayala Moren, played by Los Paraguayos, sung by Luis Alberto de Paranya. No other credits. Reviewed at Globe Theatre, N.Y., Nov. 17, 1967. Running Time, 85 MINS.
Sandra	Isabel Sarli
Joseph	Armando Bo
Chuck	Victor Bo
Shorty	Oscar Valicelli
Fernando	Juan Jose Miguez

(*Dubbed English Soundtrack*)
Isabel Sarli, the star of this Argentine-produced sexploiter being released in the U.S. by the recently-formed Prentoulis Films, is so well-endowed physically and moves her body in such total awareness of this fact that her screen presence can evoke only two impressions in the spectator: (1) she is, even judged against other sexploitation stars, an unbelievably sexy woman, or (2) she repels sexual interest because she is a caricature of her type. There should be enough adherents of position (1) to make "Woman and Temptation" on of the top-grossing entries in its class.

This is not however, another "I, a Woman." It is simply too faulty in the writing, acting and technical departments to make it with women and art-house patrons. In New York, Prentoulis opened the film daydate at an art house and a traditional sex unit; he asked for reviews, practically unheard-of for a sexploiter; and he took huge (though very old-fashioned) ads in the papers. But, as the distrib himself now admits, the business done by the film has not justified this expense. The market for "Woman and Temptation" remains the traditional sexploiter one, where (as has already been proved in other cities) it can gross sensationally.

The story itself is almost too poor for words. Miss Sarli falls overboard from a yacht traveling through the River Parana in the Argentine jungle. She finds herself in a community of five sex-starved men. One, the most civilized among them, truly loving her, but the rest go on a raping and killing rampage which is more steamy and melodramatic than anything seen North of the Border in many years. All of this is not helped by some of the worst dubbing ever. But nothing can sully the sight of the buxom Miss Sarli showering in a crude jungle stall, sucking on a grass of straw as she tries to attract a man's attention, or fondling her body in a state of rapture. Most patrons of sexploiter units should find this film well worth the admission price.

"Woman and Temptation" is badly written, acted, photographed, directed and edited. But it is a sexploitation film, and, in that context, eminently succeeds.
Byro.

Red Letter Days
(Unnepnapok)
(HUNGARIAN)

Budapest, Nov. 21.
Hungarofilm release of Mafilm Studio No. 3 production. With Janos Gorbe, Gabor Konxz, Teri Horvath, Kati Kovacs. Written and directed by Ferenc Kardos; camera, Sandor Sara; music, Andras Szollosky. Reviewed at Pushkin Cinema, Budapest. Running Time, 77 MINS.

Old Mihaly	Janos Gorbe
His Sons	Istvan Avar,
	Ferenc Kallai, Lajos Oze
Misi	Gabor Koncz
Misi's mother	Teri Horvath
Kati	Kati Kovacs

Ferenc Kardos is one of the talented young Hungarian film directors, having done two short features and the feature film, "Grimace." They all revealed his grotesque sense of humor. But this pic follows a different line. "Holidays" recalls the last months in the life of an old worker. The almost tragic road accident suffered by his grandson unexpectedly raises the question—was there any aim in his life? The old man spent many long years working at a machine in a factory, and, with great sacrifice, he managed to send all of his sons to school. These boys, who are now men with families, live a different life from what he had imagined.

The contact between the two generations separates them, and they cannot find a common language. All his hopes were placed in the son of his fourth son who died in the war, whom he raised and who he thought would be the continuation of his life. After the road accident, he begins to realize that even this boy lived in a different way and looked forward to a different future to what his grandfather expected.

The clash between the conceptions of three generations is the basic theme of this pic that needs little action. The message which is of interest to society is approached by Kardos in a strongly de-dramatized style. Instead of lusty clashes and loud action, calm conversation supplants them together with deeply intensive short episodes. This sympathetic approach sometimes causes relapses. The methods adapted from cinema verite techniques become sluggish and slow down the over-all.

However, a feature of this is its merciless frankness and the introduction of realism without any illusions. In the clash between the concept of the three generations, the director does not take a stand and demand unreachable ideals. This exact and unfalsified illustration of the merciless and decisive role of circumstances endows it with worthwhile interest.

The performances are generally good, but perhaps Janos Gorbe is slightly more colorless than his role demands. The film also offered an excellent chance for Kati Kovacs, the pop-singer to demonstrate her ability as an actress.

Because of its special topic and tone, this vehicle has only slight possibilities of being shown abroad, and then primarily in a few arty cinemas. Ban.

Guess Who's Coming to Dinner
(COLOR)

Blockbuster comedy - drama about interracial marriage. Spencer Tracy's last pic, Sidney Poitier and Katherine Hepburn also starred. Superior Stanley Kramer film headed for torrid b.o.

Hollywood, Nov. 22.
Columbia Pictures release, produced and directed by Stanley Kramer. Stars Spencer Tracy, Sidney Poitier, Katharine Hepburn; features Katharine Houghton. Screenplay, William Rose; camera (Technicolor), Sam Leavitt; editor, Robert C. Jones; music, Frank DeVol; song, Billy Hill; production design, Robert Clatworthy; sound, Charles J. Rice, Robert Martin; asst. director, Ray Gosnell. Reviewed at Columbia Studios, L.A., Nov. 21, '67. Running Time, 108 MINS.

Matt Drayton	Spencer Tracy
John Prentice	Sidney Poitier
Christina Drayton	Katharine Hepburn
Joey Drayton	Katharine Houghton
Msgr. Ryan	Cecil Kellaway
Mrs. Prentice	Beah Richards
Mr. Prentice	Roy E. Glenn, Sr.
Tillie	Isabell Sanford
Hilary St. George	Virginia Christine
Car Hop	Alexandra Hey
Dorothy	Barbara Randolph
Frankie	D'Urville Martin
Peter	Tom Heaton
Judith	Grace Gaynor
Delivery Boy	Skip Martin
Cab Driver	John Hudkins

Problem: how to tell an interracial love story in a literate, non-sensational and balanced way. Solution: make it a drama with comedy. "Guess Who's Coming To Dinner" is an outstanding Stanley Kramer production, superior in almost every imaginable way, which examines its subject matter with perception, depth, insight, humor and feeling. Spencer Tracy, Sidney Poitier and Katharine Hepburn head a perfect cast. A landmark in its tasteful introduction of sensitive material to the screen, the Columbia release can look to torrid b.o. response throughout a long-legged theatrical release.

William Rose's original screenplay demands recognition as one of the true "stars" of this superior production. Script is properly motivated at all times; dialog is punchy, adroit and free of preaching; dramatic rhythm is superb. Casting and direction by Kramer is terrific. Film can exhaust most superlatives by the time an analysis is complete. Production values are strong throughout. George Glass was associate producer.

The story covers 12 hours, from arrival in, and departure from, Frisco of Poitier and newcomer Katharine Houghton (Miss Hepburn's niece, in a whammo screen debut). Tracy and Miss Hepburn are her parents, of longtime liberal persuasion, faced with a true test of their beliefs: do they approve of their daughter marrying a Negro.

Poitier's parents, Beah Richards and Roy E. Glenn Sr., also are faced with the question when they fly up for dinner (hence, the title). Peripheral characters, all of whom add a dimension to the well-developed exposition, include priest Cecil Kellaway, a family friend, Isabell Sanford, the Tracy-Hepburn Negro maid, and Virginia Christine, a biz partner to Miss Hepburn.

Between the lovers and two sets of parents, every possible inter-action is explored admidst comedy angles which range from drawing-room sophistication to sight gag, from bitter cynicism to telling irony. Film must be seen to be believed.

Apart from the pic itself, there are several plus angles. This is the ninth teaming of Tracy and Hepburn, and the last, unfortunately; Tracy died shortly after principal photography was complete. Older audiences who remember their successful prior pix will be drawn to this one, while younger crowds will be attracted by the interracial romance.

Also, for Poitier, film marks a major step forward, not just in his proven acting ability, but in the opening-up of his script character. In many earlier films, he seemed to come from nowhere; he was a symbol. But herein, he has a family, a professional background, likes, dislikes, humor, temper. In other words, he is a whole human being. This alone is a major achievement in screenwriting, and for Poitier himself, his already recognized abilities now have expanded casting horizons.

To point out acting highlights would be to repeat the cast listing; suffice it to say that Kramer cast with care and directed in the same sure manner. Miss Houghton is an attractive, talented girl who is off to a running start. Miss Sanford, the maid, has not been in pix before, according to associate producer Glass; well, she's off to a strong start, too.

Recurring theme, interpolated nicely by Frank DeVol, is the late Billy Hill's "The Glory Of Love" ("You've Got to Give a Little, Take A Little . . ."). Jacqueline Fontaine sings it at one point. Over 30 years old, the Shapiro-Bernstein copyright gets a deserved new lease on life. Rest of the score is good.

Production credits rate a big nod —Robert Clatworthy's production design and the Jean Louis wardrobe in particular. What appears to be some poor process work may be attributed to the exigencies of production vis-a-vis Tracy's terminal illness. Robert C. Jones executed the sharp editing to a very good 108 minutes.

Story ends on an upbeat note, leaving audiences not only entertained but with many a new thought on how they would face similar situations. Almost every familiar racial prejudice is brought up and, if ont demolished, at least illuminated in detail to spark definite word of mouth. Certain Dixie areas may not dig the film, sight-unseen, but it is big enough, and important enough, to command screen time in those regions. Murf.

The Producers
(COLOR)

Pie-in-the-face farce spoofs Broadway flopmaker. Turns loose Zero Mostel. Some "in" humor, but also broad appeal. Okay prospects.

Washington, Dec. 1.
Embassy release of Sidney Glazier production. Stars Zero Mostel, features Gene Wilder and Dick Shawn. Written and directed by Mel Brooks. Camera (Pathecolor), Joe Coffey. Reviewed at Playhouse, Washington, Nov. 30, '67. Running Time, 100 MINS.

Max Bialystock	Zero Mostel
Leo Bloom	Gene Wilder
Franz Liebkind	Kenneth Mars
Old Lady	Estelle Winwood
Eva Braun	Renee Taylor
Roger DeBris	Christopher Hewitt
Ulla	Lee Meredith
Carmen Giya	Andreas Voutsina
L.S.D.	Dick Shawn

Caught in a Washington, D.C. theatre, this release has never been tradeshown by Embassy.

Mel Brooks has turned a funny idea into a slapstick film, thanks to the performers, particularly Zero Mostel. Playing a Broadway producer of flops who survives (barely) by suckering little old ladies, he teams with an emotionally retarded accountant portrayed by Gene Wilder in a scheme to produce a flop. By selling 25,000% of production, they figure to be rich when it flops. For the twist, the musical comedy "Hitler in Springtime," penned by a shell-shocked Nazi, is a smash.

(*Basic situation of the legit promoter - scoundrel embarrassed by an unintended hit, and therefore obligated to pay dividends to suckers is part of the Broadway legend. It takes off from reality, in that some promoters have lived off flops, and nothing but flops. But whether accidental success ever actually ensued is not verifiable. It is believed that several short stories have dealt with the plot of a fluke hit.—Ed.*)

Lack of a big name may hamper b.o. prospects. Also, flaws creep in about half-way through. There is a weak and pretty sentimental climax and ending. Scene that shows how Dick Shawn as Hitler turns the show into a hit isn't convincing. At least Brooks doesn't shy away from showing what happens rather than just talk-about it, however, and the Third Reich production number is hilarious.

The film is unmatched in the scenes featuring Mostel and Wilder alone together, and several episodes with other actors are truly rare. When the producers approach the most atrocious director on Broadway, they find Christopher Hewitt in drag exchanging catty comments with his secretary, Andreas Voutsinas. Estelle Winwood is a winner as a salacious little old lady, and Kenneth Mars has his moments as the Nazi scripter.

Fortunately, "The Producers" is fast-paced and doesn't linger over the multiple puns, etc., that dot the script more frequently than punctuation marks. The characters' names are mostly jokes—someday there probably will be a director named DeBris. It's possible Brooks conceived of "The Producers" as a play, then decided it would be too hard to put over on stage. That's true, but it makes a very entertaining film. Mick.

Horl, Ma Panenko
(Song of the Firemen)
(CZECH — COLOR)

Paris, Dec. 5.
Czech State Film production and release. With Jan Vostrcil, Josef Sebanek, Josef Valnoha, Josef Kolb. Directed by Milos Forman. Screenplay, Forman, Ivan Passer; camera (Eastmancolor), Miroslav Ondricek; editor, Miroslav Hajek; music, Karel Mares. Previewed in Paris. Running Time, 73 MINS.

Jan	Jan Vostrcil
Josef	Josef Sebanek
Adjutant	Josef Valnoha
Assistant	Josef Kolb

Milos Forman, one of the Czech filmmakers who helped make the buffs, critics and film audiences around the world mindful of the Czechoslovak film renaissance, now comes up with another funny, human but never sentimental pic after his "Loves of a Blonde." Czech forthrightness in gently skeptical, socially probing and wittily provocative comedies and dramas on contemporary life is evident here.

In this film, a group of elderly firemen of a small town are planning to bring off a farewell ball for their retiring director. Filmmaker Forman has cannily used a bevy of non-actors to flesh out a practically plotless vehicle if a lively, brimming comedy on human conduct and smalltown life.

An attempt to pick girls for a Miss Fireman prize leads to heavy searching in the dancing, drinking crowds. This ends with a group too timid to go up to present the gift for the retiring director. The latter is a slightly deaf old man, who generally is lost in the varied proceedings.

A scuffle, when the girls are being rounded up to parade, is interrupted by a real fire. And a house burns down when the fire truck is caught in a snowdrift. Here Forman avoids bathos and undue sentimentality without sacrificing a serious strain that is inherent in all good comedy. An old homeless man prays as his house goes up in flames, and the local cafe owner shows enterprise by selling drinks to the crowd.

Back at the ball, the lottery prizes are found to have been stolen. Petty larceny is tut-tutted by the fire chief and he has the lights put out to have the culprits return the prizes. But when they are turned on again, a fireman is the only one returning a plate his wife has taken.

Forman uses the basic timidity and uneasiness of many of his non-actors while also utilizing personal traits to create robust portraits that ring true in an acceptable comedic larger-than-life fashion. The probing camera of Miroslav Ondricek, with his finely-honed hues, is a big help as well as the sprightly music and well-paced editing.

Earthy on the surface, this still has a universal appeal and could be helped by word-of-mouth in some foreign spots. Arty and playoff attributes are there, with good prospects apparent abroad for this beguiling, human comedy.

Title is actually a Czech folk song about firemen. Forman makes it all look easy, and belies the brilliance in conception, pacing and unending comic twists. A couple making haphazard love under a table during a search for a spilled string of pearls is never milked, but adds to the quilt of criss-cross characters and liveliness.

And the invention rarely flags if its deceptive simplicity makes it look spontaneous rather than practically a tour-de-force of comedic knowhow. The only cavil might be Forman's insistence on the plainness and eccentricity of most of his characters. But an obvious sincerity and tenderness towards them remove the dangers of patronizing   *Mosk.*

School for Sex
(Nikutai No Gakko)
(JAPANESE)

Divorcee meets male prostie in modern Japan. Artsy effects and lack of motivation do not help fair story. Mild U.S. art house prospects.

Toho International release of a Masakatsu Kaneko production. Stars Kyoko Kishida, Tsutomu Yamazaki. Directed by Ryo Kinashita. Screenplay, Toshiro Ide, from story by Yukio Mishima; camera, Jo Aizawa; music, Shigeru Ikeno. No other credits. Previewed in N.Y., Nov. 30, 1967. Running Time, 95 MINS.
Taeko .... Kyoko Kishida
Senkichi ....:.. Tsutomu Yamazaki

As far it goes, the Japanese "School for Sex" tells an interesting story of an affair between a young divorcee and a male prostie but it is marred by a succession of theatrical effects and a moral imbalance which defeat its essential sobriety. Though it came in on rubber heels, film has garnered some excellent reviews and could be in for a good run at N.Y.'s 55th St. Playhouse. Its general b.o. prospects on the art house circuit, however, must be rated mild.

Divorce is still a rare thing in Japan and this film follows a successful dress shop owner (Kyoko Kishida of "Woman in the Dunes") as she struggles to find love with a handsome gigolo several years her junior. Oddly enough, she meets him in a homosexual bar, where he has been working as a bartender and often selling his favors to its clientele. The scenes in this establishment, incidentally, are the longest such than can be remembered in any previous pic, east or west. If the film is to be believed, such bars are quite popular with U.S. servicemen in Japan!

The young man, played by Tsutomu Yamazaki, eventually betrays his lover via an affair and eventual engagement to the daughter of one of the divorcee's rich friends. But there's revenge available when the divorcee obtains some incriminating photos from one of his former "gay" companions. The point seems to be that having gone through all this the woman will now approach life in a more mature, realistic fashion.

The problem with Toshiro Ide's screenplay, based on a story by Yukio Mishima, is its total lack of sympathy with the male character. His poverty background is mentioned, but apparently it is not meant to even partially explain his actions, which are seen as evil in the impurest sense. True, the film is a kind of male "Of Human Bondage" and it could be argued that W. Somerset Maugham had little interest in his Mildred's motives—but at least the character herself was fascinating. Same cannot be said for Senkichi, the boy-man played by Yamazaki.

Director Ryo Kinashita has compounded these inadequacies with some of the more pseudo-poetic effects seen in recent days. They are, moreover, the kind done on set—e.g. the lighting is suddenly dimmed on everything but a character's face, a row of pinball machines is made unrealistically endless, etc. Not only do they add nothing to the story, but they are unbearably contrived in a way

that remains unassimilable on film.

The acting by the two leads is undistinguished. Technical credits are no more than adequate.
                Byro.

The Glory Stompers
(COLOR—SCOPE)

Routine motorcycle meller, with moderate sex and violence, for exploitation duals.

Hollywood, Nov. 28.
American International Pictures release of Norman T. Herman production; executive producers, Maurice Smith, Arthur Gilbert; produced by John Lawrence. Stars Dennis Hopper, Jody McCrea, Chris Noel, Jock Mahoney. Directed by Anthony Lanza. Screenplay, James Gordon White, John Lawrence; camera, (Pathecolor), Mario Tossi; editor, Len Miller; music, Sidewalk Prods. Inc.; sound, Arthur Names; asst. director, Rudy Kaddo. Reviewed at Academy Award Theatre, L.A., Nov. 27, 1967. Running Time, 84 MINS.
Chino .... Dennis Hopper
Darryl .... Jody McCrea
Chris .... Chris Noel
Smiley .... Jock Mahoney
Paul .... Jim Reader
Jo Ann .... Saundra Gale
Magoo .... Robert Tessier
Doreen .... Astrid Warner
Pony .... Gary Wood
Monk .... Lindsay Crosby
Mouth .... Casey Kasem

The 400 or so exhibs, who played American International's "The Glory Stompers" five days before AIP unleashed its latest protest pic on the Hollywood trade press, already know it for what it is. The Norman T. Herman production is another motorcycle gang meller, far from the best but not the worst. Sluggish pacing, dull acting-direction, and unexciting sex and violence mark this pic for fast, fast playoff, on exploitation duals where one of AIP's past leather-shocking sagas can shore up the bill.

Indie-made pic has the usual signs — multiplicity of producers (a Herman production, produced by John Lawrence, exec producers, Maurice Smith and Arthur Gilbert, plus three associate producers); padded and repetitive transitional footage (motorcycles on highways); and an overused camera angle (low-angle, fish-eye lens).

James Gordon White and producer Lawrence are credited with the story. Dennis Hopper, head of one motorcycle gang which includes gal friend Saundra Gale, brute Robert Tessier, Lindsay Crosby and local deejay Casey Kasem, kidnaps Chris Noel from arms of Jody McCrea, head of a rival gang and left for dead after beating by Hopper's crew.

Jock Mahony, who once was a gang member but now rides alone, helps McCrea rescue Miss Noel. Latter, between consistent resistance to Hopper's advances, fakes an interest in Jim Reader in hopes of escape. Reader, the most intriguing character in the plot, is killed by Tessier in a climactic fight, after which audience learns he was Hopper's brother.

Script is formula — no depth to anyone — and acting is dull. Anthony Lanza's direction is partly to blame. Mario Tossi's camera work, despite the overused angle, has some bright moments. Excuse for the pic seems to be a love-in sequence, lovingly described in production notes as a "wild orgy."

(Promises, promises.) Pathecolor hues are generally consistent and the anamorphic process used is something called Colorscope. Other credits blah.   *Murf.*

Mise a Sac
(Pillaged)
(FRENCH-COLOR)

Paris, Nov. 28.
United Artists release of Ariane Films-UA-Registi Produttori Associati production. Stars Michel Constantin, Franco Interlenghi, Daniel Ivernel, Irene Tunc. Directed by Alain Cavalier. Screenplay, Claude Sautet, Cavalier, Oscar Dancigers from book by Robert Stark; camera (Eastmancolor), Pierre Lhomme; editor, Pierre Gillette. At Balzac, Paris. Running Time, 85 MINS.
Georges .... Michel Constantin
Edgar .... Daniel Ivernel
Maurice .... Franco Interlenghi
Marie-Ange .... Irene Tunc
Assistant .... Paul Le Persen

A group of well-organized criminals move into a small town one night and calmly take over its police station and post office, and proceed to rob its banks and factory coffers. All the latest tools are used and only a personal quirk of one of the instigators sets things awry. Crime may not pay, but a couple of gangsters escape unharmed.

This routine but carefully made and generally interest-sustaining pic is original if nothing else. It appears feasible that a smalltown could be taken over this way. Even the few who stay up late are easily handled when they phone the police since one of the hoods is answering all calls.

The only thing is that the characterizations are kept surface. There is some intimation that it's all the vengeance of the man who masterminds this raid on his home town and this makes it seem plausible. It seems the head of the town factory had run off with his wife and ditched her. His attempt at revenge louses up a solidly prepared criminal outing.

Alain Cavalier shows a good feel for movement, timing and keeping this interesting, although he is not able to generate desired suspense because of its mainly telegraphed and familiar story. However, nothing is forced and even a romantic interlude between one of the gang and a telephone operator is tastefully handled. Acting is properly sober and direct. It is technically good, with a neat production dress. UA has a good programmer for abroad, with good tele possibilities, if the more intense edge and character probings are missing for arty theatre legs.
                Mosk.

In Cold Blood
(PANAVISION)

Outstanding Richard Brooks film from Truman Capote's book. Solid word of mouth and b.o. prospects.

Hollywood, Dec. 2.

Columbia Pictures release, adapted, produced and directed by Richard Brooks. Features Robert Blake, Scott Wilson, John Forsythe. Based on the book by Truman Capote; camera, Conrad Hall; editor, Peter Zinner; music, Quincy Jones; art direction, Robert Boyle; sound, William Randall, Jr., Jack Haynes, A. Piantadosi, Richard Tyler; asst. director, Tom Shaw. Reviewed at Columbia Studios, L.A., Dec. 1, '67. Running Time, **133 MINS.**

Perry Smith	Robert Blake
Dick Hickock	Scott Wilson
Alvin Dewey	John Forsythe
Reporter	Paul Stewart
Harold Nye	Gerald S. O'Loughlin
Mr. Hickock	Jeff Corey
Roy Church	John Gallaudet
Clarence Duntz	James Flavin
Mr. Smith	Charles McGraw
Officer Rohleder	James Lantz
Prosecutor	Will Geer
Herbert Clutter	John McLiam
Bonnie Clutter	Ruth Storey
Nancy Clutter	Brenda C. Currin
Kenyon Clutter	Paul Hough
Good Samaritan	Vaughn Taylor
Young Reporter	Duke Hobbie
Rev. Post	Sheldon Allman
Mrs. Smith	Sammy Thurman
Mrs. Sadie Truitt, Myrtle Clare	Themselves
Young Hitchhiker	Teddy Eccles
Old Hitchhiker	Raymond Hatton
Susan Kidwell	Mary-Linda Rapelye
Nancy's Friend	Ronda Fultz
Sheriff	Al Christy
Salesman	Don Sollars
Mrs. Hartman	Harriet Levitt
Insurance Man	Stan Levitt

In the skillful hands of adapter-director-producer Richard Brooks, Truman Capote's "In Cold Blood," the non-fiction novel-like account about two Kansas killers, becomes on screen a probing, sensitive, tasteful, balanced and suspenseful documentary-drama. Solid pre-sell from the book, plus word of mouth from initial exclusive runs in key cities, will propel the Columbia release into top b.o. brackets. Initial exploitation campaign, of the institutional genre, should be broadened for maximum b.o. in the later general playoff.

Film has the look and sound of reality, in part from use of actual locales in six states and non-pros as atmosphere players, the rest from Brooks' own filmmaking professionalism. Planned as a $3,000,000, 124-day pic, it came in for $2,200,000 in 80 days. If costs are recouped in two years, film may not be on tv for five years; with a growing public awareness of shorter pix-to-tv clearances, it might be advisable, before general playoff, to ballyhoo the determined no-tv angle.

Heading the competent cast are Robert Blake and Scott Wilson, bearing a striking resemblance to the now-dead Kansas drifters who, in the course of a burglary on Nov. 15, 1959, murdered four of a family. Almost six years later, after an exhausted appeal route, they were hanged. John Forsythe plays the chief investigator who broke the case.

Brooks' screenplay and direction are remarkable in that pic avoids so many pitfalls: it is not a crime meller, told either from the police or criminal viewpoint; it is not social tract against capital punishment; it is not cheap exploitation material; and it is not amateurish in technical execution, despite its realistic flavor.

Instead, Brooks gives careful exposition to his main characters and their motivations, and by shrewd story-telling and underplaying of climactic events, appeals to the viewer's intellect as well as his senses, never to excess. Although millions know that the murders really took place, a hefty amount of suspense is generated. No small factor in character delineation is the technical assistance from Dr. Joseph Satten of the Menninger Foundation's law and psychiatry division.

Blake (a former serial star as a youngster, and latterday tv player) seems assured of a renewed and bigtime career from his portrayal of the fantasy-ridden Perry Smith, who did the actual murdering. Laconic, latently violent, child-like, pitiable, sympathetic, virile, submissive—all these facets emerge from his excellent performance.

Wilson, too, proves that his small, but meaty, part in "In The Heat Of The Night" cannot be credited in totality to the machinations of direction and editing. A basic talent is there, rest assured, and herein he excels in a well-rounded portrayal of Dick Hickock, who had a grudge against the world, a fear of sexual inadequacy, but a remarkable knowledge of human nature.

Forsythe, a fine actor not seen enough, also makes his part three-dimensional: stunned at the brutal crime, deliberate in investigatory procedures, he avoids the extremes of emotional vengeance and "Dragnet" monotone. Paul Stewart, who, conceivably, could be a fictional Capote, plays an important role as the detached outsider in pulling together plot angles.

Jeff Corey, as Wilson's father, Charles McGraw, as Blake's dad, prosecutor Will Geer, clergyman Sheldon Allman, and salesman Don Sollars give strong support in brief footage. Also, young Teddy Eccles and vet Raymond Hatton, playing hitchhikers, stand out in a sequence which accomplishes a threefold purpose: creating suspense, relieving tension, and illuminating character. Entire cast was selected with apparent care, results of which are obvious.

Film is nicely organized in its just-right 133 minutes, as edited by Peter Zinner: first 29 minutes introduce Blake and Wilson, and take them up to the murder house; next 63 minutes jump ahead to flight, pursuit, near-capture, final apprehension in Las Vegas, and interrogation; then, via a Blake-narrated flashback, the circumstances of the murder take the next 18 minutes; final 23 minutes depict trial, appeal and death.

Atmosphere is heightened by black-and-white lensing, supervised in outstanding fashion by Conrad Hall who used crisp Panavision lenses. There may be debate on b&w usage, as opposed to subdued color lensing which would have been possible, no doubt. But such debate would be merely pounding sand; Brooks chose b&w, and, through Hall, used the entire black-to-white spectrum to superior dramatic advantage. Technicolor Corp. supervised the top-notch print work.

For those who equate filmmaking excellence with jerky, eye-irritating hand-held camera movements, focused on leaves and furniture, it is a pleasure to report that none of this apparent. But, it is a further pleasure to have found out that extensive use was made of modern, lightweight camera equipment, although the viewer is not made aware—properly so—of this fact via pretentious and distracting setups.

Aside from a passing instance of poor looping, the sound team—William Randall Jr., Jack Haynes, A. Piantadosi and Richard Tyler—has complemented the visual feel of authenticity with an aural liveliness. Quincy Jones has provided an excellent and spare score, with an emphasis on percussion, which incorporates a valid usage of the Doppler principle of acoustics. Flashbacks, via direct cuts, are almost silent and, gratifyingly, are most lucid.

Fadeout scene is socko: the hanged Blake; the sound of a beating heart slowing, slowing, stopped; then black film, no end titles whatsoever. Columbia must alert boothmen to this vital point, and proper firstrun exhibition would seem to demand that nothing follow the film's end but a silent intermission. All other technical film credits are firstrate. Incidentally, nowhere in credits is the word "producer" used, nor is this a Brooks "production."

Brooks, who obviously did produce, takes only adaptation and director credit. *Murf.*

Poor Cow
(BRITISH—COLOR)

Brutal sex life among British underworldlings. Redeemed by some compassion. Good b.o. probable though lacks names for U.S.

London, Dec. 6.

National General (in U.S.) and Warner-Pathe release of Joseph Janni production for Vic Films from Anglo Amalgamated. Stars Carol White, Terence Stamp. Directed by Kenneth Loach. Screenplay, Nell Dunn and Loach, based on Miss Dunn's novel; camera (Eastmancolor), Brian Probyn; music, Donovan; editor, Roy Watts; asst. director, Andrew Grieve. Reviewed at London Pavilion, Dec. 5, '67. Running Time, **101 MINS.**

Joy	Carol White
Dave	Terence Stamp
Tom	John Bindon
Beryl	Kate Williams
Aunt Emm	Queenie Watts
Trixie	Geraldine Sherman
Tom's Mate	James Beckett
Tom's Mate	Billy Murray
Solicitor	Ellis Dale
Judge	Gerald Young
Governor in studio	Paddy Joyce
Bet	Gladys Dawson
Petal	Ron Pember
Billy	Malcolm McDowell

The team of director Kenneth Loach, writer Nell Dunn, and actress Carol White meet up for the first time for a feature, but they drew attention in the realistic vidcast "Up the Junction," a seamy look at the amoral poor whose salty lingo and no-holds-barred toughness garnered a huge tv audience. Producer Joseph Janni exploits the anything goes of today's uninhibited candour, and reassembled the group. The result should pay off in big b.o. grosses, and registers Miss White as potential marquee bait. Release is unlikely to have the shock appeal of "Junction" or the similar-toned "Cathy Come Home" (also involving Loach and the girl) on tv, for theatrical films have established a wider theme license for themselves over the past decade. But it still packs a potent punch, and the squeamish may wriggle over its adjectival liberty and certain unclad scenes.

It has a jolting opening, with Joy, the hapless heroine, shown in full detail giving birth to a baby, with the infant emerging from the womb in its natural state. This leads into a portrait of Joy, who has married a brutal crook (John Bindon) and, after he is nabbed by the cops, shacks up with another thief (Terence Stamp), a gentler type who is himself put inside for robbery with violence. But the incidents of the plot are an excuse for an examination of promiscuous Joy. Left to fend for herself, she snatches happiness where she can find it, for her temperament is heedless. While visiting her lover in jail and ensuring him of her fidelity, she takes the baker into bed and encourages the customers in the pub where she works as a barmaid. To make money, she poses nude for amateur photographers, and the only firm emotion she possesses is her love for the toddling child.

Kenneth Loach uses an improvisatory technique in all this, and it largely works. Thesps were given the gist and trend of the dialog, and permitted to embroider it with their own words. It's a method made familiar by the features of the likes of Jean-Luc Godard, and Loach shows himself an astute imitator, even down to captions to split up each episode. It results in a sort of private scrapbook of a personality, with touches of the confessional. And Loach brings off some episodes with notable wit and point, such as the nude-posing sequence and Joy's enquiries about a divorce from a polysyllabic solicitor. Somewhat less happy are the romantic episodes involving Terence Stamp, who is slightly uncertain when he's groping for words. But the general air of haphazard squalor is effective, and contributory performances from Queenie Watts (as Joy's philosophical Aunt Emm, who has a dismissive attitude to men as creatures to be used and discarded) and from Geraldine Sherman, as Joy's friend, teetering on the brink of turning prostie. John Bindon, recruited from this sort of environment, shows promise as Joy's husband, with a passionate monologue about everyone being "bent" from the cops to the shopkeepers.

But it is Miss White's film, and she scores with a flow of varied emotion, ranging from fetching happiness to a sudden spurt of tears in the final minutes, when she recalls straight to camera her affection for her baby. She passes from beauty to bedraggled wretchedness with equal conviction, and she wins sympathy for a character who might easily be deeply uninteresting, because shallow and inexplicit.

The color lensing is okay, but adds nothing to settings and moods that would be starker in black-&-white, but the film, though derivative, is strong in compassion that occasionally laps over into sentimentality. *Otta.*

Bedazzled
(BRITISH-PANAVISION-COLOR)

Way-out British comedy based on Faust legend. Well enough done but with limited appeal for American audiences, where best chance is either art or highly selected situation. Some chance of church resentment of irreverence.

Hollywood, Dec. 6.
Twentieth-Fox release of Stanley Donen production, directed by Donen. Stars Peter Cook, Dudley Moore, Eleanor Bron; features Raquel Welch. Screenplay, Cook, Moore, from story by Cook; music, Moore; camera (DeLuxe Color), Austin Dempster; editor, Richard Marden; asst. director, John Quested; art direction, Terence Knight; sound, John Purchese, Doug Turney. Reviewed at 20th-Fox Studios, Dec. 5, '67. Running Time, 104 MINS.
George Spiggot .... Peter Cook
Stanley Moon .... Dudley Moore
Margaret .... Eleanor Bron
Lillian Lust .... Raquel Welch
Vanity .... Alba
Anger .... Robert Russell
Envy .... Barry Humphries
Gluttony .... Parnell McGarry
Avarice .... Daniele Noel
Sloth .... Howard Goorney
Inspector Clarke .... Michael Bates
Irving Moses .... Bernard Spear
Randolph .... Robin Hawdon
Lord Dowdy .... Michael Trubshawe
Mrs. Wisby .... Evelyn Moore
Vicar .... Charles Lloyd Pack
St. Peter .... Lockwood West
Sister Phoebe .... Betty Cooper

"Bedazzled" is smartly-styled & typical of certain types of high British comedy. Fantasy of a London short-order cook madly in love with a waitress, who is offered seven wishes by the Devil in return for his soul, there is farce, and irreverence bordering on what some may regard as the sacrilegious. For American audiences- it will require hard sell, best suited for more select situations where demand is for the unusual.

Stanley Donen production is pretty much the work of two of its three stars, Peter Cook and Dudley Moore, who previously were responsible for the much-touted satirical revue, "Beyond the Fringe," which enjoyed a long run on the London stage and later produced on Broadway. Pair scripted from Cook's original story, and Moore also composed music score. Eleanor Bron, prominent as a British comedienne, is third star and for domestic marquee lure there is Raquel Welch, whose brief appearance is equalled only by her scant attire.

Mephistophelean overtones are inserted in this modern-day Faust legend tacked onto Moore, who would give his soul to possess Margaret, the waitress (Miss Bron), Cook (Mephistopheles parading under the mundane name of George Spiggot, appears mysteriously in Moore's flat as he flubs a suicide attempt—latest of his many failures in life—and grants all of the cook's wishes. Power, wealth, adulation, learning, love, they're all his, but they all have the knack of turning sour on him, with his last wish running out while he is converted to a nun in a cloister and unable to resume his true identity.

Donen, who also directs, maintains a speedy pace as the chef and the devil go through their paces in trying to win Margaret. Both Cook and Moore play their characters broad and Miss Bron matches their style. Expectedly,

Miss Welch strips, which is pleasant gandering, and even has a few lines.

Technical departments are well handled, including Austin Dempster's color photography, Terence Knight's art direction, Richard Marden's editing.   *Whit.*

The Fox
(COLOR)

Lesbian theme and Sandy Dennis prime marquee bait in artie situations. Visually interesting but uneven film from D. H. Lawrence's novella. Urban b.o. good.

Hollywood, Dec. 8.
Claridge Pictures (Warner Bros.-Seven Arts) release of Raymond Stross-Motion Pictures Intl. production. Features Sandy Dennis, Keir Dullea, Anne Heywood. Directed by Mark Rydell. Screenplay, Lewis John Carlino, Howard Koch, based on the D. H. Lawrence novella; camera (DeDuxe Color), William Fraker; editor, Thomas Stanford; music, Lalo Schifrin; song, Oscar Brand; art direction, Charles Bailey; sound, Des Dollery; asst. director, Burtt Harris. Reviewed at Academy Award Theatre, L.A., Dec. 7, '67. Running Time, 110 MINS.
Jill .... Sandy Dennis
Paul .... Keir Dullea
March .... Anne Heywood
Realtor .... Glyn Morris

D. H. Lawrence's lesbian-themed novella, "The Fox," nas been turned into a beautifully photographed, dramatically uneven Canadian-made film, produced by Raymond Stross in association with Steve Broidy's Motion Pictures International, indie. The sensitive subject matter is, in the main, handled with taste, although pic at times vacillates between dainty skirting of the problem and crudity reminiscent of low-grade foreign imports. Sandy Dennis and the lesbo theme are the prime bait for good, if uneven, b.o. in special situations. Pic is the second release of Claride Pictures; if not listed in the phone book, try the Warner Bros.-Seven Arts exchange.

Screenplay is credited to Lewis John Carlino and Howard Koch (latter also associate producer. Miss Dennis and Anne Heywood, a British actress now working in domestic pix, are cast as lesbian lovers who have exiled themselves to a lonely farm. Arrival of Keir Dullea, whose grandfather once owned the farm, cues a disintegration of the femme relationship and eventual tragedy.

Title derives from a four-legged neighborhood predator who disrupts the tranquility of the hen house; Miss Heywood, who gets an opportunity to kill the animal, does not. Parallel between the fox and Dullea is quite evident; so presumably is the phallic symbology — shotgun, axe, carving knife, tree, pitchfork, etc.

In early reels, Miss Heywood (whose looks, hair and voice remind strongly of Ruth Roman) seems the dominant female. She is inwardly uneasy, perhaps afraid of eventual old age. Or maybe she really wants a man; not necessarily a lasting heterosexual relationship, but just a physical encounter — as near-climactic development suggests.

In any case, before film is 13 minutes over, there is a nude, and crude, bathroom scene in

which Miss Heywood is depicted as masturbating, after self-stimulation in a mirror. This scene — overlong as is most of the film — is gratuitously "sexsational." Overall, actress does a creditable job, particularly in reacting.

Miss Dennis, who emerges as the more strong-willed, has the greater acting burden, and her performance is uneven. Her daffiness in early reels seems overdone, result of which is that her later, plaintive remarks — which should evoke pity — may draw unwanted smiles, even chuckles, from audiences. Miss Dennis, it will be recalled, made a smooth transition from superficial giddiness to pitiable bewilderment in "Who's Afraid Of Virginia Woolf?" She does not repeat here.

Dullea plays his part with quiet determination to snare Miss Heywood. Whether or not he suspects or comprehends the lesbian relationship is debatable, from script and actions. First sexual encounter between him and Miss Heywood, in a woodshed, at her insistence, is awkward, too — the gaspings, the clutching of turf, etc. — but effect is mitigated by cross-cutting to a hysterical Miss Dennis.

A later romantic scene between the two gals, by contrast, is excellent. Dullea, not to be thwarted, returns to the house for his intended, and climax finds Miss Dennis deliberately in danger from a falling tree. She knows it; Dullea knows it; everybody knows it. Ironically, just like in the now-derogated old-fashioned pix where deus ex machina killed the heavy, we have not yet escaped such pat solutions in the new cinema, either.

Director Mark Rydell, in his feature debut after telepix directing, shows meritorious pictorial ability. Handling of Miss Dennis and Dullea, the two dynamic characters, is less sure. Outstanding mood is established, however, and one never knows for sure where other things seem to have gone awry — script, editing, etc. On latter score, the 110 minutes is too much, as executed by Thomas Stanford.

William Fraker's excellent De-Luxe Color camera, and Charles Bailey's adroit art direction, are big assets. Lalo Schifrin's score also is firstrate, and an Oscar Brand song, "Roll It Over," is a telling plot mover. Don Record is credited with montages and titles, another very big plus factor which must not be overlooked in appreciation of the setting. Film was shot last winter near Toronto.
          Murf.

Doctor Dolittle
(70M—TODD-AO—COLOR)

Highly entertaining unsophisticated music fantasy rates as hardticket winner with lengthy runs indicated in most situations. Rex Harrison excellent.

20th Century-Fox release of Apjac (Arthur P. Jacobs) production. Stars Rex Harrison, Samantha Eggar, Anthony Newley; features Richard Attenborough, Peter Bull, William Dix, Geoffrey Holder. Directed by Richard Fleischer. Screenplay, music and lyrics, Leslie Bricusse, based on the Hugh Lofting stories; camera (De Luxe Color), Robert Surtees; editors, Samuel E. Beetley, Marjorie Fowler; production design, Mario Chiari; special effects, L. B. Abbott, Art Cruickshank, Emil Kosa Jr., Howard Lydecker; sound, James Corcoran, Murray Spivack, Douglas Williams, Bernard Freericks, John Myers; music, scored and conducted by Lionel Newman, Alexander Courage; animals and birds, Jungleland; asst. director, Richard Lang. Reviewed at Loew's State, N.Y., Dec. 18, '67. Running Time, (not including intermission): 152 MINS.
Doctor Dolittle .... Rex Harrison
Emma Fairfax .... Samantha Eggar
Matthew Mugg .... Anthony Newley
Albert Blossom .. Richard Attenborough
General Bellowes .... Peter Bull
Mrs. Blossom .... Muriel Landers
Tommy Stubbins .... William Dix
Willie Shakespeare .... Geoffrey Holder
Sarah Dolittle .... Portia Nelson
Lady Petherington .... Norma Varden

The overall entertainment value of "Doctor Dolittle" is rather difficult to pinpoint. The hardcore sophisticates (who go to the "cinema") probably won't like it; the average man (who goes to the "movies") and his family will love it. Fortunately for 20th Century-Fox and producer Arthur P. Jacobs, the latter far outnumbers the former.

There's sufficient reason to believe that, properly handled, this handsomely mounted, stylishly acted musical fantasy could pick up the crown that must be dropped eventually by "Sound of Music." While an imperfect gem, it has sufficient values going for it to survive any barbs aimed at it by the critics. (It will be recalled that "Sound of Music" drew so-so "initial" reviews.)

A reported negative cost of $16,000,000 means that "Dolittle" must not only come up with successful initial runs, it must maintain them in all situations. Holiday openings and heavy advance sales (reportedly close to $400,000 in New York), should enable it to establish strong roots for runs in these and other key situations. An added value is its inherent reissue worth. If 20th has the courage to withdraw it completely after a couple of years (as Metro does "Wind" and Disney most of its films), "Dolittle" could be a giltedge security for many years. The wish for a quick payoff could prevent this.

Is it a "good" motion picture? The answer varies according to what the individual expects for his money. Action fans won't "dig" it and there's even a bit of dissension to be expected from loyal readers of the original Hugh Lofting stories. Rex Harrison, physically, is not at all like the rotund original; but histrionically, he's perfect. Gentle and loving with animals, patient and kind with obtuse and very young friends, he can become a veritable holocaust when confronted with cruel and uncomprehending adults who threaten his animal world. That he's attractive enough to intrigue a pretty young thing, obviously half his age, only a churl could doubt. Heroic in his deeds and befuddled in his home life, Harrison's "Dolittle" is a type seen rarely these days. He's a charmer.

Lesley Bricusse's adaptation of the Lofting stories has, generally, retained the delightful aspects while taking considerable liberty with the plot. He interjects a suggested love story (that doesn't really help but at least doesn't get in the way) and occasionally adds dollops of wit that, because they're unexpected in such a wholesome film, are mostly enjoyed in retrospect.

His music and lyrics, while containing no smash hits of the "Stop The World" genre, are admirably suited to the scenario. Some, such as the title tune, are getting plenty of exposure, a plus asset for the pic's promotion. The considerable editing on the film has resulted in excision of one entire number, Harrison's "Something In Your Smile," and a truncated version of Anthony Newley's "Beautiful Things," which may befuddle purchasers of the soundtrack album and souvenir programs.

Director Richard Fleischer, an old hand at the special effects bit after "Fantastic Voyage," nearly succeeds in perfectly merging his **real-life and unreal segments. There can be no complaint about the remarkable animal work (the complexity of the training by the Jungleland people is made to seem effortless), or Harrison's work with them. It is understood that Fleischer instructed his human actors to follow the lead of the animals in most scenes as the latter couldn't be expected to be familiar with the script.**

There are some slow periods and some insufficiently defined plot elements. Introducing the girl (not in the original stories) was evidently a problem. As a result there's some confusion initially as to whether she's romantically inclined towards Newley or Harrison. Samantha Eggar, while attractive and talented, has actually the least demanding (and the least rewarding) major role in the film.

The few key supporting roles (and despite the official billing, only Harrison is an authentic star) are handled by top talent. Anthony Newley, as far as American audiences are concerned, debuts with this role and comes over as a very strong personality. He has another, unreleased, feature for another company (Warners' "Sweet November") and long-memory fans will remember his Artful Dodger in David Lean's "Oliver Twist," but he's probably best known in the U.S., as is Bricusse, from the legit "Stop The World" and "Roar of the Greasepaint."

Outstanding, considering his brief appearance, is Richard Attenborough as Albert Blossom, the circus owner. He comes on so strong in his one song-and-dance bit (considering he's thought of only as a dramatic actor) that it's nearly a perfect example of why important cameo roles should be turned over to important talents. Peter Bull's villainous magistrate, the "straightest" part in the film, beautifully complements the gentleness of "Dolittle," while William Dix, as the tyke who accompanies Harrison and Newley, and Geoffrey Holder as one of the screen's most bizarre and hilarious native chieftains, are also outstanding. Muriel Landers, Portia Nelson and Norma Varden, briefly seen, are impressive, especially Miss Varden's mouse sequence.

There are few bellylaughs in "Doctor Dolittle" but a myriad chuckles (evidently the reaction author Lofting was aiming for) and whether this will prove enough for today's extreme-emotion demanding general audience remains to be seen. The overall editing by Samuel K. Beetley and Marjorie Fowler could perhaps still be tightened in a few spots and the intermission break, which presently follows the trial scene, would be more effective after the action-laden jailbreak, which would enable the second half to open up with the sea voyage.

Most of the budget has evidently gone into the production and it shows. The lengthy location work in England and the West Indies for the exteriors blend perfectly with the studio-shot interiors and merges gracefully, for the most part, into the fantasy sequences. The entire film is a tribute to the production design of Mario Chiari, the art direction of Jack Martin Smith and Ed Graves, the costumes of Ray Aghayan, the set decorations of Walter M. Scott and Stuart A. Reiss and, particularly, the special effects of L. B. Abbott, Art Cruckshank, Emil Kosa Jr. and Howard Lydecker.

Aided by Todd-AO and De Luxe Color, cameraman Robert Surtees has given the film a lush patina that is a very valuable asset to the film's production values, as are the clever, animated main titles by Don Record and Pacific Title. The Bricusse tunes, arranged and conducted by Lionel Newman and Alexander Courage, are never allowed to dominate, but are skillfully used to supplement and underscore the dialog and songs. The transition from spoken to sung dialog is uniformly smooth.

"Doctor Dolittle," an expensive piece of film, will, it seems certain, not be everyone's cup of tea but, as Newley says, *"Maybe what the Doctor tells me isn't altogether true, but I don't know any better one, do you?"* *Robe.*

Valley of the Dolls
(PANAVISION-COLOR)

Talky, sudsy version of the book. Handsome production, otherwise dull. Pre-sell from book is biggest asset for strong initial b.o.

Hollywood, Nov. 30.

Twentieth Century-Fox release of Red Lion (Mark Robson) production, produced by David Weisbart. Features entire cast. Directed by Robson. Screenplay, Helen Deutsch, Dorothy Kingsley, based on the novel by Jacqueline Susann; camera (DeLuxe Color), William H. Daniels; editor, Dorothy Spencer; music, John Williams; songs, Andre and Dory Previn; art direction; Jack Martin Smith, Richard Day; sound, Don J. Bassman, David Dockendorf; asst. director, Eli Dunn. Reviewed at 20th-Fox Studios, L.A. Nov. 29, '67. Running time, **123 MINS.**

Anne Welles .... Barbara Perkins
Neely O'Hara .... Patty Duke
Lyon Burke .... Paul Burke
Jennifer North .... Sharon Tate
Tony Polar .... Tony Scotti
Mel Anderson .... Martin Milner
Kevin Gillmore Charles Drake
Ted Casablanca .... Alex Davison
Miriam Polar .... Lee Grant
Lawyer's Secretary .... Naomi Stevens
Lawyer .... Robert H. Harris
Reporter .... Jacqueline Susann
Director .... Robert Viharo
Telethon M. C. .... Joey Bishop
Awards M.C. .... George Jessel
Helen Lawson .... Susan Hayward

If "Valley Of The Dolls" had been an original screenplay, or based on some obscure or unpublished work, it would be properly dismissed as a slick, undistinguished, high-budget programmer. Not that it's anything else, but the notoriety of the book has created a drooling pre-sell for Fox which is bound to stir up hot b.o. action, at least in first stages of release. Few assets, many liabilities mark this sex-teasing, talky sudser.

The film trade used to call such potboilers "women's pictures," market for which has diminished due to combination of near-extinct matinee weeper biz, plus over-explicit documentation of sexual mores and hang-ups in contemporary films. Jacqueline Susann's book, however, has a very good chance as a pic because of the carried-over "guess-who?" publicity gimmicks—about showbiz personalities — which helped the novel.

But word of mouth may work against the pic and heavy exploitation will help. As reported in these pages, 20th has placed, before its corporate logo, a disclaimer about similarity to real persons; this might well be exploited in advertising, too. In any case, lotsa ballyhoo is needed.

Helen Deutsch and, later, Dorothy Kingsley wrestled with the screenplay, and both are credited. The late David Weisbart endowed pic with handsome, lush production values, and Mark Robson's direction occasionally elicits sparks from the female performers. As written and directed, almost every male character is weak cardboard.

Plot meanders between New England country girl Barbara Parkins, who comes to the big city and eventually is seduced by urban social patterns; Patty Duke, rising young singing star who gets hung up on pills (Miss Susann used the word "dolls" to describe pep-calm pills; to date, she is about the only one to use the word); and Sharon Tate, playing a big-breasted, untalented, but basically sensitive girl who never finds happiness and, faced with impending breast removal because of cancer, kills herself with pills—dolls.

The misses Parkins and Tate, the latter particularly good, suffer from under-emphasis in early reels, **and corny plot resolution; Miss Parkins, for example, returns to her rural origins, presumably where life is pure and serene. Main body of the story concerns the rise, plateau and erratic performance of Miss Duke's character. For her, this is a very good role by which to command greater casting attention.**

Susan Hayward, who replaced Judy Garland in cast, does an excellent job in giving acting depth to the role of the older legit star, ever alert to remove threats to her supremacy. Her scenes with Miss Duke are particularly lively. Lee Grant again impresses with her forte of playing twitchy, nervous characters. Miss Susann herself has a bit as an inquiring newshen.

Lawyer Paul Burke, biologically-defective Tony Scotti, weak publicist Martin Milner, cosmetics manufacturer Charles Drake, and allegedly homosexual dress designer Alex Davison (whose scene involves some strictly heterosexual dalliance) are stock characters out of pulp fiction. But showbiz lawyer Robert H. Harris and foreign artie pix producer Richard Angarola give life to their minor parts. Joey Bishop and George Jessel appear as themselves in bits.

Some salty dialog is evident, and a few sex scenes are shot in silhouette. Special effects — a very amusing satire on sexy foreign pix, fictional teleblurbs, and some transitional montages—are excellent.

Cameraman William H. Daniels has caught all the inherent visual values in crisp Panavision-DeLuxe Color lensing. Art direction by Jack Martin Smith and Richard Day, and associates, is superior, ditto Travilla's wardrobe.

John (ex-Johnny) Williams' music adaptation is good. Five songs, including title theme, by Andre and Dory Previn are interpolated nicely, and logically, into plot. Dionne Warwick regularly warbles title tune.

Dorothy Spencer executed editing to a fizzling-out 123 minutes. Other credits are pro. *Murf.*

La Mujer De Otro
(Another Man's Wife)
(SPANISH-COLOR)

Madrid, Dec. 12.

Paramount release of Coral production. Directed by Rafael Gil. Screenplay, Jose Lopez Rubio, Torcuato Luca de Tena, based on novel of same title by Luca de Tena; camera (Eastmancolor), Jose F. Aguayo; music, Ernesto Halfther. Reviewed at Cine Gran Via, Madrid. Running Time, **95 MINS.**

Ana Maria .... Martha Hyer
Andres .... John Ronane
Pepa .... Analia Gade
Enrique .... Angel del Pozo
Father .... Fosco Giachetti

At least on paper, this Paramount release should have had an even chance: a new theme for Spanish films (adultery), based on a prize winning novel, directed by veteran Rafael Gil and with an American star, Martha Hyer. Unfortunately it does not come close to its promise. Too many trite situations, teary closeups and heavy-handed flashbacks will appeal mainly to less demanding Spanish audiences. Outside of Spain, only similar Latino situations might seem indicated.

Plot is fairly conventional: rich housewife and mother Ana Maria (Martha Hyer) whose husband is too interested in business, meets her old college boyfriend Andres (John Ronane), also married and now a successful painter. He wants to begin again where they left off.

Unfortunately the mood and plausibility are broken by the appearance of Ana Maria's long lost father, now a pauper, who left the family when she was just a little girl and whom she has not seen since. Just as she is about to run away with Andres to Paris, the father, alerted by a friend of Ana Maria's, shows up and, after a tearful reunion, convinces her to return to her family. He goes along to live in luxury.

As usual director Rafael Gil has tried to mix humor into a basically serious story—the busybody girl friend, salt-of-the-earth taxidriver and smart-alecky kids seem right out of his latest musical comedy. Just when the story demands some treatment in depth, the comic relief appears to divert the audience and avoid a confrontation with any meaning. By fadeout there is no resolution, since the wronged husband and wife do not even know they have been deceived and neither adulterer has righted the home situation that drove them into sin. Given the banality of some of the lines, the acting is okay. Technical credits are pro.

Lyon.

The Graduate
(PANAVISION—COLOR)

Excellent comedy directed by Mike Nichols. Hot b.o. in the young market.

Hollywood, Dec. 9.
Embassy Pictures release, produced by Lawrence Turman. Features Anne Bancroft, Dustin Hoffman, Katharine Ross. Directed by Mike Nichols. Screenplay, Calder Willingham, Buck Henry, based on novel by Charles Webb; camera (Technicolor), Robert Surtees; editor, Sam O'Steen; music, Dave Grusin; songs, Paul Simon; production design, Richard Sylbert; sound, Jack Solomon; asst. director, Don Kranze. Reviewed at Samuel Goldwyn Studios, L.A., Dec. 8, '67. Running Time, **105 MINS.**

Mrs. Robinson	Anne Bancroft
Ben Braddock	Dustin Hoffman
Elaine Robinson	Katharine Ross
Mr. Braddock	William Daniels
Mr. Robinson	Murray Hamilton
Mrs. Braddock	Elizabeth Wilson
Carl Smith	Brian Avery
Mr. Maguire	Walter Brooke
Mr. McCleery	Norman Fell
Second Lady	Elizabeth Fraser
Mrs. Singleman	Alice Ghostley
Room Clerk	Buck Henry
Miss De Witt	Marion Lorne

"The Graduate" is a delightful, satirical comedy-drama about a young man's seduction by an older woman, and the measure of maturity which he attains from the experience. Anne Bancroft, Katharine Ross and relative newcomer Dustin Hoffman head a very competent cast. Mike Nichols directed in modern, uptight fashion, which wears well for two-thirds of the pic, and producer Lawrence Turman has supplied all the necessary props of a materialistic society. The young market, particularly, will dig this Embassy release (overseas, United Artists), and older audiences also will be amused. Strong b.o. prospects are likely in initial exclusive bookings, as a setup for a hotsy general playoff.

An excellent screenplay by Calder Willingham and comedy specialist Buck Henry, based on the Charles Webb novel, focuses on Hoffman, just out of college and wondering what it's all about. Predatory Miss Bancroft, wife of Murray Hamilton, introduces Hoffman to mechanical sex, reaction to which evolves into true love with Miss Ross, Miss Bancroft's daughter.

Had the story been told in terms of straight drama, it would have been one of those boring modern mellers — the hippie equivalent of a woman's pic — in which vacant stares are supposed to convey emotion and plot action, and jazzed up cinematics become obvious and pretentious. To be sure, Nichols, in his second feature film, has laid on, with a trowel, most of th current gimmicks, but, thanks to a strong script, they are not noticeable for most of the film.

In the 70 minutes which elapse from Hoffman's arrival home from school to the realization by Miss Ross that he has had an affair with her mother, pic is loaded with hilarious comedy and, because of this, the intended commentary on materialistic society is most effective. Only in retrospect does one realize a basic, but not overly damaging, flaw: Hoffman's achievements in school are not credible in light of his basic shyness. No matter, or not much, anyway.

Miss Bancroft, feline and slinky in a manner very much like Lauren Bacall, is excellent, as is Miss Ross, an exciting, fresh actress, from the Universal stable, who has a long career ahead of her. Hoffman is perfect in his role. William Daniels and Elizabeth Wilson play his parents in top fashion. Small, but well-cast, supporting contingent includes co-scripter Henry, as a room clerk.

Only in the final 35 minutes, as Hoffman drives up and down the L.A.-Frisco route in pursuit of Miss Ross, does film falter in pacing, result of which the switched-on cinematics become obvious, and therefore tiring. Vet cameraman Robert Surtees used Panavision and Technicolor to desired advantage. It would be wrong to say that Surtees has "turned on" to new techniques; more precisely, and more importantly, he is responsive to the desire for a modern look. In other words, he is a professional craftsman.

Richard Sylbert's production design is outstanding, again. Paul Simon wrote the good songs, sung by Simon & Garfunkel, and Dave Grusin's incidental music is equally adroit. Sam O'Steen's editing is sharp, and other technical credits are strong. Count this one a winner for Joseph E. Levine, Turman and Nichols.

Murf.

The President's Analyst
(PANAVISION—COLOR)

Excellent satire of modern U.S. politics and espionage. Strongest appeal in youth market.

Hollywood, Dec. 13.
Paramount Pictures release of a Panpiper Production; executive producer, Howard W. Koch; produced by Stanley Rubin. Stars James Coburn. Written and directed by Theodore J. Flicker. Camera (Technicolor), William A. Fraker; editor, Stuart Pappe; music, Lalo Schifrin; songs, Barry Maguire, Paul Potash, The Clear Light; production design, Pato Guzman; sound, Robert L. Post, John Wilkinson; asst. director, Kurt Neumann. Reviewed at Directors Guild of America, L.A., Dec. 12, '67. Running Time, **103 MINS.**

Dr. Schaefer	James Coburn
Don Masters	Godfrey Cambridge
Kropotkin	Severn Darden
Nan Butler	Joan Delaney
Arlington Hewes	Pat Harrington
Old Wrangler	Barry Maguire
Snow White	Jill Banner
Ethan Allan Cocket	Eduard Franz
Henry Lux	Walter Burke
Dr. Evans	Will Geer
Wynn Quantrill	William Daniels
Jeff Quantrill	Joan Darling
Bing Quantrill	Sheldon Collins
Sullivan	Arte Johnson
Puddlians	Martin Horsey, William Beckley
Tourist	Kathleen Hughes

"The President's Analyst" is a superior satire on some sacred cows of contemporary society, principally the lightly camouflaged FBI, hippies, psychiatry, liberal and conservative politics—and the telephone company. Inventive story peg—James Coburn starring as the personal analyst to the President of the U.S.—is fleshed out with hilarious incdents which zero in on, and hit, their targets. So telling is the commentary that the Paramount release may find its major, market among anti-establishment youth. Best thing that could happen, b.o.-wise, would be for film to be blasted by the Old Guard.

A significant amount of guts has been demonstrated by exec producer Howard W. Koch, producer Stanley Rubin, writer-director Theodore J. Flicker, Coburn (and his own Panpiper indie), as well as bankrolling Paramount, to make such a film. The funny, ironic, and even terrifying side of contemporary American life, as well as the bland public relations by which so many loose ends are (or were) tidied up, get an analysis which reveals the patent non sequiturs. Not that the pic will change anything, but there is a measure of relief engendered by such an expose.

Despite a facetious disclaimer (right after the Par logo) of resemblance to existing groups, the real-life counterparts are obvious, if not in name, (FBR, CEA are used) at least by type. Coburn, a practicing psychiatrist, is selcted to be the President's analyst so that the latter can have someone to talk to. This serves to introduce Walter Burke, as the J. Edgar Hoover counterpart, and Eduard Franz, obvious head of the CIA.

The Burke and Franz dialog and acting capture perfectly the images which, rightly or wrongly, persist in the minds of many.

William Daniels also scores as an upper-middle class compulsive liberal, whose family practices marksmanship, karate and eavesdropping because of right-wing neighbors. Barry Maguire and Jill Banner are hippies, and Miss Banner's sex scene with Coburn—in fields of flowers right out of some cosmetics teleblurb—is a comedy highlight in which several foreign and domestic spies kill each other off as they plot Coburn's demise.

Eventually Coburn, pursued by multiple agents, finds that the prime heavy is the telephone company. Pat Harrington excels as the glib automaton (his words are fed in via a plug connection to his heel) who wants Coburn to intercede with the President for a money-making scheme. Joan Delaney plays Coburn's mistress, herself an agent. Fadeout finds all hands, including Coburn, still enjoying the System, and just as much victims of it as before.

Pic probably will offend some audience segments, particularly those who tend to rationalize conduct on the basis of who are the official "good" and "bad" guys, of the moment, that is. Sophisticated audiences and questioning youth will be more appreciative. Flicker's script and direction are very good. Coburn's strong performance is a vital asset, since his character is the only one who questions what this madness is all about.

William A. Fraker' excellent Panavision Technicolor lensing, Pato Guzman's colorful production design, and other technical credits enhance overall impact. Lalo Schifrin's score, and incidental songs by Maguire, Paul Potash, The Clear Light, Schifrin and Flicker, create a modern sound. Stuart Pappe edited to a good 103 minutes, perrhaps a bit long in final reel.

Murf.

The Hippie Revolt
(DOCUMENTARY—COLOR)

Superficial and tedious visit to Haight-Ashbury and environs which emphasizes the most spectacular manifestations of the hippie movement. Initial b.o. promise, but word-of-mouth will hurt.

Belish-Fremont release of Art Lieberman production. Directed and photographed (Technicolor) by Edgar Beatty. Commentary, improvised; music, Tom Bahler, John Bahler, performed by The Love Generation; editor, Robert Springer. Previewed in N.Y., Dec. 11, '67. Running Time, **85 MINS.**

This superficial and tedious film purports to "tell it like it is" about hippie life on the West Coast, but director Edgar Beatty has chosen to let his cameras film only the most spectacular and public manifestations of the movement. Consequently the picture presents little not already seen numerous times on television news reports. Strong initial response on basis of subject matter can be expected from urban youth, but word-of-mouth should dissipate audiences. "The Hippie Revolt" is a drag.

Would-be hippies or older members of the "straight" world will have few of their questions answered by this film. When not turning on with drugs, dancing the frug on the grass or strolling on Haight St., how do hippies live? How do they sleep, eat, get money, etc.? A motion picture which took us "inside" this sub-culture would be most welcome, but Beatty concentrates on drug sessions, freakouts, demonstrations, etc. Not only do these become unbearably boring to a non-participant, but the motivational information communicated is miniscule.

Beatty tries to make up for this via a continuous commentary by the hippies themselves in which they rationalize their way of life, defend drug usage, etc. Usually only one sentence per person is heard before the next chimes in. Most often what is being heard on the soundtrack has no direct relationship with the concurrent visuals. And the words are so abstract and general that they too convey little to the spectator. The boredom becomes complete.

A director of television commercials for eight years, Beatty tries some fancy camerawork in the film. There's a long dance sequence during which the lights flick on and off in discotheque fashion. Once the "psychedelic" message is received, the scene becomes eye-strainingly endless.

Sequences were shot during four months this spring and summer in San Francisco, Los Angeles and a rural commune monickered Strawberry Fields. This last is especially disappointing as Beatty displays no interest in the economics and living conditions involved but instead shows a round-table discussion on philosophies of life. Potential talking points in "The Hippie Revolt" include a body-painting session and several hippie "marriages." *Byro.*

The Ambushers
(COLOR)

Third Matt Helm spy pic with Dean Martin. Okay exploitation item on duals.

Hollywood, Dec. 12.

Columbia Pictures release of Meadway-Claude (Irving Allen) Production. Stars Dean Martin. Directed by Henry Levin. Screenplay, Herbert Baker, based on the book by Donald Hamilton; camera (Technicol), Burnett Guffey, Edward Colman; second unit camera, Jack Marta, Tony Braun; editor, Harold F. Kress; music, Hugo Montenegro; title song, Baker, Montenegro; art direction, Joe Wright; sound, Charles J. Rice, James Flaster, Jack Haynes, asst. director, Jerome M. Siegel; second unit director, James Havens. Reviewed at Columbia Studios, L.A., Dec. 11, '67. Running Time, 101 MINS.
Matt Helm .... Dean Martin
Francesca .... Senta Berger
Sheila .... Janice Rule
MacDonald .... James Gregory
Ortega .... Albert Salmi
Quintana .... Kurt Kasznar
Lovey .... Beverly Adams
Nassim .... David Mauro
Karl .... Roy Jenson
Rocco .... John Brascia
Linda .... Linda Foster

The warnings are clear from "The Ambushers:" if the Dean Martin gumshoe series is to merit uppercase continuation, it had better shape up better in the script and direction departments. This third Matt Helm pic, in which violence is soft-pedalled, starts out with silly double entendre, then shifts for last half to tedious plot resolution right out of old serials. While production values remain strong, acting, writing and direction are pedestrian. Irving Allen's production needs big exploitation and fast playoff, plus a good dual bill mate, for satisfactory b.o.

Film re-teams from "Murderer's Row," second in series, director Henry Levin, adapter (from Donald Hamilton's books) Herbert Baker, and thesps James Gregory (Martin's dour espionage boss) and Beverly Adams (Martin's secretary). Gone from the days of "The Silencers," first in series, are action director Phil Karlson, and scripter Oscar Saul.

Plot is simple: U.S. flying saucer-ess Janice Rule is kidnapped by despicable beast Albert Salmi; Gregory sends Martin to find out why; Senta Berger reps another foreign government (lucky place, too); Kurt Kasznar is a funny bad guy — a Mexican beer baron; assorted heavies get their deserts. Not a bad story line for a formula pic, as long as the filmmakers do not make audiences too consciously aware of the formula.

Baker's script adds no new clever ideas. The same old leery wheezes crop up to the point of being ludicrous. Martin at times becomes a caricature of himself playing himself, and comes across as a male Mae West. Gadgets and gimmicks are in less profusion than before. Final reels are little more than distended, predictable serial episodes.

Although visual aspects — the Oleg Cassini wardrobe and overall fashion supervision — are very

good, pic at same time has that slapdash quickie look. Second unit lensing, in Mexico, is poorly matched to soundstage mountain greenery. Title song has a good bounce. Other credits (see box) are adequate. *Murf.*

Knives of the Avenger
(I Coltelli dei Vendicatori)
(ITALIAN—COLOR—TECHNISCOPE)

A real surprise: a beautifully-designed and exciting Viking tale from a pseudonymous Mario Bava. Only subject and cast make this a programmer —but it's a top one.

World Entertainment release of a Sider Films (P. Tagliaferri) production. Features Cameron Mitchell. Directed by John Hold (Mario Bava). Screenplay, Alberto Liberati; camera (Technicolor), Anthony (Antonio) Renaldi; music, Marcello Giambini; editor, Othello; asst. director, Robert Glands; sound, Peter Danielson. Reviewed at Selwyn Theatre, N.Y., Nov. 28, '67. Running Time, 86 MINS.
Rurik .... Cameron Mitchell
Aghen .... Fausto Tozzi
Moki .... Luciana Polletin
Karen .... Elissa Picelli
Arald .... Jack Stewart

(Dubbed English Soundtrack)

This Viking tale shot in Italy with Yank actor Cameron Mitchell is one of the real surprises of the year. Its careful craftsmanship and really original and exciting action sequences put it head and and shoulders above any other programmer recently put on the U.S. market, and it should be a top choice for any exhib seeking strong supporter fare. In fact it is only the film's subject matter, poor marquee values and Italian nationality which condemn it to this status, plus an often unintelligible dubbing job. Otherwise "Knives of the Avenger" puts much of Hollywood's high-budget action product to shame.

Of the scores of new Italian directors who have emerged as a result of the recent spear-and-sandal and current oater booms, only two or three have shown any real distinction, and Mario Bava has long been recognized as being one of them. The "John Hold" who is credited with "Knives of the Avenger" is actually Bava working under his *nom de service*, and this former director of photography has brought to the film a real eye for lighting and settings.

Rarely has a "barbarian" world been seen in such beauty. With certain dramatic exceptions, the film has been entirely decorated in "burnt" shades of gold, brown and green. The interior of one house is a veritable jungle of hanging objects (vegetables, knives, etc.), and there is a richly-detailed wedding ceremony. One fight scene is set against an ocean at dusk, and Bava's use of light and shadow here is most impressive. Even the well-known graininess of the Techniscope process when used on exteriors works to an advantage in this and other scenes: a certain "diffused" quality emerges which is consistent with the film's visual style.

Story has Mitchell as a stranded king who defends a woman and child against villanous enemies;

the woman, played by Elissa Picelli, awaits her husband, who has been at sea three years and is presumed lost. Mitchell's amorous advances are foiled when the husband (Jack Stewart) suddenly returns, but he remains to defeat the chief antagonist (Fausto Tozzi).

What is so curious about all this is that the film is more a "western" in the Hollywood sense than is any oater ground out at Cinecitta — for it presents the serviceable western legend of the tired fighter who must perform one last moral mission even though he wishes to give up the life of action. The genuine gentleness of the scenes between Mitchell and the young boy (Luciana Polletin) are obviously inspired by "Shane," as is the finale when the hero, alone once more, rides away into the distance.

Mitchell often achieves that deep, brooding, fatalistic quality which Gary Cooper or Alan Ladd sometimes brought to this kind of role.

It's hard to judge the other players, all of whom spoke Italian on set, but they seem adequate and Miss Picelli is quite beautiful.

Under Bava's direction the camerawork of Antonio Renaldi is a knockout and other technical credits are fine. The film's action set piece is a lengthy fight in a tavern in which Mitchell produces and throws scores of knives in a fashion even more rapid-fire than Clint Eastwood shoots bullets. It, like everything else, is expertly handled by Bava. *Byro.*

Good Morning . . . And Goodbye
(COLOR)

Well made Russ Meyer sexploitation drama, better scripted than usual. Good b.o. prospects in its market.

Hollywood, Dec. 1.

Eve Productions release, produced, directed and photographed by Russ Meyer. Features entire cast. Screenplay, John E. Moran, based on a story by Meyer; editors, Meyer, Richard Brummer; music, Igo Kantor; sound, Brummer, Moran; asst. director, George Costello. Reviewed at Samuel Goldwyn Studios, L.A., Nov. 30, '67. Running Time, 78 MINS.
Angel .... Alaina Capri
Burt .... Stuart Lancaster
Stone .... Pat Wright
Witch .... Haji
Lana .... Karen Ciral
Ray .... Don Johnson
Herb .... Tom Howland
Lottie .... Megan Timothy
Betty .... Toby Adler
Dancer .... Sylvia Tedemar
Nude .... Carol Peters

Russ Meyer, whose latterday films have relied on largely unmotivated, gratuitous sex and violence, has a stronger script in "Good Morning...And Good Bye." Violence is sparse, but logically developed, while emphasis is on sexual promiscuity. Producer-director-photographer Meyer filmed his latest in color for about the usual $60,000, and with the usual camera and live sound craftsmanship. Another strong b.o. bet for male-oriented situations, as well as houses which occasionally depart from regular film policy.

Among American indie filmmakers, Meyer is somewhat unique. He has a solid commercial reputation among patrons of raw film fare for his frank pix, yet he is largely un-

discovered by aesthetes who fawn over much lesser product from foreign and domestic obscurities.

At the same time, as some major studio product becomes more violent and sexy, without defensible script motivation, Meyer is paying greater attention to character development and dramatic structure. Meyer, who qualifies as an auteur, is making definite progress.

John E. Moran is credited with the screenplay, from a Meyer story, which turns on the marital sex frustration of Alaina Capri and Stuart Lancaster. Latter, abandoned earlier by first wife but left with daughter Karen Ciral, is not sufficiently sexy to satisfy the new wife, who is giving it away all over the county. Pat Wright, a construction boss, is her favored playmate but also finds time to make it with Megan Timothy, wife of his helper, Tom Howland. Surfer-type Don Johnson enters as Miss Ciral's boyfriend.

Script is flawed by a supernatural character, played by Haji, who turns on Lancaster so he can become the compleat husband. Role seems little more than an excuse to get another good looker into the film, and the dramatic backlash affects Lancaster's part. He, a Meyer regular, is an excellent character actor not showcased to good effect here.

Surprise in the plotting is that some key characters have depth: Miss Capri, admittedly promiscuous, repeatedly and consistently shows a love-hate duality; Wright, a gutsy actor of merit, is seen as a pitiable stud who has all the dames he wants, but nothing ahead of him except old age; Miss Ciral has some good moments as a teenager who is confused, understandably, about sex and love.

Film suffers from overabundance of double entendre (at times so Mae West-ian as to draw unwanted laughs), over-modulated music excerpts, supervised by Igo Kantor, which get heavy-handed, and overdone narration in prolog. Camera work, on bodies, breasts, buttocks and also in dramatic scenes, is excellent. Meyer's wife, Eve, once his camera subject, now serves as associate producer and femme film salesman in their Eve Prods. releasing indie. *Murf.*

The Catalina Caper
(COLOR—SONGS)

Last (?) of the beach-party imitations is an inane bore. A possible programmer in those markets where the genre still draws.

Crown International release of Executive Pictures (Bond Blackman and Jack Bartlett) production; executive producer, Sherman H. Dryer. Features Tommy Kirk, Del Moore, Peter Duryea, Robert Donner, Ulla Stromstedt. Directed by Lee Sholem. Screenplay, Clyde Ware, from story by Sam Pierce; camera (no color process credited), Ted Mikels; music, Jerry Long; editor, Herman Freedman; asst. dir., Dick Dixon; sound, Rod Sutton. Reviewed at UA Riverside Theatre, N.Y., Dec. 14, '67. Running Time, 84 MINS.
Don .... Tommy Kirk
Arthur Duvall .... Del Moore
Tad .... Peter Duryea
Fingers .... Robert Donner
Katrina .... Ulla Stromstedt
Larry .... Jim Bagg
Bob Draper .... Mike Blodgett
Tina .... Venita Wolf

Borman .... Peter Mamakos
Themselves .... Little Richard, Carol Connors, The Cascades

This is pretty insubstantial of its kind but even if it had been done better "The Catalina Caper" would face an unresponsive market. The "beach party" cycle ended about a year-and-a-half ago and there's already a quaintness and curio value about "Caper." Exhibs who want a change of pace from westerns and spypix might try the film as second feature fare; it'll work in those territories where the grosses for the last few beach-party epics weren't disappointing.

American International's Frankie Avalon-Annette Funicello beach series had its share of drivel, but at least there was a kookiness sometimes apparent, some charming (if repetitive) sarcasm of adult mores and a general esprit de corps. "The Catalina Caper" takes on whole some aspects of the AIP formula (the criminals are all "creeps," for example), but it is labored and boring because the kids themselves are all of the healthy, handsome variety and there are no character juveniles of the likes of Jody McCrea, who used to provide comic relief in the AIP productions.

Actually, film's cast is headed by AIP's own Tommy Kirk. He's his usual goody-good self, helping a group of frugging teenyboppers on Catalina to nab two gangs of art thieves. But everything's been underehearsed and/or done in one take, with result that all lines are read with little inflection. The girls, per usual, are gorgeous and the men good-looking.

Some well-known recording stars of a couple of years back were brought along, and interrupt the proceedings at awkward moments in order to perform a rock tune. These include Little Richard ("Scuba Party"), Carol Connors ("Book of Love") and the Cascades ("There's a New World Opening for Me"). In addition, Mary Wells warbles a number over the main titles — the best thing in the film, incidentally, as executed by Hollywood's Murakami-Wolf Productions.

Producers Bond Blackman and Jack Bartlett entrusted direction of the Clyde Ware screenplay to Hollywood vet Lee Sholem. The touch of William Asher, the (relatively) young director who created the "beach party" series for AIP, is sorely missing. *Byro.*

A Man Called Dagger
(COLOR)

Lowercase secret agent spoof.

Hollywood, Dec. 14.

Metro release of Lewis M. Horwitz production. Stars Terry Moore, Jan Murray, Paul Mantee, Sue Ane Langdon; features Eileen O'Neill, Maureen Arthur. Directed by Richard Rush. Screenplay, James Peatman, Robert S. Weekley; based on idea by W. L. Riffs; camera (Metrocolor), Leslie Kovacs; editor, Len Miller; music, Steve Allen; art direction, Mike McCloskey; sound, Franklin Milton; asst. director, Steve Bernhardt. Reviewed at Metro Studios, Dec. 13, '67. Running Time, **88 MINS.**

Harper Davis .... Terry Moore
Rudolph Koffman .... Jan Murray
(SS Obergruppenfuhrer Hans Leitel)
Ingrid Toren .... Sue Ane Langdon
Richard Dagger .... Paul Mantee
Erica .... Eileen O'Neill
Joy .... Maureen Arthur
Dr. Rainer .... Leonard Stone
Melissa .... Mimi Dillard
Otto .... Richard Kiel
Dr. Grulik .... Bruno Ve Sota

Avalanche of secret agent spoofs that has surefeited the market in wake of James Bond success on screen is not materially advanced in this Metro release. Acts which the man called Dagger, probably world's most indestructible and expressionless agent (but whose agent, that's the question), performs, are surpassed only by what the audience is called upon to swallow. In short, for the least discriminating action houses.

Lewis M. Horwitz production unfolds mostly in Los Angeles, where Dagger has followed an ex-Nazi scientist from Europe. Latter has made trek to join a former SS colonel and concentration camp commandant whose plan is to conquer the world by mentally subjecting leaders of the various world governments and others in key positions. Operation calls for him first to kidnap and brainwash them, then implant small radio receivers in their teeth which will give him total control over them. Dagger, as you can see, has his work cut out for him, but Dagger wins out and the erstwhile SSer winds up on a meat hook.

Credibility is a quality unheard of in script by James Peatman and Robert S. Weekley, based on an idea by W. L. Riffs. Bond, Flint and all the rest wouldn't stand a chance with Dagger, who makes use of wondrous weapons as he surmounts all odds. Direction by Richard Rush is as good as script will permit in fast movement, but his handling of people is unsure.

Cast gives stock performances, with no standouts. Terry Moore, top-billed, is in for marquee dressing only and in her few scenes is nearly unrecognizable. Paul Mantee plays Dagger, and Jan Murray the ex-Nazi leader. Eileen O'Neill and Maureen Arthur are additional distaffers, Sue Ane Langdon is unbievable.

Technical credits are okay.
Whit.

Les Tetes Brulees
(The Hotheads)
(FRENCH)
(COLOR)

Paris, Dec. 12.

Valoria release of Sport Films, Valoria Films, Cocifra, Kalender production. Stars Lang Jeffries, Estella, Blain; features Philippe Clay, Jacques Dufilho, Carnardel, Irene Cabas. Directed by Willy Rozier. Screenplay, Rozier, Xavier Walter from book by Jean-Louis Cotte; camera (Eastmancolor), Michel Rocca; editor, Madeleine Cretolle. At Lutetia, Paris. Running Time, **100 MINS.**

Jonathon .... Lang Jeffries
Lucia .... Estella Balin
Precheur .... Philippe Clay
Dante .... Jacques Dufilho
Sebastien .... Carnardel
Therese .... Irene Cabas

Average adventure opus concerns some truckers in Africa getting caught between the French and some warring Arab factions. They are just out for the money and are mainly destroyed as they get between the two fighting groups. But lacklustre direction, ordinary thesping and stilted scripting make this primarily a home item, with perhaps some dualer use possible elsewhere via its action segments.

The truckers go off to deliver some trucks to an Arab group in revolt but are made prisoners and finally nearly wiped out when the fighting starts. There is a comely blonde widow, an American adventurer and some assorted French types. Love blossoms between widow and the Yank before they are both shot down as a few survivors trek off into the distance.

Stereotyped characters, surface characterization and a vague storyline keep this crawling along. Lang Jefferies is the Yank but can't do much with the callow character he plays. Estella Blain, a blonde French actress, looks out of place and too well groomed for her desert adventures. This is technically passable. *Mosk.*

Les Grands Vacances
(The Big Vacation)
(FRENCH—COLOR)

Paris, Dec. 19.

Valoria release of Copernic, Fida Cinematografica production. Stars Louis De Funes; features Ferdy Mayne, Claude Gensac, Martine Kelly, Francois Leccia, Olivier De Funes. Directed by Jean Girault. Screenplay, Marcel Grignon; editor, Jean-Michel Gautier. At Ambassade-Gaumont, Paris. Running Time, **95 MINS.**

Bosquier .... Louis De Funes
Wife .... Claude Gensac
Girl .... Martine Kelly
Father .... Ferdy Mayne
Gerard .... Olivier De Funes
Philippe .... Francois Leccia

Louis De Funes now has three pix in firstrun situations here and all are doing big biz. He is a middleaged comic actor, who manages to be overbearing and seemingly selfish and yet show some human weaknesses to keep his pix from being smug or nasty. They do bowl along, have good production dress and this, like the others, have enough invention and comic imbroglios to make it good fodder here. But does not look meaty enough for much offshore chances.

Here, De Funes runs a private boarding school where he rules tyrannically with the help of an informer son and a silly wife. But an older son goes off on a cruise rather than to England, where he is replaced by another student. This is the main thread of the yarn to keep the situations perking. Usual French and British stereotypes abound as De Funes tries to find his runaway son and the daughter of a rich Britisher.

There are some good comic chases and fights. De Funes is funny in his own right as he sputters and asserts his ways with the vulnerable undertones that is the mark of knockabout comedy. Others are mainly foils for De Funes's tantrums, with Martine Kelley, a Yank, playing a British ingenue with freshness. Others are acceptable as they feel the wrath or shy pacification of De Funes's ways. If he ever gets the right vehicle De Funes may well make a dent on world marts just as he has at home.
Mosk.

Fitzwilly
(PANAVISION-COLOR)

So-so comedy starring Dick Van Dyke as gentleman robber. Needs good lowercase partner in general situations.

Hollywood, Nov. 18.

United Artists release of a Mirisch Corp.-Dramatic Features Inc. presentation, produced by Walter Mirisch. Stars Dick Van Dyke. Directed by Delbert Mann. Screenplay, Isobel Lennart, based on the novel, "A Garden of Cucumbers," by Poyntz Tyler; camera (DeLuxe Color), Joseph Biroc; editor, Ralph Winters; music, Johnny Williams; song lyric, Alan and Marilyn Bergman; art direction, Robert F. Boyle; sound, Robert Martin, Robert A. Reich, Clem Portman; asst. director, Terry Nelson. Reviewed at Academy Award Theatre, L.A., Nov. 17, '67. Running Time, **102 MINS.**

Fitzwilliam .... Dick Van Dyke
Juliet .... Barbara Feldon
Victoria .... Edith Evans
Albert .... John McGiver
Mr. Nowell .... Harry Townes
Mr. Dunne .... John Fiedler
Oderblatz .... Norman Fell
Buckmaster .... Cecil Kellaway
Casey .... Stephen Strimpell
Grimsby .... Anne Seymour
Mrs. Mortimer .... Helen Kleeb
Oliver .... Sam Waterston
Prettikin .... Paul Reed
Cotty .... Laurence Naismith

Dick Van Dyke is the major selling point in the title role of "Fitzwilly," an okay, but sluggish, comedy about a butler who masterminds robberies. Potential in the screenplay, the very good cast, and the handsome Walter Mirisch production, is not realized due to generally tame direction by Delbert Mann. A zesty climactic sequence, however, is an asset, but it's a long time in coming. Year-end b.o. surge will help the United Artists release to achieve satisfactory results on general duals.

Isobel Lennart adapted Poyntz Tyler's novel, "A Garden of Cucumbers," in which Van Dyke is the devoted butler to Edith Evans, one of those lovable biddies who, in this case, is not at all as wealthy as she thinks. Van Dyke and crew keep planning heists in order to support her fantasies, and philanthropies. Arrival of new secretary Barbara Feldon upsets the smooth-running machinery.

Film opens strongly with a neat, artistically economical establishment of Van Dyke's character, the basic situation, and Miss Evans' warm-hearted daffiness. But after first reel, pace limps along for about an hour as Miss Feldon (in her film debut, according to production notes) becomes romantically attached to Van Dyke after N.Y. department store—is excellent film comedy.

Accomplices in Van Dyke's plans include footman John McGiver (whose conscience pangs—he's an ex-minister—sparks the fadeout), maids Anne Seymour and Helen Kleeb, and chauffer Sam Waterston. Victims of the various heists include music store clerk John Fiedler, cashier Norman Fell, and chief guard Paul Reed. Harry Townes plays Miss Feldon's scholarly dad, whose friend, publisher Lawrence Naismith, has a hand in the happy ending. Cecil Kellaway and Stephen Strimpell have okay bits.

Results of the flat direction is a pic that, in the main, draws smiles, not outright laughs, until the department store panic scene, staged in top fashion. In the plugola department, a sporting goods line gets a strong play, and a low-calorie beverage push is as chilling in its callousness as the drink says it is in its own, paid advertising.

Joseph Biroc's Panavision-DeLuxe Color lensing is good, as are other technical credits. Johnny Williams' score, and the Alan and Marilyn Bergman song, are bright spots. Ralph Winters executed editing to mopey 102 minutes.
Murf.

Fantasterne
(Dreamers)
(DANISH)

Paris, Dec. 12.

Teatrenes Films, Kontor A/S production and release. With Sisse Reingard, Per Bentzon, Peter Bierlich, Gertie Jung. Directed by Kirsten Stenbaek. Screenplay, Bent Grasten, Stenbaek; music, Erik Moseholm; camera, Mikael Slaomon; editor, Kasper Schyberg. Previewed in Paris. Running Time, 87 MINS.

Else	Sisse Reingard
Harald	Per Bentzon
William	Peter Bierlich
Isabella	Gertie Jung

The Danes have usually contributed sagas, sex pix, solid comedies or sagacious dramas to the film scene. Here a femme director goes against the tide with a fairly zany, madcap comedy about a trio of outsiders who represent all the former types, with songs and dances to boot, plus well assimilated influences of Yank musicals and comedies plus French New Wave techniques.

All this does not jell completely, and there is a tendency to be a bit too determinedly offbeat, using the idea of this trio writing a script in lieu of any true thread of story, more discernible satire and needed characterization. So a couple has a tagalong friend who seduces the girl, but then goes off enticed by another girl.

Based on Danish eccentrics, it has them thumbing their noses at Scandanavian sobriety, sex anxieties and most so-called social taboos. Love scenes are frisky if to the point, dialog is brash and an undulating nudie keeps reppearing throughout the film. Some of the songs have parodic point but some are just thrown in for their own sake. But the music is catchy and the players personable. This is technically fine.

This is a specialized offbeater but has handles for arty and even exploitation use abroad on its brashness and good spirits. It is just that director Kirsten Stenbaek is sometimes too obscure for outlanders in many national allusions and needs more coherence, point and theme in the future for more chances in offshore spots. But this is a promising film from Denmark.

Mosk.

Follow That Camel
(BRITISH—COLOR)

Phil Silvers joins Britain's 'Carry On' series. Latest is hokum formula as before.

London, Dec. 15.

Rank release of Peter Rogers production. Stars Phil Silvers, Kenneth Williams, Jim Dale, Charles Hawtrey, Joan Sims, Angela Douglas, Peter Butterworth, Bernard Bresslaw, Anita Harris. Directed by Gerald Thomas. Screenplay, Talbot Rothwell; camera (Eastmancolor), Alan Hume; music, Eric Rogers; editor, Alfred Roome; asst. director, David Bracknell. Reviewed at Leicester Square Theatre, London, Dec. 14, '67. Running Time, 95 MINS.

Sergeant Nocker	Phil Silvers
Bertram Oliphant West	Jim Dale
Simpson	Peter Butterworth
Captain Le Pice	Charles Hawtrey
Commandant Burger	Kenneth Williams
Corktip	Anita Harris
Zigzig	Joan Sims
Abdul	Bernard Bresslaw
Lady Jane Ponsonby	Angela Douglas
Corporal Clotski	John Bluthal
Riff	Larry Taylor
Raff	William Hurndell
Algerian Spiv	Gertan Klauber
Bagshaw	Peter Gilmore
Doctor	Julian Orchard
Ponsonby	William Mervyn
Ticket Collector	Julian Holloway
Ship's Officer	Vincent Ball
Hotel Manager	David Glover

Coming from the tried-and-true stable still turning out the "Carry On" features, this one has all the same ingredients, stirred with plenty of salt and spice. With the familiar farsical team practically intact and a script that goes even further in the direction of healthy punning vulgarity, good b.o. grosses are predictable in Britain. For the U.S. mart, additional marquee bait is the inclusion of Phil Silvers, and, though he doesn't happily fit this peculiarly British idiom, he adds some relish.

Talbot Rothwell's story line provides adequate excuse for a foray into the Foreign Legion territory, with a young hero (Jim Dale), accused of cheating at cricket, enlisting with his manservant to exculpate his disgrace. There he encounters Phil Silvers, as a Sergeant who invents acts of heroism and is much decorated (a close relation of the Bilko character, but less well applied with witty patter), Kenneth Williams as the German commanding officer, Charles Hawtrey, as his deft adjutant, and Joan Simps, as a much-cleavage siren. They are involved in running skirmishes with an Arab chieftain, serivrng a master called Mustapha Leak, and the farrago climaxes in a hilarious battle at a desert fort, after a forced march through waterless wastes.

It all works with considerable bounce, with elements of parody of "Beau Geste"-style movies for those alert to them. All the regular comics are on first-rate form, though Hawtrey's role is diminished to give him fewer chances. Williams, in particular, is especially funny as the spended commander, with his fluting voice and foolish dignity. Joan Sims scores as the local available lady, hand on hip and looking sultry—a witty sendup of every gal who took a soldier's mind off his ammunition. Bernard Bresslaw also makes the utmost of his native desperade, and Jim Dale makes a suitably craven hero.

But one chief asset of this one is the delicious performance by Angela Douglas, as Dale's English girl who follows him out to the desert and takes attacks on her virginity with superb aplomb. Typical of the gags is the entrance of the ship's steward, on her voyage out, who turns out the lights with a view to "closing the porthole." There's a teeming host of such double entendres, some so close to the knuckle that the very innocent won't grab the point.

Peter Rogers' production effectively disguises the fact that the company didn't stray from Britain even for its sandy vistas, and Gerald Thomas's skilled and able direction gives the whole thing a spanking pace, and points up the puns. In fact the only disappointment of major proportions is the hiring of Silvers, who is, as indicated, out of his element, largely because he depends on a machine-gun rattle of lines and the tempo is necessarily slower, and less verbal, in this type of trousers-down jape.

Otta.

Half a Sixpence
(BRITISH—COLOR—PANAVISION)

Big outlook. Beautiful production values against Edwardian England. A fun picture.

London, Dec. 21.

Paramount release of Charles H. Schneer-George Sidney Production. Executive producer, John Dark. Stars Tommy Steele; features Julia Foster, Cyril Ritchard, Penelope Horner, Grover Dale. Directed by Sidney. Screenplay, Beverley Cross, based on the musical "Half a Sixpence" adapted from the novel "Kipps" by H. G. Wells; camera (Technicolor), Geoffrey Unsworth; music and lyrics, David Heneker, supervised by Irwin Kostal; choreography, Gillian Lynne; editors, Bill Lewthwaite, Frank Santillo. Reviewed at Astoria Theatre, London, Dec. 19, '67. Running Time, 148 MINS.

Arthur Kipps	Tommy Steele
Ann	Julia Foster
Chitterlow	Cyril Ritchard
Helen	Penelope Horner
Pearce	Grover Dale
Kate	Elaine Taylor
Shalford	Hilton Edwards
Flo	Julia Sutton
Buggins	Leslie Meadows
Victoria	Sheila Falconer
Sid	Christopher Sandford
Mrs. Walsingham	Pamela Brown
Hubert	James Villiers
Lady Botting	Jean Anderson
Wilkins	Allan Cuthbertson
Laura	Aleta Morrison

With its legit renown and the vital repeat performance by Tommy Steele, "Half a Sixpence" seems set for big b.o. dividends. The attack and buoyancy of the original have been retained, and often enhanced, in George Sidney's production, and the whole thing looks gorgeous, conveying the atmosphere of Edwardian England in which H. G. Well's basic Kipps story was set. Without tampering over much with the original libretto, Sidney has managed both to open it up and to keep the fantasy air of a not-quite-lifelike setting, so that the musical spots emerge from it with spontaneous ease.

As with all good musicals, the story has a simple moral — that money can be a troublesome thing — and it is told in a straightforward narrative, without too much complication of character. Thus Kipps is projected as a likable lad, temporarily aberrated by his coming into a fortune, and returning to the true common virtues when he loses it. The snobs he encounters are satirical thumbnails, and his girl friend a lively maiden with a virtuous dedication to her man. Despite some languishing in the middle stretches, the story retains its charm throughout, and it is far more pertinent than most librettos. Beverley Cross's book, skilfully adapted by Dorothy Kingsley, has the merit of being literate and workable without the song-and-dance routines.

But the cohesive force is certainly that of Tommy Steele, who takes hold of his part like a terrier and never lets go. It's a tribute to the hard work he's put into his transformation from rock inger to allrounder that there's no hint that he's a disker masquerading out of his class. His assurance is overwhelming, and he leads the terping with splendid vigor and elan. Of course, the haunting title song and the ebullient "Flash, Bang, Wallop!" remain the showstoppers, and David Heneker's score is a little short of socko tunes elsewhere. But it uses recitative to excellent dramatic effect, and even the soso numbers get a gloss in the performance.

Highspots of the show are the photographic wedding routine, and the Henley regatta, a superb period evocation of the river and the elegant dames and the excitement of the boat race. Equally dashing is Kipp's encounter with Chitterlow and the theatrical troupe, also a visual delight in delicate colours, a further tribute to Geoffrey Unsworth's dulcet, often soft-focus lensing which gives an air of dream to many episodes. Steele makes the most of his comic chances, especially in a farcical interlude where he endeavors to cope with the cutlery and decorum of a dinner party, and his Cockney verve gives a poignancy to his performance even greater than when he delivered it on stage.

Another standout piece of casting is Julia Foster as the girl friend who gets the half sixpence as a token of his love. Known as an individual and striking straight actress, she takes to the idiom with fine abandon, and adds many sympathetic touches to a role that might easily have declined into a conventional swoony musicomedy heroine. Cyril Ritchard is somewhat subdued to start with as Chitterlow, but gives a subtle performance that would have benefited from rather more extravagance, a strange point vis-a-vis Ritchard. All the other casting is exact, though the aristocratic gal who purloins Kipps's affections is too much a cold stereotype in Penelope Horner's impersonation, as directed.

But the whole thing maintains a style and a flavor that take hold of the imagination, and it adds up to firstrate entertainment for most brows who can respond to the essential romance and good nature of it.

Otta.

Inside North Vietnam
(DOCUMENTARY—COLOR)

Dissenting docu demonstrates civilian damage by U.S. but offers recruiting-poster propaganda of North Vietnam. Preaches to the converted.

Felix Greene production and release, directed, photographed (Eastman Color) and narrated by Greene. Editor, Gordon Mueller. Reviewed at Carnegie Hall Cinema, N.Y., Dec. 10, '67. Running Time, 80 MINS.

This filmed report on Ho Chi Minh's domain by Felix Greene, longtime leftist dissident from many Western policies, proves the following: (1) War is hell; (2) U.S. bombing of North Vietnam has meant killing and wounding civilians and destroying their habitats; (3) In their day-to-day life, the North Vietnamese people, like most Asians, are charming and gentle. But the film does not prove (1) whether, as the U.S. contends, these charming and gentle people, like the Japanese before them, can be aggressive and warlike in their public actions, or (2) whether, in a guerilla war, there can be meaningful distinctions between military and civilian targets.

Of what use is a film like this? Greene, former head (circa 1939) of the British Broadcasting Co. in New York and now a freelance journalist-filmmaker domiciled in San Francisco, spent three-and-a-half months (Feb.-May '67) in North Vietnam on assignment from the San Francisco Chronicle and CBS Television News. His "Inside North Vietnam" is well-photographed and an adroit bit of pro-Hanoi propaganda, but it will affect only the converted. A motion picture on this subject in which the word "'Communist" is never once mentioned in re the government of North Vietnam obviously leaves too many unanswered questions.

Those Americans who believe in the wrongness of U.S. involvement in Vietnam don't have to go for Hanoi's recruiting-poster viewpoint. As a political act this Greene film is perhaps meaningful, but as a film it's almost beneath discussion. In towns with sizable blocs of dovish sentiment, it can make a small b.o. impact.

Greene mostly avoids Hanoi to concentrate on the smaller cities and villages. There are scenes of rice-growing via primitive irrigation, a group of happy teenagers who repair roads and bridges, hospitals, Haiphong harbor, and more. Many interviews are meant to express the unanimity of the North Vietnamese feeling (or propaganda line?) that they will fight and win even if it takes 100 years. There is also a talk with a downed U.S. airman who disputes Yank policy in the country. He seems well-cared for and not brainwashed. Cities made uninhabitable by constant air raids are displayed, as are the "foxhole" shelters which are everywhere in North Vietnam. The point is made that raids are so frequent they have become routine—though the damage as shown as frightening.

A long closeup of a wounded youngster falls under the category of what Francois Truffaut calls "abuse of cinematic power": unless one is a pacifist (which the North Vietnamese are not), it proves nothing and substitutes emotion for thought.

Considering the primitive conditions under which the film was made (Greene had no crew), "Inside North Vietnam" is well-photographed. The North Vietnamese countryside comes through in luscious greens, which reinforces Greene's point that this is a "peaceful" country transgressed by the United States. *Byro.*

I'll Never Forget What's 'is Name
(BRITISH—COLOR)

Jumpy pacing and cutting. Sexual promiscuity of non-hero probable b.o. advantage. Spoof on success spoiled by excesses.

London, Dec. 21.

Universal release of Scimitar Films production. Produced and directed by Michael Winner. Stars Orson Welles, Oliver Reed, Carol White, Harry Andrews; features Michael Hordern, Wendy Craig, Norman Rodway, Marianne Faithfull, Lyn Ashley, Frank Finlay; screenplay, Peter Draper; camera (Technicolor), Otto Heller; editor, Bernard Gribble; music, Frances Lai; asst. directors, Michael Dryhurst, Michael Guest. Reviewed at Rialto Theatre, London, Dec. 18, '67. Running Time, **97 MINS.**

Johnathan Lute .... Orson Welles
Andrew Quint .... Oliver Reed
Georgina .... Carol White
Gerald Sater .... Harry Andrews
Headmaster .... Michael Hordern
Louise Quint .... Wendy Craig
Josie .... Marianne Faithfull
Nicholas .... Norman Rodway
Chaplain .... Frank Finlay
Maccabee .... Harvey Hall
Carla .... Ann Lynn
Susannah .... Lyn Ashley
Anna .... Veronica Clifford
Walter .... Edward Fox
Lewis Force .... Stuart Cooper
Eldrich .... Roland Curran
Bankman .... Peter Graves
Michael Cornwall .... Mark Burns
Kellaway .... Mark Eden
Marian .... Josephine Rueg
Vietnamese Girl .... Mona Chong
Galloway .... Robert Mill
Pinchin .... Terence Seward

Michael Winner, who made the likable "The Jokers" with a background of modish London, follows up with a more jaundiced look at the same vistas, but this one suffers from a stereotyped plot which all his helming frenzy can't generate into life. But the hectic style, the sexual freedom, and the presence of Carol White (currently gathering plaudits for her "Poor Cow" role) should help its b.o. chances. Additional asset is the now mountainous appearance of Orson Welles, as an ad agency chief of super-cunning. Given the sharpest lines in Peter Draper's script, he scores easily in his most unpremeditated style.

Story concerns a successful and resentful whizkid of the advertising game (Oliver Reed), who opts out to join a pal in running an esoteric literary magazine. Separated from his wife, he is a womanizer of perpetual appetite, taking one off to a lonely and disused railroad station for undraped capers, and establishing a flighty relationship with a secretary (Carol White), who is prim at heart and takes it all seriously. Thus the theme is the aridity of fashionable achievement, and the sour smell of success is hammered home by Winner with an insistence that destroys its own claims and closes with a final scene — where Reed makes a sendup commercial, using Belsen clips and the nuclear mushroom — of stunning vulgarity.

Oliver Reed, an ugly-fascinating thesp of perpetual potential, looks grim and disenchanted throughout, but hasn't the power to suggest that there's much talent going to waste. And the best parts of the film are incidental. In addition to Welles, Miss White registers as the girl torn between her virginal upbringing and her beckoning by Reed. The role is inconclusive, but she gives it the stamp of charm and unforced sweetness. Wendy Craig, as the deserted wife, and Norman Rodway, as the literary gent who talks of fulfilment and then sells out for money, are also effective, and there are sharp small cameos from Frank Finlay and Michael Hordern.

Winner's jumpy directional style manages to avoid monotony, at the expense of conviction, and Otto Heller's lensing is colorful and precisely evocative of its London locales. Peter Draper's script has moments of brittle wit, but suffers from its treatment, which is over-indulgent in farcical tricks, so that its point, however conventional, is blunted.

In fact, it's a feature about success that is spoilt by its excesses, and lacks the fluent charm that made "The Jokers" so engaging. *Otta.*

The Good, The Bad and The Ugly
(Il Buono, Il Brutto, Il Cattivo) (ITALIAN—TECHNISCOPE—(COLOR)

Visually stunning but overly violent oater. Too long by 40 minutes. If cut, could do solid biz in action houses and later subrun double features.

United Artists release of Alberto Grimaldi production. Stars Clint Eastwood. Directed by Sergio Leone. Screenplay, Luciano Vincenzoni, Leone, based on story by Age-Scarpelli, Vincenzoni, Leone; English version, Mickey Knox; camera (Technicolor), Tonino Del Colli; editors, Nino Baragli, Eugenio Alabiso; music, Ennio Moricone. Reviewed at N.Y. homeoffice, Dec. 22, '67. Running Time, **161 MINS.**

Joe .... Clint Eastwood
Tuco .... Eli Wallach
Setenza .... Lee Van Cleef

"The Good, The Bad and The Ugly" is exactly that — a curious amalgam of the visually striking, the dramatically feeble and the offensively sadistic. Commercially, this third in the Clint Eastwood series of Italo westerns is seriously handicapped by its 161-minute running time, a length that complicates double-feature bookings. Lack of a "Dollars" handle on the current pic, as had originally been planned, would suggest the first two entries did not live up to United Artists' expectations in their U.S. dates, and the outsize running time must be counted a major liability for what is at heart a programmer, notwithstanding its top-grade production values.

Trimming 40 minutes from the film would seem an easy matter, unless UA's contract with director Sergio Leone forbids such distrib interference. Unfortunately the most expendable sequence — a lengthy episode that finds Eastwood and Mexican bandit Eli Wallach stranded in the midst of a Civil War battle — is also the most spectacular. A repetitious and flat-footed introduction to the three protagonists could also be excised to good advantage.

Story concerns search for buried treasure by "Good" Eastwood, "Ugly" Wallach and "Bad" Lee Van Cleef (making his second appearance in an Eastwood western). Along the way they taunt and torture each other and also contribute a total of 20 dead bodies to the western landscape, reasonably well-faked by European exteriors. As befits his star status, Eastwood kills 10 of these; as befits his titular Goodness, his victims all draw first. Unlike the earlier Leone efforts, however, the violence here has little of the balletic, even erotic quality that equally fascinated non-sadomasochistic filmgoers. One sequence in particular, a five-minute torture session that climaxes in an attempted eye-gouging, may well serve as the battle cry for opponents of screen violence.

Leone's visual sense is as strong as ever, however, and his effective alternation of extreme closeups and long shots renders much of the pic graphically electric. Unfortunately, his eye is not matched by his mind, as he allows several excursions into laughably sentimental characterization, or his hand, as his three actors (especially Wallach) overplay to the point of absurdity. Even with these defects, he is undeniably a unique stylist, and much of Tonino Del Colli's photography is a knockout.

Ennio Moricone's insistent music and Carlo Simi's baroque art direction further contribute to the pic's too-muchness. Still, if UA can intelligently abbreviate the film to a manageable running time, "The Good, The Bad and The Ugly" could emerge a real b.o. winner in action markets. *Beau.*

Four Stars
(COLOR—SONGS)

Still conducting his own private education in public, Warhol shows technical finesse but no narrative sense. Psychedelic use of color. Mild b.o. for way-outs.

Filmmakers' release of an Andy Warhol production, directed, photographed and edited by Warhol. Features Nico, International Velvet, Ivy Nicholson, Viva, Edie Sedgewick, Ingrid Superstar, Brigit Polk, Katrina, Alan Midgette, Ultra Violet, Ondine; introduces Tiger Morse; music, The Velvet Underground. Reviewed at New Cinema Playhouse, N.Y., Dec. 22, '67. Running Time, **102 MINS.**

Andy Warhol, always the one for gimmicks, uses star-symbol in title. This refers to the highest rating awarded by the film critics of the N.Y. Daily News. Film is a real advance technically for Warhol though commercially it's probably the least promising of his more recent efforts. Version now being shown first-run in New York is actually the first 102 minutes of what officially is a 25-hour film; out of the rest of the footage, Warhol says, will come at least five more feature-length releases. The painter-director obviously has higher hopes for this one than he's had for some other late productions; whereas he handled such as "I, a Man" and "Bike Boy" himself, he's turned over "Four Stars" to the Filmmakers' Distribution Centre for national release, hoping perhaps to repeat the success of "The Chelsea Girls."

But "Girls" could at least be seen as a "vision of hell" as lived by the residents of a hotel; the films following it all centered on one character and provided personality sketches if not always stories. This latest, on the other hand, seems random footage with no narrative or thematic framework whatsoever. It appears merely as a kind of exercise for Warhol in which he can experiment with color and sound. Whether paying patrons will abide this self-indulgence is doubtful.

Film as shown at New Cinema Playhouse in N.Y. is on 16m reels which begin on the hour and half-hour. At 15 minutes past each hour, a second projector begins unspooling other footage, so that part of the time two images are being projected simultaneously on screen. In fact, Warhol has sometimes double-printed each strip of film so that there are even triple and quadruple exposures. This makes effects which are alternately hypnotic, annoying, beautiful and pointless.

Various things are shown, all of them featuring Warhol's usual bevy of fancily-named actors. Two young people make love; a boy relates a hitchhiking exeprience; a girl, probably a model, strenuously applies makeup while her boyfriend feeds her inane questions; there's a kind of rape; Ondine (the "pope" in "Chelsea Girls") describes a homosexual encounter, and so on. Some of it is vaguely amusing and interesting, some is bring and sleep-inducing — but most of it has such wonderful and controlled use of color that this alone maintains awareness. Rarely has there been such "psychedelic" use of reds, greens and blues.

Film is completely edited, and for the first time in Warhol the voices emerging from the screen do not correspond exactly to the concurrent images. The last 15 minutes, indeed, consist entirely of a folk song being sung while shots of youngsters playing on the beach are projected. Some of it, including final shot of a sunset, is beautiful in a surprisingly conventional way. This represents one of the few times Warhol has gone outdoors and it's amazing how well he responds to the freedom of natural environments. Another bravura sequence, that of Tiger Morse surrounded by tinsel, is too reminiscent of the late Ron Rice's "Chumlum," one of the few really exciting "underground" films.

"Four Stars" shows that Warhol can conquer the technical side of filmmaking. Now if he can only combine this new knowledge with his thematic insight, he may well come up with an important statement. But he should do his practicing in private. Putting such films on public display only makes Warhol tiresome in the eyes of critics and laymen. A truly finely-etched work of art — which Warhol may be capable of — would be welcome; it's not necessary that we witness every step in his thinking as Warhol approaches the making of it. Byro.

Counterpoint
(TECHNISCOPE—COLOR)

Offbeat World War II meller. Okay prospects for general market.

Hollywood, Dec. 12.
Universal release of Dick Berg production. Stars Charlton Heston, Maximilian Schell; features Kathryn Hays, Leslie Nielsen. Directed by Ralph Nelson. Screenplay, James Lee, Joel Oliansky; from novel, "The General," by Alan Sillitoe; camera (Technicolor), Russell Metty; music, Bronislaw Kaper; editor, Howard G. Epstein; art direction, Alexander Golitzen, Carl Anderson; asst. director, Wallace Worsley; sound, Waldon O. Watson, William Russell. Reviewed at Universal Studios, Dec. 11, '67. Running Time, 105 MINS.

Evans	Charlton Heston
Schiller	Maximilian Schell
Annabelle	Kathryn Hays
Victor	Leslie Nielsen
Arndt	Anton Diffring
Long	Linden Chiles
Galloway	Pete Masterson
Klingerman	Curt Lowens
Dorothy	Neva Patterson
Tartzoff	Cyril Delevanti
Jordon	Gregory Morton
Hook	Parley Baer
Chaminant	Dan Drazer
Prescott	Ed Peck

"Counterpoint" is the story of an American symphony—on a U.S.O. tour in Belgium—taken prisoner by the Germans during the Battle of the Bulge. Some of the incidents are contrived and charac-

terizations of its two leads, as developed in trying to make them strong, are sometimes confusing, but in the main subject has been well handled and possessed of a theme which may be ballyed for okay grosses in general market. Star names of Charlton Heston and Maximilian Schell should exert marquee lure.

Script by James Lee and Joel Oliansky, based upon Alan Sillitoe's novel, "The General," packs suspense as fate of the martinet symph conductor and his 70 musicians at hands of the Germans, under order to execute every prisoner, remains uncertain until finale. Something new has been added here for a war film; parts of five major music works, recorded by Los Angeles Philharmonic Orchestra for the action, which should have particular appeal for music lovers. Symph sequences are logically inserted as integral ingredients of plot.

Heston plays the maestro, whose demands that his company be freed immediately as non-combatants are ignored. Schell is the music-loving general, who temporarily overlooks his orders to shoot all prisoners and insists that the conductor, whose work he has long admired, play a concert for him. Heston, aware that once the concert is concluded all will be shot, stalls for time. Footage becomes a battle of wills between the two. A partisans' surprise attack saves the day.

Heston appears occasionally to overplay his role but is convincing in what is for him a new type of part. Schell's motives aren't always apparent and he suffers from underexpository writing but is still strongly cast. Leslie Nielsen as the concert master whose wife, Kathryn Hays, a cellist in orch, once had an affair with conductor, fulfills the slight demands of role and Miss Hays is okay. Anton Diffring makes the most of a German colonel, constantly at odds with the general to machine-gun the prisoners.

Musical numbers, as orch plays in a chapel, carry a high level of interest. Included in quintet are Schubert's Unfinished Symphony, overture to Wagner's Tannhauser, Tchaikovsky's Swan Lake Ballet, fourth movement of Brahms' First Symphony and first movement of Beethoven's Fifth Symphony.

Direction by Ralph Nelson maintains a fast clip and Dick Berg's producer activities are expertly executed. Technical credits all rate highly, including Russell Metty's facile camera work, Bronislaw Kaper's music score, Howard G. Epstein's tight editing, atmospheric art direction by Alexander Golitzen and Carl Anderson. Whit.

Le Viol
(The Rape)
(FRENCH—SWEDISH—COLOR)

Paris, Dec. 19.
Athos Films release of Sandrews, Parc Films, Argos Films production. Stars Bibi Andersson, Bruno Cremer; features Frederic De Pasquale. Written and directed by Jacques Doniol-Valcroze. Camera (Eastmancolor), Rune Ericson; editor, M. Bhaul. At Public's, Paris. Running time, 85 MINS.

Marianne	Bibi Andersson
Walter	Bruce Cremer
Henri	Frederic De Pasquale

Tale of an erotic daydream is somewhat too mannered and fussily directed to create a needed tension and maintain interest throughout. It is glossy, clever but somewhat effete despite a torrid love scene. This appears to lack the weight and characterization for arty use and is somewhat too elegant for grinds. Playoff is there on its theme, but it needs hardsell for most markets.

Film is fortunate in having Swedish actress Bibi Andersson who gives a luminous quality to a young wife who finds herself alone one afternoon when the doorbell rings. Just about to take a bath, she slips on a robe and opens the door. In breaks a man who ties her up and informs her he is going to keep her incommunicado for several hours.

He finally unties her, they talk, there are intimations that her husband may be in danger and finally she practically seduces him. He leaves and at a dinner party that night the intruder is apparently one of the guests. So it seems she had just thought up the whole thing in an erotic, longing daydream.

All this might be acceptable and it does tend to tie up many plot loopholes. But it is also somewhat too sketchy and finally a bit precious. The script and direction play on suspense and showing the man waiting outside, etc., as a sort of duality on whether it was true or her imagination and secret desire. And this saps the film's mood and dramatic feasibility rather than heightening it by so-called breaks between illusion and reality.

Swedish-French production does have a quality that could have it taking place in any upper middleclass milieu. Pic has nice color and setting, and manages to make its one locale and practically straight time and place sequencing avoid boredom. Bruno Cremer has the right blend of menace and charm and director Jacques Doniol-Valcroze has good feeling for composition if he has a tendency to dwell on objects for their own sake.

Rather than comment on erotic cowardice, desire or psychological nuances, this tries to have both suspense and literary probings of the pysche but does not manage to blend the two adequately. It is just too elusive, straining for elegance and charm without the needed true insights. Still, there are some handles on its one love scene if it finds its right outlets and audience. Mosk.

Vernost Materi
(A Mother's Devotion)
(RUSSIAN)

Paris, Dec. 19.
Mosfilm release of Gorki Studio production. With Elena Fadeyeva, Guennady Tchertov, Rodion Nakhapetov. Directed by Mark Donskoi. Screenplay, Z. Voskrenenskaia, I. Donskoi; camera, M. Iakovitch; music, R. Khozac. Previewed in Paris. Running Time, 90 MINS.

Mother	Elena Fadeyeva
Alexandre	Guennady Tchertov
Vladimir	Rodion Nakhapetov
Maria	T. Loginova

Film is the second one in a two-part tale about Lenin's mother. The first, "A Mother's Heart," was shown at the recent New York Film Fest. This one deals more

with Lenin then the previous part, but still concentrates a lot on the mother as it takes her from her son's early imprisonments to the eve of his power, when she dies.

Veteran director Mark Donskoi manages to avoid the pitfalls of sentimentality by his deftness in handling the drama of a dedicated mother, even if she has created Lenin. It is somewhat academic, but in a good sense. There is restraint and expert acting and a deft blending of fact, poetics and legend.

Elena Fadeyeva again amply manages to show an inner strength in her looks, comportment and bearing. True, she may be somewhat too lionized, but it is in keeping with the foreshadowing of her son's destiny and the generally historical tone of the film. Not exactly realistic, it still gives a good feeling for the times and humanizes the characters enough to keep this from being pompous or stodgy.

Rodion Nakhapetov has a remarkable resemblance to the young Lenin and plays it with restraint and keeps it from being pompous. This is a warm, rich and telegraphed historical film about the Soviet's great man. However, it has the filmic knowhow and balance to overcome this and make it warm if slightly overripe hymn to a mother, be she of Lenin or any man. It is technically fine too. Mosk.

Playtime
(FRENCH—COLOR—70M)

Jacques Tati, France's painstaking creative comic, in his fourth film. Strong values but needs careful sell.

Paris, Dec. 25.
Prodis release of Specta Films production. Stars Jacques Tati; features Barbara Dennek, Georges Montant, J. Abbey. Directed by Jacques Tati. Screenplay, Tati, Jacques Lagrange; camera (Eastmancolor), Jean Badal; editor, Gerard Pollicand; music, Francis Lemargue. At Empire-Cinerama, Paris. Running Time, 145 MINS.

Hulot	Jacques Tati
Girl	Barbara Dennek
Giffard	Georges Montant
Lacs	John Abbey
Doorman	Tony Andal
German	Reinhardt Kouldehoff
Friend	Yves Barscaq
Headwaiter	Michel Francini
Pilier	Billy Bourbon
Schulz	Billy Kearns

Jacques Tati, with considerable renown as a personalized comic director-actor-writer via only three films, now makes his fourth effort after an almost 10-year hiatus. It was worth the wait. Tati has come up with a big scale, gentle comedy about people (mainly tourists) in the growing new metallic and glass cities that resemble each other. Pic takes to the 70m process with an extraordinary impressionistic outdoor set of a new Paris, and is an observant romp during a one-day stay of a group of tourists.

In his first feature pic, "Jour De Fete," 1947, Tati dealt with a rustic mailman trying to speed up delivery by emulating American knowhow. With "Mr. Hulot's Holiday," he was an innocent figure trying to enjoy himself at a beach resort and causing joy and mishaps unintentionally, and in "My Uncle" he disrupted the gadget-ridden house of his brother-in-law.

Here, Hulot wanders into a glass

and metal building ostensibly to see someone and just his presence turns all this modernism into fun. Chairs that make whooshing sounds and inflate and deflate, endless corridors, buildings that may be hospitals, airports, stores or business centres, depending on how they are lensed. All this is set as a scene for the arrival of a group of American tourists on a oneday, herded stopover in Paris.

Hulot gets mingled with them and this new modern world as he goes his almost wordless, innocent way. He meets an old friend and is taken home where people literally live in glass houses. Outside, cars pass as people are seen in their homes via large glass windows. Hulot also gets into a new nitery - eatery, Royal Gardens, which is still actually being built as the customers arrive. Hulot's doorman friend sees him and gets him in. He ends up unwittingly helping tear down the unfinished structure.

Tati is not an active satirist nor does he use slapstick. He has assimilated the greats but is an individual comic talent who builds meticulous gags founded on a gentle, anarchic individualism that is always sympathetic, personal and, above all, funny and constantly inventive.

Tati is not reactionary either but does intimate that man will have to find a way of living in the new modern cities springing up without staunching man's own personality. So in these days of pop, madcap, sexy farces as the mainstay of film comedy, Tati maintains a fresh, innocent and human observation of man coping with the new environment.

Film thus needs careful handling but should reap results on its wealth of revealing human insights and its use of color, 70m and sound to add to the essential human comedy theme. The green of neon in a modernistic French drugstore with food etc. shines on faces of people eating and almost gets Hulot sick as he thinks they are bilious from food. Footsteps echoing down the long corridors, sounds being cut by the glass walls as the camera reveals it later all blend with Hulot's own unwitting immersion in the growing new world.

Jean Badal's clear and crystaline colors also enhance this new metal, glass world.

The only cavil might be a tendency to overdo a point, as Hulot's attempt to find a man in a gigantic industrial building. The point is made but then, perhaps, a bit repeated.

Tati has been re-releasing his other pix in the last few years and spent almost three years on this film. It is a definite comic pic event and should be heard from on the world marts. The production finds its fantasy and humor in the everyday, changing world. Tati is his usual disarticulated self as he catalyses events but is never actually affected himself to any degree. The various roles are cast by type and all work effectively from the innocent American girl tourist to the harassed head waiter, the perky doorman and gnomish drunk, as well as international types adrift in a brave, risible new world.

Dialog is just functional and film is universal in its mainly visual treatment. It would need no subtitles anywhere. Added gag is that the few lines of American dialog are attributed in screen credit to the noted American humorist-newsman Art Buchwald. As in all good works it is French in feel but worldwide in appeal. Charming music and knowing editing are also assets. *Mosk.*

The Ballad Of Josie
(TECHNISCOPE—COLOR)

Mild Doris Day oater comedy for dual bills.

Hollywood, Dec. 20.
Universal Pictures release, produced by Norman MacDonnell; executive producer, Martin Melcher. Stars Doris Day. Directed by Andrew V. McLaglen. Screenplay, Harold Swanton; camera (Technicolor), Milton Krasner; editors, Otho S. Lovering, Fred A. Chulak; music, Frank DeVol; songs, Floyd Huddleston, Don Costa, Jack Lloyd, Gene de Paul; art direction, Alexander Golitzen, Addison Hehr; sound, Waldon O. Watson, Frank H. Wilkinson; asst. director, Terry Morse, Jr. Reviewed at Universal Studios, L.A., Dec. 19, '67. Running Time, 102 MINS.
Josie	Doris Day
Jason	Peter Graves
Arch	George Kennedy
Judge	Andy Devine
Charlie	William Talman
Fonse	David Hartman
Annabelle	Audrey Christie
Klugg	Timothy Scott
Bratsch	Don Stroud
Alpheus	Paul Fix

"The Ballad Of Josie" is a pleasant, innocuous Doris Day oater comedy about sheep-cattle range wars, and women's rights, in pre-1890, pre-Statehood Wyoming. Action director Andrew V. McLaglen shows his talents in the few lively scenes; elsewhere, direction and script are plodding, acting routine. Production values are good. Universal release will need strong dual bill mate for okay b.o. in general situations.

Harold Swanton's episodic and talky screenplay, which gets most laughs from low comedy sight gags, finds Miss Day (who sings not a note, by the way) as a widowed frontier mother, unable to support herself and son Teddy Quinn. Peter Graves (of the "Mission: Impossible" vidseries), and George Kennedy play the good and bad guy, respectively. Norman MacDonnell produced, and Martin Melcher was exec producer.

Frontier town officials are played by judge Andy Devine, attorney William Talman and medic David Hartman and medic Guy Raymond. Audrey Christie runs the town—ahem—"boardinghouse," in which, amid scarlet trappings, reside Karen Jensen, Elisabeth Fraser, Linda Meiklejohn and Shirley O'Hara. Timothy Scott and Don Stroud play sheepherders, a good casting of a good comedy plot angle. Paul Fix, Miss Day's stern father-in-law, Robert Lowery, her late husband, and storekeeper John Fiedler round out okay cast.

Plot situations are contrived. When the few chances arise for some action, McLaglen, along with stunt coordinator Hal Needham, put them over. Techniscope-Technicolor lensing by Milton Krasner captures the excellent visual details. Frank DeVol's adequate score is a combo of familiar folk airs and musical sound effects.

Title song and end-title tune are okay, ditto other credits. Film runs a longish 102 minutes. *Murf.*

Mennesker Moedes og Soed Musik Opstaar i Hjertet
(People Meet And Sweet Music Rises In Hearts)
(DANISH—SWEDISH)

Copenhagen, Dec. 19.
Nordisk Film Kompagni release of Henning Carlsen/Nordisk Film Kompagni, Copenhagen/ and Sandrew Film/AB, Stockholm production. Directed by Henning Carlsen. Written by Henning Carlsen, Poul Borum, based on novel by Jens August Schade. Stars Harriet Andersson, Erik Wedersoe, Preben Neergaard. Camera, Henning Kristiansen. Music, Krysztof Komeda. Reviewed at Dagmar Theatre, Copenhagen. Running Time, 105 MINS.

Henning Carlsen's "Sult" (Hunger) copped a Golden Palm award for its male star (Per Oscarsson) at last year's Cannes Film fest. His new film concentrates more on a woman (Harriet Andersson) although several men are active around and about her in this erotic comedy of the mildly absurd. "People Meet" is based on a Danish novel that was amusingly avant-garde 25 years ago. Its fame even spread to France. However, it's doubtful if the film will carry its fame further into worldwide acceptance. But the film should draw both chuckles and nostalgic sentiment in arty houses almost everywhere.

The story itself seems like a huge gag. It is also an ode to physical love in a way that entirely avoids any risk of being labelled obscene. Even so, there is much bed-hopping which is vividly described. And where beds are not available, train washrooms or any available floor will do. Every erotic scene is tempered either with humor or with madcap poetry. (An English-speaking version of the film was made right along with the Scandinavian version). There is no other plot than the hero's wanderings through many beds and bosoms and the heroine's even more vagrant dance through brothels, dancehalls and boudoirs. The two meet occasionally, and they make love when they do. It turns out that they are childhood sweethearts.

Henning Carlsen and his excellent photographer, Henning Kristiansen, handle all the sweet nonsense with a sufficiently light touch and also with some cinematic imagination all their own. The black-and-white photography is made to seem almost colorful through sudden switches from brownish prints to bluish ones. Fittingly, occasional panels in the silent film tradition are interspersed. They ask questions like "Is there anything so erotic as a train?"

Halfway through, the film grows repetitious. Were it not for Sweden's Harriet Andersson's lusty portrayal of the heroine, one might be tempted to ask: Is there anything so unerotic as this pic? However, some censors may find fault. *Kell.*

Smashing Time
(COLOR—SONGS)

Comedy may be somewhat too British for American audience; old-fashioned by American standards; best suited for selected and art situations.

Hollywood, Dec. 19.
Paramount release of Carlo Ponti-Selmur (Roy Millichip, Carlo Ponti) production. Stars Rita Tushingham, Lynn Redgrave; features Michael York, Anna Quayle, Irene Handl, Ian Carmichael. Directed by Desmond Davis. Screenplay, George Melly; camera, Manny Wynn; music, John Addison; editor, Barry Vince; art direction, Ken Bridgeman. Reviewed at Paramount Studios, Dec. 19, '67. Running Time, 96 MINS.
Brenda	Rita Tushingham
Yvonne	Lynn Redgrave
Tom Wabe	Michael York
Charlotte	Anna Quayle
Mrs. Gimble	Irene Handl
Mome-Rath	Ian Carmichael
Toni	Toni Palmer
Tove	Jeremy Lloyd
Cape Boss	Arthur Mullard
Tramp	Sydney Bromley
Hall Porter	Howard Marion Crawford
1st Exquisite	Murray Melvin
2d Exquisite	Paul Danquah
Tove's Secretary	Valery Leon
Gossiping Customer	Adele Strong
Man in Cafe No. 6	Jerold Wells

By strictly British standards, "Smashing Time" is probably just that for British audiences, but it more nearly resembles out-of-date American slapstick. Starring Rita Tushingham and Lynn Redgrave as a pair of girls from the north of England who go to London to explore its glittery side—and have themselves a smashing time—the writer and producers display an amazing memory of past Hollywood film. They draw liberally, for instance, on gags and bits of business from such immortals as Laurel & Hardy. Given smart exploitation it may enjoy certain success in U.S., but in selected and art situations only.

The Roy Millichip-Carlo Ponti production is typically British in tone, and so are its protagonists, so much so, in fact, that it is impossible for American ears to understand much of the dialog. Femmes play Laurel & Hardy characters, Miss Tushingham as the bewildered Stan, Miss Redgrave the aggressive Oliver.

George Melly's original screenplay might be the further misadventures of the late Hollywood comics in change-of-sex garb. Lasses are immediately catapulted into a series of comic calamities that would make any Hollywood producer blanch.

Extensive use is made of a swinging London background, with many of its characters, particularly the fey. Desmond Davis' direction, when it isn't focusing on hoary routines, is fast in limning the conglomerate situations in which femmes are plunged, Lynn becoming a recording star, Rita a top fashion photographer's model. With their usual flair for disaster, both find themselves out.

Stars play their roles broad, as do balance of cast. Michael York portrays the fotog, reminiscent of David Hemmings' bulber in "Blow-Up," and Anna Quayle is a quaint boutique owner. Ian Carmichael plays it slapstick all the way as a nightclub sport who entices Lynn to his flat. However, his intentions of seduction are stymied by Rita, who follows, lacing his brandy with a laxative, which is about typical of the type of humor in the piece.

Manny Wynn's color photography is luscious as he catches some interesting London backgrounds as well as interiors. John Addison's music score is spirited, Ken Bridgeman's art direction fanciful at times and Barry Vince's fast editing. *Whit.*

Gammera the Invincible
(JAPANESE—U.S.—TOTALSCOPE)

Latest in the Japanese series featuring gigantic reptiles is a monstrous yawn. For least discriminating markets.

World Entertainment Corp. release of a Harris Associates presentation of a Daiei Motion Picture Co. Ltd. Production, produced by Masaichi Nagata; executive producer, Ken Barnett. Features Albert Dekker, Brian Donlevy. Directed by Noriaki Yuasa. Screenplay, Nizo Takahashi, from an idea by Yonejiro Saito; additional dialogue, Richard Kraft; camera, Nobuo Munekawa, Julian Townsend; title song, Wes Farrell; editor, Ross-Gaffney Inc.; asst. director, Sid Cooperschmidt; art director, Hank Aldrich. Reviewed at Lyric Theatre, N.Y., Dec. 21, '67. Running Time, 86 MINS.

Secretary of Defense	Albert Dekker
Gen. Terry Arnold	Brian Donlevy
Sgt. Susan Embers	Diane Findlay
Capt. Lovell	John Baragrey
Gen. O'Neill	Dick O'Neill
Dr. Hidaka	Eiji Funakoshi
Kyoko	Harumi Kiritachi
Aoyagi	Junichiro Yamashita
Toshio	Yoshiro Uchida
Nobuyo	Michiko Sugata
Sakurai	Yoshiro Kitahara
Dr. Murase	Jun Hamamura

(*Dubbed English Soundtrack*)

If followups to "Godzilla" still mean big business in Japan, it's clear that the market has eroded in the U.S. to the point where the latest entry in the Nipponese series, "Gammera the Invincible," can be recommended only for the least discriminating situations. The title character in this instance is a huge fire-eating turtle who threatens mass destruction and cannot be felled even by nuclear devices. Surprise ending has the creature removed as a menace by a socalled Plan Z—an appropriate idea for "Gammera," a film which can be rated as Grade Z.

As with "Godzilla," the U.S. handlers of "Gammera the Invincible" have interpolated extensive footage with Yank actors. Version shown in Japan had an all-native cast, but as distributed by World Entertainment Corp. in this country there are numerous scenes taking place at a U.S. Army installation in Alaska, in the Pentagon in Washington and at U.N. headquarters in New York. They feature Brian Donlevy, Albert Dekker and others. Admittedly they are well-intergrated into the story and they do make the film more acceptable to U.S. program audiences, though, like everything else, they are primitively directed and played. The credits shown above are as they appear on pic's main credits — a cocktail of the original Japanese technicians and those who worked on the American footage. But the data is reported as given. Of particular note is that sole editing credit goes to a service rather than an individual—the New York firm of Ross-Gaffney Inc.

Script and acting throughout are on a thoroughly predictable and pedestrian level, and the only fun comes in watching the formula play itself out. There's the usual pseudo-scientific explanation for the emergence of the millenia-old creature, the incredulity on the part of the authorities, the understated panic once the menace is acknowledged ("Gammera — certainly one of the more controversial issues of our time"), the expected displays of Soviet-U.S. amity in the face of the threat to both. Routine dubbing and black-and-white cinematography will not help "Gammera the Invincible" for most spectators, who can be expected to greet even the usual extensive special effects with monstrous yawns. *Byro.*

The Crazy World of Laurel & Hardy
(COMPILATION)

Another collection of excerpts from L & H pix with plus value of sound. Includes Hal Roach's Oscar-winning "Music Box" and clips from features. For all old-days comedy fans.

Joseph Brenner Associates distribution of a Hal Roach-Jay Ward production. Stars Stan Laurel and Oliver Hardy. Narrated by Garry Moore. Executive producers, Jay Ward, Bill Scott; producer, Hal Roach; associate producer, Raymond Rohauer. Screenplay, Bill Scott; film editors, Skip Craig, Roger Donley; music, Jerry Fielding. Reviewed at Rizzoli Screening Room, N.Y., Dec. 14, '67. Running Time, 83 MINS.

With one exception, the 1927 "Bacon Grabbers," all the excerpts in this compilation of Stan Laurel and Oliver Hardy comedies are from the comedy team's sound films. As their voices proved to be as important to their portrayals as their talent for physical action and reaction, this gives "The Crazy World of Laurel and Hardy" at least one considerable jump on the other L&H compilations available.

The Joseph Brenner release, which premieres tomorrow (Thurs.) at the Kip's Bay, shows the handiwork of an assortment of producers, with the supervisory touch of Hal Roach most evident. The feature is being packaged with a 38-minute assortment, "Jay Ward's Intergalactic Film Festival," a collection of cartoons from "The Bullwinkle Show" and "George of the Jungle" plus some "Fractured Flickers." In the latter category, Lon Chaney's "Hunchback of Notre Dame" is jazzed up with an added soundtrack and retitled "Dinky Dunstan, Cheerleader at U.S.C." The fragmented format will enable theatres to eliminate sections to make it fit any schedule.

With an occasional bit of narration by Garry Moore that is admiring but never allowed to intrude on the action, "Crazy World" permits the viewer new to the Laurel & Hardy scene, to form an excellent impression of what made this dissimilar twosome click. For L&H addicts, of course, it's lagniappe. What may seem an advantage to some and a hindrance to others is the fact that, using excerpts from many comedies, the viewer becomes aware that the two comedians actually had only a few "pieces of business" which they repeated or varied only slightly, with the shoestring plots suggesting the variations. Not that this is a drawback because, as with the classic vaudeville turns, the audience quickly becomes familiar with the routine and usually resents any major changes. However, no other pair of funnymen ever got as much laugh mileage out of a pair of derby hats nor encountered so many mishaps by just going through a door.

If there is a highlight in this particular collection, it's the 1933 "Music Box," with L&H as the world's most inept piano movers, tackling one of those horribly steep set of steps peculiar to the Los Angeles suburban hillsides. The result won an Academy Award for producer Roach. Some of the shorts are included almost intact, including the 1932 "Helpmates," "Come Clean," "Dirty Work," "Towed In A Hole," "Busy Bodies" and "Any Old Port." There are also segments from such features as "Brau Hunks," "Bohemian Girl," "Way Out West" "Blockheads" and "Swiss Miss."

A delightful session with two of the screen's all-time great comics and a film that should never be allowed to go out of circulation. *Robe.*

Berserk
(BRITISH—COLOR)

Circus pic with four sensational murders. Joan Crawford stars in the melodrama thriller. Should do good b.o., especially in ozoners.

Dayton, O., Dec. 9.

Columbia Pictures release of Herman Cohen (Robert Sterne) production. Stars Joan Crawford; features Ty Hardin, Diana Dors, Michael Gough, Judy Geeson, Robert Hardy. Directed by Jim O'Connolly. Screenplay by Aben Kandel and Herman Cohen; camera (Technicolor), Desmond Dickinson; editor, Raymond Poulton; music, Patrick John Scott; art director, Maurice Pelling; production manager, Laurie Greenwood; asst. director, Barry Langley. Reviewed at Loew's Theatre, Dayton, Dec. 9, '67. Running Time, 96 MINS.

Monica Rivers	Joan Crawford
Frank Hawkins	Ty Hardin
Matilda	Diana Dors
Dorando	Michael Gough
Angela Rivers	Judy Geeson
Superintendent Brooks	Robert Hardy
Commissioner Dalby	Geoffrey Keen
Harrison Liston	Sydney Tafler
Bruno	George Claydon
Lazlo	Philip Madoc
Bearded Lady	Golda Casimir
Skeleton Man	Ted Lune
Strong Man	Milton Reid

"Berserk" was caught at Loew's Theatre here. It's for general release in January or February.

Story is full of holes, but it makes no difference. All the elements of the thrill picture are present. Promotion will bring them in.

"Berserk" doesn't have the continuous attention-holding gimmick of, say, "Invisible Man" or "House of Wax," but it fills the gap between its four sensational murders with a colorful array of circus acts and loosely constructed story line.

For Joan Crawford, owner and ringmaster (in leotard, red jacket, and top hat) of a circus plagued with brutal killings, it's more of "Whatever Happened to Baby Jane?" or "Straitjacket" effort. All good showmanship.

Ty Hardin comes in as replacement wirewalker for the first victim and works hard at conquering a share of the circus ownership.

Michael Gough as the show's business manager, becomes jealous and follows him into the big top only to be spiked through the head to a tent post. At this point Robert Hardy, as Scotland Yard superintendent, joins the puzzle.

Magician's assistant Diana Dors has a try at Hardin but finds his ambitions greater than his romantic desires. She is tossed from his caravan and brawls with another woman who ribs her lack of success. Shortly thereafter she gets dissected by a buzzsaw when someone jams her illusion equipment. The killer is identified in a surprise ending.

George Claydon, Goldia Casimir, Ted Lune, and Milton Reid offer a light note with a comedy number, "It Might Be Me," and animal acts, plus aerial ballet, grand parade and raising the big top in London keeps things moving well between murders.

Production and photography come across clean and sharp via Desmond Dickinson's color camera work adding dimension to Maurice Pelling's realistic setting (although they could have used more extras in the widely space "packed audiences.") Special effects weren't credited, but whoever dreamed up the situations and portrayed them as shown deserves a big part of the film's prospective success.

"Berserk" is an oldfashioned thriller with more circus entertainment than plot or thrill, but it's got the name, the promotion, and the nonsophisticated audience appeal that makes this type of entertainment. Offers good potential if sold right, particularly in drive-ins and houses in the south and west. *Bush.*

Rheinsberg
(GERMAN-COLOR)

Berlin, Dec. 19.

Constantin release of independent-Film (Kurt Hoffmann and Heinz Angermeyer) production. Stars Cornelia Froboess, Christian Wolff; features Werner Hinz, Willie Rose, Anita Kupsch, Agnes Windeck. Directed by Kurt Hoffmann. Screenplay, Herbert Reinecker, after same-titled novelette by Kurt Tucholsky; camera (Eastmancolor), Richard Angst; music, Hans-Martin Majewski; editors, Gisela Haller. At Gloria-Palast, West Berlin. Running time, 88 MINS.

Claire	Cornelia Froboess
Wolf	Christian Wolff
Claire's father	Werner Hinz
Claire's mother	Ehmi Bessel
Anna	Ruth Stephan
Vogler	Willie Rose
Paula	Anita Kupsch
Frau Knappke	Agnes Windeck
Carla	Monika Peitsch

The nowadays rare thing of a strictly and even typical German romantic comedy that stands a fine chance to go places. "Rheinsberg" is an intriguing pic for young and old patrons—especially those who have a romantic spot in their heart. This feature pic stands a refreshing departure from the abundance of sex and violance-loaded films currently in circulation.

It is a simple tale which has been vaguely adapted from a novelette by the late (1935) Kurt Tucholsky, one of Germany's finest raconteurs of the pre-Hitler era. Story revolves around two young people who leave the big city, Berlin, to spend secretly a few happy days in a cozy little hotel in a provincial spot called Rheinsberg. They pretend being man and wife in an attempt to find out whether they are really meant for each other.

Film which plays before the first World War has many assets. There is a good deal of humor. And there is a series of genuinely amusing dialog sequences. Handled with care, taste and directorial imagination, "Rheinsberg" is a solidly sympathetic film.

Cornelia Froboess, who plays the leading femme owes much to director Kurt Hoffmann. He has given her the chance to display her wide range of acting abilities. Miss Froboess, a former moppet star and then a successful pop singer, evidently has gained much from her recent stage experiences. She seems to have hit the jackpot with this film. She now may be in for a new and substantial screen career. She is, by all means, one of this film's big plus factors.

Christian Wolff, her partner, is less effective which, however, stems from his occasionally rather passive role. It's always he who follows her. Yet his performance also is fully adequate. Also, he is an optical delight. For a change here is a young lover with neatly combed hair. Support is excellent all down the line. In the main, Werner Hinz, as Miss Froboess' Babbitt type of stiff Prussian father, deserves mention.

Technical credits are fine. In particular, this goes for Werner Schlichting's beautiful settings and the slick lensing by vet cameraman Richard Angst.

This is Kurt Hoffmann's 42d film and one of his best in years. Hoffman shows that he is still the possessor of a light hand, a compliment which can be paid only to a few native directors. Film, incidentcost about $350,000.

Hans.

Grand Slam
(Ad Ogni Costo)
(ITALIAN-GERMAN-SPANISH COLOR)

Rome, Dec. 19.

Paramount release of Jolly Film (Rome) —Constatin Film (Munich)—Coral Producciones (Madrid) coproduction. Stars Janet Leigh, Robert Hoffman, Klaus Kinski, with Riccardo Cucciolla and George Rigaud. Guest performances by Adolfo Celi and Edward G. Robinson. Directed by Giuliano Montaldo. Screenplay by Roli, Caminito, Marcello Fondato, Antonio De La Loma, Marcello Coscia; camera, Antonio Macasoli; music, Ennio Morricone. At Appio Cinema, Rome. Running time, 101 MINS.
Prof. Anders ...... Edward G. Robinson
Mary Ann .... Janet Leigh
Playboy .... Robert Hoffman
German Sgt. .... Klaus Kinski
Mechanic .... Riccardo Cucciolla
Safe Expert .... George Rigaud
Mark Milford .... Adolfo Celi

It comes as no surprise that Jolly Film signed Giuliano Montaldo to a longterm exclusive pact after the young director completed "Grand Slam." And, by the same token, it requires no crystal ball to predict that Paramount will do good biz on a modest investment to acquire release of this three-way coproduction.

A fine, tight script is proof—in this instance at any rate—that five heads are better than one. Yarn is synched like a Swiss watch with suspense action rigged to a safecracking jewel robbery in Rio De Janiero. Prof. Anders (Edward G. Robinson) returns to N. Y. from Rio after dividing his 30-year sojourn between teaching English and drawing up a foolproof blueprint to relieve the jewelry establishment facing his classroom of a $10,000,000 gem cache. He organizes for the coup in the first 20 minutes of footage and then exits until the ingenious, ironic twist in the final sequence.

It's like a takeoff on "Rififi" though the plot benefits from global backgrounds of the crime quartet as well as from the picturesque points of Rio and its flamboyant carnival. Predecessor was staged in the hush of night; "Grand Slam" takes cover within the exotic percussion of a celebrating populace.

Each of the four specialized lawbreakers has a telltale flaw that imperils the project. Yet the plan advances unfalteringly with an equal suspenseful dose of reality and improbability up to the safecrackers' short-lived triumph. As the story unplots, jewelry house secretary Mary Ann (Janet Leigh) is a strategic barrier in hornrimmed glasses whose seduction is vital to the gem haul.

Except for a bit too much emphasis on the details of safecracking technique and George Riguad's performance, "Grand Slam" is paced like a stirring horse race. Director Montaldo grabs audience interest in the first reel and gradually draws spectators to their seat edge. He uses the beauty of Rio to storytelling advantage and cleverly balances carnival inserts without ever taking his eyes off the clock.

Performances by Robinson, Miss Leigh, Robert Hoffman, as the Playboy, Klaus Kinski, as the Teuton toughie heading the Rio operation; Riccardo Cucciolla and Adolfo Celi are all standout as the cast merges into the step-by-step rhythm of Robinson's master plan, under Montaldo's shrewd helming.

Lenser Antonio Macasoli's pastel tints and deep landscape focus, together with Ennio Morricone's tense score are added factors that help set "Grand Slam" on a par with Hollywood's best suspensers.

Werb.